TIME
ALMANAC
2011

POWERED BY

ENCYCLOPÆDIA
Britannica®

www.britannica.com

Jacob E. Safra, *Chairman of the Board*
Jorge Aguilar-Cauz, *President*

Chicago London New Delhi Paris Seoul Sydney Taipei Tokyo

Year in Review

People

Awards

Nature, Science, Medicine, & Technology

World

United States

Business

Arts, Entertainment, & Leisure

Sport

ENCYCLOPÆDIA BRITANNICA, INC.

EDITORIAL
Thad King, Editor
Michael J. Anderson
Patricia Bauer
Robert M. Lewis
Kenneth Pletcher
Barbara Schreiber
Melinda C. Shepherd
Karen Jacobs Sparks
Amy Tikkanen

PRODUCTION CONTROL
Marilyn L. Barton

WORLD DATA
Stephen Neher
Mary Kasprzak
Letricia A. Dixon

CARTOGRAPHY
Michael Nutter
Ken Chmielewski

COPY
Sylvia Wallace
Glenn Jenne
Alison Eldridge
Kimberly Jeffries
Claire Navarro

ART AND COMPOSITION
Steven N. Kapusta
Nicole DiGiacomo
Carol A. Gaines
Christine McCabe
Cate Nichols
Patrick Riley
Thomas J. Spanos

EDITORIAL LIBRARY
Henry Bolzon
Lars Mahinske

INFORMATION MANAGEMENT
Carmen-Maria Hetrea
Sheila Vasich
Mansur Abdullah
Diana Chen

MANUFACTURING
Kim Gerber

MEDIA ASSET MANAGEMENT
Jeannine Deubel
Kimberly Cleary
Kurt Heintz

ENCYCLOPÆDIA BRITANNICA, INC.
Jacob E. Safra
Chairman of the Board

Jorge Aguilar-Cauz
President

Michael Ross
Senior Vice President,
Corporate Development

Dale H. Hoiberg
Senior Vice President
and Editor

Michael Levy
Executive Editor, Core Reference

J.E. Luebering
Director, Core Reference

Rosaline Jackson-Keys
Director, Almanac and World Data

Marsha Mackenzie
Executive Director,
Media and Production

CONTRIBUTING EDITOR
Kelly Knauer

DESIGN
Anthony Wing Kosner

PICTURES
Patricia Cadley

Richard Fraiman
Publisher

Steven Sandonato
General Manager

Carol Pittard
Executive Director, Marketing
Services

Tom Mifsud
Executive Director, Retail and
Special Sales

Peter Harper
Director, New Product Development

Laura Adam
Director, Bookazine Development
& Marketing

Joy Butts
Publishing Director, Brand Marketing

Helen Wan
Assistant General Counsel

Suzanne Janso
Book Production Manager

Anne-Michelle Gallero
Design and Prepress Manager

Michela Wilde
Brand Manager

Alex Voznesenskiy
Associate Prepress Manager

Special thanks to: Christine Austin, Glenn Buonocore, Jim Childs, Susan Chodakiewicz, Rose Cirrincione, Jacqueline Fitzgerald, Carrie Frazier, Lauren Hall, Malena Jones, Brynn Joyce, Mona Li, Robert Marasco, Amy Migliaccio, Kimberly Posa, Brooke Reger, Dave Rozzelle, Ilene Schreider, Adriana Tierno, Sydney Webber

Front cover photos: Insets (left to right): Gerry Broome/AP Images; Brendan Smialowski/Getty Images; Pier Paolo Cito/AP Images; ©20th Century Fox; U.S. Coast Guard via Getty Images. Earth: Jan Rysavy/iStockphoto Back cover photos (left to right): Paul Sakuma/AP Images; Jae C. Hong/AP Images; Jeffrey Mayer/Wirelmage/Getty Images; Chip Somodevilla/Getty Images

ISBN-10: 1-60320-164-5; ISBN-13: 978-1-60320-164-3 Hardcover
ISBN-10: 1-60320-165-3; ISBN-13: 978-1-60320-165-0 Paperback
International Standard Serial Number: 0073-7860

ENCYCLOPÆDIA BRITANNICA ALMANAC 2011

Britannica.com may be accessed on the Internet at http://www.britannica.com. For information on group and bulk sales, please send an e-mail to books@eb.com.

(Trademark Reg. U.S. Pat. Off.) Printed in U.S.A.

If you would like to order any of our hardcover Collector's Edition books, please call us at 1-800-327-6388 (Monday through Friday, 7:00 A.M.–8:00 P.M. or Saturday, 7:00 A.M.–6:00 P.M. Central Time).

Business

Arts, Entertainment, & Leisure

Sport

In the US, Crisis in the Statehouses

by David von Drehle, TIME

In New Jersey, taxes are high, the budget's a mess, government is inefficiently organized, and the public pension fund is blown to kingdom come. Which makes New Jersey a lot like most other states in 2010. What makes the state unusual is its rookie governor, a human bulldozer named Chris Christie, who vowed to lead like a one-termer and is keeping his promise with brio. He has proposed chopping US$11 billion from the state's budget—more than a quarter of the total—for fiscal year 2011 (which starts 1 Jul 2010). He's backing a constitutional cap on property taxes in hopes of pushing the state's myriad villages and townships to merge into more efficient units. He's locked in an ultimate cage match with the New Jersey teachers' union. It may be the bitterest political fight in the country—and that's saying something in 2010. A union official recently circulated a humorous prayer with a punch line asking God to kill Christie. You know, New Jersey humor.

The tone of the New Jersey budget battle may be distinctive, but many of the same notes can be heard in state capitals across the country. From Hartford to Honolulu, once sturdy state governments are approaching the brink of fiscal calamity, as the crash of 2008 and its persistent aftermath have led to the reckoning of 2010. Squeezed by the end of federal stimulus money on one hand and desperate local governments on the other, states are facing the third straight year of staggering budget deficits, and the necessary cuts will cost jobs, limit services, and touch the lives of millions of Americans. Government workers have been laid off in half the states plus Puerto Rico. Twenty-two states have instituted unpaid furloughs. At least 28 states have ordered across-the-board budget cuts, with many of them adding deeper cuts in targeted agencies. And massive shortfalls in public pension plans loom as well.

Almost no one—and no place—is exempt. Nearly everywhere, tax revenue plummeted as property values tanked, incomes dwindled, and consumers stopped shopping. Falling prices for stocks and real estate have made mincemeat of often underfunded public pension plans. Unemployed workers have swelled the demand for welfare and Medicaid services. Governments that were frugal in the past are just squeaking by. Governments that were lavish in the good times, building their budgets on optimism and best-case scenarios, now risk being wrecked like a shantytown in an earthquake.

For the first time in four decades of collecting data, the National Governors Association (NGA) reports that total state spending has dropped for two years in a row. In hard-hit Arizona, for example, the state budget has sagged to 2004 levels, despite blistering growth in population and demand for government services. Starting with the 2008 fiscal year, state governments have closed more than US$300 billion in cumulative budget gaps, with another US$125 billion already projected for the coming years, said Corina Eckl, fiscal-program director at the National Conference of State Legislatures. Similar figures aren't collected for the nation's counties, villages, and towns, but when the National League of Cities surveyed mayors recently, three-fourths of them described worsening economic conditions.

Accustomed to the ups and downs of the ordinary economic cycle, elected officials and budget planners are facing something none of them have experienced before: year after year of shortfalls, steadily compounding. Ordinarily, deficits are resolved mostly through budgetary hocus-pocus. But the length and depth of the recession are forcing governments to go beyond sleight of hand to genuine cuts.

Many taxpayers might say that it's about time spending dropped. But then they start hearing the specifics. Government budgets contain a lot of fixed costs and herds of sacred cows. K-12 education absorbs nearly a third of all spending from state general funds. Add medical expenses, primarily Medicaid, and it's over half. Prisons must be maintained, colleges and universities kept open, interest on bonds and other loans paid. Real cuts provoke loud howls, and you can hear them rising in every corner of the country. College students have marched in California, firefighters have protested in Florida, and on 10 Jun 2010, Minnesota saw the largest one-day strike of nurses—some 12,000—in US history.

In August, despite polls showing strong public concern over federal deficits, Congress passed an emergency spending bill designed to help state budgets, sending US$26 billion to the states, mainly to support teachers' jobs and cover Medicaid spending. But that was a bandage designed to stop present bleeding, not a cure for what ails state budgets. Already, 11 states are projecting major budget gaps—greater than 10% of general-fund spending—well into 2013. (Only the federal government is allowed to run deficits; states and cities must balance their budgets or face default.) Such persistent budget woes are unprecedented in the era of modern US government. You'd have to go back to the 1930s to find a parallel.

WHEN MAIN STREET ACTED LIKE WALL STREET

Whether the characters are mighty or meek, this unfolding economic disaster story is in fact a series of variations on a single theme. When times were good and the future seemed bulletproof, all sorts of grand ventures were floated on waves of debt. No one cared, because everyone planned to be richer when the bills came due. The arbitrageurs of leveraged derivatives, the cash-strapped subprime home buyers, the government grandees issuing bonds and boosting pensions—all were versions of the same doom-shadowed figure. Only if the bubble burst would the bills become unpayable. How did so many people forget all at once that the bubble always bursts?

Strapped for cash, state and local governments so far have taken mostly predictable steps. They've depleted their rainy-day funds; of all the cash expected to be on hand in state treasuries by the end of the 2010 fiscal year, two-thirds of it will be held by just two states, Alaska and Texas, which enjoy income from vast energy deposits. By comparison, 14 states are expected to have reserves of less than 1% of their annual spending—basically they're living hand to mouth, hoping their checks don't bounce. And a majority of states will have reserves well below safe levels recommended by the National Association of State Budget Officers. Leery of broad tax hikes in a bad economy, governments have instead chosen to shake the sofa cushions and punish the naughty, closing loopholes, cracking down on tax evaders, and raising levies on tobacco, alcohol, gambling, soda pop, and candy—even bottled water in Washington state. Nearly half the states have hiked fees for higher education, court services, park access, business licenses—or all of the above.

These are the tried-and-true responses to dips in the business cycle, but as the woes drag on from year to year, the job of closing budget gaps grows more difficult. Now larger issues and harder choices are being laid bare, beginning with the sprawling mess that is Medicaid. Created by Congress, administered by the states, and paid for by a patchwork of federal, state, and local governments, the health care system for America's poor is a jumble in the best of times. With enrollments growing rapidly, that jumble is becoming a train wreck.

According to the NGA, the number of people covered by Medicaid will grow again in 2011 by an estimated 5.4% on average. Meanwhile, anticipated funding is expected to grow hardly at all. That might not spell disaster for a state like Nebraska, which anticipates just 2% enrollment growth. But in foreclosure-racked Arizona, officials are planning for a jump of more than 17%, and the budgetary pressure is enormous. As Gov. Jan Brewer put it in her 2010 state-of-the-state address, government revenues have sagged to 2004 levels, and "some people...say we should just adopt the 2004 budget." But Arizona's Medicaid rolls have grown by 475,000 patients since then.

What's going to give? Prepare for a free-for-all. The states are pressing Washington to maintain the emergency Medicaid supplement that was part of the stimulus package. So far, congressional moderates are blanching at the price tag. If the Beltway budget hawks win that battle, states plan to squeeze the patients, who are currently protected by strings attached to the stimulus money. No federal supplement means no more strings. Already various states are contemplating tighter eligibility rules, lower benefits, higher co-pays, and other restrictions. And then there's the ongoing fight between the states and the medical system. Governments are wringing money from doctors and hospitals coming and going: first they are cutting payments for Medicaid services, and then they are raising fees on Medicaid providers.

Just as ugly is the issue of public-employee pay and benefits. The mess in New Jersey is just an extreme example of a widespread problem: many state and local governments have made the mistake of courting the votes of public employees by fattening salaries and benefits, all the time imagining that pension-fund investments could only go up. The Pew Center on the States, a nonpartisan research group, estimates that states are at least US$1 trillion short of what it will take to keep their retirement promises to public workers. Two Chicago-area professors recently calculated the shortfall at US$3 trillion. According to Pew, half the states ran fully funded pension plans in 2000, but by 2008 that number had dwindled to four.

It's tough to cut the benefits of police officers, firefighters, and schoolteachers. But the long recession has cast a glaring light on the fact that public and private workers increasingly live in separate economies.

Private-sector employees face frequent job turnover, relentless downsizing, stagnant wages, and rising health-insurance premiums. They fund their own retirement through 401(k)s and similar plans, which rise and fall with the tides of the economy. Many public-sector workers, by contrast, enjoy relative job security, and the number of government jobs rose even as the overall unemployment rate shot just past 10%.

The B word—bankruptcy—has crept into so many conversations in communities around the country that a number of investors are worried that municipal bonds have become the latest debt-fueled bubble ready to burst. California's public-employee unions are lobbying for a bill to ban government bankruptcies entirely, so worried are they about the possibility of widespread defaults to escape pension obligations. Perhaps more worrisome, though, is the risk that all this calamity will ultimately produce little in the way of lessons learned. States are already barred from formal bankruptcy, so although many of them are broke, somehow—given enough time—they will make ends meet. But will they do it only by tweaking taxes and killing innovative programs like Kentucky's juvenile drug courts, which spend money up front on aggressive intervention and rehabilitation programs in hopes of saving the long-run expense of ruined lives in costly prisons?

A few leaders have their sights set higher, trying to shape this crisis into a moment for significant government reform. Gov. Jennifer Granholm of Michigan, a state devastated by the shrinking of the American auto industry, has called for an efficiency revolution. She has cut unneeded departments, sold excess state property, and killed hundreds of obsolete boards and commissions. Having risen to power in 2002 on the shoulders of the state teachers' union, in 2010 Democrat Granholm successfully pushed a plan to coax thousands of senior teachers into retirement, to be replaced by a smaller number of younger teachers earning less generous but more sustainable benefits. Indiana Gov. Mitch Daniels, a budget czar in the free-spending Bush administration, has proved an efficiency fiend at the state level, privatizing bureaucracies, selling a poorly managed toll road, even taking the controversial step of decertifying Indiana's public-employee unions.

Modernizing government is no less painful than globalizing industry has been. Consider the proposal by Nebraska state Sen. Rich Pahls to merge many of the state's 93 counties. The idea could mean boarding up stately old courthouses while forcing consolidation of such services as road maintenance, vehicle registration, even sheriffs' offices—and many of the jobs that go with them. The bill died, in part because it seemed too frank an acknowledgment of the passing of small-town America. Yet surely its time will come: only 16 of the counties have more than 20,000 residents, and two are home to fewer than 500 people each. "I tell these people, you don't ranch or farm the way they did 100 years ago," says Pahls. "A ranch might have had 20 hands, and now they have four. They didn't stay behind the technology."

The great reckoning of 2010 took us years to create and will be years in the fixing. It's not as if the economic crisis isn't plenty painful already. In government, as in life, there are cuts that injure and cuts that heal. As they continue to slog through the wreckage of the Great Recession, state and local leaders have a challenge to be surgeons rather than hacks and make this era of crisis into a season of fresh starts.

Unmanned Aerial Vehicles Crowd the Skies

by Peter Saracino

A little-known but important milestone in modern warfare was reached in 2009: in that year the US Air Force trained more operators of unmanned aerial vehicles (UAVs) than it did pilots. In an age when war is increasingly dominated by robots, the US military alone fields at least 7,000 of these machines, which are either remotely guided by a human using a radio link or self-guided by preprogrammed flight plans. Interest in UAVs is global, however. More than 60 manufacturers in at least 40 countries are now servicing a market that is expected to exceed tens of billions of dollars over the next decade.

A GROWING TECHNOLOGY

UAVs, also called remotely piloted vehicles (RPVs) or unmanned aircraft systems (UASs), are aircraft without a pilot onboard. Fixed-wing UAVs resemble "smart weapons" such as cruise missiles, but they are superior because they return to their base after a mission and can be reused. Also, UAVs have two decisive advantages over manned aircraft: their ... es not risk the ... aircrews, and ... loiter over ... est longer ... s of air- ... ilots. ... ition ... size ... ller- ... ed ... er- ... et- ... n-

> *Quentin Davies, the UK's defense minister, predicted in July 2009 that the world is now witnessing the last generation of manned combat aircraft and that by 2030 UAVs will have displaced them.*

... e from a few hundred thou- ... models to well over US$100

... es during World War II with ... es, and they continued to ... Vietnam era, when film ... et-powered drones for ... Truly modern UAVs ... tlefields until the ... al advancements ... vanced compos- ... airframes, and ... elopment of ... Also, full im- ... em (GPS) ... Vs with

... ring ... the ... la- ... et ... h

The Predator remains the most widely used battlefield UAV operated by the United States. The entire system consists of the vehicle itself (with built-in radar, TV and infrared cameras, and laser designator), a ground-control station, and a communication suite to link the two by satellite. Though pilotless, the Predator is operated by approximately 55 personnel, including a pilot operator and a sensor operator as well as intelligence, maintenance, and launch and recovery specialists. An updated version, designated the MQ-1, went into service in 2001 armed with two laser-guided AGM-114 Hellfire missiles, giving the UAV the ability to attack targets as well as identify them. The first time a Predator made a confirmed kill was in Yemen in 2002, when one operated by the CIA destroyed a vehicle carrying six alleged members of al-Qaeda. A significantly larger version of the Predator, called the MQ-9 Reaper, has been operational since 2007 with US forces and is also used by Britain's Royal Air Force.

THE LIMITS OF HIGH TECHNOLOGY

UAV technology may be sophisticated, but it is still in its infancy. By 2009 some 65 Predators (each costing US$4 million) had crashed. Thirty-six of the crashes were attributed to human error. Since UAVs are not yet completely autonomous, their operators must display great skill in judging distance and speed when landing, a task made more difficult by a slight delay in signal transmission between the UAV and the ground-control station. Moreover, there are occasional technical glitches, such as the one that occurred in September 2009 when a Reaper on a combat mission over Afghanistan could no longer be controlled and had to be shot down by US warplanes.

Successful attacks by UAVs depend upon the accuracy and timeliness of intelligence. This principle was demonstrated in 2009 when an al-Qaeda military planner was believed to have been killed by an American UAV in September but suddenly appeared in a media interview in October. Also, high-tech weapons may win engagements on the battlefield, but they cannot solve political problems—and on occasion they may even aggravate them. In July 2009 the Brookings Institution think tank estimated that for every militant killed by a UAV in Afghanistan and Pakistan, approximately 10 civilians were also killed, a situation that was alienating the local population and turning them against the United States and its NATO allies. UAV use also raises issues of accountability. According to the nongovernmental organization Human Rights Watch, Israeli UAVs unlawfully killed at least 29 Palestinian civilians during the Gaza incursion in late 2008 and early 2009 because UAV operators allegedly failed to verify that targets were combatants.

FUTURE USES IN WAR AND PEACE

Most UAVs remain dedicated to what the military calls ISTAR—intelligence, surveillance, target acquisition, and reconnaissance. For example, American UAVs began patrolling off the coast of Somalia in October 2009 in order to provide early warning of pirate vessels approaching merchant ships. However, the number of potential uses for UAVs is growing. In August 2009 the US Marine Corps awarded contracts to Boeing and a joint venture between Lockheed Martin and Kaman to develop cargo UAVs that would be capable of delivering supplies to troops on the battlefield. The goal is to demonstrate how such UAVs could reduce risk and expense in logistics. Currently it is expensive to operate ground supply convoys on the poor roads and in the back country of Afghanistan; also, convoys must be heavily guarded, and they continually run risks from roadside bombs and ambushes.

Besides these military uses, UAV technology is attracting interest from police forces and other civilian agencies. For example, the US Customs and Border Patrol has been using the Predator to patrol the Mexico-US border since 2005 and the Canada-US border since early 2009, and two maritime-patrol variants are scheduled to be operational in 2010. UAVs are also being developed for use in search-and-rescue operations to help locate survivors and deliver emergency supplies to them. In addition, UAVs are being evaluated for their potential in assessing damage suffered from disasters such as hurricanes, forest fires, and maritime oil spills.

As robotic vehicles become more commonplace, UAVs can be expected to be used wherever possible to minimize threats to personnel and to do tasks that exceed human strength and endurance. If current trends continue, UAVs could one day evacuate casualties from the heat of battle and mount round-the-clock surveillance missions for months and maybe even years at a time.

Peter Saracino is a freelance defense journalist.

Child Soldiers: From Recruitment to Reintegration

by Michael Wessells

When in April 2009, 112 child soldiers who had served with the rebel National Liberation Forces (FLN) were freed following the signing of a ceasefire agreement between the FLN and the government of Burundi, the existence of modern-day child soldiers was brought forcefully into the international spotlight. Worldwide, armed forces and nongovernmental armed groups recruit and exploit children, who are defined under international law as those under 18 years of age. Though the number of child soldiers is unknown, it is estimated that at any time, there are approximately 250,000 child soldiers, many of whom are girls. Children may also be born into armed groups. For example, the Lord's Resistance Army (LRA), which abducted many children and fought against the government of Uganda, maintained military camps in southern Sudan, where its leader, Joseph Kony, sired numerous children who subsequently became soldiers.

> ❝ *Although most child soldiers are teenagers, the recruits also include children as young as six or seven years of age.* ❞

Armed forces and groups recruit children for diverse reasons. Commanders often select children because they are available in large numbers and can be recruited with impunity, because they can be fashioned into effective fighters, and because commanders know that they can manipulate children easily by employing terror tactics and offering incentives for bravery and initiative in combat. Armed with small lightweight weapons, such as AK-47 assault rifles, even young children can be effective fighters. They may also serve as spies who can slip behind enemy lines without suspicion. Teenagers are often sought for their size and strength, their willingness to take risks that many adults would avoid, and their political consciousness. In Sri Lanka the Liberation Tigers of Tamil Elam fought

government forces in part by recruiting teena[...] serve as suicide bombers.

THE RECRUITMENT OF CHILDREN

Child recruitment is contextua[...] force or decisions made by the c[...] recruited as many as 60,000 c[...] and subjugating them into o[...] regime of terror. To deter escap[...]
d[...]
ro[...]
c[...]

but their choice[...] are made in d[...] mixture of "[...] example, a[...] may lea[...] of an a[...] bee[...] tion[...] hel[...] we[...] a[...] t[...]

Unmanned Aerial Vehicles Crowd the Skies

by Peter Saracino

A little-known but important milestone in modern warfare was reached in 2009: in that year the US Air Force trained more operators of unmanned aerial vehicles (UAVs) than it did pilots. In an age when war is increasingly dominated by robots, the US military alone fields at least 7,000 of these machines, which are either remotely guided by a human using a radio link or self-guided by preprogrammed flight plans. Interest in UAVs is global, however. More than 60 manufacturers in at least 40 countries are now servicing a market that is expected to exceed tens of billions of dollars over the next decade.

A GROWING TECHNOLOGY

UAVs, also called remotely piloted vehicles (RPVs) or unmanned aircraft systems (UASs), are aircraft without a pilot onboard. Fixed-wing UAVs resemble "smart weapons" such as cruise missiles, but they are superior because they return to their base after a mission and can be reused. Also, UAVs have two decisive advantages over manned aircraft: their use does not risk the lives of aircrews, and they can loiter over areas of interest longer than most types of aircraft with human pilots. The current generation of UAVs varies in size from small propeller-driven hand-launched models such as the German army's Aladin to jet-powered intercontinental-range craft such as the US Air Force's RQ-4 Global Hawk. Prices range from a few hundred thousand dollars for small models to well over US$100 million for a Global Hawk.

UAVs first took to the skies during World War II with radio-controlled target drones, and they continued to develop slowly through the Vietnam era, when film cameras were mounted onto jet-powered drones for photoreconnaissance missions. Truly modern UAVs did not begin to appear over battlefields until the 1980s, when a number of technical advancements made them much more effective. Advanced composite materials made for lighter, stronger airframes, and improved electronics permitted the development of high-resolution TV and infrared cameras. Also, full implementation of the Global Positioning System (GPS) in the 1990s made it possible to navigate UAVs with a precision that was previously unattainable.

UAVs began to garner media attention during NATO's intervention in the Yugoslav civil war of the 1990s. In 1995 the US Air Force put the RQ-1 Predator into service for airborne surveillance and target acquisition. The Predator could cruise at 140 km/h (87 mph), stay aloft for up to 16 hours, and reach altitudes of 7,600 m (25,000 ft). Predators flying over Yugoslavia tracked troop movements, monitored roads, and marked targets so that manned aircraft could attack them with laser-guided bombs.

> *Quentin Davies, the UK's defense minister, predicted in July 2009 that the world is now witnessing the last generation of manned combat aircraft and that by 2030 UAVs will have displaced them.*

The Predator remains the most widely used battlefield UAV operated by the United States. The entire system consists of the vehicle itself (with built-in radar, TV and infrared cameras, and laser designator), a ground-control station, and a communication suite to link the two by satellite. Though pilotless, the Predator is operated by approximately 55 personnel, including a pilot operator and a sensor operator as well as intelligence, maintenance, and launch and recovery specialists. An updated version, designated the MQ-1, went into service in 2001 armed with two laser-guided AGM-114 Hellfire missiles, giving the UAV the ability to attack targets as well as identify them. The first time a Predator made a confirmed kill was in Yemen in 2002, when one operated by the CIA destroyed a vehicle carrying six alleged members of al-Qaeda. A significantly larger version of the Predator, called the MQ-9 Reaper, has been operational since 2007 with US forces and is also used by Britain's Royal Air Force.

THE LIMITS OF HIGH TECHNOLOGY

UAV technology may be sophisticated, but it is still in its infancy. By 2009 some 65 Predators (each costing US$4 million) had crashed. Thirty-six of the crashes were attributed to human error. Since UAVs are not yet completely autonomous, their operators must display great skill in judging distance and speed when landing, a task made more difficult by a slight delay in signal transmission between the UAV and the ground-control station. Moreover, there are occasional technical glitches, such as the one that occurred in September 2009 when a Reaper on a combat mission over Afghanistan could no longer be controlled and had to be shot down by US warplanes.

Successful attacks by UAVs depend upon the accuracy and timeliness of intelligence. This principle was demonstrated in 2009 when an al-Qaeda military planner was believed to have been killed by an American UAV in September but suddenly appeared in a media interview in October. Also, high-tech weapons may win engagements on the battlefield, but they cannot solve political problems—and on occasion they may even aggravate them. In July 2009 the Brookings Institution think tank estimated that for every militant killed by a UAV in Afghanistan and Pakistan, approximately 10 civilians were also killed, a situation that was alienating the local population and turning them against the United States and its NATO allies. UAV use also raises issues of accountability. According to the nongovernmental organization Human Rights Watch, Israeli UAVs unlawfully killed at least 29 Palestinian civilians during the Gaza incursion in late 2008 and early 2009 because UAV operators allegedly failed to verify that targets were combatants.

FUTURE USES IN WAR AND PEACE

Most UAVs remain dedicated to what the military calls ISTAR—intelligence, surveillance, target acquisition, and reconnaissance. For example, American UAVs began patrolling off the coast of Somalia in October 2009 in order to provide early warning of pirate vessels approaching merchant ships. However, the number of potential uses for UAVs is growing. In August 2009 the US Marine Corps awarded contracts to Boeing and a joint venture between Lockheed Martin and Kaman to develop cargo UAVs that would be capable of delivering supplies to troops on the battlefield. The goal is to demonstrate how such UAVs could reduce risk and expense in logistics. Currently it is expensive to operate ground supply convoys on the poor roads and in the back country of Afghanistan; also, convoys must be heavily guarded, and they continually run risks from roadside bombs and ambushes.

Besides these military uses, UAV technology is attracting interest from police forces and other civilian agencies. For example, the US Customs and Border Patrol has been using the Predator to patrol the Mexico-US border since 2005 and the Canada-US border since early 2009, and two maritime-patrol variants are scheduled to be operational in 2010. UAVs are also being developed for use in search-and-rescue operations to help locate survivors and deliver emergency supplies to them. In addition, UAVs are being evaluated for their potential in assessing damage suffered from disasters such as hurricanes, forest fires, and maritime oil spills.

As robotic vehicles become more commonplace, UAVs can be expected to be used wherever possible to minimize threats to personnel and to do tasks that exceed human strength and endurance. If current trends continue, UAVs could one day evacuate casualties from the heat of battle and mount round-the-clock surveillance missions for months and maybe even years at a time.

Peter Saracino is a freelance defense journalist.

Child Soldiers: From Recruitment to Reintegration

by Michael Wessells

When in April 2009, 112 child soldiers who had served with the rebel National Liberation Forces (FLN) were freed following the signing of a ceasefire agreement between the FLN and the government of Burundi, the existence of modern-day child soldiers was brought forcefully into the international spotlight. Worldwide, armed forces and nongovernmental armed groups recruit and exploit children, who are defined under international law as those under 18 years of age. Though the number of child soldiers is unknown, it is estimated that at any time, there are approximately 250,000 child soldiers, many of whom are girls. Children may also be born into armed groups. For example, the Lord's Resistance Army (LRA), which abducted many children and fought against the government of Uganda, maintained military camps in southern Sudan, where its leader, Joseph Kony, sired numerous children who subsequently became soldiers.

Armed forces and groups recruit children for diverse reasons. Commanders often select children because they are available in large numbers and can be recruited with impunity, because they can be fashioned into effective fighters, and because commanders know that they can manipulate children easily by employing terror tactics and offering incentives for bravery and initiative in combat. Armed with small lightweight weapons, such as AK-47 assault rifles, even young children can be effective fighters. They may also serve as spies who can slip behind enemy lines without suspicion. Teenagers are often sought for their size and strength, their willingness to take risks that many adults would avoid, and their political consciousness. In Sri Lanka the Liberation Tigers of Tamil Elam fought

government forces in part by recruiting teenage girls to serve as suicide bombers.

THE RECRUITMENT OF CHILDREN

Child recruitment is contextual and may involve force or decisions made by the child. The LRA forcibly recruited as many as 60,000 children by abducting and subjugating them into obedience through a regime of terror. To deter escape the LRA forced abducted children to surround recaptured escapees and beat them to death. Forced recruitment was also used in Sierra Leone, where the opposition group Revolutionary United Front forced young people at gunpoint to join and often required children to kill members of their own villages or families.

> " *Although most child soldiers are teenagers, the recruits also include children as young as six or seven years of age.* "

Some children decide to join armed groups, but their choices may not be "voluntary," since they are made in desperate circumstances and involve a mixture of "push" and "pull" factors. In Colombia, for example, a boy who has been abused in his home may leave and seek an alternate "family" in the form of an armed group. In other countries youths have been lured by propaganda and an ideology of liberation into believing that by becoming soldiers, they will help to liberate their people. In Rwanda young Hutu were recruited into a youth militia (the Interahamwe) and were taught that Tutsi had to be eliminated; more than 800,000 people, mostly Tutsi, were killed in 1994 genocide.

Other pull factors may include retribution, family ties, and power. In Liberia some child[...] armed groups in an effort to avenge wrong[...] the killing of one's parents by government f[...]

dren may also be eager to earn money that they can send home to support impoverished families. In northern Afghanistan children frequently joined the Northern Alliance to fight the Taliban because their fathers, brothers, or uncles were members and because they regarded fighting as a matter of family honor and village protection. Some children seek power and prestige. Many children report that because they carry a gun and wear a uniform, they are treated with a level of respect that they never enjoyed as civilians.

Inside armed groups, children play diverse roles. A common myth is that all child soldiers are fighters, when in fact many recruits serve as porters, cooks, and bodyguards, among other roles. Another myth is that all child soldiers are boys. In conflicts in countries such as Liberia and Sierra Leone, girls were recruited to serve not only as fighters but also as sex slaves, whose refusal to provide sex often led to severe punishment or death.

THE REINTEGRATION OF FORMERLY RECRUITED CHILDREN

Because they have been socialized into lives as soldiers, child soldiers may themselves become a means of perpetuating violence and armed conflict. To break cycles of violence, a key priority has been to disarm and demobilize child soldiers and to help them to transition or reintegrate into civilian life. Having turned in their weapons (disarmament), child soldiers are demobilized by being officially stood down from armed groups. They are reintegrated through rehabilitation and work with families and communities to help them find a place in civilian society.

Rehabilitation requires attention to mental health issues that cause distress and impede reintegration. In countries such as Liberia and Sierra Leone, where commanders had plied child soldiers with drugs to make them fearless, many former child soldiers developed problems of substance abuse. In other countries some former child soldiers develop clinical problems, such as depression, anxiety, and trauma, particularly the post-traumatic stress disorder that can arise following extreme events, including exposure to deaths or active engagement in killing. Effective treatment of these problems requires specialized supports, such as counseling by well-trained psychologists or psychiatrists, few of whom are available in war zones. In addition, mental health issues may

have indigenous roots. In Angola, for example, former child soldiers were terrified because they believed that they were haunted by the unavenged spirits of the people they had killed. In this case, rather than counseling, the children benefit from the services of a traditional healer, who conducts a cleansing ritual to remove their spiritual pollution.

It is often everyday social issues, however, that cause the greatest distress and the most formidable barriers to reintegration. It is essential, when possible, to reunify former recruits with their families and to manage family conflicts. Nearly all former child soldiers struggle because they have lost years of education and lack the income needed to start a family or the social skills to assume the role of mother or father. Some develop unruly behavior, while others have difficulty meeting expectations associated with ordinary living. Many former child soldiers—particularly girls—are stigmatized and called "rebels" or are viewed as aggressive troublemakers. Media accounts sometimes support these stereotypes by referring to former child soldiers as a "Lost Generation."

Effective reintegration is possible through holistic community-based supports. It is important to mobilize communities to support the livelihood, acceptance, and education of former child soldiers and to activate protection mechanisms that guard against rerecruitment or retaliation. Nevertheless, reintegration efforts are not sufficient by themselves; equal efforts should be given to prevention, particularly to ending the impunity that allows recruitment to continue.

Recognition by the international community of the serious nature of enlisting children in warfare was highlighted in 2009 when warlord Thomas Lubanga Dyilo became the first person to be tried by the International Criminal Court. He was accused of having committed war crimes by recruiting children as soldiers in the Democratic Republic of the Congo. The UN was also at the forefront of strengthening international standards against child recruitment and urged governments to ratify the optional protocol on the involvement of children in armed conflict. The optional protocol, which was adopted in 2000 to augment the UN Convention on the Rights of the Child (1989), raises the minimum age of participation in hostilities from 15 years of age to 18. These efforts will succeed, however, only if all countries agree to abide by the optional protocol and thus safeguard the world's children.

Michael Wessells is Professor of Clinical Population and Family Health, Columbia University, New York City; he is the author of Child Soldiers: From Violence to Protection.

Electric Cars Gear Up

by Lee Hudson Teslik

In retrospect, 2009 may come to be seen as a year in which the movement toward electric automobiles gained momentum. This gathering of energy actually brought together a number of forces that had begun previously. First was a spike in oil prices, which reached US$147 per barrel in July 2008 and hovered in the US$60–US$80 range through much of 2009. Gasoline prices followed, threatening to make sport-utility vehicles (SUVs) and pickup trucks less economically viable for American consumers. Second was the severe recession that gripped first the United States and

then the rest of the world in 2008 and 2009, squeezing sales of new automobiles to their lowest levels in half a century and bringing major automotive companies to their knees. Third was a growing international awareness of the challenges posed by climate change, which led policymakers to seek ways to reduce carbon emissions such as those produced in automobile exhaust. Finally, the electric car movement was given a lift by improvements in technology and by government commitments to develop the infrastructure needed to support electric vehicles.

SOME HISTORICAL PERSPECTIVE

Electric cars in fact are nothing new. Electric motors did not have to be started manually; they were quieter than gasoline engines; and they provided a smoother ride because there were no gears to shift. But several innovations and discoveries proved enough to tilt consumers toward gasoline-powered cars. Among these were the exhaust muffler, the electric starter, the discovery of underground reserves of petroleum in the United States, and, ultimately, Henry Ford's assembly-line model for producing cars cheap enough to be owned by the common man.

The internal combustion engine dominated the 20th century, its success perpetuated by low fuel prices. Businesses helped to entrench gasoline-powered vehicles by establishing the infrastructure—gasoline stations—to support them. Electric vehicles, meanwhile, were sidelined. Generally more expensive than fuel-powered alternatives, they were unable to travel long distances without recharging. Most significantly, the infrastructure needed to support a large fleet of electric cars—battery-charging facilities—did not exist. Given the dearth of electric vehicles on the road, there was little demand for infrastructure, which in turn made it even less worthwhile to produce electric cars.

> *Indeed, in the late 19th century and the first two decades of the 20th, electricity was the preferred method of powering automobiles in Western Europe and the United States.*

During the 1990s electric vehicles briefly reentered the public sphere in response to a mandate by the California Air Resources Board (CARB) that "zero emission vehicles" make up 10% of vehicle sales in that state by 2003. General Motors introduced the first modern mass-produced electric vehicle, the EV1; Toyota followed suit with an electric version of its RAV4 SUV; and other automakers announced their own plans. By 2003, however, the vehicles had been withdrawn from production, and CARB had rescinded its stringent requirements. Critics alleged that the automakers had intentionally undermined the market for electric cars in order to protect their existing product lines—an idea popularized by the 2006 film *Who Killed the Electric Car?*

Toyota and Honda introduced hybrid electric automobiles, the Prius and the Insight, in 1997. Featuring a small gasoline engine that supplemented an electric motor when necessary for added propulsion, hybrid vehicles proved popular, in part because they did not have to be plugged into the electric power grid to be recharged.

ELECTRIC VEHICLES AND HYBRIDS TODAY

The gathering economic forces of 2008-09 prompted renewed interest not only in hybrids but also in fully electric vehicles and so-called plug-in hybrids (models with an extra capacity to recharge their batteries off the power grid). During his campaign for the US presidency in 2008, Barack Obama promised that half of all vehicles purchased by the federal government by 2012 would be plug-in hybrids or fully electric. In August 2009 Obama, now president, announced that US$2.4 billion of his economic stimulus package had been awarded to some 48 automakers or auto parts manufacturers in order to increase production of electric vehicles. Another US$400 million was laid aside to fund projects aimed at developing infrastructure.

Other countries made similar efforts. China's government announced that it would provide subsidies for research and for the purchase of electric or hybrid vehicles for use in Chinese taxi fleets and by government agencies. Britain's Prime Minister Gordon Brown said in July 2009 that he wanted all new cars sold in his country by 2020 to be electric or hybrid.

Auto companies scrambled to capitalize on new grants and subsidies. General Motors, which by July 2009 was majority-owned by the US government, announced plans to roll out its new electric car, the Chevrolet Volt, in late 2010. The Volt was an "extended range" model, one whose batteries would be recharged overnight by a plug-in connection or on the road by a small gasoline engine. In August Nissan Motor Co. announced production of the Leaf, a fully electric automobile that would boast zero tailpipe carbon emissions.

Efforts were being made on the infrastructure end as well. The mayor of London, vowing to make that city the "electric car capital of Europe," announced plans to have as many as 25,000 charging points installed by 2015. In Yokohama, Japan, the US-based company Better Place demonstrated the prototype of an automated battery-exchange station that it intended to install throughout Israel and Denmark as part of a program to encourage a mass market for electric automobiles.

CHALLENGES FOR THE FUTURE

Despite the gathering momentum of 2009, several challenges will have to be overcome if a sizable portion of the world's auto fleet is to be replaced with electric or hybrid vehicles. First, at current gasoline prices it is unclear whether fully electric vehicles can be economically viable alternatives on a broad scale. Second is the problem of range. Given the limitations of current battery capacities, and given current technologies that partly recharge batteries by using energy produced while braking, electric vehicles currently are best suited for stop-and-go, short-range driving. Before fully electric vehicles can be expected to replace fuel-powered cars or hybrids, charging and battery-exchange stations will have to be put in place everywhere cars are driven—not just in a few cities.

Finally, even assuming the establishment of networks of charging stations, technological problems would have to be addressed. For instance, many plug-in models take hours to recharge, whereas gasoline-powered cars take only minutes to refuel. Stations that are capable of charging car batteries rapidly are possible only in theory. In addition to dramatically decreasing charging time, these stations would have to be designed and operated in such a manner that they would avoid straining municipal power grids.

Lee Hudson Teslik is Senior Editor and Analyst at Roubini Global Economics.

Chronology, July 2009–June 2010

A day-by-day listing of important and interesting events, adapted from
Britannica Book of the Year. *See also Disasters.*

July 2009

1 Jul The presidency of the European Union rotates to Sweden, led by Prime Minister Fredrik Reinfeldt.

2 Jul The US Department of Labor releases figures showing that the country's unemployment rate reached 9.5% in June; stock markets drop precipitously in response.

▶ Yukiya Amano of Japan is chosen to replace Mohamed ElBaradei as director general of the International Atomic Energy Agency.

3 Jul Former vice presidential nominee Sarah Palin astounds political observers with an announcement that she will step down as governor of Alaska with a year and a half left in her term of office.

4 Jul American Serena Williams defeats her sister Venus Williams to take her third All-England (Wimbledon) women's tennis championship; the following day Roger Federer of Switzerland wins the men's title for the sixth time when he defeats American Andy Roddick for a record 15th Grand Slam victory.

▶ American radio host Casey Kasem broadcasts his final countdown of the American top 20 popular songs; *American Top 20* is a spinoff of *American Top 40*, a show he initiated on 4 Jul 1970.

5 Jul In lively legislative elections in Bulgaria, the opposition center-right Citizens for the European Development of Bulgaria, led by Boiko Borisov, wins a resounding victory over the ruling Socialist-led coalition.

QUOTE OF THE MONTH

❝ *I vote for a European Bulgaria, which has to prove that it is not the poorest and most corrupt country in Europe.* ❞

—Boyko Borisov, on the Bulgarian election that his party won, 5 July

---

6 Jul US Pres. Barack Obama meets in Moscow with Russian Pres. Dmitry Medvedev; they agree to negotiate a treaty on nuclear-arms reduction to replace the START I treaty, which will expire in December.

▶ The Italian automaker Fiat Group announces that it plans to enter into a joint venture with the Chinese state-owned Guangzhou Automobile Group.

▶ The militant organization Movement for the Emancipation of the Niger Delta (MEND) declares that the previous day it seized a chemical tanker and also destroyed a Chevron oil facility in Nigeria.

7 Jul Missiles from a US drone kill 13 Taliban and 3 Uzbek militants in Pakistan's South Waziristan province.

8 Jul The Group of 8 industrialized countries begins a summit meeting in L'Aquila, Italy; topics under discussion include the global economic recession, global warming, and the war in Afghanistan.

9 Jul Thousands of pro-democracy demonstrators take to the streets of Tehran, undeterred by tear gas and beatings from security forces.

10 Jul The reorganized car company General Motors exits bankruptcy 40 days after filing for it.

11 Jul It is reported that former US vice president Dick Cheney had ordered the Central Intelligence Agency to refrain from reporting to Congress on a counterterrorism project for eight years; the program was ended in June when the agency's new director, Leon Panetta, learned of its existence.

12 Jul Ji Eun-Hee of South Korea wins a one-stroke victory over Candie Kung of Taiwan to win the US Women's Open golf tournament in Bethlehem PA.

13 Jul Henry Okah, a leader of the MEND rebel group, is released from prison in Nigeria; on 15 July the movement leaders declare a 60-day cease-fire.

14 Jul At its triennial convention in Anaheim CA, the Episcopal Church USA votes to affirm that any level of the ministry may be filled by openly gay persons; on 17 July the convention votes to allow the blessing of same-sex unions in jurisdictions in which such unions are legal.

▶ The banking company Goldman Sachs reports its most profitable quarter ever and plans to offer US$11.4 billion in bonuses to its executives.

▶ The oil company Exxon Mobil announces that it has formed a partnership with the biotechnology company Synthetic Genomics, headed by J. Craig Venter, in a venture to create biofuel from algae.

15 Jul The space shuttle *Endeavour* takes off from the Kennedy Space Center in Florida on a mission to continue construction of the International Space Station.

16 Jul At a summit meeting of the Nonaligned Movement in Egypt, the prime ministers of Pakistan and India release a joint statement that they have agreed to cooperate to combat terrorism and will continue to engage in talks to resolve their differences.

▶ With his return to Marina del Rey CA, Zac Sunderland, age 17, becomes the youngest person to have sailed around the world solo.

17 Jul Pakistan's Supreme Court acquits former prime minister Nawaz Sharif of the crime of hijacking, of which he had been convicted following his unsuccessful attempt to prevent Pervez Musharraf from taking over the country in a coup in 1999; the ruling makes Sharif eligible to hold public office.

▶ The American television station Nickelodeon celebrates the 10th anniversary of its phenomenally popular cartoon show *SpongeBob SquarePants* with a 50-hour, three-day marathon.

18 Jul Some 5,500 Mexican soldiers are deployed to Michoacán state in Mexico after a series of horrific attacks on police by drug cartel members.

19 Jul Anthony Wesley, an amateur astronomer in Australia, finds a dark spot the size of the Pacific Ocean in Jupiter's atmosphere, which suggests that the planet was hit by a comet.

▶ Stewart Cink of the US defeats crowd favorite Tom Watson, age 59, in a four-hole playoff to win the British Open golf tournament at Turnberry in Ayrshire, Scotland.

20 Jul Four US soldiers are killed by a roadside bomb in eastern Afghanistan, which brings the total number of US troops killed in the country in July to 30, the highest number in any month since the 2001

invasion; the 56 coalition troops killed in July is also a record.

▸ The book retailer Barnes & Noble announces a store for electronic books, BN.com, that will offer more than 700,000 titles that can be downloaded onto computers or smartphones.

21 Jul Spanish Foreign Minister Miguel Ángel Moratinos enters Gibraltar for talks with British Foreign Secretary David Miliband and Gibraltar's chief minister, Peter Caruana; no Spanish minister has visited Gibraltar, which Spain ceded to Britain in 1713, in more than three centuries.

22 Jul A tribunal at the Permanent Court of Arbitration at The Hague redraws the borders of the disputed Abyei region between northern and southern Sudan; both the government of Sudan and the Sudan People's Liberation Movement accept the new borders.

23 Jul Mark Buehrle of the Chicago White Sox pitches the first perfect game since 2004 and the 18th in Major League Baseball history in his team's 5–0 victory over the Tampa Bay Rays.

▸ The Dow Jones Industrial Average closes at 9069.29, its first close above 9000 since the beginning of the year.

▸ The first fiber-optic cables between East Africa and India, the Middle East, and Europe are switched on.

24 Jul The US Army Corps of Engineers reports that it has completed a project to block off the Mississippi River–Gulf Outlet, a shipping channel that was built in the 1960s and is believed to have been a contributing factor to the flooding of New Orleans after Hurricane Katrina in 2005.

25 Jul In regional elections in Kurdistan in Iraq, the ruling coalition retains power, in spite of a surprisingly strong showing by the opposition coalition.

26 Jul Spanish cyclist Alberto Contador wins the Tour de France.

▸ The National Baseball Hall of Fame in Cooperstown NY inducts outfielders Rickey Henderson and Jim Rice and second baseman Joe Gordon.

27 Jul Eduardo Medina Mora, attorney general of Mexico, announces a new program that will make it possible for drug addicts who have committed minor crimes to be sent to rehabilitation rather than prison.

28 Jul The Virginia Tech Transportation Institute releases a study of the texting behavior of long-haul truckers that took place over a period of 18 months which found that texting while driving increases the risk of collision by a factor of 23; talking on the phone while driving increases the risk by only a factor of 4.

29 Jul Scientists from the Wildlife Conservation Society report the discovery in Laos of the first new species of bulbul in more than a century; the new songbird, which has a largely featherless head, is dubbed the bare-faced bulbul.

30 Jul The death of Mohammad Yusuf, the leader of the militant Islamist group Boko Haram, in Maiduguri, Nigeria, is confirmed; it is believed that hundreds of people may have died in several days of violence.

31 Jul The US government releases figures showing that the country's economy in the second fiscal quarter shrank at an annual rate of 1%, a significant improvement over the 6.4% contraction in the first quarter.

▸ FINA, the governing body of international swimming, announces that from 1 Jan 2010 the use of polyurethane suits in competition will be banned and that, in addition, men's suits may cover from the waist to kneecaps only, and women's suits must be limited to the area between the shoulders and the kneecaps.

August 2009

1 Aug More than 100 opposition figures go on trial in Iran, accused of having attempted to foment a revolution after the disputed June election.

▸ Days of attacks by a militant Muslim group against Christians in Gojra, in Pakistan's Punjab province, culminate in the burning and looting of more than 100 homes in the Christian quarter and the killing of six Christians.

2 Aug At the opening of its new global headquarters in Yokohama, Japan, the automobile manufacturer Nissan introduces the Leaf, an all-electric hatchback that is expected to go on sale in the US, Japan, and Europe by the end of 2010.

▸ Scottish golfer Catriona Matthew captures the Women's British Open golf tournament.

3 Aug Ayatollah Ali Khamenei, Iran's supreme leader, ceremonially approves Mahmoud Ahmadinejad as the country's president.

4 Aug The Palestinian movement Fatah opens its first party conference in 20 years in Bethlehem in the West Bank; Palestinian leader Mahmoud Abbas declares it an opportunity for a new beginning.

▸ A panel of federal judges orders California to reduce its prison population by more than 25% within the next two years.

5 Aug Former US president Bill Clinton leaves North Korea with American journalists Laura Ling and Euna Lee after having secured a pardon for them from North Korean leader Kim Jong Il; Ling and Lee

had been sentenced to 12 years of hard labor for having entered North Korean territory.

▸ Tens of thousands of Filipinos attend the funeral procession for Corazon Aquino, who restored democracy to the Philippines in 1986 and served as president in 1986–92; she died on 1 August.

6 Aug In London, robbers steal 43 pieces of diamond jewelry with an estimated value of US$65 million from the Graff jewelry store in one of Britain's largest-ever diamond heists.

7 Aug After a North Korean ship ostensibly carrying sugar to the Middle East inexplicably anchors in the Bay of Bengal, not far from Myanmar (Burma), it is seized by Indian authorities; it is the first time that a North Korean ship has been seized since UN sanctions permitting the action were enacted in June.

▸ The US Bureau of Labor Statistics reports that the country's unemployment rate fell to 9.4% in July and that the monthly loss of jobs was the smallest since August 2008.

8 Aug Sonia Sotomayor is sworn in as the first Hispanic person to become a justice of the US Supreme Court.

▸ Muscle Hill wins the Hambletonian harness race by six lengths at Meadowlands Racetrack in East Rutherford NJ.

9 Aug The 50th Edward MacDowell Medal for outstanding contribution to the arts is awarded to

American visual artist Kiki Smith at the MacDowell Colony in Peterborough NH.

10 Aug A US federal judge turns down a consent decree between the Securities and Exchange Commission and Bank of America in which Bank of America would pay a US$33 million fine for failing to disclose bonuses paid to Merrill Lynch executives; he is angered by the failure of the agreement to address the allegations in the complaint against the company.

11 Aug In Myanmar (Burma), opposition figure Aung San Suu Kyi is sentenced to 18 further months of house arrest for having allowed an American intruder into her home.

▶ Armed forces in Yemen begin an offensive against Shiʻite rebels in Saʻdah province.

12 Aug The World Trade Organization rules that China's limits on imported books, movies, and songs, which may be sold only through state-approved distributors, violate international trade rules.

▶ It is reported that the *Arctic Sea,* a Maltese-flagged, Russian-crewed cargo ship carrying timber from Finland to Algeria, was apparently hijacked off Sweden on 24 July and has not been sighted since 31 July; it was due in Algeria on 4 August.

13 Aug The journal *Cell* publishes a study by a team at the Broad Institute who found a way to identify drugs that kill cancer stem cells but not other cells; the finding could lead to more effective ways to treat cancer.

▶ The executive board of the International Olympic Committee votes to include women's boxing in the 2012 Olympic Games and recommends the inclusion of rugby sevens and golf in the 2016 Olympic Games.

14 Aug The US National Oceanic and Atmospheric Administration reports that the average temperature of the surface waters of the world's oceans in July reached 16.98 °C (62.56 °F), the highest temperature ever recorded.

15 Aug At the Bethel Woods Center for the Arts in Bethel NY, the 40th anniversary of the legendary Woodstock Music and Art Fair is celebrated with a concert by the so-called Heroes of Woodstock, bands that performed at, or otherwise had a connection with, the original three-day festival.

16 Aug At the Hazeltine National Golf Club in Chaska MN, Y.E. Yang of South Korea defeats Tiger Woods of the US by three strokes in the Professional Golfers' Association championship to become the first Asian-born man to win a major PGA golf tournament.

17 Aug Russia reports that the missing cargo ship *Arctic Sea* has been found 483 km (300 mi) off Cape Verde; the crew is reported to be safe.

18 Aug The UN World Food Programme says that in spite of its efforts to provide food to people in Kenya suffering from a lengthy drought, some 1.3 million people there are still going hungry.

19 Aug The major Swiss bank UBS agrees to disclose information to the US Internal Revenue Service on 4,450 holders of secret accounts whom the US suspects of tax evasion.

▶ Shortly before Caster Semenya of South Africa wins the women's 800-m race at the track-and-field world championships in Berlin by more than two seconds, officials from the International Association of Athletics Federations reveal that the runner, who has a masculine-appearing physique, is undergoing sex-determination testing.

20 Aug A presidential election is held in Afghanistan despite Taliban intimidation; turnout is nearly 40%.

▶ ʻAbd al-Basit al-Megrahi, the only person convicted in the 1988 bombing of Pan Am Flight 103 over Lockerbie, Scotland, returns to a hero's welcome in Libya after having been released from prison for compassionate reasons (he has terminal prostate cancer) by a magistrate in Scotland; Megrahi served 8 years of a 27-year sentence.

21 Aug Delegates to the national assembly of the Evangelical Lutheran Church in America in Minneapolis MN vote to allow people in committed same-sex relationships to serve as clergy.

22 Aug The government of Greece declares a state of emergency as wildfires that started the previous day near Grammatiko spread to Varnava and Marathon.

23 Aug England defeats Australia by 197 runs in a cricket Test match at the Oval in London to retake the Ashes series.

24 Aug The US government's popular cash-for-clunkers program ends; it provided financial incentives of up to US$4,500 to consumers who traded in old cars for new, more fuel-efficient ones.

▶ US Attorney General Eric Holder appoints John H. Durham to lead an investigation to determine whether criminal conduct may have taken place in the CIA's interrogations of prisoners in its secret rendition program.

25 Aug Palestinian Prime Minister Salam Fayad presents a plan that maps out the government of a Palestinian state; it is intended to be in place within two years and is to be pursued in parallel with peace negotiations with Israel.

▶ Stalwart liberal Sen. Edward M. Kennedy of Massachusetts dies at his home in Hyannis Port MA.

26 Aug A plan to create a system for voluntary organ donation is announced in China, where much of the need for organ transplantation goes unmet and organs that are available often come from executed prisoners or black-market sellers.

27 Aug The US Federal Deposit Insurance Corp. reports that the country's banking industry lost US$3.7 billion in the second fiscal quarter of 2009.

28 Aug North Korea and South Korea agree to resume cross-border family reunions beginning in late September.

29 Aug India's space agency loses contact with its lunar orbiter, Chandrayaan-1.

> ### QUOTE OF THE MONTH
>
> ❝ *The road ends outside Libreville. After that we eat dust. It's impossible. We can't continue like this.* ❞
>
> —Mathieu Ngoma, a voter in Gabon, on the lack of change promised in the next day's presidential election, 29 August

30 Aug A presidential election is held in Gabon; Ali Ben Bongo, the son of the late president, Omar Bongo, wins handily, though many Gabonese believe the election was rigged.

▶ The Park View team from Chula Vista CA defeats the Kuei-Shan team from Taoyuan, Taiwan, 6–3 to win baseball's 63rd Little League World Series.

31 Aug Turkey and Armenia announce that they have agreed to take steps toward establishing diplomatic relations.

September 2009

1 Sep The Afghan Electoral Complaints Commission declares that it has so far received more than 2,600 reports of vote fraud, including vote stealing.

▶ Eurostat, the European Union's statistical agency, reports that the unemployment rate in the euro zone in July rose to 9.5%, its highest level in a decade.

▶ The Commonwealth announces the suspension of Fiji's membership in the organization because of its lack of progress toward the restoration of democracy since the 2006 coup.

2 Sep In Juárez, Mexico, masked men carrying automatic guns invade a drug-rehabilitation center and slaughter 18 recovering addicts; more than 300 people in the city died violently in August alone.

3 Sep US Secretary of State Hillary Rodham Clinton announces the suspension of US$30 million in US aid to Honduras in reaction to the intransigence of the coup-led government.

4 Sep A NATO air strike near Kunduz, Afghanistan, called for by German forces, causes two fuel trucks that had been stolen by the Taliban to explode; scores of people are believed to have been killed, but it is unclear how many of them were militants and how many civilians.

▶ The US Bureau of Labor Statistics reports that that country's unemployment rate rose to 9.7% in August, its highest level in 26 years, in spite of a decreased number of job losses.

5 Sep After two days of protests by Han Chinese who say that Uighurs have been stabbing people with needles, the Communist Party secretary of Urumqi, China, is removed from his post.

6 Sep North Korea unexpectedly releases water from a dam on the Imjin River, which flows through both North and South Korea; the resultant wall of water sweeps away six South Koreans who were camping and fishing on the river.

7 Sep Mohamed ElBaradei reports to the board of the International Atomic Energy Agency that the organization has reached a stalemate with Iran, which refuses to stop enriching uranium or engage in negotiations over its nuclear program.

▶ Two German cargo ships arrive at the port of Yamburg in far northern Russia, completing a transit of the usually ice-blocked Northeast Passage.

8 Sep The price of gold rises to US$1,000 an ounce; the precious metal has risen 13.6% in value during the course of the year.

▶ The US Federal Reserve reports that the amount of money borrowed by American consumers in July fell by a record US$21.6 billion from the previous month.

9 Sep Hywind, the first full-scale floating wind turbine, opens in Norway; the turbine is attached to the seabed some 10 km (6 mi) from the island of Karmøy.

▶ The fabled jewelry maker Fabergé presents its first jewelry collection in some 90 years.

10 Sep Turkey's Higher Education Board approves the study of the Kurdish language at Mardin Artuklu University in Mardin province; Turkey had long banned the use of Kurdish.

▶ Venezuela becomes the third country, after Russia and Nicaragua, to recognize the independence of the enclaves of South Ossetia and Abkhazia in Georgia.

11 Sep The Naismith Memorial Basketball Hall of Fame in Springfield MA inducts as members National Basketball Association players Michael Jordan, John Stockton, and David Robinson, and coach Jerry Sloan and women's college coach C. Vivian Stringer.

12 Sep Salah Ezzedine, a Hezbollah-connected owner of a publishing house and a financial institution, is charged in a pyramid scheme in which members of Lebanon's Shi'ite community lost a total of hundreds of millions of dollars in investments.

13 Sep Kim Clijsters of Belgium defeats Caroline Wozniacki of Denmark to win the women's US Open tennis championship; the following day, in an astonishing upset, Juan Martín del Potro of Argentina defeats five-time winner Roger Federer of Switzerland to take the men's title.

14 Sep The UN General Assembly agrees to create a new agency focused on women.

▶ The 2009 Lasker Awards for medical research are presented: winners are John Gurdon and Shinya Yamanaka, for their contributions to stem cell research, and Brian Druker, Nicholas B. Lydon, and Charles L. Sawyers, for their work on a drug that successfully treats myeloid leukemia.

15 Sep A report on the three-week war conducted by Israel in the Gaza Strip beginning in late December 2008 is released by a UN fact-finding mission; it says that both the Israeli military and Palestinian militants engaged in war crimes.

16 Sep Election monitors from the European Union state that about one-third of the votes that were tallied for Pres. Hamid Karzai in Afghanistan's presidential election on 20 August should be examined further for possible fraud.

▶ An air strike by Yemeni military forces against al-Houthi rebels in Adi, in northern Yemen, reportedly leaves at least 80 people, many of them refugees from violence, dead.

17 Sep US Pres. Barack Obama cancels plans to base components of an antiballistic missile shield, which was intended to protect the US against attack by long-range missiles, in Poland and the Czech Republic, ordering that a different system to protect against short- and medium-range missiles from Iran be put in place.

▶ Al-Shabaab rebels bomb the headquarters of the African Union peacekeeping force in Mogadishu, Somalia, killing 21 people, among them the second in command of the peacekeeping force.

18 Sep The US Bureau of Labor Statistics reports that the unemployment rate in California in August reached 12.2%, its highest level in 70 years; the same report reveals that the unemployment rate reached at least 10% in 14 states and the District of Columbia, with the highest rate (15.2%) in Michigan.

▶ The new Liège-Guillemins railway station in Belgium, designed by Santiago Calatrava, officially opens in Liège; it will be a hub in Europe's high-speed train network, serving some 36,000 people a day.

19 Sep A statement ostensibly from Taliban leader Mullah Omar, in which he warns Western countries away from Afghanistan, is posted on a Web site used by the Taliban.

20 Sep In Yemen, al-Houthi rebels launch an attack in an attempted takeover of the presidential palace in Sa'dah, but they are driven back by the Yemeni military, which reports having killed more than 140 militants.

▸ The Emmy Awards are presented in Los Angeles; winners include the television shows *30 Rock* and *Mad Men* and the actors Alec Baldwin, Bryan Cranston, Toni Collette, Glenn Close, Jon Cryer, Michael Emerson, Kristin Chenoweth, and Cherry Jones.

21 Sep Manuel Zelaya, the deposed president of Honduras, contrives to reenter the country and takes refuge in the Brazilian embassy in Tegucigalpa.

22 Sep The US Environmental Protection Agency issues new rules that from 1 Jan 2010 will require the biggest emitters of greenhouse gases in the country to track and report to the agency their emissions; some 10,000 industrial sites and fossil-fuel suppliers will have to start reporting their emissions at the beginning of 2011.

▸ Irina Bokova of Bulgaria is elected director general of UNESCO.

23 Sep Libyan leader Muammar al-Qaddafi gives a 90-minute address before the UN General Assembly in which he demands that a seat on the Security Council be opened for Africa and raises a large number of often bizarre other issues.

24 Sep The journal *Science* publishes online a report that data from three different spacecraft indicate the presence on the Moon of water or of hydroxyl (one hydrogen atom plus one oxygen atom).

25 Sep The Group of 20 countries with industrialized and emerging economies agree to coordinate their economic strategies with each other in an effort to prevent future global meltdowns and to attempt to reach a new international trade agreement; it is also decided that global economic issues will now be discussed by the Group of 20 rather than by the Group of 7 industrialized countries.

26 Sep Typhoon Ketsana strikes the main island of Luzon in the Philippines, causing massive flooding in Manila and leaving at least 464 people dead and some 380,000 homeless.

▸ Film director Roman Polanski is arrested in Switzerland in connection with a 1977 sex-offense conviction in the US, from where he fled before being sentenced.

27 Sep The foreign ministers of India and Pakistan agree that the countries should resume negotiations over their differences but fail to agree on when such talks might begin; India wishes to see more concrete action in Pakistan against the organizers of the terrorist attack in Mumbai (Bombay) in 2008.

28 Sep As tens of thousands of people demonstrate in an association football (soccer) stadium to demand democracy in Guinea, guard troops embark on a brutal rampage during which they open fire on the rally, killing some 157 people.

▸ The large utility company Exelon announces that it will leave the US Chamber of Commerce because of the chamber's opposition to government policies to limit greenhouse-gas emissions; it is the second major utility to take the step.

QUOTE OF THE MONTH

❝ *This is a savagery that can't be explained. What's going on with us here is horrible. The people are in shock here.* ❞

—Thierno Maadjou Sow of the Guinean Organization for Human Rights, on the massacre of pro-democracy demonstrators in Conakry, 28 September

---

29 Sep A magnitude-8.0 earthquake takes place under the South Pacific Ocean about the same distance from both American Samoa and Samoa, causing a tsunami that damages both island groups as well as Tonga and leaves at least 190 people, most of them in Samoa, dead.

30 Sep A magnitude-7.6 earthquake strikes some 50 km (30 mi) off the coast of Padang, Indonesia, collapsing buildings and killing at least 1,100 people.

▸ To the shock of all concerned, the Penske Automotive Group ceases talks with the carmaker General Motors to acquire its Saturn unit; as a result, Saturn models will be discontinued, and all 350 Saturn dealerships will close.

October 2009

1 Oct In a significant constitutional development, the first-ever Supreme Court of the United Kingdom is sworn in in London; the independent body replaces the Appellate Committee of the House of Lords.

▸ The Roscoe Wind Complex, with 627 turbines the world's largest wind farm, begins operations in Texas, generating 781.5 MW of electricity.

▸ A team of scientists reports the finding of a new hominin species, exemplified by a nearly complete skeleton dating from 4.4 million years ago in Ethiopia; the skeleton, dubbed "Ardi" and classified as *Ardipithecus ramidus*, is of a species that lived after the human line diverged from that of chimpanzees and has features that resemble those of extinct apes.

2 Oct At its meeting in Copenhagen, the International Olympic Committee chooses Rio de Janeiro as the site of the Olympic Games to be held in summer 2016.

▸ Voters in Ireland take part in a second referendum on the Lisbon Treaty to change the governing structure of the European Union; this time the pact is overwhelmingly approved.

3 Oct Flood levels in the Indian states of Karnataka and Andhra Pradesh begin to recede after astonishingly heavy rains that left at least 221 people dead in Karnataka and 63 dead in Andhra Pradesh.

QUOTE OF THE MONTH

❝ *My message today is very simple: Thank you, Ireland. Ireland has given Europe a new chance.* ❞

—José Manuel Barroso, president of the European Commission, on learning that Ireland had approved the Lisbon Treaty, 3 October

---

4 Oct Mohamed ElBaradei, head of the International Atomic Energy Agency, says that Iran has agreed to allow nuclear inspectors to visit its newly disclosed facility in Qom and that it will engage in talks about exporting low-enriched uranium to be made into fuel for medical nuclear reactors.

▶ With his win in the Prix de l'Arc de Triomphe, Irish colt Sea The Stars wins his sixth consecutive Group 1 race and becomes the only horse to have won the 2,000 Guineas, the Derby, and the Prix de l'Arc de Triomphe.

5 Oct The Nobel Prize for Physiology or Medicine is awarded to Elizabeth Blackburn, Carol Greider, and Jack Szostak of the US for their discoveries about the functioning of telomeres (structures at the ends of chromosomes) and of the enzyme telomerase.

▶ The first authorized sequel to the Winnie-the-Pooh books by A.A. Milne, *Return to the Hundred Acre Wood,* written by David Benedictus and illustrated by Mark Burgess, goes on sale.

6 Oct In Stockholm the Nobel Prize for Physics is awarded to Charles Kao of the UK for his work in developing the light-carrying properties of fiber-optic cables and to Americans Willard Boyle and George Smith for their invention of the charge-coupled device, the first digital sensor.

▶ The Man Booker Prize goes to British writer Hilary Mantel for her historical novel *Wolf Hall.*

7 Oct NASA reports that its Spitzer Space Telescope has discovered a large and tenuous infrared ring around the edge of Saturn's system of rings and moons; this ring circles in the opposite direction from most of the rings and moons of the planet and is thought to be made of dust from the moon Phoebe.

▶ The Nobel Prize for Chemistry is awarded to Venkatraman Ramakrishnan of the UK, Thomas Steitz of the US, and Ada Yonath of Israel for their research on the atomic structure and function of the ribosome, a cellular structure that transcribes DNA to make protein.

8 Oct The US Department of the Interior withdraws permission to drill for gas and oil on 60 of 77 drilling sites on public land in Utah that were opened for drilling in the last few weeks of the administration of former president George W. Bush.

▶ The Nobel Prize for Literature is awarded to Romanian-born German writer Herta Müller.

9 Oct The Nobel Peace Prize is awarded to US Pres. Barack Obama.

▶ The Phoenix Mercury defeats the Indiana Fever 94–86 in game five of the finals to win the Women's National Basketball Association championship by three games to two.

10 Oct In Zürich the foreign ministers of Armenia and Turkey ceremonially sign an agreement to establish diplomatic relations and to open their borders.

▶ With his first-place finish in the Indy 300 race in Homestead FL, Scottish driver Dario Franchitti wins the overall IndyCar drivers' championship.

11 Oct Pope Benedict XVI canonizes five saints, among them Father Damien, who cared for victims of leprosy in Hawaii in 1873–89, and Jeanne Jugan, who helped found the Little Sisters of the Poor.

▶ The US defeats the International team 19½–14½ to win the Presidents Cup in team golf.

12 Oct The minister of natural resources for the Kurdistan area of Iraq posts a letter on the Kurdish government Web site stating that no further oil will be pumped in Kurdistan for export until the Iraqi government has paid the foreign companies that are pumping the oil.

▶ The Nobel Memorial Prize in Economic Sciences goes to Elinor Ostrom and to Oliver E. Williamson, both of the US, for their respective work in the area of economic governance.

13 Oct A group of government ministers from Turkey and Syria, in meetings held in Aleppo, Syria, and Gaziantep, Turkey, sign several agreements on a range of issues, including the removal of visa requirements, the use of water from the Euphrates River, and a pipeline project.

14 Oct The Dow Jones Industrial Average closes at 10,015.86, its first close above 10,000 since October 2008.

▶ The NASCAR Hall of Fame in Charlotte NC announces its first five inductees: drivers Richard Petty, Dale Earnhardt, and Junior Johnson, NASCAR founder Bill France, Sr., and his son, Bill France, Jr., who led NASCAR for close to three decades.

15 Oct Iraqi Prime Minister Nuri al-Maliki and Turkish Prime Minister Recep Tayyip Erdogan sign pacts on cooperation on oil and gas exports and sharing water from the Euphrates River, among other agreements.

▶ A family in Fort Collins CO reports that their six-year-old son is stranded inside a runaway helium balloon, and a large rescue effort is mounted; the boy is found safe at home, however, and it is later learned that the event was a hoax staged by a family that wanted to star in a reality television show.

16 Oct An official in the southern region of Sudan says that an agreement has been reached on specifications for an independence referendum to take place in January 2011.

▶ The US government reports that the budget deficit for the fiscal year that ended on 1 October reached US$1.4 trillion, some 10% of GDP; it has not been so large since 1945.

17 Oct The Pakistani military begins a long-planned major ground offensive against militants in South Waziristan.

▶ An underwater cabinet meeting is held in Maldives to dramatize the very real danger that sea-level rise caused by global warming will drown the archipelago country.

18 Oct With a fifth-place finish at the Brazilian Grand Prix, British driver Jenson Button secures the Formula 1 automobile racing drivers' championship.

19 Oct In Afghanistan the Electoral Complaints Commission orders that votes from 210 polling stations be discounted; this leaves Pres. Hamid Karzai short of 50% of votes cast, making a runoff election necessary.

20 Oct The Vatican announces that members of the Anglican Communion who are unhappy with their church may join the Roman Catholic Church in personal ordinariates, which will allow them to retain some Anglican traditions.

21 Oct The value of the US dollar falls to US$1.50 against the euro.

22 Oct In Tokyo the Japan Art Association awards the Praemium Imperiale to Austrian pianist Alfred Brendel, British sculptor Richard Long, British architect Zaha Hadid, British playwright Tom Stoppard, and Japanese photographer Hiroshi Sugimoto.

23 Oct Pres. Vaclav Klaus of the Czech Republic accepts a compromise that will exempt his country from a rule under the Lisbon Treaty that he feared could allow families of some three million Germans expelled from what was then Czechoslovakia after World War II to make property claims in the Czech Republic.

24 Oct In Melbourne celebrated trainer Bart Cummings's colt So You Think wins the Cox Plate under jockey Glen Boss.

25 Oct Sébastien Loeb of France secures a record sixth successive world rally championship automobile racing drivers' title with his first-place finish in the Wales Rally GB.

26 Oct The 12th annual Mark Twain Prize for American Humor is awarded to comedian Bill Cosby in a ceremony at the John F. Kennedy Center for the Performing Arts in Washington DC.

27 Oct The death of 8 American soldiers in combat in Afghanistan brings the total number of US troops killed in the country in October to 53; it is the highest monthly death toll since the war began in 2001.

28 Oct NASA makes a successful test launch of the Ares I-X, a prototype of a manned launcher that is being developed to replace the space shuttle.

29 Oct Under pressure from the US, Roberto Micheletti, the de facto leader of Honduras, agrees to allow ousted president Manuel Zelaya to complete his term of office as the head of a unity government.

▶ The US Department of Commerce reports that the country's economy grew 3.5% in the third fiscal quarter of 2009, which means that the US has officially emerged from recession.

30 Oct US Pres. Barack Obama signs an order ending a ban first put in place in 1987 on the entry into the US of people who test positive for HIV, the virus that causes AIDS.

▶ At its annual meeting in Seoul, the board of the Internet Corporation for Assigned Names and Numbers (ICANN) votes to permit domain names written in non-Latin alphabets.

31 Oct US Secretary of State Hillary Rodham Clinton meets separately with Palestinian leader Mahmoud Abbas and with Israeli Prime Minister Benjamin Netanyahu in an attempt to persuade them to engage in peace negotiations.

November 2009

1 Nov In Afghanistan, opposition presidential candidate Abdullah Abdullah announces his withdrawal from the runoff election scheduled for 7 November, saying that Pres. Hamid Karzai has failed to make the changes necessary to assure a free and fair election.

QUOTE OF THE MONTH

" *I hoped there would be a better process. But it is final. I will not participate in the November 7 elections.* *"*

—Opposition candidate Abdullah Abdullah, announcing his withdrawal from the runoff presidential election in Afghanistan, 1 November

---

▶ Meb Keflezighi of the US wins the New York City Marathon with a time of 2 hr 9 min 15 sec, while Ethiopia's Derartu Tulu is the fastest woman, with a time of 2 hr 28 min 52 sec.

2 Nov Hamid Karzai is officially declared the winner of the Afghan presidential election; US Pres. Barack Obama tells him that he must now take action against corruption in the government and against the drug trade in the country.

▶ The Ford Motor Co. announces earnings of US$997 million in its third fiscal quarter; the carmaker also says that it made a profit in the North American market for the first time since 2005.

3 Nov Pres. Vaclav Klaus of the Czech Republic signs the Lisbon Treaty; the Czech Republic is the last of the European Union's member states to ratify the document, which creates a new governing structure for the organization.

▶ American investor Warren Buffet agrees to buy the Burlington Northern Santa Fe railroad company.

4 Nov An Italian court convicts in absentia 23 Americans, most of them CIA operatives, of having kidnapped Muslim cleric Osama Moustafa Hassan Nasr in 2003 in Milan, whence he was sent to Egypt as part of the CIA practice of rendition.

▶ In the World Series, the New York Yankees defeat the Philadelphia Phillies 7–3 in game six to win the Major League Baseball championship.

5 Nov At the Ft. Hood US Army post in Texas, a man identified as Maj. Nidal Malik Hasan, an army psychiatrist, goes on a shooting rampage; 13 people are killed and at least 28 wounded.

▶ At the Latin Grammy Awards in Las Vegas, Puerto Rican hip-hop and reggaeton act Calle 13 wins five awards, including album of the year for *Los de atrás vienen conmigo* and record of the year for "No hay nadie como tú" (Calle 13 featuring Café Tacuba).

6 Nov The US Department of Labor releases figures showing that the country's unemployment rate rose to 10.2% in October; it is the first time since 1983 that the rate has been in double digits.

7 Nov The Yomiuri Giants defeat the Hokkaido Nippon-Ham Fighters 2–0 in game six to win baseball's Japan Series.

▶ The Breeders' Cup Classic Thoroughbred horse race is won by Zenyatta at Santa Anita Park in Arcadia CA; Zenyatta is the first female horse to win the race.

8 Nov At the Forum on China-Africa Cooperation in Ra's Nasrani (Sharm el-Sheikh), Egypt, Chinese Prime Minister Wen Jiabao offers US$10 billion in low-interest development loans to African countries and pledges assistance in addressing global warming in Africa.

9 Nov The 20th anniversary of the fall of the Berlin Wall is celebrated in Paris and in Berlin, where stylized dominoes symbolize the event.

▶ National Hockey League players Brett Hull, Luc Robitaille, Brian Leetch, and Steve Yzerman, executive Lou Lamoriello, broadcaster John Davidson, and journalist Dave Molinari are inducted into the Hockey Hall of Fame in Toronto.

10 Nov Joe Cada of Michigan wins the World Series of Poker; at 21, he is the youngest winner of the card game tournament.

11 Nov The day after the signing of an agreement between the Seychelles and the European Union to allow EU forces to seek and detain Somali pirates off the Seychelles, a Greek container ship is seized by pirates in those waters.

12 Nov Election officials of the Palestinian Authority announce that the presidential and legislative elections scheduled for January 2010 will have to be postponed because of the lack of cooperation by

Hamas, which rules Gaza, with election preparations in the territory.

13 Nov Prime Minister Recep Tayyip Erdogan of Turkey announces a plan to allow the use of the Kurdish language in broadcast media and to restore the original Kurdish names of cities that had had their names changed to Turkish ones.

▶ NASA scientists report that an experiment in which it crashed a satellite onto the surface of the Moon on 9 October yielded, among other results, evidence of at least 98.4 liters (26 gal) of water.

14 Nov In Las Vegas Manny Pacquiao of the Philippines defeats Miguel Cotto of Puerto Rico in a technical knockout in the 12th round to win the World Boxing Organization welterweight title, his seventh title in as many different weight classes.

▶ In a tournament in Moscow, Magnus Carlsen of Norway becomes at age 18 the youngest person to hold the number one ranking in chess when he defeats Peter Leko of Hungary.

15 Nov US Pres. Barack Obama attends a summit meeting of the Association of Southeast Asian Nations (ASEAN) in Singapore, where he also engages in substantive talks with Russian Pres. Dmitry Medvedev and attends Asia-Pacific Economic Cooperation (APEC) talks.

16 Nov The automobile manufacturer General Motors announces that it will begin paying back to the US government some of the US$50 billion it was given to keep it from going under.

17 Nov Israel announces that plans to build 900 housing units in a part of Jerusalem that Palestinians believe belongs to them have advanced closer to approval.

18 Nov The National Book Award for fiction is presented to Colum McCann for *Let the Great World Spin.*

19 Nov Belgian Prime Minister Herman Van Rompuy is elected to become the first president of the European Council under the Lisbon Treaty when it enters into force in December.

20 Nov Officials at Britain's University of East Anglia acknowledge that hackers have taken 13 years of e-mail messages from the servers of its Climatic Research Unit and made them public; many of the e-mails reveal contempt for those who are skeptical of the evidence for man-made global warming, and such skeptics say other e-mails show willingness on the part of the university researchers to manipulate data.

22 Nov After the final auto race of the season, Jimmie Johnson is crowned winner of the NASCAR drivers' championship for a record fourth year in a row.

▶ Real Salt Lake wins the Major League Soccer title with a 5–4 victory in a penalty shoot-out over the Los Angeles Galaxy in the MLS Cup in Seattle.

23 Nov In Maguindanao province on Mindanao island in the Philippines, in what appears to be part of a feud between clans, members of the entourage of a gubernatorial candidate, including relatives and journalists, are abducted and massacred; the dead number at least 57.

24 Nov At the National Museum of Iraq, Eric Schmidt, CEO of Internet company Google, announces a plan to make digital images of every artifact held by the museum, which is open to invited scholars but not the public, and make the images freely available.

25 Nov The government of Dubai in the United Arab Emirates and the conglomerate Dubai World ask to put off debt repayments for six months; the action causes a shock wave in the world's stock markets.

▶ Israeli Prime Minister Benjamin Netanyahu announces a planned 10-month moratorium on new construction of housing in Jewish settlements in the West Bank.

26 Nov Andal Ampatuan, Jr., the mayor of the Philippine city of Datu Unsay, surrenders to authorities in connection with the massacre of supporters of a rival politician three days earlier; 20 others have also been arrested.

▶ South Korea's Truth and Reconciliation Commission reveals that in the opening months of the Korean War, at least 4,900 civilians who had been made to join what was called the National Guidance League—for anticommunistic reeducation—were executed by the South Korean military and police forces.

27 Nov The governing board of the International Atomic Energy Agency, meeting in Vienna, passes a resolution demanding that Iran immediately stop work at its nuclear enrichment plant in Qom.

▶ Golf star Tiger Woods crashes his car into a fire hydrant and a neighbor's tree during a possible domestic dispute in Florida; in the following weeks his personal life begins to unravel as infidelities are made public.

28 Nov Rwanda becomes the 54th member of the Commonwealth of Nations.

29 Nov In a referendum, voters in Switzerland ban the construction of minarets in the country.

30 Nov A preliminary report is issued that shows the inflation rate in the euro zone In November to have reached 0.6%, its first rise above zero in five months; on 13 November data were released showing that the euro zone is no longer in recession, with 1.6% annualized growth in the third fiscal quarter.

▶ Beams of protons are sent at 1.18 trillion electron volts in the Large Hadron Collider near Geneva, setting a new record for proton acceleration; the previous record, not quite 1 trillion electron volts, was set at the Tevatron collider at Fermilab in Batavia IL.

December 2009

1 Dec US Pres. Barack Obama in a speech at the US Military Academy in West Point NY lays out his plan for the war in Afghanistan, saying that he intends to send 30,000 extra troops in the next few months but will begin pulling the US military out of the country in 2011.

▶ Hearings open at the International Court of Justice in The Hague on a petition by Serbia for the court to find that Kosovo's declaration of independence in 2008 was illegal.

2 Dec Fish and wildlife officials in Illinois begin poisoning a 9.7-km (6-mi) stretch of the Chicago Sanitary and Ship Canal, which links the Mississippi River system with Lake Michigan, in an effort to prevent the invasive Asian carp from reaching the Great Lakes.

3 Dec Shooting breaks out in Conakry, Guinea, possibly between rival factions of the military, and the country's military ruler, Moussa Dadis Camara, is wounded in an apparent assassination attempt.

▶ Gold prices close at a record high of US$1,217.40 an ounce.

4 Dec The US Department of Labor reports that the unemployment rate in November decreased to 10.0% and that only 11,000 jobs were lost during the month.

5 Dec In a case that has riveted Italy, American college student Amanda Knox and her Italian former boyfriend, Raffaele Sollecito, are found guilty of having murdered Knox's British roommate, Meredith Kercher, in 2007.

▶ Spain defeats the Czech Republic 5–0 to win the Davis Cup in men's international team tennis for the second consecutive year.

6 Dec Iraq's legislature reaches a new agreement on a law that will permit national elections to be held in 2010; the law expands the number of seats in the legislature from 275 to 325.

▶ The annual Kennedy Center Honors are presented in Washington DC to jazz musician Dave Brubeck, opera singer Grace Bumbry, filmmaker Mel Brooks, actor Robert De Niro, and rock musician Bruce Springsteen.

7 Dec Britain's Turner Prize is presented in London to artist Richard Wright for work that includes a gold-leaf wall painting; Wright stresses the ephemerality of his work, which is always to be painted over at the conclusion of its exhibition.

8 Dec The World Meteorological Organization releases a preliminary analysis indicating that the first decade of the 21st century has been the warmest decade since measurements began.

▶ In Waimea Bay, Hawaii, 28 surfers compete in the prestigious Quicksilver in Memory of Eddie Aikau big-wave competition; waves sufficiently large to hold the Eddie had not appeared since 2004.

9 Dec After Indian politician K. Chandrasekhar Rao has engaged in a fast for 10 days and people in Hyderabad have staged a general strike, the government accedes to their demands and agrees to begin the process of creating a new state of Telangana from the southern portion of Andhra Pradesh.

10 Dec Lebanon's legislature approves the new government and its policy platform, one part of which allows the militant group Hezbollah to retain its arms.

▶ The 120-m (394-ft) cable-stayed Samuel Beckett Bridge, designed by Santiago Calatrava, opens in Dublin.

11 Dec Leaders of the European Union say that they will provide US$10.5 billion to help less-developed countries address the effects of global warming.

▶ Beleaguered American golf star Tiger Woods announces on his personal Web site that he will take an "indefinite break" from playing professional golf.

12 Dec Authorities in Bangkok seize a North Korean cargo plane loaded with weapons, including missiles, that had stopped to refuel en route to an unknown destination; the UN forbids the export of such weapons from North Korea.

▶ Steer roper Trevor Brazile of Texas wins his seventh all-around cowboy world championship at the 51st annual Wrangler National Finals Rodeo in Las Vegas.

13 Dec Sergei V. Bagapsh is reelected president of the separatist region of Abkhazia in Georgia; Georgia views the election as invalid, as ethnic Georgians living in Abkhazia are denied the vote.

14 Dec Chinese Pres. Hu Jintao ceremonially opens a natural-gas pipeline that runs from Turkmenistan through Kazakhstan and Uzbekistan into China's autonomous region of Xinjiang.

15 Dec The members of the Gulf Cooperation Council at a summit meeting in Kuwait agree to launch a single currency similar to the euro in the region; the first step will be the creation of a monetary council in 2010.

▶ In return for foreign aid from Russia, Nauru becomes the fourth country to recognize Abkhazia in Georgia as an independent country; the following day it extends recognition to South Ossetia as well.

▶ In Everett WA the Boeing 787 Dreamliner makes its first test flight.

16 Dec Pakistan's Supreme Court rules as unconstitutional an amnesty created in 2007 for politicians charged with corruption; the decision affects some 6,000 people, including Pres. Asif Ali Zardari.

17 Dec The Yemeni military conducts strikes against al-Qaeda bases in the mountainous area of Abyan and in Sanaa; at least 34 militants are reportedly killed.

18 Dec At international climate talks in Copenhagen, the US, China, India, Brazil, and South Africa forge an agreement that calls for developed countries to reduce their greenhouse-gas emissions and to provide financial assistance to help less-developed countries monitor and report their greenhouse-gas emissions.

> **QUOTE OF THE MONTH**
>
> 66 *This progress did not come easily, and we know that this progress alone is not enough.* 99
>
> —US Pres. Barack Obama, announcing a limited agreement at the UN conference on climate change in Copenhagen, 18 December

▶ A law goes into effect permitting citizens of 25 of the member countries of the European Union to travel freely among those countries without the need for a visa.

19 Dec Over the objections of the US and the UN, Cambodia deports to China 20 Uighurs who had sought asylum in Cambodia.

20 Dec A large protest by Maoists and their sympathizers in Kathmandu, Nepal, is met by riot police, and fighting breaks out; some 70 people are arrested.

21 Dec Cambodia signs several agreements with China that involve investments by China in Cambodia worth some US$850 million.

▶ The legislature of Mexico City passes a law giving same-sex couples the same rights as opposite-sex couples, including the rights to marry, adopt, and inherit.

22 Dec Serbia applies for membership in the European Union.

23 Dec The UN Security Council imposes sanctions on Eritrea, saying that it supports Islamic extremist militants in Somalia.

24 Dec Greece's legislature passes an austerity budget in an attempt to rein in the budget deficit.

▶ The Yemeni military makes an air strike against what is believed to be a gathering of al-Qaeda leaders in the southern part of the country; some 30 people are killed.

25 Dec As Northwest Airlines Flight 253 from Amsterdam is approaching its destination of Detroit,

Umar Farouk Abdulmutallab of Nigeria apparently makes an attempt to ignite a powerful explosive that he had concealed in his underwear; he is immediately subdued by passengers and crew and is arrested upon the plane's safe landing in Detroit.

26 Dec During a Shiʿite holiday, clashes take place between antigovernment protesters and government forces in several public squares in Tehran.

27 Dec Legislative elections in which all parties support the government of Pres. Islam Karimov take place in Uzbekistan.

28 Dec *Alfa Romeo* is the first across the finish line and *Two True* is the overall winner of the 2009 Sydney Hobart Yacht Race in Australia.

29 Dec The Piracy Reporting Centre of the International Maritime Bureau reveals that Somali pirates in 2009 attacked 214 vessels, nearly twice the number attacked in 2008, and successfully hijacked 47 of them, 12 of which are still being held.

30 Dec A double agent viewed as a valuable informant blows himself up at a meeting with agents at a CIA base in Afghanistan's Khost province, killing eight CIA employees, a significant loss to operations working against Taliban and al-Qaeda on the border between Afghanistan and Pakistan.

31 Dec By the last bell of the year at the New York Stock Exchange, the Dow Jones Industrial Average has risen 18.8% since the beginning of the year; the Standard & Poor's 500-stock index has risen 23.5%, and the Nasdaq composite has gained 43.9%.

▶ A US federal judge dismisses charges against five former security guards working for what was then Blackwater USA in connection with the shooting deaths of 17 unarmed civilians in Baghdad in September 2007, citing prosecutorial misconduct.

January 2010

1 Jan In the third annual Winter Classic National Hockey League outdoor match, the Boston Bruins defeat the Philadelphia Flyers 2–1 in overtime before a crowd of 38,112 at Boston's Fenway Park.

▶ The yearlong celebration marking the bicentennial of composer Frédéric Chopin's birth begins with a ceremony in his birthplace, Zelazowa Wola, Poland, and a concert in Warsaw.

2 Jan A magnitude-5.3 earthquake in the eastern Pamir Mountains devastates the villages of Rog and Gishkon in Tajikistan; some 20,000 people are left homeless.

3 Jan The United States and the United Kingdom close their embassies in Sanaa, the capital of Yemen, in view of apparent threats from the terrorist organization al-Qaeda in the Arabian Peninsula.

4 Jan The price of a barrel of crude oil closes at US$81.51, its highest price since October 2008.

▶ The world's tallest building is ceremonially opened in Dubai, UAE; the 160-story, 828-m (2,717-ft)-high tower, is given the name Burj Khalifa in honor of the leader of Abu Dhabi, which gave financial assistance to Dubai at the end of 2009.

5 Jan Pres. Ólafur Ragnar Grímsson of Iceland vetoes legislation passed in 2009 to compensate the governments of Britain and the Netherlands for funds they used to repay depositors who lost money when the Icelandic banking system collapsed in late 2008.

6 Jan In Turkmenistan, Turkmen Pres. Gurbanguly Berdymukhammedov and Iranian Pres. Mahmoud Ahmadinejad ceremonially open a natural gas pipeline that runs from Turkmenistan to Iran.

7 Jan The University of Alabama defeats the University of Texas 37–21 in college football's Bowl Championship Series title game in Pasadena CA to win the NCAA Football Bowl Subdivision championship.

8 Jan Switzerland's Federal Administrative Court rules that the Financial Market Supervisory Authority overstepped its authority when it ordered the banking giant UBS to give US investigators financial data on some 300 clients suspected of tax evasion.

▶ Portugal's legislature passes a bill that allows same-sex marriage; if approved by the president, as expected, it will make Portugal the sixth European country to legalize gay marriage.

9 Jan Togo withdraws from the African Cup of Nations association football (soccer) tournament after the team bus was ambushed and three of those aboard, including an assistant coach, were killed en route to a match in Cabinda, Angola.

▶ Indianapolis Colts quarterback Peyton Manning wins a record fourth National Football League Most Valuable Player award.

10 Jan After three days of race riots in Rosarno, Italy, in southern Calabria, some 1,000 guest workers from sub-Saharan Africa have been evacuated to immigrant centers.

▶ Three Christian churches and a convent school are struck by Molotov cocktails in Malaysia, adding to the firebombing of four churches over the previous two days; resentment over a recent Supreme Court ruling that overturned a law preventing members of religions other than Islam from using the term *Allah* to refer to their supreme deity is believed to be behind the attacks.

11 Jan Figures are released showing that China has passed the US to become the largest automobile market in number of vehicles sold; data released a day earlier showed that it has also passed Germany to become the biggest exporter of manufactured goods.

▶ Former St. Louis Cardinals slugger Mark McGwire, who holds the Major League Baseball record for home runs in a single season, publicly admits that he used steroids throughout the 1990s; his record of 70 home runs was set in 1998.

12 Jan A devastating magnitude-7.0 earthquake flattens Port-au-Prince, the capital of Haiti, and the death toll eventually tops 222,570; among the buildings destroyed or heavily damaged are the national cathedral, the presidential palace, those housing the parliament, the tax office, and the Ministries of Commerce and Foreign Affairs, and the headquarters of the UN mission in the country.

▶ The Internet company Google announces that it will cease cooperating with censorship of search results in China and that it may withdraw from China entirely; it cites cyberattacks that took place the previous month, many of which appeared to target Google e-mail accounts of Chinese human rights activists.

13 Jan The UN releases a report saying that in 2009 in Afghanistan 2,412 civilians were killed—a 14% increase from the previous year—and that 1,630 of them were killed by Taliban and other insurgent groups; the figure is the highest since the fall of the Taliban regime in late 2001.

> *Parliament has collapsed. The tax office has collapsed. Schools have collapsed. Hospitals have collapsed.*
>
> —Haitian Pres. René Préval, describing effects of the previous day's earthquake, 13 January

14 Jan Aid begins to trickle in to the decimated city of Port-au-Prince, where Haitian Pres. René Préval says that 7,000 people have been buried in a mass grave, and the death toll is thought to be at least 200,000.

▸ The *Bulletin of the Atomic Scientists* announces at the New York Academy of Sciences that the Doomsday Clock, which illustrates how close mankind is to self-destruction, has been set back one minute, to 11:54 PM, citing international cooperation in nuclear disarmament and agreements to limit greenhouse gas emissions.

15 Jan American banking giant JPMorgan Chase reports that its profit in 2009 was more than double that of 2008 and that it will pay out compensation, including bonuses, totaling US$26.9 billion—about 18% more than in the previous year.

16 Jan The Dakar Rally concludes in Buenos Aires; the winners are Spanish driver Carlos Sainz in a Volkswagen automobile, French driver Cyril Despres on a KTM motorcycle, Russian driver Vladimir Chagin in a Kamaz truck, and Argentine driver Marcos Patronelli in a Yamaha ATV.

17 Jan Violent fighting between Christians and Muslims breaks out in Jos, Nigeria; over the next three days, some 400 people, most of them Muslims, are killed.

▸ At the Golden Globe Awards in Beverly Hills CA, best picture honors go to *Avatar* and *The Hangover;* best director goes to James Cameron for *Avatar.*

18 Jan In the field of children's literature, the Newbery Medal is awarded to Rebecca Stead for her novel *When You Reach Me,* and Jerry Pinkney wins the Caldecott Medal for *The Lion & the Mouse;* the Printz Award for best young-adult book goes to Libba Bray for *Going Bovine.*

▸ At Thoroughbred horse racing's 2009 Eclipse Awards, the four-year-old filly Rachel Alexandra is named Horse of the Year.

19 Jan In Massachusetts, Republican candidate Scott Brown wins election over Democrat Martha Coakley to fill the seat in the US Senate that was long held by Ted Kennedy.

20 Jan A magnitude-6.1 aftershock rattles Port-au-Prince, Haiti, where people continue to die for lack of medical attention; the dearth of infrastructure is one element hampering the efficient deployment of aid.

21 Jan In a politically explosive ruling, the US Supreme Court overturns two previous decisions and rules that spending on political campaigns by corporations is protected free speech and cannot be curtailed by the government.

▸ The carmaker Toyota Motor Corp. issues a recall for 2.3 million cars from model years 2005–10 to fix a reported problem with accelerators' becoming stuck, causing unintended acceleration; in November 2009 Toyota recalled 4.2 million vehicles to address a problem of accelerator pedals' getting stuck under floor mats.

22 Jan US government figures reveal that unemployment rates rose in December 2009 in 43 states, reaching record highs in Delaware, North Carolina, South Carolina, and Florida.

23 Jan British officials say that the owner of ATSC Ltd. has been arrested on fraud charges; hundreds of bomb detectors the company supplied to the Iraqi government have been found to be useless.

24 Jan Heavy rains cause mud slides in the area of Machu Picchu in Peru, killing some five people and cutting off road and rail access to the Inca site; hundreds of stranded visitors have to be airlifted to safety.

▸ Kelly Kulick defeats Chris Barnes 265–195 in the championship match to win the 45th Professional Bowlers Association Tournament of Champions; she is the first woman to win a PBA Tour title.

25 Jan It is reported in China that health officials have removed dairy products from store shelves in Guizhou province after finding that food companies have supplied products tainted with the toxic industrial ingredient melamine.

26 Jan The American Wind Energy Association reports that the capacity of the wind-power industry grew 39% in 2009, adding a record 9,900 MW.

▸ The ticket sales of the movie *Avatar,* directed by James Cameron, reach US$1.86 billion, making it the highest-grossing film in history.

27 Jan In San Francisco, Apple CEO Steven P. Jobs introduces a tablet computer called the iPad; it combines features of laptops, smartphones, and electronic readers.

28 Jan At an international conference on Afghanistan in London, Afghan Pres. Hamid Karzai says that he plans to attempt reconciliation with Taliban members and that it could take as long as 10 years for the Afghan military to be able to take over responsibility from US-led coalition forces.

29 Jan The US Commerce Department reveals that the country's GDP in the last fiscal quarter of 2009 expanded at an annual rate of 5.7%, its fastest expansion since the third quarter of 2003, but that the economy shrank drastically for the year as a whole.

▸ Spain's government proposes broad and deep spending cuts in an effort to decrease its budget deficit; unemployment in Spain in the last fiscal quarter of 2009 is reported at 18.8%.

30 Jan American Serena Williams defeats Justine Henin of Belgium to win the Australian Open women's tennis championship; the following day Roger Federer of Switzerland defeats Briton Andy Murray to take the men's title and extend his record string of Grand Slam victories to 16.

▸ Top awards at the annual Sundance Film Festival in Park City UT go to *Winter's Bone, Restrepo, Happythankyoumoreplease,* and *Waiting for Superman.*

31 Jan Egypt wins the African Cup of Nations in association football (soccer) for a record seventh time when it defeats Ghana 1–0 in the final match in Angola.

▸ At the Grammy Awards in Los Angeles, the top winner is Beyoncé, who wins six awards, including song of the year for "Single Ladies (Put a Ring on It)"; the award for record of the year goes to the Kings of Leon for "Use Somebody"; the album of the year is Taylor Swift's *Fearless;* and the best new artist is the Zac Brown Band.

February 2010

1 Feb UN officials announce that 55 countries, accounting for 78% of global greenhouse gas emissions from energy use, submitted emission-reduction plans to the UN Framework Convention on Climate Change by the deadline set by the Copenhagen Accord; the pledges do not include submissions from Russia or Mexico and are not enough to meet the goals of the agreement.

2 Feb In testimony before the US Senate Armed Services Committee, both Secretary of Defense Robert Gates and Adm. Mike Mullen, chairman of the Joint Chiefs of Staff, support the repeal of the "don't ask, don't tell" policy, in place since 1993, that prevents people who are openly gay from serving in the armed forces.

▶ The British medical journal *The Lancet* retracts a 1998 article that suggested that the combined measles, mumps, and rubella childhood vaccination is a cause of autism.

3 Feb *Walking Man I,* a bronze sculpture by Alberto Giacometti, sells at Sotheby's auction house for £65,001,250 (about US$103,675,000), a new world record price for a work of art sold at auction.

4 Feb The Democratic Unionist Party members of Northern Ireland's legislature approve a government agreement negotiated with Sinn Fein to transfer police and justice functions to local control on 12 April.

▶ Indian linguist Anvita Abbi reports that with the 26 January death of Boa Sr, the last known speaker of the Andamanese language of Bo, the language, thought to be among the oldest in the world and to have originated in Africa, is extinct.

5 Feb The US Department of Labor reports that the unemployment rate in January fell to 9.7% though 20,000 jobs were lost from the economy during the same period.

6 Feb In Northern Ireland, the Irish National Liberation Army declares that it has surrendered its weapons; of the groups that signed the 1997 truce bringing peace to the province, it is the last to lay down its arms.

▶ A winter storm that began the previous day leaves the mid-Atlantic US states buried in snow, with more than 51 cm (20 in) in Washington DC and a record 76 cm (30 in) in Baltimore MD; the governors of Delaware, Maryland, and Virginia declare states of emergency.

7 Feb In Miami Gardens FL, the New Orleans Saints defeat the Indianapolis Colts 31–17 to win the National Football League's Super Bowl XLIV; it is the first time the Saints have won the championship.

▶ The Escogido Lions (Leones) of the Dominican Republic defeat the Caracas Lions (Leones) of Venezuela 7–4 to win baseball's Caribbean Series.

8 Feb Nielsen figures show that some 106.5 million people watched the Super Bowl on 7 February, passing the 105.97 million people who watched the series finale of the television program *M*A*S*H* to make the football game the most-watched TV program in American history.

9 Feb Haiti's government raises the death toll from the earthquake that took place on 12 January to 230,000.

10 Feb Iran slows Internet service and shuts down text messaging in an effort to prevent large opposition demonstrations for the following day's celebration of the anniversary of the Islamic Revolution.

11 Feb At a summit meeting in Brussels, EU leaders agree to aid Greece in order to safeguard the euro but, at the behest of Germany, offer no specifics beyond monitoring the country's austerity plan.

▶ Pres. 'Ali 'Abdallah Salih of Yemen announces an immediate cease-fire with al-Houthi rebels; a rebellion had flared up in late 2009.

12 Feb The XXI Olympic Winter Games officially open in Vancouver, BC, Canada; the opening ceremony is overshadowed by the death earlier in the day of Georgian athlete Nodar Kumaritashvili during a practice run for the luge competition.

QUOTE OF THE MONTH

" *He had a dream to participate in the Olympic Games. He trained hard, and he had this fatal accident. I have no words to say what we feel.* "

—International Olympic Committee president Jacques Rogges after the accidental death of Georgian luger Nodar Kumaritashvili hours before the opening ceremony of the Vancouver Winter Olympics, 12 February

---

13 Feb Afghan, US, and British military forces begin a major offensive to take the town and area of Marjah in Afghanistan from the Taliban; Marjah is a Taliban stronghold.

▶ The first gold medal of the Vancouver Winter Olympics is awarded to Simon Ammann of Switzerland in the normal hill individual ski jump; a week later Ammann also wins gold in the large hill final.

14 Feb In Daytona Beach FL, the 52nd running of the Daytona 500 NASCAR race is won by Jamie McMurray.

▶ After two and a half years of court battles, American challenger BMW Oracle, owned by Larry Ellison, wins the America's Cup yacht race 2–0 in a head-to-head competition; its yacht, *USA-17,* comes in five minutes ahead of Swiss defender *Alinghi 5* in the final race off the coast of Valencia, Spain.

15 Feb Gov. Felix Camacho of the US territory of Guam issues an executive order to government agencies to henceforth in all official communications refer to the island territory as Guahan, which is believed to reflect the island's original name in the Chamorro language.

16 Feb The US military reports that the number of US troops in Iraq has dropped to 98,000; it is the first time since the invasion in 2003 that there have been fewer than 100,000 American soldiers in Iraq.

▶ Roundtown Mercedes of Maryscot wins Best in Show at the Westminster Kennel Club's 134th dog show; the Scottish terrier, known as Sadie, becomes the first dog to take the Triple Crown, having previously won at the National Dog Show and the AKC/Eukanuba National Championship.

17 Feb Russian Pres. Dmitry Medvedev and Sergey V. Bagapsh, president of Georgia's separatist republic of Abkhazia, announce an agreement for a Russian military base to be established in Abkhazia.

18 Feb A military coup d'état takes place in Niger, and the increasingly unpopular Pres. Mamadou Tandja is taken into military custody; the coup leader is named as Salou Djibo.

▶ A software engineer, apparently frustrated by a provision of tax law pertaining to his field, crashes his small private airplane into the office building of the US Internal Revenue Service in Austin TX, killing himself and one other person.

19 Feb Pope Benedict XVI approves sainthood for Sister Mary of the Cross (Mary Helen MacKillop), founder of the Congregation of the Sisters of St. Joseph of the Sacred Heart; she will be Australia's first Roman Catholic saint.

20 Feb Short-track speed skater Apolo Anton Ohno becomes the most decorated American Winter Olympian in history with his seventh career medal, a bronze in the men's 1,000-m final; on 26 February he adds an eighth Olympic medal, also bronze, in the men's 5,000-m relay.

▶ The Turkish-German film *Bal* (*Honey*), directed by Semih Kaplanoglu, wins the Golden Bear at the Berlin International Film Festival.

21 Feb Israel's air force introduces a fleet of Heron TP drones with wingspans of 26 m (86 ft) that are capable of remaining in the air for a full day and flying as far as the Persian Gulf.

▶ Argentine Foreign Minister Jorge Taiana asks the Rio Group of Latin American and Caribbean countries to issue a statement in condemnation of plans by Britain to drill for oil in the seabed surrounding the Falkland Islands in the South Atlantic Ocean; Argentina has opposed the plan with threats and by insisting that ships ask permission to travel through its waters en route to the Falklands.

22 Feb The publishing company Macmillan introduces DynamicBooks, an electronic textbook that professors can freely modify.

23 Feb The winner of the Emporis Skyscraper Award, given annually to a building at least 100 m (328 ft) in height and completed within the award year, is

announced as Aqua, an 81-story residential and hotel building in Chicago.

▶ Leaders of the Caribbean Community (CARICOM) agree to join with Latin American countries to create a new regional grouping provisionally called the Community of Latin American and Caribbean States; details of the proposed new bloc are to be determined at a meeting in July 2011.

24 Feb Akio Toyoda, head of the Toyota Motor Corp., testifies before the US House Committee on Oversight and Government Reform about his company's response to the problem of sticking accelerators in some models of its cars.

25 Feb The US National Medal of Arts is awarded to, among others, actor and director Clint Eastwood, musician Bob Dylan, architect Maya Lin, soprano Jessye Norman, and composer and conductor John Williams.

▶ In the first visit by a French president to Rwanda since the 1994 genocide, Pres. Nicolas Sarkozy visits Kigali, where he admits that France had been mistaken in its reaction to the genocide and agrees on cooperation on a range of subjects with Rwandan Pres. Paul Kagame.

26 Feb The US government-owned mortgage backer Fannie Mae reports that it lost US$16.3 billion in the final quarter of 2009 and asks for US$15.3 billion from the US Treasury; the number of delinquencies on mortgages continues to rise.

27 Feb A magnitude-8.8 earthquake strikes central Chile, causing major damage in the area around Concepción, and is followed by a tsunami, which devastates Talcahuano and Constitución; at least 577 people are killed and some 800,000 are left homeless.

28 Feb On the final day of the Winter Olympics in Vancouver, Canada defeats the US 3–2 in overtime to win the gold medal in men's ice hockey.

March 2010

1 Mar The UN World Food Programme reports that, last week, pirates in Somalia seized three trucks that had just unloaded food aid; it is the first incidence of land piracy in Somalia.

2 Mar Guatemala's national police chief and its antinarcotics unit leader are arrested on drug-trafficking charges stemming from a shootout the previous April between rival drug gangs over stolen cocaine.

3 Mar Meeting in Cairo, the foreign ministers of the Arab League endorse a plan for US-mediated indirect peace talks between Israeli and Palestinian officials.

4 Mar US Secretary of State Hillary Clinton announces that US aid to Honduras, which was suspended after the overthrow of its president in 2009, will be resumed.

▶ Both the Bank of England and the European Central Bank decide to leave their benchmark interest rates unchanged; the level is 0.5% for the Bank of England and 1.0% for the European Central Bank.

5 Mar A study published in the journal *Science* describes new research on Arctic undersea permafrost that has been found to be melting, causing the release of heat-trapping methane gas into the atmosphere.

▶ Biologists in California's Pinnacles National Monument confirm the presence of the first condor egg laid by wild condors within the park in more than 100 years.

6 Mar Russia's Federal Security Service reports that militant leader Aleksandr Tikhomirov (nom de guerre Said Buryatsky) was killed in a raid in the republic of Ingushetiya several days previously and that proof had been found that Tikhomirov's organization was behind several recent attacks, including the bombing of the Nevsky Express train in November 2009.

7 Mar Closely contested, pivotal legislative elections take place in Iraq; it is expected to take weeks to tally the vote.

▶ At the 82nd Academy Awards presentation, hosted by Steve Martin and Alec Baldwin, Oscars are won by, among others, *The Hurt Locker* (best picture) and its director, Kathryn Bigelow (the first woman to win the award for best director), and actors Jeff Bridges, Sandra Bullock, Christoph Waltz, and Mo'Nique.

8 Mar The government of Myanmar (Burma) declares that it has completed an election law; the law sets draconian limits on political participation, including conditions that would bar the candidacy of opposition leader Aung San Suu Kyi.

9 Mar China and India formally agree to join the Copenhagen Accord, the nonbinding international agreement to attempt to ameliorate global warming that was arrived at in December 2009.

▶ The Central and Southern Andes GPS Project reports that the 27 February earthquake in Chile caused Santiago to move 28 cm (11 in) and Concepción 3 m (10 ft) to the west.

▶ The US$250,000 A.M. Turing Award for excellence in computer science is granted to Chuck Thacker for his pioneering work as a cocreator of the early Alto personal computer and of Ethernet networking.

10 Mar China reports a 46% year-on-year increase in its exports in February; this is a much larger increase than was expected.

▶ The US Department of Labor reports that unemployment increased in 30 states in January, with new records set in California, South Carolina, Florida, North Carolina, and Georgia; the highest unemployment rate, 14.3%, is in Michigan.

11 Mar In New York City the winners of the National Book Critics Circle Awards are announced as Hilary Mantel for *Wolf Hall* (fiction), Richard Holmes for *The Age of Wonder: How the Romantic Generation Discovered the Beauty and Terror of Science* (nonfiction), Blake Bailey for *Cheever: A Life* (biography), Diana Athill for *Somewhere Towards the End: A Memoir* (autobiography), Rae Armantrout for *Versed* (poetry), and Eula Biss for *Notes from No Man's Land: American Essays* (criticism); Joyce Carol Oates is granted the Ivan Sandrof Lifetime Achievement Award.

12 Mar Russian Prime Minister Vladimir Putin meets in New Delhi with Indian Prime Minister Manmohan Singh; the leaders sign agreements to cooperate on nuclear, military, and space projects.

13 Mar US Pres. Barack Obama proposes a number of changes to the No Child Left Behind Act of 2002—changes intended to reduce the focus on testing and to reward top-performing schools, among other reforms.

14 Mar Tens of thousands of supporters of former Thai prime minister Thaksin Shinawatra, known as Red Shirts, march in Bangkok to demand the resignation of Thailand's government.

▶ Katie Spotz, age 22, lands in Georgetown, Guyana, after having left Dakar, Senegal, on 3 January and rowed for 4,533.5 km (2,817 mi) across the Atlantic Ocean to become the youngest person and first American to row solo across an entire ocean.

15 Mar The government of Haiti releases a report compiled with various international agencies that estimates that some 220,000 people died in the earthquake in January, with a further 869 people missing, that some 105,000 houses were destroyed and 1,300 schools and 50 hospitals were rendered unusable, and that it will need US$11.5 billion over the next three years for reconstruction.

▶ In a ceremony in New York City, the Rock and Roll Hall of Fame inducts musician Jimmy Cliff, the groups Abba, Genesis, the Hollies, and the Stooges, songwriters Barry Mann, Cynthia Weil, Ellie Greenwich, Jeff Barry, Jesse Stone, Mort Shuman, and Otis Blackwell, and producer David Geffen.

16 Mar Lance Mackey wins the Iditarod Trail Sled Dog Race for a record fourth consecutive year, passing under the Burled Arch in Nome, Alaska, after a journey of 8 days 23 hours 59 minutes 9 seconds.

17 Mar A US Court of Appeals upholds an injunction barring the prosecution of minor children for "sexting"—transmitting sexually suggestive text messages and images by cell phone or over the Internet.

▶ The Dresden Historians' Commission publishes a report after five years of research on the 1945 Allied bombings of Dresden, Germany, during World War II; it concluded that about 25,000 people were killed, fewer than had been widely believed.

18 Mar At a meeting in Doha, Qatar, the Convention on International Trade in Endangered Species of

Wild Fauna and Flora rejects US-backed proposals to ban international trade in the severely depleted bluefin tuna and to protect polar bears.

19 Mar India's central bank raises its benchmark repurchase interest rate to 5% from 4.75% after having not raised its rates for almost two years; both Australia and Malaysia previously raised rates in March.

20 Mar Pope Benedict XVI sends a pastoral letter to Roman Catholics in Ireland, offering a passionately worded apology for decades of abuse of children at the hands of Irish clergy and condemning church leaders for having allowed the abuse to go on.

▶ With its 12–10 defeat of England, France wins the Six Nations Rugby Union championship, having achieved a record of 5–0; the previous day the women's championship had gone to England for the fifth consecutive year.

21 Mar In London *Spring Awakening* wins four Laurence Olivier Awards: best new musical, best actor in a musical or entertainment (Aneurin Barnard), best supporting performance in a musical or entertainment (Iwan Rheon), and best sound design.

22 Mar The Internet company Google closes its online search service in mainland China, directing users there to its service in Hong Kong, where search results are not censored, as they were in mainland China.

23 Mar After a long and bruising legislative battle, a sweeping and complex health care reform bill, the Patient Protection and Affordable Care Act, is signed into law by US Pres. Barack Obama.

QUOTE OF THE MONTH

❝ *We have just now enshrined, as soon as I sign this bill, the core principle that everybody should have some basic security when it comes to their health care.* ❞

—US Pres. Barack Obama, on signing
health care reform into law, 23 March

▶ The winner of the PEN/Faulkner Award for Fiction is announced as Sherman Alexie for his story and poem collection *War Dances*.

24 Mar Japan's legislature approves a record ¥92.3 trillion (about US$1 trillion) budget intended to stimulate the economy; the government also announces a reversal of a plan started by former prime minister Junichiro Koizumi to privatize the postal banking system.

▶ A small island in the Bay of Bengal claimed by both India and Bangladesh is reported by the School of Oceanographic Studies in Kolkata (Calcutta) to have disappeared, a victim of rising sea levels.

25 Mar The countries of the euro zone agree on a rescue package for Greece that includes bilateral loans from the members of the grouping and from the International Monetary Fund (IMF), to be used if Greece cannot find funding in the commercial markets; in addition, the European Central Bank announces that it will not tighten lending rules until 2011.

▶ Francisco J. Ayala, a Spanish-born American evolutionary biologist and geneticist, is named the winner of the Templeton Prize for his contributions to affirming the roles of both science and religious faith in advancing human understanding.

26 Mar The results of the 7 March election in Iraq are announced: the Iraqiyah bloc, headed by former prime minister Ayad 'Allawi, wins 91 seats—the highest number won by any party—while the State of Law Coalition, led by Prime Minister Nuri al-Maliki, wins 89 seats; in order to form a government, a coalition must control 163 seats.

▶ A South Korean navy patrol ship near disputed waters west of the Korean peninsula is sunk by what is believed to be a torpedo attack from North Korea; 46 crew members are killed.

27 Mar Gloria De Campeao wins the Dubai World Cup, the world's richest horse race, in a photo finish with Lizard's Desire.

28 Mar Russian Pres. Dmitry Medvedev orders that the Pacific Far East time zone be eliminated and drops a second time zone in central Russia, reducing the number of time zones in the country to nine.

▶ Japanese architects Kazuyo Sejima and Ryue Nishizawa of the Tokyo-based firm SANAA are named winners of the 2010 Pritzker Architecture Prize; among their works are the 21st Century Museum of Contemporary Art in Kanazawa, Japan, and the New Museum of Contemporary Art in New York City.

29 Mar Human Rights Watch reports that in the northeastern Democratic Republic of the Congo, the brutal Ugandan militia the Lord's Resistance Army in December 2009 rounded up and kidnapped hundreds of people from villages outside Niangara, killing at least 320 of them.

▶ After FBI raids in the US states of Indiana, Michigan, and Ohio, indictments are unsealed against nine members of a Michigan-based apocalyptic Christian militia called the Hutaree; the militia is said to have planned to kill police officers in hopes of triggering an antigovernment revolution.

30 Mar For the first time, physicists succeed in creating collisions between subatomic particles in the Large Hadron Collider near Geneva.

31 Mar US Pres. Barack Obama and Secretary of the Interior Ken Salazar unveil proposals to open much of the Atlantic coastline, parts of the eastern Gulf of Mexico, and Alaska's north coast to offshore oil and natural gas drilling.

▶ The US Federal Reserve ends its program, begun in November 2008, of buying mortgage-backed securities; the program was, to date, the Fed's largest single effort to stabilize the economy.

April 2010

1 Apr A law making universal primary education both compulsory and free goes into effect in India.

▶ The US government announces new fuel-efficiency standards for cars and trucks that will require vehicles to reach an average of 35.5 mi per gallon of gas by the 2016 model year, about 10 mi per gallon more efficient than current requirements.

2 Apr The US Consumer Product Safety Commission advises owners of buildings that contain Chinese-made drywall that emits unacceptable levels of hydrogen sulfide to remove and replace not only all such drywall but also all associated electrical systems, gas piping, sprinkler systems, and other components that contain metal; hydrogen sulfide has a corrosive effect on metal.

3 Apr Tens of thousands of antigovernment Red Shirt protesters block the main commercial district in Bangkok, vowing to continue the protest until new elections have been scheduled.

▶ Shortly after departing from the port of Gladstone, the *Shen Neng 1*, a Chinese freighter carrying tons of coal and bunker fuel and traveling 14.5 km (9 mi) outside its shipping lane, runs aground on the Great Barrier Reef off Australia in what is feared to be an ecological catastrophe.

4 Apr A magnitude-7.2 earthquake with its epicenter near the Baja California city of Mexicali, Mexico, causes property damage in both Mexico and southern California and kills two people in Mexicali; though it is an unusually strong earthquake, the damage is fairly light.

5 Apr Apple Inc. reports that more than 300,000 iPads were sold on the initial day of sale of the device.

▶ The National Collegiate Athletic Association championship in men's basketball is won by Duke University, which defeats Butler University 61–59; the following day the University of Connecticut defeats Stanford University 53–47 to win the women's title and become the first team in women's college basketball to have two consecutive undefeated seasons.

6 Apr It is reported that a team of Russian and American scientists working at the Dubna cyclotron particle accelerator on the Volga River in Russia believe that by means of smashing isotopes of calcium into radioactive berkelium, they have produced six atoms of the previously unknown element 117.

7 Apr After a day of fighting in Bishkek, the capital of Kyrgyzstan, between antigovernment protesters and police in which at least 85 people are killed, opposition politicians succeed in forcing Pres. Kurmanbek Bakiyev to flee the city; former foreign minister Roza Otunbayeva is said to be in charge.

▶ Antigovernment Red Shirt protesters invade the parliament building in Bangkok; lawmakers flee, and Thai Prime Minister Abhisit Vejjajiva declares a state of emergency.

8 Apr Pakistan's National Assembly unanimously approves a change to the constitution that repeals many of the changes put in by previous military governments, transfers most authority from the president to the legislature, and gives the North-West Frontier Province a new name: Khyber Pakhtunkhwa.

▶ In a ceremony in Prague, Russian Pres. Dmitry Medvedev and US Pres. Barack Obama sign the New START nuclear arms control treaty.

9 Apr Russia suspends adoptions of Russian children by Americans the day after a seven-year-old boy who had been adopted by an American woman in Tennessee arrived alone in Russia carrying a note from his adoptive mother saying that for reasons of safety she no longer wants to be the child's parent.

▶ US Supreme Court Justice John Paul Stevens announces that he plans to retire at the end of the present term of the court, of which he has been a member since 1975.

10 Apr A Tupolev Tu-154 plane carrying Polish Pres. Lech Kaczynski to a Polish memorial for the 70th anniversary of the Katyn Massacre crashes near Smolensk, Russia, in bad weather, killing all 97 people aboard, among them Kaczynski, several legislators, the chiefs of the army and the navy, and the national bank head.

▸ Thai military forces attempt to break up the antigovernment Red Shirt occupation of the commercial center of Bangkok and are repulsed by the protesters; 25 people are killed in the violence.

11 Apr Leaders of the 16 countries of the euro zone announce that they can offer Greece as much as €30 billion (US$40.5 billion) at 5% interest, in addition to money that the IMF might be able to offer, to help the country meet its debt obligations.

▸ Phil Mickelson of the US wins the Masters golf tournament in Augusta, GA, finishing three strokes ahead of British golfer Lee Westwood.

12 Apr The Dow Jones Industrial Average rises 8.62 points to finish at 11,005.97, its first close above 11,000 points in 19 months.

13 Apr The day after the freighter *Shen Neng 1*, which ran aground on the Great Barrier Reef off Australia on 3 April, was refloated, an Australian government scientist estimates that it could take up to 20 years for the coral reef to recover from the damage; the ship left a scar 3 km (1.9 mi) long and as much as 250 m (820 ft) wide.

▸ The winner of the 2010 Ruth Lilly Poetry Prize is named as Eleanor Ross Taylor.

14 Apr China's Qinghai province, near its border with Sichuan province, is struck by a magnitude-7.1 earthquake, whose epicenter is in Yushu county; the town of Jiegu on the Plateau of Tibet is largely destroyed, and at least 2,260 people perish.

▸ The US Library of Congress announces an agreement to add the public content of the microblogging service Twitter to its archives.

15 Apr Airspace over the British Isles and some airports in France and Germany are closed because of the cloud of silicate ash drifting over Europe from the previous day's eruption of the glacial volcano Eyjafjallajökull in Iceland.

▸ US Pres. Barack Obama orders that rules be issued to hospitals that participate in Medicare or Medicaid that require them to grant designated nonfamily members, including same-sex partners, the same rights to visit hospital patients as those granted to family members.

16 Apr Volcanic ash from the volcano Eyjafjallajökull spreads eastward across northern Europe, expanding the area closed to air travel and thus stranding thousands of passengers and disrupting trade, business, and performance schedules.

▸ The US Department of Labor reports that although 33 states posted gains in employment in March, 17 states saw higher unemployment, with new records set in California, Florida, Nevada, and Georgia and the highest rate, 14.1%, in Michigan.

17 Apr The UN endorses Afghan Pres. Hamid Karzai's appointment of former Supreme Court justice Fazel Ahmed Manawi to head the country's discredited election commission and agrees to a plan to let the UN appoint two (rather than the previous three) members of the five-member Electoral Complaints Commission, whose members have veto power.

18 Apr Dervis Eroglu is elected president of the unilaterally declared Turkish Republic of Northern Cyprus.

▸ The last working sardine cannery in the US, owned by Bumble Bee Foods since 2004 but open for several decades, shuts down in Prospect Harbor ME.

19 Apr Pakistani Pres. Asif Ali Zardari signs into law an amendment to the constitution that makes Pakistan a parliamentary democracy, with more power belonging to the prime minister than to the president.

▸ Arizona's state legislature passes a bill that requires police to ask for documentation from people whom they suspect of being illegal immigrants and to arrest those who fail to produce proof of legality and that makes failure to carry such documents a crime; Gov. Jan Brewer signs it into law on 23 April.

▸ The 114th Boston Marathon is won by Robert Kiprono Cheruiyot of Kenya with a time of 2 hr 5 min 52 sec; the fastest woman is Teyba Erkesso of Ethiopia, who posts a time of 2 hr 26 min 11 sec.

20 Apr The deep-sea oil-drilling rig Deepwater Horizon, leased by energy company BP and working in the Gulf of Mexico some 80 km (50 mi) off the coast of the US state of Louisiana, suddenly explodes in what is thought to be an unprecedented accident; 17 crew members are injured and 11 are lost.

▸ Brazil's electrical regulatory authority grants a consortium of companies the right to build a controversial hydroelectric dam that will be the third largest ever built; the deal to construct the Belo Monte dam, on the Xingu River, a tributary of the Amazon, is approved just a day after a federal judge suspended bidding on the project.

21 Apr Algeria, Mauritania, Mali, and Niger open a joint military headquarters in Tamanrasset, Algeria, in order to coordinate responses to terrorism and crime related to drug trafficking.

▸ The futuristically designed city of Brasília, the capital of Brazil, celebrates its 50th anniversary; though planned for a population of 600,000, the city is home to 2.6 million.

▸ The US unveils a redesigned US$100 bill whose images—designed to make the bill difficult to counterfeit—change in appearance as the bill is manipulated.

22 Apr The oil-drilling rig Deepwater Horizon, which exploded two days previously, suffers more explosions and sinks in the Gulf of Mexico.

▸ Eurostat revises its estimate of Greece's budget deficit in 2009 to 13.6% of GDP, higher than the Greek government's estimate of 12.9%, and the rating agency Moody's downgrades its rating for Greek bonds.

23 Apr Greek Prime Minister Georgios Papandreou formally requests financial aid from his country's euro zone partners and the IMF.

QUOTE OF THE MONTH

❝ We drew up a plan. We took difficult and painful measures. But the markets did not respond. ❞

—Prime Minister Georgios Papandreou of Greece, requesting financial aid from the other euro zone countries, 23 April

---

▸ For the first time since the Eyjafjallajökull volcano in Iceland began erupting on 14 April, two airports in Iceland close because of the dangers to aircraft posed by volcanic dust; some 29% of global aviation has been disrupted by the volcano's eruption.

24 Apr The front half of the South Korean warship that sank on 26 March after an explosion believed to have been caused by a torpedo is lifted from the water; the rear half of the ship was salvaged earlier.

25 Apr Officials reveal that it has been found that the deepwater well drilled by the now-sunken oil rig

Deepwater Horizon is leaking 159,000 liters (42,000 gal) of oil a day into the Gulf of Mexico; BP is attempting to activate a blowout preventer to seal the well 1,525 m (5,000 ft) below the ocean's surface and is using chemical dispersants to break up the oil.

▸ Tsegaye Kebede of Ethiopia wins the London Marathon with a time of 2 hr 5 min 19 sec, and Liliya Shobukhova of Russia is the fastest woman in the race, with a time of 2 hr 22 min 0 sec.

26 Apr Pres. Omar al-Bashir is announced as the winner of presidential elections held in Sudan on 11–15 April; international observers say that the elections fell short of democratic standards.

27 Apr The rating agency Standard & Poor's downgrades Greece's government bonds to junk status.

▸ In spite of brawling and the throwing of eggs and smoke bombs, Ukraine's legislature agrees to extend Russia's lease on a naval base in Sevastapol, Ukraine, for 25 years in return for lower prices on natural gas from Russia.

28 Apr The US Department of the Interior authorizes the construction of the Cape Wind project, which is anticipated to be the country's first offshore wind farm; it is to be built in Nantucket Sound some eight kilometers (five miles) off the coast of Massachusetts.

▸ The IMF pledges to increase the size of the aid package for Greece from €45 billion to as much as €120 billion over three years as it attempts to negotiate deeper cuts in Greece's budget.

29 Apr The day after an announcement that oil from the undersea well drilled by the sunken oil rig Deepwater Horizon is spilling at a rate of 5,000 bbl, or 757,080 liters (200,000 gal), a day—five times the previous estimate—the US government adds resources from the US Navy to the Coast Guard and BP personnel trying to stop the spread of oil.

30 Apr Opening ceremonies for the six-month World Expo, expected to be attended by as many as 70 million people, are held in Shanghai.

May 2010

1 May A smoke-filled Nissan Pathfinder is reported to police by two street vendors who noticed it parked with its engine running near New York City's Times Square; it proves to contain a car bomb that could have caused a massive explosion if it had exploded.

▸ Super Saver, ridden by Calvin Borel, wins the Kentucky Derby by two and a half lengths.

2 May Greece signs an agreement with the European Union and the International Monetary Fund that commits it to deep cuts in the public sector, tax increases, and tax reform in return for bailout funds.

3 May United Airlines announces its purchase of Continental Airlines; the combined company will be the world's largest airline.

▸ In Sheffield, England, Neil Robertson defeats Graeme Dott of Scotland 18–13 to win the world championship in snooker; he is the first Australian to gain the title.

4 May Transportation ministers from the member countries of the EU, meeting in Belgium, agree to accelerate plans for unified control over EU airspace and to develop guidelines for determining what conditions make it unsafe to fly and for responding to such conditions.

5 May The mortgage insurer Freddie Mac, which was taken over by the US federal government in 2008, asks for US$10.6 billion in federal aid, bringing the total amount needed to bail out the entity to US$61.3 billion.

▸ The Washington Post Co. puts the weekly newsmagazine *Newsweek,* which has been published since 1933, up for sale.

6 May In legislative elections in the UK, no single party wins a ruling majority, with the Conservatives taking 306 seats, Labour 258, and the Liberal Democrats 57; this result makes a coalition government necessary for the first time since World War II.

▸ A containment dome is lowered into the Gulf of Mexico by the energy company BP; the company hopes the dome will capture most of the estimated 794,900 liters (210,000 gal) of oil spewing daily from the well drilled by the Deepwater Horizon before the rig exploded and sank in April.

7 May The US Department of Labor reports that the unemployment rate in April rose to 9.9%, although the economy added 290,000 nonfarm jobs, the biggest increase in job creation in four years.

8 May Near the encampment of antigovernment Red Shirt protesters in Bangkok, shooting and explosions kill one police officer and injure five other police officers and two civilians.

9 May The US government announces that the first round of agreed-to indirect talks between Israeli and Palestinian negotiators, with US special envoy George J. Mitchell shuttling between them, has taken place.

▸ Dallas Braden of the Oakland Athletics pitches the 19th perfect game in Major League Baseball history when he dismisses 27 consecutive batters in his team's 4–0 victory over the Tampa Bay Rays.

10 May The member countries of the European Union agree to provide US$560 billion in new loans and US$76 billion under an existing program to shore up countries suffering debt crises.

▸ US Pres. Barack Obama nominates Solicitor General Elena Kagan to replace Justice John Paul Stevens on the Supreme Court.

11 May Conservative leader David Cameron takes office as British prime minister in a Conservative–Liberal Democratic coalition government; Liberal Democratic leader Nick Clegg is to serve as deputy prime minister.

▸ US Secretary of the Interior Ken Salazar announces that the Minerals Management Service, which both regulates offshore oil drilling and leases offshore tracts to oil companies, will be split into separate agencies for the conflicting functions; the agency has been criticized as having been lax in its oversight of safety.

▸ Quarterly filings show that Bank of America, Citigroup, Goldman Sachs, and JPMorgan Chase & Co. all posted perfect quarters, in which each banking entity lost no money in trading on any day of the first quarter of 2010, a highly unusual occurrence.

12 May The price of gold reaches record heights, selling for more than US$1,240 a troy ounce in London.

▸ The Spanish association football (soccer) team Club Atlético de Madrid defeats Fulham FC of Britain 2–1 in extra time to win the inaugural Union des Associations Européennes de Football (UEFA) Europa League title in Hamburg.

13 May The UN General Assembly adds 14 new members to the Human Rights Council, including Angola, Libya, Malaysia, Thailand, and Uganda.

14 May Thai troops move against antigovernment Red Shirt protesters in Bangkok, and protesters fight back; at least 16 people are killed in the confrontation.

▸ After some 13 years of negotiations, Ethiopia, Rwanda, Tanzania, and Uganda sign the Cooperative Framework Agreement in Entebbe, Uganda; the agreement, which Egypt and Sudan declined to sign, is intended to govern the use and sharing of the waters of the Nile River system.

15 May The Thai military continues to press against the antigovernment Red Shirt protesters in Bangkok as the death toll in the three days of confrontation rises to 24; Prime Minister Abhisit Vejjajiva goes on television to explain the government crackdown.

QUOTE OF THE MONTH

❝ *The government cannot turn back. Ending the rally is the only way to prevent calamity.* ❞

—Thai Prime Minister Abhisit Vejjajiva, in a televised address to the country, as the military and Red Shirt protesters clash, 15 May

---

▸ Lookin At Lucky, under jockey Martin Garcia, wins the Preakness Stakes, the second event in US Thoroughbred horse racing's Triple Crown, by three-quarters of a length; Kentucky Derby winner Super Saver finishes eighth.

16 May Iraq's election commission declares that at the conclusion of the partial recount of votes from the 7 March election, the results remain the same, with a very narrow victory for the coalition led by former interim prime minister Ayad 'Allawi.

▸ Engineers from the energy company BP succeed in inserting a tube into the damaged wellhead pipe from which oil is leaking and are able to siphon some of the escaping oil to a drill ship on the surface of the Gulf of Mexico; it is the company's first success in stanching the flow of oil since the 22 April collapse of the drilling platform Deepwater Horizon.

17 May A team of physicists working at the Fermi National Accelerator Laboratory in Batavia IL post online a report describing their finding that particles called neutral B-mesons, which oscillate between a state of matter and a state of antimatter, appear to change to matter more quickly than to antimatter, providing a possible explanation for the apparently inexplicable preponderance of matter over antimatter in the universe.

18 May The US announces that it has reached agreement with Britain, France, Russia, China, and Germany on a new set of proposed sanctions against Iran for its continued uranium enrichment; the sanctions must be voted on by the UN Security Council.

▸ A suicide bomber kills at least five US soldiers in Kabul, bringing the number of US troops killed in the conflict in Afghanistan since the beginning of the war in 2001 above 1,000.

▸ The US National Oceanic and Atmospheric Administration (NOAA) nearly doubles the area in the Gulf of Mexico that is closed to fishing because of the impact of the oil spill unleashed by the collapse of the Deepwater Horizon oil platform in April.

19 May The Thai military moves in to put an end to what remains of the encampment of antigovernment Red Shirt protesters, and leaders of the protest are arrested; 12 people are killed in the crackdown, and rioting and arson take place in response elsewhere in Bangkok and in provinces in northeastern Thailand.

▸ *Troubles* (1970), by J.G. Farrell, is named the winner of the Lost Man Booker Prize; a change in 1971 from granting the British literary award to novels published in the previous year to granting it to those released during the year of the award had left books published in 1970 ineligible for a Booker Prize.

20 May Japanese Prime Minister Yukio Hatoyama announces that he has decided to honor a 2006 agreement to move the US air base on Okinawa to a less-populated part of that island, in spite of widespread support in Japan for Hatoyama's previous promise to insist that the base be moved off Okinawa entirely.

▸ South Korean officials publicly present the results of an investigation, based on forensic evidence, that they say proves that North Korea was responsible for the March sinking of the South Korean warship *Cheonan* in international waters near the border between the two countries.

▸ The Mars rover Opportunity, designed by NASA for a three-month mission, becomes the longest-surviving spacecraft on Mars as it continues to operate after 2,246 Sols, or Martian days (2,307 Earth days), since its arrival on 25 Jan 2004.

21 May Salva Kiir, leader of the Sudan People's Liberation Movement, is sworn in as the first president of the semiautonomous region of southern Sudan; a referendum on independence for the region is to be held in 2011.

22 May In association football (soccer), Inter Milan of Italy defeats the German team Bayern Munich 2–0 to win the UEFA Champions League title in Madrid.

23 May The Czech Republic defeats Russia 2–1 to win the men's International Ice Hockey Federation world championship.

▸ Drivers Dale Earnhardt, Junior Johnson, and Richard Petty, along with NASCAR founder Bill France and former president, chairman, and CEO Bill France, Jr., are inducted into the inaugural class of the NASCAR Hall of Fame in Charlotte NC.

24 May Four regional savings banks in Spain agree to merge some of their operations in a joint banking group in an effort to strengthen their assets; two days earlier the Spanish government had taken control of another savings bank, CajaSur, when its merger negotiations with Unicaja fell through.

25 May After a three-day standoff, police storm the Tivoli Gardens slum in Kingston, Jamaica, in an attempt to arrest the gang leader Christopher Coke, whom the government has agreed to extradite to the US, where he is wanted for drug and firearms trafficking; residents of the neighborhood, who regard Coke as a benefactor, resist, and at least 70 people die in the fighting.

26 May The energy company BP begins an attempt to fill the drill pipes of the leaking oil well in the Gulf of

Mexico with heavy drilling fluid; the maneuver, known as "top kill," has never been tried on a well at such an extreme depth as this one, and the attempt is halted the next day.

▶ As the five-year review of the Nuclear Nonproliferation Treaty comes to a close, British Foreign Secretary William Hague, in a speech to the House of Commons, reveals for the first time that the UK has a stockpile of 225 nuclear warheads; at the beginning of the review, the US disclosed an arsenal of 5,113 nuclear warheads.

▶ Apple Inc. overtakes Microsoft Corp. to become the world's most valuable technology company.

27 May US federal officials raise their estimate of the rate at which oil has been flowing into the ocean daily since the collapse of the Deepwater Horizon oil platform in April to between 12,000 and 19,000 bbl a day; the previous estimate was 5,000 bbl a day.

▶ The government of Ukraine declares that it is no longer seeking to become a member of NATO.

▶ In Oslo 58 countries represented at the Oslo Climate and Forest Conference agree to a framework convention on channeling funds from richer countries to poorer ones in order to protect forests, a vital component of efforts to reduce emissions of greenhouse gases; the previous day Norway had announced a US$1 billion package to save forests in Indonesia.

28 May The World Bank cancels Haiti's debt to the bank's International Development Association in order to help the country recover from the devastating earthquake in January.

29 May Roy Halladay of the Philadelphia Phillies pitches the 20th perfect game in Major League Baseball history in his team's 1–0 victory over the Florida Marlins only 20 days after the previous perfect game.

▶ In Oslo, German singer Lena Meyer-Landrut wins the Eurovision Song Contest with her song "Satellite."

30 May The National Museum of XXI Century Arts, also known as MAXXI, opens in Rome; the new museum, with curving walls and floor-to-ceiling windows, was designed by Zaha Hadid.

▶ The 94th Indianapolis 500 automobile race is won by Dario Franchitti of Scotland.

31 May As an aid flotilla organized by the Free Gaza Movement and a charitable Turkish organization heads toward Gaza, Israeli commandos descend from a helicopter and board one of the ships in international waters; when activists on the ship resist, the commandos open fire, and nine passengers, many Turkish, are killed.

June 2010

1 Jun The US Supreme Court rules that suspects who wish to invoke their right to remain silent must explicitly state that they are invoking that right; otherwise, any statement they make may be construed as waiving the right.

2 Jun American automobile company Ford Motor announces that it will discontinue the manufacture of the 71-year-old Mercury brand by fall; the original Mercury Eight went on sale in 1939.

▶ In a crime that shocks Britain, a cab driver in England's Lake District shoots three other drivers and then drives through the district, shooting passersby; at least 12 people are murdered and 25 injured before the gunman turns his weapon on himself.

3 Jun The energy company BP successfully places a containment dome over the gushing oil well in the Gulf of Mexico; the device allows BP to collect some of the oil and send it to a ship on the surface to be processed.

4 Jun The US Department of Labor reports that the unemployment rate in May fell to 9.7% and that the economy added 431,000 nonfarm jobs; the vast majority of those jobs are temporary hiring by the Census Bureau, however, and the stock markets fall on the news.

▶ The 83rd Scripps National Spelling Bee is won by Anamika Veeramani of Incarnate Word Academy in Parma Heights OH; she correctly spells *stromuhr.*

5 Jun Francesca Schiavone of Italy defeats Australian Samantha Stosur to win the women's French Open tennis title; the following day Rafael Nadal of Spain defeats Robin Söderling of Sweden to capture the men's championship for the fifth time.

▶ Long shot Drosselmeyer, with jockey Mike Smith aboard, wins the Belmont Stakes, the last event in Thoroughbred horse racing's US Triple Crown.

6 Jun The energy company BP finds that it must limit the amount of oil it is capturing from the gushing oil well under the Gulf of Mexico lest it overwhelm the processing capacity on hand, and Coast Guard Adm. Thad Allen warns that the oil will continue to be a problem long after the well has been capped.

> ### QUOTE OF THE MONTH
>
> " *This is a siege across the entire gulf. This spill is holding everybody hostage, not only economically but physically.* "
>
> —US Coast Guard Adm. Thad W. Allen, describing the effects of the continuing oil spill catastrophe in the Gulf of Mexico, 6 June

7 Jun The first criminal convictions stemming from the 1984 chemical leak at a Union Carbide plant that left some 5,000 people dead in Bhopal, India, occur in a courtroom in Bhopal: eight former executives of Union Carbide's Indian subsidiary are found guilty of negligence, and the seven still living are sentenced to two years in prison.

▶ German Chancellor Angela Merkel presents an austerity package intended to reduce the country's budget deficit.

8 Jun A spokeswoman for the United Nations High Commissioner for Refugees says that the agency has been told that it must leave Libya, where it has operated since 1991 and serves as the country's only asylum system.

▶ It is reported that a cache of 75 silent films that have been found in the New Zealand Film Archive will be sent to the US for restoration; the films include the only copy of *Upstream* (1927), directed by John Ford, and the earliest Mabel Normand film.

9 Jun Barbara Kingsolver wins the Orange Prize for Fiction, an award for fiction written by women and published in the UK, for her novel *The Lacuna.*

▶ The Chicago Blackhawks defeat the Philadelphia

Flyers 4–3 in sudden-death overtime to win the Stanley Cup for the first time since 1961.

10 Jun Researchers for a US government panel raise the estimate of the amount of oil that has been flowing from the oil well under the Gulf of Mexico since the explosion and sinking of the Deepwater Horizon oil platform in April to 25,000–30,000 bbl a day, nearly double the previous estimate.

11 Jun Attacks that began the previous night involving rival drug-trafficking organizations leave some 85 people dead throughout Mexico.

12 Jun US officials reveal that geologists have found in Afghanistan many previously unknown mineral deposits, including iron, copper, gold, cobalt, and lithium, worth an estimated US$1 trillion, worth to become a major component of the country's economy, which is presently based largely on opium production.

▶ Abby Sunderland, a 16-year-old girl from California who is attempting to sail solo around the world, is rescued some 3,200 km (2,000 mi) west of Australia after losing a mast in heavy seas in the Indian Ocean.

13 Jun Kyrgyzstan's national news agency reports that three days of ethnic violence in southern Kyrgyzstan, largely in and around Osh, has killed at least 114 people and that tens of thousands of ethnic Uzbeks have fled the violence.

▶ The 64th annual Tony Awards are presented in New York City; winners include *Red* (which takes six awards), *Memphis, Fences,* and *La Cage aux Folles* and the actors Denzel Washington, Catherine Zeta-Jones, Douglas Hodge, and Scarlett Johansson.

14 Jun Iraq's new legislature convenes, takes the oath of allegiance, and is immediately suspended, as no new government has been agreed on and no bloc commands a majority.

▶ Scientists head to South Australia to retrieve the capsule of the Japanese space explorer Hayabusa, which landed there overnight after a seven-year journey to collect samples from an asteroid and return them to Earth.

15 Jun Speaking before the House of Commons, British Prime Minister David Cameron apologizes for the "Bloody Sunday" killings in 1972 in which 14 unarmed demonstrators were killed in Londonderry, Northern Ireland, were killed by British soldiers, saying that the shootings had no justification.

▶ American stock markets make a sustained rise throughout the day of more than 2%; the Dow Jones Industrial Average rises 213.88 points to close at 10,404.77.

16 Jun After four days of negotiations, US Pres. Barack Obama announces that the energy company BP has agreed to set up a fund of US$20 billion to compensate people who lost their livelihoods and suffered other damage from the oil spill in the Gulf of Mexico.

▶ David Beckmann, president of the Christian advocacy organization Bread for the World, and Jo Luck, president of Heifer International, which provides animals for food and income to poor families throughout the world, are honored with the World Food Prize.

17 Jun Estonia becomes the 17th country to join the euro zone.

▶ Switzerland's legislature agrees to adhere to the terms of an agreement made in August 2009 for the bank UBS to disclose information on 4,450 accounts held by Americans suspected of tax evasion.

▶ The Los Angeles Lakers defeat the Boston Celtics 83–79 in game seven of the tournament to secure the team's 16th overall and 2nd consecutive National Basketball Association championship.

18 Jun Six member countries of the Organisation of Eastern Caribbean States sign an agreement in Castries, St. Lucia, to form an economic union; the remaining three members are expected to sign on within a few weeks.

▶ The 2010 winners of the Kyoto Prize are announced: medical scientist Shinya Yamanaka (advanced technology), mathematician Laszlo Lovasz (basic sciences), and visual artist William Kentridge (arts and philosophy).

19 Jun China announces that it will allow its currency, the renminbi, to move a little more freely in relation to the US dollar; in later days it is seen that the change is quite small.

▶ Kurdish militants attack a Turkish military post near the Iraqi border, killing 8 soldiers and triggering an attack by Turkish warplanes that leaves 12 Kurdish insurgents dead.

20 Jun Israeli Prime Minister Benjamin Netanyahu announces an easing of Israel's land blockade of Gaza, including plans to facilitate the passage of larger amounts of civilian goods and plans to issue a list of prohibited items, to replace the currently used list of permitted items.

▶ Graeme McDowell of Northern Ireland secures a one-stroke victory over Gregory Havret of France to win the US Open golf tournament in Pebble Beach CA.

21 Jun Faisal Shahzad pleads guilty in a US federal court to having created the failed car bomb found on 1 May in Times Square in New York City, explaining in detail how and why he engineered the attempted attack.

▶ The death of a British Royal Marine from wounds he received on 12 June in a bombing in Afghanistan's Helmand province marks the 300th British military death in the war in Afghanistan.

22 Jun A bighead Asian carp is caught in a fishing net in Lake Calumet, about 9.7 km (6 mi) from Lake Michigan and beyond the electric fence designed to keep the voracious invasive species out of the Great Lakes system.

23 Jun US Pres. Barack Obama fires Gen. Stanley McChrystal and replaces him as top commander in the war in Afghanistan with Gen. David Petraeus; the dismissal follows an interview published in the magazine *Rolling Stone* in which McChrystal and his staff had criticized administration officials.

▶ At a meeting of the International Whaling Commission, compromise talks aimed at controlling commercial whaling by Japan, Norway, and Iceland collapse.

24 Jun Kevin Rudd resigns as prime minister of Australia; he is replaced by Julia Gillard, who is Australia's first female prime minister.

▶ Kimberley Process negotiations over whether diamonds from Zimbabwe's Marange diamond fields should be certified as conflict-free break down; Zimbabwe's government, which has been accused of violently seizing control of the fields, threatens to market the diamonds without certification.

▶ At Wimbledon the longest match in the history of professional tennis concludes—after three days and 182 games—with a victory by American John Isner over Nicolas Mahut of France in five sets: 6–4, 3–6, 6–7, 7–6, 70–68.

25 Jun Hong Kong's Legislative Council approves a plan to expand the legislature by 10 seats beginning in 2012 and for the first time makes most of the seats subject to direct popular election; the committee that chooses the chief executive is enlarged to 1,200 members.

26 Jun A presidential election is held in Somalia's self-declared independent enclave of Somaliland; opposition candidate Ahmed M. Mohamoud Silanyo is declared the winner on 1 July.

27 Jun Free elections take place in Guinea for the first time in the country's history; they result in the need for a presidential runoff.

▸ Cristie Kerr of the US wins the Ladies Professional Golf Association Championship tournament by 12 strokes over Kim Song-Hee of South Korea.

28 Jun Five couples who were arrested in New York, Massachusetts, and Virginia the previous day are charged with conspiracy to act as unlawful agents of a foreign government as part of a Russian espi-

onage ring; an 11th person is charged but has not been apprehended.

29 Jun In Chongqing, China, representatives of China and Taiwan sign a framework trade agreement that will, among other things, remove tariffs from hundreds of goods exported from Taiwan to China as well as some goods exported from China to Taiwan.

▸ Larry King, host of the cable television talk show *Larry King Live* since 1985, announces his retirement.

30 Jun The World Trade Organization rules that the European airplane manufacturer Airbus has for some 40 years received improper subsidies in the form of low-interest and interest-free loans from European governments—subsidies that gave it an unfair advantage over its American rival Boeing.

Disasters

Listed here are major disasters between July 2009 and June 2010 The list includes natural and nonmilitary mechanical disasters that claimed 25 or more lives and/or resulted in significant damage to property.

July 2009

3 Jul Eastern Cape, South Africa. Officials report that the death toll among teenage boys so far this year from ritual circumcisions has reached 31.

5 Jul Ahmadabad, India. Hundreds of slum dwellers imbibe illegally brewed alcohol that is poisonous; by 10 July, 112 of them have died, and 225 remain hospitalized.

12 Jul Peru. It is reported that since March some 246 children have perished in mountainous areas as a result of extreme cold.

15 Jul Iran. A Caspian Airlines Tupolev Tu-154M jetliner en route from Tehran to Yerevan, Armenia,

crashes near the village of Jannatabad and explodes; all 168 people aboard perish.

24 Jul Novito, Colombia. A landslide sweeps away some 30 prospectors panning for gold in a river; five bodies are recovered, while the rest remain missing.

24 Jul Iran. An Aria Air airplane skids off the runway during an emergency landing at the airport in Mashhad; at least 17 of the 153 aboard perish.

26–27 Jul Off the Turks and Caicos Islands. A sailboat grossly overloaded with Haitian would-be migrants sinks; 15 bodies are recovered, and a further 67 people are believed to have drowned.

August 2009

5 Aug Tonga. The MV *Princess Ashika,* an inter-island ferry traveling from Nuku'alofa to Ha'afeva island, sinks; some 74 passengers drown.

8 Aug Taiwan. Typhoon Morakot inundates the island with several days of exceptionally heavy rainfall, leading to massive landslides and mud slides that leave more than 600 people dead, nearly 500 of them in the village of Hsiao-lin; earlier the typhoon killed 22 people in the Philippines.

10 Aug Slovakia. An explosion in a coal mine in Handlova kills 20 miners.

13 Aug Panama. On the outskirts of Panama City, a

truck trying to overtake another vehicle while crossing a bridge hits a bus head-on; at least 24 bus passengers die.

17 Aug Southern Siberia. At the aging Sayano-Shushenskaya hydroelectric power plant, the largest such facility in Russia, a water conduit bursts, unleashing flooding that leaves 75 workers dead.

20 Aug Off the coast of Lampedusa, Italy. Italian border police rescue five Eritreans; the Eritreans say that 75 others perished during a three-week trip from Libya, and Italy and Malta blame each other for having failed to prevent the tragedy.

September 2009

2 Sep Indonesia. A magnitude-7.0 earthquake with its epicenter in Jawa Barat province leaves at least 64 people dead and 27,000 people homeless.

8 Sep Sierra Leone. In waters off Freetown, an overloaded boat carrying children returning from school holidays encounters a storm and sinks; at least 150 passengers, many of them schoolchildren, are drowned.

13 Sep Taldykorgan, Kazakhstan. A quickly moving

fire kills at least 39 patients and staff members at a drug-treatment center with barred windows.

15 Sep North Sumatra province, Indonesia. Flash flooding submerges homes and sweeps away bridges and roads in Mandailing Natal district; at least 38 people perish, and several more are reported missing.

23 Sep Chhattisgarh state, India. In Korba a chimney being built at a power plant collapses into the building's cafeteria; at least 40 people are crushed to death, with dozens more believed to have been trapped in the rubble.

26 Sep Philippines. Typhoon Ketsana makes landfall on the main island, Luzon, and inundates much of Manila; at least 464 people lose their lives, while some 380,000 are left homeless.

29 Sep South Pacific Ocean. A magnitude-8.0 earthquake some 18 km (11 mi) under the seabed causes a tsunami that rolls into Samoa, American Samoa, and Tonga; at least 190 people, most of them in Samoa, perish.

29 Sep Vietnam. Typhoon Ketsana roars through the country, leaving behind rising floods; at least 99 people are killed.

30 Sep Kerala state, India. A sightseeing boat in Periyar Lake capsizes when the passengers flock to one side to see an elephant; at least 41 tourists die.

30 Sep Padang, Indonesia. A magnitude-7.6 undersea earthquake collapses hundreds of buildings and leaves the large city without power or communications; at least 1,100 people are killed.

October 2009

2 Oct Sicily. Near Messina, Italy, mud slides cause the collapse of dozens of buildings, leaving at least 23 people dead and a further 35 people missing.

3 Oct India. Several days of exceptionally heavy monsoon rains leave at least 221 people dead in Karnataka and 63 people dead in Andhra Pradesh.

5 Oct Southern India. After four days of heavy rains, more than 240 people have perished.

8 Oct Philippines. At least 193 people die in Benguet and Mountain Province in landslides caused by Ty-

phoon Parma as well as by intentional dam releases that were an attempt to limit flooding.

9 Oct Southern Nigeria. A fuel tanker on a highway riven with potholes falls over and is then hit by a car, causing an explosion that engulfs six commuter buses; some 70 people are thought to have been killed.

13 Oct Nepal. Flooding and landslides in the western part of the country are reported to have killed a minimum of 60 people.

November 2009

6 Nov Himachal Pradesh state, India. Near the town of Haripur, a crowded bus rolls into a gorge; at least 34 passengers are killed.

8 Nov El Salvador. Pres. Mauricio Funes declares a state of emergency, as flooding and landslides have left at least 157 people dead and more than 12,000 homeless.

10 Nov Tamil Nadu state, India. Officials report that at least 38 people have died in landslides following heavy rains over the past two days.

14 Nov North-central China. Chinese officials say that waves of snowstorms that began on 9 November have left at least 40 people dead and more than 9,000 buildings collapsed.

15 Nov Myanmar (Burma). Shortly after leaving the town of Pathein, a ferry collides with a barge in the

Ngawun River; at least 50 people are believed to have lost their lives.

21 Nov Heilongjiang province, China. A gas explosion at the state-owned Xinxing coal mine kills at least 104 miners and leaves a further 4 people trapped.

25 Nov Saudi Arabia. Rare heavy rain causes flash flooding; some 116 people in Jiddah lose their lives, and at least 4 people die in Mecca.

25 Nov Democratic Republic of the Congo. A logging boat illegally carrying passengers sinks on Lake Mai Ndombe, in the northeastern part of the country; at least 73 passengers die, and many more are missing.

27 Nov Bangladesh. An overloaded triple-deck ferry carrying passengers from Dhaka to Nazir Hat capsizes in the Tetulia River; at least 77 people perish.

December 2009

4 Dec Bangladesh. A ferry sinks on the Daira River; at least 46 passengers, most of them women and children, drown.

5 Dec Perm, Russia. As the Lame Horse nightclub celebrates its eighth anniversary, pyrotechnic fountains ignite a suspended ceiling decorated with twigs, and panicked patrons stampede the single exit; at least 152 people die.

21 Dec Europe. Three days of unusually severe winter

weather have left at least 42 people in Poland and 27 people in Ukraine dead from the cold.

24 Dec Rajasthan state, India. A section of a cable-stayed bridge that is being built some 50 m (164 ft) above the Chambal River collapses, killing at least 45 people, with many more missing.

24 Dec Peru. A passenger bus in the Andes goes off the road and falls into a ravine; 40 passengers die.

January 2010

1 Jan Brazil. Mud slides bury a resort on the island of Ilha Grande, killing at least 26 people; other mud slides on the mainland in southeastern Brazil, which follow days of torrential rain, leave at least 40 more people dead.

12 Jan Haiti. A devastating earthquake of magnitude 7.0 flattens Port-au-Prince; some 222,570 people are killed, and most buildings, among them the

presidential palace, the parliament building, the national cathedral, and the headquarters of the UN mission, are heavily damaged or destroyed.

12 Jan Papua New Guinea. At least 40 people die violently when two passenger buses collide head-on near the village of Ragiampum.

15 Jan Cuba. The Ministry of Health declares that 26 of the patients of Havana's largest psychiatric hospital died during a cold snap over the previous few days.

25 Jan Beirut. Ethiopian Airlines Flight 409 bound for Addis Ababa, Ethiopia, goes down in a storm shortly after taking off; all 90 aboard are presumed to have been killed.

February 2010

8 Feb Uttar Pradesh state, India. In the town of Sitapur a tractor that is pulling a trolley with some 70 passengers overturns; at least 23 passengers are killed.

9 Feb Afghanistan. A series of 17 avalanches that began the previous day in the Salang Pass in the Hindu Kush mountain range buries a 3.5-km (2-mi) stretch of the highway, blocking the Salang Tunnel and leaving at least 169 people dead.

9 Feb South Africa. A fire kills 15 people, 13 of them children, at an orphanage in KwaZulu-Natal province.

11 Feb Arunachal Pradesh state, India. A fire breaks out in a school dormitory in the town of Palin; some 14 schoolchildren are believed to have been killed.

13 Feb Nigeria. An electrical cable falls on a bus during a storm; at least 20 people, including bystanders, are electrocuted.

15 Feb Halle, Belgium. Two passenger trains crash into each other head-on after one of them allegedly ignores a stop signal; at least 18 people are killed.

17 Feb Uttar Pradesh state, India. A bus carrying guests from a wedding party goes off the road and plunges into a river in Jalaun district; at least 22 of the passengers expire.

17 Feb North-West Frontier Province, Pakistan. An avalanche buries a remote village in Kohistan district; at least 102 people perish.

19 Feb Meknès, Morocco. The 400-year-old minaret of the Lalla Khenata mosque collapses during Friday prayer; at least 41 worshippers perish.

20 Feb Madeira Islands. Torrential rains cause flash flooding and rock slides on the Portuguese island of Madeira in the Atlantic Ocean; at least 42 people are killed.

22 Feb Peru. Two passenger buses collide head-on on the Pan-American Highway between Rio Hondo and Virú; at least 38 passengers perish.

25 Feb Bangladesh. A fire breaks out at a clothing factory in Gazipur, leaving at least 21 people dead.

25 Feb Timbuktu, Mali. As crowds attempt to reach the Djingareyber mosque to celebrate a festival, they find access blocked by road construction; a stampede results in which 26 people are crushed to death.

27 Feb Chile. A magnitude-8.8 earthquake in the central part of the country shatters the area around Concepción and is followed by a tsunami; at least 577 people are killed and some 800,000 are left homeless.

28 Feb Europe. Officials report that the Atlantic storm Xynthia has since the previous day battered the coasts of Portugal, Spain, and France, leaving more than 60 people dead; 51 people died, mostly of drowning, in France alone.

March 2010

1 Mar Uganda. Mud slides following torrential rain sweep away buildings in villages on the slopes of Mt. Elgon; some 300 people are feared dead.

4 Mar Mangarh, India. As some 10,000 people attend a religious ceremony at a popular ashram, a structure put up for the occasion collapses, setting off a stampede in which at least 63 people, nearly all of them women and children, perish.

8 Mar Eastern Turkey. A magnitude-6.1 earthquake levels homes in three villages; at least 57 people are killed.

12 Mar Southern Kazakhstan. Two dams give way under the pressure of heavy rains and snowmelt; the resultant flooding and mud slides leave some 35 people dead and thousands homeless.

15 Mar Rajasthan state, India. A passenger bus hits a vehicle that is parked on a bridge and goes over the rail into a dry riverbed some 18 m (60 ft) below; at least 26 people are killed.

23 Mar Afghanistan. Afghan officials report that it has been learned that an avalanche took place two weeks previously in the northern province of Badakhshan and that at least 35 people were killed.

26 Mar Kentucky. On Interstate 65 near Munfordville, a truck crosses the median and crashes head-on with a van carrying a party of Mennonites on their way to a wedding; 10 people in the van, most of them members of one family, and the truck driver perish.

28 Mar Shanxi province, China. A flood in the Wangjialing coal mine traps 153 miners; 108 others are airlifted to safety, and many of the remaining miners are rescued in the ensuing days, though at least 35 perish.

April 2010

5 Apr Outside Montcoal WV. A methane gas explosion in the Upper Big Branch coal mine leaves 29 miners dead.

7 Apr Brazil. A storm that dumps some 28 cm (11 in) of rain on Rio de Janeiro causes flash flooding that leaves at least 247 people dead and 150 people missing.

7 Apr Brazil. The largest of dozens of mud slides triggered by heavy rains sweeps away hillside slums in Niterói, near Rio de Janeiro; some 200 people die.

9 Apr Peru. The Pan American Health Organization reports that heavy rains in the departments of Huánuco, Cajamarca, and Ancash have caused flooding that has left at least 30 people dead and an additional 38 others missing.

10 Apr Near Smolensk, Russia. A Tupolev Tu-154 jet carrying Polish dignitaries to a memorial observation of the Katyn Massacre crashes in the forest in heavy fog; all 97 aboard, including Polish Pres. Lech Kaczynski, the chiefs of the army and the navy, and several legislators, are killed.

13 Apr Eastern India. A cyclone makes landfall in Bihar, West Bengal, and Assam, causing great destruction and leaving at least 139 people dead and some 100,000 homeless.

14 Apr China. A magnitude-7.1 earthquake strikes Qinghai province on the Tibetan plateau; the town of Jiegu is left in ruins, and at least 2,260 people

lose their lives, while thousands more are displaced.

23 Apr Uganda. A health official declares that over the past three weeks in Kabale district some 80 people have succumbed after drinking a homemade banana gin known as *waragi* that contained methanol.

May 2010

3 May US. Parts of downtown Nashville are evacuated after 330 mm (13 in) of rain falling in two days causes the Cumberland River to overflow its banks, flooding, among other things, many of the famous music venues in the city; the flooding has caused at least 30 deaths in Tennessee, Kentucky, and Mississippi.

8 May Siberia, Russia. Two methane gas explosions, four hours apart, collapse shafts, including the main air shaft, in the large Raspadskaya coal mine in the Kemerovo region; 90 miners and rescue workers are killed.

8 May Southern Tajikistan. Two days of flooding and mud slides brought on by heavy rain leave at least 40 people dead.

12 May Libya. An Afriqiyah Airways Airbus A330-200 that took off from Johannesburg crashes on its approach in Tripoli; 103 of those aboard, 66 of whom are Dutch tourists, are killed.

16 May Democratic Republic of the Congo. A landslide caused by flooding on the slopes of the volcano Mt. Nyiragongo destroys hundreds of homes and leaves at least 54 people dead or missing.

17 May Afghanistan. A Pamir Airways Antonov-24 flying from Kunduz to Kabul disappears in heavy fog; the wreckage of the plane, which broke into four parts, is found three days later in the Hindu Kush mountain range, and it is clear that all 44 aboard perished.

17 May Turkey. An explosion in the Karadon coal mine near Zonguldak traps 32 miners deep underground; none survive.

20 May Andhra Pradesh, India. Cyclone Laila makes landfall, causing great damage and causing the deaths of at least 23 people; in addition, at least 55 fishermen are reported missing.

22 May Mangalore, India. An Air India Boeing 737-800 arriving from Dubai overshoots the runway when landing and crashes into a concrete navigational aid before falling into a valley; 158 of the 166 people aboard perish.

23 May Poland. The Vistula River bursts its banks and the mayor of Warsaw recommends that people evacuate the city as flooding from days of heavy rains spreads northward; some 15 people lose their lives in the floods.

23 May Liaoning province, China. On an expressway in Fuxin, a collision between a passenger bus and a truck leaves 32 people, all but 3 from the bus, dead.

29 May Central America. Tropical Storm Agatha roars through El Salvador, Honduras, and Guatemala, leaving at least 205 people, some 200 of them in Guatemala, dead and opening a sinkhole roughly 30 m (100 ft) in diameter and at least 60 m (200 ft) deep in Guatemala City.

June 2010

3 Jun Dhaka, Bangladesh. The explosion of an electrical transformer ignites a fire that spreads quickly; at least 117 people, including 15 members of a wedding party, perish in the conflagration.

4 Jun Zamfara state, Nigeria. Authorities report that attempts by poor villagers to leach gold from rock deposits have since the beginning of the year resulted in the deaths from lead poisoning of more than 160 people, most of them children.

11 Jun Arkansas. Flash flooding on the Caddo and Little Missouri rivers sweeps through campgrounds in the Ouachita National Forest; at least 19 campers perish.

14 Jun Northern India. A boat ferrying people to a temple sinks under the weight of its passengers in the Ganges River; at least 35 people are feared dead.

15 Jun Bangladesh. Heavy rainfall causes landslides in the area around Cox's Bazar that destroy dozens of houses and an army camp and leave at least 58 people dead.

15 Jun Southeastern France. Flash flooding said to be the worst since 1827 takes place above the French Riviera in unusually heavy rains; the town of Draguignan is particularly hard hit, and at least 25 people perish.

16 Jun Colombia. An explosion tears through the San Fernando coal mine in Amagá, killing 73 miners.

21 Jun Henan province, China. A powder magazine in

a coal mine in Pingdingshan explodes, and at least 47 miners are killed.

21 Jun Myanmar (Burma). Officials report that days of flooding and landslides in the northwestern part of the country from rains that continued for days have left at least 63 people dead and swept away homes, schools, and bridges.

21 Jun Southern and central China. Authorities say that continuing monsoon rains have inundated the previously drought-stricken area, sweeping away homes, drowning crops, and leaving at least 175 people dead.

21 Jun Republic of the Congo. A train departing Pointe-Noire en route to Brazzaville goes off the tracks and falls into a ravine; at least 60 of the passengers perish.

22 Jun Northeastern Brazil. Several days of heavy rain cause flooding that washes away whole villages in Alagoas and Pernambuco states; at least 41 people succumb, and there are hundreds reported missing.

27 Jun Ghana. An illegal gold mine in Dunkwa-on-Offin collapses after heavy rain; as many as 100 artisanal miners are thought to have lost their lives.

28 Jun Southern and central China. As monsoon rains continue to fall, a landslide buries Dazhai village in Guizhou province, burying at least 100 people; the death toll from flooding, excluding this event, is said to have reached at least 235.

People

The TIME 100, 2010

Each year the editors of TIME designate 100 individuals as the most influential persons of the year in four categories: Leaders, Artists, Thinkers, and Heroes. Those individuals chosen for 2010 include a number of Heroes who worked to aid the people of Haiti in the wake of the devastating 12 January earthquake.

LEADERS

Glenn Beck The history buff and cable-TV talker delights in assailing the powers-that-be.

Ron Bloom The US car czar got Detroit's ailing automotive industry back on track by combining a unionist's heart and a banker's soul.

Scott Brown He took on the president and an entrenched political machine to win Edward M. Kennedy's Senate seat for the Republicans.

Mark Carney The head of the Bank of Canada leads a system that didn't require a bailout.

Recep Tayyip Erdogan Turkey's PM has led his nation away from the West and has become a global spokesman for the Muslim world.

Salam Fayyad Palestine's PM has reformed his government and set the stage for nationhood.

Yukio Hatoyama Japan's PM helped end one-party rule but resigned after his controversial decision to allow a US army base to remain in Okinawa.

Sister Carol Keehan The leader of the Catholic Health Association of the US helped win passage of the controversial health-care reform bill.

John Kyl Colleagues on both sides of a divided Senate look to the US senator from Arizona for wise conservative leadership.

Christine Lagarde France's finance minister is fighting a host of skeptics to pioneer a new age of global interdependence.

Robin Li The US-educated computer geek now runs China's answer to Google, search giant Baidu.

Luiz Inácio Lula da Silva Brazil's president, a champion of the working class, now in his second term, continues to cultivate equal opportunity for all.

Jenny Beth Martin A breakout star of the Tea Party movement, the former Republican consultant helped build its ascending brand.

General Stanley McChrystal The legendary special operator lost his command in Afghanistan when his staff spoke too freely to a *Rolling Stone* reporter.

Admiral Mike Mullen The hands-on chairman of the joint chiefs of staff supports his troops and took a strong stand against Don't Ask, Don't Tell.

Sheikh Khalifah ibn Zayid al-Nahyan When neighbor Dubai's real-estate boom crashed, Abu Dhabi's ruler bailed out its 160-story skyscraper hotel.

Barack Obama Despite a mountain of obstacles, he herded cats and got health-care reform passed.

Sarah Palin Alaska's ex-governor continues to play an outsized, outspoken role in US politics.

Annise Parker Houston's Democratic mayor is focusing on fixing her city's budget shortfall.

Nancy Pelosi The first female speaker of the House is a favorite target of the GOP, but she helped make health-care reform a reality.

Manmohan Singh India's PM is the quiet engine of his nation's progress as it becomes a great power.

Dominique Strauss-Kahn Leading the International Monetary Fund, he helped keep the world economy afloat amid a global recession.

Tidjane Thiam The boss of Britain's Prudential insurance company, a native of the Côte d'Ivoire, is leading the way to a new future for Africa.

J.T. Wang The CEO of Taiwanese PC maker Acer Group listens to customers and reaps the profits.

Bo Xilai China's former commerce minister has led a strong crusade against corruption in Chongqing.

ARTISTS

Banksy The mysterious, mischievous graffiti artist creates work that's accessible, fun, and stimulating—as seen in the film *Exit Through the Gift Shop*.

Chetan Bhagat India's best-selling novelist is a one-time investment banker who followed his dream and encourages others to do the same.

Kathryn Bigelow The director of Oscar's Best Film of 2009, *The Hurt Locker*, tackles the tough topics other moviemakers won't touch.

Neill Blomkamp South Africa's vibrant storyteller won deserved acclaim for his daring science fiction/apartheid critique film *District 9*.

Sandra Bullock "America's Sweetheart" was the year's biggest box-office star and survived a very public divorce with her usual strength and class.

James Cameron He didn't just direct *Avatar*, the smash film that made 3-D mainstream; he invented the camera that he sat behind to shoot it.

David Chang His Momofuku café in New York City reinvented the casual restaurant. Now he feeds a global audience's appetite for culinary adventure.

Suzanne Collins The author of the young-adult hit *Hunger Games* trilogy is an ace literary fusioneer who's getting teens excited about reading.

Simon Cowell In nine seasons on *American Idol*, the show's bad cop made an indelible impression on global pop culture while staying true to himself.

Carlton Cuse and Damon Lindelof Having proved that prime-time TV can be challenging, the writers behind *Lost* bade farewell to their intriguing island.

Lady Gaga The pop-music phenom and international style icon, only 24, found stardom by turning her life into performance art.

Valery Gergiev The conductor of Russia's Mariinksy orchestra has led the group to new prominence and has introduced new artists to Western audiences.

Ricky Gervais The deadpan British funnyman is still willing to tackle life's touchiest subjects.

Han Han China's most popular blogger zeroes in on the ills of his society, defying the party line.

Neil Patrick Harris The comedy star emerged as the charming, sought-after host of TV award shows.

Jerry Holkins and Mike Krahulik The writer and artist of the online comic strip *Penny Arcade* have become the tastemakers of the video-game world.

Marc Jacobs Designing for Louis Vuitton or for his own line, he sets the fashions that others follow.

Elton John The pop star, now 63, is committed to protecting and advocating for the most vulnerable.

Ashton Kutcher The onetime TV pretty boy has become a smart, wired-in new-media mogul.

Lea Michele At 24, the star of the smash TV hit *Glee* is a gifted singer-actress-dancer-comedian.

Conan O'Brien He lost his *Tonight Show* gig to Jay Leno, dusted himself off, toured his comedy act around the country, and will return to a TV near you.

Robert Pattinson The star of the Twilight films, 23, is shy, bookish—and a superstar actor to-be.

Prince Deep into his career, the pop-music legend always seems to stay ahead of his times.

Taylor Swift The country princess, only 20, is now a pop-music queen with four Grammys in the barn.

Oprah Winfrey In her last year on her long-running talk show, she continues to inspire and inform.

THINKERS

Matt Berg He's leading a health revolution in Africa with a cell-phone system to track disease.

David Boies and Theodore Olsen The left loves Boies, the right Olsen. The odd couple teamed up to challenge California's ban on gay marriage.

Edna Foa The psychologist devised a new way to treat post-traumatic stress disorder, and it's been embraced by the US military to help war veterans.

Atul Gawande The doctor saved lives by making checklists essential in medical procedures.

Deborah Gist The commissioner of Rhode Island's schools isn't afraid to rock teachers' boats, as she proved when she fired an entire faculty.

Zaha Hadid The Iraqi-born architect's buildings can be compared to a gust of desert wind: they are organic, forceful, cleansing.

Lisa Jackson The head of the EPA is determined to restore public trust in her beleaguered agency.

Steve Jobs The mind behind Apple's machines gave us this year's two biggest hits in the high-stakes battle for digital dominance, the iPad and iPhone 4.

Jaron Lanier The pioneer of virtual reality casts a critical eye on today's socially networked world.

Lee Kuan Yew Singapore's venerable leader made his nation the undisputed leader of its region.

Jaime Lerner The ex-governor of Brazil's Paraná state was an early champion of green cities.

Kathleen Merrigan An activist of the dinner table, she helped chart the path for organic farming, farmers' markets, and local food.

Elon Musk A Renaissance man and rocket scientist, he designed the pioneering electric Tesla car—but can he make it affordable?

Victor Pinchuk Ukraine's top philanthropist and patron of the arts may bring his nation into the EU.

Michael Pollan His revelatory books on the US food industry have changed America's appetite. Who needs high-fructose corn syrup, anyway?

Sanjit "Bunker" Roy The Indian educator's "Barefoot College" is redefining the way the world thinks about fighting poverty.

Douglas Schwartzentruber and Larry Kwak The two researchers, working in separate labs, are racing to find a vaccine against cancer.

Amartya Sen The Indian philosopher concerns himself with both moral and material problems.

Michael Sherraden The coleader of the Global Assets Project helps people in developing countries acquire the financial smarts they need to survive.

Amy Smith An engineer and founder of MIT's innovative D-Lab, she creates simple machines that meet particular needs and can be built locally.

Sonia Sotomayor In her first full term, the new justice brought common sense to the Supreme Court bench.

Paul Volcker The former Fed chairman served as a towering voice for financial reform—and it passed.

Elizabeth Warren She oversaw the unpopular bailout of the US banking system with a powerful intellect and plainspoken articulation.

Tim Westergren The engineer behind online music phenomenon Pandora knows what you want to hear.

Tim White The veteran paleontologist's latest find is "Ardi," a 4.4 million-year-old hominid.

HEROES

Valentine Abe The activist from Côte d'Ivoire has led the effort to improve Haiti's fisheries.

Will Allen His Growing Power Inc. in Milwaukee is leading the movement toward urban farming.

Bill Clinton Increasingly admired as an advocate for the world's needy, he was named to coordinate US support for Haiti after the devastating earthquake.

Chen Shu-chu An ordinary vegetable vendor, she has become a leading philanthropist in Taiwan.

Didier Drogba The captain of Côte d'Ivoire's soccer team has plowed his earnings into improving the health of his impoverished fellow citizens.

Temple Grandin The animal scientist has become an inspiration for those suffering from autism.

Jet Li The action-movie star's One Foundation assists disaster-relief efforts in China and beyond.

Malali Joya The Afghani educator was elected to parliament, then expelled—but remains outspoken.

Liya Kebede The Ethiopian fashion model is an advocate for maternal and child health care.

Kim Yu-Na Both artist and athlete, she skated away with the gold medal at the Winter Olympics—and the hearts of her South Korean countrymen.

Nay Phone Latt The poet and blogger, 29, remains a political prisoner in his native Burma.

Tristan Lecomte The founder of France's Alter Eco company advocates trade that is fair—and green.

Graça Machel Nelson Mandela's wife is a potent voice for justice and an outspoken advocate for the rights of women, children, and refugees.

Kiran Mazumdar-Shaw The physician is leading the charge to curb cancer in her native India.

Phil Mickelson A longtime favorite of the gallery, the golfer won the 2010 Masters even as his wife and mother battled breast cancer.

Mir Hossein Mousavi His failed presidential race in Iran ignited popular protests that shook the regime.

P. Namperumalsamy The ophthalmologist perfected a fast procedure to replace cataracts, restoring the gift of vision for tens of thousands in India.

Reem Al Numery The youngster from Yemen fought an arranged marriage at 12 to a cousin, 30.

Karls Paul-Noel The highest-ranking Haitian-American firefighter in the US left Miami soon after the earthquake to lead rescue efforts in Haiti.

Zahra Rahnavard The artist and educator has become a forceful critic of Iran's harsh regime.

Rahul Singh The Canadian paramedic founded GlobalMedic to provide disaster relief and led the rapid response to Haiti's devastating earthquake.

Ben Stiller The comedian founded a charity that will provide schools for the children of Haiti.

Sachin Tendulkar India's great cricket player has become an uplifting figure for his countrymen.

Chief Master Sergeant Tony Travis The US Air Force combat air-traffic controller rapidly cleared the way for airborne relief to reach Haiti.

Serena Williams Still tops on the tennis court, she has become an outspoken and effective advocate for education around the world.

Celebrities and Newsmakers

These mini-biographies are intended to provide background information about people in the news. See also the Obituaries (below) for recently deceased persons.

50 Cent (Curtis Jackson; 6 Jul 1976, Jamaica, Queens NY), American hard-core rapper.

Shawn A-in-chut Atleo (16 Jan 1967?), Canadian First Nations activist; national chief of the Assembly of First Nations from 2009.

Eva Aariak (Arctic Bay, NT [now in NU], Canada), Canadian politician; premier of Nunavut from 2008.

Mahmoud (Ridha) Abbas (nom de guerre Abu Mazen; 26 Mar 1935, Zefat, British Palestine), Palestinian politician; secretary-general of the Palestine Liberation Organization executive committee and cofounder (with Yasir Arafat) of the Fatah movement; he served as the first prime minister of the Palestinian Authority and was its president from 2005.

Mohamed Ould Abdel Aziz (1956, Akjoujt, Mauritania), Mauritanian military leader; chairman of the high council of state, 2008–09, and president from 2009.

Paula (Julie) Abdul (19 Jun 1962, San Fernando CA), American pop singer, choreographer, and TV personality.

Abdullah ('Abdullah ibn 'Abd al-'Aziz al-Sa'ud; 1923, Riyadh, Saudi Arabia), Saudi royal; king of Saudi Arabia from 2005.

Abdullah II ('Abd Allah ibn al-Husayn; 30 Jan 1962, Amman, Jordan), Jordanian royal; king from 1999.

George Abela (22 Apr 1948, Qormi, Malta), Maltese politician; president from 2009.

Tuanku Mizan Zainal Abidin ibni al-Marhum Sultan Mahmud (22 Jan 1962, Kuala Terengganu, Malaysia), Malaysian politician; *yang di-pertuan agong* (head of state) in 2001 and again from 2006.

J(effrey) J(acob) Abrams (27 Jun 1966, New York NY), American producer and director whose credits include the TV series *Alias* (2001–06) and *Lost* (2004–10) and the film *Star Trek* (2009).

Chinua Achebe (Albert Chinualumogu Achebe; 16 Nov 1930, Ogidi, Nigeria), Nigerian novelist and poet who in 2007 won the second Man Booker International Prize for fiction.

Amy (Lou) Adams (20 Aug 1974, Aviano, Italy), American stage and film actress.

Gerry Adams (Gerard Adams; Irish: Gearóid Mac Ádhaimh; 6 Oct 1948, West Belfast, Northern Ireland), Irish resistance leader; president of Sinn Féin, the political wing of the Irish Republican Army, from 1983.

John (Coolidge) Adams (15 Feb 1947, Worcester MA), American composer.

Adele (Adele Laurie Blue Adkins; 5 May 1988, West Norwood, England), English soul and jazz singer.

Thomas Adès (27 Jun 1971, London, England), British composer, pianist, and conductor.

Chimamanda Ngozi Adichie (15 Sep 1977, Enugu, Nigeria), Nigerian novelist; winner of the 2007 Orange Broadband Prize for Fiction.

Aravind Adiga (1974, India), Indian author; recipient of the 2008 Man Booker Prize for *The White Tiger.*

Ben(jamin Geza) Affleck (15 Aug 1972, Berkeley CA), American actor, writer, and director.

(Caleb) Casey Affleck (12 Aug 1975, Falmouth MA), American film actor.

Isaias Afwerki (2 Feb 1946, Asmara, Ethiopia [now in Eritrea]), Eritrean independence leader, secretary-general of the Provisional Government, and first president of Eritrea, from 1993.

Christina (Maria) Aguilera (18 Dec 1980, Staten Island NY), American pop singer.

Liaquat Ahamed (c. 1952, Kenya), Kenyan businessman and author; his *Lords of Finance: The Bankers Who Broke the World* won the 2010 Pulitzer Prize for history.

Bertie Ahern (Bartholomew Patrick Ahern; 12 Sep 1951, Dublin, Ireland), Irish politician; prime minister (*taoiseach*) of Ireland, 1997–2008.

Mahmoud Ahmadinejad (28 Oct 1956, Garmsar, Iran), Iranian politician; president from 2005.

Sheikh Sharif Sheikh Ahmed (25 Jul 1964, Somalia), Somali politician; nominally president from 2009.

Martti Ahtisaari (23 Jun 1937, Viipuri, Finland [now Vyborg, Russia]), Finnish politician; president of Finland, 1994–2000, and winner of the 2008 Nobel Peace Prize.

Akihito (original name Tsugu Akihito; era name Heisei; 23 Dec 1933, Tokyo, Japan), Japanese royal; emperor of Japan from 1989.

Akil Akilov (1944, Tajikistan?), Tajik politician; prime minister from 1999.

Jessica (Marie) Alba (28 Apr 1981, Pomona CA), American TV and film actress.

Albert II (Albert Félix Humbert Théodore Christian Eugène Marie of Saxe-Coburg-Gotha; 6 Jun 1934, Brussels, Belgium), Belgian royal; king from 1993.

Albert II (Albert Alexandre Louis Pierre; 14 Mar 1958, Monaco), Monegasque prince and ruler of Monaco from 2005.

Claribel Alegría (12 May 1924, Estelí, Nicaragua), Nicaraguan-born Salvadoran poet, essayist, and journalist; recipient of the 2006 Neustadt Prize.

Sherman J. Alexie, Jr. (7 Oct 1966, Wellpinit, Spokane Indian Reservation, Washington), American poet and novelist who writes of his Native American upbringing; recipient of the Pen/Faulkner Award for Fiction in 2010.

Monica Ali (20 Oct 1967, Dacca, Pakistan [now Dhaka, Bangladesh]), Bangladeshi-born British writer.

Muhammad Ali (Cassius Marcellus Clay, Jr.; 17 Jan 1942, Louisville KY), American boxer, the first to win the heavyweight championship three separate times.

Samuel A. Alito, Jr. (1 Apr 1950, Trenton NJ), American jurist; associate justice of the US Supreme Court from 2006.

Ilham Aliyev (Ilham Geidar ogly Aliev; 24 Dec 1961, Baku, USSR [now in Azerbaijan]), Azerbaijani politician; prime minister briefly in 2003 and president from October 2003.

Joan Allen (20 Aug 1956, Rochelle IL), American film and theater actress.

Paul G. Allen (21 Jan 1953, Mercer Island WA), American corporate executive; cofounder (1975) of Microsoft Corp. and owner of several professional sports teams.

Thad Allen (16 Jan 1949, Tucson AZ), American military leader; commandant of the US Coast Guard (2006–10), he coordinated the federal response to Hurricane Katrina (2005) and the Deepwater Horizon oil spill (2010).

Woody Allen (Allen Stewart Konigsberg; 1 Dec 1935, Brooklyn NY), American filmmaker and actor.

Isabel Allende (2 Aug 1942, Lima, Peru), Chilean writer in the magic realist tradition.

Pedro Almodóvar (Caballero) (24 Sep 1949, Calzada de Calatrava, Spain), Spanish film director specializing in melodrama.

Alois (Alois Philipp Maria Prince von und zu Liechtenstein; 11 Jun 1968, Zürich, Switzerland), Liechtenstein crown prince.

Marin Alsop (16 Oct 1956, New York NY), American conductor and jazz violinist; music director of the Baltimore Symphony Orchestra from 2007; she was the first woman to head a major American orchestra.

Amadou (Amadou Bagayoko; 24 Oct 1954, Bamako, French West Africa [now in Mali]), Malian guitarist (for Amadou and Mariam).

Yukiya Amano (9 May 1947, Japan), Japanese international official; director general of the International Atomic Energy Agency from 2009.

Pamela (Denise) Anderson (1 Jul 1967, Ladysmith, BC, Canada), Canadian-born model and actress.

Paul Thomas Anderson (26 Jun 1970, Studio City CA), American film director.

Wes Anderson (1 May 1969, Houston TX), American film director.

Tadao Ando (13 Sep 1941, Osaka, Japan), Japanese architect; recipient of the 1995 Pritzker Prize.

André 3000 (André Benjamin; Dré; 27 May 1975, Atlanta GA), American hip-hop artist and actor.

Marc Andreessen (9 Jul 1971, Cedar Falls IA), American computer innovator; developer of Netscape.

Andrew (Andrew Albert Christian Edward Mountbatten-Windsor; 19 Feb 1960, Buckingham Palace, London, England), British prince; second son of Queen Elizabeth II and Prince Philip, duke of Edinburgh; and duke of York.

Criss Angel (Christopher Nicholas Sarantakos; 19 Dec 1967, Long Island NY), American magician and illusionist.

Maya Angelou (Marguerite Annie Johnson; 4 Apr 1928, St. Louis MO), American poet.

Jennifer Aniston (Jennifer Linn Anistassakis; 11 Feb 1969, Sherman Oaks CA), American TV and film actress.

Kofi (Atta) Annan (18 Apr 1938, Kumasi, Gold Coast [now Ghana]), Ghanaian diplomat; UN secretary-general, 1997–2006; corecipient, with the UN, of the 2001 Nobel Peace Prize.

Anne (Anne Elizabeth Alice Louise Mountbatten-Windsor; 15 Aug 1950, Clarence House, London, England), British princess; daughter of Queen Elizabeth II and Prince Philip, duke of Edinburgh.

Andrus Ansip (1 Oct 1956, Tartu, USSR [now in Estonia]), Estonian politician; prime minister from 2005.

Carmelo Anthony (29 May 1984, New York NY), American pro basketball forward.

Marc Anthony (Marco Antonio Muñiz; 16 Sep 1968, Spanish Harlem, New York NY), American salsa singer.

Apa Sherpa (c. 1960, Thami, Nepal), Nepali mountaineer; he set the record for most ascents of Mount Everest (20).

Judd Apatow (6 Dec 1967, Syosset NY), American filmmaker.

Benigno Aquino III (8 Feb 1960, Manila, Philippines), Filipino politician; president from 2010.

Martha Argerich (5 Jun 1941, Buenos Aires, Argentina), Argentine concert pianist.

Óscar Arias (Sánchez) (13 Sep 1941, Heredia, Costa Rica), Costa Rican statesman; president of Costa Rica, 1986–90 and 2006–10; recipient of the 1987 Nobel Peace Prize.

Alan (Wolf) Arkin (26 Mar 1934, Brooklyn NY), American film and TV actor.

Giorgio Armani (11 Jul 1934, Piacenza, Italy), Italian fashion designer.

Rae Armantrout (1947, Vallejo CA), American poet; her *Versed* won the 2010 Pulitzer Prize for poetry.

Billie Joe Armstrong (17 Feb 1972, Rodeo CA), American punk-rock vocalist and guitarist (for Green Day).

Lance Armstrong (18 Sep 1971, Plano TX), American cyclist who won the Tour de France seven years in succession, 1999–2005.

Courteney Cox Arquette (Courteney Bass Cox; 15 Jun 1964, Birmingham AL), American TV and film actress.

Taro Aso (20 Sep 1940, Iizuka, Fukuoka prefecture, Japan), Japanese politician (Liberal Democratic Party); prime minister, 2008–09.

Bashar al-Assad (11 Sep 1965, Damascus, Syria), Syrian politician; president from 2000.

Susan Athey (29 Nov 1970, Boston MA), American economist specializing in economic theory, empirical economics, and econometrics.

Kate Atkinson (1951, York, England), British author.

Abdul Rahman ibn Hamad al-Attiyah (1950, Qatar), Qatari international official; secretary-general of the Gulf Cooperation Council from 2002.

Margaret (Eleanor) Atwood (18 Nov 1939, Ottawa, ON, Canada), Canadian poet, novelist, and critic.

Daw Aung San Suu Kyi (19 Jun 1945, Rangoon, Burma [now Yangon, Myanmar]), Burmese human rights activist; recipient in 1991 of the Nobel Peace Prize.

David Axelrod (22 Feb 1953, New York, NY), American political consultant (Democrat); senior adviser to US Pres. Barack Obama.

Hank Azaria (25 Apr 1964, Forest Hills NY), American actor best known for comic film roles and for providing voices for TV's *The Simpsons*.

Mykola Azarov (17 Dec 1947, Kaluga, Russia), Russian-born Ukrainian politician; prime minister from 2010.

(Verónica) Michelle Bachelet (Jeria) (29 Sep 1951, Santiago, Chile), Chilean politician (Socialist); president, 2006–10.

Bob Baffert (13 Jan 1953, Nogales AZ), American trainer of Thoroughbred racehorses.

Jerry D. Bailey (29 Aug 1957, Dallas TX), American jockey.

(Josiah) Voreque ("Frank") Bainimarama (27 Apr 1954, Kiuva, Fiji), Fijian military leader; self-appointed acting prime minister from 2007.

Sheila (Colleen) Bair (3 Apr 1954, Wichita KS), American businesswoman; chair of the Federal Deposit Insurance Corporation (FDIC) from 2006.

Gordon Bajnai (5 Mar 1968, Szeged, Hungary) Hungarian politician; prime minister, 2009–10.

Kurmanbek Bakiyev (1 Aug 1949, Masadan, Kirghiz SSR, USSR [now Teyyit, Kyrgyzstan]), Kyrgyz politician; president of Kyrgyzstan, 2005–10.

John E(lias) Baldacci (30 Jan 1955, Bangor ME), American politician (Democrat); governor of Maine from 2003.

Alec Baldwin (Alexander Rae Baldwin III; 3 Apr 1958, Massapequa NY), American film and TV actor.

Christian (Charles Philip) Bale (30 Jan 1974, Haverfordwest, Pembrokeshire, Wales), British film actor.

Jan Peter Balkenende (7 May 1956, Kapelle, Netherlands), Dutch politician (Christian Democratic Appeal); prime minister from 2002.

Steven A. Ballmer (24 Mar 1956, Detroit? MI), American corporate executive; CEO of Microsoft Corp. from 2000.

Ed(ward) Balls (25 Feb 1967, Norwich, England), British public official; secretary of state for children, schools, and families, 2007-10.

Ban Ki-moon (13 Jun 1944, Umsong, Japanese-occupied Korea [now in South Korea]), Korean government and international official; secretary-general of the United Nations from 2007.

Eric Bana (Eric Banadinovich; 9 Aug 1968, Melbourne, VIC, Australia), Australian actor.

Rupiah Banda (13 Feb 1937, Gwanda, Zimbabwe), Zambian politician; president from 2008.

Russell Banks (28 Mar 1940, Newton MA), American novelist.

Tyra Banks (4 Dec 1973, Los Angeles CA), American model, actress, and TV show host.

Banksy (1974?, Bristol?, England), British graffiti artist.

Haley (Reeves) Barbour (22 Oct 1947, Yazoo City MS), American politician (Republican); governor of Mississippi from 2004.

Javier (Ángel Encinas) Bardem (1 Mar 1969, Las Palmas, Canary Islands, Spain), Spanish film actor.

Daniel Barenboim (15 Nov 1942, Buenos Aires, Argentina), Israeli pianist and conductor; recipient of a Praemium Imperiale in 2007.

Julian Barnes (pseudonyms Edward Pygge and Dan Kavanagh; 19 Jan 1946, Leicester, Leicestershire, England), British author and TV critic.

Sacha (Noam) Baron Cohen (13 Oct 1971, Hammersmith, London, England), British comedian and actor.

José Manuel Durão Barroso (23 Mar 1956, Lisbon, Portugal), Portuguese politician; prime minister, 2002-04, and president of the European Commission from 2004.

Dean (Oliver) Barrow (2 Mar 1951, Belize City, British Honduras [now Belize]), Belizean politician (United Democratic Party); prime minister from 2008.

John D(avid) Barrow (29 Nov 1952, London, England), British cosmologist, a specialist in the anthropic principle; recipient of the 2006 Templeton Prize.

Dave Barry (3 Jul 1947, Armonk NY), American humorist, newspaper columnist, and author.

Drew Barrymore (Andrew Blythe Barrymore; 22 Feb 1975, Culver City CA), American film actress.

Frederick Barthelme (10 Oct 1943, Houston TX), American writer of short stories and novels.

Bartholomew I (Dimitrios Archontonis; 29 Feb 1940, Imbros [now Gokceada], Turkey), Eastern Orthodox archbishop of Constantinople and ecumenical patriarch from 1991.

Richard Barton (2 Jun 1967, New Canaan CT), American Internet entrepreneur (Expedia.com, Zillow.com).

Jaume Bartumeu Cassany (10 Nov 1954, Andorra), Andorran chief executive from 2009.

Carol (Ann) Bartz (29 Aug 1948, Winona MN), American corporate executive; CEO and president of Yahoo! Inc. from 2009.

Mikhail (Nikolayevich) Baryshnikov (28 Jan 1948, Riga, USSR [now in Latvia]), Soviet-born American ballet dancer, director, and actor.

Traian Basescu (4 Nov 1951, Basarabi, Romania), Romanian politician; president from 2004.

Omar Hassan Ahmad al-Bashir (1944, Hosh Bannaga, Anglo-Egyptian Sudan), Sudanese military leader; president from 1989.

Sükhbaataryn Batbold (1963), Mongolian businessman and politician; prime minister from 2009.

Michael (Benjamin) Bay (17 Feb 1965, Los Angeles CA), American director and producer of action films.

Sanj(aaglyn) Bayar (1956, Ulaanbaatar, Mongolia), Mongolian diplomat; prime minister, 2007-09.

Beatrix (31 Jan 1938, Soestdijk, Netherlands), Dutch royal; queen of the Netherlands from 1980.

Glenn Beck (10 Feb 1964, Mount Vernon WA), American conservative TV commentator and author.

David (Robert) Beckham (2 May 1975, Leytonstone, East London, England), British association football (soccer) player.

Victoria Beckham (Victoria Caroline Adams; 7 Apr 1975, Goff's Oak, Hertfordshire, England), British pop singer ("Posh Spice" of the Spice Girls) and designer.

Kate Beckinsale (26 Jul 1973, London, England), British actress.

Mike Beebe (Michael Dale Beebe; 28 Dec 1946, Amagon AR), American politician (Democrat); governor of Arkansas from 2007.

Kenenisa Bekele (13 Jun 1982, near Bekoji, Ethiopia), Ethiopian cross-country runner.

Bill Belichick (William Stephen Belichick; 16 Apr 1952, Nashville TN), American football coach.

Arden L. Bement, Jr. (22 May 1932, Pittsburgh PA), American materials scientist; director of the National Science Foundation from 2004.

Zine al-Abidine Ben Ali (3 Sep 1936, Hammam-Sousse, French Tunisia), Tunisian politician and president from 1987.

Benedict XVI (Joseph Alois Ratzinger; 16 Apr 1927, Marktl am Inn, Bavaria, Germany), German Roman Catholic churchman; pope from 2005.

Raymond Benjamin (24 Nov 1945, Alexandria, Egypt), French international official; secretary-general of the International Civil Aviation Organization from 2009.

Regina (Marcia) Benjamin (26 Oct 1956, Mobile AL), American physician; US surgeon general from 2009.

Alan Bennett (9 May 1934, Leeds, England), British dramatist and writer.

Gurbanguly Berdymukhammedov (29 Jun 1957, Bararab, USSR [now in Turkmenistan]), Turkmen politician; president from 2006.

Sali (Ram) Berisha (15 Oct 1944, Tropojë, Albania), Albanian cardiologist and politician (Democratic Party); president, 1992-97, and prime minister from 2005.

Silvio Berlusconi (29 Sep 1936, Milan, Italy), Italian businessman and politician; prime minister, 1994-95, 2001-06, and again from 2008.

Ben(jamin Shalom) Bernanke (13 Dec 1953, Augusta GA), American economist; chairman of the Board of Governors of the Federal Reserve System from 2006.

Tim(othy J.) Berners-Lee (8 Jun 1955, London, England), British inventor of the World Wide Web and director of the World Wide Web Consortium (W3C) from 1994.

Halle (Maria) Berry (14 Aug 1968, Cleveland OH), American film actress and model.

Tarcisio Cardinal Bertone (2 Dec 1934, Romano Canavese, Italy), Italian Roman Catholic churchman; secretary of state of the Vatican from 2006.

Steve(n Lynn) Beshear (21 Sep 1944, Dawson Springs KY), American politician (Democrat); governor of Kentucky from 2007.

Beyoncé (Knowles) (4 Sep 1981, Houston TX), American R&B singer and actress.

Jeffrey P. Bezos (12 Jan 1964, Albuquerque NM), American corporate executive; founder and CEO of Amazon.com from 1995.

Bhumibol Adulyadej (Rama IX; 5 Dec 1927, Cambridge MA), Thai royal; king of Thailand from 1946.

Joe Biden (Joseph Robinette Biden, Jr.; 20 Nov 1942, Scranton PA), American politician (Democrat); senator from Delaware, 1973–2009, and vice president of the US from 2009.

Jessica (Claire) Biel (3 Mar 1982, Ely MN), American TV and film actress.

Kathryn Bigelow (27 Nov 1951, San Carlos CA), American film director; she was the first woman to win an Academy Award for best director.

Osama bin Laden (also spelled Usamah ibn Ladin; 10 Mar 1957, Riyadh, Saudi Arabia), Saudi Arabian–born terrorist and leader of the al-Qaeda organization.

Harrison Birtwistle (15 Jul 1934, Accrington, Lancashire, England), British composer of operas, chamber music, and orchestral music.

Paul Biya (13 Feb 1933, Mvomeka'a, Cameroon), Cameroonian politician; president from 1982.

Jack Black (28 Aug 1969, Hermosa Beach CA), American film actor and comic rock musician.

Elizabeth H. Blackburn (26 Nov 1948, Hobart, TAS, Australia), Australian-born American molecular biologist and biochemist; cowinner of the 2009 Nobel Prize for Physiology or Medicine.

Douglas A. Blackmon (6 Sep 1964, Stuttgart AR), American journalist and author; recipient of the 2009 Pulitzer Prize for general nonfiction for *Slavery by Another Name: The Re-Enslavement of Black Americans from the Civil War to World War II.*

Rod Blagojevich (Milorad R. Blagojevich; 10 Dec 1956, Chicago IL), American politician (Democrat); governor of Illinois, 2003–09; he was impeached on corruption allegations that included the attempted sale of US Pres. Barack Obama's vacated Senate seat.

Dennis C(utler) Blair (4 Feb 1947, Kittery ME), American military official; US director of national intelligence, 2009–10.

Tony Blair (Anthony Charles Lynton Blair; 6 May 1953, Edinburgh, Scotland), British politician (Labour); prime minister of the UK, 1997–2007, and special envoy to the Middle East thereafter.

Cate Blanchett (Catherine Elise Blanchett; 14 May 1969, Melbourne, VIC, Australia), Australian film actress.

Mary J. Blige (11 Jan 1971, New York NY), American hip-hop soul singer.

Amy Bloom (1953, New York NY), American writer.

Harold (Irving) Bloom (11 Jul 1930, New York NY), American literary critic.

Orlando Bloom (13 Jan 1977, Canterbury, Kent, England), British film actor.

Michael R. Bloomberg (14 Feb 1942, Medford MA), American businessman, philanthropist, and politician (independent); mayor of New York City from 2002.

Emil Boc (6 Sep 1966, Rachitele, Romania), Romanian politician, prime minister from 2008.

Andrea Bocelli (22 Sep 1958, Lajatico, Italy), Italian operatic tenor, blind from childhood.

Samuel (Wright) Bodman (26 Nov 1938, Chicago IL), American chemical engineer, corporate leader, and official; US secretary of energy, 2005–09.

Irina Bokova (12 Jul 1952, Bulgaria), Bulgarian diplomat and politician; director general of UNESCO from 2009.

Charles F(rank) Bolden, Jr. (19 Aug 1946, Columbia SC), American astronaut; administrator of NASA from 2009.

Haji Hassanal Bolkiah Mu'izzadin Waddaulah (15 Jul 1946, Brunei Town [now Bandar Seri Begawan], Brunei), Bruneian royal; sultan from 1967.

Usain Bolt (21 Aug 1986, Montego Bay, Jamaica), Jamaican sprinter.

Barry (Lamar) Bonds (24 Jul 1964, Riverside CA), American baseball player who broke the all-time home run record in 2007.

(Thomas) Yayi Boni (1952, Tchaourou, French Dahomey [now Benin]), Beninese politician (independent); president from 2006.

Jon Bon Jovi (John Francis Bongiovi, Jr.; 2 Mar 1962, Perth Amboy NJ), American rock singer, musician, and songwriter.

Bono (Paul David Hewson; also known as Bono Vox; 10 May 1960, Dublin, Ireland), Irish rock vocalist (for U2) as well as a human rights activist and mediator.

Boiko Borisov (13 Jun 1959), Bulgarian politician; prime minister from 2009.

Umberto Bossi (19 Sep 1941, Cassano Magnano, Italy), Italian politician and leader of the separatist Northern League from 1991.

Kate Bosworth (Catherine Anne Bosworth; 2 Jan 1983, Los Angeles CA), American film and TV actress.

Bouasone Bouphavanh (3 Jun 1954, Ban Tao Poun, Salavan province, French Indochina [now in Laos]), Laotian politician and prime minister from 2006.

Anthony (Michael) Bourdain (25 Jun 1956, New York NY), American chef, author, and TV personality.

Abdelaziz Bouteflika (2 Mar 1937, Tlemcen, Algeria), Algerian politician, diplomat, and president from 1999.

Dési(ré Delano) Bouterse (13 Oct 1945, Domburg, Dutch Guiana [now Suriname]), Surinamese politician; president of Suriname from 2010.

Danny Boyle (20 Oct 1956, Manchester, England), British film director.

T. Coraghessan Boyle (Thomas John Boyle; 2 Dec 1948, Peekskill NY), American author.

Willard Boyle (19 Aug 1924, Amherst, NS, Canada), Canadian American physicist; cowinner of the 2009 Nobel Prize for Physics.

François Bozizé (14 Oct 1946, Mouila, French Equatorial Africa [now in Gabon]), Central African Republic politician; president from 2003.

Dallas Braden (13 Aug 1983, Phoenix AZ), American professional baseball starting pitcher; he pitched a perfect game for the Oakland Athletics in May 2010, only the 19th player in MLB history to do so.

Tom Brady (Thomas Brady; 3 Aug 1977, San Mateo CA), American professional football quarterback.

Zach(ary Israel) Braff (6 Apr 1975, South Orange NJ), American TV and film actor.

Lakhdar Brahimi (1 Jan 1934, Algeria), Algerian statesman, diplomat, and international official.

Serge Brammertz (17 Feb 1962, Eupen, Belgium), Belgian jurist; deputy prosecutor for the International Criminal Court, 2003–07, and prosecutor for the International Tribunal for the Former Yugoslavia from 2008.

Russell Brand (4 Jun 1975, Grays, Essex, England), British comedian and actor.

Richard (Charles Nicholas) Branson (18 Jul 1950, Shamley Green, Surrey, England), British entrepreneur who founded the Virgin empire in 1973.

Anthony Braxton (4 Jun 1945, Chicago IL), American avant-garde reed player and composer.

Phil(ip Norman) Bredesen (21 Nov 1943, Oceanport NJ), American politician (Democrat); governor of Tennessee from 2003.

Alfred Brendel (5 Jan 1931, Wiesenberg, Moravia [now Czech Republic]), Austrian pianist; recipient of a Praemium Imperiale in 2009.

Abigail (Kathleen) Breslin (14 Apr 1996, New York NY), American actress.

Jan(ice K.) Brewer (26 Sep 1944, Hollywood CA), American politician (Republican), governor of Arizona from 2009.

Stephen (Gerald) Breyer (15 Aug 1938, San Francisco CA), American jurist; associate justice of the US Supreme Court from 1994.

Sergey (Mikhaylovich) Brin (21 Aug 1973, Moscow, USSR [now in Russia]), Russian-born computer scientist and Internet entrepreneur who co-founded (1998) the Google Internet search engine.

Matthew Broderick (21 Mar 1962, New York NY), American actor.

Martin Brodeur (6 May 1972, Montreal, QC, Canada), French Canadian ice-hockey player; in 2009 he became the all-time winningest goalie in the National Hockey League.

Wallace S. Broecker (29 Nov 1931, Chicago IL), American geochemist, a specialist in climate change; recipient of a National Medal of Science in 1996 and a Crafoord Prize in 2006.

Josh (J.) Brolin (12 Feb 1968, Los Angeles CA), American film and TV actor.

Kix Brooks (Leon Eric Brooks; 12 May 1955, Shreveport LA), American country-and-western singer (for Brooks & Dunn).

(Troyal) Garth Brooks (7 Feb 1962, Tulsa OK), American country-and-western singer.

Pierce (Brendan) Brosnan (16 May 1953, Navan, County Meath, Ireland), Irish actor.

Dan Brown (22 Jun 1964, Exeter NH), American novelist.

Ewart (Frederick) Brown, Jr. (1946, Bermuda), Bermudan politician; prime minister from 2006.

(James) Gordon Brown (20 Feb 1951, Glasgow, Scotland), Scottish-born politician (Labour); chancellor of the Exchequer, 1997–2007, and prime minister, 2007–10.

Jerry Bruckheimer (21 Sep 1945, Detroit MI), American film and TV producer.

Kobe Bryant (23 Aug 1978, Philadelphia PA), American basketball player.

Quentin Bryce (1942, Brisbane, QLD, Australia), Australian politician; governor-general of Australia from 2008.

Bill Bryson (1951, Des Moines IA), American-born journalist and travel writer.

Michael Bublé (9 Sep 1975, Burnaby, BC, Canada), Canadian pop singer.

Patrick J(oseph) Buchanan (2 Nov 1938, Washington DC), American conservative journalist.

Christopher (Taylor) Buckley (1952, New York NY), American satiric novelist and magazine editor.

Mark (Anthony) Buehrle (23 Mar 1979, St. Charles MO), American professional baseball starting pitcher; he pitched a perfect game for the Chicago White Sox in July 2009, only the 18th player in MLB history to do so.

Warren (Edward) Buffett (30 Aug 1930, Omaha NE), American investor; CEO of Berkshire Hathaway Inc. from 1965; named the world's richest person by *Forbes* in 2008.

Sandra (Annette) Bullock (26 Jul 1964, Arlington VA), American film actress.

Gisele (Caroline Nonnenmacher) Bündchen (20 Jul 1980, Horizontina, Rio Grande do Sul state, Brazil), Brazilian fashion model.

Daniel Buren (25 Mar 1938, Paris, France), French conceptual artist; recipient of a 2007 Praemium Imperiale.

Mark Burnett (17 Jul 1960, Myland, East London, England), English-born American reality-TV-show producer.

Ken(neth Lauren) Burns (29 Jul 1953, Brooklyn NY), American documentary filmmaker.

Tim(othy William) Burton (25 Aug 1958, Burbank CA), American film director and writer.

Steve Buscemi (13 Dec 1957, Brooklyn NY), American film actor.

Barbara Bush (Barbara Pierce; 8 Jun 1925, Rye NY), American first lady; wife of US Pres. George W. Bush (married 6 Jan 1945).

George H(erbert) W(alker) Bush (12 Jun 1924, Milton MA), American statesman; vice president of the US, 1981–89, and 41st president, 1989–93; father of US Pres. George W. Bush.

George W(alker) Bush (6 Jul 1946, New Haven CT), American politician (Republican); 43rd president of the US, 2001–09; son of US Pres. George H.W. Bush.

Laura Bush (Laura Lane Welch; 4 Nov 1946, Midland TX), American first lady; wife of US Pres. George W. Bush (married 5 Nov 1977).

Mangosuthu Gatsha Buthelezi (27 Aug 1928, Mahlabatini, Natal, Union of South Africa [now KwaZulu Natal province, South Africa]), South African Zulu chief, the founder (1975) and leader of the Inkatha Freedom Party.

Gerard (James) Butler (13 Nov 1969, Glasgow, Scotland), British actor.

A.S. Byatt (Antonia Susan Drabble; 24 Aug 1936, Sheffield, England), English literary critic and novelist.

(Mary) Rose Byrne (24 Jul 1979, Balmain, Sydney, NSW, Australia), Australian actress.

Nicolas Cage (Nicholas Kim Coppola; 7 Jan 1964, Long Beach CA), American film actor.

Cai Guo Qiang (8 Dec 1957, Quanzhou, Fujian province, China), Chinese installation artist.

Santiago Calatrava (28 Jul 1951, Valencia, Spain), Spanish architect.

Felipe (de Jesús) Calderón (Hinojosa) (18 Aug 1962, Morelia, Michoacán state, Mexico), Mexican politician (National Action Party); president from 2006.

Felix Perez Camacho (30 Oct 1957, Camp Zama, Japan), Guamanian politician (Republican); governor of Guam from 2003.

Moussa Dadis Camara (1964, Koure, Guinea), Guinean military leader, president from 2008.

David (William Donald) Cameron (9 Oct 1966, London, England), British politician (Conservative); prime minister from 2010.

James Cameron (16 Aug 1954, Kapuskasing, ON, Canada), Canadian film director whose credits include the blockbusters *Titanic* (1997) and *Avatar* (2009).

Camilla (Camilla Parker Bowles; Camilla Shand; 17 Jul 1947, London, England), British duchess of Cornwall and celebrity; wife of Charles, prince of Wales (married 9 Apr 2005).

Louis C. Camilleri (1955, Alexandria, Egypt), American corporate executive; chairman and CEO of Philip Morris International from 2008.

Gordon Campbell (12 Jan 1948, Vancouver, BC, Canada), Canadian politician (Liberal); premier of British Columbia from 2001.

Menzies Campbell (22 May 1941, Glasgow, Scotland), British politician; leader of the Liberal Democratic Party, 2006–07.

Naomi Campbell (22 May 1970, London, England), British runway and photographic model.

Fabio Cannavaro (13 Sep 1973, Naples, Italy), Italian association football (soccer) player.

Don(ald L.) Carcieri (16 Dec 1942, East Greenwich RI), American banker and politician (Republican); governor of Rhode Island from 2003.

Drew (Allison) Carey (23 May 1958, Cleveland OH), American comic TV actor and game-show host.

Mariah Carey (27 Mar 1970, Huntington, Long Island, NY), American pop singer.

Peter (Philip) Carey (7 May 1943, Bacchus Marsh, VIC, Australia), Australian author.

Carl XVI Gustaf (Carl Gustaf Folke Hubertus; 30 Apr 1946, Stockholm, Sweden), Swedish royal; king from 1973.

Robert A. Caro (30 Oct 1935, New York NY), American biographer.

Caroline (Caroline Louise Margaret Grimaldi; 23 Jan 1957, Monte Carlo, Monaco), Monegasque princess, the elder daughter of Prince Rainier III and Princess Grace.

Steve(n John) Carrell (16 Aug 1962, Concord MA), American comic actor.

Jim Carrey (James Eugene Carrey; 17 Jan 1962, Newmarket, ON, Canada), Canadian-born American comic actor.

Edwin W. Carrington (1938, Tobago, British West Indies [now in Trinidad and Tobago]), Trinidadian international official; secretary-general of the Caribbean Community (CARICOM) from 1992.

Jimmy Carter (James Earl Carter, Jr.; 1 Oct 1924, Plains GA), American statesman; 39th president of the US, 1977–81, and recipient of the 2002 Nobel Peace Prize.

Marsh(all N.) Carter (1940, Washington DC?), American corporate executive; chairman of the New York Stock Exchange from 2005.

Rosalynn Carter (18 Aug 1927, Plains GA), American first lady; wife of US Pres. Jimmy Carter (married 7 Jul 1946).

David Caruso (7 Jan 1956, Forest Hills NY), American actor.

James Carville, Jr. (25 Oct 1944, Carville LA), American political strategist and commentator.

George W. Casey, Jr. (22 Jul 1948, Sendai, Japan), American military officer; chief of staff of the US Army from 2007.

Fidel (Alejandro) Castro (Ruz) (13 Aug 1926, near Birán, Holguín province, Cuba), Cuban revolutionary; leader of Cuba, 1959–2008; he became a defiant symbol of communist revolution in Latin America.

Raúl (Modesto) Castro (Ruz) (3 Jun 1931, near Birán, Holguín province, Cuba), Cuban revolutionary leader and politician; acting president of Cuba from 2006, following the illness of his brother Fidel, and president from 2008.

Helio Castroneves (10 May 1975, São Paulo, Brazil), Brazilian race-car driver.

Kim Cattrall (21 Aug 1956, Liverpool, England), British-born film and TV actress.

Aníbal (António) Cavaco Silva (15 Jul 1939, Boliqueime, Algarve, Portugal), Portuguese politician; prime minister, 1985–95, and president from 2006.

Roberto Cavalli (15 Nov 1940, Florence, Italy), Italian fashion designer.

Michael Cera (7 Jun 1988, Brampton, ON, Canada), Canadian actor.

Vinton G(ray) Cerf (23 Jun 1943, New Haven CT), American computer scientist known as the "father of the Internet"; recipient of a Japan Prize in 2008.

Michael Chabon (24 May 1963, Washington DC), American novelist and short-story writer.

Riccardo Chailly (20 Feb 1953, Milan, Italy), Italian orchestra conductor; music director of the Leipzig Opera, 2005–08, and Leipzig's Gewandhaus Orchestra from 2005.

Martin Chalfie (15? Jan 1947, Chicago IL), American chemist; corecipient of the 2008 Nobel Prize for Chemistry.

John T. Chambers (23 Aug 1949, Cleveland OH), American corporate executive; CEO (from 1995) and chairman (from 2006) of Cisco Systems, Inc.

Jackie Chan (Chan Kwong-Sang; 7 Apr 1954, Hong Kong), Chinese actor and director of martial arts films.

Margaret Chan (1947, Hong Kong), Hong Kong–born public health officer; director general of the World Health Organization from 2007.

Elaine L. Chao (26 Mar 1953, Taipei, Taiwan), American government official; secretary of labor, 2001–09.

Dave Chappelle (David Chappelle; 24 Aug 1973, Washington DC), American film and TV comedian and actor.

Jean Charest (John James Charest; 24 Jun 1958, Sherbrooke, QC, Canada), French Canadian politician; leader of the Quebec Liberal Party from 1998 and premier of Quebec from 2003.

Charles (Charles Philip Arthur George Mountbatten-Windsor; 14 Nov 1948, Buckingham Palace, London, England), British prince of Wales; the eldest son of Queen Elizabeth II and Prince Philip, duke of Edinburgh; and heir apparent to the throne.

Hugo Chávez (Frías) (28 Jul 1954, Sabaneta, Venezuela), Venezuelan military leader and politician; president of Venezuela from 1999.

Don Cheadle (29 Nov 1964, Kansas City MO), American film and TV actor.

Chen Shui-bian (Ch'en Shui-pian; 18 Feb 1951, Hsichuang village, Tainan county, Taiwan), Taiwanese politician and president, 2000–08.

Dick Cheney (Richard Bruce Cheney; 30 Jan 1941, Lincoln NE), American politician (Republican); US secretary of defense, 1989–93, and vice president, 2001–09.

Michael Chertoff (28 Nov 1953, Elizabeth NJ), American attorney; secretary of homeland security, 2005–09.

Robert Kipkoech Cheruiyot (26 Sep 1978, Eldoret, Kenya), Kenyan long-distance runner.

Kenny Chesney (26 Mar 1968, Luttrell TN), American country-and-western singer.

Judy Chicago (Judy Cohen; 20 Jul 1939, Chicago IL), American artist.

Dale Chihuly (20 Sep 1941, Tacoma WA), American glass artist.

Lee Child (Jim Grant; 1954, Coventry, West Midlands, England), English author of thrillers.

Laura Chinchilla (28 Mar 1959, San José, Costa Rica), Costa Rican politician; first female president of Costa Rica from 2010.

Fujio Cho (1937, Tokyo, Japan), Japanese corporate executive; chairman of Toyota Motor Corp. from 2005.

Deepak Chopra (22 Oct 1946, New Delhi, British India), Indian-born American endocrinologist, alternative-medicine advocate, and best-selling author.

Choummaly Sayasone (6 Mar 1936, Attapu province, French Indochina [now in Laos]), Laotian political official; general secretary of the Lao People's Revolutionary Party from 2006, and president from 2006.

Chow Yun-Fat (Zhou Runfa; 18 May 1955, Lamma Island, Hong Kong), Hong Kong actor.

Chris Christie (6 Sep 1962, Newark NJ), American lawyer and politician (Republican); governor of New Jersey from 2010.

Julie (Frances) Christie (14 Apr 1941, Chukua, Assam, British India), British film actress.

Dimitris Christofias (29 Aug 1946, Kato Dhikomo, British Cyprus), Cypriot politician; president of Cyprus from 2008.

Steven Chu (28 Feb 1948, St. Louis MO), American physicist; corecipient of the 1997 Nobel Prize for Physics; US secretary of energy from 2009.

Ralph J(ohn) Cicerone (2 May 1943, New Castle PA), American electrical engineer and atmospheric scientist; president of the National Academy of Sciences from 2005.

Sandra Cisneros (20 Dec 1954, Chicago IL), American short-story writer and poet.

Tom Clancy (Thomas L. Clancy, Jr.; 12 Apr 1947, Baltimore MD), American best-selling novelist.

James R. Clapper, Jr. (c. 1941), American military leader; US director of national intelligence from 2010.

Eric Clapton (Eric Patrick Clapp; 30 Mar 1945, Ripley, Surrey, England), British guitarist, singer, and songwriter.

Helen Clark (26 Feb 1950, Hamilton, New Zealand), New Zealand politician (Labour); prime minister, 1999–2008, and first female administrator of the United Nations Development Programme from 2009.

Kelly Clarkson (24 Apr 1982, Burleson TX), American pop singer.

Patricia (Davies) Clarkson (29 Dec 1959, New Orleans LA), American stage, film, and TV actress.

John (Marwood) Cleese (27 Oct 1939, Weston-super-Mare, England), British comic actor.

Nick Clegg (Nicholas William Peter Clegg; 7 Jan 1967, Chalfont St. Giles, Buckinghamshire, England), British politician (Liberal Democrats); deputy prime minister from 2010.

Van Cliburn (Harvey Lavan Cliburn, Jr.; 12 Jul 1934, Shreveport LA), American pianist.

Bill Clinton (William Jefferson Blythe III; 19 Aug 1946, Hope AR), American statesman; 42nd president of the US, 1993–2001.

Hillary Rodham Clinton (Hillary Diane Rodham; 26 Oct 1947, Chicago IL), American politician (Democrat); senator from New York, 2001–09, unsuccessful candidate for president in 2008, and US secretary of state from 2009; wife of US Pres. Bill Clinton.

George Clooney (6 May 1961, Lexington KY), American film and TV actor.

Chuck Close (Charles Thomas Close; 5 Jul 1940, Monroe WA), American Photo-realist painter.

Glenn Close (19 Mar 1947, Greenwich CT), American film and stage actress.

G(erald) Wayne Clough (24 Sep 1941, Douglas GA), American educator and executive; secretary of the Smithsonian Institution from 2008.

Diablo Cody (Brooke Busey; 14 Jun 1978, Chicago IL), American stripper-turned-writer; author of several screenplays, including for the film Juno (2007).

Paulo Coelho (24 Aug 1947, Rio de Janeiro, Brazil), Brazilian novelist.

Ethan Coen (21 Sep 1958, St. Louis Park MN), American filmmaker.

Joel Coen (29 Nov 1955, St. Louis Park MN), American filmmaker.

J(ohn) M(axwell) Coetzee (9 Feb 1940, Cape Town, Union of South Africa), South African novelist and critic; recipient of the 2003 Nobel Prize for Literature.

Leonard Cohen (21 Sep 1934, Montreal, QC, Canada), Canadian singer and songwriter.

Stephen Colbert (13 May 1964, Charleston SC), American TV commentator and satirist; host of The Colbert Report from 2005.

Ornette Coleman (9 Mar 1930, Fort Worth TX), American jazz saxophonist, composer, and bandleader; his Sound Grammar won the 2007 Pulitzer Prize for music.

Toni Collette (Antonia Collette; 1 Nov 1972, Sydney, NSW, Australia), Australian film and TV actress.

Billy Collins (1941, New York NY), American poet; poet laureate of the US, 2001–03.

Francis S. Collins (14 Apr 1950, Staunton VA), American physician, geneticist, and medical administrator; director of the National Institutes of Health from 2009.

Marva Collins (Marva Delores Knight; 31 Aug 1936, Monroeville AL), American educator.

Alan Colmes (24 Sep 1950, Long Island NY), American liberal journalist and commentator on radio and TV.

Álvaro Colom (Caballeros) (15 Jun 1951, Guatemala City, Guatemala), Guatemalan politician (National Union for Hope); president from 2008.

Sean Combs ("Puffy"; Puff Daddy; P. Diddy; Diddy; 4 Nov 1970, Harlem, New York NY), American rap artist, impresario, fashion mogul, and actor.

Common (Lonnie Rashid Lynn, Jr.; Common Sense; 13 Mar 1972, Chicago IL), American hip-hop artist and actor.

Blaise Compaoré (1951, Ziniane, Upper Volta [now Burkina Faso]), Burkinabe politician; president of Burkina Faso from 1987.

Jennifer Connelly (12 Dec 1970, Round Top NY), American fashion model and film actress.

(Thomas) Sean Connery (25 Aug 1930, Edinburgh, Scotland), Scottish film actor.

Alberto Contador (6 Dec 1982, Pinto, Spain), Spanish cyclist; winner of the 2007, 2009, and 2010 Tours de France.

James T. Conway (26 Dec 1947, Walnut Ridge AR), American military officer; commandant of the US Marine Corps from 2006.

Dane (Jeffrey) Cook (18 Mar 1972, Boston MA), American comedian and actor.

Anderson (Hays) Cooper (3 Jun 1967, New York NY), American TV journalist.

Bradley Cooper (5 Jan 1975, Philadephia PA), American TV and film actor.

Chris(topher W.) Cooper (9 Jul 1951, Kansas City MO), American film and TV actor.

Cynthia Cooper (14 Apr 1963, Chicago IL), American basketball player and coach.

Francis Ford Coppola (7 Apr 1939, Detroit MI), American film director, writer, and producer.

Sofia Coppola (14 May 1971, New York NY), American film director, writer, actress, and designer; daughter of director Francis Ford Coppola.

Chick Corea (Armando Anthony Corea; 12 Jun 1941, Chelsea MA), American jazz pianist, composer, and bandleader.

Patricia Cornwell (Patricia Daniels; 9 Jun 1956, Miami FL), American author of mystery novels.

Rafael (Vicente) Correa (Delgado) (6 Apr 1963, Guayaquil, Ecuador), Ecuadorian politician; president from 2007.

Jon (Stevens) Corzine (1 Jan 1947, Willey's Station IL), American politician (Democrat); senator from New Jersey, 2001–06, and governor, 2006–10.

Bill Cosby (William Henry Cosby, Jr.; 12 Jul 1937, Philadelphia PA), American comedian, actor, and author.

Bob Costas (Robert Quinlan Costas; 22 Mar 1952, New York NY), American TV sportscaster and host.

Kevin (Michael) Costner (18 Jan 1955, Lynwood CA), American film actor and director.

Marion Cotillard (30 Sep 1975, Paris, France), French actress.

Pascal Couchepin (5 Apr 1942, Martigny, Switzerland), Swiss politician; president, 2003, and 2008–09.

Tom Coughlin (Thomas Richard Coughlin; 31 Aug 1946, Waterloo NY), American football coach.

David Coulthard (27 Mar 1971, Twynholm, Scotland), British Formula 1 race-car driver.

Katie Couric (7 Jan 1957, Arlington VA), American TV talk-show host and news anchor.

Simon (Phillip) Cowell (7 Oct 1959, Brighton, East Sussex, England), British record producer and TV personality; a judge on the *American Idol* show (2002–10).

Brian Cowen (Irish: Brian Ó Comhain; 10 Jan 1960, Tullamore, County Offaly, Ireland), Irish politician (Fianna Fáil); prime minister from 2008.

Christopher Cox (16 Oct 1952, St. Paul MN), American politician (Republican); chairman of the US Securities and Exchange Commission, 2005–09.

Tony Cragg (1949, Liverpool, England), British sculptor and installation artist; recipient of a Praemium Imperiale in 2007.

Daniel (Wroughton) Craig (2 Mar 1968, Chester, Cheshire, England), British stage and movie actor who played James Bond in films from 2006.

Bryan Cranston (7 Mar 1956, San Fernando Valley, California), American actor.

Charlie Crist (Charles Joseph Crist, Jr.; 24 Jul 1956, Altoona PA), American politician (Independent); governor of Florida from 2007.

Stanley Crouch (14 Dec 1945, Los Angeles CA), American journalist and critic.

Sheryl Crow (11 Feb 1962, Kennett MO), American singer-songwriter.

Russell (Ira) Crowe (7 Apr 1964, Wellington, New Zealand), New Zealand–born Australian film actor.

Tom Cruise (Thomas Cruise Mapother IV; 3 Jul 1962, Syracuse NY), American actor.

Nilo Cruz (1962?, Matanzas, Cuba), Cuban-born American playwright.

Penélope Cruz (Sánchez) (28 Apr 1974, Madrid, Spain), Spanish film actress.

Branko Crvenkovski (12 Oct 1962, Sarajevo, Yugoslavia [now in Bosnia and Herzegovina]), Macedonian politician; prime minister, 1992–98 and 2002–04, and president, 2004–09.

Jamie Cullum (20 Aug 1979, Essex, England), British pop, jazz, and rock pianist and vocalist.

Chet Culver (Chester John Culver; 25 Jan 1966, Washington DC), American politician (Democrat); governor of Iowa from 2007.

Joan Cusack (11 Oct 1962, New York NY), American film and TV actress.

John (Paul) Cusack (28 Jun 1966, Evanston IL), American film actor.

Mirko Cvetkovic (16 Aug 1950, Zajecar, Yugoslavia [now in Serbia]), Serbian politician; prime minister from 2008.

Miley (Ray) Cyrus (Destiny Hope Cyrus; 23 Nov 1992, Franklin TN), American TV (*Hannah Montana*) and film actress and singer.

Dalai Lama (the 14th Dalai Lama, Tenzin Gyatso; original name Lhamo Dhondrub; 6 Jul 1935, Takster, Amdo province, Tibet [now Tsinghai province, China]), Tibetan spiritual leader (enthroned in 1940) and ruler-in-exile; head of the Tibetan Buddhists; recipient of the 1989 Nobel Peace Prize.

Richard M(ichael) Daley (24 Apr 1942, Chicago IL), American politician (Democrat); mayor of Chicago from 1989.

Matt(hew Page) Damon (8 Oct 1970, Cambridge MA), American film actor.

Claire (Catherine) Danes (12 Apr 1979, New York NY), American actress.

Lee Daniels (24 Dec 1959, Philadelphia PA), American film director and producer.

Mitch(ell Elais) Daniels, Jr. (7 Apr 1949, Monongahela PA), American businessman and politician (Republican); director of the US Office of Management and Budget, 2001–03, and governor of Indiana from 2005.

Edwidge Danticat (19 Jan 1969, Port-au-Prince, Haiti), Haitian-born American author.

Larry David (2 Jul 1947, Brooklyn NY), American actor and writer.

Shani Davis (13 Aug 1982, Chicago IL), American speed skater; first black athlete to win an individual Winter Olympics gold medal.

Terry Davis (Terence Anthony Gordon Davis; 5 Jan 1938, Stourbridge, West Midlands, England), British international executive; secretary-general of the Council of Europe, 2004–09.

Viola Davis (11 Aug 1965, Saint Matthews SC), American actress.

Daniel (Michael Blake) Day-Lewis (29 Apr 1957, London, England), British film actor.

Pierre de Boissieu (1945), French statesman; secretary-general of the Council of the European Union from 2009.

Jaap de Hoop Scheffer (Jakob Gijsbert de Hoop Scheffer; 3 Apr 1948, Amsterdam, Netherlands), Dutch international official; secretary-general of NATO, 2004–09.

Danielle de Niese (1980, Melbourne, VIC, Australia), Australian-born American operatic soprano.

Robert De Niro (17 Aug 1943, New York NY), American film actor.

Howard (Brush) Dean III (17 Nov 1948, New York NY), American physician and politician (Democrat); governor of Vermont, 1991–2003, and chairman of the Democratic National Committee, 2005–09.

Idriss Déby Itno (1952, Fada, Chad, French Equatorial Africa [now in Chad]), Chadian politician; president from 1990.

Ellen DeGeneres (26 Jan 1958, Metairie LA), American comedian and TV personality.

John P. deJongh, Jr. (13 Nov 1957, St. Thomas, US Virgin Islands), Virgin Islander politician (Democrat); governor of the US Virgin Islands from 2007.

Benicio Del Toro (19 Feb 1967, San Turce, Puerto Rico), American film actor.

Bertrand Delanoë (30 May 1950, Tunis, French Tunisia), French politician (Socialist); mayor of Paris from 2001.

Don DeLillo (20 Nov 1936, New York NY), American postmodernist novelist.

Michael S. Dell (23 Feb 1965, Houston TX), American businessman; founder of Dell Computer Corp. and its CEO, 1984–2004 and again from 2007.

Yelena (Vyacheslavovna) Dementyeva (15 Oct 1981, Moscow, USSR [now in Russia]), Russian tennis player.

Patrick Dempsey (13 Jan 1966, Lewiston ME), American film and TV actor.

Judi Dench (Judith Olivia Dench; 9 Dec 1934, York, England), British stage, TV, and film actress.

Carl Dennis (17 Sep 1939, St. Louis MO), American poet.

Nick Denton (24 Aug 1966, Hampstead, London, England), British founder of Gawker Media.

Johnny Depp (John Christopher Depp II; 9 Jun 1963, Owensboro KY), American film actor.

Kiran Desai (3 Sep 1971, New Delhi, India), Indian-born American novelist; her *The Inheritance of Loss* won the 2006 Booker Prize.

Bernard d'Espagnat (22 Aug 1921, Fourmagnac, France), French physicist and philosopher of science; recipient of the 2009 Templeton Prize.

Frankie Dettori (Lanfranco Dettori; 15 Dec 1970, Milan, Italy), Italian-born English jockey.

Darrell Dexter (10 Sep 1957, Halifax, NS, Canada), Canadian politician (Nova Scotia New Democratic Party); premier of Nova Scotia from 2009.

Cameron (Michelle) Diaz (30 Aug 1972, San Diego CA), American model and actress.

Junot Díaz (31 Dec 1968, Santo Domingo, Dominican Republic), Dominican Republic-born American writer; his novel *The Brief Wondrous Life of Oscar Wao* won the 2008 Pulitzer Prize for fiction.

Kate DiCamillo (25 Mar 1965, Philadelphia PA), American author of children's books.

Leonardo (Wilhelm) DiCaprio (11 Nov 1974, Los Angeles CA), American film actor.

Joan Didion (5 Dec 1934, Sacramento CA), American author and journalist.

Vin Diesel (Mark Vincent; 18 Jul 1967, New York NY), American film actor.

Matt Dillon (18 Feb 1964, New Rochelle NY), American film actor.

Jamie Dimon (James Dimon; 13 Mar 1956, New York NY), American executive; president and CEO of JPMorgan Chase & Co. from 2005.

Céline Dion (30 Mar 1968, Charlemagne, QC, Canada), French Canadian pop singer.

Stéphane Dion (28 Sep 1955, Quebec city, QC, Canada), Canadian politician; leader of the Liberal Party of Canada, 2007–08.

El Hadj Diouf (15 Jan 1981, Dakar, Senegal), Senegalese association football (soccer) star for French and English clubs and for the Senegalese national team.

Jacques Diouf (1 Aug 1938, Saint-Louis, French West Africa [now in Senegal]), Senegalese international official; director general of the Food and Agriculture Organization of the UN from 1994.

Milo Djukanovic (15 Feb 1962, Niksic, Yugoslavia [now in Montenegro]), Montenegrin politician; president of Montenegro, 1998–2002, and prime minister, 1991–98, 2003–06, and again from 2008.

Lou Dobbs (24 Sep 1945, Childress TX), American business journalist and radio host.

E(dgar) L(aurence) Doctorow (6 Jan 1931, New York NY), American novelist.

Christopher J(ohn) Dodd (27 May 1944, Willimantic CT), American politician (Democrat); senator from Connecticut from 1981.

Mick Dodson (Michael James Dodson; 10 Apr 1950, Katherine, NT, Australia), Australian Aboriginal leader and activist; he was named Australian of the Year for 2009.

Gary Doer (31 Mar 1948, Winnipeg, MB, Canada), Canadian politician (New Democratic Party of Manitoba); premier of Manitoba, 1999–2009, and Canadian ambassador to the US from 2009.

Timothy M(ichael) Dolan (6 Feb 1950, St. Louis MO), American Roman Catholic church leader; archbishop of New York from 2009.

Domenico Dolce (13 Aug 1958, Polizzi Generosa, near Palermo, Italy), Italian fashion designer and partner of Stefano Gabbana.

Valdis Dombrovskis (5 Aug 1971, Riga, Latvia), Latvian politician, prime minister of Latvia from 2009.

Plácido Domingo (21 Jan 1941, Madrid, Spain), Spanish-born Mexican operatic tenor.

John (Joseph) Donahoe II (1960, US?), American executive; president and CEO of eBay from 2008.

Vincent (Phillip) D'Onofrio (30 Jul 1959, Brooklyn NY), American TV and film actor.

Landon Donovan (4 Mar 1982, Ontario CA), American association football (soccer) player.

Shaun Donovan (24 Jan 1966, New York NY), American architect and government official; US secretary of housing and urban development from 2009.

Jean-Marie Doré (1938?), Guinean politician; prime minister from 2010.

Jack Dorsey (4 Apr 1977, St. Louis MO), American entrepreneur; cofounder of Twitter.

José Eduardo dos Santos (28 Aug 1942, Luanda, Portuguese Angola), Angolan statesman and president from 1979.

Denzil L. Douglas (14 Jan 1953, St. Paul's, Saint Kitts, British West Indies [now in Saint Kitts and Nevis]), West Indian politician; prime minister of Saint Kitts and Nevis from 1995.

James H. Douglas (21 Jun 1951, Springfield MA), American politician (Republican); governor of Vermont from 2003.

Michael Douglas (25 Sep 1944, New Brunswick NJ), American film actor and producer.

Rita (Frances) Dove (28 Aug 1952, Akron OH), American writer and teacher; poet laureate of the US, 1993–95.

Maureen Dowd (14 Jan 1952, Washington DC), American journalist and op-ed columnist for the *New York Times*.

Robert Downey, Jr. (4 Apr 1965, New York NY), American actor.

Jim Doyle (James Edward Doyle; 23 Nov 1945, Washington DC), American politician (Democrat); governor of Wisconsin from 2003.

Dr. Dre (Andre Young; 18 Feb 1965, Los Angeles CA), American rap musician and impresario, considered a pioneer of gangsta rap.

Deborah Drattell (1956, Brooklyn NY), American composer of operas.

Paquito D'Rivera (Francisco Dejesus Rivera; 4 Jun 1948, Havana, Cuba), Cuban-born American jazz reed player and Afro-Cuban bandleader.

Didier Drogba (11 Mar 1978, Abidjan, Côte d'Ivoire), Ivorian association football (soccer) player; he was voted African Footballer of the Year for 2006 and 2009.

Matt Drudge (27 Oct 1967), American Internet journalist; editor of the Drudge Report.

David (William) Duchovny (7 Aug 1960, New York NY), American TV and film actor.

Gustavo (Adolfo) Dudamel (Ramírez) (26 Jan 1981, Barquisimeto, Venezuela), Venezuelan conductor; music director of the Göteborg (Sweden) Symphony Orchestra from 2007 and the Los Angeles Philharmonic from 2009.

Robert W. Dudley (1955, Queens NY), American corporate executive; group chief executive of BP PLC from 2010.

Hilary (Ann Lisa) Duff (28 Sep 1987, Houston TX), American TV and film actress and pop singer.

Carol Ann Duffy (23 Dec 1955, Glasgow, Scotland), British poet; first woman to serve as poet laureate of Britain, from 2009.

Mike Duke (Michael T. Duke), American corporate executive; president and CEO of Wal-Mart from 2009.

Sarah Dunant (8 Aug 1950, London, England), British crime and historical novelist, broadcaster, and critic.

Arne Duncan (6 Nov 1964, Chicago IL), American education administrator; US secretary of education from 2009.

Tim(othy Theodore) Duncan (25 Apr 1976, St. Croix, US Virgin Islands), American basketball player.

Ronnie Gene Dunn (1 Jun 1953, Coleman TX), American country-and-western singer (for Brooks & Dunn).

Kirsten (Caroline) Dunst (30 Apr 1982, Point Pleasant NJ), American film actress.

Ann E. Dunwoody (January 1953, Fort Belvoir VA), US general; first woman to reach (2008) four-star status in the US military.

Robert Duvall (5 Jan 1931, San Diego CA), American actor, producer, and screenwriter.

Bob Dylan (Robert Allen Zimmerman; 24 May 1941, Duluth MN), American singer and songwriter; he received a special citation from the Pulitzer Prize committee in 2008.

Freeman (John) Dyson (15 Dec 1923, Crowthorne, Berkshire, England), British-born American physicist and educator.

James Dyson (2 May 1947, Cromer, Norfolk, England), British inventor.

Steve Earle (Stephen Fain Earle; 17 Jan 1955, Fort Monroe VA), American country singer, guitarist, and songwriter.

(Ralph) Dale Earnhardt, Jr. (10 Oct 1974, Concord NC), American NASCAR race-car driver.

Michael F(rancis) Easley (23 Mar 1950, Nash county NC), American politician (Democrat); governor of North Carolina, 2001–09.

Clint(on) Eastwood, Jr. (31 May 1930, San Francisco CA), American film actor and moviemaker.

Martin Eberhard (15 May 1960, Berkeley CA), American entrepreneur and cofounder of Tesla Motors.

Roger Ebert (18 Jun 1942, Urbana IL), American film critic.

Marcelo (Luis) Ebrard (Casaubon) (10 Oct 1959, Mexico City, Mexico), Mexican politician (Party of the Democratic Revolution); head of government of the Federal District (mayor of Mexico City) from 2006.

Umberto Eco (5 Jan 1932, Alessandria, Italy), Italian literary critic, novelist, and semiotician.

Marian Wright Edelman (6 Jun 1939, Bennettsville SC), American attorney and civil rights advocate who founded the Children's Defense Fund.

Edward (Edward Anthony Richard Louis Mountbatten-Windsor; 10 Mar 1964, Buckingham Palace, London, England), British prince; third son of Queen Elizabeth II and Prince Philip, duke of Edinburgh; and earl of Wessex.

John Edwards (10 Jun 1953, Seneca SC), American politician (Democrat); senator from North Carolina, 1999–2005.

Tuiatua Tupua Tamasese Efi (1 Mar 1938, Samoa?), Samoan royal; O le Ao o le Malo (elective monarch) from 2007.

Zac Efron (18 Oct 1987, San Luis Obispo CA), American TV and film actor.

Edward Michael Cardinal Egan (2 Apr 1932, Oak Park IL), American Roman Catholic church leader; archbishop of New York, 2000–09, and cardinal from 2001.

Dave Eggers (8 Jan 1970, Chicago IL), American author, screenwriter, and graphic artist; founder and editor of McSweeney's, a journal and Web site, from 1998.

Michael D(ammann) Eisner (7 Mar 1942, Mount Kisco NY), American corporate executive; CEO and chairman of the Walt Disney Co., 1984–2004.

Mohamed ElBaradei (Muhammad al-Baradei; 17 Jun 1942, Cairo, Egypt), Egyptian international official; director general of the International Atomic Energy Agency, 1997–2009.

Tsakhiagiyn Elbegdorj (30 Mar 1963, Zereg, Mongolia), Mongolian politician (Democratic Party); prime minister, 1998 and 2004–06, and president from 2009.

Carmen Electra (Tara Leigh Patrick; 20 Apr 1972, Sharonville OH), American model, TV actress, and celebrity.

Olafur Eliasson (1967, Copenhagen, Denmark), Danish installation artist.

Elizabeth II (Elizabeth Alexandra Mary Windsor; 21 Apr 1926, London, England), British royal; queen of the United Kingdom of Great Britain and Northern Ireland from 1952.

George F(rancis) R(ayner) Ellis (11 Aug 1939, Johannesburg, Union of South Africa), South African applied mathematician and professor.

Lawrence J(oseph) Ellison (17 Aug 1944, Chicago IL), American corporate executive; founder and CEO of Oracle Corp. from 1977.

James Ellroy (Lee Earle Ellroy; 4 Mar 1948, Los Angeles CA), American mystery writer.

Ernie Els (Theodore Ernest Els; 17 Oct 1969, Johannesburg, South Africa), South African golfer.

Mike Eman (Michiel; 1 Sep 1961, Oranjestad, Aruba), Aruban politician; prime minister from 2009.

Rahm Emanuel (29 Nov 1959, Chicago IL), American politician (Democrat); congressman from Illinois, 2003–09, and White House chief of staff from 2009.

Eminem (Marshall Bruce Mathers III; 17 Oct 1973, St. Joseph MO), American hip-hop artist.

Emmanuel III Delly (Emmanuel-Karim Delly; 6 Oct 1927, Telkaif, Iraq), Iraqi churchman; patriarch of Babylonia and the Chaldeans (leader of the Chaldean Catholic Church) from 2003 and Roman Catholic cardinal from 2007.

Nambaryn Enkhbayar (1 Jun 1958, Ulaanbaatar, Mongolia), Mongolian politician (People's Revolutionary Party); prime minister, 2000–04, and president, 2005–09.

Anne Enright (11 Oct 1962, Dublin, Ireland), Irish writer; her novel *The Gathering* was awarded the 2007 Man Booker Prize.

Enya (Eithne Ní Bhraonáin; 17 May 1961, Gweedore, County Donegal, Ireland), Irish New Age singer.

Recep Tayyip Erdogan (26 Feb 1954, Istanbul, Turkey), Turkish politician (Justice and Development Party); prime minister from 2003.

Dervis Eroglu (1938), Turkish Cypriot politician; president of the Turkish Republic of Northern Cyprus from 2010.

Melissa Etheridge (29 May 1961, Leavenworth KS), American rock singer and songwriter.

Samuel Eto'o (Fils) (10 Mar 1981, Nkon, Cameroon), Cameroonian association football (soccer) player; he was voted African Footballer of the Year in 2003, 2004, and 2005.

Robin Eubanks (25 Oct 1955, Philadelphia PA), American jazz trombone player.

Richard D. Fairbank (18 Sep 1950, Menlo Park CA), American corporate executive; founder, chairman, and CEO of Capital One Financial Corp. from 1988.

Edie Falco (Edith Falco; 5 Jul 1963, Brooklyn NY), American film and TV actress.

Jimmy Fallon (James Thomas Fallon, Jr.; 19 Sep 1974, Brooklyn NY), American comedian and talk-show host.

(Hannah) Dakota Fanning (23 Feb 1994, Conyers GA), American film actress.

Abdirahman Mohamed Farole (1945, Italian Somaliland [now in Somalia]), Somali politician; president of the secessionist republic of Puntland from 2009.

Louis (Abdul) Farrakhan (Louis Eugene Walcott; 11 May 1933, Bronx NY), American leader of the Nation of Islam (Black Muslims) from 1978.

Colin (James) Farrell (31 May 1976, Dublin, Ireland), Irish actor.

Suzanne Farrell (Roberta Sue Ficker; 16 Aug 1945, Cincinnati OH), American ballet dancer.

Anthony S(tephen) Fauci (24 Dec 1940, Brooklyn NY), American public-health physician and AIDS researcher; director of the National Institute of Allergy and Infectious Diseases from 1984; recipient of a Lasker Medical Award in 2007.

(Catharine) Drew Gilpin Faust (18 Sep 1947, New York NY), American educator and historian; president of Harvard University from 2007.

Brett (Lorenzo) Favre (10 Oct 1969, Kiln MS), American pro football quarterback.

Werner Faymann (4 May 1960, Vienna, Austria), Austrian politician (Social Democrat); chancellor from 2008.

Salam Fayyad (1952, near Tulkarm, Jordan [West Bank]), Palestinian politician (Third Way); prime minister of the Palestinian Authority from 2007.

Roger Federer (8 Aug 1981, Basel, Switzerland), Swiss tennis player who has won the most Grand Slam tournaments in men's professional tennis history.

Russ(ell Dana) Feingold (2 Mar 1953, Janesville WI), American politician (Democrat); senator from Wisconsin from 1993.

Felipe (Felipe de Borbón y Grecia; 30 Jan 1968, Madrid, Spain), Spanish royal, prince of Asturias, and heir to the Spanish throne.

Eddie Fenech Adami (7 Feb 1934, Birkirkara, Malta), Maltese politician; prime minister, 1987–96 and 1998–2004, and president, 2004–09.

Dennis Fentie (8 Nov 1950, Edmonton, AB, Canada), Canadian businessman and politician (Yukon Party); premier of Yukon from 2002.

Craig Ferguson (17 May 1962, Glasgow, Scotland), British film and TV actor; host of TV's *The Late Late Show* from 2005.

Sarah (Margaret) Ferguson (15 Oct 1959, London, England), British celebrity; duchess of York after her marriage (23 Jul 1986) to Prince Andrew; they divorced in 1996.

Cristina (Elisabet) Fernández (Wilhelm) de Kirchner (19 Feb 1953, La Plata, Argentina), Argentine politician; president, following her husband, Néstor Kirchner, from 2007.

Leonel Fernández (Reyna) (26 Dec 1953, Santo Domingo, Dominican Republic), Dominican politician; president, 1996–2000 and again from 2004.

Gil de Ferran (11 Nov 1967, Paris, France), French-born Brazilian race-car driver.

(John) Will(iam) Ferrell (16 Jul 1967, Irvine CA), American comedian and actor.

America (Georgine) Ferrera (18 Apr 1984, Los Angeles CA), American film and TV actress.

Tina Fey (Elizabeth Stamatina Fey; 18 May 1970, Upper Darby PA), American comedian, writer, and actress.

Robert Fico (15 Sep 1964, Topolcany, Czechoslovakia [now in Slovakia]), Slovak politician (Social Democrat); prime minister of Slovakia (2006–10).

Sally (Margaret) Field (6 Nov 1946, Pasadena CA), American comic and dramatic actress.

Ralph (Nathaniel) Fiennes (22 Dec 1962, Suffolk, England), British dramatic actor.

Harvey (Forbes) Fierstein (6 Jun 1954, Brooklyn NY), American playwright and actor.

Vlad Filat (6 May 1969, Lapusna, Moldova), Moldovan politician; prime minister from 2009.

François Fillon (4 Mar 1954, LeMans, France), French politician; prime minister from 2007.

David (Leo) Fincher (28 Aug 1962, Denver CO), American film director.

Harvey V. Fineberg (15 Sep 1945, Pittsburgh PA), American public-health physician and medical administrator; president of the Institute of Medicine from 2002.

Carly Fiorina (Cara Carleton Sneed; 6 Sep 1954, Austin TX), American corporate executive and politician (Republican); president and CEO (1999–2005) and chairman (2000–05) of Hewlett-Packard.

Colin Firth (10 Sep 1960, Grayshott, Hampshire, England), British actor.

Heinz Fischer (9 Oct 1938, Graz, Austria), Austrian politician (Social Democrat); president from 2004.

Jan Fischer (2 Jan 1951, Prague, Czechoslovakia [now in the Czech Republic]), Czech politician; prime minister from 2009.

Allison Fisher (24 Feb 1968, Cheshunt, Hertfordshire, England), British pocket-billiards champion.

Isla (Lang) Fisher (3 Feb 1976, Muscat, Oman), British film actress.

Benígno (Repeki) Fitial (27 Nov 1945, Saipan, Northern Mariana Islands), Northern Marianas politician (Covenant Party); governor of the Northern Mariana Islands from 2006.

Patrick Fitzgerald (22 Dec 1960, New York NY), American special prosecutor in a number of high-profile cases.

Tim Flannery (28 Jan 1956, Melbourne, VIC, Australia), Australian zoologist and environmentalist; he was named Australian of the Year for 2007.

Leon Fleisher (23 Jul 1928, San Francisco CA), American pianist.

Renée Fleming (14 Feb 1959, Indiana PA), American operatic soprano.

Vince Flynn (6 Apr 1966, St. Paul MN), American author of thrillers.

Ken Follett (pseudonyms Zachary Stone and Simon Myles; 5 Jun 1949, Cardiff, Wales), British author of political thrillers and historical novels.

Phil Fontaine (Larry Phillip Fontaine; "Buddy"; 20 Sep 1944, Fort Alexander Reserve, MB, Canada), Canadian Ojibway First Nations activist; national chief of the Assembly of First Nations, 1997–2009.

Harrison Ford (13 Jul 1942, Chicago IL), American film actor.

Tom Ford (27 Aug 1961, Austin TX), American fashion designer and film director.

William Clay Ford, Jr. (3 May 1957, Detroit MI), American businessman; executive chairman of Ford Motor Co. from 2006.

Diego Forlán (19 May 1979, Montevideo, Uruguay), Uruguayan association football (soccer) player; won the Golden Ball award in the 2010 FIFA World Cup.

William Forsythe (1949, New York NY), American ballet dancer, choreographer, and director.

Luis G. Fortuño (31 Oct 1960, San Juan PR), Puerto Rican politician; governor of Puerto Rico from 2009.

Jodie Foster (Alicia Christian Foster; 19 Nov 1962, Los Angeles CA), American film actress.

Norman (Robert) Foster (1 Jun 1935, near Manchester, England), British architect; recipient of the 1999 Pritzker Prize and a 2002 Praemium Imperiale.

Megan (Denise) Fox (16 May 1986, Rockwood TN), American actress.

Jamie Foxx (Eric Bishop; 13 Dec 1967, Terrell TX), American actor and comedian.

Don Francisco (Mario Kreutzberger; 28 Dec 1940, Talca, Chile), Chilean-born American TV personality; host of the popular show Sábado Gigante on the Spanish-language Univision channel.

James (Edward) Franco (19 Apr 1978, Palo Alto CA), American actor.

Al Franken (21 May 1951, New York NY), American comedian, writer, and politician; senator from Minnesota from 2009.

Jonathan Franzen (17 Aug 1959, Western Springs IL), American author.

Frederik (Frederik André Henrik Christian; 26 May 1968, Copenhagen, Denmark), Danish crown prince.

Morgan Freeman (1 Jun 1937, Memphis TN), American theater and film actor.

Dawn French (11 Oct 1957, Holyhead, Wales), British actress, comedian, and writer.

Lucian Freud (8 Dec 1922, Berlin, Germany), German-born British painter.

Dave Freudenthal (David Duane Freudenthal; 12 Oct 1950, Thermopolis WY), American politician (Democrat); governor of Wyoming from 2003.

Saul Friedländer (11 Oct 1932, Prague, Czechoslovakia [now in the Czech Republic]), Czech-born French-Israeli historian and professor whose study The Years of Extermination: Nazi Germany and the Jews, 1939–1945 won the 2008 Pulitzer Prize for general nonfiction.

Thomas L. Friedman (20 Jul 1953, Minneapolis MN), American journalist and author; foreign-affairs columnist for the New York Times.

Janus Friis (1976, Denmark), Danish Internet entrepreneur; codeveloper of Joost, a popular program for receiving TV broadcasts on a personal computer, and Skype, which allows users to make phone calls over the Internet.

(Carlos) Mauricio Funes (Cartagena) (18 Oct 1959, San Salvador, El Salvador), Salvadoran journalist and politician; president from 2009.

Nelly (Kim) Furtado (2 Dec 1978, Victoria, BC, Canada), Canadian singer and songwriter.

Stefano Gabbana (14 Nov 1962, Milan, Italy), Italian fashion designer and partner of Domenico Dolce.

Zach Galifianakis (1 Oct 1969, Wilkesboro NC), American actor.

John Galliano (Juan Carlos Antonio Galliano Guillen; 28 Nov 1960, Gibraltar), British fashion designer and designer in chief at Christian Dior.

Sonia Gandhi (Sonia Maino; 9 Dec 1947, Turin, Italy), Italian-born Indian widow of Rajiv Gandhi and a political force in India.

James Gandolfini (18 Sep 1961, Westwood NJ), American TV and film actor.

Gabriel (José) García Márquez (6 Mar 1928, Aracataca, Colombia), Colombian novelist and short-story writer, a figure in the magic realism movement in Latin American literature; recipient of the 1972 Neustadt Prize and the 1982 Nobel Prize for Literature.

Alan García (Pérez) (23 May 1949, Lima, Peru), Peruvian politician; president, 1985–90 and again from 2006.

Jennifer (Anne) Garner (17 Apr 1972, Houston TX), American TV and film actress.

Kevin (Maurice) Garnett (19 May 1976, Mauldin SC), American professional basketball player.

Ivan Gasparovic (27 Mar 1941, Poltar, Czechoslovakia [now in Slovakia]), Slovak politician; president from 2004.

Bill Gates (William Henry Gates III; 28 Oct 1955, Seattle WA), American computer programmer, businessman, philanthropist, and cofounder of Microsoft Corp.; he has been named the world's richest person by Forbes numerous times, including in 2009.

Melinda Gates (Melinda French; 15 Aug 1964, Dallas TX), American philanthropist; cofounder of the Bill & Melinda Gates Foundation.

Robert M(ichael) Gates (25 Sep 1943, Wichita KS), American government official; CIA director, 1991–93, and secretary of defense from 2006.

Jean-Paul Gaultier (24 Apr 1952, Arcueil, France), French fashion designer.

Laurent Gbagbo (31 May 1945, Gagnoa, French West Africa [now in Côte d'Ivoire]), Ivorian politician; president of Côte d'Ivoire from 2000.

Haile Gebrselassie (18 Apr 1973, Assela, Ethiopia), Ethiopian runner and world record holder in the marathon.

Frank Gehry (Frank Owen Goldberg; 28 Feb 1929, Toronto, ON, Canada), Canadian-born American architect and designer whose original, sculptural, often audacious work won him worldwide renown; recipient of the 1989 Pritzker Prize.

Timothy (Franz) Geithner (18 Aug 1961, New York NY), American public official; US secretary of the treasury from 2009.

Bob Geldof (Robert Frederick Xenon Geldof; 5 Oct 1954, Dublin, Ireland), Irish singer and songwriter and humanitarian.

Julius Genachowski (19 Aug 1962, American businessman and public official; chairman of the Federal Communications Commission from 2009.

Francis (Eugene) Cardinal George (16 Jan 1937, Chicago IL), American Roman Catholic churchman; archbishop of Chicago from 1997 and cardinal from 1998.

George Tupou V (Tupouto'a; 4 May 1948, Nuku'alofa, British Tonga), Tongan royal; king from 2006.

Leo W. Gerard (1947?, Sudbury, ON, Canada), Canadian labor leader; international president of the United Steelworkers International from 2001.

Richard (Tiffany) Gere (31 Aug 1949, Philadelphia PA), American film actor.

Valery (Abisalovich) Gergiev (2 May 1953, Moscow, USSR [now in Russia]), Russian conductor; artistic and general director of the Mariinsky Theatre from 1996.

Ricky (Dene) Gervais (25 Jun 1961, Reading, Berkshire, England), British comedian and actor.

Ron(ald Anthony) Gettelfinger (1 Aug 1944, near De-Pauw IN), American labor leader; president of the United Automobile Workers from 2002.

Mohamed Ghannouchi (18 Aug 1941, Al-Hamma, French Tunisia), Tunisian politician; prime minister from 1999.

Mihai Ghimpu (19 Nov 1951, Chisinau, Moldova), Moldovan politician; acting president from 2009.

Robert Ghiz (21 Jan 1974, Charlottetown, PE, Canada), Canadian politician (Liberal); premier of Prince Edward Island from 2007.

Paul (Edward Valentine) Giamatti (6 Jun 1967, New Haven CT), American film actor.

Frida Giannini (1972, Rome, Italy), Italian fashion designer; creative director at Gucci from 2006.

Jim Gibbons (James Arthur Gibbons; 16 Dec 1944, Sparks NV), American politician (Republican); governor of Nevada from 2007.

Robert Gibbs (29 Mar 1971, Auburn AL), American political consultant and media official; White House press secretary from 2009.

Charles (deWolf) Gibson (9 Mar 1943, Evanston IL), American TV journalist and anchorman.

Mel (Columcille Gerard) Gibson (3 Jan 1956, Peekskill NY), Australian American actor, producer, and director.

(Makhdoom Syed) Yousaf Raza Gilani (9 Jun 1952, Karachi, Pakistan), Pakistani politician (PPP); prime minister from 2008.

Alan Gilbert (23 Feb 1967, New York NY), American violinist and conductor; music director of the New York Philharmonic from 2009.

Melissa Gilbert (8 May 1964, Los Angeles CA), American film and TV actress; president of the Screen Actors Guild, 2002–05.

João Gilberto (do Prado Pereira de Oliveira) (10 Jun 1931, Juazeiro, Bahia state, Brazil), Brazilian bossa-nova singer, songwriter, and guitarist.

Vince(nt Grant) Gill (12 Apr 1957, Norman OK), American country and progressive-bluegrass instrumentalist and singer.

Julia Gillard (29 Sep 1961, Barry, Vale of Galmorgan, Wales), Australian politician (Labor); the first female Australian prime minister from 2010.

Tony Gilroy (Anthony Joseph Gilroy; 11 Sep 1956, New York NY), American screenwriter and director.

Ruth Bader Ginsburg (15 Mar 1933, Brooklyn NY), American jurist; associate justice of the US Supreme Court from 1993.

Dana Gioia (24 Dec 1950, Los Angeles CA), American poet and critic; chairman of the US National Endowment for the Arts, 2003–09.

Nikki Giovanni (Yolande Cornelia Giovanni, Jr.; 7 Jun 1943, Knoxville TN), American poet.

Rudy Giuliani (Rudolph William Giuliani; 28 May 1944, Brooklyn NY), American politician (Republican) and consultant; mayor of New York City, 1994–2002.

Ira Glass (3 Mar 1959, Baltimore MD), American radio broadcaster, creator (1995) and host of *This American Life* on public radio and later also on cable TV.

Philip Glass (31 Jan 1937, Baltimore MD), American minimalist composer.

Savion Glover (19 Nov 1973, Newark NJ), American dancer and choreographer.

Louise (Elisabeth) Glück (22 Apr 1943, New York NY), American poet; US poet laureate, 2003–04.

Faure (Essozimna) Gnassingbé (Eyadéma) (6 Jun 1966, Afagnan, Togo), Togolese politician; president in February 2005 and again from May 2005.

Jean-Luc Godard (3 Dec 1930, Paris, France), French film director.

Ivars Godmanis (27 Nov 1951, Riga, USSR [now in Latvia]), Latvian politician; prime minister (1990–93, 2007–09).

Whoopi Goldberg (Caryn Elaine Johnson; 13 Nov 1955, New York NY), American comedian, film actress, and TV talk-show host.

(Orette) Bruce Golding (5 Dec 1947, Clarendon, Jamaica, British West Indies), Jamaican politician; prime minister from 2007.

Carlos Gomes, Jr. (19 Dec 1949, Bolama, Portuguese Guinea [now Guinea-Bissau]), Guinea-Bissauan politician; prime minister, 2004–05 and again from 2009.

Ralph E. Gonsalves (8 Aug 1946, Colonarie, Saint Vincent, British West Indies [now in Saint Vincent and the Grenadines]), West Indian politician; prime minister of Saint Vincent and the Grenadines from 2001.

Alejandro González Iñárritu (15 Aug 1963, Mexico City, Mexico), Mexican film director.

Lawrence Gonzi (1 Jul 1953, Valletta, Malta), Maltese politician (Nationalist); prime minister from 2004.

Roger Goodell (19 Feb 1959, Jamestown NY), American sports executive; commissioner of the National Football League from 2006.

Allegra Goodman (1967, Brooklyn NY), American writer, notably on Jewish themes.

Doris Kearns Goodwin (4 Jan 1943, Brooklyn NY), American historian, biographer, and TV commentator.

Annette Gordon-Reed (19 Nov 1958, Livingston TX), American author; recipient of the 2009 Pulitzer Prize for history for *The Hemingses of Monticello: An American Family*.

Al(bert Arnold) Gore, Jr. (31 Mar 1948, Washington DC), American statesman and environmental advocate; vice president of the US, 1993–2001, and corecipient of the 2007 Nobel Peace Prize.

Ryan (Thomas) Gosling (12 Nov 1980, London, ON, Canada), Canadian TV and film actor.

Michael Gove (26 Aug 1967, Edinburgh, Scotland), British politician (Conservative); secretary of state for education from 2010.

Shawn Graham (22 Feb 1968, Rexton, NB, Canada), Canadian politician (Liberal); premier of New Brunswick from 2006.

(Allen) Kelsey Grammer (21 Feb 1955, St. Thomas, US Virgin Islands), American TV actor, writer, and producer.

Michael Grandage (2 May 1962, Yorkshire, England), British theater director; artistic director of London's Donmar Warehouse from 2002.

Jennifer Granholm (Jennifer Mulhern; 5 Feb 1959, Vancouver, BC, Canada), Canadian-born American attorney and politician (Democrat); governor of Michigan from 2003.

Hugh Grant (9 Sep 1960, London, England), British film actor.

Günter (Wilhelm) Grass (16 Oct 1927, Danzig, Germany [now Gdansk, Poland]), German poet, novelist, playwright, sculptor, and printmaker; recipient of the 1999 Nobel Prize for Literature.

Michael Graves (9 July 1934, Indianapolis IN), American postmodernist architect and housewares designer.

Richard Greenberg (1958, Long Island NY), American playwright.

Brian Greene (9 Feb 1963, New York NY), American physicist and expert on string theory.

Paul Greengrass (13 Aug 1955, Cheam, Surrey, England), British film director.

Alan Greenspan (6 Mar 1926, New York NY), American monetary policy maker; chairman of the Board of Governors of the Federal Reserve System, 1987–2006.

Christine Gregoire (Christine O'Grady; 24 Mar 1947, Auburn WA), American politician (Democrat); governor of Washington from 2005.

Grégoire III Laham (Lutfi Laham; 15 Dec 1933, Daraya, Syria), Syrian church leader; patriarch of Antioch in the Greek Melkite Catholic Church from 2000.

Philippa Gregory (9 Jan 1954, Nairobi, Kenya), British historical novelist.

Carol W. Greider (15 Apr 1961, San Diego CA), American molecular biologist; cowinner of the 2009 Nobel Prize for Physiology or Medicine.

Brad Grey (1958?, Bronx NY), American talent agent, producer, and film executive; chairman and CEO of Paramount Motion Picture Group from 2005.

Ólafur Ragnar Grímsson (14 May 1943, Ísafjörður, Iceland), Icelandic politician; president from 1996.

John Grisham (8 Feb 1955, Jonesboro AR), American lawyer and best-selling novelist.

Matt(hew Abram) Groening (15 Feb 1954, Portland OR), American cartoonist and creator (1989) of TV's The Simpsons.

Dave Grohl (David Eric Grohl; 14 Jan 1969, Warren OH), American rock drummer, guitarist, and singer (for Nirvana and Foo Fighters).

Gilbert M. Grosvenor (5 May 1931, Washington DC), American executive; president of the National Geographic Society, 1980–96, and chairman of the board from 1987.

Jon Gruden (17 Aug 1963, Sandusky OH), American professional football coach and TV commentator.

Nikola Gruevski (31 Aug 1970, Skopje, Yugoslavia [now in Macedonia]), Macedonian politician; prime minister from 2006.

Dalia Grybauskaite (1 Mar 1956, Vilnius, USSR [now in Lithuania]), Lithuanian politician; president from 2009.

(Edward Michael) Bear Grylls (7 Jun 1974, Isle of Wight), British survival expert and TV star.

Armando (Emílio) Guebuza (20 Jan 1943, Marrupula, Portuguese Mozambique), Mozambican politician; secretary-general of the Frelimo political party from 2002 and president from 2005.

Ismail Omar Guelleh (27 Nov 1947, Diré-Dawa, Ethiopia), Djiboutian politician; president from 1999.

Guillaume (Guillaume Jean Joseph Marie; 11 Nov 1981, Château de Betzdorf, Luxembourg), Luxembourgian grand duke, prince of Nassau and Bourbon-Parma, and heir to the throne.

Ozzie Guillen (Oswaldo José Guillen Barrios; 20 Jan 1964, Ocumare del Tuy, Venezuela), Venezuelan-born professional baseball manager.

Abdullah Gul (29 Oct 1950, Kayseri, Turkey), Turkish economist and politician; prime minister, 2002–03, and president from 2007.

Natalie (Anne) Gulbis (7 Jan 1983, Sacramento CA), American golfer.

James Edward Gunn (21 Oct 1938, Livingstone TX), American cosmologist; recipient of the 2008 National Medal of Science.

Tim(othy) Gunn (29 Jul 1953, Washington DC), fashion consultant and TV personality.

José Ángel Gurría Treviño (8 May 1950, Tampico, Tamaulipas state, Mexico), Mexican economist; secretary-general of the Organisation for Economic Co-operation and Development from 2006.

Xanana Gusmão (José Alexandre Gusmão; 20 Jun 1946, Laleia, Portuguese Timor [now East Timor (Timor-Leste)]), Timorese independence leader; first president of independent East Timor, 2002–07, and prime minister from 2007.

António (Manuel de Oliveira) Guterres (30 Apr 1949, Lisbon, Portugal), Portuguese politician (Socialist); prime minister, 1995–2002, and UN high commissioner for refugees from 2005.

Carlos M. Gutierrez (4 Nov 1953, Havana, Cuba), Cuban-born American corporate executive and government official; CEO of Kellogg Company, 2000–05, and US secretary of commerce, 2005–09.

Buddy Guy (George Guy; 30 Jul 1936, Lettsworth LA), American blues guitarist and singer.

Gyanendra Bir Bikram Shah Dev (7 Jul 1947, Kathmandu, Nepal), Nepalese king, last monarch of Nepal, 2001–08.

Jake Gyllenhaal (Jacob Benjamin Gyllenhaal; 19 Dec 1980, Los Angeles CA), American film actor.

Haakon (Haakon Magnus; 20 Jul 1973, Oslo, Norway), Norwegian crown prince and heir to the throne.

Zaha Hadid (31 Oct 1950, Baghdad, Iraq), Iraqi-born architect; recipient of the 2004 Pritzker Prize.

Stephen (John) Hadley (13 Feb 1947, Toledo OH), American security official; US national security advisor, 2005–09.

William Hague (28 Mar 1961, Rotherham, Yorkshire, England), British politician (Conservative); foreign secretary from 2010.

Hilary Hahn (27 Nov 1979, Lexington VA), American violinist.

Stelios Haji-Ioannou (14 Feb 1967, Athens, Greece), Greek entrepreneur who created the easyGroup holding company, which includes easyJet.

Donald (Andrew) Hall, Jr. (20 Sep 1928, New Haven CT), American poet, essayist, and critic; US poet laureate, 2006–07.

Michael C. Hall (1 Feb 1971, Raleigh NC), American actor.

Roy Halladay (14 May 1977, Denver CO), American professional baseball starting pitcher; he pitched a perfect game for the Philadelphia Phillies in May 2010, only the 20th player in MLB history to do so.

Tarja (Kaarina) Halonen (24 Dec 1943, Helsinki, Finland), Finnish politician; president from 2000.

Jane Hamilton (13 Jul 1957, Oak Park IL), American novelist.

Richard Hamilton (24 Feb 1922, London, England), British artist; recipient of a 2008 Praemium Imperiale.

Jon(athan Daniel) Hamm (10 Mar 1971, St. Louis MO), American actor.

Herbie Hancock (Herbert Jeffrey Hancock; 12 Apr 1940, Chicago IL), American Grammy Award-winning jazz keyboardist and composer.

Daniel Handler (pseudonym Lemony Snicket; 28 Feb 1970, San Francisco CA), American children's book author.

Tom Hanks (Thomas Jeffrey Hanks; 9 Jul 1956, Concord CA), American film actor and director.

Sean (Patrick) Hannity (30 Dec 1961, New York NY), American conservative commentator and talk-show host.

Hans Adam II (14 Feb 1945, Vaduz, Liechtenstein), Liechtenstein royal; prince of Liechtenstein from 1989.

Harald V (21 Feb 1937, Skaugum, Norway), Norwegian royal; king from 1991.

Marcia Gay Harden (14 Aug 1959, La Jolla CA), American film, stage, and TV actress.

Paul Harding (c. 1967), American teacher and author; his *Tinkers* won the 2010 Pulitzer Prize for fiction.

Roy Hargrove (16 Oct 1969, Waco TX), American jazz trumpeter.

Joy Harjo (9 May 1951, Tulsa OK), American poet, musician, and Native American (Muskogee) activist.

Stephen (Joseph) Harper (30 Apr 1959, Toronto, ON, Canada), Canadian politician (Conservative); prime minister of Canada from 2006.

Padraig Harrington (31 Aug 1971, Dublin, Ireland), Irish golfer.

Ed(ward Allen) Harris (28 Nov 1950, Englewood NJ), American film and stage actor and director.

Neil Patrick Harris (15 Jun 1973, Albuquerque NM), American actor.

Harry (Henry Charles Albert David Mountbatten-Windsor; 15 Sep 1984, London, England), British prince of Wales; son of Charles and Diana, prince and princess of Wales, and third in line to the British throne.

Mary Hart (Mary Johanna Harum; 8 Nov 1950, Madison SD), American actress and cohost of *Entertainment Tonight* on TV from 1982.

Dominik Hasek (29 Jan 1965, Pardubice, Czechoslovakia [now in the Czech Republic]), Czech ice-hockey goalie.

Sheikh Hasina Wazed (28 Sep 1947, Tungipara, India [now in Bangladesh]), Bangladeshi politician; prime minister, 1996–2001 and again from 2009.

Robert Hass (1 Mar 1941, San Francisco CA), American poet; US poet laureate, 1995–97.

Anne (Jacqueline) Hathaway (12 Nov 1982, Brooklyn NY), American film actress.

Yukio Hatoyama (11 Feb 1947, Tokyo, Japan), Japanese politician (Democratic Party of Japan); prime minister, 2009–10.

Tony Hawk (Anthony Frank Hawk; 12 May 1968, San Diego CA), American professional skateboarder.

Stephen W. Hawking (8 Jan 1942, Oxford, Oxfordshire, England), British theoretical physicist, a specialist in cosmology and quantum gravity.

Michael (Vincent) Hayden (17 Mar 1945, Pittsburgh PA), American director of the National Security Agency, 1999–2005, and director of the CIA, 2006–09.

Salma Hayek (Jiménez) (2 Sep 1966, Coatzacoalcos, Veracruz state, Mexico), Mexican-born actress.

Roy Haynes (13 Mar 1926, Roxbury, Boston MA), American jazz drummer and bandleader.

Todd Haynes (2 Jan 1961, Los Angeles CA), American film director, producer, and screenwriter.

Tony Hayward (1957, Slough, England), British corporate executive; group chief executive of BP PLC (2007–10); he initially handled the company's response to the Horizon Deepwater oil spill (2010).

Seamus (Justin) Heaney (13 Apr 1939, near Castledawson, County Londonderry, Northern Ireland), Irish poet; recipient of the 1995 Nobel Prize for Literature.

Hugh M. Hefner (9 Apr 1926, Chicago IL), American magazine publisher (*Playboy*).

Katherine (Marie) Heigl (24 Nov 1978, Washington DC), American model and TV and film actress.

Dave Heineman (David Eugene Heineman; 12 May 1948, Falls City NE), American politician (Republican); governor of Nebraska from 2005.

Ed Helms (24 Jan 1974, Atlanta GA), American actor.

Frederick ("Fritz") Henderson (29 Nov 1958, Detroit MI), American businessman; president and CEO of General Motors, 2009.

Henri (16 Apr 1955, Château de Betzdorf, Luxembourg), Luxembourgian grand duke from 2000.

(Charles) Brad(ford) Henry (10 Jun 1963, Shawnee OK), American politician (Democrat); governor of Oklahoma from 2003.

Thierry (Daniel) Henry (17 Aug 1977, Châtillon, near Paris, France), French association football (soccer) player.

Gary R(ichard) Herbert (7 May 1947, American Fork UT), American politician (Republican); governor of Utah from 2009.

Seymour M(yron) Hersh (8 Apr 1937, Chicago IL), American investigative reporter and writer.

Mohamud Muse Hersi, Somali general; president of the secessionist republic of Puntland, 2005–09.

Jacques Herzog (19 Apr 1950, Basel, Switzerland), Swiss architect; corecipient of the 2001 Pritzker Prize and of a Praemium Imperiale in 2007.

Jennifer Higdon (31 Dec 1962, Brooklyn NY), American composer; her *Violin Concerto* won the 2010 Pulitzer Prize for music.

Rosalyn Higgins (Rosalyn Cohen; 2 Jun 1937, London, England), British jurist; president of the International Court of Justice, 2006–09.

Tommy Hilfiger (Thomas Jacob Hilfiger; 24 Mar 1951, Elmira NY), American fashion designer.

Faith Hill (Audrey Faith Perry; 21 Sep 1967, Jackson MS), American country singer.

Julia Butterfly Hill (18 Feb 1974, Mount Vernon MO), American environmental activist.

Paris Hilton (17 Feb 1981, New York NY), American heiress and socialite.

Sam(uel Archibald Anthony) Hinds (27 Dec 1943, Mahaicony, British Guiana [now Guyana]), Guyanese politician; president in 1997 and prime minister, 1992–97, 1997–99, and again from 1999.

Emile (Davenport) Hirsch (13 Mar 1985, Palms CA), American film actor.

Damien Hirst (1965, Bristol, England), British artist.

Christopher Hitchens (26 Apr 1949, Portsmouth, England), American cultural and political critic and journalist.

Stanley Ho (Ho Hung-sun; 25 Nov 1921, Hong Kong), Macanese gaming magnate and multibillionaire.

Susan Hockfield (1951, Chicago IL), American neuroscientist; president of the Massachusetts Institute of Technology from 2004.

David Hockney (9 Jul 1937, Bradford, Yorkshire, England), British painter, draftsman, printmaker, photographer, and stage designer.

John (Henry) Hoeven III (13 Mar 1957, Bismarck ND), American politician (Republican); governor of North Dakota from 2000.

James P(hillip) Hoffa (19 May 1941, Detroit MI), American labor leader; president of the International Brotherhood of Teamsters from 1999.

David E. Hoffman (c. 1955, Palo Alto CA), American newspaper editor and author; his *The Dead Hand: The Untold Story of the Cold War Arms Race and Its Dangerous Legacy* won the 2010 Pulitzer Prize for general nonfiction.

Dustin Hoffman (8 Aug 1937, Los Angeles CA), American film and stage actor.

Philip Seymour Hoffman (23 Jul 1967, Fairport NY), American stage and film actor and theater director.

Hulk Hogan (Terry Gene Bollea; 11 Aug 1953, Augusta GA), American professional wrestler and actor.

Eric (Himpton) Holder (Jr.) (21 Jan 1951, New York NY), American lawyer; US attorney general from 2009.

John (Paul) Holdren (1 Mar 1944, Sewickley PA), presidential science adviser and director of the Office of Science and Technology Policy from 2009.

Katie Holmes (Kate Noelle Holmes; 18 Dec 1978, Toledo OH), American TV, film, and stage actress.

(Philip) Anthony Hopkins (31 Dec 1937, Margam, West Glamorgan, Wales), British film and stage actor.

Nick Hornby (17 Apr 1957, Redhill, Surrey, England), British novelist and journalist.

Khaled Hosseini (4 Mar 1965, Kabul, Afghanistan), Afghan-born American novelist.

Whitney (Elizabeth) Houston (9 Aug 1963, Newark NJ), American pop singer and film actress.

Dwight Howard (8 Dec 1985, Atlanta GA), American basketball player.

Ken Howard (28 Mar 1944, El Centro CA), American actor; president of the Screen Actors Guild from 2009.

Ron Howard (1 Mar 1954, Duncan OK), American TV and film actor and director.

Terrence (Dashon) Howard (11 Mar 1969, Chicago IL), American TV and film actor.

Daniel Walker Howe (1937, Ogden UT), American historian and professor who won the 2008 Pulitzer Prize for history for his book *What Hath God Wrought.*

Hu Jintao (25 Dec 1942, Jixi, Anhui province, China), Chinese statesman; general secretary of the Communist Party of China from 2002 and president of China from 2003.

Jan Huber (Johannes Huber; 1947?, Netherlands), Dutch international official; executive secretary of the Antarctic Treaty system from 2004.

Mike Huckabee (Michael Dale Huckabee; 24 Aug 1955, Hope AR), American politician (Republican) and political commentator; governor of Arkansas, 1996–2007.

Jennifer (Kate) Hudson (12 Sep 1981, Chicago IL), American soul and gospel singer and film actress.

Arianna Huffington (Ariana Stassinopoulos; 1950, Athens, Greece), Greek-born American political commentator, syndicated newspaper columnist, and author; cofounder of the Huffington Post, a liberal news and commentary Web site.

Felicity (Kendall) Huffman (9 Dec 1962, Bedford NY), American TV and film actress.

Robert (Studley Forrest) Hughes (28 Jul 1938, Sydney, NSW, Australia), Australian art critic and author.

Hun Sen (4 Apr 1951, Kampong Cham province, Cambodia), Cambodian politician; prime minister from 1985.

Holly Hunter (20 Mar 1958, Conyers GA), American film and TV actress.

Jon M(eade) Huntsman, Jr. (26 Mar 1960, Palo Alto CA), American businessman (Huntsman Family Holdings), politician (Republican), and philanthropist; governor of Utah, 2005–09, and US ambassador to China from 2009.

Lubomyr Cardinal Husar (26 Feb 1933, Lwow, Poland [now Lviv, Ukraine]), Ukrainian Greek Catholic Church leader; cardinal from 2001 and major archbishop of Kyiv-Halyc from 2005.

Nicholas Hytner (7 May 1956, Didsbury, near Manchester, England), British theater director; artistic director of the National Theatre from 2003.

Ice Cube (O'Shea Jackson; 15 Jun 1969, Los Angeles CA), American rapper, songwriter, and actor.

Ice-T (Tracy Morrow; 16 Feb 1958, Newark NJ), American hip-hop artist and actor.

Apisai Ielemia (19 Aug 1955, Vaitupu?, British Ellice Islands [now Tuvalu]), Tuvaluan politician; prime minister from 2006.

Ieronymos II (Ioannis Liapis; 1938, Oinofyta, Greece), Greek Orthodox churchman; archbishop of Athens and all Greece from 2008.

Ekmeleddin Ihsanoglu (26 Dec 1943, Cairo, Egypt), Turkish professor of history; secretary-general of the Organisation of the Islamic Conference from 2005.

Toomas Hendrik Ilves (26 Dec 1953, Stockholm, Sweden), Estonian diplomat; president from 2006.

Jeffrey R(obert) Immelt (19 Feb 1956, Cincinnati OH), American corporate executive; CEO of the General Electric Co. from 2001.

Hubert (Alexander) Ingraham (4 Aug 1947, Pine Ridge, Bahamas, British West Indies), Bahamian politician; prime minister, 1992–2002 and again from 2007.

José Miguel Insulza (2 Jun 1943, Santiago, Chile), Chilean government official (Socialist); secretary-general of the Organization of American States from 2005.

Valentin Inzko (22 May 1949, Klagenfurt, Austria), Austrian diplomat; high representative for Bosnia and Herzegovina from 2009.

Bill Irwin (11 Apr 1950, Santa Monica CA), American actor and choreographer.

Walter Isaacson (20 May 1952, New Orleans LA), American corporate executive; chairman and CEO of the Cable News Network (CNN), 2001–03, and president and CEO of the Aspen Institute from 2003.

Riduan Isamuddin (Encep Nurjaman; "Hambali"; 4 Apr 1966, Pamokolan, West Java, Indonesia), Indonesian militant and leader of the Jemaah Islamiyah group; arrested in 2003 by American agents for his alleged involvement in several terrorist attacks.

Kazuo Ishiguro (8 Nov 1954, Nagasaki, Japan), Japanese-born British novelist.

Shintaro Ishihara (30 Sep 1932, Kobe, Japan), Japanese author and nationalist politician; governor of Tokyo from 1999.

Takanobu Ito (29 Aug 1953), Japanese businessman; president and CEO of Honda Motor Co. from 2009.

Gjorge Ivanov (2 May 1960, Valandovo, Yugoslavia [now in Macedonia]), Macedonian politician, president of Macedonia from 2009.

Allen (Ezail) Iverson (7 Jun 1975, Hampton VA), American basketball player.

James (Francis) Ivory (7 Jun 1928, Berkeley CA), American film director.

Hugh (Michael) Jackman (12 Oct 1968, Sydney, NSW, Australia), Australian film and stage actor.

Alan (Eugene) Jackson (17 Oct 1958, Newnan GA), American country-and-western singer and guitarist.

Janet (Damita Jo) Jackson (16 May 1966, Gary IN), American singer and film and TV actress.

Jesse (Louis) Jackson (8 Oct 1941, Greenville SC), American civil rights leader, minister, and politician.

Lisa P(erez) Jackson (8 Feb 1962, Philadelphia PA), American public official; administrator of the US Environmental Protection Agency from 2009.

Peter Jackson (31 Oct 1961, Pukerua Bay, New Zealand), New Zealand film director and producer.

Phil(ip Douglas) Jackson (17 Sep 1945, Deer Lodge MT), American basketball player and coach.

Samuel L(eroy) Jackson (21 Dec 1948, Washington DC), American film actor.

Marc Jacobs (9 Apr 1963, New York NY), American fashion designer.

Bharrat Jagdeo (23 Jan 1964, Unity village, Demarara, Guyana), Guyanese politician; president from 1999.

Mick Jagger (Michael Philip Jagger; 26 Jul 1943, Dartford, Kent, England), British rock musician and lead singer for the Rolling Stones.

Thorbjørn Jagland (5 Nov 1950, Drammen, Norway), Norwegian politician; secretary-general of the Council of Europe from 2009.

Helmut Jahn (4 Jan 1940, Nürnberg, Germany), German-born architect.

Zsuzsanna Jakab (17 May 1951, Hungary), Hungarian epidemiologist; the first director of the European Centre for Disease Prevention and Control (ECDC), from 2005.

LeBron James (30 Dec 1984, Akron OH), American professional basketball player.

Judith (Ann) Jamison (10 May 1944, Philadelphia PA), American dancer and choreographer (Alvin Ailey American Dance Theater).

Yahya Jammeh (Alphonse Jamus Jebulai Jammeh; 25 May 1965, Kanilai village, Gambia), Gambian politician; president from 1994.

Mariss Jansons (14 Jan 1943, Riga, Latvia), Latvian-born American director; conductor of the Royal Concertgebouw Orchestra of Amsterdam from 2004.

Jim Jarmusch (22 Jan 1953, Akron OH), American avant-garde filmmaker.

Neeme Järvi (7 Jun 1937, Tallinn, Estonia), Estonian conductor; music director of the Detroit Symphony Orchestra, 1990–2005, and of the New Jersey Symphony Orchestra, 2005–09, and chief conductor of the Hague Philharmonic from 2005.

D(isanayaka) M(udiyanselage) Jayaratne (4 Jun 1936), Sri Lankan politician; prime minister from 2010.

Jay-Z (Shawn Corey Carter; 4 Dec 1970, Brooklyn NY), American rapper.

Michaëlle Jean (6 Sep 1957, Port-au-Prince, Haiti), Haitian-born Canadian journalist; governor-general of Canada from 2005.

Katharine Jefferts Schori (26 Mar 1954, Pensacola FL), American church leader; presiding bishop of the US Episcopal Church from 2006.

Derek (Sanderson) Jeter (26 Jun 1974, Pequannock NJ), American baseball player.

Bobby Jindal (Piyush Jindal; 10 Jun 1971, Baton Rouge LA), American politician (Republican); governor of Louisiana from 2008.

Steven (Paul) Jobs (24 Feb 1955, San Francisco CA), American inventor and corporate executive; co-founder of Apple Computer and CEO from 1997.

Scarlett Johansson (22 Nov 1984, New York NY), American film and stage actress.

Elton John (Reginald Kenneth Dwight; 25 Mar 1947, Pinner, Middlesex, England), British singer, composer, and pianist.

Jasper Johns (15 May 1930, Augusta GA), American painter and graphic artist, a pioneer of Pop art.

(Alexander) Boris (de Pfeffel) Johnson (19 Jun 1964, New York NY), American-born British journalist, editor (Spectator), and MP (Conservative); mayor of London from 2008.

Denis Johnson (1949, Munich, West Germany), American novelist, short-story writer, and poet.

Dwayne (Douglas) Johnson ("The Rock"; 2 May 1972, Hayward CA), American professional wrestler-turned-actor.

Robert L. Johnson (8 Apr 1946, Hickory MS), American entrepreneur; founder (1980) of BET (Black Entertainment Television).

Stephen L. Johnson (21 Mar 1951, Washington DC), American government official; administrator of the US Environmental Protection Agency, 2005–09.

Ellen Johnson Sirleaf (29 Oct 1938, Monrovia, Liberia), Liberian government and international official; president of Liberia from 2006.

Angelina Jolie (Voight) (4 Jun 1975, Los Angeles CA), American film actress and philanthropist.

Goodluck Jonathan (20 Nov 1957, Otuoke, Nigeria), Nigerian politician; vice president, 2007–10, and president from 2010.

Bill T. Jones (William Tass Jones; 15 Feb 1952, Steuben county NY), American dancer, choreographer, and director.

Carwyn Jones (1967, Swansea, Wales), Welsh politician; first minister of Wales from 2009.

Edward P(aul) Jones (5 Oct 1950, Washington DC), American short-story writer and novelist.

James Earl Jones (Todd Jones; 17 Jan 1931, Arkabutla MS), American actor.

James L(ogan) Jones (19 Dec 1943, Kansas City MO), American military officer; US national security advisor from 2009.

January Jones (5 Jan 1978, Sioux Falls SD), American actress.

Marion Jones (12 Oct 1975, Los Angeles CA), American sprinter, long jumper, and basketball player.

Norah Jones (30 Mar 1979, New York NY), American jazz-pop vocalist and pianist.

Quincy (Delight) Jones, Jr. (14 Mar 1933, Chicago IL), American jazz and pop arranger, composer, and producer.

Tommy Lee Jones (15 Sep 1946, San Saba TX), American actor.

Michael (Jeffrey) Jordan (17 Feb 1963, Brooklyn NY), American basketball player; he was voted ESPN's Athlete of the Century and is believed by many to be the best basketball player in history; he became majority owner of the NBA Charlotte Bobcats in 2010.

Ivo Josipovic (28 Aug 1957, Zagreb, Yugoslavia [now in Croatia]), Croatian politician; president from 2010.

Juan Carlos I (Juan Carlos Alfonso Víctor María de Borbón y Borbón; 5 Jan 1938, Rome, Italy), Spanish royal; king from 1975.

Juanes (Juan Esteban Aristizábal Vásquez; 9 Aug 1972, Medellín, Colombia), Colombian singer, songwriter, and guitarist.

Anerood Jugnauth (29 Mar 1930, Mauritius), Mauritian politician; prime minister, 1982–95 and 2000–03, and president from 2003.

Jean-Claude Juncker (9 Dec 1954, Rédange-sur-Attert, Luxembourg), Luxembourgian politician; prime minister of Luxembourg from 1995.

Emilia Kabakov (3 Dec 1945, Dnipropetrovsk, USSR [now in Ukraine]), Ukrainian sculptor; recipient of a 2008 Praemium Imperiale.

Ilya Kabakov (30 Sep 1933, Dnipropetrovsk, USSR [now in Ukraine]), Ukrainian sculptor; recipient of a 2008 Praemium Imperiale.

Joseph Kabila (4 Jun 1971, Sud-Kivu province, Democratic Republic of the Congo), Congolese politician; president of the Democratic Republic of the Congo from 2001.

Ismail Kadare (28 Jan 1938, Gjirokastër, Albania), Albanian novelist and poet; recipient of the first Man Booker International Prize, in 2005.

Paul Kagame (23 Oct 1957, Gitarama, Ruanda-Urundi [now Rwanda]), Rwandan politician; president from 2000.

Elena Kagan (28 Apr 1960, New York NY), American lawyer and educator; dean of Harvard Law School (2003–09); solicitor general of the United States (2009–10); associate justice of the US Supreme Court from 2010.

Dahir Riyale Kahin (1952), Somali politician; president of the secessionist Republic of Somaliland from 2002.

Robert E(lliot) Kahn (23 Dec 1938, Brooklyn NY), American computer scientist, a key developer of the network that became the Internet; recipient of a Japan Prize in 2008.

Tim(othy Michael) Kaine (26 Feb 1958, St. Paul MN), American politician (Democrat); governor of Virginia, 2006–10, and chairman of the Democratic National Committee from 2009.

Kaká (Ricardo Izecson dos Santos Leite; 22 Apr 1982, Brasília, Brazil), Brazilian association football (soccer) player; he was voted World Player of the Year by FIFA in 2007.

Ingvar Kamprad (1926, Småland province, Sweden), Swedish businessman; founder of the home-furnishing company IKEA.

Naoto Kan (10 Oct 1946, Ube, Yamaguchi prefecture, Japan), Japanese politician (Democratic Party of Japan); prime minister from 2010.

Hiroo Kanamori (17 Oct 1936, Tokyo, Japan), Japanese seismologist; recipient of a 2007 Kyoto Prize.

Charles Kao (4 Nov 1933, Shanghai, China), English American physicist; cowinner of the 2009 Nobel Prize for Physics.

Radovan Karadzic (19 Jun 1945, Petnjica, Yugoslavia [now in Montenegro]), Bosnian Serb politician and president of Republika Srpska (Bosnia and Herzegovina), 1992–96; he was wanted as a war criminal and was arrested in 2008.

Kostas Karamanlis (Konstantinos Karamanlis; 14 Sep 1956, Athens, Greece), Greek politician (New Democracy); prime minister of Greece, 2004–09.

Donna Karan (Donna Faske; 2 Oct 1948, Forest Hills NY), American fashion designer.

Islam Karimov (30 Jan 1938, Samarkand, USSR [now in Uzbekistan]), Uzbek politician; president of Uzbekistan from 1990.

Mel(vin Alan) Karmazin (24 Aug 1943, New York NY), American media executive; CEO of Sirius XM Radio (formerly Sirius Satellite Radio) from 2004.

Hamid Karzai (24 Dec 1957, Karz, Afghanistan), Afghan statesman; president of Afghanistan from 2001.

Garry Kasparov (Garri Kimovich Kasparov; original name Garri or Harry Weinstein; 13 Apr 1963, Baku, USSR [now in Azerbaijan]), Azerbaijani-born Russian chess champion of the world, 1985–2000.

Jeffrey Katzenberg (21 Dec 1950, New York NY), American film producer and a cofounder (1994) of DreamWorks SKG.

Takashi Kawamura (19 Dec 1939, Japan?), Japanese businessman; CEO of Hitachi Corp. from 2009.

Diane Keaton (Diane Hall; 5 Jan 1946, Los Angeles CA), American actress and director.

Keb' Mo' (Kevin Moore; 3 Oct 1951, Los Angeles CA), American blues musician.

Garrison Keillor (Gary Edward Keillor; 7 Aug 1942, Anoka MN), American humorist and writer best known for his long-running radio variety show, *A Prairie Home Companion*.

Toby Keith (Covel) (8 Jul 1961, Clinton OK), American country-and-western singer.

Bill Keller (18 Jan 1949), American journalist; managing editor of the *New York Times*, 1997–2001, and executive editor from 2003.

Tim(othy J.) Keller (1950, Pennsylvania), American churchman and author; founding pastor (1989) of Redeemer Presbyterian Church, New York City.

Ellsworth Kelly (31 May 1923, Newburgh NY), American painter and sculptor.

R. Kelly (Robert S. Kelly; 8 Jan 1969, Chicago IL), American R&B performer.

William M. Kelso (30 Mar 1941, Chicago IL), American archaeologist; director of archaeology for the Jamestown Rediscovery Project.

Thomas (Michael) Keneally (pseudonym William Coyle; 7 Oct 1935, Sydney, NSW, Australia), Australian novelist.

Anthony (McCleod) Kennedy (23 Jul 1936, Sacramento CA), American jurist; associate justice of the US Supreme Court from 1988.

R(ichard) Gil Kerlikowske (1949, Fort Myers FL), American law enforcement official; director of national drug control policy ("drug czar") from 2009.

Lee Kernaghan (15 Apr 1964, Corryong, VIC, Australia), Australian country singer; he was named Australian of the Year for 2008.

John F(orbes) Kerry (11 Dec 1943, Fitzsimmons Army Hospital [now in Aurora CO]), American politician (Democrat) and senator from Massachusetts from 1985.

John (Phillip) Key (9 Aug 1961, Auckland, New Zealand), New Zealand politician (National Party); prime minister of New Zealand from 2008.

Alicia Keys (Alicia Augello Cook; 25 Jan 1981, New York NY), American R&B singer and pianist.

Hamad ibn Isa al-Khalifah (28 Jan 1950, Bahrain), Bahraini sheikh; emir and chief of state from 1999; he proclaimed himself king in 2002.

Zalmay (Mamozy) Khalilzad (22 Mar 1951, Mazar-i-Sharif, Afghanistan), Afghan-born American diplomat; ambassador to Afghanistan, 2003–05, to Iraq, 2005–07, and to the United Nations, 2007–09.

(Seretse Khama) Ian Khama (27 Feb 1953, Bechuanaland [now Botswana]), Botswanan military officer; president of Botswana from 2008.

Hojatolislam Sayyed Ali Khamenei (15 Jul 1939, Meshed, Iran), Iranian Shi'ite clergyman and politician who served as president, 1981–89, and as that country's *rahbar*, or leader, from 1989.

Mikhail (Borisovich) Khodorkovsky (26 Jun 1963, Moscow, USSR [now in Russia]), Russian businessman, the imprisoned former billionaire head of Yukos Oil Co.

Mwai Kibaki (15 Nov 1931, Gatuyaini village, Central province, Kenya), Kenyan politician; president of Kenya from 2002.

Angelique Kidjo (14 Jul 1960, Ouidah, Dahomey [now Benin]), Beninese pop singer.

* Nicole (Mary) Kidman (20 Jun 1967, Honolulu HI), American-born Australian actress.

Anselm Kiefer (8 Mar 1945, Donaueschingen, Germany), German Neo-Expressionist painter.

Jakaya (Mrisho) Kikwete (7 Oct 1950, Msoga, British Tanganyika [now in Tanzania]), Tanzanian military officer and government official; president from 2005.

Val (Edward) Kilmer (31 Dec 1959, Los Angeles CA), American film actor.

Jeong H. Kim (1961, Seoul, South Korea), Korean-born American electronics industry executive who was founder (1992) of Yurie Systems, Inc., and president of Alcatel-Lucent's Bell Labs from 2005.

Kim Jong II (16 Feb 1941, near Khabarovsk, USSR [now in Russia]), North Korean leader and successor to his father, Kim Il-Sung, as general secretary of the Central Committee of the Workers' Party of Korea (North Korea) from 1997.

Jimmy Kimmel (13 Nov 1967, Brooklyn NY), American comedian and TV talk-show host.

Jamaica Kincaid (Elaine Potter Richardson; 25 May 1949, Saint John's, Antigua, British West Indies [now in Antigua and Barbuda]), Antiguan American writer.

B.B. King (Riley B. King; 16 Sep 1925, Itta Bena, near Indianola MS), American blues guitarist and singer.

Larry King (Lawrence Harvey Zeiger; 19 Nov 1933, Brooklyn NY), American TV journalist.

Stephen (Edward) King (pseudonym Richard Bachman; 21 Sep 1947, Portland ME), American writer of novels combining horror, fantasy, and science fiction.

Stephenson King (13 Nov 1958, Saint Lucia, British West Indies?), West Indian politician (United Workers Party); prime minister of Saint Lucia from 2007.

Barbara Kingsolver (8 Apr 1955, Annapolis MD), American author and political activist; winner of the 2010 Orange Prize for Fiction for The Lacuna.

Galway Kinnell (1 Feb 1927, Providence RI), American poet.

Michael Kinsley (9 Mar 1951, Detroit MI), American political commentator and editor.

Kirill I (20 Nov 1946, Leningrad, USSR [now St. Petersburg, Russia]), Russian Orthodox patriarch of Moscow and All Russia from 2009.

Ron Kirk (1954, Austin TX), American politician (Democrat); mayor of Dallas, 1995–2001, and US trade representative from 2009.

Philippe Kirsch (1 Apr 1947, Namur, Belgium), Belgian-born Canadian jurist; president of the International Criminal Court, 2003–09.

Mari Kiviniemi (27 Sep 1968, Seinäjoki, Finland), Finnish politician; prime minister of Finland from 2010.

Vaclav Klaus (19 Jun 1941, Prague, Czechoslovakia [now in the Czech Republic]), Czech politician who served as prime minister, 1992–97, and president of the Czech Republic for one month in 1993 and again from 2003.

Calvin (Richard) Klein (19 Nov 1942, Bronx NY), American fashion designer.

August Kleinzahler (1949, Jersey City NJ), American poet.

Mirsolav Klose (9 Jun 1978, Opole, Poland), German association football (soccer) player.

Heidi Klum (1 Jun 1973, Bergisch Gladbach, West Germany), German American supermodel and TV-show host.

Bobby Knight (Robert Montgomery Knight; 25 Oct 1940, Massillon OH), American basketball coach and TV commentator; the winningest coach in men's collegiate basketball.

Keira Knightley (26 Mar 1985, Teddington, London, England), British film actress.

Makoto Kobayashi (7 Apr 1944, Nagoya, Japan), Japanese scientist; cowinner of the 2008 Nobel Prize in Physics.

Samuel Kobia (20 Mar 1947, Miathene, British Kenya), Kenyan Methodist church leader; general secretary of the World Council of Churches from 2004.

Horst Köhler (22 Feb 1943, Skierbieszow, Poland), German international economic official; president of Germany, 2004–10.

Yorihiko Kojima (1941, Tokyo, Japan), Japanese businessman; president and CEO of Mitsubishi Corp. from 2004.

Kabiné Komara (1950, French West Africa [now in Guinea]), Guinean businessman and politician; prime minister of Guinea, 2009–10.

Bronislaw Komorowski (4 Jun 1952, Oborniki Slaskie, Poland), Polish politician; president of Poland from 2010.

Zeljko Komsic (20 Jan 1964, Sarajevo, Yugoslavia [now in Bosnia and Herzegovina]), Bosnia and Herzegovinian politician; chairman of the presidency of the republic, 2007–08 and 2009–10.

Yusef Komunyakaa (29 Apr 1947, Bogalusa LA), American poet.

Alpha Oumar Konaré (2 Feb 1946, Kayes, French West Africa [now in Mali]), Malian statesman; president of Mali, 1992–2002, and chairman of the Commission of the African Union, 2003–08.

Maxim Kontsevich (25 Aug 1964, Khimki, USSR [now in Russia]), Russian mathematician; recipient of the Fields Medal in 1998 and a Crafoord Prize in 2008.

Joseph Kony (1964?, Odek, Uganda), Ugandan rebel commander; leader of the Lord's Resistance Army.

Rem Koolhaas (17 Nov 1944, Rotterdam, Netherlands), Dutch architect; recipient of the 2000 Pritzker Prize.

Jeff Koons (21 Jan 1955, York PA), American Pop-art painter and sculptor.

Dean (Ray) Koontz (9 Jul 1945, Everett PA), American novelist.

Ted Kooser (Theodore Kooser; 25 Apr 1939, Ames IA), American poet; US poet laureate, 2004–06.

Ernest Bai 'Koroma (2 Oct 1953, Makeni, British Sierra Leone), Sierra Leonean politician; president from 2007.

Michael (David) Kors (Karl Anderson, Jr.; 1959, Merrick, Long Island NY), American fashion designer.

Jadranka Kosor (1 Jul 1953, Pakrac, Yugoslavia [now in Croatia]), Croatian politician; prime minister from 2009.

Vojislav Kostunica (24 Mar 1944, Belgrade, Yugoslavia [now in Serbia]), Serbian politician; president of Yugoslavia, 2000–03; prime minister of Serbia, 2004–08.

Bernard Kouchner (1 Nov 1939, Avignon, France), French foreign minister from 2007.

Jon Krakauer (12 Apr 1954, Brookline MA), American author of nonfiction.

Alison Krauss (23 Jul 1971, Decatur IL), American bluegrass fiddle player and singer.

Lenny Kravitz (26 May 1964, Brooklyn NY), American rock musician.

Gidon Kremer (27 Feb 1947, Riga, USSR [now in Latvia]), Latvian-born violinist and conductor.

William Kristol (23 Dec 1952, New York NY), American editor and columnist.

Paul Krugman (28 Feb 1953, New York NY), American economist and journalist; winner of the 2008 Nobel Prize for Economics.

Andrius Kubilius (8 Dec 1956, Vilnius, USSR [now in Lithuania]), Lithuanian politician; prime minister of Lithiuania, 1999–2000 and again from 2008.

Dennis J. Kucinich (8 Oct 1946, Cleveland OH), American politician (Democrat); mayor of Cleveland, 1977–79; congressman from Ohio from 1997.

Ted Kulongoski (Theodore R. Kulongoski; 5 Nov 1940, Missouri), American politician (Democrat); governor of Oregon from 2003.

Yayoi Kusama (22 Mar 1929, Matsumoto, Nagano prefecture, Japan), Japanese artist; recipient of a 2006 Praemium Imperiale.

Tony Kushner (16 Jul 1956, New York NY), American playwright.

Shia LaBeouf (11 Jun 1986, Los Angeles CA), American actor.

Lady Gaga (Stefani Joanne Angelina Germanotta; 28 Mar 1986, Yonkers NY), American singer.

Christine Lagarde (1 Jan 1956, Paris, France), French lawyer; minister of finance from 2007.

Emeril (John) Lagasse (15 Oct 1959, Fall River MA), American TV chef, restaurateur, and media personality.

Karl Lagerfeld (10 Sep 1938, Hamburg, Germany), German-born French fashion designer.

Ray LaHood (6 Dec 1945, Peoria IL), American politician (Republican); congressman from Illinois, 1995–2009, and US secretary of transportation from 2009.

Miroslav Lajcak (20 Mar 1963, Poprad, Czechoslovakia [now in Slovakia]), Slovak diplomat and government official; high representative for Bosnia and Herzegovina, 2007–09.

Anthony Lake (1939), American diplomat and author; executive director of UNICEF from 2010.

Guy Laliberté (1959, Quebec city, QC, Canada), Canadian circus performer and founder of Cirque du Soleil.

Edward S. Lampert (19 Jul 1962, Roslyn NY), American business executive; founder (1988) of ESL Investments and chairman of Sears Holdings Corp. from 2005.

Pascal Lamy (8 Apr 1947, Levallois-Perret, Paris, France), French financial and government official; EU trade commissioner, 1999–2004, and director general of the World Trade Organization from 2005.

Rocco Landesman (20 Jul 1947, St. Louis MO), American theater producer; chairman of the US National Endowment for the Arts from 2009.

Mitch Landrieu (16 Aug 1960, New Orleans LA), American politician (Democrat); mayor of New Orleans from 2010.

Diane Lane (22 Jan 1965, New York NY), American film actress.

Nathan Lane (Joseph Lane; 3 Feb 1956, Jersey City NJ), American stage and film actor.

David Lang (8 Jan 1957, Los Angeles CA), American opera composer whose *The Little Match Girl Passion* won the 2008 Pulitzer Prize for music.

Helmut Lang (10 Mar 1956, Vienna, Austria), Austrian fashion designer.

Jessica Lange (20 Apr 1949, Cloquet MN), American film, stage, and TV actress.

Frank Langella (1 Jan 1940, Bayonne NJ), American film actor.

Anthony M. LaPaglia (31 Jan 1959, Adelaide, SA, Australia), Australian film and TV actor.

Lewis H. Lapham (8 Jan 1935, San Francisco CA), American liberal political commentator and author; editor of *Harper's Magazine,* 1976–81 and 1983–2006.

Lyndon (Hermyle) LaRouche, Jr. (8 Sep 1922, Rochester NH), American economist, populist politician, and perennial presidential candidate.

John Lasseter (12 Jan 1957, Hollywood CA), American animator and director; chief creative officer at Pixar Animation Studios from 2006.

Matt(hew Todd) Lauer (30 Dec 1957, New York NY), American TV journalist and news anchor.

Ralph Lauren (Ralph Lipschitz; 14 Oct 1939, New York NY), American fashion designer.

(James) Hugh (Calum) Laurie (11 Jun 1959, Oxford, England), British TV and film actor.

Taylor Lautner (11 Feb 1992, Grand Rapids MI), American actor.

Sergey (Viktorovich) Lavrov (21 Mar 1950, Moscow, USSR [now in Russia]), Russian politician; foreign minister from 2004.

Jude Law (29 Dec 1972, Blackheath, London, England), British stage and screen actor.

Martin Lawrence (16 Apr 1965, Frankfurt am Main, West Germany), American TV actor and comedian.

Nigella (Lucy) Lawson (6 Jan 1960), British cook and author of food-related books.

John Le Carré (David John Moore Cornwell; 19 Oct 1931, Poole, Dorset, England), English spy novelist.

Jean-Marie Gustave Le Clézio (13 Apr 1940, Nice, France), French author; winner of the 2008 Nobel Prize for Literature.

Ursula K(roeber) Le Guin (21 Oct 1929, Berkeley CA), American science-fiction and fantasy writer.

Meave Leakey (28 Jul 1942, London, England), British-born Kenyan paleoanthropologist.

Richard (Erskine Frere) Leakey (19 Dec 1944, Nairobi, Kenya), Kenyan physical anthropologist, paleontologist, conservationist, and politician.

Michael O. Leavitt (11 Feb 1951, Cedar City UT), American politician (Republican) and official; governor of Utah, 1993–2003, EPA administrator, 2003–05, and US secretary of health and human services, 2005–09.

Ang Lee (23 Oct 1954, P'ing-Tung county, Taiwan), Taiwanese-born film director.

Jason (Michael) Lee (25 Apr 1970, Orange CA), American skateboarder and film and TV actor.

Spike Lee (Shelton Lee; 20 Mar 1957, Atlanta GA), American film director.

Stan Lee (Stanley Martin Lieber; 28 Dec 1922, New York NY), American comic-book artist; creator of Spider-Man and other superheroes.

Lee Hsien Loong (10 Feb 1952, Singapore), Singaporean politician and economic expert; prime minister from 2004.

Lee Kun Hee (9 Jan 1942, Uiryung, Japanese-occupied Korea [now in South Korea]), South Korean corporate executive; chairman of the Samsung Group, 1987–2008 and again from 2010.

Lee Myung-bak (19 Dec 1941, Osaka, Japan), South Korean politician (Grand National Party); mayor of Seoul, 2002–06, and president of South Korea from 2008.

John Leguizamo (22 Jul 1964, Bogotá, Colombia), Colombian-born American comedian and actor.

Dennis Lehane (4 Aug 1966, Dorchester, Boston MA), American crime novelist.

Jim Lehrer (James C. Lehrer; 19 May 1934, Wichita KS), American TV journalist and author.

Annie Leibovitz (Anna-Lou Leibovitz; 2 Oct 1949, Westbury CT), American portrait photographer and photojournalist.

Jean Lemierre (6 Jun 1950, Sainte Adresse, France), French international banking executive and president of the European Bank for Reconstruction and Development from 2000.

Jay Leno (James Douglas Muir Leno; 28 Apr 1950, Short Hills NJ), American comedian and TV talk-show host.

Robert Lepage (12 Dec 1957, Quebec, QC, Canada), Canadian actor, director, and playwright.

Doris Lessing (Doris May Thaler; 22 Oct 1919, Kermanshah, Persia [now Bakhtaran, Iran]), British novelist and short-story writer; recipient of the 2007 Nobel Prize for Literature.

Jonathan (Allen) Lethem (19 Feb 1964, Brooklyn NY), American novelist, short-story writer, and essayist.

Letsie III (David Mohato; 17 Jul 1963, Morija, Basutoland [now Lesotho]), Lesotho royal; king of Lesotho, 1990–95 and again from 1996.

David (Michael) Letterman (12 Apr 1947, Indianapolis IN), American TV talk-show host.

Tracy Letts (4 Jul 1965, Tulsa OK), American playwright and actor whose *August: Osage County* won the 2008 Pulitzer Prize for drama.

Doris Leuthard (10 Apr 1963, Merenschwand, Switzerland), Swiss politician; president from 2010.

James Levine (23 Jun 1943, Cincinnati OH), American conductor and pianist; music director of the Metropolitan Opera from 1976 and principal conductor of the Boston Symphony Orchestra from 2004.

Bernard-Henri Lévy (5 Nov 1948, Béni-Saf, French Algeria), Algerian-born French media darling and author of best-selling "enhanced nonfiction" books.

Eugene Levy (17 Dec 1946, Hamilton, ON, Canada), Canadian comic actor and writer.

Jacob J. Lew (29 Aug 1955, New York NY), American economist; Pres. Barack Obama's nominee to become director of the US Office of Management and Budget.

Kenneth D. Lewis (9 Apr 1947, Meridian MS), American corporate executive; CEO of the Bank of America Corp., 2001–10.

(Diane) Monique Lhuillier (1971, Cebu, Philippines), American couturier.

Jet Li (Li Lian Jie; 26 Apr 1963, Beijing, China), Chinese-born *wushu* (acrobatic martial arts) champion and film actor.

Daniel Libeskind (12 May 1946, Lodz, Poland), Polish-born Israeli American architect.

Nicklas (Erik) Lidström (28 Apr 1970, Västerås, Sweden), Swedish ice-hockey defenseman.

Joseph I. Lieberman (24 Feb 1942, Stamford CT), American politician (Independent Democrat); senator from Connecticut from 1989.

Lil' Kim (Kimberly Denise Jones; 11 Jul 1975, Bedford-Stuyvesant, Brooklyn NY), American hip-hop performer.

Rush Limbaugh (12 Jan 1951, Cape Girardeau MO), American radio talk-show host and conservative commentator.

Linda Lingle (Linda Cutter; 4 Jun 1953, St. Louis MO), American politician (Republican); governor of Hawaii from 2002.

Laura Linney (5 Feb 1964, New York NY), American film and stage actress.

John Lithgow (19 Oct 1945, Rochester NY), American film and TV actor.

Lucy (Alexis) Liu (2 Dec 1968, Jackson Heights, Queens NY), American TV and film actress.

Liu Chao-shiuan (10 May 1943, Hengyang, Hunan province, China), Taiwanese politician; president of the Executive Yuan (premier), 2008–09.

Nicholas (Joseph Orville) Liverpool (9 Sep 1934, Dominica, British West Indies), West Indian politician; president of Dominica from 2003.

Kenneth Livingstone (17 Jun 1945, Lambeth, London, England), British politician (Labour); mayor of London, 2000–08.

Tzipi Livni (Tzipora Malka Livni; 8 Jul 1958, Tel Aviv–Yafo, Israel), Israeli politician (Kadima); foreign minister of Israel, 2006–09, and leader of the Kadima party from 2008.

LL Cool J (James Todd Smith; 14 Jan 1968, Queens NY), American hip-hop artist and actor.

Andrew Lloyd Webber (22 Mar 1948, London, England), British composer of stage musicals; recipient of a Praemium Imperiale in 1995 and a 2006 Kennedy Center Honor.

Porfirio Lobo (Sosa) (22 Dec 1947, Trujillo, Honduras), Honduran politician; president from 2010.

Gary Locke (21 Jan 1950, Seattle WA), American politician (Democrat); governor of Washington, 1997–2005, and US secretary of commerce from 2009.

Keith Alan Lockhart (7 Nov 1959, Poughkeepsie NY), American conductor of the Boston Pops from 1993.

John Logan (24 Sep 1961, Chicago IL), American screenwriter and playwright.

Lindsay (Morgan) Lohan (2 Jul 1986, New York NY), American actress and film starlet.

Jonah Tali Lomu (12 May 1975, Auckland, New Zealand), New Zealand rugby winger.

Letitia A. Long (1959?, Annapolis MD), American intelligence official; director of the National Geospatial-Intelligence Agency from 2010, the first female to head one of the major US intelligence agencies.

Richard Long (1945, Bristol, England), British sculptor; recipient of a Praemium Imperiale in 2009.

Eva (Jacqueline) Longoria Parker (15 Mar 1975, Corpus Christi TX), American TV actress.

Jennifer Lopez (24 Jul 1970, Bronx NY), American pop singer, actress, and fashion designer.

Peter Löscher (17 Sep 1957, Villach, Austria), Austrian corporate executive; president and CEO of Siemens AG from 2007.

Trent Lott (9 Oct 1941, Grenada MS), American politician (Republican); senator from Mississippi, 1989–2007, Senate leader, 1996–2003, and Senate whip, 1995–96 and again in 2007.

Christian Louboutin (7 Jan 1963, Paris, France), French high-fashion shoe designer.

Julia Louis-Dreyfus (13 Jan 1961, New York NY), American actress.

Henri Loyrette (31 May 1952, Neuilly-sur-Seine, France), French museum curator; director of the Louvre from 2001.

George (Walton) Lucas, Jr. (14 May 1944, Modesto CA), American film producer.

Susan Lucci (23 Dec 1947, Scarsdale NY), American TV soap opera star.

Fernando (Armindo) Lugo (Méndez) (30 May 1951, San Pedro del Paraná, Paraguay), Paraguayan Roman Catholic bishop; president from 2008.

Baz(mark Anthony) Luhrmann (17 Sep 1962, near Sydney, NSW, Australia), Australian film and stage director and producer.

Alyaksandr (Hrygorevich) Lukashenka (30 Aug 1954, Kopys, Vitebsk oblast, Belorussian SSR, USSR [now Belarus]), Belarusian politician; president of Belarus from 1994.

Luiz Inácio Lula da Silva (27 Oct 1945, Garanhuns, Pernambuco state, Brazil), Brazilian labor leader and politician (Workers Party); president of Brazil from 2003.

Hilary Lunke (7 Jun 1979, Edina MN), American golfer.

Jane Lynch (14 Jul 1960, Dolton IL), American film and television actress.

John (H.) Lynch (25 Nov 1952, Waltham MA), American businessman and politician (Democrat); governor of New Hampshire from 2005.

Evan Lysacek (4 Jun 1985, Chicago IL), American Olympic champion figure skater.

Yo-Yo Ma (7 Oct 1955, Paris, France), American cellist.

Ma Ying-jeou (Ma Yingjiu; 13 Jul 1950, Hong Kong), Taiwanese politician and government official; mayor of Taipei, 1998–2006, and president from 2008.

Lorin Maazel (6 Mar 1930, Neuilly, France), French-born American conductor and violinist; music director of the New York Philharmonic, 2002–09.

Gloria (Macaraeg) Macapagal Arroyo (5 Apr 1947, San Juan, Philippines), Philippine politician; president, 2001–10.

Alistair MacLeod (20 Jul 1936, North Batteford, SK, Canada), Canadian writer.

Rachel Maddow (1 Apr 1973, Castro Valley CA), American liberal television commentator.

Bernard L. Madoff (29 Apr 1938, Queens NY), American financier; convicted in 2009 of having operated one of the world's largest Ponzi schemes.

Madonna (Madonna Louise Veronica Ciccone; 16 Aug 1958, Bay City MI), American singer, songwriter, actress, and entrepreneur.

Tobey Maguire (Tobias Vincent Maguire; 27 Jun 1975, Santa Monica CA), American film actor.

Bill Maher (20 Jan 1956, New York NY), American TV comedian and personality.

Roger Michael Cardinal Mahony (27 Feb 1936, Hollywood CA), American Roman Catholic churchman; archbishop of Los Angeles from 1985 and cardinal from 1991.

Natalie Maines (14 Oct 1974, Lubbock TX), American country vocalist (for the Dixie Chicks).

Mohammed ibn Rashid al-Maktum (1949, Dubai, British Trucial States [now in United Arab Emirates]?), UAE sheikh; crown prince from 1995 and ruler of Dubai from 2006.

Tuilaepa Sailele Malielegaoi (14 Apr 1945, Lepa, Samoa), Samoan politician; prime minister of Samoa from 1998.

Nuri (Kamal) al-Maliki (Jawad al-Maliki; Abu Isra; 1 Jul 1950, near Karbala, Iraq), Iraqi politician (Shiʻite); prime minister of Iraq from 2006.

Evgeni Malkin (31 Jul 1986, Magnitogorsk, Russia), Russian ice-hockey player.

John (Gavin) Malkovich (9 Dec 1953, Christopher IL), American film actor and filmmaker.

David (George Joseph) Malouf (20 Mar 1934, Brisbane, QLD, Australia), Australian poet and novelist; recipient of the 2000 Neustadt Prize.

David (Alan) Mamet (30 Nov 1947, Chicago IL), American playwright, director, and screenwriter.

Joe Manchin (Joseph Manchin III; 24 Aug 1947, Farmington WV), American businessman and politician (Democrat); governor of West Virginia from 2005.

Nelson (Rolihlahla) Mandela (18 Jul 1918, Umtata, Cape of Good Hope, Union of South Africa [now Mthatha, South Africa]), South African black nationalist leader and statesman; he was a political prisoner, 1962–90, president of South Africa (1994–99), and corecipient of the 1993 Nobel Peace Prize.

Barry Manilow (Barry Alan Pincus; 17 Jun 1946, Brooklyn NY), American pop singer and songwriter.

Michael (Kenneth) Mann (5 Feb 1943, Chicago IL), American film director.

Eli(sha Nelson) Manning (3 Jan 1981, New Orleans LA), American pro football quarterback.

Patrick (Augustus Merving) Manning (17 Aug 1946, San Fernando, Trinidad, British West Indies [now in Trinidad and Tobago]), Trinidadian politician; prime minister of Trinidad and Tobago, 1991–95 and 2001–10.

Peyton (Williams) Manning (24 Mar 1976, New Orleans LA), American pro football quarterback.

Hilary Mantel (6 Jul 1952, Hadfield, Derbyshire, England), English writer; winner of the 2009 Man Booker Prize.

John H. Marburger III (1941?, Staten Island NY), American physicist; presidential science adviser and head of the Office of Science and Technology Policy, 2001–09.

Sergio Marchionne (17 Jun 1952, Chieti, Italy), Italian Canadian businessman; CEO of Chrysler Group LLC.

Brice Marden (15 Oct 1938, Bronxville NY), American minimalist painter and printmaker.

Margrethe II (Margrethe Alexandrine Thorhildur Ingrid; 16 Apr 1940, Copenhagen, Denmark), Danish royal; queen from 1972.

Julianna Margulies (8 Jun 1966, Spring Valley NY), American actress.

Mariam (Mariam Doumbia; 15 Apr 1958), Malian singer (of Amadou and Mariam).

Mariza (Mariza Nunes; 1974?, Mozambique), Portuguese fado singer.

Mary Ellen Mark (20 Mar 1940, Philadelphia PA), American photojournalist.

Jack Markell (26 Nov 1940, Newark DE), American politician (Democrat); governor of Delaware from 2009.

Branford Marsalis (26 Aug 1960, Breaux Bridge LA), American jazz saxophonist, bandleader, and producer.

Wynton Marsalis (18 Oct 1961, New Orleans LA), American jazz trumpeter and composer.

Yann Martel (25 Jun 1963, Salamanca, Spain), Spanish-born Canadian novelist.

Kevin Martin (14 Dec 1966, Charlotte NC), American politician and chairman of the Federal Communications Commission, 2005–09.

Steve Martin (14 Aug 1945, Waco TX), American comedic actor, screenwriter, playwright, and author.

Ricardo (Alberto) Martinelli (Berrocal) (11 Mar 1952, Panama City, Panama), Panamanian politician; president of Panama from 2009.

Mary (Mary Donaldson; 5 Feb 1972, Hobart, TAS, Australia), Australian-born marketing executive and crown princess of Denmark; wife of Crown Prince Frederik (married 14 May 2004).

Masako (Masako Owada; 9 Dec 1963, Tokyo, Japan), Japanese royal; princess consort of Crown Prince Naruhito (married 9 Jun 1993).

Toshihide Maskawa (7 Feb 1940, Nagoya, Japan), Japanese physicist; cowinner of the 2008 Nobel Prize for Physics.

Mathilde (Mathilde d'Udekem d'Acoz; 21 Jan 1973, Uccle, Belgium), Belgian royal; princess consort of Prince Philippe (married 4 Dec 1999) and heir to the throne.

Hideki Matsui (12 Jun 1974, Ishikawa prefecture, Japan), Japanese baseball outfielder.

Daisuke Matsuzaka (13 Sep 1980, Tokyo, Japan), Japanese baseball player.

Dave Matthews (David John Matthews; 9 Jan 1967, Johannesburg, South Africa), American rock musician (of the Dave Matthews Band).

James Mattis (1950?, Pullman WA), American military leader; commander of US Central Command from 2010.

Máxima (Máxima Zorreguieta Cerruti; 17 May 1971, Buenos Aires, Argentina), Argentine-born Dutch investment banker and princess consort of Crown Prince Willem-Alexander (married 2 Feb 2002).

John (Clayton) Mayer (16 Oct 1977, Bridgeport CT), American singer and songwriter.

Thom Mayne (19 Jan 1944, Waterbury CT), American architect; recipient of the 2005 Pritzker Prize.

Floyd Mayweather, Jr. ("Pretty Boy"; 24 Feb 1977, Grand Rapids MI), American boxing champion in several weight classes, from lightweight to super welterweight.

Kiran Mazumdar-Shaw (1954?, Bangalore [now Bengaluru], India), Indian business executive; founder (1978) of Biocon India, India's first biotechnology company.

Thabo (Mvuyelwa) Mbeki (18 Jun 1942, Idutywa, Cape of Good Hope, Union of South Africa [now in Eastern Cape province, South Africa]), South African politician; president, 1999–2008.

Mary (Patricia) McAleese (27 Jun 1951, Belfast, Northern Ireland), Irish politician; president from 1997.

James (Andrew) McAvoy (21 Apr 1979, Glasgow, Scotland), British actor.

John (Sidney) McCain III (29 Aug 1936, Panama Canal Zone), American politician (Republican); senator from Arizona from 1987.

Cormac McCarthy (Charles McCarthy, Jr.; 20 Jul 1933, Providence RI), American novelist in the Southern gothic tradition.

(James) Paul McCartney (18 Jun 1942, Liverpool, England), British singer, songwriter, and former member of the Beatles.

Stella (Nina) McCartney (13 Sep 1971, London, England), British fashion designer.

Matthew McConaughey (4 Nov 1969, Uvalde TX), American film actor.

Mike McConnell (John Michael McConnell; 26 Jul 1943, Greenville SC), American military intelligence officer; director of the National Security Agency, 1992–96, and director of national intelligence, 2007–09.

(Addison) Mitch(ell) McConnell (Jr.) (20 Feb 1942, Tuscumbia, AL), American politician (Republican); senator from Kentucky from 1985, Senate whip, 2003–07, and Senate minority leader from 2007.

David McCullough (7 Jul 1933, Pittsburgh PA), American biographer and historian.

Audra (Ann) McDonald (3 Jul 1970, West Berlin, West Germany [now in Berlin, Germany], American theater actress.

Robert F(rancis) McDonnell (15 Jun 1954, Philadelphia PA), American politician (Republican); governor of Virginia from 2010.

Frances McDormand (23 Jun 1957, Chicago IL), American film actress.

John (Patrick) McEnroe, Jr. (16 Feb 1959, Wiesbaden, West Germany), American tennis player and TV sportscaster.

Reba McEntire (28 Mar 1954, McAlester OK), American country singer and TV and film actress.

Ian (Russell) McEwan (21 Jun 1948, Aldershot, England), British novelist.

Patrick McGorry (1952?, Dublin, Ireland), Australian psychiatrist and educator; he was named Australian of the Year for 2010.

Glenn (Donald) McGrath (9 Feb 1970, Dubbo, NSW, Australia), Australian cricket fast bowler.

Phil(lip C.) McGraw (1 Sep 1950, Vinita OK), American talk-show host, author, and psychologist-educator.

(Samuel) Tim(othy) McGraw (1 May 1967, Delhi LA), American country-and-western singer.

Dalton McGuinty (19 Jul 1955, Ottawa, ON, Canada), Canadian lawyer and politician (Liberal); premier of Ontario from 2003.

Kevin McKenzie (29 Apr 1954, Burlington VT), American ballet dancer, choreographer, and director.

Beverley McLachlin (7 Sep 1943, Pincher Creek, AB, Canada), Canadian Supreme Court justice from 1989 and chief justice from 2000.

Vince(nt Kennedy) McMahon (Jr.) (24 Aug 1945, Pinehurst NC), American wrestling promoter; owner of World Wrestling Entertainment, Inc., from 1982.

Larry McMurtry (3 Jun 1936, Wichita Falls TX), American novelist.

W. James McNerney, Jr. (22 Aug 1949, Providence RI), American corporate executive; chairman of the board, president, and CEO of the Boeing Co. from 2005.

Marian McPartland (Margaret Marian Turner; 20 Mar 1918, Slough, England), English-born jazz pianist and composer.

James M. McPherson (11 Oct 1936, Valley City ND), American historian of slavery and the antislavery movement.

Ian McShane (29 Sep 1942, Blackburn, Lancashire, England), British film and TV actor.

Jon Meacham (1969, Chattanooga TN), American author, political commentator, and magazine editor.

Russell (Charles) Means (10 Nov 1939, Pine Ridge SD), American Lakota Sioux activist.

Dmitry (Anatolyevich) Medvedev (14 Sep 1965, Leningrad, USSR [now St. Petersburg, Russia]), Russian lawyer and politician; president of Russia from 2008.

Zubin Mehta (29 Apr 1936, Bombay, British India [now Mumbai, India]), Indian orchestral conductor; music director of the Israel Philharmonic from 1977.

John Mellencamp (Johnny Cougar; John Cougar Mellencamp; 7 Oct 1951, Seymour IN), American singer and songwriter.

Eva Mendes (5 Mar 1974, Miami FL), American model and film actress.

Sam(uel Alexander) Mendes (1 Aug 1965, Reading, England), British film director.

Paulo Mendes da Rocha (25 Oct 1928, Vitória, Espírito Santo state, Brazil), Brazilian architect and professor; recipient of the 2006 Pritzker Prize.

Fradique de Menezes (1942), Sao Tome and Principe politician; president, 2001–03 and again from 2003.

Angela Merkel (Angela Dorothea Kasner; 17 Jul 1954, Hamburg, West Germany), German politician (Christian Democratic Union); chancellor of Germany from 2005.

W(illiam) S(tanley) Merwin (30 Sep 1927, New York NY), American poet and translator; US poet laureate for 2010–11.

Hans-Rudolf Merz (10 Nov 1942, Herisau, Switzerland), Swiss politician; president, 2009.

Stipe Mesic (Stjepan Mesic; 24 Dec 1934, Orahovica, Yugoslavia [now in Croatia]), Croatian politician; president, 2000–10.

Lionel (Andrés) Messi (24 Jun 1987, Rosario, Argentina), Argentine association football (soccer) player; he was voted World Player of the Year by FIFA in 2009.

Mette-Marit (Mette-Marit Tjessem Høiby; 19 Aug 1973, Kristiansand, Norway), Norwegian royal; princess consort of Crown Prince Haakon (married 25 Aug 2001).

Pierre de Meuron (8 May 1950, Basel, Switzerland), Swiss architect; corecipient of the 2001 Pritzker Prize and of a Praemium Imperiale in 2007.

Stephenie Meyer (24 Dec 1973, Hartford CT), American author of fiction for young adults.

Lena Meyer-Landrut (23 May 1991, Hannover, Germany), German pop singer; winner of the 2010 Eurovision Song Contest.

Jonathan Rhys Meyers (Jonathan Michael Francis O'Keefe; 27 Jul 1977, Dublin, Ireland), Irish film actor.

M.I.A. (Maya Arulpragasam; 18 Jul 1975, London, England), British-born Sri Lankan singer and rapper.

Michael (Michael Hohenzollern-Sigmaringen; ruled as Mihai I; 25 Oct 1921, Sinaia, Romania), Romanian king, 1927–30 (under regency) and 1940–47.

Jillian Michaels (18 Feb 1974, Los Angeles CA), American fitness expert and TV personality.

Lorne Michaels (Lorne Michael Lipowitz; 17 Nov 1944, Toronto, ON, Canada), Canadian-born TV and film producer.

James (Alix) Michel (16 Aug 1944, Mahe Island, Seychelles), Seychelles politician; president from 2004.

Lea Michele (29 Aug 1986, Bronx NY), American actress.

Roberto Micheletti (Baín) (13 Aug 1948, El Progreso, Honduras), Honduran politician; de facto president, 2009–10.

Michiko (Michiko Shoda; 20 Oct 1934, Tokyo, Japan), Japanese royal; empress consort of Emperor Akihito (married 10 Apr 1959).

Bette Midler (1 Dec 1945, Honolulu HI), American comedian, singer, and actress.

David (Wright) Miliband (15 Jul 1965, London, England), British politician (Labour); foreign secretary, 2007–10.

David (Raymond) Miller (26 Dec 1958, San Francisco CA), American-born Canadian politician (independent); mayor of Toronto from 2003.

Dennis Miller (3 Nov 1953, Pittsburgh PA), American TV comedian, radio talk-show host, and writer.

(Samuel) Bode Miller (12 Oct 1977, Easton NH), American Alpine skier.

Sienna (Rose) Miller (28 Dec 1981, New York NY), American-born British stage and film actress.

Sue Miller (29 Nov 1943, Chicago IL), American novelist.

John Atta Mills (21 Jul 1944, Tarkwa, Gold Coast [now Ghana]), Ghanaian politician; president from 2009.

Ruth Ann Minner (Ruth Ann Coverdale; 17 Jan 1935, Milford DE), American politician (Democrat); governor of Delaware (2001–09).

Kylie (Ann) Minogue (28 May 1968, Melbourne, VIC, Australia), Australian actress and pop singer.

Helen Mirren (Ilyena Lydia Mironoff; 26 Jul 1945, Chiswick, London, England), British stage, TV, and film actress.

Joni Mitchell (Roberta Joan Anderson; 7 Nov 1943, Fort Macleod, AB, Canada), Canadian singer, songwriter, and painter.

Efthimios E. Mitropoulos (30 May 1939, Piraeus, Greece), Greek international official; secretary-general of the International Maritime Organization from 2004.

Lakshmi (Narayan) Mittal (15 Jun 1950, Sadulpur, Rajasthan state, India), Indian-born British steel magnate.

Satoshi Miura (3 Apr 1944, Japan?), Japanese corporate executive; CEO and president of Nippon Telephone & Telegraph from 2007.

Ratko Mladic (12 Mar 1943, Kalinovik village, Bosnia, Yugoslavia [now in Bosnia and Herzegovina]), Bosnian Serb military officer sought as a war criminal.

N(avarre) Scott Momaday (27 Feb 1934, Lawton OK), American writer of Kiowa heritage.

Mo'Nique (Mo'Nique Imes-Hicks; 11 Dec 1967, Woodlawn MD), American comedian and actress.

Thomas S(pencer) Monson (21 Aug 1927, Salt Lake City UT), American church leader; president of the Church of Jesus Christ of Latter-day Saints from 2008.

Luc Montagnier (18 Aug 1932, Chabris, France), French scientist; cowinner of the 2008 Nobel Prize for Physiology or Medicine.

Alan Moore (18 Nov 1953), British author and creator of graphic novels.

Demi Moore (Demetria Gene Guynes; 11 Nov 1962, Roswell NM), American film actress.

Julianne Moore (Julie Anne Smith; 3 Dec 1960, Fayetteville NC), American film actress.

Lorrie Moore (Marie Lorena Moore; 13 Jan 1957, Glens Falls NY), American short-story writer and novelist.

Mandy Moore (Amanda Leigh Moore; 10 Apr 1984, Nashua NH), American pop singer and film actress.

Michael Moore (23 Apr 1954, Davison MI), American film director and author.

(Juan) Evo Morales (Ayma) (26 Oct 1959, Orinoca, Bolivia), Bolivian farm-union leader; president from 2006.

Jason Moran (21 Jan 1975, Houston TX), American jazz pianist and bandleader.

Luis Moreno Ocampo (4 Jun 1952, Buenos Aires, Argentina), Argentine lawyer; the first chief prosecutor of the International Criminal Court, from 2003.

Rhodri Morgan (29 Sep 1939, Cardiff, Wales), Welsh politician (Labour); first minister of Wales, 2000–09.

Manny Mori (Emanuel Mori; 1948, Chuuk state?, Micronesia), Micronesian politician; president of Micronesia from 2007.

Mark Morris (29 Aug 1956, Seattle WA), American dancer and choreographer.

Matthew Morrison (30 Oct 1978, Fort Ord CA), American actor.

Toni Morrison (Chloe Anthony Wofford; 18 Feb 1931, Lorain OH), American novelist; recipient of the 1993 Nobel Prize for Literature.

Viggo (Peter) Mortensen (20 Oct 1958, New York NY), American film actor.

Walter Mosley (12 Jan 1952, Los Angeles CA), American writer of science fiction and mystery novels.

Kate Moss (16 Jan 1974, Addiscombe, Surrey, England), British model.

Andrew Motion (26 Oct 1952, London, England), English poet, teacher, editor, and biographer; poet laureate of Britain, 1999–2009.

Kgalema (Petrus) Motlanthe (19 Jul 1949, Johannesburg, Union of South Africa), South African politician (African National Congress); president, 2008–09, and deputy president from 2009.

Markos Moulitsas (Zúniga) ("Kos"; 11 Sep 1971, Chicago IL), American populist journalist and blogger; founder and editor of the Daily Kos blog from 2002.

Amr Muhammad Moussa (3 Oct 1936, Cairo, Egypt), Egyptian secretary-general of the League of Arab States from 2001.

Bill Moyers (Billy Don Moyers; 5 Jun 1934, Hugo OK), American TV journalist, former government official, and author.

Brian T. Moynihan (9 Oct 1959, Marietta OH), American businessman; president and CEO of Bank of America from 2010.

Mswati III (19 Apr 1968, Swaziland), Swazi royal; king of Swaziland from 1986.

(Muhammed) Hosni Mubarak (4 May 1928, Al-Minufiyah governorate, Egypt), Egyptian politician; president of Egypt from 1981.

Edward A. Mueller (1947, St. Louis MO), American corporate executive; chairman and CEO of Qwest Communications International Inc. from 2007.

Lisel Mueller (Lisel Neumann; 8 Feb 1924, Hamburg, Germany), German-born American poet.

Robert S(wan) Mueller III (7 Aug 1944, New York NY), American government official; FBI director from 2001.

Robert (Gabriel) Mugabe (21 Feb 1924, Kutama, Southern Rhodesia [now Zimbabwe]), Zimbabwean politician; the first prime minister (1980–87) of the reconstituted state of Zimbabwe and president from 1987.

Muhammad VI (Muhammad ibn al-Hassan; 21 Aug 1963, Rabat, Morocco), Moroccan royal; king from 1999.

Ali Muhammad Mujawar (1953, Shabwah, British-protected Aden [now in Yemen]), Yemeni politician; prime minister from 2007.

José (Alberto) Mujica (Cordano) (20 May 1935, Montevideo, Uruguay), Uruguayan politician (Broad Front); president from 2010.

Michael (Bernard) Mukasey (28 Jul 1941, Bronx NY), American jurist; US attorney general, 2007–09.

Pranab Mukherjee (11 Dec 1935, Mirati village, West Bengal, British India), Indian politician (Indian National Congress); foreign minister, 1995–96 and 2006–09, and finance minister from 2009.

Alan Mulally (4 Aug 1945, Oakland CA), American businessman; president and CEO of Ford Motor Co. from 2006.

Paul Muldoon (20 Jun 1951, Portadown, Northern Ireland), Irish-born American poet.

Herta Müller (17 Aug 1953, Nitchidorf, Romania), Romanian-born German writer; winner of the 2009 Nobel Prize for Literature.

Thomas Müller (13 Sep 1989, Weilheim, West Germany), German association football (soccer) player; won the Golden Boot award in the 2010 FIFA World Cup.

Carey Mulligan (28 May 1985, London, England), British actress.

Alice Munro (Alice Anne Laidlaw; 10 Jul 1931, Wingham, ON, Canada), Canadian short-story writer; recipient of the 2009 Man Booker International Prize.

(Keith) Rupert Murdoch (11 Mar 1931, Melbourne, VIC, Australia), Australian-born British newspaper publisher and media entrepreneur; founder of the global media holding company News Corporation Ltd.

Eddie Murphy (3 Apr 1961, Brooklyn NY), American comedian and film actor.

Cormac Cardinal Murphy-O'Connor (24 Aug 1932, Reading, Berkshire, England), British church leader; archbishop of Westminster (leader of the Roman Catholic Church in the UK), 2000–09, and cardinal from 2001.

Narayana Murthy (20 Aug 1946, Kolar, British India), Indian international business executive and pioneer in India's high-tech industry; cofounder and chairman of Infosys Technologies Ltd., a technology and consulting firm.

Yoweri (Kaguta) Museveni (15 Aug 1944, Mbarra district, Uganda), Ugandan politician; president from 1986.

Pervez Musharraf (Nish-i-Imtiaz) (11 Aug 1943, New Delhi, British India), Pakistani military leader and politician; head of Pakistan's government, 1999–2001, and president, 2001–08.

Bingu wa Mutharika (24 Feb 1934, Thyolo district, British Nyasaland [now Malawi]), Malawian politician (United Democratic Front); president of Malawi from 2004.

Riccardo Muti (28 Jul 1941, Naples, Italy), Italian conductor; music director of La Scala Orchestra in Milan, 1986–2005; music director of the Chicago Symphony Orchestra from 2010.

Mike Myers (25 May 1963, Scarborough, ON, Canada), Canadian comedian and actor.

James Nachtwey (14 Mar 1948, Syracuse NY), American news photographer.

Rafael Nadal (Parera) (3 Jun 1986, Manacor, Mallorca, Spain), Spanish tennis player.

Ralph Nader (27 Feb 1934, Winsted CT), American social activist and politician; he was a presidential candidate in 2000, 2004, and 2008.

(Clarence) Ray Nagin, Jr. (11 Jun 1956, New Orleans LA), American politician (Democrat); mayor of New Orleans, 2002–10.

Khalifah ibn Zayid al-Nahyan (c. 1948, Al-ʿAyn, Abu Dhabi, British Trucial States [now United Arab Emirates]), UAE sheikh; ruler of Abu Dhabi and president of the United Arab Emirates from 2004.

Ratu Epeli Nailatikau (5 Jul 1941), Fijian politician; president from 2009.

V(idiadhar) S(urajprasad) Naipaul (17 Aug 1932, Chaguanas, Trinidad, British West Indies [now in Trinidad and Tobago]), Trinidadian-born British writer; recipient of the 2001 Nobel Prize for Literature.

Datuk Seri Najib Tun Razak (23 Jul 1953, Kuala Lipis, Malaysia), Malaysian politician; prime minister from 2009.

Yoichiro Nambu (18 Jan 1921, Tokyo, Japan), American physicist; cowinner of the 2008 Nobel Prize for Physics.

Giorgio Napolitano (29 Jun 1925, Naples, Italy), Italian politician (Communist); president of Italy from 2006.

Janet Napolitano (29 Nov 1957, New York NY), American politician (Democrat); governor of Arizona, 2003–09, and US secretary of homeland security from 2009.

Robert (Louis) Nardelli (17 May 1948, Old Forge PA), American corporate executive; CEO of the Home Depot, Inc., 2000–07, and of Chrysler Corp., 2007–09.

Naruhito (23 Feb 1960, Tokyo, Japan), Japanese crown prince.

Nas (Nasir bin Olu Dara Jones; "Nasty Nas"; "Nas Escobar"; 14 Sep 1973, Queens NY), American hiphop artist.

Mohamed Nasheed (17 May 1967, Male, Maldives), Maldivian politician; president from 2008.

Sayyed Hassan Nasrallah (31 Aug 1960, Borj Hammoud, Beirut, Lebanon), Lebanese Islamic extremist military leader; secretary-general of Hezbollah from 1992.

Taslima Nasrin (25 Aug 1962, Mymensingh, Bangladesh), Bangladeshi Islamic feminist writer.

S(ellapan) R(amanathan) Nathan (3 Jul 1924, Singapore?), Singaporean politician; president from 1999.

Bruce Nauman (6 Nov 1941, Fort Wayne IN), American sculptor and installation and performance artist.

Nursultan Nazarbayev (6 Jul 1940, Chemolgan, USSR [now in Kazakhstan]), Kazakh politician; president from 1990.

Youssou N'Dour (1 Oct 1959, Dakar, French West Africa [now in Senegal]), Senegalese singer and songwriter.

Petr Necas (19 Nov 1964, Uherské Hradiste, Czechoslovakia [now in Czech Republic]), Czech politician; prime minister from 2010.

Liam Neeson (William Neeson; 7 Jun 1952, Ballymena, Northern Ireland), British film actor.

Willie (Hugh) Nelson (30 Apr 1933, Fort Worth TX), American songwriter and guitarist.

Madhav Kumar Nepal (9 Mar 1953, Gaur, Nepal), Nepalese politician; prime minister from 2009.

Nerses Bedros XIX (Boutros Tarmouni; 17 Jan 1940, Cairo, Egypt), Armenian churchman; patriarch of the Catholic Armenians from 1999.

Benjamin Netanyahu (21 Oct 1949, Tel Aviv [now Tel Aviv–Yafo], Israel), Israeli politician; prime minister, 1996–99 and again from 2009.

Randy Newman (Randall Stuart Newman; 28 Nov 1943, Los Angeles CA), American songwriter, singer, and pianist.

Marc Newson (1963, Sydney, NSW, Australia), Australian industrial designer.

Thandie Newton (Thandiwe Newton; 6 Nov 1972, Zambia), Zambian-born British TV and film actress.

Teodoro Obiang Nguema Mbasogo (1942, Acoacan, Río Muni [now Equatorial Guinea]), Equatorial Guinean politician; president of Equatorial Guinea from 1979.

Nguyen Minh Triet (8 Oct 1942, Ben Cat district, French Indochina [now in Vietnam]), Vietnamese politician; president of Vietnam from 2006.

Nguyen Tan Dung (17 Nov 1949, Ca Mau, French Indochina [now in Vietnam]), Vietnamese politician; prime minister of Vietnam from 2006.

Vincent Gerard Nichols (8 Nov 1945, Crosby, Merseyside, England), British church leader; archbishop of Westminster (leader of the Roman Catholic Church in the UK) from 2009.

Jack Nicholson (John Joseph Nicholson; 22 Apr 1937, Neptune NJ), American film actor.

Takashi Nishioka (1936?, Japan?), Japanese corporate executive; chairman of Mitsubishi Motors Corp. from 2005.

Ryue Nishizawa (7 Feb 1966, Kanagawa prefecture, Japan), Japanese architect; corecipient of the 2010 Pritzker Prize.

Jay Nixon (Jeremiah W. Nixon; 13 Feb 1956, De Soto MO), American politician (Democrat); governor of Missouri from 2008.

Pierre Nkurunziza (18 Dec 1963, Ngozi province, Burundi), Burundian Hutu rebel leader; president from 2005.

Ronald K(enneth) Noble (1957?, New Jersey), American law professor and government official; secretary-general of Interpol from 2000.

Christopher (Jonathan James) Nolan (30 Jul 1970, London, England), British film director.

Indra Nooyi (28 Oct 1955, Madras [now Chennai], Tamil Nadu state, India), Indian-born American businesswoman; chairman and CEO of PepsiCo from 2007.

Norodom Sihamoni (14 May 1953, Phnom Penh, Cambodia), Cambodian royal; king from 2004.

Norodom Sihanouk (Preah Baht Samdach Preah Norodom Sihanuk Varman; 31 Oct 1922, Phnom Penh, Cambodia), Cambodian king, 1941–55 and 1993–2004; head of state, 1960–70 and 1991–93.

Chris Noth (13 Nov 1954, Madison WI), American film and TV actor.

Lynn Nottage (1964, Brooklyn NY), American playwright.

Jean Nouvel (12 Aug 1945, Fumel, France), French architect; recipient of a Praemium Imperiale in 2001 and the 2008 Pritzker Prize.

Jim Nussle (James Allen Nussle; 27 Jun 1960, Des Moines IA), American politician (Republican); director of the Office of Management and Budget, 2007–09.

Michael A(nthony) Nutter (29 Jun 1957, Philadelphia PA), American politician (Democrat); mayor of Philadelphia from 2008.

Joyce Carol Oates (16 Jun 1938, Lockport NY), American novelist, short-story writer, and essayist.

Thoraya Obaid (2 Mar 1945, Baghdad, Iraq), Iraqi-born Saudi Arabian civil servant; executive director of the UN Population Fund from 2001.

Barack (Hussein) Obama (II) (4 Aug 1961, Honolulu HI), American politician (Democrat); 44th president of the US, from 2009, and winner of the 2009 Nobel Peace Prize.

Michelle Obama (Michelle LaVaughn Robinson; 17 Jan 1964, Chicago IL), American first lady; wife of Pres. Barack Obama (married 3 Oct 1992).

Conan O'Brien (18 Apr 1963, Brookline MA), American TV talk-show host.

Chad Ocho Cinco (Chad Javon Johnson; 9 Jan 1978, Miami FL), American professional football player.

Lorena Ochoa (15 Nov 1981, Guadalajara, Jalisco state, Mexico), Mexican golfer.

Mark O'Connor (5 Aug 1961, Seattle WA), American country fiddle player.

Sandra Day O'Connor (26 Mar 1930, El Paso TX), American jurist; associate justice of the US Supreme Court, 1981–2005, the first woman appointed to the court.

Piermaria J. Oddone (26 Mar 1944, Arequipa, Peru), Peruvian-born American experimental particle physicist and administrator; director of the Fermi National Accelerator Laboratory from 2005.

Raila (Amollo) Odinga (7 Jan 1945, Maseno, Nyanza province, British Kenya), Kenyan politician (Liberal Democratic); prime minister from 2008.

Kenzaburo Oe (31 Jan 1935, Ose, Ehime prefecture, Japan), Japanese novelist; recipient of the 1994 Nobel Prize for Literature.

Apollo (Anton) Ohno (22 May 1982, Seattle WA), American short-track speed skater; he was the most decorated American athlete in the history of Winter Olympics.

Masahiro Okafuji (c. 1950), Japanese businessman; president and CEO of ITOCHU Corp. from 2010.

Keith Olbermann (27 Jan 1959, New York NY), American TV sportscaster and commentator.

Claes (Thure) Oldenburg (28 Jan 1929, Stockholm, Sweden), Swedish-born Pop-art sculptor.

Sharon Olds (19 Nov 1942, San Francisco CA), American poet.

Jamie Oliver (27 May 1975, Essex, England), British chef and TV personality.

Ehud Olmert (30 Sep 1945, Binyamina, British Palestine [now in Israel]), Israeli politician (Kadima); prime minister, 2006–09.

Ashley (Fuller) Olsen (13 Jun 1986, Sherman Oaks CA), American former child star and a marketing phenomenon in modeling, films, TV, and music videos.

Mary-Kate Olsen (13 Jun 1986, Sherman Oaks CA), American former child star and a marketing phenomenon in modeling, films, TV, and music videos.

Martin (Joseph) O'Malley (18 Jan 1963, Washington DC), American politician (Democrat); mayor of Baltimore, 1999–2007, and governor of Maryland from 2007.

Sean Patrick O'Malley (29 Jun 1944, Lakewood OH), American Roman Catholic churchman; archbishop of Boston from 2003; cardinal from 2006.

Marc Ona Essangui (1964?, Gabon?), Gabonese environmental activist; winner of the 2009 Goldman Environmental Prize.

(Philip) Michael Ondaatje (12 Sep 1943, Colombo, British Ceylon [now Sri Lanka]), Canadian novelist and poet.

Shaquille (Rashaun) O'Neal (6 Mar 1972, Newark NJ), American basketball center.

Viktor Orbán (31 May 1963, Alcsútdoboz, Hungary), Hungarian politician; prime minister, 1998–2002, and from 2010.

Bill O'Reilly (William James O'Reilly, Jr.; 10 Sep 1949, New York NY), American TV journalist and talk-show host.

Suze Orman (5 Jun 1951, Chicago IL), American financial adviser and best-selling author.

Peter Orszag (16 Dec 1968, Boston MA), American economist; director of the US Office of Management and Budget, 2009–10.

(José) Daniel Ortega (Saavedra) (11 Nov 1945, La Libertad, Nicaragua), Nicaraguan guerrilla leader and politician; president, 1984–90 and again from 2007.

Joel Osteen (5 Mar 1963, Houston TX), American evangelist; head of the Lakewood Church in Houston.

Elinor Ostrom (7 Aug 1933, Los Angeles CA), American political scientist; cowinner of the 2009 Nobel Prize for Economics.

Paul S. Otellini (12 Oct 1950, San Francisco CA), American corporate executive; president of Intel Corp. from 2002 and CEO from 2005.

Peter (Seamus) O'Toole (2 Aug 1932, Connemara, County Galway, Irish Free State), British stage and film actor.

Butch Otter (Clement Leroy Otter; 3 May 1942, Caldwell ID), American politician (Republican); governor of Idaho from 2007.

Roza Otunbayeva (23 Aug 1950, Osh, Kirghiz SSR, USSR [now in Kyrgyzstan], Kyrgyz politician; head of the interim government of Kyrgyzstan from 2010.

Alexander (Mikhailovich) Ovechkin (17 Sep 1985, Moscow, USSR [now in Russia]), Russian professional hockey player.

Hisashi Owada (18 Sep 1932, Niigata, Japan), Japanese jurist; president of the International Court of Justice from 2009.

Clive Owen (3 Oct 1964, Keresley, Coventry, Warwickshire, England), British actor.

Amos Oz (4 May 1939, Jerusalem, British Palestine), Israeli novelist, short-story writer, and essayist.

Mehmet Oz (11 Jun 1960, Cleveland OH), American cardiac surgeon, TV medical expert, and author.

Cynthia Ozick (17 Apr 1928, New York NY), American novelist, short-story writer, and playwright.

Rajendra K. Pachauri (20 Aug 1940, Nainital, Uttar Pradesh [now in Uttarakhand state], British India), Indian businessman; head of the Intergovernmental Panel on Climate Change from 2002.

Al(fredo James) Pacino (25 Apr 1940, New York NY), American film actor.

Larry Page (Lawrence Edward Page; 1972, East Lansing MI), American computer scientist and Internet entrepreneur who cofounded (1998) the Google Internet search engine.

Borut Pahor (2 Nov 1963, Postojna, Yugoslavia [now in Slovenia]), Slovenian politician; prime minister of Slovenia from 2008.

Brad Paisley (28 Oct 1972, Glen Dale WV), American contemporary country-and-western singer.

Ian (Richard Kyle) Paisley (6 Apr 1926, Armagh, County Armagh, Northern Ireland), Northern Irish Protestant leader and politician; first minister of Northern Ireland, 2007–08.

Sarah Palin (Sarah Heath; 11 Feb 1964, Sandpoint ID), American politician (Republican); governor of Alaska, 2006–09, and the Republican nominee for vice president in 2008.

Eddie Palmieri (15 Dec 1936, New York NY), American jazz-salsa pianist.

Samuel J. Palmisano (29 Jul 1951), American corporate executive; president and CEO of the International Business Machines (IBM) Corp. from 2002.

Gwyneth Paltrow (28 Sep 1972, Los Angeles CA), American film and stage actress.

Orhan Pamuk (7 Jun 1952, Istanbul, Turkey), Turkish novelist; winner of the 2006 Nobel Prize for Literature.

Leon Panetta (28 Jun 1938, Monterey CA), American politician; congressman from California, 1977–93, director of the Office of Management and Budget, 1993–94, White House chief of staff, 1994–97, and director of the CIA from 2009.

Paola (Paola dei Principi Ruffo di Calabria; 11 Sep 1937, Forte dei Marmi, Italy), Italian-born Belgian royal; queen consort of King Albert II (married 2 Jul 1959).

George Papandreou (16 Jun 1952, St. Paul MN), American-born Greek politician; prime minister of Greece from 2009.

Karolos Papoulias (4 Jun 1929, Ioannina, Greece), Greek politician; president of Greece from 2005.

Anna (Helene) Paquin (24 Jul 1982, Winnipeg, MB, Canada), New Zealand film actress.

Sara Paretsky (8 Jun 1947, Ames IA), American mystery writer.

Nick Park (Nicholas Wulstan Park; 6 Dec 1958, Preston, Lancashire, England), British film animator.

Alan (William) Parker (14 Feb 1944, Islington, London, England), British advertising copywriter and film director.

Mary-Louise Parker (2 Aug 1964, Fort Jackson SC), American actress on stage, in film, and on TV.

Sarah Jessica Parker (25 Mar 1965, Nelsonville OH), American TV and film actress.

Mark Parkinson (24 Jun 1957, Wichita KS), American politician (Democrat); governor of Kansas from 2009.

Suzan-Lori Parks (10 May 1963, Fort Knox KY), American playwright.

Sean R. Parnell (19 Nov 1962, Hanford CA), American politician (Republican); governor of Alaska from 2009.

Anja Pärson (25 Apr 1981, Umeå, Sweden), Swedish downhill skier.

Richard D(ean) Parsons (4 Apr 1949, Bedford-Stuyvesant, Brooklyn NY), American corporate executive; CEO of Time Warner (formerly AOL Time Warner), 2002–07, and chairman of Citigroup from 2009.

Dolly (Rebecca) Parton (19 Jan 1946, Locust Ridge TN), American country-and-western singer, songwriter, and actress.

Amy Pascal (1959, Los Angeles CA), American film executive; chairman of Sony Pictures Entertainment Motion Picture Group from 2003 and cochairman of Sony Pictures Entertainment from 2006.

Ann Patchett (2 Dec 1963, Los Angeles CA), American novelist.

David A. Paterson (20 May 1954, Brooklyn NY), American politician (Democrat); governor of New York from 2008.

Pratibha Patil (19 Dec 1934, Jalgaon, British India), Indian politician; the country's first female president, from 2007.

Danica (Sue) Patrick (25 Mar 1982, Beloit WI), American race-car driver.

Deval (Laurdine) Patrick (31 Jul 1956, Chicago IL), American politician (Democrat); governor of Massachusetts from 2007.

Robert Pattinson (13 May 1986, London, England), British actor.

Ron(ald Ernest) Paul (20 Aug 1935, Pittsburgh PA), American physician and libertarian politician; congressman from Texas from 1997.

Henry M(erritt) Paulson, Jr. (28 Mar 1946, Palm Beach FL), American corporate executive and government official; CEO of Goldman Sachs Group, 1999–2006, and US secretary of the treasury, 2006–09.

Tim(othy James) Pawlenty (21 Nov 1960, St. Paul MN), American politician (Republican); governor of Minnesota from 2003.

James (Benjamin) Peake (18 Jun 1944, St. Louis MO), American army medical officer; US secretary of veterans affairs, 2007–09.

Amanda Peet (11 Jan 1972, New York NY), American film and TV actress.

Pelé (Edson Arantes do Nascimento; 23 Oct 1940, Três Corações, Minas Gerais state, Brazil), Brazilian association football (soccer) legend.

Cesar Pelli (12 Oct 1926, Tucumán, Argentina), Argentine architect.

Nancy Pelosi (Nancy D'Alesandro; 26 Mar 1940, Baltimore MD), American politician (Democrat); congresswoman from California from 1987, House Democratic leader, 2003–07, and speaker of the House from 2007.

Sean (Justin) Penn (17 Aug 1960, Santa Monica CA), American film actor and director.

Murray Perahia (19 Apr 1947, New York NY), American concert pianist.

Bev(erly Eaves) Perdue (14 Jan 1947, Grundy VA), American politician (Democrat); governor of North Carolina from 2009.

Sonny Perdue (George Ervin Perdue III; 20 Dec 1946, Perry GA), American agribusinessman and politician (Republican); governor of Georgia from 2003.

Shimon Peres (Shimon Perski; 2 Aug 1923, Wolozyn, Poland [now Valozhyn, Belarus]), Israeli statesman, prime minister, 1984–86 and 1995–96, and president from 2007; he won the Nobel Peace Prize in 1994 for his efforts to work with the Palestinian Liberation Organization.

Grayson Perry (24 Mar 1960, Chelmsford, Essex, England), British artist; recipient of the 2003 Turner Prize.

Rick Perry (James Richard Perry; 4 Mar 1950, West Texas), American politician (Republican); governor of Texas from 2000.

Kamla Persad-Bissessar (22 Apr 1952, Siparia, Trinidad, British West Indies [now in Trinidad and Tobago]), Trinidadian politician; prime minister of Trinidad and Tobago from 2010.

Mary E. Peters (4 Dec 1948, Phoenix AZ), American transportation official; US secretary of transportation, 2006–09.

David (Howell) Petraeus (7 Nov 1952, Cornwall-on-Hudson NY), American military leader; commander of Multinational Force Iraq, 2007–08, US Central Command, 2008–10, and US and NATO forces in Afghanistan from 2010.

Michelle Pfeiffer (29 Apr 1958, Santa Ana CA), American film actress.

Michael Phelps (30 Jun 1985, Baltimore MD), American swimmer.

Regis (Francis Xavier) Philbin (25 Aug 1934, New York NY), American TV personality.

Philip (Prince Philip of Greece and Denmark; 10 Jun 1921, Corfu, Greece), British duke of Edinburgh; prince consort of Queen Elizabeth II (married 20 Nov 1947).

Danny Philip (1951, Solomon Islands?), Solomon Islands politician; prime minister from 2010.

Philippe (Philippe Leopold Louis Marie; 15 Apr 1960, Brussels, Belgium), Belgian royal; duke of Brabant and crown prince of Belgium.

(Matthew) Ryan Phillippe (10 Sep 1974, New Castle DE), American TV and film actor.

Stone Phillips (2 Dec 1954, Texas City TX), American TV host and anchorman.

Ellen (Philpotts-) Page (21 Feb 1987, Halifax, NS, Canada), Canadian TV and film actress.

Joaquin Phoenix (Joaquin Raphael Bottom; 28 Oct 1974, San Juan, Puerto Rico), American film actor.

Renzo Piano (14 Sep 1937, Genoa, Italy), Italian architect; winner of the 1998 Pritzker Prize and the 2002 UIA Gold Medal for Architecture.

T(homas) Boone Pickens (22 May 1928, Holdenville OK), American billionaire oilman; advocate of aggressive investment in alternative energy.

Jodi Picoult (19 May 1966, Neconset, NY), American author.

DBC Pierre (Peter Warren Finlay; June 1961, Reynella, SA, Australia), Australian-born British novelist; winner of the 2003 Man Booker Prize.

Navanethem Pillay (23 Sep 1941, Durban, Union of South Africa), South African judge; UN high commissioner for human rights from 2008.

Sebastián Piñera (1 Dec 1949, Santiago, Chile), Chilean politician (National Renewal); president of Chile from 2010.

Jean Ping (24 Nov 1942, Omboué, French Gabon), Gabonese statesman; UN General Assembly president, 2004, and chairman of the Commission of the African Union from 2008.

Pink (Alecia Beth Moore; 8 Sep 1979, Doylestown PA), American pop singer.

Jada Pinkett Smith (Jada Koren Pinkett; 18 Sep 1971, Baltimore MD), American actress, video director, and clothing designer.

Robert Pinsky (20 Oct 1940, Long Branch NJ), American poet and critic; poet laureate of. the US, 1997–2000.

Pedro (Verona Rodrigues) Pires (April 1934, Ilha do Fogo, Cape Verde), Cape Verdean politician; president from 2001.

Surin Pitsuwan (28 Oct 1949, Nakhon Si Thammarat, Thailand), Thai intellectual and government official; secretary-general of the Association of Southeast Asian Nations from 2008.

(William) Brad(ley) Pitt (18 Dec 1963, Shawnee OK), American film actor.

Yevgeny (Viktorovich) Plushchenko (also spelled Evgeni Plushenko; 3 Nov 1982, Solnechny, USSR [now in Russia]), Russian figure skater.

Amy Poehler (16 Sep 1971, Burlington MA), American actress and comedian on TV and in films.

Hifikepunye (Lucas) Pohamba (18 Aug 1935, Okanghudi, South West Africa [now Namibia]), Namibian independence leader and politician; president from 2005.

Sidney Poitier (20 Feb 1927?, Miami FL), Bahamian American stage and film actor and director.

Roman Polanski (Raimund Liebling; 18 Aug 1933, Paris, France), Polish film director, scriptwriter, and actor.

Judit Polgar (23 Jul 1976, Budapest, Hungary), Hungarian chess grand master.

Gregg Popovich (28 Jan 1949, East Chicago IN), American professional basketball coach.

Natalie Portman (Natalie Hershlag; 9 Jun 1981, Jerusalem, Israel), American film actress.

Zac(hary E.) Posen (24 Oct 1980, Brooklyn NY), American fashion designer.

John E. Potter (1956, Bronx NY), American corporate executive; CEO and postmaster general of the US Postal Service from 2001.

Earl A. ("Rusty") Powell III (24 Oct 1943, Spartanburg SC), American museum official; director of the National Gallery of Art in Washington DC from 1992.

Samantha Power (1970, Ireland), Irish-born American writer and political adviser; foreign-policy adviser to the National Security Council from 2009.

Miuccia Prada (1949, Milan, Italy), Italian fashion designer.

Steve(n Clyde) Preston (1961?, Janesville WI?), American government official; US secretary of housing and urban development, 2008–09.

René (García) Préval (17 Jan 1943, Port-au-Prince, Haiti), Haitian politician; president, 1996–2001 and again from 2006.

André (George) Previn (6 Apr 1929, Berlin, Germany), German-born American pianist, composer, and conductor.

Richard Price (12 Oct 1949, Bronx NY), American novelist and screenwriter.

Prince (Prince Rogers Nelson; 7 Jun 1958, Minneapolis MN), American singer and songwriter.

Birgit Prinz (25 Oct 1977, Frankfurt am Main, West Germany), German association football (soccer) player.

Romano Prodi (9 Aug 1939, Scandiano, Italy), Italian politician; president of the European Commission, 1999–2004, and prime minister of Italy, 1996–98 and 2006–08.

E(dna) Annie Proulx (22 Aug 1935, Norwich CT), American writer.

(José) Albert(o) Pujols (16 Jan 1980, Santo Domingo, Dominican Republic), Dominican baseball player.

Georgi Purvanov (28 Jun 1957, Kovachevtsi, Bulgaria), Bulgarian politician; president from 2002.

Vladimir (Vladimirovich) Putin (7 Oct 1952, Leningrad, USSR [now St. Petersburg, Russia]), Russian intelligence officer; prime minister of Russia, 1999–2000, president, 1999–2008, and prime minister again from 2008.

(Sayyid) Qabus ibn Saʿid (18 Nov 1940, Salalah, Oman), Omani head of state; sultan of Oman from 1970 and prime minister from 1972.

Muammar al-Qaddafi (also spelled Muammar Khadafy, Moammar Gadhafi, or Muʿammar al-Qadhdhafi; spring 1942, near Surt, Libya), Libyan military leader and Arab statesman; de facto chief of state from 1969.

Dennis Quaid (9 Apr 1954, Houston TX), American film actor.

Thomas Quasthoff (9 Nov 1959, Hildesheim, West Germany), German bass-baritone.

Queen Latifah (Dana Elaine Owens; 18 Mar 1970, Newark NJ), American rap musician, film actress, and TV personality.

Anna (Marie) Quindlen (8 Jul 1953, Philadelphia PA), American political commentator and author.

Pat Quinn (16 Dec 1948, Hinsdale IL), American politician (Democrat); governor of Illinois from 2009.

Daniel Radcliffe (23 July 1989, Fulham, London, England), British film and stage actor.

Paula Radcliffe (17 Dec 1973, Northwich, Cheshire, England), British marathon runner.

Iveta Radicová (7 Dec 1956, Bratislava, Czechoslovakia [now in Slovakia]), Slovak politician; prime minister from 2010.

Nebojsa Radmanovic (1 Oct 1949, Gracanica, Yugoslavia [now in Bosnia and Herzegovina]), Bosnia and Herzegovinian politician; chairman of the presidency of the republic, 2008–09.

Aishwarya Rai (1 Nov 1973, Mangalore, Karnataka state, India), Indian beauty queen and film actress.

Sam(uel M.) Raimi (23 Oct 1959, Franklin MI), American cult filmmaker.

Rain (Jeong Ji-hoon; 25 Jun 1982, Seoul, South Korea), Korean pop singer and actor.

Mahinda Rajapakse (18 Nov 1945, British Ceylon [now Sri Lanka]), Sri Lankan politician; prime minister, 2004–05, and president from 2005.

Andry Rajoelina (30 May 1974), Malagasy politician; president of Madagascar from 2009.

Imomali Rakhmonov (5 Oct 1952, Dangara, Tadzhik SSR, USSR [now Tajikistan]), Tajik politician; president from 1992.

Venkatraman Ramakrishnan (1952, Chidambaram, India), Indian-born American physicist and molecular biologist; cowinner of the 2009 Nobel Prize for Chemistry.

José Ramos-Horta (26 Dec 1949, Dili, Portuguese Timor [now East Timor (Timor-Leste)]), Timorese nationalist leader; prime minister, 2006–07, and president from 2007; corecipient of the 1996 Nobel Peace Prize.

Gordon (James) Ramsay (8 Nov 1966, Glasgow, Scotland), British chef and TV personality.

Rania al-Abdullah (Rania al-Yaseen; 31 Aug 1970, Kuwait), Kuwaiti-born Jordanian royal; queen consort of King Abdullah II (married 10 Jun 1993).

Ian Rankin (28 Apr 1960, Cardenden, Fife, Scotland), British crime novelist.

Phylicia Rashad (Phylicia Ayers-Allen; 19 Jun 1948, Houston TX), American TV and stage actress.

Anders Fogh Rasmussen (26 Jan 1953, Ginnerup, Denmark), Danish politician; prime minister, 2001–09, and secretary-general of NATO from 2009.

Lars Løkke Rasmussen (15 May 1964, Vejle, Denmark) Danish politician; prime minister from 2009.

Simon (Denis) Rattle (19 Jan 1955, Liverpool, England), British orchestra conductor; principal conductor and artistic director of the Berlin Philharmonic from the 2002–03 season.

Marc Ravalomanana (1949, near Atananarivo, French Madagascar), Malagasy politician; president of Madagascar, 2002–09.

Rachael (Domenica) Ray (25 Aug 1968, Cape Cod MA), American TV cook and cookbook author.

(Charles) Robert Redford, Jr. (18 Aug 1937, Santa Monica CA), American film actor and director.

Vanessa Redgrave (30 Jan 1937, London, England), British stage and screen actress and political activist.

Joshua Redman (1 Feb 1969, Berkeley CA), American jazz saxophone player.

Sumner Redstone (Sumner Murray Rothstein; 27 May 1923, Boston MA), American media executive.

David Rees (1973?), American comic artist.

Martin J(ohn) Rees (23 Jun 1942, Shropshire, England), British astronomer royal; recipient of the Craoford Prize in 2005.

Keanu (Charles) Reeves (2 Sep 1964, Beirut, Lebanon), American actor.

Steve Reich (3 Oct 1936, New York NY), American composer.

Harry Reid (2 Dec 1939, Searchlight NV), American politician (Democrat); senator from Nevada from 1987, Senate whip, 1998–2005, and Senate leader from 2005.

John C(hristopher) Reilly (24 May 1965, Chicago IL), American stage and film actor.

Rob Reiner (6 Mar 1947, Bronx NY), American actor, director, writer, and producer.

(John) Fredrik Reinfeldt (4 Aug 1965, Österhaninge, Sweden), Swedish politician (Moderate Party); prime minister from 2006.

Jason Reitman (19 Oct 1977, Montreal, QC, Canada), Canadian actor, director, and writer.

M(argaret) Jodi Rell (Mary Carolyn Reavis; 16 Jun 1946, Norfolk VA), American politician (Republican); governor of Connecticut from 2004.

Edward (Gene) Rendell (5 Jan 1944, New York NY), American politician (Democrat); mayor of Philadelphia, 1992–2000, and governor of Pennsylvania from 2003.

Ruth Rendell (Baroness Rendell of Babergh; pseudonym Barbara Vine; 17 Feb 1930, London, England), British mystery novelist.

Jeremy Renner (7 Jan 1971, Modesto CA), American actor.

Ryan Reynolds (23 Oct 1976, Vancouver, BC, Canada), Canadian film actor.

Yasmina Reza (1 May 1959, Paris, France), French playwright.

Christina Ricci (12 Feb 1980, Santa Monica CA), American film actress.

Anne Rice (Howard Allen O'Brien; pseudonyms A.N. Roquelaure and Anne Rampling; 4 Oct 1941, New Orleans LA), American Gothic novelist.

Condoleezza Rice (14 Nov 1954, Birmingham AL), American academic and government official; national security advisor, 2001–05, and US secretary of state, 2005–09.

Adrienne (Cecile) Rich (16 May 1929, Baltimore MD), American poet.

(George) Maxwell Richards (1931, San Fernando, Trinidad, British West Indies [now in Trinidad and Tobago]), Trinidadian chemical engineer and university professor; president of Trinidad and Tobago from 2003.

Keith Richards (18 Dec 1943, Dartford, Kent, England), British rock guitarist and singer (for the Rolling Stones).

Bill Richardson (William Blaine Richardson; 15 Nov 1947, Pasadena CA), American politician (Democrat); governor of New Mexico from 2003.

Nicole Richie (15 Sep 1981, Berkeley CA), American celebrity entertainer.

Gerhard Richter (9 Feb 1932, Dresden, Germany), German Capitalist Realist artist.

Sally K(risten) Ride (26 May 1951, Encino CA), American astronaut and astrophysicist.

Rihanna (Robyn Rihanna Fenty; 20 Feb 1988, Saint Michael parish, Barbados), West Indian pop singer and entertainer.

Robert R. Riley (3 Oct 1944, Ashland AL), American politician (Republican); governor of Alabama from 2003.

LeAnn Rimes (28 Aug 1982, Jackson MS), American country-and-western singer.

Kelly Ripa (2 Oct 1970, Stratford NJ), American talk-show host and actress.

Bill Ritter (August William Ritter, Jr.; 6 Sep 1956, Denver CO), American politician (Democrat); governor of Colorado from 2007.

Geraldo (Miguel) Rivera (4 Jul 1943, Brooklyn NY), American TV journalist and talk-show host.

Tim Robbins (16 Oct 1958, West Covina CA), American actor.

Cecil E(dward) Roberts, Jr. (31 Oct 1946, Kayford WV), American labor leader; president of the United Mine Workers of America from 1995.

John G(lover) Roberts (27 Jan 1955, Buffalo NY), American jurist; chief justice of the US from 2005.

Julia Roberts (Julie Fiona Roberts; 28 Oct 1967, Smyrna GA), American film actress.

Nora Roberts (Eleanor Marie Robertson; 10 Oct 1950, Silver Spring MD), American novelist.

Marilynne Robinson (1947, Sandpoint ID), American author.

Peter (David) Robinson (29 Dec 1948, Belfast, Northern Ireland), Northern Irish Protestant loyalist politician; first minister of Northern Ireland from 2008.

Chris Rock (7 Feb 1966, Georgetown SC), American stand-up comedian and actor.

Kid Rock (Robert James Ritchie; 17 Jan 1971, Romeo MI), American rap-rock artist.

Andy Roddick (30 Aug 1982, Omaha NE), American tennis player.

Alex Rodriguez (27 Jul 1975, New York NY), American baseball shortstop and third baseman.

Narciso Rodríguez (January 1961, New Jersey), American fashion designer.

Robert (Anthony) Rodriguez (20 Jun 1968, San Antonio TX), Mexican American filmmaker.

Seth Rogen (15 Apr 1982, Vancouver, BC, Canada), Canadian film actor.

James E. Rogers (20 Sep 1947, Birmingham AL), American corporate executive; president and CEO (from 2006) and chairman of the board (from 2007) of Duke Energy.

Richard (George) Rogers (23 Jul 1933, Florence, Italy), British architect; recipient of a Praemium Imperiale in 2000 and the Pritzker Prize in 2007.

Jacques Rogge (2 May 1942, Ghent, Belgium), Belgian Olympic yachtsman, surgeon, and sports executive; president of the International Olympic Committee from 2001.

Floyd Roland (23 Nov 1961, Inuvik, NT, Canada), Canadian politician; premier of the Northwest Territories from 2007.

Sonny Rollins (Theodore Walter Rollins; 7 Sep 1930, Harlem, New York NY), American jazz saxophonist.

Ray Romano (21 Dec 1957, Queens NY), American comic actor.

(Willard) Mitt Romney (12 Mar 1947, Bloomfield MI), American businessman, sports executive, and politician (Republican); governor of Massachusetts, 2003–07.

Tony Romo (21 Apr 1980, San Diego CA), American pro football quarterback.

Ronaldo (Ronaldo Luiz Nazario de Lima; 22 Sep 1976, Itaguai, Rio de Janeiro state, Brazil), Brazilian association football (soccer) player.

Cristiano Ronaldo (dos Santos Aveiro) (5 Feb 1985, Funchal, Madeira, Portugal), Portuguese association football (soccer) player; he was voted World Player of the Year by FIFA in 2008.

Charlie Rose (5 Jan 1942, Henderson NC), American TV journalist and interviewer.

Derrick Rose (4 Oct 1988, Chicago IL), American basketball player.

Alan Rosenberg (4 Oct 1950, Passaic NJ), American actor; president of the Screen Actors Guild, 2005–09.

Wilbur Ross (28 Nov 1937, North Bergen NJ), American financier and turnaround specialist.

Philip (Milton) Roth (19 Mar 1933, Newark NJ), American novelist and short-story writer.

Mike Rounds (Marion Michael Rounds; 24 Oct 1954, Huron SD), American politician (Republican); governor of South Dakota from 2003.

Mickey Rourke (16 Sep 1952, Schenectady NY), American actor.

Karl Rove (25 Dec 1950, Denver CO), American right-wing political operative, consultant, and commentator; former chief strategist for Pres. George W. Bush.

J(oanne) K(athleen) Rowling (31 Jul 1965, Chipping Sodbury, near Bristol, Gloucestershire, England), British author, creator of the Harry Potter series.

Rick Rubin (Frederick Jay Rubin; 10 Mar 1963, Lido Beach NY), American record producer.

Kevin (Michael) Rudd (21 Sep 1957, Nambour, QLD, Australia), Australian politician (Labor); prime minister, 2007–10.

Geoffrey Rush (6 Jul 1951, Toowoomba, QLD, Australia), Australian film actor.

(Ahmed) Salman Rushdie (19 Jun 1947, Bombay, British India [now Mumbai, India]), Anglo-Indian novelist.

Richard Russo (15 Jul 1949, Johnstown NY), American author; winner of the 2002 Pulitzer Prize for fiction.

Burt Rutan (Elbert L. Rutan; 17 Jun 1943, Portland OR), American test pilot, aerospace engineer, and designer of specialized aircraft.

John Rutter (24 Sep 1945, London, England), British composer and conductor; founder (1981) and leader of the Cambridge Singers.

Kay Ryan (11 Sep 1945, San Jose CA), American poet; recipient of the 2004 Ruth Lilly Poetry Prize and US poet laureate (2008–10).

Meg Ryan (Margaret Mary Emily Anne Hyra; 19 Nov 1961, Fairfield CT), American film actress.

Alexander Rybak (13 May 1986, Minsk, USSR [now in Belarus]), Norwegian pop singer; winner of the 2009 Eurovision Song Contest.

Winona Ryder (Winona Laura Horowitz; 29 Oct 1971, Winona MN), American film actress.

Mikhail Saakashvili (21 Dec 1967, Tbilisi, USSR [now in Georgia]), Georgian politician; president from 2004.

Charles Saatchi (9 Jun 1943, Baghdad, Iraq), Iraqi-born British advertising executive and art patron.

Sabah al-Ahmad al-Jabir Al Sabah (1929?, Kuwait city, Kuwait), Kuwaiti sheikh; emir from 2006.

Jeffrey D(avid) Sachs (5 Nov 1954, Detroit MI), American economist; involved in efforts to eradicate poverty on a global scale.

Oliver (Wolf) Sacks (9 Jul 1933, London, England), British-born American neurologist and author of books on medical topics.

Muqtada al-Sadr (1974, Al-Najaf, Iraq), Iraqi Shi'ite Muslim cleric, a charismatic figure in the anti-American and anti-Western insurrection in Iraq following the US-led occupation of March 2003.

Ken Salazar (2 March 1955, Alamosa CO), American lawyer and politician (Democrat); senator from Colorado, 2005–09, and US secretary of the interior from 2009.

Sebastião (Ribeiro) Salgado (8 Feb 1944, Aimorés, Minas Gerais state, Brazil), Brazilian photographer.

'Ali 'Abdallah Salih (21 Mar 1942, Beit al-Ahmar, Yemen), Yemeni politician; president of Yemen (San'a), 1978–90, and of the unified Yemen since.

Alex(ander Elliot Anderson) Salmond (31 Dec 1954, Linlithgow, Scotland), Scottish politician (Scottish National Party); first minister of Scotland from 2007.

Esa-Pekka Salonen (30 Jun 1958, Helsinki, Finland), Finnish conductor; musical director of the Los Angeles Philharmonic, 1992–2009, and principal conductor and artistic adviser of the Philharmonia Orchestra, London, from 2008.

Ahmed Abdallah Sambi (5 Jun 1958, Mutsamudu, Anjouan, French Comoro Islands), Comoran Muslim religious leader; president from 2006.

Adam Sandler (9 Sep 1966, Brooklyn NY), American comic actor.

Mark Sanford (Marshall Clement Sanford, Jr.; 15 Jan 1960, Fort Lauderdale FL), American politician (Republican); governor of South Carolina from 2003.

Malam Bacai Sanhá (5 May 1947, Darsalame, Portuguese Guinea [now Guinea-Bissau]), Guinea-Bissauan politician; president from 2009.

Johan (Alexander) Santana (Araque) (13 Mar 1979, Tovar, Venezuela), Venezuelan pro baseball starting pitcher.

Juan Manuel Santos Calderón (10 Aug 1951, Bogotá, Colombia), Colombian politician; finance minister (2000–02), defense minister (2006–09), and president of Colombia from 2010.

Cristina Saralegui (29 Jan 1948, Havana, Cuba), Cuban-born American Spanish-language TV talk-show host.

Susan Sarandon (Susan Abigail Tomalin; 4 Oct 1946, New York NY), American film actress.

Serzh (Azati) Sarkisyan (30 Jun 1954, Stepanakert, Nagorno-Karabakh autonomous oblast, USSR [now in Azerbaijan]), Armenian politician; prime minister, 2007–08, and president from April 2008.

Tigran Sarkisyan (29 Jan 1960, Kirovakan, USSR [now Vanadzor, Armenia]), Armenian economist and politician; prime minister from 2008.

Nicolas Sarkozy (Nicolas Paul-Stéphane Sarközy de Nagy-Bocsa; 28 Jan 1955, Paris, France), French conservative politician; interior minister, 2005–07, and president from 2007.

Denis Sassou-Nguesso (1943, Edou, French Equatorial Africa [now in the Republic of the Congo]), Congolese politician; president of the Republic of Congo, 1979–92 and again from 1997.

Marjane Satrapi (22 Nov 1969, Rasht, Iran), Iranian-born French graphic novelist; author of the Persepolis books, her memoirs of Iran during the last decades of the 20th century.

al-Walid ibn Talal ibn Abdulaziz al-Saud (1954, Riyadh, Saudi Arabia), Saudi prince and billionaire businessman.

Diane K. Sawyer (Lila Sawyer; 22 Dec 1945, Glasgow KY), American TV journalist.

Antonin Scalia (11 Mar 1936, Trenton NJ), American jurist; associate justice of the US Supreme Court from 1986.

Joe Scarborough (Charles Joseph Scarborough; 9 Apr 1963, Atlanta GA), American conservative TV host and commentator.

Edward T(homas) Schafer (8 Aug 1946, Bismarck ND), American businessman and politician (Republican); US secretary of agriculture, 2008–09.

Mary L. Schapiro (19 Jun 1955, New York NY), American finance administrator; chairman of the Securities and Exchange Commission from 2009.

Eric E. Schmidt (1955?), American computer scientist and corporate executive; CTO of Sun Microsystems, Inc., 1983–97, chairman and CEO of Novell, Inc., 1997–2001, and chairman and CEO of Google, Inc., from 2001.

Julian Schnabel (26 Oct 1951, Brooklyn NY), American Neo-Expressionist artist and film director.

Daniel Schorr (31 Aug 1916, New York NY), American TV and radio journalist and political commentator.

Howard Schultz (19 Jul 1953, Brooklyn NY), American businessman; CEO of Starbucks Corp. from 1987.

Philip Schultz (1945, Rochester NY), American poet.

Michael Schumacher (3 Jan 1969, Hürth-Hermülheim, West Germany), German Formula 1 race-car driver.

Susan (Carol) Schwab (23 Mar 1955, Washington DC), American trade official; US trade representative, 2006–09.

Arnold (Alois) Schwarzenegger (30 Jul 1947, Thal bei Graz, Austria), Austrian-born American bodybuilder, film actor, and politician (Republican); governor of California from 2003.

Brian (David) Schweitzer (4 Sep 1955, Havre MT), American politician (Democrat); governor of Montana from 2005.

David Schwimmer (2 Nov 1966, Astoria, Queens NY), American TV and film actor.

Jon Scieszka (8 Sep 1954, Flint MI), American author of books for children.

John Scofield (26 Dec 1951, Dayton OH), American jazz electric guitarist, composer, and bandleader.

Martin Scorsese (17 Nov 1942, Flushing, Long Island NY), American film director, writer, and producer.

Ridley Scott (30 Nov 1937, South Shields, Durham, England), British film director and producer.

Kristin Scott Thomas (24 May 1960, Redruth, Cornwall, England), British actress.

Vincent J(ames) Scully, Jr. (1930, New Haven CT), American architectural historian and critic.

Ryan (John) Seacrest (24 Dec 1974, Atlanta GA), American TV program host (*American Idol*).

Seal (Sealhenry Olusegun Olumide Samuel; 19 Feb 1963, Kilburn, London, England), British soul singer.

Sean Paul (Ryan Francis Henriques) (8 Jan 1973, St. Andrew, Jamaica), Jamaican reggae and rap musician.

Kathleen Sebelius (Kathleen Gilligan; 15 May 1948, Cincinnati OH), American politician (Democrat); governor of Kansas, 2003–09, and US secretary of health and human services from 2009.

Alice Sebold (1963, Madison WI), American novelist.

Amy Sedaris (29 Mar 1961, Endicott NY), American comic actress and writer.

David Sedaris (26 Dec 1956, Johnson City NY), American writer and humorist.

Kyra (Minturn) Sedgwick (19 Aug 1965, New York NY), American film and TV actress.

Ivan G. Seidenberg (1947?, Bronx NY), American corporate executive; CEO of Verizon Communications from 2002.

Jerry Seinfeld (Jerome Seinfeld; 29 Apr 1954, Brooklyn NY), American comic and TV personality.

Fatmir Sejdiu (23 Oct 1951, Pakashtice, Yugoslavia [now in Kosovo]), Kosovar professor and politician; president of Kosovo from 2006.

Kazuyo Sejima (29 Oct 1956, Mito, Japan), Japanese architect; corecipient of the 2010 Pritzker Prize.

Bud Selig (Allan H. Selig; 30 Jul 1934, Milwaukee WI), American sports executive; Major League Baseball commissioner from 1998.

Greg Selinger (c. 1951), Canadian politician (New Democratic Party of Manitoba); premier of Manitoba from 2009.

Paul Sereno (11 Oct 1957, Aurora IL), American paleontologist.

Richard Serra (2 Nov 1939, San Francisco CA), American minimalist sculptor of large outdoor works; recipient of a Praemium Imperiale in 1994.

Nasrallah Pierre Cardinal Sfeir (Nasrallah Boutros Pierre Sfeir; 15 May 1920, Reyfoun, Lebanon), Lebanese (Maronite Catholic) patriarch of Antioch and all the East from 1986 and Roman Catholic cardinal from 1994.

Gil Shaham (19 Feb 1971, Champaign-Urbana IL), American violinist.

Shakira (Shakira Isabel Mebarak Ripoll; 2 Feb 1977, Barranquilla, Colombia), Colombian-born pop singer.

Tony Shalhoub (Anthony Marcus Shalhoub; 9 Oct 1953, Green Bay WI), American TV and film actor.

John Patrick Shanley (1950, Bronx NY), American screenwriter and playwright.

Mariya (Yuryevna) Sharapova (19 Apr 1987, Nyagan, USSR [now in Russia]), Russian tennis player.

Kamalesh Sharma (30 Sep 1941), Indian diplomat; secretary-general of the Commonwealth from 2008.

Al Sharpton (3 Oct 1954, New York NY), American politician (Democrat), political activist, and civil rights leader.

William Shatner (22 Mar 1931, Montreal, QC, Canada), Canadian TV actor.

Charlie Sheen (Carlos Irwin Estevez; 3 Sep 1965, New York NY), American film and TV actor.

Martin Sheen (Ramon Estevez; 3 Aug 1940, Dayton OH), American stage, film, and TV actor.

Judith Sheindlin (21 Oct 1942, Brooklyn NY), American TV judge (of *Judge Judy*).

Sam(uel) Shepard (Rogers) (5 Nov 1943, Fort Sheridan IL), American playwright and actor.

Cindy Sherman (Cynthia Morris Sherman; 19 Jan 1954, Glen Ridge NJ), American photographer.

Osamu Shimomura (27 Aug 1928, Kyoto, Japan), Japanese chemist; cowinner of the 2008 Nobel Prize for Chemistry.

Eric K. Shinseki (28 Nov 1942, Lihue HI), American army officer; US secretary of veterans affairs from 2009.

Masaaki Shirakawa (27 Sep 1949, Kitakyushu, Japan), Japanese banker; governor of the Bank of Japan from 2008.

Vandana Shiva (5 Nov 1952, Dehra Dun, Uttar Pradesh [now in Uttarakhand] state, India), Indian biologist and social activist against the "biological theft" of the resources of poor countries by the richer ones.

Will Shortz (26 Aug 1952, Crawfordsville IN), American "enigmatologist" and "puzzlemaster"; crossword-puzzle editor at the New York Times.

Than Shwe (2 Feb 1933, Kyaukse, Burma [now Myanmar]), Burmese military officer; head of government in Myanmar, 1992–2003, and chairman of the State Peace and Development Council (head of state) from 1992.

M(anoj) Night Shyamalan (6 Aug 1970, Pondicherry, India), Indian-born film director and screenwriter.

Gabourey Sidibe (6 May 1983, Brooklyn NY), American actress.

Malick Sidibé (1935/36, Soloba, French Sudan [now Mali]), Malian photographer.

Jóhanna Sigurðardóttir (4 Oct 1942, Reykjavik, Iceland), Icelandic politician; prime minister from 2009.

(David) Derek Sikua (10 Sep 1959, Guadalcanal province, British-protected Solomon Islands), Solomon Islands politician; prime minister, 2007–10.

Haris Silajdzic (1 Oct 1945, Sarajevo, Yugoslavia [now in Bosnia and Herzegovina]), Bosnia and Herzegovinian politician; chairman of the presidency of the republic in 2008 and from 2010.

Sarah (Kate) Silverman (1 Dec 1970, Bedford NH), American comedian, TV actress, and writer.

Silvia (Silvia Renate Sommerlath; 23 Dec 1943, Heidelberg, Germany), Swedish royal and social activist; queen consort of King Carl XVI Gustaf (married 19 Jun 1976).

Charles Simic (9 May 1938, Belgrade, Yugoslavia [now in Serbia]), Yugoslav-born American poet; US poet laureate, 2007–08.

Russell Simmons (4 Oct 1957, Queens NY), American hip-hop impresario and cofounder of Def Jam Records.

Jessica Simpson (10 Jul 1980, Dallas TX), American pop singer and actress.

Lorna Simpson (13 Aug 1960, Brooklyn NY), American multimedia artist.

Ashlee Simpson-Wentz (3 Oct 1984, Dallas TX), American actress and singer.

Hammerskjoeld Simwinga (17 Nov 1964, Isoka, Zambia), Zambian environmentalist; recipient of the 2007 Goldman Environmental Prize for Africa.

Manmohan Singh (26 Sep 1932, Gah, Punjab, British India [now in Pakistan]), Indian economist; prime minister from 2004.

Gary Sinise (17 Mar 1955, Blue Island IL), American TV and film actor and producer.

(Sayyid) Ali (Hussaini) al-Sistani (4 Aug 1930?, near Meshed, Iran), Iranian Shi'ite Muslim cleric.

Jeffrey S. Skoll (16 Jan 1965, Montreal, QC, Canada), Canadian entrepreneur; cofounder of eBay and, from 1999, the president of the philanthropic Skoll Foundation.

Leonard (Edward) Slatkin (1 Sep 1944, Los Angeles CA), American conductor; music director of the Detroit Symphony Orchestra from 2008.

Carlos Slim (Helú) (28 Jan 1940, Mexico City, Mexico), Mexican investor; head of Grupo Carso, SA de CV, and longtime chairman and CEO of the national telephone monopoly, Teléfonos de México (Telmex); he was named the world's richest person by Forbes in 2010.

Tavis Smiley (13 Sep 1964, Gulfport MS), American advocacy journalist on radio and TV.

Alexander McCall Smith (24 Aug 1948, Bulawayo, Southern Rhodesia [now Zimbabwe]), British author of crime novels and works for children.

Anna Deavere Smith (18 Sep 1950, Baltimore MD), American playwright, actress, and professor.

George E. Smith (10 May 1930, White Plains NY), American physicist; cowinner of the 2009 Nobel Prize for Physics.

Marc (Kelly) Smith (195?, Chicago IL), American performance poet; originator of the poetry slam.

Michael W. Smith (7 Oct 1957, Kenova WV), American Christian singer.

Patti (Lee) Smith (30 Dec 1946, Chicago IL), American musician, poet, and visual artist.

Stephen Smith (12 Dec 1955, Narrogin, WA, Australia), Australian politician (Labor); foreign minister from 2007.

Will(ard Christopher) Smith, Jr. (25 Sep 1968, Philadelphia PA), American rapper and actor.

Zadie Smith (Sadie Smith; 27 Oct 1975, Willesden Green, London, England), British novelist.

Snoop Dogg (Calvin Broadus; 20 Oct 1972, Long Beach CA), American gangsta rap musician.

Gary (Sherman) Snyder (8 May 1930, San Francisco CA), American poet.

José Sócrates (Carvalho Pinto de Sousa) (6 Sep 1957, Vilar de Maçada, Portugal), Portuguese civil engineer and politician (Socialist); prime minister from 2005.

Steven Soderbergh (14 Jan 1963, Atlanta GA), American film director.

Sofia (Princess Sophie of Greece; Sofia de Grecia y Hannover; 2 Nov 1938, Athens, Greece), Spanish royal; queen consort of King Juan Carlos I (married 12 May 1962).

Javier Solana (Madariaga) (14 Jul 1942, Madrid, Spain), Spanish statesman; NATO secretary-general, 1995–99, and secretary-general of the Council of the European Union, 1999–2009.

Hilda Solis (20 Oct 1957, Los Angeles CA), American politician (Democrat); congresswoman from California, 2001–09, and US secretary of labor from 2009.

László Sólyom (3 Jan 1942, Pécs, Hungary), Hungarian jurist and politician; president from 2005.

Michael (Thomas) Somare (9 Apr 1936, Rabaul, Australian-mandated New Guinea [now Papua New Guinea]), Papua New Guinean politician; prime minister, 1975–80, 1982–85, and again from 2002.

Juan (Octavio) Somavia (21 Apr 1941, Chile), Chilean international official; director general of the International Labour Organization from 1999.

Stephen (Joshua) Sondheim (22 Mar 1930, New York NY), American composer and lyricist for musical theater.

Sang Hyun Song (21 Dec 1941, Japanese-occupied Korea [now in South Korea]), South Korean jurist; president of the International Criminal Court from 2009.

Sonja (Sonja Haraldsen; 4 Jul 1937, Oslo, Norway), Norwegian royal; queen consort of King Harald V (married 29 Aug 1968).

Sophie (Sophie Helen Rhys-Jones; 20 Jan 1965, Oxford, England), British royal; wife of Prince Edward (married 19 Jun 1999) and countess of Wessex.

Annika Sörenstam (9 Oct 1970, Stockholm, Sweden), Swedish golfer.

Aaron Sorkin (9 Jun 1961, Scarsdale NY), American screenwriter, playwright, and TV producer.

Guillaume Soro (8 May 1972, Kofiplé, Côte d'Ivoire), Ivorian politician; prime minister from 2007.

Sonia (Maria) Sotomayor (25 Jun 1954, Bronx NY), American jurist; associate justice of the US Supreme Court from 2009.

David H(ackett) Souter (17 Sep 1939, Melrose MA), American jurist; associate justice of the US Supreme Court, 1990–2009.

Wole Soyinka (Akinwande Oluwole Soyinka; 13 Jul 1934, Abeokuta, Nigeria), Nigerian playwright, poet, novelist, and critic; recipient of the 1986 Nobel Prize for Literature.

Kevin Spacey (Kevin Matthew Fowler; 26 Jul 1959, South Orange NJ), American stage and film actor and artistic director of the Old Vic theater in London.

Nicholas Sparks (31 Dec 1965, Omaha NE), American novelist.

Britney (Jean) Spears (2 Dec 1981, Kentwood LA), American pop singer and celebrity.

Margaret Spellings (30 Nov 1957, Michigan), American political adviser, education expert, and secretary of education, 2005–09.

W(inston) Baldwin Spencer (8 Oct 1948), West Indian politician; prime minister of Antigua and Barbuda from 2004.

Steven Spielberg (18 Dec 1947, Cincinnati OH), American film director and producer.

Nikola Spiric (4 Sep 1956, Drvar, Yugoslavia [now in Bosnia and Herzegovina]), Bosnia and Herzegovinian politician; chairman of the Council of Ministers (prime minister) from 2007.

Eliot (Laurence) Spitzer (10 Jun 1959, Riverdale, Bronx NY), American attorney and politician (Democrat); governor of New York, 2007–08.

Bruce Springsteen (23 Sep 1949, Freehold NJ), American rock singer and songwriter.

(Michael) Sylvester (Enzio) Stallone ("Sly"; 6 Jul 1946, New York NY), American film actor and director.

Albert Starr (1 Jun 1926, New York NY), American cardiovascular surgeon and inventor of an artificial heart valve; recipient of a 2007 Lasker Medical Prize.

James G. Stavridis (15 Feb 1955, West Palm Beach FL), American military official; Supreme Allied Commander, Europe (SACEUR) from 2009 and commander of the US European Command from 2009.

Danielle (Fernande Schuelein-) Steel (14 Aug 1947, New York NY), American romance novelist.

Michael Steele (19 Oct 1958, Andrews AFB, Prince George's county MD), American politician (Republican); first African American chairman of the Republican National Committee from 2009.

Gwen Stefani (3 Oct 1969, Fullerton CA), American rock and pop vocalist.

Gregg Steinhafel (1955), American businessman; president of Target Corp. from 1999 and its CEO from 2008.

Ralph M(arvin) Steinman (14 Jan 1943, Montreal, QC, Canada), American immunologist and specialist in immune response in cells; recipient of a 2007 Lasker Medical Prize.

Frank-Walter Steinmeier (5 Jan 1956, Detmold, West Germany), German politician (Social Democrat); foreign minister, 2005–09, and vice-chancellor, 2007–09.

Thomas Steitz (23 Aug 1940, Milwaukee WI), American biophysicist and biochemist; cowinner of the 2009 Nobel Prize for Chemistry.

Frank P(hilip) Stella (12 May 1936, Malden MA), American painter.

Ed Stelmach (11 May 1951, Lamont, AB, Canada), Canadian politician (Progressive Conservative); premier of Alberta from 2006.

Stephanie (Stéphanie Marie Elizabeth Grimaldi; 1 Feb 1965, Monaco), Monegasque princess; the youngest child of Prince Rainier III and Grace Kelly.

Marcus Stephen (1 Oct 1969, Nauru?), Nauruan weight lifter and politician; president from 2007.

Howard Stern (12 Jan 1954, Roosevelt NY), American radio and TV personality.

John Paul Stevens (20 Apr 1920, Chicago IL), American jurist; associate justice of the US Supreme Court, 1975–2010.

Ellen Stewart (7 Nov 1919, Chicago IL), American theater director and producer, the founder (1961) of La MaMa Experimental Theater Club in New York City; recipient of a Praemium Imperiale in 2007.

Jon Stewart (Jonathan Stewart Leibowitz; 28 Nov 1962, New York NY), American actor, writer, and comedian; anchor of TV's The Daily Show from 1999.

Kristen Stewart (9 April 1990, Los Angeles CA), American actress.

Patrick Stewart (13 Jul 1940, Mirfield, Yorkshire, England), British actor.

T.J. Stiles (Minnesota), American author; his The First Tycoon: The Epic Life of Cornelius Vanderbilt won the 2010 Pulitzer Prize for biography or autobiography.

Ben Stiller (30 Nov 1965, New York NY), American comedian, actor, and film director.

Sting (Gordon Matthew Sumner; 2 Oct 1951, Wallsend, Newcastle upon Tyne, England), British singer, songwriter, and actor.

Jens Stoltenberg (16 Mar 1959, Oslo, Norway), Norwegian economist and politician (Norwegian Labor Party); prime minister, 2000–01 and from 2005.

Biz Stone (Christopher Isaac Stone; 10 Mar 1974, Massachusetts), American entrepreneur; cofounder of Twitter.

Joss Stone (Joscelyn Eve Stoker; 11 Apr 1987, Dover, Kent, England), English soul singer.

Oliver (William) Stone (15 Sep 1946, New York NY), American director, writer, and producer.

Tom Stoppard (Tomas Straussler; 3 Jul 1937, Zlin, Moravia, Czechoslovakia [now in the Czech Republic]), Czech-born British playwright and screenwriter.

Dominique Strauss-Kahn (25 Apr 1949, Neuilly-sur-Seine, France), French politician (Socialist); managing director of the International Monetary Fund from 2007.

Jack Straw (John Whitaker Straw; 3 Aug 1946, Brentwood, Essex, England), British politician; home secretary, 1997–2001, foreign secretary, 2001–06, and secretary of state for justice and lord high chancellor, 2007–10.

Meryl Streep (Mary Louise Streep; 22 Jun 1949, Summit NJ), American film actress.

Barbra Streisand (Barbara Joan Streisand; 24 Apr 1942, Brooklyn NY), American singer, actress, and film director.

Ted Strickland (4 Aug 1941, Lucasville OH), American politician (Democrat); governor of Ohio from 2007.

Howard Stringer (19 Feb 1942, Cardiff, Wales), Welsh-born business executive; chairman and CEO of Sony Corp. from 2005.

Susan Stroman (17 Oct 1954, Wilmington DE), American theater director.

Elizabeth Strout (6 Jan 1956, Portland ME), American author.

(Christopher) Ruben Studdard (12 Sep 1978, Frankfurt am Main, West Germany), American singer.

Juan Manuel Suárez del Toro Rivero (1952, Spain), Spanish international official; president of the International Federation of Red Cross and Red Crescent Societies from 2001.

Hiroshi Sugimoto (1948, Tokyo, Japan), Japanese photographer; recipient of a Praemium Imperiale in 2009.

Arthur Ochs Sulzberger, Jr. (22 Sep 1951, Mount Kisco NY), American newspaper executive, publisher of the New York Times from 1992 and CEO from 1997.

Pat Summitt (Patricia Head; 14 Jun 1952, Henrietta TN), American women's basketball coach; the winningest coach in NCAA basketball history.

Rashid Sunyaev (Rashid [Aliyevich] Syunyayev; 1 Mar 1943, Tashkent, USSR [now in Uzbekistan]), Russian astrophysicist; director of the Max Planck Institute for Astrophysics from 1996; recipient of the 2000 Bruce Medal and a 2008 Crafoord Prize.

Kiefer Sutherland (William Frederick Dempsey George Sutherland; 21 Dec 1966, London, England), Canadian film and TV actor.

Ichiro Suzuki (22 Oct 1973, Kasugai, Aichi prefecture, Japan), Japanese baseball player.

Hilary Swank (30 Jul 1974, Lincoln NE), American film actress.

Taylor Swift (13 Dec 1989, Reading PA), American country singer.

Tilda Swinton (Katherine Matilda Swinton; 5 Nov 1960, London, England), British actress.

Wanda Sykes (7 Mar 1964, Portsmouth VA), American comedian and actress.

Jack W. Szostak (9 Nov 1952, London, England), English-born American biochemist and geneticist; cowinner of the 2009 Nobel Prize for Physiology and Medicine.

Boris Tadic (15 Jan 1958, Sarajevo, Yugoslavia [now in Bosnia and Herzegovina]), Serbian politician and government official; president of Serbia from 2004.

Jalal Talabani (1933, Kalkan, Iraq), Iraqi Kurdish politician; president of Iraq from 2005.

Mehmet Ali Talat (6 Jul 1952, Girne, British Cyprus), Turkish Cypriot politician; prime minister of the Turkish Republic of Northern Cyprus, 2004–05, and president, 2005–10.

Mamadou Tandja (1938, Maïné-Soroa, French West Africa [now in Niger]), Nigerois politician; president, 1999–2010.

Quentin (Jerome) Tarantino (27 Mar 1963, Knoxville TN), American film director and screenwriter.

Marc Tarpenning (1 Jun 1964, Sacramento CA), American entrepreneur and cofounder of Tesla Motors.

Ratan (Naval) Tata (28 Dec 1937, Bombay, British India [now Mumbai, India]), Indian corporate executive; chairman of the Tata Group and its several subsidiary companies.

Audrey Tautou (9 Aug 1978, Beaumont, France), French film actress.

John Tavener (28 Jan 1944, London, England), British composer.

Charles M(argrave) Taylor (5 Nov 1931, Montreal, QC, Canada), Canadian philosopher and professor; recipient of the 2007 Templeton Prize.

Elizabeth (Rosemond) Taylor (27 Feb 1932, London, England), American film actress.

Julie Taymor (15 Dec 1952, Newton MA), American theater and film director.

Oscar Temaru (1 Nov 1944, Faaa, Tahiti, French Polynesia), French Polynesian politician; president, 2004, 2005–06, 2007–08, and 2009.

Hashim Thaci (24 Apr 1969, Buroja, Yugoslavia [now in Kosovo]), Kosovar politician; prime minister from 2008.

Bal (Keshav) Thackeray (23 Jan 1927), Indian politician who established the Shiv Sena party.

John A. Thain (26 May 1955, Antioch IL), American financial official; CEO of the New York Stock Exchange, 2004–07, and the last CEO of Merrill Lynch, 2007–09.

Hamad ibn Khalifah al-Thani (1950, Doha, Qatar), Qatari sheikh; emir from 1995.

Twyla Tharp (1 Jul 1941, Portland IN), American dancer, director, and choreographer.

Charlize Theron (7 Aug 1975, Benoni, South Africa), South African actress.

Thich Nhat Hanh (11 Oct 1926, central Vietnam), Vietnamese Buddhist monk, pacifist, and teacher.

Lyonchen Jigme (Yoeser) Thinley (1952, Bumthang district, Bhutan), Bhutanese prime minister, 1998–99, 2003–04, and again from 2008.

Clarence Thomas (23 Jun 1948, Pinpoint community, near Savannah GA), American jurist; associate justice of the US Supreme Court from 1991.

Michael Tilson Thomas (21 Dec 1944, Hollywood CA), American conductor and composer; music director of the San Francisco Symphony from 1995.

Tillman (Joseph) Thomas (13 Jun 1945, Hermitage, St. Patrick, Grenada, British West Indies), West Indian politician; prime minister of Grenada from 2008.

David (John Howard) Thompson (December 1961, London, England), Barbadian politician; prime minister from 2008.

Emma Thompson (15 Apr 1959, London, England), British film actress.

Robert Thomson (11 Mar 1961, Echuca, VIC, Australia), Australian journalist; editor of The Times of London, 2002–07, and managing editor of The Wall Street Journal from 2008.

Billy Bob Thornton (4 Aug 1955, Hot Springs AR), American director and actor.

Uma (Karuna) Thurman (29 Apr 1970, Boston MA), American film actress.

Rex W. Tillerson (23 Mar 1952, Wichita Falls TX), American petroleum company executive; president (from 2004) and CEO (from 2006) of Exxon Mobil Corp.

Timbaland (Timothy Z. Mosley; 10 Mar 1972, Norfolk VA), American R&B and rap composer, record producer, and performer.

Justin (Randall) Timberlake (31 Jan 1981, Memphis TN), American pop singer.

Sakata Tojuro (31 Dec 1931, Kyoto, Japan), Japanese actor; recipient of a 2008 Praemium Imperiale.

Claire Tomalin (Claire Delavenay; 20 Jun 1933, London, England), English biographer and author.

(Iroij) Litokwa Tomeing (14 Oct 1939, Wotje atoll, Japanese-mandated Marshall Islands), Marshallese politician; president of the Marshall Islands, 2008–09.

Anote Tong (1952), Kiribati politician; president of Kiribati from 2003.

Gaston Tong Sang (7 Aug 1949, Bora-Bora, Tahiti, French Polynesia), French Polynesian politician; president of French Polynesia, 2006–07, 2008–09, and again from November 2009.

Bamir Topi (24 Apr 1957, Tiranë, Albania), Albanian biologist and politician; president from 2007.

Mirek Topolanek (15 May 1956, Vsetin, Moravia, Czechoslovakia [now in the Czech Republic]), Czech industrial engineer, businessman, and politician; prime minister, 2006–09.

Johnson Toribiong (1946, Airai, US-occupied Palau), Palauan politician, president of Palau from 2009.

Martín Torrijos (Espino) (18 Jul 1963, Panama City, Panama), Panamanian politician (Democratic Revolutionary Party); president, 2004–09.

Daniel Tosh (29 May 1975, Germany), American comedian and TV actor.

Amadou Toumani Touré (4 Nov 1948, Mpoti, French Sudan [now in Mali]), Malian politician; president, 1991–92 and again from 2002.

Hamadoun Touré (3 Sep 1953, French Sudan [now Mali]), Malian international official; secretary-general of the International Telecommunication Union from 2007.

Randy Travis (Randy Traywick; 4 May 1959, Marshville NC), American country-and-western singer, songwriter, and actor.

John (Joseph) Travolta (18 Feb 1955, Englewood NJ), American TV and film actor.

Natasha Trethewey (26 Apr 1966, Gulfport MS), American poet.

Jean-Claude Trichet (20 Dec 1942, Lyons, France), French banker, governor of the Banque de France, 1993–2003, and president of the European Central Bank from 2003.

Libby Trickett (Lisbeth Lenton; 28 Jan 1985, Townsville, QLD, Australia), Australian swimmer.

Lars von Trier (30 Apr 1956, Copenhagen, Denmark), Danish film director and cinematographer.

Calvin Trillin (5 Dec 1935, Kansas City MO), American author, commentator, and occasional poet.

Travis Tritt (9 Feb 1963, Marietta GA), American country-and-western singer.

Robert L. Trivers (19 Feb 1943, Washington DC), American evolutionary biologist and sociobiologist; recipient of a 2007 Crafoord Prize.

Garry R. Trudeau (21 Jul 1948, New York NY), American cartoonist; creator of the durable Doonesbury syndicated comic strip.

Richard L. Trumka (24 Jul 1949, Nemacolin PA), American labor leader; president of the AFL-CIO from 2009.

Donald (John) Trump (14 Jun 1946, New York NY), American real-estate developer and reality-TV personality.

Ronald A. Tschetter (4 Oct 1941, Huron SD), American investment executive; director of the Peace Corps from 2006.

Roger Y. Tsien (1 Feb 1952, New York NY), American chemist; cowinner of the 2008 Nobel Prize for Chemistry.

Morgan Tsvangirai (10 Mar 1952, Gutu, Southern Rhodesia [now Zimbabwe]), Zimbabwean labor leader and politician; head of the Movement for Democratic Change (from 1999), main opposition leader to the regime of Pres. Robert Mugabe, and prime minister of Zimbabwe in a historic power-sharing agreement from 2009.

Togiola T(alalei) A. Tulafono (28 Feb 1947, Aunu'u Island, American Samoa), American Samoan politician (Democrat); governor of American Samoa from 2003.

Tommy Tune (28 Feb 1939, Wichita Falls TX), American musical-comedy dancer and actor.

Danilo Turk (19 Feb 1952, Maribor, Yugoslavia [now in Slovenia]), Slovenian law professor and diplomat; president from 2007.

Ted Turner (Robert Edward Turner III; 19 Nov 1938, Cincinnati OH), American TV executive, the founder of Turner Broadcasting System (TBS) and Cable News Network (CNN); sports club owner (of the Atlanta Braves, the Atlanta Hawks, and the Atlanta Thrashers); yachtsman; and philanthropist.

John Turturro (27 Feb 1957, Brooklyn NY), American stage, film, and TV actor.

Donald (Franciszek) Tusk (22 Apr 1957, Gdansk, Poland), Polish politician (Civic Platform); prime minister from 2007.

Desmond (Mpilo) Tutu (7 Oct 1931, Klerksdorp, South Africa), South African Anglican cleric who in 1984 received the Nobel Peace Prize for his role in the opposition to apartheid in South Africa.

Cy Twombly (Edwin Parker Twombly, Jr.; 25 Apr 1928, Lexington VA), American abstract artist and sculptor.

Anne Tyler (25 Oct 1941, Minneapolis MN), American novelist and short-story writer.

Liv Tyler (Liv Rundgren; 1 Jul 1977, Portland ME), American actress and model.

Yuliya (Volodymyrivna) Tymoshenko (27 Nov 1960, Dnipropetrovsk, USSR [now in Ukraine]), Ukrainian businesswoman and politician (Yuliya Tymoshenko Bloc); prime minister, 2005 and 2007–10.

(Alfred) McCoy Tyner (Sulaimon Saud; 11 Dec 1938, Philadelphia PA), American jazz pianist and composer.

João Ubaldo (Osório Pimentel) Ribeiro (23 Jan 1941, Itaparica, Bahia state, Brazil), Brazilian novelist.

Carrie Underwood (10 Mar 1983, Muskogee OK), American country singer.

Keith (Lionel) Urban (26 Oct 1967, Whangerei, New Zealand), New Zealand–born Australian country singer.

Álvaro Uribe (Vélez) (4 Jul 1952, Medellín, Colombia), Colombian politician; president of Colombia, 2002–10.

Usher (Usher Raymond IV; 14 Oct 1978, Chattanooga TN), American R&B singer.

Herman Van Rompuy (31 Oct 1947, Etterbeek, Belgium), Belgian politician (Christian Democratic and Flemish); prime minister, 2008–09; president of the European Council from 2010.

Gus van Sant (24 Jul 1952, Louisville KY), American film director.

Matti Vanhanen (4 Nov 1955, Jyväskylä, Finland), Finnish politician; prime minister, 2003–10.

Harold (Eliot) Varmus (18 Dec 1939, Oceanside NY), American virologist; corecipient of the 1989 Nobel Prize for Physiology or Medicine; director of the National Institutes of Health, 1993–99, president of Memorial Sloan-Kettering Cancer Center in New York City from 2000, and director of the National Cancer Institute from 2010.

Vince(nt Anthony) Vaughn (28 Mar 1970, Minneapolis MN), American actor.

Tabaré (Ramón) Vázquez (Rosas) (17 Jan 1940, Barrio La Teja, Montevideo, Uruguay), Uruguayan physician and politician (Socialist); president, 2005–10.

Eddie Vedder (Edward Louis Severson III; 23 Dec 1964, Evanston IL), American rock vocalist and songwriter (for Pearl Jam).

Abhisit Vejjajiva (3 Aug 1964, Newcastle upon Tyne, England), Thai politician; prime minister of Thailand from 2008.

Jaci Velasquez (Jacquelyn Davette Velasquez; 15 Oct 1979, Houston TX), American Latin and gospel singer.

Ann M. Veneman (29 Jun 1949, Modesto CA), American government official; US secretary of agriculture, 2001–05, and executive director of UNICEF, 2005–10.

(Runaldo) Ronald Venetiaan (18 Jun 1936, Paramaribo, Dutch Guiana [now Suriname]), Surinamese mathematician and politician; president of Suriname, 1991–96 and 2000–10.

Maxim Vengerov (Maksim Aleksandrovich Vengerov; 20 Aug 1974, Novosibirsk, USSR [now in Russia]), Russian-born concert violinist.

J. Craig Venter (14 Oct 1946, Salt Lake City UT), American geneticist and researcher into the human genome; he was the founder of Celera Genomics and the J. Craig Venter Institute.

Guy Verhofstadt (11 Apr 1953, Dendermonde, Belgium), Belgian politician (VLD); prime minister, 1999–2008.

Donatella Versace (2 May 1955, Reggio di Calabria, Italy), Italian fashion designer; creative director at the Versace design house from 1997.

Ben Verwaayen (11 Feb 1952, Driebergen, Netherlands), Dutch corporate executive; CEO of Alcatel-Lucent from 2008.

Charles M. Vest (9 Sep 1941, Morgantown WV), American scientist and educator; president of the Massachusetts Institute of Technology, 1990–2004, and president of the National Academy of Engineering from 2007.

Jack Vettriano (Jack Hoggan; 17 Nov 1951, St. Andrews, Fife, Scotland), British painter.

Victoria (Victoria Ingrid Alice Desirée; 14 Jul 1977, Stockholm, Sweden), Swedish crown princess and duchess of Västergötland.

David Villa (3 Dec 1981, Tuilla, Spain), Spanish association football (soccer) player.

Antonio Villaraigosa (Antonio Ramón Villar, Jr.; 23 Jan 1953, East Los Angeles CA), American politician (Democrat); mayor of Los Angeles from 2005.

Tom Vilsack (13 Dec 1950, Pittsburgh PA), American politician (Democrat); governor of Iowa, 1999–2007, and US secretary of agriculture from 2009.

Diana Vishneva (Diana Viktorovna Vishnyova; 13 Jun 1976, Leningrad, USSR [now St. Petersburg, Russia]), Russian ballerina with the Mariinsky Ballet and, from 2003, the American Ballet Theatre.

Lindsey Vonn (Lindsey Kildow; 18 Oct 1984, St. Paul MN), American Alpine skier.

Vladimir Voronin (25 May 1941, Corjova, Moldavian SSR, USSR [now Moldova]), Moldovan politician; president, 2001–09.

Peter Voser (29 Aug 1958, Switzerland), Swiss businessman; CEO of Royal Dutch Shell from 2009.

Filip Vujanovic (1 Sep 1954, Belgrade, Yugoslavia [now in Serbia]), Montenegrin politician; president of the Republic of Montenegro, before and after its independence, 2002–03 (acting) and again from 2003.

Abdoulaye Wade (29 May 1926, Kébémer, French West Africa [now in Senegal]), Senegalese politician; president from 2000.

G. Richard Wagoner, Jr. (9 Feb 1953, Wilmington DE), American corporate executive; CEO of General Motors Corp., 2000–09.

Mark (Robert Michael) Wahlberg (5 Jun 1971, Dorchester, Boston MA), American actor.

Rufus Wainwright (22 Jul 1973, Rhinebeck NY), Canadian singer and songwriter.

Ted Waitt (18 Jan 1963, Sioux City IA), American computer executive and philanthropist; cofounder of Gateway Inc. in 1985 and chairman and president of the charitable Waitt Family Foundation from 1993.

Derek (Alton) Walcott (23 Jan 1930, Castries, Saint Lucia, British West Indies), West Indian poet and playwright; recipient of the 1992 Nobel Prize for Literature.

Jimmy (Donal) Wales (7 Aug 1966, Huntsville AL), American Internet publisher; founder of *Wikipedia*.

Alice (Malsenior) Walker (9 Feb 1944, Eatonton GA), American novelist, poet, and short-story writer.

Brad Wall (24 Nov 1965, Swift Current, SK, Canada), Canadian businessman and politician (Progressive Conservative); premier of Saskatchewan from 2007.

Mike Wallace (Myron Leon Wallace; 9 May 1918, Brookline MA), American TV journalist, interviewer, and coeditor of CBS's *60 Minutes*.

Mark Walport (1953, England), British immunologist; director of the Wellcome Trust from 2003.

Barbara (Ann) Walters (25 Sep 1931, Boston MA), American television personality, broadcast journalist, and interviewer.

John P. Walters (1951?), American civic and government official; director of national drug control policy ("drug czar"), 2001–09.

Alice L. Walton (c. 1949), American heiress of part of the Wal-Mart fortune.

Jim C. Walton (c. 1948), American business executive; chairman and CEO of the Arvest Bank Group.

Christoph Waltz (4 Oct 1956, Vienna, Austria), Austrian actor.

Vera Wang (27 Jun 1949, New York NY), American fashion designer.

Jigme Khesar Namgyal Wangchuk (21 Feb 1980, Thimphu, Bhutan), Bhutanese royal; king from 2006.

Shane Keith Warne (13 Sep 1969, Ferntree Gully, VIC, Australia), Australian cricketer, a spin bowler named one of *Wisden*'s Five Cricketers of the Century.

Rick Warren (1954, San Jose CA), American evangelist minister.

Denzel Washington, Jr. (28 Dec 1954, Mount Vernon NY), American film, stage, and TV actor.

(Chaudhry) Wasim Akram (3 Jun 1966, Lahore, Pakistan), Pakistani cricket left-handed fast bowler.

Alice Waters (28 Apr 1944, Chatham NJ), American chef and restaurant owner (Chez Panisse, Berkeley CA).

John Waters (22 Apr 1946, Baltimore MD), American filmmaker.

John S. Watson (c. 1957), American business executive; chairman and CEO of Chevron Corp. from 2010.

Naomi Watts (28 Sep 1968, Shoreham, Kent, England), Australian film actress.

George (Manneh Oppong Ousman) Weah (1 Oct 1966, Monrovia, Liberia), Liberian-born association football (soccer) star, named in 1998 African Player of the Century.

Hugo Weaving (4 Apr 1900, Austin, Nigeria), Australian film actor.

Karrie Webb (21 Dec 1974, Ayr, QLD, Australia), Australian golfer.

Andrew (Thomas) Weil (8 Jun 1942, Philadelphia PA), American physician and champion of alternative medicine.

Bob Weinstein (18 Oct 1954, Queens NY), American film executive; cofounder of Miramax Films and the Weinstein Co.

Harvey Weinstein (19 Mar 1952, Queens NY), American film executive; cofounder of Miramax Films and the Weinstein Co.

Rachel Weisz (7 Mar 1971, London, England), British film actress.

Gillian Welch (2 Oct 1967, New York NY), American folk and country-and-western singer.

Wen Jiabao (September 1942, Tianjin, China), Chinese geologist and party and state official; premier from 2003.

Jann S. Wenner (7 Jan 1946, New York NY), American journalist; originator (1967) and publisher of *Rolling Stone* magazine.

Kanye West (8 Jun 1977, Atlanta GA), American rapper and music producer.

Guido Westerwelle (27 Dec 1961, Bad Honnef, Germany), German politician (Free Democrat); foreign minister and vice-chancellor from 2009.

Randy Weston (Randolph Edward Weston; 6 Apr 1926, Brooklyn NY), American jazz pianist and composer.

Vivienne Westwood (Vivienne Swire; 8 Apr 1941, Tintwistle, Derbyshire, England), British fashion designer.

Forest (Steven) Whitaker (15 Jul 1961, Longview TX), American film actor and director.

Betty (Marion) White (17 Jan 1922, Oak Park IL), American actress.

Jack White (John Anthony Gillis; 9 Jul 1975, Detroit MI), American alternative-rock guitarist, drummer, vocalist (for the White Stripes, the Raconteurs, and the Dead Weather), and record producer.

Shaun White (3 Sep 1986, San Diego CA), American snowboarder.

Ratnasiri Wickremanayake (5 May 1933, British Ceylon [now Sri Lanka]), Sri Lankan politician; prime minister, 2000–01 and 2005–10.

John Edgar Wideman (14 Jun 1941, Washington DC), American novelist.

Richard (Purdy) Wilbur (1 Mar 1921, New York NY), American poet associated with the New Formalist movement; poet laureate of the US, 1987–88, and recipient of the 2006 Ruth Lilly Poetry Prize.

Tom Wilkinson (Thomas Jeffery Wilkinson, Jr.; 12 Dec 1948, Leeds, West Yorkshire, England), British character actor.

George F(rederick) Will (4 May 1941, Champaign IL), American conservative political commentator and columnist.

Willem-Alexander (27 Apr 1967, Utrecht, Netherlands), Dutch crown prince.

William (William Arthur Philip Louis Mountbatten-Windsor; 21 Jun 1982, London, England), British prince of Wales; son of Charles and Diana, prince and princess of Wales, and second in line to the British throne.

Brian (Douglas) Williams (5 May 1959, Elmira NY), American TV newsman; anchor of *NBC Nightly News* from 2004.

C(harles) K(enneth) Williams (4 Nov 1936, Newark NJ), American poet.

Danny Williams (4 Aug 1950, St. John's, NF [now NL], Canada), Canadian lawyer and politician (Progressive Conservative); premier of Newfoundland and Labrador from 2003.

Evan Williams (31 Mar 1972, Nebraska), American entrepreneur; cofounder of Twitter.

John Williams (24 Apr 1941, Melbourne, VIC, Australia), Australian-born classical guitarist.

John (Towner) Williams (8 Feb 1932, Queens NY), American conductor and composer of movie sound tracks.

Lucinda Williams (26 Jan 1953, Lake Charles LA), American contemporary folk and country singer and songwriter.

Pharrell Williams ("Skateboard P"; 5 Apr 1973, Virginia Beach VA), American hip-hop artist, songwriter, and producer.

Robbie Williams (Robert Peter Maximillian Williams; 13 Feb 1974, Tunstall, Stoke-on-Trent, Staffordshire, England), British singer.

Robin Williams (21 Jul 1952, Chicago IL), American comedian and actor.

Rowan (Douglas) Williams (14 Jun 1950, Swansea, Wales), Welsh-born Anglican clergyman; archbishop of Canterbury from 2003.

Serena Williams (26 Sep 1981, Saginaw MI), American tennis player and clothing designer.

Vanessa (Lynn) Williams (18 Mar 1963, Tarrytown NY), American singer and actress.

Venus Williams (17 Jun 1980, Lynwood CA), American tennis player and businesswoman.

Oliver E. Williamson (27 Sep 1932, Superior WI), American social scientist; cowinner of the 2009 Nobel Prize for Economics.

Bruce Willis (Walter Bruce Willison; 19 Mar 1955, Idar-Oberstein, West Germany), American actor.

Brian Wilson (20 Jun 1942, Inglewood CA), American pop music songwriter and producer (for the Beach Boys); recipient of a 2007 Kennedy Center Honor.

Lanford Wilson (13 Apr 1937, Lebanon MO), American playwright.

Luke (Cunningham) Wilson (21 Sep 1971, Dallas TX), American actor.

Owen (Cunningham) Wilson (18 Nov 1968, Dallas TX), American actor.

Robert Wilson (4 Oct 1941, Waco TX), American avant-garde theater director.

Amy (Jade) Winehouse (14 Sep 1983, Enfield, Middlesex, England), British singer and songwriter.

Oprah Winfrey (29 Jan 1954, Kosciusko MS), American TV personality; host and producer of *The Oprah Winfrey Show* from 1985.

Kate Winslet (5 Oct 1975, Reading, England), British film actress.

Anna Wintour (3 Nov 1949, London, England), British-born fashion magazine editor, editor in chief of American *Vogue* from 1988.

(Laura Jean) Reese Witherspoon (22 Mar 1976, Baton Rouge LA), American film actress.

Edward Witten (26 Aug 1951, Baltimore MD), American mathematician and specialist in superstring theory; recipient of the 1990 Fields Medal and a 2008 Crafoord Prize.

Patricia A(nn) Woertz (17 Mar 1953, Pittsburgh PA), American corporate executive; CEO of Archer Daniels Midland from 2006.

Girma Wolde-Giorgis (December 1924, Addis Ababa, Ethiopia), Ethiopian military officer; president from 2001.

Nathan Wolfe (24 Aug 1970, Detroit MI), American virologist and professor, a specialist in the transfer of viruses from animals to humans.

Tom Wolfe (Thomas Kennerly Wolfe, Jr.; 2 Mar 1930, Richmond VA), American novelist, journalist, and social commentator.

Tobias (Jonathan Ansell) Wolff (19 Jun 1945, Birmingham AL), American writer.

Stevie Wonder (Steveland Judkins; Steveland Morris; 13 May 1950, Saginaw MI), American pop songwriter and singer.

Elijah (Jordan) Wood (28 Jan 1981, Cedar Rapids IA), American film actor.

Tiger Woods (Eldrick Woods; 30 Dec 1975, Cypress CA), American golfer.

Klaus Wowereit (1 Oct 1953, West Berlin, West Germany [now in Berlin, Germany]), German politician (Social Democrat); mayor of Berlin from 2001.

Stephen Wozniak (11 Aug 1950, San Jose CA), American electrical engineer, cofounder of Apple Computer Corp., and youth leader.

Wu Den-yih (30 Jan 1948, Caotun, Taiwan), Taiwanese politician; president of the Executive Yuan (premier) from 2009.

Christian Wulff (19 Jun 1959, Osnabrück, West Germany), German politician; president of Germany from 2010.

Ken Wyatt (1953?, Australia), Australian physician and politician; the first Aboriginal man elected to the Australian House of Representatives (in 2010).

Xavi (Xavier Hernández Creus; 25 Jan 1980, Terrassa, Spain), Spanish association football (soccer) player.

Ram Baran Yadav (4 Feb 1948, Sapahi, Dhanukha, Nepal), Nepalese politician; the first president of Nepal, from 2008.

Shinya Yamanaka (4 Sep 1962, Osaka, Japan), Japanese physician and stem-cell researcher; recipient of a 2009 Lasker Medical Prize.

Yang Jiechi (May 1950, Shanghai, China), Chinese foreign minister from 2007.

Viktor Yanukovych (9 Jul 1950, Yenakiyeve, Ukraine), Ukrainian politician; president from 2010.

Yao Ming (12 Sep 1980, Shanghai, China), Chinese basketball player.

Catherine Yass (1963, London, England), British photographic artist.

Trisha Yearwood (Patricia Lynn Yearwood; 19 Sep 1964, Monticello GA), American country singer.

Michelle Yeoh (Yang Zi Chong or Yeoh Chu-keng; 6 Aug 1962, Ipoh, Malaysia), Malaysian-born film actress.

Gloria Yerkovich (1942), American child-welfare advocate; founder of Child Find, an organization that helps to locate missing children. ·

Francis Yip (Yip Lai Yee; 1948, Hong Kong), Hong Kong Chinese pop singer.

Ada Yonath (22 Jun 1939, Jerusalem), Israeli protein crystallographer; cowinner of the 2009 Nobel Prize for Chemistry.

Banana Yoshimoto (Yoshimoto Mahoko; 24 Jul 1964, Tokyo, Japan), Japanese writer of best-selling fiction.

Will(iam Robert) Young (20 Jan 1979, Hungerford, Berkshire, England), British pop singer.

Susilo Bambang Yudhoyono (9 Sep 1949, Pacitan, East Java, Indonesia), Indonesian military officer; president from 2004.

Muhammad Yunus (28 Jun 1940, Chittagong, East Bengal, British India [now in Bangladesh]), Bangladeshi economist specializing in microcredit and founder of the Grameen Bank; corecipient of the 2006 Nobel Peace Prize.

Viktor (Andriyovych) Yushchenko (23 Feb 1954, Khoruzhivka, Sumy oblast, USSR [now in Ukraine]), Ukrainian banker and politician (Our Ukraine); prime minister, 1999–2001, and president, 2005–10.

Sadi Yusuf (1934, near Basra, Iraq), Iraqi-born poet.

Adam Zagajewski (21 Jun 1945, Lwow, Poland [now Lviv, Ukraine]), Polish poet, novelist, and essayist; recipient of the 2004 Neustadt Prize.

José Luis Rodríguez Zapatero (4 Aug 1960, Valladolid, Spain), Spanish politician (Socialist Workers Party); prime minister from 2004.

Asif Ali Zardari (21 Jul 1956, Nawabshah, Pakistan), Pakistani politician and widower of Benazir Bhutto; cochairman of the Pakistan People's Party from 2007 and president of Pakistan from 2008.

Valdis Zatlers (22 Mar 1955), Latvian politician; president from 2007.

Ayman al-Zawahiri (19 Jun 1951, Maadi, Egypt), Egyptian-born physician and militant Islamic extremist leader, the chief lieutenant of Osama bin Laden.

Jurelang Zedkaia (13 Jul 1950, Majuro Atoll, Marshall Islands), Marshallese politician; president of the Marshall Islands from 2009.

(José) Manuel Zelaya (Rosales) (20 Sep 1952, Catacamas, Honduras), Honduran politician (Liberal Party); president, 2006–09.

Sam Zell (Samuel Zielonka; 28 Sep 1941, Chicago IL), American real-estate tycoon.

Renée (Kathleen) Zellweger (25 Apr 1969, Katy TX), American actress.

Robert Zemeckis (14 May 1952, Chicago IL), American film director.

Meles Zenawi (8 May 1955, Adoua, Ethiopia), Ethiopian politician; prime minister from 1995.

Niklas Zennström (1966, Sweden), Swedish Internet entrepreneur; codeveloper of Joost, a popular program for receiving TV broadcasts on a personal computer, and Skype, software for communication over the Internet.

Catherine Zeta-Jones (Catherine Jones; 25 Sep 1969, Swansea, West Glamorgan, Wales), Welsh-born actress.

Zhang Ziyi (9 Feb 1979, Beijing, China), Chinese actress.

Mary (Alice) Zimmerman (23 Aug 1960, Lincoln NE), American stage director.

Slavoj Zizek (21 Mar 1949, Ljubljana, Yugoslavia [now in Slovenia]), Slovenian political philosopher and social critic.

Robert B. Zoellick (25 Jul 1953, Evergreen Park IL), American businessman and government official; US trade representative, 2001–05, deputy secretary of state, 2005–06, and president of the World Bank from 2007.

Mark Zuckerberg (14 May 1984, Dobbs Ferry NY), American Internet entrepreneur; founder and CEO of Facebook, a social networking Web site.

Mortimer B. Zuckerman (4 Jun 1937, Montreal, QC, Canada), Canadian-born American publisher, columnist, and editor in chief of U.S. News & World Report.

Jacob (Gedleyihlekisa) Zuma (12 Apr 1942, Inkandla, Natal, Union of South Africa [now in KwaZulu Natal province, South Africa]), South African politician; deputy president of South Africa, 1999–2005, president of the African National Congress from 2007, and president of South Africa from 2009.

Peter Zumthor (26 Apr 1943, Basel, Switzerland), Swiss architect; recipient of the 2009 Pritzker Prize.

Harald zur Hausen (11 Mar 1936, Gelsenkirchen, Germany), German virologist; cowinner of the 2008 Nobel Prize for Physiology or Medicine.

Obituaries

Death of notable people since 1 July 2009

Dede Allen (Dorothea Corothers Allen; 3 Dec 1923, Cleveland OH—17 Apr 2010, Los Angeles CA), American film editor who helped to revolutionize film editing in Hollywood in such movies as *The Hustler* (1961) and *Bonnie and Clyde* (1967); she received the American Cinema Editors' Career Achievement Award in 1994 and the Motion Picture Editors Guild's Fellowship and Service Award in 2007.

Hédi Annabi (4 Sep 1944, Stains, France—12 Jan 2010, Port-au-Prince, Haiti), Tunisian diplomat who served in the United Nations Department of Peacekeeping Operations from its inception in 1992, from 2007 leading the United Nations Stabilization Mission in Haiti; he was killed by the collapse of the building housing his office in the massive earthquake that devastated the country.

Corazon Aquino (Maria Corazon Cojuangco Aquino; 25 Jan 1933, Tarlac province, Philippines—1 Aug 2009, Makati, Philippines), Philippine political leader who, as president (1986–92) of the Philippines, restored democratic rule in that country after the long dictatorship of Ferdinand Marcos. Her husband, Benigno Simeon Aquino, Jr., a prominent opposition leader, was jailed by Marcos for eight years (1972–80), and her husband's assassination in 1983 galvanized opposition to the Marcos government; when Marcos called for presidential elections in February 1986, Aquino became the unified opposition's candidate, and though she was officially reported to have lost to Marcos, high officials in the military publicly renounced Marcos and proclaimed Aquino the rightful president. She appointed a commission to write a new constitution, which restored the bicameral Congress abolished by Marcos in 1973, held elections to the new Congress, and broke up the monopolies held by Marcos's allies over the economy.

Alexis Argüello ("El Flaco Explosivo"; 19 Apr 1952, Managua, Nicaragua—found dead 1 Jul 2009, Managua, Nicaragua), Nicaraguan boxer who held world titles in three different divisions—featherweight, junior lightweight (now super featherweight), and lightweight—between 1974 and 1982; in 90 bouts as a professional, he compiled an impressive record of 82 victories (64 by knockout) and 8 losses, and he was inducted into the International Boxing Hall of Fame in 1992.

Fabian Bachrach (Louis Fabian Bachrach, Jr.; 9 Apr 1917, Newton MA—26 Feb 2010, Newton MA), American photographer who snapped the iconic image of US Pres. John F. Kennedy that became the official presidential portrait most widely recognized by the public; Bachrach also photographed such famous subjects as baseball player Joe DiMaggio, actor Vincent Price, and oceanographer Jacques Cousteau.

Gene Barry (Eugene Klass; 14 Jun 1919, New York NY—9 Dec 2009, Woodland Hills CA), American actor who glamorized the role of the lawman as the debonair star of the television series *Bat Masterson* (1958–61) and as a millionaire who solved crimes in Los Angeles in *Burke's Law* (1963–65, 1994–95), for which he won the 1965 Golden Globe best actor award.

Alec Victor Bedser (4 Jul 1918, Reading, Berkshire, England—4 Apr 2010, Woking, Surrey, England), English cricketer who was one of the all-time greatest of English fast-medium bowlers and the mainstay of the England attack during the post-World War II years.

James Whyte Black (14 Jun 1924, Uddingston, Scotland—21 Mar 2010), Scottish pharmacologist who received the Nobel Prize for Physiology or Medicine in 1988 (along with George H. Hitchings and Gertrude B. Elion) for his insights into the pharmacotherapeutic potential of receptor-blocking drugs and his development of two such drugs, propranolol (the first clinically useful beta-receptor blocking drug) and cimetidine (a drug that could block histamine receptors), which revolutionized the treatment of coronary heart disease and of gastric and duodenal ulcers, respectively.

Aage Niels Bohr (19 Jun 1922, Copenhagen, Denmark—8 Sep 2009, Copenhagen, Denmark), Danish physicist who shared the 1975 Nobel Prize for Physics with American James Rainwater and American-born Ben R. Mottelson for their work in determining the asymmetrical shapes of certain atomic nuclei; from 1946 he was associated with the Institute for Theoretical Physics (later named the Niels Bohr Institute), founded in Copenhagen by his father (1922 Nobel physics laureate Niels Bohr), whom he succeeded as director (1963–70).

Manute Bol (16 Oct 1962, southern Sudan—19 Jun 2010, Charlottesville VA), Sudanese basketball player and political activist who used his tremendous height—variously identified as 2.31 m (7 ft 7 in) or 2.29 m (7 ft 6 in)—to great effect as one of the NBA's best defensive players throughout his 10-year (1985–95) NBA career with the Washington Bullets, the Golden State Warriors, the Philadelphia 76ers, and the Miami Heat; in 624 games he made 2,086 blocks, for an average of 3.34 per game, the second best in NBA history.

Norman Ernest Borlaug (25 Mar 1914, Cresco IA—12 Sep 2009, Dallas TX), American agricultural scientist and plant pathologist who won the Nobel Prize for Peace in 1970 for his contributions in laying the groundwork of the so-called Green Revolution, the agricultural technological advance that promised to alleviate world hunger.

Louise Bourgeois (25 Dec 1911, Paris, France—31 May 2010, New York NY), French-born American sculptor who was famous for her monumental abstract and often biomorphic works that deal with the relationships of men and women; she was perhaps best known for *Maman* (1999), which was commissioned as the centerpiece of the inaugural exhibit in the vast Turbine Hall at the opening (2000) of London's Tate Modern museum.

Algirdas Mykolas Brazauskas (22 Sep 1932, Rokiskis, Lithuania—26 Jun 2010, Vilnius, Lithuania), Lithuanian politician who was the first elected president (1993–98) of his homeland after it withdrew from the USSR.

Himan Brown (21 Jul 1910, New York NY—4 Jun 2010, New York NY), American radio producer, actor, and director who pioneered early radio drama, notably with the use of sound effects such as the distinct train whistle of *Grand Central Station* (1937–54) and the eerie creaking door on *Inner Sanctum Mysteries* (1941–52); he was inducted into the Radio Hall of Fame in 1990 and earned an American Broadcast Pioneer Award in 1997.

Dennis Vincent Brutus (28 Nov 1924, Salisbury, Southern Rhodesia [now Harare, Zimbabwe]—26 Dec 2009, Cape Town, South Africa), South African poet and antiapartheid activist who penned works that centered on his sufferings and those of his fellow blacks in South Africa; in part owing to his continued pressure on the International Olympic Committee, South Africa was suspended from the 1964 Olympic Games and later was officially expelled from the Olympics, not to compete again until 1992.

Robert Carlyle Byrd (Cornelius Calvin Sale, Jr.; 20 Nov 1917, North Wilkesboro NC—28 Jun 2010, Falls Church VA), American politician who achieved a historical landmark during his tenure as a US Democratic senator (1959–2010) from West Virginia when he became (2006) the longest-serving US senator, and, combined with his three terms (1953–59) as a US representative, he claimed the record in 2009 as the longest-serving member of Congress. He held such Senate leadership positions as Democratic whip (1971–77), majority leader (1977–80, 1987–88), minority leader (1981–86), and president pro tempore (1989–95, 2001–03, and 2007–10); he was a supporter of Pres. Barack Obama's efforts to overhaul health care.

Rafael Antonio Caldera Rodríguez (24 Jan 1916, San Felipe, Venezuela—24 Dec 2009, Caracas, Venezuela), Venezuelan politician who served as president of Venezuela (1969–74; 1994–99) and helped to establish democratic stability; during his first term as president, he restored ties with the Soviet Union, Cuba, and Latin American military dictatorships (Argentina, Panama, and Peru) and granted amnesty to leftist revolutionaries, encouraging them to enter politics peacefully.

Rodrigo Carazo Odio (27 Dec 1926, Cartago, Costa Rica—9 Dec 2009, San José, Costa Rica), Costa Rican politician who served (1978–82) as president of Costa Rica during a time in which he faced both domestic and foreign crises.

Jim Carroll (James Dennis Carroll; 1 Aug 1949, New York NY—11 Sep 2009, New York NY), American author and rock musician who wrote several acclaimed collections of poems but was best known for *The Basketball Diaries* (1978; filmed 1995), an unvarnished account of his drug-addled adolescence in 1960s New York City.

Dixie (Virginia) Carter (25 May 1939, McLemoresville TN—10 Apr 2010, Houston TX), American stage and television actress who often portrayed independent, successful Southern women and was best known for her role as Julia Sugarbaker on the television comedy *Designing Women* (1986–93).

Jacques Chessex (1 Mar 1934, Payerne, Switzerland—9 Oct 2009, Yverdon-les-Bains, Switzerland), Swiss novelist who was honored as the first non-French winner of the Prix Goncourt for his novel *L'Ogre* (1973; *A Father's Love*, 1975), a semiautobiographical account of the troubled relationship between a son and his (recently deceased) father.

Alex Chilton (William Alexander Chilton; 28 Dec 1950, Memphis TN—17 Mar 2010, New Orleans LA), American singer and songwriter who, as the frontman of the seminal power pop band Big Star, crafted a body of work whose influence far outstripped its output; he began his musical career as the lead singer of the Box Tops, whose song "The Letter" spent four weeks in 1967 at the top of the *Billboard* Hot 100 chart, but many considered the song "September Gurls" (1974) to be Chilton's masterpiece.

Liam Clancy (William Clancy; 2 Sep 1935, Carrick-on-Suir, Ireland—4 Dec 2009, Cork, Ireland), Irish folk musician who was the youngest member of the singing Clancy Brothers, who, along with Tommy Makem, helped to popularize traditional Celtic folk music in the US and elsewhere in the 1960s.

Lucille Clifton (Thelma Lucille Sayles; 27 Jun 1936, Depew NY—13 Feb 2010, Baltimore MD), American poet who examined family life, racism, and gender in such books of verse as *Good Times* (1969) and *Blessing the Boats: New and Selected Poems, 1988–2000* (2000), which won the National Book Award; in 2007 Clifton was awarded the Ruth Lilly Poetry Prize.

the Rev. John Bowen Coburn (27 Sep 1914, Danbury CT—8 Aug 2009, Bedford MA), American clergyman who led (1967–76) the Episcopal House of Deputies, part of the Episcopal Church's governing legislative body, during a period of change, in which a new Book of Common Prayer was adopted and women were officially ordained.

Gary Wayne Coleman (8 Feb 1968, Zion IL—28 May 2010, Provo UT), American actor who achieved early stardom in the television sitcom *Diff'rent Strokes* (1978–86) with his portrayal of the younger of two impoverished African American brothers adopted by a wealthy white businessman after their mother, a domestic worker in his household, dies; his trademark catchphrase from the show was, "Whatchoo talkin' 'bout, Willis?"

Walter (Leland) Cronkite (Jr.) (4 Nov 1916, St. Joseph MO—17 Jul 2009, New York NY), American journalist who was a pioneer of television news programming and became known as "the most trusted man in America" as the longtime anchor of the *CBS Evening News with Walter Cronkite* (1962–81); from the anchor chair, he reported on the assassination (1963) of US Pres. John F. Kennedy, the Apollo 11 Moon landing (1969), the Watergate Scandal (1972–75), the resignation (1974) of US Pres. Richard M. Nixon, the historic peace negotiations (1977–78) between Egyptian Pres. Anwar el-Sadat and Israeli Prime Minister Menachem Begin, and the Vietnam War, which he famously denounced as unwinnable in 1968. He won several Emmy and Peabody awards, and in 1981 US Pres. Jimmy Carter awarded him the Presidential Medal of Freedom.

Robert Martin Culp (16 Aug 1930, Oakland CA—24 Mar 2010, Los Angeles CA), American actor who starred as Bill Cosby's partner in the trailblazing espionage television drama *I Spy* (1965–68), the first program to feature a black actor (Cosby) in a leading role.

Evelyn Cunningham (Evelyn Elizabeth Long; 25 Jan 1916, Elizabeth City NC—28 Apr 2010, New York NY), American journalist who, as a pathbreaking newspaperwoman for the *Pittsburgh Courier*, a black weekly, covered some of the most prominent stories of the civil rights era, notably the numerous lynchings that occurred in the segregated South; in 1998 she was one of five reporters who accepted the George Polk Award on behalf of the *Courier* for that newspaper's civil rights coverage.

Merce Cunningham (Mercier Philip Cunningham; 16 Apr 1919, Centralia WA—26 Jul 2009, New York NY), American dancer and choreographer who made a mark on modern dance in the US and Britain by expanding the potentialities of space, time, and movement in the creation of abstract dance, especially in works for the Merce Cunningham Dance Company, which he founded in 1953;

he developed "choreography by chance," a technique in which selected isolated movements are assigned sequence by such random methods as tossing a coin.

Cahal Brendan Cardinal Daly (1 Oct 1917, Loughguile, County Antrim, Ireland—31 Dec 2009, Belfast, Northern Ireland), Irish Roman Catholic prelate who, as the archbishop of Armagh and primate of all Ireland from 1990 until he retired as archbishop emeritus in 1996, publicly denounced as "sinful" the violence advanced by the Irish Republican Army and censured Sinn Fein, the IRA's political wing; though credited as a strong voice for peace, he was criticized for not being sufficiently proactive when the church faced a series of sex scandals.

Joe Deal (Joseph Maurice Deal; 12 Aug 1947, Topeka KS—18 Jun 2010, Providence RI), American photographer who repudiated the tradition of romanticized landscape photography to focus on a detached exploration of human development and man-made structures within nature.

Jimmy (Ray) Dean (10 Aug 1928, Seth Ward TX—13 Jun 2010, Varina VA), American performer and businessman who penned (in less than two hours) and recorded the Grammy Award-winning song "Big Bad John" (1961); Dean also delighted television audiences with his folksy charm and country twang, especially on his variety program *The Jimmy Dean Show*, which ran on ABC (1963–66) after a brief run in 1957 on CBS. Dean founded (1969) the Jimmy Dean Meat Co. and served as its sausage spokesperson (until 2003); in 2010 Dean was elected to the Country Music Hall of Fame.

Roy Rudolph DeCarava (9 Dec 1919, New York NY—27 Oct 2009, New York NY), American photographer who crafted arresting images of African Americans that chronicled daily life in Harlem, the civil rights movement, and performances of such legendary jazz musicians as Louis Armstrong, John Coltrane, Duke Ellington, and Billie Holiday; DeCarava received a National Medal of Arts in 2006.

Hasan di Tiro (25 Sep 1925, Aceh province, Indonesia—3 Jun 2010, Banda Aceh, Aceh province, Indonesia), Indonesian rebel leader who founded (1976) the separatist Free Aceh Movement in the Indonesian province of Aceh, which fought the Jakarta government for more than three decades.

Ronnie James Dio (Ronald James Padavona; 10 Jul 1942, Portsmouth NH—16 May 2010, Los Angeles CA), American rock singer who fronted the heavy metal bands Rainbow, Black Sabbath, and Dio with soaring, nearly operatic vocals and a theatrical stage persona; he was also credited with popularizing the "devil's horns" hand gesture favored by heavy metal music fans.

Victoria Draves (Victoria Taylor Manalo; Vicki; 31 Dec 1924, San Francisco CA—11 Apr 2010, Palm Springs CA), American diver who became the first woman to win gold medals in both 3-m springboard and 10-m platform diving at the same Olympic Games, accomplishing this feat at the 1948 Games in London; she was inducted into the International Swimming Hall of Fame in 1969.

Jean-Louis Dumas (Jean-Louis Robert Frédéric Dumas-Hermès; 2 Feb 1938, Paris, France—1 May 2010, Paris, France), French fashion executive who transformed Hermès (founded in 1837 by his mother's great-grandfather Thierry Hermès) from a prestigious but languishing company into an international high-fashion retailer with some 300 stores and revenues of about US$2.5 billion.

Dominick Dunne (29 Oct 1925, Hartford CT—26 Aug 2009, New York NY), American writer who covered high-profile crime trials for the magazine *Vanity Fair* and wrote popular novels based on true crimes in high society; he was best known for his coverage of the 1995 murder trial of O.J. Simpson.

Guillermo Endara (Guillermo David Endara Galimany; 12 May 1936, Panama City, Panama—28 Sep 2009, Panama City, Panama), Panamanian politician who served (1989–94) as Panama's president after the United States deposed the military strongman Manuel Noriega; he was credited with leading the country back to democracy.

Natalya Khusainova Estemirova (28 Feb 1959, Saratov, Russia, USSR—15 Jul 2009, near Nazaran, Ingushetiya, Russia), Russian human rights activist who documented torture, kidnappings, and murders to give a voice and publicity to victims of political violence in the Russian republic of Chechnya.

Konstantin Petrovich Feoktistov (7 Feb 1926, Voronezh, Russia, USSR—21 Nov 2009, Moscow, Russia), Russian spacecraft designer and cosmonaut who took part, with Vladimir M. Komarov and Boris B. Yegorov, in the world's first multimanned spaceflight, Voskhod 1 (1964).

Art(hur) Ferrante (7 Sep 1921, Brooklyn NY—19 Sep 2009, Longboat Key FL), American pianist who performed with Lou Teicher in the popular two-piano act Ferrante & Teicher, which was known for lush arrangements of the theme songs from such films and Broadway shows as *The Apartment*, *West Side Story*, and *Exodus*.

Sid Fleischman (Albert Sidney Fleischman; 16 Mar 1920, Brooklyn NY—17 Mar 2010, Santa Monica CA), American children's author who used humor to inform the tall tales in his McBroom books and to relate the escapades of his characters in the 1987 Newbery Medal-winning book *The Whipping Boy*.

John Forsythe (John Lincoln Freund; 29 Jan 1918, Penns Grove NJ—1 Apr 2010, Santa Ynez CA), American actor who found fame on three television series: *Bachelor Father* (1957–62), as the guardian to his teenage niece; *Charlie's Angels* (1976–81), as the voice of a multimillionaire private eye who outlines cases via telephone to his female protégés; and particularly as oil mogul Blake Carrington in the nighttime soap opera *Dynasty* (1981–89), a role that brought him two Golden Globe Awards.

Dick Francis (Richard Stanley Francis; 31 Oct 1920, Lawrenny, Pembrokeshire, Wales—14 Feb 2010, Grand Cayman, Cayman Islands), British jockey and mystery writer who thrilled fans with more than 40 detective novels that featured realistic plots centered on the sport of horse racing; three won Edgar Awards—*Forfeit* (1968), *Whip Hand* (1979), and *Come to Grief* (1995).

Frank Frazetta (Frank Frazzetta; 9 Feb 1928, Brooklyn NY—10 May 2010, Fort Myers FL), American artist who produced images of grim warriors, scantily clad maidens, and otherworldly landscapes that graced the covers of countless science-fiction and fantasy novels.

Daryl Francis Gates (30 Aug 1926, Glendale CA—16 Apr 2010, Dana Point CA), American law-enforcement official who served (1978–92) as chief of the Los Angeles Police Department, during which time he faced harsh criticism from those who blamed his aggressive efforts to fight crime for provoking incidents of police brutality and racial unrest in the city; criticism mounted in 1991 following an incident involving four white policemen who were videotaped beating Rodney King, an African American; in April 1992, hours after the policemen's acquittal in the assault case, riots erupted in which more than 50 people were killed, and Gates was forced to resign as police chief the following June.

Larry Simon Gelbart (25 Feb 1928, Chicago IL—11 Sep 2009, Beverly Hills CA), American writer and librettist who wrote comedy hits for the stage, screen, and television but was best known for creating the pilot (1972) for the enormously influential TV smash hit program *M*A*S*H* (1972–83); he captured Tony Awards for best book of a musical for *A Funny Thing Happened on the Way to the Forum* (1962) and for *City of Angels* (1989).

Henry Gibson (James Bateman; 21 Sep 1935, Philadelphia PA—14 Sep 2009, Malibu CA), American actor and comedian who won audiences over with his deadpan delivery of ridiculous self-penned poetry in the 1960s television variety show *Rowan & Martin's Laugh-in* and went on to enjoy a long movie and television career.

Miep Gies (Hermine Santrouschitz; Hermine Santruschitz; 15 Feb 1909, Vienna, Austria-Hungary—11 Jan 2010, Hoorn, Netherlands), Austrian-born heroine who was the last surviving member of the group who concealed Anne Frank and her family from the Nazis in the secret annex above their Amsterdam office for more than two years (9 Jul 1942–4 Aug 1944); Gies rescued Anne's private diary, which she later returned to Anne's father, Otto.

Charlie Gillett (Charles Thomas Gillett; 20 Feb 1942, Morecambe, Lancashire, England—17 Mar 2010, London, England), British radio broadcaster and author who championed world music after having earlier helped to popularize in Britain classic American rock and roll in a career as an influential host of radio programs.

(Charles) David Ginsburg (20 Apr 1912, New York NY—23 May 2010, Alexandria VA), American lawyer and government official who, as a prominent liberal lawyer, wrote national policies, advised presidents and Supreme Court justices, and defended such eminent clients as Henry Kissinger, whom he represented in the high-profile case (decided in 1980) that denied reporters access to telephone transcripts collected while Kissinger served under Pres. Richard M. Nixon.

Vitaly Lazarevich Ginzburg (4 Oct [21 Sep Old Style], 1916, Moscow, Russia—8 Nov 2009, Moscow, Russia), Russian physicist and astrophysicist who won the Nobel Prize for Physics in 2003 (with Alexey A. Abrikosov of Russia and Anthony J. Leggett of Great Britain) for his pioneering work on superconductivity; he was also a member of the team that worked to develop the first Soviet thermonuclear bomb.

William Edwin Gordon (8 Jan 1918, Paterson NJ—16 Feb 2010, Ithaca NY), American engineer and scientist who designed and built the Arecibo Observatory, the world's largest radio telescope, in Puerto Rico; he was the director of the observatory from its completion in 1963 until 1965.

Alfred Gottschalk (7 Mar 1930, Oberwesel, Germany—12 Sep 2009, Cincinnati OH), American rabbi and religious scholar who, as one of the principal institutional leaders within Reform Judaism, ordained the first women rabbis in the US and Israel and oversaw the creation and development of the United States Holocaust Memorial Museum.

Bruce John Graham (1 Dec 1925, La Cumbre, Colombia—6 Mar 2010, Hobe Sound FL), American architect who designed some of the world's tallest, most iconic skyscrapers and was a dominant force behind Chicago's architectural prominence during the late 20th century; his most notable Chicago buildings include the 100-story John Hancock Center (1970), which received (1999) the American Institute of Architects' 25-Year Award; and the 108-story Sears Tower (1974; renamed Willis Tower in 2009), which was constructed by using the groundbreaking tubular frame method and stood as the world's tallest skyscraper until 1996; he was also instrumental in drafting the Chicago 21 Plan, which included the revitalization of Navy Pier as a recreation destination, the straightening of the S curve of Lake Shore Drive, and creation of the Museum Campus.

Peter Graves (Peter Duesler Aurness; 18 Mar 1926, Minneapolis MN—14 Mar 2010, Pacific Palisades CA), American actor who was best known for his portrayal of Jim Phelps, the intensely serious leader of a secret government organization charged with presenting dangerous assignments to a crew of operatives on the television drama series *Mission: Impossible* (1967–73 and 1988–90), for which he won a Golden Globe Award in 1971 as best television actor in a drama; though he was initially reluctant to appear in the wildly popular spoof film *Airplane!* (1980), he ultimately played pilot Capt. Clarence Oveur in that movie and in *Airplane II: The Sequel* (1982); he also shared an Emmy Award (as the narrator) for outstanding informational series for *Judy Garland: Beyond the Rainbow* (1997).

Kathryn Grayson (Zelma Kathryn Elisabeth Hedrick; 9 Feb 1922, Winston-Salem NC—17 Feb 2010, Los Angeles CA), American actress who showcased her coloratura voice in a string of 1940s and '50s movie musicals, notably *Anchors Aweigh* (1945), *Show Boat* (1951), and *Kiss Me Kate* (1953).

Ellie Greenwich (Eleanor Louise Greenwich; 23 Oct 1940, Brooklyn NY—26 Aug 2009, New York NY), American songwriter who harnessed the emotional earnestness of teenage love in a series of pop songs that became iconic classics of the 1960s; she wrote or cowrote such hits as "Leader of the Pack," "Chapel of Love," "(Today I Met) The Boy I'm Gonna Marry," and "River Deep—Mountain High."

Guru (Keith Elam; 17 Jul 1962, Boston MA—19 Apr 2010, New York NY), American rapper who was half (with DJ Premier [Christopher Martin]) of the acclaimed hip-hop duo Gang Starr, who were known for their pioneering fusion of hip-hop and jazz.

Charles Gwathmey (19 Jun 1938, Charlotte NC—3 Aug 2009, New York NY), American architect who was celebrated for his geometric-inspired Modernist architecture; Gwathmey Siegel & Associates, the firm that he founded in 1968 with fellow architect Robert Siegel, was noted for creating massive public buildings (especially museums).

Alexander Meigs Haig, Jr. (2 Dec 1924, Philadelphia PA—20 Feb 2010, Baltimore MD), American general and government official who achieved prominence as White House chief of staff (May 1973–September 1974) under US Pres. Richard Nixon, as commander in chief of American forces in Europe and supreme allied commander of NATO forces (1974–79), and as secretary of state (January 1981–June 1982) under Pres. Ronald Reagan; Haig was widely credited with keeping the White House functioning during the period surrounding Nixon's resignation as president in August 1974, but he left his post shortly after Pres. Gerald Ford issued a presidential pardon for Nixon.

'Abd al-'Aziz al-Hakim (1950, Al-Najaf, Iraq—26 Aug 2009, Tehran, Iran), Iraqi political leader who became head of Iraq's largest Shi'ite political party—the Supreme Council for the Islamic Revolution in Iraq—after years of opposing the regime of Saddam Hussein.

Pierre Harmel (Pierre-Charles-José-Marie Harmel; 16 Mar 1911, Uccle, Belgium—15 Nov 2009, Brussels, Belgium), Belgian statesman who was briefly prime minister of Belgium (1965–66) but who was best known for promoting NATO as a peacekeeping organization in a document that became known as the Harmel doctrine.

Ernie Harwell (William Earnest Harwell; 25 Jan 1918, Washington GA—4 May 2010, Novi MI), American sports broadcaster who was the announcer for a number of Major League Baseball teams—including the Brooklyn Dodgers, the Baltimore Orioles, the New York Giants, and the California Angels—but was indelibly identified as the beloved folksy radio voice of the Detroit Tigers during his more than four decades (1960–91 and 1993–2002) of calling the action on the field for that team; throughout his 55 years as a sportscaster, Harwell delighted listeners with his Southern inflection and unique descriptions, and in 1981 the Baseball Hall of Fame bestowed upon him the Ford C. Frick Award, which celebrates a broadcaster's major contributions to baseball.

Knut Magne Haugland (23 Sep 1917, Rjukan, Norway—25 Dec 2009, Oslo, Norway), Norwegian soldier and adventurer who played a prominent role in the Norwegian resistance during World War II and was particularly well known for his role in a daring raid in 1943 on a Norwegian hydroelectric plant feared to be sought by Germany as a source of atomic power; he later captured the public's imagination as a member of the fabled *Kon-Tiki* expedition, sailing on a balsa-wood raft from Peru to French Polynesia in 1947 to test a theory about pre-Columbian migration patterns.

Dale Hawkins (Delmar Allen Hawkins, Jr.; 22 Aug 1936, Goldmine LA—13 Feb 2010, Little Rock AR), American songwriter and singer whose rockabilly standard "Susie Q" (1957) became a bandstand classic and was chosen by the Rock and Roll Hall of Fame as one of the 500 songs that shaped rock music.

Nicolas George Hayek (19 Feb 1928, Beirut, Lebanon—28 Jun 2010, Biel, Switzerland), Lebanese-born Swiss entrepreneur who rejuvenated the failing Swiss watchmaking industry in the early 1980s when he initiated and marketed the inexpensive and collectable Swatch line of watches.

Raymond Victor Haysbert (19 Jan 1920, Cincinnati OH—24 May 2010, Baltimore MD), American businessman who blazed a trail as a member (1942–45) of the Tuskegee Airmen, the first African American flying unit in the US military, and as coowner of Parks Sausage Co., the first African American–owned business to go public (1969).

Gerald William Heaney (29 Jan 1918, Goodhue MN—22 Jun 2010, Duluth MN), American judge who issued pivotal court rulings on civil rights during his 40 years (1966–2006) on the US Court of Appeals for the 8th Circuit; he was a key figure in eight major desegregation cases.

Dorothy Irene Height (24 Mar 1912, Richmond VA—20 Apr 2010, Washington DC), American civil rights and women's rights activist who was involved in social service for some six decades, four of them as president of the National Council of Negro Women, an umbrella organization that comprises civic, church, educational, labor, community, and professional groups; her numerous honors include the Presidential Medal of Freedom (1994) and the Congressional Gold Medal (2004).

Milan Herzog (23 Aug 1908, Vrbovec, Croatia—20 Apr 2010, Los Angeles CA), Croatian-born American filmmaker who produced numerous instructional films for Encyclopædia Britannica Educational Corp. on a wide range of subjects. He pioneered the use of costumed characters in a medieval history film he produced during the 1950s and was the first to use a children's choir and orchestra to create the musical score in the film *Christmas Rhapsody* (1955).

Don(ald Shepard) Hewitt (14 Dec 1922, New York NY—19 Aug 2009, Bridgehampton NY), American television producer who was best known as the creator and longtime producer (1968–2004) of the compelling television newsmagazine *60 Minutes*, which combined hard-hitting investigative reporting with candid profiles and interviews; he also produced (1960) the first-ever televised US presidential debate; Hewitt won eight Emmy Awards and an Edward R. Murrow Award (2008).

Jeanne Marjorie Holm (23 Jun 1921, Portland OR—15 Feb 2010, Annapolis MD), major general (ret.), US Air Force, who was a pioneer of equity in the armed forces, becoming the first woman to rise to the rank of general in the US Air Force and the first female to become a two-star general in any US armed service.

Benjamin Lawson Hooks (31 Jan 1925, Memphis TN—15 Apr 2010, Memphis TN), American jurist, minister, and government official who, as executive director (1977–92) of the National Association for the Advancement of Colored People (NAACP), helped reinvigorate the flagging organization and was successful in boosting the sagging NAACP membership; he was awarded the Presidential Medal of Freedom in 2007.

Dennis Lee Hopper (17 May 1936, Dodge City KS—29 May 2010, Los Angeles CA), American actor, director, and writer who became a countercultural icon following his starring role as the long-haired Billy in the classic drug-fueled motorcycle drama *Easy Rider* (1969)—the film also marked Hopper's directorial debut and situated him at the forefront of the burgeoning youth-oriented resistance to the status quo. Hopper made his film debut as a high-school gang member in the classic *Rebel Without a Cause* (1955) opposite James Dean and went on to star in films such as *Cool Hand Luke* (1967), *Blue Velvet* (1986), and *Hoosiers* (1986); he later earned an Emmy Award nomination for the TV movie *Paris Trout* (1991). In addition to his more than 100 films, Hopper was known for his photographs and paintings, which were featured in a major retrospective in 2001.

Lena (Mary Calhoun) Horne (30 Jun 1917, Brooklyn NY—9 May 2010, New York NY), American singer and actress who was a velvety-voiced jazz songstress who broke down racial barriers as the first black performer to land a long-term contract with a major Hollywood studio and who went on to promote civil rights while she showcased her expressive vocals on the stage, on television, in films, on recordings, and in nightclubs; her one-woman show, *Lena Horne: The Lady and Her Music* (1981), garnered a Drama Critics' Circle Award and a special-achievement Tony Award; in 1984 she received a Kennedy Center Honor for lifetime contribution to the arts, and in 1989 she was the recipient of a Grammy Award for lifetime achievement.

John (Wilden) Hughes (Jr.) (18 Feb 1950, Lansing MI—6 Aug 2009, New York NY), American filmmaker who captured the essence of teen angst in comedic coming-of-age tales; he wrote and directed the iconic films *Sixteen Candles* (1984), *The Breakfast Club* (1985), *Ferris Bueller's Day Off* (1986), and *Planes, Trains, and Automobiles* (1987) and wrote the screenplays for such films as *Mr. Mom* (1983), *Pretty in Pink* (1986), and three of the four *Home Alone* movies (1990, 1992, 1997).

Ruby Hunter (1955, South Australia, Australia—17 Feb 2010, Victoria, Australia), Australian Aboriginal singer and songwriter who, with her partner, Archie Roach, embodied the spirit and experience of the "stolen generation" of Aborigines in music and performances in Australia and elsewhere.

Marvin Isley (18 Aug 1953, Cincinnati OH—6 Jun 2010, Chicago IL), American bass guitarist and songwriter who reimagined the gritty rhythm-and-blues singing trio the Isley Brothers (Kelly, Rudolph, and Ronald); after joining (1973) his older brothers (together with another brother, Ernie, and brother-in-law Chris Jasper), Marvin cowrote many of the band's greatest hits, including "That Lady (Part 1)" (1973); in 1992 the group was inducted into the Rock and Roll Hall of Fame.

Jeanne-Claude (Jeanne-Claude Denat de Guillebon; 13 Jun 1935, Casablanca, Morocco—18 Nov 2009, New York NY), French environmental artist who, with her artist husband, Christo, created controversial outdoor sculptures and huge temporary displays of fabrics and plastics, including *The Gates, Central Park, New York City, 1979–2005*, built in 2005 along 37 km (23 mi) of walkway in Central Park and featuring 7,503 steel gates standing 5 m (16 ft) high and decorated with saffron-colored cloth panels.

Lionel Charles Jeffries (10 Jun 1926, London, England—19 Feb 2010, Poole, Dorset, England), British actor and director who was a prematurely bald, mustachioed character actor and a familiar face in scores of British films and television programs, including *Camelot* (1967) and *Chitty Chitty Bang Bang* (1968), in which he convincingly played actor Dick Van Dyke's father despite actually being slightly younger than Van Dyke; Jeffries also wrote and directed *The Railway Children* (1970), which in 1999 the British Film Institute voted one of Britain's 100 best films.

Lester Johnson (27 Jan 1919, Minneapolis MN—30 May 2010, Westhampton NY), American painter who was known for bold, energetic canvases depicting human figures; his association with the Eighth Street Club, a social group that consisted mainly of Abstract Expressionists, strongly influenced his style and technique.

Hank Jones (Henry William Jones, Jr.; 31 July/Aug 1918, Vicksburg MS—16 May 2010, Bronx NY), American jazz musician who played lyrical solo piano and accompanied other musicians with such taste, sensitivity, and versatility that he became one of the most in-demand modern-jazz musicians; performing (1947–51) with the all-star Jazz at the Philharmonic troupe led to his accompanying (1947–53) Ella Fitzgerald, Charlie Parker, Lester Young, Billie Holiday, Miles Davis, and Benny Goodman, among others. Jones won a National Medal of Arts in 2008 and a Grammy Lifetime Achievement Award in 2009.

Jennifer Jones (Phylis Lee Isley; 2 Mar 1919, Tulsa OK—17 Dec 2009, Malibu CA), American actress who lit up movie screens in the 1940s and '50s with her luminous performances in roles that alternated between fresh-faced naifs and tempestuous vixens; she won (1943) a best actress Academy Award for her star-making turn as a French peasant girl in *The Song of Bernadette* (1943).

Stan(ley Paul) Jones (24 Nov 1931, Altoona PA—21 May 2010, Broomfield CO), American football player who established himself as a strong and versatile offensive and defensive lineman for the NFL's Chicago Bears (1954–65); he was one of the first NFL players to use a weightlifting regimen to build muscle; in his final college season (1953) he earned the Knute Rockne Memorial Trophy for outstanding lineman and helped the team to a place in the Orange Bowl; Jones was voted to the Pro Bowl seven times, and in 1991 he was inducted into the Pro Football Hall of Fame.

Lech Kaczynski (18 Jun 1949, Warsaw, Poland—10 Apr 2010, Smolensk, Russia), Polish politician who, as president of Poland (2005–10), was known as a fierce nationalist and religious conservative who advocated a strong central government, promoted both tax cuts and a strong economic safety net, and was often critical of the EU; in 2009, however, having secured opt-outs for Poland from EU policy on some social issues, including abortion, he initialed the Lisbon Treaty. He died in a plane crash on his way to commemorate the Katyn Massacre, the mass execution of Polish military officers by the Soviet Union during World War II.

Dorothy Kamenshek (Dottie; Kammie; 21 Dec 1925, Norwood OH—17 May 2010, Palm Desert CA), American baseball player who was a sensational left-handed first baseman and leadoff hitter for the Rockford (IL) Peaches in the All-American Girls Professional Baseball League (AAGPBL); during her professional career, she was named to seven All-Star teams, won batting titles in 1946 and 1947 (hitting .316 and .306, respectively), and held the all-time AAGPBL batting average record (.292). The exploits of Kamenshek and her teammates inspired the 1992 film *A League of Their Own,* and in 1999 *Sports Illustrated* named Kamenshek number 100 on its list of top female athletes of the century.

Ted Kennedy (Edward Moore Kennedy; 22 Feb 1932, Boston MA—25 Aug 2009, Hyannis Port MA), American politician who was a respected US senator (1962–2009), as well as a prominent figure in the Democratic Party and in liberal politics in general for more than four decades. Kennedy, the last surviving brother of Pres. John F. Kennedy, was also a noteworthy spokesman for the policies that had come to be associated with his family name—support for social-welfare legislation and active participation in world affairs; he was known as the "lion of the Senate," serving as a leading advocate for many liberal causes, including voting rights, fair housing, consumer protection, and national health insurance, and at the same time, he was recognized for his willingness to cooperate with Republicans to advance important legislation, such as the No Child Left Behind Act (2001). In the last months of his life, he was granted an honorary British knighthood (KBE) and the US Presidential Medal of Freedom.

Ted Kennedy (Theodore Kennedy; "Teeder"; 12 Dec 1925, Humberstone, ON, Canada—14 Aug 2009,

Port Colborne, ON, Canada), Canadian ice hockey player who, as the tenacious center and longtime captain of the NHL's Toronto Maple Leafs, led the team to five Stanley Cup championships (in the 1944–45, 1946–47, 1947–48, 1948–49, and 1950–51 seasons); considered by many to be the best face-off player in the NHL, he made the All-Star team five times and in 1955 was awarded the Hart Memorial Trophy as the NHL's most valuable player, and in 1966 he was inducted into the Hockey Hall of Fame.

Richard Darwin Keynes (14 Aug 1919, London, England–12 Jun 2010, Cambridge, England), British physiologist who was among the first in Britain to trace the movements of sodium and potassium during the transmission of a nerve impulse by using radioactive sodium and potassium; he also conducted research on English naturalist Charles Darwin (his maternal great-grandfather) and on economist John Maynard Keynes (his paternal uncle); he was elected in 1959 to the Royal Society, which he later served (1965–68) as vice president, and was created CBE in 1984.

Kim Dae-Jung (6 Jan 1924?, Mokp'o, Japanese-occupied Korea [now in South Korea]–18 Aug 2009, Seoul, South Korea), South Korean politician who served (1998–2003) as South Korean president, the first opposition leader to win election to that office; he was awarded (2000) the Nobel Prize for Peace for his efforts to restore democracy in South Korea and to improve relations with North Korea—his "sunshine" policy allowed South Koreans to visit relatives in the North and eased rules governing South Korean investment in the country.

Girija Prasad Koirala (1925, Bihar state, British India–20 Mar 2010, Kathmandu, Nepal), Indian-born Nepalese politician who served four times as prime minister of Nepal (1991–94, 1998–99, 2000–01, 2006–08); his administrations were plagued by persistent problems, including factional disputes between Koirala and his rivals within the ruling Nepali Congress Party, the murder in 2001 of King Birendra and subsequent clashes with his autocratic successor, King Gyanendra, and a bloody uprising (1996–2006) of Maoist insurgents.

André-Dieudonné Kolingba (12 Aug 1936, Bangui, Ubangi-Shari, French Equatorial Africa [now Bangui, Central African Republic]–7 Feb 2010, Paris, France), Central African Republic army commander and politician who held dictatorial rule over his country for 12 years, from 1981, when he overthrew Pres. David Dacko, until he reluctantly stepped down in 1993, after having lost a presidential election to Ange-Félix Patassé.

Jack Kramer (John Albert Kramer; 1 Aug 1921, Las Vegas NV–12 Sep 2009, Los Angeles CA), American tennis player who won the All-England (Wimbledon) singles (1947) and men's doubles (1946 and 1947) championships, captured the US singles (1946–47), men's doubles (1940–41, 1943, 1947), and mixed doubles (1941) titles, and in 1946 and 1947 was on the victorious American Davis Cup teams; he was also instrumental in the organization of the Association of Tennis Professionals, a union for men players, and he was named to the International Tennis Hall of Fame in 1968.

Edwin Gerhard Krebs (6 Jun 1918, Lansing IA–21 Dec 2009, Seattle WA), American biochemist who was awarded (with Edmond H. Fischer) the 1992 Nobel Prize for Physiology or Medicine for discovering reversible protein phosphorylation, which is a biochemical process that regulates the activities of proteins in cells and thus governs countless processes that are necessary for life.

Irving William Kristol (22 Jan 1920, Brooklyn NY–18 Sep 2009, Arlington VA), American essayist, editor, and publisher who was best known as an intellectual leader of the neoconservative movement in the United States; his championing of supply-side economics and conservative moral values, his aggressive anticommunism, and his insistence on using US power to shape the world "in accord with our national interests" greatly influenced the domestic and foreign policies of the Ronald Reagan, George H.W. Bush, and George W. Bush administrations.

Kjell Eugenio Laugerud García (24 Jan 1930, Guatemala City, Guatemala–9 Dec 2009, Guatemala City, Guatemala), Guatemalan politician who served (1974–78) as president of Guatemala.

Phillip Garth Law (21 Apr 1912, Tallangatta, VIC, Australia–28 Feb 2010, Melbourne, VIC, Australia), Australian polar explorer who earned the nickname "Mr. Antarctica" for his devotion to the scientific study of that continent and to the expansion of the Australian Antarctic Territory there; as director (1949–66) of the Australian Antarctic Division and leader of the Australian National Antarctic Research Expedition, he mapped more than 5,000 km (3,100 mi) of Antarctic coastline and established three permanent research stations; he was appointed Officer of the Order of Australia (1975) and advanced to Companion of the Order of Australia (1995).

Art Linkletter (Gordon Arthur Kelly; Arthur Gordon Linkletter; 17 Jul 1912, Moose Jaw, SK, Canada–26 May 2010, Los Angeles CA), Canadian-born American broadcasting host who charmed radio and television audiences for more than 20 years with his amiable ad-libs and his ability to put those he interviewed—particularly young children—at ease; he was the emcee for the variety show *House Party* (1944–67), which involved the audience in spontaneous contests and activities; he created the show's popular segment "Kids Say the Darndest Things," and he hosted another audience-participation show, *People Are Funny*, on radio (1942–59) and TV (1954–61). He was granted a lifetime achievement Emmy Award in 2003.

Oswaldo Enrique López Arellano (30 Jun 1921, Danlí, Honduras–16 May 2010, Tegucigalpa, Honduras), Honduran military and political leader who toppled two civilian governments and held power as a military strongman from 1963 to 1971 and again from 1972 to 1975; as the longtime head of the Honduran military, he first assumed presidential power after leading a coup in 1963 against Pres. José Ramón Villeda Morales, and in December 1972 he staged another coup, against Pres. Ramón Ernesto Cruz.

Ali Hassan al-Majid ("Chemical Ali"; 1941, Tikrit, Iraq–25 Jan 2010, Baghdad, Iraq), Iraqi official who, as a loyal henchman to former Iraqi strongman Saddam Hussein, earned his nickname for his leadership of a campaign in the late 1980s against Iraq's Kurdish population in which mass executions, starvation, and chemical weapons laid waste to many Kurdish villages and killed an estimated 120,000 Kurds; after the Persian Gulf War, Majid bloodily put down the Shi'ite uprising in southern Iraq and the Kurdish uprising in northern Iraq, leaving some 30,000 people dead; he was captured after Saddam's overthrow by the US-led invasion in 2003, and he was executed after having been tried and found guilty of genocide and crimes against humanity.

Karl Malden (Mladen Sekulovich; 22 Mar 1912, Chicago IL—1 Jul 2009, Los Angeles CA), American actor who won critical acclaim for his strong character roles, most notably alongside Marlon Brando in *A Streetcar Named Desire* (1951), in a role that won him the Academy Award for best supporting actor (1951), and *On the Waterfront* (1954); he reached a new audience as lead detective Mike Stone in the television show *The Streets of San Francisco* (1972–77) opposite a young Michael Douglas; Malden served (1989–92) as president of the Academy of Motion Picture Arts and Sciences, and he was presented with the 2003 Screen Actors Guild's Life Achievement Award.

Wilma Pearl Mankiller (18 Nov 1945, Tahlequah OK—6 Apr 2010, Adair county, Oklahoma), Native American leader and activist who became principal Cherokee chief in 1985, the first woman chief of a major American tribe; her administration focused on lowering the high unemployment rate and increasing educational opportunities, improving community health care, and developing the economy of northeastern Oklahoma, and she also established the Institute for Cherokee Literacy; she was inducted (1993) into the National Women's Hall of Fame, and in 1998 she received the Presidential Medal of Freedom.

Al Martino (Alfred Cini; 7 Oct 1927, Philadelphia PA—13 Oct 2009, Springfield PA), American pop singer who scored hits in the 1950s and '60s with a number of smoothly crooned romantic ballads but was perhaps best known for his film role as Johnny Fontane, the wedding singer who uses his Mafia ties to jump-start his career, in *The Godfather* (1972); notable among his successes is "Spanish Eyes" (1965), one of nine of his songs that reached the US top 40 between 1963 and 1967.

Rue McClanahan (Eddi-Rue McClanahan; 21 Feb 1934, Healdton OK—3 Jun 2010, New York NY), American actress who portrayed the liberated sensual Southern belle Blanche Devereaux on the television sitcom *The Golden Girls* (1985–92), a role for which she won an Emmy Award in 1987; Blanche's talk of her sexual exploits provided her three housemates—two middle-aged women (Betty White and Bea Arthur) and the latter's screen mother (Estelle Getty)—fodder for such comic zingers as "Your life's an open blouse." Prior to *The Golden Girls*, McClanahan starred in a series of Off-Broadway productions and captured an Obie Award in 1970 for her role as the "other woman" in *Who's Happy Now?*

Frank McCourt (Francis McCourt; 19 Aug 1930, Brooklyn NY—19 Jul 2009, New York NY), American author and teacher who was perhaps best known for the Pulitzer Prize–winning memoir *Angela's Ashes* (1996), a vivid portrayal of a Dickensian childhood amid the grinding conditions of Irish slum life that also won the National Book Critics Circle Award and was adapted into a well-received film (1999); he taught public school for 29 years.

Dick McGuire (Richard Joseph McGuire; "Tricky Dick"; 26 Jan 1926, New York NY—3 Feb 2010, Huntington NY), American basketball player and coach who enjoyed a career of more than half a century with the New York Knicks and Detroit Pistons professional NBA teams; he played in seven All-Star games and served as the floor leader of three Knicks teams

that went on to the NBA finals, and he was inducted into the Basketball Hall of Fame in 1993.

Malcolm Robert Andrew McLaren (22 Jan 1946, London, England—8 Apr 2010, Switzerland), British rock impresario and musician who helped birth punk culture in his role as the colorfully provocative manager of the punk band the Sex Pistols; after a brief stint managing and costuming the American glam rock band the New York Dolls, in 1975 he began working with a band he dubbed the Sex Pistols, and following the Sex Pistols' collapse in 1978, McLaren guided the image and career of new-wave band Adam and the Ants and formed a spin-off act, Bow Wow Wow.

Steve (LaTreal) McNair (14 Feb 1973, Mount Olive MS—4 Jul 2009, Nashville TN), American football player who played 13 NFL seasons (1995–2008) as one of a small number of high-profile African American quarterbacks; he was the third NFL draft pick in 1995, selected by the Houston Oilers (later the Tennessee Titans), whom he led in 2000 to Super Bowl XXXIV; he played in three Pro Bowls and was named joint Most Valuable Player in 2003.

Robert S(trange) McNamara (9 Jun 1916, San Francisco CA—6 Jul 2009, Washington DC), US government official who served (1961–68) as US secretary of defense and played a major role in the country's military involvement in Vietnam—though he initially advocated the deepening US military involvement in Vietnam, by 1967 he was openly seeking a way to launch peace negotiations; he later served (1968–81) as president of the World Bank.

(Lee) Alexander McQueen (17 Mar 1969, London, England—found dead 11 Feb 2010, London, England), British fashion designer who was known for his precise tailoring, shocking catwalk fashion shows, and groundbreaking clothes, including what he called "bumster" trousers (1992)—pants cut so low that they revealed the cleavage of the backside; despite his "enfant terrible" image, McQueen was named British Designer of the Year in 1996 (an honor he received three more times), and later that year he took over as the head designer of the French couture house Givenchy while maintaining his own eponymous design label in London.

Stanley Middleton (1 Aug 1919, Bulwell, Nottinghamshire, England—25 Jul 2009, Nottingham, Nottinghamshire, England), British novelist who was a prolific author—he published a book nearly every year from the 1960s through the '90s; his novel *Holiday* (1974) garnered him the Booker Prize, which he shared with South African Nobel laureate Nadine Gordimer.

Robin Milner (Arthur John Robin Gorell Milner; 13 Jan 1934, Yealmpton, Devon, England—20 Mar 2010, Cambridge, England), British computer scientist who won the A.M. Turing Award, the highest honor in computer science, in 1991 for his work with automatic theorem provers, the ML ("metalanguage") computer programming language, and a general theory of concurrency; he was elected to the Royal Society in 1988.

Reinhard Mohn (29 Jun 1921, Gütersloh, Germany—3 Oct 2009, Steinhagen, Germany), German businessman who reversed the fortunes of his family's ailing publishing house, Bertelsmann, making it into one of the world's leading media empires.

Carlos Monsiváis (4 May 1938, Mexico City, Mexico—19 Jun 2010, Mexico City, Mexico), Mexican journalist, critic, and political activist who championed leftist social causes (including feminism, minority rights, gay rights, and the 1994 Zapatista uprising for Indian rights) and explored Mexican society with a journalistic style that often emphasized his acerbic wit and satiric tone.

Hossein Ali Montazeri (Husayn-ʿAli Muntaziri; 1922, Najafabad, Iran—20 Dec 2009, Qom, Iran), Iranian cleric who became one of the highest-ranking authorities in Shiʿite Islam; Ayatollah Montazeri (grand ayatollah after 1984) was emphatic in his defense of human rights in Iran, however, and he spent long periods under arrest during both the regime of Mohammad Reza Shah Pahlavi and the Islamic republic that he himself helped to establish.

Charles Lee Moore (9 Mar 1931, Hackleburg AL—11 Mar 2010, Palm Beach Gardens FL), American photographer who documented (1958–65) civil rights struggles in gripping black-and-white images, some of the most enduring of which were published in *Life* magazine; he recorded the arrest in 1958 of Martin Luther King, Jr., the riots that occurred when in 1962 black student James Meredith integrated the University of Mississippi, and the events in 1965 when police teargassed voting-rights marchers in Selma AL.

Howard Leslie Morrison (18 Aug 1935, Rotorua, New Zealand—24 Sep 2009, Rotorua, New Zealand), New Zealand entertainer who was beloved as the leader of the often humorous Howard Morrison Quartet (1956–64) and then as a solo crooner; he was made OBE in 1976, named New Zealand's Entertainer of the Decade in 1989, and awarded a knighthood in 1990.

Robert Adam Mosbacher, Sr. (11 Mar 1927, Mount Vernon NY—24 Jan 2010, Houston TX), American business executive and government official who was a key confidante to George H.W. Bush, advising him to drop out of the US presidential race during Ronald Reagan's 1980 run for office and later taking on the role of chief fund-raiser in Bush's 1988 successful presidential campaign; afterwards, Mosbacher served as commerce secretary (1989–92) and was a leading advocate for the adoption of the North American Free Trade Agreement (NAFTA).

Ces Mountford (Cecil Mountford; "The Blackball Bullet"; 16 Jun 1919, Blackball, New Zealand—19 Jul 2009, Gold Coast, QLD, Australia), New Zealand rugby player and coach who was considered to be one of the best stand-off halves in the sport of rugby league; he was made MBE in 1987 and in 1990 was one of the inaugural inductees into the New Zealand Sports Hall of Fame.

John Patrick Murtha, Jr. (17 Jun 1932, New Martinsville WV—8 Feb 2010, Arlington VA), American politician who was respected for his support of the military and known for masterful dealmaking in his 19 terms of office as a Democratic member of the US House of Representatives from Pennsylvania; his withdrawal in 2005 of his prior support for the Iraq War was therefore notable.

Abel Tendekayi Muzorewa (14 Apr 1925, Old Umtali, Southern Rhodesia [now Zimbabwe]—8 Apr 2010, Harare, Zimbabwe), Rhodesian-born cleric and politician who served as prime minister of his homeland from 29 May to 11 Dec 1979, during the transitional period from white-ruled Southern Rhodesia to black-ruled Zimbabwe.

Patricia Neal (Patsy Louise Neal; 20 Jan 1926, Packard KY—8 Aug 2010, Edgartown MA), American motion picture actress known for her deeply intelligent performances and for her rehabilitation and triumphant return to films following a series of strokes; by 1947 she was a student at the Actors Studio and had won a Tony Award for her performance in *Another Part of the Forest*, and she delivered one of her most renowned film performances in *Hud* (1963), winning the best actress Oscar for her efforts.

Ronald Neame (23 Apr 1911, London, England—16 Jun 2010, Los Angeles CA), British filmmaker who was one of Britain's most admired cinematographers in the 1930s and '40s, notably on a series of acclaimed films with director David Lean; Neame himself later directed such hits as the drama *The Prime of Mrs. Jean Brodie* (1969) and the disaster movie *The Poseidon Adventure* (1972); he was made CBE in 1996.

Marshall Warren Nirenberg (10 Apr 1927, Brooklyn NY—15 Jan 2010, New York NY), American biochemist who was corecipient, with Robert William Holley and Har Gobind Khorana, of the 1968 Nobel Prize for Physiology or Medicine; Nirenberg was cited for his role in deciphering the genetic code; his research earned him the National Medal of Science in 1965, and in 1968 he and Khorana were recognized with an Albert Lasker Basic Medical Research Award.

Robert (David Sanders) Novak (26 Feb 1931, Joliet IL—18 Aug 2009, Washington DC), American political journalist and commentator who wrote the syndicated newspaper column "Inside Report" for more than 40 years and from 1980 espoused a conservative viewpoint on a number of political TV talk shows, notably CNN's *Crossfire*; in 2003 he controversially identified Valerie Plame as a CIA operative in a column after her husband, Joseph Wilson, had publicly asserted that the administration of Pres. George W. Bush had distorted intelligence to justify the 2003 invasion of Iraq.

Peter O'Donnell (11 Apr 1920, London, England—3 May 2010, Brighton, England), British writer who created the fictional action heroine Modesty Blaise, a glamorous and clever master-criminal-turned-secret-agent; working with a series of cartoonists, O'Donnell wrote more than 10,000 daily comic strips featuring Blaise and her devoted Cockney sidekick, Willie Garvin.

Merlin Jay Olsen (15 Sep 1940, Logan UT—11 Mar 2010, Duarte CA), American football player, sports announcer, and actor who was the left tackle (1962–76) for the NFL's Los Angeles Rams, making up a crucial part of the formidable line that was heralded as the "Fearsome Foursome"; in the 1962–63 season, Olsen was named the NFL Rookie of the Year; in 1973 he was voted the National Football Conference Defensive Lineman of the Year, and for every year but his last in the league he was voted to the Pro Bowl; he was inducted into the College Football Hall of Fame in 1980 and the Pro Football Hall of Fame in 1982. After leaving the Rams, Olsen served as an NFL commentator, television spokesperson, and TV actor, best known for his recurring role as Jonathan Garvey (1977–81) on *Little House on the Prairie* and as the star of *Father Murphy* (1981–83).

Fess Parker (Fess Elisha Parker, Jr.; 16 Aug 1924, Fort Worth TX—18 Mar 2010, Santa Ynez Valley, California), American actor who brought a folksy charm and imposing 1.98-m (6-ft 6-in) physique to the television roles of the iconic American frontiersmen Davy Crockett and Daniel Boone.

Robert (Brown) Parker (17 Sep 1932, Springfield MA—18 Jan 2010, Cambridge MA), American author who created two well-known detective series—one featuring Spenser, a hard-boiled, wise-cracking Boston-based private eye who also exhibits a sensitive side as he solves crimes and ruminates on human nature, and the other featuring Jesse Stone, a divorced alcoholic who serves as the chief of police in a Massachusetts town; Parker was the recipient in 2002 of the Grand Master Award from the Mystery Writers of America.

Arnall Patz (14 Jun 1920, Elberton GA—11 Mar 2010, Pikesville MD), American ophthalmologist who discovered the leading cause of blindness in premature infants in the 1950s and later helped develop one of the first argon laser treatments for diabetic retinopathy and other eye conditions characterized by overgrowth and leaking of blood vessels in the retina; he was a corecipient, with V. Everett Kinsey, of the Albert Lasker Clinical Medical Research Award in 1956 and was awarded the Presidential Medal of Freedom in 2004.

Les Paul (Lester William Polsfuss; 9 Jun 1915, Waukesha WI—13 Aug 2009, White Plains NY), American musician and inventor who designed a solid-body electric guitar in 1941 that acquired a devoted following—its versatility and balance made it the favored instrument of such guitarists as Eric Clapton, Jimmy Page, and Peter Frampton; in 1977 Paul earned a Grammy Award for *Chester & Lester* (1976), an instrumental duet album with country legend Chet Atkins, and in 2006 he collected two more Grammys; Paul was inducted into the Grammy Hall of Fame (1978), the Rock and Roll Hall of Fame (1988), and the National Inventors Hall of Fame (2005), and he was awarded a National Medal of Arts in 2007.

Teddy Pendergrass (Theodore DeReese Pendergrass; 26 Mar 1950, Kingstree SC—13 Jan 2010, Bryn Mawr PA), American rhythm-and-blues vocalist who embodied the smooth Philly soul sound of the 1970s as lead singer for Harold Melvin and the Blue Notes before embarking on a successful solo career.

Irving Penn (16 Jun 1917, Plainfield NJ—7 Oct 2009, New York NY), American photographer who was noted for his sophisticated fashion images, which communicated elegance and luxury through compositional refinement and clarity of line, and for his incisive celebrity portraits, in which he combined simplicity and directness with great formality.

Alan Frederick Plater (15 Apr 1935, Jarrow, England—25 Jun 2010, London, England), British dramatist and screenwriter who wrote skillful, naturalistic dialogue for television, theater, film, and radio in a prolific career spanning six decades; he was best known for his TV scripts for such shows as the influential police series *Z Cars* (1963–65) and *A Very British Coup* (1988), which won (1989) a British Academy of Film and Television Arts (BAFTA) TV award for best drama series; Plater received the Dennis Potter Writing Award from BAFTA (2005) and a lifetime achievement award from the Writers' Guild of Great Britain (2007); he was made CBE in 2005.

Walter Plowright (20 Jul 1923, Sutton Bridge, Lincolnshire, England—20 Feb 2010, Goring, Oxfordshire, England), British veterinary scientist who developed an effective and inexpensive vaccine that wiped out rinderpest (cattle plague)—an acute, highly contagious viral disease of cloven-hoofed ruminant animals, which had previously killed up to 90% of affected herds and devastated cattle and water buffalo-based African and Asian agricultural communities; his honors include a CMG (1974)

and admission to the Royal Society (1981); in 1999 he was awarded the World Food Prize.

Sigmar Polke (13 Feb 1941, Öls, Germany [now Olesnica, Poland]—10 Jun 2010, Cologne, Germany), German artist who rendered complex, layered paintings that played an important role in the resurgence of modern German art; in the 1980s he and other German artists—including Jörg Immendorff, Anselm Kiefer, and Georg Baselitz—were part of a movement known as Neo-Expressionism.

Pavel Romanovich Popovich (5 Oct 1929, Uzin, Ukraine, USSR—30 Sep 2009, Gurzuf, Ukraine), Soviet cosmonaut who became the sixth man in orbit when he piloted the Vostok 4 spacecraft (12–15 Aug 1962), and he and Andriyan G. Nikolayev, who was launched on 11 August in Vostok 3, were the first two men to be in space simultaneously; Popovich was also the commander of the Soyuz 14 mission (3–19 Jul 1974), on which he and flight engineer Yury P. Artyukhin docked their craft with Salyut 3, a military space station that had been placed in orbit on 25 June, and engaged in a 15-day program of reconnaissance of Earth's surface.

Pete(r Alexander Greenlaw) Quaife (31 Dec 1943, Tavistock, Devonshire, England—23 Jun 2010, Herlev, Denmark), British musician who was a founding member of the British Invasion rock band the Kinks and played bass guitar during their 1960s rise to fame; during his time with the Kinks, the band had 12 Top 10 songs in Britain; Quaife was inducted into the Rock and Roll Hall of Fame with the Kinks in 1990.

Corin William Redgrave (16 Jul 1939, London, England—6 Apr 2010, London, England), veteran British character actor and ardent left-wing political activist who to many people was best known as the "prince" of the renowned Redgrave family acting dynasty—he was the son of Sir Michael Redgrave and Rachel Kempson, the grandson of silent-film actor Roy Redgrave, and the brother of actresses Vanessa Redgrave and Lynn Redgrave; perhaps Corin's best role was as the brutal warden, Boss Whalen, in Tennessee Williams's *Not About Nightingales* (1998), which earned him a Laurence Olivier Award and, after the play moved to Broadway in 1999, a Tony nomination for best actor.

Lynn Rachel Redgrave (8 Mar 1943, London, England—2 May 2010, Kent CT), British-born actress who was a member of the renowned Redgrave family acting dynasty; she was the younger sister of Vanessa Redgrave and Corin Redgrave, the daughter of Sir Michael Redgrave and Rachel Kempson, and the granddaughter of silent-film actor Roy Redgrave. Lynn Redgrave made her professional debut as Helena in Shakespeare's *A Midsummer Night's Dream* in 1962 and her screen debut in *Tom Jones* in 1963, the same year she was chosen as a founding member of the National Theatre (later the Royal National Theatre) under Sir Laurence Olivier; she gained international recognition—as well as a New York Film Critics Circle Award and the first of her two Academy Award nominations—for her star turn in the romantic comedy *Georgy Girl* (1966); she was made OBE in 2002.

(Granville) Oral Roberts (24 Jan 1918, near Ada OK—15 Dec 2009, Newport Beach CA), American evangelist who was widely recognized as one of the leading figures in Christianity in the US during the latter half of the 20th century, bringing Pentecostal theology and practice into the mainstream by means of a vast business empire and a pervasive media presence. In the late 1940s he became an itinerant preacher at revival meetings, and he expanded his ministry in the 1950s through regular radio and television broadcasts, which gave him a national audience, and further extended his brand with the founding (1963) of Oral Roberts University, Tulsa OK, which eventually became the largest charismatic Christian university in the world.

Pernell Elvin Roberts, Jr. (18 May 1928, Waycross GA—24 Jan 2010, Malibu CA), American actor who was best remembered for his television portrayals of two characters: the brainy and debonair Adam Cartwright (the eldest of three sons) on the long-running western *Bonanza* (1959–73; he appeared until 1965) and the eponymous compassionate chief of surgery at a San Francisco hospital on *Trapper John, M.D.* (1979–86).

Robin Evan Roberts (30 Sep 1926, near Springfield IL—6 May 2010, Temple Terrace FL), American baseball player who was a phenomenal right-handed pitcher (1948–61) for the major league Philadelphia Phillies; as one of the famed "Whiz Kids," he led the team to the 1950 National League pennant, the franchise's first in 35 years; he led the league in victories (1952–55), innings pitched (1951–55), and complete games (1952–56), and he won at least 20 games every season from 1950 to 1955; he was inducted into the Baseball Hall of Fame in 1976.

Bobby Robson (Robert William Robson; 18 Feb 1933, Sacriston, Durham county, England—31 Jul 2009, Durham county, England), British association football (soccer) player and manager who was one of England's most respected athletes; he played 20 matches with the national team, including appearances in the 1958 and 1962 World Cup finals, and later, as the England manager (1982–90), he steered the team to two more World Cup finals tournaments (1986, 1990); he was knighted in 2002 and inducted into the English Football Hall of Fame in 2003.

Egon Ronay (24 Jul 1915?, Budapest, Austria-Hungary—12 Jun 2010, Berkshire, England), British restaurant critic who raised the standards of British cooking through his restaurant reviews and eponymous guidebooks.

Moishe Rosen (Martin Meyer Rosen; 12 Apr 1932, Kansas City MO—19 May 2010, San Francisco CA), American religious leader who founded (1973) the evangelical Christian organization Jews for Jesus, which he led until his retirement in 1996.

Dan(iel David) Rostenkowski ("Rosty"; 2 Jan 1928, Chicago IL—11 Aug 2010, Kenosha county, Wisconsin), American politician who served in the US House of Representatives for 36 years (1959–95), rising to become one of the most powerful Democratic Party members of Congress as a member (1964–81) and then chairman (1981–94) of the House Ways and Means Committee, which legislates federal taxation and other revenue-raising bills; he helped to broker such legislative deals as the landmark 1966 Medicare legislation, the 1983 overhaul to strengthen Social Security's fiscal standing, and the 1986 tax-reform act that cut nominal tax rates and eliminated many loopholes. He was compelled to step down from the Ways and Means Committee in July 1994 after he was indicted on 17 felony corruption charges; in 1996 he plead guilty to two counts of mail fraud and was sentenced to 17 months in prison; he was pardoned in 2000 by Pres. Bill Clinton.

William Safire (William Lewis Safir; 17 Dec 1929, New York NY—27 Sep 2009, Rockville MD), American writer who was known for his work as a speechwriter for Pres. Richard M. Nixon and for his fiercely opinionated conservative columns (1973–2005) for the *New York Times* as well as his witty and meticulous columns (1979–2009) in *The New York Times Magazine* that traced the origins and meanings of popular phrases; Safire won a Pulitzer Prize for commentary in 1978 and the Presidential Medal of Freedom in 2006.

Soupy Sales (Milton Supman; 8 Jan 1926, Franklinton NC—22 Oct 2009, New York NY), American television and radio personality who achieved widespread popularity in the 1960s as the zany host of the syndicated television program *The Soupy Sales Show;* he was especially known for his pie-throwing routines, and he once estimated that 20,000 pies had been hurled at him or his guests during the show's run.

J.D. Salinger (Jerome David Salinger; 1 Jan 1919, New York NY—27 Jan 2010, Cornish NH), American writer who won critical acclaim and devoted admirers for his novel *The Catcher in the Rye* (1951), which uses humor and colorful language to portray the sensitive, rebellious adolescent Holden Caulfield, who views his life with an added dimension of precocious self-consciousness as he relates his flight from the "phony" adult world, his search for innocence and truth, and his collapse on a psychiatrist's couch; at the time of his death, Salinger's entire corpus of published works consisted of that one novel and a number of short stories, only 13 of which were issued in collected book form during his lifetime.

Samak Sundaravej (13 Jun 1935, Bangkok, Thailand—24 Nov 2009, Bangkok, Thailand), Thai journalist and politician who served as prime minister of Thailand in 2008, the first Thai prime minister to be democratically elected since the ousting of Prime Minister Thaksin Shinawatra in a September 2006 military coup; Samak was forced to step down after less than nine months in office after the Constitutional Court found him guilty of having illegally accepted payment for television cooking show appearances that he had made while serving as prime minister.

Paul Anthony Samuelson (15 May 1915, Gary IN—13 Dec 2009, Belmont MA), American economist who was awarded the Nobel Memorial Prize in Economic Sciences in 1970 for his fundamental contributions to nearly all branches of economic theory.

José Saramago (16 Nov 1922, Azinhaga, Portugal—18 Jun 2010, Lanzarote, Canary Islands, Spain), Portuguese novelist and man of letters who was awarded the Nobel Prize for Literature in 1998; in many of his novels, he sets whimsical parables against realistic historical backgrounds in order to comment ironically on human foibles.

Budd Schulberg (Seymour Wilson Schulberg; 27 Mar 1914, New York NY—5 Aug 2009, Westhampton Beach NY), American novelist, screenwriter, and journalist who earned a 1954 Academy Award for his story and screenplay for the classic film *On the Waterfront.*

Mike Seeger (15 Aug 1933, New York NY—7 Aug 2009, Lexington VA), American folk musician who collected and performed traditional American music from the 1920s and '30s and was a major influence in the folk music revival of the 1960s and later; Seeger was a member of a prominent family in American folk music (his sister Peggy Seeger and half brother Pete Seeger were also renowned musicians).

Erich Wolf Segal (16 Jun 1937, Brooklyn NY—17 Jan 2010, London, England), American educator, author, and screenwriter who wrote the best-selling novel *Love Story* (1970); he also wrote the screenplay for the blockbuster film, which grossed nearly US$200 million and reportedly saved the struggling Paramount Pictures.

Eunice (Mary) Kennedy Shriver (10 Jul 1921, Brookline MA—11 Aug 2009, Hyannis MA), American social activist who worked to improve the lives of the mentally disabled and founded (1968) the Special Olympics; the sister of Pres. John F. Kennedy and Senators Robert F. Kennedy and Edward M. Kennedy, Shriver became in 1957 the director of the Joseph P. Kennedy, Jr., Foundation, the goals of which were to seek the causes of mental retardation and improve the social treatment of the mentally challenged; she was also a force behind the 1962 creation of the National Institute of Child Health and Human Development, which now bears her name. Shriver was granted the 1966 Albert Lasker Public Service Award, and in 1984 she received the Presidential Medal of Freedom.

Naomi (Ruth) Sims (30 Mar 1949, Oxford MS—1 Aug 2009, Newark NJ), American model and business executive who shattered the barrier that had prevented black models from achieving supermodel status when she became (1968) the first black model to adorn the cover of *Ladies' Home Journal.*

Frederik van Zyl Slabbert (2 Mar 1940, Pretoria, South Africa—14 May 2010, Johannesburg, South Africa), South African politician and academic who was a leading Afrikaner in the white opposition to South African apartheid and an MP for the antiapartheid Progressive Party (later renamed the Progressive Federal Party [PFP]) for 12 years (1974–86).

Carl M. Smith (15 Mar 1927, Maynardville TN—16 Jan 2010, Franklin TN), American country music singer who was one of the most popular country music recording stars of the 1950s and '60s as well as a regular fixture on television, which showcased his polished and handsome appearance and his refined ballad-style voice; during the 1950s he charted 30 Top 10 singles and 58 consecutive Top 40 hits on the *Billboard* country music chart, and he was inducted into the Country Music Hall of Fame in 2003.

David Soyer (24 Feb 1923, Philadelphia PA—25 Feb 2010, New York NY), American musician who cofounded (1964) the world-renowned Guarneri String Quartet, for which he served as cellist until his retirement in 2001; the Guarneri achieved the distinction of being the longest continually performing quartet in the world, maintaining all original members for 37 years.

George Michael Steinbrenner III ("the Boss"; 4 Jul 1930, Rocky River OH—13 Jul 2010, Tampa FL), American businessman and sports executive who was the principal owner (1973–2010) of the New York Yankees professional baseball team. Although his exacting methods and often bellicose manner established him as one of the most controversial personalities in MLB, under his ownership the Yankees became one of the most dominant teams in baseball (winning 7 World Series titles [1977, 1978, 1996, 1998, 1999, 2000, and 2009] and 11 pennants) and one of the most valuable franchises in sports (valued at about US$1.6 billion in 2010).

Ted Stevens (Theodore F. Stevens; 18 Nov 1923, Indianapolis IN—found dead 10 Aug 2010, near Dillingham AK), American politician who served as a Republican US senator from Alaska (1968–2009); in his 40 years as senator, Stevens earned a reputation as a powerful advocate for Alaskan industry, helping to draft the Alaska Native Claims Settlement Act, which enabled construction of the Trans-Alaska Pipeline (completed 1977), and brokering legislation that opened the Tongass National Forest to logging and mandated millions of dollars in federal payments to Alaska for prohibiting development in other large wilderness areas. As chair of the Senate Appropriations Committee (1997–01, 2003–05), he funneled more than US$3 billion to Alaska between 1995 and 2008.

Joseph Ezekiel Strick (6 Jul 1923, Braddock PA—1 Jun 2010, Paris, France), American independent filmmaker who drew both critical acclaim and government censorship with daring and often controversial works—most notably his *Interviews with My Lai Veterans* (1971), which recounts the experiences of former soldiers who were present at the infamous 1968 massacre of Vietnamese civilians by American troops, for which Strick won an Academy Award (1971) for best documentary short subject.

Patrick (Wayne) Swayze (18 Aug 1952, Houston TX—14 Sep 2009, Los Angeles CA), American actor and dancer who used his New York City training with the Harkness and the Joffrey Ballet schools to captivate audiences in his breakout performance as a seductive dance instructor in the smash-hit film *Dirty Dancing* (1987) and went on to even greater acclaim as the romantic lead in the box-office sensation *Ghost* (1990); he received Golden Globe nominations for both movies, which became cult classics, and such films as *The Outsiders* (1983), *Red Dawn* (1984), *Road House* (1989), *Next of Kin* (1989), and *Point Break* (1991) followed.

Mary Allin Travers (9 Nov 1936, Louisville KY—16 Sep 2009, Danbury CT), American folk singer who performed (with fellow singers Peter Yarrow and Noel Paul Stookey) as part of the popular folk music trio Peter, Paul, and Mary, which was known for smooth harmonies and earnest, often politically tinged anthems—despite the group's soft-edged sound, their lyrics addressed the issues of the civil rights movement, and in 1963 the trio performed at the Rev. Martin Luther King, Jr.'s March on Washington; the group's protest songs included covers of Bob Dylan's "Blowin' in the Wind" and "The Times They Are a-Changin'," and they scored hits with renditions of John Denver's "Leaving on a Jet Plane" and the Pete Seeger–Lee Hayes call to arms "If I Had a Hammer."

Stewart Lee Udall (31 Jan 1920, St. Johns AZ—20 Mar 2010, Santa Fe NM), American conservationist and administrator who preserved millions of hectares of wilderness while serving as interior secretary under US Presidents John F. Kennedy and Lyndon B. Johnson; he was instrumental in acquiring more than 1.5 million ha (nearly 4 million ac) of land that included Canyonlands (Utah), Guadalupe Mountains (Texas), North Cascades (Washington), and Redwood (California) national parks.

Edward George Uhl (24 Mar 1918, Elizabeth NJ—9 May 2010, Easton MD), American engineer and aerospace executive who was serving in the US Army during World War II when he helped develop (1942) a weapon, nicknamed the bazooka, that fired an explosive that was capable of penetrating several centimeters of armor; the weapon was particularly effective against the armor plate on German tanks and was credited with helping to secure victory for the Allies.

Helen (Losee) Wagner (3 Sep 1918, Lubbock TX—1 May 2010, Mount Kisco NY), American actress who portrayed Nancy Hughes, the old-fashioned housewife (later a widow) and mother in the daytime television soap opera *As the World Turns,* from the program's inception on 2 Apr 1956 until her final appearance on 5 Apr 2010; her 54-year run in the same role secured her a spot in *Guinness World Records;* in 2004 Wagner was the recipient of the Lifetime Achievement Award from the National Academy of Television Arts and Sciences.

Abdurrahman Wahid (Gus Dur; 7 Sep 1940, Denanyar, East Java, Dutch East Indies [now in Indonesia]—30 Dec 2009, Jakarta, Indonesia), Indonesian Muslim religious leader and politician who was (1999–2001) the first president of Indonesia to be elected through a vote by the People's Consultative Assembly, as opposed to the earlier, consensus-seeking process.

Gordon (Trueman Riviere) Waller (4 Jun 1945, Braemar, Aberdeenshire, Scotland—17 Jul 2009, Norwich CT), British singer who was the lower-voiced member of the pop-singing duo Peter and Gordon; between 1964 and 1968, Waller and his singing partner, Peter Asher, racked up eight top 20 hit records in the US.

Alan Rhun Watkins (3 Apr 1933, Tycroes, Carmarthenshire, Wales—8 May 2010, London, England), British journalist who covered British politics for more than 50 years, writing an insightful and witty weekly column for the *Sunday Express* (1959–64), *The Spectator* (1964–67), the *New Statesman* (1967–76), *The Observer* (1976–93), and *The Independent on Sunday* (1993–2010).

Edgar Wayburn (17 Sep 1906, Macon GA—5 Mar 2010, San Francisco CA), American conservationist who was awarded (1999) the Presidential Medal of Freedom for his leading role in helping to preserve more than 40 million ha (100 million ac) of North American wilderness; he also served five terms as president of the Sierra Club.

Robert Michael White (6 Jul 1924, New York NY—17 Mar 2010, Orlando FL), major general (ret.), US Air Force, who was a test pilot for the US Air Force when he became the first American to fly an airplane into outer space; he took the rocket-powered X-15 to new aircraft speed records of Mach 4, Mach 5, and Mach 6 (four, five, and six times the speed of sound, respectively), and on 17 Jul 1962, he flew an X-15 to an altitude of 95.9 km (59.6 mi).

Al(fonso) Williamson (21 Mar 1931, New York NY—12 Jun 2010, New York state), American comic artist who illustrated comic books and strips with a richly detailed, almost cinematic style; he was particularly noted for his work on *Flash Gordon* in the 1960s, '80s, and '90s, as well as the adaptations of the Star Wars motion picture franchise as a daily comic strip (1981–84) in the *Los Angeles Times* newspaper, as a Marvel Comics series (1979), and as a graphic novel, *Episode I: The Phantom Menace* (1999); Williamson was inducted into the Will Eisner Comic Industry Hall of Fame in 2000.

Charlie Wilson (Charles Nesbitt Wilson; 1 Jun 1933, Trinity TX—10 Feb 2010, Lufkin TX), American politician who, as a 12-term (1973–96) Democratic member of the US House of Representatives from Texas, engineered the covert supplying of billions of dollars in funding and weaponry to the mujahideen fighting the Soviet Union in Afghanistan in the 1980s, an effort that was instrumental in forcing the Soviet withdrawal from Afghanistan in 1989; his exploits were dramatized in the 2007 movie *Charlie Wilson's War.*

John Robert Wooden ("Wizard of Westwood"; 14 Oct 1910, Hall IN—4 Jun 2010, Los Angeles CA), American basketball coach who directed teams from UCLA to 10 NCAA championships in 12 seasons (1964–65, 1967–73, 1975), while as a student at Purdue University, he gained All-America honors as a basketball player for three seasons (1930–32) and won a Western Conference (Big Ten) medal for athletic and scholastic excellence. He coached at UCLA from 1948–75 and retired with a record of 620 wins and 147 losses, for an .808 percentage; his overall 40-year record was 885 wins and 203 losses, a percentage of .813. Among Wooden's most notable accomplishments at UCLA were two record winning streaks: 88 consecutive games (over four seasons, 1971–74) and 38 consecutive NCAA tournament games. He was named the NCAA's College Basketball Coach of the Year six times (1964, 1967, 1969–70, 1972–73) and was the first person to be inducted into the Naismith Memorial Basketball Hall of Fame as both a player (1961) and a coach (1973). The John R. Wooden Award, established in 1976, annually honors the nation's outstanding player as chosen by a media poll. Wooden was awarded the Presidential Medal of Freedom in 2003.

Edward (Albert Arthur) Woodward (1 Jun 1930, Croydon, Surrey, England—16 Nov 2009, Truro, Cornwall, England), British actor who received five Emmy Award nominations for his portrayal of a disillusioned intelligence agent turned good-guy vigilante in the American television show *The Equalizer* (1985–89).

(Alice) Patricia Wrightson (19 Jun 1921, Lismore, NSW, Australia—15 Mar 2010, Lismore, NSW, Australia), Australian children's book author who penned more than two dozen novels for children; she was noted for her sensitive and generally respectful use of Aboriginal figures and motifs; she was made OBE in 1977, and in 1999 New South Wales granted the first annual Patricia Wrightson Prize for Children's Literature.

Tsutomu Yamaguchi (16 Mar 1916, Nagasaki, Japan—4 Jan 2010, Nagasaki, Japan), Japanese engineer, translator, and educator who was the only officially documented survivor of both the Hiroshima (6 Aug 1945) and Nagasaki (9 Aug 1945) atomic bombings during World War II; in 2006 Yamaguchi addressed the United Nations General Assembly in New York City in support of nuclear disarmament.

Umaru Musa Yar'Adua (16 Aug 1951, Katsina, Nigeria—5 May 2010, Abuja, Nigeria), Nigerian politician who served (2007–10) as president of Nigeria; his inauguration on 29 May 2007 marked the first time in the country's history that an elected civilian head of state had transferred power to another.

Paul Charles Zamecnik (22 Nov 1912, Cleveland OH—27 Oct 2009, Boston MA), American molecular biologist who codiscovered (1956) tRNA (transfer ribonucleic acid), a molecule essential for protein synthesis, and pioneered research into antisense DNA, which selectively inhibits the activity of genes; he was elected to the National Academy of Sciences (1968) and received the National Medal of Science (1991) and the Albert Lasker Award for Special Achievement in Medical Science (1996).

Awards

TIME's Top 100 Films

There's nothing like a list to stimulate a strong discussion, so in the hopes of striking a few sparks among movie lovers, TIME asked its long-time film critics Richard Corliss and Richard Schickel to compile a list of the 100 greatest films ever made. Of course, the discussions that followed between the two critics were entirely civil at all times. Below, the films and the year they were released.

A–C
Aguirre: The Wrath of God (1972)
The Apu Trilogy (1955, 1956, 1959)
The Awful Truth (1937)
Baby Face (1933)
Bande à part (1964)
Barry Lyndon (1975)
Berlin Alexanderplatz (1980)
Blade Runner (1982)
Bonnie and Clyde (1967)
Brazil (1985)
Bride of Frankenstein (1935)
Camille (1936)
Casablanca (1942)
Charade (1963)
Children of Paradise (1945)
Chinatown (1974)
Chungking Express (1994)
Citizen Kane (1941)
City Lights (1931)
City of God (2002)
Closely Watched Trains (1966)
The Crime of Monsieur Lange (1936)
The Crowd (1928)

D–F
Day for Night (1973)
The Decalogue (1989)
Detour (1945)
The Discreet Charm of the Bourgeoisie (1972)
Dodsworth (1936)
Double Indemnity (1944)
Dr. Strangelove or: How I Learned To Stop Worrying and Love the Bomb (1964)
Drunken Master II (1994)
E.T.: The Extra-Terrestrial (1982)
8 1/2 (1963)
The 400 Blows (1959)
Farewell My Concubine (1993)
Finding Nemo (2003)
The Fly (1986)

G–J
The Godfather, Parts I and II (1972, 1974)
The Good, the Bad, and the Ugly (1966)
Goodfellas (1990)
A Hard Day's Night (1964)
His Girl Friday (1940)
Ikiru (1952)
In a Lonely Place (1950)
Invasion of the Body Snatchers (1956)
It's a Gift (1934)
It's a Wonderful Life (1946)

K–M
Kandahar (2001)
Kind Hearts and Coronets (1949)
King Kong (1933)
The Lady Eve (1941)
The Last Command (1928)
Lawrence of Arabia (1962)
Léolo (1992)
The Lord of the Rings (2001, 2002, 2003)
The Man with a Camera (1929)
The Manchurian Candidate (1962)
Meet Me in St. Louis (1944)
Metropolis (1927)
Miller's Crossing (1990)
Mon oncle d'Amérique (1980)
Mouchette (1967)

N–P
Nayakan (1987)
Ninotchka (1939)
Notorious (1946)
Olympia, Parts 1 and 2 (1938)
On the Waterfront (1954)
Once upon a Time in the West (1968)
Out of the Past (1947)
Persona (1966)
Pinocchio (1940)
Psycho (1960)
Pulp Fiction (1994)
The Purple Rose of Cairo (1985)
Pyaasa (1957)

Q–S
Raging Bull (1980)
Schindler's List (1993)
The Searchers (1956)
Sherlock, Jr. (1924)
The Shop Around the Corner (1940)
Singin' in the Rain (1952)
The Singing Detective (1986)
Smiles of a Summer Night (1955)
Some Like It Hot (1959)
Star Wars (1977)
A Streetcar Named Desire (1951)
Sunrise (1927)
Sweet Smell of Success (1957)
Swing Time (1936)

T–Z
Talk to Her (2002)
Taxi Driver (1976)
Tokyo Story (1953)
A Touch of Zen (1971)
Ugetsu (1953)
Ulysses' Gaze (1995)
Umberto D (1952)
Unforgiven (1992)
White Heat (1949)
Wings of Desire (1987)
Yojimbo (1961)

TIME's Person of the Year, 1927–2009

Every year since 1927, TIME has named a Person of the Year, identifying the individual who has done the most to affect the news in the past twelve months. The designation is often mistaken for an honor, but the magazine has always pointed out that inclusion on the list is not a recognition of good works (like the Nobel Peace prize, for example), but rather a reflection of the sheer power of one's actions, whether for good or for ill. Hence, both Adolf Hitler and Ayatollah Ruhollah Khomeini were chosen Person of the Year at the time when their actions commanded the attention of the world. Below, the complete list of Persons of the Year.

1927	Charles Lindbergh
1928	Walter Chrysler
1929	Owen Young
1930	Mahatma Gandhi
1931	Pierre Laval
1932	Franklin Delano Roosevelt
1933	Hugh Johnson
1934	Franklin Delano Roosevelt
1935	Haile Selassie
1936	Wallis Simpson
1937	Chiang Kai-Shek and Soong Mei-ling
1938	Adolf Hitler
1939	Joseph Stalin
1940	Winston Churchill
1941	Franklin Delano Roosevelt
1942	Joseph Stalin
1943	George Marshall
1944	Dwight Eisenhower
1945	Harry Truman
1946	James F. Byrnes
1947	George Marshall
1948	Harry Truman
1949	Winston Churchill ("Man of the Half-Century")
1950	The American Fighting-Man (representing US troops fighting in the Korean War; first abstract chosen)
1951	Mohammed Mossadegh
1952	Queen Elizabeth II
1953	Konrad Adenauer
1954	John Foster Dulles
1955	Harlow Curtice
1956	Hungarian Freedom Fighter (representing the citizens' uprising against Soviet domination)
1957	Nikita Khrushchev
1958	Charles De Gaulle
1959	Dwight Eisenhower
1960	US Scientists (represented by Linus Pauling, Isidor Rabi, Edward Teller, Joshua Lederberg, Donald A. Glaser, Willard Libby, Robert Woodward, Charles Draper, William Shockley, Emilio Segrè, John Enders, Charles Townes, George Beadle, James Van Allen, and Edward Purcell)
1961	John F. Kennedy
1962	Pope John XXIII
1963	Martin Luther King, Jr.
1964	Lyndon Johnson
1965	William Westmoreland
1966	The Generation Twenty-Five and Under (representing American youth)
1967	Lyndon Johnson
1968	Apollo 8 astronauts Frank Borman, Jim Lovell, and William Anders
1969	The Middle Americans (representing the American electorate's turn to the right)
1970	Willy Brandt
1971	Richard Nixon
1972	Richard Nixon and Henry Kissinger
1973	John Sirica
1974	King Faisal
1975	American Women (represented by Betty Ford, Carla Hills, Ella Grasso, Barbara Jordan, Susie Sharp, Jill Conway, Billie Jean King, Susan Brownmiller, Addie Wyatt, Kathleen Byerly, Carol Sutton, and Alison Cheek)
1976	Jimmy Carter
1977	Anwar el-Sadat
1978	Deng Xiaoping
1979	Ayatollah Ruhollah Khomeini
1980	Ronald Reagan
1981	Lech Walensa
1982	The Computer (first non-human abstract chosen; termed "Machine of the Year")
1983	Ronald Reagan and Yuri Andropov
1984	Peter Ueberroth
1985	Deng Xiaoping
1986	Corazon Aquino
1987	Mikhail Gorbachev
1988	Endangered Earth ("Planet of the Year")
1989	Mikhail Gorbachev ("Man of the Decade")
1990	George H.W. Bush
1991	Ted Turner
1992	Bill Clinton
1993	The Peacemakers (represented by Nelson Mandela and F.W. de Klerk of South Africa and Yasir Arafat and Yitzhak Rabin of the Middle East)
1994	Pope John Paul II
1995	Newt Gingrich
1996	David Ho
1997	Andy Grove
1998	Bill Clinton and Kenneth Starr
1999	Jeffrey P. Bezos
2000	George W. Bush
2001	Rudolph Giuliani
2002	The Whistleblowers (represented by Cynthia Cooper of Worldcom, Sherron Watkins of Enron, and Coleen Rowley of the FBI)
2003	The American Soldier (representing US troops fighting in Iraq and Afghanistan)
2004	George W. Bush
2005	The Good Samaritans (represented by Bono [Paul Hewson], Bill Gates, and Melinda Gates)
2006	You (representing the new age of user-generated Internet content)
2007	Vladimir Putin
2008	Barack Obama
2009	Ben Bernanke

Nobel Prizes

The Alfred B. Nobel Prizes are widely regarded as the world's most prestigious awards given for intellectual achievement. They are awarded annually from a fund bequeathed for that purpose by the Swedish inventor and industrialist Alfred Bernhard Nobel and administered by the Nobel Foundation. Nobel's will established five of the six prizes: those for physics, chemistry, literature, physiology or medicine, and peace. The prize for economic sciences was added in 1969. Each year thousands of invitations are sent out to members of scholarly institutions, scientists, Nobel laureates, members of national legislatures, and others, requesting nominations. The country given is the citizenship of the recipient at the time that the award was made. Prizes may be withheld or not awarded in years when no worthy recipient can be found or when the world situation (e.g., World Wars I and II) prevents the gathering of information needed to reach a decision. Prizes are awarded in December in Stockholm and Oslo. A cash award of SEK 10 million (about US$1,286,000), a personal diploma, and a commemorative medal are given for each prize category.

Nobel Foundation Web site: <http://nobelprize.org>.

Physics

YEAR	WINNER(S)	COUNTRY	ACHIEVEMENT
1901	Wilhelm Conrad Röntgen	Germany	discovery of X-rays
1902	Hendrik Antoon Lorentz	Neth.	} investigation of the influence
	Pieter Zeeman	Neth.	} of magnetism on radiation
1903	Henri Becquerel	France	discovery of spontaneous radioactivity
	Marie Curie	France	} investigations of radiation phenomena
	Pierre Curie	France	} discovered by Becquerel
1904	John William Strutt, 3rd Baron Rayleigh (of Terling Place)	UK	discovery of argon
1905	Philipp Lenard	Germany	research on cathode rays
1906	J.J. Thomson	UK	research into the electrical conductivity of gases
1907	A.A. Michelson	US	spectroscopic and metrological investigations
1908	Gabriel Lippmann	France	photographic reproduction of colors
1909	Ferdinand Braun	Germany	} development of
	Guglielmo Marconi	Italy	} wireless telegraphy
1910	Johannes Diederik van der Waals	Neth.	research concerning the equation of state of gases and liquids
1911	Wilhelm Wien	Germany	discoveries regarding laws governing heat radiation
1912	Nils Dalén	Sweden	invention of automatic regulators for lighting coastal beacons and light buoys
1913	Heike Kamerlingh Onnes	Neth.	investigation into the properties of matter at low temperatures; production of liquid helium
1914	Max von Laue	Germany	discovery of diffraction of X-rays by crystals
1915	Lawrence Bragg	UK	} analysis of crystal structure
	William Bragg	UK	} by means of X-rays
1917	Charles Glover Barkla	UK	discovery of the characteristic X-radiation of elements
1918	Max Planck	Germany	discovery of the elemental quanta
1919	Johannes Stark	Germany	discovery of the Doppler effect in positive ion rays and the division of spectral lines in the electric field
1920	Charles Édouard Guillaume	Switz.	discovery of anomalies in alloys
1921	Albert Einstein	Switz.	work in theoretical physics
1922	Niels Bohr	Denmark	investigation of atomic structure and radiation
1923	Robert Andrews Millikan	US	work on the elementary charge of electricity and on the photoelectric effect
1924	Karl Manne Georg Siegbahn	Sweden	work in X-ray spectroscopy
1925	James Franck	Germany	} discovery of the laws governing the
	Gustav Hertz	Germany	} impact of an electron upon an atom
1926	Jean Perrin	France	work on the discontinuous structure of matter
1927	Arthur Holly Compton	US	discovery of the wavelength change in diffused X-rays
	C.T.R. Wilson	UK	method of making visible the paths of electrically charged particles
1928	Owen Willans Richardson	UK	work on electron emission by hot metals
1929	Louis-Victor, 7e duc (duke) de Broglie	France	discovery of the wave nature of electrons
1930	Chandrasekhara Venkata Raman	India	discovery of Raman effect, light wavelength variation that occurs when a light beam is deflected by molecules
1932	Werner Heisenberg	Germany	creation of quantum mechanics

Physics (continued)

YEAR	WINNER(S)	COUNTRY	ACHIEVEMENT
1933	P.A.M. Dirac	UK	} introduction of wave equations
	Erwin Schrödinger	Austria	} in quantum mechanics
1935	James Chadwick	UK	discovery of the neutron
1936	Carl David Anderson	US	discovery of the positron
	Victor Francis Hess	Austria	discovery of cosmic radiation
1937	Clinton Joseph Davisson	US	} experimental demonstration of the interference
	George Paget Thomson	UK	} phenomenon in crystals irradiated by electrons
1938	Enrico Fermi	Italy	disclosure of artificial radioactive elements produced by neutron irradiation
1939	Ernest Orlando Lawrence	US	invention of the cyclotron
1943	Otto Stern	US	discovery of the magnetic moment of the proton
1944	Isidor Isaac Rabi	US	resonance method for the registration of various properties of atomic nuclei
1945	Wolfgang Pauli	Austria	discovery of the exclusion principle of electrons
1946	Percy Williams Bridgman	US	discoveries in the domain of high-pressure physics
1947	Edward V. Appleton	UK	discovery of the Appleton layer in the upper atmosphere
1948	Patrick M.S. Blackett	UK	discoveries in the domain of nuclear physics and cosmic radiation
1949	Hideki Yukawa	Japan	prediction of the existence of mesons
1950	Cecil Frank Powell	UK	photographic method of studying nuclear processes; discoveries concerning mesons
1951	John D. Cockcroft	UK	} work on the transmutation of atomic nuclei
	Ernest T.S. Walton	Ireland	} by accelerated particles
1952	Felix Bloch	US	} discovery of nuclear magnetic
	E.M. Purcell	US	} resonance in solids
1953	Frits Zernike	Neth.	method of phase-contrast microscopy
1954	Max Born	UK	statistical studies of atomic wave functions
	Walther Bothe	W.Ger.	invention of the coincidence method
1955	Polykarp Kusch	US	measurement of the magnetic moment of the electron
	Willis Eugene Lamb, Jr.	US	discoveries in the hydrogen spectrum
1956	John Bardeen	US	} investigations on
	Walter H. Brattain	US	} semiconductors and the
	William B. Shockley	US	} invention of the transistor
1957	Tsung-Dao Lee	China	} discovery of violations of the principle of parity, the
	Chen Ning Yang	China	} symmetry between phenomena in coordinate systems
1958	Pavel Alexeyevich Cherenkov	USSR	} discovery and interpretation of the Cherenkov effect, which indicates that electrons emit light as they
	Ilya Mikhaylovich Frank	USSR	} pass through a transparent medium at a speed
	Igor Yevgenyevich Tamm	USSR	} higher than the speed of light in that medium
1959	Owen Chamberlain	US	} confirmation of the existence
	Emilio Segrè	US	} of the antiproton
1960	Donald A. Glaser	US	development of the bubble chamber
1961	Robert Hofstadter	US	determination of the shape and size of atomic nucleons
	Rudolf Ludwig Mössbauer	W.Ger.	discovery of the Mössbauer effect, a nuclear process permitting the resonance absorption of gamma rays
1962	Lev Davidovich Landau	USSR	contributions to the understanding of condensed states of matter
1963	J. Hans D. Jensen	W.Ger.	} development of the shell model theory of
	Maria Goeppert Mayer	US	} the structure of the atomic nuclei
	Eugene Paul Wigner	US	principles governing the interaction of protons and neutrons in the nucleus
1964	Nikolay G. Basov	USSR	} work in quantum electronics leading to the
	Aleksandr M. Prokhorov	USSR	} construction of instruments based on
	Charles Hard Townes	US	} maser-laser principles
1965	Richard P. Feynman	US	} work in quantum electrodynamics, which
	Julian Seymour Schwinger	US	} describes mathematically all interactions of light with
	Shin'ichiro Tomonaga	Japan	} matter and of charged particles with one another
1966	Alfred Kastler	France	discovery of optical methods for studying Hertzian resonances in atoms
1967	Hans Albrecht Bethe	US	discoveries concerning the energy production of stars
1968	Luis W. Alvarez	US	work with elementary particles, in particular the discovery of resonance states
1969	Murray Gell-Mann	US	classification of elementary particles and their interactions
1970	Hannes Alfvén	Sweden	} work in magnetohydrodynamics and
	Louis-Eugène-Félix Néel	France	} in antiferromagnetism and ferrimagnetism
1971	Dennis Gabor	UK	invention of holography

Physics (continued)

YEAR	WINNER(S)	COUNTRY	ACHIEVEMENT
1972	John Bardeen	US	development of the theory of superconductivity, the
	Leon N. Cooper	US	disappearance of electrical resistance in various solids
	John Robert Schrieffer	US	when they are cooled below certain temperatures
1973	Leo Esaki	Japan	experimental discoveries in tunneling in
	Ivar Giaever	US	semiconductors and superconductors
	Brian D. Josephson	UK	predictions of supercurrent properties through a tunnel barrier
1974	Antony Hewish	UK	work in radio
	Martin Ryle	UK	astronomy
1975	Aage N. Bohr	Denmark	work on the atomic nucleus
	Ben R. Mottelson	Denmark	that paved the way for nuclear
	James Rainwater	US	fusion
1976	Burton Richter	US	discovery of new class of
	Samuel C.C. Ting	US	elementary particles (psi, or J)
1977	Philip W. Anderson	US	contributions to understanding the
	Nevill F. Mott	UK	behavior of electrons in
	John H. Van Vleck	US	magnetic, noncrystalline solids
1978	Pyotr L. Kapitsa	USSR	research in magnetism and low-temperature physics
	Arno Penzias	US	discovery of cosmic microwave background
	Robert Woodrow Wilson	US	radiation, providing support for the big-bang theory
1979	Sheldon Lee Glashow	US	contributions to the theory of the
	Abdus Salam	Pakistan	unified weak and electromagnetic
	Steven Weinberg	US	interactions of subatomic particles
1980	James Watson Cronin	US	demonstration of the simultaneous violation of both
	Val Logsdon Fitch	US	charge-conjugation and parity-inversion symmetries
1981	Nicolaas Bloembergen	US	applications of lasers
	Arthur L. Schawlow	US	in spectroscopy
	Kai M.B. Siegbahn	Sweden	development of electron spectroscopy
1982	Kenneth G. Wilson	US	analysis of continuous phase transitions
1983	Subrahmanyan Chandrasekhar	US	contributions to understanding the evolution and devolution of stars
	William A. Fowler	US	studies of nuclear reactions key to the formation of chemical elements
1984	Simon van der Meer	Neth.	discovery of subatomic particles W and Z,
	Carlo Rubbia	Italy	which supports the electroweak theory
1985	Klaus von Klitzing	W.Ger.	discovery of the quantized Hall effect, permitting exact measurements of electrical resistance
1986	Gerd Binnig	W.Ger.	development of the scanning tunneling
	Heinrich Rohrer	Switz.	electron microscope
	Ernst Ruska	W.Ger.	development of the electron microscope
1987	J. Georg Bednorz	W.Ger.	discoveries of superconductivity in
	Karl Alex Müller	Switz.	ceramic materials
1988	Leon Max Lederman	US	research in
	Melvin Schwartz	US	subatomic
	Jack Steinberger	US	particles
1989	Hans Georg Dehmelt	US	development of methods to isolate atoms
	Wolfgang Paul	W.Ger.	and subatomic particles for study
	Norman Foster Ramsey	US	development of the atomic clock
1990	Jerome Isaac Friedman	US	discovery of
	Henry Way Kendall	US	atomic
	Richard E. Taylor	Canada	quarks
1991	Pierre-Gilles de Gennes	France	discovery of general rules for behavior of molecules
1992	Georges Charpak	France	invention of a detector that traces subatomic particles
1993	Russell Alan Hulse	US	identification of
	Joseph H. Taylor, Jr.	US	binary pulsars
1994	Bertram N. Brockhouse	Canada	development of
	Clifford G. Shull	US	neutron-scattering techniques
1995	Martin Lewis Perl	US	discovery of the tau subatomic particle
	Frederick Reines	US	discovery of the neutrino subatomic particle
1996	David M. Lee	US	discovery of
	Douglas D. Osheroff	US	superfluidity in
	Robert C. Richardson	US	isotope helium-3
1997	Steven Chu	US	process of
	Claude Cohen-Tannoudji	France	cooling and trapping atoms with
	William D. Phillips	US	laser light
1998	Robert B. Laughlin	US	discovery of fractional quantum Hall effect, showing
	Horst L. Störmer	US	that electrons in a low-temperature magnetic field can
	Daniel C. Tsui	US	form a quantum fluid with fractional electric charges

Physics (continued)

YEAR	WINNER(S)	COUNTRY	ACHIEVEMENT
1999	Gerardus 't Hooft	Neth.	study of the quantum structure
	Martinus J.G. Veltman	Neth.	of electroweak interactions
2000	Zhores I. Alferov	Russia	development of fast semiconductors
	Herbert Kroemer	Germany	for use in microelectronics
	Jack S. Kilby	US	development of the integrated circuit (microchip)
2001	Eric A. Cornell	US	achievement of Bose-Einstein condensation in dilute
	Wolfgang Ketterle	Germany	gases of alkali atoms; early fundamental studies of
	Carl E. Wieman	US	the properties of the condensates
2002	Raymond Davis, Jr.	US	pioneering contributions to astrophysics,
	Masatoshi Koshiba	Japan	in particular the detection of cosmic neutrinos
	Riccardo Giacconi	US	pioneering contributions to astrophysics, which
			have led to the discovery of cosmic X-ray sources
2003	Alexei A. Abrikosov	US/Russia	pioneering contributions
	Vitaly L. Ginzburg	Russia	to the theory of superconductors
	Anthony J. Leggett	UK/US	and superfluids
2004	David J. Gross	US	discovery of asymptotic
	H. David Politzer	US	freedom in the theory of
	Frank Wilczek	US	the strong interaction
2005	Roy J. Glauber	US	contributions to quantum theory of optical coherence
	John L. Hall	US	contributions to the development of laser-based
	Theodor W. Hänsch	Germany	precision spectroscopy, including the optical
			frequency comb technique
2006	John C. Mather	US	discovery of the blackbody form and variability of
	George F. Smoot	US	cosmic microwave background radiation
2007	Albert Fert	France	discovery of Giant Magnetoresistance (large resistance
	Peter Grünberg	Germany	changes in materials composed of alternating layers of
			various metallic elements), a nanotechnology application
2008	Makoto Kobayashi	Japan	research on the origin of the broken symmetry in
	Toshihide Maskawa	Japan	subatomic physics that predicts three families of quarks
	Yoichiro Nambu	US	discovery of spontaneous broken symmetry
			in subatomic physics
2009	Charles K. Kao	UK/US	contributions in the transmission of light in fiber optics
	Willard S. Boyle	Canada/US	invention of the
	George E. Smith	US	CCD sensor

Chemistry

YEAR	WINNER(S)	COUNTRY	ACHIEVEMENT
1901	Jacobus H. van 't Hoff	Neth.	discovery of the laws of chemical dynamics and osmotic pressure
1902	Emil Fischer	Germany	work on sugar and purine syntheses
1903	Svante Arrhenius	Sweden	theory of electrolytic dissociation
1904	William Ramsay	UK	discovery of inert gas elements and their places in the periodic system
1905	Adolf von Baeyer	Germany	work on organic dyes and hydroaromatic compounds
1906	Henri Moissan	France	isolation of fluorine; introduction of the Moissan furnace
1907	Eduard Buchner	Germany	discovery of noncellular fermentation
1908	Ernest Rutherford	UK	investigations into the disintegration of elements and the chemistry of radioactive substances
1909	Wilhelm Ostwald	Germany	pioneer work on catalysis, chemical equilibrium, and reaction velocities
1910	Otto Wallach	Germany	pioneer work in alicyclic combinations
1911	Marie Curie	France	discovery of radium and polonium; isolation of radium
1912	Victor Grignard	France	discovery of the Grignard reagents
	Paul Sabatier	France	method of hydrogenation organic compounds
1913	Alfred Werner	Switz.	work on the linkage of atoms in molecules
1914	Theodore W. Richards	US	accurate determination of various atomic weights
1915	Richard Willstätter	Germany	research in plant pigments, especially chlorophyll
1918	Fritz Haber	Germany	synthesis of ammonia
1920	Walther Hermann Nernst	Germany	work in thermochemistry
1921	Frederick Soddy	UK	investigation into the chemistry of radioactive substances and the occurrence and nature of isotopes
1922	Francis William Aston	UK	work with mass spectrographs; formulation of the whole-number rule
1923	Fritz Pregl	Austria	method of microanalysis of organic substances
1925	Richard Zsigmondy	Austria	elucidation of the heterogeneous nature of colloidal solutions

Chemistry (continued)

YEAR	WINNER(S)	COUNTRY	ACHIEVEMENT
1926	Theodor H.E. Svedberg	Sweden	work on disperse systems
1927	Heinrich Otto Wieland	Germany	research into the constitution of bile acids
1928	Adolf Windaus	Germany	research into the constitution of sterols
1929	Hans von Euler-Chelpin	Sweden	investigations into the fermentation of sugars
	Arthur Harden	UK	and the enzyme action involved
1930	Hans Fischer	Germany	hemin, chlorophyll research; synthesis of hemin
1931	Friedrich Bergius	Germany	invention and development of
	Carl Bosch	Germany	chemical high-pressure methods
1932	Irving Langmuir	US	discoveries and investigations in surface chemistry
1934	Harold C. Urey	US	discovery of heavy hydrogen
1935	Frédéric and Irène Joliot-Curie	France	synthesis of new radioactive elements
1936	Peter Debye	Neth.	work on dipole moments and diffraction of X-rays and electrons in gases
1937	Norman Haworth	UK	research on carbohydrates and vitamin C
	Paul Karrer	Switz.	research on carotenoids, flavins, and vitamins
1938	Richard Kuhn (declined)	Germany	carotenoid and vitamin research
1939	Adolf Butenandt (declined)	Germany	work on sexual hormones
	Leopold Ruzicka	Switz.	work on polymethylenes and higher terpenes
1943	Georg Charles von Hevesy	Hungary	use of isotopes as tracers in chemical research
1944	Otto Hahn	Germany	discovery of the fission of heavy nuclei
1945	Artturi Ilmari Virtanen	Finland	invention of the fodder preservation method
1946	John Howard Northrop	US	preparation of enzymes and
	Wendell M. Stanley	US	virus proteins in pure form
	James B. Sumner	US	discovery of enzyme crystallization
1947	Robert Robinson	UK	investigation of alkaloids and other plant products
1948	Arne Tiselius	Sweden	research on electrophoresis and adsorption analysis; discoveries concerning serum proteins
1949	William Francis Giauque	US	behavior of substances at extremely low temperatures
1950	Kurt Alder	W.Ger.	discovery and development of
	Otto Paul Hermann Diels	W.Ger.	diene synthesis
1951	Edwin M. McMillan	US	discovery of and research on
	Glenn T. Seaborg	US	transuranium elements
1952	A.J.P. Martin	UK	development of partition
	R.L.M. Synge	UK	chromatography
1953	Hermann Staudinger	W.Ger.	work on macromolecules
1954	Linus Pauling	US	study of the nature of the chemical bond
1955	Vincent du Vigneaud	US	first synthesis of a polypeptide hormone
1956	Cyril N. Hinshelwood	UK	work on the kinetics of
	Nikolay N. Semyonov	USSR	chemical reactions
1957	Alexander Robertus Todd, Baron Todd (of Trumpington)	UK	work on nucleotides and nucleotide coenzymes
1958	Frederick Sanger	UK	determination of the structure of the insulin molecule
1959	Jaroslav Heyrovsky	Czecho-slovakia	discovery and development of polarography
1960	Willard Frank Libby	US	development of radiocarbon dating
1961	Melvin Calvin	US	study of chemical steps that take place during photosynthesis
1962	John C. Kendrew	UK	determination of the structure of
	Max Ferdinand Perutz	UK	hemoproteins
1963	Giulio Natta	Italy	research into the structure and synthesis of polymers
	Karl Ziegler	W.Ger.	in the field of plastics
1964	Dorothy M.C. Hodgkin	UK	determination of the structure of biochemical compounds essential in combating pernicious anemia
1965	R.B. Woodward	US	synthesis of sterols, chlorophyll, and other substances
1966	Robert S. Mulliken	US	work concerning chemical bonds and the electronic structure of molecules
1967	Manfred Eigen	W.Ger.	studies of
	Ronald G.W. Norrish	UK	extremely fast
	George Porter	UK	chemical reactions
1968	Lars Onsager	US	work on the theory of thermodynamics of irreversible processes
1969	Derek H.R. Barton	UK	work in determining the actual three-dimensional
	Odd Hassel	Norway	shape of molecules
1970	Luis Federico Leloir	Argentina	discovery of sugar nucleotides and their role in the biosynthesis of carbohydrates

Chemistry (continued)

YEAR	WINNER(S)	COUNTRY	ACHIEVEMENT
1971	Gerhard Herzberg	Canada	research in the structure of molecules
1972	Christian B. Anfinsen	US	fundamental contributions to the study of ribonuclease
	Stanford Moore	US	} fundamental contributions
	William H. Stein	US	} to enzyme chemistry
1973	Ernst Otto Fischer	W.Ger.	} studies in the field of
	Geoffrey Wilkinson	UK	} organometallic chemistry
1974	Paul J. Flory	US	studies of long-chain molecules
1975	John W. Cornforth	UK	} work in
	Vladimir Prelog	Switz.	} stereochemistry
1976	William N. Lipscomb, Jr.	US	studies on the structure of boranes
1977	Ilya Prigogine	Belgium	widening the scope of thermodynamics
1978	Peter Dennis Mitchell	UK	formulation of a theory of energy transfer processes in biological systems
1979	Herbert Charles Brown	US	} introduction of compounds of boron and
	Georg Wittig	W.Ger.	} phosphorus in the synthesis of organic substances
1980	Paul Berg	US	first preparation of a hybrid DNA
	Walter Gilbert	US	} development of chemical and
	Frederick Sanger	UK	} biological analyses of DNA structure
1981	Kenichi Fukui	Japan	} orbital symmetry interpretation
	Roald Hoffmann	US	} of chemical reactions
1982	Aaron Klug	UK	determination of the structure of biological substances
1983	Henry Taube	US	study of electron transfer reactions
1984	Bruce Merrifield	US	development of a method of polypeptide synthesis
1985	Herbert A. Hauptman	US	} development of a way to map the
	Jerome Karle	US	} chemical structure of small molecules
1986	Dudley R. Herschbach	US	} development of methods
	Yuan T. Lee	US	} for analyzing basic
	John C. Polanyi	Canada	} chemical reactions
1987	Donald J. Cram	US	} development of molecules
	Jean-Marie Lehn	France	} that can link with
	Charles J. Pedersen	US	} other molecules
1988	Johann Deisenhofer	W.Ger.	} discovery of structure
	Robert Huber	W.Ger.	} proteins needed
	Hartmut Michel	W.Ger.	} in photosynthesis
1989	Sidney Altman	US	} discovery of certain
	Thomas Robert Cech	US	} basic properties of RNA
1990	Elias James Corey	US	development of retrosynthetic analysis for synthesis of complex molecules
1991	Richard R. Ernst	Switz.	improvements in nuclear magnetic resonance spectroscopy
1992	Rudolph A. Marcus	US	explanation of how electrons transfer between molecules
1993	Kary B. Mullis	US	} invention of techniques for
	Michael Smith	Canada	} gene study and manipulation
1994	George A. Olah	US	development of techniques to study hydrocarbon molecules
1995	Paul Crutzen	Neth.	} explanation of processes
	Mario Molina	US	} that deplete Earth's
	F. Sherwood Rowland	US	} ozone layer
1996	Robert F. Curl, Jr.	US	} discovery of new
	Harold W. Kroto	UK	} carbon compounds
	Richard E. Smalley	US	} called fullerenes
1997	Paul D. Boyer	US	} explanation of the enzymatic
	John E. Walker	UK	} conversion of adenosine triphosphate
	Jens C. Skou	Denmark	discovery of sodium-potassium-activated adenosine triphosphatase
1998	Walter Kohn	US	development of the density-functional theory
	John A. Pople	UK	development of computational methods in quantum chemistry
1999	Ahmed H. Zewail	Egypt/US	study of the transition states of chemical reactions using femtosecond spectroscopy
2000	Alan J. Heeger	US	} discovery of plastics
	Alan G. MacDiarmid	US	} that conduct
	Hideki Shirakawa	Japan	} electricity
2001	William S. Knowles	US	} work on chirally catalyzed
	Ryoji Noyori	Japan	} hydrogenation reactions
	K. Barry Sharpless	US	work on chirally catalyzed oxidation reactions

Chemistry (continued)

YEAR	WINNER(S)	COUNTRY	ACHIEVEMENT
2002	John B. Fenn	US	development of soft desorption ionization methods
	Koichi Tanaka	Japan	for mass spectrometric analyses of biological macromolecules
	Kurt Wüthrich	Switz.	development of nuclear magnetic resonance spectroscopy for determining the three-dimensional structure of biological macromolecules in solution
2003	Peter Agre	US	cell membrane channel
	Roderick MacKinnon	US	discoveries
2004	Aaron Ciechanover	Israel	discovery of
	Avram Hershko	Israel	ubiquitin-mediated
	Irwin Rose	US	protein degradation
2005	Yves Chauvin	France	development of the
	Robert H. Grubbs	US	metathesis method in
	Richard R. Schrock	US	organic synthesis
2006	Roger D. Kornberg	US	studies of the molecular basis of eukaryotic transcription
2007	Gerhard Ertl	Germany	studies of chemical processes on solid surfaces
2008	Martin Chalfie	US	discovery and development
	Osamu Shimomura	US	of GFP, the green
	Roger Y. Tsien	US	fluorescent protein
2009	Venkatraman Ramakrishnan	US	studies of the structure
	Thomas A. Steitz	US	and function
	Ada E. Yonath	Israel	of the ribosome

Physiology or Medicine

YEAR	WINNER(S)	COUNTRY	ACHIEVEMENT
1901	Emil von Behring	Germany	work on serum therapy
1902	Ronald Ross	UK	discovery of how malaria enters an organism
1903	Niels Ryberg Finsen	Denmark	treatment of skin diseases with light
1904	Ivan Petrovich Pavlov	Russia	work on the physiology of digestion
1905	Robert Koch	Germany	tuberculosis research
1906	Camillo Golgi	Italy	work on the structure
	Santiago Ramón y Cajal	Spain	of the nervous system
1907	Alphonse Laveran	France	discovery of the role of protozoa in diseases
1908	Paul Ehrlich	Germany	work on
	Élie Metchnikoff	Russia	immunity
1909	Emil Theodor Kocher	Switz.	work on aspects of the thyroid gland
1910	Albrecht Kossel	Germany	researches in cellular chemistry
1911	Allvar Gullstrand	Sweden	work on dioptrics of the eye
1912	Alexis Carrel	France	work on the vascular suture; the transplantation of organs
1913	Charles Richet	France	work on anaphylaxis
1914	Robert Bárány	Austria-Hungary	work on vestibular apparatus
1919	Jules Bordet	Belgium	work on immunity factors in blood serum
1920	August Krogh	Denmark	discovery of the capillary motor-regulating mechanism
1922	A.V. Hill	UK	discoveries concerning heat production in muscles
	Otto Meyerhof	Germany	work on metabolism of lactic acid in muscles
1923	Frederick G. Banting	Canada	discovery of
	J.J.R. Macleod	UK	insulin
1924	Willem Einthoven	Neth.	discovery of the electrocardiogram mechanism
1926	Johannes Fibiger	Denmark	contributions to cancer research
1927	Julius Wagner-Jauregg	Austria	work on malaria inoculation in dementia paralytica
1928	Charles-Jules-Henri Nicolle	France	work on typhus
1929	Christiaan Eijkman	Neth.	discovery of the antineuritic vitamin
	Frederick Gowland Hopkins	UK	discovery of growth-stimulating vitamins
1930	Karl Landsteiner	US	discovery of human blood groups
1931	Otto Warburg	Germany	discovery of the nature of the respiratory enzyme
1932	Edgar Douglas Adrian, 1st Baron Adrian	UK	discoveries regarding the functions
	Charles Scott Sherrington	UK	of neurons
1933	Thomas Hunt Morgan	US	discoveries concerning chromosomal heredity functions
1934	George Richards Minot	US	discoveries concerning
	William P. Murphy	US	liver treatment
	George H. Whipple	US	for anemia

Physiology or Medicine (continued)

YEAR	WINNER(S)	COUNTRY	ACHIEVEMENT
1935	Hans Spemann	Germany	discovery of the organizer effect in embryos
1936	Henry Dale	UK	} work on the chemical
	Otto Loewi	Germany	transmission of nerve impulses
1937	Albert Szent-Gyorgyi	Hungary	work on biological combustion
1938	Corneille Heymans	Belgium	discovery of the role of sinus and aortic mechanisms in respiration regulation
1939	Gerhard Domagk (declined)	Germany	discovery of the antibacterial effect of Prontosil
1943	Henrik Dam	Denmark	discovery of vitamin K
	Edward Adelbert Doisy	US	discovery of the chemical nature of vitamin K
1944	Joseph Erlanger	US	} research on differentiated
	Herbert S. Gasser	US	functions of nerve fibers
1945	Ernst Boris Chain	UK	discovery of
	Alexander Fleming	UK	penicillin
	Howard Walter Florey, Baron Florey	Australia	and its curative value
1946	Hermann J. Muller	US	production of mutations by X-ray irradiation
1947	Carl and Gerty Cori	US	discovery of how glycogen is catalytically converted
	Bernardo A. Houssay	Argentina	discovery of the pituitary hormone function in sugar metabolism
1948	Paul Hermann Müller	Switz.	discovery of properties of DDT
1949	António Egas Moniz	Portugal	discovery of therapeutic value in leucotomy for psychoses
	Walter Rudolf Hess	Switz.	discovery of the function of the interbrain
1950	Philip Showalter Hench	US	} research on adrenal cortex
	Edward Calvin Kendall	US	hormones, their structure, and
	Tadeus Reichstein	Switz.	their biological effects
1951	Max Theiler	South Africa	yellow fever discoveries
1952	Selman A. Waksman	US	discovery of streptomycin
1953	Hans Adolf Krebs	UK	discovery of the citric-acid cycle
	Fritz Albert Lipmann	US	discovery of coenzyme A metabolism
1954	John Franklin Enders	US	} cultivation of the
	Frederick C. Robbins	US	poliomyelitis virus in
	Thomas H. Weller	US	tissue cultures
1955	Axel H.T. Theorell	Sweden	discoveries concerning oxidation enzymes
1956	André F. Cournand	US	} discoveries concerning
	Werner Forssmann	W.Ger.	heart catheterization and
	Dickinson W. Richards	US	circulatory changes
1957	Daniel Bovet	Italy	production of synthetic curare
1958	George Wells Beadle	US	} discovery of the genetic regulation
	Edward L. Tatum	US	of chemical processes
	Joshua Lederberg	US	discoveries concerning genetic recombination
1959	Arthur Kornberg	US	} work on producing nucleic
	Severo Ochoa	US	acids artificially
1960	Macfarlane Burnet	Australia	} discovery of acquired immunity to
	Peter B. Medawar	UK	tissue transplants
1961	Georg von Békésy	US	discovery of functions of the inner ear
1962	Francis H.C. Crick	UK	} discoveries concerning
	James Dewey Watson	US	the molecular structure
	Maurice Wilkins	UK	of DNA
1963	John Carew Eccles	Australia	} study of the transmission
	Alan Hodgkin	UK	of impulses along
	Andrew F. Huxley	UK	a nerve fiber
1964	Konrad Bloch	US	} discoveries concerning
	Feodor Lynen	W.Ger.	cholesterol and fatty-acid metabolism
1965	François Jacob	France	} discoveries concerning
	André Lwoff	France	regulatory activities
	Jacques Monod	France	of the body cells
1966	Charles B. Huggins	US	} research on causes and
	Peyton Rous	US	treatment of cancer
1967	Ragnar Arthur Granit	Sweden	} discoveries about chemical
	Haldan Keffer Hartline	US	and physiological visual
	George Wald	US	processes in the eye
1968	Robert William Holley	US	} deciphering
	Har Gobind Khorana	US	of the
	Marshall W. Nirenberg	US	genetic code
1969	Max Delbrück	US	} research and discoveries
	A.D. Hershey	US	concerning viruses and
	Salvador Luria	US	viral diseases

Physiology or Medicine (continued)

YEAR	WINNER(S)	COUNTRY	ACHIEVEMENT
1970	Julius Axelrod	US	discoveries concerning
	Ulf von Euler	Sweden	the chemistry of
	Sir Bernard Katz	UK	nerve transmission
1971	Earl W. Sutherland, Jr.	US	discoveries concerning the action of hormones
1972	Gerald M. Edelman	US	research on the chemical
	Rodney Robert Porter	UK	structure of antibodies
1973	Karl von Frisch	Austria	discoveries in
	Konrad Lorenz	Austria	animal behavior
	Nikolaas Tinbergen	UK	patterns
1974	Albert Claude	US	research on the structural
	Christian René de Duve	Belgium	and functional organization
	George E. Palade	US	of cells
1975	David Baltimore	US	discoveries concerning the interaction between
	Renato Dulbecco	US	tumor viruses and the genetic
	Howard Martin Temin	US	material of the cell
1976	Baruch S. Blumberg	US	studies of the origin and
	D. Carleton Gajdusek	US	spread of infectious diseases
1977	Roger C.L. Guillemin	US	research on pituitary
	Andrew Victor Schally	US	hormones
	Rosalyn S. Yalow	US	development of radioimmunoassay
1978	Werner Arber	Switz.	discovery and application
	Daniel Nathans	US	of enzymes that
	Hamilton O. Smith	US	fragment DNA
1979	Allan M. Cormack	US	development of
	Godfrey N. Hounsfield	UK	the CAT scan
1980	Baruj Benacerraf	US	investigations of genetic
	Jean Dausset	France	control of the response of the
	George Davis Snell	US	immune system to foreign substances
1981	David Hunter Hubel	US	discoveries concerning the processing of visual
	Torsten Nils Wiesel	Sweden	information by the brain
	Roger Wolcott Sperry	US	discoveries concerning cerebral hemisphere functions
1982	Sune K. Bergström	Sweden	discoveries concerning the biochemistry
	Bengt I. Samuelsson	Sweden	and physiology of
	John Robert Vane	UK	of prostaglandins
1983	Barbara McClintock	US	discovery of mobile plant genes that affect heredity
1984	Niels K. Jerne	Denmark	theory and development
	Georges J.F. Köhler	W.Ger.	of a technique
	César Milstein	UK/	for producing
		Argentina	monoclonal antibodies
1985	Michael S. Brown	US	discovery of cell receptors relating to
	Joseph L. Goldstein	US	cholesterol metabolism
1986	Stanley Cohen	US	discovery of chemical agents
	Rita Levi-Montalcini	Italy	that help regulate the growth of cells
1987	Susumu Tonegawa	Japan	study of genetic aspects of antibodies
1988	James Black	UK	development of new
	Gertrude Belle Elion	US	classes of drugs for
	George H. Hitchings	US	combating disease
1989	J. Michael Bishop	US	study of cancer-causing
	Harold Varmus	US	genes called oncogenes
1990	Joseph E. Murray	US	development of kidney and
	E. Donnall Thomas	US	bone-marrow transplants
1991	Erwin Neher	Germany	discovery of how cells
	Bert Sakmann	Germany	communicate, as related to diseases
1992	Edmond H. Fischer	US	discovery of a class of enzymes
	Edwin Gerhard Krebs	US	called protein kinases
1993	Richard J. Roberts	UK	discovery of "split," or
	Phillip A. Sharp	US	interrupted, genetic structure
1994	Alfred G. Gilman	US	discovery of cell signalers
	Martin Rodbell	US	called G-proteins
1995	Edward B. Lewis	US	identification of genes
	Christiane Nüsslein-Volhard	Germany	that control the body's
	Eric F. Wieschaus	US	early structural development
1996	Peter C. Doherty	Australia	discovery of how the immune
	Rolf M. Zinkernagel	Switz.	system recognizes virus-infected cells
1997	Stanley B. Prusiner	US	discovery of the prion, a type of disease-causing protein
1998	Robert F. Furchgott	US	discovery that nitric oxide
	Louis J. Ignarro	US	acts as a signaling molecule in
	Ferid Murad	US	the cardiovascular system

Physiology or Medicine (continued)

YEAR	WINNER(S)	COUNTRY	ACHIEVEMENT
1999	Günter Blobel	US	discovery that proteins help govern cellular organization
2000	Arvid Carlsson	Sweden	discovery of how signals
	Paul Greengard	US	are transmitted between nerve
	Eric Kandel	US	cells in the brain
2001	Leland H. Hartwell	US	discovery of key
	R. Timothy Hunt	UK	regulators of
	Paul M. Nurse	UK	the cell cycle
2002	Sydney Brenner	UK	discoveries concerning how genes
	H. Robert Horvitz	US	regulate and program organ
	John E. Sulston	UK	development and cell death
2003	Paul C. Lauterbur	US	discoveries concerning magnetic
	Peter Mansfield	UK	resonance imaging
2004	Richard Axel	US	discoveries of odorant receptors and the
	Linda B. Buck	US	organization of the olfactory system
2005	Barry J. Marshall	Australia	discovery of the bacterium *Helicobacter pylori* and its
	J. Robin Warren	Australia	role in peptic ulcer disease and gastritis
2006	Andrew Z. Fire	US	discovery of RNA interference: gene silencing
	Craig C. Mello	US	by double-stranded RNA
2007	Mario R. Capecchi	US	discoveries of principles for introducing
	Martin J. Evans	UK	specific gene modifications
	Oliver Smithies	US	using embryonic stem cells
2008	Françoise Barré-Sinoussi	France	discovery of the human
	Luc Montagnier	France	immunodeficiency virus (HIV)
	Harald zur Hausen	Germany	research supporting the theory that human papillomaviruses cause cervical cancer
2009	Elizabeth H. Blackburn	US/Australia	discovery of the protection
	Carol W. Greider	US	of chromosomes by telomeres
	Jack W. Szostak	US	and the enzyme telomerase

Literature

YEAR	WINNER(S)	COUNTRY	FIELD
1901	Sully Prudhomme	France	poetry
1902	Theodor Mommsen	Germany	history
1903	Bjørnstjerne Martinus Bjørnson	Norway	prose fiction, poetry, drama
1904	José Echegaray y Eizaguirre	Spain	drama
	Frédéric Mistral	France	poetry
1905	Henryk Sienkiewicz	Poland	prose fiction
1906	Giosuè Carducci	Italy	poetry
1907	Rudyard Kipling	UK	poetry, prose fiction
1908	Rudolf Christoph Eucken	Germany	philosophy
1909	Selma Lagerlöf	Sweden	prose fiction
1910	Paul Johann Ludwig von Heyse	Germany	poetry, prose fiction, drama
1911	Maurice Maeterlinck	Belgium	drama
1912	Gerhart Hauptmann	Germany	drama
1913	Rabindranath Tagore	India	poetry
1915	Romain Rolland	France	prose fiction
1916	Verner von Heidenstam	Sweden	poetry
1917	Karl Gjellerup	Denmark	prose fiction
	Henrik Pontoppidan	Denmark	prose fiction
1918	Erik Axel Karlfeldt (declined)	Sweden	poetry
1919	Carl Spitteler	Switzerland	poetry, prose fiction
1920	Knut Hamsun	Norway	prose fiction
1921	Anatole France	France	prose fiction
1922	Jacinto Benavente y Martínez	Spain	drama
1923	William Butler Yeats	Ireland	poetry
1924	Wladyslaw Stanislaw Reymont	Poland	prose fiction
1925	George Bernard Shaw	Ireland	drama
1926	Grazia Deledda	Italy	prose fiction
1927	Henri Bergson	France	philosophy
1928	Sigrid Undset	Norway	prose fiction
1929	Thomas Mann	Germany	prose fiction
1930	Sinclair Lewis	US	prose fiction
1931	Erik Axel Karlfeldt (posthumously)	Sweden	poetry
1932	John Galsworthy	UK	prose fiction
1933	Ivan Alekseyevich Bunin	USSR	poetry, prose fiction
1934	Luigi Pirandello	Italy	drama

Literature (continued)

YEAR	WINNER(S)	COUNTRY	FIELD
1936	Eugene O'Neill	US	drama
1937	Roger Martin du Gard	France	prose fiction
1938	Pearl Buck	US	prose fiction
1939	Frans Eemil Sillanpää	Finland	prose fiction
1944	Johannes V. Jensen	Denmark	prose fiction
1945	Gabriela Mistral	Chile	poetry
1946	Hermann Hesse	Switzerland	prose fiction
1947	André Gide	France	prose
1948	T.S. Eliot	UK	poetry, criticism
1949	William Faulkner	US	prose fiction
1950	Bertrand Russell	UK	philosophy
1951	Pär Lagerkvist	Sweden	prose fiction
1952	François Mauriac	France	poetry, prose fiction, drama
1953	Winston Churchill	UK	history, oration
1954	Ernest Hemingway	US	prose fiction
1955	Halldór Laxness	Iceland	prose fiction
1956	Juan Ramón Jiménez	Spain	poetry
1957	Albert Camus	France	prose fiction, drama
1958	Boris L. Pasternak (declined)	USSR	prose fiction, poetry
1959	Salvatore Quasimodo	Italy	poetry
1960	Saint-John Perse	France	poetry
1961	Ivo Andric	Yugoslavia	prose fiction
1962	John Steinbeck	US	prose fiction
1963	George Seferis	Greece	poetry
1964	Jean-Paul Sartre (declined)	France	philosophy, drama
1965	Mikhail A. Sholokhov	USSR	prose fiction
1966	S.Y. Agnon	Israel	prose fiction
	Nelly Sachs	Sweden	poetry
1967	Miguel Ángel Asturias	Guatemala	prose fiction
1968	Yasunari Kawabata	Japan	prose fiction
1969	Samuel Beckett	Ireland	prose fiction, drama
1970	Aleksandr I. Solzhenitsyn	USSR	prose fiction
1971	Pablo Neruda	Chile	poetry
1972	Heinrich Böll	West Germany	prose fiction
1973	Patrick White	Australia	prose fiction
1974	Eyvind Johnson	Sweden	prose fiction
	Harry Martinson	Sweden	prose fiction, poetry
1975	Eugenio Montale	Italy	poetry
1976	Saul Bellow	US	prose fiction
1977	Vicente Aleixandre	Spain	poetry
1978	Isaac Bashevis Singer	US	prose fiction
1979	Odysseus Elytis	Greece	poetry
1980	Czeslaw Milosz	US	poetry
1981	Elias Canetti	Bulgaria	prose
1982	Gabriel García Márquez	Colombia	prose fiction, journalism, social criticism
1983	William Golding	UK	prose fiction
1984	Jaroslav Seifert	Czechoslovakia	poetry
1985	Claude Simon	France	prose fiction
1986	Wole Soyinka	Nigeria	drama, poetry
1987	Joseph Brodsky	US	poetry, prose
1988	Naguib Mahfouz	Egypt	prose fiction
1989	Camilo José Cela	Spain	prose fiction
1990	Octavio Paz	Mexico	poetry, prose
1991	Nadine Gordimer	South Africa	prose fiction
1992	Derek Walcott	Saint Lucia	poetry
1993	Toni Morrison	US	prose fiction
1994	Kenzaburo Oe	Japan	prose fiction
1995	Seamus Heaney	Ireland	poetry
1996	Wislawa Szymborska	Poland	poetry
1997	Dario Fo	Italy	drama
1998	José Saramago	Portugal	prose fiction
1999	Günter Grass	Germany	prose fiction
2000	Gao Xingjian	France	prose fiction, drama
2001	V.S. Naipaul	UK	prose fiction
2002	Imre Kertész	Hungary	prose fiction
2003	J.M. Coetzee	South Africa	prose fiction
2004	Elfriede Jelinek	Austria	prose fiction, drama
2005	Harold Pinter	UK	drama

Literature (continued)

YEAR	WINNER(S)	COUNTRY	FIELD
2006	Orhan Pamuk	Turkey	prose fiction
2007	Doris Lessing	UK	prose fiction, social criticism
2008	Jean-Marie Gustave Le Clézio	France/Mauritius	prose fiction, essays
2009	Herta Müller	Germany	poetry, prose

Peace

YEAR	WINNER(S)	COUNTRY	YEAR	WINNER(S)	COUNTRY
1901	Henri Dunant	Switzerland	1952	Albert Schweitzer	France
	Frédéric Passy	France	1953	George C. Marshall	US
1902	Élie Ducommun	Switzerland	1954	Office of the United Nations	(founded 1951)
	Charles-Albert Gobat	Switzerland		High Commissioner for	
1903	Randal Cremer	UK		Refugees	
1904	Institute of International Law	(founded 1873)	1957	Lester B. Pearson	Canada
1905	Bertha, Freifrau von Suttner	Austria-Hungary	1958	Dominique Pire	Belgium
1906	Theodore Roosevelt	US	1959	Philip John Noel-Baker,	UK
1907	Ernesto Teodoro Moneta	Italy		Baron Noel-Baker (of the	
	Louis Renault	France		City of Derby)	
1908	Klas Pontus Arnoldson	Sweden	1960	Albert John Luthuli	South Africa
	Fredrik Bajer	Denmark	1961	Dag Hammarskjöld	Sweden
1909	Auguste-Marie-François	Belgium		(posthumously)	
	Beernaert		1962	Linus Pauling	US
	Paul-H.-B. d'Estournelles	France	1963	International Committee of	(founded 1863)
	de Constant			the Red Cross	
1910	International Peace Bureau	(founded 1891)		League of Red Cross	(founded 1919)
1911	Tobias Michael Carel Asser	The Netherlands		Societies	
	Alfred Hermann Fried	Austria-Hungary	1964	Martin Luther King, Jr.	US
1912	Elihu Root	US	1965	United Nations Children's	(founded 1946)
1913	Henri-Marie Lafontaine	Belgium		Fund	
1917	International Committee of	(founded 1863)	1968	René Cassin	France
	the Red Cross		1969	International Labour	(founded 1919)
1919	Woodrow Wilson	US		Organisation	
1920	Léon Bourgeois	France	1970	Norman Ernest Borlaug	US
1921	Karl Hjalmar Branting	Sweden	1971	Willy Brandt	West Germany
	Christian Lous Lange	Norway	1973	Henry Kissinger	US
1922	Fridtjof Nansen	Norway		Le Duc Tho (declined)	North Vietnam
1925	Austen Chamberlain	UK	1974	Seán MacBride	Ireland
	Charles G. Dawes	US		Eisaku Sato	Japan
1926	Aristide Briand	France	1975	Andrey Dmitriyevich	USSR
	Gustav Stresemann	Germany		Sakharov	
1927	Ferdinand-Édouard Buisson	France	1976	Mairéad Corrigan	Northern
	Ludwig Quidde	Germany			Ireland
1929	Frank B. Kellogg	US		Betty Williams	Northern
1930	Nathan Söderblom	Sweden			Ireland
1931	Jane Addams	US	1977	Amnesty International	(founded 1961)
	Nicholas Murray Butler	US	1978	Menachem Begin	Israel
1933	Norman Angell	UK		Anwar el-Sadat	Egypt
1934	Arthur Henderson	UK	1979	Mother Teresa	India
1935	Carl von Ossietzky	Germany	1980	Adolfo Pérez Esquivel	Argentina
1936	Carlos Saavedra Lamas	Argentina	1981	Office of the United Nations	(founded 1951)
1937	Robert Gascoyne-Cecil,	UK		High Commissioner for	
	1st Viscount Cecil			Refugees	
	(of Chelwood)		1982	Alfonso García Robles	Mexico
1938	Nansen International Office	(founded 1931)		Alva Myrdal	Sweden
	for Refugees		1983	Lech Walesa	Poland
1944	International Committee of	(founded 1863)	1984	Desmond Tutu	South Africa
	the Red Cross		1985	International Physicians for	(founded 1980)
1945	Cordell Hull	US		the Prevention of Nuclear	
1946	Emily Greene Balch	US		War	
	John R. Mott	US	1986	Elie Wiesel	US
1947	American Friends Service	US	1987	Oscar Arias Sánchez	Costa Rica
	Committee		1988	United Nations Peace-	
	Friends Service Council	UK		keeping Forces	
1949	John Boyd Orr, Baron Boyd-	UK	1989	Dalai Lama	Tibet
	Orr of Brechin Mearns		1990	Mikhail Gorbachev	USSR
1950	Ralph Bunche	US	1991	Aung San Suu Kyi	Myanmar
1951	Léon Jouhaux	France			(Burma)

Peace (continued)

YEAR	WINNER(S)	COUNTRY	YEAR	WINNER(S)	COUNTRY
1992	Rigoberta Menchú	Guatemala	1999	Doctors Without Borders	(founded 1971)
1993	F.W. de Klerk	South Africa	2000	Kim Dae Jung	Republic of
	Nelson Mandela	South Africa			Korea
1994	Yasir Arafat	Palestinian	2001	Kofi Annan	Ghana
		territories		United Nations	(founded 1945)
	Shimon Peres	Israel	2002	Jimmy Carter	US
	Yitzhak Rabin	Israel	2003	Shirin Ebadi	Iran
1995	Pugwash Conferences	(founded 1957)	2004	Wangari Maathai	Kenya
	Joseph Rotblat	UK	2005	Mohamed ElBaradei	Egypt
1996	Carlos Filipe Ximenes Belo	East Timor		International Atomic	(founded 1957)
	José Ramos-Horta	East Timor		Energy Agency	
1997	International Campaign to	(founded 1992)	2006	Muhammad Yunus	Bangladesh
	Ban Landmines			Grameen Bank	(founded 1976)
	Jody Williams	US	2007	Intergovernmental Panel	(founded 1988)
1998	John Hume	Northern		on Climate Change	
		Ireland		Albert Arnold (Al) Gore, Jr.	US
	David Trimble	Northern	2008	Martti Ahtisaari	Finland
		Ireland	2009	Barack H. Obama	US

Economics

YEAR	WINNER(S)	COUNTRY	ACHIEVEMENT
1969	Ragnar Frisch	Norway	work in
	Jan Tinbergen	Neth.	econometrics
1970	Paul Samuelson	US	work in scientific analysis of economic theory
1971	Simon Kuznets	US	extensive research on the economic growth of nations
1972	Kenneth J. Arrow	US	contributions to general economic
	John R. Hicks	UK	equilibrium theory and welfare theory
1973	Wassily Leontief	US	development of input-output analysis
1974	Friedrich von Hayek	UK	pioneering analysis of the interdependence of
	Gunnar Myrdal	Sweden	economic, social, and institutional phenomena
1975	Leonid V. Kantorovich	USSR	contributions to the theory of
	Tjalling C. Koopmans	US	optimum allocation of resources
1976	Milton Friedman	US	work in consumption analysis and economic stabilization
1977	James Edward Meade	UK	contributions to the theory
	Bertil Ohlin	Sweden	of international trade
1978	Herbert A. Simon	US	study of decision-making in economic organizations
1979	Arthur Lewis	UK	research into analyses of economic processes
	Theodore W. Schultz	US	in developing nations
1980	Lawrence Robert Klein	US	creation of empirical models of business fluctuations
1981	James Tobin	US	portfolio-selection theory of investment
1982	George J. Stigler	US	studies of economic effects of governmental regulation
1983	Gerard Debreu	US	mathematical proof of the supply-and-demand theory
1984	Richard Stone	UK	development of national income accounting systems
1985	Franco Modigliani	US	analyses of household savings and financial markets
1986	James M. Buchanan, Jr.	US	development of the public-choice theory bridging
			economics and political science
1987	Robert Merton Solow	US	contributions to the theory of economic growth
1988	Maurice Allais	France	study of the theory of markets and efficient resource use
1989	Trygve Haavelmo	Norway	development of statistical techniques
			for economic forecasting
1990	Harry M. Markowitz	US	study of financial
	Merton H. Miller	US	markets and investment
	William F. Sharpe	US	decision making
1991	Ronald Coase	US	application of economic principles to the study of law
1992	Gary S. Becker	US	application of economic theory to social sciences
1993	Robert William Fogel	US	contributions to
	Douglass C. North	US	economic history
1994	John C. Harsanyi	US	development
	John F. Nash	US	of game
	Reinhard Selten	Germany	theory
1995	Robert E. Lucas, Jr.	US	incorporation of rational expectations in macroeconomic theory
1996	James A. Mirrlees	UK	contributions to the theory of incentives under
	William Vickrey	US	conditions of asymmetric information
	(posthumously)		

Economics (continued)

YEAR	WINNER(S)	COUNTRY	ACHIEVEMENT
1997	Robert C. Merton	US	} method for determining the value of
	Myron S. Scholes	US	} stock options and other derivatives
1998	Amartya Sen	India	contribution to welfare economics
1999	Robert A. Mundell	Canada	analysis of optimum currency areas and of policy under different exchange-rate regimes
2000	James J. Heckman	US	} development of methods of statistical
	Daniel L. McFadden	US	} analysis of individual and household behavior
2001	George A. Akerlof	US	} analyses of
	A. Michael Spence	US	} markets with asymmetric
	Joseph E. Stiglitz	US	} information
2002	Daniel Kahneman	US/Israel	psychological study of economic decision making
	Vernon L. Smith	US	establishment of laboratory experiments for empirical economic analysis of alternative market mechanisms
2003	Robert F. Engle	US	methods of analysis of economic time series with time-varying volatility
	Clive W.J. Granger	UK	methods of analysis of economic time series with common trends
2004	Finn E. Kydland	Norway	} macroeconomic analysis of the time consistency of
	Edward C. Prescott	US	} economic policy and the driving forces behind business cycles
2005	Robert J. Aumann	Israel/US	} enhancement of the understanding of conflict and
	Thomas C. Schelling	US	} cooperation through game-theory analysis
2006	Edmund S. Phelps	US	analysis of intertemporal tradeoffs in macroeconomics
2007	Leonid Hurwicz	US	} research that
	Eric S. Maskin	US	} laid the foundations
	Roger B. Myerson	US	} of mechanism design theory
2008	Paul Krugman	US	research into trade patterns and location of economic activity
2009	Elinor Ostrom	US	research in economic governance, especially the commons
	Oliver E. Williamson	US	analysis of economic governance, especially the boundaries of the firm

Special Achievement Awards

Kennedy Center Honors

The Kennedy Center Honors are bestowed annually by the John F. Kennedy Center for the Performing Arts in Washington DC. First conferred in 1978, the honors salute several artists each year for lifetime achievement in the performing arts.
Web site: <www.kennedy-center.org/programs/specialevents/honors/>.

YEAR	NAME	FIELD
1978	Marian Anderson	opera singer
	Fred Astaire	dancer, actor
	George Balanchine	choreographer
	Richard Rodgers	composer
	Artur Rubinstein	pianist
1979	Aaron Copland	composer
	Ella Fitzgerald	singer
	Henry Fonda	actor
	Martha Graham	dancer, choreographer
	Tennessee Williams	playwright
1980	Leonard Bernstein	conductor
	James Cagney	actor
	Agnes de Mille	dancer, choreographer
	Lynn Fontanne	actress
	Leontyne Price	opera singer
1981	Count Basie	jazz pianist
	Cary Grant	actor
	Helen Hayes	actress
	Jerome Robbins	dancer, choreographer
	Rudolf Serkin	pianist

YEAR	NAME	FIELD
1982	George Abbott	theater producer, director, writer
	Lillian Gish	actress
	Benny Goodman	swing musician
	Gene Kelly	dancer, actor
	Eugene Ormandy	conductor
1983	Katherine Dunham	dancer, choreographer
	Elia Kazan	theater and film director
	Frank Sinatra	singer, actor
	James Stewart	actor
	Virgil Thomson	composer, music critic
1984	Lena Horne	singer, actress
	Danny Kaye	actor, comedian
	Gian Carlo Menotti	composer
	Arthur Miller	playwright
	Isaac Stern	violinist
1985	Merce Cunningham	dancer, choreographer
	Irene Dunne	actress
	Bob Hope	entertainer, actor

Kennedy Center Honors (continued)

YEAR	NAME	FIELD
1985 (cont.)	Alan Jay Lerner	playwright, lyricist
	Frederick Loewe	composer
	Beverly Sills	opera singer
1986	Lucille Ball	actress
	Ray Charles	soul musician
	Hume Cronyn	actor
	Jessica Tandy	actress
	Yehudi Menuhin	violinist
	Antony Tudor	choreographer
1987	Perry Como	singer
	Bette Davis	actress
	Sammy Davis, Jr.	singer, dancer, entertainer
	Nathan Milstein	violinist
	Alwin Nikolais	choreographer
1988	Alvin Ailey	dancer, choreographer
	George Burns	actor, comedian
	Myrna Loy	actress
	Alexander Schneider	violinist, conductor
	Roger L. Stevens	arts administrator
1989	Harry Belafonte	folk singer, actor
	Claudette Colbert	actress
	Alexandra Danilova	ballet dancer
	Mary Martin	actress, singer
	William Schuman	composer
1990	Dizzy Gillespie	jazz musician
	Katharine Hepburn	actress
	Risë Stevens	opera singer
	Jule Styne	composer
	Billy Wilder	film director
1991	Roy Acuff	country musician
	Betty Comden	theater and film writer
	Adolph Green	theater and film writer
	Fayard Nicholas	dancer
	Harold Nicholas	dancer
	Gregory Peck	actor
	Robert Shaw	conductor
1992	Lionel Hampton	swing musician
	Paul Newman	actor
	Joanne Woodward	actress
	Ginger Rogers	dancer, actress
	Mstislav Rostropovich	musician, conductor
	Paul Taylor	dancer, choreographer
1993	Johnny Carson	television entertainer
	Arthur Mitchell	dancer, choreographer
	Georg Solti	conductor
	Stephen Sondheim	composer, lyricist
	Marion Williams	gospel singer
1994	Kirk Douglas	actor
	Aretha Franklin	soul singer
	Morton Gould	composer
	Harold Prince	theater director, producer
	Pete Seeger	folk musician
1995	Jacques d'Amboise	dancer, choreographer
	Marilyn Horne	opera singer
	B.B. King	blues musician
	Sidney Poitier	actor
	Neil Simon	playwright
1996	Edward Albee	playwright
	Benny Carter	jazz musician
	Johnny Cash	country musician
	Jack Lemmon	actor
	Maria Tallchief	ballet dancer
1997	Lauren Bacall	actress
	Bob Dylan	singer, songwriter
	Charlton Heston	actor

YEAR	NAME	FIELD
1997 (cont.)	Jessye Norman	opera singer
	Edward Villella	dancer, choreographer
1998	Bill Cosby	actor, comedian
	Fred Ebb	lyricist
	John Kander	composer
	Willie Nelson	country musician
	André Previn	pianist, composer, conductor
	Shirley Temple Black	actress, diplomat
1999	Victor Borge	pianist, comedian
	Sean Connery	actor
	Judith Jamison	dancer, choreographer
	Jason Robards	actor
	Stevie Wonder	musician
2000	Mikhail Baryshnikov	dancer
	Chuck Berry	musician
	Plácido Domingo	opera singer
	Clint Eastwood	actor, director
	Angela Lansbury	actress
2001	Julie Andrews	actress
	Van Cliburn	pianist
	Quincy Jones	music producer, composer
	Jack Nicholson	actor
	Luciano Pavarotti	opera singer
2002	James Earl Jones	actor
	James Levine	conductor
	Chita Rivera	musical theater performer
	Paul Simon	singer
	Elizabeth Taylor	actress
2003	James Brown	musician
	Carol Burnett	actress
	Loretta Lynn	musician
	Mike Nichols	director
	Itzhak Perlman	musician
2004	Warren Beatty	film actor, director
	Ossie Davis	actor, writer, producer, director
	Ruby Dee	actress, writer
	Elton John	musician
	Joan Sutherland	opera singer
	John Williams	composer
2005	Tony Bennett	singer
	Suzanne Farrell	dancer, teacher
	Julie Harris	actress
	Robert Redford	film actor, director, producer
	Tina Turner	singer, actress
2006	Zubin Mehta	conductor
	Dolly Parton	singer, actress
	William "Smokey" Robinson	singer
	Steven Spielberg	film director, producer
	Andrew Lloyd Webber	composer
2007	Leon Fleisher	pianist, conductor
	Steve Martin	actor, writer
	Diana Ross	singer, actress
	Martin Scorsese	film director
	Brian Wilson	composer, singer
2008	Roger Daltrey	singer, composer, actor
	Morgan Freeman	actor
	George Jones	country musician
	Barbra Streisand	singer, actress, director, producer, writer
	Twyla Tharp	dancer, choreographer
	Pete Townshend	musician, composer

Kennedy Center Honors (continued)

YEAR	NAME	FIELD	YEAR	NAME	FIELD
2009	Mel Brooks	writer, actor, director, producer, composer	2009 (cont.)	Grace Bumbry	opera singer
	Dave Brubeck	pianist, composer		Robert De Niro	actor, director, producer
				Bruce Springsteen	singer, songwriter

National Medal of Arts

The National Medal of Arts, awarded annually since 1985 by the National Endowment for the Arts (NEA) and the president of the United States, honors artists and art patrons for remarkable contributions to American arts. Both the NEA and the president choose candidates for the award, and the winners are selected by the president.

Web site: <www.nea.gov/honors/medals/medalists_year.html>.

YEAR	NAME	FIELD	YEAR	NAME	FIELD
1985	Elliott Carter, Jr.	composer	1989 (cont.)	Alfred Eisenstaedt	photojournalist
	Dorothy Buffum Chandler	patron		Martin Friedman	museum director
				Leigh Gerdine	civic leader, patron
	Ralph Ellison	writer		Dizzy Gillespie	jazz musician
	José Ferrer	actor		Walker K. Hancock	sculptor
	Martha Graham	dancer, choreographer		Vladimir Horowitz[1]	pianist
	Hallmark Cards, Inc.	patron		Czeslaw Milosz	writer
	Lincoln Kirstein	patron		Robert Motherwell	painter
	Paul Mellon	patron		John Updike	writer
	Louise Nevelson	sculptor	1990	George Abbott	theater producer, director, writer
	Georgia O'Keeffe	painter			
	Leontyne Price	opera singer		Hume Cronyn	actor, director
	Alice Tully	patron		Merce Cunningham	dancer, choreographer
1986	Marian Anderson	opera singer			
	Frank Capra	film director		Jasper Johns	painter, sculptor
	Aaron Copland	composer		B.B. King	blues musician
	Willem de Kooning	painter		David Lloyd Kreeger	patron
	Dominique de Menil	patron		Jacob Lawrence	painter
	Agnes de Mille	dancer, choreographer		Harris and Carroll Sterling Masterson	patrons
	Exxon Corp.	patron			
	Seymour H. Knox	patron		Ian McHarg	landscape architect
	Eva Le Gallienne	actress, producer		Beverly Sills	opera singer
	Alan Lomax	ethnomusicologist		Southeastern Bell Corp.	patron
	Lewis Mumford	architectural critic			
	Eudora Welty	writer		Jessica Tandy	actress
1987	Romare Bearden	painter	1991	Maurice Abravanel	conductor, music director
	J.W. Fisher	patron			
	Ella Fitzgerald	singer		Roy Acuff	country musician
	Armand Hammer	patron		Pietro Belluschi	architect
	Sydney and Frances Lewis	patrons		J. Carter Brown	museum director
				Charles "Honi" Coles	tap dancer
	Howard Nemerov	writer, scholar		John O. Crosby	opera director, conductor
	Alwin Nikolais	choreographer			
	Isamu Noguchi	sculptor		Richard Diebenkorn	painter
	William Schuman	composer		R. Philip Hanes, Jr.	patron
	Robert Penn Warren	writer		Kitty Carlisle Hart	actress, singer
1988	Brooke Astor	patron		Pearl Primus	choreographer, anthropologist
	Saul Bellow	writer			
	Sydney J. Freedberg	art historian, curator		Isaac Stern	violinist
	Francis Goelet	patron		Texaco Inc.	patron
	Helen Hayes	actress	1992	AT&T	patron
	Gordon Parks	filmmaker, photographer, writer		Marilyn Horne	opera singer
				Allan Houser	sculptor
	I.M. Pei	architect		James Earl Jones	actor
	Jerome Robbins	dancer, choreographer		Minnie Pearl	Grand Ole Opry performer
	Rudolf Serkin	pianist			
	Roger L. Stevens	arts administrator		Robert Saudek	television producer, museum director
	Obert C. Tanner	patron			
	Virgil Thomson	composer, music critic		Earl Scruggs	banjo player
1989	Leopold Adler	historic preservationist, civic leader		Robert Shaw	conductor
				Billy Taylor	jazz pianist
	Dayton Hudson Corp.	patron		Robert Venturi and Denise Scott Brown	architects
	Katherine Dunham	dancer, choreographer			

National Medal of Arts (continued)

YEAR	NAME	FIELD
1992 (cont.)	Lila Wallace–Reader's Digest Fund	patron
	Robert Wise	film director
1993	Walter and Leonore Annenberg	patrons
	Cabell "Cab" Calloway	jazz musician
	Ray Charles	soul musician
	Bess Lomax Hawes	folklorist, musician
	Stanley Kunitz	poet
	Robert Merrill	opera singer
	Arthur Miller	playwright
	Robert Rauschenberg	painter
	Lloyd Richards	theater director
	William Styron	writer
	Paul Taylor	dancer, choreographer
	Billy Wilder	film director, writer
1994	Harry Belafonte	folksinger, actor
	Dave Brubeck	jazz musician
	Celia Cruz	salsa singer
	Dorothy DeLay	violin instructor
	Julie Harris	actress
	Erick Hawkins	dancer, choreographer
	Gene Kelly	dancer, actor
	Pete Seeger	folk musician
	Catherine Filene Shouse	patron
	Wayne Thiebaud	painter
	Richard Wilbur	poet
	Young Audiences	arts organization
1995	Licia Albanese	opera singer
	Gwendolyn Brooks	poet
	B. Gerald and Iris Cantor	patrons
	Ossie Davis and Ruby Dee	actors
	David Diamond	composer
	James Ingo Freed	architect
	Bob Hope	entertainer
	Roy Lichtenstein	painter
	Arthur Mitchell	dancer, choreographer
	William S. Monroe	bluegrass musician
	Urban Gateways	arts education organization
1996	Edward Albee	playwright
	Boys Choir of Harlem	choir
	Sarah Caldwell	opera conductor
	Harry Callahan	photographer
	Zelda Fichandler	theater founder, director
	Eduardo "Lalo" Guerrero	Chicano musician
	Lionel Hampton	swing musician
	Bella Lewitzky	dancer, choreographer
	Vera List	patron
	Robert Redford	actor, film director
	Maurice Sendak	illustrator, writer
	Stephen Sondheim	composer, lyricist
1997	Louise Bourgeois	sculptor
	Betty Carter	jazz singer
	Agnes Gund	patron
	Daniel Urban Kiley	landscape architect
	Angela Lansbury	actress
	James Levine	opera conductor, pianist
	MacDowell Colony	artists' colony
	Tito Puente	jazz and mambo musician
	Jason Robards	actor

YEAR	NAME	FIELD
1997 (cont.)	Edward Villella	dancer, choreographer
	Doc Watson	folk and country musician
1998	Jacques d'Amboise	dancer, choreographer
	Antoine "Fats" Domino	rock-and-roll musician
	Ramblin' Jack Elliott	folk musician
	Frank O. Gehry	architect
	Barbara Handman	patron
	Agnes Martin	painter
	Gregory Peck	actor
	Roberta Peters	opera singer
	Philip Roth	writer
	Sara Lee Corp.	patron
	Steppenwolf Theatre Company	arts organization
	Gwen Verdon	actress, dancer
1999	Irene Diamond	patron
	Aretha Franklin	soul singer
	Michael Graves	architect, designer
	The Juilliard School	performing arts school
	Norman Lear	television producer, writer
	Rosetta LeNoire	actress, theater founder
	Harvey Lichtenstein	arts administrator
	Lydia Mendoza	Tejano musician
	Odetta	folksinger
	George Segal	sculptor
	Maria Tallchief	ballet dancer
2000	Maya Angelou	poet, writer
	Eddy Arnold	country musician
	Mikhail Baryshnikov	dancer, dance company director
	Benny Carter	jazz musician
	Chuck Close	painter
	Horton Foote	dramatist
	Lewis Manilow	patron
	National Public Radio cultural programming division	broadcaster
	Claes Oldenburg	sculptor
	Itzhak Perlman	violinist
	Harold Prince	theater director
	Barbra Streisand	singer, actress
2001	Alvin Ailey Dance Foundation	modern dance company and school
	Rudolfo Anaya	writer
	Johnny Cash	country musician
	Kirk Douglas	actor
	Helen Frankenthaler	painter
	Judith Jamison	dancer, choreographer
	Yo-Yo Ma	cellist
	Mike Nichols	theater and film director
2002	Florence Knoll Bassett	designer, architect
	Trisha Brown	dancer, choreographer
	Philippe de Montebello	museum director
	Uta Hagen	actress, educator
	Lawrence Halprin	landscape architect
	Al Hirschfeld[1]	artist, caricaturist
	George Jones	singer, songwriter
	Ming Cho Lee	painter, stage designer
	William "Smokey" Robinson, Jr.	singer, songwriter

National Medal of Arts (continued)

YEAR	NAME	FIELD
2003	*Austin City Limits*	television show
	Beverly Cleary	children's book author
	Rafe Esquith	arts educator
	Suzanne Farrell	dancer, artistic director, arts educator
	Buddy Guy	blues musician
	Ron Howard	actor, director, writer
	Mormon Tabernacle Choir	choir
	Leonard Slatkin	conductor
	George Strait	singer, songwriter
	Tommy Tune	director, actor
2004	Andrew W. Mellon Foundation	patron
	Ray Bradbury	writer
	Carlisle Floyd	opera composer
	Frederick "Rick" Hart[1]	sculptor
	Anthony Hecht[1]	poet
	John Ruthven	painter
	Vincent Scully	architectural historian
	Twyla Tharp	dancer, choreographer
2005	Louis Auchincloss	writer
	James DePreist	conductor
	Paquito D'Rivera	musician
	Robert Duvall	actor
	Leonard Garment	arts advocate
	Ollie Johnston	animator, artist
	Wynton Marsalis	musician, educator
	Dolly Parton	singer, songwriter
	Pennsylvania Academy of the Fine Arts	arts academy
	Tina Ramirez	dancer, choreographer
2006	William Bolcom	composer
	Cyd Charisse	dancer
	Roy R. DeCarava	photographer
	Wilhelmina C. Holladay	patron
	Interlochen Center for the Arts	music school
	Erich Kunzel	conductor

YEAR	NAME	FIELD
2006 (cont.)	Preservation Hall Jazz Band	jazz ensemble
	Gregory Rabassa	translator
	Viktor Schreckengost	industrial designer
	Dr. Ralph Stanley	bluegrass musician
2007	Lionel Hampton International Jazz Festival	music competition, festival
	Morten Lauridsen	composer
	N. Scott Momaday	author, poet
	Roy R. Neuberger	patron
	R. Craig Noel	theater director
	Les Paul	guitarist, inventor
	Henry Steinway	patron
	George Tooker	painter
	Andrew Wyeth	painter
2008	Olivia de Havilland	actress
	Fisk Jubilee Singers	choral ensemble
	Ford's Theatre Society	theater, museum
	Hank Jones	jazz musician
	José Limón Dance Foundation	dance company
	Stan Lee	comic book writer
	Jesús Moroles	sculptor
	Presser Foundation	patron
	Sherman Brothers	songwriters
2009	Bob Dylan	singer, songwriter
	Clint Eastwood	director, actor
	Milton Glaser	graphic designer
	Maya Lin	artist, designer
	Rita Moreno	singer, dancer, actress
	Jessye Norman	soprano
	Oberlin Conservatory of Music	conservatory
	Joseph P. Riley, Jr.	patron
	School of American Ballet	ballet school
	Frank Stella	painter, sculptor
	Michael T. Thomas	conductor
	John Williams	composer, conductor

[1]*Awarded posthumously.*

Spingarn Medal

The National Association for the Advancement of Colored People (NAACP) presents the medal for distinguished achievement among African Americans. The medal is named for early NAACP activist Joel E. Spingarn.

YEAR	NAME	FIELD
1915	Ernest Everett Just	marine biologist
1916	Charles Young	army officer
1917	Harry Thacker Burleigh	singer, composer
1918	William Stanley Braithwaite	poet, literary critic
1919	Archibald Henry Grimké	lawyer, diplomat, social activist
1920	W.E.B. Du Bois	sociologist, social activist
1921	Charles S. Gilpin	actor
1922	Mary Burnett Talbert	civil rights activist
1923	George Washington Carver	agricultural chemist
1924	Roland Hayes	singer, composer
1925	James Weldon Johnson	diplomat, anthologist
1926	Carter G. Woodson	historian
1927	Anthony Overton	businessman
1928	Charles W. Chesnutt	writer

YEAR	NAME	FIELD
1929	Mordecai W. Johnson	minister, university president
1930	Henry Alexander Hunt	educator, government official
1931	Richard B. Harrison	actor
1932	Robert Russa Moton	educator, civil rights leader
1933	Max Yergan	civil rights leader
1934	William T.B. Williams	educator
1935	Mary McLeod Bethune	educator, social activist
1936	John Hope (posthumously)	educator
1937	Walter White	civil rights leader
1938	*no medal awarded*	
1939	Marian Anderson	opera singer
1940	Louis T. Wright	surgeon, civil rights leader
1941	Richard Wright	writer

Spingarn Medal (continued)

YEAR	NAME	FIELD
1942	A. Philip Randolph	labor and civil rights leader
1943	William H. Hastie	lawyer, judge
1944	Charles Richard Drew	surgeon, research scientist
1945	Paul Robeson	actor, singer, social activist
1946	Thurgood Marshall	lawyer, US Supreme Court justice
1947	Percy L. Julian	chemist
1948	Channing H. Tobias	civil rights leader
1949	Ralph Bunche	diplomat, scholar
1950	Charles Hamilton Houston (posthumously)	lawyer
1951	Mabel Keaton Staupers	nurse, social activist
1952	Harry T. Moore (posthumously)	civil rights activist, educator
1953	Paul R. Williams	architect
1954	Theodore K. Lawless	dermatologist, philanthropist
1955	Carl Murphy	journalist, civil rights activist
1956	Jackie Robinson	baseball player
1957	Martin Luther King, Jr.	civil rights leader
1958	Daisy Bates and the Little Rock Nine	school integration activists
1959	Duke Ellington	jazz musician
1960	Langston Hughes	writer
1961	Kenneth Bancroft Clark	educator
1962	Robert C. Weaver	economist, government official
1963	Medgar Evers (posthumously)	civil rights activist
1964	Roy Wilkins	civil rights leader
1965	Leontyne Price	opera singer
1966	John H. Johnson	publisher
1967	Edward W. Brooke III	lawyer, US senator
1968	Sammy Davis, Jr.	singer, dancer, entertainer
1969	Clarence M. Mitchell, Jr.	civil rights lobbyist
1970	Jacob Lawrence	painter
1971	Leon H. Sullivan	minister, civil rights activist
1972	Gordon Parks	filmmaker, photographer, writer
1973	Wilson C. Riles	educator
1974	Damon Keith	lawyer, judge
1975	Hank Aaron	baseball player
1976	Alvin Ailey	dancer, choreogrpher
1977	Alex Haley	writer
1978	Andrew Young	civil rights leader
1979	Rosa Parks	civil rights activist
1980	Rayford W. Logan	educator, writer
1981	Coleman A. Young	labor activist, politician
1982	Benjamin E. Mays	educator, minister
1983	Lena Horne	singer, actress
1984	Thomas Bradley	politician
1985	Bill Cosby	actor, comedian
1986	Benjamin L. Hooks	civil rights leader, government official
1987	Percy Ellis Sutton	civil rights activist, politician
1988	Frederick Douglass Patterson (posthumously)	educator
1989	Jesse Jackson	minister, politician, civil rights leader
1990	L. Douglas Wilder	politician
1991	Colin Powell	army general, government official
1992	Barbara Jordan	lawyer, politician
1993	Dorothy I. Height	social activist
1994	Maya Angelou	poet
1995	John Hope Franklin	historian, educator
1996	A. Leon Higginbotham	lawyer, judge, scholar
1997	Carl T. Rowan	journalist, commentator
1998	Myrlie Evers-Williams	civil rights activist
1999	Earl G. Graves	publisher
2000	Oprah Winfrey	television host, media personality
2001	Vernon E. Jordan, Jr.	lawyer, civil rights activist
2002	John Lewis	politician, civil rights activist
2003	Constance Baker Motley	judge, lawyer, civil rights activist
2004	Robert L. Carter	judge, lawyer, civil rights activist
2005	Oliver W. Hill	lawyer, civil rights activist
2006	Benjamin S. Carson	physician
2007	John Conyers, Jr.	politician
2008	Ruby Dee	actress, writer
2009	Julian Bond	statesman, civil rights activist
2010	Cicely Tyson	actress

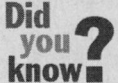

Did you know? Dalmatians were originally bred as guard dogs for stagecoaches. Because they were used to running long distances and being around horses, and because their bright white coats with black spots were easily visible, they were chosen by fire departments to run ahead of horse-drawn fire engines, barking a warning and clearing the path of onlookers. With the advent of motorized fire trucks, Dalmatians were retained as the official mascot of firehouses everywhere.

Science Honors

Fields Medal

The Fields Medal, officially known as the International Medal for Outstanding Discoveries in Mathematics, is granted every four years to between two and four mathematicians for outstanding or groundbreaking research. It is traditionally given to mathematicians under the age of 40. Prize: Can$15,000 (about US$14,200).

Fields Medal (continued)

YEAR	NAME	BIRTHPLACE	PRIMARY RESEARCH
1936	Lars Ahlfors	Helsinki, Finland	Riemann surfaces
	Jesse Douglas	New York NY	Plateau problem
1950	Laurent Schwartz	Paris, France	functional analysis
	Atle Selberg	Langesund, Norway	number theory
1954	Kunihiko Kodaira	Tokyo, Japan	algebraic geometry
	Jean-Pierre Serre	Bages, France	algebraic topology
1958	Klaus Roth	Breslau, Germany	number theory
	René Thom	Montbéliard, France	topology
1962	Lars Hörmander	Mjällby, Sweden	partial differential equations
	John Milnor	Orange NJ	differential topology
1966	Michael Atiyah	London, England	topology
	Paul Cohen	Long Branch NJ	set theory
	Alexandre Grothendieck	Berlin, Germany	algebraic geometry
	Stephen Smale	Flint MI	topology
1970	Alan Baker	London, England	number theory
	Heisuke Hironaka	Yamaguchi prefecture, Japan	algebraic geometry
	Sergey Novikov	Gorky, USSR (now in Russia)	topology
	John Thompson	Ottawa KS	group theory
1974	Enrico Bombieri	Milan, Italy	number theory
	David Mumford	Worth, Sussex, England	algebraic geometry
1978	Pierre Deligne	Brussels, Belgium	algebraic geometry
	Charles Fefferman	Washington DC	classical analysis
	Gregory Margulis	Moscow, USSR (now in Russia)	Lie groups
	Daniel Quillen	Orange NJ	algebraic K-theory
1983	Alain Connes	Darguignan, France	operator theory
	William Thurston	Washington DC	topology
	Shing-Tung Yau	Swatow, China	differential geometry
1986	Simon Donaldson	Cambridge, England	topology
	Gerd Faltings	Gelsenkirchen, West Germany	Mordell conjecture
	Michael Freedman	Los Angeles CA	Poincaré conjecture
1990	Vladimir Drinfeld	Kharkov, USSR (now in Ukraine)	algebraic geometry
	Vaughan Jones	Gisborne, New Zealand	knot theory
	Shigefumi Mori	Nagoya, Japan	algebraic geometry
	Edward Witten	Baltimore MD	superstring theory
1994	Jean Bourgain	Ostend, Belgium	analysis
	Pierre-Louis Lions	Grasse, France	partial differential equations
	Jean-Christophe Yoccoz	Paris, France	dynamical systems
	Yefim Zelmanov	Khabarovsk, USSR (now in Russia)	group theory
1998	Richard Borcherds	Cape Town, South Africa	mathematical physics
	William Gowers	Marlborough, Wiltshire, England	functional analysis
	Maksim Kontsevich	Khimki, USSR (now in Russia)	mathematical physics
	Curt McMullen	Berkeley CA	chaos theory
2002	Laurent Lafforgue	Antony, France	number theory and analysis
	Vladimir Voevodsky	Moscow, USSR (now in Russia)	algebraic geometry
2006	Andrei Okounkov	Moscow, USSR (now in Russia)	algebraic geometry
	Grigory Perelman (declined)	Leningrad, USSR (now in Russia)	Ricci flow
	Terence Tao	Adelaide, SA, Australia	prime numbers, nonlinear equations
	Wendelin Werner	Cologne, West Germany	mathematics of critical phenomena
2010	Elon Lindenstrauss	Jerusalem, Israel	measure rigidity in ergodic theory
	Ngo Bao Chau	Hanoi, Vietnam	proof of the Fundamental Lemma
	Stanislav Smirnov	Saint Petersburg, USSR (now in Russia)	statistical physics
	Cédric Villani	Brive-la-Gaillarde, France	Boltzmann equation

National Medal of Science

The National Medal of Science was established by Congress in 1959. Awarded annually since 1962 by the National Science Foundation, it recognizes notable achievements in mathematics, engineering, and the physical, natural, and social sciences.

National Science Foundation Web site: <www.nsf.gov/od/nms/medal.jsp>.

YEAR	NAME	FIELD
1962	Theodore von Karman	aerospace engineering
1963	Luis W. Alvarez	physics
	Vannevar Bush	electrical engineering

YEAR	NAME	FIELD
1963 (cont.)	John Robinson Pierce	communications engineering
	Cornelius Barnardus van Niel	biology
	Norbert Wiener	mathematics

National Medal of Science (continued)

YEAR	NAME	FIELD	YEAR	NAME	FIELD
1964	Roger Adams	chemistry	1968	B.F. Skinner	psychology
	Othmar Herman Ammann	civil engineering	(cont.)	Eugene Paul Wigner	mathematical physics
	Theodosius Dobzhansky	genetics	1969	Herbert C. Brown	chemistry
	Charles Stark Draper	aerospace engineering		William Feller	mathematics
				Robert J. Huebner	virology
	Solomon Lefschetz	mathematics		Jack Kilby	electrical engineering
	Neal Elgar Miller	psychology		Ernst Mayr	biology
	H. Marston Morse	mathematics		Wolfgang K.H. Panofsky	physics
	Marshall Warren Nirenberg	biochemistry	1970	Richard Dagobert Brauer	mathematics
	Julian Seymour Schwinger	physics		Robert H. Dicke	physics
				Barbara McClintock	genetics
	Harold C. Urey	chemistry		George E. Mueller	physics
	Robert Burns Woodward	chemistry		Albert Bruce Sabin	medicine, vaccine development
1965	John Bardeen	physics			
	Peter J.W. Debye	physical chemistry		Allan R. Sandage	astronomy
	Hugh L. Dryden	physics		John C. Slater	physics
	Clarence L. Johnson	aerospace engineering		John Archibald Wheeler	physics
	Leon M. Lederman	physics		Saul Winstein	chemistry
	Warren K. Lewis	chemical engineering	1971	no recipients named	
	Francis Peyton Rous	pathology	1972	no recipients named	
	William W. Rubey	geology	1973	Daniel I. Arnon	biochemistry
	George Gaylord Simpson	paleontology		Carl Djerassi	chemistry
				Harold E. Edgerton	electrical engineering, photography
	Donald D. Van Slyke	chemistry		Maurice Ewing	geophysics
	Oscar Zariski	mathematics		Arie Jan Haagen-Smit	biochemistry
1966	Jacob A.B. Bjerknes	meteorology		Vladimir Haensel	chemical engineering
	Subrahmanyan Chandrasekhar	astrophysics		Frederick Seitz	physics
				Earl W. Sutherland, Jr.	biochemistry
	Henry Eyring	chemistry		John Wilder Tukey	statistics
	Edward F. Knipling	entomology		Richard T. Whitcomb	aerospace engineering
	Fritz Albert Lipmann	biochemistry			
	John Willard Milnor	mathematics		Robert Rathbun Wilson	particle physics
	William C. Rose	biochemistry			
	Claude E. Shannon	mathematics, electrical engineering	1974	Nicolaas Bloembergen	physics
	John H. Van Vleck	physics		Britton Chance	biophysics
	Sewall Wright	genetics		Erwin Chargaff	biochemistry
	Vladimir Kosma Zworykin	electrical engineering		Paul J. Flory	physical chemistry
				William A. Fowler	nuclear astrophysics
1967	Jesse W. Beams	physics		Kurt Gödel	mathematics
	Francis Birch	geophysics		Rudolf Kompfner	physics
	Gregory Breit	physics		James Van Gundia Neel	genetics
	Paul Joseph Cohen	mathematics			
	Kenneth S. Cole	biophysics		Linus Pauling	chemistry
	Louis P. Hammett	chemistry		Ralph Brazelton Peck	geotechnical engineering
	Harry F. Harlow	psychology			
	Michael Heidelberger	immunology		Kenneth Sanborn Pitzer	physical chemistry
	George B. Kistiakowsky	chemistry			
	Edwin Herbert Land	physics		James Augustine Shannon	physiology
	Igor I. Sikorsky	aircraft design			
	Alfred H. Sturtevant	genetics		Abel Wolman	sanitary engineering
1968	Horace A. Barker	biochemistry	1975	John W. Backus	computer science
	Paul D. Bartlett	chemistry		Manson Benedict	nuclear engineering
	Bernard B. Brodie	pharmacology		Hans Albrecht Bethe	theoretical physics
	Detlev W. Bronk	biophysics		Shiing-shen Chern	mathematics
	J. Presper Eckert, Jr.	engineering, computer science		George B. Dantzig	mathematics
				Hallowell Davis	physiology
	Herbert Friedman	astrophysics		Paul Gyorgy	medicine, vitamin research
	Jay L. Lush	livestock genetics			
	Nathan M. Newmark	civil engineering		Sterling Brown Hendricks	chemistry
	Jerzy Neyman	statistics			
	Lars Onsager	chemistry		Joseph O. Hirschfelder	chemistry

National Medal of Science (continued)

YEAR	NAME	FIELD	YEAR	NAME	FIELD
1975 (cont.)	William Hayward Pickering	physics	1983	Howard L. Bachrach	biochemistry
	Lewis H. Sarett	chemistry		Paul Berg	biochemistry
	Frederick Emmons Terman	electrical engineering		E. Margaret Burbidge	astronomy
				Maurice Goldhaber	physics
	Orville Alvin Vogel	research agronomy		Herman H. Goldstine	computer science
	Wernher von Braun	aerospace engineering		William R. Hewlett	electrical engineering
				Roald Hoffmann	chemistry
	E. Bright Wilson, Jr.	chemistry		Helmut E. Landsberg	climatology
	Chien-Shiung Wu	physics		George M. Low	aerospace engineering
1976	Morris Cohen	materials science			
	Kurt Otto Friedrichs	mathematics		Walter H. Munk	oceanography
	Peter C. Goldmark	communications engineering		George C. Pimentel	chemistry
				Frederick Reines	physics
	Samuel Abraham Goudsmit	physics		Wendell L. Roelofs	chemistry, entomology
				Bruno B. Rossi	astrophysics
	Roger Charles Louis Guillemin	physiology		Berta V. Scharrer	neuroscience
				John Robert Schrieffer	physics
	Herbert S. Gutowsky	chemistry		Isadore M. Singer	mathematics
	Erwin W. Mueller	physics		John G. Trump	electrical engineering
	Keith Roberts Porter	cell biology		Richard N. Zare	chemistry
	Efraim Racker	biochemistry	1984	no recipients named	
	Frederick D. Rossini	chemistry	1985	no recipients named	
	Verner E. Suomi	meteorology	1986	Solomon J. Buchsbaum	physics
	Henry Taube	chemistry		Stanley Cohen	biochemistry
	George Eugene Uhlenbeck	physics		Horace R. Crane	physics
				Herman Feshbach	physics
	Hassler Whitney	mathematics		Harry Gray	chemistry
	Edward O. Wilson	biology		Donald A. Henderson	medicine, public health
1977	no recipients named				
1978	no recipients named			Robert Hofstadter	physics
1979	Robert H. Burris	biochemistry		Peter D. Lax	mathematics
	Elizabeth C. Crosby	neuroanatomy		Yuan Tseh Lee	chemistry
	Joseph L. Doob	mathematics		Hans Wolfgang Liepmann	aerospace engineering
	Richard P. Feynman	theoretical physics			
	Donald E. Knuth	computer science		T.Y. Lin	civil engineering
	Arthur Kornberg	biochemistry		Carl S. Marvel	chemistry
	Emmett N. Leith	electrical engineering		Vernon B. Mountcastle	neurophysiology
	Herman F. Mark	chemistry			
	Raymond D. Mindlin	mechanical engineering		Bernard M. Oliver	electrical engineering
				George Emil Palade	cell biology
	Robert N. Noyce	computer science		Herbert A. Simon	social science
	Severo Ochoa	biochemistry		Joan A. Steitz	molecular biology
	Earl R. Parker	materials science		Frank H. Westheimer	chemistry
	Edward M. Purcell	physics		Chen Ning Yang	theoretical physics
	Simon Ramo	electrical engineering		Antoni Zygmund	mathematics
	John H. Sinfelt	chemical engineering	1987	Philip Hauge Abelson	physical chemistry
	Lyman Spitzer, Jr.	astrophysics		Anne Anastasi	psychology
	Earl Reece Stadtman	biochemistry		Robert Byron Bird	chemical engineering
	George Ledyard Stebbins	botany, genetics		Raoul Bott	mathematics
				Michael E. DeBakey	heart surgery
	Victor F. Weisskopf	physics		Theodor O. Diener	plant pathology
	Paul Alfred Weiss	biology		Harry Eagle	cell biology
1980	no recipients named			Walter M. Elsasser	physics
1981	Philip Handler	biochemistry		Michael H. Freedman	mathematics
1982	Philip W. Anderson	physics		William S. Johnson	chemistry
	Seymour Benzer	molecular biology		Har Gobind Khorana	biochemistry
	Glenn W. Burton	genetics		Paul C. Lauterbur	chemistry
	Mildred Cohn	biochemistry		Rita Levi-Montalcini	neurology
	F. Albert Cotton	chemistry		George E. Pake	research, physics
	Edward H. Heinemann	aerospace engineering		H. Bolton Seed	civil engineering
				George J. Stigler	economics
	Donald L. Katz	chemical engineering		Walter H. Stockmayer	chemistry
	Yoichiro Nambu	theoretical physics		Max Tishler	chemistry
	Marshall H. Stone	mathematics		James Alfred Van Allen	physics
	Gilbert Stork	organic chemistry			
	Edward Teller	nuclear physics		Ernst Weber	electrical engineering
	Charles Hard Townes	physics			

National Medal of Science (continued)

YEAR	NAME	FIELD
1988	William O. Baker	chemistry
	Konrad E. Bloch	biochemistry
	David Allan Bromley	physics
	Michael S. Brown	molecular genetics
	Paul C.W. Chu	physics
	Stanley N. Cohen	genetics
	Elias James Corey	chemistry
	Daniel C. Drucker	engineering education
	Milton Friedman	economics
	Joseph L. Goldstein	molecular genetics
	Ralph E. Gomory	mathematics, research
	Willis M. Hawkins	aerospace engineering
	Maurice R. Hilleman	vaccine research
	George W. Housner	earthquake engineering
	Eric Kandel	neurobiology
	Joseph B. Keller	mathematics
	Walter Kohn	physics
	Norman Foster Ramsey	physics
	Jack Steinberger	physics
	Rosalyn S. Yalow	medical physics
1989	Arnold O. Beckman	chemistry
	Richard B. Bernstein	chemistry
	Melvin Calvin	biochemistry
	Harry G. Drickamer	chemistry, physics
	Katherine Esau	botany
	Herbert E. Grier	aerospace engineering
	Viktor Hamburger	biology
	Samuel Karlin	mathematics
	Philip Leder	genetics
	Joshua Lederberg	genetics
	Saunders Mac Lane	mathematics
	Rudolph A. Marcus	chemistry
	Harden M. McConnell	chemistry
	Eugene N. Parker	theoretical astrophysics
	Robert P. Sharp	geology
	Donald C. Spencer	mathematics
	Roger Wolcott Sperry	neurobiology
	Henry M. Stommel	oceanography
	Harland G. Wood	biochemistry
1990	Baruj Benacerraf	pathology, immunology
	Elkan R. Blout	chemistry
	Herbert W. Boyer	biochemistry, genetics
	George F. Carrier	mathematics
	Allan MacLeod Cormack	physics
	Mildred S. Dresselhaus	physics
	Karl August Folkers	chemistry
	Nick Holonyak, Jr.	electrical engineering
	Leonid Hurwicz	economics
	Stephen Cole Kleene	mathematics
	Daniel E. Koshland, Jr.	biochemistry
	Edward B. Lewis	genetics
	John McCarthy	computer science
	Edwin Mattison McMillan	nuclear physics
	David G. Nathan	pediatrics
	Robert V. Pound	physics
	Roger R.D. Revelle	oceanography

YEAR	NAME	FIELD
1990 (cont.)	John D. Roberts	chemistry
	Patrick Suppes	philosophy, statistics education
	E. Donnall Thomas	medicine
1991	Mary Ellen Avery	pediatrics
	Ronald Breslow	chemistry
	Alberto P. Calderon	mathematics
	Gertrude B. Elion	pharmacology
	George H. Heilmeier	electrical engineering
	Dudley R. Herschbach	chemistry
	G. Evelyn Hutchinson	zoology
	Elvin A. Kabat	immunology
	Robert W. Kates	geography
	Luna B. Leopold	hydrology, geology
	Salvador Luria	biology
	Paul A. Marks	hematology, cancer research
	George A. Miller	psychology
	Arthur L. Schawlow	physics
	Glenn T. Seaborg	nuclear chemistry
	Folke K. Skoog	botany
	H. Guyford Stever	aerospace engineering
	Edward C. Stone	physics
	Steven Weinberg	nuclear physics
	Paul C. Zamecnik	molecular biology
1992	Eleanor J. Gibson	psychology
	Allen Newell	computer science
	Calvin F. Quate	electrical engineering
	Eugene M. Shoemaker	planetary geology
	Howard E. Simmons, Jr.	chemistry
	Maxine F. Singer	biochemistry, administration
	Howard Martin Temin	virology
	John Roy Whinnery	electrical engineering
1993	Alfred Y. Cho	electrical engineering
	Donald J. Cram	chemistry
	Val Logsdon Fitch	particle physics
	Norman Hackerman	chemistry
	Martin D. Kruskal	mathematics
	Daniel Nathans	microbiology
	Vera C. Rubin	astronomy
	Salome G. Waelsch	molecular genetics
1994	Ray W. Clough	civil engineering
	John Cocke	computer science
	Thomas Eisner	chemical ecology
	George S. Hammond	chemistry
	Robert K. Merton	sociology
	Elizabeth F. Neufeld	biochemistry
	Albert W. Overhauser	physics
	Frank Press	geophysics, administration
1995	Thomas Robert Cech	biochemistry
	Hans Georg Dehmelt	physics
	Peter M. Goldreich	astrophysics
	Hermann A. Haus	electrical engineering
	Isabella L. Karle	chemistry
	Louis Nirenberg	mathematics
	Alexander Rich	molecular biology
	Roger N. Shepard	psychology
1996	Wallace S. Broecker	geochemistry
	Norman Davidson	chemistry, molecular biology
	James L. Flanagan	electrical engineering

National Medal of Science (continued)

YEAR	NAME	FIELD
1996 (cont.)	Richard M. Karp	computer science
	C. Kumar N. Patel	electrical engineering
	Ruth Patrick	limnology
	Paul Samuelson	economics
	Stephen Smale	mathematics
1997	William K. Estes	psychology
	Darleane C. Hoffman	chemistry
	Harold S. Johnston	chemistry
	Marshall N. Rosenbluth	theoretical plasma physics
	Martin Schwarzschild	astrophysics
	James Dewey Watson	genetics, biophysics
	Robert A. Weinberg	biology, cancer research
	George W. Wetherill	planetary science
	Shing-Tung Yau	mathematics
1998	Bruce N. Ames	biochemistry, cancer research
	Don L. Anderson	geophysics
	John N. Bahcall	astrophysics
	John W. Cahn	materials science
	Cathleen Synge Morawetz	mathematics
	Janet D. Rowley	medicine, cancer research
	Eli Ruckenstein	chemical engineering
	George M. Whitesides	chemistry
	William Julius Wilson	sociology
1999	David Baltimore	virology, administration
	Felix E. Browder	mathematics
	Ronald R. Coifman	mathematics
	James Watson Cronin	particle physics
	Jared Diamond	physiology
	Leo P. Kadanoff	theoretical physics
	Lynn Margulis	microbiology
	Stuart A. Rice	chemistry
	John Ross	chemistry
	Susan Solomon	atmospheric science
	Robert M. Solow	economics
	Kenneth N. Stevens	electrical engineering, speech
2000	Nancy C. Andreasen	psychiatry
	John D. Baldeschwieler	chemistry
	Gary S. Becker	economics
	Yuan-Cheng B. Fung	bioengineering
	Ralph F. Hirschmann	chemistry
	Willis Eugene Lamb, Jr.	physics
	Jeremiah P. Ostriker	astrophysics
	Peter H. Raven	botany
	John Griggs Thompson	mathematics
	Karen K. Uhlenbeck	mathematics
	Gilbert F. White	geography
	Carl R. Woese	microbiology
2001	Andreas Acrivos	chemical engineering
	Francisco J. Ayala	molecular biology
	George F. Bass	nautical archaeology
	Mario R. Capecchi	genetics
	Marvin L. Cohen	materials science
	Ernest R. Davidson	chemistry
	Raymond Davis, Jr.	chemistry, astrophysics
	Ann M. Graybiel	neuroscience
	Charles D. Keeling	oceanography
	Gene E. Likens	ecology
	Victor A. McKusick	medical genetics
	Calyampudi R. Rao	mathematics, statistics

YEAR	NAME	FIELD
2001 (cont.)	Gabor A. Somorjai	chemistry
	Elias M. Stein	mathematics
	Harold Varmus	virology, administration
2002	Leo L. Beranek	engineering
	John I. Brauman	chemistry
	James E. Darnell	cell biology
	Richard L. Garwin	physics
	James G. Glimm	mathematics, statistics
	W. Jason Morgan	geophysics
	Evelyn M. Witkin	genetics
	Edward Witten	mathematical physics
2003	J. Michael Bishop	microbiology
	G. Brent Dalrymple	geology
	Carl R. de Boor	mathematics
	Riccardo Giacconi	astrophysics
	R. Duncan Luce	cognitive science
	John M. Prausnitz	chemical engineering
	Solomon H. Snyder	neuroscience
	Charles Yanofsky	molecular biology
2004	Kenneth J. Arrow	economics
	Norman E. Borlaug	agriculture
	Robert N. Clayton	geochemistry
	Edwin N. Lightfoot	engineering
	Stephen J. Lippard	chemistry
	Phillip A. Sharp	molecular biology, biochemistry
	Thomas E. Starzl	medicine
	Dennis P. Sullivan	mathematics
2005	Jan D. Achenbach	mechanical engineering
	Ralph A. Alpher	astronomy
	Gordon H. Bower	psychology
	Bradley Efron	statistics
	Anthony S. Fauci	immunology
	Tobin J. Marks	chemistry
	Lonnie G. Thompson	glaciology
	Torsten N. Wiesel	neurobiology
2006	Hyman Bass	mathematics
	Marvin H. Caruthers	genetic engineering
	Rita R. Colwell	marine microbiology
	Peter B. Dervan	organic chemistry
	Nina V. Fedoroff	molecular biology
	Daniel Kleppner	atomic physics
	Robert S. Langer	medical research
	Lubert Stryer	biochemistry
2007	Fay Ajzenberg-Selove	nuclear physics
	Mostafa A. El-Sayed	laser dynamics
	Leonard Kleinrock	Internet technology
	Robert J. Lefkowitz	receptor biology
	Bert W. O'Malley	molecular biology
	Charles P. Slichter	condensed-matter physics
	Andrew J. Viterbi	wireless communications
	David J. Wineland	ionic physics
2008	Berni Alder	physical sciences
	Francis S. Collins	biology
	Joanna S. Fowler	chemistry
	Elaine Fuchs	biology
	James E. Gunn	physical sciences
	Rudolf E. Kálmán	engineering
	Michael I. Posner	behavioral and social sciences
	JoAnne Stubbe	chemistry
	J. Craig Venter	biology

Nature, Science, Medicine, & Technology

Why Start-ups Are Charging into Lithium

by Steven Grey and Bryan Walsh, TIME

In February 2010, Pres. Barack Obama told the crowd at a Henderson NV high school that not so long ago, the US made barely 2% of the advanced batteries used in the world's electric vehicles. Now, thanks to a multibillion-dollar federal investment, American companies are positioned to increase production tenfold—and potentially control 40% of the global lithium-ion-battery market by 2015. "We've created an entire new industry," Obama said.

Not quite, but certainly the beginnings of one. Demand for lithium-ion batteries is increasing strongly as electric-car technology improves and prices drop. Nissan has introduced the all-electric Leaf, and in 2010 Chevy will debut the long-anticipated gas-electric Volt. Those and future electric cars need battery packs, and at least a dozen American lithium-battery start-ups are competing with Asian companies such as Sanyo and Hitachi to provide them. "There's a tremendous amount of competition," says David Vieau, chief executive of A123 Systems, a Watertown MA start-up powered by federal money that is vying for the business.

And it's a ton of business. The consulting firm Pike Research estimates that the global market for lithium-ion batteries could grow from US$877 million this year to US$8 billion by 2015. In North America, the market is expected to expand from about US$287 million this year to US$2.2 billion in 2015.

The year brought good news for companies seeking lithium, as well. Most of the world's lithium reserves are currently found in China, Chile, and especially Bolivia, which has by far the largest known deposits in the world. But in June the *New York Times* reported that the US had discovered nearly US$1 trillion in untapped mineral deposits in Afghanistan, including huge veins of iron, copper, cobalt, gold, and lithium. Indeed, Afghanistan apparently has enough of the last mineral to become the "Saudi Arabia of lithium," according to an internal Pentagon memo. The reports were good news for the electric-car industry, especially if the new source of lithium helps break the dominance in reserves now held by one or two countries.

A123 Systems is a window on how the government's electric-vehicle gambit is working. The company was founded at MIT in 2001 with a US$100,000 grant from the Department of Energy. One of its early products was lithium-ion batteries for power-tool maker Black & Decker. Last year, A123 Systems got a US$249 million federal grant to open at least three lithium-ion-battery plants in Michigan that will employ hundreds of workers. Michigan is home to or close to many of the plants where electric vehicles are being made, of course, and the state has a surplus of skilled workers. It's not, ahem, a bad choice politically either.

Companies like A123 are busy wrestling with two key issues facing electric-car batteries: providing enough power to the car's engine and storing enough power to guarantee a defined range—say, 200 miles (about 320 km)—between charges. The goal for electric-car manufacturers is an affordable battery that can handle countless partial charge-discharge cycles over an eight-to-10-year life cycle. The battery has to absorb energy from braking and provide short bursts of power for acceleration. Lithium-ion batteries, with their high density-to-weight ratio, provide the greatest acceleration and range with the fewest batteries compared with lead-acid or nickel-metal-hydride batteries. One big problem: they can overheat and even blow up—bad enough in a single-battery laptop but potentially disastrous in a multibattery electric car. So engineers have been busy resolving the heat problem and refining the batteries' ability to handle partial charge-discharge cycles.

As for affordability, lithium-ion battery packs currently cost about US$1,000 per kilowatt-hour of capacity. Which means the GM Volt's 16-kW-h battery pack alone would cost US$16,000, according to some industry analysts. The price per kilowatt-hour has to fall below US$500 to make production viable—and it will.

Sakti3 is another company trying to create a breakthrough. The company was launched a few years ago at the University of Michigan by an ambitious young engineering professor, Ann Marie Sastry. Sakti3 is developing solid-state (as opposed to liquid) lithium-ion batteries that Sastry believes will enable cars to travel twice as far as batteries do now, allowing the cars to be used the way internal-combustion-engine-driven vehicles are. Her firm is developing prototypes to deliver to automakers late in 2010. Sastry's 20-employee firm, based in Ann Arbor, has generated millions of dollars in government grants and considerable buzz—but so far no juice.

Automakers, meanwhile, are developing their own battery capability. Ford, for one, believes that designing its own lithium-ion battery packs will help streamline the development of its electric vehicles and reduce the cost. Design experts will be brought in-house, says Nancy Gioia, Ford's director of global electrification. By developing battery packs, Gioia says, "we get the volume and scale of more than 1 million units on our battery-management systems. Our suppliers aren't in a position to do that yet."

While they wait for the US electric-auto market to develop, some new suppliers are looking toward consumer electronic goods and markets outside the US to keep their plants busy and improve quality until the big orders come in. "We're in the early stages of what will be a significant run-up," says A123's Vieau. "There's a lot of business out there." Sastry echoes that view, saying many automakers rely on engine suppliers. "If the dream I and others have is realized, we'll see batteries being treated like engines," she says. Job engines, no less.

Time

Time Zone Map

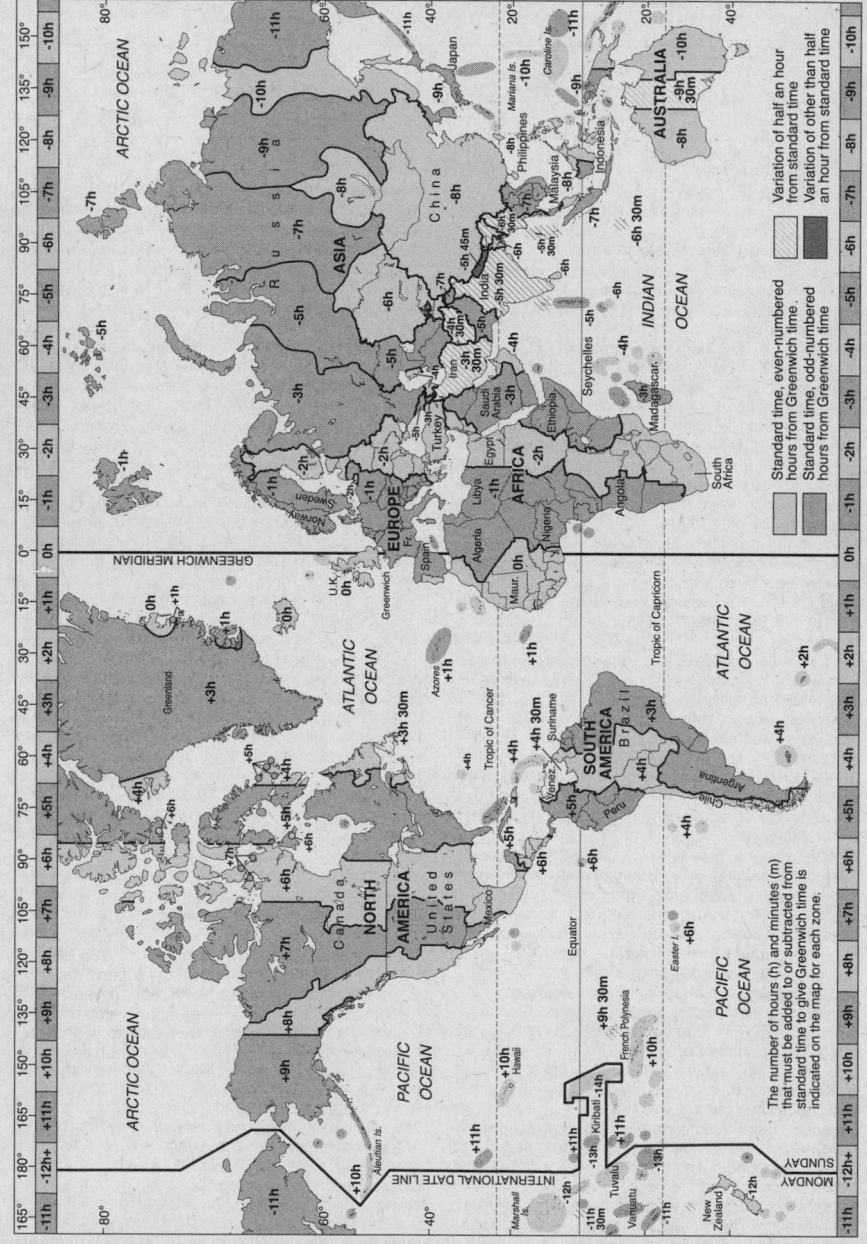

Based on data from the US Defense Mapping Agency Hydrographic/Topographic Center

Daylight Saving Time

Also called **summer time, daylight saving time** is a system for uniformly advancing clocks, especially in summer, so as to extend daylight hours during conventional waking time. In the Northern Hemisphere, clocks are usually set ahead one hour in late March or in April and are set back one hour in late September or in October; most Southern Hemisphere countries that observe daylight saving time set clocks ahead in October or November and reset them in March or April. Equatorial countries do not observe daylight saving time because daylight hours stay about the same from season to season in the lower latitudes.

The practice was first suggested in a whimsical essay by **Benjamin Franklin** in 1784. In 1907 an Englishman, William Willett, campaigned for setting the clock ahead by 80 minutes in four moves of 20 minutes each during the spring and summer months. In 1908 the British House of Commons rejected a bill to advance the clock by one hour in the spring and return to Greenwich Mean (standard) Time in the autumn.

Several countries, including Australia, Great Britain, Germany, and the United States, adopted **summer daylight saving time** during World War I to conserve fuel by reducing the need for artificial light. During World War II, clocks were kept continuously advanced by an hour in some nations—for instance, in the US from 9 Feb 1942 to 30 Sep 1945—and England used "double summer time" during part of the year, advancing clocks two hours from the standard time during the summer and one hour during the winter months.

In 2005 the US Congress changed the law governing daylight saving time, moving the start of daylight saving time from the first Sunday in April to the second Sunday in March, while moving the end date from the last Sunday in October to the first Sunday in November starting in 2007. In most of the countries of Western Europe, daylight saving time starts on the last Sunday in March and ends on the last Sunday in October.

Julian and Gregorian Calendars

The **Julian calendar**, also called the Old Style calendar, is a dating system established by Julius Caesar as a reform of the Roman republican calendar. Caesar, advised by the Alexandrian astronomer Sosigenes, made the new calendar solar, not lunar, and he took the length of the solar year as 365¼ days. The year was divided into 12 months, all of which had either 30 or 31 days except February, which contained 28 days in common (365-day) years and 29 in every fourth year (a leap year, of 366 days). Because of misunderstandings, the calendar was not established in smooth operation until AD 8. Further, Sosigenes had overestimated the length of the year by 11 minutes 14 seconds, and by the mid-1500s, the cumulative effect of this error had shifted the dates of the seasons by about 10 days from Caesar's time.

This inaccuracy led **Pope Gregory XIII** to reform the Julian calendar. His **Gregorian calendar**, also called the **New Style calendar**, is still in general use. Gregory's proclamation in 1582 restored the calendar to the seasonal dates of AD 325, an adjustment of 10 days. Although the amount of regression was some 14 days by Pope Gregory's time, Gregory based his reform on restoration of the vernal equinox, then falling on 11 March, to the date (21 March) it had in AD 325, the time of the Council of Nicaea. Advancing the calendar 10 days after 4 Oct 1582, the day following being reckoned as 15 October, effected the change.

The Gregorian calendar differs from the Julian only in that no century year is a leap year unless it is exactly divisible by 400 (e.g., 1600, 2000). A further refinement, the designation of years evenly divisible by 4,000 as common (not leap) years, will keep the Gregorian calendar accurate to within one day in 20,000 years.

Jewish Calendar

The **Jewish calendar** is lunisolar—i.e., regulated by the positions of both the Moon and the Sun. It consists usually of 12 alternating lunar months of 29 and 30 days each (except for Heshvan and Kislev, which sometimes have either 29 or 30 days), and totals 353, 354, or 355 days per year. The average lunar year (354 days) is adjusted to the solar year (365¼ days) by the periodic introduction of leap years in order to assure that the major festivals fall in their proper season. The leap year consists of an additional 30-day month called **First Adar**, which always precedes the month of (Second) Adar. (During leap year, the Adar holidays are postponed to Second Adar.) A leap year consists of either 383, 384, or 385 days and occurs seven times during every 19-year period (the so-called Metonic cycle). Among the consequences of the lunisolar structure are these: (1) The number of days in a year may vary considerably, from 353 to 385 days. (2) The first day of a month can fall on any day of the week, that day varying from year to year. Consequently, the days of the week upon which an annual Jewish festival falls vary from year to year despite the festival's fixed position in the Jewish month. The months of the Jewish calendar and their Gregorian equivalents are as follows:

JEWISH MONTH	GREGORIAN MONTH(S)	JEWISH MONTH	GREGORIAN MONTH(S)
Tishri	September–October	Nisan	March–April
Heshvan, or Marheshvan	October–November	Iyyar	April–May
Kislev	November–December	Sivan	May–June
Tevet	December–January	Tammuz	June–July
Shevat	January–February	Av	July–August
Adar	February–March	Elul	August–September

Muslim Calendar

The **Muslim calendar** (also called the **Islamic calendar**, or **Hijrah**) is a dating system used in the Muslim world that is based on a year of 12 months. Each month begins with the sighting of the crescent of the new moon as it emerges from eclipse. The **months** of the Muslim calendar are Muharram, Safar, Rabi I, Rabi II, Jumada I, Jumada II, Rajab, Sha'-ban, Ramadan, Shawwal, Dhu al-Qa'dah, and Dhu al-Hijjah.

In the standard Muslim calendar the months are alternately 30 and 29 days long except for the 12th month, Dhu al-Hijjah, the length of which is varied in a 30-year cycle intended to keep the calendar in step with the true phases of the Moon. In 11 years of this cycle, Dhu al-Hijjah has 30 days, and in the other 19 years it has 29. Thus the year has either 354 or 355 days. No months are intercalated, so that the named months do not remain in the same seasons but retrogress through the entire solar, or seasonal, year (of about 365.25 days) every 32.5 solar years.

There are some exceptions to this calendar in the Muslim world. Turkey uses the Gregorian calendar, while Iran has a Muslim calendar that is based on a solar year. The Iranian calendar still begins from the same dating point as other Muslim calendars—that is, some 10 years prior to the death of Muhammad in AD 632. Thus, the Gregorian year AD 2011 corresponds to the Hijrah years of AH 1432–33.

Chinese Calendar

The **Chinese calendar** is a dating system used concurrently with the Gregorian (Western) calendar in China and Taiwan and in neighboring countries (e.g., Japan). The calendar consists of 12 months of alternately 29 and 30 days, equal to 354 or 355 days, or approximately 12 full lunar cycles. Intercalary months have been inserted to keep the calendar year in step with the solar year of about 365 days. **Months** have no names but are instead referred to by numbers within a year and sometimes also by a series of 12 animal names that from ancient times have been attached to years and to hours of the day.

The calendar also incorporates a **meteorologic cycle** that contains 24 points, each beginning one of the periods named. The establishment of this cycle required a fair amount of astronomical understanding of Earth as a celestial body. Modern scholars acknowledge the superiority of pre-Sung **Chinese astronomy** (at least until about the 13th century AD) over that of other, contemporary nations.

The **24 points** within the meteorologic cycle coincide with points 15° apart on the ecliptic (the plane of Earth's yearly journey around the Sun or, if it is thought that the Sun turns around Earth, the apparent journey of the Sun against the stars). It takes about 15.2 days for the Sun to travel from one of these points to another (because the ecliptic is a complete circle of 360°), and the Sun needs 365¼ days to finish its journey in this cycle. Supposedly, each of the 12 months of the year contains two points, but, because a lunar month has only 29½ days and the two points share about 30.4 days, there is always the chance that a lunar month will fail to contain both points, though the distance between any two given points is only 15°. If such an occasion occurs, the intercalation of an extra month takes place. For instance, one may find a year with two "Julys" or with two "Augusts" in the Chinese calendar. In fact, as mentioned above, the exact length of the month in the Chinese calendar is either 30 days or 29 days—a phenomenon that reflects its lunar origin.

SOLAR TERMS—CHINESE (ENGLISH EQUIVALENTS)	GREGORIAN DATE (APPROXIMATE)	LUNAR MONTH (CORRESPONDENCE OF LUNAR AND SOLAR MONTHS APPROXIMATE)
Lichun (spring begins)	5 February	1—tiger
Yushui (rain water)	19 February	
Jingzhe (excited insects)	5 March	2—rabbit/hare
Chunfen (vernal equinox)	20 March	
Qingming (clear and bright)	5 April	3—dragon
Guyu (grain rains)	20 April	
Lixia (summer begins)	5 May	4—snake
Xiaoman (grain fills)	21 May	
Mangzhong (grain in ear)	6 June	5—horse
Xiazhi (summer solstice)	21 June	
Xiaoshu (slight heat)	7 July	6—sheep/ram
Dashu (great heat)	23 July	
Liqiu (autumn begins)	7 August	7—monkey
Chushu (limit of heat)	23 August	
Bailu (white dew)	8 September	8—chicken/rooster
Qiufen (autumn equinox)	23 September	
Hanlu (cold dew)	8 October	9—dog
Shuangjiang (hoar frost descends)	24 October	
Lidong (winter begins)	8 November	10—pig/boar
Xiaoxue (little snow)	22 November	
Daxue (heavy snow)	7 December	11—rat
Dongzhi (winter solstice)	22 December	
Xiaohan (little cold)	6 January	12—cow/ox
Dahan (severe cold)	20 January	

Chinese Calendar (continued)

CHINESE NEW YEAR	GREGORIAN DATE	ANIMAL	CHINESE NEW YEAR	GREGORIAN DATE	ANIMAL
4702	22 Jan 2004	monkey	4709	3 Feb 2011	rabbit/hare
4703	9 Feb 2005	chicken/rooster	4710	23 Jan 2012	dragon
4704	29 Jan 2006	dog	4711	10 Feb 2013	snake
4705	18 Feb 2007	pig/boar	4712	31 Jan 2014	horse
4706	7 Feb 2008	rat	4713	19 Feb 2015	sheep/ram
4707	26 Jan 2009	cow/ox	4714	9 Feb 2016	monkey
4708	14 Feb 2010	tiger	4715	28 Jan 2017	rooster

Religious and Traditional Holidays

The word holiday comes from "holy day," and it was originally a day of dedication to religious observance; in modern times a holiday may be of either religious or secular commemoration. All dates in this article are Gregorian.

Jewish holidays—The major holidays are the Pilgrim Festivals: **Pesah** (Passover), **Shavuot** (Feast of Weeks, or Pentecost), and **Sukkoth** (Tabernacles); and the High Holidays: **Rosh Hashana** (New Year) and **Yom Kippur** (Day of Atonement).

Pesah commemorates the Exodus from Egypt and the servitude that preceded it. As such, it is the most significant of the commemorative holidays, for it celebrates the very inception of the Jewish people—i.e., the event that provided the basis for the covenant between God and Israel. The term Pesah refers to the paschal (Passover) lamb sacrificed on the eve of the Exodus, the blood of which marked the Jewish homes to be spared from God's plague. Leaven (se'or) and foods containing leaven (hametz) are neither to be owned nor consumed during Pesah. Aside from meats, fresh fruits, and vegetables, it is customary to consume only those foods prepared under rabbinic supervision and labeled "kosher for Passover." The unleavened bread (matzo) consists entirely of flour and water. On the eve of Pesah families partake of the seder, an elaborate festival meal. The table is bedecked with an assortment of foods symbolizing the passage from slavery (e.g., bitter herbs) into freedom (e.g., wine). Pesah will begin at sundown on 18 April and end on 26 April in 2011. (All Jewish holidays begin at sundown.)

A distinctive **Rosh Hashana** observance is the sounding of the ram's horn (shofar) at the synagogue service. Symbolic ceremonies, such as eating bread and apples dipped in honey, accompanied by prayers for a "sweet" and propitious year, are performed at the festive meals. In 2011 Rosh Hashana will begin at sundown on 28 September and will end on 30 September. **Yom Kippur** is a day when sins are confessed and expiated and man and God are reconciled. It is the holiest and most solemn day of the Jewish year. It is marked by fasting, penitence, and prayer. Working, eating, drinking, washing, anointing one's body, engaging in sexual intercourse, and donning leather shoes are all forbidden. Yom Kippur begins at sundown on 7 October in 2011.

Though not as important theologically, the feast of **Hanukkah** has become socially significant, especially in Western cultures. Hanukkah commemorates the rededication (164 BCE) of the Second Temple of Jerusalem after its desecration three years earlier. Though modern Israel tends to emphasize the military victory of the general Judas Maccabeus, the dis-

tinctive rite of lighting the menorah also recalls the Talmud story of how the small supply of nondesecrated oil—enough for one day—miraculously burned in the Temple for eight full days until new oil could be obtained. During Hanukkah, in addition to the lighting of the ceremonial candles, gifts are exchanged and children play holiday games. The festival occurs 1 through 9 Dec 2010, subsequently spanning 20 through 28 Dec 2011.

Christian holidays—The major holidays celebrated by nearly all Christians are **Easter** and **Christmas**.

Easter celebrates the Resurrection of Jesus on the third day after his Crucifixion. In the Christian liturgical year, Easter is preceded by the period of Lent, the 40 days (not counting Sundays) before Easter, which traditionally were observed as a period of penance and fasting. Lent begins on **Ash Wednesday**, a day devoted to penitence. Holy Week precedes **Easter Sunday** and includes **Maundy Thursday**, the commemoration of Jesus' last supper with his disciples; **Good Friday**, the day of his Crucifixion; and **Holy Saturday**, the transition between Crucifixion and Resurrection. Easter shares with Christmas the presence of numerous customs, some of which have little to do with the Christian celebration of the resurrection but clearly derive from folk customs. In 2011 the Western churches (nearly all Christian denominations) will observe Ash Wednesday on 9 March and Easter on 24 April. For Eastern Orthodox Christians, Lent begins on 7 March in 2011.

Christmas commemorates the birth of Jesus Christ. Since the early part of the 20th century, Christmas has also become a secular family holiday, observed by non-Christians, devoid of Christian elements, and marked by an increasingly elaborate exchange of gifts. In this secular Christmas celebration, a mythical figure named Santa Claus plays the pivotal role. Christmas is held on 25 December in most Christian cultures but occurs on the following 7 January in some Eastern Orthodox churches.

Islamic holidays—**Ramadan** is the holy month of fasting for Muslims. The Islamic ordinance prescribes abstention from evil thoughts and deeds as well as from food, drink, and sexual intercourse from dawn until dusk throughout the month. The beginning and end of Ramadan are announced when one trustworthy witness testifies before the authorities that the new moon has been sighted; a cloudy sky may therefore delay or prolong the fast. The end of the fast is celebrated as the feast of **'Id al-Fitr**. Ramadan is scheduled to begin on 1 August in 2011 and 'Id al-Fitr on 31 August of that year (all Islamic holidays begin at sundown). The Muslim New Year, **Hijrah**, is on 7 December in 2010 and 26 November in 2011.

Religious and Traditional Holidays (continued)

After 'Id al-Fitr, the second major Islamic festival is **'Id al-Adha**. Throughout the Muslim world, all who are able sacrifice sheep, goats, camels, or cattle and then divide the flesh equally among themselves, the poor, and friends and neighbors to commemorate the ransom of Ishmael with a ram. This festival falls at the end of the hajj, the pilgrimage to the holy city of Mecca in Saudi Arabia, which every adult Muslim of either sex must make at least once in his or her lifetime. 'Id al-Adha will be observed on 6 November in 2011.

'Ashura was originally designated in AD 622 by Muhammad as a day of fasting from sunset to sunset, probably patterned on the Jewish Day of Atonement, Yom Kippur. Among the Shi'ites, 'Ashura is a major festival that commemorates the death of Husayn (Hussein), son of 'Ali and grandson of Muhammad. It is a period of expressions of grief and of pilgrimage to Karbala (the site of Husayn's death, in present-day Iraq). 'Ashura is on 16 December in 2010 and 5 December in 2011.

Buddhist holidays—Holidays practiced by a large number of Buddhists are *uposatha* days and days that commemorate events in the life of the Buddha.

The four monthly holy days of ancient Buddhism continue to be observed in the Theravada countries of Southeast Asia. These *uposatha* days—the new moon and full moon days of each lunar month and the eighth day following the new and full moons—have their origin, according to some scholars, in the fast days that preceded the Vedic soma sacrifices.

The three major events of the Buddha's life—his birth, Enlightenment, and entrance into final nirvana—are commemorated in all Buddhist countries but not everywhere on the same day. In the Theravada countries the three events are all observed together on **Vesak**, the full moon day of the sixth lunar month, which usually occurs in May. In Japan and other Mahayana countries, the three anniversaries of the Buddha are observed on separate days (in some countries the birth date is 8 April, the Enlightenment date is 8 December, and the death date is 15 February).

Chinese holidays—The **Chinese New Year** is celebrated with a big family meal, and presents of cash are given to children in red envelopes. In 2011 the Chinese New Year will be on 3 February.

During the **Chinese Moon Festival**, on the 15th day of the 8th month of the lunar calendar, people return to their homes to visit with their family. The traditional food is moon cakes, round pastries stuffed with food such as red bean paste. The Moon Festival will occur on 12 September in 2011.

Japanese holidays—The Japanese celebrate **7-5-3 day** (Shichi-go-san no hi), in which parents bring children of those ages to the Shinto shrine to pray for their continued health. This day is held on 15 November.

In mid-July (or mid-August, in some areas) the Japanese celebrate **Bon** (also known as Bon Matsuri, or Urabon). The festival honors the spirits of deceased householders and of the dead generally. Memorial stones are cleaned, community dances are performed, and paper lanterns and fires are lit to welcome the dead and to bid them farewell at the end of their visit. The Shinto New Year, **Gantan-sai**, is celebrated on 1–3 January.

Hindu holidays—**Dussehra** celebrates the victory of Rama over Ravana, the symbol of evil on earth. In 2011 Dussehra falls on 6 October. **Diwali** is a festival of lights devoted to Laksmi, the goddess of wealth. During the festival, small earthenware lamps filled with oil are lit and placed in rows along the parapets of temples and houses and set adrift on rivers and streams. Diwali is on 26 October in 2011. **Mahasivaratri**, the most important sectarian festival of the year for devotees of the Hindu god Shiva, occurs on 3 March in 2011. **Holi** is a spring festival, probably of ancient origin. Participants throw colored waters and powders on one another, and, on this day, the usual restrictions of caste, sex, status, and age are disregarded. It will be on 20 March in 2011.

Sikh holidays—Sikhs observe all festivals celebrated by the Hindus of northern India. In addition, they celebrate the birthdays of the first and the last Gurus and the martyrdom of the fifth (Arjun) and the ninth (Tegh Bahadur). In 2011 **Guru Nanak Dev Sahib's birthday** is celebrated on 10 November, and that of **Guru Gobind Singh Sahib** is celebrated on 5 January in 2012. On 16 June in 2012 **Arjun's martyrdom** is observed. *Kachi lassi* (sweetened milk) is offered to passersby to commemorate his death. On 24 November in 2012 the **martyrdom of Guru Tegh Bahadur** is observed.

Baha'i holidays—The Baha'i New Year (**Naw Ruz**) in 2011 will fall on 21 March (all Baha'i holidays begin at sundown). Other important observances include the **declaration of the Bab** (23 May), the **Baha Ullah's birth** (12 November), and **Ascension** (29 May).

Zoroastrian holidays—**Noruz** (New Day) is on 21 March for 2011, and the 28th of that month is **Khordad Sal**, the birth of the prophet Zarathustra.

African American holiday—**Kwanzaa** (Swahili for "First Fruits") is celebrated each year from 26 December to 1 January and is patterned after various African harvest festivals. Maulana Karenga, a black-studies professor, created Kwanzaa in 1966 as a nonreligious celebration of family and social values. Each day of Kwanzaa is dedicated to one of seven principles: unity (*umoja*), self-determination (*kujichagulia*), collective responsibility (*ujima*), cooperative economics (*ujamaa*), purpose (*nia*), creativity (*kuumba*), and faith (*imani*).

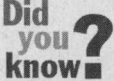

Did you know? A small-scale climatic stage that affected most parts of the world and lasted roughly from the beginning of the 16th century until the mid-19th century is known as the Little Ice Age. The harsh winters, moist, cool summers, and advancing ice sheets that characterized the Little Ice Age led to crop failures and the abandonment of the northern villages, and it necessitated the altering of oceanic sailing routes.

Perpetual Calendar

The perpetual calendar is a type of dating system that makes it possible to find the correct day of the week for any date over a wide range of years. Aspects of the perpetual calendar can be found in the Jewish religious and the Julian calendars, and some form of it has appeared in many proposed calendar reforms.

To find the day of the week for any Gregorian or Julian date in the perpetual calendar provided in this table, first find the proper dominical letter (one of the letters A through G) for the year in the upper table. Leap years have two dominical letters, the first applicable to dates in January and February, the second to dates in the remaining months. Then find the same dominical letter in the lower table, in whichever column it appears opposite the month in question. The days then fall as given in the lowest section of the column.

YEAR			CENTURY											
			JULIAN CALENDAR							GREGORIAN CALENDAR			
			0	100	200	300	400	500	600	1500**	1600	1700	1800	1900
			700	800	900	1000	1100	1200	1300		2000	2100	2200	2300
			1400	1500*										
0			DC	ED	FE	GF	AG	BA	CB	...	BA	C	E	G
1	29	57 85	B	C	D	E	F	G	A	F	G	B	D	F
2	30	58 86	A	B	C	D	E	F	G	E	F	A	C	E
3	31	59 87	G	A	B	C	D	E	F	D	E	G	B	D
4	32	60 88	FE	GF	AG	BA	CB	DC	ED	CB	DC	FE	AG	CB
5	33	61 89	D	E	F	G	A	B	C	A	B	D	F	A
6	34	62 90	C	D	E	F	G	A	B	G	A	C	E	G
7	35	63 91	B	C	D	E	F	G	A	F	G	B	D	F
8	36	64 92	AG	BA	CB	DC	ED	FE	GF	ED	FE	AG	CB	ED
9	37	65 93	F	G	A	B	C	D	E	C	D	F	A	C
10	38	66 94	E	F	G	A	B	C	D	B	C	E	G	B
11	39	67 95	D	E	F	G	A	B	C	A	B	D	F	A
12	40	68 96	CB	DC	ED	FE	GF	AG	BA	GF	AG	CB	ED	GF
13	41	69 97	A	B	C	D	E	F	G	E	F	A	C	E
14	42	70 98	G	A	B	C	D	E	F	D	E	G	B	D
15	43	71 99	F	G	A	B	C	D	E	C	D	F	A	C
16	44	72	ED	FE	GF	AG	BA	CB	DC	...	CB	ED	GF	BA
17	45	73	C	D	E	F	G	A	B	...	A	C	E	G
18	46	74	B	C	D	E	F	G	A	...	G	B	D	F
19	47	75	A	B	C	D	E	F	G	...	F	A	C	E
20	48	76	GF	AG	BA	CB	DC	ED	FE	...	ED	GF	BA	DC
21	49	77	E	F	G	A	B	C	D	...	C	E	G	B
22	50	78	D	E	F	G	A	B	C	...	B	D	F	A
23	51	79	C	D	E	F	G	A	B	...	A	C	E	G
24	52	80	BA	CB	DC	ED	FE	GF	AG	...	GF	BA	DC	FE
25	53	81	G	A	B	C	D	E	F	...	E	G	B	D
26	54	82	F	G	A	B	C	D	E	C	D	F	A	C
27	55	83	E	F	G	A	B	C	D	B	C	E	G	B
28	56	84	DC	ED	FE	GF	AG	BA	CB	AG	BA	DC	FE	AG

MONTH	DOMINICAL LETTER						
January, October	A	B	C	D	E	F	G
February, March, November	D	E	F	G	A	B	C
April, July	G	A	B	C	D	E	F
May	B	C	D	E	F	G	A
June	E	F	G	A	B	C	D
August	C	D	E	F	G	A	B
September, December	F	G	A	B	C	D	E
1 8 15 22 29	Sunday	Saturday	Friday	Thursday	Wednesday	Tuesday	Monday
2 9 16 23 30	Monday	Sunday	Saturday	Friday	Thursday	Wednesday	Tuesday
3 10 17 24 31	Tuesday	Monday	Sunday	Saturday	Friday	Thursday	Wednesday
4 11 18 25	Wednesday	Tuesday	Monday	Sunday	Saturday	Friday	Thursday
5 12 19 26	Thursday	Wednesday	Tuesday	Monday	Sunday	Saturday	Friday
6 13 20 27	Friday	Thursday	Wednesday	Tuesday	Monday	Sunday	Saturday
7 14 21 28	Saturday	Friday	Thursday	Wednesday	Tuesday	Monday	Sunday

*On and before 1582, 4 October only. **On and after 1582, 15 October only.

Source: Smithsonian Physical Tables, 9th edition, rev. 2003.

Civil Holidays

DAY	EVENT
1 January	New Year's Day, the first day of the modern calendar (various countries)
20 January	Inauguration Day, for quadrennial inauguration of US president
26 January	Australia Day, commemorates the establishment of the first British settlement in Australia
3rd Monday in January	Martin Luther King Day, for birth of US civil rights leader
2nd new moon after winter solstice (at the earliest 21 January and at the latest 19 February)	New Year, for Chinese lunar year, inaugurating a 15-day celebration
6 February	Waitangi Day, for Treaty of Waitangi, granting British sovereignty (New Zealand)
11 February	National Foundation Day, for founding by first emperor (Japan)
14 February	St. Valentine's Day, celebrating the exchange of love messages and named for either of two 3rd-century Christian martyrs (various)
3rd Monday in February	Presidents' Day, Washington-Lincoln Day, or Washington's Birthday, for birthdays of US Presidents George Washington and Abraham Lincoln
8 March	International Women's Day, celebration of the women's liberation movement
17 March	St. Patrick's Day, for patron saint of Ireland (Ireland and various)
21 or 22 March	Vernal Equinox Day, for beginning of spring (Japan)
25 March	Independence Day, for proclamation of independence from the Ottoman Empire (Greece)
4th Sunday in Lent	Mothering Day (UK)
1 April	April Fools' Day, or All Fools' Day, day for playing jokes, falling one week after the old New Year's Day of 25 March (various)
5 April	Qingming, for sweeping tombs and honoring the dead (China)
7 April	World Health Day, for founding of World Health Organization
22 April	Earth Day, for conservation and reclaiming of the natural environment (various)
25 April	ANZAC Day, for landing at Gallipoli (Australia/New Zealand/Samoa/Tonga)
29 April	Green Day, national holiday for environment and nature (Japan)
30 April	Queen's Birthday, for Queen Beatrix's investiture and former queen Juliana's birthday (The Netherlands)
1 May	May Day, celebrated as labor day or as festival of flowers (various)
3 May	Constitution Memorial Day, for establishment of democratic government (Japan)
5 May	Children's Day, honoring children (Japan/Republic of Korea)
5 May	Cinco de Mayo, anniversary of Mexico's victory over France in the Battle of Puebla (Mexico)
8/9 May	V-E Day, or Liberation Day, for end of World War II in Europe (various)
2nd Sunday in May	Mother's Day, honoring mothers (US)
Monday on or preceding 25 May	Victoria Day, for Queen Victoria's birthday (Canada)
30 or last Monday in May	Memorial Day, or Decoration Day, in honor of the deceased, especially the war dead (US)
2 June	Anniversary of the Republic, for referendum establishing republic (Italy)
5 June	Constitution Day (Denmark)
6 June	National Day, for Gustav I Vasa's ascension to the throne and adoption of Constitution (Sweden)
10 June	Portugal's Day, or Camões Memorial Day, anniversary of Luis de Camões's death
14 June	Flag Day, honoring flag (US)
3rd Saturday in June	Queen's Official Birthday, for Queen Elizabeth II (UK/New Zealand)
3rd Sunday in June	Father's Day, honoring fathers (US)
23 June	National Day, for Grand Duke Jean's official birthday (Luxembourg)
23–24 June	Midsummer Eve and Midsummer Day, celebrating the return of summer (various European)
last Sunday in June	Gay and Lesbian Pride Day, final day of weeklong advocacy of rights of gay men and lesbians (international)
1 July	Canada Day (formerly Dominion Day), for establishment of dominion
4 July	Independence Day, for Declaration of Independence from Britain (US)
12 July	Orangemen's Day, or Orange Day, anniversary of the Battle of the Boyne (Northern Ireland)
14 July	Bastille Day, for fall of the Bastille and onset of French Revolution (France)
21 July	National Day, for separation from The Netherlands (Belgium)
1 August	National Day, anniversary of the founding of the Swiss Confederation (Switzerland)
6 August	Hiroshima Day, for dropping of atomic bomb (Japan)
full-moon day of 8th lunar month	Chusok, harvest festival (Republic of Korea)
1st Monday in September	Labor Day, tribute to workers (US/Canada)
15 September	Respect-for-the-Aged Day, for the elderly (Japan)
16 September	Independence Day, for independence from Spain (Mexico)
23 or 24 September	Autumnal Equinox Day, for beginning of autumn; in honor of ancestors (Japan)

Civil Holidays (continued)

DAY	EVENT
two weeks ending on 1st Sunday in October	Oktoberfest, festival of food and drink, formerly commemorating marriage of King Louis (Ludwig) I (Germany)
3 October	Day of German Unity, for reunification of Germany
5 October	Republic Day, for founding of the republic (Portugal)
12 or 2nd Monday in October	Hispanic Day, Columbus Day, Discovery Day, or Day of the Race, for Christopher Columbus's discovery of the New World on behalf of Spain (Spain and various)
2nd Monday in October	Thanksgiving Day, harvest festival (Canada)
24 October	United Nations Day, for effective date of UN Charter (international)
26 October	National Day, for end of postwar occupation and return of sovereignty (Austria)
31 October	Halloween, or All Hallows' Eve, festive celebration of ghosts and spirits, on eve of All Saints' Day (various)
5 November	Guy Fawkes Day, anniversary of the Gunpowder Plot to blow up the king and Parliament (UK)
11 November	Armistice Day, Remembrance Day, or Veterans Day, honoring participants in past wars and recalling the Armistice of World War I (various)
23 November	Labor Thanksgiving Day, honoring workers (Japan)
4th Thursday in November	Thanksgiving Day, harvest festival (US)
16 December	Day of Reconciliation, for promoting national unity (South Africa)
23 December	Emperor's Birthday, for birthday of Emperor Akihito (Japan)
26 December	Boxing Day, second day of Christmas, for giving presents to service people (various)
31 December	New Year's Eve, celebration ushering out the old year and in the new year (various)

The Universe

Astronomical Constants

QUANTITY	SYMBOL	VALUE
astronomical unit	AU	length of the semimajor axis of the Earth's orbit around the Sun—149,597,870 km (92,955,808 mi)

measures large distances in space; equals the average distance from the Earth to the Sun

parsec	pc	one parsec equals 3.26 light-years

measures the distance at which the radius of the Earth's orbit subtends an angle of one second of arc

light-year	ly	9.46089×10^{12} km (5.8787×10^{12} mi)

measures the distance traveled by light moving in a vacuum in the course of one year

speed of light (in a vacuum)	c	$2.99792458 \times 10^{10}$ cm per sec (186,282 mi per sec)

mass of the Sun	Sun $M.$	1.989×10^{30} kg (330,000 times the mass of the Earth)

radius of the Sun	Sun $R.$	6.96×10^{8} m (109 times the radius of Earth)

Earth's mean radius		6,378 km (3,963 mi)

mean solar day (on Earth)   24 h 3 min 56.55 sec of mean sideral time

the interval between two successive passages of the Sun across the same meridian is a solar day; in practice, since the rate of the Sun's motion varies with the seasons, use is made of a fictitious Sun that always moves across the sky at an even rate

tropical (or solar) year (on Earth)   365.242 days

the time required for the Earth's orbital motion to return the Sun's position to the spring equinoctial point

synodic month (on Earth)   29.53 days

the time required for the Moon to pass through one complete cycle of phases

Definitions of Astronomical Positions

A **conjunction** is an apparent meeting or passing of two or more celestial bodies. For example, the Moon is in conjunction with the Sun at the phase of new Moon, when it moves between the Earth and Sun and the side turned toward the Earth is dark. Inferior planets—those with orbits smaller than the Earth's (namely, Venus and Mercury)—have two kinds of conjunctions with the Sun. An **inferior conjunction** occurs when the planet passes approximately between Earth and Sun; if it passes exactly between them, moving across the Sun's face as seen from Earth, it is said to be in transit (see *below*). A **superior conjunction** occurs when Earth and the other planet are on opposite sides of the Sun, but all three bodies are again nearly in a straight line. Superior planets, those having orbits larger than the Earth's, can have only superior conjunctions with the Sun.

When celestial bodies appear in opposite directions in the sky they are said to be in **opposition**. The Moon, when full, is said to be in opposition to the Sun (the Earth is then approximately between them). A superior planet (one with an orbit farther from the Sun than Earth's) is in opposition when Earth passes between it and the Sun. The opposition of a planet is a good time to observe it, because the planet is then at its nearest point to the Earth and in its full phase. The inferior planets, Venus and Mercury, can never be in opposition to the Sun.

When a celestial body as seen from the Earth makes a right angle with the direction of the Sun it is said to be in **quadrature**. The Moon at first or last quarter is said to be at east or west quadrature, respectively. A superior planet is at west quadrature when its position is 90° west of the Sun.

The east–west coordinate by which the position of a celestial body is ordinarily measured is known as the **right ascension**. Right ascension in combination with **declination** defines the position of a celestial object. Declination is the angular distance of a body north or south of the celestial equator. North declination is considered positive and south, negative. Thus, +90° declination marks the north celestial pole, 0° the celestial equator, and −90° the south celestial pole. The symbol for right ascension is the Greek letter α (alpha) and for declination the lowercase Greek letter Δ (delta).

The angular distance in celestial longitude separating the Moon or a planet from the Sun is known as **elongation**. The greatest elongation possible for the two inferior planets is about 48° in the case of Venus and about 28° in that of Mercury. Elongation may also refer to the angular distance of any celestial body from another around which it revolves or from a particular point in the sky; e.g., the extreme east or west position of a star with reference to the north celestial pole.

The point at which a planet is closest to the Sun is called the **perihelion**, and the most distant point in that planet's orbit is the **aphelion**. The term helion refers specifically to the Sun as the primary body about which the planet is orbiting.

Occultation refers to the obscuring of the light of an astronomical body, most commonly a star, by another astronomical body, such as a planet or a satellite. Hence, a solar eclipse is the occultation of the Sun by the Moon. From occultations of stars by planets, asteroids, and satellites, astronomers are able to determine the precise sizes and shapes of the latter bodies in addition to the temperatures of planetary atmospheres. For example, astronomers unexpectedly discovered the rings of Uranus during a stellar occultation on 10 Mar 1977.

A complete or partial obscuring of a celestial body by another is an **eclipse**; these occur when three celestial objects become aligned. The Sun is eclipsed when the Moon comes between it and the Earth; the Moon is eclipsed when it moves into the shadow of the Earth cast by the Sun. Eclipses of natural or artificial satellites of a planet occur as the satellites move into the planet's shadow. When the apparent size of the eclipsed body is much smaller than that of the eclipsing body, the phenomenon is known as an **occultation** (see *above*). Examples are the disappearance of a star, nebula, or planet behind the Moon, or the vanishing of a natural satellite or space probe behind some body of the solar system. A **transit** (see *above*) occurs when, as viewed from the Earth, a relatively small body passes across the disk of a larger body, usually the Sun or a planet, eclipsing only a very small area: Mercury and Venus periodically transit the Sun, and a satellite may transit its planet.

When an object orbiting the Earth is at the point in its orbit that is the greatest distance from the center of the Earth, this point is known as **apogee**; the term is also used to describe the point farthest from a planet or a satellite (as the Moon) reached by an object orbiting it. **Perigee** is the opposite of apogee.

The difference in direction of a celestial object as seen by an observer from two widely separated points is termed **parallax**. The measurement of parallax is used directly to find the distance of the body from the Earth (geocentric parallax) and from the Sun (heliocentric parallax). The two positions of the observer and the position of the object form a triangle; if the base line between the two observing points is known and the direction of the object as seen from each has been measured, the apex angle (the parallax) and the distance of the object from the observer can be determined.

An **hour angle** is the angle between an observer's meridian (a great circle passing over his head and through the celestial poles) and the hour circle (any other great circle passing through the poles) on which some celestial body lies. This angle, when expressed in hours and minutes, is the time elapsed since the celestial body's last transit of the observer's meridian. The hour angle can also be expressed in degrees, 15° of arc being equal to one hour.

Constellations

From the earliest times the star groups known as **constellations**, the smaller groups (parts of constellations) known as **asterisms**, and, also, **individual stars** have received names connoting some meteorological phenomena or symbolizing religious or mythological beliefs. At one time it was held that the constellation names and myths were of Greek origin, but it is now thought that they are primarily of Semitic or even pre-Semitic origin and that they came to the Greeks through the Phoenicians.

Constellations (continued)

The Alexandrian astronomer **Ptolemy** lists the names and orientation of 48 constellations in his *Almagest*, and, with but few exceptions, they are identical with those used at the present time. The majority of the remaining 40 constellations that are now accepted were added by European astronomers in the 17th and 18th centuries. In the 20th century the delineation of precise boundaries for all 88 constellations was undertaken by a committee of the International Astronomical Union.

NAME	GENITIVE	MEANING	NOTES
Constellations described by Ptolemy: the zodiac			(First-magnitude stars are given in italics in this column)
Aries	Arietis	Ram	
Taurus	Tauri	Bull	*Aldebaran* is the constellation's brightest star. Taurus also contains the Pleiades star cluster and the Crab Nebula.
Gemini	Geminorum	Twins	The brightest stars in Gemini are Castor and *Pollux*.
Cancer	Cancri	Crab	Cancer contains the well-known star cluster Praesepe.
Leo	Leonis	Lion	*Regulus* is the brightest star in Leo.
Virgo	Virginis	Virgin	*Spica* is the brightest star in Virgo.
Libra	Librae	Balance	
Scorpius	Scorpii	Scorpion	*Antares* is the brightest star of Scorpius.
Sagittarius	Sagittarii	Archer	The center of the Milky Way Galaxy lies in Sagittarius, with the densest star clouds of the galaxy.
Capricornus	Capricorni	Sea-goat	
Aquarius	Aquarii	Water-bearer	
Pisces	Piscium	Fishes	
Other Ptolemaic constellations			
Andromeda	Andromedae	Andromeda (an Ethiopian princess of Greek legend)	The constellation's most notable feature is the great spiral galaxy Andromeda (also called M31).
Aquila	Aquilae	Eagle	The brightest star in Aquila is *Altair*.
Ara	Arae	Altar	
Argo Navis	Argus Navis	the ship *Argo*	Argo Navis is now divided into smaller constellations that include Carina, Puppis, Pyxis, and Vela.
Auriga	Aurigae	Charioteer	The brightest star in Auriga is *Capella*. The constellation also contains open star clusters M36, M37, and M38.
Boötes	Boötis	Herdsman	*Arcturus* is the brightest star in Boötes.
Canis Major	Canis Majoris	Greater Dog	*Sirius* is the brightest star in Canis Major.
Canis Minor	Canis Minoris	Smaller Dog	*Procyon* is the brightest star in Canis Minor.
Cassiopeia	Cassiopeiae	Cassiopeia was a legendary queen of Ethiopia	Tycho's nova, one of the few recorded supernovae in the Galaxy, appeared in Cassiopeia in 1572.
Centaurus	Centauri	Centaur (possibly represents Chiron)	*Alpha Centauri* in Centaurus contains Proxima, the nearest star to the Sun.
Cepheus	Cephei	Cepheus (legendary king of Ethiopia)	Delta Cephei was the prototype for cepheid variables (a class of variable stars).
Cetus	Ceti	Whale	Mira Ceti was the first recognized variable star.
Corona Austrina	Coronae Austrinae	Southern Crown	
Corona Borealis	Coronae Borealis	Northern Crown	
Corvus	Corvi	Raven	
Crater	Crateris	Cup	
Cygnus	Cygni	Swan	Cygnus contains the asterism known as the Northern Cross; the constellation's brightest star is *Deneb*.
Delphinus	Delphini	Dolphin	Delphinus contains the asterism known as Job's Coffin.
Draco	Draconis	Dragon	Draco contains the star Thuban, which was the polestar in 3000 BC.
Equuleus	Equulei	Little Horse	
Eridanus	Eridani	River Eridanus or river god	*Achernar* is the brightest star in Eridanus.
Hercules	Herculis	Hercules (Greek hero)	Hercules contains the great globular star cluster M13.
Hydra	Hydrae	Water Snake	
Lepus	Leporis	Hare	
Lupus	Lupi	Wolf	

Constellations (continued)

NAME	GENITIVE	MEANING	NOTES
Other Ptolemaic constellations (continued)			
Lyra	Lyrae	Lyre	The brightest star in Lyra is *Vega*. In some 10,000 years, *Vega* will become the polestar. Lyra also contains the Ring Nebula (M57).
Ophiuchus	Ophiuchi	Serpent-bearer	
Orion	Orionis	Hunter	*Rigel* is the brightest star in Orion; M42 (the Great Nebula) resides in Orion.
Pegasus	Pegasi	Pegasus (winged horse)	The constellation contains stars of the Great Square of Pegasus.
Perseus	Persei	Perseus (legendary Greek hero)	
Piscis Austrinus	Piscis Austrini	Southern Fish	The brightest star in Piscis Austrinus is *Fomalhaut*.
Sagitta	Sagittae	Arrow	
Serpens	Serpentis	Serpent	
Triangulum	Trianguli	Triangle	The constellation contains M33, a nearby spiral galaxy.
Ursa Major	Ursae Majoris	Great Bear	The seven brightest stars of this constellation are the Big Dipper (also called the Plough).
Ursa Minor	Ursae Minoris	Lesser Bear	Ursa Minor contains Polaris (the north polestar).
Southern constellations, added c. 1600			
Apus	Apodis	Bird of Paradise	
Chamaeleon	Chamaeleontis	Chameleon	
Dorado	Doradus	Swordfish	The most notable object in Dorado is the Large Magellanic Cloud.
Grus	Gruis	Crane	
Hydrus	Hydri	Water Snake	
Indus	Indi	Indian	
Musca	Muscae	Fly	
Pavo	Pavonis	Peacock	
Phoenix	Phoenicis	Phoenix (mythical bird)	
Triangulum Australe	Trianguli Australis	Southern Triangle	
Tucana	Tucanae	Toucan	The most notable object in Tucana is the Small Magellanic Cloud.
Volans	Volantis	Flying Fish	
Constellations of Bartsch, 1624			
Camelopardalis	Camelopardalis	Giraffe	
Columba	Columbae	Dove	
Monoceros	Monocerotis	Unicorn	
Constellations of Hevelius, 1687			
Canes Venatici	Canum Venaticorum	Hunting Dogs	The constellation contains M51 (the Whirlpool Galaxy).
Lacerta	Lacertae	Lizard	
Leo Minor	Leonis Minoris	Lesser Lion	
Lynx	Lyncis	Lynx	
Scutum	Scuti	Shield	Scutum contains the Scutim star cloud in the Milky Way.
Sextans	Sextantis	Sextant	
Vulpecula	Vulpeculae	Fox	Vulpecula contains M27 (the Dumbbell Nebula).
Ancient asterisms that are now separate constellations			
Carina	Carinae	Keel [of the *Argo*, a legendary ship]	The brightest star in Carina is *Canopus*.
Coma Berenices	Comae Berenices	Berenice's Hair	The constellation contains both a coma (star cluster) and the north galactic pole (a point that lies perpendicular to the Milky Way).
Crux	Crucis	[Southern] Cross	
Puppis	Puppis	Stern [of the *Argo*]	
Pyxis	Pyxidis	Compass [of the *Argo*]	
Vela	Velorum	Sails [of the *Argo*]	

Constellations (continued)

NAME	GENITIVE	MEANING	NOTES
Southern constellations of Lacaille, c. 1750			
Antlia	Antliae	Pump	
Caelum	Caeli	[Sculptor's] Chisel	
Circinus	Circini	Drawing Compasses	
Fornax	Fornacis	[Chemical] Furnace	
Horologium	Horologii	Clock	
Mensa	Mensae	Table [Mountain]	
Microscopium	Microscopii	Microscope	
Norma	Normae	Square	
Octans	Octantis	Octant	Octans contains the south celestial pole.
Pictor	Pictoris	Painter's [Easel]	
Reticulum	Reticuli	Reticle	
Sculptor	Sculptoris	Sculptor's [Work-shop]	Sculptor contains the south galactic pole.
Telescopium	Telescopii	Telescope	

Astrology: The Zodiac

Signs of the zodiac are popularly used for divination as well as for designation of constellations.

NAME	SYMBOL	DATES	SEX/NATURE	TRIPLICITY	HOUSE	EXALTATION
Aries the Ram	♈	21 Mar–19 Apr	masculine/moving	fire	Mars	Sun (19°)
Taurus the Bull	♉	20 Apr–20 May	feminine/fixed	earth	Venus	Moon (3°)
Gemini the Twins	♊	21 May–21 Jun	masculine/common	air	Mercury	
Cancer the Crab	♋	22 Jun–22 Jul	feminine/moving	water	Moon	Jupiter (15°)
Leo the Lion	♌	23 Jul–22 Aug	masculine/fixed	fire	Sun	
Virgo the Virgin	♍	23 Aug–22 Sep	feminine/common	earth	Mercury	Mercury (15°)
Libra the Balance	♎	23 Sep–23 Oct	masculine/moving	air	Venus	Saturn (21°)
Scorpius the Scorpion	♏	24 Oct–21 Nov	feminine/fixed	water	Mars	
Sagittarius the Archer	♐	22 Nov–21 Dec	masculine/common	fire	Jupiter	
Capricorn the Goat	♑	22 Dec–19 Jan	feminine/moving	earth	Saturn	Mars (28°)
Aquarius the Water Bearer	♒	20 Jan–18 Feb	masculine/fixed	air	Saturn	
Pisces the Fish	♓	19 Feb–20 Mar	feminine/common	water	Jupiter	Venus (27°)

Classification of Stars

The spectral sequence O–M represents stars of essentially the same chemical composition but of different temperatures and atmospheric pressures. Stars belonging to other, more rare types of spectral classifications differ in chemical composition from those stars classified under the O–M scheme.

Each spectral class is additionally subdivided into 10 spectral types. For example, spectral class A is subdivided into spectral types A0–A9 with 0 being the hottest and 9 the coolest. (Spectral class O is unusual in that it is subdivided into O4–O9.) Between two stars of the same spectral type, the more luminous star will also be larger in diameter. Thus the Yerkes system of luminosity also tells something of a star's radius, with Ia being the largest and V the smallest. Approximately 90% of all stars are main-sequence, or type V, stars.

Based upon these systems, the Sun would be a G2 V star (a yellow, relatively hot dwarf star).

SPECTRAL CLASS	COLOR	APPROXIMATE SURFACE TEMP (°C)	EXAMPLES
O	blue	30,000 or greater	these stars are relatively rare
B	blue-white	20,000 to 30,000	Rigel, Alpha Crucis, Beta Crucis
A	white	10,000 to 20,000	Sirius, Vega, Fomalhaut
F	yellow-white	7,000 to 10,000	Canopus, Procyon
G	yellow	6,000 to 7,000	Sun
K	orange	4,500 to 6,000	Arcturus, Aldebaran
M	red	3,000 to 4,500	Betelgeuse, Antares

LUMINOSITY CLASSES (BASED UPON THE YERKES SYSTEM)

Ia	most luminous supergiants
Ib	luminous supergiants
II	bright giants
III	normal giants
IV	subgiants
V	main-sequence stars (dwarfs)

Astronomical Phenomena for 2011

Source: The Astronomical Almanac for the Year 2011.

MONTH	DAY	HOUR (GMT)	EVENT	MONTH	DAY	HOUR (GMT)	EVENT
January	2	14	Jupiter 0°.6 S of Uranus	April	2	09	Moon at apogee
	2	15	Mercury 4° N of Moon		3	15	new moon
	3	19	Earth at perihelion		4	00	Saturn at opposition
	4	09	new moon[1]		6	15	Jupiter in conjunction with Sun
	8	00	Neptune 5° S of Moon				
	8	16	Venus greatest elongation W (47°)		9	07	Pluto stationary
					9	20	Mercury in inferior conjunction
	9	15	Mercury greatest elongation W (23°)		11	12	first quarter
	10	06	Moon at apogee		17	06	Moon at perigee
	10	15	Uranus 7° S of Moon		17	08	Saturn 8° N of Moon
	10	17	Jupiter 7° S of Moon		18	03	full moon
	12	12	first quarter		19	08	Mercury 0°.8 N of Mars
	15	22	Venus 8° N of Antares		22	05	Mercury stationary
	19	21	full moon		22	19	Venus 0°.9 S of Uranus
	22	00	Moon at perigee		25	03	last quarter
	22	23	Juno stationary		27	10	Neptune 6° S of Moon
	25	10	Saturn 8° N of Moon		29	16	Juno stationary
	26	13	last quarter		29	18	Moon at apogee
	27	08	Saturn stationary		30	04	Uranus 6° S of Moon
	30	04	Venus 3° N of Moon		30	23	Venus 7° S of Moon
	31	01	Ceres in conjunction with Sun	May	1	07	Mercury 8° S of Moon
					1	11	Mars 0°.4 N of Jupiter
February	1	18	Mercury 4° S of Moon		1	19	Jupiter 6° S of Moon
	3	03	new moon		1	20	Mars 6° S of Moon
	4	17	Mars in conjunction with Sun		3	07	new moon
					7	19	Mercury greatest elongation W (27°)
	6	23	Moon at apogee				
	7	00	Uranus 6° S of Moon		10	21	first quarter
	7	10	Jupiter 7° S of Moon		10	23	Mercury 2° S of Jupiter
	11	07	first quarter		11	09	Venus 0°.6 S of Jupiter
	17	10	Neptune in conjunction with Sun		14	15	Saturn 8° N of Moon
					15	11	Moon at perigee
	18	09	full moon		17	11	full moon
	19	07	Moon at perigee		20	01	Mercury 2° S of Mars
	21	17	Saturn 8° N of Moon		22	15	Venus 1°.1 S of Mars
	24	23	last quarter		24	18	Neptune 6° S of Moon
	25	09	Mercury in superior conjunction		24	19	last quarter
					25	15	Pallas stationary
	28	00	Vesta 0°.9 N of Moon[2]		27	10	Moon at apogee
					27	13	Uranus 6° S of Moon
March	1	04	Venus 1°.6 S of Moon		29	15	Jupiter 6° S of Moon
	4	21	new moon		30	20	Mars 4° S of Moon
	6	08	Moon at apogee		31	04	Venus 4° S of Moon
	7	05	Jupiter 7° S of Moon				
	12	10	Juno at opposition	June	1	21	new moon[1]
	13	00	first quarter		3	15	Neptune stationary
	16	17	Mercury 2° N of Jupiter		9	02	first quarter
	19	18	full moon		10	21	Saturn 8° N of Moon
	19	19	Moon at perigee		12	02	Moon at perigee
	20	23	equinox		13	00	Mercury in superior conjunction
	21	00	Saturn 8° N of Moon				
	21	12	Uranus in conjunction with Sun		14	05	Saturn stationary
					15	20	full moon[1]
	23	01	Mercury greatest elongation E (19°)		18	08	Venus 5° N of Aldebaran
	26	12	last quarter		21	02	Neptune 6° S of Moon
	27	01	Venus 0°.2 S of Neptune		21	17	solstice
	28	07	Vesta 1°.2 S of Moon[2]		23	12	last quarter
	30	17	Mercury stationary		23	23	Uranus 6° S of Moon
	31	02	Neptune 5° S of Moon		24	04	Moon at apogee
	31	13	Venus 6° S of Moon		24	19	Vesta stationary

Astronomical Phenomena for 2011 (continued)

MONTH	DAY	HOUR (GMT)	EVENT	MONTH	DAY	HOUR (GMT)	EVENT
June	26	09	Jupiter 5° S of Moon	September	16	22	Pallas stationary
(continued)	28	05	Pluto at opposition	(continued)	18	02	Vesta stationary
	28	19	Mars 1°7 S of Moon		20	14	last quarter
	28	22	Mercury 5° S of Pollux		23	08	Mars 5° N of Moon
					23	09	equinox
July	1	09	new moon[1]		26	00	Uranus at opposition
	3	02	Mercury 5° N of Moon		27	11	new moon
	4	15	Earth at aphelion		28	01	Moon at perigee
	6	07	Mars 5° N of Aldebaran		28	20	Mercury in superior
	7	14	Moon at perigee				conjunction
	8	04	Saturn 8° N of Moon	October	3	12	Venus 3° N of Spica
	8	06	first quarter		4	03	first quarter
	10	08	Uranus stationary		8	02	Neptune 6° S of Moon
	15	07	full moon		10	22	Uranus 6° S of Moon
	18	10	Neptune 6° S of Moon		12	02	full moon
	20	05	Mercury greatest		12	12	Moon at apogee
			elongation E (27°)		13	20	Jupiter 5° S of Moon
	21	07	Uranus 6° S of Moon		13	21	Saturn in conjunction
	21	23	Moon at apogee				with Sun
	23	05	last quarter		20	04	last quarter
	24	01	Jupiter 5° S of Moon		22	00	Mars 6° N of Moon
	27	17	Mars 0°5 N of Moon[2]		23	01	Juno in conjunction
	29	14	Pallas at opposition				with Sun
	30	19	new moon		26	12	Moon at perigee
August	1	00	Ceres stationary		26	20	new moon
	1	11	Mercury 1°5 N of Moon		28	02	Mercury 0°2 N of
	2	07	Mercury stationary				Moon[2]
	2	21	Moon at perigee		28	05	Venus 1°8 N of Moon
	4	12	Saturn 8° N of Moon		29	02	Jupiter at opposition
	5	10	Vesta at opposition		31	05	Saturn 5° N of Spica
	6	11	first quarter	November	2	17	first quarter
	13	19	full moon		4	08	Neptune 6° S of Moon
	14	16	Neptune 6° S of Moon		7	02	Uranus 6° S of Moon
	16	12	Venus in superior		8	13	Moon at apogee
			conjunction		9	19	Jupiter 5° S of Moon
	17	01	Mercury in inferior		9	21	Neptune stationary
			conjunction		9	21	Venus 4° N of Antares
	17	13	Uranus 6° S of Moon		10	05	Mars 1°4 N of Regulus
	18	16	Moon at apogee		10	05	Mercury 1°9 N of
	20	12	Jupiter 5° S of Moon				Antares
	21	22	last quarter		10	20	full moon
	22	23	Neptune at opposition		12	06	Ceres stationary
	25	14	Mars 3° N of Moon		14	09	Mercury greatest
	26	04	Mercury stationary				elongation E (23°)
	28	01	Mercury 3° N of Moon		18	15	last quarter
	29	03	new moon		19	10	Mars 8° N of Moon
	30	17	Jupiter stationary		22	22	Saturn 7° N of Moon
	30	18	Moon at perigee		23	23	Moon at perigee
	31	23	Saturn 7° N of Moon		24	10	Mercury stationary
September	3	06	Mercury greatest		25	06	new moon[1]
			elongation W (18°)		26	10	Mercury 1°7 S of Moon
	4	18	first quarter		27	04	Venus 3° S of Moon
	9	02	Mercury 0°7 N of	December	1	15	Neptune 6° S of Moon
			Regulus		2	10	first quarter
	10	02	Mars 6° S of Pollux		4	08	Uranus 6° S of Moon
	10	21	Neptune 6° S of Moon		4	09	Mercury in inferior
	12	09	full moon				conjunction
	13	18	Uranus 6° S of Moon		6	01	Moon at apogee
	15	06	Moon at apogee		6	20	Jupiter 5° S of Moon
	16	12	Pluto stationary		10	15	full moon[1]
	16	17	Ceres at opposition		10	15	Uranus stationary
	16	18	Jupiter 5° S of Moon				

Astronomical Phenomena for 2011 (continued)

MONTH	DAY	HOUR (GMT)	EVENT	MONTH	DAY	HOUR (GMT)	EVENT
December	14	02	Mercury stationary	December	23	04	Mercury 3° N of Moon
(continued)	17	13	Mars 8° N of Moon	(continued)	24	18	new moon
	18	01	last quarter		26	11	Jupiter stationary
	20	10	Saturn 7° N of Moon		27	11	Venus 6° S of Moon
	22	03	Moon at perigee		29	01	Neptune 6° S of Moon
	22	06	solstice		29	08	Pluto in conjunction with Sun
	22	20	Mars 7° N of Antares				
	23	03	Mercury greatest elongation W (22°)		31	16	Uranus 6° S of Moon

¹Eclipse.   ²Occultation.

Morning and Evening Stars

This table gives the morning and evening stars for autumn 2010 through 2011. The morning and evening stars are actually planets visible to the naked eye during the early morning and at evening twilight.

PLANET	MORNING STAR	EVENING STAR
Mercury	23 Sep–5 Oct, 26 Dec 2010–13 Feb 2011, 18 Apr–5 Jun, 25 Aug–19 Sep, 10–31 Dec 2011	1 Nov–14 Dec 2010; 7 Mar–2 Apr, 20 Jun–9 Aug, 12 Oct–28 Nov 2011
Venus	4 Nov 2010–11 Jul 2011	23 Sep–24 Oct 2010; 23 Sep–31 Dec 2011
Mars	17 Apr–31 Dec 2011	23 Sep–5 Dec 2010
Jupiter	21 Apr–29 Oct 2011	23 Sep 2010–24 Mar 2011, 29 Oct–31 Dec 2011
Saturn	19 Oct 2010–4 Apr 2011, 31 Oct–31 Dec 2011	4 Apr–26 Sep 2011
Uranus	23 Sep–mid-December 2010; early April–late December 2011	mid-December 2010–early March 2011, late December–31 Dec 2011
Neptune	23 Sep–mid-November 2010; early March–late November 2011	mid-November 2010–late January 2011, late November–31 Dec 2011

 **Did you know?**

Efforts are ongoing in 2010 to compile the first digital "soil map" of the continents of the world. The goals of the project are to better understand the composition of the soils in different areas to maximize yields through crop selection and also to monitor the changes in the soil brought about by global warming and by native practices such as crop rotation.

Characteristics of Celestial Bodies

Mean orbital velocity indicates the average speed at which a planet orbits the Sun unless otherwise specified. *Inclination of orbit to ecliptic* indicates the angle of tilt between a planet's orbit and the plane of Earth's orbit (essentially the plane of the solar system). *Orbital period* indicates the planet's sidereal year (in Earth days except where noted). *Rotation period* indicates the planet's sidereal day (in Earth days except where noted). *Inclination of equator to orbit* indicates the angle of tilt between a planet's orbit and its equator. *Gravitational acceleration* is a measure of the body's gravitational pull on other objects. *Escape velocity* is the speed needed at the surface to escape the planet's gravitational pull. *Eccentricity of orbit* is a measure of the circularity or elongation of an orbit; 0 indicates circular orbits, and closer to 1 more elliptical ones.

Sun
diameter (at equator): 1.39 million km (863,705 mi)
mass (in 10^{20} kg): 19.8 billion
density (mass/volume, in kg/m³): 1,408
mean orbital velocity: the Sun orbits the Milky Way's center at around 220 km/sec (136.7 mi/sec)
orbital period: the Sun takes approximately 250 million Earth years to complete its orbit around the Milky Way's center
rotation period: 25–36 Earth days

gravitational acceleration: 275 m/sec² (902.2 ft/sec²)
escape velocity: 618.02 km/sec (384.01 mi/sec)
mean temperature at visible surface: 5,527 °C (9,980 °F)
probes and space missions: US—Pioneer 5–9, launched 1960–68; Skylab, 1973; Genesis, 2001; Solar Dynamics Observatory, 2010; Japan—Yohkoh, 1991; US/European Space Agency (ESA)—Ulysses, 1990–2009; SOHO, 1995.

Characteristics of Celestial Bodies (continued)

Mercury
average distance from the Sun: 58 million km (36 million mi)

diameter (at equator): 4,879 km (3,032 mi)

mass (in 10^{20} kg): 3,300

density (mass/volume, in kg/m³): 5,427

eccentricity of orbit: 0.206

mean orbital velocity: 47.9 km/sec (29.7 mi/sec)

inclination of orbit to ecliptic: 7.0°

orbital period: 88 Earth days

rotation period: 58.6 Earth days

inclination of equator to orbit: probably 0°

gravitational acceleration: 3.7 m/sec² (12.1 ft/sec²)

escape velocity: 4.3 km/sec (2.7 mi/sec)

mean temperature at surface†: 167 °C (333 °F)

satellites: none known

probes and space missions: US—Mariner 10, 1973; Messenger, 2004.

Venus
average distance from the Sun: 108.2 million km (67.2 million mi)

diameter (at equator): 12,104 km (7,521 mi)

mass (in 10^{20} kg): 48,700

density (mass/volume, in kg/m³): 5,243

eccentricity of orbit: 0.007

mean orbital velocity: 35.0 km/sec (21.8 mi/sec)

inclination of orbit to ecliptic: 3.4°

orbital period: 224.7 Earth days

rotation period: 243.0 Earth days (retrograde)

inclination of equator to orbit: 177.4°

gravitational acceleration: 8.9 m/sec² (29.1 ft/sec²)

escape velocity: 10.4 km/sec (6.4 mi/sec)

mean temperature at surface†: 464 °C (867 °F)

satellites: none known

probes and space missions: USSR—Venera 1–16, 1961–83; Vega 1 and 2, 1984; US—Mariner 2, 5, and 10, 1962, 1967, and 1973; Pioneer Venus Orbiter and Pioneer Venus Multiprobe, 1978; Galileo, 1989; Magellan, 1989; ESA—Venus Express, 2005.

Earth
average distance from the Sun: 149.6 million km (93 million mi)

diameter (at equator): 12,756 km (7,926 mi)

mass (in 10^{20} kg): 59,700

density (mass/volume, in kg/m³): 5,515

eccentricity of orbit: 0.017

mean orbital velocity: 29.8 km/sec (18.5 mi/sec)

inclination of orbit to ecliptic: 0.00°

orbital period: 365.25 days

rotation period: 23 hours, 56 minutes, and 4 seconds of mean solar time

inclination of equator to orbit: 23.5°

gravitational acceleration: 9.8 m/sec² (32.1 ft/sec²)

escape velocity: 11.2 km/sec (7.0 mi/sec)

mean temperature at surface†: 15 °C (59 °F)

satellites: 1 known—the Moon.

Moon (of Earth)
average distance from Earth: 384,401 km (238,855.7 mi)

diameter (at equator): 3,475 km (2,159 mi)

mass (in 10^{20} kg): 730

density (mass/volume, in kg/m³): 3,340

eccentricity of orbit: orbital eccentricity of Moon around Earth is 0.055

mean orbital velocity: the Moon orbits Earth at 1.0 km/sec (0.64 mi/sec)

inclination of orbit to ecliptic: 5.1°

orbital period: the Moon revolves around Earth in 27.32 Earth days

rotation period: the Moon rotates on its axis every 27.32 Earth days (synchronous with orbital period)

inclination of equator to orbit: 6.7°

gravitational acceleration: 1.6 m/sec² (5.3 ft/sec²)

escape velocity: 2.4 km/sec (1.5 mi/sec)

mean temperature at surface†: daytime: 107 °C (224.6 °F); nighttime: −153 °C (−243.4 °F)

probes and space missions: USSR, US, ESA, Japan—collectively about 70 missions since 1959, including 9 manned missions by the US. On 20 Jul 1969 humans first set foot on the Moon, from NASA's Apollo 11.

Mars
average distance from the Sun: 227.9 million km (141.6 million mi)

diameter (at equator): 6,794 km (4,222 mi)

mass (in 10^{20} kg): 6,420

density (mass/volume, in kg/m³): 3,933

eccentricity of orbit: 0.094

mean orbital velocity: 24.1 km/sec (15 mi/sec)

inclination of orbit to ecliptic: 1.9°

orbital period: 687 Earth days (1.88 Earth years)

rotation period: 24.6 Earth hours

inclination of equator to orbit: 24.9°

gravitational acceleration: 3.7 m/sec² (12.1 ft/sec²)

escape velocity: 5.0 km/sec (3.1 mi/sec)

mean temperature at surface†: −65 °C (−85 °F)

satellites: 2 known—Phobos and Deimos

probes and space missions: US—Mariner 4, 6, 7, and 9, 1964–71; Viking 1 and 2, 1975; Mars Global Surveyor, 1996; Mars Pathfinder, 1996; 2001 Mars Odyssey, 2001; Mars Exploration Rovers, 2003; Mars Reconnaissance Orbiter, 2005; USSR—Mars 2–7, 1971–73; Phobos 1 and 2, 1988; ESA—Mars Express, 2003; Phoenix, 2007.

Jupiter
average distance from the Sun: 778.6 million km (483.8 million mi)

diameter (at equator): 142,984 km (88,846 mi)

mass (in 10^{20} kg): 18.99 million

density (mass/volume, in kg/m³): 1,326

eccentricity of orbit: 0.049

mean orbital velocity: 13.1 km/sec (8.1 mi/sec)

inclination of orbit to ecliptic: 1.3°

orbital period: 11.86 Earth years

rotation period: 9.9 Earth hours

inclination of equator to orbit: 3.1°

gravitational acceleration: 23.1 m/sec² (75.9 ft/sec²)

escape velocity: 59.5 km/sec (37.0 mi/sec)

mean temperature at surface†: −110 °C (−166 °F)

satellites: at least 62 moons—including Callisto, Ganymede, Europa, and Io—plus rings

probes and space missions: US—Pioneer 10 and 11, 1972–73; Voyager 1 and 2, 1977; Galileo, 1989; Ulysses, 1990; US/ESA—Cassini-Huygens, 1997.

Saturn
average distance from the Sun: 1.433 billion km (890.8 million mi)

diameter (at equator): 120,536 km (74,897 mi)

mass (in 10^{20} kg): 5.00 million

density (mass/volume, in kg/m³): 687

eccentricity of orbit: 0.057

Characteristics of Celestial Bodies (continued)

mean orbital velocity: 9.7 km/sec (6 mi/sec)
inclination of orbit to ecliptic: 2.5°
orbital period: 29.43 Earth years
rotation period: 10.66 Earth hours
inclination of equator to orbit: 26.7°
gravitational acceleration: 9.0 m/sec^2 (29.4 ft/sec^2)
escape velocity: 35.5 km/sec (22.1 mi/sec)
mean temperature at surface†: −140 °C (−220 °F)
satellites: at least 62 moons—including Titan—plus rings
probes and space missions: US—Pioneer 11, 1973; Voyager 1 and 2, 1977; US/ESA—Cassini/Huygens, 1997.

Uranus

average distance from the Sun: 2.872 billion km (1.784 billion miles)
diameter (at equator): 51,118 km (31,763 mi)
mass (in 10^{20} kg): 868,000
density (mass/volume, in kg/m^3): 1,270
eccentricity of orbit: 0.046
mean orbital velocity: 6.8 km/sec (4.2 mi/sec)
inclination of orbit to ecliptic: 0.8°
orbital period: 84.01 Earth years
rotation period: 17.2 Earth hours (retrograde)
inclination of equator to orbit: 97.8°
gravitational acceleration: 8.7 m/sec^2 (28.5 ft/sec^2)
escape velocity: 21.3 km/sec (13.2 mi/sec)
mean temperature at surface†: −195 °C (−320 °F)
satellites: at least 27 moons, plus rings
probes and space missions: US—Voyager 2, 1977.

Neptune

average distance from the Sun: 4.495 billion km (2.793 billion mi)
diameter (at equator): 49,528 km (30,775 mi)
mass (in 10^{20} kg): 1.02 million
density (mass/volume, in kg/m^3): 1,638
eccentricity of orbit: 0.009
mean orbital velocity: 5.48 km/sec (3.40 mi/sec)
inclination of orbit to ecliptic: 1.8°
orbital period: 164.79 Earth years
rotation period: 16.1 Earth hours
inclination of equator to orbit: 28.3°
gravitational acceleration: 11.0 m/sec^2 (36.0 ft/sec^2)
escape velocity: 23.5 km/sec (14.6 mi/sec)
mean temperature at surface†: −200 °C (−330 °F)
satellites: at least 13 moons, plus rings
probes and space missions: US—Voyager 2, 1977.

Pluto

average distance from the Sun: 5.910 billion km (3.67 billion mi); Pluto lies within the Kuiper belt and can be considered its largest known member
diameter (at equator): 2,344 km (1,485 mi)
mass (in 10^{20} kg): 125
density (mass/volume, in kg/m^3): about 2,000
eccentricity of orbit: 0.249
mean orbital velocity: 4.72 km/sec (2.93 mi/sec)
inclination of orbit to ecliptic: 17.2°
orbital period: 248 Earth years
rotation period: 6.4 Earth days (retrograde)
inclination of equator to orbit: 122.5°
gravitational acceleration: 0.6 m/sec^2 (1.9 ft/sec^2)
escape velocity: 1.1 km/sec (0.7 mi/sec)

mean temperature at surface†: −225 °C (−375 °F)
satellites: 3 known—including Charon
probes and space missions: US—New Horizons, 2006.

asteroids

(several hundred thousand small rocky bodies, about 1,000 km [610 mi] or less in diameter, that orbit the Sun primarily between the orbits of Mars and Jupiter)
distance from the Sun: between approximately 300 million km (190 million mi) and 600 million km (380 million mi), with notable outliers
estimated mass (in 10^{21} kg): 2.3
probes and space missions: US—Galileo, 1989; Ulysses, 1990; NEAR Shoemaker, 1996; Deep Space 1, 1998; Stardust, 1999; Dawn, 2007; US/ESA—Cassini-Huygens, 1997; Japan—Hayabusa, 2003; ESA—Rosetta, 2004.

Comet 1P/Halley

distance from the Sun at closest point of orbit: 87.8 million km (54 million mi); farthest distance from the Sun: 5.2 billion km (3.2 billion mi).
diameter (at equator): 16 x 8 x 8 km (9.9 x 4.9 x 4.9 mi)
density (mass/volume, in kg/m^3): possibly as low as 200
eccentricity of orbit: 0.967
inclination of orbit to ecliptic: 18°
orbital period: 76.1 to 79.3 Earth years; the next appearance will be 2061. The comet's orbit is retrograde.
rotation period: 52 Earth hours
probes and space missions: USSR—Vega 1 and 2, 1984; ESA—Giotto, 1985; Japan—Sakigake and Suisei, 1985.

Comet Hale-Bopp

distance from the Sun at closest point of orbit: 136 million km (84.5 million mi); farthest distance from the Sun: 74.7 billion km (46.4 billion mi).
eccentricity of orbit: 0.995
orbital period: 4,000 Earth years; last closest pass of Sun was on 31 Mar 1997.

Kuiper belt

(a huge flat ring located beyond Neptune containing residual icy material from the formation of the outer planets)
average distance from the Sun (main concentration): 4.5–7.5 billion km (2.8–4.7 billion mi)
mass: scientists estimate there may be as many as 100,000 icy, cometlike bodies of a size greater than 100 km in the Kuiper belt; the belt is estimated to have a mass of 6,000 x 10^{20} kg.
probes and space missions: US—New Horizons, 2006.

Oort cloud

(an immense, roughly spherical cloud of icy, cometlike bodies inferred to orbit the Sun at distances roughly 1,000 times that of the orbit of Pluto)
average distance from the Sun: 3–7 trillion km (1.9–4.3 trillion mi)
mass: some trillions of the cloud's icy objects have an estimated total mass of at least 600,000 x 10^{20} kg (10 times the mass of Earth).

---

†For celestial bodies with no surface, temperature given is at a level in the atmosphere equal to 1 bar of pressure.

Solar System Superlatives

Largest planet: Jupiter (142,984 km [88,846 mi] diameter); all of the other planets in the solar system could fit inside Jupiter.

Largest moon: Jupiter's moon Ganymede (5,268 km [3,273 mi] diameter).

Smallest planet: Mercury (4,879 km [3,032 mi] diameter).

Smallest moons: Jupiter and Saturn both have numerous satellites that are smaller than 10 km (6 mi) in diameter.

Planet closest to the Sun: Mercury (average distance from the Sun 58 million km [36 million mi]).

Planet farthest from the Sun: Neptune (average distance from the Sun 4.50 billion km [2.79 billion mi]); Pluto, demoted to a dwarf planet in 2006, was the farthest planet from the Sun for all but 20 years of its 248-year orbital period.

Planet with the most eccentric (least circular) orbit: Mercury (eccentricity of 0.206).

Moon with the most eccentric orbit: Neptune's moon Nereid (eccentricity of 0.75).

Planet with the least eccentric orbit: Venus (eccentricity of 0.007).

Moon with the least eccentric orbit: Saturn's moon Tethys (eccentricity of 0.0001).

Planet most tilted on its axis: Uranus (axial tilt of 98° from its orbital plane).

Planets with the most moons: Jupiter and Saturn (at least 62).

Planets with the fewest moons: Mercury and Venus (none).

Planet with the longest day: Venus (1 day on Venus equals 243 Earth days).

Planet with the shortest day: Jupiter (1 day on Jupiter equals 9.9 Earth hours).

Planet with the longest year: Neptune (1 year on Neptune equals 165 Earth years).

Planet with the shortest year: Mercury (1 year on Mercury equals 88 Earth days).

Fastest orbiting planet: Mercury (47.9 km/sec [29.7 mi/sec] mean orbital velocity).

Slowest orbiting planet: Neptune (5.48 km/sec [3.40 mi/sec] mean orbital velocity).

Hottest planet: Venus (464 °C [867 °F] average temperature); although Mercury is closer to the Sun, Venus is hotter because Mercury has no atmosphere, whereas the atmosphere of Venus traps heat via a strong greenhouse effect.

Coldest planet: Neptune (−220 °C [−364 °F] average temperature).

Brightest visible star in the night sky: Sirius (apparent visual magnitude −1.46).

Brightest planet in the night sky: Venus (apparent visual magnitude −4.5 to −3.77).

Densest planet: Earth (density of 5,515 kg/m³).

Least dense planet: Saturn (density of 687 kg/m³); Saturn in theory would float in water.

Planet with strongest gravity: Jupiter (more than twice the gravitational force of Earth at an altitude at which one bar of atmospheric pressure is exerted).

Planet with weakest gravity: Mars (slightly more than one-third the gravitational force of Earth).

Planet with the largest mountain: Mars (Olympus Mons, an extinct volcano, stands some 21 km [13 mi] above the planet's mean radius and 540 km [335 mi] across).

Planet with the deepest valley: Mars (Valles Marineris, a system of canyons, is some 4,000 km [2,500 mi] long and from about 2 to 9 km [1 to 5.6 mi] deep).

Largest known impact crater: Valhalla, a crater on Jupiter's moon Callisto, has a bright central area that is about 600 km (370 mi) across, with concentric ridges extending about 1,500 km (900 mi) from the center. (The largest crater on Earth believed to be of impact origin is the Vredefort ring structure in South Africa, which is about 300 km [190 mi] across.)

The Sun

The Sun is the star around which Earth and the other components of the solar system revolve. It is the dominant body of the system, constituting more than 99% of the system's entire mass. The Sun, at least 90% hydrogen by number of atoms, is the source of an enormous amount of energy produced during the conversion of hydrogen atoms to helium. This energy provides Earth with the light and heat necessary to support life. In 2010 NASA's Solar Dynamics Observatory was launched to capture more details of the Sun's inner activities and its effect on everything on Earth, including satellites, power grids, GPS communications, and the climate. The geologic record of Earth and the Moon reveals that the Sun was formed about 4.5 billion years ago.

The Sun is classified as a G2 V star, where G2 stands for the second hottest stars of the yellow G class—of surface temperature about 5,500 °C (10,000 °F)—and V represents a main sequence, or dwarf, star, the typical star for this temperature class (see also "Classification of Stars"). The Sun exists in the outer part of the Milky Way Galaxy and was formed from material that had been processed inside other stars and supernovas.

The mass of the Sun is 743 times the total mass of all the planets in the solar system and 330,000 times that of Earth. All the planetary and interplanetary gravitational phenomena are negligible effects in comparison to the gravitational force exerted by the Sun. Under the force of gravity, the mass of the Sun presses inward, and to keep the star from collapsing, the central pressure outward must be great enough to support its weight. The Sun's core, which occupies approximately 25% of the star's radius, has a density about 100 times that of water (roughly 6 times that at the center of Earth), but the temperature at the core is at least 15 million °C (27 million °F), so the central pressure is at least 10,000 times greater than that at the center of Earth. In this environment atoms are stripped of their electrons, and at this high temperature the bare nuclei collide to produce the nuclear reactions that are responsible for generating the energy vital to life on Earth.

The temperature of the Sun's surface is so high that no solid or liquid can exist; the constituent materials are predominantly gaseous atoms, with a very small number of molecules. As a result, there is no fixed surface. The surface viewed from Earth, the photosphere, is approximately 400 km (250 mi) thick and

The Sun (continued)

is the layer from which most of the radiation reaches us; the radiation from below the photosphere is absorbed and reradiated, while the emission from overlying layers drops sharply, by about a factor of six every 200 km (124 mi).

While the temperature of the Sun drops from 15 million °C (27 million °F) at the core to around 5,500 °C (10,000 °F) at the photosphere, it begins to rise in the chromosphere, a layer several thousand kilometers thick. Temperatures there range from 4,200 °C (7,600 °F) to 100,000 °C (180,000 °F). Above the chromosphere is a comparatively dim, extended halo

called the corona, which has a temperature of 1 million °C (1.8 million °F) and reaches far past the planets. Beyond a distance of around 3.5 million km (2.2 million mi) from the Sun, the corona flows outward at a speed (near Earth) of 400 km/sec (250 mi/sec); this flow of charged particles is called the solar wind.

Superposed on the Sun's stable energy, however, is an 11-year cycle of magnetic activity manifested by regions of transient strong magnetic fields called sunspots. The largest sunspot can be seen on the solar surface even without a telescope.

Mercury

Mercury is the planet closest to the Sun, revolving around it at an average distance of 58 million km (36 million mi). In Sumerian times, some 5,000 years ago, it was already known in the night sky. In classical Greece the planet was called Apollo when it appeared as a morning star and Hermes, for the Greek equivalent of the Roman god Mercury, when it appeared as an evening star.

Mercury's orbit lies inside the orbit of the Earth and is more elliptical than those of most of the other planets. At its closest approach (perihelion), Mercury is only 46 million km (28.5 million mi) from the Sun, while its greatest distance (aphelion) approaches 70 million km (43.5 million mi). Mercury orbits the Sun in 88 Earth days at an average speed of 48 km per second (29.8 mi per sec), allowing it to overtake and pass Earth every 116 Earth days (synodic period).

Because of its proximity to the Sun, the surface of Mercury can become extremely hot. High temperatures at "noon" may reach 400 °C (755 °F) while the "predawn" lowest temperature is −173 °C (−280 °F). Mercury's equator is almost exactly in its orbital plane (its spin-axis inclination is nearly zero), and thus Mercury does not have seasons as does the Earth. Because of its elliptical orbit and a peculiarity of its rotational period (see below), however, certain longitudes experience cyclical variations in temperatures on a "yearly" as well as on a "diurnal" basis.

Mercury is about 4,879 km (3,032 mi) in diameter, the smallest of the planets. Mercury is only a bit larger than the Moon. Its mass, as measured by the gravitational perturbation of the path of the Mariner 10 spacecraft during close flybys in 1974–75, is about one-eighteenth

of the mass of the Earth. Escape velocity, the speed needed to escape from a planet's gravitational field, is about 4.3 km per second (2.7 mi per second)—compared with 11.2 km per sec (7 mi per sec) for the Earth.

The mean density of Mercury, calculated from its mass and radius, is about 5.43 grams per cubic cm, nearly the same as that of the Earth (5.52 grams per cubic cm).

Photographs relayed by the Mariner 10 spacecraft showed that Mercury spins on its axis (rotates) once every 58.646 Earth days, exactly two-thirds of the orbital period of 87.9694 Earth days. This observation confirmed that Mercury is in a 3:2 spin-orbit tidal resonance—i.e., that tides raised on Mercury by the Sun have forced it into a condition that causes it to rotate three times on its axis in the same time it takes to revolve around the Sun twice. The 3:2 spin-orbit coupling combines with Mercury's eccentric orbit to create very unusual temperature effects.

Although Mercury rotates on its axis once every 58.646 Earth days, one rotation does not bring the Sun back to the same part of the sky, because during that time Mercury has moved partway around the Sun. A solar day on Mercury (for example, from one sunrise to another, or one noon to another) is 176 Earth days (exactly two Mercurian years).

Mercury's low escape velocity and high surface temperatures do not permit it to retain a significant atmosphere.

In January 2008 the MESSENGER spacecraft flew by Mercury, revealing previously unseen details in photographs, and scientists approved dozens of new names for surface features such as craters.

Venus

Venus is the second planet from the Sun and the planet whose orbit is closest to that of the Earth. When visible, Venus is the brightest planet in the sky. Viewed through a telescope, it presents a brilliant, yellow-white, essentially featureless face to the observer. The obscured appearance results because the surface of the planet is hidden from sight by a continuous and permanent cover of clouds.

Venus's orbit is the most nearly circular of that of any planet, with a deviation from perfect circularity of only about 1 part in 150. The period of the orbit—that is, the length of the Venusian year—is 224.7 Earth days. The rotation of Venus is unusual in both its direction and speed. Most of the planets in the solar system rotate in a counterclockwise direction when viewed from above their north poles; Venus, however,

rotates in the opposite, or retrograde, direction. Were it not for the planet's clouds, an observer on Venus's surface would see the Sun rise in the west and set in the east.

Venus spins on its axis slowly, taking 243 Earth days to complete one rotation. Venus's spin and orbital periods are nearly synchronized with the Earth's orbit such that Venus presents almost the same face toward the Earth when the two planets are at their closest.

Venus is nearly the Earth's twin in terms of size and mass. Venus's equatorial diameter is about 95% of the Earth's diameter, while its mass is 81.5% that of the Earth. The similarities to the Earth in size and mass also produce a similarity in density; Venus's density is 5.24 grams per cubic cm, as compared with 5.52 for the Earth.

Venus (continued)

In terms of its shape, Venus is more nearly a perfect sphere than are most planets. A planet's rotation generally causes a slight flattening at the poles and bulging at the equator, but Venus's very slow rotation rate allows it to maintain its highly spherical shape.

Venus has the most massive atmosphere of all the terrestrial planets (Mercury, Venus, Earth, and Mars). Its atmosphere is composed of 96.5% carbon dioxide and 3.5% nitrogen. The atmospheric pressure at the planet's surface varies with the surface elevation but averages about 90 bars, or 90 times the atmospheric pressure at the Earth's surface. This is the same pressure found at a depth of about one kilometer in the Earth's oceans. Temperatures range between a minimum temperature of −45 °C (−49 °F) and a maximum temperature of 500 °C (932 °F); the average temperature is 464 °C (867 °F).

Earth

Earth is the third planet in distance outward from the Sun. It is the only planetary body in the solar system that has conditions suitable for life, at least as known to modern science.

The average distance of Earth from the Sun—149.6 million km (93 million mi)—is designated as the distance of the unit of measurement known as the AU (astronomical unit). Earth orbits the Sun at a speed of 29.8 km (18.5 mi) per second, making one complete revolution in 365.25 days. As it revolves around the Sun, Earth spins on its axis and rotates completely once every 23 hr 56 min 4 sec. Earth has a single natural satellite, the Moon.

The fifth largest planet of the solar system, Earth has a total surface area of roughly 509.6 million sq km (197 million sq mi), of which about 29%, or 148 million square km (57 million square mi), is land. Oceans and smaller seas cover the balance of the surface. Earth is the only planet known to have liquid water. Together with ice, the liquid water constitutes the hydrosphere. Seawater makes up more than 98% of the total mass of the hydrosphere and covers about 71% of Earth's surface. Significantly, seawater constituted the environment of the earliest terrestrial life forms.

Earth's atmosphere consists of a mixture of gases, chiefly nitrogen (78%) and oxygen (21%). Argon makes up much of the remainder of the gaseous envelope, with trace amounts of water vapor, carbon dioxide, and various other gases also present.

Earth's structure consists of an inner core of nearly solid iron, surrounded by successive layers of molten metals and solid rock, and a thin layer at the surface comprising the continental crust.

Earth is surrounded by a magnetosphere, a region dominated by Earth's magnetic field and extending upward from about 140 km (90 mi) in the upper atmosphere. In the magnetosphere, the magnetic field of Earth traps rapidly moving charged particles (mainly electrons and protons), the majority of which flow from the Sun (as solar wind). If it were not for this shielding effect, such particles would bombard the terrestrial surface and destroy life. High concentrations of the trapped particles make up two doughnut-shaped zones called the Van Allen radiation belts. These belts play a key role in certain geophysical phenomena, such as auroras.

The Moon

The Moon is the sole natural satellite of Earth. It revolves around the planet from west to east at a mean distance of about 384,400 km (238,900 mi). The Moon is less than one-third the size of Earth, having a diameter of only about 3,475 km (2,159 mi) at its equator. The Moon shines by reflecting sunlight, but its albedo—is the fraction of light received that is reflected—is only 0.073.

The Moon rotates about its own axis in about 27.32 days, which is virtually identical to the time it takes to complete its orbit around Earth. As a result, the Moon always presents nearly the same face to Earth. The rate of actual rotation is uniform, but the arc through which the Moon moves from day to day varies somewhat, causing the lunar globe (as seen by a terrestrial observer) to oscillate slightly over a period nearly equal to that of revolution.

The surface of the Moon has been a subject of continuous telescopic study from the time of Galileo's first observation in 1609. The Italian Jesuit astronomer Giovanni B. Riccioli designated the dark areas on the Moon as seas (maria), with such fanciful names as Mare Imbrium ("Sea of Showers") and Mare Nectaris ("Sea of Nectar"). During the centuries that followed the publication of these early studies, more detailed maps and, eventually, photographs were produced. A Soviet space probe photographed the side of the Moon facing away from Earth in 1959. By the late 1960s, the US Lunar Orbiter missions had yielded close-up photographs of the entire lunar surface. On 20 Jul 1969, Apollo 11 astronauts Neil Armstrong and Edwin ("Buzz") Aldrin set foot on the Moon. US explorations in late 2009 and early 2010 detected "a significant amount" of water on the Moon's surface, some in the form of ice deposits formed in craters, the most striking formations on the Moon.

These craters, which measure up to about 200 km (320 mi) or more in diameter, are scattered over the surface in great profusion and often overlap one another. Meteorites hitting the lunar surface at high velocity produced most of the large craters. Many of the smaller ones—those measuring less than 1 km (0.6 mi) across—appear to have been formed by explosive volcanic activity, however. The Moon's maria have relatively few craters. These lava outpourings spread over vast areas after most of the craters had already been formed.

Various theories for the Moon's origin have been proposed. At the end of the 19th century, the English astronomer Sir George H. Darwin advanced a hypothesis stating that the Moon had been originally part of Earth but had broken away as a result of tidal gravitational action and receded from the planet. This was proved unlikely in the 1930s. A theory that arose dur-

The Moon (continued)

ing the 1950s postulated that the Moon had formed elsewhere in the solar system and was then later captured by Earth. This idea was also proved to be physically implausible and was dismissed. Today, most investigators favor an explanation known as the giant-impact hypothesis, which postulates that a Mars-sized body struck proto-Earth early in the history of the solar system. As a result, a cloud of fragments from both bodies was ejected into orbit around Earth, and this later accreted into the Moon.

Moon Phases, 2010–2011

As the Moon orbits Earth, more or less of the half of the Moon illuminated by the Sun is visible on Earth. During the lunar month the Moon's appearance changes from dark (the new moon) to being illuminated more and more on the right side (waxing crescent, first quarter, and waxing gibbous) to the full disc being illuminated (the full moon). The phases of the Moon are completed by the Moon being illuminated less and less on the left side (waning gibbous, last quarter, and waning crescent) and end with another new moon. This cycle takes place over a period of around 29 days; the time from new moon to new moon is referred to as a lunation.

The phases of the Moon are caused by the positions of the Sun in relationship to the Moon. Thus, when the Sun and the Moon are close in the sky a dark new moon is the result (the Sun is lighting the half of the Moon not visible to Earth). When the Sun and the Moon are at opposition (in opposite parts of the sky) the full moon occurs (the Sun illuminates fully the half of the Moon seen on Earth). When the Sun and the Moon are at about a 90-degree angle, one sees either a first quarter or a last quarter moon.

The dates for the new moon, first quarter, full moon, and last quarter for late June 2010–December 2011 are given in the table below.

MONTH	NEW MOON	FIRST QUARTER	FULL MOON	LAST QUARTER
June 2010	12	19	26	(4 July)
July 2010	11	18	26	(3 August)
August 2010	10	16	24	(1 September)
September 2010	8	15	23	(1 October)
October 2010	7	14	23	30
November 2010	6	13	21	28
December 2010	5	13	21	28
January 2011	4	12	19	26
February 2011	3	11	18	24
March 2011	4	12	19	26
April 2011	3	11	18	25
May 2011	3	10	17	24
June 2011	1	9	15	23
July 2011	1	8	15	23
August 2011	(30 July)	6	13	21
September 2011	(29 August)	4	12	20
October 2011	(27 September)	4	12	20
November 2011	(26 October)	2	10	18
December 2011	(25 November)	2	10	18

Mars

Mars is the fourth planet in order of average distance from the Sun and the seventh in order of diminishing size and mass. It orbits the Sun once in 687 Earth days and spins on its axis once every 24 Earth hours and 37 minutes.

Because of its blood-red color, Mars has often been associated with warfare and slaughter. It is named for the Roman god of war; as far back as 3,000 years ago, Babylonian astronomer-astrologers called the planet Nergal for their god of death and pestilence. The Greeks called it Ares for their god of battle; the planet's two satellites, Phobos (Fear) and Deimos (Terror), were later named for the two sons of Ares and Aphrodite.

Mars moves around the Sun at a mean distance of approximately 1.52 times that of Earth from the Sun. Because the orbit of Mars is relatively elongated, the distance between Mars and the Sun varies from 206.6 to 249.2 million km (128.4 to 154.8 million mi). Mars completes a single orbit in roughly the time in which Earth completes two. At its closest approach, Mars is less than 56 million km (34.8 million mi) from Earth, but it recedes to almost 400 million km (248.5 million mi). Mars is a small planet. Its equatorial radius is about half that of Earth, and its mass is only one-tenth the terrestrial value.

The axis of rotation is inclined to the orbital plane at an angle of 24.9°, and, as on Earth, the tilt gives rise to seasons. The Martian year consists of 668.6 Martian solar days (called sols). The orientation and eccentricity of the orbit (eccentricity denotes how much the orbit deviates from a perfect circle: the more elongated, the more eccentric) leads to seasons that are quite uneven in length. The Martian atmosphere is mainly composed of carbon dioxide. It is very thin (less than 1% of Earth's atmospheric pressure). Evidence suggests that the atmosphere was much denser in the remote past and that water was once much more abundant at the surface. Only small amounts of water are found in the lower atmosphere today, occasionally forming thin ice clouds at high altitudes and, in several localities, morning ice fogs. Mars's polar caps consist of frozen

Mars (continued)

carbon dioxide and water ice. Observations confirm that water ice also is present under large areas of the Martian surface and hint that liquid water may have flowed in geologically recent times.

The characteristic temperature in the lower atmosphere is about −70 °C (−100 °F). Unlike that of Earth, the total mass (and pressure) of the atmosphere experiences large seasonal variations, as carbon dioxide "snows out" at the winter pole.

The surface of Mars shows the massive extinct volcano Olympus Mons, which stands some 21 km (13 mi) above the planet's mean radius and is 540 km (335 mi) across, and Valles Marineris, a system of canyons, is some 4,000 km (2,500 mi) long and from about 2 to 9 km (1 to 5.6 mi) deep.

The two satellites of Mars—Phobos and Deimos—were discovered in 1877 by Asaph Hall of the United States Naval Observatory. Little was known about these bodies until observations were made by NASA's orbiting Mariner 9 spacecraft nearly a century later. The moons of Mars cannot be seen from all locations on the planet because of their small size, proximity to the planet, and near-equatorial orbits.

Mars Exploration Rovers—Spirit and Opportunity—landed on Mars in January 2004. In May 2008 the spacecraft Phoenix successfully landed on the planet and began its mission to be the first spacecraft to retrieve and study water (ice) from another planet. In late July it confirmed the presence of water on Mars but ceased operations soon thereafter due to diminishing sunlight. In 2010 Opportunity continued to explore the Concepción Crater rim, while Spirit became stuck in a sand-filled crater and, through the winter, remained parked but active, taking pictures of the soil around it.

The speed of steamboats increased dramatically over the years; the run from New Orleans to Louisville KY, which took 25 days in 1816, required only 4 days by 1853. The average life span of a steamboat was only four to five years because of poor construction and maintenance, exploding boilers, and sinkings due to river construction. Spontaneous races were common and contributed greatly to the approximately 4,000 deaths in steamboat disasters between 1810 and 1850.

Jupiter

Jupiter is the most massive of the planets and is fifth in average distance from the Sun. When ancient astronomers named the planet Jupiter for the ruler of the gods in the Greco-Roman pantheon, they had no idea of the planet's true dimensions, but the name is appropriate, for Jupiter is larger than all the other planets combined. It has a narrow ring system and at least 62 known satellites, 3 larger than Earth's Moon. Jupiter also has an internal heat source—i.e., it emits more energy than it receives from the Sun. This giant has the strongest magnetic field of any planet, with a magnetosphere so large that, if it could be seen from Earth, its apparent diameter would exceed that of the Moon. Jupiter's system is the source of intense bursts of radio noise, at some frequencies occasionally radiating more energy than the Sun.

Of particular interest concerning Jupiter's physical properties is its low mean density of 1.33 grams per cubic cm—in contrast with Earth's 5.52 grams/cm^3—coupled with the large dimensions and mass and the short rotational period. The low density and large mass indicate that Jupiter's composition and structure are quite unlike those of Earth and the other inner planets, a deduction that is supported by detailed investigations of the giant planet's atmosphere and interior.

Jupiter has no solid surface; the transition from the atmosphere to its highly compressed core occurs gradually at great depths. The close-up views of Jupiter from the Voyager spacecraft revealed a variety of cloud forms, with a predominance of elliptical features reminiscent of cyclonic and anticyclonic storm systems on Earth. All these systems are in motion, appearing and disappearing on time scales dependent on their sizes and locations. Also observed to vary are the pastel shades of various colors present in the cloud layers—from the tawny yellow that seems to characterize the main layer, through browns and blue-grays, to the well-known salmon-colored Great Red Spot, Jupiter's largest, most prominent, and longest-lived feature.

Because Jupiter has no solid surface, it has no topographic features, and latitudinal currents dominate the planet's large-scale circulation. The lack of a solid surface with physical boundaries and regions with different heat capacities makes the persistence of these currents and their associated cloud patterns all the more remarkable. The Great Red Spot, for example, moves in longitude with respect to Jupiter's rotation, but it does not move in latitude.

The Voyager 1 spacecraft verified the existence of a ring system surrounding Jupiter when it crossed the planet's equatorial plane. Subsequently, images from the Galileo spacecraft revealed that the ring system consists principally of four concentric components whose boundaries are associated with the orbits of Jupiter's four innermost moons. The ring system is composed of large numbers of micrometer-sized particles that produce strong forward scattering of incident sunlight. The presence of such small particles requires a source, and the association of the ring boundaries with the four moons makes the source clear. The particles are thought to be generated by impacts on these moons (and on still smaller bodies within the main part of the ring) by micrometeoroids, cometary debris, and possibly volcanically produced material from Jupiter's moon Io.

Jovian Moons

The satellites orbiting Jupiter are numerous; there are at least 62 Jovian moons and likely additional ones to be discovered.

The first objects in the solar system discovered by means of a telescope (by Galileo in 1610) were the four brightest moons of Jupiter. Now known as the Galilean satellites, they are (in order of increasing distance from Jupiter) Io, Europa, Ganymede, and Callisto. Each is a unique world in its own right. Callisto and Ganymede, for example, are as large as or larger than the planet Mercury, but, while Callisto's icy surface is ancient and heavily cratered from impacts, Ganymede's appears to have been extensively modified by internal activity. Europa may still be geologically active and may harbor an ocean of liquid water, and possibly even life, beneath its frozen surface. Io is the most volcanically active body in the solar system; its surface is a vividly colored landcape of erupting vents, pools and solidified flows of lava, and sulfurous deposits.

Data for the first 16 known Jovian moons (discovered 1610–1979) are summarized below. The orbits of the inner eight satellites have low inclinations (they are not tilted relative to the planet's equator) and low eccentricities (their orbits are relatively circular). The orbits of the outer eight have much higher inclinations and eccentricities, and four of them are retrograde (they are opposite to Jupiter's spin and orbital motion around the Sun). The innermost four satellites are thought to be intimately associated with Jupiter's ring and are the sources of the fine particles within the ring itself.

Beginning in 1999 some 47 tiny moons (including one seen in 1975 and then lost) were discovered photographically in observations from Earth. All have high orbital eccentricities and inclinations and large orbital radii; nearly all of the orbits are retrograde. Rough size estimates based on their brightness place them between 2 and 8 km (1.2 and 5 mi) in diameter. They were assigned provisional numerical designations on discovery; many also have received official names.

In the table, "sync" denotes that the orbital period and rotational period are the same, or synchronous; hence, the moon always keeps the same face toward Jupiter. "R" following the orbital period indicates a retrograde orbit. Unspecified quantities are unknown.

NAME (DESIGNATION)	MEAN DISTANCE FROM JUPITER	DIAMETER	MASS (10^{20} KG)	ORBITAL PERIOD (EARTH DAYS)	ROTATIONAL PERIOD (EARTH DAYS)
Metis (JXVI)	128,000 km (79,500 mi)	40 km (25 mi)	0.001	0.295	sync
Adrastea (JXV)	129,000 km (80,000 mi)	20 km (12 mi)	0.0002	0.298	sync
Amalthea (JV)[1]	181,000 km (112,500 mi)	189 km (117 mi)	0.075	0.498	sync
Thebe (JXIV)	222,000 km (138,000 mi)	100 km (62 mi)	0.008	0.675	sync
Io (JI)[1]	422,000 km (262,000 mi)	3,630 km (2,256 mi)	893.2	1.769	sync
Europa (JII)[1]	671,000 km (417,000 mi)	3,130 km (1,945 mi)	480	3.551	sync
Ganymede (JIII)[1]	1,070,000 km (665,000 mi)	5,268 km (3,273 mi)	1,482	7.155	sync
Callisto (JIV)[1]	1,883,000 km (1,170,000 mi)	4,806 km (2,986 mi)	1,076	16.689	sync
Leda (JXIII)	11,127,000 km (6,914,000 mi)	10 km (6 mi)	0.00006	234	
Himalia (JVI)	11,480,000 km (7,133,000 mi)	170 km (106 mi)	0.095	251	0.4
Lysithea (JX)	11,686,000 km (7,261,300 mi)	24 km (15 mi)	0.0008	258	0.5
Elara (JVII)	11,737,000 km (7,293,000 mi)	80 km (50 mi)	0.008	256	0.5
Ananke (JXII)	21,269,000 km (13,216,000 mi)	20 km (12.5 mi)	0.0004	634 R	0.4
Carme (JXI)	23,350,000 km (14,509,000 mi)	30 km (18.6 mi)	0.001	729 R	0.4
Pasiphae (JVIII)	23,500,000 km (14,602,000 mi)	36 km (22.3 mi)	0.003	735 R	
Sinope (JIX)	23,700,000 km (14,726,500 mi)	28 km (17.3 mi)	0.0008	758 R	0.5

[1]Densities are known for these moons: Amalthea (0.86 grams/cm^3), Io (3.53 grams/cm^3), Europa (3.01 grams/cm^3), Ganymede (1.94 grams/cm^3), Callisto (1.83 grams/cm^3).

Jovian Ring

Jupiter's complex ring was discovered and first studied by the twin Voyager spacecraft during flybys of the planet in 1979 and further elucidated by images from the Galileo spacecraft in 1996–97. The ring consists of four main components: an outer gossamer ring, whose outer radius coincides with the orbital radius of the Jovian moon Thebe (221,900 km; 137,880 mi); an inner gossamer ring bounded on its outer edge by the orbit of Amalthea (181,400 km; 112,720 mi); the main ring, extending inward some 6,000 km (3,730 mi) from the orbits of Adrastea (129,000 km; 80,160 mi) and Metis (128,000 km; 79,540 mi); and a halo of particles with a thickness of 20,000 km (12,430 mi) that extends from the main ring inward to a radius of about 92,000 km (57,170 mi). For comparison, Jupiter's visible surface lies at a radius of about 71,500 km (44,430 mi) from its center. The moons involved with the ring are believed to supply the fine particles that compose it.

Saturn

Saturn is the sixth planet in order of average distance from the Sun and the second largest of the planets in mass and size. Its dimensions are almost equal to those of Jupiter, while its mass is about a third as large; it has the lowest mean density of any object in the solar system.

Both Saturn and Jupiter resemble stellar bodies in that the light gas hydrogen dominates their bulk **chemical composition.** Saturn's atmosphere is 91% hydrogen by mass and is thus the most hydrogen-rich atmosphere in the solar system. Saturn's structure and **evolutionary history,** however, differ significantly from those of its larger counterpart. Like the other giant planets—Jupiter, Uranus, and Neptune—Saturn has extensive satellite and ring systems, which may provide clues to its origin and evolution. The planet has at least 62 moons, including the second largest in the solar system. Saturn's dense and extended rings, which lie in its equatorial plane, are the most impressive in the solar system.

Saturn has no single **rotation period.** Cloud motions in its massive upper atmosphere can be used to trace out a variety of rotation periods, with periods as short as about 10 hours 10 minutes near the equator and increasing with some oscillation to about 30 minutes longer at latitudes higher than 40°. The rotation period of Saturn's deep interior can be determined from the rotation period of the magnetic field, which is presumed to be rooted in an outer core of hydrogen compressed to a metallic state. The "surface" of Saturn that is seen through telescopes and in spacecraft images is actually a complex layer of clouds.

The **atmosphere** of Saturn shows many smaller-scale time-variable features similar to those found in that of Jupiter, such as red, brown, and white spots; bands; eddies; and vortices. The atmosphere generally has a much blander appearance than Jupiter's, however, and is less active on a small scale. A spectacular exception occurred during September–November 1990, when a large white spot appeared near the equator, expanded to a size exceeding 20,000 km (12,400 mi), and eventually spread around the equator before fading.

Saturnian Moons

At least 62 natural satellites are known to circle Saturn. Data for the first 18 Saturnian moons (discovered 1655–1990) are summarized below. As with those of the other giant planets, the satellites closest to Saturn are mostly regular, meaning that their orbits are fairly circular and not greatly inclined (tilted) with respect to the planet's equator. All of the satellites in the table except distant **Phoebe** are regular.

Titan is Saturn's largest moon and the only satellite in the solar system known to have clouds and a dense atmosphere (composed mostly of nitrogen and methane). The moon is also enveloped in a reddish haze, which is thought to be composed of complex organic compounds that are produced by the action of sunlight on its clouds and atmosphere. That organic molecules may have been settling out of the haze onto Titan's surface for much of its history has encouraged some scientists to speculate on the possibility that life may have evolved there. Observations by the Cassini-Huygens spacecraft showed Titan to have a varied surface sculpted by rains of hydrocarbon compounds, flowing liquids, wind, impacts, and possibly volcanic and tectonic activity. Saturn's second largest moon is **Rhea,** followed by **Iapetus** and **Dione.**

An unusual Saturnian satellite is **Hyperion.** Because of its highly irregular shape and eccentric orbit, it does not rotate stably about a fixed axis. Unlike any other known object in the solar system, Hyperion rotates chaotically, alternating unpredictably between periods of tumbling and seemingly regular rotation.

Between 2000 and 2005 about 30 additional tiny moons occupying various (mostly distant) orbits were discovered. Like the numerous outer moons of Jupiter, nearly all of the recent finds around Saturn belong to the irregular class, meaning that their orbits are highly inclined and elliptical. More than half of them, plus Phoebe, are in retrograde orbits (they move opposite to Saturn's spin and orbital motion around the Sun).

In March 2008 it was announced that the Cassini spacecraft had taken images of Rhea in 2005 that appeared to show the first known ring around a moon.

In the table, "sync" denotes that the orbital period and rotational period are the same, or synchronous. Unspecified quantities are unknown.

NAME (DESIGNATION)	MEAN DISTANCE FROM SATURN	DIAMETER	MASS (10²⁰ KG)	DENSITY (GRAMS/CM³)	ORBITAL PERIOD (EARTH DAYS)	ROTATIONAL PERIOD (EARTH DAYS)
Pan (SXVIII)	133,580 km (82,000 mi)	20 km (12 mi)	0.00003	0.63	0.5750	
Atlas (SXV)	137,670 km (85,540 mi)	28 km (17 mi)	0.0001	0.63	0.6019	

Saturnian Moons (continued)

NAME (DESIGNATION)	MEAN DISTANCE FROM SATURN	DIAMETER	MASS (10^{20} KG)	DENSITY (GRAMS/CM³)	ORBITAL PERIOD (EARTH DAYS)	ROTATIONAL PERIOD (EARTH DAYS)
Prometheus (SXVI)	139,350 km (86,590 mi)	92 km (57 mi)	0.0033	0.63	0.6130	
Pandora (SXVII)	141,700 km (88,050 mi)	92 km (57 mi)	0.002	0.63	0.6285	
Epimetheus (SXI)	151,420 km (94,090 mi)	114 km (71 mi)	0.0054	0.60	0.6942	sync
Janus (SX)	151,470 km (94,120 mi)	178 km (111 mi)	0.0192	0.65	0.6945	sync
Mimas (SI)	185,520 km (115,280 mi)	392 km (244 mi)	0.375	1.14	0.94	sync
Enceladus (SII)	238,020 km (147,900 mi)	520 km (323 mi)	0.7	1.0	1.37	sync
Tethys (SIII)	294,660 km (183,090 mi)	1,060 km (659 mi)	6.27	1.0	1.88	sync
Telesto (SXIII)*	294,660 km (183,090 mi)	30 km (19 mi)	0.00007	1.0	1.88	
Calypso (SXIV)*	294,660 km (183,090 mi)	26 km (16 mi)	0.00004	1.0	1.88	
Dione (SIV)	377,400 km (234,510 mi)	1,120 km (696 mi)	11	1.5	2.73	sync
Helene (SXII)†	377,400 km (234,510 mi)	32 km (20 mi)	0.0003	1.5	2.73	
Rhea (SV)	527,040 km (327,490 mi)	1,530 km (951 mi)	23.1	1.24	4.51	sync
Titan (SVI)	1,221,830 km (759,210 mi)	5,150 km (3,200 mi)	1,350	1.881	15.94	sync
Hyperion (SVII)	1,481,100 km (920,310 mi)	286 km (178 mi)	0.2	1.50	21.27	chaotic
Iapetus (SVIII)	3,561,300 km (2,212,890 mi)	1,460 km (907 mi)	16	1.02	79.33	sync
Phoebe (SIX)	12,952,000 km (8,048,000 mi)	220 km (137 mi)	0.004	1.3	550.5 (retrograde)	0.4

*Telesto and Calypso occupy the same orbit as Tethys but about 60° ahead and behind, respectively.
†Helene occupies the same orbit as Dione but about 60° behind.

Saturnian Rings

Saturn's rings rank among the most spectacular phenomena in the solar system. They have intrigued astronomers ever since they were discovered telescopically by Galileo in 1610, and their mysteries have only deepened since they were photographed and studied by Voyager 1 and 2 in the early 1980s. In October 2009, researchers announced the discovery of a giant Saturnian ring that lies far beyond the planet's other rings. Sighted through NASA's Spitzer Space Telescope, it is the largest known planetary ring in the solar system, beginning about 6 million km (about 3.7 million mi) from Saturn and stretching outward 12 million km (7.5 million mi). The particles that make up the rings are composed primarily of water ice and range from dust specks to house-sized chunks. The rings exhibit a great amount of structure on many scales, from the broad A, B, and C rings visible from Earth down to myriad narrow component ringlets. Odd structures resembling spokes, braids, and spiral waves are also present. Some of this detail is explained by gravitational interaction with a number of Saturn's 62 moons (the orbits of well more than a dozen known moons, from Pan to Dione and Helene, lie within the rings), but much of it remains unaccounted for.

Numerous divisions or gaps are seen in the major ring regions. A few of the more prominent ones are named for famous astronomers who were associated with studies of Saturn.

The major rings and divisions, listed outward from Saturn, are given below. For comparison, Saturn's visible surface lies at a radius of about 60,300 km (37,500 mi).

RING (OR DIVISION)	RADIUS OF RING'S INNER EDGE	WIDTH	COMMENTS
D ring (Guerin division)	66,970 km (41,610 mi)	7,500 km (4,700 mi)	visible only in reflected light
C ring (Maxwell division)	74,490 km (46,290 mi)	17,500 km (10,900 mi)	also called Crepe ring
B ring (Cassini division, Huygens gap)	91,980 km (57,150 mi)	25,500 km (15,800 mi)	brightest ring Cassini division is the largest ring gap
A ring	122,050 km (75,840 mi)	14,600 km (9,100 mi)	the outermost ring visible from Earth

Saturnian Rings (continued)

RING (OR DIVISION)	RADIUS OF RING'S INNER EDGE	WIDTH	COMMENTS
(Encke division)			located within the A ring, near its outer edge
F ring	140,220 km (87,130 mi)	30–500 km (20–300 mi)	faint, narrowest major ring
G ring	166,000 km (103,150 mi)	8,000 km (5,000 mi)	faint
E ring	180,000 km (111,850 mi)	300,000 km (186,400 mi)	faint

Uranus

Uranus is the seventh planet in order of distance from the Sun and the first found with the aid of a telescope. Its low density and large size place it among the four giant planets, all of which are composed primarily of hydrogen, helium, water, and other volatile compounds and which thus are without solid surfaces. Absorption of red light by methane gas gives the planet a blue-green color. The planet has at least 27 satellites, ranging up to 789 km (490 mi) in radius, and 13 narrow rings.

Uranus spins on its side; its **rotation axis** is tipped at an angle of 98° relative to its orbit axis. The 98° tilt is thought to have arisen during the final stages of planetary accretion when bodies comparable in size to the present planets collided in a series of violent events that knocked Uranus onto its side.

Although Uranus is nearly featureless, extreme contrast enhancement of images taken by the Voyager spacecraft reveals faint bands oriented parallel to circles of constant latitude. Apparently the rotation of the planet and not the distribution of absorbed sunlight controls the cloud patterns.

Wind is the motion of the atmosphere relative to the rotating planet. At high latitudes on Uranus, as on the Earth, this relative motion is in the direction of the planet's rotation. At low (that is, equatorial) latitudes, the relative motion is in the opposite direction. On the Earth these directions are called east and west, respectively, but the more general terms are prograde and retrograde. The winds that exist on Uranus are several times stronger than are those of the Earth. The wind is 200 m (656 ft) per second (prograde) at a latitude of 55° S and 110 m (360.8 ft) per second (retrograde) at the equator. Neptune's equatorial winds are also retrograde, although those of Jupiter and Saturn are prograde. No satisfactory theory exists to explain these differences.

Uranus has no large **spots** like the Great Red Spot of Jupiter or the Great Dark Spot of Neptune. Since the giant planets have no solid surfaces, the spots represent atmospheric storms. For reasons that are not clear, Uranus seems to have the smallest number of storms of any of the giant planets. Most of the mass of Uranus (roughly 80%) is in the form of a liquid core made primarily of icy materials (water, methane, and ammonia).

Uranus was discovered in 1781 by the English astronomer **William Herschel**, who had undertaken a survey of all stars down to eighth magnitude—i.e., those about five times fainter than stars visible to the naked eye. Herschel suggested naming the new planet the Georgian Planet after his patron, King George III of England, but the planet was eventually named according to the tradition of naming planets for the gods of Greek and Roman mythology; Uranus is the father of Saturn, who is in turn the father of Jupiter.

After the discovery, Herschel continued to observe the planet with larger and better telescopes and eventually discovered its two largest satellites, Titania and Oberon, in 1787. Two more satellites, Ariel and Umbriel, were discovered by the British astronomer William Lassell in 1851. The names of the four satellites come from English literature—they are characters in works by Shakespeare and Pope—and were proposed by Herschel's son, John Herschel. A fifth satellite, Miranda, was discovered by Gerard P. Kuiper in 1948. The tradition of naming the satellites after characters in Shakespeare's and Pope's works continues to the present.

Uranian Moons and Rings

Uranus has 27 known **satellites** forming three distinct groups: 13 small moons orbiting quite close to the planet, 5 large moons located somewhat farther out, and finally, another 9 small and much more distant moons. The members of the first two groups are in nearly circular orbits with low inclinations with respect to the planet.

The densities of the four largest satellites, **Ariel, Umbriel, Titania,** and **Oberon**, suggest that they are about half (or more) water ice and the rest rock. Oberon and Umbriel are heavily scarred with large impact craters dating back to the very early history of the solar system, evidence that their surfaces probably have been stable since their formation. In contrast, Titania and Ariel have far fewer large craters, indicating relatively young surfaces shaped over time by internal geological activity. **Miranda**, though small compared with the other major moons, has a unique jumbled patchwork of varied surface terrain revealing surprisingly extensive past activity. Data for the major satellites are summarized below.

The 5 major moons were **discovered** telescopically from Earth between 1787 and 1948. Ten of the 13 innermost moons, with radii of about 10–80 km (6–50 mi), were found in Voyager 2 images. The rest of the moons, with radii of 5–81 km (3–50 mi), were detected in Earth-based observations between 1997 and 2003; the orbital motion of nearly all of the outermost moons is retrograde (opposite to the direction of Uranus's spin and revolution around the Sun).

Thirteen narrow rings are known to encircle Uranus, with radii from 41,837 to 51,149 km (25,996 to 31,783 mi), for the most part within the orbits of the innermost moons. For comparison, Uranus's visible surface lies at a radius of about 25,600 km (15,900 mi). The ring system was first detected in 1977 during Earth-based observations of Uranus. Subsequent observations from Earth and images from Voyager 2 and the Hubble Space Telescope clarified the number and other features of the rings.

Uranian Moons and Rings (continued)

NAME (DESIGNATION)	MEAN DISTANCE FROM URANUS	RADIUS OR RADIAL DIMENSIONS	MASS (10^{20} KG)	DENSITY (GRAMS/CM³)	ORBITAL PERIOD/ ROTATIONAL PERIOD (EARTH DAYS)*
Miranda (V)	129,900 km (80,720 mi)	240 x 234 x 233 km (149 x 145 x 145 mi)	0.66	1.2	1.413
Ariel (I)	190,900 km (118,620 mi)	581 x 578 x 578 km (361 x 359 x 359 mi)	13.5	1.67	2.52
Umbriel (II)	266,000 km (165,280 mi)	585 km (364 mi)	11.7	1.4	4.144
Titania (III)	436,300 km (271,100 mi)	789 km (490 mi)	35.2	1.71	8.706
Oberon (IV)	583,500 km (362,570 mi)	761 km (473 mi)	30.1	1.63	13.46

*The orbital period and rotational period are the same, or synchronous, for the listed moons.

Neptune

Neptune is the eighth planet in average distance from the Sun. It has 13 known satellites. It was named for the Roman god of the sea, whose trident serves as the planet's astronomical symbol.

Neptune's **distance** from the Sun varies between 29.8 and 30.4 astronomical units (AUs). Its **diameter** is about four times that of Earth, but because of its great distance Neptune cannot be seen from Earth without the aid of a telescope. Neptune's deep blue **color** is due to the absorption of red light by methane gas in its atmosphere. It receives less than half as much sunlight as Uranus, but heat escaping from its interior makes Neptune slightly warmer than the latter. The heat released may also be responsible for Neptune's stormier **atmosphere**, which exhibits the fastest winds seen on any planet in the solar system.

Neptune's **orbital period** is 164.8 Earth years. It has not completely circled the Sun since its discovery in 1846, so some refinements in calculations of its orbital size and shape are still expected. The planet's orbital eccentricity of 0.009 means that its orbit is very nearly circular; among the planets in the solar system, only Venus has a smaller eccentricity. Neptune's seasons (and the seasons of its moons) are therefore of nearly equal length, each about 41 Earth years in duration. The length of Neptune's day, as determined by Voyager 2, is 16.11 Earth hours.

As with the other giant planets of the outer solar system, Neptune's atmosphere is composed predominantly of hydrogen and helium. The **temperature** of Neptune's atmosphere varies with altitude. A minimum temperature of about −223 °C (−369 °F) occurs at pressure near 0.1 bar. The temperature increases with altitude to about 477 °C (891 °F) at 2,000 km (1,240 mi, which corresponds to a pressure of 10^{-11} bar) as measured from the one-bar level and remains uniform above that altitude. It also increases with depth to about 6,730 °C (12,140 °F) near the center of the planet.

As is the case with several of the other large planets, the **winds** on Neptune are constrained to blow generally along lines of constant latitude and are relatively invariable with time. Winds on Neptune vary from about 100 m/sec (328 ft/sec) in an easterly (prograde) direction near latitude 70° S to as high as 700 m/sec (2,300 ft/sec) in a westerly (retrograde) direction near latitude 20° S.

The high winds and relatively large contribution of escaping internal heat may be responsible for the observed turbulence in Neptune's visible atmosphere. Two large dark ovals are clearly visible in images of Neptune's southern hemisphere taken by Voyager 2 in 1989, although they are not present in Hubble Space Telescope images made two years later. The largest, called the **Great Dark Spot** because of its similarity in latitude and shape to Jupiter's Great Red Spot, is comparable to the entire Earth in size. It was near this feature that the highest wind speeds were measured. Atmospheric storms such as the Great Dark Spot may be centers where strong upwelling of gases from the interior takes place.

Neptune's mean **density** is about 30% of Earth's; nevertheless, it is the densest of the giant planets. Neptune's greater density implies that a larger percentage of its interior is composed of melted ices and molten rocky materials than is the case for the other gas giants.

Neptunian Moons and Rings

Neptune has at least 13 natural satellites, but Earth-based observations had found only 2 of them, Triton in 1846 and Nereid in 1949, before Voyager 2 flew by the planet in 1989. The spacecraft observed 5 small moons orbiting close to Neptune and verified the existence of a 6th that had been detected from Earth in 1981. Data for these 8 moons are summarized in the table below. In 2002–03, 5 additional small moons (diameters roughly 30–60 km [20–40 mi]) were discovered telescopically from Earth; they all occupy highly inclined and elliptical orbits that are comparatively far from Neptune.

Triton is Neptune's only large moon and the only large satellite in the solar system to orbit its planet in the retrograde direction (opposite the planet's rotation and orbital motion around the Sun). Thus, as is also suspected of the solar system's other retrograde moons, Triton likely was captured by its planet rather than formed in orbit with its planet from the solar nebula. Its density (2 grams/cm³) suggests that it is about 25% water ice and the rest rock. Triton has a tenuous atmosphere, mostly of nitrogen. Its varied icy surface, imaged by Voyager 2, contains giant faults and dark markings that have been interpreted as the product of geyserlike

Neptunian Moons and Rings (continued)

"ice volcanoes" in which the eruptive material may be gaseous nitrogen and methane. Nereid has the most elliptical orbit of any planet or moon in the solar system; it also is probably a captured object.

Neptune's system of six faint rings, with radii from about 42,000 to 63,000 km (26,000–39,000 mi), straddles the orbits of its 4 innermost moons. (Neptune's visible surface lies at a radius of 24,800 km, or 15,400 mi.) The outermost ring, named Adams, is

unusual in that it contains several clumps, or concentrations of material, that before Voyager 2's visit had been interpreted incorrectly as independent ring arcs. What created and has maintained this structure has not yet been fully explained; it has been suggested that the clumps resulted from the relatively recent breakup of a small moon and are being temporarily held together by the gravitational effects of the nearby moon Galatea.

NAME (DESIGNATION)	MEAN DISTANCE FROM NEPTUNE	DIAMETER	MASS (10^{20} KG)	ORBITAL PERIOD (EARTH DAYS)
Naiad (III)	48,230 km (29,970 mi)	58 km (36 mi)	0.002	0.294
Thalassa (IV)	50,070 km (31,110 mi)	80 km (50 mi)	0.004	0.311
Despina (V)	52,530 km (32,640 mi)	148 km (92 mi)	0.02	0.335
Galatea (VI)	61,950 km (38,490 mi)	158 km (98 mi)	0.04	0.429
Larissa (VII)	73,550 km (45,700 mi)	192 km (119 mi)	0.05	0.555
Proteus (VIII)	117,640 km (73,100 mi)	416 km (258 mi)	0.5	1.122
Triton (I)*	354,800 km (220,460 mi)	2,700 km (1,678 mi)	214	5.877 (retrograde)
Nereid (II)	5,509,100 km (3,423,200 mi)	340 km (211 mi)	0.2	359.632

*Among the rotational periods of Neptune's moons, only Triton's has been established; it is the same as (synchronous with) the orbital period.

Pluto

Pluto is named for the god of the underworld in Roman mythology. It was long considered the planet normally farthest from the Sun, but on 24 Aug 2006, the International Astronomical Union announced that it was downgrading the status of Pluto to a dwarf planet. The key criterion in this classification was that Pluto, which orbits in the cluttered, icy Kuiper belt, had not cleared the neighborhood around its orbit. This was a controversial decision sure to be revisited.

Pluto has three natural satellites, Charon, Hydra, and Nix. Because Charon's diameter is more than half the size of Pluto's and they orbit around a common center of gravity, it was common to speak of the Pluto-Charon system as a double planet. Charon, named for the boatman in Greek mythology who carried the souls of the dead across the river Styx, was discovered in 1978, while Hydra and Nix were both first seen in 2005. The New Horizons spacecraft, launched in January 2006 and scheduled to arrive at Pluto in 2015, will search for yet more new satellites.

Pluto is so distant (its average distance from the Sun is 39.6 astronomical units, or AU) that sunlight traveling at 299,792 km/sec (186,282.1 mi/sec) takes more than five hours to reach it. An observer standing on the dwarf planet's surface would see the Sun as an extremely bright star in the dark sky, providing Pluto with only 1/1600 the amount of sunlight reaching the Earth.

Pluto has a diameter less than half that of Mercury; it is about two-thirds the size of the Moon. Pluto's physical characteristics are unlike those of any of the planets. Pluto resembles most closely Neptune's icy satellite Triton, which implies a similar origin for these

two bodies. Most scientists now believe that Pluto and Charon are large icy planetesimals left over from the formation of the giant outer planets of the solar system. Accordingly, Pluto can be interpreted to be the largest known member of the Kuiper belt (which, as discussed, includes the outer part of Pluto's orbit). Observations of Pluto show that it appears slightly red, though not as red as Mars or Io. Thus, the surface of Pluto cannot be composed simply of pure ices. Its overall reflectivity, or albedo, ranges from 0.3 to 0.5, as compared with 0.1 for the Moon and 0.8 for Triton.

The surface **temperature** of Pluto has proved very difficult to measure. Observations made from the Infrared Astronomical Satellite suggest values in the range of −228 to −215 °C (−379 to −355 °F), whereas measurements at radio wavelengths imply a range of −238 to −223 °C (−397 to −370 °F). The temperature certainly must vary over the surface, depending on the local reflectivity and solar zenith angle. There is also expected to be a seasonal decrease in incident solar energy by a factor of roughly three as Pluto moves from perihelion to aphelion.

The detection of methane ice on Pluto's surface made scientists confident that it had an **atmosphere** before one was actually discovered. The atmosphere was finally detected in 1988 when Pluto passed in front of a star as observed from the Earth. The light of the star was dimmed before disappearing entirely behind Pluto during the occultation. This proved that a thin, greatly distended atmosphere was present. Because that atmosphere must consist of vapors in equilibrium with their ices, small changes in temperature will have a large effect on the amount of gas in the atmosphere.

Measurements and Numbers

The International System of Units (SI)

Rapid advances in science and technology in the 19th and 20th centuries fostered the development of several overlapping systems of units of measurements as scientists improvised to meet the practical needs of their disciplines. The **General Conference on Weights and Measures** was chartered by international convention in 1875 to produce standards of physical measurement based upon an earlier international standard, the meter-kilogram-second (MKS) system. The convention calls for regular General Conference meetings to consider improvements or modifications in standards, an International Committee of Weights and Measures elected by the Conference (meets annually), and several consultative committees. **The International Bureau of Weights and Measures** (Bureau International des Poids et Mesures) at Sèvres, France, serves as a depository for the primary international standards and as a laboratory for certification and intercomparison of national standard copies.

The 1960 **International System** (universally abbreviated as **SI**, from *système international*) builds upon the MKS system. Its **seven basic units**, from which other units are derived, are currently defined as

follows: the **meter**, defined as the distance traveled by light in a vacuum in 1/299,792,458 second; the **kilogram** (about 2.2 pounds avoirdupois), which equals 1,000 grams as defined by the international prototype kilogram of platinum-iridium in the keeping of the International Bureau of Weights and Measures; the **second**, the duration of 9,192,631,770 periods of radiation associated with a specified transition of the cesium-133 atom; the **ampere**, which is the current that, if maintained in two wires placed one meter apart in a vacuum, would produce a force of 2×10^{-7} newton per meter of length; the **candela**, defined as the intensity in a given direction of a source emitting radiation of frequency 540×10^{12} hertz and that has a radiant intensity in that direction of 1/683 watt per steradian; the **mole**, defined as containing as many elementary entities of a substance as there are atoms in 0.012 kilogram of carbon-12; and the **kelvin**, which is 1/273.16 of the thermodynamic temperature of the triple point (equilibrium among the solid, liquid, and gaseous phases) of pure water.

International Bureau of Weights and Measures Web site: <www.bipm.fr>.

Elemental and Derived SI Units and Symbols

Quantity	SI Units		
	UNIT	FORMULA/EXPRESSION IN BASE UNITS	SYMBOL
elemental units			
length	meter	—	m
mass	kilogram	—	kg
time	second	—	s
electric current	ampere	—	A
luminous intensity	candela	—	cd
amount of substance	mole	—	mol
thermodynamic temperature	kelvin	—	K
derived units			
acceleration	meter/second squared	m/s^2	
area	square meter	m^2	
charge	coulomb	$A \times s$	C
Celsius temperature	degree Celsius	K	°C
density	kilogram/cubic meter	kg/m^3	
electric field strength	volt/meter	V/m	
electrical potential	volt	W/A	V
energy	joule	$N \times m$	J
force	newton	$kg \times m/s^2$	N
frequency	hertz	s^{-1}	Hz
illumination	lux	lm/m^2	lx
inductance	henry	$V \times s/A$	H
kinematic viscosity	square meter/second	m^2/s	
luminance	candela/square meter	cd/m^2	
luminous flux	lumen	$cd \times sr$	lm
magnetic field strength	ampere/meter	A/m	
magnetic flux	weber	$V \times s$	Wb
magnetic flux density	tesla	Wb/m^2	T
plane angle	radian	$m \times m^{-1}=1$	rad
power	watt	J/s	W
pressure	pascal (newton/square meter)	N/m^2	Pa
resistance	ohm	V/A	Ω
stress	pascal (newton/square meter)	N/m^2	Pa
velocity	meter/second	m/s	
viscosity	newton-second/square meter	$N \times s/m^2$	
volume	cubic meter	m^3	

Conversion of Metric Weights and Measures

conversions accurate within 10 parts per million.

inches × 25.4[1] = millimeters; millimeters × 0.0393701 = inches
feet × 0.3048[1] = meters; meters × 3.28084 = feet
yards × 0.9144[1] = meters; meters × 1.09361 = yards
miles (statute) × 1.60934 = kilometers; kilometers × 0.621371 = miles (statute)
square inches × 6.4516[1] = square centimeters; square centimeters × 0.155000 = square inches
square feet × 0.0929030 = square meters; square meters × 10.7639 = square feet
square yards × 0.836127 = square meters; square meters × 1.19599 = square yards
acres × 0.404686 = hectares[2] hectares[2] × 2.47105 = acres
cubic inches × 16.3871 = cubic centimeters; cubic centimeters × 0.0610237 = cubic inches
cubic feet × 0.0283168 = cubic meters; cubic meters × 35.3147 = cubic feet
cubic yards × 0.764555 = cubic meters; cubic meters × 1.30795 = cubic yards
quarts (liquid) × 0.946353 = liters[2]; liters[2] × 1.05669 = quarts (liq)
gallons × 0.00378541 = cubic meters; cubic meters × 264.172 = gallons
ounces (avdp)[3] × 28.3495 = grams; grams × 0.0352740 = ounces (avdp)[3]
pounds (avdp)[3] × 0.453592 = kilograms; kilograms × 2.20462 = pounds (avdp)[3]
horsepower × 0.745700 = kilowatts; kilowatts × 1.34102 = horsepower

[1]Exact. [2]Common term not used in SI. [3]avdp = avoirdupois.
Source: National Institute of Standards and Technology.

Tables of Equivalents: Metric System Prefixes

prefixes designating multiples and submultiples

PREFIX	SYMBOL	FACTOR BY WHICH UNIT IS MULTIPLIED		EXAMPLES
exa-	E	10^{18}	= 1,000,000,000,000,000,000	
peta-	P	10^{15}	= 1,000,000,000,000,000	
tera-	T	10^{12}	= 1,000,000,000,000	
giga-	G	10^{9}	= 1,000,000,000	gigabyte (GB)
mega-	M	10^{6}	= 1,000,000	megaton (Mt)
kilo-	k	10^{3}	= 1,000	kilometer (km)
hecto-, hect-	h	10^{2}	= 100	hectare (ha)
deca-, dec-	da	10	= 10	decastere (das)
			1	
deci-	d	10^{-1}	= 0.1	decigram (dg)
centi-, cent-	c	10^{-2}	= 0.01	centimeter (cm)
milli-	m	10^{-3}	= 0.001	milliliter (ml)
micro-, micr-	μ	10^{-6}	= 0.000001	microgram (μg)
nano-	n	10^{-9}	= 0.000000001	nanosecond (ns)
pico-	p	10^{-12}	= 0.000000000001	
femto-	f	10^{-15}	= 0.000000000000001	
atto-	a	10^{-18}	= 0.000000000000000001	

Cooking Measurements

MEASURE	CONVENTIONAL EQUIVALENTS[1]	METRIC EQUIVALENT
drop	1/60 teaspoon	0.08 ml
dash	1/8 teaspoon	0.62 ml
teaspoon	8 dashes; 1/3 tablespoon; 1/6 fluid ounce	4.93 ml
tablespoon	3 teaspoons; 1/2 fluid ounce	14.79 ml
ounce (weight)	1/16 pound	28.35 g
fluid ounce (volume)	2 tablespoons	29.57 ml
dram	1/8 fluid ounce	3.70 ml
cup	8 fluid ounces; 16 tablespoons; 1/2 pint	236.59 ml
pound	16 ounces	453.6 g
pint	16 fluid ounces; 2 cups; 1/2 quart	473.18 ml
quart	32 fluid ounces; 4 cups; 2 pints; 1/4 gallon	946.36 ml
gallon	128 fluid ounces; 16 cups; 8 pints; 4 quarts	3.785 l
peck	2 gallons	7.57 l
bushel	8 gallons; 4 pecks	30.28 l

[1]All ounce measurements are in US ounces or fluid ounces.

Spirits Measures

Many specific volumes have varied over time and from place to place, but the proportional relationships within families of measures have generally remained the same. All ounce measures are in US fluid ounces.

MEASURE	CONVENTIONAL EQUIVALENTS	METRIC EQUIVALENT
pony	0.75 oz = ¾ shot= ½ jigger	22.17 ml
shot/ounce/finger	1 oz = 1⅓ ponies = ⅔ jigger	29.57 ml
jigger	1.5 oz = 2 ponies = 1½ shots	44.36 ml
double	2 oz = 2 shots	59.15 ml
triple	3 oz = 3 shots	88.72 ml
pint	16 oz = ⅝ fifth = ½ quart	473.2 ml
bottle (champagne or other wine)	about 25.5 oz or ⅙ imperial gallon	750 ml (industry standard)
fifth	25.6 oz = ⅘ quart = ⅕ gallon	757.1 ml
quart	32 oz = ½ magnum = ¼ gallon	946.3 ml
magnum	2 bottles (champagne or other wine)	1.5 l
magnum	64 oz = 2 quarts = ½ gallon	1.893 l
yard	80 oz = 5 pints	2.365 l
gallon/double magnum	128 oz = 4 quarts = 5 fifths = 2 magnums	3.785 l
imperial gallon	1.20 gallons = ⅖ barn gallon	4.546 l
ale/beer gallon	1.22 gallons	4.620 l
barn gallon	2½ imperial gallons	11.37 l
half keg	5 gallons (type varies)	varies
keg	10 gallons (type varies)	varies
British bottle	126 bottles = 21 imperial gallons	95.47 l
barrel (wine)	126 quarts = 31½ gallons	119.2 l
barrel (ale/beer)	144 quarts = 36 gallons	136.3 l
British hogshead (ale/beer)	54 imperial gallons = ½ butt (ale/beer) = ¼ tun (ale/beer)	245.5 l
British hogshead (wine)	63 imperial gallons = ½ butt (wine) = ¼ tun (wine)	286.4 l
butt/pipe (ale/beer)	108 imperial gallons = ½ tun (ale/beer)	491.0 l
butt/pipe (wine)	126 imperial gallons = ½ tun (wine)	572.8 l
tun (ale/beer)	216 imperial gallons = 4 British hogsheads (ale/beer) = 2 butts (ale/beer)	982.0 l
tun (wine)	252 imperial gallons = 12 British bottles = 2 butts (wine)	1,146 l

Playing Cards Chances

Blackjack

Number of two-card combinations in a 52-card deck (where aces equal 1 or 11 and face cards equal 10) for each number between 13 and 21

TOTAL WITH TWO CARDS	POSSIBLE COMBINATIONS FROM 52 CARDS
21	64
20	136
19	80
18	86
17	96
16	86
15	96
14	102
13	118

Approximate chances of various hands reaching or exceeding 21

TOTAL IN HAND BEFORE DEAL (TWO OR MORE CARDS)	CHANCE OF REACHING A COUNT OF 17 TO 21 (%)	CHANCE OF EXCEEDING 21 ONE CARD (%)	ANY NUMBER OF CARDS (%)
16	38	62	62
15	42	54	58
14	44	46	56
13	48	38	52

Poker

Number of ways to reach and odds of reaching various five-card combinations on a single deal (52-card deck, no wild cards)

HAND	NUMBER OF COMBINATIONS	ODDS OF RECEIVING ON A SINGLE DEAL
royal flush	4	1 in 649,740
straight flush	36	1 in 72,193
four of a kind	624	1 in 4,165
full house	3,744	1 in 694
flush	5,108	1 in 509
straight	10,200	1 in 255
three of a kind	54,912	1 in 47
two pairs	123,552	1 in 21
one pair	1,098,240	1 in 2

Roman Numerals

Seven numeral-characters compose the Roman numeral system. When a numeral appears with a line above it, it represents the base value multiplied by 1,000. However, because Roman numerals are now seldom utilized for values beyond 4,999, this convention is no longer in use.

ARABIC	ROMAN	ARABIC	ROMAN	ARABIC	ROMAN	ARABIC	ROMAN
1	I	15	XV	60	LX	800	DCCC
2	II	16	XVI	70	LXX	900	CM
3	III	17	XVII	80	LXXX	1,000	M
4	IV	18	XVIII	90	XC	1,001	MI
5	V	19	XIX	100	C	1,002	MII
6	VI	20	XX	101	CI	1,003	MIII
7	VII	21	XXI	102	CII	1,900	MCM
8	VIII	22	XXII	103	CIII	2,000	MM
9	IX	23	XXIII	200	CC	2,001	MMI
10	X	24	XXIV	300	CCC	2,002	MMII
11	XI	25	XXV	400	CD	2,100	MMC
12	XII	30	XXX	500	D	3,000	MMM
13	XIII	40	XL	600	DC	4,000	MMMM or $M\overline{V}$
14	XIV	50	L	700	DCC	5,000	$\overline{V}$

Mathematical Formulas

The ratio of the circumference of a circle to its diameter is π (3.141592653589793238462643383279..., generally rounded to $^{22}/_7$ or 3.1416). It occurs in various mathematical problems involving the lengths of arcs or other curves, the areas of surfaces, and the volumes of many solids.

	SHAPE	ACTION	FORMULA
circumference	circle	multiply diameter by π	πd
area	circle	multiply radius squared by π	πr^2
	rectangle	multiply height by length	hl
	sphere surface	multiply radius squared by π by 4	$4\pi r^2$
	square	length of one side squared	s^2
	trapezoid	parallel side length A + parallel side length B multiplied by height and divided by 2	$(A+B)h/2$
	triangle	multiply base by height and divide by 2	$hb/2$
volume	cone	multiply base radius squared by π by height and divide by 3	$br^2\pi h/3$
	cube	length of one edge cubed	$a3$
	cylinder	multiply base radius squared by π by height	$br^2\pi h$
	pyramid	multiply base area by height and divide by 3	$hb/3$
	sphere	multiply radius cubed by π by 4 and divide by 3	$4\pi r^3/3$

Large Numbers

The American system of numeration for denominations above one million was modeled on a French system, but subsequently the French system changed to correspond to the German and British systems. In the American system each of the denominations above 1,000 millions (the American *billion*) is 1,000 times the preceding one (one trillion = 1,000 billions; one quadrillion = 1,000 trillions). In the British system the first denomination above 1,000 millions (the British *milliard*) is 1,000 times the preceding one, but each of the denominations above 1,000 milliards (the British *billion*) is 1,000,000 times the preceding one (one trillion = 1,000,000 billions; one quadrillion = 1,000,000 trillions). In recent years, however, British usage has reflected widespread and increasing use of the values of the American system.

Source: Merriam-Webster, Inc., *Merriam-Webster's Collegiate Dictionary*, 11th ed., 2003.

AMERICAN NAME	VALUE IN POWERS OF TEN	NUMBER OF ZEROS	BRITISH NAME	VALUE IN POWERS OF TEN	NUMBER OF ZEROS
billion	10^9	9	billion	10^{12}	12
trillion	10^{12}	12	trillion	10^{18}	18
quintillion	10^{18}	18	quintillion	10^{30}	30
septillion	10^{24}	24	septillion	10^{42}	42
quattuordecillion	10^{45}	45	quattuordecillion	10^{84}	84
googol	10^{100}	100	googol	10^{100}	100
centillion	10^{303}	303	centillion	10^{600}	600
googolplex	10^{googol}	googol	googolplex	10^{googol}	googol

Periodic Table of the Elements

The periodic table arranges the elements into groups (vertically) of elements sharing common physical and chemical characteristics and into periods (horizontally) of sequentially increasing atomic number and electron-shell configuration. Elements 113–118 have been created experimentally and have temporary names. Atomic weights in parentheses indicate the number of the most common isotope of a radioactive element.

1																		18
1 H	2											13	14	15	16	17	2 He
3 Li	4 Be											5 B	6 C	7 N	8 O	9 F	10 Ne
11 Na	12 Mg	3	4	5	6	7	8	9	10	11	12	13 Al	14 Si	15 P	16 S	17 Cl	18 Ar
19 K	20 Ca	21 Sc	22 Ti	23 V	24 Cr	25 Mn	26 Fe	27 Co	28 Ni	29 Cu	30 Zn	31 Ga	32 Ge	33 As	34 Se	35 Br	36 Kr
37 Rb	38 Sr	39 Y	40 Zr	41 Nb	42 Mo	43 Tc	44 Ru	45 Rh	46 Pd	47 Ag	48 Cd	49 In	50 Sn	51 Sb	52 Te	53 I	54 Xe
55 Cs	56 Ba	57 La	72 Hf	73 Ta	74 W	75 Re	76 Os	77 Ir	78 Pt	79 Au	80 Hg	81 Tl	82 Pb	83 Bi	84 Po	85 At	86 Rn
87 Fr	88 Ra	89 Ac	104 Rf	105 Db	106 Sg	107 Bh	108 Hs	109 Mt	110 Ds	111 Rg	112 Cn	113 Uut	114 Uuq	115 Uup	116 Uuh	117 Uus	118 Uuo

Lanthanide Series	58 Ce	59 Pr	60 Nd	61 Pm	62 Sm	63 Eu	64 Gd	65 Tb	66 Dy	67 Ho	68 Er	69 Tm	70 Yb	71 Lu
Actinide Series	90 Th	91 Pa	92 U	93 Np	94 Pu	95 Am	96 Cm	97 Bk	98 Cf	99 Es	100 Fm	101 Md	102 No	103 Lr

Element	Symbol	Atomic no.	Atomic weight	Element	Symbol	Atomic no.	Atomic weight
Actinium	Ac	89	(227)	Molybdenum	Mo	42	95.94
Aluminum	Al	13	26.98154	Neodymium	Nd	60	144.242
Americium	Am	95	(243)	Neon	Ne	10	20.1797
Antimony	Sb	51	121.760	Neptunium	Np	93	(237)
Argon	Ar	18	39.948	Nickel	Ni	28	58.6934
Arsenic	As	33	74.92160	Niobium	Nb	41	92.90638
Astatine	At	85	(210)	Nitrogen	N	7	14.0067
Barium	Ba	56	137.327	Nobelium	No	102	(259)
Berkelium	Bk	97	(247)	Osmium	Os	76	190.23
Beryllium	Be	4	9.01218	Oxygen	O	8	15.9994
Bismuth	Bi	83	208.98040	Palladium	Pd	46	106.42
Bohrium	Bh	107	(272)	Phosphorus	P	15	30.97376
Boron	B	5	10.811	Platinum	Pt	78	195.084
Bromine	Br	35	79.904	Plutonium	Pu	94	(244)
Cadmium	Cd	48	112.411	Polonium	Po	84	(209)
Calcium	Ca	20	40.078	Potassium	K	19	39.0983
Californium	Cf	98	(251)	Praseodymium	Pr	59	140.90765
Carbon	C	6	12.0107	Promethium	Pm	61	(145)
Cerium	Ce	58	140.116	Protactinium	Pa	91	231.03588
Cesium	Cs	55	132.90545	Radium	Ra	88	(226)
Chlorine	Cl	17	35.453	Radon	Rn	86	(222)
Chromium	Cr	24	51.9961	Rhenium	Re	75	186.207
Cobalt	Co	27	58.93320	Rhodium	Rh	45	102.90550
Copernicium	Cn	112	(285)	Roentgenium	Rg	111	(280)
Copper	Cu	29	63.546	Rubidium	Rb	37	85.4678
Curium	Cm	96	(247)	Ruthenium	Ru	44	101.07
Darmstadtium	Ds	110	(281)	Rutherfordium	Rf	104	(267)
Dubnium	Db	105	(268)	Samarium	Sm	62	150.36
Dysprosium	Dy	66	162.500	Scandium	Sc	21	44.9559
Einsteinium	Es	99	(252)	Seaborgium	Sg	106	(271)
Erbium	Er	68	167.259	Selenium	Se	34	78.96
Europium	Eu	63	151.964	Silicon	Si	14	28.0855
Fermium	Fm	100	(257)	Silver	Ag	47	107.8682
Fluorine	F	9	18.99840	Sodium	Na	11	22.98977
Francium	Fr	87	(223)	Strontium	Sr	38	87.62
Gadolinium	Gd	64	157.25	Sulfur	S	16	32.065
Gallium	Ga	31	69.723	Tantalum	Ta	73	180.94788
Germanium	Ge	32	72.64	Technetium	Tc	43	(98)
Gold	Au	79	196.96657	Tellurium	Te	52	127.60
Hafnium	Hf	72	178.49	Terbium	Tb	65	158.92535
Hassium	Hs	108	(270)	Thallium	Tl	81	204.3833
Helium	He	2	4.00260	Thorium	Th	90	232.03806
Holmium	Ho	67	164.93032	Thulium	Tm	69	168.93421
Hydrogen	H	1	1.00794	Tin	Sn	50	118.710
Indium	In	49	114.818	Titanium	Ti	22	47.867
Iodine	I	53	126.90447	Tungsten (wolfram)	W	74	183.85
Iridium	Ir	77	192.217	Ununhexium	Uuh	116	(293)
Iron	Fe	26	55.845	Ununoctium	Uuo	118	(294)
Krypton	Kr	36	83.798	Ununpentium	Uup	115	(288)
Lanthanum	La	57	138.90547	Ununquadium	Uuq	114	(289)
Lawrencium	Lr	103	(262)	Ununseptium	Uus	117	(292)
Lead	Pb	82	207.2	Ununtrium	Uut	113	(284)
Lithium	Li	3	6.941	Uranium	U	92	238.02891
Lutetium	Lu	71	174.967	Vanadium	V	23	50.9415
Magnesium	Mg	12	24.3050	Xenon	Xe	54	131.293
Manganese	Mn	25	54.93805	Ytterbium	Yb	70	173.04
Meitnerium	Mt	109	(276)	Yttrium	Y	39	88.90585
Mendelevium	Md	101	(258)	Zinc	Zn	30	65.409
Mercury	Hg	80	200.59	Zirconium	Zr	40	91.224

Applied Science

Chemistry

Chemistry is the science that deals with the properties, composition, and structure of substances (defined as elements and compounds), the transformations that they undergo, and the energy that is released or absorbed during these processes. Every substance, whether naturally occurring or artificially produced, consists of one or more of the hundred-odd species of atoms that have been identified as elements. Although these atoms, in turn, are composed of more elementary particles, they are the basic building blocks of chemical substances; there is no quantity of oxygen, mercury, or gold, for example, smaller than an atom of that substance. Chemistry, therefore, is concerned not with the subatomic domain but with the properties of atoms and the laws governing their combinations and with how the knowledge of these properties can be used to achieve specific purposes.

Physics

Physics is the science that deals with the structure of matter and the interactions between the fundamental constituents of the observable universe. The basic physical science, its aim is the discovery and formulation of the fundamental laws of nature. In the broadest sense, physics (from the Greek *physikos*) is concerned with all aspects of nature on both the macroscopic and submicroscopic levels. Its scope of study encompasses not only the behavior of objects under the action of given forces but also the nature and origin of gravitational, electromagnetic, and nuclear force fields. Its ultimate objective is the formulation of a few comprehensive principles that bring together and explain all such disparate phenomena. Physics can, at base, be defined as the science of matter, motion, and energy. Its laws are typically expressed with economy and precision in the language of mathematics.

Weight, Mass, and Density

Mass, strictly defined, is the quantitative measure of inertia, the resistance a body offers to a change in its speed or position when force is applied to it. The greater the mass of a body, the smaller the change produced by an applied force. In more practical terms, it is the measure of the amount of material in an object, and in common usage is often expressed as weight. However, the mass of an object is constant regardless of its position, while weight varies according to gravitational pull.

In the International System of Units (SI; the metric system), the kilogram is the standard unit of mass, defined as equaling the mass of the international prototype of the kilogram, currently a platinum-iridium cylinder kept at Sèvres, near Paris, France; it is roughly equal to the mass of 1,000 cubic centimeters of pure water at the temperature of its maximum density. In the US customary system, the unit is the slug, defined as the mass which a one pound force can accelerate at a rate of one foot per second per second, which is the same as the mass of an object weighing 32.17 pounds on the earth's surface.

Weight is the gravitational force of attraction on an object, caused by the presence of a massive second object, such as the Earth or Moon. Weight is the product of an object's mass and the acceleration of gravity at the point where the object is located. A given object will have the same mass on the Earth's surface, on the Moon, or in the absence of gravity, while its weight on the Moon would be about one sixth of its weight on the Earth's surface, because of the Moon's smaller gravitational pull (due in turn to the Moon's smaller mass and radius), and in the absence of gravity the object would have no weight at all.

Weight is measured in units of force, not mass, though in practice units of mass (such as the kilogram) are often substituted because of mass's relatively constant relation to weight on the Earth's surface. The weight of a body can be obtained by multiplying the mass by the acceleration of gravity. In SI, weight is expressed in newtons, or the force required to impart an acceleration of one meter per second per second to a mass of one kilogram. In the US customary system, it is expressed in pounds.

Density is the mass per unit volume of a material substance. It offers a convenient means of obtaining the mass of a body from its volume, or vice versa; the mass is equal to the volume multiplied by the density, while the volume is equal to the mass divided by the density. In SI, density is expressed in kilograms per cubic meter.

Communications

Introduction to the Internet

The **Internet** is a dynamic collection of computer networks that has revolutionized communications and methods of commerce by enabling those networks around the world to interact with each other. Sometimes referred to as a "**network of networks**," the Internet was developed in the United States in the 1970s but was not widely used by the general public until the early 1990s. By early 2010 some 1.8 billion people, or roughly 27% of the world's population, were estimated to be regular users of the Internet. It is estimated that at least half of the world's population have some form of Internet access

Introduction to the Internet (continued)

in 2010, and it is assumed that wireless access will continue to play a growing role.

The Internet is so powerful and general that it can be used for almost any purpose that depends on the processing of information, and it is accessible by every individual who connects to one of its constituent networks. It supports human communication via electronic mail (**e-mail**), real-time "chat rooms," instant messaging (IM), newsgroups, and audio and video transmission and allows people to work collaboratively at many different locations. It supports access to information by many applications, including the **World Wide Web**, which uses text and graphical presentations. Publishing has been revolutionized, as whole novels and reference works are available on the Web, and online periodicals, including data prepared daily for an individual subscriber (such as stock market reports or news summaries), are also common. The Internet has attracted a large and growing number of "e-businesses" (including subsidiaries of traditional "brick-and-mortar" companies) that carry out most of their sales and services over the Internet.

While the precise structure of the future Internet is not yet clear, many directions of growth seem apparent. One is the increased availability of wireless access, enabling better real-time use of Web-managed information. Another future development is toward higher backbone and network access speeds. Backbone data rates of 10 billion bits (10 gigabits) per second are readily available today, but data rates of 1 trillion bits (1 terabit) per second or higher will eventually become commercially feasible. At very high data rates, high-resolution video, for example, would occupy only a small fraction of available bandwidth, and remaining bandwidth could be used to transmit auxiliary information about the data being sent, which in turn would enable rapid customization of displays and prompt resolution of certain local queries.

Communications connectivity will be a key function of a future Internet as more machines and devices are interconnected. Since the Internet Engineering Task Force published its 128-bit IP address standard in 1998, the increased number of available addresses (2^{128}, as opposed to 2^{32} under the previous standard) allowed almost every electronic device imaginable to be assigned a unique address. The Internet Corporation for Assigned Names and Numbers announced in late October 2009 that domain names in non-Latin alphabets will henceforth be allowed.

Growth of Internet Use

Source: *International Telecommunication Union, ICT Indicators Database.*

YEAR	US USERS	WORLD USERS	YEAR	US USERS	WORLD USERS
2000	124,000,000	393,446,100	2005	205,766,900	1,047,860,400
2001	142,823,000	494,134,400	2006	210,720,400	1,216,976,900
2002	172,834,300	679,819,300	2007	221,724,000	1,402,145,800
2003	183,195,700	790,121,400	2008	230,630,000	1,603,345,800
2004	194,159,000	934,952,700	2009	239,893,600	1,833,746,200

Worldwide Cellular Mobile Telephone Subscribers, 2009

Source: *International Telecommunication Union, ICT Indicators Database.*

COUNTRY	SUBSCRIBERS	SUBSCRIBERS PER 1,000 RESIDENTS	COUNTRY	SUBSCRIBERS	SUBSCRIBERS PER 1,000 RESIDENTS
China	747,000,000	555	United Kingdom	80,375,400	1,306
India	525,090,000	438	Philippines	74,489,000	810
United States	298,404,000	948	Nigeria	73,099,300	472
Russia	230,500,000	1,636	Turkey	62,779,600	839
Brazil	173,959,400	898	France	59,543,000	955
Indonesia	159,247,600	693	Egypt	55,352,200	667
Japan	114,917,000	904	Ukraine	55,333,200	1,211
Germany	105,000,000	1,278	Iran	52,555,000	708
Pakistan	102,980,000	570	Argentina	51,891,000	1,288
Italy	90,613,000	1,514	Spain	50,991,100	1,136
Vietnam	88,566,000	1,006	Bangladesh	50,400,000	311
Mexico	83,527,900	762	Republic of Korea	47,944,200	992
Thailand	83,057,000	1,226	**world**	**4,676,174,400**	**683**

Growth of Cell Phone Use in the US

Number of cellular mobile telephone subscribers in the US, 1998–2009. Source: CTIA-
The Wireless Association's Annualized Wireless Industry Survey Results, December 1985–December 2009.

YEAR	SUBSCRIBERS	YEAR	SUBSCRIBERS	YEAR	SUBSCRIBERS	YEAR	SUBSCRIBERS
1998	69,209,321	2001	128,374,512	2004	182,140,362	2007	255,395,599
1999	86,047,003	2002	140,766,842	2005	207,896,198	2008	270,333,881
2000	109,478,031	2003	158,721,981	2006	233,040,781	2009	285,646,191

Aerospace Technology
Space Exploration

Three men were the first scientists to conceive pragmatically of spaceflight: the Russian **Konstantin Tsiolkovsky**, the American **Robert Goddard**, and the German **Hermann Oberth**. By the end of World War II, the German development of rocket propulsion for aircraft and guided missiles (notably the V-2) had reached a high level. After the war the US and its allies fell heir to the technical knowledge of rocket power developed by the Germans. The technical director of the German missile effort, **Wernher von Braun**, and some 150 of his top aides surrendered to US troops. Most immigrated to the US, where they assembled and launched V-2 missiles that had been captured and shipped there. The USSR carried out an unpublicized but extensive and likely similar program; Britain and France conducted smaller programs.

In both the US and the USSR the development of **military missile technology** was essential to the achievement of satellite flight. Preparations for the International Geophysical Year (IGY, 1957–58) stimulated discussion of the possibility of launching **artificial Earth satellites** for scientific investigations. Both the US and the USSR became determined to prepare scientific satellites for launching during the IGY. While the US was still developing a space launch vehicle, the USSR startled the world by placing **Sputnik 1** in orbit on 4 Oct 1957. This was followed a month later by **Sputnik 2**, which carried a live dog. The failure by the US to launch its small payload on 6 Dec 1957 heightened that country's political discomfiture in view of its supposed advanced status in science. Following debates on the necessity of achieving parity, the US government established the **National Aeronautics and Space Administration (NASA)** in 1958. Since that time, NASA has conducted virtually all major aspects of the US space program.

The first successful US satellite, **Explorer 1**, was launched about four months after Sputnik 1. During the next decades the two countries participated in a space race, conducting thousands of successful launches of spacecraft of all varieties including scientific-research, communications, meteorological, remote-sensing, military-reconnaissance, early-warning,

and navigation satellites, lunar and planetary probes, and manned craft. The USSR launched the first human, **Yury Gagarin**, into orbit around Earth on 12 Apr 1961. On 20 July 1969, the US landed two men, **Neil Armstrong** and **Edwin ("Buzz") Aldrin**, on the surface of the Moon as part of the **Apollo 11** mission. On 12 Apr 1981, the 20th anniversary of manned space flight, the US launched the first reusable manned space transportation system, the **space shuttle**. Since the 1960s various European countries, Japan, India, China, and other countries have formed their own agencies for space exploration and development. The **European Space Agency (ESA)** consists of 18 member states. Private corporations, too, offer space launches for communications and remote-sensing satellites.

In the post-Apollo decades, while the US focused much of its manned space program on the shuttle, the USSR concentrated on launching a series of increasingly sophisticated Earth-orbiting **space stations**, beginning with the world's first in 1971. Station crews, who were carried up in two- and three-person spacecraft, carried out mostly scientific missions while gaining experience in living and working for long periods in the space environment. After the USSR was dissolved in 1991, its space program was continued by Russia on a much smaller scale owing to economic constraints. The US launched a space station in 1973 using surplus Apollo hardware and conducted shuttle missions to a Russian station, Mir, in the 1990s. In 1998, at the head of a 16-country consortium and with Russia as a major partner, the US began in-orbit assembly of the **International Space Station (ISS)**, using the shuttle and Russian expendable launch vehicles to ferry the facility's modular components and crews into space. In addition to manned and unmanned lunar exploration, space exploration programs have included deep-space robotic missions to the planets, their moons, and smaller bodies such as comets and asteroids. Also important has been the development of unmanned space-based astronomical observatories, which allow observation of near and distant cosmic objects above the filtering and distorting effects of Earth's atmosphere.

Significant space programs and missions:

Sputnik (Russian for "fellow traveler")
Years launched: 1957–58. **Country or space agency:** USSR. **Designation:** 1 through 3 (first series). **Not manned. Events of note:** Sputnik 1 was the first satellite to be successfully launched into space, and Sputnik 2 carried a small dog named Laika ("Barker").

Vanguard
Years launched: 1958–59. **Country or space agency:** US. **Designation:** 1 through 3. **Not manned. Events of note:** The first attempted Vanguard launch, hastily mounted in December 1957 after the USSR's Sputnik successes, failed with the launch vehicle's explosion.

Explorer
Years launched: 1958–75. **Country or space agency:** US. **Designation:** 1 through 55. **Not manned. Events of note:** Explorer 1, the first successful US satellite, discovered Earth's inner radiation belt.

Pioneer
Years launched: 1958–78. **Country or space agency:** US. **Designation:** 1 through 13. **Not manned. Events of note:** Pioneer 10 was the first spacecraft to travel through the asteroid belt, to fly by Jupiter, and to escape the solar system; Pioneer 11 was the first to visit Saturn.

Luna (Russian for "Moon")
Years launched: 1959–76. **Country or space agency:** USSR. **Designation:** 1 through 24. **Not manned. Events of note:** Luna 2 was the first spacecaft to crash-land on the lunar surface; Luna 3 took the first photographs of the Moon's far side; three Lunas (16, 20, and 24) returned with samples of lunar soil.

Vostok (Russian for "east")
Years launched: 1961–63. **Country or space agency:** USSR. **Designation:** 1 through 6. **Manned. Events of note:** The first man in space and to orbit Earth was Soviet cosmonaut Yury Gagarin in Vostok 1, launched

on 12 April 1961. Vostok 6 was launched with Valentina Tereshkova, the first woman in space, in 1963.

Mercury
Years launched: 1961–63 (manned missions). **Country or space agency:** US. **Designation:** Mercury spacecraft had program designations, but they were better known by the individual names bestowed on them, such as *Freedom 7*, to honor the seven NASA astronauts chosen for the program. **Events of note:** Some 20 preliminary unmanned Mercury missions took place between 1959 and 1961. Of the six manned missions, *Freedom 7* was launched in 1961 with Alan Shepard (the first American in space) aboard, and *Friendship 7* in 1962 with John Glenn (the first American to orbit Earth).

Ranger
Years launched: 1961–65. **Country or space agency:** US. **Designation:** 1 through 9. **Not manned. Events of note:** Ranger 4 was the first US spacecraft to crash-land on the Moon; the last three Rangers returned thousands of images of the lunar surface before crashing on the lunar surface as planned.

Mariner
Years launched: 1962–73. **Country or space agency:** US. **Designation:** 1 through 10. **Not manned. Events of note:** Various Mariners in the program flew by Venus, Mercury, and Mars. Mariner 9 mapped Mars in detail from orbit, becoming the first spacecraft to orbit another planet. Mariner 10 was the first spacecraft to have visited the vicinity of Mercury.

Voskhod (Russian for "sunrise" or "ascent")
Years launched: 1964–65. **Country or space agency:** USSR. **Designation:** 1 and 2. **Manned. Events of note:** Voskhod 1 was the first spacecraft to carry more than one person; Aleksey Leonov performed the first space walk, from the Voskhod 2 spacecraft, on 18 Mar 1965.

Gemini
Years launched: 1965–66. **Country or space agency:** US. **Designation:** 1 through 12. **Manned. Events of note:** Ten two-person manned missions followed two unmanned test flights. Gemini 8 was the first spacecraft to rendezvous and dock with another craft. The Gemini program showed that astronauts could live and work in space for the time needed for a round-trip to the Moon.

Lunar Orbiter
Years launched: 1966–67. **Country or space agency:** US. **Designation:** 1 through 5. **Not manned. Events of note:** Five consecutive spacecraft made detailed photographic surveys of most of the Moon's surface, providing the mapping essential for choosing landing sites for the manned Apollo missions.

Soyuz (Russian for "union")
Years launched: 1967–present. **Country or space agency:** USSR. **Designation:** 1 through 40 (first series). Three subsequent series of upgraded spacecraft received the additional suffix letters T, TM, or TMA and were renumbered from 1. **Manned. Events of note:** On 24 Apr 1967 cosmonaut Vladimir Komarov conducted the inaugural test flight (Soyuz 1) of this multiperson transport craft but died returning to Earth after the parachute system failed, becoming the first fatality during a spaceflight. Soyuz 11 ferried the crew of the first space station, Salyut 1. Soyuz TM-2 made the inaugural manned flight of this TM upgrade while transporting the second crew of the Mir space station. Soyuz TM-31 carried up the International Space Station's first three-man crew.

Apollo
Years launched: 1968–72 (manned missions). **Country or space agency:** US. **Designation:** 7 through 17. **Events of note:** Several unmanned test flights preceded 11 manned Apollo missions, including two in Earth orbit (7 and 9), two in lunar orbit (8 and 10), one lunar flyby (13), and six lunar landings (11, 12, and 14–17) in which a total of 12 astronauts walked on the Moon. Apollo 11, crewed by Neil Armstrong, Michael Collins, and Buzz Aldrin, was the first mission to land humans on the Moon, on 20 Jul 1969. Apollo 13, planned as a lunar landing mission, experienced an onboard explosion en route to the Moon; after a swing around the Moon, the crippled spacecraft made a harrowing but safe return to Earth with its crew, James Lovell, John Swigert, and Fred Haise. The landing missions collectively returned almost 382 kg (842 lb) of lunar rocks and soil for study.

Salyut (Russian for "salute")
Years launched: 1971–82. **Country or space agency:** USSR. **Designation:** 1 through 7 (two designs). **Manned. Events of note:** Salyut 1, launched 19 Apr 1971, was the world's first space station; its crew, cosmonauts Georgy Dobrovolsky, Vladislav Volkov, and Viktor Patsayev, died returning to Earth when their Soyuz spacecraft depressurized. Salyut 6 operated as a highly successful scientific space platform, supporting a series of crews over a four-year period.

Skylab
Year launched: 1973. **Country or space agency:** US. **Manned. Events of note:** Skylab, based on the outfitted and pressurized upper stage of a Saturn V Moon rocket, was the first US space station. Three successive astronaut crews carried out solar astronomy studies, materials-sciences research, and biomedical experiments on the effects of weightlessness.

Apollo-Soyuz
Year launched: 1975. **Countries or space agencies:** US and USSR. **Manned. Events of note:** As a sign of improved US-Soviet relations, an Apollo spacecraft carrying three astronauts docked in Earth orbit with a Soyuz vehicle carrying two cosmonauts. It was the first cooperative multinational space mission.

Viking
Year launched: 1975. **Country or space agency:** US. **Designation:** 1 and 2. **Not manned. Events of note:** Both probes traveled to Mars, released landers, and took photographs of large expanses of Mars from orbit. The Viking 1 lander transmitted the first pictures from the Martian surface; both landers carried experiments designed to detect living organisms or life processes but found no convincing signs of life.

Voyager
Year launched: 1977. **Country or space agency:** US. **Designation:** 1 and 2. **Not manned. Events of note:** Both Voyager spacecraft flew past Jupiter and Saturn, transmitting measurements and photographs; Voyager 2 went on to Uranus in 1986 and then to Neptune. Both craft continued out of the solar system, with Voyager 1 overtaking Pioneer 10 in 1998 to become the most distant human-made object in space.

space shuttle (Space Transportation System, or STS)
Years launched: 1981–present. **Country or space**

agency: US. **Designation:** Individual missions were designated STS with a number (and sometimes letter) suffix, though the orbiter spacecraft themselves were reused. **Manned. Events of note:** The first flight of a manned space shuttle, STS-1, was on 12 Apr 1981 with the orbiter *Columbia*. The other original operational orbiters were *Challenger, Discovery,* and *Atlantis*. During shuttle mission STS-51-L, *Challenger* exploded after liftoff on 28 Jan 1986, killing all seven astronauts aboard, including a private citizen, Christa McAuliffe; the orbiter *Endeavour* was built as a replacement vehicle. Space shuttle missions were used to deploy satellites, space observatories, and planetary probes; to carry out in-space repairs of orbiting spacecraft; and to take US astronauts to the Russian space station Mir. Beginning in 1998 a series of shuttle missions ferried components, supplies, and crews to the International Space Station during its assembly and operation. In 2003 the orbiter *Columbia* disintegrated while returning from a space mission, claiming the lives of its seven-person crew, including Ilan Ramon, the first Israeli astronaut to go into space.

Giotto
Year launched: 1985. **Country or space agency:** ESA. **Not manned. Events of note:** This first deep-space probe launched by ESA made a close flyby of Halley's Comet, collecting data and transmitting images of the icy nucleus. It was then redirected to a second comet, using a gravity-assist flyby of Earth, the first time that a spacecraft coming back from deep space had made such a maneuver.

Mir (Russian for "peace" and "world")
Years launched: 1986–96. **Country or space agency:** USSR/Russia. **Manned. Events of note:** The core of this modular space station was launched on 20 Feb 1986; five additional modules were added over the next decade to create a large, versatile space laboratory. Although intended for a five-year life, it supported human habitation between 1986 and 2000, including an uninterrupted stretch of occupancy of almost 10 years, and it hosted a series of US astronauts as part of a Mir–space shuttle cooperative endeavor. In 1995 Mir cosmonaut Valery Polyakov set a space endurance record of nearly 438 days.

Magellan
Year launched: 1989. **Country or space agency:** US. **Not manned. Events of note:** Magellan was the first deep-space probe deployed by the space shuttle. During four years in orbit above Venus, it mapped some 98% of the surface of the planet with radar at high resolution. At the end of its mission, it was sent on a gradual dive into the Venusian atmosphere, where it measured various properties before burning up.

Galileo
Year launched: 1989. **Country or space agency:** US. **Not manned. Events of note:** Galileo released an atmospheric probe into the Jovian system and then went into orbit around Jupiter for an extended study of the giant planet and its Galilean moons. Among many discoveries, Galileo found evidence of a liquid-water ocean below the moon Europa's icy surface.

NEAR Shoemaker (Near Earth Asteroid Rendezvous)
Year launched: 1996. **Country or space agency:** US. **Not manned. Events of note:** This spacecraft was the first to orbit a small body (the Earth-approaching asteroid Eros) and then to touch down on its surface. It studied Eros for a year with cameras and instruments and then made a soft landing and transmitted gamma-ray data from the surface for more than two weeks.

Mars Pathfinder
Year launched: 1996. **Country or space agency:** US. **Not manned. Events of note:** This was the first spacecraft to land on Mars since the 1976 Viking missions; the lander and its robotic surface rover, Sojourner, together successfully collected 17,000 images and other data.

Cassini-Huygens
Year launched: 1997. **Countries or space agencies:** US and ESA. **Not manned. Events of note:** Consisting of an orbiter (Cassini) and a descent probe (Huygens), the spacecraft traveled to the Saturnian system. En route it flew by Jupiter and returned detailed images. Cassini then established an orbit around Saturn for several years of studies, while the Huygens probe parachuted through the atmosphere of the moon Titan, transmitting data during its descent and from the moon's surface.

International Space Station (ISS)
Years launched: 1998–present. **Countries or space agencies:** US, Russia, ESA, Canada, Japan, and Brazil. **Manned. Events of note:** A large complex of habitat modules and laboratories, the ISS continued to be assembled in Earth orbit by means of space-shuttle and Proton and Soyuz rocket flights that brought components, crews, and supplies. The first component, called Zarya, was launched on 20 Nov 1998. The ISS received its first resident crew on 2 Nov 2000.

Chandra X-Ray Observatory
Year launched: 1999. **Country or space agency:** US. **Not manned. Events of note:** The world's most powerful X-ray telescope, it revolves in an elliptical orbit around Earth, delivering roughly 1,000 observations of the universe annually.

2001 Mars Odyssey
Year launched: 2001. **Country or space agency:** US. **Not manned. Events of note:** This spacecraft was launched to study Mars from orbit and serve as a communications relay for future landers. Some of its data suggested the presence of huge subsurface reservoirs of frozen water in both polar regions.

Mars Express
Year launched: 2003. **Country or space agency:** ESA. **Not manned. Events of note:** The spacecraft's lander, Beagle 2, which was designed to examine the rocks and soil for signs of past or present life, failed to establish radio contact after presumably reaching the Martian surface.

Mars Exploration Rovers
Year launched: 2003. **Country or space agency:** US. **Designation:** Spirit and Opportunity. **Not manned. Events of note:** Twin six-wheeled robotic rovers, each equipped with cameras, a microscopic imager, a rock-grinding tool, and other instruments, landed on opposite sides of Mars. Both rovers found evidence of past water; particularly dramatic was the discovery by Opportunity of rocks that appeared to have been laid down at the shoreline of an ancient body of salty water.

Deep Impact
Year launched: 2005. **Country or space agency:** US. **Not manned. Events of note:** Deep Impact was the first

spacecraft designed to study the interior composition of a comet. It released an instrumented impactor into the path of Comet Tempel 1's icy nucleus. A high-resolution camera and other apparatuses on the flyby portion of the probe studied the impact and the resulting crater.

Mars Reconnaissance Orbiter
Year launched: 2005. Country or space agency: US. Not manned. Events of note: It carries the most powerful camera ever flown on a space mission. The Orbiter is an important communications link between other spacecraft, Mars, and Earth.

Phoenix
Year launched: 2007. Country or space agency: US. Not manned. Events of note: Phoenix was the first spacecraft designed to measure water (ice) on a planet other than Earth. It was equipped with robotic arms and sophisticated sensors to dig under the surface of Mars, collect soil samples, and analyze them. It landed on the surface of Mars on 25 May 2008 and

quickly established communications with Earth. Before the end of its planned three-month experiment, Phoenix verifed the presence of water (ice) in the Martian subsurface.

Lunar Crater Observation and Sensing Satellite
Year launched: 2009. Country or space agency: US. Not manned. Events of note: The objective of the Lunar Crater Observation and Sensing Satellite (LCROSS) was to confirm the presence of water (ice) in a crater in the permanent shadow on the Moon's south pole. On 9 Oct 2009, LCROSS conducted experiments that successfully uncovered water on the Moon.

CryoSat-2
Year launched: 2010. Country or space agency: ESA. Not manned. Events of note: CryoSat-2 is charged with measuring precisely the thickness of the marine ice in the polar oceans and the ice sheets covering Greenland and Antarctica.

Space Exploration Firsts

EVENT	DETAILS	COUNTRY OR AGENCY	DATE ACCOMPLISHED
first person to study in detail the use of rockets for spaceflight	Konstantin Tsiolkovsky	Russia	late 19th–early 20th centuries
first launch of a liquid-fueled rocket	Robert Goddard	US	16 Mar 1926
first launch of the V-2 ballistic missile, the forerunner of modern space rockets	Wernher von Braun	Germany	3 Oct 1942
first artificial Earth satellite	Sputnik 1	USSR	4 Oct 1957
first animal launched into space	dog Laika aboard Sputnik 2	USSR	3 Nov 1957
first spacecraft to hard-land on another celestial object (the Moon)	Luna 2	USSR	14 Sep 1959
first pictures of the far side of the Moon	Luna 3	USSR	7 Oct 1959
first applications satellite launched	TIROS 1 (weather observation)	US	1 Apr 1960
first recovery of a payload from Earth orbit	Discoverer 13	US	11 Aug 1960
first piloted spacecraft to orbit Earth	Vostok 1 (piloted by Yury Gagarin)	USSR	12 Apr 1961
first US citizen in space	Alan Shepard on Freedom 7	US	5 May 1961
first piloted US spacecraft to orbit Earth	Friendship 7 (piloted by John Glenn)	US	20 Feb 1962
first active communications satellite	Telstar 1	US	10 July 1962
first data transmitted to Earth from vicinity of another planet (Venus)	Mariner 2	US	14 Dec 1962
first woman in space	Valentina Tereshkova on Vostok 6	USSR	16 Jun 1963
first satellite to operate in geostationary orbit	Syncom 2 (telecommunications satellite)	US	26 Jul 1963
first space walk	Aleksey Leonov on Voskhod 2	USSR	18 Mar 1965
first spacecraft pictures of Mars	Mariner 4	US	14 Jul 1965
first spacecraft to soft-land on the Moon	Luna 9	USSR	3 Feb 1966
first death during a space mission	Vladimir Komarov on Soyuz 1	USSR	24 Apr 1967
first humans to orbit the Moon	Frank Borman, James Lovell, and William Anders on Apollo 8	US	24 Dec 1968
first human to walk on the Moon	Neil Armstrong on Apollo 11	US	20 Jul 1969
first unmanned spacecraft to carry lunar samples back to Earth	Luna 16	USSR	24 Sep 1970
first soft landing on another planet (Venus)	Venera 7	USSR	15 Dec 1970
first space station launched	Salyut 1	USSR	19 Apr 1971
first spacecraft to orbit another planet (Mars)	Mariner 9	US	13 Nov 1971
first spacecraft to soft-land on Mars	Mars 3	USSR	2 Dec 1971
first spacecraft to fly by Jupiter	Pioneer 10	US	3 Dec 1973
first international docking in space	Apollo and Soyuz spacecraft	US/USSR	17 Jul 1975
first pictures transmitted from the surface of Mars	Viking 1	US	20 Jul 1976
first spacecraft to fly by Saturn	Pioneer 11	US	1 Sep 1979
first reusable spacecraft launched and returned from space	space shuttle Columbia	US	12–14 Apr 1981
first spacecraft to fly by Uranus	Voyager 2	US	24 Jan 1986
first spacecraft to make a close flyby of a comet's nucleus	Giotto at Halley's Comet	European Space Agency (ESA)	13 Mar 1986

Space Exploration Firsts (continued)

EVENT	DETAILS	COUNTRY OR AGENCY	DATE ACCOMPLISHED
first spacecraft to fly by Neptune	Voyager 2	US	24 Aug 1989
first large optical space telescope launched	Hubble Space Telescope	US/ESA	25 Apr 1990
first spacecraft to orbit Jupiter	Galileo	US	7 Dec 1995
first spacecraft to orbit and land on an asteroid	NEAR Shoemaker at the asteroid Eros	US	14 Feb 2000– 12 Feb 2001
first piloted Chinese spacecraft to orbit Earth	Shenzhou 5, piloted by Yang Liwei	China	15 Oct 2003
first privately funded human spaceflight (to 100 km [62 mi] height)	*SpaceShipOne*, piloted by Michael W. Melvill (private venture)	US	21 Jun 2004
first spacecraft to strike a comet's nucleus and study its interior composition	Deep Impact at Comet Tempel 1	US	4 Jul 2005
first spacecraft designed to measure water (ice) on a planet other than Earth	Phoenix	US	5 Jun 2008

Air Travel

Flight History

Humanity has been fascinated with the possibility of flight for millennia—there are historical references to a Chinese kite that used a rotary wing as a source of lift from as early as about AD 400. Toys using the principle of the helicopter were known during the Middle Ages. Near the end of the 15th century, Leonardo da Vinci made drawings pertaining to flight. In the 1700s experiments were made with the ornithopter, a machine with flapping wings.

The history of successful flight begins with the hot-air balloon. Two French brothers, Joseph and Étienne Montgolfier, experimented with a large cell contrived of paper in which they could collect heated air. On 19 Sep 1783 the Montgolfiers sent aloft a balloon with a rooster, a duck, and a sheep, and on 21 November the first manned flight was made. Balloons gained importance as their flights ranged for hundreds of miles, but they were essentially unsteerable.

Count Ferdinand von Zeppelin spent much of his retired life working with balloons, particularly on the steering problem. Hydrogen and illuminating gas eventually replaced hot air, and a motor was mounted on a bag filled with gas that had been fitted with propellers and rudders. It was Zeppelin who first saw clearly that maintaining a steerable shape was essential. On 2 Jul 1900 Zeppelin undertook the first experimental flight of what he called an airship. The development of the dirigible went well until the docking procedure at Lakehurst NJ on 6 May 1937, when the *Hindenburg* burst into flames and exploded, with a loss of 36 lives. Public reaction made further development futile.

It should be noted that neither balloons nor dirigibles had produced true flight: what they had done was harness the dynamics of the atmosphere to lift a craft off the ground, using what power (if any) they supplied primarily to steer. The first scientific exposition of the principles that ultimately led to the successful flight with a heavier-than-air device came in 1843 from Sir George Cayley, who is regarded by many as the father of fixed-wing flight. He built a successful man-carrying glider that came close to permitting real flight. His work was built upon in the experiments on gliders from the late 1800s by Otto Lilienthal of Germany and Octave Chanute of the US. The American brothers Wilbur and Orville Wright by 1902 had developed a fully practical biplane glider

that could be controlled in every direction. Fitting a small engine and two propellers to another biplane, the Wrights on 17 Dec 1903 made the world's first successful flight of a man-carrying, engine-powered, heavier-than-air craft at a site near Kitty Hawk NC.

World War I (1914–18) further accelerated the expansion of aviation. Initially used for aerial reconnaissance, aircraft were soon fitted with machine guns and bombs; military aircraft with these types of armaments became known, respectively, as fighters and bombers.

By the 1920s the first small commercial airlines had begun to carry mail, and the increased speed and range of aircraft made nonstop flights over the world's oceans, poles, and continents possible. In the 1930s more efficient monoplane aircraft with all-metal fuselages and retractable undercarriages became standard. Aircraft played a key role in World War II (1939–45), developing in size, weight, speed, power, range, and armament. The war marked the high point of piston-engined propeller craft while also introducing the first aircraft with jet engines, which could fly at higher speeds. Jet-engined craft became the norm for fighters in the late 1940s and proved their superiority as commercial transports beginning in the '50s. The high speeds and low operating costs of jet airliners led to a massive expansion of commercial air travel in the second half of the 20th century.

The next great aviation innovation was the ability to fly at supersonic speeds. The first supersonic aircraft—a Bell XS-1 rocket-powered plane piloted by Maj. Charles E. Yeager of the US Air Force—broke the sound barrier on 14 Oct 1947 at 1,066 km/hr (662 mph) and attained a top speed of 1,126 km/hr (700 mph). The first supersonic passenger-carrying commercial airplane, the Concorde, was built jointly in Great Britain and France and was in regular commercial service between 1976 and 2003. In the 21st century aircraft manufacturers strove to produce larger planes. A huge new passenger airliner, the double-decker Airbus A380, with a passenger capacity of 555 (40% greater than the next largest airplane), began commercial flights in late October 2007. The Boeing 787 Dreamliner, undergoing final tests in 2010, has a capacity of 330 but a range of 3,050 nautical miles, making it more fuel-efficient than the A380.

Airlines in the US: Best On-Time Arrival Performance

Data for 2009.
Source: US Department of Transportation, February 2010.

RANK	AIRLINE	% OF ALL FLIGHTS	RANK	AIRLINE	% OF ALL FLIGHTS	RANK	AIRLINE	% OF ALL FLIGHTS
1	Hawaiian Airlines	92.1	7	US Airways	80.9	13	Frontier Airlines	78.3
2	Southwest Airlines	83.0	8	Northwest Airlines	79.2	14	JetBlue Airways	77.5
3	Alaska Airlines	82.9	9	Mesa Airlines	79.1	15	American Eagle	77.2
4	Pinnacle Airlines	82.5	10	Continental Airlines	78.8		American Airlines	77.2
5	SkyWest Airlines	82.1	11	ExpressJet Airlines	78.7			
6	United Airlines	81.0	12	Delta Air Lines	78.6			

World's Busiest Airports

Ranked by total aircraft movement (takeoffs and landings), 2009.
Source: Airports Council International (preliminary statistics), <www.airports.org>.

RANK	AIRPORT	SERVES	AIRPORT CODE	TOTAL MOVEMENTS
1	Hartsfield-Jackson Atlanta International Airport	Atlanta GA	ATL	970,235
2	O'Hare International Airport	Chicago IL	ORD	827,679
3	Dallas/Fort Worth International Airport	Dallas/Fort Worth TX	DFW	638,782
4	Denver International Airport	Denver CO	DEN	606,006
5	George Bush Intercontinental Airport	Houston TX	IAH	578,150
6	Los Angeles International Airport	Los Angeles CA	LAX	545,210
7	Paris Charles de Gaulle International Airport	Paris, France	CDG	525,314
8	McCarran International Airport	Las Vegas NV	LAS	511,064
9	Charlotte Douglas International Airport	Charlotte NC	CLT	509,358
10	Beijing Capital International Airport	Beijing, China	PEK	488,495
11	Philadelphia International Airport	Philadelphia PA	PHL	472,668
12	Heathrow Airport	London, UK	LHR	466,393
13	Frankfurt Airport	Frankfurt, Germany	FRA	463,111
14	Phoenix Sky Harbor International Airport	Phoenix AZ	PHX	457,207
15	Madrid Barajas International Airport	Madrid, Spain	MAD	435,179
16	Minneapolis–St. Paul International Airport	Minneapolis/St. Paul MN	MSP	432,604
17	Detroit Metropolitan Wayne County Airport	Detroit MI	DTW	432,589
18	John F. Kennedy International Airport	New York NY	JFK	412,980
19	Newark Liberty International Airport	Newark NJ	EWR	411,185
20	Toronto Pearson International Airport	Toronto, ON, Canada	YYZ	407,736
21	Amsterdam Airport Schiphol	Amsterdam, Netherlands	AMS	406,969
22	Phoenix Deer Valley Airport	Phoenix AZ	DVT	402,335
23	Munich International Airport	Munich, Germany	MUC	396,805
24	San Francisco International Airport	San Francisco CA	SFO	379,751
25	Salt Lake City International Airport	Salt Lake City UT	SLC	372,354

Meteorology

World Temperature Extremes

REGION	highest recorded air temperature			lowest recorded air temperature		
	PLACE (ELEVATION)	°F	°C	PLACE (ELEVATION)	°F	°C
Africa	Al-'Aziziyah, Libya (112 m [367 ft]; 13 Sep 1922)	136.0	57.8	Ifrane, Morocco (1,635 m [5,364 ft]; 11 Feb 1935)	−11.0	−23.9
Antarctica	Vanda Station, Scott Coast (15 m [49 ft]; 5 Jan 1974)	59.0	15.0	Vostok, 78° 27' S, 106° 52' E (3,420 m [11,220 ft]; 21 Jul 1983)	−129.0	−89.4
Asia	Tirat Zevi, Israel (−220 m [−722 ft]; 22 Jun 1942)	129.0	53.9	Verkhoyansk, Russia (107 m [350 ft]; 7 Feb 1892)	−90.0	−67.8
Australia	Oodnadatta, SA (112 m ([367 ft]; 2 Jan 1960)	123.0	50.7	Charlotte Pass, NSW (1,755 m [5,758 ft]; 29 Jun 1994)	−9.4	−23.0
Europe	Seville, Spain (8 m [26 ft]; 4 Aug 1881)	122.0	50.0	Ust-Shchuger, Russia (85 m [279 ft]; exact date unknown)	−67.0	−55.0
North America	Greenland Ranch, Death Valley, California (−54 m [−178 ft]; 10 Jul 1913)	134.0	56.7	Snag, YT, Canada (646 m [2,120 ft]; 3 Feb 1947)	−81.4	−63.0

World Temperature Extremes (continued)

	highest recorded air temperature			lowest recorded air temperature		
REGION	PLACE (ELEVATION)	°F	°C	PLACE (ELEVATION)	°F	°C
South America	Rivadavia, Argentina (206 m [676 ft]; 11 Dec 1905)	120.0	48.9	Colonia, Sarmiento, Argentina (268 m [879 ft]; 1 Jun 1907)	−27.0	−32.8
Tropical Pacific	Tuguegarao, Philippines (22 m [72 ft]; 29 Apr 1912)	108.0	42.2	Haleakala, Hawaii (2,972 m [9,750 ft]; 17 May 1979)	12.0	−11.1

Did you know? The oldest detected meteorite impact on Earth occurred 3.47 billion years ago. The meteor left geochemical evidence of its impact in southern Africa and Australia and is thought to have been about 20 km (12 mi) wide. It would have taken less than two seconds to pass through the atmosphere and slam into the surface of the planet, causing immense tsunamis and devastating erosion to the ocean floor and small continents.

Indexes

Wind Chill Index

The wind chill index is based upon a formula that determines how cold the atmosphere feels by combining the temperature and wind speed and applying other factors. For more information, see <www.nws.noaa.gov/om/windchill/index.shtml>.

		TEMPERATURE (°F)													
	CALM	40	35	30	25	20	15	10	5	0	−5	−10	−15	−20	−25	−30
	5	36	31	25	19	13	7	1	−5	−11	−16	−22	−28	−34	−40	−46
	10	34	27	21	15	9	3	−4	−10	−16	−22	−28	−35	−41	−47	−53
	15	32	25	19	13	6	0	−7	−13	−19	−26	−32	−39	−45	−51	−58
	20	30	24	17	11	4	−2	−9	−15	−22	−29	−35	−42	−48	−55	−61
WIND	25	29	23	16	9	3	−4	−11	−17	−24	−31	−37	−44	−51	−58	−64
SPEED	30	28	22	15	8	1	−5	−12	−19	−26	−33	−39	−46	−53	−60	−67
(MPH)	35	28	21	14	7	0	−7	−14	−21	−27	−34	−41	−48	−55	−62	−69
	40	27	20	13	6	−1	−8	−15	−22	−29	−36	−43	−50	−57	−64	−71
	45	26	19	12	5	−2	−9	−16	−23	−30	−37	−44	−51	−58	−65	−72
	50	26	19	12	4	−3	−10	−17	−24	−31	−38	−45	−52	−60	−67	−74
	55	25	18	11	4	−3	−11	−18	−25	−32	−39	−46	−54	−61	−69	−75
	60	25	17	10	3	−4	−11	−19	−26	−33	−40	−48	−55	−62	−69	−76

Heat Index

The Heat Index shows the effects of the combination of heat and humidity. Apparent temperature is the temperature as it feels to your body. For more information see <www.jeonet.com/heat.htm>.

	AIR TEMPERATURE (°F)										
relative humidity	70	75	80	85	90	95	100	105	110	115	120
					apparent temperature						
0%	64	69	73	78	83	87	91	95	99	103	107
10%	65	70	75	80	85	90	95	100	105	111	116
20%	66	72	77	82	87	93	99	105	112	120	130
30%	67	73	78	84	90	96	104	113	123	135	148
40%	68	74	79	86	93	101	110	123	137	151	
50%	69	75	81	88	96	107	120	135	150		
60%	70	76	82	90	100	114	132	149			
70%	70	77	85	93	106	124	144				
80%	71	78	86	97	113	136	157				
90%	71	79	88	102	122	150	170				
100%	72	80	91	108	133	166					

Ultraviolet (UV) Index

The Ultraviolet (UV) Index predicts the intensity of the sun's ultraviolet rays. It was developed by the National Weather Service and the US Environmental Protection Agency to provide a daily forecast of the expected risk of overexposure to the sun. The Index is calculated on a next-day basis for dozens of cities across the US. Other local conditions, such as cloud cover, are taken into account in determining the UV Index number. UV Index numbers are: 0–2 (minimal exposure); 3–4 (low exposure); 5–6 (moderate exposure); 7–9 (high exposure); and 10 and over (very high exposure).

Some simple precautions can be taken to reduce the risk of sun-related illness: limit time in the sun between 10 AM and 4 PM, when rays are generally the strongest; seek shade whenever possible; use a broad spectrum sunscreen with an SPF of at least 15; wear a wide-brimmed hat and, if possible, tightly woven, full-length clothing; wear UV-protective sunglasses; avoid sunlamps and tanning salons; and watch for the UV Index daily. The UV Index should not be used by seriously sun-sensitive individuals, who should consult their doctors and take additional precautions regardless of the exposure level.

Hurricanes
Hurricane and Tornado Classifications

The **Saffir/Simpson Hurricane Wind Scale**[1] is used to rank tropical cyclones.
Category 1. *Barometric pressure:* 28.91 in or more; *wind speed:* 74–95 mph; *damage:* minimal.
Category 2. *Barometric pressure:* 28.50–28.91 in; *wind speed:* 96–110 mph; *damage:* extensive.
Category 3. *Barometric pressure:* 27.91–28.47 in; *wind speed:* 111–130 mph; *damage:* devastating.
Category 4. *Barometric pressure:* 27.17–27.88 in; *wind speed:* 131–155 mph; *damage:* catastrophic.
Category 5. *Barometric pressure:* less than 27.17 in; *wind speed:* 155 mph or more; *damage:* catastrophic.

Tornado classifications.
Tornadoes are assigned specific values on the Fujita Scale, or F-Scale, of tornado intensity established by meteorologist T. Theodore Fujita.
Categories:
F0. *Wind speed:* 40–72 mph; *damage:* light.
F1. *Wind speed:* 73–112 mph; *damage:* moderate.
F2. *Wind speed:* 113–157 mph; *damage:* considerable.
F3. *Wind speed:* 158–206 mph; *damage:* severe.
F4. *Wind speed:* 207–260 mph; *damage:* devastating.
F5. *Wind speed:* 261–318 mph; *damage:* incredible.

[1]*Published by permission of Herbert Saffir, consulting engineer, and Robert Simpson, meteorologist. The scale was revised in early 2010 to remove hurricane-related data, such as storm surge and flooding. Damage estimates are in part affected by building codes and duration and direction of high winds.*

Hurricane Names
Source: National Hurricane Center.

In 1953, the National Hurricane Center developed a list of given names for Atlantic tropical storms. This list is now maintained by the World Meteorological Organization (WMO). Until 1979 only women's names were used, but since then men's and women's names have alternated. There are six lists

currently in rotation, so names can be reused every six years. Any country affected by a hurricane, however, can request that its name be retired for ten years. Also, if a storm has been particularly destructive, the WMO can remove it from the list and replace it with a different name.

Deadliest Hurricanes in the US

Listed below, in order of number of deaths, are the 25 deadliest hurricanes to hit the US or its territories in 1851–2009. Hurricane names are given in parentheses after the location, when applicable.

Note: ranking numbers 10 and 20 on the list are repeated due to the equal number of fatalities in separate hurricanes. Source: National Hurricane Center. <www.nhc.noaa.gov/Deadliest_Costliest.shtml>.

	HURRICANE LOCATION	YEAR	CATEGORY	DEATHS
1	Galveston TX	1900	4	8,000[1]
2	NC; SC; Puerto Rico	1899	3	3,419
3	Lake Okeechobee, Florida	1928	4	2,500[2]
4	Cheniere Caminada LA	1893	4	2,000[3]
5	southeastern LA; MS (Katrina)	2005	3	1,500

	HURRICANE LOCATION	YEAR	CATEGORY	DEATHS
6	Sea Islands, South Carolina and Georgia	1893	3	1,000[4]
7	Puerto Rico; US Virgin Islands	1867	3	811
8	Puerto Rico	1852	1	800
9	GA; SC	1881	2	700
10	Last Island, Louisiana	1856	4	600[3]

Deadliest Hurricanes in the US (continued)

HURRICANE LOCATION	YEAR	CATEGORY	DEATHS		HURRICANE LOCATION	YEAR	CATEGORY	DEATHS
10 New Orleans LA	1915	4	600[3]	19	Galveston TX	1915	4	275
12 southwestern LA; northern TX (Audrey)	1957	4	416	20	MS; southeastern LA; VA (Camille)	1969	5	256
13 Florida Keys	1935	5	408	20	New England	1938	3	256
14 northeastern US	1944	3	390[3]	22	US Virgin Islands; Puerto Rico	1932	2	225
15 FL; MS; AL	1926	4	372					
16 Grand Isle LA	1909	3	350	23	northeastern US (Diane)	1955	1	184
17 Puerto Rico (San Felipe)	1928	5	312	24	GA; SC; NC	1898	4	179
18 Florida Keys; southern TX	1919	4	287	25	TX	1875	3	176

[1]Death toll may have been as high as 12,000.   [2]Death toll may have been as high as 3,000.   [3]Including those lost at sea.   [4]Death toll may have been as high as 2,000.

Costliest Hurricanes in the US

Listed below, in order of the highest monetary damage figures in constant 2009 US dollars, are the 25 costliest hurricanes to hit the US or its territories in 1900–2009. Locations of the damaged areas are given in parentheses after the hurricane name. Note that figures for Hurricane Hugo reflect the damage done by that storm both on the US mainland and on its Caribbean territories. Source: National Hurricane Center.
<www.nhc.noaa.gov/Deadliest_Costliest.shtml>.

RANK	HURRICANE (LOCATION)	YEAR	CATEGORY	ESTIMATED DAMAGE (US$), NOT ADJUSTED	DAMAGE IN CONSTANT 2009 US DOLLARS
1	Katrina (southeastern FL; southeastern LA; MS)	2005	3	81,000,000,000	88,978,500,000
2	Andrew (southeastern FL; southeastern LA)	1992	5	26,500,000,000	40,522,000,000
3	Ike (TX; LA)	2008	2	24,900,000,000	24,811,400,000
4	Wilma (southern FL)	2005	3	20,600,000,000	22,629,100,000
5	Charley (southwestern FL)	2004	4	15,000,000,000	17,035,800,000
6	Ivan (AL; northwestern FL)	2004	3	14,200,000,000	16,127,200,000
7	Hugo (SC; US Virgin Islands; Puerto Rico)	1989	4	8,000,000,000	13,841,100,000
8	Rita (southwestern LA; northern TX)	2005	3	11,300,000,000	12,413,100,000
9	Agnes (FL; northeastern US)	1972	1	2,100,000,000	10,778,200,000
10	Frances (FL)	2004	2	8,900,000,000	10,107,900,000
11	Betsy (southeastern FL; southeastern LA)	1965	3	1,420,500,000	9,674,600,000
12	Camille (MS; southeastern LA; VA)	1969	5	1,420,700,000	8,305,000,000
13	Jeanne (FL)	2004	3	6,900,000,000	7,836,500,000
14	Frederic (AL; MS)	1979	3	2,300,000,000	6,796,600,000
15	Diane (northeastern US)	1955	1	831,700,000	6,657,900,000
16	Allison (northern TX)	2001	TS[1]	5,000,000,000	6,057,000,000
17	Floyd (mid-Atlantic US; northeastern US)	1999	2	4,500,000,000	5,794,800,000
18	(New England)	1938	3	300,000,000	4,564,600,000
19	Fran (NC)	1996	3	3,200,000,000	4,375,500,000
20	Alicia (northern TX)	1983	3	2,000,000,000	4,308,000,000
21	Gustav (LA)	2008	2	4,300,000,000	4,284,700,000
22	Opal (northwestern FL; AL)	1995	3	3,000,000,000	4,223,200,000
23	Isabel (mid-Atlantic US)	2003	2	3,370,000,000	3,929,300,000
24	Carol (northeastern US)	1954	2	460,000,000	3,668,700,000
25	Juan (LA)	1985	1	1,500,000,000	2,990,800,000

[1]Of tropical storm intensity but included because of high damage.

Did you know? The amount of water in river systems at any given time is but a tiny fraction of the Earth's total water. The oceans contain 97% of all water. About three-quarters of all fresh water is stored as land ice; nearly all of the remainder occurs as groundwater. Lakes account for less than 0.5% of all fresh water, soil moisture 0.05%, and water in river channels only 0.025%, or about one four-thousandth of the Earth's total fresh water.

Geologic Disasters

Measuring Earthquakes

The seismologists Beno Gutenberg and Charles Francis Richter introduced measurement of the seismic energy released by earthquakes on a magnitude scale in 1935. Each increase of one unit on the scale represents a 10-fold increase in the magnitude of an earthquake. Seismographs are designed to measure the different components of seismic waves, such as wave type, intensity, and duration. This table shows the typical effects of earthquakes in various magnitude ranges. For further information, see <www.seismo.unr.edu/ftp/pub/louie/class/100/magnitude.html>.

MAGNITUDE	EARTHQUAKE EFFECTS
Less than 3.5	Generally not felt, but recorded.
3.5–5.4	Often felt, but rarely causes damage.
Less than 6.0	At most, slight damage to well-designed buildings. Can cause major damage to poorly constructed buildings over small regions.
6.1–6.9	Can be destructive in areas up to about 100 km (61 mi) across where people live.
7.0–7.9	Major earthquake. Can cause serious damage over larger areas.
8 or greater	Great earthquake. Can cause serious damage in areas several hundred km across.

Major Historical Earthquakes

Magnitudes given for pre-20th-century events are generally estimations from intensity data. In cases where no magnitude is available, the earthquake's maximum intensity, written as a Roman numeral from I to XII, is given.

YEAR (AD)	AFFECTED AREA	MAGNITUDE OR INTENSITY	DEATHS	YEAR (AD)	AFFECTED AREA	MAGNITUDE OR INTENSITY	DEATHS
365	Knossos, Crete, Greece	XI	50,000	1906	off the coast of Ecuador	8.8	1,000
				1906	Valparaíso, Chile	8.2	20,000
526	Antioch, Syria	unknown	250,000	1906	San Francisco CA	7.8	c. 3,000
844	Damascus, Syria	VIII	50,000	1907	southwestern Tajikistan	8.0	12,000
847	Damascus, Syria	X	70,000	1908	Messina, Italy	7.2	70,000
847	Mosul, Iraq	unknown	50,000	1912	Sea of Marmara, Turkey	7.8	2,800
856	Damghan, Iran	unknown	200,000	1915	Avezzano, Italy	7.0	32,610
893	Daipur, India	unknown	180,000	1920	Ningxia province, China	7.8	200,000
893	Ardabil, Iran	unknown	150,000	1923	Tokyo; Yokohama, Japan	7.9	143,000
893	Caucasus	unknown	82,000	1927	Qinghai province, China	7.6	40,900
1042	Palmyra, Syria	X	50,000	1933	Sanriku, Japan	8.4	2,990
1138	Aleppo, Syria	unknown	230,000	1935	Quetta, Pakistan	7.5	30,000
1201	Upper Egypt or Syria	IX	1,100,000	1939	Erzincan, Turkey	7.8	32,700
				1939	Chillán, Chile	7.8	28,000
1268	Cilicia, Turkey		60,000	1944	Tonankai, Japan	8.1	998
1290	Chihli, China	unknown	100,000	1944	San Juan, Argentina	7.4	c. 8,000
1556	Shaanxi province, China	8.0	830,000	1945	off the coast of Pakistan	8.0	4,000
				1946	Nankaido, Japan	8.1	1,362
1667	Shemakha, Azerbaijan	unknown	80,000	1948	Ashgabat, Turkmenistan	7.3	110,000
				1950	China-India border, near Myanmar (Burma)	8.6	1,526
1668	Shandong province, China	XII	50,000	1960	Puerto Montt, Chile	9.5	1,655– 5,700
1693	Sicily, Italy	7.5	60,000				
1703	Jeddo, Japan	unknown	200,000	1960	Agadir, Morocco	5.7	10,000– 15,000
1727	Tabriz, Iran	unknown	77,000				
1730	Hokkaido, Japan	unknown	137,000	1964	Prince William Sound, Alaska	9.2	128
1731	Beijing, China	unknown	100,000				
1739	China	X	50,000	1968	Khorasan, Iran	7.3	12,000
1755	Lisbon, Portugal; Spain; Morocco	8.7	70,000	1970	northern Peru	7.9	66,000
				1970	Yunnan province, China	7.5	10,000
1755	Kashan, Iran	unknown	40,000				
1780	Tabriz, Iran	unknown	100,000	1972	Fars, Iran	7.1	5,054
1783	Calabria, Italy	unknown	50,000	1972	Managua, Nicaragua	6.2	5,000
1811	New Madrid MO	8.6	unknown	1974	Yunnan province, China	6.8	20,000
1812	Caracas, Venezuela	7.7	26,000	1974	North-West Frontier Province, Pakistan	6.2	5,300
1835	northern Japan	7.6	28,300				
1868	Arica, Chile	9.0	25,000	1975	Liaoning province, China	7.0	2,000
1868	Ecuador; Colombia	7.7	70,000	1976	Mindanao, Philippines	7.9	8,000
1883	Java, Indonesia	unknown	100,000	1976	Tangshan, China	7.5	242,000– 655,000
1896	Sanriku, Japan	8.5	27,000				
1905	Kangra, India	7.5	19,000	1976	Guatemala City, Guatemala	7.5	23,000

Major Historical Earthquakes (continued)

YEAR (AD)	AFFECTED AREA	MAGNITUDE OR INTENSITY	DEATHS	YEAR (AD)	AFFECTED AREA	MAGNITUDE OR INTENSITY	DEATHS
1976	Turkey-Iran border	7.3	5,000	2001	Gujarat state, India	7.6	20,023
1977	Bucharest, Romania	7.2	1,500	2002	Hindu Kush mountains, Afghanistan	6.1	c. 1,000
1978	Khorasan, Iran	7.8	15,000	2003	northern Algeria	6.8	2,266
1979	Colombia; Ecuador	7.9	579	2003	Bam, Iran	6.6	c. 31,000
1980	Ech-Cheliff (El-Asnam), Algeria	7.7	5,000	2004	off the western coast of Sumatra, Indonesia	9.1	227,898
1980	southern Italy	6.5	3,114	2005	northern Sumatra, Indonesia	8.6	1,313
1985	Michoacán state, Mexico	8.0	9,500–35,000	2005	Kashmir, Pakistan	7.6	c. 86,000
1988	Gyumri (Leninakan), Armenia	6.8	25,000	2006	Bantul, Indonesia	6.3	5,749
1990	Luzon, Philippines	7.7	1,621	2007	off the coast of central Peru	8.0	514
1990	Rasht, Iran	7.4	50,000	2008	eastern Sichuan province, China	7.9	87,587
1991	northern India	6.8	2,000	2009	southern Sumatra, Indonesia	7.5	1,117
1992	Flores, Indonesia	7.5	2,500				
1993	Latur, India	6.2	9,748	2009	central Italy	6.3	295
1995	Sakhalin Island, Russia	7.1	1,989	2010	off the western coast of Chile, near Maule	8.8	577
1995	Kobe, Japan	6.9	5,502				
1997	eastern Iran	7.3	1,567	2010	southern Haiti, near Port-au-Prince	7.0	222,570
1998	Feyzabad, Afghanistan	6.6	4,000				
1999	Taiwan	7.6	2,400	2010	southern Qinghai province, China	6.9	2,267
1999	Golcuk, Turkey	7.6	17,118				
2001	El Salvador	7.7	852				

Tsunami

A tsunami is a catastrophic ocean wave, usually caused by a submarine earthquake occurring less than 30 mi (50 km) beneath the seafloor, with a magnitude greater than 6.5. Underwater or coastal landslides or volcanic eruptions also may cause a tsunami. The often-used term tidal wave is a misnomer: the wave has no connection with the tides. After the earthquake or other generating impulse, a train of simple, progressive oscillatory waves is propagated great distances at the ocean surface in ever-widening circles, much like the waves produced by a pebble falling into a shallow pool. In deep water, the wavelengths are enormous, about 60 to 125 mi (100 to 200 km), and the wave heights are very small, only 1 to 2 ft (0.3 to 0.6 m). The resulting wave steepness is extremely low; coupled with the waves' long periods that vary from five minutes to an hour, this enables normal wind waves and swell to completely obscure the waves in deep water. Thus, a ship in the open ocean experiences the passage of a tsunami as an insignificant rise and fall. As the waves approach the continental coasts, friction with the increasingly shallow bottom reduces the velocity of the waves. The period must remain constant; consequently, as the velocity lessens, the wavelengths become shortened and the wave amplitudes increase, coastal waters rising as high as 100 feet (30 m) in 10 to 15 minutes. By a poorly understood process, the continental shelf waters begin to oscillate after the rise in sea level. Between three and five major oscillations generate most of the damage; the oscillations cease, however, only several days after they begin. Occasionally, the first arrival of a tsunami at a coast may be a trough, the water receding and exposing the shallow seafloor.

Deadly Volcano Eruptions
Casualty figures are approximate.

VOLCANO (LOCATION)	YEAR	CASUALTIES	VOLCANO (LOCATION)	YEAR	CASUALTIES
Tambora (Indonesia)	1815	92,000[1]	Raung (Indonesia)	1730	3,000
Krakatoa (Indonesia)	1883	36,000[1]	Lamington (Papua New Guinea)	1951	3,000
Pelée (Martinique)	1902	30,000	Awu (Indonesia)	1856	2,800
Ruiz (Colombia)	1985	25,000[2]	Taal (Philippines)	1906	1,500
Etna (Italy)	1669	20,000	Taal (Philippines)	1911	1,300
Unzen (Japan)	1792	15,000	Etna (Italy)	1536	1,000
Kelud (Indonesia)	1586	10,000	Paricutín (Mexico)	1949	1,000
Laki (Iceland)	1783	9,000	Purace (Colombia)	1949	1,000
Kelud (Indonesia)	1919	5,000	Pinatubo (Philippines)	1991	350
Vesuvius (Italy)	79	3,360	El Chichón (Mexico)	1982	100
Awu (Indonesia)	1711	3,200	St. Helens (Washington)	1980	57
Raung (Indonesia)	1638	3,000			

[1] Includes tsunami triggered by eruption.   [2] Includes mudflow triggered by eruption.

Civil Engineering

The Seven Wonders of the Ancient World

The seven wonders of the ancient world were considered to be the preeminent architectural and sculptural achievements of the Mediterranean and Middle East. Although different lists exist, the classic list contains the following:

Pyramids of Giza. The oldest of the wonders and the only one substantially in existence today, the pyramids of Giza were erected c. 2575–c. 2465 BC on the west bank of the Nile River in northern Egypt. The designations of the pyramids—Khufu, Khafre, and Menkaure—correspond to the kings for whom they were built. Khufu (also called the Great Pyramid) is the largest of the three, the length of each side at the base averaging 230 m (755 ft). According to Herodotus, the Great Pyramid took 20 years to construct and demanded the labor of 100,000 men.

Hanging Gardens of Babylon. A series of landscaped terraces ascribed to either Queen Sammu-ramat (810–783 BC) or King Nebuchadrezzar II (c. 605–c. 561 BC), the gardens were built within the walls of the royal palace at Babylon (in present-day southern Iraq). They did not actually "hang" but were instead roof gardens laid out on a series of ziggurat terraces that were irrigated by pumps from the Euphrates River.

Statue of Zeus. An ornate figure of Zeus on his throne, this wonder was completed about 430 BC by Phidias of Athens after eight years of work. It was placed in the huge Temple of Zeus at Olympia in western Greece. The statue, almost 12 m (40 ft) high and plated with gold and ivory, represented the god sitting on an elaborate throne ornamented with ebony, ivory, gold, and precious stones. On his outstretched right hand was a statue of Nike (Victory), and in the god's left hand was a scepter on which an eagle was perched.

Temple of Artemis. The great temple was built by Croesus, king of Lydia, in about 550 BC and was rebuilt after being burned by a madman named Herostratus in 356 BC. The artemesium was famous not only for its great size (over 110 by 55 m [350 by 80 ft]) but also for the magnificent works of art that adorned it. It was destroyed by invading Goths in AD 262, and though it was never rebuilt, copies survive of the famous statue of Artemis in it. This early representation stands stiffly straight, with her hands extended outward. The original was made of gold, ebony, silver, and black stone.

Mausoleum of Halicarnassus. This monumental tomb of Mausolus, the tyrant of Caria in southwestern Asia Minor, was built between about 353 and 351 BC by Mausolus' sister and widow, Artemisia. According to the description of Pliny the Elder, the monument, designed by the architect Pythius (Pytheos), was almost square, with a total periphery of 125 m (411 ft). It was bounded by 36 columns, and the top formed a pyramid surmounted by a marble chariot. Fragments of the mausoleum's sculpture are preserved in the British Museum. The mausoleum was probably destroyed by an earthquake, and the stones were reused in local buildings.

Colossus of Rhodes. This huge bronze statue was built at the harbor of Rhodes in ancient Greece in commemoration of the raising of the siege of Rhodes (305–304 BC). The sculptor was Chares of Lyndus. The Colossus was said to be 32 m (105 ft) high, making it technically impossible that it could have straddled the harbor entrance, as was popularly believed. The Colossus took 12 years to build (c. 294–282 BC) and was toppled by an earthquake about 225 BC.

Pharos of Alexandria. This lighthouse, the most famous of the ancient world, was built by Sostratus of Cnidus about 280 BC on the island of Pharos off Alexandria, and it is said to have been more than 100 m (350 ft) high. It is the archetype of all lighthouses since. The lighthouse was destroyed by an earthquake in the 1300s. In 1994 a large amount of masonry blocks and statuary, thought to be wreckage from the lighthouse, was found in the waters off Pharos.

Tallest Buildings in the World

Building height equals the distance from the level of the lowest significant, open-air, pedestrian entrance to the architectural top of the building, including spires but not including antennas, signage, or flag poles. Only buildings that have been completed or are scheduled to be completed in 2010 are included in this table. Source: Council on Tall Buildings and Urban Habitat.

RANK	BUILDING	CITY	YEAR COMPLETED	HEIGHT IN FT/M	STORIES
1	Burj Khalifa	Dubai, UAE	2010	2,717/828	163
2	Taipei 101	Taipei, Taiwan	2004	1,667/508	101
3	Shanghai World Financial Center	Shanghai, China	2008	1,614/492	101
4	International Commerce Centre	Hong Kong, China	2010	1,588/484	108
5	Petronas Tower 1	Kuala Lumpur, Malaysia	1998	1,483/452	88
6	Petronas Tower 2	Kuala Lumpur, Malaysia	1998	1,483/452	88
7	Nanjing Greenland Financial Center	Nanjing, China	2010	1,476/450	66
8	Willis Tower (Sears Tower)	Chicago IL	1974	1,451/442	108
9	Trump International Hotel & Tower	Chicago IL	2009	1,389/423	98
10	Jin Mao Building	Shanghai, China	1999	1,380/421	88
11	Two International Finance Centre	Hong Kong, China	2003	1,352/412	88
12	CITIC Plaza	Guangzhou, China	1996	1,280/390	80
13	Shun Hing Square	Shenzhen, China	1996	1,260/384	69
14	Empire State Building	New York NY	1931	1,250/381	102
15	Central Plaza	Hong Kong, China	1992	1,227/374	78

Tallest Buildings in the World (continued)

RANK	BUILDING	CITY	YEAR COMPLETED	HEIGHT IN FT/M	STORIES
16	Bank of China Tower	Hong Kong, China	1989	1,205/367	70
17	Bank of America Tower	New York NY	2009	1,200/366	55
18	Almas Tower	Dubai, UAE	2008	1,181/360	68
19	Emirates Tower One	Dubai, UAE	2000	1,163/355	54
20	Tuntex Sky Tower	Kaohsiung, Taiwan	1997	1,140/348	85
21	Aon Centre	Chicago IL	1973	1,136/346	83
22	The Center	Hong Kong, China	1998	1,135/346	73
23	John Hancock Center	Chicago IL	1969	1,128/344	100
24	Rose Rayhaan by Rotana	Dubai, UAE	2007	1,093/333	72
25	Shimao International Plaza	Shanghai, China	2006	1,093/333	60

Longest Span Structures in the World by Type

Bridges

SUSPENSION	LOCATION	YEAR OF COMPLETION	MAIN SPAN (M)
Akashi Kaikyo	Kobe–Awaji Island, Japan	1998	1,991
part of eastern link between islands of Honshu and Shikoku			
Xihoumen	Zhoushan archipelago, China	2007	1,650
links Jintang and Cezi islands			
Store Baelt (Great Belt)	Zealand–Funen, Denmark	1998	1,624
part of link between Copenhagen and mainland Europe			
Nancha	Zhenjiang, China	2005	1,490
world's third longest suspension bridge			
Humber	near Kingston upon Hull, England	1981	1,410
crosses Humber estuary between Yorkshire and Lincolnshire			

CABLE-STAYED (STEEL)			
Sutong	Nantong, China	2008	1,088
longest main span, highest main-bridge tower, and deepest foundation piers for a cable-stayed bridge			
Stonecutters (Angchuanzhou)	Tsing Yi–Sha Tin, Hong Kong	2009	1,018
links growing areas of Northeast New Territories and Kowloon, Hong Kong			
Edong	Huangshi–Huanggang, China	2009	926
alleviates congestion on Huangshi Yangtze Bridge			
Tatara	Onomichi–Imabari, Japan	1999	890
part of western link between islands of Honshu and Shikoku			
Normandie	near Le Havre, France	1995	856
crosses Seine estuary between upper and lower Normandy			

ARCH steel			
Chaotianmen	Chongqing, China (across the Yangtze)	2009	552
world's longest steel-arch bridge			
Lupu	Shanghai, China	2003	550
crosses Huangpujiang (Huangpu River) between central Shanghai and Pudong New District			
New River Gorge	Fayetteville WV	1977	518
provides road link through scenic New River Gorge National River area			
concrete			
Wanxian	Sichuan province, China	1997	425
crosses Chang Jiang (Yangtze River) in Three Gorges area			
Krk I	Krk island, Croatia	1980	390
links scenic Krk island with mainland Croatia			
Jiangjiehe	Guizhou province, China	1995	330
spans gorge of Wujiang (Wu River)			

CANTILEVER steel truss			
Québec	Quebec City, QC, Canada	1917	549
provides rail crossing over St. Lawrence River			
Forth	Edinburgh–North Queensferry, Scotland	1890	2 spans, each 521
provides rail crossing over Firth of Forth			
Minato	Osaka–Amagasaki, Japan	1974	510
carries road traffic across Osaka's harbor			

Longest Span Structures in the World by Type (continued)

	LOCATION	YEAR OF COMPLETION	MAIN SPAN (M)
CANTILEVER (CONTINUED)			
prestressed concrete			
Shibanpo-2	Chongqing, China	2006	336
world's longest prestressed-concrete box girder bridge			
Stolmasundet	Austevoll, Norway	1998	301
links islands of Stolmen and Sjelbörn south of Bergen			
Raftsundet	Lofoten, Norway	1998	298
crosses Raft Sound in arctic Lofoten islands			
BEAM			
steel truss			
Ikitsuki Ohashi	Nagasaki prefecture, Japan	1991	400
connects islands of Iki and Hirado off northwest Kyushu			
Astoria	Astoria OR	1966	376
carries Pacific Coast Highway across Columbia River between Oregon and Washington			
Francis Scott Key	Baltimore MD	1977	366
spans Patapsco River at Baltimore harbor			
steel plate and box girder			
Presidente Costa e Silva	Rio de Janeiro state, Brazil	1974	300
crosses Guanabara Bay between Rio de Janeiro and suburb of Niterói			
Neckartalbrücke-1	Weitingen, Germany	1978	263
carries highway across Neckar River valley			
Brankova	Belgrade, Serbia	1956	261
provides road crossing of Sava River between Old and New Belgrade			
MOVABLE			
vertical lift			
Arthur Kill	Elizabeth NJ–New York NY	1959	170
provides rail link between port of Elizabeth and Staten Island			
Cape Cod Canal	Cape Cod MA	1935	166
provides rail crossing over waterway near Buzzard's Bay			
Delair	Delair NJ–Philadelphia PA	1960	165
provides rail link across Delaware River between Philadelphia and southern Jersey Shore			
swing span			
Al-Firdan (El-Ferdan)	Suez Canal, Egypt	2001	340
provides road and rail link between Sinai Peninsula and eastern Nile delta region			
Santa Fe	Fort Madison IA–Niota IL	1927	160
provides road and rail crossing of Mississippi River			
Kaiser-Wilhelm-Brücke	Wilhelmshaven, Germany	1907	159
crosses the Wupper River			
BASCULE			
South Capitol Street/Frederick Douglass Memorial	Washington DC	1949	118
carries road traffic over Anacostia River			
Sault Sainte Marie	Sault Sainte Marie MI–Ontario, Canada	1941	102
connects rail systems of United States and Canada			
Charles Berry	Lorain OH	1940	101
carries road traffic over Black River			
Market Street/Chief John Ross	Chattanooga TN	1917	94
carries road traffic over Tennessee River			

Causeways (fixed link over water only)			
Lake Pontchartrain-2	Metairie–Mandeville LA	1969	38,422
carries northbound road traffic from suburbs of New Orleans to north lakeshore			
Lake Pontchartrain-1	Mandeville–Metairie LA	1956	38,352
carries southbound road traffic from north lakeshore to suburbs of New Orleans			
Hangzhou Bay Transoceanic	near Jiaxing–near Cixi, China	2008	36,000
world's longest transoceanic bridge or causeway			
King Fahd	Bahrain–Saudi Arabia	1986	24,950
carries road traffic across Gulf of Bahrain in Persian Gulf			
Confederation	Borden-Carleton, PE–Cape Jourimain, NB, Canada	1997	12,900
carries road traffic over Northumberland Strait			

Basic Types of Bridges

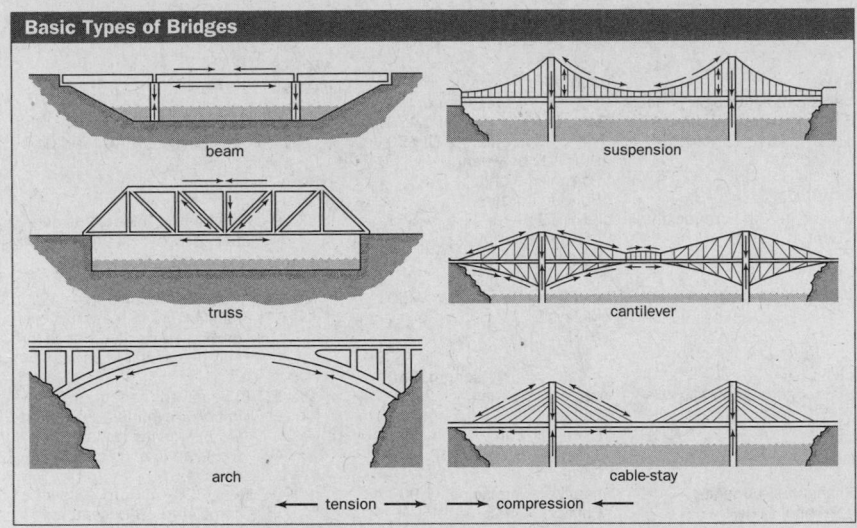

beam

suspension

truss

cantilever

arch

cable-stay

← tension →   → compression ←

Notable Civil Engineering Projects (in progress or completed as of July 2010)

NAME	LOCATION		YEAR OF COMPLETION	NOTES
airports		terminal area (sq m)		
Barcelona (El Prat) (Terminal T1)	southwest of Barcelona	544,066	2009	Opened 17 June; new second terminal building is located midfield
Miami International (North Terminal)	northwest of central Miami	316,000	2011	Largest US airport expansion under way in 2009; original terminal is being remodeled and expanded to become the North Terminal
Cairo International (new Terminal 3)	northeast of Cairo	211,000	2009	Opened 27 April; Africa's 2nd busiest airport
bridges		length (main span; m)		
Hong Kong–Zhuhai Crossing	Hong Kong to China link (via Macau) (in Pearl River estuary)	c. 50 km	2016	To include world's largest sea bridge (c. 35 km) and world's longest immersed tube tunnel (c. 5.5 km); construction began in mid-December 2009
Hangzhou Bay #2 (Jiashao)	between Jiaxing and Shaoxing, China	2,689	2012	Will be world's longest all-span cable-stayed bridge
Zambezi bridge at Caia	Caia–Chimuara, Mozambique	2,276*	2009	Opened 1 August; *total length of two sections; Africa's second longest bridge; first bridge over Mozambican part of the Zambezi River
buildings		height (m)		
Burj Khalifa	Dubai, UAE	828	2010	Opened 4 Jan 2010; became world's tallest man-made structure in April 2008; known as Burj Dubai ("Dubai Tower") prior to 4 Jan 2010
Shanghai Tower	Shanghai	632	2014	To be world's 2nd tallest building and the tallest in China
Abraj Al Bait ("Royal Clock") Towers	Mecca, Saudi Arabia	577	2011	To be world's 3rd tallest building; 6 residential/hotel towers to house 65,000 people

Notable Civil Engineering Projects (in progress or completed as of July 2010) (continued)

NAME	LOCATION	YEAR OF COMPLETION	NOTES
dams and hydrologic projects	**crest length (m)**		
Santo Antonio (SA)/Jirau (J) (2 dams on the Madeira River)	(SA): near Porto Velho, Rondônia, Brazil (J): between Porto Velho and Bolivian border	(SA) 1,173 (J) 550 → 2012 2014	Together will provide 8% of the electricity for Brazil by 2014
Merowe (earth core rockfill) Dam	on Nile, 350 km north of Khartoum, Sudan	841 / 2009	Inaugurated 3 March; to contain 20% of Nile annual flow; to double Sudan's power capacity
Bakun Hydroelectric Project	Balui River, Sarawak, Malaysia	750 / 2010	To be largest concrete-faced rockfill dam in the world; will provide electricity to Singapore and peninsular Malaysia
highways	**length (km)**		
South Interoceanic Highway	Iñapari (at Brazilian border)–Ilo/ Matarani/San Juan de Marcona, Peru	c. 2,000 / 2011	To be paved road for Brazilian imports/exports from/to Asia via 3 Peruvian ports; to link the Atlantic and Pacific oceans
Shanghai–Chongqing National Highway	Shanghai–Chongqing, China	1,900 / 2009	Final, 320-km Hurongxi section completed 19 December; links China's largest city with centrally located Chongqing via a modern expressway
Mombasa–Nairobi–Addis Ababa Road Corridor	Addis Ababa, Ethiopia–Mombasa, Kenya	1,284 / 2011?	To facilitate trade between landlocked Ethiopia and the world through the Kenyan port of Mombasa
canals and floodgates	**length (m)**		
St. Petersburg Flood Protection Barrier	Gulf of Finland embankment, Russia (Gorskaya–Bronka via Kotlin Island)	25,400 / 2010	To protect city from tidal surges; navigation channel opened October 2008; begun 1980, halted 1987, resumed 2003
New Orleans Surge Barrier	near confluence of Gulf Intercoastal Waterway and Mississippi River Gulf Outlet, east of New Orleans	2,300 / 2011	Central component of 3.2-km-long project to prevent storm-surge flooding, using 7.9-m barrier walls and floodgates
Panama Canal Expansion	between Panama City and Colón, Panama	— / 2014	Will include new wider and longer 3-chamber locks, doubling the canal's capacity and allowing the passage of world's biggest container ships
railways (heavy)	**length (km)**		
Benguela Railway (rehabilitation; closed by civil war 1975–2002)	Benguela–Luau, Angola (at the Democratic Republic of the Congo border)	1,314 / 2011	Will enable resumption of copper exports from the Democratic Republic of the Congo and Zambia
North South Rail Project (Phase A)	Al-Zubairah–Ras Al-Zour, Saudi Arabia	818 / 2010	To facilitate the export of phosphate and bauxite from mines in the interior via the Persian Gulf
Xinqiu–Bayan UI Railway	Xinqiu, Liaoning– Bayan UI, Inner Mongolia, China	487 / 2010	To be important for coal transport; future link to Mongolia expected
railways (high speed)	**length (km)**		
Jinghu High-Speed	Beijing–Shanghai	1,318 / 2012	To halve travel time between capital and financial center
Wuhan–Guangzhou High-Speed	Wuhan–Guangzhou, China	968 / 2009	Opened 26 December; average speed of 350 km/hr
Turkish High-Speed	Ankara–Istanbul	533 / 2013	To connect capital with largest city; 245-km section from Ankara to Eskisehir opened 13 Mar 2009

Notable Civil Engineering Projects (in progress or completed as of July 2010) (continued)

NAME	LOCATION	YEAR OF COMPLETION	NOTES
subways/metros/light rails		length (km)	
Dubai Metro (Red Line)	Dubai, UAE	52.1	2009	Opened 9 September; 22.5-km Green Line to open in 2010; 2 lines together will be world's longest fully automated driverless transport system
Shanghai Metro (Line 7)	Shanghai	34.5	2009	Opened 5 December; length of lines opened since 1995 equals 284.6 km
Namma Metro	Bengaluru (Bangalore), India	33.0	2011	2 lines to be built; construction began in 2007
tunnels		length (m)	
Apennine Range tunnels (9)	Bologna, Italy–Florence (high-speed railway)	73,400	2009	Rail line opened to traffic 13 December; longest tunnel (Vaglia, 18.6 km); tunnels cover 93% of railway
Brenner Base Tunnel	Innsbruck, Austria–Fortezza, Italy	55,392	2015	To ease congestion of freight travel from across Europe passing through the Alps
Marmaray railroad project tunnels	connecting European and Asian portions of Istanbul	13,600	2011	Includes 1.4-km-long bored tunnel, world's deepest sunken-tube tunnel (56 m under the Bosporus strait); completed (though not opened) 13 Oct 2008
miscellaneous		length (km)	
Eastern Africa Submarine Cable System	western Indian Ocean between South Africa and Sudan	13,700	2010	To be first underwater fiber-optic cable in Indian Ocean, providing Internet and communications services to 250 million people in Africa

1 m=3.28 ft; 1 km=0.62 mi

Life on Earth

Taxonomy

Taxonomy is the classification of living and extinct organisms. The term is derived from the Greek *taxis* ("arrangement") and *nomos* ("law") and refers to the methodology and principles of systematic botany and zoology by which the various kinds of plants and animals are arranged in hierarchies of superior and subordinate groups.

Popularly, classifications of living organisms arise according to need and are often superficial; for example, although the term fish is common to the names shellfish, crayfish, and starfish, there are more anatomical differences between a shellfish and a starfish than there are between a bony fish and a human. Also, vernacular names vary widely. Biologists have attempted to view all living organisms with equal thoroughness and thus have devised a formal classification. A formal classification supports a relatively uniform and internationally understood nomenclature, thereby simplifying cross-referencing and retrieval of information.

Carolus Linnaeus, who is usually regarded as the founder of modern taxonomy and whose books are considered the beginning of modern botanical and zoological nomenclature, drew up rules for assigning names to plants and animals and was the first to use binomial nomenclature consistently, beginning in 1758. Classification since Linnaeus has incorporated newly discovered information and more closely approaches a natural system, and the process of clarifying relationships continues to this day. The table below shows the seven ranks that are accepted as obligatory by zoologists and botanists and sample listings for animals and plants.

	ANIMALS	PLANTS
Kingdom	Animalia	Plantae
Phylum/Division	Chordata	Tracheophyta
Class	Mammalia	Pteropsida
Order	Primates	Coniferales

Taxonomy (continued)

	ANIMALS	PLANTS
Family	Hominidae	Pinaceae
Genus	*Homo*	*Pinus*
Species	*Homo sapiens* (human)	*Pinus strobus* (white pine)

Names of the Male, Female, Young, and Group of Selected Animals

ANIMAL	MALE	FEMALE	YOUNG	GROUP
ape	male	female	baby	shrewdness
bear	boar	sow	cub	sleuth, sloth
deer	buck, stag	doe	fawn	herd
donkey	jack, jackass	jennet, jenny	colt, foal	drove, herd
ferret	hob	jill	kit	business, fesynes
fox	reynard	vixen	kit, cub, pup	skulk, leash
giraffe	bull	doe	calf	herd, corps, tower
hamster	buck	doe	pup	horde
hippopotamus	bull	cow	calf	herd, bloat
horse	stallion, stud	mare, dam	foal, colt (male), filly (female)	stable, harras, herd, team (working) string or field (racing)
human	man	woman	baby, infant, toddler	clan (related), crowd, family (closely related), community, tribe
lion	lion	lioness	cub	pride
mouse	buck	doe	pup, pinkie, kitten	horde, mischief
pig	boar	sow	piglet, shoat, farrow	drove, herd, litter (of pups), sounder
quail	cock	hen	chick	bevy, covey, drift
rhinoceros	bull	cow	calf	crash
seal	bull	cow	pup	herd, pod, rookery, harem
sheep	buck, ram	ewe, dam	lamb, lambkin, cosset	drift, drove, flock, herd, mob, trip
turkey	tom	hen	poult	rafter
whale	bull	cow	calf	gam, grind, herd, pod, school

Forests of the World

This table shows the 20 countries or dependencies that lost the most forest area between 1990 and 2005 and those that gained the most, as well as forest losses or gains by continent. 1 hectare (ha) = .01 sq km, .004 sq mi. Source: State of the World's Forests 2009. Web site: <www.fao.org/forestry>.

COUNTRY/AREA	LAND AREA ('000 HA)	TOTAL FOREST IN 1990 ('000 HA)	TOTAL FOREST IN 2005 ('000 HA)	PERCENTAGE OF LAND AREA IN 2005 (%)	% CHANGE 1990–2005
Kiribati	81	28	2	3.0	−92.86
Kazakhstan	269,970	9,758	3,337	1.2	−65.80
Comoros	186	12	5	2.9	−58.33
Togo	5,439	719	386	7.1	−46.31
Lesotho	3,035	14	8	0.3	−42.86
The Bahamas	1,001	842	515	51.5	−38.84
Brunei	527	452	278	52.8	−38.50
Mozambique	78,638	31,238	19,262	24.6	−38.34
Burundi	2,568	241	152	5.9	−36.93
Nigeria	91,077	17,501	11,089	12.2	−36.64
Afghanistan	65,209	1,351	867	1.3	−35.83
Mauritania	103,070	415	267	0.3	−35.66
Niger	126,670	1,945	1,266	1.0	−34.91
Haiti	2,756	158	105	3.8	−33.54
Pakistan	77,088	2,755	1,902	2.5	−30.96
Libya	175,954	311	217	0.1	−30.23
Benin	11,062	3,349	2,351	21.3	−29.80
Uganda	19,710	5,103	3,627	18.4	−28.92
Ghana	22,754	7,535	5,517	24.2	−26.78
Albania	2,740	1,069	794	29.0	−25.72
Lebanon	1,023	37	137	13.3	+270.27
Federated States of Micronesia	70	24	63	90.6	+162.50
Ethiopia	100,000	4,996	13,000	11.9	+160.21
Cape Verde	403	35	84	20.7	+140.00
Northern Mariana Islands	46	14	33	72.4	+135.71

Forests of the World (continued)

COUNTRY/AREA	LAND AREA ('000 HA)	TOTAL FOREST IN 1990 ('000 HA)	TOTAL FOREST IN 2005 ('000 HA)	PERCENTAGE OF LAND AREA IN 2005 (%)	% CHANGE 1990–2005
Mauritius	203	17	37	18.2	+117.65
Tunisia	15,536	499	1,056	6.8	+111.62
Kuwait	1,782	3	6	0.3	+100.00
Oman	30,950	1	2	1	+100.00
Sierra Leone	7,162	1,416	2,754	38.5	+94.49
Uruguay	17,502	791	1,506	8.6	+90.39
Iceland	10,025	25	46	1	+84.00
Saudi Arabia	214,969	1,504	2,728	1.3	+81.38
Puerto Rico	887	234	408	46.0	+74.36
Uzbekistan	42,540	1,923	3,295	8.0	+71.35
St. Vincent and the Grenadines	39	7	11	27.4	+57.14
El Salvador	2,072	193	298	14.4	+54.40
Iran	162,855	7,299	11,075	6.8	+51.73
East Timor	1,487	541	798	53.7	+47.50
Cyprus	924	119	174	18.9	+46.22
South America	1,760,726	922,731	831,540	47.7	−9.88
Africa	2,963,666	702,502	635,412	21.4	−9.55
Europe	2,208,811	1,030,475	1,001,394	44.3	−2.82
North and Central America	2,112,080	555,002	699,875	33.1	+26.10
Asia	3,096,597	551,448	571,576	18.5	+3.65
Oceania	849,091	201,271	206,254	24.3	+2.48
World	13,013,868	3,963,429	3,952,025	30.3	−0.29

[1]Negligible.

Geology

The Continents

Figures given are approximate. Area and population as of 2009. Highest and lowest points listed are all given in relation to sea level.

CONTINENT	POPULATION	AREA	% OF TOTAL LAND AREA[1]	HIGHEST/LOWEST POINT
Africa	1,004,139,100	30,270,144 sq km 11,687,458 sq mi	20.2	Mt. Kilimanjaro (Tanzania): 5,895 m (19,340 ft) Lake Assal (Djibouti): −157 m (−515 ft)
Antarctica	N/A	14,200,000 sq km 5,500,000 sq mi	9.5	Vinson Massif: 4,892 m (16,050 ft) Bentley Subglacial Trench: −2,500 m (−8,200 ft)
Asia	4,110,089,000	31,788,350 sq km 12,273,581 sq mi	21.1	Mt. Everest (China/Nepal): 8,850 m (29,035 ft) Dead Sea (Israel/Jordan): −400 m (−1,312 ft)
Europe	737,062,400	23,041,268 sq km 8,896,280 sq mi	15.4	Mont Blanc (France/Italy/Switzerland); 4,807 m (15,771 ft) Caspian Sea (Russia): −27 m (−90 ft)
North America	528,435,200	24,393,963 sq km 9,418,562 sq mi	16.3	Mt. McKinley (Alaska): 6,194 m (20,320 ft) Death Valley (California): −86 m (−282 ft)
Australia (and Oceania)	35,144,650	8,515,098 sq km 3,287,699 sq mi	5.7	Jaya Peak (Indonesia): 5,030 m (16,500 ft) Lake Eyre (Australia): −15 m (−50 ft)
South America	385,813,500	17,824,370 sq km 6,882,027 sq mi	11.9	Mt. Aconcagua (Argentina/Chile): 6,959 m (22,834 ft) Valdés Peninsula (Argentina): −40 m (−131 ft)

[1]Together, the continents make up about 29.2% of the Earth's surface.

Geologic Time Scale

Eon	Era	Period	Epoch	Age	mya[1]
Phanerozoic	Cenozoic	Quaternary	Holocene		
			Pleistocene	Tarantian	0.0117
				"Ionian"	0.126
				Calabrian	0.781
				Gelasian	1.806
		Neogene	Pliocene	Piacenzian	2.588
				Zanclean	3.600
			Miocene	Messinian	5.332
				Tortonian	7.246
				Serravallian	11.608
				Langhian	13.82
				Burdigalian	15.97
				Aquitanian	20.43
		Paleogene	Oligocene	Chattian	23.03
				Rupelian	28.4 ± 0.1
			Eocene	Priabonian	33.9 ± 0.1
				Bartonian	37.2 ± 0.1
				Lutetian	40.4 ± 0.2
				Ypresian	48.6 ± 0.2
			Paleocene	Thanetian	55.8 ± 0.2
				Selandian	58.7 ± 0.2
				Danian	~61.1
	Mesozoic	Cretaceous	Upper	Maastrichtian	65.5 ± 0.3
				Campanian	70.6 ± 0.6
				Santonian	83.5 ± 0.7
				Coniacian	85.8 ± 0.7
				Turonian	~88.6
				Cenomanian	93.6 ± 0.8
			Lower	Albian	99.6 ± 0.9
				Aptian	112.0 ± 1.0
				Barremian	125.0 ± 1.0
				Hauterivian	130.0 ± 1.5
				Valanginian	~133.9
				Berriasian	140.2 ± 3.0
					145.5 ± 4.0

Eon	Era	Period	Epoch	Age	mya[1]
Phanerozoic	Mesozoic	Jurassic	Upper	Tithonian	145.5 ± 4.0
				Kimmeridgian	150.8 ± 4.0
				Oxfordian	~155.6
			Middle	Callovian	161.2 ± 4.0
				Bathonian	164.7 ± 4.0
				Bajocian	167.7 ± 3.5
				Aalenian	171.6 ± 3.0
			Lower	Toarcian	175.6 ± 2.0
				Pliensbachian	183.0 ± 1.5
				Sinemurian	189.6 ± 1.5
				Hettangian	196.5 ± 1.0
		Triassic	Upper	Rhaetian	199.6 ± 0.6
				Norian	203.6 ± 1.5
				Carnian	216.5 ± 2.0
			Middle	Ladinian	~228.7
				Anisian	237.0 ± 2.0
			Lower	Olenekian	~245.9
				Induan	~249.5
	Paleozoic	Permian	Lopingian	Changhsingian	251.0 ± 0.4
				Wuchiapingian	253.8 ± 0.7
			Guadalupian	Capitanian	260.4 ± 0.7
				Wordian	265.8 ± 0.7
				Roadian	268.0 ± 0.7
			Cisuralian	Kungurian	270.6 ± 0.7
				Artinskian	275.6 ± 0.7
				Sakmarian	284.4 ± 0.7
				Asselian	294.6 ± 0.8
		Carboniferous (Pennsylvanian[2])	Upper	Gzhelian	299.0 ± 0.8
				Kasimovian	303.4 ± 0.9
			Middle	Moscovian	307.2 ± 1.0
			Lower	Bashkirian	311.7 ± 1.1
		Carboniferous (Mississippian[2])	Upper	Serpukhovian	318.1 ± 1.3
			Middle	Visean	328.3 ± 1.6
			Lower	Tournaisian	345.3 ± 2.1
					359.2 ± 2.5

Eon	Era	Period	Epoch	Age	mya[1]
Phanerozoic	Paleozoic	Devonian	Upper	Famennian	359.2 ± 2.5
				Frasnian	374.5 ± 2.6
			Middle	Givetian	385.3 ± 2.6
				Eifelian	391.8 ± 2.7
			Lower	Emsian	397.5 ± 2.7
				Pragian	407.0 ± 2.8
				Lochkovian	411.2 ± 2.8
		Silurian	Pridoli		416.0 ± 2.8
			Ludlow	Ludfordian	418.7 ± 2.7
				Gorstian	421.3 ± 2.6
			Wenlock	Homerian	422.9 ± 2.5
				Sheinwoodian	426.2 ± 2.4
			Llandovery	Telychian	428.2 ± 2.3
				Aeronian	436.0 ± 1.9
				Rhuddanian	439.0 ± 1.8
		Ordovician	Upper	Hirnantian	443.7 ± 1.5
				Katian	445.6 ± 1.5
				Sandbian	455.8 ± 1.6
			Middle	Darriwilian	460.9 ± 1.6
				Dapingian	468.1 ± 1.6
			Lower	Floian	471.8 ± 1.6
				Tremadocian	478.6 ± 1.7
		Cambrian[3]	Furongian	Stage 10	488.3 ± 1.7
				Stage 9	~492.0
				Paibian	~496.0
			Series 3	Guzhangian	~499.0
				Drumian	~503.0
				Stage 5	~506.5
			Series 2	Stage 4	~510.0
				Stage 3	~515.0
			Terreneuvian	Stage 2	~521.0
				Fortunian	~528.0
					542.0 ± 1.0

Precambrian

Eon	Era	Period	mya[1]
Proterozoic	Neoproterozoic	Ediacaran	542.0
		Cryogenian	~635.0
		Tonian	850.0
	Mesoproterozoic	Stenian	1,000.0
		Ectasian	1,200.0
		Calymmian	1,400.0
	Paleoproterozoic	Statherian	1,600.0
		Orosirian	1,800.0
		Rhyacian	2,050.0
		Siderian	2,300.0
Archean	Neoarchean		2,500.0
	Mesoarchean		2,800.0
	Paleoarchean		3,200.0
	Eoarchean		3,600.0
	Hadean (informal)		4,000.0
			4,600.0

[1] Millions of years ago.
[2] Both the Mississippian and Pennsylvanian time units are formally designated as subperiods within the Carboniferous Period.
[3] Several Cambrian unit age boundaries are informal and are awaiting ratified definitions.

Published with permission from the International Commission on Stratigraphy (ICS). International chronostratigraphic units, ranks, names, and formal status are approved by the ICS and ratified by the International Union of Geological Sciences (IUGS). Source: 2009 International Stratigraphic Chart produced by the ICS.

Geography

Largest Islands of the World

NAME AND LOCATION	REGION	AREA[1] SQ MI	SQ KM
Greenland	North America	836,330	2,166,086
New Guinea, Papua New Guinea/Indonesia	Oceania	309,000	800,000
Borneo, Indonesia/Malaysia/Brunei	Asia	292,000	755,000
Madagascar	Africa	226,662	587,051
Baffin, Nunavut, Canada	North America	195,928	507,451
Sumatra, Indonesia	Asia	170,233	446,687
Great Britain, UK	Europe	88,394	228,938
Honshu, Japan	Asia	87,992	227,898
Victoria, Northwest Territories/Nunavut, Canada	North America	83,896	217,291
Ellesmere, Nunavut, Canada	North America	75,767	196,236
Celebes, Indonesia	Asia	74,845	193,847
South Island, New Zealand	Oceania	58,776	152,229
Java, Indonesia	Asia	49,926	129,307
North Island, New Zealand	Oceania	44,872	116,219
Cuba	North America	42,427	109,886
Newfoundland, Canada	North America	42,031	108,860
Luzon, Philippines	Asia	40,420	104,688
Iceland	Europe	39,769	103,000
Mindanao, Philippines	Asia	36,537	94,630
Ireland, Ireland/UK	Europe	32,590	84,408

[1]Area given may include small adjoining islands. Conversions for rounded figures may be rounded to the nearest hundred.

Highest Mountains of the World by Region

"I" in the name of a peak refers to the highest in a group of numbered peaks of the same name.

NAME AND LOCATION	HEIGHT IN M	HEIGHT IN FT	YEAR FIRST CLIMBED
Africa			
Kilimanjaro (Kibo peak), Tanzania	5,895	19,340	1889
Kenya (Batian peak), Kenya	5,199	17,058	1899
Margherita, Ruwenzori Range, Dem. Rep. of the Congo/Uganda	5,119	16,795	1906
Ras Dejen, Simen Mtns., Ethiopia	4,533	14,872	1841
Antarctica			
Vinson Massif, Sentinel Range, Ellsworth Mtns.	4,892	16,050	1966
Tyree, Sentinel Range, Ellsworth Mtns.	4,852	15,918	1967
Shinn, Sentinel Range, Ellsworth Mtns.	4,660	15,289	1966
Gardner, Sentinel Range, Ellsworth Mtns.	4,573	15,003	1966
Asia			
Everest (Chomolungma), Himalayas, China/Nepal	8,850	29,035	1953
K2 (Godwin Austen) (Chogori), Karakoram Range, Pakistan/China	8,611	28,251	1954
Kanchenjunga I, Himalayas, Nepal/India	8,586	28,169	1955
Lhotse I, Himalayas, Nepal/China	8,501	27,890	1956
Caucasus			
Elbrus, Russia	5,642	18,510	1874
Dykhtau, Russia	5,204	17,073	1888
Koshtantau, Russia	5,151	16,900	1889
Shkhara, Russia/Georgia	5,068	16,627	1888
Europe			
Mont Blanc, Alps, France/Italy/Switzerland	4,807	15,771	1786
Dufourspitze, Monte Rosa Massif, Alps, Switzerland/Italy	4,634	15,203	1855
Dom (Mischabel), Alps, Switzerland	4,545	14,912	1858
Weisshorn, Alps, Switzerland	4,505	14,780	1861

Highest Mountains of the World by Region (continued)

NAME AND LOCATION	HEIGHT IN M	HEIGHT IN FT	YEAR FIRST CLIMBED
North America			
McKinley, Alaska Range, Alaska	6,194	20,320	1913
Logan, St. Elias Mtns., Yukon, Canada	5,951	19,524	1925
Citlaltépetl (Orizaba), Cordillera Neo-Volcánica, Mexico	5,610	18,406	1848
St. Elias, St. Elias Mtns., Alaska/Canada	5,489	18,008	1897
Oceania			
Jaya (Sukarno) (Carstensz), Sudirman Range, Indonesia	5,030	16,500[1]	1962
Pilimsit (Idenburg), Sudirman Range, Indonesia	4,800	15,750[1]	1962
Trikora (Wilhelmina), Jayawijaya Mtns., Indonesia	4,750	15,580[1]	1912
Mandala (Juliana), Jayawijaya Mtns., Indonesia	4,700	15,420[1]	1959
South America			
Aconcagua, Andes, Argentina/Chile	6,959	22,834	1897
Ojos del Salado, Andes, Argentina/Chile	6,893	22,614	1937
Bonete, Andes, Argentina	6,872	22,546	1913
Mercedario, Andes, Argentina/Chile	6,770	22,211	1934

[1]Conversions rounded to the nearest 10 ft.

Major Caves and Cave Systems of the World by Continent

Source: Bob Gulden, National Speleological Society.

NAME AND LOCATION	DEPTH[1]		LENGTH[2]	
	FT	M	MI	KM
Africa				
Ifflis, Algeria	3,839	1,170	1.2	2.0
Boussouil, Algeria	2,641	805	2.0	3.2
Tafna (Bou Ma'za), Algeria	N/A	N/A	11.4	18.4
Tamdoun, Morocco	N/A	N/A	11.4	18.4
Asia				
Krubera, Georgia	7,188	2,191	8.2	13.2
Illyuzia-Mezhonnogo-Snezhnaya, Georgia	5,751	1,753	15.0	24.1
Air Jernih, Malaysia	1,165	355	109.2	175.7
Shuanghe Dongqun, China	1,946	593	74.4	119.8
Australia (and Oceania)				
Neide-Muruk, Papua New Guinea	4,127	1,258	10.6	17.0
Nettlebed, New Zealand	2,917	889	15.1	24.3
Bullita, Northern Territory, Australia	75	23	74.8	120.4
Bulmer, New Zealand	2,477	755	41.0	66.0
Europe				
Lamprechtsofen Vogelschacht, Austria	5,354	1,632	23.6	38.0
Gouffre Mirolda–Lucien Bouclier, France	5,335	1,626	8.1	13.0
Optimisticheskaya, Ukraine	49	15	143.0	230.1
Hölloch, Switzerland	3,079	939	121.7	195.9
North America				
Cuicateco, Mexico	4,869	1,484	16.3	26.2
Huautla, Mexico	4,839	1,475	38.6	62.1
Mammoth–Flint Ridge, Kentucky	379	116	367.0	590.6
Jewel, South Dakota	632	193	150.1	241.6
South America				
Collet, Brazil	2,201	671	N/A	N/A
Pumacocha, Peru	2,093	638	N/A	N/A
Boa Vista, Brazil	164	50	63.7	102.5
Barriguda, Brazil	200	61	18.6	30.0

[1]Below highest entrance.   [2]Explored portion of cave.

Major Deserts of the World by Continent

NAME AND LOCATION	AREA SQ KM	SQ MI	NAME AND LOCATION	AREA SQ KM	SQ MI
Africa			**Australia (continued)**		
Sahara, northern Africa	8,600,000	3,320,000	Great Sandy, northern	400,000	150,000
Kalahari, southwestern	930,000	360,000	Western Australia		
Africa			Gibson, Western Australia	156,000	60,000
Namib, southwestern	135,000	52,000	Simpson, Northern Territory	143,000	55,000
Africa					
Libyan, Libya, Egypt, and	N/A	N/A	**North America**		
Sudan			Great Basin, southwestern	492,000	190,000
			US		
Asia			Chihuahuan, northern	450,000	175,000
Arabian, southwestern Asia	2,330,000	900,000	Mexico		
Gobi, Mongolia and	1,300,000	500,000	Sonoran, southwestern US	310,800	120,000
northeastern China			and Baja California		
Rub' al-Khali, southern	650,000	250,000	Mojave, southwestern US	65,000	25,000
Arabian Peninsula					
Karakum, Turkmenistan	350,000	135,000	**South America**		
			Patagonian, southern	673,000	260,000
Australia			Argentina		
Great Victoria, Western	647,000	250,000	Atacama, northern Chile	140,000	54,000
and South Australia					

Major Volcanoes of the World by Continent

NAME AND LOCATION	ELEVATION M	FT	FIRST RECORDED ERUPTION	MOST RECENT ERUPTION
Africa				
Kilimanjaro, Tanzania[1]	5,895	19,340	N/A	N/A
Teide (Tenerife), Canary Islands	3,715	12,188	N/A	1909
Nyiragongo, Democratic Republic of the Congo	3,470	11,384	1884	2010
Nyamuragira, Democratic Republic of the Congo	3,058	10,033	1865	2010
Antarctica				
Erebus, Ross Island	3,794	12,447	1841	2010
Melbourne, Victoria Land	2,732	8,963	N/A	c. 1750
Belinda, Montagu Island	1,370	4,495	N/A	2007
Darnley, Sandwich Islands	1,100	3,609	1823	1956
Asia and Australia (and Oceania)				
Klyuchevskaya, Kamchatka, Russia	4,835	15,863	1697	2010
Mauna Kea, Hawaii	4,205	13,796	N/A	c. 2460 BC
Mauna Loa, Hawaii	4,170	13,681	N/A	1984
Kerinci, Sumatra, Indonesia	3,800	12,467	1838	2009
Europe				
Etna, Italy	3,330	10,925	N/A	2009
Eyjafjallajökull, Iceland	1,666	5,466	920	2010
Hekla, Iceland	1,491	4,892	1104	2000
Vesuvius, Italy	1,281	4,203	79	1944
North America				
Pico de Orizaba (Citlaltépetl), Mexico	5,675	18,619	N/A	1846
Popocatépetl, Mexico	5,426	17,802	1345	2010
Rainier, Washington	4,392	14,409	N/A	1894
Shasta, California	4,317	14,163	1786	1786
South America				
Guallatiri, Chile	6,071	19,918	1825	1960
Tupungatito, Chile	6,000	19,685	1829	1987
Cotopaxi, Ecuador	5,911	19,393	1532	1940
Láscar, Chile	5,592	18,346	1848	2007

[1]Includes three dormant volcanoes (Kibo, Mawensi, and Shira) that have not erupted in historic times.

Oceans and Seas

	AREA		VOLUME	
	SQ KM	SQ MI	CU KM	CU MI
Pacific Ocean				
without marginal seas	165,250,000	63,800,000	707,600,000	169,900,000
with marginal seas	179,680,000	69,370,000	723,700,000	173,700,000
Atlantic Ocean				
without marginal seas	82,440,000	31,830,000	324,600,000	77,900,000
with marginal seas	106,460,000	41,100,000	354,700,000	85,200,000
Indian Ocean				
without marginal seas	73,440,000	28,360,000	291,000,000	69,900,000
with marginal seas	74,920,000	28,930,000	291,900,000	70,100,000
Arctic Ocean	14,090,000	5,440,000	17,000,000	4,100,000
Gulf of Mexico and Caribbean Sea	4,320,000	1,670,000	9,600,000	2,300,000
Mediterranean and Black Seas	2,970,000	1,150,000	4,200,000	100,000
Bering Sea	2,304,000	890,000	3,330,000	80,000
Hudson Bay	1,230,000	470,000	160,000	40,000
North Sea	570,000	220,000	50,000	10,000
Baltic Sea	420,000	160,000	20,000	5,000
Irish Sea	100,000	40,000	6,000	1,000
English Channel	75,000	29,000	4,000	1,000

	AVERAGE DEPTH		
	M	FT	DEEPEST POINT
Pacific Ocean			
without marginal seas	4,280	14,040	Mariana Trench
with marginal seas	4,030	13,220	(11,034 m; 36,201 ft)
Atlantic Ocean			
without marginal seas	3,930	12,890	Puerto Rico Trench
with marginal seas	3,330	10,920	(8,380 m; 27,493 ft)
Indian Ocean			
without marginal seas	3,960	10,040	Sunda Deep of the Java
with marginal seas	3,900	12,790	Trench (7,450 m; 24,442 ft)
Arctic Ocean	1,205	3,950	(5,502 m; 18,050 ft)
Gulf of Mexico and Caribbean Sea	2,220	7,280	Cayman Trench (7,686 m; 25,216 ft)
Mediterranean and Black Seas	1,430	4,690	Ionian Basin (4,900 m; 16,000 ft)
Bering Sea	1,440	4,720	Bowers Basin (4,097 m; 13,442 ft)
Hudson Bay	128	420	(867 m; 2,846 ft)
North Sea	94	310	Skagerrak (700 m; 2,300 ft)
Baltic Sea	55	180	Landsort Deep (459 m; 1,506 ft)
Irish Sea	60	200	Mull of Galloway (175 m; 576 ft)
English Channel	54	180	Hurd Deep (172 m; 565 ft)

Major Natural Lakes of the World

Conversions for figures may have been rounded, thousands to the nearest hundred and hundreds to the nearest ten.

NAME	LOCATION	AREA SQ MI	AREA SQ KM	NAME	LOCATION	AREA SQ MI	AREA SQ KM
Caspian Sea	Central Asia	149,200	386,400	Tanganyika	eastern Africa	12,700	32,900
Superior	Canada/US	31,700	82,100	Great Bear	Canada	12,096	31,328
Victoria	eastern Africa	26,828	69,484	Nyasa (Malawi)	eastern Africa	11,430	29,604
Huron	Canada/US	23,000	59,600	Great Slave	Canada	11,030	28,568
Michigan	US	22,300	57,800	Erie	Canada/US	9,910	25,667

Did you know? Wall Street, which was recognized even before the Civil War as the financial capital of the US, is narrow and short, extending only about seven blocks across part of southern Manhattan in New York City. It was named for an earthen wall built by Dutch settlers in 1653 to repel an expected English invasion.

Longest Rivers of the World by Continent

This list includes both rivers and river systems. Conversions of rounded figures may be rounded to the nearest 10 or 100 miles or kilometers.

NAME	OUTFLOW	LENGTH	
		MI	KM
Africa			
Nile	Mediterranean Sea	4,132	6,650
Congo	South Atlantic Ocean	2,900	4,700
Niger	Gulf of Guinea	2,600	4,200
Zambezi	Mozambique Channel	2,200	3,540
Asia			
Yangtze	East China Sea	3,915	6,300
Yenisey-Baikal-Selenga	Kara Sea	3,442	5,539
Huang He (Yellow)	Gulf of Chihli	3,395	5,464
Ob-Irtysh	Gulf of Ob	3,362	5,410
Europe			
Volga	Caspian Sea	2,193	3,530
Danube	Black Sea	1,770	2,850
Ural	Caspian Sea	1,509	2,428
Dnieper	Black Sea	1,367	2,200
North America			
Mississippi-Missouri-Jefferson	Gulf of Mexico	3,710	5,971
Mackenzie-Slave-Peace	Beaufort Sea	2,635	4,241
Missouri-Jefferson	Mississippi River	2,540	4,088
St. Lawrence–Great Lakes	Gulf of St. Lawrence	2,500	4,000
Australia			
Darling	Murray River	1,702	2,739
Murray	Great Australian Bight	1,572	2,530
Murrumbidgee	Murray River	1,050	1,690
Lachlan	Murrumbidgee River	930	1,500
South America			
Amazon-Ucayali-Apurímac	South Atlantic Ocean	4,000	6,400
Paraná	Río de la Plata	3,032	4,880
Madeira-Mamoré-Guaporé	Amazon River	2,082	3,352
Juruá	Amazon River	2,040	3,283

Preserving Nature

US National Parks

Dates in parentheses indicate when the area was first designated a national park, in most cases under a different name. Web site: <www.nps.gov/parks.html>.

PARK	LOCATION	DESIGNATION DATE	SQ MI	SQ KM
Acadia	Bar Harbor ME	1929 (1919)	74	192
American Samoa	American Samoa	1993	14	36
Arches	Moab UT	1971	120	311
Badlands	southwestern South Dakota	1978	379	982
Big Bend	curve of the Rio Grande river, Texas	1944	1,252	3,243
Biscayne	near Miami FL	1980	270	699
Black Canyon of the Gunnison	near Montrose CO	1999	43	112
Bryce Canyon	Bryce Canyon, Utah	1928 (1924)	56	145
Canyonlands	near Moab UT	1964	527	1,366
Capitol Reef	near Torrey UT	1971	379	982
Carlsbad Caverns	near Carlsbad NM	1930	73	189
Channel Islands	Ventura CA	1980	75	194
Congaree	Hopkins SC	2003	34	88
Crater Lake	Crater Lake OR	1902	286	741
Cuyahoga Valley	near Cleveland and Akron OH	2000	51	133
Death Valley	Death Valley, California and Nevada	1994	5,219	13,518
Denali	central Alaska	1980 (1917)	9,492	24,584
Dry Tortugas	Key West FL	1992	101	262
Everglades	southern Florida	1947	2,358	6,107

US National Parks (continued)

PARK	LOCATION	DESIGNATION DATE	SQ MI	SQ KM
Gates of the Arctic	Bettles AK	1980	13,238	34,287
Glacier	northwest Montana	1910	1,584	4,102
Glacier Bay	Gustavus AK	1980	5,130	13,287
Grand Canyon	Grand Canyon, Arizona	1919	1,902	4,927
Grand Teton	Moose WY	1950 (1929)	484	1,255
Great Basin	near Baker NV	1986	121	313
Great Sand Dunes	Mosca CO	2004	132	343
Great Smoky Mountains	Tennessee and North Carolina	1934	815	2,110
Guadalupe Mountains	Salt Flat TX	1972	135	350
Haleakala	Kula, Maui HI	1960 (1916)	47	121
Hawaii Volcanoes	near Hilo HI	1961 (1916)	328	849
Hot Springs	Hot Springs AR	1921	9	22
Isle Royale	Houghton MI	1940	893	2,314
Joshua Tree	near Palm Springs CA	1994	1,591	4,120
Katmai	near King Salmon AK	1980	7,385	19,128
Kenai Fjords	Seward AK	1980	1,047	2,711
Kings Canyon	near Three Rivers CA	1940 (1890)	722	1,869
Kobuk Valley	Kotzebue AK	1980	2,672	6,920
Lake Clark	Port Alsworth AK	1980	6,297	16,309
Lassen Volcanic	Mineral CA	1916	166	430
Mammoth Cave	Mammoth Cave, Kentucky	1941	83	214
Mesa Verde	near Cortez and Mancos CO	1906	81	211
Mount Rainier	near Ashford WA	1899	368	954
North Cascades	near Marblemount WA	1968	1,069	2,769
Olympic	near Port Angeles WA	1938	1,442	3,734
Petrified Forest	Arizona	1962	146	379
Redwood	Crescent City CA	1968	172	445
Rocky Mountain	near Estes Park and Grand Lake CO	1915	415	1,076
Saguaro	Tucson AZ	1994	143	370
Sequoia	near Three Rivers CA	1890	631	1,635
Shenandoah	near Luray VA	1935	311	805
Theodore Roosevelt	Medora ND (south unit); near Watford City ND (north unit)	1978 (1947)	110	285
Virgin Islands	St. John, US Virgin Islands	1956	23	59
Voyageurs	International Falls MN	1975	341	883
Wind Cave	near Hot Springs SD	1903	44	115
Wolf Trap	Vienna VA	2002	130 acres	
Wrangell–St. Elias	near Copper Center AK	1980	20,587	53,320
Yellowstone	Idaho, Montana, and Wyoming	1872	3,468	8,983
Yosemite	in the Sierra Nevada, California	1890	1,189	3,081
Zion	Springdale UT	1919	229	593

Health

Worldwide Health Indicators

Column data as follows: **Life expectancy** in 2005; **Doctors** = persons per doctor[1]; **Infant mortality** per 1,000 births in 2005; **Water** = percentage (%) of population with access to safe drinking water in 2004; **Food** = percentage (%) of the FAO recommended minimum in 2004[2].

REGION/BLOC	LIFE EXPECTANCY		DOCTORS	INFANT MORTALITY	WATER	FOOD
	MALE	FEMALE				
World	**66.0**	**70.0**	**730**	**38.3**	**83**	**118**
Africa	**51.8**	**53.8**	**2,560**	**78.4**	**64**[3]	**103**
Central Africa	49.8	50.2	12,890	96.1	46[3]	80
East Africa	46.9	48.2	13,620	86.7	50[3]	86
North Africa	67.2	71.0	890	39.2	91	125
Southern Africa	47.8	51.2	1,610	55.1	85[3]	119
West Africa	47.7	49.7	6,260	94.3	65[3]	109
Americas	**71.5**	**77.6**	**520**	**17.1**	**91**[3]	**129**
Anglo-America[4]	75.0	80.4	370	6.2	100[3]	140
Canada	76.7	83.6	540	4.8	100	136
United States	74.8	80.1	360	6.4	100	141

Worldwide Health Indicators (continued)

REGION/BLOC	LIFE EXPECTANCY MALE	LIFE EXPECTANCY FEMALE	DOCTORS	INFANT MORTALITY	WATER	FOOD
Americas (continued)						
Latin America	69.4	76.0	690	23.6	91	123
Caribbean	67.5	71.6	380	29.4	79[3]	118
Central America	67.9	73.7	950	21.4	88[3]	106
Mexico	72.7	77.6	810	12.6	97	134
South America	68.9	76.2	710	26.3	86[3]	122
Andean Group	69.4	75.6	830	23.5	86[3]	108
Brazil	67.7	75.9	770	30.7	90	132
Other South America	72.1	79.4	410	17.5	82[3]	120
Asia	**67.2**	**70.3**	**970**	**39.6**	**81[3]**	**116**
Eastern Asia	71.2	75.0	610	22.3	78[5]	121
China	70.4	73.7	620	25.2	77	123
Japan	78.6	85.6	530	2.7	100	110
Republic of Korea	71.7	79.3	740	6.4	92	123
Other Eastern Asia	71.7	77.3	500	13.8	94[3]	93
South Asia	63.3	64.6	2,100	60.5	85[6]	108
India	63.6	65.2	1,920	56.3	86	112
Pakistan	64.7	65.5	1,840	76.2	91	100
Other South Asia	60.4	60.5	5,080	71.0	85[3]	97
Southeast Asia	66.8	71.9	3,120	33.9	82	123
Southwest Asia	67.3	71.9	610	35.5	85[3]	118
Central Asia	61.0	68.9	330	54.0	82[3]	99
Gulf Cooperation Council	73.4	77.5	620	12.7	95[3]	117
Iran	68.6	71.4	1,200	41.6	94	131
Other Southwest Asia	67.6	71.9	690	31.6	82[3]	119
Europe	**71.0**	**79.1**	**300**	**7.2**	**98[3]**	**130**
European Union (EU)	75.5	81.8	290	4.8	100[3]	137
France	76.7	83.8	330	3.6	100	142
Germany	75.8	82.0	290	4.1	100	131
Italy	77.6	83.2	180	5.9	100[3]	151
Spain	76.7	83.2	240	4.4	100	138
United Kingdom	75.9	81.0	720	5.1	100	137
Other EU	73.6	80.3	320	5.2	100[3]	133
Non-EU[7]	78.5	83.5	480	3.8	100[3]	131
Eastern Europe	62.3	73.8	290	11.7	95[3]	119
Russia	59.9	73.3	240	11.5	97	117
Ukraine	62.2	74.0	330	10.0	96	120
Other Eastern Europe	67.3	74.7	370	13.4	84[3]	121
Australia	**78.5**	**83.3**	**400**	**4.7**	**100**	**116**
Oceania	**74.5**	**79.4**	**480**	**14.7**	**50[8]**	**117**
Pacific Ocean Islands	68.3	73.3	770	30.1	67[3]	118

[1]Latest data available for individual countries. [2]The Food and Agriculture Organization of the United Nations (FAO) calculates this percentage by dividing the caloric equivalent to the known average daily supply of foodstuffs for human consumption in a given country by its population, thus arriving at a minimum daily per capita caloric intake. The higher the percentage, the more calories consumed. [3]Data for 2000. [4]Includes Canada, the US, Greenland, Bermuda, and St. Pierre and Miquelon. [5]Does not include Japan. [6]Includes Iran. [7]Western Europe only; includes Andorra, Faroe Islands, Gibraltar, Guernsey, Iceland, Isle of Man, Jersey, Liechtenstein, Monaco, Norway, San Marino, and Switzerland. [8]Does not include New Zealand.

Causes of Death, Worldwide, by Region

Global estimates for 2002 as published in the World Health Organization (WHO) World Health Report 2004. Regions are as defined by the WHO. Numbers are in thousands ('000).

LEADING CAUSES OF DEATH	ALL CATEGORIES (%)	ALL CATEGORIES	REGION AFRICA	REGION AMERICAS	REGION EASTERN MEDITERRANEAN	REGION EUROPE	REGION SOUTHEAST ASIA	REGION WESTERN PACIFIC
1 Ischemic heart disease	12.6	7,208	332	921	638	2,373	2,039	993
2 Cerebrovascular disease	9.7	5,509	309	452	227	1,447	1,069	1,957
3 Lower respiratory infections	6.8	3,884	1,104	223	348	280	1,453	471

Causes of Death, Worldwide, by Region (continued)

LEADING CAUSES OF DEATH	ALL CATE-GORIES (%)	ALL CATE-GORIES	AFRICA	AMERICAS	EASTERN MEDITER-RANEAN	EUROPE	SOUTHEAST ASIA	WESTERN PACIFIC
4 HIV disease	4.9	2,777	2,095	103	44	36	436	61
5 Chronic obstructive pulmonary disease	4.8	2,748	117	241	95	261	656	1,375
6 Perinatal conditions	4.3	2,462	554	175	303	65	1,012	349
7 Diarrheal diseases	3.2	1,798	707	57	259	16	604	154
8 Tuberculosis	2.7	1,566	348	46	138	69	599	366
9 Malaria	2.2	1,272	1,136	1	59	0	65	11
10 Trachea, bronchus, and lung cancers	2.2	1,243	17	231	27	366	174	427
11 Road traffic accidents	2.1	1,192	195	135	133	127	296	304
12 Diabetes mellitus	1.7	988	80	253	55	142	263	192
13 Hypertensive heart disease	1.6	911	60	135	97	179	152	284
14 Self-inflicted injuries	1.5	873	34	63	34	163	246	331
15 Stomach cancer	1.5	850	34	74	21	157	63	500
16 Cirrhosis of the liver	1.4	786	54	105	67	171	204	185
17 Nephritis and nephrosis	1.2	677	99	102	65	76	169	165
18 Colon and rectum cancers	1.1	622	20	109	15	228	63	186
19 Liver cancer	1.1	618	45	37	15	66	61	394
20 Measles	1.1	611	311	0	70	6	196	28
21 Violence	1.0	559	134	146	26	73	113	66
22 Congenital anomalies	0.9	493	56	58	83	38	149	108
23 Breast cancer	0.8	477	35	89	27	150	93	82
24 Esophagus cancer	0.8	446	22	32	16	48	82	245
25 Inflammatory heart disease	0.7	404	42	67	37	101	76	81

Ten Leading Causes of Death in the US, by Age

Preliminary data for 2007. Numbers in thousands. Rates per 100,000 population. Numbers are based on weighted data rounded to the nearest individual, so category percentages and rates may not add to totals given.
Source: National Vital Statistics Report, <www.cdc.gov/nchs>.

CAUSE	NUMBER	RATE	%
ALL AGES			
1 Diseases of heart	615,651	204.1	25.4
Ischemic heart disease	403,741	133.9	16.7
Heart failure	57,235	19.0	2.4
2 Malignant neoplasms	560,187	185.7	23.1
Neoplasms of the trachea, bronchus, and lung	158,258	52.5	6.5
Neoplasms of the colon, rectum, and anus	53,100	17.6	2.2
Neoplasms of the breast	40,514	13.4	1.7
3 Cerebrovascular diseases	133,990	44.4	5.5
4 Chronic lower respiratory diseases	129,311	42.9	5.3
5 Accidents	117,075	38.8	4.8
Motor-vehicle accidents	43,098	14.3	1.8
6 Alzheimer disease	74,944	24.8	3.1
7 Diabetes mellitus	70,905	23.5	2.9
8 Influenza and pneumonia	52,847	17.5	2.2
9 Nephritis, nephrotic syndrome, and nephrosis	46,095	15.3	1.9
10 Septicemia	34,851	11.6	1.4
All other causes	588,203	195.0	24.3
All causes, all ages	**2,424,059**	**803.7**	**100**
1–4 YEARS			
1 Accidents	1,566	9.5	33.7
Motor-vehicle accidents	529	3.2	11.4
All other accidents	1,037	6.3	22.3
2 Congenital malformations, deformations, and chromosomal abnormalities	506	3.1	10.9
3 Assault (homicide)	365	2.2	7.8

CAUSE	NUMBER	RATE	%
1–4 YEARS (CONTINUED)			
4 Malignant neoplasms	361	2.2	7.8
5 Diseases of heart	163	1.0	3.5
6 Influenza and pneumonia	106	0.6	2.3
7 Conditions of perinatal origin	77	0.5	1.7
8 Septicemia	74	0.4	1.6
9 Nonmalignant/unknown neoplasms	55	0.3	1.2
10 Cerebrovascular diseases	52	0.3	1.1
All other causes	1,326	8.1	28.5
All causes, 1–4 years	**4,651**	**28.2**	**100**
5–14 YEARS			
1 Accidents	2,157	5.4	35.4
Motor-vehicle accidents	1,264	3.1	20.8
All other accidents	893	2.2	14.7
2 Malignant neoplasms	929	2.3	15.3
3 Congenital malformations, deformations, and chromosomal abnormalities	356	0.9	5.8
4 Assault (homicide)	337	0.8	5.5
5 Diseases of heart	209	0.5	3.4
6 Intentional self-harm (suicide)	195	0.5	3.2
7 Influenza and pneumonia	111	0.3	1.8
8 Chronic lower respiratory diseases	98	0.2	1.6
9 Cerebrovascular diseases	85	0.2	1.4
10 Nonmalignant/unknown neoplasms	82	0.2	1.3
All other causes	1,532	3.8	25.2
All causes, 5–14 years	**6,091**	**15.2**	**100**

Ten Leading Causes of Death in the US, by Age (continued)

CAUSE	NUMBER	RATE	%
15–24 YEARS			
1 Accidents	15,356	36.1	45.4
Motor-vehicle accidents	10,507	24.7	31.1
All other accidents	4,849	11.4	14.4
2 Assault (homicide)	5,284	12.4	15.6
3 Intentional self-harm (suicide)	4,030	9.5	11.9
4 Malignant neoplasms	1,609	3.8	4.8
5 Diseases of heart	991	2.3	2.9
6 Congenital malformations, deformations, and chromosomal abnormalities	373	0.9	1.1
7 Cerebrovascular diseases	197	0.5	0.6
8 Pregnancy and childbirth	166	0.4	0.5
9 Septicemia	156	0.4	0.5
10 Influenza and pneumonia	154	0.4	0.5
All other causes	5,472	12.9	16.2
All causes, 15–24 years	**33,788**	**79.5**	**100**

CAUSE	NUMBER	RATE	%
25–44 YEARS			
1 Accidents	29,085	34.7	24.0
Motor-vehicle accidents	13,139	15.7	10.9
All other accidents	15,946	19.0	13.2
2 Malignant neoplasms	16,577	19.8	13.7
3 Diseases of heart	14,110	16.8	11.7
4 Intentional self-harm (suicide)	11,528	13.8	9.5
5 Assault (homicide)	7,457	8.9	6.2
6 HIV disease	4,552	5.4	3.8
7 Chronic liver disease and cirrhosis	2,849	3.4	2.4
8 Cerebrovascular diseases	2,568	3.1	2.1
9 Diabetes mellitus	2,495	3.0	2.1
10 Septicemia	1,191	1.4	1.0
All other causes	28,675	34.2	23.7
All causes, 25–44 years	**121,087**	**144.6**	**100**

CAUSE	NUMBER	RATE	%
45–64 YEARS			
1 Malignant neoplasms	152,059	198.5	32.4
2 Diseases of heart	100,751	131.6	21.5

CAUSE	NUMBER	RATE	%
45–64 YEARS (CONTINUED)			
3 Accidents	29,417	38.4	6.3
Motor-vehicle accidents	10,596	13.8	2.3
All other accidents	18,821	24.6	4.0
4 Chronic lower respiratory diseases	16,886	22.0	3.6
5 Diabetes mellitus	16,862	22.0	3.6
6 Cerebrovascular diseases	16,713	21.8	3.6
7 Chronic liver disease and cirrhosis	15,738	20.5	3.4
8 Intentional self-harm (suicide)	12,138	15.8	2.6
9 Septicemia	6,698	8.7	1.4
10 Nephritis, nephrotic syndrome, and nephrosis	6,604	8.6	1.4
All other causes	95,625	124.9	20.4
All causes, 45–64 years	**469,491**	**613.0**	**100**

CAUSE	NUMBER	RATE	%
65 YEARS AND OVER			
1 Diseases of heart	498,980	1,317.0	28.4
2 Malignant neoplasms	388,548	1,025.5	22.1
3 Cerebrovascular diseases	114,237	301.5	6.5
4 Chronic lower respiratory diseases	111,087	293.2	6.3
5 Alzheimer disease	74,106	195.6	4.2
6 Diabetes mellitus	51,359	135.6	2.9
7 Influenza and pneumonia	46,135	121.8	2.6
8 Nephritis, nephrotic syndrome, and nephrosis	38,249	101.0	2.2
9 Accidents	38,222	100.9	2.2
Motor-vehicle accidents	6,925	18.3	0.4
All other accidents	31,297	82.6	1.8
10 Septicemia	26,388	69.6	1.5
All other causes	372,161	982.3	21.2
All causes, 65 years and over	**1,759,472**	**4,643.9**	**100**

HIV/AIDS

Acquired immunodeficiency syndrome, or AIDS, is a fatal transmissable disorder of the immune system that is caused by the human immunodeficiency virus (HIV). HIV was first isolated in 1983. In most cases, HIV slowly attacks and destroys the **immune system**, leaving the infected individual vulnerable to malignancies and infections that eventually cause death. AIDS is the last stage of HIV infection, during which time these diseases arise. An average interval of 10 years exists between infection with HIV and development of the conditions typical of AIDS. **Pneumonia** and **Kaposi sarcoma** are two of the most common diseases seen in AIDS patients.

HIV is contracted through semen, vaginal fluid, breast milk, blood, or other body fluids containing blood. Health care workers may come into contact with other body fluids that may transmit the HIV virus, including amniotic and synovial fluids. Although it is a transmiss-

able virus, it is not contagious and cannot be spread through coughing, sneezing, or casual physical contact. Other **sexually transmitted diseases**, such as genital herpes, may increase the risk of contracting HIV through sexual contact.

The main **cellular target** of HIV is a special class of white blood cells critical to the immune system known as T4 helper cells. Once HIV has entered, it can cause these cells to function poorly or to die. A hallmark of the onset of AIDS is a drastic reduction in the number of helper T cells in the body. Two predominant strains of the virus, designated HIV-1 and HIV-2, are known. Worldwide the most common strain is HIV-1, with HIV-2 more common primarily in western Africa; the two strains act in a similar manner, but the latter causes a form of AIDS that progresses much more slowly.

Diagnosis is made on the basis of blood tests approved by the Centers for Disease Control and Pre-

HIV/AIDS (continued)

vention that may be administered by a health professional. Alternately, a home collection kit may be purchased. No vaccine or cure has yet been developed that can prevent HIV infection. Several **drugs** are now used to slow the development of AIDS, including azidothymidine (AZT). **Protease inhibitors**, such as ritonavir and indinavir, have been shown to block the development of AIDS, at least temporarily. Protease inhibitors are most effective when used in conjunction with two different reverse transcriptase inhibitors—the so-called triple-drug therapy.

HIV/AIDS is a major problem in developing countries, particularly sub-Saharan Africa. The most recent UN report states that at the end of 2008, as many as 35.8 million people were estimated to be living with HIV. In 2008 alone, as many as 3.0 million contracted the disease and up to 2.4 million died of it.

For confidential information on HIV/AIDS, call 1-800-342-AIDS.

Internet resource: <www.cdc.gov/hiv>.

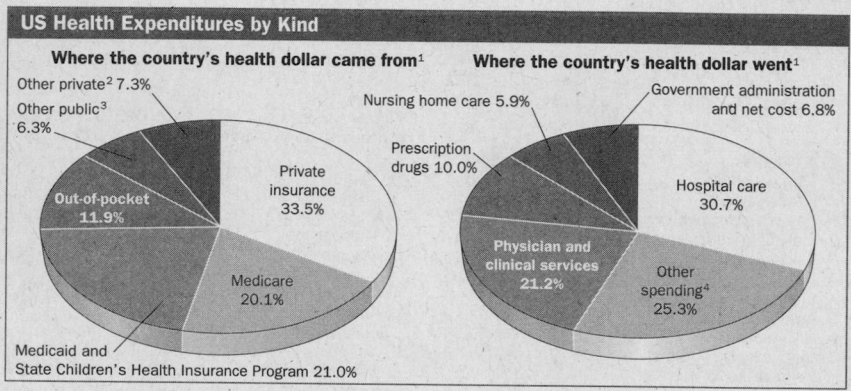

US Health Expenditures by Kind

Where the country's health dollar came from[1]

- Other private[2] 7.3%
- Other public[3] 6.3%
- Out-of-pocket 11.9%
- Private insurance 33.5%
- Medicare 20.1%
- Medicaid and State Children's Health Insurance Program 21.0%

Where the country's health dollar went[1]

- Nursing home care 5.9%
- Prescription drugs 10.0%
- Government administration and net cost 6.8%
- Hospital care 30.7%
- Physician and clinical services 21.2%
- Other spending[4] 25.3%

[1] Calendar year 2008. Detail may not add to 100% because of rounding.
[2] Other private includes industrial in-plant, privately funded construction, and non-patient revenues, including philanthropy.
[3] Other public includes programs such as workers' compensation, public health activity, US Department of Defense, US Department of Veterans Affairs, Indian Health Service, state and local hospital subsidies, and school health.
[4] Other spending includes dentist and other professional services, home health care, durable medical equipment, over-the-counter medicines and sundries, other nondurable medical products, government public health activities, and research and construction.
Source: Centers for Medicare and Medicaid Services, Office of the Actuary, National Health Statistics Group.

Sexually Transmitted Diseases (STDs)

Sexually transmitted diseases (STDs) are usually passed from person to person by direct sexual contact. They may also be transmitted from a mother to her child before or at birth or, less frequently, may be passed from person to person in nonsexual contact. STDs usually initially affect the genitals, the reproductive tract, the urinary tract, the oral cavity, the anus, or the rectum, but they may mature in the body to attack various organs and systems. Following are some of the major STDs:

Syphilis was first widely reported by European writers in the 16th century, and a virtual epidemic swept Europe around the year 1500. Syphilis is spread through direct contact with a syphilis sore (chancre); development of this sore is the first stage of the disease. The second stage manifests itself as a rash on the palms and the bottoms of the feet. In the last stage, symptoms disappear, but the disease remains in the body and may damage internal organs and lead to paralysis, blindness, dementia, and even death. For individuals infected less than a year, a single dose of penicillin will cure the disease. Larger doses are needed for those who have had it for a longer period of time.

Gonorrhea, a form of urethritis (an infection and inflammation of the urethra), is one of the most common STDs. Although spread through sexual contact, the gonorrhea infection can also be spread to other parts of the body after touching the infected area. Men manifest symptoms, which include discharge and a burning sensation when urinating, more often than women. If gonorrhea is left untreated, women may develop pelvic inflammatory disease (PID) and men may become infertile. The disease can also spread to the blood or joints and is potentially life threatening.

Chlamydia, another form of urethritis, can be transmitted during vaginal, anal, or oral sex. Since there are frequently no symptoms, most infected individuals do not know they have the disease until complications develop. Untreated chlamydia can cause pain during urination or sex in men and PID in women. Antibiotics can successfully cure the disease.

Genital herpes, a disease that became especially widespread in the 1960s and 1970s, often presents minimal symptoms upon infection. The most common sign, however, is blistering in the genital area; outbreaks can occur over many years but generally decrease in severity and number. Genital herpes is

Sexually Transmitted Diseases (STDs) (continued)

caused by the herpes simplex viruses type 1 (HSV-1) and type 2 (HSV-2). The former causes infections on and around the mouth but may be spread through the saliva to the genitals; the latter is transmitted during sexual contact with someone who has a genital infection. The HSV-2 infection can cause problems for people with suppressed immune systems and for infants who contract the disease upon delivery. Herpes can also leave individuals more susceptible to HIV infection and make those carrying the disease more infectious. A variety of treatments, including antiviral medications, have been used to help manage genital herpes, but currently there is no cure for the disease.

Internet resource:
<www.cdc.gov/nchhstp>.

Diet and Exercise

The Food and Drug Administration (FDA)

*The FDA is a division of the US Department of Health and Human Services. **FDA Web site:** <www.fda.gov>.*

Mission: To promote and protect the public health by helping safe and effective products reach the market in a timely way and monitoring products for continued safety after they are in use. **History:** The FDA celebrated its 100th anniversary in 2006, having been created by the passing of the Food and Drugs Act, or Wiley Act, in 1906. The Food, Drug, and Cosmetic Act of 1938 then brought cosmetics and medical devices under the authority of the FDA. The Food and Drug Administration Act of 1988 officially established the body as an agency of the Department of Health and Human Services, with a commissioner of food and drugs appointed by the president with the consent of the Senate. **Location:** Rockville MD (with a transfer to Silver Spring MD in progress and scheduled to be completed in 2012). **Commissioner of Food and**

Drugs: Margaret Hamburg. **Budget:** FY 2011 (requested) US$4.03 billion. **Functions:** The FDA is the agency of the US federal government authorized by Congress to inspect, test, approve, and set safety standards for foods and food additives, drugs, chemicals, cosmetics, and household and medical devices. Generally, the FDA is empowered to prevent untested products from being sold and to take legal action to halt the sale of undoubtedly harmful products or of products that involve a health or safety risk. Through court procedure, the FDA can seize products and prosecute the persons or firms responsible for legal violation. FDA authority is limited to interstate commerce. The agency cannot control prices nor directly regulate advertising except of prescription drugs and medical devices.

Body Mass Index (BMI)

The BMI is a measure expressing the relationship of weight to height determined by dividing body weight in kilograms by the square of height in meters (for convenience, the information has been converted to standard US measurements in the table below). It is more highly correlated with body fat than any other indicator of height and weight. The National Institutes of Health recommend using the BMI scale to help assess the risk of diseases and disabilities associated with an unhealthy weight. The BMI may overestimate body fat in athletes and others who have a muscular build, and it may underestimate body fat in older persons and others who have lost muscle mass.

Source: <www.nhlbi.nih.gov>.

HEIGHT (INCHES)	BODY WEIGHT (POUNDS)																				
58	91	96	100	105	110	115	119	124	129	134	138	143	148	153	158	162	167	172	177	181	186
59	94	99	104	109	114	119	124	128	133	138	143	148	153	158	163	168	173	178	183	188	193
60	97	102	107	112	118	123	128	133	138	143	148	153	158	163	168	174	179	184	189	194	199
61	100	106	111	116	122	127	132	137	143	148	153	158	164	169	174	180	185	190	195	201	206
62	104	109	115	120	126	131	136	142	147	153	158	164	169	175	180	186	191	196	202	207	213
63	107	113	118	124	130	135	141	146	152	158	163	169	175	180	186	191	197	203	208	214	220
64	110	116	122	128	134	140	145	151	157	163	169	174	180	186	192	197	204	209	215	221	227
65	114	120	126	132	138	144	150	156	162	168	174	180	186	192	198	204	210	216	222	228	234
66	118	124	130	136	142	148	155	161	167	173	179	186	192	198	204	210	216	223	229	235	241
67	121	127	134	140	146	153	159	166	172	178	185	191	198	204	211	217	223	230	236	242	249
68	125	131	138	144	151	158	164	171	177	184	190	197	203	210	216	223	230	236	243	249	256
69	128	135	142	149	155	162	169	176	182	189	196	203	209	216	223	230	236	243	250	257	263
70	132	139	146	153	160	167	174	181	188	195	202	209	216	222	229	236	243	250	257	264	271
71	136	143	150	157	165	172	179	186	193	200	208	215	222	229	236	243	250	257	265	272	279
72	140	147	154	162	169	177	184	191	199	206	213	221	228	235	242	250	258	265	272	279	287
73	144	151	159	166	174	182	189	197	204	212	219	227	235	242	250	257	265	272	280	288	295
74	148	155	163	171	179	186	194	202	210	218	225	233	241	249	256	264	272	280	287	295	303
75	152	160	168	176	184	192	200	208	216	224	232	240	248	256	264	272	279	287	295	303	311

BMI	19	20	21	22	23	24	25	26	27	28	29	30	31	32	33	34	35	36	37	38	39
			NORMAL						OVERWEIGHT							OBESE					

Food Guide Pyramid

In 2005 the USDA released an update of its food-pyramid guide to a healthy diet. It is designed to help individuals get proper nutrients while at the same time consuming the appropriate amount of calories necessary to maintain healthy weight. The 2005 pyramid also provides information about exercise and weight loss. Diets should be low in added sugars, salt, saturated fat and cholesterol and moderate in overall fat.

Find your balance between food and physical activity:

- Be sure to stay within your daily calorie needs.
- Be physically active for at least 30 minutes most days of the week.
- About 60 minutes a day of physical activity may be needed to prevent weight gain.
- For sustaining weight loss, at least 60 to 90 minutes a day of physical activity may be required.
- Children and teenagers should be physically active for 60 minutes every day or most days.

Recommended daily intake
These amounts are appropriate for individuals who get less than 30 minutes per day of moderate physical activity, beyond normal daily activities. Those who are more physically active may be able to consume more because they may have greater calorie needs.

MyPyramid.gov

	Grains	Vegetables	Fruits	Fats and Oils—limit your intake	Milk	Meat and Beans
Children 2–3 years old	3 ounce equivalents[1]	1 cup[2]	1 cup[3]		2 cups[4]	2 ounce equivalents[5]
Children 4–8 years old	4–5 ounce equivalents[1]	1.5 cups[2]	1–1.5 cups[3]		2 cups[4]	3–4 ounce equivalents
Girls 9–13 years old	5 ounce equivalents[1]	2 cups[2]	1.5 cups[3]		3 cups[4]	5 ounce equivalents
Boys 9–13 years old	6 ounce equivalents[1]	2.5 cups[2]	1.5 cups[3]		3 cups[4]	5 ounce equivalents
Girls 14–18 years old	6 ounce equivalents[1]	2.5 cups[2]	1.5 cups[3]		3 cups[4]	5 ounce equivalents[5]
Boys 14–18 years old	7 ounce equivalents[1]	3 cups[2]	2 cups[3]		3 cups[4]	6 ounce equivalents[5]
Women 19–30 years old	6 ounce equivalents[1]	2.5 cups[2]	2 cups[3]		3 cups[4]	5.5 ounce equivalents
Men 19–30 years old	8 ounce equivalents[1]	3 cups[2]	2 cups[3]		3 cups[4]	6.5 ounce equivalents
Women 31–50 years old	6 ounce equivalents[1]	2.5 cups[2]	1.5 cups[3]		3 cups[4]	5 ounce equivalents
Men 31–50 years old	7 ounce equivalents[1]	3 cups[2]	2 cups[3]		3 cups[4]	6 ounce equivalents
Women 51+ years old	5 ounce equivalents[1]	2 cups[2]	1.5 cups[3]		3 cups[4]	5 ounce equivalents
Men 51+ years old	6 ounce equivalents[1]	2.5 cups[2]	2 cups[3]		3 cups[4]	5.5 ounce equivalents

[1] 1 slice of bread, 1 cup of ready-to-eat cereal, or ½ cup of cooked rice, cooked pasta, or cooked cereal can be considered as 1 ounce equivalent from the grains group.

[2] 1 cup of raw or cooked vegetables or vegetable juice or 2 cups of raw leafy greens can be considered as 1 cup from the vegetable group.

[3] 1 cup of fruit or 100% fruit juice or ½ cup of dried fruit can be considered as 1 cup from the fruit group.

[4] 1 cup of milk or yogurt, 1½ ounces of natural cheese, or 2 ounces of processed cheese can be considered as 1 cup from the milk group.

[5] 1 ounce of meat, poultry, or fish, ¼ cup cooked dry beans, 1 egg, 1 tablespoon of peanut butter, or ½ ounce of nuts or seeds can be considered as 1 ounce equivalent from the meat and beans group.

Source: USDA.

Nutrient Composition of Selected Fruits and Vegetables

Values shown are approximations for 100 grams (3.57 oz.). Foods are raw unless otherwise noted. Source: USDA Nutrient Data Laboratory. kcal: kilocalorie; g: gram; mg: milligram; IU: international unit.

	ENERGY (KCAL)	WATER (G)	CARBO-HYDRATE (G)	PROTEIN (G)	FAT (G)	VITAMIN A (IU)	VITAMIN C (MG)	THIAMINE (MG)	RIBO-FLAVIN (MG)	NIACIN (MG)
Fruits										
Apple	59	83.93	15.25	0.19	0.36	53	5.7	0.017	0.014	0.077
Avocado	161	74.27	7.39	1.98	15.32	61	7.9	0.108	0.122	1.921
Banana	92	74.26	23.43	1.03	0.48	81	9.1	0.045	0.100	0.540
Blueberries	56	84.61	14.13	0.67	0.38	100	13.0	0.048	0.050	0.359
Cherries (sweet)	72	80.76	16.55	1.20	0.96	214	7.0	0.050	0.060	0.400
Grapes	67	81.30	17.15	0.63	0.35	100	4.0	0.092	0.057	0.300
Grapefruit	32	90.89	8.08	0.63	0.10	124	34.4	0.036	0.020	0.250
Lemon	29	88.98	9.32	1.10	0.30	29	53.0	0.040	0.020	0.100
Orange	47	86.75	11.75	0.94	0.12	205	53.2	0.087	0.040	0.282
Peach	43	87.66	11.10	0.70	0.09	535	6.6	0.017	0.041	0.990
Pear	59	83.81	15.11	0.39	0.40	20	4.0	0.020	0.040	0.100
Pineapple	49	86.50	12.39	0.39	0.43	23	15.4	0.092	0.036	0.420
Plum	55	85.20	13.01	0.79	0.62	323	9.5	0.043	0.096	0.500
Raspberries	49	86.57	11.57	0.91	0.55	130	25.0	0.030	0.090	0.900
Strawberries	30	91.57	7.02	0.61	0.37	27	56.7	0.020	0.066	0.230
Vegetables										
Asparagus[1]	24	92.20	4.23	2.59	0.31	539	10.8	0.123	0.126	1.082
Beans (snap, green)	31	90.27	7.14	1.82	0.12	668	16.3	0.084	0.105	0.752
Broccoli	28	90.69	5.24	2.98	0.35	1,542	93.2	0.065	0.119	0.638
Cabbage	25	92.15	5.43	1.44	0.27	133	32.2	0.050	0.040	0.300
Carrot	43	87.79	10.14	1.03	0.19	28,129	9.3	0.097	0.059	0.928
Cauliflower	25	91.91	5.20	1.98	0.21	19	46.4	0.057	0.063	0.526
Collards[1]	26	91.86	4.90	2.11	0.36	3,129	18.2	0.040	0.106	0.575
Corn (sweet, yellow)[1]	108	69.57	25.11	3.32	1.28	217	6.2	0.215	0.072	1.614
Mushroom[1]	27	91.08	5.14	2.17	0.47	0	4.0	0.073	0.300	4.460
Onion[1]	44	87.86	10.15	1.36	0.19	0	5.2	0.042	0.023	0.165
Pepper (sweet, red)	27	92.19	6.43	0.89	0.19	5,700	190.0	0.066	0.030	0.509
Potato[2]	93	75.42	21.56	1.96	0.10	0	12.8	0.105	0.021	1.395
Spinach	22	91.58	3.50	2.86	0.35	6,715	28.1	0.078	0.189	0.724
Sweet potato[2]	103	72.85	24.27	1.72	0.11	21,822	24.6	0.073	0.127	0.604
Tomato (red)	21	93.76	4.64	0.85	0.33	623	19.1	0.059	0.048	0.628

[1]Boiled.   [2]Baked.

Nutritional Value of Selected Foods

Values shown are approximations. Source: Home and Garden Bulletin No. 72, USDA. kcal: kilocalorie; g: gram; mg: milligram; oz: ounce; fl oz: fluid ounce.

FOOD	AMOUNT	GRAMS	ENERGY (KCAL)	CARBO-HYDRATE (G)	PROTEIN (G)	TOTAL FAT (G)	SATU-RATED FAT (G)	CALCIUM (MG)	IRON (MG)	SODIUM (MG)
Beverages										
Beer	12 fl oz	360	150	13	1	0	0	14	0.1	18
Cola, regular	12 fl oz	369	160	41	0	0	0	11	0.2	18
Cola, diet (w/aspartame and saccharine)	12 fl oz	355	0	0	0	0	0	14	0.2	32
Coffee, brewed	6 fl oz	180	0	0	0	0	0	4	0	2
Wine, table, red	3.5 fl oz	102	75	3	0	0	0	8	0.4	5
Dairy										
Butter, salted	4 oz	113	810	0	1	92	57.1	27	0.2	933
Cheese, American (pasteurized, processed)	1 oz	28.35	105	0	6	9	5.6	174	0.1	406
Cottage cheese, small curd	8 oz	210	215	6	26	9	6	126	0.3	850
Cream cheese	1 oz	28.35	100	1	2	10	6.2	23	0.3	84
Cream, sour	8 oz	230	495	10	7	48	30	268	0.1	123
Eggs, cooked, fried	1 egg	46	90	1	6	7	1.9	25	0.7	162
Ice cream, vanilla, 11% fat	8 oz	133	270	32	5	14	8.9	176	0.1	116
Milk, whole, 3.3% fat	8 oz	244	150	11	8	8	5.1	291	0.1	120

Nutritional Value of Selected Foods (continued)

FOOD	AMOUNT	GRAMS	ENERGY (KCAL)	CARBO-HYDRATE (G)	PROTEIN (G)	TOTAL FAT (G)	SATU-RATED FAT (G)	CALCIUM (MG)	IRON (MG)	SODIUM (MG)
Dairy (continued)										
Milk, low fat, 2% fat	8 oz	244	120	12	8	5	2.9	297	0.1	122
Milk, skim	8 oz	245	85	12	8	0	0.3	302	0.1	126
Yogurt, plain, low fat	8 oz	227	145	16	12	4	2.3	415	0.2	159
Fats, oils										
Margarine, hard, 80% fat	0.5 oz	14	100	0	0	11	2.2	4	0	132
Olive oil	0.5 oz	14	125	0	0	14	1.9	0	0	0
Vegetable shortening	0.5 oz	13	115	0	0	13	3.3	0	0	0
Fish										
Fish sticks, frozen	1 piece	28	70	4	6	3	0.8	11	0.3	53
Ocean perch, breaded, fried	1 piece	85	185	7	16	11	2.6	31	1.2	138
Oysters, raw	8 oz	240	160	8	20	4	1.4	226	15.6	175
Salmon, baked, red	3 oz	85	140	0	21	5	1.2	26	0.5	55
Shrimp, fried	3 oz	85	200	11	16	10	2.5	61	2	384
Tuna, canned, white, in water	3 oz	85	135	0	30	1	0.3	17	0.6	468
Fruits, fruit products										
Applesauce, canned, sweetened	8 oz	255	195	51	0	0	0.1	10	0.9	8
Pineapple, canned, heavy syrup	8 oz	255	200	52	1	0	0	36	1	3
Raisins	8 oz	145	435	115	5	1	0.2	71	3	17
Watermelon	1 piece	482	155	35	3	2	0.3	39	0.8	10
Grains										
Bagels, plain	1 bagel	68	200	38	7	2	0.3	29	1.8	245
Bread, rye, light	1 slice	25	65	12	2	1	0.2	20	0.7	175
Bread, white	1 slice	25	65	12	2	1	0.3	32	0.7	129
Bread, whole wheat	1 slice	28	70	13	3	1	0.4	20	1	180
Cereal, Cheerios	1 oz	28.35	110	20	4	2	0.3	48	4.5	307
Cereal, Kellogg's Corn Flakes	1 oz	28.35	110	24	2	0	0	1	1.8	351
Cereal, Lucky Charms	1 oz	28.35	110	23	3	1	0.2	32	4.5	201
Cereal, Post Raisin Bran	1 oz	28.35	85	21	3	1	0.1	13	4.5	185
Cake, white, w/white frosting, commercial	1 piece	71	260	42	3	9	2.1	33	1	176
Cheesecake	1 piece	92	280	26	5	18	9.9	52	0.4	204
Chocolate chip cookies, commercial	4 cookies	42	180	28	2	9	2.9	13	0.8	140
Doughnuts, cake, plain	1 doughnut	50	210	24	3	12	2.8	22	1	192
English muffins, plain	1 muffin	57	140	27	5	1	0.3	96	1.7	378
Oatmeal, instant, cooked, w/salt	8 oz	234	145	25	6	2	0.4	19	1.6	374
Popcorn, air-popped, unsalted	8 oz	8	30	6	1	0	0	1	0.2	0
Rice, brown, cooked	8 oz	195	230	50	5	1	0.3	23	1	0
Rice, white, instant, cooked	8 oz	165	180	40	4	0	0.1	5	1.3	0
Meat, poultry										
Bacon, regular, cooked	3 slices	19	110	0	6	9	3.3	2	0.3	303
Chicken, breast, roasted	3 oz	86	140	0	27	3	0.9	13	0.9	64
Chicken, drumstick, floured, fried	1.7 oz	49	120	1	13	7	1.8	6	0.7	44
Ham, roasted, lean and fat	3 oz	85	205	0	18	14	5.1	6	0.7	1009
Hamburger	4-oz patty	174	445	38	25	21	7.1	75	4.8	763
Lamb chops, braised, lean	1.7 oz	48	135	0	17	7	2.9	12	1.3	36
Turkey, roasted	8 oz	140	240	0	41	7	2.3	35	2.5	98
Nuts, legumes, seeds										
Peanuts, oil-roasted, unsalted	8 oz	145	840	27	39	71	9.9	125	2.8	22
Peanut butter	0.5 oz	16	95	3	5	8	1.4	5	0.3	75
Tofu	1 piece	120	85	3	9	5	0.7	108	2.3	8

Nutritional Value of Selected Foods (continued)

FOOD	AMOUNT	GRAMS	ENERGY (KCAL)	CARBO-HYDRATE (G)	PROTEIN (G)	TOTAL FAT (G)	SATU-RATED FAT (G)	CALCIUM (MG)	IRON (MG)	SODIUM (MG)
Sauces, dressings, condiments										
Catsup	0.5 oz	15	15	4	0	0	0	3	0.1	156
Cheese sauce w/milk, from mix	8 fl oz	279	305	23	16	17	9.3	569	0.3	1565
Mayonnaise	0.5 oz	14	100	0	0	11	1.7	3	0.1	80
Mustard, yellow	0.17 oz	5	5	0	0	0	0	4	0.1	63
Salad dressing, French	0.5 oz	16	85	1	0	9	1.4	2	0	188
Salad dressing, Italian, low calorie	0.5 oz	15	5	2	0	0	0	1	0	136
Sugars, sweets, miscellaneous snacks										
Chocolate, dark, sweet	1 oz	28.35	150	16	1	10	5.9	7	0.6	5
Potato chips	10 chips	20	105	10	1	7	1.8	5	0.2	94
Pudding, chocolate, instant	4 oz	130	155	27	4	4	2.3	130	0.3	440
Sugar, brown	8 oz	220	820	212	0	0	0	187	4.8	97
Sugar, white, granulated	8 oz	200	770	199	0	0	0	3	0.1	5

Reading Food Labels

The FDA requires most food manufacturers to provide standardized information about certain nutrients. Within strict guidelines the nutritional labels are designed to **aid the consumer in making informed dietary decisions** as well as to **regulate claims made by manufacturers** about their products.

The percent daily value is based on a 2,000-calorie-per-day diet. Some larger packages will have listings for both 2,000-calorie and 2,500-calorie diets. For products that require additional preparation before eating, such as dry cake mixes, manufacturers often provide two columns of nutritional information, one with the values of the food as purchased, the other with the values of the food as prepared.

The FDA selects mandatory label components (see sample label at right) based on current understanding of nutrition concerns, and **component order on the label is consistent with the priority of dietary recommendations**. Components that may appear in addition to the mandatory components are limited to the following: calories from saturated fat, polyunsaturated fat, monounsaturated fat, potassium, soluble fiber, insoluble fiber, sugar alcohol (for example, the sugar substitutes xylitol, mannitol, and sorbitol), other carbohydrate (the difference between total carbohydrate and the sum of dietary fiber, sugars, and sugar alcohol if declared), percent of vitamin A present as beta-carotene, and other essential vitamins and minerals. Any of these optional components that form the basis of product claims, fortification, or enrichment must appear in the nutrition facts. In 2006 labels were required to specify amounts of trans fatty acids.

Certain key descriptions are also regulated by the FDA. They include the following, in amounts per serving:

Low fat: 3 g or less
Low saturated fat: 1 g or less
Low sodium: 140 mg or less
Low cholesterol: 20 mg or less and 2 g or less of saturated fat
Low calorie: 40 calories or less

Dietary Guidelines for Americans, 2005
  Web site: <www.health.gov/dietaryguidelines>.

Nutrition Facts

Serving Size 1 cup (228g)
Servings Per Container 2

Amount Per Serving

Calories 250   Calories from Fat 110

                                        %Daily Value*

Total Fat 12g   **18%**

   Saturated Fat 3g   **15%**

   Trans Fat 3g

Cholesterol 30mg   **10%**

Sodium 470mg   **20%**

Potassium 700mg   **20%**

Total Carbohydrate 31g   **10%**

   Dietary Fiber 0g   **0%**

   Sugars 5g

Protein 5g

Vitamin A   **4%**

Vitamin C   **2%**

Calcium   **20%**

Iron   **4%**

*Percent Daily Values are based on a 2,000 calorie diet. Your Daily Values may be higher or lower depending on your calorie needs:

	Calories	2,000	2,500
Total Fat	Less than	65g	80g
Sat Fat	Less than	20g	25g
Cholesterol	Less than	300mg	300mg
Sodium	Less than	2,400mg	2,400mg
Total Carbohydrate		300g	375g
Dietary Fiber		25g	30g

Ways To Burn 150 Calories

Values shown are approximations. Activities are listed from more to less vigorous—the more vigorous an activity, the less time it takes to burn a calorie. When specific distances are given, the activity must be performed in the time shown (for example, one must run 1.5 miles in 15 minutes to burn 150 calories).

ACTIVITY	DURATION (MINUTES)	ACTIVITY	DURATION (MINUTES)
Climbing stairs	15	Raking leaves	30
Shoveling snow	15	Pushing a stroller 1.5 miles	30
Running 1.5 miles (10 minutes/mile)	15	Dancing fast	30
Jumping rope	15	Shooting baskets	30
Bicycling 4 miles	15	Walking 1.75 miles (20 minutes/mile)	35
Playing basketball	15–20	Gardening (standing)	30–45
Playing wheelchair basketball	20	Playing touch football	30–45
Swimming laps	20	Playing volleyball	45
Performing water aerobics	30	Washing windows or floors	45–60
Walking 2 miles (15 minutes/mile)	30	Washing and waxing a car or boat	45–60

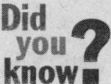

Did you know? In 17th-century Holland a speculative frenzy erupted over the sale of tulip bulbs. Tulips had been introduced into Europe from Turkey shortly after 1550. Demand for new varieties soon exceeded the supply, and prices rose to astonishing heights. The craze, known as the tulip mania, reached its peak in Holland in 1633–37. Homes, estates, and industries were mortgaged so that bulbs could be purchased; bulbs of rare varieties sold for the equivalent of hundreds of dollars each. The crash came in 1637, when almost overnight the price structure collapsed, sweeping away fortunes and leaving behind financial ruin for many Dutch families.

Target Heart Rate Training Zones

Measuring **target heart rate** involves monitoring your pulse periodically as you exercise. To use the Target Heart Rate chart:

1. Calculate your maximum heart rate by subtracting your age from 220.
2. Determine your target heart rate zone (50–70% of your maximum heart rate).
3. While exercising, monitor your pulse regularly. Count the number of beats for 10 seconds, then multiply by 6 to determine in what zone you are working.

The American Heart Association recommends using the target heart rate scale when participating in more vigorous athletic activity, such as jogging or aerobics. If your activity is moderate or taking your pulse is too bothersome, a "talk test" can be used as a substitute. If you can converse with someone with minimal effort, you are not working too hard. Alternately, if you can sing without difficulty, you are not working hard enough.

Note: For optimal cardiovascular fitness, you should work toward the middle of your 50 and 70% zones. Always check with your physician before starting any fitness routine, especially if you have heart or respiratory concerns.

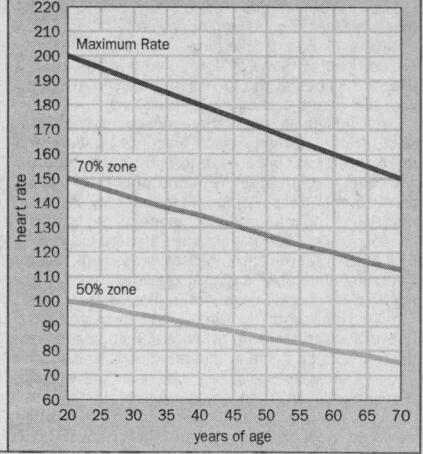

World

The World Cup and Africa's Future

by Alex Perry, TIME

When I moved with my young family to South Africa in 2006, the country was famous for three things—violent crime, AIDS, and Nelson Mandela—and the chances of encountering the first two seemed larger than meeting the third. We took a house on the outskirts of Cape Town protected by infrared beams, bars in the windows, metal "rape gates" in the doors, and, in the street outside, an armed private security patrol. After six months we were burgled; a year later it happened again.

But by then, reality was overtaking preconceptions. There was crime; a lingering, sometimes lethal racial intolerance; and an excruciating inequality between town and township. But that was offset by growing integration in the cities; rising affluence in places like Soweto, the huge African township on the edge of Johannesburg; and a new broad-mindedness that saw, for instance, the villagers of Limpopo accept as their champion the runner Caster Semenya, whose gender had been challenged after she won the world 800-m championship last year. The beauty of the place—the Cape sea, as cold and clear as ice, the stillness of the Karoo desert—lent the nation a serenity for which we were wholly unprepared.

Meanwhile, South Africa's preparations for the soccer World Cup, such as the building of new trains, rapid bus systems, and airports, spoke of a country on the move. Even the country's struggles gave it a vibrancy. Friends in England would talk property prices. Friends in South Africa would debate the country's future. After a year, we bought a house with a thatched roof and thick white-washed walls and, thinking we'd never find a better place to raise a family, decided to have another child, a third daughter born last month. When a friend used the Afrikaans phrase *vrek plek,* meaning "place to die in," to describe our new house, we understood that she was talking not about violent crime but a home.

If our ideas of the country were changing, so were my impressions of the continent. I'd read of an Africa trapped in a monotony of war, famine, genocide, and death. And the grim stories were there. But Somalia, Darfur, and Congo turned out to be the exceptions in a place where the norm was increasingly diverse, galloping opportunity. On my reporting trips, I was meeting coffee moguls in Rwanda, biofuel entrepreneurs in Liberia, offshore bankers in Mauritius, and jazz impresarios in Ethiopia. Moreover, if you were backing China, I realized, you were backing Africa, because China was backing Africa with billions a year. African growth was averaging 5% to 7%. Africa's middle class was bigger than India's.

But knowing, strangely, is not always believing. Archbishop Emeritus Desmond Tutu tells a story about visiting Nigeria from apartheid South Africa in the 1970s and the pride he felt at spotting two black pilots manning an internal flight—only to panic when the plant hit turbulence that "those blacks" would crash. Many South Africans were aware of the new reality but still imprisoned by their old perceptions. I knew Africa was changing, but making the continent's case in print was not the same as banishing the ingrained doubt from my mind.

It took an opening whistle to do that. If the big idea behind staging the World Cup in Africa was to change outside perceptions of the continent, the surprise bonus is that it has allowed Africans to believe in themselves. The arrival of hundreds of thousands of fans was sudden, giant, cacophonous confirmation. And just as our faith caught up with our facts, it got better. South Africa scored a beautiful first tournament goal. Ghana beat the US to reach the quarterfinals. Hardly a crime was reported.

Perhaps the most remarkable sight of the tournament came on its second day, outside the stadium in tiny, rural Phokeng. In the hours before the England-US game, 44,000 fans in face paint and fluorescent wigs stepped off their coaches into a dusty African village, asking if there was anywhere they could have a beer. After a few moments of hesitation, the owners of 10 houses and a local shop threw open their doors, set up giant *braais* (barbecues) of chicken in their yards, and started handing out quarts of cold beer. It was perhaps the most peaceful and gently inebriated meeting of two worlds in history.

The country had predicted a post-World Cup hangover for itself, but that didn't seem to happen, even after Nelson Mandela's grandchildren were threatened at gunpoint as they returned home from a party to celebrate his 92nd birthday in Johannesburg in a robbery gone wrong. The up mood also got an assist when Finance Minister Pravin Gordhan said the World Cup brought 38 billion rand (more than US$5 billion) into South Africa, exactly the amount the local organizing committee said staging the event cost.

After the Cup ended, Pres. Jacob Zuma unveiled plans to build 400,000 new homes by the time his term ends in 2014, to deliver improvements in the public-health system, to speed up the prosecution of corruption in the government, and to invest in more infrastructure such as power stations and public transport. "The inspiration to do more and achieve more is the primary legacy of the Cup," Zuma said.

Some of this will no doubt turn out to be puffery—particularly, more vague commitments to improve the lot of the young and of small farmers. Skeptics are also right to question the ability of a ruling party, the African National Congress, that in 16 years in power has, by its own admission, failed to deliver a better life to millions of poor, black South Africans. But in a country where, perhaps more than in any other, the word struggle describes righteous dedication as much as poverty, it seems possible that South Africans will remember the unity, jubilation, and accomplishment of the World Cup for some time to come.

Years of agonizing challenges no doubt lie ahead for Africa. But for a month, we've been living something wondrously different. At a rock concert in Soweto the night before the opening game, Tutu tried to put it into words. "Can you feel it?" he exclaimed. "You can touch it! It's unbelievable! I am in a dream!" He was—I think—talking about Africa's future. It is here.

Countries of the World

The information about the countries of the world that follows has been assembled and analyzed by *Encyclopædia Britannica* editors from hundreds of private, national, and international sources. Included are all the sovereign states of the world. The historical background sketches have been adapted, augmented, and updated from *Britannica Concise Encyclopedia* and the statistical sections from *Britannica World Data,* which is published annually in conjunction with the *Britannica Book of the Year.* The section called Recent Developments also has been adapted from material appearing in recent issues of the yearbook, as well as from other sources inside and outside Britannica. The locator maps have been prepared by Britannica's cartography department. Several countries, including those with the largest economies, are given expanded coverage in this section.

All information is the latest available to Britannica. It must be understood that in many cases it takes several years for the various countries or agencies to gather and process statistics—the most current data available will normally be dated several years earlier.

A few definitions of terms used in the articles may be useful. **GDP** (gross domestic product) is the total value of goods and services produced in a country during a given accounting period, usually a year. Typically the value is given in current prices of the year indicated. **GNI** (gross national income) is essentially GDP plus income from foreign transactions minus payments made outside the country. **Imports** are material goods legally entering a country (or customs area) and subject to customs regulations. The value of goods imported is given free on board (**f.o.b.**) unless otherwise specified; the value of goods exported and imported f.o.b. is calculated from the cost of production and excludes the cost of transport. The principal alternate basis for valuation of goods in international trade is that of cost, insurance, and freight (**c.i.f.**); its use is restricted to imports, as it comprises the principal charges needed to bring the goods to the customs house in the country of destination. **Exports** are material goods legally leaving a country and subject to customs regulations. Valuation of goods exported is virtually always f.o.b.

Afghanistan

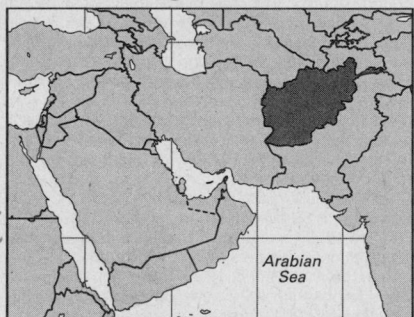

Arabian Sea

Official name: Islamic Republic of Afghanistan (Jomhuri-ye Eslami-ye Afghanestan [Dari (Persian)]; Da Afghanestan Eslami Jamhuriyat [Pashto]). **Form of government:** Islamic republic with two legislative houses (House of Elders [102]; House of the People [249]). **Head of state and government:** President Hamid Karzai (from 2002). **Capital:** Kabul. **Official languages:** Dari (Persian); Pashto; six additional languages have local official status per the 2004 constitution. **Official religion:** Islam. **Monetary unit:** 1 (new) afghani (Af) = 100 puls; valuation (1 Jul 2010) US$1 = Af 44.40.

Demography

Area: 249,347 sq mi, 645,807 sq km. **Population** (2009): 28,150,000. **Density** (2009): persons per sq mi 112.9, persons per sq km 43.6. **Urban** (2006): 21.5%. **Sex distribution** (2006): male 51.14%; female 48.86%. **Age breakdown** (2006): under 15,

44.6%; 15–29, 26.7%; 30–44, 16.0%; 45–59, 8.6%; 60–74, 3.5%; 75 and over 0.6%. **Ethnolinguistic composition** (2004): Pashtun 42%; Tajik 27%; Hazara 9%; Uzbek 9%; Chahar Aimak 4%; Turkmen 3%; other 6%. **Religious affiliation** (2004): Sunni Muslim 82%; Shi'i Muslim 17%. **Major cities** (2006): Kabul 2,536,300; Herat 349,000; Kandahar (Qandahar) 324,800; Mazar-e Sharif 300,600; Jalalabad 168,600. **Location:** southern Asia, bordering Uzbekistan, Tajikistan, China, Pakistan, Iran, and Turkmenistan.

Vital statistics

Birth rate per 1,000 population (2006): 46.6 (world avg. 20.3). **Death rate** per 1,000 population (2006): 20.3 (world avg. 8.5). **Total fertility rate** (avg. births per childbearing woman; 2006): 6.69. **Life expectancy** at birth (2006): male 43.2 years; female 43.5 years.

National economy

Budget (2006–07). *Revenue:* Af 155,394,000,000 (grants 78.1%; taxes on international trade 8.5%; nontax revenue 5.1%). *Expenditures:* Af 163,884,-000,000 (economic affairs 47.3%; general administration 10.9%; public order 9.1%; defense 7.8%). **Gross national income** (2007): US$10,137,000,000 (US$373 per capita). **Public debt** (external, outstanding; 2007): US$1,961,000,000. **Production** (metric tons except as noted). *Agriculture and fishing* (2006–07): wheat 3,363,000, barley 364,000, rice 361,000, opium poppy (2007) 8,200 (93% of world production); livestock (number of live animals) 9,259,000 sheep, 6,746,000 goats, 174,000 camels; fisheries production (2005) 1,000 (from aquaculture, none). *Mining and quarrying:* salt (2007) 123,000; chromite 6,800; gemstones, n.a.;

---

1 metric ton = about 1.1 short tons;   1 kilometer = 0.6 mi (statute);   1 metric ton-km cargo = about 0.68 short ton-mi cargo;   c.i.f.: cost, insurance, and freight;   f.o.b.: free on board

marble, n.a. *Manufacturing* (value added in Af '000,000; 2005–06): food products 48,575; chemical products 1,206; cement, bricks, and ceramics 809. *Energy production (consumption):* electricity (kW-hr; 2006–07) 916,900,000 (483,600,000); coal (metric tons; 2006) 33,000 (33,000); crude petroleum, n.a. (none); petroleum products (metric tons; 2006) none (186,000); natural gas (cu m; 2006) 20,000,000 (20,000,000). **Population economically active** (2006): total 8,207,000; activity rate of total population 31.5% (participation rates: ages 15–64, 60.3; female 23.1; unemployed [January 2009] 33%). **Selected balance of payments data.** Receipts from (US$'000,000): tourism (1998) 1.0; foreign direct investment (2005–07 avg.) 268; official development assistance (2007) 3,951.

Foreign trade

Imports (2006–07; c.i.f.): US$2,744,000,000 (machinery and apparatus 19.4%; household items and medicine 12.0%; food products 12.0%; base and fabricated metals 10.0%; mineral fuels 9.3%). *Major import sources* (2005–06): Japan 16.8%; Pakistan 15.9%; China 12.8%; Russia 9.2%; Uzbekistan 8.3%. **Exports** (2006–07; f.o.b.): US$416,000,000 (carpets and handicrafts 45.0%; dried fruits 30.3%; fresh fruits 9.4%; skins 5.5% [exports of illegal opiates equalled US$4,000,000,000 in 2007]). *Major export destinations* (2005–06): Pakistan 77.6%; India 6.0%; Russia 3.4%; UAE 2.9%.

Transport and communications

Transport. *Railroads* (2006): route length 10 km. *Roads* (2006): total length 42,150 km (paved 29%). *Vehicles* (2005): passenger cars 41,000; trucks and buses 100,000. *Air transport* (2004–05): passenger-km 681,000,000; metric ton-km cargo 20,624,000. **Communications,** in total units (units per 1,000 persons). Telephone landlines (2008): 101,000 (3.7); cellular telephone subscribers (2008): 7,899,000 (290); personal computers (2006): 1,400 (4); total Internet users (2007): 580,000 (21); broadband Internet subscribers (2007): 500 (0.02).

Education and health

Literacy (2006): total population ages 15 and over literate 28.1%; males 43.1%; females 12.6%. **Health** (2007): physicians 4,900 (1 per 5,000 persons); hospital beds 10,290 (1 per 2,381 persons); infant mortality rate per 1,000 live births (2006) 160.2.

Military

Total active duty personnel (April 2009): 82,780 (army 100%); foreign troops (April 2009): 42-country NATO-sponsored security and development force 58,400, of which US 26,200, UK 8,300, Germany 3,500, Canada 2,800, France 2,800, Italy 2,400. **Military expenditure as percentage of GDP** (2007): 1.6%; per capita expenditure US$6.

Background

The area was part of the Persian empire in the 6th century BC and was conquered by Alexander the Great in the 4th century BC. Hindu influence entered with the Hephthalites and Sasanians; Islam became entrenched about AD 870, during the rule of the Saf-

farids. Afghanistan was divided between the Mughal empire of India and the Safavid empire of Persia until the 18th century, when other Persians under Nadir Shah took control. Great Britain and Russia fought several wars in the area in the 19th century. From the 1930s Afghanistan had a stable monarchy; it was overthrown in the 1970s. The rebels' intention was to institute Marxist reforms, but the reforms sparked rebellion, and troops from the USSR invaded to establish order. Afghan guerrillas prevailed, and the Soviet Union withdrew in 1988–89. In 1992 an Islamic republic was established, and in 1996 the Taliban militia took power and enforced a harsher Islamic order. The militia's unwillingness to extradite Osama bin Laden and members of his al-Qaeda militant organization following the September 11 attacks in 2001 led to military conflict with the US and allied nations and the overthrow of the Taliban, and a multinational force continued to occupy the country in the early 21st century.

Recent Developments

The war in Afghanistan assumed a higher global profile as Taliban attacks inside Pakistan demonstrated the international character of the insurgency. US and NATO troop levels in Afghanistan rose above 140,000, most of them American. A report in September 2009 stated that civilian contractors working in the country outnumbered US troops there and that the ratio of contractors to soldiers was the highest in any war in which the US had taken part. After taking office in January, US Pres. Barack Obama authorized higher troop levels, and economic reconstruction and the training of Afghan forces became priorities. There was a new willingness on the part of the US to reach out to moderate Taliban, especially to those fighting for money rather than ideology. New strategies could not disguise growing tensions between the Afghan government and its international partners, however. NATO's air strikes continued to cause civilian casualties. Many Afghans openly criticized the foreign troops for not protecting the population. The 1,000th US soldier died in Afghanistan in May 2010. The following month—the deadliest for the US since the 2001 invasion—the war became America's longest.

Internet resource: <www.cso.gov.af>.

Albania

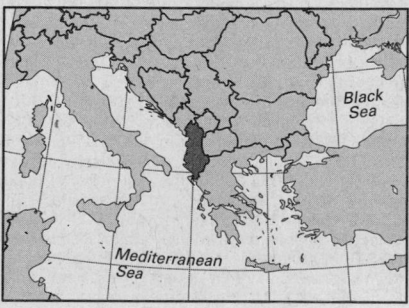

Official name: Republika e Shqipërise (Republic of Albania). **Form of government:** unitary multiparty republic with one legislative house (Assembly [140]).

Head of state: President Bamir Topi (from 2007). **Head of government:** Prime Minister Sali Berisha (from 2005). **Capital:** Tirana (Tiranë). **Official language:** Albanian. **Official religion:** none. **Monetary unit:** 1 lek = 100 qindarka; valuation (1 Jul 2010) US$1 = 111.08 leks.

Demography

Area: 11,082 sq mi, 28,703 sq km. **Population** (2009): 3,191,000. **Density** (2009): persons per sq mi 287.9, persons per sq km 111.2. **Urban** (2004) 44.5%. **Sex distribution** (2007): male 49.78%; female 50.22%. **Age breakdown** (2005): under 15, 25.3%; 15–29, 26.4%; 30–44, 19.9%; 45–59, 16.2%; 60–74, 9.2%; 75–84, 2.5%; 85 and over, 0.5%. **Ethnic composition** (2000): Albanian 91.7%; Greek 2.3%; Aromanian 1.8%; Rom 1.8%; other 2.4%. **Traditional religious groups** (2005): Muslim 68%, of which Sunni 51%, Bektashi 17%; Orthodox 22%; Roman Catholic 10%. **Major cities** (2001): Tirana (Tiranë) 343,078; Durrës 99,546; Elbasan 87,797; Shkodër 82,455; Vlorë 77,691. **Location:** southeastern Europe, bordering Montenegro, Kosovo, Macedonia, Greece, and the Mediterranean Sea.

Vital statistics

Birth rate per 1,000 population (2008): 11.4 (world avg. 20.3). **Death rate** per 1,000 population (2008): 5.1 (world avg. 8.5). **Total fertility rate** (avg. births per childbearing woman; 2008): 1.40. **Life expectancy** at birth (2008): male 72.9 years; female 77.8 years.

National economy

Budget (2006). *Revenue:* 229,444,000,000 leks (tax revenue 89.6%; nontax revenue 6.9%; grants 3.5%). *Expenditures:* 258,816,000,000 leks (social security and welfare 25.7%; transport and communications 11.8%; education 10.7%; general administration 10.3%; health 9.2%). **Gross national income** (2008): US$12,057,000,000 (US$3,840 per capita). **Public debt** (external, outstanding; end of 2007): US$2,150,000,000. **Production** (metric tons except as noted). *Agriculture and fishing* (2006): alfalfa for forage and silage 2,962,000, corn (maize) 245,400, wheat 230,900; livestock (number of live animals) 1,830,000 sheep, 940,000 goats, 634,000 cattle; fisheries production 7,699 (from aquaculture 26%). *Mining and quarrying* (2006): chromium ore 50,000. *Manufacturing* (value ▮▮▮▮ed in US$'000,000; 2005): basic chemical produ▮▮▮▮; textiles 33; base metals 32. *Energy production* (*consumption):* electricity (kW-hr; 2006) 5,094,000,000 (5,705,000,000); lignite (metric tons; 2006) 92,000 (105,000); crude petroleum (barrels; 2008) 2,190,000 ([2005] 2,950,000); petroleum products (metric tons; 2006) 271,000 (1,033,000); natural gas (cu m; 2006) 17,170,000 (17,170,000). **Population economically active** (2006): total 1,084,000; activity rate of total population 34.6% (participation rates: ages 15–64, 53.7%; female 39.6%; unemployed [2008] 13.0%). **Selected balance of payments data.** Receipts from (US$'000,000): tourism (2007) 1,002; remittances (2008) 1,495; foreign direct investment (FDI) 2005–07 avg.) 414; official development assistance (2007) 305. Disbursements for (US$'000,000):

tourism (2007) 923; remittances (2008) 10; FDI (2005–07 avg.) 10.

Foreign trade

Imports (2007; c.i.f.): 379,887,000,000 leks (machinery and apparatus 14.2%; food products 12.4%; chemical products 8.8%; refined petroleum products 7.1%; motor vehicles 6.4%; electricity 5.9%; clothing and wearing apparel 5.5%; iron and steel 5.3%). *Major import sources:* Italy 27.1%; Greece 14.6%; Turkey 7.3%; China 6.6%; Germany 5.5%. **Exports** (2007; f.o.b.): 97,456,000,000 leks (clothing and wearing apparel 26.9%; footwear 21.0%; metal ore and scrap 11.6%; mineral fuels 7.5%; locks and safes 4.4%). *Major export destinations:* Italy 68.1%; Greece 8.3%; Serbia (including Kosovo) 6.7%; China 2.6%; Germany 2.4%.

Transport and communications

Transport. *Railroads* (2007): operational route length 399 km; passenger-km 51,000,000; metric ton-km cargo 53,000,000. *Roads* (2002): total length 18,000 km (paved 39%). *Vehicles* (2007): passenger cars 237,932; trucks and buses 89,151. *Air transport* (2005; Albanian Air only): passenger-km 152,000,000. **Communications,** in total units (units per 1,000 persons). Telephone landlines (2008): 316,000 (100); cellular telephone subscribers (2008): 3,141,000 (989); personal computers (2007): 120,000 (38); total Internet users (2006): 471,000 (150); broadband Internet subscribers (2008): 36,000 (11).

Education and health

Educational attainment (2001). Population ages 20 and over having: no formal schooling/incomplete primary education 7.8%; primary 55.6%; lower secondary 2.7%; upper secondary 17.9%; vocational 8.8%; university 7.2%. **Literacy** (2006): total population ages 15 and over literate 98.7%. **Health:** physicians (2004) 3,699 (1 per 845 persons); hospital beds (2007) 9,191 (1 per 346 persons); infant mortality rate per 1,000 live births (2008) 6.0; undernourished population (2002–04) 200,000 (6% of total population based on the consumption of a minimum daily requirement of 1,980 calories).

Military

Total active duty personnel (November 2008): 14,295. **Military expenditure as percentage of GDP** (2008): 1.1%; per capita expenditure US$73.

Background

The Albanians are descended from the Illyrians, an ancient Indo-European people who lived in central Europe and migrated south by the beginning of the Iron Age. Of the two major Illyrian migrating groups, the Gegs (Ghegs) settled in the north and the Tosks in the south, along with Greek colonizers. The area was under Roman rule by the 1st century BC; after 395 AD it was connected administratively to Constantinople. Turkish invasion began in the 14th century and continued into the 15th century; though the national

1 metric ton = about 1.1 short tons; 1 kilometer = 0.6 mi (statute); 1 metric ton-km cargo = about 0.68 short ton-mi cargo; c.i.f.: cost, insurance, and freight; f.o.b.: free on board

hero, Skanderbeg, was able to resist them for a time, after his death (1468) the Turks consolidated their rule. The country achieved independence in 1912 and was admitted into the League of Nations in 1920. It was briefly a republic in 1925–28 and then became a monarchy under Zog I, whose initial alliance with Benito Mussolini led to Italy's invasion of Albania in 1939. After the war a socialist government under Enver Hoxha was installed. Gradually Albania cut itself off from the nonsocialist international community and eventually from all nations, including China, its last political ally. By 1990 economic hardship had produced antigovernment demonstrations, and in 1992 a noncommunist government was elected and Albania's international isolation ended. In the late 20th and early 21st centuries, Albania continued to experience economic uncertainty and ethnic turmoil, the latter involving Albanian minorities in Serbia and Macedonia.

Recent Developments

Albania formally applied for EU membership in April 2009. The EU considered the largely free and fair general elections held on 28 June to be a litmus test of the country's progress. In March 2010 the EU announced two projects, valued at more than US$3,850,000, to bring Albania's legal system and customs union in line with EU standards.

Internet resource: <www.instat.gov.al>.

Algeria

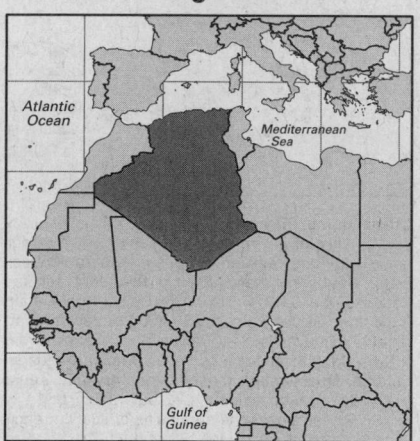

Official name: Al-Jumhuriyah al-Jazairiyah al-Dimuqratiyah al-Sha'biyah (Arabic) (People's Democratic Republic of Algeria). **Form of government:** multiparty republic with two legislative houses (Council of the Nation [144; includes 48 nonelected seats appointed by the president]; National People's Assembly [389]). **Head of state:** President Abdelaziz Bouteflika (from 1999). **Head of government:** Prime Minister Ahmed Ouyahia (from 2008). **Capital:** Algiers. **Official languages:** Arabic; Tamazight is designated as a national language. **Official religion:** Islam. **Monetary unit:** 1 Algerian dinar (DA) = 100 centimes; valuation (1 Jul 2010) US$1 = DA 75.27.

Demography

Area: 919,595 sq mi, 2,381,741 sq km. **Population** (2009): 35,369,000. **Density** (2009): persons per sq mi 38.5, persons per sq km 14.9. **Urban** (2005): 60.0%. **Sex distribution** (2008): male 50.52%; female 49.48%. **Age breakdown** (2007): under 15, 27.2%; 15–29, 32.1%; 30–44, 21.8%; 45–59, 11.9%; 60–74, 5.2%; 75–84, 1.5%; 85 and over, 0.3%. **Ethnic composition** (2000): Algerian Arab 59.1%; Berber 26.2%, of which Arabized Berber 3.0%; Bedouin Arab 14.5%; other 0.2%. **Religious affiliation** (2000): Muslim 99.7%, of which Sunni 99.1%, Ibadiyah 0.6%; Christian 0.3%. **Major cities** (2005): Algiers 1,532,000 (urban agglomeration [2007] 3,354,000); Oran 724,000; Constantine 475,000; Annaba (2004) 410,700; Batna (2004) 285,800. **Location:** northern Africa, bordering the Mediterranean Sea, Tunisia, Libya, Niger, Mali, Mauritania, Western Sahara, and Morocco.

Vital statistics

Birth rate per 1,000 population (2007): 17.1 (world avg. 20.3). **Death rate** per 1,000 population (2007): 4.6 (world avg. 8.5). **Total fertility rate** (avg. births per childbearing woman; 2007): 1.86. **Life expectancy** at birth (2007): male 71.9 years; female 75.2 years.

National economy

Budget (2007). *Revenue:* DA 3,688,500,000,000 (hydrocarbon revenue 75.8%; nonhydrocarbon revenue 24.2%). *Expenditures:* DA 3,092,700,-000,000 (current expenditures 54.1%; capital expenditures 45.9%). **Public debt** (external, outstanding; 2007): US$3,756,000,000. **Production** (metric tons except as noted). *Agriculture and fishing* (2006): wheat 2,687,930, potatoes 2,180,961, barley 1,235,880, dates 491,188, olives 364,733; livestock (number of live animals) 19,615,730 sheep, 3,754,590 goats; fisheries production 146,050 (from aquaculture, negligible). *Mining and quarrying* (2006): iron ore 1,996,000; phosphate rock 1,510,000; zinc (metal content) 572; liquid helium 15,000,000 cum. *Manufacturing* (value added in US$'000,000; 2005): food products and beverages 1,230; fabricated metal products 880; refined petroleum products and manufactured gas 720. *Energy production (consumption):* electricity (kW-hr; 2006) 35,226,-000,000 (35,308,000,000); coal (metric tons; 2006) none (948,000); crude petroleum (barrels; 2008) 485,000,000 ([2006] 148,550,000); petroleum products (metric tons; 2006) 38,294,000 (10,364,000); natural gas (cu m; 2006) 84,900,-000,000 (28,153,000,000). **Gross national income** (2008): US$146,365,000,000 (US$4,260 per capita). **Population economically active** (2006): total 10,109,600; activity rate of population 30% (participation rates: ages 15–64 [2004] 74%; female 16.9%; unemployed [June 2008] 12.3%). **Selected balance of payments data.** Receipts from (US$'000,000): tourism (2007) 219; remittances (2008) 2,202; foreign direct investment (FDI; 2005–07 avg.) 1,514; official development assistance (2007) 300. Disbursements for (US$'000,000): tourism (2007) 377; FDI (2005–07 avg.) 116.

Foreign trade

Imports (2006; c.i.f.): US$21,456,000,000 (food products and live animals 16.9%; nonelectrical machinery 16.0%; iron and steel 12.9%; motor vehicles 11.1%). *Major import sources:* France 20.4%; Italy 8.8%; China 8.0%; Germany 6.9%; US 6.6%. **Exports** (2006; f.o.b.): US$54,613,000,000 (crude petroleum 55.6%; natural gas 27.7%; manufactured gas 7.4%; refined petroleum products 7.2%). *Major export destinations:* US 27.2%; Italy 17.1%; Spain 11.0%; France 8.4%; Canada 6.6%.

Transport and communications

Transport. *Railroads* (2004): route length 3,973 km; (2003) passenger-km 946,000,000; metric ton-km cargo 2,041,000,000. *Roads* (2004): total length 108,302 km (paved 70%). *Vehicles* (2005): passenger cars 1,905,892; trucks and buses 1,068,520. *Air transport* (2007; Air Algérie only): passenger-km 3,162,000,000; metric ton-km cargo 2,420,000. **Communications,** in total units (units per 1,000 persons). Telephone landlines (2008): 3,068,000 (88); cellular telephone subscribers (2007): 27,562,000 (814); personal computers (2007): 377,000 (11); total Internet users (2007): 3,500,000 (103); broadband Internet subscribers (2007): 287,000 (8.4).

Education and health

Educational attainment (1998). Percentage of economically active population ages 6 and over having: no formal schooling 30.1%; primary education 29.9%; lower secondary 20.7%; upper secondary 13.4%; higher 4.3%; other 1.6%. **Literacy** (2005): total population ages 15 and over literate 76.3%; males literate 84.5%; females literate 68.0%. **Health:** physicians (2003) 36,347 (1 per 877 persons); hospital beds (2004) 55,089 (1 per 588 persons); infant mortality rate per 1,000 live births (2007) 29.8; undernourished population (2002–04) 1,400,000 (4% of total population based on the consumption of a minimum daily requirement of 1,870 calories).

Military

Total active duty personnel (November 2008): 147,000 (army 86.4%, navy 4.1%, air force 9.5%). **Military expenditure as percentage of GDP** (2007): 3.3%; per capita expenditure US$126.

Background

Phoenician traders settled the area early in the 1st millennium BC; several centuries later the Romans invaded, and by AD 40 they had control of the Mediterranean coast. The fall of Rome in the 5th century led to invasion by the Vandals and later by Byzantium. The Islamic invasion began in the 7th century; by 711 all of northern Africa was under the control of the Umayyad caliphate. Several Islamic Berber empires followed, most prominently the Almoravid (c. 1054–1130), which extended its domain to Spain, and the Almohad (c. 1130–1269). The Barbary Coast pirates, operating in the area, had menaced Mediterranean trade for centuries, and France seized this pretext to enter Algeria in 1830. By 1847 France had established control in the region, and by the late 19th century it had instituted civil rule. Popular movements resulted in the bloody Algerian War (1954–62); independence was achieved following a referendum in 1962. Beginning in the 1990s, Islamic fundamentalists opposing secular rule brought Algeria to a state of civil war.

Recent Developments

The group calling itself al-Qaeda in the Islamic Maghrib (formerly the Salafist Group for Preaching and Combat) continued to be a cause for concern in Algeria. At the end of May 2009, the group killed a British hostage in neighboring Mali, though it later released a Swiss hostage it had held in Mali for a US$4 million ransom. Because of such violence, Algeria joined a new 25,000-strong security force initiative with Sahel countries and the United States.

Internet resource: <www.algeria.com>.

Andorra

Official name: Principat d'Andorra (Principality of Andorra). **Form of government:** parliamentary coprincipality with one legislative house (General Council [28]). **Heads of state:** French President Nicolas Sarkozy (from 2007); Bishop of Urgell, Spain, Joan Enric Vives Sicília (from 2003). **Head of government:** Chief Executive Jaume Bartumeu Cassany (from 2009). **Capital:** Andorra la Vella. **Official language:** Catalan. **Official religion:** none. **Monetary unit:** 1 euro (€) = 100 cents; valuation (1 Jul 2010) US$1 = €0.80 (Andorra uses the euro as its official currency, even though it is not a member of the EU).

Demography

Area: 179 sq mi, 464 sq km. **Population** (2009): 85,200. **Density** (2009): persons per sq mi 476.0, persons per sq km 183.6. **Urban** (2003): 93%. **Sex distribution** (2005): male 52.16%; female 47.84%. **Age breakdown** (2007): under 15, 14.6%; 15–29, 19.0%; 30–44, 29.1%; 45–59, 20.8%; 60–74, 10.3%; 75–84, 4.2%; 85 and over, 2.0%. **Ethnic composition** (by nationality; 2007): Andorran 36.7%;

Spanish 33.0%; Portuguese 16.3%; French 6.3%; British 1.3%; Argentinian 0.8%; Moroccan 0.6%; other 5.0%. **Religious affiliation** (2000): Roman Catholic 89.1%; other Christian 4.3%; Muslim 0.6%; Hindu 0.5%; nonreligious 5.0%; other 0.5%. **Major towns** (2007): Andorra la Vella 21,556; Escaldes-Engordany 16,475; Encamp 8,704. **Location**: southwestern Europe, between France and Spain.

Vital statistics

Birth rate per 1,000 population (2007): 10.0 (world avg. 20.3). **Death rate** per 1,000 population (2007): 2.8 (world avg. 8.5). **Total fertility rate** (avg. births per childbearing woman; 2007): 1.17. **Marriage rate** per 1,000 population (2007): 3.1. **Life expectancy** at birth (2007): male 80.4 years; female 85.4 years.

National economy

Budget (2006). *Revenue*: €340,500,000 (indirect taxes 75.7%; property income 4.3%; other taxes and income 20.0%). *Expenditures*: €340,500,000 (current expenditures 53.5%; development expenditures 46.5%). **Production**. *Agriculture and fishing* (2006): tobacco 315 metric tons; other traditional crops include hay, potatoes, and grapes; livestock (number of live animals; 2007) 2,058 sheep, 1,478 cattle, 847 horses. *Quarrying*: small amounts of marble are quarried. *Manufacturing* (2006): manufactured goods include cigarettes, furniture, food products and beverages, newspapers and magazines, and worked metals. *Energy production (consumption)*: electricity (kW-hr; 2006) 73,900,000 ([2007] 577,000,000). **Population economically active** (2007): total 43,234; activity rate of total population 55% (participation rates: ages 15–64 [2003] 75.1%; female 46.6%; unemployed, n.a.). **Selected balance of payments data**. Disbursements for (US$'000,000): remittances (2001–02) 12. **Gross national income** (2007): US$3,250,000,000 (US$43,504 per capita). **Public debt** (2007): US$573,000,000.

Foreign trade

Imports (2007): €1,396,000,000 (machinery and apparatus 26.4%; food products and beverages 16.2%; motor vehicles 9.2%; wearing apparel and knitwear 9.1%; perfumes, cosmetics, and soaps 7.7%; mineral fuels 6.7%). *Major import sources*: Spain 58.7%; France 18.8%; Germany 5.1%; Italy 3.3%; Japan 2.7%. **Exports** (2007): €93,000,000 (electrical machinery and apparatus 25.0%; motor vehicles 18.5%; optical equipment, photographic equipment, and other precision instruments 10.9%; iron and steel products 6.8%; perfumes, cosmetics, and soaps 3.7%). *Major export destinations*: Spain 61.6%; France 16.2%; Germany 15.7%; Italy 2.2%.

Transport and communications

Transport. *Railroads*: none. *Roads* (1999): total length 269 km (paved 74%). *Vehicles* (2007): passenger cars 51,889; trucks and buses 5,395. **Communications**, in total units (units per 1,000 persons). Telephone landlines (2008): 37,000 (444); cellular telephone subscribers (2000): 64,000 (766); total internet users (2008): 59,000 (705); broadband Internet subscribers (2008): 21,000 (247).

Education and health

Literacy: resident population is virtually 100% literate. **Health** (2006): physicians 244 (1 per 327 persons); hospital beds 208 (1 per 385 persons); infant mortality rate per 1,000 live births (2006–07) 2.4; undernourished population, n.a.

Military

Total active duty personnel: none. France and Spain are responsible for Andorra's external security; the police force is assisted in alternate years by either French gendarmerie or Barcelona police. Andorra has no defense budget.

Background

Andorra's independence is traditionally ascribed to Charlemagne, who recovered the region from the Muslims in 803. It was placed under the joint suzerainty of the French counts of Foix and the Spanish bishops of the See of Urgell in 1278, and it was subsequently governed jointly by the Spanish bishop of Urgell and the French head of state. This feudal system of government, the last in Europe, lasted until 1993, when a constitution was adopted that transferred most of the coprinces' powers to the Andorran General Council, a body elected by universal suffrage. Andorra has long had a strong affinity with Catalonia; its institutions are based in Catalonian law, and it is part of the diocese of the See of Urgell (Spain). The traditional economy was based on sheep raising, but tourism has been very important since the 1950s.

Recent Developments

In an effort to improve fiscal and banking transparency, Andorra and France signed an agreement in September 2009 facilitating the exchange of tax information. Tourism remained the driving force of the Andorran economy, accounting for more than 80% of GDP. Andorra's unemployment rate stood officially at 0%.

Internet resource: <www.estadistica.ad>.

Angola

Official name: República de Angola (Republic of Angola). **Form of government**: unitary multiparty republic with one legislative house (National Assembly [220, excluding 3 unfilled seats reserved for Angolans living abroad]). **Head of state and government**: President José Eduardo dos Santos (from 1979). **Capital**: Luanda. **Official language**: Portuguese. **Official religion**: none. **Monetary unit**: 1 kwanza (AOA) = 100 cêntimos; valuation (1 Jul 2010) US$1 = kwanza 92.34.

Demography

Area: 481,354 sq mi, 1,246,700 sq km. **Population** (2009): 18,498,000. **Density** (2009): persons per sq mi 38.4, persons per sq km 14.8. **Urban** (2006): 55.8%. **Sex distribution** (2007): male 50.51%; female 49.49%. **Age breakdown** (2007): under 15 43.7%; 15–29, 27.1%; 30–44, 16.2%; 45–59, 8.5%; 60–74, 3.9%; 75–84, 0.6%; 85 and over, negligible. **Ethnic composition** (2000): Ovimbundu 25.2%; Kim-

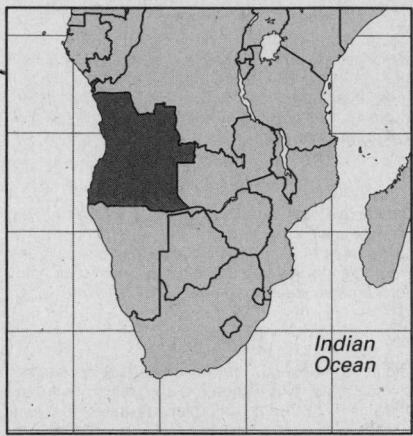

Indian
Ocean

bundu 23.1%; Kongo 12.6%; Lwena (Luvale) 8.2%; Chokwe 5.0%; Kwanyama 4.1%; Nyaneka 3.9%; Luchazi 2.3%; Ambo (Ovambo) 2.0%; Mbwela 1.7%; Nyemba 1.7%; mixed race (Eurafrican) 1.0%; white 0.9%; other 8.3%. **Religious affiliation** (2006): Roman Catholic 55%; independent Christian 30%, of which African indigenous 25%, Brazilian evangelical 5%; Protestant 10%; Muslim 0.7%; traditional beliefs/other 4.3%. **Major cities** (2004): Luanda (urban agglomeration; 2005) 2,766,000; Huambo 173,600; Lobito 137,400; Benguela 134,500; Namibe 132,900. **Location:** southern Africa, bordering the Democratic Republic of the Congo (DRC), Zambia, Namibia, and the Atlantic Ocean; the exclave of Cabinda on the Atlantic Ocean borders the Republic of the Congo and the DRC.

Vital statistics

Birth rate per 1,000 population (2007): 44.5 (world avg. 20.3). **Death rate** per 1,000 population (2007): 24.8 (world avg. 8.5). **Total fertility rate** (avg. births per childbearing woman; 2007): 6.27. **Life expectancy** at birth (2007): male 36.7 years; female 38.6 years.

National economy

Budget (2006). *Revenue:* US$20,966,000,000 (petroleum revenue 80.1%; nonpetroleum revenue 19.9%). *Expenditures:* US$14,269,000,000 (current expenditures 71.8%; development expenditures 28.2%). **Production** (metric tons except as noted). *Agriculture and fishing* (2006): cassava 8,810,000, sweet potatoes 685,000, potatoes 593,000, oil palm fruit 291,233; livestock (number of live animals) 4,150,000 cattle, 2,050,000 goats, 780,000 pigs; fisheries production 213,948 (from aquaculture, none). *Mining and quarrying* (2007): diamonds 9,702,000 carats; granite 46,000 cu m. *Manufacturing* (2005): fuel oil 609,000; diesel fuel 461,000; jet fuel 290,000. *Energy production (consumption):* electricity (kW-hr; 2006) 2,959,000,000 (2,959,-000,000); crude petroleum (barrels; 2008) 694,980,000 ([2006] 15,883,000); petroleum prod-

ucts (metric tons; 2006) 1,821,000 (2,075,000); natural gas (cu m; 2006) 793,000,000 (793,000,000). **Selected balance of payments data.** Receipts from (US$'000,000): tourism (2006) 75; foreign direct disinvestment (2005–07 avg.) −947; official development assistance (2007) 241. Disbursements for (US$'000,000): tourism (2006) 148; remittances (2008) 603; foreign direct investment (2005–07 avg.) 247. **Gross national income** (2008): US$62,113,000,000 (US$3,450 per capita). **Public debt** (external, outstanding; 2007): US$10,474,-000,000. **Population economically active** (2006): total 7,246,000; activity rate of total population 43.8% (participation rates: ages 15–64, 82.8%; female 46.7%; unemployed, n.a.).

Foreign trade

Imports (2006): US$10,776,000,000 (consumer goods 60.3%; capital goods 28.8%; intermediate goods 10.9%). *Major import sources* (2005): South Korea 20.5%; Portugal 13.4%; US 12.5%; South Africa 7.4%; Brazil 7.0%. **Exports** (2006): US$31,817,000,000 (crude petroleum 94.2%; diamonds 3.6%; refined petroleum products 0.9%). *Major export destinations* (2005): US 39.8%; China 29.6%; France 7.8%; Chile 5.4%; Taiwan 4.4%.

Transport and communications

Transport. *Railroads* (2008): route length of lines in operation 750 km; (2006; Benguela Railway only) passenger-km 69,900,000; (2006; Benguela Railway only) metric ton-km cargo 510,000. *Roads* (2006): total length 72,000 km (paved 25%). *Vehicles* (2001): passenger cars 117,200; trucks and buses 118,300. *Air transport:* passenger-km (2004) 479,000,000.

Education and health

Literacy (2006): percentage of population ages 15 and over literate 67.4%; males literate 82.9%; females literate 54.2%. **Health:** physicians (2004) 1,165 (1 per 9,890 persons); hospital beds (2005) 1,170 (1 per 10,000 persons); infant mortality rate per 1,000 live births (2007) 184.4; undernourished population (2002–04) 4,800,000 (35% of total population based on the consumption of a minimum daily requirement of 1,800 calories).

Military

Total active duty personnel (November 2008): 107,000 (army 93.5%, navy 0.9%, air force 5.6%). **Military expenditure as percentage of GDP** (2008): 3.9%; per capita expenditure US$194.

Background

An influx of Bantu-speaking peoples in the 1st millennium AD led to their dominance in the area by c. 1500. The most important Bantu kingdom was the Kongo; south of the Kongo was the Ndongo kingdom of the Mbundu people. Portuguese explorers arrived in 1483 and over time gradually extended their rule. Angola's frontiers were largely determined with other European nations in the 19th century, but not without

1 metric ton = about 1.1 short tons; 1 kilometer = 0.6 mi (statute); 1 metric ton-km cargo = about 0.68 short ton-mi cargo; c.i.f.: cost, insurance, and freight; f.o.b.: free on board

severe resistance by the indigenous peoples. Its status as a Portuguese colony was changed to that of an overseas province in 1951. Resistance to colonial rule led to the outbreak of fighting in 1961, which led ultimately to independence in 1975. Rival factions continued fighting after independence; although a peace accord was reached in 1994, forces led by Jonas M. Savimbi continued to resist government control. The killing of Savimbi in February 2002 changed the political balance and led to the signing of a cease-fire agreement in Luanda in April that effectively ended the civil war.

Recent Developments

The decline in oil prices slowed Angola's economic growth from 25% in 2008 to about 3% in 2009. Angola was one of Africa's two largest oil producers, together with Nigeria, and was China's largest oil supplier and African trading partner. Angola secured at least US$13 billion in oil-backed loans from China, a key participant in reconstructing Angola after its prolonged civil war.

Internet resource: <www.angola.org>.

Antigua and Barbuda

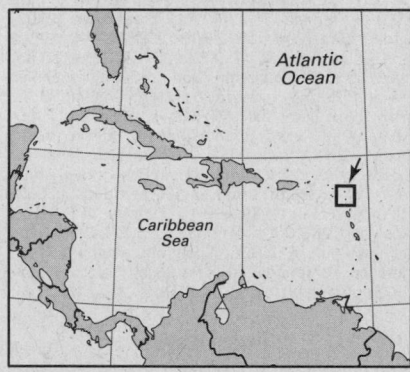

Atlantic Ocean

Caribbean Sea

Official name: Antigua and Barbuda. **Form of government:** constitutional monarchy with two legislative houses (Senate [17]; House of Representatives [17]). **Head of state:** British Queen Elizabeth II (from 1952), represented by Governor-General Louise Lake-Tack (from 2007). **Head of government:** Prime Minister Baldwin Spencer (from 2004). **Capital:** Saint John's. **Official language:** English. **Official religion:** none. **Monetary unit:** 1 Eastern Caribbean dollar (EC$) = 100 cents; valuation (1 Jul 2010) US$1 = EC$2.68.

Demography

Area: 171 sq mi, 442 sq km. **Population** (2009): 85,600. **Density** (2009): persons per sq mi 502.1, persons per sq km 193.8. **Urban** (2003): 37.7%. **Sex distribution** (2007): male 47.61%; female 52.39%. **Age breakdown** (2001): under 15, 27.0%; 15–29, 23.6%; 30–44, 23.3%; 45–59, 16.0%; 60–74, 6.7%; 75–84, 2.1%; 85 and over, 0.7%. **Ethnic composition** (2000): black 82.4%; US white 12.0%; mulatto 3.5%;

British 1.3%; other 0.8%. **Religious affiliation** (2001): Christian 74%, of which Anglican 23%, independent Christian 23%, other Protestant (including Methodist, Moravian, and Seventh-day Adventist) 28%; Rastafarian 2%; atheist/nonreligious 5%; other/unknown 19%. **Major settlements** (2006): Saint John's 25,300; All Saints 2,550; Liberta 1,680. **Location:** islands in the eastern Caribbean Sea.

Vital statistics

Birth rate per 1,000 population (2007): 17.0 (world avg. 20.3); (2001) within marriage 25.7%. **Death rate** per 1,000 population (2007): 6.4 (world avg. 8.5). **Total fertility rate** (avg. births per childbearing woman; 2007): 2.09. **Life expectancy** at birth (2007): male 71.9 years; female 75.7 years.

National economy

Budget (2007). *Revenue:* EC$718,300,000 (tax revenue 91.4%, of which taxes on international transactions 38.3%, taxes on income and profits 14.0%; current nontax revenue 5.1%; grants 2.8%; development revenue 0.7%). *Expenditures:* EC$923,800,000 (current expenditures 78.3%, of which transfers and subsidies 21.7%; development expenditures 21.7%). **Production** (metric tons except as noted). *Agriculture and fishing* (2007): mangoes, mangosteens, and guavas 1,430, melons 840, tomatoes 395, "Antiguan Black" pineapples 210; livestock (number of live animals) 19,000 sheep, 14,500 cattle; fisheries production (2006) 3,092 (from aquaculture, none). *Mining and quarrying:* crushed stone for local use. *Manufacturing:* manufactures include cement, bricks, and tiles, handicrafts, alcoholic and nonalcoholic beverages, and jams and jellies. *Energy production (consumption):* electricity (kW-hr; 2006) 116,000,000 (116,000,000); petroleum products (metric tons; 2006) none (139,000). **Population economically active** (2001): total 39,564; activity rate of total population 51.5% (participation rates: ages 15–64, 77.0%; female 50%; unemployed [2005] 4%). **Gross national income** (2008): US$1,165,000,000 (US$13,620 per capita). **Public debt** (external, outstanding; December 2007): US$615,400,000. **Selected balance of payments data.** Receipts from (US$'000,000): tourism (2007) 338; remittances (2008) 26; foreign direct investment (2005–07 avg.) 326; official development assistance (2007) 4. Disbursements for (US$'000,000): tourism (2007) 51; remittances (2008) 2.

Foreign trade

Imports (2007): US$573,000,000 (machinery and apparatus 20.3%; manufactured goods 16.3%; food products and live animals 15.0%; motor vehicles 8.1%; refined petroleum products 6.2%). *Major import sources:* US 58.2%; UK 6.4%; Japan 4.3%; Netherlands Antilles 4.2%; Trinidad and Tobago 3.9%. **Exports** (2007): US$99,000,000 (refined petroleum products 57.6%; telecommunications equipment 6.6%; generators 3.0%; sails 2.9%). *Major export destinations:* Netherlands Antilles 30.9%; US 23.5%; Barbados 8.2%; Dominica 6.1%; UK 4.2%.

Transport and communications

Transport. *Roads* (2002): total length 1,165 km (paved 33%). *Air transport* (2006): passenger-km

118,200,000; metric ton-km cargo 200,000. **Communications,** in total units (units per 1,000 persons). Telephone landlines (2008): 38,000 (450); cellular telephone subscribers (2008): 137,000 (1,616); total Internet users (2008): 65,000 (769); broadband Internet subscribers (2008): 13,000 (149).

Education and health

Educational attainment (2001). Percentage of population ages 25 and over having: no formal schooling 0.6%; incomplete primary education 2.6%; complete primary 27.9%; secondary 43.6%; higher (not university) 14.4%; university 10.9%. **Literacy** (2003): percentage of total population ages 15 and over literate 85.8%. **Health:** hospital beds (2009) 211 (1 per 420 persons); infant mortality rate per 1,000 live births (2007) 18.8.

Military

Total active duty personnel (November 2008): a 170-member defense force (army 73.5%, navy 26.5%) is part of the Eastern Caribbean regional security system. **Military expenditure as percentage of GDP** (2007): 0.5%; per capita expenditure US$61.

Background

Christopher Columbus visited Antigua in 1493 and named it after a church in Seville, Spain. It was colonized in 1632 by English settlers, who imported African slaves to grow tobacco and sugarcane. Barbuda was colonized by the English in 1678. In 1834 its slaves were emancipated. Antigua (with Barbuda) was part of the British colony of the Leeward Islands from 1871 until that colony was defederated in 1956. The islands achieved full independence in 1981.

Recent Developments

There were fears in the crucial tourism industry of Antigua and Barbuda after several high-profile crimes against tourists. In January 2009 an Australian man was murdered there, and a year later an American tourist was also killed. The murder rate—roughly 17 per 100,000 people in 2009—was worse than that of New York City, and several cruise lines rerouted their ships to avoid Antiguan stops.

Internet resource: <www.ab.gov.ag>.

Argentina

Official name: República Argentina (Argentine Republic). **Form of government:** federal republic with two legislative houses (Senate [72]; Chamber of Deputies [257]). **Head of state and government:** President Cristina Fernández de Kirchner (from 2007), assisted by Cabinet Chief Aníbal Fernández (from 2009). **Capital:** Buenos Aires. **Official language:** Spanish. **Official religion:** none (Roman Catholicism has special status and receives financial support from the state). **Monetary unit:** 1 peso (ARS) = 100 centavos; valuation (1 Jul 2010) US$1 = ARS 3.93.

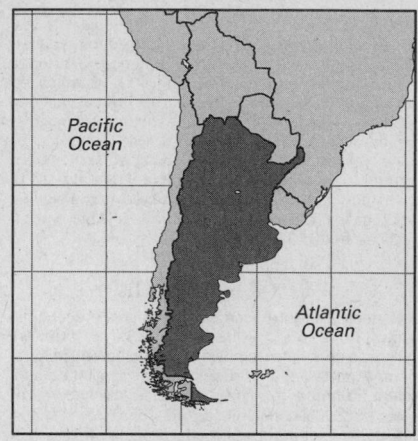

Demography

Area: 1,073,519 sq mi, 2,780,403 sq km. **Population** (2009): 40,276,000. **Density** (2009): persons per sq mi 37.5, persons per sq km 14.5. **Urban** (2005): 91.4%. **Sex distribution** (2007): male 49.23%; female 50.77%. **Age breakdown** (2007): under 15, 25.9%; 15–29, 24.9%; 30–44, 19.2%; 45–59, 15.4%; 60–74, 9.8%; 75–84, 3.6%; 85 and over, 1.2%. **Ethnic composition** (2000): European extraction 86.4%; mestizo 6.5%; Amerindian 3.4%; Arab 3.3%; other 0.4%. **Religious affiliation** (2005): Roman Catholic 70%; Protestant 9%; Muslim (mostly Sunni) 1.5%; Jewish 0.8%; nonreligious/unknown 16.2%; other (significantly Middle East–based Christian) 2.5%. **Major urban agglomerations** (2007): Buenos Aires 12,795,000; Córdoba 1,452,000; Rosario 1,203,000; Mendozá 918,000; San Miguel de Tucumán 832,000. **Location:** southern South America, bordering Bolivia, Paraguay, Brazil, Uruguay, the South Atlantic Ocean, and Chile.

Vital statistics

Birth rate per 1,000 population (2007): 18.3 (world avg. 20.3). **Death rate** per 1,000 population (2007): 7.5 (world avg. 8.5). **Total fertility rate** (avg. births per childbearing woman; 2007): 2.39. **Life expectancy** at birth (2007): male 72.9 years; female 79.6 years.

National economy

Budget (2008). *Revenue:* ARS 169,463,000,000 (indirect taxes 57.1%; social security contributions 23.7%; direct taxes 12.9%). *Expenditures:* ARS 161,486,000,000 (current expenditures 88.2%, of which social security 41.2%, debt service 11.9%, economic development 9.4%; capital expenditures 11.8%). **Public debt** (external, outstanding; 2007): US$66,110,000,000. **Gross national income** (2008): US$287,160,000,000 (US$7,200 per capita). **Production** (metric tons except as noted). *Agriculture and fishing* (2007): soybeans 45,500,000, alfalfa (2006) 38,783,332, corn (maize) 21,775,364, sunflower seeds 3,500,000, maté 270,000; livestock (number

---

1 metric ton = about 1.1 short tons;   1 kilometer = 0.6 mi (statute);   1 metric ton-km cargo = about 0.68 short ton-mi cargo;   c.i.f.: cost, insurance, and freight;   f.o.b.: free on board

of live animals) 50,750,000 cattle, 12,450,000 sheep, 3,680,000 horses; fisheries production (2006) 1,184,713 (from aquaculture, negligible). *Mining and quarrying* (2006): boron 533,535; copper (metal content) 180,144; silver 248,227 kg; gold 44,131 kg. *Manufacturing* (value added in US$'000,000; 2002): food products 10,152, of which vegetable oils and fats 3,864; base metals 4,031; industrial and agricultural chemical products 2,770; refined petroleum products 2,514. *Energy production (consumption):* electricity (kW-hr; 2007) 104,448,000,000 ([2006] 117,555,000,000); coal (metric tons; 2006) 427,000 (1,254,000); crude petroleum (barrels; 2008) 241,400,000 ([2006] 202,307,000); petroleum products (metric tons; 2006) 26,785,000 (22,541,000); natural gas (cu m; 2007) 59,484,000,000 ([2006] 45,641,000,000). **Selected balance of payments data.** Receipts from (US$'000,000): tourism (2007) 4,314; remittances (2008) 691; foreign direct investment (FDI; 2005–07 avg.) 5,341. Disbursements for (US$'000,000): tourism (2007) 3,921; remittances (2008) 732; FDI (2005–07 avg.) 1,542. **Population economically active** (2006): total 11,089,700; activity rate of total population 46.2% (participation rates: ages 15–64, 68.5%; female 43.4%; unemployed [April 2007– March 2008] 8.1%).

Foreign trade

Imports (2007; c.i.f.): US$44,707,000,000 (machinery and apparatus 30.3%; chemical products 18.5%; motor vehicles 15.0%; mineral fuels 6.0%). *Major import sources:* Brazil 32.8%; US 11.9%; China 11.4%; Germany 4.8%; Mexico 3.0%. **Exports** (2007; f.o.b.): US$55,780,000,000 (soybean animal foodstuffs 10.3%; motor vehicles 9.5%; cereals 9.3%; crude petroleum 8.4%; soybean oil 7.9%; soybeans 6.2%). *Major export destinations:* Brazil 18.8%; China 9.3%; US 7.8%; Chile 7.5%; Spain 3.7%.

Transport and communications

Transport. *Railroads* (2006): route length 30,818 km; (2005) passenger-km 8,327,000,000; (2001) metric ton-km cargo 12,262,000,000. *Roads* (2003): total length 231,374 km (paved 30%). *Vehicles* (2005): passenger cars 5,230,000; trucks and buses 1,775,000. *Air transport* (2007): passenger-km 14,616,000,000; metric ton-km cargo 130,668,000. **Communications**, in total units (units per 1,000 persons). Telephone landlines (2008): 9,631,000 (241); cellular telephone subscribers (2008): 46,509,000 (1,166); personal computers (2006): 3,500,000 (90); total Internet users (2008): 11,212,000 (281); broadband Internet subscribers (2008): 3,185,000 (80).

Education and health

Educational attainment (2001). Percentage of population ages 15 and over having: no formal schooling 3.7%; incomplete primary education 14.2%; complete primary 28.0%; secondary 37.1%; some higher 8.3%; complete higher 8.7%. **Literacy** (2005): percentage of total population ages 15 and over literate 97.5%. **Health:** physicians (2005) 120,978 (1 per 319 persons); hospital beds (2004) 76,446 (1 per 500 persons); infant mortality rate per 1,000 live births (2007) 12.1; undernourished population (2002–04) 1,200,000 (3% of total population based on the consumption of a minimum daily requirement of 1,940 calories).

Military

Total active duty personnel (November 2008): 76,000 (army 54.5%, navy 26.3%, air force 19.2%). **Military expenditure as percentage of GDP** (2008): 0.7%; per capita expenditure US$50.

Background

Little is known of Argentina's indigenous population before the Europeans' arrival. The area was explored for Spain by Sebastian Cabot in 1526–30; by 1580, Asunción, Santa Fe, and Buenos Aires had been settled. At first attached to the Viceroyalty of Peru (1620), it was later included with regions of modern Uruguay, Paraguay, and Bolivia in the Viceroyalty of the Río de la Plata, or Buenos Aires (1776). With the establishment of the United Provinces of the Río de la Plata in 1816, Argentina achieved its independence from Spain, but its boundaries were not set until the early 20th century. In 1943 the government was overthrown by the military; Col. Juan Perón took control in 1946. He in turn was overthrown in 1955. He returned to power in 1973 after two decades of turmoil. His second wife, Isabel, became president on his death in 1974 but lost power after a military coup in 1976. The military government tried to take the Falkland Islands (Islas Malvinas) in 1982 but was defeated by the British, with the result that the government returned to civilian rule in 1983. The government of Raúl Alfonsín worked to end the human rights abuses that characterized the former regimes. Hyperinflation led to public riots and Alfonsín's electoral defeat in 1989; his Peronist successor, Carlos Menem, instituted laissez-faire economic policies. Under a succession of interim presidents, Argentina experienced one of its worst economic collapses at the beginning of the 21st century. Néstor Kirchner won the 2003 presidential elections and helped to stabilize the economy. Four years later his wife became the country's first elected female president.

Did you know? The *pampas* are vast plains extending westward across central Argentina from the Atlantic coast to the Andean foothills. The plains are home to the famous gauchos, or Argentine cowboys.

Recent Developments

Another international controversy played out between Argentina and Britain over the fate of the Falkland Islands. In April 2009 the Argentinian government laid claim to a large area of ocean floor, including the area around the Falklands, South Georgia, and the South Sandwich Islands, all territories claimed by Britain. In February 2010 Argentina prevented a ship bearing pipes thought to be for petroleum exploration from travelling to the Falklands and declared that any ship desiring to visit the islands required Argentinian permission. As well, Argentina filed a complaint that month with the UN. Many Latin American leaders, including the presidents of Brazil, Mexico, Venezuela, and Nicaragua, expressed support for the Argentine claim. Nonetheless, Britain began exploratory drilling in February.

Internet resource: <www.indec.mecon.ar>.

Armenia

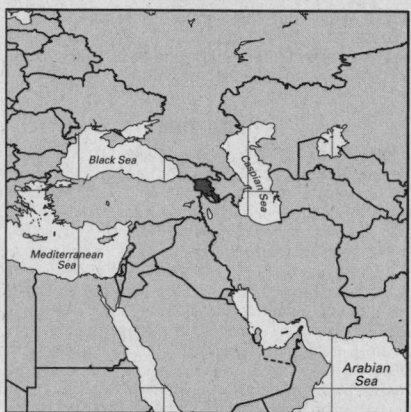

Official name: Hayastani Hanrape-tut'yun (Republic of Armenia). **Form of government:** unitary multiparty republic with a single legislative house (National Assembly [131]). **Head of state:** President Serzh Sarkisyan (from 2008). **Head of government:** Prime Minister Tigran Sarkisyan (from 2008). **Capital:** Yerevan. **Official language:** Armenian. **Official religion:** none (the Armenian Apostolic Church [Armenian Orthodox Church] has special status per 1991 religious law). **Monetary unit:** 1 dram (AMD) = 100 luma; valuation (1 Jul 2010) US$1 = 367.50 drams.

Demography

Area: 11,484 sq mi, 29,743 sq km; in addition, about 16% of neighboring Azerbaijan (including the 1,700-sq-mi [4,400-sq-km] geographic region of Nagorno-Karabakh [Armenian: Artsakh]) has been occupied by Armenian forces since 1993. **Population** (2009): 3,083,000. **Density** (2009): persons per sq mi 268.5, persons per sq km 103.7. **Urban** (2007): 64.1%. **Sex distribution** (2007): male 48.38%; female 51.62%. **Age breakdown** (2005): under 15, 20.9%; 15–29, 27.2%; 30–44, 19.5%; 45–59, 17.9%; 60–74, 10.2%; 75–84, 3.8%; 85 and over, 0.5%. **Ethnic composition** (2001): Armenian 97.9%; Kurdish 1.3%; Russian 0.5%; other 0.3%. **Religious affiliation** (2005): Armenian Apostolic (Orthodox) 72.9%; Roman Catholic 4.0%; Sunni Muslim 2.4%; other Christian 1.3%; Yazidi 1.3%; other/nonreligious 18.1%. **Major cities** (2007): Yerevan 1,107,800; Gyumri 147,000; Vanadzor 105,000; Vagharshapat 57,300; Hrazdan 52,900. **Location:** western Transcaucasia, bordering Georgia, Azerbaijan, Iran, and Turkey.

Vital statistics

Birth rate per 1,000 population (2007): 12.4 (world avg. 20.3); within marriage 64.5%. **Death rate** per 1,000 population (2007): 8.3 (world avg. 8.5). **Total fertility rate** (avg. births per childbearing woman; 2006): 1.30. **Life expectancy** at birth (2006): male 70.0 years; female 76.4 years.

National economy

Budget (2007). *Revenue:* AMD 588,080,000,000 (tax revenue 82.3%, of which VAT 42.2%, tax on profits 12.8%, income tax 8.0%, excise tax 7.1%; nontax revenue 17.7%). *Expenditures:* AMD 634,-735,000,000 (defense 15.1%; education and science 15.0%; social security 9.9%; public administration 9.8%; police 8.2%; health 7.4%). **Public debt** (external, outstanding; 2007): US$1,272,000,000. **Gross national income** (2008): US$10,320,-000,000 (US$3,350 per capita). **Production** (metric tons except as noted). *Agriculture and fishing* (2007): potatoes 540,000, tomatoes 250,000, grapes 200,000; livestock (number of live animals) 620,200 cattle, 587,200 sheep; fisheries production (2006) 1,406 (from aquaculture 75%). *Mining and quarrying* (2005): copper concentrate (metal content) 16,256; molybdenum (metal content) 3,030; gold (metal content) 1,400 kg. *Manufacturing* (value of production in AMD '000,000; 2007): food products and beverages 208,733; base metals 122,269; construction materials 40,207; 320,000 carats of cut diamonds were processed in 2004. *Energy production (consumption):* electricity (kW-hr; 2008) 6,114,000,000 ([2006] 5,145,000,000); coal (metric tons; 2005), none (negligible); petroleum products (metric tons; 2005) none (320,000); natural gas (cu m; 2005) none (1,596,000,000). **Population economically active:** total (2006) 1,181,300; activity rate of total population (2001) 49.5% (participation rates: ages 15–64 [2001] 72.1%; female 45.7%; unemployed [2008] 6.3%). **Selected balance of payments data.** Receipts from (US$'000,000): tourism (2007) 305; remittances (2008) 1,062; foreign direct investment (FDI; 2005–07 avg.) 451; official development assistance (2007) 352. Disbursements for (US$'000,000): tourism (2007) 294; remittances (2008) 185.

Foreign trade

Imports (2007; c.i.f.): US$3,053,000,000 (machinery and apparatus 14.0%; food products 12.4%; refined petroleum products 7.4%; natural gas 7.4%; iron and steel 6.7%; motor vehicles 5.7%; diamonds 5.4%; gold 4.3%). *Major import sources:* Russia 15.8%; Ukraine 8.2%; Kazakhstan 7.9%; China 6.3%; France 4.9%. **Exports** (2007; f.o.b.): US$1,121,000,000 (ferroalloys 21.0%; cut diamonds 14.0%; nonferrous metals 11.6%, of which unrefined copper 5.9%, aluminum foil 3.3%; wine and brandy 10.3%; copper ore and concentrates 7.9%). *Major export destinations:* Russia 17.7%; Germany 15.0%; Netherlands 13.9%; Belgium 8.9%; Georgia 6.2%.

Transport and communications

Transport (2007). *Railroads:* length 732 km; passenger-km 23,900,000; metric ton-km cargo 770,500,000. *Roads:* length 7,515 km (paved 68%). *Air transport* (Armavia airlines only): passenger-km 993,600,000; metric ton-km cargo 6,100,000. **Communications,** in total units (units per 1,000 persons). Telephone landlines (2005): 537,000 (180); cellular telephone subscribers (2007): 1,876,000 (611); personal computers (2007): 980,000 (319); total Inter-

---

1 metric ton = about 1.1 short tons;   1 kilometer = 0.6 mi (statute);   1 metric ton-km cargo = about 0.68 short ton-mi cargo;   c.i.f.: cost, insurance, and freight;   f.o.b.: free on board

net users (2006): 173,000 (57); broadband Internet subscribers (2006): 2,000 (0.3).

Education and health

Educational attainment (2001). Percentage of population ages 25 and over having: no formal schooling 0.7%; primary education 13.0%; completed secondary and some postsecondary 66.0%; higher 20.3%. **Literacy** (2006): total population ages 15 and over literate 99.4%; male 99.7%; female 99.2%. **Health** (2007): physicians 12,251 (1 per 264 persons); hospital beds 13,126 (1 per 246 persons); infant mortality rate per 1,000 live births 10.8; undernourished population (2002–04) 700,000 (24% of total population based on the consumption of a minimum daily requirement of 1,980 calories).

Military

Total active duty personnel (November 2008): 42,080 (army 94.7%, air force 5.3%); Russian troops (November 2008) 3,210. **Military expenditure as percentage of GDP** (2008): 3.2%; per capita expenditure US$132.

Background

Armenia is a successor state to a historical region in southwestern Asia. Historical Armenia's boundaries have varied considerably, but the region extended over what is now northeastern Turkey and the Republic of Armenia. The area was later conquered by the Medes and the Macedonians and still later allied with the Roman Empire. Armenia adopted Christianity as its national religion in AD 303. It came under the rule of the Ottoman Turks in 1514. Over the next centuries, as parts were ceded to other rulers, nationalism arose among the scattered Armenians; by the late 19th century it was causing widespread disruption. Fighting between Turks and Russians escalated when part of Armenia was ceded to Russia in 1878, and it continued through World War I, leading to Armenian deaths on a genocidal scale. With the Turkish defeat, the Russian-controlled part of Armenia was set up as a Soviet republic in 1921. Armenia became a constituent republic of the USSR in 1936. With the latter's dissolution in the late 1980s, Armenia declared its independence in 1991. It fought Azerbaijan for control over Nagorno-Karabakh until a cease-fire in 1994. About one-fifth of the population left the country beginning in 1993 because of an energy crisis. Political tension escalated, and in 1999 the prime minister and some legislators were killed in a terrorist attack on the legislature.

Recent Developments

Its relationship with Turkey continued to dominate the political landscape in Armenia. On 10 Oct 2009, Armenia and Turkey signed protocols establishing diplomatic relations and opening their mutual border, but neither country's parliament immediately ratified them. In early 2010 the US ambassador to Turkey stated that Turkey linked ratification to the successful resolution of the Nagorno-Karabakh conflict, which dampened expectations internationally.

Internet resource: <www.armstat.am>.

Australia

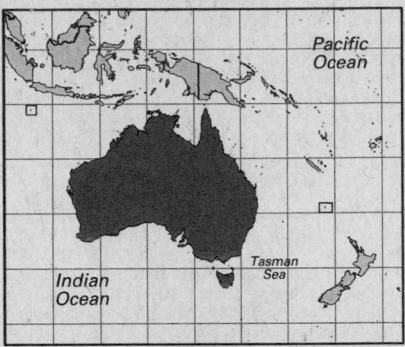

Official name: Commonwealth of Australia. **Form of government:** federal parliamentary state (formally a constitutional monarchy) with two legislative houses (Senate [76]; House of Representatives [150]). **Head of state:** British Queen Elizabeth II (from 1952), represented by Governor-General Quentin Bryce (from 2008). **Head of government:** Prime Minister Julia Gillard (from 2010). **Capital:** Canberra. **Official language:** English. **Official religion:** none. **Monetary unit:** 1 Australian dollar ($A) = 100 cents; valuation (1 Jul 2010) US$1 = $A 1.19.

Demography

Area: 2,969,978 sq mi, 7,692,208 sq km. **Population** (2009): 21,829,000. **Density** (2009): persons per sq mi 7.3, persons per sq km 2.8. **Urban** (2005): 88.2%. **Sex distribution** (2008): male 50.09%; female 49.91%. **Age breakdown** (2008): under 15, 18.7%; 15–29, 20.8%; 30–44, 22.0%; 45–59, 20.0%; 60–74, 12.2%; 75–84, 4.5%; 85 and over, 1.8%. **Ethnic composition** (2007): white and others not elsewhere classified 90.2%; Asian (excluding Middle Eastern) 7.3%; aboriginal 2.5%. **Religious affiliation** (2006): Christian 63.9%, of which Roman Catholic 25.6%, Anglican Church of Australia 18.7%, Uniting Church 5.7%, Presbyterian 2.9%, Orthodox 2.6%, Baptist 1.6%, Lutheran 1.3%; other Christian 5.5%; Buddhist 2.1%; Muslim 1.7%; Hindu 0.7%; Jewish 0.4%; no religion 18.7%; other 12.5%. **Major urban centers (metropolitan areas)** (2006): Sydney 3,641,422 (4,119,191); Melbourne 3,371,888 (3,592,590); Brisbane 1,676,389 (1,763,132); Perth 1,256,035 (1,445,077); Adelaide 1,040,719 (1,105,840); Gold Coast 454,436 (541,675); Newcastle 288,732 (493,467); Canberra 356,120 (368,128); Gosford 282,726 (n.a.); Wollongong 234,482 (263,535); Sunshine Coast 184,662 (209,578); Hobart 128,577 (200,524); Geelong 137,220 (160,992); Townsville 128,808 (143,330); Cairns 98,349 (122,731); Toowoomba 95,265 (114,480); Darwin 66,291 (105,990). **Place of birth** (2006): 70.9% native-born; 29.1% foreign-born, of which Europe 10.5% (UK 5.2%, Italy 1.0%, Greece 0.6%, Germany 0.5%, Netherlands 0.4%, Poland 0.3%), Asia and Middle East 7.3% (China [including Hong Kong] 1.4%, Vietnam 0.8%, India 0.7%), New Zealand 2.0%, Africa, the Americas, and other 0.3%. **Location:** Oceania, continent between the Indian Ocean and the South Pacific Ocean. **Mobility** (1999). Population ages 15 and over living in the same residence as in 1998: 84.4%; different residence between states, regions, and neighborhoods 15.6%. **Immigration** (2006–07): permanent immigrants admitted 140,148, from New Zealand 17.1%, UK 16.6%, India 9.6%, China 8.6%, Philippines 4.0%, South Africa 2.9%, Vietnam 2.2%, Malaysia 2.1%, Sri Lanka 1.9%, Sudan 1.8%. **Emigration** (2006–07): 72,100, to New Zealand 19.3%, UK 18.2%, US 10.0%, Hong Kong 7.5%. **Refugee arrivals** (2006–07) 13,017.

Vital statistics

Birth rate per 1,000 population (2007–08): 13.6 (world avg. 20.3); (2006) within marriage 67.3%. **Death rate** per 1,000 population (2007–08): 6.7 (world avg. 8.5). **Total fertility rate** (avg. births per childbearing woman; 2007–08): 1.93. **Life expectancy** at birth (2008): male 79.2 years; female 84.0 years.

Social indicators

Quality of working life. Average workweek (2007): 34.6 hours. Working 50 hours a week or more (2006) 22.5%. Annual rate per 100,000 workers for: accidental injury and industrial disease (2006) 1,070; death (2006) 2.0. Proportion of employed persons insured for damages or income loss resulting from: injury 100%; permanent disability 100%; death 100%. Working days lost to industrial disputes per 1,000 employees (2006): 22. Means of transportation to work (2003): private automobile 74.5%; public transportation 12.0%; motorcycle, bicycle, and foot 5.7%. Discouraged job seekers (2006): 52,900 (0.5% of labor force). **Educational attainment** (2005). Percentage of population ages 15–64 having: no formal schooling and incomplete secondary education 48.5%; completed secondary and postsecondary, technical, or other certificate/diploma 28.9%; bachelor's degree 14.2%; incomplete graduate and graduate degree or diploma 5.4%; unknown 3.0%. **Social participation.** Eligible voters participating in last national election (2007): 94.8%; voting is compulsory. Trade union membership in total workforce (2006): 20.3%. Volunteerism rate of population ages 18 and over (2006) 34.1%. **Social deviance** (2007). Offense rate per 100,000 population for: murder 1.2; sexual assault 94.1; assault 839; auto theft 364; burglary and housebreaking 1,182; robbery 85.6, of which armed robbery 36.5. Incidence per 100,000 in general population of: prisoners 129; suicide (2006) 8.7. **Material well-being** (2005). Households possessing: refrigerator 99.9%; washing machine 96.4%; dishwasher 41.5%; automobiles per 1,000 population (2006) 544.

National economy

Gross national income (2008): US$862,461,000,000 (US$40,350 per capita). **Budget** (2007–08). *Revenue:* $A 303,713,000,000 (tax revenue 94.2%, of which income tax 41.5%, indirect tax 25.6%, corporate taxes 21.3%; nontax revenue 5.8%). *Expenditures:* $A 280,108,000,000 (social security and welfare 34.9%; health 15.8%; economic services 7.4%; general administration 7.2%; education 6.6%; defense 6.3%; interest on public debt 1.3%). **Public debt** (December 2008):

US$106,300,000,000. **Production** (metric tons except as noted). *Agriculture and fishing* (2006–07): sugarcane 36,000,000, wheat 10,822,000, barley 4,257,000, grapes 1,530,000, sorghum 1,283,000, potatoes 1,212,000, oats 748,000, rapeseed 573,000, oranges 461,000, tomatoes 296,000, cotton lint 282,000, carrots 271,000, lettuce 271,000, apples 270,000, bananas 213,000; livestock (number of live animals) 85,711,000 sheep, 28,037,000 cattle, 2,605,000 pigs; fisheries production (2006) 241,456 (from aquaculture 20%); aquatic plants production 15,504 (from aquaculture, none). *Mining and quarrying* (metric tons except as noted; 2006): iron ore (metal content) 170,933,000 (world rank: 2), bauxite 62,307,000 (world rank: 1), ilmenite 2,377,000 (world rank: 1), zinc (metal content) 1,362,000 (world rank: 2), copper (metal content) 879,000 (world rank: 5), lead (metal content) 686,000 (world rank: 2), rutile 232,000 (world rank: 1), nickel (metal content) 185,000 (world rank: 3), cobalt (metal content) 7,400 (world rank: 3), opal (value of production) $A 50,000,000 (world rank: 1), diamonds 21,915,000 carats (world rank: 2), gold 247,000 kilograms (world rank: 4). *Manufacturing* (value added in $A '000,000; 2006–07): base metals 15,158; food products 14,455; machinery and apparatus 10,538; fabricated metal products 9,076; transportation equipment 9,003; chemical products 6,831; beverages and tobacco products 5,787; bricks, cement, and ceramics 5,019. **Population economically active** (July 2007): total 10,952,000; activity rate of total population 52.5% (participation rates: ages 15 and over, 65.0%; female [2006] 45.0%; unemployed [June 2008] 4.2%). *Energy production (consumption):* electricity (kW-hr; 2007) 227,496,000,000 ([2005] 251,120,000,000); coal (metric tons; 2006) 267,490,000 (36,371,000); lignite (metric tons; 2006) 102,825,000 (105,548,000); crude petroleum (barrels; 2006–07) 171,900,000 ([2006] 206,566,000); petroleum products (metric tons; 2006) 29,979,000 (36,211,000); natural gas (cu m; 2007) 37,211,000,000 ([2006] 29,256,000,000). **Selected balance of payments data.** Receipts from (US$'000,000): tourism (2007) 22,405; remittances (2008) 4,638; foreign direct investment (FDI; 2005–07 avg.) 4,236. Disbursements for (US$'000,000): tourism (2007) 14,244; remittances (2008) 2,997; FDI (2005–07 avg.) 4,441.

Foreign trade

Imports (2005–06): $A 167,603,000,000 (machinery and apparatus 29.3%, of which telecommunications equipment 5.8%, office machinery and data-processing equipment 5.3%, electrical machinery 4.8%; transportation equipment 15.8%, of which motor vehicles 12.2%; crude and refined petroleum 12.7%; chemical products 6.1%, of which medicines and pharmaceuticals 4.3%; textiles and wearing apparel 3.9%). *Major import sources* (2006–07): China 15.0%; US 13.8%; Japan 9.6%; Singapore 5.6%; Germany 5.1%; UK 4.1%; Thailand 4.0%; Malaysia 3.7%; South Korea 3.3%; New Zealand 3.1%. **Exports** (2005–06): $A 151,792,000,000 (mineral fuels 24.9%, of which coal [all forms] 16.0%, petroleum products and natural gas 8.9%; food products and

---

1 metric ton = about 1.1 short tons; 1 kilometer = 0.6 mi (statute); 1 metric ton-km cargo = about 0.68 short ton-mi cargo; c.i.f.: cost, insurance, and freight; f.o.b.: free on board

beverages 12.0%, of which meat 4.4%, cereals 3.2%; iron ore 8.2%; aluminum and aluminum ore 6.9%; gold 4.8%; machinery and apparatus 4.1%; transportation equipment 3.5%). *Major export destinations* (2006–07): Japan 19.4%; China 13.6%; South Korea 7.8%; US 5.8%; New Zealand 5.6%; UK 3.7%; Taiwan 3.7%; Singapore 2.7%; Indonesia 2.5%; Thailand 2.5%.

Transport and communications

Transport. *Railroads* (2006): route length 38,550 km; passengers carried (2004–05) 616,270,000; passenger-km (2004–05) 11,200,000,000; metric ton-km cargo (2004–05) 182,990,000,000. *Roads* (2004): total length 810,641 km (paved 42%). *Vehicles* (2008): passenger cars 11,848,326; trucks and buses 2,880,647. *Air transport* (2006): passenger-km 82,128,000,000; metric ton-km cargo 2,347,000,000. **Communications**, in total units (units per 1,000 persons). Telephone landlines (2008): 9,370,000 (437); cellular telephone subscribers (2008): 22,120,000 (1,032); personal computers (2006): 15,671,000 (757); total Internet users (2008): 11,900,000 (555); broadband Internet subscribers (2008): 5,140,000 (240).

Education and health

Literacy (2006): total population literate, virtually 100%. **Health:** physicians (2006) 55,063 (1 per 375 persons); hospital beds (2005–06) 80,828 (1 per 254 persons); infant mortality rate per 1,000 live births (2007–08): 4.1; undernourished population (2002–04) less than 2.5% of total population.

Military

Total active duty personnel (November 2008): 54,747 (army 50.2%, navy 24.1%, air force 25.7%); troops deployed abroad (November 2008): 2,858, of which to Afghanistan 1,080, to East Timor 750. **Military expenditure as percentage of GDP** (2007): 2.2%; per capita expenditure $961.

Background

Australia has long been inhabited by Aborigines, who arrived on the continent 40,000–60,000 years ago. Estimates of the population at the time of European settlement in 1788 range from 300,000 to more than 1,000,000. Widespread European knowledge of Australia began with 17th-century explorations. The Dutch landed in 1616 and the British in 1688, but the first large-scale expedition was that of James Cook in 1770, which established Britain's claim to Australia. The first English settlement, at Port Jackson (1788), consisted mainly of convicts and seamen; convicts were to make up a large proportion of the incoming settlers. By 1859 the colonial nuclei of all Australia's states had been formed, but with devastating effects on the Aborigines, whose population declined sharply with the introduction of European diseases and weaponry. Britain granted its colonies limited self-government in the mid-19th century, and Australia achieved federation in 1901. Australia fought alongside the British in World War I, notably at Gallipoli, and again in World War II, defending against the occupation of Australia by the Japanese. It joined the US in the Korean and Vietnam wars. Since the 1960s the government has sought to deal more fairly with the Aborigines, and a loosening of immigration restrictions has led to a more heterogeneous population. Constitutional links allowing British interference in government were formally abolished in 1968, and Australia has assumed a leading role in Asian and Pacific affairs. During the 1990s it experienced several debates about giving up its British ties and becoming a republic.

Recent Developments

At the beginning of 2009, Australia's national accounts were in a relatively healthy condition, largely because of mineral exports to China. By February 2010, however, unemployment had risen to 5.3%. In April 2009 the national airline Qantas announced that 1,750 jobs would be eliminated and deferred new aircraft delivery, and other major industries took similar steps. In the May budget the government followed up its previous policies of cutting interest rates and giving funding to targeted sectors of the population, including pensioners, the unemployed, and Aborigines. In his budget speech, Treasurer Wayne Swan announced a massive infrastructure program. As a result, fiscal 2009 saw a record deficit and unprecedented revenue losses. The stunning rebound of Chinese industrial production helped Australia shrug off the global financial crisis better than had been anticipated, however, and in October Australia became the first major world economy to raise interest rates since the crisis began. In a series of disputes with China, the government faced its most serious foreign crisis. Aluminum Corp. of China failed in a bid to obtain a $A 25 billion (about US$19.5 billion) stake in Anglo-Australian mining giant Rio Tinto. Shortly afterward, Stern Hu, a Chinese-born Australian citizen and head of Rio Tinto's iron ore operations in China, was arrested for industrial espionage and bribery, together with three senior Chinese employees of Rio. There was some thought in Australia that these arrests were a punishment for failing to accept the Chinese offer. In March 2010 Hu was sentenced to 10 years in prison. Relations remained frosty, as Canberra declined to refuse a visa to the exiled Uighur leader Rebiya Kadeer, even when asked to do so by Chinese Foreign Minister Yang Jiechi, and Beijing canceled a scheduled visit to Australia by Vice Minister He Yafei.

Internet resource: <www.abs.gov.au>.

Austria

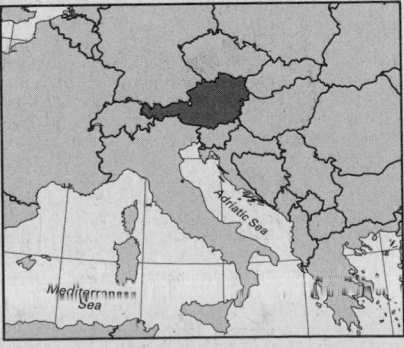

Official name: Republik Österreich (Republic of Austria). **Form of government:** federal state with two legislative houses (Federal Council [62]; National Council [183]). **Head of state:** President Heinz Fischer (from 2004). **Head of government:** Chancellor Werner Faymann (from 2008). **Capital:** Vienna. **Official language:** German. **Official religion:** none. **Monetary unit:** 1 euro (€) = 100 cents; valuation (1 Jul 2010) US$1 = €0.80.

Demography

Area: 32,386 sq mi, 83,879 sq km. **Population** (2009): 8,378,000. **Density** (2009): persons per sq mi 258.7, persons per sq km 99.9. **Urban** (2005): 66.5%. **Sex distribution** (2007): male 48.66%; female 51.34%. **Age breakdown** (2007): under 15, 15.5%; 15–29, 18.7%; 30–44, 23.3%; 45–59, 20.3%; 60–74, 14.3%; 75–84, 6.0%; 85 and over, 1.9%. **Population composition by country of birth** (2007): 84.8%; former Serbia and Montenegro 2.3%; Germany 2.2%; Turkey 1.9%; Bosnia and Herzegovina 1.6%; Poland 0.7%; Romania 0.7%; other 5.8%. **Religious affiliation** (2001): Christian 81.5%, of which Roman Catholic 73.7%, Protestant (mostly Lutheran) 4.7%, Orthodox 2.2%; Muslim 4.2%; nonreligious 12.0%; other 0.3%; unknown 2.0%. **Major cities** (2007): Vienna 1,677,867; Graz 250,653; Linz 189,069; Salzburg 149,201; Innsbruck 118,362. **Location:** central Europe, bordering the Czech Republic, Slovakia, Hungary, Slovenia, Italy, Switzerland, Liechtenstein, and Germany.

Vital statistics

Birth rate per 1,000 population (2008): 9.3 (world avg. 20.3); within marriage 61.2%. **Death rate** per 1,000 population (2008): 9.0 (world avg. 8.5). **Total fertility rate** (avg. births per childbearing woman; 2008): 1.41. **Life expectancy** at birth (2008): male 77.6 years; female 83.0 years.

National economy

Budget (2007). *Revenue:* €113,942,000,000 (tax revenue 66.4%, of which income taxes 30.5%, taxes on products 27.1%; social security contributions 33.6%). *Expenditures:* €131,126,000,000 (social protection 41.6%; health 15.5%; general administration 14.2%; education 10.7%; economic affairs 9.6%). **Public debt** (December 2007): US$220,517,000,000. **Production** (metric tons except as noted). *Agriculture and fishing* (2006): sugar beets 2,493,097, corn (maize) 1,471,668, wheat 1,396,300; livestock (number of live animals) 3,160,382 pigs, 2,002,143 cattle; fisheries production 2,863 (from aquaculture 87%). *Mining and quarrying* (2006): iron ore (metal content) 650,000; manganese (metal content) 16,000; tungsten 1,300. *Manufacturing* (value added in €'000,000; 2006): nonelectrical machinery and apparatus 6,250; fabricated metal products 5,550; food products and beverages 3,900. *Energy production (consumption):* electricity (kW-hr; 2008) 66,792,000,000 ([2006] 70,295,000,000); coal (metric tons; 2007) none (4,161,000); lignite (metric tons; 2006) none (753,000); crude petroleum (barrels; 2008)

5,660,000 ([2006] 59,642,000); petroleum products (metric tons; 2006) 7,259,000 (12,106,000); natural gas (cu m; 2008) 1,686,000,000 ([2006] 9,584,000,000). **Population economically active** (2007): total 4,213,500; activity rate of total population 51.4% (participation rates: ages 15–64 [2006] 73.7%; female 45.5%; unemployed [March 2008–February 2009] 6.0%). **Gross national income** (2008): US$386,044,000,000 (US$46,260 per capita). **Selected balance of payments data.** Receipts from (US$'000,000): tourism (2007) 18,754; remittances (2008) 3,237; foreign direct investment (FDI; 2005–07 avg.) 15,882. Disbursements for (US$'000,000): tourism (2007) 10,566; remittances (2008) 3,356; FDI (2005–07 avg.) 17,414.

Foreign trade

Imports (2007; c.i.f.): €114,010,000,000 (machinery and apparatus 23.6%; chemical products 10.9%; motor vehicles and parts 10.6%; crude petroleum 6.3%; food products 5.3%). *Major import sources:* Germany 41.5%; Italy 6.9%; Switzerland 4.2%; China 4.0%; US 3.3%. **Exports** (2007; f.o.b.): €114,400,000,000 (machinery and apparatus 28.6%, of which electrical machinery 6.9%, general industrial machinery 6.5%; motor vehicles and parts 10.9%; chemical products 9.5%; iron and steel 6.1%; fabricated metal products 4.9%). *Major export destinations:* Germany 30.1%; Italy 8.9%; US 5.1%; Switzerland 4.4%; France 3.6%.

Transport and communications

Transport. *Railroads* (2006; federal railways only): route length (2007) 5,656 km; passenger-km 8,646,000,000; metric ton-km cargo 17,871,000,000. *Roads* (2003): total length 133,718 km (paved 100%). *Vehicles* (2007): passenger cars 4,245,583; trucks and buses 363,043. *Air transport* (2007): passenger-km 17,412,000,000; metric ton-km cargo 453,756,000. **Communications,** in total units (units per 1,000 persons). Telephone landlines (2008): 3,342,000 (400); cellular telephone subscribers (2008): 10,816,000 (1,296); personal computers (2006): 5,027,000 (607); total Internet users (2008): 4,950,000 (593); broadband Internet subscribers (2008): 1,792,000 (215).

Education and health

Educational attainment (2007). Percentage of population ages 15 and over having: compulsory education through age 14, 28.3%; apprentice training/intermediate technical 48.2%; academic secondary/higher technical 13.9%; university 9.6%. **Literacy:** virtually 100%. **Health** (2007): physicians 20,318 (1 per 410 persons); hospital beds 57,646 (1 per 144 persons); infant mortality rate per 1,000 live births (2008) 3.7; undernourished population (2002–04) less than 2.5% of total population.

Military

Total active duty personnel (November 2008): 34,900 (army 80.8%, air force 19.2%). **Military expenditure as percentage of GDP** (2008): 0.7%; per capita expenditure US$330.

1 metric ton = about 1.1 short tons;　1 kilometer = 0.6 mi (statute);　1 metric ton-km cargo = about 0.68 short ton-mi cargo;　c.i.f.: cost, insurance, and freight;　f.o.b.: free on board

Background

Settlement in Austria goes back some 3,000 years, when Illyrians were probably the main inhabitants. The Celts invaded c. 400 BC and established Noricum. The Romans arrived after 200 BC and established the provinces of Raetia, Noricum, and Pannonia; prosperity followed and the population became Romanized. With the fall of Rome in the 5th century AD, many tribes invaded, including the Slavs; they were eventually subdued by Charlemagne, and the area became ethnically Germanic. The distinct political entity that would become Austria emerged in 976 with Leopold I of Babenberg as margrave. In 1278 Rudolf I of the Holy Roman Empire (formerly Rudolf IV of Habsburg) conquered the area; Habsburg rule lasted until 1918. While in power the Habsburgs created a kingdom centered on Austria, Bohemia, and Hungary. The Napoleonic Wars brought about the creation of the Austrian Empire (1804) and the end of the Holy Roman Empire (1806). Count von Metternich tried to assure Austrian supremacy among Germanic states, but war with Prussia led Austria to divide the empire into the Dual Monarchy of Austria-Hungary. Nationalist sentiment plagued the kingdom, and the assassination of Francis Ferdinand by a Serbian nationalist in 1914 triggered World War I, which destroyed the Austro-Hungarian Empire. In the postwar carving up of Austria-Hungary, Austria became an independent republic. It was annexed by Nazi Germany in 1938 and joined the Axis powers in World War II. The republic was restored in 1955 after 10 years of Allied occupation. Austria became a member of the European Union in 1995. After a half-century of military neutrality, Austria was one of the few members of the EU that was not a member of NATO at the outset of the 21st century.

Recent Developments

Austria's economy contracted sharply in 2009 because of the worldwide financial crisis. Exports declined drastically in 2009, largely as a result of a contraction in GDP growth in Germany (Austria's main trading partner) and in the rest of the euro area and Russia. Unemployment reached 8.6% at year's end. The government estimated the deficit to be 3.9% of GDP in 2009, and as a result, in October the European Commission initiated procedures against Austria for having exceeded the 3.0% of GDP threshold established in the EU's Stability and Growth Pact.

Internet resource: <www.statistik.at>.

Azerbaijan

Official name: Azerbaycan Respublikasi (Republic of Azerbaijan). Form of government: unitary multiparty republic with a single legislative house (National Assembly [125]). Head of state and government: President Ilham Aliyev (from 2003), assisted by Prime Minister Artur Rasizade (from 2003). Capital: Baku (Baki). Official language: Azerbaijanian. Official religion: none. Monetary unit: 1 (new) manat (AZN) = 100 gopik, valuation (1 Jul 2010) free rate, US$1 = AZN 0.80.

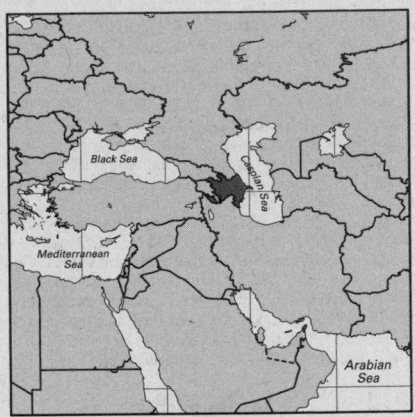

Demography

Area: 33,400 sq mi, 86,600 sq km. Population (2009): 8,832,000. Density (2009): persons per sq mi 264.1, persons per sq km 102.0. Urban (2007): 51.7%. Sex distribution (2007): male 49.34%; female 50.66%. Age breakdown (2006): under 15, 26.3%; 15–29, 27.9%; 30–44, 22.7%; 45–59, 14.1%; 60–74, 6.7%; 75–84, 1.9%; 85 and over, 0.4%. Ethnic composition (1999): Azerbaijani 90.6%; Lezgian (Dagestani) 2.2%; Russian 1.8%; Armenian 1.5%; other 3.9%. Religious affiliation (2005): Muslim 87.0%, of which Shi'i 52.8%, Sunni 34.2%; nonreligious/other 13.0%. Major cities (2007): Baku 1,145,000 (urban agglomeration 1,892,000); Ganca 307,500; Sumqayit (Sumgait) 268,800; Mingacevir (Mingechaur) 95,500; Qaracuxur 74,700. Location: eastern Transcaucasia, bordering Russia, the Caspian Sea, Iran, Turkey, Armenia, and Georgia.

Vital statistics

Birth rate per 1,000 population (2007): 17.7 (world avg. 20.3); within marriage 88.2%. Death rate per 1,000 population (2007): 6.3 (world avg. 8.5). Total fertility rate (avg. births per childbearing woman; 2007): 2.30. Life expectancy at birth (2007): male 69.7 years; female 75.1 years.

National economy

Budget (2007). Revenue: AZN 7,949,000,000 (tax revenue 70.9%, of which corporate taxes 30.9%, VAT 14.8%, income tax 7.4%, social security contributions 6.9%; nontax revenue [all petroleum fund revenues] 29.1%). Expenditures: AZN 7,356,000,000 (current expenditures 62.5%; development expenditures 37.5%). Production (metric tons except as noted). Agriculture and fishing (2006): wheat 1,460,303, potatoes 999,343, barley 399,737, seed cotton 130,123, persimmons 124,485; livestock (number of live animals) 7,304,431 sheep, 2,148,108 cattle; fisheries production 4,093 (from aquaculture 3%). Mining and quarrying (2005): limestone 1,256,000. Manufacturing (value of production in AZN '000,000; 2007): refined petroleum products 1,634; food, beverages, and tobacco products 1,457; base and fabricated metals 398. Energy production (consumption): electricity (kW-hr) 2007)

20,337,000,000 ([2006] 25,429,000,000); crude petroleum (barrels; 2007) 303,000,000 ([2006] 53,972,000); petroleum products (metric tons; 2006) 7,183,000 (3,931,000); natural gas (cu m; 2007) 9,606,000,000 ([2006] 10,662,000,000). **Population economically active** (2005): total 3,906,500; activity rate of total population 46.3% (participation rates: ages 15–61 [male], 15–56 [female] 71.8%; female 47.7%; unemployed [2007] 6.5%). **Gross national income** (2008): US$33,232,000,000 (US$3,830 per capita). **Public debt** (external, outstanding; 2007): US$1,748,000,000. **Selected balance of payments data.** Receipts from (US$'000,000): tourism (2007) 178; remittances (2008) 1,554; foreign direct investment (2005–07 avg.) 1,537; official development assistance (2007) 225. Disbursements for (US$'000,000): tourism (2007) 264; remittances (2008) 593.

Foreign trade

Imports (2007; c.i.f.): US$5,712,000,000 (machinery and apparatus 30.7%, of which civil engineering equipment and parts 6.2%; food products 11.5%, of which cereals 5.8%; motor vehicles 11.3%; iron and steel products 8.7%; chemical products 7.5%). *Major import sources:* Russia 17.6%; Turkey 10.9%; Germany 8.2%; Ukraine 8.2%; UK 7.2%. **Exports** (2008; f.o.b.): US$47,756,000,000 (crude petroleum 92.5%; refined petroleum products 4.3%; aluminum alloys 0.3%; boats and floating structures 0.3%). *Major export destinations* (2007): Turkey 17.4%; Italy 15.5%; Russia 8.7%; Iran 7.2%; Indonesia 6.4%.

Transport and communications

Transport. *Railroads* (2007): length 2,122 km; passenger-km 1,108,000,000; metric ton-km cargo 10,375,000,000. *Roads* (2004): total length 59,141 km (paved 49%). *Vehicles* (2007): passenger cars 616,853; trucks and buses 138,483. *Air transport* (2007): passenger-km 1,764,000,000; metric ton-km cargo 11,892,000. **Communications,** in total units (units per 1,000 persons), Telephone landlines (2008): 1,318,000 (151); cellular telephone subscribers (2008): 6,548,000 (750); personal computers (2007): 207,000 (24); total Internet users (2007): 1,036,000 (122); broadband Internet subscribers (2008): 60,000 (6.9).

Education and health

Educational attainment (1999). Percentage of population ages 25 and over having: primary education 4.1%; some secondary 9.3%; secondary 50.1%; vocational 4.2%; some higher 0.9%; higher 13.3%. **Literacy** (2007): 99.4%. **Health** (2007): physicians 32,400 (1 per 252 persons); hospital beds 68,100 (1 per 49 persons); infant mortality rate per 1,000 live births 11.6; undernourished population (2003–05) 100,000,000 (12% of total population based on the consumption of a minimum daily requirement of 1,920 calories).

Military

Total active duty personnel (November 2008): 66,940 (army 84.9%, navy 3.3%, air force 11.8%).

Military expenditure as percentage of GDP (2008): 2.5%; per capita expenditure US$154.

Background

Azerbaijan adjoins the Iranian region of the same name, and the origin of their respective inhabitants is the same. By the 9th century AD the area had come under Turkish influence, and in ensuing centuries it was fought over by Arabs, Mongols, Turks, and Iranians. Russia acquired the territory of what is now independent Azerbaijan in the early 19th century. After the Russian Revolution of 1917, Azerbaijan declared its independence; it was subdued by the Red Army in 1920 and became a Soviet Socialist Republic. It declared independence from the collapsing Soviet Union in 1991. Azerbaijan has two geographic peculiarities. The exclave Nakhichevan is separated from the rest of Azerbaijan by Armenian territory. Nagorno-Karabakh, which lies within Azerbaijan and is administered by it, has a Christian Armenian majority. Azerbaijan and Armenia went to war over both territories in the 1990s, causing great economic disruption. Though a cease-fire was declared in 1994, the political situation remained unresolved.

Recent Developments

In 2009 Azerbaijani Pres. Ilham Aliyev met several times with his Armenian counterpart, Pres. Serzh Sarkisyan, to discuss the Nagorno-Karabakh conflict, but the two failed to reach a settlement. The commitment in October by Armenia and Turkey to establish diplomatic relations occasioned official protests from the Azerbaijani government. President Aliyev, who had declined to attend a UN-sponsored conference in Istanbul in early April, hinted in October that Azerbaijan could choose Russia, rather than Turkey, as the route for future natural gas exports.

Internet resource: <www.azstat.org/indexen.php>.

Bahamas, The

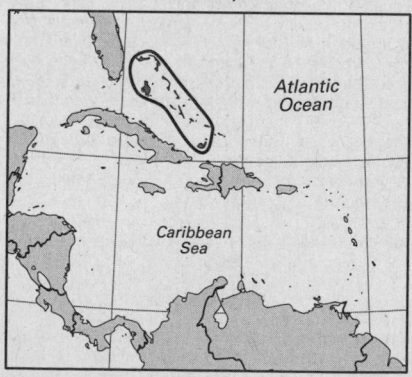

Atlantic Ocean

Caribbean Sea

Official name: The Commonwealth of The Bahamas. **Form of government:** constitutional monarchy with two legislative houses (Senate [16]; House of Assembly [41]). **Head of state:** British Queen Elizabeth

II (from 1952), represented by Governor-General Arthur Dion Hanna (from 2006). **Head of government:** Prime Minister Hubert Ingraham (from 2007). **Capital:** Nassau. **Official language:** English. **Official religion:** none. **Monetary unit:** 1 Bahamian dollar (B$) = 100 cents; valuation (1 Jul 2010) US$1 = B$1.00.

Demography

Area: 5,382 sq mi, 13,939 sq km. **Population** (2009): 342,000. **Density** (2009): persons per sq mi 87.9, persons per sq km 34.0. **Urban** (2005): 83.0%. **Sex distribution** (2008): male 48.71%; female 51.29%. **Age breakdown** (2008): under 15, 26.0%; 15–29, 24.4%; 30–44, 23.9%; 45–59, 16.8%; 60–74, 7.1%; 75–84, 1.5%; 85 and over, 0.3%. **Ethnic composition** (2007): local black/mixed race 74%; Haitian 15%; white/European 11%. **Religious affiliation** (2000): Baptist 35.4%; Anglican 15.1%; Roman Catholic 13.5%; other Protestant/independent Christian 32.3%; other/nonreligious 3.7%. **Major cities and towns** (2006): Nassau 231,500; Freeport 47,100; West End 12,900. **Location:** chain of islands in the Caribbean Sea, southeast of Florida.

Vital statistics

Birth rate per 1,000 population (2006): 13.9 (world avg. 20.3); (2000) within marriage 43.2%. **Death rate** per 1,000 population (2006): 5.3 (world avg. 8.5). **Total fertility rate** (avg. births per childbearing woman; 2006): 2.18. **Life expectancy** at birth (2006): male 62.2 years; female 69.0 years.

National economy

Budget (2008–09). *Revenue:* B$1,569,300,000 (tax revenue 90.3%, of which taxes on international trade and transactions 48.6% [including import duties 32.8%, excise taxes 14.9%], business and professional licenses 7.1%, property taxes 6.2%; nontax revenue 9.7%). *Expenditures:* B$1,672,900,000 (education 19.0%; health 16.6%; general administration 16.6%; public order 11.2%; interest on public debt 9.9%; public works and water supply 7.0%). **Public debt** (external, outstanding; September 2008): US$833,800,000. *Production* (metric tons except as noted). *Agriculture and fishing* (2006): sugarcane 55,500, fruits 33,472; livestock (number of live animals; 2007) 3,000,000 chickens; fisheries production (mainly lobsters, crayfish, and conch) 10,620 (from aquaculture, negligible). *Mining and quarrying* (2006): salt 1,150,000; aragonite 1,100. *Manufacturing* (value of export production in B$'000; 2007): polystyrene 142,200; organic chemical products 84,562; rum 20,282. *Energy production (consumption):* electricity (kW-hr; 2006–07) 2,149,000,000 ([2006] 2,090,000,000); petroleum products (metric tons; 2006) none (693,000). **Gross national income** (2007): US$7,042,000,000 (US$21,021 per capita). **Population economically active** (2007): total 186,105; activity rate of total population 56.2% (participation rates: ages 15–64, 76.2%; female 48.5%; unemployed [February 2009; New Providence only] 12.1%). **Selected balance of payments data.** Receipts from (US$'000,000): tourism (2007) 2,187; remittances, n.a.; foreign direct investment (2005–07 avg.) 1,067. Disbursements for (US$'000,000): tourism (2007) 377; remittances (2008) 143.

Foreign trade

Imports (2007; c.i.f.): B$3,103,000,000 (refined petroleum products 19.2%; machinery and apparatus 14.0%; food products 12.9%; chemical products 9.0%; motor vehicles 6.2%). *Major import sources:* US 88.5%; Netherlands Antilles 2.8%; Venezuela 2.1%; Japan 1.1%. **Exports** (2007; f.o.b.): B$670,000,000 (refined petroleum products 25.0%; polystyrene 21.2%; organic chemical products 12.7%; crayfish 12.1%; aragonite 5.3%; rum 2.9%). *Major export destinations:* US 71.6%; Canada 5.7%; Netherlands 5.6%; France 4.9%; Germany 2.4%.

Transport and communications

Transport. *Railroads:* none. *Roads* (2002): total length 2,717 km (paved 57%). *Vehicles* (2002): passenger cars 112,900; trucks and buses 19,200. *Air transport* (2006): passenger-km 275,700,000; metric ton-km cargo 600,000. **Communications,** in total units (units per 1,000 persons). Telephone landlines (2008): 133,000 (393); cellular telephone subscribers (2008): 358,000 (1,058); total Internet users (2008): 142,000 (420); broadband Internet subscribers (2008): 34,000 (101).

Education and health

Educational attainment (2000). Percentage of population ages 15 and over having: no formal schooling 1.5%; primary education 8.7%; incomplete secondary 19.9%; complete secondary 53.7%; incomplete higher 8.1%; complete higher 7.1%; not stated 1.0%. **Literacy** (2005): total percentage ages 15 and over literate 95.8%; males literate 95.0%; females literate 96.7%. **Health** (2003): physicians 523 (1 per 602 persons); hospital beds 1,068 (1 per 295 persons); infant mortality rate per 1,000 live births (2006) 16.3; undernourished population (2002–04) 25,000 (8% of total population based on the consumption of a minimum daily requirement of 1,940 calories).

Military

Total active duty personnel (November 2008): 860 (paramilitary coast guard 100%). **Military expenditure as percentage of GDP** (2007): 0.8%; per capita expenditure US$175.

Background

The islands were inhabited by Lucayan Indians when Christopher Columbus sighted them on 12 Oct 1492. He is thought to have landed on San Salvador (Watling) Island. The Spaniards made no attempt to settle but carried out slave raids that depopulated the islands; when English settlers arrived in 1648 from Bermuda, the islands were uninhabited. They became a haunt of pirates, and few of the ensuing settlements prospered. The islands enjoyed some prosperity following the American Revolution, when Loyalists fled the US and established cotton plantations. The islands were a center for blockade runners during the American Civil War. Not until the development of tourism after World War II did permanent economic prosperity arrive. The Bahamas was granted internal self-government in 1964 and became independent from Britain in 1973.

Recent Developments

In May 2009 The Bahamas submitted a claim to the UN for formal delineation of its maritime boundaries, proposing to extend the limits of its continental shelf beyond its 200-nautical-mile exclusive economic zone. Controversially, this area overlapped into US-, Haitian-, Cuban-, and Turks and Caicos-claimed waters.

Internet resource:
<http://statistics.bahamas.gov.bs>.

Bahrain

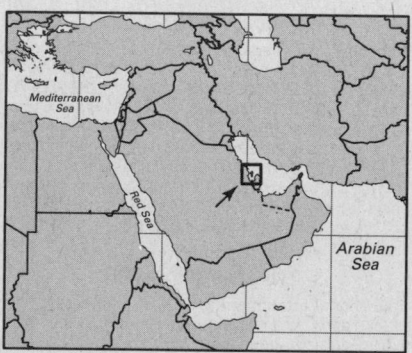

Official name: Mamlakat al-Bahrayn (Kingdom of Bahrain). **Form of government:** constitutional monarchy with two legislative houses (Shura Council [40]; Council of Representatives [40]). **Head of state:** King Sheikh Hamad ibn 'Isa al-Khalifah (from 2002). **Head of government:** Prime Minister Sheikh Khalifah ibn Sulman al-Khalifah (from 1970). **Capital:** Manama. **Official language:** Arabic. **Official religion:** Islam. **Monetary unit:** 1 Bahraini dinar (BD) = 1,000 fils; valuation (1 Jul 2010) US$1 = BD 0.38.

Demography

Area: 290 sq mi, 750 sq km. **Population** (2009): 1,168,000. **Density** (2009): persons per sq mi 4,027.6, persons per sq km 1,557.3. **Urban** (2005): 88.4%. **Sex distribution** (2007): male 60.82%; female 39.18%. **Age breakdown** (2007): under 15, 21.1%; 15–29, 29.1%; 30–44, 31.7%; 45–59, 14.3%; 60–74, 2.8%; 75–84, 0.7%; 85 and over, 0.3%. **Ethnic composition** (2000): Bahraini Arab 63.9%; Indo-Pakistani 14.8%, of which Urdu 4.5%, Malayali 3.5%; Persian 13.0%; Filipino 4.5%; British 2.1%; other 1.7%. **Religious affiliation** (2000): Muslim 82.4%, of which Shi'i 58%, Sunni 24%; Christian 10.5%; Hindu 6.3%; other 0.8%. **Major urban areas** (2001): Manama (2007) 157,000; Muharraq 91,307; Al-Rifa' 79,550; Madinat Hamad 52,718; Al-'Ali 47,529. **Location:** the Middle East, archipelago in the Persian Gulf, east of Saudi Arabia.

Vital statistics

Birth rate per 1,000 population (2007): 15.4 (world avg. 20.3). **Death rate** per 1,000 population (2007):

2.2 (world avg. 8.5). **Total fertility rate** (avg. births per childbearing woman; 2007): 2.00. **Life expectancy** at birth (2005): male 71.7 years; female 76.8 years.

National economy

Budget (2006). *Revenue:* BD 1,839,600,000 (petroleum and natural gas revenue 77.0%; other 23.0%). *Expenditures:* BD 1,558,500,000 (current expenditures 70.7%; development expenditures 29.3%). **Public debt** (2008): US$6,530,000,000. **Production** (metric tons except as noted). *Agriculture and fishing* (2007): dates 15,500, tomatoes 2,250, onions 1,300; livestock (number of live animals) 41,000 sheep, 26,500 goats, 470,000 chickens; fisheries production (2006) 15,596 (from aquaculture, negligible). *Manufacturing* (value added in BD 000,000; 2007): petroleum products 436.8; aluminum 263.3; other metal industries 115.2. *Energy production (consumption):* electricity (kW-hr; 2008) 11,657,000,000 ([2006] 9,822,-000,000); crude petroleum (barrels; 2008) 66,900,000 ([2006] 94,428,000); petroleum products (metric tons; 2006) 11,110,000 (1,447,000); natural gas (cu m; 2008) 15,241,000,000 ([2006] 7,890,000,000). **Gross national income** (2007): US$14,022,000,000 (US$12,935 per capita). **Population economically active** (2005): total 350,000; activity rate of total population 48.3% (participation rates: ages 15 and over 67.0%; female 23.2%; unemployed [Bahrainis only; October 2008] 3.6%). **Selected balance of payments data.** Receipts from (US$'000,000): tourism (2007) 1,105; foreign direct investment (FDI; 2005–07 avg.) 1,907. Disbursements for (US$'000,000): tourism (2007) 479; remittances (2008) 1,483; FDI (2005–07 avg.) 1,261.

Foreign trade

Imports (2007; c.i.f.): US$11,515,000,000 (crude petroleum 50.9%; machinery and apparatus 10.0%; motor vehicles 7.9%; aluminum oxide 5.8%; food products and live animals 4.0%). *Major import sources* (2006; excluding petroleum): Japan 11.9%; Saudi Arabia 11.6%; Australia 8.3%; China 8.2%; US 7.1%. **Exports** (2007; f.o.b.): US$13,665,000,000 (refined petroleum products 79.1%; aluminum [all forms] 9.0%; urea 2.4%; iron ore agglomerates 1.4%; methanol 1.3%). *Major export destinations* (2006; excluding petroleum): Saudi Arabia 20.9%; US 9.3%; India 6.8%; Singapore 6.5%; Qatar 3.9%.

Transport and communications

Transport. *Railroads:* none. *Roads* (2003): total length 3,498 km (paved 79%). *Vehicles* (2007): passenger cars 275,389; trucks and buses 44,075. *Air transport* (2007; Gulf Air only): passenger-km 13,999,000,000; metric ton-km cargo 498,000,000. **Communications,** in total units (units per 1,000 persons). Telephone landlines (2008): 220,000 (196); cellular telephone subscribers (2008): 1,400,000 (1,247); personal computers (2004): 121,000 (147); total Internet users (2007): 250,000 (241); broadband Internet subscribers (2008): 93,000 (83).

---

1 metric ton = about 1.1 short tons;   1 kilometer = 0.6 mi (statute);   1 metric ton-km cargo = about 0.68 short ton-mi cargo;   c.i.f.: cost, insurance, and freight;   f.o.b.: free on board

Education and health

Educational attainment (2001). Percentage of population ages 15 and over having: no formal education 24.0%; primary education 37.1%; secondary 26.4%; higher 12.5%. Literacy (2005): percentage of population ages 15 and over literate 90.0%; males literate 92.6%; females literate 86.4%. Health (2007): physicians 2,225 (1 per 467 persons); hospital beds 2,043 (1 per 509 persons); infant mortality rate per 1,000 live births (2007) 8.3.

Military

Total active duty personnel (November 2008): 8,200 (army 73.2%, navy 8.5%, air force 18.2%); US troops in Bahrain (November 2008): 1,324. Military expenditure as percentage of GDP (2008): 2.6%; per capita expenditure US$509.

Background

The area has long been an important trading center and is mentioned in Persian, Greek, and Roman references. It was ruled by Arabs from the 7th century AD but was then occupied by the Portuguese in 1521–1602. Since 1783 it has been ruled by the Khalifah family, though through a series of treaties its defense remained a British responsibility from 1820 to 1971. After Britain withdrew its forces from the Persian Gulf (1968), Bahrain declared its independence in 1971. It served as a center for the allies in the Persian Gulf War (1990–91). Since 1994 it has experienced bouts of political unrest, mainly among its large Shi'ite population. Constitutional revisions, ratified in 2002, made Bahrain a constitutional monarchy and enfranchised women.

Recent Developments

In May 2009 Bahrain announced that it would abolish the sponsorship system for its foreign workers, which had been compared to slavery. The move meant that the estimated 512,000 workers there would be able to change jobs and secure better pay without the approval of their sponsor (kafeel).

Internet resource: <www.cio.gov.bh>.

Bangladesh

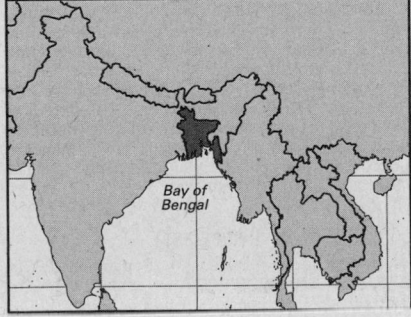

Bay of Bengal

Official name: Gana Prajatantri Bangladesh (People's Republic of Bangladesh). Form of government: unitary multiparty republic with one legislative house (Parliament [345]). Head of state: President Zillur Rahman (from 2009). Head of government: Prime Minister Sheikh Hasina Wazed (from 2009). Capital: Dhaka. Official language: Bengali (Bangla). Official religion: Islam. Monetary unit: 1 Bangladesh taka (Tk) = 100 paisa; valuation (1 Jul 2010) US$1 = Tk 69.45.

Demography

Area: 56,977 sq mi, 147,570 sq km. Population (2009): 156,051,000. Density (2009): persons per sq mi 2,900.7, persons per sq km 1,120.0. Urban (2006): 24.6%. Sex distribution (2006): male 51.21%; female 48.79%. Age breakdown (2005): under 15, 33.8%; 15–29, 30.5%; 30–44, 19.5%; 45–59, 10.6%; 60–74, 4.6%; 75–84, 0.9%; 85 and over, 0.1%. Ethnic composition (1997): Bengali 97.7%; tribal 1.9%, of which Chakma 0.4%, Saontal 0.2%, Marma 0.1%; other 0.4%. Religious affiliation (2005): Muslim (nearly all Sunni) 88.3%; Hindu 10.5%; Buddhist 0.6%; Christian (mostly Roman Catholic) 0.3%; other 0.3%. Major cities (metropolitan areas) (2008): Dhaka 7,000,940 (12,797,394); Chittagong 2,579,107 (3,858,093); Khulna 855,650 (1,388,425); Rajshahi 472,775 (775,495); Sylhet 463,198. Location: South Asia, bordering India, Myanmar (Burma), and the Bay of Bengal.

Vital statistics

Birth rate per 1,000 population (2006): 20.6 (world avg. 20.3). Death rate per 1,000 population (2006): 5.6 (world avg. 8.5). Total fertility rate (avg. births per childbearing woman; 2006): 2.41. Life expectancy at birth (2006): male 64.4 years; female 66.0 years.

National economy

Budget (2007–08). Revenue: Tk 605,400,000,000 (tax revenue 79.3%, of which VAT 28.1%, taxes on income and profits 18.8%, import duties 15.4%; nontax revenue 20.7%). Expenditures: Tk 936,100,000,000 (current expenditures 55.8%, of which interest on domestic debt 11.3%, education 9.2%, agriculture 6.5%; development expenditures 24.0%; other 20.2%). Public debt (external, outstanding; 2007): US$20,151,000,000. Production (metric tons except as noted). Agriculture and fishing (2007–08): paddy rice 28,931,000, potatoes 5,762,000, sugarcane 4,983,656, jute 832,000, rapeseed 227,930, allspice (2005) 138,000, ginger 57,000; livestock (number of live animals; 2007) 52,500,000 goats, 25,300,000 cattle; fisheries production (2006) 2,328,545 (from aquaculture 38%). Mining and quarrying (2007): granite 1,500,000; marine salt 360,000. Manufacturing (value added in Tk '000,000,000; 2004–05): marine products 28.6; medicines and pharmaceuticals 23.0; refined petroleum products 22.9. Energy production (consumption): electricity (kW-hr; 2007) 22,572,000,000 ([2006] 23,703,000,000); coal (metric tons; 2007) 1,000,000 (700,000); crude petroleum (barrels; 2007) 2,100,000 ([2006] 9,949,000); petroleum products (metric tons; 2006) 884,000 (3,462,000); natural gas (cu m; 2007) 15,225,000,000 ([2006] 15,488,000,000). Population economically active (2004 05): total 10,101,000, activity rate of total population 36.0% (participation rates: ages 15–64, 59.7%; female 24.5%; unemployed or underemployed [2008] 38%). **Gross national income** (2008): US$82,569,000,000 (US$520 per capita). **Selected balance of payments data.** Receipts from (US$'000,000): tourism (2007) 76; remittances (2008) 8,979; foreign direct investment (2005–07 avg.) 768; official development assistance (2007) 1,502. Disbursements for (US$'000,000): tourism (2007) 156; remittances (2008) 3.

Foreign trade

Imports (2006; c.i.f.): US$15,688,000,000 (machinery and apparatus 21.3%; refined petroleum products 10.9%; food products 9.6%; textile yarn and fabrics 9.2%; cotton 5.4%). *Major import sources:* China 16.4%; India 12.0%; Kuwait 9.3%; Japan 5.7%; South Korea 4.2%. **Exports** (2006; f.o.b.): US$11,697,000,000 (knitted or woven clothing and accessories 71.1%; dyed woven fabrics 5.9%; shrimp 4.1%; leather 2.1%; textile yarn 2.0%). *Major export destinations* (2006): US 26.7%; Germany 15.0%; UK 9.0%; China 6.6%; France 6.1%.

Transport and communications

Transport. *Railroads* (2002): route length 2,768 km; passenger-km 3,970,000,000; metric ton-km cargo 908,000,000. *Roads* (2003): total length 239,226 km (paved 10%). *Vehicles* (2005–06): passenger cars 97,450; trucks and buses 113,329. *Air transport* (2007; Biman Bangladesh Airlines only): passenger-km 4,186,000,000; metric ton-km cargo 116,140,000. **Communications,** in total units (units per 1,000 persons). Telephone landlines (2008): 1,345,000 (8.7); cellular telephone subscribers (2008): 44,640,000 (290); personal computers (2006): 3,050,000 (22); total Internet users (2007): 500,000 (3.5); broadband Internet subscribers (2007): 44,000 (0.3).

Education and health

Educational attainment (2004). Percentage of population ages 25 and over having: no formal schooling 48.8%; incomplete primary education 17.9%; complete primary 7.7%; incomplete secondary 15.1%; complete secondary or higher 10.5%. **Literacy** (2006): total population ages 15 and over literate 53.7%; males literate 58.5%; females literate 48.8%. **Health** (2006): physicians 44,632 (1 per 3,110 persons); hospital beds 51,044 (1 per 2,719 persons); infant mortality rate per 1,000 live births 45.0; undernourished population (2002–04) 44,000,000 (30% of total population based on the consumption of a minimum daily requirement of 1,780 calories).

Military

Total active duty personnel (November 2008): 157,053, of which UN peacekeepers 8,028 (army 80.3%, navy 10.8%, air force 8.9%). **Military expenditure as percentage of GDP** (2007): 1.5%; per capita expenditure US$7.

Background

In its early years Bangladesh was known as Bengal. When the British left the subcontinent in 1947, the area that was East Bengal became the part of Pakistan called East Pakistan. Bengali nationalist sentiment increased after the creation of an independent Pakistan. In 1971 violence erupted; some one million Bengalis were killed, and millions more fled to India, which finally entered the war on the side of the Bengalis, ensuring West Pakistan's defeat. East Pakistan became the independent nation of Bangladesh. Little of the devastation caused by the war has been repaired, and political instability, including the assassinations of two presidents, has, continued. In addition, the low-lying country has been repeatedly battered by natural disasters, notably tropical storms and flooding.

Recent Developments

A new government came into power in Bangladesh as the year 2009 began, ending the two-year rule of an unelected military-backed interim government. The parliament was suspended during this time, and many political leaders had been jailed on charges ranging from graft to the illegal possession of liquor. The country fared relatively well during the global recession, with GDP growth estimated at 5.9% and export growth in the ready-made-garment sector of more than 20.0% during the first half of the year.

Internet resource: <www.bbs.gov.bd>.

Barbados

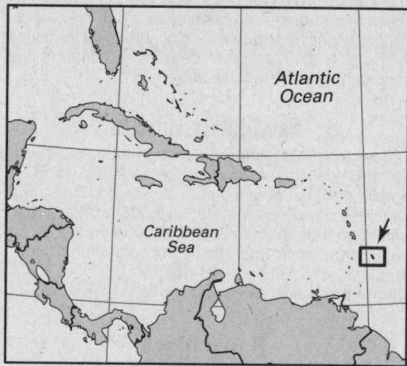

Official name: Barbados. **Form of government:** constitutional monarchy with two legislative houses (Senate [21]; House of Assembly [30]). **Head of state:** British Queen Elizabeth II (from 1952), represented by Governor-General Sir Clifford Husbands (from 1996). **Head of government:** Prime Minister David Thompson (from 2008). **Capital:** Bridgetown. **Official language:** English. **Official religion:** none. **Monetary unit:** 1 Barbados dollar (Bds$) = 100 cents; valuation (1 Jul 2010) US$1 = Bds$2.00.

Demography

Area: 166 sq mi, 430 sq km. **Population** (2009): 276,000. **Density** (2009): persons per sq mi 1,662.7, persons per sq km 641.9. **Urban** (2005):

---

1 metric ton = about 1.1 short tons;   1 kilometer = 0.6 mi (statute);   1 metric ton-km cargo = about 0.68 short ton-mi cargo;   c.i.f.: cost, insurance, and freight;   f.o.b.: free on board

38.4%. **Sex distribution** (2007): male 48.36%; female 51.64%. **Age breakdown** (2007): under 15, 19.8%; 15–29, 22.4%; 30–44, 24.7%; 45–59, 20.2%; 60–74, 8.7%; 75–84, 3.1%; 85 and over, 1.1%. **Ethnic composition** (2000): local black 87.1%; mixed race 6.0%; British expatriates 4.3%; US white 1.2%; Indo-Pakistani 1.1%; other 0.3%. **Religious affiliation** (2000): Christian 72.5%, of which Anglican 28.3%, Pentecostal 18.7%, Adventist 5.5%, Methodist 5.1%; Rastafarian 1.1%; Muslim 0.7%; Hindu 0.3%; nonreligious 17.3%; other/unknown 8.1%. **Major urban areas** (2006): Bridgetown 98,700; Speightstown 3,600; Oistins 2,300. **Location:** island at the eastern edge of the Caribbean Sea where it adjoins the North Atlantic Ocean, northeast of Venezuela.

Vital statistics

Birth rate per 1,000 population (2007): 12.8 (world avg. 20.3). **Death rate** per 1,000 population (2007): 8.5 (world avg. 8.5). **Total fertility rate** (avg. births per childbearing woman; 2007): 1.68. **Life expectancy** at birth (2007): male 71.2 years; female 75.8 years.

National economy

Budget (2006–07). *Revenue* (current revenue only): Bds$2,156,000,000 (tax revenue 95.8%, of which VAT 30.1%, corporate taxes 20.6%, income tax 13.8%, import duties 6.8%; nontax revenue 4.2%). *Expenditures:* Bds$2,351,000,000 (current expenditures 89.1%, of which education 19.0%, general public service 15.7%, debt payments 14.0%, health 12.2%; development expenditures 10.9%). **Production** (metric tons except as noted). *Agriculture and fishing* (2006): sugarcane (2007) 354,000, sweet potatoes 2,000, coconuts 1,950, okra 1,550; livestock (number of live animals) 19,000 pigs, 10,800 sheep, 3,400,000 chickens; fisheries production 1,974 (from aquaculture, none). *Mining and quarrying* (2006): limestone 1,900,000, clay and shale 145,000. *Manufacturing* (2007): cement 294,184, raw sugar 34,700, rum (2005) 132,000 hectolitres; other manufactures include industrial chemical products, electronics, garments, and wooden furniture. *Energy production (consumption):* electricity (kW-hr; 2007) 924,000,000 (924,000,000); crude petroleum (barrels; 2007) 303,000 ([2006] negligible); petroleum products (metric tons; 2006) 1,000 (252,000); natural gas (cu m; 2007) 21,100,000 ([2006] 26,857,000). **Population economically active** (December 2005): total 145,800; activity rate of total population 53.1% (participation rates: ages 15 and over, 69.0%; female 49.5%; unemployed [July–September 2008] 8.4%). **Gross national income** (2007): US$3,580,000,000 (US$12,178 per capita). **Public debt** (external, outstanding; December 2006): US$799,400,000. **Selected balance of payments data.** Receipts from (US$'000,000): tourism (2006) 967; remittances (2008) 168; foreign direct investment (FDI; 2005–07 avg.) 68; official development assistance (2007) 14. Disbursements for (US$'000,000): tourism (2006) 105; remittances (2008) 40; FDI (2005–07 avg.) 11.

Foreign trade

Imports (2007; c.i.f.): US$1,299,000,000 (machinery and apparatus 24.4%; manufactured goods 18.0%; food products 15.6%; chemical products 11.3%; motor vehicles 7.8%). *Major import sources:* US 43.7%; UK 7.8%; Trinidad and Tobago 7.7%; Japan 4.5%; Canada 4.4%. **Exports** (2007; f.o.b.): US$314,000,000 (crude petroleum 21.9%; food products 15.3%, of which raw sugar 6.0%; rum 10.8%; machinery and apparatus 7.8%; medicines 7.7%; fabricated metal products 5.7%). *Major export destinations:* Trinidad and Tobago 27.8%; US 14.2%; UK 9.1%; St. Lucia 6.6%; Jamaica 5.3%.

Transport and communications

Transport. *Railroads:* none. *Roads* (2006): total length 1,650 km (paved virtually 100%). *Vehicles* (2004): passenger cars 92,195; trucks and buses 8,597. *Air transport* (2003): metric ton-km cargo 200,000. **Communications,** in total units (units per 1,000 persons). Telephone landlines (2006): 140,000 (501); cellular telephone subscribers (2006): 237,000 (847); personal computers (2005): 40,000 (148); total Internet users (2007): 280,000 (997); broadband Internet subscribers (2006): 55,000 (202).

Education and health

Educational attainment (2003). Percentage of employed labor force having: no formal schooling 0.5%; primary education 14.9%; secondary 58.7%; technical/vocational 5.4%; university 19.6%; other/unknown 0.9%. **Literacy** (2003): total population ages 15 and over literate 99.7%. **Health** (2007): physicians (2003) 369 (1 per 751 persons); hospital beds 630 (1 per 446 persons); infant mortality rate per 1,000 live births 13.2; undernourished population (2002–04) less than 2.5% of total population.

Military

Total active duty personnel (November 2008): 610 (army 82.0%, navy 18.0%). **Military expenditure as percentage of GDP** (2008): 0.8%; per capita expenditure US$106.

Background

The island of Barbados was probably inhabited by Arawak Indians who originally came from South America. Spaniards may have landed by 1518, and by 1536 they had apparently wiped out the Indian population. Barbados was settled by the English in the 1620s. Slaves were brought in to work the sugar plantations, which were especially prosperous in the 17th–18th centuries. The British Empire abolished slavery in 1834, and all the slaves in Barbados were freed by 1838. In 1958 Barbados joined the West Indies Federation. When the latter dissolved in 1962, Barbados sought independence from Britain; it achieved it and joined the Commonwealth in 1966.

Recent Developments

The "get-tough" immigration policy of June 2009 in Barbados decreed that foreigners living there illegally must prove prior residence in the country, pass a background check, and provide evidence of employment to avoid deportation.

Internet resource: <www.barstats.gov.bb>.

Belarus

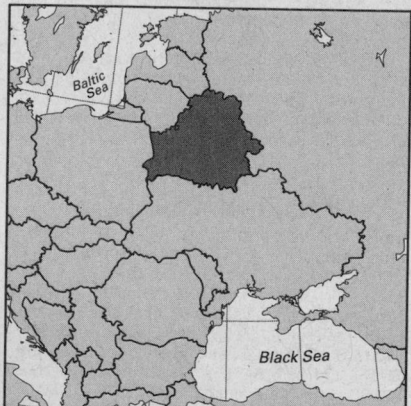

Official name: Respublika Belarus (Republic of Belarus). **Form of government:** republic with two legislative houses (Council of the Republic [64]; House of Representatives [110]). **Head of state and government:** President Alyaksandr H. Lukashenka (from 1994), assisted by Prime Minister Syarhey Sidorski (from 2003). **Capital:** Minsk. **Official languages:** Belarusian; Russian. **Official religion:** none (a 2003 concordat grants the Belarusian Orthodox Church privileged status). **Monetary unit:** Belarusian rubel (Br); valuation (1 Jul 2010) US$1 = Br 3,020.00.

Demography

Area: 80,153 sq mi, 207,595 sq km. **Population** (2009): 9,658,000. **Density** (2009): persons per sq mi 120.4, persons per sq km 46.5. **Urban** (2007): 73.4%. **Sex distribution** (2007): male 46.67%; female 53.33%. **Age breakdown** (2005): under 15, 15.7%; 15–29, 23.9%; 30–44, 22.0%; 45–59, 20.3%; 60–74, 12.5%; 75–84, 4.9%; 85 and over, 0.7%. **Ethnic composition** (1999): Belarusian 81.2%; Russian 11.4%; Polish 3.9%; Ukrainian 2.4%; Jewish 0.3%; other 0.8%. **Religious affiliation** (2007): nonreligious/atheist 50.0%; Belarusian Orthodox 40.0%; Roman Catholic 7.0%; other Christian 1.0%; Jewish 0.6%; other 1.4%. **Major cities** (2005): Minsk 1,741,000; Homyel 481,500; Mahilyow 367,700; Vitsyebsk 343,600; Hrodna 318,600. **Location:** eastern Europe, bordering Latvia, Russia, Ukraine, Poland, and Lithuania.

Vital statistics

Birth rate per 1,000 population (2008): 11.1 (world avg. 20.3); within marriage 79.9%. **Death rate** per 1,000 population (2008): 13.8 (world avg. 8.5). **Total fertility rate** (avg. births per childbearing woman; 2008): 1.42. **Life expectancy** at birth (2008): male 64.7 years; female 76.5 years.

National economy

Budget (2007). *Revenue:* Br 37,167,000,000 (taxes on goods and services 34.2%; social security contri-

butions 30.3%; taxes on trade 16.9%; corporate taxes 6.1%; other taxes 4.8%; nontax revenue 7.7%). *Expenditures:* Br 36,748,000,000 (social protection 32.9%; economic affairs 25.0%; general administration 23.8%). **Public debt** (external, outstanding; 2007): US$2,338,000,000. **Population economically active** (2007): 4,525,200; activity rate of total population 46.6% (participation rate [1999]: ages 15–64, 69.7%; female 52.8%; officially/unofficially unemployed [2008] 1.0%/15–20%). **Production** (metric tons except as noted). *Agriculture and fishing* (2007): potatoes 8,744,000, sugar beets 3,626,000, barley 1,911,000, rapeseed 240,000; livestock (number of live animals) 4,007,000 cattle, 3,598,000 pigs; fisheries production (2006) 5,050 (from aquaculture 82%). *Mining and quarrying* (2005): potash 4,844,000; peat 2,408,000. *Manufacturing* (2007): fertilizers 5,880,000; cement 3,820,000; crude steel (2005) 2,076,000. *Energy production (consumption):* electricity (kW-hr; 2007) 31,800,000,000 ([2006] 36,171,000,000); coal (metric tons; 2006) none (132,000); crude petroleum (barrels; 2007) 12,800,000 ([2006] 154,800,000); petroleum products (metric tons; 2006) 17,882,000 (5,622,000); natural gas (cu m; 2006) 219,000,000 (20,779,000,000). **Gross national income** (2008): US$52,117,000,000 (US$5,380 per capita). **Selected balance of payments data.** Receipts from (US$'000,000): tourism (2007) 324; remittances (2008) 448; foreign direct investment (2005–07 avg.) 810; official development assistance (2007) 83. Disbursements for (US$'000,000): tourism (2007) 606; remittances (2008) 142.

Foreign trade

Imports (2007; c.i.f.): US$28,693,000,000 (crude petroleum 25.2%; nonelectrical machinery 11.0%; base and fabricated metals 10.6%; chemical products 9.0%; natural gas 7.3%). *Major import sources:* Russia 60.0%; Germany 7.6%; Ukraine 5.3%; Poland 2.9%; China 2.8%. **Exports** (2007; f.o.b.): US$24,275,-000,000 (refined petroleum products 31.4%; machinery and apparatus 12.9%; motor vehicles 8.0%; food products 6.9%, of which dairy products 3.8%; potassium chloride 5.6%; iron and steel 4.9%). *Major export destinations:* Russia 36.6%; Netherlands 17.6%; UK 6.3%; Ukraine 6.1%; Poland 5.1%.

Transport and communications

Transport. *Railroads* (2007): length (2002) 5,533 km; passenger-km 9,366,000,000; metric ton-km cargo 47,933,000,000. *Roads* (2005): total length 94,797 km (paved 89%). *Vehicles* (2005): passenger cars 1,771,398. *Air transport* (2007): passenger-km 975,000,000; metric ton-km cargo 66,000,000. **Communications,** in total units (units per 1,000 persons). Telephone landlines (2007): 3,672,000 (379); cellular telephone subscribers (2007): 6,960,000 (717); personal computers (2007): 78,000 (80); broadband Internet subscribers (2006): 11,000 (1.2).

Education and health

Literacy (2007): total population ages 15 and over literate 99.7%. **Health** (2007): physicians 46,900 (1

---

1 metric ton = about 1.1 short tons;   1 kilometer = 0.6 mi (statute);   1 metric ton-km cargo = about 0.68 short ton-mi cargo;   c.i.f.: cost, insurance, and freight;   f.o.b.: free on board

per 207 persons); hospital beds 108,900 (1 per 89 persons); infant mortality rate per 1,000 live births (2008) 4.5; undernourished population (2002–04) 400,000 (4% of total population based on the consumption of a minimum daily requirement of 1,970 calories).

Military

Total active duty personnel (November 2008): 72,940 (army 40.6%, air force and air defense 24.9%, centrally controlled units 34.5%). **Military expenditure as percentage of GDP** (2008): 1.2%; per capita expenditure US$70.

Background

While Belarusians share a distinct identity and language, they did not enjoy political sovereignty until the late 20th century. The territory that is now Belarus underwent partition and changed hands often; as a result its history is entwined with those of its neighbors. In medieval times the region was ruled by Lithuanians and Poles. Following the Third Partition of Poland, it was ruled by Russia. After World War I, the western part was assigned to Poland, and the eastern part became Soviet Russian territory. After World War II, the Soviets expanded what had been the Belorussian SSR by annexing more of Poland. Much of the area suffered radiation contamination from the Chernobyl accident in 1986, forcing many to evacuate. Belarus declared its independence in 1991 and later joined the Commonwealth of Independent States.

Recent Developments

In 2009, complex international relationships grew in importance to Belarus. In May Russia cancelled the remaining US$500 million of a US$2 billion loan to Belarus. In June, after Belarus had held talks with the EU on dairy exports, Russia instituted a ban on all Belarusian milk products—a serious act, since Belarus sells 95% of its dairy exports to Russia. Belarus in turn skipped a meeting of the Collective Security Treaty Organization in Moscow, at which it was scheduled to take up the rotating chairmanship. Belarus also withstood Russian pressure to recognize the breakaway Georgian republics of South Ossetia and Abkhazia. On 7 May in Prague, Belarus was accepted as a member of the EU's Eastern Partnership project, the goal of which was to promote economic integration and enhance political links between EU border countries.

Internet resource:
<http://belstat.gov.by/homep/en/main.html>.

Belgium

Official name: Koninkrijk België (Dutch); Royaume de Belgique (French); Königreich Belgien (German) (Kingdom of Belgium). **Form of government:** federal constitutional monarchy with two legislative houses (Senate [71]; House of Representatives [150]). **Head of state:** King Albert II (from 1993). **Head of government:** Prime Minister Yves Leterme (from 2009). **Capital:** Brussels. **Official languages:** Dutch; French; German. **Official religion:** none. **Monetary unit:** 1 euro (€) = 100 cents; valuation (1 Jul 2010) US$1 = €0.80.

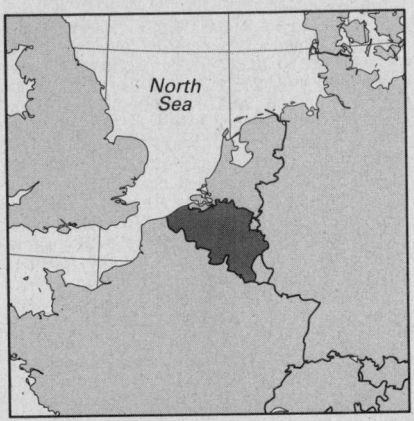

North Sea

Demography

Area: 11,787 sq mi, 30,528 sq km. **Population** (2009): 10,779,000. **Density** (2009): persons per sq mi 914.5, persons per sq km 353.1. **Urban** (2005): 97.3%. **Sex distribution** (2007): male 48.98%; female 51.02%. **Age breakdown** (2005): under 15, 17.1%; 15–29, 18.4%; 30–44, 22.0%; 45–59, 20.5%; 60–74, 14.0%; 75–84, 6.4%; 85 and over, 1.6%. **National composition** (2007): Belgian 90.9%, of which Flemish-speaking 53.6%, French-speaking 36.4%, German-speaking 0.9%; Italian 1.6%; French 1.2%; Dutch 1.2%; Moroccan 0.7%; other 4.4%. **Religious affiliation** (2000): Roman Catholic 57%; undefined Christian 15%; Muslim 4%; nonreligious 17%; other 7%. **Major cities/urban agglomerations** (2007): Brussels 148,873/1,831,496; Antwerp 472,071/955,338; Liège 190,102/641,591; Gent 237,250/423,320; Charleroi 201,593/405,236. **Location:** western Europe, bordering the Netherlands, Germany, Luxembourg, France, and the North Sea.

Vital statistics

Birth rate per 1,000 population (2008): 11.7 (world avg. 20.3); within marriage 58.0%. **Death rate** per 1,000 population (2007): 9.5 (world avg. 8.5). **Total fertility rate** (avg. births per childbearing woman; 2008): 1.82. **Life expectancy** at birth (2008): male 77.5 years; female 83.5 years.

National economy

Budget (2007). *Revenue:* €160,393,000,000 (social security contributions 28.8%; income tax 23.3%; taxes on goods and services 23.1%). *Expenditures:* €161,154,000,000 (social insurance benefits 46.3%, of which health 12.8%; wages 24.1%; interest on debt 7.8%; capital expenditure 5.9%). **Production** (metric tons except as noted). *Agriculture and fishing* (2007): sugar beets 5,746,892, potatoes 2,877,685, wheat 1,480,710, chicory roots 361,305; livestock (number of live animals) 6,270,000 pigs, 2,639,700 cattle; fisheries production (2006) 24,219 (from aquaculture 5%). *Mining and quarrying* (2007): marble 340,000. *Manufacturing* (value added in €'000,000; 2007): chemical products 9,228; base and fabricated metals 8,174; food products, beverages, and tobacco products 6,257. *Energy production (consumption):* electricity (kW-hr; 2007) 88,278,000,000 ([2005] 93,248,000,000); hard coal (metric tons; 2007) none (5,371,000); lignite (metric tons; 2006) 29,000 (313,000); crude petroleum (barrels; 2007) none ([2005] 235,000,000); petroleum products (metric tons; 2006) 28,114,000 (17,514,000); natural gas (cu m; 2007) none ([2006] 21,922,000,000). **Population economically active** (2006): total 4,647,200; activity rate 44.2% (participation rates: ages 15–64, 58.8%; female 44.4%; unemployed [2008] 7.1%). **Gross national income** (2008): US$474,467,000,000 (US$44,330 per capita). **Public debt** (September 2008; federal only): US$398,900,000,000. **Selected balance of payments data.** Receipts from (US$'000,000): tourism (2007) 10,898; remittances (2008) 9,280; foreign direct investment (FDI; 2005–07 avg.) 46,439. Disbursements for (US$'000,000): tourism (2007) 17,268; remittances (2008) 3,689; FDI (2005–07 avg.) 46,284.

Foreign trade

Imports (2007; c.i.f.): US$413,371,000,000 (machinery and apparatus 13.9%; mineral fuels 11.5%; motor vehicles and parts 10.9%; base and fabricated metals 8.5%; medicines 8.0%; organic chemical products 7.3%). *Major import sources:* Germany 17.8%; Netherlands 17.6%; France 11.2%; UK 6.3%; US 5.3%. **Exports** (2007; f.o.b.): US$430,822,000,000 (machinery and apparatus 12.3%; motor vehicles and parts 11.4%; medicines 11.0%; food products 6.9%; mineral fuels 6.6%; organic chemical products 6.5%; iron and steel 6.0%; plastic products 5.1%; diamonds 4.2% [world's leading exporter]). *Major export destinations:* Germany 19.7%; France 16.7%; Netherlands 11.9%; UK 7.6%; US 5.6%.

Transport and communications

Transport. *Railroads* (2006): route length 3,233 km; passenger-km 9,607,000,000; metric ton-km cargo 8,442,000,000. *Roads* (2004): total length 150,567 km (paved 78%). *Vehicles* (2006): passenger cars 4,976,286; trucks and buses 638,579. *Air transport* (2007; Brussels Airlines only): passenger-km 7,542,000,000; metric ton-km cargo 80,668,000. **Communications,** in total units (units per 1,000 persons). Telephone landlines (2008): 4,457,000 (416); cellular telephone subscribers (2008): 11,822,000 (1,104); personal computers (2006): 3,977,000 (377); total Internet users (2007): 7,006,000 (659); broadband Internet subscribers (2008): 2,962,000 (277).

Education and health

Educational attainment (2002). Percentage of population ages 25 and over having: no formal schooling through lower-secondary education 39%; upper secondary/higher vocational 33%; university 28%. **Health:** physicians (2007) 38,402 (1 per 278 persons); hospital beds (2005) 70,795 (1 per 148 persons); infant mortality rate per 1,000 live births (2008) 3.4; undernourished population (2002–04) less than 2.5% of total population.

Military

Total active duty personnel (November 2008): 38,844 (army 36.7%, navy 4.2%, air force 18.9%, medical service 4.9%, joint service 35.3%); foreign forces at NATO headquarters (November 2008): US 1,301; UK 400. **Military expenditure as percentage of GDP** (2007): 1.1%; per capita expenditure US$471.

Background

Inhabited in ancient times by the Belgae, a Celtic people, the area was conquered by Caesar in 57 BC; under Augustus it became the Roman province of Gallia Belgica. Conquered by the Franks, it later broke up into semi-independent territories, including Brabant and Luxembourg. By the late 15th century AD, the territories of the Netherlands, of which the future Belgium was a part, had gradually united and passed to the Habsburgs. In the 16th century, it was a center for European commerce. The basis of modern Belgium was laid in the southern Catholic provinces that split from the northern provinces after the Union of Utrecht in 1579. Overrun by the French and incorporated into France in 1801, it was reunited to Holland and with it became the independent Kingdom of the Netherlands in 1815. After the revolt of its citizens in 1830, it became the independent Kingdom of Belgium. Under Léopold II it acquired vast lands in Africa. Overrun by the Germans in World Wars I and II, Belgium was the scene of the Battle of the Bulge. Internal discord led to legislation in the 1970s and 1980s that created three nearly autonomous regions in accordance with language distribution: Flemish Flanders, French Wallonia, and bilingual Brussels. In 1993 it became a federation comprising the three regions, which gained greater autonomy at the outset of the 21st century. It is a member of the European Union.

Did you know? Belgium's population is split between the Flemings, who speak Flemish (Dutch) and live mostly in the northern half of the country, and the Walloons, who speak French and can in general be found in the south.

Recent Developments

Belgium enjoyed some much-needed political stability in 2009 after having had three governments in the previous 18 months. In January a new coalition under Herman Van Rompuy received a solid vote of confidence: 88 deputies voted in favor and 45 against. After having been forced to resign as prime minister in December 2008, Yves Leterme returned to the government in the summer of 2009 as foreign minister. In November, after it was announced that Van Rompuy would become the first-ever president of the EU, King Albert gave Leterme a second chance at the prime ministership, appointing him to succeed Van Rompuy as Belgium's head of government.

Internet resource: <www.visitbelgium.com>.

---

1 metric ton = about 1.1 short tons;   1 kilometer = 0.6 mi (statute);   1 metric ton-km cargo = about 0.68 short ton-mi cargo;   c.i.f.: cost, insurance, and freight;   f.o.b.: free on board

Belize

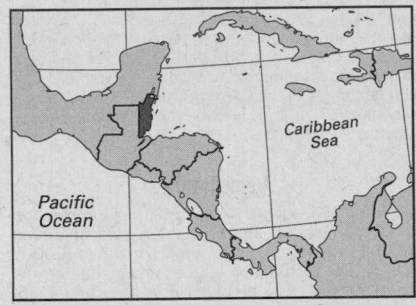

Caribbean Sea

Pacific Ocean

Official name: Belize. **Form of government:** constitutional monarchy with two legislative houses (Senate [12]; House of Representatives [31]). **Head of state:** British Queen Elizabeth II (from 1952), represented by Governor-General Colville Young (from 1993). **Head of government:** Prime Minister Dean Barrow (from 2008). **Capital:** Belmopan. **Official language:** English. **Official religion:** none. **Monetary unit:** 1 Belize dollar (BZ$) = 100 cents; valuation (1 Jul 2010) US$1 = BZ$1.93.

Demography

Area: 8,867 sq mi, 22,965 sq km. **Population** (2009): 334,000. **Density** (2009): persons per sq mi 37.7, persons per sq km 14.5. **Urban** (2008): 51.4%. **Sex distribution** (2008): male 49.95%; female 50.05%. **Age breakdown** (2007): under 15, 38.9%; 15–29, 29.4%; 30–44, 17.7%; 45–59, 8.9%; 60–74, 3.8%; 75–84, 1.1%; 85 and over, 0.2%. **Ethnic composition** (2004): mestizo (Spanish-Indian) 48.4%; Creole (predominantly black) 27.0%; Mayan Indian 10.0%; Garifuna (black-Carib Indian) 5.7%; white 3.9%, of which Mennonite 3.2%; East Indian 3.0%; Chinese 0.9%; other 1.1%. **Religious affiliation** (2000): Roman Catholic 49.6%; Protestant 31.8%, of which Pentecostal 7.4%, Anglican 5.3%, Seventh-day Adventist 5.2%, Mennonite 4.1%; other Christian 1.9%; nonreligious 9.4%; other 7.3%. **Major cities** (2008): Belize City 65,200; San Ignacio/Santa Elena 19,100; Belmopan 18,100; Orange Walk 16,300; Dangriga 12,000. **Location:** Central America, bordering Mexico, the Caribbean Sea, and Guatemala.

Vital statistics

Birth rate per 1,000 population (2007): 28.3 (world avg. 20.3); (1997) within marriage 40.3%. **Death rate** per 1,000 population (2007): 5.7 (world avg. 8.5). **Total fertility rate** (avg. births per childbearing woman; 2007): 3.52. **Life expectancy** at birth (2007): male 66.4 years; female 70.1 years.

National economy

Budget (2007). *Revenue:* BZ$765,477,000 (tax revenue 75.2%, of which taxes on goods and services 30.3%, taxes on international trade 22.8%, taxes on income and profits 21.3%; grants 11.4%; nontax revenue 9.7%; other 3.7%). *Expenditures:* BZ$794,758,000 (current expenditures 80.0%; capital expenditures 20.0%). **Production** (metric tons except as noted). *Agriculture and fishing* (2007): sugarcane (2008) 1,017,000, oranges 213,100, bananas (2008) 79,200, plantain 41,000, papayas (2008) 28,900; livestock (number of live animals) 58,500 cattle, 1,600,000 chickens; fisheries production (2006) 11,788 (from aquaculture 65%). *Mining and quarrying* (2006): limestone 287,000; sand and gravel 219,000 cu m. *Manufacturing* (value added in US$'000,000; 2007): food products and beverages (significantly citrus concentrate, flour, sugar, and beer) 77.2; textiles, wearing apparel, and footwear 3.6; other (including crude petroleum extraction) 64.3. *Energy production (consumption):* electricity (kW-hr; 2006) 191,000,000 (220,000,000); crude petroleum (barrels; 2007) 1,100,000 (n.a.); petroleum products (metric tons; 2006) none (272,000). **Population economically active** (2005): total 110,786; activity rate of total population 38.2% (participation rates: ages 15–64, 64.2%; female 36.7%; unemployed [2008] 8.1%). **Gross national income** (2008): US$1,186,000,000 (US$3,820 per capita). **Public debt** (external, outstanding; December 2008): US$954,100,000. **Selected balance of payments data.** Receipts from (US$'000,000): tourism (2007) 291; remittances (2008) 78; foreign direct investment (2005–07 avg.) 114; official development assistance (2007) 23. Disbursements for (US$'000,000): tourism (2007) 43; remittances (2008) 29.

Foreign trade

Imports (2007; c.i.f.): US$684,300,000 (refined petroleum products 14.3%; manufactured goods 11.9%; machinery and apparatus 11.7%; food products 9.9%; chemical products 7.5%; motor vehicles 5.8%). *Major import sources:* US 33.9%; Cuba 11.4%; Panama 9.7%; Mexico 9.6%; Guatemala 6.9%). **Exports** (2007; f.o.b.): US$266,600,000 (food products 63.2%, of which orange juice 19.6%, raw cane sugar 16.5%, bananas 7.8%, frozen crustaceans 7.6%, papayas and melons 4.9%; crude petroleum 26.9%). *Major export destinations:* US 26.8%; UK 18.0%; Panama 14.3%; Costa Rica 11.8%; Netherlands 7.8%.

Transport and communications

Transport. *Railroads:* none. *Roads* (2006): total length 3,007 km (paved 19%). *Vehicles* (2003): passenger cars 36,952; trucks and buses 7,380. *Air transport* (2001; Belize international airport only): passenger arrivals 256,564, passenger departures 240,900; cargo loaded 186 metric tons, cargo unloaded 1,272 metric tons. **Communications,** in total units (units per 1,000 persons). Telephone landlines (2008): 31,000 (97); cellular telephone subscribers (2008): 160,000 (497); personal computers (2002): 35,000 (132); total Internet users (2007): 32,000 (111); broadband Internet subscribers (2008): 7,700 (24).

Education and health

Educational attainment (2000). Percentage of population ages 25 and over having: no formal schooling 36.6%; primary education 40.9%; secondary 11.7%; postsecondary/advanced vocational 6.4%; university 3.8%; other/unknown 0.6%. **Literacy** (2003): total population ages 15 and over literate 76.9%; males literate 77.1%; females literate 76.7%. **Health:** physicians (2009) 262 (1 per 1,110 persons); hospital beds (2005) 436 (1 per 665 persons); infant mortality rate per 1,000 live births (2007) 21.2; undernourished population (2002–04) 10,000 (4% of total population based on the consumption of a minimum daily requirement of 1,810 calories).

Military

Total active duty personnel (November 2008): 1,050 (army 100%); foreign forces (2008): British army 30. **Military expenditure as percentage of GDP** (2007): 1.4%; per capita expenditure US$58.

Background

The area was inhabited by the Maya 300 BC–AD 900; the ruins of their ceremonial centers, including Caracol and Xunantunich, can still be seen. The Spanish claimed sovereignty from the 16th century but never tried to settle Belize, though they regarded as interlopers the British who did. British logwood cutters arrived in the mid-17th century; Spanish opposition was finally overcome in 1798. When settlers began to penetrate the interior they met with Indian resistance. In 1871 British Honduras became a crown colony, but an unfulfilled provision of an 1859 British-Guatemalan treaty led Guatemala to claim the territory. The situation had not been resolved when Belize was granted its independence in 1981. A British force, stationed there to ensure the new nation's security, was withdrawn after Guatemala officially recognized the territory's independence in 1991.

Recent Developments

Despite the Belize government's US$200 million economic stimulus package, by the end of the first quarter of the 2009 fiscal year, the economy was feeling the effects of high inflation (9.6%) and a drop in domestic exports (2.6%). The fall in the price of petroleum, the loss of tourists' dollars, and debt servicing added to the downturn.

Internet resource: <www.statisticsbelize.org.bz>.

Benin

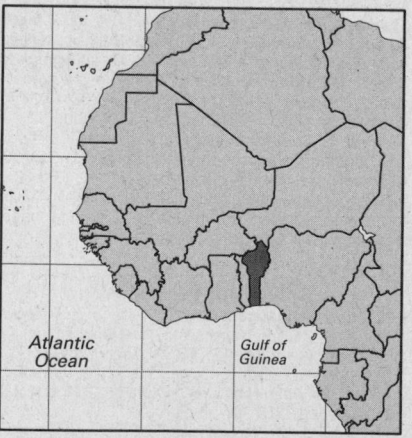

Atlantic Ocean

Gulf of Guinea

Official name: République du Bénin (Republic of Benin). **Form of government:** multiparty republic with one legislative house (National Assembly [83]). **Head of state and government:** President Yayi Boni (from 2006). **Capital:** Porto-Novo (official capital and seat of legislature; administrative seat in Cotonou). **Official language:** French. **Official religion:** none. **Monetary unit:** 1 CFA franc (CFAF) = 100 centimes; valuation (1 Jul 2010) US$1 = CFAF 527.20.

Demography

Area: 43,484 sq mi, 112,622 sq km. **Population** (2009): 8,792,000. **Density** (2009): persons per sq mi 202.2, persons per sq km 78.1. **Urban** (2005): 40.0%. **Sex distribution** (2008): male 49.99%; female 50.01%. **Age breakdown** (2008): under 15, 45.5%; 15–29, 27.3%; 30–44, 15.7%; 45–59, 7.4%; 60–74, 3.4%; 75–84, 0.6%; 85 and over 0.1%. **Ethnic composition** (2002): Fon 39.2%; Adjara 15.2%; Yoruba (Nago) 12.3%; Bariba 9.2%; Fulani 7.0%; Somba (Otomary) 6.1%; Yoa-Lokpa 4.0%; other 7.0%. **Religious affiliation** (2002): Christian 42.8%, of which Roman Catholic 27.1%, Protestant 5.4%, indigenous Christian 5.3%; Muslim 24.4%; traditional beliefs 23.3%, of which Vodou (voodoo) 17.3%; nonreligious 6.5%; other 3.0%. **Major urban localities** (2006): Cotonou 719,912; Porto-Novo 255,878; Godomey 187,836; Parakou 178,304; Abomey-Calavi 75,226. **Location:** western Africa, bordering Burkina Faso, Niger, Nigeria, the Atlantic Ocean, and Togo.

Vital statistics

Birth rate per 1,000 population (2008): 39.8 (world avg. 20.3). **Death rate** per 1,000 population (2008): 9.7 (world avg. 8.5). **Total fertility rate** (avg. births per childbearing woman; 2008): 5.58.

National economy

Budget (2007). *Revenue:* CFAF 634,000,000,000 (tax revenue 70.3%; nontax revenue 16.0%; grants 13.7%). *Expenditures:* CFAF 585,400,000,000 (current expenditures 65.6%; development expenditures 34.4%, of which externally financed expenditures 19.3%). **Public debt** (external, outstanding; 2007): US$852,000,000. **Gross national income** (2008): US$5,951,000,000 (US$690 per capita). **Production** (metric tons except as noted). *Agriculture and fishing* (2007): cassava 2,525,000, yams 2,240,000, corn (maize) 900,000, seed cotton 313,500, oil palm fruit 275,000, okra 77,500, cashews 41,500; livestock (number of live animals) 1,900,000 cattle, 1,439,600 goats, 15,050,000 chickens; fisheries production (2006) 38,436 (from aquaculture, 1%). *Mining and quarrying* (2006): clay 21,000, gold 20 kg. *Manufacturing* (value added in US$'000,000; 1999): food products 74; textiles 42; beverages 36. *Energy production (consumption):* electricity (kW-hr; 2006) 128,000,000 (718,000,000); crude petroleum (barrels; 2005) 137,000 (negligible); petroleum products (metric tons; 2006) none (972,000). **Population economically active** (2006): total 3,539,000; activity rate of total population 40.4% (participation rates: ages 15–64, 72.9%; female 40.3%; unemployed, n.a.). **Selected balance of payments data.** Re-

---

1 metric ton = about 1.1 short tons;   1 kilometer = 0.6 mi (statute);   1 metric ton-km cargo = about 0.68 short ton-mi cargo;   c.i.f.: cost, insurance, and freight;   f.o.b.: free on board

ceipts from (US$'000,000): tourism (2007) 118; remittances (2008) 271; foreign direct investment (2005–07 avg.) 51; official development assistance (2007) 470. Disbursements for (US$'000,000): tourism (2007) 35; remittances (2008) 67.

Foreign trade

Imports (2005; c.i.f.): US$898,700,000 (food products 26.2%, of which rice 11.2%, poultry cuts 4.7%; refined petroleum products 13.7%; machinery and apparatus 7.4%; electricity 6.3%; motor vehicles 4.7%; cement clinker 4.4%). Major import sources: France 18.4%; China 8.8%; Ghana 7.2%; Côte d'Ivoire 6.9%; Thailand 6.7%. Exports (2005; f.o.b. [excludes reexports—notably petroleum and food products particularly from Nigeria and Niger—valued at US$253,000,000]): US$288,200,000 (cotton 58.0%; food products 12.0%, of which cashews 6.9%; cigarettes 6.7%). Major export destinations: China 36.2%; India 6.9%; Nigeria 5.8%; Niger 5.2%; Indonesia 3.6%.

Transport and communications

Transport. Railroads (2006): length 578 km; passenger-km (2005) 17,000,000; metric ton-km cargo 28,900,000. Roads (2004): total length 19,000 km (paved 9.5%). Vehicles (2003): passenger cars 135,700; trucks and buses 19,200. Air transport (2003): metric ton-km cargo 7,000,000. Communications, in total units (units per 1,000 persons). Telephone landlines (2007): 110,000 (14); cellular telephone subscribers (2008): 3,435,000 (403); personal computers (2007): 58,000 (7); total Internet users (2008): 550,000 (64); broadband Internet subscribers (2007): 2,000 (0.2).

Education and health

Educational attainment (2002). Percentage of population ages 15 and over having: no formal schooling 63.5%; primary education 18.7%; secondary 15.9%; postsecondary 1.9%. Literacy (2005): total percentage of population ages 15 and over literate 43.2%; males literate 58.8%; females literate 28.4%. Health: physicians (2003) 1,013 (1 per 7,135 persons); hospital beds (2001) 590 (1 per 11,238 persons); infant mortality rate per 1,000 live births (2008) 66.2; undernourished population (2002–04) 800,000 (12% of total population based on the consumption of a minimum daily requirement of 1,800 calories).

Military

Total active duty personnel (November 2008): 4,750, of which UN peacekeepers 1,178 (army 90.5%, navy 4.2%, air force 5.3%). Military expenditure as percentage of GDP (2007): 0.9%; per capita expenditure US$7.

Background

In southern Benin, the Dahomey, or Fon, established the Abomey kingdom in 1625. In the 18th century, the kingdom became known as Dahomey when it expanded to include Allada and Ouidah, where French forts had been established in the 17th century. In 1857 the French reestablished themselves in the area, and eventually fighting ensued. In 1894 Dahomey became a French protectorate; it was incorporated into the federation of French West Africa in 1904. It achieved independence in 1960. The area called Dahomey was renamed Benin in 1975. Its chronically weak economy produced tension between laborers and the government into the 21st century.

Recent Developments

The government of Benin announced in February 2009 that substantial offshore oil reserves, estimated to be capable of producing 14,000 bbl a day, had been found. That month the World Bank also granted Benin US$30 million for the creation of small businesses and the provision of electricity to less-developed parts of the country.

Internet resource: <www.insae-bj.org>.

Bhutan

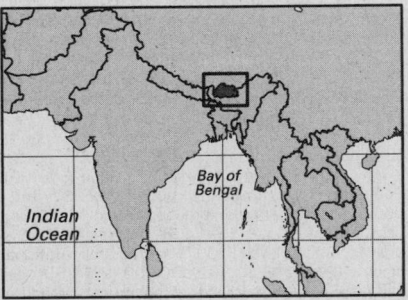

Official name: Druk-Yul (Kingdom of Bhutan). Form of government: constitutional monarchy with two legislative houses (National Council [25]; National Assembly [47]). Head of state: King Jigme Khesar Namgyal Wangchuk (from 2006). Head of government: Prime Minister Lyonchen Jigmi Thinley (from 2008). Capital: Thimphu. Official language: Dzongkha (a Tibetan dialect). Official religion: none (Mahayana Buddhism is the spiritual heritage of Bhutan according to the 2008 constitution). Monetary unit: 1 ngultrum (Nu) = 100 chetrum; valuation (1 Jul 2010) US$1 = Nu 46.49 (the Indian rupee is also accepted as legal tender).

Demography

Area: 14,824 sq mi, 38,394 sq km. Population (2009): 691,000. Density (2009): persons per sq mi 46.6, persons per sq km 18.0. Urban (2007): 26.4%. Sex distribution (2008): male 52.50%; female 47.50%. Age breakdown (2008): under 15, 30.9%; 15–29, 31.9%; 30–44, 18.6%; 45–59, 10.6%; 60–74, 6.3%; 75–84, 1.5%; 85 and over, 0.2%. Ethnic composition (2005): Bhutia (Ngalops) 50%; Nepalese (Gurung) 35%; Sharchops 15%. Religious affiliation (2005): Buddhist 74%; Hindu 25%; Christian 1%. Major towns (2005): Thimphu 79,185; Phuntsholing 20,537; Gelaphu 9,199. Location: southern Asia, bordering China and India.

Vital statistics

Birth rate per 1,000 population (2008): 20.6 (world avg. 20.3). Death rate per 1,000 population (2008):

7.5 (world avg. 8.5). **Total fertility rate** (avg. births per childbearing woman; 2008): 2.48. **Life expectancy** at birth (2008): male 64.8 years; female 66.4 years.

National economy

Budget (2007–08). *Revenue:* Nu 20,481,000,000 (grants 40.7%; nontax revenue 33.0%, of which dividends and transfers 28.4%; tax revenue 23.7%, of which corporate taxes 9.2%; other 2.6%). *Expenditures:* Nu 22,223,000,000 (capital expenditures 52.3%; current expenditures 47.7%). **Public debt** (external, outstanding; July 2008): US$779,900,000. **Production** (metric tons except as noted). *Agriculture and fishing* (2007): corn (maize) 94,500, rice 69,000, potatoes 57,000, ginger 7,350, nutmeg, mace, and cardamom 5,800, mustard seed 4,500; livestock (number of live animals) 385,000 cattle, (2005) 45,538 yaks, 26,000 horses; fisheries production (2006) 300 (from aquaculture, negligible). *Mining and quarrying* (2007): limestone 560,000; dolomite 440,000; gypsum 165,000; ferrosilicon 21,000. *Manufacturing* (value of sales in Nu '000,000; 2007): ferroalloys 1,886; cement 1,664; chemical products 1,406; wood board products (2006) 382. *Energy production (consumption):* electricity (kW-hr; 2006) 3,357,000,000 (739,000,000); coal (metric tons; 2006) 98,000 (52,000); petroleum products (metric tons; 2006) none (51,000). **Population economically active** (2005): total 256,895; activity rate of total population 38.2% (participation rates: ages 15–64, 62.7%; female 36.6%; officially unemployed [2007] 3.7%). **Gross national income** (2008): US$1,302,000,000 (US$1,900 per capita). **Selected balance of payments data.** Receipts from (US$'000,000): tourism (2007) 30; remittances (2007) 1.5; foreign direct investment (2005–07 avg.) 31; official development assistance (2007) 89.

Foreign trade

Imports (2007; c.i.f.): Nu 24,658,000,000 (machinery and apparatus 17.7%; food products and beverages 16.3%; mineral fuels 16.0%; precious stones and precious metals 10.8%; base and fabricated metals 9.2%; palm oil 6.9%). *Major import sources:* India 69.4%; Indonesia 6.0%; Singapore 5.1%; Russia 3.4%; South Korea 3.0%. **Exports** (2007; f.o.b.): Nu 27,859,000,000 (electricity to India 36.0%; unrecorded media [magnetic discs] 16.0%; copper wire 11.8%; ferroalloys 5.3%; information technology software 4.8%; vegetable fats and oils 4.5%). *Major export destinations:* India 81.6%; Hong Kong 9.9%; Thailand 3.9%; Singapore 2.5%; Bangladesh 1.7%.

Transport and communications

Transport. *Railroads:* none. *Roads* (2006): total length 4,545 km (paved 55%). *Vehicles* (2003): passenger cars 10,574; trucks and buses 3,852. *Air transport* (2004): passenger-km 69,000,000; metric ton-km cargo (including the weight of passengers and mail) 6,000,000. **Communications,** in total units (units per 1,000 persons). Telephone landlines (2008): 27,000 (40); cellular telephone subscribers

(2008): 251,000 (368); personal computers (2005): 13,000 (16); total Internet users (2008): 40,000 (59); broadband Internet subscribers (2008): 2,100 (3.1).

Education and health

Educational attainment (2007). Percentage of head of household population having: no formal schooling 73.2%; incomplete/complete primary education 16.5%; incomplete/complete secondary 5.5%; higher 4.8%. **Literacy** (2007): total population ages 6 and over literate 55.5%; males literate 65.7%; females literate 45.9%. **Health** (2006): physicians 150 (1 per 4,428 persons); hospital beds 1,133 (1 per 586 persons); infant mortality rate per 1,000 live births (2008) 51.9.

Military

Total active duty personnel (2006): about 6,000 (army 100%). **Military expenditure as percentage of GDP** (2005): 1.0%; per capita expenditure US$11.

Background

Bhutan's mountains and forests long made it inaccessible to the outside world, and its feudal rulers banned foreigners until well into the 20th century. In 1865 it came under British influence, and in 1910 it agreed to be guided by Britain in its foreign affairs. India took over Britain's role in 1949, and China's 1950 occupation of neighboring Tibet further strengthened Bhutan's ties with India. The apparent Chinese threat made Bhutan's rulers aware of the need to modernize, and it embarked on a program to build roads and hospitals and to create a system of secular education. The transition from an absolute monarchy to a parliamentary democracy was completed in March 2008, and a new constitution was promulgated in July.

Recent Developments

Bhutan remained peaceful and tranquil in 2009, following the country's first democratic elections and its transformation in 2008 from an absolute to a constitutional monarchy, but reports of outlawed Indian insurgent groups reforming inside Bhutan (near the border of the Indian state of Assam) raised alarms. Although Bhutan enjoyed robust economic growth of more than 8.0%, according to the country's Labour Ministry, the unemployment rate jumped to 4.0% in 2009, from 3.7% in 2007.

Internet resource: <www.rma.org.bt>.

Bolivia

Official name: Estado Plurinacional de Bolivia (Plurinational State of Bolivia). **Form of government:** unitary multiparty republic with two legislative houses (Chamber of Departmental Representatives [36]; Chamber of Deputies [130]). **Head of state and government:** President Evo Morales (from 2006). **Capitals:** La Paz (executive and legislative); Sucre (judicial). **Official languages:** Spanish and 36 indigenous

1 metric ton = about 1.1 short tons; 1 kilometer = 0.6 mi (statute); 1 metric ton-km cargo = about 0.68 short ton-mi cargo; c.i.f.: cost, insurance, and freight; f.o.b.: free on board

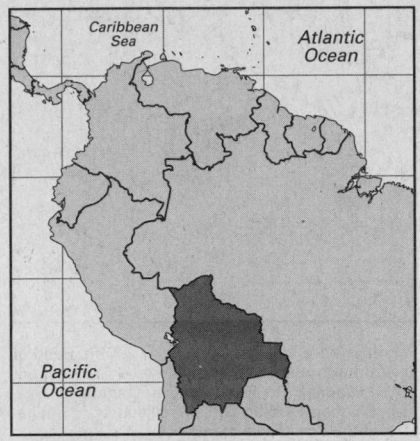

languages. **Official religion:** none. **Monetary unit:** 1 boliviano (Bs) = 100 centavos; valuation (1 Jul 2010) US$1 = Bs 6.86.

Demography

Area: 424,164 sq mi, 1,098,581 sq km. **Population** (2009): 9,775,000. **Density** (2009): persons per sq mi 23.0, persons per sq km 8.9. **Urban** (2005): 64.2%. **Sex distribution** (2008): male 49.50%; female 50.50%. **Age breakdown** (2008): under 15, 35.9%; 15–29, 29.2%; 30–44, 17.5%; 45–59, 10.8%; 60–74, 4.9%; 75–84, 1.4%; 85 and over, 0.3%. **Ethnic composition** (2006): Amerindian 55%, of which Quechua 29%, Aymara 24%; mestizo 30%; white 15%. **Religious affiliation** (2001): Roman Catholic 78%; Protestant/independent Christian 16%; other Christian 3%, of which Mormon 1.8%; nonreligious 2.5%; other 0.5%. **Major cities** (2001): Santa Cruz 1,116,059 (urban agglomeration [2007] 1,422,000); La Paz 789,585 (urban agglomeration [2007] 1,590,000); El Alto 647,350; Cochabamba 516,683; Oruro 201,230; Sucre 193,873. **Location:** central South America, bordering Brazil, Paraguay, Argentina, Chile, and Peru.

Vital statistics

Birth rate per 1,000 population (2008): 26.5 (world avg. 20.3). **Death rate** per 1,000 population (2008): 7.2 (world avg. 8.5). **Total fertility rate** (avg. births per childbearing woman; 2008): 3.26. **Life expectancy** at birth (2008): male 63.9 years; female 69.4 years.

National economy

Budget (2008). *Revenue:* Bs 58,394,500,000 (sales of hydrocarbons 45.1%; tax income [including royalties on minerals] 36.6%). *Expenditures:* Bs 54,478,200,000 (current expenditures 72.0%; capital expenditures 28.0%). **Production** (metric tons except as noted). *Agriculture and fishing* (2007): sugarcane 6,200,000, soybeans 1,900,000, potatoes 755,000, cassava 373,700, sunflower seeds 170,000, chestnuts (2006) 35,000; additionally, Bolivia was the third largest producer of coca in the world in 2008, producing an estimated 113 metric tons of cocaine; livestock (number of live animals)

8,990,000 sheep, 7,515,000 cattle, 2,490,000 pigs, (2004) 1,900,000 llamas and alpacas; fisheries production (2006) 7,130 (from aquaculture 6%). *Mining and quarrying* (metal content; 2007): zinc 214,050; tin 15,970; tungsten 1,400; silver 530; gold 8,820 kg. *Manufacturing* (value added in Bs '000,000 in constant prices of 1990; 2007): food products 1,792; beverages and tobacco products 766; petroleum products 574. *Energy production (consumption):* electricity (kW-hr; 2007) 5,550,000,000 (4,123,000,000); crude petroleum (barrels; 2007) 15,000,000 ([2006] 20,435,000); petroleum products (metric tons; 2006) 1,847,000 (2,118,000); natural gas (cu m; 2007) 14,301,000,000 ([2006] 1,446,000,000). **Population economically active** (2000): total 3,823,937; activity rate of total population 46.2% (participation rates: ages 15–64, 71.8%; female 44.6%; unemployed [2006] 8% in urban areas). **Gross national income** (2008): US$14,106,000,000 (US$1,460 per capita). **Public debt** (external, outstanding; September 2008): US$2,298,000,000. **Selected balance of payments data.** Receipts from (US$'000,000): tourism (2007) 259; remittances (2008) 927; foreign direct investment (FDI; 2005–07 avg.) 66; official development assistance (2007) 476. Disbursements for (US$'000,000): tourism (2007) 249; remittances (2008) 72.

Foreign trade

Imports (2007; c.i.f.): US$3,522,000,000 (chemical products 17.2%; motor vehicles 13.4%; specialized machinery 8.1%; food products 7.9%; refined petroleum products 7.6%; iron and steel 7.3%). *Major import sources:* Brazil 20.2%; Argentina 16.9%; US 11.7%; Japan 9.4%; China 7.6%. **Exports** (2007; f.o.b.): US$4,812,700,000 (natural gas 41.3%; zinc 14.4%; crude petroleum 5.6%; soybean foodstuffs 4.7%; silver 4.5%; tin 3.7%). *Major export destinations:* Brazil 36.7%; Argentina 8.7%; US 8.6%; Japan 8.5%; Venezuela 5.0%.

Transport and communications

Transport. *Railroads* (2007): route length 3,504 km; (2004) passenger-km 286,000,000; (2004) metric ton-km cargo 1,058,000,000. *Roads* (2004): total length 62,479 km (paved 7%). *Vehicles* (2004): passenger cars 294,000; trucks and buses 173,864. *Air transport* (2006; AeroSur, LAB, and Amazonas airlines only): passenger-km 1,056,000,000; metric ton-km cargo 7,668,000. **Communications,** in total units (units per 1,000 persons). Telephone landlines (2007): 678,000 (71); cellular telephone subscribers (2008): 4,830,000 (503); personal computers (2006): 224,000 (24); total Internet users (2007): 1,000,000 (106); broadband Internet subscribers (2007): 34,000 (3.6).

Education and health

Educational attainment (2007). Percentage of population ages 19 and over having: no formal schooling 10.7%; some to complete primary education 37.5%; some to complete secondary 27.2%; some to complete higher 24.4%; not specified 0.2%. **Literacy** (2007). Total population ages 15 and over literate 90.7%; males literate 96.0%; females literate 86.0%. **Health:** physicians (2004) 3,211 (1 per 2,806 persons); hospital beds (2007) 14,928 (1 per 658 persons); infant mortality rate per 1,000 live births (2008) 45.9; undernourished population (2002–04) 2,000,000 (23% of total population based on the consumption of a minimum daily requirement of 1,780 calories).

Military

Total active duty personnel (November 2008): 46,100 (army 75.5%, navy 10.4%, air force 14.1%). **Military expenditure as percentage of GDP** (2008): 1.4%; per capita expenditure US$27.

Background

The Bolivian highlands were the location of the advanced Tiwanaku culture in the 7th–11th centuries and, with its passing, became the home of the Aymara, an Indian group conquered by the Incas in the 15th century. The Incas were overrun by the invading Spanish under Francisco Pizarro in the 1530s. By 1600 Spain had established the cities of Charcas (now Sucre), La Paz, Santa Cruz, and what would become Cochabamba and had begun to exploit the silver wealth of Potosí. Bolivia flourished in the 17th century, and for a time Potosí was the largest city in the Americas. By the end of the century, the mineral wealth had dried up. Talk of independence began as early as 1809, but not until 1825 were Spanish forces finally defeated. Bolivia shrank in size when it lost Atacama province to Chile in 1884 at the end of the War of the Pacific and again in 1939 when it lost most of Gran Chaco to Paraguay. One of South America's poorest countries, it was plagued by governmental instability for much of the 20th century. Social and economic tension continued in the early 21st century, fueled by resistance to government efforts to eradicate the growth of coca (from which the narcotic cocaine is derived), by unrest among Bolivia's Indians, and by disagreements over how to exploit the country's vast natural gas reserves.

Recent Developments

Although the world economic downturn dampened demand for Bolivia's natural gas in 2009, fears that the nationalization of resource industries would sour relations with foreign investors proved largely unfounded. The most exciting development in natural resources concerned lithium, which is used in the batteries that power cell phones, laptops, and electric automobiles. About half of the world's known lithium deposits were located in the Salar de Uyuni, a salt desert in southwestern Bolivia, and the government continued construction of a pilot plant to process the mineral.

Internet resource: <http://boliviaweb.com>.

Bosnia and Herzegovina

Official name: Bosna i Hercegovina (Bosnia and Herzegovina). **Form of government:** emerging republic with two legislative houses (House of Peoples [15]; House of Representatives [42]). **Heads of state:** tripartite presidency with 8-month-long rotating chairmanship (final authority rests with International High

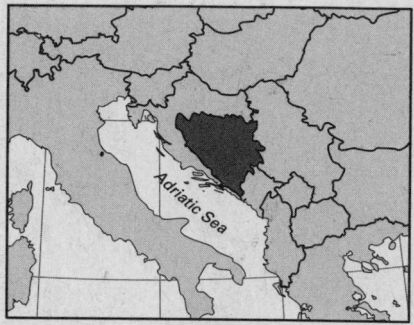

Representative Valentin Inzko [from 2009]). **Head of government:** Prime Minister Nikola Spiric (from 2007). **Capital:** Sarajevo. **Official languages:** Bosnian; Croatian; Serbian. **Official religion:** none. **Monetary unit:** 1 convertible marka (KM; plural maraka) = 100 feninga; valuation (1 Jul 2010) US$1 = KM 1.60 (the euro [€] also circulates as semiofficial legal tender).

Demography

Area: 19,772 sq mi, 51,209 sq km. **Population** (2009): 3,835,000. **Density** (2009): persons per sq mi 194.0, persons per sq km 74.9. **Urban** (2005): 45.7%. **Sex distribution** (2005): male 48.11%; female 51.89%. **Age breakdown** (2005): under 15, 16.6%; 15–29, 22.7%; 30–44, 22.6%; 45–59, 20.4%; 60–74, 13.3%; 75–84, 3.9%; 85 and over, 0.5%. **Ethnic composition** (1999): Bosniac 44.0%; Serb 31.0%; Croat 17.0%; other 8.0%. **Religious affiliation** (2002): Sunni Muslim 40%; Serbian Orthodox 31%; Roman Catholic 15%; Protestant 4%; nonreligious/other 10%. **Major cities** (2005): Sarajevo [2007] 376,000; Banja Luka 165,100; Zenica 84,300; Tuzla 84,100; Mostar 63,500. **Location:** southeastern Europe, bordered by Croatia, Serbia, Montenegro, and the Adriatic Sea.

Vital statistics

Birth rate per 1,000 population (2007): 8.8 (world avg. 20.3); (2006) within marriage 88.4%. **Death rate** per 1,000 population (2007): 9.1 (world avg. 8.5). **Total fertility rate** (avg. births per childbearing woman; 2007): 1.17. **Life expectancy** at birth (2007): male 66.9 years; female 72.5 years.

National economy

Budget (2006). *Revenue:* KM 9,075,000,000 (tax revenue 80.8%, of which VAT/sales tax 29.9%, social security contributions 26.7%, excise tax 11.4%; nontax revenue 13.7%; grants 5.5%). *Expenditures:* KM 8,655,000,000 (current expenditures 86.5%; development expenditures 13.5%). **Gross national income** (2008): US$17,001,000,000 (US$4,510 per capita). **Production** (metric tons except as noted). *Agriculture and fishing* (2007): corn (maize) 635,344, potatoes 387,239, wheat 257,112; livestock (number of live animals) 1,000,000 sheep, 712,000 pigs, 515,000 cattle,

---

1 metric ton = about 1.1 short tons;   1 kilometer = 0.6 mi (statute);   1 metric ton-km cargo = about 0.68 short ton-mi cargo;   c.i.f.: cost, insurance, and freight;   f.o.b.: free on board

in addition, 285,000 beehives; fisheries production 9,625 (from aquaculture 79%). *Mining and quarrying* (2006): iron ore (metal content) 1,700,000; bauxite 816,768; lime 180,000. *Manufacturing* (value of production in KM '000,000; 2006): base and fabricated metals 1,578; food products, beverages, and tobacco products 1,255; wood products 398. *Energy production (consumption):* electricity (kW-hr; 2006) 13,346,000,000 (11,238,000,000); coal (metric tons; 2006) 3,616,-000 (4,242,000); lignite (metric tons; 2006) 9,960,000 (9,871,000); petroleum products (metric tons; 2006) none (1,099,000); natural gas (cu m; 2006) none (396,000,000). **Public debt** (external, outstanding; 2007): US$2,981,000,000. **Population economically active** (2007): total 1,196,000; activity rate of total population 36.1% (participation rates: ages 15–64, 52.2%; female 36.5%; unemployed 29.0%). **Selected balance of payments data.** Receipts from (US$'000,000): tourism (2007) 729; remittances (2008) 2,735; foreign direct investment (2005–07 avg.) 1,108; official development assistance (2007) 443. Disbursements for (US$'000,-000): tourism (2007) 186; remittances (2008) 70.

Did you know?
A variety of fruits are commonly grown in Bosnia and Herzegovina, including apples, grapes, peaches, pears, nectarines, and especially plums. Slivovitz, distilled from plums, particularly those from the Posavina region in the far north of the country, is the liquor of choice for men in Bosnia and Herzegovina and in other Balkan countries.

Foreign trade

Imports (2007): US$9,720,000,000 (machinery and apparatus 16.8%; food products 11.8%; chemical products 10.5%; refined petroleum products 9.2%; motor vehicles 7.1%; iron and steel 5.2%). *Major import sources:* Croatia 17.6%; Germany 12.5%; Serbia 10.2%; Italy 9.0%; Slovenia 6.4%. **Exports** (2007): US$4,152,000,000 (aluminum 9.7%; fabricated metal products 8.2%; iron and steel 7.1%; metal ore/metal scrap 6.8%; footwear 5.8%; sawn wood 5.7%). *Major export destinations:* Croatia 18.4%; Serbia 13.7%; Italy 13.1%; Germany 12.8%; Slovenia 10.9%.

Transport and communications

Transport. *Railroads* (2005): length 1,028 km; passenger-km 51,396,000; metric ton-km cargo 1,159,000,000. *Roads* (2005): total length 22,419 km (paved [2001] 64%). *Air transport* (2003): passenger-km 47,000,000; metric ton-km 6,000,000. **Communications,** in total units (units per 1,000 persons). Telephone landlines (2008): 1,031,000 (268); cellular telephone subscribers (2008): 3,179,000 (827); personal computers (2007): 246,000 (64); total Internet users (2008): 1,308,000 (340); broadband Internet subscribers (2008): 188,000 (49).

Education and health

Educational attainment (2004). Percentage of population ages 18 and over having: no formal schooling 8.7%; incomplete primary education 11.4%; complete primary 21.4%; incomplete/complete secondary 49.8%; technical/university 8.7%. **Literacy** (2002): total population ages 15 and over literate 94.6%; males literate 98.4%; females literate 91.1%. **Health:** physicians (2005) 5,540 (1 per 694 persons); hospital beds (2004) 11,414 (1 per 337 persons); infant mortality rate per 1,000 live births (2007) 6.8; undernourished population (2002–04) 350,000 (9% of total population based on the consumption of a minimum daily requirement of 2,000 calories).

Military

Total active duty personnel (November 2008): 8,543; EU-sponsored (EUFOR) peacekeeping troops (March 2009): 2,153. **Military expenditure as percentage of GDP** (2008): 1.5%; per capita expenditure US$58.

Background

Habitation long predates the era of Roman rule, when much of the country was included in the province of Dalmatia. Slav settlement began in the 6th century AD. For the next several centuries, parts of the region fell under the rule of Serbs, Croats, Hungarians, Venetians, and Byzantines. The Ottoman Turks invaded Bosnia in the 14th century, and after many battles it became a Turkish province in 1463. Herzegovina, then known as Hum, was taken in 1482. In the 16th–17th centuries the area was an important Turkish outpost, constantly at war with the Habsburgs and Venice. During this period much of the native population converted to Islam. At the Congress of Berlin after the Russo-Turkish War of 1877–78, Bosnia and Herzegovina was assigned to Austria-Hungary, and it was fully annexed in 1908. Growing Serb nationalism resulted in the 1914 assassination of the Austrian archduke Francis Ferdinand at Sarajevo by a Bosnian Serb, an event that precipitated World War I. After the war the area was annexed to Serbia. Following World War II the twin territory became a republic of communist Yugoslavia. With the collapse of communist regimes in Eastern Europe, Bosnia and Herzegovina declared its independence in 1992; its Serb population objected, and conflict ensued among Serbs, Croats, and Muslims. The 1995 peace accord established a loosely federated government roughly divided between a Muslim-Croat Federation and a Serb Republic (Republika Srpska). From 1996 to 2002 an EU peacekeeping force was installed there. By the early 21st century, much of the infrastructure damaged during the conflict had been reconstructed, but ethnic tensions remained.

Recent Developments

In October 2009 Bosnia and Herzegovina submitted an application for the NATO Membership Action Plan, which prepares candidates for NATO membership. Although NATO foreign ministers did not offer Bosnia a formal plan in December, they did lay out a specific set of goals that, if achieved, would result in the offer.

Internet resource: <www.bhas.ba>.

Botswana

Official name: Republic of Botswana. **Form of government:** multiparty republic with one legislative house (National Assembly [63]). **Head of state and**

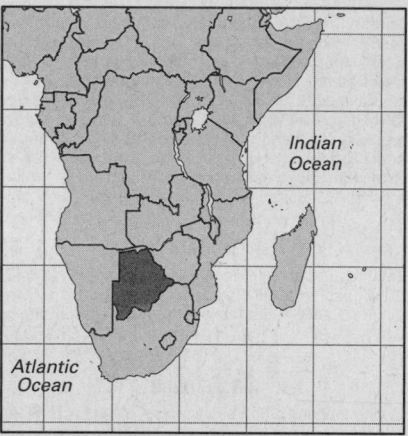

government: President Ian Khama (from 2008). **Capital:** Gaborone. **Official language:** English (Tswana is the national language). **Official religion:** none. **Monetary unit:** 1 pula (P) = 100 thebe; valuation (1 Jul 2010) US$1 = P 6.92.

Demography

Area: 224,848 sq mi, 582,356 sq km. **Population** (2009): 1,991,000. **Density** (2009): persons per sq mi 8.9, persons per sq km 3.4. **Urban** (2005): 57.4%. **Sex distribution** (2008): male 49.99%; female 50.01%. **Age breakdown** (2008): under 15, 35.3%; 15–29, 32.9%; 30–44, 17.4%; 45–59, 9.0%; 60–74, 3.9%; 75–84, 1.2%; 85 and over, 0.3%. **Ethnic composition** (2000): Tswana 66.8%; Kalanga 14.8%; Ndebele 1.7%; Herero 1.4%; San (Bushman) 1.3%; Afrikaner 1.3%; other 12.7%. **Religious affiliation** (2005): independent Christian 41.7%; traditional beliefs 35.0%; Protestant 12.8%; Muslim 0.3%; Hindu 0.2%; other 10.0%. **Major cities** (2006): Gaborone 214,400; Francistown 91,800; Molepolole 65,600; Selebi-Pikwe 54,700; Maun 51,600. **Location:** southern Africa, bordered by Namibia, Zimbabwe, and South Africa.

Vital statistics

Birth rate per 1,000 population (2008): 23.2 (world avg. 20.3). **Death rate** per 1,000 population (2008): 8.5 (world avg. 8.5). **Total fertility rate** (avg. births per childbearing woman; 2008): 2.66. **Life expectancy** at birth (2008): male 61.5 years; female 62.1 years.

National economy

Budget (2006–07). *Revenue:* P 27,397,700,000 (tax revenue 92.1%, of which mineral royalties 47.9%, customs duties and excise tax 24.1%, non-mineral income tax 11.2%; nontax revenue 6.3%; grants 1.6%). *Expenditures:* P 19,737,400,000 (general government services including defense 29.2%; education 24.5%; economic services 14.5%; health 11.3%; transfers 10.2%). **Population economically active** (2006): total 651,500; activity rate of total population 35.8% (participation rates: ages 15–59 [2001] 58.1%; female 49.1%; unemployed [2007] 7.5%). **Production** (metric tons except as noted). *Agriculture and fishing* (2007): roots and tubers 93,000, sorghum 33,000, corn (maize) 12,000, sunflower seeds 7,000; livestock (number of live animals) 3,100,000 cattle, 1,960,000 goats, 300,000 sheep; fisheries production 123 (from aquaculture, none). *Mining and quarrying* (2007): salt 165,710; nickel ore (metal content) 26,532; copper ore (metal content) 22,589; cobalt (metal content) 356; semiprecious gemstones (mostly agate) 48,000 kg; gold 2,656 kg; diamonds 33,639,000 carats (Botswana is the world's leading producer of diamonds by value). *Manufacturing* (value added in US$'000,-000; 2005): beverages 55; textiles 14; tanned and processed leather 1. *Energy production (consumption):* electricity (kW-hr; 2005) 912,000,000 (2,602,000,000); coal (metric tons; 2007) 828,000 ([2006] 938,000). **Selected balance of payments data.** Receipts from (US$'000,000): tourism (2007) 546; remittances (2008) 148; foreign direct investment (FDI; 2005–07 avg.) 422; official development assistance (2007) 104. Disbursements for (US$'000,000): tourism (2007) 281; remittances (2008) 120; FDI (2005–07 avg.) 53. **Gross national income** (2008): US$12,328,000,000 (US$6,470 per capita). **Public debt** (external, outstanding; 2007): US$380,000,000.

Foreign trade

Imports (2007; c.i.f.): US$3,987,000,000 (machinery and apparatus 18.9%; refined petroleum products 13.7%; motor vehicles 10.6%; food products 10.2%; chemical products 9.2%). *Major import sources:* South Africa 83.5%; China 1.8%; Belgium 1.6%; UK 1.4%; Zimbabwe 1.3%. **Exports** (2007; f.o.b.): US$5,073,000,000 (diamonds 62.5%; nickel matte 15.5%; wearing apparel and accessories 6.7%; copper ore/copper matte 5.8%; textiles 5.0%). *Major export destinations:* UK 65.0%; South Africa 10.2%; Norway 8.1%; Zimbabwe 7.3%; China 1.9%.

Transport and communications

Transport. *Railroads* (2006): route length 888 km; (2003) passenger-km 572,000,000; (2004) metric ton-km cargo 636,700,000. *Roads* (2007; roads maintained by central government only): total length 8,916 km (paved 72%). *Vehicles* (2007): passenger cars 104,926; trucks and buses 105,754. *Air transport* (2007; Air Botswana only): passenger-km 117,700,000. **Communications,** in total units (units per 1,000 persons). Telephone landlines (2008): 142,000 (73); cellular telephone subscribers (2008): 1,486,000 (761); personal computers (2006): 84,000 (45); total Internet users (2008): 80,000 (41); broadband Internet subscribers (2007): 3,500 (1.8).

Education and health

Literacy (2005): total population ages 15 and over literate 81.4%; males literate 78.6%; females literate 84.1%. **Health** (2007): physicians 478 (1 per 3,798 persons); hospital beds 3,704 (1 per 490 persons); infant mortality rate per 1,000 live births (2008) 13.4; undernourished population (2002–04) 600,000

1 metric ton = about 1.1 short tons; 1 kilometer = 0.6 mi (statute); 1 metric ton-km cargo = about 0.68 short ton-mi cargo; c.i.f.: cost, insurance, and freight; f.o.b.: free on board

(32% of total population based on the consumption of a minimum daily requirement of 1,860 calories).

Military

Total active duty personnel (November 2008): 9,000 (army 94.4%, air force 5.6%). **Military expenditure as percentage of GDP** (2007): 2.7%; per capita expenditure US$175.

Background

The region's earliest inhabitants were the Khoekhoe and San (Bushmen). Sites were settled as early as AD 190 during the southerly migration of Bantu-speaking farmers. Tswana dynasties, which developed in the western Transvaal in the 13th–14th centuries, moved into Botswana in the 18th century and established several powerful states. European missionaries arrived in the early 19th century, but it was the discovery of gold in 1867 that excited European interest. In 1885 the area became the British Bechuanaland Protectorate. The next year the region south of the Molopo River became a crown colony, and it was annexed by the Cape Colony 10 years later. Bechuanaland itself continued as a British protectorate until the 1960s. In 1966 the Republic of Bechuanaland (later Botswana) was proclaimed an independent member of the British Commonwealth. Independent Botswana tried to maintain a delicate balance between its economic dependence on South Africa and its relations with the surrounding black countries; the independence of Namibia in 1990 and South Africa's rejection of apartheid eased tensions.

Recent Developments

In Botswana, the world's largest diamond producer, diamond production was cut by 40%, to 20 million carats, in 2009 in response to the global economic downturn. After temporary mine closures, however, the production of base metals for East Asian markets surged ahead, as did plans for the massive expansion of coal mining at Mmamabula and the construction of an electrical power plant there.

Internet resource: <www.cso.gov.bw>.

Brazil

Official name: República Federativa do Brasil (Federative Republic of Brazil). **Form of government:** multiparty federal republic with two legislative houses (Federal Senate [81]; Chamber of Deputies [513]). **Head of state and government:** President Luiz Inácio Lula da Silva (from 2003). **Capital:** Brasília. **Official language:** Portuguese. **Official religion:** none. **Monetary unit:** 1 real (R$; plural reais) = 100 centavos; valuation (1 Jul 2010) US$1 = 1.80 reais.

Demography

Area: 3,287,612 sq mi, 8,514,877 sq km. **Population** (2009): 191,481,000. **Density** (2009): persons per sq mi 58.2, persons per sq km 22.5. **Urban** (2005): 84.2%. **Sex distribution** (2005): male 49.32%; female 50.68%. **Age breakdown** (2005): under 16, 27.0%; 15–29, 27.7%; 30–44, 21.7%; 45–59, 14.1%; 60–74, 6.6%; 75–84, 1.8%; 85 and over, 0.5%. **Racial composition** (2000): white 53.7%;

mulatto and mestizo 39.1%; black and black/Amerindian 6.2%; Asian 0.5%; Amerindian 0.4%. **Religious affiliation** (2005): Roman Catholic 65.1%; Protestant 12.7%, of which Assemblies of God 9.2%; independent Christian 10.7%, of which Universal Church of the Kingdom of God 2.2%; Spiritist (Kardecist) 1.3%; Jehovah's Witness 0.7%; African and syncretic religions 0.4%; Muslim 0.4%; nonreligious/other 8.7%. **Major cities (metropolitan areas)** (2007): São Paulo 10,238,500 (19,226,426); Rio de Janeiro 6,093,500 (11,563,302); Belo Horizonte 2,412,900 (5,450,084); Porto Alegre 1,379,100 (3,896,515); Recife 1,533,600 (3,654,534); Salvador 2,891,400 (3,598,454); Brasília 2,348,600 (3,507,662); Fortaleza 2,431,400 (3,436,515); Curitiba 1,797,400 (3,124,596); Campinas 1,022,000 (2,635,261); Belém 1,399,800 (2,043,543); Goiânia 1,236,400 (1,973,892); Manaus 1,602,100 (1,612,475); Vitória 314,000 (1,609,532). **Location:** eastern South America, bordered by Venezuela, Guyana, Suriname, French Guiana, Uruguay, Argentina, Paraguay, Bolivia, Peru, and Colombia. **Families.** Average family size (2005) 3.2; (1996) 1–2 persons 25.2%, 3 persons 20.3%, 4 persons 22.2%, 5–6 persons 22.3%, 7 or more persons 9.0%. **Emigration** (2000): Brazilian emigrants living abroad 1,887,895; in the US 42.3%, in Paraguay 23.4%, in Japan 12.0%. **Immigration** (2000): foreign-born immigrants living in Brazil 683,830; from Europe 56.3%, of which Portugal 31.2%; South/Central America 21.0%; Asia 17.8%, of which Japan 10.4%.

Vital statistics

Birth rate per 1,000 population (2008): 16.4 (world avg. 20.3). **Death rate** per 1,000 population (2008): 6.4 (world avg. 8.5). **Total fertility rate** (avg. births per childbearing woman; 2008): 1.90. **Life expectancy** at birth (2008): male 68.7 years; female 76.0 years.

Social indicators

Educational attainment (2005). Percentage of population ages 25 and over having: no formal schooling or less than one year of primary education 15.0%; 1 to 3 years of primary education 13.7%; complete primary/incomplete secondary 40.2%; complete secondary 18.8%; 1 to 3 years of higher education 3.8%; 4 years or more of higher education 8.0%; unknown 0.5%. **Quality of working life.** Proportion of employed population receiving minimum wage (2002): 53.5%. Number and percentage of children (ages 5–17) working: 5,400,000 (12.6% of age group). **Access to services.** Proportion of urban households having access to (2006): safe public (piped) water supply 93.2%; public (piped) sewage system 66.8%; garbage collection 90.3%. (Rural households have far less access to services.) **Social participation.** Trade union membership in total workforce (2001): 19,500,000. **Social deviance.** *Annual murder rate* per 100,000 population (2005): Brazil 29.6; Rio de Janeiro only (2002) 56; São Paulo only (2002) 54. **Leisure.** Favorite leisure activities include: playing soccer, dancing, practicing *capoeira,* rehearsing all year in neighborhood samba groups for celebrations of Carnival, and competing in water sports, volleyball, and basketball. **Material well-being.** Urban households possessing (2006): electricity 99.7%, color television receiver 94.8%, refrigerator 93.3%, washing machine 42.2%, computer 25.5%, Internet access 19.6%, freezer 16.1%.

National economy

Gross national income (2008): US$1,411,224,-000,000 (US$7,350 per capita). **Budget** (2006). *Revenue:* R$543,253,000,000 (tax revenue 72.3%, of which income tax 25.3%, social security contributions 17.0%, VAT on industrial products 5.2%; social welfare contributions 22.7%; other 5.0%). *Expenditures:* R$493,450,000,000 (social security and welfare 30.5%; wages and salaries 19.3%; transfers to state and local governments 17.1%; other 33.1%). **Public debt** (external, outstanding; 2007): US$79,957,000,000. **Production** ('000 metric tons except as noted). *Agriculture and fishing* (2008): sugarcane 648,921, soybeans 59,917, corn (maize) 59,018, cassava 25,878, oranges 18,390, rice 12,100, bananas 7,117, wheat 5,886, seed cotton 3,971, tomatoes 3,934, potatoes 3,676, dry beans 3,461, coffee 2,791, coconuts 2,759, pineapples 2,492, sorghum 1,966, papayas 1,900, cashew apples 1,660, grapes 1,403, dry onions 1,300, mangoes and guavas 1,272, apples 1,121, lemons and limes 1,040, tobacco 850, oil palm fruit 660, maté 436, peanuts (groundnuts) 297, cashews 240, cacao beans 208, sunflower seeds 146, natural rubber 114, garlic 92, pepper 69, Brazil nuts 30; livestock (number of live animals) 175,436,992 cattle, 40,000,000 pigs, 16,500,000 sheep, 5,650,000 horses; fisheries production (2007) 1,072,825 (from aquaculture 27%). *Mining and quarrying* (metric tons; 2007): iron ore (metal content) 235,504,000 (world rank: 1); bauxite 24,800,000 (world rank: 3); kaolin (marketable product) 2,500,000; manganese (metal content) 933,000 (world rank: 5); copper (metal content) 205,728; graphite 76,200 (world rank: 3); nickel (metal content) 58,317; tin (metal content) 10,000 (world rank: 5); tantalum 180 (world rank: 2); gold 49,613 kg; diamonds 182,000 carats. **Population economically active:** September 2006): total 97,528,000; activity rate of total population 52.1% (participation rates: ages 15–64, 73.7%; female 43.7%; unemployed [De-

cember 2007–November 2008] 7.9%). **Selected balance of payments data.** Receipts from (US$'000,000): tourism (2007) 4,953; remittances (2008) 5,089; foreign direct investment (FDI; 2005–07 avg.) 22,824; official development assistance (2007) 297. Disbursements for (US$'000,-000): tourism (2007) 8,211; remittances (2008) 1,191; FDI (2005–07 avg.) 12,595. *Energy production (consumption):* electricity (kW-hr; 2006) 412,159,000,000 (460,500,000,000); coal (metric tons; 2006) 6,380,000 (21,600,000); crude petroleum (barrels; 2007) 645,800,000 ([2006] 621,888,000); petroleum products (metric tons; 2006) 80,179,000 (74,098,000); natural gas (cu m; 2007) 18,151,000,000 ([2006] 18,609,-000,000); ethanol (litres; 2007) 19,000,000,000 (16,700,000,000).

Foreign trade

Imports (2007): US$120,618,000,000 (chemical products 19.0%, of which organic chemicals 5.0%, fertilizers 3.7%, medicines and pharmaceuticals 3.3%; mineral fuels 18.5%, of which crude petroleum 9.9%, refined petroleum products 5.0%; motor vehicles and parts 6.8%; general industrial machinery 5.4%; food products 3.9%; telecommunications equipment 3.7%; power-generating machinery 3.7%). *Major import sources:* US 15.7%; China 10.5%; Argentina 8.6%; Germany 7.2%; Nigeria 4.4%; Japan 3.8%; France 2.9%; Chile 2.9%; South Korea 2.8%; Italy 2.8%. **Exports** (2007): US$160,649,000,000 (food products 19.4%, of which meat 6.9%, coffee 2.1%, animal foodstuffs 2.1%, raw sugar 1.9%; motor vehicles and parts 7.9%; chemical products 6.6%, of which organic chemicals 2.6%; iron ore and concentrates 6.6%; iron and steel 6.3%; crude petroleum 5.5%; soybeans 4.2%; aircraft/spacecraft 3.2%; nonferrous metals 2.9%; power-generating machinery 2.7%; refined petroleum products 2.7%; specialized industrial machinery 2.6%; general industrial machinery 2.4%; wood pulp and waste paper 1.9%). *Major export destinations:* US 15.8%; Argentina 9.0%; China 6.7%; Netherlands 5.5%; Germany 4.5%; Venezuela 2.9%; Italy 2.8%; Chile 2.7%; Mexico 2.7%; Japan 2.7%.

Transport and communications

Transport. *Railroads* (2006): route length 29,605 km; (2005) passenger-km 5,852,000,000; (2005) metric ton-km cargo 154,870,000,000. *Roads* (2004): total length 1,751,868 km (paved [2000] 6%). *Vehicles* (2004): passenger cars 24,936,541; trucks and buses 6,294,502. *Air transport* (2007): passenger-km 52,044,000,000; metric ton-km cargo 1,477,824,000. **Communications,** in total units (units per 1,000 persons). Telephone landlines (2008): 41,141,000 (217); cellular telephone subscribers (2008): 150,641,000 (794); personal computers (2006): 29,340,000 (161); total Internet users (2007): 67,510,000 (360); broadband Internet subscribers (2008): 10,098,000 (53).

Education and health

Literacy (2005): total population ages 15 and over literate 89.0%; males literate 88.7%; females literate

---

1 metric ton = about 1.1 short tons;   1 kilometer = 0.6 mi (statute);   1 metric ton-km cargo = about 0.68 short ton-mi cargo;   c.i.f.: cost, insurance, and freight;   f.o.b.: free on board

89.2%. Health (2005): physicians 505;841 (1 per 356 persons); hospital beds 432,190 (1 per 416 persons); infant mortality rate per 1,000 live births (2008) 23.5; undernourished population (2002–04) 13,100,000 (7% of total population based on the consumption of a minimum daily requirement of 1,900 calories).

Military

Total active duty personnel (November 2008): 326,435 (army 58.2%, navy 20.5%, air force 21.3%). **Military expenditure as percentage of GDP** (2007): 1.6%; per capita expenditure US$111.

Background

Little is known about Brazil's early indigenous inhabitants. Though the area was theoretically allotted to Portugal by the 1494 Treaty of Tordesillas, it was not formally claimed by discovery until Pedro Álvares Cabral accidentally touched land in 1500. It was first settled by the Portuguese in the early 1530s on the southeastern coast and at São Vicente (near modern São Paulo); the French and Dutch created small settlements over the next century. A viceroyalty was established in 1640, and Rio de Janeiro became the capital in 1763. In 1808 Brazil became the refuge and the seat of the government of John VI of Portugal when Napoleon invaded Portugal; ultimately the Kingdom of Portugal, Brazil, and the Algarves was proclaimed, and John ruled from Brazil in 1815–21. On John's return to Portugal, his son Pedro I proclaimed Brazilian independence. In 1889 his successor, Pedro II, was deposed, and a constitution mandating a federal republic was adopted. The 20th century saw increased immigration and growth in manufacturing along with frequent military coups and suspensions of civil liberties. Construction of a new capital at Brasília, intended to spur development of the country's interior, worsened the inflation rate. After 1979 the military government began a gradual return to democratic practices, and in 1989 the first popular presidential election in 29 years was held.

Recent Developments

New oil discoveries continued to be made in 2009 by the Brazilian state oil company, Petrobrás, and its partners in the ultra-deepwater subsalt areas of the Santos basin. Multiple discoveries over the previous three years of multibillion-barrel reserves raised Brazil's profile as a top future oil producer and gave impetus to increased investment in ports, shipyards, naval construction, refineries, and oil and gas exploration. The government stated the goal to triple oil production by 2020. On 31 August Pres. Luiz Inácio Lula da Silva unveiled the federal government's plan for a new regulatory regime to manage this new oil wealth. He proposed the creation of a new government enterprise, called Petrosal, to manage and oversee the contracts for subsalt exploration and production. Under this regime Petrobrás would be the only operator with a guaranteed stake of 30% in each concession. Moreover, current royalty distributions would be changed, and a social and environmental fund would be created to spread oil revenues to other states outside the production areas.

Internet resource: <www.ibge.gov.br>.php>.

Brunei

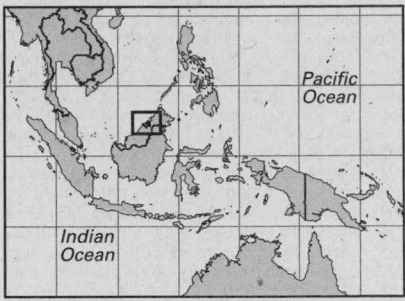

Official name: Negara Brunei Darussalam (State of Brunei Darussalam, Abode of Peace). **Form of government:** monarchy (sultanate) with one advisory house (Legislative Council [29]). **Head of state and government:** Sultan and Prime Minister Haji Hassanal Bolkiah Mu'izzadin Waddaulah (from 1967). **Capital:** Bandar Seri Begawan. **Official language:** Malay. **Official religion:** Islam. **Monetary unit:** 1 Brunei dollar (B$) = 100 sen; valuation (1 Jul 2010) US$1 = B$1.37.

Demography

Area: 2,226 sq mi, 5,765 sq km. **Population** (2009): 400,000. **Density** (2009): persons per sq mi 179.7, persons per sq km 69.4. **Urban** (2005): 73.5%. **Sex distribution** (2008): male 53.02%; female 46.98%. **Age breakdown** (2008): under 15, 27.2%; 15–29, 27.7%; 30–44, 25.1%; 45–59, 14.8%; 60–74, 4.1%; 75–84, 0.9%; 85 and over, 0.2%. **Ethnic composition** (2003): Malay 66.6%; Chinese 10.9%; other indigenous 3.6%; other 18.9%. **Religious affiliation** (2006): Muslim 80.4%; Buddhist 7.9%; Christian 3.2%; traditional beliefs/other 8.5%. **Major cities** (2006): Bandar Seri Begawan 67,100; Kuala Belait 32,000; Seria 30,700; Tutong 19,600. **Location:** southeastern Asia, bordering the South China Sea and Malaysia.

Vital statistics

Birth rate per 1,000 population (2007): 16.2 (world avg. 20.3). **Death rate** per 1,000 population (2007): 3.0 (world avg. 8.5). **Total fertility rate** (avg. births per childbearing woman; 2007): 1.70. **Life expectancy** at birth (2007): male 75.2 years; female 77.8 years.

National economy

Budget (2007–08). *Revenue:* B$9,646,000,000 (tax revenue 65.8%, of which taxes on petroleum and natural gas companies 62.5%, import duties 1.6%; nontax revenue 34.2%, of which dividends paid by petroleum companies 18.9%, petroleum and natural gas royalties 10.3%). *Expenditures:* B$5,601,000,000 (current expenditures 80.0%; capital expenditures 20.0%). **Production** (metric tons except as noted). *Agriculture and fishing* (2007): cassava 1,800, rice 1,200, pineapples 990; livestock (number of live animals) 4,580 buffalo, 15,500,000 chickens; fisheries production 2,803 (from aquaculture 22%). *Mining and quarrying:* other than petroleum and natural gas, none except sand and gravel for construction. *Manufacturing* (value added in B$'000,000; 2006–07):

liquefied natural gas 1,692; textiles and wearing apparel 122. *Energy production (consumption):* electricity (kW-hr; 2006) 2,948,000,000 (2,656,-000,000); crude petroleum (barrels; 2007) 70,800,000 ([2006] 697,000); petroleum products (metric tons; 2006) 1,207,000 (1,200,000); natural gas (cu m; 2007) 13,219,000,000 ([2006] 1,457,000,000). **Gross national income** (2007): US$12,400,000,000 (US$31,523 per capita). **Population economically active** (2008): total 188,800; activity rate of total population 47.4% (participation rates: ages 15–64 [2001] 65.9%; female 39.4%; unemployed 3.7%). **Selected balance of payments data.** Receipts from (US$'000,000): tourism (2006) 224; foreign direct investment (FDI; 2005–07 avg.) 302. Disbursements for (US$'000,000): tourism (2006) 408; remittances (2008) 405; FDI (2005–07 avg.) 34.

Foreign trade

Imports (2007; c.i.f.): US$2,101,000,000 (machinery and transportation equipment 41.4%; manufactured goods 21.8%; food products 12.8%). *Major import sources* (2006): Malaysia 21.6%; Singapore 17.4%; Japan 12.8%; US 9.0%; China 7.9%. **Exports** (2007; f.o.b.): US$7,668,000,000 (crude petroleum 66.0%; liquefied natural gas 30.1%; garments 1.5%). *Major export destinations* (2007; for crude petroleum, liquefied natural gas, and garments only): Japan 34.2%; Indonesia 24.7%; Australia 14.0%; South Korea 12.4%; US 5.0%.

Transport and communications

Transport. *Railroads* (2004): length 19 km. *Roads* (2007): total length 3,774 km (paved 76%). *Vehicles* (2003): passenger cars 212,000; trucks and buses (2002) 20,000. *Air transport* (2007): passenger-km 3,720,000,000; metric ton-km cargo 115,536,000. **Communications,** in total units (units per 1,000 persons). Telephone landlines (2006): 80,000 (210); cellular telephone subscribers (2007): 397,000 (997); personal computers (2004): 31,000 (87); total Internet users (2007): 188,000 (488); broadband Internet subscribers (2007): 12,000 (29).

Education and health

Educational attainment (1991). Percentage of population ages 25 and over having: no formal schooling/unknown 17.5%; primary education 43.3%; secondary 26.3%; postsecondary and higher 12.9%. **Literacy** (2004): percentage of total population ages 15 and over literate 92.7%; males literate 95.2%; females literate 90.2%. **Health** (2007): physicians 393 (1 per 1,013 persons); hospital beds 1,068 (1 per 373 persons); infant mortality rate per 1,000 live births 7.6; undernourished population (2002–04) 15,000 (4% of total population based on the consumption of a minimum daily requirement of 1,910 calories).

Military

Total active duty personnel (November 2008): 7,000 (army 70.0%, navy 14.3%, air force 15.7%); British troops 550; Singaporean troops 500. **Military expen-** diture as percentage of GDP (2007): 2.8%; per capita expenditure US$880.

Background

Brunei traded with China in the 6th century AD. Through allegiance to the Javanese Majapahit kingdom (13th–15th centuries), it came under Hindu influence. In the early 15th century, with the decline of the Majapahit kingdom, many people converted to Islam, and Brunei became an independent sultanate. When Ferdinand Magellan's ships visited in 1521, the sultan of Brunei controlled almost all of Borneo and its neighboring islands. Beginning in the late 16th century, Brunei lost power because of the Portuguese, Dutch, and, later, British activities in the region. By the 19th century, the sultanate of Brunei included Sarawak (present-day Brunei) and part of North Borneo (now part of Sabah). In 1841 a revolt took place against the sultan, and a British soldier, James Brooke, helped put it down; he was later proclaimed governor. In 1847 the sultanate entered into a treaty with Great Britain and by 1906 had yielded all administration to a British resident. Brunei rejected membership in the Federation of Malaysia in 1963, negotiated a new treaty with Britain in 1979, and achieved independence in 1984, with membership in the Commonwealth.

Recent Developments

According to the Asian Development Bank, the Brunei economy shrank by less than 1% in 2009. This represented a slight improvement over 2008, when GDP fell by nearly 2%. In March 2009 Malaysia and Brunei announced that they had reached a landmark agreement in resolving their border disputes; a settlement could clear the way for exploration in potentially oil-and gas-rich waters shared by both countries. In August it was announced that Malaysia's national oil company, Petronas, would participate in a joint oil-extraction venture with Brunei.

Internet resource: <www.bedb.com.bn>.

Bulgaria

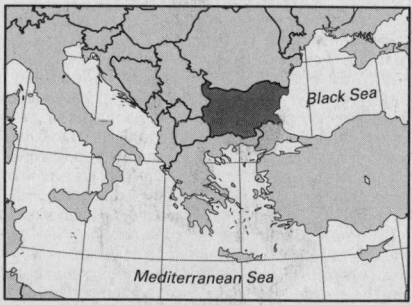

Official name: Republika Bulgaria (Republic of Bulgaria). **Form of government:** unitary multiparty republic with one legislative house (National Assembly [240]). **Head of state:** President Georgi Purvanov

---

1 metric ton = about 1.1 short tons; 1 kilometer = 0.6 mi (statute); 1 metric ton-km cargo = about 0.68 short ton-mi cargo; c.i.f.: cost, insurance, and freight; f.o.b.: free on board

(from 2002). **Head of government:** Prime Minister Boiko Borisov (from 2009). **Capital:** Sofia. **Official language:** Bulgarian. **Official religion:** none (the constitution refers to Eastern Orthodoxy as the "traditional" religion). **Monetary unit:** 1 lev (Lv; plural leva) = 100 stotinki; valuation (1 Jul 2010) US$1 = 1.57 leva.

Demography

Area: 42,858 sq mi, 111,002 sq km. **Population** (2009): 7,584,000. **Density** (2009): persons per sq mi 177.0, persons per sq km 68.3. **Urban** (2008): 71.1%. **Sex distribution** (2008): male 48.40%; female 51.60%. **Age breakdown** (2007): under 15, 13.4%; 15–29, 20.4%; 30–44, 21.5%; 45–59, 21.2%; 60–74, 16.1%; 75–84, 6.3%; 85 and over, 1.1%. **Ethnic composition** (2001): Bulgarian 83.9%; Turkish 9.4%; Rom (Gypsy) 4.7%; other 2.0%. **Religious affiliation** (2005): Bulgarian Orthodox 81%; Sunni Muslim 12%; Evangelical Protestant 2%; Catholic 1%; other 4%. **Major cities** (2007): Sofia 1,156,796; Plovdiv 345,249; Varna 313,983; Burgas 187,514; Ruse 156,761. **Location:** southeastern Europe, bordering Romania, the Black Sea, Turkey, Greece, Macedonia, and Serbia.

Vital statistics

Birth rate per 1,000 population (2008): 10.2 (world avg. 20.3); (2008) within marriage 48.9%. **Death rate** per 1,000 population (2008): 14.5 (world avg. 8.5). **Total fertility rate** (avg. births per childbearing woman; 2008): 1.48. **Life expectancy** at birth (2008): male 69.5 years; female 76.6 years.

National economy

Budget (2007). *Revenue:* 26,210,000,000 leva (tax revenue 80.6%, of which VAT 30.9%, social insurance 14.6%, excise taxes 14.5%; nontax revenue 12.2%; grants 7.2%). *Expenditures:* 24,389,000,000 leva (current expenditures 81.5%; capital expenditures 17.3%; other 1.2%). **Public debt** (external, outstanding; November 2008): US$5,207,000,000. **Gross national income** (2008): US$41,830,000,000 (US$5,490 per capita). **Production** (metric tons except as noted). *Agriculture and fishing* (2007): wheat 2,390,000, corn (maize) 1,312,900, sunflower seeds 564,447; livestock (number of live animals) 1,635,410 sheep, 1,012,655 pigs, 628,271 cattle; fisheries production 12,929 (from aquaculture 32%). *Mining and quarrying* (2004): copper (metal content) 133,000; zinc (metal content) 17,000; gold 3,818 kg. *Manufacturing* (value added in '000,000 leva; 2004): refined petroleum products, n.a.; wearing apparel 566; food products 503; nonelectrical machinery and apparatus 485. *Energy production (consumption):* electricity (kW-hr; 2008) 44,423,000,000 (34,684,000,000); coal (metric tons; 2006) 27,000 (4,259,000); lignite (metric tons; 2007) 28,308,000 ([2006] 25,775,000); crude petroleum (barrels; 2006) 205,000 (52,123,000); petroleum products (metric tons; 2006) 6,088,000 (3,944,000); natural gas (cu m; 2008) 213,000,000 (3,806,000,000). **Population economically active** (2008): total 3,504,700; activity rate of total population 46.0% (participation rates: ages 15–64 67%; female 47.0%; unemployed 5.7%). **Selected balance of payments data.** Receipts from (US$'000,000): tourism (2007) 3,131; remittances (2008) 2,634; foreign direct investment (FDI; 2005–07 avg.) 6,620. Disbursements

for (US$'000,000): tourism (2007) 1,823; remittances (2008) 74; FDI (2005–07 avg.) 249.

Foreign trade

Imports (2007): US$30,086,000,000 (manufactured goods 20.3%; machinery and apparatus 19.6%; chemical products 8.7%; motor vehicles 8.4%; metal ore and scrap 5.8%). *Major import sources* (2008): Russia 14.5%; Germany 11.8%; Italy 7.9%; Ukraine 7.2%; Romania 5.6%. **Exports** (2007): US$18,576,000,000 (base and fabricated metals 22.3%, of which copper 9.4%, iron and steel 6.8%; machinery and apparatus 13.0%; refined petroleum products 12.7%; wearing apparel 10.3%; food products 5.5%). *Major export destinations* (2008): Greece 9.9%; Germany 9.2%; Turkey 8.8%; Italy 8.5%; Romania 7.3%.

Transport and communications

Transport. *Railroads* (2004): track length 6,238 km; (2008–09) passenger-km 2,299,000,000; (2008–09) metric ton-km cargo 4,508,000,000. *Roads* (2004): length 44,033 km (paved 99%). *Vehicles* (2005): cars 2,538,000; trucks and buses 371,000. *Air transport* (2007; Hemus Air and Bulgaria Air only): passenger-km 2,001,000,000; metric ton-km cargo 3,400,000. **Communications,** in total units (units per 1,000 persons). Telephone landlines (2008): 2,258,000 (296); cellular telephone subscribers (2008): 10,633,000 (1,395); personal computers (2007): 682,000 (89); total Internet users (2007): 2,368,000 (309); broadband Internet subscribers (2008): 853,000 (112).

Education and health

Educational attainment (2004). Percentage of population ages 25–64 having: no formal schooling to complete primary education 28%; secondary 50%; higher 22%. **Literacy** (2006): total population ages 15 and over literate 98.3%; males 98.7%; females 97.9%. **Health** (2007): physicians 27,756 (1 per 274 persons); hospital beds 48,930 (1 per 155 persons); infant mortality rate per 1,000 live births (2008) 8.6; undernourished population (2002–04) 600,000 (8% of total population based on the consumption of a minimum daily requirement of 1,990 calories).

Military

Total active duty personnel (November 2008): 40,747 (army 46.1%, navy 10.1%, air force 22.9%, central staff 20.9%). **Military expenditure as percentage of GDP** (2007): 2.2%; per capita expenditure US$115.

Background

Evidence of human habitation in Bulgaria dates from prehistoric times. Thracians were its first recorded inhabitants, dating from c. 3500 BC, and their first state dates from about the 5th century BC; the area was subdued by the Romans, who divided it into the provinces of Moesia and Thrace. In the 7th century AD the Bulgars took the region to the south of the Danube. The Byzantine Empire in 681 formally recognized Bulgar control over the area between the Balkans and the Danube. In the second half of the 14th century, Bulgaria fell to the Turks and ultimately lost its independence. At the end of the Russo-Turkish War (1877–78), Bulgaria rebelled. The ensuing Treaty of San Stefano was unacceptable to the Great Powers, and the Congress of Berlin (1878) resulted. In 1908 the Bulgarian ruler, Ferdinand, declared Bulgaria's independence. After its involvement in the Balkan Wars (1912–13), Bulgaria lost territory. It sided with the Central Powers in World War I and with Germany in World War II. A communist coalition seized power in 1944, and in 1946 a people's republic was declared. Like other Eastern European countries in the late 1980s, Bulgaria experienced political unrest; its communist leader resigned in 1989. A new constitution proclaiming a republic was implemented in 1991. Bulgaria joined NATO in 2004 and the EU in 2007.

Recent Developments

Although its long-term economic outlook improved in 2009, Bulgaria dropped two spots, to 44th, on the World Bank's ranking of countries based on their attractiveness to foreign investment, and, indeed, foreign direct investment dropped precipitously during the year. Projected inflation was only 1.8%, owing in part to lower oil and raw-material prices caused by the global economic crisis, and the country's current account deficit was estimated at US$4.1 billion, compared with US$7.3 billion a year earlier. Unemployment remained at over 6%, however, and tourism revenues, which contributed 14% of GDP, declined 25% from 2008.

Internet resource: <www.nsi.bg/Index_e.htm>.

Burkina Faso

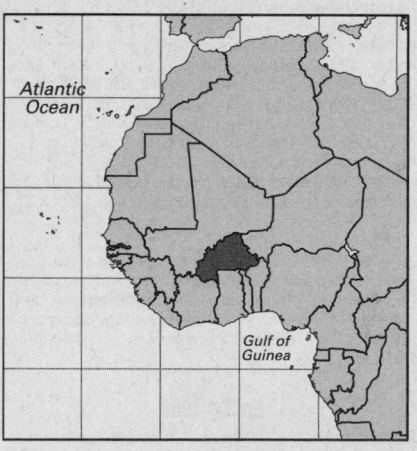

Official name: Burkina Faso. Form of government: multiparty republic with one legislative house (National Assembly [111]). Head of state: President Blaise Compaoré (from 1987). Head of government: Prime Minister Tertius Zongo (from 2007). Capital: Ouagadougou. Official language: French. Official reli-

gion: none. Monetary unit: 1 CFA franc (CFAF) = 100 centimes; valuation (1 Jul 2010) US$1 = CFAF 527.20.

Demography

Area: 103,456 sq mi, 267,950 sq km. Population (2009): 15,757,000. Density (2009): persons per sq mi 152.3, persons per sq km 58.8. Urban (2006): 22.7%. Sex distribution (2006): male 48.29%; female 51.71%. Age breakdown (2006): under 15, 46.4%; 15–29, 26.2%; 30–44, 14.3%; 45–59, 7.6%; 60–74, 3.8%; 75–84, 0.9%; 85 and over, 0.3%; unknown 0.5%. Ethnic composition (1995): Mossi 47.9%; Fulani 10.3%; Lobi 6.9%; Bobo 6.9%; Mande 6.7%; Senufo 5.3%; Grosi 5.0%; Gurma 4.8%; Tuareg 3.1%. Religious affiliation (2006): Muslim 60.5%; Roman Catholic 19.0%; traditional beliefs 15.3%; Protestant/independent Christian 4.2%; nonreligious 0.4%; other 0.6%. Major urban localities (2006): Ouagadougou 1,475,223; Bobo-Dioulasso 489,967; Koudougou 88,184; Banfora 75,917; Ouahigouya 73,153. Location: western Africa, bordering Mali, Niger, Benin, Togo, Ghana, and Côte d'Ivoire.

Vital statistics

Birth rate per 1,000 population (2007): 45.0 (world avg. 20.3). Death rate per 1,000 population (2007): 13.9 (world avg. 8.5). Total fertility rate (avg. births per childbearing woman; 2007): 6.41. Life expectancy at birth (2007): male 50.3 years; female 54.0 years.

National economy

Budget (2007). Revenue: CFAF 618,508,000,000 (tax revenue 65.4%, of which taxes on goods and services 35.2%, taxes on international transactions 12.6%; grants 29.0%; nontax revenue 5.6%). Expenditures: CFAF 839,362,000,000 (current expenditures 54.0%; development expenditures 45.8%; other 0.2%). Production (metric tons except as noted). Agriculture and fishing (2007): sorghum 1,507,000, millet 966,000, seed cotton 690,000, shea nuts (2005) 70,000, bambara beans 40,500, sesame 25,600; livestock (number of live animals) 11,295,000 goats, 7,914,000 cattle, 7,544,000 sheep; fisheries production 10,498 (from aquaculture, 3%). Mining and quarrying (2007): gold 2,250 kg; granite 300,000 cu m. Manufacturing (value added in CFAF '000,000; 1999): food products, beverages, and tobacco 126,125; textiles 46,217; chemical products 9,335. Energy production (consumption): electricity (kW-hr; 2006) 548,000,000 (687,000,000); petroleum products (metric tons; 2006) none (440,000). Population economically active (2006): total 5,412,102; activity rate 38.6% (participation rates: ages 15 and over, 72.7%; female 45.3%; officially unemployed 2.3%). Gross national income (2008): US$7,278,000,000 (US$480 per capita). Public debt (external; 2007): US$1,268,000,000. Selected balance of payments data. Receipts from (US$'000,000): tourism (2006) 53; remittances (2008) 50; foreign direct investment (2005–07 avg.) 223; official development assistance (2007) 930. Disbursements for (US$'000,000): tourism (2006) 55; remittances (2008) 44.

1 metric ton = about 1.1 short tons;   1 kilometer = 0.6 mi (statute);   1 metric ton-km cargo = about 0.68 short ton-mi cargo;   c.i.f.: cost, insurance, and freight;   f.o.b.: free on board

Foreign trade

Imports (2007; f.o.b. in commodities and c.i.f. in trading partners): CFAF 585,100,000,000 (machinery and apparatus 29.3%; refined petroleum products 24.5%; food products 10.3%). *Major import sources* (2005): France 18.7%; Côte d'Ivoire 18.0%; Togo 11.4%; Benin 6.8%; Ghana 5.9%. **Exports** (2007): CFAF 296,100,000,000 (raw cotton 55.4%; gold 5.4%; shea nuts 4.6%). *Major export destinations* (2005): Togo 41.1%; Ghana 16.7%; Côte d'Ivoire 10.5%; France 9.8%; Switzerland 9.4%.

Transport and communications

Transport. *Railroads:* route length (2007) 622 km; passenger-km (2003) 9,980,000; metric ton-km cargo (2005) 674,900,000. *Roads* (2006): total length 15,272 km (paved 17%). *Vehicles* (2005): passenger cars 84,161; trucks and buses 38,261. *Air transport* (2005; combined data for Ouagadougou and Bobo-Dioulasso airports): passenger arrivals 134,247, passenger departures 137,373; cargo unloaded 2,837 metric tons, cargo loaded 1,347 metric tons. **Communications**, in total units (units per 1,000 persons). Telephone landlines (2007): 122,000 (8.3); cellular telephone subscribers (2008): 2,553,000 (168); personal computers (2007): 88,000 (6.0); total Internet users (2008): 140,000 (9.2); broadband Internet subscribers (2006): 1,700 (0.1).

Education and health

Educational attainment (2003). Percentage of population ages 25 and over having: no formal schooling or unknown 85.4%; incomplete to complete primary education 7.9%; incomplete to complete secondary 5.5%; higher 1.2%. **Literacy** (2006): percentage of total population ages 15 and over literate 21.1%; males literate 27.9%; females literate 15.4%. **Health** (2007): physicians 441 (1 per 31,634 persons); hospital beds (2006) 12,200 (1 per 1,111 persons); infant mortality rate per 1,000 live births 87.6; undernourished population (2002–04) 2,000,000 (15% of total population based on the consumption of a minimum daily requirement of 1,800 calories).

Military

Total active duty personnel (November 2008): 10,800 (army 59.3%, air force 1.8%, gendarmerie 38.9%). **Military expenditure as percentage of GDP** (2007): 1.3%; per capita expenditure US$7.

Background

Probably in the 14th century, the Mossi and Gurma peoples established themselves in eastern and central areas of what is now Burkina Faso. The Mossi kingdoms of Yatenga and Ouagadougou existed into the early 20th century. A French protectorate was established over the region (1895–97), and its southern boundary was demarcated through an Anglo-French agreement. It was part of the Upper Senegal-Niger colony and then became a separate colony in 1919. Named Upper Volta, it was constituted an overseas territory within the French Union in 1947, became an autonomous republic within the French Community in 1958, and achieved total independence in 1960. Since then, the country has been ruled primarily by the military and has experienced several coups; following one in 1983, the country received its present name. A new constitution, adopted in 1991, restored multiparty rule.

Recent Developments

A population growth rate of 3.1% threatened to offset strong increases in Burkina Faso's economic growth in 2009. Despite record harvests, food prices remained high. In February the UN World Food Programme (WFP) launched a food-voucher scheme designed to benefit 20,000 Ouagadougou households. In August the WFP called for expansion of the emergency program, calling attention to the continued high prices and empty shelves in their warehouses. At least 30,000 more families in the capital were estimated to be in dire need of help. Additionally, September floods left more than 150,000 residents homeless.

Internet resource: <www.burkina.com>.

Burundi

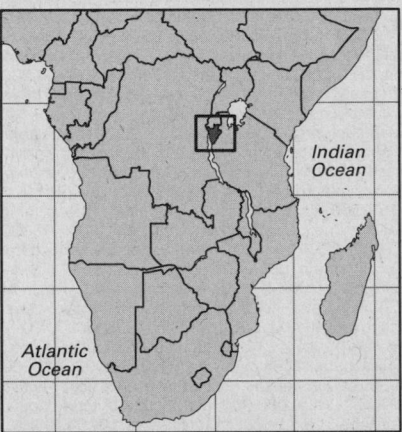

Official name: Republika y'u Burundi (Rundi); République du Burundi (French) (Republic of Burundi). **Form of government:** republic with two legislative houses (Senate [49]; National Assembly [100]). **Head of state and government:** President Pierre Nkurunziza (from 2005). **Capital:** Bujumbura. **Official languages:** Rundi; French. **Official religion:** none. **Monetary unit:** 1 Burundi franc (FBu) = 100 centimes; valuation (1 Jul 2010) US$1 = FBu 1,205.29.

Demography

Area: 10,740 sq mi, 27,816 sq km. **Population** (2009): 8,303,000. **Density** (2009): persons per sq mi 828.7, persons per sq km 320.0. **Urban** (2007): 9.9%. **Sex distribution** (2005): male 48.82%; female 51.18%. **Age breakdown** (2005): under 15, 41.4%; 15–29, 30.8%; 30–44, 14.7%; 45–59, 8.7%; 60–74, 3.5%; 75–84, 0.8%; 85 and over, 0.1%. **Ethnic composition** (2000): Hutu 80.9%; Tutsi 15.6%; Lingala 1.6%; Twa Pygmy 1.0%; other 0.9%. **Religious affiliation** (2004): Christian 67%, of which Roman Catholic 62%, Protestant 5%; traditional beliefs 23%; Muslim (mostly Sunni) 10%. **Major city and towns**

(2004): Bujumbura 374,152; Gitega 25,500; Ngozi 21,500; Bururi 20,500. **Location:** central Africa, bordering Rwanda, Tanzania, Lake Tanganyika, and the Democratic Republic of the Congo.

Vital statistics

Birth rate per 1,000 population (2005): 35.4 (world avg. 20.3). **Death rate** per 1,000 population (2005): 14.8 (world avg. 8.5). **Total fertility rate** (avg. births per childbearing woman; 2005): 5.04. **Life expectancy** at birth (2005): male 47.8 years; female 50.5 years.

National economy

Budget (2007). *Revenue:* FBu 419,600,000,000 (grants 52.9%; tax revenue 43.5%, of which taxes on goods and services 22.0%, income tax 12.7%, taxes on international trade 8.1%; nontax revenue 3.6%). *Expenditures:* FBu 407,900,000,000 (current expenditures 63.9%; capital expenditures 33.0%; other 3.1%). **Public debt** (external, outstanding; February 2008): US$1,330,000,000. **Production** (metric tons except as noted). *Agriculture and fishing* (2007): bananas 1,600,000, sweet potatoes 835,000, cassava 710,000, taros 62,000, palm oil 12,773; livestock (number of live animals) 750,000 goats, 400,000 cattle, 250,000 sheep; fisheries production 14,200 (from aquaculture 1%). *Mining and quarrying* (2007): columbite-tantalite ore 51,550 kg; gold 2,423 kg. *Manufacturing* (2007): beer 1,289,400 hectoliters; carbonated beverages 294,200 hectoliters; cottonseed oil 51,200 liters. *Energy production (consumption):* electricity (kW-hr; 2007) 117,500,000 (192,600,000); petroleum products (metric tons; 2006) none (58,000); peat (metric tons; 2007) 9,800 ([2000] 12,000). **Selected balance of payments data.** Receipts from (US$'000,000): tourism (2007) 1.3; remittances (2004) 4.1; foreign direct investment (2005–07 avg.) negligible; official development assistance (2007) 466. Disbursements for (US$'000,000): tourism (2007) 104; remittances (2008) negligible. **Gross national income** (2008): US$1,092,000,000 (US$140 per capita). **Population economically active** (2006): total 4,060,000; activity rate of total population 49.7% (participation rates: ages 15–64, 90.5%; female 51.9%; unemployed, n.a.).

Foreign trade

Imports (2007; c.i.f.): US$423,000,000 (refined petroleum products 27.5%; motor vehicles 19.8%; food products 11.0%, of which cereals 7.7%; machinery and apparatus 8.7%; iron and steel 6.4%). *Major import sources:* Saudi Arabia 27.5%; Belgium 11.3%; Uganda 10.7%; Kenya 7.9%; Japan 7.0%. **Exports** (2007; f.o.b.): US$156,200,000 (gold 34.0% [nearly all smuggled from neighboring countries]; coffee 24.6%; motor vehicles 9.2%; black tea 4.2%; raw cane sugar 4.0%; prefabricated buildings 3.0%; hides and skins 2.4%). *Major export destinations:* UAE 34.2%; Switzerland 10.9%; Democratic Republic of the Congo 9.4%; Kenya 7.2%; Rwanda 6.7%.

Transport and communications

Transport. *Railroads:* none. *Roads* (2004): total length 12,322 km (paved 7%). *Vehicles:* passenger cars

(2003) 7,000; trucks and buses (2002) 14,400. *Air transport* (2007–08; Bujumbura airport only): passenger arrivals 96,175, passenger departures 62,845; cargo unloaded 2,116 metric tons, cargo loaded 317 metric tons. **Communications,** in total units (units per 1,000 persons). Telephone landlines (2008): 30,000 (3.8); cellular telephone subscribers (2008): 481,000 (60); personal computers (2006): 57,000 (7.0); total Internet users (2008): 65,000 (8.1); broadband Internet subscribers (2008): 200 (0.02).

Education and health

Literacy (2007): percentage of total population ages 15 and over literate 56.1%; males literate 61.4%; females literate 51.1%. **Health:** physicians (2004) 200 (1 per 37,581 persons); hospital beds (2006) 5,663 (1 per 1,429 persons); infant mortality rate per 1,000 live births (2005) 102.0; undernourished population (2002–04) 4,500,000 (66% of total population based on the consumption of a minimum daily requirement of 1,800 calories).

Military

Total active duty personnel (November 2008): 20,000 (army 100%); Burundian troops in Somalia as part of African Union (AU) peacekeeping mission (December 2008): 1,700; South African troops in Burundi representing AU peacekeeping mission (February 2009): 973. **Military expenditure as percentage of GDP** (2007): 7.8%; per capita expenditure US$9.

Background

Original settlement by the Twa people was followed by Hutu settlement, which occurred gradually and was completed by the 11th century. The Tutsi arrived 300–400 years later; though a minority, they established the kingdom of Burundi in the 16th century. In the 19th century the area came within the German sphere of influence, but the Tutsi remained in power. Following World War I the Belgians took control of the area, which became a UN trusteeship after World War II. Colonial-period conditions had intensified Hutu-Tutsi ethnic animosities, and as independence neared, hostilities flared. Independence was granted in 1962 in the form of a kingdom ruled by the Tutsi. In 1965 the Hutu rebelled but were brutally repressed. The rest of the 20th century saw violent clashes between the two groups. In 2001 a power-sharing transitional government was established, paving the way to the promulgation of a new constitution and the installation of a new government in 2005.

Recent Developments

The Burundi government in early 2009 released 247 former National Liberation Forces (FNL) prisoners and the FNL responded by releasing 136 child soldiers, leading to the official implementation of a 2006 cease-fire agreement that ended the civil war between the Tutsi and the Hutu that had begun in 1993. Despite this progress some 16,000 former rebels rejected the terms of demobilization.

Internet resource: <www.burunditourisme.com/index.php?id=10&L=1>.

1 metric ton = about 1.1 short tons;   1 kilometer = 0.6 mi (statute);   1 metric ton-km cargo = about 0.68 short ton-mi cargo;   c.i.f.: cost, insurance, and freight;   f.o.b.: free on board

Cambodia

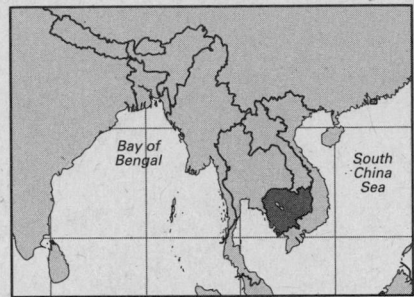

Official name: Preahreacheanachakr Kampuchea (Kingdom of Cambodia). **Form of government:** constitutional monarchy with two legislative houses (Senate [61]; National Assembly [123]). **Head of state:** King Norodom Sihamoni (from 2004). **Head of government:** Prime Minister Samdech Hun Sen (from 1998). **Capital:** Phnom Penh. **Official language:** Khmer. **Official religion:** Buddhism. **Monetary unit:** 1 riel (KHR) = 100 sen; valuation (1 Jul 2010) US$1 = 4,182.01 riels.

Demography

Area: 69,898 sq mi, 181,035 sq km. **Population** (2009): 14,494,000. **Density** (2009): persons per sq mi 210.9, persons per sq km 81.4. **Urban** (2008): 19.5%. **Sex distribution** (2008): male 48.51%; female 51.49%. **Age breakdown** (2005): under 15, 36.6%; 15–29, 30.5%; 30–44, 18.4%; 45–59, 9.4%; 60–74, 4.1%; 75–84, 0.9%; 85 and over, 0.1%. **Ethnic composition** (2000): Khmer 85.2%; Chinese 6.4%; Vietnamese 3.0%; Cham 2.5%; Lao 0.6%; other 2.3%. **Religious affiliation** (2000): Buddhist 84.7%; Chinese folk religionist 4.7%; traditional beliefs 4.3%; Muslim 2.3%; Christian 1.1%; other 2.9%. **Major urban areas** (1998): Phnom Penh (2005) 1,364,000; Battambang 124,290; Sisophon 85,382; Siemreap 83,715; Sihanoukville 66,723. **Location:** southeastern Asia, bordering Thailand, Laos, Vietnam, and the Gulf of Thailand.

Vital statistics

Birth rate per 1,000 population (2008): 25.7 (world avg. 20.3). **Death rate** per 1,000 population (2008): 8.2 (world avg. 8.5). **Total fertility rate** (avg. births per childbearing woman; 2008): 3.08. **Life expectancy** at birth (2008): male 59.7 years; female 63.8 years.

National economy

Budget (2007). *Revenue:* KHR 3,280,300,000,000 (tax revenue 58.3%; nontax revenue 17.2%; grants 20.0%; other 4.5%). *Expenditures:* KHR 3,294,700,000,000 (current expenditures 59.7%; development expenditures 40.3%). *Production* (metric tons except as noted). *Agriculture and fishing* (2007): rice 5,995,000, cassava 2,000,000, corn (maize) 380,000, rubber 22,000; livestock (number of live animals) 3,500,000 cattle, 2,790,000 pigs, 775,000 buffalo, (2005) 120,000 crocodiles; fisheries production 514,200 (from aquaculture 7%); aquatic plants production 16,000 (from aquaculture 100%). *Mining and quarrying* (2007): gold, n.a.; gem-

stones, n.a.; salt 76,700. *Manufacturing* (value added in KHR '000,000,000; 2002): wearing apparel 1,808; food products 392; base and fabricated metals 120. *Energy production (consumption):* electricity (kW-hr; 2006) 1,235,000,000 (1,345,000,000); petroleum products (metric tons; 2006) none (1,327,000). **Selected balance of payments data.** Receipts from (US$'000,000): tourism (2007) 1,284; remittances (2008) 325; foreign direct investment (2005–07 avg.) 577; official development assistance (2007) 672. Disbursements for (US$'000,000): tourism (2007) 194; remittances (2008) 164. **Gross national income** (2008): US$8,859,000,000 (US$600 per capita). **Public debt** (external, outstanding; 2007): US$3,537,000,000. **Population economically active** (2004): total 7,557,600; activity rate of total population 55.0% (participation rates: ages 15–64, 82.6%; female 49.4%; registered unemployed 7.1%).

Foreign trade

Imports (2005; c.i.f.): US$4,254,000,000 (retained imports 97.3%; imports for reexport 2.7%). *Major import sources* (2004): Thailand 23.9%; Hong Kong 15.0%; China 13.5%; Singapore 11.5%; Vietnam 7.6%. **Exports** (2005; f.o.b.): US$2,910,000,000 (domestic exports 95.3%, of which garments 77.7%, rice 6.1%, rubber 4.1%, fish 2.6%, sawn timber and logs 0.5%; reexports 4.7%). *Major export destinations* (2004): US 56.2%; Germany 11.5%; UK 7.0%; Canada 4.3%; Vietnam 3.7%.

Transport and communications

Transport. *Railroads* (2004): length 602 km; (2000) passenger-km 45,000,000; (1999) metric ton-km 76,171,000. *Roads* (2004): total length 38,257 km (paved 6%). *Vehicles* (2004): passenger cars 235,298; trucks and buses 35,448. *Air transport* (2005–06): passenger-km 198,000,000; metric ton-km cargo 1,214,000. **Communications,** in total units (units per 1,000 persons). Telephone landlines (2008): 45,000 (3.1); cellular telephone subscribers (2008): 4,237,000 (288); personal computers (2007): 56,000 (4.0); total Internet users (2007): 70,000 (4.8); broadband Internet subscribers (2007): 8,400 (0.6).

Education and health

Educational attainment (2004). Percentage of literate population ages 25 and over having: no formal schooling/unknown 4.6%; incomplete primary education 54.0%; complete primary 23.7%; incomplete secondary 11.3%; secondary/vocational 5.3%; higher 1.1%. **Literacy** (2004): percentage of total population ages 15 and over literate 74.4%; males literate 82.1%; females literate 67.4%. **Health:** physicians (2004) 2,122 (1 per 6,169 persons); hospital beds (2002) 9,800 (1 per 1,405 persons); infant mortality rate per 1,000 live births (2008) 56.6; undernourished population (2002–04) 4,600,000 (33% of total population based on the consumption of a minimum daily requirement of 1,770 calories).

Military

Total active duty personnel (November 2008): 124,300 (army 60.3%, navy 2.3%, air force 1.2%, provincial forces 36.2%). **Military expenditure as per-**

centage of GDP (2007): 1.6%; per capita expenditure US$10.

Background

In the early Christian era, what is now Cambodia was under Hindu and, to a lesser extent, Buddhist influence. The Khmer state gradually spread in the early 7th century and reached its height under Jayavarman II and his successors in the 9th–12th centuries, when it ruled the Mekong Valley and the tributary Shan states and built Angkor. Widespread adoption of Buddhism occurred in the 13th century, resulting in a script change from Sanskrit to Pali. From the 13th century Cambodia was attacked by Annam and Siamese city-states and was alternately a province of one or the other. The area became a French protectorate in 1863. It was occupied by the Japanese in World War II and became independent in 1954. Cambodia's borders were the scene of fighting in the Vietnam War from 1961, and in 1970 its northeastern and eastern areas were occupied by the North Vietnamese and penetrated by US and South Vietnamese forces. An indiscriminate US bombing campaign alienated much of the population, enabling the communist Khmer Rouge under Pol Pot to seize power in 1975. Their regime of terror resulted in the deaths of at least one million Cambodians. Vietnam invaded in 1979 and drove the Khmer Rouge into the western hinterlands, but it was unable to effect reconstruction of the country, and Cambodian infighting continued. A peace accord was reached by most Cambodian factions under UN auspices in 1991, and elections were held in 1993. In 2004 King Norodom Sihanouk abdicated, and his son Sihamoni was named his successor.

Recent Developments

International attention focused in 2009 on the first public trial held by the Khmer Rouge Tribunal (officially the Extraordinary Chambers in the Courts of Cambodia [ECCC]). The trial of 67-year-old Kaing Guek Eav (better known as Duch), who headed the notorious S-21 prison during the 1975–79 Pol Pot regime, began in February and drew to a close in November. Early in the trial, Duch dramatically confessed his responsibility for the crimes. The four remaining defendants in ECCC custody were to be tried jointly. In July 2010, Duch was found guilty of crimes against humanity and was sentenced to 35 years in prison. This was reduced for credit for time served and other factors to 19 years, with eligibility for parole in 12.

Internet resource: <www.nis.gov.kh>.

Cameroon

Official name: République du Cameroun (French); Republic of Cameroon (English). **Form of government:** unitary multiparty republic with one legislative house (National Assembly [180]). **Head of state:** President Paul Biya (from 1982). **Head of government:** Prime Minister Philemon Yang (from 2009). **Capital:** Yaoundé. **Official languages:** French; English. **Official religion:** none. **Monetary unit:** 1 CFA franc (CFAF) = 100 centimes; valuation (1 Jul 2010) US$1 = CFAF 527.20.

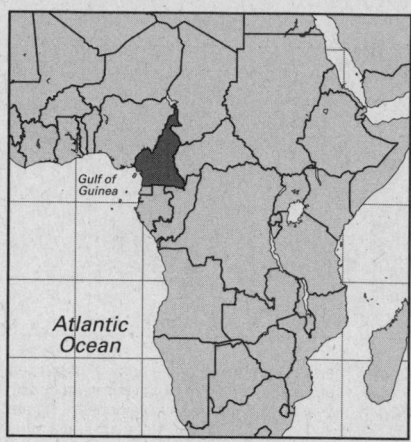

Demography

Area: 183,920 sq mi, 476,350 sq km (includes the 270-sq-mi [699-sq-km] area of Bakassi Peninsula, which was formally ceded by Nigeria to Cameroon in August 2008). **Population** (2009): 19,522,000. **Density** (2009; based on land area excluding Bakassi Peninsula): persons per sq mi 108.3, persons per sq km 41.8. **Urban** (2007): 56.0%. **Sex distribution** (2006): male 50.15%; female 49.85%. **Age breakdown** (2006): under 15, 41.5%; 15–29, 29.0%; 30–44, 15.7%; 45–59, 8.8%; 60–74, 4.1%; 75–84, 0.8%; 85 and over, 0.1%. **Ethnic composition** (2006): "western highlanders" 38.0%, including Bamileke 11.5%; "coastal tropical forest peoples" 12.0%, including Bassa 2.5%; "southern tropical forest peoples" 18.0%, including Ewondo (Yaunde) 8.0%; "mostly Islamic central highlanders" 14.0%, including Fulani 8.5%; "mostly traditional believers of central highlands and far north" or "Kirdi" 18.0%, including Mofa 2.5%. **Religious affiliation** (2005): Roman Catholic 27.4%; traditional beliefs 22.2%; Protestant 20.2%; Sunni Muslim 20.0%; nonreligious/other 10.2%. **Major urban areas** (2006): Douala 1,371,400; Yaoundé 1,344,600; Kousséri 476,600; Garoua 461,300; Bamenda 419,400. **Location:** western Africa, bordering Chad, the Central African Republic, the Republic of the Congo, Gabon, Equatorial Guinea, the Bight of Biafra, and Nigeria.

Vital statistics

Birth rate per 1,000 population (2006): 35.6 (world avg. 20.3). **Death rate** per 1,000 population (2006): 13.0 (world avg. 8.6). **Total fertility rate** (avg. births per childbearing woman; 2006): 4.58. **Life expectancy** at birth (2006): male 51.7 years; female 53.0 years.

National economy

Budget (2006). *Revenue:* CFAF 4,472,000,000,000 (grants 59.6%; non-oil revenue 26.0%, of which VAT 10.0%, direct taxes 5.9%, customs duties 4.6%, non-tax revenue 2.2%; oil revenue 14.4%). *Expenditures:*

1 metric ton = about 1.1 short tons;   1 kilometer = 0.6 mi (statute);   1 metric ton-km cargo = about 0.68 short ton-mi cargo;   c.i.f.: cost, insurance, and freight;   f.o.b.: free on board

CFAF 1,364,000,000,000 (current expenditures 80.4%; capital expenditures 19.6%). **Public debt** (external, outstanding; 2007): US$2,204,000,000. **Gross national income** (2008): US$21,781,000,000 (US$1,150 per capita). **Population economically active** (2006): total 6,857,000; activity rate of total population 37.7% (participation rates: ages 15–64, 64.7%; female 41.2%; unemployed 9.3%, underemployed 68.8%). **Production** (metric tons except as noted). *Agriculture and fishing* (2007): cassava 2,076,000, plantains 1,317,000, oil palm fruit 1,300,000, taro 1,133,000, seed cotton 225,000, cacao 179,239, natural rubber 47,000; livestock (number of live animals) 6,000,000 cattle, 3,800,000 sheep; fisheries production 138,952 (from aquaculture, negligible). *Mining and quarrying* (2007): pozzolana 600,000; limestone 100,000; gold 20,000 kg. *Manufacturing* (value added in US$'000,000; 2002): food products 97; refined petroleum products 88; beverages 78. *Energy production (consumption):* electricity (kW-hr; 2006) 3,900,000,000 (3,320,000,000); crude petroleum (barrels; 2008) 29,700,000 ([2007] 9,500,000); petroleum products (metric tons; 2005) 1,784,000 (932,000); natural gas (cu m; 2006) 20,000,000 (20,000,000). **Selected balance of payments data.** Receipts from (US$'000,000): tourism (2007) 177; remittances (2008) 167; foreign direct investment (2005–07 avg.) 273; official development assistance (2007) 1,933. Disbursements for (US$'000,000): tourism (2007) 318; remittances (2008) 103.

Foreign trade

Imports (2006; c.i.f.): US$3,150,500,000 (crude petroleum 29.4%; chemical products 11.1%; machinery and apparatus 10.9%; cereals 9.0%; motor vehicles 5.8%). *Major import sources:* Nigeria 23.3%; France 17.2%; China 6.3%; Belgium 4.1%; Equatorial Guinea 3.5%. **Exports** (2006; f.o.b.): US$3,576,400,000 (crude petroleum 49.8%; refined petroleum products 11.8%; sawn wood 9.7%; cocoa [all forms] 7.3%; aluminum 4.5%; raw cotton 2.9%; natural rubber 1.8%; coffee 1.8%). *Major export destinations:* Spain 25.9%; Italy 23.1%; France 10.7%; US 6.4%; Netherlands 6.3%.

Transport and communications

Transport. *Railroads* (2005): route length (2006) 987 km; passenger-km 323,000,000; metric ton-km cargo 1,119,000,000. *Roads* (2004): total length 50,000 km (paved 10%). *Vehicles* (2005): passenger cars 175,981; trucks and buses 59,399. *Air transport* (2005): passenger-km 646,000,000; metric ton-km cargo (2001) 23,255,000. **Communications,** in total units (units per 1,000 persons). Telephone landlines (2008): 198,000 (10); cellular telephone subscribers (2008): 6,161,000 (323); personal computers (2006): 194,000 (11); total Internet users (2007): 548,000 (29); broadband Internet subscribers (2007): 400 (0.02).

Education and health

Educational attainment (2004): Percentage of population ages 25 and over having: no formal schooling/unknown 34.3%; primary education 35.3%; secondary 26.2%; higher 4.2%. **Literacy** (2007): percentage of total population ages 15 and over literate 78.8%; males literate 84.6%; females literate

73.2%. **Health** (2004): physicians 2,966 (1 per 5,609 persons); hospital beds 26,487 (1 per 667 persons); infant mortality rate per 1,000 live births (2006) 67.2; undernourished population (2002–04) 4,200,000 (26% of total population based on the consumption of a minimum daily requirement of 1,860 calories).

Military

Total active duty personnel (November 2008): 14,100 (army 88.7%, navy 9.2%, air force 2.1%). **Military expenditure as percentage of GDP** (2007): 1.6%; per capita expenditure US$16.

Background

The Cameroon area had long been inhabited before European colonization. Bantu speakers from equatorial Africa settled in the south, followed by Muslim Fulani from the Niger River basin, who settled in the north. Portuguese explorers visited in the late 15th century and established a foothold, but they lost control to the Dutch in the 17th century. In 1884 the Germans took control and extended their protectorate over Cameroon. In World War I joint French-British action forced the Germans to retreat, and after the war the region was divided into French and British administrative zones. After World War II the two areas became UN trusteeships. In 1960 the French trust territory became an independent republic. In 1961 the southern part of the British trust territory voted for union with the new republic of Cameroon, and the northern part voted for union with Nigeria. In recent decades economic problems have produced unrest in the country.

Recent Developments

Concerns over Cameroon's human rights record continued in 2009. In January Reporters Without Borders strongly protested the three-year prison sentence given to Lewis Medjo, editor of an opposition weekly journal. Amnesty International alleged that month that the government had committed severe human rights violations, including brutal torture. In August the government's own human rights commission published a damning report on prison conditions—more than 23,000 prisoners were in facilities designed for 16,000.

Internet resource: <www.cameroon-tourism.org>.

Canada

Official name: Canada. **Form of government:** federal multiparty parliamentary state with two legislative houses (Senate [105]; House of Commons [308]). **Head of state:** British Queen Elizabeth II (from 1952), represented by Governor-General Michaëlle Jean (from 2005). **Head of government:** Prime Minister Stephen Harper (from 2006). **Capital:** Ottawa. **Official languages:** English; French. **Official religion:** none. **Monetary unit:** 1 Canadian dollar (Can$) = 100 cents; valuation (1 Jul 2010) US$1 = Can$1.06.

Demography

Area: 3,855,103 sq mi, 9,984,670 sq km. **Population** (2009): 33,687,000. **Density** (2009; based on

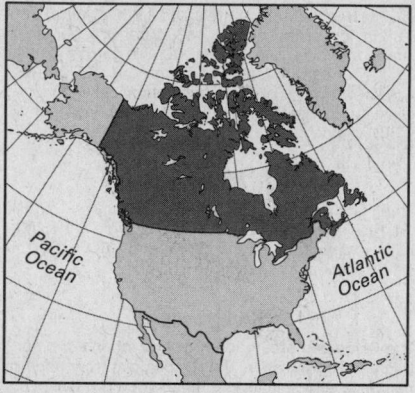

Life expectancy at birth (2006): male 76.9 years; female 83.7 years.

Social indicators

Educational attainment (2006). Percentage of population ages 25–64 having: less than complete secondary education 15.5%; complete secondary 23.9%; higher vocational 12.4%; some college/university 25.3%; bachelor's degree 14.6%; beyond bachelor's/master's 7.5%; doctorate 0.8%. **Quality of working life.** Average workweek (2007): 35.6 hours. Annual rate per 100,000 workers for (2006): injury, accident, or industrial illness 1,998; death 5.9. Average days lost to labor stoppages per 1,000 employee-workdays (2001): 0.7. Average round-trip commuting time (2005): 63 minutes; mode of transportation (2006): auto driver 72.3%, auto passenger 7.7%, public transportation 11.0%, walking 6.4%, bicycling 1.3%, other/unknown 1.3%. Labor force covered by a pension plan (2006): 38.1%. **Social participation.** Population over 18 years of age participating in voluntary work (2000): 26.7%. Trade union membership as percentage of civilian labor force (2007) 29.4%. Attendance at religious services on a weekly basis (2006): 17%. **Social deviance** (2007). Offense rate per 100,000 population for: violent crime 929.6, of which battery/aggravated battery/dangerous operation of vehicle 718.5, robbery 89.8, sexual assault 65.0, homicide 1.8; property crime 3,319.7, of which breaking and entering 700.3, auto theft 443.2, fraud 267.7. **Leisure** (1998). Favorite leisure activities (hours weekly): television (2004) 21.4; radio (2005) 19.1; social time 13.3; reading 2.8; sports and entertainment 1.4. **Material well-being** (2006). Households possessing: owned automobile 59.7%; owned truck/van 36.9%; landline telephone only (December 2007) 24.0%; cellular phone (December 2007) 72.4%; air conditioner 48.1%; cable television 65.2%; home computer 75.4%; Internet use from home 68.1%; dishwasher 57.7%.

National economy

Gross national income (2008): US$1,390,040,-000,000 (US$41,730 per capita). **Budget** (2007–08; federal government). *Revenue:* Can$256,575,-000,000 (income tax 46.2%; corporate taxes 16.3%; sales tax 13.8%; contributions to social security 8.5%; other 15.2%). *Expenditures:* Can$242,814,-000,000 (social services 37.0%; defense/police 11.8%; transfers to government subsectors 11.3%; health 10.6%; debt service 8.4%; resource conservation and industrial development 4.5%; foreign affairs/international assistance 2.4%; education 2.3%). **Production** (metric tons except as noted). *Agriculture and fishing* (2008): wheat 28,611,100, rapeseed 12,642,900, barley 11,781,400, corn (maize) 10,592,000, potatoes 4,724,460, oats 4,272,600, dry peas 3,571,300, soybeans 3,335,900, linseed 861,100, tomatoes 770,059, apples 393,435, sugar beets 344,700, rye 316,200, dry onions 202,636, canary seed 195,600, mustard seed 161,000, sunflower seeds 112,200, blueberries 94,551, mushrooms and truffles 86,946, grapes 80,959, cranberries 72,642; livestock (number of live animals) 13,895,000 cattle, 13,810,000 pigs, 165,000,000 chickens, 5,880,000 turkeys; fisheries production

land area): persons per sq mi 9.6, persons per sq km 3.7. **Urban** (2006): 80.2%. **Sex distribution** (2007): male 49.53%; female 50.47%. **Age breakdown** (2007): under 15, 17.0%; 15–29, 20.5%; 30–44, 21.9%; 45–59, 22.0%; 60–74, 12.2%; 75–84, 4.7%; 85 and over, 1.7%. **Population by mother tongue** (2006): English 57.8%; French 22.1%; other 20.1%, of which Chinese languages 3.3%, Italian 1.5%, German 1.5%, Punjabi 1.2%, Spanish 1.2%, Arabic 0.9%, Tagalog 0.9%, Portuguese 0.7%, Polish 0.7%, Urdu 0.5%, Ukrainian 0.5%. **Aboriginal population** (2006): North American Indian 1,172,790 (2.2% of total population); Métis 698,025 (1.3%); Inuit (Eskimo) 50,485 (0.2%); other/multiple 34,500 (0.1%). **Religious affiliation** (2001): Christian 77.1%, of which Roman Catholic 43.2%, Protestant 28.3%, unspecified Christian 2.6%, Orthodox 1.7%, other Christian 1.3%; Muslim 2.0%; Jewish 1.1%; Hindu 1.0%; Buddhist 1.0%; Sikh 0.9%; nonreligious 16.5%; other 0.4%. **Major metropolitan areas** (2006): Toronto 5,113,149; Montreal 3,635,571; Vancouver 2,116,581; Ottawa-Gatineau 1,130,761; Calgary 1,079,310; Edmonton 1,034,945; Quebec 715,515; Winnipeg 694,668; Hamilton 692,911; London 457,720; Kitchener 451,235; St. Catharines–Niagara 390,317. **Location:** northern North America, bordering the Arctic Ocean, the North Atlantic Ocean, the US, and the North Pacific Ocean. **Place of birth** (2006): 80.2% native-born; 19.8% foreign-born, of which Asian 8.1%, European 7.3%, Latin American 1.2%, African 1.2%. **Mobility** (2006). Population living in the same residence as in 2001: 59.1%; different residence, same municipality 22.0%; same province, different municipality 12.1%; different province 2.9%; different country 3.9%. **Immigration** (2007): permanent immigrants admitted 236,758; from Asia/Pacific 47.6%, of which China 11.4%, India 11.0%, Philippines 8.1%; Africa/Middle East 20.5%; Europe 16.5%; Latin America 10.9%; US 4.4%; refugee population (January 2008) 175,741.

Vital statistics

Birth rate per 1,000 population (2007–08): 11.0 (world avg. 20.3). **Death rate** per 1,000 population (2007–08): 7.2 (world avg. 8.5). **Total fertility rate** (avg. births per childbearing woman; 2006): 1.59.

1 metric ton = about 1.1 short tons;   1 kilometer = 0.6 mi (statute);   1 metric ton-km cargo = about 0.68 short ton-mi cargo;   c.i.f.: cost, insurance, and freight;   f.o.b.: free on board

(2007) 1,174,735 (from aquaculture 14%); aquatic plants production (2006) 11,313 (from aquaculture, none). *Mining and quarrying* (value of production in Can$'000,000; 2007): nickel 9,902 (world rank: 2); copper 4,533; potash 3,142 (world rank: 1); uranium 2,523 (world rank: 1); iron ore 2,512; gold 2,377; zinc 2,087 (world rank: 5); diamonds 1,445; stone 1,333; platinum group 543 (world rank: 3); salt 427 (world rank: 5); cobalt 223 (world rank: 2); gypsum 112 (world rank: 4); ilmenite 816,000 metric tons (world rank: 3); molybdenum (metal content) 6,841 metric tons (world rank: 5). *Manufacturing* (value added in Can$'000,000,000 in constant prices of 2002; 2008): transportation equipment 30.8; food products 19.3; base chemicals, medicines, and soaps 15.6; machinery and apparatus 13.7; fabricated metal products 13.4; base metals 11.8; wood products (excluding furniture) 9.6; paper products 9.5; rubber and plastic products 9.0; information and communication technologies 8.5. **Population economically active** (2006): total 17,825,800; activity rate of total population 55.6% (participation rates: ages 15 and over, 67.5%; female 46.7%; unemployed [January–December 2008] 6.1%). **Public debt** (March 2008): US$477,101,000,000. *Energy production (consumption):* electricity (kW-hr; 2007) 603,180,000,000 ([2005] 604,343,000,000); coal (metric tons; 2007) 32,800,000 ([2005] 15,100,000); lignite (metric tons; 2007) 36,600,000 ([2005] 45,400,000); crude petroleum (barrels; 2008) 946,000,000 (from [in 2007]: the Alberta oil sands 50%, conventional on land sources 38%, offshore Newfoundland in the Atlantic Ocean 12%) ([2006] 641,598,000); petroleum products (metric tons; 2006) 85,832,000 (78,534,000); natural gas (cu m; 2007) 187,000,000,000 (92,900,000,000). **Selected balance of payments data.** Receipts from (US$'000,000): tourism (2007) 15,614; foreign direct investment (FDI; 2005–07 avg.) 66,129. Disbursements for (US$'000,000): tourism (2007) 24,882; FDI (2005–07 avg.) 40,851.

Foreign trade

Imports (2007): Can$408,436,000,000 (machinery and apparatus 25.3%, of which nonelectrical machinery 12.2%; motor vehicles 16.6%, of which cars 6.7%, parts for motor vehicles 5.5%; chemical products 10.3%; crude petroleum 5.9%; food products 4.9%). *Major import sources:* US 54.2%; China 9.4%; Mexico 4.2%; Japan 3.8%; Germany 2.8%; UK 2.8%; South Korea 1.3%; Norway 1.3%. **Exports** (2007): Can$451,043,000,000 (mineral fuels 20.8%, of which crude petroleum 9.3%, natural gas 6.3%; motor vehicles 15.0%, of which cars 8.9%; machinery and apparatus 12.6%; chemical products 8.3%; sawn wood, wood pulp, and paper products 6.4%; food products 6.2%; base nonferrous metals 5.4%). *Major export destinations:* US 79.0%; UK 2.8%; China 2.1%; Japan 2.0%; Mexico 1.1%; Germany 0.9%; Norway 0.8%; France 0.7%.

Transport and communications

Transport. *Railroads* (2007): length 72,212 km; passenger-km 1,444,656,000; metric ton-km cargo 357,444,000,000. *Roads* (2004): total length 1,408,900 km (paved 35%). *Vehicles* (2005): passenger cars 10,120,005; trucks and buses 785,649. *Air transport* (2007; Air Canada only): passenger-km 74,400,000,000; metric ton-km cargo 1,184,921,000. **Communications,** in total units (units per 1,000 persons). Telephone landlines (2006): 21,000,000 (645); cellular telephone subscribers (2008): 21,455,000 (644); personal computers (2007): 31,051,000 (943); total Internet users (2007): 28,000,000 (852); broadband Internet subscribers (2008): 9,633,000 (289).

Education and health

Literacy (2005): total population ages 15 and over literate virtually 100%. **Health** (2005): physicians (2006) 62,307 (1 per 524 persons); hospital beds 110,113 (1 per 294 persons); infant mortality rate per 1,000 live births 5.4; undernourished population (2002–04) less than 2.5% of total population.

Military

Total active duty personnel (November 2008): 64,371 (army 52.4%, navy 17.0%, air force 30.6%); Canadian troops in Afghanistan as part of the NATO International Security Assistance Force (April 2009): 2,830. **Military expenditure as percentage of GDP** (2007): 1.3%; per capita expenditure US$559.

Background

Originally inhabited by American Indians and Inuit, Canada was visited about AD 1000 by Scandinavian explorers, whose discovery is confirmed by archaeological evidence from Newfoundland. Fishing expeditions off Newfoundland by the English, French, Spanish, and Portuguese began as early as 1500. The French claim to Canada was made in 1534 when Jacques Cartier entered the Gulf of St. Lawrence. A small settlement was made in Nova Scotia (Acadia) in 1605, and in 1608 Samuel de Champlain founded Quebec. Fur trading was the impetus behind the early colonizing efforts. In response to French activity, the English in 1670 formed the Hudson's Bay Company.

The British-French rivalry for the interior of upper North America lasted almost a century. The first French loss occurred in 1713 at the conclusion of Queen Anne's War (War of the Spanish Succession) when Nova Scotia and Newfoundland were ceded to the British. The Seven Years' War (French and Indian War) resulted in France's expulsion from continental North America in 1763. After the US War of Independence, the population was augmented by Loyalists fleeing the US, and the increasing number arriving in Quebec led the British to divide the colony into Upper and Lower Canada in 1791. The British reunited the two provinces in 1841. Canadian expansionism resulted in the confederation movement of the mid-19th century, and in 1867 the Dominion of Canada, comprising Nova Scotia, New Brunswick, Quebec, and Ontario, came into existence. After confederation, Canada entered a period of westward expansion.

The prosperity that accompanied Canada into the 20th century was marred by continuing conflict between the English and French communities. Through the Statute of Westminster (1931), Canada was recognized as an equal of Great Britain. With the Constitution Act of 1982, the British gave Canada total control over its constitution and severed the remaining legal connections between the two countries. French Canadian unrest continued to be a major concern, with a movement growing for Quebec separatism in the late 20th century. Referendums for more political autonomy for Quebec were rejected in 1992 and 1995, but the issue remained unresolved. In 1999 Canada formed the new territory of Nunavut, and in December 2001 Newfoundland was renamed Newfoundland and Labrador.

Recent Developments

In October 2009, Toronto-Dominion Bank released a report predicting a combined Canadian federal-provincial deficit of Can$90 billion–Can$100 billion for the 2009–10 fiscal year. Only one year earlier the federal government and all provincial and territorial governments had initially proposed balanced budgets for fiscal 2008–09. In spite of growing deficits, surging personal bankruptcies, and the loss of nearly 400,000 jobs from peak employment in October 2008 to August 2009, Canada remained in the best financial situation of the Group of Eight (G-8) industrialized countries, according to the federal government. The country's conservative risk-averse banking system, which had strictly controlled cash-to-credit ratios, was able to emerge from the credit crisis relatively unscathed and without the bank bailouts and extensive credit guarantees that were common in the US. Indeed, though Canada's economy declined by 2.9% in 2009, entering 2010 it had seen four consecutive months of growth. Other industrial sectors faced much more difficult conditions, however, and unemployment had reached 8.3% by the end of 2009, a rise of 2.2%. Prime Minister Stephen Harper and Ontario Premier Dalton McGuinty announced on 1 June that the federal and Ontario provincial governments would buy a 12% stake in General Motors (GM) in exchange for Can$10.5 billion. Up to 85,000 jobs would be lost, mostly in southern Ontario, if GM did not undergo government-backed restructuring. The agreement between the governments and the automaker precluded GM's Canadian operations from entering court-approved bankruptcy protection.

A ruling by Canada's Immigration and Refugee Board, which had granted a white man refugee status in Canada on the basis of the racial prejudice and violence that he claimed to have experienced in South Africa from the black majority there, prompted the federal Ministry of Immigration to announce in September a plan to appeal that decision in the face of international outrage. South African officials condemned the original ruling, made by a quasi-judicial and independent board, as one that would serve to perpetuate racism. The South African government noted that the government had made efforts to fight violence and crime against all people, regardless of ethnicity or creed. A newly enacted EU ban on a range of seal products from Canada was expected to be an irritant during trade talks between Canada and the EU. The ban—which was lodged as a protest to an annual hunt of some 300,000 harp seals that some environmentalists and EU legislators had labeled as cruel and inhumane—affected only products from Canada's Atlantic region and excluded seal products produced by the Canadian Arctic's indigenous Inuit peoples. Canada defended the hunt as being conducted in a humane manner and as essential to the livelihoods of people living in rural and isolated areas on Canada's East Coast. The EU had imported Can$2.5 million worth of seal products from Canada in 2008. Canadian military involvement

in Afghanistan remained a controversial, largely unpopular topic in the country. As Canadian deaths in the country topped 140 in February 2010, the government remained firm in its resolve to withdraw its forces from the country by August 2011.

Internet resource: <www.statcan.gc.ca>.

Cape Verde

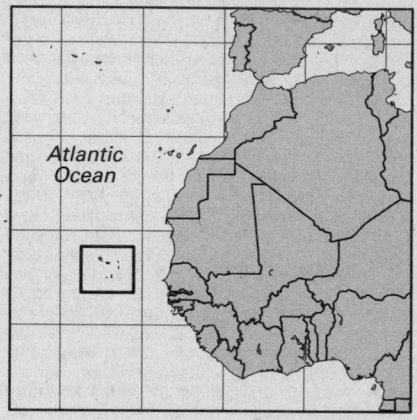

Official name: República de Cabo Verde (Republic of Cape Verde). **Form of government:** multiparty republic with one legislative house (National Assembly [72]). **Head of state:** President Pedro Pires (from 2001). **Head of government:** Prime Minister José Maria Neves (from 2001). **Capital:** Praia. **Official language:** Portuguese (Cape Verdean Creole [Crioulo] is the national language). **Official religion:** none. **Monetary unit:** 1 escudo (C.V.Esc.) = 100 centavos; valuation (1 Jul 2010) US$1 = C.V.Esc. 89.23.

Demography

Area: 1,557 sq mi, 4,033 sq km. **Population** (2009): 509,000. **Density** (2009): persons per sq mi 326.9, persons per sq km 126.2. **Urban** (2007): 59.8%. **Sex distribution** (2008): male 47.70%; female 52.30%. **Age breakdown** (2005): under 15, 39.2%; 15–29, 30.2%; 30–44, 16.9%; 45–59, 7.9%; 60–74, 4.4%; 75–84, 1.2%; 85 and over, 0.2%. **Ethnic composition** (2000): Cape Verdean *mestiço* (black-white admixture) 69.6%; Fulani 12.2%; Balanta 10.0%; Mandyako 4.6%; Portuguese white 2.0%; other 1.6%. **Religious affiliation** (2000): Christian 95.1%, of which Roman Catholic 88.1%, Protestant 3.3%, independent Christian 2.7%; Muslim 2.8%; other 2.1%. **Major urban localities** (2009): Praia 125,148; Mindelo 76,650; Santa Maria 18,780; Assomada 13,562; Pedra Badejo 11,348. **Location:** islands in the North Atlantic Ocean, off the coast of western Africa.

Vital statistics

Birth rate per 1,000 population (2007): 25.1 (world avg. 20.3). **Death rate** per 1,000 population (2007):

---

1 metric ton = about 1.1 short tons;   1 kilometer = 0.6 mi (statute);   1 metric ton-km cargo = about 0.68 short ton-mi cargo;   c.i.f.: cost, insurance, and freight;   f.o.b.: free on board

5.3 (world avg. 8.5). **Total fertility rate** (avg. births per childbearing woman; 2007): 2.89. **Life expectancy** at birth (2007): male 68.3 years; female 73.6 years.

National economy

Budget (2008). *Revenue:* C.V.Esc. 40,129,000,000 (tax revenue 73.7%, of which VAT 29.2%, taxes on income and profits 21.2%, taxes on international transactions 14.7%; grants 16.0%; nontax revenue 6.5%; other 3.8%). *Expenditures:* C.V.Esc. 41,304,000,000 (current expenditures 60.6%; capital expenditures 39.4%). **Public debt** (external, outstanding; December 2006): US$601,000,000. **Gross national income** (2008): US$1,561,000,000 (US$3,130 per capita). **Production** (metric tons except as noted). *Agriculture and fishing* (2007): sugarcane 15,400, corn (maize) 12,000, bananas 6,800; livestock (number of live animals) 217,000 pigs, 115,400 goats, 24,150 cattle; fisheries production 18,328 (from aquaculture, none). *Mining and quarrying* (2007): salt 1,600; pozzolana, n.a. *Manufacturing* (2003): cement 160,000; frozen fish 900; canned fish 200; other manufactured goods include clothing, footwear, and rum. *Energy production (consumption):* electricity (kW-hr; 2006) 252,000,000 (252,000,000); petroleum products (metric tons; 2006) none (100,000). **Population economically active** (2006): total 189,000; activity rate of total population 36.4% (participation rates: ages 15–64, 63%; female 40%; unemployed 18.3%, underemployed 26%). **Selected balance of payments data.** Receipts from (US$'000,000): tourism (2007) 346; remittances (2008) 138; foreign direct investment (2005–07 avg.) 130; official development assistance (2007) 163. Disbursements for (US$'000,000): tourism (2007) 107; remittances (2008) 6.0.

Foreign trade

Imports (2007; c.i.f.): US$737,000,000 (food and agricultural products 20.5%; machinery and apparatus 15.2%; refined petroleum products 9.3%; motor vehicles 8.0%; aircraft and parts 7.2%; chemical products 5.7%). *Major import sources:* Portugal 40.0%; Netherlands 11.5%; France 9.6%; Brazil 6.2%; Spain 4.6%. **Exports** (2007; f.o.b.): US$114,800,000 (refined petroleum products 49.8%; transport containers 15.8%; fresh fish 8.3%; wearing apparel 5.7%; footwear 4.0%). *Major export destinations:* Côte d'Ivoire 30.7%; Portugal 21.6%; Netherlands 15.2%; Spain 9.1%; France 4.1%.

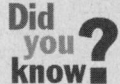 **Did you know?** Historically, Guinea-Bissau was the center of the Portuguese West African slave trade. Military posts at Cacheu from the early 17th century and at Bissau from the 18th century served as collection points. Slaves were often transported from Guinea-Bissau to the slave trading center of Cape Verde.

Transport and communications

Transport. *Railroads:* none. *Roads* (2007): total length 2,250 km (paved [mostly with cobblestones] 70%). *Vehicles* (2005): passenger cars 23,811; trucks and buses 5,032. *Air transport* (2004): passenger-km 725,000,000. **Communications,** in total units (units per 1,000 persons). Telephone landlines (2008): 72,000 (144); cellular telephone subscribers (2008): 278,000 (556); personal computers (2004): 48,000 (102); total Internet users (2008): 103,000 (206); broadband Internet subscribers (2008): 7,400 (15).

Education and health

Educational attainment (1990). Percentage of population ages 25 and over having: no formal schooling/unknown 52.3%; primary 40.9%; incomplete secondary 3.9%; complete secondary 1.4%; higher 1.5%. **Literacy** (2007): total population ages 15 and over literate 79.4%; males literate 87.5%; females literate 72.6%. **Health** (2007): physicians 230 (1 per 2,137 persons); hospital beds 1,016 (1 per 484 persons); infant mortality rate per 1,000 live births 21.7.

Military

Total active duty personnel (November 2008): 1,200 (army 83.3%, air force 8.3%, coast guard 8.4%). **Military expenditure as percentage of GDP** (2007): 0.6%; per capita expenditure US$16.

Background

When visited by the Portuguese in 1456–60, the islands were uninhabited. In 1460 Diogo Gomes sighted and named Maio and São Tiago, and in 1462 the first settlers landed on São Tiago, founding the city of Ribeira Grande. The city's importance grew with the development of the slave trade, but its wealth attracted pirates so often that it was abandoned after 1712. The prosperity of the Portuguese-controlled islands vanished with the decline of the slave trade in the 19th century but later improved because of their position on the great trade routes between Europe, South America, and southern Africa. In 1951 the colony became an overseas province of Portugal. Many islanders preferred independence, and it was granted in 1975. At one time associated politically with Guinea-Bissau, Cape Verde split from it in the wake of a 1980 coup there.

Recent Developments

When in August 2009 US Secretary of State Hillary Clinton visited Cape Verde on her African tour, she praised its successful implementation of the US$110 million Millennium Challenge compact to improve social services, increase agricultural productivity, and develop infrastructure. She also noted that progress was being made toward greater governmental transparency and that Cape Verde was the only African country where women made up more than half of the government's cabinet ministers.

Internet resource: <www.governo.cv>.

Central African Republic

Official name: République Centrafricaine (Central African Republic). **Form of government:** multiparty republic with one legislative house (National Assembly [105]). **Head of state:** President François Bozizé (from 2003). **Head of government:** Prime Minister Faustin Archange Touadéra (from 2008). **Capital:** Bangui. **Official languages:** French; Sango. **Official**

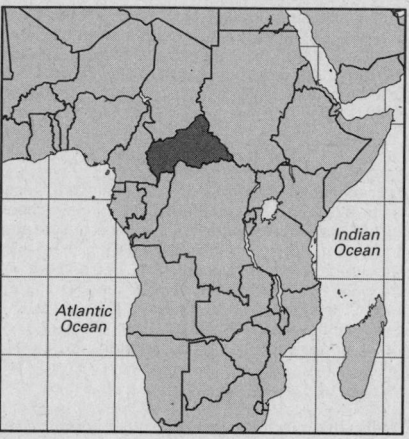

religion: none. **Monetary unit:** 1 CFA franc (CFAF) = 100 centimes; valuation (1 Jul 2010) US$1 = CFAF 527.20.

Demography

Area: 240,324 sq mi, 622,436 sq km. **Population** (2009): 4,511,000. **Density** (2009): persons per sq mi 18.8, persons per sq km 7.2. **Urban** (2007): 38.3%. **Sex distribution** (2007): male 49.44%; female 50.56%. **Age breakdown** (2007): under 15, 41.6%; 15–29, 29.6%; 30–44, 15.1%; 45–59, 7.7%; 60–74, 4.6%; 75–84, 1.2%; 85 and over, 0.2%. **Ethnolinguistic composition** (2004): Gbaya (Baya) 33%; Banda 27%; Mandjia 13%; Sara 10%; Mbum 7%; Ngbaka 4%; other 6%. **Religious affiliation** (2005): Protestant/independent Christian 51%; Roman Catholic 29%; traditional beliefs 10%; Muslim 10%. **Major urban localities** (2003): Bangui 622,771; Bimbo 124,176; Berbérati 76,918; Carnot 45,421; Bambari 41,356. **Location:** central Africa, bordering Chad, Sudan, the Democratic Republic of the Congo, the Republic of the Congo, and Cameroon.

Vital statistics

Birth rate per 1,000 population (2007): 33.5 (world avg. 20.3). **Death rate** per 1,000 population (2007): 18.3 (world avg. 8.5). **Total fertility rate** (avg. births per childbearing woman; 2007): 4.32. **Life expectancy** at birth (2007): male 43.9 years; female 44.1 years.

National economy

Budget (2006). *Revenue:* CFAF 176,300,000,000 (grants 58.4%; tax revenue 34.3%, of which taxes on goods and services 24.3%; nontax revenue 7.3%). *Expenditures:* CFAF 107,200,000,000 (current expenditures 58.3%; development expenditures 41.7%). **Public debt** (external, outstanding; 2007): US$836,000,000. **Production** (metric tons except as noted). *Agriculture and fishing* (2007): cassava 565,000, yams 346,000, peanuts (groundnuts) 137,000, sesame seeds 40,000, seed cotton (2007–08) 3,355, coffee (2007–08) 1,931; livestock (number of live animals) 3,378,000 cattle, 3,087,000 goats, 805,000 pigs; fisheries production 15,000 (from aquaculture, negligible). *Mining and quarrying* (2007–08): diamonds 326,000 carats (official figure; a roughly equal amount was thought to have been smuggled out of the country). *Manufacturing* (2004): aluminum sheets 184,100; soap 1,800; cigarettes 16,000,000 packets; other manufactures include footwear, textiles, and bicycles. *Energy production (consumption):* electricity (kW-hr; 2007–08) 94,100,000 ([2005] 110,000,000); petroleum products (metric tons; 2006) none (81,000). **Population economically active** (2006): total 1,883,000; activity rate of total population 44.2% (participation rates: ages 15–64, 77.0%; female 45.7%). **Gross national income** (2008): US$1,804,000,000 (US$410 per capita). **Selected balance of payments data.** Receipts from (US$'000,000): tourism (2005) 4.0; foreign direct investment (2005–07 avg.) 21; official development assistance (2007) 176. Disbursements for (US$'000,000): tourism (2004) 32.

Foreign trade

Imports (2005; c.i.f.): CFAF 98,300,000,000 (refined petroleum products 16.7%; logs and sawn wood 14.8%; food products 13.6%, of which cereals 6.6%; machinery and apparatus 8.6%; motor vehicles 8.3%). *Major import sources* (2007): France 16.6%; Netherlands 13.0%; Cameroon 9.7%; US 6.3%. **Exports** (2007; f.o.b.): CFAF 85,300,000,000 (wood products 49.1%; diamonds 34.9%; coffee 4.9%; cotton 0.5%). *Major export destinations:* Belgium 22.7%; Indonesia 19.3%; Italy 7.7%; France 7.1%; Spain 6.9%.

Transport and communications

Transport. *Railroads:* none. *Roads* (2005): total length (national roads only; much of the 15,600 km local road network is unusable) 10,000 km (paved 7%). *Vehicles* (2006): passenger cars 800; trucks and buses 700. *Air transport* (2003): passenger arrivals (Bangui airport only) 19,250, passenger departures (Bangui airport only) 19,107; metric ton-km cargo 7,000,000. **Communications,** in total units (units per 1,000 persons). Telephone landlines (2006): 12,000 (2.8); cellular telephone subscribers (2008): 154,000 (35); personal computers (2006): 13,000 (3.0); total Internet users (2008): 19,000 (4.3).

Education and health

Educational attainment (1994–95). Percentage of population ages 25 and over having: no formal schooling/unknown 55.1%; at least some primary education 30.5%; at least some secondary education 14.4%. **Literacy** (2007): total population ages 15 and over literate 56.6%; males literate 67.6%; females literate 46.4%. **Health:** physicians (2004) 331 (1 per 11,867 persons); hospital beds (2006) 5,118 (1 per 833 persons); infant mortality rate per 1,000 live births (2007) 83.7; undernourished population (2002–04) 1,700,000 (44% of total population based on the consumption of a minimum daily requirement of 1,800 calories).

1 metric ton = about 1.1 short tons;   1 kilometer = 0.6 mi (statute);   1 metric ton-km cargo = about 0.68 short ton-mi cargo;   c.i.f.: cost, insurance, and freight;   f.o.b.: free on board

Military

Total active duty personnel (November 2008): 3,150 (army 63.5%, air force 4.8%, gendarmerie 31.7%). Military expenditure as percentage of GDP (2007): 1.1%; per capita expenditure US$4.

Background

For several centuries before the arrival of Europeans, the territory was subjected to slave traders. The French explored and claimed central Africa and in 1889 established a post at Bangui. In 1898 they partitioned the colony among commercial concessionaires. United with Chad in 1906 to form the French colony of Ubangi-Shari, it later became part of French Equatorial Africa. It was separated from Chad in 1920 and became an overseas territory in 1946. Named an autonomous republic within the French Community in 1958, the country achieved independence in 1960. In 1966 the military overthrew a civilian government and installed Jean-Bédel Bokassa, who in 1976 declared himself Emperor Bokassa I and renamed the country the Central African Empire. The military again seized power in the 1980s. A new constitution was promulgated in 2004, and a democratically elected government was installed in 2005.

Recent Developments

Insecurity in the northern region of the Central African Republic (CAR) continued in 2009. In February government troops were accused of having carried out violent reprisals in the Ndele region against civilians who were thought to be supporting rebels. UN peacekeepers took over responsibility for the troubled border area in March amid fears that the Ugandan Lord's Resistance Army (LRA) was preparing to move across the CAR border from its bases in the Democratic Republic of the Congo. In late July the LRA attacked towns in CAR, and operations within the country continued in 2010.

Internet resource: <www.stat-centrafrique.com>.

Chad

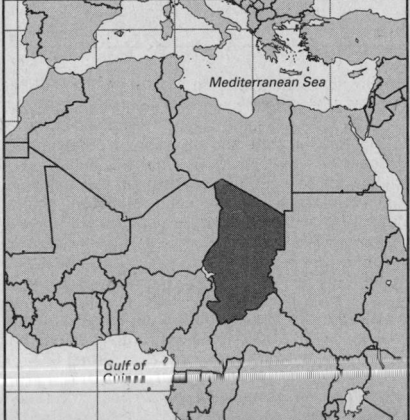

Official name: Jumhuriyah Tshad (Arabic); République du Tchad (French) (Republic of Chad). Form of government: unitary republic with one legislative house (National Assembly [155]). Head of state: President Idriss Déby (from 1990). Head of government: Prime Minister Emmanuel Nadingar (from 2010). Capital: N'Djamena. Official languages: Arabic; French. Official religion: none. Monetary unit: 1 CFA franc (CFAF) = 100 centimes; valuation (1 Jul 2010) US$1 = CFAF 527.20.

Demography

Area: 495,755 sq mi, 1,284,000 sq km. Population (2009): 10,329,000. Density (2009): persons per sq mi 20.8, persons per sq km 8.0. Urban (2007): 26.3%. Sex distribution (2007): male 47.92%; female 52.08%. Age breakdown (2007): under 15, 47.3%; 15–29, 26.4%; 30–44, 13.7%; 45–59, 8.0%; 60–74, 3.8%; 75–84, 0.7%; 85 and over, 0.1%. Ethnolinguistic composition (1993): Sara 27.7%; Sudanic Arab 12.3%; Mayo-Kebbi peoples 11.5%; Kanem-Bornu peoples 9.0%; Ouaddaï peoples 8.7%; Hadjeray (Hadjaraï) 6.7%; Tangale (Tandjilé) peoples 6.5%; Gorane peoples 6.3%; Fitri-Batha peoples 4.7%; Fulani (Peul) 2.4%; other 4.2%. Religious affiliation (2005): Muslim 57.0%; traditional beliefs 18.8%; Protestant 10.5%; other (significantly Roman Catholic and nonreligious) 13.7%. Major cities (2000): N'Djamena (urban agglomeration; 2007) 989,000; Moundou 108,728; Sarh 95,050; Abéché 63,165; Kelo 36,643. Location: central Africa, bordered by Libya, Sudan, the Central African Republic, Cameroon, Nigeria, and Niger.

Vital statistics

Birth rate per 1,000 population (2007): 42.4 (world avg. 20.3). Death rate per 1,000 population (2007): 16.7 (world avg. 8.6). Total fertility rate (avg. births per childbearing woman; 2007): 5.56. Life expectancy at birth (2007): male 46.2 years; female 48.3 years.

National economy

Budget (2007). Revenue: CFAF 764,900,000,000 (petroleum revenue 73.6%, of which taxes on profits 55.7%, royalties and dividends 17.3%; nonpetroleum tax revenue 24.7%; other 1.7%). Expenditures: CFAF 709,300,000,000 (current expenditures 65.4%; development expenditures 34.6%). Public debt (external, outstanding; December 2008): US$1,581,000,000. Production (metric tons except as noted). Agriculture, and fishing (2007): rice 1,290,000, sorghum 700,000, millet 550,000, sesame seed 35,300, gum arabic (2006) 25,000; livestock (number of live animals) 6,820,300 cattle, 6,096,390 goats, 2,981,800 sheep, 749,600 camels; fisheries production 70,000 (from aquaculture, none). Mining and quarrying (2007): aggregate (gravel) 300,000; natron 12,000; gold 150 kg. Manufacturing (2004–05): cotton fiber 88,158; refined sugar 51,823; woven cotton fabrics (2000) 1,000,000 meters. Energy production (consumption): electricity (kW-hr; 2006) 95,000,000 (88,300,000); crude petroleum (barrels; 2008) 46,500,000 (n.a.); petroleum products (metric tons; 2008) none (65,000). Selected balance of payments data. Receipts from (US$'000,000): tourism (2005) 14; foreign direct investment (2005–07 avg.) 639; official development assistance (2007) 352. Disbursements for (US$'000,000): tourism (2002) 80. **Population economically active** (2006): total 4,179,000; activity rate of total population 39.9% (participation rates: ages 15–64, 74.7%; female 48.8%). **Gross national income** (2008): US$5,916,000,000 (US$530 per capita).

Foreign trade

Imports (2007): CFAF 719,600,000,000 (petroleum sector 39.7%; nonpetroleum private sector 32.9%; public sector 12.0%). *Major import sources:* France 20.4%; Cameroon 16.1%; US 10.9%; China 10.0%; Germany 7.5%. **Exports** (2007): CFAF 1,755,300,-000,000 (crude petroleum 87.0%; live cattle 6.9%; cotton 2.5%; gum arabic 0.9%). *Major export destinations:* US 89.5%; Japan 3.7%; China 3.4%.

Transport and communications

Transport. *Railroads:* none. *Roads* (2006): total length 40,000 km (paved 2%). *Vehicles* (2006): passenger cars 18,867; trucks and buses 28,152. *Air transport* (2001): passenger-km 130,000,000; metric ton-km cargo (2004) 7,000,000. **Communications,** in total units (units per 1,000 persons). Telephone landlines (2006): 13,000 (1.3); cellular telephone subscribers (2008): 1,809,000 (179); personal computers (2006): 19,000 (2.0); total Internet users (2008): 130,000 (13).

Education and health

Educational attainment (2003). Percentage of population ages 25 and over having: no formal schooling 74.5%; primary education 17.4%; secondary education 6.8%; higher education 1.3%. **Literacy** (2007): percentage of total population ages 15 and over literate 53.7%; males literate 61.5%; females literate 46.3%. **Health:** physicians (2004) 345 (1 per 26,370 persons); hospital beds (2005) 3,760 (1 per 2,500 persons); infant mortality rate per 1,000 live births (2007) 102.1; undernourished population (2002–04) 3,000,000 (35% of total population based on the consumption of a minimum daily requirement of 1,810 calories).

Military

Total active duty personnel (November 2008): 25,350 (army 78.9%, air force 1.4%, other 19.7%). **Military expenditure as percentage of GDP** (2007): 1.1%; per capita expenditure US$7.

Background

About 800 AD the kingdom of Kanem was founded in north-central Africa, and by the early 1200s its borders had expanded to form a new kingdom, Kanem-Bornu, in the northern regions of the area. Its power peaked in the 16th century with its command of the southern terminus of the trans-Sahara trade route to Tripoli. Around this time the rival kingdoms of Baguirmi and Wadai evolved in the south. In the years 1883–93 all three kingdoms fell to the Sudanese adventurer Rabih al-Zubayr, who was in turn pushed out by the French in 1900. Extending their power, the French in 1910 made Chad a part of French Equato-

rial Africa. Chad became a separate colony in 1920 and was made an overseas territory in 1946. The country achieved independence in 1960. This was followed by decades of civil war and frequent intervention by France and Libya, resulting in political instability and a lack of economic development.

Recent Developments

Chad's chronic instability persisted throughout 2009. The governments of Sudan and Chad again agreed not to provide support to each other's rebel movements, but this had little effect. One of the rebel movements continued to launch operations from Chad into the war-torn Sudanese region of Darfur and was thought to receive much of its funding from Pres. Idriss Déby; meanwhile, Chadian rebels continued to operate from Darfur. Government forces in Chad were able to rebuff a rebel attack in May, and by mid-2009, despite a steep decline in fighting in Darfur that led some observers to declare that the region should no longer be considered a war zone, some 250,000 refugees from the region remained in eastern Chad.

Internet resource: <www.chadembassy.us>.

Chile

Official name: República de Chile (Republic of Chile). **Form of government:** multiparty republic with two legislative houses (Senate [38]; Chamber of Deputies [120]). **Head of state and government:** President Sebastián Piñera (from 2010). **Capital:** Santiago (legislative bodies meet in Valparaíso). **Official language:** Spanish. **Official religion:** none. **Monetary unit:** 1 peso (Ch$) = 100 centavos; valuation (1 Jul 2010) US$1 = Ch$541.35.

Demography

Area: 291,930 sq mi, 756,096 sq km. **Population** (2009): 16,602,000. **Density** (2009): persons per sq mi 56.9, persons per sq km 22.0. **Urban** (2007):

---

1 metric ton = about 1.1 short tons;   1 kilometer = 0.6 mi (statute);   1 metric ton-km cargo = about 0.68 short ton-mi cargo;   c.i.f.: cost, insurance, and freight;   f.o.b.: free on board

89.0%. Sex distribution (2008): male 49.46%; female 50.54%. Age breakdown (2005): under 15, 24.9%; 15–29, 24.3%; 30–44, 23.0%; 45–59, 16.2%; 60–74, 8.3%; 75–84, 2.5%; 85 and over, 0.8%. Ethnic composition (2002): mestizo 72%; white 22%; Amerindian 5%, of which Araucanian (Mapuche) 4%; other 1%. Religious affiliation (2002): Roman Catholic 70.0%; Protestant/independent Christian 15.1%; atheist/nonreligious 8.3%; other 6.6%. Major cities (urban agglomerations) (2002): Santiago 4,656,690 (5,428,590); Valparaíso 263,499 (803,683); Concepción 212,003 (666,381); La Serena 147,815 (296,253); Antofagasta 285,255. Location: southern South America, bordering Peru, Bolivia, Argentina, the South Atlantic Ocean, and the South Pacific Ocean.

Vital statistics

Birth rate per 1,000 population (2006): 14.8 (world avg. 20.3). Death rate per 1,000 population (2006): 5.2 (world avg. 8.5). Total fertility rate (avg. births per childbearing woman; 2006): 2.00. Life expectancy at birth (2006): male 74.8 years; female 80.8 years.

National economy

Budget (2007). Revenue: Ch$23,534,000,-000,000 (tax revenue 78.1%; nontax revenue 17.0%; other 4.9%). Expenditures: Ch$15,996,-000,000,000 (social protection 28.8%; education 17.2%; health 15.9%; transportation 8.8%; defense 6.5%). Public debt (external, outstanding; 2007): US$9,975,000,000. Population economically active (2007): total 7,078,000; activity rate of total population 42.5% (participation rates: ages 15–64, 61.7%; female 36.8%; unemployed [November 2007–October 2008] 7.7%). Production (metric tons except as noted). Agriculture and fishing (2007): grapes 2,350,000, sugar beets 1,806,600, corn (maize) 1,557,100, kiwi fruit 170,000, avocados 167,000; livestock (number of live animals) 4,350,000 cattle, 3,480,000 pigs, 3,420,000 sheep; fisheries production (2006) 4,635,927 (from aquaculture 18%); aquatic plants production 359,770 (from aquaculture 6%). Mining (2007): copper (metal content) 5,557,000; iron ore (metal content) 4,195,000; lithium carbonate (2006) 50,035; molybdenum (metal content) 44,900; iodine 15,500; silver 1,936,000 kg; gold 41,500 kg. Manufacturing (value added in US$'000,000; 2005): nonferrous base metals 20,677; refined petroleum products 6,245; food products 5,239. Energy production (consumption): electricity (kW-hr; 2007) 57,576,000,000 ([2006] 59,840,000,000); coal (metric tons; 2007) 288,000 ([2006] 5,402,000); crude petroleum (barrels; 2008) 963,000 ([2006] 80,800,000); petroleum products (metric tons; 2006) 10,701,000 (9,630,000); natural gas (cu m; 2007) 2,015,000,000 (4,191,000,000). Gross national income (2008): US$157,460,000,000 (US$9,400 per capita). Selected balance of payments data. Receipts from (US$'000,000): tourism (2007) 1,419; remittances (2008) 3; foreign direct investment (FDI; 2005–07 avg.) 9,600; official development assistance (2007) 120. Disbursements for (US$'000,000): tourism (2007) 1,762; remittances (2008) 6; FDI (2005–07 avg.) 2,963.

Foreign trade

Imports (2007; c.i.f.): US$42,732,000,000 (crude petroleum 22.7%; machinery and apparatus 21.4%; chemical products 11.1%; motor vehicles 9.9%; food products 6.5%). Major import sources: US 17.0%; China 11.4%; Brazil 10.5%; Argentina 10.1%; South Korea 7.2%. Exports (2007; f.o.b.): US$65,739,000,000 (refined copper 36.4%; copper ore 20.5%; food products 12.5%, of which fruits 4.0%, fish 3.8%; other base metal ores 5.4%). Major export destinations: China 15.2%; US 12.8%; Japan 10.8%; Netherlands 5.9%; South Korea 5.9%.

Transport and communications

Transport. Railroads (2006): route length 5,034 km; passenger-km 843,131,000; metric ton-km cargo 3,660,000,000. Roads (2003): total length 80,505 km (paved 22%). Vehicles (2006): passenger cars 1,514,220; trucks and buses 735,901. Air transport (2007): passenger-km 16,056,000,000; metric ton-km cargo 1,294,968,000. Communications, in total units (units per 1,000 persons). Telephone landlines (2008): 3,526,000 (214); cellular telephone subscribers (2008): 14,797,000 (899); personal computers (2006): 2,277,000 (141); total Internet users (2008): 5,456,000 (332); broadband Internet subscribers (2008): 1,426,000 (87).

Education and health

Educational attainment (2002). Percentage of population ages 25 and over having: no formal schooling/other 5.4%; incomplete primary education 24.6%; complete primary 8.7%; secondary 43.9%; higher technical 4.9%; university 12.5%. Literacy (2006): total population ages 15 and over literate 96.4%. Health (2006): physicians 21,100 (1 per 765 persons); hospital beds 37,374 (1 per 432 persons); infant mortality rate per 1,000 live births 7.6; undernourished population (2002–04) 600,000 (4% of total population based on the consumption of a minimum daily requirement of 1,920 calories).

Military

Total active duty personnel (November 2008): 60,560 (army 57.8%, navy 29.4%, air force 12.8%). Military expenditure as percentage of GDP (2008): 3.0%; per capita expenditure US$286.

Background

Originally inhabited by native peoples, including the Mapuche, the Chilean coast was invaded by the Spanish in 1536. A settlement begun at Santiago in 1541 was governed under the Viceroyalty of Peru but became a separate captaincy general in 1778. It revolted against Spanish rule in 1810; its independence was finally assured by the victory of José de San Martín in 1818, and the area was then governed by Bernardo O'Higgins to 1823. In the War of the Pacific against Peru and Bolivia, it won the rich nitrate fields on the coast of Bolivia, effectively forcing that country into a landlocked position. Chile remained neutral in World War I and World War II but severed diplomatic ties with the Axis powers in 1943. In 1970 Salvador Allende was elected president, becoming the first avowed Marxist to be elected chief of state in Latin America. Following economic upheaval, he was ousted in 1973 in a coup led by Gen. Augusto Pinochet, whose military junta for many years harshly suppressed all internal opposition. A national referendum in 1988 rejected Pinochet, and elections held in 1989 returned the country to civilian rule. Chile's economy maintained steady growth through most of the 1990s and in the early 21st century remained one of the strongest in Latin America.

Recent Developments

A magnitude-8.8 earthquake—thought to be the fifth strongest ever recorded—struck Chile on 27 Feb 2010. The epicenter was located some 200 miles southwest of the capital of Santiago, and the focus occurred at a depth of about 22 miles below the surface of the Pacific Ocean. The temblor was the strongest to strike the region since a magnitude-9.5 event of 1960, considered to be the most powerful earthquake ever recorded. The initial event was succeeded in the following weeks by hundreds of aftershocks, many of them of magnitude 5.0 or greater, including one in March that registered 7.2. A NASA computer model ascertained that the powerful force of the subducting plate had shifted Earth's axis sufficiently to shorten the day by more than a microsecond. Though damage to structures within the zone of the earthquake was likely limited by stringent building codes instituted in the wake of the 1960 earthquake and revised several times during the 1990s, many buildings still sustained significant damage, including approximately 500,000 homes. Chilean government officials estimated that two million people had been directly affected by the quake. The death toll rose to at least 577 people, and an estimated US$30 billion in damage was sustained.

Internet resource: <www.bcentral.cl>.

China

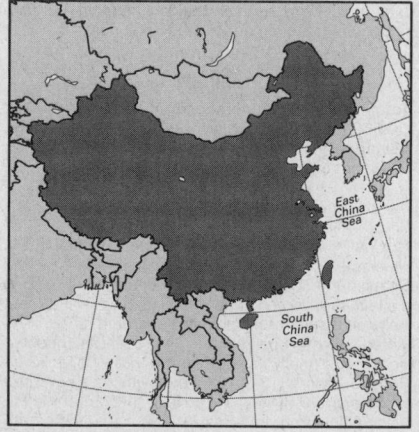

Official name: Zhonghua Renmin Gongheguo (People's Republic of China). **Form of government:** single-party people's republic with one legislative house (National People's Congress [3,000]). **Head of state:** President Hu Jintao (from 2003). **Head of government:** Premier Wen Jiabao (from 2003). **Capital:** Beijing (Peking). **Official language:** Mandarin Chinese. **Official religion:** none. **Monetary unit:** 1 renminbi (yuan) (Y) = 10 jiao = 100 fen; valuation (1 Jul 2010) US$1 = Y 6.78.

Demography

Area: 3,696,100 sq mi, 9,572,900 sq km. **Population** (2009): 1,331,433,000. **Density** (2009): persons per sq mi 360.2, persons per sq km 139.1. **Urban** (2008): 45.7%. **Sex distribution** (2008): male 51.47%; female 48.53%. **Age breakdown** (2007): under 15, 17.9%; 15–29, 21.4%; 30–44, 26.8%; 45–59, 20.3%; 60–74, 10.4%; 75–84, 2.7%; 85 and over, 0.5%. **Ethnic composition** (2005): Han (Chinese) 90.95%; Chuang 1.37%; Manchu 0.82%; Yi 0.79%; Hui 0.77%; Miao 0.75%; Uighur 0.74%; Tuchia 0.65%; Tibetan 0.57%; Mongolian 0.49%; Tung 0.28%; Puyi 0.26%; Yao 0.24%; Korean 0.14%; Pai 0.14%; Hani 0.12%; Li 0.11%; Kazakh 0.09%; Tai 0.08%; other 0.64%. **Religious affiliation** (2005): nonreligious 39.2%; Chinese folk-religionist 28.7%; Christian 10.0%, of which unregistered Protestant 7.7%, registered Protestant 1.2%, unregistered Roman Catholic 0.5%, registered Roman Catholic 0.4%; Buddhist 8.4%; atheist 7.8%; traditional beliefs 4.4%; Muslim 1.5%. **Major urban agglomerations** (2007): Shanghai 14,987,000; Beijing 11,106,000; Guangzhou 8,829,000; Shenzhen 7,581,000; Wuhan 7,243,000; Tianjin 7,180,000; Chongqing 6,461,000; Shenyang 4,787,000; Dongguan 4,528,000; Chengdu 4,123,000; Xi'an 4,009,000; Nanjing 3,679,000; Guiyang 3,662,000; Harbin 3,621,000; Changchun 3,183,000; Dalian 3,167,000; Zibo 3,061,000; Hangzhou 3,007,000; Kunming 2,931,000; Taiyuan 2,913,000; Qingdao 2,866,000; Jinan 2,798,000; Zhengzhou 2,636,000; Fuzhou 2,606,000; Changsha 2,604,000; Lanzhou 2,561,000; Xiamen 2,519,000; Jinxi 2,426,000. **Location:** eastern Asia, bordering Mongolia, Russia, North Korea, the Yellow Sea, the East China Sea, the South China Sea, Vietnam, Laos, Myanmar (Burma), India, Bhutan, Nepal, Pakistan, Afghanistan, Tajikistan, Kyrgyzstan, and Kazakhstan. **Mobility** (2007). Population residing in registered enumeration area 90.4%; population not residing in registered enumeration area 9.6%.

Vital statistics

Birth rate per 1,000 population (2008): 12.1 (world avg. 20.3). **Death rate** per 1,000 population (2008): 7.1 (world avg. 8.5). **Total fertility rate** (avg. births per childbearing woman; 2007): 1.77. **Life expectancy** at birth (2007): male 71.3 years; female 74.8 years.

Social indicators

Educational attainment (2007). Percentage of population ages 6 and over having: no formal schooling 8.0%; incomplete/complete primary education 31.8%; some secondary 40.2%; complete secondary 13.4%; some postsecondary through advanced degree 6.6%. **Quality of working life.** Average workweek (November 2007): 45.5 hours. Annual rate per 100,000 workers for (2008): death in mining, indus-

1 metric ton = about 1.1 short tons;   1 kilometer = 0.6 mi (statute);   1 metric ton-km cargo = about 0.68 short ton-mi cargo;   c.i.f.: cost, insurance, and freight;   f.o.b.: free on board

trial, or commercial enterprises 2.82. Death toll from work accidents (2008) 91,172. **Access to services.** Percentage of population having access to electricity (2005) 99.4%. Percentage of total (urban, rural) population with safe public water supply (2002) 83.6% (94.0%, 73.0%). Sewage system (1999): total (urban, rural) households with flush apparatus 20.7% (50.0%, 4.3%), with pit latrines 69.3% (33.6%, 86.7%), with no latrine 5.3% (7.8%, 4.1%). **Social participation.** Trade union membership in total labor force (2006): 169,942,200 (22%). Percentage of population who consider themselves religious (2005–06) 31.4%. **Social deviance.** Annual reported arrest rate per 100,000 population (2007) for: thievery 248.0; robbery 22.2; fraud 16.6; injury 12.3; rape 2.4; homicide 1.2. **Material well-being.** Urban households possessing (number per household; 2004): bicycles 1.4; color televisions (2007) 1.4; washing machines 1.0; refrigerators 0.9; air conditioners 0.7; cameras 0.5; computers (2007) 0.5. Rural families possessing (number per household; 2004): bicycles 1.2; color televisions (2007) 0.9; washing machines 0.4; refrigerators 0.2; air conditioners 0.05; cameras 0.04; computers (2007) 0.04.

National economy

Gross national income (2008): US$3,678,488,-000,000 (US$2,770 per capita). **Budget** (2007). *Revenue:* Y 5,132,178,000,000 (tax revenue 88.9%, of which VAT 30.1%, corporate taxes 17.1%, business tax 12.8%, income tax 6.2%; nontax revenue 11.1%). *Expenditures:* Y 4,978,135,000,000 (general administration 17.1%; education 14.3%; social security 10.9%; manufacturing, trade, and finance 8.6%; defense 7.1%; public security/police 7.0%; agriculture and forestry 6.8%; health 4.0%). **Public debt** (external, outstanding; 2007): US$87,653,000,000. **Production** (metric tons except as noted). *Agriculture and fishing* (2007): grains—rice 185,490,000, corn (maize) 151,830,000, wheat 109,860,000, barley 3,851,000; oilseeds—soybeans 15,600,000, peanuts (groundnuts) 13,016,000, rapeseed 10,375,000, sunflower seeds 1,800,000; fruits and nuts—apples 27,500,000, citrus 19,617,100, cantaloupes 13,650,000, pears 12,500,000, bananas 7,100,000; other—sugarcane 105,651,000, sweet potatoes 102,000,000, potatoes 72,000,000, cabbage 36,000,000, tomatoes 33,500,000, cucumbers 28,000,000, seed cotton 22,872,000, onions 20,500,000, eggplants 18,000,000, chilies and peppers 14,000,000, garlic 12,000,000, spinach 12,000,000, asparagus 6,250,000, tobacco leaves 2,395,000, tea 1,186,500, silkworm cocoons (2003) 667,000; livestock (number of live animals) 501,475,621 pigs, 197,267,883 goats, 171,961,000 sheep, 116,859,793 cattle, 22,717,000 water buffalo, 4,509,633,000 chickens, 736,912,000 ducks; fisheries production 46,079,311 (from aquaculture 68%); aquatic plants production 10,081,245 (from aquaculture 97%). *Mining and quarrying* (2005; by world rank): metal content of mine output—iron ore 138,000,000 (3), zinc 2,450,000 (1), manganese 1,100,000 (5), lead 1,000,000 (1), copper 740,000 (7), antimony 120,000 (1), tin 110,000 (1), tungsten 61,000 (1), silver 2,500 (3), gold 225 (2); metal ores—bauxite 18,000,000 (3), vanadium 17,000 (1); nonmetals—salt 44,547,000 (2), phosphate rock 9,130,000 (2), magnesite 1,700,000 (1), barite 4,200,000 (1), talc 3,000,000 (1), fluorspar 2,700,000 (1), asbestos 520,000 (2), strontium

140,000 (2). *Energy production (consumption):* electricity (kW-hr; 2008) 3,392,304,000,000 (3,450,200,000,000); coal (metric tons; 2007) 2,430,000,000 ([2008] 2,740,000,000 [including lignite]); lignite (metric tons; 2007) 120,000 (n.a.); crude petroleum (barrels; 2008) 1,450,000,000 (2,635,-000,000); petroleum products (metric tons; 2006) 238,365,000 (256,345,000); natural gas (cu m; 2008) 80,314,000,000 (80,700,000,000). **Population economically active** (2006): total 792,324,000; activity rate of total population 59.6% (participation rates: ages 15–64, 81.2%; female 45.8%; registered unemployed in urban areas [2008] 4.0%; urban unemployed including migrants [2008] up to 9.0%; rural unemployment is substantial). **Selected balance of payments data.** Receipts from (US$'000,000): tourism (2007) 37,233; remittances (2008) 40,641; foreign direct investment (FDI; 2005–07 avg) 76,214; official development assistance (2007) 1,439. Disbursements for (US$'000,000): tourism (2007) 29,786; remittances (2008) 5,737; FDI (2005–07 avg.) 18,630.

Foreign trade

Imports (2007; c.i.f.): US$955,956,000,000 (machinery and apparatus 39.4%, of which electronic integrated circuits and micro-assemblies 13.4%, computers and office machines 4.8%, telecommunications equipment and parts 3.7%; chemical products 11.2%, of which organic chemicals 4.0%; mineral fuels 11.0%, of which crude petroleum 8.4%; metal ore and metal scrap 7.3%; optical instruments and apparatus 4.8%. *Major import sources:* Japan 14.0%; South Korea 10.9%; Taiwan 10.6%; China free trade zones 9.0%; US 7.3%; Germany 4.7%; Malaysia 3.0%; Australia 2.7%; Thailand 2.4%; Philippines 2.4%. **Exports** (2007; f.o.b.): US$1,217,776,000,000 (machinery and apparatus 43.0%, of which computers and office machines and parts 13.6%, electrical machinery and electronics 10.6%, telecommunications equipment and parts 8.4%; wearing apparel and accessories 9.5%; chemical products 4.9%; textile yarn, fabrics, and made-up articles 4.6%; iron and steel 4.2%). *Major export destinations:* US 19.1%; Hong Kong 15.1%; Japan 8.4%; South Korea 4.6%; Germany 4.0%; Netherlands 3.4%; UK 2.6%; Singapore 2.4%; Russia 2.3%; India 2.0%.

Transport and communications

Transport. *Railroads* (2008): route length (2007) 78,000 km; passenger-km 777,860,000,000; metric ton-km cargo 2,511,180,000,000. *Roads* (2005): total length 1,930,544 km (paved 82%). *Vehicles* (2007): passenger cars 31,959,900; trucks 10,540,600. *Air transport* (2008): passenger-km 288,280,000,000; metric ton-km cargo 11,960,000,000. **Communications**, in total units (units per 1,000 persons). Telephone landlines (2008) 340,810,000 (256); cellular telephone subscribers (2008) 641,230,000 (482); personal computers (2007) 75,118,000 (57); total Internet users (2008) 298,000,000 (225); broadband Internet subscribers (2008) 83,366,000 (63).

Education and health

Literacy (2007): total population ages 15 and over literate 91.6%; males literate 95.7%; females literate 87.6%. **Health** (2008): physicians 2,050,000 (1 per 650 persons); hospital beds 3,690,000 (1 per 361

persons); infant mortality rate per 1,000 live births (2007) 22.9; undernourished population (2002–04) 150,000,000 (12% of total population based on the consumption of a minimum daily requirement of 1,930 calories).

Military

Total active duty personnel (November 2008): 2,185,000 (army 73.2%, navy 11.7%, air force 15.1%). **Military expenditure as percentage of GDP** (2007): 3.0%; per capita expenditure US$97.

Background

The discovery of Peking man (*Homo erectus*) in 1927 dated the advent of early humans in what is now China to the Middle Pleistocene, about 900,000 to 130,000 years ago. Chinese civilization probably spread from the Huang He (Yellow River) valley, where it existed about 3000 BC. The first dynasty for which there is definite historical material is the Shang (c. 16th century BC), which had a writing system and a calendar. The Zhou overthrew its Shang rulers in the 11th century BC and ruled until the 3rd century BC. Daoism and Confucianism were founded in this era.

A time of conflict, called the Warring States period, lasted from the 5th century BC until 221 BC, when the Qin (Ch'in) dynasty (from whose name China is derived) was established after its rulers had conquered rival states and created a unified empire. The Han dynasty was established in 206 BC and ruled until AD 220. A time of turbulence followed, and Chinese reunification was not achieved until the Sui dynasty was established in 581.

After the founding of the Song dynasty in 960, the capital was moved to the south because of northern invasions. In 1279 this dynasty was overthrown and Mongol (Yuan) domination began. During this time Marco Polo visited Kublai Khan. The Ming dynasty followed the period of Mongol rule and lasted from 1368 to 1644, cultivating antiforeign feelings to the point that China closed itself off from the rest of the world. Peoples from Manchuria overran China in 1644 and established the Qing (Manchu) dynasty. Ever-increasing incursions by Western and Japanese interests led in the 19th century to the Opium Wars, the Taiping Rebellion, and the Sino-Japanese War, all of which weakened the Manchus.

The dynasty fell in 1911, and a republic was proclaimed in 1912 by Sun Yat-sen. The power struggles of warlords weakened the republic. Under Sun's successor, Chiang Kai-shek, some national unification was achieved in the 1920s, but Chiang soon broke with the Communists, who had formed their own armies. Japan invaded northern China in 1937; its occupation lasted until 1945. The Communists gained support after the Long March (1934–35), in which Mao Zedong emerged as their leader.

Upon Japan's surrender at the end of World War II, a fierce civil war began; in 1949 the Nationalists fled to the island of Taiwan and the Communists proclaimed the People's Republic of China. The Communists undertook extensive reforms, but pragmatic policies alternated with periods of revolutionary upheaval, most notably in the Great Leap Forward and the Cultural Revolution. The anarchy, terror, and eco-

nomic paralysis of the latter led, after Mao's death in 1976, to a turn to moderation under Deng Xiaoping, who undertook economic reforms and renewed China's ties to the West; the country established diplomatic ties with the US in 1979. The economy has been in transition since the late 1970s, moving from central planning and state-run industries to a mixture of state-owned and private enterprises in manufacturing and services, in the process growing dramatically and transforming Chinese society. The Tiananmen Square incident in 1989 was a challenge to an otherwise increasingly stable political environment after 1980. The death of Deng in 1997 marked the end of a political era, but power passed peacefully to Jiang Zemin. In 1997 Hong Kong reverted to Chinese rule, as did Macao in 1999.

Recent Developments

The strength of China's economy was credited with helping to stave off a worldwide economic collapse in 2009. In the face of the global downturn, China's GDP grew 10.7% in the fourth quarter compared with the fourth quarter of 2008. It grew 8.7% for the entire year, while industrial production rose 18.5%. The Chinese economy, the output of which was US$4.9 trillion in 2009, was slated to become the world's second largest by the end of 2010. Although China recorded its first trade deficit in six years in March 2010, it still saw a trade surplus of US$14.5 billion for that first quarter.

China continued to try to secure more access to vital mineral resources. The Aluminum Corporation of China attempted to buy the Australian-based mining conglomerate Rio Tinto for US$19.2 billion in February 2009, but by June the deal had collapsed under political pressure from the Australian public not to sell control of strategic minerals to China. In the spring, however, Chinese concerns successfully acquired stakes in two other Australian mining companies. In November China pledged US$10 billion in loans to Africa, with which it had greatly expanded trade for the past decade, mostly in the form of minerals going to China. Construction continued in 2010 on a massive copper mine that China was developing in Afghanistan, part of a multi-billion dollar effort that also involved oil, natural gas, coal, and other mineral resources.

China's relations with the US got off to an inauspicious start in 2009 when the US protested to Beijing in March about what it claimed was harassment of a US naval intelligence vessel, the USNS *Impeccable*, by Chinese ships in international waters. Throughout the year the US cautiously pressed China to allow its currency, the renminbi, to appreciate, though with little success. In November US Pres. Barack Obama visited China on an official state visit. Many critics called the visit unsuccessful because he failed to extract commitments from China on issues of importance to Washington, such as sanctions against Iran, unified policy toward North Korea, or cooperation on global warming. In January 2010 the Chinese completed a successful test of a missile-defense system, which many saw as a warning to the US for having sold Patriot missile-defense systems to Taiwan earlier in the month.

Internet resource: <www.stats.gov.cn>.

---

1 metric ton = about 1.1 short tons;   1 kilometer = 0.6 mi (statute);   1 metric ton-km cargo = about 0.68 short ton-mi cargo;   c.i.f.: cost, insurance, and freight;   f.o.b.: free on board

Colombia

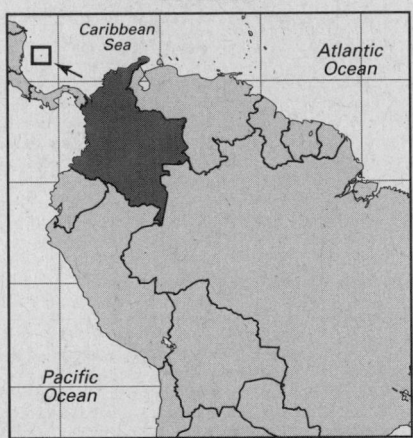

Official name: República de Colombia (Republic of Colombia). Form of government: unitary multiparty republic with two legislative houses (Senate [102]; House of Representatives [166]). Head of state and government: President Juan Manuel Santos Calderón (from 2010). Capital: Bogotá. Official language: Spanish. Official religion: none. Monetary unit: 1 peso (Col$) = 100 centavos; valuation (1 Jul 2010) US$1 = Col$1,897.50.

Demography

Area: 440,832 sq mi, 1,141,749 sq km. Population (2009): 44,972,000. Density (2009): persons per sq mi 102.0, persons per sq km 39.4. Urban (2005): 73.6%. Sex distribution (2007): male 49.01%; female 50.99%. Age breakdown (2007): under 15, 29.8%; 15–29, 25.4%; 30–44, 22.3%; 45–59, 14.4%; 60–74, 6.2%; 75–84, 1.6%; 85 and over, 0.3%. Ethnic composition (2006): mestizo 58%; white 20%; mulatto 14%; black 4%; black-Amerindian 3%; Amerindian 1%. Religious affiliation (2007): Roman Catholic 80.0%; Protestant/independent Christian 13.5%; Mormon 0.3%; nonreligious 2.0%; other 4.2%. Major cities (2007): Bogotá 7,033,914; Medellín 2,248,912; Cali 2,139,535; Barranquilla 1,144,470; Cartagena 871,342. Location: northern South America, bordering the Caribbean Sea, Venezuela, Brazil, Peru, Ecuador, the Pacific Ocean, and Panama.

Vital statistics

Birth rate per 1,000 population (2007): 20.2 (world avg. 20.3). Death rate per 1,000 population (2007): 5.5 (world avg. 8.5). Total fertility rate (avg. births per childbearing woman; 2007): 2.51. Life expectancy at birth (2007): male 68.4 years; female 76.2 years.

National economy

Budget (2007). Revenue: Col$103,986,000,-000,000 (tax revenue 56.4%, of which taxes on goods and services 26.1%, income tax 16.7%; nontax revenue 39.3%; other 4.3%). Expenditures: Col$110,014,000,000,000 (interest on debt 25.1%;

other 74.9%). Population economically active (2006): total 20,177,100; activity rate 44.5% (participation rates: ages 12–55, 63.2%; female 43.0%; unemployed [April 2008–March 2009] 11.5%). Production (metric tons except as noted). Agriculture and fishing (2007): sugarcane 40,000,000, plantains 3,600,000, rice 2,250,000, coffee 710,000; Colombia is a leading producer of coca, with 430 metric tons of illegal cocaine production in 2008; livestock (number of live animals) 26,000,000 cattle, 3,400,000 sheep, 2,500,000 horses; fisheries production 156,100 (from aquaculture 38%). Mining and quarrying (2006): nickel (metal content) 94,100; gold 15,700 kg; emeralds 5,734,000 carats. Manufacturing (value added in US$'000,000; 2005): processed food products 3,471; refined petroleum products 2,873; medicines, fertilizers, and soaps 1,956. Energy production (consumption): electricity (kW-hr; 2006) 51,830,000,000 (52,963,000,000); coal (metric tons; 2007) 71,700,000 (4,480,000); crude petroleum (barrels; 2008) 214,400,000 ([2007] 105,500,000); petroleum products (metric tons; 2006) 13,247,000 (9,442,000); natural gas (cu m; 2006) 6,600,000,000 (9,298,000,000). Gross national income (2008): US$207,425,-000,000 (US$4,660 per capita). Public debt (external, outstanding; December 2008): US$24,855,-000,000. Selected balance of payments data. Receipts from (US$'000,000): tourism (2007) 1,669; remittances (2008) 4,884; foreign direct investment (FDI; 2005–07 avg.) 8,577; official development assistance (2007) 731. Disbursements for (US$'000,000): tourism (2007) 1,537; remittances (2008) 88; FDI (2005–07 avg.) 2,043.

Foreign trade

Imports (2007; c.i.f.): US$32,897,000,000 (machinery and apparatus 26.5%; chemical products 18.5%; motor vehicles 12.0%; base and fabricated metals 9.8%). Major import sources: US 26.2%; China 10.1%; Mexico 9.3%; Brazil 7.3%; Venezuela 4.2%. Exports (2007; f.o.b.): US$29,991,000,000 (crude petroleum 18.5%; coal 11.1%; refined petroleum products 5.8%; coffee 5.7%; ferronickel 5.6%; wearing apparel and accessories 4.5%; motor vehicles and parts 3.9%; cut flowers 3.7%). Major export destinations: US 35.4%; Venezuela 17.4%; Ecuador 4.3%; Switzerland 3.0%; Netherlands 2.8%.

Transport and communications

Transport. Railroads (2006): route length 2,030 km; passenger-km (2004) 25,000,000; metric ton-km cargo (2005) 8,236,000,000. Roads (2006): total length 164,278 km (paved [2000] 23%). Vehicles (2005): cars 1,606,880; trucks and buses 1,079,247. Air transport (2007): passenger-km 9,552,000,000; metric ton-km cargo 189,804,000. Communications, in total units (units per 1,000 persons). Telephone landlines (2008): 6,820,000 (153); cellular telephone subscribers (2008): 41,365,000 (931); personal computers (2007): 3,513,000 (80); total Internet users (2008): 17,117,000 (385); broadband Internet subscribers (2008): 1,903,000 (43).

Education and health

Educational attainment (2005). Percentage of population ages 25 and over having: no formal schooling/unknown 10.2%; primary education 40.1%; secondary 34.2%; higher 15.5%. **Literacy** (2006): population ages 15 and over literate 92.3%; males literate 92.4%; females literate 92.2%. **Health:** physicians (2006) 51,095 (1 per 849 persons); hospital beds (2004) 50,824 (1 per 833 persons); infant mortality rate per 1,000 live births (2007) 20.1; undernourished population (2002–04) 5,900,000 (13% of total population based on the consumption of a minimum daily requirement of 1,830 calories).

Military

Total active duty personnel (November 2008): 267,231 (army 84.7%, navy 11.5%, air force 3.8%). **Military expenditure as percentage of GDP** (2008): 4.7%; per capita expenditure US$186.

Military

Total active duty personnel (2007): 254,259 (army 85.3%, navy 10.9%, air force 3.8%). **Military expenditure as percentage of GDP** (2005): 3.7%; per capita expenditure US$106.

Background

The Spanish arrived in what is now Colombia c. 1500 and by 1538 had defeated the area's Chibchan-speaking Indians and made the area subject to the Viceroyalty of Peru. After 1740 authority was transferred to the newly created Viceroyalty of New Granada. Parts of Colombia threw off Spanish jurisdiction in 1810, and full independence came after Spain's defeat by Simón Bolívar in 1819. Civil war in 1840 checked development. Conflict between the Liberal and Conservative parties led to the War of a Thousand Days (1899–1903). Years of relative peace followed, but hostility erupted again in 1948; the two parties agreed in 1958 to a scheme for alternating governments. A new constitution was adopted in 1991, but democratic power remained threatened by civil unrest. Many leftist rebels and right-wing paramilitary groups funded their activities through kidnappings and narcotics trafficking.

Recent Developments

There were a number of government scandals in Colombia in 2009. In the so-called parapolitics scandal, more than 70 members of Congress—most of them supporters of the president—were placed under investigation for alleged connections to right-wing paramilitary groups. A second scandal involved allegations that soldiers had killed innocent citizens and—in an attempt to boost the soldiers' chances for promotion—had reported those killed as guerrillas or drug traffickers. The government's close relations with the US continued to cause trouble for it in the region. The announcement that the US military would be allowed to use seven Colombian military bases as part of the battle against drug trafficking and related armed groups met with opposition from some governments in the region. Venezuelan Pres. Hugo Chávez and Ecuadoran Pres. Rafael Correa were the most vociferous critics, with Venezuela going so far as to suspend relations with Colombia.

Internet resource: <www.dane.gov.co>.

Comoros

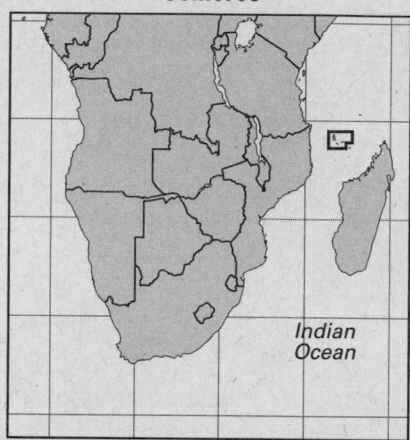

Indian Ocean

Official names: Udzima wa Komori (Comorian); Jumhuriyat al-Qamar al-Muttahidah (Arabic); Union des Comores (French) (Union of the Comoros). **Form of government:** republic with one legislative house (Assembly of the Union [33]). **Head of state and government:** President Ahmed Abdallah Mohamed Sambi (from 2006). **Capital:** Moroni. **Official languages:** Comorian (Shikomor); Arabic; French. **Official religion:** Islam. **Monetary unit:** 1 Comorian franc (CF) = 100 centimes; valuation (1 Jul 2010) US$1 = CF 401.10.

Demography

Area: 719 sq mi, 1,862 sq km. **Population** (2009): 676,000 (excludes Comorians living abroad in France or Mayotte [about 150,000 people]). **Density** (2009): persons per sq mi 940.2, persons per sq km 363.1. **Urban** (2008): 28.1%. **Sex distribution** (2006): male 49.61%; female 50.39%. **Age breakdown** (2006): under 15, 42.7%; 15–29, 26.6%; 30–44, 17.8%; 45–59, 8.2%; 60–74, 3.9%; 75 and over, 0.8%. **Ethnic composition** (2000): Comorian (a mixture of Bantu, Arab, Malay, and Malagasy peoples) 97.1%; Makua 1.6%; French 0.4%; other 0.9%. **Religious affiliation** (2005): Muslim (nearly all Sunni) 98.4%; other 1.6%. **Major cities** (2002): Moroni (2007) 46,000; Mutsamudu 21,558; Domoni 13,254; Fomboni 13,053; Tsémbéhou 10,552. **Location:** islands in the western Indian Ocean, between Madagascar and Mozambique.

Vital statistics

Birth rate per 1,000 population (2008): 32.6 (world avg. 20.3). **Death rate** per 1,000 population (2008): 6.3 (world avg. 8.5). **Total fertility rate** (avg. births per childbearing woman; 2006): 5.03. **Life expectancy** at birth (2006): male 60.0 years; female 64.7 years.

National economy

Budget (2007). *Revenue:* CF 33,945,000,000 (tax revenue 49.1%, of which taxes on international trade

1 metric ton = about 1.1 short tons;   1 kilometer = 0.6 mi (statute);   1 metric ton-km cargo = about 0.68 short ton-mi cargo;   c.i.f.: cost, insurance, and freight;   f.o.b.: free on board

17.6%, taxes on goods and services 11.5%; grants 37.7%; nontax revenue 13.2%). *Expenditures:* CF 37,314,000,000 (current expenditures 72.5%, of which interest on debt 2.2%; development expenditures 27.5%). **Public debt** (external, outstanding; 2008): US$277,000,000. **Production** (metric tons except as noted). *Agriculture and fishing* (2007): coconuts 77,000, bananas 65,000, cassava 58,000, cloves 2,500, vanilla 90, ylang-ylang essence 25; livestock (number of live animals) 115,000 goats, 45,000 cattle, 21,000 sheep; fisheries production 16,000 (from aquaculture, none). *Mining and quarrying* (2009): sand, gravel, and crushed stone from coral mining for local construction. *Manufacturing* (2009): products of small-scale industries include processed vanilla and ylang-ylang, cement, handicrafts, soaps, soft drinks, woodwork, and wearing apparel. *Energy production (consumption):* electricity (kW-hr; 2006) 50,600,000 (22,000,000); petroleum products (metric tons; 2006) none (32,000). **Population economically active** (2006): total 348,000; activity rate of total population 42.5% (participation rates: ages 15–64, 73.8%; female 43.1%; unemployed [2005] 13.3%). **Gross national income** (2007): US$425,000,000 (US$680 per capita). **Selected balance of payments data.** Receipts from (US$'000,000): tourism (2006) 27; remittances (2007) 12; foreign direct investment (2005–07 avg.) 1; official development assistance (2007) 44. Disbursements for (US$'000,000): tourism (2006) 11.

Foreign trade

Imports (2007; c.i.f.): CF 49,716,000,000 (refined petroleum products 21.4%; rice 10.4%; meat 6.8%; cement 4.9%; iron and steel 2.3%). *Major import sources* (2005): South Africa 15.4%; France 13.8%; Pakistan 3.1%; Mauritius 3.0%; Belgium-Luxembourg 2.4%. **Exports** (2007; f.o.b.): CF 4,965,000,000 (cloves 57.7%; vanilla 25.7%; ylang-ylang 14.3%). *Major export destinations* (2005): France 73.3%; Germany 10.4%.

Transport and communications

Transport. *Railroads:* none. *Roads* (2004): total length 793 km (paved 70%). *Vehicles* (1996): passenger cars 9,100; trucks and buses 4,950. *Air transport* (2001): passengers arriving or departing Moroni 108,000. **Communications,** in total units (units per 1,000 persons). Telephone landlines (2005): 17,000 (28); cellular telephone subscribers (2007): 40,000 (48); personal computers (2004): 5,000 (6.3); total Internet users (2006): 21,000 (26).

Education and health

Educational attainment (1996). Percentage of population ages 25 and over having: no formal schooling/unknown 73.9%; primary education 11.0%; secondary 15.1%. **Literacy** (2007): total population ages 15 and over literate 57.1%; males literate 64.2%; females literate 50.1%. **Health:** physicians (2004) 48 (1 per 12,417 persons); hospital beds (1995) 1,450 (1 per 342 persons); infant mortality rate per 1,000 live births (2006) 72.9.

Military

Total active duty personnel (2008): the 1,100-member national army is not necessarily accepted by each of the islands; each island also has its own armed security. France provides training for military personnel. **Military expenditure as percentage of GDP** (2005): 3.5%; per capita expenditure US$21.

Background

The Comoro Islands were known to European navigators from the 16th century. In 1843 France officially took possession of Mayotte and in 1886 placed the other three islands under protection. Subordinated to Madagascar in 1912, Comoros became an overseas territory of France in 1947. In 1961 it was granted autonomy. In 1974 majorities on three of the islands voted for independence, which was granted in 1975. The following decade saw several coup attempts, which culminated in the assassination of the president in 1989. French intervention permitted multiparty elections in 1990, but the country remained in a state of chronic instability. Anjouan and Mohéli seceded from the Comoros federation in 1997. The army took control of the government in 1999. A referendum at the end of 2001 renamed the country the Union of the Comoros and granted the three main islands partially autonomous status.

Recent Developments

In 2009 Comoros faced a referendum that had significant impact on the political future of the country. On 17 May Comorans voted to modify the framework of the power-sharing government that had been in place since 2001. The constitutional change pared down the governmental structure; federal presidents became governors of the semiautonomous Grande Comore, Anjouan, and Moheli islands, and the term of the union presidency was extended (from four) to five years.

Internet resource:
<www.comores-online.com/pagegb.htm>.

Congo, Democratic Republic of the

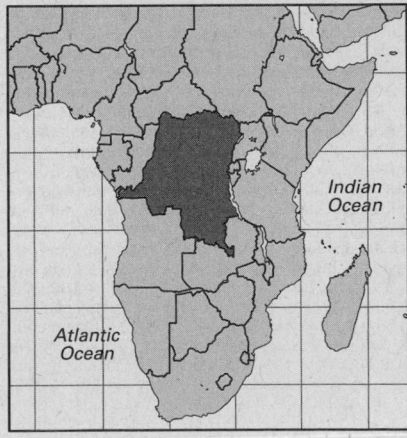

Official name: République Democratique du Congo (Democratic Republic of the Congo). **Form of government:** unitary multiparty republic with two legislative houses (Senate [108]; National Assembly [500]). **Head of state:** President Joseph Kabila (from 2001). **Head of government:** Prime Minister Adolphe Muzito (from 2008). **Capital:** Kinshasa. **Official languages:** French (Kongo, Lingala, Swahili, and Tshiluba are national languages). **Official religion:** none. **Monetary unit:** Congo franc (FC) = 100 centimes; valuation (1. Jul 2010) US$1 = FC 885.05.

Demography

Area: 905,355 sq mi, 2,344,858 sq km. **Population** (2009): 66,020,000. **Density** (2009): persons per sq mi 72.9, persons per sq km 28.2. **Urban** (2005): 32.1% **Sex distribution** (2005): male 49.48%; female 50.52%. **Age breakdown** (2005): under 15, 47.2%; 15–29, 27.1%; 30–44, 14.2%; 45–59, 7.4%; 60–74, 3.4%; 75–84, 0.6%; 85 and over, 0.1%. **Ethnic composition** (1983): Luba 18.0%; Kongo 16.1%; Mongo 13.5%; Rwanda 10.3%; Azande 6.1%; Bangi and Ngale 5.8%; Rundi 3.8%; Teke 2.7%; Boa 2.3%; Chokwe 1.8%; Lugbara 1.6%; Banda 1.4%; other 16.6%. **Religious affiliation** (2004): Roman Catholic 50%; Protestant 20%; Kimbanguist (indigenous Christian) 10%; Muslim 10%; traditional beliefs and syncretic sects 10%. **Major urban areas** (2004): Kinshasa 7,273,947; Lubumbashi 1,283,380; Mbuji-Mayi 1,213,726; Kananga 720,362; Kisangani 682,599. **Location:** central Africa, bordering the Central African Republic, Sudan, Uganda, Rwanda, Burundi, Tanzania, Zambia, Angola, the South Atlantic Ocean, and the Republic of the Congo.

Vital statistics

Birth rate per 1,000 population (2007): 43.4 (world avg. 20.3). **Death rate** per 1,000 population (2007): 11.9 (world avg. 8.5). **Total fertility rate** (avg. births per childbearing woman; 2007): 6.37. **Life expectancy** at birth (2007): male 51.9 years; female 55.4 years.

National economy

Budget (2005). *Revenue:* FC 564,900,000,000 (grants 31.1%; customs and excise taxes 25.7%; direct and indirect taxes 19.7%; petroleum royalties and taxes 17.4%). *Expenditures:* FC 655,500,-000,000 (current expenditures 65.3%, of which interest on external debt 14.8%; capital expenditures 17.4%; expenditures on demobilization and reintegration 14.8%). **Public debt** (external, outstanding; 2007): US$10,853,000,000. **Production** (metric tons except as noted). *Agriculture and fishing* (2007): cassava 15,000,000, sugarcane 1,550,000, plantains 1,200,000, (2005) pimento and allspice 33,000, coffee 21,300; livestock (number of live animals) 4,000,000 goats, 957,000 pigs; fisheries production 238,970 (from aquaculture 1%). *Mining and quarrying* (2006): copper (metal content) 130,000; cobalt (metal content) 28,400; tin (metal content) 3,500; silver 67,633 kg; gold 10,000 kg; diamonds 28,540,000 carats. *Manufacturing* (2004): cement 402,500; flour 199,000; steel 130,000. *Energy production (consumption):* electricity (kW-hr; 2006) 7,240,000,000 (5,160,000,000)); coal (metric tons; 2007) 116,000 (296,000); crude petroleum (barrels; 2008) 7,290,000 (negligible); petroleum products

(metric tons; 2006) none (373,000). **Gross national income** (2008): US$9,843,000,000 (US$150 per capita). **Population economically active** (2003): total 21,718,000; activity rate 40.0% (participation rates: ages 15–64, 77.1%; female 41.1%). **Selected balance of payments data.** Receipts from (US$'000,000): tourism (2005) 1.0; foreign direct investment (2004–06 avg.) 37; official development assistance (2005) 1,828. Disbursements for (US$'000,000): tourism (1997) 7.0.

Foreign trade

Imports (2005): US$2,465,000,000 (aid-related imports 22.9%; other imports 77.1%). *Major import sources* (2004): South Africa 18.5%; Belgium 15.6%; France 10.9%; US 6.2%; Germany 5.9%. **Exports** (2005): US$2,042,000,000 (diamonds 48.4%; crude petroleum 20.0%; cobalt [2004] 15.0%; copper [2004] 3.3%; coffee [2004] 0.9%; gold [2004] 0.7%). *Major export destinations:* Belgium 42.5%; Finland 17.8%; Zimbabwe 12.2%; US 9.2%; China 6.5%.

Transport and communications

Transport. *Railroads* (2003): length (2004) 5,138 km; passenger-km 152,930,000; metric ton-km cargo 506,010,000. *Roads* (2004): total length 153,497 km (paved 2%). *Vehicles* (1999): passenger cars 172,600; trucks and buses 34,600. *Air transport* (1999): passenger-km 263,000,000; metric ton-km cargo 39,000,000. **Communications,** in total units (units per 1,000 persons). Telephone landlines (2008): 37,000 (0.6); cellular telephone subscribers (2008): 9,263,000 (143); total Internet users (2008): 290,000 (4.5); broadband Internet subscribers (2007): 1,500 (0.02).

Education and health

Literacy (2003): percentage of total population ages 15 and over literate 65.5%; males literate 76.2%; females literate 55.1%. **Health:** physicians (2004) 5,827 (1 per 9,585 persons); infant mortality rate per 1,000 live births (2005) 116.5; undernourished population (2002–04) 39,000,000 (74% of total population based on the consumption of a minimum daily requirement of 1,830 calories).

Military

Total active duty personnel (November 2008): 145,000 (army 79.0%, central staff 9.5%, republican guard 5.0%, air force 2.0%, navy 4.5%); UN peacekeepers (March 2009): 16,600 troops, 1,100 police. **Military expenditure as percentage of GDP** (2007): 1.7%; per capita expenditure US$3.

Background

Prior to European colonization, several native kingdoms had emerged in the Congo region, including the 16th-century Luba kingdom and the Kuba federation, which reached its peak in the 18th century. European development began late in the 19th century when King Léopold II of Belgium financed Henry Morton Stanley's exploration of the Congo River. The 1884–85 Berlin West Africa Conference recognized

1 metric ton = about 1.1 short tons; 1 kilometer = 0.6 mi (statute); 1 metric ton-km cargo = about 0.68 short ton-mi cargo; c.i.f.: cost, insurance, and freight; f.o.b.: free on board

the Congo Free State with Léopold as its sovereign. The growing demand for rubber helped finance the exploitation of the Congo, but abuses against native peoples outraged Western nations and forced Léopold to grant the Free State a colonial charter as the Belgian Congo in 1908. Independence was granted in 1960, and the country's name was changed to Zaire in 1971. The postindependence period was marked by unrest, culminating in a military coup that brought Gen. Mobutu Sese Seko to power in 1965. Mismanagement, corruption, and increasing violence devastated the infrastructure and economy. Mobutu was deposed in 1997 by Laurent Kabila, who restored the country's name to Democratic Republic of the Congo (DRC). Instability in neighboring countries, an influx of refugees from Rwanda, and a desire for Congo's mineral wealth led to military involvement by various African countries. Unrest continued in the early 21st century.

Recent Developments

The situation in the DRC remained grim throughout 2009. Despite vast mineral wealth, mining production declined because of mismanagement, corruption, endemic civil unrest, the global recession, and a lack of new investment. Early in the year the government forged an unexpected alliance with Rwanda to conduct a joint military operation in the DRC's North Kivu province to eliminate the influence of the Democratic Forces for the Liberation of Rwanda, a major factor in destabilizing the area for 12 years. In a joint operation with the Ugandan government, the army engaged Lord's Resistance Army (LRA) insurgents near the border, but that mission also met with limited success. In March 2010 it was reported that at least 321 civilians were massacred by LRA rebels in northeastern DRC in December 2009, and that many others were horribly mutilated.

Internet resource: <www.bcc.cd>.

Congo, Republic of the

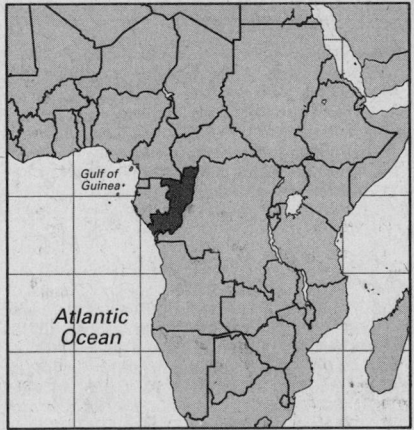

Gulf of Guinea

Atlantic Ocean

Official name. République du Congo (Republic of the Congo). **Form of government:** republic with two legislative houses (Senate [72]; National Assembly

[137]). **Head of state and government:** President Denis Sassou-Nguesso (from 1997). **Capital:** Brazzaville. **Official language:** French (Lingala and Monokutuba are national languages). **Official religion:** none. **Monetary unit:** 1 CFA franc (CFAF) = 100 centimes; valuation (1 Jul 2010) US$1 = CFAF 527.20.

Demography

Area: 132,047 sq mi, 342,000 sq km. **Population** (2009): 3,683,000. **Density** (2009): persons per sq mi 27.9, persons per sq km 10.8. **Urban** (2007): 61.0%. **Sex distribution** (2008): male 49.72%; female 50.28%. **Age breakdown** (2008): under 15, 46.1%; 15–29, 27.4%; 30–44, 14.8%; 45–59, 7.4%; 60–74, 3.4%; 75–84, 0.8%; 85 and over, 0.1%. **Ethnic composition** (2000): Kongo 21.2%; Yombe 11.5%; Teke 10.7%; Kougni 8.0%; Mboshi 5.4%; Ngala 4.2%; Sundi 4.0%; other 35.0%. **Religious affiliation** (2005): Roman Catholic 49%; independent Christian 13%; Protestant 11%; Muslim 2%; other (mostly traditional beliefs and nonreligious) 25%. **Major cities** (2007): Brazzaville 1,308,700; Pointe-Noire 647,152; Dolisie 118,562; Nkayi 60,453; Ouesso 26,994. **Location:** west-central Africa, bordering Cameroon, the Central African Republic, the Democratic Republic of the Congo, Angola, the South Atlantic Ocean, and Gabon.

Vital statistics

Birth rate per 1,000 population (2008): 41.8 (world avg. 20.3). **Death rate** per 1,000 population (2008): 12.3 (world avg. 8.5). **Total fertility rate** (avg. births per childbearing woman; 2008): 5.92. **Life expectancy** at birth (2008): male 52.5 years; female 55.0 years.

National economy

Budget (2005). *Revenue:* CFAF 1,300,100,000,000 (petroleum revenue 80.6%; nonpetroleum revenue 16.9%; grants 2.5%). *Expenditures:* CFAF 736,400,000,000 (current expenditures 77.0%, of which interest 20.4%, wages and salaries 17.7%; capital expenditures 23.0%). **Public debt** (external, outstanding; 2006): US$5,328,000,000. **Gross national income** (2008): US$7,134,000,000 (US$1,970 per capita). **Production** (metric tons except as noted). *Agriculture and fishing* (2007): cassava 915,000, sugarcane 550,000, oil palm fruit 90,000; livestock (number of live animals) 290,000 goats, 110,000 cattle, 99,000 sheep; fisheries production 59,966 (from aquaculture, negligible). *Mining and quarrying* (2007): gold 100 kg; diamonds, n.a. *Manufacturing* (2001): residual fuel oil (2000) 206,000; refined sugar 71,814; distillate fuel oils (2000) 62,000. *Energy production (consumption):* electricity (kW-hr; 2006) 453,000,000 (864,000,-000); crude petroleum (barrels; 2007) 82,600,000 ([2006] 4,909,000); petroleum products (metric tons; 2006) 625,000 (355,000); natural gas (cu m; 2006) 23,600,000 (23,700,000). **Population economically active** (2006): total 1,482,000; activity rate of total population 40.2% (participation rates: ages 15–64, 69.5%; female 41.3%). **Selected balance of payments data.** *Receipts from* (US$'000,000): tourism (2007) 54; remittances (2008) 15; foreign direct investment (2005–07 avg.) 473; official development assistance (2007) 127.

Disbursements for (US$'000,000): tourism (2007) 168; remittances (2008) 102.

Foreign trade

Imports (2005): CFAF 746,400,000,000 (nonpetroleum sector 85.9%; petroleum sector 14.1%). *Major import sources* (2002): France 26%; US 11%; Italy 8%; Lebanon 6%; Netherlands 5%. **Exports** (2005): CFAF 2,484,300,000,000 (crude petroleum 92.5%; wood products 4.6%; refined petroleum products 1.2%). *Major export destinations* (2002): Taiwan 27%; North Korea 11%; US 10%; South Korea 7%; France 7%.

Transport and communications

Transport. *Railroads* (1998): length 894 km; passenger-km 242,000,000; metric ton-km cargo 135,000,000. *Roads* (2004): total length 17,289 km (paved 5%). *Vehicles:* passenger cars (2002) 30,000; trucks and buses (1997) 15,500. *Air transport* (2002): passenger-km 27,000,000; metric ton-km cargo 3,000,000. **Communications,** in total units (units per 1,000 persons). Telephone landlines (2005): 16,000 (4); cellular telephone subscribers (2008): 1,807,000 (470); personal computers (2006): 17,000 (5); total Internet users (2008): 155,000 (40).

Education and health

Educational attainment (2005). Percentage of population ages 15–49 having: no formal schooling 5.6%; primary education 28.1%; lower secondary 47.2%; upper secondary/higher 19.1%. **Literacy** (2005): total population ages 15 and over literate 87.4%; males literate 92.3%; females literate 82.9%. **Health:** physicians (2000) 540 (1 per 5,745 persons); hospital beds (2001) 5,195 (1 per 623 persons); infant mortality rate per 1,000 live births (2008) 81.7; undernourished population (2003–05) 800,000 (22% of total population based on the consumption of a minimum daily requirement of 1,800 calories).

Military

Total active duty personnel (November 2008): 10,000 (army 80.0%, navy 8.0%, air force 12.0%). **Military expenditure as percentage of GDP** (2007): 1.1%; per capita expenditure US$26.

Background

In precolonial days the Congo area was home to several thriving kingdoms, including the Kongo, which had its beginnings in the 1st millennium AD. The slave trade began in the 15th century with the arrival of the Portuguese; it supported the local kingdoms and dominated the area until its suppression in the 19th century. The French arrived in the mid-19th century and established treaties with two of the kingdoms, placing them under French protection prior to their becoming part of the colony of French Congo. In 1910 the French possessions were renamed French Equatorial Africa, and Congo became known as Middle (Moyen) Congo. In 1946 Middle Congo became a French overseas territory and in 1958 voted to become an autonomous republic within the French Community. Full independence came two years later. The area has suffered from political instability since independence. Congo's first president was ousted in 1963. A Marxist party, the Congolese Labor Party, gained strength, and in 1968 another coup, led by Maj. Marien Ngouabi, created the People's Republic of the Congo. Ngouabi was assassinated in 1977, and a series of military rulers followed. Fighting between local militias that began in 1997 badly disrupted the economy, and though a 2003 peace agreement largely ended the conflict, sporadic violence continued.

Recent Developments

A food and nutrition security program was initiated in the Republic of the Congo in February 2009, designed to provide incentives for farmers to increase production for the market (only 5% of the country's arable land was currently under cultivation). Negotiations with South African farmers to lease some 200,000 ha (about 494,200 ac) of Congolese farmland for the production of food and fiber crops were successfully concluded in October.

Internet resource: <www.cnsee.org>.

Costa Rica

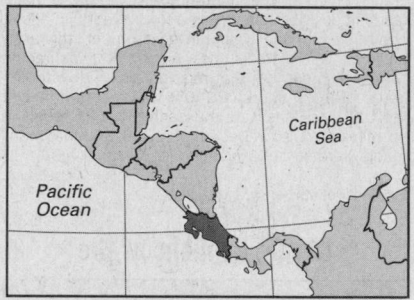

Official name: República de Costa Rica (Republic of Costa Rica). **Form of government:** unitary multiparty republic with one legislative house (Legislative Assembly [57]). **Head of state and government:** President Laura Chinchilla (from 2010). **Capital:** San José. **Official language:** Spanish. **Official religion:** Roman Catholicism. **Monetary unit:** 1 Costa Rican colón (₡) = 100 céntimos; valuation (1 Jul 2010) US$1 = ₡530.70.

Demography

Area: 19,730 sq mi, 51,100 sq km. **Population** (2009): 4,509,000. **Density** (2009): persons per sq mi 228.5, persons per sq km 88.2. **Urban** (2003): 60.6%. **Sex distribution** (2006): male 50.76%; female 49.24%. **Age breakdown** (2005): under 15, 28.4%; 15–29, 28.1%; 30–44, 21.5%; 45–59, 13.7%; 60–74, 5.9%; 75–84, 1.8%; 85 and over, 0.6%. **Ethnic composition** (2000): white 77.0%; mestizo 17.0%; black/mulatto 3.0%; East Asian (mostly

---

1 metric ton = about 1.1 short tons;   1 kilometer = 0.6 mi (statute);   1 metric ton-km cargo = about 0.68 short ton-mi cargo;   c.i.f.: cost, insurance, and freight;   f.o.b.: free on board

Chinese) 2.0%; Amerindian 1.0%. **Religious affiliation** (2004): Roman Catholic (practicing) 47%; Roman Catholic (nonpracticing) 25%; Evangelical Protestant 13%; nonreligious 10%; other 5%. **Major cities** (2009): San José 356,174; Limón 65,600; Alajuela 50,989; San Francisco 48,036; Cinco Esquinas 43,100. **Location:** Central America, bordering Nicaragua, the Caribbean Sea, Panama, and the North Pacific Ocean.

Vital statistics

Birth rate per 1,000 population (2008): 16.9 (world avg. 20.3); within marriage (2007) 40.1%. **Death rate** per 1,000 population (2008): 4.1 (world avg. 8.5). **Total fertility rate** (avg. births per childbearing woman; 2008): 1.97. **Life expectancy** at birth (2008): male 76.7 years; female 81.7 years.

National economy

Budget (2007). *Revenue:* ₡2,106,400,000,000 (taxes on goods and services 59.1%; income tax 25.2%; taxes on international trade 7.9%). *Expenditures:* ₡2,025,500,000,000 (education 31.8%; interest on debt 20.7%; social protection 16.0%; public order 11.4%; transportation 10.7%). **Public debt** (external, outstanding; 2007): US$3,750,000,000. **Gross national income** (2008): US$27,447,000,000 (US$6,060 per capita). **Production** (metric tons except as noted). *Agriculture and fishing* (2007): sugarcane 4,300,000, bananas 2,240,000, pineapples 1,225,000, green coffee 110,400; livestock (number of live animals) 1,000,000 cattle, 550,000 pigs, 19,500,000 chickens; fisheries production 47,500 (from aquaculture 54%). *Mining and quarrying* (2006): limestone 900,000; gold 1,210 kg. *Manufacturing* (value added in US$'000,000; 2003): food products 734; beverages 188; paints, soaps, and pharmaceuticals 169. *Energy production (consumption):* electricity (kW-hr; 2006) 8,697,000,000 (8,786,000,000); coal (metric tons; 2006) none (60,000); crude petroleum (barrels; 2006) none (4,911,000); petroleum products (metric tons; 2006) 637,000 (2,132,000). **Population economically active** (2008): total 2,059,613; activity rate of total population 45.4% (participation rates: ages 12–59 [2005] 60.8%; female [2005] 36.2%; unemployed 4.9%). **Selected balance of payments data.** Receipts from (US$'000,000): tourism (2007) 2,029; remittances (2008) 635; foreign direct investment (FDI; 2005–07 avg.) 1,409; foreign development assistance (2007) 53. Disbursements for (US$'000,000): tourism (2007) 628; remittances (2008) 271; FDI (2005–07 avg.) 106.

Foreign trade

Imports (2005; c.i.f.): US$9,640,100,000 (machinery and apparatus 34.2%; chemical products 11.0%; mineral fuels 10.5%; plastic products 7.0%; fabricated metal products 6.8%). *Major import sources:* US 40.1%; Japan 5.8%; Mexico 5.0%; Venezuela 4.9%; Ireland 4.5%. **Exports** (2005; f.o.b.): US$7,150,690,000 (machinery and apparatus 29.8%; food products 24.8%, of which bananas 6.8%, pineapples 4.6%, coffee 3.7%; professional and scientific equipment 8.1%; textiles 7.5%; chemical products 8.0%). *Major export destinations:* US 40.2%; Hong Kong 6.8%; Netherlands 6.3%; Guatemala 4.0%; Nicaragua 3.9%.

Transport and communications

Transport. *Railroads* (2004): 278 km. *Roads* (2006): total length 35,983 km (paved 25%). *Vehicles* (2004): passenger cars 620,992; trucks and buses 220,456. *Air transport* (2005; Lacsa [Costa Rican Airlines] only): passenger-km 2,284,000,000; metric ton-km cargo 10,351,000. **Communications,** in total units (units per 1,000 persons). Telephone landlines (2008): 1,438,000 (317); cellular telephone subscribers (2008): 1,887,000 (416); personal computers (2005): 1,000,000 (233); total Internet users (2007): 1,500,000 (336); broadband Internet subscribers (2008): 176,000 (39).

Education and health

Educational attainment (2004). Percentage of population ages 5 and over having: no formal schooling/unknown 12.8%; incomplete primary education 23.3%; complete primary 24.5%; incomplete secondary 18.2%; complete secondary 8.5%; higher 12.7%. **Literacy** (2003): total population ages 15 and over literate 96.0%; males literate 95.9%; females literate 96.1%. **Health:** physicians (2004) 6,600 (1 per 644 persons); hospital beds (2003) 5,908 (1 per 714 persons); infant mortality rate per 1,000 live births (2008) 9.0; undernourished population (2003–05) less than 5% of total population.

Military

Paramilitary expenditure as percentage of GDP (2008): 0.7%; per capita expenditure US$43. The army was officially abolished in 1948. Paramilitary (police) forces (November 2008): 9,800.

Background

Christopher Columbus landed in Costa Rica in 1502 in an area inhabited by a number of small, independent Indian tribes. These peoples were not easily dominated, and it took almost 60 years for the Spanish to establish a permanent settlement. Ignored by the Spanish crown because of its lack of mineral wealth, the colony grew slowly. Coffee exports and the construction of a rail line improved its economy in the 19th century. It joined the short-lived Mexican Empire in 1821, was a member of the United Provinces of Central America (1823–38), and adopted a constitution in 1871. In 1890 Costa Ricans held what is considered to be the first free and honest election in Central America, beginning a tradition of democracy for which Costa Rica is renowned. In 1987 then president Óscar Arias Sánchez was awarded the Nobel Peace Prize. In the early 21st century, many Costa Ricans looked to increasingly free trade with the US as a solution to the country's economic woes.

Recent Developments

National elections were held on 7 Feb 2010 in Costa Rica, and the political parties spent 2009 in nominating conventions. On 31 May the opposition Citizen Action Party (PAC) selected Ottón Solís in a closed primary. The governing National Liberation Party (PLN) held an open primary on 7 June. The winner, Laura Chinchilla Miranda, had served in the incumbent government as vice president and minister of justice; she defeated Johnny Araya, former mayor of San José. In the 2010 election, Chinchilla won nearly twice as many votes as her rivals, becoming the first female president in Costa Rican history.

Internet resource: <www.tourism.co.cr>.

Côte d'Ivoire

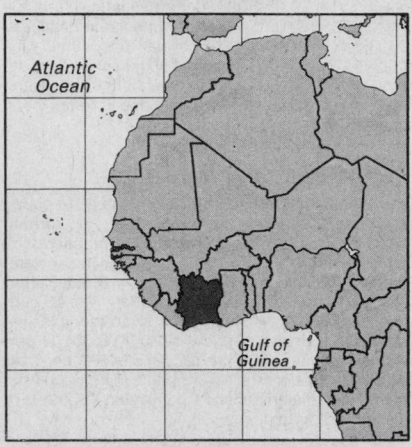

Atlantic Ocean

Gulf of Guinea

Official name: République de Côte d'Ivoire (Republic of Côte d'Ivoire). **Form of government:** transitional regime with one legislative house (National Assembly [225]). **Head of state and government:** President Laurent Gbagbo (from 2000), assisted by Prime Minister Guillaume Soro (from 2007). **Capital:** Abidjan. **Official language:** French. **Official religion:** none. **Monetary unit:** 1 CFA franc (CFAF) = 100 centimes; valuation (1 Jul 2010) US$1 = CFAF 527.20.

Demography

Area: 123,863 sq mi, 320,803 sq km. **Population** (2009): 20,617,000. **Density** (2009): persons per sq mi 166.5, persons per sq km 64.3. **Urban** (2008): 49.0%. **Sex distribution** (2007): male 50.75%; female 49.25%. **Age breakdown** (2007): under 15, 41.2%; 15–29, 29.2%; 30–44, 16.5%; 45–59, 8.4%; 60–74, 3.9%; 75–84, 0.6%; 85 and over, 0.2%. **Ethnolinguistic composition** (1998; local population only [in 1998 foreigners constituted 26% of the population]): Akan 42.1%; Mande 26.5%; other 31.4%. **Religious affiliation** (2005): traditional beliefs 37%; Christian 32%, of which Roman Catholic 17%, Protestant 8%, independent Christian 7%; Muslim 28%; other 3%. **Major cities** (2005): Abidjan (urban agglomeration) 3,576,000; Bouaké 573,700; Daloa 215,100; Yamoussoukro (2003) 185,600; Korhogo (2003) 115,000. **Location:** western Africa, bordering Mali, Burkina Faso, Ghana, the Atlantic Ocean, Liberia, and Guinea.

Vital statistics

Birth rate per 1,000 population (2008): 37.1 (world avg. 20.3). **Death rate** per 1,000 population (2008): 13.6 (world avg. 8.5). **Total fertility rate** (avg. births per childbearing woman; 2007): 4.33. **Life expectancy** at birth (2008): male 50.3 years; female 53.7 years.

National economy

Budget (2005). *Revenue:* CFAF 1,566,000,000,000 (tax revenue 79.9%; nontax revenue 14.1%; grants 6.0%). *Expenditures:* CFAF 1,536,600,000,000 (current expenditures 78.4%; interest on public debt 11.5%; other 10.1%). **Public debt** (external, outstanding; 2006): US$10,830,000,000. **Production** (metric tons except as noted). *Agriculture and fishing* (2007): yams 4,900,000, cassava 2,110,000, plantains 1,590,000, cacao beans 1,300,000, coffee 171,000, cashew nuts 130,000, natural rubber 128,000, fonio 9,700; livestock (number of live animals) 1,523,000 sheep, 1,500,000 cattle; fisheries production 33,416 (from aquaculture 2%). *Mining and quarrying* (2007): gold 1,243 kg; diamonds 300,000 carats. *Manufacturing* (value added in CFAF '000,000,000; 1997): food products 156.6, of which cocoa and chocolate 72.4; chemical products 60.2; wood products 55.9; refined petroleum products 46.0. *Energy production (consumption):* electricity (kW-hr; 2006) 5,510,300 ([2005] 4,181,000,000); crude petroleum (barrels; 2007) 18,800,000 ([2005] 30,000,000); petroleum products (metric tons; 2005) 3,136,000 (974,000); natural gas (cu m; 2005) 1,661,000,000 (1,661,000,000). **Population economically active** (2006): total 6,937,000; activity rate of total population 36.7% (participation rates: ages 15–64, 66.2%; female 30.5%). **Selected balance of payments data.** Receipts from (US$'000,000): tourism (2007) 104; remittances (2008) 215; foreign direct investment (2005–07 avg.) 353; official development assistance (2007) 165. Disbursements for (US$'000,000): tourism (2007) 396; remittances (2008) 19. **Gross national income** (2008): US$20,257,000,000 (US$980 per capita).

Foreign trade

Imports (2005): CFAF 2,687,000,000,000 (machinery and transportation equipment 40.1%; crude petroleum and refined petroleum products 32.3%; food products 17.0%). *Major import sources* (2004): France 24.3%; Nigeria 19.2%; UK 4.0%; China 4.0%; Italy 3.8%. **Exports** (2005): CFAF 3,950,000,000,000 (cacao beans and products 27.5%; crude petroleum and refined petroleum products 26.9%; wood products 3.8%; coffee 2.1%). *Major export destinations* (2004): US 11.6%; Netherlands 10.3%; France 9.5%; Italy 5.5%; Belgium 4.7%.

Transport and communications

Transport. *Railroads* (1999): route length (2004) 660 km; passenger-km 93,100,000; metric ton-km cargo 537,600,000. *Roads* (2004): total length 80,000 km (paved 8%). *Vehicles:* passenger cars (2002) 114,000; trucks and buses (2001) 54,900. *Air transport* (2002; Abidjan airport only): passenger arrivals and departures 821,400; cargo unloaded and loaded 16,699 metric tons. **Communications,** in total units (units per 1,000 persons). Telephone landlines (2008): 357,000 (18); cellular telephone subscribers (2008): 10,449,000 (533); personal computers

(2004): 262,000 (16); total Internet users (2008): 66,000 (34); broadband Internet subscribers (2005): 1,200 (0.07).

Education and health

Educational attainment (1998–99). Percentage of population ages 25 and over having: no formal schooling/unknown 63.0%; primary education 19.4%; secondary 14.3%; higher 3.3%. **Literacy** (2007): percentage of population ages 15 and over literate 55.5%; males literate 65.1%; females literate 45.5%. **Health:** physicians (2004) 2,081 (1 per 8,143 persons); hospital beds (2001) 5,981 (1 per 2,660 persons); infant mortality rate per 1,000 live births (2008) 98.3; undernourished population (2003–05) 2,600,000 (14% of total population based on the consumption of a minimum daily requirement of 1,780 calories).

Military

Total active duty personnel (November 2008): 17,050 (army 38.1%, navy 5.3%, air force 4.1%, presidential guard 7.9%, gendarmerie 44.6%); peacekeeping troops: UN (March 2009): 7,800, French (November 2008): 1,800. **Military expenditure as percentage of GDP** (2007): 1.4%; per capita expenditure US$15.

Background

Europeans came to the area to trade in ivory and slaves beginning in the 15th century, and local kingdoms gave way to French influence in the 19th century. The French colony of Côte d'Ivoire was founded in 1893, and full occupation took place during 1908–18. In 1946 it became a territory in the French Union; in 1947 the northern part of the country separated and became part of Upper Volta (now Burkina Faso). Côte d'Ivoire peacefully achieved autonomy in 1958 and independence in 1960, when Félix Houphouët-Boigny was elected president. The country's first multiparty presidential elections were held in 1990. Political turmoil has persisted since Houphouët-Boigny died in 1993, and a civil war in 2002 left the country divided into northern and southern sections. Attempts at reconciliation were initiated over the following years, including a 2007 power-sharing agreement signed by both sides.

Recent Developments

Seven years after the civil war that divided Côte d'Ivoire in half (the rebel-held north and the government-controlled south), progress was marked by the redeployment of 4,000 police to the north in 2009. In April the IMF agreed to cancel one-quarter of the country's US$12.8 billion national debt, and in May the Paris Club restructured the country's foreign debt and wrote off some of its scheduled loan repayments.

Internet resource: <www.ins.ci>.

Croatia

Official name: Republika Hrvatska (Republic of Croatia). **Form of government:** multiparty republic with one legislative house (Croatian Parliament [153]).

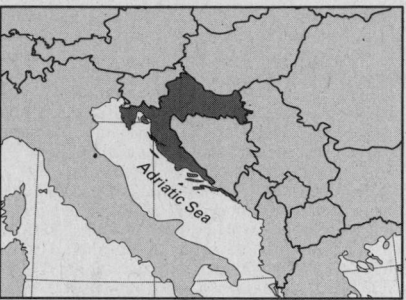

Head of state: President Ivo Josipovic (from 2010). **Head of government:** Prime Minister Jadranka Kosor (from 2009). **Capital:** Zagreb. **Official language:** Croatian. **Official religion:** none (Roman Catholicism receives state financial support through concordats with the Vatican). **Monetary unit:** 1 kuna (kn; plural kune) = 100 lipa; valuation (1 Jul 2010) US$1 = kn 5.78.

Demography

Area: 21,831 sq mi, 56,542 sq km. **Population** (2009): 4,431,000. **Density** (2009): persons per sq mi 203.0, persons per sq km 78.4. **Urban** (2005): 56.5%. **Sex distribution** (2006): male 48.17%; female 51.83%. **Age breakdown** (2004): under 15, 16.1%; 15–29, 20.2%; 30–44, 20.9%; 45–59, 20.7%; 60–74, 15.9%; 75–84, 5.3%; 85 and over, 0.9%. **Ethnic composition** (2001): Croat 89.6%; Serb 4.5%; Bosniac 0.5%; Italian 0.4%; Hungarian 0.4%; other 4.6%. **Religious affiliation** (2001): Christian 92.6%, of which Roman Catholic 87.8%, Eastern Orthodox 4.4%; Muslim 1.3%; nonreligious/atheist 5.2%; other 0.9%. **Major cities** (2001): Zagreb 691,724; Split 175,140; Rijeka 143,800; Osijek 90,411; Zadar 69,556. **Location:** southeastern Europe, bordering Slovenia, Hungary, Serbia, Montenegro, Bosnia and Herzegovina, and the Adriatic Sea.

Vital statistics

Birth rate per 1,000 population (2007): 9.4 (world avg. 20.3); within marriage 88.5%. **Death rate** per 1,000 population (2007): 11.8 (world avg. 8.5). **Total fertility rate** (avg. births per childbearing woman; 2007): 1.40. **Life expectancy** at birth (2007): male 72.3 years; female 79.2 years.

National economy

Budget (2007). *Revenue:* kn 108,321,000,000 (tax revenue 59.3%, of which VAT 35.0%, excise taxes 11.2%; social security contributions 34.3%; nontax revenue 6.0%; grants 0.4%). *Expenditures:* kn 108,008,000,000 (social security and welfare 44.6%; wages and salaries 25.5%; goods and services 4.2%). **Population economically active** (2005): total (1,802,000); activity rate 40.5% (participation rates: ages 15–64, 58.3%; female 45.5%; unemployed [July 2005–June 2006] 12.7%). *Production* (metric tons except as noted). *Agriculture and fishing* (2007): sugar beets 1,582,606, corn (maize) 1,424,599, wheat 950,000, sunflower seeds 54,303; livestock (number of live animals) 1,489,000 pigs, 680,000 sheep, 483,000 cattle; fisheries production (2006) 52,750 (from aquaculture 28%). *Mining and quarrying* (2005): ceramic clay 200,000; ornamental stone 1,000,000 sq m. *Manufacturing* (value added in kn '000,000; 2004): food products and beverages 7,112; refined petroleum products 4,005;· chemical products 2,774. *Energy production (consumption):* electricity (kW-hr; 2007) 12,540,000,000 ([2006] 18,052,000,000); coal (metric tons; 2006) none (1,071,000); crude petroleum (barrels; 2007) 6,710,000 ([2006] 34,300,000); petroleum products (metric tons; 2006) 4,537,000 (4,490,000); natural gas (cu m; 2007) 2,713,000,000 ([2006] 2,802,000,000). **Gross national income** (2008): US$60,192,000,000 (US$13,570 per capita). **Public debt** (external, outstanding; 2007): US$14,212,000,000. **Selected balance of payments data.** Receipts from (US$'000,000): tourism (2007) 9,233; remittances (2008) 1,602; foreign direct investment (FDI; 2004–06 avg.) 2,191; official development assistance (2006) 200. Disbursements for (US$'000,000): tourism (2007) 985; remittances (2008) 110; FDI (2004–06 avg.) 267.

Foreign trade

Imports (2007; c.i.f.): US$23,658,000,000 (basic manufactures 20.0%; mineral fuels 15.0%; chemical products 11.0%; motor vehicles and parts 9.3%). *Major import sources:* Italy 16.3%; Germany 14.4%; Russia 9.9%; China 6.2%; Slovenia 6.0%. **Exports** (2007; f.o.b.): US$11,294,000,000 (basic manufactures 15.7%; mineral fuels 12.7%; ships and boats [particularly tankers] 11.5%; chemical products 9.4%; food products 8.0%). *Major export destinations:* Italy 19.2%; Bosnia and Herzegovina 14.4%; Germany 10.1%; Slovenia 8.3%; Austria 6.2%.

Transport and communications

Transport. *Railroads* (2007): length (2004) 2,726 km; passenger-km 1,611,000,000; metric ton-km cargo 3,574,000,000. *Roads* (2005): total length 28,472 km (paved [2003] 85%). *Vehicles* (2008): passenger cars 1,529,271; trucks and buses 175,455. *Air transport* (2007): passenger-km 1,080,000,000; metric ton-km cargo 2,220,000. **Communications,** in total units (units per 1,000 persons). Telephone landlines (2008): 1,851,000 (407); cellular telephone subscribers (2008): 5,924,000 (1,302); personal computers (2004): 842,000 (191); total Internet users (2008): 2,244,000 (493); broadband Internet subscribers (2008): 525,000 (115).

Education and health

Educational attainment (2001). Percentage of population ages 15 and over having: no formal schooling/unknown 3.5%; incomplete primary education 15.8%; primary 21.7%; secondary 47.1%; postsecondary and higher 11.9%. **Literacy** (2003): population ages 15 and over literate 98.5%; males literate 99.4%; females literate 97.8%. **Health** (2005): physicians 8,216 (1 per 541 persons); hospital beds

24,000 (1 per 185 persons); infant mortality rate per 1,000 live births 5.7; undernourished population (2002–04) 300,000 (7% of total population based on the consumption of a minimum daily requirement of 2,010 calories).

Military

Total active duty personnel (November 2008): 18,600 (army 61.2%, navy 10.0%, air force 18.8%, joint staff 10.0%). **Military expenditure as percentage of GDP** (2008): 1.7%; per capita expenditure US$217.

 **Did you know?** Split, a popular tourist destination on Croatia's Adriatic seacoast, is home to the ruins of the Roman city of Spalato ("little palace"), so called because it was here that the Roman emperor Diocletian (AD 284–305) constructed his palace.

Background

The Croats, a southern Slavic people, arrived in the area in the 7th century AD and in the 8th century came under Charlemagne's rule. They converted to Christianity soon afterward and formed a kingdom in the 10th century. Most of Croatia was taken by the Turks in 1526; the rest voted to accept Austrian rule. In 1867 it became part of Austria-Hungary, with Dalmatia and Istria ruled by Vienna and Croatia-Slavonia a Hungarian crown land. In 1918, after the defeat of Austria-Hungary in World War I, it joined other southern Slavic territories to form the Kingdom of Serbs, Croats, and Slovenes, renamed Yugoslavia in 1929. During World War II an independent state of Croatia was established by Germany and Italy, embracing Croatia-Slavonia, part of Dalmatia, and Bosnia and Herzegovina; after the war Croatia was rejoined to Yugoslavia as a people's republic. It declared its independence in 1991, sparking insurrections by Croatian Serbs, who carved out autonomous regions with Serbian-led Yugoslav army help; Croatia had taken back most of these regions by 1995 and regained full control of its territory in 2002. With some stability returning, Croatia's economy began to revive in the early 21st century. The country joined NATO in 2009.

Recent Developments

Developments in Croatia's accession negotiations with the European Union dominated the political scene in 2009. By midyear Croatia had made progress on only one of the thorny issues hindering its EU accession bid: the reform of its shipbuilding industry. The government in June set out its program for restructuring and privatizing the six state-owned shipyards. The EU accepted the plan and thereby allowed Croatia to open accession talks on competition policy. By October the European Commission had announced that Croatia could complete its accession talks by the end of 2010.

Internet resource: <www.dzs.hr>.

---

1 metric ton = about 1.1 short tons;   1 kilometer = 0.6 mi (statute);   1 metric ton-km cargo = about 0.68 short ton-mi cargo;   c.i.f.: cost, insurance, and freight;   f.o.b.: free on board

Cuba

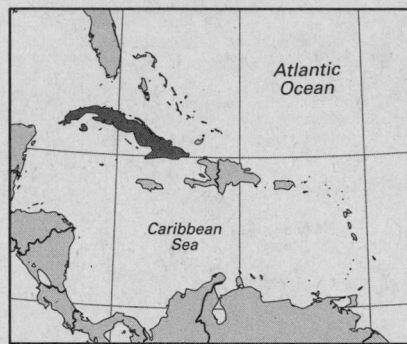

Atlantic
Ocean

Caribbean
Sea

Official name: República de Cuba (Republic of Cuba). **Form of government:** unitary socialist republic with one legislative house (National Assembly of the People's Power [614]). **Head of state and government:** President Raúl Castro Ruz (from 2008). **Capital:** Havana. **Official language:** Spanish. **Official religion:** none. **Monetary unit:** 1 Cuban peso (CUP) = 100 centavos; valuation (1 Jul 2010) US$1 = 22.22 CUP.

Demography

Area: 42,427 sq mi, 109,886 sq km. **Population** (2009): 11,235,000. **Density** (2009): persons per sq mi 264.8, persons per sq km 102.2. **Urban** (2005): 75.5%. **Sex distribution** (2008): male 50.09%; female 49.91%. **Age breakdown** (2005): under 15, 19.2%; 15–29, 20.5%; 30–44, 27.6%; 45–59, 17.0%; 60–74, 10.8%; 75–84, 3.6%; 85 and over, 1.3%. **Ethnic composition** (1994): mixed 51.0%; white 37.0%; black 11.0%; other 1.0%. **Religious affiliation** (2005): Roman Catholic 47%; Protestant 5%; nonreligious 22%; other 26% (as much as 70% of the population also practice Santería). **Major cities** (2006): Havana 2,174,790; Santiago de Cuba 425,990; Camagüey 306,702; Holguín 274,805; Santa Clara 208,739. **Location:** island southeast of Florida (US), between the North Atlantic Ocean and the Caribbean Sea.

Vital statistics

Birth rate per 1,000 population (2008): 10.9 (world avg. 20.3). **Death rate** per 1,000 population (2008): 7.6 (world avg. 8.5). **Total fertility rate** (avg. births per childbearing woman; 2008): 1.50. **Life expectancy** at birth (2005–07): male 76.0 years; female 80.0 years.

National economy

Budget (2008). *Revenue:* CUP 42,055,600,000 (tax revenue 61.5%; nontax revenue 38.5%). *Expenditures:* CUP 46,255,600,000 (current revenue 90.3%, of which education 16.2%, health 15.5%, social security contributions 9.5%, public safety and defense 4.4%; capital expenditures 9.7%). **Public debt** (external, outstanding; 2004): US$12,000,000,000. **Production** (metric tons except as noted). *Agriculture and fishing* (2007): sugarcane 11,100,000, tomatoes 640,000, plan-

tains 540,000, tobacco leaves 30,000; livestock (number of live animals) 3,750,000 cattle, 2,765,000 sheep, 1,765,000 pigs; fisheries production 62,144 (from aquaculture 50%). *Mining and quarrying* (2006): nickel (metal content) 75,000; cobalt (metal content) 4,300. *Manufacturing* (2006): cement 1,713,900; steel 257,- 200; cigarettes (2004) 12,800,000,000 units. *Energy production (consumption):* electricity (kW-hr; 2008) 17,957,100,000 (17,957,100,000); coal (metric tons; 2006) none (11,000); crude petroleum (barrels; 2006) 18,700,000 (39,400,- 000); petroleum products (metric tons; 2006) 1,861,000 (4,527,000); natural gas (cu m; 2006) 1,085,000,000 (1,085,000,000). **Population economically active** (2008): total 5,027,800; activity rate 44.7% (participation rates: ages 15 and over [2004] 52.3%; female 38.0%; unemployed 1.6%). **Gross national income** (2007): US$51,167,000,000 (US$4,541 per capita). **Selected balance of payments data.** Receipts from (US$'000,000): tourism (2007) 2,141; remittances (2003) 1,200; foreign direct investment (2005–07 avg.) 20; official development assistance (2007) 92.

Foreign trade

Imports (2004; c.i.f.): US$5,610,000,000 (food products 18.4%, of which cereals 8.0%; machinery and apparatus 17.5%; refined petroleum products 12.8%; chemical products 9.6%; crude petroleum 9.4%). *Major import sources* (2006): Venezuela 23.5%; China 16.7%; Spain 9.0%; Germany 6.5%; US 5.1%. **Exports** (2004; f.o.b.): US$2,332,000,000 (nickel oxide 45.5%; food products 19.7%, of which raw cane sugar 11.5%; cigars 8.7%; medicine 6.0%). *Major export destinations* (2006): Netherlands 28.0%; Canada 19.8%; Venezuela 10.7%; China 8.9%; Spain 5.4%.

Transport and communications

Transport. *Railroads* (2003; Cuban Railways only): length 4,226 km; (2001) passenger-km 1,766,600; metric ton-km cargo 806,900,000. *Roads* (2000): total length 60,856 km (paved 49%). *Vehicles* (1998): passenger cars 172,574; trucks and buses 185,495. *Air transport* (2003; Cubana airline only): passenger-km 2,044,000,000; metric ton-km cargo 40,933,000. **Communications,** in total units (units per 1,000 persons). Telephone landlines (2008): 1,104,000 (98); cellular telephone subscribers (2008): 332,000 (29); personal computers (2005): 377,000 (33); total Internet users (2008): 1,450,000 (129); broadband Internet subscribers (2007): 1,900 (0.2).

Education and health

Educational attainment (2002): Percentage of population ages 25 and over having: no formal schooling 14.1%; primary education 17.2%; secondary 26.6%; vocational/teacher training 32.8%; university 9.3%. **Literacy** (2004): total population ages 15 and over literate 96.9%; males literate 97.0%; females literate 96.8%. **Health:** physicians (2006) 70,594 (1 per 160 persons); hospital beds (2004) 70,079 (1 per 160 persons); infant mortality rate per 1,000 live births (2008) 4.7; undernourished population (2003–04) less than 5% of total population.

Military

Total active duty personnel (November 2008): 49,000 (army 77.6%, navy 6.1%, air force 16.3%); US military forces at Naval Base Guantanamo Bay (November 2008): 903. **Military expenditure as percentage of GDP** (2005): 3.8%; per capita expenditure US$151.

Background

Several Indian groups, including the Ciboney, the Taino, and the Arawak, inhabited Cuba at the time of the first Spanish contact. Christopher Columbus claimed the island for Spain in 1492, and the Spanish conquest began in 1511, when the settlement of Baracoa was founded. The native Indians were eradicated over the succeeding centuries, and African slaves, from the 18th century until slavery was abolished in 1886, were imported to work the sugar plantations. Cuba revolted unsuccessfully against Spain in the Ten Years' War (1868–78); a second war of independence began in 1895. In 1898 the US entered the war; Spain relinquished its claim to Cuba, which was occupied by the US for three years before gaining its independence in 1902. The US invested heavily in the Cuban sugar industry in the first half of the 20th century, and this, combined with tourism and gambling, caused the economy to prosper. In 1958–59 the communist revolutionary Fidel Castro overthrew Cuba's longtime dictator, Fulgencio Batista, and established a socialist state aligned with the Soviet Union, abolishing capitalism and nationalizing foreign-owned enterprises. Relations with the US deteriorated, reaching a low point with the 1961 Bay of Pigs invasion and the 1962 Cuban missile crisis. In 1980 about 125,000 Cubans, including many that their government officially labeled "undesirables," were shipped to the US in what became known as the "Mariel boatlift." When communism collapsed in the USSR, Cuba lost important financial backing and its economy suffered greatly. In the early 21st century, Cuba benefited from a petroleum-trade agreement with Venezuela and eased some of its restrictive economic and social policies. Castro officially stepped down as president in 2008, ending his 49-year rule of Cuba; his younger brother Raúl replaced him as Cuba's leader.

Recent Developments

US-Cuban relations began to experience a greater degree of openness after Barack Obama was inaugurated as president of the US at the beginning of 2009, the year in which Cuba commemorated the 50th anniversary of the revolution. In April the US repealed all restrictions on the ability of Cuban Americans living in the US to visit Cuba or send money to their relatives there. In June the US joined with the other countries in the Western Hemisphere to approve a path for Cuba's entry into the Organization of American States, though the Castro administration rebuffed the measure. Bilateral migration talks that had broken down in 2003 were restarted, as were negotiations on the resumption of direct postal service between the two countries. Obama did extend the trade embargo in September, however.

Internet resource: <www.one.cu>.

Cyprus

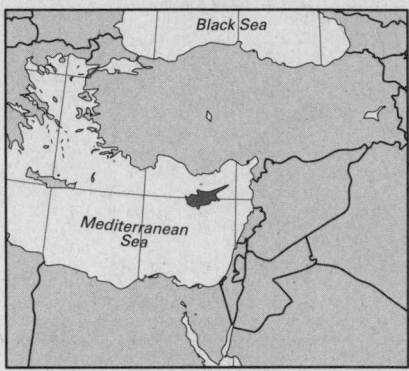

Two de facto states currently exist on the island of Cyprus: the Republic of Cyprus (ROC), predominantly Greek in character, occupying the southern two-thirds of the island, which is the original and still the internationally recognized de jure government of the whole island; and the Turkish Republic of Northern Cyprus (TRNC), proclaimed unilaterally 15 Nov 1983, on territory originally secured for the Turkish Cypriot population by the 20 Jul 1974 intervention of Turkey. Only Turkey recognizes the TRNC, and the two ethnic communities have failed to reestablish a single state. Provision of separate data below does not imply recognition of either state's claims but is necessitated by the lack of unified data.

Area: 3,572 sq mi, 9,251 sq km. **Population** (2009): 1,084,000 (includes 140,000–150,000 immigrants [mostly from Turkey]; excludes 3,050 British military in the Sovereign Base Areas (SBA) in the ROC and 869 UN peacekeeping troops). **Location:** the Middle East, island in the Mediterranean Sea, south of Turkey.

Republic of Cyprus

Official name: Kipriaki Dhimokratia (Greek); Kibris Cumhuriyeti (Turkish) (Republic of Cyprus). **Form of government:** unitary multiparty republic with one legislative house (House of Representatives [80; 24 seats reserved for Turkish Cypriots are not occupied]). **Head of state and government:** President Dimitris Christofias (from 2008). **Capital:** Lefkosia (Nicosia). **Official languages:** Greek; Turkish. **Monetary unit:** 1 euro (€) = 100 cents; valuation (1 Jul 2010) US$1 = €0.80 (the euro replaced the Cyprus pound [£C] on 1 Jan 2008, at the rate of €1 = £C 0.59).

Demography

Area: 2,276 sq mi, 5,896 sq km (includes 99 sq mi [256 sq km] of British military SBAs and 107 sq mi [278 sq km] of the UN Buffer Zone). **Population** (2009): 808,000 (excludes British and UN military forces). **Age breakdown** (2007): under 15, 17.5%; 15–29, 24.0%; 30–44, 21.6%; 45–59, 19.6%; 60–74, 12.2%; 75 and over, 5.1%. **Ethnic composition** (2000): Greek Cypriot 91.8%; Armenian 3.3%;

1 metric ton = about 1.1 short tons;   1 kilometer = 0.6 mi (statute);   1 metric ton-km cargo = about 0.68 short ton-mi cargo;   c.i.f.: cost, insurance, and freight;   f.o.b.: free on board

Arab 2.9%, of which Lebanese 2.5%; British 1.4%; other 0.6%. **Religious affiliation** (2001): Greek Orthodox 94.8%; Roman Catholic 2.1%, of which Maronite 0.6%; Anglican 1.0%; Muslim 0.6%; other 1.5%. **Urban areas** (2007): Lefkosia (ROC only) 231,800; Limassol 183,000; Larnaca 81,700.

Vital statistics

Birth rate per 1,000 population (2007): 10.9 (world avg. 20.3). **Death rate** per 1,000 population (2007): 6.8 (world avg. 8.5). **Total fertility rate** (avg. births per childbearing woman; 2007): 1.39. **Life expectancy** at birth (2006–07): male 78.3 years; female 81.9 years.

National economy

Budget (2005). *Revenue:* £C 3,273,700,000 (excises and import duties 41.4%; income tax 22.3%; social security contributions 19.9%). *Expenditures:* £C 3,459,300,000 (current expenditures 91.3%; development expenditures 8.7%). **Gross national income** (2007): US$19,617,000,000 (US$24,940 per capita). **Production** (metric tons except as noted). *Agriculture and fishing* (2008; island of Cyprus): potatoes 131,695, barley 46,806, oranges 43,910, grapes 35,976, grapefruit 26,900, olives 18,025; livestock (number of live animals) 464,900 pigs, 318,400 goats, 267,300 sheep; fisheries production (2007) 4,950 (from aquaculture 51%). *Manufacturing* (value added in US$'000,000; 2005): food products, beverages, and tobacco products 281; cement, bricks, and ceramics 98; base metals and fabricated metal products 67. *Energy production (consumption):* electricity (kW-hr; 2006) 4,652,000,000 (4,652,000,000). **Selected balance of payments data.** Receipts from (US$'000,000): tourism (2007) 2,687; remittances (2008) 279; foreign direct investment (FDI; 2005–07 avg.) 1,590. Disbursements for (US$'000,000): tourism (2007) 1,479; remittances (2008) 577; FDI (2005–07 avg.) 826.

Foreign trade

Imports (2006; c.i.f.): US$7,046,000,000 (refined petroleum products 17.2%; machinery and apparatus 16.4%; motor vehicles 11.0%; food products 9.2%). *Major import sources:* Greece 17.3%; Italy 11.4%; UK 8.9%; Germany 8.9%; Israel 6.2%. **Exports** (2006; f.o.b.): US$1,414,900,000 (refined petroleum products 18.2%; telecommunications equipment 9.9%; motor vehicles 9.8%; vegetables and fruit 8.9%; medicine 8.6%; cigars and cigarettes 4.5%). *Major export destinations:* UK 14.6%; Greece 13.2%; France 7.4%; Germany 4.5%.

Transport and communications

Transport. *Roads* (2004): total length 12,059 km (paved 65%). *Vehicles* (2007): cars 410,936; trucks and buses 120,790. *Air transport* (2008): passenger-km 3,384,000,000; metric ton-km cargo 46,000,000. **Communications,** in total units (island of Cyprus unless otherwise noted; units per 1,000 persons). Telephone landlines (2008): 413,000 (479); cellular telephone subscribers (2008): 1,017,000 (1,177); personal computers (ROC only; 2001): 210,000 (000); total Internet users (2007): 380,000 (445); broadband Internet subscribers (2008): 104,000 (120).

Education and health

Educational attainment (2008). Percentage of population ages 20 and over having: no formal schooling/incomplete primary education 7%; complete primary 18%; secondary 47%; higher education 28%. **Health** (2006): physicians 1,950 (1 per 395 persons); hospital beds 2,864 (1 per 269 persons); infant mortality rate per 1,000 live births (2007) 3.1.

Military

Total active duty personnel (2008): 10,000 (national guard 100%); Greek troops (2008): 950. **Military expenditure as percentage of GDP** (2007): 2.3%; per capita expenditure US$635.

Turkish Republic of Northern Cyprus

Official name: Kuzey Kibris Turk Cumhuriyeti (Turkish) (Turkish Republic of Northern Cyprus). **Capital:** Lefkosa (Nicosia). **Official language:** Turkish. **Monetary unit:** new Turkish lira (YTL); valuation (1 Jul 2010) US$1 = YTL 1.58. **Population** (2009): 276,000 (includes 140,000–150,000 immigrants [mostly from Turkey]; excludes 3,050 British military in the Sovereign Base Areas (SBA) in the ROC and 869 UN peacekeeping troops) (Lefkosa [2006] 49,237; Magusa [Famagusta] [2006] 34,803; Girne [Kyrenia] [2006] 24,122; Güzelyurt [Morphou] [2006] 12,425). **Sex distribution** (2006): male 53.99%; female 46.01%. **Ethnic composition** (2006): Turkish Cypriot/Turkish 96.8%; other 3.2%. **Birth rate** per 1,000 population (2007): 15.0 (world avg. 20.3). **Death rate** per 1,000 population (2007): 6.8 (world avg. 8.5). **Total fertility rate** (avg. births per childbearing woman; 2007) 1.80. **Budget** (2007). *Revenue:* YTL 1,912,021,000 (indirect taxes 29.4%; direct taxes 20.5%; foreign aid 14.8%). *Expenditures:* YTL 2,125,064,000 (social transfers 39.8%; wages and salaries 35.6%; investments 10.7%; defense 5.6%). **Imports** (2004): US$853,100,000 (machinery and transportation equipment 35.7%; food products 9.4%). *Major import sources:* Turkey 60.1%; UK 10.7%. **Exports** (2004): US$62,000,000 (citrus fruits 32.4%; wearing apparel 18.9%). *Major export destinations:* Turkey 46.3%; UK 21.8%. **Health** (2007): physicians 474 (1 per 529 persons); hospital beds 1,380 (1 per 194 persons); infant mortality rate per 1,000 live births 15.0.

Background

By the late Bronze Age Cyprus had been visited and settled by Mycenaeans and Achaeans, who introduced Greek culture and language, and it became a trading center. By 800 BC Phoenicians had begun to settle there. Ruled over the centuries by the Assyrian, Persian, and Ptolemaic empires, it was annexed by Rome in 58 BC. It was part of the Byzantine Empire in the 4th–12th centuries AD. Cyprus was conquered by the English king Richard I in 1191. A part of the Venetian empire from 1489, it was taken by Ottoman Turks in 1571. In 1878 the British assumed control, and Cyprus became a British crown colony in 1925. It gained independence in 1960. Conflict between Greek and Turkish Cypriots led to the establishment of a UN peacekeeping mission in 1964. In 1974, fearing a movement to unite Cyprus with Greece, Turkish soldiers occupied the northern third of the country, and Turkish Cypriots established a government, which obtained recognition only from Turkey. Conflict has continued to the present, and the UN peacekeeping mission has remained in place. The Republic of Cyprus joined the European Union in 2004 and adopted the euro as its official currency in 2008.

Recent Developments

In 2009 Cyprus remained a divided island, though the open, if controlled, border allowed significant movement of people crossing in both directions. The two Cypriot presidents met in August and September to discuss a range of issues that included power sharing and governance, land tenure arrangements, security, and the future of the Turkish force in Northern Cyprus. The UK offered to hand over half of its sovereign territory in Cyprus to help move negotiations along. UN Secretary-General Ban Ki-moon also visited the island in early 2010 to encourage the process.

Internet resource: <www.visitcyprus.com>.

Czech Republic

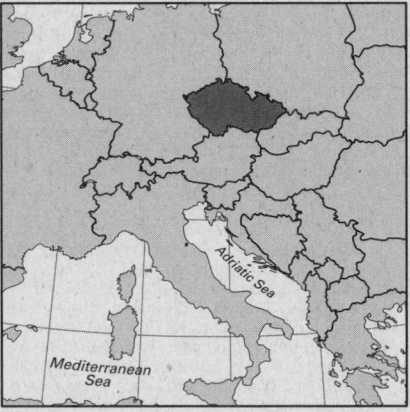

Official name: Ceska Republika (Czech Republic). **Form of government:** unitary multiparty republic with two legislative houses (Senate [81]; Chamber of Deputies [200]). **Head of state:** President Vaclav Klaus (from 2003). **Head of government:** Prime Minister Petr Necas (from 2010). **Capital:** Prague. **Official language:** Czech. **Official religion:** none. **Monetary unit:** 1 koruna (Kc) = 100 haleru; valuation (1 Jul 2010) US$1 = 20.68 Kc.

Demography

Area: 30,451 sq mi, 78,867 sq km. **Population** (2009): 10,504,000. **Density** (2009): persons per sq mi 344.9, persons per sq km 133.2. **Urban** (2003): 74.3%. **Sex distribution** (2006): male 48.83%; female 51.17%. **Age breakdown** (2004): under 15, 14.9%; 15–29, 22.1%; 30–44, 21.3%; 45–59, 22.0%; 60–74, 13.6%; 75–84, 5.2%; 85 and over, 0.9%. **Ethnic composition** (2001): Czech 90.4%;

Moravian 3.7%; Slovak 1.9%; Polish 0.5%; German 0.4%; Silesian 0.1%; Rom (Gypsy) 0.1%; other 2.9%. **Religious affiliation** (2000): Christian 63.0%, of which Roman Catholic 40.4%, unaffiliated Christian 16.0%, Protestant (mostly Lutheran) 3.1%, independent Christian (mostly independent Catholic [Hussite Church of the Czech Republic]) 2.6%; atheist 5.0%; Jewish 0.1%; nonreligious 31.9%. **Major cities** (2008): Prague 1,233,211; Brno 370,592; Ostrava 307,767; Plzen 169,273; Liberec 100,914. **Location:** central Europe, bordering Germany, Poland, Slovakia, and Austria.

Vital statistics

Birth rate per 1,000 population (2008): 11.5 (world avg. 20.3); within marriage 58.6%. **Death rate** per 1,000 population (2008): 10.1 (world avg. 8.5). **Total fertility rate** (avg. births per childbearing woman; 2008): 1.50. **Life expectancy** at birth (2007): male 73.7 years; female 79.9 years.

National economy

Budget (2007). *Revenue:* Kc 1,151,050,000,000 (tax revenue 92.0%, of which social security contributions 45.3%, taxes on goods and services 26.9%, taxes on income and profits 18.8%; grants 4.3%; nontax revenue 3.7%). *Expenditures:* Kc 1,210,270,000,000 (social security and welfare 33.7%; health 16.1%; education 9.4%; transportation and communications 7.0%; defense 3.8%). **Production** (metric tons except as noted). *Agriculture and fishing* (2007): wheat 3,955,437, sugar beets 2,598,676, barley 1,919,712, rapeseed 1,038,400; livestock (number of live animals) 2,741,300 pigs, 1,389,600 cattle; fisheries production 24,723 (from aquaculture 83%). *Mining and quarrying* (2007): kaolin 3,604,000; feldspar 514,000. *Manufacturing* (value added in Kc '000,000; 2003): base and fabricated metals 93,380; food products, beverages, and tobacco products 81,440; electrical and optical equipment 70,800. *Energy production (consumption):* electricity (kW-hr; 2007) 88,187,000,000 ([2006] 71,730,000,000); coal (metric tons; 2007) 12,900,000 ([2005] 9,220,000); lignite (metric tons; 2007) 49,300,000 ([2005] 47,600,000); crude petroleum (barrels; 2006) 2,332,000 (53,800,-000); petroleum products (metric tons; 2006) 5,578,000 (6,761,000); natural gas (cu m; 2007) 223,000,000 ([2006] 10,661,000,000). **Population economically active** (2007): total 5,198,300; activity rate of total population 50.4% (participation rates: ages 15–64, 69.8%; female 43.6%; unemployed 6.0%). **Public debt** (external, outstanding; 2004): US$12,020,000,000. **Gross national income** (2008): US$173,154,000,000 (US$16,600 per capita). **Selected balance of payments data.** Receipts from (US$'000,000): tourism (2007) 6,637; remittances (2008) 1,415; foreign direct investment (FDI; 2005–07 avg.) 8,931. Disbursements for (US$'000,000): tourism (2007) 3,647; remittances (2008) 3,826; FDI (2005–07 avg.) 927.

Foreign trade

Imports (2006; c.i.f.): Kc 2,111,100,000,000 (machinery and apparatus 31.9%; chemical products

10.2%; mineral fuels 9.0%; motor vehicles and parts 8.5%). *Major import sources:* Germany 28.5%; China 6.1%; Russia 6.0%; Poland 5.6%; Slovakia 5.4%. **Exports** (2006; f.o.b.): Kc 2,149,800,000,000 (machinery and apparatus 34.7%, of which computers and office machines and parts 7.8%, general industrial machinery 6.8%; motor vehicles and parts 15.7%; chemical products 5.8%; fabricated metal products 5.5%). *Major export destinations:* Germany 31.9%; Slovakia 8.4%; Poland 5.7%; France 5.5%; Austria 5.1%.

Transport and communications

Transport. *Railroads* (2005): route length (2004) 9,441 km; passenger-km 6,667,000; metric ton-km cargo 14,866,000,000. *Roads* (2006): total length 128,512 km (paved [2004] 100%). *Vehicles* (2005): passenger cars 3,958,708; trucks and buses 435,235. *Air transport* (2008): passenger-km 6,300,000,000; metric ton-km cargo 27,180,000. **Communications,** in total units (units per 1,000 persons). Telephone landlines (2008): 2,278,000 (224); cellular telephone subscribers (2008): 13,780,000 (1,353); personal computers (2004): 5,100,000 (500); total Internet users (2007): 4,400,000 (432); broadband Internet subscribers (2008): 1,760,000 (173).

Education and health

Educational attainment (2001). Percentage of population ages 15 and over having: no formal schooling 0.2%; primary education 21.6%; secondary 68.7%; higher 9.5%. **Literacy** (2001): 99.8%. **Health** (2005): physicians 36,381 (1 per 282 persons); hospital beds 65,022 (1 per 158 persons); infant mortality rate per 1,000 live births (2008) 2.8; undernourished population (2003–05) less than 5% of total population.

Military

Total active duty personnel (November 2008): 24,083 (army 55.5%, air force 20.5%, joint staff 24.0%). **Military expenditure as percentage of GDP** (2008): 1.5%; per capita expenditure US$279.

Background

Until 1918 the history of what is now the Czech Republic was largely that of Bohemia. In that year the independent republic of Czechoslovakia was born through the union of Bohemia and Moravia with Slovakia. Czechoslovakia came under the domination of the Soviet Union after World War II, and from 1948 to 1989 it was ruled by a communist government. Its growing political liberalization was suppressed by a Soviet invasion in 1968. After communist rule collapsed in 1989–90, separatist sentiments emerged among the Slovaks, and in 1992 the Czechs and the Slovaks agreed to break up their federated state. On 1 Jan 1993 the Czechoslovakian republic was peacefully dissolved and replaced by two new countries, the Czech Republic and Slovakia, with the region of Moravia remaining in the former. In 1999 the Czech Republic entered NATO and in 2004 the EU.

Recent Developments

Relations between the Czech Republic and Brussels were damaged not only by the country's political instability during its EU presidency in the first half of 2009 but also by its delay in approving the Lisbon Treaty to reform EU institutions. Pres. Vaclav Klaus initially refused to sign the treaty, even after it was backed by the Czech legislature. He finally backed down in early November, however, allowing the treaty to take effect throughout the EU on 1 December. In relations with the United States, Prague received a much-publicized visit from US Pres. Barack Obama in early April. In September the Obama administration canceled the controversial missile defense shield that was to have been built in the Czech Republic and Poland.

Internet resource: <www.czso.cz>.

Denmark

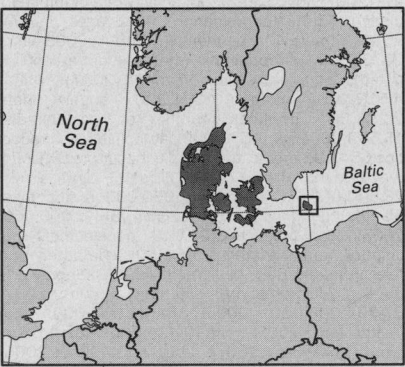

Official name: Kongeriget Danmark (Kingdom of Denmark). **Form of government:** constitutional monarchy with one legislative house (Folketing [179]). **Head of state:** Queen Margrethe II (from 1972). **Head of government:** Prime Minister Lars Løkke Rasmussen (from 2009). **Capital:** Copenhagen. **Official language:** Danish. **Official religion:** Evangelical Lutheran. **Monetary unit:** 1 Danish krone (DKK; plural kroner) = 100 øre; valuation (1 Jul 2010) US$1 = DKK 5.99.

Demography

Area: 16,640 sq mi, 43,098 sq km (excludes the Faroe Islands and Greenland). **Population** (2009): 5,523,000. **Density** (2009): persons per sq mi 331.9, persons per sq km 128.1. **Urban** (2004): 85.4%. **Sex distribution** (2008): male 49.57%; female 50.43%. **Age breakdown** (2006): under 15, 18.6%; 15–29, 17.3%; 30–44, 21.9%; 45–59, 20.2%; 60–74, 15.0%; 75–84, 5.1%; 85 and over, 1.9%. **Ethnic composition** (2006): Danish 91.9%; Turkish 0.6%; German 0.5%; Iraqi 0.4%; Swedish 0.4%; Norwegian 0.3%; Bosnian 0.3%; other 5.6%. **Religious affiliation** (2006): Evangelical Lutheran 83.0%; other Christian 1.3%; Muslim 3.7%; nonreligious 5.4%; atheist 1.5%; other 5.1%. **Major urban areas** (2007): Greater Copenhagen 1,153,615; Århus 237,551; Odense 158,163; Ålborg 121,818; Esbjerg 70,880. **Location:** northern Europe, bordering the North Sea, the Baltic Sea, and Germany.

Vital statistics

Birth rate per 1,000 population (2008): 11.8 (world avg. 20.3); within marriage 53.8%. **Death rate** per 1,000 population (2008): 9.9 (world avg. 8.5). **Total fertility rate** (avg. births per childbearing woman; 2008): 1.89. **Life expectancy** at birth (2007–08): male 76.3 years; female 80.7 years.

National economy

Budget (2007). *Revenue:* DKK 694,084,000,000 (taxes on income and profits 44.4%; taxes on goods and services 39.8%). *Expenditures:* DKK 613,412,000,000 (social protection 35.1%; education 11.4%; economic affairs 5.8%; defense 4.3%; health 0.2%). **National debt** (December 2006): US$57,887,000,000. **Population economically active** (2007): total 2,893,200; activity rate of total population 53.0% (participation rates: ages 15–64, 80.2%; female 47.1%; unemployed [July 2005–June 2006] 5.0%). **Production** (metric tons except as noted). *Agriculture and fishing* (2007): wheat 4,519,200, barley 3,104,200, sugar beets 2,255,300; livestock (number of live animals) 13,599,000 pigs, 1,579,000 cattle; fisheries production 684,191 metric tons (from aquaculture 5%). *Mining and quarrying* (2007): sand and gravel 28,600,000 cu m; chalk 1,950,000 metric tons. *Manufacturing* (value of sales in DKK '000,000; 2005): food products 121,040; nonelectrical machinery and apparatus 66,050; computer and telecommunications equipment 49,078. *Energy production (consumption):* electricity (kW-hr; 2007) 37,394,000,000 ([2006] 38,781,000,000); coal (metric tons; 2006) none (9,436,000); crude petroleum (barrels; 2007) 111,300,000 ([2006] 59,111,000); petroleum products (metric tons; 2006) 7,840,000 (6,800,000); natural gas (cu m; 2006) 10,053,000,000 (4,918,000,000). **Gross national income** (2008): US$325,060,000,000 (US$59,130 per capita). **Selected balance of payments data.** Receipts from (US$'000,000): tourism (2007) 6,218; remittances (2008) 1,087; foreign direct investment (FDI; 2005–07 avg.) 9,243. Disbursements for (US$'000,000): tourism (2007) 8,791; remittances (2008) 3,227; FDI (2005–07 avg.) 13,914.

Foreign trade

Imports (2006; c.i.f.): DKK 502,587,000,000 (machinery and apparatus 25.9%; chemical products 10.8%; food products 9.2%; motor vehicles 8.5%). *Major import sources:* Germany 21.5%; Sweden 14.3%; Netherlands 6.2%; UK 5.8%; China 5.3%. **Exports** (2006; f.o.b.): DKK 535,933,000,000 (machinery and apparatus 23.3%, of which general industrial machinery 6.4%, power-generating machinery 4.5%; food products 16.1%, of which meat 5.6%; crude petroleum 9.3%; medicine and pharmaceuticals 7.3%). *Major export destinations:* Germany 15.5%; Sweden 13.8%; UK 8.4%; US 6.0%; Norway 5.7%.

Transport and communications

Transport. *Railroads* (2004): route length 2,644 km; passenger-km 6,132,000,000; metric ton-km cargo 1,976,000,000. *Roads* (2006): total length 72,362 km (paved 100%). *Vehicles* (2006): passenger cars 2,020,013; trucks and buses 508,788. *Air transport* (2008; Danish share of Scandinavian Airlines System): passenger-km 5,316,000,000; metric ton-km cargo (2007) 8,748,000. **Communications,** in total units (units per 1,000 persons). Telephone landlines (2008): 2,487,000 (456); cellular telephone subscribers (2008): 6,551,000 (1,201); personal computers (2004): 3,543,000 (659); total Internet users (2008): 4,630,000 (849); broadband Internet subscribers (2008): 2,006,000 (369).

Education and health

Educational attainment (2004). Percentage of population ages 25–69 having: completed lower secondary or not stated 30.3%; completed upper secondary or vocational 43.9%; undergraduate 19.6%; graduate 6.2%. **Literacy:** 100%. **Health:** physicians (2004) 19,450 (1 per 278 persons); hospital beds (2005) 20,487 (1 per 265 persons); infant mortality rate per 1,000 live births (2008) 4.0; undernourished population (2003–05) less than 5% of total population.

Military

Total active duty personnel (November 2008): 29,550 (army 48.2%, air force 12.1%, navy 11.8%, joint staff 27.9%). **Military expenditure as percentage of GDP** (2008): 1.3%; per capita expenditure US$746.

Background

The Danes, a Scandinavian branch of the Teutons, settled the area c. the 6th century AD. During the Viking period the Danes expanded their territory, and by the 11th century the united Danish kingdom included parts of what are now Germany, Sweden, England, and Norway. Scandinavia was united under Danish rule from 1397 until 1523, when Sweden became independent; a series of debilitating wars with Sweden in the 17th century resulted in the Treaty of Copenhagen (1660), which established the modern Scandinavian frontiers. Denmark gained and lost various other territories, including Norway, in the 19th and 20th centuries; it went through three constitutions between 1849 and 1915 and was occupied by Nazi Germany in 1940–45. A founding member of NATO (1949), Denmark adopted its current constitution in 1953. It became a member of the European Community in 1973 and of the EU in 1993, but it negotiated exemptions from certain EU provisions in response to some Danes' concerns regarding environmental protection and social welfare.

Recent Developments

Denmark was sharply criticized in 2009 by both the UN High Commissioner for Refugees and Amnesty International for the government's plan to forcibly repatriate rejected Iraqi asylum seekers. In August police ousted about 20 such Iraqis from the crypt of the Copenhagen church where they had been living for three months. Violent clashes broke out between protesters and the police as the Iraqis were arrested and bused to an asylum center, where they faced depor-

---

1 metric ton = about 1.1 short tons;   *1 kilometer = 0.6 mi (statute);*   *1 metric ton-km cargo = about 0.68 short ton-mi cargo;*   *c.i.f.: cost, insurance, and freight;*   *f.o.b.: free on board*

tation. By far the most important event of the year in Denmark was the 15th Conference of the Parties to the UN Framework Convention on Climate Change, or COP15, held in Copenhagen in December. The gathering, which was attended by some 15,000 participants from 170 countries, conducted crucial international negotiations on a successor plan to the Kyoto Protocol on global warming.

Internet resource: <www.dst.dk>.

Djibouti

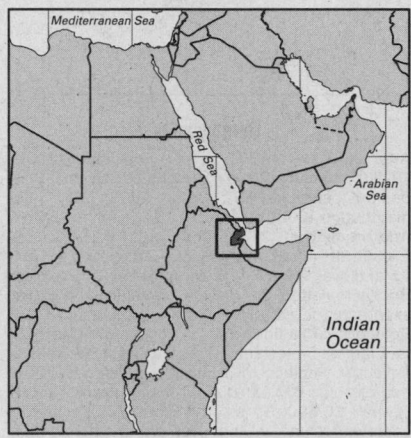

Official name: Jumhuriyah Jibuti (Arabic); République de Djibouti (French) (Republic of Djibouti). **Form of government:** multiparty republic with one legislative house (National Assembly [65]). **Head of state and head of government:** President Ismail Omar Guelleh (from 1999). **Capital:** Djibouti. **Official languages:** Arabic; French. **Official religion:** Islam. **Monetary unit:** 1 Djibouti franc (FDJ) = 100 centimes; valuation (1 Jul 2010) US$1 = FDJ 174.74.

Demography

Area: 8,950 sq mi, 23,200 sq km. **Population** (2009): 864,000. **Density** (2009): persons per sq mi 96.5, persons per sq km 37.2. **Urban** (2007): 86.9%. **Sex distribution** (2006): male 51.19%; female 48.81%. **Age breakdown** (2006): under 15, 43.3%; 15–29, 28.0%; 30–44, 13.7%; 45–59, 9.2%; 60–74, 5.1%; 75 and over, 0.7%. **Ethnic composition** (2000): Somali 46.0%; Afar 35.4%; Arab 11.0%; mixed African and European 3.0%; French 1.6%; other/unspecified 3.0%. **Religious affiliation** (2000): Muslim (nearly all Sunni) 94.1%; Christian 4.5%, of which Orthodox 3.0%, Roman Catholic 1.4%; nonreligious 1.3%; other 0.1%. **Major city and towns** (2009): Djibouti (2007) 583,000; Ali Sabieh 23,000; Dikhil 16,700; Arta 11,600. **Location:** the Horn of Africa, bordering Eritrea, the Red Sea, the Gulf of Aden, Somalia, and Ethiopia.

Vital statistics

Birth rate per 1,000 population (2006): 39.5 (world avg. 20.3). **Death rate** per 1,000 population (2006):

19.3 (world avg. 8.5). **Total fertility rate** (avg. births per childbearing woman; 2006): 5.31. **Life expectancy** at birth (2006): male 41.9 years; female 44.5 years.

National economy

Budget (2005). *Revenue:* FDJ 46,710,000,000 (tax revenue 65.8%, of which indirect taxes 26.3%, direct taxes 24.8%, transit taxes, harbor dues, and other registration fees 14.7%; nontax revenue 17.5%; grants 16.7%). *Expenditures:* FDJ 46,378,000,000 (current expenditures 74.7%; capital expenditures 25.3%). **Public debt** (external, outstanding; February 2006): US$474,000,000. **Production** (metric tons except as noted). *Agriculture and fishing* (2007): lemons and limes 1,800, dry beans 1,500, tomatoes 1,200; livestock (number of live animals) 512,000 goats, 466,000 sheep, 297,000 cattle, 69,000 camels; fisheries production 265 (from aquaculture, none). *Mining and quarrying:* mineral production limited to locally used construction materials such as basalt and evaporated salt (2006) 138,000. *Manufacturing* (2003): products of limited value include furniture, nonalcoholic beverages, meat and hides, light electromechanical goods, and mineral water. *Energy production (consumption):* electricity (kW-hr; 2006) 280,000,000 (280,000,000); petroleum products (metric tons; 2006) none (139,000); natural gas (cu m; 2004) none (4,380,000); geothermal, wind, and solar resources are substantial but largely undeveloped. **Population economically active** (2003): total 299,000; activity rate of total population 39.1% (participation rates: ages 15–64, 69.0%; female 39.5%; unemployed [2006] 60%). **Gross national income** (2008): US$957,000,000 (US$1,030 per capita). **Selected balance of payments data.** Receipts from (US$'000,000): tourism (2006) 9.2; remittances (2008) 29; foreign direct investment (2005–07 avg.) 139; official development assistance (2006) 117. Disbursements for (US$'000,000): tourism (2006) 3.5; remittances (2008) 5.

Foreign trade

Imports (1999; total and commodities data exclude Ethiopian trade via rail): US$152,700,000 (food products and beverages 25.0%; machinery and electric appliances 12.5%; khat 12.2%; refined petroleum products 10.9%; transportation equipment 10.3%). *Major import sources* (2004): Saudi Arabia 21.9%; India 18.7%; China 10.2%; Ethiopia 4.8%; France 4.7%. **Exports** (2001; total and commodities data exclude Ethiopian trade via rail): US$10,200,000 (aircraft parts 24.5%; hides and skins of cattle, sheep, goats, and camels 20.6%; leather products 7.8%; live animals 6.9%). *Major export destinations* (2005): Somalia 66.4%; Ethiopia 21.5%; Yemen 3.4%.

Transport and communications

Transport. *Railroads* (2006): length 100 km; (1999) passenger-km 81,000,000; (2002) metric ton-km cargo 201,000,000. *Roads* (2002): total length 2,890 km (paved 13%). *Vehicles* (2002): passenger cars 15,700; trucks and buses 3,200. *Air transport* (2005): passenger arrivals and departures 219,119; metric tons of freight loaded and unloaded 10,473. **Communications,** in total units (units per 1,000 persons). Telephone landlines (2005): 11,000 (23); cellular telephone subscribers (2007): 45,000 (54); personal computers (2005): 19,000 (41); total Internet users (2006): 11,000 (23); broadband Internet subscribers (2005): 40 (0.09).

Education and health

Literacy (2007): percentage of population ages 15 and over literate 72.2%; males literate 81.2%; females literate 63.8%. **Health:** physicians (2004) 129 (1 per 3,619 persons); hospital beds (2000) 694 (1 per 621 persons); infant mortality rate per 1,000 live births (2006) 102.4; undernourished population (2002–04) 200,000 (24% of total population based on the consumption of a minimum daily requirement of 1,770 calories).

Military

Total active duty personnel (November 2008): 10,450 (army 76.6%, navy 1.9%, air force 2.4%, national security force 19.1%); foreign troops (November 2008): French Foreign Legion 2,850; US 1,900; German 100. **Military expenditure as percentage of GDP** (2007): 1.9%; per capita expenditure US$20.

Background

Settled around the 3rd century BC by the Arab ancestors of the Afars, Djibouti was later populated by Somali Issas. In AD 825 Islam was brought to the area by missionaries. Arabs controlled the trade in this region until the 16th century; it became the French protectorate of French Somaliland in 1888. In 1946 it became a French overseas territory, and in 1977 it gained its independence. In the late 20th century, the country received refugees from the Ethiopian-Somali war and from civil conflicts in Eritrea. In the 1990s it suffered from political unrest.

Recent Developments

Djibouti partnered with the European Union and with Japan in 2009 to help combat the increasingly serious problem of piracy in the waters off of the Horn of Africa. The EU force, the Atalanta mission, was mandated by the UN World Food Programme to protect food-aid shipments into Somalia; under it, roughly 1,200 EU forces would be based in Djibouti. Food prices on the continent had spiked, owing in large part to pirate attacks on these aid ships.

Internet resource: <www.ministere-finances.dj>.

Dominica

Official name: Commonwealth of Dominica. **Form of government:** multiparty republic with one legislative house (House of Assembly [32]). **Head of state:** President Nicholas Liverpool (from 2003). **Head of government:** Prime Minister Roosevelt Skerrit (from 2004). **Capital:** Roseau. **Official language:** English. **Official religion:** none. **Monetary unit:** 1 East Caribbean dollar (EC$) = 100 cents; valuation (1 Jul 2010) US$1 = EC$2.68.

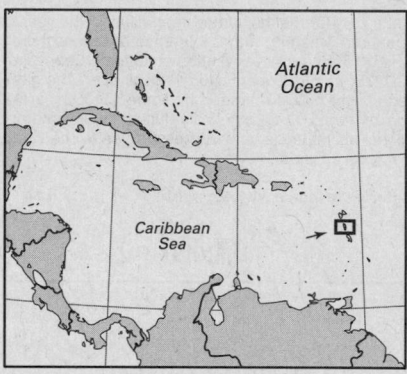

Demography

Area: 290 sq mi, 751 sq km. **Population** (2009): 71,900. **Density** (2009): persons per sq mi 247.9, persons per sq km 95.7. **Urban** (2003): 72.0%. **Sex distribution** (2006): male 50.34%; female 49.66%. **Age breakdown** (2006): under 15, 26.1%; 15–29, 23.8%; 30–44, 27.4%; 45–59, 12.4%; 60–74, 7.0%; 75 and over, 3.3%. **Ethnic composition** (2000): black 88.3%; mulatto 7.3%; black-Amerindian 1.7%; British expatriates 1.0%; Indo-Pakistani 1.0%; other 0.7%. **Religious affiliation** (2001): Roman Catholic 61%; four largest Protestant groups (including Seventh-day Adventist, Pentecostal groups, and Methodist) 28%; nonreligious 6%; other 5%. **Major towns** (2006): Roseau 16,600; Portsmouth 3,600; Marigot 2,900. **Location:** island in the southern Caribbean Sea, south of Guadeloupe and north of Martinique.

Vital statistics

Birth rate per 1,000 population (2006): 15.3 (world avg. 20.3); (1991) within marriage 24.1%. **Death rate** per 1,000 population (2006): 6.7 (world avg. 8.5). **Total fertility rate** (avg. births per childbearing woman; 2006): 1.94. **Life expectancy** at birth (2006): male 72.0 years; female 77.9 years.

National economy

Budget (2008). *Revenue:* EC$467,600,000 (tax revenue 65.7%, of which VAT 24.4%, taxes on international trade and transactions 14.7%, taxes on income and profits 11.1%; grants 27.8%; nontax revenue 6.5%). *Expenditures:* EC$458,300,000 (current expenditures 66.2%, of which wages and salaries 26.2%, transfers 13.9%, debt service 7.2%; development expenditures and net lending 33.8%). **Public debt** (external, outstanding; 2005): US$208,400,000. **Gross national income** (2007): US$310,000,000 (US$4,250 per capita). **Population economically active** (2001): total 27,865; activity rate of total population 40.0% (participation rates: ages 15–64, 64.7%; female 38.9%; unemployed [2002] 25%). **Production** (metric tons except as noted). *Agriculture and fishing* (2007): bananas 30,000, grapefruit and pomelos 17,000, coconuts 12,000; livestock (number of live animals) 13,500 cattle, 9,700 goats, 7,600 sheep; fisheries produc-

1 metric ton = about 1.1 short tons; 1 kilometer = 0.6 mi (statute); 1 metric ton-km cargo = about 0.68 short ton-mi cargo; c.i.f.: cost, insurance, and freight; f.o.b.: free on board

tion 776 (from aquaculture, negligible). *Mining and quarrying:* pumice, limestone, and sand and gravel are quarried primarily for local consumption. *Manufacturing* (value of production in EC$'000; 2004): toilet and laundry soap 24,588; toothpaste 8,774; crude coconut oil (2001) 1,758; other products include fruit juices, beer, garments, bottled spring water, and cardboard boxes. *Energy production (consumption):* electricity (kW-hr; 2006) 85,000,-000 (85,000,000); petroleum products (metric tons; 2006) none (38,000). **Selected balance of payments data.** Receipts from (US$'000,000): tourism (2007) 71; remittances (2008) 30; foreign direct investment (2005–07 avg.) 31; official development assistance (2007) 19. Disbursements for (US$'000,000): tourism (2007) 10; remittances (2008) negligible.

Foreign trade

Imports (2006; c.i.f.): US$166,900,000 (machinery and apparatus 17.1%; food products 15.5%; refined petroleum products 14.2%; chemical products 12.2%; motor vehicles 5.9%). *Major import sources:* US 36.1%; Trinidad and Tobago 22.1%; UK 5.8%; Japan 4.0%; China 3.9%. **Exports** (2006; f.o.b.): US$41,500,000 (food products 32.8%, of which bananas 21.2%; soap 25.3%; dental and oral hygiene preparations 13.5%; stone, sand, and gravel 6.7%). *Major export destinations:* UK 18.6%; Jamaica 15.2%; Antigua and Barbuda 13.0%; France (including overseas departments) 8.2%; Trinidad and Tobago 7.5%.

Transport and communications

Transport. *Railroads:* none. *Roads* (1999): total length 780 km (paved 50%). *Vehicles* (1998): passenger cars 8,700; trucks and buses 3,400. *Air transport* (1997): passenger arrivals and departures 74,100; cargo unloaded 575 metric tons, cargo loaded 363 metric tons. **Communications,** in total units (units per 1,000 persons). Telephone landlines (2004): 21,000 (295); cellular telephone subscribers (2004): 42,000 (589); personal computers (2004): 13,000 (182); total Internet users (2005): 26,000 (372); broadband Internet subscribers (2004): 3,300 (46).

Education and health

Educational attainment (2002). Percentage of population ages 15 and over having: primary education 62%; secondary 31%; vocational/university 7%. **Literacy** (1996): total population ages 15 and over literate, 94.0%. **Health:** physicians (2004) 38 (1 per 1,824 persons); hospital beds (2002) 270 (1 per 257 persons); infant mortality rate per 1,000 live births (2006) 13.7; undernourished population (2003–05) less than 5% of total population.

Military

Total active duty personnel (2006): none (a 300-member police force includes a coast guard unit).

Background

At the time of the arrival of Christopher Columbus in 1493, Dominica was inhabited by the Caribs. With its steep coastal cliffs and inaccessible mountains, it was one of the last islands to be explored by Europeans, and the Caribs remained in possession until the 18th century; it was then settled by the French and ultimately taken by Britain in 1783. Subsequent hostilities between the settlers and the native inhabitants resulted in the Caribs' near extinction. Incorporated with the Leeward Islands in 1883 and with the Windward Islands in 1940, it became a member of the West Indies Federation in 1958. Dominica became independent in 1978.

Recent Developments

For several years Dominica had voted alongside Japan to overturn the International Whaling Commission's ban on commercial whale hunting—which caused critics to suggest that Japan was "buying" its vote with aid. In March 2009, however, Prime Minister Roosevelt Skerrit announced that Dominica would no longer support Japan's efforts to reestablish commercial whaling.

Internet resource: <www.dominica.gov.dm>.

Dominican Republic

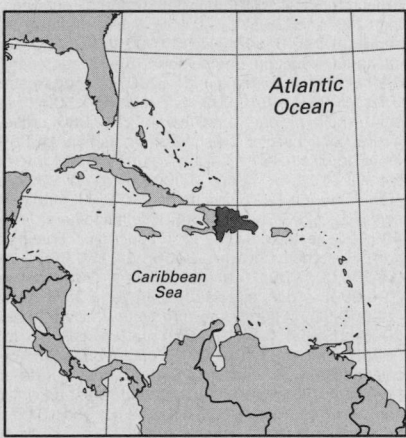

Official name: República Dominicana (Dominican Republic). **Form of government:** multiparty republic with two legislative houses (Senate [32]; Chamber of Deputies [183]). **Head of state and government:** President Leonel Fernández Reyna (from 2004). **Capital:** Santo Domingo. **Official language:** Spanish. **Official religion:** none (Roman Catholicism is the state religion per concordat with Vatican City). **Monetary unit:** 1 Dominican peso (RD$) = 100 centavos; valuation (1 Jul 2010) US$1 = RD$36.90.

Demography

Area: 18,792 sq mi, 48,671 sq km. **Population** (2009): 9,749,000. **Density** (2009): persons per sq mi 518.8, persons per sq km 200.3. **Urban** (2005): 66.8%. **Sex distribution** (2005): male 50.18%; female 49.82%. **Age breakdown** (2003): under 15, 33.5%; 15–29, 26.6%; 30–44, 20.2%; 45–59, 11.7%; 60–74, 5.9%; 75–84, 1.6%; 85 and over, 0.5%. **Ethnic composition** (2003): mulatto 73%;

white 16%; black 11%. **Religious affiliation** (2004): Roman Catholic 64.4%; other Christian 11.4%; non-religious 22.5%; other 1.7%. **Major urban centers** (2002): Santo Domingo 1,887,586; Santiago 507,418; San Pedro de Macorís 193,713; La Romana 191,303; San Cristóbal 137,422. **Location:** eastern two-thirds of the island of Hispaniola, bordered by the North Atlantic Ocean, the Caribbean Sea, and Haiti.

Vital statistics

Birth rate per 1,000 population (2007): 20.4 (world avg. 20.3). **Death rate** per 1,000 population (2007): 3.6 (world avg. 8.5). **Total fertility rate** (avg. births per childbearing woman; 2006): 2.83. **Life expectancy** at birth (2006): male 71.0 years; female 74.5 years.

National economy

Budget (2005). *Revenue:* RD$157,585,000,000 (tax revenue 94.2%, of which taxes on goods and services 49.0%, import duties 24.0%, income taxes 18.8%; nontax revenue 5.8%). *Expenditures:* RD$161,612,-000,000 (current expenditures 75.7%; development expenditures 24.3%). **Public debt** (external, outstanding; 2006): US$6,571,000,000. **Gross national income** (2008): US$43,207,000,000 (US$4,390 per capita). **Production** (metric tons except as noted). *Agriculture and fishing* (2007): sugarcane 5,700,000, rice 710,000, bananas 552,500; livestock (number of live animals) 2,210,000 cattle, 47,500,000 chickens; fisheries production 14,689 (from aquaculture 7%). *Mining* (2007): nickel (metal content) 47,125; marble 6,000 cu m; gold, none. *Manufacturing* (2005): cement 2,779,000; refined sugar 139,203; beer 4,541,000 hectoliters; rum 499,000 hectoliters. *Energy production (consumption):* electricity (kW-hr; 2006) 14,150,000,000 (14,150,000,000); coal (metric tons; 2006) none (704,000); crude petroleum (barrels; 2006) none (14,800,000); petroleum products (metric tons; 2006) 1,936,000 (5,190,000); natural gas (cu m; 2006) none (331,400,000). **Population economically active** (2007): total 4,204,800; activity rate of total population 45.2% (participation rates: ages 15 and over, 64.3%; female 38.7%; unemployed 10.0%). **Selected balance of payments data.** Receipts from (US$'000,000): tourism (2007) 4,082; remittances (2008) 3,487; foreign direct investment (2005–07 avg.) 1,427; official development assistance (2007) 128. Disbursements for (US$'000,000): tourism (2007) 326; remittances (2008) 28.

Foreign trade

Imports (2006): US$8,745,000,000 (consumer goods 50.7%, of which refined petroleum products 21.0%, food products 5.8%; capital goods 15.4%; crude petroleum 10.9%). *Major import sources* (2005): US 50.0%; Colombia 6.2%; Mexico 5.8%. **Exports** (2006): US$6,440,000,000 (reexports of free zones 70.0%, of which wearing apparel 24.8%, electronics 10.3%, jewelry 9.8%; ferronickel 11.0%; mineral fuels 5.6%; raw sugar 1.6%). *Major export destinations* (2005): US 78.9%; Netherlands 2.4%; Mexico 1.9%.

Transport and communications

Transport. *Railroads* (2004): route length 615 km. *Roads* (2002): total length 19,705 km (paved 51%). *Vehicles* (2008): passenger cars 630,815; trucks and buses 383,869. *Air transport:* (1999) passenger-km 4,900,000; (2003) metric ton-km cargo 200,000. **Communications,** in total units (units per 1,000 persons). Telephone landlines (2008): 986,000 (100); cellular telephone subscribers (2008): 7,211,000 (728); personal computers (2007): 331,000 (35); total Internet users (2008): 2,563,000 (259); broadband Internet subscribers (2008): 226,000 (23).

Education and health

Educational attainment (2002). Percentage of population ages 25 and older having: no formal education/unknown 4.1%; incomplete/complete primary education 53.1%; secondary 25.9%; undergraduate 15.9%; graduate 1.0%. **Literacy** (2003): total population ages 15 and over literate 84.7%. **Health** (2005): physicians (public sector only) 12,966 (1 per 730 persons); hospital beds 9,640 (1 per 982 persons); infant mortality rate per 1,000 live births (2006) 29.0; undernourished population (2003–05) 2,000,000 (21% of total population based on the consumption of a minimum daily requirement of 1,840 calories).

Military

Total active duty personnel (November 2008): 49,910 (army 81.0%, navy 8.0%, air force 11.0%). **Military expenditure as percentage of GDP** (2008): 0.6%; per capita expenditure US$30.

Background

The Dominican Republic was originally part of the Spanish colony of Hispaniola. In 1697 the western third of the island, which later became Haiti, was ceded to France; the remainder of the island passed to France in 1795. The eastern two-thirds of the island was returned to Spain in 1809, and the colony declared its independence in 1821. Within a matter of weeks it was overrun by Haitian troops and occupied until 1844. Since then the country has been under the rule of a succession of dictators, except for short interludes of democratic government, and the US has frequently been involved in its affairs. The termination of the dictatorship of Rafael Trujillo in 1961 led to civil war in 1965 and US military intervention. The country frequently suffered from severe hurricanes, as in 1979 and 1998.

Recent Developments

For a country whose economy was heavily dependent on trade with the US, remittances from the US, nickel mining, tourism, and duty-free industrial zones, the Dominican Republic weathered the financial storms of 2009 better than expected. Economic indicators declined significantly when contrasted with previous years, but at the end of 2009, GDP had grown a surprising 6.5%. Inflation closed out the year at 5.8%,

---

1 metric ton = about 1.1 short tons;   1 kilometer = 0.6 mi (statute);   1 metric ton-km cargo = about 0.68 short ton-mi cargo;   c.i.f.: cost, insurance, and freight;   f.o.b.: free on board

and tourism numbers were resilient, with figures similar to those in 2007. Government commitments to tackle endemic corruption, the erosion of educational standards, increasing drug addiction, and lingering extreme poverty rang hollow. A low minimum daily wage of US$2.52—which was lower by 10 cents than that of Nicaragua, the second poorest country in the Western Hemisphere—exacerbated existing labor tensions.

Internet resource:
<www.godominicanrepublic.com>.

East Timor (Timor-Leste)

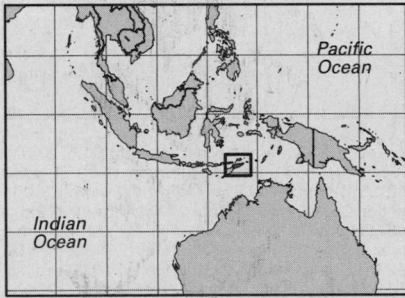

Official name: República Democrática de Timor-Leste (Portuguese); Republika Demokratika Timor Lorosa'e (Tetum); (Democratic Republic of Timor-Leste [East Timor]). **Form of government:** republic with one legislative house (National Parliament [65]). **Head of State:** President José Ramos-Horta (from 2007). **Head of government:** Prime Minister Xanana Gusmão (from 2007). **Capital:** Dili. **Official languages:** Portuguese; Tetum. **Official religion:** none. **Monetary unit:** 1 US dollar (US$) = 100 centavos.

Demography

Area: 5,760 sq mi, 14,919 sq km. **Population** (2009): 1,110,000. **Density** (2009): persons per sq mi 192.7, persons per sq km 74.4. **Urban** (2005): 7.8%. **Sex distribution** (2008): male 50.79%; female 49.21%. **Age breakdown** (2008): under 15, 45.0%; 15–29, 25.3%; 30–44, 15.1%; 45–59, 9.6%; 60–74, 4.0%; 75 and over, 1.0%. **Ethnic composition** (1999): East Timorese 80%; other (nearly all Indonesian, and particularly West Timorese) 20%. **Religious affiliation** (2005): Roman Catholic 98%; Protestant 1%; Muslim 1%. **Major urban areas** (2004): Dili 151,026; Los Palos (Lospalos) 12,612; Same 9,966. **Location:** southeast Asia, eastern end of the island of Timor plus an exclave on the western end, bordered by the Timor Sea and Indonesia.

Vital statistics

Birth rate per 1,000 population (2008): 40.9 (world avg. 20.3). **Death rate** per 1,000 population (2008): 10.0 (world avg. 8.5). **Total fertility rate** (avg. births per childbearing woman; 2008): 6.50. **Life expectancy** at birth (2006): male 64.0 years; female 68.7 years.

National economy

Budget (2005–06). *Revenue:* US$485,000,000 (oil and gas revenue 93.1%, of which taxes 74.8%, royalties 15.5%; domestic revenue 6.9%). *Expenditures:* US$93,000,000 (current expenditures 71.3%; capital expenditures 16.9%; previous year spending 11.8%). **Production** (metric tons except as noted). *Agriculture and fishing* (2007): corn (maize) 63,430, cassava 49,720, rice 41,386, coffee 14,000, candlenut (2001) 1,063, cinnamon 75; livestock (number of live animals) 346,000 pigs, 171,000 cattle, 110,000 buffalo; sandalwood exports were formerly more significant; fisheries production 350 (from aquaculture, none). *Mining and quarrying* (2006): commercial quantities of marble are exported. *Manufacturing* (2001): principally the production of textiles, garments, handicrafts, bottled water, and processed coffee. *Energy production (consumption):* electricity (kW-hr; 2006) 320,000,000 (320,000,000); crude petroleum (barrels; 2006) 1,142,000 (negligible); petroleum products (metric tons; 2006) 6,735,000 (97,000). **Population economically active** (2006): total 427,000; activity rate of total population 38% (participation rates: ages 15–64, 71%; female 40%; unemployed [2000] 50%). **Gross national income** (2008): US$2,706,000,000 (US$2,460 per capita). **Selected balance of payments data.** Receipts from (US$'000,000): foreign direct investment (2005–07 avg.) 1; official development assistance (2007) 278.

Foreign trade

Imports (2008): US$268,583,000 (mineral fuels 26.5%; motor vehicles 16.3%; cereals 9.5%; electrical equipment 6.5%; machinery and apparatus 6.5%). *Major import sources:* Indonesia 42.5%; Singapore 17.1%; Australia 13.8%; Vietnam 7.0%; Japan 4.5%. **Exports** (2008): US$49,206,000 (domestic exports 26.2%, of which coffee 25.7%; reexports 73.8%). *Major export destinations* (excluding reexports): Germany 26.9%; US 26.8%; Indonesia 16.6%; Singapore 10.0%; Portugal 6.4%.

 Sandalwood trees, the wood and fragrant oils of which are popular in carpentry and for perfumes and soaps, have historically been one of the primary sources of wealth to the country of East Timor.

Transport and communications

Transport. *Railroads:* none. *Roads* (2005): total length 5,000 km (paved 50%). *Vehicles* (1998): passenger cars 3,156; trucks and buses 7,140. **Communications,** in total units (units per 1,000 persons). Telephone landlines (2003): 2,000 (2.4); cellular telephone subscribers (2007): 69,000 (60); total Internet users (2004): 1,000 (1.1).

Education and health

Educational attainment (2002). Percentage of population ages 15 and over having no formal education 54.3%, some primary education 14.4%, complete primary 6.2%, lower secondary 10.4%, upper secondary and higher 14.7%. **Literacy** (2005): percentage of population ages 15 and over literate 49%; males literate 54%; females literate 45%. **Health** (2008): physicians 347 (1 per 3,107 persons); hospital beds (1999) 560 (1 per 1,277 persons); infant mortality rate per 1,000 live births 83.5.

Military

Total active duty personnel (November 2008): 1,286 (army 97%, navy 3%); foreign peacekeeping troops (March 2009): Australian 650; New Zealander 140.

Background

The Portuguese first settled on the island of Timor in 1520 and were granted rule over Timor's eastern half in 1860. The Timorese political party Fretilin declared East Timor independent in 1975 after Portugal withdrew its troops. It was invaded by Indonesian forces and was incorporated as a province of Indonesia in 1976. The takeover, which resulted in thousands of East Timorese deaths during the next two decades, was disputed by the UN. In 1999 an independence referendum won overwhelmingly; civilian militias, armed by the military and led by local supporters of integration, then rampaged through the province, killing 1,000–2,000 people. The Indonesian parliament rescinded Indonesia's annexation of the territory, and East Timor was returned to its preannexation status as a non-self-governing territory, though this time under UN supervision. Preparation for independence got under way in 2001, with East Timorese voting by universal suffrage in August for a Constituent Assembly of 88 members. Independence was officially declared on 20 May 2002 and was followed by the swearing in of Xanana Gusmão as the first president of the country.

Recent Developments

East Timor celebrated 10 years of independence in 2009 with an international bicycle ride, Tour de Timor, which was designed to show the world that Dili was safe and had returned to normal life after the attempted assassination in 2008 of Pres. José Ramos-Horta. It was underscored that East Timor had one of the lowest per capita crime rates in the world.

Internet resource: <http://dne.mof.gov.tl>.

Ecuador

Official name: República del Ecuador (Republic of Ecuador). **Form of government:** unitary multiparty republic with one legislative house (National Assembly [124]). **Head of state and government:** President Rafael Correa Delgado (from 2007). **Capital:** Quito. **Official language:** Spanish (Quechua and Shuar are also official languages for the indigenous peoples). **Official religion:** none. **Monetary unit:** 1 US dollar (US$) = 100 centavos.

Demography

Area: 105,037 sq mi, 272,045 sq km. **Population** (2009): 14,005,000. **Density** (2009): persons per

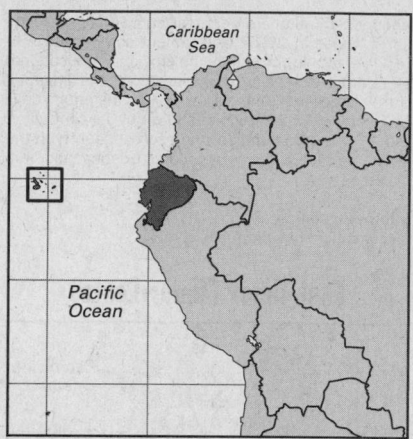

sq mi 133.3, persons per sq km 51.5. **Urban** (2005): 62.8%. **Sex distribution** (2005): male 50.15%; female 49.85%. **Age breakdown** (2005): under 15, 32.6%; 15–29, 27.4%; 30–44, 19.5%; 45–59, 12.1%; 60–74, 6.1%; 75–84, 1.8%; 85 and over, 0.5%. **Ethnic composition** (2000): mestizo 42.0%; Amerindian 40.8%; white 10.6%; black 5.0%; other 1.6%. **Religious affiliation** (2005): Roman Catholic (practicing) 35%; Roman Catholic (non-practicing) 50%; other (significantly Evangelical Protestant) 15%. **Major cities** (2003): Guayaquil (urban agglomeration; 2005) 2,387,000; Quito (urban agglomeration; 2005) 1,514,000; Cuenca 303,994; Machala 217,266; Santo Domingo de los Colorados 211,689. **Location:** northwestern South America, bordering Colombia, Peru, and the Pacific Ocean.

Vital statistics

Birth rate per 1,000 population (2008): 14.9 (world avg. 20.3). **Death rate** per 1,000 population (2008): 4.3 (world avg. 8.5). **Total fertility rate** (avg. births per childbearing woman; 2005): 2.70. **Life expectancy** at birth (2005): male 71.7 years; female 77.6 years.

National economy

Budget (2006). *Revenue:* US$6,895,000,000 (nonpetroleum revenue 75.1%, of which VAT 32.3%, income tax 15.5%, customs duties 9.0%; petroleum export revenue 24.9%). *Expenditures:* US$7,011,000,000 (current expenditures 76.2%; capital expenditures 23.8%). **Production** (metric tons except as noted). *Agriculture and fishing* (2007): sugarcane 7,300,000, bananas 6,130,000, oil palm fruit 2,100,000, plantains 590,000, pyrethrum and dried flowers (2004) 105; livestock (live animals) 5,050,000 cattle, 1,300,000 pigs, 1,050,000 sheep; fisheries production 554,745 (from aquaculture 31%). *Mining and quarrying* (2007): limestone 5,374,000; gold 3,186 kg. *Manufacturing* (value added in US$'000,000; 2004): refined petroleum products 1,794; food products 870; beverages 845. *Energy production (consumption):* electricity (kW-hr;

---

1 metric ton = about 1.1 short tons;   *1 kilometer = 0.6 mi (statute);*   *1 metric ton-km cargo = about 0.68 short ton-mi cargo;*   *c.i.f.: cost, insurance, and freight;*   *f.o.b.: free on board*

2006) 14,814,000,000 (16,383,000,000); crude petroleum (barrels; 2007) 187,000,000 ([2006] 55,500,000); petroleum products (metric tons; 2006) 7,453,000 (8,218,000); natural gas (cu m; 2006) 687,000,000 (687,000,000). **Population economically active** (2006): total 4,204,800; activity rate of total population 45.2% (participation rates: ages 15–64, 69.6%; female 38.7%; unemployed [March 2006–February 2007] 10.1%). **Public debt** (external, outstanding; December 2006): US$10,108,000,000. **Gross national income** (2008): US$49,105,000,000 (US$3,640 per capita). **Selected balance of payments data.** Receipts from (US$'000,000): tourism (2007) 623; remittances (2008) 3,200; foreign direct investment (2005–07 avg.) 314; official development assistance (2007) 215. Disbursements for (US$'000,000): tourism (2007) 504; remittances (2008) 83.

Foreign trade

Imports (2006; c.i.f.): US$12,114,000,000 (mineral fuels 21.1%; machinery and apparatus 20.0%; chemical products 15.3%; motor vehicles and parts 11.5%; iron and steel 6.0%). *Major import sources* (2008): US 19.0%; Colombia 9.6%; Brazil 4.8%; Japan 3.6%; Mexico 3.5%. **Exports** (2006; f.o.b.): US$12,728,000,000 (crude petroleum 54.5%; bananas and plantains 9.5%; fish 5.4%; shrimp 4.6%; refined petroleum products 3.9%; cut flowers 3.4%). *Major export destinations* (2008): US 45.3%; Peru 9.2%; Chile 8.2%; Colombia 4.2%; Venezuela 3.8%.

Transport and communications

Transport. *Railroads* (2006): route length (2005) 965 km; passenger-km 4,000,000; metric ton-km cargo 2,000. *Roads* (2006): total length 43,670 km (paved 15%). *Vehicles* (2006): passenger cars 519,041; trucks and buses 357,514. *Air transport* (2005): passenger-km 867,100,000; metric ton-km cargo 5,400,000. **Communications,** in total units (units per 1,000 persons). Telephone landlines (2008): 1,910,000 (142); cellular telephone subscribers (2008): 11,595,000 (860); personal computers (2005): 866,000 (65); total Internet users (2008): 1,310,000 (97); broadband Internet subscribers (2008): 35,000 (2.6).

Education and health

Educational attainment (1995). Percentage of population ages 25 and over having: no formal schooling/incomplete primary education 18.8%; complete primary/incomplete secondary 47.2%; complete secondary 16.1%; higher 17.9%. **Literacy** (2003): total population ages 15 and over literate 92.5%; males literate 94.0%; females literate 91.0%. **Health:** physicians (2004) 21,625 (1 per 603 persons); hospital beds (2007) 20,523 (1 per 663 persons); infant mortality rate per 1,000 live births (2008) 16.4; undernourished population (2003–05) 1,900,000 (15% of total population based on the consumption of a minimum daily requirement of 1,770 calories).

Military

Total active duty personnel (November 2008): 57,983 (army 80.2%, navy 12.6%, air force 7.2%).

Military expenditure as percentage of GDP (2007): 1.8%; per capita expenditure US$57.

Background

Ecuador was conquered by the Incas in AD 1450 and came under Spanish control in 1534. Under the Spaniards it was a part of the Viceroyalty of Peru until 1740, when it became a part of the Viceroyalty of New Granada. It gained its independence from Spain in 1822 as part of the republic of Gran Colombia, and in 1830 it became a sovereign state. A succession of authoritarian governments ruled into the mid-20th century, and economic hardship and social unrest prompted the military to take a strong role. Border disputes led to war between Peru and Ecuador in 1941; the two fought periodically until agreeing to a final demarcation in 1998. The economy, booming in the 1970s with petroleum profits, was depressed in the 1980s by reduced oil prices and earthquake damage. A new constitution was adopted in 1979. In the 1990s social unrest caused political instability and several changes of heads of state. In a controversial move to help stabilize the economy, the US dollar replaced the sucre as the national currency in 2000.

Recent Developments

Ecuadoran Pres. Rafael Correa was reelected handily in April 2009; vowing to push ahead with his vision of "21st century socialism," he expanded programs aimed at improving life for the poor and challenged foreign companies and investors to accept new terms of engagement with Ecuador. Relations with the United States and neighboring Colombia continued to be strained in 2009. Colombia maintained that Ecuador provided tacit support to guerrillas of the Revolutionary Armed Forces of Colombia (FARC). In September the last US personnel left the military base at Manta after Ecuador declined to renew a lease allowing them to conduct antidrug operations; these were then shifted to Colombian bases.

Internet resource: <www.ecuador.com>.

Egypt

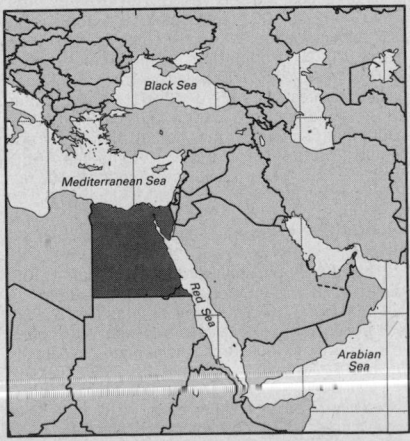

Official name: Jumhuriah Misr al-ʿArabiyah (Arab Republic of Egypt). **Form of government:** republic with two legislative houses (Consultative Assembly [264]; People's Assembly [454]). **Head of state:** President Hosni Mubarak (from 1981). **Head of government:** Prime Minister Ahmed Nazif (from 2004). **Capital:** Cairo. **Official language:** Arabic. **Official religion:** Islam. **Monetary unit:** 1 Egyptian pound (LE) = 100 piastres; valuation (1 Jul 2010) US$1 = LE 5.70.

Demography

Area: 386,874 sq mi, 1,002,000 sq km. **Population** (2009): 82,999,000. **Density** (2009): persons per sq mi 214.5, persons per sq km 82.8. **Urban** (2006): 43.1%. **Sex distribution** (2006): male 51.11%; female 48.89%. **Age breakdown** (2005): under 15, 33.0%; 15–29, 28.0%; 30–44, 19.8%; 45–59, 12.3%; 60–74, 5.7%; 75 and over, 1.2%. **Ethnic composition** (2000): Egyptian Arab 84.1%; Sudanese Arab 5.5%; Arabized Berber 2.0%; Bedouin 2.0%; Rom (Gypsy) 1.6%; other 4.8%. **Religious affiliation** (2000): Muslim 84.4% (nearly all Sunni; Shiʿi make up less than 1% of population); Christian 15.1%, of which Orthodox 13.6%, Protestant 0.8%, Roman Catholic 0.3%; nonreligious 0.5%. **Major cities** (2006): Cairo 6,759,000 ([urban agglomeration; 2007] 11,893,000); Alexandria 4,085,000; Al-Jizah 2,891,000; Shubra al-Khaymah 1,026,000; Port Said 571,000. **Location:** northern Africa, bordering the Mediterranean Sea, the Gaza Strip, Israel, the Red Sea, Sudan, and Libya.

Vital statistics

Birth rate per 1,000 population (2008–09): 25.0 (world avg. 20.3). **Death rate** per 1,000 population (2008–09): 6.3 (world avg. 8.5). **Total fertility rate** (avg. births per childbearing woman; 2006): 2.83. **Life expectancy** at birth (2007–08): male 71.0 years; female 74.0 years.

National economy

Budget (2006–07). *Revenue:* LE 205,655,000,000 (nontax revenue 42.6%; corporate taxes 23.7%; taxes on goods and services 19.2%). *Expenditures:* LE 239,602,000,000 (social protection 35.8%; general administration 24.4%; education 11.6%; defense 7.5%). **Population economically active** (2005): total 22,310,000; activity rate 31.3% (participation rates: ages 15–64 [2001] 46.9%; female 23.3%; unemployed [2008] 8.7%). **Production** ('000; metric tons except as noted). *Agriculture and fishing* (2007): sugarcane 16,200, tomatoes 7,550, wheat 7,379, dates 1,130, seed cotton 560, figs 170; livestock ('000; number of live animals) 5,180 sheep, 4,550 cattle, 3,950 buffalo, 120 camels; fisheries production 1,008,007 (from aquaculture 63%). *Mining and quarrying* (2006): gypsum 3,300; iron ore 2,600; phosphate rock 2,200; salt 1,200; kaolin 416. *Manufacturing* (value added in US$'000,000; 2002): chemical products 2,823; food products 1,016; textiles and wearing apparel 618. *Energy production (consumption):* electricity ('000,000 kW-hr; 2008) 128,105 ([2006]

118,058); coal (metric tons; 2006) 25,000 (1,713,000); crude petroleum (barrels; 2008) 241,500,000 ([2006] 205,400,000); petroleum products (metric tons; 2006) 30,700,000 (30,977,000); natural gas (cu m; 2007) 47,488,000,000 (31,800,000,000). **Gross national income** (2008): US$146,851,000,000 (US$1,800 per capita). **Public debt** (external, outstanding; 2007): US$26,940,000,000. **Selected balance of payments data.** Receipts from (US$'000,000): tourism (2007) 9,303; remittances (2008) 9,476; foreign direct investment (FDI; 2005–07 avg.) 8,999; official development assistance (2007) 1,083. Disbursements for (US$'000,000): tourism (2007) 2,446; remittances (2008) 180; FDI (2005–07 avg.) 302.

Foreign trade

Imports (2007; c.i.f.): US$26,928,000,000 (food products 15.7%, of which wheat 5.8%; machinery and apparatus 14.9%; mineral fuels 14.7%; chemical products 9.8%; iron and steel 4.5%). *Major import sources:* free zones 15.2%; US 9.5%; Saudi Arabia 8.3%; Germany 6.6%; China 6.0%. **Exports** (2007; f.o.b.): US$16,101,000,000 (refined petroleum products 25.4%; liquefied natural gas 16.6%; food products 7.7%; crude petroleum 6.5%; iron and steel 4.6%). *Major export destinations:* free zones 16.3%; India 11.3%; Italy 9.8%; Spain 6.4%; bunkers and ships' stores 6.0%.

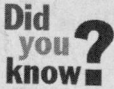 **Did you know?** Somalia has been a lively trading center for millennia. The area was known to ancient Egyptians as the land of aromatics and incense, and later was the source of exotic products as varied as ostrich feathers, clarified butter, and precious vegetable gums.

Transport and communications

Transport. *Railroads* (2005): length 9,525 km; passenger-km 54,853,000,000; metric ton-km cargo 4,234,000,000. *Roads* (2004): total length 92,370 km (paved 81%). *Vehicles:* passenger cars (2004) 1,960,000; trucks and buses (2002) 650,000. *Inland water* (2007): Suez Canal, number of transits 20,384; metric ton cargo 710,098,000. *Air transport* (2006): passenger-km 10,332,000,000; metric ton-km cargo 323,160,000. **Communications,** in total units (units per 1,000 persons). Telephone landlines (2008): 12,011,000 (147); cellular telephone subscribers (2008): 41,272,000 (506); personal computers (2007): 3,923,000 (49); total Internet users (2008): 12,569,000 (154); broadband Internet subscribers (2008): 769,000 (9.4).

Education and health

Educational attainment (2006). Percentage of population ages 10 and over having: no formal schooling 41.6%; incomplete primary education/incomplete

---

1 metric ton = about 1.1 short tons;   1 kilometer = 0.6 mi (statute);   1 metric ton-km cargo = about 0.68 short ton-mi cargo;   c.i.f.: cost, insurance, and freight;   f.o.b.: free on board

secondary 20.7%; complete secondary/some higher 28.1%; university 9.4%; advanced degree 0.2%. **Literacy** (2001): total population ages 15 and over literate 56.1%; males literate 67.2%; females literate 44.8%. **Health:** physicians (2006) 161,000 (1 per 451 persons); hospital beds (2007) 185,000 (1 per 393 persons); infant mortality rate per 1,000 live births (2007–08) 16.0; undernourished population (2002–04) 2,600,000 (4% of total population based on the consumption of a minimum daily requirement of 1,900 calories).

Military

Total active duty personnel (November 2008): 468,500 (army 72.6%, navy 3.9%, air force [including air defense] 23.5%). **Military expenditure as percentage of GDP** (2007): 3.5%; per capita expenditure US$58.

Background

Egypt is home to one of the world's oldest continuous civilizations. Upper and Lower Egypt were united about 3000 BC, beginning a period of cultural achievement and a line of native rulers that lasted nearly 3,000 years. Egypt's ancient history is divided into the Old, Middle, and New Kingdoms, spanning 31 dynasties and lasting to 332 BC. The pyramids date from the Old Kingdom, the cult of Osiris and the refinement of sculpture from the Middle Kingdom, and the era of empire and the Exodus of the Jews from the New Kingdom. An Assyrian invasion occurred in the 7th century BC, and the Persian Achaemenids established a dynasty in 525 BC. The invasion by Alexander the Great in 332 BC inaugurated the Macedonian Ptolemaic period and the ascendancy of Alexandria. The Romans held Egypt from 30 BC to AD 395; later it was placed under the control of Constantinople. Constantine's granting of tolerance in 313 to the Christians began the development of a formal Egyptian (Coptic) church. Egypt came under Arab control in 642 and ultimately was transformed into an Arabic-speaking state, with Islam as the dominant religion. Held by the Umayyad and Abbasid dynasties, in 969 it became the center of the Fatimid dynasty. In 1250 the Mamluks established a dynasty that lasted until 1517, when Egypt fell to the Ottoman Turks. An economic decline ensued, and with it a decline in Egyptian culture. Egypt became a British protectorate in 1914 and received nominal independence in 1922, when a constitutional monarchy was established. A coup overthrew the monarchy in 1952, with Gamal Abdel Nasser taking power. Following three wars with Israel, Egypt, under Nasser's successor, Anwar el-Sadat, ultimately played a leading role in Middle East peace talks. Sadat was succeeded by Hosni Mubarak, who followed Sadat's peace initiatives and in 1982 regained Egyptian sovereignty (lost in 1967) over the Sinai Peninsula. Although Egypt took part in the coalition against Iraq during the Persian Gulf War (1991), it later made peace overtures to Iraq and other countries in the region.

Recent Developments

The impact of the international financial crisis on the Egyptian economy was harsh. By the end of the 2008–09 fiscal year, inflation was estimated at 9.9% (and 13.6% in January 2010), remittances by Egyptian expatriates had declined by 8.8%, Suez Canal receipts had dropped by 8.4%, and tourism revenues had declined by 3.1%. In July representatives of the Nile River basin countries met in Alexandria to discuss an agreement regulating the distribution of water and conditions for future projects. Egypt, one of the downstream countries, demanded full recognition of its historical water rights, an annual water quota, and prior notification of any projects in the Nile basin that could affect water resources.

Internet resource: <www.capmas.gov.eg>.

El Salvador

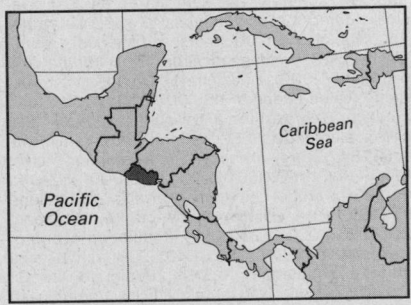

Official name: República de El Salvador (Republic of El Salvador). **Form of government:** republic with one legislative house (Legislative Assembly [84]). **Head of state and government:** President Mauricio Funes (from 2009). **Capital:** San Salvador. **Official language:** Spanish. **Official religion:** none (Roman Catholicism, though not official, enjoys special recognition in the constitution). **Monetary unit:** 1 colón (₡) = 100 centavos; valuation (1 Jul 2010) US$1 = ₡8.55 (the US dollar [US$] has also been legal tender since 1 Jan 2001; the colón is rarely in use).

Demography

Area: 8,124 sq mi, 21,041 sq km. **Population** (2009): 6,192,000. **Density** (2009): persons per sq mi 762.2, persons per sq km 294.3. **Urban** (2008): 64.8%. **Sex distribution** (2008): male 47.39%; female 52.61%. **Age breakdown** (2008): under 15, 32.6%; 15–29, 27.2%; 30–44, 18.3%; 45–59, 11.9%; 60–69, 5.0%; 70 and over, 5.0%. **Ethnic composition** (2000): mestizo 88.3%; Amerindian 9.1%, of which Pipil 4.0%; white 1.6%; other/unknown 1.0%. **Religious affiliation** (2005): Roman Catholic 71%; independent Christian 11%; Protestant 10%; Jehovah's Witness 2%; other 6%. **Major cities** (2007): San Salvador 316,090 (urban agglomeration 1,433,000); Santa Ana 245,421; Soyapango 241,403; San Miguel 218,410; Mejicanos 140,751. **Location:** Central America, bordering Guatemala, Honduras, and the North Pacific Ocean.

Vital statistics

Birth rate per 1,000 population (2008): 22.5 (world avg. 20.3); (2003) within marriage 27%.

Death rate per 1,000 population (2008): 5.9 (world avg. 8.5). **Total fertility rate** (avg. births per childbearing woman; 2006): 3.12. **Life expectancy** at birth (2006): male 67.9 years; female 75.3 years.

National economy

Budget (2007). *Revenue:* US$3,077,600,000 (VAT 53.9%; income tax 31.4%; import duties 6.6%; grants 1.4%; other 6.7%). *Expenditures:* US$2,928,900,000 (education 18.4%; defense and public security 18.3%; public health and welfare 9.7%; other 53.6%). **Public debt** (external, outstanding; 2007): US$5,444,000,000. **Production** (metric tons except as noted). *Agriculture and fishing* (2007): sugarcane 5,400,000, corn (maize) 836,695, sorghum 181,694, coffee 94,514; livestock (number of live animals) 1,380,112 cattle, 451,482 pigs, 96,000 horses; fisheries production 52,368 (from aquaculture 7%). *Mining and quarrying* (2006): limestone 1,200,000. *Manufacturing* (value added in US$'000,000; 2004): food products 875; textiles and wearing apparel 262; chemical products 262; refined petroleum products 234. *Energy production (consumption):* electricity (kW-hr; 2006) 5,293,000,000 (5,204,-000,000); crude petroleum (barrels; 2006) none (6,348,000); petroleum products (metric tons; 2006) 811,000 (1,857,000). **Population economically active** (2008): total 2,495,908; activity rate of total population 40.8% (participation rates: ages 16–64, 62.9%; female 41.3%; unemployed 5.9%). **Gross national income** (2008): US$21,361,000,000 (US$3,480 per capita). **Selected balance of payments data.** Receipts from (US$'000,000): tourism (2007) 847; remittances (2008) 3,804; foreign direct investment (FDI; 2005–07 avg.) 752; official development assistance (2006) 157. Disbursements for (US$'000,000): tourism (2007) 605; remittances (2008) 29; FDI (2005–07 avg.) 62.

Foreign trade

Imports (2006; c.i.f.): US$7,627,000,000 (food products, beverages, and tobacco 16.2%; imports for reexport 15.8%; machinery and apparatus 14.4%; crude petroleum 13.7%). *Major import sources:* US 40.5%; Guatemala 8.0%; Mexico 7.7%; Brazil 4.0%; Costa Rica 2.9%. **Exports** (2006; f.o.b.): US$3,513,000,000 (reexports [mostly clothing] 45.6%; fabricated metal products 5.9%; coffee 5.4%; distilled spirits 4.5%; paper products 4.2%). *Major export destinations:* US 57.1%; Guatemala 13.0%; Honduras 8.0%; Nicaragua 4.8%; Costa Rica 3.4%.

Transport and communications

Transport. *Railroads* (2007; rail service was suspended in 2005): length 562 km. *Roads* (2002): total length 11,458 km (paved 23%). *Vehicles* (2000): passenger cars 148,000; trucks and buses 250,800. *Air transport* (2005; TACA International Airlines only): passenger-km 8,117,465,000; metric ton-km cargo 37,883,000. **Communications,** in total units (units per 1,000 persons). Telephone landlines (2008):

1,077,000 (155); cellular telephone subscribers (2008): 6,951,000 (1,000); personal computers (2007): 359,000 (52); total Internet users (2007): 763,000 (111); broadband Internet subscribers (2008): 124,000 (18).

Education and health

Educational attainment (2004). Percentage of population over ages 25 having: no formal schooling 22.0%; primary education: grades 1–3 19.1%, grades 4–6 19.9%; secondary: grades 7–9 13.9%, grades 10–12 14.6%; higher 10.5%. **Literacy** (2008): total population ages 10 and over literate 85.9%; males literate 88.5%; females literate 83.6%. **Health** (2005): physicians 8,670 (1 per 794 persons); hospital beds 4,816 (1 per 1,429 persons); infant mortality rate per 1,000 live births (2004) 10.5; undernourished population (2002–04) 700,000 (11% of total population based on the consumption of a minimum daily requirement of 1,800 calories).

Military

Total active duty personnel (November 2008): 15,500 (army 89.4%, navy 4.5%, air force 6.1%). **Military expenditure as percentage of GDP** (2008): 0.4%; per capita expenditure US$20.

Background

The Spanish arrived in the area in 1524 and subjugated the Pipil Indian kingdom of Cuzcatlán by 1539. The country was divided into two districts, San Salvador and Sonsonate, both attached to Guatemala. When independence came in 1821, San Salvador was incorporated into the Mexican Empire; upon its collapse in 1823, Sonsonate and San Salvador combined to form the new state of El Salvador within the United Provinces of Central America. From its founding, El Salvador experienced a high degree of political turmoil and was under military rule from 1931 to 1979, when the government was ousted in a coup. Elections held in 1982 set up a new government, and in 1983 a new constitution was adopted, but civil war continued through the 1980s. An accord in 1992 brought an uneasy truce.

Recent Developments

Television journalist Mauricio Funes won the hard-fought presidential election in El Salvador in March 2009. Although sympathetic to other leftist governments in the hemisphere, Funes emphasized that he did not want ideological confrontation with the US and that he was not a part of the more extreme left represented by Venezuelan Pres. Hugo Chávez. One of Funes's first acts upon taking office was to restore diplomatic relations with Cuba. In the realm of domestic policy, he launched new aid programs for the elderly poor and began implementing dramatic improvements in education and children's health benefits. He provided free education, meals, and uniforms for poor public-school students.

Internet resource: <www.bcr.gob.sv>.

---

1 metric ton = about 1.1 short tons;   1 kilometer = 0.6 mi (statute);   1 metric ton-km cargo = about 0.68 short ton-mi cargo;   c.i.f.: cost, insurance, and freight;   f.o.b.: free on board

Equatorial Guinea

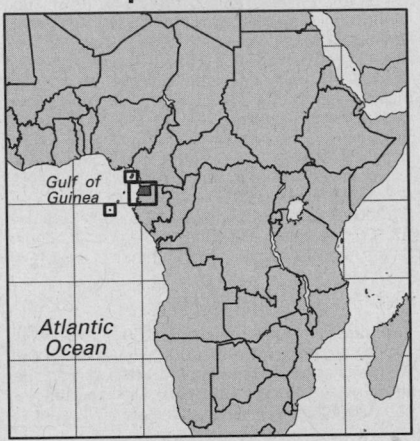

Gulf of Guinea

Atlantic Ocean

Official name: República de Guinea Ecuatorial (Spanish); République du Guinée Équatoriale (French) (Republic of Equatorial Guinea). **Form of government:** republic with one legislative house (House of People's Representatives [100]). **Head of state and government:** President Teodoro Obiang Nguema Mbasogo (from 1979), assisted by Prime Minister Ignacio Milam Tang (from 2008). **Capital:** Malabo. **Official languages:** Spanish; French. **Official religion:** none. **Monetary unit:** 1 CFA franc (CFAF) = 100 centimes; valuation (1 Jul 2010) US$1 = CFAF 527.20.

Demography

Area: 10,831 sq mi, 28,051 sq km. **Population** (2009): 633,000. **Density** (2009): persons per sq mi 58.4, persons per sq km 22.6. **Urban** (2008): 60.8%. **Sex distribution** (2008): male 49.57%; female 50.43%. **Age breakdown** (2008): under 15, 42.0%; 15–29, 26.6%; 30–44, 16.6%; 45–59, 8.7%; 60–74, 5.0%; 75–84, 1.0%; 85 and over, 0.1%. **Ethnic composition** (2000): Fang 56.6%; migrant laborers from Nigeria 12.5%, of which Yoruba 8.0%, Igbo 4.0%; Bubi 10.0%; Seke 2.9%; Spaniard 2.8%; other 15.2%. **Religious affiliation** (2000): Roman Catholic 79.9%; Sunni Muslim 4.1%; independent Christian 3.7%; Protestant 3.2%; traditional beliefs 2.1%; nonreligious/atheist 4.9%; other 2.1%. **Major cities** (2003): Malabo 92,900; Bata 66,800; Mbini 11,600. **Location:** western Africa, the mainland portion bordering Cameroon, Gabon, and the Bight of Biafra.

Vital statistics

Birth rate per 1,000 population (2008): 37.1 (world avg. 20.3). **Death rate** per 1,000 population (2008): 9.7 (world avg. 8.5). **Total fertility rate** (avg. births per childbearing woman; 2008): 5.16. **Life expectancy** at birth (2008): male 60.4 years; female 62.1 years.

National economy

Budget (2007). *Revenue:* CFAF 2,308,500,000,000 (oil revenue 90.0%, of which profit sharing 10.0%; roy-alties 20.3%; non-oil revenue 9.1%, of which tax revenue 3.3%). *Expenditures:* CFAF 1,151,900,-

000,000 (infrastructure 43.3%; social services 18.3%; public administration 17.0%). **Public debt** (external, outstanding; 2006): US$156,800,000. **Gross national income** (2008): US$9,875,000,000 (US$14,980 per capita). **Production** (metric tons except as noted). *Agriculture and fishing* (2007): cassava 45,000, sweet potatoes 36,000, oil palm fruit 35,000; livestock (number of live animals) 37,600 sheep, 9,000 goats, 6,100 pigs; fisheries production 3,583 (from aquaculture, none). *Mining and quarrying* (2007): gold 200 kg. *Manufacturing* (2004): methanol 1,027,300; processed timber 31,200 cu m. *Energy production (consumption):* electricity (kW-hr; 2006) 29,000,000 (29,000,000); crude petroleum (barrels; 2007) 133,000,000 ([2006] negligible); petroleum products (metric tons; 2006) none (51,000); natural gas (cu m; 2006) 480,000,000 (480,000,000). **Population economically active** (2006): total 193,000; activity rate of total population 38.9% (participation rates: ages 15–64, 69.5%; female 33.7%; unemployed [1998] 30%). **Selected balance of payments data.** Receipts from (US$'000,000): tourism (2005) 5; foreign direct investment (2005–07 avg.) 1,752; official development assistance (2007) 31.

Foreign trade

Imports (2007): CFAF 1,325,000,000,000 (petroleum sector 35.6%; nonpetroleum sector 64.4%). *Major import sources* (2005): US 26.8%; Côte d'Ivoire 21.4%; Spain 13.6%; France 8.8%; UK 7.8%. **Exports** (2007): CFAF 4,893,200,000,000 (crude petroleum 83.1%; methanol 15.9%; timber 0.7%). *Major export destinations* (2005): US 24.6%; China 21.8%; Spain 10.8%; Canada 7.3%; Netherlands 5.2%.

Transport and communications

Transport. *Railroads:* none. *Roads* (2000): total length 2,880 km (paved 13%). *Vehicles* (2002): passenger cars 8,380; trucks and buses 6,618. **Communications**, in total units (units per 1,000 persons). Telephone landlines (2005): 10,000 (20); cellular telephone subscribers (2008): 346,000 (666); personal computers (2004): 7,000 (3.3); total Internet users (2008): 12,000 (23); broadband Internet subscribers (2007): 200 (0.04).

Education and health

Literacy (2006): percentage of total population ages 15 and over literate 87.0%; males literate 93.4%; females literate 80.5%. **Health:** physicians (2004) 101 (1 per 5,020 persons); hospital beds (1998) 907 (1 per 472 persons); infant mortality rate per 1,000 live births (2008) 83.8.

Military

Total active duty personnel (November 2008): 1,320 (army 83.3%, navy 9.1%, air force 7.6%).

Background

The first inhabitants of the mainland region appear to have been Pygmies. The now-prominent Fang and Bubi reached the mainland region in the 17th century Bantu migrations. Equatorial Guinea was ceded by the Portuguese to the Spanish in the late 18th century; it was frequented by slave traders, as well as by British, German, Dutch, and French merchants. Independence was declared in 1968, followed by a reign of terror and economic chaos under the dictatorial president Macías Nguema, who was overthrown by a military coup in 1979 and later executed. A new constitution was adopted in 1982, but political unrest persisted into the 21st century despite the country's oil wealth.

Recent Developments

In 2009 Equatorial Guinea was one of the largest oil producers in sub-Saharan Africa, yet infant and child mortality was increasing and the majority of the country's population remained very poor and without access to any social services. A Human Rights Watch report released in July detailed the misappropriation of oil revenue by Pres. Teodoro Obiang Nguema Mbasogo, and two months earlier a French judge agreed to launch a formal investigation into issues raised in a lawsuit filed by the global anticorruption organization Transparency International, which accused Obiang and two other African presidents of having misused public funds, embezzled, and engaged in money laundering. A maritime border dispute with Gabon over the island of Mbanie in the Gulf of Guinea, where oil had been discovered, remained unresolved.

Internet resource: <http://guinea-equatorial.com>.

Eritrea

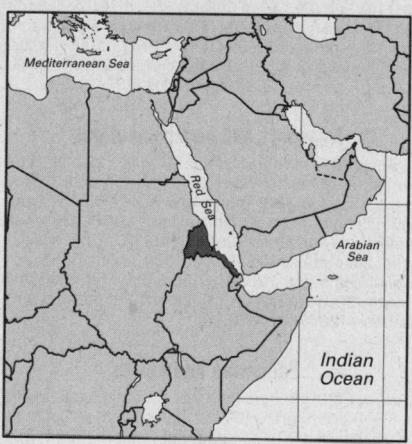

Mediterranean Sea

Red Sea

Arabian Sea

Indian Ocean

Official name: State of Eritrea. **Form of government:** transitional regime with one interim legislative house (transitional National Assembly [150]). **Head of state and government:** President Isaias Afwerki (from 1993). **Capital:** Asmara. **Official language:** none. **Official religion:** none. **Monetary unit:** 1 nakfa (Nfa) = 100 cents; valuation (1 Jul 2010) US$1 = Nfa 15.00.

Demography

Area: 46,774 sq mi, 121,144 sq km. **Population** (2009): 5,073,000. **Density** (2009; based on land

area only): persons per sq mi 130.1, persons per sq km 50.2. **Urban** (2006): 21.3%. **Sex distribution** (2006): male 49.84%; female 50.16%. **Age breakdown** (2006): under 15, 44.0%; 15–29, 27.9%; 30–44, 14.3%; 45–59, 8.2%; 60–74, 4.5%; 75 and over, 1.1%. **Ethnolinguistic composition** (2004): Tigrinya (Tigray) 50.0%; Tigré 31.4%; Afar 5.0%; Saho 5.0%; Beja 2.5%; Bilen 2.1%; other 4.0%. **Religious affiliation** (2004): Muslim (virtually all Sunni) 50%; Christian 48%, of which Eritrean Orthodox 40%, Roman Catholic 5%, Protestant 2%; traditional beliefs 2%. **Major cities** (2003): Asmara 435,000; Keren 57,000; Assab 28,000; Afabet 25,000; Massawa 25,000. **Location:** the Horn of Africa, bordering Sudan, the Red Sea, Djibouti, and Ethiopia.

Vital statistics

Birth rate per 1,000 population (2006): 34.3 (world avg. 20.3). **Death rate** per 1,000 population (2006): 9.6 (world avg. 8.5). **Total fertility rate** (avg. births per childbearing woman; 2006): 5.08. **Life expectancy** at birth (2006): male 57.4 years; female 60.7 years.

National economy

Budget (2002). *Revenue:* Nfa 3,409,800,000 (tax revenue 45.1%, of which import duties 18.1%, sales tax 10.8%, corporate taxes 9.9%; grants 32.8%; nontax revenue 21.2%; extraordinary revenue 0.9%). *Expenditures:* Nfa 6,138,200,000 (defense 34.3%; health 9.6%; humanitarian assistance 7.9%; education 7.6%; debt service 5.7%). **Public debt** (external, outstanding; 2007): US$856,000,000. **Gross national income** (2008): US$1,492,000,000 (US$300 per capita). **Production** (metric tons except as noted). *Agriculture and fishing* (2007): sorghum 130,000, millet 20,000, sesame seeds 19,000; livestock (number of live animals) 2,120,000 sheep, 1,960,000 cattle, 1,720,000 goats, 76,000 camels; fisheries production 1,932 (from aquaculture, none). *Mining and quarrying* (2007): coral 67,332, basalt 45,335, granite 21,394. *Manufacturing* (value added in US$'000,000; 2004): beverages 31; tobacco products 8; furniture 7. *Energy production (consumption):* electricity (kW-hr; 2006) 269,000,000 (269,000,000); petroleum products (metric tons; 2006) none (173,000). **Population economically active** (2006): 1,881,000; activity rate of total population 40.1% (participation rates: ages 15–64, 71.4%; female 41.3%). **Selected balance of payments data.** Receipts from (US$'000,000): tourism (2007) 60; remittances (2003) 150; foreign direct disinvestment (2005–07 avg.) −2; official development assistance (2007) 155.

Foreign trade

Imports (2003; c.i.f.): US$432,800,000 (food products and live animals 40.5%, of which cereals 25.5%; machinery and apparatus 14.8%; motor vehicles 7.3%; chemical products 6.1%). *Major import sources* (2008): Italy 16.9%; UAE 15.7%; China 13.0%; India 9.4%; US 6.7%. **Exports** (2003; f.o.b.): US$6,600,000 (food products and live animals 36.4%, of which fresh fish 22.7%; leather products 10.6%; corals and shells 9.1%). *Major export destinations* (2008): India 31.7%; Italy 18.6%; Kenya 11.9%; China 11.5%; France 5.4%.

---

1 metric ton = about 1.1 short tons;   1 kilometer = 0.6 mi (statute);   1 metric ton-km cargo = about 0.68 short ton-mi cargo;   c.i.f.: cost, insurance, and freight;   f.o.b.: free on board

Transport and communications

Transport. *Railroads* (2005): route length 306 km. *Roads* (2004): total length 4,000 km (paved 20%). *Vehicles* (1996): automobiles 5,940. *Air transport* (2001; Asmara airport only): passenger arrivals 39,266, passenger departures 46,448; freight loaded 202 metric tons, freight unloaded 1,548 metric tons. **Communications,** in total units (units per 1,000 persons). Telephone landlines (2008): 40,000 (8.2); cellular telephone subscribers (2008): 109,000 (22); personal computers (2007): 38,000 (8); total Internet users (2008): 150,000 (30).

Education and health

Educational attainment (2002). Percentage of population ages 25 and over having: no formal education/unknown 67.6%, incomplete primary education 16.6%, complete primary 1.3%, incomplete secondary 5.8%, complete secondary 5.7%, higher 3.0%. **Literacy** (2006): total population ages 15 and over literate 61.4%; males literate 72.3%; females literate 50.7%. **Health** (2006): physicians (2004) 215 (1 per 20,791 persons); hospital beds 5,500 (1 per 833 persons); infant mortality rate per 1,000 live births 46.3; undernourished population (2002–04) 3,100,000 (75% of total population based on the consumption of a minimum daily requirement of 1,730 calories).

Military

Total active duty personnel (November 2008): 201,750 (army 99.1%, navy 0.7%, air force 0.2%); mandate for the UN peacekeeping force along the Eritrean-Ethiopian border was terminated in July 2008. **Military expenditure as percentage of GDP** (2003): 24.1%; per capita expenditure US$49.

Background

As the site of the main ports of the Aksumite empire, Eritrea was linked to the beginnings of the Ethiopian kingdom, but it retained much of its independence until it came under Ottoman rule in the 16th century. From the 17th to the 19th centuries, control of the territory was disputed between Ethiopia, the Ottomans, the kingdom of Tigray, Egypt, and Italy; it became an Italian colony in 1890. Eritrea was used as the base for the Italian invasions of Ethiopia (1896 and 1935–36) and in 1936 became part of Italian East Africa. It was captured by the British in 1941, federated to Ethiopia in 1952, and made a province of Ethiopia in 1962. Thirty years of guerrilla warfare by Eritrean secessionist groups ensued. A provisional Eritrean government was established in 1991, and independence came in 1993. A border war with Ethiopia that began in 1998 ended in an Ethiopian victory in 2000.

Recent Developments

The small and impoverished country of Eritrea remained one of the world's most militarized countries in 2009, with a strict program of military conscription aimed at maintaining high troop levels at its disputed border with Ethiopia. Eritrea ended the year with an active army of about 200,000 soldiers.

During the year Kenya and Western countries, including the US and the UK, accused Eritrea of aiding Islamic extremist insurgents involved in a civil war in Somalia. The UN Security Council voted to impose sanctions on Eritrea in December, claiming that the country was destabilizing the Horn of Africa.

Internet resource: <www.shabait.com>.

Estonia

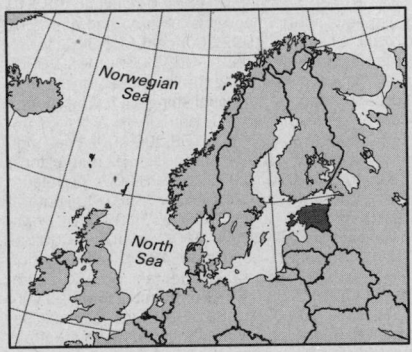

Official name: Eesti Vabariik (Republic of Estonia). **Form of government:** unitary multiparty republic with a single legislative house (Riigikogu [101]). **Head of state:** President Toomas Hendrik Ilves (from 2006). **Head of government:** Prime Minister Andrus Ansip (from 2005). **Capital:** Tallinn. **Official language:** Estonian. **Official religion:** none. **Monetary unit:** 1 kroon (EEK; plural krooni) = 100 senti; valuation (1 Jul 2010) US$1 = EEK 12.58.

Demography

Area: 17,462 sq mi, 45,227 sq km. **Population** (2009): 1,340,000. **Density** (2009; based on land area only): persons per sq mi 81.9, persons per sq km 31.6. **Urban** (2005): 69.3%. **Sex distribution** (2008): male 46.05%; female 53.95%. **Age breakdown** (2005): under 15, 15.1%; 15–29, 22.7%; 30–44, 20.5%; 45–59, 20.2%; 60–74, 14.7%; 75–84, 5.7%; 85 and over, 1.1%. **Ethnic composition** (2005): Estonian 68.6%; Russian 25.7%; Ukrainian 2.1%; Belarusian 1.2%; Finnish 0.8%; other 1.6%. **Religious affiliation** (2000): Christian 63.5%, of which unaffiliated Christian 25.6%, Protestant (mostly Lutheran) 17.2%, Orthodox 16.5%, independent Christian 3.3%; nonreligious 25.1%; atheist 10.9%; other 0.5%. **Major cities** (2006): Tallinn 396,852; Tartu 101,965; Narva 66,712; Kohtla-Järve 45,399; Pärnu 44,074. **Location:** eastern Europe, bordering the Gulf of Finland, Russia, Latvia, the Gulf of Riga, and the Baltic Sea.

Vital statistics

Birth rate per 1,000 population (2008): 12.0 (world avg. 20.3); within marriage 40.9%. **Death rate** per 1,000 population (2008): 12.4 (world avg. 8.5). **Total fertility rate** (avg. births per childbearing woman, 2008): 1.66. **Life expectancy** at birth (2008): male 67.6 years; female 79.2 years.

National economy

Budget (2006). *Revenue:* EEK 57,735,000,000 (tax revenue 58.7%, of which taxes on goods and services 46.6%, taxes on income and profits 12.1%; social contributions 20.9%). *Expenditures:* EEK 53,149,000,000 (social protection 30.2%; general administration 17.8%; economic affairs 11.9%; education 8.5%; health 6.6%; defense 5.3%). **Production** (metric tons except as noted). *Agriculture and fishing* (2007): barley 372,800, wheat 322,000, potatoes 173,700; livestock (number of live animals) 345,800 pigs, 244,800 cattle; fisheries production 98,614 (from aquaculture, negligible). *Mining and quarrying* (2007): oil shale 13,992,000; peat 900,800. *Manufacturing* (value added in US$'000,000; 2006): wood products (excluding furniture) 211; food products 197; printing and publishing 141. *Energy production (consumption):* electricity (kW-hr; 2008) 10,524,000,000 ([2006] 8,758,000,000); coal (metric tons; 2006) none (70,000); lignite (metric tons; 2008) 16,044,000 ([2006] 14,028,000); petroleum products (metric tons; 2006) none (858,000); natural gas (cu m; 2007) none ([2006] 963,000,000). **Population economically active** (2005): total 659,600; activity rate of total population 48.8% (participation rates: ages 15–64, 69.6%; female 50.1%; unemployed [2008] 5.5%). **Gross national income** (2008): US$19,131,000,000 (US$14,270 per capita). **Selected balance of payments data.** Receipts from (US$'000,000): tourism (2007) 1,036; remittances (2008) 422; foreign direct investment (FDI; 2005–07 avg.) 2,345. Disbursements for (US$'000,000): tourism (2007) 670; remittances (2008) 113; FDI (2005–07 avg.) 1,088.

Foreign trade

Imports (2007; c.i.f.): EEK 164,451,000,000 (machinery and apparatus 20.2%; refined petroleum products 11.5%; motor vehicles 11.1%; chemical products 8.6%; food products 5.6%; iron and steel 5.1%). *Major import sources:* Finland 15.9%; Germany 12.8%; Russia 10.2%; Sweden 10.1%; Latvia 7.6%. **Exports** (2006; f.o.b.): EEK 117,121,000,000 (machinery and apparatus 20.1%; refined petroleum products 9.8%; motor vehicles and parts 7.1%; food products 5.6%; sawn wood 5.3%; furniture 4.3%). *Major export destinations:* Finland 18.0%; Sweden 13.3%; Latvia 11.4%; Russia 8.9%; Lithuania 5.8%.

Transport and communications

Transport. *Railroads* (2005): route length (2004) 958 km; passenger-km 246,951,000; metric ton-km cargo 10,629,398,000. *Roads* (2005): total length 57,016 km (paved 23%). *Vehicles* (2005): passenger cars 493,800; trucks and buses 91,400. *Air transport* (2007): passenger-km 756,000,000; metric ton-km cargo 1,044,000. **Communications,** in total units (units per 1,000 persons). Telephone landlines (2008): 498,000 (372); cellular telephone subscribers (2008): 2,524,000 (1,883); personal computers (2007): 700,000 (522); total Internet users (2007): 854,000 (637); broadband Internet subscribers (2008): 318,000 (237).

Education and health

Educational attainment (2000). Percentage of population ages 10 and over having: no formal schooling/incomplete primary education 6.7%; complete primary/lower secondary 31.6%; complete secondary 29.2%; higher vocational 17.5%; undergraduate 12.3%; advanced degree 0.4%; unknown 2.3%. **Health** (2007): physicians 4,504 (1 per 298 persons); hospital beds 7,473 (1 per 179 persons); infant mortality rate per 1,000 live births (2008) 5.0; undernourished population (2002–04) less than 2.5% of total population.

Military

Total active duty personnel (November 2008): 5,300 (army 88.7%, navy 5.7%, air force 5.6%). **Military expenditure as a percentage of GDP** (2008): 1.8%; per capita expenditure US$317.

Background

The lands on the eastern shores of the Baltic Sea were invaded by Vikings in the 9th century AD, but the Estonians were able to withstand the assaults until the Danes took control in 1219. In 1346 the Danes sold their sovereignty to the Teutonic Order, which was then in possession of Livonia (southern Estonia and Latvia). In the mid-16th century Estonia was once again divided, with northern Estonia capitulating to Sweden and Poland gaining Livonia, which it surrendered to Sweden in 1629. Russia acquired Livonia and Estonia in 1721. Serfdom was abolished, and from 1881 Estonia underwent intensive Russification. In 1918 Estonia obtained independence from Russia, which lasted until the Soviet Union occupied the country in 1940 and forcibly incorporated it into the USSR. Germany held the region (1941–44) during World War II, but the Soviet regime was restored in 1944, after which Estonia's economy was collectivized and integrated into that of the Soviet Union. In 1991, along with other parts of the former USSR, it proclaimed its independence and subsequently held elections. Estonia continued negotiations with Russia to settle their common border, and, along with the other Baltic states, Estonia joined the EU and NATO in 2004.

Recent Developments

Most of the economic indicators in Estonia were negative in 2009. There was a massive decline in GDP and real-estate values, while unemployment rose to 15.5% by the end of the year. Nonetheless, the government made painful budget cuts in an effort to keep the deficit below 3% of GDP as required by the EU for euro adoption.

Internet resource: <www.stat.ee>.

Ethiopia

Official name: Federal Democratic Republic of Ethiopia. **Form of government:** federal republic with two legislative houses (House of the Federation [112]; House of Peoples' Representatives [547]).

---

1 metric ton = about 1.1 short tons;   1 kilometer = 0.6 mi (statute);   1 metric ton-km cargo = about 0.68 short ton-mi cargo;   c.i.f.: cost, insurance, and freight;   f.o.b.: free on board

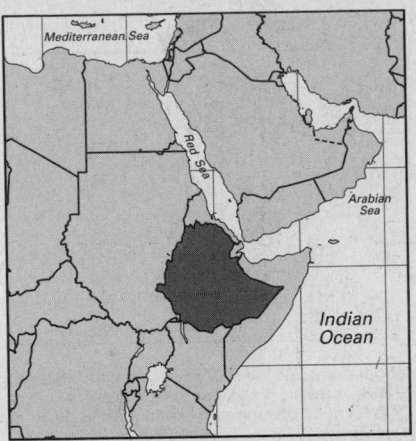

Mediterranean Sea

Arabian Sea

Indian Ocean

Head of state: President Girma Wolde-Giorgis (from 2001). **Head of government:** Prime Minister Meles Zenawi (from 1995). **Capital:** Addis Ababa. **Official language:** none (Amharic is the "working" language). **Official religion:** none. **Monetary unit:** 1 birr (Br) = 100 cents; valuation (1 Jul 2010) US$1 = Br 13.40.

Demography

Area: 435,186 sq mi, 1,127,127 sq km. **Population** (2009): 82,825,000. **Density** (2009): persons per sq mi 190.3, persons per sq km 73.5. **Urban** (2007): 16.2%. **Sex distribution** (2007): male 50.46%; female 49.54%. **Age breakdown** (2007): under 15, 45.0%; 15–29, 28.3%; 30–44, 14.7%; 45–59, 7.2%; 60–74, 3.7%; 75–84, 0.8%; 85 and over, 0.3%. **Ethnic composition** (2007): Oromo 34.5%; Amhara 26.9%; Somali 6.2%; Tigray 6.1%; Sidamo 4.0%; Gurage 2.5%; Welaita 2.3%; other 17.5%. **Religious affiliation** (2007): Orthodox 43.5%; Muslim 33.9%; Protestant 18.6%; traditional beliefs 2.7%; Roman Catholic 0.7%; other 0.6%. **Major cities** (2007): Addis Ababa 2,738,248; Adama (Nazret) 222,035; Dire Dawa 222,000; Mekele 215,546; Gonder 206,987. **Location:** the Horn of Africa, bordering Eritrea, Djibouti, Somalia, Kenya, and Sudan.

Vital statistics

Birth rate per 1,000 population (2008): 44.0 (world avg. 20.3). **Death rate** per 1,000 population (2008): 11.8 (world avg. 8.5). **Total fertility rate** (avg. births per childbearing woman; 2008): 6.17. **Life expectancy** at birth (2008): male 52.5 years; female 57.5 years.

National economy

Budget (2006–07). *Revenue:* Br 30,274,000,000 (tax revenue 57.3%, of which import duties 27.0%, income and profits tax 16.1%, sales tax 9.5%; grants 28.0%; nontax revenue 14.7%). *Expenditures:* Br 35,564,000,000 (capital expenditures 51.7%, of which economic development 32.0%; current expenditures 48.3%, of which education 13.8%, defense 8.4%). **Public debt** (external, outstanding;

2007–08): US$2,753,600,000. **Gross national income** (2008): US$22,742,000,000 (US$280 per capita). **Production** (metric tons except as noted). *Agriculture and fishing* (2007): corn (maize) 4,000,000, wheat 3,000,000, teff (2006–07) 2,437,700, coffee 325,800, maté 260,000, chickpeas 190,000, sesame seeds 164,000; leading producer of beeswax, honey, cut flowers, and khat; livestock (number of live animals) 43,000,000 cattle, 23,700,000 sheep, 18,000,000 goats, 2,300,000 camels, (1998) 3,037 civets; fisheries production 13,253 (from aquaculture, none). *Mining and quarrying* (2007): rock salt 230,000; tantalum 77,000 kg; niobium 12,000 kg; gold 3,400 kg. *Manufacturing* (value added in US$'000,000; 2004): food products 157; beverages 118; bricks, cement, and ceramics 69. *Energy production (consumption):* electricity (kW-hr; 2007–08) 3,530,280,000 ([2005] 2,872,000,000); crude petroleum (barrels; 2005) none (5,640,000); petroleum products (metric tons; 2006) n.a. (1,680,000). **Population economically active** (2005): total 32,158,392; activity rate of total population 50.9% (participation rates: ages 10 and over, 78.4%; female [1999] 45.5%; unemployed 5.0%). **Selected balance of payments data.** Receipts from (US$'000,000): tourism (2007) 177; remittances (2008) 358; foreign direct investment (2005–07 avg.) 355; official development assistance (2007) 2,422. Disbursements for (US$'000,000): tourism (2007) 107; remittances (2008) 15.

Foreign trade

Imports (2006; c.i.f.): US$5,207,000,000 (machinery and apparatus 20.7%; refined petroleum products 19.5%; motor vehicles 14.1%; chemical products 11.0%; food products 6.7%). *Major import sources:* Saudi Arabia 17.9%; China 12.3%; Italy 7.7%; UAE 7.6%; India 5.8%. **Exports** (2006; f.o.b.): US$1,043,000,000 (coffee and khat 40.8%; sesame seeds 15.4%; gum products, cut flowers, and foliage 12.4%; gold 6.2%; leather products 4.2%; chickpeas 3.5%). *Major export destinations:* Germany 12.6%; China 9.7%; Japan 8.4%; Switzerland 6.4%; Saudi Arabia 6.3%.

Transport and communications

Transport. *Railroads* (2003): length 781 km; (2006–07) passenger-km 28,200,000. *Roads* (2007–08): total length 44,359 km (paved [2004] 19%). *Vehicles* (2003): passenger cars 71,311; trucks and buses 65,557. *Air transport* (2008): passenger-km 9,300,000,000; metric ton-km cargo 227,760,000. **Communications,** in total units (units per 1,000 persons). Telephone landlines (2008): 909,000 (11); cellular telephone subscribers (2008): 3,168,000 (37); personal computers (2007): 551,000 (7.0); total Internet users (2008): 360,000 (4.2); broadband Internet subscribers (2007): 300.

Education and health

Educational attainment (2000). Percentage of population ages 15 and over having: no formal schooling 63.8%; incomplete primary education 21.6%; primary 2.6%; incomplete secondary 8.1%; secondary 2.5%; post-secondary 1.4%. **Literacy** (2007): total population ages 15 and over literate 47.5%. **Health.** physicians (2004–05) 1,077 (1 per 66,236 persons); hospital beds (2007–08) 13,145 (1 per 6,062 persons);

infant mortality rate per 1,000 live births (2008) 82.6; undernourished population (2003-05) 35,200,000 (46% of total population based on the consumption of a minimum daily requirement of 1,680 calories).

Military

Total **active duty personnel** (November 2008): 138,000 (army 97.8%, air force 2.2%); mandate for the UN peacekeeping force along the Eritrean-Ethiopian border was terminated in July 2008. **Military expenditure as percentage of GDP** (2008): 1.6%; per capita expenditure US$4.

Background

Ethiopia, the Biblical land of Cush, was inhabited from earliest antiquity and was once under ancient Egyptian rule. Ge'ez-speaking agriculturalists established the kingdom of Da'amat in the 2nd millennium BC. After 300 BC they were superseded by the kingdom of Aksum, whose King Menilek I, according to legend, was the son of King Solomon and the Queen of Sheba. Christianity was introduced in the 4th century AD and became widespread. Ethiopia's prosperous Mediterranean trade was cut off by the Muslim Arabs in the 7th and 8th centuries, and the area's interests were directed eastward. Contact with Europe resumed in the late 15th century with the arrival of the Portuguese. Modern Ethiopia began with the reign of Tewodros II, who began the consolidation of the country. In the wake of European encroachment, the coastal region was made an Italian colony in 1890, but under Emperor Menilek II the Italians were defeated and ousted in 1896. Ethiopia prospered under his rule, and his modernization programs were continued by Emperor Haile Selassie in the 1930s. In 1936 Italy again gained control of the country, and it was held as part of Italian East Africa until 1941, when it was liberated by the British. Ethiopia incorporated Eritrea in 1952. In 1974 Haile Selassie was deposed, and a Marxist government, plagued by civil wars and famine, controlled the country until 1991. In 1993 Eritrea gained its independence, but there were continuing border conflicts with it and neighboring Somalia into the 21st century.

Recent Developments

The border dispute between Ethiopia and Eritrea remained at a stalemate in 2009. Neither had taken steps to demarcate the border in line with the 2002 ruling of the Eritrea-Ethiopia Boundary Commission, which Ethiopia had rejected. In August the Eritrea-Ethiopia Claims Commission ruled that compensation should be paid by each country to the other for damages inflicted during the 1998-2000 war. In early 2009 Ethiopia formally withdrew its armed forces from neighboring Somalia, where they had been serving since December 2006 in support of the Transitional Federal Government of Somalia, but reports of Ethiopian troop activity inside the country continued throughout the year.

Internet resource: <www.csa.gov.et>.

Fiji

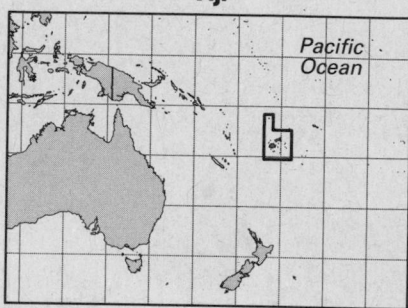

Official name: Republic of the Fiji Islands; Matanitu Tu-Vaka-i-koya ko Viti (Fijian); Fiji Ripablik (Hindustani). **Form of government:** interim regime. **Head of state:** President Ratu Epeli Nailatikau (from 2009). **Head of government:** Prime Minister Voreque Bainimarama (from 2007). **Capital:** Suva. **Official languages:** English, Fijian, and Hindustani have equal status per constitution. **Official religion:** none. **Monetary unit:** 1 Fiji dollar (F$) = 100 cents; valuation (1 Jul 2010) US$1 = F$2.00.

Demography

Area: 7,055 sq mi, 18,272 sq km. **Population** (2009): 845,000. **Density** (2009): persons per sq mi 119.8, persons per sq km 46.2. **Urban** (2007): 50.7%. **Sex distribution** (2007): male 51.02%; female 48.98%. **Age breakdown** (2007): under 15, 29.0%; 15-29, 27.9%; 30-44, 21.1%; 45-59, 14.5%; 60-74, 6.1%; 75 and over, 1.4%. **Ethnic composition** (2007): Fijian 56.8%; Indian 37.5%; other Pacific islanders 3.0%, of which Rotuman (Polynesian/other) 1.2%; European/part-European 1.7%; Chinese 0.6%; other 0.4%. **Religious affiliation** (2007): Christian 64.4%, of which Methodist 34.6%, Roman Catholic 9.1%, Assemblies of God 5.7%; Hindu 27.9%; Muslim 6.3%; other 1.4%. **Major urban areas** (2007): Nasinu 87,446; Suva 85,691 (urban agglomeration, 241,432); Lautoka 52,220; Nausori 47,604; Nadi 42,284. **Location:** Oceania, archipelago in the South Pacific Ocean, between Hawaii (US) and New Zealand.

Vital statistics

Birth rate per 1,000 population (2007): 20.7 (world avg. 20.3). **Death rate** per 1,000 population (2007): 7.1 (world avg. 8.5). **Total fertility rate** (avg. births per childbearing woman; 2006): 2.73. **Life expectancy** at birth (2006): male 67.3 years; female 72.5 years.

National economy

Budget (2006). *Revenue:* F$1,373,000,000 (tax revenue 90.7%, of which taxes on goods and services 40.9%, income tax 32.5%; other 9.3%). *Expenditures:* F$1,530,000,000 (general administration 25.0%; education 22.4%; economic affairs 14.2%; public order 9.4%; health 9.3%; defense 5.4%). **Public debt** (external, outstanding; June

---

1 metric ton = about 1.1 short tons;   1 kilometer = 0.6 mi (statute);   1 metric ton-km cargo = about 0.68 short ton-mi cargo;   c.i.f.: cost, insurance, and freight;   f.o.b.: free on board

2009): US$273,000,000. **Production** (metric tons except as noted). *Agriculture and fishing* (2007): sugarcane 3,200,000, coconuts 140,000, taro 38,000, cassava 34,500, rice 15,000, ginger 4,300, yaqona (kava) (2006) 2,259; livestock (number of live animals) 315,000 cattle, 4,300,000 chickens; fisheries production (2006) 47,319 (from aquaculture 1%). *Mining and quarrying* (2005): gold 3,800 kg; silver 1,500 kg. *Manufacturing* (value added in US$'000,000; 2004): food products 63; textiles and wearing apparel 53; beverages 46. *Energy production (consumption):* electricity (kW-hr; 2006) 840,000,000 (841,000,000); coal (metric tons; 2006) none (12,000); petroleum products (metric tons; 2006) none (489,000). **Population economically active** (2007): total 334,787; activity rate of total population 40.0% (participation rates: ages 15–64, 57.0%; female 33.9%; unemployed 8.6%). **Gross national income** (2008): US$3,300,000,000 (US$3,930 per capita). **Selected balance of payments data.** Receipts from (US$'000,000): tourism (2006) 433; remittances (2008) 175; foreign direct investment (2005–07 avg.) 268; official development assistance (2007) 57. Disbursements for (US$'000,000): tourism (2006) 101; remittances (2008) 32.

Foreign trade

Imports (2008; c.i.f.): F$3,601,000,000 (mineral fuels 33.9%; machinery and transportation equipment 20.2%; food products 14.4%). *Major import sources* (2007): Singapore 34.2%; Australia 22.8%; New Zealand 17.7%; China 3.3%; US 3.2%. **Exports** (2008; f.o.b.): F$1,471,000,000 (reexports [mostly refined petroleum products] 33.2%; sugar 16.9%; fish 9.1%; mineral water [2007] 9.1%; wearing apparel 6.9%; lumber 4.0%). *Major export destinations* (2007): Singapore 18.6%; US 14.7%; UK 14.2%; Australia 13.3%; New Zealand 6.9%.

Transport and communications

Transport. *Railroads* (2003; owned by the Fiji Sugar Corporation): length 597 km. *Roads* (1999): total length 3,440 km (paved 49%). *Vehicles* (2005): passenger cars 76,273; trucks and buses 42,311. *Air transport* (2004–05; Air Pacific only): passenger-km 2,360,000,000; metric ton-km cargo 92,108,000. **Communications,** in total units (units per 1,000 persons). Telephone landlines (2007): 108,000 (130); cellular telephone subscribers (2007): 437,000 (524); personal computers (2004): 44,000 (52); total Internet users (2007): 91,000 (110); broadband Internet subscribers (2007): 12,000 (14).

Education and health

Educational attainment (1996). Percentage of population ages 25 and over having: no formal schooling 4.4%; some education 22.3%; incomplete secondary 47.7%; complete secondary 17.0%; some higher 6.7%; university degree 1.9%. **Literacy** (2003): total population ages 15 and over literate 93.7%; males literate 95.5%; females literate 91.9%. **Health** (2007): physicians 318 (1 per 2,622 persons); hospital beds 1,727 (1 per 483 persons); infant mortality rate per 1,000 live births 18.4; undernourished population (2002–04) 40,000 (5% of total population based on the consumption of a minimum daily requirement of 1,920 calories).

Military

Total active duty personnel (November 2008): 3,500 (army 91.4%, navy 8.6%, air force, none); reserve 6,000. **Military expenditure as percentage of GDP** (2007): 1.6%; per capita expenditure US$60.

Background

Archaeological evidence shows that the islands of Fiji were occupied in the late 2nd millennium BC. The first European sighting was by the Dutch in the 17th century AD; in 1774 the islands were visited by Capt. James Cook, who found a mixed Melanesian-Polynesian population with a complex society. Traders and the first missionaries arrived in 1835. In 1857 a British consul was appointed, and in 1874 Fiji was proclaimed a crown colony. It became independent as a member of the Commonwealth in 1970 and was declared a republic in 1987 following a military coup. Elections in 1992 restored civilian rule. A new constitution was approved in 1997. Coups in 2000 and 2006 created continuing political instability in the early 21st century.

Recent Developments

In April 2009 Fiji's Court of Appeal ruled that under the 1997 Constitution, Pres. Ratu Josefa Iloilovatu Uluivuda did not have the power to dismiss the previous government or to install the interim government that had seized power in 2006. President Iloilo immediately abrogated the 1997 constitution, dismissed the judges, and appointed himself head of state with power to rule by decree. With the backing of the military, he announced that he would install an interim government for a five-year period.

Internet resource: <www.statsfiji.gov.fj>.

Finland

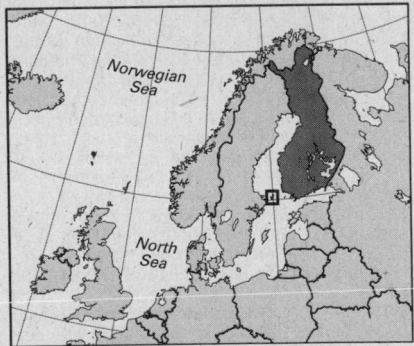

Official names: Suomen Tasavalta (Finnish); Republiken Finland (Swedish) (Republic of Finland). **Form of government:** multiparty republic with one legislative house (Parliament [200]). **Head of state:** President Tarja Halonen (from 2000). **Head of government:** Prime Minister Mari Kiviniemi (from 2010). **Capital:** Helsinki. **Official languages:** none (Finnish and Swedish are national [not official] languages). **Official**

religion: none. **Monetary unit:** 1 euro (€) = 100 cents; valuation (1 Jul 2010) US$1 = €0.80.

Demography

Area: 130,667 sq mi; 338,425 sq km. **Population** (2009): 5,339,000. **Density** (2009; based on land area only): persons per sq mi 45.5, persons per sq km 17.6. **Urban** (2004): 62.1%. **Sex distribution** (2008): male 49.03%; female 50.97%. **Age breakdown** (2008): under 15, 16.7%; 15–29, 18.8%; 30–44, 19.0%; 45–59, 21.7%; 60–74, 15.9%; 75–84, 5.9%; 85 and over, 2.0%. **Linguistic composition** (2008): Finnish 90.9%; Swedish 5.4%; Russian 0.9%; other 2.8%. **Religious affiliation** (2005): Evangelical Lutheran 83.1%; nonreligious 14.7%; Finnish (Greek) Orthodox 1.1%; Muslim 0.4%; other 0.7%. **Major cities** (2008): Helsinki 576,632 (urban agglomeration [2007] 1,115,000); Espoo 241,565; Tampere 209,552; Vantaa 195,397; Turku 175,582. **Location:** northern Europe, bordering Norway, Russia, the Gulf of Finland, the Baltic Sea, the Gulf of Bothnia, and Sweden.

Vital statistics

Birth rate per 1,000 population (2008): 11.2 (world avg. 20.3); within marriage 59.3%. **Death rate** per 1,000 population (2008): 9.2 (world avg. 8.5). **Total fertility rate** (avg. births per childbearing woman; 2008): 1.85. **Life expectancy** at birth (2008): male 76.3 years; female 83.0 years.

National economy

Budget (2008). *Revenue:* €45,522,000,000 (income and property taxes 34.2%; turnover taxes 33.3%; excise duties 11.0%). *Expenditures:* €45,522,000,000 (social security and health 31.0%; education 15.4%; public debt service 9.3%; agriculture and forestry 6.2%; defense 5.3%). **Public debt** (2008): US$74,700,000,000. **Production** (metric tons except as noted). *Agriculture and fishing* (2007): barley 1,984,000, oats 1,222,000, wheat 797,000; livestock (number of live animals) 1,448,000 pigs, 927,000 cattle, 193,000 reindeer; fisheries production (2006) 162,341 (from aquaculture 8%). *Mining and quarrying* (2006): chromite 320,000; zinc (metal content) 66,109; gold 5,292 kg. *Manufacturing* (value added in €'000,000; 2007): electrical and optical equipment (largely telephone apparatus) 10,291; nonelectrical machinery and apparatus 4,707; chemical products 4,129. *Energy production (consumption):* electricity (kW-hr; 2008) 74,052,-000,000 ([2006] 93,705,000,000); coal (metric tons; 2006) none (7,612,000); crude petroleum (barrels; 2008) none ([2006] 76,800,000); petroleum products (metric tons; 2006) 12,849,000 (10,541,000); natural gas (cu m; 2007) none (4,587,000,000). **Population economically active** (2008): total 2,725,600; activity rate of total population 51.3% (participation rates: ages 15–64, 76.1%; female 47.8%; unemployed [May 2008–April 2009] 8.0%). **Gross national income** (2008): US$255,678,000,000 (US$48,120 per capita). **Selected balance of payments data.** Receipts from (US$'000,000): tourism (2008) 3,127;

remittances (2008) 772; foreign direct investment (FDI; 2005–07 avg.) 6,236. Disbursements for (US$'000,000): tourism (2008) 4,350; remittances (2008) 391; FDI (2005–07 avg.) 5,336.

Foreign trade

Imports (2007; c.i.f.): €59,600,000,000 (machinery and apparatus 26.2%; crude petroleum 10.8%; chemical products 10.1%; motor vehicles and parts 8.5%; metal ore and scrap metal 7.2%). *Major import sources:* Russia 14.1%; Germany 14.0%; Sweden 9.8%; China 7.5%; UK 4.8%. **Exports** (2007; f.o.b.): €65,607,000,000 (telecommunications equipment and parts 13.6%; paper products and cardboard 12.3%; iron and steel 7.8%; specialized machinery 6.7%; refined petroleum products 5.1%; general industrial machinery 5.0%; nonferrous base metals 4.7%). *Major export destinations:* Germany 10.9%; Sweden 10.7%; Russia 10.2%; US 6.4%; UK 5.8%.

Transport and communications

Transport. *Railroads* (2008): route length 5,919 km; passenger-km 4,100,000,000; metric ton-km cargo 10,800,000,000. *Roads* (2008): total length 78,141 km (paved [2005] 65%). *Vehicles* (2005): passenger cars 2,430,345; trucks and buses 363,644. *Air transport* (2007): passenger-km 15,564,000,000; metric ton-km cargo 489,672,000. **Communications,** in total units (units per 1,000 persons). Telephone landlines (2008): 1,650,000 (311); cellular telephone subscribers (2008): 6,830,000 (1,285); personal computers (2007): 2,644,000 (500); total Internet users (2007): 4,169,000 (788); broadband Internet subscribers (2008): 1,617,000 (304).

Education and health

Educational attainment (2003). Percentage of population ages 25 and over having: incomplete upper-secondary education 35.6%; complete upper secondary or vocational 35.8%; higher 28.6%. **Literacy:** virtually 100%. **Health** (2007): physicians 18,843 (1 per 281 persons); hospital beds 36,095 (1 per 147 persons); infant mortality rate per 1,000 live births (2008) 2.6; undernourished population (2002–04) less than 2.5% of total population.

Military

Total active duty personnel (November 2008): 31,900 (army 67.4%, navy 17.9%, air force 14.7%); reserves 237,000. **Military expenditure as percentage of GDP** (2007): 1.3%; per capita expenditure US$596.

Background

Recent archaeological discoveries have led some to suggest that human habitation in Finland dates back at least 100,000 years. Ancestors of the Sami apparently were present in Finland by about 7000 BC. The ancestors of the present-day Finns came from the southern shore of the Gulf of Finland in the 1st millennium BC. The area was gradually Christianized from the 11th century. From the 12th century Swe-

---

1 metric ton = about 1.1 short tons;   1 kilometer = 0.6 mi (statute);   1 metric ton-km cargo = about 0.68 short ton-mi cargo;   c.i.f.: cost, insurance, and freight;   f.o.b.: free on board

den and Russia contested for supremacy in Finland, but by 1323 Sweden ruled most of the country. Russia was ceded part of Finnish territory in 1721; in 1808 Alexander I of Russia invaded Finland, which in 1809 was formally ceded to Russia. The subsequent period saw the growth of Finnish nationalism. Russia's losses in World War I and the Russian Revolution of 1917 set the stage for Finland's independence in 1917. It was defeated by the Soviet Union in the Russo-Finnish War (1939–40) but then sided with Nazi Germany against the Soviets during World War II and regained the territory it had lost. Facing defeat again by the advancing Soviets in 1944, it reached a peace agreement with the USSR, ceding territory and paying reparations. Finland's economy recovered after World War II. It joined the EU in 1995.

Recent Developments

The Finnish economy continued to plunge. The economy was heavily dependent on exports, which had accounted for over 44.0% of GDP in 2008. The value of exported goods dropped by 28.6% in 2009. At the same time, the value of imports, most notably raw materials and other items needed in manufacturing, decreased by 27.9%. Accordingly, industrial production was at its lowest in years, registering a 20.4% drop for the year. GDP fell 7.8% in 2009; the unemployment rate grew to 9.5% in January 2010; and inflation dropped by 4.1% in 2009.

Internet resource: <www.stat.fi/index_en.html>.

France

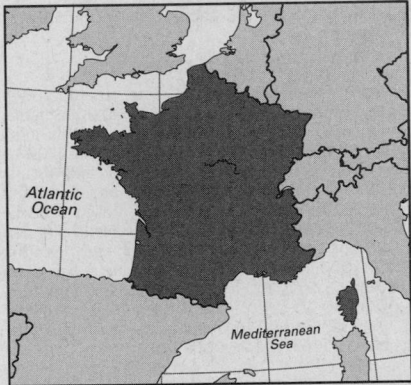

Official name: République Française (French Republic). **Form of government:** republic with two legislative houses (Senate [343], National Assembly [577]). **Head of state:** President Nicolas Sarkozy (from 2007). **Head of government:** Prime Minister François Fillon (from 2007). **Capital:** Paris. **Official language:** French. **Official religion:** none. **Monetary unit:** 1 euro (€) = 100 cents; valuation (1 Jul 2010) US$1 = €0.80.

Demography

Area: 210,026 sq mi, 543,965 sq km. **Population** (2000): 62,500,000 (excludes the populations of French Guiana, Guadeloupe, Martinique, and Réunion, totaling 1,861,000 people in mid-2009). **Den-**sity (2009): persons per sq mi 298.0, persons per sq km 115.1. **Urban** (2003): 76.3%. **Sex distribution** (2006): male 48.60%; female 51.40%. **Age breakdown** (2005): under 15, 18.4%; 15–29, 19.1%; 30–44, 21.1%; 45–59, 20.4%; 60–74, 12.7%; 75–84, 6.3%; 85 and over, 2.0%. **Ethnic composition** (2000): French 76.9%; Algerian and Moroccan Berber 2.2%; Italian 1.9%; Portuguese 1.5%; Moroccan Arab 1.5%; Fleming 1.4%; Algerian Arab 1.3%; Basque 1.3%; Jewish 1.2%; German 1.2%; Vietnamese 1.0%; Catalan 0.5%; other 8.1%. **Religious affiliation** (2004): Roman Catholic 64.3%, of which practicing 8.0%; nonreligious/atheist 27.0%; Muslim 4.3%; Protestant 1.9%; Buddhist 1.0%; Jewish 0.6%; Jehovah's Witness 0.4%; Orthodox 0.2%; other 0.3%. **Major cities (urban agglomerations)** (2006): Paris 2,181,371 (10,142,977); Marseille 839,043 (1,418,481); Lyon 472,305 (1,417,463); Lille 226,014 (1,016,205); Nice 347,060 (940,017); Toulouse 437,715 (850,873); Bordeaux 232,260 (803,117); Nantes 282,853 (568,743); Toulon 167,816 (543,065); Douai-Lens: Douai (2005) 40,094, Lens (2005) 34,872 (512,462); Strasbourg 272,975 (440,265); Grenoble 156,107 (427,658); Rouen 107,904 (388,798); Valenciennes (2005) 41,506 (355,660); Nancy 105,468 (331,279); Metz 124,435 (322,946); Montpellier 251,634 (318,225); Tours 136,942 (306,974); Saint-Étienne 177,480 (286,400); Rennes 209,613 (282,550). **Location:** western Europe, bordering the North Atlantic Ocean, Belgium, Luxembourg, Germany, Switzerland, Italy, the Mediterranean Sea, Spain, and Andorra. **Immigration:** total immigrant population (2004) 4,850,000; immigrants admitted (2002) 205,707, of which North African 30.7%, EU 20.8%, sub-Saharan African 15.2%, Asian 14.1%, other European 11.8%.

Vital statistics

Birth rate per 1,000 population (2008): 12.9 (world avg. 20.3); (2007) within marriage 48.3%. **Death rate** per 1,000 population (2008): 8.6 (world avg. 8.5). **Total fertility rate** (avg. births per childbearing woman; 2008): 2.00. **Life expectancy** at birth (2008): male 77.6 years; female 84.4 years.

Social indicators

Educational attainment (2002). Percentage of population ages 25–64 with no formal schooling through lower-secondary education 35%, upper secondary/higher vocational 41%, university 24%. **Quality of working life.** Legally worked week for full-time employees (2005) 36.0 hours. Rate of fatal injuries per 100,000 insured workers (2004): 3.7. Average days lost to labor stoppages per 1,000 workers (2004): 13. Trade union membership (2003): 1,900,000 (8% of labor force). **Access to services** (2004). Proportion of principal residences having: electricity 97.4%; indoor toilet 94.6%; indoor kitchen with sink 94.2%; hot water 60.3%; air conditioner 15.4%. **Social participation.** Population ages 15 and over participating in voluntary associations (1997): 28.0%. Percentage of population who "never" or "almost never" attend church services (2000) 60%; percentage of Roman Catholic population who attend Mass weekly (2003) 12%. **Social deviance.** Offense rate per 100,000 population (2000) for: murder 1.5, rape 16.0, other assault 269.2; theft (including burglary and housebreaking) 3,403.8. Incidence per 100,000 in general population of: homicide (2001)

0.8; suicide (2001) 16.1. **Leisure.** Members of sports federations (2007): 16,254,000, of which football (soccer) 2,321,000. Movie tickets sold (2005): 174,200,000. Average daily hours of television viewing for population ages 4 and over (2007): 3.45. **Material well-being** (2004). Households possessing: automobile (2007) 82%; color television 95%; personal computer 45%; washing machine 92%; microwave 74%; dishwasher (2001) 39%.

National economy

Gross national income (2008): US$2,702,180,-000,000 (US$42,250 per capita). **Budget** (2007). *Revenue:* €369,600,000,000 (tax revenue 80.0%, of which taxes on goods and services 43.6%; social contributions 10.9%; grants 4.5%). *Expenditures:* €411,410,000,000 (social protection 20.0%; education 19.4%; economic affairs 13.8%; debt service 11.1%; defense 8.2%). **Public debt** (2007): US$1,655,000,000,000. **Production** (metric tons except as noted). *Agriculture and fishing* (2008): wheat 39,001,700, sugar beets 30,306,300, corn (maize) 15,818,500, barley 12,171,300, potatoes 6,808,210, grapes 5,664,195, rapeseed 4,719,053, apples 1,940,200, triticale 1,820,950, sunflower seeds 1,607,977, tomatoes 714,635, oats 471,960, dry peas 446,850, lettuce and chicory 420,400, green peas 337,488, string beans 337,488, dry onions 189,992, pears 162,000, mushrooms and truffles 150,450, spinach 143,487, chicory roots 125,475, flax fibre and tow 95,000, kiwi fruit 65,670; livestock (number of live animals) 19,887,458 cattle, 14,805,557 pigs, 8,187,329 sheep, 175,000,000 chickens, 25,253,000 turkeys, 22,848,000 ducks, 420,238 horses; fisheries production (2007) 749,903 (from aquaculture 31%); aquatic plants production (2007) 76,678 (from aquaculture, negligible). *Mining and quarrying* (2006): gypsum 3,500,000; kaolin 300,000; gold 1,500 kg. *Manufacturing* (value added in US$'000,000; 2003): food products 27,023; pharmaceuticals, soaps, and paints 22,675; motor vehicles, trailers, and motor vehicle parts 20,269; fabricated metal products 14,264; general purpose machinery 10,595; plastic products 8,754; medical, measuring, and testing appliances 7,551; aircraft and spacecraft 7,476; publishing 6,911; special purpose machinery 6,605; bricks, cement, and ceramics 5,922; basic chemical products 5,843; base metals 5,547, of which iron and steel 4,117; paper products 5,532; beverages 5,509; furniture 4,218. *Energy production (consumption):* electricity (kW-hr; 2006) 574,473,000,000 (511,138,000,000 [including Monaco]); coal (metric tons; 2007) 168,000 ([2005] 19,069,000); lignite (metric tons; 2006) negligible (36,000 [including Monaco]); crude petroleum (barrels; 2007) 7,430,000 ([2006; including Monaco] 606,000,000); petroleum products (metric tons; 2006 [including Monaco]) 74,659,000 (75,921,000); natural gas (cu m; 2007) 1,079,000,000 ([2006; including Monaco] 49,155,000,000). *Retail trade* (value of sales in €'000,000; 2004): large food stores 162,600; large nonfood stores 136,400; auto repair shops 120,400; pharmacies and stores selling orthopedic equipment 32,600; shops selling bread, pastries, or meat 31,800; small food stores and boutiques 15,300. **Population economically active** (2005): total 27,635,800; activity rate of total population 45.5% (participation rates: ages 15–64, 69.1%; female 46.4%; unemployed [April 2007] 8.2%). **Selected balance of payments data.** Receipts from (US$'000,000): tourism (2007) 54,165; remittances (2008) 15,133; foreign direct investment (FDI; 2005–07 avg.) 107,025. Disbursements for (US$'000,000): tourism (2007) 36,743; remittances (2008) 4,541; FDI (2005–07 avg.) 153,666.

Foreign trade

Imports (2006; c.i.f. [including Monaco]): US$529,902,000,000 (machinery and apparatus 22.1%, of which electrical machinery and parts 5.4%, general industrial machinery 3.9%, office machines and computers 3.5%; mineral fuels 14.8%, of which crude petroleum 7.5%, refined petroleum products 3.5%; chemical products 12.7%, of which medicines and pharmaceuticals 3.5%; motor vehicles and parts 10.2%; wearing apparel and accessories 3.5%; iron and steel 3.2%). *Major import sources:* Germany 16.3%; Italy 8.5%; Belgium 8.3%; Spain 6.9%; UK 6.1%; US 6.0%; China 5.7%; Netherlands 4.1%; Japan 2.4%; Russia 2.4%. **Exports** (2006; f.o.b. [including Monaco]): US$479,013,000,000 (machinery and apparatus 22.1%, of which electrical machinery and parts 6.2%, general industrial machinery 4.8%, power-generating machinery 3.7%, telecommunications equipment 3.1%; chemical products 15.7%, of which medicines and pharmaceuticals 5.1%, perfumery and cosmetics 2.3%; motor vehicles and parts 12.1%; food products 6.1%; aircraft and parts 6.0%; mineral fuels 4.3%; iron and steel 3.7%; alcoholic beverages [mostly wine] 2.4%). *Major export destinations:* Germany 14.5%; Spain 9.9%; Italy 9.1%; UK 8.5%; Belgium 7.4%; US 6.9%; Netherlands 4.1%; Switzerland 2.7%; China 2.1%; Poland 1.8%.

Transport and communications

Transport. *Railroads* (2006): route length (2004) 29,085 km; passenger-km 92,000,000,000; metric ton-km cargo 41,000,000,000. *Roads* (2006): total length 951,500 km (paved 100%). *Vehicles* (2006): passenger cars 30,400,000; trucks and buses 6,262,000. *Air transport* (2008): passenger-km 131,664,000,000; metric ton-km cargo 5,838,-300,000. **Communications,** in total units (units per 1,000 persons). Telephone landlines (2008): 35,000,000 (565); cellular telephone subscribers (2008): 57,972,000 (936); personal computers (2007): 40,400,000 (652); total Internet users (2007): 31,571,000 (512); broadband Internet subscribers (2008): 17,691,000 (286).

Education and health

Health: physicians (2007) 212,700 (1 per 291 persons); hospital beds (2004) 457,132 (1 per 132 persons); infant mortality rate per 1,000 live births (2008) 3.6; undernourished population (2002–04) less than 2.5% of total population.

Military

Total active duty personnel (November 2008): 352,771 (army 38.0%, navy 12.5%, air force 16.3%, headquarters staff 1.5%, health services 2.4%, gen-

---

1 metric ton = about 1.1 short tons;   1 kilometer = 0.6 mi (statute);   1 metric ton-km cargo = about 0.68 short ton-mi cargo;   c.i.f.: cost, insurance, and freight;   f.o.b.: free on board

darmerie 29.3%). **Military expenditure as percentage of GDP** (2007): 2.4%; per capita expenditure US$980.

Background

Archaeological excavations in France indicate continuous settlement from Paleolithic times. About 1200 BC the Gauls migrated into the area, and in 600 BC Ionian Greeks established several settlements, including one at Marseille. Julius Caesar completed the Roman conquest of Gaul in 50 BC. During the 6th century AD, the Salian Franks ruled; by the 8th century power had passed to the Carolingians, the greatest of whom was Charlemagne. The Hundred Years' War (1337–1453) resulted in the return to France of land that had been held by the British; by the end of the 15th century, France approximated its modern boundaries. The 16th century was marked by the Wars of Religion between Protestants (Huguenots) and Roman Catholics. Henry IV's Edict of Nantes (1598) granted substantial religious toleration, but this was revoked in 1685 by Louis XIV, who helped to raise monarchical absolutism to new heights. In 1789 the French Revolution proclaimed the rights of the individual and destroyed the ancien régime. Napoleon ruled from 1799 to 1814, after which a limited monarchy was restored until 1871, when the Third Republic was created. World War I (1914–18) ravaged the northern part of France. After Nazi Germany's invasion during World War II, the collaborationist Vichy regime governed. Liberated by Allied and Free French forces in 1944, France restored parliamentary democracy under the Fourth Republic. A costly war in Indochina and rising nationalism in French colonies during the 1950s overwhelmed the Fourth Republic. The Fifth Republic was established in 1958 under Charles de Gaulle, who presided over the dissolution of most of France's overseas colonies. In 1981 François Mitterrand became France's first elected Socialist president. At various times from 1986 through the beginning of the 21st century, France balanced a form of divided government known as "cohabitation," with a president and prime minister of different political parties.

Recent Developments

France was affected by the global recession of 2009, but in ways that reflected its political strengths and weaknesses. The downturn's impact was softened by the French state's traditionally large role in the economy of spending and providing welfare. Yet with only a weak parliamentary opposition to air their complaints, many French took part in national street demonstrations to protest the government's inability to do even more to protect jobs and wages. The French model of regulated capitalism was hailed for steering the country clear of the excesses of Anglo-Saxon lending and borrowing. Pres. Nicolas Sarkozy's very active governing style invited people to lay the blame for most problems at his door. The year's big concern was the economy: GDP was expected to fall by more than 2.0%. Although this decline was smaller than that in many other countries, it was the first drop in France's annual GDP since 1993. As the unemployment rate began to increase toward the 10.0% mark, both the government and workers began to adopt unorthodox tactics to stem its rise. Days before authorizing loans to Renault and Peugeot-Citroën to sustain their car businesses, Sarkozy urged Peugeot to close its factories in the Czech Republic or Slovakia rather than in France. The economy improved somewhat in the second quarter, partly as a result of the French government's relatively small but swift stimulus program of about US$33 billion. Sarkozy also planned a "national bond" issue for investment of more than US$50 billion in long-term research projects and the national infrastructure.

Internet resource: <www.insee.fr>.

Gabon

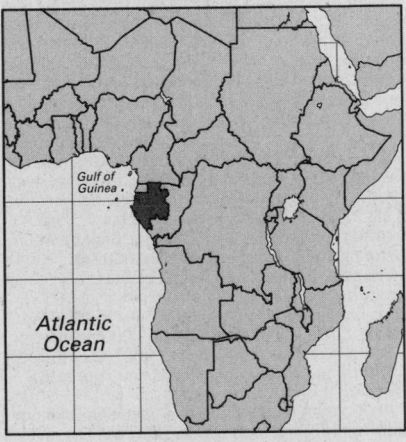

Gulf of Guinea

Atlantic Ocean

Official name: République Gabonaise (Gabonese Republic). **Form of government:** unitary multiparty republic with two legislative houses (Senate [102]; National Assembly [120]). **Head of state:** President Ali Bongo Ondimba (from 2009). **Head of government:** Prime Minister Paul Biyoghé Mba (from 2009). **Capital:** Libreville. **Official language:** French. **Official religion:** none. **Monetary unit:** 1 CFA franc (CFAF) = 100 centimes; valuation (1 Jul 2010) US$1 = CFAF 527.20.

Demography

Area: 103,347 sq mi, 267,667 sq km. **Population** (2009): 1,475,000. **Density** (2009): persons per sq mi 14.3, persons per sq km 5.5. **Urban** (2006): 85.7%. **Sex distribution** (2006): male 49.67%; female 50.33%. **Age breakdown** (2005): under 15, 40.0%; 15–29, 28.3%; 30–44, 16.1%; 45–59, 9.3%; 60–74, 4.6%; 75–84, 1.4%; 85 and over, 0.3%. **Ethnic composition** (2000): Fang 28.6%; Punu 10.2%; Nzebi 8.9%; French 6.7%; Mpongwe 4.1%; Teke 4.0%; other 37.5%. **Religious affiliation** (2005): Christian 73%, of which Roman Catholic 45%, Protestant/independent Christian 28%; Muslim 12%; traditional beliefs 10%; nonreligious 5%. **Major urban areas** (2003): Libreville 661,600; Port-Gentil 116,200; Franceville 41,300. **Location:** western Africa, bordering Cameroon, the Republic of the Congo, the South Atlantic Ocean, and Equatorial Guinea.

Vital statistics

Birth rate per 1,000 population (2006): 36.2 (world avg. 20.3). **Death rate** per 1,000 population (2006):

12.3 (world avg. 8.5). **Total fertility rate** (avg. births per childbearing woman; 2006): 4.74. **Life expectancy** at birth (2006): male 53.2 years; female 55.8 years.

National economy

Budget (2006). *Revenue:* CFAF 1,582,600,000,000 (oil revenues 64.0%; taxes on international trade 15.2%; direct taxes 10.0%; indirect taxes 7.2%; other revenues 3.6%). *Expenditures:* CFAF 1,066,300,-000,000 (current expenditures 77.6%, of which transfers 27.3%, wages and salaries 23.7%, debt service 10.9%; capital expenditures 22.4%). **Public debt** (external, outstanding; 2007): US$5,177,000,000. **Gross national income** (2008): US$10,490,000,000 (US$7,240 per capita). **Production** (metric tons except as noted). *Agriculture and fishing* (2007): plantains 275,000, cassava 240,000, sugarcane 220,000, natural rubber 12,000; livestock (number of live animals) 213,000 pigs, 3,100,000 chickens; fisheries production 39,124 (from aquaculture, negligible). *Mining and quarrying* (2005): manganese ore 2,859,000; gold 300 kg (excludes about 400 kg of illegally mined gold smuggled out of Gabon). *Manufacturing* (value added in CFAF '000,000,000; 2004): agricultural products 48.0; wood products (excluding furniture) 31.3; refined petroleum products 18.1. *Energy production (consumption):* electricity (kW-hr; 2006) 1,726,000,000 (1,726,000,000); crude petroleum (barrels; 2007) 83,900,000 ([2006] 5,749,000); petroleum products (metric tons; 2006) 684,000 (497,000); natural gas (cu m; 2006) 126,000,000 (126,000,000). **Population economically active** (2003): total 570,000; activity rate of total population 42.5% (participation rates: ages 15–64, 74.1%; female 43.0%; unemployed 21%). **Selected balance of payments data.** Receipts from (US$'000,000): tourism (2005) 15; remittances (2008) 11; foreign direct investment (FDI; 2005–07 avg.) 199; official development assistance (2006) 31. Disbursements for (US$'000,000): tourism (2004) 214; remittances (2008) 186; FDI (2005–07 avg.) 76.

Foreign trade

Imports (2006; c.i.f.): US$1,725,000,000 (machinery and apparatus 27.6%, of which general industrial machinery 8.8%; food products 13.0%; motor vehicles and parts 9.9%; chemical products 9.2%). *Major import sources:* France 39.9%; Belgium 14.2%; US 7.3%; Cameroon 3.5%; Japan 3.0%. **Exports** (2006; f.o.b.): US$6,015,000,000 (crude petroleum 84.4%; rough wood 5.1%; manganese ore and concentrate 3.1%; veneer and plywood 2.0%; refined petroleum products 1.2%). *Major export destinations:* US 58.4%; China 10.6%; France 7.1%; Singapore 5.3%; Switzerland 2.6%.

Transport and communications

Transport. *Railroads* (2002): route length (2005) 814 km; passenger-km 97,500,000; metric ton-km cargo 1,553,000,000. *Roads* (2004): total length 9,170 km (paved 10%). *Vehicles* (1997): passenger cars 24,750; trucks and buses 16,490. *Air transport* (2002): passenger-km 643,000,000. **Communica-

tions,** in total units (units per 1,000 persons). Telephone landlines (2007): 27,000 (18); cellular telephone subscribers (2008): 1,300,000 (963); personal computers (2007): 46,000 (36); total Internet users (2008): 90,000 (68); broadband Internet subscribers (2007): 2,000 (1.3).

Education and health

Educational attainment (2000): no formal schooling 6.2%; incomplete primary and complete primary education 32.7%; lower secondary 41.3%; upper secondary 14.2%; higher 5.6%. **Literacy** (2000): total population ages 15 and over literate 71%; males literate 80%; females literate 62%. **Health** (2003–04): physicians 270 (1 per 5,006 persons); hospital beds 4,460 (1 per 303 persons); infant mortality rate per 1,000 live births (2006) 54.5; undernourished population (2002–04) 60,000 (5% of total population based on the consumption of a minimum daily requirement of 1,850 calories).

Military

Total active duty personnel (November 2008): 4,700 (army 68.1%, navy 10.6%, air force 21.3%); French troops (2008): 800. **Military expenditure as percentage of GDP** (2007): 1.1%; per capita expenditure US$86.

Background

Artifacts dating from late Paleolithic and early Neolithic times have been found in Gabon, but it is not known when the Bantu speakers who established Gabon's ethnic composition arrived. Pygmies were probably the original inhabitants. The Fang arrived in the late 18th century and were followed by the Portuguese and by French, Dutch, and English traders. The slave trade dominated commerce in the 18th and much of the 19th century. The French then took control, and Gabon was administered (1843–86) with French West Africa. In 1886 the colony of French Congo was established to include both Gabon and the Congo; in 1910 Gabon became a separate colony within French Equatorial Africa. An overseas territory of France from 1946, it became an autonomous republic within the French Community in 1958 and declared its independence in 1960. Rule by a sole political party was established in the 1960s, but discontent with it led to riots in Libreville in 1989. Legalization of opposition parties led to new elections in 1990. The country continued to face economic difficulties despite large revenues from petroleum exports.

Recent Developments

Gabonese Pres. Omar Bongo suffered a heart attack and died on 8 Jun 2009. In power for 41 years, at the time of his death he was Africa's longest-serving head of state. French Pres. Nicolas Sarkozy, in attendance at the state funeral, was jeered by crowds protesting a French government investigation launched in May into Bongo's finances.

Internet resource: <www.legabon.org>.

1 metric ton = about 1.1 short tons;   1 kilometer = 0.6 mi (statute);   1 metric ton-km cargo = about 0.68 short ton-mi cargo;   c.i.f.: cost, insurance, and freight;   f.o.b.: free on board

Gambia, The

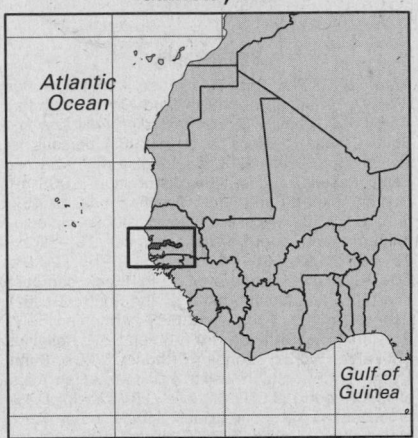

Atlantic Ocean

Gulf of Guinea

Official name: Republic of The Gambia. **Form of government:** multiparty republic with one legislative house (National Assembly [53]). **Head of state and government:** President Col. Yahya Jammeh (from 1994). **Capital:** Banjul. **Official language:** English. **Official religion:** none. **Monetary unit:** 1 dalasi (D) = 100 bututs; valuation (1 Jul 2010) US$1 = D 28.57.

Demography

Area: 4,491 sq mi, 11,632 sq km. **Population** (2009): 1,705,000. **Density** (2009): persons per sq mi 379.6, persons per sq km 146.6. **Urban** (2006): 54.3%. **Sex distribution** (2007): male 49.92%; female 50.08%. **Age breakdown** (2007): under 15, 44.1%; 15–29, 26.9%; 30–44, 15.6%; 45–59, 8.8%; 60–74, 3.8%; 75–84, 0.7%; 85 and over, 0.1%. **Ethnic composition** (2003): Malinke 42%; Fulani 18%; Wolof 16%; Diola 10%; Soninke 9%; other 5%. **Religious affiliation** (2005): Muslim 90%; Christian (mostly Roman Catholic) 9%; traditional beliefs/other 1%. **Major cities** (2006): Banjul 33,131 (Greater Banjul [2003] 523,589); Serekunda 335,700; Brikama 80,700; Bakau 45,500; Farafenni 30,400. **Location:** western Africa, bordering Senegal and the North Atlantic Ocean.

Vital statistics

Birth rate per 1,000 population (2007): 39.0 (world avg. 20.3). **Death rate** per 1,000 population (2007): 13.0 (world avg. 8.5). **Total fertility rate** (avg. births per childbearing woman; 2007): 5.2. **Life expectancy** at birth (2006): male 52.3 years; female 56.0 years.

National economy

Budget (2007). *Revenue:* D 3,663,500,000 (tax revenue 82.9%, of which taxes on goods and services 36.7%, taxes on income and profits 24.1%; nontax revenue 11.8%; grants 5.3%). *Expenditures:* D 3,635,000,000 (current expenditures 71.1%, of which interest payments 22.4%; capital expenditures 26.9%; net lending 2.1%). *Production (metric tons except as noted). Agriculture and fishing* (2007): millet 160,000, peanuts (groundnuts) 100,000, sorghum 40,000, findo (local cereal; 2005) 600; livestock (number of live animals) 334,000 cattle, 280,000 goats, 150,000 sheep; fisheries production 43,574 (from aquaculture, negligible). *Mining and quarrying* (2007): clay 14,000; sand and gravel are also excavated for local use. *Manufacturing* (value added in US$; 1995): food products and beverages 6,000,000; textiles, wearing apparel, and footwear 750,000; wood products 550,000. *Energy production (consumption):* electricity (kW-hr; 2007) 213,000,000 ([2006] 166,000,000); petroleum products (metric tons; 2006) none (109,000). **Population economically active** (2006): total 754,000; activity rate of total population 45.3% (participation rates: ages 15–64, 77.1%; female 45.6%). **Public debt** (external, outstanding; 2007): US$704,000,000. **Gross national income** (2008): US$653,000,000 (US$390 per capita). **Selected balance of payments data.** Receipts from (US$'000,000): tourism (2007) 75; remittances (2008) 64; foreign direct investment (2005–07 avg.) 60; official development assistance (2007) 72. Disbursements for (US$'000,000): tourism (2007) 7; remittances (2008) 12.

Foreign trade

Imports (2007; c.i.f.): US$262,900,000 (imports for domestic use 70.0%, of which refined petroleum products 10.8%; imports for reexport [principally to Senegal] 30.0%). *Major import sources:* Denmark 14%; US 13%; China 11%; Germany 8%; UK 8%. **Exports** (2007; f.o.b.): US$91,400,000 (reexports 86.3%; peanut [groundnut] oil 3.3%; peanuts [groundnuts] 2.7%; fish 2.0%). *Major export destinations:* reexports (principally to Senegal) 86.3%; domestic exports 13.7%, of which to Senegal 3.5%, to UK 2.7%, to France 1.9%.

Transport and communications

Transport. *Railroads:* none. *Roads* (2004): total length 3,742 km (paved 19%). *Vehicles* (2004): passenger cars 8,109; trucks and buses 2,961. *Air transport* (2001; Yumdum International Airport at Banjul only): passenger arrivals 300,000, passenger departures 300,000; cargo loaded and unloaded 2,700 metric tons. **Communications,** in total units (units per 1,000 persons). Telephone landlines (2008): 49,000 (30); cellular telephone subscribers (2008): 1,166,000 (702); personal computers (2007): 53,000 (33); total Internet users (2008): 114,000 (69); broadband Internet subscribers (2007): 300 (0.2).

Education and health

Literacy (2007): total population ages 15 and over literate 44.9%; males literate 52.3%; females literate 37.8%. **Health:** physicians (2003) 156 (1 per 9,769 persons); hospital beds (2005) 1,221 (1 per 1,250 persons); infant mortality rate per 1,000 live births (2007) 72.0; undernourished population (2002–04) 450,000 (29% of total population based on the consumption of a minimum daily requirement of 1,850 calories).

Military

Total active duty personnel (November 2008): 800 (army 100%). **Military expenditure as percentage of GDP** (2007): 0.6%; per capita expenditure US$2.

Background

Beginning about the 13th century AD, the Wolof, Malinke, and Fulani peoples settled in different parts of what is now The Gambia and established villages and then kingdoms in the region. European exploration began when the Portuguese sighted the Gambia River in 1455. Britain and France both settled in the area in the 17th century. The British Ft. James, on an island about 20 mi (32 km) from the river's mouth, was an important collection point for the slave trade. In 1783 the Treaty of Versailles reserved the Gambia River for Britain. After the British abolished slavery in 1807, they built a fort at the mouth of the river to block the continuing slave trade. In 1889 The Gambia's boundaries were agreed upon by Britain and France; the British declared a protectorate over the area in 1894. Independence was proclaimed in 1965, and The Gambia became a republic within the Commonwealth in 1970. It formed a limited confederation with Senegal in 1982 that was dissolved in 1989. During the 1990s the government was in turmoil.

Recent Developments

Suppression of freedom of expression and arbitrary kidnappings and beatings of citizens by state agents continued to be problems in The Gambia in 2009. In March Amnesty International reported that approximately 1,000 Gambians had been detained and tortured in state-sanctioned witch hunts.

Internet resource: <www.gambia.gm>.

Georgia

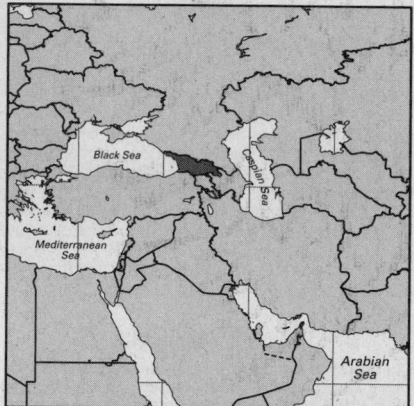

Black Sea

Caspian Sea

Mediterranean Sea

Arabian Sea

Official name: Sakartvelo (Georgia). **Form of government:** unitary multiparty republic with a single legislative house (Parliament [150]). **Head of state and government:** President Mikheil Saakashvili (from 2008), assisted by Prime Minister Nika Gilauri (from 2009). **Capital:** Tbilisi (T'bilisi). **Official language:** Georgian. **Official religion:** none (special recognition is given to the Georgian Orthodox Church). **Monetary**

unit: 1 Georgian lari (GEL) = 100 tetri; valuation (1 Jul 2010) US$1 = 1.85 lari.

Demography

Area: 27,086 sq mi, 70,152 sq km. **Population** (2009; excluding Abkhazia and South Ossetia): 4,368,000. **Density** (2009; excluding Abkhazia and South Ossetia): persons per sq mi 196.4, persons per sq km 75.8. **Urban** (2008; excluding Abkhazia and South Ossetia): 52.7%. **Sex distribution** (2008; excluding Abkhazia and South Ossetia): male 47.45%; female 52.55%. **Age breakdown** (2008; excluding Abkhazia and South Ossetia): under 15, 17.1%; 15–29, 23.9%; 30–44, 20.7%; 45–59, 20.0%; 60–74, 12.4%; 75 and over, 5.9%. **Ethnic composition** (2002; excluding Abkhazia and South Ossetia): Georgian 83.8%; Azerbaijani 6.5%; Armenian 5.7%; Russian 1.5%; Ossetian 0.9%; other 1.6%. **Religious affiliation** (2005): Georgian Orthodox 54.8%; Sunni Muslim 14.5%; Shiʿi Muslim 5.0%; Armenian Apostolic (Orthodox) 3.9%; Catholic 0.8%; Yazidi 0.4%; Protestant 0.4%; nonreligious 13.0%; other 7.2%. **Major cities** (2008): Tbilisi (T'bilisi) 1,106,500; Kutaisi 188,600; Batumi 122,200; Rustavi 117,300; Zugdidi 72,100. **Location:** northern Transcaucasia, bordering Russia, Azerbaijan, Armenia, Turkey, and the Black Sea.

Vital statistics

Birth rate per 1,000 population (2008; excluding Abkhazia and South Ossetia): 12.9 (world avg. 20.3); within marriage 65.7%. **Death rate** per 1,000 population (2008; excluding Abkhazia and South Ossetia): 9.8 (world avg. 8.5). **Total fertility rate** (avg. births per childbearing woman; 2007; excluding Abkhazia and South Ossetia): 1.45. **Life expectancy** at birth (2008; excluding Abkhazia and South Ossetia): male 69.3 years; female 79.0 years.

National economy

Budget (2007). *Revenue:* GEL 5,158,600,000 (tax revenue 72.4%, of which VAT 38.3%, social tax 14.0%, corporate taxes 8.4%, excise tax 8.3%; nontax revenue 23.3%; grants 4.3%). *Expenditures:* GEL 5,237,100,000 (defense 28.6%; social security and welfare 14.8%; general public service 14.6%; public order 13.1%; education 7.3%). **Population economically active** (2008): total 1,917,800; activity rate of total population 43.8% (participation rates: ages 15 and over, 62.6%; female 46.4%; unemployed 16.5%). **Production** (metric tons except as noted). *Agriculture and fishing* (2007): potatoes 174,500, grapes 93,000, wheat 92,300, apples 42,500, walnuts 12,400; livestock (number of live animals) 1,318,800 cattle, 509,700 pigs; fisheries production 18,377 (from aquaculture 1%). *Mining and quarrying* (2005): manganese ore 251,800. *Manufacturing* (value of production in US$'000,000; 2006): food products and beverages 95; chemical products 41; cement, bricks, and ceramics 26. *Energy production (consumption):* electricity (kW-hr; 2006) 7,599,000,000 (8,373,000,000); coal (metric tons; 2006) 11,000 (23,000); crude petroleum (barrels; 2007) 357,300 (4,737,700); petroleum products (metric tons; 2006) 4,000 (658,000); natural gas (cu m; 2007) 10,000,000 (1,490,000,000). **Gross national income** (2008): US$10,788,-000,000 (US$2,470 per capita). **Public debt** (external, outstanding; March 2009): US$2,170,-032,000. **Selected balance of payments data.** Receipts from (US$'000,000): tourism (2007) 385; remittances (2008–09) 907; foreign direct investment (2006–08 avg.) 1,192; official development assistance (2007) 382. Disbursements for (US$'000,000): tourism (2007) 176; remittances (2008–09) 77.

Foreign trade

Imports (2008; c.i.f.): US$6,304,557,300 (mineral fuels 18.5%; motor vehicles 13.9%; food products and beverages 13.7%; nonelectrical machinery 9.1%; electrical machinery 8.2%; chemical products 7.0%). *Major import sources:* Turkey 14.9%; Ukraine 10.4%; Azerbaijan 9.6%; Germany 7.9%; Russia 6.8%. **Exports** (2008; f.o.b.): US$1,496,060,400 (iron and steel 27.4%; food products and beverages [including wine] 16.7%; chemical products 13.6%; mineral fuels 11.3%). *Major export destinations:* Turkey 17.6%; Azerbaijan 13.7%; Ukraine 9.0%; Canada 8.8%; Armenia 8.2%.

Transport and communications

Transport. *Railroads* (2007): 1,559 km; passenger-km 773,900,000; metric ton-km cargo 6,927,500,000. *Roads* (2007): 20,329 km (paved [2006] 39%). *Vehicles* (2008): passenger cars 466,900; trucks and buses 105,100. *Air transport* (2007): passenger-km 474,800,000; metric ton-km cargo 3,600,000. **Communications**, in total units (units per 1,000 persons). Telephone landlines (2008): 556,000 (129); cellular telephone subscribers (2008): 3,283,000 (762); personal computers (2007): 228,000 (52); total Internet users (2008): 388,000 (90); broadband Internet subscribers (2007): 47,000 (11).

Education and health

Educational attainment (2004). Percentage of population ages 15 and over having: no formal education/unknown 1.6%; primary education 4.1%; incomplete secondary 10.5%; secondary 48.2%; incomplete higher 12.3%; higher 23.3%. **Literacy** (2008): virtually 100%. **Health** (2008): physicians 20,253 (1 per 216 persons); hospital beds 14,100 (1 per 310 persons); infant mortality rate per 1,000 live births 17.0; undernourished population (2002–04) 500,000 (9% of total population based on the consumption of a minimum daily requirement of 1,960 calories).

Military

Total active duty personnel (November 2008): 21,150 (army 84.0%, national guard 7.5%, navy 2.3%, air force 6.2%); Russian troops in Abkhazia and South Ossetia (November 2008): 3,800 in each. **Military expenditure as percentage of GDP** (2007): 7.6%; per capita expenditure US$250.

Background

Ancient Georgia was the site of the kingdoms of Iberia and Colchis, whose wealth was known to the ancient Greeks. The area was part of the Roman Empire by 65 BC and became Christian in AD 337. For the next three centuries it was involved in the conflicts between the Byzantine and Persian empires; after 654 it was controlled by Arab caliphs, who established an emirate in Tbilisi. It was controlled by the Bagratids from the 8th to the 12th century, and the zenith of Georgia's power was reached in the reign of Queen Tamara, whose realm stretched from Azerbaijan to Circassia, forming a pan-Caucasian empire. Invasions by Mongols and Turks in the 13th and 14th centuries disintegrated the kingdom, and the fall of Constantinople (now Istanbul) to the Ottoman Turks in 1453 isolated it from Western Christendom. The next three centuries saw repeated invasions by the Armenians, Turks, and Persians. Georgia sought Russian protection in 1783, and in 1801 it was annexed to Russia. After the Russian Revolution of 1917, the area was briefly independent; in 1921 a Soviet regime was installed, and in 1936 Georgia became the Georgian SSR, a full member of the Soviet Union. In 1990 a noncommunist coalition came to power in the first free elections ever held in Soviet Georgia, and in 1991 Georgia declared independence. In the 1990s, while Pres. Eduard Shevardnadze tried to steer a middle course, internal dissension resulted in conflicts with the northwestern republic of Abkhazia and the northern republic of South Ossetia, and external distrust of Russian motives in the area grew. In 1992 Abkhazia reinstated its 1925 constitution and declared independence, which Georgia refused to recognize. After several weeks of sporadic exchanges of gunfire between Georgian soldiers and rebel forces in South Ossetia, Georgian troops entered the republic on 7 Aug 2008. In response, Russian tanks and troops advanced into South Ossetia on 8 August, bombed the port of Poti and several military bases, and occupied Gori. Several hundred servicemen and civilians died during the fighting, and tens of thousands were forced to flee their homes. Following the deployment of international observers in October, Russian troops withdrew from the conflict zones.

Recent Developments

Tensions continued in Georgia in 2009 concerning Abkhazia and South Ossetia. In July Russia blocked an extension of the mandate of the UN Observer Mission in Georgia, and the mission's 130 members were forced to leave Abkhazia. In violation of the previous year's armistice agreements, in September Russia signed military cooperation pacts with both republics. That month an international group tasked with evaluating the events leading to the August 2008 war concluded that Georgia had begun the hostilities but condemned Russia's disproportionate response and its failure to prevent ethnic cleansing by South Ossetian forces. One positive sign came in late December when Georgia and Russia reopened their main border crossing, closed since 2006. By April 2010 only Nicaragua, Venezuela, and Nauru had joined Russia in officially recognizing the independence of Abkhazia and South Ossetia.

Internet resource:
<www.statistics.ge/index.php?plang=1>.

Germany

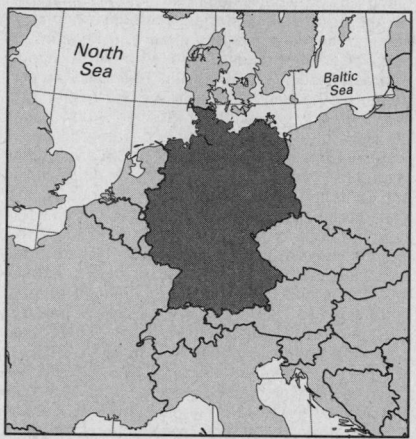

North Sea

Baltic Sea

Official name: Bundesrepublik Deutschland (Federal Republic of Germany). **Form of government:** federal multiparty republic with two legislative houses (Federal Council [69]; Federal Diet [622; statutory number is 598]). **Head of state:** President Christian Wulff (from 2010). **Head of government:** Chancellor Angela Merkel (from 2005). **Capital:** Berlin; some ministries remain in Bonn, the previous capital of West Germany, and the federal supreme court meets in Karlsruhe. **Official language:** German. **Official religion:** none. **Monetary unit:** 1 euro (€) = 100 cents; valuation (1 Jul 2010) US$1 = €0.80.

Demography

Area: 137,882 sq mi, 357,114 sq km. **Population** (2009): 82,000,000. **Density** (2009): persons per sq mi 594.7, persons per sq km 229.6. **Urban** (2003): 88.1%. **Major cities (urban agglomerations)** (2005): Dortmund 588,168 (5,746,018); Essen 585,430 (5,746,018); Duisburg 501,564 (5,746,018); Berlin 3,395,189 (4,200,072); Stuttgart 592,569 (2,625,690); Hamburg 1,743,627 (2,549,339); Munich 1,259,677 (1,940,477); Frankfurt am Main 651,899 (1,915,002); Cologne 983,347 (1,846,241); Mannheim 307,900 (1,579,252); Düsseldorf 574,514 (1,318,512); Nuremberg (Nürnberg) 499,237 (1,030,168); Hannover 515,729 (1,001,580); Saarbrücken 178,914 (942,594); Bonn 312,818 (899,753); Bremen 546,852 (858,488); Wuppertal 359,237 (832,685); Wiesbaden 274,611 (795,725); Dresden 495,181 (695,680); Karlsruhe 285,263 (600,161); Aachen 258,208 (599,676); Bielefeld 326,925 (585,145); Leipzig 502,651 (580,050); Darmstadt 140,562 (531,077). **Location:** central Europe, bordering Denmark, the Baltic Sea, Poland, the Czech Republic, Austria, Switzerland, France, Luxembourg, Belgium, the Netherlands, and the North Sea. **Sex distribution** (2007): male 48.98%; female 51.02%. **Sex distribution** (2007): male 48.98%; female 51.02%. **Ethnic composition** (by nationality; 2000): German 88.2%; Turkish 3.4% (including Kurdish 0.7%); Italian 1.0%; Greek 0.7%; Serb

0.6%; Russian 0.6%; Polish 0.4%; other 5.1%. **Age breakdown** (2006): under 15, 13.9%; 15–29, 17.6%; 30–44, 22.4%; 45–59, 21.1%; 60–74, 16.7%; 75–84, 6.3%; 85 and over, 2.0%. **Religious affiliation** (2005): Protestant 35.0%, of which Lutheran/Reformed churches 34%; Roman Catholic 32.5%; Sunni Muslim 4.3%; Orthodox 1.7%; New Apostolic 0.5%; Buddhist 0.3%; Jewish 0.2%; nonreligious 18.0%; atheist 2.0%; other 5.5%. **Resident foreign population** (2007): 6,744,900; *region/country of birth:* EU countries 34.7%, of which Italy 7.8%, Poland 5.7%, Greece 4.4%, Austria 2.6%; Turkey 25.4%; Asian countries 12.1%; former Serbia and Montenegro 4.9%; African countries 4.0%; Croatia 3.3%; Russia 2.8%; Bosnia and Herzegovina 2.3%; US 1.5%; other 9.0%. **Population with immigrant background** (2008): 14,800,000 (18% of total population). **Immigration/emigration trends** (2007): foreigners arriving 680,000; Germans departing 165,000.

Vital statistics

Birth rate per 1,000 population (2008): 8.2 (world avg. 20.3); within marriage 68.2%. **Death rate** per 1,000 population (2008): 10.3 (world avg. 8.5). **Total fertility rate** (avg. births per childbearing woman; 2008): 1.37. **Life expectancy** at birth (2008): male 77.2 years; female 82.5 years.

Social indicators

Educational attainment (2006). Percentage of population ages 25–64 having: no formal schooling through primary education 3%; lower secondary 14%; upper secondary 52%; post-secondary non-tertiary 7%; higher vocational 9%; university 14%; advanced degree 1%. **Quality of working life.** Average workweek (2007): 38.4 hours. Annual rate per 100,000 workers (2007) for: injuries or accidents at work 2,803; deaths 2.16. Proportion of labor force insured for damages of income loss resulting from: injury, virtually 100%; permanent disability, virtually 100%; death, virtually 100%. Average days lost to labor stoppages per 1,000 workers (2008): 3.7. **Access to services.** Proportion of dwellings (2002) having: electricity, virtually 100%; piped water supply, virtually 100%; flush sewage disposal (1993) 98.4%; public fire protection, virtually 100%. **Social participation.** Trade union membership in total workforce (2008): 6,441,045 (15.4%). Population "religious"/"deeply religious" (2007): in western Germany 78%/21%; in eastern Germany 36%/8%; 15% of Roman Catholics "regularly" attend religious services. **Social deviance** (2006; excluding eastern Germany except for the former East Berlin). Conviction rate per 100,000 population for: murder, manslaughter, and attempted murder 0.8; sexual abuse of children 3.1; rape 2.7; assault and battery 91.3; theft 195.3; fraud 132.4. **Leisure.** Favorite leisure activities include playing football (soccer; registered participants, 2004) 6,272,804, as well as watching television, using the computer, going to the cinema, attending theatrical and musical performances, visiting museums, and taking part in package tours. **Material well-being** (2008). Households possessing: automobile (2005) 76.8%; refrigerator 98.6%; freezer 52.4%; dishwasher 62.5%; microwave oven 69.6%; washing machine (2004) 95.5%; clothes dryer 38.5%; television

---

1 metric ton = about 1.1 short tons;   1 kilometer = 0.6 mi (statute);   1 metric ton-km cargo = about 0.68 short ton-mi cargo;   c.i.f.: cost, insurance, and freight;   f.o.b.: free on board

(2004) 95.0%; DVD player (2006) 59%; personal computer (2006) 71.6%; Internet access (2006) 57.9%; MP3 player (2006) 23%.

National economy

Budget (2007; general government). *Revenue:* €1,064,730,000,000 (tax revenue 54.5%, of which income tax 21.6%, general taxes on goods and services 15.6%, excise taxes 6.0%; social security contributions 37.6%; nontax revenue 7.5%; other 0.4%). *Expenditures:* €1,061,590,000,000 (social protection 45.7%; health 14.0%; education 9.1%; economic affairs 7.2%; public debt payments 6.3%; public order 3.5%; defense 2.4%). **Total public debt** (May 2009): US$2,052,000,000,000. **Production** (metric tons except as noted). *Agriculturé and fishing* (2008): wheat 25,988,600, sugar beets 23,002,600, barley 11,967,100, potatoes 11,369,000, rapeseed 5,154,700, corn (maize) 5,105,900, rye 3,744,200, triticale 2,381,500, grapes 1,428,776, apples 1,046,995, cabbages 806,078, oats 793,200, dry onions 407,602, strawberries 150,854, dry peas 140,600, sunflower seeds 48,900, gooseberries 40,000, hops 39,700, currants 10,587; livestock (number of live animals) 26,686,800 pigs, 12,969,674 cattle, 2,437,000 sheep, 114,625,000 chickens; fisheries production (2007) 293,757 (from aquaculture 15%). *Mining and quarrying* (metric tons; 2006): potash 3,625,000; bentonite 364,000; feldspar 167,332; barite 85,524. *Energy production (consumption):* electricity (kW-hr; 2007) 594,660,000,000 ([2006] 619,784,000,000); coal (metric tons; 2008) 17,200,000 ([2006] 65,500,000); lignite (metric tons; 2008) 175,300,000 ([2006] 176,400,000); crude petroleum (barrels; 2008) 34,100,000 ([2006] 817,800,000); petroleum products (metric tons; 2006) 104,605,000 (100,068,000); natural gas (cu m; 2008) 20,337,000,000 ([2006] 94,772,000,000) (in 2009 Germany was a world leader in the production of wind and solar power). **Gross national income** (2008): US$3,485,674,000,000 (US$42,440 per capita). **Population economically active** (2008): total 41,875,000; activity rate of total population 51.0% (participation rates: ages 15–64, 76.0%; female 45.4%; unemployed [April 2008–March 2009] 8.7%. **Selected balance of payments data.** Receipts from (US$'000,000): tourism (2007) 36,092; remittances (2008) 11,064; foreign direct investment (FDI; 2005–07 avg.) 49,355. Disbursements for (US$'000,000): tourism (2007) 82,966; remittances (2008) 14,976; FDI (2005–07 avg.) 110,338.

Foreign trade

Imports (2007; c.i.f.): US$1,059,308,000,000 (machinery and apparatus 23.0%, of which electrical machinery 6.7%, office machines and computers 4.0%; manufactured goods 14.4%, of which iron and steel 3.6%; mineral fuels 10.5%, of which crude petroleum 5.2%; motor vehicles and parts 8.2%; food products 5.2%; medicines and pharmaceuticals 3.9%). *Major import sources:* France 8.4%; Netherlands 8.3%; China 7.1%; US 5.9%; Italy 5.7%; UK 5.6%; Belgium 5.0%; Austria 4.2%; Switzerland 3.9%; Russia 3.7%. **Exports** (2007; f.o.b.): US$1,328,841,000,000 (machinery and apparatus 28.4%, of which electrical machinery and electronics 7.3%, general industrial machinery 7.0%; transportation equipment 19.0%, of which motor vehicles 16.4%; manufactured goods 14.1%, of

which iron and steel, non-ferrous metals, and fabricate metal products 8.6%; chemical products 13.8%, of which medicines and pharmaceuticals 4.2%). *Major export destinations:* France 9.7%; US 7.6%; UK 7.3%; Italy 6.7%; Netherlands 6.4%; Austria 5.4%; Belgium 5.3%; Spain 5.0%; Switzerland 3.8%; Poland 3.7%.

Transport and communications

Transport. *Railroads* (2005): track length 76,473 km (route length 38,206 km); passenger-km 74,946,-000,000; metric ton-km cargo 95,421,000,000. *Roads* (2005): total length 231,480 km (paved [2003] 100%). *Vehicles* (2006): passenger cars 46,090,300; trucks and buses 2,573,100. *Air transport* (2007): passenger-km 206,112,000,000; metric ton-km cargo 8,345,976,000. **Communications,** in total units (units per 1,000 persons). Telephone landlines (2008): 51,500,000 (627); cellular telephone subscribers (2008): 107,245,000 (1,308); personal computers (2007): 53,967,000 (656); total Internet users (2008): 62,500,000 (761); broadband Internet subscribers (2008): 22,600,000 (275).

Education and health

Health (2006): physicians 311,000 (1 per 265 persons); hospital beds 510,767 (1 per 161 persons); infant mortality rate per 1,000 live births (2008) 4.0; undernourished population (2002–04) less than 2.5% of total population.

Military

Total active duty personnel (November 2008): 244,324 (army 65.8%, navy 9.4%, air force 24.8%); German peacekeeping troops abroad (November 2008): 7,300, including 3,300 in Afghanistan; US troops in Germany (November 2008): 40,000; British troops (November 2008): 22,000; French troops (November 2008): 2,800. **Military expenditure as percentage of GDP** (2007): 1.3%; per capita expenditure US$512.

Background

Germanic tribes entered the region about the 2nd century BC, displacing the Celts. The Romans failed to conquer the region, which became a political entity only with the division of the Carolingian empire in the 9th century AD. The monarchy's control was weak, and power increasingly devolved upon the nobility, organized in feudal states. The monarchy was restored under Saxon rule in the 10th century, and the Holy Roman Empire, centering on Germany and northern Italy, was revived. Continuing conflict between the Holy Roman emperors and the Roman Catholic popes undermined the empire, and its dissolution was accelerated by Martin Luther's revolt in 1517, which divided Germany, and ultimately Europe, into Protestant and Roman Catholic camps, culminating in the Thirty Years' War (1618–48). Germany's population and borders were greatly reduced, and its numerous feudal princes gained virtually full sovereignty. In 1862 Otto von Bismarck came to power in Prussia and over the next decade reunited Germany in the German Empire. It was dissolved in 1918 after the German defeat in World War I. Germany was stripped of much of its territory and all of its colonies. In 1933 Adolf Hitler came chancellor and established a totalitarian state, the Third Reich, dominated by the Nazi Party. Hitler's invasion of Poland in 1939 plunged the world into

World War II. Following its defeat in 1945, Germany was divided by the Allied Powers into four zones of occupation. Disagreement with the USSR over the reunification of the zones led to the creation in 1949 of the Federal Republic of Germany (West Germany) and the German Democratic Republic (East Germany). Berlin, the former capital, remained divided. West Germany became a prosperous parliamentary democracy and East Germany a one-party state under Soviet control. The East German Communist government was brought down peacefully in 1989, and Germany was reunited in 1990. After the initial euphoria over unity, the former West Germany sought to incorporate the former East Germany both politically and economically, resulting in heavy financial burdens for the wealthier western Germans. The country continued to move toward deeper political and economic integration with Western Europe through its membership in the European Union.

Recent Developments

In February the German government approved a second economic stimulus package of more than US$65 billion. (The first had been passed in November 2008.) Many criticized their government for this action, which they thought pushed Germany too far into debt and would be of dubious efficacy. Later decreases in unemployment and reports from economic research institutes that the German economy was emerging from recession seemed to prove the doubters wrong. At the end of 2008, the car manufacturer Opel had been suffering because of the economic difficulties of its owner, General Motors (GM). In early 2009 Opel requested financial aid from the government because it was facing the possibility of plant closures. The government granted the aid, and in March 2010 GM agreed to provide roughly US$2.6 billion in additional funding to the car manufacturer.

Internet resource: <www.destatis.de>.

Ghana

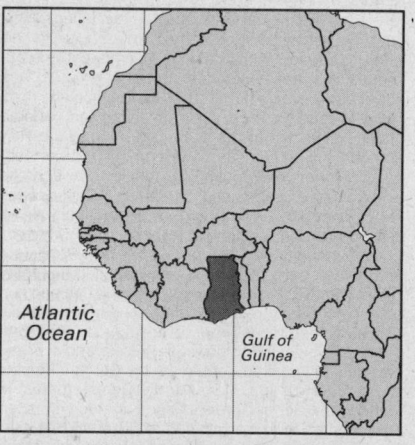

Atlantic Ocean

Gulf of Guinea

Official name: Republic of Ghana. Form of government: unitary multiparty republic with one legislative house (Parliament [230]). Head of state and government: President John Atta Mills (from 2009). Capital: Accra. Official language: English. Official religion: none. Monetary unit: 1 Ghana cedi (GH¢) = 100 pesewas; valuation (1 Jul 2010) US$1 = GH¢1.41 (the Ghana cedi replaced the cedi [¢] 1 Jul 2007, at the rate of 1 GH¢ = ¢10,000).

Demography

Area: 92,098 sq mi, 238,533 sq km. Population (2009): 23,832,000. Density (2009): persons per sq mi 258.8, persons per sq km 99.9. Urban (2008): 50.1%. Sex distribution (2008): male 50.02%; female 49.98%. Age breakdown (2008): under 15, 37.7%; 15–29, 29.4%; 30–44, 18.3%; 45–59, 9.5%; 60–74, 4.1%; 75–84, 0.9%; 85 and over, 0.1%. Ethnic composition (2000): Akan 41.6%; Mossi 23.0%; Ewe 10.0%; Ga-Adangme 7.2%; Gurma 3.4%; Nzima 1.8%; Yoruba 1.6%; other 11.4%. Religious affiliation (2005): Protestant 23.7%; traditional beliefs 21.5%; Sunni Muslim 20.1%; independent Christian 15.9%; Roman Catholic 12.2%; other 6.6%. Major cities (2002): Accra (2003) 1,847,432; Kumasi 627,600; Tamale 269,200; Tema 237,700; Obuasi 122,600. Location: western Africa, bordering Burkina Faso, Togo, the Atlantic Ocean, and Côte d'Ivoire.

Vital statistics

Birth rate per 1,000 population (2008): 29.4 (world avg. 20.3). Death rate per 1,000 population (2008): 9.3 (world avg. 8.5). Total fertility rate (avg. births per childbearing woman; 2008): 3.78. Life expectancy at birth (2008): male 58.5 years; female 60.8 years.

National economy

Budget (2006). Revenue: ¢31,917,680,000,000 (tax revenue 77.2%, of which VAT 18.4%, trade tax 17.0%, petroleum tax 12.8%, income tax 9.7%, corporate tax 9.4%; grants 19.9%; nontax revenue 2.9%). Expenditures: ¢38,734,730,000,000 (current expenditures 63.9%, of which transfers 14.7%, debt service 10.2%; capital expenditures 36.1%). Public debt (external, outstanding; December 2008): US$3,982,600,000. Gross national income (2008): US$15,744,000,000 (US$670 per capita). Production (metric tons except as noted). Agriculture and fishing (2007): cassava 9,650,000, yams 3,550,000, plantains 2,930,000, cacao beans 690,000; livestock (number of live animals) 3,704,700 goats, 3,420,000 sheep, 1,427,100 cattle; fisheries production 321,875 (from aquaculture, negligible). Mining and quarrying (2007): bauxite 748,000; manganese (metal content) 410,000; gold (legal production only) 77,349 kg; gem diamonds 720,000 carats. Manufacturing (value added in US$'000,000; 2003): wood products 157; chemical products 115; food products 108; refined petroleum products 55; precious and nonferrous metal products (including gold) 47. Energy production (consumption): electricity (kW-hr; 2006) 8,435,000,000 (8,309,000,000); crude petroleum (barrels; 2006) none (12,500,000); petroleum products (metric tons;

1 metric ton = about 1.1 short tons;   1 kilometer = 0.6 mi (statute);   1 metric ton-km cargo = about 0.68 short ton-mi cargo;   c.i.f.: cost, insurance, and freight;   f.o.b.: free on board

2006) 920,000 (1,909,000). **Population economically active** (2006): total 10,218,000; activity rate of total population 44.4% (participation rates: ages 15–64, 73.3%; female 49.4%; unemployed [2001] 20.3%). **Selected balance of payments data.** Receipts from (US$'000,000): tourism (2007) 908; remittances (2008) 128; foreign direct investment (2005–07 avg.) 545; official development assistance (2007) 1,151. Disbursements for (US$'000,000): tourism (2007) 558; remittances (2008) 6.

Foreign trade

Imports (2006; c.i.f.): US$5,329,000,000 (machinery and apparatus 19.1%; motor vehicles 14.8%; crude petroleum 12.9%; food products 12.2%; chemical products 10.8%). *Major import sources:* Nigeria 9.6%; China 9.5%; UK 8.9%; US 6.6%; Belgium 5.6%. **Exports** (2006; f.o.b.): US$3,614,000,000 (cocoa 34.3%; gold 31.3%; woven cotton fabrics 6.3%; wood products [excluding furniture] 5.5%). *Major export destinations:* South Africa 25.8%; Burkina Faso 12.6%; Netherlands 11.1%; Switzerland 6.8%; France 4.6%.

Transport and communications

Transport. *Railroads* (2002): route length (2005) 953 km; passenger-km 238,000,000; metric ton-km cargo , 168,000,000. *Roads* (2005): total length 57,614 km (paved 15%). *Vehicles* (2006): passenger cars 275,424; trucks and buses 135,819. *Air transport* (2003; Ghana Airways only): passenger-km 906,000,000; metric ton-km cargo 16,630,000. **Communications,** in total units (units per 1,000 persons). Telephone landlines (2008): 144,000 (6); cellular telephone subscribers (2008): 11,570,000 (483); personal computers (2004): 112,000 (5.2); total Internet users (2008): 997,000 (42); broadband Internet subscribers (2008): 17,000 (0.7).

Education and health

Educational attainment (2003). Percentage of population ages 25 and over having: no formal schooling/unknown 41.8%; incomplete primary education 9.6%; primary 3.6%; incomplete secondary 35.0%; secondary 5.4%; higher 4.6%. **Literacy** (2007): total population ages 15 and over literate 65.0%; males literate 71.7%; females literate 58.3%. **Health:** physicians (2004) 3,240 (1 per 6,631 persons); hospital beds (2001) 18,448 (1 per 1,089 persons); infant mortality rate per 1,000 live births (2008) 52.5; undernourished population (2003–05) 1,900,000 (9% of total population based on the consumption of a minimum daily requirement of 1,800 calories).

Military

Total active duty personnel (November 2008): 10,913 (army 74.1%, navy 14.8%, air force 11.1%); UN peacekeepers (November 2008): 2,587. **Military expenditure as percentage of GDP** (2007): 0.7%; per capita expenditure US$5.

Background

The modern state of Ghana is named after the ancient Ghana empire that flourished until the 13th century AD in the western Sudan, about 000 km (500 mi) northwest of the modern state. The Akan peoples then founded their first states in modern Ghana.

Gold-seeking Mande traders arrived by the 14th century, and Hausa merchants arrived by the 16th century. During the 15th century the Mande founded the states of Dagomba and Mamprussi in the northern half of the region. The Asante, an Akan people, originated in the central forest region and formed a strongly centralized empire that was at its height in the 18th and 19th centuries. European exploration of the region began early in the 15th century, when the Portuguese landed on the Gold Coast; they later established a settlement at Elmina as headquarters for the slave trade. By the mid-18th century the Gold Coast was dominated by numerous forts controlled by Dutch, British, and Danish merchants. Britain made the Gold Coast a crown colony in 1874, and British protectorates over Asante and the northern territories were established in 1901. In 1957 the Gold Coast became the independent state of Ghana.

Recent Developments

On 7 Jan 2009, John Atta Mills was inaugurated as president of Ghana, the second time in the country's history that the presidency had gone to an opposition politician. Six months later US Pres. Barack Obama highlighted Ghana's importance as an emergent democracy when he made it the destination for his first official state visit to sub-Saharan Africa. Bypassing other influential African states, notably Kenya and Nigeria, he made it clear that he chose Ghana because it promoted democratic principles and transparency.

Internet resource: <www.touringghana.com>.

Greece

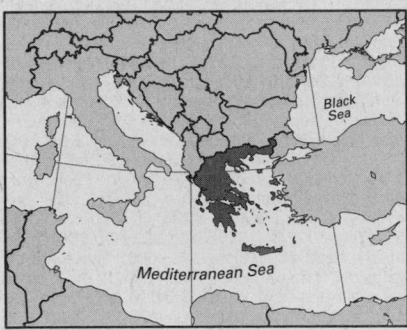

Official name: Ellinikí Dhimokratía (Hellenic Republic). **Form of government:** unitary multiparty republic with one legislative house (Hellenic Parliament [300]). **Head of state:** President Karolos Papoulias (from 2005). **Head of government:** Prime Minister Georgios Papandreou (from 2009). **Capital:** Athens. **Official language:** Greek. **Official religion:** none (the autocephalous Greek Orthodox Church receives special recognition per the constitution). **Monetary unit:** 1 euro (€) = 100 cents; valuation (1 Jul 2010) US$1 = €0.80.

Demography

Area: 50,949 sq mi, 131,957 sq km. **Population** (2009): 11,285,000. **Density** (2009): persons per sq mi 221.5, persons per sq km 85.5. **Urban** (2005): 60.4%. **Sex distribution** (2006): male 49.51%; female 50.49%. **Age breakdown** (2006): under 15, 14.3%; 15–29, 19.3%; 30–44, 22.9%; 45–59, 19.7%; 60–74, 15.8%; 75–84, 6.6%; 85 and over, 1.4%. **Ethnic composition** (2000; unofficial source; the government states there are no ethnic divisions in Greece): Greek 90.4%; Macedonian 1.8%; Albanian 1.5%; Turkish 1.4%; Pomak 0.9%; Rom (Gypsy) 0.9%; other 3.1%. **Religious affiliation** (2005): Orthodox 90%; Sunni Muslim 5%; Roman Catholic 2%; other 3%. **Major cities** (2001): Athens 745,514 (urban agglomeration 3,187,734); Thessaloníki 363,987 (urban agglomeration 800,764); Piraeus (Piraiévs) 175,697; Pátrai 161,114; Peristérion 137,918. **Location:** southern Europe, bordering Albania, Macedonia, Bulgaria, Turkey, and the Mediterranean Sea.

Vital statistics

Birth rate per 1,000 population (2008): 10.3 (world avg. 20.3); within marriage 93.5%. **Death rate** per 1,000 population (2008): 9.5 (world avg. 8.5). **Total fertility rate** (avg. births per childbearing woman; 2008): 1.45. **Life expectancy** at birth (2008): male 77.2 years; female 82.2 years.

National economy

Budget (2007). *Revenue:* €89,100,000,000 (tax revenue 51.0%, of which VAT 28.8%, income tax 19.2%; social contributions 35.7%; other revenue 13.3%). *Expenditures:* €95,398,000,000 (social benefits 41.1%; wages and salaries 23.8%; goods and services 10.5%; interest payments 10.4%). **Production** (metric tons except as noted). *Agriculture and fishing* (2007): olives 2,600,000, corn (maize) 1,767,500, tomatoes 1,450,000, oranges 1,000,000, grapes 950,000, peaches and nectarines 700,000; livestock (number of live animals) 8,803,350 sheep, 5,570,885 goats, 1,315,000 beehives; fisheries production 209,356 (from aquaculture 54%). *Mining and quarrying* (2007): bauxite 2,163,000; nickel (metal content) 18,000; marble 150,000 cu m. *Manufacturing* (value added in US$'000,000; 2005): food products and beverages 5,300; textiles 1,950; chemical products 1,750; refined petroleum products and coal derivatives 1,500. *Energy production (consumption):* electricity (kW-hr; 2007) 59,776,000,000 ([2006] 64,991,000,000); coal (metric tons; 2006) none (463,000); lignite (metric tons; 2007) 63,448,000 ([2006] 64,332,000); crude petroleum (barrels; 2006) 760,000 (136,000,000); petroleum products (metric tons; 2006) 20,627,000 (19,158,000); natural gas (cu m; 2006) 16,000,000 (3,275,000,000). **Population economically active** (2007): total 4,917,900; activity rate of total population 44.1% (participation rates: ages 15–64 [2006] 66.9%; female 40.9%; unemployed [April 2007–March 2008] 8.1%). **Gross national income** (2008): US$321,972,000,000 (US$28,650 per capita). **Public debt** (general government; 2008): US$347,416,000,000. **Selected balance of payments data.** Receipts from (US$'000,000): tourism (2007) 15,550; remittances (2008) 2,687; foreign direct investment (FDI; 2005–07 avg.) 2,629. Disbursements for (US$'000,000): tourism (2007) 3,423; remittances (2008) 1,912; FDI (2005–07 avg.) 3,652.

Foreign trade

Imports (2006; c.i.f.): US$63,739,000,000 (machinery and apparatus 14.4%; crude petroleum 13.1%; food products 8.7%; motor vehicles and parts 8.5%; medicine and pharmaceuticals 5.8%; ships and tankers 5.3%). *Major import sources:* Germany 12.5%; Italy 11.6%; Russia 7.1%; France 5.9%; Netherlands 5.2%. **Exports** (2006; f.o.b.): US$20,943,000,000 (food products 14.0%, of which vegetables and fruit 7.2%; refined petroleum products 12.4%; machinery and apparatus 10.6%; wearing apparel 7.4%; medicine and pharmaceuticals 5.3%; aluminum 4.4%). *Major export destinations:* Germany 11.3%; Italy 11.2%; Bulgaria 6.3%; UK 6.0%; Cyprus 5.3%.

Transport and communications

Transport. *Railroads* (2006): length 2,509 km; passenger-km 1,811,000,000; metric ton-km cargo 662,000,000. *Roads* (2005): total length 34,863 km (paved 93%). *Vehicles* (2007): passenger cars 4,798,530; trucks and buses 1,283,047. *Air transport* (2008): passenger-km 6,612,000,000; metric ton-km cargo 69,660,000. **Communications,** in total units (units per 1,000 persons). Telephone landlines (2008): 5,975,000 (535); cellular telephone subscribers (2008): 13,799,000 (1,235); personal computers (2007): 1,058,000 (94); total Internet users (2008): 3,631,000 (325); broadband Internet subscribers (2008): 1,507,000 (135).

Education and health

Educational attainment (2001). Percentage of population ages 25 and over having: no formal schooling 12.7%; primary education 34.3%; lower secondary 8.5%; upper secondary 25.7%; higher 18.8%. **Literacy** (2007): total population ages 15 and over literate 97.1%; males literate 98.2%; females literate 96.0%. **Health** (2006): physicians (public health institutions only) 21,038 (1 per 436 persons); hospital beds (public health institutions only) 44,307 (1 per 207 persons); infant mortality rate per 1,000 live births (2008) 3.5; undernourished population (2003–05) less than 5% of total population.

Military

Total active duty personnel (November 2008): 156,600 (army 59.7%, navy 12.8%, air force 20.1%, joint staff 7.4%); Greek troops in Cyprus (November 2008): 1,150. **Military expenditure as percentage of GDP** (2007): 2.8%; per capita expenditure US$773.

Background

The earliest urban society in Greece was the palace-centered Minoan civilization, which reached its height on Crete about 2000 BC. It was succeeded by the mainland Mycenaean civilization, which arose about 1600 BC following a wave of Indo-European invasions. About 1200 BC a second wave of invasions destroyed the Bronze Age cultures, and a dark age followed, known mostly through the epics of Homer. At the end of this time, classical Greece began to emerge (c. 750 BC) as a collection of independent city-states, including Sparta in the Peloponnese and Athens in Attica. The

---

1 metric ton = about 1.1 short tons;   1 kilometer = 0.6 mi (statute);   1 metric ton-km cargo = about 0.68 short ton-mi cargo;   c.i.f.: cost, insurance, and freight;   f.o.b.: free on board

civilization reached its zenith after repelling the Persians at the beginning of the 5th century BC and began to decline after the civil strife of the Peloponnesian War at the century's end. In 338 BC the Greek city-states were taken over by Philip II of Macedon, and Greek culture was spread by Philip's son Alexander the Great throughout his empire. The Romans, themselves heavily influenced by Greek culture, conquered the Greek states in the 2nd century BC. After the fall of Rome, Greece remained part of the Byzantine Empire until the mid-15th century AD, when it became part of the expanding Ottoman Empire; it gained its independence in 1832. It was occupied by Nazi Germany during World War II. Civil war followed and lasted until 1949, when communist forces were defeated. In 1952 Greece joined NATO. A military junta ruled the country from 1967 to 1974, when democracy was restored and a referendum declared an end to the Greek monarchy. In 1981 Greece joined the European Community, the first Eastern European country to do so. Upheavals in the Balkans in the 1990s strained Greece's relations with some neighboring states, notably the former Yugoslav entity that took the name Republic of Macedonia.

Recent Developments

The global economic crisis seriously weakened the Greek economy in 2009. The economy contracted by 0.7%. Inflation dropped to below 2.0%, while unemployment increased to 11.3% in January 2010. The crisis threatened to bankrupt the country, and in April 2010 the head of the German Bundesbank stated that Greece could require an aid program of €80 billion to ensure recovery. In December 2009 the government announced tough measures to deal with the country's high deficit, including major cuts in government spending. On the social front, the influx of illegal immigrants continued, but there was no consensus among the political parties on how to address the issue.

Internet resource:
<www.statistics.gr/portal/page/portal/ESYE>.

Greenland

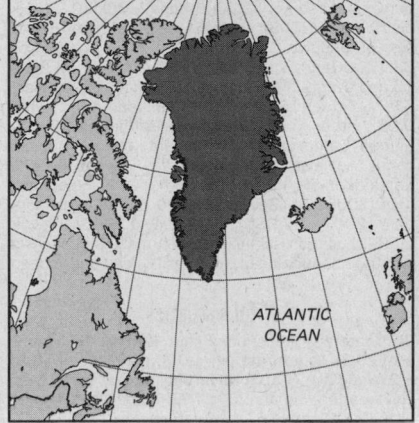

ATLANTIC
OCEAN

Official name: Kalaallit Nunaat (Greenlandic) (Greenland). **Political status:** self-governing overseas admin-

istrative division of Denmark with one legislative house (Parliament [31]). **Head of state:** Danish Queen Margrethe II (from 1972). **Heads of government:** High Commissioner (for Denmark) Søren Hald Møller (from 2005); Prime Minister (for Greenland) Kuupik Kleist (from 2009). **Capital:** Nuuk (Godthåb). **Official language:** Greenlandic (Danish was an official language prior to 21 Jun 2009). **Official religion:** Evangelical Lutheran (Lutheran Church of Greenland). **Monetary unit:** 1 Danish krone (DKK; plural kroner) = 100 øre; valuation (1 Jul 2010) US$1 = DKK 5.99.

Demography

Area: 836,330 sq mi, 2,166,086 sq km. **Population** (2009): 56,100. **Density** (2009; calculated with reference to ice-free area only): persons per sq mi 0.35, persons per sq km 0.14. **Urban** (2008): 83.8%. **Sex distribution** (2008): male 53.05%; female 46.95%. **Age breakdown** (2007): under 15, 23.7%; 15–29, 22.1%; 30–44, 23.3%; 45–59, 20.4%; 60–74, 8.7%; 75 and over, 1.8%. **Ethnic composition** (2008): Inuit (Greenland Eskimo) 89%; Danish and others 11%. **Religious affiliation** (2000): Protestant 69.2%, of which Evangelical Lutheran 64.2%, Pentecostal 2.8%; other Christian 27.4%; other/nonreligious 3.4%. **Major towns** (2008): Nuuk (Godthåb) 15,105; Sisimiut (Holsteinsborg) 5,458; Ilulissat (Jakobshavn) 4,528. **Location:** island in the North Atlantic Ocean, east of northern Canada.

Vital statistics

Birth rate per 1,000 population (2007): 14.9 (world avg. 20.3); (1993) within marriage 29.2%. **Death rate** per 1,000 population (2007): 7.8 (world avg. 8.5). **Total fertility rate** (avg. births per childbearing woman; 2007): 2.28. **Life expectancy** at birth (2006): male 66.4 years; female 73.6 years.

National economy

Budget (general government; 2007). *Revenue:* DKK 8,625,000,000 (block grant from Danish government 44.8%; taxes on income and wealth 33.9%; import duties 6.5%). *Expenditures:* DKK 8,239,000,000 (social welfare 26.0%; education 19.3%; health 12.1%; general administration 11.7%; economic affairs 11.6%). **Production** (metric tons except as noted). *Agriculture, fishing, other marine:* locally grown broccoli, cauliflower, potatoes, and cabbage sold commercially for the first time in 2007; fish catch (2006) 213,600 (of which prawn 132,500, Greenland halibut 44,900, Atlantic cod 10,600, lumpfish 10,000, crab 3,600); number of other marine catch (2006): narwhals 411, minke whales 181, beluga whales 137, porpoises 2,923, seals 187,613, walrus 45; livestock (number of live animals; 2007) 21,704 sheep, 2,441 tame reindeer, 216 horses; number of animals killed (2006) reindeer 15,002, musk ox 2,393, polar bear 118. *Mining* (2007): gold 1,639 kg. *Manufacturing:* principally fish and prawn processing, handicrafts, hides and skins, and ship repair. *Energy production (consumption):* electricity (kW-hr; 2006) 344,000,000 (268,000,000); petroleum products (metric tons; 2006) none (184,000). **Tourism** (2008): number of overnight stays at hotels 236,913, of which visitors from within Greenland 115,289, from Denmark 79,396, from the US 6,532. **Gross national income** (2007): US$1,834,000,000 (US$32,429 per capita). **Population economically active** (2003): total 32,119; activity rate of total population 56.5% (participation rates: ages 15–62, 83.5%; female [2006] 48.6%; unemployed [2007; urban only] 6.8%). **Public debt** (2008): none.

Foreign trade

Imports (2007): DKK 3,643,000,000 (mineral fuels [mostly refined petroleum products] 24.2%; machinery and transportation equipment 22.8%; food products 16.4%; manufactured products 13.3%). *Major import sources:* Denmark 70.1%; Sweden 22.6%; Norway 1.7%; Canada 0.9%. **Exports** (2007): DKK 2,322,000,000 (prawn 48.5%; Greenland halibut 19.0%; gold 9.9%; cod 7.7%; crab 1.6%). *Major export destinations:* Denmark 85.1%; Canada 10.0%; Iceland 1.5%; UK 1.2%.

Transport and communications

Transport. *Railroads:* none. *Roads* (1998): total length 150 km (paved 60%). *Vehicles* (2007): passenger cars 4,819; trucks and buses 423. Air transport (2006; Air Greenland A/S only): passenger-km 441,422,000; metric ton-km cargo 49,485,000. **Communications,** in total units (units per 1,000 persons). Telephone landlines (2008): 23,000 (405); cellular telephone subscribers (2008): 56,000 (991); total Internet users (2007): 52,000 (920).

Education and health

Educational attainment (2002). Two-thirds of labor force has no formal education. **Literacy** (2001): total population ages 15 and over literate: virtually 100%. **Health:** physicians (2004) 91 (1 per 626 persons); hospital beds (2005) 411 (1 per 139 persons); infant mortality rate per 1,000 live births (2007) 8.2.

Military

Total active duty personnel. Denmark is responsible for Greenland's defense—Greenlanders are not liable for military service; US Air Force personnel at Thule Air Base (December 2008): 138.

Background

The Inuit probably crossed to Greenland from North America, along the islands of the Canadian Arctic, from 4000 BC to AD 1000. The Norwegian Erik the Red visited Greenland in 982; his son, Leif Eriksson, introduced Christianity. Greenland came under joint Danish-Norwegian rule in the late 14th century. The original Norse settlements became extinct in the 15th century, but Greenland was recolonized by Denmark. In 1776 Denmark closed the Greenland coast to foreign trade; it was not reopened until 1950. Greenland became part of Denmark in 1953. Home rule was established in 1979. In the early 21st century, the movement for full independence gained support, as did the belief that global warming was responsible for the accelerated melting of the Greenlandic ice.

Recent Developments

On 21 Jun 2009, Greenland celebrated the implementation of an expanded self-government agreement, under which Greenland would keep half of the income from oil and mineral sales, with the ultimate goal of full independence. In October the world's largest-known reserve of rare-earth metals—the Ilimaussaq field—was discovered in Greenland. It could meet 25% of global demand for the next 50 years and double Greenland's GDP.

Internet resource: <www.stat.gl>.

Grenada

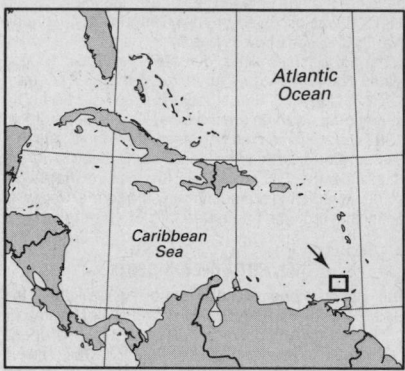

Atlantic Ocean

Caribbean Sea

Official name: Grenada. **Form of government:** constitutional monarchy with two legislative houses (Senate [13]; House of Representatives [15]). **Head of state:** British Queen Elizabeth II (from 1952), represented by Governor-General Carlyle Glean (from 2008). **Head of government:** Prime Minister Tillman Thomas (from 2008). **Capital:** St. George's. **Official language:** English. **Official religion:** none. **Monetary unit:** 1 Eastern Caribbean dollar (EC$) = 100 cents; valuation (1 Jul 2010) US$1 = EC$2.68.

Demography

Area: 133 sq mi, 344 sq km. **Population** (2009): 107,000. **Density** (2009): persons per sq mi 804.5, persons per sq km 311.0. **Urban** (2008): 30.9%. **Sex distribution** (2008): male 51.96%; female 48.04%. **Age breakdown** (2008): under 15, 32.4%; 15–29, 33.7%; 30–44, 21.6%; 45–59, 8.2%; 60–74, 3.1%; 75 and over, 1.0%. **Ethnic composition** (2000): black 51.7%; mixed 40.0%; Indo-Pakistani 4.0%; white 0.9%; other 3.4%. **Religious affiliation** (2005): Roman Catholic 41%; Protestant (of which significantly Anglican and Seventh-day Adventist) 30%; Rastafarian 5%; nonreligious/other 24%. **Major localities** (2006): St. George's 4,300 (urban agglomeration [2007] 32,000); Gouyave 3,400; Grenville 2,500. **Location:** island between the Caribbean Sea and the Atlantic Ocean, north of Trinidad and Tobago.

Vital statistics

Birth rate per 1,000 population (2008): 18.1 (world avg. 20.3). **Death rate** per 1,000 population (2008): 8.2 (world avg. 8.5). **Total fertility rate** (avg. births per childbearing woman; 2008): 2.30. **Life expectancy** at birth (2008): male 67.1 years; female 70.5 years.

1 metric ton = about 1.1 short tons;   1 kilometer = 0.6 mi (statute);   1 metric ton-km cargo = about 0.68 short ton-mi cargo;   c.i.f.: cost, insurance, and freight;   f.o.b.: free on board

National economy

Budget (2008). *Revenue:* EC$516,100,000 (tax revenue 84.1%, of which tax on international trade 45.5%, corporate taxes 13.8%; grants 10.0%; nontax revenue 5.9%). *Expenditures:* EC$627,500,000 (current expenditures 65.9%, of which wages and salaries 32.0%, transfers 14.9%, debt service 5.6%; capital expenditures 34.1%). **Public debt** (external, outstanding; 2007): US$249,740,000. **Gross national income** (2008): US$603,000,000 (US$5,710 per capita). **Production** (metric tons except as noted). *Agriculture and fishing* (2007): sugarcane 7,200, coconuts 7,000, bananas 4,300, nutmeg 2,800, cacao beans 1,000, cinnamon 50, cloves 20; livestock (number of live animals) 13,200 sheep, 7,200 goats, 2,650 pigs; fisheries production 2,407 (from aquaculture, none). *Mining and quarrying:* excavation of limestone, sand, and gravel for local use. *Manufacturing* (value of production in EC$'000; 1997): wheat flour 13,390; soft drinks 9,798; beer 7,072. *Energy production (consumption):* electricity (kW-hr; 2008) 169,568,000 ([2006] 171,000,000); petroleum products (metric tons; 2006) none (78,000). **Population economically active** (2004): total 37,000; activity rate of total population 35% (participation rate: ages 15–64 [1998] 78%; female [1998] 43.5%; unemployed [2005] 18.0%). **Selected balance of payments data.** Receipts from (US$'000,000): tourism (2007) 110; remittances (2008) 64; foreign direct investment (2005–07 avg.) 98; official development assistance (2007) 23. Disbursements for (US$'000,000): tourism (2007) 10; remittances (2008) 4.

Foreign trade

Imports (2006; c.i.f.): US$298,900,000 (machinery and transportation equipment 22.1%; food products and live animals 16.1%; chemical products 9.6%; mineral fuels 5.9%). *Major import sources:* US 39.3%; Trinidad and Tobago 19.2%; UK 5.6%; China 5.3%; Japan 3.9%. **Exports** (2006; f.o.b.): US$25,400,000 (food products and live animals 51.6%, of which fish 14.6%, spices [nearly all nutmeg and mace] 11.0%; machinery and transportation equipment 11.8%; chemical products 4.7%). *Major export destinations:* US 27.6%; Saint Lucia 13.0%; Dominica 9.4%; St. Kitts and Nevis 7.5%; Trinidad and Tobago 7.1%.

Transport and communications

Transport. *Railroads:* none. *Roads* (2000): total length 1,127 km (paved 61%). *Vehicles* (2001): passenger cars 15,800; trucks and buses 4,200. *Air transport* (2001; Point Salines airport only): passengers 331,000; cargo 2,747 metric tons. **Communications**, in total units (units per 1,000 persons). Telephone landlines (2008): 29,000 (276); cellular telephone subscribers (2008): 60,000 (580); personal computers (2004): 16,000 (155); total Internet users (2008): 24,000 (232); broadband Internet subscribers (2008): 10,000 (98).

Education and health

Educational attainment (2001). Percentage of population ages 18 and over having: no formal schooling/unknown 7.0%, primary education 65.1%; secondary 21.7%; higher 5.6%, of which university 1.5%. **Literacy** (2004): total population ages 15 and over lit-

erate 98.0%. **Health** (2007): physicians (2006) 96 (1 per 1,111 persons); hospital beds 279 (1 per 385 persons); infant mortality rate per 1,000 live births 11.0; undernourished population (2002–04) 7,000 (7% of total population based on the consumption of a minimum daily requirement of 1,910 calories).

Military

Total active duty personnel (2006): paramilitary and coast guard units only.

Background

The warlike Carib Indians dominated Grenada when Christopher Columbus sighted the island in 1498 and named it Concepción; they ruled it for the next 150 years. In 1674 it became subject to the French crown and remained so until 1762, when British forces captured it. In 1833 the island's black slaves were freed. Grenada was the headquarters of the government of the British Windward Islands (1885–1958) and a member of the West Indies Federation (1958–62). It became a self-governing state in association with Britain in 1967 and gained its independence in 1974. In 1979 a left-wing government took control in a bloodless coup. Relations with its US-oriented Latin American neighbors became strained as Grenada leaned toward Cuba and the Soviet bloc. In order to counteract this trend, the US invaded the island in 1983; democratic self-government was reestablished in 1984. Grenada's relations with Cuba, once suspended, were restored in 1997.

Recent Developments

In 2009 the government of Grenada instituted a number of reforms aimed at increasing oversight of the country's offshore financial sector, including the creation of a new regulatory financial agency.

Internet resource: <www.grenadagrenadines.com>.

Guatemala

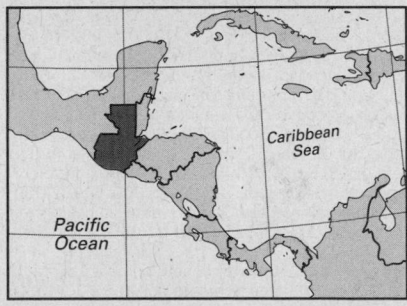

Official name: República de Guatemala (Republic of Guatemala). **Form of government:** republic with one legislative house (Congress of the Republic [158]). **Head of state and government:** President Álvaro Colom Caballeros (from 2008). **Capital:** Guatemala City. **Official language:** Spanish. **Official religion:** none. **Monetary unit:** 1 quetzal (Q) = 100 centavos; valuation (1 Jul 2010) US$1 = Q 7.87.

Demography

Area: 42,130 sq mi, 109,117 sq km. **Population** (2009): 14,027,000. **Density** (2009): persons per sq mi 332.9, persons per sq km 128.6. **Urban** (2005): 47.2%. **Sex distribution** (2008): male 48.79%; female 51.21%. **Age breakdown** (2006): under 15, 41.5%; 15–29, 28.6%; 30–44, 14.7%; 45–59, 9.6%; 60–74, 4.4%; 75–84, 1.1%; 85 and over, 0.1%. **Ethnic composition** (2002): mestizo 60.0%; Maya 39.3%, of which Quiché 11.3%, Kekchi 7.6%, Cakchiquel 7.4%, Mam 5.5%; other 0.7%. **Religious affiliation** (2005): Roman Catholic 57%; Protestant/ independent Christian 40%; traditional Mayan religions 1%; other 2%. **Major urban agglomerations** (2002): Guatemala City 942,348; Mixco 277,400; Villa Nueva 187,700; Quetzaltenango 106,700; Escuintla 65,400. **Location:** Central America, bordering Mexico, Belize, the Caribbean Sea, Honduras, El Salvador, and the Pacific Ocean.

Vital statistics

Birth rate per 1,000 population (2007): 29.1 (world avg. 20.3). **Death rate** per 1,000 population (2007): 5.3 (world avg. 8.5). **Total fertility rate** (avg. births per childbearing woman; 2007): 3.70. **Life expectancy** at birth (2007): male 66.7 years; female 73.8 years.

National economy

Budget (2006). *Revenue:* Q 29,102,000,000 (tax revenue 93.6%, of which taxes on goods and services 55.3%, corporate taxes 18.0%; nontax revenue 3.1%). *Expenditures:* Q 33,600,000,000 (general administration 18.8%; education 18.6%; housing 13.8%; transportation 12.8%; public order 9.4%; health 7.7%). **Public debt** (external, outstanding; 2008): US$4,382,400,000. **Production** (metric tons except as noted). *Agriculture and fishing* (2007): sugarcane 18,000,000, corn (maize) 1,100,000, bananas 1,010,000, coffee 216,600, cardamom and nutmeg 19,000; livestock (number of live animals) 2,800,000 cattle, 265,000 sheep, 27,000,000 chickens; fisheries production 33,987 (from aquaculture 48%). *Mining and quarrying* (2007): silver 70,000 kg; gold 7,100 kg. *Manufacturing* (value added in Q '000,000; 2007): food products, beverages, and tobacco products 24,429; textiles, wearing apparel, and footwear 8,340; cement, bricks, and rubber or plastic products 4,284. *Energy production (consumption):* electricity (kW-hr; 2006) 7,911,000,000 (7,832,000,000); coal (metric tons; 2006) none (428,000); crude petroleum (barrels; 2008) 5,670,000 ([2006] 930,000); petroleum products (metric tons; 2006) 23,000 (2,952,000). **Selected balance of payments data.** Receipts from (US$'000,000): tourism (2007) 1,055; remittances (2008) 4,446; foreign direct investment (FDI; 2005–07 avg.) 608; official development assistance (2007) 450. Disbursements for (US$'000,000): tourism (2007) 597; remittances (2008) 18; FDI (2005–07 avg.) 54. **Gross national income** (2008): US$36,634,000,000 (US$2,680 per capita). **Population economically active** (2006): total 5,565,200; activity rate of total population 42.8% (participation rates: ages 15–64, 68.0%; female 38.1%).

Foreign trade

Imports (2007; c.i.f.): US$12,731,000,000 (machinery and apparatus 17.3%; refined petroleum products 15.8%; chemical products 14.8%; food products 9.8%; motor vehicles and parts 7.8%). *Major import sources:* US 34.1%; Mexico 8.8%; China 5.7%; El Salvador 4.8%; South Korea 3.6%. **Exports** (2007; f.o.b.): US$6,900,000,000 (food products 33.0%, of which coffee 8.4%, raw sugar 5.2%, bananas 4.7%; wearing apparel and accessories 20.1%; crude petroleum 3.6%; toiletries and perfumery 3.6%; silver 3.0%). *Major export destinations:* US 42.6%; El Salvador 12.2%; Honduras 8.6%; Mexico 6.7%; Nicaragua 3.9%.

Transport and communications

Transport. *Railroads* (2004): route length 886 km. *Roads* (2002): total length 14,044 km (paved 39%). *Vehicles* (2004): passenger cars 1,328,100; trucks and buses (2000) 53,236. *Air transport* (1999): passenger-km 341,700,000; metric ton-km cargo (2003) 200,000. **Communications,** in total units (units per 1,000 persons). Telephone landlines (2008): 1,449,000 (106); cellular telephone subscribers (2008): 14,949,000 (1,092); personal computers (2005): 262,000 (21); total Internet users (2008): 1,920,000 (143); broadband Internet subscribers (2005): 27,000 (2.1).

Education and health

Educational attainment (2002). Percentage of heads of households having: no formal schooling 33.3%; incomplete/complete primary education 46.1%; incomplete/complete secondary 15.0%; higher 5.6%. **Literacy** (2005): total population ages 15 and over literate 71.8%; males literate 79.1%; females literate 64.6%. **Health** (2005): physicians 12,273 (1 per 1,049 persons); hospital beds 8,894 (1 per 1,429 persons); infant mortality rate per 1,000 live births (2006) 30.8; undernourished population (2002–04) 2,800,000 (22% of total population based on the consumption of a minimum daily requirement of 1,760 calories).

Military

Total active duty personnel (November 2008): 15,500 (army 86.7%, navy 6.4%, air force 6.9%). **Military expenditure as percentage of GDP** (2008): 0.3%; per capita expenditure US$13.

Background

From simple farming villages dating to 2500 BC, the Maya of Guatemala and the Yucatán developed an impressive civilization. The civilization of the Maya declined after AD 900, and the Spanish began the subjugation of their descendants in 1523. The Central American colonies declared independence from Spain in Guatemala City in 1821, and Guatemala became part of the Mexican Empire until its collapse in 1823. In 1839 Guatemala became an independent republic under the first of a series of dictators who held power almost continuously for the next century. In 1945 a liberal-democratic coalition came to power and instituted sweeping reforms. Attempts to expropriate land belonging to American business interests

1 metric ton = about 1.1 short tons; 1 kilometer = 0.6 mi (statute); 1 metric ton-km cargo = about 0.68 short ton-mi cargo; c.i.f.: cost, insurance, and freight; f.o.b.: free on board

prompted the US government in 1954 to sponsor an invasion. In the following years Guatemala's social revolution came to an end and most of the reforms were reversed. Chronic political instability and violence thenceforth marked Guatemalan politics; most of the 200,000 deaths that resulted were blamed on government forces. In 1991 the country abandoned its long-standing claims of sovereignty over Belize, and the two established diplomatic relations. It continued to experience violence as guerrillas sought to seize power. A peace treaty was signed in 1996, and the country started slowly to recover from its civil war.

Recent Developments

The murder of prominent Guatemalan attorney Rodrigo Rosenberg in May 2009 caused international headlines when shortly after his death a video appeared in which the victim declared, "If you are hearing or seeing this message, it is because I was assassinated by President Álvaro Colom." Rosenberg also claimed knowledge of Colom's involvement in two other killings. Colom denied the accusations and invited the UN to assist in the investigation. In a bizarre twist, the UN body investigating the murder cleared Colom in February 2010, concluding that Rosenberg had actually arranged for his own execution.

Internet resource:
<www.visitguatemala.com/web/index.php>.

Guinea

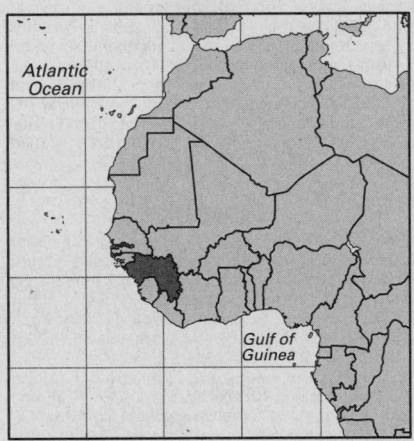

Official name: République de Guinée (Republic of Guinea). **Form of government:** transitional military regime. **Head of state and government:** President Moussa Dadis Camara (from 2008), assisted by Prime Minister of caretaker government Jean-Marie Doré (from 2010). **Capital:** Conakry. **Official language:** French. **Official religion:** none. **Monetary unit:** 1 Guinean franc (FG) = 100 centimes; valuation (1 Jul 2010) US$1 = FG 4,996.94.

Demography

Area: 94,918 sq mi, 245,836 sq km. **Population** (2009): 10,069,000. **Density** (2009): persons per sq mi 106.1, persons per sq km 41.0. **Urban** (2008): 28.0%. **Sex distribution** (2008): male 50.00%; female 50.00%. **Age breakdown** (2008): under 15, 42.9%; 15–29, 26.5%; 30–44, 16.0%; 45–59, 9.2%; 60–74, 4.4%; 75 and over, 1.0%. **Ethnic composition** (2000): Fulani 38.3%; Malinke 25.6%; Susu 12.2%; Kpelle 5.2%; Kisi 4.8%; other 13.9%. **Religious affiliation** (2005): Muslim (nearly all Sunni) 85%; Christian 8%; traditional beliefs 7%. **Major cities** (2004): Conakry 1,851,800; Kankan 113,900; Labé (2001) 64,500; Kindia (2001) 56,000; Nzérékoré (2001) 55,000. **Location:** western Africa, bordering Guinea-Bissau, Senegal, Mali, Côte d'Ivoire, Liberia, Sierra Leone, and the North Atlantic Ocean.

Vital statistics

Birth rate per 1,000 population (2008): 37.8 (world avg. 20.3). **Death rate** per 1,000 population (2008): 11.3 (world avg. 8.5). **Total fertility rate** (avg. births per childbearing woman; 2008): 5.25. **Life expectancy** at birth (2008): male 55.1 years; female 58.1 years.

National economy

Budget (2008). *Revenue:* FG 3,854,400,000,000 (tax revenue 81.9%, of which taxes on domestic production and trade 29.8%, mining sector revenue taxes 22.0%, taxes on international trade 18.5%; grants 12.7%). *Expenditures:* FG 3,735,600,000,000 (current expenditures 65.2%, of which wages and salaries 23.0%, interest on debt 14.6%; capital expenditures 34.6%; net lending and restructuring 0.2%). **Public debt** (external, outstanding; January 2009): US$3,527,000,000. **Production** (metric tons except as noted). *Agriculture and fishing* (2007): rice 1,401,592, cassava 1,122,171, oil palm fruit 883,000, fonio 243,361, coffee 18,600, cacao beans 15,000; livestock (number of live animals) 4,180,965 cattle, 1,590,400 goats, 1,330,600 sheep; fisheries production 100,000 (from aquaculture, none). *Mining and quarrying* (2008–09): bauxite 16,865,960; gold 508,980 troy oz; diamonds 459,370 carats. *Manufacturing* (2008–09): cement 292,130; flour 21,630; paints 1,340. *Energy production (consumption):* electricity (kW-hr; 2008–09) 683,091,000 ([2006] 836,000,000); petroleum products (metric tons; 2006) none (385,000); natural gas (cu m; 2008–09) 84,460 ([2006] none). **Population economically active** (2007): total 4,500,000; activity rate of total population (2003) 49.0% (participation rates: ages 15 and over, 85.0%; female 47.2%). **Gross national income** (2007): US$3,722,000,000 (US$400 per capita). **Selected balance of payments data.** Receipts from (US$'000,000): tourism (2007) 0.2; remittances (2008) 151; foreign direct investment (2005–07 avg.) 108; official development assistance (2007) 224. Disbursements for (US$'000,000): tourism (2007) 29; remittances (2008) 119.

Foreign trade

Imports (2006): US$942,000,000 (machinery and apparatus 33.7%; refined petroleum products 23.7%; food products 17.5%). *Major import sources:* China 8.6%; France 8.0%; Belgium 4.4%; Côte d'Ivoire 3.5%; India 3.2%. **Exports** (2006): US$1,011,100,000 (bauxite 40.0%; gold 31.6%; alumina 14.0%; diamonds 4.2%; fish 4.2%; coffee 0.1%). *Major export destinations:* Russia 11.6%; Ukraine 9.6%; Spain 9.0%; South Korea 8.8%; US 7.7%.

Transport and communications

Transport. *Railroads* (2008): route length (mostly for bauxite transport) 1,185 km; metric ton-km cargo (1993) 710,000,000. *Roads* (2003): total length 44,348 km (paved 10%). *Vehicles* (2003): passenger cars 47,524; trucks and buses 26,467. *Air transport* (1999): passenger-km 94,000,000; metric ton-km cargo 10,000,000. **Communications,** in total units (units per 1,000 persons). Telephone landlines (2008): 50,000 (5.1); cellular telephone subscribers (2008): 2,600,000 (264); personal computers (2006): 47,000 (5); total Internet users (2008): 90,000 (9.2).

Education and health

Educational attainment of those ages 25 and over having attended school (1999): none/unknown 81.4%; primary education 7.8%; secondary 6.8%; higher 4.0%. **Literacy** (2006): percentage of total population ages 15 and over literate 29.5%; males literate 42.6%; females literate 18.1%. **Health:** physicians (2006) 689 (1 per 13,660 persons); hospital beds (2005) 2,766 (1 per 3,333 persons); infant mortality rate per 1,000 live births (2008) 67.4; undernourished population (2002–04) 2,000,000 (24% of total population based on the consumption of a minimum daily requirement of 1,830 calories).

Military

Total active duty personnel (November 2008): 12,300 (army 69.1%, navy 3.3%, air force 6.5%, gendarmerie 8.1%, republican guard 13.0%). **Military expenditure as percentage of GDP** (2007): 1.1%; per capita expenditure US$5.

Background

About AD 900 successive migrations of the Susu swept down from the desert and pushed the original inhabitants of Guinea, the Baga, to the Atlantic coast. Small kingdoms of the Susu rose in importance in the 13th century and later extended their rule to the coast. In the mid-15th century, the Portuguese visited the coast and developed a slave trade. In the 16th century, the Fulani established domination over the Fouta Djallon region; they ruled into the 19th century. In the early 19th century, the French arrived and in 1849 proclaimed the coastal region a French protectorate. In 1895 French Guinea became part of the federation of French West Africa. In 1946 it was made an overseas territory of France, and in 1958 it achieved independence. Following a military coup in 1984, Guinea began implementing Westernized government systems. A new constitution was adopted in 1991, and the first multiparty elections were held in 1993. During the 1990s Guinea accommodated several hundred thousand war refugees from neighboring Liberia and Sierra Leone, and conflicts between these countries and Guinea have continued to flare up over the refugee population into the early 21st century.

Recent Developments

Despite Guinea's suspension from both the African Union and the Economic Community of West African

States, presidential elections to replace its interim regime were scheduled to take place at the end of June 2010.

Internet resource: <www.stat-guinee.org>.

Guinea-Bissau

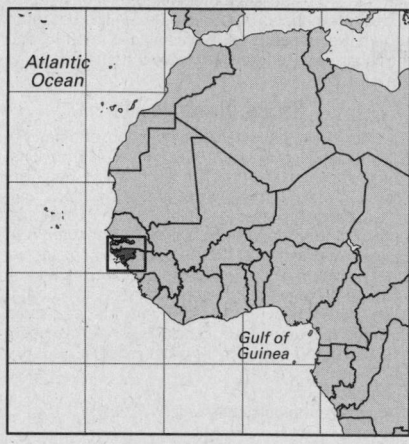

Official name: República da Guiné-Bissau (Republic of Guinea-Bissau). **Form of government:** republic with one legislative house (National People's Assembly [102]). **Head of state and government:** President Malam Bacai Sanhá (from 2009), assisted by Prime Minister Carlos Gomes Júnior (from 2009). **Capital:** Bissau. **Official language:** Portuguese. **Official religion:** none. **Monetary unit:** 1 CFA franc (CFAF) = 100 centimes; valuation (1 Jul 2010) US$1 = CFAF 527.20.

Demography

Area: 13,948 sq mi, 36,125 sq km. **Population** (2009): 1,534,000. **Density** (2009; based on land area of 10,859 sq mi [28,125 sq km]): persons per sq mi 141.3, persons per sq km 54.5. **Urban** (2005): 29.6%. **Sex distribution** (2009): male 48.82%; female 51.18%. **Age breakdown** (2005): under 15, 41.6%; 15–29, 28.1%; 30–44, 16.1%; 45–59, 9.4%; 60–74, 4.1%; 75 and over, 0.7%. **Ethnic composition** (2000): Balante 25.0%; Fulani (locally Fulakunda) 17.1%; Mandyako 12.0%; Malinke 10.0%; Guinean mestiço (Portuguese-black) 9.2%; Pepel 6.3%; nonindigenous Cape Verdean mulatto 1.0%; other 19.4%. **Religious affiliation** (2005): traditional beliefs 49%; Muslim 42%; Christian/other 9%. **Major cities** (2004): Bissau 305,700; Bafatá 15,000; Cacheu 14,000; Gabú 10,000. **Location:** western Africa, bordering Senegal, Guinea, and the North Atlantic Ocean.

Vital statistics

Birth rate per 1,000 population (2005): 37.6 (world avg. 20.3). **Death rate** per 1,000 population (2005):

---

1 metric ton = about 1.1 short tons;   1 kilometer = 0.6 mi (statute);   1 metric ton-km cargo = about 0.68 short ton-mi cargo;   c.i.f.: cost, insurance, and freight;   f.o.b.: free on board

16.7 (world avg. 8.5). **Total fertility rate** (avg. births per childbearing woman; 2005): 4.93. **Life expectancy** at birth (2005): male 44.8 years; female 48.5 years.

National economy

Budget (2007). *Revenue:* CFAF 53,800,000,000 (grants 50.6%; tax revenue 34.9%; nontax revenue 14.5%). *Expenditures:* CFAF 73,700,000,000 (current expenditures 66.9%; capital expenditures 33.1%). **Production** (metric tons except as noted). *Agriculture and fishing* (2008): rice 148,757; cashew nuts 81,000, oil palm fruit 80,000, sugarcane 6,000; livestock (number of live animals) 599,200 cattle, 401,300 pigs; fisheries production (2007) 6,200 (from aquaculture, none). *Mining and quarrying:* small-scale production of clays, limestone, and granite. *Manufacturing* (2003): processed wood 11,000; bakery products 7,900; wood products 4,400. *Energy production (consumption):* electricity (kW-hr; 2006) 66,000,000 (66,000,000); petroleum products (metric tons; 2006) none (91,000). **Selected balance of payments data.** Receipts from (US$'000,000): tourism (2006) 2.8; remittances (2008) 30; foreign direct investment (2005–07 avg.) 11; official development assistance (2007) 123. Disbursements for (US$'000,000): tourism (2006) 16; remittances (2008) 5. **Population economically active** (2006): total 618,000; activity rate of total population 37.5% (participation rates: ages 15–64, 73.0%; female 38.8%). **Public debt** (external, outstanding; 2007): US$730,000,000. **Gross national income** (GNI; 2008): US$386,000,000 (US$250 per capita) (formal economy only; in 2009 most of Guinea-Bissau's income was derived from trafficking South American cocaine into Europe).

Foreign trade

Imports (2007): US$136,000,000 (agricultural products 55.1%, of which refined sugar 12.5%; cereals 11.1%, beverages 7.9%). *Major import sources* (2008): Portugal 25%; Senegal 17%; Pakistan 5%; France 5%; Cuba 4%. **Exports** (2007): US$85,000,000 (cashews 64.3%; refined sugar 11.2%). *Major export destinations* (2008): India 75%; Nigeria 21%.

Transport and communications

Transport. *Railroads:* none. *Roads* (2003): total length 2,755 km (paved 28%). *Vehicles* (2002): passenger cars, trucks, and buses 1,985. *Air transport* (2003): passenger arrivals 17,834, passenger departures 18,528. **Communications,** in total units (units per 1,000 persons). Telephone landlines (2008): 4,600 (3.1); cellular telephone subscribers (2008): 500,000 (333); personal computers (2007): 2,900 (2); total Internet users (2008): 37,000 (25).

Education and health

Literacy (2007): total population ages 15 and over literate 64.6%; males literate 75.1%; females literate 54.4%. **Health** (2005): physicians 188 (1 per 7,522 persons); hospital beds 1,686 (1 per 839 persons); infant mortality rate per 1,000 live births 107.2; undernourished population (2002–04) 600,000 (39% of total population based on the consumption of a minimum daily requirement of 1,800 calories).

Military

Total active duty personnel (November 2008): 6,500 (army 62%, navy 5%, air force 2%, gendarmerie 31%). **Military expenditure as percentage of GDP** (2007): 4.2%; per capita expenditure US$10.

Background

More than 1,000 years ago the coast of Guinea-Bissau was occupied by iron-using agriculturists. They grew irrigated and dry rice and were also the major suppliers of marine salt to the western Sudan. At about the same time, the region came under the influence of the Mali empire and became a tributary kingdom known as Kaabu. After 1546 Kaabu was virtually autonomous; vestiges of the kingdom lasted until 1867. The earliest overseas contacts came in the 15th century with the Portuguese, who imported slaves from the Guinea area to the offshore Cape Verde Islands. Portuguese control of Guinea-Bissau was marginal despite claims to sovereignty there. The end of the slave trade forced the Portuguese inland in search of new profits. Their subjugation of the interior was slow and sometimes violent; it was not effectively achieved until 1915, though sporadic resistance continued until 1936. Guerrilla warfare in the 1960s led to the country's independence in 1974, but political turmoil continued and the government was overthrown by a military coup in 1980. A new constitution was adopted in 1984, and the first multiparty elections were held in 1994. A destructive civil war in 1998 was followed by a military coup in 1999, but the coup was followed by elections. A bloodless coup in 2003 was also followed by elections.

Recent Developments

Hours after a bomb blast killed Gen. Batista Tagme Na Waie, the head of the armed forces and longtime rival of Guinea-Bissau Pres. João Bernardo Vieira, Vieira himself was shot dead on 2 Mar 2009 by renegade soldiers in an apparent revenge attack. The expected political chaos did not follow, and the military did not seize power. Malam Bacai Sanhá won the June election to become president of the country ranked third from last on the United Nations 2008 Human Development Index.

Internet resource: <www.republica-da-guine-bissau.org/index.php?id=1>.

Guyana

Official name: Co-operative Republic of Guyana. **Form of government:** unitary multiparty republic with one legislative house (National Assembly [65]). **Head of state and government:** President Bharrat Jagdeo (from 1999). **Capital:** Georgetown. **Official language:** English. **Official religion:** none. **Monetary unit:** 1 Guyanese dollar (G$) = 100 cents; valuation (1 Jul 2010) US$1 = G$203.24.

Demography

Area: 83,012 sq mi, 214,999 sq km. **Population** (2009): 760,000. **Density** (2009, based on land area only): persons per sq mi 10.1, persons per sq km 3.9. **Urban** (2005): 38.5%. **Sex distribution** (2008): male 50.06%; female 49.94%. **Age breakdown** (2005):

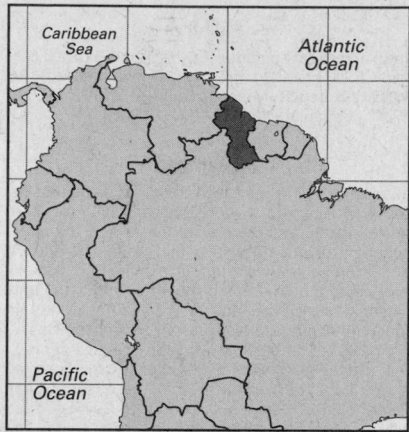

under 15, 26.5%; 15–29, 29.7%; 30–44, 23.0%; 45–59, 13.3%; 60–74, 5.6%; 75 and over, 1.9%. **Ethnic composition** (2002): East Indian 43.5%; 'black 30.2%; mixed race 16.7%; Amerindian 9.2%; other 0.4%. **Religious affiliation** (2002): Christian 57.3%, of which Protestant/independent Christian 48.2% (including Anglican 6.9%), Roman Catholic 8.0%, Jehovah's Witness 1.1%; Hindu 28.4%; Muslim 7.2%; Rastafarian 0.5%; nonreligious 4.3%; other/unknown 2.3%. **Major urban areas** (2006): Georgetown 236,900; Linden 44,900; New Amsterdam 35,700; Corriverton 12,700; Bartica 11,300. **Location:** northern South America, bordering the North Atlantic Ocean, Suriname, Brazil, and Venezuela.

Vital statistics

Birth rate per 1,000 population (2008): 18.5 (world avg. 20.3). **Death rate** per 1,000 population (2008): 7.9 (world avg. 8.5). **Total fertility rate** (avg. births per childbearing woman; 2008): 2.60. **Life expectancy** at birth (2005): male 62.9 years; female 68.3 years.

National economy

Budget (2008): *Revenue:* G$99,513,000,000 (current revenue 82.9%, of which VAT 24.1%; corporate taxes 18.7%, excise tax 13.2%, income tax 12.7%; grants 13.7%). *Expenditures:* G$105,838,000,000 (current expenditures 59.5%; development expenditures 40.5%). **Production** (metric tons except as noted). *Agriculture and fishing* (2007): sugarcane 3,250,000, rice 475,000, coconuts 45,000, cassava (manioc) 29,000, mangoes 12,000; livestock (number of live animals) 130,000 sheep, 110,000 cattle, 21,500,000 chickens; fisheries production 48,100 (from aquaculture 1%), of which shrimp or prawns (2006) 19,860. *Mining and quarrying* (2008): bauxite 1,995,000; gold 8,131 kg; diamonds 169,000 carats. *Manufacturing* (2008): flour 35,700; margarine 1,528; rum 142,000 hectoliters. *Energy production (consumption):* electricity (kW-hr; 2006) 867,000,000 (867,000,000); petroleum products (metric tons; 2006) none (491,000). **Population economically active** (2006):

total 279,100; activity rate of total population 37% (participation rates: ages 15–65, 60%; female [2002] 34.1%; unemployed [2002] 11.7%). **Gross national income** (2008): US$1,081,000,000 (US$1,420 per capita). **Public debt** (external, outstanding; 2008): US$833,000,000. **Selected balance of payments data.** Receipts from (US$'000,000): tourism (2007) 50; remittances (2008) 278; foreign direct investment (2005–07 avg.) 110; official development assistance (2007) 124. Disbursements for (US$'000,000): tourism (2007) 58; remittances (2008) 61.

Foreign trade

Imports (2007; c.i.f.): US$1,028,800,000 (refined petroleum products 22.9%; machinery and apparatus 20.2%; food products 11.3%; chemical products 9.8%). *Major import sources:* Trinidad and Tobago 25.1%; US 25.1%; China 8.5%; UK 6.1%; Netherlands Antilles 3.9%. **Exports** (2007; f.o.b.): US$784,700,000 (gold 20.2%; raw sugar 19.2%; bauxite 12.2%; rice 9.6%; sawn wood 5.0%; shrimp 4.7%; diamonds 4.2%). *Major export destinations:* Canada 21.6%; UK 15.9%; US 14.4%; Barbados 5.9%; Netherlands 5.6%.

Transport and communications

Transport. *Railroads:* none. *Roads* (2000): total length 7,970 km (paved 7%). *Vehicles* (2001): passenger cars 61,300; trucks and buses 15,500. *Air transport* (2001; scheduled traffic only): passenger-km 174,800,000; metric ton-km cargo 1,600,000. **Communications**, in total units (units per 1,000 persons). Telephone landlines (2008): 125,000 (164); cellular telephone subscribers (2005): 281,000 (375); personal computers (2005): 29,000 (39); total Internet users (2008): 205,000 (269); broadband Internet subscribers (2005): 2,000 (2.6).

Education and health

Educational attainment (2002). Percentage of population ages 15 and over having: no formal schooling/unknown 3.4%; primary education 26.0%; secondary 62.1%; post-secondary 3.7%; higher 4.8%. **Literacy** (2005): total population ages 15 and over literate 99.0%; males literate 99.2%; females literate 98.7%. **Health** (2005): physicians 323 (1 per 2,325 persons); hospital beds (2004–05) 1,887 (1 per 401 persons); infant mortality rate per 1,000 live births 33.3; undernourished population (2002–04) 60,000 (8% of total population based on the consumption of a minimum daily requirement of 1,880 calories).

Military

Total active duty personnel (November 2008): 1,100 (army 81.8%, navy 9.1%, air force 9.1%). **Military expenditure as percentage of GDP** (2004): 1.8%; per capita expenditure US$19.

Background

Guyana was colonized by the Dutch in the 17th century. During the Napoleonic Wars the British occupied the territory and afterward purchased the colonies of

1 metric ton = about 1.1 short tons;   1 kilometer = 0.6 mi (statute);   1 metric ton-km cargo = about 0.68 short ton-mi cargo;   c.i.f.: cost, insurance, and freight;   f.o.b.: free on board

Demerara, Berbice, and Essequibo, united in 1831 as British Guiana. The slave trade was abolished in 1807, but emancipation of the 100,000 slaves in the colonies was not completed until 1838. From the 1840s East Indian and Chinese indentured servants were brought to work the plantations; by 1917 almost 240,000 East Indians had migrated to British Guiana. It was made a crown colony in 1928 and granted home rule in 1953. Political parties began to emerge, developing on racial lines as the People's Progressive Party (largely East Indian) and the People's National Congress (largely black). The PNC formed a coalition government and led the country into independence as Guyana in 1966. In 1970 Guyana became a republic within the Commonwealth; in 1980 it adopted a new constitution. Venezuela has long claimed land west of the Essequibo River, and the UN continued to arbitrate the issue in the early 21st century.

Recent Developments

Guyana received continued interest from international petroleum companies. In November 2009 Canadian company CGX Energy reported that it would drill its Corentyne offshore license, and in February 2010 it announced its progress in acquiring a rig for the field.

Internet resource: <www.statisticsguyana.gov.gy>.

Haiti

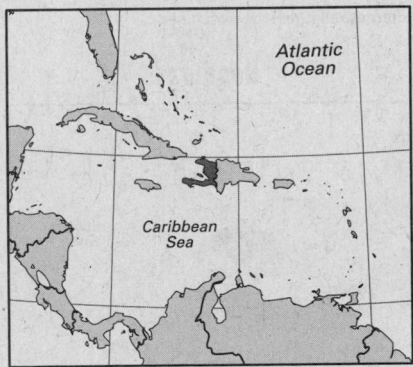

Atlantic Ocean

Caribbean Sea

Official name: Repiblik d' Ayiti (Haitian Creole); République d'Haïti (French) (Republic of Haiti). Form of government: republic with two legislative houses (Senate [30]; Chamber of Deputies [99]). Head of state: President René Préval (from 2006). Head of government: Prime Minister Jean-Max Bellerive (from 2009). Capital: Port-au-Prince. Official languages: Haitian Creole; French. Official religions: Roman Catholicism has special recognition per concordat with the Vatican; Vodou (Voodoo) became officially sanctioned per governmental decree of April 2003. Monetary unit: 1 gourde (G) = 100 centimes; valuation (1 Jul 2010) US$1 = G 38.94.

Demography

Area: 10,695 sq mi, 27,700 sq km. Population (2009): 9,521,000. Density (2009): persons per sq mi 890.2, persons per sq km 343.7. Urban (2007):

40.1%. Sex distribution (2005): male 49.29%; female 50.71%. Age breakdown (2005): under 15, 42.6%; 15–29, 30.5%; 30–44, 14.2%; 45–59, 7.5%; 60–74, 4.2%; 75 and over, 1.0%. Ethnic composition (2000): black 94.2%; mulatto 5.4%; other 0.4%. Religious affiliation (2003): Roman Catholic 54.7% (about 80% of all Roman Catholics also practice Vodou [Voodoo]); Protestant/independent Christian 28.5%, of which Baptist 15.4%, Pentecostal 7.9%; Vodou (Voodoo) 2.1%; nonreligious 10.2%; other/unknown 4.5%. Major cities (2003): Port-au-Prince 703,023 (urban agglomeration 1,977,036); Carrefour (1999) 336,222; Delmas (1999) 284,079; Cap-Haïtien 111,094; Gonaïves 104,825. Location: western third of the island of Hispaniola, bordered by the North Atlantic Ocean, the Caribbean Sea, and the Dominican Republic.

Vital statistics

Birth rate per 1,000 population (2007): 27.9 (world avg. 20.3). Death rate per 1,000 population (2007): 9.2 (world avg. 8.5). Total fertility rate (avg. births per childbearing woman; 2007): 3.50. Life expectancy at birth (2007): male 59.1 years; female 62.8 years.

National economy

Budget (2007). Revenue: G 25,323,750,000 (customs duties 53.1%; sales tax 27.5%; taxes on income and profits 17.8%). Expenditures: G 29,534,070,000 (current expenditures 77.1%, of which wages and salaries 33.9%, transfers 4.2%, interest on public debt 2.3%; capital expenditures 22.9%). Gross national income (2008): US$6,464,000,000 (US$660 per capita). Production (metric tons except as noted). Agriculture and fishing (2007): sugarcane 1,000,000, cassava (manioc) 330,000, bananas 293,000, mangoes 260,000, cacao beans 4,500; livestock (number of live animals) 1,900,000 goats, 1,450,000 cattle, 1,000,000 pigs; fisheries production 10,000 (from aquaculture, none). Mining and quarrying (2007): sand 2,000,000 cu m. Manufacturing (value added in G '000,000 at constant prices of 1986–87; 2002): food products and beverages 484.5; textiles, wearing apparel, and footwear 195.7; chemical and rubber products 63.8. Energy production (consumption): electricity (kW-hr; 2007) 241,990,000 (215,380,000 [excluding December]); petroleum products (metric tons; 2006) none (541,000). Population economically active (2006): total 3,539,000; activity rate of total population 37.5% (participation rates: ages 15–64, 60.4%; female 33.3%; officially unemployed [2003] 32.7%). Public debt (external, outstanding; December 2007): US$1,478,000,000. Selected balance of payments data. Receipts from (US$'000,000): tourism (2007) 140; remittances (2008) 1,300; foreign direct investment (2005–07 avg.) 87; official development assistance (2007) 701. Disbursements for (US$'000,000): tourism (2007) 55; remittances (2008) 96.

Foreign trade

Imports (2008): US$2,107,750,000 (food products 27.2%; mineral fuels 26.6%; machinery and transportation equipment 8.2%; chemical products 3.5%). Major import sources (2004): US 52.9%; Dominican Republic 6.0%; Japan 2.9%. Exports (2008): US$490,100,000 (reexports to US 86.7%, of which wearing apparel and accessories 85.5%; essential oils 3.7%; mangoes 2.0%; cocoa 1.5%; rock lobster

1.1%). *Major export destinations* (2004): US 81.8%; Dominican Republic 7.2%; Canada 4.2%.

Transport and communications

Transport. *Railroads:* none. *Roads* (2000): total length 4,160 km (paved 24%). *Vehicles* (1999): passenger cars 93,000; trucks and buses 61,600. **Communications,** in total units (units per 1,000 persons). Telephone landlines (2006): 150,000 (17); cellular telephone subscribers (2008): 3,200,000 (328); personal computers (2007): 499,000 (52); total Internet users (2007): 1,000,000 (104).

Education and health

Educational attainment (2000). Percentage of population ages 25 and over having: no formal education/unknown 46.1%; incomplete primary education 28.9%; primary 5.3%; incomplete secondary 15.6%; secondary 1.8%; higher 2.3%. **Literacy** (2007): total population ages 15 and over literate 62.1%; males literate 60.1%; females literate 64.0%. **Health:** physicians (1999) 1,910 (1 per 4,000 persons); hospital beds (2000) 6,431 (1 per 1,234 persons); infant mortality rate per 1,000 live births (2007) 71.0; undernourished population (2003–05) 5,300,000 (58% of total population based on the consumption of a minimum daily requirement of 1,860 calories).

Military

Total active duty personnel (2008). The national police force had 2,000 personnel; UN peacekeepers (March 2009): 7,044 troops, 2,011 police.

Background

Haiti gained its independence when the former slaves of the island rebelled against French rule in 1791–1804. The new republic encompassed the entire island of Hispaniola, but the eastern portion was restored to Spain in 1809. The island was reunited under Haitian Pres. Jean-Pierre Boyer (1818–43); after his overthrow the eastern portion revolted and formed the Dominican Republic. Haiti's government was marked by instability, with frequent coups and assassinations. It was occupied by the US in 1915–34. In 1957 the dictator François ("Papa Doc") Duvalier came to power. Despite an economic decline and civil unrest, Duvalier ruled until his death in 1971. He was succeeded by his son, Jean-Claude ("Baby Doc") Duvalier, who was forced into exile in 1986. Haiti's first free presidential elections, held in 1990, were won by Jean-Bertrand Aristide. He was deposed by a military coup in 1991, after which tens of thousands of Haitians attempted to flee to the US in small boats. The military government stepped down in 1994, and Aristide returned from exile and resumed the presidency. Economic and political instability continued to plague Haiti in the early 21st century.

Recent Developments

A large-scale earthquake occurred 12 Jan 2010 on Hispaniola. Most severely affected was Haiti. The earthquake hit some 15 miles (25 km) southwest of Port-au-Prince. The initial shock registered a magnitude of 7.0 and was soon followed by two aftershocks of magnitudes 5.9 and 5.5. More aftershocks occurred in the following days, including another one of magnitude 5.9 that struck on 20 January. The densely populated region around Port-au-Prince, located on the Gulf of Gonâve, was among those most heavily affected. It was estimated that at least 222,570 people died and 1.6 million were displaced. The collapsed buildings defining the landscape of the disaster area came as a consequence of Haiti's lack of building codes. Without adequate reinforcement, the buildings disintegrated under the force of the quake, killing or trapping their occupants. In Port-au-Prince the cathedral and the National Palace were both heavily damaged, as were the United Nations headquarters, national penitentiary, and parliament building.

A significant portion of Haiti's debt had been cancelled the previous year as part of the Heavily Indebted Poor Countries initiative of the International Monetary Fund and World Bank, but the country still owed more than US$1 billion to a range of creditors. With its economy barely functioning, the country appeared unlikely to meet those obligations. In February the G7 countries forgave the remaining portion of Haiti's debt to them, and in March the Inter-American Development Bank forgave US$447 million and pledged over US$30 million in further support. A UN donor conference in New York City in late March generated pledges of US$9.9 billion.

Internet resource: <www.brh.net>.

Honduras

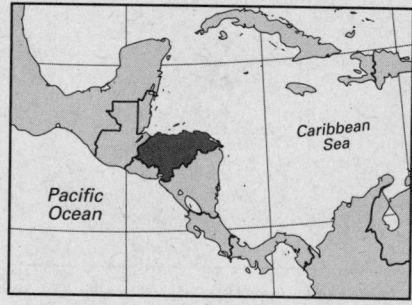

Official name: República de Honduras (Republic of Honduras). **Form of government:** multiparty republic with one legislative house (National Congress [128]). **Head of state and government:** President Porfirio Lobo (from 2010). **Capital:** Tegucigalpa. **Official language:** Spanish. **Official religion:** none. **Monetary unit:** 1 lempira (L) = 100 centavos; valuation (1 Jul 2010) US$1 = L 18.49.

Demography

Area: 43,433 sq mi, 112,492 sq km. **Population** (2009): 7,466,000. **Density** (2009): persons per sq mi 171.9, persons per sq km 66.4. **Urban** (2008):

---

1 metric ton = about 1.1 short tons;   1 kilometer = 0.6 mi (statute);   1 metric ton-km cargo = about 0.68 short ton-mi cargo;   c.i.f.: cost, insurance, and freight;   f.o.b.: free on board

47.9%. **Sex distribution** (2008): male 49.95%; female 50.05%. **Age breakdown** (2005): under 15, 40.5%; 15–29, 29.2%; 30–44, 16.7%; 45–59, 8.6%; 60–74, 3.9%; 75 and over, 1.1%. **Ethnic composition** (2000): mestizo 86.6%; Amerindian 5.5%; black (including Black Carib) 4.3%; white 2.3%; other 1.3%. **Religious affiliation** (2002): Roman Catholic 63%; Evangelical Protestant 23%; other 14%. **Major cities** (2008): Tegucigalpa 967,200; San Pedro Sula 623,100; Choloma 212,400; La Ceiba 167,300; El Progreso 118,200. **Location:** Central America, bordering the Caribbean Sea, Nicaragua, the North Pacific Ocean, El Salvador, and Guatemala.

Vital statistics

Birth rate per 1,000 population (2008): 27.4 (world avg. 20.3). **Death rate** per 1,000 population (2008): 5.6 (world avg. 8.5). **Total fertility rate** (avg. births per childbearing woman; 2008): 3.20. **Life expectancy** at birth (2008): male 67.2 years; female 73.9 years.

National economy

Budget (2008). *Revenue:* L 52,343,000,000 (tax revenue 80.5%; nontax revenue 8.5%; grants 11.0%). *Expenditures:* L 58,650,000,000 (current expenditures 78.7%, of which wages and salaries 41.8%; capital expenditures 21.3%). **Public debt** (external, outstanding; January 2009): US$2,900,000,000. *Production* (metric tons except as noted). *Agriculture and fishing* (2008): sugarcane 5,958,300, oil palm fruit 1,112,118, bananas 910,000, coffee 217,951, tobacco 6,500; livestock (number of live animals) 2,544,888 cattle, 490,000 pigs, 34,000,000 chickens; fisheries production (2007) 67,567 (from aquaculture 81%). *Mining and quarrying* (2007): gypsum (2005) 60,000; zinc (metal content) 38,000; silver 50,000 kg; gold 4,100 kg. *Manufacturing* (value added in L '000,000; 2008): food products, beverages, and tobacco products 21,997; textiles and wearing apparel 15,624; fabricated metal products 4,905. *Energy production (consumption):* electricity (kW-hr; 2008) 6,589,300,000 (6,589,300,000); coal (metric tons; 2006) none (190,000); petroleum products (metric tons; 2006) none (2,256,000). **Selected balance of payments data.** Receipts from (US$'000,000): tourism (2007) 557; remittances (2008) 2,824; foreign direct investment (FDI; 2005–07 avg.) 697; official development assistance (2007) 464. Disbursements for (US$'000,000): tourism (2007) 306; remittances (2008) 2.0; FDI (2005–07 avg.) 1.0. **Population economically active** (2006): total 2,811,800; activity rate of total population 40.0% (participation rates: ages 15 and over, 60.0%; female 34.7%; officially unemployed [2008] 3.5%). **Gross national income** (2008): US$13,026,000,000 (US$1,800 per capita).

Foreign trade

Imports (2008; c.i.f.): US$11,088,100,000 (mineral fuels and lubricants 18.0%; textiles and wearing apparel 17.5%; machinery and electrical equipment 15.4%; food products and live animals 11.9%; chemical products 10.8%; fabricated metal products 7.1%; transportation equipment 5.9%). *Major import sources:* US 40.4%; Guatemala 8.6%; Mexico 5.5%; El Salvador 5.4%; Costa Rica 3.9%. **Exports** (2008; f.o.b.): US$5,984,200,000 (textiles and wearing apparel 49.3%; coffee 10.4%; bananas 6.4%; shrimp

2.4%; tobacco products 2.3%). *Major export destinations:* US 40.5%; El Salvador 9.3%; Guatemala 6.9%; Mexico 6.1%; Belgium 5.9%.

Transport and communications

Transport. *Railroads* (2008): serviceable lines 75 km; most tracks are out of use but not dismantled. *Roads* (2008): total length 14,239 km (paved 22%). *Vehicles* (2003): passenger cars 386,468; trucks and buses 113,744. *Air transport* (1995): passenger-km 341,000,000; metric ton-km cargo 33,000,000. **Communications,** in total units (units per 1,000 persons). Telephone landlines (2008): 826,000 (113); cellular telephone subscribers (2008): 6,211,000 (849); personal computers (2007): 143,000 (20); total Internet users (2008): 659,000 (90).

Education and health

Educational attainment (2005–06). Percentage of population ages 25 and over having: no formal schooling/unknown 16.7%; incomplete primary education 37.0%; complete primary 22.7%; secondary 17.6%; higher 6.0%. **Literacy** (2007): total population ages 15 and over literate 83.1%; males literate 82.4%; females literate 83.7%. **Health:** physicians (2006) 5,977 (1 per 1,176 persons); hospital beds (2008) 6,929 (1 per 1,056 persons); infant mortality rate per 1,000 live births (2007) 20.0; undernourished population (2002–04) 1,600,000 (23% of total population based on the consumption of a minimum daily requirement of 1,780 calories).

Military

Total active duty personnel (November 2008): 12,000 (army 69.2%, navy 11.7%, air force 19.1%); US troops (December 2008): 418. **Military expenditure as percentage of GDP** (2008): 0.7%; per capita expenditure US$13.

Background

Early residents of Honduras were part of the Mayan civilization that flourished in the 1st millennium AD. Christopher Columbus reached Honduras in 1502, and permanent settlement followed. A major war between the Spanish and the Indians broke out in 1537, culminating in the decimation of the Indian population through disease and enslavement. After 1570 Honduras was part of the captaincy general of Guatemala until Central American independence in 1821. Part of the United Provinces of Central America, Honduras withdrew in 1838 and declared its independence. In the 20th century, under military rule, there was constant civil war and some intervention by the US. A civilian government assumed office in 1982.

Recent Developments

In March 2009 Honduran Pres. Manuel Zelaya ordered a referendum to ask voters to approve a constituent assembly that would reform the constitution and allow him to run again for office. The Supreme Court, Congress, and the electoral tribunal declared the referendum illegal. On 28 June, the day of the proposed election, Zelaya was arrested and transported to Costa Rica. Congress appointed its leader, Roberto Micheletti, to complete Zelaya's term, and the Supreme Court charged Zelaya with having violated the constitution. Zelaya returned to Honduras in September, taking refuge in the Brazilian embassy. He did not participate in the November general elections, however, in which Porfirio Lobo of the opposition won the presidency. In January 2010 Zelaya went into exile in the Dominican Republic.

Internet resource: <www.honduras.com>.

Hong Kong

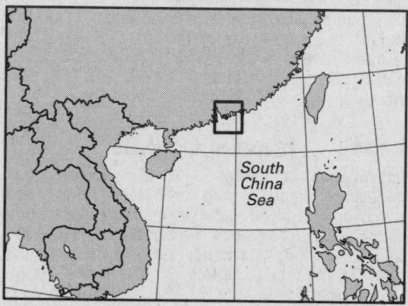

South China Sea

Official name: Xianggang Tebie Xingzhengqu (Chinese); Hong Kong Special Administrative Region (English). **Political status:** special administrative region of the People's Republic of China with one legislative house (Legislative Council [60]). **Head of state:** Chinese President Hu Jintao (from 2003). **Head of government:** Chief Executive Donald Tsang (from 2005). **Government offices:** Central & Western District. **Official languages:** Chinese; English. **Official religion:** none. **Monetary unit:** 1 Hong Kong dollar (HK$) = 100 cents; valuation (1 Jul 2010) US$1 = HK$7.80.

Demography

Area: 426 sq mi, 1,104 sq km. **Population** (2009): 7,038,000. **Density** (2009): persons per sq mi 16,521, persons per sq km 6,375. **Urban** (2003): 100%. **Sex distribution** (2008): male 47.26%; female 52.74%. **Age breakdown** (2008): under 15, 12.8%; 15–29, 20.4%; 30–44, 24.7%; 45–59, 24.9%; 60–74, 11.0%; 75–84, 4.6%; 85 and over, 1.6%. **Ethnic composition** (2006): Chinese 95.0%; Filipino 1.6%; Indonesian 1.3%; assorted Caucasian 0.5%; Indian 0.3%; Nepalese 0.2%; other 1.1%. **Religious affiliation** (2002): nonreligious/non-practitioner of religion 57%; participant of religious practice 43%, of which Protestant 4.5%, Roman Catholic 3.5%, Muslim 1.5%, remainder (mostly Buddhist, Taoist, or Confucianist) 33.5%. **Major built-up areas** (2006): Kowloon 2,019,533; Victoria 981,714; Tuen Mun 488,249; Shaʻ Tin 425,140; Tseung Kwan O 344,872. **Location:** eastern Asia, bordering China and the South China Sea.

Vital statistics

Birth rate per 1,000 population (2008): 11.3 (world avg. 20.3). **Death rate** per 1,000 population (2008): 5.9 (world avg. 8.5). **Total fertility rate** (avg. births per childbearing woman; 2008): 1.06. **Life expectancy** at birth (2008): male 79.4 years; female 85.5 years.

National economy

Budget (2007–08). *Revenue:* HK$358,465,000,000 (earnings and profits taxes 37.3%; indirect taxes 26.9%; capital revenue 22.9%). *Expenditures:* HK$252,400,000,000 (education 21.3%; social welfare 13.8%; health 13.3%; police 11.1%; housing 5.7%; economic services 5.3%). **Public debt** (external, outstanding; January 2007): US$1,673,-000,000. **Gross national income** (2008): US$219,255,000,000 (US$31,420 per capita). **Production** (metric tons except as noted). *Agriculture and fishing* (2007): vegetables 18,900, fruits 1,617; cut flowers are also produced; livestock (number of live animals) 269,100 pigs, 7,273,000 chickens; fisheries production 158,661 (from aquaculture 3%). *Quarrying* (2006): stone and aggregates 6,000,000. *Manufacturing* (value added in HK$'000,000; 2006): publishing and printed materials 11,954; textiles 5,580; food products 5,548. *Energy production (consumption):* electricity (kW-hr; 2006) 38,613,000,000 (44,982,000,000); coal (metric tons; 2006) none (10,878,000); petroleum products (metric tons; 2006) none (3,432,000); natural gas (cu m; 2006) none (2,322,000,000). **Selected balance of payments data.** Receipts from (US$'000,000): tourism (2007) 13,566; remittances (2008) 355; foreign direct investment (FDI; 2005–07 avg.) 46,190. Disbursements for (US$'000,000): tourism (2007) 15,086; remittances (2008) 394; FDI (2005–07 avg.) 41,789. **Population economically active** (2008): total 3,648,900; activity rate of total population 52.3% (participation rates: ages 15–64, 70.2%; female 46.5%; unemployed [March–May 2009] 5.3%).

Foreign trade

Imports (2008; c.i.f.): HK$3,025,288,000,000 (capital goods 30.2%; consumer goods 26.8%; mineral fuels and lubricants 3.7%; food products 3.2%). *Major import sources:* China 46.6%; Japan 9.8%; Singapore 6.4%; Taiwan 6.3%; US 5.0%. **Exports** (2008; f.o.b.): HK$2,824,151,000,000 (reexports 96.8%, of which capital goods 32.2%, consumer goods 30.6%; domestic exports 3.2%, of which wearing apparel and accessories 0.8%). *Major export destinations:* China 48.5%; US 12.7%; Japan 4.3%; Germany 3.3%.

Transport and communications

Transport. *Railroads* (2003): route length 64 km. *Roads* (2008): total length 2,040 km (paved 100%). *Vehicles* (2008): passenger cars 401,000; trucks and buses 128,000. *Air transport* (2005; Cathay Pacific and Dragonair only): passenger-km 71,595,000,000; metric ton-km cargo 8,026,729,000. **Communications,** in total units (units per 1,000 persons). Telephone landlines (2008): 4,108,000 (564); cellular telephone subscribers (2008): 11,374,000 (1,563); personal computers (2007): 4,751,000 (686); total Internet users (2008): 4,124,000 (567); broadband Internet subscribers (2008): 1,948,000 (268).

1 metric ton = about 1.1 short tons;   1 kilometer = 0.6 mi (statute);   1 metric ton-km cargo = about 0.68 short ton-mi cargo;   c.i.f.: cost, insurance, and freight;   f.o.b.: free on board

Education and health

Educational attainment (2008). Percentage of population ages 15 and over having: no formal schooling 5.4%; primary education 18.2%; secondary 46.3%; matriculation 5.4%; nondegree higher 8.2%; higher degree 16.5%. Literacy (2000): total population ages 15 and over literate 93.5%; males literate 96.5%; females literate 90.2%. Health (2005): physicians 11,775 (1 per 588 persons) (additionally, there were 4,848 practitioners of traditional Chinese medicine in Hong Kong at the beginning of 2006); hospital beds 33,939 (1 per 204 persons); infant mortality rate per 1,000 live births (2008) 1.7.

Military

Total active duty personnel (November 2007): 7,000 troops of Chinese military (including elements of army, navy, and air force); Hong Kong residents are exempted from military service.

Background

The island of Hong Kong and adjacent islets were ceded by China to the British in 1842, and the Kowloon Peninsula and the New Territories were later leased by the British from China for 99 years (1898–1997). A joint Chinese-British declaration, signed on 19 Dec 1984, paved the way for the entire territory to be returned to China, which occurred on 1 Jul 1997.

Recent Developments

Although not as seriously affected as some of the other Asian economic powerhouses, Hong Kong struggled during the international financial crisis in 2009. While the unemployment rate stayed level, at 4.6%, production in the key wearing apparel and textiles sectors dropped by 29.8% and 22.1%, respectively. There was a 12.6% decline in exports and an 11.0% drop in imports, and the value of construction fell by 3.4%.

Internet resource: <www.censtatd.gov.hk>.

Hungary

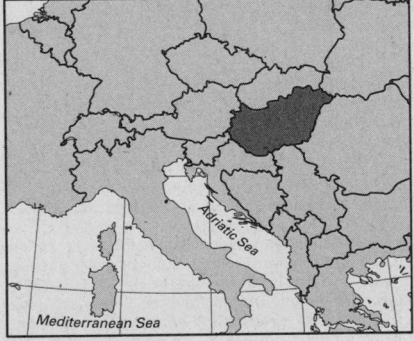

Official name: Magyar Köztársaság (Republic of Hungary). Form of government: unitary multiparty republic with one legislative house (National Assembly

[386]). Head of state: President László Sólyom (from 2005). Head of government: Prime Minister Viktor Orbán (from 2010). Capital: Budapest. Official language: Hungarian. Official religion: none. Monetary unit: 1 forint (Ft) = 100 filler; valuation (1 Jul 2010) US$1 = Ft 230.75.

Demography

Area: 35,919 sq mi, 93,030 sq km. Population (2009): 10,021,000. Density (2009): persons per sq mi 279.0, persons per sq km 107.7. Urban (2004): 64.8%. Sex distribution (2008): male 47.46%; female 52.54%. Age breakdown (2008): under 15, 14.9%; 15–29, 19.8%; 30–44, 22.4%; 45–59, 20.8%; 60–74, 14.9%; 75–84, 5.7%; 85 and over, 1.5%. Ethnic composition (2000): Hungarian 84.4%; Rom 5.3%; Ruthenian 2.9%; German 2.4%; Romanian 1.0%; Slovak 0.9%; Jewish 0.6%; other 2.5%. Religious affiliation (2001): Roman Catholic 51.9%; Reformed 15.9%; Lutheran 3.0%; Greek Catholic 2.6%; Jewish 0.1%; nonreligious 14.5%; other/unknown 12.0%. Major cities (2007): Budapest 1,702,297; Debrecen 205,084; Miskolc 171,096; Szeged 167,039; Pécs 156,664. Location: central Europe, bordering Slovakia, Ukraine, Romania, Serbia, Croatia, Slovenia, and Austria.

Vital statistics

Birth rate per 1,000 population (2008): 9.9 (world avg. 20.3); within marriage 60.5%. Death rate per 1,000 population (2008): 13.0 (world avg. 8.5). Total fertility rate (avg. births per childbearing woman; 2008): 1.35. Life expectancy at birth (2007): male 69.2 years; female 77.3 years.

National economy

Budget (2006). Revenue: Ft 8,653,000,000,000 (social security contributions 34.6%; taxes on goods and services 34.0%; income tax 13.2%). Expenditures: Ft 10,710,700,000,000 (social protection 38.0%; economic affairs 12.5%; health 11.6%; public debt 8.6%; education 8.6%; defense 3.1%). Production (metric tons except as noted). Agriculture and fishing (2007): corn (maize) 8,400,000, wheat 3,988,177, sugar beets 1,676,000, sunflower seeds 1,043,000, Hungarian red paprika (2006) 32,633; livestock (number of live animals) 3,987,000 pigs, 702,000 cattle, 2,708,000 geese; fisheries production 22,888 (from aquaculture 69%). Mining and quarrying (2007): bauxite 546,000. Manufacturing (value added in US$'000,000; 2005): electrical machinery and apparatus 2,436; food products and beverages 2,363; motor vehicles and parts 2,129; refined petroleum products 1,436. Energy production (consumption): electricity ('000,000 kW-hr; 2008) 33,586 ([2006] 43,066); coal ('000 metric tons; 2006) none (1,851); lignite ('000 metric tons; 2008) 9,333 ([2006] 10,184); crude petroleum ('000 barrels; 2008) 5,180 ([2006] 50,700); petroleum products ('000 metric tons; 2006) 6,184 (6,408); natural gas ('000,000 cu m; 2008) 2,691 ([2006] 14,689). Selected balance of payments data. Receipts from (US$'000,000): tourism (2007) 4,739; remittances (2008) 2,946; foreign direct investment (FDI; 2005–07 avg.) 6,090. Disbursements for (US$'000,000): tourism (2007) 2,949; remittances (2008) 1,407; FDI (2005–07 avg.) 3,314. Population economically active (2008): total 4,208,600;

activity rate of total population 41.9% (participation rates: ages 15–64, 61.5%; female 45.7%; unemployed [August 2008–July 2009] 8.7%). **Gross national income** (2008): US$128,581,000,000 (US$12,810 per capita). **Public debt** (2008): US$107,200,000,000.

Foreign trade

Imports (2007; c.i.f.): US$94,660,000,000 (electrical machinery and electronic devices 13.5%; nonelectrical machinery 12.5%; mineral fuels 9.4%; motor vehicles 8.6%). *Major import sources:* Germany 26.8%; Russia 6.9%; Austria 6.1%; China 5.4%; Italy 4.5%. **Exports** (2007; f.o.b.): US$94,591,-000,000 (nonelectrical machinery 15.4%, of which engines and parts 8.1%; telecommunications equipment 11.0%; motor vehicles and parts 11.0%; electrical machinery 9.8%). *Major export destinations:* Germany 28.4%; Italy 5.6%; France 4.7%; Austria 4.5%; UK 4.5%.

Transport and communications

Transport. *Railroads* (2008): route length 7,269 km; passenger-km (2007) 8,751,000,000; metric ton-km cargo (2008) 9,817,000,000. *Roads* (2007; national public roads only): total length 31,183 km (paved 99%). *Vehicles* (2008): passenger cars 3,055,000; trucks and buses 442,000. *Air transport* (2007; Malév Hungarian Airlines only): passenger-km (2007) 4,537,000,000; metric ton-km cargo (2008) 17,000,000. **Communications,** in total units (units per 1,000 persons). Telephone landlines (2008): 3,094,000 (308); cellular telephone subscribers (2008): 12,224,000 (1,218); personal computers (2007): 2,574,000 (256); total Internet users (2008): 5,500,000 (548); broadband Internet subscribers (2008): 1,542,000 (154).

Education and health

Educational attainment (2007). Population ages 25–64 having: no formal schooling through lower-secondary education 20%; upper secondary/higher vocational 61%; university 17%; unknown 2%. **Health** (2007): physicians 28,189 (1 per 357 persons); hospital beds 71,902 (1 per 140 persons); infant mortality rate per 1,000 live births (2008) 5.6.

Military

Total active duty personnel (November 2008): 25,207 (army 43.4%, air force 22.5%, joint staff 34.1%). **Military expenditure as percentage of GDP** (2008): 1.2%; per capita expenditure US$161.

Background

The western part of Hungary was incorporated into the Roman Empire in 14 BC. The Magyars, a nomadic people, occupied the middle basin of the Danube River in the late 9th century AD. Stephen I, crowned in 1000, Christianized the country and organized it into a strong and independent state. Invasions by the Mongols in the 13th century and by the Ottoman Turks in the 14th century devastated the country, and by 1568 the territory of modern Hungary had been divided into three parts: Royal Hungary went to the Habsburgs; Transylvania gained autonomy in 1566 under the Turks; and the central plain remained under Turkish control until the late 17th century, when the Austrian Habsburgs took over. Hungary declared its independence from Austria in 1849, and in 1867 the dual monarchy of Austria-Hungary was established. Its defeat in World War I resulted in the dismemberment of Hungary, leaving it only those areas in which Magyars predominated. In an attempt to regain some of this lost territory, Hungary cooperated with the Germans against the Soviet Union during World War II. After the war, a pro-Soviet provisional government was established, and in 1949 the Hungarian People's Republic was formed. Opposition to this Stalinist regime broke out in 1956 but was suppressed. Nevertheless, from 1956 to 1988 communist Hungary grew to become the most tolerant of the Soviet-bloc nations of Eastern Europe. It gained its independence in 1989 and soon attracted the largest amount of direct foreign investment in east-central Europe. In 1999 it joined NATO and in 2004 the European Union.

Recent Developments

Hungary's economy in 2009 was on the verge of collapse, with a public debt standing at 77% of GDP. The forint had lost 20% of its value against the euro, which made it difficult for the government to service its foreign-currency-denominated debt. Although exports to the EU collapsed and industrial production plummeted, GDP contracted by 7%, and unemployment rose to more than 10%, an austerity program—which included radical cuts in all areas of public spending and a reform of the health care, pension, and education systems—eased investors' fears about the country's prospects for riding out the global financial crisis.

Internet resource: <http://portal.ksh.hu>.

Iceland

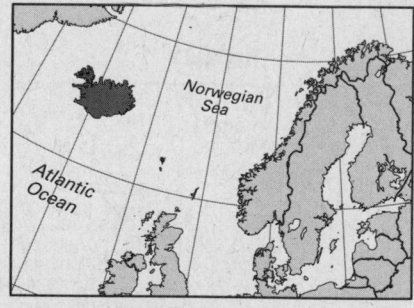

Official name: Lýdhveldidh Ísland (Republic of Iceland). **Form of government:** unitary multiparty republic with one legislative house (Althingi [63]). **Head of state:** President Ólafur Ragnar Grímsson (from 1996). **Head of government:** Prime Minister Jóhanna Sigurðardóttir (from 2009). **Capital:** Reykjavík. **Offi-**

---

1 metric ton = about 1.1 short tons; 1 kilometer = 0.6 mi (statute); 1 metric ton-km cargo = about 0.68 short ton-mi cargo; c.i.f.: cost, insurance, and freight; f.o.b.: free on board

cial language: Icelandic. Official religion: Evangelical Lutheran. Monetary unit: 1 króna (ISK; plural krónur) = 100 aurar; valuation (1 Jul 2010) US$1 = ISK 126.87.

Demography

Area: 39,769 sq mi, 103,000 sq km. Population (2009): 318,000. Density (2009): persons per sq mi 34.6, persons per sq km 13.4. Urban (2007): 93.1%. Sex distribution (2007): male 50.89%; female 49.11%. Age breakdown (2007): under 15, 21.0%; 15–29, 22.3%; 30–44, 21.4%; 45–59, 19.2%; 60–74, 10.4%; 75–84, 4.3%; 85 and over, 1.4%. Ethnic composition by citizenship (2008): Icelandic 93.2%; European 5.5%, of which Polish 2.7%, Nordic 0.6%; Asian 0.8%; other 0.5%. Religious affiliation (2007): Evangelical Lutheran 80.7%; Roman Catholic 2.5%; other Christian 6.8%; other/not specified 10.0%. Major cities (2008): Reykjavík 119,547 (urban agglomeration [2007] 195,840); Kópavogur 29,976; Hafnarfjördhur 25,850; Akureyri 17,541; Gardhabær 10,358. Location: northern Europe, island between the Greenland Sea, the Norwegian Sea; and the North Atlantic Ocean.

Vital statistics

Birth rate per 1,000 population (2008): 15.2 (world avg. 20.3); within marriage 35.9%. Death rate per 1,000 population (2008): 6.3 (world avg. 8.5). Total fertility rate (avg. births per childbearing woman; 2008): 2.14. Life expectancy at birth (2008): male 79.6 years; female 83.0 years.

National economy

Budget (2007). Revenue: ISK 454,588,000,000 (tax revenue 78.4%, of which VAT 42.9%, income tax 31.5%; nontax revenue 21.6%). Expenditures: ISK 403,199,000,000 (social security and health 48.8%; education 10.6%; social affairs 9.4%; interest payment 6.9%). Production (metric tons except as noted). Agriculture and fishing (2007): potatoes 13,000, tomatoes 1,603, hay 1,993,773 cu m; livestock (number of live animals) 454,812 sheep, 70,660 cattle, 41,497 mink; fisheries production (value in ISK '000,000): 80,251, of which cod 29,585, haddock 14,538, redfish 7,646, herring 5,700, saithe 4,263, capelin 4,247, blue whiting 3,022; fisheries production by tonnage 1,404,066 (from aquaculture, negligible). Mining and quarrying (2007): pumice 95,000. Manufacturing (value of sales in ISK '000,000; 2008): base metals (nearly all aluminum and ferrosilicon) 196,547; preserved and processed fish 162,252; other food products and beverages 72,049. Energy production (consumption): electricity (kW-hr; 2007) 11,976,000,000 (11,976,000,000); coal (metric tons; 2006) none (91,000); petroleum products (metric tons; 2006) none (797,000). Selected balance of payments data. Receipts from (US$'000,000): tourism (2007) 640; remittances (2008) 46; foreign direct investment (FDI; 2005–07 avg.) 3,385. Disbursements for (US$'000,000): tourism (2007) 1,341; remittances (2008) 100; FDI (2005–07 avg.) 8,180. Population economically active (2007): total 181,500; activity rate of total population 58.3% (participation rates: ages 16–64, 87.7%; female 46.6%) unemployed [April–June 2009] 9.1%). Gross national income (2008): US$12,702,000,000 (US$40,070

per capita). Public debt (December 2008): US$9,906,000,000.

Foreign trade

Imports (2007; c.i.f.): ISK 428,509,000,000 (machinery and apparatus 22.6%; motor vehicles 11.5%; refined petroleum products 8.2%; aircraft and parts 6.6%; food products 6.3%; alumina 4.8%). Major import sources: US 13.5%; Germany 12.1%; Sweden 10.0%; Denmark 7.4%; Netherlands 5.6%. Exports (2007; f.o.b.): ISK 305,670,000,000 (fresh fish 26.6%; aluminum 26.3%; aircraft 14.6%; dried and salted fish 8.2%; fish foodstuff for animals 3.5%; ferrosilicon 2.6%). Major export destinations: Netherlands 21.3%; Germany 13.4%; UK 13.2%; Ireland 7.6%; US 7.5%.

Transport and communications

Transport. Railroads: none. Roads (2006): total length 13,038 km (paved 33%). Vehicles (2007): passenger cars 207,513; trucks and buses 33,038. Air transport (2007; Icelandair only): passenger-km 4,252,000; metric ton-km cargo [2005] 121,591,000. Communications, in total units (units per 1,000 persons). Telephone landlines (2007): 187,000 (600); cellular telephone subscribers (2007): 348,000 (1,117); personal computers (2005): 142,000 (481); total Internet users (2007): 202,000 (648); broadband Internet subscribers (2008): 100,000 (315).

Education and health

Educational attainment (2007). Percentage of population ages 25–64 having: primary education 3%; lower secondary 33%; upper secondary 23%; postsecondary non-tertiary 11%; higher vocational 4%; university 25%; advanced degree 1%. Literacy: virtually 100%. Health: physicians (2007) 1,157 (1 per 270 persons); hospital beds (2002) 2,162 (1 per 133 persons); infant mortality rate per 1,000 live births (2008) 2.5; undernourished population (2002–04) less than 2.5% of total population.

Military

Total active duty personnel (November 2008): 130 coast guard (paramilitary) personnel; Iceland has no military. Coast guard expenditure as percentage of GDP (2008): 0.3%; per capita expenditure US$109.

Background

Iceland was settled by Norwegian seafarers in the 9th century and was Christianized by 1000. Its legislature, the Althing, was founded in 930, making it one of the oldest legislative assemblies in the world. Iceland united with Norway in 1262. It became an independent state of Denmark in 1918 but severed those ties to become an independent republic in 1944. Vigdís Finnbogadóttir became the world's first female elected president in 1980.

Recent Developments

In 2009 Iceland's economy struggled following the collapse of the country's banking system a year earlier. Real GDP contracted by an estimated 8–10%, and unemployment increased to more than 10%. A US$2.1 billion line of credit was extended to Iceland by the IMF and was supplemented by loans from the other Nordic states as well as from Poland and the Faroe Islands. Reversing years of resistance to the idea, the government filed Iceland's formal application for EU membership in July.

Internet resource: <www.statice.is>.

India

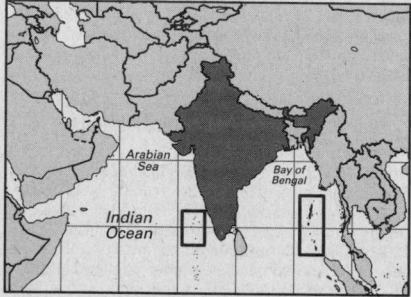

Official name: Bharat (Hindi); Republic of India (English). **Form of government:** multiparty federal republic with two legislative houses (Council of States [245], House of the People [545]). **Head of state:** President Pratibha Patil (from 2007). **Head of government:** Prime Minister Manmohan Singh (from 2004). **Capital:** New Delhi. **Official languages:** Hindi; English. **Official religion:** none. **Monetary unit:** 1 Indian rupee (Re; plural abbreviated Rs) = 100 paise; valuation (1 Jul 2010) US$1 = Rs 46.82.

Demography

Area: 1,222,559 sq mi, 3,166,414 sq km (excludes 46,660 sq mi [120,849 sq km] of territory claimed by India as part of Jammu and Kashmir but occupied by Pakistan or China). **Population** (2009): 1,198,003,000. **Density** (2009): persons per sq mi 979.9, persons per sq km 378.3. **Urban** (2008): 29.0%. **Sex distribution** (2008): male 51.87%; female 48.13%. **Age breakdown** (2008): under 15, 30.9%; 15–29, 26.9%; 30–44, 21.2%; 45–59, 13.1%; 60–74, 6.4%; 75–84, 1.3%; 85 and over, 0.2%. **Major cities (urban agglomerations)** (2006 [2007]): Mumbai (Bombay) 12,880,000 (18,978,-000); Delhi 11,220,000 (15,926,000); Kolkata (Calcutta) 4,640,000 (14,787,000); Chennai (Madras) 4,350,000 (7,163,000); Bengaluru (Bangalore) 5,100,000 (6,787,000); Hyderabad 3,630,000 (6,376,000); Ahmadabad 3,770,000 (5,375,000); Pune (Poona) 3,040,000 (4,672,000); Surat 3,020,000 (3,842,000); Kanpur 2,900,000 (3,162,000); Jaipur 2,820,000 (2,917,000); Lucknow 2,540,000 (2,695,000); Nagpur 2,270,000 (2,454,000); Patna 1,660,000 (2,158,000); Vadodara (2001) 1,306,227; Bhopal 1,640,000 (1,727,000); Coimbatore (2001) 930,882; Ludhiana 1,580,000 (1,649,000); New Delhi 302,363. **Location:** southern Asia, bordering Pakistan, China,

Nepal, Bhutan, Myanmar (Burma), Bangladesh, and the Indian Ocean. *Linguistic composition* (2001): Hindi 41.03%; Bengali 8.11%; Telugu 7.19%; Marathi 6.99%; Tamil 5.91%; Urdu 5.01%; Gujarati 4.48%; Kannada 3.69%; Malayalam 3.21%; Oriya 3.21%; Punjabi 2.83%; Assamese 1.28%; Maithili 1.18%; Bhili/Bhilodi 0.93%; Santhali 0.63%; Kashmiri 0.54%; Nepali 0.28%; Gondi 0.26%; Sindhi 0.25%; Konkani 0.24%; Dogri 0.22%; Khandeshi 0.20%; Tulu 0.17%; Kurukh/Oraon 0.17%; Manipuri 0.14%; Bodo 0.13%; Khasi 0.11%; Mundari 0.10%; Ho 0.10%; Sanskrit 0.0013%; other 1.41%. Hindi (roughly 66%) and English (roughly 33%) are also spoken as lingua francas. **Castes/tribes** (2001): number of Scheduled Castes (formerly referred to as "Untouchables") 166,635,700; number of Scheduled Tribes (aboriginal peoples) 84,326,240. **Religious affiliation** (2005): Hindu 72.04%; Muslim 12.26%, of which Sunni 8.06%, Shi'i 4.20%; Christian 6.81%, of which independent 3.23%, Protestant 1.74%, Roman Catholic 1.62%, Orthodox 0.22%; traditional beliefs 3.83%; Sikh 1.87%; Buddhist 0.67%; Jain 0.51%; Baha'i 0.17%; Zoroastrian (Parsi) (2000 estimate) 0.02%; nonreligious 1.22%; atheist 0.17%; other 0.43%.

Vital statistics

Birth rate per 1,000 population (2008): 22.8 (world avg. 20.3). **Death rate** per 1,000 population (2008): 8.2 (world avg. 8.5). **Total fertility rate** (avg. births per childbearing woman; 2008): 2.80. **Life expectancy** at birth (2008): male 63.0 years; female 67.0 years.

Social indicators

Educational attainment (2001). Percentage of population ages 25 and over having: no formal schooling 48.1%; incomplete primary education 9.0%; complete primary 22.1%; secondary 13.7%; higher 7.1%. **Quality of working life.** Average workweek (2006): 46.9. Rate of fatal injuries per 100,000 employees (2006) 38. Agricultural workers in servitude to creditors (early 1990s) 10–20%. Children ages 5–14 working as child laborers (2003): 35,000,000 (14% of age group). Percentage of population living below the poverty line (2004–05): 21.7%. **Access to services** (2005–06). Percentage of total (urban, rural) households having access to: electricity for lighting purposes 67.9% (93.1%, 55.7%), kerosene for lighting purposes (2001) 36.9% (8.3%, 46.6%), water closets 24.3% (50.8%, 11.4%), pit latrines 7.9% (7.0%, 8.6%), no latrines 55.3% (16.8%, 74.0%), closed drainage for waste water (2001) 12.5% (34.5%, 3.9%), open drainage for waste water (2001) 33.9% (43.4%, 30.3%), no drainage for waste water (2001) 53.6% (22.1%, 65.8%). Type of fuel used for cooking in households: firewood 54.4% (23.0%, 69.6%), LPG (liquefied petroleum gas) 24.7% (58.7%, 8.2%), dung 10.6% (2.8%, 14.4%), kerosene 3.2% (8.2%, 0.8%), coal 1.9% (4.3%, 0.8%). Source of drinking water: hand pump or tube well 42.8% (21.3%, 53.2%), piped water 24.5% (50.7%, 11.8%), well 9.3% (2.9%, 12.4%), river, canal, spring, public tank, pond, or lake 1.5% (0.8%, 1.8%). **Social participation.** Registered trade unions (2005): 78,465. **Social deviance** (2003). Offense rate per 100,000 population for: murder 3.1; rape 1.5; dacoity (gang

---

1 metric ton = about 1.1 short tons;   1 kilometer = 0.6 mi (statute);   1 metric ton-km cargo = about 0.68 short ton-mi cargo;   c.i.f.: cost, insurance, and freight;   f.o.b.: free on board

robbery) 0.5; theft 23.0; riots 5.4. Rate of suicide per 100,000 population (2007): 10.5. **Material well-being** (2005–06). Total (urban, rural) households possessing: television receivers 44.2% (73.2%, 30.1%), cellular telephones 16.8% (36.3%, 7.4%), scooters, motorcycles, or mopeds 17.2% (30.5%, 10.8%), cars, jeeps, or vans 2.7% (6.1%, 1.0%). Households availing banking services (2001) 35.5% (49.5%, 30.1%).

National economy

Gross national income (2008): US$1,215,485,-000,000 (US$1,070 per capita). **Budget** (2008–09). *Revenue:* Rs 9,009,530,000,000 (tax revenue 51.7%, of which corporate taxes 18.3%, income tax 10.0%, excise taxes 9.8%; capital revenue 37.6%; nontax revenue 10.7%). *Expenditures:* Rs 9,009,530,000,000 (current expenditures 89.2%, of which public debt payments 21.4%, subsidies 14.3%, defense 8.2%; capital expenditures 10.8%). **Public debt** (external, outstanding; 2007): US$74,419,000,000. **Production** (in '000 metric tons except as noted). *Agriculture and fishing* (2008): sugarcane 348,188, rice 148,260, wheat 78,570, potatoes 34,463, bananas 23,205, corn [maize] 19,290, mangoes 13,649, millet 11,340, seed cotton 11,305, coconuts 10,894, tomatoes 10,261, cassava 9,054, soybeans 9,045, eggplants 8,450, dry onions 8,178, sorghum 7,926, peanuts [groundnuts] 7,338, rapeseed 5,833, chickpeas 5,749, cauliflower 5,015, oranges 4,397, dry beans 3,930, okra 3,497, pigeon peas 3,076, papayas 2,686, lemons and limes 2,429, peas 2,293, apples 2,001, jute 1,846, grapes 1,677, pineapples 1,306, sweet potatoes 1,146, castor beans 1,123, sunflower seeds 1,112, natural rubber 819, tea 805, sesame 666, cashews 665, garlic 645, tobacco 520, ginger 370; livestock (number of live animals) 174,510,000 cattle, 125,732,000 goats, 98,595,000 water buffalo, 64,989,000 sheep, 14,000,000 pigs, 632,000 camels; fisheries production (2007) 7,308 (from aquaculture 46%). *Mining and quarrying* (2007): mica 1.7; iron ore (metal content) 129,000; bauxite 19,221; chromium 3,320; barite 1,000; manganese (metal content) 900; zinc (metal content) 314; lead (metal content) 77.6; copper (metal content) 34.7; silver 79,300 kg; gold 3,000 kg; gem diamonds 15,000 carats. *Manufacturing* (value added in US$'000,000; 2004): chemical products 10,804; base metals 10,109; refined petroleum products 7,214; transportation equipment 6,473; textiles and wearing apparel 5,430; food products 4,300; nonelectrical machinery 3,222; cements, bricks, and ceramics 2,958; other metals 2,120; electrical machinery 1,962. *Energy production (consumption):* electricity (kW-hr; 2008–09) 724,000,000,000 ([2006] 746,829,-000,000); coal (metric tons; 2008–09) 493,220,000 ([2007–08] 502,660,000); lignite (metric tons; 2008–09) 33,364,000 ([2007–08] 34,657,000); crude petroleum (barrels; 2008–09) 254,638,000 ([2007–08] 1,186,382,800); petroleum products (metric tons; 2008–09) 149,519,000 ([2007–08] 140,697,000); natural gas (cu m; 2008–09) 31,804,000,000 ([2007–08] 34,328,000,000). **Population economically active** (2001): total 402,234,724; activity rate of total population 39.1% (participation rates: ages 15–69, 60.2%; female 31.6%; unemployed [2008] 6.8%). **Selected balance of payments data.** Receipts from (US$'000,000)) tourism (2007) 10,729; remittances (2008) 51,974; foreign direct investment (FDI; 2006–09 avg.)

30,785; official development assistance (2007) 1,298. Disbursements for (US$'000,000): tourism (2006) 7,352; remittances (2008) 1,580; FDI (2005–07 avg.) 9,823. **Service enterprises** (net value added in Rs '000,000,000; 1998–99): wholesale and retail trade 1,562; finance, real estate, and insurance 1,310; transport and storage 804; community, social, and personal services 763; construction 545.

Foreign trade

Imports (2007–08): US$251,654,000,000 (crude petroleum and refined petroleum products 31.6%; electronics 8.2%; transportation equipment 8.0%; nonelectrical machinery 7.9%; gold 6.6%; chemical products 4.6%; base metals 3.5%; precious stones [significantly diamonds] 3.2%; metal ores [significantly copper ore and concentrates] 3.1%; coal 2.6%). *Major import sources:* China 10.8%; US 8.4%; Saudi Arabia 7.7%; UAE 5.4%; Iran 4.3%; Germany 3.9%; Switzerland 3.9%; Singapore 3.2%; Australia 3.1%; Kuwait 3.1%. **Exports** (2007–08): US$163,132,100,000 (refined petroleum products 17.4%; gems and jewelry [significantly diamonds] 12.1%; textiles and wearing apparel 11.9%; food products, beverages, and tobacco products 11.3%; chemical products 9.1%; machinery and apparatus 5.6%; fabricated metal products 4.3%; transportation equipment 4.3%; iron ore 3.6%). *Major export destinations:* US 12.7%; UAE 9.6%; China 6.6%; Singapore 4.5%; UK 4.1%; Hong Kong 3.9%; Netherlands 3.2%; Germany 3.1%; Belgium 2.6%; Italy 2.4%.

Transport and communications

Transport. *Railroads* (2007–08): route length 63,000 km; passenger-km 735,980,000,000; metric ton-km cargo 511,854,000,000. *Roads* (2002): total length 3,319,644 km (paved 46%). *Vehicles* (2004): passenger cars 9,451,000; trucks and buses 4,516,000. *Air transport* (2008–09): passenger-km 75,932,000,000; metric ton-km cargo 1,071,000,000. **Communications,** in total units (units per 1,000 persons). Telephone landlines (2008): 37,900,000 (32); cellular telephone subscribers (2008): 346,890,000 (294); personal computers (2007): 38,434,000 (33); total Internet users (2007): 81,000,000 (69); broadband Internet subscribers (2008): 5,280,000 (4.5).

Education and health

Literacy (2007): percentage of total population ages 15 and over literate 66.0%; males literate 76.9%; females literate 54.5%. **Health** (2007): physicians (government hospitals only) 696,700 (1 per 1,696 persons); hospital beds (government hospitals only) 482,500 (1 per 2,449 persons); infant mortality rate per 1,000 live births (2008) 54.0; undernourished population (2002–04) 209,500,000 (20% of total population based on the consumption of a minimum daily requirement of 1,820 calories).

Military

Total active duty personnel (November 2008): 1,281,200 (army 85.8%, navy 4.3%, air force 9.4%, coast guard 0.5%); paramilitary 1,009,000, reserve 1,155,000. **Military expenditure as percentage of GDP** (2008): 2.3%; per capita expenditure US$21.

Background

Agriculture in India dates back to at least the 7th millennium BC, and an urban civilization, that of the Indus valley, was established by 2600 BC. Buddhism and Jainism arose in the 6th century BC in reaction to the caste-based society created by the Vedic religion and its successor, Hinduism. Muslim invasions began about AD 1000, establishing the long-lived Delhi sultanate in 1206 and the Mughal dynasty in 1526. Vasco da Gama's voyage to India in 1498 initiated several centuries of commercial rivalry among the Portuguese, Dutch, English, and French. British conquests in the 18th and 19th centuries led to the rule of the British East India Co., and direct administration by the British Empire began in 1858. After Mohandas K. Gandhi helped end British rule in 1947, Jawaharlal Nehru became India's first prime minister, and he, Indira Gandhi (his daughter), and Rajiv Gandhi (his grandson) guided the nation's destiny for all but a few years until 1989. The subcontinent was partitioned into two countries—India, with a Hindu majority, and Pakistan, with a Muslim majority—in 1947. A later clash with Pakistan resulted in the creation of Bangladesh in 1971. In the 1980s and '90s, Sikhs sought to establish an independent state in Punjab, and ethnic and religious conflicts took place in other parts of the country as well. In 2004 Manmohan Singh, a Sikh, became the country's first non-Hindu prime minister. The Kashmir region in the northwest has been a source of constant tension.

Recent Developments

While relations with Pakistan as usual dominated India's foreign policy in 2009, renewed differences between India and China on the status of the Indian state of Arunachal Pradesh caused some friction between the Asian giants. China continued to claim Arunachal Pradesh as its territory, while India rejected this claim, having held regular elections to the provincial government there, including in October 2009. India's plans to step up infrastructure development in the state met with strong Chinese disapproval on the board of the Asian Development Bank, which India had approached for a loan to fund this investment. Although China tried to block the loan, it was ultimately approved. India-China trade and business relations continued to flourish nonetheless; China emerged as India's biggest trade partner, despite Indian allegations of dumping and nontransparent pricing of Chinese goods. India and Russia signed a number of important agreements, including ones in March 2010 in which Russia agreed to build 16 nuclear reactors for India and sell it a refitted aircraft carrier and 29 fighter aircraft.

Internet resource: <http://mospi.nic.in>.

Indonesia

Official name: Republik Indonesia (Republic of Indonesia). **Form of government:** multiparty republic with two legislative houses (Regional Representatives Council [128]; House of Representatives [560]). **Head of state and government:** President Susilo Bambang Yudhoyono (from 2004). **Capital:** Jakarta.

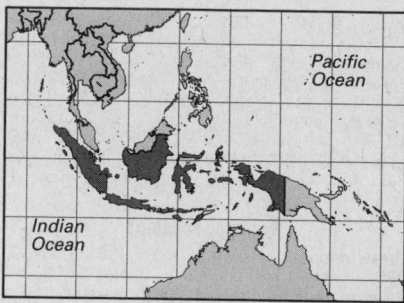

Official language: Indonesian (Bahasa Indonesia). **Official religion:** monotheism. **Monetary unit:** 1 Indonesian rupiah (Rp) = 100 sen; valuation (1 Jul 2010) US$1 = Rp 9,070.00.

Demography

Area: 718,289 sq mi, 1,860,360 sq km. **Population** (2009): 229,965,000. **Density** (2009): persons per sq mi 320.2, persons per sq km 123.6. **Urban** (2003): 45.6%. **Sex distribution** (2006): male 50.01%; female 49.99%. **Age breakdown** (2006): under 15, 29.1%; 15–29, 27.0%; 30–44, 22.2%; 45–59, 13.5%; 60–74, 6.7%; 75–84, 1.4%; 85 and over, 0.1%. **Ethnic composition** (2000): Javanese 36.4%; Sundanese 13.7%; Malay 9.4%; Madurese 7.2%; Han Chinese 4.0%; Minangkabau 3.6%; other 25.7%. **Religious affiliation** (2005): Muslim (excluding syncretists) 55.8%; Neoreligionists (syncretists) 21.2%; Christian 13.2%; Hindu 3.2%; traditional beliefs 2.6%; nonreligious 1.8%; other 2.2%. **Major municipalities** (2005): Jakarta 8,603,349; Surabaya 2,611,506; Bandung 2,288,570; Medan 2,029,797; Bekasi 1,940,308; Tangerang 1,451,595; Semarang 1,352,869; Depok 1,339,263; Palembang 1,323,169; Makasar 1,168,258. **Location:** archipelago in southeastern Asia, bordering Malaysia, the Pacific Ocean, Papua New Guinea, the Indian Ocean, and East Timor (Timor-Leste).

Vital statistics

Birth rate per 1,000 population (2006): 20.1 (world avg. 20.3). **Death rate** per 1,000 population (2006): 6.3 (world avg. 8.5). **Total fertility rate** (avg. births per childbearing woman; 2006): 2.41. **Life expectancy** at birth (2006): male 67.4 years; female 72.4 years.

National economy

Budget (2005). *Revenue:* Rp 495,444,000,000,000 (tax revenue 70.0%, of which income tax 35.4%, VAT 20.4%; nontax revenue 30.0%, of which revenue from petroleum 14.7%). *Expenditures:* Rp 509,419,000,-000,000 (current expenditures 58.5%; regional expenditures 29.5%; developmental expenditures 12.0%). **Public debt** (external, outstanding; December 2007): US$80,609,000,000. **Population economically active** (2006): total 106,388,935; activity rate 46.5% (participation rates: ages 16 and over, 66.2%; unemployed 10.3%). **Production** (metric tons except as noted). *Agriculture and fishing* (2008): oil palm fruit 85,000,000,

1 metric ton = about 1.1 short tons; 1 kilometer = 0.6 mi (statute); 1 metric ton-km cargo = about 0.68 short ton-mi cargo; c.i.f.: cost, insurance, and freight; f.o.b.: free on board

rice 60,251,072, sugarcane 26,000,000, cassava 21,593,052, coconuts 19,500,000, corn (maize) 16,323,922, natural rubber 2,921,872, cacao beans 792,761, cloves 80,929, cinnamon 60,000; livestock (number of live animals) 15,805,900 goats, 11,869,200 cattle, 8,355,764 sheep; fisheries production (2007) 6,329,533 (from aquaculture 22%); aquatic plants production (2007) 1,733,705 (from aquaculture 99%). *Mining and quarrying* (2007): bauxite 1,251,000; copper (metal content) 796,000; nickel (metal content) 229,200; silver 268,967 kg; gold 117,851 kg. *Manufacturing* (value added in US$'000,000; 2003): textiles, wearing apparel, and footwear 5,011; tobacco products 4,584; transportation equipment 4,189; food products 3,970; chemical products 3,464; paper products 1,774. *Energy production (consumption):* electricity (kW-hr; 2006) 133,108,000,000 (133,108,000,000); coal (metric tons; 2007) 174,800,000 ([2006] 21,201,000); crude petroleum (barrels; 2007) 357,500,000 ([2006] 329,040,000); petroleum products (metric tons; 2006) 42,347,000 (52,700,000); natural gas (cu m; 2007) 85,200,000,000 (37,700,000,000). **Gross national income** (2008): US$458,159,000,000 (US$2,010 per capita). **Selected balance of payments data.** Receipts from (US$'000,000): tourism (2007) 5,346; remittances (2008) 6,795; foreign direct investment (FDI; 2005–07 avg.) 6,726; official development assistance (2006) 1,404. Disbursements for (US$'000,000): tourism (2007) 4,446; remittances (2008) 1,766; FDI (2005–07 avg.) 3,519.

Foreign trade

Imports (2005–06; c.i.f.): US$65,712,154,000 (crude petroleum and natural gas 23.7%; machinery and apparatus 16.8%; chemical products 10.4%; base metals 8.8%; transportation equipment 6.5%). *Major import sources* (2006): Singapore 16.4%; China 10.9%; Japan 9.0%; US 6.7%; Saudi Arabia 5.5%. **Exports** (2005–06; f.o.b.): US$78,740,892,000 (crude petroleum and natural gas 27.4%; rubber products 15.7%; machinery and apparatus 14.5%; textiles 10.8%; base metals 7.0%; paper products 4.2%). *Major export destinations* (2006): Japan 21.6%; US 11.2%; Singapore 8.9%; China 8.3%; South Korea 7.6%.

Transport and communications

Transport. *Railroads* (2007): route length 4,803 km; passenger-km 15,872,000,000; metric ton-km cargo 4,425,000,000. *Roads* (2007): length 396,362 km (paved 56%). *Vehicles* (2007): passenger cars 52,902,100; trucks and buses 4,845,900. *Air transport* (2005): passenger-km 22,986,000,000; metric ton-km cargo (2004) 248,000,000. **Communications,** in total units (units per 1,000 persons). Telephone landlines (2008): 30,378,000 (134); cellular telephone subscribers (2008): 140,578,000 (618); personal computers (2005): 3,285,000 (15); total Internet users (2008): 30,000,000 (132); broadband Internet subscribers (2007): 257,000 (1.1).

Education and health

Educational attainment (2002–03). Percentage of population ages 15–64 having: no schooling or incomplete primary education 19.2%; primary and some secondary 57.2%; complete secondary 19.3%; higher 4.2%. **Literacy** (2007): total population ages 15 and over literate 91.9%; males literate 95.2%; females literate 88.6%. **Health:** physicians (2003) 29,499 (1 per 7,368 persons); hospital beds (2001) 124,834 (1 per 1,697 persons); infant mortality rate per 1,000 live births (2006) 33.3; undernourished population (2003–05) 37,100,000 (17% of total population based on the consumption of a minimum daily requirement of 1,810 calories).

Military

Total active duty personnel (November 2008): 302,000 (army 77.2%, navy 14.9%, air force 7.9%). **Military expenditure as percentage of GDP** (2007): 1.0%; per capita expenditure US$19.

Background

Proto-Malay peoples migrated to Indonesia from mainland Asia before 1000 BC. Commercial relations were established with China in about the 5th century AD, and Hindu and Buddhist cultural influences from India began to take hold. Arab traders brought Islam to the islands in the 13th century; the religion took hold throughout the islands, except for Bali, which retained its Hindu religion and culture. European influence began in the 16th century, and the Dutch ruled Indonesia from the late 17th century until 1942, when the Japanese invaded. Independence leader Sukarno declared Indonesia's sovereignty in 1945, which the Dutch granted, with nominal union to the Netherlands, in 1949; Indonesia dissolved this union in 1954. The suppression of an alleged coup attempt in 1965 resulted in the deaths of more than 300,000 people the government claimed to be communists, and by 1968 Gen. Suharto had taken power. His government forcibly incorporated East Timor (Timor-Leste) into Indonesia in 1975–76, with much loss of life; East Timor became independent in 2002. In the 1990s the country was beset by political, economic, and environmental problems, and Suharto was deposed in 1998.

Recent Developments

In 2009 Indonesia consolidated its reputation as Southeast Asia's most democratic country. Simultaneous elections were held in April for the national, provincial, and district legislatures, and those were followed by direct presidential elections in July. The elections were largely peaceful and, in the opinion of most observers, reasonably fair. Indonesia also had one of the strongest-performing economies in the region, with an annual growth rate of 4.2% that ranked behind only China and India. Robust domestic consumer demand and high export commodity prices were chief drivers of Indonesia's economic expansion. Proving particularly popular with voters was a range of direct government payments to lower-income families to compensate for the effects of rising prices. In late September and early October, several earthquakes struck western Indonesia, causing devastation and heavy loss of life in the Padang region of West Sumatra. The confirmed death toll exceeded 1,100. The collapse of many public buildings prompted calls for tighter construction standards, particularly given that scientists were warning of more severe quakes over the next two decades.

Internet resource: <www.bps.go.id>.

Iran

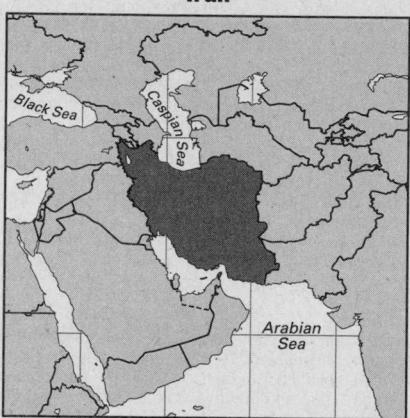

Official name: Jomhuri-ye Eslami-ye Iran (Islamic Republic of Iran). **Form of government:** unitary Islamic republic with one legislative house (Islamic Consultative Assembly [290]). **Supreme political/religious authority:** *Rahbar* (Spiritual Leader) Ayatollah Sayyed Ali Khamenei (from 1989). **Head of state and government:** President Mahmoud Ahmadinejad (from 2005). **Capital:** Tehran. **Official language:** Farsi (Persian). **Official religion:** Islam. **Monetary unit:** 1 rial (Rls) = 100 dinars; valuation (1 Jul 2010) US$1 = Rls 10,007.99.

Demography

Area (land area only): 628,874 sq mi, 1,628,777 sq km. **Population** (2009): 74,196,000. **Density** (2009): persons per sq mi 116.6, persons per sq km 45.0. **Urban** (2007–08): 69.3%. **Sex distribution** (2006–07): male 50.88%; female 49.12%. **Age breakdown** (2006–07): under 15, 25.1%; 15–29, 35.4%; 30–44, 20.6%; 45–59, 11.6%; 60–74, 5.4%; 75–84, 1.6%; 85 and over, 0.3%. **Ethnic composition** (2000): Persian 34.9%; Azerbaijani 15.9%; Kurd 13.0%; Luri 7.2%; Gilaki 5.1%; Mazandarani 5.1%; Afghan 2.8%; other 16.0%. **Religious affiliation** (2005): Muslim 98.2% (Shi'i 86.1%, Sunni 10.1%, other 2.0%); Baha'i 0.5%; Christian 0.4%; Zoroastrian 0.1%; other 0.8%. **Major cities** (2006): Tehran 7,797,520; Mashhad 2,427,316; Esfahan 1,602,110; Tabriz 1,398,060; Karaj 1,386,030. **Location:** the Middle East, bordering the Caspian Sea, Turkmenistan, Afghanistan, Pakistan, the Gulf of Oman, the Persian Gulf, Iraq, Turkey, Azerbaijan, and Armenia.

Vital statistics

Birth rate per 1,000 population (2006–07): 17.8 (world avg. 20.3). **Death rate** per 1,000 population (2006–07): 5.8 (world avg. 8.5). **Total fertility rate** (avg. births per childbearing woman; 2007): 1.83. **Life expectancy** at birth (2007): male 70.0 years; female 72.7 years.

National economy

Budget (2007–08). *Revenue:* Rls 791,199,000,-000,000 (petroleum and natural gas revenue 69.4%; taxes 20.5%, of which taxes on income and profits 12.3%). *Expenditures:* Rls 691,225,000,000,000 (current expenditures 72.8%; development expenditures 21.4%). **Public debt** (external, outstanding; 2007): US$11,146,000,000. **Gross national income** (2007): US$251,486,000,000 (US$3,540 per capita). **Production** (metric tons except as noted). *Agriculture and fishing* (2007): wheat 15,000,000, sugarcane 5,700,000, sugar beets 5,300,000, dates 1,000,000, pistachios 230,000; livestock (number of live animals) 52,220,000 sheep, 25,860,000 goats, 9,776,000 cattle, 146,000 camels; fisheries production 562,424 (from aquaculture 28%). *Mining and quarrying* (2007): iron ore (metal content) 11,000,000; copper ore (metal content) 260,000; chromite 225,000; zinc (metal content) 100,000. *Manufacturing* (value added in US$'000,000; 2005): base metals 3,032; motor vehicles and parts 2,850; refined petroleum products 2,210. *Energy production (consumption):* electricity (kW-hr; 2008) 206,300,000,000 ([2006] 200,794,000,000); coal (metric tons; 2006) 1,520,000 (1,930,000); crude petroleum (barrels; 2008) 1,486,000,000 ([2006] 517,000,000); petroleum products (metric tons; 2006) 75,336,000 (67,265,000); natural gas (cu m; 2007) 111,909,000,000 ([2006] 104,082,000,000). **Population economically active** (2006–07): total 23,469,000; activity rate of total population 33.3% (participation rates: ages 10 and over, 39.4%; female 15.5%; unemployed [October–December 2008] 9.5%). **Selected balance of payments data.** Receipts from (US$'000,000): tourism (2007) 1,486; remittances (2008) 1,115; foreign direct investment (FDI; 2005–07 avg.) 663; official development assistance (2007) 102. Disbursements for (US$'000,000): tourism (2007) 6,002; FDI (2005–07 avg.) 380.

Foreign trade

Imports (2005–06): US$40,969,000,000 (nonelectrical machinery 23.5%; base metals 13.8%; motor vehicles 13.0%; chemical products 10.7%). *Major import sources:* UAE 19.7%; Germany 13.1%; France 6.8%; Italy 6.0%; China 5.5%. **Exports** (2005–06): US$60,013,000,000 (crude petroleum 73.1%; chemical products 5.2%; fruits and nuts 2.2%, of which pistachios 1.4%; wool carpets 0.8%). *Major export destinations:* Japan 16.9%; China 11.9%; Turkey 5.8%; Italy 5.7%; South Korea 5.7%.

Transport and communications

Transport. *Railroads* (2006–07): route length 8,565 km; passenger-km 12,549,000,000; metric ton-km cargo 20,542,000,000. *Roads* (2006–07): length 72,611 km (paved 92%). *Vehicles* (2006–07): passenger cars 920,136; trucks and buses 184,629. *Air transport* (2008; Iran Air, Iran Aseman Airlines, and Mahan Air only): passenger-km 11,760,610,000; metric ton-km cargo 110,843,000. **Communications,** in total units (units per 1,000 persons). Telephone landlines (2008): 24,800,000 (338); cellular telephone subscribers (2008): 43,000,000 (587); personal computers (2007): 7,678,000 (106); total In-

---

1 metric ton = about 1.1 short tons;   1 kilometer = 0.6 mi (statute);   1 metric ton-km cargo = about 0.68 short ton-mi cargo;   c.i.f.: cost, insurance, and freight;   f.o.b.: free on board

ternet users (2008): 23,000,000 (314); broadband Internet subscribers (2008): 300,000 (4:1).

Education and health

Literacy (2006–07): total population ages 6 and over literate 84.6%; males literate 88.7%; females literate 80.3%. **Health** (2006–07): physicians (public sector only) 29,937 (1 per 2,355 persons); hospital beds 116,474 (1 per 605 persons); infant mortality rate per 1,000 live births (2007) 29.1; undernourished population (2002–04) 2,500,000 (4% of total population based on the consumption of a minimum daily requirement of 1,850 calories).

Military

Total active duty personnel (November 2008): 523,000 (revolutionary guard corps 23.9%, army 66.9%, navy 3.5%, air force 5.7%). **Military expenditure as percentage of GDP** (2007): 2.9%; per capita expenditure US$103.

Background

Habitation in Iran dates to 100,000 BC, but recorded history began with the Elamites in 3000 BC. The Medes flourished from about 728 BC but were overthrown (550 BC) by the Persians, who were in turn conquered by Alexander the Great in the 4th century BC. The Parthians created a Greek-speaking empire that lasted from 247 BC to AD 226, when control passed to the Sasanians. Arab Muslims conquered them in 640 and ruled Iran for 850 years. In 1502 the Safavids established a dynasty that lasted until 1736. The Qajars ruled from 1779, but in the 19th century the country was controlled economically by the Russian and British empires. Reza Khan seized power in a coup (1921). His son Mohammad Reza Shah Pahlavi alienated religious leaders with a program of modernization and Westernization and was overthrown in 1979; Shi'ite cleric Ruhollah Khomeini then set up a fundamentalist Islamic republic, and Western influence was suppressed. The destructive Iran-Iraq War of the 1980s ended in a stalemate. Among the most contentious of Iran's foreign policy issues at the beginning of the 21st century was the ongoing question of the development of its nuclear capabilities. Iran insisted that its nuclear pursuits were intended for peaceful purposes, but the international community, expressing deep suspicion that Iran's activities included the development of nuclear weapons, advocated efforts to suspend them.

Recent Developments

Although US Pres. Barack Obama had sent a Noruz (New Year) message in 2009 to the Iranian people and had offered wide-ranging diplomatic dialogue with the regime, the harsh treatment of peaceful demonstrators following June elections evinced a sharp rebuff from Obama. The US also claimed a direct role in negotiations over Iran's nuclear program. US Secretary of State Hillary Clinton responded to Iran's continuing failure to desist from developing nuclear capacity and promised US protection to the Arab states of the Persian Gulf against any Iranian threat. The meeting of the UN General Assembly in September endorsed Obama's proposals for an end to the proliferation of nuclear weapons. Nevertheless, Iran pressed on with its nuclear program, including plans to inaugurate the Bushehr atomic power station, expand capacity at Natanz, and secretly create a new underground facility near Qom. Negotiations toward external monitoring of the nuclear program made little progress. In February 2010 Iran claimed to have produced its first batch of 20% enriched uranium, a step, some experts believed, on the way to 90% enriched weapons-grade uranium.

Internet resource: <www.cbi.ir>.

Iraq

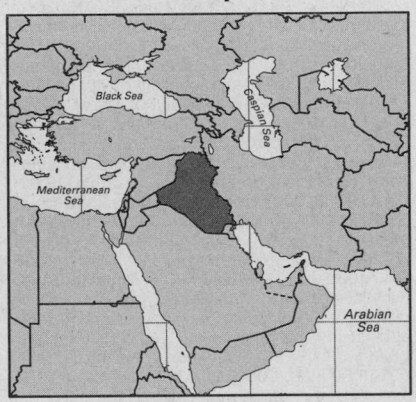

Official name: Al-Jumhuriyah al-'Iraqiyah (Republic of Iraq). **Form of government:** multiparty republic with one legislative house (Council of Representatives of Iraq [325]). **Head of state:** President Jalal Talabani (from 2005). **Head of government:** Prime Minister Nuri al-Maliki (from 2006). **Capital:** Baghdad. **Official languages:** Arabic; Kurdish. **Official religion:** Islam. **Monetary unit:** 1 Iraqi dinar (ID) = 1,000 fils; valuation (1 Jul 2010) US$1 = ID 1,168.50.

Demography

Area: 167,618 sq mi, 434,128 sq km. **Population** (2009): 30,747,000. **Density** (2009): persons per sq mi 183.4, persons per sq km 70.8. **Urban** (2007): 66.5%. **Sex distribution** (2007): male 50.35%; female 49.65%. **Age breakdown** (2007): under 15, 43.1%; 15–29, 27.9%; 30–44, 16.4%; 45–59, 8.2%; 60–74, 3.3%; 75 and over, 1.0%. **Ethnic composition** (2000): Arab 64.7%; Kurd 23.0%; Turkmen/Azerbaijani 6.8%; other 5.5%. **Religious affiliation** (2000): Shi'i Muslim 62.0%; Sunni Muslim 34.0%; Christian (primarily Chaldean rite and Syrian rite Catholic and Nestorian) 3.2%; other (primarily Yazidi syncretist) 0.8%. **Major urban agglomerations** (2007): Baghdad 5,054,000; Mosul 1,316,000; Irbil 926,000; Al-Basrah 870,000; Karkuk (2003) 750,000. **Location:** the Middle East, bordering Turkey, Iran, the Persian Gulf, Kuwait, Saudi Arabia, Jordan, and Syria.

Vital statistics

Birth rate per 1,000 population (2008): 30.7 (world avg. 20.3). **Death rate** per 1,000 population (2008):

5.1 (world avg. 8.5). **Total fertility rate** (avg. births per childbearing woman; 2008): 3.97. **Life expectancy** at birth (2008): male 68.3 years; female 71.0 years.

National economy

Budget (2007). *Revenue:* ID 58,714,000,000,000 (crude oil export revenue 80.3%; oil-related public enterprises 9.8%; grants 4.9%). *Expenditures:* ID 48,153,000,000,000 (current expenditures 79.6%; development expenditures 20.4%). **Public debt** (external, outstanding; September 2009): US$70,000,-000,000–US$120,000,000,000. **Production** (metric tons except as noted). *Agriculture and fishing* (2008): wheat 2,228,000, tomatoes 830,000, potatoes 598,000, dates 440,000; livestock (number of live animals) 6,200,000 sheep, 1,650,000 goats, 1,500,000 cattle, 9,500 camels; fisheries production (2007) 73,589 (from aquaculture 21%). *Mining and quarrying* (2007): salt 25,000. *Manufacturing* (2007): gasoline 19,000,000 barrels; distillate fuels 19,000,000 barrels; residual fuels 58,000,000 barrels. *Energy production (consumption):* electricity (kW-hr; 2006) 31,869,000,000 (33,170,000,000); crude petroleum (barrels; 2008) 884,000,000 ([2006] 178,900,000); petroleum products (metric tons; 2006) 19,703,000 (21,896,000); natural gas (cu m; 2006) 3,408,000,000 (3,408,000,000). **Population economically active** (2006): total 7,002,000; activity rate of total population 24.6% (participation rates: ages 15–64, 43.3%; female 16.8%; unemployed [2009] 18.0%). **Gross national income** (2007): US$69,800,000,000 (US$2,367 per capita). **Selected balance of payments data.** Receipts from (US$'000,000): remittances (2008) 389; foreign direct investment (FDI; 2005–07 avg.) 449; official development assistance (2007) 9,115. Disbursements for (US$'000,000): remittances (2008) 781; FDI (2005–07 avg.) 180.

Foreign trade

Imports (2007): US$18,289,000,000 (private sector imports 55.7%, of which capital goods 41.8%, consumer goods 13.9%; government imports 44.3%, of which refined petroleum products 7.9%). *Major import sources* (2008): Syria 27.6%; Turkey 20.6%; US 11.2%; China 6.2%; Jordan 4.7%. **Exports** (2007): US$39,590,000,000 (crude petroleum 95.4%; refined petroleum products 4.0%; other 0.6%). *Major export destinations* (2008): US 43.5%; Italy 11.0%; South Korea 7.3%; Canada 4.5%; France 4.1%.

Transport and communications

Transport. *Railroads* (2006): route length 580 sq km. *Roads* (2002): total length 45,550 km (paved 84%). *Vehicles* (2001): passenger cars 754,066; trucks and buses 372,241. *Air transport:* n.a. (Iraqi Airways resumed international flights in September 2004 after 14 years of being grounded by war and sanctions). **Communications,** in total units (units per 1,000 persons). Telephone landlines (2008): 1,082,000 (36); cellular telephone subscribers (2009): 17,700,000 (585); total Internet users (2007): 275,000 (9.3).

Education and health

Educational attainment (2004). Percentage of population ages 25 and over having: no formal schooling 28%; incomplete primary education 12%; primary 36%; secondary 9%; higher 15%. **Literacy** (2003): total population ages 15 and over literate 40.4%; males literate 55.9%; females literate 24.4%. **Health** (2008): physicians 16,000 (1 per 1,901 persons); hospital beds (2003) 34,505 (1 per 778 persons); infant mortality rate per 1,000 live births 46.2.

Military

Total active duty personnel (November 2008): 577,056 (army/national guard 32.4%, navy 0.3%, air force 0.3%, ministry of interior/police 67.0%); US forces (August 2009): 130,000.

Background

Called Mesopotamia in Classical times, the region gave rise to the world's earliest civilizations, including those of Sumer, Akkad, and Babylon. Conquered by Alexander the Great in 330 BC, the area later became a battleground between Romans and Parthians and then between Sasanians and Byzantines. Arab Muslims conquered it in the 7th century AD and ruled until the Mongols took over in 1258. The Ottomans took control in the 16th century and ruled until 1917. The British occupied the country during World War I and created the kingdom of Iraq in 1921. The British occupied Iraq again during World War II. A king was restored following the war, but a revolution ended the monarchy in 1958. Following a series of military coups, the socialist Baʿth Party, led by Saddam Hussein, took control and established totalitarian rule in 1968. The Iran-Iraq War of the 1980s and the Persian Gulf War (precipitated by the Iraqi invasion of Kuwait in 1990) brought heavy casualties and disrupted the economy. The 1990s were dominated by economic and political turmoil. In response to increasingly willful and autocratic behavior by Saddam and the contention that Iraq was in possession of weapons of mass destruction (none were ever found), on 19 Mar 2003 air attacks on Baghdad began, and soon afterward US and British ground forces invaded southern Iraq from Kuwait; within a month most of the country was under the control of coalition forces. Saddam was taken into custody in December. In July 2003 US authorities established an Iraqi Governing Council, and a new interim constitution was agreed upon in late February 2004. Almost immediately after the occupation began, however, various forms of Iraqi opposition arose, and resistance attacks grew in frequency and violence in the years that followed.

Recent Developments

Although Iraq still suffered from a lack of security, 2009 saw some improvement. The reduction in violence helped the US to withdraw its troops from Iraqi urban areas by the end of June and to regroup in less visible camps in the countryside. Some joint US-Iraqi military operations continued against al-Qaeda and other insurgents, especially in and around Baghdad and the northern province of Nineveh. December 2009 was the first month since the invasion in 2003

---

1 metric ton = about 1.1 short tons;   1 kilometer = 0.6 mi (statute);   1 metric ton-km cargo = about 0.68 short ton-mi cargo;   c.i.f.: cost, insurance, and freight;   f.o.b.: free on board

in which no US troops were killed in combat. Iraq continued to face many problems: high unemployment (18–20%), low standards of living, and a lack of potable water and electricity. Corruption remained very high, as did common crimes such as robbery, murder, and kidnapping for ransom. All those social ills created a deep sense of discontent and unease among Iraqis and prevented many Iraqi emigrants from returning from neighboring Syria and Jordan. Despite repeated delays by the parliament in approving the new oil law, the Iraqi government signed an important agreement on 3 November, with a consortium of BP and the China National Petroleum Corp. to develop the giant oil field of Al-Rumaylah in southern Iraq, a step forward for the Iraqi oil industry. BP had been expelled from Iraq in 1972 when the former Ba'th regime nationalized the oil industry. Relations with Syria deteriorated after Iraq accused the Syrian government of tolerating al-Qaeda militants and former Ba'thists living in Syria whom Iraqi officials blamed for major explosions in Baghdad. These explosions, on 19 August and 25 October, killed hundreds of Iraqis and severely damaged several government buildings. Syria denied any involvement in the bombings, but Iraq insisted on a UN investigation and rejected any mediation by Arab or other countries. Iraq's relations with Kuwait remained tense. Iraq hoped for the cancellation of some US$25 billion in UN-required reparations for the country's 1990 invasion of Kuwait. Those requests had been systematically rejected by Kuwait, which insisted on full payment. By fall 2009 Kuwait had become more inclined to accept a UN-sponsored solution suggesting that Kuwait invest those reparations in diverse development projects in Iraq. Iraq had also asked other Arab countries, including Saudi Arabia, to cancel its outstanding debts. Settling the Kuwaiti reparations issue was essential to removing Iraq from obligations imposed under Chapter VII of the UN Charter after the country's failed invasion of Kuwait, which in turn was vital to Iraq's ability to trade freely with the rest of the world.

Internet resource: <www.cbi.iq>.

Ireland

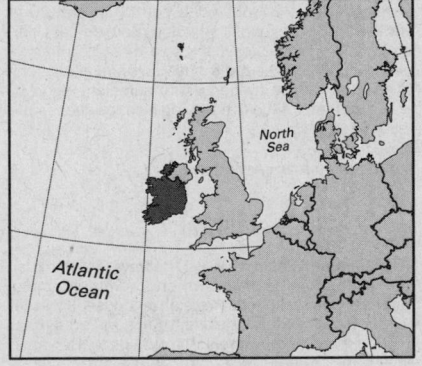

North Sea

Atlantic Ocean

Official name: Éire (Irish); Ireland (English). Form of government: unitary multiparty republic with two legislative houses (Senate [60]; House of Representa-

tives [166]). Head of state: President Mary McAleese (from 1997). Head of government: Prime Minister Brian Cowen (from 2008). Capital: Dublin. Official languages: Irish; English. Official religion: none. Monetary unit: 1 euro (€) = 100 cents; valuation (1 Jul 2010) US$1 = €0.80.

Demography

Area: 27,133 sq mi, 70,273 sq km. Population (2009): 4,553,000. Density (2009): persons per sq mi 167.8, persons per sq km 64.8. Urban (2005): 60.5%. Sex distribution (2008): male 49.89%; female 50.11%. Age breakdown (2008): under 15, 20.6%; 15–29, 23.4%; 30–44, 23.1%; 45–59, 17.5%; 60–74, 10.6%; 75–84, 3.6%; 85 and over, 1.2%. Ethnic composition (2000): Irish 95.0%; British 1.7%, of which English 1.4%; Ulster Irish 1.0%; US white 0.8%; other 1.5%. Religious affiliation (2006): Roman Catholic 86.8%; Church of Ireland (Anglican) 3.0%; other Christian 2.7%; nonreligious 4.4%; other 3.1%. Major cities (2006): Dublin 506,211 (urban agglomeration 1,186,159); Cork 119,418; Galway 72,414; Limerick 52,539; Waterford 45,748. Location: western Europe, bordering the UK (Northern Ireland), the Irish Sea, the Celtic Sea, and the North Atlantic Ocean.

Vital statistics

Birth rate per 1,000 population (2008): 16.9 (world avg. 20.3); (2006) within marriage 66.8%. Death rate per 1,000 population (2007): 6.4 (world avg. 8.5). Total fertility rate (avg. births per childbearing woman; 2007): 2.03. Life expectancy at birth (2006): male 76.8 years; female 81.6 years.

National economy

Budget (2005). Revenue: €39,849,000,000 (VAT 30.3%; income tax 28.3%; corporate taxes 13.5%). Expenditures: €33,496,000,000 (current expenditures 88.4%; capital expenditures 11.6%). Total public debt (2008): US$90,000,000,000. Gross national income (2008): US$221,158,000,000 (US$49,590 per capita). Production (metric tons except as noted). Agriculture and fishing (2007): barley 1,125,000, wheat 713,000, potatoes 399,000; livestock (number of live animals) 6,704,000 cattle, 5,522,000 sheep, 1,588,000 pigs; fisheries production 284,246 (from aquaculture 20%). Mining and quarrying (2005): zinc ore (metal content) 428,596; lead ore (metal content) 63,810. Manufacturing (gross value added in €'000,000; 2005): chemical products 12,000; electrical and optical equipment 7,097; food products, beverages, and tobacco products 6,391. Energy production (consumption): electricity (kW-hr; 2007) 27,888,000,000 ([2006] 29,824,000,000); coal (metric tons; 2006) none (2,597,000); crude petroleum (barrels; 2006) none (22,974,000); petroleum products (metric tons; 2006) 3,223,000 (7,384,000); natural gas (cu m; 2007) 498,000,000 ([2006] 4,784,000,000); peat (metric tons; 2006) 4,300,000 (n.a.). Population economically active (2005): total 2,014,800; activity rate 48.8% (participation rates: ages 15–64, 70.2%; female 42.3%; unemployed [March 2005–February 2006] 4.4%). Selected balance of payments data. Receipts from (US$'000,000): tourism (2007) 6,140; remittances (2008) 643; foreign direct disinvestment (2005–07 avg.) −2,213. Disbursements for

(US$'000,000): tourism (2007) 8,682; remittances (2008) 2,691; foreign direct investment (2005–07 avg.) 16,804.

Foreign trade

Imports (2007; c.i.f.): €62,173,000,000 (machinery and transportation equipment 40.2%, of which office machines and parts 14.8%; motor vehicles 7.0%; electrical machinery 5.2%; chemical products 13.2%; mineral fuels 7.9%; food products 7.2%). *Major import sources* (2006): UK 30.1%; US 11.3%; Germany 8.7%; China 8.3%; Netherlands 4.2%. **Exports** (2007; f.o.b.): €88,581,000,000 (organic chemical products 21.9%; medicinal and pharmaceutical products 16.5%; office machines and parts 14.2%; food products 8.3%). *Major export destinations* (2007): UK 18.7%; US 17.8%; Belgium 14.3%; Germany 7.5%; France 5.8%.

Transport and communications

Transport. *Railroads* (2007): route length (2004) 3,312 km; passenger-km 2,007,065,000; metric ton-km cargo 128,908,000. *Roads* (2003): length 96,602 km (paved 100%). *Vehicles* (2006): passenger cars 1,778,861; trucks 318,604. *Air transport* (2007; Aer Lingus only): passenger-km 14,807,000,000; metric ton-km cargo 75,400,000. **Communications,** in total units (units per 1,000 persons). Telephone landlines (2008): 2,202,000 (503); cellular telephone subscribers (2008): 5,048,000 (1,503); personal computers (2007): 2,536,000 (582); total Internet users (2008): 2,830,000 (646); broadband Internet subscribers (2008): 891,000 (203).

Education and health

Educational attainment (2006). Percentage of population ages 15–64 having: no formal schooling/primary education 15.1%; some/complete secondary 46.5%; post secondary certificate 9.4%; some higher 9.5%; complete higher 16.8%; unknown 2.7%. **Health:** physicians (2004) 11,141 (1 per 365 persons); hospital beds (2006) 12,051 (publicly funded acute hospitals only) (1 per 352 persons); infant mortality rate per 1,000 live births (2007) 2.9; undernourished population (2002–04) less than 2.5% of total population.

Military

Total active duty personnel (November 2008): 10,460 (army 81.3%, navy 10.5%, air force 8.2%); reserve 14,875. **Military expenditure as percentage of GDP** (2008): 0.5%; per capita expenditure US$303.

Background

Human settlement in Ireland began about 6000 BC, and Celtic migration dates from c. 300 BC. St. Patrick is credited with Christianizing the country in the 5th century AD. Norse domination began in 795 and ended in 1014, when the Norse were defeated by Brian Boru. Gaelic Ireland's independence ended in 1171, when English King Henry II proclaimed himself overlord of the island. Beginning in the 16th century, Irish Catholic landowners fled religious persecution by the English and were replaced by English and Scottish Protestants. The United Kingdom of Great Britain and Ireland was established in 1801. The Great Famine of the 1840s led over two million people to emigrate and built momentum for Irish Home Rule. The Easter Rising (1916) was followed by the Anglo-Irish War (1919–21), during which the Irish Republican Army used guerrilla tactics to force the British government to negotiate. The signing of the Anglo-Irish Treaty on 6 Dec 1921, when ratified by the Dáil the following month, granted southern Ireland dominion status as the Irish Free State. Internecine struggle between supporters and opponents of the treaty culminated in the Irish Civil War (1922–23). In 1937 the Free State adopted the name Éire (Ireland) and became a sovereign independent country. In 1948 the Dáil passed the Republic of Ireland Act, which took effect in April 1949, declaring Ireland a republic and removing it from the British Commonwealth of Nations. Britain recognized the new status of Ireland but declared that unity with the six counties of Northern Ireland could not occur without consent of the parliament of Northern Ireland. In 1973 Ireland joined the European Economic Community (later the European Community); it is now a member of the EU. The late 20th century was dominated by sectarian hostilities. The Irish government played a pivotal role in winning public support for the Belfast Agreement (1998), which removed Ireland's constitutional claim to the entire island's territory. Ireland continued to play an important consultative role in Northern Ireland, such as helping to negotiate an agreement between the Democratic Union Party and Sinn Féin coalition government in 2010, under which policing and justice powers were to be devolved to Northern Ireland's government.

Recent Developments

The Commission to Inquire into Child Abuse, which was established in 2000 to investigate the abuse of children in Catholic-run residential institutions in Ireland from the 1930s onward, published its final report in May 2009. The report concluded that beatings and neglect were routine and that sexual abuse was "endemic" in many institutions and also that church authorities were often aware of the abuse and made efforts to protect offenders from legal charges. A separate inquiry into child-abuse allegations against clergy members in Dublin between 1975 and 2004 ended in July; the inquiry's findings caused considerable public disquiet over the role of senior churchmen, who were criticized for not pursuing allegations of child sex abuse by clergy with sufficient vigor. By year's end four of the five serving bishops cited in the report had resigned.

Internet resource: <www.cso.ie>.

Israel

Official name: Medinat Yisrael (Hebrew); Dawlat Israil (Arabic) (State of Israel). **Form of government:** multiparty republic with one legislative house (Knesset [120]). **Head of state:** President Shimon Peres (from 2007). **Head of government:** Prime Minister Benjamin Netanyahu (from 2009). **Capital:** Jerusalem is the proclaimed capital of Israel and the actual seat of gov-

---

1 metric ton = about 1.1 short tons;   1 kilometer = 0.6 mi (statute);   1 metric ton-km cargo = about 0.68 short ton-mi cargo;   c.i.f.: cost, insurance, and freight;   f.o.b.: free on board

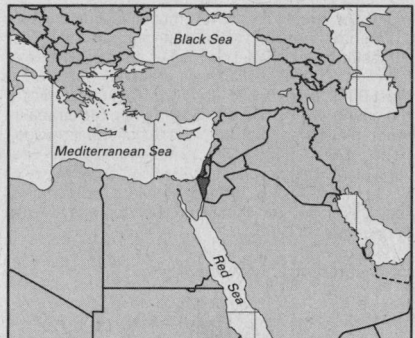

(2007) 26,236 (from aquaculture 85%). *Mining and quarrying* (2007): phosphate rock 3,069,000, potash 2,150,000, gypsum 82,974, diamonds 526,000 carats. *Manufacturing* (value added in US$'000,000; 2005): chemical products 3,427; medical, measuring, and testing appliances 2,270; electronics and telecommunications equipment 2,259. *Energy production (consumption):* electricity ₄ (kW-hr; 2008) 54,504,000,000 ([2006] 49,967,000,000); coal (metric tons; 2008) none (12,882,000); lignite (metric tons; 2006) 452,000 (452,000); crude petroleum (barrels; 2007) 8,200 ([2006] 73,310,000); petroleum products (metric tons; 2006) 10,687,000 (11,572,000); natural gas (cu m; 2007) 2,758,000,000 ([2008] 1,847,000,000). **Population economically active** (2008): total 2,957,100; activity rate 42.1% (participation rates: ages 15 and over, 56.5%; female 46.6%; unemployed [July 2008–June 2009] 7.0%). **Selected balance of payments data.** Receipts from (US$'000,000): tourism (2007) 3,059; remittances (2008) 1,422; foreign direct investment (FDI; 2005–07 avg.) 9,869. Disbursements for (US$'000,000): tourism (2007) 3,260; remittances (2008) 3,537; FDI (2005–07 avg.) 8,364.

ernment, but recognition of its status as capital by the international community has largely been withheld. **Official languages:** Hebrew; Arabic. **Official religion:** none. **Monetary unit:** 1 new (Israeli) sheqel (NIS) = 100 agorot; valuation (1 Jul 2010) US$1 = NIS 3.90.

Demography

Area: 8,357 sq mi, 21,643 sq km (excludes the West Bank and the Gaza Strip; includes the Golan Heights and East Jerusalem). **Population** (2009; excludes estimated mid-year Jewish population of West Bank [305,000]): 7,128,000. **Density** (2009; excludes estimated mid-year Jewish population of West Bank): persons per sq mi 852.9, persons per sq km 329.3. **Urban** (2008): 91.7%. **Sex distribution** (2008): male 49.44%; female 50.56%. **Age breakdown** (2008): under 15, 28.4%; 15–29, 23.4%; 30–44, 19.4%; 45–59, 15.2%; 60–74, 9.0%; 75–84, 3.5%; 85 and over, 1.1%. **Ethnic composition** (2008): Jewish 75.5%; Arab 20.2%; other 4.3%. **Religious affiliation** (2008): Jewish 75.5%; Muslim 16.8%; Christian 2.1%; Druze 1.7%; other 3.9%. **Major cities** (2008): Jerusalem 763,600; Tel Aviv–Yafo 392,500 (urban agglomeration [2006] 3,040,400); Haifa 264,800 (urban agglomeration [2006] 996,000); Rishon LeZiyyon 226,100. **Location:** Middle East, bordering Lebanon, Syria, Jordan, the West Bank, Egypt, the Gaza Strip, and the Mediterranean Sea.

Vital statistics

Birth rate per 1,000 population (2008): 21.5 (world avg. 20.3). **Death rate** per 1,000 population (2008): 5.4 (world avg. 8.5). **Total fertility rate** (avg. births per childbearing woman; 2008): 2.96. **Life expectancy** at birth (2008): male 79.1 years; female 83.0 years.

National economy

Budget (2007). *Revenue:* NIS 294,399,000,000 (current revenue 67.3%, of which income tax 31.0%, VAT 18.3%; capital revenue 29.2%, of which loans and grants 19.7%). *Expenditures:* NIS 307,240,000,000 (debt service 32.5%; defense 18.2%; social security and welfare 12.8%; education 11.3%; health 5.5%). **Public debt** (January 2009): US$86,080,000,000. **Gross national income** (2008): US$180,499,000,000 (US$24,700 per capita). **Production** (metric tons except as noted). *Agriculture and fishing* (2008): potatoes 592,001, tomatoes 421,721, oranges 117,804, dates 22,000, livestock (number of live animals) 430,000 sheep, 416,000 cattle; fisheries production

Foreign trade

Imports (2008; c.i.f.) (excluding the import of military goods [equaling US$2,493,000,000 in 2006]): US$65,173,200,000 (machinery and apparatus 19.7%; crude petroleum 16.7%; diamonds 13.6%; chemical products 11.0%; transportation equipment 8.0%). *Major import sources:* US 12.3%; Belgium and Luxembourg 6.8%; China 6.5%; Switzerland 6.1%; Germany 6.0%. **Exports** (2008; f.o.b.): US$61,339,-100,000 (machinery and apparatus 22.4%; chemical products 21.5%; polished diamonds 10.3%; rough diamonds 5.4%; crude petroleum and refined petroleum products 5.0%; professional and scientific equipment 3.6%). *Major export destinations:* US 32.6%; Belgium and Luxembourg 7.6%; Hong Kong 6.8%; India 3.8%; Netherlands 3.3%.

Transport and communications

Transport. *Railroads* (2008): route length 949 km; passenger-km 1,968,000,000, metric ton-km cargo 1,056,000,000. *Roads* (2008): total length 18,096 km (paved 100%). *Vehicles* (2008): passenger cars 1,875,765; trucks and buses 372,268. *Air transport* (2008; El Al only): passenger-km 17,388,000,000; metric ton-km cargo 606,000,000. *Communications,* in total units (units per 1,000 persons). Telephone landlines (2008): 2,900,000 (411); cellular telephone subscribers (2008): 8,982,000 (1,274); personal computers (2004): 5,037,000 (734); total Internet users (2008): 2,106,000 (299); broadband Internet subscribers (2008): 1,600,000 (227).

Education and health

Educational attainment (2007). Percentage of population ages 25–64 having: no formal schooling/unknown 1%; primary 12%; secondary 44%; postsecondary, vocational, and higher 43%. **Literacy** (2004): total population ages 15 and over literate 97.1%; males literate 98.5%; females literate 95.9%. **Health** (2008): physicians (2007) 25,314 (1 per 273 persons); hospital beds 42,178 (1 per 166 persons); infant mortality rate per 1,000 live births 3.8; undernourished population (2002–04) less than 2.5% of total population.

Military

Total active duty personnel (November 2008): 176,500 (army 75.4%, navy 5.4%, air force 19.2%); reserve 565,000. **Military expenditure as percentage of GDP** (2007): 7.2%; per capita expenditure US$1,681.

Background

The record of human habitation in Israel is at least 100,000 years old. Efforts by Jews to establish a national state there began in the late 19th century. Britain supported Zionism and in 1922 assumed political responsibility for what was Palestine. Migration of Jews there during Nazi persecution led to deteriorating relations with Arabs. In 1947 the UN voted to partition the region into separate Jewish and Arab states, a decision opposed by neighboring Arab countries. The State of Israel was proclaimed in 1948, and Egypt, Transjordan, Syria, Lebanon, and Iraq immediately declared war on it. Israel won this war as well as the 1967 Six-Day War, in which it claimed the West Bank from Jordan and the Gaza Strip from Egypt. Another war with its Arab neighbors followed in 1973, but the Camp David Accords led to the signing of a peace treaty between Israel and Egypt in 1979. Israel invaded Lebanon to quell the Palestine Liberation Organization (PLO) in 1982, and in the late 1980s a Palestinian resistance movement arose in the occupied territories. Peace negotiations between Israel and the Arab states and Palestinians began in 1991. Israel and the PLO agreed in 1993 upon a five-year extension of self-government to the Palestinians of the West Bank and the Gaza Strip. Israel signed a full peace treaty with Jordan in 1994. Israeli soldiers and Lebanon's Hezbollah forces clashed in 1997. Following numerous contentious talks between Israel and Lebanon, Israeli troops abruptly withdrew from Lebanon in 2000, and negotiations between Israel and the Palestinians broke down amid violence that claimed hundreds of lives. In an effort to stem the fighting, Israel in 2005 withdrew its soldiers and settlers from parts of the West Bank and from all of the Gaza Strip, which came under Palestinian control.

Recent Developments

In a speech in June, Israeli prime minister Benjamin Netanyahu committed himself to an independent Palestinian state alongside Israel. Netanyahu's offer, however, bore conditions: the Palestinian state would have to be demilitarized; the Palestinians would have to recognize Israel as a "Jewish state"; no Palestinian refugees would return to Israel-proper; and no part of Jerusalem would serve as the capital of the Palestinian state. The Palestinians, who had been offered far more by outgoing prime minister Ehud Olmert, demanded that Netanyahu freeze Jewish settlement construction in the West Bank. US Pres. Barack Obama led a dynamic US resolve to promote comprehensive Israeli-Arab peace, which he saw as the key to stability in the region. In a seminal speech made in Cairo in June, he set down conditions for the resumption of Israeli-Palestinian negotiations, including a freeze on the construction of Jewish settlements in the West Bank, and urged the Arab world to encourage peacemaking by taking initial steps toward nor-

malization with Israel. In November Israel agreed to a 10-month freeze, with construction in East Jerusalem, which Israel claimed as an integral area of its capital but Palestinians considered part of the West Bank, excepted. In March 2010, during a visit to the country by US Vice Pres. Joe Biden, the Israeli interior ministry announced plans to construct an additional 1,600 homes for Israeli settlers in East Jerusalem. This development, which US Secretary of State Hillary Clinton termed "insulting," brought Israeli-US relations to what some asserted was the lowest point in 35 years.

Internet resource: <www.cbs.gov.il>.

Italy

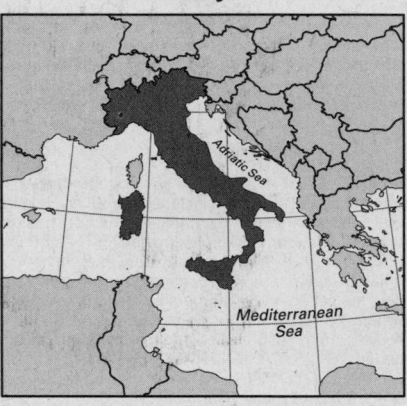

Official name: Repubblica Italiana (Italian Republic). **Form of government:** republic with two legislative houses (Senate [322]; Chamber of Deputies [630]). **Head of state:** President Giorgio Napolitano (from 2006). **Head of government:** Prime Minister Silvio Berlusconi (from 2008). **Capital:** Rome. **Official language:** Italian (in addition, German is locally official in the region of Trentino–Alto Adige and French is locally official in the region of Valle d'Aosta). **Official religion:** none. **Monetary unit:** 1 euro (€) = 100 cents; valuation (1 Jul 2010) US$1 = €0.80.

Demography

Area: 116,346 sq mi, 301,336 sq km. **Population** (2009): 60,325,000. **Density** (2009): persons per sq mi 518.5, persons per sq km 200.2. **Urban** (2005): 67.6%. **Sex distribution** (2007): male 48.56%; female 51.44%. **Age breakdown** (2007): under 15, 14.1%; 15–29, 16.3%; 30–44, 23.8%; 45–59, 20.1%; 60–74, 16.1%; 75–84, 7.2%; 85 and over, 2.4%. **Ethnolinguistic composition** (2000): Italian 96.0%; North African Arab 0.9%; Italo-Albanian 0.8%; Albanian 0.5%; German 0.4%; Austrian 0.4%; other 1.0%. **Religious affiliation** (2005): Roman Catholic 83%, of which practicing 28%; Muslim 2%; nonreligious/atheist 14%; other 1%. **Major cities (urban agglomerations)** (2007): Rome 2,718,768 (3,339,000); Milan 1,299,633 (2,945,000); Naples

1 metric ton = about 1.1 short tons;   1 kilometer = 0.6 mi (statute);   1 metric ton-km cargo = about 0.68 short ton-mi cargo;   c.i.f.: cost, insurance, and freight;   f.o.b.: free on board

973,132 (2,250,000); Turin 908,263 (1,652,000); Palermo 663,173 (863,000); Genoa 610,887; Bologna 372,256; Florence 364,710; Bari 322,511; Catania 298,957; Venice 268,993; Verona 264,191; Messina 243,997; Padua 210,173; Trieste 205,356. **Location:** southern Europe, bordering Switzerland, Austria, Slovenia, the Mediterranean Sea, and France; wholly contained within Italy are the countries of San Marino and Vatican City. **Immigration** (2007): resident foreigners 3,432,651, of which from EU countries 17.7%, other Europe 23.0%, North African countries 15.2%, other Africa 6.6%, Asian countries 7.7%, other 29.8%.

Vital statistics

Birth rate per 1,000 population (2008): 9.6 (world avg. 20.3); (2007) within marriage 79.3%. **Death rate** per 1,000 population (2008): 9.8 (world avg. 8.5). **Total fertility rate** (avg. births per childbearing woman; 2007): 1.37. **Life expectancy** at birth (2007): male 78.6 years; female 84.1 years.

Social indicators

Educational attainment (2007). Percentage of population ages 25 to 64 having: no formal schooling through primary education 15%; lower secondary 33%; upper secondary 37%; university 13%; other 2%. **Quality of working life.** Average workweek (2008): 34.6 hours. Annual rate per 100,000 workers (2007) for: nonfatal injury 2,647; fatal injury 4. Number of working days lost to labor stoppages per 1,000 workers (2007): 52.6. **Material well-being.** Rate per 100 households possessing (2008): mobile phone 88.5; personal computer 50.1; Internet access 42.0; satellite dish 30.7. **Transport used for work** per 100 employees (includes double-counting; 2008): car 75.7%, walking 11.1%, bus 4.9%, motorcycle/motorbike 4.6%, bicycle 3.1%, train 2.9%, underground 2.5%, other 2.9%. **Social participation.** Trade union membership in total workforce (2004): 30%. **Social deviance** (2007). Offense rate per 100,000 population for: murder/manslaughter 4.6; rape 8.2; theft 2,756; battery 132.2; robbery 86.2. **Access to services** (2002). Nearly 100% of dwellings have access to electricity, a safe water supply, and toilet facilities. **Leisure** (2006). Favorite leisure activities (attendance per 100 people ages 6 and over): cinema 48.9; museum or art exhibition 27.7; sporting events 27.3; discotheque 24.8; archaeological sites or monuments 21.1.

National economy

Gross national income (2008): US$2,109,075,-000,000 (US$35,240 per capita). **Budget** (2006). *Revenue:* €672,610,000,000 (taxes on goods and services 27.6%; social security contributions 27.6%; income tax 24.4%; nontax revenue 6.7%; corporate taxes 6.4%). *Expenditures:* €722,750,000,000 (social protection 37.2%; health 14.4%; economic affairs 12.0%; public debt 9.5%; education 9.2%; defense 2.8%). **Public debt** (May 2009): US$2,137,581,000,000. *Energy production (consumption):* electricity (kW-hr; 2008) 316,719,-000,000 ([2006] 359,106,000,000); coal (metric tons; 2006) 21,000 (24,806,000); crude petroleum (barrels; 2008) 36,400,000 ([2006] 601,000,000); petroleum products (metric tons; 2006) 89,810,000 (77,681,000); natural gas (cu m; 2008) 9,103,-

000,000 ([2006] 82,488,000,000). **Production** (metric tons except as noted). *Agriculture and fishing* (2008): corn (maize) 9,491,203, wheat 8,855,440, grapes 7,793,301, tomatoes 5,976,912, sugar beets 3,800,000, olives 3,512,660, oranges 2,527,453, apples 2,208,227, potatoes 1,603,828, peaches and nectarines 1,589,118, pears 770,100, artichokes 483,561, kiwi fruit 473,955, sunflower seeds 260,927, hazelnuts 111,841, almonds 118,723; livestock (number of live animals) 9,273,000 pigs, 8,237,000 sheep, 6,283,000 cattle; fisheries production (2007) 465,637 (from aquaculture 38%). *Mining and quarrying* (2007): limestone 32,953,000; feldspar 4,727,000 [world rank: 1]; marble and travertine 4,643,000; pozzolana 4,000,000 [world rank: 1]. *Manufacturing* (value added in US$'000,000; 2005): fabricated metal products 34,849; food products 21,119; general purpose machinery 19,782; paints, soaps, pharmaceuticals 14,945; special purpose machinery 13,548; bricks, cement, ceramics 12,684; printing and publishing 10,567; plastic products 9,205; textiles 9,063; motor vehicles and parts 8,533; wearing apparel 8,317; furniture 8,195; iron and steel 7,298; footwear and leather products 6,643. **Population economically active** (2008): total 25,096,600; activity rate of total population 42.2% (participation rates: ages 15–64, 63.0%; female 40.7%; unemployed [April 2008–March 2009] 7.0%). **Selected balance of payments data.** Receipts from (US$'000,000): tourism (2007) 42,660; remittances (2008) 3,136; foreign direct investment (FDI; 2005–07 avg.) 33,138. Disbursements for (US$'000,000): tourism (2007) 27,329; remittances (2008) 12,718; FDI (2005–07 avg.) 58,225.

Foreign trade

Imports (2007; c.i.f.): US$504,582,000,000 (machinery and apparatus 16.4%; chemical products 12.6%; motor vehicles and parts 11.0%; crude petroleum 9.0%; food products 6.4%; iron and steel 5.8%; nonferrous metals 4.0%). *Major import sources:* Germany 16.7%; France 9.0%; China 5.9%; Netherlands 5.2%; Belgium 4.3%; Spain 4.2%; Libya 3.3%; UK 3.2%; US 3.0%; Switzerland 3.0%. **Exports** (2007; f.o.b.): US$492,058,000,000 (assorted manufactured goods 20.9%, of which iron and steel 5.2%, fabricated metal products 4.4%; nonelectrical machinery 20.7%, of which general industrial machinery 10.0%; specialized machinery 6.3%; chemical products 10.1%; motor vehicles and parts 8.0%; electrical machinery 5.3%; wearing apparel and accessories 4.6%; food products 4.5%). *Major export destinations:* Germany 12.8%; France 11.4%; Spain 7.3%; US 6.8%; UK 5.8%; Switzerland 3.7%; Belgium 2.9%; Russia 2.7%; Poland 2.4%; Austria 2.3%.

Transport and communications

Transport. *Railroads:* (2007) route length 16,356 km; (2006) passenger-km 46,439,000,000; (2005) metric ton-km cargo 22,760,000,000. *Roads* (2003): total length 484,688 km (paved 100%). *Vehicles* (2006): passenger cars 35,297,282; trucks and buses 4,427,846. *Air transport* (2008; Air One, Alitalia, Livingston S.P.A., and Meridiana airlines only): passenger-km 39,121,000,000; metric ton-km cargo 1,201,000,000. **Communications,** in total units (units per 1,000 persons). Telephone landlines (2008): 20,031,000 (335); cellular telephone subscribers (2008): 88,580,000 (1,480); personal computers (2007): 21,791,000 (367); total Internet users (2008): 29,118,000 (486); broadband Internet subscribers (2008): 11,283,000 (189).

Education and health

Literacy (2007): total population ages 15 and over literate 98.9%; males literate 99.1%; females literate 98.6%. **Health**: physicians (2006) 215,000 (1 per 274 persons); hospital beds (2005) 234,428 (1 per 250 persons); infant mortality rate per 1,000 live births (2007) 3.8; undernourished population (2002–04) less than 2.5% of total population.

Military

Total active duty personnel (November 2008): 292,983 (army 36.9%, navy 11.6%, air force 14.7%, carabinieri 36.8%); US military forces (December 2008): 9,160. **Military expenditure as percentage of GDP** (2007): 1.8%; per capita expenditure US$635.

Background

The Etruscan civilization arose in the 9th century BC and was overthrown by the Romans in the 4th–3rd centuries BC. Barbarian invasions of the 4th and 5th centuries AD destroyed the Western Roman Empire. Italy's political fragmentation lasted for centuries but did not diminish its impact on European culture, notably during the Renaissance. From the 15th to the 18th century, Italian lands were ruled by France, the Holy Roman Empire, Spain, and Austria. When Napoleonic rule ended in 1815, Italy was again a grouping of independent states. The Risorgimento successfully united most of Italy, including Sicily and Sardinia, by 1861, and the unification of peninsular Italy was completed by 1870. Italy joined the Allies during World War I, but social unrest in the 1920s brought to power the Fascist movement of Benito Mussolini, and Italy allied itself with Nazi Germany in World War II. Defeated by the Allies in 1943, Italy proclaimed itself a republic in 1946. It was a charter member of NATO (1949) and of the European Community. It completed the process of setting up regional legislatures with limited autonomy in the 1970s. Since World War II it has experienced rapid changes of government but has remained socially stable. It worked with other European countries to establish the European Union.

Recent Developments

On 6 Apr 2009, an earthquake with a magnitude of 6.3 devastated a mountainous stretch of the Abruzzi region, severely damaging the 13th-century city of L'Aquila. Aftershocks from the country's worst earthquake in 30 years rippled through central Italy for more than a month. At least 294 people died, and an estimated 60,000 were left homeless. The Group of Eight summit that had been scheduled to take place on Maddalena Island was held instead in L'Aquila in July. Scientists remained concerned about the high potential for future seismic activity along Italy's geologically vulnerable eastern spine, the Apennine Mountains, where the quake had occurred. Though

seismologists reiterated the need for stricter adherence to building codes, Italy had thousands of centuries-old structures that were difficult to modify.

Internet resource: <www.istat.it>.

Jamaica

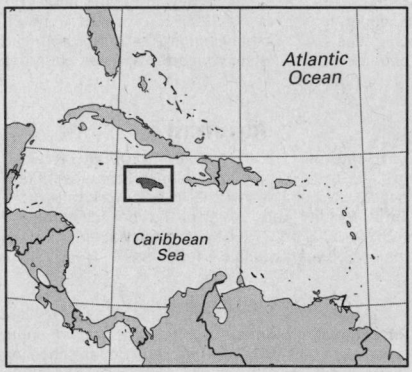

Atlantic Ocean

Caribbean Sea

Official name: Jamaica. **Form of government:** constitutional monarchy with two legislative houses (Senate [21]; House of Representatives [60]). **Head of state:** British Queen Elizabeth II (from 1952), represented by Governor-General Patrick Allen (from 2009). **Head of government:** Prime Minister Bruce Golding (from 2007). **Capital:** Kingston. **Official language:** English. **Official religion:** none. **Monetary unit:** 1 Jamaican dollar (J$) = 100 cents; valuation (1 Jul 2010) US$1 = J$85.35.

Demography

Area: 4,244 sq mi, 10,991 sq km. **Population** (2009): 2,702,000. **Density** (2009): persons per sq mi 636.7, persons per sq km 245.8. **Urban** (2008): 53.3%. **Sex distribution** (2008): male 49.28%; female 50.72%. **Age breakdown** (2008): under 15, 27.9%; 15–29, 25.0%; 30–44, 23.8%; 45–59, 12.4%; 60–74, 7.1%; 75 and over, 3.8%. **Ethnic composition** (2001): black 91.6%; mixed race 6.2%; East Indian 0.9%; Chinese 0.2%; white 0.2%; other/unknown 0.9%. **Religious affiliation** (2001): Protestant 61.2%, of which Church of God 23.8%, Seventh-day Adventist 10.8%, Pentecostal 9.5%; Roman Catholic 2.6%; other Christian 1.7%; Rastafarian 0.9%; nonreligious 20.9%; other 12.7%. **Major cities** (2006): Kingston 585,300; Spanish Town 148,800; Portmore 103,900; Montego Bay 82,700; Mandeville 47,700. **Location:** island in the Caribbean Sea, south of Cuba.

Vital statistics

Birth rate per 1,000 population (2008): 16.7 (world avg. 20.3). **Death rate** per 1,000 population (2008): 6.3 (world avg. 8.5). **Total fertility rate** (avg. births per childbearing woman; 2008): 2.30. **Life expectancy** at birth (2008): male 71.9 years; female 75.4 years.

---

1 metric ton = about 1.1 short tons; 1 kilometer = 0.6 mi (statute); 1 metric ton-km cargo = about 0.68 short ton-mi cargo; c.i.f.: cost, insurance, and freight; f.o.b.: free on board

National economy

Budget (2008–09). *Revenue:* J$276,199,800,000 (tax revenue 89.1%; nontax revenue 5.8%; grants and other revenue 5.1%). *Expenditures:* J$351,521,400,000 (public debt service 35.6%; wages and salaries 31.7%; capital expenditures 11.8%). **Production** (metric tons except as noted). *Agriculture and fishing* (2007): sugarcane 2,000,000, coconuts 170,000, oranges 142,000, pimiento and allspice (2005) 10,400, coffee 2,700; livestock (number of live animals) 430,000 cattle, 12,500,000 chickens; fisheries production 22,164 (from aquaculture 25%). *Mining and quarrying* (2008): bauxite 14,697,000; alumina 3,991,000; limestone (2007) 2,950,000; gypsum 238,000. *Manufacturing* (2008): cement 724,600,000; animal feeds (2005) 367,600; sugar 140,000; molasses 62,654; rum [and other distilled spirits] 265,349 hectoliters. *Energy production (consumption):* electricity (kW-hr; 2006) 7,473,000,000 (7,473,000,000); coal (metric tons; 2006) none (32,000); crude petroleum (barrels; 2006) none (7,440,000); petroleum products (metric tons; 2006) 995,000 (3,806,000). **Population economically active** (2008): total 1,302,400; activity rate of total population 48.4% (participation rates: ages 14 and over [2006] 64.6%; female 45.4%; unemployed 10.3%). **Gross national income** (2008): US$13,098,-000,000 (US$4,870 per capita). **Public debt** (external, outstanding; May 2009): US$6,297,000,000. **Selected balance of payments data.** Receipts from (US$'000,000): tourism (2008) 1,984; remittances (2008–09) 1,860; foreign direct investment (2006–08 avg.) 1,062; official development assistance (2007) 26. Disbursements for (US$'000,000): tourism (2007) 298; remittances (2008–09) 262; foreign direct disinvestment (2005–07 avg.) −77.

Foreign trade

Imports (2006; c.i.f.): US$5,041,000,000 (crude petroleum 23.6%; machinery and apparatus 15.5%; food products 12.5%; chemical products 11.3%; motor vehicles 6.1%). *Major import sources:* US 36.8%; Trinidad and Tobago 11.5%; Venezuela 10.7%; Japan 4.2%; China 4.1%. **Exports** (2006; f.o.b.): US$1,989,000,000 (alumina 52.3%; refined petroleum products 13.5%; food products 12.0%, of which raw sugar 4.5%, vegetables and fruit 2.9%, coffee 1.5%; alcoholic beverages 4.2%). *Major export destinations:* US 30.4%; Canada 15.6%; China 15.1%; UK 10.3%; Netherlands 7.0%.

Transport and communications

Transport. *Railroads* (2004): route length 201 km. *Roads* (2005): total length 21,532 km (paved 74%). *Vehicles* (2004): passenger cars 357,660; trucks and buses 128,239. *Air transport* (2006; Air Jamaica only): passenger-km 3,907,530,000; metric ton-km cargo 20,192,000. **Communications**, in total units (units per 1,000 persons). Telephone landlines (2008): 317,000 (117); cellular telephone subscribers (2008): 2,723,000 (1,006); personal computers (2005): 179,000 (68); total Internet users (2008): 1,540,000 (569); broadband Internet subscribers (2008): 98,000 (36).

Education and health

Educational attainment (2001). Percentage of population ages 15 and over having: no formal schooling/unknown 6.7%; primary education 25.5%; secondary 55.5%; higher 12.3%, of which university 4.2%. **Literacy** (2007): population ages 15 and over literate 86.0%; males literate 80.5%; females literate 91.1%. **Health:** physicians (2005) 2,253 (1 per 1,176 persons); hospital beds (2006) 5,326 (1 per 500 persons); infant mortality rate per 1,000 live births (2008) 15.6; undernourished population (2002–04) 250,000 (9% of total population based on the consumption of a minimum daily requirement of 1,930 calories).

Military

Total active duty personnel (November 2008): 2,830 (army 88.3%, coast guard 6.7%, air force 5.0%). **Military expenditure as percentage of GDP** (2007): 1.0%; per capita expenditure US$40.

Background

The island of Jamaica was settled by Arawak Indians c. AD 600. It was sighted by Christopher Columbus in 1494; Spain colonized it in the early 16th century but neglected it because it lacked gold reserves. Britain gained control in 1655, and by the end of the 18th century Jamaica had become a prized colonial possession due to the volume of sugar produced by slave laborers. Slavery was abolished in the late 1830s, and the plantation system collapsed. Jamaica gained full internal self-government in 1959 and became an independent country within the British Commonwealth in 1962.

Recent Developments

In July 2009 the Jamaican government confirmed that it had applied to the IMF to borrow money under a stand-by agreement. In February 2010 the IMF formally approved the US$1.27 billion loan. The 27-month agreement gave Jamaica immediate access to roughly US$640 million. The country also completed a restructuring of some US$8 billion in government debt.

Internet resource: <www.statinja.com>.

Japan

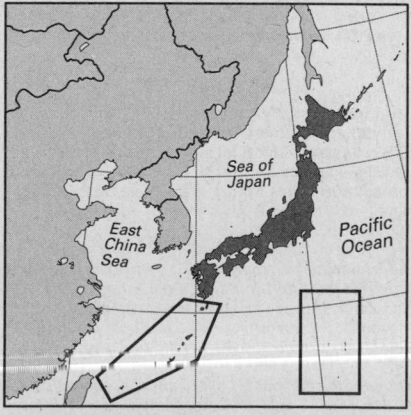

Official name: Nihon, Nippon (Japan). **Form of government:** constitutional monarchy with a national Diet consisting of two legislative houses (House of Councillors [242]; House of Representatives [480]). **Symbol of state:** Emperor Akihito (from 1989). **Head of government:** Prime Minister Naoto Kan (from 2010). **Capital:** Tokyo. **Official language:** Japanese. **Official religion:** none. **Monetary unit:** 1 yen (¥) = 100 sen; valuation (1 Jul 2010) US$1 = ¥87.61.

Demography

Area: 145,898 sq mi, 377,873 sq km. **Population** (2009): 127,556,000. **Density** (2009): persons per sq mi 874.2, persons per sq km 337.5. **Urban** (2005): 66.0%. **Sex distribution** (2009): male 48.72%; female 51.28%. **Age breakdown** (2009): under 15, 13.4%; 15–29, 16.2%; 30–44, 21.1%; 45–59, 19.4%; 60–74, 19.3%; 75–84, 7.8%; 85 and over, 2.8%. **Composition by nationality** (2004): Japanese 98.5%; Korean 0.5%; Chinese 0.4%; Brazilian 0.2%; other 0.4%. **Immigration/Emigration** (2006): permanent immigrants/registered aliens in Japan 2,084,919, from North or South Korea 28.7%, from Taiwan, Hong Kong, Macau, or China 26.9%, from Brazil 15.0%, from the Philippines 9.3%, from Peru 2.8%, from the US 2.5%, from Thailand 1.9%, from Vietnam 1.6%, other 11.3%. Japanese nationals living abroad 1,063,695, in the US 34.8%, in China 11.8%, in Brazil 6.1%, in the UK 5.7%, in Australia 5.6%, in Thailand 3.8%, in Germany 3.2%, other 29.0%. Permanent expatriates (including those with dual nationality) 328,317, of which living in the US 37.6%, in Brazil 19.1%, in Australia 8.5%, in Canada 8.3%. **Major cities** (2008): Tokyo 8,731,000; Yokohama 3,648,000; Osaka 2,651,000; Nagoya 2,246,000; Sapporo 1,898,000; Kobe 1,533,000; Kyoto 1,467,000; Fukuoka 1,437,000; Kawasaki 1,388,000; Saitama 1,210,000; Hiroshima 1,166,000; Sendai 1,031,000. **Major metropolitan areas** (2007): Tokyo 35,676,000; Osaka-Kobe 11,294,000; Nagoya 3,230,000; Fukuoka–Kita-Kyushu 2,792,000; Sapporo 2,544,000; Sendai 2,250,000; Hiroshima 2,045,000; Kyoto 1,805,000. **Location:** eastern Asia, island chain between the North Pacific Ocean and the Sea of Japan. **Religious affiliation** (2003): Shinto and related beliefs 84.2%; Buddhism and related beliefs 73.6% (many Japanese practice both Shintoism and Buddhism); Christian 1.7%; Muslim 0.1%; other 7.8%. **Mobility** (2007). Percentage of total population moving: within a prefecture 2.3%; between prefectures 2.0%.

Vital statistics

Birth rate per 1,000 population (2008): 8.6 (world avg. 20.3). **Death rate** per 1,000 population (2008): 8.8 (world avg. 8.5). **Total fertility rate** (avg. births per childbearing woman; 2008): 1.37. **Life expectancy** at birth (2008): male 79.3 years; female 86.1 years.

Social indicators

Educational attainment (2007). Percentage of population ages 25–64 having: no formal schooling through upper secondary education 59%; higher vocational 18%; university 23%. **Quality of working life.** Average hours worked per week (2008): 40.7. Annual rate of deaths/nonfatal injuries per 100,000 workers (2008): 1.9/177.5. Proportion of labor force insured for damages or income loss resulting from injury, permanent disability, and death (2005): 53.1%. Average man-days lost to labor stoppages per 1,000 workdays (2006): 1.8. Average duration of journey to work (2003): 34.2 minutes. **Access to services** (2004). Proportion of households having access to: safe public water supply 96.9%; public sewage system 68.0%. **Social participation.** Adult population working as volunteers at least once in the year (2006) 26.2%. Trade union membership in total workforce (2007): 15.1%. **Social deviance** (2005). Offense rate per 100,000 population for: homicide 1.0; robbery 3.0; larceny and theft 151.6. Incidence in general population of: drug and substance abuse 0.1. Rate of suicide per 100,000 population (2007): 24.1. **Material well-being** (2003–04). Households possessing: automobile 81.6%; air conditioner (2002) 87.2%; personal computer 77.5%.

National economy

Gross national income (2008): US$4,879,171,-000,000 (US$38,210 per capita). **Budget** (2007–08). *Revenue:* ¥83,000,000,000,000 (government bonds 30.5%; corporate taxes 20.1%; income tax 19.6%; VAT 12.8%). *Expenditures:* ¥83,000,000,000,000 (social security 26.2%; debt service 24.3%; public works 8.1%; education and science 6.4%; national defense 5.8%). **Public debt** (July 2009): US$8,602,560,000,000. *Energy production (consumption):* electricity (kW-hr; 2008) 990,864,000,000 ([2007] 959,660,000,000); coal (metric tons; 2007) 1,340,000 ([2006] 179,075,000); crude petroleum (barrels; 2008) 6,180,000 ([2006] 1,461,000,000); petroleum products (metric tons; 2006) 169,502,000 (173,182,000); natural gas (cu m; 2008) 3,864,000,000 ([2006] 92,352,000,000). Composition of energy supply by source (2002): crude oil and petroleum products 49.7%, coal 19.5%, natural gas 13.5%, nuclear power 11.6%, hydroelectric power 3.2%, solar power and other new energy supplies 2.4%, geothermal 0.1%. **Population economically active** (2008): total 66,620,000; activity rate of total population 52.2% (participation rates: ages 15 and over, 60.3%; female 41.7%; unemployed [September 2008–August 2009] 4.7%). **Production** (metric tons except as noted). *Agriculture and fishing* (2007): rice 11,028,750, sugar beets 4,297,000, potatoes 2,800,000, cabbages 2,390,000, sugarcane 1,500,000, green onions 1,265,000, dry onions 1,165,000, tangerines and mandarin oranges 1,066,000, sweet potatoes 968,400, wheat 882,300, apples 840,100, tomatoes 750,300, carrots 750,000, pears 326,400, spinach 302,000, persimmons 244,800, soybeans 226,700, grapes 209,100, taro 195,000, strawberries 193,000, peaches 150,200, chilies 149,600, tea 94,100, mushrooms 67,000, ginger 42,000, kiwi fruit 32,800, chestnuts 22,100, cherries 16,600; livestock (number of live animals) 9,745,000 pigs, 4,423,000 cattle, 284,651,000 chickens; fisheries production (2008) 5,588,000, of which mackerel 514,000, bonito 304,000, squid 291,000, tuna 217,000, pollack 212,000 (from aquaculture [including aquatic plants] 21% [of which laver 338,000, oys-

---

1 metric ton = about 1.1 short tons;   1 kilometer = 0.6 mi (statute);   1 metric ton-km cargo = about 0.68 short ton-mi cargo;   c.i.f.: cost, insurance, and freight;   f.o.b.: free on board

ters 190,000, yellowtail 158,000, wakame 55,000, pearls 25,000]); whales caught (2005) 815. *Mining and quarrying* (2007): limestone 165,982,000; silica 4,600,000 [world rank: 9]; dolomite 3,655,000; pyrophyllite 345,000; magnesium 12,000; iodine 8,700 [world rank: 2]; silver 11,000 kg; gold 8,869 kg. **Selected balance of payments data.** Receipts from (US$'000,000): tourism (2007) 9,345; remittances (2008) 1,929; foreign direct investment (FDI; 2005–07 avg.) 6,273. Disbursements for (US$'000,000): tourism (2007) 26,511; remittances (2008) 4,743; FDI (2005–07 avg.) 56,532.

Foreign trade

Imports (2006; c.i.f.): ¥67,345,000,000,000 (mineral fuels 27.9%, of which crude petroleum 20.1%, natural gas 5.3%, coal 2.5%; machinery and apparatus 21.1%, of which heavy machinery 4.8%, office machines and computers 4.6%, electronic integrated circuits and micro-assemblies 3.7%; food products 7.4%, of which marine products 2.3%; chemical products 7.1%; metal ores and metal scrap 4.2%; wearing apparel and accessories 4.1%; nonferrous base metals [particularly aluminum and platinum-group] 3.1%; professional and scientific equipment 2.7%; motor vehicles 2.4%). *Major import sources:* China 20.5%; US 12.0%; Saudi Arabia 6.4%; UAE 5.5%; Australia 4.8%; South Korea 4.7%; Indonesia 4.2%; unspecified Asia (probably Taiwan) 3.5%; Germany 3.2%; Thailand 2.9%. **Exports** (2006; f.o.b.): ¥75,214,000,000,000 (machinery and apparatus 39.5%, of which microcircuits and transistors 6.5%, specialized machinery 5.9%, general industrial machinery 5.4%, telecommunications equipment 5.2%, office machines and computers 3.7%, power-generating machinery 3.7%; motor vehicles 21.6%, of which passenger cars 14.6%; chemical products 8.9%; iron and steel 4.6%). *Major export destinations:* US 22.8%; China 14.3%; South Korea 7.8%; unspecified Asia (probably Taiwan) 6.8%; Hong Kong 5.6%; Thailand 3.5%; Germany 3.2%; Singapore 3.0%; UK 2.4%; Netherlands 2.3%.

Transport and communications

Transport. *Railroads* (2007): length (2004) 23,577 km; passenger-km 395,908,000,000; metric ton-km cargo 23,191,000,000. *Roads* (2006): total length 1,197,000 km (paved 79%). *Vehicles* (2008): passenger cars 57,617,000; trucks and buses 16,490,000. *Air transport* (2007): passengers carried 112,543,000; passenger-km 162,954,000,000; metric ton-km cargo 9,449,850,000. **Communications**, in total units (units per 1,000 persons). Telephone landlines (2007): 51,232,000 (401); cellular telephone subscribers (2008): 110,395,000 (864); personal computers (2005): 86,389,000 (675); total Internet users (2007): 88,110,000 (690); broadband Internet subscribers (2008): 30,107,000 (236). *Radio and television broadcasting* (2003): total radio stations 1,612, of which commercial 723; total television stations 15,021, of which commercial 8,276. Commercial broadcasting hours (by percentage of programs): reports—radio 12.3%, television 19.8%; education—radio 2.4%, television 12.3%; culture—radio 13.3%, television 25.1%, entertainment—radio 69.3%, television 37.5%. Advertisements (daily average): radio 149, television 445.

Education and health

Literacy: total population ages 15 and over literate, virtually 100%. **Health** (2006): physicians 275,127 (1 per 464 persons); dentists 95,944 (1 per 1,332 persons); nurses and assistant nurses 1,194,129 (1 per 107 persons); pharmacists 234,429 (1 per 545 persons); midwives (2004) 25,257 (1 per 5,059 persons); hospital beds (2007) 1,620,173 (1 per 79 persons); infant mortality rate per 1,000 live births (2008) 2.6; undernourished population (2002–04) less than 2.5% of total population.

Military

Total active duty personnel (November 2008): 230,300 (army 60.1%, navy 19.1%, air force 19.8%, central staff 1.0%); US troops (December 2008): 34,039 (including 2,850 troops deployed in Afghanistan and Iraq). **Military expenditure as percentage of GDP** (2008): 0.9%; per capita expenditure US$370.

Background

Japan's history began with the accession of the legendary first emperor, Jimmu, in 660 BC. The Yamato court established the first unified Japanese state in the 4th–5th centuries AD; during this period Buddhism arrived in Japan by way of Korea. For centuries Japan borrowed heavily from Chinese culture, but it began to sever its links with the mainland by the 9th century. In 1192 Minamoto Yoritomo established Japan's first bakufu, or shogunate. Unification was achieved in the late 1500s under the leadership of Oda Nobunaga, Toyotomi Hideyoshi, and Tokugawa Ieyasu. During the Tokugawa shogunate, beginning in 1603, the government imposed a policy of isolation. Under the leadership of Emperor Meiji (1868–1912), it adopted a constitution (1889) and began a program of modernization and Westernization. Japanese imperialism led to war with China (1894–95) and Russia (1904–05) as well as to the annexation of Korea (1910) and Manchuria (1931). During World War II, Japan attacked US forces in Hawaii and the Philippines (December 1941) and occupied European colonial possessions in South Asia. In 1945 the US dropped atomic bombs on Hiroshima and Nagasaki, and Japan surrendered to the Allied powers. US postwar occupation of Japan led to a new democratic constitution in 1947. In rebuilding Japan's ruined industrial plant, new technology was used in every major industry. A tremendous economic recovery followed, and Japan became one of the world's wealthiest countries.

Recent Developments

In Japan's general election held in August 2009, the Liberal Democratic Party (LDP) was forced from office for only the second time in 54 years as the opposition Democratic Party of Japan (DPJ) ascended to power under the leadership of Yukio Hatoyama. The DPJ achieved an even greater landslide victory than political forecasters had predicted, increasing its seat total in the 480-seat lower house of the Diet (parliament) from 115 to 308 while the LDP slid from 300 seats to just 119. The election originally had been scheduled for late 2008. It was delayed, however, as the global financial crisis hit Japan hard, causing a sharp contraction of economic activity that saw GDP shrink by 6.1% and value of exports fall 26.6% by the end of 2009. The government responded to the crisis with three stimulus packages amounting to roughly US$275 billion, but this stimulus failed to reverse the unemployment rate, which crept steadily upward to 5.1% by the end of 2009. Hatoyama officially took office on 16 September, and it was announced the next day that the government was suspending construction on the US$5.2 billion Yamba Dam in Gunma prefecture; work on another 47 central-government-funded dams was later suspended as well. The government also announced that it would be trimming the third stimulus package from US$147 billion to US$115 billion.

The DPJ victory posed challenges for the US-Japan alliance. The DPJ had campaigned on a platform that called for improved relations with China and a "more equal" partnership with the US. In its early days in office, Hatoyama's administration declared its intention to end Japan's naval refueling mission in the Indian Ocean, which involved the use of Japanese vessels to refuel US ships engaged in the war in Afghanistan, though it would at the same time offer US$5 billion in aid to Afghanistan. The new administration also indicated its desire to renegotiate a deal on relocating a US military base in Okinawa that the two governments had reached earlier in the year. In mid-2010, however, Hatoyama agreed to accept the relocation of the base, despite widespread public opposition. After apologizing to the people of Japan, he resigned in June, leading to the election of Naoto Kan, the country's fifth prime minister in the last three years.

Internet resource: <www.stat.go.jp>.

Jordan

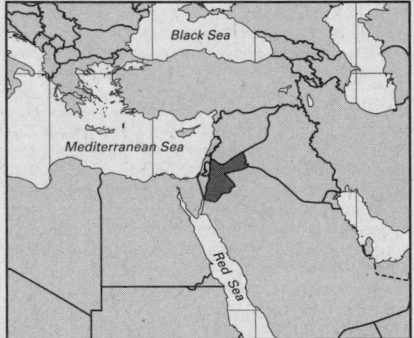

Official name: Al-Mamlakah al-Urduniyah al-Hashimiyah (Hashemite Kingdom of Jordan). **Form of government:** constitutional monarchy with two legislative houses (Senate [55]; House of Representatives [110]). **Head of state and government:** King ʿAbdullah II (from 1999), assisted by Prime Minister Samir al-Rifai (from 2009). **Capital:** Amman. **Official language:** Arabic. **Official religion:** Islam. **Monetary unit:** 1 Jordanian dinar (JD) = 1,000 fils; valuation (1 Jul 2010) US$1 = JD 0.71.

Demography

Area: 34,277 sq mi, 88,778 sq km. **Population** (2009): 5,981,000. **Density** (2009): persons per sq mi 174.5, persons per sq km 67.4. **Urban** (2004): 82.6%. **Sex distribution** (2008): male 51.05%; female 48.95%. **Age breakdown** (2005): under 15, 37.2%; 15–29, 28.9%; 30–44, 20.7%; 45–59, 8.2%; 60–74, 4.2%; 75–84, 0.7%; 85 and over, 0.1%. **Ethnic composition** (2000): Arab 97.8%, of which Jordanian 32.4%, Palestinian 32.2%, Iraqi 14.0%, Bedouin 12.8%; Circassian 1.2%; other 1.0%. **Religious affiliation** (2005): Sunni Muslim 95%; Christian 3%; other (mostly Shiʿi Muslim and Druze) 2%. **Major cities** (2004): Amman 1,036,330; Al-Zarqa 395,227; Irbid 250,645; Al-Rusayfah 227,735; Al-Quwaysimah 135,500. **Location:** the Middle East, bordering Syria, Iraq, Saudi Arabia, the Gulf of Aqaba, Israel, and the West Bank.

Vital statistics

Birth rate per 1,000 population (2007): 28.0 (world avg. 20.3). **Death rate** per 1,000 population (2007): 7.0 (world avg. 8.5). **Total fertility rate** (avg. births per childbearing woman; 2008): 3.50. **Life expectancy** at birth (2008): male 71.6 years; female 74.4 years.

National economy

Budget (2007). *Revenue:* JD 3,971,500,000 (tax revenue 75.4%, of which taxes on goods and services 39.5%, corporate taxes 10.0%, customs duties 9.3%, property taxes 7.7%; nontax revenue 15.5%; grants 8.6%). *Expenditures:* JD 4,540,100,000 (social protection 28.0%; defense 16.7%; education 13.9%; public order 8.8%; economic affairs 7.6%; health 7.1%; public debt 7.1%). **Public debt** (external, outstanding; 2007): US$7,318,000,000. **Production** (metric tons except as noted). *Agriculture and fishing* (2007): tomatoes 550,000, potatoes 170,000, cucumbers 140,000, olives 115,000, eggplants 95,000; livestock (number of live animals) 2,100,000 sheep, 434,000 goats, 25,000,000 chickens; fisheries production 1,015 (from aquaculture 50%). *Mining and quarrying* (2007): phosphate ore 5,552,000; potash 1,796,000; bromine 85,105. *Manufacturing* (value added in US$'000,000; 2006): bricks, cement, and ceramics 423; food products 280; paints, soaps, and pharmaceuticals 260. *Energy production (consumption):* electricity (kW-hr; 2008) 12,682,000,000 ([2006] 11,598,000,000); crude petroleum (barrels; 2007) 9,300 ([2006] 30,900,000); petroleum products (metric tons; 2006) 4,067,000 (4,710,000); natural gas (cu m; 2006) 199,000,000 (2,150,000,000). **Population economically active** (2006): total 1,627,000; activity rate of total population 28.4% (participation rates: ages 15–64, 46.8%; female 17.0%; unemployed [2007] 13.1%). **Gross national income** (2008): US$19,526,000,000 (US$3,310 per capita). **Selected balance of payments data.** Receipts from (US$'000,000): tourism (2007) 2,312; remittances (2007) 3,737; foreign direct investment (FDI; 2005–07 avg.) 2,276; official development assistance (2007) 504. Disbursements for (US$'000,000): tourism (2007) 883; remittances (2007) 479; FDI (2005–07 avg.) 24.

1 metric ton = about 1.1 short tons;   1 kilometer = 0.6 mi (statute);   1 metric ton-km cargo = about 0.68 short ton-mi cargo;   c.i.f.: cost, insurance, and freight;   f.o.b.: free on board

Foreign trade

Imports (2007; c.i.f.): US$13,531,000,000 (machinery and apparatus 17.4%; crude petroleum 15.3%; food products 13.0%; chemical products 9.3%; motor vehicles and parts 7.2%). *Major import sources:* Saudi Arabia 21.0%; China 9.7%; Germany 7.5%; US 4.7%; Egypt 4.4%. **Exports** (2007; f.o.b.): US$5,700,000,000 (wearing apparel and accessories 21.3%; fertilizers 14.5%; food products 10.9%, of which tomatoes 3.1%; medicaments 7.5%; telecommunications equipment and parts 5.9%). *Major export destinations:* US 21.8%; Iraq 12.7%; India 8.3%; Saudi Arabia 7.2%; UAE 6.8%.

Transport and communications

Transport. *Railroads* (2004): route length (2006) 506 km; passenger-km 1,000,000; metric ton-km cargo 563,000,000. *Roads* (2005): total length 7,601 km (paved 100%). *Vehicles* (2006): passenger cars 482,042; trucks and buses 216,905. *Air transport* (2006; Royal Jordanian airlines only): passenger-km 5,521,000,000; metric ton-km cargo 210,000,000. **Communications,** in total units (units per 1,000 persons). Telephone landlines (2008): 519,000 (89); cellular telephone subscribers (2008): 5,314,000 (908); personal computers (2007): 383,000 (67); total Internet users (2008): 1,501,000 (257); broadband Internet subscribers (2008): 128,000 (22).

Education and health

Educational attainment (2004). Percentage of population ages 25 and over having: no formal schooling: illiterate 14.0%, literate 4.8%; primary/lower secondary education 36.6%; upper secondary 19.4%; some higher 25.1%, of which advanced degree 2.1%; unknown 0.1%. **Literacy** (2007): percentage of population ages 15 and over literate 92.1%; males literate 95.7%; females literate 88.4%. **Health** (2007): physicians 15,280 (1 per 375 persons); hospital beds 11,029 (1 per 519 persons); infant mortality rate per 1,000 live births (2008) 19.0; undernourished population (2002–04) 300,000 (6% of total population based on the consumption of a minimum daily requirement of 1,810 calories).

Military

Total active duty personnel (November 2008): 100,500 (army 84.6%, navy 0.5%, air force 14.9%). **Military expenditure as percentage of GDP** (2008): 10.6%; per capita expenditure US$332.

Background

Jordan shares much of its history with Israel, since both occupy the area known historically as Palestine. Much of present-day eastern Jordan was incorporated into Israel under Kings David and Solomon c. 1000 BC. It fell to the Seleucids in 330 BC and to Muslim Arabs in the 7th century AD. The Crusaders extended the kingdom of Jerusalem east of the Jordan River in 1099. Jordan submitted to Ottoman Turkish rule during the 16th century. In 1920 the area comprising Jordan (then known as Transjordan) was established within the British mandate of Palestine. Transjordan became an independent state in 1927, although the British mandate did not end until 1948. After hostilities with the new state of Israel ceased in 1949, Jordan annexed the West Bank of the Jordan River, administering the territory until Israel gained control of it in the Six-Day War of 1967. In 1970–71 Jordan was wracked by fighting between the government and guerrillas of the Palestine Liberation Organization (PLO), a struggle that ended in the expulsion of the PLO from Jordan. In 1988 King Hussein renounced all Jordanian claims to the West Bank in favor of the PLO. In 1994 Jordan and Israel signed a full peace agreement. Upon the death of King Hussein in 1999, his son 'Abdullah took over the throne.

Recent Developments

Proposals for Jordan's becoming an alternative homeland for the 2.3 million Palestinians from the Israeli-occupied West Bank troubled the kingdom throughout 2009. In early January, amid Israel's 22-day war with Hamas militants in the Gaza Strip, King 'Abdullah II voiced concern over the future of the Palestinians and spoke of a "conspiracy" against them. This was interpreted as a warning against an earlier Israeli scenario involving passing administrative control of the Gaza Strip to Egypt and forcibly transferring Palestinians in the West Bank to Jordan.

Internet resource:
<www.dos.gov.jo/dos_home_e/main/index.htm>.

Kazakhstan

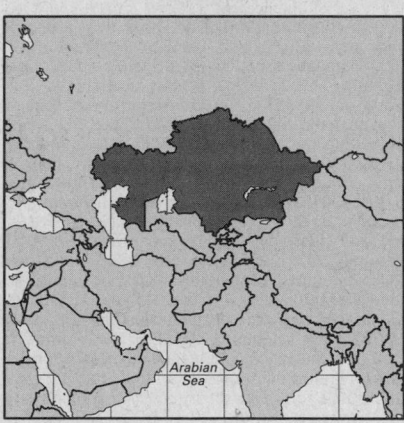

Official name: Qazaqstan Respublikasy (Kazakh); Respublika Kazakhstan (Russian) (Republic of Kazakhstan). **Form of government:** unitary republic with two legislative houses (Senate [47]; House of Representatives [107]). **Head of state and government:** President Nursultan Nazarbayev (from 1990), assisted by Prime Minister Karim Masimov (from 2007). **Capital:** Astana. **Official languages:** Kazakh; Russian. **Official religion:** none. **Monetary unit:** 1 tenge (T) = 100 tiyn; valuation (1 Jul 2010) US$1 = T 144.95.

Demography

Area: 1,052,090 sq mi 2,724,900 sq km. **Population** (2009): 15,881,000. **Density** (2009): persons per sq mi 15.1, persons per sq km 5.8. **Urban** (2007): 53.1%. **Sex distribution** (2008): male 47.59%; female 52.41%. **Age breakdown** (2005): under 15, 23.7%; 15–29, 28.7%; 30–44, 20.7%; 45–59, 16.4%; 60–74, 7.9%; 75–84, 2.3%; 85 and over, 0.3%. **Ethnic composition** (2003): Kazakh 57.2%; Russian 27.2%; Ukrainian 3.1%; Uzbek 2.7%; German 1.6%; Tatar 1.6%; Uighur 1.5%; other 5.1%. **Religious affiliation** (2000): Muslim (mostly Sunni) 42.7%; nonreligious 29.3%; Christian 16.7%, of which Orthodox 8.6%; atheist 10.9%; other 0.4%. **Major cities** (2005): Almaty 1,247,896; Astana 550,438; Shymkent (Chimkent) 526,140; Qaraghandy (Karaganda) 446,139; Taraz 336,057. **Location:** central Asia, bordering Russia, China, Kyrgyzstan, Uzbekistan, the Aral Sea, Turkmenistan, and the Caspian Sea.

Vital statistics

Birth rate per 1,000 population (2008): 22.6 (world avg. 20.3). **Death rate** per 1,000 population (2008): 9.7 (world avg. 8.5). **Total fertility rate** (avg. births per childbearing woman; 2008): 1.88. **Life expectancy** at birth (2008): male 61.9 years; female 72.6 years.

National economy

Budget (2007). *Revenue:* T 2,895,975,900,000 (tax revenue 81.4%; transfers 8.9%; capital revenue 3.2%). *Expenditures:* T 2,678,280,300,000 (social security 18.8%; education 17.0%; health 11.2%; transportation and communications 10.8%; public order 9.0%). **Public debt** (external, outstanding; July 2009): US$2,254,900,000. **Population economically active** (2008): total 8,415,100; activity rate of total population 53.7% (participation rates: ages 15–64, 78.2%; female 49.6%; unemployed [July 2008–June 2009] 6.7%). **Production** (metric tons except as noted). *Agriculture and fishing* (2008): wheat 12,538,200, potatoes 2,354,400, barley 2,059,000, cotton 317,500; livestock (number of live animals) 16,770,400 sheep and goats, 5,991,600 cattle, 148,300 camels; fisheries production (2007) 41,628 (from aquaculture 1%). *Mining and quarrying* (2006): iron ore 18,600,000; bauxite 4,800,000; chromite 3,600,000 (world rank: 2); copper (metal content) 457,000; zinc (metal content) 400,000; silver 830,000 kg; gold 18,000 kg. *Manufacturing* (value of production in T '000,000; 2008): base metals 1,408,325; food products 757,757; machinery and apparatus 297,501; coke, refined petroleum products, and nuclear fuel 235,309. *Energy production (consumption):* electricity (kW-hr; 2008–09) 77,556,000,000 ([2006] 72,488,000,000); coal (metric tons; 2008–09) 95,011,000 ([2006] 63,765,000); lignite (metric tons; 2008–09) 4,478,000 ([2006] 4,207,000); crude petroleum (barrels; 2008–09) 515,758,000 ([2006] 92,615,000); petroleum products (metric tons; 2006) 11,524,000 (9,048,000); natural gas (cu m; 2008) 33,382,500,000 ([2007] 30,580,000,000). **Gross national income** (2008): US$96,240,000,000 (US$6,140 per capita). **Selected balance of payments data.** Receipts from (US$'000,000): tourism (2007) 1,013; remittances (2008) 192; foreign direct investment (FDI; 2006–08 avg.) 10,337; official development assistance (2007) 202. Disbursements for (US$'000,000): tourism (2007) 1,041; remittances (2008) 3,559; FDI (2005–07 avg.) 876.

Foreign trade

Imports (2008; c.i.f.): US$37,889,000,000 (mineral fuels 15.0%; fabricated metal products 12.4%; transportation equipment 9.3%; machinery and apparatus 7.6%; chemical products 3.6%; iron and steel 3.1%). *Major import sources:* Russia 36.3%; China 12.0%; Germany 6.8%; Ukraine 5.6%; US 5.1%. **Exports** (2008; f.o.b.): US$71,183,500,000 (mineral fuels 72.1%; iron and steel 8.8%; nonferrous metals 6.0%, of which refined copper 4.1%). *Major export destinations:* Italy 16.7%; Switzerland 15.8%; China 10.8%; Russia 8.7%; France 7.6%.

Transport and communications

Transport. *Railroads* (2008): route length 13,700 km; passenger-km 14,130,000,000; metric ton-km cargo 215,110,600,000. *Roads* (2008): total length 93,600 km (paved 90%). *Vehicles* (2007): passenger cars 2,183,100; trucks and buses 442,572. *Air transport:* passenger-km (2008) 5,550,000,000; metric ton-km cargo (2007) 85,700,000. **Communications,** in total units (units per 1,000 persons). Telephone landlines (2008): 3,410,000 (220); cellular telephone subscribers (2008): 14,911,000 (961); total Internet users (2008): 2,300,000 (148); broadband Internet subscribers (2008): 661,000 (43).

Education and health

Educational attainment (1999). Population ages 25 and over having: no formal schooling/some primary education 9.1%; primary education 23.1%; secondary/some postsecondary 57.8%; higher 10.0%. **Literacy** (2007): percentage of total population ages 15 and over literate, virtually 100%. **Health** (2008): physicians 58,945 (1 per 266 persons); hospital beds 120,840 (1 per 130 persons); infant mortality rate per 1,000 live births 20.5; undernourished population (2002–04) 900,000 (6% of total population based on the consumption of a minimum daily requirement of 1,950 calories).

Military

Total active duty personnel (November 2008): 49,000 (army 61.2%, navy 6.1%, air force 24.5%, Ministry of Defense staff 8.2%). **Military expenditure as percentage of GDP** (2007): 1.1%; per capita expenditure US$75.

Background

Named for its earliest inhabitants, the Kazakhs, the area came under Mongol rule in the 13th century. The Kazakhs consolidated a nomadic empire in the 15th–16th centuries. Under Russian rule by the mid-19th century, it became part of the Kirgiz Autonomous Republic formed by the Soviets in 1920, and in 1925 its name was changed to the Kazakh Autonomous Soviet Socialist Republic. Kazakhstan obtained its independence in 1991, and during the 1990s it attempted to stabilize its economy.

---

1 metric ton = about 1.1 short tons; 1 kilometer = 0.6 mi (statute); 1 metric ton-km cargo = about 0.68 short ton-mi cargo; c.i.f.: cost, insurance, and freight; f.o.b.: free on board

Recent Developments

As the Central Asian state whose economy was most closely integrated into the world financial system, Kazakhstan in 2009 experienced significant negative effects from the global financial crisis. In addition, Kazakhstan assumed the annual chairmanship of the Organization for Security and Co-operation in Europe in 2010, the first Commonwealth of Independent States member—and the first Asian state—to assume the position. Questions arose, however, about the Kazakh government's stand on Internet freedom (and media freedom in general) and restrictions on freedom of belief, expression, and association.

Internet resource: <www.eng.stat.kz>.

Kenya

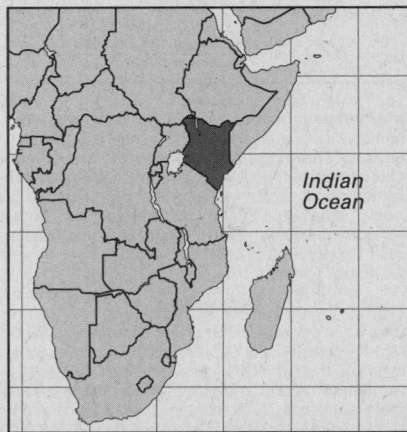

Indian Ocean

Official name: Jamhuri ya Kenya (Swahili); Republic of Kenya (English). **Form of government:** unitary multiparty republic with one legislative house (National Assembly [224]). **Head of state and government:** President Mwai Kibaki (from 2002), assisted by Prime Minister Raila Odinga (from 2008). **Capital:** Nairobi. **Official languages:** Swahili; English. **Official religion:** none. **Monetary unit:** 1 Kenya shilling (K Sh) = 100 cents; valuation (1 Jul 2010) US$1 = K Sh 81.65.

Demography

Area: 224,961 sq mi, 582,646 sq km. **Population** (2009): 39,802,000. **Density** (2009): persons per sq mi 176.9, persons per sq km 68.3. **Urban** (2005): 20.7%. **Sex distribution** (2006): male 48.90%; female 51.10%. **Age breakdown** (2006): under 15, 43.1%; 15–29, 30.2%; 30–44, 15.2%; 45–59, 7.0%; 60–74, 3.5%; 75 and over, 1.0%. **Ethnic composition** (2004): Kikuyu 21%; Luhya 14%; Luo 13%; Kalenjin 11%; Kamba 11%; Gusii 6%; Meru 5%; other 19%. **Religious affiliation** (2006): Protestant/independent Christian 66%; Roman Catholic 23%; Muslim 8%; nonreligious 2%; traditional beliefs 1%. **Major cities** (2006): Nairobi 2,864,700; Mombasa 823,500; Nakuru 260,500; Eldoret 227,000; Kisumu 220,000. **Location:** eastern Africa, bordering Ethiopia, Somalia, the Indian Ocean, Tanzania, Uganda, and Sudan.

Vital statistics

Birth rate per 1,000 population (2006): 39.7 (world avg. 20.3). **Death rate** per 1,000 population (2006): 11.5 (world avg. 8.5). **Total fertility rate** (avg. births per childbearing woman; 2006): 4.91. **Life expectancy** at birth (2006): male 54.3 years; female 54.2 years.

National economy

Budget (2008–09). *Revenue:* K Sh 511,355,-000,000 (tax revenue 85.5%, of which income and profit taxes 39.9%, VAT 24.8%, excise tax 13.7%; nontax revenue 11.0%; grants 3.5%). *Expenditures:* K Sh 621,909,000,000 (current expenditures 74.3%, of which interest payments 8.4%; development expenditures 25.7%). **Production** (metric tons except as noted). *Agriculture and fishing* (2007): sugarcane (2008) 4,991,907, corn (maize) 3,240,000, cassava 850,000, tea (2008) 345,818, pigeon peas 105,000, coffee (2008) 38,705, supplier of cut flowers to EU; livestock (number of live animals) 12,500,000 cattle, 9,300,000 sheep; fisheries production 136,005 (from aquaculture 3%). *Mining and quarrying* (2007): soda ash 386,598; fluorspar 82,000; salt 64,000; tourmaline 8,800 carats; ruby 5,600 carats. *Manufacturing* (value added in US$'000,000; 2006): food products 473; coke oven products (nearly all soda ash) 268; glass and glass products 244. *Energy production (consumption):* electricity (kW-hr; 2008) 5,694,000,000 (5,301,000,000); coal (metric tons; 2006) none (120,000); crude petroleum (barrels; 2006) none (12,800,000); petroleum products (metric tons; 2006) 1,586,000 (3,365,000). **Population economically active** (2006): total 16,944,000; activity rate of total population 46.4% (participation rates: ages 15–64, 82.1%; female 46.5%; unemployed [2008] 40%). **Gross national income** (2008): US$29,541,000,000 (US$770 per capita). **Public debt** (external, outstanding; 2007): US$6,122,-000,000. **Selected balance of payments data.** Receipts from (US$'000,000): tourism (2007) 910; remittances (2008) 1,692; foreign direct investment (FDI; 2005–07 avg.) 267; official development assistance (2007) 1,275. Disbursements for (US$'000,000): tourism (2007) 262; remittances (2008) 16; FDI (2005–07 avg.) 23.

Foreign trade

Imports (2007; c.i.f.): K Sh 605,142,000,000 (crude petroleum 20.9%; machinery and apparatus 16.1%; chemical products 12.8%; motor vehicles 8.5%; food products 6.1%; aircraft 5.6%). *Major import sources:* UAE 14.8%; India 9.4%; China 7.6%; US 7.4%; Japan 6.8%. **Exports** (2007; f.o.b.): K Sh 274,711,000,000 (tea 17.1%; cut flowers 7.7%; wearing apparel and accessories 5.9%; vegetables 5.7%; refined petroleum products 4.0%; coffee 3.8%; soda ash, none). *Major export destinations:* Uganda 12.2%; UK 10.5%; Tanzania 8.1%; Netherlands 8.0%; US 7.0%.

Transport and communications

Transport. *Railroads.* route length 2,778 km; passenger-km 489,000,000; metric ton-km cargo 1,358,000,000. *Roads* (2004): total length 63,265 km (paved 14%). *Vehicles* (2004): passenger cars 307,772; trucks and buses 299,317. *Air transport*

(2008; Kenya Airways and African Express only): passenger-km 8,829,000,000; metric ton-km cargo 238,451,000. **Communications**, in total units (units per 1,000 persons). Telephone landlines (2008): 252,000 (6.5); cellular telephone subscribers (2008): 16,234,000 (419); personal computers (2007): 529,000 (14); total Internet users (2008): 3,360,000 (87); broadband Internet subscribers (2006): 18,000 (0.5).

Education and health

Educational attainment (1998–99). Percentage of population ages 6 and over having: no formal schooling/unknown 20.2%; primary education 59.0%; secondary 19.7%; university 1.1%. **Literacy** (2000): total population ages 16 and over literate 73.6%; males literate 77.7%; females literate 70.2%. **Health** (2006): physicians (2007) 6,271 (1 per 5,886 persons); hospital beds 51,481 (1 per 714 persons); infant mortality rate per 1,000 live births 59.0; undernourished population (2002–04) 9,900,000 (31% of total population based on the consumption of a minimum daily requirement of 1,840 calories).

Military

Total active duty personnel (November 2008): 24,120 (army 82.9%, navy 6.7%, air force 10.4%). **Military expenditure as percentage of GDP** (2008): 2.1%; per capita expenditure US$17.

Background

The coastal region of East Africa was dominated by Arabs until it was seized by the Portuguese in the 16th century. The Masai people held sway in the north and moved into central Kenya in the 18th century, while the Kikuyu expanded from their home region in south-central Kenya. The interior was explored by European missionaries in the 19th century. After the British took control, Kenya was established as a British protectorate (1890) and a crown colony (1920). The Mau Mau rebellion of the 1950s was directed against European colonialism. In 1963 the country became fully independent, and a year later a republican government under Jomo Kenyatta was elected. In 1992 Kenyan Pres. Daniel arap Moi allowed the country's first multiparty elections in three decades, though the balloting was marred by violence and fraud. Political turmoil occurred over the following years.

Recent Developments

The global recession impeded export growth and reduced tourism receipts, remittances, and private capital flows in Kenya in 2009. GDP growth dropped from 6% in 2004–07 to 2.5% in 2009. Crop production declined steeply as Kenya suffered from the worst drought to hit East Africa since 2000; production of corn (maize), the country's staple food crop, dropped by nearly 28%. The UN World Food Programme estimated that nearly four million Kenyans—some 10% of the population—required emergency assistance, which was slow to materialize. In the northern pastoral districts, massive cattle deaths caused widespread hunger and spawned interethnic hostilities. Throughout the drought-affected areas, rising prices of food and water bred antigovernment sentiments, which led many observers to fear the possible resurgence of armed militias.

Internet resource: <www.knbs.or.ke>.

Kiribati

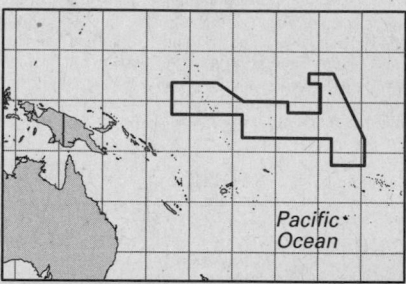

Pacific Ocean

Official name: Republic of Kiribati. **Form of government:** unitary republic with one legislative house (House of Assembly [46]). **Head of state and government:** President Anote Tong (from 2003). **Capital:** Bairiki (executive); Ambo (legislative); Betio (judicial). **Official language:** English. **Official religion:** none. **Monetary unit:** 1 Australian dollar ($A) = 100 cents; valuation (1 Jul 2010) US$1 = $A 1.19.

Demography

Area: 312.9 sq mi, 810.5 sq km. **Population** (2009): 99,000. **Density** (2009): persons per sq mi 353.6, persons per sq km 136.4. **Urban** (2005): 47.5%. **Sex distribution** (2007): male 49.64%; female 50.36%. **Age breakdown** (2007): under 15, 38.2%; 15–29, 27.7%; 30–44, 18.0%; 45–59, 10.7%; 60–74, 4.5%; 75 and over, 0.9%. **Ethnic composition** (2000): Micronesian 98.8%; Polynesian 0.7%; European 0.2%; other 0.3%. **Religious affiliation** (2005): Roman Catholic 55.3%; Kiribati Protestant (Congregational) 35.7%; Mormon 3.1%; Baha'i 2.2%; other/nonreligious 3.7%. **Major villages** (2005): Betio 12,509; Bikenibeu 6,170; Teaoraereke 3,939. **Location:** Oceania, islands in the western Pacific Ocean, south of the Hawaiian Islands (US).

Vital statistics

Birth rate per 1,000 population (2007): 30.5 (world avg. 20.3). **Death rate** per 1,000 population (2007): 8.1 (world avg. 8.5). **Total fertility rate** (avg. births per childbearing woman; 2007): 4.12. **Life expectancy** at birth (2007): male 59.4 years; female 65.7 years.

National economy

Budget (2008). *Revenue:* $A 161,700,000 (nontax revenue 24.1%, of which fishing license fees 19.9%; tax revenue 18.4%; grants 57.5%). *Expenditures:* $A 183,000,000 (development expenditures 50.9%; current expenditures 49.1%). **Public debt** (external, outstanding; 2008): US$10,100,000.

1 metric ton = about 1.1 short tons;   1 kilometer = 0.6 mi (statute);   1 metric ton-km cargo = about 0.68 short ton-mi cargo;   c.i.f.: cost, insurance, and freight;   f.o.b.: free on board

Production (metric tons except as noted). *Agriculture and fishing* (2007): coconuts 110,000, bananas 5,800, taro 2,200; livestock (number of live animals) 12,600 pigs, 480,000 chickens; fisheries production 21,603 (from aquaculture, negligible); aquatic plants (all seaweed) production 1,112 (from aquaculture 100%). *Mining and quarrying*: small amounts of salt. *Manufacturing* (2008): copra 9,135; processed fish, wearing apparel, and handicrafts are also made. *Energy production (consumption)*: electricity (kW-hr; 2006) 15,000,000 (15,000,000); petroleum products (metric tons; 2006) none (10,000). **Selected balance of payments data.** Receipts from (US$'000,000): tourism (2001) 3.2; remittances (2008) 9; foreign direct investment (2005–07 avg.) 8; official development assistance (2007) 27. Disbursements for (US$'000,000): tourism (1999) 2.0. **Population economically active** (2005): total 36,969; activity rate of total population 38.8% (participation rates: ages 16 and over, 63.4%; female 45.9%; unemployed 6.1%). **Gross national income** (2008): US$193,000,000 (US$2,000 per capita).

Foreign trade

Imports (2005): $A 96,900,000 (food products 29.6%, of which rice 10.7%, meat 6.4%; refined petroleum products 16.8%; machinery and apparatus 14.6%, of which generators 6.2%; motor vehicles 5.7%). *Major import sources* (2007): Fiji 35.1%; Australia 33.5%; Japan 6.3%; New Zealand 5.9%; China 4.3%. **Exports** (2007): $A 11,655,000 (domestic exports 81.0%, of which crude coconut oil 45.7%, copra and copra cake 14.4%, fish 10.7%, seaweed 1.9%; reexports 19.0%). *Major export destinations* (2005): Australia 22%; Fiji 17%; other Asia (probably Taiwan) 14%; Hong Kong 8%.

Transport and communications

Transport. *Roads* (2000): total length 670 km. *Vehicles* (2004; registered vehicles in South Tarawa only): passenger cars 610; trucks and buses 808. *Air transport*: domestic air service only from 2004. **Communications**, in total units (units per 1,000 persons). Telephone landlines (2008): 4,000 (41);* cellular telephone subscribers (2008): 1,000 (10); personal computers (2005): 1,000 (11); total Internet users (2008): 2,000 (21).

Education and health

Educational attainment (2005). Percentage of population ages 5 and over having: no schooling/unknown 9.2%; primary education 40.3%; secondary 47.6%; higher 2.9%. **Literacy** (2001): population ages 15 and over literate 94.0%; males literate 93.0%; females literate 95.0%. **Health:** physicians (2006) 30 (1 per 3,120 persons); hospital beds (2005) 140 (1 per 681 persons); infant mortality rate per 1,000 live births (2007) 45.9; undernourished population (2002–04) 5,000 (7% of total population based on the consumption of a minimum daily requirement of 1,810 calories).

Military

Total active duty personnel (November 2008): none; defense assistance is provided by Australia and New Zealand.

Background

The islands were settled by Austronesian-speaking peoples before the 1st century AD. In 1765 the British discovered the island of Nikunau; the first permanent European settlers arrived in 1837. In 1916 the Gilbert and Ellice islands and Banaba became a crown colony of Britain; they were later joined by the Phoenix and Line islands. The Ellice Islands declared independence (as Tuvalu) in 1978, and in 1979 the remaining islands became the nation of Kiribati.

Recent Developments

Predictions by the Asian Development Bank of economic deterioration in Kiribati proved correct in 2009. The worsening situation led to large drawdowns from the Revenue Equalization Reserve Fund to finance budget deficits. The fund was already shrinking; its investments in offshore financial markets posted negative returns, and this led to warnings that government expenditures would need to be cut to ensure that the fund could continue to finance development in Kiribati.

Internet resource: <www.kiribatitourism.gov.ki>.

Korea, North

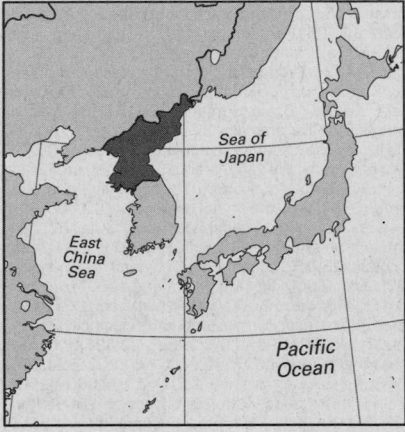

Official name: Choson Minjujuui In'min Konghwaguk (Democratic People's Republic of Korea). **Form of government:** unitary single-party republic with one legislative house (Supreme People's Assembly [687]). **Head of state and government:** Supreme Leader and Chairman of the National Defense Commission Kim Jong II (from 1998). **Capital:** P'yongyang. **Official language:** Korean. **Official religion:** none. **Monetary unit:** 1 (new) North Korean won (W) = 100 chon; valuation (1 Jul 2010) US$1 = 135.00 (new) won (the currency was revalued on 1 Dec 2009; as of this date, 100 (old) North Korean won = 1 (new) North Korean won. The approximate value of the won on the black market in February 2009 was about US$1 = 3,500 [old] won.

Demography

Area: 47,399 sq mi, 122,762 sq km. **Population** (2009): 24,162,000. **Density** (2009): persons per sq mi 509.8, persons per sq km 196.8. **Urban** (2005): 61.6%. **Sex distribution** (2008): male 48.73%; female 51.27%. **Age breakdown** (2007): under 15, 22.1%; 15–29, 23.6%; 30–44, 25.6%; 45–59, 15.5%; 60–74, 11.0%; 75–84, 2.0%; 85 and over, 0.2%. **Ethnic composition** (1999): Korean 99.8%; Chinese 0.2%. **Religious affiliation** (2005): mostly nonreligious/atheist; autonomous religious activities are almost nonexistent. **Major urban agglomerations** (2007): P'yongyang 3,300,000; Namp'o 1,127,000; Hamhung 773,000; Ch'ongjin (1993) 582,480; Kaesong (1993) 334,433. **Location:** eastern Asia, bordering China, Russia, the Sea of Japan (East Sea), the Republic of Korea, and the Yellow Sea.

Vital statistics

Birth rate per 1,000 population (2007): 15.5 (world avg. 20.3). **Death rate** per 1,000 population (2007): 10.4 (world avg. 8.5). **Total fertility rate** (avg. births per childbearing woman; 2007): 1.99. **Life expectancy** at birth (2007): male 60.6 years; female 65.8 years.

National economy

Budget (1999). *Revenue:* 19,801,000,000 [old] won (turnover tax and profits from state enterprises). *Expenditures:* 20,018,200,000 [old] won (1994; national economy 67.8%; social and cultural affairs 19.0%; defense 11.6%). **Population economically active** (2006): total 12,305,000; activity rate of total population 51.9% (participation rates: ages 15–64, 53.7%; female 44.0%). **Production** (metric tons except as noted). *Agriculture and fishing* (2007): rice 2,165,000, potatoes 1,900,000, corn (maize) 1,645,000; livestock (number of live animals) 3,300,000 pigs, 2,760,000 goats, 576,000 cattle; fisheries production 268,700 (from aquaculture 24%); aquatic plants production 444,300 (from aquaculture 100%). *Mining and quarrying* (2007): iron ore (metal content) 1,400,000; magnesite 1,000,000; phosphate rock 300,000; zinc (metal content) 70,000; sulfur 42,000; lead (metal content) 13,000; copper (metal content) 12,000; silver 20; gold 2,000 kg. *Manufacturing* (2007): cement 6,415,000; coke 2,000,000; crude steel 1,279,000. *Energy production (consumption):* electricity (kW-hr; 2007) 25,460,000,000 ([2006] 22,436,000,000); coal (metric tons; 2007) 25,060,000 ([2006] 24,860,-000); lignite (metric tons; 2007) 7,000,000 ([2006] 7,946,000); crude petroleum (barrels; 2006) none (2,690,000); petroleum products (metric tons; 2006) 352,000 (701,000). **Public debt** (external, outstanding; 2001): US$12,500,000,000. **Gross national income** (2008): US$24,815,000,000 (US$1,033 per capita). **Selected balance of payments data.** Receipts from (US$'000,000): foreign direct disinvestment (2005–07 avg.) −1; official development assistance (2007) 98.

Foreign trade

Imports (2005): US$2,718,472,000 ([2002; data for commodities exclude trade with South Korea (US$1,525,400,000)] food products, beverages, and other agricultural products 19.3%; mineral fuels and lubricants 15.5%; machinery and apparatus 15.4%; textiles and wearing apparel 10.4%). *Major import sources:* China 39.8%; South Korea 26.3%; Russia

8.2%; Thailand 7.6%; Singapore 2.7%. **Exports** (2005): US$1,338,281,000 ([2002; data for commodities exclude trade with South Korea (US$735,000,000)] live animals and agricultural products 39.3%; textiles and wearing apparel 16.7%; machinery and apparatus 11.6%; mineral fuels and lubricants 9.5%). *Major export destinations:* China 37.3%; South Korea 25.4%; Japan 9.8%; Thailand 9.3%; Russia 0.6%.

Transport and communications

Transport. *Railroads* (2007): length 5,242 km. *Roads* (2007): total length 16,033 mi, 25,802 km (paved [2006] 3%). *Vehicles* (1990): passenger cars 248,000. *Air transport* (2004): passenger-km 39,000,000; metric ton-km cargo (including the weight of mail and passengers) 6,000,000. **Communications,** in total units (units per 1,000 persons). Telephone landlines (2008): 1,180,000 (49).

Education and health

Educational attainment (1987–88). Percentage of population ages 16 and over having attended or graduated from postsecondary-level school: 13.7%. **Literacy** (1997): percentage of total population ages 15 and over literate, 95%. **Health:** physicians (2003) 74,597 (1 per 299 persons); infant mortality rate per 1,000 live births (2007) 53.8; undernourished population (2002–04) 7,600,000 (33% of total population based on the consumption of a minimum daily requirement of 1,900 calories).

Military

Total active duty personnel (November 2008): 1,106,000 (army 85.9%, navy 4.2%, air force 9.9%); reserve 4,700,000. **Military expenditure as percentage of GNI** (2004): 8.1%; per capita expenditure US$80.

Background

According to tradition, the ancient kingdom of Choson was established in the northern part of the Korean peninsula, probably by peoples from northern China, in the 3rd millennium BC and was conquered by China in 108 BC. The kingdom was ruled by the Yi dynasty from AD 1392 to 1910. That year Korea was formally annexed by Japan. It was freed from Japanese control in 1945, at which time the USSR occupied the area north of latitude 38° N and the US occupied the area south of it. The Democratic People's Republic of Korea was established as a communist state in 1948. North Korea launched an invasion of South Korea in 1950, initiating the Korean War, which ended with an armistice in 1953. Under Kim Il-sung, North Korea became one of the most harshly regimented societies in the world, with a state-owned economy that failed to produce adequate food. In the late 1990s, under Kim Il-sung's successor, Kim Jong Il, the country endured a serious famine; as many as one million Koreans may have died. In October 2006 North Korea conducted an underground nuclear test.

Recent Developments

North Korea's leader, the reclusive Kim Jong Il, who had recovered from a suspected stroke, made a

1 metric ton = about 1.1 short tons;   1 kilometer = 0.6 mi (statute);   1 metric ton-km cargo = about 0.68 short ton-mi cargo;   c.i.f.: cost, insurance, and freight;   f.o.b.: free on board

record 150-plus public appearances in 2009. He celebrated his renewed vigor with a long-range missile test and satellite launch in April; the effort failed. The following month North Korea appeared to conduct its second underground nuclear test, which seemed to have been more successful than its first test. Most analysts believed, however, that it would be at least a decade before the country could marry its missile and nuclear programs. North Korea also began rebuilding a nuclear reactor that it had partially dismantled as part of a 2005 nuclear accord and resumed plutonium production. In December a UN envoy visited the country bearing a letter from US Pres. Barack Obama in an attempt to revive the moribund nuclear talks, but North Korea appeared to be in no hurry to return to the negotiating table. Days later Thai authorities interdicted a 35-ton North Korean arms shipment believed to have been bound for the Middle East in contravention of UN Security Council resolutions.

Internet resource: <www.kcna.co.jp/index-e.htm>.

Korea, South

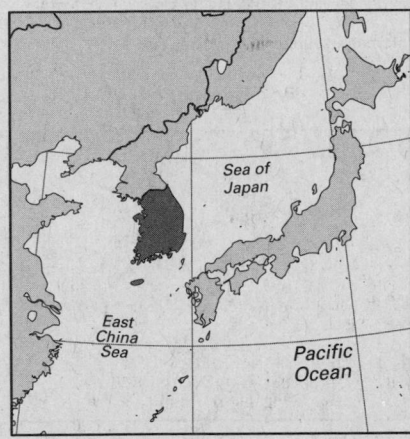

Official name: Taehan Min'guk (Republic of Korea). **Form of government:** unitary multiparty republic with one legislative house (National Assembly [299]). **Head of state and government:** President Lee Myung Bak (from 2008), assisted by Prime Minister Chung Un Chan (from 2009). **Capital:** Seoul. **Official language:** Korean. **Official religion:** none. **Monetary unit:** 1 South Korean won (W) = 100 chon; valuation (1 Jul 2010) US$1 = W 1,230.20.

Demography

Area: 38,486 sq mi, 99,678 sq km. **Population** (2009): 48,333,000. **Density** (2009): persons per sq mi 1,255.9, persons per sq km 484.9. **Urban** (2008): 81.0%. **Sex distribution** (2008): male 50.23%; female 49.77%. **Age breakdown** (2005): under 15, 18.6%; 15–29, 22.5%; 30–44, 26.0%; 45–59, 19.2%; 60 74, 10.7%; 75–04, 2.5%, 85 and over, 0.5%. **Ethnic composition** (2000): Korean 97.7%; Japanese 2.0%; US white 0.1%; Han Chinese 0.1%; other 0.1%. **Religious affiliation** (2005): Christian 43%, of which Protestant 17%, independent Christian 16%, Roman Catholic 9%; traditional beliefs 15%; Buddhist 14%; New Religionist 14%; Confucianist 10%; other 4%. **Major cities** (2008): Seoul 10,456,034; Pusan 3,596,076; Inch'on 2,741,217; Taegu 2,512,601; Taejon 1,494,951. **Location:** eastern Asia, bordering the Democratic People's Republic of Korea, the Sea of Japan (East Sea), and the Yellow Sea.

Vital statistics

Birth rate per 1,000 population (2008): 9.4 (world avg. 20.3). **Death rate** per 1,000 population (2008): 5.0 (world avg. 8.5). **Total fertility rate** (avg. births per childbearing woman; 2008): 1.19. **Life expectancy** at birth (2007): male 76.1 years; female 82.7 years.

National economy

Budget (2006). *Revenue:* W 209,574,000,000,000 (current revenue 99.3%, of which tax revenue 78.9%, nontax revenue 20.4%; capital revenue 0.7%). *Expenditures:* W 205,928,000,000,000 (current expenditures 84.3%, of which defense 11.4%; capital expenditures 15.7%). **Public debt** (June 2009): US$380,116,000,000. **Production** (metric tons except as noted). *Agriculture and fishing* (2007): rice 5,959,500, cabbages 3,000,000, tangerines, mandarins, satsumas 615,000, persimmons 345,000, garlic 325,000; livestock (number of live animals; 2008) 9,087,000 pigs, 2,876,000 cattle, 119,784,000 chickens; fisheries production 2,464,328 (from aquaculture 25%); aquatic plants production 811,142 (from aquaculture 98%). *Mining and quarrying* (2007): zinc (metal content) 674,400; feldspar 398,513; iron ore (metal content) 163,000; silver (metal content) 1,393,935 kg. *Manufacturing* (value added in US$'000,000; 2006): televisions, radios, telecommunications equipment, and electronic parts 70,085; transportation equipment 52,349, of which automobiles 20,987, automobile parts 16,175, ships and boats 12,771; machinery and apparatus 30,704; chemical products 27,076; iron and steel 20,064; food products 19,928; fabricated metal products 19,172; textiles and wearing apparel 16,913; refined petroleum products 12,161. *Energy production (consumption):* electricity (kW-hr; 2008–09) 425,174,000,000 ([2008] 385,100,000,000); coal (metric tons; 2008–09) 2,604,000 ([2006] 81,003,000); lignite (metric tons; 2006) none (3,706,000); crude petroleum (barrels; 2006) 329,850 (868,150,000); petroleum products (metric tons; 2006) 94,555,000 (55,248,000); natural gas (cu m; 2007) 640,000,-000 (37,000,000,000). **Gross national income** (2008): US$1,046,285,000,000 (US$21,530 per capita). **Population economically active** (2009): total 24,525,000; activity rate 50.7% (participation rates: ages 15 and older 61.1%; female 41.3%; unemployed [September 2008–August 2009] 3.3%. **Selected balance of payments data.** Receipts from (US$'000,000): tourism (2007) 5,797; remittances (2008) 3,062; foreign direct investment (FDI; 2005–07 avg.) 3,641. Disbursements for (US$'000,000): tourism (2007) 20,890; remittances (2008) 3,472; FDI (2005–07 avg.) 7,083.

Foreign trade

Imports (2008; c.i.f.): US$435,274,737,000 (mineral fuels 32.7%, of which crude petroleum 24.1%, natural gas 5.7%; machinery and apparatus 23.5%, of which electrical machinery 11.2%; chemical products 8.4%; iron and steel 7.7%). *Major import sources:* China 17.7%; Japan 14.0%; US 8.8%; Saudi Arabia 7.8%; UAE 4.4%. **Exports** (2008; f.o.b.): US$422,007,328,000 (machinery and apparatus 34.0%, of which telecommunications equipment 11.7%, electrical equipment 11.7%; transportation equipment 21.4%; chemical products 10.1%; crude petroleum and refined petroleum products 9.1%; professional and scientific equipment 6.0%). *Major export destinations:* China 21.7%; US 11.0%; Japan 6.8%; Hong Kong 4.9%; Singapore 3.9%.

Transport and communications

Transport. *Railroads* (2005): length (2008) 3,381 km; passenger-km 31,004,200,000; metric ton-km cargo 9,336,000,000. *Roads* (2008): total length 103,029 km (paved 78%). *Vehicles* (2006): passenger cars 11,607,000; trucks and buses 4,239,200. *Air transport* (2008): passenger-km 82,236,000,000; metric ton-km cargo 8,786,809,000. **Communications,** in total units (units per 1,000 persons). Telephone landlines (2008): 21,325,000 (443); cellular telephone subscribers (2008): 45,607,000 (947); personal computers (2007): 27,736,000 (578); total Internet users (2008): 34,476,000 (778); broadband Internet subscribers (2008): 15,475,000 (321).

Education and health

Educational attainment (2008). Percentage of population ages 15 and older having: no formal schooling through lower secondary education 31.7%; upper secondary/higher vocational 39.2%; college 9.1%; university 20.0%. **Literacy** (2002): total population ages 15 and over literate 97.9%; males literate 99.2%; females literate 96.6%. **Health** (2008): physicians 95,013 (1 per 507 persons); hospital beds (2006) 417,387 (1 per 114 persons); infant mortality rate per 1,000 live births 3.4; undernourished population (2002–04) less than 2.5% of total population.

Military

Total active duty personnel (November 2008): 692,000 (army 80.9%, navy 9.8%, air force 9.3%); US military forces (January 2009): 24,655. **Military expenditure as percentage of GDP** (2008): 4.0%; per capita expenditure US$594.

Background

Civilization in the Korean peninsula dates to the 3rd millennium BC. The Republic of Korea was established in AD 1948 in the southern portion of the Korean peninsula. In 1950 North Korean troops invaded South Korea, precipitating the Korean War. UN forces sided with South Korea, while Chinese troops backed North Korea in the war, which ended with an armistice in 1953. The devastated country was rebuilt with US aid, and South Korea prospered in the postwar era, developing a strong export-oriented economy. It experienced an economic downturn in the mid-1990s that affected many Asian economies. Efforts at reconciliation between North and South

Korea, including the first-ever summit between their leaders (2000) and reunions of families from both countries, were accompanied by periods of continuing tension.

Recent Developments

By the end of 2009, South Korea had come through the global economic downturn in surprisingly good shape. After three straight quarters of year-on-year decline, the South Korean economy started to come back to life. Unemployment ended the year at a modest 3.5%. The Hyundai-Kia Automotive Group led the way in economic growth, with the partners expanding their global market share from 6.5% to 7.8% in the first nine months of 2009, while by February 2010 the group held a record-setting 8.4% of the US market share. Pres. Lee Myung-Bak continued to improve relations with the US, exchanging state visits with US Pres. Barack Obama in 2009, and he controversially decided to redeploy several hundred troops and reconstruction personnel to Afghanistan. Relations with North Korea, however, remained frosty, and a military engagement was not ruled out in March 2010 when a South Korean navy ship sank near their maritime border, leaving 46 sailors and a rescue diver dead.

Internet resource: <www.nso.go.kr>.

Kosovo

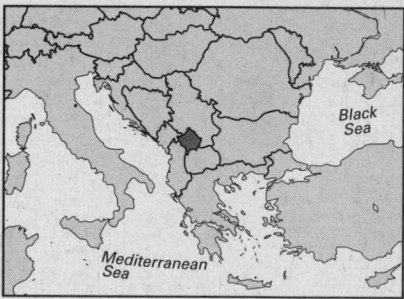

Official name: Republika e Kosovës (Albanian); Republika Kosovo (Serbian) (Republic of Kosovo). **Form of government:** multiparty transitional republic with one legislative house (Assembly of Kosovo [120]). **International authority:** UN Interim Administrator Lamberto Zannier (from 2008), assisted by EU Special Representative Pieter Feith (from 2008). **Head of state:** President Fatmir Sejdiu (from 2006). **Head of government:** Prime Minister Hashim Thaçi (from 2008). **Capital:** Pristina. **Official languages:** Albanian; Serbian. **Official religion:** none. **Monetary unit:** 1 euro (€) = 100 cents; valuation (1 Jul 2010) US$1 = €0.80 (Kosovo uses the euro as its official currency, even though it is not a member of the EU).

Demography

Area: 4,212 sq mi, 10,908 sq km. **Population** (2009): 1,805,000. **Density** (2009): persons per sq mi 428.5, persons per sq km 165.5. **Urban** (2006):

---

1 metric ton = about 1.1 short tons;　1 kilometer = 0.6 mi (statute);　1 metric ton-km cargo = about 0.68 short ton-mi cargo;　c.i.f.: cost, insurance, and freight;　f.o.b.: free on board

37%. **Sex distribution** (2007): male 50.52%; female 49.48%. **Age breakdown** (2003): under 15, 32.2%; 15–59, 58.7%; 60 and over, 9.1%. **Ethnic composition** (2008): Albanian 92.0%; Serb 5.3%; other 2.7%. **Religious affiliation** (2006): Muslim (including nominal population) 91.0%; Orthodox 5.5%; Roman Catholic 3.0%; Protestant 0.5%. **Major cities** (2003): Pristina 165,844; Prizren 107,614; Ferizaj 71,758; Mitrovicë (Mitrovica) 68,929; Gjakovë 68,645. **Location**: southeastern Europe, bordering Serbia, Macedonia, Albania, and Montenegro.

Vital statistics

Birth rate per 1,000 population (2008): 16.0 (world avg. 20.3); within marriage 59.8%. **Death rate** per 1,000 population (2008): 3.2 (world avg. 8.5). **Total fertility rate** (avg. births per childbearing woman; 2003): 3.0. **Life expectancy** at birth (2004; Albanian population only): male 69.8 years; female 71.4 years.

National economy

Budget (2007–08). *Revenue:* €2,148,400,000 (tax revenue 79.7%, of which border taxes [including customs duties and VAT] 59.8%; domestic taxes [mostly income and corporate taxes] 19.9%; nontax revenue 20.3%). *Expenditures:* €1,523,000,000 (current expenditures 81.1%; capital expenditures 18.9%). **Production** (metric tons except as noted). *Agriculture and fishing* (2006): wheat 239,464, hay 184,677, corn (maize) 138,248; livestock (number of live animals) 381,995 cattle, 100,814 sheep, 2,337,086 chickens. *Manufacturing* (2006): cement, bricks, and tiles for reconstruction of housing; food products; beverages. *Energy production (consumption):* electricity (kW-hr; 2008) 4,506,000,000 (2,941,000,000); lignite (metric tons; 2008) 7,842,000 (n.a.). **Gross national income** (2007): US$3,780,000,000 (US$2,117 per capita). **Population economically active** (2007): total 633,000; activity rate of total population 30% (participation rates: ages 15–64, 47%; female 28%; unofficially unemployed [2007] 40%). **Selected balance of payments data.** Receipts from (US$'000,000): tourism (2008) 42; remittances (2008) 785; foreign direct investment (FDI; 2005–07 avg.) 322. Disbursements for (US$'000,000): tourism (2008) 82; remittances (2006) 126; FDI (2006–08 avg.) 15.

Foreign trade

Imports (2008; c.i.f.): €1,927,900,000 (food products and live animals 24.6%; mineral fuels 20.1%; machinery and apparatus 12.2%; base metals 9.3%; chemical products 7.2%; transportation equipment 6.7%). *Major import sources:* Macedonia 18.0%; Serbia 11.1%; Germany 10.2%; Turkey 6.6%; China 6.3%. **Exports** (2008; f.o.b.): €195,900,000 (iron and steel [all forms] 63.3%; food products 11.0%; mineral fuels 9.1%). *Major export destinations:* Belgium 14.3%; Italy 13.0%; India 12.0%; Albania 10.8%; Macedonia 9.9%.

Transport and communications

Transport. *Railroads* (2007): route length 430 km. *Roads* (2008): total length 1,924 km (paved 87%). *Vehicles* (2006): passenger cars 146,744; trucks and buses 20,000. *Air transport* (2007; Pristina airport only). passenger arrivals 483,330; passenger departures 506,962. **Communications**, in total units (units per

1,000 persons). Telephone landlines (2006): 106,000 (60); cellular telephone subscribers (2007): 562,000 (315); total Internet users (2006): 50,000 (28); broadband Internet subscribers (2005): 4,700 (2.3).

Education and health

Educational attainment (2003). Percentage of population ages 25–49 having: no formal schooling 3.5%; incomplete/complete primary 46.0%; incomplete/ complete secondary 45.0%; higher 5.5%. **Literacy** (2004): total population ages 15 and over literate 94.1%; males literate 97.3%; females literate 91.3%. **Health:** physicians (2006) 1,534 (1 per 1,368 persons); hospital beds (2005) 5,308 (1 per 387 persons); infant mortality rate per 1,000 live births (2008) 9.7.

Military

Total active duty personnel (February 2010): NATO-led Kosovo Force 10,200.

Background

The Kingdom of the Serbs, Croats, and Slovenes was created after the collapse of Austria-Hungary at the end of World War I. The country signed treaties with Czechoslovakia and Romania in 1920–21, marking the beginning of the Little Entente. In 1929 an absolute monarchy was established, the country's name was changed to Yugoslavia, and it was divided into regions without regard to ethnic boundaries. Axis powers invaded Yugoslavia in 1941, and German, Italian, Hungarian, and Bulgarian troops occupied it for the rest of World War II. In 1945 the Socialist Federal Republic of Yugoslavia was established; it included the republics of Bosnia and Herzegovina, Croatia, Macedonia, Montenegro, Serbia, and Slovenia. Its independent form of communism under Josip Broz Tito's leadership provoked the USSR. Internal ethnic tensions flared up in the 1980s, causing the country's ultimate collapse. In 1991–92 independence was declared by Croatia, Slovenia, Macedonia, and Bosnia and Herzegovina; the new Federal Republic of Yugoslavia (containing roughly 45% of the population and 40% of the area of its predecessor) was proclaimed by Serbia and Montenegro. Still fueled by long-standing ethnic tensions, hostilities continued into the 1990s. Despite the approval of the Dayton Peace Agreement (1995), sporadic fighting continued and was followed in 1998–99 by Serbian repression and expulsion of ethnic populations in the province of Kosovo. In September–October 2000, the battered nation of Yugoslavia ended the autocratic rule of Pres. Slobodan Milosevic. In April 2001 he was arrested and in June extradited to The Hague to stand trial for war crimes, genocide, and crimes against humanity committed during the fighting in Kosovo. In February 2003 both houses of the Yugoslav federal legislature voted to accept a new state charter and change the name of the country from Yugoslavia to Serbia and Montenegro. Henceforth, defense, international political and economic relations, and human rights matters would be handled centrally, while all other functions would be run from the republican capitals, Belgrade and Podgorica, respectively. The move was seen as an acknowledgment that Serbia and Montenegro had little in common, and a provision was included for both states to vote on independence after three years; Serbia declared its independence in June 2006, shortly after Montenegro severed its federal union with Serbia. From 1999 an autonomous region administered by the UN, Kosovo declared its independence from Serbia on 17 Feb 2008. That December the UN transferred most of its powers of oversight to the EU.

Recent Developments

By mid-2010, 69 countries, including the US and most European countries, had recognized Kosovo's independence, and in July the International Court of Justice ruled that Kosovo's declaration of independence had been legal. Remittances from Kosovo's diaspora fell 8.0% in 2009; these sums constituted 14.1% of Kosovo's GDP, 2.7% more than exports. Unemployment remained the highest in Europe, at 45.0% in 2009. The IMF forecast GDP growth of 3.8% for 2009, down from 5.4% in 2008.

Internet resource: <www.ks-gov.net/ESK>.

Kuwait

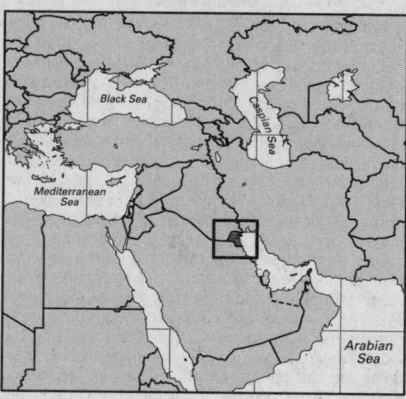

Official name: Dawlat al-Kuwayt (State of Kuwait). Form of government: constitutional monarchy with one legislative house (National Assembly [50]). Head of state and government: Emir Sheikh Sabah al-Ahmad al-Jabir al-Sabah (from 2006), assisted by Prime Minister Sheikh Nasir al-Muhammad al-Ahmad al-Jabir al-Sabah (from 2006). Capital: Kuwait (city). Official language: Arabic. Official religion: Islam. Monetary unit: 1 Kuwaiti dinar (KD) = 1,000 fils; valuation (1 Jul 2010) US$1 = KD 0.29.

Demography

Area: 6,880 sq mi, 17,818 sq km. Population (2009): 3,442,000. Density (2009): persons per sq mi 500.3, persons per sq km 193.2. Urban (2005): 98.3%. Sex distribution (2007): male 59.34%; female 40.66%. Age breakdown (2005): under 15, 24.3%; 15–29, 26.8%; 30–44, 34.2%; 45–59, 11.6%; 60–74, 2.7%; 75–84, 0.3%; 85 and over, 0.1%. Ethnic composition (2005): Arab 57%, of which Kuwaiti 35%; Bedouin 4%; non-Arab (primarily Asian) 39%. Religious affiliation (2005): Muslim 74%, of

which Sunni 59%, Shi'i 15%; Christian 13%, of which Roman Catholic 9%; Hindu 10%; Buddhist 3%. Major cities (2005): Qalib al-Shuyukh 179,264; Al-Salimiyah 145,328; Hawalli 106,992; Kuwait (city) 32,403 (urban agglomeration [2007] 2,063,000). Location: the Middle East, bordering Iraq, the Persian Gulf, and Saudi Arabia.

Vital statistics

Birth rate per 1,000 population (2008): 21.9 (world avg. 20.3). Death rate per 1,000 population (2008): 2.3 (world avg. 8.5). Total fertility rate (avg. births per childbearing woman; 2008): 2.81. Life expectancy at birth (2008): male 76.4 years; female 78.7 years.

National economy

Budget (2006–07). Revenue: KD 15,509,300,000 (oil revenue 93.6%; tax revenue 1.9%). Expenditures: KD 12,568,700,000 (social security and welfare 29.1%; general public administration 15.8%; oil and electricity 13.4%; defense 10.3%; education 10.1%; health 5.3%). Public debt (external, outstanding; 2008): US$7,719,000,000. Gross national income (2007): US$125,016,000,000 (US$38,015 per capita). Production (metric tons except as noted). Agriculture and fishing (2007): tomatoes 55,500, cucumbers and gherkins 35,000, potatoes 23,500, dates 14,500; livestock (number of live animals) 900,000 sheep, 160,000 goats, 28,000 cattle, 5,000 camels; fisheries production 4,721 (from aquaculture 7%). Mining and quarrying (2007): sulfur 660,000; lime 50,000. Manufacturing (value added in KD '000,000; 2006): refined petroleum products 829; basic chemical products 230; bricks, cement, and tiles 98. Energy production (consumption): electricity (kW-hr; 2006) 47,607,000,000 (47,607,000,000); crude petroleum (barrels; 2008) 979,300,000 ([2006] 331,600,000); petroleum products (metric tons; 2006) 38,505,000 (12,365,000); natural gas (cu m; 2006) 14,064,000,000 (14,064,000,000). Population economically active (2007): total 2,092,509, of which Kuwaiti 15.5%, non-Kuwaiti 84.5%; activity rate of total population 61.6% (participation rates: ages 15–64 [2005] 70.8%; female [2005] 25.2%; unemployed [2006; Kuwaiti nationals only] 4.0%). Selected balance of payments data. Receipts from (US$'000,000): tourism (2008) 256; foreign direct investment (FDI; 2005–07 avg.) 160. Disbursements for (US$'000,000): tourism (2008) 7,571; remittances (2008) 5,558; FDI (2005–07 avg.) 9,184.

Foreign trade

Imports (2007; c.i.f.): KD 5,106,000,000 (industrial requirements 29.1%; machinery and capital equipment 21.4%; durable consumer goods 10.7%; food products and beverages 10.2%). Major import sources: Germany 11.5%; US 10.6%; China 10.0%; Japan 8.0%; Italy 6.4%. Exports (2007; f.o.b.): KD 18,099,000,000 (crude petroleum 61.5%; refined petroleum products 29.7%; liquefied petroleum gas 3.1%; ethylene products 2.2%). Major export destinations (2008): Japan 21%; South Korea 15%; US 10%; Singapore 9%; China 7%.

---

1 metric ton = about 1.1 short tons;   1 kilometer = 0.6 mi (statute);   1 metric ton-km cargo = about 0.68 short ton-mi cargo;   c.i.f.: cost, insurance, and freight;   f.o.b.: free on board

Transport and communications

Transport. *Railroads:* none. *Roads* (2004): total length 5,749 km (paved 85%). *Vehicles* (2004): passenger cars 858,055; trucks and buses 180,940. *Air transport* (2008; Kuwait Airways only): passenger-km 7,447,000,000; metric ton-km cargo 280,346,000. **Communications,** in total units (units per 1,000 persons). Telephone landlines (2008): 541,000 (158); cellular telephone subscribers (2008): 2,907,000 (850); personal computers (2007): 779,000 (237); total Internet users (2008): 1,000,000 (292); broadband Internet subscribers (2005): 25,000 (8.7).

Education and health

Educational attainment (2005). Percentage of population ages 10 and over having: no formal schooling: illiterate 6.2%, literate 37.9%; primary education 12.7%; lower secondary 20.8%; upper secondary 11.7%; some higher 4.1%; completed undergraduate 6.6%. **Literacy** (2005): total population ages 15 and over literate 84.4%; males literate 85.7%; females literate 82.8%. **Health** (2006): physicians 4,775 (1 per 646 persons); hospital beds 5,760 (1 per 535 persons); infant mortality rate per 1,000 live births (2008) 9.2; undernourished population (2002–04) 120,000 (5% of total population based on the consumption of a minimum daily requirement of 1,980 calories).

Military

Total active duty personnel (November 2008): 15,500 (army 71.0%, navy/coast guard 12.9%, air force 16.1%); US troops for Iraqi support (May 2009): 15,000. **Military expenditure as percentage of GDP** (2008): 2.8%; per capita expenditure US$1,441.

Background

Faylakah Island, in Kuwait Bay, had a civilization dating back to the 3rd millennium BC that flourished until 1200 BC. Greek colonists resettled the island in the 4th century BC. Abd Rahim of the Sabah dynasty became sheikh in AD 1756, the first of a family that continues to rule Kuwait. In 1899, to thwart German and Ottoman influences, Kuwait gave Britain control of its foreign affairs. Following the outbreak of war in 1914, Britain established a protectorate there. In 1961, after Kuwait became independent, Iraq laid claim to it. British troops defended Kuwait, the Arab League recognized its independence, and Iraq dropped its claim. Iraqi forces invaded and occupied Kuwait in 1990, and a US-led military coalition drove them out in 1991. Iraqi forces set fire to most of Kuwait's oil wells, but these were extinguished, and petroleum production soon returned to prewar levels.

Recent Developments

In 2009 Kuwait suffered the effects of the global financial crisis. The government was obliged to shore up Gulf Bank, the country's second largest bank, and fully guarantee all bank deposits. The Kuwait stock exchange and real-estate prices tumbled, but by the beginning of the second half of the year, the economy was showing signs of recovery. Tense relations between Kuwait and Iraq continued over border issues, shared oil fields, and war reparations owed by Iraq to Kuwait. While Kuwait insisted upon fulfillment of Iraq's international obligations, including payment of reparations, Iraq sought the cancellation of about US$25 billion of the UN-mandated reparations for destruction wrought by Saddam Hussein's 1990 invasion of Kuwait.

Internet resource: <www.cbk.gov.kw>.

Kyrgyzstan

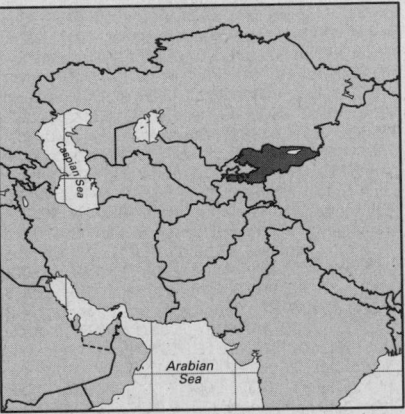

Official name: Kyrgyz Respublikasy (Kyrgyz); Respublika Kirgizstan (Russian) (Kyrgyz Republic). **Form of government:** interim caretaker regime (caretaker government to end with parliamentary elections in October 2010) with one legislative house (Supreme Council [90]). **Head of state and government:** President Kurmanbek Bakiyev (from 2005) (caretaker). **Capital:** Bishkek. **Official languages:** Kyrgyz; Russian. **Official religion:** none. **Monetary unit:** 1 som (KGS) = 100 tyiyn; valuation (1 Jul 2010) US$1 = KGS 46.38.

Demography

Area: 77,182 sq mi, 199,900 sq km. **Population** (2009): 5,345,000. **Density** (2009): persons per sq mi 69.3, persons per sq km 26.7. **Urban** (2007): 34.7%. **Sex distribution** (2008): male 49.34%; female 50.66%. **Age breakdown** (2005): under 15, 31.3%; 15–29, 29.3%; 30–44, 19.9%; 45–59, 12.2%; 60–74, 5.2%; 75–84, 1.9%; 85 and over, 0.2%. **Ethnic composition** (2005): Kyrgyz 67.4%; Uzbek 14.2%; Russian 10.3%; Hui 1.1%; Uighur 1.0%; other 6.0%. **Religious affiliation** (2000): Muslim (mostly Sunni) 60.8%; Christian 10.4%, of which Russian Orthodox 7.7%; nonreligious 21.6%; atheist 6.3%; other 0.9%. **Major cities** (2006): Bishkek 794,300; Osh 224,300; Jalal-Abad 85,100; Karakol 61,900; Tokmok 54,900. **Location:** central Asia, bordering Kazakhstan, China, Tajikistan, and Uzbekistan.

Vital statistics

Birth rate per 1,000 population (2008): 24.1 (world avg. 20.3); (1994) within marriage 83.2%. **Death rate** per 1,000 population (2008): 7.1 (world avg. 8.5). **Total fertility rate** (avg. births per childbearing woman; 2005): 2.69. **Life expectancy** at birth (2007): male 63.6 years; female 72.2 years.

National economy

Budget (2008). *Revenue:* KGS 45,479,000,000 (tax revenue 79.0%, of which VAT 36.4%, customs duties 10.2%, income tax 8.6%; nontax revenue 17.9%; grants 3.1%). *Expenditures:* KGS 36,944,000,000 (education 26.0%; general administration 18.3%; defense and public order 14.8%; social security 12.6%; health 11.8%). **Public debt** (external, outstanding; 2008): US$1,918,000,000. **Population economically active** (2006): total 2,285,000; activity rate of total population 44.1% (participation rates: ages 15–64, 70.4%; female 42.4%; unemployed [November 2007] 8.2%). **Production** (metric tons except as noted). *Agriculture and fishing* (2008): potatoes 1,334,900, wheat 746,200, corn (maize) 462,100; livestock (number of live animals) 3,379,097 sheep, 1,168,026 cattle, 355,533 horses, 338 camels; fisheries production (2007) 141 (from aquaculture 76%). *Mining and quarrying* (2007): mercury 250; gold 10,636 kg. *Manufacturing* (value of production in KGS '000,000; 2008): base metals and fabricated metal products 36,360; food products and tobacco products 11,186; cement, bricks, and ceramics 8,505. *Energy production (consumption):* electricity (kW-hr; 2008) 11,223,000,000 ([2006] 14,561,000,000); coal (metric tons; 2008) 58,000 ([2006] 818,000); lignite (metric tons; 2008) 364,000 ([2006] 436,000); crude petroleum (barrels; 2008) 480,000 ([2006] 516,000); petroleum products (metric tons; 2006) 83,000 (547,000); natural gas (cu m; 2008) 16,000,000 ([2006] 769,000,000). **Gross national income** (2008): US$3,932,000,000 (US$740 per capita). **Selected balance of payments data.** Receipts from (US$'000,000): tourism (2007) 346; remittances (2008) 1,232; foreign direct investment (FDI; 2005–07 avg.) 144; official development assistance (2007) 274. Disbursements for (US$'000,000): tourism (2007) 90; remittances (2008) 196.

Foreign trade

Imports (2007; c.i.f.): US$2,417,000,000 (refined petroleum products 25.2%; machinery and apparatus 14.4%; food products 11.6%; chemical products 10.6%; motor vehicles and parts 4.8%). *Major import sources:* Russia 40.5%; China 14.7%; Kazakhstan 12.9%; Uzbekistan 5.0%; US 4.0%. **Exports** (2007; f.o.b.): US$1,134,200,000 (refined petroleum products 20.8%; gold 19.8%; machinery and apparatus 6.2%; outerwear 5.5%; vegetables 4.2%; glass 3.5%; portland cement 3.5%). *Major export destinations:* Russia 20.7%; Switzerland 19.9%; Kazakhstan 18.0%; Afghanistan 10.4%; Uzbekistan 7.6%.

Transport and communications

Transport. *Railroads* (2007): route length (2008) 470 km; passenger-km 59,900,000; metric ton-km cargo 853,700,000. *Roads* (2000): total length 18,500 km (paved 91%). *Vehicles* (2005): passenger cars 201,430. *Air transport* (2008): passenger-km 585,000,000; metric ton-km cargo 2,314,000. **Communications,** in total units (units per 1,000 persons). Telephone landlines (2008): 494,000 (94); cellular telephone subscribers (2008): 3,394,000 (643); personal computers (2007): 99,000 (19); total Internet users (2008): 850,000 (161); broadband Internet subscribers (2008): 2,900 (0.5).

Education and health

Educational attainment (1999). Percentage of population ages 15 and over having: primary education 6.3%; some secondary 18.3%; completed secondary 50.0%; some postsecondary 14.9%; higher 10.5%. **Literacy** (2006): total population ages 15 and over literate 98.7%. **Health** (2006): physicians 12,710 (1 per 406 persons); hospital beds 26,339 (1 per 196 persons); infant mortality rate per 1,000 live births (2007) 30.6; undernourished population (2002–04) 200,000 (4% of total population based on the consumption of a minimum daily requirement of 1,930 calories).

Military

Total active duty personnel (November 2008): 10,900 (army 78.0%, air force 22.0%); Russian troops (November 2008): 500. **Military expenditure as percentage of GDP** (2007): 1.1%; per capita expenditure US$7.

Background

The Kyrgyz, a nomadic people of Central Asia, settled in the Tian Shan region in ancient times. They were conquered by Genghis Khan's son Jochi in 1207. The area became part of the Qing empire of China in the mid-18th century. The region came under Russian control in the 19th century, and its rebellion against Russia in 1916 resulted in a long period of brutal repression. Kirgiziya became an autonomous province of the USSR in 1924 and was made the Kirghiz Soviet Socialist Republic in 1936. Kyrgyzstan gained independence in 1991. It subsequently struggled with creating a democratic process and with establishing a stable economy.

Recent Developments

After meeting with Russian Pres. Dmitry Medvedev in February 2009, Kyrgyz Pres. Kurmanbek Bakiyev announced that the agreement that permitted US and NATO forces fighting in Afghanistan to use Kyrgyzstan's Manas airfield would be terminated. At the same time, Bakiyev received a promise of US$2 billion in financial assistance from Russia, primarily to finance construction of the Kambarata hydropower station. The promised Russian aid was slow to materialize, however, and on 22 June an agreement was signed under which the US would continue to use Manas as a transit shipment center for nonmilitary deliveries to forces in Afghanistan.

Internet resource:
<www.nbkr.kg/index.jsp?lang=ENG>.

Laos

Official name: Sathalanalat Paxathipatai Paxaxon Lao (Lao People's Democratic Republic). **Form of government:** unitary single-party people's republic with one legislative house (National Assembly [115]). **Head of state:** President Choummaly Sayasone (from 2006). **Head of government:** Prime Minister Bouasone Bouphavanh (from 2006). **Capital:** Vientiane (Viangchan). **Official language:** Lao. **Official religion:**

---

1 metric ton = about 1.1 short tons; 1 kilometer = 0.6 mi (statute); 1 metric ton-km cargo = about 0.68 short ton-mi cargo; c.i.f.: cost, insurance, and freight; f.o.b.: free on board

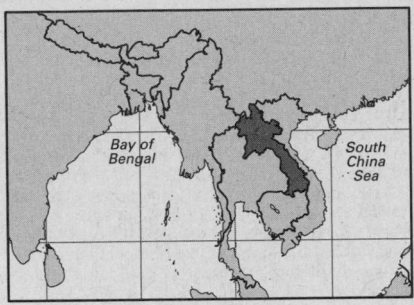

Bay of Bengal

South China Sea

none. **Monetary unit:** 1 kip (KN) = 100 at; valuation (1 Jul 2010) US$1 = KN 8,160.14.

Demography

Area: 91,429 sq mi, 236,800 sq km. **Population** (2009): 6,320,000. **Density** (2009): persons per sq mi 69.1, persons per sq km 26.7. **Urban** (2007): 29.7%. **Sex distribution** (2007): male 49.86%; female 50.14%. **Age breakdown** (2007): under 15, 38.7%; 15–29, 28.9%; 30–44, 17.0%; 45–59, 9.7%; 60–74, 4.3%; 75 and over, 1.4%. **Ethnic composition** (2005): Lao 54.6%; Khmou 10.9%; Hmong 8.0%; Tai 3.8%; Phu Tai (Phouthay) 3.3%; Lue 2.2%; Katang 2.1%; Makong 2.1%; other 13.0%. **Religious affiliation** (2005): traditional beliefs 49%; Buddhist 43%; Christian 2%; nonreligious/other 6%. **Major cities** (2003): Vientiane (Viangchan) 194,200 (urban agglomeration [2007] 745,000); Savannakhet 58,200; Pakxe 50,100; Xam Nua 40,700; Muang Khammouan 27,300. **Location:** southeastern Asia, bordering China, Vietnam, Cambodia, Thailand, and Myanmar (Burma).

Vital statistics

Birth rate per 1,000 population (2008): 34.5 (world avg. 20.3). **Death rate** per 1,000 population (2008): 11.0 (world avg. 8.5). **Total fertility rate** (avg. births per childbearing woman; 2008): 4.50. **Life expectancy** at birth (2008): male 54.1 years; female 58.4 years.

National economy

Budget (2007–08). *Revenue:* KN 7,035,000,000,000 (tax revenue 80.0%, of which turnover tax 17.5%, excise tax 16.9%, tax on mining sector 11.4%, import duties 9.6%; nontax revenue 11.5%; grants 8.5%). *Expenditures:* KN 7,952,000,000,000 (current expenditures 58.1%; capital expenditures 41.9%). **Public debt** (external, outstanding; 2007): US$2,446,000,000. **Population economically active** (2005): total 2,778,000; activity rate of total population 66.6% (participation rates: ages 15–64, 81.3%; female 50.2%; officially unemployed [2005] 2.4%). **Production** (metric tons except as noted). *Agriculture and fishing* (2008): rice 2,710,050, corn (maize) 1,107,780, sugarcane 749,295, natural rubber (hectares; 2006) 11,778; livestock (number of live animals) 2,548,000 pigs, 1,499,000 cattle, 1,155,000 water buffalo, 21,983,000 chickens, 3,200,000 ducks; fisheries production (2007) 104,925 (from aquaculture 74%). *Mining and quarrying* (2007): gypsum 775,000; limestone 750,000; copper (metal content) 99,040; tin (metal content)

450; gold 4,161 kg. *Manufacturing* (2007): plastic products 7,383; nails 2,168; plywood 952,000,000 sheets. *Energy production (consumption):* electricity (kW-hr; 2008) 3,705,000,000 ([2006] 1,021,000,000); coal (metric tons; 2008) 392,000 ([2006] 305,000); lignite (metric tons; 2006) 319,000 (96,000); petroleum products (metric tons; 2006) none (133,000). **Gross national income** (2008): US$4,674,000,000 (US$750 per capita). **Selected balance of payments data.** Receipts from (US$'000,000): tourism (2008) 275; remittances (2008) 1.0; foreign direct investment (2005–07 avg.) 180; official development assistance (2007) 396. Disbursements for (US$'000,000): remittances (2007) 1.0.

Foreign trade

Imports (2008): US$2,816,100,000 (capital goods 41.6%; crude petroleum 15.0%; materials for garment assembly 5.1%). *Major import sources:* Thailand 68.6%; China 11.3%; Vietnam 4.7%; South Korea 2.5%; Japan 2.5%. **Exports** (2008): US$1,638,600,000 (copper 37.9%; garments 11.6%; timber 8.0%; gold 7.3%; electricity 7.2%). *Major export destinations:* Thailand 34.7%; Vietnam 13.2%; China 8.6%; South Korea 4.5%; UK 3.3%.

Transport and communications

Transport. *Railroads:* none. *Roads* (2007): total length 36,831 km (paved 14%). *Vehicles* (2002): passenger cars, trucks, and buses 315,000. *Air transport* (2007): passenger-km 245,400,000; metric ton-km cargo 200,000. **Communications,** in total units (units per 1,000 persons). Telephone landlines (2008): 98,000 (16); cellular telephone subscribers (2008): 1,822,000 (294); personal computers (2007): 110,000 (18); total Internet users (2008): 130,000 (21); broadband Internet subscribers (2007): 3,600 (0.6).

Education and health

Educational attainment (2005). Percentage of population ages 25 and over having: no formal schooling 32.8%; incomplete primary education 21.6%; complete primary 18.2%; lower secondary 11.4%; upper secondary 6.2%; higher 9.8%. **Literacy** (2005): total population ages 15 and over literate 72.7%; males literate 82.5%; females literate 63.2%. **Health** (2005): physicians 5,000 (1 per 1,129 persons); hospital beds (2007) 6,955 (1 per 838 persons); infant mortality rate per 1,000 live births 79.5; undernourished population (2002–04) 1,100,000 (19% of total population based on the consumption of a minimum daily requirement of 1,730 calories).

Military

Total active duty personnel (November 2008): 29,100 (army 88.0%, air force 12.0%). **Military expenditure as percentage of GDP** (2007): 0.4%; per capita expenditure US$2.

Background

The Lao people migrated into Laos from southern China after the 8th century AD, displacing indigenous tribes. In the 14th century Fa Ngum founded the first Laotian state, Lan Xang. Except for a period of rule by Burma (1574–1637), the Lan Xang kingdom ruled Laos until

1713, when it split into three kingdoms. France gained control of the region in 1893. In 1945 Japan seized it and declared Laos independent. The area reverted to French rule after World War II. The Geneva Conference of 1954 unified and granted independence to Laos. Communist forces took control in 1975, establishing the Lao People's Democratic Republic. Laos held its first election in 1989 and promulgated a new constitution in 1991. Although its economy was adversely affected by the mid-1990s Asian monetary crises, it realized a longtime goal in 1997 when it joined the Association of Southeast Asian Nations.

Recent Developments

China continued to invest heavily in several of Laos's key economic sectors in 2009. Chinese investments in the country were valued at about US$3.5 billion in early 2009. The fast-growing Chinese presence, however, raised concerns among local residents and international organizations. In recent years the Lao government had granted a large number of land and mining concessions to Chinese companies. Many observers worried about the social, economic, and environmental impacts of these companies' activities on Laos's rural areas. The global financial crisis also affected this dynamic. The Sepon copper and gold mine was sold in April 2009 to the Chinese state company China Minmetals Corp after having laid off hundreds of workers the previous December.

Internet resource: <www.nsc.gov.la>.

Latvia

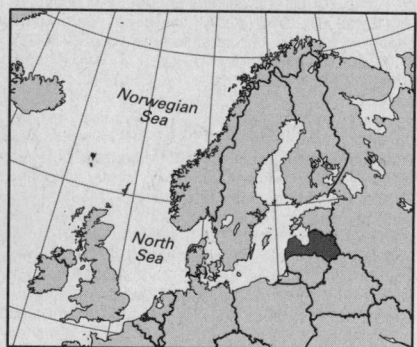

Official name: Latvijas Republika (Republic of Latvia). **Form of government:** unitary multiparty republic with a single legislative house (Parliament, or Saeima [100]). **Head of state:** President Valdis Zatlers (from 2007). **Head of government:** Prime Minister Valdis Dombrovskis (from 2009). **Capital:** Riga. **Official language:** Latvian. **Official religion:** none. **Monetary unit:** 1 lats (Ls; plural lati) = 100 santimi; valuation (1 Jul 2010) US$1 = 0.58 Ls.

Demography

Area: 24,926 sq mi, 64,559 sq km. **Population** (2009): 2,256,000. **Density** (2009): persons per sq mi 90.5, persons per sq km 34.9. **Urban** (2008): 67.8%. **Sex distribution** (2008): male 46.13%; female 53.87%. **Age breakdown** (2008): under 15, 13.7%; 15–29, 22.6%; 30–44, 20.8%; 45–59, 20.6%; 60–74, 15.0%; 75–89, 6.9%; 90 and over, 0.4%. **Ethnic composition** (2008): Latvian 59.3%; Russian 27.8%; Belarusian 3.6%; Ukrainian 2.5%; Polish 2.4%; Lithuanian 1.3%; other 3.1%. **Religious affiliation** (2005): Orthodox 29%, of which Russian 16%; Roman Catholic 19%; Lutheran 14%; nonreligious 26%; atheist/other 12%. **Major cities** (2008): Riga 713,016; Daugavpils 104,857; Liepaja 84,747; Jelgava 65,419; Jurmala 55,870. **Location:** eastern Europe, bordering Estonia, Russia, Belarus, Lithuania, and the Baltic Sea.

Vital statistics

Birth rate per 1,000 population (2008): 10.6 (world avg. 20.3); within marriage 56.9%. **Death rate** per 1,000 population (2008): 13.7 (world avg. 8.5). **Total fertility rate** (avg. births per childbearing woman; 2007): 1.45. **Life expectancy** at birth (2008): male 67.2 years; female 77.9 years.

National economy

Budget (2008–09). *Revenue:* Ls 5,203,700,000 (taxes on products 29.4%; social security contributions 25.3%; income tax 24.7%; VAT 17.4%). *Expenditures:* Ls 6,602,100,000 (wages and salaries 28.5%; social security and welfare 23.3%; transfers 12.5%). **Public debt** (external, outstanding; June 2009): US$4,308,600,000. **Production** (metric tons except as noted). *Agriculture and fishing* (2008): wheat 989,600, potatoes 673,000, barley 277,000; livestock (number of live animals) 384,000 pigs, 380,000 cattle; fisheries production 158,500 (from aquaculture, negligible). *Mining and quarrying* (2008): peat 865,500; limestone 515,900; gypsum 349,100. *Manufacturing* (value added in Ls '000,000; 2008): food products 313.6; wood products (excluding furniture) 270.1; fabricated metal products 131.0. *Energy production (consumption):* electricity (kW-hr; 2008–09) 4,895,000,000 (7,276,000,000); coal (metric tons; 2008–09) none (137,000); petroleum products (metric tons; 2008–09) none (1,377,000); natural gas (cu m; 2008–09) none (1,573,000,000). **Selected balance of payments data.** Receipts from (US$'000,000): tourism (2007) 671; remittances (2008) 601; foreign direct investment (FDI; 2005–07 avg.) 1,517. Disbursements for (US$'000,000): tourism (2007) 927; remittances (2008) 58; FDI (2005–07 avg.) 178. **Gross national income** (2008): US$26,883,000,000 (US$11,860 per capita). **Population economically active** (2008): total 1,215,800; activity rate of total population 53.7% (participation rates: ages 15–74, 67.7%; female 48.9%; unemployed [July 2008–June 2009] 12.3%).

Foreign trade

Imports (2008; c.i.f.): Ls 7,527,687,000 (machinery and apparatus 18.3%; mineral fuels 15.6%, of which diesel oil 5.3%; food products and beverages 13.7%; transportation equipment 10.7%; base and fabricated metals 10.3%; chemical products 9.7%). *Major import sources:* Lithuania 16.5%; Germany 13.0%;

---

1 metric ton = about 1.1 short tons;   1 kilometer = 0.6 mi (statute);   1 metric ton-km cargo = about 0.68 short ton-mi cargo;   c.i.f.: cost, insurance, and freight;   f.o.b.: free on board

Russia 10.6%; Poland 7.2%; Estonia 7.1%. **Exports** (2008; f.o.b.): Ls 4,428,945,000 (food products and beverages 16.7%; base and fabricated metals 16.7%; wood products 16.6%; machinery and apparatus 12.5%; chemical products 8.4%; textiles and wearing apparel 5.5%). *Major export destinations:* Lithuania 16.7%; Estonia 14.0%; Russia 10.0%; Germany 8.1%; Sweden 6.6%.

Transport and communications

Transport. *Railroads* (2008): length 2,263 km; passenger-km 951,000,000; metric ton-km cargo 19,581,000,000. *Roads* (2008): total length 51,300 km (paved 39%). *Vehicles* (2008): passenger cars 932,800; trucks and buses 140,300. *Air transport* (2008): passenger-km 3,498,000,000; metric ton-km cargo 15,000,000. **Communications**, in total units (units per 1,000 persons). Telephone landlines (2008): 644,000 (285); cellular telephone subscribers (2008): 2,234,000 (989); personal computers (2005): 566,000 (245); total Internet users (2007): 1,252,000 (552); broadband Internet subscribers (2007): 146,000 (64).

Education and health

Educational attainment (2007). Percentage of population ages 15–74 having: none/unknown through complete primary education 26.1%; secondary 25.5%; vocational 30.1%; higher 18.3%. **Literacy** (2007): total population ages 15 and over literate, virtually 100%. **Health** (2008): physicians 8,437 (1 per 268 persons); hospital beds 17,001 (1 per 133 persons); infant mortality rate per 1,000 live births 6.7; undernourished population (2002–04) 70,000 (3% of total population based on the consumption of a minimum daily requirement of 1,960 calories).

Military

Total active duty personnel (November 2008): 5,187 (army 29.4%, navy 13.5%, air force 9.3%, headquarters/administrative/other 47.8%). **Military expenditure as percentage of GDP** (2008): 1.6%; per capita expenditure US$226.

Background

Latvia was settled by the Balts in ancient times. It was conquered by the Vikings in the 9th century and later dominated by its German-speaking neighbors, who Christianized the people in the 12th–13th centuries. By 1230 German rule was established. From the mid-16th to the early 18th century, the region was split between Poland and Sweden, but by the end of the 18th century all of Latvia had been annexed by Russia. Latvia declared its independence after the Russian Revolution of 1917, but in 1940 the Soviet Red Army invaded. Held by Nazi Germany in 1941–44, the country was recaptured by the Soviets and incorporated into the Soviet Union. Latvia gained its independence in 1991 with the breakup of the Soviet Union; subsequently it sought to build ties with Western Europe (becoming a member of both the EU and NATO in 2004).

Recent Developments

The global economic downturn was Latvia's principal concern in 2009. The Ministry of Finance estimated

that GDP fell by about 18% for the year and unemployment climbed to nearly 20%. The principal source of political discord and popular discontent was balancing the budget so as to avoid bankruptcy and to meet the preconditions for borrowing US$10 billion from the IMF, the EU, the World Bank, and other international sources. This required restructuring of the economy, including raising taxes, curtailing spending, cutting welfare payments and public workers' salaries, systematically repaying loans, and meeting the requirements for the adoption of the euro by 2014. The budget was adopted on 1 Dec 2010.

Internet resource: <www.csb.lv/avidus.cfm?lng=en>.

Lebanon

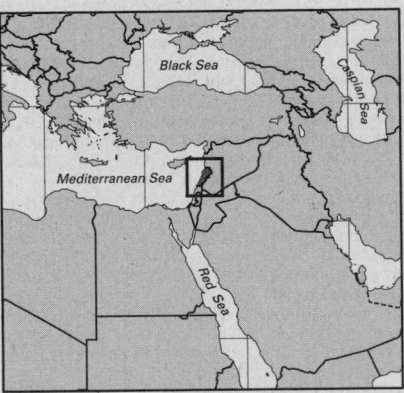

Official name: Al-Jumhuriyah al-Lubnaniyah (Lebanese Republic). **Form of government:** unitary multiparty republic with one legislative house (National Assembly [128]). **Head of state:** President Michel Suleiman (from 2008). **Head of government:** Prime Minister Saad Hariri (from 2009). **Capital:** Beirut. **Official language:** Arabic. **Official religion:** none. **Monetary unit:** 1 Lebanese pound (LBP) = 100 piastres; valuation (1 Jul 2010) US$1 = LBP 1,502.50.

Demography

Area: 4,016 sq mi, 10,400 sq km. **Population** (2009): 4,224,000. **Density** (2009): persons per sq mi 1,051, persons per sq km 406.2. **Urban** (2005): 86.6%. **Sex distribution** (2008): male 48.97%; female 51.03%. **Age breakdown** (2005): under 15, 27.6%; 15–29, 27.1%; 30–44, 21.7%; 45–59, 13.6%; 60–74, 7.7%; 75–84, 2.0%; 85 and over, 0.3%. **Ethnic composition** (2000): Arab 84.5%, of which Lebanese 71.2%, Palestinian 12.1%; Armenian 6.8%; Kurd 6.1%; other 2.6%. **Religious affiliation** (2005): Muslim 56%, of which Shi'i 28%, Sunni 28%; Maronite (Eastern-rite Roman Catholic) 22%; Greek Orthodox 8%; Druze 5%; Greek Catholic 4%; other 5%. **Major cities** (2003): Beirut 395,000 (urban agglomeration [2007] 1,846,000); Tripoli 212,900; Sidon 149,000; Tyre (Sur) 117,100; Al-Nabatiyah 89,400. **Location:** the Middle East, bordering Syria, Israel, and the Mediterranean Sea.

Vital statistics

Birth rate per 1,000 population (2008): 20.2 (world avg. 20.3). **Death rate** per 1,000 population (2008): 5.0 (world avg. 8.5). **Total fertility rate** (avg. births per childbearing woman; 2007): 2.21. **Life expectancy** at birth (2007): male 69.9 years; female 74.2 years.

National economy

Budget (2007). *Revenue:* LBP 8,390,000,000,000 (tax revenue 66.7%, of which taxes on goods and services 34.8%, customs duties 6.7%; nontax revenue 26.5%; grants 5.9%; social contributions 0.9%). *Expenditures:* LBP 12,599,000,000,000 (public debt 37.3%; fuel/electricity 11.2%; defense 9.2%; social protection 7.5%; education 6.9%; health 2.2%). **Public debt** (external, outstanding; July 2009): US$21,294,000,000. **Gross national income** (2008): US$26,297,000,000 (US$6,350 per capita). **Production** (metric tons except as noted). *Agriculture and fishing* (2007): potatoes 490,000, tomatoes 255,000, oranges 195,000, olives 83,000, almonds 27,000; livestock (number of live animals) 495,000 goats, 340,000 sheep, 77,000 cattle; fisheries production 4,614 (from aquaculture 17%). *Manufacturing* (value added in US$'000,000; 1998): food products 345; cement, bricks, and ceramics 212; wood products 188. *Energy production (consumption):* electricity (kW-hr; 2008) 11,188,000,000 ([2007] 10,590,000,000); coal (metric tons; 2006) none (200,000); petroleum products (metric tons; 2006) none (4,009,000). **Population economically active** (2007): total 1,228,800; activity rate of total population 32.7% (participation rates: ages 15–64, 47.6%; female 25.0%; unemployed 9.2%). **Selected balance of payments data.** Receipts from (US$'000,000): tourism (2007) 4,993; remittances (2008) 6,000; foreign direct investment (FDI; 2005–07 avg.) 2,792; official development assistance (2007) 939. Disbursements for (US$'000,000): tourism (2007) 3,114; remittances (2008) 3,022; FDI (2005–07 avg.) 142.

Foreign trade

Imports (2008): US$16,137,000,000 (mineral products [significantly crude petroleum] 26.5%; food products and live animals 13.2%; transportation equipment 10.6%; electrical machinery 10.5%). *Major import sources:* US 11.5%; China 8.6%; France 8.3%; Italy 6.9%; Germany 6.4%. **Exports** (2008): US$3,478,000,000 (precious metal jewelry and stones [significantly gold and diamonds] 16.5%; electrical machinery 15.4%; base and fabricated metals 15.2%; chemical products 12.5%). *Major export destinations:* UAE 10.0%; Switzerland 9.5%; Iraq 7.7%; Syria 6.4%; Saudi Arabia 6.0%.

Transport and communications

Transport. *Railroads:* (2009) 401 km. *Roads* (2005): total length 6,970 km. *Vehicles* (2001): passenger cars 1,370,897; trucks and buses 102,394. *Air transport* (2008; Middle East Airlines only): passenger-km 2,748,000,000; metric ton-km cargo 38,524,000. **Communications,** in total units (units per 1,000 persons). Telephone landlines (2008):

714,000 (170); cellular telephone subscribers (2008): 1,430,000 (341); personal computers (2007): 433,000 (104); total Internet users (2008): 2,190,000 (522); broadband Internet subscribers (2007): 200,000 (48).

Education and health

Educational attainment (2004). Percentage of population ages 4 and over having: no formal education/unknown 13.7%; incomplete primary education 3.2%; primary 54.2%; secondary/vocational 15.5%; upper vocational 1.7%; higher 11.7%. **Literacy** (2005): total population ages 15 and over literate 88.3%; males literate 93.6%; females literate 83.4%. **Health** (2005): physicians 10,538 (1 per 387 persons); hospital beds (2006) 12,037 (1 per 343 persons); infant mortality rate per 1,000 live births 23.6; undernourished population (2002–04) 120,000 (3% of total population based on the consumption of a minimum daily requirement of 1,920 calories).

Military

Total active duty personnel (November 2008): 56,000 (army 96.2%, navy 2.0%, air force 1.8%); estimated strength of Hezbollah (November 2008): 2,000; UN peacekeeping troops (March 2009): 12,261. **Military expenditure as percentage of GDP** (2008): 3.1%; per capita expenditure US$179.

Background

Much of present-day Lebanon corresponds to ancient Phoenicia, which was settled about 3000 BC. In the 6th century AD, Christians fleeing Syrian persecution settled in what is now northern Lebanon and founded the Maronite Church. Arab tribesmen settled in southern Lebanon and by the 11th century had founded the Druze faith. Lebanon was later ruled by the Mamluks. In 1516 the Ottoman Turks seized control; the Turks ended the local rule of the Druze Shihab princes in 1842. After the massacre of Maronites by Druze in 1860, France forced the Ottomans to form an autonomous province for the Christian area, known as Mount Lebanon. Following World War I, it was administered by the French military, but by 1946 it was fully independent. After the Arab-Israeli War of 1948–49, Palestinian refugees settled in southern Lebanon. In 1970 the Palestine Liberation Organization (PLO) moved its headquarters there and began raids into northern Israel. Political and religious divisions and a growing Palestinian "state within a state" fueled a descent into civil war. In 1976 Syria intervened on behalf of the Christians, and in 1982 Israeli forces attempted to drive Palestinian fighters out of southern Lebanon. Israeli troops had withdrawn from all but a narrow buffer zone in the south by 1985; thereafter, guerrillas from the Lebanese Shi'ite militia Hezbollah clashed with the Israelis regularly. Israeli soldiers completely withdrew from Lebanon in 2000, and Syrian forces disengaged from the country in 2005. In mid-2006 Hezbollah and Israel engaged in a 34-day war, primarily fought in Lebanon, in which more than 1,000 people were killed. Israeli troops subsequently withdrew from most of Lebanon in October 2006.

1 metric ton = about 1.1 short tons;   1 kilometer = 0.6 mi (statute);   1 metric ton-km cargo = about 0.68 short ton-mi cargo;   c.i.f.: cost, insurance, and freight;   f.o.b.: free on board

Recent Developments

Lebanon's external debt and fiscal deficits remained high at more than US$50 billion, but the country reduced the debt-to-GDP ratio from 180% to 154% by the end of 2009. The budget deficit was 26.2% of spending. In spite of increased spending on electricity—which accounted for US$1.4 billion annually—revenues in the first half of 2009 reached US$4.27 billion, up 23.4% from the same period in 2008. Lebanon's defense and security spending was estimated to increase by 22% in 2009. The important banking sector showed resilience to the ongoing global financial crisis. Total assets increased by US$13 billion in 2008, up by 13%. The IMF revised its estimate of Lebanon's GDP growth in 2009 from 4% to 7%. The World Bank put the per capita income in 2008 at US$10,880, which made Lebanon ranked 94th among world countries and 6th among Middle Eastern and North African countries.

Internet resource: <www.lebanon-tourism.gov.lb>.

Lesotho

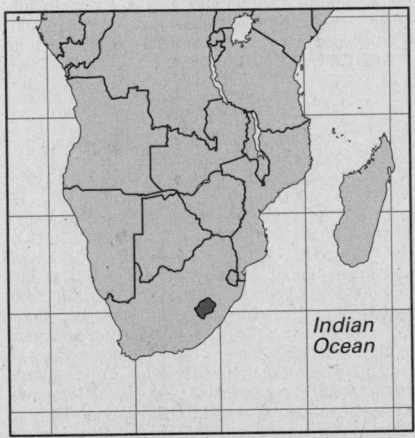

Indian Ocean

Official name: Musa oa Lesotho (Sotho); Kingdom of Lesotho (English). **Form of government:** constitutional monarchy with two legislative houses (Senate [33]; National Assembly [120]). **Head of state:** King Letsie III (from 1996). **Head of government:** Prime Minister Bethuel Pakalitha Mosisili (from 1998). **Capital:** Maseru. **Official languages:** Sotho; English. **Official religion:** Christianity. **Monetary unit:** 1 loti (plural maloti [M]) = 100 licente; valuation (1 Jul 2010) US$1 = M 7.54 (the South African rand is also accepted as legal tender).

Demography

Area: 11,720 sq mi, 30,355 sq km. **Population** (2009): 2,067,000. **Density** (2009): persons per sq mi 176.4, persons per sq km 68.1. **Urban** (2006): 23.8%. **Sex distribution** (2006): male 48.72%; female 51.28%. **Age breakdown** (2006): under 15, 40.7%; 15–29, 31.1%; 30–44, 15.0%; 45–59, 9.0%; 60–74, 5.0%; 75 and over, 2.0%. **Ethnic composition** (2000): Sotho 80.3%; Zulu 14.4%; other 5.3%. **Reli-**

gious affiliation (2000): Christian 91.0%, of which Roman Catholic 37.5%, unaffiliated Christian 23.9%, Protestant (mostly Reformed and Anglican) 17.7%, independent Christian 11.8%; traditional beliefs 7.7%; other 1.3%. **Major urban centers** (2006): Maseru 116,300; Mafeteng 61,600; Hlotse 50,900; Mohale's Hoek 44,500; Maputsoe 32,800. **Location:** southern Africa, surrounded by South Africa.

Vital statistics

Birth rate per 1,000 population (2008): 24.4 (world avg. 20.3). **Death rate** per 1,000 population (2008): 22.3 (world avg. 8.5). **Total fertility rate** (avg. births per childbearing woman; 2008): 3.13. **Life expectancy** at birth (2008): male 41.0 years; female 39.3 years.

National economy

Budget (2007–08). *Revenue:* M 7,169,700,000 (tax revenue 88.3%, of which customs receipts 57.2%, VAT 11.8%, income tax 11.0%; nontax revenue 9.3%; grants 2.4%). *Expenditures:* M 5,334,400,000 (wages and salaries 33.2%; grants 14.5%; transfers 6.2%; debt service 5.5%; social benefits 4.2%). **Production** (metric tons except as noted). *Agriculture and fishing* (2007): potatoes 96,000, corn (maize) 50,800, sorghum 11,200; livestock (number of live animals) 1,025,000 sheep, 715,000 goats, 695,000 cattle; fisheries production 179 (from aquaculture 73%). *Mining and quarrying* (2008): diamonds 216,546 carats. *Manufacturing* (value added in M '000,000; 2007): textiles and wearing apparel 376.8; food products and beverages 59.4; leather products and footwear 30.8. *Energy production (consumption):* electricity (kW-hr; 2006) 200,000,000 (226,000,000); petroleum products (metric tons; 2003) none (100,000). **Population economically active** (2008): total 788,541; activity rate of total population 38.5% (participation rates: ages 15 and older, 63.5%; female 55.3%; unemployed 22.7%). **Gross national income** (2008): US$2,179,000,000 (US$1,080 per capita). **Public debt** (external, outstanding; January 2009): US$619,000,000. **Selected balance of payments data.** Receipts from (US$'000,000): tourism (2007) 43; remittances (2008) 443; foreign direct investment (2005–07 avg.) 85; official development assistance (2007) 130. Disbursements for (US$'000,000): tourism (2007) 16; remittances (2008) 21.

Foreign trade

Imports (2008; c.i.f.): M 13,237,230,000 ([2006] assorted manufactured goods 40%; food products 24%; chemical products 13%; machinery and transportation equipment 13%). *Major import sources* (2007): other Southern African Customs Union (SACU) countries 76.5%; Asia 21.4%. **Exports** (2008; f.o.b.): M 7,256,070,000 (textiles and wearing apparel 50.4%; diamonds 24.0%; machinery and transportation equipment 14.0%; food products, beverages, and tobacco products 6.6%). *Major export destinations:* other SACU countries 37.7%; North America (mostly US) 35.0%; European Union 24.0%.

Transport and communications

Transport. Railroads (2001): length 1.0 km. Roads (2006): total length 2,370 km (paved 57%). *Vehicles* (1996): passenger cars 12,610; trucks and buses

25,000. *Air transport* (1999): passenger-km, negligible (less than 500,000); metric ton-km cargo, negligible. **Communications,** in total units (units per 1,000 persons). Telephone landlines (2008): 65,000 (32); cellular telephone subscribers (2008): 581,000 (284); personal computers (2005): 1,000 (0.5); total Internet users (2008): 73,000 (36); broadband Internet subscribers (2005): 50 (0.02).

Education and health

Educational attainment (2004). Percentage of population ages 25 and over having: no formal education/unknown 18%; incomplete primary education 44%; complete primary 15%; secondary 20%; vocational and higher 3%. **Literacy** (2007): total population ages 15 and over literate 86.5%; males literate 77.1%; females literate 95.6%. **Health:** physicians (2005) 124 (1 per 16,089 persons); hospital beds (2006) 2,618 (1 per 769 persons); infant mortality rate per 1,000 live births (2008) 78.6; undernourished population (2002–04) 250,000 (13% of total population based on the consumption of a minimum daily requirement of 1,850 calories).

Military

Total active duty personnel (November 2008): 2,000 (army 100%). **Military expenditure as percentage of GDP** (2007): 2.3%; per capita expenditure US$20.

Background

Bantu-speaking farmers created a number of chiefdoms in the area in the 16th century. The most powerful organized the Basotho in 1824 and obtained British protection in 1843 as tension between the Basotho and the South African Boers increased. The area became a British territory in 1868 and was annexed to the Cape Colony in 1871. The colony's effort to disarm the Basotho resulted in revolt in 1880, and four years later it separated from the colony and became a British High Commission Territory. In 1966 it gained independence. A new constitution (1993) ended seven years of military rule. At the beginning of the 21st century, Lesotho suffered from a deteriorating economy and one of the world's highest HIV/AIDS infection rates.

Recent Developments

The South Africa–Lesotho Joint Bilateral Commission announced in April 2009 that the South African government had approved 7.4 billion rand (about US$950 million) for the second phase of the massive Lesotho Highlands Water Project, with construction to begin in 2011. Meanwhile, a South African decision on textiles threatened to undermine Lesotho's garment sector, which directly employed almost 40,000 people and contributed roughly 20% of the GDP.

Internet resource: <www.bos.gov.ls>.

Liberia

Official name: Republic of Liberia. **Form of government:** multiparty republic with two legislative houses

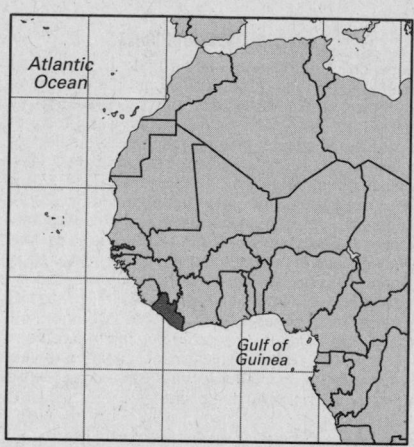

(Senate [30]; House of Representatives [64]). **Head of state and government:** President Ellen Johnson Sirleaf (from 2006). **Capital:** Monrovia. **Official language:** English. **Official religion:** none. **Monetary unit:** 1 Liberian dollar (L$) = 100 cents; valuation (1 Jul 2010) US$1 = L$72.00.

Demography

Area: 37,466 sq mi, 97,036 sq km. **Population** (2009): 3,955,000. **Density** (2009): persons per sq mi 105.6, persons per sq km 40.8. **Urban** (2008): 47.0%. **Sex distribution** (2008): male 50.05%; female 49.95%. **Age breakdown** (2008): under 15, 41.9%; 15–29, 29.1%; 30–44, 16.7%; 45–59, 7.4%; 60–74, 3.4%; 75–84, 1.0%; 85 and over, 0.5%. **Ethnic composition** (2008): Kpelle 20.3%; Bassa 13.4%; Grebo 10.0%; Gio (Dan) 8.0%; Mano 7.9%; Kru 6.0%; Loma (Lorma) 5.1%; Kissi 4.8%; Gola 4.4%; Krahn 4.0%; Vai 4.0%; other 12.1%. **Religious affiliation** (2005): traditional beliefs 40%; Christian (mostly Protestant/independent Christian) 40%; Muslim 20%. **Major urban areas** (2008): Monrovia 1,010,970; Ganta 41,106; Buchanan 34,270; Gbarnga 34,046; Kakata 33,945. **Location:** western Africa, bordering Guinea, Côte d'Ivoire, the North Atlantic Ocean, and Sierra Leone.

Vital statistics

Birth rate per 1,000 population (2007): 43.8 (world avg. 20.3). **Death rate** per 1,000 population (2007): 22.2 (world avg. 8.5). **Total fertility rate** (avg. births per childbearing woman; 2007): 5.94. **Life expectancy** at birth (2007): male 38.9 years; female 41.9 years.

National economy

Budget (2007). *Revenue:* L$10,222,400,000 (customs and excise duties 44.3%; direct taxes 32.1%; indirect taxes 12.6%; maritime revenue 7.6%). *Expenditures:* L$9,498,000,000 (general administration 41.5%; social and community services 19.8%; economic services 6.9%). **Population economically active**

---

1 metric ton = about 1.1 short tons;   1 kilometer = 0.6 mi (statute);   1 metric ton-km cargo = about 0.68 short ton-mi cargo;   c.i.f.: cost, insurance, and freight;   f.o.b.: free on board

(2006): total 1,324,000; activity rate 37.0% (participation rates: ages 15–64, 70.7%; female 39.8%; unemployed [2007] 80%). **Production** (metric tons except as noted). *Agriculture and fishing* (2008): cassava 560,000, sugarcane 265,000, oil palm fruit 183,000, natural rubber 81,000, coffee 3,000, cacao beans 3,000; livestock (number of live animals) 285,000 goats, 241,000 sheep, 199,500 pigs; fisheries production (2007) 16,245 (from aquaculture, none). *Mining and quarrying* (2008): diamonds 60,536 carats; gold 624 kg. *Manufacturing* (value of sales in L$'000; 2007): cement 1,308,767; beer 1,023,734; carbonated beverages 429,776. *International maritime licensing* (registration fees earned; 2007): more than US$12,000,000. *Energy production (consumption):* electricity (kW-hr; 2006) 351,000,000 (351,000,000); petroleum products (metric tons; 2006) none (230,000). **Gross national income** (2008): US$634,000,000 (US$170 per capita). **Public debt** (external, outstanding; 2007): US$910,000,000. **Selected balance of payments data.** Receipts from (US$'000,000): remittances (2007) 303; foreign direct disinvestment (2005–07 avg.) –517; official development assistance (2007) 696. Disbursements for (US$'000,000): remittances (2007) 139; foreign direct investment (2005–07 avg.) 382.

Foreign trade

Imports (2008, excluding December): US$798,000,000 (food products 25.7%, of which rice 15.8%; machinery and transportation equipment 25.6%; refined petroleum products 19.5%). *Major import sources* (2008): South Korea 27%; Singapore 25%; Japan 12%; China 11%. **Exports** (2008, excluding December): US$239,000,000 (rubber products 86.1%; gold 5.1%; diamonds 4.1%; cacao beans and coffee 1.2%). *Major export destinations* (2008): Malaysia 38%; US 16%; Poland 12%; Germany 9%; Belgium 6%.

Transport and communications

Transport. *Railroads* (2009): operational route length, none. *Vehicles* (2002): passenger cars 17,100; trucks and buses 12,800. **Communications,** in total units (units per 1,000 persons). Telephone landlines (2008): 2,000 (0.5); cellular telephone subscribers (2008): 732,000 (193); total Internet users (2008): 20,000 (5.3).

Education and health

Educational attainment (2008). Percentage of population ages 25 and over having: no formal schooling 55.3%; incomplete primary education 7.5%; complete primary 3.3%; incomplete secondary 16.2%; complete secondary 11.3%; vocational 1.2%; higher 5.2%. **Literacy** (2008): total population ages 15 and over literate 54.0%; males literate 65.6%; females literate 42.6%. **Health:** physicians (2009) 122 (1 per 32,418 persons); hospital beds (2001) 2,751 (1 per 1,075 persons); infant mortality rate per 1,000 live births (2007) 149.7; undernourished population (2002–04) 1,700,000 (50% of total population based on the consumption of a minimum daily requirement of 1,820 calories).

Military

Total active duty personnel (November 2008): 2,400; UN peacekeeping troops (August 2009): 10,046. **Mil-**itary expenditure as percentage of GDP (2003): 11%; per capita expenditure US$16.

Background

Africa's oldest republic, Liberia was established as a home for freed American slaves under the American Colonization Society, which founded a colony at Cape Mesurado in 1821. Joseph Jenkins Roberts, Liberia's first nonwhite governor, proclaimed Liberian independence in 1847. In 1980 a coup led by Samuel K. Doe marked the end of the Americo-Liberians' long political dominance over the descendants of indigenous Africans. A destructive civil war consumed the 1990s. A National Transitional Government, supported by UN peacekeeping troops, was established in 2003. Presidential elections were held in 2005, and Ellen Johnson Sirleaf was declared the winner, the first woman to be elected head of state in Africa.

Recent Developments

Liberia's economy grew in 2009; public services noticeably improved; and progress was made in the regulation of the rubber, timber, and diamond trades. The World Bank named Liberia the best global and regional reformer, citing it as a model for how other post-conflict countries should use the private sector to rebuild markets. In February Pres. Ellen Johnson Sirleaf apologized to the Truth and Reconciliation Commission (TRC) "for being fooled" into providing financial support to now-imprisoned former president Charles Taylor at the beginning of the country's 14-year civil war in 1989. The TRC recommended that she be banned from holding elective office for 30 years. Immediate local and international response, however, demonstrated widespread support for the president.

Internet resource: <www.cbl.org.lr>.

Libya

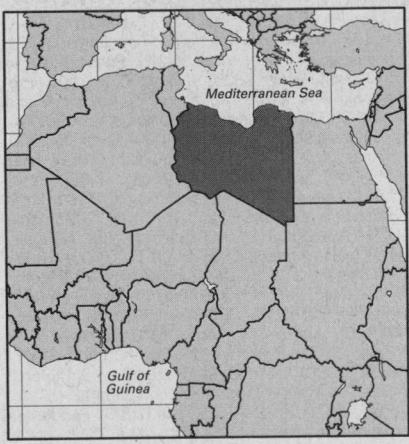

Mediterranean Sea

Gulf of Guinea

Official name: Al-Jamahiriyah al-ʿArabiyah al-Libiyah al-Shaʿbiyah al-Ishtirakiyah al ʿUzma (Great Socialist People's Libyan Arab Jamahiriya). **Form of government:** authoritarian state with one policy-making house (General People's Congress [468]). **Head of**

state: Muammar al-Qaddafi (de facto; from 1969); Secretary of the General People's Congress Muhammad Abul-Qasim al-Zwai (de jure; from 2010). **Head of government:** Secretary of the General People's Committee (Prime Minister) Al-Baghdadi Ali al-Mahmudi (from 2006). **Capital:** Tripoli. **Official language:** Arabic. **Official religion:** Islam. **Monetary unit:** 1 Libyan dinar (LD) = 1,000 dirhams; valuation (1 Jul 2010) US$1 = LD 1.30.

Demography

Area: 686,127 sq mi, 1,777,060 sq km. **Population** (2009): 6,420,000. **Density** (2009): persons per sq mi 9.4, persons per sq km 3.6. **Urban** (2005): 84.8%. **Sex distribution** (2006): male 51.93%; female 48.07%. **Age breakdown** (2005): under 15, 30.1%; 15–29, 32.2%; 30–44, 19.8%; 45–59, 11.4%; 60–74, 5.3%; 75–84, 1.0%; 85 and over, 0.2%. **Ethnic composition** (2000): Arab 87.1%, of which Libyan 57.2%, Bedouin 13.8%, Egyptian 7.7%, Sudanese 3.5%, Tunisian 2.9%; Amazigh (Berber) 6.8%, of which Arabized 4.2%; other 6.1%. **Religious affiliation** (2000): Muslim (nearly all Sunni) 96.1%; Orthodox 1.9%; Roman Catholic 0.8%; other 1.2%. **Major cities (urban agglomerations)** (2006 [2007]): Tripoli (Tarabulus) 1,065,405 (2,189,000); Banghazi 670,797 ([2005] 1,113,000); Misratah (2003) 121,669. **Location:** northern Africa, bordering the Mediterranean Sea, Egypt, Sudan, Chad, Niger, Algeria, and Tunisia.

Vital statistics

Birth rate per 1,000 population (2005): 26.8 (world avg. 20.3). **Death rate** per 1,000 population (2005): 3.5 (world avg. 8.5). **Total fertility rate** (avg. births per childbearing woman; 2005): 3.34. **Life expectancy** at birth (2005): male 74.3 years; female 78.8 years.

National economy

Budget (2008). *Revenue:* LD 72,741,200,000 (oil revenues 88.6%; other 11.4%). *Expenditures:* LD 44,115,000,000 (development expenditures 65.5%; administrative expenditures 26.9%). **Public debt** (external outstanding; 2005): US$3,900,000,000. **Production** (metric tons except as noted). *Agriculture and fishing* (2007): potatoes 196,000, tomatoes 190,000, dry onions 181,000, dates 175,000, olives 165,000, almonds 25,000; livestock (number of live animals) 4,500,000 sheep, 1,265,000 goats, 130,000 cattle, 47,000 camels; fisheries production 32,161 (from aquaculture 1%). *Mining and quarrying* (2006): lime 250,000; gypsum 175,000; salt 40,000. *Manufacturing* (value of production in LD '000,000; 1996): base metals 212; electrical machinery 208; petrochemicals 175. *Energy production (consumption):* electricity (kW-hr; 2006) 23,992,000,000 (24,025,-000,000); coal (metric tons; 2002) none (4,000); crude petroleum (barrels; 2008) 643,800,000 ([2006] 114,800,000); petroleum products (metric tons; 2008) 15,860,000 (10,244,000); natural gas (cu m; 2006) 14,413,000,000 (6,223,000,000). **Population economically active** (2003): total 2,137,000; activity rate of total population 37.9% (participation rates: ages 15 to 64, 56.7%; female 24.7%; unemployed [2004] 30.0%). **Gross national income** (2008):

US$72,735,000,000 (US$11,590 per capita). **Selected balance of payments data.** Receipts from (US$'000,000): tourism (2007) 74; remittances (2008) 16; foreign direct investment (2005–07 avg.) 1,864; official development assistance (2007) 19. Disbursements for (US$'000,000): tourism (2007) 888; remittances (2008) 762.

Foreign trade

Imports (2004): US$8,768,000,000 (machinery and transportation equipment 48.0%; food products and live animals 14.1%; chemical products 4.0%). *Major import sources* (2006): Europe 58.7%, of which Italy 9.9%, Germany 8.5%, UK 3.7%; Arab countries 11.3%; Japan 5.7%. **Exports** (2004): US$20,600,-000,000 (hydrocarbons [mostly crude petroleum] 95.7%). *Major export destinations* (2006): Europe 82.3%, of which Italy 42.5%, Germany 9.8%, Spain 8.5%, France 4.8%; Asian countries 5.4%.

Transport and communications

Transport. *Railroads:* none. *Roads* (2000): total length 83,200 km (paved 57%). *Vehicles* (2005): passenger cars 1,356,987; trucks and buses 145,935. *Air transport* (2003): passenger-km 825,000,000; metric ton-km cargo (2001) 259,000. **Communications,** in total units (units per 1,000 persons). Telephone landlines (2008): 1,033,000 (164); cellular telephone subscribers (2008): 4,828,000 (767); personal computers (2005): 130,000 (21); total Internet users (2008): 323,000 (51); broadband Internet subscribers (2006): 9,600 (1.6).

Education and health

Literacy (2006): percentage of total population ages 15 and over literate 88.1%; males literate 93.0%; females literate 83.1%. **Health:** physicians (2004) 7,405 (1 per 775 persons); hospital beds (2002) 21,400 (1 per 256 persons); infant mortality rate per 1,000 live births (2005) 24.6; undernourished population (2002–04) less than 2.5% of total population.

Military

Total active duty personnel (November 2008): 76,000 (army 65.6%, navy 10.5%, air force 23.7%). **Military expenditure as percentage of GDP** (2007): 1.1%; per capita expenditure US$113.

Background

Greeks and Phoenicians settled the area in the 7th century BC. It was conquered by Rome in the 1st century BC and by Arabs in the 7th century AD. In the 16th century, the Ottoman Turks combined Libya's three regions under one regency in Tripoli. In 1911 Italy claimed control of Libya, and by the outbreak of World War II, 150,000 Italians lived there. It became an independent state in 1951. The discovery of oil in 1959 brought wealth to Libya. A decade later a group of army officers led by Muammar al-Qaddafi deposed the king and made the country an Islamic republic. Under Qaddafi's rule it supported the Palestinian Liberation Organization and terrorist groups, bringing protests from many countries, particularly the US. In-

1 metric ton = about 1.1 short tons; 1 kilometer = 0.6 mi (statute); 1 metric ton-km cargo = about 0.68 short ton-mi cargo; c.i.f.: cost, insurance, and freight; f.o.b.: free on board

termittent warfare with Chad during the 1970s and '80s ended with Chad's defeat of Libya in 1987. International relations in the 1990s were dominated by the consequences of the 1988 bombing of an American airliner over Lockerbie, Scotland; the US accused Libyan nationalists of the deed and imposed a trade embargo on Libya, endorsed by the UN in 1992. This sanction was lifted in 2003.

Recent Developments

In August 2009 Libya and Scotland reached a deal to release 'Abd al-Basit al-Megrahi, the convicted bomber of the 1988 Pan Am disaster over Lockerbie. Scottish officials said that Megrahi's release was arranged on compassionate grounds, as he suffered from terminal cancer, though Muammar al-Qaddafi's son claimed that Megrahi's case was repeatedly raised in talks with the British government pertaining to gas and oil. Although British officials denied this, the release and possible deal triggered speculations regarding the UK's oil and gas interests in Libya. Megrahi's continued survival in 2010, staying with his family in a state-supplied luxury villa, further enraged many in the West, who felt that his release was an affront to the memory of those who had died in the terrorist bombing. In 2009 Libya produced 1.8 million bbl of oil daily, compared with 1.3 million bbl in 2003, the year before the US lifted its sanctions on Libya. While international companies raced to explore investment opportunities in Libya, Qaddafi's visits in June to Rome and in September to New York City—where he addressed the UN General Assembly for the first time—marked Libya's return to the international community.

Internet resource: <www.cbi.gov.ly>.

Liechtenstein

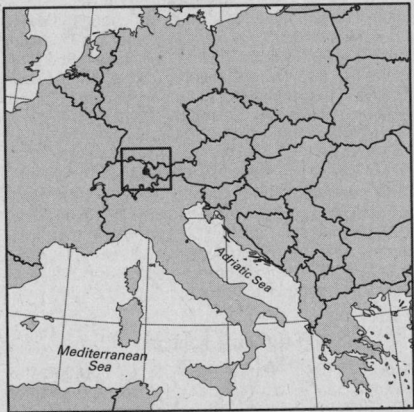

Mediterranean Sea

Adriatic Sea

Official name: Fürstentum Liechtenstein (Principality of Liechtenstein). **Form of government:** constitutional monarchy with one legislative house (Diet [25]). **Head of state:** Prince Hans Adam II (from 1989). **Head of government:** Prime Minister Klaus Tschütscher (from 2009). **Capital:** Vaduz. **Official language:** German. **Official religion:** none. **Monetary unit:** 1 Swiss franc (CHF) = 100 centimes; valuation (1 Jul 2010) US$1 = CHF 1.07.

Demography

Area: 62.0 sq mi, 160.5 sq km. **Population** (2009): 35,700. **Density** (2009): persons per sq mi 575.8, persons per sq km 222.4. **Urban** (2005): 14.3%. **Sex distribution** (2007): male 49.35%; female 50.65%. **Age breakdown** (2007): under 15, 16.8%; 15–29, 19.9%; 30–44, 22.5%; 45–59, 22.6%; 60–74, 13.1%; 75–84, 3.8%; 85 and over, 1.3%. **Ethnic composition** (2006): Liechtensteiner 66.1%; Swiss 10.3%; Austrian 5.8%; Italian 3.4%; German 3.4%; other 11.0%. **Religious affiliation** (2002): Christian 83.9%, of which Roman Catholic 76.0%, Protestant 7.0%, Orthodox 0.8%; Muslim 4.1%; nonreligious/other 12.0%. **Major cities** (2007): Schaan 5,690; Vaduz 5,109; Triesen 4,713. **Location:** central Europe, between Austria and Switzerland.

Vital statistics

Birth rate per 1,000 population (2008): 9.9 (world avg. 20.3); within marriage 86.0%. **Death rate** per 1,000 population (2008): 5.8 (world avg. 8.5). **Total fertility rate** (avg. births per childbearing woman; 2008): 1.40. **Life expectancy** at birth (2006): male 78.9 years; female 83.1 years.

National economy

Budget (2007). *Revenue:* CHF 1,010,300,000 (current revenue 98.2%, of which taxes and duties 75.7%, investment income 16.5%; capital revenue and other 1.8%). *Expenditures:* CHF 1,029,200,000 (current expenditures 89.7%, of which wages and salaries 18.2%, financial affairs 17.1%; depreciation on portfolio securities 7.2%; capital expenditures 10.3%). **Public debt:** none. **Tourism** (2007): 59,603 tourist arrivals. **Population economically active** (2007): total 16,193; activity rate of total population 45.3% (participation rates: ages 15 and over [2005] 54.3%; female [2003] 41.4%; unemployed [2007] 2.7%). **Production** (metric tons except as noted). *Agriculture and fishing* (2007): grapes 200; other crops include cereals and apples; livestock (number of live animals) 6,037 cattle, 3,683 sheep, 1,735 pigs; *Manufacturing* (2007): small-scale precision manufacturing includes optical lenses, electron microscopes, electronic equipment, and high-vacuum pumps; metal manufacturing, construction machinery, and ceramics are also important. *Energy production (consumption):* electricity (kW-hr; 2007) 72,273,000 (379,013,000); coal (metric tons; 2004) none ([2003] 13); petroleum products (metric tons; 2004) none (50,000).

Foreign trade

Imports (2007; excludes trade with Switzerland and transshipments through Switzerland): CHF 2,416,000,000 (fabricated metal products and iron and steel 36.8%; machinery and electronic goods 31.9%; mineral fuels and chemical products 15.2%; glass products, ceramics, and textiles 8.5%). *Major import sources:* Germany 40.2%; Austria 36.9%; Italy 5.2%; US 1.8%; France 1.8%. **Exports** (2007; excludes trade with Switzerland and transshipments through Switzerland): CHF 4,182,000,000 (machinery and electronic goods 34.0%; fabricated metal products and precision tools 33.2%; transportation equipment and parts 8.6%; glass products, ceramics, and textiles [including lead crystal and specialized dental products] 7.3%). *Major export destinations:* Germany 20.0%; US 14.3%; Austria 11.5%; France 9.9%; Italy 6.3%.

Transport and communications

Transport. *Railroads* (2006): length 18.5 km. *Roads* (2007): total length 380 km (paved 100%). *Vehicles* (2007): passenger cars 24,368; trucks and buses 7,532. *Air transport:* the nearest scheduled airport service is through Zürich, Switzerland. **Communications,** in total units (units per 1,000 persons). Telephone landlines (2008): 20,000 (550); cellular telephone subscribers (2008): 34,000 (954); total Internet users (2008): 23,000 (646); broadband Internet subscribers (2007): 14,000 (396).

Education and health

Educational attainment (2000). Percentage of population ages 25 and over having: incomplete compulsory education (schooling to age 16) 3.0%; complete compulsory 22.9%; lower vocational 44.5%; higher vocational, teacher training 13.8%; university 6.6%; unknown 9.2%. **Literacy:** virtually 100%. **Health:** physicians (2005) 79 (1 per 441 persons); hospital beds (1997) 108 (1 per 288 persons); infant mortality rate per 1,000 live births (2006) 5.5.

Military

Total active duty personnel: none; Liechtenstein has had no standing army since 1868; defense is the responsibility of Switzerland. **Military expenditure as percentage of GDP:** none.

Background

The Rhine plain was occupied for centuries by two independent lordships of the Holy Roman Empire, Vaduz and Schellenberg. The principality of Liechtenstein, consisting of these two lordships, was founded in 1719 and remained part of the Holy Roman Empire. It was included in the German Confederation (1815–66). In 1866 it became independent, recognizing Vaduz and Schellenberg as unique regions forming separate electoral districts. An almost 60-year ruling coalition dissolved in 1997, and the prince won the passage of constitutional reforms in 2003 that greatly strengthened royal power.

Recent Developments

In 2009 Prince Alois set a tone of moderation in Liechtenstein by offering to cooperate with other countries to combat tax evasion and fraud. He agreed to follow the rules of the Organisation for Economic Co-operation and Development and signed separate agreements easing bank secrecy with Germany in July and with Britain in August.

Internet resource: <www.liechtenstein.li/en>.

Lithuania

Official name: Lietuvos Respublika (Republic of Lithuania). **Form of government:** unitary multiparty

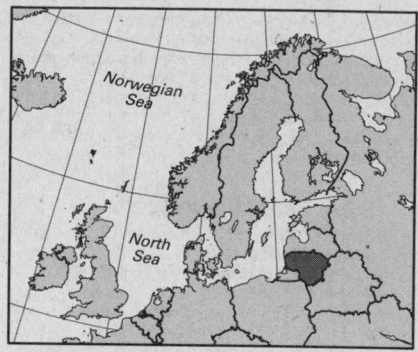

republic with one legislative house (Seimas [141]). **Head of state:** President Dalia Grybauskaite (from 2009). **Head of government:** Prime Minister Andrius Kubilius (from 2008). **Capital:** Vilnius. **Official language:** Lithuanian. **Official religion:** none. **Monetary unit:** 1 litas (LTL; plural litai) = 100 centai; valuation (1 Jul 2010) US$1 = LTL 2.82.

Demography

Area: 25,212 sq mi, 65,300 sq km. **Population** (2009): 3,339,000. **Density** (2009): persons per sq mi 132.4, persons per sq km 51.1. **Urban** (2008): 66.9%. **Sex distribution** (2008): male 46.55%; female 53.45%. **Age breakdown** (2008): under 15, 15.1%; 15–29, 22.7%; 30–44, 21.1%; 45–59, 20.4%; 60–74, 13.8%; 75–84, 5.7%; 85 and over, 1.2%. **Ethnic composition** (2008): Lithuanian 84.1%; Polish 6.1%; Russian 4.9%; Belarusian 1.1%; Ukrainian 0.6%; Jewish 0.1%; other/unknown 3.1%. **Religious affiliation** (2007): Roman Catholic 80.2%; Orthodox 4.9%, of which Old Believers 0.8%; Lutheran/Reformed 0.8%; other Christian 3%; Jewish 0.1%; Muslim 0.1%; nonreligious/other 10.9%. **Major cities** (2008): Vilnius 558,165; Kaunas 352,279; Klaipeda 183,433; Siauliai 126,215; Panevezys 112,619. **Location:** eastern Europe, bordering Latvia, Belarus, Poland, Russia, and the Baltic Sea.

Vital statistics

Birth rate per 1,000 population (2008): 10.4 (world avg. 20.3); within marriage 71.5%. **Death rate** per 1,000 population (2008): 13.1 (world avg. 8.5). **Total fertility rate** (avg. births per childbearing woman; 2008): 1.47. **Life expectancy** at birth (2008): male 66.3 years; female 77.6 years.

National economy

Budget (2007). *Revenue:* LTL 30,067,000,000 (tax revenue 58.4%, of which tax on goods and services 36.8%, income tax 13.0%; social security contributions 30.4%; grants 5.8%; nontax revenue 5.4%). *Expenditures:* LTL 30,933,000,000 (social security and welfare 33.1%; general administration 23.7%; health 11.4%; economic affairs 11.1%; education 6.9%; defense 5.8%). **Gross national income** (2008): US$39,866,000,000 (US$11,870 per capita). **Production** (metric tons except as noted). *Agriculture and*

---

1 metric ton = about 1.1 short tons;   1 kilometer = 0.6 mi (statute);   1 metric ton-km cargo = about 0.68 short ton-mi cargo;   c.i.f.: cost, insurance, and freight;   f.o.b.: free on board

fishing (2007): wheat 1,390,700, barley 1,013,700, sugar beets 799,900; livestock (number of live animals) 1,127,100 pigs, 838,800 cattle; fisheries production 190,890 (from aquaculture 2%). *Mining and quarrying* (2006): limestone 1,776,300; peat 471,400. *Manufacturing* (value added in US$'000,000; 2006): food products and beverages 664, of which dairy products 170; wood products 372; bricks, tiles, and ceramics 192; refined petroleum products 174. *Energy production (consumption)*: electricity (kW·hr; 2008) 13,101,000,000 ([2006] 12,054,000,000); coal (metric tons; 2006) none (399,000); crude petroleum (barrels; 2008) 938,000 ([2006] 58,800,000); petroleum products (metric tons; 2006) 7,957,000 (2,486,000); natural gas (cu m; 2006) none (2,926,000,000). **Public debt** (December 2008):. US$7,099,000,000. **Population economically active** (2007): total 1,603,100; activity rate of total population 47.6% (participation rates: ages 15–64, 67.9%; female 49.3%; registered unemployed [2008] 5.8%). **Selected balance of payments data.** Receipts from (US$'000,000): tourism (2007) 1,153; remittances (2008) 1,537; foreign direct investment (FDI; 2005–07 avg.) 1,602. Disbursements for (US$'000,000): tourism (2007) 1,143; remittances (2008) 567; FDI (2005–07 avg.) 411.

Foreign trade

Imports (2007; c.i.f.): US$24,445,000,000 (machinery and apparatus 18.1%; mineral fuels 16.2%, of which crude petroleum 9.2%; motor vehicles 14.5%; chemical products 12.6%). *Major import sources:* Russia 18.0%; Germany 15.0%; Poland 10.6%; Latvia 5.5%; Netherlands 4.3%. **Exports** (2007; f.o.b.): US$17,162,000,000 (food products 14.0%; machinery and apparatus 12.8%; refined petroleum products 11.6%; motor vehicles and parts 8.5%; furniture 5.1%; fertilizers 4.9%; wearing apparel and accessories 4.3%). *Major export destinations:* Russia 15.0%; Latvia 12.9%; Germany 10.5%; Poland 6.3%; Estonia 5.8%.

Transport and communications

Transport. *Railroads* (2007): length 2,180 km; passenger-km 408,710,000; metric ton-km cargo 14,372,677,000. *Roads* (2007): total length 80,715 km (paved 88%). *Vehicles* (2007): passenger cars 1,587,903; trucks and buses 140,995. *Air transport* (2007): passenger-km 1,521,700,000; metric ton-km cargo 5,777,000. **Communications**, in total units (units per 1,000 persons). Telephone landlines (2008): 785,000 (234); cellular telephone subscribers (2008): 5,023,000 (1,496); personal computers (2007): 618,000 (183); total Internet users (2008): 1,777,000 (529); broadband Internet subscribers (2008): 590,000 (176).

Education and health

Educational attainment (2005). Percentage of population ages 15 and over having: no schooling through complete primary education 14.7%; lower secondary 18.0%; higher secondary 28.2%; vocational/technical 19.3%; higher 19.8%. **Literacy** (2007): total population ages 15 and over literate 99.7%. **Health** (2008): physicians 13,403 (1 per 250 persons); hospital beds 27,362 (1 per 122 persons); infant mortality rate per 1,000 live births 4.5, undernourished population (2002–04) less than 2.5% of total population.

Military

Total active duty personnel (November 2008): 8,850 (army 83.4%, navy 5.3%, air force 11.3%). **Military expenditure as percentage of GDP** (2008): 1.1%; per capita expenditure US$149.

Background

Lithuanian tribes united in the mid-13th century to oppose the Teutonic knights. Gediminas, one of the grand dukes, expanded Lithuania into an empire that dominated much of Eastern Europe in the 14th through 16th centuries. In 1386 the Lithuanian grand duke became the king of Poland, and the two countries remained closely associated until Lithuania was acquired by Russia in the Third Partition of Poland in 1795. Occupied by Germany during World War I, it declared its independence in 1918. In 1940 the Soviet Red Army gained control of Lithuania. Germany occupied it again in 1941–44, but the USSR regained control in 1944. With the breakup of the USSR, Lithuania became independent in 1991. It signed a border treaty with Russia in 1997, and it joined the European Union and NATO in 2004.

Recent Developments

In 2009 Lithuania celebrated the 1,000th year of its first mention in historical records. Its economy, however, was severely affected by the global banking crisis, particularly by the significant reduction in local businesses' access to credit. As a result, GDP fell 20.2%, exports plunged 32.2%, and unemployment soared to 13.8%. The conservative government was forced to cut public spending and also sold US$1.5 billion in state bonds in the US.

Internet resource: <www.stat.gov.lt/en>.

Luxembourg

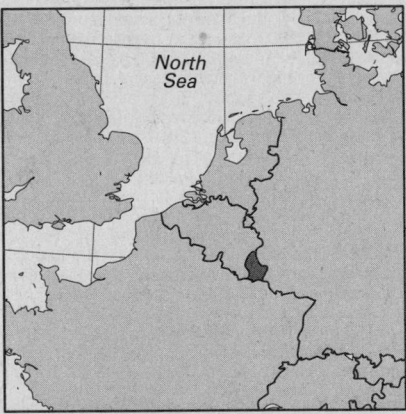

North Sea

Official name: Groussherzogtum Lëtzebuerg (Luxembourgish); Grand-Duché de Luxembourg (French); Grossherzogtum Luxemburg (German) (Grand Duchy of Luxembourg). **Form of government:** constitutional monarchy with one legislative house (Chamber of Deputies [60]). **Head of state:** Grand Duke Henri (from 2000). **Head of government:** Prime Minister Jean-Claude Juncker (from 1995). **Capital:** Luxembourg. **Official language:** none (Luxembourgish is the national language; French and German are both languages of administration). **Official religion:** none. **Monetary unit:** 1 euro (€) = 100 cents; valuation (1 Jul 2010) US$1 = €0.80.

Demography

Area: 999 sq mi, 2,586 sq km. **Population** (2009): 498,000. **Density** (2009): persons per sq mi 498.5, persons per sq km 192.6. **Urban** (2008): 82.0%. **Sex distribution** (2008): male 49.61%; female 50.39%. **Age breakdown** (2008): under 15, 17.9%; 15–29, 18.7%; 30–44, 24.0%; 45–59, 20.6%; 60–74, 12.2%; 75–84, 5.2%; 85 and over, 1.4%. **Ethnic composition** (nationality; 2008): Luxembourger 56.3%; Portuguese 16.2%; French 5.8%; Italian 3.9%; Belgian 3.4%; German 2.4%; other 12.0%. **Religious affiliation** (2005): Roman Catholic 90%; Protestant 3%; Muslim 2%; Orthodox 1%; other 4%. **Major communes (urban agglomerations)** (2007): Luxembourg 85,467 (125,594); Esch-sur-Alzette 29,515 (72,437); Pétange 15,151 (22,379); Differdange 20,443; Dudelange 18,052. **Location:** western Europe, bordering Belgium, Germany, and France.

Vital statistics

Birth rate per 1,000 population (2008): 11.3 (world avg. 20.3); within marriage 69.8%. **Death rate** per 1,000 population (2008): 7.3 (world avg. 8.5). **Total fertility rate** (avg. births per childbearing woman; 2008): 1.60. **Life expectancy** at birth (2007): male 77.6 years; female 82.7 years.

National economy

Budget (2008; general government [consolidated] budget). *Revenue:* €15,864,000,000 (indirect taxes 33.2%; direct taxes 29.7%; social contributions 27.0%). *Expenditures:* €14,920,300,000 (social benefits 47.7%; development expenditure 9.7%). **Public debt** (2007): negligible. **Gross national income** (2008): US$41,406,000,000 (US$84,890 per capita). **Production** (metric tons except as noted). *Agriculture and fishing* (2008): wheat 97,760, barley 52,816, potatoes 21,756; livestock (number of live animals) 195,855 cattle, 81,407 pigs. *Mining and quarrying* (2007): limited quantities of limestone and slate. *Manufacturing* (value added in €'000,000; 2008): base metals 1,031.9; rubber and plastic products 320.8; fabricated metal products 304.9. *Energy production (consumption):* electricity (kW-hr; 2008–09) 3,508,000,000 ([2006] 7,890,000,000); coal (metric tons; 2006) none (153,000); petroleum products (metric tons; 2006) none (2,498,000); natural gas (cu m; 2007) none (1,403,300,000). **Population economically active** (2008): total 218,100; activity rate of total population 44.6% (participation rates: ages 15–64, 67.0%; female 43.5%; unemployed [September 2008–August 2009] 5.2%). **Selected balance of payments data.** Receipts from (US$'000,000): tourism (2007) 4,009; remittances (2008) 1,737; foreign direct disinvestment (2005–07 avg.) −670. Disbursements for (US$'000,000): tourism (2007) 3,552; remittances

(2008) 10,922; foreign direct investment (2005–07 avg.) 21,446.

Foreign trade

Imports (2008; c.i.f.): €17,290,280,000 (transportation equipment 15.5%; mineral fuels 15.2%; machinery and apparatus 14.1%; base and fabricated metals 11.2%; chemical products 9.8%; food products and live animals 7.0%). *Major import sources:* Belgium 34.8%; Germany 29.8%; France 12.7%; Netherlands 6.1%; US 2.4%. **Exports** (2008; f.o.b.): €11,890,410,000 (base and fabricated metals 36.2%; machinery and apparatus 15.9%; chemical products 7.1%; transportation equipment 7.0%; food products and live animals 5.0%). *Major export destinations:* Germany 27.5%; France 17.2%; Belgium 12.8%; Netherlands 6.2%; UK 4.9%.

Transport and communications

Transport. *Railroads* (2008): route length 275 km; passenger-km 316,000,000; metric ton-km cargo 294,000,000. *Roads* (2008): total length 2,894 km (paved 100%). *Vehicles* (2008): passenger cars 329,038; trucks and buses 30,116. *Air transport* (2008; Luxair only): passenger-km 1,368,000,000; metric ton-km cargo, negligible. **Communications,** in total units (units per 1,000 persons). Telephone landlines (2008): 261,000 (542); cellular telephone subscribers (2008): 707,000 (1,471); personal computers (2005): 290,000 (634); total Internet users (2008): 387,000 (805); broadband Internet subscribers (2008): 143,000 (298).

Education and health

Educational attainment (2007). Percentage of population ages 25–64 having: no formal schooling through primary education 18%; lower secondary 9%; upper secondary/higher vocational 47%; higher 26%. **Literacy** (2008): virtually 100% literate. **Health** (2007): physicians 1,672 (1 per 287 persons); hospital beds 2,743 (1 per 175 persons); infant mortality rate per 1,000 live births (2008) 2.0; undernourished population (2002–04) less than 2.5% of total population.

Military

Total active duty personnel (November 2008): 900 (army 100%). **Military expenditure as percentage of GDP** (2007): 0.7%; per capita expenditure US$750.

Background

At the time of Roman conquest (57–50 BC), Luxembourg was inhabited by a Belgic tribe. After AD 400, Germanic tribes invaded the region. Made a duchy in 1354, it was ceded to the house of Burgundy in 1443 and to the Habsburgs in 1477. In the mid-16th century it became part of the Spanish Netherlands. It was made a grand duchy in 1815. After an uprising in 1830, its western portion became part of Belgium, while the remainder was held by the Netherlands. In 1867 the European powers guaranteed the neutrality and independence of Luxembourg. In the late 19th century it exploited its extensive iron-ore deposits. It

---

1 metric ton = about 1.1 short tons;   1 kilometer = 0.6 mi (statute);   1 metric ton-km cargo = about 0.68 short ton-mi cargo;   c.i.f.: cost, insurance, and freight;   f.o.b.: free on board

was invaded and occupied by Germany in both world wars. It abandoned its neutrality by joining NATO in 1949; it had joined the Benelux Economic Union in 1944. A member of the European Union, its economy has continued to expand. On 7 Oct 2000, Grand Duke Jean abdicated power in favor of his son, Crown Prince Henri, after 36 years on the throne.

Recent Developments

Luxembourg's economy continued to flourish in 2009, owing in large part to the banking and financial services sector, which accounted for roughly 28% of GDP. Diverse industries included chemicals and rubber as well as steel. Luxembourg's GDP per capita was the third highest in the world, trailing only that of Qatar and Liechtenstein.

Internet resource: <www.ont.lu>.

Macedonia

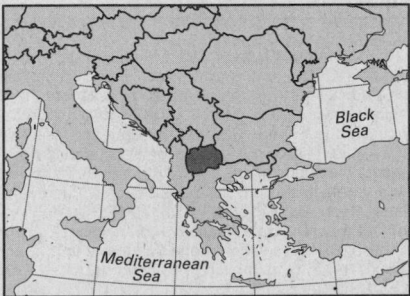

Official name: Republika Makedonija (Macedonian); Republika e Maqedonisë (Albanian) (Republic of Macedonia [member of the UN under the name The Former Yugoslav Republic of Macedonia]). **Form of government:** unitary multiparty republic with one legislative house (Assembly [120]). **Head of state:** President Gjorge Ivanov (from 2009). **Head of government:** Prime Minister Nikola Gruevski (from 2006). **Capital:** Skopje. **Official languages:** Macedonian; Albanian. **Official religion:** none. **Monetary unit:** 1 denar (MKD) = 100 deni; valuation (1 Jul 2010) US$1 = 49.93 MKD.

Demography

Area: 9,928 sq mi, 25,713 sq km. **Population** (2009): 2,052,000. **Density** (2009): persons per sq mi 206.7, persons per sq km 79.8. **Urban** (2005): 68.9%. **Sex distribution** (2005): male 49.95%; female 50.05%. **Age breakdown** (2005): under 15, 20.5%; 15–29, 23.8%; 30–44, 21.8%; 45–59, 18.8%; 60–74, 11.5%; 75–84, 3.2%; 85 and over, 0.4%. **Ethnic composition** (2002): Macedonian 64.2%; Albanian 25.2%; Turkish 3.9%; Rom (Gypsy) 2.7%; Serbian 1.8%; Bosniac 0.8%; other 1.4%. **Religious affiliation** (2005): Orthodox 65%; Sunni Muslim 32%; Roman Catholic 1%; other (mostly Protestant) 2%. **Major city/municipalities** (2008): Skopje (city) 488,600; Bitola 73,300; Kumanovo 71,700; Prilep 66,000; Tetovo 54,500. **Location:** southeastern Europe, bordering Kosovo, Serbia, Bulgaria, Greece, and Albania.

Vital statistics

Birth rate per 1,000 population (2008): 11.2 (world avg. 20.3); within marriage 87.8%. **Death rate** per 1,000 population (2008): 9.3 (world avg. 8.5). **Total fertility rate** (avg. births per childbearing woman; 2007): 1.46. **Life expectancy** at birth (2007): male 71.1 years; female 75.9 years.

National economy

Budget (2008). *Revenue:* MKD 136,412,000,000 (tax revenue 84.4%, of which social contributions 28.1%, VAT 26.5%, income and profit tax 12.7%, excise taxes 10.5%; nontax revenue 15.6%). *Expenditures:* MKD 140,265,000,000 (current expenditures 85.7%, of which transfers 55.6%, wages and salaries 14.5%, interest 1.9%; capital expenditures 14.3%). **Production** (metric tons except as noted). *Agriculture and fishing* (2007): grapes 225,000, potatoes 192,500, wheat 157,400; livestock (number of live animals) 817,500 sheep, 253,800 cattle; fisheries production 1,218 (from aquaculture 90%). *Mining and quarrying* (metal content; 2007): lead 32,000; zinc 20,000; copper 7,300. *Manufacturing* (value added in US$'000,000; 2006): food products and beverages 297; cement, bricks, and glass products 177; iron and steel (including ferronickel) 103; refined petroleum products 53. *Energy production (consumption):* electricity (kW-hr; 2006) 7,006,000,000 (8,801,000,000); coal (metric tons; 2006) none (57,000); lignite (metric tons; 2006) 6,639,000 (6,823,000); crude petroleum (barrels; 2006) none (7,821,000); petroleum products (metric tons; 2006) 1,026,000 (893,000); natural gas (cu m; 2006) none (80,000,000). **Population economically active** (2006): total 891,679; activity rate 55.1% (participation rates: ages 15–64, 61.4%; female 39.5%; unemployed 36.0%). **Gross national income** (2008): US$8,432,000,000 (US$4,140 per capita). **Public debt** (external, outstanding; 2007): US$1,520,000,000. **Selected balance of payments data.** Receipts from (US$'000,000): tourism (2007) 186; remittances (2008) 408; foreign direct investment (2005–07 avg.) 280; official development assistance (2007) 213. Disbursements for (US$'000,000): tourism (2007) 102; remittances (2008) 25.

Foreign trade

Imports (2006; c.i.f.): US$3,763,000,000 (crude petroleum 14.3%; machinery and apparatus 12.2%; iron and steel 9.9%; food products 9.8%; chemical products 9.7%). *Major import sources:* Russia 15.1%; Germany 9.8%; Greece 8.5%; Serbia 7.5%; Bulgaria 6.6%. **Exports** (2006; f.o.b.): US$2,401,000,000 (iron and steel 27.8%, of which flat-rolled products 9.1%; ferronickel 8.4%; wearing apparel and accessories 21.2%; refined petroleum products 8.4%; food products 8.0%; tobacco products 4.7%). *Major export destinations:* Serbia 23.2%; Germany 15.6%; Greece 15.0%; Italy 9.9%; Bulgaria 5.4%.

Transport and communications

Transport. *Railroads* (2007): length (2004) 699 km; passenger-km 109,000,000; metric ton-km cargo 799,000,000. *Roads* (2007): length 13,840 km (paved [2000] 58%). *Vehicles* (2007): passenger cars 248,774; trucks and buses 28,842. *Air transport* (2005; Macedonian Airlines only): passenger-km 266,000,000; metric ton-km cargo 111,000. **Communications**, in total units (units per 1,000 persons). Telephone landlines (2008): 457,000 (224); cellular telephone subscribers (2008): 2,502,000 (123); personal computers (2005): 451,000 (221); total Internet users (2008): 876,000 (429); broadband Internet subscribers (2008): 179,000 (88).

Education and health

Educational attainment (2002). Percentage of population ages 15 and over having: less than full primary education 18.1%; primary 35.0%; secondary 36.9%; postsecondary and higher 10.0%. **Literacy** (2003): total population ages 10 and over literate 96.1%; males literate 98.2%; females literate 94.1%. **Health** (2006): physicians 5,134 (1 per 397 persons); hospital beds 9,343 (1 per 218 persons); infant mortality rate per 1,000 live births (2008) 9.7; undernourished population (2003–05) less than 5% of the total population.

Military

Total active duty personnel (November 2008); 10,890 (army 89.6%, air force 10.4%). **Military expenditure as percentage of GDP** (2008): 2.0%; per capita expenditure US$80.

Background

Macedonia has been inhabited since before 7000 BC. Part of it was incorporated into a Roman province in AD 29. It was settled by Slavic tribes by the mid-6th century AD. Seized by the Bulgarians in 1185, it was ruled by the Ottoman Empire from 1371 to 1912. The north and center of the region were annexed by Serbia in 1913 and in 1918 became part of what was later known as Yugoslavia. When Yugoslavia was partitioned by the Axis powers in 1941, Yugoslav Macedonia was occupied principally by Bulgaria. Macedonia again became part of Yugoslavia in 1946. After Croatia and Slovenia seceded from Yugoslavia, fear of Serbian dominance drove Macedonia to declare its independence in 1991. Because of Greek objections over using the name of an ancient Greek province, it entered the UN in 1993 as "The Former Yugoslav Republic of Macedonia." It normalized relations with Greece in 1995.

Recent Developments

The UN-mediated talks between Macedonia and Greece over the former's name continued without a resolution in 2009. A major incentive for Macedonia to resolve the name issue came on 14 October when the European Commission recommended that the country begin negotiations in 2010 to join the EU. In November the EU announced that citizens of Macedonia, Serbia, and Montenegro would be allowed to travel without a visa within the EU's Schengen zone.

Internet resource: <www.stat.gov.mk>.

Madagascar

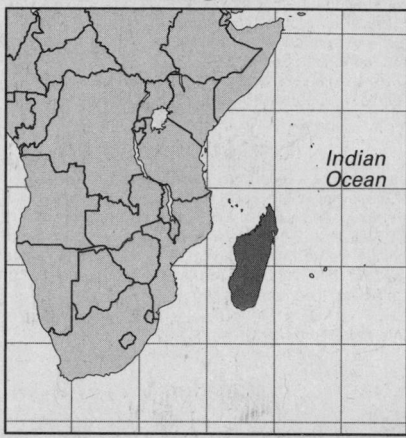

Indian Ocean

Official name: Repoblikan'i Madagasikara (Malagasy); République de Madagascar (French) Republic of Madagascar (English). **Form of government:** transitional regime (from March 2009 the two legislative houses, the Senate [33] and the National Assembly [127], are dissolved). **Heads of state and government:** President of the High Authority of Transition Andry Rajoelina (from 2009), assisted by Prime Minister Albert Camille Vital (from 2009). **Capital:** Antananarivo. **Official languages:** Malagasy; French; English. **Official religion:** none. **Monetary unit:** 1 ariary (MGA) = 5 iraimbilanja; valuation (1 Jul 2010) US$1 = MGA 2,219.30.

Demography

Area: 226,662 sq mi, 587,051 sq km. **Population** (2009): 19,625,000. **Density** (2009): persons per sq mi 86.6, persons per sq km 33.4. **Urban** (2006): 27.3%. **Sex distribution** (2005): male 49.72%; female 50.28%. **Age breakdown** (2006): under 15, 44.1%; 15–29, 27.1%; 30–44, 15.7%; 45–59, 8.4%; 60–74, 3.7%; 75–84, 0.9%; 85 and over, 0.1%. **Ethnic composition** (2000): Malagasy 95.9%, of which Merina 24.0%, Betsimisaraka 13.4%, Betsileo 11.3%, Tsimihety 7.0%, Sakalava 5.9%; Makua 1.1%; French 0.6%; Comorian 0.5%; Reunionese 0.4%; other 1.5%. **Religious affiliation** (2005): traditional beliefs 42%; Protestant (significantly Lutheran) 27%; Roman Catholic 20%; Sunni Muslim 2%; other 9%. **Major cities** (2001): Antananarivo 1,403,449; Toamasina 179,045; Antsirabe 160,356; Fianarantsoa 144,225; Mahajanga 135,660. **Location:** island in the Indian Ocean, east of Mozambique.

Vital statistics

Birth rate per 1,000 population (2006): 38.8 (world avg. 20.3). **Death rate** per 1,000 population (2006): 8.7 (world avg. 8.5). **Total fertility rate** (avg. births per childbearing woman; 2006): 5.29. **Life expectancy** at birth (2006): male 59.9 years; female 63.7 years.

---

1 metric ton = about 1.1 short tons;   1 kilometer = 0.6 mi (statute);   1 metric ton-km cargo = about 0.68 short ton-mi cargo;   c.i.f.: cost, insurance, and freight;   f.o.b.: free on board

National economy

Budget (2007). *Revenue:* MGA 2,251,000,000,000 (tax revenue 67.76%; grants 31.1%; nontax revenue 1.3%). *Expenditures:* MGA 2,818,000,000,000 (current expenditures 50.1%; capital expenditures 49.9%). **Public debt** (external, outstanding; 2007): US$1,425,000,000. **Production** (metric tons except as noted). *Agriculture and fishing* (2007): paddy rice 3,596,000, sugarcane 2,700,000, cassava 2,400,000, cloves (whole and stem) 10,000, vanilla 2,600; livestock (number of live animals) 9,600,000 cattle, 1,610,000 pigs, 3,000,000 geese; fisheries production 159,035 (from aquaculture 7%). *Mining and quarrying* (2007): chromite ore 95,000; graphite 15,000; sapphires 4,700 kg; rubies 920 kg; gold 210 kg (illegally smuggled, 2,000 kg). *Manufacturing* (value in US$'000,000; 2004): beverages 107; wearing apparel 57; fabricated metal products 35. *Energy production (consumption):* electricity (kW-hr; 2006) 1,065,000,000 (1,065,000,000); coal (metric tons; 2006) none (10,000); crude petroleum (barrels; 2006) none (3,518,000); petroleum products (metric tons; 2006) 325,000 (746,000). **Population economically active** (2005): total 9,844,100; activity rate of total population 52.8% (participation rates: ages 15–64, 88.1%; female 49.6%; unemployed 2.8%). **Selected balance of payments data.** Receipts from (US$'000,000): tourism (2007) 262; remittances (2008) 11; foreign direct investment (2005–07 avg.) 459; official development assistance (2007) 892. Disbursements for (US$'000,000): tourism (2007) 94; remittances (2008) 21. **Gross national income** (2008): US$7,766,000,000 (US$410 per capita).

Foreign trade

Imports (2006; c.i.f.): US$1,760,300,000 (refined petroleum products 17.7%; machinery and apparatus 12.8%; food products 11.4%, of which cereals 4.3%; fabrics 9.3%; chemical products 8.6%; motor vehicles 5.0%; wool 4.8%). *Major import sources:* China 17.8%; Bahrain 16.4%; France 13.2%; South Africa 5.7%; US 3.6%. **Exports** (2006; f.o.b.): US$1,008,200,000 (food products and spices 32.4%, of which shrimp 12.0%, vanilla 4.7%; fish 4.4%, cloves 2.7%; wearing apparel and accessories 25.0%; refined petroleum products 7.9%; precious and semiprecious stones 2.6%). *Major export destinations:* France 39.5%; US 15.0%; Germany 6.0%; Italy 4.2%; UK 3.0%.

Transport and communications

Transport. *Railroads* (2000): route length (2003) 901 km; passenger-km 24,471,000; metric ton-km cargo 27,200,000. *Roads* (2000): total length 49,827 km (paved 12%). *Vehicles* (1998): passenger cars 64,000; trucks and buses 9,100. *Air transport* (2007): passenger-km 1,248,000,000; metric ton-km cargo (2006) 18,768,000. **Communications**, in total units (units per 1,000 persons). Telephone landlines (2008): 165,000 (8.6); cellular telephone subscribers (2008): 4,835,000 (253); personal computers (2005): 102,000 (5.5); total Internet users (2008): 316,000 (17); broadband Internet subscribers (2008): 6,200 (0.3).

Education and health

Educational attainment (2003–04). Percentage of population ages 25–59 (male) and 25–49 (female) having: no formal schooling 20.4%; incomplete primary education 33.6%; complete primary 13.2%; incomplete secondary 23.0%; complete secondary 6.4%; higher 3.4%. **Literacy** (2006): percentage of total population ages 15 and over literate 70.7%; males literate 76.5%; females literate 65.3%. **Health** (2004): physicians 1,861 (1 per 9,998 persons); hospital beds 9,303 (1 per 2,000 persons); infant mortality rate per 1,000 live births (2006) 58.5; undernourished population (2002–04) 6,600,000 (38% of total population based on the consumption of a minimum daily requirement of 1,800 calories).

Military

Total active duty personnel (November 2008): 13,500 (army 92.6%, navy 3.7%, air force 3.7%). **Military expenditure as percentage of GDP** (2007): 1.1%; per capita expenditure US$4.

Background

Indonesians migrated to Madagascar about AD 700. The first European to visit the island was Portuguese navigator Diogo Dias in 1500. Trade in arms and slaves allowed the development of Malagasy kingdoms at the beginning of the 17th century. The Merina kingdom became dominant in the 18th century and in 1868 signed a treaty granting France control over the northwestern coast. In 1895 French troops took the island, and Madagascar became a French overseas territory in 1946. As the Malagasy Republic, it gained independence in 1960. It severed ties with France in the 1970s. A new constitution was adopted in 1992, and the country was named the Republic of Madagascar. The country has since been both politically and economically unstable.

Recent Developments

The early months of 2009 in Madagascar saw more than 100 people killed in weeks of violent street protests against Pres. Marc Ravalomanana, who was accused of having ruled in an authoritarian way and having misspent public money. The protests culminated in what was widely regarded as a coup in March, when soldiers pledged their support to Andry Rajoelina, a former mayor of Antananarivo who had led the opposition to Ravalomanana. Ravalomanana handed power to the military and then fled to the African mainland. The military transferred power in a matter of hours to Rajoelina, who was quickly sworn in as president. The international community refused to accept the new government because it had come to power illegitimately, and Madagascar was suspended from both the African Union and the Southern African Development Community. In August international mediators led by former Mozambican president Joaquim Chissano met with Rajoelina and Ravalomanana, and an agreement was reached on a power-sharing government for a transitional period of 15 months, during which legislative and presidential elections would be held. Rajoelina did not participate in a final round of power-sharing talks, and he formally abandoned the power-sharing deal altogether on 20 December.

Internet resource: <www.wildmadagascar.org>.

Malawi

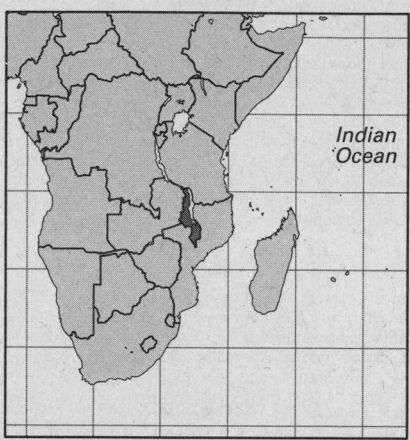

Indian Ocean

Official name: Republic of Malawi. **Form of government:** multiparty republic with one legislative house (National Assembly [193]). **Head of state and government:** President Bingu wa Mutharika (from 2004). **Capital:** Lilongwe (the judiciary meets in Blantyre). **Official language:** none. **Official religion:** none. **Monetary unit:** 1 Malawian kwacha (MK) = 100 tambala; valuation (1 Jul 2010) US$1 = MK 149.17.

Demography

Area: 45,747 sq mi, 118,484 sq km. **Population** (2009): 15,029,000. **Density** (2009; based on land area): persons per sq mi 412.9, persons per sq km 159.4. **Urban** (2008): 15.0% **Sex distribution** (2008): male 48.72%; female 51.28%. **Age breakdown** (2007): under 15, 45.7%; 15–29, 28.4%; 30–44, 14.1%; 45–59, 7.6%; 60–74, 3.5%; 75–84, 0.6%; 85 and over, 0.1%. **Ethnic composition** (2000): Chewa 34.7%; Maravi 12.2%; Ngoni 9.0%; Yao 7.9%; Tumbuka 7.9%; Lomwe 7.7%; Ngonde 3.5%; other 17.1%. **Religious affiliation** (2005): Protestant/independent Christian 55%; Roman Catholic 20%; Muslim 20%; traditional beliefs 3%; other 2%. **Major cities** (2008): Lilongwe 669,021; Blantyre 661,444; Mzuzu 128,432; Zomba 87,366; Kasungu 42,351. **Location:** southeastern Africa, bordering Tanzania, Mozambique, and Zambia.

Vital statistics

Birth rate per 1,000 population (2008): 42.1 (world avg. 20.3). **Death rate** per 1,000 population (2008): 14.9 (world avg. 8.5). **Total fertility rate** (avg. births per childbearing woman; 2008): 5.67. **Life expectancy** at birth (2008): male 48.4 years; female 49.5 years.

National economy

Budget (2008–09). *Revenue:* MK 187,402,000,000 (tax revenue 62.4%, of which VAT 21.0%, excises 9.7%, corporate taxes 8.1%; grants 29.3%; nontax

revenue 6.9%; other 1.4%). *Expenditures:* MK 223,502,000,000 (current expenditures 82.0%; capital expenditures 18.0%). **Public debt** (external, outstanding; March 2009): US$664,000,000. **Production** (metric tons except as noted). *Agriculture and fishing* (2007): corn (maize) 3,444,700, sugarcane 2,500,000, cassava 2,150,000, tobacco leaves 118,000, pigeon peas 79,000, tea 39,000, sunflower seeds 5,913; livestock (number of live animals) 1,900,000 goats, 752,000 cattle, 458,000 pigs; fisheries production 68,000 (from aquaculture 2%). *Mining and quarrying* (2007): limestone 31,490; gemstones (significantly rubies and sapphires) 3,710 kg. *Manufacturing* (value added in US$'000,000; 2001): food products 62; beverages 28; chemical products 11. *Energy production (consumption):* electricity (kW-hr; 2006) 1,556,000,000 (1,546,000,000); coal (metric tons; 2007) 58,550 ([2006] 50,000); petroleum products (metric tons; 2006) none (263,000). **Population economically active** (2006): total 5,585,000; activity rate 41.2% (participation rates: ages 15–64, 77.1%; female 50.2%). **Gross national income** (2008): US$4,107,000,000 (US$290 per capita). **Selected balance of payments data.** Receipts from (US$'000,000): tourism (2007) 27; remittances (2008) 1.0; foreign direct investment (2005–07 avg.) 37; official development assistance (2007) 735. Disbursements for (US$'000,000): tourism (2007) 73; remittances (2008) 1.0.

Foreign trade

Imports (2007; c.i.f.): MK 192,833,000,000 (chemical products 27.8%, of which fertilizers 13.7%; refined petroleum products 13.1%; machinery and apparatus 11.8%; motor vehicles 10.4%; food products 5.9%). *Major import sources:* South Africa 29.1%; Mozambique 12.2%; UAE 7.0%; UK 5.0%; India 5.0%. **Exports** (2007; f.o.b.): MK 121,567,000,000 (unmanufactured tobacco 48.7%; corn (maize) 11.5%; raw sugar 7.0%; tea 6.4%; sunflower seeds 3.7%; wearing apparel and accessories 3.7%). *Major export destinations:* Zimbabwe 15.2%; South Africa 14.8%; Belgium 8.0%; UK 6.6%; Germany 5.8%.

Transport and communications

Transport. *Railroads* (2007): route length 797 km; (2004) passenger-km 29,523,000; metric ton-km cargo 18,438,000. *Roads* (2003): total length 15,451 km (paved 45%). *Vehicles* (2001): passenger cars 22,500; trucks and buses 57,600. *Air transport* (2007; Air Malawi only): passenger-km 165,000,000. **Communications,** in total units (units per 1,000 persons). Telephone landlines (2008): 236,000 (16); cellular telephone subscribers (2008): 1,781,000 (122); personal computers (2007): 28,000 (2); total Internet users (2008): 316,000 (22); broadband Internet subscribers (2007): 1,600 (0.1).

Education and health

Educational attainment (2004). Percentage of population ages 25 and over having: no formal education/unknown 33.5%; incomplete primary education 24.2%; complete primary 27.9%; secondary and university 14.4%. **Literacy** (2007): total population ages 15 and over literate 65.9%; males literate 78.1%; fe-

---

1 metric ton = about 1.1 short tons;   1 kilometer = 0.6 mi (statute);   1 metric ton-km cargo = about 0.68 short ton-mi cargo;   c.i.f.: cost, insurance, and freight;   f.o.b.: free on board

males literate 53.9%. **Health** (2008): physicians 260 (1 per 56,246 persons); hospital beds (2007) 15,658 (1 per 909 persons); infant mortality rate per 1,000 live births 88.1; undernourished population (2002–04) 4,200,000 (35% of total population based on the consumption of a minimum daily requirement of 1,790 calories).

Military

Total active duty personnel (November 2008): 5,300 (army 100%). **Military expenditure as percentage of GDP** (2007): 1.7%; per capita expenditure US$3.

Background

Inhabited since at least 8000 BC, the region was settled by Bantu-speaking peoples between the 1st and the 4th century AD. About 1480 they founded the Maravi Confederacy, which encompassed most of central and southern Malawi. In northern Malawi the Ngonde people established a kingdom about 1600. The slave trade flourished during the 18th–19th centuries. Britain established colonial authority in 1891, and the area became known as Nyasaland in 1907. The colonies of Northern and Southern Rhodesia and Nyasaland formed (1951–53) a federation, which was dissolved in 1963. The next year Malawi achieved independence. In 1966 it became a republic, with Hastings Banda as president. In 1971 Banda was designated president for life, and he ruled until he was defeated in multiparty elections in 1994. A new constitution was adopted in 1995.

Recent Developments

Malawi in 2009 had one of the world's fastest-growing economies, one that successfully dodged most of the effects of the global financial crisis. According to the Reserve Bank of Malawi, GDP growth for 2009 was 16.6%. Helping to boost the economy was the government's Agricultural Input Subsidy Program, which benefited two million small-scale producers of corn (maize), tobacco, coffee, and tea. In June the government announced a record corn harvest that was expected to more than meet internal consumption needs.

Internet resource: <www.nso.malawi.net>.

Malaysia

Indian Ocean

Official name: Malaysia. **Form of government:** federal constitutional monarchy with two legislative houses (Senate [70]; House of Representatives [222]). **Head of state:** Yang di-Pertuan Agong (Paramount Ruler) Tuanku Mizan Zainal Abidin ibni al-Marhum Sultan Mahmud (from 2006). **Head of government:** Prime Minister Datuk Seri Najib Tun Razak (from 2009). **Capital:** Kuala Lumpur (location of the first royal palace and both houses of parliament). **Administrative center:** Putrajaya (location of the second royal palace, the prime minister's office, and the supreme court). **Official language:** Malay. **Official religion:** Islam. **Monetary unit:** 1 ringgit, or Malaysian dollar (RM) = 100 sen; valuation (1 Jul 2010) US$1 = RM 3.23.

Demography

Area: 127,366 sq mi, 329,876 sq km. **Population** (2009): 27,468,000. **Density** (2009): persons per sq mi 215.7, persons per sq km 83.3. **Urban** (2008): 63.5%. **Sex distribution** (2008): male 50.90%; female 49.10%. **Age breakdown** (2008): under 15, 32.0%; 15–29, 26.6%; 30–44, 20.4%; 45–59, 14.0%; 60–74, 5.6%; 75 and over, 1.4%. **Ethnic composition** (2008): Malay 50.8%; other indigenous 11.0%; Chinese 22.9%; Indian 6.9%; other citizen 1.2%; noncitizen 7.2%. **Religious affiliation** (2000): Muslim 60.4%; Buddhist 19.2%; Christian 9.1%; Hindu 6.3%; Chinese folk religionist 2.6%; animist 0.8%; other 1.6%. **Major cities** (2006): Kuala Lumpur 1,482,400; Subang Jaya 954,300; Klang 636,700; Johor Bahru 838,900; Ipoh 692,200; Putrajaya 55,000. **Location:** southeastern Asia, on the Malay Peninsula and the northern third of the island of Borneo, bordering Thailand, the South China Sea, Brunei, and Indonesia.

Vital statistics

Birth rate per 1,000 population (2008): 17.5 (world avg. 20.3). **Death rate** per 1,000 population (2008): 4.2 (world avg. 8.5). **Total fertility rate** (avg. births per childbearing woman; 2008): 2.57. **Life expectancy** at birth (2008): male 72.1 years; female 76.8 years.

National economy

Budget (2008). *Revenue:* RM 159,793,000,000 (tax revenue 70.7%, of which corporate taxes 23.6%, taxes on petroleum 15.1%, income tax 9.4%; nontax revenue 29.3%). *Expenditures:* RM 196,346,000,000 (current expenditures 78.2%, of which wages and salaries 20.9%; development expenditures 21.8%). **Population economically active** (2008): total 11,028,100; activity rate 40.8% (participation rates: ages 15–64, 62.6%; female 35.8%; unemployed [April 2008–March 2009] 3.4%). **Production** (metric tons except as noted). *Agriculture and fishing* (2008): oil palm fruit 83,000,000, rice 2,384,000, natural rubber 1,072,400, sugarcane 693,850, coconuts 555,120, bananas 530,000, cassava 430,000, cacao beans 30,000; livestock (number of live animals) 790,000 cattle, 131,000 buffalo; fisheries production (2007) 1,783,739 (from aquaculture 19%). *Mining and quarrying* (2008–09): iron ore 1,023,434; tin (metal content) 2,646 gold 2,427 kg. *Manufacturing* (value added in RM '000,000; 2006): electrical machinery and electronics 32,017; chemical products 19,035; refined petroleum and coal products 16,577; transportation equipment 6,796. *Energy production (consumption):* electricity (kW-hr; 2008–09) 103,734,200,000 (92,662,100,000); coal (metric tons; 2008–09) 1,433,341 ([2006] 11,143,000); crude petroleum (barrels; 2008–09) 248,239,000 ([2006] 185,607,500); petroleum products (metric tons; 2008–09) 23,380,000 ([2006] 23,718,000); natural gas (cu m; 2008–09) 56,794,675,000 ([2007] 32,900,000,000). **Gross national income** (2008): US$188,061,000,000 (US$6,970 per capita). **Public debt** (external, outstanding; 2007): US$18,441,000,000. **Selected balance of payments data.** Receipts from (US$'000,000): tourism (2007) 12,905; remittances (2008) 1,920; foreign direct investment (FDI; 2006–08 avg.) 7,256; official development assistance (2007) 200. Disbursements for (US$'000,000): tourism (2007) 5,252; remittances (2008) 6,385; FDI (2005–07 avg.) 6,667.

Foreign trade

Imports (2006; c.i.f.): RM 481,000,000,000 (microcircuits and transistors 23.9%; crude petroleum 8.3%; office machines, computers, and parts 7.8%; chemical products 7.8%; base metals 6.8%). *Major import sources:* Japan 13.2%; US 12.5%; China 12.1%; Singapore 11.7%; Thailand 5.5%. **Exports** (2006; f.o.b.): RM 589,367,000,000 (computers, office machines, and parts 17.4%; microcircuits and transistors 15.9%; crude petroleum 8.9%; telecommunications equipment 5.7%; natural gas 4.8%; palm oil 3.2%). *Major export destinations:* US 18.8%; Singapore 15.4%; Japan 8.9%; China 7.2%; Thailand 5.3%.

Transport and communications

Transport. *Railroads* (2008–09): route length (2008) 1,849 km; passenger-km 1,466,892,000; metric ton-km cargo 1,267,935,000. *Roads* (2006): total length 90,127 km (paved 79%). *Vehicles* (2006): passenger cars 7,024,043; trucks and buses 896,570. *Air transport* (2008–09): passenger-km 32,297,000,000; metric ton-km cargo 2,142,483,000. **Communications,** in total units (units per 1,000 persons). Telephone landlines (2008): 4,292,000 (159); cellular telephone subscribers (2008): 27,743,000 (1,027); personal computers (2006): 6,106,000 (234); total Internet users (2008): 16,903,000 (626); broadband Internet subscribers (2008): 1,302,000 (48).

Education and health

Educational attainment (2002). Percentage of population ages 25–64 having: no formal schooling/unknown 8.4%; primary education 28.7%; lower secondary 20.7%; upper secondary 31.1%; higher 11.1%. **Literacy** (2007): total population ages 15 and over literate 91.9%; males literate 94.2%; females literate 89.6%. **Health** (2008): physicians 25,102 (1 per 1,076 persons); hospital beds (2007) 47,784 (1 per 556 persons); infant mortality rate per 1,000 live births 6.7; undernourished population (2002–04) 600,000 (3% of total population based on the consumption of a minimum daily requirement of 1,850 calories).

Military

Total active duty personnel (November 2008): 109,000 (army 73.4%, navy 12.8%, air force 13.8%). **Military expenditure as percentage of GDP** (2008): 1.9%; per capita expenditure US$146.

Background

Malaya has been inhabited for 6,000–8,000 years, and small kingdoms existed in the 2nd–3rd centuries AD, when adventurers from India first arrived. Sumatran exiles founded the city-state of Malacca about 1400, and it flourished as a trading and Islamic religious center until its capture by the Portuguese in 1511. Malacca passed to the Dutch in 1641. The British founded a settlement on Singapore Island in 1819, and by 1867 they had established the Straits Settlements, including Malacca, Singapore, and Penang. During the late 19th century the Chinese began to migrate to Malaya. Japan invaded in 1941. Opposition to British rule led to the creation of the United Malays National Organization (UNMO) in 1946, and in 1948 the peninsula was federated with Penang. Malaya gained independence in 1957, and the Federation of Malaysia was established in 1963. Its economy expanded greatly from the late 1970s, but it suffered from the economic slump that struck the area in the mid-1990s.

Recent Developments

Malaysia's economy was hit hard by the global recession in 2009. GDP shrank at a rate of 8.7%—a far slide from the 15.5% growth during 2008. The crucial manufacturing and mining sectors suffered the largest drops. The value of Malaysian exports posted a year-on-year decline of 16.6%; the drop was reflected in higher-than-average unemployment in manufacturing. The production of natural rubber, long an important export commodity for Malaysia, fell by 19.6%, though production of crude palm oil remained steady. General unemployment leveled off at 3.5% nationally, and the inflation rate increased by only 0.7%. Malaysia's central bank predicted that the economy would strengthen, buoyed by more stable global conditions and two economic stimulus packages amounting to more than US$18 billion. Indeed, exports in January 2010 showed a 37.0% increase over those of January 2009.

Internet resource: <www.statistics.gov.my>.

Maldives

Official name: Dhivehi Raajjeyge Jumhooriyyaa (Republic of Maldives). **Form of government:** multiparty republic with one legislative house (People's Majlis [77]). **Head of state and government:** President Mohamed Nasheed (from 2008). **Capital:** Male. **Official language:** Dhivehi (Maldivian). **Official religion:** Islam. **Monetary unit:** 1 rufiyaa (Rf) = 100 laari; valuation (1 Jul 2010) US$1 = Rf 12.63.

---

1 metric ton = about 1.1 short tons;   1 kilometer = 0.6 mi (statute);   1 metric ton-km cargo = about 0.68 short ton-mi cargo;   c.i.f.: cost, insurance, and freight;   f.o.b.: free on board

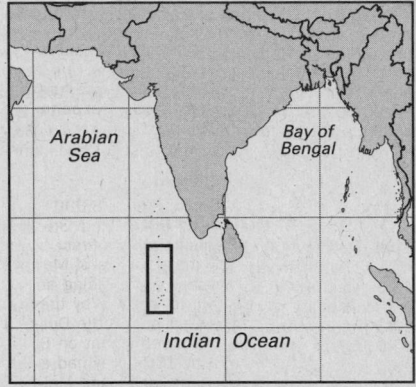

Arabian Sea

Bay of Bengal

Indian Ocean

Demography

Area: 115 sq mi, 298 sq km. **Population** (2009): 315,000. **Density** (2009; based on areas of inhabited islets only): persons per sq mi 6,984, persons per sq km 2,697. **Urban** (2006): 34.7%. **Sex distribution** (2006): male 50.66%; female 49.34%. **Age breakdown** (2006): under 15, 31.1%; 15–29, 33.2%; 30–44, 18.3%; 45–59, 9.2%; 60–74, 5.2%; 75–84, 1.1%; 85 and over, 0.2%; unknown 1.7%. **Ethnic composition** (2000): Maldivian 98.5%; Sinhalese 0.7%; other 0.8%. **Religious affiliation:** virtually 100% Sunni Muslim. **Major islets** (2006): Male 103,693; Hithadhoo 9,465; Fuvammulah 7,636. **Location:** islands in the Indian Ocean, south of India.

Vital statistics

Birth rate per 1,000 population (2008): 22 (world avg. 20.3). **Death rate** per 1,000 population (2008): 3 (world avg. 8.5). **Total fertility rate** (avg. births per childbearing woman; 2006): 2.1. **Life expectancy** at birth (2007): male 72.3 years; female 73.7 years.

National economy

Budget (2008). *Revenue:* Rf 7,757,000,000 (nontax revenue 48.6%, of which resort lease rent 19.5%; tax revenue 43.7%, of which import duties 31.7%; grants 7.2%; other 0.5%). *Expenditures:* Rf 9,789,000,000 (general administration 21.8%; community programs 20.5%; education 15.6%; health 12.8%; police and security 9.1%; defense 5.6%). **Public debt** (external, outstanding; 2008): US$471,700,000. **Production** (metric tons except as noted). *Agriculture and fishing* (2007): vegetables 28,526, bananas 11,000, coconuts 2,625; fisheries production 144,169, of which skipjack tuna 97,342, yellowfin tuna 24,415 (from aquaculture, none). *Mining and quarrying:* coral for construction materials. *Manufacturing:* n.a.; however, major industries include boat building and repairing, coir yarn and mat weaving, coconut and fish processing, lacquerwork, garment manufacturing, and handicrafts. *Energy production (consumption):* electricity (kW-hr; 2008) 301,000,000 ([2006] 212,000,000); petroleum products (metric tons; 2006) none (203,000). Selected balance of payments data. Receipts from (US$'000,000): tourism (2007) 586; remittances (2008) 3; foreign direct investment (2005–07 avg.)

13; official development assistance (2007) 37. Disbursements for (US$'000,000): tourism (2007) 92; remittances (2008) 103. **Population economically active** (2006): total 128,836; activity rate of total population 43.1% (participation rates: ages 15–64, 65.8%; female 41.3%; unemployed 14.4%). **Gross national income** (2008): US$1,126,000,000 (US$3,630 per capita).

Foreign trade

Imports (2008; c.i.f.): US$1,388,000,000 (refined petroleum products 22.6%; food products 15.3%; goods for construction 14.1%; transportation equipment and parts 10.4%). *Major import sources:* Singapore 21.3%; UAE 18.0%; India 10.4%; Malaysia 7.7%; Sri Lanka 5.9%. **Exports** (2008; f.o.b.): US$330,500,000 (reexports [mostly jet fuel] 61.6%; fish 37.3%, of which fresh skipjack tuna 16.7%, fresh yellowfin tuna 13.2%, dried fish 3.0%). *Major export destinations* (domestic exports only): Thailand 49.4%; Sri Lanka 9.5%; France 8.8%; Italy 8.3%; UK 7.7%.

Transport and communications

Transport. *Railroads:* none. *Vehicles* (2008): passenger cars 3,917; trucks and buses 2,314. *Air transport* (2008; Male airport only): passenger arrivals 1,275,993, passenger departures 1,264,572; cargo unloaded 20,561 metric tons, cargo loaded 13,029 metric tons. **Communications,** in total units (units per 1,000 persons). Telephone landlines (2008): 47,000 (151); cellular telephone subscribers (2008): 436,000 (1,407); personal computers (2005): 45,000 (152); total Internet users (2008): 72,000 (231); broadband Internet subscribers (2008): 16,000 (51).

Education and health

Educational attainment (2006). Population ages 6 and over 267,283; percentage with bachelor's degree 0.6%; master's degree 0.3%. **Literacy** (2006): total population ages 15 and over literate 93.5%; males literate 92.5%; females literate 94.5%. **Health** (2008): physicians 575 (1 per 539 persons); hospital beds 785 (1 per 395 persons); infant mortality rate per 1,000 live births 11; undernourished population (2002–04) 30,000 (10% of total population based on the consumption of a minimum daily requirement of 1,840 calories).

Military

Total active duty personnel (2006): 2,000-member paramilitary incorporates coast guard duties. **Paramilitary expenditure as percentage of GDP** (2008): 4.9%; per capita expenditure US$139.

Background

The archipelago was settled in the 5th century BC by Buddhists from Sri Lanka and southern India, and Islam was adopted there in 1153. The Portuguese held sway in Male in 1558–73. The islands were a sultanate under the Dutch rulers of Ceylon (now Sri Lanka) during the 17th century. After the British gained control of Ceylon in 1796, the area became a British protectorate, a status formalized in 1887. The islands won full independence from Britain in 1965, and in 1968 a republic was founded. The Maldives joined the Commonwealth in 1982.

Recent Developments

Maldives continued to be concerned about the grave threat facing the islands as a result of sea level rise. The government considered climate change to be a human rights issue, because peoples' right to life was threatened. In March 2009 Maldives declared its intention to become the first carbon-neutral country in the world by 2020, and in early 2010 it officially sent the pledge to the UN. In October 2009, in an effort to draw the attention of the world to the need to reduce global warming, Pres. Mohamed Nasheed and his cabinet members donned scuba gear and held a meeting underwater.

Internet resource: <http://planning.gov.mv>.

Mali

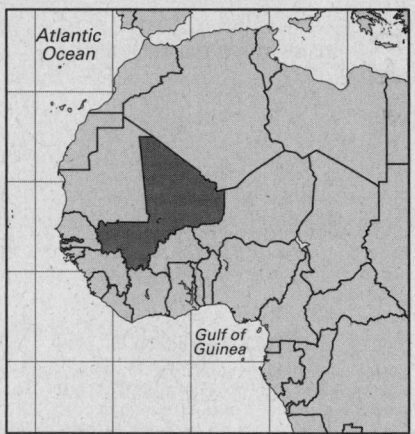

Atlantic Ocean

Gulf of Guinea

Official name: République du Mali (Republic of Mali). **Form of government:** multiparty republic with one legislative house (National Assembly [147]). **Head of state:** President Amadou Toumani Touré (from 2002). **Head of government:** Prime Minister Modibo Sidibé (from 2007). **Capital:** Bamako. **Official language:** French. **Official religion:** none. **Monetary unit:** 1 CFA franc (CFAF) = 100 centimes; valuation (1 Jul 2010) US$1 = CFAF 527.20.

Demography

Area: 482,077 sq mi, 1,248,574 sq km. **Population** (2009): 13,443,000. **Density** (2009): persons per sq mi 27.9, persons per sq km 10.8. **Urban** (2008): 32.4%. **Sex distribution** (2006): male 49.67%; female 50.33%. **Age breakdown** (2006): under 15, 48.1%; 15–29, 27.7%; 30–44, 12.9%; 45–59, 6.4%; 60–74, 4.1%; 75–84, 0.7%; 85 and over, 0.1%. **Ethnic composition** (2000): Bambara 30.6%; Senufo 10.5%; Fula Macina (Niafunke) 9.6%; Soninke 7.4%; Tuareg 7.0%; Maninka 6.6%; Songhai 6.3%; Dogon

4.3%; Bobo 3.5%; other 14.2%. **Religious affiliation** (2005): Muslim (nearly all Sunni) 90%; Christian (mostly Roman Catholic) 5%; traditional beliefs/non-religious 5%. **Major cities** (1998): Bamako (urban agglomeration; 2007) 1,494,000; Sikasso 113,803; Ségou 90,898; Mopti 79,840; Koutiala 74,153. **Location:** western Africa, bordering Algeria, Niger, Burkina Faso, Côte d'Ivoire, Guinea, Senegal, and Mauritania.

Vital statistics

Birth rate per 1,000 population (2008): 46.8 (world avg. 20.3). **Death rate** per 1,000 population (2008): 15.3 (world avg. 8.5). **Total fertility rate** (avg. births per childbearing woman; 2008): 6.70. **Life expectancy** at birth (2008): male 49.9 years; female 53.0 years.

National economy

Budget (2008). *Revenue:* CFAF 757,700,000,000 (tax revenue 74.3%; grants 22.4%; nontax revenue 3.3%). *Expenditures:* CFAF 913,500,000,000 (current expenditures 59.8%; capital expenditures 40.2%). **Public debt** (external, outstanding; 2007): US$1,989,000,000. **Selected balance of payments data.** Receipts from (US$'000,000): tourism (2006) 175; remittances (2008) 344; foreign direct investment (2005–07 avg.) 222; official development assistance (2007) 1,017. Disbursements for (US$'000,000): tourism (2006) 120; remittances (2008) 83. **Population economically active** (2004): total 2,598,200; activity rate of total population 23% (participation rates: ages 15–64, 51.1%; female 42.5%; officially unemployed 8.8%). **Production** (metric tons except as noted). *Agriculture and fishing* (2007): millet 1,074,440, rice 955,300, sorghum 907,966, seed cotton 414,965, karite nuts (2005) 85,000, cowpeas 70,000; livestock (number of live animals) 13,010,000 goats, 8,595,000 sheep, 7,917,000 cattle, 476,000 camels; fisheries production 100,640 (from aquaculture 1%). *Mining and quarrying* (2007): salt (2005) 6,000; gold 52,800 kg. *Manufacturing* (2005): beef and veal 98,000; goat meat (2001) 49,000; sheep meat 36,000. *Energy production (consumption):* electricity (kW-hr; 2006) 489,000,000 (489,000,000); petroleum products (metric tons; 2006) none (185,000). **Gross national income** (2008): US$7,360,000,000 (US$580 per capita).

Foreign trade

Imports (2007): CFAF 842,700,000,000 (machinery and apparatus 30.3%; refined petroleum products 28.9%; food products 19.7%). *Major import sources* (2004): France 15.9%; Senegal 12.2%; Côte d'Ivoire 9.4%; Togo 8.5%; Benin 7.4%. **Exports** (2007): CFAF 705,600,000,000 (gold 73.0%; raw cotton and cotton products 15.2%; livestock 4.3%). *Major export destinations* (2004): South Africa 30.9%; Switzerland 20.4%; Senegal 6.3%; China 4.7%; Côte d'Ivoire 4.7%.

Transport and communications

Transport. *Railroads* (2002): route length (2004) 729 km; passenger-km 196,000,000; metric ton-km

1 metric ton = about 1.1 short tons;   1 kilometer = 0.6 mi (statute);   1 metric ton-km cargo = about 0.68 short ton-mi cargo;   c.i.f.: cost, insurance, and freight;   f.o.b.: free on board

cargo 188,000,000. *Roads* (2004): total length 18,709 km (paved 18%). *Vehicles* (2007): passenger cars 86,967; trucks and buses 26,759. **Communications,** in total units (units per 1,000 persons). Telephone landlines (2008): 83,000 (6.5); cellular telephone subscribers (2008): 3,267,000 (257); personal computers (2007): 98,000 (8); total Internet users (2008): 125,000 (9.8); broadband Internet subscribers (2008): 5,300 (0.4).

Education and health

Educational attainment (2001). Population ages 25 and over having: no formal schooling/unknown 82.1%; incomplete primary education 7.7%; complete primary 2.0%; secondary 6.5%; higher 1.7%. **Literacy** (2007): percentage of total population ages 15 and over literate 23.3%; males literate 31.4%; females literate 16.0%. **Health:** physicians (2004) 1,053 (1 per 10,566 persons); hospital beds (2001) 1,664 (1 per 6,203 persons); infant mortality rate per 1,000 live births (2008) 118.1; undernourished population (2003–05) 1,200,000 (11% of total population based on the consumption of a minimum daily requirement of 1,720 calories).

Military

Total active duty personnel (November 2008): 7,350 (army 100%). **Military expenditure as percentage of GDP** (2007): 2.1%; per capita expenditure US$12.

Background

Inhabited since prehistoric times, the region was situated on a caravan route across the Sahara. In the 12th century, the Malinke empire of Mali was founded on the Upper and Middle Niger. In the 15th century, the Songhai empire in the Timbuktu-Gao region gained control. In 1591 Morocco invaded the area, and Timbuktu remained under the Moors for two centuries. In the mid-19th century, the French conquered the area, which became a part of French West Africa known as the French Sudan. In 1946 it became an overseas territory of the French Union. It was proclaimed the Sudanese Republic in 1958, briefly joined with Senegal (1959–60) to form the Mali Federation, and became the Republic of Mali in 1960. The government was overthrown by military coups in 1968 and 1991. Democratic multiparty elections have been held every five years since 1992.

Recent Developments

Progress toward the peaceful reconciliation of the Malian government and the Tuareg people continued in 2009, as in February an estimated 700 Tuaregs turned in their arms at a ceremony in the town of Kidal. In July the main Tuareg former rebel group, Alliance for Democracy and Change, announced that it would join with Mali's army to fight insurgents allied with al-Qaeda.

Internet resource: <www.tourisme.gov.ml>.

Malta

Official name: Repubblika ta' Malta (Maltese); Republic of Malta (English). **Form of government:** unitary multiparty republic with one legislative house

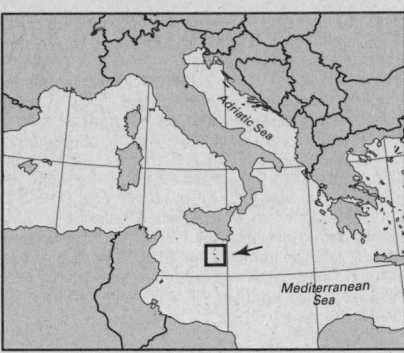

(Kamra tad-Deputati, or House of Representatives [69; statutory number is 65]). **Head of state:** President George Abela (from 2009). **Head of government:** Prime Minister Lawrence Gonzi (from 2004). **Capital:** Valletta. **Official languages:** Maltese; English. **Official religion:** Roman Catholicism. **Monetary unit:** 1 euro (€) = 100 cents; valuation (1 Jul 2010) US$1 = €0.80 (the euro replaced the Maltese lira [Lm] 1 Jan 2008, at the rate of €1 = Lm 0.43).

Demography

Area: 121.9 sq mi, 315.6 sq km. **Population** (2009): 414,000. **Density** (2009): persons per sq mi 3,396, persons per sq km 1,312. **Urban** (2005): 95.3%. **Sex distribution** (2008): male 49.77%; female 50.23%. **Age breakdown** (2008): under 15, 15.9%; 15–29, 21.6%; 30–44, 19.8%; 45–59, 21.5%; 60–74, 15.1%; 75–84, 4.8%; 85 and over, 1.3%. **Ethnic composition** (2005): Maltese 97.0%; other European 2.3%, of which British 1.2%; other 0.7%. **Religious affiliation** (2004): Roman Catholic 95%, of which practicing 63%; other Christian 0.5%; Muslim 0.7%; nonreligious/atheist 2%; other 1.8%. **Major localities** (2007): Birkirkara 22,241; Mosta 19,018; Qormi 16,625; Zabbar 14,849; Valletta 6,319 (urban agglomeration 81,204). **Location:** islands in the Mediterranean Sea, south of Sicily (Italy).

Vital statistics

Birth rate per 1,000 population (2008): 10.0 (world avg. 20.3); within marriage 74.6%. **Death rate** per 1,000 population (2008): 7.9 (world avg. 8.5). **Total fertility rate** (avg. births per childbearing woman; 2008): 1.43. **Life expectancy** at birth (2008): male 76.7 years; female 82.3 years.

National economy

Budget (2008). *Revenue:* €2,132,200,000 (income tax 34.5%; VAT 21.4%; social security contributions 16.0%; nontax revenue and grants 9.6%). *Expenditures:* €2,365,300,000 (recurrent expenditures 90.1%; capital expenditures 9.9%). **Public debt** (December 2008): US$5,052,000,000. **Production** (metric tons except where noted). *Agriculture and fishing* (2007): potatoes 25,000, tomatoes 16,600, wheat 9,200; livestock (number of live animals) 73,683 pigs, 19,233 cattle, 1,100,000 chickens; fisheries production 2,783 (from aquaculture 87%). *Mining and quarrying* (2008): salt 6,000, limestone 1,200,000 cu m. *Manufacturing* (value added in

US$'000,000; 2005): electronics 153; food products 109; printing and publishing 99. *Energy production (consumption):* electricity (kW-hr; 2006/07) 2,266,000,000 ([2006] 2,296,000,000); petroleum products (metric tons; 2006) none (815,000). **Population economically active** (2006): total 164,400; activity rate of total population 40.5% (participation rates: ages 15–64, 59.1%; female 32.1%; unemployed [April 2008–March 2009] 10.6%). **Gross national income** (2008): US$8,028,000,000 (US$19,512 per capita). **Selected balance of payments data.** Receipts from (US$'000,000): tourism (2008) 947; remittances (2008) 50; foreign direct investment (2005–07 avg.) 1,170. Disbursements for (US$'000,000): tourism (2008) 435; remittances (2008) 60.

Foreign trade

Imports (2007; c.i.f.): US$4,748,000,000 (machinery and apparatus 33.4%, of which electronic integrated circuits and micro-assemblies 20.0%; refined petroleum products 11.8%; food products 10.9%; chemical products 9.7%). *Major import sources:* Italy 24.9%; UK 14.4%; France 9.1%; Germany 8.4%; US 6.0%. **Exports** (2007; f.o.b.): US$3,067,000,000 (machinery and apparatus 57.4%, of which semiconductor devices 44.6%; medicinal and pharmaceutical products 6.8%; food products 4.8%; printed matter 4.2%; children's toys 3.1%; professional and scientific equipment 3.0%). *Major export destinations:* Germany 13.6%; Singapore 13.6%; France 12.0%; US 11.0%; UK 9.9%.

Transport and communications

Transport. *Railroads:* none. *Roads* (2004): total length 2,254 km (paved 88%). *Vehicles* (2008): passenger cars 222,775; trucks and buses 48,210. *Air transport* (2008; Air Malta only): passenger-km 2,604,000,000; metric ton-km cargo 8,027,000. **Communications,** in total units (units per 1,000 persons). Telephone landlines (2008): 241,000 (586); cellular telephone subscribers (2008): 386,000 (937); personal computers (2005): 67,000 (166); total Internet users (2008): 200,000 (487); broadband Internet subscribers (2008): 99,000 (240).

Education and health

Educational attainment (2005). Percentage of population ages 15 and over having: no formal schooling 2.4%; special education for disabled 0.3%; primary education 25.9%; secondary 45.3%; some postsecondary 16.5%; undergraduate or professional qualification 7.2%; graduate 2.4%. **Literacy** (2005): total population ages 10 and over literate 92.8%; males literate 91.7%; females literate 93.9%. **Health** (2008): physicians 1,374 (1 per 299 persons); hospital beds (2007) 1,967 (1 per 210 persons); infant mortality rate per 1,000 live births 9.9; undernourished population (2002–04) less than 2.5% of total population.

Military

Total active duty personnel (November 2008): 1,954 (armed forces includes air and marine elements); Ital-

ian military (November 2008): 49 troops. **Military expenditure as percentage of GDP** (2007): 0.6%; per capita expenditure US$107.

Background

Inhabited as early as 3800 BC, Malta was ruled by the Carthaginians from the 6th century BC until it came under Roman control in 218 BC. In AD 60 the apostle Paul converted the inhabitants to Christianity. It was under Byzantine rule until the Arabs seized control in 870. In 1091 the Normans defeated the Arabs, and Malta was ruled by feudal lords until it came under the Knights of Malta in 1530. Napoleon seized control in 1798; the British took it in 1800 and returned it to the Knights in 1802. The Maltese protested and acknowledged the British as sovereign, an arrangement ratified in 1814. It became self-governing in 1921 but reverted to a colonial regime in 1936. Malta was severely bombed by Germany and Italy during World War II, and in 1942 it received the George Cross, Britain's highest civilian decoration. In 1964 it gained independence within the Commonwealth and in 1974 became a republic. In 2004 it joined the EU, and it adopted the euro as its official currency in 2008.

Recent Developments

Massive immigration from Africa remained controversial in Malta in 2009. The Italian and Maltese governments argued in the summer after surviving migrants from a drifting dinghy were rescued in Italian waters after having earlier been intercepted by Malta. In December Malta was chosen to host the European Asylum Support Office, an agency created to distribute resources and craft policy in the realm of refugees and other immigrants.

Internet resource: <www.nso.gov.mt>.

Marshall Islands

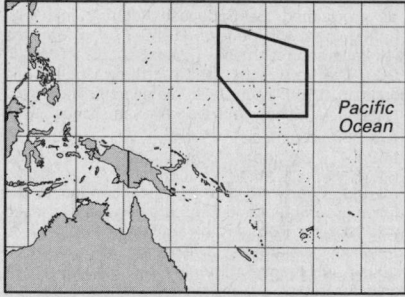

Pacific Ocean

Official name: Majol (Marshallese) (Republic of the Marshall Islands). **Form of government:** unitary republic with one legislative house (Nitijela [33]). **Head of state and government:** President Jurelang Zedkaia (from 2009). **Capital:** Majuro. **Official language:** Marshallese (Kajin-Majol). **Official religion:** none. **Monetary unit:** 1 US dollar (US$) = 100 cents.

---

1 metric ton = about 1.1 short tons;   1 kilometer = 0.6 mi (statute);   1 metric ton-km cargo = about 0.68 short ton-mi cargo;   c.i.f.: cost, insurance, and freight;   f.o.b.: free on board

Demography

Area: 70.05 sq mi, 181.43 sq km. **Population** (2009): 53,800. **Density** (2009): persons per sq mi 768.0, persons per sq km 296.5. **Urban** (2008): 68.0%. **Sex distribution** (2008): male 50.99%; female 49.01%. **Age breakdown** (2008): under 15, 38.5%; 15–29, 29.6%; 30–44, 16.8%; 45–59, 10.5%; 60–74, 3.6%; 75–84, 0.8%; 85 and over, 0.2%. **Ethnic composition** (2006): Marshallese 92.1%; other Pacific Islanders 1.0%; East Asians 0.5%; US white 0.3%; other 6.1%. **Religious affiliation** (1999): Protestant 85.0%, of which United Church of Christ 54.8%, Assemblies of God 25.8%; Roman Catholic 8.4%; Mormon 2.1%; nonreligious 1.5%; other 3.0%. **Major towns** (1999): Majuro (2004) 20,800; Ebeye 9,345; Laura 2,256. **Location:** Oceania, group of atolls and reefs in the North Pacific Ocean, halfway between Hawaii (US) and Papua New Guinea.

Vital statistics

Birth rate per 1,000 population (2008): 31.5 (world avg. 20.3). **Death rate** per 1,000 population (2008): 4.6 (world avg. 8.5). **Total fertility rate** (avg. births per childbearing woman; 2008): 3.68. **Life expectancy** at birth (2008): male 68.9 years; female 73.0 years.

National economy

Budget (2007). *Revenue:* US$98,900,000 (US government grants 63.6%; tax revenue 25.0%, of which income tax 11.0%, import duties 8.9%; nontax revenue 11.4%). *Expenditures:* US$99,900,000 (current expenditures 79.0%; capital expenditures 21.0%). **Public debt** (external, outstanding; 2008): US$87,000,000. **Production** (metric tons except as noted). *Agriculture and fishing* (2002–03): copra (2007) 5,491, breadfruit 4,536, coconuts 885, pandanus 114; livestock (number of live animals) 12,900 pigs, 86,000 chickens; fisheries production (2006) 42,019, of which skipjack 37,661 (from aquaculture, none). *Mining and quarrying:* for local construction only. *Manufacturing* (2007): copra 5,491; coconut oil and processed (chilled or frozen) fish are important products; the manufacture of handicrafts and personal items (clothing, mats, boats, etc.) by individuals is also significant. *Energy production (consumption):* electricity (kW-hr; 2006) 104,000,000 (104,000,000); petroleum products (metric tons; 2006) none (30,000). **Population economically active** (1999): total 14,677; activity rate of total population 28.9% (participation rates: ages 15–64, 52.1%; female 34.1%; unemployed [2007] 30.9%). **Gross national income** (2008): US$195,000,000 (US$3,270 per capita). **Selected balance of payments data.** Receipts from (US$'000,000): tourism (2007) 4.5; remittances (2005) 0.4; foreign direct investment (FDI; 2005–07 avg.) 272; official development assistance (2007) 52. Disbursements for (US$'000,000): tourism (2006) 0.4; FDI (2005–07 avg.) 24.

Foreign trade

Imports (2006; c.i.f.): US$67,700,000 ([2000] mineral fuels and lubricants 43.6%; machinery and transportation equipment 16.9%; food products, beverages, and tobacco products 10.9%). *Major import sources:* US 45.8%; Australia 8.4%; Japan 8.1%; New Zealand 3.2%; Hong Kong 1.8%. **Exports** (2006–07;

f.o.b.): US$20,300,000 ([2005] reexports of diesel fuel 80.9%; crude coconut oil 15.4%). *Major export destinations* (2005): mostly the US.

Transport and communications

Transport. *Roads* (2007): 75 km (only Majuro and Kwajalein have paved roads). *Vehicles* (2004): passenger cars 1,694; trucks and buses 602. *Air transport* (2006; Air Marshall Islands only): passenger-km 31,236,000; metric ton-km cargo 348,000. **Communications,** in total units (units per 1,000 persons). Telephone landlines (2008): 4,400 (73); cellular telephone subscribers (2008): 1,000 (17); personal computers (2005): 4,600 (88); total Internet users (2008): 2,200 (36).

Education and health

Educational attainment (2006). Percentage of population ages 25 and over having: no formal schooling 2.1%; elementary education 28.0%; secondary 55.8%; some higher 7.9%; undergraduate degree 5.1%; advanced degree 1.1%. **Literacy** (2000): total population ages 15 and over literate 92.0%; males literate 92.0%; females literate 92.0%. **Health** (2008): physicians 38 (1 per 1,401 persons); hospital beds (2004) 140 (1 per 411 persons); infant mortality rate per 1,000 live births 26.4.

Military

The US provides for the defense of the Republic of the Marshall Islands under the 1984 and 2003 compacts of free association; the US Army's premier ballistic missile test site is at Kwajalein.

Background

The islands were sighted in 1529 by the Spanish navigator Álvaro Saavedra. Germany purchased them from Spain in 1899, and Japan seized them in 1914. During World War II the US took Kwajalein and Enewetak, and the Marshall Islands were made part of a UN trust territory under US jurisdiction in 1947. Bikini and Enewetak atolls served as testing grounds for US nuclear weapons from 1946 to 1958. The country became an internally self-governing republic in 1979. In 1986 it became fully self-governing when it entered into a Compact of Free Association with the US, which was renewed in 2003.

Recent Developments

The Marshall Islands Nuclear Claims Tribunal, which was established to compensate those who were made ill or whose property was damaged by the nuclear weapons tested (1946–58) by the US in the Marshall Islands, ran low on funds and stopped making payments in July 2009.

Internet resource: <www.rmiembassyus.org>.

Mauritania

Official name: Al-Jumhuriyah al-Islamiyah al-Muritaniyah (Islamic Republic of Mauritania). **Form of government:** republic with two legislative houses (Senate [56]; National Assembly [95]). **Head of state and government:** President Mohamed Ould Abdel

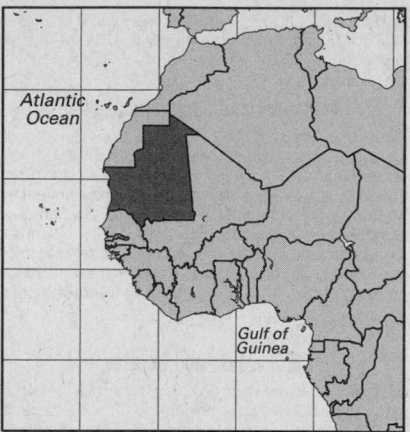

Aziz (from 2009), assisted by Prime Minister Moulaye Ould Mohamed Laghdaf (from 2008). **Capital:** Nouakchott. **Official language:** Arabic (Arabic, Fulani, Soninke, and Wolof are national languages). **Official religion:** Islam. **Monetary unit:** 1 ouguiya (UM) = 5 khoums; valuation (1 Jul 2010) US$1 = UM 279.63.

Demography

Area: 398,000 sq mi, 1,030,700 sq km. **Population** (2009): 3,129,000. **Density** (2009): persons per sq mi 7.9, persons per sq km 3.0. **Urban** (2006): 65.5%. **Sex distribution** (2006): male 49.50%; female 50.50%. **Age breakdown** (2006): under 15, 45.6%; 15–29, 27.2%; 30–44, 15.6%; 45–59, 8.0%; 60–74, 3.1%; 75 and over, 0.5%. **Ethnic composition** (2003): black African-Arab-Berber (Black Moor) 40%; Arab-Berber (White Moor) 30%; black African (mostly Wolof, Tukulor, Soninke, and Fulani) 30%. **Religious affiliation** (2000): Sunni Muslim 99.1%; traditional beliefs 0.5%; Christian 0.3%; other 0.1%. **Major cities** (2005): Nouakchott 743,500; Nouadhibou 94,700; Rosso (2000) 48,922; Boghe (2000) 37,531; Adel Bagrou (2000) 36,007. **Location:** northern Africa, bordering Western Sahara, Algeria, Mali, Senegal, and the North Atlantic Ocean.

Vital statistics

Birth rate per 1,000 population (2008): 34.6 (world avg. 20.3). **Death rate** per 1,000 population (2008): 9.3 (world avg. 8.5). **Total fertility rate** (avg. births per childbearing woman; 2008): 4.52. **Life expectancy** at birth (2008): male 57.9 years; female 62.2 years.

National economy

Budget (2005). *Revenue:* UM 131,300,000,000 (tax revenue 57.9%, of which VAT 20.3%, corporate taxes 17.0%; nontax revenue 34.3%, of which fishing royalties 26.9%; grants 7.8%). *Expenditures:* UM 166,100,000,000 (current expenditures 76.2%, of which goods and services 36.5%, wages and salaries 13.5%, defense 10.7%; capital expenditures 23.8%). **Public debt** (external, outstanding; January 2008): US$1,751,000,000. **Production** (metric tons except as noted). *Agriculture and fishing* (2007): rice 77,000, sorghum 58,000, dates 22,000, cowpeas 7,200; livestock (number of live animals) 8,850,000 sheep, 5,600,000 goats, 1,692,000 cattle, 1,600,000 camels; fisheries production 201,588, of which octopuses 11,525 (from aquaculture, none). *Mining and quarrying* (gross weight; 2006–07): iron ore 11,439,000; gypsum (2005) 39,000; copper 5,000. *Manufacturing* (value added in US$'000,000; 1997): food products, beverages, and tobacco products 5.2; machinery, transportation equipment, and fabricated metal products 3.8; bricks, tiles, and cement 1.6. *Energy production (consumption):* electricity (kW-hr; 2006–07) 404,000,000 (290,000,000); coal (metric tons; 2004) none (7,000); crude petroleum (barrels; 2006–07) 9,600,000 ([2004] 8,830,000); petroleum products (metric tons; 2006–07) none (431,000). **Selected balance of payments data.** Receipts from (US$'000,000): tourism (2005) 11; remittances (2008) 2; foreign direct investment (2005–07 avg.) 374; official development assistance (2007) 364. Disbursements for (US$'000,000): tourism (1999) 55. **Population economically active** (2006): total 1,238,000; activity rate of total population 39.2% (participation rates: ages 16 and over, 68.8%; female 40.4%; unemployed [2005] 32.5%). **Gross national income** (2007): US$2,636,000,000 (US$840 per capita).

Foreign trade

Imports (2007): US$1,198,800,000 (imports for extractive industries 28.3%; refined petroleum products 23.1%). *Major import sources* (2006): France 11.9%; China 8.2%; US 6.8%; Belgium 6.7%; Italy 5.9%. **Exports** (2007): US$1,342,500,000 (iron ore 39.7%; crude petroleum 23.1%; fish products 15.3%). *Major export destinations* (2006): China 26.3%; Italy 11.8%; France 10.2%; Belgium 6.8%; Spain 6.7%.

Transport and communications

Transport. *Railroads* (2005): route length 697 km; metric ton-km cargo (2000) 7,766,000,000. *Roads* (2006): total length 11,066 km (paved 27%). *Vehicles* (2001): passenger cars 12,200; trucks and buses 18,200. **Communications,** in total units (units per 1,000 persons). Telephone landlines (2008): 76,000 (24); cellular telephone subscribers (2008): 2,092,000 (651); personal computers (2005): 42,000 (14); total Internet users (2006): 100,000 (33); broadband Internet subscribers (2008): 5,900 (1.8).

Education and health

Educational attainment (2000). Percentage of population ages 6 and over having: no formal schooling 43.9%; no formal schooling but literate 2.5%; Islamic schooling 18.4%; primary education 23.2%; lower secondary 5.3%; upper secondary 4.6%; higher technical 0.4%; higher 1.7%. **Literacy** (2007): percentage of total population ages 15 and over literate 43.6%; males literate 53.2%; females literate 34.3%. **Health**

---

1 metric ton = about 1.1 short tons;   1 kilometer = 0.6 mi (statute);   1 metric ton-km cargo = about 0.68 short ton-mi cargo;   c.i.f.: cost, insurance, and freight;   f.o.b.: free on board

(2006): physicians (2005) 477 (1 per 6,212 persons); hospital beds 1,826 (1 per 1,667 persons); infant mortality rate per 1,000 live births (2008) 64.9; undernourished population (2003–05) 200,000 (8% of total population based on the consumption of a minimum daily requirement of 1,790 calories).

Military

Total active duty personnel (November 2008): 15,870 (army 94.5%, navy 3.9%, air force 1.6%). **Military expenditure as percentage of GDP** (2007): 0.5%; per capita expenditure US$6.

Background

Inhabited in ancient times by Sanhadja Berbers, in the 11th and 12th centuries Mauritania was the center of the Berber Almoravid movement, which imposed Islam. Arab tribes arrived in the 15th century and formed powerful confederations; the Portuguese also arrived then. France gained control of the coast in 1817 and in 1903 made the territory a protectorate. In 1904 it was added to French West Africa, and later it became a colony. In 1960 Mauritania achieved independence. Its first president was ousted in a 1978 military coup. After a series of military rulers, in 1991 a new constitution was adopted, and multiparty elections were held in 1992. The country faced continued economic hardship and political unrest, including coups, in the late 20th and early 21st centuries.

Recent Developments

In 2009 the African Union refused to lift sanctions imposed on the leaders of the August 2008 coup that overthrew Sidi Mohamed Ould Cheikh Abdallahi, Mauritania's first democratically elected president, until late June, after opposition leaders signed an agreement with the government that called for an interim unity government until the 18 July presidential elections.

Internet resource:
<http://mauritania.embassyhomepage.com>.

Mauritius

Official name: Republic of Mauritius. **Form of government:** republic with one legislative house (National Assembly [69]). **Head of state:** President Sir Anerood Jugnauth (from 2003). **Head of government:** Prime Minister Navin Ramgoolam (from 2005). **Capital:** Port Louis. **Official language:** English. **Official religion:** none. **Monetary unit:** 1 Mauritian rupee (Mau Re; plural Mau Rs) = 100 cents; valuation (1 Jul 2010) US$1 = Mau Rs 31.50.

Demography

Area: 788 sq mi, 2,040 sq km. **Population** (2009): 1,276,000. **Density** (2009): persons per sq mi 1,619, persons per sq km 625.5. **Urban** (2008): 41.9%. **Sex distribution** (2009): male 49.35%; female 50.65%. **Age breakdown** (2008): under 15, 22.7%; 15–29, 24.6%; 30–44, 23.2%; 45–59, 19.2%; 60–74, 7.7%; 75–84, 2.1%; 85 and over, 0.5%. **Ethnic composition** (2000): Indo-Pakistani 67.0%; Creole (mixed Caucasian, Indo-Pakistani, and

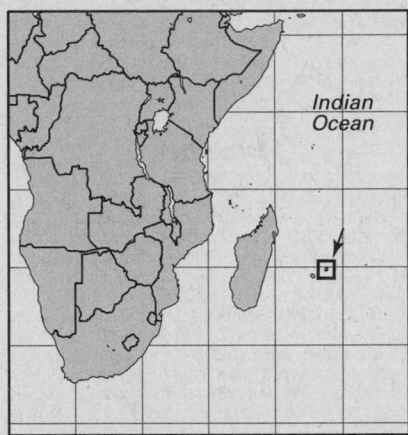

African) 27.4%; Chinese 3.0%; other 2.6%. **Religious affiliation** (2000): Hindu 49.6%; Christian 32.2%, of which Roman Catholic 23.6%; Muslim 16.6%; Buddhist 0.4%; other 1.2%. **Major municipalities** (2007): Port Louis 148,939; Beau Bassin–Rose Hill 109,701; Vacoas-Phoenix 106,865; Curepipe 83,754; Quatre Bornes 80,780. **Location:** island in the Indian Ocean, east of Madagascar.

Vital statistics

Birth rate per 1,000 population (2008): 12.9 (world avg. 20.3). **Death rate** per 1,000 population (2008): 7.1 (world avg. 8.5). **Total fertility rate** (avg. births per childbearing woman; 2006): 1.73. **Life expectancy** at birth (2007): male 69.1 years; female 75.8 years.

National economy

Budget (2007–08). *Revenue:* Mau Rs 57,593,-500,000 (tax revenue 86.7%, of which taxes on goods and services 46.1%, taxes on trade 11.5%, corporate taxes 10.8%; nontax revenue and grants 13.3%). *Expenditures:* Mau Rs 55,781,200,000 (social security 22.6%; education 14.8%; interest on debt 14.3%; health 8.4%; police and defense 8.1%). **Public debt** (external, outstanding; 2007): US$572,000,000. **Gross national income** (2008): US$8,122,000,000 (US$6,400 per capita). **Production** (metric tons except as noted). *Agriculture and fishing* (2007): sugarcane 4,400,000, tomatoes 13,000, potatoes 13,000; livestock (number of live animals) 28,500 cattle, 10,000,000 chickens; fisheries production 8,476 (from aquaculture 7%). *Mining* (2007): basalt, n.a.; marine salt 6,650. *Manufacturing* (value added in Mau Rs '000,000; 2005): wearing apparel 8,823; food products 6,220; beverages and tobacco products 3,053. *Energy production (consumption):* electricity (kW-hr; 2008) 2,512,000,000 ([2006] 2,350,000,000); coal (metric tons; 2006) none (484,000); petroleum products (metric tons; 2006) none (835,000). **Population economically active** (2004): total 549,600; activity rate of total population 44.5% (participation rates: ages 15 and over 60.2%, female 35.0%, unemployed [2008] 7.2%). **Selected balance of payments data.** Receipts from (US$'000,000): tourism (2007) 1,304;

remittances (2008) 215; foreign direct investment (FDI; 2005–07 avg.) 162; official development assistance (2007) 75. Disbursements for (US$'000,000): tourism (2007) 361; remittances (2008) 14; FDI (2005–07 avg.) 39.

Foreign trade

Imports (2007; c.i.f.): Mau Rs 121,037,000,000 (machinery and transportation equipment 23.5%, of which motor vehicles 6.7%; food products 16.6%, of which fish 5.8%; refined petroleum products 15.7%; fabrics and yarn 7.4%). *Major import sources:* India 21.2%; China 11.4%; France 10.6; South Africa 7.4%; Japan 3.6%. Exports (2007; f.o.b.): Mau Rs 69,708,000,000 (wearing apparel and accessories 35.5%; food products 24.8%, of which raw sugar 13.7%; textile yarns, fabrics, and wearing apparel 2.6%). *Major export destinations:* UK 32.4%; France 10.1%; US 6.4%; UAE 3.5%; Madagascar 2.6%.

Transport and communications

Transport. *Railroads:* none. *Roads* (2005): total length 2,020 km (paved 98%). *Vehicles* (2008): passenger cars 109,500; trucks and buses 61,500. *Air transport* (2005; Air Mauritius only): passenger-km 6,274,000,000; metric ton-km cargo 211,716,000. Communications, in total units (units per 1,000 persons). Telephone landlines (2008): 365,000 (285); cellular telephone subscribers (2008): 1,033,000 (807); personal computers (2005): 210,000 (169); total Internet users (2008): 380,000 (297); broadband Internet subscribers (2008): 73,000 (57).

Education and health

Educational attainment (2000). Percentage of population ages 25 and over having: no formal education/unknown 12.8%; primary 44.1%; lower secondary 23.2%; upper secondary/some higher 17.3%; complete higher 2.6%. Literacy (2000): percentage of total population ages 12 and over literate 85.1%; males literate 88.7%; females literate 81.6%. Health (2008): physicians 1,450 (1 per 875 persons); hospital beds (2007) 3,756 (1 per 336 persons); infant mortality rate per 1,000 live births 14.4; undernourished population (2002–04) 60,000 (5% of total population based on the consumption of a minimum daily requirement of 1,910 calories).

Military

Total active duty personnel (November 2008): none; a 2,000-person paramilitary force includes a 500-person coast guard unit. Paramilitary expenditure as percentage of GDP (2008): 0.3%; per capita expenditure US$26.

Background

The island was visited by the Portuguese in the early 16th century. The Dutch took possession in 1598 and made attempts to settle it (1638–58 and 1664–1710) before abandoning it to pirates. The French East India Company occupied Mauritius in 1721 and administered it until the French government took over in 1767. Sugar production allowed the colony to prosper. The British captured the island in 1810 and were granted formal control in 1814. In the late 19th century, competition from beet sugar and the opening of the Suez Canal caused an economic decline. After World War II, Mauritius adopted political and economic reforms, and in 1968 it became an independent state within the Commonwealth. In 1992 it became a republic. It experienced political unrest during the 1990s.

Recent Developments

In February 2009 Mauritius unveiled a plan to preserve about 650,000 sq km (250,000 sq mi) of marine habitat surrounding the Chagos Archipelago. The plan included the habitat of the archipelago's largest island, Diego Garcia, a British protectorate from which some 2,000 residents had been displaced 40 years earlier to clear the island for use as a military base by the US. The reef conservation plan included the repatriation of Chagossians to serve as the nature reserve's wardens.

Internet resource: <www.gov.mu/portal/site/cso>.

Mexico

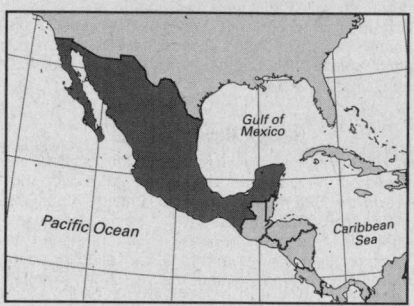

Official name: Estados Unidos Mexicanos (United Mexican States). Form of government: federal republic with two legislative houses (Senate [128]; Chamber of Deputies [500]). Head of state and government: President Felipe Calderón Hinojosa (from 2006). Capital: Mexico City. Official language: Spanish. Official religion: none. Monetary unit: 1 Mexican peso (Mex$) = 100 centavos; valuation (1 Jul 2010) US$1 = Mex$13.05.

Demography

Area: 758,450 sq mi, 1,964,375 sq km. Population (2009): 107,551,000. Density (2009): persons per sq mi 141.8, persons per sq km 54.8. Urban (2008): 77.2%. Sex distribution (2008): male 49.20%; female 50.80%. Age breakdown (2008): under 15, 29.6%; 15–29, 27.0%; 30–44, 21.6%; 45–59, 13.1%; 60–74, 6.4%; 75–89, 2.1%; 90 and over, 0.2%. Ethnic composition (2000): mestizo 64.3%; Amerindian 18.0%, of which detribalized 10.5%; Mexican white 15.0%; Arab 1.0%; Mexican black 0.5%; Spaniard 0.3%; US white 0.2%; other 0.7%. Religious affiliation (2000): Christian 96.3%, of which Roman

Catholic 87.0%, Protestant 3.2%, independent Christian 2.7%, unaffiliated Christian 1.4%, other Christian (mostly Mormon and Jehovah's Witness) 2.0%; Muslim 0.3%; nonreligious 3.1%; other 0.3%. **Major cities (urban agglomerations)** (2005 [2007]): Mexico City 8,463,906 (19,028,000); Guadalajara 1,600,894 (4,198,000); Monterrey 1,133,070 (3,712,000); Puebla 1,399,519 (2,195,000); Ecatepec 1,687,549; Toluca 467,712 (1,584,000); Tijuana 1,286,187 (1,553,000); León 1,137,465 (1,488,000); Juárez 1,301,452 (1,343,000); Torreon 548,723 (1,201,000); Ciudad Netzahualcóyotl 1,136,300; San Luis Potosí 685,934 (1,050,000); Querétaro 596,450 (1,032,000); Zapopan 1,026,492; Mérida 734,153 (1,017,000); Mexicali 653,046 (935,000); Aguascalientes 663,671 (927,000); Chihuahua 748,518 (841,000); Culiacán 605,304 (837,000); Saltillo 633,667 (802,000); Naucalpan 792,226; Guadelupe 691,434; Tlalnepantla 674,417; Hermosillo 641,791; Acapulco 616,394. **Location:** southern North America, bordering the US, the Gulf of Mexico, the Caribbean Sea, Belize, Guatemala, and the North Pacific Ocean. **Migration.** Legal Mexican immigrants entering the US in 2004: 173,664; total number of illegal Mexican immigrants in US (2006) 6,600,000.

Vital statistics

Birth rate per 1,000 population (2008): 19.1 (world avg. 20.3); (2003) within marriage 62%. **Death rate** per 1,000 population (2008): 4.8 (world avg. 8.5). **Total fertility rate** (avg. births per childbearing woman; 2008): 2.10. **Life expectancy** at birth (2008): male 74.0 years; female 78.8 years.

Social indicators

Educational attainment (2005). Percentage of population ages 15 and over having: no formal schooling/unknown 10.9%; incomplete primary education 14.3%; complete primary 17.6%; secondary 25.2%; vocational/professional 31.3%; advanced university (master's or doctorate degree) 0.7%. **Access to services** (2005). Proportion of dwellings having: electricity 96.6%; piped water supply 87.8%; piped sewage 84.8%. **Material well-being.** Percentage of households possessing (2005): television 91.0%; refrigerator 79.0%; washing machine 62.7%; computer 19.6%. **Quality of working life** (2008). Average workweek 44.5 hours. Annual rate per 100,000 insured workers for: injury 3,569; death 10. Labor stoppages: 21, involving 13,242 workers. **Social participation.** Trade union membership in total workforce (2000): formal sector only, less than 20%; both formal and informal sectors, 17%. Practicing religious population (1995–97): percentage of adult population attending church services at least once per week 46%. **Social deviance** (2007). Formally registered offense rate per 100,000 population for: murder 6.2; property damage 14.5; rape 4.3; battery 30.2; robbery 69.3; illegal narcotics possession 16.0; fraud 4.4; squatting 3.3; breaking and entering 2.5. Incidence per 100,000 in general population of: alcoholism (2000) 7.6; suicide 4.2.

National economy

Gross national income (2008): US$1,061,444,-000,000 (US$9,980 per capita). **Budget** (2008). *Revenue:* Mex$2,857,100,000,000 (nontax rev-

enue 36.9%; tax revenue 34.8%, of which income tax 21.3%; other revenue, from PEMEX state oil company 12.6%, other state-owned organizations or companies 15.7%). *Expenditures:* Mex$2,865,-300,000,000 (current expenditures 58.3%; extrabudgetary expenditures 23.2%; capital expenditures 18.5%). **Public debt** (external, outstanding; 2007): US$105,379,000,000. **Production** (metric tons except as noted). *Agriculture and fishing* (2008): sugarcane 51,106,900, corn (maize) 24,320,100, sorghum 6,610,900, oranges 4,306,633, wheat 4,019,400, tomatoes 2,936,773, lemons and limes 2,224,382, bananas 2,159,280, chilies and green peppers 2,054,968, mangoes and guavas 1,855,359, potatoes 1,670,480, dry onions 1,252,441, coconuts 1,246,400, avocados 1,124,565, dry beans 1,122,720, blue agave (2006) 778,000, papayas 638,237, pineapples 685,805, apples 524,755, grapefruit and pomelos 394,865, seed cotton 365,227, grapes 307,478, oil palm fruit 292,499, coffee (green) 265,817; livestock (number of live animals) 32,565,200 cattle, 15,527,600 pigs, 8,831,000 goats, 7,825,000 sheep, 6,350,000 horses, 504,300,000 chickens; fisheries production (2007) 1,496,002 (from aquaculture 10%); aquatic plants production 4,500 (from aquaculture, none). *Mining and quarrying* (2008): fluorspar 980,000 [world rank: 2]; bismuth (metal content) 1,200 [world rank: 2]; silver (metal content) 3,000,000 kg [world rank: 2]; strontium 96,900 [world rank: 3]; lead (metal content) 145,000 [world rank: 5]; zinc (metal content) 460,000 [world rank: 6]; cadmium (metal content) 1,620 [world rank: 6]; gypsum 5,800,000 [world rank: 7]; iron ore (metal content) 12,000,000; sulfur 1,800,000; copper (metal content) 270,000; gold (metal content) 41,000 kg. *Manufacturing* (value added in Mex$'000,000; 2007): food products and beverages 994,797; transportation equipment 146,839, of which motor vehicles 84,137, motor vehicle parts 58,470; mineral fuels 130,233, of which refined petroleum products 121,740; chemical products 125,629, of which pharmaceutical products 58,561; base metals 74,005; bricks, cement, and ceramics 66,932; electrical machinery and equipment 28,962; paper products 28,773; fabricated metal products 26,355; rubber and plastic products 25,690; textiles and wearing apparel 23,195; nonelectrical machinery and apparatus 21,529; electronics 6,442; printing and publishing 6,085; wood products 5,780. *Energy production (consumption):* electricity (kW-hr; 2008) 129,948,000,000 ([2006] 248,872,000,000); coal (metric tons; 2008–09) 10,679,000 ([2006] 1,920,000); lignite (metric tons; 2006) 9,573,000 (14,936,000); crude petroleum (barrels; 2008–09) 913,369,200 ([2006] 495,699,000); petroleum products (metric tons; 2006) 64,836,000 (74,439,000); natural gas (cu m; 2008–09) 74,360,122,000 ([2006] 51,054,509,000). **Population economically active** (2008): total 45,460,000; activity rate of total population 42.6% (participation rates: ages 15–64, 63.6%; female 37.7%; unemployed [April 2008–March 2009] 4.3%). **Selected balance of payments data.** Receipts from (US$'000,000): tourism (2008) 13,289, of which border shoppers only 2,695; remittances (2008) 26,304; foreign direct investment (FDI; 2008) 27 avg.) 21,041, official development assistance (2007) 121. Disbursements for (US$'000,000): tourism (2008) 8,526, of which border shoppers only 4,001; FDI (2005–06 avg.) 6,829.

Foreign trade

Imports (2006): US$256,130,000,000 (non-maquiladora sector 65.8%, of which imports for automotive industry 10.9%, special machinery for industries 9.8%, imports for extractive industries 8.2%, electrical and electronic equipment 6.3%, imports for chemical industry 5.6%; maquiladora sector 34.2%, of which electrical and electronic equipment 15.5%). *Major import sources:* US 50.9%; China 9.5%; Japan 6.0%; South Korea 4.2%; Germany 3.7%; Canada 2.9%; Brazil 2.2%; Taiwan 1.9%; Malaysia 1.7%; Italy 1.6%. **Exports** (2006): US$249,997,000,000 (non-maquiladora sector 55.3%, of which motor vehicles and parts 15.1%, crude petroleum 13.9%, special machinery for industries 3.1%, electrical and electronic equipment 2.5%, food products, beverages, and tobacco products 2.4%; maquiladora sector 44.7%, of which electrical and electronic equipment 20.1%, exports of automotive industry 6.1%, professional and scientific equipment 2.6%). *Major export destinations:* US 84.7%; Canada 2.1%; Spain 1.3%; Germany 1.2%; Colombia 0.9%; Venezuela 0.7%; China 0.7%.

Transport and communications

Transport. *Railroads* (2008): route length 26,722 km; passenger-km 147,000,000; metric ton-km cargo 78,872,000,000. *Roads* (2008): total length 360,352 km (paved 35%). *Vehicles* (2007): passenger cars 17,533,245; trucks and buses 8,152,942. *Air transport* (2008): passenger-km 28,514,000,000; metric ton-km cargo 223,958,000. **Communications,** in total units (units per 1,000 persons). Telephone landlines (2008): 20,668,000 (190); cellular telephone subscribers (2008): 75,304,000 (694); personal computers (2006): 14,578,000 (139); total Internet users (2008): 23,260,000 (214); broadband Internet subscribers (2008): 7,597,000 (70).

Education and health

Literacy (2007): total population ages 15 and over literate 92.8%; males literate 94.4%; females literate 91.4%. **Health** (2008): physicians (public health institutions only; 2007) 171,193 (1 per 618 persons); hospital beds (public health institutions only) 84,813 (1 per 1,258 persons); infant mortality rate per 1,000 live births 15.2; undernourished population (2002–04) 5,300,000 (5% of total population based on the consumption of a minimum daily requirement of 1,900 calories).

Military

Total active duty personnel (November 2008): 255,506 (army 73.6%, navy 21.9%, air force 4.5%). **Military expenditure as percentage of GDP** (2007): 0.4%; per capita expenditure US$38.

Background

Inhabited for more than 20,000 years, Mexico produced great civilizations in AD 100–900, including the Olmec, Toltec, Mayan, and Aztec. The Aztec were conquered in 1521 by Spanish explorer Hernán Cortés, who established Mexico City on the site of the Aztec capital, Tenochtitlán. Francisco de Montejo conquered the remnants of Mayan civilization in the mid-16th century, and Mexico became part of the Viceroyalty of New Spain. In 1821 rebels negotiated a status quo independence from Spain, and in 1823 a new congress declared Mexico a republic. In 1845 the US voted to annex Texas, initiating the Mexican-American War. Under the Treaty of Guadalupe Hidalgo in 1848, Mexico ceded a vast territory in what is now the western and southwestern US. The Mexican government endured several rebellions and civil wars in the late 19th and early 20th centuries. During World War II it declared war on the Axis powers (1942), and in the postwar era it was a founding member of the UN (1945) and the Organization of American States (1948). In 1993 it ratified the North American Free Trade Agreement. The election of Vicente Fox to the presidency in 2000 ended 71 years of rule by the Institutional Revolutionary Party.

Recent Developments

Mexico faced daunting economic and social challenges in 2009. Although Mexico had in recent years somewhat reduced its heavy trade dependence on the US, the US market was still the destination for approximately four-fifths of all Mexican exports. As a consequence, the country's manufacturing sector was badly affected by the sharp decline in US import demand during the year. The automobile and auto parts sector, which constituted Mexico's most important source of manufactured exports, suffered severely because of the broader crisis in the North American automotive industry. The flow of migrant remittances to Mexico (which, after petroleum, were the country's largest source of legal export earnings) fell by more than 10% between 2008 and 2009, and the number of households reporting the receipt of remittances declined by approximately one-fifth between 2005 and 2009. Although the administration of Pres. Felipe Calderón had committed enormous financial and human resources (including approximately 45,000 army troops) since 2006 to the battle against drug-smuggling cartels, the Mexican public had grown increasingly weary of the protracted violence—approximately 22,700 people have died in that period, and 2009 was the deadliest year, with 9,635 deaths, including in such previously spared tourist enclaves as Acapulco, where 17 were killed in March 2010. In further signs of the escalation of the conflict, that same month an American employee of the US consulate in Ciudad Juárez and her husband were assassinated, and in April the US Department of Homeland Security issued a warning that the Mexican cartels had authorized the killing of American police officers. The administration retained broad support for its efforts, but only about half of respondents to public opinion surveys believed that the government would win the fight.

Internet resource: <www.visitmexico.com>.

---

1 metric ton = about 1.1 short tons; 1 kilometer = 0.6 mi (statute); 1 metric ton-km cargo = about 0.68 short ton-mi cargo; c.i.f.: cost, insurance, and freight; f.o.b.: free on board

Micronesia, Federated States of

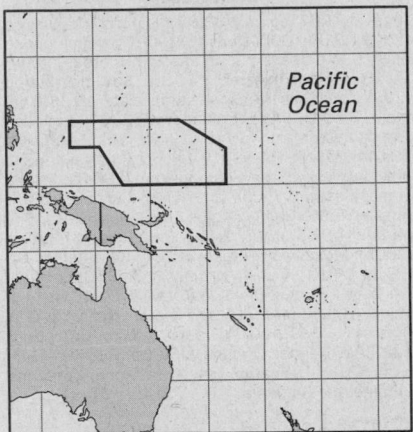

Pacific
Ocean

Official name: Federated States of Micronesia. **Form of government:** federal nonparty republic in free association with the US with one legislative house (Congress [14]). **Head of state and government:** President Emanuel Mori (from 2007). **Capital:** Palikir. **Official language:** none (English is the language of the Congress). **Official religion:** none. **Monetary unit:** 1 US dollar (US$) = 100 cents.

Demography

Area: 270.6 sq mi, 700.9 sq km. **Population** (2009): 111,000. **Density** (2009): persons per sq mi 409.9, persons per sq km 158.3. **Urban** (2007): 22.0%. **Sex distribution** (2008): male 50.32%; female 49.68%. **Age breakdown** (2008): under 15, 36.9%; 15–29, 26.9%; 30–44, 17.0%; 45–59, 13.1%; 60–74, 4.7%; 75 and over, 1.4%. **Ethnic composition** (2000): Chuukese/Mortlockese 33.6%; Pohnpeian 24.9%; Yapese 10.6%; Kosraean 5.2%; US white 4.5%; Asian 1.3%; other 19.9%. **Religious affiliation** (2005): Roman Catholic 50%; Protestant 47%; other 3%. **Major towns** (2000): Weno 13,802; Palikir 6,444; Nett 6,158. **Location:** Oceania, island group in the North Pacific Ocean, northeast of New Guinea.

Vital statistics

Birth rate per 1,000 population (2007): 25.5 (world avg. 20.3); (2006) within marriage 83.2%. **Death rate** per 1,000 population (2007): 5.5 (world avg. 8.5). **Total fertility rate** (avg. births per childbearing woman; 2006): 2.68. **Life expectancy** at birth (2007): male 67.4 years; female 68.0 years.

National economy

Budget (2006–07; for consolidated general government). *Revenue:* US$145,200,000 (external grants 63.7%; tax revenue 19.1%; nontax revenue 17.2%, of which fishing access revenue 10.3%). *Expenditures:* US$153,000,000 (current expenditures 91.4%; capital expenditures 8.6%). **Public debt** (external, outstanding; September 2007): US$67,200,000. **Population economically active** (2000): total 37,414;

activity rate of total population 35.0% (participation rates: ages 15–64, 60.7%; female 42.9%; unemployed 22.0%). **Production** (metric tons except as noted). *Agriculture and fishing* (2007): coconuts 41,000, cassava 12,000, sweet potatoes 3,200, betel nuts (2005) 228, kava (*sakau*) n.a.; livestock (number of live animals) 33,000 pigs, 14,000 cattle; fisheries production 16,990, of which significantly skipjack tuna (from aquaculture, negligible); foreign fishing in the Exclusive Economic Zone (200-mile limit; 2007) 111,512 metric tons, of which Taiwanese 53,767 metric tons, Japanese 32,431 metric tons. *Mining and quarrying:* quarrying of sand and aggregate for local construction only. *Manufacturing:* copra and coconut oil are traditionally important products; the manufacture of handicrafts and personal items (garments, mats, boats, etc.) is also important. *Energy production (consumption):* electricity (kW-hr; 2007) 67,300,000 (n.a.). **Gross national income** (2008): US$260,000,000 (US$2,340 per capita). **Selected balance of payments data.** Receipts from (US$'000,000): tourism (2006) 18; remittances (2005) 6.0; foreign direct investment (2005–06 avg.) 0.5; official development assistance (2007) 115. Disbursements for (US$'000,000): tourism (2006) 5.7.

Foreign trade

Imports (2007; c.i.f.): US$142,659,000 (food products and beverages 29.8%; mineral fuels 22.1%; machinery and apparatus 14.4%; transportation equipment 6.0%; chemical products 5.4%). *Major import sources:* US 41.2%; Singapore 8.7%; Japan 8.5%; Hong Kong 6.3%; Australia 4.1%. **Exports** (2007; f.o.b.): US$16,190,000 (tuna 69.9%; betel nuts 13.7%; reef fish 5.2%; cooked food 4.9%; kava 2.6%). *Major export destinations:* Guam 22.5%; US 17.2%; Northern Marianas 4.3%; Japan 4.1%; unspecified 51.2%.

Transport and communications

Transport. *Railroads:* none. *Roads* (2000): total length 240 km (paved 18%). *Vehicles* (2007): passenger cars 3,916; trucks and buses 3,849. *Air transport* (2006; Continental Micronesia only): passenger-km 4,762,000,000; metric ton-km cargo 102,000,000. **Communications,** in total units (units per 1,000 persons). Telephone landlines (2008): 8,700 (79); cellular telephone subscribers (2008): 34,000 (308); personal computers (2005): 6,000 (55); total Internet users (2008): 16,000 (145).

Education and health

Educational attainment (2000). Percentage of population ages 25 and over having: no formal schooling/unknown 13.4%; primary education 37.0%; some secondary 18.3%; secondary 12.9%; some college 18.4%. **Literacy** (2000): total population ages 10 and over literate 72,140 (92.4%); males literate 36,528 (92.9%); females literate 35,612 (91.9%). **Health:** physicians (2005) 62 (1 per 1,774 persons); hospital beds (2006) 365 (1 per 301 persons); infant mortality rate per 1,000 live births (2007) 37.5.

Military

External security is provided by the US.

Background

The islands of Micronesia were probably settled by people from eastern Melanesia some 3,500 years ago. Europeans first landed on the islands in the 16th century. Spain took control of the islands in 1886 and then sold them to Germany in 1899. The islands came under Japanese rule after World War I. They were captured by US forces during World War II, and in 1947 they became a UN trust territory administered by the US. The group of islands centered on the Caroline Islands became an internally self-governing federation in 1979. In 1986 the Federated States of Micronesia (FSM) entered into a Compact of Free Association with the US, which was amended in 2003. In the early 21st century, Micronesia found itself threatened by rising water levels.

Recent Developments

Faced with intensified environmental degradation from climate change, the Federated States of Micronesia took an active role in environmental politics in 2009. As lead entity in the Alliance of Small Island States, it pushed for a 45% reduction in greenhouse-gas emissions by 2020 and, with Mauritius, filed an application for an amendment to the Montreal Protocol to limit the use of hydrofluorocarbons.

Internet resource:
<www.spc.int/prism/country/fm/stats>.

Moldova

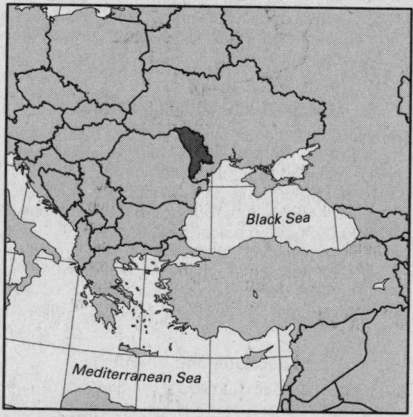

Black Sea

Mediterranean Sea

Official name: Republica Moldova (Republic of Moldova). Form of government: unitary parliamentary republic with a single legislative house (Parliament [101]). Head of state: President Mihai Ghimpu (from 2009). Head of government: Prime Minister Vlad Filat (from 2009). Capital: Chisinau. Official language: Moldovan. Official religion: none. Monetary unit: 1 Moldovan leu (plural lei) = 100 bani; valuation (1 Jul 2010) free rate, US$1 = 12.63 Moldovan lei.

Demography

Area: 13,067 sq mi, 33,843 sq km. Population (2009): 3,604,000. Density (2009): persons per sq mi 275.8, persons per sq km 106.5. Urban (2007; excludes Transdniestria): 41.3%. Sex distribution (2007; excludes Transdniestria): male 48.06%; female 51.94%. Age breakdown (2004; excludes Transdniestria): under 15, 19.1%; 15–29, 26.3%; 30–44, 20.9%; 45–59, 19.1%; 60 and over, 14.3%; unknown 0.3%. Ethnic composition (2004; excludes Transdniestria): Moldovan 75.8%; Ukrainian 8.4%; Russian 5.9%; Gagauz 4.4%; Rom (Gypsy) 2.2%; Bulgarian 1.9%; other 1.4%. Religious affiliation (2005): Moldovan Orthodox 31.8%; Bessarabian Orthodox 16.1%; Russian Orthodox 15.4%; Sunni Muslim 5.5%; Protestant 1.7%; Jewish 0.6%; nonreligious 19.9%; other 9.0%. Major cities (2007): Chisinau 630,300; Tiraspol 155,000; Balti 122,200; Bender (Tighina) 95,000; Rybnitsa (Ribnita) 52,000. Location: eastern Europe, bordering Ukraine and Romania.

Vital statistics

Birth rate per 1,000 population (2008): 10.9 (world avg. 20.3); within marriage 77.7%. Death rate per 1,000 population (2008): 11.7 (world avg. 8.5). Total fertility rate (avg. births per childbearing woman; 2008): 1.28. Life expectancy at birth (2008): male 65.6 years; female 73.2 years.

National economy

Budget (2007). Revenue: 14,004,000,000 Moldovan lei (tax revenue 75.0%, of which VAT 53.9%; nontax revenue 18.5%; grants 6.5%). Expenditures: 14,211,000,000 Moldovan lei (health care 12.9%; education 10.3%; public order 7.5%; social fund transfers 6.2%; transportation and communications 6.0%; interest payments 4.3%; defense 1.9%). Public debt (external, outstanding; 2007): US$779,000,000. Production (metric tons except as noted). Agriculture and fishing (2008): corn (maize) 1,478,560, wheat 1,286,330, sugar beets 960,712, grapes 635,513, sunflower seeds 371,935, walnuts 13,742; livestock (number of live animals) 753,903 sheep, 298,675 pigs, 231,716 cattle; fisheries production (2007) 5,860 (from aquaculture 80%). Mining and quarrying (2006): gypsum 725,900. Manufacturing (value of production in '000,000 Moldovan lei; 2004; excludes Transdniestria): alcoholic beverages 4,013, of which wine 3,098; food products 3,461; nonmetallic mineral products 1,273. Energy production (consumption): electricity (kW-hr; 2006) 3,829,000,000 (7,341,000,000); coal (metric tons; 2006) none (194,000); crude petroleum (barrels; 2006) 29,000 (negligible); petroleum products (metric tons; 2006) none (607,000); natural gas (cu m; 2006) none (2,696,000,000). Population economically active (2005; excludes Transdniestria): total 1,422,300; activity rate of total de facto population 39.5% (participation rates: ages 15–64, 53.2%; female 51.5%; unemployed [2008] 4.0%). Gross national income (2008; excludes Transdniestria): US$5,338,000,000 (US$1,470 per capita). Selected balance of payments data. Receipts from (US$'000,000): tourism (2007) 164; remittances

---

1 metric ton = about 1.1 short tons;   1 kilometer = 0.6 mi (statute);   1 metric ton-km cargo = about 0.68 short ton-mi cargo;   c.i.f.: cost, insurance, and freight;   f.o.b.: free on board

(2008) 1,897; foreign direct investment (2005–07 avg.) 299; official development assistance (2007) 269. Disbursements for (US$'000,000): tourism (2007) 213; remittances (2008) 115.

Foreign trade

Imports (2006; c.i.f.): US$2,693,000,000 (machinery and apparatus 13.8%; refined petroleum products 12.6%, chemical products 11.9%, natural gas 8.1%; food products 7.4%). *Major import sources:* Ukraine 19.2%; Russia 15.5%; Romania 12.8%; Germany 7.9%; Italy 7.3%. **Exports** (2006; f.o.b.): US$1,051,000,000 (food products 19.8%, of which cereals 4.3%, walnuts 3.6%; wearing apparel and accessories 19.1%; wine and grape must 15.4%; machinery and apparatus 5.2%). *Major export destinations:* Russia 17.3%; Romania 14.8%; Ukraine 12.2%; Italy 11.1%; Belarus 7.0%.

Transport and communications

Transport. *Railroads* (2007): length 1,154 km; passenger-km 468,000,000; metric ton-km cargo 3,120,000,000. *Roads* (2007): total length 9,337 km (paved 94%). *Vehicles* (2003): passenger cars 252,490; trucks and buses 77,534. *Air transport* (2007): passenger-km 550,000,000; metric ton-km cargo 1,300,000. **Communications,** in total units (units per 1,000 persons). Telephone landlines (2008): 1,115,000 (307); cellular telephone subscribers (2008): 2,420,000 (666); personal computers (2005): 348,000 (83); total Internet users (2008): 800,000 (220); broadband Internet subscribers (2008): 115,000 (32).

Education and health

Literacy (2003): total population ages 15 and over literate 99.1%. **Health** (2008): physicians (excludes Transdniestria) 12,665 (1 per 287 persons); hospital beds (excludes Transdniestria) 21,798 (1 per 167 persons); infant mortality rate per 1,000 live births 12.1; undernourished population (2002–04) 450,000 (11% of total population based on the consumption of a minimum daily requirement of 1,970 calories).

Military

Total active duty personnel (November 2008): 6,000 (army 85.8%, air force 14.2%); opposition forces (excluding Russian troops) in Transdniestria (2008): 7,500; Russian troops in Transdniestria (November 2008): 1,500. **Military expenditure as percentage of GDP** (2008): 0.4%; per capita expenditure US$7.

Background

Moldova, once part of the principality of Moldavia, was founded by the Vlachs in the 14th century. In the mid-16th century, it was under Ottoman rule. In 1774 it came under Russian control and lost portions of its territory. In 1859 it joined with the principality of Walachia to form the state of Romania, and in 1918 some of the territory it had ceded earlier also joined Romania. Romania was compelled in 1940 to cede some of the Moldavian area to Russia in 1940, and that area combined with what Russia already controlled to become the Moldavian SSR. In 1991

Moldavia declared independence from the Soviet Union. It adopted the Romanian spelling of Moldova after having legitimized the use of the Roman rather than the Cyrillic alphabet in 1989. It was admitted to the UN in 1992. In 2000 it abandoned its semipresidential form of government to become a parliamentary republic.

 **Did you know?** Cricova and Milestii Mici, underground wine cellars that form a part of Moldova's important alcohol industry, are so large that they are toured by automobile.

Recent Developments

Moldova's international relations seemed to be improving. In December 2009 the country's economy minister visited Russia to promote ties and to seek the first payment of a US$500 million loan offered in June. In January 2010 Prime Minister Vlad Filat visited the United States to finalize a US$262 million financial aid package. The next month a legislative delegation visited Romania. A treaty detailing Moldovan-Romanian cooperation and future integration with Europe was discussed. In March Romania began issuing travel documents allowing Moldovans visa-free travel to and the right to temporarily stay in Romania.

Internet resource:
<www.statistica.md/index.php?l=en>.

Monaco

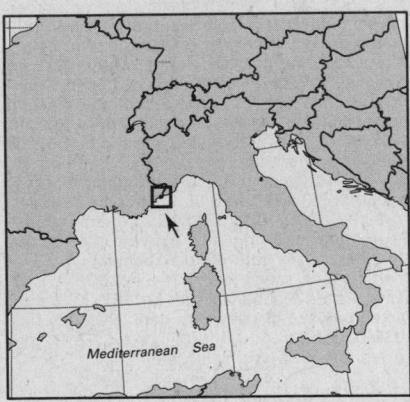

Mediterranean Sea

Official name: Principauté de Monaco (Principality of Monaco). **Form of government:** constitutional monarchy with one legislative house (National Council [24]). **Head of state:** Prince Albert II (from 2005). **Head of government:** Minister of State Jean-Paul Proust (from 2005), assisted by the Council of Government. **Capital:** no separate area is distinguished as such. **Official language:** French. **Official religion:** Roman Catholicism. **Monetary unit:** 1 euro (€) = 100 centimes; valuation (1 Jul 2010) US$1 = €0.80 (Monaco uses the euro as its official currency, even though it is not a member of the EU).

Demography

Area: 0.78 sq mi, 2.02 sq km. **Population** (2009): 35,400. **Density** (2009): persons per sq mi 45,385, persons per sq km 17,525. **Urban** (2008): 100%. **Sex distribution** (2008): male 47.94%; female 52.06%. **Age breakdown** (2008): under 15, 12.8%; 15–29, 12.7%; 30–44, 19.2%; 45–59, 21.8%; 60–74, 19.1%; 75–84, 7.9%; 85 and over, 4.2%; unknown 2.3%. **Ethnic composition** (2008): French 28.4%; Monegasque 21.6%; Italian 18.7%; British 7.5%; Belgian 2.8%; Swiss 2.5%; German 2.5%; US 1.0%; other 15.0% (including Asian countries 2.5%, African countries 2.2%). **Religious affiliation** (2000): Christian 93.2%, of which Roman Catholic 89.3%; Jewish 1.7%; nonreligious and other 5.1%. **Location:** western Europe, bordering the Mediterranean Sea and France.

Vital statistics

Birth rate per 1,000 population (2007): 26.2 (world avg. 20.3); (2005) within marriage 61.4%. **Death rate** per 1,000 population (2007): 14.2 (world avg. 8.5). **Total fertility rate** (avg. births per childbearing woman; 2007): 1.75. **Life expectancy** at birth (2007): male 76.0 years; female 83.9 years.

National economy

Budget (2007). *Revenue:* €845,600,700 (taxes on hotels, banks, and the industrial sector 47.4%; property taxes 12.9%; state-run monopolies 10.0%; customs duties 3.1%). *Expenditures:* €843,119,681 (current expenditures 65.1%; capital expenditures 34.9%). **Production.** *Agriculture and fishing:* limited horticulture and greenhouse cultivation; fisheries production (2007; metric tons) 1 (from aquaculture, none). *Mining and quarrying* (2009): none. *Manufacturing* (value of sales in €'000; 2007): chemical products, cosmetics, perfumery, and pharmaceuticals 364,077; plastic products 266,366; light electronics and precision instruments 86,113. *Energy production (consumption):* electricity (kW-hr; 2001) n.a. (475,000,000 [imported from France]). **Gross national income** (2008): US$6,919,000,000 (US$195,717 per capita). **Population economically active** (2005): total 40,289; activity rate of total population 58.4% (participation rates: ages 17–64 [2000] 61.1%; female 41.4%; unemployed [2000] 3.6%). **Selected balance of payments data.** Receipts from (US$'000,000): tourism (2007) n.a.; 2,773 hotel rooms, 327,985 overnight visitors.

Foreign trade

Imports (2007; excludes trade with France; Monaco has participated in a customs union with France since 1963): €850,202,845 (nonelectrical machinery and apparatus 40.2%; pharmaceuticals, perfumes, wearing apparel, and publishing 19.2%; rubber and plastic products, glass products, construction materials, organic chemical products, and paper products 15.7%; food products 7.4%). *Major import sources:* China 34.9%; Italy 18.6%; Japan

8.5%; UK 7.1%; Belgium 5.3%. **Exports** (2007; excludes trade with France; Monaco has participated in a customs union with France since 1963): €834,108,693 (rubber and plastic products, glass products, construction materials, organic chemical products, and paper products 39.9%; products of the automobile industry 12.7%; pharmaceuticals, perfumes, wearing apparel, and publishing 12.2%; nonelectrical machinery and apparatus 12.1%). *Major export destinations:* Germany 10.7%; Italy 8.4%; Spain 7.9%; UK 6.6%; Lithuania 5.2%.

Transport and communications

Transport. *Railroads* (2001): length 1.7 km; passengers 2,171,100; cargo 3,357 tons. *Roads* (2007): total length 77 km (paved 100%). *Vehicles* (1997): passenger cars 21,120; trucks and buses 2,770. *Air transport* (2004; charter service of Monacair): passenger-km 414,000. **Communications**, in total units (units per 1,000 persons). Telephone landlines (2008): 35,000 (990); cellular telephone subscribers (2008): 22,000 (622); total Internet users (2008): 22,000 (622); broadband Internet subscribers (2007): 12,000 (348).

Education and health

Educational attainment (2000). Percentage of population ages 17 and over having: primary/lower secondary education 24.7%; upper secondary 27.6%; vocational 12.7%; university 35.0%. **Literacy:** virtually 100%. **Health** (2002): physicians 156 (1 per 207 persons); hospital beds 521 (1 per 62 persons); infant mortality rate per 1,000 live births (2007) 5.2.

Military

Defense responsibility lies with France according to the terms of the Versailles Treaty of 1919.

Background

Inhabited since prehistoric times, Monaco was known to the Phoenicians, Greeks, Carthaginians, and Romans. In 1191 the Genoese took possession of it; in 1297 the reign of the Grimaldi family began. The Grimaldis allied themselves with France except for the period 1524–1641, when they were under the protection of Spain. France annexed Monaco in 1793, and it remained under French control until the fall of Napoleon, when the Grimaldis returned. In 1815 it was put under the protection of Sardinia. A treaty in 1861 called for the sale of the towns of Menton and Roquebrune to France and the establishment of Monaco's independence. It joined the UN in 1993. In 1997 the 700-year rule of the Grimaldis, then under Prince Rainier III, was celebrated. Although not a member of the EU, Monaco adopted the euro as its currency in 2002.

Recent Developments

Monaco's Prince Albert II remained an advocate for the environment in 2009. In January he visited sev-

---

1 metric ton = about 1.1 short tons;   1 kilometer = 0.6 mi (statute);   1 metric ton-km cargo = about 0.68 short ton-mi cargo;   c.i.f.: cost, insurance, and freight;   f.o.b.: free on board

eral scientific bases in Antarctica, and in September he gave a speech calling for international action to protect the Arctic from climate change.

Internet resource: <www.monte-carlo.mc>.

Mongolia

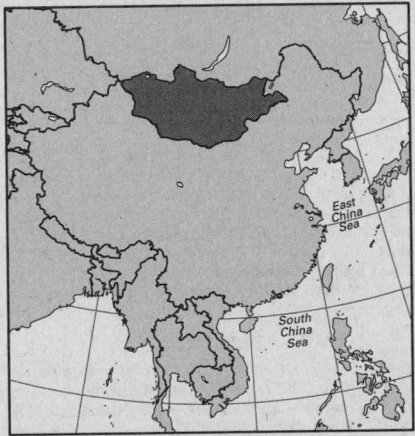

Official name: Mongol Uls (Mongolia). **Form of government:** unitary multiparty republic with one legislative house (State Great Hural [76]). **Head of state:** President Tsakhiagiyn Elbegdorj (from 2009). **Head of government:** Prime Minister Sukhbaataryn Batbold (from 2009). **Capital:** Ulaanbaatar (Ulan Bator). **Official language:** Khalkha Mongolian. **Official religion:** none. **Monetary unit:** 1 tugrik (Tug) = 100 mongo; valuation (1 Jul 2010) US$1 = Tug 1,372.00.

Demography

Area: 603,930 sq mi, 1,564,160 sq km. **Population** (2009): 2,704,000. **Density** (2009): persons per sq mi 4.5, persons per sq km 1.7. **Urban** (2006): 60.9%. **Sex distribution** (2004): male 49.60%; female 50.40%. **Age breakdown** (2005): under 15, 28.9%; 15–29, 32.3%; 30–44, 22.6%; 45–59, 10.3%; 60–74, 4.5%; 75–84, 1.1%; 85 and over, 0.3%. **Ethnic composition** (2000): Khalkha Mongol 81.5%; Kazakh 4.3%; Dörbed Mongol 2.8%; Bayad 2.1%; Buryat Mongol 1.7%; Dariganga Mongol 1.3%; Zakhchin 1.3%; Tuvan (Uriankhai) 1.1%; other 3.9%. **Religious affiliation** (2005): traditional beliefs (shamanism) 32%; Buddhist (Lamaism) 23%; Muslim 5%; Christian 1%; nonreligious 30%; atheist/other 9%. **Major cities** (2007): Ulaanbaatar (Ulan Bator) 1,031,200; Erdenet 74,300; Darhan 72,400; Choybalsan (2000) 40,123; Mörön (2000) 28,903. **Location:** north-central Asia, bordering Russia and China.

Vital statistics

Birth rate per 1,000 population (2008): 23.8 (world avg. 20.3); (2001) within marriage 81.1%. **Death rate** per 1,000 population (2008): 5.6 (world avg. 8.5). **Total fertility rate** (avg. births per childbearing

woman; 2005): 1.97. **Life expectancy** at birth (2004): male 61.6 years; female 67.8 years.

National economy

Budget (2006). *Revenue:* Tug 1,360,400,000,000 (tax revenue 83.0%, of which income tax 35.0%, taxes on goods and services 25.9%; nontax revenue 16.6%; other 0.4%). *Expenditures:* Tug 1,237,000,-000,000 (economic services 26.1%; social security 20.8%; general administration 19.6%; education 15.6%; health 8.0%; defense and public order 3.7%). **Population economically active** (2004): total 986,100; activity rate of total population 39.3% (participation rates: ages 16–59, 63.7%; female 51.0%; registered unemployed [December 2008] 2.8%). **Production** (metric tons except as noted). *Agriculture and fishing* (2007): hay 930,405, potatoes 114,490, wheat 109,560; livestock (number of live animals) 15,451,700 goats, 14,815,100 sheep, 2,167,900 cattle, 2,114,800 horses, 253,500 camels; fisheries production 185 (from aquaculture, none). *Mining and quarrying* (2007): fluorspar 381,000; copper (metal content) 130,160; molybdenum (metal content) 1,978; gold 17,473 kg. *Manufacturing* (value of production in Tug '000,000; 2006): textiles 93,475; base metals 74,879; food products 71,428. *Energy production (consumption):* electricity (kW-hr; 2006) 3,544,000,000 (3,691,000,000); coal (metric tons; 2006) 1,316,000 (1,316,000); lignite (metric tons; 2006) 6,758,000 (4,301,000); crude petroleum (barrels; 2005) 201,000 (n.a.); petroleum products (metric tons; 2006) none (635,000). **Gross national income** (2008): US$4,411,000,000 (US$1,680 per capita). **Public debt** (external; 2007): US$1,566,-000,000. **Selected balance of payments data.** Receipts from (US$'000,000): tourism (2006) 225; remittances (2008) 200; foreign direct investment (2005–07 avg.) 267; official development assistance (2007) 228. Disbursements for (US$'000,000): tourism (2006) 188; remittances (2008) 77.

Foreign trade

Imports (2006; c.i.f.): US$1,489,200,000 (mineral fuels 30.0%; machinery and apparatus 18.2%; food and agricultural products 12.4%; transportation equipment 10.3%). *Major import sources:* Russia 36.6%; China 27.5%; Japan 6.8%; South Korea 5.6%; Kazakhstan 3.5%. **Exports** (2006; f.o.b.): US$1,528,800,000 (copper concentrate 42.7%; gold 18.1%; refined copper 7.2%; combed goat down 5.3%; raw [greasy] cashmere 4.2%; molybdenum 3.2%). *Major export destinations:* China 68.1%; Canada 11.2%; US 7.8%; Russia 2.9%; UK 2.5%.

Transport and communications

Transport. *Railroads* (2006): route length 1,810 km; passenger-km 1,287,000,000; metric ton-km cargo 10,513,000,000. *Roads* (2002): total length 49,250 km (paved 4%). *Vehicles* (2007): passenger cars 110,153; trucks and buses 50,216. *Air transport* (2006): passenger-km 835,800,000; metric ton-km cargo 86,400,000. **Communications**, in total units (units per 1,000 persons). Telephone landlines (2008): 165,000 (63); cellular telephone subscribers (2008): 999,000 (378); personal computers (2005): 340,000 (133); total Internet users (2008): 330,000 (125); broadband Internet subscribers (2007): 7,400 (2.8).

Education and health

Educational attainment (2000). Percentage of population ages 10 and over having: no formal education 11.6%; primary education 23.5%; secondary 46.1%; vocational secondary 11.2%; higher 7.6%. **Literacy** (2004): percentage of total population ages 15 and over literate 97.8%; males 98.0%; females 97.5%. **Health** (2004): physicians 6,590 (1 per 384 persons); hospital beds 18,400 (1 per 138 persons); infant mortality rate per 1,000 live births (2008) 19.6; undernourished population (2003–05) 800,000 (29% of total population based on the consumption of a minimum daily requirement of 1,840 calories).

Military

Total active duty personnel (November 2008): 10,000 (army 89.0%, air force 8.0%, other 3.0%); reserve 137,000. **Military expenditure as percentage of GDP** (2007): 1.1%; per capita expenditure US$16.

Background

In Neolithic times Mongolia was inhabited by small groups of nomads. During the 3rd century BC it became the center of the Xiongnu empire. Turkic-speaking peoples held sway in the 4th–10th centuries AD. In the early 13th century Genghis Khan united the Mongol tribes and conquered central Asia. His successor, Ogodei, conquered the Chin dynasty of China in 1234. Kublai Khan established the Yuan, or Mongol, dynasty in China in 1279. After the 14th century the Ming dynasty of China confined the Mongols to their homeland in the steppes; later they became part of the Chinese Ch'ing dynasty. Inner Mongolia was incorporated into China in 1644. After the fall of the Ch'ing dynasty in 1911, Mongol princes declared Mongolia's independence from China, and in 1921 Russian forces helped drive off the Chinese. The Mongolian People's Republic was established in 1924 and recognized by China in 1946. The nation adopted a new constitution in 1992 and shortened its name to Mongolia.

Recent Developments

After five years of serious disagreements about windfall taxes and what Mongolia's stake in the mine should be, in July 2009 the Great Khural authorized the government to conclude an agreement with the Ivanhoe Mines and Rio Tinto companies to exploit the rich gold and copper deposits at Oyuutolgoi. Government ministers signed the Oyuutolgoi contract in October, and in December the companies announced a 2010 budget of more than US$750 million for work on the mine complex.

Internet resource: <www.nso.mn/v3/index2.php>.

Montenegro

Official name: Crna Gora (Montenegro). **Form of government:** multiparty republic with one legislative house (Parliament [81]). **Head of state:** President Filip Vujanovic (from 2003). **Head of government:**

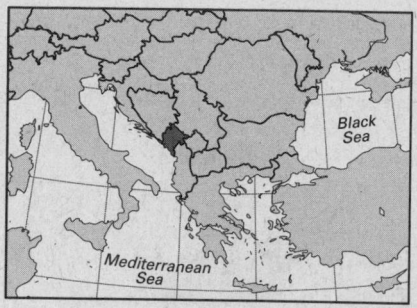

Prime Minister Milo Djukanovic (from 2008). **Capital:** Podgorica; Cetinje is the old royal capital. **Official language:** Montenegrin (according to the constitution, Serbian, Bosnian, Albanian, and Croatian may also be used as official languages). **Official religion:** none. **Monetary unit:** 1 euro (€) = 100 cents; valuation (1 Jul 2010) US$1 = €0.80 (Montenegro uses the euro as its official currency, even though it is not a member of the EU).

Demography

Area: 5,333 sq mi, 13,812 sq km. **Population** (2009): 630,000. **Density** (2009): persons per sq mi 118.1, persons per sq km 45.6. **Urban** (2005): 61.2%. **Sex distribution** (2006): male 49.28%; female 50.72%. **Age breakdown** (2005): under 15, 19.6%; 15–29, 23.6%; 30–44, 19.8%; 45–59, 19.1%; 60–74, 12.8%; 75–84, 4.3%; 85 and over, 0.8%. **Ethnic composition** (2003): Montenegrin 43.2%; Serb 32.0%; Bosniac/Muslim 11.8%; Albanian 5.0%; undeclared 4.0%; other 4.0%. **Religious affiliation** (2003): Orthodox 70%; Muslim 21%; Roman Catholic 4%; other 5%. **Major settlements** (2003): Podgorica 136,473; Niksic 58,212; Pljevlja 21,377; Bijelo Polje 15,883; Cetinje 15,137. **Location:** southeastern Europe, bordering Bosnia and Herzegovina, Serbia, Kosovo, Albania, the Mediterranean Sea, and Croatia.

Vital statistics

Birth rate per 1,000 population (2008): 13.1 (world avg. 20.3); within marriage 82.6%. **Death rate** per 1,000 population (2008): 9.1 (world avg. 8.5). **Total fertility rate** (avg. births per childbearing woman; 2007): 1.69. **Life expectancy** at birth (2007): male 71.2 years; female 76.1 years.

National economy

Budget (2006). *Revenue:* €582,258,287 (tax revenue 85.8%, of which VAT 44.5%, income tax 12.5%, excise tax 12.4%, taxes on international trade 9.7%; nontax revenue 14.2%). *Expenditures:* €579,780,129 (wages and salaries 27.4%; transfers 20.7%; debt service 20.0%). **Public debt** (external, outstanding; December 2008): US$670,400,000. **Production** (metric tons except as noted). *Agriculture and fishing* (2007): potatoes 130,000, grapes 41,000, tomatoes 22,000, tobacco 400; livestock (number of live animals) 249,281 sheep, 114,922 cattle, 13,294 pigs; fisheries production 911 (from aquaculture 1%). *Mining and quarrying* (2007): baux-

1 metric ton = about 1.1 short tons;   1 kilometer = 0.6 mi (statute);   1 metric ton-km cargo = about 0.68 short ton-mi cargo;   c.i.f.: cost, insurance, and freight;   f.o.b.: free on board

ite 667,053; sea salt 20,000. *Manufacturing* (gross value added in €'000; 2005): base metals and fabricated metal products (mostly of aluminum) 60,766; food products, beverages, and tobacco products 56,607; paper products, publishing, and printing 7,044. *Energy production (consumption):* electricity (kW-hr; 2007) 2,144,000,000 (2,654,000,000 [industrial consumption only]); lignite (metric tons; 2007) 1,195,500 (29,000 [industrial consumption only]). **Population economically active** (2007): total 269,500; activity rate 43.2% (participation rates: ages 16 and over, 52.9%; female 43.0%; unemployed [September 2008–August 2009] 14.1%). **Gross national income** (2008): US$4,008,000,000 (US$6,440 per capita). **Selected balance of payments data.** Receipts from (US$'000,000): tourism (2008) 725; remittances (2006) 100; foreign direct investment (FDI; 2005–07 avg.) 657; official development assistance (2007) 106. Disbursements for (US$'000,000): tourism (2008) 43; FDI (2005–07 avg.) 98.

Foreign trade

Imports (2007; c.i.f.): €2,134,377,900 (mineral fuels 11.6%; motor vehicles 11.4%; nonelectrical machinery and apparatus 9.0%; electrical machinery and apparatus 8.8%; base and fabricated metals 7.1%). *Major import sources:* Serbia 29.9%; Germany 10.0%; Italy 9.8%; Croatia 3.9%; Greece 3.5%. **Exports** (2007; f.o.b.): €599,020,700,000 (aluminum and aluminum products 47.0%; base metals 11.9%; beverages and tobacco products 8.9%; mineral fuels 8.1%). *Major export destinations:* Serbia 28.3%; Italy 27.4%; Greece 12.3%; Hungary 11.1%; Bosnia and Herzegovina 5.1%.

Transport and communications

Transport. *Railroads* (2007): length (2006) 250 km; passenger-km 110,000,000; metric ton-km cargo 184,957,000. *Roads* (2006): total length 7,368 km (paved 64%). *Vehicles* (2007): passenger cars 178,449. *Air transport* (2007): passengers 1,024,491; freight 1,320 metric tons. **Communications**, in total units (units per 1,000 persons). Telephone landlines (2008): 362,000 (577); cellular telephone subscribers (2008): 735,000 (1,171); total Internet users (2008): 294,000 (468); broadband Internet subscribers (2006): 26,000 (42).

Education and health

Educational attainment (2005). Percentage of population ages 15 and over having: no formal education 3.2%; incomplete primary education 6.8%; complete primary 22.5%; secondary 55.0%; higher 12.5%. **Literacy** (2003): total population ages 15 and over literate 97.6%; males literate 99.6%; females literate 95.7%. **Health** (2007): physicians 1,277 (1 per 490 persons); hospital beds 3,948 (1 per 159 persons); infant mortality rate per 1,000 live births (2008) 7.5.

Military

Total active duty personnel (November 2008): 4,500 (army 55.6%, navy 44.4%). **Military expenditure as**

percentage of GDP (2007): 2.3%; per capita expenditure US$94.

Background

The Kingdom of the Serbs, Croats, and Slovenes was created after the collapse of Austria-Hungary at the end of World War I. The country signed treaties with Czechoslovakia and Romania in 1920–21, marking the beginning of the Little Entente. In 1929 an absolute monarchy was established, the country's name was changed to Yugoslavia, and it was divided into regions without regard to ethnic boundaries. Axis powers invaded Yugoslavia in 1941, and German, Italian, Hungarian, and Bulgarian troops occupied it for the rest of World War II. In 1945 the Socialist Federal Republic of Yugoslavia was established; it included the republics of Bosnia and Herzegovina, Croatia, Macedonia, Montenegro, Serbia, and Slovenia. Its independent form of communism under Josip Broz Tito's leadership provoked the USSR. Internal ethnic tensions flared up in the 1980s, causing the country's ultimate collapse. In 1991–92 independence was declared by Croatia, Slovenia, Macedonia, and Bosnia and Herzegovina; the new Federal Republic of Yugoslavia (containing roughly 45% of the population and 40% of the area of its predecessor) was proclaimed by Serbia and Montenegro. Still fueled by long-standing ethnic tensions, hostilities continued into the 1990s. Despite the approval of the Dayton Peace Agreement (1995), sporadic fighting continued and was followed in 1998–99 by Serbian repression and expulsion of ethnic populations in the province of Kosovo. In September–October 2000, the battered nation of Yugoslavia ended the autocratic rule of Pres. Slobodan Milosevic. In April 2001 he was arrested and in June extradited to The Hague to stand trial for war crimes, genocide, and crimes against humanity committed during the fighting in Kosovo. In February 2003 both houses of the Yugoslav federal legislature voted to accept a new state charter and change the name of the country from Yugoslavia to Serbia and Montenegro. Henceforth, defense, international political and economic relations, and human rights matters would be handled centrally, while all other functions would be run from the republican capitals, Belgrade and Podgorica, respectively. A provision was included for both states to vote on independence after three years, and in June 2006 Montenegro's parliament declared the republic's independence, severing some 88 years of union with Serbia.

Recent Developments

The Montenegrin parliament adopted more than 100 laws in 2009 in an effort to build the country's legal framework and to address European integration issues. In December 2008 Montenegro had submitted its application for membership in the EU, and it hoped for admission in 2012. In its annual report the European Commission noted that Montenegro had made progress in addressing the political criteria needed for EU membership but warned that the government needed to consolidate the rule of law and combat corruption and organized crime. In March 2010 a project was launched to reform the country's customs system in an effort to help address the problem with organized crime. In December NATO offered the country a formal plan to join the alliance, and in March 2010 a contingent of 31 soldiers was deployed to join NATO forces in Afghanistan.

Internet resource: <www.monstat.org>.

Morocco

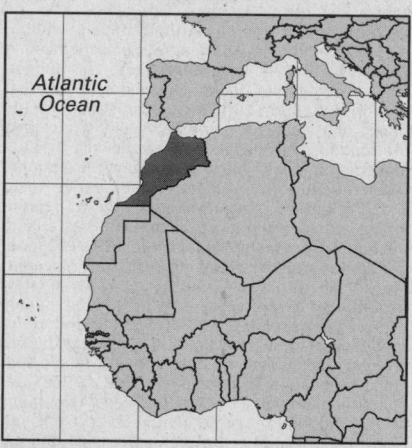

Official name: Al-Mamlakah al-Maghribiyah (Kingdom of Morocco). **Form of government:** constitutional monarchy with two legislative houses (House of Councillors [270]; House of Representatives [325]). **Head of state and government:** King Muhammad VI (from 1999), assisted by Prime Minister Abbas El Fassi (from 2007). **Capital:** Rabat. **Official language:** Arabic. **Official religion:** Islam. **Monetary unit:** 1 Moroccan dirham (DH) = 100 santimat; valuation (1 Jul 2010) US$1 = DH 8.87.

Demography

Area: 274,461 sq mi, 710,850 sq km (includes Western Sahara, annexure of Morocco whose political status has been unresolved since 1991; Western Sahara area: 97,344 sq mi, 252,120 sq km). **Population** (2009; includes Western Sahara, population [2009 est.] 405,000): 31,690,000 (in addition, about 90,000 Western Saharan refugees live in camps near Tindouf). **Density** (2009; includes Western Sahara): persons per sq mi 115.5, persons per sq km 44.6. **Urban** (2007): 56.4%. **Sex distribution** (2008; excludes Western Sahara): male 49.28%; female 50.72%. **Age breakdown** (2008; excludes Western Sahara): under 15, 29.1%; 15–29, 28.6%; 30–44, 21.0%; 45–59, 13.1%; 60–74, 6.0%; 75–84, 1.8%; 85 and over, 0.4%. **Ethnic composition** (2000): Amazigh (Berber) 45%, of which Arabized 24%; Arab 44%; Moors originally from Mauritania 10%; other 1%. **Religious affiliation** (2004): Muslim more than 99% (including Sunni 97%; Shi'i 2%); other less than 1%. **Major urban agglomerations** (2007):

Casablanca 3,181,000; Rabat 1,705,000; Fès 1,002,000; Marrakech 872,000; Tangier (2004) 669,685. **Location:** northern Africa, bordering the Mediterranean Sea, the Spanish exclaves of Ceuta and Melilla, Algeria, Mauritania, and the North Atlantic Ocean.

Vital statistics

Birth rate per 1,000 population (2008; excludes Western Sahara): 20.0 (world avg. 20.3). **Death rate** per 1,000 population (2008; excludes Western Sahara): 4.7 (world avg. 8.5). **Total fertility rate** (avg. births per childbearing woman; 2008; excludes Western Sahara): 2.31. **Life expectancy** at birth (2008; excludes Western Sahara): male 72.2 years; female 78.4 years.

National economy

Budget. *Revenue* (2007): DH 167,904,000,000 (VAT 29.6%; corporate taxes 18.1%; income tax 16.5%; nontax revenue 8.8%). *Expenditures* (2007): DH 168,959,000,000 (current expenditures 78.5%; capital expenditures 16.3%). **Public debt** (external, outstanding; 2007): US$15,670,000,000. **Population economically active** (2006): total 10,990,000; activity rate 36.0% (participation rates: ages 15 and over, 51.3%; female [2005] 27.5%; unemployed [April 2008–March 2009] 9.7%). **Production** (metric tons except as noted). *Agriculture and fishing* (2008): wheat 3,769,450, sugar beets 2,925,700, potatoes 1,536,560, olives 765,380, clementines (2006–07) 336,000, grapes 290,794; livestock (number of live animals) 17,077,700 sheep, 2,814,000 cattle, 45,000 camels; fisheries production (2007; roughly 60% of Morocco's fisheries production comes from Atlantic waters off of Western Sahara) 882,079 (from aquaculture, negligible). *Mining and quarrying* (2007): phosphate rock 27,834,000; barite 664,708; fluorite 78,817; zinc (metal content) 68,000; lead (metal content) 44,800; cobalt (metal content) 1,100; silver 246,000 kg. *Manufacturing* (value added in US$'000,000; 2005): food products and beverages 1,467; tobacco products 1,307; wearing apparel 697. *Energy production (consumption):* electricity (kW-hr; 2008) 18,646,000,000 ([2006] 25,190,000,000); coal (metric tons; 2006) none (5,877,000); crude petroleum (barrels; 2007) 81,000 ([2006] 46,000,000); petroleum products (metric tons; 2006) 5,221,000 (7,467,000); natural gas (cu m; 2007) 61,000,000 ([2006] 571,000,000). **Selected balance of payments data.** Receipts from (US$'000,000): tourism (2007) 7,181; remittances (2008) 6,730; foreign direct investment (FDI; 2005–07 avg.) 2,277; official development assistance (2007) 1,090. Disbursements for (US$'000,000): tourism (2007) 880; remittances (2008) 52; FDI (2005–07 avg.) 390. **Gross national income** (2008): US$80,544,000,000 (US$2,580 per capita).

Foreign trade

Imports (2008; c.i.f.): DH 321,931,000,000 (mineral fuels 22.2%, of which crude petroleum 9.6%; machinery and apparatus 22.0%; food products and beverages 9.6%). *Major import sources:*

1 metric ton = about 1.1 short tons; 1 kilometer = 0.6 mi (statute); 1 metric ton-km cargo = about 0.68 short ton-mi cargo; c.i.f.: cost, insurance, and freight; f.o.b.: free on board

France 15.0%; Spain 11.1%; Italy 6.7%; China 5.7%; US 5.0%. **Exports** (2008; f.o.b.): DH 154,493,000,000 (wearing apparel and accessories 16.6%; phosphoric acid 14.6%; phosphate rock 11.2%; fish, shrimp, and octopuses 8.0%; fertilizer 7.1%; electricity distribution equipment 5.8%; vegetables and fruit 5.7%; cannabis is an important illegal export—Morocco was the world's number 2 producer in 2008). *Major export destinations:* France 20.0%; Spain 17.8%; India 6.6%; Brazil 5.1%; Italy 4.7%.

Transport and communications

Transport. *Railroads* (2007): route length (2005) 1,907 km; passenger-km 3,659,000,000; metric ton-km cargo 5,835,000,000. *Roads* (2007): total length 57,799 km (paved 62%). *Vehicles* (2007): passenger cars 1,644,523; trucks and buses 528,175. *Air transport* (2008; Royal Air Maroc only): passenger-km 9,901,000,000; metric ton-km cargo 55,477,000. **Communications,** in total units (units per 1,000 persons). Telephone landlines (2008): 2,991,000 (95); cellular telephone subscribers (2008): 22,816,000 (728); personal computers (2007): 1,115,000 (36); total Internet users (2008): 10,300,000 (329); broadband Internet subscribers (2008): 484,000 (15).

Education and health

Educational attainment (2004). Percentage of population ages 10 and over having: no formal education through incomplete primary education 45.5%; complete primary 40.8%; secondary 8.7%; higher 5.0%. **Literacy** (2007): total population ages 11 and over literate 58.7%; males literate 70.6%; females literate 47.3%. **Health** (2006): physicians 18,248 (1 per 1,678 persons); hospital beds (public hospitals only) 26,649 (1 per 1,149 persons); infant mortality rate per 1,000 live births (2008; excludes Western Sahara) 30.9; undernourished population (2002–04) 1,800,000 (6% of total population based on the consumption of a minimum daily requirement of 1,870 calories).

Military

Total active duty personnel (November 2008): 195,800 (army 89.4%, navy 4.0%, air force 6.6%). **Military expenditure as percentage of GDP** (2008): 3.4%; per capita expenditure US$115.

Background

The Berbers entered Morocco near the end of the 2nd millennium BC. Phoenicians established trading posts along the Mediterranean during the 12th century BC, and Carthage had settlements along the Atlantic in the 5th century BC. After the fall of Carthage, Morocco became a loyal ally of Rome, and in AD 42 it was annexed by Rome as part of the province of Mauretania. It was invaded by Muslims in the 7th century. Beginning in the mid-11th century, the Almoravids, Almohads, and Marinids ruled successively. After the fall of the Marinids in the mid-15th century, the Sa'dis ruled for a century beginning in 1550. The French fought Morocco over the Algerian boundary in the 1840s, and the Spanish seized part of Moroccan territory in 1859. It was a French protectorate from 1912

until its independence in 1956. In the mid-1970s it reasserted claim to the Western Sahara, and in 1976 Spanish troops withdrew from the region, leaving behind the Algerian-supported Saharan guerrillas of the Polisario movement. Relations with Mauritania and Algeria deteriorated, and fighting over the region continued. Attempts at mediation have repeatedly been made by the international community.

Recent Developments

Although Morocco's economy reflected the effects of the global downturn, it was estimated to grow by 2.6% in 2009. The number of tourists rose by 9.0% in the first half of 2009, and consumer prices fell by 3.4%. There was also a bumper harvest, which raised the agricultural GDP—itself 16.0% of the overall GDP—by 23.0%. Nonetheless, with unemployment at 10.5% and migrants returning from Europe, popular discontent led public-sector unions to organize strikes in January and February in favor of a wage increase.

Internet resource: <www.visitmorocco.com>.

Mozambique

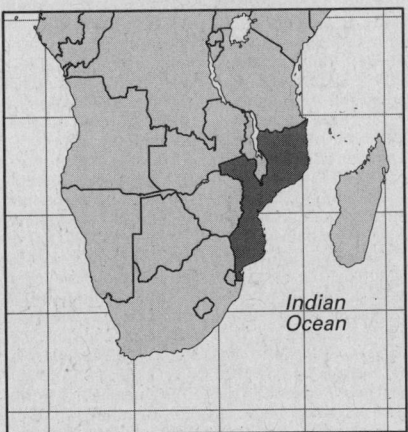

Indian Ocean

Official name: República de Moçambique (Republic of Mozambique). **Form of government:** multiparty republic with one legislative house (Assembly of the Republic [250]). **Head of state and government:** President Armando Guebuza (from 2005). **Capital:** Maputo. **Official language:** Portuguese. **Official religion:** none. **Monetary unit:** 1 (new) metical (MTn; plural meticais) = 100 centavos; valuation (1 Jul 2010) US$1 = MTn 33.55 (the [new] metical replaced the [old] metical [MT] on 1 Jul 2006, at the rate of 1 MTn = MT 1,000).

Demography

Area. 308,042 sq mi, 799,379 sq km. **Population** (2009): 22,894,000. **Density** (2009): persons per sq mi 74.2, persons per sq km 28.6. **Urban** (2008): 36.9%. **Sex distribution** (2007): male 47.67%; female 52.33%. **Age breakdown** (2005): under 15, 43.1%; 15–29, 26.8%; 30–44, 16.5%; 45–59, 9.0%; 60–74, 3.9%; 75 and over, 0.7%. **Ethnic composition** (2000): Makuana 15.3%; Makua 14.5%; Tsonga 8.6%; Sena 8.0%; Lomwe 7.1%; Tswa 5.7%; Chwabo 5.5%; other 35.3%. **Religious affiliation** (2005): traditional beliefs 46%; Christian 37%, of which Roman Catholic 19%, Protestant 11%; Muslim 9%; other 8%. **Major cities** (2007): Maputo 1,094,315 (urban agglomeration 1,766,823); Matola 672,508; Nampula 477,900; Beira 431,583; Chimoio 237,278. **Location:** southern Africa, bordering Tanzania, the Indian Ocean, South Africa, Swaziland, Zimbabwe, Zambia, and Malawi.

Vital statistics

Birth rate per 1,000 population (2008): 38.7 (world avg. 20.3). **Death rate** per 1,000 population (2008): 19.5 (world avg. 8.5). **Total fertility rate** (avg. births per childbearing woman; 2006): 5.35. **Life expectancy** at birth (2006): male 41.2 years; female 40.4 years.

National economy

Budget (2008). *Revenue:* MTn 69,107,000,000 (tax revenue 47.3%; grants 45.4%; nontax revenue 7.3%). *Expenditures:* MTn 83,220,000,000 (capital expenditures 48.6%; current expenditures 45.5%). **Public debt** (external, outstanding; 2007): US$2,533,000,000. **Production** (metric tons except as noted). *Agriculture and fishing* (2007): cassava 7,350,000, sugarcane 2,650,000, corn (maize) 1,579,400, peanuts (groundnuts) 105,000, cashews 58,000, tobacco 11,000; livestock (number of live animals) 1,330,000 cattle, 393,000 goats, 28,500,000 chickens; fisheries production 93,108 (from aquaculture 1%). *Mining and quarrying* (2007): bauxite 12,000; limestone 250,000 cu m; tantalite 28,000 kg; garnet 7,200 kg; gold 450 kg (official figures; unofficial artisanal production is 360–480 kg per year). *Manufacturing* (value added in MT '000,000,000; 2003): aluminum 19,067; beverages 4,773; food products 2,577. *Energy production (consumption):* electricity (kW-hr; 2006) 14,737,000,000 (11,751,000,000); coal (metric tons; 2006) 41,000 (negligible); petroleum products (metric tons; 2006) none (490,000); natural gas (cu m; 2006) 2,700,000,000 (84,500,000). **Population economically active** (2003): total 8,981,000; activity rate 47.1% (participation rates: ages 15–64, 84.4%; female 53.8%; unemployed [2004–05] 18.7%). **Gross national income** (2008): US$8,119,000,000 (US$370 per capita). **Selected balance of payments data.** Receipts from (US$'000,000): tourism (2007) 163; remittances (2008) 116; foreign direct investment (2005–07 avg.) 230; official development assistance (2007) 1,777. Disbursements for (US$'000,000): tourism (2007) 180; remittances (2008) 52.

Foreign trade

Imports (2006; c.i.f.): US$2,869,000,000 (machinery and apparatus 14.5%; refined petroleum prod-

ucts 13.1%; food products 11.4%, of which cereals 6.7%; motor vehicles 9.4%). *Major import sources:* South Africa 37.4%; Netherlands 15.8%; India 4.6%; UAE 4.2%; US 3.5%. **Exports** (2006; f.o.b.): US$2,381,000,000 (aluminum 58.9%; food products 10.2%, of which shrimp 3.6%; electricity 7.5%; natural gas 4.6%; tobacco products 4.6%). *Major export destinations:* Netherlands 59.7%; South Africa 14.1%; Zimbabwe 3.2%; Switzerland 2.2%.

Transport and communications

Transport. *Railroads* (2003): route length (2002) 3,123 km; passenger-km 167,000,000; metric ton-km cargo 1,362,000,000. *Roads* (2000): total length 30,400 km (paved 19%). *Vehicles* (2001): passenger cars 81,600; trucks and buses 76,000. *Air transport* (2007; LAM [Linhas Aéreas de Moçambique] only): passenger-km 440,000,000; metric ton-km cargo 6,000,000. **Communications,** in total units (units per 1,000 persons). Telephone landlines (2008): 78,000 (3.5); cellular telephone subscribers (2008): 4,405,000 (197); personal computers (2005): 283,000 (14); total Internet users (2008): 350,000 (16).

Education and health

Educational attainment (1997). Percentage of population ages 15 and over having: no formal schooling/unknown 79.0%; primary education 18.4%; secondary 2.0%; technical 0.4%; higher 0.2%. **Literacy** (2007): percentage of total population ages 15 and over literate 53.0%; males literate 67.9%; females literate 38.6%. **Health** (2003): physicians 635 (1 per 30,525 persons); hospital beds 16,493 (1 per 1,175 persons); infant mortality rate per 1,000 live births (2006) 112.1; undernourished population (2003–05) 7,500,000 (38% of total population based on the consumption of a minimum daily requirement of 1,800 calories).

Military

Total active duty personnel (November 2008): 11,200 (army 89.3%, navy 1.8%, air force 8.9%). **Military expenditure as percentage of GDP** (2007): 0.7%; per capita expenditure US$3.

Background

Mozambique was settled by Bantu peoples about the 3rd century AD. Arab traders occupied the coastal region from the 14th century, and the Portuguese controlled the area from the early 16th century. The slave trade later became an important part of the economy. In the late 19th century private trading companies began to administer parts of the inland areas. It became an overseas province of Portugal in 1951. After years of war beginning in the 1960s, the country was granted independence in 1975. It was wracked by civil war in the 1970s and '80s. In 1990 a new constitution was promulgated, and a peace treaty was signed with the rebels in 1992. The first multiparty elections were held two years later.

1 metric ton = about 1.1 short tons;   1 kilometer = 0.6 mi (statute);   1 metric ton-km cargo = about 0.68 short ton-mi cargo;   c.i.f.: cost, insurance, and freight;   f.o.b.: free on board

Recent Developments

The 2009 quality-of-life index published by the United Nations Development Programme indicated that Mozambique had made the most progress among less-developed countries, scoring nearly 50% higher than in 1990. Attendance in primary schools had risen more than 33% from 2000 to 2006, and a significant reduction in mortality rates among children under the age of five was reported. Economic growth registered at 4.5%, and inflation dropped below 6.0%.

Internet resource: <www.ine.gov.mz>.

Myanmar (Burma)

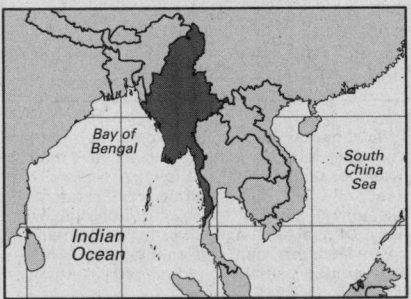

Bay of Bengal

South China Sea

Indian Ocean

Official name: Pyidaungzu Myanma Nainngngandaw (Union of Myanmar). **Form of government:** military regime. **Head of state and government:** Chairman of the State Peace and Development Council Gen. Than Shwe (from 1997), assisted by Prime Minister Thein Sein (from 2007). **Capital:** Naypyidaw (Nay Pyi Taw) (a site near Pyinmana was officially proclaimed the new capital on 27 Mar 2006). **Official language:** Burmese. **Official religion:** none. **Monetary unit:** 1 Myanmar kyat (K) = 100 pyas; valuation (1 Jul 2010) US$1 = K 6.30.

Demography

Area: 261,228 sq mi, 676,577 sq km. **Population** (2009): 48,138,000. **Density** (2009): persons per sq mi 184.3, persons per sq km 71.1. **Urban** (2007): 32.0%. **Sex distribution** (2008): male 49.49%; female 50.51%. **Age breakdown** (2008): under 15, 25.7%; 15–29, 28.6%; 30–44, 23.4%; 45–59, 14.3%; 60–74, 6.2%; 75–89, 1.7%; 90 and over, 0.1%. **Ethnic composition** (2000): Burman 55.9%; Karen 9.5%; Shan 6.5%; Han Chinese 2.5%; Mon 2.3%; Yangbye 2.2%; Kachin 1.5%; other 19.6%. **Religious affiliation** (2005): Buddhist 74%; Protestant 6%; Muslim 3%; Hindu 2%; traditional beliefs 11%; other 4%. **Major urban agglomerations** (2007): Yangon (Rangoon) 4,088,000; Mandalay 961,000; Naypyidaw (Nay Pyi Taw) 930,000; Mawlamyine (Moulmein) (city population; 2004) 405,800; Pathein (Bassein) (city population; 2004) 215,600. **Location:** southeastern Asia, bordering China, Laos, Thailand, the Andaman Sea, the Bay of Bengal, Bangladesh, and India.

Vital statistics

Birth rate per 1,000 population (2008): 17.2 (world avg. 20.3). **Death rate** per 1,000 population (2008): 9.2 (world avg. 8.5). **Total fertility rate** (avg. births per childbearing woman; 2008): 1.92. **Life expectancy** at birth (2008): male 60.7 years; female 65.3 years.

National economy

Budget (2005–06). *Revenue:* K 819,534,000,000 (tax revenue 58.2%, of which taxes on goods and services 30.7%, income tax 25.2%; nontax revenue 41.8%). *Expenditures:* K 1,008,785,000,000 (economic affairs 34.3%; transportation 19.7%; defense 19.6%; education 6.8%; health 2.2%). **Public debt** (external, outstanding; 2007): US$5,516,000,000. **Production** (metric tons except as noted). *Agriculture and fishing* (2007): rice 32,610,000, sugarcane 7,450,000, dry beans 1,765,000, sesame seeds 600,000, pigeon peas 540,000, sunflower seeds 365,000, chickpeas 225,000, garlic 128,000; livestock (number of live animals) 12,500,000 cattle, 6,300,000 pigs, 94,500,000 chickens; fisheries production 2,840,240 (from aquaculture 21%). *Mining and quarrying* (2008–09): copper (2007; metal content) 14,700; jade 32,311,589 kg; rubies 1,751,355 carats; sapphires 1,313,723 carats; spinel 339,894 carats. *Manufacturing* (value added in US$'000,000; 2003): nonelectrical machinery and equipment 728; transportation equipment 483; fabricated metal products 254. *Energy production (consumption):* electricity (kW-hr; 2008–09) 6,654,630,000 ([2006] 6,164,000,000); coal (metric tons; 2006) 1,006,000 (128,000); lignite (metric tons; 2006) 380,000 (111,000); crude petroleum (barrels; 2008–09) 7,058,000 ([2006] 6,035,600); petroleum products (metric tons; 2006) 790,000 (1,633,000); natural gas (cu m; 2008–09) 11,591,300,000 ([2006] 2,119,600,000). **Selected balance of payments data.** Receipts from (US$'000,000): tourism (2006) 46; remittances (2008) 150; foreign direct investment (2005–07 avg.) 202; official development assistance (2007) 190. Disbursements for (US$'000,000): tourism (2006) 37; remittances (2008) 32. **Gross national income** (2008): US$28,663,000,000 (US$578 per capita). **Population economically active** (2008): total 28,361,000; activity rate of total population 57.6% (participation rates: ages 15–64, 79.3%; female 45.5%; officially unemployed 4.9%).

Foreign trade

Imports (2006–07; c.i.f.): K 16,835,000,000 (mineral fuels 24.8%; nonelectrical machinery and transportation equipment 15.9%; base and fabricated metals 7.0%; synthetic fabrics 6.5%). *Major import sources:* Singapore 36.5%; China 24.4%; Thailand 10.3%; India 5.3%; Japan 4.9%. **Exports** (2006–07; f.o.b.): K 30,026,000,000 (natural gas 42.6%; pulses [mostly beans] 11.1%; hardwood 10.0%, of which teak 6.0%; garments 5.3%). *Major export destinations:* Thailand 48.9%; India 13.7%; Hong Kong 8.2%; China 7.9%; Singapore 3.5%.

Transport and communications

Transport. *Railroads* (2008–09): route length 3,955 km; passenger-km 5,466,155,000; metric ton-km cargo 883,650,000. *Roads* (1999): total length 27,966 km (paved 11%). *Vehicles* (2009): passenger cars 244,609; trucks and buses 79,025. *Air transport* (2007–08): passenger-km 124,885,000; metric ton-km cargo (2006) 245,000,000. **Communications**, in total units (units per 1,000 persons). Telephone landlines (2008): 811,000 (16); cellular telephone subscribers (2008): 367,000 (7.4); personal computers (2005): 400,000 (8.6); total Internet users (2008): 109,000 (2.2); broadband Internet subscribers (2008): 10,000.

Education and health

Literacy (2003): total population ages 15 and over literate 89.7%; males literate 93.7%; females literate 86.2%. **Health** (2004–05): physicians 17,564 (1 per 2,660 persons); hospital beds 34,654 (1 per 1,350 persons); infant mortality rate per 1,000 live births (2008) 49.1; undernourished population (2002–04) 2,400,000 (5% of total population based on the consumption of a minimum daily requirement of 1,820 calories).

Military

Total active duty personnel (November 2008): 406,000 (army 92.4%, navy 3.9%, air force 3.7%).

Background

Myanmar, until 1989 known as Burma, has long been inhabited, with the Mon and Pyu states dominant between the 1st century BC and the 9th century AD. It was united in the 11th century under a Burmese dynasty that was overthrown by the Mongols in the 13th century. The Portuguese, Dutch, and English traded there in the 16th–17th centuries. The modern Burmese state was founded in the 18th century. It fell to the British in 1885 and became a province of India. It was occupied by Japan in World War II and became independent in 1948. A military coup took power in 1962 and nationalized major economic sectors. Civilian unrest in the 1980s led to antigovernment rioting. In 1990 opposition parties won in national elections, but the army remained in control. Trying to negotiate for a freer government amid the unrest, Aung San Suu Kyi, the National League for Democracy leader, was awarded the Nobel Peace Prize in 1991. She spent extended periods of the 1990s and 2000s under house arrest.

Recent Developments

The regime in Myanmar announced no legislative preparations ahead of scheduled elections in 2010, and more than 2,100 political dissidents remained in prison. In May 2009 pro-democracy leader Aung San Suu Kyi was placed on trial for having breached the terms of her 2003 house arrest order; her trial stemmed from an uninvited visit by an American man to her residence in Yangon (Rangoon). She was found guilty and sentenced to three years' hard labor in prison; this was immediately commuted to 18 months of additional home detention.

Internet resource: <www.myanmar-tourism.com>.

Namibia

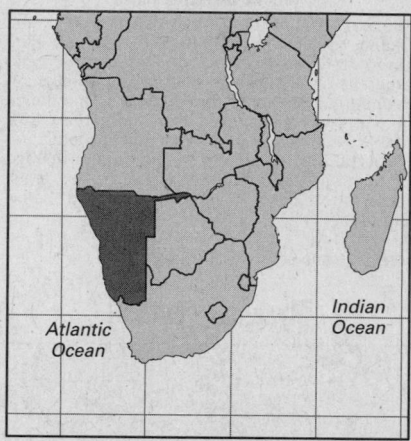

Official name: Republic of Namibia. **Form of government:** republic with two legislative houses (National Council [26]; National Assembly [78]). **Head of state and government:** President Hifikepunye Pohamba (from 2005). **Capital:** Windhoek. **Official language:** English. **Official religion:** none. **Monetary unit:** 1 Namibian dollar (N$) = 100 cents; valuation (1 Jul 2010) US$1 = N$7.38.

Demography

Area: 318,193 sq mi, 824,116 sq km. **Population** (2009): 2,109,000. **Density** (2009): persons per sq mi 6.6, persons per sq km 2.6. **Urban** (2007): 36.3%. **Sex distribution** (2006): male 50.13%; female 49.87%. **Age breakdown** (2006): under 15, 38.2%; 15–29, 31.3%; 30–44, 15.6%; 45–59, 9.2%; 60–74, 4.5%; 75 and over 1.2%. **Ethnic composition** (2000): Ovambo 34.4%; mixed race (black/white) 14.5%; Kavango 9.1%; Afrikaner 8.1%; San (Bushmen) and Bergdama 7.0%; Herero 5.5%; Nama 4.4%; Kwambi 3.7%; German 2.8%; other 10.5%. **Religious affiliation** (2000): Protestant (mostly Lutheran) 49.3%; Roman Catholic 17.7%; unaffiliated Christian 14.1%; independent Christian 10.8%; traditional beliefs 6.0%; other 2.1%. **Major urban localities** (2006): Windhoek 277,300; Rundu 62,300; Walvis Bay 54,900; Oshakati 34,900; Swakopmund 26,700. **Location:** southwestern Africa, bordering Angola, Zambia, Botswana, South Africa, and the South Atlantic Ocean.

Vital statistics

Birth rate per 1,000 population (2008): 25.5 (world avg. 20.3). **Death rate** per 1,000 population (2008): 12.5 (world avg. 8.5). **Total fertility rate** (avg. births per childbearing woman; 2006): 3.06. **Life expectancy** at birth (2006): male 44.5 years; female 42.3 years.

---

1 metric ton = about 1.1 short tons;   *1 kilometer = 0.6 mi (statute);*   *1 metric ton-km cargo = about 0.68 short ton-mi cargo;*   *c.i.f.: cost, insurance, and freight;*   *f.o.b.: free on board*

National economy

Budget (2008–09). *Revenue:* N$21,973,000,000 (tax revenue 91.9%, of which customs duties and excises 40.4%, income tax 33.4%, VAT 16.8%; nontax revenue 7.0%; grants 1.1%). *Expenditures:* N$22,469,100,000 (current expenditures 76.9%; capital expenditures 23.1%). **Production** (metric tons except as noted). *Agriculture and fishing* (2007): millet 58,000, corn (maize) 40,000, wheat 10,000, seed cotton 5,200; livestock (number of live animals) 2,700,000 sheep, 2,500,000 cattle, 2,000,000 goats; fisheries production 415,543 (from aquaculture, negligible). *Mining and quarrying* (2007): salt 800,000; fluorite 118,766; zinc (metal content) 52,000; lead (metal content) 11,900; copper (metal content) 8,500; uranium oxide 3,395; amethyst 40,000 kg; silver 30,000 kg; gold 2,600 kg; gem diamonds 2,266,000 carats. *Manufacturing* (value added in N$'000,000; 2006): food products 2,633 (of which fish processing 620, meat processing 101); other manufactures, which include fur products (from Karakul sheep), textiles, carved wood products, and refined metals 2,962. *Energy production (consumption):* electricity (kW-hr; 2006) 1,606,000,000 ([2004] 2,819,000,000). **Selected balance of payments data.** Receipts from (US$'000,000): tourism (2007) 434; remittances (2008) 16; foreign direct investment (2005–06 avg.) 477; official development assistance (2007) 205. Disbursements for (US$'000,000): tourism (2007) 132; remittances (2008) 16; foreign direct disinvestment (2005–07 avg.) −9. **Population economically active** (2006): total 656,000; activity rate of total population 32.0% (participation rates: ages 16 and over, 54.0%; female 43.4%; officially unemployed 5.3%). **Public debt** (external, outstanding; 2006–07): US$2,526,000,000. **Gross national income** (GNI; 2008): US$8,880,000,000 (US$4,200 per capita).

Did you know? Portions of two of the world's major deserts—the Kalahari Desert and the Namib Desert—can be found in the modern country of Namibia, in the southwestern end of the African continent.

Foreign trade

Imports (2006; c.i.f.): N$21,719,000,000 (refined petroleum products 18.3%; transportation equipment 16.0%; chemical, rubber, and plastic products 12.1%; food products, beverages, and tobacco products 11.5%; machinery and apparatus 9.8%). *Major import sources* (2004): South Africa 85.4%; UK 2.6%; Germany 1.9%; China 1.2%; Zimbabwe 0.8%. **Exports** (2006; f.o.b.): N$20,605,000,000 (diamonds 33.0%; fish 18.2%; other minerals [mainly gold, zinc, copper, lead, and silver] 12.4%; refined zinc 12.2%; meat preparations [mostly beef] 7.8%). *Major export destinations* (2004): South Africa 27.8%; UK 14.9%; Angola 13.8%; US 11.0%; Spain 9.6%.

Transport and communications

Transport. *Railroads:* route length (2006) 2,382 km; (1995–96) passenger-km 48,300,000; (2003–04) metric ton-km 1,247,400. *Roads* (2004): total length 42,237 km (paved 13%). *Vehicles* (2008): passenger cars 107,825; trucks and buses 119,806. *Air transport* (2006; Air Namibia only): passenger-km 1,588,466,000; metric ton-km cargo (2005) 60,429,000. **Communications,** in total units (units per 1,000 persons). Telephone landlines (2008): 140,000 (66); cellular telephone subscribers (2008): 1,052,000 (494); personal computers (2007): 504,000 (240); total Internet users (2008): 114,000 (53); broadband Internet subscribers (2007): 300.

Education and health

Educational attainment (2000). Percentage of population ages 25 and over having: no formal schooling/unknown 26.5%; incomplete primary education 25.5%; complete primary 8.0%; incomplete secondary 24.9%; complete secondary 11.4%; higher 3.7%. **Literacy** (2007): total population ages 15 and over literate 86.6%; males literate 86.5%; females literate 86.7%. **Health:** physicians (2004) 598 (1 per 3,201 persons); hospital beds (2004–05; public sector only) 6,811 (1 per 283 persons); infant mortality rate per 1,000 live births (2006) 48.1; undernourished population (2003–05) 400,000 (19% of total population based on the consumption of a minimum daily requirement of 1,790 calories).

Military

Total active duty personnel (November 2008): 9,200 (army 97.8%, navy 2.2%). **Military expenditure as percentage of GDP** (2008): 4.4%; per capita expenditure US$112.

Background

Long inhabited by indigenous peoples, Namibia was explored by the Portuguese in the late 15th century. In 1884 it was annexed by Germany as German South West Africa. It was captured in World War I by South Africa, which received it as a mandate from the League of Nations in 1920 and refused to give it up after World War II. A UN resolution in 1966 ending the mandate was challenged by South Africa in the 1970s and '80s. Through long negotiations involving many factions and interests, Namibia achieved independence in 1990. The country has been severely affected by the AIDS epidemic.

Recent Developments

The government of Namibia in 2009 continued to be sympathetic to Zimbabwean Pres. Robert Mugabe and refrained from criticizing continued human rights abuses in that country. In August, on the 10th anniversary of the attempt by people in the Caprivi region to secede from Namibia, it was notable that more than 100 of those involved remained on trial.

Internet resource: <www.npc.gov.na/cbs/index.htm>.

Nauru

Official name: Naoero (Republic of Nauru). **Form of government:** republic with one legislative house (Parliament [18]). **Head of state and government:** President Marcus Stephen (from 2007). **Capital:** there is

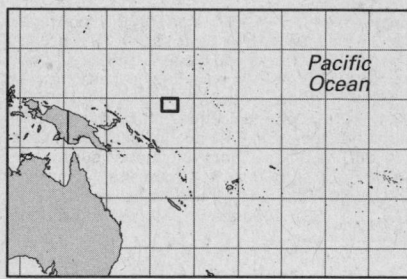

Pacific
Ocean

no official capital; government offices are located in Yaren district. **Official language:** none (Nauruan is the national language; English is the language of business and government). **Official religion:** none. **Monetary unit:** 1 Australian dollar ($A) = 100 cents; valuation (1 Jul 2010) US$1 = $A 1.19.

Demography

Area: 8.2 sq mi, 21.2 sq km. **Population** (2009): 9,800. **Density** (2009): persons per sq mi 1,195, persons per sq km 462.3. **Urban** (2006): 100%. **Sex distribution** (2006): male 50.78%; female 49.22%. **Age breakdown** (2005): under 15, 37.5%; 15–29, 29.5%; 30–44, 17.8%; 45–59, 11.8%; 60–74, 3.1%; 75 and over, 0.3%. **Ethnic composition** (2006): Nauruan 95.8%; Kiribertese (Gilbertese) 1.5%; Asian 1.4%; other Pacific Islanders 0.3%; other/unknown 1.0%. **Religious affiliation** (2005): Protestant 49%, of which Congregational 29%; Roman Catholic 24%; Chinese folk-religionist 10%; other 17%. **Major cities:** none; population of Yaren urban area (2007) 4,616. **Location:** Oceania, island in the western Pacific Ocean, near the equator east of Papua New Guinea.

Vital statistics

Birth rate per 1,000 population (2009): 29.8 (world avg. 20.3). **Death rate** per 1,000 population (2009): 9.0 (world avg. 8.5). **Total fertility rate** (avg. births per childbearing woman; 2007): 3.4. **Life expectancy** at birth (2008): male 52.5 years; female 58.2 years.

National economy

Budget (2007). *Revenue:* $A 17,751,000 (grants 38.2%; property income 35.3%; sales of goods and services 13.1%; other taxes 13.4%). *Expenditures:* $A 21,769,000. *Total public and private debt* (July 2007): US$854,000,000. **Gross national income** (2008): US$34,933,000 (US$3,650 per capita). **Production** (metric tons except as noted). *Agriculture and fishing* (2007): coconuts 1,800, tropical fruit, coffee, almonds, figs, and pandanus (screw pine) are also cultivated; livestock (number of live animals) 2,900 pigs, 5,000 chickens; fisheries production 39 (from aquaculture, none). *Mining and quarrying* (2007): phosphate rock (gross weight) 45,000 (phosphate extraction, the backbone of the Nauruan economy, halted in 2003 but resumed in 2006; phosphate extraction is expected for the next 5 to 20 years using

processing refurbishments). *Manufacturing* (2009): none; virtually all consumer manufactures are imported. *Energy production (consumption):* electricity (kW-hr; 2006) 33,000,000 (33,000,000); petroleum products (metric tons; 2006) none (46,000). **Population economically active** (2002): 3,280; activity rate of total population 32.6% (participation rates: ages 16 and over, 76.7%; female 45.5%; unemployed [2006] 26.7%). **Selected balance of payments data.** Receipts from (US$'000,000): foreign direct investment (2005–07 avg.) 0.67; official development assistance (2007) 26.

Foreign trade

Imports (2005–06): $A 32,300,000 (unspecified [mostly personal material needs] 100%). *Major import sources* (2005): South Korea 48%; Australia 36%; US 6%; Germany 5%. **Exports** (2005–06): $A 1,500,000 (phosphate and coral gravel, a by-product of phosphate extraction, virtually 100%). *Major export destinations* (2005): South Korea 30%; Canada 24%.

Transport and communications

Transport. *Railroads* (2001): length 5 km. *Roads* (2004): total length 40 km (paved 73%). *Air transport* (2004): passenger-km 338,000,000; metric ton-km cargo (including weight of passengers and mail) 34,000,000. **Communications,** in total units (units per 1,000 persons). Telephone landlines (2008): 1,800 (188).

Education and health

Educational attainment (2007). Percentage of population ages 15–49 and over having: incomplete/complete primary education 4%; incomplete secondary 71%; complete secondary 17%; more than secondary 8%. **Literacy** (2007): total population ages 15–49 literate 98%; males literate 96.1%; females literate 99.3%. **Health** (2008): physicians 10 (1 per 957 persons); hospital beds 51 (1 per 188 persons); infant mortality rate per 1,000 live births (2003–07) 37.9.

Military

Total active duty personnel (2008): Nauru does not have any military establishment. Its defense is assured by Australia, but no formal agreement exists.

Background

Nauru was inhabited by Pacific islanders when British explorers arrived in 1798. Annexed by Germany in 1888, in 1919 it was placed under a joint mandate of Britain, Australia, and New Zealand. During World War II it was occupied by the Japanese. Made a UN trust territory under Australian administration in 1947, it gained independence in 1968 and became a member of the Commonwealth and the UN in 1999. Nauru once had the world's largest concentration of phosphate and became wealthy from mining and processing it. The deposits have been severely depleted, however, and the economy has been converting to fishing activities.

1 metric ton = about 1.1 short tons;   1 kilometer = 0.6 mi (statute);   1 metric ton-km cargo = about 0.68 short ton-mi cargo;   c.i.f.: cost, insurance, and freight;   f.o.b.: free on board

Recent Developments

In December 2009 Nauru established formal diplomatic relations with Abkhazia and South Ossetia, reportedly in exchange for some US$50 million in aid from Moscow. Nauru joined Russia, Venezuela, and Nicaragua as the only governments to officially recognize the two breakaway Georgian republics. This followed the establishment of diplomatic ties with China exclusively in 2002, followed by the breaking of those ties in favor of relations with Taiwan in 2005.

Internet resource:
<www.spc.int/prism/country/nr/stats>.

Nepal

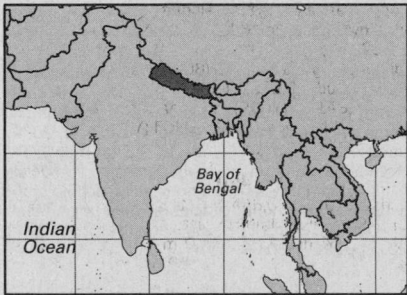

Official name: Sanghiya Loktantrik Ganatantra Nepal (Federal Democratic Republic of Nepal). **Form of government:** multiparty republic with interim legislature (Constituent Assembly [601]). **Head of state:** President Ram Baran Yadav (from 2008). **Head of government:** Prime Minister Madhav Kumar Nepal (from 2009). **Capital:** Kathmandu. **Official language:** Nepali. **Official religion:** none. **Monetary unit:** 1 Nepalese rupee (NR; plural NRs) = 100 paisa; valuation (1 Jul 2010) US$1 = NRs 72.88.

Demography

Area: 56,827 sq mi, 147,181 sq km. **Population** (2009): 28,563,000. **Density** (2009): persons per sq mi 502.6, persons per sq km 194.1. **Urban** (2006): 16.7%. **Sex distribution** (2007): male 50.10%; female 49.90%. **Age breakdown** (2005): under 15, 39.0%; 15–29, 27.9%; 30–44, 17.2%; 45–59, 10.2%; 60–74, 4.7%; 75–84, 0.9%; 85 and over, 0.1%. **Ethnic composition** (2000): Nepalese 55.8%; Maithili 10.8%; Bhojpuri 7.9%; Tharu 4.4%; Tamang 3.6%; Newar 3.0%; Awadhi 2.7%; Magar 2.5%; Gurkha 1.7%; other 7.6%. **Religious affiliation** (2001): Hindu 80.6%; Buddhist 10.7%; Muslim 4.2%; Kirat (local traditional belief) 3.6%; Christian 0.5%; other 0.4%. **Major cities** (2001): Kathmandu 671,846; Biratnagar 166,674; Lalitpur 162,991; Pokhara 156,312; Birganj 112,484. **Location:** south-central Asia, bordering China and India.

Vital statistics

Birth rate per 1,000 population (2008): 27.7 (world avg. 20.3). **Death rate** per 1,000 population (2008): 8.3 (world avg. 8.5). **Total fertility rate** (avg. births per childbearing woman; 2007): 3.10. **Life expectancy** at birth (2008): male 63.6 years; female 64.5 years.

National economy

Budget (2007–08). *Revenue:* NRs 104,865,300,000 (tax revenue 81.1%, of which VAT 28.4%, customs duties 20.1%, corporate taxes 12.6%; nontax revenue 18.9%). *Expenditures:* NRs 151,969,500,000 (current expenditures 64.6%, of which education 16.8%, defense 6.7%, health 6.1%; capital expenditures 35.4%). **Production** (metric tons except as noted). *Agriculture and fishing* (2008): rice 4,299,264, sugarcane 2,485,437, potatoes 2,054,817, ginger 176,602, mustard seed 134,286, garlic 32,317, jute 16,988; livestock (number of live animals) 8,135,880 goats, 7,090,714 cattle, 4,496,507 buffalo; fisheries production (2007) 46,779 (from aquaculture 57%). *Mining and quarrying* (2007): limestone 822,042; talc 9,043; marble 22,110 sq m. *Manufacturing* (value added in US$'000,000; 2002): food products 83; textiles and wearing apparel 73; tobacco products 55. *Energy production (consumption):* electricity (kW-hr; 2006) 2,684,000,000 (2,755,000,000); coal (metric tons; 2006) 11,963 (420,000); petroleum products (metric tons; 2006) none (645,000). **Gross national income** (2008): US$11,537,000,000 (US$400 per capita). **Population economically active** (2003): total 9,981,000; activity rate of total population 38.3% (participation rates: ages 15–64, 66.3%; female 41.0%; unofficially unemployed [2004] 42%). **Public debt** (external, outstanding; 2007): US$3,485,000,000. **Selected balance of payments data.** Receipts from (US$'000,000): tourism (2007) 200; remittances (2008) 2,735; foreign direct investment (2005–07 avg.) 0.3; official development assistance (2007) 598. Disbursements for (US$'000,000): tourism (2007) 274; remittances (2008) 4.

Foreign trade

Imports (2006–07; c.i.f.): NRs 191,709,000,000 (basic manufactures [including fabrics, yarns, and wearing apparel] 24.8%; mineral fuels [mostly refined petroleum products] 19.0%; machinery and transportation equipment 18.6%; chemical products 13.5%). *Major import sources* (2006): India 48%; China 13%; UAE 12%; Saudi Arabia 5%; Kuwait 4%. **Exports** (2006–07; f.o.b.): NRs 60,796,000,000 (ready-made garments 9.8%; woolen carpets 9.2%; vegetable ghee 6.8%; thread 6.7%; zinc sheets 5.9%; textiles 5.0%; jute goods 4.5%). *Major export destinations* (2006): India 58%; US 14%; Germany 6%; UK 3%; France 2%.

Transport and communications

Transport. *Railroads* (2006): route length 59 km; passengers carried (2002) 1,600,000; freight handled 22,000 metric tons. *Roads* (2007): total length 17,782 km (paved 30%). *Vehicles* (2007): passenger cars 93,266; trucks and buses 64,959. *Air transport:* passenger-km (2003) 652,000,000; metric ton-km cargo (2005) 7,000,000. **Communications,** in total units (units per 1,000 persons). *Telephone landlines* (2008): 805,000 (28); cellular telephone subscribers (2008): 4,200,000 (146); personal computers (2005): 132,000 (4.9); total internet users (2008):

499,000 (17); broadband Internet subscribers (2007): 14,000 (0.5).

Education and health

Educational attainment (2005–06). Percentage of population having: unknown through literate 15.4%; primary education 22.0%; secondary 44.0%; higher 18.6%. **Literacy** (2003–04): total population ages 15 and over literate 48.0%; males literate 64.5%; females literate 33.8%. **Health** (2006): physicians (public health system only) 1,259 (1 per 21,737 persons); hospital beds 9,881 (1 per 2,801 persons); infant mortality rate per 1,000 live births (2007) 48.0; undernourished population (2003–05) 4,000,000 (15% of total population based on the consumption of a minimum daily requirement of 1,760 calories).

Military

Total active duty personnel (November 2008): 69,000 (army 100%). **Military expenditure as percentage of GDP** (2007): 2.1%; per capita expenditure US$6.

Background

Nepal developed under early Buddhist influence, and dynastic rule dates from about the 4th century AD. It was formed into a single kingdom in 1769 and fought border wars with China, Tibet, and British India in the 18th–19th centuries. Its independence was recognized by Britain in 1923. A new constitution in 1990 restricted royal authority and accepted a democratically elected parliamentary government. The Communist Party of Nepal (Maoist) began an armed insurgency in 1996. Nepal signed trade agreements with India in 1997. On 1 Jun 2001, King Birendra, the queen, and seven other members of the royal family were fatally shot by Crown Prince Dipendra, who then turned the gun on himself. After a historic vote by a constituent assembly in 2008, the monarchy was abolished and Nepal became a multiparty republic.

Recent Developments

In January 2010 the tenure of the UN Mission in Nepal was extended to mid-May 2010, coincident with the deadline for the promulgation of a new constitution. The UN achieved a major breakthrough the previous July when Nepal began discharging the 4,008 former Maoist child soldiers and noncombatants who had been detained in military camps. Despite relative peace in most of the hill area, violence was increasing, along with the number of armed groups, in parts of the eastern hill area and in the southern plains.

Internet resource: <www.welcomenepal.com>.

Netherlands

Official name: Koninkrijk der Nederlanden (Kingdom of the Netherlands). **Form of government:** constitutional monarchy with a parliament (States General)

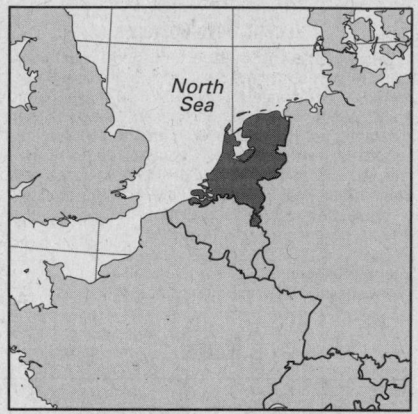

comprising two legislative houses (Senate [75]; House of Representatives [150]). **Head of state:** Queen Beatrix (from 1980). **Head of government:** Prime Minister Jan Peter Balkenende (from 2002). **Capital:** Amsterdam. **Seat of government:** The Hague. **Official language:** Dutch (Frisian is officially recognized in Friesland but not legally codified by the national government). **Official religion:** none. **Monetary unit:** 1 euro (€) = 100 cents; valuation (1 Jul 2010) US$1 = €0.80.

Demography

Area: 16,040 sq mi, 41,543 sq km. **Population** (2009): 16,522,000. **Density** (2009; based on land area): persons per sq mi 1,267, persons per sq km 489.1. **Urban** (2005): 80.2%. **Sex distribution** (2008): male 49.48%; female 50.52%. **Age breakdown** (2008): under 15, 17.7%; 15–29, 18.2%; 30–44, 21.5%; 45–59, 21.3%; 60–74, 14.5%; 75–84, 5.1%; 85 and over, 1.7%. **Ethnic composition** (by place of origin; 2008): Netherlander 80.0%; from EU countries 5.3%; Indonesian 2.3%; Turkish 2.3%; Surinamese 2.1%; Moroccan 2.1%; Netherlands Antillean/Aruban 0.8%; other 5.1%. **Religious affiliation** (2004): Roman Catholic 30%; Reformed/Lutheran tradition 20%; Muslim 6%; nonreligious/atheist 40%; other 4%. **Major urban agglomerations** (2007): Amsterdam 1,482,287; Rotterdam 1,169,800; The Hague 997,323; Utrecht 592,463; Haarlem 407,521. **Location:** northwestern Europe, bordering the North Sea, Germany, and Belgium.

Vital statistics

Birth rate per 1,000 population (2008): 11.2 (world avg. 20.3); within marriage 58.8%. **Death rate** per 1,000 population (2008): 8.2 (world avg. 8.5). **Total fertility rate** (avg. births per childbearing woman; 2008): 1.77. **Life expectancy** at birth (2008): male 78.4 years; female 82.4 years.

National economy

Budget (2007). *Revenue:* €261,628,000,000 (social security contributions 31.3%; indirect taxes 28.3%;

---

1 metric ton = about 1.1 short tons;   1 kilometer = 0.6 mi (statute);   1 metric ton-km cargo = about 0.68 short ton-mi cargo;   c.i.f.: cost, insurance, and freight;   f.o.b.: free on board

direct taxes 26.0%; nontax revenue 7.3%; sales tax 7.1%). *Expenditures:* €259,526,000,000 (current expenditures 92.3%, of which social security and welfare 45.3%; development expenditures 7.7%). **Production** (metric tons except as noted). *Agriculture and fishing* (2007): potatoes 7,200,000, sugar beets 5,400,000, wheat 990,000; flowering bulbs and tubers 80,000 acres (32,400 hectares), of which tulips 27,200 acres (11,000 hectares), cut flowers and plants under glass 10,900 acres (4,400 hectares); livestock (number of live animals) 11,663,000 pigs, 3,763,000 cattle, 1,369,000 sheep; fisheries production 470,363 (from aquaculture 12%). *Mining:* limestone, n.a. *Manufacturing* (value added in €'000,000; 2008): food products, beverages, and tobacco products 16,198; refined petroleum products 8,094; base chemical products and man-made fibers 7,975. *Energy production (consumption):* electricity (kW-hr; 2008) 107,645,000,000 ([2006] 118,192,000,000); coal (metric tons; 2008) none ([2006] 12,683,000); crude petroleum (barrels; 2008) 12,200,000 ([2006] 357,600,000); petroleum products (metric tons; 2006) 61,361,000 (25,334,000); natural gas (cu m; 2008) 79,771,000,000 ([2006] 50,416,000,000). **Gross national income** (2008): US$824,636,000,000 (US$50,150 per capita). **Public debt** (December 2008): US$392,000,000,000. **Population economically active** (2005): total 8,308,000; activity rate of total population 51% (participation rates: ages 15–64, 75.1%; female 45.1%; unemployed [April 2008–March 2009] 2.8%. **Selected balance of payments data.** Receipts from (US$'000,000): tourism (2007) 13,339; remittances (2008) 3,006; foreign direct investment (FDI; 2005–07 avg.) 51,705. Disbursements for (US$'000,000): tourism (2007) 19,110; remittances (2008) 8,431; FDI (2005–07 avg.) 71,354.

Foreign trade

Imports (2007; c.i.f.): €307,851,000,000 (machinery and apparatus 25.7%, of which office machines, computers, and parts 8.7%; mineral fuels 13.6%, of which crude petroleum 7.0%; chemical products 12.1%; food products 7.0%; motor vehicles 5.4%). *Major import sources:* Germany 20.1%; Belgium 10.8%; China 8.6%; US 7.9%; UK 6.4%. **Exports** (2007; f.o.b.): €348,964,000,000 (machinery and apparatus 26.3%, of which office machines, computers, and parts 8.3%; nonelectrical machinery and equipment 7.3%; chemical products 15.2%; food products 9.8%; refined petroleum products 8.0%). *Major export destinations:* Germany 23.6%; Belgium 11.9%; UK 9.1%; France 8.2%; US 5.0%.

Transport and communications

Transport. *Railroads* (2006): length 2,797 km; passenger-km (2004) 14,097,000,000; metric ton-km cargo (2001) 4,293,000,000. *Roads* (2006): total length 134,981 km (paved 90%). *Vehicles* (2006): passenger cars 7,230,178; trucks and buses 1,064,846. *Air transport* (2007): passenger-km 75,012,000,000; metric ton-km cargo 4,735,500,000. **Communications,** in total units (units per 1,000 persons). Telephone landlines (2008): 7,324,000 (446); cellular telephone subscribers (2008): 19,927,000 (1,212); personal computers (2007): 14,934,000 (912); total Internet users (2008): 14,273,000 (868); broadband Internet subscribers (2008): 5,756,000 (350).

Education and health

Educational attainment (2007). Percentage of population ages 25–64 having: primary/lower secondary education 27%; upper secondary 39%; higher vocational 2%; university 29%; other 3%. **Health:** physicians (2005) 60,519 (1 per 270 persons); hospital beds (2006) 48,000 (1 per 340 persons); infant mortality rate per 1,000 live births (2008) 3.8.

Military

Total active duty personnel (November 2008): 40,537 (army 53.0%, navy 23.4%, air force 23.6%). **Military expenditure as percentage of GDP** (2007): 1.5%; per capita expenditure US$700.

Background

Celtic and Germanic tribes inhabited the Netherlands at the time of the Roman conquest. Under the Romans, trade and industry flourished, but by the mid-3rd century AD Roman power had waned, eroded by resurgent German tribes and the encroachment of the sea. A Germanic invasion (406–07) ended Roman control. The Merovingian dynasty followed the Romans but was supplanted in the 7th century by the Carolingian dynasty, which converted the area to Christianity. After Charlemagne's death in 814, the area was increasingly the target of Viking attacks. It became part of the kingdom of Lotharingia, which established an Imperial Church. In the 12th–14th centuries dike building occurred on a large scale. The dukes of Burgundy gained control in the late 14th century. By the early 16th century the Low Countries were ruled by the Spanish Habsburgs. In 1581 the seven northern provinces, led by Calvinists, declared their independence from Spain, and in 1648, following the Thirty Years' War, Spain recognized Dutch independence. The 17th century was the golden age of Dutch civilization. The Dutch East India Company secured Asian colonies, and the country's standard of living soared. In the 18th century the region was conquered by the French and became the Kingdom of Holland under Napoleon (1806). It remained neutral in World War I and declared neutrality in World War II but was occupied by Germany. It joined NATO in 1949, was a founding member of what is now the European Community, and is part of the EU. At the outset of the 21st century the Netherlands benefitted from a strong, highly regulated mixed economy but struggled with the social and economic challenges of immigration.

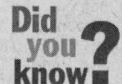

Did you know? The Keeshond was long kept on Dutch barges as a guard and companion. Popular with working-class people, the Keeshond is now the national dog of the Netherlands.

Recent Developments

In the area of foreign relations in 2009, the Dutch government found itself in the midst of controversy over past treaties it had made with Belgium. One of the treaties' provisions concerned the Western Schelde estuary, which lies within the Netherlands but gives the Belgian city of Antwerp access to the North Sea. The 2005 agreement stipulated that the Dutch would deepen the estuary in order to accommodate the largest oceangoing vessels 24 hours a day. The dredging work was to begin in 2007 and to be completed in 2009. While the Belgian government had agreed to a two-year delay, patience ran thin when the Dutch Council of State blocked the start of the work, citing possible environmental consequences. The initial agreement had proposed to mitigate the negative environmental effects of dredging by returning polders (areas of reclaimed land) along the estuary to their natural flooded state; this strategy, however, was opposed by many local residents.

Internet resource: <www.cbs.nl>.

New Zealand

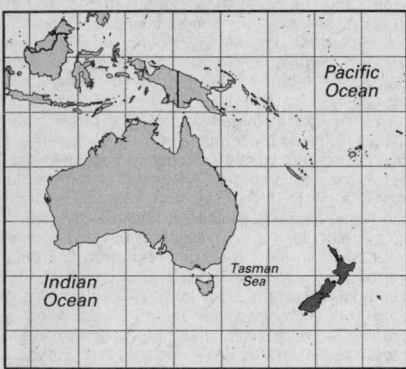

Official name: New Zealand (English); Aotearoa (Maori). Form of government: constitutional monarchy with one legislative house (House of Representatives [122; statutory number is 120 seats]). Head of state: British Queen Elizabeth II (from 1952), represented by Governor-General Anand Satyanand (from 2006). Head of government: Prime Minister John Key (from 2008). Capital: Wellington. Official languages: English; Maori. Official religion: none. Monetary unit: 1 New Zealand dollar (NZ$) = 100 cents; valuation (1 Jul 2010) US$1 = NZ$1.45.

Demography

Area: 104,515 sq mi, 270,692 sq km. Population (2009): 4,317,000. Density (2009): persons per sq mi 41.3, persons per sq km 15.9. Urban (2007): 86.0%. Sex distribution (2006): male 48.96%; female 51.04%. Age breakdown (2006): under 15, 21.1%; 15–29, 20.8%; 30–44, 21.8%; 45–59, 19.5%; 60–74, 11.2%; 75 and over, 5.6%. Ethnic composition (2006): European 67.6%; Maori (local Polynesian) 14.6%; Asian 9.2%, of which Chinese

3.7%; other Pacific peoples (mostly other Polynesian) 6.9%; other 1.7%. Religious affiliation (2006): Christian 51.1%, of which Anglican 13.3%, Roman Catholic 12.2%, Presbyterian 9.2%, Methodist 2.9%, Maori (indigenous) Christian 1.6%; Hindu 1.6%; Buddhist 1.3%; Muslim 1.0%; nonreligious 31.1%; other 1.0%; unknown 12.9%. Major urban agglomerations (2008): Auckland 1,313,200; Christchurch 382,200; Wellington 381,900; Hamilton 197,300; Napier 122,600. Location: Oceania, islands between the South Pacific Ocean and the Tasman Sea, southeast of Australia.

Vital statistics

Birth rate per 1,000 population (2008): 15.1 (world avg. 20.3); within marriage 51.9%. Death rate per 1,000 population (2008): 6.8 (world avg. 8.5). Total fertility rate (avg. births per childbearing woman; 2008): 2.18. Life expectancy at birth (2006): male 78.0 years; female 82.2 years.

National economy

Budget (2007). *Revenue:* NZ$65,859,000,000 (tax revenue 85.3%, of which income tax 41.3%; nontax revenue 14.5%; social contributions 0.2%). *Expenditures:* NZ$60,247,000,000 (social protection 33.9%; education 16.7%; health 16.7%; defense 3.2%). Production (metric tons except as noted). *Agriculture and fishing* (2007): potatoes 505,000, barley 400,000, apples 380,000, kiwifruit 315,000, grapes 190,000; livestock (number of live animals) 40,000,000 sheep, 9,650,000 cattle; fisheries production 600,868 (from aquaculture 19%); aquatic plants 192 (from aquaculture, none). *Mining and quarrying* (2007): limestone and marl 5,092,000; gold 10,762 kg; silver 10,568 kg. *Manufacturing* (value added in US$'000,000; 2005): food products 4,175; fabricated metal products 1,350; printing and publishing 1,250. *Energy production (consumption):* electricity (kW-hr; 2007–08) 42,728,000,000 ([2006] 37,390,000,000); coal (metric tons; 2007–08) 2,178,000 ([2006] 196,000); lignite (metric tons; 2007–08) 2,855,000 ([2006] 4,783,000); crude petroleum (barrels; 2007–08) 20,607,500 ([2006] 35,016,000); petroleum products (metric tons; 2007–08) 5,187,000 ([2006] 6,026,000); natural gas (cu m; 2007–08) 4,290,200,000 ([2006] 3,700,000,000). Population economically active (2007): total 2,235,400; activity rate 52.8% (participation rates: ages 15–64, 76.9%; female 46.3%; unemployed [July 2007–June 2008] 3.6%). Gross national income (2008): US$119,246,000,000 (US$27,940 per capita). Selected balance of payments data. Receipts from (US$'000,000): tourism (2007) 5,406; remittances (2008) 626; foreign direct investment (FDI; 2005–07 avg.) 4,163. Disbursements for (US$'000,000): tourism (2007) 3,066; remittances (2008) 1,202; FDI (2005–07 avg.) 961.

Foreign trade

Imports (2006; c.i.f.): NZ$40,774,000,000 (machinery and apparatus 21.4%; mineral fuels 14.9%; motor vehicles 11.7%; aircraft 4.2%; plastic products 3.8%). *Major import sources:* Aus-

---

1 metric ton = about 1.1 short tons;   1 kilometer = 0.6 mi (statute);   1 metric ton-km cargo = about 0.68 short ton-mi cargo;   c.i.f.: cost, insurance, and freight;   f.o.b.: free on board

tralia 20.1%; China 12.2%; US 12.1%; Japan 9.1%; Germany 4.4%. **Exports** (2006; f.o.b.): NZ$34,619,000,000 (dairy products 20.6%; beef and sheep meat 12.1%; wood and paper products 9.4%; machinery and apparatus 8.6%; aluminum 4.3%; fish 3.7%; fruit 3.7%). *Major export destinations:* Australia 20.5%; US 13.1%; Japan 10.3%; China 5.4%; UK 4.9%.

Transport and communications

Transport. *Railroads* (2006): route length 4,128 km; metric ton-km cargo (1999–2000) 4,040,000,000. *Roads* (2007): total length 93,748 km (paved 65%). *Vehicles* (2007): passenger cars 2,775,717; trucks and buses 558,412. *Air transport* (2007; Air New Zealand only): passenger-km 28,423,000,000; metric ton-km cargo 906,000,000. **Communications**, in total units (units per 1,000 persons). Telephone landlines (2008): 1,750,000 (414); cellular telephone subscribers (2008): 4,620,000 (1,092); personal computers (2005): 2,077,000 (507); total Internet users (2008): 3,047,000 (720); broadband Internet subscribers (2008): 915,000 (216).

Education and health

Educational attainment (2007). Percentage of population ages 15 and over having: no formal schooling to incomplete primary education 26.8%; primary 9.0%; vocational 29.8%; secondary 15.0%; higher 19.4%. **Literacy:** virtually 100%. **Health:** physicians (2006) 9,547 (1 per 434 persons); hospital beds (2002) 23,825 (1 per 165 persons); infant mortality rate per 1,000 live births (2008) 5.0; undernourished population (2002–04) less than 2.5% of total population.

Military

Total active duty personnel (November 2008): 9,278 (army 51.2%, navy 21.8%, air force 27.0%). **Military expenditure as percentage of GDP** (2008): 1.1%; per capita expenditure US$286.

Background

Polynesian occupation of New Zealand dates to about AD 1000. First sighted by Dutch explorer Abel Janszoon Tasman in 1642, the main islands were charted by Capt. James Cook in 1769. Named a British crown colony in 1840, the area, was the scene of warfare between colonists and native Maori through the 1860s. In 1907 the colony became the Dominion of New Zealand. It administered Western Samoa during 1919–62 and participated in both world wars. New Zealand took a strong stand against nuclear proliferation, since the mid-1980s banning nuclear-powered ships or those carrying nuclear weapons from its waters. There has been a revival of traditional Maori culture and art, and Maori social and economic activism have been central to political developments in the country since the late 20th century.

Recent Developments

The unemployment rate in New Zealand reached 7.3% by the end of 2009, and employment ini-tiatives and fiscal policies to cushion the recession dominated the first full year of New Zealand Prime Minister John Key's fledgling government. To preserve and create jobs, the government offered subsidies to businesses that adopted an average workweek of four and a half days, funded infrastructure projects, and initiated the construction of a bikeway network intended eventually to span the country. With New Zealand facing reduced tax revenues and mounting welfare expenditures, the country's budget called for a deficit of some US$4.8 billion in 2009–10 and deficits exceeding US$5.5 billion in each of the following two years. Planned borrowing of about US$25 billion from 2009 to 2013 would effectively double government debt.

Internet resource: <www.stats.govt.nz>.

Nicaragua

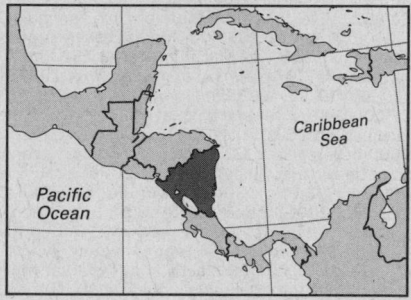

Official name: República de Nicaragua (Republic of Nicaragua). **Form of government:** unitary multiparty republic with one legislative house (National Assembly [92]). **Head of state and government:** President Daniel Ortega (from 2007). **Capital:** Managua. **Official language:** Spanish. **Official religion:** none. **Monetary unit:** 1 córdoba (C$) = 100 centavos; valuation (1 Jul 2010) US$1 = C$20.94.

Demography

Area: 50,337 sq mi, 130,373 sq km; land area alone equals 46,464 sq mi, 120,340 sq km. **Population** (2009): 5,743,000. **Density** (2009; based on land area): persons per sq mi 123.6, persons per sq km 47.7. **Urban** (2005): 55.9%. **Sex distribution** (2008): male 50.03%; female 49.97%. **Age breakdown** (2008): under 15, 34.6%; 15–29, 31.3%; 30–44, 19.3%; 45–59, 9.8%; 60–74, 3.1%; 75–84, 0.9%; 85 and over, 1.0%. **Ethnic composition** (2000): mestizo (Spanish/Indian) 63.1%; white 14.0%; black 8.0%; multiple ethnicities 5.0%; other 9.9%. **Religious affiliation** (2005): Roman Catholic 58.5%; Protestant/independent Christian 23.2%, of which Evangelical 21.6%, Moravian 1.6%; nonreligious 15.7%; other 2.6%. **Major cities** (2005): Managua 908,892; León 139,433; Chinandega 95,614; Masaya 92,500; Estelí 90,294. **Location:** Central America, bordering Honduras, the Caribbean Sea, Costa Rica, and the North Pacific Ocean.

Vital statistics

Birth rate per 1,000 population (2008): 23.7 (world avg. 20.3). **Death rate** per 1,000 population (2008): 4.3 (world avg. 8.5). **Total fertility rate** (avg. births per childbearing woman; 2008): 2.63. **Life expectancy** at birth (2008): male 69.1 years; female 73.4 years.

National economy

Budget (2008). *Revenue:* US$1,209,700,000 (tax revenue 92.6%, of which taxes on goods and services 32.7%, taxes on international trade 30.0%, taxes on income and profits 29.8%; nontax revenue 7.4%). *Expenditures:* US$1,641,600,000 (education 20.7%; health 14.4%; economic services 14.4%; defense and public order 11.4%). **Public debt** (external, outstanding; 2007): US$2,144,000,000. **Production** (metric tons except as noted). *Agriculture and fishing* (2007): sugarcane 4,875,000, corn (maize) 569,948, rice 302,697, peanuts (groundnuts) 116,682, coffee 81,818; livestock (number of live animals) 3,600,000 cattle, 268,000 horses; fisheries production 37,959, of which lobster 3,752 (from aquaculture 30%). *Mining and quarrying* (2007): gold 2,059 kg. *Manufacturing* (value added in C$'000,000 in constant prices of 1994; 2003): food products 1,917; textiles and wearing apparel 969; beverages 713. *Energy production (consumption):* electricity (kW-hr; 2006) 2,958,-000,000 (3,011,000,000); crude petroleum (barrels; 2006) none (5,989,000); petroleum products (metric tons; 2006) 763,000 (1,286,000). **Population economically active** (2006): total 2,204,300; activity rate of total population 39.9% (participation rates: ages 10 and over [2005] 55.0%; female [2005] 35.2%; officially unemployed [2008] 6.1%). **Gross national income** (2008): US$6,126,000,000 (US$1,080 per capita). **Selected balance of payments data.** Receipts from (US$'000,000): tourism (2007) 255; remittances (2008) 818; foreign direct investment (FDI; 2005–07 avg.) 279; official development assistance (2007) 834. Disbursements for (US$'000,000): tourism (2007) 121; FDI (2005–07 avg.) 16.

Foreign trade

Imports (2006; c.i.f.): US$2,741,000,000 (chemical products 16.7%; machinery and apparatus 15.6%; crude petroleum 13.2%; refined petroleum products 10.8%; food products 9.7%). *Major import sources:* US 22.8%; Mexico 14.8%; China 7.6%; Venezuela 6.8%; Costa Rica 5.4%. **Exports** (2006; f.o.b.): US$759,000,000 (coffee 26.4%; cattle meat 10.3%; crustaceans 9.3%; gold 7.7%; raw sugar 6.6%; peanuts [groundnuts] 5.2%). *Major export destinations:* US 46.5%; Mexico 6.2%; Canada 6.0%; Spain 4.5%; Honduras 4.4%.

Transport and communications

Transport. *Railroads* (2004): 6 km. *Roads* (2004): total length 18,669 km (paved [2002]

11%). *Vehicles* (2007): passenger cars 101,899; trucks and buses 187,526. *Air transport* (2000): passenger-km 72,200,000; metric ton-km cargo (2003) 200,000. **Communications,** in total units (units per 1,000 persons). Telephone landlines (2008): 312,000 (55); cellular telephone subscribers (2008): 3,039,000 (536); personal computers (2005): 220,000 (43); total Internet users (2008): 185,000 (33); broadband Internet subscribers (2006): 19,000 (3.6).

Education and health

Educational attainment (2005). Percentage of population ages 10 and over having: no formal schooling/unknown 20.5%; 1–3 years 16.6%; 4–6 years 27.0%; 7–9 years 16.1%; 10–12 years 10.5%; vocational 2.3%; incomplete university 2.6%; complete university 4.4%. **Literacy** (2005): total population ages 15 and over literate 78.0%; males literate 78.1%; females literate 77.9%. **Health** (2003): physicians 2,076 (1 per 2,538 persons); hospital beds 5,030 (1 per 1,047 persons); infant mortality rate per 1,000 live births (2005) 26.4; undernourished population (2003–05) 1,200,000 (22% of total population based on the consumption of a minimum daily requirement of 1,770 calories).

Military

Total active duty personnel (November 2008): 12,000 (army 83.3%, navy 6.7%, air force 10.0%). **Military expenditure as percentage of GDP** (2008): 0.6%; per capita expenditure US$7.

Background

Nicaragua has been inhabited for thousands of years, most notably the Maya. Christopher Columbus arrived in 1502, and Spanish explorers discovered Lake Nicaragua soon thereafter. Nicaragua was governed by Spain until 1821, when it declared its independence. It was part of Mexico and then the United Provinces of Central America until 1838, when full independence was achieved. The US intervened in political affairs by maintaining troops there in 1912–33. Ruled by the dictatorial Somoza dynasty from 1936 to 1979, it was taken over by the Sandinistas after a popular revolt. They were opposed by armed insurgents, the US-backed contras, from 1981. The Sandinista government nationalized several sectors of the economy. They lost the national elections in 1990, but Sandinista leader Daniel Ortega returned to power after winning the presidential election of 2006.

Recent Developments

In the face of the global economic crisis, the government's decision in 2009 to offset social expenditures with cuts to capital expenditures helped keep Nicaragua's budget within IMF parameters. Allegations of electoral fraud and corruption, however, resulted in reduced foreign assistance from the US and Europe. The

1 metric ton = about 1.1 short tons;   1 kilometer = 0.6 mi (statute);   1 metric ton-km cargo = about 0.68 short ton-mi cargo;   c.i.f.: cost, insurance, and freight;   f.o.b.: free on board

worldwide economic downturn led to a contraction in Nicaragua's economy, with GDP estimated to decline by 3.7% in 2009 and exports projected to drop by at least 17.0%. Inflation stood at just 2.8%, down from a high of 13.8% in 2008. Lower inflation allowed for a loosening of monetary policy and increased access to credit.

Internet resource: <www.visitanicaragua.com>.

Niger

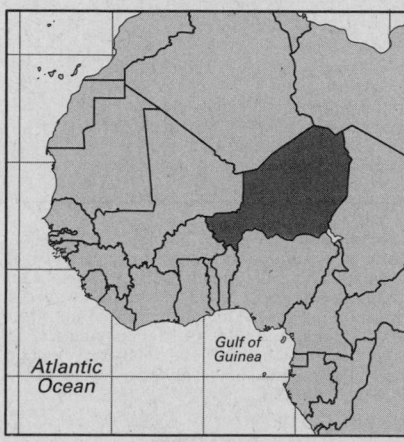

Gulf of Guinea

Atlantic Ocean

Official name: République du Niger (Republic of Niger). **Form of government:** military regime (per the military coup of February 2010, which resulted in the dissolution of the country's constitution). **Head of state and government:** President of the Supreme Council for the Restoration of Democracy Salou Djibo (from 2010), assisted by Prime Minister Mahamadou Danda (from 2010). **Capital:** Niamey. **Official language:** French. **Official religion:** none. **Monetary unit:** 1 CFA franc (CFAF) = 100 centimes; valuation (1 Jul 2010) US$1 = CFAF 527.20.

Demography

Area: 459,286 sq mi, 1,189,546 sq km. **Population** (2009): 15,306,000. **Density** (2009): persons per sq mi 33.3, persons per sq km 12.9. **Urban** (2008): 18.4%. **Sex distribution** (2008): male 50.02%; female 49.98%. **Age breakdown** (2008): under 15, 49.6%; 15–29, 25.6%; 30–44, 13.7%; 45–59, 7.2%; 60–74, 3.3%; 75 and over, 0.6%. **Ethnolinguistic composition** (2001): Hausa 55.4%; Zarma-Songhai-Dendi 21.0%; Tuareg 9.3%; Fulani (Peul) 8.5%; Kanuri 4.7%; other 1.1%. **Religious affiliation** (2005): Muslim 90%, of which Sunni 85%, Shiʻi 5%; traditional beliefs 9%; other 1%. **Major cities** (2001): Niamey 707,951 (urban agglomeration [2007] 915,000); Zinder 170,575; Maradi 148,017; Agadez 78,289; Tahoua 73,002. **Location:** western Africa, bordering Algeria, Libya, Chad, Nigeria, Benin, Burkina Faso, and Mali.

Vital statistics

Birth rate per 1,000 population (2008): 52.2 (world avg. 20.3). **Death rate** per 1,000 population (2008): 15.2 (world avg. 8.5). **Total fertility rate** (avg. births per childbearing woman; 2008): 7.83. **Life expectancy** at birth (2008): male 51.0 years; female 53.4 years.

National economy

Budget (2008): *Revenue:* CFAF 584,100,000,000 (tax revenue 48.1%; nontax revenue 27.2%; external aid and grants 24.3%; other 0.4%). *Expenditures:* CFAF 546,000,000,000 (current expenditures 53.1%, of which wages and salaries 15.3%; capital expenditures 46.9%). **Public debt** (external, outstanding; 2008): US$795,000,000. **Selected balance of payments data.** Receipts from (US$'000,000): tourism (2007) 37; remittances (2008) 78; foreign direct investment (2005–07 avg.) 36; official development assistance (2007) 542. Disbursements for (US$'000,000): tourism (2007) 30; remittances (2008) 29; foreign direct disinvestment (2005–07 avg.) −2. **Gross national income** (2008): US$4,823,000,000 (US$330 per capita). **Production** (metric tons except as noted). *Agriculture and fishing* (2008): millet 3,489,400, cowpeas 1,548,000, sorghum 1,311,100, dry onions 373,600, pimento 25,800; livestock (number of live animals) 12,641,500 goats, 10,191,400 sheep, 8,737,400 cattle, 1,630,500 camels; fisheries production (2007) 29,768 (from aquaculture, negligible). *Mining and quarrying* (2008): uranium 2,993; salt (2007) 1,300; gold 2,314 kg. *Manufacturing* (value added in CFAF '000,000; 2008): food products 6,797; paper products, printing, and publishing 2,604; soaps and other chemical products 1,625. *Energy production (consumption):* electricity (kW-hr; 2006) 179,000,000 (535,000,000); coal (metric tons; 2008) 182,912 ([2006] 183,000); petroleum products (metric tons; 2006) none (138,000). **Population economically active** (2006): total 6,139,000; activity rate of total population 42.6% (participation rates: ages 16 and over, 83.5%; female 41.9%).

Foreign trade

Imports (2008): CFAF 501,605,000,000 (food products 25.1%; refined petroleum products 15.5%; machinery and apparatus 15.1%; chemical products 14.9%; transportation equipment 6.8%). *Major import sources:* France 13.7%; China 13.3%; Netherlands 7.6%; US 7.4%; Nigeria 4.9%. **Exports** (2008): CFAF 316,412,000,000 (uranium 62.6%; livestock 23.7%, of which cattle 9.5%; gold 5.6%; onions 4.2%). *Major export destinations:* France 36.8%; Nigeria 25.0%; US 14.2%; Japan 10.4%; Switzerland 5.6%.

Transport and communications

Transport. *Railroads:* none. *Roads* (2008): total length 18,949 km (paved 21%). *Vehicles* (2005): passenger cars 21,360. *Air transport* (2007; Niamey airport only): passenger arrivals 64,904, passenger departures 60,297; cargo unloaded 1,394 metric tons, cargo loaded 149 metric tons. *Communications, in total units (units per 1,000 persons).* Telephone landlines (2008): 65,000 (4.4); cellular telephone subscribers (2008):

1,898,000 (129); personal computers (2005): 10,000 (0.8); total Internet users (2008): 80,000 (5.4); broadband Internet subscribers (2008): 600 (0.04).

Education and health

Educational attainment (2006; Niamey only). Percentage of population ages 25 and over having: no formal schooling/unknown 86.2%; incomplete primary education 6.9%; complete primary 1.0%; incomplete secondary 3.7%; complete secondary 0.4%; higher 0.9%. **Literacy** (2007–08): total population ages 15 and over literate 29.0%; males literate 42.8%; females literate 17.1%. **Health** (2008): physicians (public health institutions only) 427 (1 per 34,548 persons); hospital beds (2007) 2,934 (1 per 4,845 persons); infant mortality rate per 1,000 live births 118.9; undernourished population (2002–04) 3,900,000 (32% of total population based on the consumption of a minimum daily requirement of 1,800 calories).

Military

Total active duty personnel (November 2008): 5,300 (army 98.1%, air force 1.9%). **Military expenditure as percentage of GDP** (2007): 1.0%; per capita expenditure US$3.

Background

In the territory of Niger, there is evidence of Neolithic culture, and several kingdoms existed there before the colonialists arrived. First explored by Europeans in the late 18th century, it became a French colony in 1922. It became an overseas territory of France in 1946 and gained independence in 1960. The first multiparty elections were held in 1993.

Recent Developments

In June 2009 Niger's Pres. Mamadou Tandja issued a decree that called for a referendum on a new constitution that would include a three-year extension of his rule and would eliminate presidential term limits. The Constitutional Court annulled the decree, and Tandja responded by assuming emergency powers and dissolving the court. His actions were met with international condemnation and public demonstrations. Opposition parties called for a boycott of the referendum, which contributed to a massive win for the president. The legislative election to replace the National Assembly, held in October, was also boycotted by the opposition and resulted in victory for the ruling party. On the day of the election, Niger was suspended from the Economic Community of West African States for having ignored its call to postpone the poll. In February 2010 a military junta known as the Supreme Council for the Restoration of Democracy seized Tandja and overthrew his government.

Internet resource: <www.stat-niger.org>.

Nigeria

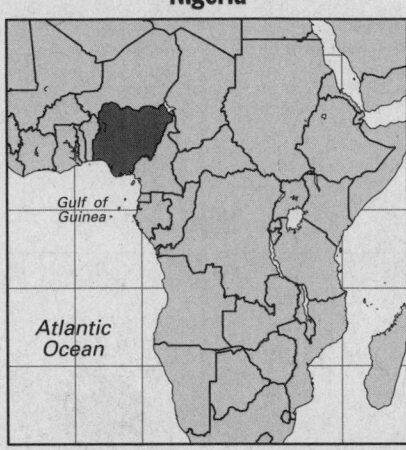

Official name: Federal Republic of Nigeria. **Form of government:** federal republic with two legislative houses (Senate [109]; House of Representatives [360]). **Head of state and government:** President Goodluck Jonathan (from 2010). **Capital:** Abuja. **Official language:** English. **Official religion:** none. **Monetary unit:** 1 naira (N) = 100 kobo; valuation (1 Jul 2010) US$1 = N148.56.

Demography

Area: 356,669 sq mi, 923,768 sq km. **Population** (2009): 154,729,000. **Density** (2009): persons per sq mi 433.8, persons per sq km 167.5. **Urban** (2007): 47.7%. **Sex distribution** (2006): male 50.80%; female 49.20%. **Age breakdown** (2005): under 15, 43.1%; 15–29, 28.2%; 30–44, 15.3%; 45–59, 8.6%; 60–74, 4.0%; 75–84, 0.7%; 85 and over, 0.1%. **Ethnic composition** (2000): Yoruba 17.5%; Hausa 17.2%; Igbo (Ibo) 13.3%; Fulani 10.7%; Ibibio 4.1%; Kanuri 3.6%; Egba 2.9%; Tiv 2.6%; Igbira 1.1%; Nupe 1.0%; Edo 1.0%; Ijo 0.8%; detribalized 0.9%; other 23.3%. **Religious affiliation** (2003): Muslim (predominantly Sunni) 50.5%; Christian 48.2%, of which Protestant 15.0%, Roman Catholic 13.7%, other (mostly independent Christian) 19.5%; other 1.3%. **Major urban agglomerations** (2007): Lagos 9,466,000; Kano 3,140,000; Ibadan 2,628,000; Abuja 1,576,000; Kaduna 1,442,000. **Location:** western Africa, bordering Niger, Chad, Cameroon, the Atlantic Ocean, and Benin.

Vital statistics

Birth rate per 1,000 population (2007): 39.9 (world avg. 20.3). **Death rate** per 1,000 population (2007): 16.8 (world avg. 8.5). **Total fertility rate** (avg. births per childbearing woman; 2007): 5.30. **Life expectancy** at birth (2007): male 46.4 years; female 47.3 years.

1 metric ton = about 1.1 short tons;   1 kilometer = 0.6 mi (statute);   1 metric ton-km cargo = about 0.68 short ton-mi cargo;   c.i.f.: cost, insurance, and freight;   f.o.b.: free on board

National economy

Budget (2008; federal budget). *Revenue:* N2,411,000,000,000 (petroleum revenue 83.3%, of which tax on profits and royalties 39.8%; nonpetroleum revenue 16.7%, of which corporate taxes 6.3%). *Expenditures:* N2,451,000,000,000 (current expenditures 65:3%; capital expenditures 34.7%). **Production** (metric tons except as noted). *Agriculture and fishing* (2007): cassava 45,750,000, yams 37,150,000, sorghum 10,500,000, peanuts (groundnuts) 3,835,600, cowpeas 3,150,000, cashews 660,000, cacao beans 500,000, melon seeds 488,500, ginger 138,000, sesame seeds 100,000; livestock (number of live animals) 28,583,000 goats, 23,993,500 sheep, 16,258,560 cattle; fisheries production 615,507 (from aquaculture 14%). *Mining and quarrying* (2007): limestone 3,300,000; marble 200,000. *Manufacturing* (value added in N'000,000; 2008): refined petroleum products 44,297; cement 18,036; other unspecified (particularly food products, beverages, and textiles) 543,259. *Energy production (consumption):* electricity (kW-hr; 2006) 23,110,000,000 (23,110,000,000); coal (metric tons; 2007) 530,000 ([2006] 8,000); crude petroleum (barrels; 2008) 767,700,000 ([2006] 43,800,000); petroleum products (metric tons; 2006) 5,319,000 (10,344,000); natural gas (cu m; 2007) 46,046,000,000 ([2006] 10,730,000,000). **Gross national income** (2008): US$175,622,000,000 (US$1,160 per capita). **Public debt** (external, outstanding; December 2008): US$3,704,000,000. **Population economically active** (2006): total 44,112,000; activity rate 30.5% (participation rates: ages 15–64, 55.5%; female 35.5%; unofficially unemployed [2007] 60%). **Selected balance of payments data.** Receipts from (US$'000,000): tourism (2007) 215; remittances (2008) 9,980; foreign direct investment (FDI; 2005–07 avg.) 10,463; official development assistance (2007) 2,042. Disbursements for (US$'000,000): tourism (2007) 2,444; remittances (2008) 103; FDI (2005–07 avg.) 230.

Foreign trade

Imports (2008): N4,991,000,000,000 (basic manufactures 33.0%; chemical products 25.0%; machinery and transportation equipment 22.0%; food products and live animals 6.0%). *Major import sources* (nonpetroleum imports only [81.6% of all imports]): US 14.4%; China 10.5%; France 9.4%; UK 7.9%; Netherlands 7.4%. **Exports** (2008): N9,495,000,000,000 (crude petroleum 92.2%; other petroleum sector 6.8%; cacao beans 0.3%). *Major export destinations* (crude petroleum exports only): US 23.0%; Spain 9.3%; China 6.0%; Brazil 5.0%; Italy 4.1%.

Transport and communications

Transport. *Railroads* (2005): length (2006) 3,505 km; passenger-km 75,170,000; metric ton-km cargo 18,027,000. *Roads* (2004): total length 193,200 km (paved 15%). *Vehicles* (2007): passenger cars 4,560,000. *Air transport* (2008): passenger-km 2,136,000,000; metric ton-km cargo 7,368,000. **Communications,** in total units (units per 1,000 persons). Telephone landlines (2008): 1,308,000 (8.7); cellular telephone subscribers (2008): 62,989,000 (417); personal computers (2007): 1,182,000 (8); total Internet users (2008): 11,000,000 (73); broadband Internet subscribers (2008): 26,000 (0.2).

Education and health

Educational attainment (2003). Percentage of population ages 25 and over having: no formal schooling/unknown 50.4%; primary education 20.4%; secondary 20.1%; higher 9.1%. **Literacy** (2007): total population ages 15 and over literate 73.1%; males literate 79.4%; females literate 67.0%. **Health** (2005): physicians 42,563 (1 per 3,234 persons); hospital beds 85,523 (1 per 1,609 persons); infant mortality rate per 1,000 live births (2007) 109.0; undernourished population (2002–04) 11,400,000 (9% of total population based on the consumption of a minimum daily requirement of 1,830 calories).

Military

Total active duty personnel (November 2008): 80,000 (army 77.5%, navy 10.0%, air force 12.5%). **Military expenditure as percentage of GDP** (2007): 0.7%; per capita expenditure US$7.

Background

Inhabited for thousands of years, Nigeria was the center of the Nok culture from 500 BC to AD 200 and of several precolonial empires, including the state of Kanem-Bornu and the Songhai, Hausa, and Fulani kingdoms. Visited in the 15th century by Europeans, it became a center for the slave trade. The area began to come under British control in 1861; by 1903 British rule was total. Nigeria gained independence in 1960 and became a republic in 1963. Ethnic strife soon led to military coups, and military groups ruled the country from 1966 to 1979 and from 1983 to 1999. A civil war between the central government and the former Eastern Region—which seceded and called itself Biafra—began in 1967 and ended in 1970 with Biafra's surrender after widespread starvation and civilian deaths. In 1991 the capital was moved from Lagos to Abuja. The government's execution of environmental activist Ken Saro-Wiwa in 1995 led to international sanctions, and civilian rule was finally reestablished in 1999. Ethnic conflicts continued in the early 21st century, as did violent protests over oil production in the Niger delta. Friction also increased between Muslims and Christians after some of the northern and central states adopted Islamic law.

Recent Developments

Turbulence in the Niger delta remained a major stumbling block to peace in Nigeria. In May 2009 the government launched a sweeping military offensive against rebel groups in the region, including the Movement for the Emancipation of the Niger Delta (MEND); though the operation killed and wounded hundreds, it failed to subdue the militants, who later in the year were able to strike beyond the delta, setting fire to an oil depot and several tankers in Lagos. On 4 August the government announced a 60-day amnesty for any militant who agreed to surrender his weapons in exchange for a daily stipend, education, and retraining. Between 7,000 and 15,000 militants accepted the amnesty. MEND announced a unilateral cease-fire in late October. In March 2010, however, MEND detonated several bombs outside a government building, the first acts of violence after they had announced the end of the cease-fire in January. A number of outbreaks of sectarian unrest also occurred. In February 2009 and again in December, Christians and Muslims clashed in the city of Bauchi. Intense fighting took place between Muslim militants belonging to the group Boko Haram and security forces, leaving between 800 and 1,000 people dead—most of them members of Boko Haram. In January 2010 about 300 Muslim herdsmen were killed in the central city of Jos, and in reprisal herdsmen killed an estimated 500 Christians, mostly farmers from surrounding villages, in March.

Internet resource: <http://nigerianstat.gov.ng>.

Norway

Official name: Kongeriket Norge (Kingdom of Norway). Form of government: constitutional monarchy with one legislative house (Storting, or Parliament [169]). Head of state: King Harald V (from 1991). Head of government: Prime Minister Jens Stoltenberg (from 2005). Capital: Oslo. Official language: Norwegian (Sami is official locally). Official religion: Evangelical Lutheran. Monetary unit: 1 Norwegian krone (NOK; plural kroner) = 100 øre; valuation (1 Jul 2010) US$1 = NOK 6.48.

Demography

Area: 148,718 sq mi, 385,179 sq km. Population (2009): 4,828,000. Density (2009): persons per sq mi 37.9, persons per sq km 14.6. Urban (2005): 77.4%. Sex distribution (2008): male 49.90%; female 50.10%. Age breakdown (2008): under 15, 19.0%; 15-29, 19.1%; 30-44, 21.7%; 45-59, 19.5%; 60-74, 13.3%; 75-84, 5.1%; 85 and over, 2.3%. Ethnic composition (2008): Norwegian (nonimmigrant) 89.4%; other 10.6%, of which from Europe 4.2%, Asia 3.9%, Africa 1.3%. Religious affiliation (2003): Evangelical Lutheran 85.7%; other Christian

4.5%; Muslim 1.8%; other/nonreligious 8.0%. Major cities (2007): Oslo 560,484 (urban agglomeration 856,915); Bergen 247,746; Trondheim 165,191; Stavanger 119,586; Bærum 108,144. Location: northern Europe, bordering the Barents Sea, Russia, Finland, Sweden, the North Sea, and the Norwegian Sea.

Vital statistics

Birth rate per 1,000 population (2008): 12.7 (world avg. 20.3); within marriage 45.0%. Death rate per 1,000 population (2008): 8.7 (world avg. 8.5). Total fertility rate (avg. births per childbearing woman; 2008): 1.96. Life expectancy at birth (2008): male 78.3 years; female 83.0 years.

National economy

Budget (2007). Revenue: NOK 1,146,890,-000,000 (tax revenue 57.5%; nontax revenue 24.5%; social security 18.0%). Expenditures: NOK 736,004,000,000 (social security and welfare 41.5%; general public services 17.5%; health 16.6%; education 5.8%; defense 5.0%; transportation 4.5%). Public debt (June 2009): US$101,447,000,000. Production (metric tons except as noted). Agriculture and fishing (2007): barley 580,000, wheat 380,000, potatoes 380,000; livestock (number of live animals) 2,400,000 sheep, 930,000 cattle; fisheries production 3,209,140 (from aquaculture 26%); aquatic plants production 134,671 (from aquaculture, none). Mining and quarrying (2007): olivine sand 3,000,000, ilmenite concentrate 882,000, iron ore (metal content) 630,000. Manufacturing (value added in NOK '000,000; 2008): machinery and apparatus 55,474; food products, beverages, and tobacco products 34,589; ships and oil platforms 26,139. Energy production (consumption): electricity (kW-hr; 2008) 142,632,000,000 ([2006] 22,518,000,-000); coal (metric tons; 2007) 3,995,000 (1,115,000); crude petroleum (barrels; 2008) 743,700,000 ([2006] 94,800,000); petroleum products (metric tons; 2006) 22,993,000 (11,936,000); natural gas (cu m; 2008) 99,403,-000,000 ([2007] 6,512,000,000). Selected balance of payments data. Receipts from (US$'000,000): tourism (2007) 4,222; remittances (2008) 684; foreign direct investment (FDI; 2005-07 avg.) 4,163. Disbursements for (US$'000,000): tourism (2007) 14,032; remittances (2008) 4,776; FDI (2005-07 avg.) 18,092. Population economically active (2006): total 2,446,000; activity rate of total population 52.5% (participation rates: ages 15-64, 80.8%; female 47.1%; unemployed [July 2008-June 2009] 2.9%). Gross national income (2008): US$415,249,000,000 (US$87,070 per capita).

Foreign trade

Imports (2007; c.i.f.): NOK 470,681,000,000 (machinery and apparatus 24.8%, of which nonelectrical machinery and equipment 11.6%; base and fabricated metals 10.7%; motor vehicles 10.2%; chemical products 8.6%; metal ore and metal scrap

6.7%). *Major import sources:* Sweden 14.7%; Germany 13.6%; UK 6.9%; Denmark 6.4%; China 6.0%. **Exports** (2007; f.o.b.): NOK 799,284,000,000 (crude petroleum 39.9%; natural gas 19.3%; machinery and apparatus 6.8%; refined petroleum products 4.8%; aluminum 4.4%; fish 3.6%; nickel 2.4%). *Major export destinations:* UK 26.2%; Germany 12.3%; Netherlands 10.3%; France 8.0%; Sweden 6.5%.

Transport and communications

Transport. *Railroads* (2007): route length 4,087 km; passenger-km 3,432,000,000; metric ton-km cargo 2,476,000,000. *Roads* (2007): total length 92,920 km (paved 80%). *Vehicles* (2007): passenger cars 2,153,730; trucks and buses 538,225. *Air transport* (2008; SAS [Norwegian part] and Widerøe only): passenger-km 8,194,000,000; metric ton-km cargo 7,646,000. **Communications,** in total units (units per 1,000 persons). Telephone landlines (2008): 1,928,000 (404); cellular telephone subscribers (2008): 5,287,000 (1,109); personal computers (2007): 2,959,000 (629); total Internet users (2008): 4,237,000 (889); broadband Internet subscribers (2008): 1,608,000 (337).

Education and health

Educational attainment (2007). Percentage of population ages 16 and over having: primary and lower secondary education 29.6%; higher secondary 41.3%; higher 24.8%; unknown 4.3%. **Literacy** (2000): virtually 100% literate. **Health:** physicians (2006) 17,523 (1 per 266 persons); hospital beds (2007) 22,882 (1 per 206 persons); infant mortality rate per 1,000 live births (2008) 2.7; undernourished population (2002–04) less than 2.5% of total population.

Military

Total active duty personnel (November 2008): 19,100 (army 34.0%, navy 16.5%, air force 14.2%, central support 31.4%, other 3.9%). **Military expenditure as percentage of GDP** (2008): 1.2%; per capita expenditure US$1,013.

Background

Several principalities were united into the kingdom of Norway in the 11th century. From 1380 it had the same king as Denmark until it was ceded to Sweden in 1814. The union with Sweden was dissolved in 1905, and Norway's economy grew rapidly. The country remained neutral during World War I, though its shipping industry played a vital role in the conflict. It declared its neutrality in World War II but was invaded and occupied by German troops. Norway is a member of NATO but turned down membership in the EU in 1994. Its economy grew consistently during the 1990s, aided particularly by its North Sea petroleum industry.

Recent Developments

Relying on the country's US$400 billion Government Pension Fund–Global (the former Petroleum Fund), the Norwegian government insulated its economy from the effects of the global financial crisis in 2009. Norwegian oil companies, facing dwindling North Sea reserves, were eager to drill in the Arctic waters around Norway's Lofoten and Vesteralen islands, and seismic surveys to determine potential deposits were conducted in the summer. Strong protests followed from fishermen's organizations and environmentalists, citing the potential for disruption of the important cod-fishing industry and the catastrophic environmental damage that could occur.

Internet resource: <www.ssb.no>.

Oman

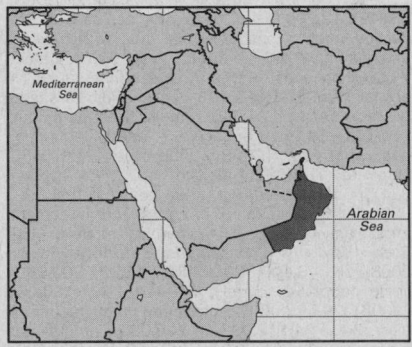

Official name: Saltanat 'Uman (Sultanate of Oman). **Form of government:** monarchy with two advisory bodies (State Council [70]; Consultative Council [84]). **Head of state and government:** Sultan (from 1970) and Prime Minister (from 1972) Qabus ibn Sa'id. **Capital:** Muscat. **Official language:** Arabic. **Official religion:** Islam. **Monetary unit:** 1 rial Omani (RO) = 1,000 baiza; valuation (1 Jul 2010) US$1 = RO 0.38.

Demography

Area: 119,500 sq mi, 309,500 sq km. **Population** (2009): 2,845,000. **Density** (2009): persons per sq mi 23.8, persons per sq km 9.2. **Urban** (2005): 71.5%. **Sex distribution** (2008): male 50.54%; female 49.46%. **Age breakdown** (2008): under 15, 35.2%; 15–29, 38.5%; 30–44, 16.3%; 45–59, 6.3%; 60–74, 3.1%; 75 and over, 0.6%. **Ethnic composition** (2000): Omani Arab 48.1%; Indo-Pakistani 31.7%, of which Balochi 15.0%, Bengali 4.4%, Tamil 2.5%; other Arab 7.2%; Persian 2.8%; Zanzibari (blacks originally from Zanzibar) 2.5%; other 7.7%. **Religious affiliation** (2005): Muslim 89%, of which Ibadiyah 75%, Sunni 8%, Shi'i 6%; Hindu 5%; Christian 5%; other 1%. **Major cities** (populations of districts; 2007): Muscat 28,987 (urban agglomeration 620,000); Al-Sib 268,259; Matrah 203,159; Bawshar 193,778; Salalah 185,780. **Location:** the Middle East, bordering the Gulf of Oman, the Arabian Sea, Yemen, Saudi Arabia, and the UAE; the Ru'us al-Jibal exclave occupies the northern tip of the Musandam Peninsula and borders the UAE, the Persian Gulf, and the Strait of Hormuz.

Vital statistics

Birth rate per 1,000 population (2008): 24.2 (world avg. 20.3). **Death rate** per 1,000 population (2008): 2.5 (world avg. 8.5). **Total fertility rate** (avg. births per childbearing woman; 2008): 3.19. **Life expectancy** at birth (2008): male 73.2 years; female 75.4 years.

National economy

Budget (2008). *Revenue:* RO 7,829,400,000 (oil revenue 67.5%; natural gas revenue 11.6%; nontax revenue 11.0%). *Expenditures:* RO 7,556,700,000 (current expenditures 58.5%, of which defense 23.5%, education 9.8%, social security and welfare 6.6%, health 3.4%; capital expenditures 30.2%). **Public debt** (external, outstanding; 2006): US$819,000,000. **Gross national income** (2008): US$49,812,200,000 (US$17,884 per capita). **Production** (metric tons except as noted). *Agriculture and fishing* (2007): dates 260,000, tomatoes 41,000, bananas 26,000; livestock (number of live animals; 2008) 1,652,400 goats, 373,500 sheep, 319,900 cattle, 124,500 camels; fisheries production 151,834 (from aquaculture, negligible). *Mining and quarrying* (2008): limestone 3,604,452; chromite 784,082; marble 457,146; gypsum 321,746. *Manufacturing* (value added in US$'000,-000; 2006): petroleum products 1,754; cement, bricks, and ceramics 367; chemical products 333. *Energy production (consumption):* electricity (kW-hr; 2008) 16,048,100,000 ([2007] 11,191,000,000); crude petroleum (barrels; 2008–09) 277,100,000 ([2008] 29,565,000); petroleum products (metric tons; 2006) 4,172,000 (4,265,000); natural gas (cu m; 2008) 30,288,712,000 (13,460,000,000). **Population economically active** (2007): total 968,782; activity rate of total population 35.5% (participation rates: ages 15–64, 55.2%; female 19.6%; unemployed [2004] 15%). **Selected balance of payments data.** Receipts from (US$'000,000): tourism (2007) 645; remittances (2008) 39; foreign direct investment (FDI; 2005–07 avg.) 1,896. Disbursements for (US$'000,000): tourism (2007) 744; remittances (2008) 5,181; FDI (2005–07 avg.) 377.

Foreign trade

Imports (2008; c.i.f.): RO 8,814,500,000 ([2007] motor vehicles and parts 24.1%; nonelectrical machinery and equipment 17.8%; food products and live animals 8.3%; iron and steel 8.2%; chemical products 6.4%). *Major import sources:* UAE 27.2%; Japan 15.6%; US 5.7%; China 4.6%; India 4.5%. **Exports** (2008; f.o.b.): RO 14,503,000,000 (domestic exports 89.5%, of which crude petroleum 58.0%, liquefied natural gas 11.0%, refined petroleum products 6.9%; reexports 10.5%, of which motor vehicles and parts 9.1%). *Major export destinations:* China 28.4%; UAE 10.9%; Japan 8.1%; Thailand 6.7%; South Korea 6.3%.

Transport and communications

Transport. *Railroads:* none. *Roads* (2008): total length 53,556 km (paved 44%). *Vehicles* (2003): passenger cars 308,663; trucks and buses 109,118. *Air transport* (2008; Oman Air only): passenger-km 3,551,000,000; metric ton-km cargo 20,000,000. **Communications,** in total units (units per 1,000 persons). Telephone landlines (2008): 274,000 (98); cellular telephone subscribers (2008): 3,219,000 (1,156); personal computers (2006): 180,000 (67); total Internet users (2008): 465,000 (167); broadband Internet subscribers (2008): 32,000 (12).

Education and health

Educational attainment (2003). Percentage of population ages 10 and over having: no formal schooling (illiterate) 15.9%; no formal schooling (literate) 22.3%; primary 35.3%; secondary 17.0%; higher technical 3.3%; higher undergraduate 5.2%; higher graduate 0.7%; other 0.3%. **Literacy** (2007): percentage of total population ages 15 and over literate 84.4%; males literate 89.4%; females literate 77.5%. **Health** (2008): physicians 5,194 (1 per 536 persons); hospital beds 5,473 (1 per 509 persons); infant mortality rate per 1,000 live births 10.3.

Military

Total active duty personnel (November 2008): 42,600 (army 58.7%, navy 9.9%, air force 11.7%, royal household/foreign troops 19.7%). **Military expenditure as percentage of GDP** (2007): 8.1%; per capita expenditure US$1,185.

Background

Oman has been inhabited for at least 10,000 years. Arabs began migrating there in the 9th century BC. Tribal warfare was endemic until the conversion to Islam in the 7th century AD. It was ruled by Ibadi imams until 1154, when a royal dynasty was established. The Portuguese controlled the coastal areas from about 1507 to 1650, when they were expelled. The Al Bu Sa'id dynasty, founded in the mid-18th century, still rules Oman. Oil was discovered in 1964. In 1970 the sultan was deposed by his son, who began a policy of modernization, and under him the country joined the Arab League and the UN. In the Persian Gulf War, Oman cooperated with the allied forces against Iraq. It subsequently continued to expand its foreign relations.

Recent Developments

Oman weathered the global economic slowdown in 2009 better than most. The reasons were several—the cushion provided by earlier robust levels of revenue accrued from exceptionally high petroleum prices, increased oil production (to about 805,000 bbl per day), sustained income from exports of natural gas, and conservative local practices of lending and investment. A new oil field was also discovered off the Musandam Peninsula. The country's tourism industry was also booming, providing a reliable source of foreign currency.

Internet resource: <www.mone.gov.om/index.asp>.

1 metric ton = about 1.1 short tons; 1 kilometer = 0.6 mi (statute); 1 metric ton-km cargo = about 0.68 short ton-mi cargo; c.i.f.: cost, insurance, and freight; f.o.b.: free on board

Pakistan

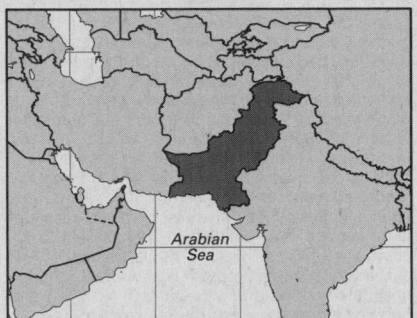

Arabian
Sea

Official name: Islamic Republic of Pakistan. **Form of government:** federal republic with two legislative houses (Senate [100]; National Assembly [342]). **Head of state:** President Asif Ali Zardari (from 2008). **Head and government:** Prime Minister Yousaf Raza Gilani (from 2008). **Capital:** Islamabad. **Official language:** none (Urdu is the national language). **Official religion:** Islam. **Monetary unit:** 1 Pakistan rupee (PKR) = 100 paisa; valuation (1 Jul 2010) US$1 = PKR 85.61.

Demography

Area data exclude the 33,125-sq-mi (85,793-sq-km) area of Pakistani-administered Jammu and Kashmir (comprising both Azad Kashmir [AK] and Gilgit-Baltistan [GB]); population and density data include Afghan refugees and the 2009 populations of AK (3,890,000) and GB (1,009,000). **Area:** 307,374 sq mi, 796,096 sq km. **Population** (2009): 174,579,000. **Density** (2009): persons per sq mi 512.7, persons per sq km 198.0. **Urban** (2008): 35.3%. **Sex distribution** (2007): male 51.89%; female 48.11%. **Age breakdown** (2005): under 15, 37.2%; 15–29, 29.9%; 30–44, 16.8%; 45–59, 10.2%; 60–74, 4.7%; 75–84, 1.0%; 85 and over, 0.2%. **Ethnic composition** (2000): Punjabi 52.6%; Pashtun 13.2%; Sindhi 11.7%; Urdu-speaking muhajirs 7.5%; Balochi 4.3%; other 10.7%. **Religious affiliation** (2000): Muslim 96.1%; Christian 2.5%; Hindu 1.2%; others (including Ahmadiyah) 0.2%. **Major urban agglomerations** (2007): Karachi 12,130,000; Lahore 6,577,000; Faisalabad 2,617,000; Rawalpindi 1,858,000; Multan 1,522,000. **Location:** southern Asia, bordering China, India, the Arabian Sea, Iran, and Afghanistan.

Vital statistics

Birth rate per 1,000 population (2008): 25.0 (world avg. 20.3). **Death rate** per 1,000 population (2008): 7.7 (world avg. 8.5). **Total fertility rate** (avg. births per childbearing woman; 2007): 3.13. **Life expectancy** at birth (2007): male 64.3 years; female 64.4 years.

National economy

Budget (2007–08). *Revenue:* PKR 1,368,139,-000,000 (tax revenue 75.3%, of which corporate taxes 28.4%, sales taxes 27.4%, customs 11.3%; nontax revenue 24.7%). *Expenditures:* PKR 1,353,660,000,000 (general public service 47.4%; defense 20.3%; economic affairs 5.8%; public order and police 1.8%; education 1.8%). **Public debt** (external, outstanding; June 2008): US$40,243,-000,000. **Production** (metric tons except as noted). *Agriculture and fishing* (2007): sugarcane 54,752,000, wheat 23,520,000, rice 8,300,000, seed cotton 6,500,000, mangoes 2,250,000, chickpeas 842,000, sunflower seeds 560,000, dates 510,000; livestock (number of live animals) 53,800,000 goats, 29,600,000 cattle, 27,300,000 buffalo, 900,000 camels; fisheries production (2007–08) 640,000 (from aquaculture 23%). *Mining and quarrying* (2007–08): limestone 30,825,000; rock salt 1,872,000; gypsum 682,000; kaolin (2007) 39,000. *Manufacturing* (value of production in PKR '000,000,000; 2000–01): textiles 321; food products 189; refined petroleum products and coke 94. *Energy production (consumption) in '000:* electricity (kW-hr; 2007–08) 109,021,000 ([2006–07] 72,712,000); coal (metric tons; 2007–08) 3,482 ([2006–07] 7,894); crude petroleum (barrels; 2007–08) 25,610 ([2006] 84,000); petroleum products (metric tons; 2006) 9,793 ([2006–07] 16,847); natural gas (cu m; 2007–08) 40,981,000 ([2006–07] 34,601,000). **Population economically active** (2007): total 50,331,000; activity rate of total population 31.8% (participation rates: ages 15–64, 53.7%; female 20.7%; officially unemployed 5.3%). **Gross national income** (2008): US$162,930,000,000 (US$980 per capita). **Selected balance of payments data.** Receipts from (US$'000,000): tourism (2007) 276; remittances (2008) 7,032; foreign direct investment (FDI; 2005–07 avg.) 3,936; official development assistance (2007) 2,212. Disbursements for (US$'000,-000): tourism (2007) 1,593; remittances (2008) 3.0; FDI (2005–07 avg.) 84.

Foreign trade

Imports (2007–08): US$35,417,333,000 (refined petroleum products 17.4%; machinery and apparatus 16.2%; chemical products 14.4%; crude petroleum 12.2%; food products 10.0%). *Major import sources:* UAE 14.5%; Saudi Arabia 10.2%; China 8.6%; Kuwait 6.9%; Singapore 4.8%. **Exports** (2007–08): US$20,122,394,000 (textiles 49.8%, of which woven cotton fabric 11.5%, knitwear 10.5%, bedding 6.9%, ready-made garments 5.5%, cotton yarn 5.3%; rice 5.6%; refined petroleum products 3.7%). *Major export destinations:* US 18.6%; UAE 8.6%; UK 5.3%; Afghanistan 5.1%; Germany 4.1%.

Transport and communications

Transport. *Railroads* (2007): length (2005–06) 11,515 km; passenger-km 25,821,000,000; metric ton-km cargo 5,876,000,000. *Roads* (2007–08): total length 264,853 km (paved 67%). *Vehicles* (2007): passenger cars 1,440,072; trucks and buses 357,455. *Air transport* (2008): passenger-km 13,920,000,000; metric ton-km cargo 319,800,000. **Communications,** in total units (units per 1,000 persons). Telephone landlines (2008): 4,416,000 (25); cellular telephone subscribers (2008): 88,020,000 (497); personal computers (2005): 803,000 (5.2); total Internet users (2008): 18,500,000 (105); broadband Internet subscribers (2008): 168,000 (0.9).

Education and health

Literacy (2006–07): total population ages 15 and over literate 52%; males literate 65%; females literate 38%. **Health** (2007): physicians 127,859 (1 per 1,280 persons); hospital beds (2006) 103,285 (1 per 1,585 persons); infant mortality rate per 1,000 live births 68.0; undernourished population (2003–05) 35,000,000 (23% of total population based on the consumption of a minimum daily requirement of 1,750 calories).

Military

Total active duty personnel (November 2008): 617,000 (army 89.1%, navy 3.6%, air force 7.3%). **Military expenditure as percentage of GDP** (2008): 2.8%; per capita expenditure US$21.

Background

Pakistan has been inhabited since about 3500 BC. From the 3rd century BC to the 2nd century AD, it was part of the Mauryan and Kushan kingdoms. The first Muslim conquests were in the 8th century AD. The British East India Company subdued the reigning Mughal dynasty in 1757. During the period of British colonial rule, what is now Pakistan was part of India. When the British withdrew in 1947, the new state of Pakistan came into existence by act of the British Parliament. Kashmir remained a disputed territory between Pakistan and India, resulting in full-scale war in 1965 and continued military clashes. Civil war between East Pakistan and West Pakistan resulted in independence for the former, which became Bangladesh, in 1971. Many Afghan refugees migrated to Pakistan during the Soviet-Afghan war in the 1980s. Pakistan elected Benazir Bhutto prime minister in 1988; she was the first woman to head a modern Islamic state. She was ousted in 1990 on charges of corruption and incompetence. During the 1990s border flare-ups with India continued, and Pakistan conducted tests of nuclear weapons. Pakistan's political landscape changed dramatically after the terrorist attacks of September 11. It was quickly determined that they had been staged by the Muslim militant organization al-Qaeda, which was operating out of Afghanistan with the support of the Taliban regime, with which Pakistan had diplomatic relations. As the US prepared to move militarily against both organizations, Pakistan chose to provide support to the US-led coalition.

Recent Developments

Terrorism and counterterrorism dominated developments in Pakistan in 2009. CIA drones struck South Waziristan, killing Usama al-Kini and Sheikh Ahmed Salim Swedan (who were al-Qaeda leaders on the FBI's most-wanted list in connection with the 1998 bombings of US embassies in Kenya and Tanzania) in January, and in August drones killed Baitullah Mehsud, the leader of Tehrik-i-Taliban (a coalition of Pakistani Taliban groups). US Pres. Barack Obama's decision to increase the number of US troops in Afghanistan heightened debate in Pakistan, as implementation of Obama's new strategy was demonstrated by the ratcheting up of drone attacks in Bajaur as well as in South and North Waziristan. Given the public outrage over the increased drone attacks, James Jones, Obama's national security adviser; Gen. David Petraeus, head of the US Central Command; and Adm. Mike Mullen, chairman of the US Joint Chiefs of Staff, made visits to Islamabad to try to ease deepening strains in US-Pakistan relations. The US Congress in September approved a bill making available US$7.5 billion over five years to rebuild Pakistan's roads, schools, and democratic institutions. Pakistan's higher military officials, however, registered alarm at the bill's linkage of the funding to the country's war on terrorism. The US transfer of F-16 aircraft to Pakistan proceeded without interruption, despite concerns over Pakistan's near completion of two additional nuclear weapons reactors.

Internet resource: <www.statpak.gov.pk>.

Palau

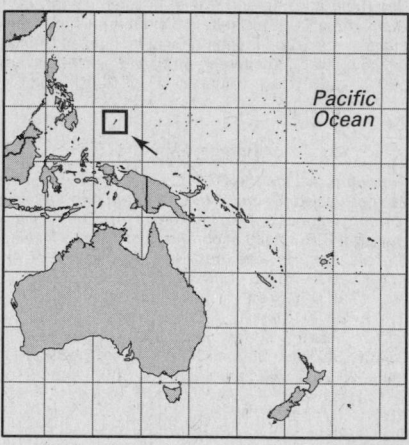

Official name: Beluu er a Belau (Palauan); Republic of Palau (English). **Form of government:** republic with two legislative houses (Senate [13]; House of Delegates [16]). **Head of state and government:** President Johnson Toribiong (from 2009). **Capital:** Melekeok. **Official languages:** Palauan; English. **Official religion:** none. **Monetary unit:** 1 US dollar (US$) = 100 cents.

Demography

Area: 188 sq mi, 488 sq km. **Population** (2009): 20,400. **Density** (2009): persons per sq mi 108.5, persons per sq km 41.8. **Urban** (2005): 70.0%. **Sex distribution** (2007): male 53.53%; female 46.47%. **Age breakdown** (2007): under 15, 24.1%; 15–29, 22.8%; 30–44, 28.0%; 45–59, 16.8%; 60–74, 5.3%; 75–84, 2.4%; 85 and over, 0.6%. **Ethnic composition** (2005; population ages 18 and over only): Palauan (Micronesian/Malay/Melanesian admixture) 65.2%; Asian 30.3%, of which Filipino 21.6%, Vietnamese

2.3%; other Micronesian 3.1%; white 1.1%; other 0.3%. **Religious affiliation** (2005; population ages 18 and over only): Roman Catholic 51.0%; Protestant 26.7%; Modekngei (marginal Christian sect) 8.9%; other Christian 1.8%; other 11.6%. **Major towns** (2005): Koror 10,743; Meyuns 1,153; Kloulklubed 680. **Location:** Oceania, island group in the North Pacific Ocean, east of the Philippines.

Vital statistics

Birth rate per 1,000 population (2007): 12.4 (world avg. 20.3). **Death rate** per 1,000 population (2007): 7.9 (world avg. 8.5). **Total fertility rate** (avg. births per childbearing woman; 2007): 2.00. **Life expectancy** at birth (2008): male 66.3 years; female 72.1 years.

National economy

Budget (2007–08). *Revenue:* US$80,900,000 (grants 48.4%; tax revenue 42.1%; nontax revenue 9.5%). *Expenditures:* US$98,800,000 (current expenditures 77.4%; capital expenditures 22.6%). **Production** (metric tons except as noted). *Agriculture and fishing* (value of sales in US$; 2001): eggs (2003) 638,750, cabbages 116,948, cucumbers 44,009; livestock (number of live animals; 2001) 702 pigs, 21,189 poultry; fisheries production (2007) 1,003 (from aquaculture 2%). *Manufacturing:* includes handicrafts and small items. *Energy production (consumption):* electricity (kW-hr; 2006) 151,000,000 (151,000,000); petroleum products (metric tons; 2006) none (66,000). **Selected balance of payments data.** Receipts from (US$'000,000): tourism (2006) 90; foreign direct investment (FDI; 2005–07 avg.) 1.67; official development assistance (2007) 22. Disbursements for (US$'000,000): tourism (2006) 1.4. **Population economically active** (2005): total 10,203; activity rate of total population 51.3% (participation rates: ages 16 and over, 69.1%; female 39.1%; unemployed 4.2%). **Gross national income** (2008): US$175,000,000 (US$8,650 per capita). **Public debt** (gross external debt; 2006–07): US$22,857,000.

Foreign trade

Imports (2006–07): US$91,287,000 (mineral fuels and lubricants 37.5%; machinery and transportation equipment 17.6%; beverages and tobacco products 14.9%; food products and live animals 9.4%; chemical products 8.7%). *Major import sources:* US 33.2%; Singapore 24.8%; Guam 11.2%; Japan 9.6%; Philippines 7.6%. **Exports** (2006–07): US$10,081,000 (mostly high-grade tuna and garments). *Major export destinations* (2003): Japan 86.7%; Vietnam 5.9%; Zambia 4.6%.

 **Did you know?** The 10th season of the popular television show *Survivor* was filmed in Palau. The season, which aired in 2005, featured 20 contestants carrying out various challenges over the course of 39 days.

Transport and communications

Transport. *Railroads:* none. *Roads* (2004): total length 61 km (paved 59%). *Vehicles* (2004): passenger cars and trucks 7,247. *Air transport* (2003): passenger arrivals 80,017, passenger departures 78,608. **Communications,** in total units (units per 1,000 persons). Telephone landlines (2008): 7,500 (370); cellular telephone subscribers (2008): 12,000 (592); total Internet users (2007): 5,400 (268); broadband Internet subscribers (2007): 100 (5).

Education and health

Educational attainment (2005). Percentage of population ages 25 and over having: no formal schooling 1.9%; incomplete primary education 9.0%; complete primary 3.9%; incomplete secondary 14.9%; complete secondary 42.2%; some postsecondary 10.0%; vocational 4.1%; higher 14.0%. **Literacy** (2005): total population ages 15 and over literate, virtually 100%. **Health:** physicians (2006) 26 (1 per 771 persons); hospital beds (2004) 135 (1 per 147 persons); infant mortality rate per 1,000 live births (2007) 7.2.

Military

The US is responsible for the external security of Palau, as specified in the Compact of Free Association of 1 Oct 1994.

Background

Palau's inhabitants began arriving 3,000 years ago in successive waves from the Indonesian and Philippine archipelagos and from Polynesia. The islands had been under nominal Spanish ownership for more than three centuries when they were sold to Germany in 1899. They were seized by Japan in 1914 and taken by Allied forces in 1944 during World War II. Palau became part of the UN Trust Territory of the Pacific Islands in 1947 and became a sovereign state in 1994; the US provides economic assistance and maintains a military presence in the islands.

Recent Developments

Pres. Johnson Toribiong controversially agreed that several Chinese Uighurs detained at a US military prison at Guantánamo Bay, Cuba, could be temporarily resettled in Palau. In November 2009 six of them arrived in Palau.

Internet resource: <www.palaugov.net/stats>.

Panama

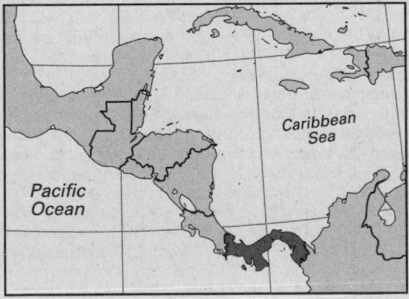

Caribbean Sea

Pacific Ocean

Official name: República de Panamá (Republic of Panama). **Form of government:** multiparty republic

with one legislative house (National Assembly [71]). **Head of state and government:** President Ricardo Martinelli (from 2009). **Capital:** Panama City. **Official language:** Spanish. **Official religion:** none. **Monetary unit:** 1 balboa (B) = 100 centésimos; valuation (1 Jul 2010) US$1 = B 0.98.

Demography

Area: 29,119 sq mi, 75,417 sq km. **Population** (2009): 3,454,000. **Density** (2009): persons per sq mi 118.6, persons per sq km 45.8. **Urban** (2005): 70.8%. **Sex distribution** (2007): male 50.43%; female 49.57%. **Age breakdown** (2007): under 15, 29.9%; 15–29, 25.7%; 30–44, 21.9%; 45–59, 13.5%; 60–74, 6.7%; 75 and over, 2.3%. **Ethnic composition** (2000): mestizo 58.1%; black and mulatto 14.0%; white 8.6%; Amerindian 6.7%; Asian 5.5%; other 7.1%. **Religious affiliation** (2008): Roman Catholic 75%; Protestant/independent Christian 20%; Mormon 1%; Jewish 0.3%; Muslim 0.3%; other 3.4%. **Major cities (districts)** (2000): Panama City 415,964 (845,684); San Miguelito 352,936; Colón 52,286 (205,557); Arraiján 63,753 (203,207); La Chorrera 54,823 (153,778). **Location:** Central America, bordering the Caribbean Sea, Colombia, the North Pacific Ocean, and Costa Rica.

Vital statistics

Birth rate per 1,000 population (2007): 20.2 (world avg. 20.3); (2006) within marriage 17.3%. **Death rate** per 1,000 population (2007): 4.4 (world avg. 8.5). **Total fertility rate** (avg. births per childbearing woman; 2007): 2.62. **Life expectancy** at birth (2007): male 73.7 years; female 79.5 years.

National economy

Budget (2007). *Revenue:* B 4,433,000,000 (tax revenue 48.1%, of which indirect taxes 22.5%, income tax 22.2%; nontax revenue 32.9%, of which revenue from Panama Canal 10.5%; capital revenue 16.9%). *Expenditures:* B 4,432,000,000 (current expenditures 78.1%, of which debt servicing 30.7%, education 14.4%, health 13.5%, public order 5.6%; development expenditures 21.9%). **Production** (metric tons except as noted). *Agriculture and fishing* (2007): sugarcane 1,800,000, bananas 440,000, rice 280,000, cantaloupes and other melons 130,000, pineapples 71,002; *livestock* (number of live animals) 1,650,000 cattle, 300,000 pigs, 190,000 horses; fisheries production 215,569 (from aquaculture 4%). *Mining and quarrying* (2007): limestone 270,000; gold 2,059 kg. *Manufacturing* (value added in B '000,000; 2006): food products 468; beverages 167; cement, bricks, and ceramics 82. *Energy production (consumption):* electricity (kW-hr; 2006) 5,962,000,000 (5,913,000,000); petroleum products (metric tons; 2006) none (1,922,000). **Selected balance of payments data.** Receipts from (US$'000,000): tourism (2007) 1,185; remittances (2008) 196; foreign direct investment (FDI; 2005–07 avg.) 1,787. Disbursements for (US$'000,000): tourism (2007) 307; remittances (2008) 198; FDI (2005–07 avg.) 2,095. **Population economically active** (2006): total 1,332,059; activity rate of total population 39.8% (participation

rates: ages 15–64, 66.9%; female 37.1%; unemployed [October 2009] 6.6%). **Gross national income** (2008): US$20,973,000,000 (US$6,180 per capita). **Public debt** (external, outstanding; 2007): US$8,267,000,000.

Foreign trade

Imports (2007; c.i.f.) (excludes trade passing through the Colón Free Zone [2007 imports US$7,633,000,000]): US$6,868,000,000 (machinery and apparatus 19.7%; refined petroleum products 17.2%; motor vehicles 11.5%; food products 9.1%; iron and steel 4.2%). *Major import sources:* US 30.8%; free zones 16.0%; Netherlands Antilles 7.1%; China 5.2%; Japan 4.8%. **Exports** (2007; f.o.b.) (excludes trade passing through the Colón Free Zone [2007 reexports US$8,523,000,000, of which textiles and wearing apparel 24.2%; machinery and apparatus 23.9%]): US$1,120,000,000 (fish 24.4%, of which tuna 7.2%; melons and papayas 18.1%; crustaceans and mollusks 10.1%; bananas 10.0%; pineapples 3.8%). *Major export destinations:* US 35.7%; France 10.2%; Sweden 5.6%; China 5.6%; UK 5.5%.

Transport and communications

Transport. *Railroads* (2005; Panama Canal Railway): route length (2007) 77 km; passenger-km 44,734,000,000; metric ton-km cargo 138,104,-000,000. *Roads* (2006): total length 13,365 km (paved 34%). *Vehicles* (2007): passenger cars 436,205; trucks and buses 194,615. Panama Canal traffic (2007–08): oceangoing transits 13,048; cargo 213,081,000 metric tons. *Air transport* (2007; COPA only): passenger-km 7,944,000,000; metric ton-km cargo (2005) 37,226,000. **Communications,** in total units (units per 1,000 persons). Telephone landlines (2008): 496,000 (146); cellular telephone subscribers (2008): 3,805,000 (1,119); personal computers (2007): 154,000 (46); total Internet users (2008): 779,000 (229); broadband Internet subscribers (2008): 158,000 (46).

Education and health

Educational attainment (2000). Percentage of population ages 25 and over having: no formal schooling/unknown 13.8%; primary education 36.4%; secondary 33.9%; undergraduate 14.4%; graduate 1.5%. **Literacy** (2005): total population ages 15 and over literate 93.0%; males literate 93.6%; females literate 92.4%. **Health** (2007): physicians 4,524 (1 per 739 persons); hospital beds 7,689 (1 per 435 persons); infant mortality rate per 1,000 live births 14.7; undernourished population (2002–04) 700,000 (23% of total population based on the consumption of a minimum daily requirement of 1,830 calories).

Military

Total active duty personnel (November 2008): none; a 12,000-member paramilitary includes air and maritime units. **Paramilitary expenditure as percentage of GDP** (2008): 0.9%; per capita expenditure US$66.

1 metric ton = about 1.1 short tons;   1 kilometer = 0.6 mi (statute);   1 metric ton-km cargo = about 0.68 short ton-mi cargo;   c.i.f.: cost, insurance, and freight;   f.o.b.: free on board

Background

Panama was inhabited by Native Americans when the Spanish arrived in 1501. The first successful Spanish settlement was founded by Vasco Núñez de Balboa in 1510. Panama was part of the Viceroyalty of New Granada until it declared its independence from Spain in 1821 to join the Gran Colombia union. In 1903 it revolted and was recognized by the US, to which it ceded the Canal Zone. The completed Panama Canal was opened in 1914; its jurisdiction reverted from the US to Panama in 1999. An invasion by US troops in 1989 overthrew the de facto ruler, Gen. Manuel Noriega. In 2007 a project to expand the canal began.

Recent Developments

Panama's economy was affected by the sharp decline in global trade in 2009. The economy contracted 2.4% during the year and unemployment increased. The US-Panama free-trade agreement remained unratified by the US Congress, despite support from the administration of US Pres. Barack Obama; some US representatives insisted that Panama first tighten its banking laws to discourage tax evasion and money laundering. The US$5.3 billion canal-expansion project, slated for completion in 2014, was well under way, however.

Internet resource:
<www.visitpanama.com/?id=&lang=en>.

Papua New Guinea

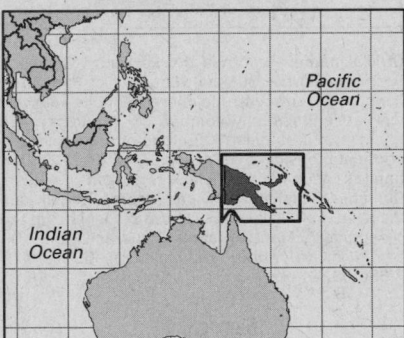

Pacific Ocean

Indian Ocean

Official names: Independent State of Papua New Guinea (English); Gau Hedinarai ai Papua-Matamata Guinea (Hiri Motu); Papua-Niugini (Tok Pisin). **Form of government:** constitutional monarchy with one legislative house (National Parliament [109]). **Head of state:** British Queen Elizabeth II (from 1952), represented by Governor-General Paulias Matane (from 2004). **Head of government:** Prime Minister Michael Somare (from 2002). **Capital:** Port Moresby. **Official languages:** English; Hiri Motu; Tok Pisin. **Official religion:** none. **Monetary unit:** 1 kina (K) = 100 toea; valuation (1 Jul 2010) US$1 = K 2.68.

Demography

Area: 178,704 sq mi, 462,840 sq km. **Population** (2009): 5,941,000. **Density** (2009): persons per sq mi 33.2, persons per sq km 12.8. **Urban** (2008): 12.0%. **Sex distribution** (2008): male 51.49%; female 48.51%. **Age breakdown** (2008): under 15, 37.7%; 15–29, 27.2%; 30–44, 19.4%; 45–59, 10.3%; 60–74, 4.5%; 75–84, 0.8%; 85 and over, 0.1%. **Ethnic composition** (1983): New Guinea Papuan 84.0%; New Guinea Melanesian 15.0%; other 1.0%. **Religious affiliation** (2005): Protestant/independent Christian 44%; Roman Catholic 22%; traditional beliefs 34%. **Major cities** (2006): Port Moresby 289,900; Lae 75,600; Arawa 40,300; Mount Hagen 34,900; Popondetta 30,400. **Location:** Oceania, group of islands, including the eastern half of the island of New Guinea, in the South Pacific Ocean near the Equator to the north of Australia, bordering Indonesia.

Vital statistics

Birth rate per 1,000 population (2008): 29.3 (world avg. 20.3). **Death rate** per 1,000 population (2008): 9.6 (world avg. 8.5). **Total fertility rate** (avg. births per childbearing woman; 2008): 3.7. **Life expectancy** at birth (2008): male 55.0 years; female 60.0 years.

National economy

Budget (2008). *Revenue:* K 7,128,000,000 (tax revenue 77.4%, of which corporate taxes 38.0%, income tax 14.8%, excise duties 6.6%; grants 15.8%; nontax revenue 6.8%). *Expenditures:* K 7,003,400,000 (current expenditures 52.0%, of which interest payments 5.3%; capital expenditures 26.9%). **Public debt** (external, outstanding; June 2009): US$1,044,390,000. **Production** (metric tons except as noted). *Agriculture and fishing* (2007): oil palm fruit 1,400,000, bananas 870,000, coconuts 677,000, coffee 75,400, cacao 50,300, natural rubber 4,700; livestock (number of live animals) 1,800,000 pigs; fisheries production 263,960 (from aquaculture, negligible). *Mining and quarrying* (2007): copper (metal content) 169,184; gold 65,000 kg; silver 51,300 kg. *Manufacturing* (value of exports in K '000,000; 2008–09): palm oil 788.8; refined petroleum products 486.5; forest products 367.9. *Energy production (consumption):* electricity (kW-hr; 2007) 2,885,000,000 (2,683,000,000); coal (metric tons; 2004) none (1,000); crude petroleum (barrels; 2008) 13,906,500 (12,045,000); natural gas (cu m; 2008) 100,000,000 (100,000,000); petroleum products (metric tons; 2006) 842,000 (1,242,000). **Population economically active** (2007): total 3,100,000; activity rate 54.5% (participation rates: ages 15–64 [2000] 73.2%; female 49.2%; officially unemployed [2004] 1.9%). **Gross national income** (2008): US$6,509,000,000 (US$1,010 per capita). **Selected balance of payments data.** Receipts from (US$'000,000): tourism (2005) 3.6; remittances (2008) 13; foreign direct investment (FDI; 2005–07 avg.) 41; official development assistance (2007) 317. Disbursements for (US$'000,000): tourism (2005) 56; remittances (2008) 135; FDI (2005–07 avg.) 5.

Foreign trade

Imports (2008; c.i.f. in commodities and f.o.b. in trading partners): K 8,413,300,000 ([2003] nonelectrical machinery 18.5%; food products 14.8%, of which cereals 7.3%; refined petroleum products 12.9%; transportation equipment 8.8%; chemical products 8.4%; fabricated metal products 6.3%). *Major import sources:* Australia 42.0%; US 22.7%; Singapore 11.3%; Japan 4.7%; China 3.5%. **Exports** (2008): K 15,423,400,000 (gold 30.3%; copper 23.4%; crude petroleum 22.7%; palm oil 6.6%; coffee 3.4%; refined petroleum products 3.3%; logs 3.0%; cocoa 2.2%). *Major export destinations:* Australia 44.3%; Japan 13.3%; Philippines 7.8%; Germany 4.8%; South Korea 4.7%.

Transport and communications

Transport. *Railroads:* none. *Roads* (2000): total length 19,600 km (paved 4%). *Vehicles* (2002): passenger cars 24,900; trucks and buses 87,800. *Air transport:* passenger-km (2006; Air Niugini only) 748,000,000; metric ton-km cargo (2007) 23,000,000. **Communications,** in total units (units per 1,000 persons). Telephone landlines (2008): 60,000 (9.1); cellular telephone subscribers (2008): 600,000 (91); personal computers (2005): 391,000 (64); total Internet users (2008): 120,000 (18).

Education and health

Educational attainment (1990). Percentage of population ages 25 and over having: no formal schooling 82.6%; some primary education 8.2%; completed primary 5.0%; some secondary 4.2%. **Literacy** (2007): total population ages 15 and over literate 57.8%; males literate 62.1%; females literate 53.4%. **Health:** physicians (2005) 750 (1 per 7,849 persons); hospital beds (2000) 14,516 (1 per 371 persons); infant mortality rate per 1,000 live births (2008) 60.0.

Military

Total active duty personnel (November 2008): 3,100 (army 80.6%, maritime element [coastal patrol] 12.9%, air force 6.5%). **Military expenditure as percentage of GDP** (2008): 0.6%; per capita expenditure US$7.

Background

Papua New Guinea (PNG) has been inhabited since prehistoric times. The Portuguese sighted the coast of New Guinea in 1512. The first colony was founded in 1793 by the British. In 1828 the Dutch claimed the western half as part of the Dutch East Indies. In 1884 Britain annexed the southeastern part and Germany took over the northeastern sector. The British part became the Territory of Papua in 1906 and passed to Australia, which also governed the German sector after World War I. After World War II, Australia governed both sectors as the Territory of Papua and New Guinea. Dutch New Guinea was annexed to Indonesia in 1969. Papua New Guinea achieved independence in 1975 and joined the British Commonwealth. It moved to resolve its war with independence fighters on the island of Bougainville in the 1990s. The decadelong war ended when final terms for peace were negotiated on 1 Jun 2001; Bougainville became an autonomous region in 2005.

Recent Developments

In 2009 Papua New Guinea pressed forward with a plan to exploit its natural gas reserves. Two proposals were put forth to construct pipelines from wells to liquefaction plants. The liquefied natural gas would then be shipped to Chinese, Japanese, and Taiwanese customers already signed up under a US$15 billion deal.

Internet resource: <www.nso.gov.pg>.

Paraguay

Official name: República del Paraguay (Spanish); Tetã Paraguáype (Guaraní) (Republic of Paraguay). **Form of government:** multiparty republic with two legislative houses (Chamber of Senators [45]; Chamber of Deputies [80]). **Head of state and government:** President Fernando Lugo (from 2008). **Capital:** Asunción. **Official languages:** Spanish; Guaraní. **Official religion:** none (Roman Catholicism, though not official, enjoys special recognition in the constitution). **Monetary unit:** 1 guaraní (₲) = 100 céntimos; valuation (1 Jul 2010) US$1 = ₲ 4,680.00.

Demography

Area: 157,048 sq mi, 406,752 sq km. **Population** (2009): 6,349,000. **Density** (2009): persons per sq mi 40.4, persons per sq km 15.6. **Urban** (2006): 57.1%. **Sex distribution** (2006): male 50.57%; female 49.43%. **Age breakdown** (2006): under 15, 35.4%; 15–29, 28.8%; 30–44, 17.4%; 45–59, 11.4%; 60–74, 5.2%; 75 and over, 1.8%. **Ethnic composition** (2000): mixed (white/Amerindian) 85.6%; white 9.3%, of which German 4.4%, Latin American 3.4%; Amerindian 1.8%; other 3.3%. **Religious affiliation** (2002): Roman Catholic 89.6%; Protestant (including all Evangelicals) 6.2%; other Christian 1.1%; nonreligious/atheist 1.1%; traditional beliefs 0.6%; other/unknown 1.4%. **Major urban areas** (2002): Asunción (2006) 519,361 (urban agglomeration

1 metric ton = about 1.1 short tons;   1 kilometer = 0.6 mi (statute);   1 metric ton-km cargo = about 0.68 short ton-mi cargo;   c.i.f.: cost, insurance, and freight;   f.o.b.: free on board

[2007] 1,870,000); Ciudad del Este 222,274; San Lorenzo 204,356; Luque 170,986; Capiatá 154,274. **Location:** central South America, bordering Brazil, Argentina, and Bolivia.

Vital statistics

Birth rate per 1,000 population (2007): 25.0 (world avg. 20.3). **Death rate** per 1,000 population (2007): 5.6 (world avg. 8.5). **Total fertility rate** (avg. births per childbearing woman; 2005): 3.30. **Life expectancy** at birth (2007): male 69.6 years; female 73.8 years.

National economy

Budget (2006–07): *Revenue:* ₲10,174,723,-000,000 (tax revenue 65.2%, of which VAT 28.5%, income tax 10.9%, taxes on international trade 8.5%; nontax revenue and grants 34.8%). *Expenditures:* ₲9,682,282,000,000 (current expenditures 77.3%, of which wages and salaries 42.9%; capital expenditures 22.7%). **Public debt** (external, outstanding; December 2007): US$2,197,000,000. **Population economically active** (2006): total 2,735,646; activity rate 46.0% (participation rates: ages 15–64 [2002] 61.4%; female 38.5%; unemployed 11.1%). **Production** (metric tons except as noted). *Agriculture and fishing* (2007): cassava 5,100,000, soybeans 3,900,000, sugarcane 3,400,000, maté 87,500, sesame seed 53,000; livestock (number of live animals) 10,000,000 cattle, 1,600,000 pigs, 17,000,000 chickens; fisheries production 22,100 (from aquaculture 10%). *Mining and quarrying* (2007): dimension stone 70,000; kaolin 66,000. *Manufacturing* (value added in US$'000,000; 2002): food products 253; chemical products 77; beverages 67. *Energy production (consumption):* electricity (kW-hr; 2006) 53,774,000,000 (Paraguay is the world's second largest net exporter of electricity) (8,076,000,000); petroleum products (metric tons; 2006) negligible (1,201,000). **Gross national income** (2008): US$13,574,000,000 (US$2,180 per capita). **Selected balance of payments data.** Receipts from (US$'000,000): tourism (2007) 102; remittances (2008) 503; foreign direct investment (FDI; 2005–07 avg.) 138; official development assistance (2007) 108. Disbursements for (US$'000,000): tourism (2007) 109; FDI (2005–07 avg.) 6.

Foreign trade

Imports (2006): US$5,254,271,000 (machinery and apparatus 35.9%; mineral fuels 13.2%; transportation equipment 11.5%; chemical products 6.3%; food products, beverages, and tobacco products 6.1%). *Major import sources:* China 27.0%; Brazil 20.0%; Argentina 13.6%; Japan 8.3%; US 6.4%. **Exports** (2006; electricity exports are excluded): US$1,906,367,000 (soybeans 23.0%; meat 22.3%; cereals 11.4%; flour 7.5%; vegetable oils 6.2%; wood products 5.2%). *Major export destinations:* Uruguay 22.0%; Brazil 17.2%; Russia 11.9%; Argentina 8.8%; Chile 6.9%.

Transport and communications

Transport. *Railroads* (2006): operational route length 36 km. *Roads* (2000): total length 29,500 km (paved 51%). *Vehicles* (2007): passenger cars 240,728, trucks 248,086. *Air transport* (2005; Transportes Aéreos del Mercosur only): passenger-km

501,000,000; metric ton-km cargo, none. **Communications,** in total units (units per 1,000 persons). Telephone landlines (2008): 363,000 (58); cellular telephone subscribers (2008): 5,791,000 (928); personal computers (2005): 460,000 (78); total Internet users (2008): 694,000 (111); broadband Internet subscribers (2008): 94,000 (15).

Education and health

Educational attainment (2003). Percentage of population ages 15 and over having: no formal schooling 4.1%; incomplete primary education 30.2%; complete primary 30.8%; secondary 26.9%; higher 8.0%. **Literacy** (2005): percentage of total population ages 15 and over literate 94.9%; males literate 95.9%; females literate 93.9%. **Health** (2007): physicians (2005) 5,517 (1 per 873 persons); hospital beds 5,766 (1 per 1,063 persons); infant mortality rate per 1,000 live births 32.4; undernourished population (2003–05) 700,000 (11% of total population based on the consumption of a minimum daily requirement of 1,810 calories).

Military

Total active duty personnel (November 2008): 10,650 (army 71.4%, navy 18.3%, air force 10.3%). **Military expenditure as percentage of GDP** (2008): 0.9%; per capita expenditure US$22.

Background

Seminomadic tribes speaking Guaraní were in Paraguay long before it was settled by Spain in the 16th and 17th centuries. Paraguay was part of the Viceroyalty of the Río de la Plata until it became independent in 1811. It suffered from dictatorial governments in the 19th century and from the 1865 war with Brazil, Argentina, and Uruguay. The Chaco War with Bolivia over disputed territory was settled primarily in Paraguay's favor by the peace treaty of 1938. Military governments, including that of Alfredo Stroessner, predominated in the mid-20th century until the election of a civilian president, Juan Carlos Wasmosy, in 1993. Paraguay suffered political unrest and a financial crisis beginning in the 1990s and continuing into the 21st century.

Recent Developments

In 2009 high political expectations faced Paraguayan Pres. Fernando Lugo, the former Roman Catholic bishop whose election had ended 61 years of rule by the Colorado Party. Although his efforts to deliver on campaign promises were hobbled by the global recession and resistance from Colorado Party functionaries in the government, he did achieve some successes. In April he and Bolivian Pres. Evo Morales signed an agreement ending a border dispute that dated from the 1932–35 Chaco War. In July Lugo finalized a deal with Brazilian Pres. Luiz Inácio Lula da Silva in which Brazil, after years of resistance, agreed to triple the amount it paid to Paraguay for energy from the Itaipú hydroelectric dam, which was jointly operated by the two countries. Lugo's administration also succeeded in significantly increasing financial and medical assistance to Paraguayans in poverty.

Internet resource: <http://country.paraguay.com>.

Peru

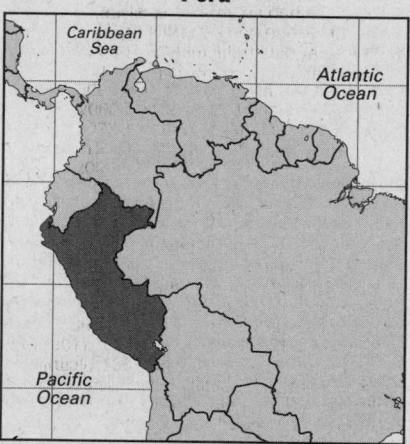

Official name: República del Perú (Spanish) (Republic of Peru). **Form of government:** unitary multiparty republic with one legislative house (Congress [120]). **Head of state and government:** President Alan García (from 2006), assisted by Prime Minister Javier Velásquez (from 2009). **Capital:** Lima. **Official languages:** Spanish (Quechua and Aymara are official locally). **Official religion:** none (the state recognizes Roman Catholicism as an important element in the historical and cultural development of Peru). **Monetary unit:** 1 nuevo sol (S/.) = 100 céntimos; valuation (1 Jul 2010) US$1 = S/. 2.83.

Demography

Area: 496,218 sq mi, 1,285,198 sq km. **Population** (2009): 28,887,000. **Density** (2009): persons per sq mi 58.2, persons per sq km 22.5. **Urban** (2007): 75.9%. **Sex distribution** (2007): male 49.68%; female 50.32%. **Age breakdown** (2007): under 15, 30.5%; 15–29, 27.5%; 30–44, 20.4%; 45–59, 12.5%; 60–74, 6.4%; 75–84, 2.0%; 85 and over, 0.7%. **Ethnic composition** (2000): Quechua 47.0%; mestizo 31.9%; white 12.0%; Aymara 5.4%; Japanese 0.5%; other 3.2%. **Religious affiliation** (2005): Roman Catholic 85%, of which practicing weekly 15%; Protestant 7%; independent Christian 4%; other 4%. **Major cities** (2007): Lima (urban agglomeration) 8,472,935; Arequipa 749,291; Trujillo 682,834; Chiclayo 524,442; Piura 377,496. **Location:** western South America, bordering Ecuador, Colombia, Brazil, Bolivia, Chile, and the South Pacific Ocean.

Vital statistics

Birth rate per 1,000 population (2007): 20.2 (world avg. 20.3). **Death rate** per 1,000 population (2007): 6.2 (world avg. 8.5). **Total fertility rate** (avg. births per childbearing woman; 2007): 2.46. **Life expectancy** at birth (2007): male 68.3 years; female 72.0 years.

National economy

Budget (2008). *Revenue:* S/. 68,352,000,000 (tax revenue 85.2%, of which VAT 46.2%, taxes on income and profits 35.3%; nontax revenue 14.8%). *Expenditures:* S/. 60,073,000,000 (current expenditures 76.9%; capital expenditures 14.6%; debt service 8.5%). **Production** (metric tons except as noted). *Agriculture and fishing* (2008): sugarcane 8,228,623, potatoes 3,383,020, rice 2,793,980, quinoa 31,824 (in 2008 Peru ranked second in the world in coca production; an estimated 302 metric tons of cocaine were produced); livestock (number of live animals) 14,580,200 sheep, 5,420,860 cattle, (2007) 4,962,000 llamas and alpacas; fisheries production (2007) 7,250,075 (from aquaculture 1%). *Mining and quarrying* (2008; metal content): iron ore 5,243,000; zinc 1,371,000; copper 1,036,700; lead 317,700; molybdenum 16,100; silver 3,465; gold (all forms) 174,700 kg. *Manufacturing* (value in US$'000,000; 2007): food products 4,066; wearing apparel 1,326; paints, soaps, pharmaceuticals 1,233; refined petroleum products 862. *Energy production (consumption):* electricity (kW-hr; 2006) 27,358,000,000 (27,358,000,000); coal (metric tons; 2007) 127,900 (1,192,000); crude petroleum (barrels; 2008) 28,000,000 ([2006] 56,600,000); petroleum products (metric tons; 2006) 9,193,000 (6,412,000); natural gas (cu m; 2006) 2,249,000,000 (2,249,000,000). **Selected balance of payments data.** Receipts from (US$'000,000): tourism (2007) 1,938; remittances (2008) 2,200; foreign direct investment (FDI; 2005–07 avg.) 3,796; official development assistance (2007) 263. Disbursements for (US$'000,000): tourism (2007) 1,007; remittances (2008) 137; FDI (2005–07 avg.) 470. **Population economically active** (2006): total 13,762,000; activity rate of total population 49.9% (participation rates: ages 15–64, 74.7%; female 44.7%; officially unemployed [metropolitan Lima only; August 2008–July 2009] 8.5%). **Gross national income** (2008): US$114,960,000,000 (US$3,990 per capita). **Public debt** (external, outstanding; 2007): US$19,669,000,000.

Foreign trade

Imports (2007; c.i.f.): US$20,494,000,000 (machinery and apparatus 23.0%; chemical products 14.6%; crude petroleum 13.4%; food products 8.4%; base and fabricated metals 8.3%). *Major import sources:* US 17.7%; China 12.1%; Brazil 9.2%; Ecuador 7.4%; Argentina 5.5%. **Exports** (2007; f.o.b.): US$27,800,000,000 (ores and concentrates 32.3%, of which copper 16.5%, zinc 8.3%, molybdenum 3.5%; gold 15.0%; food products 12.8%, of which fish meal 4.6%; crude petroleum 8.7%; refined copper 8.6%; wearing apparel and accessories 5.1%). *Major export destinations:* US 19.4%; China 10.9%; Switzerland 8.4%; Japan 7.8%; Canada 6.6%.

Transport and communications

Transport. *Railroads* (2006): route length 1,720 km; (2005) passenger-km 125,756,000; metric ton-km cargo 1,164,378,000. *Roads* (2006): total length 78,986 km (paved 14%). *Vehicles* (2007): passenger

---

1 metric ton = about 1.1 short tons;   1 kilometer = 0.6 mi (statute);   1 metric ton-km cargo = about 0.68 short ton-mi cargo;   c.i.f.: cost, insurance, and freight;   f.o.b.: free on board

cars 917,110; trucks and buses 525,277. *Air transport* (2007): passenger-km 6,472,300,000; metric ton-km cargo 148,600,000. **Communications**, in total units (units per 1,000 persons). Telephone landlines (2008): 2,878,000 (101); cellular telephone subscribers (2008): 20,952,000 (734); personal computers (2005): 2,800,000 (103); total Internet users (2008): 7,128,000 (250); broadband Internet subscribers (2008): 726,000 (25).

Education and health

Educational attainment (2005). Percentage of population ages 15 and over having: no formal schooling 11.8%; less than complete primary education 24.3%; complete primary 11.5%; incomplete secondary 15.3%; complete secondary 19.0%; higher 18.1%. **Literacy** (2005): total population ages 15 and over literate 91.6%; males literate 95.6%; females literate 87.7%. **Health** (2007): physicians 41,788 (1 per 672 persons); hospital beds 44,195 (1 per 635 persons); infant mortality rate per 1,000 live births 30.5; undernourished population (2002–04) 3,300,000 (12% of total population based on the consumption of a minimum daily requirement of 1,820 calories).

Military

Total active duty personnel (November 2008): 114,000 (army 64.9%, navy 20.2%, air force 14.9%). **Military expenditure as percentage of GDP** (2008): 1.1%; per capita expenditure US$47.

Background

Peru was the center of the Inca empire, which was established about 1230 with its capital at Cuzco. In 1533 it was conquered by Francisco Pizarro, and it was dominated by Spain for almost 300 years as the Viceroyalty of Peru. It declared its independence in 1821, and freedom was achieved in 1824. Peru was defeated in the War of the Pacific with Chile (1879–83). A boundary dispute with Ecuador erupted into war in 1941 and gave Peru control over a larger part of the Amazon basin; further disputes ensued until the border was demarcated again in 1998. The government was overthrown by a military junta in 1968, and civilian rule was restored in 1980. The government of Alberto Fujimori dissolved the legislature in 1992 and promulgated a new constitution the following year. It later successfully combated the Sendero Luminoso (Shining Path) and Tupac Amarú rebel movements. Fujimori won a second term in 1995 and a controversial third term in 2000, but he left office and the country late that year amid allegations of corruption. Fujimori was succeeded by Alejandro Toledo (2001–06), Peru's first democratically elected president of Quechuan ethnicity.

Recent Developments

Much attention in Peru was focused on the numerous protests that occurred in 2009, many of them related to the issues of land use and indigenous rights. The most notable of these was an indigenous uprising in the Peruvian Amazon region near Bagua Grande. During the first week of June, members of indigenous groups opposed to two recently enacted laws allowing the country's rainforest to be opened to exploration and development blockaded highways and became involved in deadly clashes with police. The fighting claimed the lives of at least 24 protesters and 10 policemen. The political fallout from the violence was considerable—on 18 June Congress rescinded the laws. Protests were also staged by the local populations in other parts of the Peruvian Amazon and in the Andean highlands, where many complained of deforestation that was ruining tribal hunting grounds, numerous oil spills that had contaminated water supplies, and widespread pollution that had been caused by mining and smelting operations.

Internet resource: <www.peru.info>.

Philippines

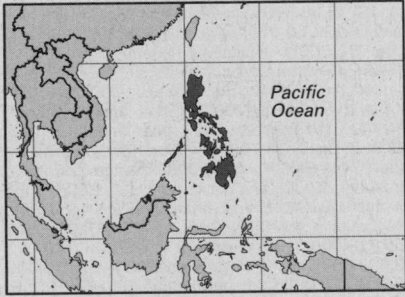

Pacific Ocean

Official name: Republika ng Pilipinas (Filipino); Republic of the Philippines (English). **Form of government:** unitary republic with two legislative houses (Senate [24]; House of Representatives [287]). **Head of state and government:** President Benigno Aquino (from 2010). **Capital:** Manila; other government offices and ministries are located in Quezon City and other Manila suburbs. **Official languages:** Filipino; English. **Official religion:** none. **Monetary unit:** 1 Philippine piso (peso; P) = 100 sentimos; valuation (1 Jul 2010) US$1 = P 46.46.

Demography

Area: 122,121 sq mi, 316,294 sq km. **Population** (2009): 91,983,000. **Density** (2009): persons per sq mi 794.1, persons per sq km 306.6. **Urban** (2007): 64.0%. **Sex distribution** (2005): male 50.38%; female 49.62%. **Age breakdown** (2005): under 15, 35.6%; 15–29, 28.4%; 30–44, 18.8%; 45–59, 11.2%; 60–74, 4.9%; 75–84, 1.0%; 85 and over, 0.1%. **Ethnic composition** (2000): Tagalog 20.9%; Visayan (Cebu) 19.0%; Ilocano 11.1%; Hiligaynon (Visaya) 9.4%; Waray-Waray (Binisaya) 4.7%; Central Bikol (Naga) 4.6%; Filipino mestizo 3.5%; Pampango 3.1%; other 23.7%. **Religious affiliation** (2005): Roman Catholic 64.9%; independent Christian 17.7%; Muslim 5.1%; Protestant 5.5%; traditional beliefs 2.2%; other 5.1%. **Major cities** (2007): Manila 1,660,714 (National Capital Region 11,553,427); Quezon City 2,679,450; Caloocan 1,378,856; Davao 1,363,337; Cebu City 798,809. **Location:** southeastern Asia, archipelago between the Philippine Sea and the South China Sea, east of Vietnam.

Vital statistics

Birth rate per 1,000 population (2005): 24.1 (world avg. 20.3). **Death rate** per 1,000 population (2005): 5.6 (world avg. 8.5). **Total fertility rate** (avg. births per childbearing woman; 2005): 3.41. **Life expectancy** at birth (2005): male 67.0 years; female 72.9 years.

National economy

Budget (2007). *Revenue:* P 1,047,500,000,000 (tax revenue 89.1%, of which income tax 40.7%, taxes on international trade 20.0%; nontax revenues 10.9%). *Expenditures:* P 1,145,030,000,000 (debt service 24.2%; education 14.3%; transportation and communications 10.0%; public order 5.7%; social protection 4.8%; defense 4.7%; health 1.6%). **Production** (metric tons except as noted). *Agriculture and fishing* (2007): sugarcane 25,300,000, rice 16,000,000, coconuts 15,580,000; livestock (number of live animals) 13,250,000 pigs, 3,365,000 buffalo, 136,000,000 chickens; fisheries production 3,209,349 (from aquaculture 22%); aquatic plants production 1,505,421 (from aquaculture 100%). *Mining and quarrying* (2007): nickel (metal content) 84,740; chromite 31,592; copper (metal content) 22,862; gold 38,792 kg. *Manufacturing* (value added in US$'000,000; 2003): refined petroleum products 1,980; electronic products 1,696; food products 1,338. *Energy production (consumption):* electricity (kW-hr; 2006) 56,818,000,000 (56,818,000,000); coal (metric tons; 2006) 180,000 (3,600,000); lignite (metric tons; 2006) 3,072,000 (6,401,000); crude petroleum (barrels; 2006) 182,000 (78,262,000); petroleum products (metric tons; 2006) 9,823,000 (11,852,000); natural gas (cu m; 2006) 2,969,000,000 (2,969,000,000). **Selected balance of payments data.** Receipts from (US$'000,000): tourism (2007) 4,931; remittances (2008) 18,643; foreign direct investment (FDI; 2005–07 avg.) 2,568. Disbursements for (US$'000,000): tourism (2007) 1,615; remittances (2008) 44; FDI (2005–07 avg.) 1,245. **Gross national income** (2008): US$170,410,000,000 (US$1,890 per capita). **Public debt** (external, outstanding; June 2008): US$35,019,000,000. **Population economically active** (2007): total 36,434,000; activity rate 41% (participation rates: ages 15 and over, 63.6%; female [2006] 39.4%; unemployed [April 2007–March 2008] 7.2%).

Did you know? A protection ritual called "mother roasting," which involved a mother being placed for some days over or near a fire, survives today in altered form in the rural Philippines, where it is regarded as having therapeutic value.

Foreign trade

Imports (2006; c.i.f.): US$54,078,000,000 (electronic components 33.6%; crude petroleum 14.1%; chemical products 7.4%; parts for office machines and computers 6.6%; food products 5.9%). *Major import sources:* US 16.2%; Japan 14.2%; Singapore 8.4%; Taiwan 7.9%; China 7.2%. **Exports** (2006; f.o.b.): US$47,410,000,000 (microcircuits and transistors 35.8%; office machines and computers and parts 17.2%; wearing apparel and accessories 5.5%; food products 3.8%). *Major export destinations:* US 18.3%; Japan 16.7%; Netherlands 10.1%; China 9.8%; Hong Kong 7.8%.

Transport and communications

Transport. *Railroads* (2004): route length 897 km; passenger-km 83,400,000; metric ton-km cargo (2000) 660,000,000. *Roads* (2003): total length 200,037 km (paved 10%). *Vehicles* (2007): passenger cars 751,100; trucks and buses 311,400. *Air transport* (2008): passenger-km 17,868,000,000; metric ton-km cargo 265,380,000. **Communications,** in total units (units per 1,000 persons). Telephone landlines (2008): 3,905,000 (43); cellular telephone subscribers (2008): 68,102,000 (754); personal computers (2005): 4,521,000 (54); total Internet users (2008): 5,618,000 (62); broadband Internet subscribers (2007): 968,000 (11).

Education and health

Educational attainment (2000). Percentage of population ages 25 and over having: no formal schooling/unknown 6.1%; primary education 38.5%; incomplete secondary 12.5%; complete secondary 17.2%; technical 5.9%; incomplete undergraduate 11.8%; complete undergraduate 7.3%; graduate 0.7%. **Literacy** (2003): total population ages 15 and over literate 92.6%. **Health** (2007): physicians (2005) 98,210 (1 per 865 persons); hospital beds 92,561 (1 per 956 persons); infant mortality rate per 1,000 live births 21.9; undernourished population (2003–05) 13,300,000 (16% of total population based on the consumption of a minimum daily requirement of 1,750 calories).

Military

Total active duty personnel (November 2008): 106,000 (army 62.3%, navy 22.6%, air force 15.1%). **Military expenditure as percentage of GDP** (2008): 0.7%; per capita expenditure US$12.

Background

Waves of diverse immigrants from the Asian mainland occupied the Philippines in ancient times. Ferdinand Magellan arrived in 1521. The islands were colonized by the Spanish, who retained control until the islands were ceded to the US in 1898 following the Spanish-American War. The Commonwealth of the Philippines was established in 1935 to prepare the country for political and economic independence, which was delayed by World War II and the Japanese invasion. The islands were liberated by US forces during 1944–45, and the Republic of the Philippines was proclaimed in 1946, with a government patterned on that of the US. In 1965 Ferdinand Marcos was elected president. He declared martial law in 1972, and it lasted until 1981. After 20 years of dictatorial rule, he was driven from power in 1986. Corazon Aquino became president

1 metric ton = about 1.1 short tons; 1 kilometer = 0.6 mi (statute); 1 metric ton-km cargo = about 0.68 short ton-mi cargo; c.i.f.: cost, insurance, and freight; f.o.b.: free on board

and instituted democratic rule. The government has tried to come to terms with Muslim independence fighters in the south by establishing the Muslim Mindanao autonomous region in Mindanao and nearby islands, but violent conflict continued into the 21st century.

Recent Developments

In one of the worst examples of political violence in the Philippines, 57 people were killed in an ambush on 23 Nov 2009 as they traveled in a convoy that had been sent to file the election papers of Ismael Mangudadatu, a candidate for governor of Maguindanao province on the island of Mindanao. A local mayor, Andal Ampatuan, Jr., was accused of having led the ambush and was charged with multiple counts of murder. His father, a former governor of the province and the leader of a clan that had long ruled Maguindanao, and his brother were among 24 people charged with rebellion. Mangudadatu indicated that Ampatuan, Jr., had threatened to kill him if he sought the governorship, so he had sent female relatives to file the papers for his candidacy, thinking that they—along with some lawyers and supporters and 30 journalists who accompanied them—would not be harmed. The victims were mutilated and buried in mass graves that had been dug in advance of the massacre. Pres. Gloria Macapagal Arroyo declared martial law in the province, and her political party expelled the Ampatuan clan.

Internet resource: <www.nscb.gov.ph>.

Poland

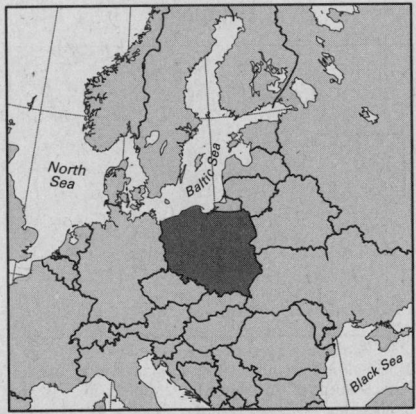

Official name: Rzeczpospolita Polska (Republic of Poland). Form of government: unitary multiparty republic with two legislative houses (Senate [100]; Sejm [460]). Head of state: President Bronislaw Komorowski (from 2010). Head of government: Prime Minister Donald Tusk (from 2007). Capital: Warsaw. Official language: Polish. Official religion: none (Roman Catholicism has special recognition per 1997 concordat with Vatican City). Monetary unit: 1 zloty (zl) = 100 groszy; valuation (1 Jul 2010) US$1 = zl 3.35.

Demography

Area: 120,726 sq mi, 312,679 sq km. Population (2009): 38,146,000. Density (2009): persons per sq mi 316.0, persons per sq km 122.0. Urban (2009): 61.1%. Sex distribution (2008): male 48.29%; female 51.71%. Age breakdown (2008): under 15, 15.2%; 15–29, 23.4%; 30–44, 20.7%; 45–59, 22.1%; 60–74, 12.4%; 75–84, 5.0%; 85 and over, 1.2%. Ethnic composition (2000): Polish 90.0%; Ukrainian 4.0%; German 4.0%; Belarusian 0.5%; Kashubian 0.4%; other 1.1%. Religious affiliation (2007): Roman Catholic 88.6%; other Catholic 0.1%; Polish Orthodox 1.3%; Protestant 0.4%; Jehovah's Witness 0.3%; other (mostly nonreligious) 9.3%. Major cities (2008): Warsaw 1,709,781; Krakow 754,624; Lodz 747,152; Wroclaw 632,162; Poznan 557,264. Location: central Europe, bordering the Baltic Sea, the Russian exclave of Kaliningrad, Lithuania, Belarus, Ukraine, Slovakia, Czech Republic, and Germany.

Vital statistics

Birth rate per 1,000 population (2008): 10.9 (world avg. 20.3); within marriage 80.1%. Death rate per 1,000 population (2008): 10.0 (world avg. 8.5). Total fertility rate (avg. births per childbearing woman; 2008): 1.39. Life expectancy at birth (2008): male 71.3 years; female 80.0 years.

National economy

Budget (2008). Revenue: zl 253,547,000,000 (VAT 40.1%; excise tax 19.9%; income tax 15.2%; corporate taxes 10.7%). Expenditures: zl 277,893,-000,000 (social security and welfare 29.6%; public debt 9.0%; national defense 5.0%; education 4.8%; public safety 4.5%). Gross national income (2008): US$453,034,000,000 (US$11,880 per capita). Production (metric tons except as noted). Agriculture and fishing (2008): potatoes 10,462,000, wheat 9,275,000, sugar beets 8,715,000, sour cherries 202,000, currants 197,000; livestock (number of live animals; 2009) 14,279,000 pigs, 5,700,000 cattle, (2007) 1,450,000 beehives; fisheries production (2007) 187,448 (from aquaculture 19%). Mining and quarrying (2007): sulfur (2008–09) 494,800; copper ore (metal content) 505,900; silver (metal content) 1,250. Manufacturing (value of sales in zl '000,000; 2008): food products 127,127; transportation equipment 94,790; mineral fuels 59,077. Energy production (consumption): electricity ('000,000 kW-hr; 2008–09) 151,968 ([2007] 154,000); coal ('000 metric tons; 2008–09) 81,441 ([2007] 85,337); lignite ('000 metric tons; 2008–09) 59,322 ([2007] 57,528); crude petroleum (barrels; 2008) 5,593,000 ([2007] 148,538,000); petroleum products (metric tons; 2008–09) 26,507,000 ([2007] 25,322,000); natural gas (cu m; 2008–09) 5,263,280,900 ([2007] 16,549,000,000). Public debt (external, outstanding; August 2009): US$53,287,900,000. Population economically active (2008): total 17,202,000; activity rate of total population 45.1% (participation rates: ages 15–64, 64.4%; female 45.2%; unemployed [October 2008–September 2009] 10.4%). Selected balance of payments data. Receipts from (US$'000,000): tourism (2007) 10,599; remittances (2008) 10,727; foreign direct investment (FDI; 2005–07 avg.) 15,714. Disbursements for (US$'000,000): tourism (2007) 7,753; remittances (2008) 1,716; FDI (2005–07 avg.) 5,210.

Foreign trade

Imports (2008; c.i.f.): zl 497,028,300,000 (electrical equipment 13.2%; chemical products 13.0%; mineral fuels 11.2%; transportation equipment 11.2%; machinery and apparatus 11.0%; base and fabricated metals 10.9%). *Major import sources:* Germany 23.0%; Russia 9.7%; China 8.1%; Italy 6.5%; France 4.7%. **Exports** (2008; f.o.b.): zl 405,383,100,000 (transportation equipment 17.4%; base and fabricated metals 12.9%; electrical equipment 12.4%; machinery and apparatus 12.3%; food products 10.1%; chemical products 5.9%; furniture 5.7%). *Major export destinations:* Germany 25.0%; France 6.2%; Italy 6.0%; UK 5.8%; Czech Republic 5.7%.

Transport and communications

Transport. *Railroads* (2008): length 20,196 km; passenger-km 20,389,000,000; metric ton-km cargo 52,043,000,000. *Roads* (2007; public roads only): total length 383,100 km (paved 68%). *Vehicles* (2008): passenger cars 16,080,000; trucks and buses 2,802,000. *Air transport* (2008): passenger-km 9,438,000,000; metric ton-km cargo 106,000,000. **Communications,** in total units (units per 1,000 persons). Telephone landlines (2008): 8,690,000 (228); cellular telephone subscribers (2008): 44,086,000 (1,156); personal computers (2004): 7,362,000 (191); total Internet users (2008): 18,679,000 (490); broadband Internet subscribers (2008): 4,791,000 (126).

Education and health

Educational attainment (2007). Percentage of population ages 13 and over having: no formal schooling/incomplete primary education 2.0%; complete primary 20.2%; lower secondary/vocational 27.9%; upper secondary and postsecondary 33.4%; university 16.5%. **Literacy** (2008): virtually 100%. **Health** (2007): physicians 78,229 (1 per 487 persons); hospital beds 227,845 (1 per 167 persons); infant mortality rate per 1,000 live births (2008) 5.6; undernourished population (2002–04) less than 2.5% of total population.

Military

Total active duty personnel (November 2008): 121,808 (army 51.5%, navy 8.9%, air force 19.2%, joint staff 20.4%). **Military expenditure as percentage of GDP** (2008): 1.8%; per capita expenditure US$224.

Background

Established as a kingdom in 922 under Mieszko I, Poland united with Lithuania in 1386 under the Jagiellon dynasty (1386–1572) to become the dominant power in east-central Europe. In 1466 it wrested western and eastern Prussia from the Teutonic Order, and its lands eventually stretched to the Black Sea. Wars with Sweden and Russia in the late 17th century led to the loss of considerable territory. In 1697 the electors of Saxony became kings of Poland, virtually ending Polish independence. In the late 18th century, Poland was divided among Prussia, Russia, and Austria. After 1815 the former Polish lands came under Russian domination, and from 1863 Poland was a Russian province. After World War I, an independent Poland was established by the Allies. The invasion of Poland in 1939 by the USSR and Germany precipitated World War II, during which the Nazis sought to purge its culture and its large Jewish population. Reoccupied by Soviet forces in 1945, it was controlled by a Soviet-dominated government from 1947. In the 1980s the Solidarity labor movement led by Lech Walesa achieved major political reforms, and free elections were held in 1989. An economic austerity program instituted in 1990 sped the transition to a market economy. Poland became a member of NATO in 1999 and the EU in 2004.

Recent Developments

Though slowed by the global recession, Poland's economy registered GDP growth of 1.7% in 2009, making it the best-performing economy in the EU and the only one to have grown in the year. Consumer price inflation increased by 4.0%, and the country's unemployment rate during the last quarter was 11.9%–2.4% higher than during the same period the previous year. The government's 2012 target date for joining the euro zone was canceled, however, and it was suggested that 2014 or 2015 might be a more realistic goal. Despite the economic slowdown, Poland was still perceived as a relatively safe haven in terms of economic development; this view was supported by the decision of the IMF to grant Poland a flexible credit line of US$20.5 billion.

Internet resource: <www.stat.gov.pl>.

Portugal

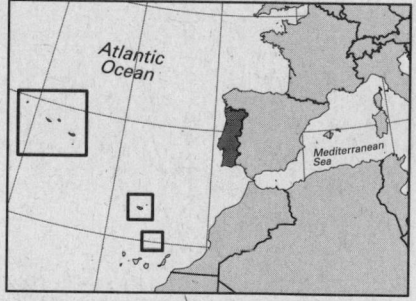

Official name: República Portuguesa (Portuguese Republic). **Form of government:** republic with one legislative house (Assembly of the Republic [230]). **Head of state:** President Aníbal Cavaco Silva (from 2006). **Head of government:** Prime Minister José Sócrates (from 2005). **Capital:** Lisbon. **Official language:** Portuguese. **Official religion:** none (a 2004 concordat with the Vatican acknowledges the special role of the Roman Catholic Church in Portugal). **Monetary unit:** 1 euro (€) = 100 cents; valuation (1 Jul 2010) US$1 = €0.80.

1 metric ton = about 1.1 short tons;   1 kilometer = 0.6 mi (statute);   1 metric ton-km cargo = about 0.68 short ton-mi cargo;   c.i.f.: cost, insurance, and freight;   f.o.b.: free on board

Demography

Area: 35,556 sq mi, 92,090 sq km. **Population** (2009): 10,639,000. **Density** (2009): persons per sq mi 299.2, persons per sq km 115.5. **Urban** (2005): 57.6%. **Sex distribution** (2008): male 48.40%; female 51.60%. **Age breakdown** (2005): under 15, 15.7%; 15–29, 20.4%; 30–44, 22.6%; 45–59, 19.2%; 60–74, 14.8%; 75–84, 5.9%; 85 and over, 1.4%. **Ethnic composition** (2000): Portuguese 91.9%; mixed race people from Angola, Mozambique, and Cape Verde 1.6%; Brazilian 1.4%; Marrano 1.2%; other European 1.2%; Han Chinese 0.9%; other 1.8%. **Religious affiliation** (2000): Christian 92.4%, of which Roman Catholic 87.4%, independent Christian 2.7%, Protestant 1.3%, other Christian 1.0%; nonreligious/atheist 6.5%; Buddhist 0.6%; other 0.5%. **Major cities** (2001): Lisbon 564,657 (urban agglomeration [2005] 2,761,000); Porto 263,131 (urban agglomeration [2005] 1,309,000); Braga 164,192; Coimbra 148,443; Funchal 103,961. **Location:** southwestern Europe, bordering Spain and the North Atlantic Ocean.

Vital statistics

Birth rate per 1,000 population (2008): 9.8 (world avg. 20.3); within marriage 63.8%. **Death rate** per 1,000 population (2008): 9.8 (world avg. 8.5). **Total fertility rate** (avg. births per childbearing woman; 2008): 1.37. **Life expectancy** at birth (2008): male 75.5 years; female 81.7 years.

National economy

Budget (2005). *Revenue:* €56,498,000,000 (tax revenue 56.2%, of which taxes of goods and services 33.7%, income tax 20.3%; social contributions 32.9%). *Expenditures:* €65,096,000,000 (social protection 35.6%; education 16.1%; health 15.9%; public order 4.5%; defense 3.2%). **Public debt** (2007): US$158,000,000,000. **Production** (metric tons except as noted). *Agriculture and fishing* (2007): grapes 1,050,000, tomatoes 1,000,000, corn (maize) 646,500, olives 375,000, cork (2008) 165,000; livestock (number of live animals) 3,549,000 sheep, 2,295,450 pigs, 1,407,270 cattle; fisheries production 260,275 (from aquaculture 3%). *Mining and quarrying* (2007): marble (2006) 837,000; kaolin (2006) 167,792; copper (metal content) 90,247; tungsten (metal content) 1,067. *Manufacturing* (value added in US$'000,000; 2003): food products 2,148; cement, tiles, and ceramics 1,611; fabricated metal products 1,536. *Energy production (consumption):* electricity (kW-hr; 2006) 49,041,000,000 (54,482,000,000); coal (metric tons; 2006) none (5,467,000); crude petroleum (barrels; 2006) none (97,108,000); petroleum products (metric tons; 2006) 12,036,000 (10,851,000); natural gas (cu m; 2006) none (4,339,000,000). **Population economically active** (2006): total 5,587,300; activity rate of total population 52.5% (participation rates: ages 15–64, 73.9%; female 46.6%; unemployed [2008] 7.6%). **Gross national income** (2008): US$218,405,000,000 (US$20,560 per capita). **Selected balance of payments data.** Receipts from (US$'000,000): tourism (2007) 10,162; remittances (2008) 4,057; foreign direct investment (FDI; 2005–07 avg.) 6,956. Disbursements for (US$'000,000): tourism (2007) 3,922; remittances (2008) 1,410; FDI (2005–07 avg.) 5,100.

Foreign trade

Imports (2006; c.i.f.): €53,162,000,000 (machinery and apparatus 18.7%; chemical products 10.9%; motor vehicles 10.3%; crude petroleum 9.5%; food products 9.3%). *Major import sources* (2007): Spain 29.5%; Germany 12.9%; France 8.4%; Italy 5.2%; Netherlands 4.5%. **Exports** (2006; f.o.b.): €34,561,000,000 (machinery and apparatus and electronics 18.6%; textiles, wearing apparel, and footwear 14.2%; motor vehicles and parts 12.5%; base and fabricated metals 7.4%; chemical products 6.5%; food products 4.5%). *Major export destinations* (2007): Spain 27.1%; Germany 12.9%; France 12.3%; UK 5.9%; US 4.8%.

Transport and communications

Transport. *Railroads* (2007): length 2,838 km; passenger-km 3,987,000,000; metric ton-km cargo 2,586,000,000. *Roads* (2005): total length 76,802 km (paved [2004] 86%). *Vehicles* (2006): passenger cars 5,234,477; trucks and buses 148,706. *Air transport* (2008): passenger-km 22,860,000,000; metric ton-km cargo 344,628,000. **Communications,** in total units (units per 1,000 persons). Telephone landlines (2008): 4,121,000 (386); cellular telephone subscribers (2008): 14,910,000 (1,396); personal computers (2007): 1,823,000 (172); total Internet users (2008): 4,451,000 (417); broadband Internet subscribers (2008): 1,692,000 (159).

Education and health

Educational attainment (2002). Percentage of population ages 25–64 having: no formal schooling through complete primary 67%; complete lower secondary 13%; complete upper secondary 11%; higher 9%. **Literacy** (2002): total population ages 15 and over literate 92.5%; males literate 95.2%; females literate 90.3%. **Health** (2007): physicians 37,904 (1 per 280 persons); hospital beds 36,178 (1 per 294 persons); infant mortality rate per 1,000 live births (2008) 3.3; undernourished population (2002–04) less than 2.5% of total population.

Military

Total active duty personnel (November 2008): 42,910 (army 62.2%, navy 21.2%, air force 16.6%); US troops (November 2008): 792. **Military expenditure as percentage of GDP** (2007): 1.5%; per capita expenditure US$319.

Background

Celtic peoples settled the Iberian Peninsula in the 1st millennium BC. They were conquered about 140 BC by the Romans, who ruled until the 5th century AD, when the area was invaded by Germanic tribes. A Muslim invasion in 711 left only the northern part of Portugal in Christian hands. In 1139 it became the kingdom of Portugal and expanded as it reconquered the Muslim-held sectors. The boundaries of modern continental Portugal were completed in 1270 under King Afonso III. In the 15th and 16th centuries, exploration took Portuguese navigators to Africa, India, Indonesia, China, the Middle East, and South America, where colonies were established. António de Oliveira Salazar ruled Portugal as a dictator in the mid-20th century; he died in office in 1970, and his successor was ousted in a coup in 1974. A new constitution was adopted in 1976 (revised 1982), and civilian rule resumed. The government returned Macau, its last overseas territory, to Chinese rule in 1999. Portugal was a charter member of NATO and is a member of the EU.

Recent Developments

The international economic crisis continued to impact the Portuguese economy in 2009. While GDP collapsed in the first two quarters of the year, dropping 3.7% compared with the same period in 2008, by late summer there were signs that the worst of the storm had passed, and for the year the drop was only 1.7%. It helped that inflation eased steadily, thanks to lower energy prices, and that the government unleashed a full slate of crisis-busting efforts—enough to increase the budget deficit to nearly 6.0% of GDP. This prompted the EU, which limits the budget gap to 3.0% of GDP, to subject Portugal to a largely symbolic excessive-deficit procedure, but it also led the legislature to pass a severe austerity budget in March 2010 in an attempt to bring the deficit down to acceptable levels. Alarmingly, the unemployment rate rose steadily to levels that had not been seen in more than a decade, hitting 10.1% by the end of 2009.

Internet resource: <www.ine.pt>.

Puerto Rico

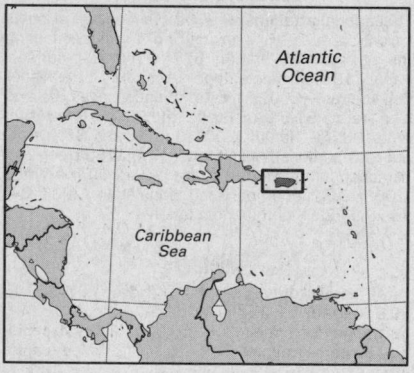

Official name: Estado Libre Asociado de Puerto Rico (Spanish); Commonwealth of Puerto Rico (English). **Political status:** self-governing commonwealth in association with the United States, with two legislative houses (Senate [27]; House of Representatives [51]). **Head of state:** US President Barack Obama (from 2009). **Head of government:** Governor Luis Fortuño (from 2009). **Capital:** San Juan. **Official languages:** Spanish; English. **Monetary unit:** 1 US dollar (US$) = 100 cents.

Demography

Area: 3,515 sq mi, 9,104 sq km. **Population** (2009): 3,966,000. **Density** (2009): persons per sq

mi 1,128, persons per sq km 435.6. **Urban** (2005): 97.6%. **Sex distribution** (2008): male 47.99%; female 52.01%. **Age breakdown** (2008): under 15, 20.3%; 15–29, 21.7%; 30–44, 20.3%; 45–59, 18.6%; 60–74, 13.1%; 75–84, 4.3%; 85 and over, 1.7%. **Ethnic composition** (2000): local white 72.1%; black 15.0%; mixed black/white 10.0%; US white 2.2%; other 0.7%. **Religious affiliation** (2000): Roman Catholic 74%; Protestant 13%; independent Christian 6%; Jehovah's Witness 2%; nonreligious/atheist 2%; Spiritist 1%; other 2%. **Major metropolitan areas** (2008): San Juan 2,608,375; Aguadilla 339,523; Ponce 262,943; San Germán 147,242; Yauco 124,566. **Location:** island in the Caribbean Sea, east of Cuba.

Vital statistics

Birth rate per 1,000 population (2008): 12.1 (world avg. 20.3). **Death rate** per 1,000 population (2008): 7.3 (world avg. 8.5). **Total fertility rate** (avg. births per childbearing woman; 2008): 1.65. **Life expectancy** at birth (2008): male 74.8 years; female 82.3 years.

National economy

Budget. *Revenue* (2006–07): US$14,988,600,-000 (income tax 42.6%; federal grants 34.5%; excise taxes 9.8%; charges for services 5.1%). *Expenditures:* US$17,158,000,000 (education 25.6%; public housing and welfare 17.8%; general government services 14.8%; health 11.4%; public safety 10.9%; interest on debt 4.7%). **Public debt** (June 2009): US$61,790,000,000. **Production** (in metric tons except as noted). *Agriculture and fishing* (2007): plantains 80,000; bananas 53,500; oranges 19,500; coffee 8,100; livestock (number of live animals) 380,000 cattle, 50,000 pigs, 13,000,000 chickens; fisheries production 1,719 (from aquaculture 3%). *Mining and quarrying* (2006): crushed stone 8,790,000. *Manufacturing* (value added in US$'000,000; 2004): chemical products (nearly all drugs and medicine) 20,276; nonelectrical machinery 3,271; professional and scientific equipment 3,211. *Energy production (consumption):* electricity (kW-hr; 2006) 25,800,000,000 (25,800,-000,000); coal, none (1,499,000); crude petroleum (barrels; 2008) none ([2005] 70,800,000); natural gas (cu m; 2007) none (736,000,000). **Gross national income** (2008): US$60,800,-000,000 (US$15,399 per capita). **Population economically active** (2005): total 1,410,000; activity rate of total population 36.0% (participation rates: ages 16–64, 56.1%; female 43.7%; unemployed [October 2008–September 2009] 14.4%). **Selected balance of payments data.** Receipts from (US$'000,000): tourism (2008) 3,450; foreign direct investment (2005–07 avg.) 27. Disbursements for (US$'000,000): tourism (2007) 1,192.

Foreign trade

Imports (2007–08): US$44,928,000,000 (pharmaceutical products 33.5%; refined petroleum products

---

1 metric ton = about 1.1 short tons;　1 kilometer = 0.6 mi (statute);　1 metric ton-km cargo = about 0.68 short ton-mi cargo;　c.i.f.: cost, insurance, and freight;　f.o.b.: free on board

and coal 11.5%; base chemical products 7.3%; computers and electronics 6.6%; food products 5.8%). *Major import sources* (2006–07): US 50.1%; Ireland 21.0%; Japan 3.7%. **Exports** (2007–08): US$63,954,000,000 (pharmaceuticals and medicine 66.0%; food products 7.0%; computers and electronics 6.4%). *Major export destinations* (2006–07): US 77.2%; Netherlands 4.6%; Germany 3.4%.

Transport and communications

Transport. *Railroads:* none. *Roads* (2008): total length 26,676 km (paved 99%). *Vehicles* (2007): passenger cars 2,421,055; trucks and buses 110,144. *Air transport* (2006): passenger arrivals and departures 11,450,700; cargo loaded and unloaded 352,396 metric tons. **Communications**, in total units (units per 1,000 persons). Telephone landlines (2008): 1,038,000 (263); cellular telephone subscribers (2005): 3,354,000 (858); total Internet users (2008): 1,000,000 (253); broadband Internet subscribers (2006): 118,000 (30).

Education and health

Educational attainment (2000). Percentage of population ages 25 and over having: no formal schooling to lower secondary education 25.4%; some upper secondary to some higher 56.3%; undergraduate or graduate degree 18.3%. **Literacy** (2002): total population ages 15 and over literate 94.1%. **Health:** physicians (2001) 7,623 (1 per 504 persons); hospital beds (2002) 12,351 (1 per 312 persons); infant mortality rate per 1,000 live births (2008) 8.3; undernourished population, n.a.

Military

Total active duty US personnel (December 2008): 191.

Background

Puerto Rico was inhabited by Arawak Indians when it was settled by the Spanish in the early 16th century. It remained largely undeveloped economically until the late 18th century. After 1830 it gradually developed a plantation economy based on the export crops of sugarcane, coffee, and tobacco. The independence movement began in the late 19th century, and Spain ceded the island to the US in 1898, after the Spanish-American War. In 1917 Puerto Ricans were granted US citizenship, and in 1952 the island became a commonwealth with autonomy in internal affairs. The question of Puerto Rican statehood has been a political issue, with commonwealth status approved by voters in 1967, 1993, and 1998.

Recent Developments

The Puerto Rican government offered strong support for the development of renewable energy when in January 2009 it canceled a US$74 million natural gas pipeline being built for the state-owned Puerto Rico Electric Power Authority.

Internet resource: <www.gotopuertorico.com>.

Qatar

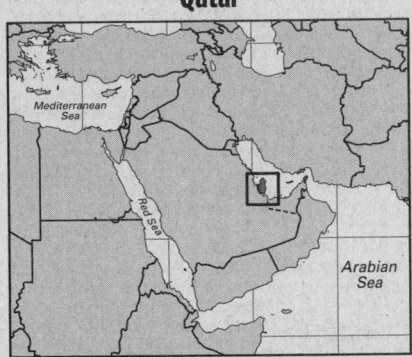

Official name: Dawlat Qatar (State of Qatar). **Form of government:** constitutional emirate with one advisory body (Advisory Council [35]). **Head of state and government:** Emir Sheikh Hamad ibn Khalifah al-Thani (from 1995), assisted by Prime Minister Sheikh Hamad ibn Jassim ibn Jabr al-Thani (from 2007). **Capital:** Doha. **Official language:** Arabic. **Official religion:** Islam. **Monetary unit:** 1 Qatari riyal (QR) = 100 dirhams; valuation (1 Jul 2010) US$1 = QR 3.64.

Demography

Area: 4,184 sq mi, 10,836 sq km. **Population** (2009): 1,661,000. **Density** (2009): persons per sq mi 397.0, persons per sq km 153.3. **Urban** (2007): 95.4%. **Sex distribution** (2007): male 75.60%; female 24.40%. **Age breakdown** (2005): under 15, 21.8%; 15–29, 25.5%; 30–44, 33.7%; 45–59, 16.3%; 60–74, 2.4%; 75 and over, 0.3%. **Ethnic composition** (2000): Arab 52.5%, of which Palestinian 13.4%, Qatari 13.3%, Lebanese 10.4%, Syrian 9.4%; Persian 16.5%; Indo-Pakistani 15.2%; black African 9.5%; other 6.3%. **Religious affiliation** (2000): Muslim 83%, of which Sunni 73%, Shi'i 10%; Christian 10%, of which Roman Catholic 6%; Hindu 3%; Buddhist 2%; nonreligious 2%. **Major cities** (2004): Al-Dawhah (Doha) 339,847; Al-Rayyan 258,193; Al-Wakrah 26,993; Umm Salal Muhammad 25,413; Al-Khawr 18,036. **Location:** the Middle East, bordering the Persian Gulf and Saudi Arabia.

Vital statistics

Birth rate per 1,000 population (2008): 11.9 (world avg. 20.3). **Death rate** per 1,000 population (2008): 1.3 (world avg. 8.5). **Total fertility rate** (avg. births per childbearing woman; 2005): 2.80. **Life expectancy** at birth (2005): male 74.4 years; female 75.8 years.

National economy

Budget (2007–08). *Revenue:* QR 117,790,000,000 (petroleum and natural gas revenue 60.1%; investment income 25.8%; corporate taxes 7.6%). *Expenditures:* QR 84,727,000,000 (public utilities 11.4%; defense 7.5%; communications 5.6%; health 5.2%; education 5.1%; roads 3.2%; interest payments 2.2%). **Production** (metric tons except as noted). *Agriculture and fishing* (2007): dates 21,000, tomatoes 5,400, barley 5,000; livestock (number of live animals) 160,000 goats, 120,000 sheep, 14,000 camels; fisheries production 15,226 (from aquaculture, negligible). *Mining and quarrying* (2007): limestone 1,100,000; gypsum, sand and gravel, and clay are also produced. *Manufacturing* (value added in QR '000,000; 2005): refined petroleum products 4,502; chemical products 2,168; base metals 1,959. *Energy production (consumption):* electricity (kW-hr; 2006) 15,325,000,000 (15,325,000,000); crude petroleum (barrels; 2007) 308,600,000 ([2006] 41,797,000); petroleum products (metric tons; 2006) 4,723,000 (2,059,000); natural gas (cu m; 2006) 49,500,000,000 (19,092,000,000). **Population economically active** (2004): total 444,133; activity rate of total population 59.7% (participation rates: ages 15 and over, 77.1%; female 15.1%; unemployed 1.5%). **Gross national income** (2008): US$113,984,000,000 (US$88,990 per capita). **Selected balance of payments data.** Receipts from (US$'000,000): tourism (2006) 874; foreign direct investment (FDI; 2005–07 avg.) 865. Disbursements for (US$'000,000): tourism (2006) 3,751; remittances (2006–07) 5,000; FDI (2005–07 avg.) 1,914.

Foreign trade

Imports (2006; c.i.f.): US$16,440,000,000 (nonelectrical machinery and equipment 23.5%; iron and steel 13.7%; electrical machinery and apparatus [including parts] 8.6%; motor vehicles 6.8%; chemical products 5.1%; fabricated metal products 4.9%). *Major import sources:* Japan 12.0%; US 9.9%; Germany 9.3%; Italy 9.3%; UAE 6.0%. **Exports** (2006; f.o.b.): US$34,051,000,000 (crude petroleum 46.9%; liquefied natural gas 34.8%; refined petroleum products 4.6%; liquefied propane and butane 3.4%; polyethylene 3.3%; urea 2.0%). *Major export destinations:* Japan 41.5%; South Korea 13.9%; Singapore 9.5%; India 4.9%; UAE 4.3%.

Transport and communications

Transport. *Railroads:* none. *Roads* (2006): total length 7,790 km. *Vehicles* (2004): passenger cars 265,609; trucks and buses 114,115. *Air transport* (2008): passenger-km 36,204,000,000; metric ton-km cargo 1,639,000,000. **Communications**, in total units (units per 1,000 persons). Telephone landlines (2008): 263,000 (206); cellular telephone subscribers (2008): 1,683,000 (1,314); personal computers (2005): 145,000 (182); total Internet users (2008): 436,000 (340); broadband Internet subscribers (2008): 103,000 (81).

Education and health

Educational attainment (2004). Percentage of population ages 10 and over having: no formal education/unknown 34.9%, of which illiterate 10.2%; primary 13.0%; preparatory (lower secondary) 16.2%; secondary 20.0%; postsecondary 15.9%. **Literacy** (2006): total population ages 15 and over literate 89.0%; males literate 89.1%; females literate 88.6%. **Health** (2007): physicians (public sector only) 1,775

(1 per 691 persons); hospital beds (public sector only) 1,651 (1 per 743 persons); infant mortality rate per 1,000 live births (2008) 7.7.

Military

Total active duty personnel (November 2008): 11,800 (army 72.0%, navy 15.3%, air force 12.7%); US troops (November 2008): 444. **Military expenditure as percentage of GDP** (2007): 1.5%; per capita expenditure US$889.

Background

Qatar was partly controlled by Bahrain in the 18th and 19th centuries and was part of the Ottoman Empire until World War I. In 1916 it became a British protectorate. Oil was discovered in 1939, and the country rapidly modernized. Qatar declared independence in 1971, when the British protectorate ended. In 1991 it served as a base for air strikes against Iraq in the Persian Gulf War.

Recent Developments

In 2009 Qatar continued to have one of the world's fastest-growing economies and one of its richest, as measured by income per capita. The country's material well-being was buttressed by the growth of the government's sovereign wealth fund and ongoing fiscal surpluses. In addition, Qatar remained the world leader in natural gas exports, which for the first time exceeded its foreign sales of petroleum. Plans for the construction of the strategic Qatar-Bahrain Friendship Bridge continued throughout 2009.

Internet resource: <www.qsa.gov.qa>.

Romania

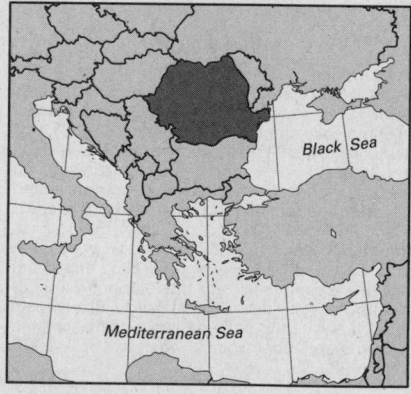

Official name: Romania. **Form of government:** unitary republic with two legislative houses (Senate [137]; Chamber of Deputies [334]). **Head of state:** President Traian Basescu (from 2004). **Head of government:** Prime Minister Emil Boc (from 2008). **Capi-**

---

1 metric ton = about 1.1 short tons; 1 kilometer = 0.6 mi (statute); 1 metric ton-km cargo = about 0.68 short ton-mi cargo; c.i.f.: cost, insurance, and freight; f.o.b.: free on board

tal: Bucharest. **Official language:** Romanian. **Official religion:** none. **Monetary unit:** 1 Romanian (new) leu (RON; plural lei) = 100 bani; valuation (1 Jul 2010) US$1 = 3.54 (new) lei.

Demography

Area: 92,043 sq mi, 238,391 sq km. **Population** (2009): 21,481,000. **Density** (2009): persons per sq mi 233.4, persons per sq km 90.1. **Urban** (2008): 55.1%. **Sex distribution** (2008): male 48.71%; female 51.29%. **Age breakdown** (2008): under 15, 15.2%; 15–29, 22.0%; 30–44, 23.3%; 45–59, 19.8%; 60–74, 13.5%; 75–84, 5.2%; 85 and over, 1.0%. **Ethnic composition** (2002): Romanian 89.5%; Hungarian 6.6%; Rom (Gypsy) 2.5%; Ukrainian 0.3%; German 0.3%; other 0.8%. **Religious affiliation** (2002): Romanian Orthodox 86.7%; Protestant 6.3%; Roman Catholic 4.7%; Greek Catholic 0.9%; Muslim 0.3%; other 1.1%. **Major cities** (2008): Bucharest 1,944,367; Timisoara 311,586; Iasi 308,843; Cluj-Napoca 306,474; Constanta 302,171. **Location:** southeastern Europe, bordering Ukraine, Moldova, the Black Sea, Bulgaria, Serbia, and Hungary.

Vital statistics

Birth rate per 1,000 population (2008): 10.3 (world avg. 20.3); within marriage 72.6%. **Death rate** per 1,000 population (2008): 11.8 (world avg. 8.5). **Total fertility rate** (avg. births per childbearing woman; 2008): 1.35. **Life expectancy** at birth (2008): male 69.5 years; female 76.7 years.

National economy

Budget (in US$'000,000; 2009). *Revenue:* 50,780. *Expenditures:* 61,510. **Public debt** (external, outstanding; June 2009): US$13,768,100,000. **Population economically active** (2008): total 9,944,700; activity rate 46.2% (participation rates: ages 15–64, 62.9%; female 44.4%; unemployed [September 2008–August 2009] 5.2%). **Production** (metric tons except as noted). *Agriculture and fishing* (2008): corn (maize) 7,849,000, wheat 7,181,000, potatoes 3,649,000, sunflower seeds 1,170,000; livestock (number of live animals) 8,882,000 sheep, 6,174,000 pigs, 2,684,000 cattle; fisheries production (2007) 16,496 (from aquaculture 63%). *Mining and quarrying* (2006; metal content of mine output): copper 12,200; zinc 9,574; lead 7,500. *Manufacturing* (value added in US$'000,000; 2006): food products 1,333; wearing apparel 1,257; transportation equipment 978. *Energy production (consumption):* electricity (kW-hr; 2008–09) 61,415,000,000 ([2006] 58,424,000,000); coal (metric tons; 2008–09) 2,356,000 ([2006] 2,796,000); lignite (metric tons; 2008–09) 32,251,000 (31,941,000); crude petroleum (barrels; 2008–09) 33,250,000 ([2006] 106,585,200); petroleum products (metric tons; 2008–09) 12,985,000 ([2006] 8,904,000); natural gas (cu m; 2008–09) 9,594,400,000 ([2008] 16,920,000,000). **Gross national income** (2008): US$170,560,000,000 (US$7,930 per capita). **Selected balance of payments data.** Receipts from (US$'000,000): tourism (2007) 1,467; remittances (2008) 9,395; foreign direct investment (FDI; 2005–07 avg.) 9,208. Disbursements for (US$'000,000): tourism (2007) 1,535; remittances (2008) 436; FDI (2005–07 avg.) 110.

Foreign trade

Imports (2006; c.i.f. in commodities and f.o.b. in trading partners): US$51,106,000,000 (mineral fuels 13.5%, of which crude petroleum 7.7%; nonelectrical machinery and equipment 11.1%; motor vehicles 10.6%; chemical products 10.6%; base and fabricated metals 9.7%; electrical machinery and electronics 7.5%). *Major import sources:* Germany 15.2%; Italy 14.6%; Russia 7.9%; France 6.5%; Turkey 5.0%. **Exports** (2006): US$32,336,000,000 (wearing apparel and accessories 13.7%; base and fabricated metals 12.6%; refined petroleum products 8.9%; nonelectrical machinery and equipment 8.0%; motor vehicles and parts 6.2%; insulated wire and fiber-optic cables 6.0%; footwear 5.3%). *Major export destinations:* Italy 18.1%; Germany 15.7%; Turkey 7.7%; France 7.5%; Hungary 4.9%.

Transport and communications

Transport. *Railroads* (2008): route length 10,788 km; passenger-km 6,958,000; metric ton-km cargo 15,000,000,000. *Roads* (2004; public roads only): length 79,454 km (paved 26%). *Vehicles* (2008): cars 4,027,000; trucks and buses 687,000. *Air transport* (2008–09): passenger-km 3,835,000,000; metric ton-km cargo 5,466,000,000. **Communications,** in total units (units per 1,000 persons). Telephone landlines (2008): 5,036,000 (236); cellular telephone subscribers (2008): 24,467,000 (1,145); personal computers (2007): 4,137,000 (192); total Internet users (2008): 6,132,000 (287); broadband Internet subscribers (2008): 2,510,000 (118).

Education and health

Educational attainment (2002). Percentage of population ages 10 and over having: no formal schooling 5.5%; primary education 20.1%; lower secondary 27.6%; upper secondary/vocational 36.7%; higher vocational 3.0%; university 7.1%. **Literacy** (2007): total population ages 15 and over literate 97.6%; males literate 98.3%; females literate 96.9%. **Health** (2008): physicians 50,238 (1 per 428 persons); hospital beds 137,984 (1 per 156 persons); infant mortality rate per 1,000 live births 11.0; undernourished population (2002–04) less than 2.5% of total population.

Military

Total active duty personnel (November 2008): 73,200 (army 58.8%, navy 8.9%, air force 13.9%, joint staff 18.4%). **Military expenditure as percentage of GDP** (2007): 1.9%; per capita expenditure US$146.

Background

Romania was formed in 1862 by the unification of the principalities Moldavia and Walachia, which had once been part of the ancient country of Dacia. During World War I, Romania sided with the Allies and doubled its territory in 1918 with the addition of Transylvania, Bukovina, and Bessarabia. Allied with Germany in World War II, it was occupied by Soviet troops in 1944 and became a satellite country of the USSR in 1948. During the 1960s Romania's foreign policy was frequently independent of the Soviet Union's. The communist regime of Nicolae Ceausescu was overthrown in 1989, and free elections were held in

1990. In 2004 it joined NATO, and in 2007 it became a member of the EU.

Recent Developments

Romania slid into a deep recession in 2009, its economy contracting by 7.1%, with the construction sector enduring the biggest drop. The unemployment rate in January 2010 had risen to 8.1%, a rise of 3.2% compared with January 2009. Facing an impending revenue crisis, Prime Minister Emil Boc negotiated a US$27 billion loan with the IMF and other lenders. The aid, which was approved in May, was conditional on Romania's making deep cuts in the public sector, which employed one-third of the labor force. The IMF also demanded that steps be taken to increase the efficiency of the bureaucracy. Unsatisfied with the pace of reform, the IMF withheld payment of the third tranche of the loan until February 2010.

Internet resource: <www.insse.ro>.

Russia

Official name: Rossiyskaya Federatsiya (Russian Federation). **Form of government:** federal multiparty republic with two legislative houses (Federation Council [178]; State Duma [450]). **Head of state:** President Dmitry Medvedev (from 2008). **Head of government:** Prime Minister Vladimir Putin (from 2008). **Capital:** Moscow. **Official language:** Russian. **Official religion:** none. **Monetary unit:** 1 ruble (RUB) = 100 kopecks; valuation (1 Jul 2010) market rate, US$1 = RUB 31.16.

Demography

Area: 6,592,800 sq mi, 17,075,400 sq km. **Population (2009):** 141,852,000. **Density (2009):** persons per sq mi 21.5, persons per sq km 8.3. **Urban (2006):** 73.0%. **Sex distribution (2007):** male 46.22%; female 53.78%. **Age breakdown (2007):** under 15, 14.6%; 15–29, 23.9%; 30–44, 21.3%; 45–59, 22.8%; 60–74, 11.9%; 75–84, 4.7%; 85 and over, 0.8%. **Ethnic composition (2002):** Russian 79.82%; Tatar 3.83%; Ukrainian 2.03%; Bashkir 1.15%; Chuvash 1.13%; Chechen 0.94%; Armenian 0.78%; Mordvin 0.58%; Belarusian 0.56%; Avar 0.52%; Kazakh 0.45%; Udmurt 0.44%; Azerbaijani 0.43%;

Mari 0.42%; German 0.41%; Kabardinian 0.36%; Ossetian 0.35%; Dargin 0.35%; Buryat 0.31%; Sakha 0.31%; other 4.83%. **Religious affiliation (2005):** Christian 58.4%, of which Russian Orthodox 53.1%, Roman Catholic 1.0%, Ukrainian Orthodox 0.9%, Protestant 0.9%; Muslim 8.2%; traditional beliefs 0.8%; Jewish 0.6%; nonreligious 25.8%; atheist 5.0%; other 1.2%. **Major cities (2007):** Moscow 10,470,318; St. Petersburg 4,568,047; Novosibirsk 1,390,513; Yekaterinburg 1,322,954; Nizhny Novgorod 1,274,708; Samara 1,135,422; Omsk 1,131,100; Kazan 1,120,238; Chelyabinsk 1,092,495; Rostov-na-Donu 1,048,714; Ufa 1,021,458. **Location:** eastern Europe and northern Asia, bordering the Arctic Ocean, the North Pacific Ocean, North Korea, China, Mongolia, Kazakhstan, the Caspian Sea, Azerbaijan, Georgia, the Black Sea, Ukraine, Belarus, Latvia, Estonia, Finland, and Norway; the exclave of Kaliningrad on the Baltic Sea borders Lithuania and Poland. **Migration (2006):** immigrants 186,380; emigrants 54,061. **Refugees (2007):** 159,500, of which from Afghanistan 84,500, Georgia 45,000.

Vital statistics

Birth rate per 1,000 population (2008): 12.1 (world avg. 20.3); within marriage 73.1%. **Death rate** per 1,000 population (2008): 14.7 (world avg. 8.5). **Total fertility rate** (avg. births per childbearing woman; 2008): 1.51. **Life expectancy** at birth (2008): male 61.7 years; female 74.2 years.

Social indicators

Educational attainment (2002). Percentage of population ages 15 and over having: no formal schooling 2.1%; primary education 7.7%; some secondary 18.1%; complete secondary/basic vocational 53.0%; incomplete higher 3.1%; complete higher 16.0%, of which advanced degrees 0.3%. **Quality of working life (2006).** Average workweek (2004): 40 hours. Annual rate per 100,000 workers of: injury or accident 290; industrial illness 16.0; death 11.8. Average working days lost to labor strikes per 1,000 employees 0.2. **Social participation.** Trade union membership in total workforce (2003) 45%. **Social deviance.** Offense rate per 100,000 population (2007) for: murder and attempted murder 15.6; rape and attempted rape 4.9; serious injury 33.3; burglary 207.6; drug abuse 162.6; robbery 31.9; theft 1,102.7. Incidence per 100,000 population of: suicide (2007) 29.0.

National economy

Public debt (external, outstanding; March 2008): US$35,200,000,000. **Budget (2007).** *Revenue:* RUB 7,443,900,000,000 (VAT 30.0%; taxes on natural resources 15.0%; corporate taxes 8.5%; income tax 5.2%). *Expenditures:* RUB 6,531,400,000,000 (transfers 29.7%; social and cultural services 14.1%; defense 12.8%; national economy 11.2%; public security 10.3%). **Gross national income (2008):** US$1,364,500,000,000 (US$9,620 per capita). **Production** (metric tons except as noted). *Agriculture and fishing* (2007): wheat 49,389,860, potatoes 36,784,200, sugar beets 29,000,000, barley 15,663,110 (world rank: 1), sunflower seeds

---

1 metric ton = about 1.1 short tons;   1 kilometer = 0.6 mi (statute);   1 metric ton-km cargo = about 0.68 short ton-mi cargo;   c.i.f.: cost, insurance, and freight;   f.o.b.: free on board

5,656,500 (world rank: 1), oats 5,407,000 (world rank: 1), cabbages 4,054,000, corn (maize) 3,953,240, rye 3,910,290 (world rank: 1), tomatoes 2,393,000, apples 2,211,000, carrots and turnips 1,900,000, dry onions 1,770,000, currants 600,000 (world rank: 1), raspberries (2005) 175,000 (world rank: 1), sour cherries 153,000 (world rank: 1); livestock (number of live animals) 21,466,000 cattle, 17,508,000 sheep, 15,793,000 pigs, camels (2008) 6,356; fisheries production 3,559,717 (from aquaculture 3%); aquatic plants production 28,594 (from aquaculture 1%). *Mining and quarrying* (2006): nickel (metal content) 320,000 (world rank: 1); platinum-group metals 138,300 (world rank: 2), of which palladium 96,800 (world rank: 1); mica 100,000 (world rank: 1); gem diamonds 23,400,000 carats (world rank: 2); vanadium (metal content) 15,100 (world rank: 3); industrial diamonds 15,000,000 carats (world rank: 3); iron ore (metal content) 59,100,000 (world rank: 5); cobalt (metal content) 5,100 (world rank: 5); copper ore (metal content) 725,000 (world rank: 6); molybdenum (metal content) 3,100 (world rank: 6); gold 159,340 kg (world rank: 7). *Manufacturing* (value added in US$'000,000; 2005): refined petroleum products 28,950; food products 12,942; iron and steel 11,904; nonferrous base metals 9,981; base chemical products 8,524; cement, bricks, and ceramics 4,892; beverages 4,532; general purpose machinery 4,075; motor vehicles 3,423; fabricated metal products 2,831; special purpose machinery 2,802; rubber products 2,313; paints, soaps, and pharmaceuticals 2,155; professional and scientific equipment 2,151; paper products 1,982; publishing 1,733. *Energy production (consumption):* electricity (kW-hr; 2007) 1,015,872,000,000 ([2006] 979,973,000,000); coal (metric tons; 2007) 242,100,000 ([2006] 145,771,000); lignite (metric tons; 2007) 72,200,000 ([2006] 73,929,000); crude petroleum (barrels; 2007) 3,568,000,000 ([2006] 1,523,000,000); petroleum products (metric tons; 2006) 197,412,000 (101,794,000); natural gas (cu m; 2007) 654,000,000,000 ([2006] 362,393,000,000). **Population economically active** (2006): total 74,146,000; activity rate of total population 52.0% (participation rates: ages 15–64, 73.0%; female 49.4%; unemployed [October 2007] 6.1%). **Selected balance of payments data.** Receipts from (US$'000,000): tourism (2007) 9,607; remittances (2008) 6,033; foreign direct investment (FDI; 2005–07 avg.) 32,583. Disbursements for (US$'000,000): tourism (2007) 22,258; remittances (2008) 26,145; FDI (2005–07 avg.) 27,190.

Foreign trade

Imports (2006; c.i.f.): US$137,728,000,000 (machinery and apparatus 27.6%, of which telecommunications equipment and television receivers 6.3%, general industrial machinery 6.2%, specialized machinery 5.4%, electrical machinery and electronics 5.3%; motor vehicles and parts 13.4%; chemical products 12.2%, of which pharmaceuticals and medicine 4.6%; food products 11.9%; base and fabricated metals 6.9%, of which iron and steel 3.6%). *Major import sources:* Germany 13.4%; China 9.4%; Ukraine 6.7%; Japan 5.7%; Belarus 5.0%; South Korea 4.9%; US 4.7%; France 4.3%; Italy 4.0%; Finland 2.9%. **Exports** (2006; f.o.b.): US$301,551,000,000 (crude petroleum 32.1%; refined petroleum products 14.7%;

natural gas 14.2%; nonferrous base metals 6.2%, of which aluminum 2.5%, nickel 2.0%, copper 1.5%; iron and steel 5.7%; chemical products 3.8%, of which fertilizers 1.4%; machinery and apparatus 2.4%; coal and coke 1.5%; food products 1.2%). *Major export destinations:* Netherlands 11.9%; Italy 8.3%; Germany 8.1%; China 5.2%; Ukraine 5.0%; Turkey 4.7%; Belarus 4.3%; Switzerland 4.0%; Poland 3.8%; UK 3.4%.

Transport and communications

Transport. *Railroads* (2007): length (2007) 85,000 km; passenger-km 174,100,000,000; metric ton-km cargo 2,090,000,000,000. *Roads* (2006): total length 854,000 km (paved 85%). *Vehicles* (2007): passenger cars 29,249,000; trucks and buses 5,591,000. *Air transport* (2006–07): passenger-km 97,510,000,000; metric ton-km cargo 2,980,000,000. **Communications,** in total units (units per 1,000 persons). Telephone landlines (2008): 44,200,000 (313); cellular telephone subscribers (2008): 187,500,000 (1,326); personal computers (2005): 17,400,000 (121); total Internet users (2008): 45,400,000 (321); broadband Internet subscribers (2008): 9,280,000 (66).

Education and health

Health (2007): physicians 707,000 (1 per 201 persons); hospital beds 1,522,000 (1 per 93 persons); infant mortality rate per 1,000 live births (2008) 8.5; undernourished population (2002–04) 3,900,000 (3% of total population based on the consumption of a minimum daily requirement of 1,980 calories).

Military

Total active duty personnel (November 2008): 1,027,000 (army 38.5%, navy 13.8%, air force 15.6%, strategic deterrent forces 7.8%, command and support 24.3%); troops abroad 31,713, of which in Ukraine 13,300, in Georgia 7,600, in Tajikistan 5,500, in Armenia 3,214 (an additional 449,000 personnel in paramilitary forces include railway troops, special construction troops, federal border guards, interior troops, and other federal guard units). **Military expenditure as percentage of GDP** (2007): 2.5%; per capita expenditure US$256.

Background

The region between the Dniester and Volga rivers was inhabited from ancient times by various peoples, including the Slavs. The area was overrun from the 8th century BC to the 6th century AD by successive nomadic peoples, including the Sythians, Sarmatians, Goths, Huns, and Avars. Kievan Rus, a confederation of principalities ruled from Kiev, emerged in the 10th century. It lost supremacy in the 11th and 12th centuries to independent principalities, including Novgorod and Vladimir. Novgorod ascended in the north and was the only Russian principality to escape the domination of the Mongol Golden Horde in the 13th century. In the 14th–15th centuries, the princes of Moscow gradually overthrew the Mongols under Ivan IV Russia began to expand. The Romanov dynasty arose in 1613. Expansion continued under Peter I (the Great) and Catherine II (the Great). The area was invaded by Napoleon in 1812; after his defeat, Russia received most of the grand duchy of Warsaw (1815). Russia annexed Georgia, Armenia, and other Caucasian territories in the 19th century. The Russian southward advance against the Ottoman Empire was of key importance to Europe. Russia was defeated in the Crimean War. It sold Alaska to the US in 1867. Russia's defeat in the Russo-Japanese War led to an unsuccessful uprising in 1905. In World War I it fought against the Central Powers.

The Russian Revolution that overthrew the czarist regime in 1917 marked the beginning of a government of soviets (councils). The Bolsheviks brought the main part of the former empire under communist control and organized it as the Russian Soviet Federated Socialist Republic (RSFSR; coextensive with present-day Russia). The RSFSR joined other soviet republics in 1922 to form the Union of Soviet Socialist Republics (USSR). Although it fought with the Allies in World War II, after the war tensions with the West led to the decades-long Cold War. Upon the dissolution of the USSR in 1991, the RSFSR was renamed Russia and became the leading member of the Commonwealth of Independent States. It adopted a new constitution in 1993. During the 1990s and into the 21st century, it struggled on several fronts, beset with economic difficulties, political corruption, and independence movements.

Recent Developments

Russia was severely hit by the global financial crisis of 2009; falling oil prices and the general economic slowdown both took their toll. In the first half of the year, GDP declined by more than 10%. Since this downturn followed a decade of rapid economic growth fueled by high energy prices, Russia entered the crisis with a strong budget, balance of payments, and reserves. Policy makers were thus able to cover a budget deficit on the order of 8% of GDP, mainly by drawing down the reserve fund that had been built up from oil and gas revenues in preceding years. The impact of the recession was exacerbated, however, by Russia's structural vulnerabilities: a dependence on oil, gas, and metals; a narrow industrial base; and a limited small- and medium-sized business sector. It appeared that many investors had reacted to the crisis by reducing their investment activity in Russia because they perceived underlying weaknesses in its economic institutions—in particular, the weak rule of law and the poor protection of property rights. The value of exports dropped by almost 36% in 2009, and the unemployment rate rose from less than 6% in the summer of 2008 to more than 8% in December 2009.

The main focus of attention throughout the year was on efforts to improve the strained relations between Russia and the US. When US Pres. Barack Obama visited Moscow in July 2009, he and Russian Pres. Dmitry Medvedev signed an agreement by which Moscow would allow the transit of supplies across Russian territory to US troops in Afghanistan. Russia also responded to Obama's September decision to halt plans to establish ballistic missile defenses in Poland and the Czech Republic by announcing that Moscow would suspend its threat to deploy short-range nuclear missiles to its Kaliningrad exclave. After Obama and Medvedev met in London in April 2009, the two countries began serious negotiations over renewing the Strategic Arms Reduction Talks I (START I) treaty. In April 2010 the two leaders signed a historic New START arms-control pact that would limit the number of deployed warheads from each country to 1,550.

Internet resource: <www.gks.ru>.

Rwanda

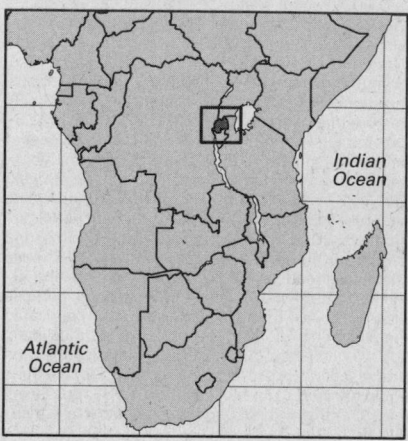

Official name: Republika y'u Rwanda (Rwanda); République Rwandaise (French); Republic of Rwanda (English). **Form of government:** multiparty republic with two legislative houses (Senate [26]; Chamber of Deputies [80]). **Head of state and government:** President Maj. Gen. Paul Kagame (from 2000), assisted by Prime Minister Bernard Makuza (from 2000). **Capital:** Kigali. **Official languages:** Rwanda; French; English. **Official religion:** none. **Monetary unit:** 1 Rwandan franc (RF); valuation (1 Jul 2010) US$1 = RF 579.26.

Demography

Area: 10,185 sq mi, 26,379 sq km. **Population** (2009): 9,998,000. **Density** (2009; based on area excluding Rwandan part of Lake Kivu): persons per sq mi 1,023, persons per sq km 395.0. **Urban** (2007): 17.6%. **Sex distribution** (2008): male 49.75%; female 50.25%. **Age breakdown** (2008): under 15, 42.4%; 15–29, 29.6%; 30–44, 16.0%; 45–59, 8.2%; 60–74, 3.0%; 75–84, 0.7%; 85 and over, 0.1%. **Ethnic composition** (2002): Hutu 85%; Tutsi 14%; Twa 1%. **Religious affiliation** (2005): Roman Catholic 44%; Protestant 25%; Muslim 13%; other 18%. **Major cities** (2002): Kigali (urban agglomeration; 2007) 860,000; Gitarama 84,669; Butare 77,449; Ruhengeri 71,511; Gisenyi 67,766. **Location:** east-central Africa, bordering Uganda, Tanzania, Burundi, and the Democratic Republic of the Congo.

Vital statistics

Birth rate per 1,000 population (2008): 38.9 (world avg. 20.3). **Death rate** per 1,000 population (2008): 11.1 (world avg. 8.5). **Total fertility rate** (avg. births per childbearing woman; 2008): 5.25. **Life expectancy** at birth (2008): male 54.6 years; female 57.1 years.

National economy

Budget (2008). *Revenue:* RF 660,800,000,000 (grants 42.3%; taxes on goods and services 24.4%; income tax 18.6%; nontax revenue 7.9%; import and export duties 6.6%). *Expenditures:* RF 649,700,000,000 (current expenditures 56.7%; capital expenditures 41.2%; net lending 2.1%). **Public debt** (external, outstanding; 2008): US$656,800,000. **Production** (metric tons except as noted). *Agriculture and fishing* (2007): plantains 2,580,000, potatoes 1,200,000, sweet potatoes 940,000, tea 19,000, coffee 18,900, pyrethrum 15; livestock (number of live animals) 1,300,000 goats, 950,000 cattle, 470,000 sheep; fisheries production 13,088 (from aquaculture 31%). *Mining and quarrying* (2007): cassiterite (tin content) 3,100; tungsten (wolframite content) 1,534; niobium 80,000 kg; tantalum 50,000 kg. *Manufacturing* (value added in RF '000,000; 2008): beverages and tobacco products 24,300; food products 16,200; furniture and unspecified products 13,200. *Energy production (consumption):* electricity (kW-hr; 2008) 194,000,000 ([2006] 220,000,000); petroleum products (metric tons; 2006) none (190,000); natural gas (cu m; 2007) none ([2006] 615,000). **Population economically active** (2006): total 4,325,000; activity rate of total population 45.7% (participation rates: ages 15–64, 81.5%; female 53.4%). **Gross national income** (2008): US$3,955,000,000 (US$410 per capita). **Selected balance of payments data.** Receipts from (US$'000,000): tourism (2007) 65; remittances (2008) 51; foreign direct investment (FDI; 2005–07 avg.) 32; official development assistance (2007) 713. Disbursements for (US$'000,000): tourism (2007) 69; remittances (2008) 68; FDI (2006–07 avg.) 13.

Did you know? The American zoologist Dian Fossey established the Karisoke Research Center in 1967 and began a hermitlike existence in the Virunga Mountains of Rwanda, one of the last bastions of the endangered mountain gorilla.

Foreign trade

Imports (2007; c.i.f.): US$696,900,000 (machinery and apparatus 17.8%; motor vehicles 12.9%; food products 9.6%; refined petroleum products 8.5%; medicaments 6.8%). *Major import sources:* Kenya 17.8%; Uganda 14.0%; UAE 7.8%; Tanzania 6.8%; Belgium 6.3%. **Exports** (2008; f.o.b.): US$261,800,000 (coffee 17.9%; cassiterite [major ore of tin] 15.7%; tea 15.3%; columbite/tantalite 14.2%; tungsten 4.9%). *Major export destinations* (2007): Kenya 18.7%; UK 18.7%; Belgium 14.0%; Hong Kong 12.5%; Switzerland 7.2%.

Transport and communications

Transport. *Railroads:* none. *Roads* (2004): total length 14,008 km (paved 19%). *Vehicles* (2008): passenger cars 21,350; trucks and buses 16,470. *Air transport* (2006; Kigali airport only): passengers embarked and disembarked 180,000; cargo loaded and unloaded (2000) 4,300 metric tons. **Communications**, in total units (units per 1,000 persons). Telephone landlines (2008): 17,000 (1.7); cellular telephone subscribers (2008): 1,323,000 (136); personal computers (2007): 28,000 (3); total Internet users (2008): 300,000 (31); broadband Internet subscribers (2008): 4,200 (0.4).

Education and health

Educational attainment (2005). Percentage of population ages 15–49 having: no formal education/unknown 21.4%; primary education 68.2%; secondary 9.6%; higher 0.8%. **Literacy** (2007): percentage of total population ages 15 and over literate 74.7%; males literate 79.3%; females literate 70.2%. **Health** (2007): physicians 540 (1 per 17,509 persons); hospital beds 14,246 (1 per 664 persons); infant mortality rate per 1,000 live births (2008) 55.9; undernourished population (2002–04) 2,800,000 (33% of total population based on the consumption of a minimum daily requirement of 1,750 calories).

Military

Total active duty personnel (November 2008): 33,000 (army 97.0%, air force 3.0%). **Military expenditure as percentage of GDP** (2007): 2.1%; per capita expenditure US$7.

Background

Originally inhabited by the Twa, a Pygmy people, Rwanda became home to the Hutu, who were well established there when the Tutsi appeared in the 14th century. The Tutsi conquered the Hutu and in the 15th century founded a kingdom near Kigali. The Belgians occupied Rwanda in 1916, and the League of Nations created Ruanda-Urundi as a Belgian mandate in 1923. The Tutsi retained their dominance until shortly before Rwanda reached independence in 1962, when the Hutu took control of the government and stripped the Tutsi of much of their land. Many Tutsi fled Rwanda, and the Hutu dominated the country's political system, waging sporadic civil wars until mid-1994, when the death of the country's leader in a plane crash—apparently shot down—led to massive violence. The Tutsi-led Rwandan Patriotic Front took over the country by force after the massacre of almost one million Tutsi and Tutsi sympathizers by the Hutu. A transitional government was replaced in 2003 following the country's first multiparty elections.

Recent Developments

By 2009—15 years after the 1994 genocide—Rwanda had become a model of postconflict recovery. In December Rwanda was declared free of land mines, the first country to realize this status. Rwanda's economy showed remarkable resilience, growing at an estimated rate of 8–9% during the year, fueled mainly by an expanding industrial base and excellent crop harvests. In November Rwanda was admitted to the Commonwealth, becoming only the second member country (after Mozambique) with no formal historical ties to Britain. In September the World Bank ranked Rwanda as the top global business reformer for 2010.

Internet resource: <www.statistics.gov.rw>.

Saint Kitts and Nevis

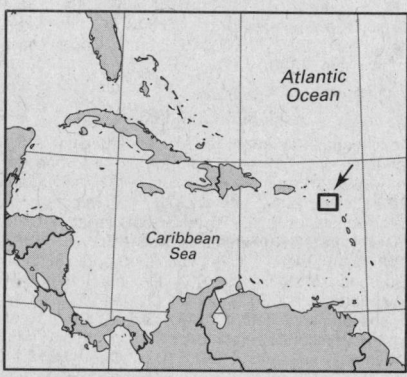

Atlantic Ocean

Caribbean Sea

Official name: Federation of Saint Kitts and Nevis (Federation of Saint Christopher and Nevis is the alternate official long-form name). **Form of government:** federated constitutional monarchy with one legislative house (National Assembly [15]). **Head of state:** British Queen Elizabeth II (from 1952), represented by Governor-General Cuthbert Sebastian (from 1996). **Head of government:** Prime Minister Denzil Douglas (from 1995). **Capital:** Basseterre. **Official language:** English. **Official religion:** none. **Monetary unit:** 1 Eastern Caribbean dollar (EC$) = 100 cents; valuation (1 Jul 2010) US$1 = EC$2.68.

Demography

Area: 104.0 sq mi, 269.4 sq km. **Population** (2009): 51,900. **Density** (2009): persons per sq mi 499.0, persons per sq km 192.7. **Urban** (2005): 33%. **Sex distribution** (2008): male 49.70%; female 50.30%. **Age breakdown** (2008): under 15, 26.7%; 15–29, 25.9%; 30–44, 19.8%; 45–59, 17.3%; 60–74, 6.3%; 75–84, 2.9%; 85 and over, 1.1%. **Ethnic composition** (2000): black 90.4%; mulatto 5.0%; Indo-Pakistani 3.0%; white 1.0%; other 0.6%. **Religious affiliation** (2005): Protestant 75%, of which Anglican 24%, Methodist 23%; Roman Catholic 11%; other 14%. **Major towns** (2006): Basseterre 12,900; Charlestown 1,500; St. Paul's 1,200. **Location:** islands in the Caribbean Sea, between the US Virgin Islands and Antigua and Barbuda.

Vital statistics

Birth rate per 1,000 population (2008): 17.7 (world avg. 20.3). **Death rate** per 1,000 population (2008):

8.2 (world avg. 8.5). **Total fertility rate** (avg. births per childbearing woman; 2008): 2.28. **Life expectancy** at birth (2008): male 70.1 years; female 78.0 years.

National economy

Budget (2008). *Revenue:* EC$641,200,000 (tax revenue 64.9%, of which taxes on international trade 30.3%, taxes on income and profits 20.5%, taxes on domestic goods and services 13.1%; nontax revenue 18.4%; grants 8.4%). *Expenditures:* EC$634,-400,000 (current expenditures 87.8%, of which interest payments 20.6%; development expenditures 12.2%). **Production** (metric tons except as noted). *Agriculture and fishing* (2007): sugarcane (2005) 100,000, coconuts 1,000, pineapples (2006) 55; livestock (number of live animals) 16,000 goats, 12,600 sheep, 4,850 cattle; fisheries production 450 (from aquaculture, negligible). *Mining and quarrying:* excavation of sand and crushed stone for local use. *Manufacturing* (2003): raw sugar 22,000; carbonated beverages (2002) 32,000 hectoliters; beer (2002) 20,000 hectoliters; other manufactures include electronic components, garments, and cement. *Energy production (consumption):* electricity (kW-hr; 2006) 135,000,000 (135,000,000); petroleum products (metric tons; 2006) none (77,000). **Gross national income** (2008): US$539,000,000 (US$10,960 per capita). **Public debt** (external, outstanding; 2007): US$272,000,000. **Population economically active** (1995): total 18,170; activity rate of total population 41.7% (participation rates [1991]: ages 15–64, 70.5%; female 44.4%; unemployed [2006] 5.1%). **Selected balance of payments data.** Receipts from (US$'000,000): tourism (2007) 106; remittances (2008) 37; foreign direct investment (2005–07 avg.) 115; official development assistance (2007) 3. Disbursements for (US$'000,000): tourism (2007) 15; remittances (2008) 6.

Foreign trade

Imports (2006; c.i.f.): US$249,500,000 (machinery and apparatus 23.1%, of which electrical machinery and parts 10.6%; food products 15.5%; base and fabricated metals 9.2%; refined petroleum products 6.6%; motor vehicles 6.5%). *Major import sources:* US 58.3%; Trinidad and Tobago 12.5%; UK 5.3%; Japan 4.3%; Canada 2.6%. **Exports** (2006; f.o.b.): US$39,700,000 (electrical switches 43.8%; telecommunications equipment and parts 25.4%; generators 9.8%; beverages [primarily bottled water and beer] 5.5%). *Major export destinations:* US 89.3%; UK 2.3%; Trinidad and Tobago 1.5%.

Transport and communications

Transport. *Railroads* (2003): length 58 km. *Roads* (2002): total length 383 km (paved [2001] 44%). *Vehicles* (2002): passenger cars 6,900; trucks and buses 2,500. *Air transport* (2001; Saint Kitts airport only): passenger arrivals 135,237, passenger departures 134,937; cargo handled 1,802. **Communications**, in total units (units per 1,000 persons). Telephone landlines (2008): 20,000 (400); cellular telephone subscribers (2008): 80,000 (1,567); personal computers (2004): 11,000 (226); total Internet

---

1 metric ton = about 1.1 short tons;   1 kilometer = 0.6 mi (statute);   1 metric ton-km cargo = about 0.68 short ton-mi cargo;   c.i.f.: cost, insurance, and freight;   f.o.b.: free on board

users (2008): 16,000 (313); broadband Internet subscribers (2008): 11,000 (217).

Education and health

Educational attainment (1991). Percentage of population ages 25 and over having: no formal schooling/unknown 6.8%; primary education 45.9%; secondary 38.4%; higher 8.9%. **Literacy** (2004): total population ages 15 and over literate 97.8%. **Health** (2008): physicians (2005) 62 (1 per 796 persons); hospital beds 208 (1 per 247 persons); infant mortality rate per 1,000 live births 14.3; undernourished population (2002–04) 5,000 (10% of total population based on the consumption of a minimum daily requirement of 1,910 calories).

Military

Total active duty personnel (2006): the defense force includes coast guard and police units.

Background

Saint Kitts became the first British colony in the West Indies in 1623. Anglo-French rivalry grew in the 17th century and lasted more than a century. In 1783, by the Treaty of Versailles, the islands became wholly British possessions. They were united with Anguilla from 1882 to 1980 but became an independent federation within the British Commonwealth in 1983.

Recent Developments

Renewable energy made a major leap forward in Saint Kitts and Nevis when in April 2009 work began to install two 5.8-MW generators at a geothermal site at Spring Hill, Nevis. It was the first time that a geothermal source had been used to generate electricity in the Caribbean.

Internet resource: <www.stkittsnevishta.org>.

Saint Lucia

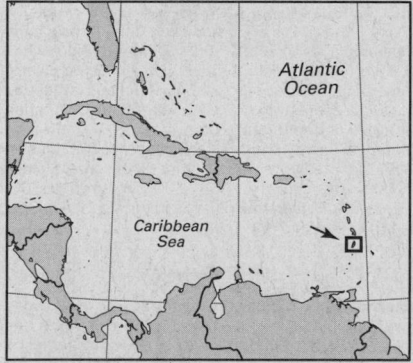

Official name: Saint Lucia. **Form of government:** constitutional monarchy with two legislative houses (Senate [11]; House of Assembly [17]). **Head of state:** British Queen Elizabeth II (from 1952), represented by Governor-General Pearlette Louisy (from 1997).

Head of government: Prime Minister Stephenson King (from 2007). **Capital:** Castries. **Official language:** English. **Official religion:** none. **Monetary unit:** 1 Eastern Caribbean dollar (EC$) = 100 cents; valuation (1 Jul 2010) US$1 = EC$2.68.

Demography

Area: 238 sq mi, 617 sq km. **Population** (2009): 178,000. **Density** (2009): persons per sq mi 747.9, persons per sq km 288.5. **Urban** (2008): 27.8%. **Sex distribution** (2008): male 49.01%; female 50.99%. **Age breakdown** (2008): under 15, 26.4%; 15–29, 28.9%; 30–44, 21.6%; 45–59, 13.7%; 60–74, 6.6%; 75 and over, 2.8%. **Ethnic composition** (2000): black 50%; mulatto 44%; East Indian 3%; white 1%; other 2%. **Religious affiliation** (2001): Roman Catholic 67.5%; Protestant 22.0%, of which Seventh-day Adventist 8.4%, Pentecostal 5.6%; Rastafarian 2.1%; nonreligious 4.5%; other 3.9%. **Major towns** (2006): Castries 65,000; Vieux Fort 4,600; Micoud 3,400. **Location:** island between the Caribbean Sea and North Atlantic Ocean, north of Saint Vincent and the Grenadines.

Vital statistics

Birth rate per 1,000 population (2008): 13.7 (world avg. 20.3); within marriage 14.0%. **Death rate** per 1,000 population (2008): 7.6 (world avg. 8.5). **Total fertility rate** (avg. births per childbearing woman; 2008): 2.2. **Life expectancy** at birth (2008): male 72.0 years; female 75.8 years.

National economy

Budget (2008–09). *Revenue:* EC$815,950,000 (tax revenue 90.3%, of which consumption taxes 17.5%, corporate taxes 13.9%, import duties 12.7%, income tax 9.3%; nontax revenue 6.4%; grants 3.3%). *Expenditures:* EC$959,100,000 (current expenditures 67.8%, of which wages and salaries 31.8%, interest payments 9.5%; capital expenditures 32.2%). **Public debt** (external, outstanding; January 2009): US$372,950,000. **Production** (metric tons except as noted). *Agriculture and fishing* (2007): bananas (2008) 38,359, coconuts 14,000, plantains 750, pepper 260, ginger 70, cacao beans 40; livestock (number of live animals) 15,000 pigs, 12,500 sheep, 12,500 cattle; fisheries production (2008) 1,695, of which tuna 492, dolphin 341 (from aquaculture, none). *Mining and quarrying:* excavation of sand for local construction and pumice. *Manufacturing* (value of production in EC$'000; 2008): food products, beverages (significantly alcoholic beverages), and tobacco products 73,638; electrical products 35,121; paper products and cardboard boxes 28,066. *Energy production (consumption):* electricity (kW-hr; 2008) 352,337,000 (352,337,000); petroleum products (metric tons; 2006) none (124,000). **Population economically active** (2007): total 85,260; activity rate of total population 49.8% (participation rates: ages 15 and over [2004] 68.6%; female 46.6%; unemployed 14.6%). **Gross national income** (2008): US$940,000,000 (US$5,530 per capita). **Selected balance of payments data.** Receipts from (US$'000,000): tourism (2007) 296; remittances (2008) 31; foreign direct investment (2005–07 avg.) 151; official development assistance (2007) 24. Disbursements for (US$'000,000): tourism (2007) 41; remittances (2008) 4.

Foreign trade

Imports (2006; c.i.f.): US$592,300,000 (food products 15.9%; machinery and apparatus 15.3%; motor vehicles 10.2%; chemical products 6.9%; base and fabricated metals 6.2%; refined petroleum products 5.7%). *Major import sources:* US 39.2%; Trinidad and Tobago 16.8%; UK 6.9%; Japan 6.3%; Barbadós 4.4%. **Exports** (2005; f.o.b.): US$64,200,000 (bananas 24.1%; beer 16.2%; refined petroleum products 15.4%; nonelectrical machinery and equipment 6.7%; paperboard cartons 5.1%). *Major export destinations* (2005): UK 26.0%; Trinidad and Tobago 22.4%; US 14.0%; Barbados 10.1%; Grenada 5.1%.

Transport and communications

Transport. *Railroads:* none. *Roads* (2002): total length 1,210 km (paved 5%). *Vehicles* (2008): passenger cars 38,504; trucks and buses 11,577. *Air transport* (2008; Castries and Vieux Fort airports only): passenger arrivals and departures 872,032; cargo unloaded and loaded 3,363 metric tons. **Communications,** in total units (units per 1,000 persons). Telephone landlines (2008): 49,000 (240); cellular telephone subscribers (2008): 170,000 (995); personal computers (2004): 26,000 (173); total Internet users (2008): 100,000 (587); broadband Internet subscribers (2008): 14,000 (82).

Education and health

Educational attainment (2007). Percentage of population ages 15 and over having: no formal schooling/unknown 8.8%; incomplete primary education 5.6%; complete primary 43.1%; secondary 32.0%; higher vocational 7.1%; university 3.4%. **Literacy** (2004): 94.8%. **Health** (2008): physicians (2005) 83 (1 per 1,983 persons); hospital beds 470 (1 per 374 persons); infant mortality rate per 1,000 live births 25.2; undernourished population (2002–04) 8,000 (5% of total population based on the consumption of a minimum daily requirement of 1,900 calories).

Military

Total active duty personnel (2006): none; a 300-member police force includes a specially trained paramilitary unit and a coast guard unit.

Background

Caribs replaced early Arawak inhabitants on the island about AD 800–1300. Settled by the French in 1650, it was ceded to Great Britain in 1814 and became one of the Windward Islands in 1871. It became fully independent as Saint Lucia in 1979. The economy is based on agriculture and tourism.

Recent Developments

With a GDP expected to contract by 2.5% in 2009, Saint Lucia approached the IMF for assistance in July, requesting access to about US$10.7 million under the rapid-access component of the Exogenous Shocks Facility. The program and its funds were designed to ease balance-of-payments pressures and shore up external reserves.

Internet resource: <www.stats.gov.lc>.

Saint Vincent and the Grenadines

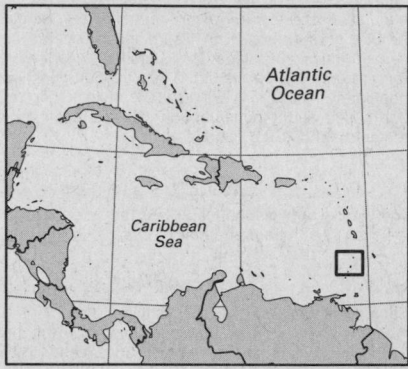

Official name: Saint Vincent and the Grenadines. **Form of government:** constitutional monarchy with one legislative house (House of Assembly [22]). **Head of state:** British Queen Elizabeth II (from 1952), represented by Governor-General Frederick Ballantyne (from 2002). **Head of government:** Prime Minister Ralph Gonsalves (from 2001). **Capital:** Kingstown. **Official language:** English. **Official religion:** none. **Monetary unit:** 1 Eastern Caribbean dollar (EC$) = 100 cents; valuation (1 Jul 2010) US$1 = EC$2.68.

Demography

Area: 150.3 sq mi, 389.3 sq km. **Population** (2009): 105,000. **Density** (2009): persons per sq mi 698.6, persons per sq km 269.7. **Urban** (2006): 46.3%. **Sex distribution** (2007): male 50.61%; female 49.39%. **Age breakdown** (2007): under 15, 27.3%; 15–29, 26.2%; 30–44, 21.6%; 45–59, 14.6%; 60–74, 7.1%; 75–84, 2.6%; 85 and over, 0.6%. **Ethnic composition** (2000): black 65.1%; mixed black-white 19.9%; Indo-Pakistani 5.5%; British 3.0%; black-Amerindian 2.0%; other 4.5%. **Religious affiliation** (2000): Protestant 47.0%; unaffiliated Christian 20.3%; independent Christian 11.7%; Roman Catholic 8.8%; Hindu 3.4%; Spiritist 1.8%; Muslim 1.5%; nonreligious 2.3%; other 3.2%. **Major cities** (2006): Kingstown 18,200; Georgetown 1,700; Byera 1,400. **Location:** islands in the Caribbean Sea, north of Trinidad and Tobago.

Vital statistics

Birth rate per 1,000 population (2007): 16.0 (world avg. 20.3); (2003) within marriage 15.6%. **Death rate** per 1,000 population (2007): 6.9 (world avg. 8.5). **Total fertility rate** (avg. births per childbearing woman; 2007): 2.06. **Life expectancy** at birth (2007): male 71.4 years; female 75.0 years.

1 metric ton = about 1.1 short tons;   1 kilometer = 0.6 mi (statute);   1 metric ton-km cargo = about 0.68 short ton-mi cargo;   c.i.f.: cost, insurance, and freight;   f.o.b.: free on board

National economy

Budget (2008). *Revenue:* EC$525,000,000 (tax revenue 84.2%, of which VAT 28.7%, tax on international trade 19.0%, income tax 10.7%, corporate taxes 8.9%; nontax revenue 7.9%; grants 7.6%). *Expenditures:* EC$558,500,000 (current expenditures 78.2%; development expenditures 21.8%). **Production** (metric tons except as noted). *Agriculture and fishing* (2007): bananas 51,000, sugarcane 20,000, roots and tubers (significantly eddoes and dasheens [varieties of taro roots]) 15,320, nutmegs 160, soursops and papayas are also grown; livestock (number of live animals) 12,000 sheep, 9,150 pigs, 7,200 goats; fisheries production 5,250 (from aquaculture, none). *Mining and quarrying:* sand and gravel for local use. *Manufacturing* (value added in EC$'000,000; 2000): beverages and tobacco products 17.4; food products 15.6; paper products and publishing 3.6. *Energy production (consumption):* electricity (kW-hr; 2008) 139,000,000 ([2006] 127,000,000); petroleum products (metric tons; 2006) none (64,000). **Selected balance of payments data.** Receipts from (US$'000,000): tourism (2008) 90; remittances (2007) 31; foreign direct investment (2005–07 avg.) 80; official development assistance (2007) 66. Disbursements for (US$'000,000): tourism (2007) 17; remittances (2007) 7. **Gross national income** (2008): US$561,000,000 (US$5,140 per capita). **Population economically active** (2006): total 58,000; activity rate of total population 48.3% (participation rates: ages 15–64, 75.3%; female 41.4%). **Public debt** (external, outstanding; December 2008): US$210,600,000.

Foreign trade

Imports (2008; c.i.f.): US$373,200,000 (machinery and apparatus 23.1%; food products and beverages 22.6%; refined petroleum products 12.5%). *Major import sources* (2006): US 32.7%; Trinidad and Tobago 25.9%; UK 7.1%; Japan 3.9%; Canada 3.6%. **Exports** (2008; f.o.b.): US$52,200,000 (food products 61.7%, of which bananas 15.9%, wheat flour 15.1%, rice 12.1%, roots and tubers 7.1%; machinery and apparatus 23.0%, of which telecommunications equipment 10.7%). *Major export destinations* (2008): Grenada 18.2%; Trinidad and Tobago 17.4%; St. Lucia 14.8%; Barbados 10.7%; UK 9.0%.

Transport and communications

Transport. *Railroads:* none. *Roads* (2004): total length 829 km (paved 70%). *Vehicles* (2008): passenger cars 9,247; trucks and buses 13,019. *Air transport* (2003): passenger arrivals 133,769; passenger departures 137,899. **Communications,** in total units (units per 1,000 persons). Telephone landlines (2008): 23,000 (217); cellular telephone subscribers (2008): 130,000 (1,239); personal computers (2005): 16,000 (152); total Internet users (2008): 66,000 (629); broadband Internet subscribers (2008): 9,400 (90).

Education and health

Educational attainment (2001). Percentage of employed population having: no formal schooling/unknown 1.7%; primary education 55.6%; secondary 27.3%; higher vocational 15.1%; university 0.3%. Literacy (2004): total population ages 15 and over literate 88.1%. **Health:** physicians (2005) 72 (1 per 1,458 persons); hospital beds (2008) 280 (1 per 375 persons); infant mortality rate per 1,000 live births (2007) 16.1; undernourished population (2002–04) 10,000 (10% of total population based on the consumption of a minimum daily requirement of 1,900 calories).

Military

Total active duty personnel (November 2007): none; a paramilitary includes coast guard and police units.

Background

The French and the British contested for control of Saint Vincent and the Grenadines until 1763, when it was ceded to England by the Treaty of Paris. The original inhabitants, the Caribs, recognized British sovereignty but revolted in 1795. Most of the Caribs were deported; many who remained were killed in volcanic eruptions in 1812 and 1902. In 1969 Saint Vincent and the Grenadines became a self-governing state in association with the United Kingdom, and in 1979 it achieved full independence.

Recent Developments

In April 2009 Saint Vincent and the Grenadines was accepted as a member of Venezuelan Pres. Hugo Chávez's Bolivarian Alliance for the Americas group, promoted by Chávez as a more "socialist" path to development than US-led free trade based on market principles.

Internet resource: <http://discoversvg.com>.

Samoa

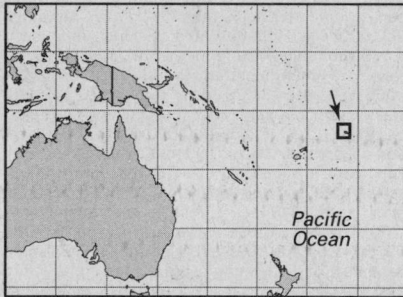

Pacific Ocean

Official name: Malo Sa'oloto Tuto'atasi o Samoa (Samoan); Independent State of Samoa (English). **Form of government:** mix of parliamentary democracy and Samoan customs with one legislative house (Legislative Assembly [49]). **Head of state:** Head of State Tuiatua Tupua Tamasese Efi (from 2007). **Head of government:** Prime Minister Tuilaepa Sailele Malielegaoi (from 1998). **Capital:** Apia. **Official languages:** Samoan; English. **Official religion:** none. **Monetary unit:** 1 tala (SAT) = 100 sene; valuation (1 Jul 2010) US$1 = SAT 2.53.

Demography

Area: 1,075 sq mi, 2,785 sq km. **Population** (2009): 183,000. **Density** (2009): persons per sq mi 170.2, persons per sq km 65.7. **Urban** (2007): 23.0%. **Sex distribution** (2006): male 51.83%; female 48.17%. **Age breakdown** (2006): under 15, 39.3%; 15–29, 24.6%; 30–44, 18.2%; 45–59, 11.0%; 60–74, 5.2%; 75 and over, 1.7%. **Ethnic composition** (2006): Samoan (Polynesian) 92.6%; Euronesian (European and Polynesian) 7.0%; European and US white 0.4%. **Religious affiliation** (2006): Congregational 33.8%; Roman Catholic 19.6%; Methodist 14.3%; Mormon 13.3%; Assemblies of God 6.9%; other Christian 9.8%; other 2.3%. **Major towns** (2006): Apia 37,237 (urban agglomeration 60,702); Vaitele 6,294; Faleasi'u 3,548. **Location:** Oceania, group of islands in the South Pacific Ocean, about halfway between Hawaii (US) and New Zealand.

Vital statistics

Birth rate per 1,000 population (2006): 27.3 (world avg. 20.3). **Death rate** per 1,000 population (2006): 4.0 (world avg. 8.5). **Total fertility rate** (avg. births per childbearing woman; 2006): 4.2. **Life expectancy** at birth (2006): male 71.5 years; female 74.2 years.

National economy

Budget (2005–06). *Revenue:* SAT 387,200,000 (tax revenue 70.5%, of which VAT 28.0%, excise taxes 17.8%, income tax 12.2%; grants 18.6%; nontax revenue 10.9%). *Expenditures:* SAT 391,700,000 (current expenditures 72.0%, of which general services 22.9%, economic services 14.4%, education 14.1%, health 12.1%; development expenditures 22.0%). **Public debt** (external, outstanding; March 2008): US$192,000,000. **Production** (metric tons except as noted). *Agriculture and fishing* (2007): coconuts 146,000, bananas 23,000, taro 17,600, noni (fruit known locally as *nonu;* also known as Indian mulberry), n.a.; livestock (number of live animals) 202,000 pigs, 29,000 cattle; fisheries production 4,609 (from aquaculture, negligible). *Manufacturing* (value of manufactured exports in SAT '000; 2006–07): beer 3,520; noni juice 3,130; coconut cream 2,130. *Energy production (consumption):* electricity (kW-hr; 2006) 113,000,000 (90,000,000); petroleum products (metric tons; 2006) none (51,000). **Population economically active** (2003): total 64,000; activity rate of total population 35% (participation rates: ages 15–64, 63%; female 32%; unemployed [2006] 1.1%). **Gross national income** (2008): US$504,000,000 (US$2,780 per capita). **Selected balance of payments data.** Receipts from (US$'000,000): tourism (2007–08) 110; remittances (2008) 135; foreign direct investment (FDI; 2005–07 avg.) 8; official development assistance (2007) −31. Disbursements for (US$'000,000): tourism (2007) 5; remittances (2008) 13; FDI (2005–07 avg.) 1.

Foreign trade

Imports (2007): SAT 593,000,000 (refined petroleum products 20.6%; products for government 5.1%). *Major import sources* (2005–06): New Zealand 29.3%; Australia 18.8%; US 10.6%; Fiji 7.0%; China 5.3%. **Exports** (2007): SAT 36,000,000 (fresh fish 55.3%; noni juice 10.6%; beer 8.6%; coconut cream 6.5%; noni fruit 1.9%). *Major export destinations* (2005–06): American Samoa 49.1%; US 32.6%; New Zealand 9.4%; Australia 3.4%; Japan 3.1%.

Transport and communications

Transport. *Railroads:* none. *Roads* (2001): total length 2,337 km (paved 14%). *Vehicles* (2005): passenger cars 4,638; trucks and buses 4,894. *Air transport* (2004; Polynesian Airlines only): passenger-km 326,090,000; metric ton-km cargo 2,709,000. **Communications,** in total units (units per 1,000 persons). Telephone landlines (2008): 29,000 (161); cellular telephone subscribers (2008): 124,000 (493); personal computers (2005): 4,000 (22); total Internet users (2008): 9,000 (50); broadband Internet subscribers (2005): 100 (0.5).

Education and health

Educational attainment (2002). Percentage of population ages 25 and over having: no formal schooling 1.8%; primary education 32.4%; secondary 55.4%; higher 10.4%. **Literacy** (2003): total population ages 16 and over literate 99.7%. **Health** (2005): physicians 50 (1 per 3,570 persons); hospital beds 229 (1 per 780 persons); infant mortality rate per 1,000 live births (2006) 20.4; undernourished population (2002–04) 7,000 (4% of total population based on the consumption of a minimum daily requirement of 1,870 calories).

Military

No military forces are maintained; informal defense ties exist with New Zealand, and Australia assists with maritime surveillance training.

Background

Polynesians inhabited the islands of the Samoan archipelago for thousands of years before they were visited by Europeans in the 18th century. Control of the islands was contested by the US, Britain, and Germany until 1899, when they were divided between the US and Germany. In 1914 Western Samoa was occupied by New Zealand, which received it as a League of Nations mandate in 1920. After World War II, it became a UN trust territory administered by New Zealand, and it achieved independence in 1962. In 1997 the word Western was dropped from the country's name.

Recent Developments

In 2009, for the first time in 10 years, Samoa's well-managed economy contracted. Contributing to the situation were an inflation rate of 13%, a decline in tourism and in remittances from expatriate Samoans, and the closure of American Samoan tuna canneries. On 29 September a magnitude-8.1 earthquake near Samoa generated a tsunami that killed some 142 people.

Internet resource: <www.visitsamoa.ws>.

1 metric ton = about 1.1 short tons;   1 kilometer = 0.6 mi (statute);   1 metric ton-km cargo = about 0.68 short ton-mi cargo;   c.i.f.: cost, insurance, and freight;   f.o.b.: free on board

San Marino

Official name: Repubblica di San Marino (Republic of San Marino). **Form of government:** unitary multiparty republic with one legislative house (Great and General Council [60]). **Heads of state and government:** two captains-regent who serve six-month terms beginning in April and October. **Capital:** San Marino. **Official language:** Italian. **Official religion:** none. **Monetary unit:** 1 euro (€) = 100 cents; valuation (1 Jul 2010) US$1 = €0.80 (San Marino uses the euro as its official currency, even though it is not a member of the EU).

Demography

Area: 23.63 sq mi, 61.20 sq km. **Population** (2009): 31,500. **Density** (2009): persons per sq mi 1,333, persons per sq km 514.7. **Urban** (2005): 96%. **Sex distribution** (2008): male 49.07%; female 50.93%. **Age breakdown** (2008): under 15, 15.0%; 15–29, 14.9%; 30–44, 26.4%; 45–59, 21.5%; 60–74, 14.1%; 75–84, 5.8%; 85 and over, 2.3%. **Ethnic composition** (2006): Sammarinesi 87.0%; Italian 11.4%; other 1.6%. **Religious affiliation** (2000): Roman Catholic 88.7%; other Christian 3.5%; nonreligious 5.1%; other 2.7%. **Major municipalities** (2008): Serravalle 10,051; Borgo Maggiore 6,198; San Marino 4,376. **Location:** southern Europe, surrounded by Italy.

Vital statistics

Birth rate per 1,000 population (2008): 11.2 (world avg. 20.3); within marriage 77.9%. **Death rate** per 1,000 population (2008): 6.1 (world avg. 8.5). **Total fertility rate** (avg. births per childbearing woman; 2008): 1.50. **Life expectancy** at birth (2008): male 80.1 years; female 85.7 years.

National economy

Budget (2005). *Revenue:* €504,800,000 (VAT 23.6%; social contributions 21.3%; income tax 20.2%). *Expenditures:* €433,100,000 (wages and salaries 35.4%; social benefits 30.5%). **Public debt** (2003): US$52,900,000. **Tourism:** number of visitor arrivals (2008) 2,111,736. **Population economically active** (2008): total 22,708; activity rate of total population 73.2% (participation rates: ages 15–64 [2002] 72.1%; female 42.0%; unemployed 3.1%). **Production** (metric tons except as noted). *Agriculture and fishing:* small amounts of wheat, grapes, and barley; livestock (number of live animals; 2005) 991 cattle, 91 sheep, 32 pigs. *Quarry-*

ing: building stone is an important export product. *Manufacturing* (2005): processed meats 283,674 kg, of which beef 270,616 kg, veal 8,549 kg, pork 3,615 kg; cheese 56,610 kg; butter 8,110 kg; other major products include electrical appliances, musical instruments, printing ink, paint, cosmetics, furniture, floor tiles, gold and silver jewelry, clothing, and postage stamps. *Energy production (consumption):* all electrical power is imported via electrical grid from Italy (kW-hr; consumption [2007] 239,983,250); crude petroleum, none (none); natural gas (cu m; 2007) none (52,785,000). **Gross national income** (2008): US$1,899,900,000 (US$60,925 per capita).

Foreign trade

Imports (2005): US$2,582,000,000 (manufactured goods of all kinds, refined petroleum products, natural gas, electricity, and gold). *Major import source* (2004): significantly Italy (a customs union with Italy has existed since 1862). **Exports** (2005): US$2,531,000,000 (electronics, postage stamps, leather products, ceramics, wine, wood products, and building stone). *Major export destinations* (2004): Italy 90% (a customs union with Italy has existed since 1862).

Transport and communications

Transport. *Railroads:* none. *Roads* (2001): total length 252 km. *Vehicles* (2008): passenger cars 34,025; trucks and buses 6,370. *Air transport:* a heliport provides passenger and cargo service between San Marino and Rimini, Italy, during the summer months. **Communications,** in total units (units per 1,000 persons). Telephone landlines (2008): 21,000 (683); cellular telephone subscribers (2008): 24,000 (797); personal computers (2003): 23,000 (819); total Internet users (2008): 21,000 (545); broadband Internet subscribers (2008): 4,900 (157).

Education and health

Educational attainment (2007). Percentage of population ages 15 and over having: basic literacy or primary education 55.3%; secondary or vocational 34.5%; higher degree 10.2%. **Literacy** (2001): total population ages 15 and over literate 98.7%; males literate 98.9%; females literate 98.4%. **Health** (2002): physicians 117 (1 per 230 persons); hospital beds 134 (1 per 191 persons); infant mortality rate per 1,000 live births (2008) 2.9.

Military

Total active duty personnel: none; defense is the responsibility of Italy; a small voluntary military force performs ceremonial duties and provides limited assistance to police.

Background

According to tradition, San Marino was founded in the early 4th century AD by St. Marinus. By the 12th century it had developed into a commune and remained independent despite challenges from neighboring rulers, including the Malatesta family in nearby Rimini, Italy. San Marino survived the Renaissance as a relic of the self-governing Italian city-state and remained an independent republic after the unification of Italy in 1861. It is one of the smallest republics in the world, and it may be the oldest one in Europe.

Recent Developments

Tax revenues fell in San Marino in 2009, and a decline in imports hurt state revenues deriving from them. Tourist arrivals decreased by 2.7%. In response the government earmarked funds for hospitality resources and the revitalization of the historic center, which had been declared a UNESCO World Heritage site in 2008.

Internet resource: <www.visitsanmarino.com>.

Sao Tome and Principe

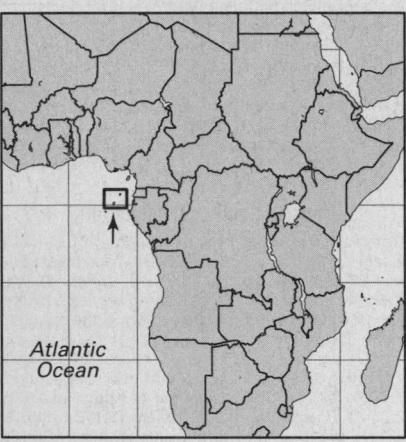

Atlantic Ocean

Official name: República Democrática de São Tomé e Príncipe (Democratic Republic of Sao Tome and Principe). **Form of government:** multiparty republic with one legislative house (National Assembly [55]). **Head of state:** President Fradique de Menezes (from 2003). **Head of government:** Prime Minister Joaquim Rafael Branco (from 2008). **Capital:** São Tomé. **Official language:** Portuguese. **Official religion:** none. **Monetary unit:** 1 dobra (Db) = 100 cêntimos; valuation (1 Jul 2010) US$1 = Db 19,888.10.

Demography

Area: 386 sq mi, 1,001 sq km. **Population** (2009): 163,000. **Density** (2009): persons per sq mi 422.3, persons per sq km 162.8. **Urban** (2008): 60.8%. **Sex distribution** (2006): male 48.63%, female 51.37%. **Age breakdown** (2006): under 15, 41.2%; 15–29, 30.8%; 30–44, 14.6%; 45–59, 7.8%; 60–74, 4.1%; 75 and over, 1.5%. **Ethnic composition** (2000): black-white admixture 79.5%; Fang 10.0%; Angolares (descendants of former Angolan slaves) 7.6%; Portuguese 1.9%; other 1.0%. **Religious affiliation** (2005): Roman Catholic 80%; Protestant 15%; Muslim 3%; other 2%. **Major urban agglomerations** (2001): São Tomé 49,957; Neves 6,635; Santana

6,228. **Location:** islands in the Gulf of Guinea, straddling the Equator west of Gabon.

Vital statistics

Birth rate per 1,000 population (2008): 31.8 (world avg. 20.3). **Death rate** per 1,000 population (2008): 7.4 (world avg. 8.5). **Total fertility rate** (avg. births per childbearing woman; 2006): 5.62. **Life expectancy** at birth (2006): male 63.5 years; female 68.5 years.

National economy

Budget (2007). *Revenue:* Db 3,144,000,000,000 (grants 75.0%; petroleum exploration bonuses 13.1%; tax revenue 10.2%; nontax revenue 1.7%). *Expenditures:* Db 780,000,000,000 (current expenditures 64.9%; capital expenditures 28.6%). **Public debt** (external, outstanding; October 2008): US$109,000,000. **Production** (metric tons except as noted). *Agriculture and fishing* (2007): oil palm fruit 40,000, coconuts 28,000, taro 27,000, cacao beans 3,500, cinnamon 30, coffee 20; livestock (number of live animals) 5,000 goats, 4,600 cattle, 350,000 chickens; fisheries production 4,150 (from aquaculture, none). *Mining and quarrying:* limited quarrying of clay and volcanic rock. *Manufacturing* (2007): small processing plants produce beer, soft drinks, soap, and textiles. *Energy production (consumption):* electricity (kW-hr; 2006) 19,000,000 (19,000,000); petroleum products (metric tons; 2006) none (34,000). **Population economically active** (2006): total 53,266; activity rate of total population 35.1% (participation rates: ages 15–64, 59.5%; female 41.6%). **Gross national income** (2008): US$164,000,000 (US$1,020 per capita). **Selected balance of payments data.** Receipts from (US$'000,000): tourism (2007) 3.4; remittances (2008) 2; foreign direct investment (FDI; 2005–07 avg.) 30; official development assistance (2007) 36. Disbursements for (US$'000,000): tourism (2007) 0.1; remittances (2008) 1; FDI (2005–07 avg.) 7.

Foreign trade

Imports (2008): US$114,094,000 (mineral fuels 23.3%; food products 19.7%; machinery and apparatus 14.1%; transportation equipment 7.9%; construction materials 7.2%). *Major import sources:* Portugal 61.3%; Angola 22.9%; Gabon 3.0%; Nigeria 2.3%. **Exports** (2008): US$5,631,000 (cacao beans 89.4%; coconuts 0.6%; coffee 0.2%). *Major export destinations:* Portugal 49.2%; Netherlands 28.2%; Belgium 7.9%; France 6.8%.

Transport and communications

Transport. *Railroads:* none. *Roads* (2000): total length 320 km (paved 68%). *Vehicles* (1996): passenger cars 4,040; trucks and buses 1,540. *Air transport* (2004): passenger-km 8,000,000. **Communications,** in total units (units per 1,000 persons). Telephone landlines (2008): 7,700 (48); cellular telephone subscribers (2008): 49,000 (306); personal computers (2005): 6,000 (38); total Internet users (2008): 25,000 (155); broadband Internet subscribers (2007): 2,500 (16).

1 metric ton = about 1.1 short tons;   1 kilometer = 0.6 mi (statute);   1 metric ton-km cargo = about 0.68 short ton-mi cargo;   c.i.f.: cost, insurance, and freight;   f.o.b.: free on board

Education and health

Educational attainment (2001). Percentage of population ages 25 and over having: no formal schooling/unknown 22.9%; primary education 41.4%; lower secondary 25.0%; upper secondary/vocational 8.8%; higher 1.9%. Literacy (2006): total population ages 15 and over literate 85%; males literate 92%; females literate 78%. Health (2006): physicians 58 (1 per 2,621 persons); hospital beds (2003) 474 (1 per 313 persons); infant mortality rate per 1,000 live births 43.9; undernourished population (2002–04) 15,000 (10% of total population based on the consumption of a minimum daily requirement of 1,770 calories).

Military

Total active duty personnel (2005): 460 (army and coast guard 65.2%; presidential guard 34.8%). Military expenditure as percentage of GDP (2005): 1.2%; per capita expenditure US$4.

Background

First visited by European navigators in the 1470s, the islands of Sao Tome and Principe were colonized by the Portuguese in the 16th century and were used in the trade and transshipment of slaves. Sugarcane and cacao were the main cash crops. The islands became an overseas province of Portugal in 1951 and achieved independence in 1975. Principe became autonomous in 1995. During recent decades the country's economy has been heavily dependent on international assistance.

Recent Developments

Although Nigeria remained Sao Tome and Principe's leading oil-production partner in the joint Development Zone in 2009, the US showed increasing interest in the potential for extracting oil from the Gulf of Guinea. The amount of oil and gas that could be obtained from the waters off the archipelago, however, remained unclear.

Internet resource: <www.saotome.st>.

Saudi Arabia

Official name: Al-Mamlakah al-'Arabiyah al-Su'udiyah (Kingdom of Saudi Arabia). Form of government: monarchy, assisted by the Consultative Council consisting of 150 appointed members. Head of state and government: King 'Abd Allah (from 2005). Capital: Riyadh. Official language: Arabic. Official religion: Islam. Monetary unit: 1 Saudi riyal (SR) = 100 halala; valuation (1 Jul 2010) US$1 = SR 3.75.

Demography

Area: 830,000 sq mi, 2,149,690 sq km. Population (2009): 25,316,000. Density (2009): persons per sq mi 30.5, persons per sq km 11.8. Urban (2007): 82.6%. Sex distribution (2008): male 55.20%; female 44.80%. Age breakdown (2008): under 15, 32.3%; 15–29, 27.1%; 30–44, 25.5%;. 45–59, 10.8%; 60–74, 3.3%; 75 and over, 1.0%. Ethnic composition (2005): Saudi Arab 74%; expatriates 26%, of which Indian 5%, Bangladeshi 3.5%, Pakistani 3.5%,

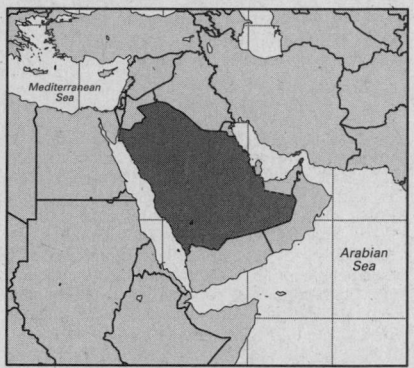

Filipino 3%, Egyptian 3%, Palestinian 1%, other 7%. Religious affiliation (2000): Muslim 94%, of which Sunni 84%, Shi'i 10%; Christian 3.5%, of which Roman Catholic 3%; Hindu 1%; nonreligious/other 1.5%. Major urban agglomerations (2007): Riyadh 4,465,000; Jiddah 3,012,000; Mecca 1,385,000; Medina 1,010,000; Al-Dammam 822,000. Location: the Middle East, bordering Iraq, Kuwait, the Persian Gulf, Qatar, the UAE, Oman, Yemen, the Red Sea, the Gulf of Aqaba, and Jordan.

Vital statistics

Birth rate per 1,000 population (2008): 24.1 (world avg. 20.3). Death rate per 1,000 population (2008): 3.9 (world avg. 8.5). Total fertility rate (avg. births per childbearing woman; 2008): 3.10. Life expectancy at birth (2007): male 70.9 years; female 75.3 years.

National economy

Budget (2008). Revenue: SR 1,100,993,000,000 (petroleum revenues 89.3%). Expenditures: SR 520,069,000,000 (current expenditures 74.8%; capital expenditures 25.2%). National debt (public only; January 2009): US$62,649,000,000. Production (metric tons except as noted). Agriculture and fishing (2007): wheat 2,700,000, alfalfa (2006) 1,644,661, dates 970,000; livestock (number of live animals) 7,000,000 sheep, 2,200,000 goats, 372,000 cattle, 260,000 camels; fisheries production 88,410 (from aquaculture 21%). Mining and quarrying (2008): gypsum 2,300,000; silver 7,513 kg; gold 4,139 kg. Manufacturing (value added in US$'000,000; 2006): industrial chemical products 6,207; food products 4,447; glass products 2,078; refined petroleum products (1998) 1,806. Energy production (consumption): electricity (kW-hr; 2008) 181,097,000,000 (179,272,185,000); crude petroleum (barrels; 2008–09) 3,210,100,000 ([2008] 838,400,000); petroleum products (metric tons; 2006) 114,437,000 (68,194,000); natural gas (cu m; 2008) 80,440,000,000 (80,440,000,000). Population economically active (2007): total 8,229,665, of which 4,029,966 Saudi workers and 4,199,699 foreign nationals; activity rate of total population 34.0% (participation rates: ages 15–64, 51.8%; female 15.4%; unemployed [2008] 5.0%). Gross national income (2008): US$471,692,446,000 (US$18,718 per capita). Selected balance of payments data. Receipts from (US$'000,000): tourism (2008) 9,756; foreign direct investment (FDI; 2005–07 avg.)

18,236. Disbursements for (US$'000,000): tourism (2008) 5,891; remittances (2008) 16,068; FDI (2005–07 avg.) 4,816.

Foreign trade

Imports (2008; c.i.f.): SR 431,753,000,000 (machinery and apparatus 27.2%; transportation equipment 18.0%; base and fabricated metals 15.3%; food products and live animals 14.4%; chemical products 12.3%). *Major import sources:* US 13.7%; China 11.0%; Japan 8.2%; Germany 7.4%; South Korea 4.5%. **Exports** (2008; f.o.b.): SR 1,175,354,000,000 (crude petroleum 78.8%; refined petroleum products 10.8%; other mineral fuels [mostly natural gas] 5.3%). *Major export destinations:* US 16.3%; Japan 15.2%; China 8.9%; South Korea 8.6%; India 7.3%.

Transport and communications

Transport. *Railroads* (2007): route length (2008) 1,423 km; passenger-km 343,000,000; metric ton-km cargo 1,257,000,000. *Roads* (2008): total length 183,925 km (paved 29%). *Vehicles* (2001): passenger cars 4,452,793; trucks and buses 4,110,271. *Air transport* (2008; scheduled flights on Saudi Arabian Airlines only): passenger-km 27,736,000,000; metric ton-km cargo 1,391,000,000. **Communications,** in total units (units per 1,000 persons). Telephone landlines (2008): 4,100,000 (163); cellular telephone subscribers (2008): 36,000,000 (1,429); personal computers (2005): 8,184,000 (354); total Internet users (2008): 7,762,000 (308); broadband Internet subscribers (2008): 1,048,000 (42).

Education and health

Educational attainment (2007). Percentage of Saudi ([2000] non-Saudi) population ages 10 and over who: are illiterate 13.7% (12.1%); are literate/have primary education 34.0% (40.6%); have some/completed secondary 42.1% (36.0%); have at least begun university 10.2% (11.3%). **Literacy** (2007): percentage of total population ages 15 and over literate 85.0%; males literate 89.1%; females literate 79.4%. **Health** (2007): physicians 47,919 (1 per 506 persons); hospital beds 53,519 (1 per 453 persons); infant mortality rate per 1,000 live births 17.9; undernourished population (2002–04) 1,000,000 (4% of total population based on the consumption of a minimum daily requirement of 1,860 calories).

Military

Total active duty personnel (November 2008): 221,500 (army 33.9%, navy 6.1%, air force 9.0%, air defense forces 1.8%, industrial security force 4.1%, national guard 45.1%); US troops (November 2008): 287. **Military expenditure as percentage of GDP** (2008): 8.6%; per capita expenditure US$1,540.

Background

Saudi Arabia is the historical home of Islam, founded by Muhammad in Medina in 622. During medieval times, local and foreign rulers fought for control of the Arabian Peninsula; in 1517 the Ottomans prevailed.

In the 18th–19th centuries Islamic leaders supporting religious reform struggled to regain Saudi territory, all of which was restored by 1904. The British held Saudi lands as a protectorate from 1915 to 1927; then they acknowledged the sovereignty of the Kingdom of the Hejaz and Najd. The two kingdoms were unified as the Kingdom of Saudi Arabia in 1932. Since World War II, it has supported the Palestinian cause in the Middle East and maintained close ties with the US.

Recent Developments

In April 2009 Saudi King 'Abd Allah attended the G-20 summit in London. The IMF ranked Saudi Arabia first among the Arab countries in economic position. In 2009 inflation subsided from around 9.0% to 5.2%. Saudi Arabia's non-oil sector expanded by 3.3%, while its oil revenue declined by 10.3%. In June Saudi Aramco and France Total agreed to invest US$9.6 billion to build the Jubayl oil refinery, expected to produce 400,000 bbl daily. The refinery was one of four planned refineries meant to boost domestic capacity from 2.1 million to 3.7 million bbl daily. The beginning of production from the Khurays oil field increased production capacity to 12 million bbl daily, amplifying Riyadh's leverage in OPEC. Saudi Arabia sacrificed billions of dollars in revenue in 2009 by cutting output to prop up the price of crude oil.

Internet resource: <www.planning.gov.sa>.

Senegal

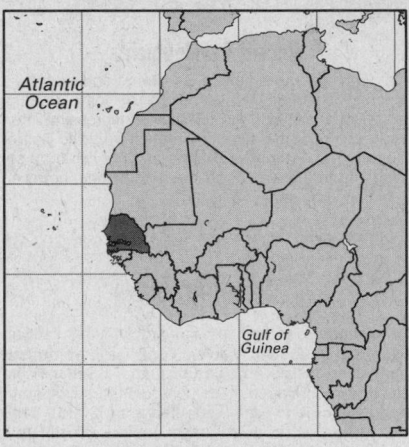

Official name: République du Sénégal (Republic of Senegal). **Form of government:** multiparty republic with two legislative houses (Senate [100]; National Assembly [150]). **Head of state and government:** President Abdoulaye Wade (from 2000), assisted by Prime Minister Souleymane Ndéné Ndiaye (from 2009). **Capital:** Dakar. **Official language:** French. **Official religion:** none. **Monetary unit:** 1 CFA franc (CFAF) = 100 centimes; valuation (1 Jul 2010) US$1 = CFAF 527.20.

1 metric ton = about 1.1 short tons;   1 kilometer = 0.6 mi (statute);   1 metric ton-km cargo = about 0.68 short ton-mi cargo;   c.i.f.: cost, insurance, and freight;   f.o.b.: free on board

Demography

Area: 75,955 sq mi, 196,722 sq km. **Population** (2009): 12,534,000. **Density** (2009): persons per sq mi 165.0, persons per sq km 63.7. **Urban** (2008): 42.4%. **Sex distribution** (2006): male 49.99%; female 50.01%. **Age breakdown** (2006): under 15, 42.2%; 15–29, 28.4%; 30–44, 16.0%; 45–59, 8.7%; 60–74, 3.9%; 75–84, 0.7%; 85 and over, 0.1%. **Ethnic composition** (2000): Wolof 34.6%; Peul (Fulani) and Tukulor 27.1%; Serer 12.0%; Malinke (Mandingo) 9.7%; other 16.6%. **Religious affiliation** (2005): Muslim 94%; Christian (mostly Roman Catholic) 4%; other 2%. **Major cities** (2007): Dakar (urban agglomeration) 2,243,400; Touba 529,200; Thiès 263,500; Kaolack 186,000; Mbour 181,800. **Location:** western Africa, bordering Mauritania, Mali, Guinea, Guinea-Bissau, the North Atlantic Ocean, and The Gambia.

Vital statistics

Birth rate per 1,000 population (2008): 34.5 (world avg. 20.3). **Death rate** per 1,000 population (2008): 8.9 (world avg. 8.5). **Total fertility rate** (avg. births per childbearing woman; 2006): 5.13. **Life expectancy** at birth (2006): male 55.0 years; female 57.7 years.

National economy

Budget (2008). *Revenue:* CFAF 1,350,900,000,000 (tax revenue 86.0%; grants 10.5%; nontax revenue 3.5%). *Expenditures:* CFAF 1,678,561,000,000 (current expenditures 67.1%; development expenditures 32.9%). **Public debt** (external, outstanding; 2007): US$2,029,000,000. **Production** (metric tons except as noted). *Agriculture and fishing* (2008): cassava 918,117, sugarcane 836,000, peanuts (groundnuts) 646,964, seed cotton 45,000; livestock (number of live animals) 5,241,352 sheep, 4,470,562 goats, 3,207,697 cattle, 4,634 camels; fisheries production (2007) 421,517 (from aquaculture, negligible). *Mining and quarrying* (2007): calcium phosphate (crude rock) 691,000. *Manufacturing* (value added in US$'000,000; 2002): food products 108; industrial chemical products 70; cement, bricks, and ceramics 31. *Energy production (consumption):* electricity (kW-hr; 2006) 2,433,000,000 (2,433,000,000); coal (metric tons; 2006) none (167,000); crude petroleum (barrels; 2006) none (2,419,000); petroleum products (metric tons; 2006) 336,000 (775,000); natural gas (cu m; 2006) 12,380,000 (12,380,000). **Population economically active** (2003): total 4,383,000; activity rate of total population 39.4% (participation rates: ages 15–64, 71.5%; female 42.0%; unemployed [2005] 40%). **Selected balance of payments data.** Receipts from (US$'000,000): tourism (2006) 250; remittances (2008) 1,288; foreign direct investment (2005–07 avg.) 114; official development assistance (2007) 843. Disbursements for (US$'000,000): tourism (2006) 54; remittances (2008) 143. **Gross national income** (2008): US$11,825,000,000 (US$970 per capita).

Foreign trade

Imports (2006; c.i.f.): US$3,671,000,000 (mineral fuels 25.9%, of which refined petroleum products 18.4%; food products 19.0%, of which cereals 8.8%; chemical products 9.4%; nonelectrical machinery 9.0%). *Major import sources:* France 24.4%; UK 6.0%; China 4.3%; Thailand 4.0%; Spain 3.8%. **Ex**ports (2006; f.o.b.): US$1,492,000,000 (food products 27.8%, of which fish 10.7%, crustaceans and mollusks 6.9%; refined petroleum products 24.3%; portland cement 5.3%; phosphoric acid and related products 5.2%). *Major export destinations:* Mali 20.2%; bunker and ships' stores 16.2%; France 7.6%; The Gambia 5.6%; India 5.3%.

Transport and communications

Transport. *Railroads* (2004): route length (2005) 906 km; passenger-km 122,000,000; metric ton-km cargo 358,000,000. *Roads* (2006): total length 14,805 km (paved 29%). *Vehicles* (2007): passenger cars 187,998; trucks and buses 64,537. *Air transport* (2006; Air Sénégal International only): passenger-km 937,000,000; metric ton-km cargo, none. **Communications**, in total units (units per 1,000 persons). Telephone landlines (2008): 238,000 (19); cellular telephone subscribers (2008): 5,389,000 (441); personal computers (2005): 250,000 (21); total Internet users (2008): 1,020,000 (84); broadband Internet subscribers (2008): 47,000 (3.9).

Education and health

Educational attainment (2005). Percentage of population ages 25 and over having: no formal schooling/unknown 70.0%; incomplete primary education 13.0%; complete primary 3.7%; incomplete secondary 9.5%; complete secondary 1.4%; higher 2.4%. **Literacy** (2007): percentage of total population ages 15 and over literate 44.0%; males literate 53.4%; females literate 34.9%. **Health:** physicians (2005) 693 (1 per 17,115 persons); hospital beds (1998) 3,582 (1 per 2,500 persons); infant mortality rate per 1,000 live births (2006) 61.4; undernourished population (2003–05) 3,000,000 (26% of total population based on the consumption of a minimum daily requirement of 1,770 calories).

Military

Total active duty personnel (November 2008): 13,620 (army 87.4%, navy 7.0%, air force 5.6%); French troops (November 2008): 841. **Military expenditure as percentage of GDP** (2007): 1.6%; per capita expenditure US$16.

Background

Links between the peoples of Senegal and North Africa were established in the 10th century AD. Islam was introduced in the 11th century, though animism retained a hold on the country into the 19th century. The Portuguese explored the coast in 1445, and in 1638 the French established a trading post—the Europeans exported slaves, ivory, and gold from Senegal. The French gained control over the coast in the early 19th century, checking the expansion of the Tukulor empire; in 1895 Senegal became part of French West Africa. Its inhabitants were made French citizens in 1946, and it became an overseas territory of France. It became an autonomous republic in 1958 and was federated with Mali in 1959–60. It became an independent state in 1960. In 1982 it entered a confederation with The Gambia, called Senegambia, which was dissolved in 1989. Separatists fighting in the south since the early 1980s signed a peace accord with the government in 2004.

Recent Developments

The EU announced in early August 2009 that it would give nearly US$16 million to Senegal to assist the estimated 460,000 people unable to afford adequate food. In September the US Millennium Challenge Corporation approved a five-year, US$540 million grant to Senegal for improvements in agriculture and infrastructure.

Internet resource: <www.senegal-tourism.com>.

Serbia

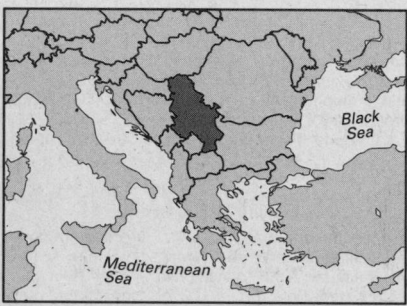

Some of these statistics include Kosovo, which declared its independence in February 2008. **Official name:** Republika Srbija (Republic of Serbia). **Form of government:** republic with one legislative house (National Assembly [250]). **Head of state:** President Boris Tadic (from 2004). **Head of government:** Prime Minister Mirko Cvetkovic (from 2008). **Capital:** Belgrade. **Official language:** Serbian. **Official religion:** none. **Monetary unit:** 1 Serbian dinar (CSD) = 100 paras; valuation (1 Jul 2010) US$1 = CSD 84.95.

Demography

Area: 29,922 sq mi, 77,498 sq km. **Population** (2009): 7,320,000. **Density** (2009): persons per sq mi 244.6, persons per sq km 94.5. **Urban** (2002): 56.4%. **Sex distribution** (2007): male 48.62%; female 51.38%. **Age breakdown** (2007): under 15, 15.8%; 15–29, 19.7%; 30–44, 20.4%; 45–59, 22.4%; 60–74, 14.9%; 75–84, 5.9%; 85 and over, 0.9%. **Ethnic composition** (2002): Serb 82.9%; Hungarian 3.9%; Bosniac 1.8%; Rom (Gypsy) 1.4%; Yugoslav 1.1%; Croat 0.9%; Montenegrin 0.9%; other 7.1%. **Religious affiliation** (2002): Orthodox 85.0%; Roman Catholic 5.5%; Muslim 3.2%; Protestant 1.1%; other 5.2%. **Major cities** (2002): Belgrade (urban agglomeration) 1,120,092; Novi Sad 191,405; Nis 173,724; Kragujevac 146,373; Subotica 99,981. **Location:** southeastern Europe, bordering Romania, Bulgaria, Macedonia, Kosovo, Montenegro, Bosnia and Herzegovina, Croatia, and Hungary.

Vital statistics

Birth rate per 1,000 population (2008): 9.4 (world avg. 20.3); (2007) within marriage 77.7%. **Death rate** per 1,000 population (2008): 14.0 (world avg. 8.5).

Total fertility rate (avg. births per childbearing woman; 2007): 1.40. **Life expectancy** at birth (2008): male 71.1 years; female 76.3 years.

National economy

Budget (2007). *Revenue:* CSD 913,488,000,000 (tax revenue 58.8%; social contributions 34.3%; nontax revenue 6.9%). *Expenditures:* CSD 935,573,000,000 (social protection 38.2%; health 15.5%; economic affairs 11.3%; general public services 9.7%; education 8.1%; public order 6.1%; defense 6.1%). **Public debt** (external, outstanding; August 2009): US$9,803,000,000. **Population economically active** (2008): total 3,267,100; activity rate of total population 43.4% (participation rates: ages 15–64, 62.7%; female 44.0%; unemployed [September 2008–August 2009] 29.7%). **Production** (metric tons except as noted). *Agriculture and fishing* (2007; includes Kosovo): corn (maize) 3,904,825, sugar beets 3,206,380, wheat 1,863,811, sunflower seeds 294,502; livestock (number of live animals) 3,998,927 pigs, 1,106,000 cattle; fisheries production (includes Kosovo) 9,159 (from aquaculture 71%). *Mining and quarrying* (2007): copper (metal content) 32,000; silver (metal content) 4,150; selenium 7,500 kg. *Manufacturing* (value added in CSD '000,000 in constant prices of 2002; 2006): food products and beverages 52,302; chemical products 23,813; cement, bricks, and ceramics 11,532. *Energy production (consumption):* electricity (kW-hr; 2008) 37,392,000,000 ([2006] 35,671,000,000); coal (metric tons; 2008) 72,000 ([2006] 160,000); lignite (metric tons; 2008) 38,520,000 ([2006] 37,367,000); crude petroleum (barrels; 2008) 4,660,000 ([2006] 23,000,000); petroleum products (metric tons; 2006) 2,488,000 (3,588,000); natural gas (cu m; 2007) 271,000,000 ([2006] 2,374,000,000). **Gross national income** (2008): US$41,929,-000,000 (US$5,710 per capita). **Selected balance of payments data.** Receipts from (US$'000,000): tourism (2007) 866; remittances (2008) 5,538; foreign direct investment (FDI; 2005–07 avg.) 3,073; official development assistance (2007) 834. Disbursements for (US$'000,000): tourism (2007) 1,042; remittances (2008) 254; FDI (2005–07 avg.) 361.

Foreign trade

Imports (2007; c.i.f.): US$18,554,000,000 (machinery and apparatus 20.3%; mineral fuels 17.2%; chemical products 14.0%; base metals 9.0%; motor vehicles 8.2%). *Major import sources:* Russia 14.2%; Germany 11.8%; Italy 9.7%; China 7.4%; Hungary 3.9%. **Exports** (2007; f.o.b.): US$8,825,000,000 (food products 15.4%, of which fruits and vegetables 5.3%; iron and steel 12.4%; machinery and apparatus 11.3%; nonferrous metals 7.9%). *Major export destinations:* Italy 12.4%; Bosnia and Herzegovina 11.8%; Montenegro 10.8%; Germany 10.6%; Russia 5.1%.

Transport and communications

Transport. *Railroads* (2006): route length (2004) 3,809 km; passenger-km 684,000,000; metric ton-km cargo 4,232,000,000. *Roads* (2007): total length 39,184 km (paved [2006] 62%). *Vehicles* (2007):

---

1 metric ton = about 1.1 short tons;   1 kilometer = 0.6 mi (statute);   1 metric ton-km cargo = about 0.68 short ton-mi cargo;   c.i.f.: cost, insurance, and freight;   f.o.b.: free on board

passenger cars 1,491,216; trucks and buses 164,566. *Air transport* (2008; Jat Airways only): passenger-km 1,434,000,000; metric ton-km cargo 3,492,000. **Communications,** in total units (units per 1,000 persons). Telephone landlines (2008): 3,085,000 (420); cellular telephone subscribers (2008): 9,619,000 (1,309); personal computers (2007): 1,801,000 (244); total Internet users (2008): 2,361,000 (321); broadband Internet subscribers (2008): 451,000 (61).

Education and health

Educational attainment (2002). Percentage of population ages 15 and over having: no formal education/unknown 7.8%; incomplete primary education 16.2%; complete primary 23.9%; secondary 41.1%; higher 11.0%. **Health** (2007): physicians (public health institutions only) 20,066 (1 per 368 persons); hospital beds (public health institutions only) 41,100 (1 per 180 persons); infant mortality rate per 1,000 live births (2008) 6.7; undernourished population (2002–04; includes Kosovo and Montenegro) 900,000 (9% of total population based on the consumption of a minimum daily requirement of 2,000 calories).

Military

Total active duty personnel (November 2008): 24,257 (army 46.1%, air force/air defense 17.1%, training/ministry of defense 36.8%). **Military expenditure as percentage of GDP** (2008) 2.1%; per capita expenditure US$128.

Background

The Kingdom of the Serbs, Croats, and Slovenes was created after the collapse of Austria-Hungary at the end of World War I. The country signed treaties with Czechoslovakia and Romania in 1920–21, marking the beginning of the Little Entente. In 1929 an absolute monarchy was established, the country's name was changed to Yugoslavia, and it was divided into regions without regard to ethnic boundaries. Axis powers invaded Yugoslavia in 1941, and German, Italian, Hungarian, and Bulgarian troops occupied it for the rest of World War II. In 1945 the Socialist Federal Republic of Yugoslavia was established; it included the republics of Bosnia and Herzegovina, Croatia, Macedonia, Montenegro, Serbia, and Slovenia. Its independent form of communism under Josip Broz Tito's leadership provoked the USSR. Internal ethnic tensions flared up in the 1980s, causing the country's ultimate collapse. In 1991–92 independence was declared by Croatia, Slovenia, Macedonia, and Bosnia and Herzegovina; the new Federal Republic of Yugoslavia (containing roughly 45% of the population and 40% of the area of its predecessor) was proclaimed by Serbia and Montenegro. Fueled by long-standing ethnic tensions, hostilities continued into the 1990s. Despite the approval of the Dayton Peace Agreement (1995), sporadic fighting continued and was followed in 1998–99 by Serbian repression and expulsion of ethnic populations in the province of Kosovo. In September–October 2000, the battered nation of Yugoslavia ended the autocratic rule of Pres. Slobodan Milosevic. In April 2001 he was arrested and in June extradited to The Hague to stand trial for war crimes, genocide, and crimes against humanity committed during the fighting in Kosovo. In February 2003 the government accepted a new state charter and changed the name of the country from Yugoslavia to Serbia and Montenegro. Henceforth, defense, international political and economic relations, and human rights matters would be handled centrally, while all other functions would be run from the republican capitals, Belgrade and Podgorica, respectively. A provision was included for both states to vote on independence after three years; Serbia declared its independence in June 2006, shortly after Montenegro severed its federal union with Serbia. In 2008 Kosovo formally seceded, but Serbia refused to recognize it as an independent country.

Recent Developments

In December 2009 Serbia remained undecided on whether to open its mission to NATO, in accordance with its membership in the Partnership for Peace program. Interim trade provisions in the agreement were initially blocked by the Netherlands, which demanded that Serbia first arrest two indicted war criminals: Bosnian Serb Gen. Ratko Mladic and Croatian Goran Hadzic. At the EU foreign ministers meeting in December, however, the Dutch government lifted its opposition after a report by the International Criminal Tribunal for the Former Yugoslavia's chief prosecutor stated that Serbia made "constant progress" in efforts to cooperate with the court. The move thus enabled Serbia to attract more foreign investment and expand trade with EU member states. Belgrade submitted an application for EU candidacy late in December, and in March 2010 the government announced plans to open its NATO office.

Internet resource: <www.serbia.travel>.

Seychelles

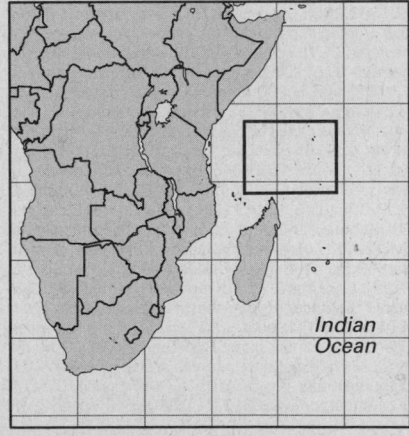

Indian
Ocean

Official name: Repiblik Sesel (Creole); République des Seychelles (French); Republic of Seychelles (English). **Form of government:** multiparty republic with one legislative house (National Assembly [34]). **Head of state and government:** President James Michel (from 2004). **Capital:** Victoria. **Official languages:**

none (Creole, French, and English are national languages per the constitution). **Official religion:** none. **Monetary unit:** 1 Seychelles rupee (roupi; SR) = 100 cents; valuation (1 Jul 2010) US$1 = SR 11.16.

Demography

Area: 174 sq mi, 452 sq km. **Population** (2009): 87,800. **Density** (2009): persons per sq mi 503.4, persons per sq km 194.4. **Urban** (2008): 53.8%. **Sex distribution** (2008): male 51.75%; female 48.25%. **Age breakdown** (2008): under 15, 22.7%; 15–29, 26.0%; 30–44, 24.5%; 45–59, 16.2%; 60–74, 7.3%; 75 and over, 3.3%. **Ethnic composition** (2000): Seychellois Creole (mixture of Asian, African, and European) 93.2%; British 3.0%; French 1.8%; Chinese 0.5%; Indian 0.3%; other 1.2%. **Religious affiliation** (2002): Roman Catholic 82.3%; Anglican 6.4%; other Christian 4.5%; Hindu 2.1%; Muslim 1.1%; other 3.6%. **Major towns** (2006): Victoria 22,600; Anse Royale (2004) 3,800. **Location:** group of islands in the Indian Ocean, northeast of Madagascar.

Vital statistics

Birth rate per 1,000 population (2007): 17.6 (world avg. 20.3); within marriage 20.8%. **Death rate** per 1,000 population (2007): 7.4 (world avg. 8.5). **Total fertility rate** (avg. births per childbearing woman; 2007): 2.24. **Life expectancy** at birth (2007): male 68.9 years; female 77.7 years.

National economy

Budget (2007). *Revenue:* SR 2,487,300,000 (tax revenue 64.7%, of which taxes on goods and services 37.2%, taxes on international trade 13.0%; social contributions 18.1%). *Expenditures:* SR 2,854,900,000 (social protection 21.5%; public debt interest charges 14.5%; education 9.9%; health 7.0%; public order 4.8%; defense 3.9%). **Public debt** (2008): US$254,000,000. **Gross national income** (2008): US$889,000,000 (US$10,290 per capita). **Production** (metric tons except as noted). *Agriculture and fishing* (2007): coconuts 3,200, bananas 2,000, cinnamon 315; livestock (number of live animals) 18,700 pigs, 5,200 goats, 575,000 chickens; fisheries production 66,239 (from aquaculture 6%). *Mining and quarrying* (2007): granite 149,000. *Manufacturing* (2006): canned tuna 40,222; fish meal 14,821; copra 253. *Energy production (consumption):* electricity (kW-hr; 2006) 251,000,000 (227,000,000); petroleum products (metric tons; 2006) none (243,000). **Population economically active** (2002): total 43,859; activity rate of total population 53.6% (participation rates: ages 15–64, 80.1%; female [1997] 47.6%; unemployed [2006] 2.6%). **Selected balance of payments data.** Receipts from (US$'000,000): tourism (2007) 278; remittances (2008) 12; foreign direct investment (FDI; 2005–07 avg.) 160; official development assistance (2007) 3. Disbursements for (US$'000,000): tourism (2007) 40; remittances (2008) 21; FDI (2005–07 avg.) 8.

Foreign trade

Imports (2007; c.i.f.): SR 5,728,000,000 (mineral fuels 25.1%; machinery and apparatus 22.4%;

food products 19.5%, of which marine products 11.9%; transportation equipment 4.1%; iron and steel 3.4%). *Major import sources:* Saudi Arabia 24.8%; Germany 9.5%; Singapore 8.5%; France 7.8%; Spain 6.6%. **Exports** (2007; f.o.b.): SR 2,435,000,000 (domestic exports 55.3%, of which canned tuna 50.6%, fish meal 1.2%, medicine and medical appliances 1.2%; reexports 44.7%, of which refined petroleum products to ships and aircraft 43.1%). *Major export destinations* (domestic exports only): UK 40.1%; France 34.7%; Italy 10.0%; Germany 3.2%.

Transport and communications

Transport. *Railroads:* none. *Roads* (2006): total length 502 km (paved 96%). *Vehicles* (2006): passenger cars 7,070; trucks and buses 2,796. *Air transport* (2006–07; Air Seychelles only): passenger-km 1,593,000,000; metric ton-km cargo 31,000,000. **Communications,** in total units (units per 1,000 persons). Telephone landlines (2008): 22,000 (266); cellular telephone subscribers (2008): 94,000 (1,115); personal computers (2005): 16,000 (193); total Internet users (2008): 68,000 (382); broadband Internet subscribers (2008): 3,400 (41).

Education and health

Educational attainment (2003). Percentage of population ages 12 and over having: less than primary or primary education 23.2%; secondary 73.4%; higher 3.4%. **Literacy** (2006): total population ages 15 and over literate 91.8%; males literate 91.4%; females literate 92.3%. **Health** (2007): physicians 91 (1 per 934 persons); hospital beds 401 (1 per 212 persons); infant mortality rate per 1,000 live births 10.7; undernourished population (2002–04) 7,000 (9% of total population based on the consumption of a minimum daily requirement of 1,810 calories).

Military

Total active duty personnel (November 2008): 200 (army 100%); there is also a 450-member paramilitary, which includes both a coast guard and a national guard. **Military expenditure as percentage of GDP** (2007): 1.9%; per capita expenditure US$129.

Background

The first recorded landing on the uninhabited Seychelles was made in 1609 by an expedition of the British East India Co. The archipelago was claimed by the French in 1756 and surrendered to the British in 1810. Seychelles became a British crown colony in 1903 and a republic within the Commonwealth in 1976. A one-party socialist state since 1979, Seychelles began moving toward democracy in the 1990s; it adopted a new constitution in 1993.

Recent Developments

In support of the international effort to stem an increase in Indian Ocean piracy, which accounted for 214 attacked ships in 2009, the Seychelles coast guard opened a monitoring and rescue center in

1 metric ton = about 1.1 short tons;   1 kilometer = 0.6 mi (statute);   1 metric ton-km cargo = about 0.68 short ton-mi cargo;   c.i.f.: cost, insurance, and freight;   f.o.b.: free on board

cooperation with the International Maritime Organization.

Internet resource: <www.nsb.gov.sc>.

Sierra Leone

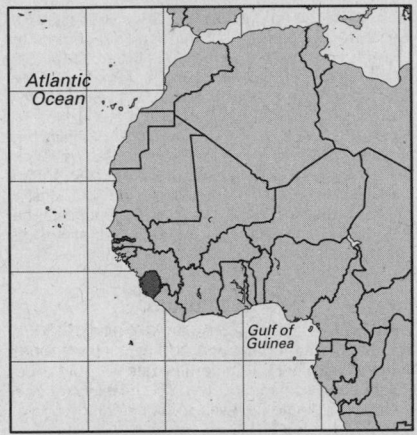

Official name: Republic of Sierra Leone. **Form of government:** republic with one legislative house (Parliament [124]). **Head of state and government:** President Ernest Bai Koroma (from 2007). **Capital:** Freetown. **Official language:** English. **Official religion:** none. **Monetary unit:** 1 leone (Le) = 100 cents; valuation (1 Jul 2010) US$1 = Le 3,850.00.

Demography

Area: 27,699 sq mi, 71,740 sq km. **Population** (2009): 5,696,000. **Density** (2009): persons per sq mi 205.6, persons per sq km 79.4. **Urban** (2008): 37.7%. **Sex distribution** (2005): male 49.23%; female 50.77%. **Age breakdown** (2005): under 15, 42.8%; 15–29, 26.1%; 30–44, 16.0%; 45–59, 9.6%; 60–74, 4.7%; 75–84, 0.7%; 85 and over, 0.1%. **Ethnic composition** (2000): Mende 26.0%; Temne 24.6%; Limba 7.1%; Kuranko 5.5%; Kono 4.2%; Fulani 3.8%; Bullom-Sherbro 3.5%; other 25.3%. **Religious affiliation** (2005): Muslim 65%; Christian 25%; traditional beliefs/other 10%. **Major towns** (2006): Freetown 818,700; Bo 181,800; Kenema 148,800; Makerli 90,400; Koidu 87,300. **Location:** western Africa, bordering Guinea, Liberia, and the North Atlantiç Ocean.

Vital statistics

Birth rate per 1,000 population (2008): 45.8 (world avg. 20.3). **Death rate** per 1,000 population (2008): 21.8 (world avg. 8.5). **Total fertility rate** (avg. births per childbearing woman; 2005): 6.49. **Life expectancy** at birth (2005): male 40.1 years; female 43.5 years.

National economy

Budget (2007). **Revenue:** Le 1,179,000,000,000 (grants 42.7%; import duties 21.8%; corporate taxes 7.7%; income tax 7.1%; excise duties on refined petroleum products 6.6%). *Expenditures:* Le 1,222,000,000,000 (current expenditures 63.4%; capital expenditures 36.6%). **Gross national income** (2008): US$1,785,000,000 (US$320 per capita). **Production** (metric tons except as noted). *Agriculture and fishing* (2007): rice 650,000, cassava 370,000, oil palm fruit 195,000, cacao beans 12,000; livestock (number of live animals) 300,000 cattle, 7,500,000 chickens; fisheries production 144,535 (from aquaculture, negligible). *Mining and quarrying* (2008): bauxite 954,370; rutile 78,910; ilmenite 17,260; diamonds 371,290 carats; gold (2007) 212 kg. *Manufacturing* (2006): soap 467,360; cement 234,440; paint 142,730 gallons. *Energy production (consumption):* electricity (kW-hr; 2006) 99,000,000 (99,000,000); crude petroleum (barrels; 2006) none (1,980,000); petroleum products (metric tons; 2006) 166,000 (200,000). **Public debt** (external, outstanding; 2007): US$308,000,000. **Population economically active** (2003–04): total 2,005,900; activity rate of total population 40.0% (participation rates: ages 15–64, 68.2%; female 53.6%; unofficially unemployed [2007] 65%). **Selected balance of payments data.** Receipts from (US$'000,000): tourism (2007) 22; remittances (2008) 150; foreign direct investment (2005–07 avg.) 74; official development assistance (2007) 535. Disbursements for (US$'000,000): tourism (2007) 14; remittances (2008) 136.

Foreign trade

Imports (2007; c.i.f.): Le 1,333,189,000,000 (mineral fuels 37.7%; machinery and transportation equipment 16.8%; food products 15.2%, of which rice 5.4%). *Major import sources* (2005): Germany 19%; Côte d'Ivoire 11%; UK 8%; US 7%; China 6%. **Exports** (2007; f.o.b.): Le 733,407,000,000 (diamonds 57.8%; rutile 15.5%; bauxite 13.3%; cocoa 4.6%; gold 1.2%). *Major export destinations:* Belgium 49.5%; US 20.6%; Netherlands 4.6%; Canada 4.0%.

Transport and communications

Transport. *Railroads* (2002; Marampa Mineral Railway; there are no passenger railways): length 84 km. *Roads* (2002): total length 11,300 km (paved 8%). *Vehicles* (2007): passenger cars 16,396; trucks and buses 14,444. *Air transport* (2004): passenger-km 85,000,000; metric ton-km cargo 8,000,000. **Communications,** in total units (units per 1,000 persons). Telephone landlines (2008): 32,000 (5.7); cellular telephone subscribers (2008): 1,009,000 (181); personal computers (1999): 100; total Internet users (2008): 14,000 (2.5).

Education and health

Educational attainment (2004). Percentage of total population having: no formal schooling 62.2%; primary education 24.6%; lower secondary 6.4%; upper secondary 4.2%; vocational 2.0%; higher 0.6%. **Literacy** (2007): total population ages 15 and over literate 38.1%; males literate 50.0%; females literate 26.8%. **Health:** physicians (2004) 168 (1 per 32,083 persons); hospital beds (2001) 2,770 (1 per 1,698 persons); infant mortality rate per 1,000 live births (2005) 163.0; undernourished population (2003–05) 2,500,000 (47% of total population based on the consumption of a minimum daily requirement of 1,750 calories).

Military

Total active duty personnel (November 2008): c. 10,500 (army 98%, navy 2%, air force, none). Military expenditure as percentage of GDP (2007): 1.7%; per capita expenditure US$5.

Background

The earliest inhabitants of Sierra Leone were probably the Buloms; the Mende and Temne peoples arrived in the 15th century. The coastal region was visited by the Portuguese in the 15th century, and by 1495 there was a Portuguese fort on the site of modern Freetown. European ships visited the coast regularly to trade for slaves and ivory, and the English built trading posts on offshore islands in the 17th century. British abolitionists and philanthropists founded Freetown in 1787 as a private venture for freed and runaway slaves. In 1808 the coastal settlement became a British colony. The region became a British protectorate in 1896. It achieved independence in 1961 and became a republic in 1971. Since independence Sierra Leone experienced a series of military coups. An 11-year civil war, which was marked by horrific atrocities and further devastated the country, ended in 2002.

Recent Developments

Hampered by the global recession, Sierra Leone's economic growth slowed to roughly 4.0% in 2009, down from 5.5% a year earlier. Two IMF missions to Sierra Leone commended the government, however, for staying on course with its monetary policies despite the challenging economic conditions worldwide. The discovery of a deepwater oil field off the coast of Sierra Leone also held the promise of relief from the country's dependence on the diamond industry.

Internet resource: <www.statistics.sl>.

Singapore

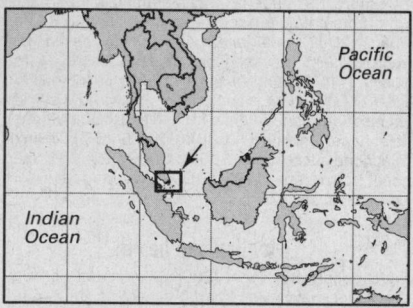

Pacific Ocean

Indian Ocean

Official name: Xinjiapo Gongheguo (Mandarin Chinese); Republik Singapura (Malay); Cingkappur Kudiyarasu (Tamil); Republic of Singapore (English). Form of government: unitary multiparty republic with one legislative house (Parliament [94]). Head of state: President Sellapan Rama (S.R.) Nathan (from 1999). Head of state government: Prime Minister Lee Hsien Loong (from 2004). Capital: Singapore. Official languages: Mandarin Chinese; Malay; Tamil; English. Official religion: none. Monetary unit: 1 Singapore dollar (S$) = 100 cents; valuation (1 Jul 2010) US$1 = S$1.40.

Demography

Area: 274.2 sq mi, 710.2 sq km. Population (2009): 4,954,000. Density (2009): persons per sq mi 18,067, persons per sq km 6,975. Urban: 100%. Sex distribution (2009): male 49.41%; female 50.59%. Age breakdown (2009): under 15, 17.9%; 15–29, 20.9%; 30–44, 24.8%; 45–59, 23.0%; 60–74, 10.0%; 75–84, 2.6%; 85 and over, 0.8%. Ethnic composition (2009): Chinese 74.2%; Malay 13.4%; Indian 9.2%; other 3.2%. Religious affiliation (2000): Buddhist/Taoist/Chinese folk-religionist 51.0%; Muslim 14.9%; Christian 14.6%; Hindu 4.0%; traditional beliefs 0.6%; nonreligious 14.9%. Location: southeastern Asia, islands between Malaysia and Indonesia.

Vital statistics

Birth rate per 1,000 population (2008): 10.2 (world avg. 20.3). Death rate per 1,000 population (2008): 4.4 (world avg. 8.5). Total fertility rate (avg. births per childbearing woman; 2008): 1.28. Life expectancy at birth (2008): male 78.4 years; female 83.2 years.

National economy

Budget (2008). Revenue: S$41,376,700,000 (income tax 44.9%; goods and services tax 16.0%; fees and charges 9.0%; assets taxes 7.0%; customs and excise duties 5.0%). Expenditures: S$37,470,-200,000 (security and external relations 36.3%; education 19.5%; health 6.1%; community development 3.1%). Production (metric tons except as noted). Agriculture and fishing (2008): vegetables 18,967, orchids (roughly 15% of the world market) and other ornamental plants are cultivated for export; livestock (number of live animals) 260,000 pigs, 2,000,000 chickens; fisheries production (2007) 8,025 (from aquaculture 56%); aquarium fish farming is also an important economic pursuit—Singapore produces roughly 30% of the world's ornamental fish. Quarrying: limestone, n.a. Manufacturing (value added in S$'000,000; 2008): pharmaceuticals 9,443; professional and scientific equipment 7,898; semiconductors 7,894; refined petroleum products and petrochemicals 2,639. Energy production (consumption): electricity (kW-hr; 2008–09) 40,964,000,000 ([2008] 37,940,300,000); crude petroleum (barrels; 2008) 3,121,845 (327,040,000); petroleum products (metric tons; 2006) 36,501,000 (7,781,000); natural gas (cu m; 2008) none (8,270,000,000). Gross national income (2008): US$168,227,-000,000 (US$34,760 per capita). Population economically active (2008): total 1,928,300; activity rate of total population 52.9% (participation rates: ages 15–64, 71.7%; female 43.3%; unemployed [October 2008–September 2009] 3.1%). Public debt (2006): US$122,000,000,000. Selected balance of payments data. Receipts from (US$'000,000): tourism (2007) 8,680; foreign direct investment (FDI; 2005–07 avg.) 20,937. Disbursements for

1 metric ton = about 1.1 short tons;   1 kilometer = 0.6 mi (statute);   1 metric ton-km cargo = about 0.68 short ton-mi cargo;   c.i.f.: cost, insurance, and freight;   f.o.b.: free on board

(US$'000,000): tourism (2007) 11,844; FDI (2005–07 avg.) 10,495.

Foreign trade

Imports (2008; c.i.f.): S$450,892,600,000 (crude petroleum and refined petroleum products 27.4%; nonelectrical machinery and equipment 16.1%; integrated circuits 13.4%; other electronics 10.2%; chemical products 5.3%; base metals 4.2%). *Major import sources:* Malaysia 11.9%; US 11.7%; China 10.6%; Japan 8.1%; South Korea 5.6%. **Exports** (2008; f.o.b.): S$476,762,100,000 (crude petroleum and refined petroleum products 24.1%; integrated circuits 16.8%; nonelectrical machinery and equipment 14.3%; other electronics 13.2%; chemical products 10.2%). *Major export destinations:* Malaysia 12.1%; Indonesia 10.6%; Hong Kong 10.4%; China 9.2%; US 7.0%.

Transport and communications

Transport. *Railroads* (2006): length 39 km. *Roads* (2008; public roads only): total length 3,325 km (paved 100%). *Vehicles* (2009): passenger cars 566,520; trucks and buses 173,178. *Air transport* (2008–09): passenger-km 92,249,000,000; metric ton-km cargo 6,845,262,000. **Communications,** in total units (units per 1,000 persons). Telephone landlines (2008): 1,857,000 (402); cellular telephone subscribers (2008): 6,376,000 (1,382); personal computers (2007): 3,409,000 (743); total Internet users (2008): 3,370,000 (730); broadband Internet subscribers (2008): 1,003,000 (217).

Education and health

Educational attainment (2005). Percentage of population ages 15 and over having: no schooling 16.4%; primary education 22.0%; lower secondary 21.3%; upper secondary 15.1%; technical 8.2%; university 17.0%. **Literacy** (2008): total population ages 15 and over literate 96.0%. **Health** (2008): physicians 7,841 (1 per 617 persons); hospital beds 11,457 (1 per 422 persons); infant mortality rate per 1,000 live births 2.1.

Military

Total active duty personnel (November 2008): 72,500 (army 69.0%, navy 12.4%, air force 18.6%). **Military expenditure as percentage of GDP** (2008): 4.1%; per capita expenditure US$1,517.

Background

Long inhabited by fishermen and pirates, Singapore was an outpost of the Sumatran empire of Srivijaya until the 14th century, when it passed to Java and then to Siam. It became part of the Malacca empire in the 15th century. In the 16th century the Portuguese controlled the area, followed by the Dutch. In 1819 Singapore was ceded to the British East India Co., becoming part of the Straits Settlements and the center of British colonial activity in Southeast Asia. The Japanese occupied the islands in 1942–45. In 1946 it became a crown colony. It achieved full internal self-government in 1959, became a part of Malaysia in 1963, and gained independence in 1965. It is influential in the affairs of the Association of Southeast Asian Nations and has become a re-gional economic powerhouse. The country's dominant voice in politics for 30 years after independence was Lee Kuan Yew.

Recent Developments

Like most countries, Singapore was in recession in 2009, but government grants to subsidize the wage bills of employers managed to stave off some retrenchments, keeping unemployment under 5% for most of the year. A S$20.5 billion (about US$13.8 billion) assistance package introduced in January included measures to encourage bank lending and spur employers to send workers for skills training. Thanks partly to these stimulus measures, economic contraction in 2009 amounted to only one-third of the level that had been feared at the beginning of the year.

Internet resource: <www.singstat.gov.sg>.

Slovakia

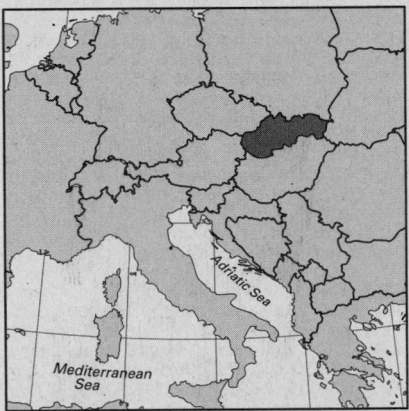

Official name: Slovenska Republika (Slovak Republic). **Form of government:** unitary multiparty republic with one legislative house (National Council [150]). **Head of state:** President Ivan Gasparovic (from 2004). **Head of government:** Prime Minister Iveta Radicová (from 2010). **Capital:** Bratislava. **Official language:** Slovak. **Official religion:** none. **Monetary unit:** 1 euro (€) = 100 cents; valuation (1 Jul 2010) US$1 = €0.80 (the euro replaced the Slovak koruna [Sk] on 1 Jan 2009, at the rate of €1 = Sk 30.126).

Demography

Area: 18,932 sq mi, 49,034 sq km. **Population** (2009): 5,418,000. **Density** (2009): persons per sq mi 286.2, persons per sq km 110.5. **Urban** (2006): 55.4%. **Sex distribution** (2008): male 48.52%; female 51/48%. **Age breakdown** (2008): under 15, 16.3%; 15–29, 24.0%; 30–44, 22.2%; 45–59, 21.1%; 60–74, 11.4%; 75–84, 4.0%; 85 and over, 1.0%. **Ethnic composition** (2001): Slovak 85.8%; Hungarian 9.7%; Rom (Gypsy) 1.7%; Czech 0.8%; Ruthenian and Ukrainian 0.7%; other 1.3%. **Religious affiliation** (2001): Roman Catholic 68.9%; Protestant 9.2%, of which Lutheran 6.9%, Reformed Christian

2.0%; Greek Catholic 4.1%; Eastern Orthodox 0.9%; nonreligious 13.0%; other 3.9%. **Major cities** (2007): Bratislava 426,927; Kosice 234,237; Presov 91,498; Zilina 85,370; Nitra 84,444. **Location:** central Europe, bordering Poland, Ukraine, Hungary, Austria, and the Czech Republic.

Vital statistics

Birth rate per 1,000 population (2008): 10.6 (world avg. 20.3); within marriage 69.9%. **Death rate** per 1,000 population (2008): 9.8 (world avg. 8.5). **Total fertility rate** (avg. births per childbearing woman; 2008): 1.33. **Life expectancy** at birth (2008): male 70.9 years; female 78.7 years.

National economy

Budget (2007). *Revenue:* Sk 546,660,000,000 (tax revenue 47.9%, of which taxes on goods and services 35.6%; social security contributions 39.8%; nontax revenue 10.9%; grants 1.4%). *Expenditures:* Sk 580,610,000,000 (social protection 33.0%; health 20.0%; general administration 18.9%; economic affairs 11.8%; police 5.9%; defense 4.5%; education 3.7%). **Production** (metric tons except as noted). *Agriculture and fishing* (2007): wheat 1,440,637, sugar beets 855,343, barley 695,042, sunflower seeds 135,376; livestock (number of live animals) 1,104,830 pigs, 507,820 cattle; fisheries production 4,071 (from aquaculture 29%). *Mining and quarrying* (2007): magnesite 457,763; kaolin 30,000; barite 13,000. *Manufacturing* (value added in US$'000,000; 2006): fabricated metal products 1,200; nonelectrical machinery and apparatus 1,165; motor vehicles and parts 1,000. *Energy production (consumption):* electricity (kW-hr; 2008) 28,908,000,000 ([2006] 29,087,000,000); coal (metric tons; 2006) none (5,148,000); lignite (metric tons; 2008) 2,412,000 ([2006] 3,168,000); crude petroleum (barrels; 2007) 170,000 ([2006] 41,400,000); petroleum products (metric tons; 2006) 5,330,000 (2,953,000); natural gas (cu m; 2007) 142,000,000 ([2006] 6,411,000,000). **Population economically active** (2008): total 2,691,200; activity rate of total population 49.8% (participation rates: ages 15–64, 68.9%; female 44.7%; unemployed [July 2008–June 2009] 9.1%). **Public debt** (external, outstanding; December 2008): US$10,313,000,000. **Gross national income** (2008): US$78,607,000,000 (US$14,540 per capita). **Selected balance of payments data.** Receipts from (US$'000,000): tourism (2007) 2,026; remittances (2008) 1,500; foreign direct investment (FDI; 2005–07 avg.) 3,179. Disbursements for (US$'000,000): tourism (2007) 1,533; remittances (2008) 73; FDI (2005–07 avg.) 303.

Foreign trade

Imports (2007): US$57,754,000,000 (machinery and apparatus 29.6%, of which telecommunications equipment and parts 9.6%; motor vehicles and parts 13.8%; mineral fuels 11.0%; base and fabricated metals 10.3%; chemical products 8.7%). *Major import sources:* Germany 19.9%; Czech Republic 11.5%; Russia 9.4%; Hungary 5.4%; China 5.2%. **Exports** (2008): US$57,802,000,000 (machinery and

apparatus 28.7%, of which color television receivers 10.3%; motor vehicles and parts 24.3%, of which passenger cars 17.9%; base and fabricated metals 12.9%, of which iron and steel 7.5%; refined petroleum products 4.5%). *Major export destinations:* Germany 21.5%; Czech Republic 12.4%; France 6.8%; Italy 6.4%; Poland 6.2%.

Transport and communications

Transport. *Railroads* (2006): length 3,658 km; passenger-km 2,213,000,000; metric ton-km cargo 9,988,000,000. *Roads* (2006): total length 43,770 km (paved 87%). *Vehicles* (2007): passenger cars 1,468,616; trucks and buses 255,089. *Air transport* (2008; SkyEurope airlines only): passenger-km 3,733,000,000; metric ton-km cargo, none. **Communications**, in total units (units per 1,000 persons). Telephone landlines (2008): 1,098,000 (203); cellular telephone subscribers (2008): 5,520,000 (1,021); personal computers (2007): 2,774,000 (514); total Internet users (2008): 2,771,000 (513); broadband Internet subscribers (2008): 619,000 (114).

Education and health

Educational attainment (2007). Percentage of population ages 25–64 having: primary education 1%; lower secondary 12%; upper secondary 73%; higher vocational 1%; university 13%. **Literacy** (2007): total population ages 15 and over literate nearly 100%. **Health:** physicians (2006) 17,031 (1 per 317 persons); hospital beds (2007) 36,426 (1 per 148 persons); infant mortality rate per 1,000 live births (2008) 5.9; undernourished population (2002–04) 400,000 (7% of total population based on the consumption of a minimum daily requirement of 2,030 calories).

Military

Total active duty personnel (November 2008): 17,445 (army 41.8%, air force 24.0%, headquarters staff 13.3%, support/training 20.9%). **Military expenditure as percentage of GDP** (2008): 1.5%; per capita expenditure US$255.

Background

Slovakia was inhabited in the first centuries AD by Illyrian, Celtic, and Germanic tribes. Slovaks settled there around the 6th century. It became part of Great Moravia in the 9th century but was conquered by the Magyars c. 907. It remained in the kingdom of Hungary until the end of World War I, when the Slovaks joined the Czechs to form the new state of Czechoslovakia in 1918. Slovakia was nominally independent under German protection in 1939–45. After the expulsion of the Germans, Slovakia joined a reconstituted Czechoslovakia, which came under Soviet domination in 1948. In 1969 a partnership between the Czechs and the Slovaks established the Slovak Socialist Republic. The fall of the communist regime in 1989 led to a revival of interest in autonomy, and Slovakia became an independent nation in 1993. It joined both NATO and the EU in 2004.

---

1 metric ton = about 1.1 short tons;   1 kilometer = 0.6 mi (statute);   1 metric ton-km cargo = about 0.68 short ton-mi cargo;   c.i.f.: cost, insurance, and freight;   f.o.b.: free on board

Recent Developments

Slovakian industrial production and exports fell dramatically in 2009 amid the global economic crisis, and the unemployment rate soared to more than 12% in the second half of the year, a year-on-year increase of more than 4%. Domestic industry was also hit by a halt in January in gas supplies during the Russian-Ukrainian price dispute. Tensions between Slovaks and Hungarians were heightened when on 21 August Bratislava banned Hungarian Pres. Laszlo Solyom from entering the country to attend the unveiling of a statue honoring a Hungarian king, in part because the visit coincided with the anniversary of the 1968 invasion by Warsaw Pact troops (including Hungarian soldiers) that crushed Czechoslovakia's Prague Spring liberalization movement.

Internet resource: <http://portal.statistics.sk>.

Slovenia

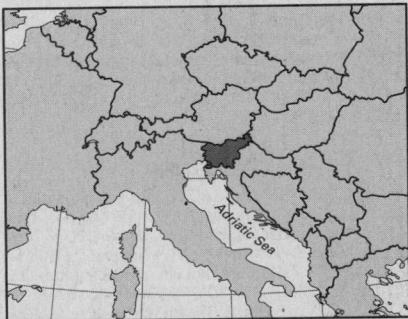

Official name: Republika Slovenija (Republic of Slovenia). Form of government: unitary multiparty republic with two legislative houses (National Council [40]; National Assembly [90]). Head of state: President Danilo Turk (from 2007). Head of government: Prime Minister Borut Pahor (from 2008). Capital: Ljubljana. Official language: Slovene. Official religion: none. Monetary unit: 1 euro (€) = 100 cents; valuation (1 Jul 2010) US$1 = €0.80.

Demography

Area: 7,827 sq mi, 20,273 sq km. Population (2009): 2,037,000. Density (2009): persons per sq mi 260.3, persons per sq km 100.5. Urban (2005): 51.0%. Sex distribution (2008): male 49.64%; female 50.36%. Age breakdown (2007): under 15, 13.9%; 15–29, 20.0%; 30–44, 22.6%; 45–59, 22.4%; 60–74, 14.1%; 75–84, 5.7%; 85 and over, 1.3%. Ethnic composition (2002): Slovene 91.2%; Serb 2.2%; Croat 2.0%; Bosniac (Muslim) 1.8%; other 2.8%. Religious affiliation (2002): Roman Catholic 57.8%; Muslim 2.4%; Orthodox 2.3%; Protestant 0.8%; nonreligious/atheist 10.2%; other 26.5%. Major cities (2008): Ljubljana 268,423; Maribor 96,408; Celje 38,047; Kranj 36,357; Velenje 25,935. Location: southeastern Europe, bordering Austria, Hungary, Croatia, the Adriatic Sea, and Italy.

Vital statistics

Birth rate per 1,000 population (2008): 10.8 (world avg. 20.3); within marriage 47.1%. Death rate per 1,000 population (2008): 9.1 (world avg. 8.5). Total fertility rate (avg. births per childbearing woman; 2008): 1.53. Life expectancy at birth (2007): male 75.0 years; female 82.3 years.

National economy

Budget (2007). Revenue: €13,658,091,000 (tax revenue 59.7%, of which taxes on goods and services 32.9%, income tax 13.2%; social security contributions 33.7%; nontax revenue 5.2%; other [including grants] 1.4%). Expenditures: €13,092,376,000 (current expenditures 88.8%, of which social protection 46.9%, wages and salaries 21.5%; capital expenditures 11.2%). Public debt (2007): US$10,875,000,000. Production (metric tons except as noted). Agriculture and fishing (2007): corn (maize) 308,259, sugar beets 260,000, wheat 133,339, hops 2,157; livestock (number of live animals) 575,120 pigs, 451,293 cattle, 212,000 beehives; fisheries production 2,463 (from aquaculture 55%). Mining and quarrying (2007): sand and gravel 11,008,600; salt (2005) 125,000. Manufacturing (value added in €'000,000; 2007): chemical products 971; fabricated metal products 961; nonelectrical machinery and equipment 776. Energy production (consumption): electricity (kW-hr; 2008) 15,357,000,000 (12,945,-000,000); coal (metric tons; 2006) none (46,000); lignite (metric tons; 2008) 4,032,000 (4,161,000); crude petroleum (barrels; 2007) 2,199 (negligible); petroleum products (metric tons; 2007) none (2,296,000); natural gas (cu m; 2007) 3,400,000 (1,124,000,000). Gross national income (2008): US$48,973,000,000 (US$24,010 per capita). Population economically active (2007): total 1,041,600; activity rate 51.8% (participation rates: ages 15–64, 71.7%; female 46.0%; unemployed [2008] 7.0%). Selected balance of payments data. Receipts from (US$'000,000): tourism (2007) 2,218; remittances (2008) 331; foreign direct investment (FDI; 2005–07 avg.) 883. Disbursements for (US$'000,000): tourism (2007) 1,103; remittances (2008) 371; FDI (2005–07 avg.) 1,038.

Foreign trade

Imports (2007; c.i.f.): €21,487,000,000 (base and fabricated metals 14.1%; motor vehicles 13.2%; chemical products 12.1%; nonelectrical machinery and equipment 10.6%; mineral fuels 9.4%; food products 5.6%). Major import sources: Germany 19.4%; Italy 18.3%; Austria 12.5%; France 5.4%; Croatia 4.0%. Exports (2007; f.o.b.): €19,385,000,000 (motor vehicles and parts 15.9%; base and fabricated metals 13.6%; nonelectrical machinery and equipment 12.5%; electrical machinery, electronics, and parts 9.6%; medicine and pharmaceuticals 7.2%; furniture 4.3%). Major export destinations: Germany 18.9%; Italy 13.2%; Croatia 8.1%; Austria 7.8%; France 6.5%.

Transport and communications

Transport. Railroads (2008): length 1,228 km; passenger-km 834,000,000; metric ton-km cargo 3,520,000,000. Roads (2006): total length 38,562 km (paved 100%). *Vehicles* (2008): passenger cars 1,045,183; trucks and buses 83,909. *Air transport* (2008): passenger-km 1,008,000,000; metric ton-km cargo 1,944,000. **Communications**, in total units (units per 1,000 persons). Telephone landlines (2008): 1,010,000 (501); cellular telephone subscribers (2008): 2,055,000 (1,020); personal computers (2007): 850,000 (425); total Internet users (2008): 1,126,000 (559); broadband Internet subscribers (2008): 427,000 (212).

Education and health

Educational attainment (2006). Percentage of population ages 15 and over having: no formal schooling through complete primary education 27.7%; secondary 6.0%; vocational 55.1%; some higher 2.9%; undergraduate 7.1%; advanced degree 1.2%. **Literacy** (2007): total population ages 15 and over literate, virtually 100%. **Health** (2007): physicians 4,441 (1 per 453 persons); hospital beds 9,414 (1 per 214 persons); infant mortality rate per 1,000 live births (2008) 2.4; undernourished population (2002–04) 60,000 (3% of total population based on the consumption of a minimum daily requirement of 1,990 calories).

Military

Total active duty personnel (November 2008): 7,200 (army 100%). **Military expenditure as percentage of GNI** (2007): 1.7%; per capita expenditure US$373.

Background

The Slovenes settled the region in the 6th century AD. In the 8th century it was incorporated into the Frankish empire of Charlemagne, and in the 10th century it came under Germany as part of the Holy Roman Empire. Except for 1809–14, when Napoleon ruled the area, most of the lands belonged to Austria until the formation of the Kingdom of Serbs, Croats, and Slovenes in 1918. It became a constituent republic of Yugoslavia in 1946. In 1990 Slovenia held the first contested multiparty elections in Yugoslavia since before World War II. In 1991 it seceded from Yugoslavia. Subsequently it sought to privatize the economy and build ties with Western Europe, joining both the EU and NATO in 2004.

Recent Developments

Slovenia, the wealthiest of the countries that had joined the EU since 2004, fell into recession in early 2009. Once the fastest-growing member of the euro zone, Slovenia became the worst performing. Industrial production improved by August, indicating that Slovenia was emerging from recession. In October, however, the European Commission initiated an excessive-deficit procedure for budgetary shortfalls above 3.0% of GDP for Slovenia, whose gap reached 5.5% by the end of the year. Waning demand for Slovenian exports—which made up two-thirds of total GDP—falling taxes, and a government stimulus program contributed.

Internet resource: <www.stat.si/eng/index.asp>.

Solomon Islands

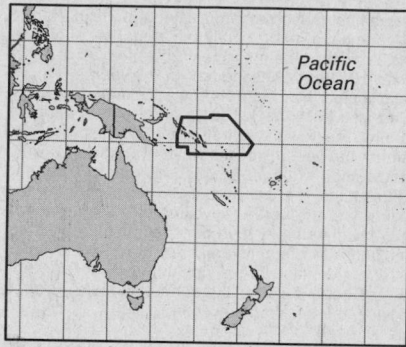

Pacific Ocean

Official name: Solomon Islands. **Form of government:** constitutional monarchy with one legislative house (National Parliament [50]). **Head of state:** British Queen Elizabeth II (from 1952), represented by Governor-General Frank Kabui (from 2009). **Head of government:** Prime Minister Derek Sikua (from 2007). **Capital:** Honiara. **Official language:** English. **Official religion:** none. **Monetary unit:** 1 Solomon Islands dollar (SI$) = 100 cents; valuation (1 Jul 2010) US$1 = SI$7.41.

Demography

Area: 10,954 sq mi, 28,370 sq km. **Population** (2009): 523,000. **Density** (2009): persons per sq mi 47.7, persons per sq km 18.4. **Urban** (2005–06): 16.0%. **Sex distribution** (2008): male 50.63%; female 49.37%. **Age breakdown** (2008): under 15, 40.1%; 15–29, 29.4%; 30–44, 17.4%; 45–59, 8.0%; 60–74, 4.0%; 75–84, 1.0%; 85 and over, 0.1%. **Ethnic composition** (2002): Melanesian 93.0%; Polynesian 4.0%; Micronesian 1.5%; other 1.5%. **Religious affiliation** (2005): Protestant 70%, of which Anglican 32%, Adventist 10%; Roman Catholic 18%; traditional beliefs 5%; other 7%. **Major towns** (2006): Honiara 57,400; Gizo 6,300; Auki 4,400. **Location:** Oceania, island group in the South Pacific Ocean, east of Papua New Guinea.

Vital statistics

Birth rate per 1,000 population (2008): 28.5 (world avg. 20.3). **Death rate** per 1,000 population (2008): 3.8 (world avg. 8.5). **Total fertility rate** (avg. births per childbearing woman; 2008): 3.65. **Life expectancy** at birth (2008): male 70.9 years; female 76.1 years.

National economy

Budget (2006). *Revenue:* SI$946,200,000 (tax revenue 73.0%, of which VAT 17.9%, logging duties 13.6%, import duties 9.3%, corporate taxes 8.2%; nontax revenue 13.9%; grants 13.1%). *Expenditures:* SI$911,100,000 (current expenditures 90.5%, of which wages and salaries 27.3%, debt service 13.9%; capital expenditures 9.5%). **Public debt** (external, outstanding; 2007): US$147,300,000. **Gross national income** (2008): US$598,000,000

---

1 metric ton = about 1.1 short tons;   1 kilometer = 0.6 mi (statute);   1 metric ton-km cargo = about 0.68 short ton-mi cargo;   c.i.f.: cost, insurance, and freight;   f.o.b.: free on board

(US$1,180 per capita). **Population economically active** (2006): total 201,000; activity rate of total population 41.0% (participation rates: ages 15 and over 68.8%; female 38.3%; unemployed [2003] 15.2%). **Production** (metric tons except as noted). *Agriculture and fishing* (2007): coconuts 276,000, oil palm fruit 155,000, sweet potatoes 86,000, cacao beans 5,300; livestock (number of live animals) 54,000 pigs, 13,600 cattle, 235,000 chickens; fisheries production 31,272 (from aquaculture, negligible); aquatic plants production 120 (from aquaculture 100%). *Mining and quarrying* (2005): gold 10 kg. *Manufacturing* (2006): coconut oil 59,000; vegetable oils and fats (2002) 50,000; copra 21,214. *Energy production (consumption):* electricity (kW-hr; 2008) 78,000,000 (57,000,000); petroleum products (metric tons; 2006) none (58,000). **Selected balance of payments data.** Receipts from (US$'000,000): tourism (2007) 4; remittances (2008) 20; foreign direct investment (2005–07 avg.) 26; official development assistance (2007) 248. Disbursements for (US$'000,000): tourism (2007) 8; remittances (2008) 3.

Foreign trade

Imports (2006; c.i.f.): US$250,613,000 (machinery and transportation equipment 24.7%; petroleum [all forms] 21.7%; food products 14.1%; construction materials 10.0%; chemical products 5.2%). *Major import sources:* Australia 25.3%; Singapore 23.4%; Japan 7.8%; New Zealand 5.0%; Fiji 4.2%. **Exports** (2007; f.o.b.): US$156,008,000 (logs 63.7%; palm oil 8.6%; frozen fish 7.2%; cacao beans 5.8%; copra 3.7%; sawn wood 3.2%). *Major export destinations* (2006): China 45.7%; South Korea 14.0%; Japan 8.5%; Thailand 4.4%; Philippines 4.0%.

Transport and communications

Transport. *Railroads:* none. *Roads* (2007): total length 1,500 km (paved 2.7%). *Vehicles* (1993): passenger cars 2,052; trucks and buses 2,574. *Air transport* (2006; Solomon Airlines only): passenger-km 74,870,000; metric ton-km cargo 648,000. **Communications,** in total units (units per 1,000 persons). Telephone landlines (2008): 8,000 (16); cellular telephone subscribers (2008): 14,000 (27); personal computers (2005): 22,000 (47); total Internet users (2008): 10,000 (20); broadband Internet subscribers (2008): 1,500 (2.9).

Education and health

Educational attainment (2005–06). Percentage of population ages 15 and over having: no schooling/unknown 15.6%; primary education 46.7%; secondary 32.8%; vocational 4.0%; higher 0.9%. **Literacy** (2004): total population ages 15 and over literate 76.6%. **Health** (2005): physicians 89 (1 per 5,293 persons); hospital beds 691 (1 per 682 persons); infant mortality rate per 1,000 live births (2008) 19.7; undernourished population (2002–04) 90,000 (21% of total population based on the consumption of a minimum daily requirement of 1,780 calories).

Military

Total active duty personnel (2008): none; 200–300 military troops and police in an Australian-led multi-

national regional intervention force (from mid-2003) maintain civil and political order.

Background

The Solomon Islands were settled c. 2000 BC by Austronesian people. Visited by the Spanish in AD 1568, the islands were subsequently explored by the French and the British. They came under British protection in 1893. During World War II, the Japanese invasion of 1942 ignited three years of the most bitter fighting in the Pacific, particularly on Guadalcanal. The protectorate became self-governing in 1976 and fully independent in 1978. In the late 20th and early 21st centuries, ethnic tensions led to political instability; a multinational force led by Australia helped restore order.

Recent Developments

In 2009 the economy of the Solomon Islands began to derive significant benefits from the 2005 Foreign Investment Act, which increased investment in fisheries, agriculture, mining, tourism, and engineering. The government also lodged claims with the UN for recognition of the Solomon Islands' extended continental shelf, where massive seafloor sulphide reserves were thought to exist.

Internet resource: <www.visitsolomons.com.sb>.

Somalia

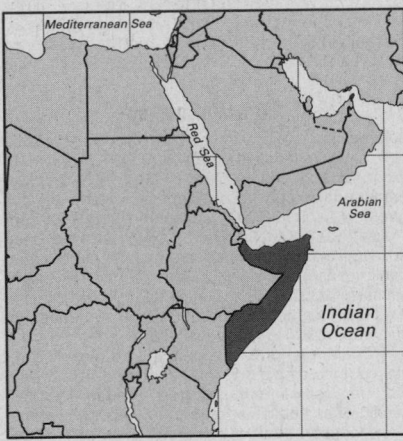

Proclamation of the "Republic of Somaliland" in May 1991 on territory corresponding to the former British Somaliland (which unified with the former Italian Trust Territory of Somalia to form Somalia in 1960) had not received international recognition as of 2010. This entity represented about a quarter of Somalia's territory. **Official name:** Soomaaliya (Somali); Al-Sumal (Arabic) (Somalia). **Form of government:** transitional regime (the "new transitional government" from October 2004 lacked effective control in mid-2010) with one legislative house (Transitional Federal Assembly [550]). At present Somalia is divided into three autonomous regions: Somaliland in the northwest, Puntland in the northeast, and Somalia in the south. **Head of state and government:** President Sheikh Sharif Sheikh Ahmed (from 2009), assisted by Prime Minister Omar Abdirashid Ali Sharmarke (from 2009). **Capital:** Mogadishu. **Official languages:** Somali; Arabic. **Official religion:** Islam. **Monetary unit:** 1 Somali shilling (Shilin Soomaali; So.Sh.) = 100 cents; valuation (1 Jul 2010) US$1 = So.Sh. 1,549.96 (the So.Sh. had limited availability and circulation in 2009; US$1 = 34,000 So.Sh. at the "black market" rate of May 2008).

Demography

Area: 246,201 sq mi, 637,657 sq km. **Population** (2009): 9,133,000. **Density** (2009): persons per sq mi 37.1, persons per sq km 14.3. **Urban** (2006): 36.5%. **Sex distribution** (2008): male 49.57%; female 50.43%. **Age breakdown** (2005): under 15, 44.6%; 15–29, 26.3%; 30–44, 16.1%; 45–59, 8.6%; 60–74, 3.6%; 75–84, 0.7%; 85 and over, 0.1%. **Ethnic composition** (2000): Somali 92.4%; Arab 2.2%; Afar 1.3%; other 4.1%. **Religious affiliation** (2005): Muslim (nearly all Sunni) 99%; other 1%. **Major cities** (2008): Mogadishu (2007) 1,100,000; Hargeysa 436,232; Burao 151,451; Belet Weyne 108,125; Boosaaso 108,016. **Location:** the Horn of Africa, bordering Djibouti, the Gulf of Aden, the Indian Ocean, Kenya, and Ethiopia.

Vital statistics

Birth rate per 1,000 population (2005): 45.0 (world avg. 20.3). **Death rate** per 1,000 population (2005): 16.0 (world avg. 8.5). **Total fertility rate** (avg. births per childbearing woman; 2005): 6.45. **Life expectancy** at birth (2005): male 48.0 years; female 51.0 years.

National economy

Budget: n.a. UN assistance (2007): US$175,000,-000, of which food aid US$50,000,000. **Public debt** (external, outstanding; 2007): US$1,979,000,000. **Production** (metric tons except as noted). *Agriculture and fishing* (2007): sugarcane 215,000, corn (maize) 99,000, cassava 82,000, sesame seed 30,000; other tree/bush products include khat, frankincense, and myrrh; livestock (number of live animals) 13,100,000 sheep, 12,700,000 goats, 7,000,000 camels, 5,350,000 cattle; fisheries production 30,000 (from aquaculture, none). *Mining and quarrying* (2007): small quantities of gemstones (including garnet and opal) and salt. *Manufacturing:* small manufacturers produce textiles, handicrafts, and processed meat. *Energy production (consumption):* electricity (kW-hr; 2006) 295,000,000 (295,000,000); crude petroleum (barrels; 2006) none (425,000); petroleum products (metric tons; 2006) 176,000 (174,000). **Population economically active** (2006): total 3,343,000; activity rate of total population 39.6% (participation rates: ages 15 and over, 72.1%; female 38.8%). **Gross national income** (2008): US$2,570,000,000 (US$288 per capita). **Selected balance of payments data.** Receipts from (US$'000,000): remittances (2008) 1,000; foreign direct investment (2005–07 avg.) 87; official development assistance (2007) 384.

Foreign trade

Imports (2007): US$793,000,000 (agricultural products 48.1%, of which sugar [all forms] 12.3%, cereals 12.0%, vegetable and animal oils 6.6%). *Major import sources* (2008): Djibouti 29%; India 12%; Kenya 8%; US 6%; Oman 6%. **Exports** (2007): US$299,000,000 (goats 12.0%; sheep 6.4%; cattle 5.5%; other agricultural products 1.4%). *Major export destinations* (2008): UAE 56%; Yemen 21%; Saudi Arabia 4%.

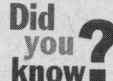

Did you know? Somalia has been a lively trading center for millennia. The area was known to ancient Egyptians as the land of aromatics and incense and later was the source of exotic products as varied as ostrich feathers, clarified butter, and precious vegetable gums.

Transport and communications

Transport. *Railroads:* none. *Roads* (2003): total length 22,000 km (paved 12%). *Air transport* (2003; four Somaliland airports only): passenger arrivals 50,096, passenger departures 41,979; cargo unloaded 3,817 metric tons, cargo loaded 152 metric tons. **Communications,** in total units (units per 1,000 persons). Telephone landlines (2008): 100,000 (11); cellular telephone subscribers (2008): 627,000 (70); personal computers (2007): 79,000 (9); total Internet users (2008): 102,000 (11).

Education and health

Literacy (2002): percentage of total population ages 15 and over literate 19.2%; males literate 25.1%; females literate 13.1%. **Health:** physicians, n.a. (in 2008, 18 doctors graduated from a Somali medical institution for the first time since 1990); infant mortality rate per 1,000 live births (2005) 110.1.

Military

Total active duty personnel: none; Ethiopian forces backing the transitional government fought Islamic extremists from December 2006 to December 2008 and from June 2009 onward; AU peacekeeping troops (September 2009): 4,300.

Background

Muslim Arabs and Persians first established trading posts along the coasts of Somalia in the 7th–10th centuries. By the 10th century Somali nomads occupied the area inland from the Gulf of Aden, and the south and west were inhabited by various groups of pastoral Oromo peoples. Intensive European exploration began after the British occupation of Aden in 1839, and in the late 19th century Britain and Italy set up protectorates in the region. During World War II the Italians invaded British Somaliland (1940); a year later British troops retook the area, and Britain administered the region until 1950, when Italian Somaliland became a UN trust territory. In 1960 it was

---

1 metric ton = about 1.1 short tons;   1 kilometer = 0.6 mi (statute);   1 metric ton-km cargo = about 0.68 short ton-mi cargo;   c.i.f.: cost, insurance, and freight;   f.o.b.: free on board

united with the former British Somaliland, and the two became the independent Republic of Somalia. Since then it has suffered political and civil strife, including military dictatorship, civil war, drought, and famine. No effective central government has existed since the early 1990s. In 1991 a Republic of Somaliland was proclaimed by a breakaway group on territory corresponding to the former British Somaliland, and in 1998 the autonomous region of Puntland in the northeast was self-proclaimed; neither received international recognition, but both were more stable than the rest of Somalia. Several attempts have been made to end the conflict and create a new central government; Somalia's most recent transitional government was approved in 2004, but the country subsequently remained in turmoil. Incidents of piracy increased along the country's coast in the early 21st century and were the focus of international concern.

Recent Developments

In 2009 fears that Somalia could become a breeding ground for terrorism escalated with the strengthening of al-Shabaab, an Islamic extremist youth movement with ties to al-Qaeda. The Transitional Federal Government, which had been shored up by support from the Ethiopian military, struggled to assert control over the country following the withdrawal of Ethiopian troops in January. Piracy also continued to dominate international news stories on Somalia, with a record 214 attempted hijackings in 2009 (nearly twice the number reported for 2008), 47 of which were successful.

Internet resource: <www.unsomalia.net>.

South Africa

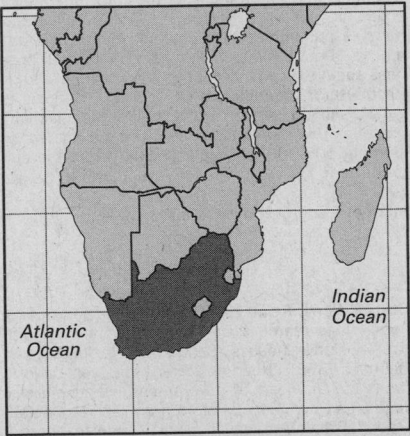

Indian Ocean

Atlantic Ocean

Official name: Republic of South Africa. Form of government: multiparty republic with two legislative houses (National Council of Provinces [90]; National Assembly [400]). Head of state and government: President Jacob Zuma (from 2009). Capitals (de facto): Pretoria/Tshwane (executive); Bloemfontein/Mangaung (judicial); Cape Town (legislative).

Official languages: Afrikaans; English; Ndebele; Pedi; Sotho; Swazi; Tsonga; Tswana; Venda; Xhosa; Zulu. Official religion: none. Monetary unit: 1 rand (R) = 100 cents; valuation (1 Jul 2010) US$1 = R 7.75.

Demography

Area: 471,359 sq mi, 1,220,813 sq km. Population (2009): 49,321,000. Density (2009): persons per sq mi 104.6, persons per sq km 40.4. Urban (2005): 59.28%. Sex distribution (2009): male 48.40%; female 51.60%. Age breakdown (2009): under 15, 31.4%; 15–29, 29.5%; 30–44, 19.5%; 45–59, 12.0%; 60–74, 6.0%; 75 and over, 1.6%. Ethnic composition (2009): black 79.3%, of which Zulu 24%, Xhosa 18%, Pedi 9%, Tswana 8%, Sotho 8%, Tsonga 4%, Swazi 3%, other black 5%; white 9.1%; mixed white/black 9.0%; Asian/other 2.6%. Religious affiliation (2005): independent Christian 37.1%, of which Zion Christian 9.5%; Protestant 26.1%; traditional beliefs 8.9%; Roman Catholic 6.7%; Muslim 2.5%; Hindu 2.4%; nonreligious 3.0%; other 13.3%. Major urban agglomerations (2007): Johannesburg 3,435,000; Cape Town 3,215,000; Ekurhuleni (East Rand) 2,986,000; eThekwini (Durban) 2,729,000; Tshwane (Pretoria) 1,338,000. Location: southern Africa, bordering Namibia, Botswana, Zimbabwe, Mozambique, Swaziland, and the Indian and South Atlantic oceans; wholly contained within South Africa is the country of Lesotho.

Vital statistics

Birth rate per 1,000 population (2005): 23.2 (world avg. 20.3). Death rate per 1,000 population (2005): 14.2 (world avg. 8.5). Total fertility rate (avg. births per childbearing woman; 2009): 2.38. Life expectancy at birth (2009): male 53.5 years; female 57.2 years.

National economy

Budget (2005–06). Revenue: R 411,085,100,000 (income tax 30.6%; VAT 28.0%; corporate taxes 23.5%). Expenditures: R 417,819,200,000 (transfers to provinces 36.0%; debt payments 12.7%; police and prisons 9.0%; defense 5.4%; education 3.0%; health 2.4%). Production (in metric tons except as noted). Agriculture and fishing (2007): sugarcane 20,500,000, corn (maize) 7,338,738, potatoes 1,900,000; livestock (number of live animals) 25,000,000 sheep, 13,500,000 cattle; fisheries production 673,360 (from aquaculture, negligible); aquatic plants production 9,600 (from aquaculture 31%). Mining and quarrying (value of sales in R '000,000,000; 2007): platinum-group metals 79.9; coal 43.1; gold 39.0; iron ore 13.4; rough diamond production 15,249,000 carats. Manufacturing (value of sales in R '000,000; 2005): food products and beverages 153,496; transportation equipment 137,870; chemical products 81,240; refined petroleum products 57,697. Energy production (consumption) (data include Botswana, Lesotho, Namibia, and Swaziland): electricity (kW-hr; 2006) 256,882,000,-000 (257,454,000,000); coal (metric tons; 2006) 246,236,000 (178,336,000); crude petroleum (barrels; 2006) 10,198,000 (180,640,000); petroleum products (metric tons; 2006) 27,024,000 (21,042,000); natural gas (cu m; 2006) 1,936,000,000 (4,551,000,000). Population economically active (2007): total 17,232,000; activity rate of total population 36.0% (participation rates: ages 15–64, 56.7%; female 46.1%; unemployed 21.0%). **Gross national income** (2008): US$283,-310,000,000 (US$5,820 per capita). **Public debt** (external, outstanding; 2007): US$13,868,000,000. **Selected balance of payments data.** Receipts from (US$'000,000): tourism (2007) 8,443; remittances (2008) 823; foreign direct investment (FDI; 2005–07 avg.) 3,936; official development assistance (2006) 718. Disbursements for (US$'000,000): tourism (2007) 3,927; remittances (2008) 1,133; FDI (2005–07 avg.) 3,794.

Foreign trade

Imports (2006): US$69,185,000,000 (machinery and apparatus 26.5%; crude petroleum 13.9%; motor vehicles 9.6%; chemical products 8.9%. *Major import sources:* Germany 12.5%; China 10.0%; US 7.6%; Japan 6.5%; Saudi Arabia 5.3%. **Exports** (2006): US$53,170,000,000 (excluding gold export earnings estimated at US$5,400,000,000) (platinum-group metals 15.3%; iron and steel 10.8%; motor vehicles 9.0%; metal ores 7.4%; coal 6.0%; pumps and compressors 4.7%; diamonds 4.6%). *Major export destinations:* Japan 11.9%; US 11.5%; UK 8.8%; Germany 7.5%; Netherlands 5.2%.

Transport and communications

Transport. *Railroads* (2001): route length (2005) 20,872 km; passenger-km 3,930,000,000; metric ton-km cargo 106,786,000,000. *Roads* (2002): length 362,099 km (paved 20%). *Vehicles* (2005): passenger cars 4,574,972; trucks and buses 2,112,601. *Air transport* (2007): passenger-km 27,576,000,000; metric ton-km cargo 935,600,000. **Communications,** in total units (units per 1,000 persons). Telephone landlines (2008): 4,425,000 (89); cellular telephone subscribers (2008): 45,000,000 (906); personal computers (2005): 3,966,000 (85); total Internet users (2008): 4,187,000 (84); broadband Internet subscribers (2007): 378,000 (7.8).

Education and health

Educational attainment (2006). Percentage of population ages 20 and over having: no formal schooling 10.4%; some primary education 21.1%; complete primary/some secondary 34.0%; complete secondary 24.9%; higher 9.1%. **Literacy** (2007): total population ages 15 and over literate 87.8%. **Health:** physicians (2006) 33,220 (1 per 1,427 persons); hospital beds (2004) 153,465 (1 per 303 persons); infant mortality rate per 1,000 live births (2009) 45.7; undernourished population (2002–04) less than 2.5% of total population.

Military

Total active duty personnel (November 2008): 62,082 (army 59.8%, navy 10.1%, air force 17.2%, military health service 12.9%). **Military expenditure as percentage of GDP** (2007): 1.4%; per capita expenditure US$78.

Background

San and Khoikhoi peoples roamed southern Africa as hunters and gatherers in the Stone Age, and the latter had developed a pastoralist culture by the time of European contact. By the 14th century AD, Bantu-speaking peoples had settled in the area and developed gold and copper mining and an active East African trade. In 1652 the Dutch established a colony at the Cape of Good Hope; the Dutch settlers became known as Boers and later as Afrikaners, after their Afrikaans language. In 1795 British forces captured the Cape, and in the 1830s, to escape British rule, Dutch settlers began the Great Trek northward and established the independent Boer republics of the Orange Free State and the South African Republic (later the Transvaal region), which the British annexed as colonies by 1902 as a result of the 30-month-long Boer War. In 1910 the British colonies of Cape Colony, Transvaal, Natal, and Orange River were unified into the new Union of South Africa. It became independent and withdrew from the Commonwealth in 1961. Throughout the 20th century, South African politics were dominated by the issue of maintaining white supremacy over the country's black majority, and in 1948 apartheid was formally instituted. Faced by increasing worldwide condemnation, it began dismantling the apartheid laws in 1990. In free elections in 1994, Nelson Mandela became the country's first black president. The country also rejoined the Commonwealth in 1994. A permanent nonracial constitution was promulgated in 1997.

Recent Developments

Following national elections in April 2009, African National Congress (ANC) president Jacob Zuma was elected president of South Africa. In the election campaign the ANC had promised to halve poverty and unemployment by 2014 and maintained that creating employment would be the core mandate for economic policy. In February a framework agreement responding to the global economic crisis was reached between the government, labor, and business sectors, which reaffirmed a commitment to infrastructural spending as the core of a stimulus to growth and job creation. In his state of the nation address in June, Zuma committed the government to creating 500,000 job opportunities before the end of the year.

Internet resource: <www.statssa.gov.za>.

Spain

Official name: Reino de España (Kingdom of Spain). **Form of government:** constitutional monarchy with two legislative houses (Senate [264]; Congress of Deputies [350]). **Head of state:** King Juan Carlos I (from 1975). **Head of government:** Prime Minister José Luis Rodríguez Zapatero (from 2004). **Capital:** Madrid. **Official language:** Castilian Spanish (per constitution, Euskera [Basque], Catalan, Galician, and all other Spanish languages are also official in their autonomous communities). **Official religion:** none. **Monetary unit:** 1 euro (€) = 100 cents; valuation (1 Jul 2010) US$1 = €0.80.

---

1 metric ton = about 1.1 short tons;　1 kilometer = 0.6 mi (statute);　1 metric ton-km cargo = about 0.68 short ton-mi cargo;　c.i.f.: cost, insurance, and freight;　f.o.b.: free on board

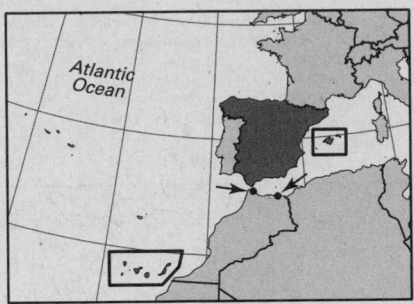

Demography

Area: 195,364 sq mi, 505,991 sq km. **Population** (2009): 46,059,000. **Density** (2009): persons per sq mi 235.8, persons per sq km 91.0. **Urban** (2005): 76.7%. **Sex distribution** (2008): male 49.38%; female 50.62%. **Age breakdown** (2008): under 15, 14.7%; 15–29, 18.9%; 30–44, 25.4%; 45–59, 19.2%; 60–74, 13.4%; 75–84, 6.3%; 85 and over, 2.1%. **Ethnic composition** (2000): Spaniard 44.9%; Catalonian 28.0%; Galician 8.2%; Basque 5.5%; Aragonese 5.0%; Rom (Gypsy) 2.0%; other 6.4%. **Religious affiliation** (2006): Roman Catholic 77%, of which practicing weekly 19%; Muslim 2.5%; Protestant 1%; other (mostly nonreligious) 19.5%. **Major cities** (2008): Madrid 3,213,271.(urban agglomeration [2007] 5,764,000); Barcelona 1,615,908 (urban agglomeration [2007] 5,057,000); Valencia 807,200; Sevilla 699,759; Zaragoza 666,129. **Location:** southwestern Europe, bordering France, Andorra, the Mediterranean Sea, the British overseas territory of Gibraltar, the Atlantic Ocean, and Portugal; the North African exclaves of Ceuta and Melilla border Morocco.

Vital statistics

Birth rate per 1,000 population (2008): 11.4 (world avg. 20.3); within marriage 67.9%. **Death rate** per 1,000 population (2008): 8.5 (world avg. 8.5). **Total fertility rate** (avg. births per childbearing woman; 2008): 1.46. **Life expectancy** at birth (2008): male 79.1 years; female 85.2 years.

National economy

Budget (2007). *Revenue:* €297,701,000,000 (tax revenue 49.1%; social contributions 45.6%). *Expenditures:* €270,293,000,000 (social protection 45.3%; debt service 4.9%; public safety 4.1%; defense 4.0%; health 1.6%; education 0.6%). **Public debt** (2007): US$520,918,000,000. **Gross national income** (2008): US$1,456,488,000,000 (US$31,960 per capita). **Production** (metric tons except as noted). *Agriculture and fishing* (2007): barley 11,684,000, wheat 6,376,900, grapes 6,013,000, olives 5,787,600, oranges 2,691,400, sunflower seeds 743,400, almonds 201,100, garlic 142,400; livestock (number of live animals) 26,034,000 pigs, 21,847,050 sheep, 6,456,350 cattle, 2,500,000 beehives; fisheries production 1,089,922 (from aquaculture 26%). *Mining and quarrying* (2007): slate 1,200,000; sepiolite 800,000; fluorite 132,753; gold 3,100 kg. *Manufacturing* (value

added in US$'000,000; 2004): food products 15,786; fabricated metal products 15,717; transportation equipment 14,508. *Energy production (consumption):* electricity (kW-hr; 2007–08) 303,278,000,000 (279,709,000,000); coal (metric tons; 2007) 10,995,000 (36,281,000); lignite (metric tons; 2007) 6,016,000 (6,016,000); crude petroleum (barrels; 2007–08) 1,133,400 (453,309,900); petroleum products (metric tons; 2007–08) 55,886,000 ([2006] 60,308,000); natural gas (cu m; 2007–08) 15,447,500 (39,414,926,000). **Population economically active** (2007): total 22,189,900; activity rate of total population 49.7% (participation rates: ages 16–64, 72.6%; female 42.3%; unemployed [October 2007–September 2008] 10.0%). **Selected balance of payments data.** Receipts from (US$'000,000): tourism (2007–08) 62,905; remittances (2008) 11,772; foreign direct investment (FDI; 2005–07 avg.) 35,098. Disbursements for (US$'000,000): tourism (2007–08) 21,277; remittances (2008) 14,656; FDI (2005–07 avg.) 87,228.

Foreign trade

Imports (2006; c.i.f.): €263,024,000,000 (machinery and apparatus 19.7%; mineral fuels 15.7%; motor vehicles and parts 14.6%; chemical products 11.0%; base and fabricated metals 7.6%). *Major import sources* (2007): Germany 15.2%; France 12.2%; Italy 8.7%; China 6.7%; UK 4.7%. **Exports** (2006; f.o.b.): €170,628,000,000 (motor vehicles and parts 20.7%; machinery and apparatus 15.2%; food products 10.9%, of which fruits and vegetables 5.8%; base and fabricated metals 8.9%). *Major export destinations* (2007): France 18.6%; Germany 10.8%; Portugal 8.6%; Italy 8.5%; UK 7.5%.

Transport and communications

Transport. *Railroads* (2007–08): route length (2006) 15,212 km; passenger-km 22,794,600,000; metric ton-km cargo 10,839,100,000. *Roads* (2006): length 681,224 km (paved 100%). *Vehicles* (2008): cars 21,440,700; trucks, vans, and buses 5,273,000. *Air transport* (2007–08): passenger-km 81,252,000,-000; metric ton-km cargo 1,169,204,000. **Communications,** in total units (units per 1,000 persons). Telephone landlines (2008): 20,200,000 (454); cellular telephone subscribers (2008): 49,678,000 (1,117); personal computers (2007): 17,646,000 (393); total Internet users (2008): 25,240,000 (567); broadband Internet subscribers (2008): 8,995,000 (202).

Education and health

Educational attainment (2007). Percentage of population ages 16 and over having: no formal schooling through incomplete primary education 11.6%; complete primary 20.9%; secondary 44.4%; undergraduate degree 14.2%; graduate degree 8.9%. **Literacy** (2003): total population ages 15 and over literate 97.9%; males literate 98.7%; females literate 97.2%. **Health** (2008): physicians 213,977 (1 per 214 persons); hospital beds (2007) 160,292 (1 per 283 persons); infant mortality rate per 1,000 live births 3.5; undernourished population (2002–04) less than 2.5% of total population.

Military

Total active duty personnel (November 2008): 221,750 (army 43.1%, navy 10.5%, air force 9.4%, joint 4.3%, civil guard 32.7%). **Military expenditure as percentage of GDP** (2008): 0.7%; per capita expenditure US$241.

Background

Remains of Stone Age populations dating back some 35,000 years have been found in Spain. Celtic peoples arrived in the 9th century BC, followed by the Romans, who dominated Spain from about 200 BC until the Visigoth invasion in the early 5th century AD. In the early 8th century, most of the peninsula fell to Muslims (Moors) from North Africa, and it remained under their control until it was gradually reconquered by the Christian kingdoms of Castile, Aragon, and Portugal. Spain was reunited in 1479 following the marriage of Ferdinand II (of Aragon) and Isabella I (of Castile). The last Muslim kingdom, Granada, was reconquered in 1492, and around this time Spain also established a colonial empire in the Americas. In 1516 the throne passed to the Habsburgs, whose rule ended in 1700 when Philip V became the first Bourbon king of Spain. His ascendancy caused the War of the Spanish Succession, which resulted in the loss of numerous European possessions and sparked revolution in most of Spain's American colonies. Spain lost its remaining overseas possessions to the US in the Spanish-American War (1898). It became a republic in 1931. The Spanish Civil War (1936–39) ended in victory for the Nationalists under Gen. Francisco Franco, who ruled as dictator until his death in 1975. His successor as head of state, King Juan Carlos I, restored the monarchy; a new constitution in 1978 established a parliamentary monarchy. Spain joined NATO in 1982 and the European Community in 1986. In the late 20th and early 21st centuries, Basque separatists continued to resort to violence as they pressed for independence, but it was Islamic militants who were responsible for the 11 Mar 2004 bombings in Madrid that killed 191 people—the worst terrorist incident in Europe since World War II.

Recent Developments

After officially entering into recession in the final quarter of 2008, the Spanish economy nose-dived in 2009. The year ended with GDP down 3.4%, unemployment at 18.8% (and at more than 27.0% among the country's immigrant population), and a budget deficit of almost 10.0% (compared with 3.8% in 2008). The number of bankruptcy proceedings increased by 80.0%. Spain not only was one of the worst-hit EU economies but also was expected to be one of the last to recover from the downturn. The economic reality shook the government out of its initial complacency. Several policies were implemented to try to improve the economic outlook, including spending the equivalent of 2.3% of GDP in measures to stimulate the economy and create jobs, introducing subsidies for new car purchases, and extending welfare provision for the unemployed. The 2010 budget approved in the fall included higher capital gains taxes, a 2.0% hike in the general VAT, and the elimi-

nation of a nearly US$600 across-the-board annual income-tax rebate that had been promised before the 2008 elections.

Internet resource: <www.ine.es>.

Sri Lanka

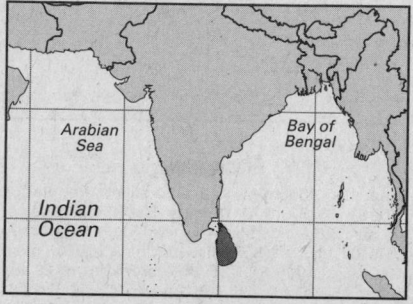

Arabian Sea

Bay of Bengal

Indian Ocean

Official name: Sri Lanka Prajatantrika Samajavadi Janarajaya (Sinhala); Ilangai Jananayaka Socialisa Kudiarasu (Tamil) (Democratic Socialist Republic of Sri Lanka). **Form of government:** unitary multiparty republic with one legislative house (Parliament [225]). **Head of state and government:** President Mahinda Rajapakse (from 2005), assisted by Prime Minister D.M. Jayaratne (from 2010). **Capitals:** Colombo (executive and judicial); Sri Jayewardenepura Kotte (Colombo suburb; legislative). **Official languages:** Sinhala; Tamil (English has official status as "the link language" between Sinhala and Tamil). **Official religion:** none (Buddhism has special recognition). **Monetary unit:** 1 Sri Lankan rupee (LKR) = 100 cents; valuation (1 Jul 2010) US$1 = LKR 113.47.

Demography

Area: 25,332 sq mi, 65,610 sq km. **Population** (2009): 20,238,000. **Density** (2009): persons per sq mi 798.9, persons per sq km 308.5. **Urban** (2008): 15.1%. **Sex distribution** (2008): male 49.36%; female 50.64%. **Age breakdown** (2008): under 15, 26.3%; 15–29, 27.0%; 30–44, 22.0%; 45–59, 15.4%; 60–74, 7.1%; 75 and over, 2.2%. **Ethnic composition** (2001): Sinhalese 81.9%; Tamil 9.4%; Sri Lankan Moor 8.0%; other 0.7%. **Religious affiliation** (2005): Buddhist 70%; Hindu 15%; Christian (mostly Roman Catholic) 8%; Muslim (nearly all Sunni) 7%. **Major cities** (2007): Colombo 672,743 (greater Colombo [2004] 2,490,300); Dehiwala–Mount Lavinia 219,827; Moratuwa 185,668; Jaffna 151,612; Negombo 150,364. **Location:** island in the Indian Ocean, southeast of India.

Vital statistics

Birth rate per 1,000 population (2008): 18.8 (world avg. 20.3). **Death rate** per 1,000 population (2008): 5.9 (world avg. 8.5). **Total fertility rate** (avg. births per childbearing woman; 2008): 1.88. **Life expectancy** at birth (2008): male 68.8 years; female 76.3 years.

1 metric ton = about 1.1 short tons;   1 kilometer = 0.6 mi (statute);   1 metric ton-km cargo = about 0.68 short ton-mi cargo;   c.i.f.: cost, insurance, and freight;   f.o.b.: free on board

National economy

Budget (2008). *Revenue:* LKR 775,477,000,000 (tax revenue 84.2%, of which VAT 32.5%, excises 15.8%; nontax revenue 12.1%; foreign grants 3.7%). *Expenditures:* LKR 1,516,330,000,000 (debt service 38.5%; transfers 15.9%; wages and salaries 11.1%). **Selected balance of payments data.** Receipts from (US$'000,000): tourism (2008) 320; remittances (2008) 2,947; foreign direct investment (FDI; 2005–07 avg.) 427; official development assistance (2007) 589. Disbursements for (US$'000,000): tourism (2007) 393; remittances (2008) 385; FDI (2005–07 avg.) 54. **Production** (metric tons except as noted). *Agriculture and fishing* (2008): rice 3,875,000, coconuts (2007) 954,000, sugarcane 799,447, tea 318,470, natural rubber 129,240, peppercorns 22,870, cinnamon 13,430, ginger 10,053; livestock (number of live animals) 1,196,000 cattle, 319,000 buffalo; fisheries production (2007) 317,988 (from aquaculture 3%). *Mining and quarrying* (2008): kaolin 11,000; graphite 10,000; sapphires 770,000 carats; rubies 23,000 carats; diamonds, n.a. *Manufacturing* (value added in LKR '000,000; 2008): food products, beverages, and tobacco products 348,358; textiles and wearing apparel 147,822; rubber and plastic products 60,680; coal and refined petroleum products 42,666. *Energy production (consumption):* electricity (kW-hr; 2008–09) 9,727,000,000 ([2006] 9,389,000,000); coal (metric tons; 2006) none (95,000); crude petroleum (barrels; 2006) none (15,766,800); petroleum products (metric tons; 2006) 1,875,000 (3,409,000). **Gross national income** (2008): US$35,854,000,000 (US$1,790 per capita). **Public debt** (external, outstanding; June 2009): US$12,737,600,000. **Population economically active** (2008): total 7,568,700; activity rate 37.7% (participation rates: ages 15–59 [2000] 60.6%; female 36.1%; unemployed [May 2008–April 2009] 5.2%).

Foreign trade

Imports (2007; c.i.f.): LKR 1,251,135,000,000 (cotton yarn and textiles 14.4%; machinery and apparatus 13.9%; refined petroleum products 13.0%; crude petroleum 9.1%; food products and beverages 7.3%; base metals 7.3%). *Major import sources:* India 22.3%; Singapore 9.6%; China 7.9%; Iran 7.2%; Hong Kong 6.2%. **Exports** (2007; f.o.b.): LKR 856,808,000,000 (garments 40.6%; tea 13.3%, of which black 11.5%; gemstones 5.7%, of which diamonds 4.5%; rubber tires 4.5%; coconut products 1.8%; fish 1.6%; rubber products 1.4%; cinnamon 1.0%). *Major export destinations:* US 24.5%; UK 12.7%; India 6.4%; Germany 5.5%; Belgium 5.0%.

Transport and communications

Transport. *Railroads* (2008–09): route length (2007) 1,449 km; passenger-km 4,515,916,000; metric ton-km cargo 115,313,000. *Roads* (2003): total length 97,286 km (paved 81%). *Vehicles* (2008): passenger cars 381,448; trucks and buses 552,474. *Air transport* (2008–09): passenger-km 8,248,000,000; metric ton-km cargo 300,611,000. **Communications**, in total units (units per 1,000 persons). Telephone landlines (2008): 3,446,000 (172); cellular telephone subscribers (2008): 11,083,000 (552); personal computers (2005): 734,000 (35); total Internet users (2008): 1,164,000 (58); broadband Internet subscribers (2008): 102,000 (5.1).

Education and health

Literacy (2007): percentage of population ages 5 and over literate 91.5%; males literate 93.2%; females literate 89.9%. **Health** (2007): physicians 11,023 (1 per 1,804 persons); hospital beds 68,694 (1 per 289 persons); infant mortality rate per 1,000 live births (2006) 11.0; undernourished population (2002–04) 4,200,000 (22% of total population based on the consumption of a minimum daily requirement of 1,860 calories).

Military

Total active duty personnel (November 2008): 150,900 (army 78.1%, navy 9.9%, air force 12.0%). **Military expenditure as percentage of GDP** (2008): 3.6%; per capita expenditure US$77.

Background

The Sinhalese people of Sri Lanka (Ceylon) probably originated with the blending of aboriginal inhabitants and migrating Indo-Aryans from India about the 5th century BC. The Tamils were later immigrants from Dravidian India, migrating over a period from the early centuries AD to about 1200. Buddhism was introduced during the 3rd century BC. As Buddhism spread, the Sinhalese kingdom extended its political control over Ceylon but lost it to invaders from southern India in the 10th century AD. Between 1200 and 1505 Sinhalese power gravitated to southwestern Ceylon, while a southern Indian dynasty seized power in the north and established the Tamil kingdom in the 14th century. Foreign invasions from India, China, and Malaya occurred in the 13th–15th centuries. In 1505 the Portuguese arrived, and by 1619 they controlled most of the island. The Sinhalese enlisted the Dutch to help oust the Portuguese and eventually came under the control of the Dutch East India Co., which relinquished power in 1796 to the British. In 1802 Ceylon became a crown colony, gaining independence in 1948. It became the Republic of Sri Lanka in 1972 and took its current name in 1978. Civil strife between Tamil and Sinhalese groups has beset the country in recent years, with the Tamils demanding a separate autonomous state in northern Sri Lanka. A prolonged insurrection by the Liberation Tigers of Tamil Eelam (LTTE; Tamil Tigers) guerrilla group was defeated by government forces in 2009.

Recent Developments

Ironically, Sri Lanka's economic growth, which had held up remarkably well during the long civil war, slumped in 2009 as the war ended but the global recession continued. After growing at 6% in 2008, GDP was estimated to rise by only 3% in 2009. While the end of fighting engendered a spirit of optimism and halted an outflow of private capital, Sri Lanka's industrial exports, particularly garments, suffered badly. The important tourist industry began to revive, however, and a US$2.6 billion loan from the International Monetary Fund, agreed to in July, helped to stabilize the country's economic position.

Internet resource: <www.statistics.gov.lk>.

Sudan

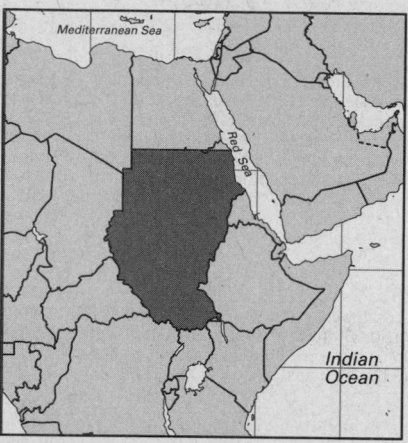

Official name: Jumhuriyat al-Sudan (Republic of the Sudan). **Form of government:** military-backed interim regime with two legislative houses (Council of States [50]; National Assembly [450]). **Head of state and government:** President Omar Hassan Ahmad al-Bashir (from 1989). **Capitals:** Khartoum (executive); Omdurman (legislative); Juba is an "alternating seat" of the interim power-sharing government. **Official languages:** Arabic; English. **Official religion:** Islamic law and custom are applicable to Muslims only. **Monetary unit:** 1 Sudanese pound (SDG); valuation (1 Jul 2010) US$1 = SDG 2.37.

Demography

Area: 967,499 sq mi, 2,505,810 sq km. **Population** (2009): 42,272,000. **Density** (2009): persons per sq mi 43.7, persons per sq km 16.9. **Urban** (2006): 37.6%. **Sex distribution** (2008): male 51.27%; female 48.73%. **Age breakdown** (2008): under 15, 42.6%; 15–29, 27.7%; 30–44, 16.8%; 45–59, 7.7%; 60–74, 3.8%; 75–84, 1.0%; 85 and over, 0.4%. **Ethnic composition** (2003): black 52%; Arab 39%; Beja 6%; foreigners 2%; other 1%. **Religious affiliation** (2005): Sunni Muslim 68.4%; traditional beliefs 10.8%; Roman Catholic 9.5%; Protestant 8.8%, of which Anglican 5.4%; other 2.5%. **Major cities** (2008): Khartoum 1,410,858 (urban agglomeration [2008] 4,272,728); Omdurman 1,849,659; Khartoum North 1,012,211; Nyala 492,984; Port Sudan 394,561. **Location:** northeastern Africa, bordering Egypt, the Red Sea, Eritrea, Ethiopia, Kenya, Uganda, the Democratic Republic of the Congo, the Central African Republic, Chad, and Libya.

Vital statistics

Birth rate per 1,000 population (2006): 35.3 (world avg. 20.3). **Death rate** per 1,000 population (2006): 15.2 (world avg. 8.5). **Total fertility rate** (avg. births per childbearing woman; 2006): 4.79. **Life expectancy** at birth (2006): male 47.1 years; female 48.8 years.

National economy

Budget (2008). *Revenue:* SDG 26,424,000,000 (nontax revenue 68.8%, of which export receipts for crude petroleum 52.3%; tax revenue 29.0%, of which taxes on goods and services 18.0%; grants 2.2%). *Expenditures:* SDG 24,331,000,000 (federal government 52.5%; transfers to: Southern Sudan 25.3%; northern states 22.2%). **Public debt** (external, outstanding; 2007): US$12,337,000,000. **Gross national income** (2008): US$46,520,000,000 (US$1,130 per capita). **Production** (metric tons except as noted). *Agriculture and fishing* (2007): sugarcane 7,500,000, sorghum 5,048,000, millet 792,000, dates 330,000, sesame seeds 260,000, seed cotton 240,000, gum arabic (2006–07) 11,242; livestock (number of live animals) 49,000,000 sheep, 42,000,000 goats, 39,500,000 cattle, 3,700,000 camels; fisheries production 67,459 (from aquaculture 3%). *Mining and quarrying* (2007): marble 26,000 cu m; gold 2,787 kg. *Manufacturing* (2006): diesel 1,817,000; flour 1,200,000; benzene 1,139,000. *Energy production (consumption):* electricity (kW-hr; 2007) 5,021,000,000 (3,836,000,000); crude petroleum (barrels; 2008) 174,400,000 ([2006] 35,500,000); petroleum products (metric tons; 2006) 4,943,000 (3,714,000). **Population economically active** (2006): total 11,504,000; activity rate of total population 30.5% (participation rates: ages 15–64, 52.0%; female 30.3%). **Selected balance of payments data.** Receipts from (US$'000,000): tourism (2007) 262; remittances (2008) 1,850; foreign direct investment (2005–07 avg.) 2,761; official development assistance (2007) 2,104. Disbursements for (US$'000,000): tourism (2007) 1,477; remittances (2008) 2.

Foreign trade

Imports (2008; c.i.f.): US$9,351,000,000 (machinery and apparatus 32.7%; transportation equipment 11.9%; wheat and wheat flour 7.6%; refined petroleum products 7.6%). *Major import sources:* China 23.1%; India 9.5%; Saudi Arabia 8.0%; UAE 6.7%; Italy 3.3%. **Exports** (2008; f.o.b.): US$11,670,000,000 (crude petroleum 92.9%; refined petroleum products 2.1%; sesame seeds 1.2%; gold 1.0%; cotton 0.5%; gum arabic 0.5%; livestock [mainly sheep and camels] 0.4%). *Major export destinations:* China 75.0%; Japan 9.7%; UAE 4.1%; Saudi Arabia 0.9%.

Transport and communications

Transport. *Railroads* (2006): route length 4,578 km; passenger-km 49,000,000; metric ton-km cargo 893,000,000. *Roads* (2000): total length 11,900 km (paved 36%). *Vehicles* (2002): passenger cars 47,300; trucks and buses 62,500. *Air transport* (2004): passenger-km 758,000,000; metric ton-km cargo (including the weight of passengers and mail) 100,000,000. **Communications,** in total units (units per 1,000 persons). Telephone landlines (2008): 356,000 (8.6); cellular telephone subscribers (2008): 11,186,000 (271); personal computers (2007): 4,528,000 (112); total Internet users (2008): 3,800,000 (92); broadband Internet subscribers (2007): 43,000 (1.1).

1 metric ton = about 1.1 short tons;   1 kilometer = 0.6 mi (statute);   1 metric ton-km cargo = about 0.68 short ton-mi cargo;   c.i.f.: cost, insurance, and freight;   f.o.b.: free on board

Education and health

Literacy (2003): total population ages 15 and over literate 60.9%; males literate 71.6%; females literate 50.4%. **Health** (2007): physicians 9,573 (1 per 4,224 persons); hospital beds 27,438 (1 per 1,474 persons); infant mortality rate per 1,000 live births (2006) 96.8; undernourished population (2002–04) 8,700,000 (26% of total population based on the consumption of a minimum daily requirement of 1,840 calories).

Military

Total active duty personnel (November 2008): 109,300 (army 96.1%, navy 1.2%, air force 2.7%); foreign troops (September 2009): Southern Sudan—UN peacekeeping force 8,800; Darfur—African Union/UN hybrid peacekeeping force 14,600. **Military expenditure as percentage of GDP** (2005): 1.8%; per capita expenditure US$13.

Background

From the end of the 4th millennium BC, Nubia (now northern Sudan) periodically came under Egyptian rule, and it was part of the kingdom of Cush from the 11th century BC to the 4th century AD. Christian missionaries converted the area's three principal kingdoms during the 6th century; these black Christian kingdoms coexisted with their Muslim Arab neighbors in Egypt for centuries, until the influx of Arab immigrants brought about their collapse in the 13th–15th centuries. Egypt had conquered all of the Sudan region by 1874 and encouraged British interference there; this aroused Muslim opposition and led to the revolt of al-Mahdi, who captured Khartoum in 1885 and established a Muslim theocracy in the Sudan that lasted until 1898, when Mahdist forces were defeated by the British. The British ruled, generally in partnership with Egypt, until the region achieved independence in 1956. Since then the country has fluctuated between ineffective parliamentary government and unstable military rule. The non-Muslim population of the south began rebellion against the Muslim-controlled government of the north in the early 1980s, leading to famines and the displacement of millions of people. Meanwhile, fighting broke out in 2003 between non-Arab Muslims in the Darfur region of western Sudan and government-backed Arab militias known as Janjaweed; tens of thousands of people were killed and hundreds of thousands more were displaced.

Recent Developments

Conflict, displacement, and insecurity persisted throughout Sudan in 2009. In Darfur hostilities continued between armed opposition factions, government armed forces, militias, and ethnic groups. The UN estimated that the total of internally displaced persons across the country had risen to 4.9 million. In February and March 2010, however, the government of Sudan signed cease-fire agreements with two rebel factions in Darfur, the Justice and Equality Movement and the Movement for Liberation and Justice. UN and local officials expressed apprehension that ongoing conflict could impede preparations for national elections, originally scheduled for July 2009 but postponed until April 2010. The elections were a crucial part of the 2005 Comprehensive Peace Agreement that ended more than two decades of civil war between the north and the south. Despite evidence of vote rigging and the boycott of the election by major opposition members, however, the national election was held in April 2010, the first multiparty election in the country in 24 years, and Pres. Omar Hassan Ahmad al-Bashir was reelected.

Internet resource: <http://cbs.gov.sd>.

Suriname

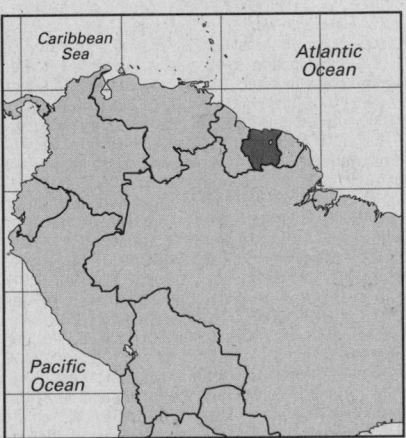

Official name: Republiek Suriname (Republic of Suriname). **Form of government:** multiparty republic with one legislative house (National Assembly [51]). **Head of state and government:** President Dési Bouterse (from 2010). **Capital:** Paramaribo. **Official language:** Dutch. **Official religion:** none. **Monetary unit:** 1 Suriname dollar (SRD) = 100 cents; valuation (1 Jul 2010) US$1 = SRD 2.71.

Demography

Area: 63,251 sq mi, 163,820 sq km. **Population** (2009): 520,000. **Density** (2009): persons per sq mi 8.2, persons per sq km 3.2. **Urban** (2005): 73.9%. **Sex distribution** (2006): male 49.71%; female 50.29%. **Age breakdown** (2006): under 15, 28.5%; 15–29, 26.8%; 30–44, 24.3%; 45–59, 12.0%; 60–74, 6.2%; 75 and over, 2.2%. **Ethnic composition** (2004): Indo-Pakistani ("Hindustani") 27.4%; Suriname Creole ("Afro-Surinamese") 17.7%; Maroon (descendants of runaway slaves living in the interior) 14.7%; Javanese ("Indonesian") 14.6%; mixed race 12.5%; Amerindian 1.5%; other 11.6%. **Religious affiliation** (2004): Christian (mostly Roman Catholic and Moravian) 40.7%; Hindu 19.9%; Muslim 13.5%; nonreligious 4.4%; traditional beliefs 3.3%; other 2.5%; unknown 15.7%. **Major towns** (2004): Paramaribo 242,946; Nieuw Nickerie 13,842; Nieuw Amsterdam 5,489. **Location:** northern South America, bordering the North Atlantic Ocean, French Guiana, Brazil, and Guyana.

Vital statistics

Birth rate per 1,000 population (2006): 17.6 (world avg. 20.3). **Death rate** per 1,000 population (2006): 5.5 (world avg. 8.5). **Total fertility rate** (avg. births per childbearing woman; 2006): 2.05. **Life expectancy** at birth (2006): male 70.3 years; female 75.8 years.

National economy

Budget (2007). *Revenue:* SRD 2,002,000,000 (tax revenue 79.1%, of which corporate taxes 22.0%, taxes on international trade 21.5%, income tax 15.4%; nontax revenue 16.0%; grants 4.9%). *Expenditures:* SRD 1,806,500,000 (current expenditures 87.5%, of which wages and salaries 37.6%, transfers 12.0%, debt interest 5.2%; capital expenditures 12.5%). **Production** (metric tons except as noted). *Agriculture and fishing* (2007): rice 195,000, sugarcane 120,000, bananas 44,000; livestock (number of live animals) 137,000 cattle, 24,500 pigs, 3,800,000 chickens; fisheries production 29,679 (from aquaculture 1%). *Mining and quarrying* (2007): bauxite 5,331,000; alumina 2,152,000; gold 9,362 kg (recorded production; unrecorded production may be as high as 30,000 kg). *Manufacturing* (value of production at factor cost in SRG; 1993): food products 992,000,000; beverages 558,000,000; tobacco products 369,000,000. *Energy production (consumption):* electricity (kW-hr; 2006) 1,618,000,000 (1,618,000,000); crude petroleum (barrels; 2006) 4,800,000 (3,478,000); petroleum products (metric tons; 2006) 401,000 (624,000). **Population economically active** (2004): total 173,130; activity rate of total population 35.1% (participation rates: ages 15–64, 56.0%; female 36.7%; unemployed 9.5%). **Gross national income** (2008): US$2,570,000,000 (US$4,990 per capita). **Public debt** (external, outstanding; 2007): US$161,100,000. **Selected balance of payments data.** Receipts from (US$'000,000): tourism (2007) 67; remittances (2008) 140; foreign direct investment (FDI; 2005–07 avg.) 346; official development assistance (2007) 151. Disbursements for (US$'000,000): tourism (2007) 22; remittances (2008) 65.

Foreign trade

Imports (2005; c.i.f.): US$1,099,900,000 (machinery and transportation equipment 26.8%; mineral fuels 15.6%; food products 9.1%; chemical products 6.9%). *Major import sources* (2007): US 31.7%; Netherlands 20.4%; Trinidad and Tobago 17.9%; China 5.5%; Japan 3.6%. **Exports** (2005; f.o.b.): US$929,100,000 (alumina 48.1%; gold 36.4%; shrimp and fish 6.1%; crude petroleum 5.8%; rice 1.5%). *Major export destinations* (2007): Canada 23.0%; Norway 14.4%; US 12.1%; Trinidad and Tobago 7.2%; France 5.4%.

Transport and communications

Transport. *Railroads:* none. *Roads* (2003): total length 4,304 km (paved 26%). *Vehicles* (2006): passenger cars 81,778; trucks and buses 28,774. *Air transport* (2008; Surinam Airways only): passenger-

km 958,323,000; metric ton-km cargo 25,794,000. **Communications**, in total units (units per 1,000 persons). Telephone landlines (2008): 82,000 (158); cellular telephone subscribers (2008): 416,000 (808); personal computers (2001): 20,000 (45); total Internet users (2008): 50,000 (97); broadband Internet subscribers (2008): 5,800 (11).

Did you know? Suriname is known for its dense tropical rainforest. Located on the Equator and receiving a significant amount of rainfall during its wet season, Suriname provides an ideal habitat for many species of monkeys, toucans, and tree frogs.

Education and health

Literacy (2004): total population ages 15 and over literate 89.6%; males literate 92.0%; females literate 87.2%. **Health:** physicians (2001) 236 (1 per 2,000 persons); hospital beds (2005) 1,797 (1 per 278 persons); infant mortality rate per 1,000 live births (2006) 20.8; undernourished population (2002–04) 40,000 (8% of total population based on the consumption of a minimum daily requirement of 1,910 calories).

Military

Total active duty personnel (November 2008): 1,840 (all services are officially part of the army) (army 76.1%, navy 13.0%, air force 10.9%). **Military expenditure as percentage of GDP** (2007): 1.0%; per capita expenditure US$43.

Background

Suriname was inhabited by various native peoples prior to European settlement. Spanish explorers claimed it in 1593, but the Dutch began to settle there in 1602, followed by the English in 1651. It was ceded to the Dutch in 1667, and in 1682 the Dutch West India Co. introduced coffee and sugarcane plantations and African slaves to cultivate them. Slavery was abolished in 1863, and indentured servants were brought from China, Java, and India to work the plantations, adding to the population mix. Except for brief interludes of British rule (1799–1802, 1804–15), it remained a Dutch colony. It gained internal autonomy in 1954 and independence in 1975. A military coup in 1980 ended civilian control until the electorate approved a new constitution in 1987. Military control resumed after a coup in 1990. Elections were held in 1992, and democratic government returned. By the early 21st century, a vast criminal economy, including drug trafficking and gold smuggling, had developed.

Recent Developments

In 2009 Suriname continued to suffer the corrosive impact of organized crime and revenue losses resulting from illegal gold mining. Economic growth fell to 2.5%, down from 6.0% in 2008. The revenue from

---

1 metric ton = about 1.1 short tons;   1 kilometer = 0.6 mi (statute);   1 metric ton-km cargo = about 0.68 short ton-mi cargo;   c.i.f.: cost, insurance, and freight;   f.o.b.: free on board

legal gold mining and oil production continued to rise, however, and the year ended with a 0.1% drop in inflation.

Internet resource: <www.statistics-suriname.org>.

Swaziland

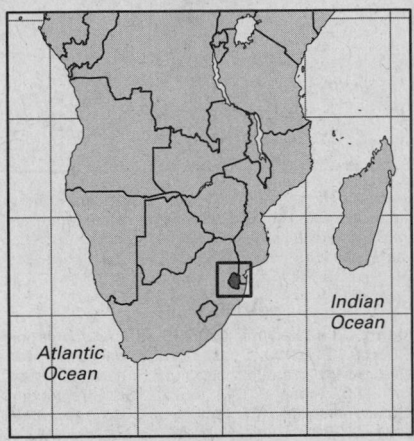

Indian
Ocean

Atlantic
Ocean

Official name: Umbuso weSwatini (Swati); Kingdom of Swaziland (English). **Form of government:** monarchy with two legislative houses (Senate [30]; House of Assembly [66]). **Head of state and government:** King Mswati III (from 1986), assisted by Prime Minister Barnabas Sibusiso Dlamini (from 2008). **Capitals:** Mbabane (administrative and judicial); Lobamba (legislative); Lozitha and Ludzidzini are royal residences that have national symbolic significance. **Official languages:** Swati (Swazi); English. **Official religion:** none. **Monetary unit:** 1 lilangeni (plural emalangeni [E]) = 100 cents; valuation (1 Jul 2010) US$1 = E 7.58.

Demography

Area: 6,704 sq mi, 17,364 sq km. **Population** (2009): 1,337,000. **Density** (2009): persons per sq mi 199.4, persons per sq km 77.0. **Urban** (2007): 22.1%. **Sex distribution** (2008): male 49.60%; female 50.40%. **Age breakdown** (2008): under 15, 38.9%; 15–29, 31.5%; 30–44, 15.8%; 45–59, 8.6%; 60–74, 4.2%; 75–84, 0.9%; 85 and over, 0.1%. **Ethnic composition** (2000): Swazi 82.3%; Zulu 9.6%; Tsonga 2.3%; Afrikaner 1.4%; mixed (black-white) 1.0%; other 3.4%. **Religious affiliation** (2006): Protestant 35%; syncretistic Christianity/traditional beliefs 30%; Roman Catholic 25%; Muslim 1%; other (including Baha'i and Mormon) 9%. **Major towns** (2006): Manzini (urban agglomeration) 115,200; Mbabane 78,700; Lobamba 11,000; Big Bend 10,400; Malkerns 10,000. **Location:** southern Africa, bordering South Africa and Mozambique.

Vital statistics

Birth rate per 1,000 population (2008): 29.1 (world avg. 20.3). **Death rate** per 1,000 population (2008): 14.9 (world avg. 8.5). **Total fertility rate** (avg. births per childbearing woman; 2008): 3.45. **Life expectancy** at birth (2008): male 47.8 years; female 48.2 years.

National economy

Budget (2008–09). *Revenue:* E 9,208,400,000 (receipts from the Customs Union of Southern Africa 65.3%; income tax 10.9%; sales taxes 8.2%; corporate taxes 5.8%). *Expenditures:* E 9,538,000,000 (general administration 31.5%; education 19.9%; transportation and communications 11.8%; police and defense 11.0%; agriculture 9.2%; health 8.8%). **Public debt** (external; March 2009): US$379,700,000. **Gross national income** (2008): US$2,945,000,000 (US$2,520 per capita). **Population economically active** (2006): total 337,200; activity rate of total population 32.8% (unemployed, 30%). **Production** (metric tons except as noted). *Agriculture and fishing* (2007): sugarcane 5,000,000, corn (maize) 68,000, grapefruit and pomelos 37,000; livestock (number of live animals) 585,000 cattle, 276,000 goats, 3,200,000 chickens; fisheries production 70 (from aquaculture, negligible). *Mining and quarrying* (2008): ferrovanadium 500; crushed stone 300,000 cu m. *Manufacturing* (value of exports in US$'000; 2007): wearing apparel and accessories (2002) 173,500; sugar 159,821; unbleached wood pulp 97,099. *Energy production (consumption):* electricity (kW-hr; 2008) 212,000,000 (1,001,700,000); coal (metric tons; 2008) 250,000 ([2007] 223,000). **Selected balance of payments data.** Receipts from (US$'000,000): tourism (2007) 32; remittances (2008) 100; foreign direct investment (2005–07 avg.) 8; official development assistance (2007) 63. Disbursements for (US$'000,000): tourism (2007) 51; remittances (2008) 8.

Foreign trade

Imports (2007; c.i.f.): US$1,164,200,000 (food products 18.2%, of which cereals and flour 7.6%; chemical products 13.6%; refined petroleum products 13.4%; machinery and apparatus 12.5%; motor vehicles and parts 6.5%). *Major import sources:* South Africa 92.9%; Namibia 2.2%; Lesotho 1.4%. **Exports** (2007; f.o.b.): US$1,082,300,000 (essential oils for food and beverage industries 29.4%; food products 21.0%, of which raw sugar 14.1%; silicates 19.9%; wearing apparel and accessories 4.4%; organic chemical products 4.3%; rough and sawn wood 4.2%). *Major export destinations:* South Africa 45.2%; Botswana 31.6%; UK 14.2%; US 3.2%.

Transport and communications

Transport. *Railroads* (2006): route length 301 km; passenger-km, n.a. (passenger service is for tourists and private charter only); metric ton-km cargo (2004) 710,000,000. *Roads* (2002): total length 3,594 km (paved 30%). *Vehicles* (2003): passenger cars 44,113; trucks and buses 47,761. **Communications,** in total units (units per 1,000 persons). Telephone landlines (2008): 44,000 (33); cellular telephone subscribers (2008): 457,000 (346); personal computers (2006): 47,000 (37); total Internet users (2008): 48,000 (37).

Education and health

Educational attainment (2006–07). Percentage of population ages 25 and over having: no formal schooling/unknown 23.5%; incomplete primary education 23.9%; complete primary 10.1%; incomplete/complete secondary 33.6%; higher 8.9%. **Literacy** (2007): total population ages 15 and over literate 84.0%; males literate 84.7%; females literate 83.4%. **Health:** physicians (2004) 171 (1 per 7,240 persons); hospital beds (2006) 2,688 (1 per 476 persons); infant mortality rate per 1,000 live births (2008) 72.4; undernourished population (2002–04) 250,000 (22% of total population based on the consumption of a minimum daily requirement of 1,840 calories).

Military

Total active duty personnel (2006): 3,000. **Military expenditure as percentage of GDP** (2004): 1.8%; per capita expenditure US$39.

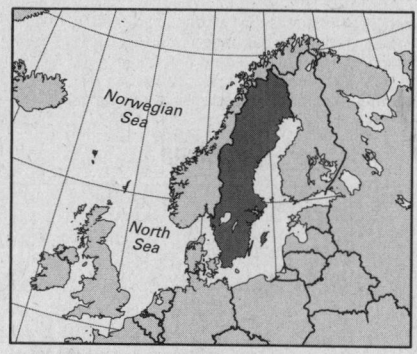

Background

Stone tools and rock paintings indicate prehistoric habitation in the region, but it was not settled until the Bantu-speaking Swazi people migrated there in the 18th century. The British gained control in the 19th century after the Swazi king sought their aid against the Zulus. Following the South African War, the British governor of Transvaal administered Swaziland; his powers were transferred to the British high commissioner in 1906. In 1949 the British rejected the Union of South Africa's request to control Swaziland. The country gained limited self-government in 1963 and achieved independence in 1968. In the 1970s new constitutions were framed based on the supreme authority of the king. During the 1990s forces demanding democracy arose, but the kingdom remained in place. In 2005 a new constitution was signed that contained a bill of rights, but it retained the ban on political parties. Swaziland has one of the highest rates of HIV infection in the world.

Recent Developments

In 2009 Swaziland experienced economic uncertainty as a result of the global recession. The shrinking of Southern African Customs Union benefits for the country had worsened the situation. Official estimates put GDP growth at 1.9%. Two major constitutional provisions were realized: a program of free primary education, which was to be introduced gradually beginning in 2010, was effected, and the Commission on Human Rights and Public Administration was appointed in September.

Internet resource: <www.gov.sz/home.asp?pid=75>.

Sweden

Official name: Konungariket Sverige (Kingdom of Sweden). **Form of government:** constitutional monarchy with one legislative house (Riksdag, or Parliament [349]). **Head of state:** King Carl XVI Gustaf (from 1973). **Head of government:** Prime Minister Fredrik

Reinfeldt (from 2006). **Capital:** Stockholm. **Official language:** Swedish. **Official religion:** none. **Monetary unit:** 1 Swedish krona (SEK; plural kronor) = 100 ore; valuation (1 Jul 2010) US$1 = SEK 7.72.

Demography

Area: 173,860 sq mi, 450,295 sq km. **Population** (2009): 9,290,000. **Density** (2009; based on land area only): persons per sq mi 58.6, persons per sq km 22.6. **Urban** (2008): 85.0%. **Sex distribution** (2008): male 49.74%; female 50.26%. **Age breakdown** (2008): under 15, 16.7%; 15–29, 19.3%; 30–44, 20.4%; 45–59, 19.1%; 60–74, 15.9%; 75–89, 7.8%; 90 and over, 0.8%. **Ethnic composition** (2008): Swedish 86.2%; other European 7.9%, of which Finnish 1.9%; Asian 3.9%, of which Iraqi 1.2%; other 2.0%. **Religious affiliation** (2005): Church of Sweden (including nonpracticing) 77%; other Protestant 4.5%; Muslim 4%; Roman Catholic 1.5%; Orthodox 1%; other 12%. **Major cities** (2008): Stockholm 810,120; Göteborg 500,197; Malmö 286,535; Uppsala 190,668; Linköping 141,863. **Location:** northern Europe, bordering Finland, the Gulf of Bothnia, the Baltic Sea, and Norway.

Vital statistics

Birth rate per 1,000 population (2008): 11.8 (world avg. 20.3); (2008) within marriage 45.4%. **Death rate** per 1,000 population (2008): 9.9 (world avg. 8.5). **Total fertility rate** (avg. births per childbearing woman; 2008): 1.91. **Life expectancy** at birth (2008): male 79.1 years; female 83.2 years.

National economy

Budget (2007). *Revenue:* SEK 857,200,000,000 (current revenue 95.2%, of which tax revenue 87.7%; capital revenue 2.1%). *Expenditures:* SEK 768,604,000,000 (social insurance 37.6%; defense 6.0%; health 5.9%; education 5.7%; debt service 5.4%). **Public debt** (October 2009): US$157,935,000,000. **Production** (metric tons except as noted). *Agriculture and fishing* (2008): wheat 2,241,600, sugar beets 1,975,000, barley 1,671,600; livestock (number of live animals) 1,609,289 pigs, 1,558,381 cattle, 524,780 sheep, (2006) 254,893 reindeer; fisheries production (2007) 243,618 (from aquaculture 2%). *Mining and*

---

1 metric ton = about 1.1 short tons;   1 kilometer = 0.6 mi (statute);   1 metric ton-km cargo = about 0.68 short ton-mi cargo;   c.i.f.: cost, insurance, and freight;   f.o.b.: free on board

quarrying (metal content; 2007): iron ore 16,100,000; zinc 214,576; copper 62,905; silver 323,171 kg. Manufacturing (value added in SEK '000,000 at constant prices of 2000; 2007): electrical machinery, telecommunications equipment, and electronics 243,346; transportation equipment 81,295; nonelectrical machinery 70,506. Energy production (consumption): electricity (kW-hr; 2008–09) 136,553,000,000 ([2008] 159,114,000,000); coal (metric tons; 2006) none (3,235,000); crude petroleum (barrels; 2008) none (128,417,950); petroleum products (metric tons; 2006) 17,682,000 (11,390,000); natural gas (cu m; 2008) none (913,000,000). Gross national income (2008): US$469,744,000,000 (US$50,940 per capita). Population economically active (2008): total 4,898,000; activity rate of total population 53.2% (participation rates: ages 15–74, 71.2%; female 47.4%; unemployed [October 2009] 8.1%). Selected balance of payments data. Receipts from (US$'000,000): tourism (2007) 12,004; remittances (2008) 822; foreign direct investment (FDI; 2005–07 avg.) 18,094. Disbursements for (US$'000,000): tourism (2007) 13,972; remittances (2008) 912; FDI (2005–07 avg.) 28,747.

Foreign trade

Imports (2006; c.i.f.): SEK 908,300,000,000 (motor vehicles 10.9%; crude petroleum and refined petroleum products 10.8%; nonelectrical machinery and equipment 10.1%; office machines and telecommunications equipment 9.9%; base metals 6.8%). Major import sources: Germany 17.9%; Denmark 9.4%; Norway 8.7%; Netherlands 6.3%; UK 6.2%. Exports (2006; f.o.b.): SEK 1,067,600,000,000 (nonelectrical machinery and equipment 14.4%; motor vehicles 13.6%; telecommunications equipment 8.5%; paper products 6.8%; medicines and pharmaceuticals 6.0%; iron and steel 5.7%). Major export destinations: Germany 9.9%; US 9.4%; Norway 9.3%; UK 7.2%; Denmark 7.0%.

Transport and communications

Transport. Railroads (2006): length (2008) 11,633 km; passenger-km 9,642,000,000; metric ton-km cargo 22,271,000,000. Roads (2008): total length 425,440 km (paved 33%). Vehicles (2008): passenger cars 4,270,031; trucks and buses 522,313. Air transport (2008–09): passenger-km 4,721,000,000; metric ton-km cargo 1,603,000. Communications, in total units (units per 1,000 persons). Telephone landlines (2008): 5,323,000 (578); cellular telephone subscribers (2008): 10,892,000 (1,183); personal computers (2005): 7,548,000 (836); total Internet users (2008): 8,086,000 (878); broadband Internet subscribers (2008): 3,791,000 (412).

Education and health

Educational attainment (2008). Percentage of population ages 16–74 having: incomplete or complete primary education 7.6%; lower secondary 15.0%; upper secondary 44.5%; vocational and higher 30.9%; unknown 2.0%. Health (2007): physicians 29,400 (1 per 311 persons); hospital beds 26,184 (1 per 349 persons); infant mortality rate per 1,000 live births (2008) 2.5; undernourished population (2002–04) less than 2.5% of total population.

Military

Total active duty personnel (November 2008): 16,900 (army 60.4%, navy 18.3%, air force 21.3%); reserve 262,000. Military expenditure as percentage of GDP (2008): 1.2%; per capita expenditure US$570.

Background

The first inhabitants of Sweden were apparently hunters who crossed the land bridge from Europe c. 9000 BC. During the Viking era (9th–10th centuries AD) the Swedes controlled river trade in eastern Europe between the Baltic Sea and the Black Sea and also raided western European lands. Sweden was loosely united and Christianized in the 11th–12th centuries. It conquered the Finns in the 12th century and in the 14th united with Norway and Denmark under a single monarchy. It broke away in 1523 under Gustav I Vasa. In the 17th century it emerged as a great European power in the Baltic region, but its dominance declined after its defeat in the Second Northern War (1700–21). Sweden became a constitutional monarchy in 1809 and united with Norway in 1814; it acknowledged Norwegian independence in 1905. It maintained its neutrality during both world wars. It was a charter member of the UN but abstained from membership in the European Union until 1995 and in NATO altogether. A new constitution drafted in 1975 reduced the monarch's role to that of ceremonial head of state. By the early 21st century, Sweden had emerged as a European center of telecommunications and information technology.

Recent Developments

As an export-oriented economy, Sweden suffered greatly from the global economic downturn in 2009. In fact, it was the most difficult year for the Swedish economy since World War II. The GDP contracted by 4.9%, after having been at a virtual standstill the year before. The production of key Swedish exports, such as cars, trucks, specialty steel, household appliances, and forest products, diminished rapidly, and the unemployment rate rose to 8.3% by the end of 2009.

Internet resource: <www.scb.se>.

Switzerland

Official name: Confédération Suisse (French); Schweizerische Eidgenossenschaft (German); Confederazione Svizzera (Italian); Confederaziun Svizra (Romansh) (Swiss Confederation). Form of government: federal state with two legislative houses (Council of States [46]; National Council [200]). Head of state and government: President Doris Leuthard (from 2010). Capitals: Bern (administrative); Lausanne (judicial). Official languages: French; German; Italian; Romansh (locally). Official religion: none. Monetary unit: 1 Swiss franc (CHF) = 100 centimes; valuation (1 Jul 2010) US$1 = CHF 1.07.

Demography

Area: 15,940 sq mi, 41,285 sq km. Population (2009): 7,739,000. Density (2009): persons per sq mi 485.5, persons per sq km 187.5. Urban (2005):

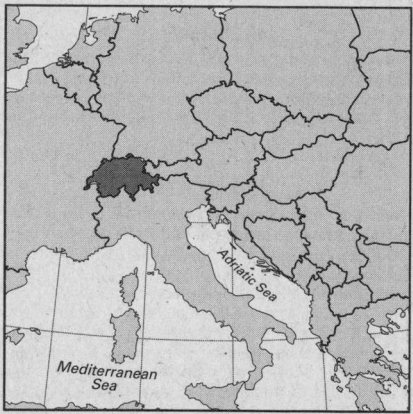

2007) 65,918,000,000 ([2006] 66,741,000,000); coal (metric tons; 2006) none (152,000); crude petroleum (barrels; 2006) none (39,800,000); petroleum products (metric tons; 2006) 5,418,000 (10,924,000); natural gas (cu m; 2006) none (3,226,000,000). **Population economically active** (2006): total 4,220,000; activity rate of total population 55.8% (participation rates: ages 15–64, 81.2%; female 45.7%; unemployed [May 2007–April 2008] 2.6%). **Gross national income** (2008): US$498,534,000,000 (US$65,330 per capita). **Public debt** (December 2006): US$188,701,000,000. **Selected balance of payments data.** Receipts from (US$'000,000): tourism (2007) 12,185; remittances (2008) 2,358; foreign direct investment (FDI; 2005–07 avg.) 21,708. Disbursements for (US$'000,000): tourism (2007) 10,265; remittances (2008) 18,954; FDI (2005–07 avg.) 57,429.

75.2%. **Sex distribution** (2007): male 49.08%; female 50.92%. **Age breakdown** (2007): under 15, 15.5%; 15–29, 18.3%; 30–44, 23.0%; 45–59, 20.9%; 60–74, 14.4%; 75–84, 5.7%; 85 and over, 2.2%. **National composition** (2007): Swiss 78.9%; Italian 3.8%; German 2.7%; Serb/Montenegrin 2.5%; Portuguese 2.4%; Turkish 1.0%; other 8.7%. **Religious affiliation** (2000): Roman Catholic 41.8%; Protestant 33.0%; Muslim 4.3%; Orthodox 1.8%; Jewish 0.2%; other Christian 2.7%; nonreligious 11.1%; other 0.8%; unknown 4.3%. **Major urban agglomerations** (2007): Zürich 1,132,200; Geneva 503,600; Basel 489,900; Bern 346,300; Lausanne 317,000. **Location:** central Europe, bordering Germany, Austria, Liechtenstein, Italy, and France.

Vital statistics

Birth rate per 1,000 population (2008): 10.1 (world avg. 20.3); within marriage 83.0%. **Death rate** per 1,000 population (2008): 8.1 (world avg. 8.5). **Total fertility rate** (avg. births per childbearing woman; 2008): 1.48. **Life expectancy** at birth (2008): male 79.7 years; female 84.4 years.

National economy

Budget (combined federal, cantonal, and communal budgets; 2007). *Revenue:* CHF 165,097,000,000 (tax revenue 59.1%, of which taxes on income and wealth 39.6%; nontax revenue 22.2%; social security obligations 18.7%). *Expenditures:* CHF 170,738,-000,000 (social security 19.0%; social welfare 16.2%; education 16.2%; health 11.3%; transportation 8.4%; defense 2.9%). **Production** (metric tons except as noted). *Agriculture and fishing* (2007): sugar beets 1,584,000, wheat 562,200, potatoes 490,000; livestock (number of live animals) 1,650,000 pigs, 1,565,000 cattle; fisheries production 2,594 (from aquaculture 47%). *Mining and quarrying* (2007): salt 560,000. *Manufacturing* (value added in CHF '000,000; 2006): chemical products and refined petroleum products 18,260; professional and scientific equipment and watches 13,488; nonelectrical machinery and equipment 12,804. *Energy production (consumption):* electricity (kW-hr;

Foreign trade

Imports (2006; c.i.f.): CHF 177,287,000,000 (machinery and apparatus 18.8%; medicine and pharmaceuticals 10.5%; base and fabricated metals [excluding gold] 10.2%; mineral fuels 7.9%; motor vehicles 6.5%). *Major import sources* (2008): Germany 34.7%; Italy 11.4%; France 9.7%; US 5.1%; Netherlands 4.8%. **Exports** (2006; f.o.b.): CHF 185,382,000,000 (medicine and pharmaceuticals 21.1%; nonelectrical machinery and equipment 15.1%; wrist watches 6.9%; organic chemical products 6.8%). *Major export destinations* (2008): Germany 20.3%; US 9.4%; Italy 8.8%; France 8.6%; UK 4.7%.

Transport and communications

Transport. *Railroads* (2005): length (2006) 5,062 km; passenger-km 16,144,000,000; metric ton-km cargo 10,149,000,000. *Roads* (2006): total length 71,353 km. *Vehicles* (2007): passenger cars 3,955,787; trucks and buses 324,153. *Air transport* (2008): passenger-km 28,140,000,000; metric ton-km cargo 1,142,000,000. **Communications,** in total units (units per 1,000 persons). Telephone landlines (2008): 4,835,000 (641); cellular telephone subscribers (2008): 8,897,000 (1,180); personal computers (2007): 6,977,000 (918); total Internet users (2008): 5,739,000 (761); broadband Internet subscribers (2008): 2,576,000 (342).

Education and health

Educational attainment (2008). Percentage of resident Swiss and resident alien population ages 25–64 having: compulsory education 13.2%; secondary 53.1%; higher 33.7%. **Health:** physicians (2005) 28,251 (1 per 263 persons); hospital beds (2006) 40,347 (1 per 185 persons); infant mortality rate per 1,000 live births (2008) 4.0; undernourished population (2002–04) less than 2.5% of total population.

Military

Total active duty personnel (November 2008): 22,823; additionally, there are 218,200 reservists and an 85,000-member civil defense force. **Military**

---

1 metric ton = about 1.1 short tons;   *1 kilometer = 0.6 mi (statute);*   *1 metric ton-km cargo = about 0.68 short ton-mi cargo;*   *c.i.f.: cost, insurance, and freight;*   *f.o.b.: free on board*

expenditure as percentage of GDP (2008): 0.9%; per capita expenditure US$515.

Background

The original inhabitants of Switzerland were the Helvetians, who were conquered by the Romans in the 1st century BC. Germanic tribes penetrated the region from the 3rd to the 6th century AD, and Muslim and Magyar raiders ventured in during the 10th century. It came under the Holy Roman Empire in the 11th century. In 1291 three cantons formed an anti-Habsburg league that became the nucleus of the Swiss Confederation. It was a center of the Reformation, which divided the confederation and led to a period of political and religious conflict. The French organized Switzerland as the Helvetic Republic in 1798. In 1815 the Congress of Vienna recognized Swiss independence and guaranteed its neutrality. A new federal state was formed in 1848 with Bern as the capital. It remained neutral in both world wars and thereafter. With the formation of the EU, Switzerland took steps toward provisional association with the European economic area, and it joined the UN in 2002.

Recent Developments

In 2009 Switzerland relaxed its banking secrecy for foreigners—though not for Swiss residents—under pressure from its European neighbors and the US to clamp down on tax evaders. The country was placed on a "gray list" of uncooperative tax havens published in April by the Organisation for Economic Co-operation and Development. Switzerland scrambled to have its name removed from the list by signing double-taxation agreements with 12 countries, offering to share previously confidential bank documents, and in September the country was removed from the list. The signing of the treaty with the US followed an agreement in August for Switzerland's biggest bank, UBS, to turn over information on 4,450 accounts of Americans suspected of holding undeclared assets. Switzerland faced international condemnation after a November referendum unexpectedly backed proposals to ban the construction of minarets. This was seen as an embarrassment for a country that hosts the European headquarters of the United Nations and where about 4.0% of the population is Muslim.

Internet resource: <www.bfs.admin.ch>.

Syria

Official name: Al-Jumhuriyah al-'Arabiyah al-Suriyah (Syrian Arab Republic). **Form of government:** unitary multiparty republic with one legislative house (People's Assembly [250]). **Head of state and government:** President Bashar al-Assad (from 2000). **Capital:** Damascus. **Official language:** Arabic. **Official religion:** none (Islam is the required religion of the head of state and is the basis of the legal system). **Monetary unit:** 1 Syrian pound (S.P) = 100 piastres; valuation (1 Jul 2010) US$1 = S.P 45.97.

Demography

Area: 71,498 sq mi, 185,180 sq km. **Population** (2009): 21,763,000 (includes 1,200,000 Iraqi refugees and 450,000 long-term Palestinian refugees in mid-2009). **Density** (2009): persons per

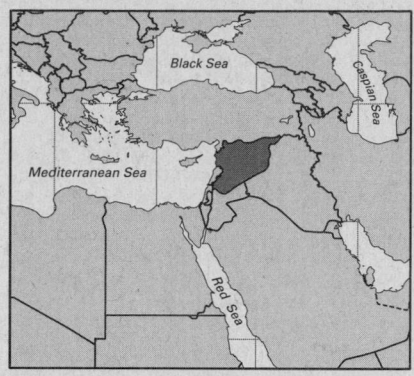

sq mi 304.4, persons per sq km 117.5. **Urban** (2005): 50.6%. **Sex distribution** (2008): male 50.85%; female 49.15%. **Age breakdown** (2008): under 15, 37.0%; 15–29, 30.8%; 30–44, 17.8%; 45–59, 9.1%; 60–74, 4.0%; 75–84, 1.1%; 85 and over, 0.2%. **Ethnic composition** (2000): Syrian Arab 74.9%; Bedouin Arab 7.4%; Kurd 7.3%; Palestinian Arab 3.9%; Armenian 2.7%; other 3.8%. **Religious affiliation** (2000): Muslim 86%, of which Sunni 74%, 'Alawite (Shi'i) 11%; Christian 8%, of which Orthodox 5%, Roman Catholic 2%; Druze 3%; nonreligious/atheist 3%. **Major cities** (2004): Aleppo 2,181,061; Damascus 1,552,161; Hims (Homs) 750,501; Hamah 467,807; Latakia 424,392. **Location:** the Middle East, bordering Turkey, Iraq, Jordan, Israel, Lebanon, and the Mediterranean Sea.

Vital statistics

Birth rate per 1,000 population (2008): 25.6 (world avg. 20.3). **Death rate** per 1,000 population (2008): 3.7 (world avg. 8.5). **Total fertility rate** (avg. births per childbearing woman; 2008): 3.23. **Life expectancy** at birth (2008): male 71.6 years; female 76.4 years.

National economy

Budget (2007). *Revenue:* S.P 458,571,000,000 (nonpetroleum nontax revenues 30.0%; petroleum royalties and taxes 21.7%; nonpetroleum tax on income and profits 16.2%; taxes on international trade 7.3%). *Expenditures:* S.P 520,531,000,000 (current expenditures 62.6%; capital expenditures 37.4%). **Public debt** (external, outstanding; 2008): US$5,678,000,000. **Gross national income** (2008): US$44,439,000,000 (US$2,090 per capita). **Production** (metric tons except as noted). *Agriculture and fishing* (2008): wheat 4,041,100, sugar beets 1,150,000, seed cotton 711,497, olives 495,310, almonds 76,093, pistachios 52,066; livestock (number of live animals) 22,865,400 sheep, 1,561,260 goats, 1,168,330 cattle, 24,500 camels; fisheries production (2007) 17,881 (from aquaculture 47%). *Mining and quarrying* (2007): phosphate rock 3,678,000; gypsum 447,900. *Manufacturing* (value added in S.P '000,000; 2007): textiles and wearing apparel 35,953; food products, beverages, and tobacco products 28,975; fabricated metal products 20,003. *Energy production (consumption):* electricity (kW-hr; 2007) 38,784,000,000 (38,784,000,000); crude petroleum (barrels; 2008) 134,800,000

([2006] 95,700,000); petroleum products (metric tons; 2006) 11,229,000 (11,988,000); natural gas (cu m; 2006) 6,087,000,000 (6,087,000,000). **Population economically active** (2007): total 5,400,800; activity rate of total population 27.5% (participation rates: ages 15 and over 45.7%; female 15.7%; unemployed 8.4%). **Selected balance of payments data.** Receipts from (US$'000,000): tourism (2007) 3,199; remittances (2008) 850; foreign direct investment (FDI; 2005–07 avg.) 662; official development assistance (2007) 75. Disbursements for (US$'000,000): tourism (2007) 719; remittances (2008) 235; FDI (2005–07 avg.) 57.

Foreign trade

Imports (2006; c.i.f.): US$11,488,000,000 (refined petroleum products 24.4%; food products 10.7%; motor vehicles 8.6%; iron and steel 8.3%; nonelectrical machinery and equipment 7.3%). *Major import sources:* Russia 10.2%; China 6.5%; Ukraine 5.3%; Egypt 5.2%; Saudi Arabia 5.1%. **Exports** (2006; f.o.b.): US$10,919,000,000 (crude petroleum 33.6%; food products and live animals 14.9%, of which vegetables and fruit 6.0%; wearing apparel and accessories 7.9%; textile yarn, fabrics, and made-up articles 7.5%; refined petroleum products 6.7%). *Major export destinations* (2007): Italy 23.7%; France 11.5%; Saudi Arabia 10.6%; Iraq 5.6%; Turkey 5.2%.

Transport and communications

Transport. *Railroads* (2007): length 2,833 km; passenger-km 744,110,000; metric ton-km cargo 2,550,742,000. *Roads* (2007): total length 55,041 km (paved 93%). *Vehicles* (2007): passenger cars 446,132; trucks and buses 566,976. *Air transport* (2008; SyrianAir only): passenger-km 2,448,000,000; metric ton-km cargo (2006) 16,000,000. **Communications,** in total units (units per 1,000 persons). Telephone landlines (2008): 3,633,000 (170); cellular telephone subscribers (2008): 7,056,000 (331); personal computers (2007): 1,844,000 (90); total Internet users (2008): 3,565,000 (167); broadband Internet subscribers (2008): 11,000 (0.5).

Education and health

Educational attainment (2003–04). Percentage of population having: no formal education (illiterate) 14.3%; no formal education (literate) 9.9%; primary education 45.8%; secondary 22.5%; incomplete higher 3.9%; higher 3.6%. **Literacy** (2005): percentage of population ages 15 and over literate 78.4%; males literate 90.6%; females literate 66.1%. **Health** (2007): physicians 29,506 (1 per 694 persons); hospital beds 28,750 (1 per 713 persons); infant mortality rate per 1,000 live births (2008) 17.3; undernourished population (2002–04) 600,000 (4% of total population based on the consumption of a minimum daily requirement of 1,840 calories).

Military

Total active duty personnel (November 2008): 292,600 (army 73.5%, navy 2.6%, air force 10.3%, air defense 13.6%); UN peacekeeping troops in Golan Heights (June 2009): 1,043. **Military expenditure as percentage of GDP** (2007): 3.9%; per capita expenditure US$68.

Background

Syria has been inhabited for several thousand years. From the 3rd millennium BC it was under the control variously of Sumerians, Akkadians, Amorites, Egyptians, Hittites, Assyrians, and Babylonians. In the 6th century BC it became part of the Persian Achaemenian dynasty, which fell to Alexander the Great in 330 BC. Seleucid rulers governed it from 301 BC to c. 164 BC; Parthians and Nabataean Arabs then divided the region. It flourished as a Roman province (64 BC–AD 300) and as part of the Byzantine Empire (300–634) until Muslims invaded and established control. It came under the Ottoman Empire in 1516, which held it, except for brief rules by Egypt, until the British invaded in World War I. After the war it became a French mandate; it achieved independence in 1945. It united with Egypt in the United Arab Republic (1958–61). During the Six-Day War (1967), it lost the Golan Heights to Israel. Syrian troops frequently clashed with Israeli troops in Lebanon during the 1980s and '90s. Hafez al-Assad's long and harsh regime (1971–2000) was marked also by antagonism toward Syria's neighbors Turkey and Iraq.

Did you know? Syria's Olympic history has been limited to participation in the Summer Games only. It won its first Olympic medal—a silver in heavyweight freestyle wrestling—at the 1984 Games in Los Angeles and its first gold medal—in women's javelin—in 1996 in Atlanta.

Recent Developments

Syria's relations with the international community improved for the most part in 2009. The foreign ministers of Syria and Saudi Arabia exchanged visits early in the year, and Pres. Bashar al-Assad traveled to Jiddah in September to attend the opening of the King Abdullah University of Science and Technology. King 'Abd Allah then capped the rapprochement by flying to Damascus in October. That month Syria's finance minister told reporters that taxes on Saudi imports would be eliminated as a way to stimulate bilateral trade. New economic protocols with Turkey were signed throughout the year. In April unprecedented joint military exercises took place, and an agreement was signed to augment cooperation between the Syrian and Turkish defense industries. US Pres. Barack Obama announced that he would name an ambassador to Syria for the first time since 2005, and in March 2010 Robert Ford was appointed. In early September 2009, however, a cluster of bombings in Baghdad prompted Iraqi officials to accuse Syria of having provided safe haven for the Ba'thist militants responsible for the attacks. The Iraqi government infuriated Damascus by demanding that the UN form a commission to look into the incident.

Internet resource: <www.cbssyr.org>.

---

1 metric ton = about 1.1 short tons;   1 kilometer = 0.6 mi (statute);   1 metric ton-km cargo = about 0.68 short ton-mi cargo;   c.i.f.: cost, insurance, and freight;   f.o.b.: free on board

Taiwan

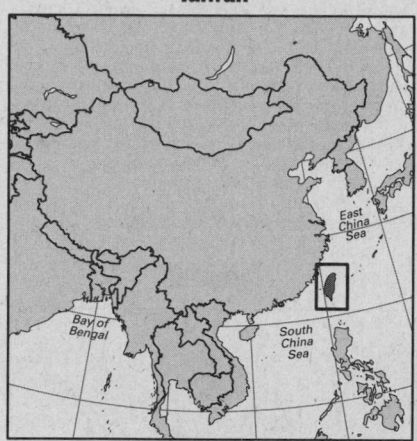

Official name: Chung-hua Min-kuo (Republic of China). **Form of government:** multiparty republic with one legislative house (Legislative Yuan [113]). **Head of state:** President Ma Ying-jeou (from 2008). **Head of government:** Premier Wu Den-yih (from 2009). **Seat of government:** Taipei. **Official language:** Mandarin Chinese. **Official religion:** none. **Monetary unit:** 1 New Taiwan dollar (NT$) = 100 cents; valuation (1 Jul 2010) US$1 = NT$32.24.

Demography

Area: 13,973 sq mi, 36,190 sq km. **Population** (2009): 23,069,000. **Density** (2009): persons per sq mi 1,651, persons per sq km 637.4. **Urban** (2005): 81%. **Sex distribution** (2007): male 50.57%; female 49.43%. **Age breakdown** (2007): under 15, 17.6%; 15–29, 23.2%; 30–44, 24.4%; 45–59, 21.2%; 60–74, 9.3%; 75–84, 3.5%; 85 and over, 0.8%. **Ethnic composition** (2003): Taiwanese 84%; mainland Chinese 14%; indigenous tribal peoples 2%, of which Ami 0.6%. **Religious affiliation** (2002): Buddhism 23.8%; Taoism 19.7%; Christian 4.5%, of which Protestant 2.6%, Roman Catholic 1.3%; I-kuan Tao 3.7% (syncretistic religion); Muslim 0.6%; other (mostly Chinese folk-religionist or non-religious) 47.7%. **Major cities (metropolitan areas)** (2007): Taipei 2,629,269 (6,698,319); Kao-hsiung 1,520,555 (2,767,655); T'ai-chung 1,055,898 (2,218,527); T'ao-yüan 391,822 (1,905,973); T'ai-nan 764,658 (1,255,-450). **Location:** island between the East China Sea, the Philippine Sea, and the South China Sea, north of the Philippines and southeast of mainland China.

Vital statistics

Birth rate per 1,000 population (2008): 8.6 (world avg. 20.3); (2007) within marriage 95.6%. **Death rate** per 1,000 population (2008): 6.2 (world avg. 8.5). **Total fertility rate** (avg. births per childbearing woman; 2008): 1.05. **Life expectancy** at birth (2007): male 75.1 years; female 81.9 years.

National economy

Budget (2006; general government). *Revenue:* NT$2,172,436,000,000 (tax revenue 71.7%; income from public enterprises 14.3%; fees 4.2%). *Expenditures:* NT$2,261,958,000,000 (education, science, and culture 21.6%; economic development 17.0%; general administration 15.3%; social welfare 13.6%; defense 10.5%). **Population economically active** (2006): total 10,522,000; activity rate of total population 46.3% (participation rates: ages 15–64, 57.9%; female 42.4%; unemployed [2007] 3.9%). **Production** (metric tons except as noted). *Agriculture and fishing* (2007): rice 1,363,458, pineapples 476,811, bamboo shoots 291,709, betel nuts 134,497; livestock (number of live animals; 2006) 7,068,621 pigs, 134,793 cattle; fisheries production 1,498,197 (from aquaculture 22%). *Mining and quarrying* (2008): marble 25,811,000. *Manufacturing* (value added in NT$'000,000,000; 2006): electronic parts and components 610; base metals 288; base chemical products 230; refined petroleum products and coal 206. *Energy production (consumption):* electricity (kW-hr; 2005) 210,300,000,000 (201,580,000,000); coal (metric tons; 2006) none (66,000,000); crude petroleum (barrels; 2007) 292,000 ([2006] 347,000,-000); natural gas (cu m; 2007) 396,000,000 (11,298,000,000). **Gross national income** (2008): US$401,806,000,000 (US$17,542 per capita). **Selected balance of payments data.** Receipts from (US$'000,000): tourism (2007) 5,137; remittances (2006) 355; foreign direct investment (FDI; 2005–07 avg.) 5,737. Disbursements for (US$'000,000): tourism (2007) 9,070; remittances (2006) 1,370; FDI (2005–07 avg.) 8,178.

Foreign trade

Imports (2007; c.i.f.): US$219,252,000,000 (mineral fuels 20.9%; electronic parts and components 16.6%; base and fabricated metals 12.1%; chemical products 11.3%). *Major import sources:* Japan 21.0%; US 12.1%; China 11.3%; South Korea 6.9%; Saudi Arabia 4.5%. **Exports** (2007; f.o.b.): US$246,677,000,000 (nonelectrical machinery, electrical machinery, and electronic goods 47.8%; base and fabricated metals 11.3%; precision instruments, watches, and musical instruments 8.1%; plastics and rubber products 7.7%). *Major export destinations:* China 21.0%; Hong Kong 15.4%; US 13.0%; Japan 6.5%; Singapore 4.3%.

Transport and communications

Transport. *Railroads* (2008; Taiwan Railway Administration only): route length (2006) 1,118 km; passenger-km 19,066,000,000; metric ton-km cargo 933,000,000. *Roads* (2006): total length 39,286 km. *Vehicles* (2008): passenger cars 5,674,000; trucks and buses 1,000,000. *Air transport* (2006; China Airlines, EVA, and Far Eastern Air transport only): passenger-km 59,108,000,000; metric ton-km cargo 11,470,000,000. **Communications,** in total units (units per 1,000 persons). Telephone landlines (2008): 14,273,000 (620); cellular telephone subscribers (2008): 25,413,000 (1,103); personal computers (2005): 13,098,000 (575); total Internet users (2008): 15,143,000 (657); broadband Internet subscribers (2008): 5,024,000 (218).

Education and health

Educational attainment (2003). Percentage of population ages 15 and over having: no formal schooling 4.6%; primary 19.8%; vocational 23.7%; secondary 26.8%; some college 12.0%; higher 13.1%. **Literacy** (2007): population ages 15 and over literate 97.6%. **Health** (2007): physicians 35,849 (excludes 4,862 doctors of traditional Chinese medicine) (1 per 639 persons); hospital beds 150,628 (1 per 152 persons); infant mortality rate per 1,000 live births 4.7.

Military

Total active duty personnel (November 2008): 290,000 (army 69.0%, navy 15.5%, air force 15.5%); reserve 1,657,000. **Military expenditure as percentage of GDP** (2008): 2.4%; per capita expenditure US$456.

Background

Known to the Chinese as early as the 7th century, Taiwan was widely settled by them early in the 17th century. In 1646 the Dutch seized control of the island, only to be ousted in 1661 by a large influx of Chinese refugees from the Ming dynasty. Taiwan fell to the Manchus in 1683 and was not open to Europeans again until 1858. In 1895 it was ceded to Japan following the Sino-Japanese War. A Japanese military center in World War II, it was frequently bombed by US planes. After Japan's defeat it was returned to China, which was then governed by the Nationalists. When the Communists took over mainland China in 1949, the Nationalist government fled to Taiwan and made it their seat of government, with Gen. Chiang Kai-shek as president. In 1954 he and the US signed a mutual defense treaty, and Taiwan received US support for almost three decades, developing its economy in spectacular fashion. It was recognized by many noncommunist countries as the representative of all China until 1971, when it was replaced in the UN by the People's Republic of China. Martial law was lifted in Taiwan in 1987 and travel restrictions with mainland China were removed in 1988. In 1989 opposition parties were legalized. The relationship with the mainland became increasingly close in the 1990s.

Recent Developments

In 2009 Taiwan continued its economic and political opening to China. After breakthroughs in 2008 that involved increasing Chinese tourism in Taiwan and expanding direct flights and trade between the two countries, Taiwan opened 192 sectors of its economy to direct Chinese investment in late June 2009. Chinese investors were also permitted to purchase real estate in Taiwan, and institutional investors (known as Chinese qualified domestic institutional investors) were allowed to invest in Taiwan's stock market. Rounding out this series of economic breakthroughs, Taiwan and China's financial regulators in November signed a memorandum of understanding on financial services that would eventually allow Taiwanese securities firms, banks, and insurance companies to set up operations in China, and vice versa. Taiwan claimed a diplomatic victory in May when, after reaching an agreement with China, it was able to send observers to the World Health Assembly, the general policy-making body of the World Health Organization; the observers attended the assembly under the name "Chinese Taipei." The significance of this was that for the first time in decades, Taiwan was able to participate in the deliberations of a UN body, albeit not as a formal member.

Internet resource: <http://eng.stat.gov.tw>.

Tajikistan

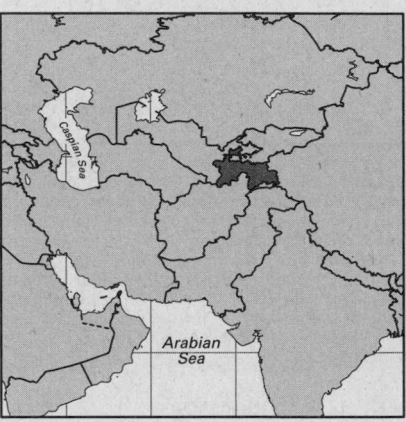

Official name: Jumhurii Tojikiston (Republic of Tajikistan). **Form of government:** republic with two legislative houses (National Assembly [34]; Assembly of Representatives [63]). **Head of state:** President Imomalii Rakhmon (from 1994). **Head of government:** Prime Minister Akil Akilov (from 1999). **Capital:** Dushanbe. **Official language:** Tajik. **Official religion:** none. **Monetary unit:** 1 somoni (TJS) = 100 dirams; valuation (1 Jul 2010) US$1 = TJS 4.38.

Demography

Area: 55,300 sq mi, 143,100 sq km. **Population** (2009): 6,952,000. **Density** (2009): persons per sq mi 125.7, persons per sq km 48.6. **Urban** (2007): 26.3%. **Sex distribution** (2007): male 49.74%; female 50.26%. **Age breakdown** (2007): under 15, 35.0%; 15–29, 31.5%; 30–44, 18.8%; 45–59, 9.7%; 60–74, 3.8%; 75 and over, 1.2%. **Ethnic composition** (2000): Tajik 80.0%; Uzbek 15.3%; Russian 1.1%; Tatar 0.3%; other 3.3%. **Religious affiliation** (2005): Sunni Muslim 78%; Shiʻi Muslim 6%; nonreligious 12%; other (mostly Christian) 4%. **Major cities** (2007): Dushanbe 679,400; Khujand 155,900; Kulyab 93,900; Kurgan-Tyube 71,000; Istaravshan (Ura-Tyube) 60,200. **Location:** central Asia, bordering Kyrgyzstan, China, Afghanistan, and Uzbekistan.

1 metric ton = about 1.1 short tons;   1 kilometer = 0.6 mi (statute);   1 metric ton-km cargo = about 0.68 short ton-mi cargo;   c.i.f.: cost, insurance, and freight;   f.o.b.: free on board

Vital statistics

Birth rate per 1,000 population (2007): 27.3 (world avg. 20.3). **Death rate** per 1,000 population (2007): 7.0 (world avg. 8.5). **Total fertility rate** (avg. births per childbearing woman; 2007): 3.09. **Life expectancy** at birth (2007): male 61.6 years; female 67.8 years.

National economy

Budget (2008). *Revenue:* TJS 3,436,000,000 (tax revenue 95.8%; nontax revenue 4.2%). *Expenditures:* TJS 5,058,000,000 (current expenditures 54.5%; capital expenditures 43.8%; net lending 1.7%). **Production** (metric tons except as noted). *Agriculture and fishing* (2007): potatoes 659,900, wheat 612,000, raw seed cotton 419,700; livestock (number of live animals) 1,922,000 sheep, 1,418,000 cattle, 1,250,000 goats, 42,000 camels; fisheries production 172 (from aquaculture 15%). *Mining and quarrying* (2006): antimony (metal content) 2,000; silver 5,000 kg; gold 3,000 kg. *Manufacturing* (value of production in TJS '000,000 at constant prices of 1998; 2007): nonferrous metals (nearly all aluminum) 585,103; food products 301,156; textiles 209,375. *Energy production (consumption):* electricity (kW-hr; 2008) 16,127,000,000 ([2007] 17,600,000,000); coal (metric tons; 2008) 216,000 ([2006] 94,000); lignite (metric tons; 2006) 15,000 (15,000); crude petroleum (barrels; 2008) 185,000 ([2006] 117,000); petroleum products (metric tons; 2006) none (1,542,000); natural gas (cu m; 2008) 12,000,000 (510,000,000). **Population economically active** (2007): total 2,201,000; activity rate of total population 30.5% (participation rates: ages 15–62 [male], 15–57 [female] 51.7%; female [2004] 41.7%; officially unemployed 2.3%). **Selected balance of payments data.** Receipts from (US$'000,000): tourism (2004) 1.0; remittances (2008) 1,750; foreign direct investment (2005–07 avg.) 265; official development assistance (2007) 221. Disbursements for (US$'000,000): tourism (2004) 3.0; remittances (2008) 184. **Gross national income** (2008): US$4,074,000,000 (US$600 per capita). **Public debt** (external, outstanding; 2007): US$1,065,000,000.

Foreign trade

Imports (2007; c.i.f.): US$2,547,000,000 (refined petroleum products 10.8%; grain and flour 5.3%; electricity 2.6%; natural gas 2.6%; other [significantly alumina] 78.7%). *Major import sources* (2008): China 25.9%; Russia 24.8%; Kazakhstan 10.6%; Uzbekistan 6.8%; Turkey 5.4%. **Exports** (2007; f.o.b.): US$1,468,000,000 (cotton fiber 9.4%; electricity 4.1%; other [significantly aluminum] 86.5%). *Major export destinations* (2008): Israel 39.6%; Turkey 8.7%; Russia 7.6%; Italy 7.4%; Norway 7.2%.

Transport and communications

Transport. *Railroads* (2005): length (2006) 482 km; passenger-km 46,000,000; metric ton-km cargo 1,066,000,000. *Roads* (2000): total length 27,767 km (paved [1996] 83%). *Vehicles* (2007): passenger cars 192,973; trucks and buses 64,324. *Air transport* (2005; Tajikistan Airlines only): passenger-km 1,030,000,000; metric ton-km cargo 7,031,000. **Communications**, in total units (units per 1,000 persons). Telephone landlines (2008): 360,000 (53); cellular telephone subscribers (2008): 2,459,000 (360); personal computers (2007): 87,000 (13); total Internet users (2008): 600,000 (88).

Education and health

Literacy (2007): percentage of total population ages 15 and over literate, virtually 100%. **Health** (2007): physicians 13,400 (1 per 505 persons); hospital beds 38,800 (1 per 175 persons); infant mortality rate per 1,000 live births 43.6; undernourished population (2002–04) 3,500,000 (56% of total population based on the consumption of a minimum daily requirement of 1,910 calories).

Military

Total active duty personnel (November 2008): 8,800 (army 83%, air force 17%); Russian troops (November 2008): 5,500. **Military expenditure as percentage of GDP** (2007): 2.4%; per capita expenditure US$13.

Background

Settled by the Persians c. the 6th century BC, Tajikistan was part of the empires of the Persians and of Alexander the Great and his successors. In the 7th–8th centuries AD it was conquered by the Arabs, who introduced Islam. The Uzbeks controlled the region in the 15th–18th centuries. In the 1860s Russia took over much of Tajikistan. In 1924 it became an autonomous republic under the administration of the Uzbek Soviet Socialist Republic, and it gained republic status in 1929. It achieved independence with the collapse of the Soviet Union in 1991. Civil war raged through much of the 1990s between government forces and an opposition of mostly Islamic forces. Peace was achieved in 1997.

Recent Developments

Though Tajikistan's financial structure was largely protected from the direct effects of the global economic crisis because of its weak integration into the international financial system, in 2009 the country experienced severe secondary effects. Tajikistan's national economy was heavily dependent on remittances from migrants working abroad, and these sharply declined as migrants lost their jobs in the economic downturn in Russia and Kazakhstan. The Tajik government drafted a package of anticrisis measures, but most of them, while highly beneficial if implemented, were designed for future needs. Among the long-term proposals was a revival of the vocational-technical education system, which could provide young people with much-needed technical skills.

Internet resource: <www.stat.tj>.

Tanzania

Official name: Jamhuri ya Muungano wa Tanzania (Swahili); United Republic of Tanzania (English). **Form of government:** unitary multiparty republic with one

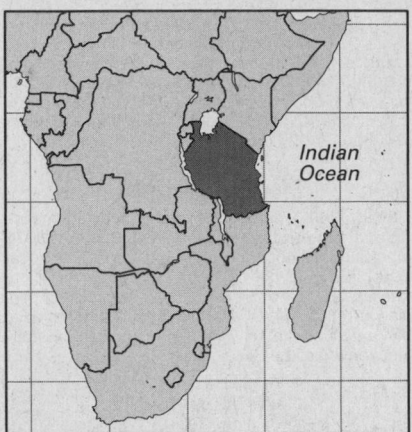

Indian Ocean

legislative house (National Assembly [323]). **Head of state and government:** President Jakaya Kikwete (from 2005). **Capital:** Dar es Salaam (Dodoma is the capital designate). **Official languages:** Swahili; English. **Official religion:** none. **Monetary unit:** 1 Tanzanian shilling (TZS) = 100 cents; valuation (1 Jul 2010) US$1 = TZS 1,440.90.

Demography

Area: 364,901 sq mi, 945,090 sq km. **Population** (2009): 41,049,000. **Density** (2009; based on land area only): persons per sq mi 120.3, persons per sq km 46.4. **Urban** (2008): 25.6%. **Sex distribution** (2006): male 49.46%; female 50.54%. **Age breakdown** (2006): under 15, 44.3%; 15–29, 29.1%; 30–44, 14.6%; 45–59, 7.6%; 60–74, 3.6%; 75–84, 0.7%; 85 and over, 0.1%. **Ethnolinguistic composition** (2000): 130 different Bantu tribes 95%, of which Sukuma 9.5%, Hehe and Bena 4.5%, Gogo 4.4%, Haya 4.2%, Nyamwezi 3.6%, Makonde 3.3%, Chagga 3.0%, Ha 2.9%; other 5%. **Religious affiliation** (2005): Muslim 35%, of which Sunni 30%, Shi'i 5%; Christian 35%; other (significantly traditional beliefs) 30%; Zanzibar only is 99% Muslim. **Major urban areas** (2006): Dar es Salaam 2,805,500; Mwanza 458,100; Zanzibar (Unguja) 422,300; Arusha 362,900; Mbeya 304,200. **Location:** eastern Africa, bordering Kenya, the Indian Ocean, Mozambique, Malawi, Zambia, the Democratic Republic of the Congo, Burundi, Rwanda, and Uganda.

Vital statistics

Birth rate per 1,000 population (2008): 38.3 (world avg. 20.3). **Death rate** per 1,000 population (2008): 12.6 (world avg. 8.5). **Total fertility rate** (avg. births per childbearing woman; 2006): 4.93. **Life expectancy** at birth (2006): male 48.5 years; female 50.9 years.

National economy

Budget (2006–07). *Revenue:* TZS 3,691,247,-900,000 (tax revenue 68.5%, of which excise tax 27.6%, income tax 19.4%; nontax revenue 5.7%). *Expenditures:* TZS 4,474,680,900,000 (current expenditures 70.1%, of which interest payments on debt 4.8%; capital expenditures 29.9%). **Gross national income** (2008; mainland Tanzania only): US$18,350,000,000 (US$440 per capita). **Public debt** (external, outstanding; 2007): US$3,684,000,000. **Production** (metric tons except as noted). *Agriculture and fishing* (2007): cassava 6,600,000, corn (maize) 3,400,-000, rice 1,240,000, cashew nuts 92,000, tobacco leaves 53,000, coffee 52,000, cloves 9,900; livestock (number of live animals) 18,000,000 cattle, 12,550,000 goats, 3,550,000 sheep; fisheries production 328,827 (from aquaculture, negligible). *Mining and quarrying* (2007): gold 40,193 kg; garnets 5,900 kg; tanzanites 3,400 kg; rubies 2,700 kg; diamonds 282,786 carats. *Manufacturing* (2005): cement 1,281,-000; wheat flour 347,296; sugar 202,200; *konyagi* (a Tanzanian liquor) 41,050 hectoliters. *Energy production (consumption):* electricity (kW-hr; 2006) 2,776,000,000 (2,899,000,000); coal (metric tons; 2006) 80,000 (80,000); petroleum products (metric tons; 2006) none (1,216,000); natural gas (cu m; 2006) 374,000,000 (374,000,000). **Population economically active** (2002): total 14,841,000; activity rate of total population 43.1% (participation rates: ages 10 and over, 64.9%; female 48.0%; officially unemployed 3.7%). **Selected balance of payments data.** Receipts from (US$'000,000): tourism (2007) 1,037; remittances (2008) 15; foreign direct investment (2005–07 avg.) 563; official development assistance (2007) 2,811. Disbursements for (US$'000,000): tourism (2007) 645; remittances (2008) 46.

Foreign trade

Imports (2006; c.i.f.): TZS 5,558,000,000,000 (refined petroleum products 23.7%; nonelectrical machinery and equipment 12.0%; chemical products 11.5%; motor vehicles 9.9%; food products 6.5%). *Major import sources* (2008): UAE 12.4%; India 11.9%; South Africa 11.0%; China 9.9%; Singapore 6.1%. **Exports** (2006; f.o.b.): TZS 2,116,000,000,000 (gold 34.9%; other metal ores [including copper and silver] 11.0%; fish 10.2%; tobacco products 6.2%; vegetables and fruit 4.7%;.coffee 4.3%). *Major export destinations* (2008): Switzerland 20.8%; Kenya 8.6%; South Africa 8.5%; China 8.2%; India 6.3%.

Transport and communications

Transport. *Railroads* (2003): length (2001) 3,690 km; passenger-km 1,305,000,000; metric ton-km cargo 4,461,000,000. *Roads* (2008): length 78,892 km (paved 6%). *Vehicles* (2007): passenger cars 80,913; trucks and buses 393,005. *Air transport* (2008): passenger-km 156,000,000; metric ton-km cargo 1,452,000. **Communications,** in total units (units per 1,000 persons). Telephone landlines (2008): 124,000 (2.9); cellular telephone subscribers (2008): 13,007,000 (306); personal computers (2005): 356,000 (9.3); total Internet users (2008): 520,000 (12).

1 metric ton = about 1.1 short tons; 1 kilometer = 0.6 mi (statute); 1 metric ton-km cargo = about 0.68 short ton-mi cargo; c.i.f.: cost, insurance, and freight; f.o.b.: free on board

Education and health

Educational attainment (2002). Percentage of population ages 25 and over having: no formal schooling/unknown 49.6%; primary education 44.0%; secondary 5.5%; postsecondary 0.9%. **Literacy** (2007): percentage of population ages 15 and over literate 72.3%; males literate 79.0%; females literate 65.9%. **Health** (2002): physicians 822 (1 per 42,085 persons); hospital beds 36,853 (1 per 939 persons); infant mortality rate per 1,000 live births (2006) 73.0; undernourished population (2003–05) 13,000,000 (35% of total population based on the consumption of a minimum daily requirement of 1,730 calories).

Military

Total active duty personnel (November 2008): 27,000 (army 85.2%, navy 3.7%, air force 11.1%). **Military expenditure as percentage of GDP** (2007): 1.1%; per capita expenditure US$4.

Background

Inhabited from the 1st millennium BC, Tanzania was occupied by Arab and Indian traders and Bantu-speaking peoples by the 10th century AD. The Portuguese gained control of the coastline in the late 15th century, but they were driven out by the Arabs of Oman and Zanzibar in the late 18th century. German colonists entered the area in the 1880s, and in 1891 the Germans declared the region a protectorate as German East Africa. In World War I, Britain captured the German holdings, which became a British mandate (1920) under the name Tanganyika. Britain retained control of the region after World War II when it became a UN trust territory (1947). Tanganyika gained independence in 1961 and became a republic in 1962. In 1964 it united with Zanzibar under the name Tanzania. The country subsequently experienced both political and economic struggles; it held its first multiparty elections in 1995.

Recent Developments

Tanzania experienced weakened demand for exports of goods (cash crops) and services (tourism) and a contraction of foreign investment in 2009. GDP growth dropped 2–3%. The country continued to rank in the lowest 10% of the world's economies in terms of annual per capita income—it was estimated that at least 52% of the population lived in poverty. The government's poverty-reduction strategy prioritized the agricultural sector, which accounted for more than 40% of GDP, 85% of exports, and 80% of the workforce. In the industrial sector, gold mining was increasingly important; Tanzania became Africa's third largest gold producer.

Internet resource: <www.nbs.go.tz>.

Thailand

Official name: Ratcha Anachak Thai (Kingdom of Thailand). **Form of government:** constitutional monarchy with two legislative houses (Senate [150]; House of Representatives [480]). **Head of state:**

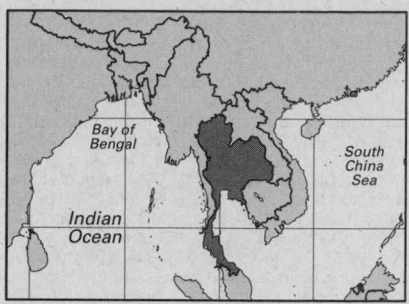

King Bhumibol Adulyadej (from 1946). **Head of government:** Prime Minister Abhisit Vejjajiva (from 2008). **Capital:** Bangkok. **Official language:** Thai. **Official religion:** none. **Monetary unit:** 1 baht (THB) = 100 satang; valuation (1 Jul 2010) US$1 = THB 32.39.

Demography

Area: 198,117 sq mi, 513,120 sq km. **Population** (2009): 65,998,000. **Density** (2009): persons per sq mi 333.1, persons per sq km 128.6. **Urban** (2008): 33.8%. **Sex distribution** (2008): male 49.44%; female 50.56%. **Age breakdown** (2008): under 15, 21.2%; 15–29, 23.9%; 30–44, 24.5%; 45–59, 18.2%; 60–74, 9.2%; 75–89, 2.9%; 90 and over, 0.1%. **Ethnic composition** (2000): Tai peoples 81.4%, of which Thai (Siamese) 34.9%, Lao 26.5%; Han Chinese 10.6%; Malay 3.7%; Khmer 1.9%; other 2.4%. **Religious affiliation** (2005): Buddhist 83%; Muslim (nearly all Sunni) 9%;* traditional beliefs 2.5%; nonreligious 2%; other (significantly Christian) 3.5%. **Major cities** (2000): Bangkok (2007) 6,704,000; Samut Prakan 378,741; Nonthaburi 291,555; Udon Thani 222,425; Nakhon Ratchasima 204,641. **Location:** southeastern Asia, bordering Laos, Cambodia, the Gulf of Thailand, Malaysia, and Myanmar (Burma).

Vital statistics

Birth rate per 1,000 population (2008): 13.6 (world avg. 20.3). **Death rate** per 1,000 population (2008): 7.1 (world avg. 8.5). **Total fertility rate** (avg. births per childbearing woman; 2008): 1.64. **Life expectancy** at birth (2008): male 70.5 years; female 75.3 years.

National economy

Budget (2008). *Revenue:* THB 1,839,600,000,000 (tax revenue 89.9%, of which VAT 27.4%, corporate taxes 25.0%, excise tax 15.1%, income tax 11.1%; nontax revenue 10.1%). *Expenditures:* THB 1,633,300,000,000 (current expenditures 79.9%; capital expenditures 20.1%). **Production** (metric tons except as noted). *Agriculture and fishing* (2008): sugarcane 76,018,410, rice 32,119,350, cassava 23,809,670, natural rubber 3,166,840; livestock (number of live animals) 7,845,346 pigs, 6,699,999 cattle, 1,699,469 buffalo; fisheries production (2007) 3,858,815 (from aquaculture 36%). *Mining and quarrying* (2007): gypsum (2008) 8,500,401; dolomite 1,123,425; feldspar 684,668; zinc [metal content] 32,921; gemstones (significantly rubies and sapphires) 102,000 carats; silver 7,400 kg; gold 3,000 kg. *Manufacturing* (value added in US$'000,000; 2000): textiles and wearing apparel 1,905; electronics 1,817; food products 1,311. *Energy production (consumption)*: electricity (kW-hr; 2007) 142,538,000,000 (138,609,000,000); coal (metric tons; 2006) none (6,252,000); lignite (metric tons; 2008) 18,171,950 ([2006] 18,852,000); crude petroleum (barrels; 2008–09) 79,899,830 ([2008] 340,545,000); petroleum products (metric tons; 2006) 43,459,000 (37,489,000); natural gas (cu m; 2008) 28,760,000,000 (37,310,000,000). **Population economically active** (2008; end of 3rd quarter): total 38,344,700; activity rate of total population 58.5% (participation rates: ages 15–59, 79.3%; female 46.0%; unemployed [April 2008–March 2009] 1.5%). **Gross national income** (2008): US$191,650,000,000 (US$2,840 per capita). **Public debt** (external, outstanding; 2007): US$9,841,000,000. **Selected balance of payments data.** Receipts from (US$'000,000): tourism (2007) 16,667; remittances (2008) 1,800; foreign direct investment (FDI; 2006–08 avg.) 10,258. Disbursements for (US$'000,000): tourism (2007) 5,143; FDI (2005–07 avg.) 1,097.

Foreign trade

Imports (2008; c.i.f.): THB 5,946,311,060,000 (mineral fuels 20.7%, of which crude petroleum 16.2%; chemical products 10.1%; electronic parts 8.5%; electrical machinery and equipment 8.3%; iron and steel 7.6%; nonelectrical machinery and equipment 6.5%; fabricated metal products 5.7%). *Major import sources:* Japan 18.8%; China 11.3%; US 6.4%; UAE 6.2%; Malaysia 5.4%. **Exports** (2008; f.o.b.): THB 5,851,371,140,000 (computers and parts 9.4%; transportation equipment 9.4%; agricultural products 9.0%; integrated circuits and parts 8.7%; electrical machinery and equipment 6.8%; refined petroleum products 5.4%; nonelectrical machinery and equipment 4.9%). *Major export destinations:* US 11.4%; Japan 11.3%; China 9.1%; Singapore 5.7%; Hong Kong 5.7%.

Transport and communications

Transport. *Railroads* (2008): route length 4,071 km; passenger-km 8,570,000,000; metric ton-km cargo 3,139,000,000. *Roads* (2007): total length 51,538 km (paved 99%). *Vehicles* (2007): passenger cars 3,560,222; trucks and buses 3,615,153. *Air transport* (2008–09): passenger-km 51,852,000,000; metric ton-km cargo 2,050,901,000. **Communications,** in total units (units per 1,000 persons). Telephone landlines (2008): 7,024,000 (104); cellular telephone subscribers (2008): 62,000,000 (920); personal computers (2007): 4,039,000 (62); total Internet users (2008): 16,100,000 (239); broadband Internet subscribers (2008): 950,000 (14).

Education and health

Educational attainment (2007). Percentage of employed population having: no formal schooling/un-

known 5.4%; incomplete primary education 32.4%; complete primary 21.2%; lower secondary 29.6%; upper secondary/higher 11.4%. **Literacy** (2007): population ages 15 and over literate 94.1%; males literate 95.9%; females literate 92.6%. **Health** (2005): physicians 19,546 (1 per 3,287 persons); hospital beds 134,016 (1 per 470 persons); infant mortality rate per 1,000 live births (2008) 18.1; undernourished population (2002–04) 13,800,000 (22% of total population based on the consumption of a minimum daily requirement of 1,870 calories).

Military

Total active duty personnel (November 2008): 306,600 (army 62.0%, navy 23.0%, air force 15.0%). **Military expenditure as percentage of GDP** (2007): 1.4%; per capita expenditure US$51.

Background

The region of Thailand has been occupied continuously for 20,000 years. It was part of the Mon and Khmer kingdoms from the 9th century AD. Thai-speaking peoples emigrated from China in the 10th century. During the 13th century two Thai states emerged: the Sukhothai kingdom, founded about 1220 after a successful revolt against the Khmer, and Chiang Mai, founded in 1296 after the defeat of the Mon. In 1350 the Thai kingdom of Ayutthaya succeeded Sukhothai. The Burmese were its most powerful rivals, occupying it briefly in the 16th century and destroying the kingdom in 1767. The Chakri dynasty came to power in 1782, moving the capital to Bangkok and extending the empire along the Malay Peninsula and into Laos and Cambodia. The country was named Siam in 1856. Though Western influence increased during the 19th century, Siam's rulers avoided colonization by granting concessions to European countries; it was the only Southeast Asian nation able to do so. In 1917 it entered World War I on the side of the Allies. It became a constitutional monarchy following a military coup in 1932 and was officially renamed Thailand in 1939. It was occupied by Japan in World War II. It participated in the Korean War as a UN forces member and was allied with South Vietnam in the Vietnam War. The country subsequently became a regional economic powerhouse, though serious social problems also emerged, including a growing gap between rich and poor and a major AIDS epidemic.

Recent Developments

Thailand faced international criticism in January 2009 following reports that its military had mistreated Muslim refugees from Myanmar (Burma) and Bangladesh. In April, Thai and Cambodian troops clashed near the Temple of Prear Vihear—a source of long-standing land disputes between the two countries; the skirmish left two Thai soldiers dead. In November former Thai prime minister Thaksin Shinawatra was made an economic adviser to Cambodian Prime Minister Hun Sen. Thailand responded by recalling its ambassador. At the

---

1 metric ton = about 1.1 short tons; 1 kilometer = 0.6 mi (statute); 1 metric ton-km cargo = about 0.68 short ton-mi cargo; c.i.f.: cost, insurance, and freight; f.o.b.: free on board

end of the year, Thailand again raised international ire when it forcibly repatriated 4,000 Hmong refugees to Laos. The country's economy remained sluggish. The tourist industry, a major source of income for Thailand, was negatively affected by persistent political unrest and by the rapid spread of the H1N1 flu, which in 2009 claimed at least 190 lives.

Internet resource: <http://web.nso.go.th>.

Togo

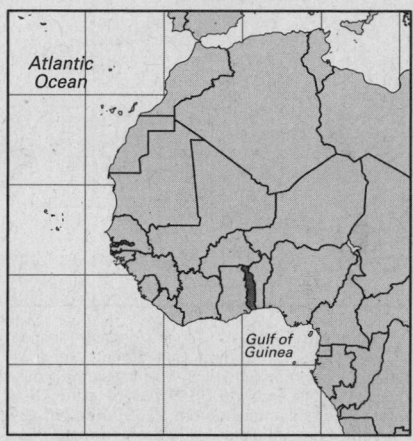

Official name: République Togolaise (Togolese Republic). **Form of government:** multiparty republic with one legislative house (National Assembly [81]). **Head of state and government:** President Faure Gnassingbé (from 2005), assisted by Prime Minister Gilbert Houngbo (from 2008). **Capital:** Lomé. **Official language:** French. **Official religion:** none. **Monetary unit:** 1 CFA franc (CFAF) = 100 centimes; valuation (1 Jul 2010) US$1 = CFAF 527.20.

Demography

Area: 21,925 sq mi, 56,785 sq km. **Population** (2009): 6,032,000. **Density** (2009): persons per sq mi 275.1, persons per sq km 106.2. **Urban** (2007): 41.4%. **Sex distribution** (2008): male 49.12%; female 50.88%. **Age breakdown** (2008): under 15, 41.6%; 15–29, 30.0%; 30–44, 15.9%; 45–59, 8.1%; 60–74, 3.6%; 75–84, 0.7%; 85 and over, 0.1%. **Ethnic composition** (2000): Ewe 22.2%; Kabre 13.4%; Wachi 10.0%; Mina 5.6%; Kotokoli 5.6%; Bimoba 5.2%; Losso 4.0%; Gurma 3.4%; Lamba 3.2%; Adja 3.0%; other 24.4%. **Religious affiliation** (2004): Christian 47.2%, of which Roman Catholic 27.8%, Protestant 9.5%, independent and other Christian 9.9%; traditional beliefs 33.0%; Muslim 13.7%; nonreligious 4.9%; other 1.2%. **Major cities** (2005): Lomé 921,000 (urban agglomeration [2007] 1,452,000); Sokodé 106,300; Kara 100,400; Atakpamé 72,700; Kpalimé 71,400. **Location:** western Africa, bordering Burkina Faso, Benin, the Atlantic Ocean, and Ghana.

Vital statistics

Birth rate per 1,000 population (2008): 36.7 (world avg. 20.3). **Death rate** per 1,000 population (2008): 9.1 (world avg. 8.5). **Total fertility rate** (avg. births per childbearing woman; 2008): 4.85. **Life expectancy** at birth (2008): male 57.0 years; female 61.6 years.

National economy

Budget (2008). *Revenue:* CFAF 249,900,000,000 (tax revenue 84.5%, of which taxes on international trade 66.5%; grants 11.7%; nontax revenue 3.8%). *Expenditures:* CFAF 253,300,000,000 (current expenditures 80.2%; capital expenditures 19.8%). **Production** (metric tons except as noted). *Agriculture and fishing* (2008): cassava 881,011, yams 638,087, corn (maize) 595,311, cacao beans 80,000, seed cotton 32,500; livestock (number of live animals) 2,001,500 sheep, 1,508,100 goats, 582,400 pigs; fisheries production (2007) 24,905 (from aquaculture 20%). *Mining and quarrying* (2007): limestone 2,400,000; phosphate rock (2008; gross weight) 686,472; diamonds 17,362 carats. *Manufacturing* (value added in CFAF '000,000; 2006): food products, beverages, and tobacco products 33,800; bricks, cement, and ceramics 19,300; base and fabricated metals 10,800. *Energy production (consumption):* electricity (kW-hr; 2006) 221,000,000 (726,000,000); petroleum products (metric tons; 2006) none (268,000). **Population economically active** (2006): total 2,521,000; activity rate of total population 39.3% (participation rates: ages 15–64, 70.0%; female 38.4%; unemployed [2004] 32%). **Gross national income** (2008): US$2,607,000,000 (US$400 per capita). **Public debt** (external, outstanding; 2007): US$1,655,000,000. **Selected balance of payments data.** Receipts from (US$'000,000): tourism (2006) 21; remittances (2008) 229; foreign direct investment (2005–07 avg.) 74; official development assistance (2007) 121. Disbursements for (US$'000,000): tourism (2006) 5; remittances (2008) 35.

Foreign trade

Imports (2007; c.i.f.): US$787,100,000 (refined petroleum products 26.7%; food products 10.6%, of which cereals 5.2%; machinery and apparatus 9.4%; cement clinker 7.9%; medicinal and pharmaceutical products 6.2%). *Major import sources:* France 19.2%; China 15.8%; Netherlands 11.1%; US 4.2%; Belgium 3.7%. **Exports** (2007; f.o.b.): US$280,000,000 (portland cement 24.1%; cement clinker 19.6%; iron and steel 12.5%; crude fertilizer 11.2%; food products 9.5%; cotton 8.9%). *Major export destinations:* Niger 12.7%; Benin 10.9%; India 9.8%; Burkina Faso 9.8%; Mali 7.1%.

Transport and communications

Transport. *Railroads* (2006): route length 568 km; passenger-km, none; metric ton-km cargo (2001) 440,000,000. *Roads* (2001): total length 7,500 km (paved 24%). *Vehicles* (2007): passenger cars 10,611; trucks and buses 2,412. **Communications,** in total units (units per 1,000 persons). Telephone landlines (2008): 141,000 (24); cellular telephone subscribers (2008):

1,547,000 (264); personal computers (2007): 171,000 (30); total Internet users (2008): 350,000 (60); broadband Internet subscribers (2008): 1,900 (0.3).

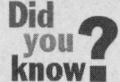

Did you know? Togo's flag, consisting of three green stripes, two yellow stripes, a red canton, and a white star, represents the country's reliance on agriculture, love, fidelity, and purity.

Education and health

Educational attainment (1998). Percentage of population ages 25 and over having: no formal education/unknown 57.2%; primary education 24.5%; secondary and higher 18.3%. **Literacy** (2007): total population ages 15 and over literate 65.8%; males literate 79.1%; females literate 52.8%. **Health:** physicians (2004) 225 (1 per 23,364 persons); hospital beds (2005) 4,862 (1 per 1,111 persons); infant mortality rate per 1,000 live births (2008) 58.2; undernourished population (2002–04) 1,200,000 (24% of total population based on the consumption of a minimum daily requirement of 1,830 calories).

Military

Total active duty personnel (November 2008): 8,550 (army 94.7%, navy 2.3%, air force 3.0%). **Military expenditure as percentage of GDP** (2007): 1.6%; per capita expenditure US$7.

Background

Until 1884 what is now Togo was an intermediate zone between the black African military states of Asante and Dahomey, and its various ethnic groups lived in general isolation from each other. In 1884 it became part of the Togoland German protectorate, which was occupied by British and French forces in 1914. In 1922 the League of Nations assigned eastern Togoland to France and the western portion to Britain. In 1946 the British and French governments placed the territories under UN trusteeship. Ten years later British Togoland was incorporated into the Gold Coast, and French Togoland became an autonomous republic within the French Union. Togo gained independence in 1960. It suspended its constitution in 1967–80. A multiparty constitution was approved in 1992, but the political situation remained unstable.

Recent Developments

In early 2010 the IMF reported on the state of Togo's economy as part of its Poverty Reduction and Growth Facility program in the country. It estimated that GDP growth stagnated in 2009 and that the value of both imports and exports dropped significantly. The budget deficit increased by CFAF 29.6 billion. Despite this the IMF declared Togo to be meeting the program's goals and recommended its continuation. In other positive news, in 2009 Togo became the 15th state of the African Union to abolish the death penalty.

Internet resource: <www.togo-tourisme.com/index-eng.php>.

Tonga

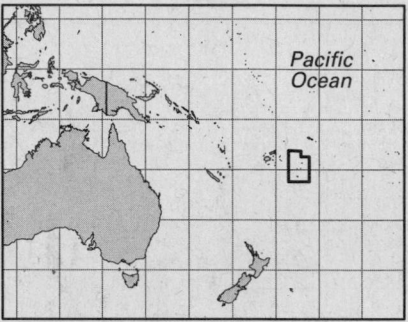

Pacific Ocean

Official name: Fakatu'i 'o Tonga (Tongan); Kingdom of Tonga (English). **Form of government:** hereditary constitutional monarchy with one legislative house (Legislative Assembly [32]). **Head of state:** King Siaosi (George) Tupou V (from 2006). **Head of government:** Prime Minister Feleti Sevele (from 2006). **Capital:** Nuku'alofa. **Official languages:** Tongan; English. **Official religion:** none. **Monetary unit:** 1 pa'anga (T$) = 100 seniti; valuation (1 Jul 2010) US$1 = T$1.97.

Demography

Area: 289 sq mi, 748 sq km. **Population** (2009): 103,000. **Density** (2009; based on land area): persons per sq mi 371.8, persons per sq km 143.5. **Urban** (2006): 23.2%. **Sex distribution** (2006): male 50.76%; female 49.24%. **Age breakdown** (2006): under 15, 38.2%; 15–29, 26.3%; 30–44, 17.2%; 45–59, 10.1%; 60–74, 6.1%; 75 and over, 2.1%. **Ethnic composition** (2006): Tongan 96.6%; Tongan/other 1.6%; white 0.6%; Chinese 0.4%; other 0.8%. **Religious affiliation** (2006): Protestant 64.9%, of which Methodist-related denominations 55.9%; Mormon 16.8%; Roman Catholic 15.6%; Baha'i 0.7%; unknown 1.4%; other 0.6%. **Major towns** (2006): Nuku'alofa 23,658 (Greater Nuku'alofa 34,311); Neiafu 4,123; Haveloloto 3,405. **Location:** Oceania, archipelago in the South Pacific Ocean between Hawaii (US) and New Zealand.

Vital statistics

Birth rate per 1,000 population (2008): 25.3 (world avg. 20.3). **Death rate** per 1,000 population (2008): 5.7 (world avg. 8.5). **Total fertility rate** (avg. births per childbearing woman; 2008): 3.76. **Life ex-**

---

1 metric ton = about 1.1 short tons;   1 kilometer = 0.6 mi (statute);   1 metric ton-km cargo = about 0.68 short ton-mi cargo;   c.i.f.: cost, insurance, and freight;   f.o.b.: free on board

pectancy at birth (2008): male 72.4 years; female 74.4 years.

National economy

Budget (2005–06). *Revenue:* T$172,446,000 (tax revenue 72.9%; grants 15.1%; nontax revenue 12.0%). *Expenditures:* T$166,031,000 (current expenditures 93.0%; development expenditures 7.0%). **Public debt** (external, outstanding; 2007): US$89,600,000. **Gross national income** (2008): US$265,000,000 (US$2,560 per capita). **Production** (metric tons except as noted). *Agriculture and fishing* (2007): coconuts 58,500, pumpkins, squash, and gourds 21,000, cassava 9,700, yams 4,700, plantains 3,300, vanilla 150; livestock (number of live animals) 81,200 pigs, 12,600 goats, 11,500 horses; fisheries production 2,549 (from aquaculture, negligible); aquatic plants production 107 (from aquaculture, negligible). *Mining and quarrying:* coral and sand for local use. *Manufacturing* (value of production in T$'000; 2005): food products and beverages 19,722; bricks, cement, and ceramics 4,109; chemical products 2,044. *Energy production (consumption):* electricity (kW-hr; 2008) 55,000,000 (47,000,000); petroleum products (metric tons; 2006) none (56,000). **Population economically active** (2003): total 36,450; activity rate 34.1% (participation rates: ages 15–64 (1996) 60.4%; female 41.9%; unemployed 5.2%). **Selected balance of payments data.** Receipts from (US$'000,000): tourism (2007) 15; remittances (2008) 100; foreign direct investment (2005–07 avg.) 17; official development assistance (2007) 30. Disbursements for (US$'000,000): tourism (2007) 10; remittances (2008) 12.

Foreign trade

Imports (2006–07; c.i.f.): T$245,200,000 (food products and beverages 31.4%; refined petroleum products 29.5%; machinery and transportation equipment 14.2%). *Major import sources:* New Zealand 33.5%; Fiji 27.3%; Australia 13.8%; US 10.3%. **Exports** (2006–07; f.o.b.): T$20,900,000 (fish 40.2%; squash 26.8%; root crops 13.9%; kava 6.7%). *Major export destinations:* Japan 35.2%; New Zealand 20.2%; US 12.2%; Australia 6.1%.

Transport and communications

Transport. *Railroads:* none. *Roads* (2000): total length 680 km (paved 27%). *Vehicles* (2004): passenger cars 7,705; trucks and buses 5,297. *Air transport* (2002): passenger-km 14,000,000; metric ton-km cargo 1,000,000. **Communications,** in total units (units per 1,000 persons). Telephone landlines (2008): 26,000 (247); cellular telephone subscribers (2008): 51,000 (487); personal computers (2005): 5,000 (50); total Internet users (2008): 8,400 (81); broadband Internet subscribers (2008): 700 (7).

Education and health

Educational attainment (2006). Percentage of population ages 25 and over having: no formal schooling/unknown 1.8%; primary education 29.5%; lower secondary 46.7%; upper secondary 11.0%; higher 11.0%, of which university 3.6%. **Literacy** (2007): percentage of population ages 15 and over literate, virtually 100%. **Health** (2004): physicians 41 (1 per 2,447 persons); hospital beds 296 (1 per 332 persons); infant mortality rate per 1,000 live births (2006) 20.0.

Military

Total active duty personnel (October 2007): 450-member force includes air and coast guard elements. Tonga has defense cooperation agreements with both Australia and New Zealand. **Military expenditure as percentage of GDP** (2004): 1.0%; per capita expenditure US$23.

Background

Tonga was inhabited at least 3,000 years ago by people of the Lapita culture. The Tongans developed a stratified social system headed by a paramount ruler whose dominion by the 13th century extended as far as the Hawaiian Islands. The Dutch visited the islands in the 17th century; in 1773 Capt. James Cook arrived and named the archipelago the Friendly Islands. The modern kingdom was established during the reign (1845–93) of King George Tupou I. It became a British protectorate in 1900. This was dissolved in 1970 when Tonga, the only ancient kingdom surviving from the pre-European period in Polynesia, achieved complete independence within the Commonwealth. King George Tupou V ceded much of the monarchy's formerly absolute power in 2008 and agreed to make most governmental decisions in consultation with the prime minister.

Recent Developments

Tonga was hurt in 2009 by declines in revenue from overseas remittances, which had dropped by 10% because of the global recession. In addition, government tax revenues were expected to plummet by 8% as a result of lower levels of spending and a decline in imports.

Internet resource:
<www.spc.int/prism/country/to/stats>.

Trinidad and Tobago

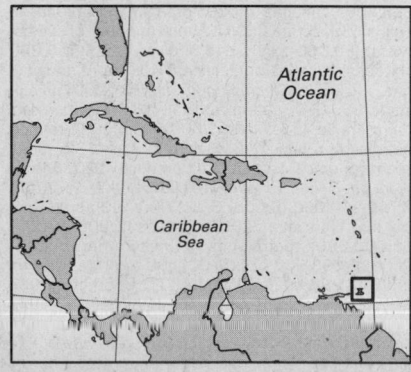

Official name: Republic of Trinidad and Tobago. **Form of government:** multiparty republic with two legislative houses (Senate [31]; House of Representatives [41]). **Head of state:** President George Maxwell Richards (from 2003). **Head of government:** Prime Minister Kamla Persad-Bissessar (from 2010). **Capital:** Port of Spain. **Official language:** English. **Official religion:** none. **Monetary unit:** 1 Trinidad and Tobago dollar (TT$) = 100 cents; valuation (1 Jul 2010) US$1 = TT$6.34.

Demography

Area: 1,990 sq mi, 5,155 sq km. **Population** (2009): 1,302,000. **Density** (2009): persons per sq mi 654.3, persons per sq km 252.6. **Urban** (2005): 12.2%. **Sex distribution** (2007): male 50.59%; female 49.41%. **Age breakdown** (2007): under 15, 20.1%; 15–29, 28.3%; 30–44, 21.8%; 45–59, 18.7%; 60–74, 8.4%; 75–84, 2.2%; 85 and over, 0.5%. **Ethnic composition** (2000): black 39.2%; East Indian 38.6%; mixed 16.3%; Chinese 1.6%; white 1.0%; other 3.3%. **Religious affiliation** (2005): Roman Catholic 29%; Hindu 24%; Protestant 19%; independent and other Christian 7%; Muslim 7%; nonreligious 2%; other 12%. **Major towns** (2006): Port of Spain 49,800 (greater Port of Spain [2004] 264,000); Chaguanas 73,100; San Juan 57,100; San Fernando 56,600; Arima 35,600. **Location:** islands northeast of Venezuela, between the North Atlantic Ocean and the Caribbean Sea.

Vital statistics

Birth rate per 1,000 population (2008): 14.1 (world avg. 20.3). **Death rate** per 1,000 population (2008): 7.7 (world avg. 8.5). **Total fertility rate** (avg. births per childbearing woman; 2007): 1.73. **Life expectancy** at birth (2007): male 67.6 years; female 73.5 years.

National economy

Budget (2008). *Revenue:* TT$55,584,400,000 (taxes on petroleum and natural gas corporations 47.5%; nonoil corporate taxes 12.1%; VAT 11.9%; income tax 7.5%; nontax revenue 4.8%; import duties 4.3%). *Expenditures:* TT$45,767,000,000 (current expenditures 78.0%; development expenditures and net lending 22.0%). **Production** (metric tons except as noted). *Agriculture and fishing* (2007): sugarcane 358,000, bananas 7,000, oranges 5,250, cacao beans 639, coffee 250; livestock (number of live animals) 60,000 goats, 45,000 pigs, 28,500,000 chickens; fisheries production 8,406 (from aquaculture, negligible). *Mining and quarrying* (2007): limestone 850,000; natural asphalt 16,200. *Manufacturing* (value added in US$'000,000; 2003): refined petroleum products and natural gas 732; base chemical products 515; food products 129. *Energy production (consumption):* electricity (kW-hr; 2008) 7,760,000,000 ([2006] 6,901,000,000); crude petroleum (barrels; 2008) 41,800,000 ([2006] 56,500,000); petroleum products (metric tons; 2006) 8,093,000 (1,209,000); natural gas (cu m; 2008) 41,839,000,000 ([2006] 14,688,000,000). **Selected balance of payments data.** Receipts from

(US$'000,000): tourism (2007) 463; remittances (2008) 109; official development assistance (2007) 18; foreign direct investment (FDI; 2005–07 avg.) 921. Disbursements for (US$'000,000): tourism (2007) 94; FDI (2005–07 avg.) 330. **Gross national income** (2008): US$22,123,000,000 (US$16,540 per capita). **Population economically active** (2008): total 626,600; activity rate of total population 48% (participation rates: ages 15–64, 70.2%; female 41.5%; unemployed 4.6%). **Public debt** (external, outstanding; March 2009): US$1,494,000,000.

Foreign trade

Imports (2007; c.i.f.): US$7,663,000,000 (crude petroleum 31.0%; nonelectrical machinery and equipment 11.4%; base and fabricated metals 8.6%; food products 7.1%; iron ore agglomerates 5.8%; motor vehicles 5.5%). *Major import sources:* US 25.1%; Brazil 10.6%; Colombia 8.8%; Gabon 6.8%; Republic of the Congo 5.7%. **Exports** (2007; f.o.b.): US$13,396,-000,000 (liquefied natural gas 30.8%; refined petroleum products 16.2%; crude petroleum 12.8%; ammonia 8.9%; methanol 7.2%). *Major export destinations:* US 57.7%; Jamaica 4.6%; Spain 4.0%; Dominican Republic 2.6%; Germany 2.2%.

Transport and communications

Transport. *Railroads:* none. *Roads* (2000): total length 8,320 km (paved 51%). *Vehicles* (2005): passenger cars 320,000; trucks and buses 71,000. *Air transport* (2008; Caribbean Airlines only): passenger-km 2,285,000,000; metric ton-km cargo 19,696,000. **Communications,** in total units (units per 1,000 persons). Telephone landlines (2008): 307,000 (236); cellular telephone subscribers (2008): 1,505,000 (1,155); personal computers (2007): 172,000 (132); total Internet users (2008): 227,000 (174); broadband Internet subscribers (2007): 36,000 (27).

Education and health

Educational attainment (2000). Percentage of population ages 15 and over having: no formal schooling/unknown 8.0%; primary education 35.4%; secondary 52.0%; university 4.6%. **Literacy** (2002): total population ages 15 and over literate 98.5%; males literate 99.0%; females literate 97.9%. **Health** (2008): physicians 1,735 (1 per 751 persons); hospital beds 3,499 (1 per 372 persons); infant mortality rate per 1,000 live births (2007) 32.2; undernourished population (2002–04) 130,000 (10% of total population based on the consumption of a minimum daily requirement of 1,950 calories).

Military

Total active duty personnel (November 2008): 4,063 (army 73.8%, coast guard 26.2%). **Military expenditure as percentage of GNI** (2007): 0.3%; per capita expenditure US$42.

Background

When Christopher Columbus visited Trinidad in 1498, it was inhabited by the Arawak Indians;

---

1 metric ton = about 1.1 short tons;   1 kilometer = 0.6 mi (statute);   1 metric ton-km cargo = about 0.68 short ton-mi cargo;   c.i.f.: cost, insurance, and freight;   f.o.b.: free on board

Caribs inhabited Tobago. The islands were settled by the Spanish in the 16th century. In the 17th and 18th centuries African slaves were imported for plantation labor to replace the original Indian population, which had been worked to death by the Spanish. Trinidad was surrendered to the British in 1797. The British attempted to settle Tobago in 1721, but the French captured the island in 1781 and transformed it into a sugar-producing colony; the British acquired it in 1802. After slavery ended in the islands in 1834–38, immigrants from India were brought in to work the plantations. The islands of Trinidad and Tobago were administratively combined in 1889. Granted limited self-government in 1925, the islands became an independent state within the Commonwealth in 1962 and a republic in 1976. Political unrest was followed in 1990 by an attempted Muslim fundamentalist coup against the government.

Recent Developments

Trinidad and Tobago was in the international spotlight in April 2009 when it hosted regional leaders at the Fifth Summit of the Americas, held in Port of Spain; the visit by US Pres. Barack Obama marked his first trip to the Caribbean as the US head of state. In November, Trinidad and Tobago again hosted an international gathering when it presided over the biennial Commonwealth Heads of Government Conference.

Internet resource: <www.cso.gov.tt>.

Tunisia

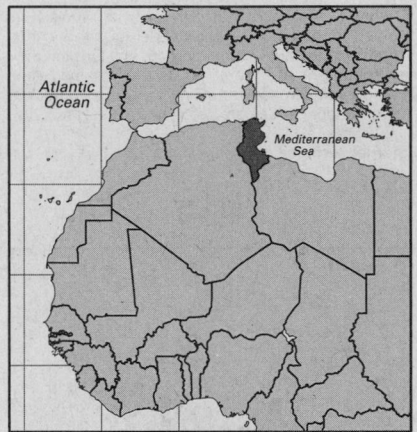

Atlantic Ocean

Mediterranean Sea

Official name: Al-Jumhuriyah al-Tunisiyah (Tunisian Republic). **Form of government:** multiparty republic with two legislative houses (Chamber of Councillors [126, statutory number]; Chamber of Deputies [214]). **Head of state:** President Zine al-Abidine Ben Ali (from 1987). **Head of government:** Prime Minister Mohamed Ghannouchi (from 1999). **Capital:** Tunis. **Official language:** Arabic. **Official religion:** Islam. **Monetary unit:** 1 dinar (TND) = 1,000 millimes; valuation (1 Jul 2010) US$1 = TND 1.50.

Demography

Area: 63,170 sq mi, 163,610 sq km. **Population** (2009): 10,272,000. **Density** (2009): persons per sq mi 162.6, persons per sq km 62.8. **Urban** (2008): 66.5%. **Sex distribution** (2008): male 50.30%; female 49.70%. **Age breakdown** (2005): under 15, 25.9%; 15–29, 30.1%; 30–44, 22.1%; 45–59, 13.2%; 60–74, 6.6%; 75–84, 1.8%; 85 and over, 0.3%. **Ethnic composition** (2000): Tunisian Arab 67.2%; Bedouin Arab 26.6%; Algerian Arab 2.4%; Amazigh (Berber) 1.4%; other 2.4%. **Religious affiliation** (2005): Muslim 99%, of which Sunni 97%; other 1%. **Major cities** (2004): Tunis (2007) 745,000; Safaqis 265,131; Al-Arianah 240,749; Susah 173,047; Ettadhamen 118,487. **Location:** northern Africa, bordering the Mediterranean Sea, Libya, and Algeria.

Vital statistics

Birth rate per 1,000 population (2008–09): 15.3 (world avg. 20.3). **Death rate** per 1,000 population (2008–09): 4.3 (world avg. 8.5). **Total fertility rate** (avg. births per childbearing woman; 2007): 2.03. **Life expectancy** at birth (2007): male 72.4 years; female 76.3 years.

National economy

Budget (2007). *Revenue:* TND 13,880,700,000 (tax revenue 68.6%, of which VAT 19.2%, income tax 9.8%; grants and loans 17.5%; nontax revenue 13.9%). *Expenditures:* TND 15,089,000,000 (social services 40.9%; debt service 26.0%; economic services 17.4%). **Production** (metric tons except as noted). *Agriculture and fishing* (2008): tomatoes 1,200,000, olives 1,000,000, wheat 918,800, chilies and peppers 291,000, dates 127,000, almonds (2007) 58,000; livestock (live animals; 2007) 7,618,350 sheep, 1,550,650 goats, 710,130 cattle, 230,000 camels; fisheries production 92,982 (from aquaculture [2007] 3%). *Mining and quarrying* (2008–09): phosphate rock 8,017,200; iron ore 178,900. *Manufacturing* (value added in TND '000,000; 2008): crude petroleum, refined petroleum products, and natural gas 4,033; electrical machinery and equipment 2,144; textiles, leather, and wearing apparel 2,133. *Energy production (consumption):* electricity (kW-hr; 2008–09) 13,854,200,000 (11,861,200,000); crude petroleum (barrels; 2008–09) 31,975,500 (12,739,100); petroleum products (metric tons; 2008–09) 1,710,800 (3,336,900); natural gas (cu m; 2008–09) 2,789,000,000 (4,256,900,000). **Population economically active** (2008): total 3,677,700; activity rate of total population 36.2% (participation rates: ages 15 and over [2007] 46.8%; female [2007] 25.3%; unemployed 14.2%). **Gross national income** (2008): US$33,998,000,000 (US$3,290 per capita). **Public debt** (external, outstanding; June 2009): US$14,673,200,000. **Selected balance of payments data.** Receipts from (US$'000,000): tourism (2008) 2,658; remittances (2008) 1,870; foreign direct investment (FDI; 2005–07 avg.) 1,904; official development assistance (2007) 310. Disbursements for (US$'000,000): tourism (2007) 437; remittances (2008) 15; FDI (2005–07 avg.) 22.

Foreign trade

Imports (2008; c.i.f.): TND 30,241,200,000 (mineral fuels 16.2%, of which refined petroleum products 10.2%; textiles and wearing apparel 13.5%, of which fabric 7.0%; food products 11.0%; chemical products 8.2%; base metals 6.8%; transportation equipment 6.7%). *Major import sources:* France 18.5%; Italy 17.2%; Germany 7.0%; Libya 4.4%; Spain 3.9%. **Exports** (2008; f.o.b.): TND 23,673,000,000 (textiles and wearing apparel 25.8%, of which clothing 19.3%; mineral fuels 17.2%, of which crude petroleum 13.6%, refined petroleum products 3.6%; electrical machinery and equipment 16.3%; phosphate products [mostly fertilizers] 12.3%; food products 9.1%). *Major export destinations:* France 28.5%; Italy 20.6%; Germany 6.9%; Spain 4.9%; UK 4.6%.

Transport and communications

Transport. *Railroads* (2008–09): route length (2008) 2,165 km; passenger-km 1,509,700,000; metric ton-km cargo 1,854,200,000. *Roads* (2004): total length 19,232 km (paved 66%). *Vehicles* (2004): passenger cars 825,990; trucks and buses 119,064. *Air transport* (2008): passenger-km 3,357,000,000; metric ton-km cargo 15,380,000. **Communications,** in total units (units per 1,000 persons). Telephone landlines (2008): 1,239,000 (122); cellular telephone subscribers (2008): 8,602,000 (846); personal computers (2008): 997,000 (98); total Internet users (2008): 2,800,000 (275); broadband Internet subscribers (2008): 227,000 (22).

Education and health

Educational attainment (2005). Percentage of population ages 10 and over having: no formal schooling 22.0%; primary education 36.5%; secondary 33.1%; higher 8.4%. **Literacy** (2007): total population ages 10 and over literate 77.9%; males literate 87.0%; females literate 68.7%. **Health** (2008): physicians (2007) 10,554 (1 per 969 persons); hospital beds 18,851 (1 per 539 persons); infant mortality rate per 1,000 live births 19.3; undernourished population (2002–04) less than 2.5% of total population.

Military

Total active duty personnel (November 2008): 35,800 (army 75.4%, navy 13.4%, air force 11.2%). **Military expenditure as percentage of GDP** (2007): 1.3%; per capita expenditure US$47.

Background

From the 12th century BC the Phoenicians had a series of trading posts on the northern African coast. By the 6th century BC the Carthaginian kingdom encompassed most of present-day Tunisia. The Romans ruled from 146 BC until the Muslim Arab invasions in the mid-7th century AD. The area was fought over, won, and lost by many, including the Abbasids, the Almohads, the Spanish, and the Ottoman Turks, who finally conquered it in 1574 and held it until the late 19th century. For a time it maintained autonomy as the French, the British, and the Italians contended for the region. In 1881 Tunisia became a French protectorate. In World War II, US and British forces captured it (1943) to end a brief German occupation. In 1956 France granted it full independence; Habib Bourguiba assumed power and remained in office until 1987.

Recent Developments

US Gen. David Petraeus, head of the US military's Central Command, told a US congressional committee in April 2009 that four recent suicide bombers in Iraq had been Tunisian and that a network had been reactivated in Tunisia six months earlier to recruit militants for attacks in Iraq and Afghanistan. Tunisia also sought the repatriation of two Tunisian prisoners held in US military facilities, one at Bagram, Afghanistan, and the other at Guantánamo Bay, Cuba, who had been charged in absentia for terrorism offenses. Despite objections from the European Court of Human Rights, European states persisted in returning illegal migrants to Tunisia. Italy sent back five migrants during the year, and all of them were subsequently sentenced to prison. Despite minor amendments, Tunisia's 2003 antiterrorism law continued to be used to imprison the regime's opponents, especially those who sympathized with Salafi jihadism. By 2009 as many as 1,200 persons had been sent to prison under the law. Sadok Chourou, the former leader of the banned Islamist political party Al-Nahdah, was sentenced to an additional year in prison for a new offense one month after his release in January from an 18-year sentence. In June the Tunisian journalists' union submitted to the government a memorandum complaining of official harassment. In Middle Eastern relations, Tunisia remained a member of the moderate Arab camp, standing with Saudi Arabia, Jordan, and Egypt in their confrontations with Iran. Tunisia also retained good relations with France, obtaining support for a nuclear power station, to be completed by 2020.

Internet resource: <www.ins.nat.tn>.

Turkey

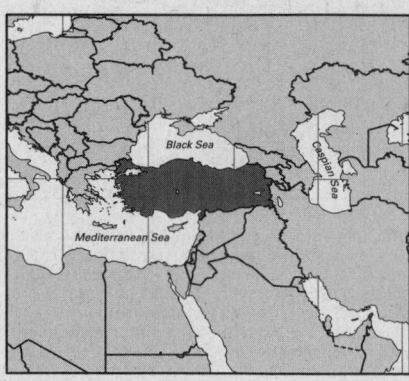

Official name: Turkiye Cumhuriyeti (Republic of Turkey). **Form of government:** multiparty republic with one legislative house (Grand National Assembly of Turkey [550]). **Head of state:** President Abdullah Gul (from 2007). **Head of government:** Prime Minister Recep Tayyip Erdogan (from 2003). **Capital:** Ankara. **Official language:** Turkish. **Official religion:** none. **Monetary unit:** 1 new Turkish lira (YTL) = 100 kurus; valuation (1 Jul 2010) US$1 = YTL 1.58.

Demography

Area: 303,224 sq mi, 785,347 sq km. **Population** (2009): 71,983,000. **Density** (2009): persons per sq mi 237.4, persons per sq km 91.7. **Urban** (2007): 70.5%. **Sex distribution** (2008): male 50.20%; female 49.80%. **Age breakdown** (2008): under 15, 26.3%; 15–29, 26.5%; 30–44, 22.2%; 45–59, 15.1%; 60–74, 7.2%; 75–84, 2.4%; 85 and over, 0.3%. **Ethnic composition** (2000): Turk 65.1%; Kurd 18.9%; Crimean Tatar 7.2%; Arab 1.8%; Azerbaijani 1.0%; Yoruk 1.0%; other 5.0%. **Religious affiliation** (2005): Muslim 97.5%, of which Sunni 82.5%, Shi'i (mostly nonorthodox Alevi) 15.0%; nonreligious 2.0%; other (mostly Christian) 0.5%. **Major cities** (2007): Istanbul 10,757,327; Ankara 3,763,591; Izmir 2,606,294; Bursa 1,431,172; Adana 1,366,027. **Location:** southwestern Asia and southeastern Europe, bordering the Black Sea, Georgia, Armenia, Azerbaijan, Iran, Iraq, Syria, the Mediterranean Sea, Greece, and Bulgaria.

Vital statistics

Birth rate per 1,000 population (2008): 17.9 (world avg. 20.3). **Death rate** per 1,000 population (2008): 6.4 (world avg. 8.5). **Total fertility rate** (avg. births per childbearing woman; 2008): 2.14. **Life expectancy** at birth (2008): male 71.4 years; female 75.8 years.

National economy

Budget (2007). *Revenue:* YTL 218,858,000,000 (tax revenue 72.1%, of which taxes on goods and services 42.2%, income tax 16.2%; nontax revenue and grants 27.9%). *Expenditures:* YTL 206,965,000,000 (public debt transactions 24.1%; other 75.9%). **Production** (in '000 metric tons except as noted). *Agriculture and fishing* (2008): wheat 17,782, sugar beets 15,488, tomatoes 10,985, barley 5,923, corn (maize) 4,274, potatoes 4,225, grapes 3,918, apples 2,504, seed cotton 1,820, olives 1,464, sunflower seeds 992, hazelnuts 801, chickpeas 518, cherries 338, walnuts 171, pistachios 120, tobacco 100; livestock (number of live animals) 23,974,600 sheep, 11,036,753 cattle, (2007) 191,066 angora goats, 1,057 camels; fisheries production (2007) 772 (from aquaculture 18%). *Mining and quarrying* (2007): magnesite 2,100; refined borates 1,093; chromite 466; copper ore (metal content) 49; marble 2,802,000 cu m; silver 198,000 kg. *Manufacturing* (value added in US$'000,000; 2005): food products 8,800; telecommunications equipment, electronics 7,450; chemical products 7,400; base metals 7,000; motor vehicles and parts 6,500, textiles 6,100. *Energy production (consumption):* electricity (kW-hr; 2008) 198,600,000,000 ([2006] 174,636,000,000); coal (metric tons; 2008)

3,340,000 ([2006] 22,800,000); lignite (metric tons; 2008) 86,100,000 ([2006] 60,800,000); crude petroleum (barrels; 2008) 15,600,000 ([2006] 194,100,000); petroleum products (metric tons; 2006) 21,563,000 (24,383,000); natural gas (cu m; 2007) 906,000,000 (36,586,000,000). **Population economically active** (2006): total 24,775,000; activity rate of total population 34.2% (participation rates: ages 15–64, 51.1%; female 26.1%; unemployed [July 2008–June 2009] 13.1%). **Gross national income** (2008): US$690,-706,000,000 (US$9,340 per capita). **Public debt** (external; outstanding; December 2008): US$74,917,000,000. **Selected balance of payments data.** Receipts from (US$'000,000): tourism (2007) 18,487; remittances (2008) 1,360; foreign direct investment (FDI; 2005–07 avg.) 17,350; official development assistance (2007) 797. Disbursements for (US$'000,000): tourism (2007) 3,260; remittances (2008) 111; FDI (2005–07 avg.) 1,365.

Foreign trade

Imports (2007; c.i.f.): US$170,057,000,000 (machinery and apparatus 21.1%; mineral fuels 20.6%; base and fabricated metals 15.2%; transportation equipment 8.5%). *Major import sources:* Russia 13.8%; Germany 10.3%; China 7.8%; Italy 5.9%; US 4.8%. **Exports** (2007; f.o.b.): US$107,213,000,000 (textiles and wearing apparel 21.4%; transportation equipment 17.0%; machinery and apparatus 15.1%; base and fabricated metals 14.6%; vegetables, fruits, and nuts 4.1%). *Major export destinations:* Germany 11.2%; UK 8.1%; Italy 7.0%; France 5.6%; Russia 4.4%.

Transport and communications

Transport. *Railroads* (2007): length 8,697 km; passenger-km 5,553,000; metric ton-km cargo 9,921,000,000. *Roads* (2006): total length 427,099 km (paved [2004] 45%). *Vehicles* (2007): passenger cars 6,472,156; trucks and buses 3,181,390. *Air transport* (2008; Atlasjet, Turkish, Pegasus, and Onur airlines only): passenger-km 51,183,000,000; metric ton-km cargo 533,-501,000. **Communications,** in total units (units per 1,000 persons). Telephone landlines (2008): 17,502,000 (246); cellular telephone subscribers (2008): 65,824,000 (926); personal computers (2007): 4,207,000 (60); total Internet users (2008): 24,483,000 (345); broadband Internet subscribers (2008): 5,750,000 (81).

Education and health

Educational attainment (2007). Percentage of population ages 25–64 having: no formal schooling through primary education 61%; lower secondary 10%; upper secondary 18%; university 11%. **Literacy** (2006): total population ages 15 and over literate 88.1%; males literate 96.0%; females literate 80.4%. **Health:** physicians (2006) 114,583 (1 per 604 persons); hospital beds (2007) 184,983 (1 per 379 persons); infant mortality rate per 1,000 live births (2008) 16.0; undernourished population (2002–04) 2,100,000 (3% of total population based on the consumption of a minimum daily requirement of 1,970 calories).

Military

Total active duty personnel (November 2008): 510,600 (army 78.7%, navy 9.5%, air force 11.8%); Turkish troops in the Turkish Republic of Northern Cyprus (November 2008): 36,000; US troops in Turkey (November 2008): 1,570. **Military expenditure as percentage of GDP** (2007): 2.1%; per capita expenditure US$195.

Background

Turkey's early history corresponds to that of Asia Minor, the Byzantine Empire, and the Ottoman Empire. Byzantine rule emerged when Constantine the Great made Constantinople (now Istanbul) his capital. The Ottoman Empire, begun in the 12th century, dominated for more than 600 years; it ended in 1918 after the Young Turk revolt. Under the leadership of Mustafa Kemal Ataturk, a republic was proclaimed in 1923, and the caliphate was abolished in 1924. Turkey remained neutral throughout most of World War II, siding with the Allies in 1945. It has since alternated between civil and military governments and has had several conflicts with Greece over Cyprus. The early 21st century saw political and civic turmoil between fundamentalist Muslims and secularists and ongoing violent conflict with Kurdish separatists.

Recent Developments

On 10 Oct 2009, the Turkish and Armenian foreign ministers signed two protocols that called for the establishment of full diplomatic relations and the opening of the frontier between the two countries. Achieving those goals remained problematic, however, as opposition emerged on numerous fronts. Turkey's relations with Syria and Iraq were upgraded to "strategic partnerships," and visa-free travel between Turkey and Syria began in September. Relations with Israel deteriorated. In January Prime Minister Recep Tayyip Erdogan quit a panel at the World Economic Forum in Davos, Switzerland, after he was not allowed to respond to a speech by Israeli Pres. Shimon Peres rejecting Turkish criticism of an Israeli operation in Gaza. In October Turkey withdrew an invitation to the Israeli air force to take part in joint maneuvers in Turkey. US Pres. Barack Obama visited Turkey in April and expressed support for Turkey's aspirations to join the EU. Turkey withdrew its ambassador to the US for a month in March 2010, however, in protest of the passing of a resolution in the US House Foreign Affairs Committee that labeled the killing of Armenians by Turks in the early 20th century "genocide."

Internet resource: <www.turkstat.gov.tr>.

Turkmenistan

Official name: Turkmenistan. **Form of government:** unitary republic with one legislative house (Mejlis, or Assembly [125]). **Head of state and government:** President Gurbanguly Berdymukhammedov (from 2006). **Capital:** Ashgabat. **Official language:** Turkmen. **Official religion:** none. **Monetary unit:** 1 (new)

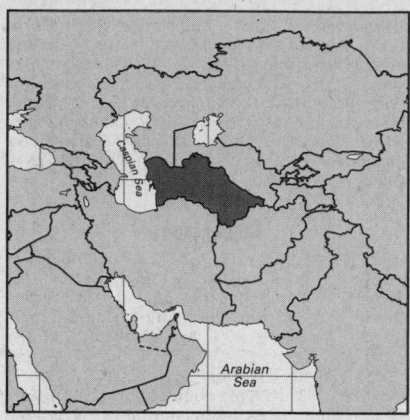

manat (TMT) = 100 tennesi; valuation (1 Jul 2010) US$1 = TMT 2.85 (the [new] manat replaced the [old] manat 1 Jan 2009, at the rate of [new] TMT 1 = [old] TMM 5,000).

Demography

Area: 188,500 sq mi, 488,100 sq km. **Population** (2009): 4,885,000. **Density** (2009): persons per sq mi 25.9, persons per sq km 10.0. **Urban** (2008): 48.2%. **Sex distribution** (2005): male 49.24%; female 50.76%. **Age breakdown** (2005): under 15, 31.8%; 15–29, 30.0%; 30–44, 20.6%; 45–59, 11.4%; 60–74, 4.6%; 75–84, 1.4%; 85 and over, 0.2%. **Ethnic composition** (2000): Turkmen 79.2%; Uzbek 9.0%; Russian 3.0%; Kazakh 2.5%; Tatar 1.1%; other 5.2%. **Religious affiliation** (2000): Muslim (mostly Sunni) 87.2%; Russian Orthodox 1.7%; nonreligious 9.0%; other 2.1%. **Major cities** (2004): Ashgabat (2007) 744,000; Turkmenabat 256,000; Dasoguz 210,000; Mary 159,000; Balkanabat 139,000. **Location:** central Asia, bordering Kazakhstan, Uzbekistan, Afghanistan, Iran, and the Caspian Sea.

Vital statistics

Birth rate per 1,000 population (2008): 21.8 (world avg. 20.3); (1998) within marriage 96.2%. **Death rate** per 1,000 population (2008): 8.2 (world avg. 8.5). **Total fertility rate** (avg. births per childbearing woman; 2008): 2.48. **Life expectancy** at birth (2008): male 59.1 years; female 67.4 years.

National economy

Budget (2006; excluding significant amounts of extra-budgetary funds). *Revenue:* TMM 22,474,-000,000,000 (tax revenue 93.8%; nontax revenue 6.2%). *Expenditures:* TMM 16,631,000,000,000 (current expenditures 94.2%; development expenditures 5.8%). **Public debt** (external, outstanding; 2007): US$648,000,000. **Production** (metric tons except as noted). *Agriculture and fishing* (2007): wheat 2,700,000, seed cotton 946,000, tomatoes 256,000; livestock (number of live animals)

---

1 metric ton = about 1.1 short tons;   1 kilometer = 0.6 mi (statute);   1 metric ton-km cargo = about 0.68 short ton-mi cargo;   c.i.f.: cost, insurance, and freight;   f.o.b.: free on board

15,500,000 sheep, 1,948,000 cattle; fisheries production 15,016 (from aquaculture, negligible). *Mining and quarrying* (2006): iodine 270,000, salt 215,000, gypsum 100,000. *Manufacturing* (2004): distillate fuel (gas-diesel oil) 2,511,000; residual fuel oils 1,745,000; motor spirits (gasoline) 1,265,000. *Energy production (consumption):* electricity (kW-hr; 2006) 13,650,000,000 (12,310,-000,000); crude petroleum (barrels; 2007) 65,700,000 (40,200,000); petroleum products (metric tons; 2006) 7,702,000 (4,191,000); natural gas (cu m; 2006) 62,000,000,000 (14,677,000,000). **Population economically active** (2006): total 2,181,000; activity rate of total population 44.5% (participation rates: ages 15–64, 68.5%; female 46.9%; unofficially unemployed [2004] 60%). **Gross national income** (2008): US$14,260,000,000 (US$2,840 per capita). **Selected balance of payments data.** Receipts from (US$'000,000): foreign direct investment (2005–07 avg.) 651; official development assistance (2007) 28.

Foreign trade

Imports (2003; c.i.f.): US$2,450,000,000 (machinery and transportation equipment 45.9%; chemical products 11.1%; food products 5.3%). *Major import sources* (2007): UAE 15%; Turkey 11%; China 10%; Ukraine 9%; Russia 8%. **Exports** (2003; f.o.b.): US$3,720,000,000 (natural gas 49.7%; petrochemicals 18.3%; crude petroleum 8.9%; cotton fiber 3.2%; cotton yarn 2.2%). *Major export destinations* (2007): Ukraine 49%; Iran 18%; Azerbaijan 5%; Turkey 5%.

Transport and communications

Transport. *Railroads* (2006): length 2,980 km; (1999) passenger-km 701,000,000; (2002) metric ton-km cargo 7,476,000,000. *Roads* (2001): total length 22,000 km (paved 82%). *Vehicles* (1995): passenger cars 220,000; trucks and buses 58,200. *Air transport* (2005; Turkmenistan Airlines only): passenger-km 1,913,000,000; metric ton-km cargo 25,997,000. **Communications,** in total units (units per 1,000 persons). Telephone landlines (2008): 478,000 (95); cellular telephone subscribers (2008): 1,135,000 (225); personal computers (2005): 348,000 (72); total Internet users (2008): 75,000 (15).

Education and health

Educational attainment (2000). Percentage of population ages 25 and over having: no formal schooling/unknown 3.2%; incomplete primary to complete standard secondary education 60.1%; vocational secondary 23.5%; higher 13.2%. **Literacy** (2007): total population ages 15 and over literate, virtually 100%. **Health** (2006): physicians 12,210 (1 per 387 persons); hospital beds 20,296 (1 per 233 persons); infant mortality rate per 1,000 live births 55.2; undernourished population (2003–05) 300,000 (6% of total population based on the consumption of a minimum daily requirement of 1,880 calories).

Military

Total active duty personnel (November 2008): 22,000 (army 84.1%, navy 2.3%, air force 13.6%).

Military expenditure as percentage of GDP (2007): 1.7%; per capita expenditure US$44.

Background

The earliest traces of human settlement in central Asia, dating back to Paleolithic times, have been found in Turkmenistan. The nomadic, tribal Turkmen probably entered the area in the 11th century AD. They were conquered by the Russians in the early 1880s, and the region became part of Russian Turkistan. It was organized as the Turkmen Soviet Socialist Republic in 1924 and became a constituent republic of the USSR in 1925. The country gained full independence from the USSR in 1991 under the name Turkmenistan. From 1990 to 2006 the country was ruled by the ever more autocratic and mercurial strongman Saparmurad Niyazov.

Recent Developments

The Turkmenistan government responded to the decrease in exports brought on by the global financial crisis in 2009 by issuing redenominated banknotes, creating a stabilization fund, and seeking to make the Turkmen economy even less dependent on the outside world. This last endeavor was made easier because Turkmenistan had no foreign debts. In June, however, the country received a US$3 billion loan from China to develop the South Yolotan natural gas deposit, from which gas would be exported to China through a new pipeline that opened in December. Turkmenistan also expressed interest during the year in participating in the Nabucco pipeline project, an international scheme to export gas to Europe via Iran, bypassing Russia. Foreign observers suggested that Turkmen interest was at least partly intended to irritate the Russian state-owned energy giant Gazprom, with whom Ashgabat had had several disagreements over gas deliveries from Turkmenistan to Russia.

Internet resource: <www.turkmenistanembassy.org>.

Tuvalu

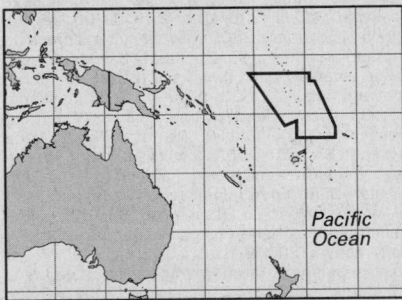

Pacific Ocean

Official name: Tuvalu. **Form of government:** constitutional monarchy with one legislative house (Parliament [15]). **Head of state:** British Queen Elizabeth II (from 1952), represented by Governor-General Filoimea Telito (from 2005). **Head of government:** Prime Minister Apisai Ielemia (from 2006). **Capital:** government offices are at Vaiaku. **Official language:**

none. **Official religion:** none. **Monetary units:** 1 Tuvaluan dollar ($T) = 1 Australian dollar ($A) = 100 Tuvaluan and Australian cents; valuation (1 Jul 2010) US$1 = $T 1.19.

Demography

Area: 9.90 sq mi, 25.63 sq km. **Population** (2009): 11,100. **Density** (2009): persons per sq mi 1,121, persons per sq km 433.1. **Urban** (2007): 49.0%. **Sex distribution** (2009): male 49.73%; female 50.27%. **Age breakdown** (2007): under 15, 29.7%; 15–29, 27.9%; 30–44, 20.0%; 45–59, 14.9%; 60–74, 5.7%; 75 and over, 1.8%. **Ethnic composition** (2004–05): Tuvaluan (Polynesian) 95.1%; mixed (Tuvaluan/other) 3.4%; I-Kiribati 1.1%; other 0.4%. **Religious affiliation** (2002): Christian 97.0%, of which Church of Tuvalu (Congregational) 91.0%, Seventh-day Adventist 2.0%, Roman Catholic 1.0%; Baha'i 1.9%; other 1.1%. **Major villages** (2002): Alapi 1,024; Fakaifou 1,007; Vaiaku 516. **Location:** Oceania, group of islands in the South Pacific Ocean, east of Papua New Guinea.

Vital statistics

Birth rate per 1,000 population (2008): 21.8 (world avg. 20.3); (2005) within marriage 92.7%. **Death rate** per 1,000 population (2008): 9.5 (world avg. 8.5). **Total fertility rate** (avg. births per childbearing woman; 2008): 3.70. **Life expectancy** at birth (2007): male 66.4 years; female 71.0 years.

National economy

Budget (2007). *Revenue:* $A 19,126,000 (tax revenue 33.1%; nontax revenue [including remittances from phosphate miners in Nauru and seafarers on German ships, rentals of fishing resources to Japan, Taiwan, and the US, and the leasing of the country's Internet domain "tv."] 48.1%; grants 18.8%). *Expenditures:* $A 23,682,000 (current expenditures 91.6%; development expenditures 8.4%). **Public debt** (external; 2007): US$8,600,000. **Gross national income** (2008): US$31,800,000 (US$2,889 per capita). **Production** (metric tons except as noted). *Agriculture and fishing* (2007): coconuts 1,700, vegetables 540, bananas 280; other agricultural products include breadfruit, *pulaka* (taro), pandanus fruit, sweet potatoes, and pawpaws; livestock (number of live animals) 13,600 pigs, 45,000 chickens, 15,000 ducks; fisheries production 2,201 (from aquaculture, negligible). *Manufacturing* (value added in $A '000; 2002): local cigarettes 755; cottage industries (including handicrafts and garments) 158. *Energy production (consumption):* electricity (kW-hr; 2006) n.a. (4,235,100); petroleum products, none (none). **Population economically active** (2004): total 4,302; activity rate of total population 44.8% (participation rates: ages 15 and over [2002] 58.2%; female [2002] 43.4%; unemployed 16.3%). **Selected balance of payments data.** Receipts from (US$'000,000): tourism (1998) 0.2; remittances (2007) 1.5; foreign direct investment (FDI; 2005–07 avg.) 2; official development assistance (2007) 12.

Foreign trade

Imports (2007; c.i.f.): $A 18,386,120 (food products [including live animals] 30.2%; mineral fuels 16.1%, of which diesel fuel 9.1%; telecommunications equipment 4.4%; wearing apparel 4.1%; base and fabricated metals 3.9%; wood products 3.4%). *Major import sources:* Australia 24.9%; Fiji 24.6%; Singapore 13.5%; New Zealand 11.3%; China 7.7%. **Exports** (2007; f.o.b.): $A 109,413 ([2005] precision instruments 18.6%; machinery and apparatus 17.4%; base and fabricated metals 15.4%; wood products 12.5%; transportation equipment 11.6%). *Major export destinations:* Fiji 93.1%; El Salvador 4.6%; New Zealand 2.2%; UK 0.1%.

Transport and communications

Transport. *Railroads:* none. *Roads* (2002): total length 8 km (paved 100%). *Vehicles* (2007): passenger cars 15; trucks and buses 2. **Communications,** in total units (units per 1,000 persons). Telephone landlines (2008): 1,500 (136); cellular telephone subscribers (2008): 2,000 (182); total Internet users (2008): 4,200 (382); broadband Internet subscribers (2007): 400 (37).

Education and health

Educational attainment (2004–05). Percentage of population ages 15 and over having: no formal education/unknown 8.8%; primary education 52.4%; secondary 29.8%; higher 9.0%. **Literacy** (2004): total population literate 95%. **Health:** physicians (2008) 7 (1 per 1,573 persons); hospital beds (2001) 56 (1 per 170 persons); infant mortality rate per 1,000 live births (2007) 19.5.

Military

Total active duty personnel: none; Tuvalu has nonformal security arrangements with Australia and New Zealand.

Background

The original Polynesian settlers of Tuvalu probably came mainly from Samoa or Tonga. The islands were sighted by the Spanish in the 16th century. Europeans settled there in the 19th century and intermarried with Tuvaluans. During this period Peruvian slave traders, known as "blackbirders," decimated the population. In 1856 the US claimed the four southern islands for guano mining. Missionaries from Europe arrived in 1865 and rapidly converted the islanders to Christianity. In 1892 Tuvalu joined the British Gilbert Islands, a protectorate that became the Gilbert and Ellice Islands Colony in 1916. Tuvaluans voted in 1974 for separation from the Gilberts (now Kiribati), whose people are Micronesian. Tuvalu gained independence in 1978, and in 1979 the US relinquished its claims. Elections were held in 1981, and a revised constitution was adopted in 1986. In recent decades, the government has tried to find overseas job opportunities for its citizens.

---

1 metric ton = about 1.1 short tons;　1 kilometer = 0.6 mi (statute);　1 metric ton-km cargo = about 0.68 short ton-mi cargo;　c.i.f.: cost, insurance, and freight;　f.o.b.: free on board

Recent Developments

Following successful experiments with solar and wind energy, Tuvalu announced in 2009 its intention to generate all of Tuvalu's energy from renewable sources by 2020. At the Copenhagen Climate Summit held in December, the country put political pressure on larger countries whose emissions were producing rises in sea level that were starting to salinate Tuvalu's soil and continuing to degrade its coasts, which were only 4.3 m (about 14 ft) above sea level at the highest point.

Internet resource: <www.timelesstuvalu.com>.

Uganda

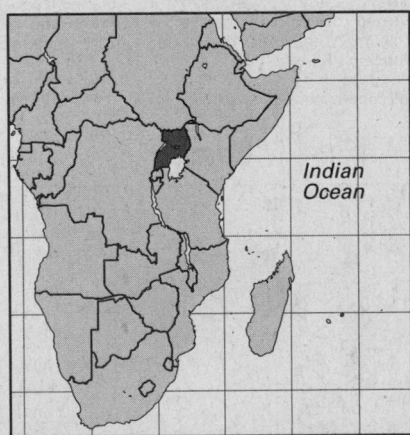

Indian Ocean

Official name: Republic of Uganda. Form of government: multiparty republic with one legislative house (Parliament [327]). Head of state and government: President Yoweri Museveni (from 1986), assisted by Prime Minister Apolo Nsibambi (from 1999). Capital: Kampala. Official languages: English; Swahili. Official religion: none. Monetary unit: 1 Ugandan shilling (UGX) = 100 cents; valuation (1 Jul 2010) US$1 = UGX 2,244.00.

Demography

Area: 93,263 sq mi, 241,551 sq km. Population (2009): 32,710,000. Density (2009; based on land area only): persons per sq mi 424.0, persons per sq km 163.7. Urban (2009): 14.8%. Sex distribution (2009): male 48.71%; female 51.29%. Age breakdown (2009): under 15, 50.2%; 15–29, 27.2%; 30–44, 13.9%; 45–59, 6.3%; 60–74, 2.1%; 75 and over, 0.3%. Ethnolinguistic composition (2002): Ganda 17.3%; Nkole 9.8%; Soga 8.6%; Kiga 7.0%; Teso 6.6%; Lango 6.2%; Acholi 4.8%; Gisu 4.7%. Religious affiliation (2002): Christian 85.3%, of which Roman Catholic 41.9%, Anglican 35.9%, Pentecostal 4.6%, Seventh-day Adventist 1.5%; Muslim 12.1%; traditional beliefs 1.0%; nonreligious 0.9%; other 0.7%. Major cities (2009): Kampala 1,533,600; Kira 164,700; Gulu

146,600; Lira 102,200; Mbale 86,200. Location: eastern Africa, bordering Sudan, Kenya, Tanzania, Rwanda, and the Democratic Republic of the Congo.

Vital statistics

Birth rate per 1,000 population (2008): 48.2 (world avg. 20.3). Death rate per 1,000 population (2008): 12.3 (world avg. 8.5). Total fertility rate (avg. births per childbearing woman; 2008): 6.81. Life expectancy at birth (2008): male 51.3 years; female 53.4 years.

National economy

Budget (2006–07). Revenue: UGX 3,574,000,-000,000 (tax revenue 63.3%, of which VAT and sales tax 21.7%, petroleum taxes 10.1%, income tax 6.9%; grants 25.4%; nontax revenue 11.3%). Expenditures: UGX 4,031,900,000,000 (current expenditures 60.6%, of which public administration 14.7%, defense 9.3%, public order 4.6%, education 3.9%, health 2.3%; capital expenditures 39.4%). Public debt (external, outstanding; January 2009): US$1,835,000,000. Production (metric tons except as noted). Agriculture and fishing (2008): plantains 9,371,000, cassava 5,072,000, sweet potatoes 2,707,000, coffee 211,762, sesame 173,000, pigeon peas 90,000, cowpeas 79,000, tobacco 29,040; livestock (number of live animals) 8,523,000 goats, 7,398,000 cattle, 2,186,000 pigs; fisheries production (2007) 551,110 (from aquaculture 9%). Mining and quarrying (2007): cobalt 698; columbite-tantalite (ore and concentrate) 275 kg. Manufacturing (value added in US$'000,000; 2002): food products 109; chemical products 59; beverages 53; tobacco products 15. Energy production (consumption): electricity (kW-hr; 2007) 2,256,000,000 (2,068,000,000); crude petroleum (barrels; 2008) none (4,745,000); petroleum products (metric tons; 2006) none (766,000). Gross national income (2008): US$13,254,000,000 (US$420 per capita). Population economically active (2005–06): total 10,848,000; activity rate of total population 37.2% (participation rates: ages 15 and older, 81.6%; female 51.4%; officially unemployed 1.9%). Selected balance of payments data. Receipts from (US$'000,000): tourism (2007) 356; remittances (2008) 489; foreign direct investment (2005–07 avg.) 383; official development assistance (2007) 1,728. Disbursements for (US$'000,000): tourism (2007) 112; remittances (2008) 281.

Foreign trade

Imports (2008; c.i.f.): US$4,525,859,000 (refined petroleum products 18.5%; chemical products 14.1%; food products 11.7%, of which cereals 3.8%; electrical machinery and equipment 11.4%; nonelectrical machinery and equipment 8.5%; transportation equipment 7.8%; base metals 7.4%). Major import sources: UAE 11.4%; Kenya 11.3%; India 10.4%; China 8.1%; South Africa 6.7%. Exports (2008; f.o.b.): US$1,724,300,000 (food products and beverages 49.6%, of which coffee 23.4%, fresh fish 7.2%; base metals 6.2%; electrical machinery and equipment 5.1%; cement, bricks, and ceramics 5.0%; tobacco products 4.0%). Major export destinations: Sudan 14.3%; Kenya 9.5%; Switzerland 9.0%; Rwanda 7.9%; UAE 7.4%.

Transport and communications

Transport. *Railroads* (2008): route length 1,244 km; metric ton-km cargo (2005) 185,559,000. *Roads* (2008; national roads only): total length 10,965 km (paved 28%). *Vehicles* (2008): passenger cars 90,856; trucks and buses 137,290. *Air transport* (2004): passenger-km 272,000,000; metric ton-km cargo 27,000,000. **Communications,** in total units (units per 1,000 persons). Telephone landlines (2008): 169,000 (5.3); cellular telephone subscribers (2008): 8,555,000 (270); personal computers (2005): 300,000 (10); total Internet users (2008): 2,500,000 (79); broadband Internet subscribers (2008): 4,800 (0.2).

Education and health

Educational attainment (2005–06). Percentage of population ages 15 and over having: no formal schooling/unknown 20.0%; incomplete primary education 43.3%; complete primary 14.1%; incomplete secondary 18.1%; complete secondary (some higher) 1.1%; complete higher (including vocational) 3.4%. **Literacy** (2007): population ages 15 and over literate 73.2%; males literate 81.7%; females literate 64.8%. **Health:** physicians (2004) 2,209 (1 per 11,947 persons); hospital beds (2006) 32,617 (1 per 909 persons); infant mortality rate per 1,000 live births (2008) 66.0; undernourished population (2002–04) 4,800,000 (19% of total population based on the consumption of a minimum daily requirement of 1,770 calories).

Military

Total active duty personnel (November 2008): 45,000 (army 100%); Ugandan peacekeeping troops in Somalia (November 2008): 1,700. **Military expenditure as percentage of GDP** (2007): 2.2%; per capita expenditure US$8.

Background

By the 19th century the region around Uganda comprised several separate kingdoms inhabited by various peoples, including Bantu- and Nilotic-speaking tribes. Arab traders reached the area in the 1840s. The native kingdom of Buganda was visited by the first European explorers in 1862. Protestant and Roman Catholic missionaries arrived in the 1870s, and the development of religious factions led to persecution and civil strife. In 1894 Buganda was formally proclaimed a British protectorate. As Uganda, it gained its independence in 1962, and in 1967 it adopted a republican constitution. The civilian government was overthrown in 1971 and replaced by a military regime under Idi Amin. His invasion of Tanzania in late 1978 resulted in the collapse of his regime. In 1985 the civilian government was again deposed by the military, which in turn was overthrown in 1986. A constituent assembly enacted a new constitution in 1995.

Recent Developments

The Ugandan economy withstood the world financial crisis in 2009 better than expected. Growth declined only slightly, from 7.1% to 6.3%. The regional drought that devastated neighboring countries initially led to increased Ugandan exports of food, which offset diminished external demand for established exports such as coffee. Although the government consolidated and expanded the gains of poverty-reduction efforts of recent years, the per capita GDP (US$440) still ranked among the lowest in Africa. At the beginning of the year, two British oil companies announced "world-class" discoveries in the Lake Albert region. The finds were later estimated to hold 800 million bbl of oil, which was roughly comparable to the reserves of Chad or Equatorial Guinea. Mindful of endemic political instability in the oil-bearing area, the government was eager to avoid the mistakes of other African oil-producing countries in unplanned development and lack of transparency. Early discussions for future planning concerned the construction of a refinery and a pipeline to the coast to end the country's dependence on Kenya.

Internet resource: <www.ubos.org>.

Ukraine

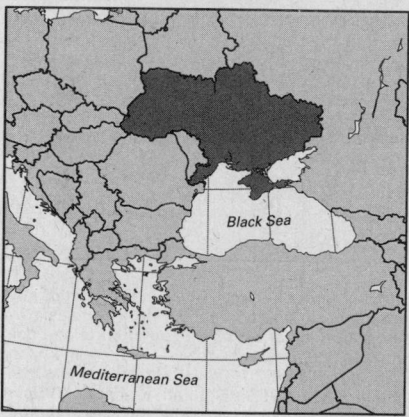

Official name: Ukrayina (Ukraine). **Form of government:** unitary multiparty republic with a single legislative house (Supreme Council [450]). **Head of state:** President Viktor Yanukovych (from 2010). **Head of government:** Prime Minister Mykola Azarov (from 2010). **Capital:** Kiev (Kyiv). **Official language:** Ukrainian. **Official religion:** none. **Monetary unit:** 1 hryvnya (UAH) = 100 kopiykas; valuation (1 Jul 2010) US$1 = UAH 7.79.

Demography

Area: 233,062 sq mi, 603,628 sq km. **Population** (2009): 46,029,000. **Density** (2009): persons per sq mi 197.5, persons per sq km 76.3. **Urban** (2008): 68.3%. **Sex distribution** (2005): male 45.97%; female 54.03%. **Age breakdown** (2006): under 15,

14.3%; 15–29, 23.0%; 30–44, 21.1%; 45–59, 21.2%; 60–74, 14.1%; 75–84, 5.5%; 85 and over, 0.8%. **Ethnic composition** (2001): Ukrainian 77.8%; Russian 17.3%; Belarusian 0.6%; Moldovan 0.5%; Crimean Tatar 0.5%; other 3.3%. **Religious affiliation** (2004): Ukrainian Orthodox, of which "Kiev patriarchy" 19%, "no particular patriarchy" 16%, "Moscow patriarchy" 9%, Ukrainian Autocephalous Orthodox 2%; Ukrainian Catholic 6%; Protestant 2%; Latin Catholic 2%; Muslim 1%; Jewish 0.5%; nonreligious/atheist/other 42.5%. **Major cities** (2008): Kiev 2,765,531; Kharkiv 1,455,964; Dnipropetrovsk 1,017,514; Odesa (Odessa) 1,008,627; Donetsk 974,598. **Location:** eastern Europe, bordering Belarus, Russia, the Black Sea, Romania, Moldova, Hungary, Slovakia, and Poland.

Vital statistics

Birth rate per 1,000 population (2008): 11.1 (world avg. 20.3); within marriage 79.1%. **Death rate** per 1,000 population (2008): 16.4 (world avg. 8.6). **Total fertility rate** (avg. births per childbearing woman; 2007): 1.30. **Life expectancy** at birth (2007): male 62.5 years; female 74.2 years.

National economy

Budget (2007). *Revenue:* UAH 165,942,000,000 (tax revenue 70.3%, of which VAT 35.8%, tax on profits of enterprises 20.5%, excise tax 6.3%; nontax revenue 25.4%). *Expenditures:* UAH 174,236,000,000 (social security 16.8%; education and health 13.4%; transportation and communications 6.7%; energy and construction 4.7%; agriculture 4.6%). **Public debt** (external; April 2008): US$15,100,000,000. **Production** (metric tons except as noted). *Agriculture and fishing* (2007): potatoes 19,102,300, sugar beets 16,978,000, wheat 13,800,000, sunflower seeds 4,173,700, sour cherries 126,000; livestock (number of live animals) 8,055,000 pigs, 6,175,400 cattle, 145,600,000 chickens; fisheries production 241,349 (from aquaculture 12%). *Mining and quarrying* (2006): iron ore (2007) 77,952,000; manganese (metal content) 550,000; ilmenite concentrate 470,000. *Manufacturing* (value of sales in UAH '000,000,000; 2007): base and fabricated metals 157.5; food products, beverages, and tobacco products 110.0; coke and refined petroleum products 52.5. *Energy production (consumption):* electricity (kW-hr; 2007) 195,230,-000,000 ([2006] 182,944,000,000); coal (metric tons; 2007) 58,742,000 ([2006] 68,470,000); crude petroleum (barrels; 2007) 31,700,000 ([2006] 100,960,000); petroleum products (metric tons; 2006) 13,941,000 (13,133,000); natural gas (cu m; 2007) 20,200,000,000 ([2006] 69,445,-600,000). **Population economically active** (2005): total 22,280,800; activity rate of total population 47% (participation rates [2003]: ages 15–64, 65.8%; female 48.9%; unemployed [2007] 6.9%). **Gross national income** (2008): US$148,643,-000,000 (US$3,210 per capita). **Selected balance of payments data.** Receipts from (US$'000,000): tourism (2007) 4,597; remittances (2008) 5,769; foreign direct investment (FDI; 2005–07 avg.) 7,700, official development assistance (2007) 106. Disbursements for (US$'000,000): tourism (2007) 3,293; remittances (2008) 54.

Foreign trade

Imports (2006; c.i.f.): US$45,022,000,000 (machinery and apparatus 17.7%; crude petroleum 15.2%; chemical products 12.1%; natural gas 10.6%; motor vehicles and parts 10.5%). *Major import sources:* Russia 30.6%; Germany 9.5%; Turkmenistan 7.8%; China 5.1%; Poland 4.7%. **Exports** (2006; f.o.b.): US$38,368,000,000 (iron and steel 38.5%, of which ingots 11.4%; machinery and apparatus 8.8%; crude petroleum 5.0%; cereals 3.9%; metal ore and scrap metal 3.9%). *Major export destinations:* Russia 22.5%; Italy 6.5%; Turkey 6.2%; Poland 3.5%; Germany 3.3%.

Transport and communications

Transport. *Railroads* (2008): length 21,700 km; passenger-km 53,100,000,000; metric ton-km cargo 257,000,000,000. *Roads* (2008): total length 169,500 km (paved 98%). *Vehicles* (2005): passenger cars 5,538,972; trucks and buses 490,495. *Air transport* (2008): passenger-km 6,528,000,000; metric ton-km cargo 63,360,000,000. **Communications,** in total units (units per 1,000 persons). Telephone landlines (2008): 13,177,000 (287); cellular telephone subscribers (2008): 55,695,000 (1,211); total Internet users (2008): 10,354,000 (225); broadband Internet subscribers (2008): 1,600,000 (35).

Education and health

Educational attainment (2001). Percentage of population ages 25 and over having: no formal schooling 0.7%; incomplete primary education 2.8%; complete primary/incomplete secondary 22.7%; complete secondary 35.9%; incomplete higher 21.7%; complete higher 16.2%. **Literacy** (2004): total population ages 15 and over literate, virtually 100%. **Health** (2006): physicians 225,000 (1 per 208 persons); hospital beds 444,000 (1 per 105 persons); infant mortality rate per 1,000 live births (2008) 9.9; undernourished population (2002–04) less than 2.5% of total population.

Military

Total active duty personnel (November 2008): 129,925 (army 54.5%, air force/air defense 34.8%, navy 10.7%); reserve 1,000,000; Russian naval forces at Sevastopol (November 2008): 13,000. **Military expenditure as percentage of GDP** (2008): 1.7%; per capita expenditure US$66.

Background

The area around Ukraine was invaded and occupied in the 1st millennium BC by the Cimmerians, Scythians, and Sarmatians and in the 1st millennium AD by the Goths, Huns, Bulgars, Avars, Khazars, and Magyars. Slavic tribes settled there after the 4th century. Kiev was the chief town of Kievan Rus. The Mongol conquest in the mid-13th century decisively ended Kievan power. Ruled by Lithuania in the 14th century and Poland in the 16th century, it fell to Russian rule in the 18th century. The Ukrainian National Republic, established in 1917, declared its independence from Soviet Russia in 1918 but was reconquered in 1919; it was made the Ukrainian Soviet Socialist Republic of the USSR in 1922. The

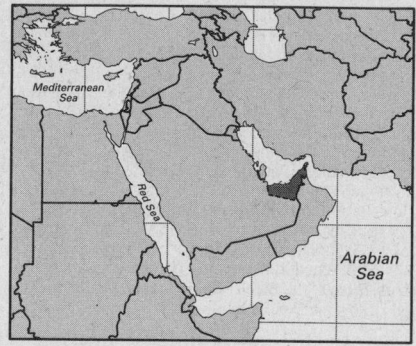

northwestern region was held by Poland from 1919 to 1939. Ukraine suffered a severe famine in 1932–33 under Soviet leader Joseph Stalin; over five million Ukrainians died of starvation. Overrun by Axis armies in 1941 in World War II, it was further devastated before being retaken by the Soviets in 1944. It was the site of the 1986 accident in Chernobyl, at a Soviet-built nuclear power plant. Ukraine declared independence in 1991. The turmoil it experienced in the 1990s as it attempted to implement economic and political reforms culminated in the disputed presidential election of 2004; mass protests over the results came to be known as the Orange Revolution.

Recent Developments

The year 2009 began with a gas dispute after the breakdown of talks over prices and back payments between Russia's Gazprom and Ukraine's national oil and gas company. By 7 January Russia had halted all gas transit through Ukraine on the main pipeline to Europe. The dispute ended after Prime Minister Yuliya Tymoshenko met with her Russian counterpart, Vladimir Putin, on 18 January. Ukraine's economic crisis, sparked by the worldwide financial recession, deepened. Construction was cut in half and GDP fell 3.7%. The unemployment rate reached 9.6%. The International Monetary Fund (IMF) released US$10.6 billion of a US$16.4 billion loan after Tymoshenko agreed to keep the country's budget deficit at less than 6.0% in 2009 and less than 4.0% in 2010. Conversely, in the parliament the opposition, led by Viktor Yanukovych, responded to the economic crisis with a bill that substantially increased both the minimum wage and pensions. Despite warnings by Tymoshenko that the bill ran counter to Ukraine's agreement with the IMF, the president signed it into law. The IMF subsequently delayed further disbursement from the country's loan. In February 2010 Yanukovych, who was seen as pro-Russian, defeated Tymoshenko in presidential elections. In April he disbanded the commissions in charge of trying to join NATO and of advancing Ukraine's Euro-Atlantic integration. The same month he controversially extended the Russian navy's lease to use the Ukrainian base at Sevastopol by 25 years.

Internet resource: <www.ukrstat.gov.ua>.

United Arab Emirates

Official name: Al-Imarat al-ʿArabiyah al-Muttahidah (United Arab Emirates). **Form of government:** federation of seven emirates with one advisory body (Federal National Council [40]). **Head of state:** President Sheikh Khalifah ibn Zayid al-Nahyan (from 2004). **Head of government:** Prime Minister Sheikh Muhammad ibn Rashid al-Maktum (from 2006). **Capital:** Abu Dhabi. **Official language:** Arabic. **Official religion:** Islam. **Monetary unit:** 1 UAE dirham (AED) = 100 fils; valuation (1 Jul 2010) US$1 = AED 3.67.

Demography

Area: 32,280 sq mi, 83,600 sq km. **Population** (2009): 4,765,000. **Density** (2009): persons per sq mi 147.6, persons per sq km 57.0. **Urban** (2008): 80.0%. **Sex distribution** (2008): male 68.96%; female 31.04%. **Age breakdown** (2008): under 15, 19.1%; 15–29, 32.3%; 30–44, 36.6%; 45–59, 10.5%; 60–74, 1.2%; 75 and over, 0.3%. **Ethnic composition** (2000): Arab 48.1%, of which UAE Arab 12.2%, UAE Bedouin 9.4%, Egyptian Arab 6.2%, Omani Arab 4.1%, Saudi Arab 4.0%; South Asian 35.7%, of which Pashtun 7.1%, Balochi 7.1%, Malayali 7.1%; Persian 5.0%; Filipino 3.4%; white 2.4%; other 5.4%. **Religious affiliation** (2005): Muslim 62% (mostly Sunni); Hindu 21%; Christian 9%; Buddhist 4%; other 4%. **Major cities** (2006): Dubai 1,354,980; Sharjah 685,000; Abu Dhabi 630,000; Al-ʿAyn 350,000; ʿAjman 202,244. **Location:** the Middle East, bordering the Persian Gulf, the Gulf of Oman, Oman, and Saudi Arabia.

Vital statistics

Birth rate per 1,000 population (2007): 16.1 (world avg. 20.3). **Death rate** per 1,000 population (2007): 2.2 (world avg. 8.5). **Total fertility rate** (avg. births per childbearing woman; 2007): 2.43. **Life expectancy** at birth (2007): male 73.2 years; female 78.3 years.

National economy

Budget (2007). *Revenue:* AED 228,750,000,000 (royalties on hydrocarbons 77.1%; tax revenue 6.0%). *Expenditures:* AED 159,726,000,000 (current expenditures 76.0%; loans, net equity, and foreign grants -13.2%; development expenditures 10.8%). **Gross national income** (2008): US$272,053,000,000 (US$57,094 per capita). **Public debt** (2008): US$117,000,000,000. **Production** (metric tons except as noted). *Agriculture and fishing* (2007): dates 755,000, tomatoes 215,000, alfalfa for forage and silage (2005) 210,000; livestock (number of live animals) 1,570,000 goats, 615,000 sheep, 260,000 camels; fisheries production 87,570 (from aquaculture 1%). *Mining and quarrying* (2007): gypsum 150,000; lime 60,000. *Manufacturing* (2007): cement 15,000,000; aluminum 890,000; steel 90,000; refined and unrefined gold (total foreign trade value) US$19,000,000,000; worked and unworked diamonds (total foreign trade value) US$11,230,000,000. *Energy production (consump-*

---

1 metric ton = about 1.1 short tons;　1 kilometer = 0.6 mi (statute);　1 metric ton-km cargo = about 0.68 short ton-mi cargo;　c.i.f.: cost, insurance, and freight;　f.o.b.: free on board

tion): electricity (kW-hr; 2007) 76,532,000,000 (74,717,000,000); crude petroleum (barrels; 2008) 978,600,000 ([2006] 135,100,000); petroleum products (metric tons; 2006) 21,592,000 (10,071,000); natural gas (cu m; 2008) 50,200,-000,000 ([2007] 38,900,000,000). **Population economically active** (2005): total 2,559,668; activity rate of total population 54.6% (participation rates: ages 15–64, 78.1%; female 13.5%; unemployed [2008] 4%). **Selected balance of payments data.** Receipts from (US$'000,000): tourism (2008) 7,162; foreign direct investment (FDI; 2005–07 avg.) 12,320. Disbursements for (US$'000,000): tourism (2008) 13,288; remittances (2007) 5,000; FDI (2005–07 avg.) 7,089.

Foreign trade

Imports (2006; c.i.f.): US$97,864,000,000 (machinery and apparatus 19.4%; base and fabricated metals 9.9%; motor vehicles 8.1%; gold 7.6%; food products 5.4%). *Major import sources* (2008): China 13.2%; India 10.4%; US 8.8%; Germany 6.5%; Japan 6.1%. **Exports** (2006; f.o.b.): US$142,505,000,000 (crude petroleum 37.9%; refined petroleum products 11.4%; gold [not jewelry] 3.4%; motor vehicles and parts 2.5%; natural gas 1.7%; telecommunications equipment 1.4%; diamonds 1.3%). *Major export destinations* (2008): Japan 23.0%; South Korea 9.4%; India 7.9%; Iran 6.5%; Thailand 5.3%.

Transport and communications

Transport. *Railroads:* none. *Roads* (2008): total length (paved roads only) 4,080 km. *Vehicles* (2007): passenger cars 1,279,098; trucks and buses 48,205. *Air transport* (2007): passenger-km 90,530,000,000; metric ton-km cargo 5,497,-149,000. **Communications,** in total units (units per 1,000 persons). Telephone landlines (2008): 1,508,000 (317); cellular telephone subscribers (2008): 9,358,000 (1,964); personal computers (2006): 1,396,000 (330); total Internet users (2008): 2,922,000 (613); broadband Internet subscribers (2008): 529,000 (111).

Education and health

Educational attainment (2005). Percentage of population ages 10 and over having: no formal schooling (illiterate/unknown) 9.4%, (literate) 13.9%; primary education 14.6%; incomplete/complete secondary 43.7%; postsecondary 4.0%; undergraduate 12.8%; graduate 1.6%. **Literacy** (2007): total population ages 10 and over literate 90.4%; males literate 90.9%; females literate 89.2%. **Health** (2007): physicians 8,662 (1 per 518 persons); hospital beds 8,348 (1 per 538 persons); infant mortality rate per 1,000 live births 7.8; undernourished population (2002–04) less than 2.5% of total population.

Military

Total active duty personnel (November 2008): 51,000 (army 86.3%, navy 4.9%, air force 8.8%); US troops (June 2009): 104; French military base for up to 500 troops officially opened in May 2009. **Military expenditure as percentage of GDP** (2007): 5.5%; per capita expenditure US$2,246.

Background

The Persian Gulf was the location of important trading centers as early as Sumerian times. Its people converted to Islam in Muhammad's lifetime. The Portuguese entered the region in the early 16th century, and the British East India Company arrived about 100 years later. In 1820 the British exacted a peace treaty with local rulers along the coast of the eastern Arabian Peninsula. The area formerly called the Pirate Coast became known as the Trucial Coast. In 1892 the rulers agreed to entrust foreign relations to Britain. Though the British administered the region from 1853, they never assumed sovereignty; each state maintained full internal control. The states formed the Trucial States Council in 1960. In 1971 the sheikhs terminated defense treaties with Britain and established the six-member federation. Ras al-Khaymah joined it in 1972. The United Arab Emirates (UAE) aided coalition forces against Iraq in the Persian Gulf War (1990–91).

Recent Developments

The global economic downturn of 2009 affected all of the emirates composing the United Arab Emirates. The formerly booming emirate of Dubayy, however, suffered the most. Dubayy's stock exchange, real-estate values, and construction industry declined markedly. In November Dubayy asked to delay interest payments for six months, and Abu Dhabi was forced to extend US$10 billion in bailout funds. In January 2010 the world's tallest building was opened in Dubai, and it was renamed the Burj Khalifa, after the ruler of Abu Dhabi, in recognition of this.

Internet resource: <www.economy.ae>.

United Kingdom

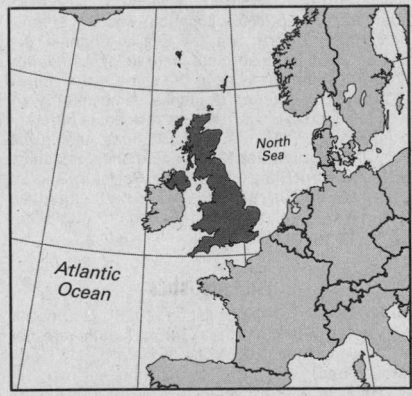

Official name: United Kingdom of Great Britain and Northern Ireland. **Form of government:** constitutional monarchy with two legislative houses (House of Lords [724]; House of Commons [646]). **Head of state:** Queen Elizabeth II (from 1952). **Head of government:** Prime Minister Gordon Brown (from 2007). **Capital:** London. **Official languages:** English (also Scots Gaelic in Scotland and Welsh in Wales). **Official reli-**

gion: none (the Church of England is "established" [protected by the state but not "official"]; the Church of Scotland is "national" [with exclusive jurisdiction in spiritual matters]; there is no established church in Northern Ireland or Wales). **Monetary unit:** 1 pound sterling (£) = 100 new pence; valuation (1 Jul 2010) US$1 = £0.66.

Demography

Area: 93,851 sq mi, 243,073 sq km (England 50,302 sq mi, 130,281 sq km; Wales 8,005 sq mi, 20,732 sq km; Scotland 30,087 sq mi, 77,925 sq km; Northern Ireland 5,457 sq mi, 14,135 sq km). **Population** (2009): 61,855,000. **Density** (2009): persons per sq mi 659.1, persons per sq km 254.5. **Urban** (2008): 90.0%. **Sex distribution** (2008): male 49.12%; female 50.88%. **Age breakdown** (2007): under 15, 17.6%; 15–29, 19.9%; 30–44, 21.6%; 45–59, 19.2%; 60–74, 14.0%; 75–84, 5.6%; 85 and over, 2.1%. **Ethnic composition** (2007): white 86.8%, of which British 81.6%; Asian 5.3%, of which Indian 2.0%, Pakistani 1.6%, Bangladeshi 0.6%, Chinese 0.4%; black 2.5%, of which from Africa 1.3%, from the Caribbean 1.1%; mixed race 1.1%; other 4.3%. **Religious affiliation** (2001): Christian 71.8%, of which Anglican-identified 29%, other Protestant-identified (significantly Presbyterian) 14%, Roman Catholic-identified 10%; Muslim 2.8%; Hindu 1.0%; Sikh 0.6%; Jewish 0.5%; nonreligious 15.0%; other 8.3%. **Major cities (urban agglomerations)** (2008 [2007]): London 7,619,800 (8,567,000); Birmingham 1,010,400 (2,285,000); Manchester 465,900 (2,230,000); Leeds 477,600 (1,529,000); Glasgow 637,000 (1,160,000); Newcastle upon Tyne 200,200 (882,000); Liverpool 464,200 (811,000); Bristol 465,500; Sheffield 458,100; Edinburgh 452,200; Leicester 348,000; Kingston upon Hull 320,100; Bradford 315,100; Coventry 312,500; Cardiff 310,800; Nottingham 273,300; Belfast 268,400; Stoke-on-Trent 258,600; Plymouth 256,000; Southampton 252,700. **Location:** western Europe, bordering the North Sea, the English Channel, the Celtic Sea, the Irish Sea, and Ireland. **Mobility** (2001). Population living in the same residence as 2000, 88.6%; different residence, same country/region (of the UK) 8.6%; different residence, different country/region (of the UK) 2.1%; from outside the UK 0.7%. **Immigration** (2007): permanent residents 527,000, from Bangladesh, India, Pakistan, and Sri Lanka 16.9%; Australia 3.0%; US 2.8%; South Africa 2.5%; New Zealand 1.5%; Canada 0.8%; other 72.5%, of which EU 31.5%.

Vital statistics

Birth rate per 1,000 population (2008): 12.9 (world avg. 20.3); within marriage 54.6%. **Death rate** per 1,000 population (2008): 9.4 (world avg. 8.5). **Total fertility rate** (avg. births per childbearing woman; 2008): 1.94. **Life expectancy** at birth (2007): male 77.6 years; female 81.7 years.

Social indicators

Educational attainment (2007). Percentage of population ages 25–64 having: unknown through lower

secondary education 13%; upper secondary 55%; higher 32%, of which at least some university 22%. **Quality of working life.** Average full-time workweek (hours; 2008): male 39.0, female 33.8. Annual rate per 100,000 workers for (2007–08): injury or accident 474.1; death 0.8. Proportion of employed labor force insured for damages or income loss resulting from (2004): injury 100%; permanent disability 100%; death 100%. Average days lost to labor stoppages per 1,000 employee workdays (2008): 28. **Social participation.** Population ages 16 and over participating in voluntary work (2001; Great Britain [England, Scotland, and Wales] only): 39%. Trade union membership in total workforce (2007–08) 26%. Percentage of population attending weekly church services (2001) 8%. **Social deviance** (2008–09; England and Wales only). Offense rate per 100,000 population for: theft and handling stolen goods 2,714; criminal damage 1,520; violence against a person 1,467; burglary 1,207; drug offenses 394; fraud and forgery 265; robbery 130; sex offenses 84. **Leisure** (2008). Favorite leisure activities: watching television, videos, and DVDs, listening to the radio, watching sporting events, and attending the cinema; the common free-time activity outside of the home is a visit to the pub; favorite sporting activities: for men—walking, golf, snooker, and billiards, for women—walking, swimming, fitness classes, and yoga. **Material well-being** (2007). Households possessing: automobile 75%, of which two cars 25%, three cars 6%; refrigerator/freezer 97%; washing machine 96%; central heating 95%; digital, cable, or satellite television receiver 77%; computer 70%; Internet connection 61%; dishwasher 37%.

National economy

Budget (2007–08). *Revenue:* £548,000,000,000 (income tax 26.9%; production and import taxes 24.1%; social security contributions 18.3%). *Expenditures:* £557,800,000,000 (social protection 33.5%; health 18.4%; education 14.1%; defense 6.1%; public order 5.8%). **Public debt** (December 2008): US$1,155,620,000,000. **Production** (metric tons except as noted). *Agriculture and fishing* (2008): wheat 17,227,000, sugar beets 7,500,000, barley 6,144,000, potatoes 5,999,000, rapeseed 1,973,030, oats 784,000, carrots 732,400, onions 349,200, apples 242,900, cauliflower 118,500, mushrooms and truffles 43,752; livestock (number of live animals) 33,131,000 sheep, 10,107,000 cattle, 4,714,000 pigs; fisheries production (2007) 793,894 (from aquaculture 22%). *Mining and quarrying* (2007): sand and gravel 95,000,000; rock salt 2,000,000; china clay (kaolin) 1,671,000; slate 870,000; potash 716,000. *Manufacturing* (value added in US$'000,000; 2006): chemical products 42,400; food products and beverages 39,100; nonelectrical machinery and equipment 26,000; printing and publishing 24,800; fabricated metal products 23,900; motor vehicles and parts 19,400; rubber and plastic products 13,300; bricks, cement, and ceramics 11,800; radio, television, and communications equipment 11,800. **Gross national income** (2008): US$2,787,159,000,000 (US$45,390 per capita). *Energy production (consumption):* electric-

---

1 metric ton = about 1.1 short tons;   1 kilometer = 0.6 mi (statute);   1 metric ton-km cargo = about 0.68 short ton-mi cargo;   c.i.f.: cost, insurance, and freight;   f.o.b.: free on board

ity (kW-hr; 2008–09) 347,214,000,000 ([2007] 345,800,000,000); coal (metric tons; 2008–09) 18,321,000 ([2008] 58,900,000); crude petroleum (barrels; 2008–09) 481,183,700 ([2008] 568,909,000); petroleum products (metric tons; 2008) 80,435,000 (70,249,000); natural gas (cu m; 2008–09) 78,306,700,000 ([2008] 108,143,- 200,000). **Population economically active** (2008): total 31,118,000; activity rate of total population 50.7% (participation rates: ages 16 and over, 62.5%; female 45.8%; unemployed [April 2008– March 2009] 6.2%). **Selected balance of payments data.** Receipts from (US$'000,000): tourism (2007) 37,690; remittances (2008) 8,234; foreign direct investment (FDI; 2005–07 avg.) 183,352. Disbursements for (US$'000,000): tourism (2007) 72,436; remittances (2008) 5,048; FDI (2005–07 avg.) 144,188.

Foreign trade

Imports (2008; c.i.f.): £343,964,000,000 (mineral fuels 13.9%, of which crude petroleum and refined petroleum products 10.8%; electrical machinery and equipment 13.8%; transportation equipment 12.9%; chemical products 11.0%, of which pharmaceuticals 3.2%; nonelectrical machinery and equipment 8.4%; food products and live animals 7.4%; wearing apparel 3.8%; base metals 3.8%). *Major import sources:* Germany 13.0%; Netherlands 7.5%; US 7.5%; China 6.7%; France 6.7%; Norway 6.3%; Belgium and Luxembourg 5.0%; Italy 4.0%; Ireland 3.6%; Spain 3.1%. **Exports** (2008; f.o.b.): £251,088,000,000 (chemical products 17.5%, of which pharmaceuticals 6.9%; mineral fuels 13.9%, of which crude petroleum and refined petroleum products 12.6%; nonelectrical machinery and equipment 12.8%; transportation equipment 12.6%; electrical machinery and equipment 10.1%; base metals 5.5%; food products and live animals 3.5%). *Major export destinations:* US 13.9%; Germany 11.2%; Netherlands 7.8%; Ireland 7.6%; France 7.2%; Belgium and Luxembourg 5.3%; Spain 4.1%; Italy 3.7%; Sweden 2.1%; China 2.0%.

Did you know? Before World World II, the UK was the largest formal empire in history. With colonies on every inhabited continent, it comprised nearly one-quarter of the land on Earth.

Transport and communications

Transport. *Railroads* (2007–08): length (2008) 16,454 km; passenger-km (Great Britain [England, Scotland, and Wales] only) 49,007,000,000; metric ton-km cargo (Great Britain [England, Scotland, and Wales] only) 21,200,000,000. *Roads* (2008; Great Britain [England, Scotland, and Wales] only): total length 394,467 km (paved 100%). *Vehicles* (2008; Great Britain [England, Scotland, and Wales] only): passenger cars 30,324,000, trucks and buses (2004) 3,522,424. *Air transport* (2008–09): passenger-km 229,710,000,000; metric ton-km cargo 6,029,510,000. **Communications,** in total units (units per 1,000 persons). Telephone landlines (2008): 33,209,000 (542); cellular telephone subscribers (2008): 77,361,000 (1,263); personal computers (2006): 48,591,000 (802);

total Internet users (2008): 46,684,000 (762); broadband Internet subscribers (2008): 17,276,000 (282).

Education and health

Literacy (2006): total population literate, about 99%. **Health** (2008): physicians (England and Scotland only) 138,878 (1 per 405 persons); hospital beds (2007) 208,413 (1 per 293 persons); infant mortality rate per 1,000 live births 4.7; undernourished population (2002–04) less than 2.5% of total population.

Military

Total active duty personnel (November 2008): 160,280 (army 59.7%, navy 19.3%, air force 21.0%); reserve 199,280); UK troops deployed abroad (November 2008): 41,700; US troops in the UK (July 2009): 9,367. **Military expenditure as percentage of GDP** (2008): 2.3%; per capita expenditure US$972.

Background

The early pre-Roman inhabitants of Britain were Celtic-speaking peoples, including the Brythonic people of Wales, the Picts of Scotland, and the Britons of Britain. Celts also settled in Ireland about 500 BC. Julius Caesar invaded and took control of the area in 55–54 BC. The Roman province of Britannia endured until the 5th century AD and included present-day England and Wales. Germanic tribes, including Angles, Saxons, and Jutes, invaded Britain in the 5th century. The invasions had little effect on the Celtic peoples of Wales and Scotland. Christianity began to flourish in the 6th century. During the 8th–9th centuries, Vikings, particularly Danes, raided the coasts of Britain. In the late 9th century Alfred the Great repelled a Danish invasion, which helped bring about the unification of England under Athelstan. The Scots attained dominance in Scotland, which was finally unified under Malcolm II (1005–34).

William of Normandy took England in 1066. The Norman kings established a strong central government and feudal state. The French language of the Norman rulers eventually merged with the Anglo-Saxon of the common people to form the English language. From the 11th century, Scotland came under the influence of the English throne. Henry II conquered Ireland in the late 12th century. His sons Richard I and John had conflicts with the clergy and nobles, and eventually John was forced to grant the nobles concessions in the Magna Carta (1215). The concept of community of the realm developed during the 13th century, providing the foundation for parliamentary government. During the reign of Edward I, statute law developed to supplement English common law, and the first Parliament was convened. In 1314 Robert the Bruce won independence for Scotland.

The Tudors became the ruling family of England following the Wars of the Roses (1455–85). Henry VIII established the Church of England and made Wales part of his realm. The reign of Elizabeth I began a period of colonial expansion; 1588 brought the defeat of the Spanish Armada. In 1603 James VI of Scotland ascended to the English throne, becoming James I, and established a personal union of the two kingdoms.

The English Civil Wars erupted in 1642 between Royalists and Parliamentarians, ending in the execution of Charles I (1649). After 11 years of Puritan rule under Oliver Cromwell and his son (1649–60), the monarchy was restored with Charles II. In 1707 England and Scotland assented to the Act of Union, forming the kingdom of Great Britain. The Hanoverians ascended to the English throne in 1714, when George Louis, elector of Hanover, became George I of Great Britain. During the reign of George III, Great Britain's American colonies won independence (1783). This was followed by a period of war with revolutionary France and later with the empire of Napoleon (1789–1815). In 1801 legislation united Great Britain with Ireland to create the United Kingdom of Great Britain and Ireland. Britain was the birthplace of the Industrial Revolution in the late 18th century, and it remained the world's foremost economic power until the late 19th century. During the reign of Queen Victoria, Britain's colonial expansion reached its zenith, though the older dominions, including Canada and Australia, were granted independence (1867 and 1901, respectively).

The UK entered World War I allied with France and Russia in 1914. Following the war, revolutionary disorder erupted in Ireland, and in 1921 the Irish Free State was granted dominion status. The six counties of Ulster, however, remained in the UK as Northern Ireland. The UK entered World War II in 1939. Following the war the Irish Free State became the Irish Republic and left the Commonwealth. India gained independence from the UK in 1947. Throughout the postwar period and into the 1970s, the UK continued to grant independence to its overseas colonies and dependencies. With UN forces, it participated in the Korean War (1950–53). In 1956 it intervened militarily in Egypt during the Suez Crisis. It joined the European Economic Community, a forerunner of the European Union, in 1973. In 1982 it defeated Argentina in the Falkland Islands War. As a result of continuing social strife in Northern Ireland, it joined with Ireland in several peace initiatives, which eventually resulted in an agreement to establish an assembly in Northern Ireland. In 1997 referenda approved in Scotland and Wales devolved power to both countries, though both remained part of the UK. In 1991 the UK joined an international coalition to reverse Iraq's conquest of Kuwait. In 2003 the UK and the US attacked Iraq and overthrew the government of Saddam Hussein. Terrorist bombings in London on 7 Jul 2005 killed more than 50 people.

Recent Developments

Amid the global recession of 2009, the announcement of a third-quarter slide of 0.2% in the UK's GDP, the sixth quarterly decline in GDP in succession, meant that the recession was the longest since quarterly GDP data were first collected in 1955. Despite signs of economic recovery in the final months of the year—including a steady rise in property values—unemployment continued to rise, reaching 8.0% of the labor force by the end of the year. For the quarter ending in February 2010, the rate remained at 8.0%, the highest quarterly rate since 1996. The Bank of England (BOE) acted aggressively in the early months of 2009 to revive de-

mand. Its benchmark interest rate started the year at 2.0%; by March it had fallen to just 0.5%, the lowest in the BOE's 300-year history, and it remained there a year later. Government measures that had been announced in 2008 to support the economy, combined with rapidly falling tax revenues, led the chancellor of the Exchequer to forecast in April that government borrowing in fiscal 2009–10 was likely to reach £175 billion (about US$260 billion), or 12.4% of GDP, the highest peacetime figure for the UK in recent decades.

The UK's military involvement in Iraq ended in 2009. As UK forces were leaving Iraq, they were arriving in Afghanistan, and by April 2010 they numbered 9,500 there, mainly in Helmand province. Amid accusations that British troops lacked some of the equipment that they needed to operate effectively, UK casualties increased sharply. In February 2010 the number of British troops killed in Afghanistan since 2001 rose to 256, reaching the number that were killed during the Falkland Islands War in 1982. In June the total reached 300. Another international controversy played out between Argentina and Britain over the fate of the Falkland Islands. In April 2009 the Argentinian government laid claim to a large area of ocean floor, including the area around the Falklands, South Georgia, and the South Sandwich Islands, all territories claimed by Britain. In February 2010 Argentina prevented a ship bearing pipes thought to be for petroleum exploration from travelling to the Falklands and declared that any ship desiring to visit the islands required Argentinian permission. As well, Argentina filed a complaint that month with the UN. Nonetheless, Britain began exploratory drilling in February.

In May 2010, British voters delivered the first hung Parliament in 36 years, after which David Cameron of the Conservatives and Nick Clegg of the Liberal Democrats formed the country's first coalition government since World War II.

Internet resource: <www.visitbritain.com>.

United States

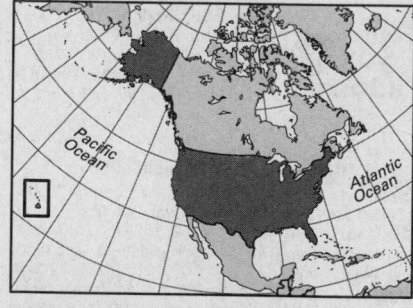

Official name: United States of America. **Form of government:** federal republic with two legislative houses (Senate [100]; House of Representatives [435, excluding 5 nonvoting delegates from the District of Columbia, the US Virgin Islands, American Samoa, the Northern Mariana Islands, and Guam and a nonvot-

---

1 metric ton = about 1.1 short tons;   1 kilometer = 0.6 mi (statute);   1 metric ton-km cargo = about 0.68 short ton-mi cargo;   c.i.f.: cost, insurance, and freight;   f.o.b.: free on board

ing resident commissioner from Puerto Rico]). **Head of state and government:** President Barack Obama (from 2009). **Capital:** Washington DC. **Official language:** none. **Official religion:** none. **Monetary unit:** 1 US dollar (US$) = 100 cents.

Demography

Area: 3,676,486 sq mi, 9,522,055 sq km; inland water area equals 78,797 sq mi (204,083 sq km), and Great Lakes water area equals 60,251 sq mi (156,049 sq km). **Population** (2009): 307,226,000. **Density** (2009; based on land area only): persons per sq mi 86.8, persons per sq km 33.5. **Urban** (2005): 80.8%. **Sex distribution** (2005): male 49.26%; female 50.74%. **Age breakdown** (2005): under 15, 20.5%; 15–29, 20.9%; 30–44, 21.6%; 45–59, 20.2%; 60–74, 10.7%; 75–84, 4.4%; 85 and over, 1.7%. **Population by race and Hispanic origin** (persons of Hispanic origin may be of any race) (2006): non-Hispanic white 66.4%; Hispanic 14.8%; non-Hispanic black 12.8%; Asian and Pacific Islander 4.6%; American Indian and Eskimo 1.0%; other 0.4%. **Religious affiliation** (2005): Christian 83.3%, of which independent Christian 23.2%, Roman Catholic 19.6%, Protestant (including Anglican) 18.9%, unaffiliated Christian 16.5%, Orthodox 1.8%, other Christian (primarily Mormon and Jehovah's Witness) 3.3%; Jewish 1.9%; Muslim 1.6%; Buddhist 0.9%; New Religionists 0.5%; Hindu 0.4%; traditional beliefs 0.4%; Baha'i 0.3%; Sikh 0.1%; nonreligious 9.8%; atheist 0.5%; other 0.3%. **Mobility** (2005). Reported gross percentage of population living in the same residence as in 2004: 86%; different residence, same county 8%; different county, same state 3%; different state 3%; moved from abroad 1%. **Place of birth** (2007): native-born 259,545,000 (87.4%); foreign-born 37,279,000 (12.6%), of which (2004) Mexico 10,011,000, the Philippines 1,222,000, China and Hong Kong 1,067,000, India 1,007,000, Cuba 952,000, Vietnam 863,000, El Salvador 765,000, South Korea 701,000. **Immigration** (2007–08): permanent immigrants admitted 1,107,126, from Mexico 17.2%, China 7.3%, India 5.7%, Philippines 4.9%, Cuba 4.5%, Dominican Republic 2.9%, Vietnam 2.8%, Colombia 2.7%, South Korea 2.4%, Haiti 2.3%, Pakistan 1.8%, El Salvador 1.8%, Jamaica 1.7%, other 42.0%. **Refugees** (2005) 380,000. **Location:** North America, bordering Canada, the North Atlantic Ocean, the Gulf of Mexico, Mexico, and the North Pacific Ocean; the outlying state of Alaska nearly touches eastern Russia and borders the Arctic Ocean, Canada, and the North Pacific Ocean; Hawaii is an island group in the North Pacific Ocean.

Vital statistics

Birth rate per 1,000 population (2008): 14.0 (world avg. 20.3); within marriage (2006) 64.2%. **Death rate** per 1,000 population (2008): 8.1 (world avg. 8.5). **Total fertility rate** (avg. births per childbearing woman; 2007): 2.09. **Life expectancy** at birth (2005): male 75.2 years, of which white male 78.3 years, black male 69.5 years; female 80.4 years, of which white female 80.8 years, black female 76.5 years.

Social indicators

Educational attainment (2007). Percentage of population ages 25 and over having: unknown/primary and incomplete secondary education 14.3%; secondary 31.6%; some postsecondary 25.3%; 4-year higher degree 18.9%; advanced degree 9.9%. Number of earned degrees (2006): associate's degree 713,066; bachelor's degree 1,485,242; master's degree 594,065; doctor's degree 56,067; first-professional degrees (in fields such as medicine, theology, and law) 87,655. **Quality of working life** (2006). Average workweek (2007): 41.3 hours. Annual death rate per 100,000 workers: 3.4; leading causes of occupational deaths: transportation incidents 42%, assaults and violent acts 13%, falls 14%, struck by object 10%. Annual occupational injury rate per 100,000 workers: 4.4. Average duration of journey to work (2006): 25.0 minutes (private automobile 86.7%, of which drive alone 76.0%, carpool 10.7%; take public transportation 4.8%; walk 2.5%; work at home 4.0%; other 2.0%). Rate per 1,000 employed workers of discouraged workers (unemployed no longer seeking work): 3.1. **Access to services** (2005). Proportion of occupied dwellings having access to: electricity 100%; safe public water supply 100%; public sewage collection 79.8%; septic tanks 20.2%. **Social participation** (2007). Population ages 16 and over volunteering for an organization 26.2%; median annual hours 52. Trade union membership in total workforce 12.1%. **Social deviance** (2007). Offense rate per 100,000 population for: murder 5.6; rape 30.0; robbery 147.6; aggravated assault 283.8; motor-vehicle theft 363.3; burglary and housebreaking 722.5; larceny-theft 2,177.8; drug-abuse violation (2005) 560.1; drunkenness (2003) 149.1. Estimated drug and substance users (population ages 12 and over; 2005): cigarettes 24.9%; binge alcohol (drinking five or more drinks on the same occasion on at least one day in the past 30 days) 22.7%; marijuana or hashish 6.0%. Rate per 100,000 population of suicide (2005): 10.7. **Leisure** (2006). Favorite leisure activities (percentage of total population ages 18 and over that undertook activity at least once in the previous year): dining out 48.6%, entertaining friends or relatives at home 40.2%, reading books 38.7%, barbecuing 33.9%, going to the beach 22.9%. **Material well-being** (2005). Occupied dwellings with householder possessing: automobiles, trucks, or vans 91.5%, 1 car with or without trucks or vans 47.5%, 2 cars 23.9%, only trucks and vans 12.7%, no cars, trucks, or vans 8.5%, 3 or more cars 7.4%; telephone 97.1%; television receiver 98.2%; video 90.2%; washing machine 82.0%; clothes dryer 79.1%; air conditioner 89.5%; cable television 67.5%; personal computers (2003) 61.8%; Internet connections (2003) 54.6%; broadband Internet (2003) 19.9%. **Recreational expenditures** (2006): US$791,100,000,000 (television and radio receivers, computers, and video equipment 19.2%; golfing, bowling, and other participatory activities 14.6%; sports supplies 10.0%; nondurable toys and sports equipment 9.0%; magazines, newspapers, and sheet music 5.7%; books and maps 5.5%).

National economy

Budget (2009). *Revenue:* US$2,699,900,000,000 (income tax 46.6%; social-insurance taxes and contributions 35.1%; corporate taxes 12.6%). *Expenditures:* US$3,107,400,000,000 (social security and medicare 37.1%; defense 21.7%; health 9.6%; interest on debt 8.4%). *Total outstanding national debt* (September 2009):

US$11,898,000,000,000, of which debt held by the public US$7,552,000,000,000, intragovernment holdings US$4,346,000,000,000. **Gross national income** (2008): US$14,466,112,000,000 (US$47,580 per capita). **Production.** *Agriculture and fishing* (value of production in US$'000,000 except as noted; 2007): corn (maize) 52,090, soybeans 26,752, wheat 13,669, alfalfa hay 8,972, cotton 5,197, grapes 3,381, potatoes 3,198, lettuce 2,751, apples 2,398, almonds 2,325, rice 2,274, tomatoes 2,179, oranges 2,111, sorghum 1,951, strawberries 1,746, sugar beets (2006) 1,526, tobacco 1,310, cottonseed 1,061, mushrooms 956, sugarcane (2006) 897, barley 852, onions 840, broccoli 764, peanuts (groundnuts) 763, cherries 651, carrots 614, sunflowers 607, blueberries 589, peppers 588, walnuts (2006) 564, pistachios 549, peaches 499, watermelons 476, cabbage 413, lemons 403, pecans 376, sweet potatoes 374, pears 346, cantaloupe 313; livestock (number of live animals; 2008) 96,669,000 cattle, 65,110,000 pigs, 9,500,000 horses, 6,100,000 sheep, 2,050,-000,000 chickens; fisheries production 5,293,877 metric tons (from aquaculture 10%); aquatic plants production 2,272 (from aquaculture, none). *Metals mining* (metal content in metric tons unless otherwise noted; 2008): molybdenum 61,400 (world rank: 1); beryllium 155 (world rank: 1); copper 1,310,000 (world rank: 2); lead 440,000 (world rank: 3); gold 230,000 kg (world rank: 3); zinc 770,000 (world rank: 4); palladium 12,400 kg (world rank: 4); platinum 3,700 kg (world rank: 5); iron 54,000,000 (world rank: 7); silver 1,120,000 kg (world rank: 7). *Nonmetals mining* (metric tons; 2008): diatomite 653,000 (world rank: 1); bromine 235,000 (world rank: 1); boron (2006) 1,150,000 (world rank: 2); perlite 449,000 (world rank: 2); kyanite 90,000 (world rank: 2); vermiculite 100,000 (world rank: 3); barite 615,000 (world rank: 3); silicon 166,000 (world rank: 5); feldspar 600,000 (world rank: 6). *Quarrying* (metric tons; 2008): gypsum 12,700,000 (world rank: 2); salt 46,000,000 (world rank: 2); phosphate rock 30,900,000 (world rank: 2); lime 19,800,000 (world rank: 2). *Manufacturing* (value added in US$'000,000; 2005): chemical products 328,440, of which pharmaceuticals and medicine 124,586; transportation equipment 254,665, of which motor vehicle parts 81,600, motor vehicles 78,772, aerospace products and parts 71,221; food products 235,673; electronics 226,319, of which navigational, measuring, medical, and scientific equipment 68,730, computers and related components 36,407, communications equipment 32,413; fabricated metal products 154,928; nonelectrical machinery and equipment 142,488; refined petroleum products and coal 117,541; plastic and rubber products 96,348; beverages and tobacco products 80,716; base metals 77,179; paper products 75,889; cement, bricks, and ceramics 64,545; printing and publishing 58,930; electrical machinery and equipment 54,318; furniture 46,801; wood products 44,763; textiles 32,395. *Construction* (completed; 2006): private US$937,047,000,000, of which residential US$641,332,000,000, nonresidential US$295,715,000,000; public US$255,191,000,-000. *Energy production (consumption):* electricity (kW-hr; 2006) 4,300,103,000,000 (4,318,523,-000,000); coal (metric tons; 2006) 523,971,000

(499,724,000); lignite (metric tons; 2006) 543,931,000 (517,337,000); crude petroleum (barrels; 2006) 1,857,000,000 (5,802,000,000); petroleum products (metric tons; 2006) 815,278,000 (834,999,000); natural gas (cu m; 2006) 525,481,000,000 (610,698,000,000). Domestic production of energy by source (2005): coal 33.3%, natural gas 27.2%, crude petroleum 15.7%, nuclear power 11.8%, renewable energy 8.8%, other 3.2%. *Energy consumption by source* (2007): crude petroleum and refined petroleum products 39.8%, natural gas 23.3%, coal 22.4%, nuclear electric power 8.3%, hydroelectric and thermal 3.2%, other renewable energy 3.0%; by end use: industrial 32.0%, residential and commercial 39.3%, transportation 28.7%. **Population economically active** (December 2009): total 153,059,000 (civilian population only); activity rate of total population 49.6% (participation rates: ages 16–64, 64.6%; female [2007] 46.5%; unemployed 10.0%). **Selected balance of payments data.** Receipts from (US$'000,000): tourism (2007) 119,223; remittances (2008) 3,049; foreign direct investment (FDI; 2005–07 avg.) 191,438. Disbursements for (US$'000,000): tourism (2007) 81,092; remittances (2008) 47,182; FDI (2005–07 avg.) 183,606. Number of foreign visitors (2007) 56,716,277 (17,735,000 from Canada, 15,089,000 from Mexico, 11,406,000 from Europe); number of nationals traveling abroad (2007) 64,052,000 (19,453,000 to Mexico, 13,371,000 to Canada, 12,304,000 to Europe).

Foreign trade

Imports (2008): US$2,100,141,200,000 (crude petroleum and refined petroleum products 21.1%; motor vehicles 9.1%; chemical products 8.4%; telecommunications equipment 6.3%; electrical machinery and equipment 5.4%; computers and office equipment 4.6%; wearing apparel 3.8%; industrial machinery 3.2%; food products and beverages 3.2%). *Major import sources:* China 16.1%; Canada 16.0%; Mexico 10.3%; Japan 6.6%; Germany 4.6%; UK 2.8%; Saudi Arabia 2.6%; Venezuela 2.4%; South Korea 2.3%; France 2.1%; Nigeria 1.8%; Taiwan 1.7%; Italy 1.7%; Ireland 1.5%; Malaysia 1.5%. **Exports** (2008): US$1,300,135,700,000 (transportation equipment 14.2%, of which motor vehicles and parts 8.2%; chemical products 13.8%; electrical machinery and equipment 8.1%; agricultural commodities 6.6%; mineral fuels 5.9%; crude materials [inedible] 5.9%; power-generating machinery 4.5%; general industrial machinery 4.5%; specialized industrial machinery 4.3%; scientific and precision equipment 3.9%; computers and office equipment 3.5%; telecommunications equipment 3.2%). *Major export destinations:* Canada 20.1%; Mexico 11.7%; China 5.5%; Japan 5.1%; Germany 4.2%; UK 4.1%; Netherlands 3.1%; South Korea 2.7%; Brazil 2.5%; France 2.2%; Singapore 2.2%; Taiwan 1.9%; Australia 1.7%; Hong Kong 1.7%; Switzerland 1.7%.

Transport and communications

Transport. *Railroads* (2006): route length 151,947 km, of which Amtrak operates 34,733 km; (2004) passenger-km 41,574,000,000; metric ton-km cargo

2,835,000,000,000. *Roads* (2008): total length 6,531,276 km (paved 67%). *Vehicles* (2007): passenger cars 135,933,000; trucks and buses 111,331,000. *Merchant marine* (2006): vessels (1,000 gross tons and over) 625; total deadweight tonnage 10,172,000. *Navigable channels* (2004) 41,843 km. *Oil pipeline length* (2005) 210,824 km; *gas pipeline length* (2004; excluding service pipelines) 2,353,300 km. *Air transport* (2007): passenger-km 1,334,199,200,000; metric ton-km cargo 43,104,300,000. *Certified route passenger/cargo air carriers* (2005) 80; operating revenue (US$'000,000; 2007) 173,104; operating expenses (US$'000,000; 2007) 163,894. **Communications,** in total units (units per 1,000 persons). Telephone landlines (2008): 150,000,000 (481); cellular telephone subscribers (2008): 270,500,000 (868); personal computers (2005): 223,810,000 (755); total Internet users (2008): 230,630,000 (740); broadband Internet subscribers (2008): 79,014,000 (254).

Education and health

Literacy (2003): percentage of population ages 16 and over: "illiterate" (able to perform no more than the most simple literacy skills—14% [30,000,000 people]); "basically literate" (able to perform simple and everyday literacy activities—29% [63,000,000 people]); "intermediately and proficiently literate" (able to perform moderately challenging to complex literacy activities—57% [123,000,000 people]). An additional 6,500,000 people were not interviewed for this 2003 survey because they did not speak English or had cognitive or mental disabilities. **Food** (2005): daily per capita caloric intake 3,754 (vegetable products 72.2%, animal products 27.8%); 143% of FAO recommended minimum requirement. Per capita consumption of major food groups (kilograms annually; 2005): milk 256.4; fresh vegetables 125.5; cereal products 177.2; fresh fruits 122.7; red meat 62.7; potatoes 54.7; poultry products 55.8; fats and oil 31.6; sugar 30.2; fish and shellfish 23.4; undernourished population (2002–04) less than 2.5% of total population. **Health** (2006): doctors of medicine 921,900 (1 per 329 persons), of which office-based practice 560,400—male 72.2%; female 27.8% (including specialties in internal medicine 16.9%, general and family practice 10.1%, pediatrics 8.1%, obstetrics and gynecology 4.6%, psychiatry 4.5%, anesthesiology 4.5%, general surgery 4.1%, emergency medicine 3.3%, diagnostic radiology 2.7%, orthopedic surgery 2.6%, cardiovascular diseases 2.4%, pathology 2.1%, ophthalmology 2.0%); doctors of osteopathy (2008) 64,000; nurses 2,417,150 (1 per 123 persons); dentists (2007) 184,000 (1 per 1,639 persons); hospital beds 947,000 (1 per 315 persons), of which nonfederal 95.3% (community hospitals 84.7%, psychiatric 8.9%, long-term general and special 1.7%), federal 4.9%; infant mortality rate per 1,000 live births (2008) 6.5.

Military

Total active duty personnel (November 2009): 1,417,747 (army 38.7%, navy 23.4%, air force 23.5%, marines 14.4%, coast guard [November 2008] 2.6%). *Total reserve duty personnel* (November 2008): 979,378 (army 55.9%, navy

12.9%, air force 19.5%, marines 10.6%, coast guard 1.1%). **Military expenditure as percentage of GDP** (2008): 4.2%; per capita expenditure US$1,994. *Major overseas deployment* (December 2008): 283,589, of which in support of Operation Iraqi Freedom 63%, in support of Operation Enduring Freedom (in Afghanistan) 11%. *Foreign military sales deliveries* (September 2004–September 2007): US$35,611,000,000, of which to Israel 11.5%, to Egypt 11.1%, to Taiwan 9.2%, to Saudi Arabia 8.6%, to Poland 5.6%, to Japan 5.2%, to South Korea 5.1%, to Australia 4.2%.

Background

The territory that is now the United States was originally inhabited for several thousand years by numerous American Indian peoples who had probably emigrated from Asia. European exploration and settlement from the 16th century began displacement of the Indians. The first permanent European settlement, by the Spanish, was at St. Augustine FL in 1565; the British settled Jamestown VA (1607), Plymouth MA (1620), Maryland (1632), and Pennsylvania (1681). They took New York, New Jersey, and Delaware from the Dutch in 1664, a year after the Carolinas had been granted to British noblemen. The British defeat of the French in 1763 ensured British political control over the 13 colonies.

Political unrest caused by British colonial policy culminated in the American Revolution (1775–83) and the Declaration of Independence (1776). The US was first organized under the Articles of Confederation (1781) and then finally under the Constitution (1787) as a federal republic. Boundaries extended west to the Mississippi River, excluding Spanish Florida. Land acquired from France by the Louisiana Purchase (1803) nearly doubled the country's territory. The US fought the War of 1812 with the British and acquired Florida from Spain in 1819. In 1830 it legalized removal of American Indians to lands west of the Mississippi River. Settlement expanded to the West Coast in the mid-19th century, especially after the discovery of gold in California in 1848. Victory in the Mexican-American War (1846–48) brought the territory of seven more future states (including California and Texas) into US hands. The northwestern boundary was established by treaty with Great Britain in 1846. The US acquired southern Arizona by the Gadsden Purchase (1853). It suffered disunity during the conflict between the slavery-based plantation economy in the South and the free industrial and agricultural economy in the North, culminating in the American Civil War (1861–65) and the abolition of slavery under the 13th Amendment.

After Reconstruction (1865–77), the US experienced rapid growth, urbanization, industrial development, and European immigration. In 1877 it authorized allotment of Indian reservation land to individual tribesmen, resulting in widespread loss of land to whites. By the beginning of the 20th century, it had acquired outlying territories, including Alaska, the Midway Islands, the Hawaiian Islands, the Philippines, Puerto Rico, Guam, Wake Island, American Samoa, the Panama Canal Zone, and part of the Virgin Islands. The US participated in World War I during 1917–18. It granted suffrage to women in 1920 and citizenship to American Indians in 1924. The stock market crash of 1929 led to the Great Depression. The US entered World War II after the Japanese bombing of Pearl Harbor (7 Dec 1941). The explosion of the first atomic bomb (6 Aug 1945), on Hiroshima, Japan, brought about the end of the war and set the US apart as a military power. After the war the US was involved in the reconstruction of Europe and Japan and embroiled in a rivalry with the Soviet Union that became known as the Cold War. It participated in the Korean War (1950-53). In 1952 it granted autonomous commonwealth status to Puerto Rico.

Racial segregation in schools was declared unconstitutional in 1954. Alaska and Hawaii were made states in 1959, bringing the total to 50. In 1964 Congress passed the Civil Rights Act and authorized full-scale intervention in the Vietnam War. The mid- to late 1960s were marked by widespread civil disorder, including race riots and antiwar demonstrations. The US accomplished the first manned lunar landing in 1969. All US troops were withdrawn from Vietnam by 1973. With the dissolution of the Soviet Union in 1991, the US assumed the status of sole world superpower. The US led a coalition of forces against Iraq in the Persian Gulf War (1990-91). Administration of the Panama Canal was turned over to Panama in 1999. After the September 11 attacks on the US in 2001 destroyed the World Trade Center and part of the Pentagon, the US attacked Afghanistan's Taliban government for harboring and refusing to extradite the mastermind of the terrorist acts, Osama bin Laden. In 2003 the US attacked Iraq, with British support, and overthrew the government of Saddam Hussein.

Recent Developments

New US president Barack Obama entered office in January 2009 vowing to reduce partisanship in Washington, but he made little progress in his first year. Democrats held substantial majorities in both houses of Congress for much of the year, and in Obama's first month in office they pushed a number of major bills through Congress with minimal or no Republican support. One reauthorized and expanded the State Children's Health Insurance Program, a measure that had been vetoed twice by former president George W. Bush. The House of Representatives passed a US$787 billion stimulus spending measure without any Republican votes. The bill was strongly tilted toward projects supported by Democratic Party constituencies, including renewable energy incentives and union construction jobs. In the Senate, where 60 votes were effectively required for most legislative action, several Republicans crossed the aisle and helped to pass the stimulus bill in February. The president was able to accomplish numerous changes through executive order. In January he rescinded the "Mexico City policy"—which had been reinstated by Bush in 2001—to allow the resumption of US funding for international family planning groups that facilitated abortion services or abortion counseling. In March Obama removed restrictions on federal funding for stem cell research that

had been established by the Bush administration eight years earlier. Obama's overall approval rating, as measured by public-opinion polls, topped 65% in early 2009 but dropped steadily to around 50% in late December, weighed down by rising unemployment and perceived federal overreaching. At year's end he obtained a major victory on his top domestic policy priority when Congress approved national health-care reform bills after contentious legislative bargaining. Republicans labeled the measure a government takeover of health care, and no GOP member voted for either bill. The Senate dropped a provision setting up a government-run insurance option to compete with private firms, angering liberal Democrats, and also watered down a strict House measure prohibiting public funds from being spent on abortion services. The two versions were reconciled in early 2010, and Obama signed the new law in March. It extended access to health insurance to an additional 30 million Americans, prohibited denial of coverage by insurers, and required most Americans to obtain insurance or face financial penalties. It would pay for expanded care in part through tax increases on higher-income earners and reductions in payments to providers of Medicare and Medicaid services.

The military focus shifted from Iraq to Afghanistan. In his presidential campaign, Obama had criticized US involvement in Iraq and suggested that Afghanistan pacification efforts were wrongly shortchanged as a result. As security conditions in Iraq continued to improve (December 2009 was the first month since the 2003 invasion in which no US troops were killed), the new administration began slowly removing US military personnel, with an announced goal of ending US combat operations by mid-2010 and exiting the country entirely by late 2011. The military outlook in Afghanistan deteriorated rapidly, however, as Taliban insurgents regrouped and stepped up attacks on US and NATO forces (US troop fatalities in the country doubled in 2009 compared with the previous year, and the country suffered its 1,000th military death in Afghanistan in May 2010). In February 2009 Obama announced plans to send 17,000 additional US troops to Afghanistan, bringing the total troop commitment to 68,000, and he later announced that he would send 30,000 more soldiers in an attempt to blunt the insurgency. Obama also called for a drawdown of combat forces to begin after 18 months, however, leading many conservatives to question the commitment. Obama defended his path as he accepted the Nobel Peace Prize in Oslo in December. "Evil does exist in the world," he said. "There will be times when nations—acting individually or in concert—will find the use of force not only necessary but morally justified."

The new administration worked to project a more cooperative and tolerant image of the US abroad during 2009, acknowledging past errors and seeking to repair strained US diplomatic relationships in many parts of the world. In April Obama sought a "fresh start" with Russia, telling Russian Pres. Dmitry Medvedev that "the relationship between our two countries has been allowed to drift." Russia authorized the US to use its airspace to resupply allied military forces in Afghanistan. Russia also responded to Obama's September decision to halt plans to establish ballistic missile defenses in Poland and the Czech Republic by suspending its threat to deploy short-range nuclear missiles to its Kaliningrad exclave. After Obama and Medvedev met in London in April 2009, the two countries began serious negotiations over renewing the Strategic Arms Reduction Talks I (START I) treaty. In April 2010 the two leaders signed a historic New START arms-control pact that would limit the number of deployed warheads from each country to 1,550.

Internet resource: <www.fedstats.gov>.

Uruguay

Atlantic Ocean

Official name: República Oriental del Uruguay (Oriental Republic of Uruguay). **Form of government:** republic with two legislative houses (Senate [31]; Chamber of Representatives [99]). **Head of state and government:** President José Alberto Mujica Cordano (from 2010). **Capital:** Montevideo. **Official language:** Spanish. **Official religion:** none. **Monetary unit:** 1 peso uruguayo (UYU) = 100 centésimos; valuation (1 Jul 2010) US$1 = UYU 20.47.

Demography

Area: 68,679 sq mi, 177,879 sq km. **Population** (2009): 3,361,000. **Density** (2009): persons per sq mi 48.9, persons per sq km 18.9. **Urban** (2007): 93.7%. **Sex distribution** (2007): male 48.30%; female 51.70%. **Age breakdown** (2007): under 15, 23.4%; 15–29, 22.8%; 30–44, 19.6%; 45–59, 16.5%; 60–74, 11.5%; 75–84, 4.7%; 85 and over, 1.5%. **Ethnic composition** (2006): white (mostly Spanish, Italian, or mixed Spanish-Italian) 87.4%; black/part-black 8.4%; Amerindian/part-Amerindian 3.0%; other 1.2%. **Religious affiliation** (2004): Roman Catholic 54%; Protestant 11%; Mormon 3%; Jewish 0.8%; nonreligious/atheist 26%; other 5.2%. **Major cities** (2004): Montevideo 1,269,552; Salto 99,072; Paysandú 73,272; Las Piedras 69,222; Rivera 64,426. **Location:** southern South America, bordering Brazil, the South Atlantic Ocean, and Argentina.

Vital statistics

Birth rate per 1,000 population (2008): 14.6 (world avg. 20.3); (2002) within marriage 42.9%. **Death rate** per 1,000 population (2008): 9.4 (world avg. 8.5). **Total fertility rate** (avg. births per childbearing woman; 2007): 2.02. **Life expectancy** at birth (2008): male 72.4 years; female 79.7 years.

National economy

Budget (2006). *Revenue:* UYU 111,321,000,000 (taxes on goods and services 59.1%; corporate taxes 12.3%; property taxes 7.1%; nontax revenue 6.7%; income tax 5.6%). *Expenditures:* UYU 117,225,-000,000 (social security and welfare 27.6%; government transfers including debt servicing 20.7%; public administration 13.9%; education 12.3%; health 7.4%; defense 4.4%). **Production** (metric tons except as noted). *Agriculture and fishing* (2007): rice 1,200,000, soybeans 800,000, wheat 620,000, sunflower seeds 60,000, honey 13,200; livestock (number of live animals) 12,000,000 cattle, 11,000,000 sheep; fisheries production 108,750 (from aquaculture, negligible). *Mining and quarrying* (2007): limestone 1,200,000; clays 82,200; gold 2,820 kg. *Manufacturing* (value added in UYU '000,000; 2005): food products and beverages 17,390; refined petroleum products 5,945; textiles, hides, and leather goods 4,633. *Energy production (consumption):* electricity (kW-hr; 2006) 5,618,000,000 (8,437,000,000); coal (metric tons; 2006) none (2,000); crude petroleum (barrels; 2006) none (13,900,000); petroleum products (metric tons; 2006) 1,758,000 (1,889,000); natural gas (cu m; 2006) none (110,000,000). **Population economically active** (2006): total 1,580,400; activity rate 47.7% (participation rates: ages 14–64, 72.7%; female 43.5%; unemployed [2007] 9.2%). **Gross national income** (2008): US$27,536,000,000 (US$8,260 per capita). **Public debt** (external, outstanding; 2007): US$9,616,000,000. **Selected balance of payments data.** Receipts from (US$'000,000): tourism (2007) 809; remittances (2008) 104; foreign direct investment (FDI; 2005–07 avg.) 1,042; official development assistance (2007) 34. Disbursements for (US$'000,000): tourism (2007) 239; remittances (2008) 5; FDI (2005–07 avg.) 13.

Foreign trade

Imports (2006; c.i.f.): US$4,775,000,000 (crude petroleum and refined petroleum products 27.5%; machinery and appliances 16.0%; chemical products 12.7%; food products, beverages, and tobacco products 8.7%; transportation equipment 7.4%). *Major import sources:* Argentina 22.6%; Brazil 22.6%; Venezuela 12.6%; China 7.3%; US 6.8%. **Exports** (2006; f.o.b.): US$3,952,000,000 (beef 23.7%; hides and leather goods 8.6%; dairy products, eggs, and honey 6.9%; textiles and wearing apparel 6.8%; rice 5.5%; plastics and rubber products 5.1%). *Major export destinations:* Brazil 14.7%; US 13.2%; Argentina 7.6%; Russia 5.7%; Germany 4.2%.

Transport and communications

Transport. *Railroads* (2006): route length 2,073 km; passenger-km (2004) 11,000,000; metric ton-km cargo (2005) 331,000,000. *Roads* (2007): length

16,398 km (paved 22%). *Vehicles* (2006): passenger cars 553,204; trucks and buses 91,007. *Air transport* (2008; PLUNA only): passenger-km 809,094,000; metric ton-km cargo, none. **Communications**, in total units (units per 1,000 persons). Telephone landlines (2008): 959,000 (286); cellular telephone subscribers (2008): 3,308,000 (1,047); personal computers (2005): 450,000 (135); total Internet users (2008): 1,340,000 (400); broadband Internet subscribers (2008): 245,000 (73).

Education and health

Educational attainment (2006). Percentage of population ages 25 and over having: no formal schooling 1.9%; incomplete primary education 15.1%; complete primary 25.8%; incomplete secondary 20.8%; complete secondary 17.6%; incomplete higher 7.2%; complete higher 11.6%. **Literacy** (2003): population ages 15 and over literate 98.0%; males literate 97.6%; females literate 98.4%. **Health:** physicians (2006) 13,603 (1 per 245 persons); hospital beds (2003) 6,661 (1 per 499 persons); infant mortality rate per 1,000 live births (2007) 12.0; undernourished population (2002–04) less than 2.5% of total population.

Military

Total active duty personnel (November 2008): 25,382 (army 66.6%, navy/coast guard 21.6%, air force 11.8%). **Military expenditure as percentage of GDP** (2007): 1.3%; per capita expenditure US$91.

Background

The Spanish navigator Juan Díaz de Solís sailed into the Río de la Plata in 1516. The Portuguese established Colonia in 1680. Subsequently, the Spanish established Montevideo in 1726, driving the Portuguese from their settlement; 50 years later Uruguay became part of the Viceroyalty of the Río de la Plata. It gained independence from Spain in 1811. The Portuguese regained it in 1821, incorporating it into Brazil as a province. A revolt against Brazil in 1825 led to its being recognized as an independent state in 1828. It battled Paraguay in 1865–70. For much of World War II, Uruguay remained neutral. The presidential office was abolished in 1951 but restored in 1966. A military coup occurred in 1973, but the country returned to civilian rule in 1985. The 1990s brought a general upturn in the economy, largely the result of reform measures and membership in Mercosul, the Southern Common Market, from 1991.

Recent Developments

In 2009 a program to provide laptop computers to all primary schoolchildren in Uruguay was successfully implemented. The ability of same-sex couples to adopt children was also legalized during the year. Health care was made more fully accessible to the poor through a somewhat controversial increase in the personal income tax. Even with a slowdown in economic growth brought on by the worldwide financial crisis, Uruguay was estimated to have posted a modest gain in GDP for the year. Unem-

ployment remained historically low, and foreign investment was especially strong. A new container terminal at the port of Montevideo was opened late in the year.

Internet resource: <www.turismo.gub.uy>.

Uzbekistan

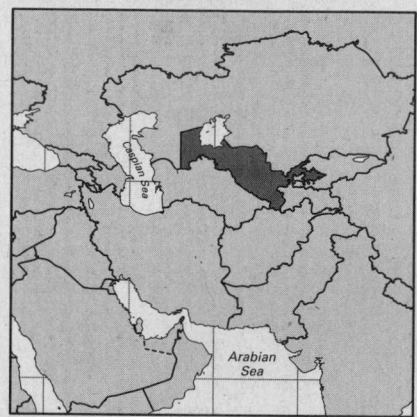

Official name: Uzbekiston Respublikasi (Republic of Uzbekistan). **Form of government:** republic with two legislative houses (Senate [150]; Legislative Chamber [120]). **Head of state and government:** President Islam Karimov (from 1990), assisted by Prime Minister Shavkat Mirziyayev (from 2003). **Capital:** Tashkent (Toshkent). **Official language:** Uzbek. **Official religion:** none. **Monetary unit:** sum (UZS; plural sumy); valuation (1 Jul 2010) US$1 = UZS 1,595.00.

Demography

Area: 172,700 sq mi, 447,400 sq km. **Population** (2009): 27,606,000. **Density** (2009): persons per sq mi 159.8, persons per sq km 61.7. **Urban** (2006): 35.9%. **Sex distribution** (2006): male 49.56%; female 50.44%. **Age breakdown** (2006): under 15, 32.9%; 15–29, 30.3%; 30–44, 19.6%; 45–59, 11.2%; 60–74, 4.3%; 75 and over, 1.7%. **Ethnic composition** (2000): Uzbek 78.3%; Tajik 4.7%; Kazakh 4.1%; Tatar 3.3%; Russian 2.5%; Karakalpak 2.1%; other 5.0%. **Religious affiliation** (2000): Muslim (mostly Sunni) 76.2%; Russian Orthodox 0.8%; Jewish 0.2%; nonreligious 18.1%; other 4.7%. **Major cities** (2007): Tashkent (Toshkent) 1,959,190; Namangan 446,237; Andijon 321,622; Samarkand 312,863; Bukhara 249,037. **Location:** central Asia, bordering Kazakhstan, Kyrgyzstan, Tajikistan, Afghanistan, and Turkmenistan.

Vital statistics

Birth rate per 1,000 population (2008): 23.6 (world avg. 20.3). **Death rate** per 1,000 population (2008):

1 metric ton = about 1.1 short tons;   1 kilometer = 0.6 mi (statute);   1 metric ton-km cargo = about 0.68 short ton-mi cargo;   c.i.f.: cost, insurance, and freight;   f.o.b.: free on board

5.0 (world avg. 8.5). **Total fertility rate** (avg. births per childbearing woman; 2006): 2.91. **Life expectancy** at birth (2006): male 61.2 years; female 68.1 years.

National economy

Budget (2006; general government consolidated budget). *Revenue:* UZS 6,406,000,000,000 (taxes on income and profits 20.2%; VAT 17.3%; taxes on property and resources 12.2%; excise taxes 10.2%). *Expenditures:* UZS 6,331,000,000,000 (health and education 34.4%; social security 27.0%; national economy 9.0%; centralized investments 8.1%). **Public debt** (external, outstanding; 2007): US$3,086,000,000. **Production** (metric tons except as noted). *Agriculture and fishing* (2007): wheat 5,900,000, seed cotton 3,300,000, tomatoes 1,327,000, raw silk 487; livestock (number of live animals) 10,450,000 sheep, 7,042,500 cattle, 1,974,300 goats, 16,500 camels; fisheries production 6,226 (from aquaculture 55%). *Mining and quarrying* (metal content; 2006): copper 115,000; uranium 2,260; gold (all forms) 85,000 kg. *Manufacturing* (value of production in UZS '000,000,000; 2006): nonferrous metals 2,705; mineral fuels 2,487; machinery and metalworking products 1,986. *Energy production (consumption):* electricity (kW-hr; 2008) 50,100,000,000 ([2006] 47,000,000,000); lignite (metric tons; 2006) 3,126,000 (3,050,000); crude petroleum (barrels; 2006) 39,465,000 (24,078,000); petroleum products (metric tons; 2006) 4,685,000 (4,461,000); natural gas (cu m; 2006) 62,500,000,000 (48,400,000,000). **Population economically active** (2004): total 9,945,500; activity rate of total population 38.7% (participation rates [2001]: ages 16–59 [male], 16–54 [female] 70.4%; female 44.0%; unemployed [official rate; 2007] 0.8%). **Gross national income** (2008): US$24,738,000,000 (US$910 per capita). **Selected balance of payments data.** Receipts from (US$'000,000): tourism (2007) 51; remittances (2005) 790; foreign direct investment (2005–07 avg.) 182; official development assistance (2007) 166.

Foreign trade

Imports (2006; c.i.f.): US$4,395,900,000 (machinery and metalworking products 40.3%; chemical products 15.0%; base metals 10.4%; food products 8.1%). *Major import sources:* Russia 27.8%; South Korea 15.2%; China 10.4%; Kazakhstan 7.3%; Germany 7.1%. **Exports** (2006; f.o.b.): US$6,389,800,000 (cotton fiber 17.2%; energy products [including natural gas and crude petroleum] 13.1%; base metals 12.9%; machinery and apparatus 10.1%; gold, n.a.; uranium, n.a.). *Major export destinations:* Russia 23.7%; Poland 11.7%; China 10.4%; Turkey 7.7%; Kazakhstan 5.9%.

Transport and communications

Transport. *Railroads* (2008): length (2006) 3,950 km; passenger-km 2,500,000,000; metric ton-km cargo 23,400,000,000. *Roads* (2005): total length 84,400 km (paved 85%). *Vehicles* (1994): passenger cars 865,300; buses 14,500. *All transport* (2008): passenger-km 5,600,000,000; metric ton-km cargo 83,300,000. **Communica-**

tions, in total units (units per 1,000 persons). Telephone landlines (2008): 1,850,000 (68); cellular telephone subscribers (2008): 12,734,000 (468); total Internet users (2008): 2,469,000 (91); broadband Internet subscribers (2008): 66,000 (2.4).

Education and health

Educational attainment (2002). Percentage of population ages 25 and over having: no formal education/unknown 2.5%; incomplete primary education 9.0%; primary 7.3%; secondary 66.0%; higher 15.2%. **Literacy** (2003): percentage of total population ages 15 and over literate, virtually 100%. **Health** (2005): physicians 70,159 (1 per 371 persons); hospital beds 135,143 (1 per 193 persons); infant mortality rate per 1,000 live births (2008) 12.6; undernourished population (2003–05) 3,600,000 (14% of total population based on the consumption of a minimum daily requirement of 1,870 calories).

Military

Total active duty personnel (November 2008): 67,000 (army 74.6%, air force 25.4%); German troops (November 2008): 163. **Military expenditure as percentage of GDP** (2007): 0.5%; per capita expenditure US$3.

Background

Genghis Khan's grandson Shibaqan received the territory of Uzbekistan as his inheritance in the 13th century AD. His Mongols ruled over nearly 100 mainly Turkic tribes, who would eventually intermarry with the Mongols to form the Uzbeks and other Turkic peoples of central Asia. In the early 16th century, a federation of Mongol-Uzbeks invaded and occupied settled regions, including an area called Transoxania that would become the Uzbeks' permanent homeland. By the early 19th century the region was dominated by the khanates of Khiva, Bukhara, and Ququon, all of which eventually succumbed to Russian domination. The Uzbek Soviet Socialist Republic was created in 1924. In June 1990 Uzbekistan became the first Central Asian republic to declare sovereignty. It achieved full independence from the USSR in 1991. During the 1990s its economy was considered the strongest in Central Asia, though its political system was deemed harsh.

Recent Developments

Uzbekistan's relations with its neighbors Kyrgyzstan and Tajikistan worsened during 2009. Uzbekistan remained fiercely opposed to the construction of large-scale hydroelectric projects in those two countries, and in February Turkmenistan was persuaded to join in the opposition to construction of the two dams, thereby infuriating the Tajiks. Uzbek-Tajik relations began to deteriorate at the very beginning of the year when Uzbekistan stopped transmission of power purchased by Tajikistan from Turkmenistan. In September an Uzbek expert questioned the safety of the large power plants built in Tajikistan and Kyrgyzstan during the Soviet era. This event marked an escalation of the verbal feud between Uzbekistan and its upstream neighbors. Relations between Uzbekistan and Kyrgyzstan were strained by the occasionally high-handed behavior of Uzbek border guards and the Uzbek reinforcement of the common border after an armed attack in May on a police post in the town of Khonobod near the Kyrgyz frontier. The attack was initially attributed to the militant Islamic Movement of Uzbekistan; the Kyrgyz Border Service denied Uzbek assertions that the group had come from Kyrgyzstan.

Internet resource: <www.stat.uz>.

Vanuatu

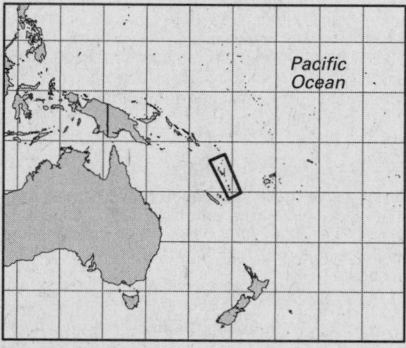

Official name: Ripablik blong Vanuatu (Bislama); République de Vanuatu (French); Republic of Vanuatu (English). **Form of government:** republic with a single legislative house (Parliament [52]). **Head of state:** President Iolu Abil (from 2009). **Head of government:** Prime Minister Edward Natapei (from 2008). **Capital:** Port-Vila. **Official languages:** Bislama; French; English. **Official religion:** none. **Monetary unit:** vatu (Vt); valuation (1 Jul 2010) US$1 = Vt 99.82.

Demography

Area: 4,707 sq mi, 12,190 sq km. **Population** (2009): 240,000. **Density** (2009): persons per sq mi 51.0, persons per sq km 19.7. **Urban** (2009): 24.3%. **Sex distribution** (2009): male 51.27%; female 48.73%. **Age breakdown** (2005): under 15, 40.1%; 15–29, 27.7%; 30–44, 17.5%; 45–59, 9.7%; 60–74, 4.1%; 75 and over, 0.9%. **Ethnic composition** (1999): Ni-Vanuatu (Melanesian) 98.7%; European and other Pacific Islanders 1.3%. **Religious affiliation** (2005): Protestant 70%, of which Presbyterian 32%, Anglican 13%, Adventist 11%; Roman Catholic 13%; traditional beliefs (significantly the John Frum cargo cult) 5%; other 12%. **Major towns** (2009): Port-Vila 45,694; Luganville 13,484; Norsup (2006) 3,000. **Location:** Oceania, island group between the South Pacific Ocean and the Coral Sea.

Vital statistics

Birth rate per 1,000 population (2008): 31.1 (world avg. 20.3). **Death rate** per 1,000 population (2008):

5.5 (world avg. 8.5). **Total fertility rate** (avg. births per childbearing woman; 2008): 4.40. **Life expectancy** at birth (2008): male 65.6 years; female 69.0 years.

National economy

Budget (2008). *Revenue:* Vt 16,997,000,000 (tax revenue 69.5%, of which VAT 26.9%, import duties 22.5%; grants 23.4%; nontax revenue 7.1%). *Expenditures:* Vt 15,121,000,000 (current expenditures 77.6%; development expenditures 22.4%). **Production** (metric tons except as noted). *Agriculture and fishing* (2007): coconuts 322,000, copra 21,644, bananas 14,500, cacao beans 1,400, kava (2004) 825; livestock (number of live animals) 174,137 cattle, 88,694 pigs, 8,792 goats; fisheries production 85,387 (from aquaculture, negligible). *Mining and quarrying:* small quantities of coral-reef limestone, crushed stone, sand, and gravel. *Manufacturing* (value added in Vt '000,000; 1995): food products, beverages, and tobacco products 645; wood products 423; fabricated metal products 377. *Energy production (consumption):* electricity (kW-hr; 2008) 55,000,000 (55,000,000); petroleum products (metric tons; 2006) none (30,000). **Population economically active** (2006): total 112,000; activity rate of total population 50.7% (participation rates: ages 15–64, 84.3%; female 46.4%; officially unemployed [1999] 1.7%). **Gross national income** (2008): US$539,000,000 (US$2,330 per capita). **Public debt** (external, outstanding; 2007): US$71,600,000. **Selected balance of payments data.** Receipts from (US$'000,000): tourism (2007) 119; remittances (2008) 7; foreign direct investment (FDI; 2005–07 avg.) 30; official development assistance (2007) 57. Disbursements for (US$'000,000): tourism (2007) 11; remittances (2008) 3; FDI (2005–07 avg.) 1.

Foreign trade

Imports (2008; c.i.f.): Vt 29,023,000,000 (machinery and transportation equipment 30.7%; mineral fuels 16.6%; food products and live animals 15.3%; chemical products 7.0%). *Major import sources* (2007): Australia 31.1%; New Zealand 16.8%; Singapore 12.4%; Fiji 9.1%; China 6.6%. **Exports** (2008; f.o.b.): Vt 4,249,000,000 (domestic exports 84.4%, of which copra 25.3%, coconut oil 17.1%, kava 11.5%, beef 9.1%, cocoa 5.6%; reexports 15.6%). *Major export destinations* (2007): Philippines 14.0%; New Caledonia 9.7%; Fiji 6.7%; Japan 5.4%; Singapore 5.4%.

Transport and communications

Transport. *Railroads:* none. *Roads* (2000): total length 1,070 km (paved 24%). *Vehicles* (2001): passenger cars 2,600; trucks and buses 4,400. *Air transport* (2008; Air Vanuatu only): passenger-km 457,518,000; metric ton-km cargo 1,714,000. **Communications,** in total units (units per 1,000 persons). Telephone landlines (2008): 10,000 (44); cellular telephone subscribers (2008): 36,000 (154); personal computers (2005): 3,000 (14); total Internet users (2008): 17,000 (73); broadband Internet subscribers (2007): 100 (0.4).

1 metric ton = about 1.1 short tons;   1 kilometer = 0.6 mi (statute);   1 metric ton-km cargo = about 0.68 short ton-mi cargo;   c.i.f.: cost, insurance, and freight;   f.o.b.: free on board

Education and health

Educational attainment (1999). Percentage of population ages 15 and over having: no formal schooling 18.0%; incomplete primary education 20.6%; completed primary 35.5%; some secondary 12.2%; completed secondary 8.5%; higher 5.2%, of which university 1.3%. **Literacy** (2007): total population ages 15 and over literate, 74%. **Health** (2005): physicians (2008) 26 (1 per 9,000 persons); hospital beds 885 (1 per 244 persons); infant mortality rate per 1,000 live births 55.2; undernourished population (2002–04) 20,000 (11% of total population based on the consumption of a minimum daily requirement of 1,790 calories).

Military

Total active duty personnel (2008): none; Australia and New Zealand assist paramilitary forces through defense assistance programs.

Background

The islands of Vanuatu were inhabited for at least 3,000 years by Melanesian peoples before being discovered in 1606 by the Portuguese. They were rediscovered by French navigator Louis-Antoine de Bougainville in 1768 and then explored by English mariner Capt. James Cook in 1774 and named the New Hebrides. Sandalwood merchants and European missionaries arrived in the mid-19th century; they were followed by British and French cotton planters. Control of the islands was sought by both the French and the British, who agreed in 1906 to form a condominium government. During World War II a major Allied naval base was on Espíritu Santo; the island group escaped Japanese invasion. The New Hebrides became the independent Republic of Vanuatu in 1980. Much of the nation's housing was ravaged by a hurricane in 1987.

Recent Developments

Pressure by the Group of 20 and the US on Vanuatu to end its tax havens led to declines in activity in Vanuatuan offshore financial centers in 2009. Though regional source economies contracted, tourism grew significantly, and the numbers of visiting cruise ships increased. In July France financed the construction of a new airport on Pentecost, which would exploit the island's tourist potential and reduce its isolation. Increases in quotas for Vanuatuan horticultural workers in New Zealand and Australia were also producing useful revenues.

Internet resource: <http://vanuatu.travel>.

Vatican City State

Official name: State of the Vatican City (Holy See). **Form of government:** ecclesiastical. **Head of state:** Pope Benedict XVI (from 2005). **Head of government:** Secretary of State Tarcisio Cardinal Bertone (from 2006). **Capital:** Vatican City. **Languages:** Italian; Latin. **Religion:** Roman Catholic. **Monetary unit:** 1 euro (€) = 100 cents; valuation (1 Jul 2010).

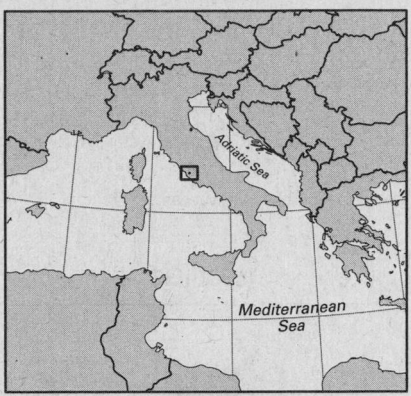

US$1 = €0.80 (Vatican City uses the euro as its official currency, even though it is not a member of the EU).

Demography

Area: 0.17 sq mi, 0.44 sq km. **Population** (2008): 930. **Density** (2008): persons per sq mi 5,471, persons per sq km 2,114. **Location:** southern Europe, within the commune of Rome, Italy. **Annual budget:** US$209,000,000. **Industries:** banking and finance; printing; production of a small amount of mosaics and uniforms; tourism.

Background

Vatican City, the independent papal state, is the smallest independent state in the world. Its medieval and Renaissance walls form its boundaries except on the southeast, at St. Peter's Square. Within the walls is a miniature nation, with its own diplomatic missions, newspaper, post office, radio station, banking system, army of more than 100 Swiss Guards, and publishing house. Extraterritoriality of the state extends to Castel Gandolfo, summer home of the Pope, and to several churches and palaces in Rome proper. Its independent sovereignty was recognized in the Lateran Treaty of 1929. The pope has absolute executive, legislative, and judicial powers within the city. He appoints the members of the Vatican's government organs, which are separate from those of the Holy See. The state's many imposing buildings include St. Peter's Basilica, the Vatican Palace, and the Vatican Museums. Frescoes by Michelangelo and Pinturicchio (in the Sistine Chapel) and Raphael's Stanze are also there. The Vatican Library contains a priceless collection of manuscripts from the pre-Christian and Christian eras.

Recent Developments

Controversy hit the Vatican when the Holy See announced in October 2009 that it would in some cases admit married Anglican priests into the Catholic priesthood. This was seen as part of an effort to encourage the conversion of conservative Anglicans dissatisfied with the acceptance of women into the priesthood and the ordaining of a gay bishop and recognition of same-sex marriages. Another controversy erupted over Pope Benedict's public claim—made during his official visit to Africa in March—that the distribution of condoms could not arrest the spread of AIDS; he instead advocated sexual abstinence and marital fidelity. A growing child-abuse scandal emerged in early 2010, with allegations of cover-ups coming from Germany, Austria, and Ireland, among other countries.

Internet resource: <www.vatican.va>.

Venezuela

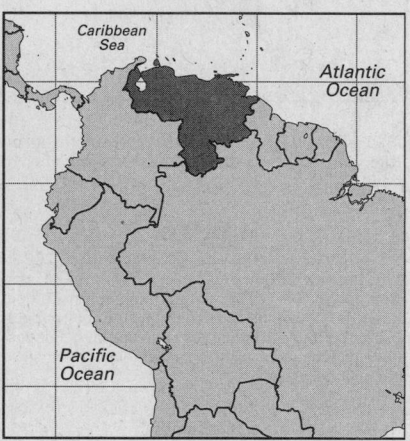

Official name: República Bolivariana de Venezuela (Bolivarian Republic of Venezuela). Form of government: federal multiparty republic with one legislative house (National Assembly [167]). Head of state and government: President Hugo Chávez Frías (from 2002). Capital: Caracas. Official language: Spanish (31 indigenous Indian languages are also official). Official religion: none. Monetary unit: 1 bolívar fuerte (VEF) = 100 céntimos; valuation (1 Jul 2010) US$1 = VEF 4.30 (the bolívar fuerte replaced the bolívar [VEB] 1 Jan 2008, at the rate of 1 VEF = VEB 1,000).

Demography

Area: 353,841 sq mi, 916,445 sq km. Population (2009): 28,583,000. Density (2009): persons per sq mi 80.8, persons per sq km 31.2. Urban (2005): 93.4%. Sex distribution (2007): male 50.19%; female 49.81%. Age breakdown (2006): under 15, 32.1%; 15–29, 26.9%; 30–44, 20.5%; 45–59, 13.2%; 60–74, 5.5%; 75–84, 1.5%; 85 and over, 0.3%. Ethnic composition (2000): mestizo 63.7%; local white 20.0%; local black 10.0%; other white 3.3%; Amerindian 1.3%; other 1.7%. Religious affiliation (2005): Roman Catholic 84.5%; Protestant 4.0%; other 11.5%. Major cities (urban agglomerations) (2009 [2007]): Caracas 2,097,400 (2,985,000); Maracaibo 1,891,800 (2,072,000); Valencia 1,408,400 (1,770,000); Barquisimeto 1,018,900

(1,116,000); Ciudad Guayana 789,500. Location: northern South America, bordering the Caribbean Sea, the North Atlantic Ocean, Guyana, Brazil, and Colombia.

Vital statistics

Birth rate per 1,000 population (2007): 21.5 (world avg. 20.3). Death rate per 1,000 population (2007): 5.1 (world avg. 8.5). Total fertility rate (avg. births per childbearing woman; 2007): 2.58. Life expectancy at birth (2007): male 70.7 years; female 76.6 years.

National economy

Budget (2006). Revenue: VEB 117,326,000,000,-000 (petroleum income 52.9%, of which royalties 37.5%, taxes 13.0%; nonpetroleum income 47.1%, of which VAT 22.4%). Expenditures: VEB 117,255,000,000,000 (current expenditures 75.0%; development expenditures 22.8%; other 2.2%). Production (metric tons except as noted). Agriculture and fishing (2007): sugarcane 9,300,000, corn (maize) 2,104,000, rice 800,000; livestock (number of live animals) 16,700,000 cattle, 120,000,000 chickens; fisheries production 477,210 (from aquaculture 5%). Mining and quarrying (2008): iron ore (metal content) 15,200,000; bauxite 5,500,000; phosphate rock 400,000; gold 10,100 kg; gem diamonds 45,000 carats. Manufacturing (value added in VEB '000,000,000; 2004): food products 8,122; iron and steel 3,022; refined petroleum products 2,890. Energy production (consumption): electricity (kW-hr; 2006) 110,357,000,000 (109,815,000,000); coal (metric tons; 2006) 7,338,000 (52,000); crude petroleum (barrels; 2008) 874,000,000 ([2006] 371,000,000); petroleum products (metric tons; 2006) 58,031,000 (26,320,000); natural gas (cu m; 2006) 24,530,000,000 (24,530,000,-000). Selected balance of payments data. Receipts from (US$'000,000): tourism (2007) 817; remittances (2008) 130; foreign direct investment (FDI; 2005–07 avg.) 882; official development assistance (2007) 71. Disbursements for (US$'000,000): tourism (2007) 1,394; remittances (2008) 771; FDI (2005–07 avg.) 1,827. Gross national income (2008): US$257,794,000,000 (US$9,230 per capita). Public debt (external, outstanding; 2007): US$27,494,000,000. Population economically active (2006): total 12,379,700; activity rate 45.9% (participation rates: ages 15–64, 68.7%; female 38.6%; unemployed [July 2006–June 2007] 9.4%).

Foreign trade

Imports (2006): US$30,559,000,000 (machinery and apparatus 26.6%; motor vehicles 12.1%; chemical products 11.0%; food products 5.9%). Major import sources: US 30.6%; Colombia 10.2%; Brazil 10.1%; Mexico 5.9%; China 4.9%. Exports (2006): US$61,385,000,000 (crude petroleum 91.6%; iron and steel 2.8%; aluminum 1.7%; organic chemical products 0.6%). Major export destinations: US 46.2%; Netherlands Antilles 13.5%; China 3.2%.

---

1 metric ton = about 1.1 short tons;   1 kilometer = 0.6 mi (statute);   1 metric ton-km cargo = about 0.68 short ton-mi cargo;   c.i.f.: cost, insurance, and freight;   f.o.b.: free on board

Transport and communications

Transport. *Railroads* (2008): route length 806 km; metric ton-km cargo (2004) 22,000,000. *Roads* (2004): total length 96,200 km (paved 34%). *Vehicles* (2007): passenger cars 2,952,129; trucks and buses 1,091,883. *Air transport* (2005): passenger-km 2,578,700,000; metric ton-km cargo 2,100,000. **Communications,** in total units (units per 1,000 persons). Telephone landlines (2008): 6,304,000 (224); cellular telephone subscribers (2008): 27,084,000 (963); personal computers (2005): 2,475,000 (98); total Internet users (2008): 7,167,000 (255); broadband Internet subscribers (2008): 1,330,000 (47).

Education and health

Educational attainment (2003). Percentage of head-of-household population having: no formal schooling 10.2%; primary education or less 38.5%; some secondary 36.9%; completed secondary/higher 14.4%. **Literacy** (2003): total population ages 15 and over literate, 93.0%. **Health** (2003): physicians 35,756 (1 per 722 persons); hospital beds 74,866 (1 per 345 persons); infant mortality rate per 1,000 live births (2006) 23.0; undernourished population (2003–05) 3,200,000 (12% of total population based on the consumption of a minimum daily requirement of 1,830 calories).

Military

Total active duty personnel (November 2008): 115,000 (army 54.8%, navy 15.2%, air force 10.0%, national guard 20.0%). **Military expenditure as percentage of GDP** (2007): 1.2%; per capita expenditure US$101.

Background

In 1498 Christopher Columbus sighted Venezuela; in 1499 the navigators Alonso de Ojeda, Amerigo Vespucci, and Juan de la Cosa traced the coast. A Spanish missionary established the first European settlement at Cumaná in about 1520. In 1718 it was included in the Viceroyalty of New Granada and was made a captaincy general in 1731. Venezuelan Creoles led by Francisco de Miranda and Simón Bolívar spearheaded the South American independence movement, and though Venezuela declared independence from Spain in 1811, that status was not assured until 1821. Military dictators generally ruled the country from 1830 until the overthrow of Marcos Pérez Jiménez in 1958. A new constitution adopted in 1961 marked the beginning of democracy. As a founding member of OPEC, Venezuela enjoyed relative economic prosperity from oil production during the 1970s, and its economy has remained dependent on the world petroleum market. The leftist president Hugo Chávez promulgated a new constitution in 1999, and he was reelected in 2002; a period of great political and economic tumult ensued.

Recent Developments

Venezuelan Pres. Hugo Chávez continued to maneuver to create the hybrid military-socialist regime that he touted as "twenty-first century socialism." In the international arena, Venezuela's burgeoning ties with Russia continued to be very important. In September 2009 Venezuela announced its acceptance of a US$2 billion loan for the purchase of Russian military equipment. On a visit to Russia that month, Chávez declared Venezuela's recognition of the Russia-supported Georgian breakaway republics of Abkhazia and South Ossetia. Earlier in the year, the two countries signed agreements detailing Russian assistance in developing a nuclear power program for Venezuela, and in April 2010 Russian Prime Minister Vladimir Putin signed additional agreements to provide assistance to Venezuela's space program and to establish a development bank to finance joint petroleum exploration projects. Chávez was angered by Colombian Pres. Álvaro Uribe's decision to allow the US to use military installations in Colombia as bases from which to hunt down drug traffickers, as relations between Venezuela and the US remained frosty.

Internet resource: <www.venezuelatuya.com/index-eng.htm>.

Vietnam

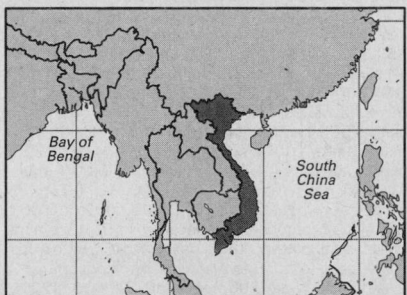

Official name: Cong Hoa Xa Hoi Chu Nghia Viet Nam (Socialist Republic of Vietnam). **Form of government:** socialist republic with one legislative house (National Assembly [493]). **Head of state:** President Nguyen Minh Triet (from 2006). **Head of government:** Prime Minister Nguyen Tan Dung (from 2006). **Capital:** Hanoi. **Official language:** Vietnamese. **Official religion:** none. **Monetary unit:** 1 dong (VND) = 10 hao = 100 xu; valuation (1 Jul 2010) US$1 = VND 19,025.00.

Demography

Area: 127,882 sq mi, 331,212 sq km. **Population** (2009): 88,577,000. **Density** (2009): persons per sq mi 692.6, persons per sq km 267.4. **Urban** (2009): 29.6%. **Sex distribution** (2009): male 49.52%; female 50.48%. **Age breakdown** (2008): under 15, 26.6%; 15–29, 29.8%; 30–44, 22.2%; 45–59, 13.8%; 60–74, 5.3%; 75–84, 1.9%; 85 and over, 0.4%. **Ethnic composition** (1999): Vietnamese 86.2%; Tho (Tay) 1.9%; Montagnards 1.7%; Thai 1.7%; Muong 1.5%; Khmer 1.4%; Nung 1.1%; Miao (Hmong) 1.0%; Dao 0.8%; other 2.7%. **Religious affiliation** (2005): Buddhist 48%; New-Religionist (mostly Cao Dai and Hoa Hao) 11%; traditional beliefs 10%; Roman Catholic 7%; Protestant 1%; nonreligious/

atheist 20%; other 3%. **Major cities (urban agglomerations)** (2009 [2007]): Ho Chi Minh City 5,929,479; Hanoi 2,632,087 (4,723,000); Haiphong 847,058 (2,129,000); Da Nang 770,499. **Location:** southeastern Asia, bordering China, the Gulf of Tonkin, the South China Sea, the Gulf of Thailand, Cambodia, and Laos.

Vital statistics

Birth rate per 1,000 population (2008): 18.1 (world avg. 20.3). **Death rate** per 1,000 population (2008): 6.0 (world avg. 8.5). **Total fertility rate** (avg. births per childbearing woman; 2008): 2.02. **Life expectancy** at birth (2008): male 69.0 years; female 74.2 years.

National economy

Budget (2008). *Revenue:* VND 323,000,000,000,-000 (tax revenue 89.0%, of which petroleum related 20.3%; nontax revenue 9.9%; grants 1.1%). *Expenditures:* VND 364,000,000,000,000 (current expenditures 72.6%; capital expenditures 27.4%). **Public debt** (external, outstanding; 2007): US$19,372,000,000. **Gross national income** (2008): US$77,031,000,000 (US$890 per capita). **Production** (metric tons except as noted). *Agriculture and fishing* (2007): rice 35,566,800, sugarcane 16,000,000, cassava 8,900,000, coffee 1,060,000, cashews 961,000, natural rubber 550,000, tea 153,000, black pepper 82,000, cinnamon 9,500; livestock (number of live animals) 26,500,000 pigs, 6,840,000 cattle, 2,921,100 buffalo, 62,800,000 ducks; fisheries production 4,277,900 (from aquaculture 50%); aquatic plants production 38,000 (from aquaculture 100%). *Mining and quarrying* (2007): phosphate rock 1,360,000; kaolin 650,000; barite 120,000; tin (metal content) 3,500. *Manufacturing* (value of production in VND '000,000,000,000; 2004): food products and beverages 156.1; cement, bricks, and pottery 46.2; paints, soaps, and pharmaceuticals 43.9. *Energy production (consumption):* electricity (kW-hr; 2007) 66,900,000,000 ([2006] 56,494,000,000); coal (metric tons; 2007) 41,200,000 ([2006] 15,700,000); crude petroleum (barrels; 2008) 100,800,000 ([2006] negligible); petroleum products (metric tons; 2006) 483,000,-000 (11,743,000); natural gas (cu m; 2007) 6,834,000,000 ([2006] 5,953,000,000). **Population economically active** (2004): total 43,242,000; activity rate of total population 52.9% (participation rates: ages 15–64, 77.7%; female 49.0%; unemployed [2008] 4.7%). **Selected balance of payments data.** Receipts from (US$'000,000): tourism (2006) 3,200; remittances (2008) 7,200; foreign direct investment (FDI; 2005–07 avg.) 3,707; official development assistance (2007) 2,497. Disbursements for (US$'000,000): FDI (2005–07 avg.) 100.

Foreign trade

Imports (2006; c.i.f.): US$44,891,000,000 (machinery and apparatus 21.3%; chemical products 14.0%; refined petroleum products 13.9%; textile yarn, fabrics, and made-up articles 8.9%; iron and steel 7.7%). *Major import sources:* China 16.5%; Singapore 14.0%; Taiwan 10.7%; Japan 10.5%; South Korea 8.7%. **Exports** (2006; f.o.b.):

US$39,826,000,000 (crude petroleum 20.9%; garments and accessories 14.0%; footwear 9.2%; furniture 4.5%; electrical machinery and equipment 3.7%; crustaceans 3.3%; rice 3.2%; coffee 3.1%; natural rubber 2.9%). *Major export destinations* (2007): US 20.8%; Japan 12.5%; Australia 7.8%; China 7.5%; Singapore 4.6%.

Transport and communications

Transport. *Railroads* (2007): route length (2005) 2,600 km; passenger-km 4,659,000,000; metric ton-km cargo 3,883,000,000. *Roads* (2007): total length 160,089 km (paved 48%). *Vehicles* (2007): passenger cars 1,146,312. *Air transport* (2008): passenger-km 15,768,000,000; metric ton-km cargo 295,764,000. **Communications**, in total units (units per 1,000 persons). Telephone landlines (2008): 29,591,000 (338); cellular telephone subscribers (2008): 70,000,000 (799); personal computers (2007): 8,306,000 (96); total Internet users (2008): 20,834,000 (238); broadband Internet subscribers (2008): 2,049,000 (23).

Education and health

Educational attainment (1999). Percentage of population ages 18 and over having: no formal education 9.0%; primary education 29.2%; lower secondary 32.5%; upper secondary 24.9%; incomplete/complete higher 4.3%; advanced degree 0.1%. **Literacy** (2003): percentage of population ages 15 and over literate 94.0%; males literate 95.8%; females literate 92.3%. **Health** (2007): physicians 54,798 (1 per 1,579 persons); hospital beds 210,800 (1 per 410 persons); infant mortality rate per 1,000 live births (2008) 23.0; undernourished population (2002–04) 13,000,000 (16% of total population based on the consumption of a minimum daily requirement of 1,840 calories).

Military

Total active duty personnel (November 2008): 455,000 (army 90.5%, navy 2.9%, air force 6.6%). **Military expenditure as percentage of GDP** (2007): 5.3%; per capita expenditure US$43.

Background

A distinct Vietnamese group began to emerge c. 200 BC in the independent kingdom of Nam Viet, which was annexed to China in the 1st century BC. The Vietnamese were under continuous Chinese control until the 10th century AD. The southern region was gradually overrun by Vietnamese from the north in the late 15th century. The area was divided into two parts in the early 17th century, with the northern part known as Tonkin and the southern part as Cochin China. In 1802 the northern and southern parts of Vietnam were unified under a single dynasty. Following several years of attempted French colonial expansion in the region, the French captured Saigon in 1859 and later the rest of the area, controlling it until World War II. The Japanese occupied Vietnam in 1940–45 and declared it independent at the end of World War II, a move the French opposed. The French and Vietnamese fought

1 metric ton = about 1.1 short tons;   1 kilometer = 0.6 mi (statute);   1 metric ton-km cargo = about 0.68 short ton-mi cargo;   c.i.f.: cost, insurance, and freight;   f.o.b.: free on board

the First Indochina War until French forces with US financial backing were defeated at Dien Bien Phu in 1954; evacuation of French troops ensued. Following an international conference at Geneva, Vietnam was partitioned along the 17th parallel, with the northern part under Ho Chi Minh and the southern part under Bao Dai; the partition was to be temporary, but the reunification elections scheduled for 1956 were never held. Bao Dai declared the independence of South Vietnam (Republic of Vietnam), while the Communists established North Vietnam (Democratic Republic of Vietnam). The activities of North Vietnamese guerrillas and pro-communist rebels in South Vietnam led to US intervention and the Vietnam War. A cease-fire agreement was signed in 1973, and US troops were withdrawn. The civil war soon resumed, and in 1975 North Vietnam invaded South Vietnam and the South Vietnamese government collapsed. In 1976 the two Vietnams were united as the Socialist Republic of Vietnam. From the mid-1980s the government enacted a series of economic reforms and began to open up to Asian and Western nations. In 1995 the US officially normalized relations with Vietnam.

Recent Developments

Relations with China became a domestic issue in 2009 when Beijing unilaterally declared a moratorium on fishing in the South China Sea from mid-May until August, the height of Vietnam's fishing season. Chinese fishery vessels aggressively chased Vietnamese fishermen out of the area by seizing catches and detaining and fining boat crews. Security authorities continued to arrest and detain prominent pro-democracy activists. In October Vietnam tried and convicted six persons for their role in 2008 in hanging banners in Haiphong calling for political freedom. Three other dissidents received separate trials in Hanoi. In December former army officer Tran Anh Kim, one of five dissidents arrested in June, was convicted and sentenced to more than five years in prison for subversion.

Internet resource: <www.gso.gov.vn>.

Yemen

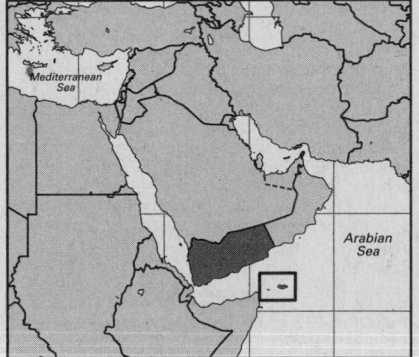

Official name: Al-Jumhuriyah al-Yamaniyah (Republic of Yemen). **Form of government:** multiparty republic with two legislative houses (Consultative Council [111]; House of Representatives [301]). **Head of state:** President Major General 'Ali 'Abdallah Salih (from 1990). **Head of government:** Prime Minister Ali Muhammad Mujawar (from 2007). **Capital:** Sanaa. **Official language:** Arabic. **Official religion:** Islam. **Monetary unit:** 1 Yemeni rial (YR) = 100 fils; valuation (1 Jul 2010): US$1 = YR 224.50.

Demography

Area: 203,891 sq mi, 528,076 sq km. **Population** (2009): 22,858,000. **Density** (2009): persons per sq mi 112.1, persons per sq km 43.3. **Urban** (2008): 31.0%. **Sex distribution** (2008): male 50.81%; female 49.19%. **Age breakdown** (2008): under 15, 44.3%; 15–29, 29.9%; 30–44, 14.0%; 45–59, 7.8%; 60–74, 3.1%; 75 and over, 0.9%. **Ethnic composition** (2000): Arab 92.8%; Somali 3.7%; black 1.1%; Indo-Pakistani 1.0%; other 1.4%. **Religious affiliation** (2005): Muslim nearly 100%, of which Sunni 58%, Shi'i 42%. **Major cities** (2004): Sanaa (2007) 2,006,619; Aden 588,938; Ta'izz 466,968; Al-Hudaydah 409,994; Ibb 212,992. **Location:** the Middle East, bordering Saudi Arabia, Oman, the Arabian Sea, the Gulf of Aden, and the Red Sea.

Vital statistics

Birth rate per 1,000 population (2008): 36.2 (world avg. 20.3). **Death rate** per 1,000 population (2008): 7.7 (world avg. 8.5). **Total fertility rate** (avg. births per childbearing woman; 2008): 5.20. **Life expectancy** at birth (2008): male 60.7 years; female 64.7 years.

National economy

Budget (2007). *Revenue:* YR 1,406,400,000,000 (petroleum revenue 69.1%; tax revenue 21.9%; nontax revenue and grants 9.0%). *Expenditures:* YR 1,748,300,000,000 (transfers and subsidies 29.7%; wages and salaries 27.9%; interest on debt 5.7%). **Public debt** (external, outstanding; January 2009): US$5,977,000,000. **Population economically active** (2008): total 5,206,000; activity rate of total population 23.4% (participation rates: ages 15 and older, 42.7%; female 11.8%; unemployed 15.0%). **Production** (metric tons except as noted). *Agriculture and fishing* (2008): mangoes 387,906, sorghum 376,728, alfalfa 290,370, khat (qat) 165,668 [khat [qat] contributes roughly 2.5% of total GDP; khat cultivation employs nearly 15% of the labor force), dates 55,204, chickpeas 54,000, sesame 23,895; livestock (number of live animals) 8,889,000 sheep, 8,708,000 goats, 1,531,000 cattle, 373,000 camels; fisheries production 132,062 (from aquaculture, none). *Mining and quarrying* (2007): salt 100,000; gypsum 44,000. *Manufacturing* (value added in YR '000,000; 2008): food products and beverages 112,090; plastic products 60,299; paper products 46,850; refined petroleum products 10,509. *Energy production (consumption):* electricity (kW-hr; 2008) 6,545,830,000 (4,496,700,000); crude petroleum (barrels; 2008–09) 102,041,700 ([2006] 29,150,000); petroleum products (metric tons; 2008) 3,307,000 ([2006]

5,394,000); natural gas (cu m; 2007) 25,000,-000,000 (25,000,000,000). **Gross national income** (2008): US$21,901,000,000 (US$950 per capita). **Selected balance of payments data.** Receipts from (US$'000,000): tourism (2007) 425; remittances (2008) 1,420; foreign direct investment (FDI; 2005–07 avg.) 428; official development assistance (2007) 225. Disbursements for (US$'000,000): tourism (2008) 184; remittances (2008) 319; FDI (2005–07 avg.) 58.

Foreign trade

Imports (2008; c.i.f.): YR 2,087,876,317,000 (crude petroleum and refined petroleum products 29.1%; food products and live animals 22.3%, of which grains 13.2%; transportation equipment 7.0%; base and fabricated metals 6.5%; chemical products 6.4%). *Major import sources:* UAE 28.9%; China 7.0%; Saudi Arabia 6.7%; Kuwait 6.4%; India 3.9%. **Exports** (2008; f.o.b.): YR 1,519,162,467,000 (refined petroleum products 77.3%; crude petroleum 9.9%; food products and live animals 5.0%, of which fish 2.6%; transportation equipment 1.9%; chemical products 1.7%). *Major export destinations:* China 31.1%; Thailand 23.8%; UAE 9.5%; India 8.0%; South Korea 6.3%.

Transport and communications

Transport. *Railroads:* none. *Roads* (2007): total length 71,300 km (paved 9%). *Vehicles* (2004): passenger cars 522,437; trucks and buses 506,766. *Air transport* (2007): passenger-km (2004) 2,473,000,000; metric ton-km cargo 41,000,000. **Communications,** in total units (units per 1,000 persons). Telephone landlines (2008): 1,117,000 (49); cellular telephone subscribers (2008): 3,700,000 (161); personal computers (2006): 587,000 (28); total Internet users (2008): 370,000 (16).

Education and health

Educational attainment (2005–06). Percentage of population ages 10 and over having: no formal schooling/unknown 42.3%; reading and writing ability 33.6%; primary education 13.1%; secondary 8.7%; higher 2.3%. **Literacy** (2007): percentage of total population ages 15 and over literate 58.9%; males literate 77.0%; females literate 40.5%. **Health** (2008): physicians 6,187 (1 per 3,592 persons); hospital beds 15,184 (1 per 1,464 persons); infant mortality rate per 1,000 live births 60.1; undernourished population (2002–04) 7,600,000 (38% of total population based on the consumption of a minimum daily requirement of 1,770 calories).

Military

Total active duty personnel (November 2008): 66,700 (army 90.0%, navy 2.5%, air force/air defense 7.5%). **Military expenditure as percentage of GDP** (2007): 4.2%; per capita expenditure US$42.

Background

Yemen was the home of ancient Minaean, Sabaean, and Himyarite kingdoms. The Romans invaded the region in the 1st century AD. In the 6th century, it was conquered by Ethiopians and Persians. Following conversion to Islam in the 7th century, it was ruled nominally under a caliphate. The Egyptian Ayyubid dynasty ruled there from 1173 to 1229, after which the region passed to the Rasulids. From 1517 through 1918, the Ottoman Empire maintained varying degrees of control, especially in the northwestern section. A boundary agreement was reached in 1934 between the northwestern imam-controlled territory, which subsequently became the Yemen Arab Republic (North Yemen), and the southeastern British-controlled territory, which subsequently became the People's Democratic Republic of Yemen (South Yemen). Relations between the two Yemens remained tense and were marked by conflict throughout the 1970s and 1980s. Reaching an accord, the two officially united as the Republic of Yemen in 1990. Its 1993 elections were the first free, multiparty general elections held in the Arabian Peninsula, and they were the first in which women participated. In 1994, after a two-month civil war, a new constitution was approved.

Recent Developments

Security challenges faced Yemen in 2009 and 2010. The al-Houthis—tribal clans that belonged to the Zaydi branch of Shi'ite Islam along the mountainous northern border with Saudi Arabia—revolted for the sixth time since 2004, claiming that they were politically marginalized. A cease-fire was signed in February 2010. On Christmas Day, 2009, however, a Nigerian who had allegedly received training in Yemen tried to blow up a passenger plane landing in Detroit. Weeks earlier, the US government had sent special forces to Yemen to help train soldiers to fight extremists such as al-Qaeda in the Arabian Peninsula, and Britain did the same after the failed bombing attempt. In February 2010 the US announced US$150 million in military assistance to Yemen for fiscal year 2010.

Internet resource: <www.cso-yemen.org>.

Zambia

Official name: Republic of Zambia. **Form of government:** multiparty republic with one legislative house (National Assembly [158]). **Head of state and government:** President Rupiah Banda (from 2008). **Capital:** Lusaka. **Official language:** English. **Official religion:** none (Zambia is a Christian nation per the preamble of a constitutional amendment). **Monetary unit:** 1 Zambian kwacha (K) = 100 ngwee; valuation (1 Jul 2010) US$1 = K 5,175.01.

Demography

Area: 290,585 sq mi, 752,612 sq km. **Population** (2009): 12,935,000. **Density** (2009): persons per

---

1 metric ton = about 1.1 short tons;   1 kilometer = 0.6 mi (statute);   1 metric ton-km cargo = about 0.68 short ton-mi cargo;   c.i.f.: cost, insurance, and freight;   f.o.b.: free on board

11 Jul 2010, Johannesburg, South Africa: Spain's national football (soccer) team celebrates its 1–0 victory over the Netherlands in the 19th FIFA World Cup. In a taut final contest, Spain scored in overtime in the 116th minute to win that nation's first world championship. The tournament was widely hailed as a triumph for the host country, even though South Africa's national team was eliminated in the first round. The final match attracted an audience estimated at 700 million viewers, one of the largest in TV history.

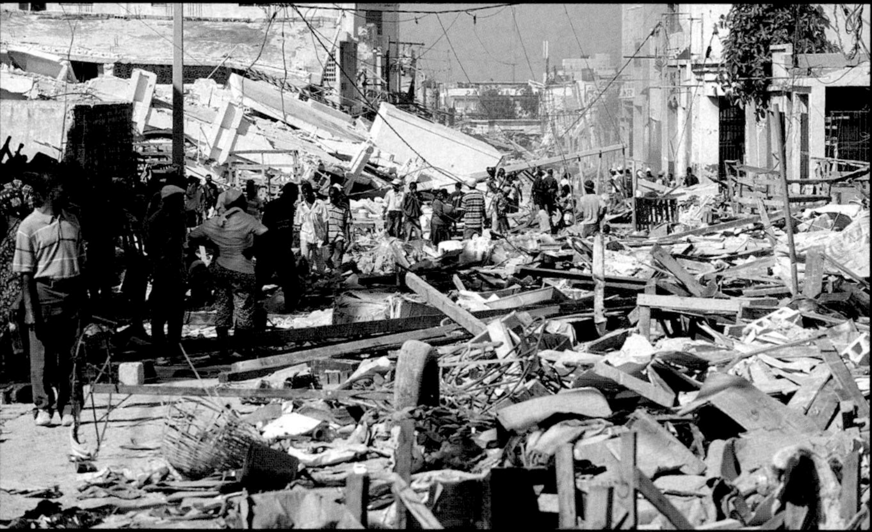

12 Jan 2010, Port-au-Prince, Haiti: The island nation was rocked by a magnitude-7.0 earthquake in the late afternoon of 12 January, reducing much of the capital city to rubble. The government estimated that some 222,570 people had died, 300,000 had been injured, and at least 1.6 million were made homeless by the quake. Above, the capital is a shambles on 14 January; at right, Mac Fenieh struggles in his attempt to free a teacher trapped in the rubble of a collapsed school building. Aid efforts were hampered by the damage done to Haiti's roads and communications systems.

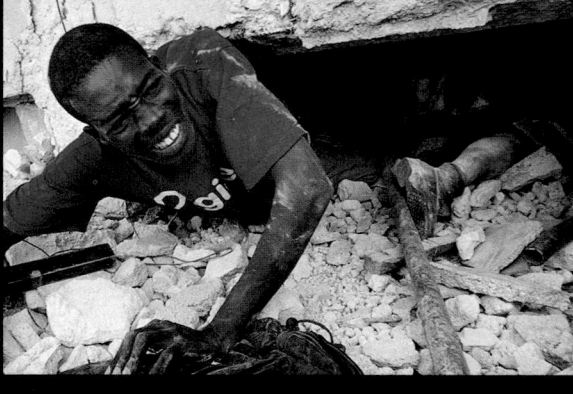

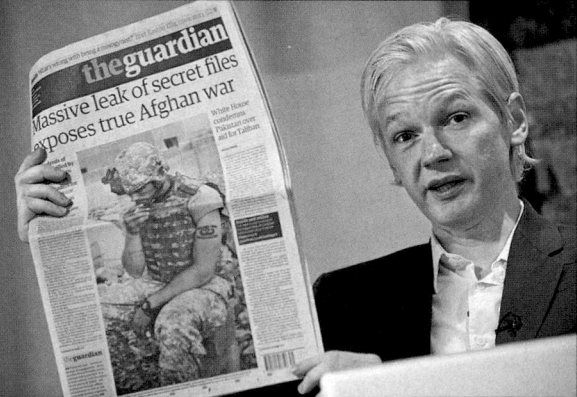

26 Jul 2010, London, England: Julian Assange, founder of the controversial whistle-blowing Web site Wikileaks, holds a newspaper that published excerpts from some 92,000 pages of secret US documents recording events in the war in Afghanistan dating from 2004 to 2009. The leaked reports documented Pakistani aid to the Taliban and anti-NATO forces in Afghanistan; they were published in the *Manchester Guardian,* the *New York Times,* and *Der Spiegel.* The US government denounced the leaks; Australian journalist Assange defended them as offering a truthful account of the conflict.

TOP TO BOTTOM: JUAN BARRETO/AFP/GETTY IMAGES; CAROL GUZY/THE WASHINGTON POST VIA GETTY IMAGES; LEON NEAL/AFP/GETTY IMAGES

24 Jun 2010, Kandahar, Afghanistan: At right, US soldiers carry a wounded colleague to receive medical aid during a major US offensive in the nation's second largest city. The escalation of US troops ordered by Pres. Barack Obama in 2009 bore mixed results, and polls showed an increasing number of Americans questioned the wisdom of the US commitment to the government of Afghan president Hamid Karzai, shown below meeting with US Secretary of State Hillary Clinton on 20 July.

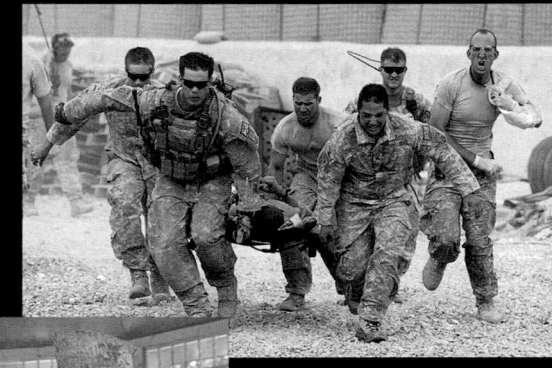

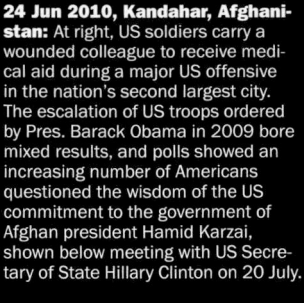

1 Mar 2010, Baghdad, Iraq: Campaign banners and posters blanketed Iraq's capital as voters prepared to cast ballots in a 7 March parliamentary election. The contest did not yield a clear majority for any single party, resulting in months of negotiation to form a government. Despite ongoing political upheaval and occasional, if less frequent, acts of violence against Iraq's government, President Obama met his goal of removing all US combat troops from Iraq by the end of August 2010.

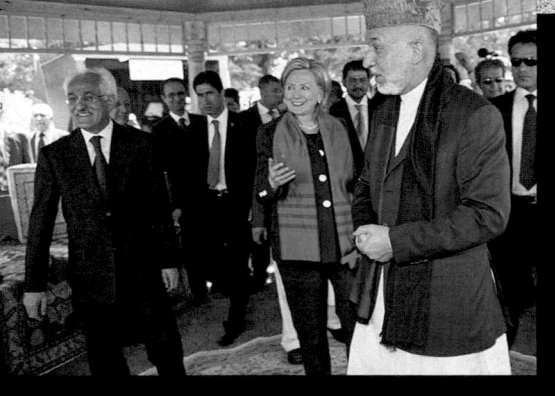

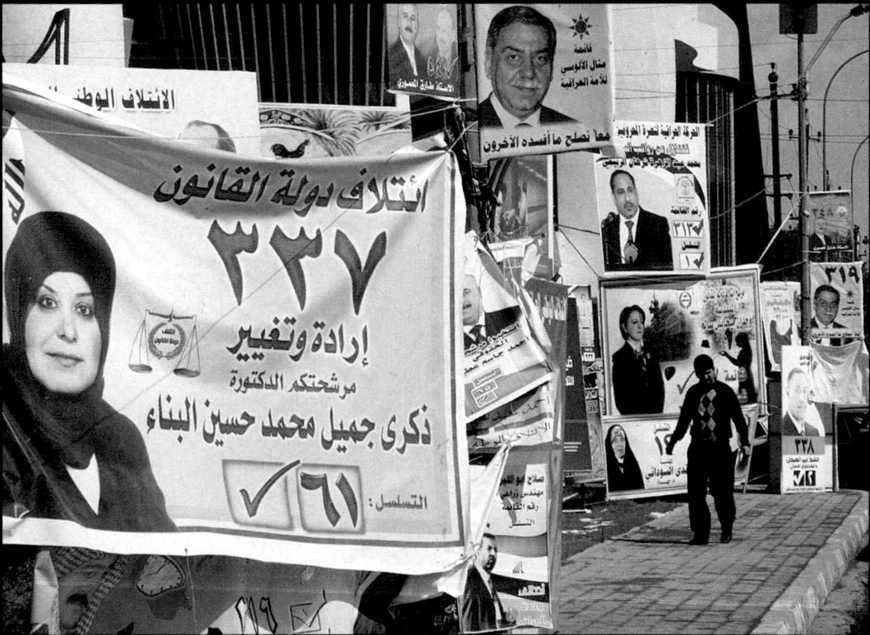

TOP TO BOTTOM: JUSTIN SULLIVAN/GETTY IMAGES; PAUL J. RICHARDS/AFP/GETTY IMAGES; KHALID MOHAMMED/AP IMAGES

Plate 4   WORLD EVENTS

31 May 2010, Mediterranean Sea: When ships bound from Turkey to Gaza with stores of aid supplies tried to run an Israeli blockade, Israeli commandos boarded and seized them. On the lead ship, the *Mavi Marmara*, nine people were killed and dozens wounded. Above, Palestinian supporters aboard the *Mavi Marmara* before the raid; at left, Israeli forces intercept a ship.

12 May 2010, London, England: British voters ousted the Labour Party and current PM Gordon Brown after 13 years in power in a 6 May election in the United Kingdom. When no single party received a majority, Conservative leader David Cameron, left, formed a coalition government with the Social Democrats and leader Nick Clegg. Above, the two prepare to take command of the government outside No. 10 Downing Street.

29 Mar 2010, Moscow, Russia: A subway rider shows the effects of one of a pair of suicide bombings carried out during rush hour, which killed at least 38 people and wounded more than 60. The bombers were believed to be rebels from the Caucasus region retaliating for Russian attacks on Islamic militants in that area.

2 Jun 2010, Tokyo, Japan: Yukio Hatoyama resigned as PM after eight months in office. He had promised to relocate a US military base on Okinawa but failed to persuade the US to do so.

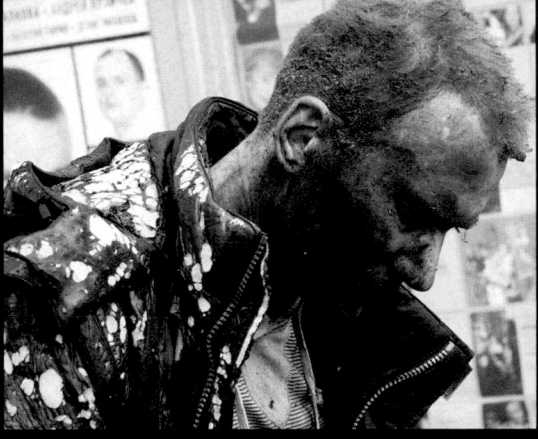

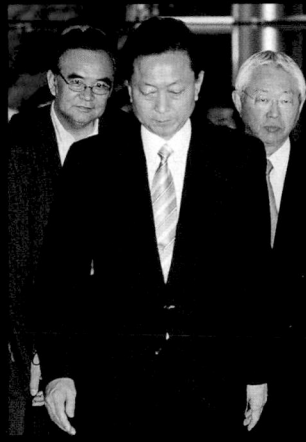

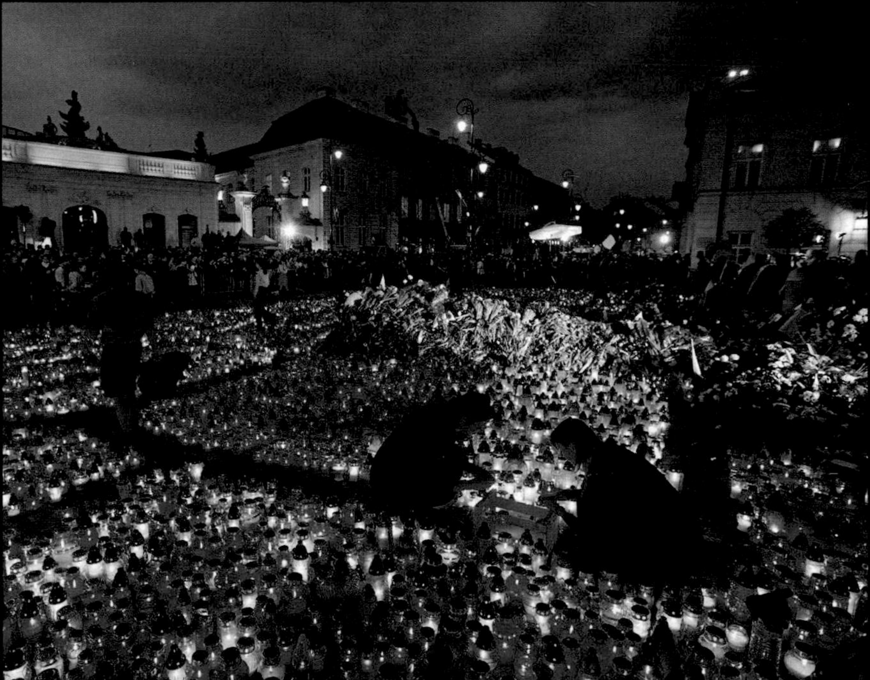

13 Apr 2010, Warsaw, Poland: Poles light candles outside the presidential palace following the 10 April crash of a Polish Air Force jetliner carrying many of the nation's political and military leaders to Smolensk, Russia. All aboard were killed; among the 96 victims were Pres. Lech Kaczynski and wife Maria. The group was traveling to a service honoring the victims of a 1940 Russian slaughter of Poles during World War II.

CLOCKWISE FROM TOP LEFT: EGOR BARBATUNOV/AP IMAGES; KYODO/AP IMAGES; SEAN GALLUP/GETTY IMAGES

Plate 6   UNITED STATES

20 Apr 2010, Gulf of Mexico:
America's Gulf Coast states, still recovering from the havoc wrought by Hurricane Katrina in 2005, took another beating in 2010. On 20 April, the Deepwater Horizon oil rig (top), leased by British Petroleum (BP) and drilling some 50 miles (80.5 km) off the Louisiana coast, exploded, killing 11 workers and injuring 17. The blast set off a gusher of oil on the seabed floor that BP was unable to contain until 15 July, during which time an estimated 4.9 million barrels of crude oil leaked into the gulf, damaging fisheries, wildlife (at left, an oil-soaked pelican), and the coastal environment. The US government insisted that BP would pay all costs of cleaning up and restoring the region.

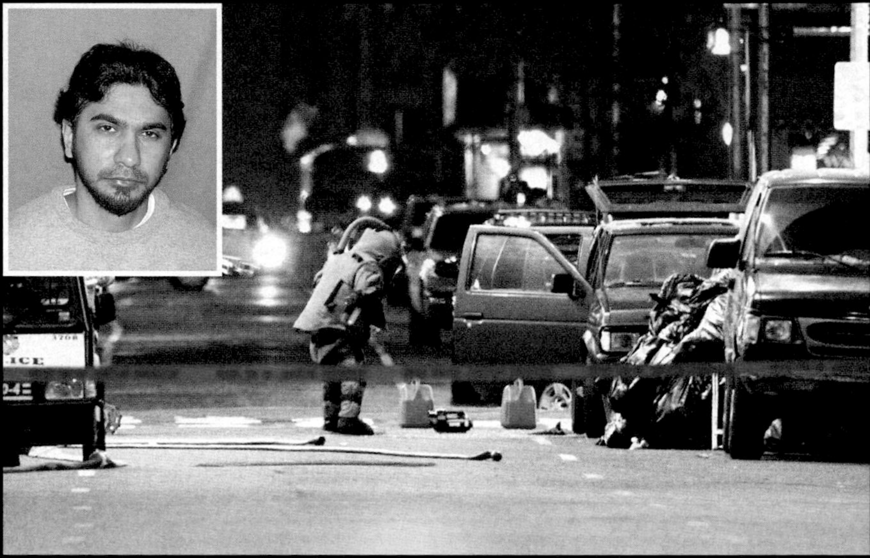

1 May 2010, New York NY: Authorities evacuated New York City's busy Times Square district after sidewalk vendors reported suspicious activity by the driver of an SUV, and police found an "amateurish" but potentially deadly bomb in the vehicle. Above, a member of the bomb squad investigates the SUV later that night. A suspect, Faisal Shahzad (inset), 30, a Pakistan-born resident of Connecticut and a US citizen since April 2009, was quickly arrested; police said he confessed to the deed and claimed he had trained for it in Pakistan.

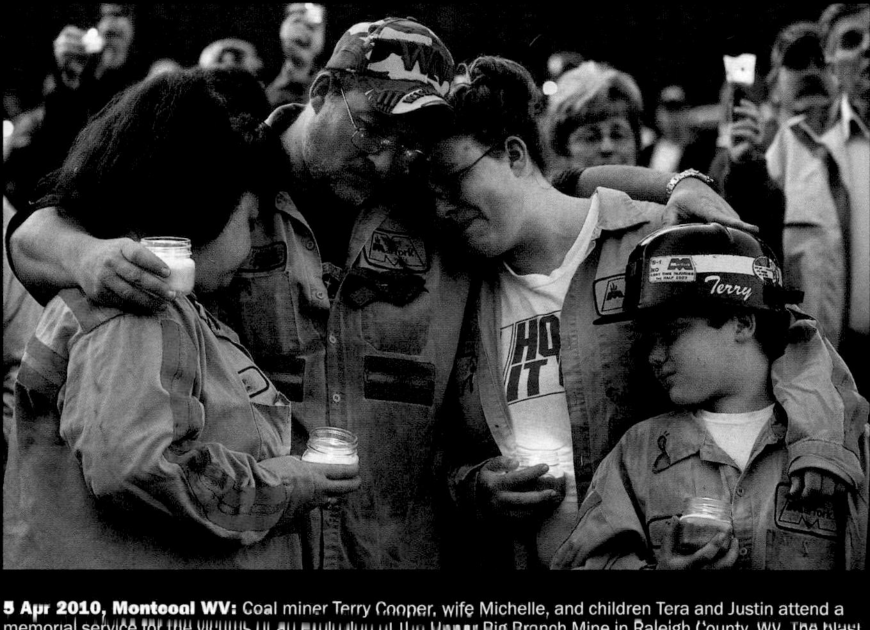

5 Apr 2010, Montcoal WV: Coal miner Terry Cooper, wife Michelle, and children Tera and Justin attend a memorial service for the victims of an explosion at the Upper Big Branch Mine in Raleigh County, WV. The blast killed 29 miners, making it the deadliest such accident in the US since 1970. The mine, operated by Massey Energy, had received 1,342 safety violations from federal regulators in the five years before the explosion.

CLOCKWISE FROM TOP LEFT: U.S. MARSHALS SERVICE/AP IMAGES; KEN GOLDFIELD/NEW YORK DAILY NEWS/AP IMAGES; MARK WILSON/GETTY IMAGES

Plate 8   UNITED STATES

23 Mar 2010, Washington DC: Pres. Barack Obama achieved his top domestic policy goal when he signed a 2,409-page health-care reform bill (inset) into law. Many Americans opposed the bill, which they viewed as a bold extension of federal power; Obama and his supporters called it an essential corrective to a broken system. Months later, on 21 July, the President signed a financial-reform law that he said would prevent future economic meltdowns like that of 2008. Below, Democratic Senators Chris Dodd, left, and majority leader Harry Reid hail the bill's passage.

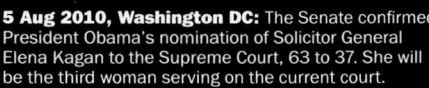

5 Aug 2010, Washington DC: The Senate confirmed President Obama's nomination of Solicitor General Elena Kagan to the Supreme Court, 63 to 37. She will be the third woman serving on the current court.

23 Apr 2010, Phoenix AZ: Arizona legislators passed a bill written to stem illegal immigration, calling on police to demand identity papers of those stopped for questioning who raised "reasonable suspicion" of being illegal. The law divided Americans, though polls showed most favored it. Before it went into effect, a federal judge issued an injunction blocking its most controversial aspects. Above, citizens take sides at rallies in late May.

23 Jun 2010, Washington DC: General Stanley McChrystal, commander of the US forces in Afghanistan, resigned his post after *Rolling Stone* magazine published quotes from the general and his staff that derided members of the administration. President Obama named General David Petraeus to assume the command.

27 Mar 2010, Searchlight NV: Former Alaska governor Sarah Palin, who resigned her position in 2009, spoke at a Tea Party rally. The 2008 GOP vice presidential candidate stumped the country to rally those opposed to the Obama administration, but she did not commit to running for the presidency in 2012.

Plate 10   BUSINESS & SOCIETY

9 Feb 2010, Norwood MA: Toyota, the top-selling auto line in the US, weathered a series of bumps in late 2009 and early 2010. The company issued multiple recalls for its popular models, two of which addressed problems with floor mats and gas pedals that resulted in unexpected acceleration. More than 8 million vehicles were recalled, but even so, the big automaker posted a profit of US$2.2 billion in the second quarter of 2010. Below, a mechanic works on the brake system of a recalled 2010 Prius model.

2 Apr 2010, Vatican City: Pope Benedict XVI prayed at a service during Holy Week, as the Roman Catholic Church continued to be battered by allegations that its leaders had sheltered priests who sexually abused young people in the past. The pope made his most explicit statements condemning such acts in 2010, but even his own decisions as a high-ranking prelate in Germany before his papacy came under fire during the year.

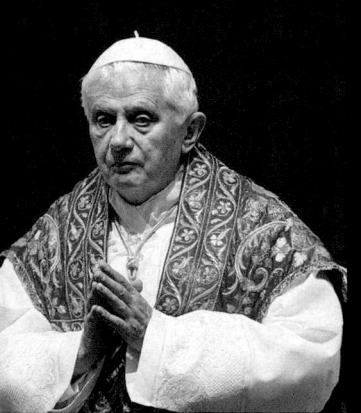

27 Jan 2010, San Francisco CA: Apple Computer CEO Steve Jobs unveils the new iPad tablet computer, operated by a touchscreen control system; it sold 3 million units in its first 80 days of release. In 2010 Apple's book value topped Microsoft's to make it the world's No. 1 technology company.

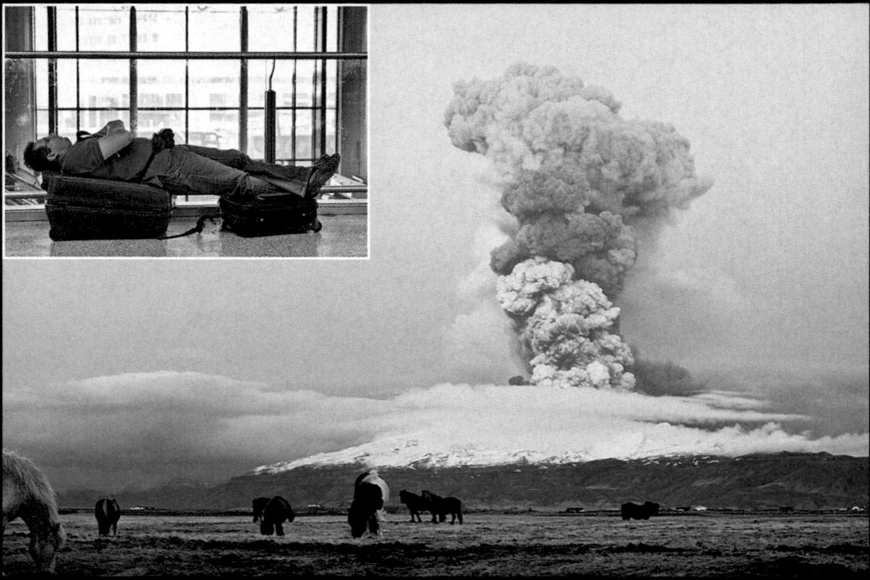

16 Apr 2010, Fimmvorduhals, Iceland: Horses graze in the foreground as a cloud of effluvia rises from the Eyjafjallajokull volcano two days after it first began explosive eruptions. The grit and ash rose to some 30,000 ft (9.1 km) and remained trapped in the airspace over the European continent, resulting in the delay or cancellation of thousands of flights across the globe and leaving travelers stranded in airports (inset).

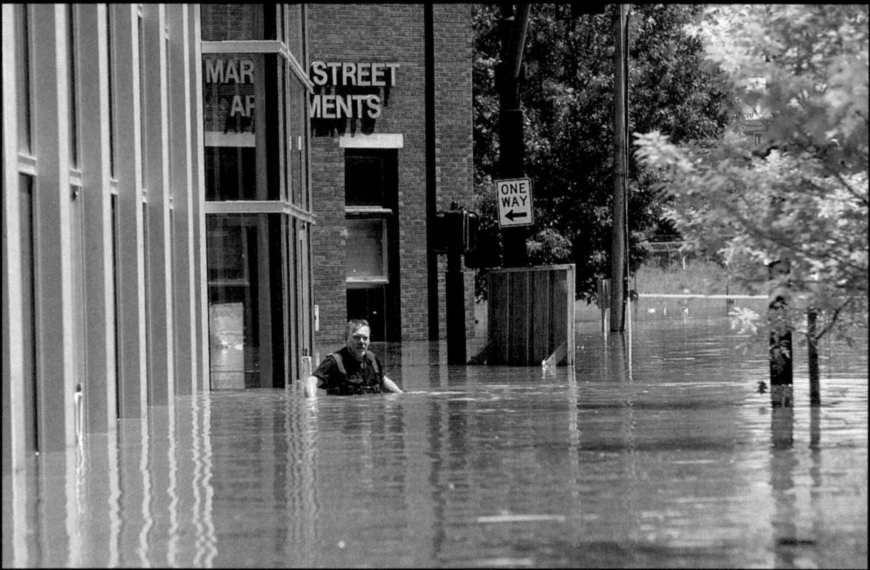

3 May 2010, Nashville TN: Torrential rains in early May caused deadly floods across a wide swath of Tennessee, northern Mississippi, and western Kentucky. Record crests were recorded throughout the region, and Nashville was particularly hard hit by flooding of the Cumberland River. Above, the city's downtown is chest-deep in floodwaters after Nashville received 13 inches of rain on May 1–2. At least 31 people died.

CLOCKWISE FROM TOP LEFT: ANDREAS SOLARO/AFP/GETTY IMAGES; SIGNY ASTA GUDMUNDSDOTTIR/NORDICPHOTOS/GETTY IMAGES; RUSTY RUSSELL/GETTY IMAGES

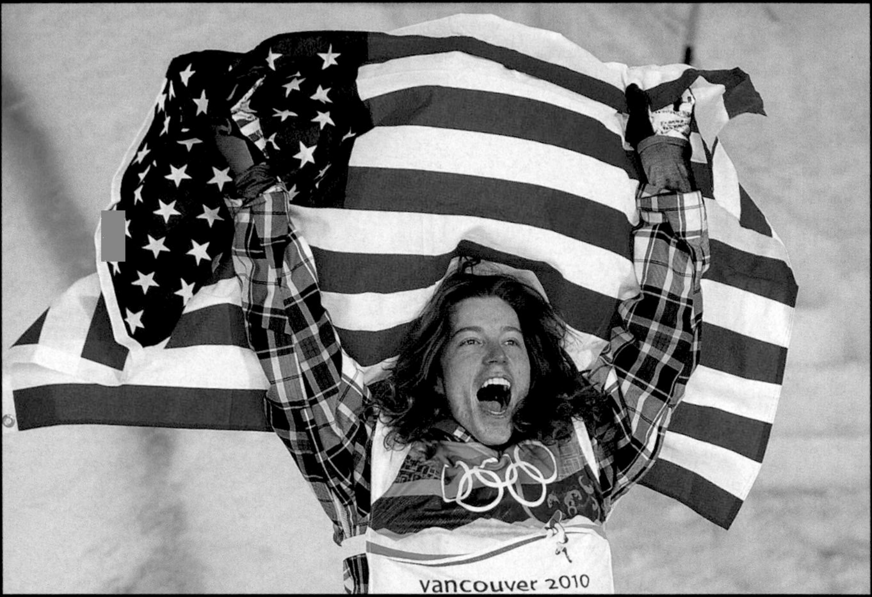

17 Feb 2010, Cypress Mountain, BC, Canada: US snowboarder Shaun White celebrates after winning the gold medal in the halfpipe competition at the 2010 Olympic Winter Games, which were held in and around Vancouver and Whistler in British Columbia. Host team Canada won the most gold medals, 14, including those for the national sports of hockey and curling. US athletes won the most medals overall, a total of 37.

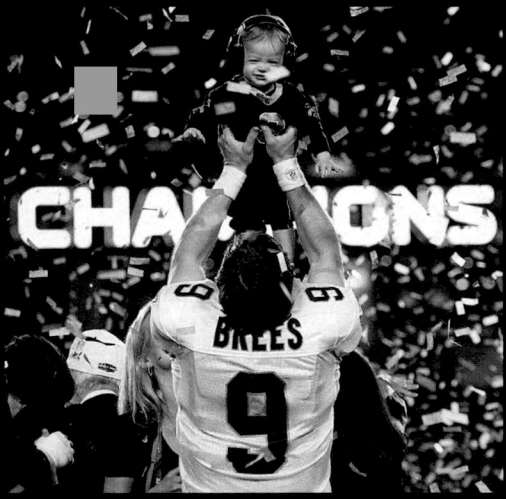

7 Feb 2010, Miami FL: New Orleans Saints quarterback Drew Brees hoists son Baylen after the Saints defeated the Indianapolis Colts, 31–17, to win the NFL title in Super Bowl XLIV. Brees was named MVP of the game. It was the Saints' first Super Bowl appearance; they were sentimental favorites among many fans, as the nation watched New Orleans recover from the devastation caused by Hurricane Katrina in 2005.

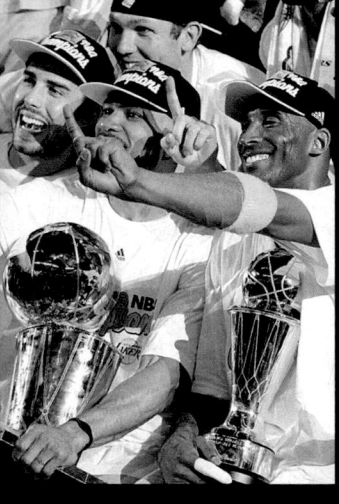

17 Jun 2010, Los Angeles CA: Led by Kobe Bryant, right, the Los Angeles Lakers topped the Boston Celtics, 83–79, in game 7 of the finals to become NBA champions for the 16th time. Bryant was named the series MVP. It was the 12th time that the two teams had fought for the league title.

CLOCKWISE FROM TOP: ADRIAN DENNIS/AFP/GETTY IMAGES; MARK J. TERRILL/AP IMAGES; ERIC GAY/AP IMAGES

4 Jun 2010, Paris, France: Spain's Rafael Nadal won the French Open for the fifth time; a month later, he won the Wimbledon tournament in England.

3 Jul 2010, Wimbledon, England: Serena Williams won the Wimbledon title for the second year in a row and fourth time in her career, defeating Russia's Vera Zvonareva in two sets.

19 Jul 2010, St. Andrews, Scotland: South Africa's Louis Oosthuizen won Britain's Open championship. Phil Mickelson won the Masters for the third time, Graeme McDowell of Northern Ireland won the US Open, and Germany's Martin Kaymer won the PGA tournament.

13 Jun 2010, Inglewood CA: Thoroughbred mare Zenyatta ran her unbeaten streak to 17 as she won the Vanity Handicap at Hollywood Park near Los Angeles. The 6-year-old has become a fan favorite with her signature style, in which she trails the entire field early in the race, then comes from last place in the closing stretch to win. A big horse with a big personality, Zenyatta went on to win her 18th straight victory in August.

Plate 14　　　ARTS, ENTERTAINMENT, & LEISURE

22 Feb 2010, Los Angeles CA: Directed by James Cameron and released late in 2009, science-fiction film *Avatar* showcased a new form of 3-D technology. It became one of the highest-grossing films of all time but garnered only three Academy Awards, all related to the movie's visuals.

11 Jun 2010, Los Angeles CA: Pixar Films, a unit of the Walt Disney Company, released the computer-generated *Toy Story 3*, a major box-office hit around the world.

20 Apr 2010, New York NY: The three members of acclaimed punk-rock band Green Day take a bow after the Broadway debut of the musical *American Idiot*, based on their 2004 album. From left are Billy Joe Armstrong, Tre Cool, and Mike Dirnt. TIME's Richard Zoglin hailed the show's "irresistible musical energy."

25 May 2010, Los Angeles CA: After its spring season ended in late May, Fox TV's hit *American Idol* entered a new era. Bad-cop judge Simon Cowell, center, and new judge Ellen DeGeneres, second from left, departed. Judges Randy Jackson, at left, and Kara DioGuardi, at right, seemed poised to stay on, as did host Ryan Seacrest, second from right.

22 Feb 2010, Los Angeles CA: Actor Sandra Bullock's three films made her the top box-office draw of 2009. The longtime fan favorite won the Academy Award for Best Actress for her role in *The Blind Side.*

31 Jan 2010, Los Angeles CA: Lady Gaga, a.k.a. Stefani Germanotta, 24, holds her two 2009 Grammy Awards. A glam-rocker in the tradition of David Bowie, Elton John, and Madonna, Gaga won fame for her danceable pop songs as well as her fashion-forward, tongue-in-cheek sense of style.

22 Jun 2010, Nashville TN: Pop-country star Taylor Swift sings at Nashville Rising, a benefit show that followed the floods in country music's capital city in early May. Swift, 20 in 2010, writes most of her songs and has made a rapid ascent to stardom: she was one of the top-selling recording artists in the US in 2009 and won four Grammy Awards in 2009. By 2010, she had sold more than 11 million albums.

Plate 16 **OBITUARIES**

J.D. Salinger: The famously reclusive author of *The Catcher in the Rye,* the great American coming-of-age novel of the 20th century, died on 19 January at 91 in Cornish NH, where he had lived in seclusion since the early 1960s.

Robert Byrd: The Democrat from West Virginia served 51 years in the US Senate, a record; he was also the longest-serving member of the US Congress in history. Famed for steering federal money to his impoverished state and for his command of Senate lore, the courtly solon died on 28 June at 92.

Dennis Hopper: The career of the great Hollywood iconoclast stretched from the beatnik era of the 1950s through the hippie days of 1969's *Easy Rider,* which he directed, to starring roles in a host of later, more mainstream films, in which he often portrayed off-beat villains. He died on 29 May at 74.

George Steinbrenner: The owner of the New York Yankees since 1973 was loved and hated in equal measure, but his famed temper mellowed in later years. "The Boss" was larger than life, and no one doubted his devotion to high standards. He died at 80 on 13 July.

Alexander Haig: A decorated veteran who rose to high command in the US Army, he later served in the Nixon, Ford, and Reagan White Houses. He died on 20 February at 85.

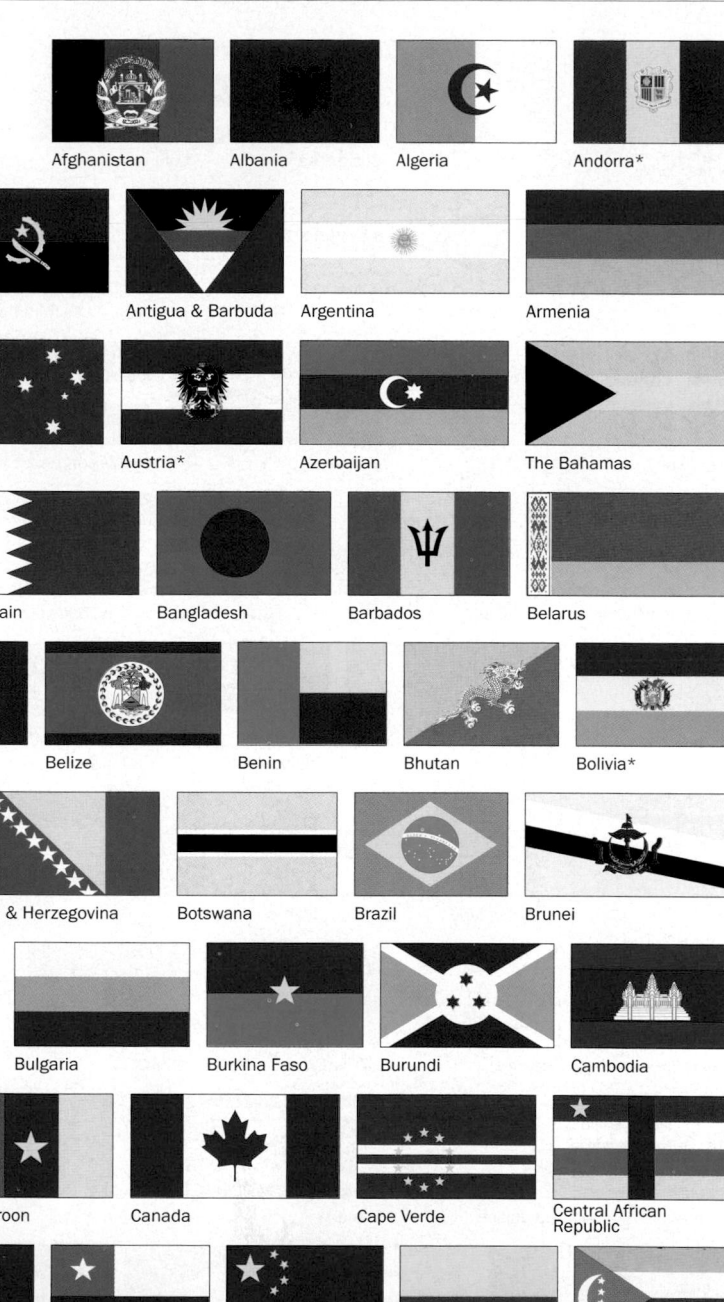

Afghanistan Albania Algeria Andorra*

Angola Antigua & Barbuda Argentina Armenia

Australia Austria* Azerbaijan The Bahamas

Bahrain Bangladesh Barbados Belarus

Belgium Belize Benin Bhutan Bolivia*

Bosnia & Herzegovina Botswana Brazil Brunei

Bulgaria Burkina Faso Burundi Cambodia

Cameroon Canada Cape Verde Central African Republic

Chad Chile China Colombia Comoros

Civil flags are shown except where marked thus (*); in these cases, government flags are shown in order to illustrate emblems. Both styles are official national flags.

Plate 18   FLAGS OF THE WORLD

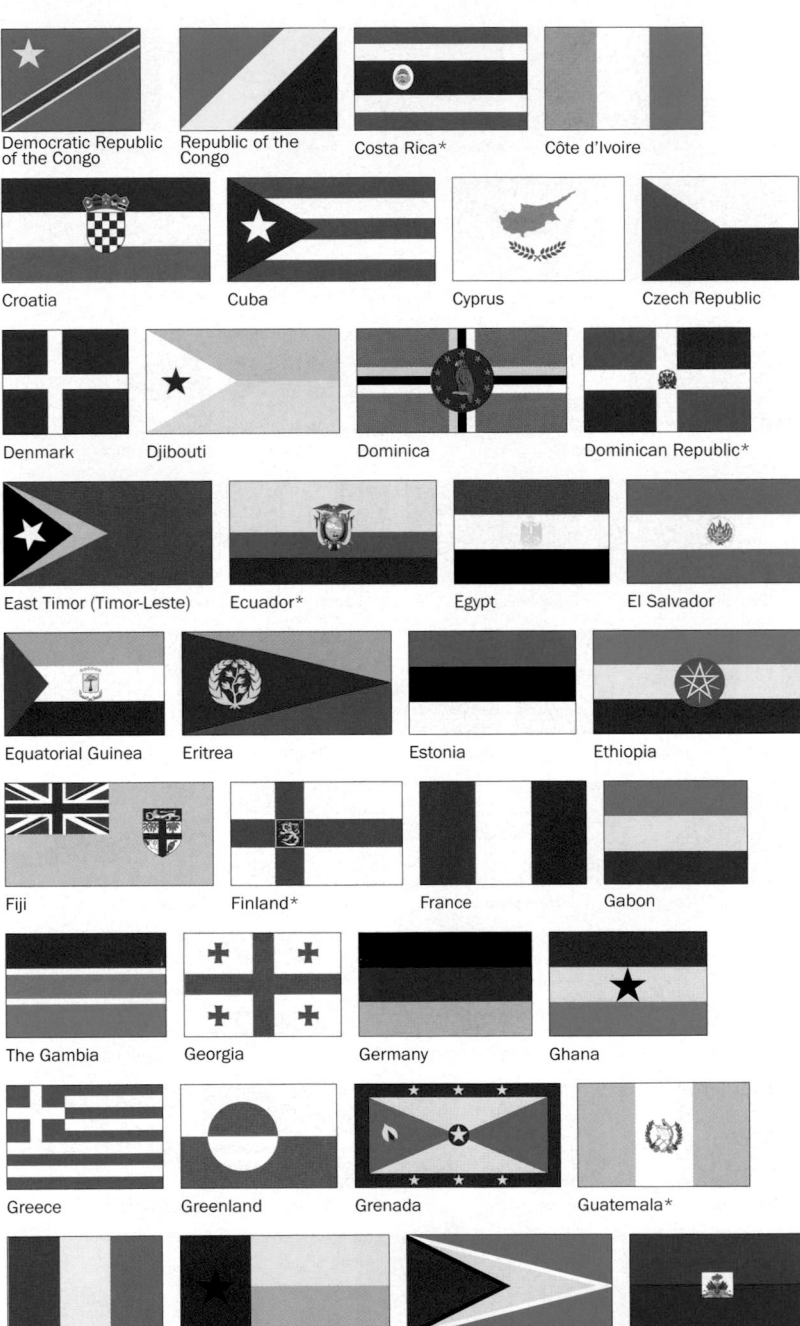

Democratic Republic of the Congo

Republic of the Congo

Costa Rica*

Côte d'Ivoire

Croatia

Cuba

Cyprus

Czech Republic

Denmark

Djibouti

Dominica

Dominican Republic*

East Timor (Timor-Leste)

Ecuador*

Egypt

El Salvador

Equatorial Guinea

Eritrea

Estonia

Ethiopia

Fiji

Finland*

France

Gabon

The Gambia

Georgia

Germany

Ghana

Greece

Greenland

Grenada

Guatemala*

Guinea

Guinea-Bissau

Guyana

Haiti*

Civil flags are shown except where marked thus (*); in these cases, government flags are shown in order to illustrate emblems. Both styles are official national flags.

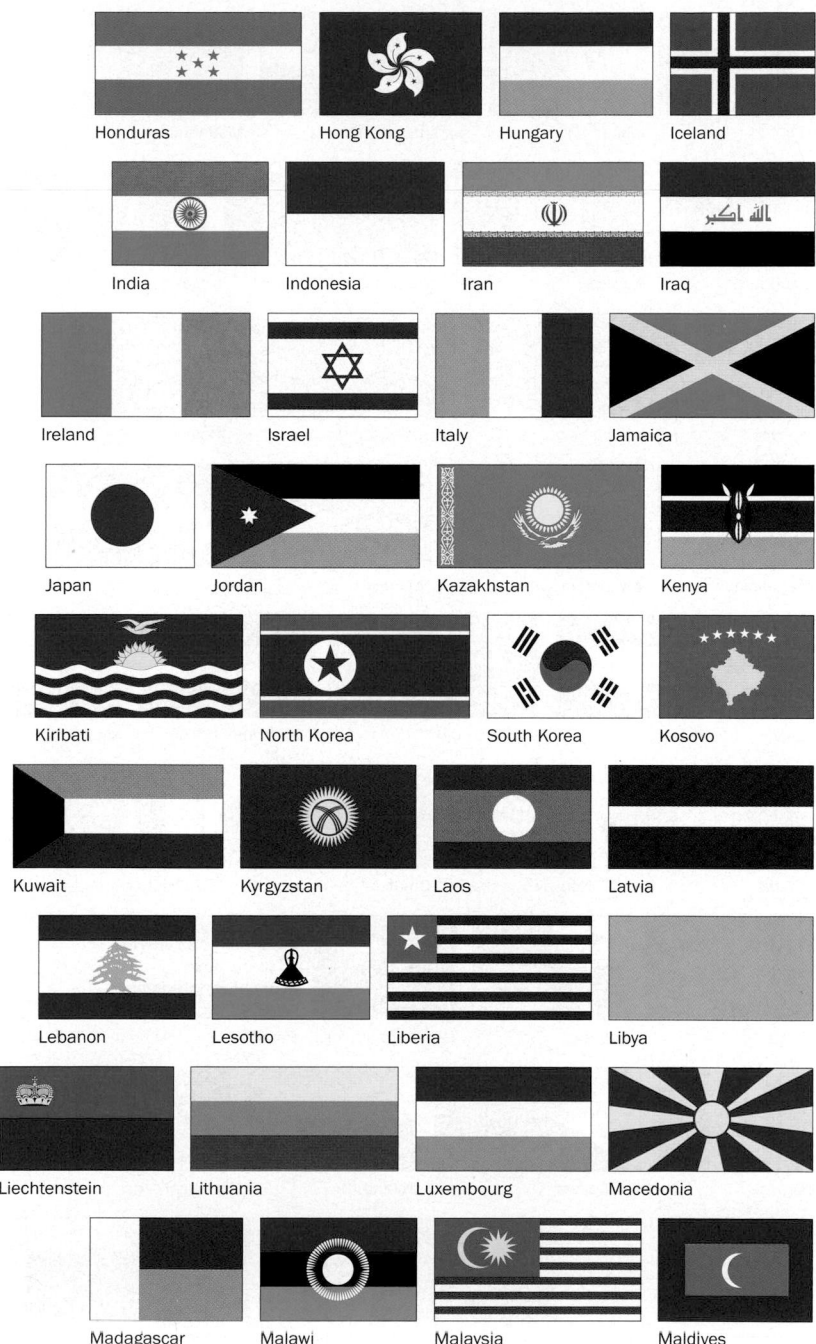

Honduras   Hong Kong   Hungary   Iceland

India   Indonesia   Iran   Iraq

Ireland   Israel   Italy   Jamaica

Japan   Jordan   Kazakhstan   Kenya

Kiribati   North Korea   South Korea   Kosovo

Kuwait   Kyrgyzstan   Laos   Latvia

Lebanon   Lesotho   Liberia   Libya

Liechtenstein   Lithuania   Luxembourg   Macedonia

Madagascar   Malawi   Malaysia   Maldives

Civil flags are shown except where marked thus (*); in these cases, government flags are shown in order to illustrate emblems. Both styles are official national flags.

Plate 20   FLAGS OF THE WORLD

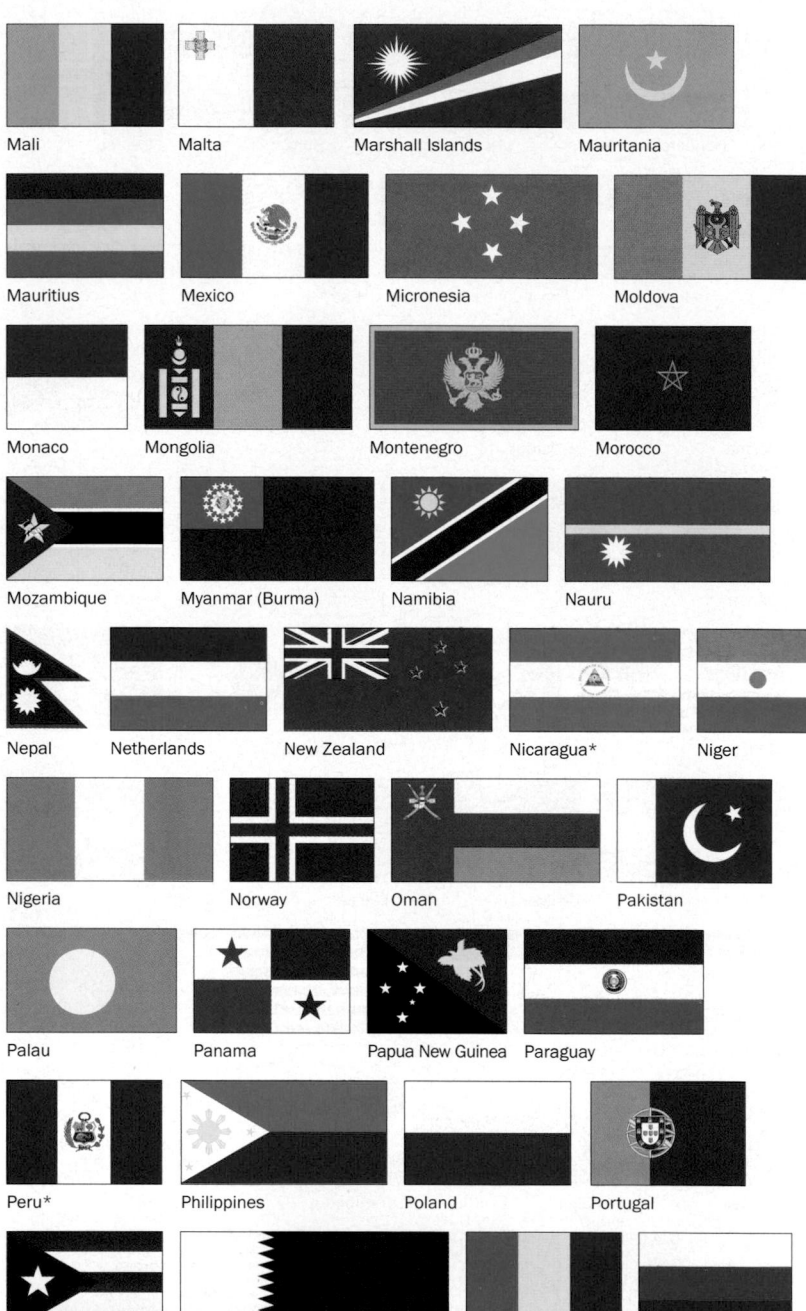

Mali   Malta   Marshall Islands   Mauritania

Mauritius   Mexico   Micronesia   Moldova

Monaco   Mongolia   Montenegro   Morocco

Mozambique   Myanmar (Burma)   Namibia   Nauru

Nepal   Netherlands   New Zealand   Nicaragua*   Niger

Nigeria   Norway   Oman   Pakistan

Palau   Panama   Papua New Guinea   Paraguay

Peru*   Philippines   Poland   Portugal

Puerto Rico   Qatar   Romania   Russia

Civil flags are shown except where marked thus (*); in these cases, government flags are shown in order to illustrate emblems. Both styles are official national flags.

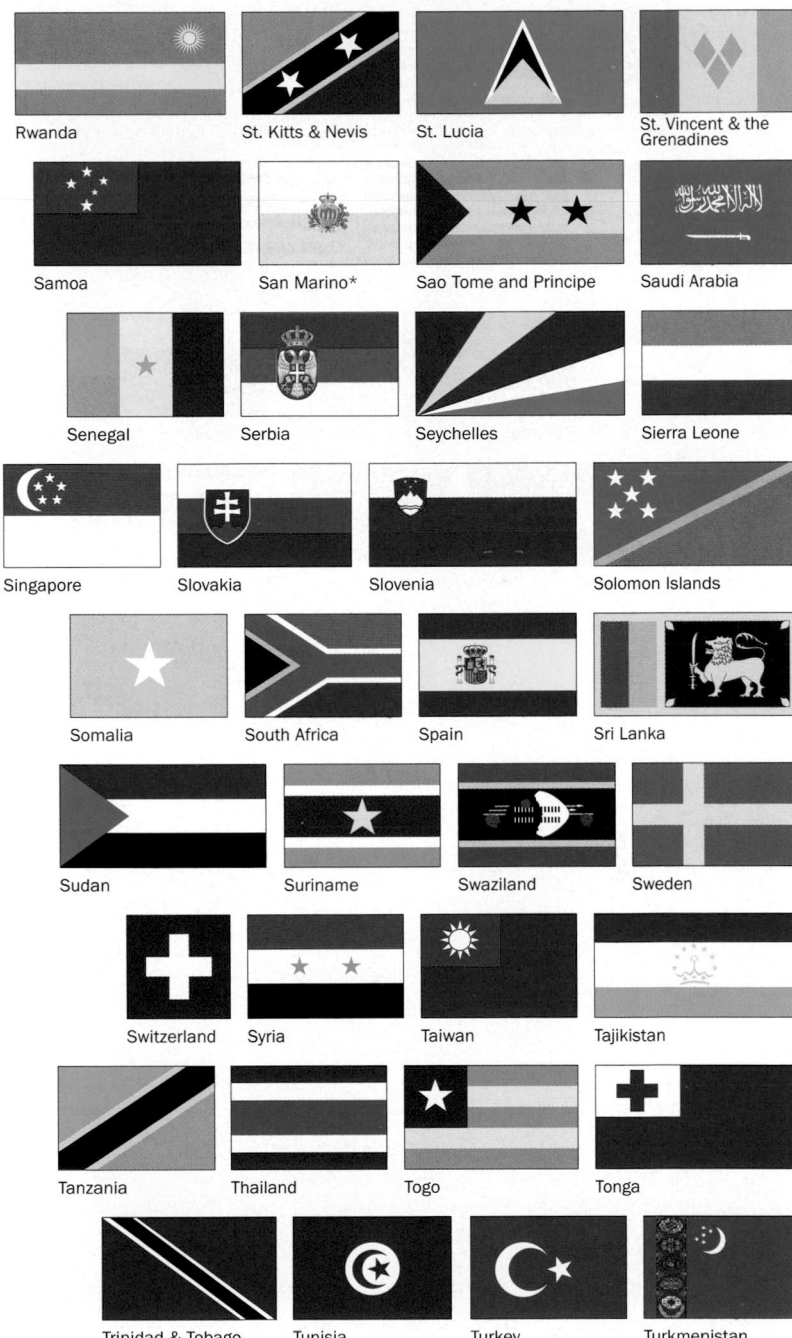

Rwanda

St. Kitts & Nevis

St. Lucia

St. Vincent & the Grenadines

Samoa

San Marino*

Sao Tome and Principe

Saudi Arabia

Senegal

Serbia

Seychelles

Sierra Leone

Singapore

Slovakia

Slovenia

Solomon Islands

Somalia

South Africa

Spain

Sri Lanka

Sudan

Suriname

Swaziland

Sweden

Switzerland

Syria

Taiwan

Tajikistan

Tanzania

Thailand

Togo

Tonga

Trinidad & Tobago

Tunisia

Turkey

Turkmenistan

Civil flags are shown except where marked thus (*); in these cases, government flags are shown in order to illustrate emblems. Both styles are official national flags.

Plate 22 **FLAGS OF THE WORLD**

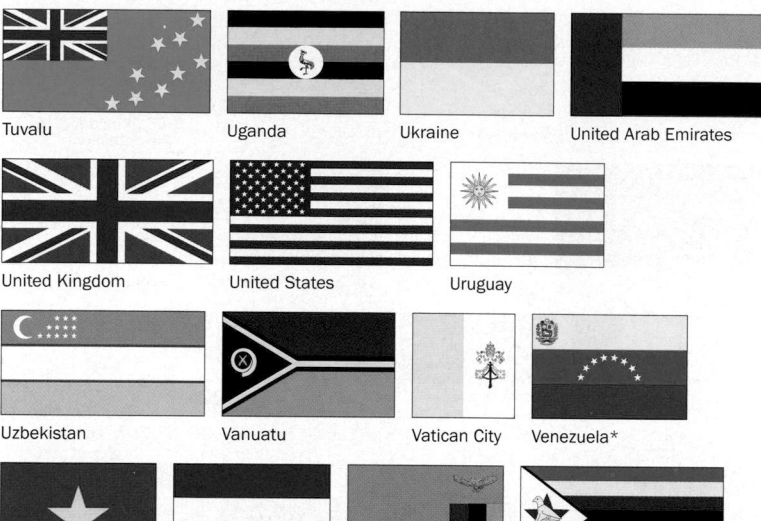

Tuvalu Uganda Ukraine United Arab Emirates

United Kingdom United States Uruguay

Uzbekistan Vanuatu Vatican City Venezuela*

Vietnam Yemen Zambia Zimbabwe

Civil flags are shown except where marked thus (*); in these cases, government flags are shown in order to illustrate emblems. Both styles are official national flags.

World Religions

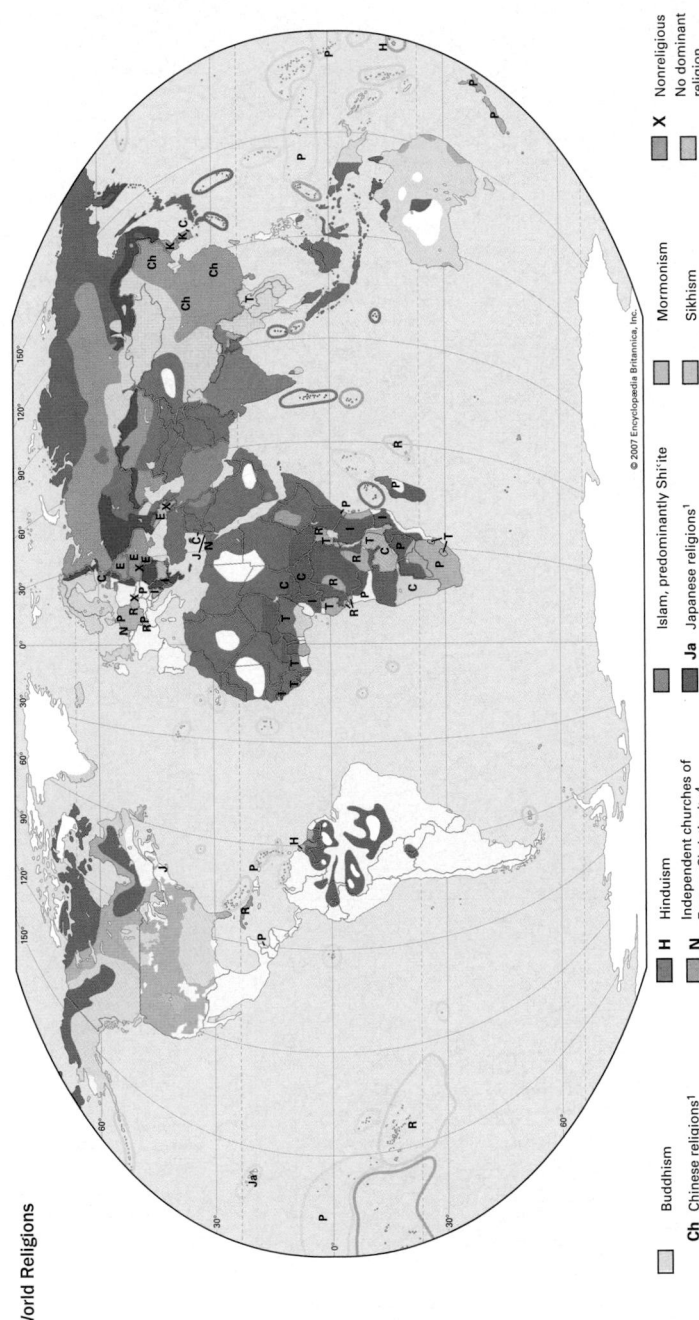

© 2007 Encyclopædia Britannica, Inc.

Buddhism

Ch Chinese religions[1]

Christianity, undifferentiated by branch[2]

E Eastern Orthodoxy[3]

H Hinduism

N Independent churches of Eastern Christianity[4]

Indigenous (tribal) religions

I Islam, predominantly Sunni

Islam, predominantly Shi'ite

Ja Japanese religions[1]

J Judaism

K Korean religions[1]

Mormonism

Sikhism

P Protestantism

R Roman Catholicism

X Nonreligious

No dominant religion

Uninhabited

Note:

The majority of the inhabitants in each of the areas colored on the map share the religious tradition indicated. Letter symbols show religious traditions shared by at least 25 percent of the inhabitants within areas no smaller than 1,000 square miles. Therefore minority religions of city dwellers have generally not been represented.

Footnotes:

[1] In certain eastern Asian areas, many of the people have plural religious affiliations. Religions in China and Korea include Buddhism, Taoism, Confucianism, and folk cults. The Japanese religions include Shinto and Buddhism.

[2] Chiefly mingled Protestantism and Roman Catholicism, neither predominant.

[3] Including Greek and Russian Orthodox Christianity.

[4] Including Armenian, Coptic, Ethiopian, East and West Syrian.

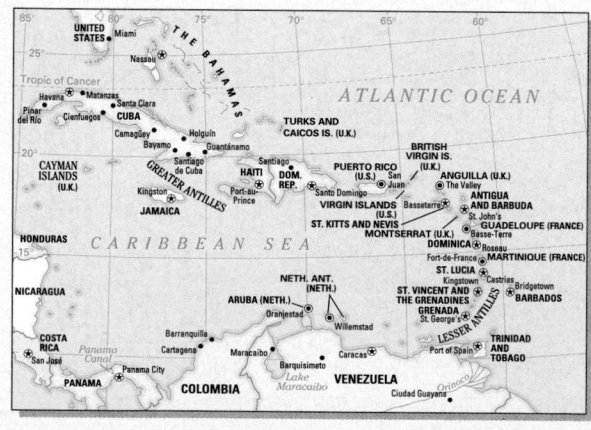
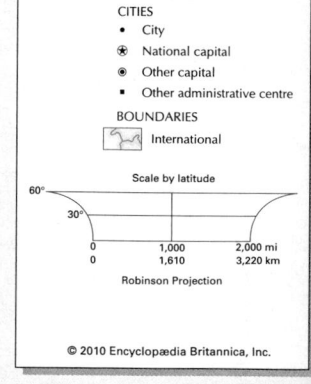

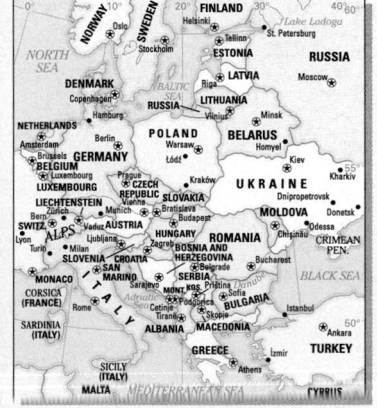

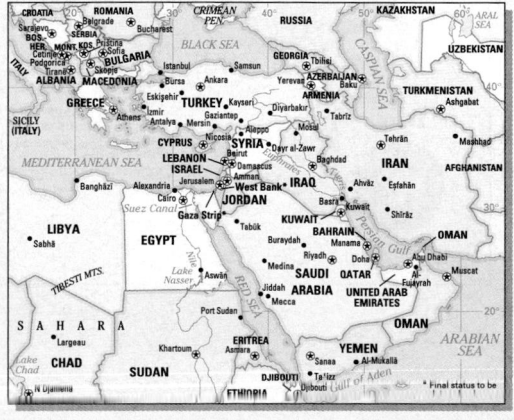

Plate 26

WORLD MAPS

Africa

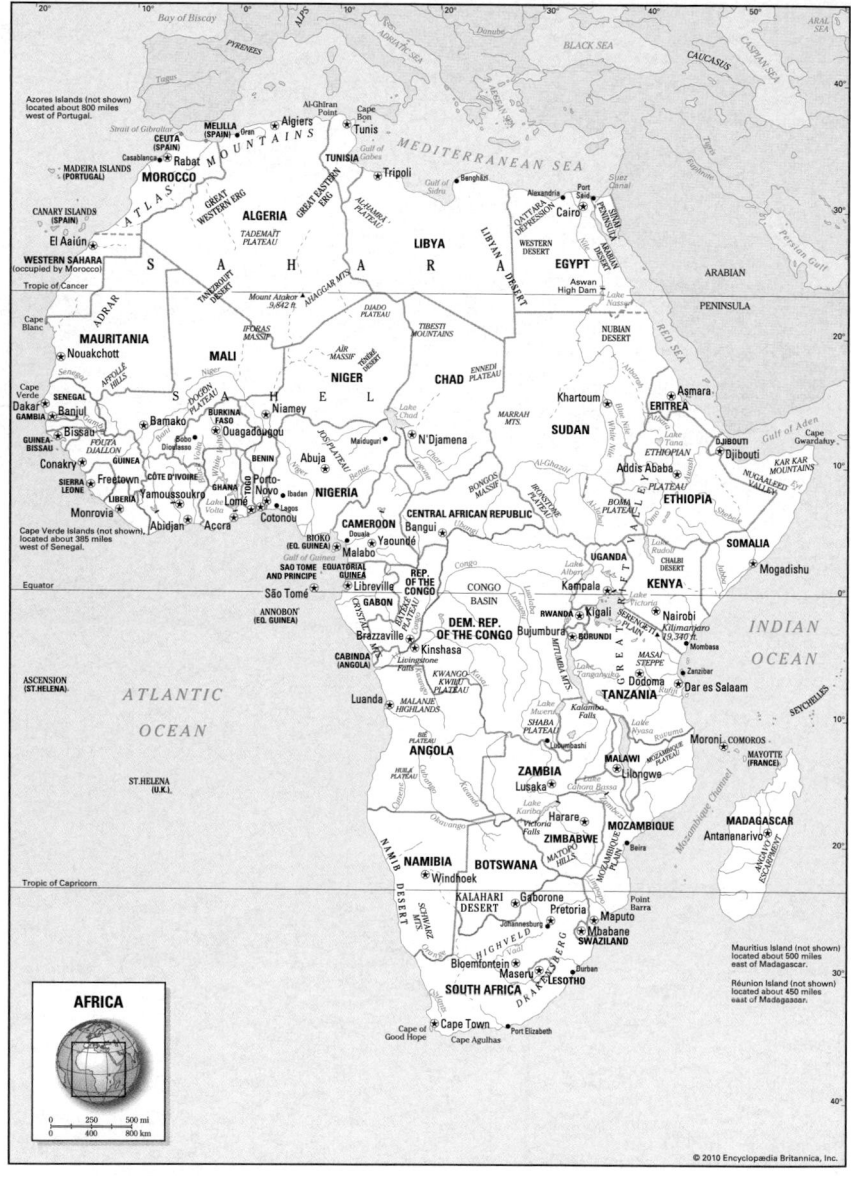

Azores Islands (not shown) located about 800 miles west of Portugal.

Cape Verde Islands (not shown), located about 385 miles west of Senegal.

Mauritius Island (not shown) located about 500 miles east of Madagascar.

Réunion Island (not shown) located about 450 miles east of Madagascar.

© 2010 Encyclopædia Britannica, Inc.

| 0 | 250 | 500 mi |
| 0 | 400 | 800 km |

Asia

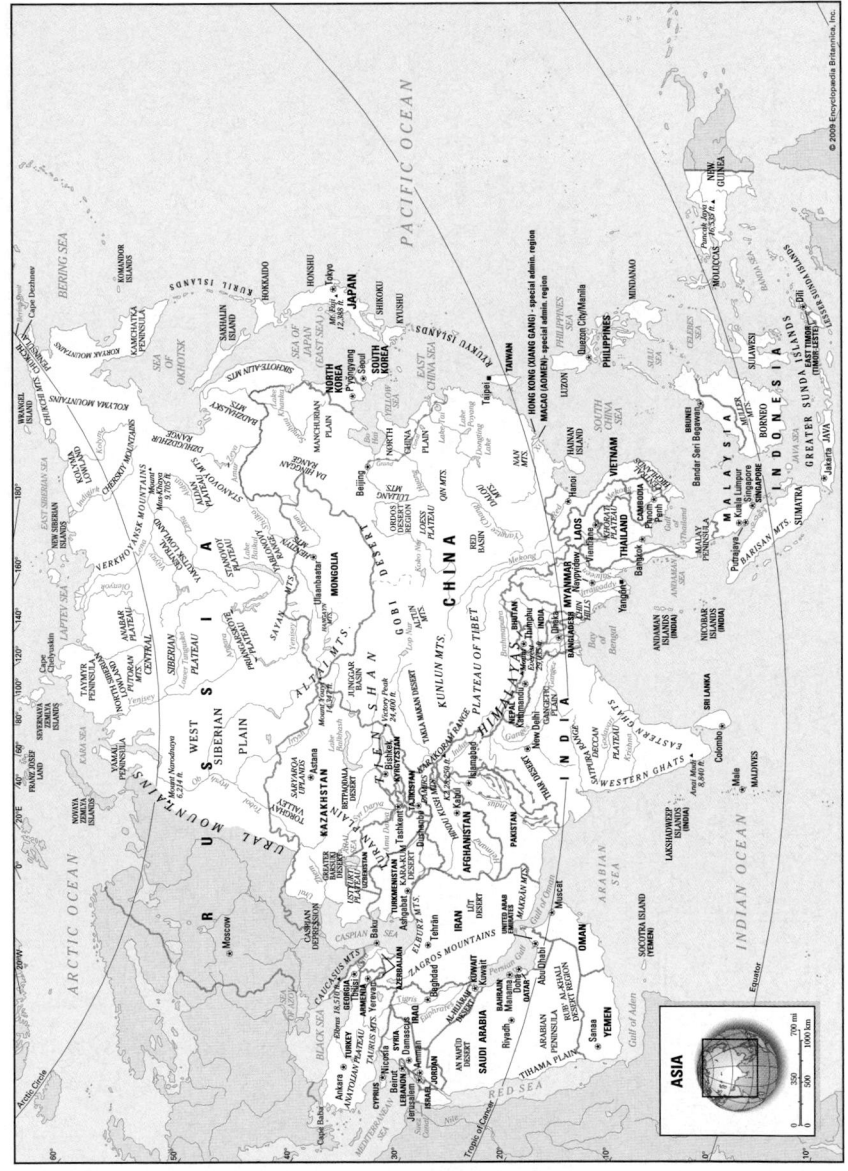

Plate 28　　WORLD MAPS

Europe

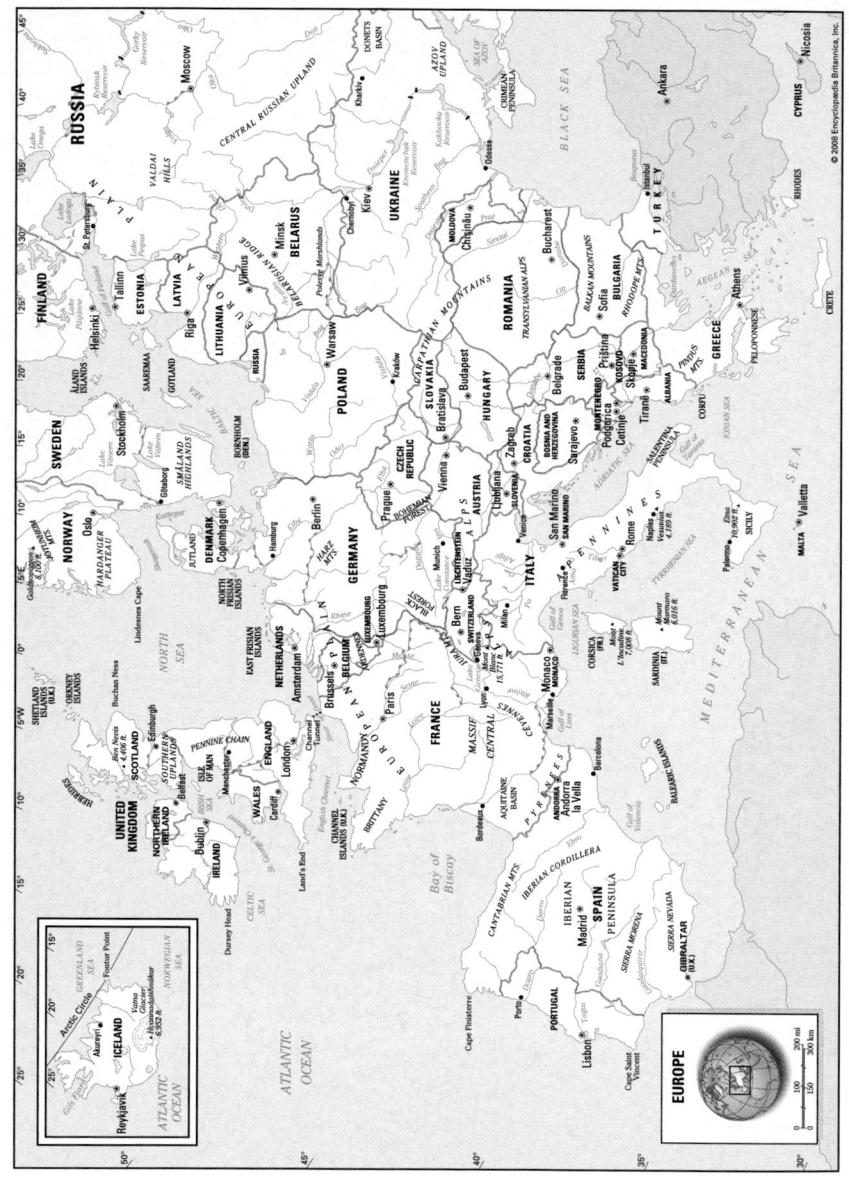

North America

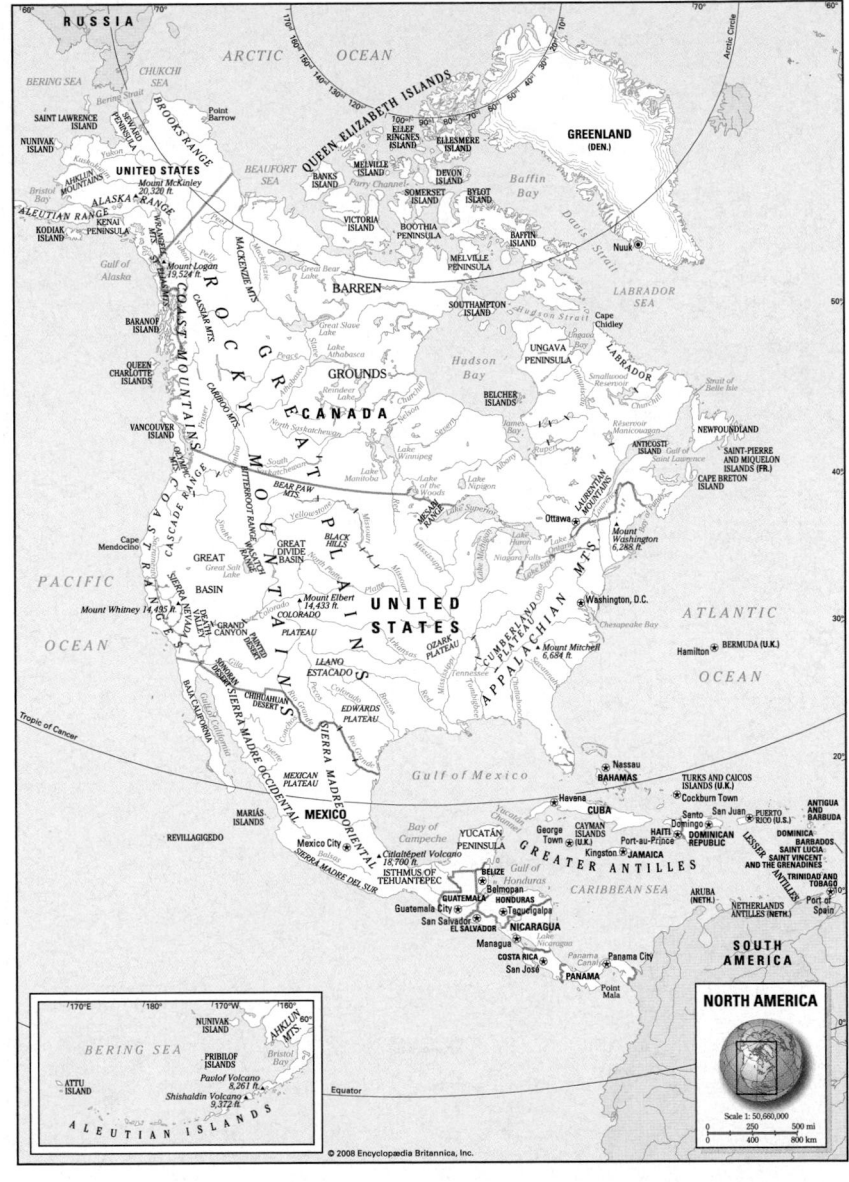

© 2008 Encyclopædia Britannica, Inc.

Plate 30 | WORLD MAPS

South America

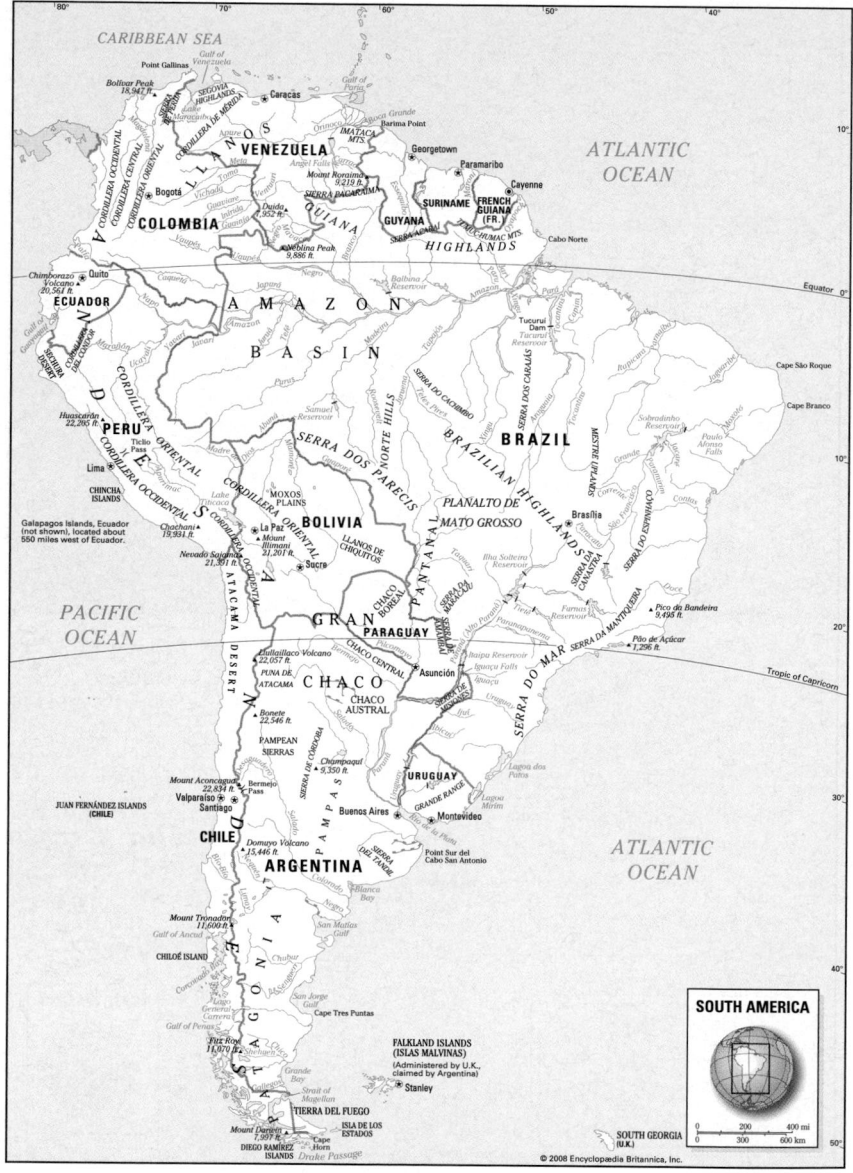

© 2008 Encyclopædia Britannica, Inc.

Australia

© 2008 Encyclopædia Britannica, Inc.

Plate 32

WORLD MAPS

Oceania/Pacific Islands

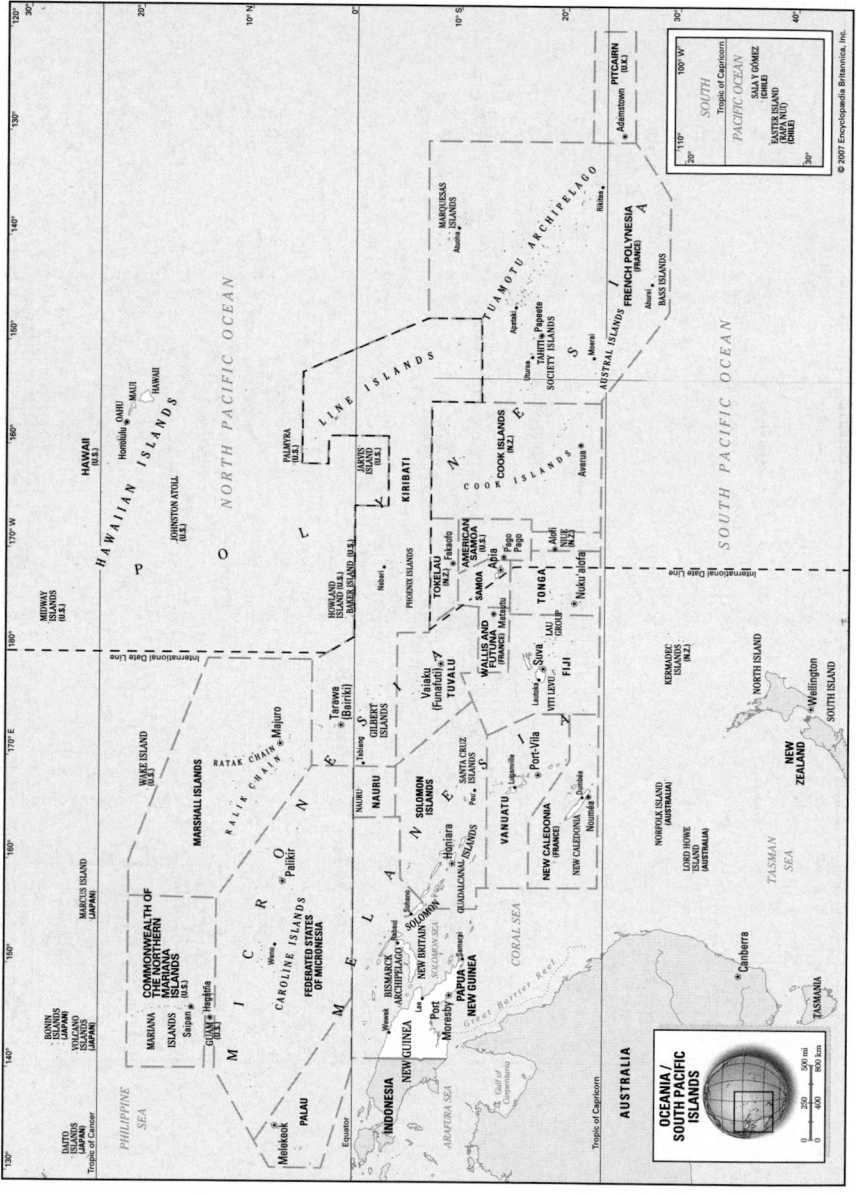

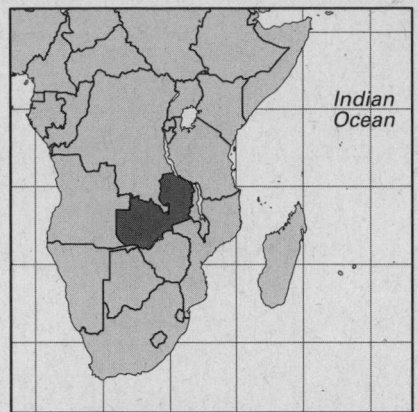

Indian Ocean

sq mi 44.5, persons per sq km 17.8. **Urban** (2008): 35.4%. **Sex distribution** (2005): male 49.75%; female 50.25%. **Age breakdown** (2005): under 15, 46.2%; 15–29, 30.6%; 30–44, 13.4%; 45–59, 6.1%; 60–74, 3.0%; 75–84, 0.6%; 85 and over, 0.1%. **Ethnic composition** (2000): Bemba 21.5%; Tonga 11.3%; Lozi 5.2%; Nsenga 5.1%; Tumbuka 4.3%; Ngoni 3.8%; Chewa 2.9%; other 45.9%. **Religious affiliation** (2000): Christian 82.4%, of which Roman Catholic 29.7%, Protestant (including Anglican) 28.2%, independent Christian 15.2%, unaffiliated Christian 5.5%; traditional beliefs 14.3%; Baha'i 1.8%; Muslim 1.1%; other 0.4%. **Major cities** (2006): Lusaka 1,306,600; Kitwe 408,300; Ndola 398,100; Kabwe 191,100; Chingola 148,600. **Location:** southern Africa, bordering Tanzania, Malawi, Mozambique, Zimbabwe, Botswana, Namibia, Angola, and the Democratic Republic of the Congo.

Vital statistics

Birth rate per 1,000 population (2008): 38.8 (world avg. 20.3). **Death rate** per 1,000 population (2008): 18.5 (world avg. 8.5). **Total fertility rate** (avg. births per childbearing woman; 2006): 5.39. **Life expectancy** at birth (2006): male 38.0 years; female 38.2 years.

National economy

Budget (2007). *Revenue:* K 10,094,600,000,000 (tax revenue 77.3%, of which income tax 33.1%, VAT 24.1%; grants 20.4%; nontax revenue 2.3%). *Expenditures:* K 12,034,400,000,000 (education 16.9%; economic affairs 14.1%; housing and community amenities 12.2%; defense 8.2%; public order 6.8%; public debt 6.0%; health 3.8%). **Production** (metric tons except as noted). *Agriculture and fishing* (2007): sugarcane 2,500,000, corn (maize) 1,366,158, cassava 940,000, seed cotton 160,000, sunflower seeds 8,200, fresh-cut flowers (value of sales; 2000) US$21,000,000; livestock (number of live animals) 2,610,000 cattle, 1,275,000 goats, 340,000 pigs; fisheries production 70,125 (from aquaculture 7%). *Mining and quarrying* (2007): copper (metal content) 520,000,000, cobalt (metal content) 7,600; amethyst 1,200,000 kg; emeralds 2,500 kg. *Manufacturing*

(2005): cement 435,000; refined copper 399,000; vegetable oils (2001) 11,800; refined cobalt 5,422. *Energy production (consumption):* electricity (kW-hr; 2006) 9,385,000,000 (9,130,000,000); coal (metric tons; 2006) 244,000 (171,000); crude petroleum (barrels; 2006) none (4,266,000); petroleum products (metric tons; 2006) 525,000 (577,000). **Selected balance of payments data.** Receipts from (US$'000,000): tourism (2007) 138; remittances (2008) 59; foreign direct investment (FDI; 2005–07 avg.) 652; official development assistance (2007) 1,045. Disbursements for (US$'000,000): tourism (2007) 56; remittances (2008) 124. **Population economically active** (2000): total 3,165,200; activity rate of total population 32.0% (participation rates: ages 12–64, 55.8%; female 41.3%; unemployed 12.7%). **Gross national income** (2008): US$11,986,000,000 (US$950 per capita). **Public debt** (external, outstanding; 2007): US$1,136,000,000.

Foreign trade

Imports (2006; c.i.f.): US$3,074,000,000 (machinery and apparatus 29.7%, of which industrial machinery and equipment 19.5%; chemical products 14.6%; crude petroleum 13.6%; motor vehicles 10.0%). *Major import sources:* South Africa 47.0%; UAE 10.4%; Zimbabwe 5.7%; Norway 4.0%; UK 3.7%. **Exports** (2006; f.o.b.): US$3,770,000,000 (refined copper 67.9%; copper ore and concentrate 11.2%; cobalt 3.8%; food products 3.8%). *Major export destinations:* Switzerland 39.8%; South Africa 11.0%; Thailand 7.7%; China 6.8%; Egypt 4.2%.

Transport and communications

Transport. *Railroads* (1998): length (2006) 2,157 km; passenger-km 586,000,000; metric ton-km cargo 702,000,000. *Roads* (2001): total length 91,440 km (paved 22%). *Vehicles* (2008): passenger cars 172,670; trucks and buses 91,835. *Air transport* (2006; Zambian Airways Limited only): passenger-km 56,609,000; metric ton-km cargo, none. **Communications,** in total units (units per 1,000 persons). Telephone landlines (2008): 91,000 (7.2); cellular telephone subscribers (2008): 3,539,000 (280); personal computers (2005): 131,000 (11); total Internet users (2008): 700,000 (56); broadband Internet subscribers (2007): 5,700 (0.4).

Education and health

Educational attainment (2001–02). Percentage of population ages 15 and over having: no formal schooling/unknown 14.7%; some primary education 33.4%; completed primary 19.7%; some secondary 22.0%; completed secondary 5.9%; higher 4.3%. **Literacy** (2007): population ages 15 and over literate 83.5%; males literate 88.5%; females literate 78.6%. **Health** (2004): physicians 1,264 (1 per 8,672 persons); hospital beds 21,924 (1 per 500 persons); infant mortality rate per 1,000 live births (2008) 90.4; undernourished population (2003–05) 5,100,000 (40% of total population based on the consumption of a minimum daily requirement of 1,750 calories).

Military

Total active duty personnel (November 2008): 15,100 (army 89.4%; navy, none; air force 10.6%). Military expenditure as percentage of GDP (2007): 2.2%; per capita expenditure US$20.

Background

Archaeological evidence suggests that early humans roamed present-day Zambia one to two million years ago. Ancestors of the modern Tonga tribe reached the region early in the 2nd millennium BC, but other modern peoples from Congo and Angola reached the country only in the 17th and 18th centuries AD. Portuguese trading missions were established early in the 18th century. Emissaries of Cecil Rhodes and the British South Africa Co. concluded treaties with most of the Zambian chiefs during the 1890s. The company administered the region known as Northern Rhodesia until 1924, when it became a British protectorate. It was part of the Central African Federation of Rhodesia and Nyasaland in 1953–63. In 1964 Northern Rhodesia became the independent republic of Zambia. A constitutional amendment was passed in 1990 allowing opposition parties; the following years were filled with political tension.

Recent Developments

The effects of the global recession on Zambia's economy in 2009 were mitigated by high copper prices, which were driven by strong demand from China, the world's largest consumer. Global electronics manufacturers also sustained demand and investment in mining. By the end of the year, copper prices had more than doubled. To reduce overdependence on the mining sector, which supplied most of the country's foreign earnings, the World Bank and other international agencies urged Zambia to develop alternative sources of revenue, including tourism and agriculture. Although poverty continued to be a serious problem, the economy had strengthened. Inflation topped 12%, but economic growth was anticipated to exceed 5% in 2009–10.

Internet resource: <www.zambiatourism.com>.

Zimbabwe

Official name: Republic of Zimbabwe. Form of government: transitional regime with two legislative houses (Senate [93]; House of Assembly [210]). Heads of state and government: President Robert Mugabe (from 1987), assisted by Prime Minister Morgan Tsvangirai (from 2009). Capital: Harare. Official language: English. Official religion: none. Monetary unit: 1 (redenominated) Zimbabwe dollar (Z$) = 100 cents; the use of the Zimbabwe dollar as legal currency was suspended indefinitely on 12 Apr 2009, because of long-term hyperinflation. Multiple foreign currencies (including the US dollar and South African rand) became legal tender in January 2009.

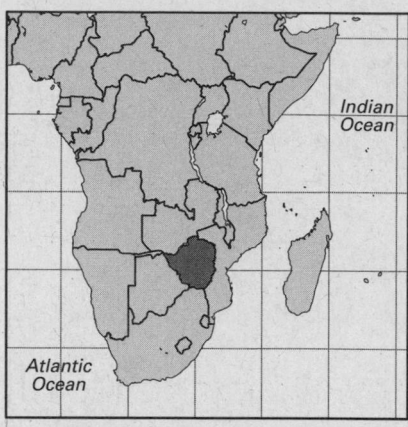

Demography

Area: 150,872 sq mi, 390,757 sq km. Population (2009): 12,523,000 (includes 3 million Zimbabweans living outside of the country, many of whom are in South Africa). Density (2009): persons per sq mi 83.0, persons per sq km 32.0. Urban (2008): 37.2%. Sex distribution (2008): male 47.40%; female 52.60%. Age breakdown (2008): under 15, 43.9%; 15–29, 28.8%; 30–44, 13.9%; 45–59, 7.9%; 60–74, 4.1%; 75 and over, 1.4%. Ethnic composition (2003): Shona 71%; Ndebele 16%; other African 11%; white 1%; mixed race/Asian 1%. Religious affiliation (2005): African independent Christian 38%; traditional beliefs 25%; Protestant 14%; Roman Catholic 8%; Muslim 1%; other (mostly unaffiliated Christian) 14%.. Major cities (2002): Harare (2007) 1,572,000; Bulawayo 676,787; Chitungwiza 321,782; Mutare 170,106; Gweru 141,260. Location: southern Africa, bordering Mozambique, South Africa, Botswana, Namibia, and Zambia.

Vital statistics

Birth rate per 1,000 population (2008): 31.6 (world avg. 20.3). Death rate per 1,000 population (2008): 17.3 (world avg. 8.5). Total fertility rate (avg. births per childbearing woman; 2008): 3.72. Life expectancy at birth (2008): male 45.1 years; female 43.5 years.

National economy

Budget (2008). Revenue: US$133,000,000 (tax revenue 96.2%, of which customs duties 33.8%, VAT 24.1%, income tax 16.5%, corporate taxes 13.5%; nontax revenue 3.8%). Expenditures: US$255,-000,000 (current expenditures 94.5%, of which debt service 54.5%, wages and salaries 20.4%, transfer payments 7.1%; capital expenditures 5.5%). Public debt (external, outstanding; 2007): US$3,735,-000,000. Population economically active (2008): total 5,836,000; activity rate of total population 46.8% (participation rates: ages 15–64 [2003] 74.0%; female 43.2%; unofficially unemployed

[2009] 95.0%). **Production** (metric tons except as noted). *Agriculture and fishing* (2007): sugarcane 3,600,000, corn (maize) 952,600, seed cotton 235,000; livestock (number of live animals) 5,400,000 cattle, 3,000,000 goats, 630,000 pigs; fisheries production 12,950 (from aquaculture 19%). *Mining and quarrying* (2007): chromite 650,000; asbestos 100,000; nickel (metal content) 7,100; cobalt (metal content) 50; platinum-group metals (palladium, platinum, rhodium, ruthenium, and iridium) 11,150 kg; gold 6,750 kg; diamonds 695,015 carats. *Manufacturing* (value added in US$'000,000; 1998): beverages 171; food products 148; textiles 99. *Energy production (consumption):* electricity (kW-hr; 2008) 8,890,000,000 (10,890,000,000); coal (metric tons; 2006) 3,447,000 (3,521,000); petroleum products (metric tons; 2006) none (624,000). **Gross national income** (2008): US$3,892,117,285 (US$312 per capita). **Selected balance of payments data.** Receipts from (US$'000,000): tourism (2007) 365; remittances (2008) 361; foreign direct investment (FDI; 2005–07 avg.) 71; official development assistance (2007) 465. Disbursements for (US$'000,000): tourism (1998) 131; FDI (2005–07 avg.) 1.3.

Foreign trade

Imports (2007; c.i.f.): US$3,594,400,000 (refined petroleum products 15.7%; chemical products 12.6%; transportation equipment 9.3%; food products and live animals 7.9%; base metals 4.7%). *Major import sources:* South Africa 42.8%; Botswana 11.4%; China 5.7%; Mozambique 4.8%; Malawi 4.8%. **Exports** (2007; f.o.b.): US$3,310,200,000 (base metals 18.8%, of which iron and steel 12.6%, nickel 5.9%; machinery and apparatus 10.7%, of which transportation equipment 5.4%; food products and live animals 8.6%; beverages and tobacco products 8.4%; textile fibers 4.0%). *Major export destinations:* South Africa 37.4%; Mozambique 13.0%; UK 7.4%; Botswana 6.1%; Netherlands 4.6%.

Transport and communications

Transport. *Railroads:* route length (2008) 3,077 km; passenger-km (1998) 408,223,000; metric ton-km cargo (2004) 1,377,000. *Roads* (2002): total length 97,267 km (paved 19%). *Vehicles* (2002): passenger cars 570,866; trucks and buses 84,456. *Air transport:* passenger-km (2006; Air Zimbabwe only) 671,185,000; metric ton-km cargo (2007) 8,000,000. **Communications,** in total units (units per 1,000 persons). Telephone landlines (2008): 348,000 (28); cellular telephone subscribers (2008): 1,655,000 (133); personal computers (2007): 1,257,000 (101); total Internet users (2008): 1,421,000 (114); broadband Internet subscribers (2008): 17,000 (1.4).

Education and health

Educational attainment (2005–06). Percentage of population ages 25 and over having: no formal schooling/unknown 13.6%; incomplete primary education 32.8%; complete primary 5.1%; incomplete secondary 42.0%; complete secondary 1.2%; vocational/higher 5.3%. **Literacy** (2007): percentage of total population ages 15 and over literate 92.8%; males literate 95.8%; females literate 89.9%.

Health: physicians (2004) 2,086 (1 per 5,792 persons); hospital beds (2006) 37,377 (1 per 333 persons); infant mortality rate per 1,000 live births (2008) 33.9; undernourished population (2002–04) 6,000,000 (47% of total population based on the consumption of a minimum daily requirement of 1,840 calories).

Military

Total active duty personnel (November 2008): 29,000 (army 86.2%; navy, none; air force 13.8%). **Military expenditure as percentage of GDP** (2005): 2.3%; per capita expenditure US$11.

Background

Remains of Stone Age cultures dating back 500,000 years have been found in the Zimbabwe area. The first Bantu-speaking peoples reached it during the 5th–10th centuries AD, driving the San (Bushmen) inhabitants into the desert. A second migration of Bantu speakers began about 1830. During this period the British and the Afrikaners moved up from the south, and the area came under the administration of the British South Africa Co. in 1889–1923. Called Southern Rhodesia (1911–64), it became a self-governing British colony in 1923. The colony united in 1953 with Nyasaland (Malawi) and Northern Rhodesia (Zambia) to form the Central African Federation of Rhodesia and Nyasaland. The federation dissolved in 1963, and Southern Rhodesia reverted to its former colonial status; beginning in 1964 it called itself Rhodesia. In 1965 it issued a unilateral declaration of independence considered illegal by the British government, which led to economic sanctions against it. The country proclaimed itself a republic in 1970. In 1979 it instituted limited majority rule and changed its name to Zimbabwe Rhodesia. It was granted independence by Britain in 1980 and became Zimbabwe. A multiparty system was established in 1990. The economy began to experience a decline in the 1990s that accelerated dramatically in the 2000s. In 2008 long-simmering political tensions between the ruling party and the opposition led to a hotly contested presidential election that sparked a protracted political crisis and exacerbated the country's economic troubles and deteriorating health and welfare conditions. An agreement for a power-sharing government, reached in September 2008, was implemented in February 2009.

Did you know? The Rhodesian ridgeback hails from what is now the country of Zimbabwe. Bred to be hunters and protectors, these dogs are famous for their skill in hunting lions.

Recent Developments

Zimbabwe had set an unenviable record at the end of 2008 as the second most extreme example of hyperinflation in world history (after Hungary in 1946). In February 2009 the government devalued the Zimbabwe dollar, dropping 12 zeros to make Z$1 trillion of the old currency redenominated to Z$1.00. Then in April the government suspended the Zimbabwe dollar, opting to allow the use of selected foreign currencies, notably the South African rand and the US dollar, in financial transactions. This gambit proved to be effective, as by year's end GDP was projected to grow by 6–7% in 2010.

Internet resource: <www.rbz.co.zw>.

Antarctica

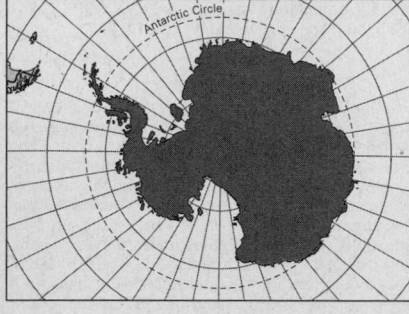

Background

The Russian F.G. von Bellingshausen, the Englishman Edward Bransfield, and the American Nathaniel Palmer all claimed first sightings of the continent in 1820. The period from the 1760s to 1900 was dominated by the exploration of Antarctic and subantarctic seas. In the early 20th century, the "heroic era" of Antarctic exploration, Robert Scott and, later, Ernest Shackleton made expeditions deep into the interior. Roald Amundsen reached the South Pole in December 1911, and Scott followed in 1912. The first half of the 20th century was also Antarctica's colonial period. Seven nations claimed sectors of the continent, while many other nations carried out explorations. In 1957–58, 12 nations established over 50 stations on the continent for cooperative study. In 1961 the Antarctic Treaty, which reserved Antarctica for free and nonpolitical scientific study, was enacted. A 1991 agreement imposed a 50-year ban on mineral exploitation.

Recent Developments

At the 32nd Antarctic Treaty Consultative Meeting, held in Baltimore MD in April 2009, more than 400 diplomats, Antarctic program managers, and polar scientists from 47 countries agreed to prohibit landings by tourists from ships carrying more than 500 passengers and to require that ships land no more than 100 passengers at a time. During the 2008–09 austral summer, 37,858 tourists visited the continent, 26,933 in the Antarctic Treaty area. In May British scientists suggested that if the West Antarctic Ice Sheet were to collapse, the sea level would rise by only half as much as had been estimated—3 m (10 ft) rather than 6 m (20 ft). In October, however, NASA scientists reported that over the past seven years ice sheets in Antarctica appeared to be shrinking more than twice as fast as originally thought.

Internet resource: <www.antarctica.org>.

Arctic Regions

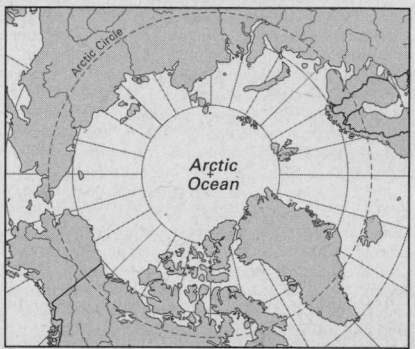

The Arctic regions may be defined in physical terms (astronomical [north of the Arctic Circle], climatic [above the 10 °C (50 °F) July isotherm], or vegetational [above the northern limit of the tree line]) or in human terms (the territory inhabited by the circumpolar cultures—Inuit [Eskimo] and Aleut in North America and Russia, Sami [Lapp] in northern Scandinavia and Russia, and 29 other peoples of the Russian North, Siberia, and East Asia). The region includes portions of Canada, the United States, Russia, Finland, Sweden, Norway, Iceland, and Greenland (part of Denmark). The Arctic Ocean, 14.09 million sq km (5.44 million sq mi) in area, constitutes about two-thirds of the region. The land area consists of permanent ice cap, tundra, or taiga. At 5.1 million sq km (1.97 million sq mi) of coverage, the 2009 Arctic summer sea ice annual minimum was the third lowest on record. Interest in Arctic oil and gas continued to grow in 2009, and the countries bordering the Arctic region continued the process of establishing rights to territory and undersea resources under the aegis of the UN Convention on the Law of the Sea. In April Norway became the first country to receive international backing when the UN confirmed its 2006 claim, extending the boundary of its continental shelf some 235,000 sq km (91,000 sq mi). In May Russia began construction on the world's first nuclear power plant on an offshore platform, with three additional offshore nuclear plants planned for coming years. One of the intended uses of the platforms was to supply power for exploration for and development of petroleum and natural-gas reserves. Earlier in the spring, Norway had launched two new offshore semisubmersible rigs designed for harsh environmental conditions and ultra-deepwater drilling. In August the US introduced a moratorium on commercial fishing in its exclusive economic zone off the Arctic coast of Alaska. Two German cargo ships successfully completed the transit of the Northeast Passage in Eurasia in September, becoming the first cargo ships to do so.

1 metric ton = about 1.1 short tons;   1 kilometer = 0.6 mi (statute);   1 metric ton-km cargo = about 0.68 short ton-mi cargo;   c.i.f.: cost, insurance, and freight;   f.o.b.: free on board

Membership in International Organizations

African Union (AU)
Founded: 1963. **Members:** 52 countries of Africa (all except Morocco), Western Sahara (Guinea was suspended in December 2008; Madagascar was suspended in March 2009; Niger was suspended in February 2010).
Web site: <www.africa-union.org>.

Asia-Pacific Economic Cooperation (APEC)
Founded: 1989. **Members:** Australia, Brunei, Canada, Chile, China, Hong Kong, Indonesia, Japan, Malaysia, Mexico, New Zealand, Papua New Guinea, Peru, Philippines, Republic of Korea, Russia, Singapore, Taiwan, Thailand, US, Vietnam.
Web site: <www.apec.org>.

Association of Southeast Asian Nations (ASEAN)
Founded: 1967. **Members:** Brunei, Cambodia, Indonesia, Laos, Malaysia, Myanmar (Burma), Philippines, Singapore, Thailand, Vietnam.
Web site: <www.aseansec.org>.

Caribbean Community (Caricom)
Founded: 1973. **Members:** Antigua and Barbuda, The Bahamas, Barbados, Belize, Dominica, Grenada, Guyana, Haiti, Jamaica, Montserrat, Saint Kitts and Nevis, Saint Lucia, Saint Vincent and the Grenadines, Suriname, Trinidad and Tobago; associate members Anguilla, Bermuda, British Virgin Islands, Cayman Islands, Turks and Caicos Islands.
Web site: <www.caricom.org>.

Commonwealth (also called Commonwealth of Nations)
Founded: 1931. **Members:** United Kingdom and 53 other countries, all of which were once under British rule or administratively connected to another member country (Fiji was suspended in September 2009; Nauru is a Member in Arrears).
Web site: <www.thecommonwealth.org>.

Commonwealth of Independent States (CIS)
Founded: 1991. **Members:** Armenia, Azerbaijan, Belarus, Kazakhstan, Kyrgyzstan, Moldova, Russia, Tajikistan, Turkmenistan, Ukraine, Uzbekistan.
Web site: <www.cisstat.com>.

Community of Portuguese Language Countries (CPLP)
Founded: 1996. **Members:** Angola, Brazil, Cape Verde, East Timor (Timor-Leste), Guinea-Bissau, Mozambique, Portugal, Sao Tome and Principe; observer states Equatorial Guinea, Mauritius, Senegal.
Web site: <www.cplp.org>.

Economic Community of West African States (ECOWAS)
Founded: 1975. **Members:** Benin, Burkina Faso, Cape Verde, Côte d'Ivoire, The Gambia, Ghana, Guinea, Guinea-Bissau, Liberia, Mali, Niger, Nigeria, Senegal, Sierra Leone, Togo (Guinea was suspended in January 2009; Niger was suspended in October 2009).
Web site: <www.ecowas.int>.

European Union (EU)
Founded: 1950. **Members:** Austria, Belgium, Bulgaria, Cyprus, Czech Republic, Denmark, Estonia, Finland, France, Germany, Greece, Hungary, Ireland, Italy, Latvia, Lithuania, Luxembourg, Malta, Netherlands, Poland, Portugal, Romania, Slovakia, Slovenia, Spain, Sweden, UK.
Web site: <http://europa.eu>.

Group of Twenty (G20)
Founded: 1999. **Members:** Argentina, Australia, Brazil, Canada, China, France, Germany, India, Indonesia, Italy, Japan, Mexico, Republic of Korea, Russia, Saudi Arabia, South Africa, Turkey, UK, US, European Union.
Web site: <www.g20.org>.

Gulf Cooperation Council (GCC)
Founded: 1981. **Members:** Bahrain, Kuwait, Oman, Qatar, Saudi Arabia, UAE.
Web site: <www.gccsg.org/eng/index.php>.

League of Arab States (LAS; also called Arab League)
Founded: 1945. **Members:** Algeria, Bahrain, Comoros, Djibouti, Egypt, Iraq, Jordan, Kuwait, Lebanon, Libya, Mauritania, Morocco, Oman, Palestinian Authority, Qatar, Saudi Arabia, Somalia, Sudan, Syria, Tunisia, UAE, Yemen; observer states Brazil, Eritrea, India, Venezuela.
Web site:
<www.arableagueonline.org>.

North Atlantic Treaty Organization (NATO)
Founded: 1949. **Members:** Albania, Belgium, Bulgaria, Canada, Croatia, Czech Republic, Denmark, Estonia, France, Germany, Greece, Hungary, Iceland, Italy, Latvia, Lithuania, Luxembourg, Netherlands, Norway, Poland, Portugal, Romania, Slovakia, Slovenia, Spain, Turkey, UK, US.
Web site: <www.nato.int>.

Organisation for Economic Co-operation and Development (OECD)
Founded: 1961. **Members:** Australia, Austria, Belgium, Canada, Chile, Czech Republic, Denmark, Finland, France, Germany, Greece, Hungary, Iceland, Ireland, Italy, Japan, Luxembourg, Mexico, Netherlands, New Zealand, Norway, Poland, Portugal, Republic of Korea, Slovakia, Spain, Sweden, Switzerland, Turkey, UK, US.
Web site: <www.oecd.org>.

Organization for Security and Co-operation in Europe (OSCE)
Founded: 1972. **Members:** 54 countries of Europe and Central Asia, plus Canada and the US.
Web site: <www.osce.org>.

Organization of American States (OAS)
Founded: 1948. **Members:** all 35 independent countries of the Western Hemisphere (Honduras was suspended in July 2009); 64 permanent observer states (including the EU).
Web site: <www.oas.org>.

Organization of the Islamic Conference (OIC)
Founded: 1969. **Members:** 56 Islamic countries (mainly in Africa and Asia), Palestinian Authority; observer states Bosnia and Herzegovina, Central African Republic, Russia, Thailand, Turkish Republic of Northern Cyprus.
Web site: <www.oic-oci.org>.

Membership in International Organizations (continued)

Organization of the Petroleum Exporting Countries (OPEC)
Founded: 1960. **Members:** Algeria, Angola, Ecuador, Iran, Iraq, Kuwait, Libya, Nigeria, Qatar, Saudi Arabia, UAE, Venezuela.
Web site: <www.opec.org>.

Secretariat of the Pacific Community (SPC)
Founded: 1947. **Members:** American Samoa, Australia, Cook Islands, Federated States of Micronesia, Fiji, France, French Polynesia, Guam, Kiribati, Marshall Islands, Nauru, New Caledonia, New Zealand, Niue, Northern Mariana Islands, Palau, Papua New Guinea, Pitcairn Islands, Samoa, Solomon Islands, Tokelau, Tonga, Tuvalu, US, Vanuatu, Wallis and Futuna.
Web site: <www.spc.int>.

Southern African Development Community (SADC)
Founded: 1979. **Members:** Angola, Botswana, Democratic Republic of the Congo, Lesotho, Madagascar, Malawi, Mauritius, Mozambique, Namibia, Seychelles, South Africa, Swaziland, Tanzania, Zambia, Zimbabwe (Madagascar was suspended in March 2009).
Web site: <www.sadc.int>.

Union of South American Nations (UNASUR/UNASUL)
Founded: 2004. **Members:** Argentina, Bolivia, Brazil, Chile, Colombia, Ecuador, Guyana, Paraguay, Peru, Suriname, Uruguay, Venezuela.
Web site: <www.comunidadandina.org>.

World Trade Organization (WTO)
Founded: 1995. **Members:** 153 member countries worldwide; 31 observer states as of July 2008.
Web site: <www.wto.org>.

United Nations Membership by Date of Admission

COUNTRY	DATE OF ADMISSION	COUNTRY	DATE OF ADMISSION	COUNTRY	DATE OF ADMISSION
Argentina	24 Oct 1945	Ecuador	21 Dec 1945	Gabon	20 Sep 1960
Belarus	24 Oct 1945	Iraq	21 Dec 1945	Madagascar	20 Sep 1960
Brazil	24 Oct 1945	Belgium	27 Dec 1945	Niger	20 Sep 1960
Chile	24 Oct 1945	Afghanistan	19 Nov 1946	Somalia	20 Sep 1960
China[1]	24 Oct 1945	Iceland	19 Nov 1946	Togo	20 Sep 1960
Cuba	24 Oct 1945	Sweden	19 Nov 1946	Mali	28 Sep 1960
Denmark	24 Oct 1945	Thailand	16 Dec 1946	Senegal	28 Sep 1960
Dominican Rep.	24 Oct 1945	Pakistan	30 Sep 1947	Nigeria	7 Oct 1960
Egypt	24 Oct 1945	Yemen	30 Sep 1947	Sierra Leone	27 Sep 1961
El Salvador	24 Oct 1945	Myanmar	19 Apr 1948	Mauritania	27 Oct 1961
France	24 Oct 1945	Israel	11 May 1949	Mongolia	27 Oct 1961
Haiti	24 Oct 1945	Indonesia	28 Sep 1950	Tanzania	14 Dec 1961
Iran	24 Oct 1945	Albania	14 Dec 1955	Burundi	18 Sep 1962
Lebanon	24 Oct 1945	Austria	14 Dec 1955	Jamaica	18 Sep 1962
Luxembourg	24 Oct 1945	Bulgaria	14 Dec 1955	Rwanda	18 Sep 1962
New Zealand	24 Oct 1945	Cambodia	14 Dec 1955	Trinidad and Tobago	18 Sep 1962
Nicaragua	24 Oct 1945	Finland	14 Dec 1955	Algeria	8 Oct 1962
Paraguay	24 Oct 1945	Hungary	14 Dec 1955	Uganda	25 Oct 1962
Philippines	24 Oct 1945	Ireland	14 Dec 1955	Kuwait	14 May 1963
Poland	24 Oct 1945	Italy	14 Dec 1955	Kenya	16 Dec 1963
USSR (later Russia)	24 Oct 1945	Jersey	14 Dec 1955	Malawi	1 Dec 1964
Saudi Arabia	24 Oct 1945	Jordan	14 Dec 1955	Malta	1 Dec 1964
Syria	24 Oct 1945	Laos	14 Dec 1955	Zambia	1 Dec 1964
Turkey	24 Oct 1945	Libya	14 Dec 1955	The Gambia	21 Sep 1965
Ukraine	24 Oct 1945	Nepal	14 Dec 1955	Maldives	21 Sep 1965
UK	24 Oct 1945	Portugal	14 Dec 1955	Singapore	21 Sep 1965
US	24 Oct 1945	Romania	14 Dec 1955	Guyana	20 Sep 1966
Greece	25 Oct 1945	Spain	14 Dec 1955	Lesotho	17 Oct 1966
India	30 Oct 1945	Sri Lanka	14 Dec 1955	Botswana	17 Oct 1966
Peru	31 Oct 1945	Morocco	12 Nov 1956	Barbados	9 Dec 1966
Australia	1 Nov 1945	Sudan	12 Nov 1956	Mauritius	24 Apr 1968
Costa Rica	2 Nov 1945	Tunisia	12 Nov 1956	Swaziland	24 Sep 1968
Liberia	2 Nov 1945	Japan	18 Dec 1956	Equatorial Guinea	12 Nov 1968
Colombia	5 Nov 1945	Ghana	8 Mar 1957	Fiji	13 Oct 1970
Mexico	7 Nov 1945	Malaysia	17 Sep 1957	Bahrain	21 Sep 1971
South Africa	7 Nov 1945	Guinea	12 Dec 1958	Bhutan	21 Sep 1971
Canada	9 Nov 1945	Benin	20 Sep 1960	Qatar	21 Sep 1971
Ethiopia	13 Nov 1945	Burkina Faso	20 Sep 1960	Oman	7 Oct 1971
Panama	13 Nov 1945	Cameroon	20 Sep 1960	United Arab Emirates	9 Dec 1971
Bolivia	14 Nov 1945	Central African Rep.	20 Sep 1960	The Bahamas	18 Sep 1973
Venezuela	15 Nov 1945	Chad	20 Sep 1960	Germany	18 Sep 1973
Guatemala	21 Nov 1945	Dem. Rep. of the Congo	20 Sep 1960	Bangladesh	17 Sep 1974
Norway	27 Nov 1945	Congo		Grenada	17 Sep 1974
Netherlands	10 Dec 1945	Rep. of the Congo	20 Sep 1960	Guinea-Bissau	17 Sep 1974
Honduras	17 Dec 1945	Côte d'Ivoire	20 Sep 1960	Cape Verde	16 Sep 1975
Uruguay	18 Dec 1945	Cyprus	20 Sep 1960	Mozambique	16 Sep 1975

United Nations Membership by Date of Admission (continued)

COUNTRY	DATE OF ADMISSION	COUNTRY	DATE OF ADMISSION	COUNTRY	DATE OF ADMISSION
Sao Tome and Principe	16 Sep 1975	Brunei	21 Sep 1984	Bosnia and Herzegovina	22 May 1992
Papua New Guinea	10 Oct 1975	Namibia	23 Apr 1990	Croatia	22 May 1992
Comoros	12 Nov 1975	Liechtenstein	18 Sep 1990	Slovenia	22 May 1992
Suriname	4 Dec 1975	Estonia	17 Sep 1991	Georgia	31 Jul 1992
Seychelles	21 Sep 1976	Dem. People's Republic of Korea	17 Sep 1991	Czech Republic	19 Jan 1993
Angola	1 Dec 1976	Republic of Korea	17 Sep 1991	Slovakia	19 Jan 1993
Samoa	15 Dec 1976	Latvia	17 Sep 1991	Macedonia[2]	8 Apr 1993
Djibouti	20 Sep 1977	Lithuania	17 Sep 1991	Eritrea	28 May 1993
Vietnam	20 Sep 1977	Marshall Islands	17 Sep 1991	Monaco	28 May 1993
Solomon Islands	19 Sep 1978	Federated States of Micronesia	17 Sep 1991	Andorra	28 Jul 1993
Dominica	18 Dec 1978			Palau	15 Dec 1994
St. Lucia	18 Sep 1979	Armenia	2 Mar 1992	Kiribati	14 Sep 1999
Zimbabwe	25 Aug 1980	Azerbaijan	2 Mar 1992	Nauru	14 Sep 1999
St. Vincent and the Grenadines	16 Sep 1980	Kazakhstan	2 Mar 1992	Tonga	14 Sep 1999
		Kyrgyzstan	2 Mar 1992	Tuvalu	5 Sep 2000
Vanuatu	15 Sep 1981	Moldova	2 Mar 1992	Serbia	1 Nov 2000
Belize	25 Sep 1981	San Marino	2 Mar 1992	Switzerland	10 Sep 2002
Antigua and Barbuda	11 Nov 1981	Tajikistan	2 Mar 1992	East Timor (Timor-Leste)	27 Sep 2002
		Turkmenistan	2 Mar 1992		
St. Kitts and Nevis	23 Sep 1983	Uzbekistan	2 Mar 1992	Montenegro	28 Jun 2006

[1]The Republic of China (Taiwan) held the seat until 25 Oct 1971, when UN Res. 2758 gave the membership and a seat on the Security Council to the People's Republic of China. [2]Macedonia is known in the UN as The Former Yugoslav Republic of Macedonia.

Secretaries-General of the United Nations

The UN General Assembly appoints the Secretary-General to a five-year term on the recommendation of the 15-member Security Council; permanent members of the Security Council have veto power over nominees. The Secretary-General balances diverse and sometimes conflicting duties in the various roles of diplomat, advocate, administrator, and civil servant. The Secretary-General has a broad mandate, being able to marshal resources and advocacy on issues as various as peace efforts around the globe and disease prevention and treatment. United Nations Web site: <www.un.org>.

SECRETARY GENERAL	TERM	COMMENTS
Sir Gladwyn Jebb (acting) (UK)	1945–1946	
Trygve Lie (Norway)	1946–1952	resigned in November 1952
Dag Hammarskjöld (Sweden)	1953–1961	died in September 1961
U Thant (Burma, now Myanmar)	1962–1971	acting Secretary-General November 1961; elected 1962
Kurt Waldheim (Austria)	1972–1981	China vetoed a third term
Javier Pérez de Cuéllar (Peru)	1982–1991	
Boutros Boutros-Ghali (Egypt)	1992–1996	US vetoed a second term
Kofi Annan (Ghana)	1997–2006	
Ban Ki-moon (Republic of Korea)	2007–	

International Criminal Court

The International Criminal Court (ICC) was established by the Rome Statute of the International Criminal Court on 17 Jul 1998. The statute that created the ICC went into force on 1 Jul 2002; the court was fully operational as of July 2003. As of 24 Mar 2010, the ICC has 111 member countries.

President
Song Sang-Hyun (Republic of Korea)

First Vice President
Fatoumata Dembele Diarra (Mali)

Second Vice President
Hans-Peter Kaul (Germany)

Chief Prosecutor
Luis Moreno-Ocampo (Argentina)

Judges
List A—elected as experts in criminal law and procedure
Joyce Aluoch (Kenya)
Bruno Cotte (France)
Fatoumata Dembele Diarra (Mali)
Silvia Alejandra Fernández de Gurmendi (Argentina)
Adrian Fulford (United Kingdom)
Daniel David Ntanda Nsereko (Uganda)
Elizabeth Odio Benito (Costa Rica)
Song Sang-Hyun (Republic of Korea)
Sylvia Steiner (Brazil)

International Criminal Court (continued)

Judges—List A (continued)
Cuno Tarfusser (Italy)
Ekaterina Trendafilova (Bulgaria)
Christine Van den Wyngaert (Belgium)

List B—elected as experts in international law and human rights law
René Blattmann (Bolivia)
Hans-Peter Kaul (Germany)

Judges—List B (continued)
Erkki Kourula (Finland)
Akua Kuenyehia (Ghana)
Sanji Mmasenono Monageng (Botswana)
Kuniko Ozaki (Japan)
Anita Usacka (Latvia)

Registrar
Silvana Arbia (Italy)

Rulers and Regimes

Europe

Roman Emperors

Overlapping reigns denote corulers. Diocletian (284–305) laid the foundation for the Byzantine Empire in the East when he appointed Maximian (286–305) to rule over the Western portion of the empire. Rome thus remained a unified state but was divided administratively. Theodosius I (379–395) was the last emperor to rule over a unified Roman Empire. When he died, Rome split into Eastern and Western empires. For a complete list of the Eastern emperors after the fall of Rome, see "Byzantine Empire."

REIGN	BYNAME	FULL NAME
27 BC–AD 14	Augustus	Caesar Augustus
14–37	Tiberius	Tiberius Caesar Augustus
37–41	Caligula	Gaius Caesar Augustus Germanicus
41–54	Claudius	Tiberius Claudius Caesar Augustus Germanicus
54–68	Nero	Nero Claudius Caesar Augustus Germanicus
68–69	Galba	Servius Galba Caesar Augustus
69	Otho	Marcus Otho Caesar Augustus
69	Vitellius	Aulus Vitellius Germanicus
69–79	Vespasian	Caesar Vespasianus Augustus
79–81	Titus	Titus Vespasianus Augustus
81–96	Domitian	Caesar Domitianus Augustus
96–98	Nerva	Nerva Caesar Augustus
98–117	Trajan	Caesar Nerva Traianus Augustus
117–138	Hadrian	Caesar Traianus Hadrianus Augustus
138–161	Antoninus Pius	Caesar Titus Aelius Hadrianus Antoninus Augustus Pius
161–180	Marcus Aurelius	Marcus Aurelius Antoninus
161–169	Lucius Verus	Lucius Aurelius Verus
177–192	Commodus	Lucius Aelius Aurelius Commodus
193	Pertinax	Publius Helvius Pertinax
193	Didius Julianus	Marcus Didius Severus Julianus
193–211	Septimius Severus	Lucius Septimius Severus Pertinax
198–217	Caracalla	Marcus Aurelius Severus Antoninus
209–212	Geta	Publius Septimius Geta
217–218	Macrinus	Marcus Opellius Severus Macrinus
218–222	Elagabalus	Sacerdos dei invicti solis Elagabali Marcus Aurelius Antoninus
222–235	Alexander Severus	Marcus Aurelius Severus Alexander
235–238	Maximin	Gaius Julius Verus Maximinus
238	Gordian I	Marcus Antonius Gordianus Sempronianus Romanus Africanus
238	Gordian II	Marcus Antonius Gordianus Sempronianus Romanus Africanus
238	Maximus	Marcus Clodius Pupienus Maximus
238	Balbinus	Decius Caelius Calvinus Balbinus
238–244	Gordian III	Marcus Antonius Gordianus
244–249	Philip	
249–251	Decius	Galus Messius Quintus Trianus Decius
251	Hostilian	Gaius Valens Hostilianus Messius Quintus
251–253	Gallus	Gaius Vibius Trebonianus Gallus
253	Aemilian	Marcus Aemilius Aemilianus
253–260	Valerian	Publius Licinius Valerianus
253–268	Gallienus	Publius Licinius Egnatius Gallienus
268–270	Claudius II Gothicus	Marcus Aurelius Valerius Claudius
269–270	Quintillus	Marcus Aurelius Claudius Quintillus
270–275	Aurelian	Lucius Domitius Aurelianus
275–276	Tacitus	Marcus Claudius Tacitus

Roman Emperors (continued)

REIGN	BYNAME	FULL NAME
276	Florian	Marcus Annius Florianus
276–282	Probus	Marcus Aurelius Probus
282–283	Carus	Marcus Aurelius Carus
283–285	Carinus	Marcus Aurelius Carinus
283–284	Numerian	Marcus Aurelius Numerius Numerianus
284–305[1]	Diocletian	Gaius Aurelius Valerius Diocletianus
286–305[2]	Maximian	Marcus Aurelius Valerius Maximianus Heraclius
305–311[1]	Galerius	Gaius Galerius Valerius Maximianus
305–306[2]	Constantius I Chlorus	Flavius Valerius Constantius
306–307[2]	Severus	Flavius Valerius Severus
306–312[2]	Maxentius	Marcus Aurelius Valerius Maxentius
308–324[1]	Licinius	Valerius Licinianus Licinius
312–337[2]	Constantine I	Flavius Valerius Constantinus
337–340[2]	Constantine II	Flavius Claudius [or Julius] Constantinus
337–350[2]	Constans I	Flavius Julius Constans
337–361[2]	Constantius II	Flavius Julius [or Valerius] Constantius
350–353[2]	Magnentius	Flavius Magnus Magnentius
361–363[2]	Julian	Flavius Claudius Julianus
363–364[2]	Jovian	Flavius Jovianus
364–375[2]	Valentinian I	Flavius Valentinianus
364–378[1]	Valens	Flavius Valens
365–366[1]	Procopius	
375–383[2]	Gratian	Flavius Gratianus Augustus
375–392[2]	Valentinian II	Flavius Valentinianus
379–395[2]	Theodosius I	Flavius Theodosius
395–408[1]	Arcadius	Flavius Arcadius
395–423[2]	Honorius	Flavius Honorius
408–450[1]	Theodosius II	
421[2]	Constantius III	
425–455[2]	Valentinian III	Flavius Placidius Valentinianus
450–457[1]	Marcian	Marcianus
455[2]	Petronius Maximus	Flavius Ancius Petronius Maximus
455–456[2]	Avitus	Flavius Maccilius Eparchus Avitus
457–474[1]	Leo I	Leo Thrax Magnus
457–461[2]	Majorian	Julius Valerius Majorianus
461–467[2]	Libius Severus	Libius Severianus Severus
467–472[2]	Anthemius	Procopius Anthemius
472[2]	Olybrius	Anicius Olybrius
473–474[2]	Glycerius	
474–475[2]	Julius Nepos	
474[1]	Leo II	
474–491[1]	Zeno	
475–476[2]	Romulus Augustulus	Flavius Momyllus Romulus Augustulus

[1]*Ruled in the East only.*   [2]*Ruled in the West only.*

Sovereigns of Britain

SOVEREIGN	DYNASTY OR HOUSE	REIGN	SOVEREIGN	DYNASTY OR HOUSE	REIGN
Kings of Wessex (West Saxons)			**Sovereigns of England (continued)**		
Egbert	Saxon	802–839	Ethelred II the Unready (Aethelred)	Saxon	978–1013
Aethelwulf (Ethelwulf)	Saxon	839–856/858	Sweyn Forkbeard	Danish	1013–14
Aethelbald (Ethelbald)	Saxon	855/856–860	Ethelred II the Unready (restored)	Saxon	1014–16
Aethelberht (Ethelbert)	Saxon	860–865/866			
Aethelred I (Ethelred)	Saxon	865/866–871	Edmund II Ironside	Saxon	1016
Alfred the Great	Saxon	871–899	Canute	Danish	1016–35
Edward the Elder	Saxon	899–924	Harold I Harefoot	Danish	1035–40
			Hardecanute	Danish	1040–42
Sovereigns of England			Edward the Confessor	Saxon	1042–66
Athelstan[1]	Saxon	925–939	Harold II	Saxon	1066
Edmund I	Saxon	939–946	William I the Conqueror	Norman	1066–87
Eadred (Edred)	Saxon	946–955	William II	Norman	1087–1100
Eadwig (Edwy)	Saxon	955–959	Henry I	Norman	1100–35
Edgar	Saxon	959–975	Stephen	Blois	1135–54
Edward the Martyr	Saxon	975–978			

Sovereigns of Britain (continued)

SOVEREIGN	DYNASTY OR HOUSE	REIGN	SOVEREIGN	DYNASTY OR HOUSE	REIGN
Sovereigns of England (continued)			**Sovereigns of Great Britain and the United Kingdom**[2, 3]		
Henry II	Plantagenet	1154–89	James I (VI of Scotland)[2]	Stuart	1603–25
Richard I	Plantagenet	1189–99	Charles I	Stuart	1625–49
John	Plantagenet	1199–1216			
Henry III	Plantagenet	1216–72	**Commonwealth**		
Edward I	Plantagenet	1272–1307	Oliver Cromwell, Lord		1653–58
Edward II	Plantagenet	1307–27	Protector		
Edward III	Plantagenet	1327–77	Richard Cromwell, Lord		1658–59
Richard II	Plantagenet	1377–99	Protector		
Henry IV	Plantagenet: Lancaster	1399–1413			
Henry V	Plantagenet: Lancaster	1413–22	**Sovereigns of Great Britain and the United Kingdom (restored)**		
Henry VI	Plantagenet: Lancaster	1422–61	Charles II	Stuart	1660–85
			James II	Stuart	1685–88
Edward IV	Plantagenet: York	1461–70	William III and Mary II[4]	Orange/ Stuart	1689–1702
Henry VI (restored)	Plantagenet: Lancaster	1470–71	Anne	Stuart	1702–14
			George I	Hanover	1714–27
Edward IV (restored)	Plantagenet: York	1471–83	George II	Hanover	1727–60
			George III[3]	Hanover	1760–1820
Edward V	Plantagenet: York	1483	George IV[5]	Hanover	1820–30
			William IV	Hanover	1830–37
Richard III	Plantagenet: York	1483–85	Victoria	Hanover	1837–1901
			Edward VII	Saxe-Coburg-Gotha	1901–10
Henry VII	Tudor	1483–1509			
Henry VIII	Tudor	1509–47	George V[6]	Windsor	1910–36
Edward VI	Tudor	1547–53	Edward VIII[7]	Windsor	1936
Mary I	Tudor	1553–58	George VI	Windsor	1936–52
Elizabeth I	Tudor	1558–1603	Elizabeth II	Windsor	1952–

[1]Athelstan was king of Wessex and the first king of all England.   [2]James VI of Scotland became also James I of England in 1603. Upon accession to the English throne he styled himself "King of Great Britain" and was so proclaimed. Legally, however, he and his successors held separate English and Scottish kingships until the Act of Union of 1707, when the two kingdoms were united as the Kingdom of Great Britain.   [3]The United Kingdom was formed on 1 Jan 1801, with the union of Great Britain and Ireland. After 1801 George III was styled "King of the United Kingdom of Great Britain and Ireland."   [4]William and Mary, as husband and wife, reigned jointly until Mary's death in 1694. William then reigned alone until his own death in 1702.   [5]George IV was regent from 5 Feb 1811.   [6]In 1917, during World War I, George V changed the name of his house from Saxe-Coburg-Gotha to Windsor.   [7]Edward VIII succeeded upon the death of his father, George V, on 20 Jan 1936, but abdicated on 11 Dec 1936, before coronation.

British Prime Ministers

The origin of the term prime minister and the question of to whom it should originally be applied have long been issues of scholarly and political debate. Although the term was used as early as the reign of Queen Anne (1702–14), it acquired wider currency during the reign of George II (1727–60), when it began to be used as a term of reproach toward Robert Walpole. The title prime minister did not become official until 1905, to refer to the leader of a government.

Before the development of the Conservative and Liberal parties in the mid-19th century, parties in Britain were, for the most part, simply alliances of prominent groups or aristocratic families. The designations Whig and Tory tend often to be approximate. In all cases, the party designation is that of the prime minister; he or she might lead a coalition government, as did David Lloyd George and Winston Churchill (in his first term).

PRIME MINISTER	PARTY	TERM	PRIME MINISTER	PARTY	TERM
Robert Walpole	Whig	1721–42	Frederick North		1770–82
Spencer Compton	Whig	1742–43	Charles Watson Went-worth	Whig	1782
Henry Pelham	Whig	1743–54			
Thomas Pelham-Holles	Whig	1754–56	William Petty-Fitzmaurice		1782–83
William Cavendish	Whig	1756–57	William Henry Cavendish-Bentinck	Whig	1783
Thomas Pelham-Holles	Whig	1757–62			
John Stuart		1762–63	William Pitt	Tory	1783–1801
George Grenville		1763–65	Henry Addington	Tory	1801–04
Charles Watson Went-worth	Whig	1765–66	William Pitt	Tory	1804–06
			William Wyndham Gren-ville		1806–07
William Pitt		1766–68			
Augustus Henry Fitzroy		1768–70			

British Prime Ministers (continued)

PRIME MINISTER	PARTY	TERM	PRIME MINISTER	PARTY	TERM
William Henry Cavendish-Bentinck	Whig	1807–09	Archibald Philip Primrose	Liberal	1894–95
			Robert Cecil	Conservative	1895–1902
Spencer Perceval	Tory	1809–12	Arthur James Balfour	Conservative	1902–05
Robert Banks Jenkinson	Tory	1812–27	Henry Campbell-Bannerman	Liberal	1905–08
George Canning	Tory	1827			
Frederick John Robinson	Tory	1827–28	H.H. Asquith	Liberal	1908–16
Arthur Wellesley	Tory	1828–30	David Lloyd George	Liberal	1916–22
Charles Grey	Whig	1830–34	Bonar Law	Conservative	1922–23
William Lamb	Whig	1834	Stanley Baldwin	Conservative	1923–24
Arthur Wellesley	Tory	1834	Ramsay Macdonald	Labour	1924
Robert Peel	Tory	1834–35	Stanley Baldwin	Conservative	1924–29
William Lamb	Whig	1835–41	Ramsay Macdonald	Labour	1929–35
Robert Peel	Conservative	1841–46	Stanley Baldwin	Conservative	1935–37
John Russell	Whig-Liberal	1846–52	Neville Chamberlain	Conservative	1937–40
Edward Geoffrey Stanley	Conservative	1852	Winston Churchill	Conservative	1940–45
George Hamilton-Gordon		1852–55	Clement Attlee	Labour	1945–51
Henry John Temple	Liberal	1855–58	Winston Churchill	Conservative	1951–55
Edward Geoffrey Stanley	Conservative	1858–59	Anthony Eden	Conservative	1955–57
Henry John Temple	Liberal	1859–65	Harold Macmillan	Conservative	1957–63
John Russell	Liberal	1865–66	Alec Douglas-Home	Conservative	1963–64
Edward Geoffrey Stanley	Conservative	1866–68	Harold Wilson	Labour	1964–70
Benjamin Disraeli	Conservative	1868	Edward Heath	Conservative	1970–74
William Ewart Gladstone	Liberal	1868–74	Harold Wilson	Labour	1974–76
Benjamin Disraeli	Conservative	1874–80	James Callaghan	Labour	1976–79
William Ewart Gladstone	Liberal	1880–85	Margaret Thatcher	Conservative	1979–90
Robert Cecil	Conservative	1885–86	John Major	Conservative	1990–97
William Ewart Gladstone	Liberal	1886	Tony Blair	Labour	1997–2007
Robert Cecil	Conservative	1886–92	Gordon Brown	Labour	2007–10
William Ewart Gladstone	Liberal	1892–94	David Cameron	Conservative	2010–

Rulers of France

RULER	REIGN	RULER	REIGN
Carolingian dynasty		**Capetian dynasty (continued)**	
Pippin III the Short	751–768	Louis VI	1108–37
Charles I (Charlemagne, Kingdom of the Franks)	768–814	Louis VII	1137–80
		Philip II (Philippe)	1180–1223
Louis I (Kingdom of the Franks)	814–840	Louis VIII	1223–26
civil war	840–843	Louis IX (Saint Louis)	1226–70
Charles II (Kingdom of the West Franks)	843–877	Philip III (Philippe)	1270–85
Louis II (Kingdom of the West Franks)	877–879	Philip IV (Philippe)	1285–1314
Louis III (Kingdom of the West Franks)	879–882	Louis X	1314–16
Carloman (Kingdom of the West Franks)	879–884	John I (Jean)	1316
Charles (III) (Charles III, Holy Roman Empire)	884–887	Philip V (Philippe)	1316–22
		Charles IV	1322–28
Robertian (Capetian) dynasty		**Valois dynasty**	
Eudes	888–898	Philip VI (Philippe)	1328–50
		John II (Jean)	1350–64
Carolingian dynasty		Charles V	1364–80
Charles III	893/898–923	Charles VI	1380–1422
		Charles VII	1422–61
Robertian (Capetian) dynasty		Louis XI	1461–83
Robert I	922–923	Charles VIII	1483–98
Rudolf (Raoul, or Rodolphe)	923–936		
		Valois dynasty (Orléans branch)	
Carolingian dynasty		Louis XII	1498–1515
Louis IV	936–954		
Lothair (Lothaire)	954–986	**Valois dynasty (Angoulême branch)**	
Louis V	986–987	Francis I (François)	1515–47
		Henry II (Henri)	1547–59
Capetian dynasty		Francis II (François)	1559–60
Hugh Capet (Hugues Capet)	987–996	Charles IX	1560–74
Robert II	996–1031	Henry III (Henri)	1574–89
Henry I (Henri)	1031–60		
Philip I (Philippe)	1060–1108		

Rulers of France (continued)

RULER	REIGN
House of Bourbon	
Henry IV (Henri)	1589–1610
Louis XIII	1610–43
Louis XIV	1643–1715
Louis XV	1715–74
Louis XVI	1774–92
Louis (XVII)	1793–95
First Republic	
National Convention	1792–95
Directorate	1795–99
Consulate (Napoléon Bonaparte)	1799–1804
First Empire (emperors)	
Napoleon I (Napoléon Bonaparte)	1804–14, 1815
Napoleon (II)	1815
House of Bourbon	
Louis XVIII	1814–24
Charles X	1824–30
House of Orléans	
Louis-Philippe	1830–48
Second Republic (president)	
Louis-Napoléon Bonaparte	1848–52
Second Empire (emperor)	
Napoleon III (Louis-Napoléon Bonaparte)	1852–70

RULER	REIGN
Third Republic (presidents)	
Adolphe Thiers	1871–73
Marie-Edmé-Patrice-Maurice	1873–79
Jules Grévy	1879–87
Sadi Carnot	1887–94
Jean Casimir-Périer	1894–95
Félix Faure	1895–99
Émile Loubet	1899–1906
Armand Fallières	1906–13
Raymond Poincaré	1913–20
Paul Deschanel	1920
Alexandre Millerand	1920–24
Gaston Doumergue	1924–31
Paul Doumer	1931–32
Albert Lebrun	1932–40
French State (État Français, or Vichy France)	
Philippe Pétain	1940–44
Provisional government	1944–47
Fourth Republic (presidents)	
Vincent Auriol	1947–54
René Coty	1954–59
Fifth Republic (presidents)	
Charles de Gaulle	1959–69
Georges Pompidou	1969–74
Valéry Giscard d'Estaing	1974–81
François Mitterrand	1981–95
Jacques Chirac	1995–2007
Nicolas Sarkozy	2007–

Rulers of Germany

On 25 Jul 1806 the Confederation of the Rhine was founded, with Karl Theodor von Dalberg as prince primate (1806–13). After the dissolution of the Rhine Confederation, there was no true central power until 1815, when the German Confederation was founded. In 1867 the governing structure became the North German Confederation, and in 1871 the German Reich. For rulers of Germany before the Confederation of the Rhine, see Holy Roman Emperors.

RULER	REIGN OR TERM
Emperors	
Hohenzollern dynasty	
Wilhelm I	1871–88
Friedrich III	1888
Wilhelm II	1888–1918
Presidents	
Richard Müller	1918
Robert Leinert	1918–19
Wilhelm Pfannkuch	1919
Eduard David	1919
Friedrich Ebert	1919–25
Paul von Hindenburg	1925–34
Adolf Hitler (Führer)	1934–45
Karl Dönitz	1945
Chancellors	
Otto Fürst von Bismarck	1871–90
Leo Graf von Caprivi	1890–94
Chlodwig Fürst zu Hohenlohe-Schillingsfürst	1894–1900
Bernhard Graf Fürst von Bülow	1900–09
Theobald von Bethmann Hollweg	1909–17
Georg Michaelis	1917

RULER	REIGN OR TERM
Chancellors (continued)	
Georg Graf von Hertling	1917–18
Maximilian Prinz von Baden	1918
Friedrich Ebert	1918
Philipp Scheidemann	1919
Gustav Bauer	1919–20
Wolfgang Kapp (in rebellion)	1920
Hermann Müller	1920
Konstantin Fehrenbach	1920–21
Joseph Wirth	1921–22
Wilhelm Cuno	1922–23
Gustav Stresemann	1923
Wilhelm Marx	1923–24
Hans Luther	1925–26
Wilhelm Marx	1926–28
Hermann Müller	1928–30
Heinrich Brüning	1930–32
Franz von Papen	1932
Kurt von Schleicher	1932–33
Adolf Hitler	1933–45
Joseph Goebbels	1945
Lutz Graf Schwerin von Krosigk (chairman of interim government)	1945

Rulers of Germany (continued)

Allied occupation   1945–49

German Democratic Republic (East Germany)[1]

Presidents		Chairmen of the Council of State (continued)	
Wilhelm Pieck	1949–60	Erich Honecker	1976–89
		Egon Krenz	1989
Chairmen of the Council of State		Sabine Bergmann-Pohl	1990
Walter Ulbricht	1960–73		
Willi Stoph	1973–76		

Federal Republic of Germany (West Germany)[1]

Presidents		Chancellors	
Theodor Heuss	1949–59	Konrad Adenauer	1949–63
Heinrich Lübke	1959–69	Ludwig Erhard	1963–66
Gustav Heinemann	1969–74	Kurt Georg Kiesinger	1966–69
Walter Scheel	1974–79	Willy Brandt	1969–74
Karl Carstens	1979–84	Helmut Schmidt	1974–82
Richard von Weizsäcker	1984–94	Helmut Kohl	1982–98
Roman Herzog	1994–99	Gerhard Schröder	1998–2005
Johannes Rau	1999–2004	Angela Merkel	2005–
Horst Köhler	2004–		

[1]*After World War II, Germany was split into four occupational zones, governed by the French, British, American, and Soviet powers. The Western zones were merged and, on 23 May 1949, became the independent Federal Republic of Germany. On 7 October of the same year, the Soviet zone was proclaimed the German Democratic Republic. On 3 Oct 1990, the latter was incorporated into the Federal Republic of Germany.*

Holy Roman Emperors

The Holy Roman Empire encompassed a varying complex of lands in Western and Central Europe. Ruled over by Frankish and then German kings, the empire officially dissolved on 6 Aug 1806, when Francis II resigned his title.

EMPEROR	REIGN	EMPEROR	REIGN
Carolingian dynasty		**Salian dynasty (continued)**	
Charlemagne (Charles I)	800–814	Henry IV	1056–1106
Louis I	814–840	Rival claimants:	
Civil War	840–843	Rudolf	1077–80
Lothair I	843–855	Hermann	1081–93
Louis II	855–875	Conrad	1093–1101
Charles II	875–877	Henry V	1105/06–25
Interregnum	877–881		
Charles III	881–887	**House of Supplinburg**	
interregnum	887–891	Lothair II	1125–37
House of Spoleto		**House of Hohenstaufen**	
Guy	891–894	Conrad III	1138–52
Lambert	894–898	Frederick I (Barbarossa)	1152–90
		Henry VI	1190–97
Carolingian dynasty		Philip	1198–1208
Arnulf	896–899		
Louis III	901–905	**Welf dynasty**	
		Otto IV	1198–1214
House of Franconia			
Conrad I	911–918	**House of Hohenstaufen**	
		Frederick II	1215–50
Carolingian dynasty		Rival claimants:	
Berengar	915–924	Henry (VII)	1220–35
		Henry Raspe	1246–47
House of Saxony (Liudolfings)		William of Holland	1247–56
Henry I	919–936	Conrad IV	1250–54
Otto I	936–973	*Great Interregnum*	1254–73
Otto II	973–983	Richard	1257–72
Otto III	983–1002	Alfonso (Alfonso X of Castile)	1257–75
Henry II	1002–24		
		House of Habsburg	
Salian dynasty		Rudolf I	1270–01
Conrad II	1024–39		
Henry III	1039–56		

Holy Roman Emperors (continued)

EMPEROR	REIGN
House of Nassau	
Adolf	1292–98
House of Habsburg	
Albert I	1298–1308
House of Luxembourg	
Henry VII	1308–13
House of Habsburg	
Frederick (III)	1314–26
House of Wittelsbach	
Louis IV	1314–46
House of Luxembourg	
Charles IV	1346–78
Wenceslas	1378–1400
House of Wittelsbach	
Rupert	1400–10
House of Luxembourg	
Jobst	1410–11
Sigismund	1410–37

EMPEROR	REIGN
House of Habsburg	
Albert II	1438–39
Frederick III	1440–93
Maximilian I	1493–1519
Charles V	1519–56
Ferdinand I	1556–64
Maximilian II	1564–76
Rudolf II	1576–1612
Matthias	1612–19
Ferdinand II	1619–37
Ferdinand III	1637–57
Leopold I	1658–1705
Joseph I	1705–11
Charles VI	1711–40
House of Wittelsbach	
Charles VII	1742–45
House of Habsburg	
Francis I	1745–65
Joseph II	1765–90
Leopold II	1790–92
Francis II	1792–1806

Rulers of Russia[1]

RULER	REIGN
Princes and Grand Princes of Moscow	
(Muscovy): Danilovich dynasty[2]	
Daniel (son of Alexander Nevsky)	c. 1276–1303
Yury	1303–25
Ivan I	1325–40
Semyon (Simeon)	1340–53
Ivan II	1353–59
Dmitry Donskoy	1359–89
Vasily I	1389–1425
Vasily II	1425–62
Ivan III	1462–1505
Vasily III	1505–33
Ivan IV	1533–47
Tsars of Russia: Danilovich dynasty	
Ivan IV	1547–84
Fyodor I	1584–98
Tsars of Russia: Time of Troubles	
Boris Godunov	1598–1605
Fyodor II	1605
False Dmitry	1605–06
Vasily (IV)	1606–10
Interregnum	1610–12
Tsars and Empresses of Russia and the	
Russian Empire: Romanov dynasty[3]	
Michael III	1613–45
Alexis	1645–76
Fyodor III	1676–82
Peter I (Ivan V coruler 1682–96)	1682–1725
Catherine I	1725–27

RULER	REIGN
Tsars and Empresses of Russia and the	
Russian Empire: Romanov dynasty[3] (continued)	
Peter II	1727–30
Anna	1730–40
Ivan VI	1740–41
Elizabeth	1741–61 (O.S.)
Peter III[4]	1761–62 (O.S.)
Catherine II	1762–96
Paul	1796–1801
Alexander I	1801–25
Nicholas I	1825–55
Alexander II	1855–81
Alexander III	1881–94
Nicholas II	1894–1917
Provisional government	1917
Chairmen (or First Secretaries) of the	
Communist Party of the Soviet Union	
Vladimir Lenin	1917–24
Joseph Stalin	1924–53
Georgy Malenkov	1953
Nikita Khrushchev	1953–64
Leonid Brezhnev	1964–82
Yury Andropov	1982–84
Konstantin Chernenko	1984–85
Mikhail Gorbachev	1985–91
Presidents of Russia	
Boris Yeltsin	1990–99
Vladimir Putin	2000–08
Dmitry Medvedev	2008–

[1]This table includes leaders of Muscovy, Russia, the Russian Empire, and the Soviet Union.   [2]The Danilovich dynasty is a late branch of the Rurik dynasty, named after its progenitor, Daniel.   [3]On 22 Oct (Old Style) 1721, Peter I the Great took the title of "emperor." However, despite the official titling, conventional usage took an odd

Rulers of Russia[1] (continued)

turn. Every male sovereign continued usually to be called tsar, but every female sovereign was conventionally called empress. [4]The direct line of the Romanov dynasty came to an end in 1761 with the death of Elizabeth, daughter of Peter I, but subsequent rulers of the "Holstein-Gottorp dynasty" (the first, Peter III, was son of Charles Frederick, duke of Holstein-Gottorp, and Anna, daughter of Peter I) took the family name of Romanov.

Middle East

Byzantine Emperors

The Byzantine Empire comprised what was previously the eastern half of the Roman Empire. It survived for nearly 1,000 years after the western half had crumbled into various feudal kingdoms; it finally fell to Ottoman Turkish onslaughts in 1453. For emperors of the Eastern Roman Empire (at Constantinople) before the fall of Rome, see "Roman Emperors."

EMPEROR	REIGN
Zeno	474–491
Anastasius I	491–518
Justin I	518–527
Justinian I	527–565
Justin II	565–578
Tiberius II Constantine	578–582
Maurice Tiberius	582–602
Phocas	602–610
Heraclius	610–641
Heraclius Constantine	641
Heraclonas (or Heraclius)	641
Constans II (Constantine Pogonatus)	641–668
Constantine IV	668–685
Justinian II Rhinotmetus	685–695
Leontius	695–698
Tiberius III	698–705
Justinian II Rhinotmetus (restored)	705–711
Philippicus	711–713
Anastasius II	713–715
Theodosius III	715–717
Leo III	717–741
Constantine V Copronymus	741–775
Leo IV	775–780
Constantine VI	780–797
Irene (empress)	797–802
Nicephorus I	802–811
Stauracius	811
Michael I Rhangabe	811–813
Leo V	813–820
Michael II Balbus	820–829
Theophilus	829–842
Michael III	842–867
Basil I	867–886
Leo VI	886–912
Alexander	912–913
Constantine VII Porphyrogenitus	913–959
Romanus I Lecapenus	920–944
Romanus II	959–963
Nicephorus II Phocas	963–969
John I Tzimisces	969–976
Basil II Bulgaroctonus	976–1025
Constantine VIII	1025–28
Romanus III Argyrus	1028–34
Michael IV	1034–41
Michael V Calaphates	1041–42
Zoe (empress)	1042–56
Constantine IX Monomachus	1042–55

EMPEROR	REIGN
Theodora (empress)	1055–56
Michael VI Stratioticus	1056–57
Isaac I Comnenus	1057–59
Constantine X Ducas	1059–67
Romanus IV Diogenes	1067–71
Michael VII Ducas	1071–78
Nicephorus III Botaniates	1078–81
Alexius I Comnenus	1081–1118
John II Comnenus	1118–43
Manuel I Comnenus	1143–80
Alexius II Comnenus	1180–83
Andronicus I Comnenus	1183–85
Isaac II Angelus	1185–95
Alexius III Angelus	1195–1203
Isaac II Angelus (restored) and Alexius IV Angelus (joint ruler)	1203–04
Alexius V Ducas Murtzuphlus	1204

Latin emperors	
Baldwin I	1204–06
Henry	1206–16
Peter	1217
Yolande (empress)	1217–19
Robert	1221–28
Baldwin II	1228–61
John	1231–37

Nicaean emperors	
Constantine (XI) Lascaris	1204–05?
Theodore I Lascaris	1205?–22
John III Ducas Vatatzes	1222–54
Theodore II Lascaris	1254–58
John IV Lascaris	1258–61

Greek emperors restored	
Michael VIII Palaeologus	1261–82
Andronicus II Palaeologus	1282–1328
Andronicus III Palaeologus	1328–41
John V Palaeologus	1341–76
John VI Cantacuzenus	1347–54
Andronicus IV Palaeologus	1376–79
John V Palaeologus (restored)	1379–90
John VII Palaeologus	1390
John V Palaeologus (restored)	1390–91
Manuel II Palaeologus	1391–1425
John VIII Palaeologus	1421–48
Constantine XI Palaeologus	1449–53

Caliphs

When Muhammad died on 8 Jun 632, Abu Bakr, his father-in-law, succeeded to his political and administrative functions. He and his three immediate successors are known as the "perfect" or "rightly guided" caliphs. After them, the title was borne by the 14 Umayyad caliphs of Damascus (from 661–750) and subsequently by the 38 'Abbasid caliphs of Baghdad (both are named after their clans of origin). The empire of the caliphate grew rapidly through conquest during its first two centuries to include most of southwestern Asia, North Africa, and Spain. 'Abbasid power ended in 945, when the Buyids took Baghdad under their rule. They retained the 'Abbasid caliphs as figureheads; other dynasties in Central Asia and the Ganges River basin acknowledged the 'Abbasid caliphs as spiritual leaders. The Fatimids, however, proclaimed a new caliphate in 920 in their capital of al-Mahdiyah in Tunisia; it lasted until 1171, by which time opposition within the sect caused it to disintegrate. 'Abbasid authority was partially restored in the 12th century, but the caliphate ceased to exist with the Mongol destruction of Baghdad in 1258. Some principal caliphs are listed below.

CALIPH	REIGN
"Perfect" caliphs	
Abu Bakr	632–634
'Umar I	634–644
'Uthman ibn 'Affan	644–656
'Ali	656–661
Umayyad caliphs (Damascus)	
Mu'awiyah I	661–680
'Abd al-Malik	685–705
al-Walid	705–715
Hisham	724–743
Marwan II	744–750
'Abbasid caliphs (Baghdad)	
al-Saffah	749–754
Harun al-Rashid	786–809
al-Mamun	813–833

CALIPH	REIGN
Fatimid caliphs (al-Mahdiyah)	
al-Mahdi	909–934
al-Qaim	934–946
al-Mansur	946–953
al-Mu'izz	953–975
al-Hakim	996–1021
al-Mustansir	1036–94
al-Musta'li	1094–1101
'Abbasid caliph (Baghdad)	
al-Nasir	1180–1225

Sultans of the Ottoman Empire

One of the most powerful states in the world during the 15th and 16th centuries, the Ottoman empire was created by Turkish tribes in Anatolia and spanned more than 600 years. It came to an end in 1922, when it was replaced by the Turkish Republic and various successor states in southeastern Europe and the Middle East. At its height the empire included most of southeastern Europe, the Middle East as far east as Iraq, North Africa as far west as Algeria, and most of the Arabian Peninsula. The term Ottoman is a dynastic appellation derived from Osman (Arabic: 'Uthman), the nomadic Turkmen chief who founded both the dynasty and the empire.

SULTAN	REIGN
Osman I	c. 1300–1324
Orhan	1324–1360
Murad I	1360–1389
Bayezid I	1389–1402
Mehmed I	1413–1421
Murad II	1421–1444
Mehmed II	1444–1446
Murad II (second reign)	1446–1451
Mehmed II (second reign)	1451–1481
Bayezid II	1481–1512
Selim I	1512–1520
Suleyman I	1520–1566
Selim II	1566–1574
Murad III	1574–1595
Mehmed III	1595–1603
Ahmed I	1603–1617
Mustafa I	1617–1618
Osman II	1618–1622
Mustafa I (second reign)	1622–1623
Murad IV	1623–1640

SULTAN	REIGN
Ibrahim	1640–1648
Mehmed IV	1648–1687
Suleyman II	1687–1691
Ahmed II	1691–1695
Mustafa II	1695–1703
Ahmed III	1703–1730
Mahmud I	1730–1754
Osman III	1754–1757
Mustafa III	1757–1774
Abdulhamid I	1774–1789
Selim III	1789–1807
Mustafa IV	1807–1808
Mahmud II	1808–1839
Abdulmecid I	1839–1861
Abdulaziz	1861–1876
Murad V	1876
Abdulhamid II	1876–1909
Mehmed V	1909–1918
Mehmed VI	1918–1922

Persian Dynasties

Dates given are approximate and may overlap.

DYNASTY/KINGDOM	PERIOD	DYNASTY/KINGDOM	PERIOD
Median	728–550 BC	Seljuqs	1038–1157
Achaemenian	559–330 BC	Mongols[4]	1220–1335
Hellenistic period of Alexander		Timurids and Ottoman Turks	1380–1501
and the Seleucids[1]	330 BC–247 BC	Safavid	1502–1736
Parthian period (Arsacid dynasty)[2]	247 BC–AD 224	Afghan interlude	1723–36
Sasanian	224–651	Nader Shah	1736–47
Arab invasion and the advent of		Zand	1750–79
Islam	640–829	Qajars	1794–1925
Iranian intermezzo[3]	821–1055	Pahlavi	1925–79

[1]Dates from the death of Darius III, the last Achaemenian king, and the invasion of Alexander the Great. [2]Dates from the year in which the Parnian chief Arsaces first battled the Seleucids. [3]Includes the Tahirid, Samanid, Ghaznavids, and Buyid dynasties. [4]Mainly the Il-Khanid dynasty (1256–1353).

Asia

Indian Dynasties

Dates given are approximations.

DYNASTY	LOCATION	DATES	DYNASTY	LOCATION	DATES
Nanda	Ganges Valley	400 BC	Pala	Bengal	800–1100
Maurya	India, barring the area south of Mysore (Karnataka)	400–200 BC	Pratihara	western India and upper Ganges Valley	900–1100
Indo-Greeks	northern India	200–100 BC	Rastrakuta	western and central Deccan	800–1100
Sunga	Ganges Valley and parts of central India	200–100 BC	Cola	Tamil Nadu	900–1300
			Candella	Bundelkhand	1000–1200
Satavahana	northern Deccan	100 BC–AD 300	Cauhan	Rajasthan	1000–1200
Saka	western India	100 BC–AD 400	Caulukya	Gujarat	1000–1300
Kusana	northern India and Central Asia	AD 100–300	Paramara	western and central India	1000–1100
Gupta	northern India	400–600	Later Calukya	western and central Deccan	1000–1200
Harsa	northern India	700	Hoysala	central and southern Deccan	1200–1400
Pallava	Tamil Nadu	400–900			
Calukya	western and central Deccan	600–800	Yadava	northern Deccan	1200–1300
			Pandya	Tamil Nadu	1300–1400

Japanese Historical Periods and Rulers

PERIOD	DATES	PERIOD	DATES
Asuka	552–710	Muromachi (or Ashikaga)	1338–1573
Nara	710–784	Azuchi-Momoyama	1574–1600
Heian	794–1185	Edo (or Tokugawa)	1603–1867
Kamakura	1192–1333	Meiji	1868–1912

Reign dates for the first 28 sovereigns (Jimmu through Senka) are taken from the *Nihon shoki* ("Chronicles of Japan"). The first 14 sovereigns are considered legendary, and while the next 14 are known to have existed, their exact reign dates have not been verified historically. When the year of actual accession and year of formal coronation are different, the latter is placed in parentheses after the former. If the two events took place in the same year, no special notation is used. If only the coronation year is known, it is placed in parentheses.

EMPEROR	REIGN	EMPEROR	REIGN
Jimmu	(660)–585 BC	Kogen	(214)–158 BC
Suizei	(581)–549 BC	Kaika	158–98 BC
Annei	549–511 BC	Sujin	(97)–30 BC
Itoku	(510)–477 BC	Suinin	(29 BC)–AD 70
Kosho	(475)–393 BC	Keiko	(71)–130
Koan	(392)–291 BC	Seimu	(131)–190
Korei	(290)–215 BC	Chuai	(192)–200

Japanese Historical Periods and Rulers (continued)

EMPEROR	REIGN	EMPEROR	REIGN
Jingu Kogo (regent)	201–269	Toba	1107–23
Ojin	(270)–310	Sutoku	1123–41
Nintoku	(313)–399	Konoe	1141–55
Richu	(400)–405	Go-Shirakawa	1155–58
Hanzei	(406)–410	Nijo	1158–65
Ingyo	(412)–453	Rokujo	1165–68
Anko	453–456	Takakura	1168–80
Yuryaku	456–479	Antoku	1180–85[1]
Seinei	(480)–484	Go-Toba	1183 (1184)–98
Kenzo	(485)–487	Tsuchimikado	1198–1210
Ninken	(488)–498	Juntoku	1210 (1211)–21
Buretsu	498–506	Chukyo	1221
Keitai	(507)–531	Goshirakawa	1221 (1222)–32
Ankan	531 (534)–535	Shijo	1232 (1233)–42
Senka	535–539	Go-Saga	1242–46
Kimmei	539–571	Go-Fukakusa	1246–59/60
Bidatsu	(572)–585	Kameyama	1259/60–74
Yomei	585–587	Gouda	1274–87
Sushun	587–592	Fushimi	1287 (1288)–98
Suiko (empress regnant)	593–628	Go-Fushimi	1298–1301
Jomei	(629)–641	Go-Nijo	1301–08
Kogyoku (empress regnant)	(642)–645	Hanazono	1308–18
Kotoku	645–654	Go-Daigo	1318–39
Saimei (empress regnant: Kogyoku rethroned)	(655)–661	Go-Murakami	1339–68
Tenji	661 (668)–672	Chokei	1368–83
Kobun	672	Go-Kameyama	1383–92
Temmu	672 (673)–686		
Jito (empress regnant)	686 (690)–697	**The Northern court[2]**	
Mommu	697–707	Kogon	1331 (1332)–33
Gemmei (empress regnant)	707–715	Komyo	1336 (1337/38)–48
Gensho (empress regnant)	715–724	Suko	1348 (1349/50)–51
Shomu	724–749	Go-Kogon	1351 (1353/54)–71
Koken (empress regnant)	749–758	Go-Enyu	1371 (1374/75)–82
Junnin	758–764	Go-Komatsu	1382–92
Shotoku (empress regnant: Koken rethroned)	764 (765)–770	Go-Komatsu	1392–1412
Konin	770–781	Shoko	1412 (1414)–28
Kammu	781–806	Go-Hanazono	1428 (1429/30)–64
Heizei	806–809	Go-Tsuchimikado	1464 (1465/66)–1500
Saga	809–823	Go-Kashiwabara	1500 (1521)–26
Junna	823–833	Go-Nara	1526 (1536)–57
Nimmyo	833–850	Ogimachi	1557 (1560)–86
Montoku	850–858	Go-Yozei	1586 (1587)–1611
Seiwa	858–876	Go-Mizunoo	1611–29
Yozei	876 (877)–884	Meisho (empress regnant)	1629 (1630)–43
Koko	884–887	Go-Komyo	1643–54
Uda	887–897	Go-Sai	1654/55 (1656)–63
Daigo	897–930	Reigen	1663–87
Suzaku	930–946	Higashiyama	1687–1709
Murakami	946–967	Nakamikado	1709 (1710)–35
Reizei	967–969	Sakuramachi	1735–47
En'yu	969–984	Momozono	1747–62
Kazan	984–986	Go-Sakuramachi (empress regnant)	1762 (1763)–71
Ichijo	986–1011	Go-Momozono	1771–79
Sanjo	1011–16	Kokaku	1780–1817
Go-Ichijo	1016–36	Ninko	1817–46
Go-Suzaku	1036–45	Komei	1846 (1847)–66
Go-Reizei	1045–68	Meiji (personal name: Mutsuhito; era name: Meiji)	1867 (1868)–1912
Go-Sanjo	1068–72	Taisho (personal name: Yoshihito; era name: Taisho)	1912 (1915)–26
Shirakawa	1072–86	Hirohito (era name: Showa)	1926 (1928)–1989
Horikawa	1086–1107	Akihito (era name: Heisei)	1989 (1990)–

[1]Antoku's reign overlaps that of Go-Toba. Go-Toba was placed on the throne by the Minamoto clan after the rival Taira clan had fled Kyoto with Antoku.   [2]From 1336 until 1392 Japan witnessed the spectacle of two contending Imperial courts—the Southern court of Go-Daigo and his descendants, whose sphere of influence was restricted to the immediate vicinity of the Yoshino Mountains, and the Northern court of Kogon and his descendants, which was under the domination of the Ashikaga family.

Chinese Dynasties

Dates given for early dynasties are approximate and may overlap.

DYNASTY	ALTERNATE NAME	DATES	DYNASTY	ALTERNATE NAME	DATES
Hsia[1]	Xia	c. 2205–1766 BC	Six Dynasties[2] (continued)		
Shang		c. 1760–1030 BC	Southern Qi		479–502
Western Zhou	Chou	c. 1050–771 BC	Southern Liang		502–57
Eastern Zhou	Chou	c. 771–255 BC	Southern Chen		557–89
Qin	Ch'in	221–206 BC	Sui		581–618
Han		206 BC–AD 220	T'ang	Tang	618–907
Western Jin	Chin	265–317	Five Dynasties[3]	Ten Kingdoms[3]	907–960
Eastern Jin[2]	Chin	317–420	Sung	Song	960–1279
Six Dynasties[2]		220–589	Yüan	Yuan, Mongol	1206–1368
Wu		222–80	Ming		1368–1644
Eastern Jin[2]		317–420	Ch'ing	Qing, Manchu	1644–1911/12
Liusong		420–79			

[1]The Hsia Dynasty is mentioned in legends but is of undetermined historicity. [2]Between the fall of the Han and the establishment of the Sui, China was divided into two societies, northern and southern. The Six Dynasties had their capital at Nanjing in the south. The Eastern Jin is considered one of these six dynasties and so is listed twice. [3]Period of time between the fall of the T'ang dynasty and the founding of the Sung dynasty, when five would-be dynasties followed one another in quick succession in North China. The era is also known as the period of the Ten Kingdoms because 10 regimes dominated separate regions of South China during the same period.

Leaders of the People's Republic of China Since 1949

Chinese Communist Party leaders

NAME	TITLE	DATES
Mao Zedong	CCP chairman	1949–1976
Hua Guofeng	CCP chairman	1976–1981
Hu Yaobang	CCP chairman; after September 1982, general secretary of the CCP	1981–1987
Zhao Ziyang	CCP general secretary	1987–1989
Jiang Zemin	CCP general secretary	1989–2002
Hu Jintao	CCP general secretary	2002–

premiers

NAME	DATES
Zhou Enlai	1949–1976
Hua Guofeng	1976–1980
Zhao Ziyang	1980–1987
Li Peng	1987–1998
Zhu Rongji	1998–2003
Wen Jiabao	2003–

Note: although he held no top party or state position, Deng Xiaoping was de facto leader of China from 1977 to 1997.

Dalai Lamas

The Dalai Lama is the head of the dominant Dge-lugs-pa (Yellow Hat) order of Tibetan Buddhists and, until 1959, was both spiritual and temporal ruler of Tibet. In accordance with the belief in reincarnate lamas, which began to develop in the 14th century, the successors of the first Dalai Lama were considered his rebirths and came to be regarded as physical manifestations of the compassionate bodhisattva ("buddha-to-be"), Avalokitesvara.

DALAI LAMA	NAME	LIVED	DALAI LAMA	NAME	LIVED
first	Dge-'dun-grub-pa	1391–1475	eighth	'Jam-dpal-rgya-mtsho	1758–1804
second	Dge-'dun-rgya-mtsho	1475–1542	ninth	Lung-rtogs-rgya-mtsho	1806–1815[1]
third	Bsod-nams-rgya-mtsho	1543–1588	tenth	Tshul-khrims-rgya-mtsho	1816–1837[1]
fourth	Yon-tan-rgya-mtsho	1589–1617	eleventh	Mkhas-grub-rgya-mtsho	1838–1856[1]
fifth	Ngag-dbang-rgya-mtsho	1617–1682	twelfth	'Phrin-las-rgya-mtsho	1856–1875[1]
sixth	Tshangs-dbyangs-rgya-mtsho	1683–1706	thirteenth	Thub-bstan-rgya-mtsho	1875–1933[2]
seventh	Bskal-bzang-rgya-mtsho	1708–1757	fourteenth	Bstan-'dzin-rgya-mtsho	1935–[3]

[1]Dalai Lamas 9–12 all died young, and the country was ruled by regencies. [2]Reigned as head of a sovereign state from 1912. [3]Ruled from exile in Dharmsala, India, from 1960.

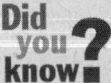
Did you know?

One of Africa's least-explored regions, the northern part of the Republic of the Congo, an area of huge swamps and nearly impenetrable forests, was traversed by foot in 1999. Dr. Michael Fay, an ecologist with the Wildlife Conservation Society, and a team of 12 others undertook a 1,200-mi (1,900-km) survey of this area as well as similar areas in neighboring Gabon. The team concluded that this wilderness is seriously threatened.

The Americas

Pre-Columbian Civilizations

Various aboriginal American Indian cultures evolved in Meso-America (part of Mexico and Central America) and the Andean region (western South America) prior to Spanish exploration and conquest in the 16th century. These pre-Columbian civilizations were extraordinary developments in human society and culture, characterized by kingdoms and empires, great monuments and cities, and refinements in the arts, metallurgy, and writing. Dates given below are approximations.

CULTURE	LOCATION	DATES
Meso-American civilizations		
Olmec	Gulf coast of southern Mexico	1150 BC–800 BC
Zapotec	Oaxaca, particularly Monte Albán	500 BC–AD 900
Totonac	east-central Mexico	500 BC–AD 900
Teotihuacán	Teotihuacán, in the Valley of Mexico	AD 400–600
Maya	southern Mexico and Guatemala	250–900
Toltec	central Mexico	900–1200
Aztec	central and southern Mexico	1400–early 1500s
Andean civilizations		
Nazca	southern coast of Peru	200 BC–AD 600
Recuay	northern highlands of Peru	200 BC–AD 600
Tiwanaku	Lake Titicaca, Bolivia	200 BC–AD 1000
Moche (Mochica)	northern coast of Peru	AD 1–700
Inca	Pacific coast of South America	1100–1532

Africa

Historic Sub-Saharan African States

STATE	LOCATION IN PRESENT-DAY COUNTRIES	FLOURISHED
Aksumite kingdom	Ethiopia, Sudan	1st–10th centuries
Asante empire	Ghana	18th–19th centuries
Basuto kingdom	Lesotho	19th century
Benin kingdom	Nigeria	12th–19th centuries
kingdom of Buganda	Uganda	14th–20th centuries
kingdom of Bunyoro	Uganda	15th–19th centuries
kingdom of Burundi	Burundi	17th–20th centuries
kingdom of Dahomey	Benin	17th–19th centuries
Darfur	Sudan	17th–19th centuries
kingdom of Dongola	Sudan	7th–14th centuries
Fulani empire	Cameroon, Niger, Nigeria	19th–20th centuries
Ghana empire	Mali, Mauritania	4th–13th centuries
Hausa states	Nigeria	14th–19th centuries
Kanem-Bornu	Nigeria, Chad, Cameroon, Niger, Libya	9th–19th centuries
Kongo kingdom	Angola, Dem. Rep. of Congo	14th–17th centuries
Kuba kingdom	Dem. Rep. of Congo	17th–19th centuries
kingdom of Kush	Egypt, Sudan	c. 850 BC–c. AD 325
Luba empire	Dem Rep. of Congo	16th–19th centuries
Lunda empire	Dem. Rep. of Congo, Angola, Zambia	17th–19th centuries
Mali empire	Mali, Mauritania, Senegal, Gambia, Guinea-Bissau	13th–16th centuries
Ndongo kingdom	Angola	14th–17th centuries
kingdom of Nubia	Egypt, Sudan	4th–7th centuries
Oyo empire	Nigeria	16th–19th centuries
Rozwi empire	Zimbabwe, Botswana	17th–19th centuries
Shewa empire	Ethiopia	15th–19th centuries
Songhai empire	Nigeria, Niger	6th–17th centuries
Tukulor empire	Mali	19th century
Wolof empire	Senegal	14th–19th centuries
Zeng empire	Somalia, Kenya, Tanzania, Mozambique	10th–16th centuries
Zulu kingdom	South Africa	19th century

Populations

Largest Urban Agglomerations

Agglomerations include a central city and associated neighboring communities.
Source: <www.citypopulation.de>.

RANK	AGGLOMERATION	COUNTRY	POPULATION (JANUARY 2010)	RANK	AGGLOMERATION	COUNTRY	POPULATION (JANUARY 2010)
1	Tokyo	Japan	34,000,000	16	Cairo	Egypt	15,200,000
2	Guangzhou	China	24,200,000	17	Beijing	China	13,600,000
	Seoul	Rep. of Korea	24,200,000		Dhaka	Bangladesh	13,600,000
4	Mexico City	Mexico	23,400,000		Moscow	Russia	13,600,000
5	Delhi	India	23,200,000	20	Buenos Aires	Argentina	13,300,000
6	Mumbai (Bombay)	India	22,800,000	21	Istanbul	Turkey	12,800,000
7	New York City	US	22,200,000		Tehran	Iran	12,800,000
8	São Paulo	Brazil	20,900,000	23	Rio de Janeiro	Brazil	12,600,000
9	Manila	Philippines	19,600,000	24	London	UK	12,400,000
10	Shanghai	China	18,400,000	25	Lagos	Nigeria	11,800,000
11	Los Angeles	US	17,900,000	26	Paris	France	10,400,000
12	Osaka	Japan	16,800,000	27	Chicago	US	9,850,000
13	Kolkata (Calcutta)	India	16,300,000	28	Shenzhen	China	9,150,000
14	Karachi	Pakistan	16,200,000	29	Lima	Peru	9,050,000
15	Jakarta	Indonesia	15,400,000	30	Wuhan	China	8,950,000

Migration of Foreigners into Selected Countries

Percentages of foreign-born populations in selected Organisation for Economic Co-operation and Development countries. N/A means not available. Source: OECD in Figures 2009.

	FOREIGN-BORN AS % OF TOTAL POPULATION			FOREIGN-BORN AS % OF TOTAL POPULATION	
COUNTRY	2000	2007	COUNTRY	2000	2007
Luxembourg	37.3	36.2	Germany	8.9	12.9[1]
Australia	23.0	25.0	Netherlands	10.1	10.7
Switzerland	21.9	24.9	UK	7.9	10.2
New Zealand	17.2	21.6	Norway	6.8	9.5
Canada	18.1	20.1	France	7.4	8.5
Ireland	8.7	15.7	Denmark	5.8	6.9
Austria	10.5	14.2	Slovakia	N/A	6.8
US	11.0	13.6	Czech Republic	4.2	6.2
Spain	4.9	13.4	Portugal	5.1	6.1
Sweden	11.3	13.4	Italy[2]	2.4	5.8
Belgium	10.3	13.0	Greece[2]	2.9	5.7

[1]2003. [2]Foreign population.

Persons of Concern Worldwide

The Office of the UN High Commissioner for Refugees (UNHCR) attempts to ease the plight of various "persons of concern," including refugees and asylum seekers. Detail may not add to total given because of statistical discrepancy. Sources: UNHCR, 2009 Global Trends: Refugees, Asylum-seekers, Returnees, Internally Displaced and Stateless Persons; Internal Displacement Monitoring Centre.

Persons of Concern to UNHCR by Region and Category (estimates as of 1 Jan 2010)

REGION	REFUGEES	ASYLUM SEEKERS	RETURNED REFUGEES	INTERNALLY DISPLACED PERSONS (IDPs)[1]	STATELESS AND OTHER	TOTAL[2]
Asia and Oceania	5,656,060	70,518	97,584	5,434,532	5,820,357	18,605,209
Africa	2,300,062	436,930	149,480	6,468,788	100,064	10,475,567
Europe	1,628,086	282,214	4,319	420,758	639,034	3,069,248
Northern America	444,895	124,973	—	—	—	569,868
Latin America and the Caribbean	367,437	68,785	70	3,303,979	118	3,740,389
total[2]	10,396,540	983,420	251,478	15,628,057	6,559,573	36,460,306

Persons of Concern Worldwide (continued)

Total Number of Refugees (estimates as of 1 January of each year)

YEAR	REFUGEES	YEAR	REFUGEES
2001	12,062,500	2006	8,394,400
2002	12,029,900	2007	9,877,700
2003	10,389,600	2008	11,390,670
2004	9,671,800	2009	10,478,621
2005	9,236,500	2010	10,396,540

Origin of Major Refugee Populations[3] (estimates as of 1 Jan 2010)

COUNTRY OF ORIGIN	TOTAL	COUNTRY OF ORIGIN	TOTAL
Afghanistan	2,887,123	Colombia	389,753
Iraq	1,785,212	Sudan	368,195
Somalia	678,309	Vietnam	339,289
Democratic Republic of the Congo	455,852	Eritrea	209,168
Myanmar (Burma)	406,669	Serbia	195,626

Host Country of Major Refugee Populations (estimates as of 1 Jan 2010)

COUNTRY OF ASYLUM	TOTAL	COUNTRY OF ASYLUM	TOTAL
Pakistan	1,740,711	Kenya	358,928
Iran	1,070,488	Chad	338,495
Syria	1,054,466	China	300,989
Germany	593,799	United States	275,461
Jordan	450,756	United Kingdom	269,363

Internally Displaced Persons (estimates as of 1 Jan 2010)

COUNTRY	TOTAL	COUNTRY	TOTAL
Sudan	4,900,000	Ethiopia	300,000–350,000
Colombia	3,300,000–4,900,000	Afghanistan	297,000+
Iraq	2,764,000	Georgia	230,000+
Democratic Republic of the Congo	1,900,000	Serbia	225,000–230,000
Somalia	1,500,000	Yemen	175,000+
Pakistan	1,230,000+	Chad	168,000
Turkey	954,000–1,201,000	Central African Republic	162,000
Azerbaijan	586,000	Peru	150,000
Zimbabwe	570,000–1,000,000	Philippines	125,000–188,000
India	500,000+	Bosnia and Herzegovina	114,000
Myanmar (Burma)	470,000+	Cyprus	100,000–201,000
Uganda	437,000+	Burundi	100,000
Syria	433,000	Lebanon	90,000–390,000
Sri Lanka	400,000	Indonesia	70,000–120,000
		Bangladesh	60,000–500,000

[1]Data include only those IDPs to whom UNHCR extends protection and/or assistance. [2]Includes unlisted returned IDPs and various unclassified persons. [3]A separate mandate of the UN Relief and Works Agency for Palestine Refugees in the Near East (UNRWA) covers more than 4,700,000 Palestinans. Palestinian refugees in the West Bank and the Gaza Strip outside of the UNRWA mandate numbered 95,201 in 2010.

Language

Most Widely Spoken Languages

Listing the languages spoken by approximately 1% of humankind (those spoken by more than 60,000,000 people), this table enumerates speakers of each tongue as a primary language. Source: Ethnologue: Languages of the World (2009), M. Paul Lewis, editor.

LANGUAGE	NUMBER OF SPEAKERS (MILLIONS)	% OF WORLD POPULATION (APPROXIMATE)	LANGUAGE FAMILY
Mandarin	845	12.4	Sino-Tibetan (Chinese)
Spanish	329	4.8	Indo-European (Romance)
English	328	4.8	Indo-European (Germanic)

Most Widely Spoken Languages (continued)

LANGUAGE	NUMBER OF SPEAKERS (MILLIONS)	% OF WORLD POPULATION (APPROXIMATE)	LANGUAGE FAMILY
Arabic	221	3.3	Afro-Asiatic (Semitic)
Hindi[1]	182	2.7	Indo-European (Indo-Aryan)
Bengali	181	2.7	Indo-European (Indo-Aryan)
Portuguese	178	2.6	Indo-European (Romance)
Russian	144	2.1	Indo-European (Slavic)
Japanese	122	1.8	isolated language
Punjabi	91	1.3	Indo-European (Indo-Aryan)
German	90	1.3	Indo-European (Germanic)
Javanese	85	1.2	Austronesian (Malayo-Polynesian)
Wu	77	1.1	Sino-Tibetan (Chinese)
Telugu	70	1.0	Dravidian
Vietnamese	69	1.0	Mon-Khmer (Vietic)
Marathi	68	1.0	Indo-European (Indo-Aryan)
French	68	1.0	Indo-European (Romance)
Korean	66	1.0	isolated language
Tamil	66	1.0	Dravidian
Italian	62	0.9	Indo-European (Romance)
Urdu[1]	61	0.9	Indo-European (Indo-Aryan)

[1]*Although Hindi and Urdu use different writing systems, these languages are branches of Hindustani and are orally mutually intelligible.*

English Neologisms

New entries from Merriam-Webster's Collegiate Dictionary, 11th ed. (2011). The date in parentheses is the date of the word's earliest recorded use in English. Italics are used to signify new definitions of established words.

Amber Alert *n* (1997): a widely publicized bulletin that alerts the public to a recently abducted or missing child

boomerang child *n* (1988): a young adult who returns to live at his or her family home especially for financial reasons

bromance *n* (2004): a close nonsexual friendship between men

cougar *n* (1774): *a middle-aged woman seeking a romantic relationship with a younger man*

crowdsourcing *n* (2006): the practice of obtaining needed services, ideas, or content by soliciting contributions from a large group of people and especially from the online community rather than from traditional employees or suppliers

cyberbullying *n* (2000): the electronic posting of mean-spirited messages about a person (as a student) often done anonymously

fair trade *n* (1932): *a movement whose goal is to help producers in developing countries to get a fair price for their products so as to reduce poverty, provide for the ethical treatment of workers and farmers, and promote environmentally sustainable practices*

fist bump *n* (1996): a gesture in which two people bump their fists together (as in greeting or celebration)

helicopter parent *n* (1989): a parent who is overly involved in the life of his or her child

hypermiling *n* (2006): the use of fuel-saving techniques (as lower speeds and frequent coasting) to maximize a vehicle's fuel mileage

kettle chip *n* (1983): a type of potato chip made so as to be thicker and crunchier than the typical potato chip

Kobe beef *n* (1889): highly marbled premium beef from Japanese cattle that is noted for exceptional tenderness and flavor

labradoodle *n* (1970): a dog that is a cross between a Labrador retriever and a poodle

microblogging *n* (2005): blogging done with severe space or size constraints typically by posting frequent brief messages about personal activities

netbook *n* (2007): a small portable computer designed primarily for wireless Internet access

parcour *n* (2002): the sport of traversing environmental obstacles by running, climbing, or leaping rapidly and efficiently

quant *n* (1979): an expert at analyzing and managing quantitative data

robocall *n* (1993): a telephone call from an automated source that delivers a prerecorded message to a large number of people

sippy cup *n* (1986): a cup that has a detachable lid with a projecting hole designed to help a young child sip liquid from the cup without spilling it

slider *n* (1530): *a very small meat sandwich typically served on a bun; especially: a small hamburger*

smartphone *n* (1997): a cell phone that includes additional software functions (as e-mail or an Internet browser)

social media *n* (2004): forms of electronic communication (as Web sites for social networking and microblogging) through which users create online communities to share information, ideas, personal messages, and other content (as videos)

tweet *n* (1768): *a post made on the Twitter online message service*

viral *adj* (1937): *quickly and widely spread or popularized especially by person-to-person electronic communication*

walk-off *adj* (1984): *ending a baseball game immediately by causing the winning run to score for the home team in the bottom of the last inning*

Scholarship

National Libraries of the World

The national libraries listed below are generally open to the public. National libraries are usually the primary repository for a nation's printed works. Sources: "National Libraries of the World: An Address List," IFLA Publications; *International Dictionary of Library Histories*, 2001, Fitzroy Dearborn Publishers.

LIBRARY	LOCATION	YEAR FOUNDED[1]	SPECIAL COLLECTIONS, ARCHIVES, PAPERS
Biblioteca Nacional de España	Madrid, Spain	1836	manuscripts, Miguel de Cervantes
Biblioteca Nacional de México	Mexico City	1867	Jesuit works, early Mexican printing
Biblioteca Nacional de Portugal	Lisbon	1796	Luís de Camões, Desiderius Erasmus
Biblioteca Nacional de Venezuela	Caracas	1833	politics and diplomacy, Simón Bolívar
Biblioteca Nazionale Centrale di Firenze	Florence, Italy	1861	Reformation, Galileo Galilei
Biblioteca Nazionale Centrale di Roma	Rome, Italy	1876	Jesuit collections, Gabriele D'Annunzio
Biblioteka Narodowa	Warsaw, Poland	1928	engravings, music
Bibliotheca Alexandrina	Alexandria, Egypt	2002[2]	ancient manuscripts, Egyptian heritage
Bibliothèque Nationale de France	Paris	1461	Denis Diderot, Jean-Paul Sartre
British Library	London	1973[3]	Charles Dickens, George B. Shaw
Deutsche Nationalbibliothek Frankfurt am Main	Germany	2006	bibliographies, exile literature (1933–45)
Deutsche Nationalbibliothek Leipzig	Germany	2006	socialism, Anne-Frank-Shoah-Bibliothek
Fundação Biblioteca Nacional	Rio de Janeiro, Brazil	1810	botany, Latin American music
Jewish National and University Library	Jerusalem, Israel	1892	world Jewish history, Albert Einstein
Koninklijke Bibliotheek	The Hague, Netherlands	1798	Hugo Grotius, Constantijn Huygens
Library and Archives Canada	Ottawa	2004	hockey, portraits of Canadians
Library of Congress	Washington DC	1800	Americana, folk music, early motion pictures
National Agricultural Library	Beltsville MD	1962	research reports
National Diet Library[4]	Tokyo, Japan	1948	Japanese culture, Allied occupation
National Library of Australia	Canberra	1960	Asian and Pacific area
National Library of China[5]	Beijing	1909	art, early communism
National Library of Education	Washington DC	1994	research reports
National Library of Greece[6]	Athens	1866[7]	incunabula
National Library of India	Kolkata (Calcutta)	1903	rare journals of vernacular languages
National Library of Ireland	Dublin	1877	biography, Gaelic manuscripts
National Library of Medicine	Bethesda MD	1956	history of medicine
National Library of New Zealand[8]	Wellington	1965	European exploration, missionary activity
National Library of Pakistan	Islamabad	1993	manuscripts, censuses
National Library of Russia[9]	St. Petersburg	1795	rare books, Russian history
National Library of Scotland	Edinburgh	1925	mountaineering, witchcraft
National Library of South Africa	Pretoria; Cape Town	1999	Africana, cookery
National Library of Sweden[10]	Stockholm	1661	Scandinavian cartography and manuscripts
National Library of Wales	Aberystwyth	1907	publications of overseas Welsh settlements

[1]*In present institutional form.* [2]*Originally founded in the 3rd century* BC. [3]*Originally founded in 1753 as the British Museum Library.* [4]*Kokuritsu Kokkai Toshokan.* [5]*Zhongguo Guojia Tushuguan.* [6]*Ethnike Bibliotheke tes Hellados.* [7]*Originally founded in 1832 as the Public Library.* [8]*Te Puna Matauranga o Aotearoa.* [9]*Rossyskaya Natsionalnaya Biblioteka.* [10]*Kungliga Biblioteket.*

World Education Profile

This table provides comparative data about the education systems in selected countries. Definitions as well as information gathering and reporting methods vary widely from country to country, so the statistics presented here are not always exactly comparable. Some statistics are rounded estimates.

Compulsory education = the number of years of education and ages of pupils required by the system; **enrollment ratio** for primary and secondary education = the actual number of children attending primary school or secondary school as a percentage of all children in the primary school or secondary school age group as defined by the country (number may exceed 100%); **enrollment ratio** for higher education = the total enrollment in higher education, regardless of age, as a percentage of all persons of school-leaving age to five years thereafter; **student/teacher ratio** = the number of pupils or students per teacher at each level; **expenditure** = the total public expenditure on education as a percentage of GDP in 2008.

Sources: *Encyclopædia Britannica World Data*, 2010; UNESCO Institute for Statistics; World Bank.

World Education Profile (continued)

COUNTRY	YEAR	% LITERACY RATE OF THOSE 15 AND OLDER			COMPULSORY EDUCATION		ENROLLMENT RATIO (2008)			STUDENT/TEACHER RATIO (2007)			EXPEN-DITURE
		TOTAL	M	F	# YEARS	AGES	PRI.	SEC.	HIGHER	PRI.	SEC.	HIGHER	
Africa													
Egypt	2007	72.0	83.6	60.7	9	6–14	100[1]	79[2]	28	27.1	17.1[2]	31.2[3]	3.7
Senegal	2007	42.6	53.1	32.3	6	7–12	84	31	8	36.4[4]	26.4[3]	24.6[3]	4.8[5]
South Africa	2008	89.0	89.9	88.1	9	7–15	105[1]	95[1]	15[5]	31.0	29.0	16.7[6]	5.1
Asia													
China	2008	93.7	96.7	90.5	9	6–14	113	76	23	17.7	16.4	15.5[2]	—
India	2007	66.0	76.9	54.5	9	6–14	113[1]	57[1]	13[1]	40.2[2]	32.7[2]	26.4[2]	3.2[5]
Indonesia	2007	91.4	94.9	88.0	9	7–15	119	74	21	18.8	13.0	14.1	3.5[1]
Iran	2007	84.7	90.0	79.4	8	6–13	128	80	36	20.0[4]	24.2[2]	23.6[4]	4.8
Israel	2004	97.1	98.5	95.9	11	5–15	111	90	60	13.4	11.9	—	6.2[5]
Japan	2008	100	100	100	10	6–15	102	101	58	18.5	12.2	7.8	3.5[5]
Turkey	2007	88.7	96.2	81.3	9	6–14	99	82	38	26.9	20.7	27.5	3.1[2]
Europe													
France	2003	99.0	99.0	99.0	11	6–16	110	113	55	19.0	12.1	25.4[5]	5.6[5]
Germany	2003	99.0	99.0	99.0	13	6–18	105	102	51[6]	13.6	13.5	12.1[5]	4.4[5]
Italy	2008	98.8	99.1	98.5	9	6–14	104[1]	100[1]	67[1]	10.3	10.1	19.5	4.7[5]
Russia	2008	99.5	99.7	99.4	10	6–15	97	85	77	17.1	8.6	13.8	3.9[5]
United Kingdom	2006	100	100	100	12	5–16	106	99	57	17.2	14.0	18.2	5.6[5]
Latin America													
Argentina	2008	97.7	97.6	97.7	10	5–14	116[1]	85[1]	68[1]	16.3[5]	12.8[5]	10.2[7]	4.5[5]
Brazil	2007	90.0	89.8	90.2	8	7–14	127	101	34	23.9	18.6	19.6[6]	5.0[5]
Cuba	2008	99.8	99.8	99.8	9	6–14	104[8]	90[8]	118[8]	9.6[4]	9.7[4]	6.7[4]	13.3[1]
Mexico	2008	92.9	94.6	91.5	10	6–15	114	90	27	28.0	17.9	9.2	4.8[5]
Northern America													
Canada	2005	100	100	100	11	6–16	99[5]	101[5]	62[2]	17.4[9]	18.4[2]	19.8[2]	4.9[3]
United States	2003	99.0	99.0	99.0	12	6–17	99	94	83	13.8	14.6	13.6	5.7[5]
Oceania													
Australia	2006	100	100	100	11	5–15	106	149	77	16.0[5]	12.1[5]	10.6[5]	5.2[5]

[1]2007 data.   [2]2004 data.   [3]2005 data.   [4]2008 data.   [5]2006 data.   [6]2003 data.   [7]2001 data.   [8]2009 data.   [9]2002 data.

Religion

Chronological List of Popes

According to Roman Catholic doctrine, the pope is the successor of St. Peter, who was head of the Apostles. The pope thus is seen to have full and supreme power of jurisdiction over the universal church in matters of faith and morals, as well as in church discipline and government. Until the 4th century, the popes were usually known only as bishops of Rome. From 1309–77, the popes' seat was at Avignon, France. In the table, **antipopes**, who opposed the legitimately elected bishop of Rome and endeavored to secure the papal throne, are listed in italics. The elections of several antipopes are greatly obscured by incomplete or biased records, and at times even their contemporaries could not decide who was the true pope. It is impossible, therefore, to establish an absolutely definitive list of antipopes.

POPE	REIGN	POPE	REIGN	POPE	REIGN
Peter	?–c. 64	Eleutherius	c. 175–189	Dionysius	259–268
Linus	c. 67–76/79	Victor I	c. 189–199	Felix I	269–274
Anacletus	76–88 or 79–91	Zephyrinus	c. 199–217	Eutychian	275–283
Clement I	88–97 or 92–101	Calixtus I (Callistus)	217?–222	Gaius	283–296
				Marcellinus	291/296–304
		Hippolytus	217, 218–235	Marcellus I	308–309
Evaristus	c. 97–c. 107	Urban I	222–230	Eusebius	309/310
Alexander I	105–115 or 109–119	Pontian	230–235	Miltiades (Melchiades)	311–314
		Anterus	235–236		
Sixtus I	c. 115–c. 125	Fabian	236–250	Sylvester I	314–335
Telesphorus	c. 125–c. 136	Cornelius	251–253	Mark	336
Hyginus	c. 136–c. 140	*Novatian*	251	Julius I	337–352
Pius I	c. 140–155	Lucius I	253–254	Liberius	352–366
Anicetus	c. 155–c. 166	Stephen I	254–257	*Felix (II)*	355–358
Soter	c. 166–c. 175	Sixtus II	257–258	Damasus I	366–384

Chronological List of Popes (continued)

POPE	REIGN	POPE	REIGN	POPE	REIGN
Ursinus	366–367	Adrian I	772–795	Benedict IX	1047–48
Siricius	384–399	Leo III	795–816	(3rd time)	
Anastasius I	399–401	Stephen IV (or V)[2]	816–817	Damasus II	1048
Innocent I	401–417	Paschal I	817–824	Leo IX	1049–54
Zosimus	417–418	Eugenius II	824–827	Victor II	1055–57
Boniface I	418–422	Valentine	827	Stephen IX (or X)[2]	1057–58
Eulalius	418–419	Gregory IV	827–844	*Benedict X*	1058–59
Celestine I	422–432	*John*	844	Nicholas II	1059–61
Sixtus III	432–440	Sergius II	844–847	Alexander II	1061–73
Leo I	440–461	Leo IV	847–855	*Honorius (II)*	1061–72
Hilary	461–468	Benedict III	855–858	Gregory VII	1073–85
Simplicius	468–483	*Anastasius*	855	*Clement (III)*	1080–1100
Felix III (or II)[1]	483–492	*(Anastasius*		Victor III	1086–87
Gelasius I	492–496	*the Librarian)*		Urban II	1088–99
Anastasius II	496–498	Nicholas I	858–867	Paschal II	1099–1118
Symmachus	498–514	Adrian II	867–872	*Theodoric*	1100–02
Laurentius	498, 501–	John VIII	872–882	*Albert (Aleric)*	1102
	c. 505/507	Marinus I	882–884	*Sylvester (IV)*	1105–11
Hormisdas	514–523	Adrian III	884–885	Gelasius II	1118–19
John I	523–526	Stephen V (or VI)[2]	885–891	*Gregory (VIII)*	1118–21
Felix IV (or III)[1]	526–530	Formosus	891–896	Calixtus II	1119–24
Dioscorus	530	Boniface VI	896	(Callistus)	
Boniface II	530–532	Stephen VI (or VII)[2]	896	Honorius II	1124–30
John II	533–535	Romanus	897	*Celestine (II)*	1124
Agapetus I	535–536	Theodore II	897	Innocent II	1130–43
Silverius	536–537	John IX	898–900	*Anacletus (II)*	1130–38
Vigilius	537–555	Benedict IV	900	*Victor (IV)*	1138
Pelagius I	556–561	Leo V	903	Celestine II	1143–44
John III	561–574	*Christopher*	903–904	Lucius II	1144–45
Benedict I	575–579	Sergius III	904–911	Eugenius III	1145–53
Pelagius II	579–590	Anastasius III	911–913	Anastasius IV	1153–54
Gregory I	590–604	Lando	913–914	Adrian IV	1154–59
Sabinian	604–606	John X	914–928	Alexander III	1159–81
Boniface III	604	Leo VI	928	*Victor (IV)*	1159–64
Boniface IV	608–615	Stephen VII (or VIII)[2]	929–931	*Paschal (III)*	1164–68
Deusdedit	615–618	John XI	931–935	*Calixtus (III)*	1168–78
(Adeodatus I)		Leo VII	936–939	*Innocent (III)*	1179–80
Boniface V	619–625	Stephen VIII (or IX)[2]	939–942	Lucius III	1181–85
Honorius I	625–638	Marinus II	942–946	Urban III	1185–87
Severinus	640	Agapetus II	946–955	Gregory VIII	1187
John IV	640–642	John XII	955–964	Clement III	1187–91
Theodore I	642–649	Leo VIII[3]	963–965	Celestine III	1191–98
Martin I	649–655	Benedict V[3]	964–966?	Innocent III	1198–1216
Eugenius I	654–657	John XIII	965–972	Honorius III	1216–27
Vitalian	657–672	Benedict VI	973–974	Gregory IX	1227–41
Adeodatus II	672–676	*Boniface VII*	974	Celestine IV	1241
Donus	676–678	*(1st time)*		Innocent IV	1243–54
Agatho	678–681	Benedict VII	974–983	Alexander IV	1254–61
Leo II	682–683	John XIV	983–984	Urban IV	1261–64
Benedict II	684–685	*Boniface VII*	984–985	Clement IV	1265–68
John V	685–686	*(2nd time)*		Gregory X	1271–76
Conon	686–687	John XV (or XVI)[4]	985–996	Innocent V	1276
Sergius I	687–701	Gregory V	996–999	Adrian V	1276
Theodore	687	*John XVI (or XVII)[4]*	997–998	John XXI[4]	1276–77
Paschal	687	Sylvester II	999–1003	Nicholas III	1277–80
John VI	701–705	John XVII (or XVIII)[4]	1003	Martin IV[5]	1281–85
John VII	705–707	John XVIII (or XIX)[4]	1004–09	Honorius IV	1285–87
Sisinnius	708	Sergius IV	1009–12	Nicholas IV	1288–92
Constantine	708–715	*Gregory (VI)*	1012	Celestine V	1294
Gregory II	715–731	Benedict VIII	1012–24	Boniface VIII	1294–1303
Gregory III	731–741	John XIX (or XX)[4]	1024–32	Benedict XI	1303–04
Zacharias (Zachary)	741–752	Benedict IX	1032–44	Clement V (at	1305–14
Stephen (II)[2]	752	*(1st time)*		Avignon from	
Stephen II (or III)[2]	752–757	Sylvester III	1045	1309)	
Paul I	757–767	Benedict IX	1045	John XXII[4]	1316–34
Constantine (II)	767–768	*(2nd time)*		(at Avignon)	
Philip	768	Gregory VI	1045–46	*Nicholas (V)*	1328–30
Stephen III (or IV)[2]	768–772	Clement II	1046–47	*(at Rome)*	

Chronological List of Popes (continued)

POPE	REIGN	POPE	REIGN	POPE	REIGN
Benedict XII	1334–42	Calixtus III	1455–58	Alexander VII	1655–67
(at Avignon)		(Callistus)		Clement IX	1667–69
Clement VI	1342–52	Pius II	1458–64	Clement X	1670–76
(at Avignon)		Paul II	1464–71	Innocent XI	1676–89
Innocent VI	1352–62	Sixtus IV	1471–84	Alexander VIII	1689–91
(at Avignon)		Innocent VIII	1484–92	Innocent XII	1691–1700
Urban V	1362–70	Alexander VI	1492–1503	Clement XI	1700–21
(at Avignon)		Pius III	1503	Innocent XIII	1721–24
Gregory XI	1370–78	Julius II	1503–13	Benedict XIII	1724–30
(at Avignon, then		Leo X	1513–21	Clement XII	1730–40
Rome from 1377)		Adrian VI	1522–23	Benedict XIV	1740–58
Urban VI	1378–89	Clement VII	1523–34	Clement XIII	1758–69
Clement (VII)	1378–94	Paul III	1534–49	Clement XIV	1769–74
(at Avignon)		Julius III	1550–55	Pius VI	1775–99
Boniface IX	1389–1404	Marcellus II	1555	Pius VII	1800–23
Benedict (XIII)	1394–1423	Paul IV	1555–59	Leo XII	1823–29
(at Avignon)		Pius IV	1559–65	Pius VIII	1829–30
Innocent VII	1404–06	Pius V	1566–72	Gregory XVI	1831–46
Gregory XII	1406–15	Gregory XIII	1572–85	Pius IX	1846–78
Alexander (V)	1409–10	Sixtus V	1585–90	Leo XIII	1878–1903
(at Bologna)		Urban VII	1590	Pius X	1903–14
John (XXIII)	1410–15	Gregory XIV	1590–91	Benedict XV	1914–22
(at Bologna)		Innocent IX	1591	Pius XI	1922–39
Martin V[5]	1417–31	Clement VIII	1592–1605	Pius XII	1939–58
Clement (VIII)	1423–29	Leo XI	1605	John XXIII	1958–63
Eugenius IV	1431–47	Paul V	1605–21	Paul VI	1963–78
Felix (V) (Amadeus	1439–49	Gregory XV	1621–23	John Paul I	1978
VIII of Savoy)		Urban VIII	1623–44	John Paul II	1978–2005
Nicholas V	1447–55	Innocent X	1644–55	Benedict XVI	2005–

[1]The higher number is used if Felix (II), who reigned from 355 to 358 and is ordinarily classed as an antipope, is counted as a pope.   [2]Though elected on 23 Mar 752, Stephen (II) died two days later before he could be consecrated and thus is ordinarily not counted. The issue has made the numbering of subsequent Stephens somewhat irregular.   [3]Either Leo VIII or Benedict V may be considered an antipope.   [4]A confusion in the numbering of popes named John after John XIV (reigned 983–984) resulted because some 11th-century historians mistakenly believed that there had been a pope named John between antipope Boniface VII and the true John XV (reigned 985–996). Therefore they mistakenly numbered the real popes John XV to XIX as John XVI to XX. These popes have since customarily been renumbered XV to XIX, but John XXI and John XXII continue to bear numbers that they themselves formally adopted on the assumption that there had indeed been 20 Johns before them. In current numbering there thus exists no pope by the name of John XX.   [5]In the 13th century the papal chancery misread the names of the two popes Marinus as Martin, and as a result of this error Simon de Brie in 1281 assumed the name of Pope Martin IV instead of Martin II. The enumeration has not been corrected, and thus there exist no Martin II and Martin III.

World Religions

At the beginning of the 21st century, one-third of the world's population is Christian, one-fifth is Muslim, one-eighth is Hindu, and one-eighth is nonreligious. Most people living in Europe and the Americas are Christian, while the vast majority of Muslims and Hindus are found in Asia. The plurality of Christians are Roman Catholics, of Muslims are Sunnis, and of Hindus are Vaishnavites. Africa hosts slightly more Christians than Muslims, with much of the rest of the population listed as ethnic religionists, which describes followers of local, tribal, animistic, or shamanistic religions.

In addition to the adherents of the predominant world religions (Christianity, Islam, Hinduism), there are small but noticeable percentages of Chinese folk religionists, Buddhists, other ethnic religionists, atheists, and new religionists. Among adherents of the remaining distinct religions, Sikhs, Spiritists, Jews, Baha'is, Confucianists, Jains, Shintoists, Daoists (Taoists) and Zoroastrians each make up less than one-half of one percent of religious adherents.

Christianity

Christianity traces its origins to the 1st century AD and to Jesus of Nazareth, whom it affirms to be the chosen one (Christ) of God. Geographically the most widely diffused of all faiths, it has a constituency of more than two billion people. Its largest groups are the Roman Catholic Church, the Eastern Orthodox churches, and the Protestant churches; in addition, there are several independent churches of Eastern Christianity as well as numerous sects throughout the world.

Christianity's sacred scripture is the Bible, particularly the New Testament. Its principal tenets are that Jesus is the son of God (the second figure of the Holy Trinity), that God's love for the world is the essential component of his being, and that Jesus died to redeem humankind.

Christianity was originally a movement of Jews who accepted Jesus as the Messiah, but the movement
(continued on page 511)

The 2010 Annual Megacensus of Religions

David B. Barrett, Todd M. Johnson, and Peter F. Crossing

Each year since 1750, churches and religions around the world have generated increasing volumes of new statistical data. Much of this information is uncovered in decennial governmental censuses; half the countries of the world have long asked their populations to state their religions, if any, and they still do today. The other major source of data each year consists of the decentralized censuses undertaken by many religious headquarters. Each year almost all Christian denominations ask and answer statistical questions on major religious subjects. A third annual source is

Worldwide Adherents of All Religions, mid-2010

	AFRICA	ASIA	EUROPE	LATIN AMERICA
Christians	488,880,000	350,822,000	584,809,000	544,592,000
Affiliated	463,320,000	346,770,000	559,393,000	538,553,000
Roman Catholics	170,484,000	139,526,000	276,688,000	470,622,000
Protestants	136,631,000	88,765,000	67,710,000	58,769,000
Independents	98,239,000	146,423,000	10,839,000	42,669,000
Orthodox	44,507,000	15,832,000	200,620,000	1,038,000
Anglicans	50,215,000	865,000	26,428,000	865,000
Marginal Christians	3,667,000	3,136,000	4,113,000	11,239,000
Doubly affiliated	−40,423,000	−47,777,000	−27,005,000	−46,649,000
Unaffiliated	25,560,000	4,052,000	25,416,000	6,039,000
Muslims	421,938,820	1,083,354,900	40,174,000	1,599,000
Hindus	2,945,000	935,753,000	991,000	789,000
Nonreligious (agnostics)	5,995,000	504,352,000	84,652,000	16,941,410
Buddhists	258,000	455,412,000	1,777,000	760,000
Chinese folk-religionists	133,000	452,762,000	438,000	189,000
Ethnoreligionists	109,592,000	153,565,000	1,150,000	3,802,000
Atheists	594,000	116,204,000	15,390,000	2,901,000
New religionists	117,000	59,611,000	364,000	1,744,000
Sikhs	74,000	22,496,000	500,000	6,900
Jews	134,000	5,980,000	1,914,000	963,000
Spiritists	2,900	2,100	143,000	13,330,000
Daoists (Taoists)	0	8,412,000	0	0
Baha'is	2,178,000	3,433,000	142,000	902,000
Confucianists	20,200	6,433,000	15,500	490
Jains	95,100	5,056,000	18,800	1,400
Shintoists	0	2,700,000	0	7,800
Zoroastrians	980	148,000	5,700	0
Other religionists	85,000	245,000	275,000	120,000
Total population	**1,033,043,000**	**4,166,741,000**	**732,759,000**	**588,649,000**

Continents. These follow current UN demographic terminology, which now divides the world into the six major areas shown above. *See* United Nations, *World Population Prospects: The 2008 Revision* (New York: UN, 2009), with populations of all continents, regions, and countries covering the period 1950–2050, with 100 variables for every country each year. Note that "Asia" includes the former Soviet Central Asian states, and "Europe" includes all of Russia eastward to the Pacific.

Change rate. This column documents the annual change in 2010 (calculated as an average annual change from 2000 to 2010) in worldwide religious and nonreligious adherents. Note that in 2010 the annual growth of world population was 1.19%, or a net increase of 79,284,600 persons.

Countries. The last column enumerates sovereign and nonsovereign countries in which each religion or religious grouping has a numerically significant and organized following.

Adherents. As defined in the 1948 Universal Declaration of Human Rights, a person's religion is what he or she professes, confesses, or states that it is. Totals are enumerated for each of the world's 232 countries following the methodology of the *World Christian Encyclopedia*, 2nd ed. (2001), and *World Christian Trends* (2001), using recent censuses, polls, surveys, yearbooks, reports, Web sites, literature, and other data. *See* the World Christian Database <www.worldchristiandatabase.org> and World Religion Database <www.worldreligiondatabase.org> for more detail. Religions (including nonreligious and atheists) are ranked in order of worldwide size in mid-2010.

Atheists. Persons professing atheism, skepticism, disbelief, or irreligion, including the militantly antireligious (opposed to all religion). A flurry of recent books have outlined the Western philosophical and scientific basis for atheism. Ironically, the vast majority of atheists today are found in Asia (primarily Chinese communists).

Buddhists. 56% Mahayana, 38% Theravada (Hinayana), 6% Tantrayana (Lamaism).

Chinese folk-religionists. Followers of a unique complex of beliefs and practices that may include universism (yin/yang cosmology with dualities earth/heaven, evil/good, darkness/light), ancestor cult, Confucian ethics, divination, festivals, folk religion, goddess worship, household gods, local deities, mediums, metaphysics, monasteries, neo-Confucianism, popular religion, sacrifices, shamans, spirit-writing, and Daoist (Taoist) and Buddhist elements.

the total of 27,000 new books on the religious situation in each single country, as well as some 9,000 printed annual yearbooks or official handbooks. Together, these three major sources of data constitute a massive annual megacensus, though decentralized and uncoordinated. The two tables below combine all these data on religious affiliation. The first table summarizes worldwide adherents by religion. The second goes into more detail for the United States of America. There are two recent publications both supporting and mapping the data below. First, the *Atlas of Global Christianity* (Edinburgh University Press, 2009) puts Christian data in the context of 1910–2010. Second, the World Religion Database <www.worldreligiondatabase.org> offers sources and a detailed analysis of global religious dynamics.

Detail may not add to total given because of rounding.

NORTHERN AMERICA	OCEANIA	WORLD	%	CHANGE RATE (%)	NUMBER OF COUNTRIES
283,308,000	28,205,000	2,280,616,000	33.0	1.20	232
229,796,000	23,759,000	2,161,591,000	31.3	1.24	232
84,400,000	8,941,000	1,150,661,000	16.7	1.06	231
60,206,000	7,714,000	419,795,000	6.1	1.48	229
71,227,000	1,271,000	370,668,000	5.4	2.04	220
7,262,000	968,000	270,227,000	3.9	0.34	136
2,795,000	4,883,000	86,051,000	1.2	1.44	161
11,820,000	668,000	34,643,000	0.5	1.74	217
−7,914,000	686,000	−170,454,000	−2.5	1.06	174
53,512,000	4,446,000	119,025,000	1.7	0.64	226
5,598,000	524,000	1,553,188,720	22.5	1.79	209
1,867,000	526,000	942,871,000	13.6	1.38	125
43,211,700	4,629,100	659,781,210	9.6	0.48	231
3,845,000	573,000	462,625,000	6.7	0.86	150
781,000	101,000	454,404,000	6.6	0.56	119
1,246,000	368,000	269,723,000	3.9	1.44	145
2,013,000	462,000	137,564,000	2.0	−0.17	220
1,747,000	101,000	63,684,000	0.9	0.21	119
613,000	48,600	23,738,500	0.3	1.42	55
5,720,000	113,000	14,824,000	0.2	0.69	139
247,000	7,600	13,732,600	0.2	0.89	57
12,700	4,400	8,429,100	0.1	0.52	6
572,000	110,000	7,337,000	0.1	1.56	221
0	47,600	6,516,790	0.1	0.45	16
102,000	3,200	5,276,500	0.1	−0.04	19
64,200	0	2,772,000	0.0	1.32	8
21,400	2,500	178,580	0.0	0.83	27
690,000	12,000	1,427,000	0.0	1.31	79
351,659,000	35,838,000	6,908,689,000	100.0	1.19	232

Christians. Followers of Jesus Christ, enumerated here under **Affiliated**, those affiliated with churches (church members, with names written on church rolls, usually total number of baptized persons including children baptized, dedicated, or undedicated): total in 2010 being 2,161,591,000, shown above divided among the six standardized ecclesiastical megablocs and with (negative and italicized) figures for those **Doubly affiliated** persons (all who are baptized members of two denominations) and **Unaffiliated,** who are persons professing or confessing in censuses or polls to be Christians though not so affiliated. **Independents.** This term here denotes members of Christian churches and networks that regard themselves as postdenominationalist and neoapostolic and thus independent of historical, mainstream, organized, institutionalized, confessional, denominationalist Christianity. **Marginal Christians.** Members of denominations who define themselves as Christians but on the margins of organized mainstream Christianity (e.g., Unitarians, Mormons, Jehovah's Witnesses, Christian Science, and Religious Science).

Confucianists. Non-Chinese followers of Confucius and Confucianism, mostly Koreans in Korea.

Ethnoreligionists. Followers of local, tribal, animistic, or shamanistic religions, with members restricted to one ethnic group.

Hindus. 68% Vaishnavites, 27% Shaivites, 2% neo-Hindus and reform Hindus.

Jews. Adherents of Judaism. For detailed data on "core" Jewish population, see the annual "World Jewish Populations" article in the American Jewish Committee's *American Jewish Year Book.*

Muslims. 84% Sunnites, 14% Shi'ites, 2% other schools.

New religionists. Followers of Asian 20th-century neoreligions, neoreligious movements, radical new crisis religions, and non-Christian syncretistic mass religions.

Nonreligious (agnostics). Persons professing no religion, nonbelievers, agnostics, freethinkers, uninterested, or dereligionized secularists indifferent to all religion but not militantly so.

Other religionists. Including a handful of religions, quasi-religions, pseudoreligions, parareligions, religious or mystic systems, and religious and semireligious brotherhoods of numerous varieties.

Total population. UN medium variant figures for mid-2010, as given in *World Population Prospects: The 2008 Revision.*

Religious Adherents in the United States of America, 1900–2010

For categories not described below, see notes to Worldwide Adherents of All Religions, pp. 508-09.

	1900	%	MID-1970	%	MID-1990	%
Christians	73,260,000	96.4	189,873,000	90.6	217,487,600	85.3
Affiliated	54,425,000	71.6	152,754,000	72.9	175,182,600	68.7
Independents	5,850,000	7.7	34,702,000	16.6	66,900,000	26.2
Roman Catholics	10,775,000	14.2	48,305,000	23.1	56,500,000	22.2
Protestants	35,000,000	46.1	58,568,000	28.0	60,216,000	23.6
Marginal Christians	800,000	1.1	6,114,000	2.9	8,940,000	3.5
Orthodox	400,000	0.5	4,395,000	2.1	5,150,000	2.0
Anglicans	1,600,000	2.1	3,196,000	1.5	2,450,000	1.0
Doubly affiliated	0	0.0	-2,526,000	-1.2	-24,973,400	-9.8
Evangelicals	32,068,000	42.2	35,117,000	16.8	38,400,000	15.1
evangelicals	11,000,000	14.5	45,500,000	21.7	90,656,000	35.6
Unaffiliated	18,835,000	24.8	37,119,000	17.7	42,305,000	16.6
Nonreligious (agnostics)	1,000,000	1.3	10,270,000	4.9	21,442,000	8.4
Jews	1,500,000	2.0	6,700,000	3.2	5,535,000	2.2
Muslims	10,000	0.0	800,000	0.4	3,500,000	1.4
Black Muslims	0	0.0	200,000	0.1	1,250,000	0.5
Buddhists	30,000	0.0	200,000	0.1	1,880,000	0.7
New religionists	10,000	0.0	560,000	0.3	1,155,000	0.5
Hindus	1,000	0.0	100,000	0.0	750,000	0.3
Atheists	1,000	0.0	200,000	0.1	770,000	0.3
Ethnoreligionists	100,000	0.1	70,000	0.0	780,000	0.3
Baha'is	2,800	0.0	138,000	0.1	600,000	0.2
Sikhs	0	0.0	10,000	0.0	160,000	0.1
Spiritists	0	0.0	0	0.0	120,000	0.0
Chinese folk-religionists	70,000	0.1	90,000	0.0	76,000	0.0
Shintoists	0	0.0	3,000	0.0	5,000	0.0
Zoroastrians	0	0.0	0	0.0	50,000	0.0
Daoists (Taoists)	0	0.0	0	0.0	14,400	0.0
Jains	0	0.0	0	0.0	10,000	0.0
Other religionists	10,200	0.0	450,000	0.2	530,000	0.2
U.S. population	75,995,000	100.0	209,464,000	100.0	254,865,000	100.0

Methodology. This table extracts and analyzes a microcosm of the world religion table. It depicts the United States, the country with the largest number of adherents to Christianity, the world's largest religion. Statistics at five points in time from 1900 to 2010 are presented. Each religion's **Annual Change** for 2000-2010 is also analyzed by **Natural** increase (births minus deaths, plus immigrants minus emigrants) per year and **Conversion** increase (new converts minus new defectors) per year, which together constitute the **Total** increase per year. **Rate** increase is then computed as percentage per year.

Structure. Vertically the table lists 30 major religious categories. The major categories (including nonreligious) in the US are listed with largest (Christians) first. Indented names of groups in the "Adherents" column are subcategories of the groups above them and are also counted in these unindented totals, so they should not be added twice into the column total. Figures in italics draw adherents from all categories of Christians above and so cannot be added together with them. Figures for Christians are built upon detailed head counts by churches, often to the last digit. Totals are then rounded to the nearest 1,000. Because of rounding, the corresponding percentage figures may sometimes not total exactly to 100%. Religions are ranked in order of size in 2010.

Christians. All persons who profess publicly to follow Jesus Christ as God and Savior. This category is subdivided into **Affiliated** (church members) and **Unaffiliated** (nominal) Christians (professing Christians not affiliated with any church). See also the note on Christians below the world religion table. The first six lines under "Affiliated Christians" are ranked by size in 2010 for each of the six megablocs (Anglican, Independent, Marginal Christian, Orthodox, Protestant, Roman Catholic).

Evangelicals/evangelicals. These two designations—italicized and enumerated separately here—cut across all of the six Christian traditions or ecclesiastical blocs listed above and should be considered separately from them. The **Evangelicals** (capitalized "E") are mainly Protestant churches, agencies, and individuals who call themselves by this term (for example, members of the National Association of Evangelicals); they usually emphasize 5 or more of 7, 9, or 21 fundamental doctrines (salvation by faith, personal acceptance, verbal inspiration of Scripture, depravity of man, Virgin Birth, miracles of Christ, atonement, evangelism, Second Advent, et al.). The **evangelicals** (lowercase "e") are Christians of evangelical conviction from all traditions who are committed to the evangel (gospel) and involved in personal witness and mission in the world.

Jews. Core Jewish population relating to Judaism, excluding Jewish persons professing a different religion.

Other categories. Definitions are as given under the world religion table.

| MID-2000 | % | MID-2010 | % | ANNUAL CHANGE, 2000-2010 | | | |
				NATURAL	CONVERSION	TOTAL	RATE (%)
236,127,200	82.0	257,334,700	81.0	2,444,500	−323,700	2,120,800	0.86
192,704,000	66.9	209,433,000	65.9	1,995,000	−322,100	1,672,900	0.84
63,877,000	22.2	70,169,000	22.1	661,300	−32,100	629,200	0.94
62,970,000	21.9	70,465,000	22.2	651,900	97,600	749,500	1.13
57,544,000	20.0	56,716,000	17.9	595,700	−678,500	−82,800	−0.14
10,085,000	3.5	11,296,000	3.6	104,400	16,700	121,100	1.14
5,516,000	1.9	6,254,000	2.0	57,100	16,700	73,800	1.26
2,300,000	0.8	2,191,000	0.7	23,800	−34,700	−10,900	−0.48
−9,588,000	−3.3	−7,658,000	−2.4	−99,300	292,300	193,000	−2.22
39,588,000	13.8	40,957,000	12.9	409,800	−272,900	136,900	0.34
95,900,000	33.3	106,063,000	33.4	992,800	23,500	1,016,300	1.01
43,423,200	15.1	47,901,700	15.1	449,500	−1,600	447,900	0.99
33,083,000	11.5	39,395,000	12.4	332,100	329,100	661,200	1.89
5,442,000	1.9	5,242,000	1.7	56,300	−76,300	−20,000	−0.37
4,034,000	1.4	4,806,000	1.5	41,800	35,400	77,200	1.77
1,650,000	0.6	1,850,000	0.6	17,100	2,900	20,000	1.15
2,522,000	0.9	3,348,000	1.1	36,500	16,100	52,600	1.40
1,503,000	0.5	1,663,000	0.5	15,600	400	16,000	1.02
1,245,000	0.4	1,479,000	0.5	12,900	10,500	23,400	1.74
1,178,000	0.4	1,329,000	0.4	12,200	2,900	15,100	1.21
988,000	0.3	1,110,000	0.3	10,200	2,000	12,200	1.17
439,000	0.2	525,000	0.2	4,500	4,100	8,600	1.81
242,000	0.1	286,000	0.1	2,500	1,900	4,400	1.68
197,000	0.1	230,000	0.1	2,000	1,300	3,300	1.56
101,000	0.0	111,000	0.0	1,000	0	1,000	0.95
74,800	0.0	87,400	0.0	800	500	1,300	1.57
58,100	0.0	64,200	0.0	600	0	600	1.00
16,400	0.0	18,000	0.0	200	0	200	0.94
11,500	0.0	12,700	0.0	100	0	100	1.00
580,000	0.2	600,000	0.2	6,000	−4,000	2,000	0.34
287,842,000	100.0	317,641,000	100.0	2,980,000	0	2,980,000	0.99

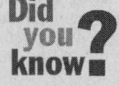

Did you know? The first sale of a military airplane was made on 8 Feb 1908, when Orville and Wilbur Wright contracted to supply one Wright Model A flyer to the US Army Signal Corps, plus a US$5,000 bonus should it exceed the speed requirement of 40 miles (65 km) per hour. The next year the plane completed its trial flights and met the condition for the bonus.

World Religions (continued)

(continued from page 507)
quickly became predominantly Gentile. Nearly all Christian churches have an ordained clergy, who lead group worship services and are viewed as intermediaries between the laity and the divine in some churches. Most Christian churches administer at least two sacraments: baptism and the Lord's Supper.

Islam

Islam is a religion that originated in the Middle East and was promulgated by the Prophet Muhammad in Arabia in the 7th century AD. The Arabic term *islam,* literally "surrender," illuminates the fundamental religious idea of Islam—that the believer (called a Muslim, from the active particle of *islam*) accepts "surrender to the will of Allah" (Arabic: "God"). Allah's will is made known through the sacred scriptures, the Qur'an, which Allah revealed to his messenger, Muhammad. In Islam, Muhammad is considered the last of a series of prophets (including Adam, Noah, Jesus, and others), and his message simultaneously consummates and abrogates the "revelations" attributed to earlier prophets.

The religious obligations of all Muslims are summed up in the Five Pillars of Islam. The fundamental concept in Islam is the Shari'ah, or Law, which embraces the total way of life commanded by God. Observant Muslims pray five times a day and join in community worship on Fridays at the mosque, where worship is led by an imam. Every believer is required to make a pilgrimage to Mecca, the holiest city, at least once in a lifetime, barring poverty or physical incapacity. The month of Ramadan is set aside for fasting. Jihad, considered a sixth pillar by some sects, is not accepted by most of the Islamic community as a call to wage physical war against unbelievers.

Divisions occurred early in Islam, brought about by disputes over the succession to the caliphate, resulting in various sects (Sunnis, Shi'ites, Isma'ilis, Sufis). From the 19th century, the concept of the Islamic community inspired Muslim peoples to cast off Western colonial rule, and in the late 20th century fundamentalist movements toppled a number of secular Middle Eastern governments. A movement of African American Muslims emerged in the 20th century in the US.

Hinduism

Hinduism is the oldest of the world's major religions, dating back more than 3,000 years, though its pres-

World Religions (continued)

ent forms are of more recent origin. It evolved from Vedism, the religion of the Indo-European peoples who settled in India at the end of the 2nd millennium BC. The vast majority of the world's Hindus live in India, though significant minorities may be found in Pakistan and Sri Lanka, and smaller numbers live in Myanmar (Burma), South Africa, Trinidad, Europe, and the US.

Though the various Hindu sects each rely on their own set of scriptures, they all revere the ancient Vedas, which were brought to India by Aryan invaders after 1200 BC. The philosophical Vedic texts called the Upanishads explore the search for knowledge that will allow mankind to escape the cycle of reincarnation. Fundamental to Hinduism is the belief in a cosmic principle of ultimate reality, called brahman, and its identity with the individual soul, or atman. All creatures go through a cycle of rebirth, or samsara, which can be broken only by spiritual self-realization, after which liberation, or moksha, is attained. The principle of karma determines a being's status within the cycle of rebirth.

The greatest Hindu deities are Brahma, Vishnu, and Shiva. The major sources of classical mythology are the Mahabharata (which includes the Bhagavadgita, the most important religious text of Hinduism), the Ramayana, and the Puranas. The hierarchical social structure of the caste system is important in Hinduism; it is supported by the principle of dharma. During the 20th century Hinduism was blended with Indian nationalism to become a potent political force.

Other major religions
Buddhism, a religion concentrated in Asia with some representation in North America, was founded by the Buddha (Siddhartha Gautama, or Gotama) in northeast India in the 5th century BC. By adhering to the Buddha's teachings, the believer can alleviate suffering through an understanding of the transitory nature of existence, in the hopes of achieving enlightenment. Distinct from Buddhism, **Shinto** is the indigenous religion of Japan and has no founder, sacred scriptures, or fixed dogmas. Also based in Asia,

Chinese folk religions worship local deities and teach ancestor worship and divination. They also adhere to Confucian ethics, though statistically only non-Chinese (mostly Korean) followers of Confucius, a Chinese philosopher of the 6th century BC, are categorized as followers of **Confucianism**. Confucianism is not an organized religion as much as it is a political and social ideology. Also in the Confucian tradition, adherents of **Daoism** seek the correct path of human conduct and an understanding of the Absolute Dao.

Zoroastrianism is an ancient pre-Islamic religion of Iran that survives there and in India. It was founded by the Iranian prophet Zoroaster in the 6th century BC and has both monotheistic and dualistic features. Also founded in Iran is the **Baha'i** faith, created as a universal religion in the mid-19th century AD for the worship of Baha' Ullah and his forerunner, the Bab; it has no priesthood or formal sacraments and is chiefly concerned with social ethics.

Jainism was founded in India in the 6th century BC by Vardhamana, or Mahavira, a monastic reformer in the Vedic, or early Hindu, tradition. Jainism emphasizes a path to spiritual purity and enlightenment through a disciplined mode of life founded upon the tradition of ahimsa, nonviolence to all living creatures.

Sikhism is a monotheistic religion founded in the late 15th century AD in India, historically associated with the Punjab region, though it includes representation in Europe and North America.

Judaism, like Christianity and Islam, is monotheistic and maintains the manifestation of God in human events, particularly through Moses in the Torah at Mount Sinai in the 13th century BC. Jews, who come together in both religious and ethnic communities, have worldwide representation, with the greatest concentration in North America and the Middle East.

New Religious Movements and non-Christian syncretistic mass religions also have significant followings.

Terrorism
International Terrorist Organizations

"Terrorism" is a subjective term. The list of organizations included here is that of the US Department of State, issued on 19 Jan 2010. The list is updated periodically. Translations and acronyms of organizations' names are given in bold parenthetically; names and acronyms by which organizations are also known follow and are not in bold.

Abu Nidal Organization (ANO) (Fatah Revolutionary Council, Arab Revolutionary Brigades, Black September, Revolutionary Organization of Socialist Muslims)
    founded in 1974 as a splinter group from the Palestinian Liberation Organization (PLO); led by Sabri al-Banna
    country or region of operation: Middle East, primarily Iraq and Lebanon; has also operated in Asia and Europe
    primary goals: elimination of Israel, establishment of a Palestinian state
Abu Sayyaf Group (ASG)
    founded in the early 1990s as a splinter group from Moro National Liberation Front by Abdurajak Abubakar Janjalani; mainly made up of semiautonomous factions
    country or region of operation: Philippines, Malaysia
    primary goals: establishment of an independent Islamic state in the southern Philippines
Ansar al-Islam (Partisans of Islam)
    founded in 2001 as an offshoot of the Islamic Movement in Iraqi Kurdistan by Najmeddin Faraj Ahmed
    country or region of operation: Iraq
    primary goals: establishment of an Islamic state in the Kurdish areas of northern Iraq

International Terrorist Organizations (continued)

al-Aqsa Martyrs Brigade
founded in 2000 as an offshoot of Fatah; diffuse cell-based leadership structure
country or region of operation: Gaza Strip, West Bank, Israel
primary goals: establishment of a Palestinian state with Jerusalem as its capital

Armed Islamic Group (GIA)
founded in 1992; leadership uncertain; fewer than 50 active members thought to be at large
country or region of operation: Algeria
primary goals: replacement of secular Algerian government with an Islamic state

Asbat al-Ansar
founded in the late 1980s; led by Abou Mahjan, aka Abdel Karim al-Saadi
country or region of operation: Lebanon
primary goals: replacement of secular Lebanese government with an Islamic state

AUM Shinrikyo (AUM Supreme Truth, Aleph)
founded in 1987 by Shoko Asahara; led by Fumihiro Joyu
country or region of operation: Japan
primary goals: takeover of Japan and the world

Basque Fatherland and Liberty (Euzkadi Ta Askatasuna, ETA)
founded in 1959; allegedly led by Jurdan Martitegi Lizaso (arrested in April 2009)
country or region of operation: Basque autonomous regions of northern Spain and southwestern France
primary goals: establishment of an independent Basque state based on Marxism

Communist Party of the Philippines/New People's Army (CPP/NPA)
founded in 1969 as a Maoist movement; led from exile by José María Sisón
country or region of operation: Philippines
primary goals: overthrow of the Philippine government

Continuity Irish Republican Army (CIRA)
founded in 1994 as a splinter group of Irish Republican Army (IRA) after the latter declared its first cease-fire
country or region of operation: Northern Ireland, Republic of Ireland
primary goals: removal of British forces from Northern Ireland

Hamas (Islamic Resistance Movement)
founded in 1987 by Sheikh Ahmed Yasin as an offshoot of Muslim Brotherhood; led by Khalid Mesha
country or region of operation: Gaza Strip, West Bank, Israel; also present throughout the Middle East
primary goals: elimination of Israel, establishment of an Islamic Palestinian state

Harakat ul-Jihad-i-Islami/Bangladesh (HUJI-B)
founded in the 1990s; affiliated with al-Qaeda
country or region of operation: Bangladesh
primary goals: establishment of Bangladesh as an Islamic state

Harakat ul-Mujahidin (HUM) (Movement of Holy Warriors)
founded in the mid-1980s or early 1990s; led by Farooq Kashmiri
country or region of operation: the Kashmir region of Pakistan and India
primary goals: establishment of Kashmir as part of an Islamic state

Hezbollah (Party of God) (Islamic Jihad, Revolutionary Justice Organization, Organization of the Oppressed on Earth, Islamic Jihad for the Liberation of Palestine)
founded in 1982; spiritual leader Sheikh Muhammad Hussein Fadlallah
country or region of operation: Lebanon; also has cells worldwide
primary goals: establishment of Islamic rule in Lebanon, elimination of Israel, liberation of occupied Arab lands

Islamic Jihad Group (IJG)
founded in 2004; offshoot of Islamic Movement of Uzbekistan (IMU)
country or region of operation: Central Asia
primary goals: replacement of the secular Uzbek government with an Islamic state

Islamic Movement of Uzbekistan (IMU)
founded in 1996; led by Tohir Yoldashev
country or region of operation: primarily Uzbekistan, Tajikistan, Kyrgyzstan, Afghanistan, Iran, and Pakistan
primary goals: replacement of the secular Uzbek government with an Islamic state

Jaish-e-Mohammed (JEM) (Army of Muhammad)
founded in 2000 as a spin-off from Harakat ul-Mujahidin; led by Maulana Masood Azhar
country or region of operation: South Asia, primarily Pakistan and India
primary goals: establishment of Pakistani control over India-administered Kashmir

al-Jama'ah al-Islamiyah (Islamic Group, IG)
founded in the late 1970s; loosely organized in two factions led by Mustafa Hamza (currently in custody in Egypt) and Rifai Taha Musa; spiritual leader Sheikh Umar Abd al-Rahman
country or region of operation: Egypt; also operates in several countries worldwide
primary goals: replacement of Egyptian government with an Islamic state

Jemaah Islamiyah (JI)
founded in the mid-1990s as a successor to Darul Islam; led by Abu Bakar Baasyir
country or region of operation: Southeast Asia, particularly Indonesia, Singapore, and Malaysia
primary goals: establishment of a pan-Islamic state in Southeast Asia

International Terrorist Organizations (continued)

Kahane Chai (Kach)
 founded in 1971 by Meir Kahane; Kahane Chai founded as follow-up group after Meir's assassination in 1990
 country or region of operation: Israel, West Bank
 primary goals: expansion of Israel, removal of Palestinians
Kata'ib Hizballah (KH) (Hezbollah Brigades)
 founded in 2007
 country or region of operation: Iraq
 primary goals: expulsion of American and allied forces from Iraq
Kongra-Gel (KGK) (formerly Kurdistan Workers' Party, PKK, KADEK)
 founded in 1974; led by Abdullah Ocalan (imprisoned since 1999)
 country or region of operation: Turkey; also operates in Europe and the Middle East
 primary goals: establishment of independent Kurdish state
Lashkar-e-Taiba (LT, Army of the Righteous)
 founded in 1990; led by Abdul Wahid Kashmiri
 country or region of operation: South Asia, primarily Pakistan and India
 primary goals: establishment of Pakistani control over India-administered Kashmir
Lashkar I Jhangvi
 founded in 1996; decentralized leadership structure
 country or region of operation: Pakistan
 primary goals: replacement of the Pakistani government with an Islamic state
Liberation Tigers of Tamil Eelam (LTTE)
 founded in 1976; led by Velupillai Prabhakaran (until his death in May 2009)
 country or region of operation: Sri Lanka
 primary goals: establishment of an independent Tamil state
Libyan Islamic Fighting Group (LIFG)
 founded in 1995 among Libyans who had fought against Soviet forces in Afghanistan; led by Anas Sebai
 country or region of operation: Libya, various Middle Eastern and European countries
 primary goals: overthrow of the government of Libyan leader Muammar al-Qaddafi
Moroccan Islamic Combatant Group (GICM)
 founded in the 1990s as an offshoot of the Moroccan organization Shabiba Islamiya (Islamic Youth)
 country or region of operation: Afghanistan, Belgium, Denmark, Egypt, France, Morocco, Spain, Turkey, UK
 primary goals: creation of an Islamic state in Morocco
Mojahedin-e Khalq Organization (MEK)
 founded in the 1960s; led by Maryam and Masud Rajavi
 country or region of operation: Iran, Iraq
 primary goals: establishment of a secular government in Iran
National Liberation Army (ELN)
 founded in 1965; led by Nicolas Rodríguez Bautista
 country or region of operation: Colombia
 primary goals: replacement of the ruling Colombian government with a Marxist state
Palestine Liberation Front (PLF)
 founded in the mid-1970s as splinter group from PFLP–GC
 country or region of operation: Israel, Iraq
 primary goals: elimination of Israel, establishment of a Palestinian state
Palestinian Islamic Jihad (PIJ)
 founded in the 1970s; most active faction led by Ramadan Shallah
 country or region of operation: primarily Israel, West Bank, Gaza Strip, Lebanon, and Syria
 primary goals: elimination of Israel, establishment of an Islamic Palestinian state
Popular Front for the Liberation of Palestine (PFLP)
 founded in 1967 by George Habash; led by Ahmed Sadat (imprisoned by Israel since 2006)
 country or region of operation: Syria, Lebanon, Israel, West Bank, Gaza Strip
 primary goals: revitalization of the PLO, opposition to peace negotiations with Israel
Popular Front for the Liberation of Palestine–General Command (PFLP–GC)
 founded in 1968 as splinter group from PFLP; led by Ahmad Jibril
 country or region of operation: Syria, Lebanon, Israel, West Bank, Gaza Strip
 primary goals: opposition to the PLO and to peace negotiations with Israel
al-Qaeda
 founded in the late 1980s; established and led by Osama bin Laden
 country or region of operation: worldwide
 primary goals: establishment of worldwide Islamic rule, overthrow of non-Islamic governments, expulsion of
 Western influences from Muslim states, killing of US citizens
al-Qaeda Organization in the Arabian Peninsula (AQAP) (formerly al-Qaeda in Yemen)
 founded in 2009; led by Nasir al-Wahishi
 country or region of operation: Yemen and Saudi Arabia
 primary goals: establishment of an Islamic state on the Arabian Peninsula
al-Qaeda Organization in the Islamic Maghreb (formerly Salafist Group for Call and Combat, GSPC)
 founded in 1996 as a splinter of the Armed Islamic Group; led by Abou Mossaab Abdelouadoud
 country or region of operation: primarily Algeria, with significant activity elsewhere in North Africa and in Europe
 primary goals: replacement of the Algerian government with an Islamic state

International Terrorist Organizations (continued)

Real IRA (True IRA)
    founded in 1998 as a splinter group of the Irish Republican Army (IRA); led by Michael ("Mickey") McKevitt (imprisoned since 2001)
    country or region of operation: Northern Ireland; also elsewhere in Great Britain and in Ireland
    primary goals: removal of British forces from Northern Ireland, unification of Ireland

Revolutionary Armed Forces of Colombia (FARC)
    founded in 1964 as the military branch of the Colombian Communist Party; governed by a group led by Alfonso Cano and including Jorge Briceño and five others
    country or region of operation: Colombia; also some operations in Venezuela, Ecuador, and Panama
    primary goals: replacement of the ruling Colombian government with a Marxist state

Revolutionary Organization 17 November
    founded in 1975; allegedly led by Alexandros Giotopoulos (imprisoned in Greece since 2002)
    country or region of operation: Greece, primarily Athens
    primary goals: elimination of US military bases in Greece, removal of Turkish forces from Cyprus, opposition to capitalism and NATO/EU membership

Revolutionary People's Liberation Party/Front (DHKP/C) (Devrimci Sol, Revolutionary Left, Dev Sol)
    founded in 1978 as a splinter group from Turkish People's Liberation Party/Front
    country or region of operation: Turkey, primarily Istanbul
    primary goals: promotion of Marxism, opposition to US and NATO

Revolutionary Struggle (Epanastatikos Aghonas; EA)
    founded in 2003; leadership unknown
    country or region of operation: Greece
    primary goals: opposition to Greece's political and economic climate

al-Shabaab
    founded in 2006 by fighters from the recently ousted Islamic Courts Union
    country or region of operation: Somalia
    primary goals: ejection of foreign troops from Somalia, reestablishment of an Islamic government in the country

Shining Path (Sendero Luminoso, SL)
    founded in the late 1960s by Abimael Guzman; led by Macario Ala
    country or region of operation: Peru, primarily rural areas
    primary goals: replacement of the Peruvian government with a communist state

Tanzim Qaidat al-Jihad fi Bilad al-Rafidayn (QJBR, al-Qaeda in Iraq) (formerly Jamaat al-Tawhid waal-Jihad, JTJ, al-Zarqawi Network)
    founded in April 2004 by Abu Musab al-Zarqawi shortly after the commencement of Operation Iraqi Freedom (OIF); adopted current name in October 2004 after merging with Osama bin Laden's al-Qaeda
    country or region of operation: Iraq
    primary goals: expulsion of OIF coalition from Iraq, establishment of Islamic state in Iraq

United Self-Defense Forces of Colombia (Autodefensas Unidas de Colombia, AUC)
    founded in 1997 as an umbrella organization of paramilitary groups
    country or region of operation: Colombia
    primary goals: opposition to and defense against leftist guerrilla groups

Military Affairs

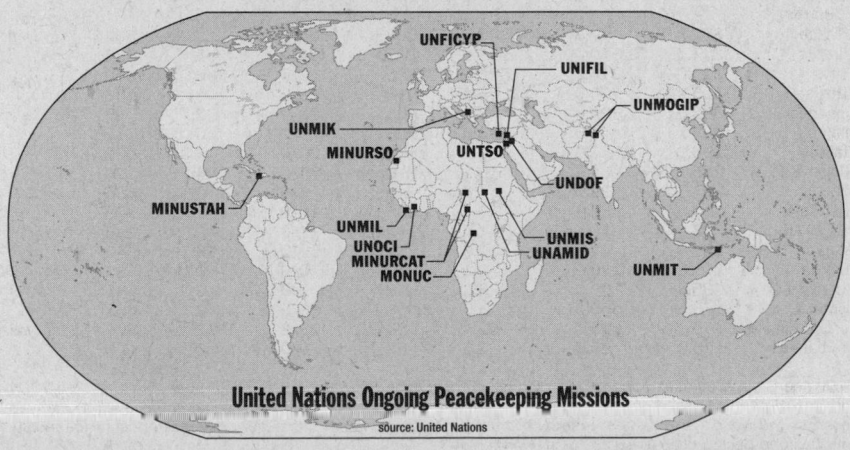

United Nations Ongoing Peacekeeping Missions

source: United Nations

United Nations Ongoing Peacekeeping Missions (continued)

MINURCAT   United Nations Mission in the Central African Republic and Chad—since September 2007 (3,671)

MINURSO   United Nations Mission for the Referendum in Western Sahara—since April 1991 (222)

MINUSTAH   United Nations Stabilization Mission in Haiti—since June 2004 (10,565)

MONUC   United Nations Organization Mission in the Democratic Republic of the Congo—since November 1999 (20,819)

UNAMID   African Union/United Nations Hybrid Operation in Darfur—since July 2007 (21,993)

UNDOF   United Nations Disengagement Observer Force (in the Golan Heights)—since May 1974 (1,043)

UNFICYP   United Nations Peacekeeping Force in Cyprus—since March 1964 (925)

UNIFIL   United Nations Interim Force in Lebanon—since March 1978 (11,871)

UNMIK   United Nations Interim Administration Mission in Kosovo—since June 1999 (9[1])

UNMIL   United Nations Mission in Liberia—since September 2003 (9,644)

UNMIS   United Nations Mission in Sudan—since March 2005 (10,571)

UNMIT   United Nations Integrated Mission in Timor-Leste—since August 2006 (1,565)

UNMOGIP   United Nations Military Observer Group in India and Pakistan—since January 1949 (44)

UNOCI   United Nations Operation in Côte d'Ivoire—since April 2004 (8,503)

UNTSO   United Nations Truce Supervision Organization (in the Middle East)—since May 1948 (152)

Parenthetical figures indicate military personnel as of 30 Apr 2010. Civilian forces, including police officers, are not included in this table. [1]Data are as of 15 Mar 2010.

Nations with Largest Armed Forces

The top 30 countries in terms of active-personnel military strength are included. Personnel numbers are in thousands ('000) and reflect November 2009 data; spending totals are from 2009 budgets except where noted. Source: The International Institute of Strategic Studies, The Military Balance 2010.

COUNTRY	MILITARY PERSONNEL		DEFENSE SPENDING (US$ BILLIONS)	BATTLE TANKS	MAJOR WARSHIPS/ CARRIERS	SUB-MARINES	COMBAT AIRCRAFT	STRATEGIC NUCLEAR WEAPONS
	ACTIVE	RESERVES						
China	2,285.0	510.0	70.3	7,650+	80/0	65	1,907	yes
United States	1,580.3	864.5	693.6	6,253	110/11	71	1,368	yes
India	1,325.0	1,155.0	35.9	4,047+	45/1	16	655	yes
D.P.R. Korea	1,106.0	4,700.0	2.3[1]	4,060+	8/0	63	620	yes
Russia	1,027.0	20,000.0	41.1	24,471	57/1	66	2,408	yes
Rep. of Korea	687.0	4,500.0	24.5	2,810	47/0	13	498	
Pakistan	617.0	304.0[2]	4.1	2,461+	7/0	8	395	yes
Iraq	578.3	0.0	N/A	149+	0/0	0	0	
Iran	523.0	350.0	9.6[3]	1,693+	6/0	3	312	
Turkey	510.6	378.7	9.9	4,503	23/0	14	426	
Egypt	468.5	479.0	4.6[3]	3,723	10/0	4	461	
Vietnam	455.0	5,000.0	2.8	1,935	11/0	2	219	
Myanmar (Burma)	406.0	107.3[2]	7.0[4]	255	3/0	0	125	
France	352.8	70.3	47.8	665	33/2	9	364	yes
Brazil	327.7	1,340.0	27.8	389+	16/1	5	357	
Syria	325.0	314.0	1.9	4,950	2/0	0	555	
Thailand	305.9	200.0	5.1	848	20/1	0	186	
Indonesia	302.0	400.0	3.5	405	30/0	2	96	
Italy	293.2	41.9	23.0	320	26/2	6	262	
Taiwan	290.0	1,657.0	9.8	1,831+	26/0	4	509	
Colombia	285.2	61.9	10.1	0	4/0	4	90	
Mexico	267.5	39.9	4.4	0	6/0	0	85	
Germany	250.6	161.8	46.5	1,385	18/0	12	303	
Saudi Arabia	233.5	15.5+[2]	41.2	910	11/0	0	280	
Japan	230.3	41.8	52.6	880	52/0	16	340	
Eritrea	201.8	120.0	0.1[5]	270	0/0	0	31	
Morocco	195.8	150.0	3.2	696	3/0	0	89	
Israel	176.5	565.0	13.0	3,501	3/0	3	461	[6]
United Kingdom	175.7	199.3	62.4	386	25/2	12	300	yes
Sri Lanka	160.9	5.5	1.6	62	0/0	0	22	

N/A means not available. [1]Spending based on 2006 budget. [2]Paramilitary forces. [3]Spending based on 2008 budget. [4]Spending based on 2007 budget. [5]Spending based on 2005 budget. [6]Although believed by many to possess the world's sixth largest arsenal of nuclear weapons, Israel has never declared a nuclear capability nor has one been proven to exist.

United States

Exit Justice Stevens, Enter Justice Kagan

by David von Drehle and Michael Scherer, TIME

The retirement of Justice John Paul Stevens in 2010 at age 90 was the end of an era for the US Supreme Court, and we're not talking about just his signature bow ties. Stevens is likely the last link to a time when presidents typically chose justices who weren't raised in ideological petri dishes. When Gerald Ford nominated Stevens in 1975, he couldn't have known much more about his choice than Stevens's reputation for integrity, brilliance, and impeccable manners. The genus was Republican, true, but the species was country club. And Ford had played enough golf to know that gentlemen don't ask other gentlemen about their politics.

That's all finished, and Stevens helped finish it. Along with Earl Warren, William J. Brennan, Harry Blackmun, and David Souter, Stevens is part of a small army of modern-era justices who marched leftward after being elevated to the court by Republican patrons. If presidents and political parties now put a premium on ideological purity, it's because they have seen what can happen when a justice decides to migrate. The art of today's Supreme Court nominations comes down to finding candidates who can talk the talk of open-mindedness—then, once safely confirmed by the Senate, wage the court's ideological battles with tireless consistency.

The surprising thing about Stevens, given his moderate beginnings and his undisputed charm, is how central he became to those ideological battles during the last decade of his long career. Only three justices in history have served longer than Stevens, led by William O. Douglas, whom Stevens replaced. Taken together, Douglas and Stevens have filled their seat since before World War II. A strong writer who insisted on drafting his own opinions, Stevens wound up as the clarion of the court's left wing. No one in the high tribunal blew a louder bugle in warning against conservative trends, which he often denounced.

Take this example: "Although we may never know with complete certainty the identity of the winner of this year's presidential election, the identity of the loser is perfectly clear. It is the nation's confidence in the judge as an impartial guardian of the rule of law." Thus Stevens excoriated the conservative majority that ruled in favor of George W. Bush against Vice Pres. Al Gore in 2000. In 2010's controversial campaign-finance case, Stevens accused the majority of pursuing their own "agenda" at the expense of "the common sense of the American people."

No one would have predicted back in the days of disco and three-piece polyester suits that Stevens would become a darling of the American left. Born into a wealthy Chicago family in 1920, he was a distinguished corporate antitrust lawyer before Republican Pres. Richard Nixon appointed him to the Seventh Circuit Court of Appeals in 1970. Elevated to the Supreme Court five years later, Stevens fit easily into the center of the Republican-dominated court. He wrote the famous opinion banning the broadcast of comedian George Carlin's seven dirty words. He opposed affirmative action and joined a group of swing justices to reinstate the death penalty. Like several of his colleagues in that period, Stevens had no grand constitutional theory to guide his decision making; instead, he drilled deeply into the facts of each file and tried to go where the case law took him. Critics called him quirky. Admirers have praised his work as an example of conservative common-law judging. His 1984 opinion in *Chevron* v. *NRDC*, balancing the legislative intent of Congress with the rule-making authority of the executive-branch agencies, has been called the most cited Supreme Court decision in history.

In recent interviews Stevens has insisted that he never changed; the court did. He's halfway correct. The court did change. It now decides fewer cases, in more heated terms. The center of gravity hasn't moved much (back then it was conservative Lewis Powell who was the swing vote; now it's conservative Anthony Kennedy), but in the 1970s the court was led from the center, while today the loudest voices are on the extremes.

Stevens did change, though. In 2008 he suggested that the death penalty was unconstitutional, joining Blackmun and Powell in repudiating the legal contraption they were instrumental in creating. He changed tack on affirmative action and resisted limits on Internet content that might have made even George Carlin blush.

History may conclude that Stevens did his most important work in recent years, as he led the court in limiting a president's power to detain suspected terrorists indefinitely, with scant access to judicial review. In those opinions he probed what is arguably the essence of the Constitution: its checks and balances on excessive concentrations of power. If his long career stands for any principle, it is that an independent judiciary starts with truly independent judges.

To fill Stevens's seat, Pres. Barack Obama nominated Solicitor General Elena Kagan, who was approved by the US Senate on 5 August by a vote of 63–37. When Kagan was sworn in by Chief Justice John Roberts on 7 August, she became the fourth female justice in the history of the Supreme Court, the eighth Jewish justice to sit on the court, and the first nominee since 1972 with no prior experience as a judge.

At 50, Kagan will also be the youngest judge on the court. Raised on the Upper West Side of Manhattan, Kagan strongly resembles the rest of the members of the court: a graduate of the Ivy League, schooled at Princeton and Harvard Law School. Kagan will assume her seat as a bit of a cipher: because she lacks a judicial record that would illuminate her views—and because during her Senate hearings she followed the recent practice of revealing as little as possible about her political leanings—observers will be scrutinizing her early votes to determine how her presence will sway the court to the right or the left, where the absence of Stevens will leave a large void in the court's more liberal wing.

United States History
United States Chronology

1492 Christopher Columbus, sailing under the Spanish flag, arrives in the Americas, 12 October.

1513 Ponce de León of Spain lands in Florida and gives that region its name.

1534 France sends Jacques Cartier to find a route to the Far East; he explores along the St. Lawrence River, and France lays claim to part of North America.

1541 Hernando de Soto of Spain sights the Mississippi River near the location of present-day Memphis.

1565 St. Augustine, the oldest permanent settlement in the US, is founded by Spaniards.

1587 A party under John White lands at Roanoke Island (now in North Carolina); when White returns three years later, the entire settlement has disappeared.

1607 The English make the first permanent settlement in the New World at Jamestown; Virginia becomes the first of the 13 English colonies.

1619 The first representative assembly in America, the House of Burgesses, meets in Virginia.

1620 Pilgrims from the ship *Mayflower* found a settlement at Plymouth.

1649 The Act Concerning Religion passed by Maryland's legislature is the first law of religious toleration in the English colonies.

1682 The Sieur de La Salle explores the lower Mississippi valley and claims the entire region for France.

1733 Georgia, the 13th and last of the English colonies in America, is founded.

1754 The French and Indian War between France and England begins in America.

1763 The Treaty of Paris ends the French and Indian War; Florida is ceded to Britain.

1765 The Quartering Act and the Stamp Act anger Americans; nine colonies are represented at the Stamp Act Congress.

1770 British troops fire on a crowd, killing five people in the so-called Boston Massacre.

1773 The Boston Tea Party, the first action in a chain leading to war with Britain, takes place.

1774 The First Continental Congress meets at Philadelphia and protests the five Intolerable Acts.

1775 The battles of Lexington and Concord and Bunker Hill occur; the Second Continental Congress meets.

1776 The Declaration of Independence is adopted.

1778–79 Gen. George Rogers Clark leads a victorious expedition into the Northwest Territory.

1781 George Washington accepts the surrender of Charles Cornwallis at Yorktown VA; the Articles of Confederation become the government of the US.

1783 A treaty of peace with Great Britain is signed at Paris, formally ending the Revolutionary War.

1786–87 Shays's Rebellion in Massachusetts shows weaknesses of the Confederation government.

1787 The Northwest Territory is organized by Congress; a convention meets to draft a new constitution.

1788 The US Constitution is ratified by the necessary nine states to ensure adoption.

1789 The new US government goes into effect; Washington is inaugurated president; the first Congress meets in New York City.

1791 The Bill of Rights is added to the Constitution; Vermont is the first new state admitted to the Union.

1793 Eli Whitney invents the cotton gin, which leads to large-scale cotton growing in the South.

1800 The national capital is moved from Philadelphia to Washington DC.

1803 Louisiana is purchased from France; the Supreme Court makes its *Marbury* v. *Madison* decision, establishing judicial review; Congress halts the importation of slaves into the US after 1807.

1804–06 Meriwether Lewis and William Clark blaze an overland trail to the Pacific and return.

1807 Robert Fulton's steamboat makes a successful journey from New York City to Albany NY.

1812–14 The US maintains its independence in a conflict with Britain, the War of 1812.

1820 The Missouri Compromise settles the problem of slavery in new states for the next 30 years.

1823 The Monroe Doctrine warns European nations that the US will protect the Americas.

1825 The Erie Canal, from the Hudson River to the Great Lakes, becomes a great water highway to the Middle West.

1829 The inauguration of Pres. Andrew Jackson introduces the era of Jacksonian Democracy.

1836 Texas wins its independence from Mexico.

1843 The first migration begins on the Oregon Trail.

1845 Texas is annexed and admitted as a state.

1846 The Oregon boundary dispute is settled with Britain; the Mexican War begins.

1847 Brigham Young leads a party of Mormons into the Salt Lake valley, Utah.

1848 The Mexican War ends; the US gains possession of the California and New Mexico regions.

1849 The gold rush to California begins.

1850 The Compromise of 1850 admits California as a free state, postponing war between the North and South.

1853 The Gadsden Purchase adds 117,935 sq km (45,535 sq mi) to what is now the southwestern US.

1854 The Republican Party is organized in opposition to slavery.

1857 The Dred Scott decision of the Supreme Court declares that the Missouri Compromise is illegal.

1860 Abraham Lincoln is elected president; South Carolina secedes from the Union.

1861 The Confederate States of America is formed; the Civil War begins; telegraph links New York City with San Francisco.

1862 Gen. Ulysses S. Grant launches a Union attack in the West; the Confederate invasion of Maryland is halted at Antietam; the Homestead Act grants 160 acres to each settler.

1863 Federal forces win decisive battles at Gettysburg PA, Vicksburg MS, and Chattanooga TN; the Emancipation Proclamation is delivered.

1864 Gen. William Tecumseh Sherman captures Atlanta and marches across Georgia.

1865 Gen. Robert E. Lee surrenders to Grant at Appomattox (VA) Court House, ending the Civil War; Lincoln is assassinated.

1867 Reconstruction acts impose military rule on the South; Alaska is purchased from Russia.

1869 The first transcontinental railroad is completed as two lines meet at Promontory UT.

1876 The telephone is invented; the Centennial Exposition in Philadelphia celebrates the 100th birthday of the US.

1877 The withdrawal of the last federal troops from the South ends the Reconstruction period.

1879 The first practical electric light is invented by Thomas A. Edison.

1884-85 The first skyscraper, the Home Insurance Building, is erected in Chicago.

1886 The American Federation of Labor (AFL) is organized; its first president is Samuel Gompers.

1887 The Interstate Commerce Act is adopted to control railroads that cross state lines.

1889-90 The first pan-American conference is held in Washington DC.

1890 The Sherman Anti-Trust Act is passed in an effort to curb the growth of monopolies.

1896 Henry Ford's first car is driven on the streets of Detroit.

1898 The US wins the Spanish-American War and gains the Philippines, Puerto Rico, and Guam.

1903 The air age begins with the successful airplane flight by the Wright brothers.

1906 The Federal Food and Drug Act is passed to protect the public from impure food and drugs.

1913 Federal income tax is authorized by the 16th Amendment.

1914 The Panama Canal is opened under the control of the US; World War I breaks out in Europe; Pres. Woodrow Wilson appeals for neutrality in the US.

1915 A German submarine sinks the British ship *Lusitania* with the loss of 124 American lives; a telephone line is established coast-to-coast.

1917 The US declares war against Germany.

1918 Pres. Wilson proposes "Fourteen Points" as the basis for peace; Americans fight at Château-Thierry, Belleau Wood, Saint-Mihiel, and Argonne Forest in France; an armistice ends the war.

1918-19 Pres. Wilson attends the Paris Peace Conference of victorious nations.

1919 The US Senate rejects the League of Nations; prohibition is established by the 18th Amendment.

1920 The right to vote is given to women by the 19th Amendment.

1921 National immigration quotas are introduced.

1921-22 The Washington Conference restricts warship construction among the chief naval powers.

1924 The army plane *Chicago* makes the first flight around the world.

1927 Charles A. Lindbergh makes the first nonstop solo flight across the Atlantic.

1928 The Kellogg-Briand Pact outlaws war.

1929 The stock market reaches a new high and then crashes; the panic marks the beginning of the Great Depression; millions of workers are unemployed.

1932 Franklin Delano Roosevelt is elected president.

1933 The New Deal is launched; the gold standard is suspended; bank deposits are insured; the Tennessee Valley Authority is organized; the 21st Amendment repeals prohibition.

1934 Congress tightens control over securities, passes the first Reciprocal Trade Agreement Act, and launches the federal housing program.

1935 The National Labor Relations (Wagner) Act guarantees collective bargaining to labor; the Congress of Industrial Organizations (CIO) is founded; the Social Security Act is passed.

1936 The Boulder Dam (now Hoover Dam) is completed across the Colorado River.

1938 The Fair Labor Standards Act provides a federal yardstick for wages and hours of workers.

1939 Germany invades Poland, beginning World War II.

1940 The US begins a huge rearmament program; the first peacetime draft takes effect; Roosevelt defies tradition and accepts the presidential nomination for a third term.

1941 The Japanese attack on Pearl Harbor, Hawaii, brings the US into World War II.

1942 Americans launch a counteroffensive in the Pacific; the Allies invade North Africa.

1943 The invasion of Italy is the Allies' first landing on the European continent.

1944 The Allies launch the greatest sea-to-land assault in history in the invasion of France; the GI Bill of Rights is passed.

1945 Germany surrenders, 8 May; the US drops atomic bombs on Japan at Hiroshima, 6 August, and Nagasaki, 9 August; Japan surrenders, 2 September; the Cold War begins between the US and the Soviet Union.

1946 The Philippines is granted independence by the US; the Atomic Energy Commission is created.

1947 The Truman Doctrine, offering aid to counter communism in Greece and Turkey, is declared; the Department of Defense consolidates the army, navy, and air force.

1948 The European Recovery Program is enacted.

1949 The Fair Deal program of social reform is announced; the US and its allies force the Soviet Union to lift the Berlin blockade; the North Atlantic Treaty Organization (NATO) is founded.

1950 The US and several other members of the UN send military forces to the aid of the Republic of Korea; bitter war develops.

1951 A two-term limit is put on the presidency by ratification of the 22nd Amendment.

1952 The US and its allies end the occupation of West Germany; the election of Dwight D. Eisenhower ends 20 years of Democratic governance.

1953 The Korean War ends; the Department of Health, Education, and Welfare becomes the 10th cabinet post.

1954 Racial segregation of public schools is declared illegal by the Supreme Court.

1955 The two largest labor organizations merge into one group—the AFL-CIO; the Salk poliomyelitis vaccine is proved successful.

1956 Legislation is passed providing funding for the US Interstate Highway System.

1957 The Eisenhower Doctrine to strengthen the US position in the Middle East is adopted.

1958 The first US artificial Earth satellite is launched; the US joins the International Atomic Energy Agency.

1959 Alaska becomes the 49th state, Hawaii the 50th.

1960 A US spy plane is downed over the Soviet Union, leading to the capture of Francis Gary Powers.

1961 The CIA is involved in an unsuccessful invasion of Cuba at the Bay of Pigs; Alan Shepard becomes the first American to make spaceflight; American troops are sent to defend West Berlin.

1962 The Cuban missile crisis erupts; the Soviets remove missiles from Cuba at the urging of the US.

1963 The March on Washington for Jobs and Freedom takes place; Pres. John F. Kennedy is assassinated in Dallas TX; a nuclear test-ban treaty is signed.

1964 The landmark Civil Rights Act is passed.

1965 US combat forces fight in Vietnam; the Medicare Act is signed; the Department of Housing and Urban Development becomes the 11th cabinet post.

1966 The Department of Transportation becomes the 12th cabinet post.

1967 The 25th Amendment to the Constitution provides for presidential succession.

1968 The assassinations of Martin Luther King, Jr, and Robert F. Kennedy provoke riots.

1969 US astronauts land on the Moon.

1970 Four students at Kent State University in Ohio are killed by National Guard soldiers during anti-Vietnam War protests.

1971 The 26th Amendment to the Constitution gives 18-year-olds the right to vote in all elections.

1972 Pres. Richard M. Nixon visits China and the Soviet Union.

1973 The US withdraws its troops from Vietnam; gas prices soar as OPEC raises the price of oil 400%.

1974 The Watergate Scandal and the threat of impeachment force Nixon to resign.

1977 The Department of Energy becomes a new cabinet post; a treaty is signed to return the Panama Canal to Panama by the year 2000.

1978 Pres. Jimmy Carter hosts the Camp David talks between Israel's Menachem Begin and Egypt's Anwar el-Sadat.

1979 The second Strategic Arms Limitation Talks (SALT II) treaty is signed by the US and the Soviet Union; militants seize 66 American hostages in a takeover of the US embassy in Iran.

1980 The Department of Health, Education, and Welfare is separated into the Department of Health and Human Services and the Department of Education.

1981 Sandra Day O'Connor is appointed the first woman Supreme Court justice.

1983 Pres. Ronald Reagan announces the Star Wars missile-defense program; the US invades Grenada.

1985 A summit between Reagan and Soviet leader Mikhail Gorbachev is held in Geneva, Switzerland.

1986 The space shuttle *Challenger* explodes shortly after liftoff; the US bombs targets in Libya.

1987 The Iran-Contra hearings are held; the stock market collapses; Reagan and Gorbachev sign the Intermediate-Range Nuclear Forces (INF) Treaty.

1988 The Department of Veterans Affairs is approved as a cabinet post.

1989 The *Exxon Valdez* supertanker spills 10 million gallons of crude oil off the Alaskan coast; the US invades Panama; the Berlin Wall ceases to divide the two Germanys, signaling the end of the Cold War.

1990 US troops are sent to Saudi Arabia in response to Iraq's invasion of Kuwait.

1991 An air and ground war leads to the Iraqi surrender and withdrawal from Kuwait; the Soviet Union comes apart.

1992 Riots erupt in Los Angeles after white policemen accused of beating African American Rodney King are acquitted; the North American Free Trade Agreement (NAFTA) is signed by the US, Canada, and Mexico.

1993 Janet Reno becomes the first woman attorney general; the World Trade Center in New York City is bombed.

1995 Timothy McVeigh detonates a bomb in a terrorist attack on the Alfred P. Murrah Federal Building in Oklahoma City, killing 168 people.

1998 Pres. Bill Clinton is impeached for perjury and obstruction of justice; he is acquitted by the Senate the following year.

2000 The results of the presidential election are challenged by Vice Pres. Al Gore; the US Supreme Court overrules the Florida Supreme Court's order for a statewide manual recount of ballots; George W. Bush wins the presidency.

2001 On 11 September, two hijacked airplanes demolish the World Trade Center in New York City, another crashes into the Pentagon outside Washington DC, and a fourth crashes in the southern Pennsylvania countryside; Pres. Bush calls for a global "war on terror" and sends US troops into Afghanistan, eventually displacing the Taliban regime.

2002 Republicans take control of both houses of Congress, holding both the legislative and executive branches of government for the first time since 1952.

2003 The US launches a war to depose the Saddam Hussein regime in Iraq and takes control of the country after just weeks of fighting; Congress passes a US$350 billion tax cut; the Department of Homeland Security is created as a cabinet post.

2004 Scandal erupts with the publication of photos of prisoner abuse at Abu Ghraib prison in Iraq; the independent 9/11 Commission finds no credible evidence of a connection between Iraq and al-Qaeda's attacks of 11 Sep 2001; Bush is reelected president.

2005 Hurricane Katrina strikes the Gulf Coast, destroying much of New Orleans and killing more than 1,500 people.

2006 Conservative lawyer John G. Roberts, Jr., is appointed to the Supreme Court as chief justice; Democrats gain control of both houses of Congress.

2007 In an effort to quell a persistent insurrection against the US-backed government of Iraq, Pres. Bush orders a "surge" of 20,000 additional US troops.

2008 A crisis in the subprime mortgage industry, leading to foreclosures and falling home values, together with record-high prices of petroleum, pushes the US economy into recession.

2009 In a historic ceremony on 20 January, Barack Obama is sworn in as the first African American president of the United States; two of the Big Three automobile manufacturers—Chrysler and General Motors—declare bankruptcy; American troops meet the 30 June deadline to withdraw from Iraqi cities under an agreement that calls for all American forces to leave Iraq by the end of 2011.

2010 Soon after the milestone of 1,000 US soldiers killed is passed, the war in Afghanistan becomes the longest in US history; a deep-water oil-drilling platform explodes in US waters in the Gulf of Mexico, killing 11 workers and causing a leak of as much as 2.5 million gallons of oil into the gulf per day, creating one of the world's worst environmental disasters.

Important Documents in US History

Mayflower Compact

On 21 Nov 1620 (11 November, Old Style), 41 male passengers on the Mayflower signed the following compact prior to their landing at Plymouth (now Massachusetts). The compact resulted from the fear that some members of the company might leave the group and settle on their own. The Mayflower Compact bound the signers into a body politic for the purpose of forming a government and pledged them to abide by any laws and regulations that would later by established. The document was not a constitution but rather an adaptation of the usual church covenant to a civil situation. It became the foundation of Plymouth's government.

In the name of God, Amen.

We whose names are underwritten, the loyal subjects of our dread sovereign Lord, King James, by the grace of God, of Great Britain, France and Ireland king, defender of the faith, etc., having undertaken, for the glory of God, and advancement of the Christian faith, and honor of our king and country, a voyage to plant the first colony in the Northern parts of Virginia, do by these presents solemnly and mutually in the presence of God, and one of another, covenant and combine ourselves together into a civil body politic, for our better ordering and preservation and furtherance of the ends aforesaid; and by virtue hereof to enact, constitute, and frame such just and equal laws, ordinances, acts, constitutions, and offices, from time to time, as shall be thought most meet and convenient for the general good of the colony, unto which we promise all due submission and obedience.

In witness whereof we have hereunder subscribed our names at Cape-Cod the 11 of November, in the year of the reign of our sovereign lord, King James, of England, France, and Ireland the eighteenth, and of Scotland the fifty-fourth. Anno Domine 1620.

Declaration of Independence

On 4 Jul 1776 the Continental Congress officially adopted the Declaration of Independence. Two days before, the Congress had "unanimously" voted (with New York abstaining) to be free and independent from Britain. The Declaration of Independence was written largely by Thomas Jefferson. After modifications by the Congress, the document was prepared and voted upon. New York delegates voted to accept it on 15 July, and on 19 July the Congress ordered the document to be engrossed as "The Unanimous Declaration of the Thirteen United States of America." It was accordingly put on parchment, and members of the Congress present on 2 August affixed their signatures to this parchment copy on that day, and others later. The last signer was Thomas McKean of Delaware, whose name was not placed on the document before 1777.

The Unanimous Declaration of the Thirteen United States of America

When in the Course of human events, it becomes necessary for one people to dissolve the political bands which have connected them with another, and to assume among the powers of the earth, the separate and equal station to which the Laws of Nature and of Nature's God entitle them, a decent respect to the opinions of mankind requires that they should declare the causes which impel them to the separation.—We hold these truths to be self-evident, that all men are created equal, that they are endowed by their Creator with certain unalienable Rights, that among these are Life, Liberty and the pursuit of Happiness.—That to secure these rights, Governments are instituted among Men, deriving their just powers from the consent of the governed,—That whenever any Form of Government becomes destructive of these ends, it is the Right of the People to alter or to abolish it, and to institute new Government, laying its foundation on such principles and organizing its powers in such form, as to them shall seem most likely to effect their Safety and Happiness. Prudence, indeed, will dictate that Governments long established should not be changed for light and transient causes; and accordingly all experience hath shown, that mankind are more disposed to suffer, while evils are sufferable, than to right themselves by abolishing the forms to which they are accustomed. But when a long train of abuses and usurpations, pursuing invariably the same Object evinces a design to reduce them under absolute Despotism, it is their right, it is their duty, to throw off such Government, and to provide new Guards for their future security.— Such has been the patient sufferance of these Colonies; and such is now the necessity which constrains them to alter their former Systems of Government. The history of the present King of Great Britain is a history of repeated injuries and usurpations, all having in direct object the establishment of an absolute Tyranny over these States.

To prove this, let Facts be submitted to a candid world.—He has refused his Assent to Laws, the most wholesome and necessary for the public good.—He has forbidden his Governors to pass Laws of immediate and pressing importance, unless suspended in their operation till his Assent should be obtained; and when so suspended, he has utterly neglected to attend to them.—He has refused to pass other Laws for the accommodation of large districts of people, unless those people would relinquish the right of Representation in the Legislature, a right inestimable to them and formidable to tyrants only.—He has called together legislative bodies at places unusual, uncomfortable, and distant from the depository of their public Records, for the sole purpose of fatiguing them into compliance with his measures.—He has dissolved Representative Houses repeatedly, for opposing with manly firmness his invasions on the rights of the people.—He has refused for a long time, after such dissolutions, to cause others to be elected; whereby the Legislative powers, incapable of Annihilation, have returned to the People at large for their exercise; the State remaining in the mean time exposed to all the dangers of invasion from without, and convulsions within.—He has endeavoured to prevent the population of these States; for that purpose obstructing the Laws for Naturalization of Foreigners; refusing to pass others to encourage their migration hither, and raising the conditions of new Appropriations of Lands.—He has obstructed the Administration of Justice, by refusing his Assent to Laws for establishing Judiciary powers.—He has made judges dependent on his Will alone, for the tenure of their offices, and the amount and payment of their salaries.—He has erected a multitude of New Offices, and sent hither swarms of Officers to harrass our people, and eat out their substance.—He has kept among us, in times of peace, Standing Armies, without the Consent of our legislatures.—He has affected to render the Military independent of and superior to the Civil power.—He has combined with others to subject us to a jurisdiction foreign to our constitution, and unacknowledged by our laws, giving his Assent to their Acts of pretended Legislation:—For quartering large bodies of armed troops among us:—For protecting them, by a mock Trial, from punishment for any Murders which they should commit on the Inhabitants of these States:—For cutting off our Trade with all parts of the world:—For imposing Taxes on us without our Consent:—For depriving us in many cases, of the benefits of Trial by Jury:—For transporting us beyond Seas to be tried for pretended offences:—For abolishing the free System of English Laws in a neighbouring Province, establishing therein an Arbitrary government, and enlarging its Boundaries so as to render it at once an example and fit instrument for introducing the same absolute rule into these Colonies:—For taking away our Charters, abolishing our most valuable Laws, and altering fundamentally the Forms of our Governments:—For suspending our own Legislatures, and declaring themselves invested with power to legislate for us in all cases whatsoever.—He has abdicated Government here, by declaring us out of his Protection and waging War against us.—He has plundered our seas, ravaged our Coasts, burnt our towns, and destroyed the lives of our people.—He is at this time transporting large Armies of foreign Mercenaries to compleat the works of death, desolation and tyranny, already begun with circumstances of Cruelty & perfidy scarcely paralleled in the most barbarous ages, and totally unworthy the Head of a civilized nation.—He has constrained our fellow Citizens taken Captive on the high Seas to bear Arms against their Country, to become the executioners of their friends and Brethren, or to fall themselves by their Hands.—He has excited domestic insurrections amongst us, and has endeavoured to bring on the inhabitants of our frontiers, the merciless Indian Savages, whose known rule of warfare, is an undistinguished destruction of all ages, sexes and conditions. In every stage of these Oppressions We have Petitioned for Redress in the most humble terms: Our repeated Petitions have been answered only by repeated injury. A Prince, whose character is thus marked by every act which may define a Tyrant, is unfit to be the ruler of a free people. Nor have We been wanting in attentions to our Brittish brethren. We have warned them from time to time of attempts by their legislature to extend an unwarrantable jurisdiction over us. We have reminded them of the circumstances of our emigration and settlement here. We have appealed to their native justice and magnanimity, and we have conjured them by the ties of our common kindred to disavow these usurpations, which, would inevitably interrupt our connections and correspondence. They too have been deaf to the voice of justice and of consanguinity. We must, therefore, acquiesce in the necessity, which denounces our Separation, and hold them, as we hold the rest of mankind, Enemies in War, in Peace Friends.—

We, therefore, the Representatives of the United States of America, in General Congress, Assembled, appealing to the Supreme Judge of the world for the rectitude of our intentions, do, in the Name, and by Authority of the good People of these Colonies, solemnly publish and declare, That these United Colonies are, and of Right ought to be Free and Independent States; that they are Absolved from all Allegiance to the British Crown, and that all political connection between them and the State of Great Britain, is and ought to be totally dissolved; and that as Free and Independent States, they have full Power to levy War, conclude Peace, contract Alliances, establish Commerce, and to do all other Acts and Things which Independent States may of right do.—And for the support of this Declaration, with a firm reliance on the protection of Divine Providence, we mutually pledge to each other our Lives, our Fortunes and our sacred Honor.

Signers of the Declaration of Independence

Connecticut
Samuel Huntington
Roger Sherman
William Williams
Oliver Wolcott

Delaware
Thomas McKean
George Read
Caesar Rodney

Georgia
Button Gwinnett
Lyman Hall
George Walton

Maryland
Charles Carroll
Samuel Chase
William Paca
Thomas Stone

Massachusetts
John Adams
Samuel Adams
Elbridge Gerry
John Hancock
Robert Treat Paine

New Hampshire
Josiah Bartlett
Matthew Thornton
William Whipple

New Jersey
Abraham Clark
John Hart
Francis Hopkinson
Richard Stockton
John Witherspoon

New York
William Floyd
Francis Lewis
Philip Livingston
Lewis Morris

North Carolina
Joseph Hewes
William Hooper
John Penn

Pennsylvania
George Clymer
Benjamin Franklin
Robert Morris
John Morton
George Ross
Benjamin Rush
James Smith
George Taylor
James Wilson

Rhode Island
William Ellery
Stephen Hopkins

South Carolina
Thomas Heyward, Jr.
Thomas Lynch, Jr.
Arthur Middleton
Edward Rutledge

Virginia
Carter Braxton
Thomas Jefferson
Benjamin Harrison
Francis Lightfoot Lee
Richard Henry Lee
Thomas Nelson, Jr.
George Wythe

Did you know? Thomas Jefferson was the first governor of a US state—Virginia—to go on to serve as president of the United States (1801–09). Sixteen governors since have been elected president, including 4 of the last 6 executives. William Henry Harrison and Andrew Jackson served as territorial governors of Indiana (1800–12) and Florida (1821) prior to their elections to the presidency.

The Constitution of the United States

The Constitution was written during the summer of 1787 in Philadelphia by 55 delegates to a Constitutional Convention that was called ostensibly to amend the Articles of Confederation. It was submitted for ratification to the 13 states on 28 Sep 1787. In June 1788, after the Constitution had been ratified by nine states (as required by Article VII), Congress set 4 Mar 1789 as the date for the new government to commence proceedings.

Preamble

We the People of the United States, in Order to form a more perfect Union, establish Justice, insure domestic Tranquility, provide for common defence, promote the general Welfare, and secure the Blessings of Liberty to ourselves and our Posterity, do ordain and establish this Constitution for the United States of America.

Article I

Section 1—

All legislative Powers herein granted shall be vested in a Congress of the United States, which shall consist of a Senate and House of Representatives.

Section 2—

The House of Representatives shall be composed of Members chosen every second Year by the People of the several States, and the Electors in each State shall have the Qualifications requisite for Electors of the most numerous Branch of the State Legislature.

No Person shall be a Representative who shall not have attained to the Age of twenty five Years, and been seven Years a Citizen of the United States, and who shall not, when elected, be an Inhabitant of that State in which he shall be chosen.

Representatives and direct Taxes shall be apportioned among the several States which may be included within this Union, according to their respective Numbers, which shall be determined by adding to the whole Number of free Persons, including those bound to Service for a Term of Years, and excluding Indians not taxed, three fifths of all other Persons. The actual Enumeration shall be made within three Years after the first Meeting of the Congress of the United States, and within every subsequent Term of ten Years, in such Manner as they shall by Law direct. The Number of Representatives shall not exceed one for every thirty Thousand, but each State shall have at Least one Representative; and until such enumeration shall be made, the State of New Hampshire shall be entitled to chuse three, Massachusetts eight, Rhode-Island and Providence Plantations one, Connecticut five, New-York six, New Jersey four, Pennsylvania eight, Delaware one, Maryland six, Virginia ten, North Carolina five, South Carolina five, and Georgia three.

When vacancies happen in the Representation from any State, the Executive Authority thereof shall issue Writs of Election to fill such Vacancies.

The House of Representatives shall chuse their speaker and other Officers; and shall have the sole Power of Impeachment.

Section 3—

The Senate of the United States shall be composed of two Senators from each State, chosen by the Legislature thereof for six Years; and each Senator shall have one Vote.

Immediately after they shall be assembled in Consequence of the first Election, they shall be divided as equally as may be into three Classes. The Seats of the Senators of the first Class shall be vacated at the Expiration of the second Year, of the second Class at the Expiration of the fourth Year, and of the third Class at the Expiration of the sixth Year, so that one third may be chosen every second Year; and if Vacancies happen by Resignation, or otherwise, during the Recess of the Legislature of any State, the Executive thereof may make temporary Appointments until the next Meeting of the Legislature, which shall then fill such Vacancies.

No Person shall be a Senator who shall not have attained to the Age of thirty Years, and been nine Years a Citizen of the United States, and who shall not, when elected, be an Inhabitant of that State for which he shall be chosen.

The Vice President of the United States shall be President of the Senate, but shall have no Vote, unless they be equally divided.

The Senate shall chuse their other Officers, and also a President pro tempore, in the Absence of the Vice President, or when he shall exercise the Office of President of the United States.

The Senate shall have the sole Power to try all Impeachments. When sitting for that Purpose, they shall be on Oath or Affirmation. When the President of the United States is tried, the Chief Justice shall preside: And no Person shall be convicted without the concurrence of two thirds of the Members present. Judgment in Cases of Impeachment shall not extend further than to removal from Office, and disqualification to hold and enjoy any Office of honor, Trust or Profit under the United States: but the Party convicted shall nevertheless be liable and subject to Indictment, Trial, Judgment and Punishment, according to law.

Section 4—

The Times, Places and Manner of holding Elections for Senators and Representatives, shall be prescribed in each State by the Legislature thereof; but the Congress may at any time by Law make or alter such Regulations, except as to the Places of chusing Senators.

The Congress shall assemble at least once in every Year, and such Meeting shall be on the first Monday in December, unless they shall by Law appoint a different Day.

Section 5—

Each House shall be the Judge of the Elections, Returns and Qualifications of its own Members, and a Majority of each shall constitute a Quorum to do business; but a smaller Number may adjourn from day to day, and may be authorized to compel the Attendance of absent Members, in such Manner, and under such Penalties as each House may provide.

Each House may determine the Rules of its Proceedings, punish its Members for disorderly Behaviour, and, with the Concurrence of two thirds, expel a Member.

Each House shall keep a journal of its Proceedings, and from time to time publish the same, excepting such Parts as may in their Judgment require Secrecy; and the yeas and Nays of the Members of either House on any question shall, at the Desire of one fifth of those Present, be entered on the journal.

Neither House, during the Session of Congress, shall, without the Consent of the other, adjourn for more than three days, nor to any other place than that in which the two Houses shall be sitting.

Section 6—

The Senators and Representatives shall receive a Compensation for their Services, to be ascertained by Law, and paid out of the Treasury of the United States. They shall in all Cases, except Treason, Felony and Breach of the Peace, be privileged from Arrest during their Attendance at the Session of their respective Houses, and in going to and returning from the same; and for any Speech or Debate in either House, they shall not be questioned in any other Place.

No Senator or Representative shall, during the Time for which he was elected, be appointed to any civil Office under the Authority of the United States, which shall have been created, or the Emoluments whereof shall have been encreased during such time; and no Person holding any Office under the United States, shall be a Member of either House during his Continuance in Office.

Section 7—

All Bills for raising Revenue shall originate in the House of Representatives; but the Senate may propose or concur with Amendments as on other Bills.

Every Bill which shall have passed the House of Representatives and the Senate, shall, before it become a Law, be presented to the President of the United States; If he approve he shall sign it, but if not he shall return it, with his Objections to that House in which it shall have originated, who shall enter the Objections at large on their Journal, and proceed to reconsider it. If after such Reconsideration two thirds of that House shall agree to pass the Bill, it shall be sent, together with the Objections, to the other House, by which it shall likewise be reconsidered, and if approved by two thirds of that House, it shall become a Law. But in all such Cases the Votes of both Houses shall be determined by yeas and Nays, and the Names of the Persons voting for and against the Bill shall be entered on the Journal of each House respectively. If any Bill shall not be returned by the President within ten Days (Sundays excepted) after it shall have been presented to him, the Same shall be a Law, in like Manner as if he had signed it, unless the Congress by their Adjournment prevent its Return, in which Case it shall not be a Law.

Every Order, Resolution, or Vote to which the Concurrence of the Senate and House of Representatives may be necessary (except on a question of Adjournment) shall be presented to the President of the United States; and before the Same shall take Effect, shall be approved by him, or being disapproved by him, shall be repassed by two thirds of the Senate and House of Representatives, according to the Rules and Limitations prescribed in the Case of a Bill.

Section 8—

The Congress shall have Power To lay and collect Taxes, Duties, Imposts and Excises, to pay the Debts and provide for the common Defence and general Welfare of the United States; but all Duties, Imposts and Excises shall be uniform throughout the United States;

To borrow Money on the credit of the United States;

To regulate Commerce with foreign Nations, and among the several States, and with the Indian Tribes;

To establish an uniform Rule of Naturalization, and uniform Laws on the subject of Bankruptcies throughout the United States;

To coin Money, regulate the Value thereof, and of foreign Coin, and fix the Standard of Weights and Measures;

To provide for the Punishment of counterfeiting the Securities and current Coin of the United States;

To establish Post Offices and post Roads;

To promote the Progress of Science and useful Arts, by securing for limited Times to Authors and Inventors the exclusive Right to their respective Writings and Discoveries;

To constitute Tribunals inferior to the supreme Court;

To define and punish Piracies and Felonies committed on the high Seas, and Offences against the Law of Nations;

To declare War, grant Letters of Marque and Reprisal, and make rules concerning Captures on Land and Water;

To raise and support Armies, but no Appropriation of Money to that Use shall be for a longer Term than two Years;

To provide and maintain a Navy;

To make Rules for the Government and Regulation of the land and naval Forces;

To provide for calling forth the Militia to execute the Laws of the Union, suppress Insurrections and repel Invasions;

To provide for organizing, arming, and disciplining, the Militia, and for governing such Part of them as may be employed in the Service of the United States, reserving to the States respectively, the Appointment of the Officers, and the Authority of training the Militia according to the discipline prescribed by Congress;

To exercise exclusive Legislation in all Cases whatsoever, over such District (not exceeding ten Miles square), as may, by Cession of particular States, and the Acceptance of Congress, become the Seat of the Government of the United States, and to exercise like Authority over all Places purchased by the Consent of the Legislature of the State in which the Same shall be for the Erection of Forts, Magazines, Arsenals, dock-Yards, and other needful Buildings; — And

To make all Laws which shall be necessary and proper for carying into Execution the foregoing Powers, and all other Powers vested by this Constitution in the Government of the United States, or in any Department or Officer thereof.

Section 9—

The Migration or Importation of such Persons as any of the States now existing shall think proper to admit, shall not be prohibited by the Congress prior to the Year one thousand eight hundred and eight, but a Tax or duty may be imposed on such Importation, not exceeding ten dollars for each Person.

The Privilege of the Writ of Habeas Corpus shall not be suspended, unless when in Cases of Rebellion or Invasion the public Safety may require it.

No Bill of Attainder or ex post facto Law shall be passed.

No Capitation, or other direct, Tax shall be laid, unless in Proportion to the Census or Enumeration herein before directed to be taken.

No Tax or Duty shall be laid on Articles exported from any State.

No Preference shall be given by any Regulation of Commerce or Revenue to the Ports of one State over those of another; nor shall Vessels bound to, or from, one State, be obliged to enter, clear or pay Duties in another.

No money shall be drawn from the Treasury, but in Consequence of Appropriations made by Law; and a regular Statement and Account of the Receipts and Expenditures of all public Money shall be published from time to time.

No Title of Nobility shall be granted by the United States: And no Person holding any Office of Profit or Trust under them, shall, without the Consent of the Congress, accept of any present, Emolument, Office, or Title, of any kind whatever, from any King, Prince, or foreign State.

Section 10—

No State shall enter into any Treaty, Alliance, or Confederation; grant Letters of Marque and Reprisal; coin Money; emit Bills of Credit; make any Thing but gold and silver Coin a Tender in Payment of Debts; pass any Bill of Attainder, ex post facto Law, or Law impairing the Obligation of Contracts, or grant any Title of Nobility.

No State shall, without the Consent of the Congress, lay any Imposts or Duties on Imports or Exports, except what may be absolutely necessary for executing it's inspection Laws: and the net Produce of all Duties and Imposts, laid by any State on Imports or Exports, shall be for the Use of the Treasury of the United States; and all such Laws shall be subject to the Revision and Controul of the Congress.

No State shall, without the Consent of Congress, lay any Duty of Tonnage, keep Troops, or Ships of War in time of Peace, enter into any Agreement or Compact with another State, or with a foreign Power, or engage in War, unless actually invaded, or in such imminent Danger as will not admit of delay.

Article II
Section 1—

The executive Power shall be vested in a President of the United States of America. He shall hold his Office during the Term of four Years, and, together with the Vice President, chosen for the same Term, be elected, as follows

Each State shall appoint, in such Manner as the Legislature thereof may direct, a Number of Electors, equal to the whole Number of Senators and Representatives to which the State may be entitled in the Congress: but no Senator or Representative, or Person holding an Office of Trust or Profit under the United States, shall be appointed an Elector.

The Electors shall meet in their respective States, and vote by Ballot for two Persons, of whom one at least shall not be an Inhabitant of the same State with themselves. And they shall make a List of all the Persons voted for, and of the Number of Votes for each; which List they shall sign and certify, and transmit sealed to the Seat of the Government of the United States, directed to the President of the Senate. The President of the Senate shall, in the Presence of the Senate and House of Representatives, open all the Certificates, and the Votes shall then be counted. The Person having the greatest Number of Votes shall be the President, if such Number be a Majority of the whole Number of Electors appointed; and if there be more than one who have such Majority, and have an equal Number of Votes, then the House of Representatives shall immediately chuse by Ballot one of them for President: and if no Person have a Majority, then from the five highest on the List the said House shall in like Manner chuse the President. But in chusing the President, the Votes shall be taken by States, the Representation from each State having one Vote; A quorum for this Purpose shall consist of a Member or Members from two thirds of the States, and a Majority of all the States shall be necessary to a Choice. In every Case, after the Choice of the President, the Person having the greatest Number of Votes of the Electors shall be the Vice President. But if there should remain two or more who have equal Votes, the Senate shall chuse from them by Ballot the Vice President.

The Congress may determine the Time of chusing the Electors, and the Day on which they shall give their Votes; which Day shall be the same throughout the United States.

No Person except a natural born Citizen, or a Citizen of the United States, at the time of the Adoption of this Constitution, shall be eligible to the Office of President; neither shall any Person be eligible to that Office who shall not have attained to the Age of thirty five Years, and been fourteen Years a Resident within the United States.

In Case of the Removal of the President from Office, or of his Death, Resignation, or Inability to discharge the Powers and Duties of the said Office, the Same shall devolve on the Vice President, and the Congress may by Law provide for the Case of Removal, Death, Resignation or Inability, both of the President and Vice President, declaring what Officer shall then act as President, and such Officer shall act accordingly, until the Disability be removed, or a President shall be elected.

The President shall, at stated Times, receive for his Services, a Compensation, which shall neither be encreased nor diminished during the Period for which he shall have been elected, and he shall not receive within that Period any other Emolument from the United States, or any of them.

Before he enter on the Execution of his Office, he shall take the following Oath or Affirmation: "I do solemnly swear (or affirm) that I will faithfully execute the Office of President of the United States, and will to the best of my Ability, preserve, protect and defend the Constitution of the United States."

Section 2—

The President shall be Commander in Chief of the Army and Navy of the United States, and of the Militia of the several States, when called into the actual Service of the United States; he may require the Opinion, in writing, of the principal Officer in each of the executive Departments, upon any Subject relating to the Duties of their respective Offices, and he shall have Power to grant Reprieves and Pardons for Offences against the United States, except in Cases of Impeachment.

He shall have Power, by and with the Advice and Consent of the Senate, to make Treaties, provided two thirds of the Senators present concur; and he shall nominate, and by and with the Advice and Consent of the Senate, shall appoint Ambassadors, other public Ministers and Consuls, Judges of the supreme Court, and all other Officers of the United States, whose Appointments are not herein otherwise provided for, and which shall be established by Law: but the Congress may by Law vest the Appointment of such inferior Officers, as they think proper, in the President alone, in the Courts of Law, or in the Heads of Departments.

The President shall have Power to fill up all Vacancies that may happen during the Recess of the Senate, by granting Commissions which shall expire at the End of their next Session.

Section 3—

He shall from time to time give to the Congress Information of the State of the Union, and recommend to their Consideration such Measures as he shall judge necessary and expedient; he may, on extraordinary Occasions, convene both Houses, or either of them, and in Case of Disagreement between them, with Respect to the Time of Adjournment, he may adjourn them to such Time as he shall think proper; he shall receive Ambassadors and other public Ministers; he shall take Care that the Laws be faithfully executed, and shall Commission all the Officers of the United States.

Section 4—

The President, Vice President and all civil Officers of the United States, shall be removed from Office on Impeachment for, and Conviction of, Treason, Bribery, or other High Crimes and Misdemeanors.

Article III

Section 1—

The judicial Power of the United States, shall be vested in one supreme Court, and in such inferior Courts as the Congress may from time to time ordain and establish. The Judges, both of the supreme and inferior Courts, shall hold their Offices during good Behaviour, and shall, at stated Times, receive for their Services, a Compensation, which shall not be diminished during their Continuance in Office.

Section 2—

The judicial Power shall extend to all Cases, in Law and Equity, arising under this Constitution, the Laws of the United States, and Treaties made, or which shall be made, under their Authority; — to all Cases affecting Ambassadors, other public Ministers and Consuls; — to all Cases of admiralty and maritime jurisdiction; — to Controversies to which the United States shall be a Party; — to Controversies between two or more States;-between a State and Citizens of another State; — between Citizens of different States; — between Citizens of the same State claiming Lands under Grants of different States, and between a State, or the Citizens thereof, and foreign States, Citizens or Subjects.

In all Cases affecting Ambassadors, other public Ministers and Consuls, and those in which a State shall be Party, the supreme Court shall have original Jurisdiction. In all the other Cases before mentioned, the supreme Court shall have appellate Jurisdiction, both as to Law and Fact, with such Exceptions, and under such Regulations as the Congress shall make.

The Trial of all Crimes, except in Cases of Impeachment, shall be by Jury; and such Trial shall be held in the State where the said Crimes shall have been committed; but when not committed within any State, the Trial shall be at such Place or Places as the Congress may by Law have directed.

Section 3—

Treason against the United States, shall consist only in levying War against them, or in adhering to their Enemies, giving them Aid and Comfort. No Person shall be convicted of Treason unless on the Testimony of two Witnesses to the same overt Act, or on Confession in open Court.

The Congress shall have Power to declare the Punishment of Treason, but no Attainder of Treason shall work Corruption of Blood, or Forfeiture except during the Life of the Person attainted.

Article IV

Section 1—

Full Faith and Credit shall be given in each State to the public Acts, Records, and judicial Proceedings of every other State. And the Congress may by general Laws prescribe the Manner in which such Acts, Records and Proceedings shall be proved, and the Effect thereof.

Section 2—

The Citizens of each State shall be entitled to all Privileges and Immunities of Citizens in the several States.

A person charged in any State with Treason, Felony, or other Crime, who shall flee from justice, and be found in another State, shall on Demand of the executive Authority of the State from which he fled, be delivered up, to be removed to the State having Jurisdiction of the Crime.

No Person held to Service or Labour in one State, under the Laws thereof, escaping into another, shall in Consequence of any Law or Regulation therein, be discharged from such Service or Labour, but shall be delivered upon on Claim of the Party to whom such Service or Labour may be due.

Section 3—

New States may be admitted by the Congress into this Union; but no new State shall be formed or erected within the Jurisdiction of any other State; nor any State be formed by the Junction of two or more States, or Parts of States, without the Consent of the Legislatures of the States concerned as well as of the Congress.

The Congress shall have Power to dispose of and make all needful Rules and Regulations respecting the Territory or other Property belonging to the United States; and nothing in this Constitution shall be so construed as to Prejudice any Claims of the United States, or of any particular State.

Section 4—

The United States shall guarantee to every State in this Union a Republican Form of Government, and shall protect each of them against Invasion; and on Application of the Legislature, or of the Executive (when the Legislature cannot be convened) against domestic Violence.

Article V

The Congress, whenever two thirds of both Houses shall deem it necessary, shall propose Amendments to this Constitution, or, on the Application of the Legislatures of two thirds of the several States, shall call a Convention for proposing Amendments, which, in either Case, shall be valid to all Intents and Purposes, as Part of this Constitution, when ratified by the Legislatures of three fourths of the several States, or by Conventions in three fourths thereof, as the one or the other Mode of Ratification may be proposed by the Congress; Provided that no Amendment which may be made prior to the Year One thousand eight hundred and eight shall in any Manner affect the first and fourth Clauses in the Ninth Section of the first

Article; and that no State, without its Consent, shall be deprived of its equal Suffrage in the Senate.

Article VI

All Debts contracted and Engagements entered into, before the Adoption of this Constitution, shall be as valid against the United States under this Constitution, as under the Confederation.

This Constitution, and the Laws of the United States which shall be made in Pursuance thereof; and all Treaties made, or which shall be made, under the Authority of the United States, shall be the supreme Law of the Land; and the Judges in every State shall be bound thereby, any Thing in the Constitution or Laws of any State to the Contrary notwithstanding.

The Senators and Representatives before mentioned, and the Members of the several State Legislatures, and all executive and judicial Officers, both of the United States and of the several States, shall be bound by Oath or Affirmation, to support this Constitution; but no religious Test shall ever be required as a Qualification to any Office or public Trust under the United States.

Article VII

The Ratification of the Conventions of nine States, shall be sufficient for the Establishment of this Constitution between the States so ratifying the Same.

Done in Convention by the Unanimous Consent of the States present the Seventeenth Day of September in the Year of our Lord one thousand seven hundred and Eighty seven and of the Independence of the United States of America the Twelfth
IN WITNESS whereof We have hereunto subscribed our Names,

G° Washington—
*Presid*ᵗ*, and deputy from Virginia*

New Hampshire
John Langdon
Nicholas Gilman

Massachusetts
Nathaniel Gorham
Rufus King

Connecticut
Wm. Saml. Johnson
Roger Sherman

New York
Alexander Hamilton

New Jersey
Wil: Livingston
David Brearley
Wm. Paterson
Jona: Dayton

Pennsylvania
B. Franklin
Thomas Mifflin
Robᵗ Morris
Geo. Clymer
Thos. FitzSimons
Jared Ingersoll
James Wilson
Gouv Morris

Delaware
Geo: Read
Gunning Bedford jun
John Dickinson
Richard Bassett
Jaco: Broom

Maryland
James McHenry
Dan of Sᵗ Thos. Jenifer
Danˡ Carroll

Virginia
John Blair—
James Madison Jr.

North Carolina
Wm. Blount
Rich'd Dobbs Spaight
Hu Williamson

South Carolina
J. Rutledge
Charles Cotesworth Pinckney
Charles Pinckney
Pierce Butler

Georgia
William Few
Abr Baldwin

Attest:
William Jackson, *Secretary*

[*Rhode Island and the Providence Plantations*
Rhode Island did not send delegates to the Constitutional Convention.]

Bill of Rights

The first 10 amendments to the Constitution were adopted as a single unit on 15 Dec 1791. Together, they constitute a collection of mutually reinforcing guarantees of individual rights and of limitations on federal and state governments.

Amendment I

Congress shall make no law respecting an establishment of religion, or prohibiting the free exercise thereof; or abridging the freedom of speech, or of the press; or the right of the people peaceably to assemble, and to petition the Government for a redress of grievances.

Amendment II

A well regulated Militia, being necessary to the security of a free State, the right of the people to keep and bear Arms, shall not be infringed.

Amendment III

No Soldier shall, in time of peace be quartered in any house, without the consent of the Owner, nor in time of war, but in a manner to be prescribed by law.

Amendment IV

The right of the People to be secure in their persons, houses, papers, and effects, against unreasonable searches and seizures, shall not be violated, and no Warrants shall issue, but upon probable cause, supported by Oath or affirmation, and particularity describing the place to be searched, and the persons or things to be seized.

Amendment V

No person shall be held to answer for a capital, or otherwise infamous crime, unless on a presentment or indictment of a Grand Jury, except in cases arising in the land or naval forces, or in the Militia, when in actual service in time of War or public danger; nor shall any person be subject for the same offence to be twice put in jeopardy of life or limb; nor shall be compelled in any criminal case to be a witness against himself, nor be deprived of life, liberty, or property, without due process of law; nor shall private property be taken for public use, without just compensation.

Amendment VI

In all criminal prosecutions, the accused shall enjoy the right to a speedy and public trial, by an impartial jury of the State and district wherein the crime shall have been committed, which district shall have been previously ascertained by law, and to be informed of the nature and cause of the accusation; to be confronted with the witnesses against him; to have compulsory process for obtaining witnesses in his favor, and to have Assistance of Counsel for his defence.

Amendment VII

In Suits at common law, where the value in controversy shall exceed twenty dollars, the right of trial by jury shall be preserved, and no fact tried by a jury, shall be otherwise re-examined in any Court of the United States, than according to the rules of the common law.

Amendment VIII

Excessive bail shall not be required, nor excessive fines imposed, nor cruel and unusual punishments inflicted.

Amendment IX

The enumeration in the Constitution, of certain rights, shall not be construed to deny or disparage others retained by the people.

Amendment X

The powers not delegated to the United States by the Constitution, nor prohibited by it to the States, are reserved to the States respectively, or to the people.

Further Amendments

Amendment XI
(ratified 7 Feb 1795)

The Judicial power of the United States shall not be construed to extend to any suit in law or equity, commenced or prosecuted against one of the United States by Citizens of another State, or by Citizens or Subjects of any Foreign State.

Amendment XII
(ratified 15 Jun 1804)

The Electors shall meet in their respective states and vote by ballot for President and Vice-President, one of whom, at least, shall not be an inhabitant of the same state with themselves; they shall name in their ballots the person voted for as President, and in distinct ballots the person voted for as Vice-President, and they shall make distinct lists of all persons voted for as President, and of all persons voted for as Vice-President, and of the number of votes for each, which lists they shall sign and certify, and transmit sealed to the seat of the government of the United States, directed to the President of the Senate; — The President of the Senate shall, in the presence of the Senate and House of Representatives, open all the certificates and the votes shall then be counted; — The person having the greatest number of votes for President, shall be the President, if such number be a majority of the whole number of Electors appointed; and if no person have such majority, then from the persons having the highest numbers not exceeding three on the list of those voted for as President, the House of Representatives shall choose immediately, by ballot, the President. But in choosing the President, the votes shall be taken by states, the representation from each state having one vote; a quorum for this purpose shall consist of a member or members from two-thirds of the states, and a majority of all the states shall be necessary to a choice. And if the House of Representatives shall not choose a President whenever the right of choice shall devolve upon then, before the fourth day of March next following, then the Vice-President shall act as President, as in the case of the death or other constitutional disability of the President. — The person having the greatest number of votes as Vice-President, shall be the Vice-President, if such number be a majority of the whole number of Electors appointed, and if no person have a majority, then from the two highest numbers on the list, the Senate shall choose the Vice-President; a quorum for the purpose shall consist of two-thirds of the whole number of Senators, and a majority of the whole number shall be necessary to a choice. But no person constitutionally ineligible to the office of President shall be eligible to that of Vice-President of the United States.

Amendment XIII
(ratified 6 Dec 1865)

Section 1—
Neither slavery nor involuntary servitude, except as a punishment for crime whereof the party shall have been duly convicted, shall exist within the United States, or any place subject to their jurisdiction.

Section 2—
Congress shall have power to enforce this article by appropriate legislation.

Amendment XIV
(ratified 9 Jul 1868)

Section 1—
All persons born or naturalized in the United States, and subject to the jurisdiction thereof, are citizens of the United States and of the State wherein they reside. No State shall make or enforce any law which shall abridge the privileges or immunities of citizens of the United States; nor shall any State deprive any person of life, liberty, or property, without due process of law; nor deny to any person within its jurisdiction the equal protection of the laws.

Section 2—

Representatives shall be apportioned among the several States according to their respective numbers, counting the whole number of persons in each State, excluding Indians not taxed. But when the right to vote at any election for the choice of electors for President and Vice President of the United States, Representatives in Congress, the Executive and Judicial officers of a State, or the members of the Legislature thereof, is denied to any of the male inhabitants of such State, being twenty-one years of age, and citizens of the United States, or in any way abridged, except for participation in rebellion, or other crime, the basis of representation therein shall be reduced in the proportion which the number of such male citizens shall bear to the whole number of male citizens twenty-one years of age in such State.

Section 3—

No person shall be a Senator or Representative in Congress, or elector of President and Vice President, or hold any office, civil or military, under the United States, or under any State, who, having previously taken an oath, as a member of Congress, or as an officer of the United States, or as a member of any State legislature, or as an executive or judicial officer of any State, to support the Constitution of the United States, shall have engaged in insurrection or rebellion against the same, or given aid or comfort to the enemies thereof. But Congress may by a vote of two-thirds of each House, remove such disability.

Section 4—

The validity of the public debt of the United States, authorized by law, including debts incurred for payment of pensions and bounties for services in suppressing insurrection or rebellion, shall not be questioned. But neither the United States nor any State shall assume or pay any debt or obligation incurred in aid of insurrection or rebellion against the United States, or any claim for the loss or emancipation of any slave; but all such debts, obligations and claims shall be held illegal and void.

Section 5—

The Congress shall have power to enforce, by appropriate legislation, the provisions of this article.

Amendment XV
(ratified 8 Feb 1870)

Section 1—

The right of citizens of the United States to vote shall not be denied or abridged by the United States or by any State on account of race, color, or previous condition of servitude.

Section 2—

The Congress shall have power to enforce this article by appropriate legislation.

Amendment XVI
(ratified 3 Feb 1913)

The Congress shall have power to lay and collect taxes on incomes, from whatever source derived, without apportionment among the several States, and without regard to any census or enumeration.

Amendment XVII
(ratified 13 Feb 1913)

The Senate of the United States shall be composed of two Senators from each State, elected by the people thereof for six years; and each Senator shall have one vote. The electors in each State shall have the qualifications requisite for electors of the most numerous branch of the State legislatures.

When vacancies happen in the representation of any State in the Senate, the executive authority of such State shall issue writs of election to fill such vacancies: Provided, That the legislature of any State may empower the executive thereof to make temporary appointments until the people fill the vacancies by election as the legislature may direct.

This amendment shall not be so construed as to affect the election or term of any Senator chosen before it becomes valid as part of the Constitution.

Amendment XVIII
(ratified 16 Jan 1919; repealed 5 Dec 1933
by Amendment XXI)

Section 1—

After one year from the ratification of this article the manufacture, sale, or transportation of intoxicating liquors within, the importation thereof into, or the exportation thereof from the United States and all territory subject to the jurisdiction thereof for beverage purposes is hereby prohibited.

Section 2—

The Congress and the several States shall have concurrent power to enforce this article by appropriate legislation.

Section 3—

This article shall be inoperative unless it shall have been ratified as an amendment to the Constitution by the legislatures of the several States as provided in the Constitution, within seven years from the date of the submission hereof to the States by the Congress.

Amendment XIX
(ratified 18 Aug 1920)

The right of citizens of the United States to vote shall not be denied or abridged by the United States or by any State on account of sex.

Congress shall have power to enforce this article by appropriate legislation.

Amendment XX
(ratified 23 Jan 1933)

Section 1—

The terms of the President and Vice President shall end at noon on the 20th day of January, and the terms of Senators and Representatives at noon on the 3d day of January, of the years in which such terms would have ended if this article had not been ratified; and the terms of their successors shall then begin.

Section 2—

The Congress shall assemble at least once in every year, and such meeting shall begin at noon on the 3d day of January, unless they shall by law appoint a different day.

Section 3—

If, at the time fixed for the beginning of the term of the President, the President elect shall have died, the Vice President elect shall become President. If a President shall not have been chosen before the time fixed for the beginning of his term, or if the President elect shall have failed to qualify, then the Vice President elect shall act as President until a President shall have qualified; and the Congress may by law provide for the case wherein neither a President elect nor a Vice President elect shall have qualified, declaring who shall then act as President, or the manner in which one who is to act shall be selected, and such person shall act accordingly until a President or Vice President shall have qualified.

Section 4—
The Congress may by law provide for the case of the death of any of the persons from whom the House of Representatives may choose a President whenever the right of choice shall have devolved upon them, and for the case of the death of any of the persons from whom the Senate may choose a Vice President whenever the right of choice shall have devolved upon them.

Section 5—
Sections 1 and 2 shall take effect on the 15th day of October following the ratification of this article.

Section 6—
This article shall be inoperative unless it shall have been ratified as an amendment to the Constitution by the legislatures of three-fourths of the several States within seven years from the date of its submission.

Amendment XXI
(ratified 5 Dec 1933)
Section 1—
The eighteenth article of amendment to the Constitution of the United States is hereby repealed.

Section 2—
The transportation or importation into any State, Territory, or possession of the United States for delivery or use therein of intoxicating liquors, in violation of the laws thereof, is hereby prohibited.

Section 3—
This article shall be inoperative unless it shall have been ratified as an amendment to the Constitution by conventions in the several States, as provided in the Constitution, within seven years from the date of the submission hereof to the States by the Congress.

Amendment XXII
(ratified 27 Feb 1951)
Section 1—
No person shall be elected to the office of the President more than twice, and no person who has held the office of President, or acted as President, for more than two years of a term to which some other person was elected President shall be elected to the office of the President more than once. But this Article shall not apply to any person holding the office of President when this Article was proposed by the Congress, and shall not prevent any person who may be holding the office of President, or acting as President, during the term within which this Article becomes operative from holding the office of President or acting as President during the remainder of such term.

Section 2—
This Article shall be inoperative unless it shall have been ratified as an amendment to the Constitution by the legislatures of three-fourths of the several States within seven years from the date of its submission to the States by the Congress.

Amendment XXIII
(ratified 29 Mar 1961)
Section 1—
The District constituting the seat of Government of the United States shall appoint in such manner as the Congress may direct:

A number of electors of President and Vice President equal to the whole number of Senators and Representatives in Congress to which the District would be entitled if it were a State, but in no event more than the least populous State; they shall be in addition to those appointed by the States, but they shall be considered, for the purposes of the election of President and Vice President, to be electors appointed by a State; and they shall meet in the District and perform such duties as provided by the twelfth article of amendment.

Section 2—
The Congress shall have power to enforce this article by appropriate legislation.

Amendment XXIV
(ratified 23 Jan 1964)
Section 1—
The right of citizens of the United States to vote in any primary or other election for President or Vice President, for electors for President or Vice President, or for Senator or Representative in Congress, shall not be denied or abridged by the United States or any State by reason of failure to pay any poll tax or other tax.

Section 2—
The Congress shall have power to enforce this article by appropriate legislation.

Amendment XXV
(ratified 23 Jan 1967)
Section 1—
In case of the removal of the President from office or of his death or resignation, the Vice President shall become President.

Section 2—
Whenever there is a vacancy in the office of the Vice President, the President shall nominate a Vice President who shall take office upon confirmation by a majority vote of both Houses of Congress.

Section 3—
Whenever the President transmits to the President pro tempore of the Senate and the Speaker of the House of Representatives his written declaration that he is unable to discharge the powers and duties of his office, and until he transmits to them a written declaration to the contrary, such powers and duties shall be discharged by the Vice President as Acting President.

Section 4—
Whenever the Vice president and a majority of either the principal officers of the executive departments or of such other body as Congress may by law provide, transmit to the President pro tempore of the Senate and the Speaker of the House of Representatives their written declaration that the President is unable to discharge the powers and duties of his office, the Vice President shall immediately assume the powers and duties of the office as Acting President.

Thereafter, when the President transmits to the President pro tempore of the Senate and the Speaker of the House of Representatives his written declaration that no inability exists, he shall resume the powers and duties of his office unless the Vice President and a majority of either the principal officers of the executive department or of such other body as Congress may by law provide, transmit within four days to the President pro tempore of the Senate and the Speaker of the House of Representatives their written declaration that the President is unable to discharge the powers and duties of his office. Thereupon Congress shall decide the issue, assembling within forty-eight hours for that purpose if not in session. If the Congress, within twenty-one days after receipt of the latter written declaration, or, if Congress is not in session, within twenty-one days after Congress is required to assemble, determines by two-thirds vote of both Houses that the President is unable to discharge the powers and duties of his office, the Vice President shall continue to discharge the same as Acting President; otherwise, the President shall resume the powers and duties of his office.

Amendment XXVI
(ratified 1 Jul 1971)

Section 1—
The right of citizens of the United States, who are eighteen years of age or older, to vote shall not be denied or abridged by the United States or by any State on account of age.

Section 2—
The Congress shall have power to enforce this article by appropriate legislation.

Amendment XXVII
(ratified 7 May 1992)
No law, varying the compensation for the services of the Senators and Representatives, shall take effect, until an election of representatives shall have intervened.

Confederate States and Secession Dates

In the months following Abraham Lincoln's election as president in 1860, seven states of the Deep South held conventions and approved secession, thus precipitating the Civil War. After the attack on Fort Sumter SC on 12 Apr 1861, Virginia, Arkansas, North Carolina, and Tennessee also seceded (Tennessee was the only state to hold a popular referendum without a convention on secession). The Confederacy operated as a separate government, with Jefferson Davis as president and Alexander H. Stephens as vice president. Its principal goals were the preservation of states' rights and the institution of slavery. Although it enjoyed a series of military victories in the first two years of fighting, the surrender at Appomattox VA by Gen. Robert E. Lee on 9 Apr 1865 signaled its dissolution.

STATE	DATE	STATE	DATE	STATE	DATE
South Carolina	20 Dec 1860	Georgia	19 Jan 1861	Arkansas	6 May 1861
Mississippi	9 Jan 1861	Louisiana	26 Jan 1861	North Carolina	20 May 1861
Florida	10 Jan 1861	Texas	1 Feb 1861	Tennessee	8 Jun 1861
Alabama	11 Jan 1861	Virginia	17 Apr 1861		

Emancipation Proclamation

The Emancipation Proclamation was issued by Pres. Abraham Lincoln and freed the slaves of the Confederate states in rebellion against the Union. After the Battle of Antietam (17 Sep 1862), Lincoln issued his proclamation calling on the revolted states to return to their allegiance before the next year, otherwise their slaves would be declared free men. No state returned, and the threatened declaration was issued on 1 Jan 1863.

By the President of the United States of America:

A Proclamation.

Whereas, on the twenty-second day of September, in the year of our Lord one thousand eight hundred and sixty-two, a proclamation was issued by the President of the United States, containing, among other things, the following, to wit:

"That on the first day of January, in the year of our Lord one thousand eight hundred and sixty-three, all persons held as slaves within any State or designated part of a State, the people whereof shall then be in rebellion against the United States, shall be then, thenceforward, and forever free; and the Executive Government of the United States, including the military and naval authority thereof, will recognize and maintain the freedom of such persons, and will do no act or acts to repress such persons, or any of them, in any efforts they may make for their actual freedom.

"That the Executive will, on the first day of January aforesaid, by proclamation, designate the States and parts of States, if any, in which the people thereof, respectively, shall then be in rebellion against the United States; and the fact that any State, or the people thereof, shall on that day be, in good faith, represented in the Congress of the United States by members chosen thereto at elections wherein a majority of the qualified voters of such State shall have participated, shall, in the absence of strong countervailing testimony, be deemed conclusive evidence that such State, and the people thereof, are not then in rebellion against the United States."

Now, therefore I, Abraham Lincoln, President of the United States, by virtue of the power in me vested as Commander-in-Chief, of the Army and Navy of the

United States in time of actual armed rebellion against the authority and government of the United States, and as a fit and necessary war measure for suppressing said rebellion, do, on this first day of January, in the year of our Lord one thousand eight hundred and sixty-three, and in accordance with my purpose so to do publicly proclaimed for the full period of one hundred days, from the day first above mentioned, order and designate as the States and parts of States wherein the people thereof respectively, are this day in rebellion against the United States, the following, to wit:

Arkansas, Texas, Louisiana, (except the Parishes of St. Bernard, Plaquemines, Jefferson, St. John, St. Charles, St. James Ascension, Assumption, Terrebonne, Lafourche, St. Mary, St. Martin, and Orleans, including the City of New Orleans) Mississippi, Alabama, Florida, Georgia, South Carolina, North Carolina, and Virginia, (except the forty-eight counties designated as West Virginia, and also the counties of Berkley, Accomac, Northampton, Elizabeth City, York, Princess Ann, and Norfolk, including the cities of Norfolk and Portsmouth[)], and which excepted parts, are for the present, left precisely as if this proclamation were not issued.

And by virtue of the power, and for the purpose aforesaid, I do order and declare that all persons held as slaves within said designated States, and parts of States, are, and henceforward shall be free; and that the Executive government of the United States, including the military and naval authorities thereof, will recognize and maintain the freedom of said persons.

And I hereby enjoin upon the people so declared to be free to abstain from all violence, unless in necessary self-defence; and I recommend to them that, in all cases when allowed, they labor faithfully for reasonable wages.

And I further declare and make known, that such persons of suitable condition, will be received into the armed service of the United States to garrison forts, positions, stations, and other places, and to man vessels of all sorts in said service.

And upon this act, sincerely believed to be an act of justice, warranted by the Constitution, upon military necessity, I invoke the considerate judgment of mankind, and the gracious favor of Almighty God.

In witness whereof, I have hereunto set my hand and caused the seal of the United States to be affixed.

Done at the City of Washington, this first day of January, in the year of our Lord one thousand eight hundred and sixty three, and of the Independence of the United States of America the eighty-seventh.

By the President: Abraham Lincoln.
William H. Seward, Secretary of State.

Gettysburg Address

On 19 Nov 1863, Pres. Abraham Lincoln delivered this speech at the consecration of the National Cemetery at Gettysburg PA, the site of one of the most decisive battles of the American Civil War.

Four score and seven years ago our fathers brought forth on this continent a new nation, conceived in Liberty, and dedicated to the proposition that all men are created equal. Now we are engaged in a great civil war, testing whether that nation or any nation so conceived and so dedicated, can long endure. We are met on a great battle-field of that war. We have come to dedicate a portion of that field, as a final resting place for those who here gave their lives that that nation might live. It is altogether fitting and proper that we should do this. But, in a larger sense, we can not dedicate—we can not consecrate—we can not hallow—this ground. The brave men, living and dead, who struggled here, have consecrated it, far above our poor power to add or detract. The world will little note, nor long remember what we say here, but it can never forget what they did here. It is for us the living, rather, to be dedicated here to the unfinished work which they who fought here have thus far so nobly advanced. It is rather for us to be here dedicated to the great task remaining before us—that from these honored dead we take increased devotion to that cause for which they gave the last full measure of devotion—that we here highly resolve that these dead shall not have died in vain—that this nation, under God, shall have a new birth of freedom—and that government of the people, by the people, for the people, shall not perish from the earth.

Government

The US Presidency at a Glance

	PRESIDENT	POLITICAL PARTY	TIME IN OFFICE	VICE PRESIDENT
1	George Washington	Federalist	1789–1797	John Adams
2	John Adams	Federalist	1797–1801	Thomas Jefferson
3	Thomas Jefferson	Jeffersonian Republican	1801–1809	Aaron Burr George Clinton
4	James Madison	Jeffersonian Republican	1809–1817	George Clinton Elbridge Gerry
5	James Monroe	Jeffersonian Republican	1817–1825	Daniel D. Tompkins
6	John Quincy Adams	National Republican	1825–1829	John C. Calhoun

The US Presidency at a Glance (continued)

	PRESIDENT	POLITICAL PARTY	TIME IN OFFICE	VICE PRESIDENT
7	Andrew Jackson	Democratic	1829–1837	John C. Calhoun Martin Van Buren
8	Martin Van Buren	Democratic	1837–1841	Richard M. Johnson
9	William Henry Harrison*	Whig	4 Mar–4 Apr 1841	John Tyler
10	John Tyler	Whig	1841–1845	none
11	James K. Polk	Democratic	1845–1849	George Mifflin Dallas
12	Zachary Taylor*	Whig	1849–1850	Millard Fillmore
13	Millard Fillmore	Whig	1850–1853	none
14	Franklin Pierce	Democratic	1853–1857	William Rufus de Vane King
15	James Buchanan	Democratic	1857–1861	John C. Breckinridge
16	Abraham Lincoln*†	Republican	1861–1865	Hannibal Hamlin Andrew Johnson
17	Andrew Johnson	Democratic (Union)	1865–1869	none
18	Ulysses S. Grant	Republican	1869–1877	Schuyler Colfax Henry Wilson
19	Rutherford B. Hayes	Republican	1877–1881	William A. Wheeler
20	James A. Garfield*†	Republican	4 Mar–19 Sep 1881	Chester A. Arthur
21	Chester A. Arthur	Republican	1881–1885	none
22	Grover Cleveland	Democratic	1885–1889	Thomas A. Hendricks
23	Benjamin Harrison	Republican	1889–1893	Levi Parons Morton
24	Grover Cleveland	Democratic	1893–1897	Adlai E. Stevenson
25	William McKinley*†	Republican	1897–1901	Garret A. Hobart Theodore Roosevelt
26	Theodore Roosevelt	Republican	1901–1909	Charles Warren Fairbanks
27	William Howard Taft	Republican	1909–1913	James Schoolcraft Sherman
28	Woodrow Wilson	Democratic	1913–1921	Thomas R. Marshall
29	Warren G. Harding*	Republican	1921–1923	Calvin Coolidge
30	Calvin Coolidge	Republican	1923–1929	Charles G. Dawes
31	Herbert Hoover	Republican	1929–1933	Charles Curtis
32	Franklin D. Roosevelt*	Democratic	1933–1945	John Nance Garner Henry A. Wallace Harry S. Truman
33	Harry S. Truman	Democratic	1945–1953	Alben W. Barkley
34	Dwight D. Eisenhower	Republican	1953–1961	Richard M. Nixon
35	John F. Kennedy*†	Democratic	1961–1963	Lyndon B. Johnson
36	Lyndon B. Johnson	Democratic	1963–1969	Hubert H. Humphrey
37	Richard M. Nixon**	Republican	1969–1974	Spiro T. Agnew Gerald R. Ford
38	Gerald R. Ford	Republican	1974–1977	Nelson A. Rockefeller
39	Jimmy Carter	Democratic	1977–1981	Walter F. Mondale
40	Ronald Reagan	Republican	1981–1989	George H.W. Bush
41	George H.W. Bush	Republican	1989–1993	Dan Quayle
42	Bill Clinton	Democratic	1993–2001	Albert Gore
43	George W. Bush	Republican	2001–2009	Richard B. Cheney
44	Barack Obama	Democratic	2009–	Joe Biden

*Died in office.   **Resigned from office.   †Assassinated.

US Presidential Biographies

George Washington (22 Feb [11 Feb, Old Style] 1732, Westmoreland county VA–14 Dec 1799, Mount Vernon, in Fairfax county VA), American Revolutionary commander-in-chief (1775–83) and first president of the US (1789–97). Born into a wealthy family, he inherited his brother's estate at Mount Vernon, including 18 slaves whose ranks grew to 49 by 1760. In the French and Indian War he was commissioned a colonel and sent to the Ohio Territory, and later he became commander of all Virginia forces, entrusted with defending the western frontier (1755–58). He resigned to manage his estate and in 1759 married Martha Dandridge Custis (1731–1802), a widow. He served in the House of Burgesses (1759–74), where he sup-ported the colonists' cause, and in the Continental Congress (1774–75). In 1775 he was elected to command the Continental Army. In the ensuing American Revolution, he proved a brilliant commander and stalwart leader despite several defeats. With the war effectively ended by the capture of Yorktown (1781), he resigned his commission and returned to Mount Vernon. He was a delegate to and presiding officer of the Constitutional Convention (1787) and helped secure ratification of the Constitution in Virginia. When the state electors met to select the first president (1789), Washington was the unanimous choice. He formed a cabinet to balance sectional and political differences but was committed to a strong central government.

Elected to a second term, he followed a middle course between the political factions that became the Federalist Party and Democratic Party. He proclaimed a policy of neutrality in the war between Britain and France (1793) and sent troops to suppress the Whiskey Rebellion (1794). He declined to serve a third term, setting a 144-year precedent, and retired in 1797. Known as the "father of his country," he is regarded as one of the greatest figures in US history.

John Adams (30 Oct [19 Oct, Old Style] 1735, Braintree [now in Quincy] MA—4 Jul 1826, Quincy MA), first vice president (1789–97) and second president (1797–1801) of the US. He practiced law in Boston and in 1764 married Abigail Smith. Active in the American independence movement, he was elected to the Massachusetts legislature and served as a delegate to the Continental Congress (1774–78), where he was appointed to a committee with Thomas Jefferson and others to draft the Declaration of Independence. He served as a diplomat in France, The Netherlands, and England (1778–88). In the first US presidential election, he received the second largest number of votes and became vice president under George Washington. Adams's term as president was marked by controversy over his signing the Alien and Sedition Acts in 1798 and by his alliance with the conservative Federalist Party. In 1800 he was defeated for reelection by Thomas Jefferson and retired to live a secluded life in Massachusetts. In 1812 he began an illuminating correspondence with Jefferson. Both men died on 4 Jul 1826, the Declaration's 50th anniversary. Pres. John Quincy Adams was his son.

Thomas Jefferson (13 Apr [2 Apr, Old Style] 1743, Shadwell VA—4 Jul 1826, Monticello VA), third president of the US (1801–9). He was a planter and lawyer from 1767, as well as a slaveholder. While a member of the House of Burgesses (1769–75), he initiated the Committee of Correspondence (1773) with Richard Henry Lee and Patrick Henry. In 1774 he wrote the influential *Summary View of the Rights of British America*, stating that the British Parliament had no authority to legislate for the colonies. A delegate to the Second Continental Congress, he was appointed to the committee to draft the Declaration of Independence and became its primary author. He was elected governor of Virginia (1779–81) but was unable to organize effective opposition when British forces invaded the colony (1780–81). Again a member of the Continental Congress (1783–85), he proposed territorial provisions later incorporated in the Northwest Ordinances. He became minister to France (1785–89), and George Washington made him secretary of state (1790–93). He soon became embroiled in conflict with Alexander Hamilton over their opposing interpretations of the Constitution. This led to the rise of factions and political parties, with Jefferson representing the Democratic-Republicans. He served as vice president (1797–1801) but opposed the Alien and Sedition Acts enacted under Pres. John Adams. In 1801 he became president after an electoral-vote tie with Aaron Burr was settled by the House of Representatives. Jefferson oversaw the Louisiana Purchase and authorized the Lewis and Clark Expedition. He sought to avoid involvement in the Napoleonic Wars by signing the Embargo Act. He retired to his plantation, Monticello, where he pursued his many interests in science, philosophy, and architecture, and in 1819 he

founded and designed the University of Virginia. In January 2000, the Thomas Jefferson Memorial Foundation accepted the conclusion, supported by DNA evidence, that Jefferson had fathered at least one, and perhaps as many as six, children with Sally Hemings, one of his house slaves.

James Madison (16 Mar [5 Mar, Old Style] 1751, Port Conway VA—28 Jun 1836, Montpelier VA), fourth president of the US (1809–17). At the Constitutional Convention (1787), his active participation and his careful notes on the debates earned him the title "father of the Constitution." To promote ratification, he collaborated with Alexander Hamilton and John Jay on the Federalist papers. In the House of Representatives (1789–97), he sponsored the Bill of Rights, was a leading Jeffersonian Republican, and split with Hamilton over funding state war debts. He was appointed secretary of state (1801–09) by Thomas Jefferson, with whom he developed US foreign policy. Elected president in 1808, he was occupied by the trade and shipping embargo problems caused by France and Britain that led to the War of 1812. He was reelected in 1812; his second term was marked principally by the war, during which he reinvigorated the Army. He retired to his Virginia estate, Montpelier, with his wife, Dolley (1768–1849), whose political acumen he had long prized. He served as rector of the University of Virginia until his death (1826–36).

James Monroe (28 Apr 1758, Westmoreland county VA—4 Jul 1831, New York NY), fifth president of the US (1817–25). He fought in the American Revolution and studied law under Thomas Jefferson. He became minister to France (1794–96), where he misled the French about US politics and was recalled. He served as governor of Virginia (1799–1802). President Jefferson sent him to France to help negotiate the Louisiana Purchase (1803), then named him minister to Britain (1803–07). He returned to Virginia and became governor (1811), but he resigned to become US secretary of state (1811–17) and secretary of war (1814–15). He served two terms as president, presiding in a period that became known as the Era of Good Feelings. He oversaw the First Seminole War (1817–18) and the acquisition of the Floridas (1819–21) and signed the Missouri Compromise (1820). With Secretary of State John Quincy Adams, he developed the principles of US foreign policy later called the Monroe Doctrine.

John Quincy Adams (11 Jul 1767, Braintree [now in Quincy] MA—23 Feb 1848, Washington DC), sixth president of the US (1825–29). He was the eldest son of Pres. John Adams and Abigail. He accompanied his father to Europe on diplomatic missions (1778–80) and was later appointed minister to The Netherlands (1794) and Prussia (1797). In 1801 he returned to Massachusetts and served in the Senate (1803–8). Resuming his diplomatic service, he became minister to Russia (1809–11) and Britain (1815–17). Appointed secretary of state (1817–24), he was instrumental in acquiring Florida from Spain and in drafting the Monroe Doctrine. He was one of three candidates in the 1824 presidential election, in which none received a majority of the electoral votes, though Andrew Jackson received a plurality. The decision went to the House of Representatives, where Adams received crucial support from Henry Clay and the electoral votes necessary to elect him president. He appointed Clay secretary of state, which further angered Jackson. Adams's presidency was unsuccessful; when he ran for reelection, Jackson defeated him. In 1830 he was elected to the House of Representatives, where he served until his death. He was outspoken in his opposition to slavery and in 1839 proposed a constitutional amendment forbidding slavery in any new state admitted to the Union. In 1841 he successfully defended the slaves in the Amistad mutiny case.

Andrew Jackson (15 Mar 1767, Waxhaws region, South Carolina–8 Jun 1845, the Hermitage, near Nashville TN), seventh president of the US (1829–37). He fought briefly in the American Revolution near his frontier home, where his family was killed. He studied law and in 1788 was appointed prosecuting attorney for western North Carolina. When the region became the state of Tennessee, he was elected to the House of Representatives (1796–97) and Senate (1797–98). He served on the state supreme court (1798–1804) and in 1802 was elected major general of the Tennessee militia. When the War of 1812 began, he offered the US the services of his 50,000-volunteer militia. He was sent to fight the Creek Indians in Mississippi Territory. After a lengthy battle (1813–14), he defeated them at the Battle of Horseshoe Bend. After capturing Pensacola FL from the British-allied Spanish, he marched overland to engage the British in Louisiana. A decisive victory at the Battle of New Orleans made him a national hero, dubbed "Old Hickory" by the press. After US acquisition of Florida, he was named governor of the territory (1821). In 1828 Jackson defeated Adams after a fierce campaign and became the first president elected from west of the Appalachian Mountains. He replaced many federal officeholders with his supporters, a process that became known as the spoils system. He pursued a policy of moving Native Americans westward with the Indian Removal Acts. During his tenure a strong Democratic Party developed that led to a vigorous two-party system.

Martin Van Buren (5 Dec 1782, Kinderhook NY–24 Jul 1862, Kinderhook NY), eighth president of the US (1837–41). He practiced law and served in the NY state senate (1812–20) and as state attorney general (1816–19). He was elected to the US Senate (1821–28), where he supported states' rights and opposed a strong central government. After John Quincy Adams became president, Van Buren joined with Andrew Jackson and others to form a group that later became the Democratic Party. He was elected governor of New York (1828) but resigned to become US secretary of state (1829–31). He was nominated for vice president at the first Democratic Party convention (1832) and served under Jackson (1833–37). As Jackson's chosen successor, he defeated William H. Harrison to win the 1836 election. His presidency was marked by an economic depression, the Maine-Canada border dispute, the Second Seminole War in Florida, and debate over the annexation of Texas. He was defeated in his bid for reelection and failed to win the Democratic nomination in 1844 because of his antislavery views. In 1848 he was nominated for president by the Free Soil Party but failed to win the election and retired.

William Henry Harrison (9 Feb 1773, Charles City county VA–4 Apr 1841, Washington DC), ninth president of the US (1841). Born into a political family, he enlisted in the army at 18 and served under Anthony Wayne at the Battle of Fallen Timbers. In 1798 he became secretary of the Northwest Territories and in 1800 governor of the new Indiana Territory. In response to pressure from white settlers, he negotiated treaties with the Native Americans that ceded millions of acres of land to the US. When the chief Tecumseh organized an uprising in 1811, Harrison led a US force to defeat the Indians at the Battle of Tippecanoe, a victory that largely established his reputation in the public mind. In the War of 1812 he was made a brigadier general and defeated the British and their Indian allies at the Battle of the Thames in Ontario. He served in the House of Representatives (1816–19) and Senate (1825–28). As the Whig party candidate in the 1836 presidential election, he lost narrowly. In 1840 he and his running mate, John Tyler, won election with a slogan emphasizing Harrison's frontier triumph: "Tippecanoe and Tyler too!" The 68-year-old Harrison delivered his inaugural speech without a hat or overcoat in a cold drizzle, contracted pneumonia, and died one month later, the first president to die in office.

John Tyler (29 Mar 1790, Charles City county VA–18 Jan 1862, Richmond VA), 10th president of the US (1841–45). He practiced law before serving as governor of Virginia (1825–27). In the House of Representatives (1817–21) and Senate (1827–36), he was a states-rights supporter. Though a slaveholder, he sought to prohibit the slave trade in the District of Columbia, provided Maryland and Virginia concurred. He resigned from the Senate rather than acquiesce to state instructions to change his vote on a censure of Pres. Andrew Jackson. After breaking with the Democratic Party, he was nominated by the Whig Party for vice president under William Henry Harrison. They won the 1840 election, carefully avoiding the issues and stressing party loyalty and the slogan "Tippecanoe and Tyler too!" Harrison died a month after taking office, and Tyler became the first to attain the presidency "by accident." He vetoed a national bank bill supported by the Whigs, and all but one member of the cabinet resigned, leaving him without party support. Nonetheless, he reorganized the navy, settled the second of the Seminole Wars in Florida, and oversaw the annexation of Texas. Committed to states' rights but opposed to secession, he organized the Washington Peace Conference (1861) to resolve sectional differences.

James Knox Polk (2 Nov 1795, Mecklenburg county NC–15 Jun 1849, Nashville TN), 11th president of the US (1845–49). He became a lawyer in Tennessee and a friend and supporter of Andrew Jackson, who helped Polk win election to the House of Representatives (1825–39). He left the House to become governor of Tennessee (1839–41). At the deadlocked 1844 Democratic convention Polk was nominated as the compromise candidate; he is considered the first dark-horse presidential candidate. A proponent of western expansion, he campaigned with the slogan "Fifty-four Forty or Fight," to bring a solution to the Oregon Question. Elected at 49, the youngest president to that time, he successfully concluded the Oregon border dispute with Britain (1846) and secured passage of the Walker Tariff Act (1846), which lowered import duties and helped foreign trade. He led the prosecution of the Mexican-American War, which resulted in large territorial gains but reopened the debate over the extension of slavery. His administration established the US Naval Academy and the Smithsonian Institution, oversaw revision of the treasury system, and proclaimed the validity of the Monroe Doctrine. He died three months after leaving office.

Zachary Taylor (24 Nov 1784, Montebello VA–9 Jul 1850, Washington DC), 12th president of the US (1849–50). Born in Virginia, he grew up on the Kentucky frontier. He fought in the War of 1812, the Black Hawk War (1832), and the Second Seminole War in Florida (1835–42), earning the nickname "Old Rough-and-Ready" for his indifference to hardship. Sent to Texas in anticipation of war with Mexico, he defeated the Mexican invaders at the Battles of Palo Alto and Resaca de la Palma (1846). After the Mexican-American War formally began, he captured Monterrey and granted the Mexican army an eight-week armistice. Displeased, Pres. James Polk moved Taylor's best troops to serve under Winfield Scott in the invasion of Veracruz. Taylor ignored orders to remain in Monterrey and marched south to defeat a large Mexican force at the Battle of Buena Vista (1847). He became a national hero and won the presidency as the Whig candidate (1848). His brief term was marked by a controversy over the new territories that produced the Compromise of 1850. He died, probably of cholera, after only 16 months in office.

Millard Fillmore (7 Jan 1800, Locke Township NY–8 Mar 1874, Buffalo NY), 13th president of the US (1850–53). Born into poverty, he became an indentured apprentice at 15. Initially identified with the Anti-Masonic Party (1828–34), he followed his political mentor, Thurlow Weed, to the Whigs and was soon a leader of the party's northern wing. He served in the House of Representatives (1833–35, 1837–43), where he became a follower of Henry Clay. In 1848 the Whigs nominated Fillmore as vice president, and he was elected with Zachary Taylor. He became president on Taylor's death in 1850. Though he abhorred slavery, he supported the Compromise of 1850 and insisted on federal enforcement of the Fugitive Slave Act. His stand, which alienated the North, led to his defeat by Winfield Scott at the Whigs' nominating convention in 1852 and effectively led to the death of the party. In 1853 he sent Matthew Perry with a US fleet to Japan, forcing its isolationist government to enter into trade and diplomatic relations. He was nominated for president by the third-party Know-Nothing Party in 1856, but he was defeated by Democrat James Buchanan.

Franklin Pierce (23 Nov 1804, Hillsboro NH–8 Oct 1869, Concord NH), 14th president of the US (1853–57). He served in the House of Representatives (1833–37) and Senate (1837–42) and briefly fought in the Mexican-American War. At the deadlocked Democratic convention of 1852, he was nominated as the compromise candidate; though largely unknown nationally, he unexpectedly trounced Winfield Scott in the general election. For the sake of harmony and business prosperity, he was inclined to oppose antislavery agitation so as to placate Southern opinion. He promoted US territorial expansion, resulting in the diplomatic controversy of the Ostend Manifesto, which urged the seizure of Cuba from Spain. He encouraged plans for a transcontinental railroad and approved the Gadsden Purchase. To promote northwestern migration and conciliate sectional demands, he approved the Kansas-Nebraska Act but was unable to settle the resultant problems. Defeated for renomination by James Buchanan in 1856, he retired from politics.

James Buchanan (23 Apr 1791, near Mercersburg PA–1 Jun 1868, near Lancaster PA), 15th president of the US (1857–61). He served in the House of Representatives (1821–31), as minister to Russia (1832–34), and in the Senate (1834–45). He was secretary of state in James Polk's cabinet (1845–49). As minister to Britain (1853–56), he helped draft the Ostend Manifesto. In 1856 he secured the Democratic nomination and election as president, defeating John C. Fremont. He equivocated on the question of Kansas's status as a slaveholding state, and the ensuing split within his party allowed Abraham Lincoln to win the election of 1860. He denounced the secession of South Carolina following the election and sent reinforcements to Fort Sumter, but he failed to respond further to the mounting crisis.

Abraham Lincoln (12 Feb 1809, near Hodgenville KY–15 Apr 1865, Washington DC), 16th president of the US (1861–65). Born in a Kentucky log cabin, he moved to Indiana in 1816 and to Illinois in 1830. He worked as a storekeeper, rail-splitter, postmaster, and surveyor and then enlisted as a volunteer in the Black Hawk War and became a captain. Though largely self-taught, he practiced law in Springfield IL and served in the state legislature (1834–40). He was elected as a Whig to the House of Representatives (1847–49). He later became one of the state's most successful lawyers, noted for his shrewdness and honesty (earning him the nickname "Honest Abe"). In 1856 he joined the Republican Party, which nominated him as its candidate in the 1858 Senate election. In a series of seven debates with Stephen A. Douglas (the Lincoln-Douglas Debates), he argued against the extension of slavery into the territories, though not against slavery itself. Although morally opposed to slavery, he was not an abolitionist. During the campaign, he attempted to rebut Douglas's charge that he was a dangerous radical by reassuring audiences that he did not favor political equality for blacks. Despite his loss in the election, the debates brought him national attention. He again ran against Douglas in the 1860 presidential election, which he won by a large margin. But the South opposed his position on slavery in the territories, and before his inauguration seven Southern states had seceded from the Union. The ensuing American Civil War completely consumed Lincoln's administration. He excelled as a wartime leader, combining statecraft and overall command of the armies with what some have called military genius. However, his abrogation of some civil liberties, especially the writ of habeas corpus, and the closing of several newspapers by his generals disturbed both Democrats and Republicans. To unite the North and influence foreign opinion, he issued the Emancipation Proclamation (1863); his Gettysburg Address (1863) further ennobled the war's purpose. His platform for reelection in 1864 included passage of the 13th Amendment outlawing slavery (ratified 1865), and he easily defeated George B. McClellan. At his second inaugural, with victory in sight, he spoke of moderation in reconstructing the South and building a harmonious Union. On 14 April, five days after the war ended, he was shot by John Wilkes Booth and soon after died.

Andrew Johnson (29 Dec 1808, Raleigh NC–31 Jul 1875, near Carter Station TN), 17th president of the US (1865–69). Born in North Carolina and reared in Tennessee, he organized a working-man's party and was elected to the state legislature (1835–43). He served in the House of Representatives (1843–53) and as governor of Tennessee (1853–57). Elected to the Senate (1857–62), he opposed antislavery agitation, but in 1860 he opposed Southern secession, even after Tennessee seceded in 1861, and during the Civil War he was the only Southern senator who refused to join the Confederacy. In 1862 he was appointed military governor of Tennessee, then under Union control. In 1864 he ran for vice president with Pres. Abraham Lincoln; he assumed the presidency after Lincoln's assassination. During Reconstruction he favored a moderate policy that readmitted former Confederate states to the Union with few provisions for reform or civil rights for freedmen. In 1867 the Radical Republicans in Congress passed civil rights legislation and established the Freedmen's Bureau. His veto angered Congress, which passed the Tenure of Office Act requiring congressional approval for the removal of any civil officers. In 1868, in defiance of the act, Johnson dismissed secretary of war Edwin M. Stanton, an ally of the Radicals, and the House responded by impeaching the president for the first time in US history. In the subsequent Senate trial, the charges proved weak and the necessary two-thirds vote needed for conviction failed by one vote. Johnson remained in office until 1869, but his effectiveness had ended. He returned to Tennessee, where he won reelection to the Senate shortly before he died.

Ulysses S. Grant (Hiram Ulysses Grant; 27 Apr 1822, Point Pleasant OH—23 Jul 1885, Mount McGregor NY), 18th president of the US (1869–77). He served in the Mexican-American War under Zachary Taylor. Allegations that he became a drunkard after the war, though never proved, would affect his reputation. When the Civil War began (1861), he was appointed brigadier general; his 1862 attack on Ft. Donelson in Tennessee produced the first major Union victory. He drove off a Confederate attack at Shiloh but was criticized for heavy Union losses. He devised the campaign to take the stronghold of Vicksburg MS in 1863, cutting the Confederacy in half from east to west. Following his victory at the Battle of Chattanooga in 1864, he was appointed commander of the Union army. While William T. Sherman made his famous march across Georgia, Grant attacked Robert E. Lee's forces in Virginia, bringing the war to an end in 1865. His successful Republican presidential campaign made him, at 46, the youngest man yet elected president. His two terms were marred by administrative inaction and political scandal involving members of his cabinet, including the Crédit Mobilier scandal and the Whiskey Ring operation. He supported amnesty for Confederate leaders and protection for black civil rights. His veto of a bill to increase the amount of legal tender (1874) diminished the currency crisis in the next 25 years. His memoirs were published by his friend Mark Twain.

Rutherford Birchard Hayes (4 Oct 1822, Delaware OH—17 Jan 1893, Fremont OH), 19th president of the US (1877–81). After fighting in the Union army, he served in the House of Representatives (1865–67). As governor of Ohio (1868–72, 1875–76), he advocated a sound currency backed by gold. In 1876 he won the Republican nomination for president. His opponent, Samuel Tilden, won a larger popular vote, but Hayes's managers contested the electoral-vote returns in four states, and a special

Electoral Commission awarded the election to Hayes. As part of a secret compromise reached with Southerners, he withdrew the remaining federal troops from the South, ending Reconstruction, and promised not to interfere with elections there, ensuring the return of white Democratic supremacy. At the request of state governors, he used federal troops against strikers in the railroad strikes of 1877. He declined to run for a second term.

James Abram Garfield (19 Nov 1831, near Orange [in Cuyahoga county] OH—19 Sep 1881, Elberon [now in Long Branch] NJ), 20th president of the US (1881). In the Civil War he led the 42nd Ohio Volunteers and fought at Shiloh and Chickamauga. He resigned as a major general to serve in the House of Representatives (1863–80). A Radical Republican during Reconstruction, he was the House Republican leader from 1876 to 1880, when he was elected to the Senate. At the 1880 Republican nominating convention, the delegates supporting Ulysses S. Grant and James Blaine became deadlocked. On the 36th ballot, Garfield was nominated as a compromise presidential candidate, with Chester Arthur as vice president, and he won by a narrow margin. His term was brief—less than 150 days. On 2 July he was shot at Washington's railroad station by Charles J. Guiteau, an Arthur supporter. He died on 19 September after 11 weeks of public debate over the ambiguous constitutional conditions for presidential succession (later clarified by the 20th and 25th Amendments).

Chester Alan Arthur (5 Oct 1829, North Fairfield VT—18 Nov 1886, New York NY), 21st president of the US (1881–85). Active in New York City Republican politics, he was appointed customs collector for the port of New York (1871–78), an office long known for its employment of the spoils system. He conducted the business of the office with integrity but continued to pad its payroll with loyalists of Sen. Roscoe Conkling. At the Republican National Convention in 1880, Arthur was the compromise choice for vice president on the ticket with James Garfield, and he became president upon Garfield's assassination. As president, Arthur displayed unexpected independence by vetoing measures that rewarded political patronage and signing the Pendleton Act, which created a civil-service system based on merit. He also recommended the appropriations for rebuilding the navy toward the strength it later achieved in the Spanish-American War (1898), but he failed to win his party's nomination for a second term.

(Stephen) Grover Cleveland (18 Mar 1837, Caldwell NJ—24 Jun 1908, Princeton NJ), 22nd and 24th president of the US (1885–89, 1893–97). As mayor of Buffalo NY (1881–82), he was known as a foe of corruption. As governor of New York (1883–85), he earned the hostility of Tammany Hall with his independence, but in 1884 he won the Democratic nomination for president and the election. The first Democratic president since 1856, he supported civil-service reform and opposed high protective tariffs, which became an issue in the 1888 election, when he was narrowly defeated by Benjamin Harrison. In 1892 he was reelected by a huge popular plurality. In 1893 he attributed the US's severe economic depression to the Sherman Silver Purchase Act of 1890 and strongly urged Congress to repeal the act. By 1896, however, supporters of the Free Silver Movement controlled the

Democratic Party, which nominated William Jennings Bryan instead of Cleveland for president.

Benjamin Harrison (20 Aug 1833, North Bend OH—13 Mar 1901, Indianapolis IN), 23rd president of the US (1889–93). The grandson of Pres. William H. Harrison, he served in the Union army in the Civil War, rising to brigadier general. He served a term in the Senate (1881–87) and, even though he lost reelection, was nominated for president by the Republicans. He went on to defeat the incumbent, Grover Cleveland, who lost despite winning more of the popular vote. As president, his domestic policy was marked by passage of the Sherman Antitrust Act, and his foreign policy expanded US influence abroad. His administration oversaw the conference that led to the establishment of the Pan-American Union, resisted pressure to abandon US interests in the Samoa Islands (1889), and negotiated a treaty with Britain in the Bering Sea Dispute (1891). He was defeated for reelection by Cleveland in 1892. In 1898–99 he was the leading counsel for Venezuela in its boundary dispute with Britain.

William McKinley (29 Jan 1843, Niles OH—14 Sep 1901, Buffalo NY), 25th president of the US (1897–1901). He served in the Civil War as an aide to Col. Rutherford B. Hayes, who later encouraged his political career. He was elected to the House of Representatives (1877–91), where he sponsored the McKinley Tariff of 1890, and he served as elected governor of Ohio (1892–96). In 1896 he won the Republican presidential nomination and the general election, defeating William Jennings Bryan. He was soon embroiled in events in Cuba and responses to the sinking of the USS *Maine*, which led to the Spanish-American War. At the war's end, he advocated US dependency status for the Philippines, Puerto Rico, and other former Spanish territories. He again defeated Bryan by a large majority in 1900. In Buffalo NY on 6 Sep 1901, he was fatally shot by an anarchist, Leon Czolgosz.

Theodore Roosevelt (27 Oct 1858, New York NY—6 Jan 1919, Oyster Bay NY), 26th president of the US (1901–09). He was elected to the New York legislature in 1882, where he became a Republican leader opposed to the Democratic political machine, and he went on to serve on the US Civil Service Commission (1889–95) and as head of New York City's board of police commissioners (1895–97). A supporter of William McKinley, he served as assistant secretary of the navy (1897–98). When the Spanish-American War was declared, he resigned to organize a cavalry unit, the Rough Riders. He returned to New York a hero and was elected governor in 1899. As the Republican vice-presidential nominee, he took office when McKinley was reelected, and he became president on McKinley's assassination in 1901. One of his early initiatives was to urge enforcement of the Sherman Antitrust Act against business monopolies. He won election in his own right in 1904, and at his urging, Congress regulated railroad rates and passed the Pure Food and Drug Act and Meat Inspection Act (both 1906) to provide new consumer protections. He set aside national forests, parks, and mineral, oil, and coal lands for conservation. For mediating an end to the Russo-Japanese War, he received the 1906 Nobel Peace Prize. He secured a treaty with Panama for construction of a trans-isthmus canal. Declining to seek reelection, he secured the nomination for William H. Taft. He tried to win the Republican presidential nomination

in 1912; when he was rejected, he organized the Bull Moose Party and ran on a policy of New Nationalism, but he failed to win the election.

William Howard Taft (15 Sep 1857, Cincinnati OH—8 Mar 1930, Washington DC), 27th president of the US (1909–13). He served as US solicitor general (1890–92) and as US appellate judge (1892–1900). He was appointed head of the Philippine Commission to set up a civilian government in the islands and was its first civilian governor (1901–04). He served as US secretary of war (1904–08) under Pres. Theodore Roosevelt, who supported Taft's nomination for president in 1908. He won the election but became allied with the conservative Republicans, causing a rift with party progressives. He was again the nominee in 1912, but the split with Roosevelt and the Bull Moose Party resulted in the electoral victory of Woodrow Wilson. Taft later was a supporter of the League of Nations. As chief justice of the Supreme Court (1921–30), he secured passage of the Judges Act of 1925, which gave the Court wider discretion in accepting cases.

(Thomas) Woodrow Wilson (28 Dec 1856, Staunton VA—3 Feb 1924, Washington DC), 28th president of the US (1913–21). He taught political science at Princeton University (1890–1902) and was its president (1902–10). With the support of progressives, he was elected governor of New Jersey. His reform measures attracted national attention, and he became the Democratic presidential nominee in 1912. His campaign emphasized the progressive measures of his New Freedom policy, and he defeated Theodore Roosevelt and William H. Taft to win the presidency. As president, he approved legislation that created the Federal Reserve System, established the Federal Trade Commission, and strengthened labor unions. In foreign affairs he promoted self-government for the Philippines and sought to contain the Mexican civil war. He maintained US neutrality in World War I, offering to mediate a settlement and initiate peace negotiations. Campaigning on the theme that he had "kept us out of war," he was narrowly reelected in 1916, defeating Charles Evans Hughes. Germany's continued submarine attacks on unarmed passenger ships caused Wilson to ask for a declaration of war in April 1917. In a continuing effort to negotiate a peace agreement, he led the US delegation to the Paris Peace Conference, where he attempted to stand on his original principles but was forced to compromise by the demands of various countries. The Treaty of Versailles faced opposition in the Senate from the Republican majority. In search of popular support for the treaty and its League of Nations, Wilson began a cross-country speaking tour, but he collapsed and returned to Washington DC, where a stroke left him partially paralyzed. He rejected any attempts to compromise his version of the League of Nations and as a result eventually urged his Senate followers to vote against ratification of the treaty, which was defeated in 1920. He was awarded the 1919 Nobel Peace Prize for his work on the League of Nations.

Warren Gamaliel Harding (2 Nov 1865, Caledonia [now Blooming Grove] OH—2 Aug 1923, San Francisco CA), 29th president of the US (1921–23). He served successively as Ohio state senator (1899–1902), lieutenant governor (1903–04), and US senator (1915–21), supporting conservative policies. At the deadlocked 1920 Republican presidential convention, he was chosen as the compromise candidate. Pledging a "return to normalcy" after World War I, he defeated James Cox with over 60% of the popular vote, the largest margin to that time. On his recommendation Congress established a budget system for the federal government, passed a high protective tariff, revised wartime taxes, and restricted immigration. His ill-advised cabinet and patronage appointments led to the Teapot Dome Scandal and characterized his administration as corrupt. While in Alaska he received word of the corruption about to be exposed and headed back. He arrived in San Francisco exhausted, reportedly suffering from food poisoning and other ills, and died there under unclear circumstances, to be succeeded by his vice president, Calvin Coolidge.

(John) Calvin Coolidge (4 Jul 1872, Plymouth VT—5 Jan 1933, Northampton MA), 30th president of the US (1923–29). He served as lieutenant governor of Massachusetts before being elected governor in 1918. He gained national attention by calling out the state guard during the Boston police strike in 1919. At the 1920 Republican convention, "Silent Cal" was nominated for vice president on Warren G. Harding's winning ticket. When Harding died in office in 1923, Coolidge became president. He restored confidence in an administration discredited by scandals and won the presidential election in 1924, defeating Robert La Follette. His presidency was marked by apparent prosperity. Congress maintained a high protective tariff and instituted tax reductions that favored capital. Coolidge declined to run for a second full term. His conservative policies of domestic and international inaction have come to symbolize the era between World War I and the Great Depression.

Herbert Hoover (10 Aug 1874, West Branch IA—20 Oct 1964, New York NY), 31st president of the US (1929–33). He headed Allied relief operations in England and Belgium prior to World War I, at which time he was appointed national food administrator (1917–19) and instituted programs that furnished food to famine-stricken areas of Europe. Appointed secretary of commerce (1921-27), he oversaw commissions to build Boulder (later Hoover) Dam and the St. Lawrence Seaway. In 1928, as the Republican presidential candidate, he soundly defeated Alfred E. Smith. His hopes for a "New Day" program were quickly overwhelmed by the Great Depression. As a believer in individual freedom, he vetoed bills to create a federal unemployment agency and to fund public-works projects, instead favoring private charity. In 1932 he finally allowed relief to farmers through the Reconstruction Finance Corp., but he was overwhelmingly defeated in 1932 by Franklin Roosevelt.

Franklin Delano Roosevelt (30 Jan 1882, Hyde Park NY—12 Apr 1945, Warm Springs GA), 32nd president of the US (1933-45). He was attracted to politics as an admirer of his cousin Pres. Theodore Roosevelt and became active in the Democratic Party. In 1905 he married distant cousin Eleanor Roosevelt, who would become a valued adviser in future years. He served as assistant secretary of the navy (1913-20). In 1920 he was nominated for vice president. The next year he was stricken with polio; though unable to walk, he remained active in politics. As governor of New York (1929-33), he set up the first state relief agency in the US. In 1932 he won the Democratic presidential nomination and

easily defeated Pres. Herbert Hoover. In his inaugural address to a nation of more than 13 million unemployed, he pronounced that "the only thing we have to fear is fear itself." Congress passed most of the changes he sought in his New Deal program in the first hundred days of his term. He was overwhelmingly reelected in 1936 over Alf Landon. By the late 1930s economic recovery had slowed, but Roosevelt was more concerned with the growing threat of war. In 1940 he was reelected to an unprecedented third term, defeating Wendell Willkie. He maintained US neutrality toward the war in Europe but approved the principle of lend-lease and in 1941 met with Winston Churchill to draft the Atlantic Charter. With US entry into World War II, he mobilized industry for military production and formed an alliance with Britain and the Soviet Union; he met with Churchill and Joseph Stalin to form war policy at Tehran (1943) and Yalta (1945). Despite declining health, he won reelection for a fourth term against Thomas Dewey (1944) but served only briefly before his death.

Harry S. Truman (8 May 1884, Lamar MO—26 Dec 1972, Kansas City MO), 33rd president of the US (1945–53). He served with distinction in World War I, and he later entered Democratic Party politics in Missouri. His reputation for honesty and good management gained him bipartisan support. In the Senate (1935–45), he led a committee that exposed fraud in defense production. In 1944 he was chosen to replace the incumbent Henry Wallace as vice-presidential nominee and was elected with Pres. Franklin Roosevelt. After only 82 days as vice president, he became president on Roosevelt's death (April 1945). He quickly made final arrangements for the San Francisco charter-writing meeting of the UN; helped arrange Germany's unconditional surrender on 8 May, which ended World War II in Europe; and in July attended the Potsdam Conference. The Pacific war ended officially on 2 September, after he ordered atomic bombs dropped on Hiroshima and Nagasaki; his justification was a report that 500,000 US troops would be lost in a conventional invasion of Japan. He announced the Truman Doctrine to aid Greece and Turkey (1947), established the Central Intelligence Agency, and pressed for passage of the Marshall Plan to aid European countries. In 1948 he defeated Thomas Dewey to gain reelection. He hewed to a foreign policy of containment to restrict the Soviet Union's sphere of influence and initiated the Berlin airlift and the NATO pact of 1949. In the Korean War he sent troops under Gen. Douglas MacArthur to head the United Nations forces. Though he was often criticized during his presidency, Truman's reputation grew steadily in later years.

Dwight David Eisenhower (14 Oct 1890, Denison TX—28 Mar 1969, Washington DC), 34th president of the US (1953-61). He graduated from West Point (1915) and then served in the Panama Canal Zone (1922-24) and in the Philippines under Douglas MacArthur (1935-39). In World War II, Gen. George Marshall chose him to command US forces in Europe (1942). After planning the invasions of North Africa, Sicily, and Italy, he was appointed supreme commander of Allied forces (1943). He planned the Normandy campaign (1944) and the conduct of the war in Europe until the German surrender (1945). He was promoted to five-star general (1944) and was named army chief of staff in 1945 and supreme commander of NATO in 1951. Both

Democrats and Republicans courted Eisenhower as a presidential candidate; in 1952, as the Republican candidate, he defeated Adlai Stevenson with the largest popular vote up to that time. He defeated Stevenson again in 1956 in an even larger landslide. His achievements included efforts to contain communism with the Eisenhower Doctrine. He sent federal troops to Little Rock AR to enforce integration of a city high school (1957). When the Soviet Union launched Sputnik 1 (1957), he was criticized for having failed to develop the US space program and responded by creating NASA (1958). In his last weeks in office the US broke diplomatic relations with Cuba.

John Fitzgerald Kennedy (29 May 1917, Brookline MA—22 Nov 1963, Dallas TX), 35th president of the US (1961–63). He joined the navy in World War II, where he earned medals for heroism. Elected to the House of Representatives (1947–53) and the Senate (1953–60), he supported social legislation and became increasingly committed to civil rights legislation. In 1960 he won the Democratic nomination for president; after a vigorous campaign, managed by his brother Robert F. Kennedy, he narrowly defeated Richard Nixon. He was the youngest person and the first Roman Catholic elected president. In his inaugural address he called on Americans to "ask not what your country can do for you, ask what you can do for your country." He proposed tax-reform and civil rights legislation but received little congressional support. He established the Peace Corps and the Alliance for Progress. His foreign policy began with the abortive Bay of Pigs invasion (1961), which emboldened the Soviet Union to move missiles to Cuba, sparking the Cuban missile crisis. In 1963 he successfully concluded the Nuclear Test-Ban Treaty. In November 1963 he was assassinated by a sniper, allegedly Lee Harvey Oswald, while riding in a motorcade in Dallas. The killing is considered the most notorious political murder of the 20th century. Kennedy's youth, energy, and charming family brought him world adulation and sparked the idealism of a generation, for whom the Kennedy White House became known as "Camelot."

Lyndon Baines Johnson (27 Aug 1908, Gillespie county TX—22 Jan 1973, San Antonio TX), 36th president of the US (1963–69). He won a seat in the House of Representatives (1937–49) as the New Deal was under conservative attack. His loyalty impressed Pres. Franklin Roosevelt, who made Johnson a protégé. He won election to the Senate in 1949 in a vicious campaign that saw fraud on both sides. As Democratic whip (1951–55) and majority leader (1955–61), he developed a talent for consensus building among dissident factions with methods both tactful and ruthless. He was largely responsible for passage of the civil rights bills of 1957 and 1960, the first in the 20th century. In 1960 he was elected vice president; he became president after the assassination of John F. Kennedy. In his first few months in office he won from Congress passage of a huge quantity of important civil rights, tax-reduction, antipoverty, and conservation legislation. He defeated Barry Goldwater in the 1964 election by the largest popular majority to that time and announced his Great Society program, which never came to fruition because of the escalation of US involvement in the Vietnam War, beginning with the Gulf of Tonkin Resolution. His approval ratings

diminished markedly and led to his decision not to seek reelection in 1968.

Richard Milhous Nixon (9 Jan 1913, Yorba Linda CA—22 Apr 1994, New York NY), 37th president of the US (1969–74). After serving in World War II, he was elected to the House of Representatives in 1947, employing harsh campaign tactics, and to the Senate in 1951, again following a bitter campaign. He won the vice presidency in 1952 on a ticket with Dwight D. Eisenhower; they were reelected easily in 1956. As presidential candidate in 1960, he lost narrowly to John F. Kennedy. He reentered politics by running for president in 1968, and he defeated Hubert H. Humphrey with his "Southern strategy" of seeking votes from Southern and Western conservatives in both parties. As president, he began to gradually withdraw US military forces in an effort to end the Vietnam War while ordering the secret bombing of North Vietnamese military centers in Laos and Cambodia, which drew widespread protest. Economic problems included the largest US budget to date, and in 1971 Nixon established unprecedented peacetime controls on wages and prices. He won reelection in 1972 with a landslide victory over George McGovern. Assisted by Henry A. Kissinger, he concluded the Vietnam War. He reopened communications with China and made a state visit there. On his visit to the Soviet Union, the first by a US president, he signed the bilateral Strategic Arms Limitation Talks (SALT) agreements. The Watergate Scandal overshadowed his second term; his complicity in efforts to cover up his involvement and the likelihood of impeachment led to his becoming, in August 1974, the first president to resign from office.

Gerald Rudolph Ford, Jr. (Leslie Lynch King, Jr.; 14 Jul 1913, Omaha NE—26 Dec 2006, Rancho Mirage CA), 38th president of the US (1974–77). He served in the House of Representatives (1948–73), becoming minority leader in 1965. After Spiro Agnew resigned as vice president in 1973, Richard Nixon nominated Ford to fill the vacant post. When the Watergate Scandal forced Nixon's departure, Ford became the first president who had not been elected to either the vice presidency or the presidency. A month later he pardoned Nixon; to counter widespread outrage, he voluntarily appeared before a House subcommittee to explain his action. His administration gradually lowered the high inflation rate it inherited. Ford's relations with the Democratic-controlled Congress were typified by his more than 50 vetoes, of which more than 40 were sustained. In the final days of the Vietnam War in 1975, he ordered an airlift of 237,000 anticommunist Vietnamese refugees, most of whom came to the US. Reaction against Watergate contributed to his defeat by James Earl Carter, Jr., in 1976.

James Earl Carter, Jr. (1 Oct 1924, Plains GA), 39th president of the US (1977–81). As governor (1971–75) he opened Georgia's government offices to blacks and women and introduced stricter budgeting procedures for state agencies. In 1976, though lacking a national political base or major backing, he won the Democratic nomination and the presidency, defeating the sitting president, Gerald Ford. As president, Carter helped negotiate a peace treaty between Egypt and Israel, signed a treaty with Panama to make the Panama Canal a neutral zone after 1999, and established full diplomatic relations with China. In 1979–80 the Iran hostage crisis became a major political liability. He responded forcefully to the USSR's invasion of

Afghanistan in 1979, embargoing the shipment of US grain to that country and leading a boycott of the 1980 Summer Olympics in Moscow. Hampered by high inflation and a recession engineered to tame it, he lost his bid for reelection to Ronald Reagan. He subsequently became involved in international diplomatic negotiations and helped oversee elections in countries with insecure democratic traditions. Carter was awarded the Nobel Peace Prize in 2002.

Ronald Wilson Reagan (6 Feb 1911, Tampico IL–5 Jun 2004, Bel Air CA), 40th president of the US (1981–89). In his career as a Hollywood movie actor, he had roles in 50 films and was twice president of the Screen Actors Guild (1947–52, 1959–60). Having gradually changed his political affiliation from liberal Democrat to conservative Republican, he served as governor of California (1967–75). In 1980 he defeated incumbent Pres. Jimmy Carter to become president. Shortly after taking office, he was wounded in an assassination attempt. Reagan adopted supply-side economics to promote rapid economic growth and reduce the federal deficit. Congress approved most of his proposals in 1981, which succeeded in lowering inflation but doubled the national debt by 1986. He began the largest peacetime military buildup in US history and in 1983 proposed construction of the Strategic Defense Initiative to place antimissile technology in space. His foreign policy decisions included signing the Intermediate-Range Nuclear Forces (INF) Treaty to restrict intermediate-range nuclear weapons and invading Grenada. In 1984 Reagan defeated Walter Mondale in a landslide for reelection. Details of his administration's involvement in the Iran-Contra Affair emerged in 1986 and significantly weakened his popularity and authority. Though his intellectual capacity for governing was often disparaged (and in 1994 he revealed that he had Alzheimer disease), his artful communication skills enabled him to pursue numerous conservative policies with conspicuous success.

George Herbert Walker Bush (12 Jun 1924, Milton MA), 41st president of the US (1989–93). He served in World War II, graduated from Yale University, and started an oil business in Texas. He served in the House of Representatives (1966–70) as a Republican. He then served as ambassador to the UN (1971–72), chief liaison to China (1974–76), and head of the CIA (1976–77). In 1980 he ran for president but lost the nomination to Ronald Reagan. Bush served as vice president with Reagan (1981–89), whom he succeeded as president, defeating Michael Dukakis. He made no dramatic departures from Reagan's policies. In 1989 he ordered a brief military invasion of Panama, which toppled that country's leader, Gen. Manuel Noriega. He helped impose a UN-approved embargo against Iraq in 1990 to force its withdrawal from Kuwait. When Iraq refused, he authorized a US-led air offensive that began the Persian Gulf War. Despite general approval of his foreign policy, an economic recession led to his defeat by Bill Clinton in 1992. His son George W. Bush was elected president in 2000 and reelected in 2004.

William Jefferson Clinton (William Jefferson Blythe III; 19 Aug 1946, Hope AR), 42nd president of the US (1993–2001). He served as state attorney general (1977–79) and served several terms as governor (1979–81, 1983–92), during which he reformed Arkansas's educational system and encouraged the growth of industry through favorable tax policies. He won the Democratic presidential nomination in 1992, after withstanding charges of personal impropriety, and defeated the incumbent, George H.W. Bush. As president he obtained approval of the North American Free Trade Agreement (NAFTA) in 1993. He and his wife, Hillary Rodham Clinton, strongly advocated their plan to overhaul the US health care system, but Congress rejected it. He committed US forces to a peacekeeping initiative in Bosnia and Herzegovina. In 1994 the Democrats lost control of Congress for the first time since 1954. Clinton defeated Robert Dole to win reelection in 1996. He faced renewed charges of personal impropriety, this time involving Monica Lewinsky, and as a result, in 1998 he became the second president in history to be impeached. Charged with perjury and obstruction of justice, he was acquitted at his Senate trial in 1999. His two terms saw sustained economic growth and successive budget surpluses, the first in three decades.

George Walker Bush (6 Jul 1946, New Haven CT), 43rd president of the US (2001–09). The eldest child of Pres. George H.W. Bush, he served as governor of Texas (1995–2000). Despite losing the national popular vote to Vice President Al Gore by more than 500,000 votes in 2000, he gained the electoral college and the presidency when a Supreme Court ruling ended a recount of ballots in Florida. His response to the terrorist attacks on 11 Sep 2001 gave shape to his administration. The invasion of Iraq by US-led forces in March 2003 was followed by a problematic occupation during which a burgeoning insurgency threatened Iraqi efforts to stabilize a democratically elected government. Bush won reelection in 2004. The loss of Republican control of Congress in elections in November 2006 limited his power to steer legislation to passage at the end of his time in the White House.

Barack Hussein Obama II (4 Aug 1961, Honolulu HI), 44th president of the US (from 2009). He graduated from Columbia University (1983) and magna cum laude from Harvard Law School (1991), where he was the first African American to serve as president of the *Harvard Law Review*. He served as a community organizer on Chicago's largely impoverished Far South Side and lectured in constitutional law at the University of Chicago. He was elected (1996) to the Illinois Senate as a member of the Democratic Party. In 2004 he was elected to the US Senate, the third African American to be elected to that body since the end of Reconstruction. He quickly became a major national political figure. In 2008 Obama won an upset victory in the Democratic primary over US senator and former first lady Hillary Clinton to become the Democratic presidential nominee. He easily defeated Republican candidate John McCain to become the first African American president, capturing nearly 53 percent of the popular vote and 365 electoral votes. Not only did he hold all the states that John Kerry had won in the 2004 election, but he also captured a number of states (e.g., Colorado, Florida, Nevada, Ohio, and Virginia) that the Republicans had carried in the previous two presidential elections. He is the author of two books, the memoir *Dreams from My Father* (1995) and *The Audacity of Hope* (2006), a mainstream polemic on his vision for the United States.

US Presidents' Spouses and Children
Maiden names of the presidents' wives appear in small capital letters.

DATE OF MARRIAGE	PRESIDENTS, SPOUSES, AND CHILDREN

George Washington
6 Jan 1759 **Martha DANDRIDGE Custis** (2 Jun 1731–22 May 1802)
no children

John Adams
25 Oct 1764 **Abigail SMITH** (22 Nov 1744–28 Oct 1818)
▸ Abigail Amelia Adams (1765–1813), ▸ John Quincy Adams (1767–1848), ▸ Susanna Adams (1768–70), ▸ Charles Adams (1770–1800), ▸ Thomas Boylston Adams (1772–1832)

Thomas Jefferson
1 Jan 1772 **Martha WAYLES Skelton** (30 Oct 1748–6 Sep 1782)
▸ Martha Washington Jefferson (1772–1836), ▸ Jane Randolph Jefferson (1774–75), ▸ infant son (1777), ▸ Mary Jefferson (1778–1804), ▸ Lucy Elizabeth Jefferson (1780–81), ▸ Lucy Elizabeth Jefferson (1782–84)

James Madison
15 Sep 1794 **Dolley PAYNE Todd** (20 May 1768–12 Jul 1849)
no children

James Monroe
16 Feb 1786 **Elizabeth KORTRIGHT** (30 Jun 1768–23 Sep 1830)
▸ Eliza Kortright Monroe (1786–1835), ▸ James Spence Monroe (1799–1800), ▸ Maria Hester Monroe (1803–50)

John Quincy Adams
26 Jul 1797 **Louisa Catherine JOHNSON** (12 Feb 1775–15 May 1852)
▸ George Washington Adams (1801–29), ▸ John Adams (1803–34), ▸ Charles Francis Adams (1807–86), ▸ Louisa Catherine Adams (1811–12)

Andrew Jackson
Aug 1791 **Rachel DONELSON Robards** (15? Jun 1767–22 Dec 1828)
no children

Martin Van Buren
21 Feb 1807 **Hannah HOES** (8 Mar 1783–5 Feb 1819)
▸ Abraham Van Buren (1807–73), ▸ John Van Buren (1810–66), ▸ Martin Van Buren (1812–55), ▸ Smith Thompson Van Buren (1817–76)

William Henry Harrison
25 Nov 1795 **Anna Tuthill SYMMES** (25 Jul 1775–25 Feb 1864)
▸ Elizabeth Bassett Harrison (1796–1846), ▸ John Cleves Symmes Harrison (1798–1830), ▸ Lucy Singleton Harrison (1800–26), ▸ William Henry Harrison (1802–38), ▸ John Scott Harrison (1804–78), ▸ Benjamin Harrison (1806–40), ▸ Mary Symmes Harrison (1809–42), ▸ Carter Bassett Harrison (1811–39), ▸ Anna Tuthill Harrison (1813–65), ▸ James Findlay Harrison (1814–17)

John Tyler
29 Mar 1813 **Letitia CHRISTIAN** (12 Nov 1790–10 Sep 1842)
▸ Mary Tyler (1815–48), ▸ Robert Tyler (1816–77), ▸ John Tyler (1819–96), ▸ Letitia Tyler (1821–1907), ▸ Elizabeth Tyler (1823–50), ▸ Anne Contesse Tyler (1825), ▸ Alice Tyler (1827–54), ▸ Tazewell Tyler (1830–74)
26 Jun 1844 **Julia GARDINER** (4 May 1820–10 Jul 1889)
▸ David Gardiner Tyler (1846–1927), ▸ John Alexander Tyler (1848–83), ▸ Julia Gardiner Tyler (1849?–71), ▸ Lachlan Tyler (1851–1902), ▸ Lyon Gardiner Tyler (1853–1935), ▸ Robert Fitzwalter Tyler (1856–1927), ▸ Pearl Tyler (1860–1947)

James K. Polk
1 Jan 1824 **Sarah CHILDRESS** (4 Sep 1803–14 Aug 1891)
no children

Zachary Taylor
21 Jun 1810 **Margaret Mackall SMITH** (21 Sep 1788–14 Aug 1852)
▸ Anne Margaret Mackall Taylor (1811–75), ▸ Sarah Knox Taylor (1814–35), ▸ Octavia Pannel Taylor (1816–20), ▸ Margaret Smith Taylor (1819–20), ▸ Mary Elizabeth Taylor (1824–1909), ▸ Richard Taylor (1826–79)

US Presidents' Spouses and Children (continued)

DATE OF MARRIAGE	PRESIDENTS, SPOUSES, AND CHILDREN

Millard Fillmore

5 Feb 1826   **Abigail POWERS** (13 Mar 1798–30 Mar 1853)
▸ Millard Powers Fillmore (1828–89), ▸ Mary Abigail Fillmore (1832–54)

10 Feb 1858   **Caroline CARMICHAEL McIntosh** (21 Oct 1813–11 Aug 1881)
no children

Franklin Pierce

10 Nov 1834   **Jane Means APPLETON** (12 Mar 1806–2 Dec 1863)
▸ Franklin Pierce (1836), ▸ Frank Robert Pierce (1839–43), ▸ Benjamin Pierce (1841–53)

James Buchanan
never married

Abraham Lincoln

4 Nov 1842   **Mary Ann TODD** (13 Dec 1818–16 Jul 1882)
▸ Robert Todd Lincoln (1843–1926), ▸ Edward Baker Lincoln (1846–50), ▸ William Wallace Lincoln (1850–62), ▸ Thomas Lincoln (1853–71)

Andrew Johnson

17 May 1827   **Eliza McCARDLE** (4 Oct 1810–15 Jan 1876)
▸ Martha Johnson (1828–1901), ▸ Charles Johnson (1830–63), ▸ Mary Johnson (1832–83), ▸ Robert Johnson (1834–69), ▸ Andrew Johnson (1852–79)

Ulysses S. Grant

22 Aug 1848   **Julia Boggs DENT** (26 Jan 1826–14 Dec 1902)
▸ Frederick Dent Grant (1850–1912), ▸ Ulysses Simpson Grant (1852–1929), ▸ Ellen Wrenshall Grant (1855–1922), ▸ Jesse Root Grant (1858–1934)

Rutherford B. Hayes

30 Dec 1852   **Lucy Ware WEBB** (28 Aug 1831–25 Jun 1889)
▸ Birchard Austin Hayes (1853–1926), ▸ James Webb Cook Hayes (1856–1934), ▸ Rutherford Platt Hayes (1858–1927), ▸ Joseph Thompson Hayes (1861–63), ▸ George Crook Hayes (1864–66), ▸ Frances Hayes (1867–1950), ▸ Scott Russell Hayes (1871–1923), ▸ Manning Force Hayes (1873–74)

James A. Garfield

11 Nov 1858   **Lucretia RUDOLPH** (19 Apr 1832–13 Mar 1918)
▸ Eliza Arabella Garfield (1860–63), ▸ Harry Augustus Garfield (1863–1942), ▸ James Rudolph Garfield (1865–1950), ▸ Mary Garfield (1867–1947), ▸ Irvin McDowell Garfield (1870–1951), ▸ Abram Garfield (1872–1958), ▸ Edward Garfield (1874–76)

Chester A. Arthur

25 Oct 1859   **Ellen Lewis HERNDON** (30 Aug 1837–12 Jan 1880)
▸ William Lewis Herndon Arthur (1860–63), ▸ Chester Alan Arthur (1864–1937), ▸ Ellen Herndon Arthur (1871–1915)

Grover Cleveland

2 Jun 1886   **Frances FOLSOM** (21 Jul 1864–29 Oct 1947)
▸ Ruth Cleveland (1891–1904), ▸ Esther Cleveland (1893–1980), ▸ Marion Cleveland (1895–1977), ▸ Richard Folsom Cleveland (1897–1974), ▸ Francis Grover Cleveland (1903–95)

Benjamin Harrison

20 Oct 1853   **Caroline Lavinia SCOTT** (1 Oct 1832–25 Oct 1892)
▸ Russell Benjamin Harrison (1854–1936), ▸ Mary Scott Harrison (1858–1930)

6 Apr 1896   **Mary Scott LORD Dimmick** (30 Apr 1858–5 Jan 1948)
▸ Elizabeth Harrison (1897–1955)

William McKinley

25 Jan 1871   **Ida SAXTON** (8 Jun 1847–26 May 1907)
▸ Katherine McKinley (1871–75), ▸ Ida McKinley (1873)

US Presidents' Spouses and Children (continued)

DATE OF MARRIAGE	PRESIDENTS, SPOUSES, AND CHILDREN

Theodore Roosevelt

27 Oct 1880 **Alice Hathaway** LEE (29 Jul 1861–14 Feb 1884)
  ▶ Alice Lee Roosevelt (1884–1980)

2 Dec 1886 **Edith Kermit** CAROW (6 Aug 1861–30 Sep 1948)
  ▶ Theodore Roosevelt (1887–1944), ▶ Kermit Roosevelt (1889–1943), ▶ Ethel Carow Roosevelt (1891–1977), ▶ Archibald Bulloch Roosevelt (1894–1979), ▶ Quentin Roosevelt (1897–1918)

William Howard Taft

19 Jun 1886 **Helen** HERRON (2 Jun 1861–22 May 1943)
  ▶ Robert Alphonso Taft (1889–1953), ▶ Helen Herron Taft (1891–1987), ▶ Charles Phelps Taft (1897–1983)

Woodrow Wilson

24 Jun 1885 **Ellen Louise** AXSON (15 May 1860–6 Aug 1914)
  ▶ Margaret Woodrow Wilson (1886–1944), ▶ Jessie Woodrow Wilson (1887–1933), ▶ Eleanor Randolph Wilson (1889–1967)

18 Dec 1915 **Edith** BOLLING **Galt** (15 Oct 1872–28 Dec 1961)
  no children

Warren G. Harding

8 Jul 1891 **Florence Mabel** KLING **DeWolfe** (15 Aug 1860–21 Nov 1924)
  no children

Calvin Coolidge

4 Oct 1905 **Grace Anna** GOODHUE (3 Jan 1879–8 Jul 1957)
  ▶ John Coolidge (1906–2000), ▶ Calvin Coolidge (1908–24)

Herbert Hoover

10 Feb 1899 **Lou** HENRY (29 Mar 1874–7 Jan 1944)
  ▶ Herbert Clark Hoover (1903–69), ▶ Allan Henry Hoover (1907–93)

Franklin D. Roosevelt

17 Mar 1905 **Anna Eleanor (Eleanor)** ROOSEVELT (11 Oct 1884–7 Nov 1962)
  ▶ Anna Eleanor Roosevelt (1906–75), ▶ James Roosevelt (1907–91), ▶ Franklin Delano Roosevelt (1909), ▶ Elliott Roosevelt (1910–90), ▶ Franklin Delano Roosevelt (1914–88), ▶ John Aspinwall Roosevelt (1916–81)

Harry S. Truman

28 Jun 1919 **Elizabeth Virginia (Bess)** WALLACE (13 Feb 1885–18 Oct 1982)
  ▶ Mary Margaret Truman (1924–2008)

Dwight D. Eisenhower

1 Jul 1916 **Mamie Geneva** DOUD (14 Nov 1896–1 Nov 1979)
  ▶ Doud Dwight Eisenhower (1917–21), ▶ John Sheldon Doud Eisenhower (1922–   )

John F. Kennedy

12 Sep 1953 **Jacqueline Lee** BOUVIER (28 Jul 1929–19 May 1994)
  ▶ Caroline Bouvier Kennedy (1957–   ), ▶ John Fitzgerald Kennedy (1960–99), ▶ Patrick Bouvier Kennedy (1963)

Lyndon B. Johnson

17 Nov 1934 **Claudia Alta (Lady Bird)** TAYLOR (22 Dec 1912–11 Jul 2007)
  ▶ Lynda Bird Johnson (1944–   ), ▶ Lucy Baines Johnson (1947–   )

Richard M. Nixon

21 Jun 1940 **Thelma Catherine (Pat)** RYAN (16 Mar 1912–22 Jun 1993)
  ▶ Patricia Nixon (1946–   ), ▶ Julie Nixon (1948–   )

Gerald R. Ford

15 Oct 1948 **Elizabeth Ann (Betty)** BLOOMER **Warren** (8 Apr 1918–   )
  ▶ Michael Gerald Ford (1950–   ), ▶ John Gardner Ford (1952–   ), ▶ Steven Meigs Ford (1956–   ), ▶ Susan Elizabeth Ford (1957–   )

Jimmy Carter

7 Jul 1946 **Eleanor Rosalynn (Rosalynn)** SMITH (18 Aug 1927–   )
  ▶ John William Carter (1947–   ), ▶ James Earl Carter (1950–   ), ▶ Donnel Jeffrey Carter (1952–   ), ▶ Amy Lynn Carter (1967–   )

US Presidents' Spouses and Children (continued)

DATE OF MARRIAGE	PRESIDENTS, SPOUSES, AND CHILDREN
	Ronald Reagan
24 Jan 1940	**Jane Wyman** (née Sarah Jane Mayfield [Fulks]) (4 Jan 1914–10 Sep 2007)
	▸ Maureen Elizabeth Reagan (1941–2001), ▸ Michael Edward Reagan (1945–), ▸ Christine Reagan (1947)
4 Mar 1952	**Nancy Davis** (née Anne Frances Robbins) (6 Jul 1921–)
	▸ Patricia Ann Reagan (1952–), ▸ Ronald Prescott Reagan (1958–)
	George H.W. Bush
6 Jan 1945	**Barbara Pierce** (8 Jun 1925–)
	▸ George Walker Bush (1946–), ▸ Pauline Robinson Bush (1949–53), ▸ John Ellis Bush (1953–), ▸ Neil Mallon Bush (1955–), ▸ Marvin Pierce Bush (1956–), ▸ Dorothy Walker Bush (1959–)
	Bill Clinton
11 Oct 1975	**Hillary Diane Rodham** (26 Oct 1947–)
	▸ Chelsea Victoria Clinton (1980–)
	George W. Bush
5 Nov 1977	**Laura Lane Welch** (4 Nov 1946–)
	▸ Barbara Pierce Bush (1981–), ▸ Jenna Bush Hager (1981–)
	Barack Obama
18 Oct 1992	**Michelle LaVaughn Robinson** (17 Jan 1964–)
	▸ Malia Ann Obama (1998–), ▸ Natasha Obama (2001–)

Did you know? Whitcomb L. Judson invented the zipper in the early 1900s; it was further refined by Swedish inventor Gideon Sundback in his 1917 patent, and it was first called a "zipper" when the B.F. Goodrich company began using the device in its rubber boots and galoshes. Most zippers have the letters "YKK" on them, which stands for the Yoshida Kogyo Kabushililaisha corporation of Japan, the world's leading zipper manufacturer.

US Presidential Cabinets

The cabinet is composed of the heads of executive departments chosen by the president with the consent of the Senate. Cabinet officials do not hold seats in Congress and are not regulated by the US Constitution, which makes no mention of such a body. The existence of the cabinet is a matter of custom dating back to George Washington, who consulted regularly with his department heads as a group. Original dates of service are given for officials appointed midterm and for newly created posts. Interim officials are not listed. Presidencies and new positions are indicated in bold.

George Washington

30 APR 1789–3 MARCH 1793 (TERM 1)

State	Thomas Jefferson
Treasury	Alexander Hamilton
War	Henry Knox
Attorney General	Edmund Randolph

4 MAR 1793–3 MAR 1797 (TERM 2)

State	Thomas Jefferson; Edmund Randolph (2 Jan 1794); Timothy Pickering (20 Aug 1795)
Treasury	Alexander Hamilton; Oliver Wolcott, Jr. (2 Feb 1795)
War	Henry Knox; Timothy Pickering (2 Jan 1795); James McHenry (6 Feb 1796)
Attorney General	Edmund Randolph; William Bradford (29 Jan 1794); Charles Lee (10 Dec 1795)

John Adams

4 MAR 1797–3 MAR 1801

State	Timothy Pickering; John Marshall (6 Jun 1800)
Treasury	Oliver Wolcott, Jr.; Samuel Dexter (1 Jan 1801)
War	James McHenry; Samuel Dexter (12 Jun 1800)
Navy	Benjamin Stoddert (18 Jun 1798)
Attorney General	Charles Lee

US Presidential Cabinets (continued)

Thomas Jefferson

4 MAR 1801–3 MAR 1805 (TERM 1)

State	James Madison
Treasury	Samuel Dexter; Albert Gallatin (14 May 1801)
War	Henry Dearborn
Navy	Benjamin Stoddert; Robert Smith (27 Jul 1801)
Attorney General	Levi Lincoln

4 MAR 1805–3 MAR 1809 (TERM 2)

State	James Madison
Treasury	Albert Gallatin
War	Henry Dearborn
Navy	Robert Smith
Attorney General	John Breckenridge; Caesar Augustus Rodney (20 Jan 1807)

James Madison

4 MAR 1809–3 MAR 1813 (TERM 1)

State	Robert Smith
Treasury	Albert Gallatin
War	John Smith; William Eustis (8 Apr 1809); John Armstrong (5 Feb 1813)
Navy	Robert Smith; Paul Hamilton (15 May 1809); William Jones (19 Jan 1813)
Attorney General	Caesar Augustus Rodney; William Pinkney (6 Jan 1812)

4 MAR 1813–3 MAR 1817 (TERM 2)

State	James Monroe
Treasury	Albert Gallatin; George Washington Campbell (9 Feb 1814); Alexander James Dallas (14 Oct 1814); William Harris Crawford (22 Oct 1816)
War	John Armstrong; James Monroe (1 Oct 1814); William Harris Crawford (8 Aug 1815)
Navy	William Jones; Benjamin Williams Crowninshield (16 Jan 1815)
Attorney General	William Pinkney; Richard Rush (11 Feb 1814)

James Monroe

4 MAR 1817–3 MAR 1821 (TERM 1)

State	John Quincy Adams
Treasury	William Harris Crawford
War	John C. Calhoun
Navy	Benjamin Williams Crowninshield; Smith Thompson (1 Jan 1819)
Attorney General	Richard Rush; William Wirt (15 Nov 1817)

4 MAR 1821–3 MAR 1825 (TERM 2)

State	John Quincy Adams
Treasury	William Harris Crawford
War	John C. Calhoun
Navy	Smith Thompson; Samuel Lewis Southard (16 Sep 1823)
Attorney General	William Wirt

John Quincy Adams

4 MAR 1825–3 MAR 1829

State	Henry Clay
Treasury	Richard Rush
War	James Barbour; Peter Buell Porter (21 Jun 1828)
Navy	Samuel Lewis Southard
Attorney General	William Wirt

Andrew Jackson

4 MAR 1829–3 MAR 1833 (TERM 1)

State	Martin Van Buren; Edward Livingston (24 May 1831)
Treasury	Samuel Delucenna Ingham; Louis McLane (8 Aug 1831)
War	John Henry Eaton; Lewis Cass (8 Aug 1831)
Navy	John Branch; Levi Woodbury (23 May 1831)
Attorney General	John Macpherson Berrien; Roger Brooke Taney (20 Jul 1831)

US Presidential Cabinets (continued)

Andrew Jackson (continued)

4 MAR 1833–3 MAR 1837 (TERM 2)

State	Edward Livingston; Louis McLane (29 May 1833); John Forsyth (1 Jul 1834)
Treasury	Louis McLane; William John Duane (1 Jun 1833); Roger Brooke Taney (23 Sep 1833); Levi Woodbury (1 Jul 1834)
War	Lewis Cass
Navy	Levi Woodbury; Mahlon Dickerson (30 Jun 1834)
Attorney General	Roger Brooke Taney; Benjamin Franklin Butler (18 Nov 1833)

Martin Van Buren

4 MAR 1837–3 MAR 1841

State	John Forsyth
Treasury	Levi Woodbury
War	Joel Roberts Poinsett
Navy	Mahlon Dickerson; James Kirke Paulding (1 Jul 1838)
Attorney General	Benjamin Franklin Butler; Felix Grundy (1 Sep 1838); Henry Dilworth Gilpin (11 Jan 1840)

William Henry Harrison

4 MAR 1841–4 APR 1841

State	Daniel Webster
Treasury	Thomas Ewing
War	John Bell
Navy	George Edmund Badger
Attorney General	John Jordan Crittenden

John Tyler

6 APR 1841–3 MAR 1845

State	Daniel Webster; Abel Parker Upshur (24 Jul 1843); John C. Calhoun (1 Apr 1844)
Treasury	Thomas Ewing; Walter Forward (13 Sep 1841); John Canfield Spencer (8 Mar 1843); George Mortimer Bibb (4 Jul 1844)
War	John Bell; John Canfield Spencer (12 Oct 1841); James Madison Porter (8 Mar 1843); William Wilkins (20 Feb 1844)
Navy	George Edmund Badger; Abel Parker Upshur (11 Oct 1841); David Henshaw (24 Jul 1843); Thomas Walker Gilmer (19 Feb 1844); John Young Mason (26 Mar 1844)
Attorney General	John Jordan Crittenden; Hugh Swinton Legaré (20 Sep 1841); John Nelson (1 Jul 1843)

James K. Polk

4 MAR 1845–3 MAR 1849

State	James Buchanan
Treasury	Robert James Walker
War	William Learned Marcy
Navy	George Bancroft; John Young Mason (9 Sep 1846)
Attorney General	John Young Mason; Nathan Clifford (17 Oct 1846); Isaac Toucey (29 Jun 1848)

Zachary Taylor

4 MAR 1849–9 JUL 1850

State	John Middleton Clayton
Treasury	William Morris Meredith
War	George Washington Crawford
Navy	William Ballard Preston
Attorney General	Reverdy Johnson
Interior	Thomas Ewing (8 Mar 1849)

Millard Fillmore

10 JUL 1850–3 MAR 1853

State	Daniel Webster; Edward Everett (6 Nov 1852)
Treasury	Thomas Corwin
War	George Washington Crawford; Charles Magill Conrad (15 Aug 1850)
Navy	William Alexander Graham; John Pendleton Kennedy (26 Jul 1852)
Attorney General	Reverdy Johnson; John Jordan Crittenden (14 Aug 1850)
Interior	Thomas Ewing; Thomas McKean Thompson McKennan (15 Aug 1850); Alexander Hugh Holmes Stuart (16 Sep 1850)

US Presidential Cabinets (continued)

Franklin Pierce

4 MAR 1853–3 MAR 1857

State	William Learned Marcy
Treasury	James Guthrie
War	Jefferson Davis
Navy	James Cochran Dobbin
Attorney General	Caleb Cushing
Interior	Robert McClelland

James Buchanan

4 MAR 1857–3 MAR 1861

State	Lewis Cass; Jeremiah Sullivan Black (17 Dec 1860)
Treasury	Howell Cobb; Philip Francis Thomas (12 Dec 1860); John Adams Dix (15 Jan 1861)
War	John Buchanan Floyd
Navy	Isaac Toucey
Attorney General	Jeremiah Sullivan Black; Edwin McMasters Stanton (22 Dec 1860)
Interior	Jacob Thompson

Abraham Lincoln

4 MAR 1861–3 MAR 1865 (TERM 1)

State	William Henry Seward
Treasury	Salmon Portland Chase; William Pitt Fessenden (5 Jul 1864)
War	Simon Cameron; Edwin McMasters Stanton (20 Jun 1862)
Navy	Gideon Welles
Attorney General	Edward Bates; James Speed (5 Dec 1864)
Interior	Caleb Blood Smith; John Palmer Usher (8 Jan 1863)

4 MAR 1865–15 APR 1865 (TERM 2)

State	William Henry Seward
Treasury	Hugh McCulloch
War	Edwin McMasters Stanton
Navy	Gideon Welles
Attorney General	James Speed
Interior	John Palmer Usher

Andrew Johnson

15 APR 1865–3 MAR 1869

State	William Henry Seward
Treasury	Hugh McCulloch
War	Edwin McMasters Stanton; John McAllister Schofield (1 Jun 1868)
Navy	Gideon Welles
Attorney General	James Speed; Henry Stanbery (23 Jul 1866); William Maxwell Evarts (20 Jul 1868)
Interior	John Palmer Usher; James Harlan (15 May 1865); Orville Hickman Browning (1 Sep 1866)

Ulysses S. Grant

4 MAR 1869–3 MAR 1873 (TERM 1)

State	Elihu Benjamin Washburne; Hamilton Fish (17 Mar 1869)
Treasury	George Sewall Boutwell
War	John Aaron Rawlins; William Tecumseh Sherman (11 Sep 1869); William Worth Belknap (1 Nov 1869)
Navy	Adolph Edward Borie; George Maxwell Robeson (25 Jun 1869)
Attorney General	Ebenezer Rockwood Hoar; Amos Tappan Akerman (8 Jul 1870); George Henry Williams (10 Jan 1872)
Interior	Jacob Dolson Cox; Columbus Delano (1 Nov 1870)

4 MAR 1873–3 MAR 1877 (TERM 2)

State	Hamilton Fish
Treasury	William Adams Richardson; Benjamin Helm Bristow (4 Jun 1874); Lot Myrick Morrill (7 Jul 1876)
War	William Worth Belknap; Alphonso Taft (11 Mar 1876); James Donald Cameron (1 Jun 1876)
Navy	George Maxwell Robeson
Attorney General	George Henry Williams; Edward Pierrepont (15 May 1875); Alphonso Taft (1 Jun 1876)
Interior	Columbus Delano; Zachariah Chandler (19 Oct 1875)

US Presidential Cabinets (continued)

Rutherford B. Hayes

4 MAR 1877–3 MAR 1881
State	William Maxwell Evarts
Treasury	John Sherman
War	George Washington McCrary; Alexander Ramsey (12 Dec 1879)
Navy	Richard Wigginton Thompson; Nathan Goff, Jr. (6 Jan 1881)
Attorney General	Charles Devens
Interior	Carl Schurz

James A. Garfield

4 MAR 1881–19 SEP 1881
State	James Gillespie Blaine
Treasury	William Windom
War	Robert Todd Lincoln
Attorney General	(Isaac) Wayne MacVeagh
Navy	William Henry Hunt
Interior	Samuel Jordan Kirkwood

Chester A. Arthur

20 SEP 1881–3 MAR 1885
State	James Gillespie Blaine; Frederick Theodore Frelinghuysen (19 Dec 1881)
Treasury	William Windom; Charles James Folger (14 Nov 1881); Walter Quintin Gresham (24 Sep 1884); Hugh McCulloch (31 Oct 1884)
War	Robert Todd Lincoln
Navy	William Henry Hunt; William Eaton Chandler (17 Apr 1882)
Attorney General	(Isaac) Wayne MacVeagh; Benjamin Harris Brewster (3 Jan 1882)
Interior	Samuel Jordan Kirkwood; Henry Moore Teller (17 Apr 1882)

Grover Cleveland

4 MAR 1885–3 MAR 1889
State	Thomas Francis Bayard
Treasury	Daniel Manning; Charles Stebbins Fairchild (1 Apr 1887)
War	William Crowninshield Endicott
Navy	William Collins Whitney
Attorney General	Augustus Hill Garland
Interior	Lucius Quintus Cincinnatus Lamar; William Freeman Vilas (16 Jan 1888)
Agriculture	Norman Jay Colman (13 Feb 1889)

Benjamin Harrison

4 MAR 1889–3 MAR 1893
State	James Gillespie Blaine; John Watson Foster (29 Jun 1892)
Treasury	William Windom; Charles Foster (24 Feb 1891)
War	Redfield Proctor; Stephen Benton Elkins (24 Dec 1891)
Navy	Benjamin Franklin Tracy
Attorney General	William Henry Harrison Miller
Interior	John Willock Noble
Agriculture	Jeremiah McLain Rusk

Grover Cleveland

4 MAR 1893–3 MAR 1897
State	Walter Quintin Gresham; Richard Olney (10 Jun 1895)
Treasury	John Griffin Carlisle
War	Daniel Scott Lamont
Navy	Hilary Abner Herbert
Attorney General	Richard Olney; Judson Harmon (11 Jun 1895)
Interior	Hoke Smith; David Rowland Francis (4 Sep 1896)
Agriculture	Julius Sterling Morton

William McKinley

4 MAR 1897–3 MAR 1901 (TERM 1)
State	John Sherman; William Rufus Day (28 Apr 1898); John Hay (30 Sep 1898)
Treasury	Lyman Judson
War	Russell Alexander Alger; Elihu Root (1 Aug 1899)
Navy	John Davis Long
Attorney General	Joseph McKenna; John William Griggs (1 Feb 1898)
Interior	Cornelius Newton Bliss; Ethan Allen Hitchcock (20 Feb 1899)
Agriculture	James Wilson

US Presidential Cabinets (continued)

William McKinley (continued)

4 MAR 1901–14 SEP 1901 (TERM 2)

State	John Hay
Treasury	Lyman Judson Gage
War	Elihu Root
Navy	John Davis Long
Attorney General	John William Griggs; Philander Chase Knox (10 Apr 1901)
Interior	Ethan Allen Hitchcock
Agriculture	James Wilson

Theodore Roosevelt

14 SEP 1901–3 MAR 1905 (TERM 1)

State	John Hay
Treasury	Lyman Judson Gage; Leslie Mortier Shaw (1 Feb 1902)
War	Elihu Root; William Howard Taft (1 Feb 1904)
Navy	John Davis Long; William Henry Moody (1 May 1902); Paul Morton (1 Jul 1904)
Attorney General	Philander Chase Knox; William Henry Moody (1 Jul 1904)
Interior	Ethan Allen Hitchcock
Agriculture	James Wilson
Commerce and Labor	George Bruce Cortelyou (16 Feb 1903); Victor Howard Metcalf (1 Jul 1904)

4 MAR 1905–3 MAR 1909 (TERM 2)

State	John Hay; Elihu Root (19 Jul 1905); Robert Bacon (27 Jan 1909)
Treasury	Leslie Mortier Shaw; George Bruce Cortelyou (4 Mar 1907)
War	William Howard Taft; Luke Edward Wright (1 Jul 1908)
Navy	Paul Morton; Charles Joseph Bonaparte (1 Jul 1905); Victor Howard Metcalf (17 Dec 1906); Truman Handy Newberry (1 Dec 1908)
Attorney General	William Henry Moody; Charles Joseph Bonaparte (17 Dec 1906)
Interior	Ethan Allen Hitchcock; James Rudolph Garfield (4 Mar 1907)
Agriculture	James Wilson
Commerce and Labor	Victor Howard Metcalf; Oscar Solomon Straus (17 Dec 1906)

William Howard Taft

4 MAR 1909–3 MAR 1913

State	Philander Chase Knox
Treasury	Franklin MacVeagh
War	Jacob McGavock Dickinson; Henry Lewis Stimson (22 May 1911)
Navy	George von Lengerke Meyer
Attorney General	George Woodward Wickersham
Interior	Richard Achilles Ballinger; Walter Lowrie Fisher (7 Mar 1911)
Agriculture	James Wilson
Commerce and Labor	Charles Nagel

Woodrow Wilson

4 MAR 1913–3 MAR 1917 (TERM 1)

State	William Jennings Bryan; Robert Lansing (23 Jun 1915)
Treasury	William Gibbs McAdoo
War	Lindley Miller Garrison; Newton Diehl Baker (9 Mar 1916)
Navy	Josephus Daniels
Attorney General	James Clark McReynolds; Thomas Watt Gregory (3 Sep 1914)
Interior	Franklin Knight Lane
Agriculture	David Franklin Houston
Commerce	William Cox Redfield
Labor	William Bauchop Wilson

4 MAR 1917–3 MAR 1921 (TERM 2)

State	Robert Lansing; Bainbridge Colby (23 Mar 1920)
Treasury	William Gibbs McAdoo; Carter Glass (16 Dec 1918); David Franklin Houston (2 Feb 1920)
War	Newton Diehl Baker
Navy	Josephus Daniels
Attorney General	Thomas Watt Gregory; Alexander Mitchell Palmer (5 Mar 1919)
Interior	Franklin Knight Lane; John Barton Payne (13 Mar 1920)
Agriculture	David Franklin Houston; Edwin Thomas Meredith (2 Feb 1920)
Commerce	William Cox Redfield; Joshua Willis Alexander (16 Dec 1919)
Labor	William Bauchop Wilson

US Presidential Cabinets (continued)

Warren G. Harding

4 MAR 1921–2 AUG 1923

State	Charles Evans Hughes
Treasury	Andrew William Mellon
War	John Wingate Weeks
Navy	Edwin Denby
Attorney General	Harry Micajah Daugherty
Interior	Albert Bacon Fall; Hubert Work (5 Mar 1923)
Agriculture	Henry Cantwell Wallace
Commerce	Herbert Hoover
Labor	James John Davis

Calvin Coolidge

3 AUG 1923–3 MAR 1925 (TERM 1)

State	Charles Evans Hughes
Treasury	Andrew William Mellon
War	John Wingate Weeks
Navy	Edwin Denby; Curtis Dwight Wilbur (18 Mar 1924)
Attorney General	Harry Micajah Daugherty; Harlan Fiske Stone (9 Apr 1924)
Interior	Hubert Work
Agriculture	Henry Cantwell Wallace; Howard Mason Gore (21 Nov 1924)
Commerce	Herbert Hoover
Labor	James John Davis

4 MAR 1925–3 MAR 1929 (TERM 2)

State	Frank Billings Kellogg
Treasury	Andrew William Mellon
War	John Wingate Weeks; Dwight Filley Davis (14 Oct 1925)
Navy	Curtis Dwight Wilbur
Attorney General	John Garibaldi Sargent
Interior	Hubert Work; Roy Owen West (21 Jan 1929)
Agriculture	William Marion Jardine
Commerce	Herbert Hoover; William Fairfield Whiting (11 Dec 1928)
Labor	James John Davis

Herbert Hoover

4 MAR 1929–3 MAR 1933

State	Henry Lewis Stimson
Treasury	Andrew William Mellon; Ogden Livingston Mills (13 Feb 1932)
War	James William Good; Patrick Jay Hurley (9 Dec 1929)
Navy	Charles Francis Adams
Attorney General	William De Witt Mitchell
Interior	Ray Lyman Wilbur
Agriculture	Arthur Mastick Hyde
Commerce	Robert Patterson Lamont; Roy Dikeman Chapin (14 Dec 1932)
Labor	James John Davis; William Nuckles Doak (9 Dec 1930)

Franklin D. Roosevelt

4 MAR 1933–20 JAN 1937 (TERM 1)

State	Cordell Hull
Treasury	William Hartman Woodin; Henry Morgenthau, Jr. (8 Jan 1934)
War	George Henry Dern
Navy	Claude Augustus Swanson
Attorney General	Homer Stille Cummings
Interior	Harold LeClaire Ickes
Agriculture	Henry Agard Wallace
Commerce	Daniel Calhoun Roper
Labor	Frances Perkins

20 JAN 1937–20 JAN 1941 (TERM 2)

State	Cordell Hull
Treasury	Henry Morgenthau, Jr.
War	Harry Hines Woodring; Henry Lewis Stimson (10 Jul 1940)
Attorney General	Homer Stille Cummings; Frank Murphy (17 Jan 1939); Robert Houghwout Jackson (18 Jan 1940)
Navy	Claude Augustus Swanson; Charles Edison (11 Jan 1940); Frank Knox (10 Jul 1940)
Interior	Harold LeClaire Ickes
Agriculture	Henry Agard Wallace; Claude Raymond Wickard (5 Sep 1940)

US Presidential Cabinets (continued)

Franklin D. Roosevelt (continued)

20 JAN 1937–20 JAN 1941 (TERM 2) (CONTINUED)

Commerce	Daniel Calhoun Roper; Harry Lloyd Hopkins (23 Jan 1939); Jesse Holman Jones (19 Sep 1940)
Labor	Frances Perkins

20 JAN 1941–20 JAN 1945 (TERM 3)

State	Cordell Hull; Edward Reilly Stettinius (1 Dec 1944)
Treasury	Henry Morgenthau, Jr.
War	Henry Lewis Stimson
Navy	Frank Knox; James Vincent Forrestal (18 May 1944)
Attorney General	Robert Houghwout Jackson; Francis Biddle (5 Sep 1941)
Interior	Harold LeClaire Ickes
Agriculture	Claude Raymond Wickard
Commerce	Jesse Holman Jones
Labor	Frances Perkins

20 JAN 1945–12 APR 1945 (TERM 4)

State	Edward Reilly Stettinius
Treasury	Henry Morgenthau, Jr.
War	Henry Lewis Stimson
Navy	James Vincent Forrestal
Attorney General	Francis Biddle
Interior	Harold LeClaire Ickes
Agriculture	Claude Raymond Wickard
Commerce	Jesse Holman Jones; Henry Agard Wallace (2 Mar 1945)
Labor	Frances Perkins

Harry S. Truman

12 APR 1945–20 JAN 1949 (TERM 1)

State	Edward Reilly Stettinius; James Francis Byrnes (3 Jul 1945); George Catlett Marshall (21 Jan 1947)
Treasury	Henry Morgenthau, Jr.; Frederick Moore (23 Jul 1945); John Wesley Snyder (25 Jun 1946)
War	Henry Lewis Stimson; Robert Porter Patterson (27 Sep 1945); Kenneth Claiborne Royall (25 Jul 1947–17 Sep 1947)
Defense	James Vincent Forrestal (17 Sep 1947)
Navy	James Vincent Forrestal (–17 Sep 1947)
Attorney General	Francis Biddle; Thomas Campbell Clark (1 Jul 1945)
Interior	Harold LeClaire Ickes; Julius Albert Krug (18 Mar 1946)
Agriculture	Claude Raymond Wickard; Clinton Presba Anderson (30 Jun 1945); Charles Franklin Brannan (2 Jun 1948)
Commerce	Henry Agard Wallace; William Averell Harriman (28 Jan 1947); Charles Sawyer (6 May 1948)
Labor	Frances Perkins; Lewis Baxter Schwellenbach (1 Jul 1945)

20 JAN 1949–20 JAN 1953 (TERM 2)

State	Dean Gooderham Acheson
Treasury	John Wesley Snyder
Defense	James Vincent Forrestal; Louis Arthur Johnson (28 Mar 1949); George Catlett Marshall (21 Sep 1950); Robert Abercrombie Lovett (17 Sep 1951)
Attorney General	Thomas Campbell Clark; James Howard McGrath (24 Aug 1949)
Interior	Julius Albert Krug; Oscar Littleton Chapman (19 Jan 1950)
Agriculture	Charles Franklin Brannan
Commerce	Charles Sawyer
Labor	Maurice Joseph Tobin

Dwight D. Eisenhower

20 JAN 1953–20 JAN 1957 (TERM 1)

State	John Foster Dulles
Treasury	George Magoffin Humphrey
Defense	Charles Erwin Wilson
Attorney General	Herbert Brownell
Interior	Douglas McKay; Frederick Andrew Seaton (8 Jun 1956)
Agriculture	Ezra Taft Benson
Commerce	Sinclair Weeks
Labor	Martin Patrick Durkin; James Paul Mitchell (9 Oct 1953)
Health, Education, and Welfare	Oveta Culp Hobby (11 Apr 1953); Marion Bayard Folson (1 Aug 1955)

US Presidential Cabinets (continued)

Dwight D. Eisenhower (continued)

20 JAN 1957–20 JAN 1961 (TERM 2)

State	John Foster Dulles; Christian Archibald Herter (22 Apr 1959)
Treasury	George Magoffin Humphrey; Robert Bernard Anderson (29 Jul 1957)
Defense	Charles Erwin Wilson; Neil Hosler McElroy (9 Oct 1957); Thomas Sovereign Gates, Jr. (2 Dec 1959)
Attorney General	Herbert Brownell, Jr.; William Pierce Rogers (27 Jan 1958)
Interior	Frederick Andrew Seaton
Agriculture	Ezra Taft Benson
Commerce	Sinclair Weeks; Frederick Henry Mueller (10 Aug 1959)
Labor	James Paul Mitchell
Health, Education, and Welfare	Marion Bayard Folsom; Arthur Sherwood Flemming (1 Aug 1958)

John F. Kennedy

20 JAN 1961–22 NOV 1963

State	David Dean Rusk
Treasury	C. Douglas Dillon
Defense	Robert S. McNamara
Attorney General	Robert F. Kennedy
Interior	Stewart L. Udall
Agriculture	Orville Lothrop Freeman
Commerce	Luther H. Hodges
Labor	Arthur J. Goldberg; W. Willard Wirtz (25 Sep 1962)
Health, Education, and Welfare	Abraham Ribicoff; Anthony J. Celebrezze (31 Jul 1962)

Lyndon B. Johnson

22 NOV 1963–20 JAN 1965 (TERM 1)

State	David Dean Rusk
Treasury	C. Douglas Dillon
Defense	Robert S. McNamara
Attorney General	Robert F. Kennedy
Interior	Stewart L. Udall
Agriculture	Orville Lothrop Freeman
Commerce	Luther H. Hodges
Labor	W. Willard Wirtz
Health, Education, and Welfare	Anthony J. Celebrezze

20 JAN 1965–20 JAN 1969 (TERM 2)

State	David Dean Rusk
Treasury	C. Douglas Dillon; Henry H. Fowler (1 Apr 1965); Joseph W. Barr (21 Dec 1968)
Defense	Robert S. McNamara; Clark M. Clifford (1 Mar 1968)
Attorney General	Nicholas Katzenbach; Ramsey Clark (10 Mar 1967)
Interior	Stewart L. Udall
Agriculture	Orville Lothrop Freeman
Commerce	John T. Connor; Alexander B. Trowbridge (14 Jun 1967); C.R. Smith (6 Mar 1968)
Labor	W. Willard Wirtz
Health, Education, and Welfare	Anthony J. Celebrezze; John W. Gardner (18 Aug 1965); Wilbur J. Cohen (9 May 1968)
Housing and Urban Development	Robert C. Weaver (18 Jan 1966); Robert C. Wood (7 Jan 1969)
Transportation	Alan Stephenson Boyd (16 Jan 1967)

Richard M. Nixon

20 JAN 1969–20 JAN 1973 (TERM 1)

State	William Pierce Rogers
Treasury	David M. Kennedy; John B. Connally (11 Feb 1971); George P. Shultz (12 Jun 1972)
Defense	Melvin R. Laird
Attorney General	John N. Mitchell; Richard G. Kleindienst (12 Jun 1972)
Interior	Walter Hickel; Rogers C.B. Morton (29 Jan 1971)
Agriculture	Clifford Morris Hardin; Earl Lauer Butz (2 Dec 1971)
Commerce	Maurice H. Stans; Peter G. Peterson (21 Feb 1972)
Labor	George P. Shultz; James D. Hodgson (2 Jul 1970)
Health, Education, and Welfare	Robert H. Finch; Elliot L. Richardson (24 Jun 1970)
Housing and Urban Development	George W. Romney
Transportation	John Anthony Volpe

US Presidential Cabinets (continued)

Richard M. Nixon (continued)

20 JAN 1973–9 AUG 1974 (TERM 2)

State	William Pierce Rogers; Henry Alfred Kissinger (22 Sep 1973)
Treasury	George P. Shultz; William E. Simon (8 May 1974)
Defense	Elliot L. Richardson; James R. Schlesinger (2 Jul 1973)
Attorney General	Richard G. Kleindienst; Elliot L. Richardson (25 May 1973); William B. Saxbe (4 Jan 1974)
Interior	Rogers C.B. Morton
Agriculture	Earl Lauer Butz
Commerce	Frederick B. Dent
Labor	Peter J. Brennan
Health, Education, and Welfare	Caspar W. Weinberger
Housing and Urban Development	James T. Lynn
Transportation	Claude Stout Brinegar

Gerald R. Ford

9 AUG 1974–20 JAN 1977

State	Henry Alfred Kissinger
Treasury	William E. Simon
Defense	James R. Schlesinger; Donald H. Rumsfeld (20 Nov 1975)
Attorney General	William B. Saxbe; Edward H. Levi (7 Feb 1975)
Interior	Rogers C.B. Morton; Stanley K. Hathaway (13 Jun 1975); Thomas S. Kleppe (17 Oct 1975)
Agriculture	Earl Lauer Butz; John Albert Knebel (4 Nov 1976)
Commerce	Frederick B. Dent; Rogers C.B. Morton (1 May 1975); Elliot L. Richardson (2 Feb 1976)
Labor	Peter J. Brennan; John T. Dunlop (18 Mar 1975); W.J. Usery, Jr. (10 Feb 1976)
Health, Education, and Welfare	Caspar W. Weinberger; David Mathews (8 Aug 1975)
Housing and Urban Development	James T. Lynn; Carla A. Hills (10 Mar 1975)
Transportation	Claude Stout Brinegar; William Thaddeus Coleman, Jr. (7 Mar 1975)

Jimmy Carter

20 JAN 1977–20 JAN 1981

State	Cyrus Roberts Vance; Edmund Sixtus Muskie (8 May 1980)
Treasury	W. Michael Blumenthal; G. William Miller (6 Aug 1979)
Defense	Harold Brown
Attorney General	Griffin B. Bell; Benjamin R. Civiletti (16 Aug 1979)
Interior	Cecil D. Andrus
Agriculture	Robert Selmer Bergland
Commerce	Juanita M. Kreps; Philip M. Klutznick (9 Jan 1980)
Labor	Ray Marshall
Health, Education, and Welfare	Joseph A. Califano, Jr.; Patricia Roberts Harris (3 Aug 1979–4 May 1980)
Health and Human Services	Patricia Roberts Harris (4 May 1980)
Housing and Urban Development	Patricia Roberts Harris; Moon Landrieu (24 Sep 1979)
Transportation	Brockman Adams; Neil Edward Goldschmidt (24 Sep 1979)
Energy	James R. Schlesinger (1 Oct 1977); Charles W. Duncan, Jr. (24 Aug 1979)
Education	Shirley M. Hufstedler (6 Dec 1979)

Ronald Reagan

20 JAN 1981–20 JAN 1985 (TERM 1)

State	Alexander Meigs Haig, Jr.; George P. Shultz (16 Jul 1982)
Treasury	Donald T. Regan
Defense	Caspar W. Weinberger
Attorney General	William French Smith
Interior	James G. Watt; William P. Clark (21 Nov 1983)
Agriculture	John Rusling Block
Commerce	Malcolm Baldrige
Labor	Raymond J. Donovan
Health and Human Services	Richard S. Schweiker; Margaret M. Heckler (9 Mar 1983)
Housing and Urban Development	Samuel R. Pierce, Jr.
Transportation	Andrew Lindsay Lewis, Jr.; Elizabeth Hanford Dole (7 Feb 1983)
Energy	James B. Edwards; Donald Paul Hodel (8 Dec 1982)
Education	Terrel H. Bell

20 JAN 1985–20 JAN 1989 (TERM 2)

State	George P. Shultz
Treasury	James A. Baker III; Nicholas F. Brady (18 Aug 1988)

US Presidential Cabinets (continued)

Ronald Reagan (continued)

20 JAN 1985–20 JAN 1989 (TERM 2) (CONTINUED)

Defense	Caspar W. Weinberger; Frank C. Carlucci (21 Nov 1987)
Attorney General	William French Smith; Edwin Meese III (25 Feb 1985); Richard Thornburgh (11 Aug 1988)
Interior	Donald Paul Hodel
Agriculture	John Rusling Block; Richard Edmund Lyng (7 Mar 1986)
Commerce	Malcolm Baldrige; C. William Verity (19 Oct 1987)
Labor	Raymond J. Donovan; William E. Brock (29 Apr 1985); Ann Dore McLaughlin (17 Dec 1987)
Health and Human Services	Margaret M. Heckler; Otis R. Bowen (13 Dec 1985)
Housing and Urban Development	Samuel R. Pierce, Jr.
Transportation	Elizabeth Hanford Dole; James Horace Burnley IV (3 Dec 1987)
Energy	John S. Herrington
Education	William J. Bennett; Lauro F. Cavazos, Jr. (20 Sep 1988)

George H.W. Bush

20 JAN 1989–20 JAN 1993

State	James A. Baker III; Lawrence Sidney Eagleburger (8 Dec 1992)
Treasury	Nicholas F. Brady
Defense	Richard B. Cheney
Attorney General	Richard Thornburgh; William Barr (20 Nov 1991)
Interior	Manuel Lujan, Jr.
Agriculture	Clayton Keith Yeutter; Edward Rell Madigan (7 Mar 1991)
Commerce	Robert A. Mosbacher; Barbara H. Franklin (27 Feb 1992)
Labor	Elizabeth Hanford Dole; Lynn Morley Martin (7 Feb 1991)
Health and Human Services	Louis W. Sullivan
Housing and Urban Development	Jack F. Kemp
Transportation	Samuel Knox Skinner; Andrew Hill Card, Jr. (22 Jan 1992)
Energy	James D. Watkins
Education	Lauro F. Cavazos, Jr.; Lamar Alexander (14 Mar 1991)
Veterans Affairs	Edward J. Derwinski (15 Mar 1989)

Bill Clinton

20 JAN 1993–20 JAN 1997 (TERM 1)

State	Warren Minor Christopher
Treasury	Lloyd M. Bentsen; Robert E. Rubin (10 Jan 1995)
Defense	Les Aspin; William J. Perry (3 Feb 1994)
Attorney General	Janet Reno
Interior	Bruce Babbitt
Agriculture	Alphonso Michael Espy; Daniel Robert Glickman (30 Mar 1995)
Commerce	Ronald H. Brown; Mickey Kantor (12 Apr 1996)
Labor	Robert B. Reich
Health and Human Services	Donna E. Shalala
Housing and Urban Development	Henry G. Cisneros
Transportation	Federico Fabian Peña
Energy	Hazel R. O'Leary
Education	Richard W. Riley
Veterans Affairs	Jesse Brown

20 JAN 1997–20 JAN 2001 (TERM 2)

State	Madeleine Korbel Albright
Treasury	Robert E. Rubin; Lawrence H. Summers (2 Jul 1999)
Defense	William S. Cohen
Attorney General	Janet Reno
Interior	Bruce Babbitt
Agriculture	Daniel Robert Glickman
Commerce	William M. Daley; Norman Y. Mineta (21 Jul 2000)
Labor	Alexis Herman
Health and Human Services	Donna E. Shalala
Housing and Urban Development	Andrew M. Cuomo
Transportation	Rodney Earl Slater
Energy	Federico Fabian Peña; Bill Richardson (18 Aug 1998)
Education	Richard W. Riley
Veterans Affairs	Togo D. West, Jr.

US Presidential Cabinets (continued)

George W. Bush

20 JAN 2001–20 JAN 2005 (TERM 1)

State	Colin L. Powell
Treasury	Paul H. O'Neill; John W. Snow (3 Feb 2003)
Defense	Donald H. Rumsfeld
Attorney General	John Ashcroft
Interior	Gale A. Norton
Agriculture	Ann M. Veneman
Commerce	Donald L. Evans
Labor	Elaine L. Chao
Health and Human Services	Tommy G. Thompson
Housing and Urban Development	Mel Martinez; Alphonso Jackson (1 Apr 2004)
Transportation	Norman Y. Mineta
Energy	Spencer Abraham
Education	Rod Paige
Veterans Affairs	Anthony J. Principi
Homeland Security	Tom Ridge (8 Oct 2001)

20 JAN 2005–20 JAN 2009 (TERM 2)

State	Condoleezza Rice
Treasury	John W. Snow; Henry M. Paulson, Jr. (10 Jul 2006)
Defense	Donald Rumsfeld; Robert M. Gates (18 Dec 2006)
Attorney General	Alberto R. Gonzales; Michael Mukasey (9 Nov 2007)
Interior	Gale A. Norton; Dirk Kempthorne (26 May 2006)
Agriculture	Mike Johanns; Ed Schafer (28 Jan 2008)
Commerce	Carlos M. Gutierrez
Labor	Elaine L. Chao
Health and Human Services	Michael O. Leavitt
Housing and Urban Development	Alphonso Jackson; Steve Preston (5 Jun 2008)
Transportation	Norman Y. Mineta; Mary E. Peters (30 Sep 2006)
Energy	Samuel W. Bodman
Education	Margaret Spellings
Veterans Affairs	R. James Nicholson; James B. Peake (20 Dec 2007)
Homeland Security	Michael Chertoff

Barack Obama

20 JAN 2009–

		WEB SITE
State	Hillary Clinton	\<www.state.gov\>
Treasury	Tim Geithner	\<www.ustreas.gov\>
Defense	Robert M. Gates	\<www.defenselink.mil\>
Attorney General	Eric Holder	\<www.usdoj.gov\>
Interior	Ken Salazar	\<www.doi.gov\>
Agriculture	Tom Vilsack	\<www.usda.gov\>
Commerce	Gary Locke	\<www.commerce.gov\>
Labor	Hilda Solis	\<www.dol.gov\>
Health and Human Services	Kathleen Sebelius	\<www.hhs.gov\>
Housing and Urban Development	Shaun Donovan	\<www.hud.gov\>
Transportation	Ray LaHood	\<www.dot.gov\>
Energy	Steven Chu	\<www.energy.gov\>
Education	Arne Duncan	\<www.ed.gov\>
Veterans Affairs	Eric Shinseki	\<www.va.gov\>
Homeland Security	Janet Napolitano	\<www.dhs.gov\>

Additionally, the White House lists the following as cabinet-rank members: Vice President Joe Biden, Chief of Staff Rahm Emanuel, Environmental Protection Agency Administrator Lisa P. Jackson, US Trade Representative Ron Kirk, Office of Management and Budget Director Peter Orszag, Council of Economic Advisers Chair Christina Romer, and United States Ambassador to the United Nations Susan Rice.

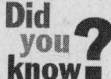

Did you know? Joseph Valachi, who turned informer in 1962, was the first member ever to describe the history, membership, and inner workings of the national crime syndicate popularly called the Mafia, which Valachi termed La Cosa Nostra ("Our Thing"). Attorney General Robert Kennedy called Valachi's testimony the "biggest single intelligence breakthrough yet in combating organized crime and racketeering in the United States."

United States Supreme Court

Justices of the Supreme Court of the United States

Listed under presidents who made appointments (bold). Chief justices' names appear in italics.

NAME	TERM OF SERVICE[1]
George Washington	
John Jay	1789–95
James Wilson	1789–98
John Rutledge	1790–91
William Cushing	1790–1810
John Blair	1790–96
James Iredell	1790–99
Thomas Johnson	1792–93
William Paterson	1793–1806
John Rutledge[2]	1795
Samuel Chase	1796–1811
Oliver Ellsworth	1796–1800
John Adams	
Bushrod Washington	1799–1829
Alfred Moore	1800–04
John Marshall	1801–35
Thomas Jefferson	
William Johnson	1804–34
Brockholst Livingston	1807–23
Thomas Todd	1807–26
James Madison	
Gabriel Duvall	1811–35
Joseph Story	1812–45
James Monroe	
Smith Thompson	1823–43
John Quincy Adams	
Robert Trimble	1826–28
Andrew Jackson	
John McLean	1830–61
Henry Baldwin	1830–44
James M. Wayne	1835–67
Roger Brooke Taney	1836–64
Philip P. Barbour	1836–41
Martin Van Buren	
John Catron	1837–65
John McKinley	1838–52
Peter V. Daniel	1842–60
John Tyler	
Samuel Nelson	1845–72
James K. Polk	
Levi Woodbury	1845–51
Robert C. Grier	1846–70
Millard Fillmore	
Benjamin R. Curtis	1851–57
Franklin Pierce	
John Archibald Campbell	1853–61
James Buchanan	
Nathan Clifford	1858–81
Abraham Lincoln	
Noah H. Swayne	1862–81
Samuel Freeman Miller	1862–90
David Davis	1862–77
Stephen Johnson Field	1863–97
Salmon P. Chase	1864–73

NAME	TERM OF SERVICE[1]
Ulysses S. Grant	
William Strong	1870–80
Joseph P. Bradley	1870–92
Ward Hunt	1873–82
Morrison Remick Waite	1874–88
Rutherford B. Hayes	
John Marshall Harlan	1877–1911
William B. Woods	1881–87
James A. Garfield	
Stanley Matthews	1881–89
Chester A. Arthur	
Horace Gray	1882–1902
Samuel Blatchford	1882–93
Grover Cleveland	
Lucius Q.C. Lamar	1888–93
Melville Weston Fuller	1888–1910
Benjamin Harrison	
David J. Brewer	1890–1910
Henry B. Brown	1891–1906
George Shiras, Jr.	1892–1903
Howell E. Jackson	1893–95
Grover Cleveland	
Edward Douglass White	1894–1910
Rufus Wheeler Peckham	1896–1909
William McKinley	
Joseph McKenna	1898–1925
Theodore Roosevelt	
Oliver Wendell Holmes	1902–32
William R. Day	1903–22
William H. Moody	1906–10
William Howard Taft	
Horace H. Lurton	1910–14
Charles Evans Hughes	1910–16
Willis Van Devanter	1911–37
Joseph R. Lamar	1911–16
Edward Douglass White	1910–21
Mahlon Pitney	1912–22
Woodrow Wilson	
James C. McReynolds	1914–41
Louis Brandeis	1916–39
John H. Clarke	1916–22
Warren G. Harding	
William Howard Taft	1921–30
George Sutherland	1922–38
Pierce Butler	1923–39
Edward T. Sanford	1923–30
Calvin Coolidge	
Harlan Fiske Stone	1925–41
Herbert Hoover	
Charles Evans Hughes	1930–41
Owen Roberts	1930–45
Benjamin N. Cardozo	1932–38

NAME	TERM OF SERVICE[1]
Franklin D. Roosevelt	
Hugo L. Black	1937–71
Stanley F. Reed	1938–57
Felix Frankfurter	1939–62
William O. Douglas	1939–75
Frank Murphy	1940–49
Harlan Fiske Stone	1941–46
James F. Byrnes	1941–42
Robert H. Jackson	1941–54
Wiley B. Rutledge	1943–49
Harry S. Truman	
Harold H. Burton	1945–58
Fred M. Vinson	1946–53
Tom C. Clark	1949–67
Sherman Minton	1949–56
Dwight D. Eisenhower	
Earl Warren	1953–69
John Marshall Harlan	1955–71
William J. Brennan, Jr.	1956–90
Charles E. Whittaker	1957–62
Potter Stewart	1958–81
John F. Kennedy	
Byron R. White	1962–93
Arthur J. Goldberg	1962–65
Lyndon B. Johnson	
Abe Fortas	1965–69
Thurgood Marshall	1967–91
Richard M. Nixon	
Warren E. Burger	1969–86
Harry A. Blackmun	1970–94
Lewis F. Powell, Jr.	1972–87
William H. Rehnquist	1972–86
Gerald Ford	
John Paul Stevens	1975–2010
Ronald Reagan	
Sandra Day O'Connor	1981–2006
William H. Rehnquist	1986–2005
Antonin Scalia	1986–
Anthony M. Kennedy	1988–
George H.W. Bush	
David H. Souter	1990–2009
Clarence Thomas	1991–
Bill Clinton	
Ruth Bader Ginsburg	1993–
Stephen G. Breyer	1994–
George W. Bush	
John G. Roberts	2005–
Samuel Anthony Alito, Jr.	2006–
Barack Obama	
Sonia Sotomayor	2009–
Elena Kagan	2010–

[1]The year the justice took the judicial oath is here used as the beginning date of service, for until that oath is taken the justice is not vested with the prerogatives of the office. Justices, however, receive their commissions ("letters patent") before taking their oaths—in some instances, in the preceding year.   [2]John Rutledge was acting chief justice; the US Senate refused to confirm him.

Milestones of US Supreme Court Jurisprudence

Information includes cases' short names, citation, year of release, and a short description of the Supreme Court's findings and importance for US law.

Marbury v. Madison, 5 U.S. 137 (1803): the first instance in which the high court declared an act of Congress (the Judiciary Act of 1789) to be unconstitutional, thus establishing judicial review.

Martin v. Hunter's Lessee, 14 U.S. 304 (1816): asserted the US Supreme Court's power of appellate review of state Supreme Court decisions.

Dred Scott v. Sandford, 60 U.S. 393 (1857): ruled that blacks, free or enslaved, were not citizens under the Constitution, and further determined that only states, and not Congress or territorial governments, had the power to prohibit slavery, thus overturning the Missouri Compromise of 1820 and legalizing slavery in all US territories.

Plessy v. Ferguson, 163 U.S. 537 (1896): permitted racial segregation in "separate but equal" public facilities.

Lochner v. New York, 198 U.S. 45 (1905): found that a state labor law limiting the number of hours in the work week violated due process because the "right of contract between the employer and employees" is protected under the Fourteenth Amendment.

Standard Oil Co. of New Jersey et al. v. United States, 221 U.S. 1 (1911): ruled that the activities of the Standard Oil Company of New Jersey, a holding company that through its subsidiaries controlled most of the US petroleum industry, constituted an undue restraint of trade and ordered the company's dissolution under the Sherman Antitrust Act.

Brown v. Board of Education of Topeka, 349 U.S. 294 (1954): ruled that racial segregation in public schools violated the Fourteenth Amendment, overturning the doctrine of "separate but equal" facilities reached in *Plessy v. Ferguson.*

Mapp v. Ohio, 367 U.S. 643 (1961): found that the Fourth Amendment prohibition of unreasonable search and seizure, and the inadmissibility of evidence obtained in violation of it, applied to state as well as to federal government.

Gideon v. Wainwright, 372 U.S. 335 (1963): declared that the Sixth Amendment right to counsel applies to defendants in state as well as federal courts.

New York Times Co. v. Sullivan, 376 U.S. 254 (1964): protected the press from the prospects of large damage awards in libel cases by requiring that "actual malice" be demonstrated; public officials who sue for damages must prove that a falsehood had been issued with knowledge that it was false or in reckless disregard of whether it was false or not.

Heart of Atlanta Motel v. United States, 379 U.S. 241; Katzenbach v. McClung, 379 U.S. 294 (1964): upheld Title II of the Civil Rights Act of 1964 (which prohibits segregation or discrimination in places of public accommodation involved in interstate commerce) in the cases of an Atlanta motel and a Birmingham AL restaurant, both of which discriminated against blacks. The court ruled that both engaged in transactions affecting interstate commerce, and thus were within the purview of congressional regulation, and that the Civil Rights Act itself was constitutional.

Griswold v. Connecticut, 381 U.S. 479 (1965): ruled that a state law prohibiting the use of contraceptives (including providing information, advice, or prescriptions for them) violated "the right of marital privacy" implied within the Bill of Rights.

Miranda v. Arizona, 384 U.S. 436 (1966): ruled that the prosecution may not use statements made by a person in police custody unless minimum procedural safeguards were followed and established guidelines to guarantee arrested persons' Fifth Amendment right not to be compelled to incriminate themselves. These guidelines included informing arrestees prior to questioning that they have the right to remain silent, that anything they say may be used against them as evidence, and that they have the right to the counsel of an attorney.

Loving v. Virginia, 388 U.S. 1 (1967): declared that antimiscegenation laws (prohibitions of interracial marriage) have no legitimate purpose and thus violate the Fourteenth Amendment.

New York Times Co. v. United States, 403 U.S. 713 (1971): in what was known as the "Pentagon Papers" case, the court vacated a US Justice Department injunction that restrained the *New York Times* and *Washington Post* from publishing excerpts of a top-secret report on the Vietnam War, ruling that such prior restraint of the press was subject to a "heavy burden of...justification," which the government failed to meet.

Roe v. Wade, 410 U.S. 113 (1973): held that overly restrictive state regulation of abortion is unconstitutional. In balancing the "compelling state interest[s]" in protecting the health of pregnant women and the potential life of fetuses, the court ruled that regulation of abortion could begin no sooner than about the end of the first trimester, with increasing regulation permissible in the second and third trimesters; the state's interest in protecting the fetus was found to increase with the fetus's "capability for meaningful life outside the mother's womb."

Gregg v. Georgia, 428 U.S. 153; Proffitt v. Florida, 428 U.S. 242; Jurek v. Texas, 428 U.S. 262 (1976): ruled that the death penalty, in and of itself, does not violate the Eighth Amendment if applied under certain guidelines in first-degree murder cases.

Cruzan by Cruzan v. Director, Missouri Department of Health, 497 U.S. 261 (1990): found that, in the absence of "clear and convincing evidence" of a person's desire to refuse medical treatment or not to live on life support, a state could require that such treatment continue.

Planned Parenthood of Southeastern Pennsylvania v. Casey, 505 U.S. 833 (1992): softened the ruling in *Roe v. Wade* by finding that some state regulation of abortion prior to fetal viability, including a 24-hour waiting period, mandatory counseling, and a parental-consent requirement for minors, is permissible as long as the regulations do not place an "undue burden" on the woman.

Romer v. Evans, 517 U.S. 620 (1996): invalidated a Colorado referendum passed by popular vote that prohibited conferral of protected status on the basis of sexual orientation; the court ruled that the referendum was overbroad and violated the Fourteenth Amendment of the US Constitution.

Oncale v. Sundowner Offshore Services, Inc., et al., 523 U.S. 75 (1998): found that Title VII's prohibition of workplace sexual discrimination applied equally in cases when the harasser and victim are of the same sex.

Boy Scouts of America v. Dale, 530 U.S. 640 (2000): ruled that the Boy Scouts, because it is a private organization, was within its rights when it dismissed a scoutmaster expressly because of his avowed homosexuality. The court reasoned that a state statute banning discrimination on the basis of sexual orientation in places of public accommodation was outweighed by the Scouts' First Amendment right to freedom of association.

Stenberg v. Carhart, 530 U.S. 914 (2000): ruled that a state law criminalizing the performance of dilation and extraction—or "partial-birth"—abortions violated the Constitution (following the same reasoning as in *Roe v. Wade*) because it allowed no consideration of the health of the woman in choosing the procedure.

Bush v. Gore, 531 U.S. 98 (2000): stopped the manual recounts, then under way in certain Florida counties at the demand of Al Gore, of disputed ballots from the November 2000 presidential election on the grounds that inconsistent vote-counting standards among the several counties involved amounted to a violation of the Fourteenth Amendment's equal protection clause. Because George W. Bush at the time led Al Gore in the number of officially recognized Florida votes, the decision meant that he would win the state and thus the general election, despite having lost the popular vote.

Atkins v. Virginia, 536 U.S. 304 (2002): ruled that the death penalty, when applied to mentally retarded individuals, constitutes a "cruel and unusual punishment" prohibited by the Eighth Amendment.

Lockyer v. Andrade, 538 U.S. 63; Ewing v. California, 538 U.S. 11 (2003): upheld a "three-strikes" law that imposes long prison sentences for a third offense, even nonviolent crimes.

State Farm Mutual Auto Insurance Co. v. Campbell, 538 U.S. 408 (2003): placed limits on "irrational and arbitrary" punitive damages and established new guidelines that generally bar consideration of a defendant's wealth or conduct outside the state's borders and lower the ratio of punitive to compensatory damages.

United States v. American Library Association, 539 U.S. 194 (2003): upheld the Children's Internet Protection Act, which conditions access to federal grants and subsidies upon the installation of antipornography filters on all Internet-connected computers.

Lawrence v. Texas, 539 U.S. 558 (2003): explicitly overruling *Bowers v. Hardwick*, 478 U.S. 186 (1986), the court declared that gay men and lesbians are "entitled to respect for their private lives" under the due process clause of the Fourteenth Amendment and rendered unconstitutional state statutes outlawing sex between adults of the same gender.

Blakely v. Washington, 542 U.S. 296 (2004): held that the Washington state system permitting judges to make independent findings that increase a convicted defendant's sentence beyond the ordinary range for the crime violated the Sixth Amendment guarantee of a right to trial by jury and to a higher standard of proof.

Cheney v. US District Court, 542 U.S. 367 (2004): sent the Sierra Club and Judicial Watch back to the lower court in a dispute over the level of executive privilege the vice president's energy-policy task force exercised in the face of discovery orders. The court held that "[s]pecial considerations control when the Executive's interests in maintaining its autonomy and safeguarding its communications' confidentiality are implicated."

Hamdi v. Rumsfeld, 542 U.S. 507; Rasul v. Bush, 542 U.S. 466 (2004): ruled that while Congress may empower the executive branch to detain even US citizens as enemy combatants, any enemy combatant in US custody may challenge detention as illegal in federal court with the assistance of counsel. The court declared that "a state of war is not a blank check for the president when it comes to the rights of the nation's citizens."

United States v. Booker and United States v. Fanfan, 543 U.S. 220 (2005): ruled that mandatory federal sentencing guidelines violated defendants' Sixth Amendment right to jury trials because they require judges to make decisions affecting prison time.

Roper v. Simmons, 543 U.S. 551 (2005): held that the execution of a felon who had committed a capital crime while a juvenile violates the Eighth Amendment prohibition of cruel and unusual punishment, noting that "the State cannot extinguish [the juvenile defendant's] life and his potential to attain a mature understanding of his own humanity."

Kelo v. City of New London, 545 U.S. 469 (2005): found that governmental entities may exercise the power of eminent domain over private property and cede the property to private developers to promote economic growth.

Gonzales v. Oregon, 546 U.S. 243 (2006): ruled that an Oregon law permitting physicians to provide lethal drugs to terminally ill patients did not violate the Controlled Substances Act.

Hamdan v. Rumsfeld, 548 U.S. 557 (2006): ruled that the government's special military commissions were not lawful courts. The commissions were to have tried some of the prisoners who had been captured in the "global war on terror."

Gonzales v. Carhart, 550 U.S. 124 (2007): held that a federal law banning "partial-birth" abortion was not unconstitutional.

Parents Involved in Community Schools v. Seattle School District No. 1, 551 U.S. 701 (2007): held that using a student's race in determining the availability of a spot at a desired school, even for the purpose of preventing resegregation, violated the 14th Amendment.

Hein v. Freedom from Religion Foundation, 551 U.S. 587 (2007): ruled that taxpayers had no standing to challenge the use of federal money to support the Office of Faith-Based and Community Initiatives, despite questions about the separation of church and state.

District of Columbia v. Heller, 554 U.S. 290 (2008): ruled that citizens have the right to bear arms without the need to be in service to a militia. This decision struck down a Washington DC handgun ban and threatened scores of other such bans nationwide.

Boumediene v. Bush, 553 U.S. 723 (2008): ruled that foreign prisoners held at Guantánamo Bay, Cuba, have the right to challenge their detention in US courts.

District Attorney's Office for the Third Judicial District v. Osborne, 557 U.S. ___ (2009): ruled that persons convicted of crimes do not have the constitutionally protected right to order advanced post-conviction DNA testing of evidence, even in the face of technological advances that may prove the innocence of the convicted person.

Ricci v. DeStefano, 557 U.S. ___ (2009): held that Title VII of the Civil Rights Act of 1964 prohibiting intentional acts of employment discrimination based on, among other factors, race, was violated by a ruling giving employment to minority candidates who had scored lower on employment tests than had white candidates.

McDonald v. *City of Chicago*, 561 U.S. ___ (2010): extended *District of Columbia* v. *Heller* in holding that the Second Amendment protection of the right to bear arms applies to state and local governments as well as to the federal government, calling into question the constitutionality of a Chicago handgun ban.

Citizens United v. *Federal Election Commission*, 558 U.S. ___ (2010): struck down a provision of the Federal Election Campaign Act (1971) that prohibited corporate and union expenditures in connection with political elections and a provision of the Bipartisan Campaign Reform Act (2002) that banned direct corporate or union funding of political ads.

United States Congress

Parties: Democratic (D); Republican (R); Independent (I).

Senate, 111th Congress

Party totals: Democrats: 57; Republicans: 41; Independents: 2.

According to Article I, Section 3 of the US Constitution, a US senator must be at least 30 years old, must reside in the state he or she represents at the time of the election, and must have been a citizen of the United States for at least nine years. Voters elect two senators from each state; terms are for six years and begin on 3 January. Each current senator's annual salary is US$174,000. The majority and minority leaders and the president pro tempore receive US$193,400 per year.

Senate leadership

president:	Joe Biden
president pro tempore:	Daniel K. Inouye
majority leader:	Harry Reid
minority leader:	Mitch McConnell
asst. majority leader (majority whip):	Dick Durbin
asst. minority leader (minority whip):	Jon Kyl

US Senate Web site: <www.senate.gov>.

STATE	NAME (PARTY)	SERVICE BEGAN	TERM ENDS
Alabama	Richard Shelby (R)	1987	2011
	Jeff Sessions (R)	1997	2015
Alaska	Lisa Murkowski (R)	2002	2011
	Mark Begich (D)	2009	2015
Arizona	John McCain (R)	1987	2011
	Jon Kyl (R)	1995	2013
Arkansas	Blanche Lincoln (D)	1999	2011
	Mark Pryor (D)	2003	2015
California	Dianne Feinstein (D)	1992[1]	2013
	Barbara Boxer (D)	1993	2011
Colorado	Mark Udall (D)	2009	2015
	Michael F. Bennet (D)	2009[2]	2011
Connecticut	Chris Dodd (D)	1981	2011
	Joe Lieberman (ID)	1989	2013
Delaware	Tom Carper (D)	2001	2013
	Ted Kaufman (D)	2009[3]	2011
Florida	Bill Nelson (D)	2001	2013
	George LeMieux (R)	2009[4]	2011
Georgia	Saxby Chambliss (R)	2003	2015
	Johnny Isakson (R)	2005	2011
Hawaii	Daniel K. Inouye (D)	1963	2011
	Daniel Kahikina Akaka (D)	1990[5]	2013
Idaho	Mike Crapo (R)	1999	2011
	James E. Risch (R)	2009	2015
Illinois	Dick Durbin (D)	1997	2015
	Roland W. Burris (D)	2009[6]	2011
Indiana	Richard G. Lugar (R)	1977	2013
	Evan Bayh (D)	1999	2011
Iowa	Chuck Grassley (R)	1981	2011
	Tom Harkin (D)	1985	2015
Kansas	Sam Brownback (R)	1996[7]	2011
	Pat Roberts (R)	1997	2015
Kentucky	Mitch McConnell (R)	1985	2015
	Jim Bunning (R)	1999	2011
Louisiana	Mary L. Landrieu (D)	1997	2015
	David Vitter (R)	2005	2011
Maine	Olympia J. Snowe (R)	1995	2013
	Susan Collins (R)	1997	2015
Maryland	Barbara Mikulski (D)	1987	2011
	Benjamin L. Cardin (D)	2007	2013

Senate, 111th Congress (continued)

STATE	NAME (PARTY)	SERVICE BEGAN	TERM ENDS
Massachusetts	John Kerry (D)	1985	2015
	Scott Brown (R)	2010[8]	2013
Michigan	Carl Levin (D)	1979	2015
	Debbie Stabenow (D)	2001	2013
Minnesota	Amy Klobuchar (D)	2007	2013
	Al Franken (D)	2009	2015
Mississippi	Thad Cochran (R)	1979	2015
	Roger Wicker (R)	2007[9]	2015
Missouri	Kit Bond (R)	1987	2011
	Claire McCaskill (D)	2007	2013
Montana	Max Baucus (D)	1979	2015
	Jon Tester (D)	2007	2013
Nebraska	Ben Nelson (D)	2001	2013
	Mike Johanns (R)	2009	2015
Nevada	Harry Reid (D)	1987	2011
	John Ensign (R)	2001	2013
New Hampshire	Judd Gregg (R)	1993	2011
	Jeanne Shaheen (D)	2009	2015
New Jersey	Frank R. Lautenberg (D)	2003	2015
	Robert Menendez (D)	2006[10]	2013
New Mexico	Jeff Bingaman (D)	1983	2013
	Tom Udall (D)	2009	2015
New York	Charles E. Schumer (D)	1999	2011
	Kirsten Gillibrand (D)	2009[11]	2011
North Carolina	Richard Burr (R)	2005	2011
	Kay Hagan (D)	2009	2015
North Dakota	Kent Conrad (D)	1987	2013
	Byron L. Dorgan (D)	1993	2011
Ohio	George V. Voinovich (R)	1999	2011
	Sherrod Brown (D)	2007	2013
Oklahoma	James M. Inhofe (R)	1994[12]	2015
	Tom Coburn (R)	2005	2011
Oregon	Ron Wyden (D)	1996[13]	2011
	Jeff Merkley (D)	2009	2015
Pennsylvania	Arlen Specter (D)	1981	2011
	Robert P. Casey (D)	2007	2013
Rhode Island	Jack Reed (D)	1997	2015
	Sheldon Whitehouse (D)	2007	2013
South Carolina	Lindsey Graham (R)	2003	2015
	Jim DeMint (R)	2005	2011
South Dakota	Tim Johnson (D)	1997	2015
	John Thune (R)	2005	2011
Tennessee	Lamar Alexander (R)	2003	2015
	Bob Corker (R)	2007	2013
Texas	Kay Bailey Hutchison (R)	1993[14]	2013
	John Cornyn (R)	2002	2015
Utah	Orrin G. Hatch (R)	1977	2013
	Bob Bennett (R)	1993	2011
Vermont	Patrick Leahy (D)	1975	2011
	Bernie Sanders (I)	2007	2013
Virginia	Jim Webb (D)	2007	2013
	Mark R. Warner (D)	2009	2015
Washington	Patty Murray (D)	1993	2011
	Maria Cantwell (D)	2001	2013
West Virginia	Jay Rockefeller (D)	1985	2015
	Carte Goodwin (D)	2010[15]	2013
Wisconsin	Herb Kohl (D)	1989	2013
	Russ Feingold (D)	1993	2011
Wyoming	Mike Enzi (R)	1997	2015
	John Barrasso (R)	2007[16]	2015

[1]Dianne Feinstein was elected in November 1992 to complete the term of Pete Wilson, who resigned in 1991 to become California's governor. [2]Michael F. Bennet was appointed in January 2009 to complete the term of Ken Salazar, who resigned to become secretary of the interior. [3]Ted Kaufman was appointed in January 2009 to replace Joe Biden, who resigned to become vice president. [4]George LeMieux was appointed in September 2009 to complete the term of Mel Martinez, who resigned. [5]Daniel Kahikina Akaka was appointed in April 1990 and took office in May 1990 to fill the vacancy caused by the death of Spark M. Matsunaga. [6]Roland W. Burris was appointed in December 2008 and took office in January 2009 to complete the term of Barack Obama, who resigned

Senate, 111th Congress (continued)

to become president. [7]Sam Brownback was elected in November 1996 to complete the term of Bob Dole, who resigned to campaign for the presidency. [8]Scott Brown was elected in January 2010 to fill the vacancy caused by the death of Edward M. Kennedy. [9]Roger Wicker was appointed in December 2007 to fill the vacancy caused by the resignation of Trent Lott. [10]Robert Menendez was appointed in January 2006 to fill the vacancy caused by the resignation of Jon S. Corzine. [11]Kirsten Gillibrand was appointed in January 2009 to replace Hillary Rodham Clinton, who resigned to become secretary of state. [12]James M. Inhofe was elected in November 1994 to complete the term of David Boren, who resigned to become president of the University of Oklahoma. [13]Ron Wyden was elected in January 1996 to complete the term of Bob Packwood, who resigned in 1995. [14]Kay Bailey Hutchison was elected in June 1993 to complete the term of Lloyd Bentsen, Jr., who resigned to become secretary of the treasury. [15]Carte Goodwin was appointed in July 2010 to fill the vacancy caused by the death of Robert C. Byrd. [16]John Barrasso was appointed in June 2007 to fill the vacancy caused by the death of Craig Thomas.

Senate Standing Committees

COMMITTEE	CHAIRMAN (PARTY–STATE)	RANKING MINORITY MEMBER (PARTY–STATE)	NUMBER OF MEMBERS MAJORITY[1]	MINORITY	NUMBER OF SUBCOMMITTEES
Agriculture, Nutrition, and Forestry	Blanche Lincoln (D-AR)	Saxby Chambliss (R-GA)	12	9	5
Appropriations	Daniel K. Inouye (D-HI)	Thad Cochran (R-MS)	17	12	12
Armed Services	Carl Levin (D-MI)	John McCain (R-AZ)	15	12	6
Banking, Housing, and Urban Affairs	Chris Dodd (D-CT)	Richard Shelby (R-AL)	13	10	5
Budget	Kent Conrad (D-ND)	Judd Gregg (R-NH)	12	10	none
Commerce, Science, and Transportation	Jay Rockefeller (D-WV)	Kay Bailey Hutchison (R-TX)	14	11	7
Energy and Natural Resources	Jeff Bingaman (D-NM)	Lisa Murkowski (R-AK)	13	10	4
Environment and Public Works	Barbara Boxer (D-CA)	James M. Imhofe (R-OK)	12	7	7
Finance	Max Baucus (D-MT)	Chuck Grassley (R-IA)	13	10	5
Foreign Relations	John Kerry (D-MA)	Richard G. Lugar (R-IN)	11	8	7
Health, Education, Labor, and Pensions	Tom Harkin (D-IA)	Mike Enzi (R-WY)	13	10	3
Homeland Security and Governmental Affairs	Joe Lieberman (ID-CT)	Susan Collins (R-ME)	10	7	6
Judiciary	Patrick Leahy (D-VT)	Jeff Sessions (R-AL)	12	7	7
Rules and Administration	Charles E. Schumer (D-NY)	Bob Bennett (R-UT)	10	8	none
Small Business and Entrepreneurship	Mary L. Landrieu (D-LA)	Olympia J. Snowe (R-ME)	11	8	none
Veterans' Affairs	Daniel Kahikina Akaka (D-HI)	Richard Burr (R-NC)	10	6	none

[1]Joe Lieberman and Bernie Sanders are Independents but caucus with the Democratic Party.

Senate Special, Select, and Other Committees

COMMITTEE	CHAIRMAN (PARTY–STATE)	RANKING MINORITY MEMBER (PARTY–STATE)	NUMBER OF MEMBERS MAJORITY	MINORITY
Special Committee on Aging	Herb Kohl (D-WI)	Bob Corker (R-TN)	13	8
Select Committee on Ethics	Barbara Boxer (D-CA)	Johnny Isakson (R-GA)	3	3
Committee on Indian Affairs	Byron L. Dorgan (D-ND)	John Barrasso (R-WY)	9	6
Select Committee on Intelligence	Dianne Feinstein (D-CA)	Kit Bond (R-MO)	10	9

House of Representatives, 111th Congress

Party totals: Democrats 255, Republicans 178; vacancies: 2.

According to Article I, Section 2 of the US Constitution, a US representative must be at least 25 years old, must reside in the state he or she represents at the time of the election, and must have been a citizen of the United States for at least seven years. Each state is entitled to at least one representative, with additional seats apportioned based on population. Each congressperson originally represented 30,000 people; the range in 2008 was from 469,262 (Louisiana 2nd district) to 991,439 (Arizona 2nd district) persons per representative. Terms are for two years and begin on 3 January (unless otherwise noted). The current representative's salary is US$174,000 per year. The majority and minority leaders receive US$193,400 per year; the speaker of the House receives US$223,500 per year.

American Samoa, the District of Columbia, Guam, the Northern Mariana Islands, and the Virgin Islands

House of Representatives, 111th Congress (continued)

elect delegates; Puerto Rico elects a resident commissioner. Their formal duties are the same, but the resident commissioner serves a four-year term. They may participate in debate and serve on committees but are not permitted to vote.

Numbers preceding the names refer to districts. Certain states gained (+) or lost (−) districts by reapportionment since the 107th Congress.

House leadership

speaker of the House:	Nancy Pelosi
majority leader:	Steny H. Hoyer
minority leader:	John A. Boehner
majority whip:	James E. Clyburn
minority whip:	Eric Cantor

US House Web site: <www.house.gov>.

STATE	REPRESENTATIVES	SERVICE BEGAN
Alabama	1. Jo Bonner (R)	Jan 2003
	2. Bobby Bright (D)	Jan 2009
	3. Mike Rogers (R)	Jan 2003
	4. Robert B. Aderholt (R)	Jan 1997
	5. Parker Griffith (R)	Jan 2009
	6. Spencer Bachus (R)	Jan 1993
	7. Artur Davis (D)	Jan 2003
Alaska	Don Young (R)	Mar 1973
Arizona (+2)	1. Ann Kirkpatrick (D)	Jan 2009
	2. Trent Franks (R)	Jan 2003
	3. John B. Shadegg (R)	Jan 1995
	4. Ed Pastor (D)	Sep 1991
	5. Harry E. Mitchell (D)	Jan 2007
	6. Jeff Flake (R)	Jan 2001
	7. Raúl M. Grijalva (D)	Jan 2003
	8. Gabrielle Giffords (D)	Jan 2007
Arkansas	1. Marion Berry (D)	Jan 1997
	2. Vic Snyder (D)	Jan 1997
	3. John Boozman (R)[1]	Nov 2001
	4. Mike Ross (D)	Jan 2001
California (+1)	1. Mike Thompson (D)	Jan 1999
	2. Wally Herger (R)	Jan 1987
	3. Daniel E. Lungren (R)	Jan 2005
	4. Tom McClintock (R)	Jan 2009
	5. Doris O. Matsui (D)[2]	Mar 2005
	6. Lynn C. Woolsey (D)	Jan 1993
	7. George Miller (D)	Jan 1975
	8. Nancy Pelosi (D)	Jun 1987
	9. Barbara Lee (D)	Apr 1998
	10. John Garamendi (D)[3]	Nov 2009
	11. Jerry McNerney (D)	Jan 2007
	12. Jackie Speier (D)[4]	Apr 2008
	13. Fortney ("Pete") Stark (D)	Jan 1973
	14. Anna G. Eshoo (D)	Jan 1993
	15. Michael M. Honda (D)	Jan 2001
	16. Zoe Lofgren (D)	Jan 1995
	17. Sam Farr (D)	Jun 1993
	18. Dennis A. Cardoza (D)	Jan 2003
	19. George Radanovich (R)	Jan 1995
	20. Jim Costa (D)	Jan 2005
	21. Devin Nunes (R)	Jan 2003
	22. Kevin McCarthy (R)	Jan 2007
	23. Lois Capps (D)	Mar 1998
	24. Elton Gallegly (R)	Jan 1987
	25. Howard P. ("Buck") McKeon (R)	Jan 1993
	26. David Dreier (R)	Jan 1981
	27. Brad Sherman (D)	Jan 1997
	28. Howard L. Berman (D)	Jan 1983
	29. Adam B. Schiff (D)	Jan 2001
	30. Henry A. Waxman (D)	Jan 1975
	31. Xavier Becerra (D)	Jan 1993
	32. Judy Chu (D)[5]	Jul 2009
	33. Diane E. Watson (D)[6]	Jun 2001
	34. Lucille Roybal-Allard (D)	Jan 1993

STATE	REPRESENTATIVES	SERVICE BEGAN
California (cont.)	35. Maxine Waters (D)	Jan 1991
	36. Jane Harman (D)[7]	Jan 1993
	37. Laura Richardson (D)[8]	Sep 2007
	38. Grace F. Napolitano (D)	Jan 1999
	39. Linda T. Sánchez (D)	Jan 2003
	40. Edward R. Royce (R)	Jan 1993
	41. Jerry Lewis (R)	Jan 1979
	42. Gary G. Miller (R)	Jan 1999
	43. Joe Baca (D)	Nov 1999
	44. Ken Calvert (R)	Jan 1993
	45. Mary Bono Mack (R)	Apr 1998
	46. Dana Rohrabacher (R)	Jan 1989
	47. Loretta Sanchez (D)	Jan 1997
	48. John Campbell (R)[9]	Dec 2005
	49. Darrell E. Issa (R)	Jan 2001
	50. Brian P. Bilbray (R)[10]	Jan 1995
	51. Bob Filner (D)	Jan 1993
	52. Duncan Hunter (R)	Jan 2009
	53. Susan A. Davis (D)	Jan 2001
Colorado (+1)	1. Diana DeGette (D)	Jan 1997
	2. Jared Polis (D)	Jan 2009
	3. John T. Salazar (D)	Jan 2005
	4. Betsy Markey (D)	Jan 2009
	5. Doug Lamborn (R)	Jan 2007
	6. Mike Coffman (R)	Jan 2009
	7. Ed Perlmutter (D)	Jan 2007
Connecticut (−1)	1. John B. Larson (D)	Jan 1999
	2. Joe Courtney (D)	Jan 2007
	3. Rosa L. DeLauro (D)	Jan 1991
	4. James A. Himes (D)	Jan 2009
	5. Christopher S. Murphy (D)	Jan 2007
Delaware	Michael N. Castle (R)	Jan 1993
Florida (+2)	1. Jeff Miller (R)[11]	Oct 2001
	2. Allen Boyd (D)	Jan 1997
	3. Corrine Brown (D)	Jan 1993
	4. Ander Crenshaw (R)	Jan 2001
	5. Ginny Brown-Waite (R)	Jan 2003
	6. Cliff Stearns (R)	Jan 1989
	7. John L. Mica (R)	Jan 1993
	8. Alan Grayson (D)	Jan 2009
	9. Gus M. Bilirakis (R)	Jan 2007
	10. C.W. Bill Young (R)	Jan 1971
	11. Kathy Castor (D)	Jan 2007
	12. Adam H. Putnam (R)	Jan 2001
	13. Vern Buchanan (R)	Jan 2007
	14. Connie Mack (R)	Jan 2005
	15. Bill Posey (R)	Jan 2009
	16. Thomas J. Rooney (R)	Jan 2009
	17. Kendrick B. Meek (D)	Jan 2003
	18. Ileana Ros-Lehtinen (R)	Aug 1989
	19. Theodore E. Deutch (D)[12]	Apr 2010
	20. Debbie Wasserman Schultz (D)	Jan 2005
	21. Lincoln Diaz-Balart (R)	Jan 1993
	22. Ron Klein (D)	Jan 2007

House of Representatives, 111th Congress (continued)

STATE	REPRESENTATIVES	SERVICE BEGAN
Florida (cont.)	23. Alcee L. Hastings (D)	Jan 1993
	24. Suzanne M. Kosmas (D)	Jan 2009
	25. Mario Diaz-Balart (R)	Jan 2003
Georgia (+2)	1. Jack Kingston (R)	Jan 1993
	2. Sanford D. Bishop, Jr. (D)	Jan 1993
	3. Lynn A. Westmoreland (R)	Jan 2005
	4. Henry C. ("Hank") Johnson, Jr. (D)	Jan 2007
	5. John Lewis (D)	Jan 1987
	6. Tom Price (R)	Feb 2005
	7. John Linder (R)	Jan 1993
	8. Jim Marshall (D)	Jan 2003
	9. Tom Graves (R)[13]	Jun 2010
	10. Paul C. Broun (R)[14]	Jul 2007
	11. Phil Gingrey (R)	Jan 2003
	12. John Barrow (D)	Jan 2005
	13. David Scott (D)	Jan 2003
Hawaii	1. Charles Djou (R)[15]	May 2010
	2. Mazie K. Hirono (D)	Jan 2007
Idaho	1. Walt Minnick (D)	Jan 2009
	2. Michael K. Simpson (R)	Jan 1999
Illinois (−1)	1. Bobby L. Rush (D)	Jan 1993
	2. Jesse L. Jackson, Jr. (D)	Dec 1995
	3. Daniel Lipinski (D)	Jan 2005
	4. Luis V. Gutierrez (D)	Jan 1993
	5. Mike Quigley (D)[16]	Apr 2009
	6. Peter J. Roskam (R)	Jan 2007
	7. Danny K. Davis (D)	Jan 1997
	8. Melissa L. Bean (D)	Jan 2005
	9. Janice D. Schakowsky (D)	Jan 1999
	10. Mark Steven Kirk (R)	Jan 2001
	11. Deborah L. Halvorson (D)	Jan 2009
	12. Jerry F. Costello (D)	Aug 1988
	13. Judy Biggert (R)	Jan 1999
	14. Bill Foster (D)[17]	Mar 2008
	15. Timothy V. Johnson (R)	Jan 2001
	16. Donald A. Manzullo (R)	Jan 1993
	17. Phil Hare (D)	Jan 2007
	18. Aaron Schock (R)	Jan 2009
	19. John Shimkus (R)	Jan 1997
Indiana (−1)	1. Peter J. Visclosky (D)	Jan 1985
	2. Joe Donnelly (D)	Jan 2007
	3. vacant[18]	
	4. Steve Buyer (R)	Jan 1993
	5. Dan Burton (R)	Jan 1983
	6. Mike Pence (R)	Jan 2001
	7. André Carson (D)[19]	Mar 2008
	8. Brad Ellsworth (D)	Jan 2007
	9. Baron P. Hill (D)[20]	Jan 1999
Iowa	1. Bruce L. Braley (D)	Jan 2007
	2. David Loebsack (D)	Jan 2007
	3. Leonard L. Boswell (D)	Jan 1997
	4. Tom Latham (R)	Jan 1995
	5. Steve King (R)	Jan 2003
Kansas	1. Jerry Moran (R)	Jan 1997
	2. Lynn Jenkins (R)	Jan 2009
	3. Dennis Moore (D)	Jan 1999
	4. Todd Tiahrt (R)	Jan 1995
Kentucky	1. Ed Whitfield (R)	Jan 1995
	2. Brett Guthrie (R)	Jan 2009

STATE	REPRESENTATIVES	SERVICE BEGAN
Kentucky (cont.)	3. John A. Yarmuth (D)	Jan 2007
	4. Geoff Davis (R)	Jan 2005
	5. Harold Rogers (R)	Jan 1981
	6. Ben Chandler (D)[21]	Feb 2004
Louisiana	1. Steve Scalise (R)[22]	May 2008
	2. Anh ("Joseph") Cao (R)	Jan 2009
	3. Charlie Melancon (D)	Jan 2005
	4. John Fleming (R)	Jan 2009
	5. Rodney Alexander (R)	Jan 2003
	6. Bill Cassidy (R)	Jan 2009
	7. Charles W. Boustany, Jr. (R)	Jan 2005
Maine	1. Chellie Pingree (D)	Jan 2009
	2. Michael H. Michaud (D)	Jan 2003
Maryland	1. Frank M. Kratovil, Jr. (D)	Jan 2009
	2. C.A. ("Dutch") Ruppersberger (D)	Jan 2003
	3. John P. Sarbanes (D)	Jan 2007
	4. Donna F. Edwards (D)[23]	Jun 2008
	5. Steny H. Hoyer (D)	May 1981
	6. Roscoe G. Bartlett (R)	Jan 1993
	7. Elijah E. Cummings (D)	Apr 1996
	8. Chris Van Hollen (D)	Jan 2003
Massa-chusetts	1. John W. Olver (D)	Jun 1991
	2. Richard E. Neal (D)	Jan 1989
	3. James P. McGovern (D)	Jan 1997
	4. Barney Frank (D)	Jan 1981
	5. Niki Tsongas (D)[24]	Oct 2007
	6. John F. Tierney (D)	Jan 1997
	7. Edward J. Markey (D)	Nov 1976
	8. Michael E. Capuano (D)	Jan 1999
	9. Stephen F. Lynch (D)[25]	Oct 2001
	10. Bill Delahunt (D)	Jan 1997
Michigan (−1)	1. Bart Stupak (D)	Jan 1993
	2. Peter Hoekstra (R)	Jan 1993
	3. Vernon J. Ehlers (R)	Dec 1993
	4. Dave Camp (R)	Jan 1991
	5. Dale E. Kildee (D)	Jan 1977
	6. Fred Upton (R)	Jan 1987
	7. Mark H. Schauer (D)	Jan 2009
	8. Mike Rogers (R)	Jan 2001
	9. Gary C. Peters (D)	Jan 2009
	10. Candice S. Miller (R)	Jan 2003
	11. Thaddeus G. McCotter (R)	Jan 2003
	12. Sander M. Levin (D)	Jan 1983
	13. Carolyn C. Kilpatrick (D)	Jan 1997
	14. John Conyers, Jr. (D)	Jan 1965
	15. John D. Dingell (D)	Dec 1955
Minnesota	1. Timothy J. Walz (D)	Jan 2007
	2. John Kline (R)	Jan 2003
	3. Erik Paulsen (R)	Jan 2009
	4. Betty McCollum (D)	Jan 2001
	5. Keith Ellison (D)	Jan 2007
	6. Michele Bachmann (R)	Jan 2007
	7. Collin C. Peterson (D)	Jan 1991
	8. James L. Oberstar (D)	Jan 1975
Mississippi (−1)	1. Travis W. Childers (D)[26]	May 2008
	2. Bennie G. Thompson (D)	Apr 1993
	3. Gregg Harper (R)	Jan 2009
	4. Gene Taylor (D)	Oct 1989

House of Representatives, 111th Congress (continued)

STATE	REPRESENTATIVES	SERVICE BEGAN	STATE	REPRESENTATIVES	SERVICE BEGAN
Missouri	1. William Lacy Clay (D)	Jan 2001	New York	27. Brian Higgins (D)	Jan 2005
	2. W. Todd Akin (R)	Jan 2001	(cont.)	28. Louise McIntosh	Jan 1987
	3. Russ Carnahan (D)	Jan 2005		Slaughter (D)	
	4. Ike Skelton (D)	Jan 1977		29. vacant[30]	
	5. Emanuel Cleaver (D)	Jan 2005			
	6. Sam Graves (R)	Jan 2001	North	1. G.K. Butterfield (D)[31]	Jul 2004
	7. Roy Blunt (R)	Jan 1997	Carolina	2. Bob Etheridge (D)	Jan 1997
	8. Jo Ann Emerson (R)	Nov 1996	(+1)	3. Walter B. Jones (R)	Jan 1995
	9. Blaine Luetkemeyer (R)	Jan 2009		4. David E. Price (D)	Jan 1997
				5. Virginia Foxx (R)	Jan 2005
Montana	Denny Rehberg (R)	Jan 2001		6. Howard Coble (R)	Jan 1985
				7. Mike McIntyre (D)	Jan 1997
Nebraska	1. Jeff Fortenberry (R)	Jan 2005		8. Larry Kissell (D)	Jan 2009
	2. Lee Terry (R)	Jan 1999		9. Sue Wilkins Myrick (R)	Jan 1995
	3. Adrian Smith (R)	Jan 2007		10. Patrick T. McHenry (R)	Jan 2005
				11. Heath Shuler (D)	Jan 2007
Nevada	1. Shelley Berkley (D)	Jan 1999		12. Melvin L. Watt (D)	Jan 1993
(+1)	2. Dean Heller (R)	Jan 2007		13. Brad Miller (D)	Jan 2003
	3. Dina Titus (D)	Jan 2009			
			North Dakota	Earl Pomeroy (D)	Jan 1993
New	1. Carol Shea-Porter (D)	Jan 2007			
Hampshire	2. Paul W. Hodes (D)	Jan 2007	Ohio	1. Steve Driehaus (D)	Jan 2009
			(−1)	2. Jean Schmidt (R)	Sep 2005
New Jersey	1. Robert E. Andrews (D)	Nov 1990		3. Michael R. Turner (R)	Jan 2003
	2. Frank A. LoBiondo (R)	Jan 1995		4. Jim Jordan (R)	Jan 2007
	3. John H. Adler (D)	Jan 2009		5. Robert E. Latta (R)[32]	Dec 2007
	4. Christopher H. Smith (R)	Jan 1981		6. Charles A. Wilson (D)	Jan 2007
	5. Scott Garrett (R)	Jan 2003		7. Steve Austria (R)	Jan 2009
	6. Frank Pallone, Jr. (D)	Nov 1988		8. John A. Boehner (R)	Jan 1991
	7. Leonard Lance (R)	Jan 2009		9. Marcy Kaptur (D)	Jan 1983
	8. Bill Pascrell, Jr. (D)	Jan 1997		10. Dennis J. Kucinich (D)	Jan 1997
	9. Steven R. Rothman (D)	Jan 1997		11. Marcia L. Fudge (D)[33]	Nov 2008
	10. Donald M. Payne (D)	Jan 1989		12. Patrick J. Tiberi (R)	Jan 2001
	11. Rodney P. Freling-	Jan 1995		13. Betty Sutton (D)	Jan 2007
	huysen (R)			14. Steven C. LaTourette (R)	Jan 1995
	12. Rush D. Holt (D)	Jan 1999		15. Mary Jo Kilroy (D)	Jan 2009
	13. Albio Sires (D)[27]	Nov 2006		16. John A. Boccieri (D)	Jan 2009
				17. Tim Ryan (D)	Jan 2003
New Mexico	1. Martin Heinrich (D)	Jan 2009		18. Zachary T. Space (D)	Jan 2007
	2. Harry Teague (D)	Jan 2009			
	3. Ben Ray Luján (D)	Jan 2009	Oklahoma	1. John Sullivan (R)[34]	Feb 2002
			(−1)	2. Dan Boren (D)	Jan 2005
New York	1. Timothy H. Bishop (D)	Jan 2003		3. Frank D. Lucas (R)	May 1994
(−2)	2. Steve Israel (D)	Jan 2001		4. Tom Cole (R)	Jan 2003
	3. Peter T. King (R)	Jan 1993		5. Mary Fallin (R)	Jan 2007
	4. Carolyn McCarthy (D)	Jan 1997			
	5. Gary L. Ackerman (D)	Mar 1983	Oregon	1. David Wu (D)	Jan 1999
	6. Gregory W. Meeks (D)	Feb 1998		2. Greg Walden (R)	Jan 1999
	7. Joseph Crowley (D)	Jan 1999		3. Earl Blumenauer (D)	May 1996
	8. Jerrold Nadler (D)	Nov 1992		4. Peter A. DeFazio (D)	Jan 1987
	9. Anthony D. Weiner (D)	Jan 1999		5. Kurt Schrader (D)	Jan 2009
	10. Edolphus Towns (D)	Jan 1983			
	11. Yvette D. Clarke (D)	Jan 2007	Penn-	1. Robert A. Brady (D)	May 1998
	12. Nydia M. Velázquez (D)	Jan 1993	sylvania	2. Chaka Fattah (D)	Jan 1995
	13. Michael E. McMahon (D)	Jan 2009	(−2)	3. Kathleen A. Dahlkemper	Jan 2009
	14. Carolyn B. Maloney (D)	Jan 1993		(D)	
	15. Charles B. Rangel (D)	Jan 1971		4. Jason Altmire (D)	Jan 2007
	16. José E. Serrano (D)	Mar 1990		5. Glenn Thompson (R)	Jan 2009
	17. Eliot L. Engel (D)	Jan 1989		6. Jim Gerlach (R)	Jan 2003
	18. Nita M. Lowey (D)	Jan 1989		7. Joe Sestak (D)	Jan 2007
	19. John J. Hall (D)	Jan 2007		8. Patrick J. Murphy (D)	Jan 2007
	20. Scott Murphy (D)[28]	Apr 2009		9. Bill Shuster (R)	May 2001
	21. Paul Tonko (D)	Jan 2009		10. Christopher P. Carney (D)	Jan 2007
	22. Maurice D. Hinchey (D)	Jan 1993		11. Paul E. Kanjorski (D)	Jan 1985
	23. William Owens (D)[29]	Nov 2009		12. Mark S. Critz (D)[35]	May 2010
	24. Michael A. Arcuri (D)	Jan 2007		13. Allyson Y. Schwartz (D)	Jan 2005
	25. Daniel B. Maffei (D)	Jan 2009		14. Michael F. Doyle (D)	Jan 1995
	26. Christopher John Lee (R)	Jan 2009		15. Charles W. Dent (R)	Jan 2005

House of Representatives, 111th Congress (continued)

STATE	REPRESENTATIVES	SERVICE BEGAN	STATE	REPRESENTATIVES	SERVICE BEGAN
Penn-sylvania (cont.)	16. Joseph R. Pitts (R)	Jan 1997	Texas (cont.)	27. Solomon P. Ortiz (D)	Jan 1983
	17. Tim Holden (D)	Jan 1993		28. Henry Cuellar (D)	Jan 2005
	18. Tim Murphy (R)	Jan 2003		29. Gene Green (D)	Jan 1993
	19. Todd Russell Platts (R)	Jan 2001		30. Eddie Bernice Johnson (D)	Jan 1993
Rhode Island	1. Patrick J. Kennedy (D)	Jan 1995		31. John R. Carter (R)	Jan 2003
	2. James R. Langevin (D)	Jan 2001		32. Pete Sessions (R)	Jan 1997
South Carolina	1. Henry E. Brown, Jr. (R)	Jan 2001	Utah	1. Rob Bishop (R)	Jan 2003
	2. Joe Wilson (R)[36]	Dec 2001		2. Jim Matheson (D)	Jan 2001
	3. J. Gresham Barrett (R)	Jan 2003		3. Jason Chaffetz (R)	Jan 2009
	4. Bob Inglis (R)	Jan 2005	Vermont	Peter Welch (D)	Jan 2007
	5. John M. Spratt, Jr. (D)	Jan 1983			
	6. James E. Clyburn (D)	Jan 1993	Virginia	1. Robert J. Wittman (R)[41]	Dec 2007
South Dakota	Stephanie Herseth Sandlin (D)[37]	Jun 2004		2. Glenn C. Nye (D)	Jan 2009
				3. Robert C. ("Bobby") Scott (D)	Jan 1993
Tennessee	1. David P. Roe (R)	Jan 2009		4. J. Randy Forbes (R)[42]	Jun 2001
	2. John J. Duncan, Jr. (R)	Nov 1988		5. Thomas S.P. Perriello (D)	Jan 2009
	3. Zach Wamp (R)	Jan 1995		6. Bob Goodlatte (R)	Jan 1993
	4. Lincoln Davis (D)	Jan 2003		7. Eric Cantor (R)	Jan 2001
	5. Jim Cooper (D)[38]	Jan 1983		8. James P. Moran (D)	Jan 1991
	6. Bart Gordon (D)	Jan 1985		9. Rick Boucher (D)	Jan 1983
	7. Marsha Blackburn (R)	Jan 2003		10. Frank R. Wolf (R)	Jan 1981
	8. John S. Tanner (D)	Jan 1989		11. Gerald E. Connolly (D)	Jan 2009
	9. Steve Cohen (D)	Jan 2007			
			Washington	1. Jay Inslee (D)[43]	Jan 1993
Texas (+2)	1. Louie Gohmert (R)	Jan 2005		2. Rick Larsen (D)	Jan 2001
	2. Ted Poe (R)	Jan 2005		3. Brian Baird (D)	Jan 1999
	3. Sam Johnson (R)	May 1991		4. Doc Hastings (R)	Jan 1995
	4. Ralph M. Hall (R)	Jan 1981		5. Cathy McMorris Rodgers (R)	Jan 2005
	5. Jeb Hensarling (R)	Jan 2003		6. Norman D. Dicks (D)	Jan 1977
	6. Joe Barton (R)	Jan 1985		7. Jim McDermott (D)	Jan 1989
	7. John Abney Culberson (R)	Jan 2001		8. David G. Reichert (R)	Jan 2005
	8. Kevin Brady (R)	Jan 1997		9. Adam Smith (D)	Jan 1997
	9. Al Green (D)	Jan 2005			
	10. Michael T. McCaul (R)	Jan 2005	West Virginia	1. Alan B. Mollohan (D)	Jan 1983
	11. K. Michael Conaway (R)	Jan 2005		2. Shelley Moore Capito (R)	Jan 2001
	12. Kay Granger (R)	Jan 1997		3. Nick J. Rahall II (D)	Jan 1977
	13. Mac Thornberry (R)	Jan 1995			
	14. Ron Paul (R)	Jan 1997	Wisconsin (−1)	1. Paul Ryan (R)	Jan 1999
	15. Rubén Hinojosa (D)	Jan 1997		2. Tammy Baldwin (D)	Jan 1999
	16. Silvestre Reyes (D)	Jan 1997		3. Ron Kind (D)	Jan 1997
	17. Chet Edwards (D)	Jan 2005		4. Gwen Moore (D)	Jan 2005
	18. Sheila Jackson-Lee (D)	Jan 1995		5. F. James Sensen-brenner, Jr. (R)	Jan 1979
	19. Randy Neugebauer (R)[39]	Jun 2003			
	20. Charles A. Gonzalez (D)	Jan 1999		6. Thomas E. Petri (R)	Apr 1979
	21. Lamar Smith (R)	Jan 1987		7. David R. Obey (D)	Apr 1969
	22. Pete Olson (R)	Jan 2009		8. Steve Kagen (D)	Jan 2007
	23. Ciro D. Rodriguez (D)[40]	Apr 1997			
	24. Kenny Marchant (R)	Jan 2005	Wyoming	Cynthia M. Lummis (R)	Jan 2009
	25. Lloyd Doggett (D)	Jan 2005			
	26. Michael C. Burgess (R)	Jan 2003			

JURISDICTION	REPRESENTATIVES	SERVICE BEGAN
American Samoa	(Delegate) Eni F.H. Faleomavaega (D)	Jan 1989
District of Columbia	(Delegate) Eleanor Holmes Norton (D)	Jan 1991
Guam	(Delegate) Madeleine Z. Bordallo (D)	Jan 2003
Northern Mariana Islands	(Delegate) Gregorio Kilili Camacho Sablan (D)	Jan 2009
Puerto Rico	(Resident Commissioner) Pedro R. Pierluisi (New Progressive)	Jan 2009
US Virgin Islands	(Delegate) Donna M. Christensen (D)	Jan 1997

[1]*John Boozman was elected 20 Nov 2001 following the resignation of Asa Hutchinson.* [2]*Doris O. Matsui was elected 8 Mar 2005 following the death of Robert T. Matsui.* [3]*John Garamendi was elected 3 Nov 2009 following the resignation of Ellen O. Tauscher.* [4]*Jackie Speier was elected 8 Apr 2008 following the death of Tom Lantos.* [5]*Judy Chu was elected 14 Jul 2009 following the resignation of Hilda L. Solis.* [6]*Diane E. Watson was*

House of Representatives, 111th Congress (continued)

elected 5 Jun 2001 following the death of Julian C. Dixon. [7]*Jane Harman did not serve 3 Jan 1999–3 Jan 2001.* [8]*Laura Richardson was elected 21 Aug 2007 following the death of Juanita Millender-McDonald.* [9]*John Campbell was elected 6 Dec 2005 following the resignation of Christopher Cox.* [10]*Brian P. Bilbray did not serve 3 Jan 2001–6 Jun 2005. He was elected 6 Jun 2005 following the resignation of Randall ("Duke") Cunningham.* [11]*Jeff Miller was elected 16 Oct 2001 following the resignation of Joe Scarborough.* [12]*Theodore Deutch was elected 13 Apr 2010 following the resignation of Robert Wexler.* [13]*Tom Graves was elected 8 Jun 2010 following the resignation of Nathan Deal.* [14]*Paul C. Broun was elected 17 Jul 2007 following the death of Charlie Norwood.* [15]*Charles Djou was elected 22 May 2010 following the resignation of Neil Abercrombie.* [16]*Mike Quigley was elected 7 Apr 2009 following the resignation of Rahm Emanuel.* [17]*Bill Foster was elected 8 Mar 2008 following the resignation of J. Dennis Hastert.* [18]*Vacant following the resignation of Mark E. Souder, 21 May 2010.* [19]*André Carson was elected 11 Mar 2008 following the death of Julia Carson.* [20]*Baron P. Hill did not serve 3 Jan 2005–3 Jan 2007.* [21]*Ben Chandler was elected 17 Feb 2004 following the resignation of Ernie Fletcher.* [22]*Steve Scalise was elected 3 May 2008 following the resignation of Bobby Jindal.* [23]*Donna F. Edwards was elected 17 Jun 2007 following the resignation of Albert Russell Wynn.* [24]*Niki Tsongas was elected 16 Oct 2007 following the resignation of Martin T. Meehan.* [25]*Stephen F. Lynch was elected 16 Oct 2001 following the death of John Joseph Moakley.* [26]*Travis W. Childers was elected 13 May 2008 following the resignation of Roger F. Wicker.* [27]*Albio Sires was elected 7 Nov 2006 following the resignation of Robert Menendez.* [28]*Scott Murphy was elected 31 Mar 2009 following the resignation of Kirsten E. Gillibrand.* [29]*William Owens was elected 3 Nov 2009 following the resignation of John McHugh.* [30]*Vacant following the resignation of Eric. J.J. Massa, 8 Mar 2010.* [31]*G.K. Butterfield was elected 20 Jul 2004 following the resignation of Frank Ballance.* [32]*Robert E. Latta was elected 11 Dec 2007 following the death of Paul E. Gillmor.* [33]*Marcia L. Fudge was elected 18 Nov 2008 following the death of Stephanie Tubbs Jones.* [34]*John Sullivan was elected 8 Jan 2002 following the resignation of Steve Largent.* [35]*Mark S. Critz was elected 18 May 2010 following the death of John P. Murtha.* [36]*Joe Wilson was elected 18 Dec 2001 following the death of Floyd Spence.* [37]*Stephanie Herseth Sandlin was elected 1 Jun 2004 following the resignation of William Janklow.* [38]*Jim Cooper did not serve 3 Jan 1995–3 Jan 2003.* [39]*Randy Neugebauer was elected 3 Jun 2003 following the resignation of Larry Combest.* [40]*Ciro D. Rodriguez took office 12 Apr 1997 following the death of Frank Tejada. He did not serve 3 Jan 2005–3 Jan 2007.* [41]*Robert J. Wittman was elected 11 Dec 2007 following the death of Jo Ann Davis.* [42]*J. Randy Forbes was elected 19 Jun 2001 following the death of Norman Sisisky.* [43]*Jay Inslee did not serve 3 Jan 1995–3 Jan 1999.*

House of Representatives Standing and Select Committees

COMMITTEE	CHAIRMAN (PARTY-STATE)	RANKING MINORITY MEMBER (PARTY-STATE)	NUMBER OF MEMBERS		NUMBER OF SUBCOM-MITTEES
			MAJORITY	MINORITY	
Agriculture	Collin C. Peterson (D-MN)	Frank D. Lucas (R-OK)	28	18	6
Appropriations	David R. Obey (D-WI)	Jerry Lewis (R-CA)	37	23	12
Armed Services	Ike Skelton (D-MO)	Howard P. "Buck" McKeon (R-CA)	37	25	7
Budget	John M. Spratt, Jr. (D-SC)	Paul Ryan (R-WI)	24	15	none
Education and Labor	George Miller (D-CA)	John Kline (R-MN)	30	19	5
Energy and Commerce	Henry A. Waxman (D-CA)	Joe Barton (R-TX)	36	23	5
Financial Services	Barney Frank (D-MA)	Spencer Bachus (R-AL)	42	29	6
Foreign Affairs	Howard L. Berman (D-CA)	Ileana Ros-Lehtinen (R-FL)	28	19	7
Homeland Security	Bennie G. Thompson (D-MS)	Peter T. King (R-NY)	21	13	6
House Administration	Robert A. Brady (D-PA)	Daniel E. Lungren (R-CA)	6	3	2
Judiciary	John Conyers, Jr. (D-MI)	Lamar S. Smith (R-TX)	24	16	5
Natural Resources	Nick J. Rahall II (D-WV)	Doc Hastings (R-WA)	29	20	4
Oversight and Government Reform	Edolphus Towns (D-NY)	Darrell E. Issa (R-CA)	25	16	5
Rules	Louise McIntosh Slaughter (D-NY)	David Dreier (R-CA)	9	4	2
Science and Technology	Bart Gordon (D-TN)	Ralph M. Hall (R-TX)	27	17	5
Small Business	Nydia M. Velázquez (D-NY)	Sam Graves (R-MO)	17	12	5
Standards of Official Conduct	Zoe Lofgren (D-CA)	Jo Bonner (R-AL)	5	5	none
Transportation and Infrastructure	James L. Oberstar (D-MN)	John L. Mica (R-FL)	45	30	6
Veterans' Affairs	Bob Filner (D-CA)	Steve Buyer (R-IN)	18	11	4
Ways and Means	Sander M. Levin (D-MI) (acting)	Dave Camp (R-MI)	26	15	6
Permanent Select Committee on Intelligence	Silvestre Reyes (D-TX)	Peter Hoekstra (R-MI)	13	9	4
Select Committee on Energy Independence and Global Warming	Edward J. Markey (D-MA)	F. James Sensenbrenner, Jr. (R-WI)	9	6	none

Joint Committees of Congress

The joint committees of Congress include members from both the Senate and the House of Representatives. They function as overseeing entities but do not have the power to approve appropriations or legislation. Chairmanship of the Joint Economic Committee is determined by seniority and alternates between the Senate and the House every Congress. The Joint Committee on the Library of Congress is evenly made up of members from the House Administration Committee and the Senate Rules and Administration Committee. Chairmanship and vice-chairmanship of the Joint Committee on Printing alternate between the House and the Senate every Congress. The Joint Committee on Taxation is composed of five members from the Senate Committee on Finance and four members from the House Committee on Ways and Means (three majority and two minority members from each).

COMMITTEE	CHAIRMAN (PARTY-STATE)	VICE-CHAIRMAN (PARTY-STATE)	NUMBER OF MEMBERS MAJORITY	MINORITY
Economic	Rep. Carolyn B. Maloney (D-NY)	Sen. Charles E. Schumer (D-NY)	12	8
Library	Rep. Robert A. Brady (D-PA)	Sen. Charles E. Schumer (D-NY)	6	4
Printing	Sen. Charles E. Schumer (D-NY)	Rep. Robert A. Brady (D-PA)	6	4
Taxation	Sen. Max Baucus (D-MT)	Rep. Sander M. Levin (D-MI)	6	4

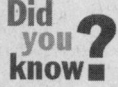

Did you know? Henri Matisse's painting *Le Bateau* (*The Boat*) was accidentally hung upside down in New York's Museum of Modern Art for 47 days in 1961. During that time 116,000 visitors saw it, but it was not until stockbroker Genevieve Habert called the *New York Times* about the mistake that the director of exhibitions was notified and the work was rehung properly.

Electoral Votes by State

Each state receives one electoral vote for each of its representatives and one for each of its two senators, ensuring at least three votes for each state, as the Constitution guarantees at least one representative regardless of population. Allocations are based on the 2000 census and are applicable for subsequent elections.

Total: 538; Majority needed to elect president and vice president: 270

STATE	NUMBER OF VOTES	STATE	NUMBER OF VOTES	STATE	NUMBER OF VOTES
Alabama	9	Kentucky	8	North Dakota	3
Alaska	3	Louisiana	9	Ohio	20
Arizona	10	Maine	4	Oklahoma	7
Arkansas	6	Maryland	10	Oregon	7
California	55	Massachusetts	12	Pennsylvania	21
Colorado	9	Michigan	17	Rhode Island	4
Connecticut	7	Minnesota	10	South Carolina	8
Delaware	3	Mississippi	6	South Dakota	3
District of Columbia	3	Missouri	11	Tennessee	11
Florida	27	Montana	3	Texas	34
Georgia	15	Nebraska	5	Utah	5
Hawaii	4	Nevada	5	Vermont	3
Idaho	4	New Hampshire	4	Virginia	13
Illinois	21	New Jersey	15	Washington	11
Indiana	11	New Mexico	5	West Virginia	5
Iowa	7	New York	31	Wisconsin	10
Kansas	6	North Carolina	15	Wyoming	3

Congressional Apportionment

The US Constitution requires a decennial census to determine the apportionment of representatives for each state in the House of Representatives.

STATE	REPRESENTATIVES	STATE	REPRESENTATIVES	STATE	REPRESENTATIVES
Alabama	7	Georgia	13	Maine	2
Alaska	1	Hawaii	2	Maryland	8
Arizona	8	Idaho	2	Massachusetts	10
Arkansas	4	Illinois	19	Michigan	15
California	53	Indiana	9	Minnesota	8
Colorado	7	Iowa	5	Mississippi	4
Connecticut	5	Kansas	4	Missouri	9
Delaware	1	Kentucky	6	Montana	1
Florida	25	Louisiana	7	Nebraska	3

Congressional Apportionment (continued)

STATE	REPRESENTATIVES	STATE	REPRESENTATIVES	STATE	REPRESENTATIVES
Nevada	3	Oklahoma	5	Utah	3
New Hampshire	2	Oregon	5	Vermont	1
New Jersey	13	Pennsylvania	19	Virginia	11
New Mexico	3	Rhode Island	2	Washington	9
New York	29	South Carolina	6	West Virginia	3
North Carolina	13	South Dakota	1	Wisconsin	8
North Dakota	1	Tennessee	9	Wyoming	1
Ohio	18	Texas	32	**Total**	**435**

United States Military Affairs

US Military Leadership

President, Commander in Chief:	Barack Obama (20 Jan 2009)
Secretary of Defense:	Robert M. Gates (18 Dec 2006)
Chairman, Joint Chiefs of Staff:	Adm. Mike Mullen (1 Oct 2007)
Vice Chairman, Joint Chiefs of Staff:	Gen. James E. Cartwright (31 Aug 2007)

RANK/POSITION	NAME (DATE ASSUMED POST)
Army	
Chief of Staff	Gen. George W. Casey, Jr. (10 Apr 2007)
Vice Chief of Staff	Gen. Peter W. Chiarelli (4 Aug 2008)
Sergeant Major	Kenneth O. Preston (15 Jan 2004)
Sec. of the Army	John M. McHugh (21 Sep 2009)
Under Sec. of the Army	Joseph W. Westphal (21 Sep 2009)
Navy	
Chief of Naval Operations	Adm. Gary Roughead (29 Sep 2007)
Vice Chief of Naval Operations	Adm. Jonathan W. Greenert (13 Aug 2009)
Master Chief Petty Officer	Rick D. West (12 Dec 2008)
Sec. of the Navy	Ray Mabus (19 May 2009)
Under Sec. of the Navy	Robert O. Work (19 May 2009)

RANK/POSITION	NAME (DATE ASSUMED POST)
Air Force	
Chief of Staff	Gen. Norton A. Schwartz (12 Aug 2008)
Vice Chief of Staff	Gen. Carrol H. Chandler (28 Aug 2009)
Chief Master Sgt.	James A. Roy (30 Jun 2009)
Sec. of the Air Force	Michael B. Donley (2 Oct 2008)
Under Sec. of the Air Force	Erin C. Conation (15 Mar 2010)
Marine Corps	
Commandant	Gen. James T. Conway (13 Nov 2006)
Asst. Commandant	Gen. James F. Amos (2 Jul 2008)
Sergeant Major	Carlton W. Kent (25 Apr 2007)
Coast Guard	
Commandant	Adm. Robert J. Papp, Jr. (25 May 2010)
Vice Commandant	Vice Adm. Sally Brice-O'Hara (24 May 2010)
Chief of Staff	Vice Adm. John P. Currier (August 2009)
Master Chief Petty Officer	Michael P. Leavitt (21 May 2010)

Unified Combatant Commands

The Unified Combatant Commands provide operational control of US combat forces and are organized geographically to a significant extent. Unified Commanders receive orders through the chairman of the Joint Chiefs of Staff. Although the number of commands may vary, each command must be composed of forces from at least two of the armed services. Information is current as of May 2010.

COMMAND	HEADQUARTERS	COMMANDER
US European Command	Stuttgart-Vaihingen, Germany	Adm. James G. Stavridis, USN
US Pacific Command	Camp H.M. Smith, Hawaii	Adm. Robert F. Willard USN
US Joint Forces Command	Norfolk VA	Gen. Raymond Odierno, USA
US Southern Command	Doral FL	Gen. Douglas M. Fraser, USAF
US Central Command	MacDill Air Force Base, Florida	Gen. James N. Mattis, USMC
US Northern Command	Peterson Air Force Base, Colorado	Adm. James A. Winnefeld, Jr., USN
US Special Operations Command	MacDill Air Force Base, Florida	Adm. Eric T. Olson, USN
US Transportation Command	Scott Air Force Base, Illinois	Gen. Duncan J. McNabb, USAF
US Strategic Command	Offutt Air Force Base, Nebraska	Gen. Kevin P. Chilton, USAF
US Africa Command	Stuttgart-Möhringen, Germany	Gen. William E. Ward, USA

North Atlantic Treaty Organization (NATO) International Commands

The NATO military command structure comprises two main strategic commands, Allied Command Operations (ACO) and Allied Command Transformation (ACT, which works closely with the US Joint Forces Command). Their subordinate centers, also listed, change as their security measures evolve.

ALLIED COMMAND OPERATIONS (ACO)
Headquarters: Casteau, Belgium
Supreme Allied Commander, Europe (SACEUR):
　Adm. James G. Stavridis, USN (2 Jul 2009–)

SUBORDINATE OPERATIONAL COMMANDS
Allied Joint Force Command (JFC) Brunssum,
　JFC Headquarters: Brunssum, Netherlands
Commander in Chief: Gen. Egon Ramms (Army,
　Germany) (26 Jan 2007–)

Allied Joint Force Command (JFC) Naples,
　JFC Headquarters: Naples, Italy
Commander in Chief: Adm. Mark Fitzgerald (USN)
　(30 Nov 2007–)

Allied Joint Command (JC) Lisbon,
　JC Headquarters: Oeiras, Portugal
Commander in Chief: Gen. Philippe Stoltz (Army,
　France) (20 Jul 2009–)

ALLIED COMMAND TRANSFORMATION (ACT)
Headquarters: Norfolk VA
Supreme Allied Commander, Transformation (SACT):
　Gen. Stéphane Abrial (Air Force, France)
　(29 Jul 2009–)

SUBORDINATE CENTERS AND SCHOOLS
Joint Analysis and Lessons Learned Centre (JALLC),
　Monsanto, Portugal
Joint Force Training Centre (JFTC), Bydgoszcz, Poland
Joint Warfare Centre (JWC), Stavanger, Norway
NATO Communications and Information Systems
　School (NCISS), Latina, Italy
NATO Defense College (NDC), Rome, Italy
NATO Maritime Interdiction Operational Training
　Centre (NMIOTC), Chania, Greece
NATO School, Oberammergau, Germany
NATO Undersea Research Centre (NURC), La Spezia,
　Italy

Chairmen of the Joint Chiefs of Staff

The 1949 amendments to the National Security Act of 1947 created the position of chairman of the Joint Chiefs of Staff, the principal military adviser to the president, the secretary of defense, and the National Security Council. The president appoints the chairman for a two-year term with the advice and consent of the Senate. In 1986 the chairman's eligibility for service increased from two to three reappointments (there is no limit on reappointment during wartime). The Joint Chiefs of Staff consist of the chairman, a vice chairman, the chief of staff of the Army, the chief of staff of the Air Force, the chief of naval operations, and the commandant of the Marine Corps. Acting chairmen are not included in this table.

NAME	MILITARY BRANCH	DATES OF SERVICE
Gen. of the Army Omar N. Bradley	US Army	16 Aug 1949–14 Aug 1953
Adm. Arthur W. Radford	US Navy	15 Aug 1953–14 Aug 1957
Gen. Nathan F. Twining	US Air Force	15 Aug 1957–30 Sep 1960
Gen. Lyman L. Lemnitzer	US Army	1 Oct 1960–30 Sep 1962
Gen. Maxwell D. Taylor	US Army	1 Oct 1962–1 Jul 1964
Gen. Earle G. Wheeler	US Army	3 Jul 1964–1 Jul 1970
Adm. Thomas H. Moorer	US Navy	2 Jul 1970–30 Jun 1974
Gen. George S. Brown	US Air Force	1 Jul 1974–20 Jun 1978
Gen. David C. Jones	US Air Force	21 Jun 1978–17 Jun 1982
Gen. John W. Vessey, Jr.	US Army	18 Jun 1982–30 Sep 1985
Adm. William J. Crowe, Jr.	US Navy	1 Oct 1985–30 Sep 1989
Gen. Colin L. Powell	US Army	1 Oct 1989–30 Sep 1993
Gen. John M. Shalikashvili	US Army	25 Oct 1993–30 Sep 1997
Gen. Harry Shelton	US Army	1 Oct 1997–30 Sep 2001
Gen. Richard B. Myers	US Air Force	1 Oct 2001–29 Sep 2005
Gen. Peter Pace	US Marine Corps	30 Sep 2005–30 Sep 2007
Adm. Mike Mullen	US Navy	1 Oct 2007–

Worldwide Deployment of the US Military

Deployments of active duty military personnel as of 1 Jan 2010. Regional totals include countries and areas not shown in the table. N/A stands for not available. Source: US Department of Defense.

COUNTRY/REGIONAL AREA	TOTAL	ARMY	NAVY	MARINE CORPS	AIR FORCE
US and territories[1]					
contiguous US	941,629	441,143	108,755	132,551	259,180
Alaska	20,450	12,684	76	24	7,666

Worldwide Deployment of the US Military (continued)

COUNTRY/REGIONAL AREA	TOTAL	ARMY	NAVY	MARINE CORPS	AIR FORCE
US and territories[1] (continued)					
Hawaii	37,245	21,116	5,468	6,132	4,529
Guam	2,972	43	962	11	1,956
Puerto Rico	179	85	47	23	24
transients	50,625	11,239	8,522	25,834	5,030
afloat	84,461	0	84,461	0	0
total ashore and afloat	**1,137,568**	**486,310**	**208,291**	**164,578**	**278,389**
Europe					
Belgium	1,253	673	108	26	446
Germany[1]	52,440	37,302	248	333	14,557
Greece	370	11	291	11	57
Greenland	138	0	0	0	138
Italy[1]	9,660	3,244	2,323	54	4,039
Netherlands	505	244	23	16	222
Portugal	700	26	29	10	635
Spain	1,262	93	705	93	371
Turkey	1,592	58	8	29	1,497
United Kingdom[1]	9,015	334	295	89	8,297
afloat	511	0	511	0	0
total ashore and afloat	**77,917**	**42,087**	**4,570**	**837**	**30,423**
East Asia and Pacific					
Australia	134	33	20	22	59
Japan[1]	35,688	2,541	3,740	17,009	12,398
Republic of Korea	N/A	N/A	N/A	N/A	N/A
Philippines	453	10	5	429	9
Singapore	118	7	83	15	13
Thailand	110	42	9	35	24
afloat	10,541	0	6,796	3,745	0
total ashore and afloat	**47,236**	**2,695**	**10,673**	**21,344**	**12,524**
Africa, Near East, and South Asia					
Afghanistan (Operation Enduring Freedom)[2]	71,000	46,400	3,500	13,000	8,100
Iraq (Operation Iraqi Freedom)[2]	151,000	108,300	18,300	6,800	17,600
Bahrain	1,337	19	1,230	64	24
Diego Garcia	245	0	209	0	36
Djibouti	1,055	40	660	84	271
Egypt	269	206	6	27	30
Qatar	466	233	4	37	192
Saudi Arabia	270	138	24	30	78
afloat	412	0	412	0	0
total ashore and afloat (excluding Iraq and Afghanistan)	**5,129**	**764**	**2,592**	**565**	**796**
Western Hemisphere					
Canada	130	6	28	9	87
Cuba (Guantánamo Bay)	880	294	457	129	0
Honduras	415	223	2	7	183
total ashore and afloat	**1,941**	**678**	**595**	**329**	**339**
all foreign countries (excluding Iraq and Afghanistan)					
ashore	266,452	67,016	107,324	35,830	56,282
afloat	17,648	0	13,903	3,745	0
total ashore and afloat	**284,100**	**67,016**	**121,227**	**39,575**	**56,282**
worldwide (excluding Iraq and Afghanistan)					
ashore	1,319,559	553,326	231,154	200,408	334,671
afloat	102,109	0	98,364	3,745	0
total ashore and afloat	**1,421,668**	**553,326**	**329,518**	**204,153**	**334,671**

[1]*Includes service members deployed to Operation Iraqi Freedom and Operation Enduring Freedom.*   [2]*Includes deployed Reserve/National Guard.*

Number of Living US Veterans[1]

Source: Statistical Abstract of the United States: 2009.

AGE IN YEARS	KOREAN CONFLICT	VIETNAM ERA	GULF WAR[2]	TOTAL WARTIME[3,4]	TOTAL PEACETIME	TOTAL VETERANS[4]
under 35	—	—	1,894,000	1,894,000	6,000	1,900,000
35–39	—	—	1,064,000	1,064,000	196,000	1,259,000
40–44	—	—·	727,000	727,000	851,000	1,578,000
45–49	—	23,000	535,000	556,000	1,320,000	1,876,000
50–54	—	883,000	364,000	1,155,000	796,000	1,950,000
55–59	—	2453,000	237,000	2,540,000	179,000	2,718,000
60–64	—	2,981,000	105,000	3,003,000	230,000	3,233,000
65 and over	2,961,000	1,545,000	41,000	6,802,000	2,500,000	·9,302,000
female, total	71,000	258,000	795,000	1,226,000	555,000	1,780,000
total[5]	2,961,000	7,884,000	4,966,000	17,739,000	6,077,000	23,816,000

[1]As of 30 Sep 2007. Includes those living outside of the US. Estimated.   [2]Service from 2 Aug 1990 to the present.   [3]Veterans who served in more than one wartime period are counted only once.   [4]Includes an estimated 2,912,000 veterans of World War II, all 65 or over, of which 137,000 are female.   [5]Detail may not add to total given because of rounding.

US Casualties of War

Data prior to World War I are based on incomplete records. Casualty data exclude personnel captured or missing in action. N/A means not available. Sources: US Department of Defense and US Coast Guard.

WAR	SERVICE BRANCH	NUMBER OF COMBATANTS	WOUNDED[1]	BATTLE DEATHS	OTHER DEATHS	TOTAL DEATHS
Revolutionary War	Army	N/A	6,004	4,044	N/A	N/A
(1775–83)	Navy	N/A	114	342	N/A	N/A
	Marines	N/A	70	49	N/A	N/A
	total	184,000–250,000[2]	6,188	4,435	20,000[2]	24,435
War of 1812	Army	N/A	4,000	1,950	N/A	N/A
(1812–15)	Navy	N/A	439	265	N/A	N/A
	Marines	N/A	66	45	N/A	N/A
	Coast Guard	100	N/A	0	N/A	N/A
	total	286,830	4,505[3]	2,260	N/A	N/A
Indian Wars (about 1817–98)	total	106,000[2]	N/A	1,000[2]	N/A	N/A
Mexican-American War	Army	N/A	4,102	1,721	11,550	13,271
(1846–48)	Navy	N/A	3	1	N/A	1
	Marines	N/A	47	11	N/A	11
	Coast Guard	71	N/A	N/A	N/A	N/A
	total	78,789	4,152[3]	1,733[3]	11,550[3]	13,283
Civil War (1861–65)	Army	2,128,948	280,040	138,154	221,374	359,528
Union	Navy	N/A	1,710	2,112	2,411	4,523
	Marines	84,415	131	148	312	460
	Coast Guard	219	N/A	1	N/A	N/A
	total	N/A	281,881[3]	140,415	224,097[3]	364,512[3]
Confederate[4]	total	600,000–1,500,000	137,000[2]	74,524	124,000[2]	198,524
Spanish-American War	Army	280,564	1,594	369	2,061	2,430
(1898)	Navy	22,875	47	10	N/A	10
	Marines	3,321	21	6	N/A	6
	Coast Guard	660	N/A	0	N/A	0
	total	307,420	1,662[3]	385	2,061[3]	2,446[3]
World War I	Army[5]	4,057,101	193,663	50,510	55,868	106,378
(1917–18)	Navy	599,051	819	431	6,856	7,287
	Marines	78,839	9,520	2,461	390	2,851
	Coast Guard	8,835	N/A	111	81	192
	total	4,743,826	204,002[3]	53,513	63,195	116,708
World War II	Army[5]	11,260,000	565,861	234,874	83,400	318,274
(1941–46)	Navy	4,183,466	37,778	36,950	25,664	62,614
	Marines	669,100	67,207	19,733	4,778	24,511
	Coast Guard	241,093	N/A	574	1,343	1,917
	total	16,353,659	670,846[3]	292,131	115,185	407,316
Korean War	Army	2,834,000	77,596	27,731	2,125	29,856
(1950–53)	Navy	1,177,000	1,576	503	154	657
	Marines	424,000	23,744	4,267	242	4,509

US Casualties of War (continued)

WAR	SERVICE BRANCH	NUMBER OF COMBATANTS	CASUALTIES			
			WOUNDED[1]	BATTLE DEATHS	OTHER DEATHS	TOTAL DEATHS
Korean War	Air Force	1,285,000	368	1,238	314	1,552
(1950–53) (cont.)	Coast Guard	8,500[6]	0	0	0	0
	total	5,764,143	103,284	33,739	2,835	36,574
Vietnam War	Army	4,368,000	96,802	30,963	7,261	38,224
(1964–73)	Navy	1,842,000	4,178	1,631	935	2,566
	Marines	794,000	51,392	13,095	1,749	14,844
	Air Force	1,740,000	931	1,745	841	2,586
	Coast Guard	8,000	60	7	N/A	7
	total	8,752,000	153,363[7]	47,441	10,786[3]	58,227
Persian Gulf War[8]	Army	338,636	354	98	126	224
(1990–91)	Navy	152,419	12[9]	6[9]	50[9]	56[9]
	Marines	97,878	92	24	44	68
	Air Force	76,543	9	20	15	35
	Coast Guard	400	N/A	N/A	N/A	N/A
	total	665,876	467	148	235	383
War on Terrorism[10]	Army	N/A	2,600	558	189	747
(2001–)	Navy[9]	N/A	54	35	21	56
	Marines	N/A	406	135	42	177
	Air Force	N/A	102	23	23	46
	Coast Guard	N/A	N/A	N/A	N/A	N/A
	total	N/A	3,162	751	275	1,026
Iraq War[11]	Army	N/A	21,759	2,526	676	3,202
(2003–)	Navy[9]	N/A	631	65	38	103
	Marines	N/A	8,622	851	171	1,022
	Air Force	N/A	418	29	22	51
	Coast Guard	N/A	N/A	N/A	N/A	N/A
	total	N/A	31,430	3,471	907	4,378
other[12]						

[1]Data in this column account for the total number of wounds, except for Marine Corps data for World War II, the Spanish-American War, and earlier wars, which represent the number of combatants wounded. [2]Estimate. [3]Excluding unavailable data from one or more service branches. [4]US service members only. [5]Includes air service. [6]Number eligible for Korean Service Medal. [7]Excludes 150,341 wounded who did not require hospital care. [8]Data for military personnel serving in the theater of operation. [9]Includes Coast Guard. [10]Operation Enduring Freedom; data for 7 Oct 2001–3 Apr 2010. [11]Operation Iraqi Freedom; data for 19 Mar 2003–3 Apr 2010. [12]US casualties of other recent military operations: in Grenada (1983) 119 wounded, 19 battle deaths; in Panama (1989) 324 wounded, 23 battle deaths; in Somalia (1992–94) 153 wounded, 43 battle deaths.

Leading Department of Defense Contractors

Top 40 Department of Defense contractors listed according to net value of prime contract awards, fiscal year 2008. Source: <www.fpds.gov>.

RANK	CONTRACTOR	AMOUNT (US$)
1	Lockheed Martin	29,091,044,406
2	Boeing	21,794,832,402
3	Northrop Grumman	19,464,937,010
4	BAE Systems	15,038,101,347
5	General Dynamics	14,771,896,697
6	Raytheon	14,313,645,582
7	Emerson Construction	13,931,307,017
8	United Technologies	8,201,621,967
9	L-3 Communications Holdings	6,006,831,672
10	KBR[1]	5,997,089,900
11	Navistar Defense	4,727,948,333
12	MacAndrews & Forbes Holdings	4,712,820,926
13	ITT	4,182,766,764
14	Science Applications International	3,881,758,597
15	General Electric	3,439,895,609
16	Humana	2,959,865,102
17	Bell Boeing Joint Project Office	2,801,354,948
18	Textron	2,793,285,550
19	Computer Sciences	2,772,927,223
20	Health Net	2,438,342,941
21	TriWest Healthcare Alliance	2,366,975,634
22	Public Warehousing	2,141,188,027
23	Bechtel Group	2,033,961,609
24	URS	2,019,716,428
25	Finmeccanica	1,982,775,250
26	Hewlett-Packard	1,914,397,306
27	Oshkosh	1,863,470,025
28	Booz Allen Hamilton	1,857,118,081
29	Harris	1,807,033,159
30	Federal Express Charter Program Team Arrangement	1,785,873,190
31	BP	1,719,803,123
32	Honeywell International	1,605,129,063
33	Royal Dutch Shell	1,594,279,311
34	Evergreen International Airlines	1,445,897,765
35	DynCorp International	1,427,082,560
36	Force Protection	1,360,427,188

Leading Department of Defense Contractors (continued)

RANK	CONTRACTOR	AMOUNT (US$)	RANK	CONTRACTOR	AMOUNT (US$)
37	Hensel Phelps Construction	1,279,912,143	39	CACI International	1,253,887,843
38	AmerisourceBergen	1,270,761,740	40	Alliant Techsystems	1,246,757,328

[1]Until April 2007 KBR was a subsidiary of Halliburton.

CIA Directors

The National Security Act of 26 Jul 1947 established the Central Intelligence Agency (CIA) on 18 Sep 1947. The director coordinates the nation's intelligence activities and informs the president on issues of national security. Acting directors are not included in this table.

NAME	DATES OF SERVICE
Rear Adm. Sidney W. Souers, USNR	23 Jan 1946–9 Jun 1946
Lt. Gen. Hoyt S. Vandenberg, USA	10 Jun 1946–30 Apr 1947
Rear Adm. Roscoe H. Hillenkoetter, USN	1 May 1947–6 Oct 1950
Gen. Walter Bedell Smith, USA	7 Oct 1950–9 Feb 1953
Allen W. Dulles	26 Feb 1953–28 Nov 1961
John A. McCone	29 Nov 1961–27 Apr 1965
Vice Adm. William F. Raborn, Jr., USN	28 Apr 1965–29 Jun 1966
Richard M. Helms	30 Jun 1966–1 Feb 1973
James R. Schlesinger	2 Feb 1973–2 Jul 1973
William E. Colby	4 Sep 1973–29 Jan 1976
George H.W. Bush	30 Jan 1976–20 Jan 1977
Adm. Stansfield Turner, USN	9 Mar 1977–20 Jan 1981
William J. Casey	28 Jan 1981–29 Jan 1987
William H. Webster	26 May 1987–31 Aug 1991
Robert M. Gates	6 Nov 1991–20 Jan 1993
R. James Woolsey	5 Feb 1993–10 Jan 1995
John M. Deutch	10 May 1995–15 Dec 1996
George J. Tenet	11 Jul 1997–11 Jul 2004
Porter J. Goss	24 Sep 2004–26 May 2006
Gen. Michael V. Hayden, USAF	30 May 2006–12 Feb 2009
Leon E. Panetta	13 Feb 2009–

National Security Council (NSC)

The National Security Act of 1947 established the NSC to advise the president on issues relating to national security.

chair	Barack Obama (president)
members	Joe Biden (vice president)
	Hillary Clinton (secretary of state)
	Robert M. Gates (secretary of defense)
	Steven Chu (secretary of energy)
	Tim Geithner (secretary of the treasury)
	Eric Holder (attorney general)
	Janet Napolitano (secretary of homeland security)
	Susan Rice (US ambassador to the United Nations)
	Rahm Emanuel (chief of staff to the president)
	James L. Jones (assistant to the president for national security affairs)
military adviser	Mike Mullen (chairman of the Joint Chiefs of Staff)
intelligence adviser	James Clapper (director of national intelligence)
additional participants[1]	Robert F. Bauer (counsel to the president)
	Thomas E. Donilon (deputy assistant to the president for national security affairs)

In 1953 Pres. Dwight D. Eisenhower established the office of assistant to the president for national security affairs (commonly referred to as the national security advisor). Holders of this office are listed below.

NAME	DATES OF SERVICE
Robert Cutler	23 Mar 1953–1 Apr 1955
Dillon Anderson	2 Apr 1955–1 Sep 1956
Robert Cutler	7 Jan 1957–23 Jun 1958
Gordon Gray	24 Jun 1958–13 Jan 1961
McGeorge Bundy	20 Jan 1961–28 Feb 1966
Walt W. Rostow	1 Apr 1966–1 Dec 1968
Henry A. Kissinger	2 Dec 1968–2 Nov 1975[2]
Brent Scowcroft	3 Nov 1975–19 Jan 1977
Zbigniew Brzezinski	20 Jan 1977–20 Jan 1981
Richard V. Allen	21 Jan 1981–4 Jan 1982
William P. Clark	4 Jan 1982–16 Oct 1983
Robert C. McFarlane	17 Oct 1983–3 Dec 1985
John M. Poindexter	4 Dec 1985–25 Nov 1986
Frank C. Carlucci	2 Dec 1986–22 Nov 1987
Colin L. Powell	23 Nov 1987–19 Jan 1989
Brent Scowcroft	20 Jan 1989–19 Jan 1993
W. Anthony Lake	20 Jan 1993–13 Mar 1997
Samuel R. Berger	14 Mar 1997–20 Jan 2001
Condoleezza Rice	22 Jan 2001–25 Jan 2005
Stephen Hadley	26 Jan 2005–19 Jan 2009
James L. Jones	20 Jan 2009–

[1]Regular attendees include the secretary of commerce, the US trade representative, the assistant to the president for economic policy, the chair of the Council of Economic Advisers, and the assistant to the president for homeland security and counterterrorism. [2]Kissinger served concurrently as secretary of state from 21 Sep 1973.

United States Population

US Population by Race, Sex, Median Age, and Residence

Numbers are in thousands ('000) except for the median age figures and the residency percentages. N/A means not available. Source: US Census Bureau.

| | RACE | | | SEX | | MEDIAN | RESIDENCE[2] | |
YEAR	WHITE	BLACK	OTHER[1]	MALE	FEMALE	AGE	URBAN (%)	RURAL (%)
1790	3,172	757	N/A	N/A	N/A	N/A	5.1	94.9
1800	4,306	1,002	N/A	N/A	N/A	N/A	6.1	93.9
1810	5,862	1,378	N/A	N/A	N/A	N/A	7.3	92.7
1820	7,867	1,772	N/A	4,897	4,742	16.7	7.2	92.8
1830	10,537	2,329	N/A	6,532	6,334	17.2	8.8	91.2
1840	14,196	2,874	N/A	8,689	8,381	17.8	10.8	89.2
1850	19,553	3,639	N/A	11,838	11,354	18.9	15.4	84.6
1860	26,923	4,442	79	16,085	15,358	19.4	19.8	80.2
1870	34,337	5,392	89	19,494	19,065	20.2	25.7	74.3
1880	43,403	6,581	172	25,519	24,637	20.9	28.2	71.8
1890	55,101	7,489	358	32,237	30,711	22.0	35.1	64.9
1900	66,809	8,834	351	38,816	37,178	22.9	39.6	60.4
1910	81,732	9,828	413	47,332	44,640	24.1	45.6	54.4
1920	94,821	10,463	427	53,900	51,810	25.3	51.2	48.8
1930	110,287	11,891	597	62,137	60,638	26.4	56.1	43.9
1940	118,215	12,866	589	66,062	65,608	29.0	56.5	43.5
1950	134,942	15,042	713	74,833	75,864	30.2	64.0	36.0
1960	158,832	18,872	1,620	88,331	90,992	29.5	69.9	30.1
1970	178,098	22,581	2,557	98,926	104,309	28.0	73.6	26.3
1980	194,713	26,683	5,150	110,053	116,493	30.0	73.7	26.3
1990	199,686	29,986	9,233	121,271	127,494	32.8	78.0	22.0
2000	211,461	34,658	13,118	138,054	143,368	35.3	79.0	21.0
2009	244,298	39,641	23,067	151,449	155,557	36.8	N/A	N/A

[1]*"Other" refers to Asians, Native Hawaiians, other Pacific Islanders, American Indians, Alaska Natives, and those belonging to two or more races. Data for Alaska and Hawaii are not included until 1960, the first census after they became states in 1959.* [2]*The census definitions for urban and rural areas have changed through the decades.*

US Population by Race and Hispanic Origin

Census 2000 was the first US census in which individuals could report themselves as being of more than one race. For the comparison between these census results and the 2009 data, this table uses the

2000 census information that was revised in April 2000. Hispanic or Latino people may be of any race.

Source: US Census Bureau.

| | 2000 CENSUS | | 2009 | | % DIFFERENCE |
RACE	NUMBER[1]	%[1]	NUMBER[1]	%[1]	2000/2009[1]
white	228,104,485	81.1	244,298,393	79.6	+7.1
black or African American	35,704,124	12.7	39,641,060	12.9	+11.0
American Indian or Alaska Native	2,663,818	0.9	3,151,284	1.0	+18.3
Asian	10,589,265	3.8	14,013,954	4.6	+32.3
Native Hawaiian or other Pacific Islander	462,534	0.2	578,353	0.2	+25.0
two or more races	3,897,680	1.4	5,323,506	1.7	+36.6
total population	**281,421,906**	**100.0**	**307,006,550**	**100.0**	**+9.1**

| | 2000 CENSUS | | 2009 | | % DIFFERENCE |
HISPANIC OR LATINO POPULATION	NUMBER[1]	%[1]	NUMBER[1]	%[1]	2000/2009[1]
Hispanic or Latino (of any race)	35,305,818	12.5	48,419,324	15.8	+37.1
not Hispanic or Latino	246,116,088	87.5	258,587,226	84.2	+5.1
total population	**281,421,906**	**100.0**	**307,006,550**	**100.0**	**+9.1**

[1]*Detail may not add to total given because of rounding.*

State Populations, 1790–2009

Resident population of the states and the District of Columbia. Numbers are in thousands ('000)[1].
Source: US Census Bureau.

STATE	1790	1800	1810	1820	1830	1840	1850	1860	1870	1880	1890	1900
AL		1	9	128	310	591	772	964	997	1,263	1,513	1,829
AK										33	32	64
AZ									10	40	88	123
AR			1	14	30	98	210	435	484	803	1,128	1,312
CA							93	380	560	865	1,213	1,485
CO								34	40	194	413	540
CT	238	251	262	275	298	310	371	460	537	623	746	908
DE	59	64	73	73	77	78	92	112	125	147	168	185
DC		8	15	23	30	34	52	75	132	178	230	279
FL					35	54	87	140	188	269	391	529
GA	83	163	252	341	517	691	906	1,057	1,184	1,542	1,837	2,216
HI												154
ID									15	33	89	162
IL			12	55	157	476	851	1,712	2,540	3,078	3,826	4,822
IN		6	25	147	343	686	988	1,350	1,681	1,978	2,192	2,516
IA						43	192	675	1,194	1,625	1,912	2,232
KS								107	364	996	1,428	1,470
KY	74	221	407	564	688	780	982	1,156	1,321	1,649	1,859	2,147
LA			77	153	216	352	518	708	727	940	1,119	1,382
ME	97	152	229	298	399	502	583	628	627	649	661	694
MD	320	342	381	407	447	470	583	687	781	935	1,042	1,188
MA	379	423	472	523	610	738	995	1,231	1,457	1,783	2,239	2,805
MI			5	9	32	212	398	749	1,184	1,637	2,094	2,421
MN							6	172	440	781	1,310	1,751
MS		8	31	75	137	376	607	791	828	1,132	1,290	1,551
MO			20	67	140	384	682	1,182	1,721	2,168	2,679	3,107
MT									21	39	143	243
NE								29	123	452	1,063	1,066
NV								7	42	62	47	42
NH	142	184	214	244	269	285	318	326	318	347	377	412
NJ	184	211	246	278	321	373	490	672	906	1,131	1,445	1,884
NM							62	94	92	120	160	195
NY	340	589	959	1,373	1,919	2,429	3,097	3,881	4,383	5,083	6,003	7,269
NC	394	478	556	639	738	753	869	993	1,071	1,400	1,618	1,894
ND									5	2	37	191	319
OH		45	231	581	938	1,519	1,980	2,340	2,665	3,198	3,672	4,158
OK										12	259	790
OR							12	52	91	175	318	414
PA	434	602	810	1,049	1,348	1,724	2,312	2,906	3,522	4,283	5,258	6,302
RI	69	69	77	83	97	109	148	175	217	277	346	429
SC	249	346	415	503	581	594	669	704	706	996	1,151	1,340
SD									12	98	349	402
TN	36	106	262	423	682	829	1,003	1,110	1,259	1,542	1,768	2,021
TX							213	604	819	1,592	2,236	3,049
UT							11	40	87	144	211	277
VT	85	154	218	236	281	292	314	315	331	332	332	344
VA	692	808	878	938	1,044	1,025	1,119	1,220	1,225	1,513	1,656	1,854
WA							1	12	24	75	357	518
WV	56	79	105	137	177	225	302	377	442	618	763	959
WI						31	305	776	1,055	1,315	1,693	2,069
WY									9	21	63	93
US total[2]	3,929	5,308	7,240	9,638	12,866	17,069	23,192	31,443	39,818[3]	50,156	62,948	75,995

[1]*Detail may not add to total given because of rounding.* [2]*Data for Alaska and Hawaii are not included until 1960,*

State Populations, 1790–2009 (continued)

1910	1920	1930	1940	1950	1960	1970	1980	1990	2000	2009 EST.
2,138	2,348	2,646	2,833	3,062	3,267	3,444	3,894	4,040	4,452	4,709
64	55	59	73	129	226	300	402	550	627	698
204	334	436	499	750	1,302	1,771	2,718	3,665	5,167	6,596
1,574	1,752	1,854	1,949	1,910	1,786	1,923	2,286	2,351	2,678	2,889
2,378	3,427	5,677	6,907	10,586	15,717	19,953	23,668	29,811	33,999	36,962
799	940	1,036	1,123	1,325	1,754	2,207	2,890	3,294	4,328	5,025
1,115	1,381	1,607	1,709	2,007	2,535	3,032	3,108	3,287	3,412	3,518
202	223	238	267	318	446	548	594	666	786	885
331	438	487	663	802	764	757	638	607	572	600
753	968	1,468	1,897	2,771	4,952	6,789	9,746	12,938	16,047	18,538
2,609	2,896	2,909	3,124	3,445	3,943	4,590	5,463	6,478	8,230	9,829
192	256	368	423	500	633	769	965	1,108	1,211	1,295
326	432	445	525	589	667	713	944	1,007	1,299	1,546
5,639	6,485	7,631	7,897	8,712	10,081	11,114	11,427	11,431	12,438	12,910
2,701	2,930	3,239	3,428	3,934	4,662	5,194	5,490	5,544	6,091	6,423
2,225	2,404	2,471	2,538	2,621	2,758	2,824	2,914	2,777	2,928	3,008
1,691	1,769	1,881	1,801	1,905	2,179	2,247	2,364	2,478	2,693	2,819
2,290	2,417	2,615	2,846	2,945	3,038	3,219	3,661	3,687	4,049	4,314
1,656	1,799	2,102	2,364	2,684	3,257	3,641	4,206	4,222	4,469	4,492
742	768	797	847	914	969	992	1,125	1,228	1,277	1,318
1,295	1,450	1,632	1,821	2,343	3,101	3,922	4,217	4,781	5,310	5,699
3,366	3,852	4,250	4,317	4,691	5,149	5,689	5,737	6,016	6,363	6,594
2,810	3,668	4,842	5,256	6,372	7,823	8,875	9,262	9,295	9,955	9,970
2,076	2,387	2,564	2,792	2,982	3,414	3,805	4,076	4,376	4,934	5,266
1,797	1,791	2,010	2,184	2,179	2,178	2,217	2,521	2,575	2,848	2,952
3,293	3,404	3,629	3,785	3,955	4,320	4,677	4,917	5,117	5,606	5,988
376	549	538	559	591	675	694	787	799	903	975
1,192	1,296	1,378	1,316	1,326	1,411	1,483	1,570	1,578	1,713	1,797
82	77	91	110	160	285	489	800	1,202	2,018	2,643
431	443	465	492	533	607	738	921	1,109	1,240	1,325
2,537	3,156	4,041	4,160	4,835	6,067	7,168	7,365	7,748	8,431	8,708
327	360	423	532	681	951	1,016	1,303	1,515	1,821	2,010
9,114	10,385	12,588	13,479	14,830	16,782	18,237	17,558	17,991	18,998	19,541
2,206	2,559	3,170	3,572	4,062	4,556	5,082	5,882	6,632	8,079	9,381
577	647	681	642	620	632	618	653	639	641	647
4,767	5,759	6,647	6,908	7,947	9,706	10,652	10,798	10,847	11,364	11,543
1,657	2,028	2,396	2,336	2,233	2,328	2,559	3,025	3,146	3,454	3,687
673	783	954	1,090	1,521	1,769	2,091	2,633	2,842	3,431	3,826
7,665	8,720	9,631	9,900	10,498	11,319	11,794	11,864	11,883	12,285	12,605
543	604	687	713	792	859	947	947	1,003	1,051	1,053
1,515	1,684	1,739	1,900	2,117	2,383	2,591	3,122	3,486	4,023	4,561
584	637	693	643	653	681	666	691	696	756	812
2,185	2,338	2,617	2,916	3,292	3,567	3,924	4,591	4,877	5,703	6,296
3,897	4,663	5,825	6,415	7,711	9,580	11,197	14,229	16,986	20,946	24,782
373	449	508	550	689	891	1,059	1,461	1,723	2,244	2,785
356	352	360	359	378	390	444	511	563	610	622
2,062	2,309	2,422	2,678	3,319	3,967	4,648	5,347	6,189	7,104	7,883
1,142	1,357	1,563	1,736	2,379	2,853	3,409	4,132	4,867	5,911	6,664
1,221	1,464	1,729	1,902	2,006	1,860	1,744	1,950	1,793	1,807	1,820
2,334	2,632	2,939	3,138	3,435	3,952	4,418	4,706	4,892	5,374	5,655
146	194	226	251	291	330	332	470	454	494	544
91,972	105,711	122,775	131,669	150,697	179,323	203,302[3]	226,546[3]	248,791[3]	282,172[3]	307,008

the first census after they became states in 1959. [3]Figures were revised by the Census Bureau after the census.

Population of US Territories

Total midyear population. Source: US Census Bureau.

YEAR	PUERTO RICO	GUAM	VIRGIN ISLANDS	AMERICAN SAMOA	NORTHERN MARIANA ISLANDS
1960	2,358,000	66,900	32,500	20,000	8,861
1965	2,596,774	74,100	43,500	24,600	10,465
1970	2,721,754	86,470	63,476	27,267	12,359
1975	2,935,124	102,110	94,484	29,640	14,938
1980	3,209,648	106,869	99,636	32,418	16,890
1985	3,382,106	120,615	100,760	38,633	21,386
1990	3,536,910	134,125	103,963	47,199	44,037
1995	3,683,103	144,190	107,817	53,906	57,229
2000	3,814,413	155,324	108,639	57,771	69,706
2005	3,910,707	168,614	109,600	62,399	70,636
2010	3,977,663	180,865	109,775	66,432	48,317

Foreign-Born Population in the US, 1850–2008

The foreign-born population consists of persons born outside the United States to parents who were not US citizens. Populations of Alaska and Hawaii were included starting in 1960. In 1850 and 1860 data, the entire slave population was considered native-born.

Source: Statistical Abstract of the United States: 2010.

YEAR	POPULATION TOTAL	FOREIGN-BORN	% OF TOTAL	YEAR	POPULATION TOTAL	FOREIGN-BORN	% OF TOTAL
1850	23,191,876	2,244,602	9.7	1940	131,669,275	11,594,896	8.8
1860	31,443,321	4,138,697	13.2	1950	150,216,110	10,347,395	6.9
1870	38,558,371	5,567,229	14.4	1960	179,325,671	9,738,091	5.4
1880	50,155,783	6,679,943	13.3	1970	203,210,158	9,619,302	4.7
1890	62,622,250	9,249,547	14.8	1980	226,545,805	14,079,906	6.2
1900	75,994,575	10,341,276	13.6	1990	248,709,873	19,767,316	7.9
1910	91,972,266	13,515,886	14.7	2000	281,421,906	31,107,889	11.1
1920	105,710,620	13,920,692	13.2	2007[1]	296,824,000	37,279,000	12.6
1930	122,775,046	14,204,149	11.6	2008[1]	299,106,000	37,264,000	12.5

[1]As of March.

Total Immigrants Admitted to the US, 1901–2009

Numbers shown include only immigrant aliens admitted for permanent residence and are for fiscal years. Currently the fiscal year begins 1 October and ends 30 September. Prior to 1976, the fiscal year began 1 July and ended 30 June.

Source: Yearbook of Immigration Statistics, 2009.

YEAR	NUMBER	YEAR	NUMBER	YEAR	NUMBER	YEAR	NUMBER
1901	487,918	1911	878,587	1921	805,228	1931	97,139
1902	648,743	1912	838,172	1922	309,556	1932	35,576
1903	857,046	1913	1,197,892	1923	522,919	1933	23,068
1904	812,870	1914	1,218,480	1924	706,896	1934	29,470
1905	1,026,499	1915	326,700	1925	294,314	1935	34,956
1906	1,100,735	1916	298,826	1926	304,488	1936	36,329
1907	1,285,349	1917	295,403	1927	335,175	1937	50,244
1908	782,870	1918	110,618	1928	307,255	1938	67,895
1909	751,786	1919	141,132	1929	279,678	1939	82,998
1910	1,041,570	1920	430,001	1930	241,700	1940	70,756
totals 1901–10	8,795,386	1911–20	5,735,811	1921–30	4,107,209	1931–40	528,431
1941	51,776	1951	205,717	1961	271,344	1971	370,478
1942	28,781	1952	265,520	1962	283,763	1972	384,685
1943	23,725	1953	170,434	1963	306,260	1973	398,515
1944	28,551	1954	208,177	1964	292,248	1974	393,919
1945	38,119	1955	237,790	1965	296,697	1975	385,378
1946	108,721	1956	321,625	1966	323,040	1976[1]	499,093
1947	147,292	1957	326,867	1967	361,972	1977	458,755
1948	170,570	1958	253,265	1968	454,448	1978	589,810
1949	188,317	1959	260,686	1969	358,579	1979	394,244
1950	249,187	1960	265,398	1970	373,326	1980	524,295
totals 1941–50	1,035,039	1951–60	2,515,479	1961–70	3,321,677	1971–80	4,399,172

Total Immigrants Admitted to the US, 1901–2009 (continued)

YEAR	NUMBER	YEAR	NUMBER	YEAR	NUMBER
1981	595,014	1991	1,826,595	2001	1,058,902
1982	533,624	1992	973,445	2002	1,059,356
1983	550,052	1993	903,916	2003	703,542
1984	541,811	1994	803,993	2004	957,883
1985	568,149	1995	720,177	2005	1,122,257
1986	600,027	1996	915,560	2006	1,266,129
1987	599,889	1997	797,847	2007	1,052,415
1988	641,346	1998	653,206	2008	1,107,126
1989	1,090,172	1999	644,787	2009	1,130,818
1990	1,535,872	2000	841,002		
totals 1981–90	7,255,956	1991–2000	9,080,528	2001–09	9,458,428

totals 1901–2009: 56,233,116

[1]Includes the 15 months from 1 Jul 1975 through 30 Sep 1976.

Immigrants Admitted to the US by State of Residence and Country of Birth
Fiscal year 2009. Korea used to designate both North and South Korea.
Source: <www.dhs.gov>.

STATE OF RESIDENCE	TOTAL IMMIGRANTS	TOP FIVE COUNTRIES OF BIRTH (NUMBER OF IMMIGRANTS)
Alabama	3,891	Mexico (450), India (291), Korea (245), China (240), Philippines (175)
Alaska	1,608	Philippines (564), Korea (71), Mexico (71), Thailand (67), China (65)
Arizona	20,997	Mexico (9,168), Philippines (877), Iraq (751), India (553), Somalia (509)
Arkansas	2,942	Mexico (1,129), El Salvador (197), India (175), Philippines (164), China (110)
California	227,876	Mexico (59,814), Philippines (24,937), China (17,139), India (12,826), Iran (11,227)
Colorado	12,841	Mexico (3,433), Ethiopia (718), Somalia (475), China (466), Vietnam (428)
Connecticut	13,632	Jamaica (1,031), India (866), Dominican Republic (733), China (616), Brazil (552)
Delaware	2,184	India (231), Mexico (190), Kenya (126), China (117), Haiti (97)
District of Columbia	2,934	Ethiopia (506), El Salvador (263), Nigeria (108), Dominican Republic (103), United Kingdom (87)
Florida	127,006	Cuba (31,928), Haiti (13,403), Colombia (11,139), Jamaica (6,655), Venezuela (6,381)
Georgia	28,396	Mexico (3,325), India (1,856), Korea (1,350), Nigeria (1,176), Vietnam (1,011)
Hawaii	6,929	Philippines (4,013), China (605), Japan (534), Korea (264), Vietnam (213)
Idaho	3,120	Mexico (989), Uzbekistan (138), Philippines (123), Iraq (116), Myanmar (Burma) (97)
Illinois	41,889	Mexico (9,202), India (3,946), Poland (2,902), Philippines (2,553), China (1,739)
Indiana	9,087	Myanmar (Burma) (1,430), Mexico (1,312), India (657), China (434), Philippines (363)
Iowa	3,963	Mexico (890), Sudan (198), India (174), Vietnam (167), China (152)
Kansas	5,319	Mexico (1,448), Vietnam (358), India (281), Kenya (192), China (191)
Kentucky	5,260	Cuba (616), Mexico (339), Somalia (271), India (270), China (245)
Louisiana	4,299	Mexico (393), Vietnam (358), Honduras (276), India (242), China (228)
Maine	1,675	Somalia (422), Kenya (177), Canada (82), China (71), Sudan (66)
Maryland	26,722	Nigeria (1,878), El Salvador (1,635), India (1,518), Ethiopia (1,440), China (1,195)
Massachusetts	32,607	Dominican Republic (4,048), China (2,202), Brazil (2,025), Haiti (1,948), India (1,666)
Michigan	18,919	Iraq (2,691), India (1,294), Mexico (1,168), Bangladesh (908), Lebanon (829)
Minnesota	18,020	Somalia (4,173), Ethiopia (1,614), Kenya (1,159), Liberia (1,013), Mexico (869)
Mississippi	1,652	Mexico (260), India (204), Philippines (124), China (102), Vietnam (70)
Missouri	7,142	Mexico (651), China (405), India (377), Philippines (316), Vietnam (282)
Montana	553	Canada (67), Philippines (66), Mexico (50), China (39), Ethiopia (24)

Immigrants Admitted to the US by State of Residence and Country of Birth (continued)

STATE OF RESIDENCE	TOTAL IMMIGRANTS	TOP FIVE COUNTRIES OF BIRTH (NUMBER OF IMMIGRANTS)
Nebraska	3,989	Mexico (866), Somalia (420), Myanmar (Burma) (260), Sudan (249), Vietnam (170)
Nevada	12,334	Mexico (3,207), Philippines (2,080), Cuba (735), China (518), Ethiopia (508)
New Hampshire	2,483	Dominican Republic (197), China (151), India (148), Kenya (110), Brazil (87)
New Jersey	58,879	Dominican Republic (7,445), India (7,080), Colombia (2,867), Philippines (2,509), Peru (2,352)
New Mexico	3,887	Mexico (2,137), Philippines (151), China (133), Cuba (114), Vietnam (75)
New York	150,722	Dominican Republic (23,793), China (19,921), Bangladesh (8,529), Jamaica (7,104), Pakistan (4,798)
North Carolina	18,562	Mexico (2,923), Vietnam (1,158), India (1,026), China (709), Colombia (575)
North Dakota	843	Somalia (112), Kěnya (68), Canada (65), Iraq (46), Liberia (43)
Ohio	15,375	Somalia (1,470), India (1,101), China (774), Philippines (614), Ghana (538)
Oklahoma	5,007	Mexico (1,614), India (312), Vietnam (240), Myanmar (Burma) (226), Philippines (224)
Oregon	9,026	Mexico (2,043), Vietnam (567), Ukraine (552), Philippines (476), China (454)
Pennsylvania	24,105	India (2,142), Dominican Republic (1,848), China (1,620), Liberia (1,277), Vietnam (816)
Rhode Island	4,156	Dominican Republic (1,047), Cape Verde (436), Liberia (284), Guatemala (254), Colombia (223)
South Carolina	4,747	Mexico (654), India (309), Colombia (288), Philippines (232), China (210)
South Dakota	1,271	Ethiopia (136), Eritrea (73), Myanmar (Burma) (61), Tanzania (57), Somalia (55)
Tennessee	9,042	Mexico (1,010), Egypt (667), India (550), China (407), Somalia (364)
Texas	95,384	Mexico (38,597), India (4,716), Vietnam (3,361), Philippines (2,797), El Salvador (2,632)
Utah	6,466	Mexico (1,386), Peru (283), Myanmar (Burma) (259), Thailand (214), Vietnam (202)
Vermont	792	Somalia (60), Canada (52), China (46), United Kingdom (39), Iraq (30)
Virginia	29,825	India (1,944), El Salvador (1,646), Pakistan (1,514), Philippines (1,503), Korea (1,446)
Washington	27,562	Mexico (2,710), Philippines (2,169), India (1,670), Ukraine (1,540), Vietnam (1,539)
West Virginia	734	Philippines (67), China (58), India (55), Pakistan (40), Mexico (31)
Wisconsin	6,727	Mexico (1,276), India (509), China (361), Philippines (286), Thailand (233)
Wyoming	429	Mexico (109), China (36), Philippines (34), India (19), Cǎnada (18)

Americans 65 and Older, 1900–2010

Data for Hawaii and Alaska are included after 1950. Source: US Census Bureau.

CENSUS YEAR	NUMBER OF PEOPLE 65 AND OLDER	% OF TOTAL POPULATION	CENSUS YEAR	NUMBER OF PEOPLE 65 AND OLDER	% OF TOTAL POPULATION
1900	3,080,498	4.1	1960	16,559,580	9.2
1910	3,949,524	4.3	1970	20,065,502	9.8
1920	4,933,215	4.7	1980	25,549,427	11.3
1930	6,633,805	5.4	1990	31,241,831	12.6
1940	9,019,314	6.8	2000	34,991,753	12.4
1950	12,269,537	8.1	2010	40,228,712	13.0

Poverty Level by State, 1980–2008

Source: US Census Bureau. Detail may not add to total given because of rounding.

STATE	% OF PEOPLE IN POVERTY			NUMBER OF PEOPLE IN POVERTY ('000)		
	1980	1990	2008	1980	1990	2008
Alabama	21.2	19.2	14.3	810	779	675
Alaska	9.6	11.4	8.2	36	57	55

Poverty Level by State, 1980–2008 (continued)

STATE	% OF PEOPLE IN POVERTY			NUMBER OF PEOPLE IN POVERTY ('000)		
	1980	1990	2008	1980	1990	2008
Arizona	12.8	13.7	18.0	354	484	1,172
Arkansas	21.5	19.6	15.3	484	472	431
California	11.0	13.9	14.6	2,619	4,128	5,344
Colorado	8.6	13.7	11.0	247	461	541
Connecticut	8.3	6.0	8.1	255	196	276
Delaware	11.8	6.9	9.6	68	48	82
District of Columbia	20.9	21.1	16.5	131	120	98
Florida	16.7	14.4	13.1	1,692	1,896	2,370
Georgia	13.9	15.8	15.5	727	1,001	1,477
Hawaii	8.5	11.0	9.9	81	121	125
Idaho	14.7	14.9	12.2	138	157	185
Illinois	12.3	13.7	12.3	1,386	1,606	1,564
Indiana	11.8	13.0	14.3	645	714	901
Iowa	10.8	10.4	9.5	311	289	285
Kansas	9.4	10.3	12.7	215	259	346
Kentucky	19.3	17.3	17.1	701	628	724
Louisiana	20.3	23.6	18.2	868	952	788
Maine	14.6	13.1	12.0	158	162	158
Maryland	9.5	9.9	8.7	389	468	481
Massachusetts	9.5	10.7	11.3	542	626	727
Michigan	12.9	14.3	13.0	1,194	1,315	1,273
Minnesota	8.7	12.0	9.9	342	524	506
Mississippi	24.3	25.7	18.1	591	684	525
Missouri	13.0	13.4	13.3	625	700	780
Montana	13.2	16.3	12.9	102	134	125
Nebraska	13.0	10.3	10.6	199	167	188
Nevada	8.3	9.8	10.8	70	119	278
New Hampshire	7.0	6.3	7.0	63	68	91
New Jersey	9.0	9.2	9.2	659	711	787
New Mexico	20.6	20.9	19.3	268	319	381
New York	13.8	14.3	14.2	2,391	2,571	2,734
North Carolina	15.0	13.0	13.9	877	829	1,285
North Dakota	15.5	13.7	11.8	99	87	74
Ohio	9.8	11.5	13.7	1,046	1,256	1,557
Oklahoma	13.9	15.6	13.6	406	481	484
Oregon	11.5	9.2	10.6	309	267	403
Pennsylvania	9.8	11.0	11.0	1,142	1,328	1,335
Rhode Island	10.7	7.5	12.7	97	71	132
South Carolina	16.8	16.2	14.0	534	548	624
South Dakota	18.8	13.3	13.1	127	93	104
Tennessee	19.6	16.9	15.0	884	833	924
Texas	15.7	15.9	15.9	2,247	2,684	3,834
Utah	10.0	8.2	7.6	148	143	209
Vermont	12.0	10.9	9.0	62	61	55
Virginia	12.4	11.1	10.3	647	705	799
Washington	12.7	8.9	10.4	538	434	680
West Virginia	15.2	18.1	14.5	297	328	260
Wisconsin	8.5	9.3	9.8	403	448	544
Wyoming	10.4	11.0	10.1	49	51	54
all US	13.0	13.5	13.2	29,272	33,585	39,830

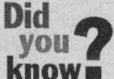

Did you know? Ouroboros was the emblematic serpent of ancient Egypt and Greece, represented with its tail in its mouth as continually devouring itself and being reborn. It represented the eternal cycle of destruction and re-creation. In the 19th century, a vision of Ouroboros gave the German chemist Friedrich August Kekule von Stradonitz the idea of linked carbon atoms forming the benzene ring.

States and Other Areas of the United States

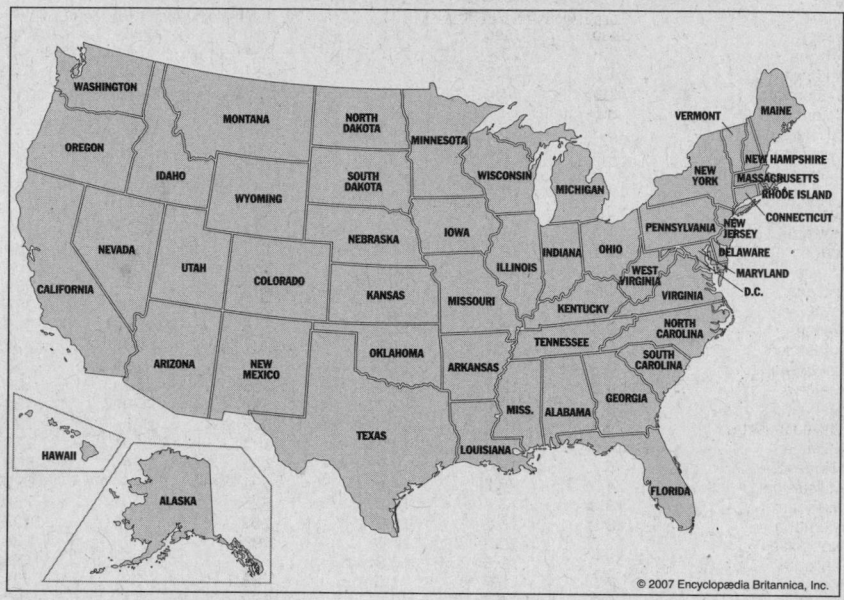

© 2007 Encyclopædia Britannica, Inc.

Alabama

Name: Alabama, from the Choctaw language, meaning "thicket clearers." **Nickname:** Heart of Dixie. **Capital:** Montgomery. **Rank:** population: 23rd; area: 30th. **Motto:** "Audemus jura nostra defendere" ("We dare defend our rights"). **Song:** "Alabama," words by Julia S. Tutwiler and music by Edna Gockel Gussen. **Amphibian:** Red Hills salamander. **Bird:** yellowhammer. **Fish:** largemouth bass (freshwater); tarpon (saltwater). **Flower:** camellia. **Fossil:** *Basilosaurus cetoides.* **Gemstone:** star blue quartz. **Insect:** monarch butterfly. **Mineral:** hematite. **Reptile:** Alabama red-bellied turtle. **Rock:** marble. **Tree:** southern longleaf pine.

Natural features

Land area: 51,700 sq mi, 133,902 sq km. **Mountain ranges:** Appalachian, Raccoon, Lookout. **Highest point:** Cheaha Mountain, 734 m (2,407 ft). **Largest lake:** Lake Guntersville. **Major rivers:** Mobile, Alabama, Tombigbee, Tennessee, Chattahoochee. **Natural regions:** the Appalachian Plateaus, extending across the north-central region; Interior Low Plateaus, far north; Valley and Ridge Province and small portion of the Piedmont Province, covering the east; Coastal Plain, covering the southern half of the state. **Land use:** forest, 64.4%; agricultural, 7.5%; pasture, 0.2%; other, 27.9%.

People

Population (2009): 4,708,708; persons per sq mi 91.1, persons per sq km 35.2. **Vital statistics** (2007; per 1,000 population): birth rate, 14.0; death rate, 10.1; marriage rate, 9.2; divorce rate, 4.3. **Major cities** (2008): Birmingham 228,798; Montgomery 202,696; Mobile 191,022; Huntsville 176,645; Tuscaloosa 90,221.

Government

Statehood: entered the Union on 14 Dec 1819 as the 22nd state. **State constitution:** adopted 1901. **Representation in US Congress:** 2 senators; 7 representatives. **Electoral college:** 9 votes. **Political divisions:** 67 counties.

Economy

Employment (2008): services 30.6%; government 15.6%; trade 14.4%; finance, insurance, real estate 13.8%; manufacturing 11.1%. **Production** (2008): finance, insurance, real estate 21.4%; manufacturing 17.2%; government 16.3%; services 15.5%; trade 13.5%. **Chief agricultural products:** *Crops:* cotton, corn (maize), soybeans, peanuts (groundnuts), potatoes, sweet potatoes, peaches, pecans, winter wheat. *Livestock:* cattle and calves, poultry, hogs. *Fish catch:* catfish, shrimp, crab, mussels, oysters. **Chief manufactured products:** food products; textiles; wearing apparel; wood products; mobile homes; refined petroleum products; plastics and rubber products; base metals.

Internet resources: <www.alabama.travel>; <www. alabama.gov>.

Alaska

Name: Alaska, from the Aleut words *alaxsxa* and *alaxsxix*, meaning "mainland" or "great land." **Nickname:** The Last Frontier. **Capital:** Juneau. **Rank:** population: 47th; area: 1st. **Motto:** "North to the future." **Song:** "Alaska's Flag," words by Marie Drake and music by Elinor Dusenbury. **Bird:** willow ptarmigan. **Fish:** giant king salmon. **Flower:** forget-me-not. **Fossil:** *Mammuthus primigenius* (woolly mammoth). **Gemstone:** jade. **Insect:** four-spot skimmer dragonfly. **Mammal:** moose. **Marine mammal:** bowhead whale. **Mineral:** gold. **Tree:** sitka spruce.

Natural features

Land area: 589,194 sq mi, 1,526,005 sq km. **Mountain ranges:** Wrangell, Chugach, Alaska, Brooks, Aleutian, Boundary. **Highest point:** Mt. McKinley (Denali), 6,194 m (20,320 ft). **Largest lake:** Iliamna Lake. **Major rivers:** Yukon, Porcupine, Tanana, Koyukuk, Noataks. **Natural regions:** panhandle, a narrow strip of land that includes portions of the Coast Mountains; coastal archipelago and the Gulf of Alaska islands; the Alaska Peninsula and Aleutian island chain that separates the North Pacific from the Bering Sea; the Alaska Range, extending across the south-central region; the Interior Plateau, including the basin of the Yukon River, the central plains and tablelands of the interior, the Seward Peninsula to the west, and the Brooks Range, sometimes called the North Slope, to the north; the Arctic Coastal Plain, a treeless region of tundra lying at the northernmost edge of the state; tundra-covered islands of the Bering Sea. **Land use:** forest, 24.1%; pasture, 0.0%; other, 75.9%.

People

Population (2009): 698,473; persons per sq mi 1.2, person per sq km 0.5. **Vital statistics** (2007; per 1,000 population): birth rate, 16.2; death rate, 5.1; marriage rate, 8.4; divorce rate, 4.3. **Major cities** (2008): Anchorage 279,243; Fairbanks 35,132; **Juneau 30,988;** Wasilla 10,256; Sitka 8,889.

Government

Statehood: entered the Union on 3 Jan 1959 as the 49th state. **State constitution:** adopted 1956. **Representation in US Congress:** 2 senators; 1 representative. **Electoral college:** 3 votes. **Political divisions:** 16 boroughs.

Economy

Employment (2008): services 28.9%; government 23.5%; finance, insurance, real estate 12.0%; trade 11.9%; transportation, public utilities 7.7%. **Production** (2008): mining 31.7%; government 17.6%; finance, insurance, real estate 13.9%; transportation, public utilities 12.7%; services 11.5%. **Chief agricultural products:** *Crops:* hay, milk, potatoes, timber. *Livestock:* cattle and calves, pigs. *Fish catch:* salmon, herring, groundfish, shellfish, crab, shrimp. **Chief manufactured products:** processed fish and seafood (fresh, frozen, canned, and cured); wood products; paper products; transportation products.

Internet resources: <www.travelalaska.com>; <www.alaska.gov>.

Arizona

Name: Arizona, derived from the Basque term for "place of oaks" or "the good oak tree." **Nickname:** Grand Canyon State. **Capital:** Phoenix. **Rank:** population: 14th; area: 6th. **Motto:** "Ditat Deus" ("God enriches"). **Song:** "Arizona March Song," words by Margaret Rowe Clifford and music by Maurice Blumenthal. **Amphibian:** Arizona treefrog. **Bird:** cactus wren. **Fish:** Arizona trout. **Flower:** saguaro blossom. **Fossil:** petrified wood. **Gemstone:** turquoise. **Mammal:** ringtail. **Reptile:** Arizona ridgenose rattlesnake. **Tree:** palo verde.

Natural features

Land area: 113,999 sq mi, 295,256 sq km. **Mountain ranges:** Black, Gila Bend, Chuska, Hualapai, San Francisco, White. **Highest point:** Humphreys Peak, 3,851 m (12,633 ft). **Largest lake:** Lake Roosevelt. **Major rivers:** Colorado, Little Colorado, Verde, Salt, Gila. **Natural regions:** the Colorado Plateaus, northeast third of the state, include the Grand Canyon and the Painted Desert; the Basin and Range Province, south, east, central, and northwest, includes the Sonoran Desert in the southwest corner and part of the Great Basin Desert to the northwest. **Land use:** pasture, 44.2%; forest, 5.7%; agricultural, 1.3%; other, 48.8%.

People

Population (2009): 6,595,778; persons per sq mi 57.9, persons per sq km 22.3. **Vital statistics** (2007; per 1,000 population): birth rate, 16.2; death rate, 7.2; marriage rate, 6.2; divorce rate, 3.9. **Major cities** (2008): **Phoenix 1,567,924;** Tucson 541,811; Mesa 463,552; Glendale 251,522; Chandler 247,140; Scottsdale 235,371; Gilbert 216,449; Tempe 175,523.

Government

Statehood: entered the Union on 14 Feb 1912 as the 48th state. **State constitution:** adopted 1911. **Representation in US Congress:** 2 senators; 8 representatives. **Electoral college:** 10 votes. **Political divisions:** 15 counties.

Economy

Employment (2008): services 33.6%; finance, insurance, real estate 18.9%; trade 14.9%; government 13.3%; construction 7.2%. **Production** (2008): finance, insurance, real estate 30.8%; services 19.4%; trade 13.4%; government 13.0%; manufacturing 7.8%. **Chief agricultural products:** *Crops:* cotton and cottonseed, wheat, sorghum, hay, barley, corn (maize), potatoes, grapes, apples, dairy products. *Livestock:* cattle and calves, hogs and pigs, sheep and lambs, angora goats. **Chief manufactured products:** semiconductors; telecommunications equipment; electrical equipment; transportation equipment; soap products; nonferrous metal products.

Internet resources: <www.arizonaguide.com>; <http://az.gov>.

Did you know? Tombstone AZ was ironically named by Ed Schieffelin, who discovered silver there after being told that all he would find would be his tombstone.

For details about state governments, see pages 608–613; for energy data, see pages 627–628.

Arkansas

Name: Arkansas, from *akansea,* an Illinois Indian word describing the Quapaw tribe (also known as the Arkansaw), meaning "people who live downstream." **Nickname:** Natural State. **Capital:** Little Rock. **Rank:** population: 32nd; area: 27th. **Motto:** "Regnat populus" ("The people rule"). **Songs:** "Arkansas," words and music by Wayland Holyfield; "Oh, Arkansas," words and music by by Terry Rose and Gary Klaff. **Bird:** mockingbird. **Flower:** apple blossom. **Gemstone:** diamond. **Insect:** honeybee. **Mammal:** white-tailed deer. **Mineral:** quartz crystal. **Rock:** bauxite. **Tree:** pine tree.

Natural features

Land area: 53,178 sq mi, 137,730 sq km. **Mountain ranges:** Ozark, Ouachita. **Highest point:** Mt. Magazine, 839 m (2,753 ft). **Largest lake:** Lake Chicot. **Major rivers:** Arkansas, Red, Ouachita, White. **Natural regions:** the Ozark Plateaus, including the Boston Mountains, north and northwest regions; the Ouachita Province, including the Arkansas valley and the Ouachita Mountains, central region; the Coastal Plain, extends from southwest to northeast. **Land use:** forest, 44.1%; agricultural, 22.1%; pasture, 0.1%; other, 33.7%.

People

Population (2009): 2,889,450; persons per sq mi 54.3, persons per sq km 21.0. **Vital statistics** (2007; per 1,000 population): birth rate, 14.6; death rate, 9.9; marriage rate, 11.9; divorce rate, 5.9. **Major cities** (2008): **Little Rock 189,515;** Fort Smith 84,716; Fayetteville 73,372; Springdale 68,180; Jonesboro 63,960.

Government

Statehood: entered the Union on 15 Jun 1836 as the 25th state. **State constitution:** adopted 1874. **Representation in US Congress:** 2 senators; 4 representatives. **Electoral college:** 6 votes. **Political divisions:** 75 counties.

Economy

Employment (2008): services 29.3%; government 14.5%; trade 13.7%; finance, insurance, real estate 12.6%; manufacturing 11.7%. **Production** (2008): finance, insurance, real estate 18.9%; manufacturing 17.4%; services 15.8%; government 13.9%; trade 13.9%. **Chief agricultural products:** *Crops:* corn (maize), cotton, soybeans, wheat, apples, blueberries, grapes, peaches, pecans, strawberries. *Livestock:* cattle and calves, hogs and pigs, poultry. *Fish catch:* catfish. **Chief manufactured products:** food products; lumber and paper products; refined petroleum products; chemical products; plastic and rubber products; base metals; fabricated metal products; machinery and apparatus; transportation equipment.

Internet resources: <www.arkansas.com>; <www.arkansas.gov>.

California

Name: California, from unknown origins. **Nickname:** Golden State. **Capital:** Sacramento. **Rank:** population: 1st; area: 3rd. **Motto:** "Eureka" ("I have found it"). **Song:** "I Love You, California," words by F.B. Silverwood and music by A.F. Frankenstein. **Bird:** California quail. **Fish:** golden trout (freshwater); garibaldi (saltwater). **Flower:** California poppy. **Fossil:** saber-tooth cat. **Gemstone:** benitoite. **Insect:** California dogface butterfly. **Mammal:** California grizzly bear. **Marine mammal:** California gray whale. **Mineral:** gold. **Reptile:** desert tortoise. **Rock:** serpentine. **Tree:** California redwood.

Natural features

Land area: 158,633 sq mi, 410,858 sq km. **Mountain ranges:** Coast, Sierra Nevada, Cascade, Santa Lucia, Klamath, Tehachapi, San Gabriel, San Bernardino. **Highest point:** Mt. Whitney, 4,418 m (14,494 ft). **Largest lake:** Lake Tahoe. **Major rivers:** Colorado, Sacramento, Pit, San Joaquin. **Natural regions:** Basin and Range Province, northeast corner, also eastern border with Arizona and southern Nevada; Cascade-Sierra Mountains, running from north to south along the east-central region; Pacific Border Province, west, including the Coast Ranges to the west, the Klamath Mountains to the north, the Los Angeles Ranges to the south, and the California Trough (commonly referred to as the Central Valley) to the east; Lower Californian Province, southwestern tip. **Land use:** pasture, 17.5%; forest, 13.7%; agricultural, 9.3%; other, 59.5%.

People

Population (2009): 36,961,664; persons per sq mi 233.0, persons per sq km 90.0. **Vital statistics** (2007; per 1,000 population): birth rate, 15.5; death rate, 6.4; marriage rate, 6.2; divorce rate (2001), 6.6. **Major cities** (2008): Los Angeles 3,833,995; San Diego 1,279,329; San Jose 948,279; San Francisco 808,976; Fresno 476,050; **Sacramento 463,794;** Long Beach 463,789; Oakland 404,155.

Government

Statehood: entered the Union on 9 Sep 1850 as the 31st state. **State constitution:** adopted 1879. **Representation in US Congress:** 2 senators; 53 representatives. **Electoral college:** 55 votes. **Political divisions:** 58 counties.

Economy

Employment (2008): services 32.5%; finance, insurance, real estate 19.7%; trade 13.7%; government 13.1%; manufacturing 7.2%. **Production** (2008): finance, insurance, real estate 33.6%; services 16.5%; trade 12.1%; government 11.7%; transportation; public utilities 10.2%. **Chief agricultural products:** *Crops:* wheat, oats, rice, apples, apricots, cherries, grapes, olives, peaches, pears, strawberries, onions, lima beans, artichokes, broccoli, snap beans, dairy products, eggs. *Livestock:* cattle and calves, sheep and lambs. *Fish catch:* bonito, halibut, mackerel, groundfish, rockfish (Pacific red snapper), sablefish (black cod), soles and sand dabs, sardines, white sea bass, shark, swordfish, tuna, crab, California spiny lobster, Pacific Ocean shrimp, prawns, squid. **Chief manufactured products:** food products; soft drinks; beer and wine; textiles; wearing apparel; lumber and wood products; paper products; printing; refined petroleum products; asphalt;

chemical products; plastic and rubber products; glass products; construction materials; base metals; fabricated metal products; machinery and apparatus; telecommunications equipment; semiconductors and computers; electronics; transportation equipment; furniture; medical equipment; sporting goods.

Internet resources: <www.visitcalifornia.com>; <www.ca.gov>.

Colorado

Name: Colorado, from a Spanish word meaning "red." Nickname: Centennial State. Capital: Denver. Rank: population: 22nd; area: 8th. Motto: "Nil sine numine" ("Nothing without Providence"). Songs: "Where the Columbines Grow," words and music by A.J. Flynn; "Rocky Mountain High," words and music by John Denver. Bird: lark bunting. Fish: greenback cutthroat trout. Flower: white and lavender columbine. Fossil: stegosaurus. Gemstone: aquamarine. Insect: Colorado hairstreak butterfly. Mammal: Rocky Mountain bighorn sheep. Tree: Colorado blue spruce.

Natural features

Land area: 104,094 sq mi, 269,602 sq km. Mountain ranges: Rocky, Front, Medicine Bow, Park, Rabbit Ears, San Juan, Sangre de Cristo, Sawatch. Highest point: Mt. Elbert, 4,399 m (14,433 ft). Largest lakes: Blue Mesa Reservoir (man-made); Grand Lake (natural). Major rivers: Colorado, Arkansas, South Platte, Rio Grande. Natural regions: the Great Plains Province, eastern half of state, includes the High Plains to the east, Colorado Piedmont to the west, and Raton Section to the south; Southern Rocky Mountains, running down the middle of the state; Middle Rocky Mountains and Wyoming Basin, northwest corner; Colorado Plateaus, western and southwestern border, include the Uinta Basin to the north, the Canyon Lands in the middle, and the Navajo Section to the south. Land use: pasture, 37.2%; agricultural, 12.5%; forest, 4.9%; other, 45.4%.

People

Population (2009): 5,024,748; persons per sq mi 48.3, persons per sq km 18.6. Vital statistics (2007; per 1,000 population): birth rate, 14.6; death rate, 6.2; marriage rate, 6.0; divorce rate, 4.4. Major cities (2008): Denver 598,707; Colorado Springs 380,307; Aurora 319,057; Lakewood 140,989; Fort Collins 136,509.

Government

Statehood: entered the Union on 1 Aug 1876 as the 38th state. State constitution: adopted 1876. Representation in US Congress: 2 senators; 7 representatives. Electoral college: 9 votes. Political divisions: 64 counties.

Economy

Employment (2008): services 31.1%; finance, insurance, real estate 21.1%; trade 13.3%; government 13.3%; construction 7.6%. Production (2008): finance, insurance, real estate 30.0%; services 16.7%; transportation, public utilities 12.4%; government 12.3%; trade 11.5%. Chief agricultural products: Crops: millet, corn (maize), potatoes, onions, sugar beets, sunflowers, wheat, dairy products, eggs, greenhouse products. Livestock: cattle and calves, hogs and pigs, sheep and lambs. Chief manufactured products: meat products; beverages; printing; semiconductors; computer and electronic products.

Internet resources: <www.colorado.com>; <www.colorado.gov>.

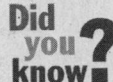 **Did you know?** Colorado's Rocky Mountains, which make up part of the North American Cordillera stretching more than 3,000 miles from Alaska to Mexico, contain some of the highest peaks in North America. The most impressive of these, perhaps, are the "Fourteeners," which is the name that mountain climbers give to the peaks that top 14,000 feet. In the state of Colorado, there are more than 50 "Fourteeners."

Connecticut

Name: Connecticut, from the Algonquian Indian word Quinnehtukqut, meaning "land on the long tidal river." Nickname: Constitution State. Capital: Hartford. Rank: population: 29th; area: 48th. Motto: "Qui transtulit sustinet" ("He who transplanted still sustains"). Song: "Yankee Doodle," words and music from folk tradition. Bird: robin. Flower: mountain laurel. Fossil: Eubrontes giganteus. Insect: praying mantis. Mammal: sperm whale. Mineral: garnet. Shellfish: eastern oyster. Tree: white oak.

Natural features

Land area: 5,006 sq mi, 12,965 sq km. Mountain range: Berkshire Hills. Highest point: Mt. Frissell, 725 m (2,380 ft). Largest lake: Candlewood Lake. Major rivers: Connecticut, Housatonic, Thames. Natural regions: the New England Province covers the state, divided into the Western Upland, Central Lowland (Connecticut Valley), and Eastern Upland. Land use: forest, 53.4%; agricultural, 5.4%; other, 41.2%.

People

Population (2009): 3,518,288; persons per sq mi 702.8, persons per sq km 271.4. Vital statistics (2007; per 1,000 population): birth rate, 11.9; death rate, 8.2; marriage rate, 4.9; divorce rate, 3.1. Major cities (2008): Bridgeport 136,405; Hartford 124,062; New Haven 123,669; Stamford 119,303; Waterbury 107,037.

Government

Statehood: entered the Union on 9 Jan 1788 as the 5th state. State constitution: adopted 1965. Representation in US Congress: 2 senators; 5 representatives. Electoral college: 7 votes. Political divisions: 8 counties.

For details about state governments, see pages 608–613; for energy data, see pages 627–628.

Economy

Employment (2008): services 33.4%; finance, insurance, real estate 21.8%; trade 13.5%; government 11.9%; manufacturing 8.6%. **Production** (2008): finance, insurance, real estate 39.0%; services 17.1%; manufacturing 13.4%; trade 10.7%; government 9.5%. **Chief agricultural products:** *Crops:* corn (maize), silage, hay, tobacco, apples, pears, dairy products, eggs. *Livestock:* poultry, cattle and calves, sheep and lambs, horses. *Fish catch:* lobster, clams, oysters, shad. **Chief manufactured products:** printing; pharmaceutical products; soap and cleaning products; plastic products; fabricated metal products; machinery and apparatus; telecommunications equipment; electronics; aerospace products; aircraft engines.

Internet resources: <www.ctvisit.com>; <www.ct.gov>.

Delaware

Name: Delaware, from Delaware River and Bay; named in turn for Sir Thomas West, Baron De La Warr. **Nickname:** First State. **Capital:** Dover. **Rank:** population: 45th; area: 49th. **Motto:** "Liberty and independence." **Song:** "Our Delaware," words by George B. Hynson and music by Will M.S. Brown. **Bird:** Blue Hen chicken. **Fish:** weakfish. **Flower:** peach blossom. **Insect:** ladybug. **Mineral:** sillimanite. **Tree:** American holly.

Natural features

Land area: 2,026 sq mi, 5,247 sq km. **Highest point:** Ebright Azimuth, 137 m (448 ft). **Largest lake:** Red Mill Pond. **Major rivers:** Delaware, Nanticoke, Pocomoke. **Natural regions:** the Piedmont Province, including the Piedmont Upland, covers the northernmost tip of the state; the remainder consists of the Coastal Plain. **Land use:** agricultural, 29.8%; forest, 22.2%; other, 48.0%.

People

Population (2009): 885,122; persons per sq mi 436.9, persons per sq km 168.7. **Vital statistics** (2007; per 1,000 population): birth rate, 14.1; death rate, 8.5; marriage rate, 5.5; divorce rate, 4.5. **Major cities** (2008): Wilmington 72,592; **Dover 36,107;** Newark 29,886; Middletown 12,152; Smyrna 8,603.

Government

Statehood: entered the Union on 7 Dec 1787 as the 1st state. **State constitution:** adopted 1897. **Representation in US Congress:** 2 senators; 1 representative. **Electoral college:** 3 votes. **Political divisions:** 3 counties.

Economy

Employment (2008): services 32.3%; finance, insurance, real estate 22.7%; trade 14.2%; government 12.9%; construction 6.7%. **Production** (2008): finance, insurance, real estate 54.8%; services 12.4%; government 8.7%; trade 7.5%; manufacturing 7.4%. **Chief agricultural products:** *Crops:* corn (maize), soybeans, wheat, barley, peas, dairy products. *Livestock:* poultry, cattle and calves, hogs. *Fish catch:* crustaceans, crab, clams. **Chief manufactured products:** chemical products; food products; paper products; rubber and plastics products; fabricated metal products; printing.

Internet resources: <www.visitdelaware.com>; <www.delaware.gov>.

District of Columbia

Name: District of Columbia, named in honor of Christopher Columbus. **Motto:** "Justitia omnibus" ("Justice for all"). **Bird:** woodthrush. **Flower:** American Beauty rose. **Tree:** scarlet oak.

Natural features

Land area: 68 sq mi, 176 sq km. **Major river:** Potomac.

People

Population (2009): 599,657; persons per sq mi 8,818.5, persons per sq km 3,407.1. **Vital statistics:** (2007; per 1,000 population): birth rate, 15.1; death rate, 8.8; marriage rate, 3.6; divorce rate, 1.6.

Government

Representation in US Congress: 1 congressional delegate. **Political divisions:** 8 wards.

Economy

Employment (2008): services 37.8%; government 31.0%; finance, insurance, real estate 21.7%; transportation, public utilities 4.0%; trade 3.4%. **Production** (2008): finance, insurance, real estate 36.6%; government 32.7%; services 20.1%; transportation, public utilities 7.1%; trade 2.1%. **Chief manufactured products:** printing and publishing products.

Internet resources: <www.washington.org>; <www.dc.gov>.

Florida

Name: Florida, in honor of Pascua Florida ("feast of the flowers"), Spain's Easter celebration. **Nickname:** Sunshine State. **Capital:** Tallahassee. **Rank:** population: 4th; area: 24th. **Motto:** "In God we trust." **Song:** "Old Folks at Home" ("Swanee River"), words and music by Stephen Foster. **Bird:** mockingbird. **Butterfly:** zebra longwing. **Fish:** sailfish (saltwater); largemouth bass (freshwater). **Flower:** orange blossom. **Gemstone:** moonstone. **Animal:** Florida panther. **Marine mammal:** manatee. **Saltwater mammal:** porpoise. **Reptile:** alligator. **Rock:** agatized coral. **Tree:** sabal palm.

Natural features

Land area: 58,599 sq mi, 151,771 sq km. **Highest point:** Britton Hill 105 m (345 ft). **Largest lake:** Lake Okeechobee. **Major rivers:** Kissimmee, Suwannee, St. Johns, Caloosahatchee, Indian. **Natural regions:** Western Highlands, a region at the westernmost end of the panhandle; Marianna Lowlands, east of the Western Highlands; Tallahassee Hills, covering the northern border with Georgia; Central Highlands, extending down the middle two-thirds of the peninsula;

Coastal Lowlands, curving along the eastern, southern, and western coasts of the peninsula; the Everglades, far southern quarter of the peninsula. **Land use:** forest, 33.9%; agricultural, 7.7%; pasture, 7.2%; other, 51.2%.

People

Population (2009): 18,537,969; persons per sq mi 316.4, persons per sq km 122.1. **Vital statistics** (2007; per 1,000 population): birth rate, 13.1; death rate, 9.2; marriage rate, 8.6; divorce rate, 4.7. **Major cities** (2008): Jacksonville 807,815; Miami 413,201; Tampa 340,882; St. Petersburg 245,314; Orlando 230,519; Hialeah 210,542; Fort Lauderdale 183,126; **Tallahassee 171,922.**

Government

Statehood: entered the Union on 3 Mar 1845 as the 27th state. **State constitution:** adopted 1968. **Representation in US Congress:** 2 senators; 25 representatives. **Electoral college:** 27 votes. **Political divisions:** 67 counties.

Economy

Employment (2008): services 37.3%; finance, insurance, real estate 18.8%; trade 14.8%; government 11.6%; construction 6.8%. **Production** (2008): finance, insurance, real estate 32.6%; services 21.1%; trade 13.8%; government 12.2%; transportation, public utilities 8.9%. **Chief agricultural products:** *Crops:* citrus fruit, cotton, peanuts (groundnuts), soybeans, sugarcane, tobacco, honey, dairy products, eggs, nursery plants and flowers. *Livestock:* cattle and calves, poultry, hogs and pigs. *Fish catch:* catfish, crab, shrimp, oysters. **Chief manufactured products:** food products; soft drinks; wearing apparel; paper products; pesticides and fertilizers; agricultural chemicals; plastic products; construction materials; fabricated metal products; machinery and apparatus; telecommunications equipment; semiconductors; electronics; aerospace products; airplane engines; ships and boats; medical and surgical equipment.

Internet resources: <www.flausa.com>; <www.myflorida.com>.

Georgia

Name: Georgia, named for George II, king of England at the time the colony of Georgia was founded. **Nicknames:** Empire State of the South; Peach State. **Capital:** Atlanta. **Rank:** population: 9th; area: 23rd. **Mottoes:** "Wisdom, justice, and moderation"; "Agriculture and commerce, 1776." **Song:** "Georgia on My Mind," words by Stuart Gorrell and music by Hoagy Carmichael. **Bird:** brown thrasher. **Fish:** largemouth bass. **Flower:** Cherokee rose. **Fossil:** shark tooth. **Gemstone:** quartz. **Insect:** honeybee. **Marine mammal:** right whale. **Mineral:** staurolite. **Reptile:** gopher tortoise. **Tree:** live oak.

Natural features

Land area: 58,922 sq mi, 152,607 sq km. **Mountain range:** Blue Ridge. **Highest point:** Brasstown Bald, 1,458 m (4,784 ft). **Largest lake:** Lanier. **Major**

rivers: Chattahoochee, Flint, Apalachicola, Ocmulgee, Oconee. **Natural regions:** Blue Ridge Province, north-central edge; Valley and Ridge Province, northwest corner; Piedmont Province, northern half of state; Coastal Plain, southern half of state, divided into the Sea Island Section (southeast) and the East Gulf Coastal Plain (southwest). **Land use:** forest, 58.0%; agricultural, 11.0%; other, 31.0%.

People

Population (2009): 9,829,211; persons per sq mi 166.8, persons per sq km 64.4. **Vital statistics** (2007; per 1,000 population): birth rate, 15.9; death rate, 7.2; marriage rate, 6.7; divorce rate (2001), 3.8. **Major cities** (2008): **Atlanta 537,958;** Augusta 194,149; Columbus 186,984; Savannah 132,410; Athens 113,398.

Government

Statehood: entered the Union on 2 Jan 1788 as the 4th state. **State constitution:** adopted 1982. **Representation in US Congress:** 2 senators; 13 representatives. **Electoral college:** 15 votes. **Political divisions:** 159 counties.

Economy

Employment (2008): services 32.3%; finance, insurance, real estate 16.4%; government 14.5%; trade 14.5%; manufacturing 7.7%. **Production** (2008): finance, insurance, real estate 26.4%; services 16.2%; trade 14.3%; government 13.9%; transportation, public utilities 12.6%. **Chief agricultural products:** *Crops:* peanuts (groundnuts), pecans, cotton and cottonseed, tobacco, peaches, apples, blueberries, grapes, honey, dairy products. *Livestock:* poultry, pigs, cattle and calves. *Fish catch:* catfish, trout. **Chief manufactured products:** food products; soft drinks; textiles; wood products; paper products; chemical products; transportation equipment.

Internet resources: <www.georgia.org>; <www.georgia.gov>.

Hawaii

Name: Hawaii, from the Polynesian Hawaiki, the name for the ancestral home of Polynesians. **Nickname:** Aloha State. **Capital:** Honolulu. **Rank:** population: 42nd; area: 47th. **Motto:** "Ua mau ke ea o ka aina i ka pono" ("The life of the land is perpetuated in righteousness"). **Song:** "Hawai'i Pono'i" ("Our Hawaii"), words by King David Kalakaua and music by Henry Berger. **Bird:** nene, or Hawaiian goose. **Fish:** rectangular triggerfish. **Flower:** yellow hibiscus. **Gemstone:** black coral. **Marine mammal:** humpback whale. **Tree:** candlenut.

Natural features

Land area: 6,461 sq mi, 16,734 sq km; the eight largest islands: *Hawaii:* 4,028 sq mi, 10,433 sq km; *Maui:* 728 sq mi, 1,886 sq km; *Oahu:* 607 sq mi, 1,574 sq km; *Kauai:* 552 sq mi, 1,430 sq km; *Molokai,* 200 sq mi, 726 sq km; *Lanai* 140 sq mi

For details about state governments, see pages 608–613; for energy data, see pages 627–628.

363 sq km; *Niihau:* 72 sq mi, 186 sq km; *Kahoolawe:* 45 sq mi, 117 sq km. **Mountain ranges:** Koolau, Waianae (both Oahu). **Highest point:** Mauna Kea (Hawaii), 4,205 m (13,796 ft). **Major rivers:** Wailuku (Hawaii); Waimea, Hanalei (Kauai). **Natural regions:** The eight major islands at the eastern end of the 1,500-mile-long chain of islands are, from west to east, Niihau, Kauai, Oahu, Molokai, Lanai, Kahoolawe, Maui, and Hawaii; each island contains regions of mountains, deeps, ridges, and wide beaches; active volcanoes are found on the island of Hawaii. **Land use:** forest, 28.9%; pasture, 23.4%; agricultural, 7.1%; other, 40.6%.

People

Population (2009): Total, 1,295,178; persons per sq mi 200.5, persons per sq km 77.4. **Vital statistics** (2007; per 1,000 population): birth rate, 14.9; death rate, 7.4; marriage rate, 21.3; divorce rate (2001), 3.8. **Major cities** (2000): **Honolulu (2008) 374,676;** Hilo 40,759; Kailua 36,513; Kaneohe 34,970; Waipahu 33,108.

Government

Statehood: entered the Union on 21 Aug 1959 as the 50th state. **State constitution:** adopted 1950. **Representation in US Congress:** 2 senators; 2 representatives. **Electoral college:** 4 votes. **Political divisions:** 4 counties.

Economy

Employment (2008): services 37.0%; government 20.7%; finance, insurance, real estate 14.4%; trade 12.8%; construction 5.8%. **Production** (2008): finance, insurance, real estate 27.6%; government 23.7%; services 22.9%; trade 10.3%; transportation, public utilities 7.4%. **Chief agricultural products:** *Crops:* pineapples, sugarcane, cut flowers, macadamia nuts, coffee, dairy products, eggs. *Livestock:* cattle and calves. *Fish catch:* fish, shellfish. **Chief manufactured products:** food products, including processed sugar, canned pineapple, and preserved fruits and vegetables; wearing apparel; textiles; printing and publishing.

Internet resources: <www.hawaiitourismauthority.org>; <www.ehawaii.gov>.

Did you know? Any island not named as part of a specific county in Hawaii is considered part of the city of Honolulu, making this the city with the longest borders in the entire world. Containing all of the islands in the Hawaiian and Pacific Islands National Wildlife Refuge, Honolulu officially stretches more than 1,300 miles.

Idaho

Name: Idaho, from a Shoshone Indian phrase meaning "gem of the mountains." **Nickname:** Gem State. **Capital:** Boise. **Rank:** population: 39th; area: 14th. **Motto:** "Esto perpetua" ("It is forever"). **Song:** "Here We Have Idaho," words by McKinley Helm and Albert J. Tompkins and music by Sallie

Hume Douglas. **Bird:** mountain bluebird. **Fish:** cutthroat trout. **Flower:** syringa. **Fossil:** Hagerman horse fossil (*Equus simplicidens*). **Gemstone:** star garnet. **Horse:** Appaloosa. **Insect:** monarch butterfly. **Tree:** western white pine.

Natural features

Land area: 83,570 sq mi, 216,445 sq km. **Mountain ranges:** Northern Rocky, Middle Rocky, Sawtooth, Pioneer, Continental Divide, Beaverhead, Clearwater, Bitterroot, Salmon River, Lost River, Lemhi. **Highest point:** Borah Peak, 3,859 m (12,662 ft). **Largest lake:** Lake Pend Oreille. **Major rivers:** Snake, Salmon. **Natural regions:** Northern Rocky Mountains, covering most of the northern half of the state; Columbia Plateau, extending across the south-central and southwestern regions; Great Basin region of the Basin and Range Province, southeast; Middle Rocky Mountains, extreme southeastern tip. **Land use:** pasture, 12.0%; agricultural, 10.2%; forest, 7.5%; other, 70.3%.

People

Population (2009): 1,545,801; persons per sq mi 18.5, persons per sq km 7.1. **Vital statistics** (2007; per 1,000 population): birth rate, 16.7; death rate, 7.2; marriage rate, 10.3; divorce rate, 4.9. **Major cities** (2008): **Boise 205,314;** Nampa 80,362; Meridian 66,916; Pocatello 54,901; Idaho Falls 54,334.

Government

Statehood: entered the Union on 3 Jul 1890 as the 43rd state. **State constitution:** adopted 1889. **Representation in US Congress:** 2 senators; 2 representatives. **Electoral college:** 4 votes. **Political divisions:** 44 counties.

Economy

Employment (2008): services 29.5%; finance, insurance, real estate 15.8%; trade 14.9%; government 13.8%; construction 8.1%. **Production** (2008): finance, insurance, real estate 26.0%; services 16.9%; government 14.3%; trade 13.8%; manufacturing 9.9%. **Chief agricultural products:** *Crops:* potatoes, timber, sugar beets, alfalfa, Kentucky bluegrass seed, hops, onions, peas, honey, dairy products. *Livestock:* cattle and calves, sheep and lambs. *Fish catch:* trout. **Chief manufactured products:** food products; lumber and wood products; paper products; printing; chemical products; plastics and rubber products; cement, bricks, and ceramics; fabricated metal products; machinery and apparatus; computers and electronics.

Internet resources: <www.visitidaho.org>; <www.idaho.gov>.

Illinois

Name: Illinois, from a Native American word meaning "tribe of superior men." **Nickname:** Prairie State. **Capital:** Springfield. **Rank:** population: 5th; area: 25th. **Motto:** "State sovereignty, national union." **Slogan:** Land of Lincoln. **Song:** "Illinois," words by Charles H. Chamberlain and music by Archibald

Johnston. **Bird:** cardinal. **Fish:** bluegill. **Flower:** violet. **Fossil:** Tully monster. **Insect:** monarch butterfly. **Mammal:** white-tailed deer. **Mineral:** fluorite. **Tree:** white oak.

Natural features

Land area: 57,915 sq mi, 149,999 sq km. **Highest point:** Charles Mound, 376 m (1,235 ft). **Largest lake:** Carlyle Lake. **Major rivers:** Mississippi, Ohio, Wabash. **Natural regions:** Central Lowland, a region of sloping hills and broad, shallow river valleys covering almost the entire state; Ozark Plateaus, extreme southwest; Interior Low Plateaus and Coastal Plain, extreme southeastern tip. **Land use:** agricultural, 66.5%; forest, 11.0%; other, 22.5%.

People

Population (2009): 12,910,409; persons per sq mi 222.9, persons per sq km 86.1. **Vital statistics** (2007; per 1,000 population): birth rate, 14.1; death rate, 7.8; marriage rate, 5.9; divorce rate, 2.6. **Major cities** (2008): Chicago 2,853,114; Aurora 171,782; Rockford 157,272; Joliet 146,125; Naperville 143,117; **Springfield 117,352**.

Government

Statehood: entered the Union on 3 Dec 1818 as the 21st state. **State constitution:** adopted 1970. **Representation in US Congress:** 2 senators; 20 representatives. **Electoral college:** 21 votes. **Political divisions:** 102 counties.

Economy

Employment (2008): services 33.6%; finance, insurance, real estate 18.7%; trade 14.1%; government 11.8%; manufacturing 8.9%. **Production** (2008): finance, insurance, real estate 33.5%; services 17.1%; trade 12.5%; manufacturing 12.4%; government 9.7%. **Chief agricultural products:** *Crops:* corn (maize), soybeans, wheat, oats, sorghum, apples, peaches, snap beans, sweet corn, potatoes, cabbage, dairy products, eggs. *Livestock:* pigs, cattle and calves, horses, poultry. **Chief manufactured products:** food products; beverages; textiles; leather goods; wearing apparel; wood products; paper products; printing; refined petroleum and coal products; asphalt; chemical products; plastics and rubber products; cement, bricks, and ceramics; base metals; fabricated metal products; machinery and apparatus; computers and electronics; transportation equipment.

Internet resources: <www.enjoyillinois.com>; <www.illinois.gov>.

Indiana

Name: Indiana, generally thought to mean "land of the Indians." **Nickname:** Hoosier State. **Capital:** Indianapolis. **Rank:** population: 16th; area: 38th. **Motto:** "The crossroads of America." **Song:** "On the Banks of the Wabash, Far Away," words and music by Paul Dresser. **Bird:** cardinal. **Flower:** peony **Rock:** limestone. **Tree:** tulip tree (yellow poplar).

Natural features

Land area: 36,418 sq mi, 94,322 sq km. **Highest point:** Hoosier Hill, 383 m (1,257 ft). **Largest lake:** Lake Monroe. **Major rivers:** Wabash, Ohio. **Natural regions:** Central Lowland comprises most of the state and includes the Eastern Lake Section to the north and the Till Plains in the center; Interior Low Plateaus, including the Highland Rim Section, cover the southern quarter of the state. **Land use:** agricultural, 57.5%; forest, 16.5%; other, 26.0%.

People

Population (2009): 6,423,113; persons per sq mi 176.4, persons per sq km 68.1. **Vital statistics** (2007; per 1,000 population): birth rate, 14.2; death rate, 8.5; marriage rate, 8.1; divorce rate, N/A. **Major cities** (2008): **Indianapolis 798,382;** Fort Wayne 251,591; Evansville 116,309; South Bend 103,807; Gary 95,920.

Government

Statehood: entered the Union on 11 Dec 1816 as the 19th state. **State constitution:** adopted 1851. **Representation in US Congress:** 2 senators; 10 representatives. **Electoral college:** 11 votes. **Political divisions:** 92 counties.

Economy

Employment (2008): services 32.3%; trade 14.4%; manufacturing 14.4%; finance, insurance, real estate 12.7%; government 12.3%. **Production** (2008): manufacturing 25.0%; finance, insurance, real estate 20.6%; services 17.6%; trade 11.9%; government 10.2%. **Chief agricultural products:** *Crops:* corn (maize), soybeans, wheat, popcorn, tobacco, peppermint, spearmint, blueberries, apples, eggs. *Livestock:* pigs, cattle and calves, poultry. **Chief manufactured products:** base metals; fabricated metal products; motor vehicle parts; machinery and apparatus; food products; dairy products; soft drinks; wood products; paper products; mobile homes.

Internet resources: <www.visitindiana.net>; <www.in.gov>.

Iowa

Name: Iowa, named for the Iowa (or Ioway) Indians who once inhabited the area. **Nickname:** Hawkeye State. **Capital:** Des Moines. **Rank:** population: 30th; area: 26th. **Motto:** "Our liberties we prize and our rights we will maintain." **Song:** "The Song of Iowa," words by S.H.M. Byers, to the tune of "O Tannenbaum." **Bird:** eastern goldfinch. **Flower:** wild rose. **Rock:** geode. **Tree:** oak.

Natural features

Land area: 56,271 sq mi, 145,741 sq km. **Highest point:** Hawkeye Point, 509 m (1,670 ft). **Largest lake:** Spirit Lake. **Major rivers:** Des Moines, Mississippi, Missouri, Big Sioux. **Natural regions:** overall, Central Lowland, including the Western Lake Section, north and central regions; Dissected Till Plains, south; Wisconsin

Driftless Section, northeast corner. **Land use:** agricultural, 70.8%; forest, 6.4%; other, 22.8%.

People

Population (2009): 3,007,856; persons per sq mi 53.5, persons per sq km 20.6. **Vital statistics** (2007; per 1,000 population): birth rate, 13.7; death rate, 9.1; marriage rate, 6.7; divorce rate, 2.6. **Major cities** (2008): **Des Moines 197,052;** Cedar Rapids 128,056; Davenport 100,827; Sioux City 82,807; Iowa City 67,831.

Government

Statehood: entered the Union on 28 Dec 1846 as the 29th state. **State constitution:** adopted 1857. **Representation in US Congress:** 2 senators; 5 representatives. **Electoral college:** 7 votes. **Political divisions:** 99 counties.

Economy

Employment (2008): services 29.8%; trade 14.8%; finance, insurance, real estate 13.4%; government 13.2%; manufacturing 11.6%. **Production** (2008): finance, insurance, real estate 22.3%; manufacturing 20.8%; services 14.9%; government 11.6%; trade 11.5%. **Chief agricultural products:** *Crops:* corn (maize), soybeans, oats, milk, eggs, butter, honey, popcorn, sorghum. *Livestock:* poultry, hogs and pigs, beef cattle, sheep and lambs. **Chief manufactured products:** food products; dairy products; pesticides, fertilizers, and other agricultural chemicals; farm machinery; construction machinery; motor vehicle parts.

Internet resources: <www.traveliowa.com>; <www.iowa.gov>.

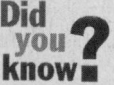 **Did you know** The geodetic center of North America, the center point from which all maps of the continent base their coordinates and borders, was located in 1901 on Meade's Ranch in north-central Kansas. Some 40 miles north, near the town of Lebanon KS, lies the geographic center of the 48 coterminous US states.

Kansas

Name: Kansas, from the Sioux word *kansa* ("people of the south wind") for the Native Americans who lived in the region. **Nickname:** Sunflower State. **Capital:** Topeka. **Rank:** population: 33rd; area: 15th. **Motto:** "Ad astra per aspera" ("To the stars through difficulties"). **Song:** "Home on the Range," words by Brewster Higley and music by Dan Kelly. **Amphibian:** barred tiger salamander. **Bird:** western meadowlark. **Flower:** wild native sunflower. **Insect:** honeybee. **Mammal:** American buffalo. **Reptile:** ornate box turtle. **Tree:** cottonwood.

Natural features

Land area: 82,277 sq mi, 213,096 sq km. **Highest point:** Mt. Sunflower, 1,231 m (4,039 ft). **Largest lake:** Milford Lake. **Major rivers:** Kansas, Arkansas,

Big Blue, Republican, Solomon. **Natural regions:** the Great Plains Province, covering the western half of the state, consists of the High Plains to the west and the Plains Border to the east; the Central Lowland covers the eastern half of the state and consists of the Dissected Till Plains to the north and the Osage Plains to the south. **Land use:** agricultural, 50.3%; pasture, 30.1%; forest, 2.9%; other, 16.7%.

People

Population (2009): 2,818,747; persons per sq mi 34.3, persons per sq km 13.2. **Vital statistics** (2007; per 1,000 population): birth rate, 15.1; death rate, 8.8; marriage rate, 6.7; divorce rate, 3.3. **Major cities** (2008): Wichita 366,046; Overland Park 171,231; Kansas City 142,562; **Topeka 123,446;** Olathe 119,993.

Government

Statehood: entered the Union on 29 Jan 1861 as the 34th state. **State constitution:** adopted 1859. **Representation in US Congress:** 2 senators; 4 representatives. **Electoral college:** 6 votes. **Political divisions:** 105 counties.

Economy

Employment (2008): services 29.4%; government 15.9%; finance, insurance, real estate 14.0%; trade 13.8%; manufacturing 10.3%. **Production** (2008): finance, insurance, real estate 21.0%; services 15.9%; manufacturing 15.2%; government 14.2%; trade 12.8%. **Chief agricultural products:** *Crops:* wheat, corn (maize), sorghum, soybeans, sunflower seed and oil, apples, peaches, pecans. *Livestock:* beef cattle, dairy cattle, hogs, sheep and lambs, horses and other equines. **Chief manufactured products:** food products; printing; refined petroleum products; soap and cleaning products; plastic products; aerospace products and parts; aircraft.

Internet resources: <www.travelks.com>; <www.kansas.gov>.

Kentucky

Name: Kentucky, possibly from the Iroquois Indian word for "prairie." **Nickname:** Bluegrass State. **Capital:** Frankfort. **Rank:** population: 26th; area: 37th. **Motto:** "United we stand, divided we fall." **Song:** "My Old Kentucky Home," words and music by Stephen Foster. **Bird:** cardinal. **Butterfly:** viceroy butterfly. **Fish:** Kentucky bass. **Flower:** goldenrod. **Horse:** Thoroughbred. **Tree:** tulip poplar. **Wild animal:** gray squirrel.

Natural features

Land area: 40,409 sq mi, 104,659 sq km. **Mountain ranges:** Cumberland, Pine. **Highest point:** Black Mountain, 1,263 m (4,145 ft). **Largest lake:** Kentucky Lake. **Major rivers:** Mississippi, Ohio, Big Sandy, Licking, Kentucky. **Natural regions:** Appalachian Plateaus cover the eastern third of the state; Interior Low Plateaus, including the Highland Rim Section and the Lexington Plain, cover the remainder, with the exception of the Coastal Plain, which covers the extreme southwestern tip. **Land use:** forest, 40.6%; agricultural, 21.2%; other, 38.2%.

People

Population (2009): 4,314,113; persons per sq mi 106.8, persons per sq km 41.2. **Vital statistics** (2007; per 1,000 population): birth rate, 14.0; death rate, 9.5; marriage rate, 7.9; divorce rate, 4.6. **Major cities** (2008): Louisville 557,224; Lexington 282,114; Owensboro 55,516; Bowling Green 55,097; Covington 43,235; **Frankfort 27,322.**

Government

Statehood: entered the Union on 1 Jun 1792 as the 15th state. **State constitution:** adopted 1891. **Representation in US Congress:** 2 senators; 6 representatives. **Electoral college:** 8 votes. **Political divisions:** 120 counties.

Economy

Employment (2008): services 30.3%; government 15.1%; trade 14.0%; finance, insurance, real estate 12.7%; manufacturing 10.4%. **Production** (2008): finance, insurance, real estate 19.0%; manufacturing 18.4%; services 16.8%; government 15.7%; trade 12.8%. **Chief agricultural products:** Crops: tobacco, soybeans, corn (maize), wheat, hay, sorghum, eggs, dairy products. Livestock: racing and show horses, beef cattle, dairy cattle, hogs, poultry, sheep and lambs. **Chief manufactured products:** food products; meatpacking; beverages; tobacco; wearing apparel; paper products; printing; chemical products; resin and synthetic rubber products; plastic products; iron and steel; aluminum; fabricated metal products; machinery; appliances; motor vehicles.

Internet resources: <www.kentuckytourism.com>; <www.kentucky.gov>.

Louisiana

Name: Louisiana, named for Louis XIV, king of France. **Nickname:** Pelican State. **Capital:** Baton Rouge. **Rank:** population: 25th; area: 31st. **Motto:** "Union, justice, and confidence." **Songs:** "Give Me Louisiana," words and music by Doralice Fontane; "You Are My Sunshine," words and music by Jimmy H. Davis and Charles Mitchell. **Amphibian:** green tree frog. **Bird:** brown pelican. **Crustacean:** crawfish. **Fish:** white perch (freshwater); spotted sea trout, or speckled trout (saltwater). **Flower:** magnolia. **Fossil:** petrified palmwood. **Gemstone:** agate. **Insect:** honeybee. **Mammal:** black bear. **Reptile:** alligator. **Tree:** bald cypress.

Natural features

Land area: 47,716 sq mi, 123,584 sq km. **Highest point:** Driskill Mountain, 163 m (535 ft). **Largest lake:** Lake Pontchartrain. **Major rivers:** Mississippi, Red, Sabine. **Natural regions:** the entire state consists of the Coastal Plain and is divided into the West Gulf Coastal Plain to the west, the Mis-

sissippi Alluvial Plain to the northeast, and the East Gulf Coastal Plain in the southeast. **Land use:** forest, 42.5%; agricultural, 17.3%; pasture, 0.9%; other, 39.3%.

People

Population (2009): 4,492,076; persons per sq mi 94.1, persons per sq km 36.3. **Vital statistics** (2007; per 1,000 population): birth rate, 15.4; death rate, 9.3; marriage rate, 7.6; divorce rate, N/A. **Major cities** (2008): New Orleans 311,853; **Baton Rouge 223,689;** Shreveport 199,729; Lafayette 113,656; Lake Charles 71,061.

Government

Statehood: entered the Union on 30 Apr 1812 as the 18th state. **State constitution:** adopted 1974. **Representation in US Congress:** 2 senators; 5 representatives. **Electoral college:** 9 votes. **Political divisions:** 64 parishes.

Economy

Employment (2008): services 33.0%; government 15.4%; finance, insurance, real estate 13.7%; trade 13.7%; construction 7.9%. **Production** (2008): manufacturing 18.2%; mining 16.4%; finance, insurance, real estate 15.7%; services 14.6%; government 11.1%. **Chief agricultural products:** Crops: soybeans, cotton, sorghum, sugarcane, rice, wheat, sweet potatoes, pecans, strawberries, peaches. Livestock: cattle and calves, chickens, hogs. Fish catch: catfish, crawfish, shrimp, oysters. **Chief manufactured products:** industrial chemicals; agricultural chemicals; plastics; refined petroleum products; cane sugar products; paper products; fabricated metal products; wood products; telecommunications equipment; ships, boats, and nautical equipment.

Internet resources: <www.louisianatravel.com>; <www.louisiana.gov>.

Maine

Name: Maine, possibly named for the former French province of Maine, or used to distinguish the mainland portion of the territory from offshore islands. **Nickname:** Pine Tree State. **Capital:** Augusta. **Rank:** population: 41st; area: 39th. **Motto:** "Dirigo" ("I direct"). **Song:** "State of Maine Song," words and music by Roger Vinton Snow. **Bird:** chickadee. **Fish:** landlocked salmon. **Flower:** white pine cone and tassel. **Fossil:** Pertica quadrifaria. **Gemstone:** tourmaline. **Insect:** honeybee. **Mammal:** moose. **Tree:** white pine.

Natural features

Land area: 33,126 sq mi, 85,796 sq km. **Mountain ranges:** Appalachian, Longfellow. **Highest point:** Mt. Katahdin, 1,606 m (5,268 ft). **Largest lake:** Moosehead Lake. **Major rivers:** Saco, Androscoggin, Kennebec, Penobscot, St. John's. **Natural regions:** entire state is part of the larger New England Province, subdivided into the White Moun-

For details about state governments, see pages 608–613; for energy data, see pages 627–628.

tain section (southwest), Seaboard Lowland Section (southeast coastline), and New England Upland Section (north and central regions). **Land use:** forest, 84.0%; agricultural, 1.8%; other 14.2%.

People

Population (2009): 1,318,301; persons per sq mi 39.8, persons per sq km 15.4. **Vital statistics** (2007; per 1,000 population): birth rate, 10.7; death rate, 9.5; marriage rate, 7.7; divorce rate, 4.5. **Major cities** (2008): Portland 62,561; Lewiston 35,131; Bangor 31,756; South Portland 23,803; Auburn 23,177; **Augusta 18,282.**

Government

Statehood: entered the Union on 15 Mar 1820 as the 23rd state. **State constitution:** adopted 1819. **Representation in US Congress:** 2 senators; 2 representatives. **Electoral college:** 4 votes. **Political divisions:** 16 counties.

Economy

Employment (2008): services 34.6%; trade 15.4%; finance, insurance, real estate 13.8%; government 13.5%; manufacturing 7.6%. **Production** (2008): finance, insurance, real estate 26.6%; services 21.1%; government 14.1%; trade 13.9%; manufacturing 11.1%. **Chief agricultural products:** *Crops:* potatoes, blueberries, apples, cranberries, oats, honey, corn (maize), dairy products, eggs. *Livestock:* poultry, cattle and calves, sheep and lambs. *Fish catch:* salmon, rainbow trout, lobster, shrimp, crab, clams, haddock, cod, mackerel. **Chief manufactured products:** paper products; leather products; lumber and wood products; food products; semiconductors; wearing apparel; printing and publishing; plastic products; ships and boats.

Internet resources: <www.visitmaine.com>; <www.maine.gov>.

Maryland

Name: Maryland, in honor of Henrietta Maria, queen of England at the time the colony of Maryland was founded. **Nickname:** Old Line State. **Capital:** Annapolis. **Rank:** population: 19th; area: 42nd. **Motto:** "Fatti maschii, parole femine" ("Manly deeds, womanly words"). **Song:** "Maryland, My Maryland," words by James Ryder Randall, to the tune of "O Tannenbaum." **Bird:** Baltimore oriole. **Crustacean:** Maryland blue crab. **Dinosaur:** *Astrodon johnstoni.* **Fish:** rockfish (striped bass). **Flower:** black-eyed Susan. **Insect:** Baltimore checkerspot. **Reptile:** diamondback terrapin. **Tree:** white oak.

Natural features

Land area: 10,454 sq mi, 27,076 sq km. **Mountain ranges:** Allegheny, Appalachian. **Highest point:** Backbone Mountain, 1,024 m (3,360 ft). **Largest lake:** Deep Creek Lake. **Major rivers:** Potomac, Patuxent, Susquehanna. **Natural regions:** Coastal Plain, eastern half of the state, includes the Embayed Section near the southwest corner of the peninsula; Piedmont Province, central, includes the Piedmont Upland to the north and

the Piedmont Lowlands to the west; Blue Ridge Province, northwest; Valley and Ridge Province, part of western neck; Appalachian Plateau, extreme western neck. **Land use:** forest, 30.1%; agricultural, 19.3%; other, 50.6%.

People

Population (2009): 5,699,478; persons per sq mi 545.2, persons per sq km 210.5. **Vital statistics** (2007; per 1,000 population): birth rate, 13.9; death rate, 7.8; marriage rate, 6.3; divorce rate, 3.1. **Major cities** (2008): Baltimore 636,919; Rockville 60,734; Frederick 59,213; Gaithersburg 58,744; Bowie 52,544; **Annapolis 36,524.**

Government

Statehood: entered the Union on 28 Apr 1788 as the 7th state. **State constitution:** adopted 1867. **Representation in US Congress:** 2 senators; 8 representatives. **Electoral college:** 10 votes. **Political divisions:** 23 counties.

Economy

Employment (2008): services 33.9%; finance, insurance, real estate 20.3%; government 15.9%; trade 13.2%; construction 7.2%. **Production** (2008): finance, insurance, real estate 32.0%; government 18.7%; services 18.2%; trade 10.8%; transportation, public utilities 8.9%. **Chief agricultural products:** *Crops:* corn (maize), soybeans, wheat, potatoes, tobacco, dairy products, eggs. *Livestock:* cattle and calves, pigs, poultry. *Fish catch:* hybrid striped bass, catfish, tilapia, trout, oysters, blue crab, other crustaceans, oysters, mollusks. **Chief manufactured products:** base metals; food products; transportation equipment, including motor vehicles and ships and boats; chemical products; plastics and rubber products; fabricated metal products; machinery and apparatus; computers and electronics.

Internet resources: <www.mdisfun.org>; <www.maryland.gov>.

Massachusetts

Name: Massachusetts, named for the Massachuset tribe of Native Americans who lived in the Great Blue Hill region south of Boston; the word *massachuset* means "near the great hill." **Nickname:** Bay State. **Capital:** Boston. **Rank:** population: 15th; area: 45th. **Motto:** "Ense petit placidam sub libertate quietem" ("By the sword we seek peace, but peace only under liberty"). **Song:** "All Hail to Massachusetts," words and music by Arthur J. Marsh. **Bird:** black-capped chickadee. **Fish:** cod. **Flower:** mayflower. **Fossil:** theropod dinosaur tracks. **Gemstone:** rhodonite. **Insect:** ladybug. **Marine mammal:** right whale. **Mineral:** babingtonite. **Rock:** Roxbury puddingstone. **Tree:** American elm.

Natural features

Land area: 8,263 sq mi, 21,401 sq km. **Mountain ranges:** Berkshire Mountains, Hoosac Range, Taconic Range. **Highest point:** Mt. Greylock, 1,064 m (3,491 ft). **Largest lake:** Webster Lake. **Major rivers:** Connecticut, Charles, Merrimack,

Housatonic, Taunton. **Natural regions:** the New England Province, comprising most of the state, subdivided into the Taconic Section along the west, the New England Upland Section in the central region, and the Seaboard Lowland Section, covering the eastern third of the state; Coastal Plain, comprising the peninsula region. **Land use:** forest, 49.9%; agricultural, 4.7%; other, 45.4%.

People

Population (2009): 6,593,587; persons per sq mi 798.0, persons per sq km 308.1. **Vital statistics** (2007; per 1,000 population): birth rate, 12.1; death rate, 8.2; marriage rate, 6.0; divorce rate, 2.2. **Major cities** (2008): **Boston 609,023;** Worcester 175,011; Springfield 150,640; Cambridge 105,596; Lowell 103,615.

Government

Statehood: entered the Union on 6 Feb 1788 as the 6th state. **State constitution:** adopted 1780. **Representation in US Congress:** 2 senators; 10 representatives. **Electoral college:** 12 votes. **Political divisions:** 14 counties.

Economy

Employment (2008): services 37.1%; finance, insurance, real estate 21.1%; trade 13.1%; government 10.6%; manufacturing 7.0%. **Production** (2008): finance, insurance, real estate 38.4%; services 20.6%; trade 10.5%; manufacturing 9.5%; government 9.1%. **Chief agricultural products:** *Crops:* tobacco, cranberries, potatoes, sweet corn, dairy products, eggs. *Livestock:* cattle and calves, poultry. *Fish catch:* lobster, crab, mollusks, oysters, quahogs, soft-shelled clams, scallops. **Chief manufactured products:** food products; dairy products; soft drinks; textiles; paper products; printing; pharmaceuticals; plastic products; cement, bricks, and ceramics; fabricated metal products.

Internet resources: <www.mass-vacation.com>; <www.mass.gov>.

Michigan

Name: Michigan, from the Ojibwa Indian word *michi-gama,* meaning "large lake." **Nicknames:** Wolverine State; Great Lake State. **Capital:** Lansing. **Rank:** population: 8th; area: 11th. **Motto:** "Si quaeris peninsulam amoenam, circumspice" ("If you seek a pleasant peninsula, look around you"). **Song:** "Michigan, My Michigan," words by Giles Kavanagh and music by H.J. O'Reilly Clint. **Bird:** robin. **Fish:** brook trout. **Flower:** apple blossom. **Gemstone:** chlorastrolite. **Mammal:** white-tailed deer (game mammal). **Reptile:** painted turtle. **Rock:** Petoskey stone. **Tree:** white pine.

Natural features

Land area: 96,716 sq mi, 250,493 sq km. **Highest point:** Mt. Arvon, 603 m (1,979 ft). **Largest lake:** Houghton Lake. **Major rivers:** Montreal, Brule, Menominee, Ou Clain. **Natural regions:** the Central

Lowland, Eastern Lake Section, covers all of Lower Michigan and part of the Upper Peninsula region; the western half of the Upper Peninsula consists of Superior Upland, as do two small areas at the eastern end. **Land use:** forest, 44.7%; agricultural, 21.7%; other, 33.6%.

People

Population (2009): 9,969,727; persons per sq mi 103.1, persons per sq km 39.8. **Vital statistics** (2007; per 1,000 population): birth rate, 12.4; death rate, 8.6; marriage rate, 5.9; divorce rate, 3.5. **Major cities** (2008): Detroit 912,062; Grand Rapids 193,396; Warren 133,939; Sterling Heights 127,160; Ann Arbor 114,386; **Lansing 113,968.**

Government

Statehood: entered the Union on 26 Jan 1837 as the 26th state. **State constitution:** adopted 1963. **Representation in US Congress:** 2 senators; 15 representatives. **Electoral college:** 17 votes. **Political divisions:** 83 counties.

Economy

Employment (2008): services 34.6%; finance, insurance, real estate 16.4%; trade 14.3%; government 12.3%; manufacturing 11.2%. **Production** (2008): finance, insurance, real estate 28.2%; services 18.7%; manufacturing 16.1%; trade 12.8%; government 11.6%. **Chief agricultural products:** *Crops:* apples, asparagus, blueberries, cherries, flowers, grapes and wine, honey, maple syrup, mint, plums. *Livestock:* beef cattle, dairy cattle, pigs, poultry, sheep and lambs. *Fish catch:* rainbow, brook, and brown trout, yellow perch, catfish. **Chief manufactured products:** motor vehicles; plastic products; pharmaceuticals; soaps; milled grain and dry cereals; agricultural machinery; furniture; dairy products; printing; electrical equipment.

Internet resources: <www.michigan.org>; <www.michigan.gov>.

Minnesota

Name: Minnesota, from a Dakota Indian word meaning "sky-tinted water." **Nickname:** North Star State. **Capital:** St. Paul. **Rank:** population: 21st; area: 12th. **Motto:** "L'Étoile du nord" ("The star of the north"). **Song:** "Hail! Minnesota," first verse and music by Truman E. Rickard, second verse by Arthur E. Upson. **Bird:** common loon. **Fish:** walleye pike. **Flower:** pink and white lady slipper. **Gemstone:** Lake Superior agate. **Insect:** monarch butterfly. **Tree:** Norway pine.

Natural features

Land area: 86,939 sq mi, 225,171 sq km. **Mountain ranges:** Mesabi, Vermillion, Cuyuna. **Highest point:** Eagle Mountain, 701 m (2,301 ft). **Largest lake:** Red Lake. **Major rivers:** Minnesota, St. Croix, Mississippi. **Natural regions:** Superior Upland, northeast corner; Central Lowland, covering most of the state; Western Lake Section, center; Dis-

For details about state governments, see pages 608–613; for energy data, see pages 627–628.

sected Till Plains, extreme southwest corner and south-central edge; Wisconsin Driftless Section, extreme southeast. **Land use:** agricultural, 39.1%; forest, 30.3%; other, 30.6%.

People

Population (2009): 5,266,214; persons per sq mi 60.6, persons per sq km 23.4. **Vital statistics** (2007; per 1,000 population): birth rate, 14.2; death rate, 7.2; marriage rate, 5.7; divorce rate (2004), 2.8. **Major cities** (2008): Minneapolis 382,605; **St. Paul 279,590;** Rochester 100,413; Duluth 84,284; Bloomington 81,280.

Government

Statehood: entered the Union on 11 May 1858 as the 32nd state. **State constitution:** adopted 1857. **Representation in US Congress:** 2 senators; 8 representatives. **Electoral college:** 10 votes. **Political divisions:** 87 counties.

Economy

Employment (2008): services 32.8%; finance, insurance, real estate 17.7%; trade 14.4%; government 11.8%; manufacturing 9.8%. **Production** (2008): finance, insurance, real estate 32.0%; services 17.3%; manufacturing 12.8%; trade 12.7%; government 10.6%. **Chief agricultural products:** *Crops:* corn (maize), green peas, onions, apples, spring wheat, barley, potatoes, sugar beets, flaxseed, dairy products. *Livestock:* pigs, cattle and calves, poultry, sheep and lambs. **Chief manufactured products:** food products; malt beverages and other alcoholic products; dairy products; machinery and apparatus; computers and office machinery; electronics and electrical equipment; precision instruments; printing and publishing; information technology; lumber and wood products.

Internet resources: <www.exploreminnesota.com>; <www.state.mn.us>.

Did you know? The original name of Saint Paul, the capital of the state of Minnesota, was Pig's Eye Landing. Named after Pierre ("Pig's Eye") Parrant, a French-Canadian tavern owner who in 1838 made the first official land claim on the area, the community that was to become Minnesota's second largest city did not receive its current name until 1841.

Mississippi

Name: Mississippi, from a Native American word meaning "great waters" or "father of waters." **Nickname:** Magnolia State. **Capital:** Jackson. **Rank:** population: 31st; area: 32nd. **Motto:** "Virtute et armis" ("By valor and arms"). **Song:** "Go, Mississippi," words and music by Houston Davis. **Bird:** mockingbird. **Fish:** largemouth bass. **Flower:** magnolia. **Fossil:** prehistoric whale. **Insect:** honeybee. **Mammal:** white-tailed deer. **Marine mammal:** bottle-nosed dolphin (porpoise). **Rock:** petrified wood. **Tree:** magnolia tree.

Natural features

Land area: 47,692 sq mi, 123,522 sq km. **Highest point:** Woodall Mountain, 246 m (806 ft). **Major rivers:** Mississippi, Pearl, Big Black, Yazoo, Tombigbee. **Natural regions:** the entire state consists of the Coastal Plain, subdivided into the Mississippi Alluvial Plain, in the west, and the East Gulf Coastal Plain, comprising the central and eastern regions. **Land use:** forest, 54.9%; agricultural, 16.3%; other, 28.8%.

People

Population (2009): 2,951,996; persons per sq mi 61.9, persons per sq km 23.9. **Vital statistics** (2007; per 1,000 population): birth rate, 15.9; death rate, 9.7; marriage rate, 5.4; divorce rate, 4.9. **Major cities** (2008): **Jackson 173,861;** Gulfport 70,055; Hattiesburg 51,993; Biloxi 45,670; Southaven 44,076.

Government

Statehood: entered the Union on 10 Dec 1817 as the 20th state. **State constitution:** adopted 1890. **Representation in US Congress:** 2 senators; 5 representatives. **Electoral college:** 6 votes. **Political divisions:** 82 counties.

Economy

Employment (2008): services 30.1%; government 18.3%; trade 13.6%; finance, insurance, real estate 10.9%; manufacturing 10.6%. **Production** (2008): government 17.5%; services 17.5%; finance, insurance, real estate 17.2%; manufacturing 15.0%; trade 13.0%. **Chief agricultural products:** *Crops:* cotton, soybeans, rice, wheat, corn (maize), greenhouse and nursery plants, sweet potatoes, pecans. *Livestock:* cattle and calves. *Fish catch:* catfish, pearls, shrimp, oysters, crustaceans. **Chief manufactured products:** food products; transportation equipment; wearing apparel; textiles; electrical equipment; rubber products.

Internet resources: <www.visitmississippi.org>; <www.mississippi.gov>.

Missouri

Name: Missouri, named for a Native American tribe that lived in the region; the name means "town of the large canoes." **Nickname:** Show Me State. **Capital:** Jefferson City. **Rank:** population: 18th; area: 20th. **Motto:** "Salus populi suprema lex esto" ("The welfare of the people shall be the supreme law"). **Song:** "Missouri Waltz," words by J.R. Shannon and music by John Valentine Eppel. **Aquatic animal:** paddlefish. **Bird:** bluebird. **Fish:** channel catfish. **Flower:** white hawthorn blossom. **Fossil:** crinoid. **Insect:** honeybee. **Mammal:** Missouri mule. **Mineral:** galena. **Rock:** mozarkite. **Tree:** flowering dogwood.

Natural features

Land area: 69,704 sq mi, 180,533 sq km. **Mountain ranges:** Ozark Plateau, St. Francois. **Highest point:** Taum Sauk Mountain, 540 m (1,772 ft). **Largest lake:** Truman Lake. **Major rivers:** Missouri, Mississippi, Des Plaines. **Natural regions:** Central Lowland, northwestern, subdivided into the Dissected Till Plains to the north and the Osage Plains to the west; Ozark Plateaus, including the Springfield-Salem Plateaus, southeast; Coastal Plain, including the Mississippi Alluvial Plain, extreme southeastern tip. **Land use:** agricultural, 30.7%; forest, 28.1%; pasture, 0.2%; other, 41.0%.

People

Population (2009): 5,987,580; persons per sq mi 85.9, persons per sq km 33.2. **Vital statistics** (2007; per 1,000 population): birth rate, 13.9; death rate, 9.2; marriage rate, 6.7; divorce rate, 3.8. **Major cities** (2008): Kansas City 451,572; St. Louis 354,361; Springfield 156,206; Independence 110,440; Columbia 100,733; **Jefferson City 40,771.**

Government

Statehood: entered the Union on 10 Aug 1821 as the 24th state. **State constitution:** adopted 1945. **Representation in US Congress:** 2 senators; 9 representatives. **Electoral college:** 11 votes. **Political divisions:** 114 counties.

Economy

Employment (2008): services 32.3%; finance, insurance, real estate 16.2%; trade 14.3%; government 13.4%; manufacturing 8.2%. **Production** (2008): finance, insurance, real estate 25.5%; services 19.0%; manufacturing 13.5%; trade 13.2%; government 12.4%. **Chief agricultural products:** Crops: soybeans, corn (maize), rice, sorghum, wheat, dairy products. Livestock: cattle and calves, pigs, sheep and lambs, poultry. **Chief manufactured products:** industrial machinery; transportation equipment; food products; malt beverages and other alcoholic products; soft drinks; soaps and detergents; agricultural chemicals; pharmaceuticals; printing and publishing; base metals.

Internet resources: <www.visitmo.com>; <www.missouri.gov>.

Montana

Name: Montana, from the Spanish word montaña ("mountain," or "mountainous region"). **Nickname:** Treasure State. **Capital:** Helena. **Rank:** population: 44th; area: 4th. **Motto:** "Oro y plata" ("Gold and silver"). **Song:** "Montana," words by Charles C. Cohan and music by Joseph E. Howard. **Bird:** western meadowlark. **Fish:** cutthroat trout. **Flower:** bitterroot. **Fossil:** Maiasaura. **Gemstones:** agate; sapphire. **Mammal:** grizzly bear. **Tree:** ponderosa pine.

Natural features

Land area: 147,042 sq mi, 380,837 sq km. **Mountain ranges:** Rocky, Grand Teton. **Highest point:** Granite Peak, 3,901 m (12,799 ft). **Largest lake:** Flathead Lake. **Major rivers:** Kootenai, Clark Fork, Flathead, Missouri, Yellowstone. **Natural regions:** Northern Rocky Mountains, western two-fifths of the state; Middle Rocky Mountains, small area along the south-central border; Missouri Plateau re-

gion of the Great Plains Province, eastern three-fifths of the state. **Land use:** pasture, 39.0%; agricultural, 15.4%; forest, 5.7%; other, 39.9%.

People

Population (2009): 974,989; persons per sq mi 6.6, persons per sq km 2.6. **Vital statistics** (2007; per 1,000 population): birth rate, 13.0; death rate, 9.0; marriage rate, 7.4; divorce rate, 3.7. **Major cities** (2008): Billings 103,994; Missoula 68,202; Great Falls 59,251; Bozeman 39,442; Butte–Silver Bow 32,119; **Helena 29,351.**

Government

Statehood: entered the Union on 8 Nov 1889 as the 41st state. **State constitution:** adopted 1972. **Representation in US Congress:** 2 senators; 1 representative. **Electoral college:** 3 votes. **Political divisions:** 56 counties.

Economy

Employment (2008): services 32.7%; trade 14.6%; government 14.4%; finance, insurance, real estate 14.4%; construction 8.1%. **Production** (2008): finance, insurance, real estate 21.1%; services 19.1%; government 15.6%; trade 12.2%; transportation, public utilities 11.1%. **Chief agricultural products:** Crops: wheat, safflowers, sunflowers, mustard, sugar beets, grapes, garlic, potatoes, honey, cherries. Livestock: beef cattle, dairy cattle, sheep and lambs, poultry, horses, llamas. **Chief manufactured products:** food products; lumber and wood products; fabricated metal products; refined petroleum products; chemical products; cement, bricks, and ceramics; machinery and apparatus.

Internet resources: <www.visitmt.com>; <www.mt.gov>.

Nebraska

Name: Nebraska, from the Oto Indian word nebrathka, meaning "flat water," a reference to the Platte River. **Nickname:** Cornhusker State. **Capital:** Lincoln. **Rank:** population: 38th; area: 16th. **Motto:** "Equality before the law." **Song:** "Beautiful Nebraska," words by Jim Fras and Guy Gage Miller and music by Jim Fras. **Bird:** western meadowlark. **Fish:** channel catfish. **Flower:** goldenrod. **Fossil:** mammoth. **Gemstone:** blue agate. **Insect:** honeybee. **Mammal:** white-tailed deer. **Rock:** prairie agate. **Tree:** cottonwood.

Natural features

Land area: 77,353 sq mi, 200,343 sq km. **Highest point:** Panorama Point 1,653 m (5,424 ft). **Largest lake:** Lake McConaughy. **Major rivers:** Missouri, Platte, Elkhorn, Loup, Republican. **Natural regions:** Great Plains Province, western three-quarters of the state; Missouri Plateau, at the northern corners; High Plains, central and north central; Plains Border, southern border; Central Lowland, including the Dissected Till Plains, eastern quarter of the state. **Land use:** pasture, 46.6%; agricultural, 39.5%; forest, 1.6%; other, 12.3%.

For details about state governments, see pages 608–613; for energy data, see pages 627–628.

People

Population (2009): 1,796,619; persons per sq mi 23.2, persons per sq km 9.0. **Vital statistics** (2007; per 1,000 population): birth rate, 15.2; death rate, 8.6; marriage rate, 7.0; divorce rate, 3.1. **Major cities** (2008): Omaha 438,646; **Lincoln 251,624;** Bellevue 49,699; Grand Island 45,801; Kearney 30,417.

Government

Statehood: entered the Union on 1 Mar 1867 as the 37th state. **State constitution:** adopted 1875. **Representation in US Congress:** 2 senators; 3 representatives. **Electoral college:** 5 votes. **Political divisions:** 93 counties.

Economy

Employment (2008): services 30.0%; finance, insurance, real estate 15.7%; trade 14.4%; government 13.8%; manufacturing 8.4%. **Production** (2008): finance, insurance, real estate 22.6%; services 15.3%; government 14.0%; transportation, public utilities 13.9%; manufacturing 11.8%. **Chief agricultural products:** *Crops:* corn (maize), soybeans, wheat, sorghum, dry beans, sugar beets. *Livestock:* beef cattle, dairy cattle, pigs, sheep and lambs, poultry. **Chief manufactured products:** food products, including canned and frozen fruits and vegetables, flour, cereal, grain products, and livestock feeds; beverages; dairy products; transportation equipment; printing and publishing; plastics and rubber goods; fabricated metal products; base metals.

Internet resources: <www.visitnebraska.org>; <www.nebraska.gov>.

Nevada

Name: Nevada, from the Spanish *nevada* ("snow-clad"), a reference to the high mountain scenery of the Sierra Nevada on the southwestern border with California. **Nicknames:** Sagebrush State; Silver State. **Capital:** Carson City. **Rank:** population: 35th; area: 7th. **Motto:** "All for our country." **Song:** "Home Means Nevada," words and music by Bertha Raffeto. **Bird:** mountain bluebird. **Fish:** Lahontan cutthroat trout. **Flower:** sagebrush. **Fossil:** ichthyosaur. **Gemstones:** fire opal; turquoise. **Mammal:** desert bighorn sheep. **Metal:** silver. **Reptile:** desert tortoise. **Rock:** sandstone. **Trees:** single-leaf piñon; bristlecone pine.

Natural features

Land area: 110,561 sq mi, 286,352 sq km. **Mountain ranges:** Snake, Schell Creek, Monitor, Toiyabe, Shoshone, Humboldt, Santa Rosa. **Highest point:** Boundary Peak, 4,006 m (13,143 ft). **Largest lakes:** Pyramid Lake (natural); Lake Mead (man-made). **Major rivers:** Humboldt, Truckee, Carson, Walker, Muddy. **Natural regions:** the Basin and Range Province covers all of the state, except for the southwestern corner, which consists of the Cascade-Sierra Mountains, and the northeastern corner, which comprises part of the Columbia Plateau. **Land use:** pasture, 11.7%; agricultural, 0.9%; forest, 0.4%; other, 87.0%.

People

Population (2009): 2,643,085; persons per sq mi 23.9, persons per sq km 9.2. **Vital statistics** (2007; per 1,000 population): birth rate, 16.1; death rate, 7.3; marriage rate, 49.3; divorce rate, 6.5. **Major cities** (2008): Las Vegas 558,383; Henderson 252,064; North Las Vegas 217,253; Reno 217,016; Sparks 88,602; **Carson City 54,867.**

Government

Statehood: entered the Union on 31 Oct 1864 as the 36th state. **State constitution:** adopted 1864. **Representation in US Congress:** 2 senators; 3 representatives. **Electoral college:** 5 votes. **Political divisions:** 16 counties; 1 independent city.

Economy

Employment (2008): services 40.0%; finance, insurance, real estate 18.3%; trade 12.9%; government 10.6%; construction 8.5%. **Production** (2008): finance, insurance, real estate 29.6%; services 27.1%; trade 11.4%; government 10.2%; construction 8.1%. **Chief agricultural products:** *Crops:* wheat, corn (maize), potatoes, rye, alfalfa, barley, dairy products. *Livestock:* cattle and calves, horses, sheep and lambs, hogs, poultry. **Chief manufactured products:** food products, including candy and frozen desserts; dairy products; soft drinks; paper products; chemical products, notably pharmaceuticals; plastics; construction materials; machinery and apparatus, significantly agricultural equipment; printing and publishing.

Internet resources: <http://travelnevada.com>; <www.nevada.gov>.

New Hampshire

Name: New Hampshire, named for Hampshire, England, by Captain John Mason. **Nickname:** Granite State. **Capital:** Concord. **Rank:** population: 40th; area: 44th. **Motto:** "Live free or die." **Songs:** "Old New Hampshire," words by John F. Holmes and music by Maurice Hoffmann; "New Hampshire, My New Hampshire," words by Julius Richelson and music by Walter P. Smith. **Amphibian:** red-spotted newt. **Bird:** purple finch. **Fish:** brook trout (freshwater); striped bass (saltwater). **Flower:** purple lilac. **Gemstone:** smoky quartz. **Insect:** ladybug. **Mammal:** white-tailed deer. **Mineral:** beryl. **Rock:** granite. **Tree:** white birch.

Natural features

Land area: 9,282 sq mi, 24,040 sq km. **Mountain ranges:** White, Ossipee, Sandwich, Presidential. **Highest point:** Mt. Washington, 1,917 m (6,288 ft). **Largest lake:** Lake Winnipesaukee. **Major rivers:** Merrimack, Salmon Falls, Connecticut, Saco, Piscataqua. **Natural regions:** the New England Province covers the entire state and is subdivided into the White Mountain Section in the northern third, the New England Upland Section in the south-central region, and the Seaboard Lowland Section in the southeast corner. **Land use:** forest, 65.6%; agricultural, 2.1%; other, 32.3%.

People

Population (2009): 1,324,575; persons per sq mi 142.7, persons per sq km 55.1. **Vital statistics** (2007; per 1,000 population): birth rate, 10.8; death rate, 7.8; marriage rate, 7.1; divorce rate, 3.9. **Major cities** (2008): Manchester 108,586; Nashua 86,576; **Concord 42,255**; Rochester 30,654; Dover 28,609.

Government

Statehood: entered the Union on 21 Jun 1788 as the 9th state. **State constitution:** adopted 1784. **Representation in US Congress:** 2 senators; 2 representatives. **Electoral college:** 4 votes. **Political divisions:** 10 counties.

Economy

Employment (2008): services 33.1%; trade 17.3%; finance, insurance, real estate 16.7%; government 11.2%; manufacturing 9.4%. **Production** (2008): finance, insurance, real estate 31.8%; services 20.4%; trade 14.1%; manufacturing 10.9%; government 9.7%. **Chief agricultural products:** Crops: apples, honey, ornamental horticulture, Christmas trees, dairy products, eggs, maple syrup. Livestock: horses, dairy cattle, sheep and lambs. **Chief manufactured products:** machinery and apparatus; computers and software; electrical equipment; semiconductors; food products; medical, surgical, and precision instruments; fabricated metal products; plastics and rubber products; printing and publishing; paper products.

Internet resources: <www.visitnh.gov>; <www.nh.gov>.

New Jersey

Name: New Jersey, named for the island of Jersey in the English Channel. **Nickname:** Garden State. **Capital:** Trenton. **Rank:** population: 11th; area: 46th. **Motto:** "Liberty and prosperity." **Bird:** eastern goldfinch. **Fish:** brook trout. **Flower:** violet. **Fossil:** Hadrosaurus foulkii. **Insect:** honeybee. **Mammal:** horse. **Tree:** red oak.

Natural features

Land area: 7,813 sq mi, 20,236 sq km. **Mountain range:** Appalachian. **Highest point:** Kittatinny Mountain, 550 m (1,803 ft). **Largest lake:** Lake Hopatcong. **Major rivers:** Delaware, Hudson, Passaic, Hackensack, Raritan. **Natural regions:** the Valley and Ridge Province, Middle Section, northwest corner; the New England Province, consisting of the New England Upland Section, east of the Valley and Ridge area; the Piedmont Province, including the Piedmont Lowlands, extending from the northeast corner to part of the border with Pennsylvania; the Coastal Plain, Embayed Section, southern half of the state. **Land use:** forest, 30.8%; agricultural, 10.1%; other, 59.1%.

People

Population (2009): 8,707,739; persons per sq mi 1,114.5, persons per sq km 430.3. **Vital statistics**
(2007; per 1,000 population): birth rate, 13.4; death rate, 8.0; marriage rate, 5.2; divorce rate, 3.0. **Major cities** (2008): Newark 278,980; Jersey City 241,114; Paterson 145,643; Elizabeth 124,755; Edison 99,706; **Trenton 82,883.**

Government

Statehood: entered the Union on 18 Dec 1787 as the 3rd state. **State constitution:** adopted 1947. **Representation in US Congress:** 2 senators; 13 representatives. **Electoral college:** 15 votes. **Political divisions:** 21 counties.

Economy

Employment (2008): services 32.3%; finance, insurance, real estate 21.8%; trade 15.3%; government 12.7%; transportation, public utilities 6.4%. **Production** (2008): finance, insurance, real estate 35.5%; services 17.3%; trade 14.2%; government 10.4%; transportation, public utilities 9.6%. **Chief agricultural products:** Crops: cranberries, blueberries, peaches, asparagus, bell peppers, spinach, sweet corn, escarole and endive, eggplants, nursery and greenhouse products. Livestock: horses, cattle, poultry. Fish catch: bluefish, tilefish, flounder, hake, shellfish. **Chief manufactured products:** chemical products, including pharmaceuticals; electronics and electrical equipment; telecommunications equipment; semiconductors; industrial equipment; refined petroleum products; fabricated metal products; cement, bricks, and ceramics; food products.

Internet resources: <www.visitnj.org>; <www.newjersey.gov>.

New Mexico

Name: New Mexico, named for the country of Mexico. **Nickname:** Land of Enchantment. **Capital:** Santa Fe. **Rank:** population: 36th; area: 5th. **Motto:** "Crescit eundo" ("It grows as it goes"). **Songs:** "O, Fair New Mexico," words and music by Elizabeth Garrett; "Así es Nuevo Mexico," words and music by Amadeo Lucero. **Bird:** roadrunner. **Fish:** New Mexico cutthroat trout. **Flower:** yucca. **Fossil:** coelophysis. **Gemstone:** turquoise. **Insect:** tarantula hawk wasp. **Tree:** piñon pine.

Natural features

Land area: 121,590 sq mi, 314,917 sq km. **Mountain ranges:** Rocky, Sangre de Cristo. **Highest point:** Wheeler Peak, 4,011 m (13,161 ft). **Largest lake:** Elephant Butte Reservoir. **Major rivers:** Rio Grande, Pecos, Canadian, San Juan, Gila. **Natural regions:** Great Plains Province, eastern third of the state, subdivided into the Raton Section to the north, the High Plains along the eastern edge, and the Pecos Valley to the west; Southern Rocky Mountains, north-central region; Colorado Plateau, northwest corner, including the Navajo Section and Datil Section; Basin and Range Province, central region and southwest corner, with the Sacramento Section to the east and the Mexican Highland to the south. **Land use:** pasture, 51.3%; forest, 7.0%; agricultural, 2.0%; other, 39.7%.

For details about state governments, see pages 608–613; for energy data, see pages 627–628.

People

Population (2009): 2,009,671; persons per sq mi 16.5, persons per sq km 6.4. **Vital statistics** (2007; per 1,000 population): birth rate, 15.5; death rate, 7.8; marriage rate, 5.7; divorce rate, 4.3. **Major cities** (2008): Albuquerque 521,999; Las Cruces 91,865; Rio Rancho 79,655; **Santa Fe 71,831;** Roswell 46,198.

Government

Statehood: entered the Union on 6 Jan 1912 as the 47th state. **State constitution:** adopted 1911. **Representation in US Congress:** 2 senators; 3 representatives. **Electoral college:** 5 votes. **Political divisions:** 33 counties.

Economy

Employment (2008): services 31.9%; government 19.0%; finance, insurance, real estate 15.2%; trade 13.4%; construction 7.1%. **Production** (2008): finance, insurance, real estate 21.1%; government 17.3%; services 15.8%; mining 15.6%; trade 9.9%. **Chief agricultural products:** *Crops:* pecans, apples, potatoes, onions, chilies, peanuts (groundnuts), sorghum, corn (maize), wheat, eggs. *Livestock:* dairy cattle, beef cattle, poultry, sheep and lambs. **Chief manufactured products:** electronics; semiconductors; printing and publishing; food products.

Internet resources: <www.newmexico.org>; <www.newmexico.gov>.

New York

Name: New York, named in honor of the English duke of York. **Nickname:** Empire State. **Capital:** Albany. **Rank:** population: 3rd; area: 28th. **Motto:** "Excelsior" ("Ever upward"). **Song:** "I Love New York," words and music by Steve Karmen. **Bird:** bluebird. **Fish:** brook trout. **Flower:** rose. **Fossil:** *Eurypterus remipes.* **Gemstone:** garnet. **Mammal:** beaver. **Tree:** sugar maple.

Natural features

Land area: 53,097 sq mi, 137,521 sq km. **Mountain ranges:** Adirondack, Catskill, Shawangunk, Taconic. **Highest point:** Mt. Marcy, 1,629 m (5,344 ft). **Largest lake:** Oneida Lake. **Major rivers:** Hudson, Mohawk, Genesee, Oswego, Delaware. **Natural regions:** Central Lowland, Eastern Lake Section, extends along the northern coast of Lake Ontario; St. Lawrence Valley, Northern Section, extends along the northern border with Canada; Adirondack Province, northeast; Appalachian Plateaus, including the Mohawks, Southern New York, and Catskill Sections, extend along the southern border with Pennsylvania and up halfway through the state; Valley and Ridge Province, southeastern edge bordering Connecticut and Massachusetts; Coastal Plain, Embayed Section, covers the islands of Manhattan and Long Island. **Land use:** forest, 56.1%; agricultural, 17.1%; other, 26.8%.

People

Population (2009): 19,541,453; persons per sq mi 368.0, persons per sq km 142.1. **Vital statistics** (2007; per 1,000 population): birth rate, 13.1; death rate, 7.7; marriage rate, 6.8; divorce rate, 2.9. **Major**

cities (2008): New York 8,363,710; Buffalo 270,919; Rochester 206,886; Yonkers 201,588; Syracuse 138,068; **Albany 93,539.**

Government

Statehood: entered the Union on 26 Jul 1788 as the 11th state. **State constitution:** adopted 1894. **Representation in US Congress:** 2 senators; 29 representatives. **Electoral college:** 31 votes. **Political divisions:** 62 counties.

Economy

Employment (2008): services 35.8%; finance, insurance, real estate 21.2%; government 13.5%; trade 12.9%; transportation, public utilities 6.1%. **Production** (2008): finance, insurance, real estate 43.4%; services 16.8%; transportation, public utilities 10.5%; government 10.3%; trade 9.7%. **Chief agricultural products:** *Crops:* apples, cabbage, corn (maize), potatoes, onions, grapes, snap beans, cherries, strawberries, maple syrup, horticultural products, milk, other dairy products, eggs. *Livestock:* cattle and calves, chickens. **Chief manufactured products:** food products; chemical products; wearing apparel; base metals; machinery and apparatus; computers and software; scientific and measuring instruments; transportation equipment; electronics and electrical equipment; printing and publishing; biotechnology products.

Internet resources: <www.iloveny.com>; <www.ny.gov>.

North Carolina

Name: North Carolina, named in honor of Charles I of England. **Nickname:** Old North State. **Capital:** Raleigh. **Rank:** population: 10th; area: 29th. **Motto:** "Esse quam videri" ("To be rather than to seem"). **Song:** "The Old North State," words by William Gaston, to the tune of a traditional German melody. **Bird:** cardinal. **Fish:** channel bass. **Flower:** dogwood. **Gemstone:** emerald. **Insect:** honeybee. **Mammal:** gray squirrel. **Reptile:** eastern box turtle. **Rock:** granite. **Tree:** pine.

Natural features

Land area: 52,671 sq mi, 136,417 sq km. **Mountain ranges:** Appalachian, Great Smoky, Blue Ridge. **Highest point:** Mt. Mitchell, 2,037 m (6,684 ft). **Largest lake:** Lake Mattamuskeet. **Major rivers:** Roanoke, Yadkin, Pee Dee. **Natural regions:** Valley and Ridge Province, far western edge; Piedmont Province, consisting of the Piedmont Upland, extending in a southwest to northeast direction through the center of the state; Coastal Plain, eastern third, divided into the Sea Island Section to the south and the Embayed Section to the north. **Land use:** forest, 45.9%; agricultural, 16.4%; other, 37.7%.

People

Population (2009): 9,380,884; persons per sq mi 178.1, persons per sq km 68.8. **Vital statistics** (2007; per 1,000 population): birth rate, 14.5; death rate, 8.4; marriage rate, 7.5; divorce rate, 4.1. **Major cities** (2008): Charlotte 687,456; **Raleigh 392,552;**

Greensboro 250,642; Durham 223,284; Winston-Salem 217,600; Fayetteville 174,091; Cary 129,545; High Point 101,835.

Government

Statehood: entered the Union on 21 Nov 1789 as the 12th state. **State constitution:** adopted 1970. **Representation in US Congress:** 2 senators, 13 representatives. **Electoral college:** 15 votes. **Political divisions:** 100 counties.

Economy

Employment (2008): services 31.9%; government 15.5%; finance, insurance, real estate 15.4%; trade 13.9%; manufacturing 9.8%. **Production** (2008): finance, insurance, real estate 26.9%; manufacturing 19.5%; services 15.5%; government 14.0%; trade 11.7%. **Chief agricultural products:** *Crops:* tobacco, peanuts (groundnuts), apples, blueberries, grapes, peaches, pecans, strawberries, sweet potatoes, Christmas trees. *Livestock:* cattle and calves, chickens, pigs, horses. *Fish catch:* catfish, trout. **Chief manufactured products:** textiles; cotton and synthetic fibers, yarns, and threads; cigarettes and tobacco products; chemical products; electronics and electrical equipment; furniture; lumber; paper products; food products.

Internet resources: <www.visitnc.com>; <www.northcarolina.gov>.

North Dakota

Name: North Dakota, from the Dakota division of the Sioux, the Native American tribe that inhabited the plains before the arrival of Europeans; *dakota* may be the Sioux word for "friend." **Nickname:** Peace Garden State. **Capital:** Bismarck. **Rank:** population: 48th; area: 18th. **Motto:** "Liberty and union now and forever, one and inseparable." **Song:** "North Dakota Hymn," words by James W. Foley and music by C.S. Putnam. **Bird:** western meadowlark. **Fish:** northern pike. **Flower:** wild prairie rose. **Fossil:** Teredo petrified wood. **Tree:** American elm.

Natural features

Land area: 70,700 sq mi, 183,112 sq km. **Highest point:** White Butte, 1,069 m (3,506 ft). **Largest lake:** Devils Lake. **Major rivers:** Red, Souris, Missouri, Little Missouri, James. **Natural regions:** Central Lowland covers eastern half of the state, with the Western Lake Section lying in the east-central region; Great Plains Province covers western half of the state, including sections of the Missouri Plateau to the north and south. **Land use:** agricultural, 53.6%; pasture, 24.5%; forest, 1.0%; other, 20.9%.

People

Population (2009): 646,844; persons per sq mi 9.1, persons per sq km 3.5. **Vital statistics** (2007; per 1,000 population): birth rate, 13.8; death rate, 8.7; marriage rate, 6.6; divorce rate, 2.4. **Major cities** (2008): Fargo 93,531; **Bismarck 60,389;** Grand Forks 51,313; Minot 35,419; West Fargo 23,708.

Government

Statehood: entered the Union on 2 Nov 1889 as the 39th state. **State constitution:** adopted 1889. **Representation in US Congress:** 2 senators; 1 representative. **Electoral college:** 3 votes. **Political divisions:** 53 counties.

Economy

Employment (2008): services 29.4%; government 16.3%; trade 15.2%; finance, insurance, real estate 12.9%; agriculture, forestry, fishing 7.2%. **Production** (2008): finance, insurance, real estate 17.8%; services 15.4%; government 14.1%; trade 13.6%; agriculture, forestry, fishing 10.9%. **Chief agricultural products:** *Crops:* spring wheat, durum wheat, flaxseed, canola, dry beans, sunflowers, barley, honey, potatoes, dairy products. *Livestock:* cattle and calves, sheep and lambs, pigs. **Chief manufactured products:** food products; wood products; refined petroleum products; transportation equipment; machinery and apparatus.

Internet resources: <www.ndtourism.com>; <www.nd.gov>.

Did you know? A 12-foot-tall bronze statue of Sakakawea (Sacagawea), the Shoshone woman who traveled thousands of miles providing indispensable aid to the famous Lewis and Clark Expedition (1804–06), stands on the grounds of the North Dakota Heritage Center in Bismarck.

Ohio

Name: Ohio, from an Iroquois Indian word meaning "great water." **Nickname:** Buckeye State. **Capital:** Columbus. **Rank:** population: 7th; area: 34th. **Motto:** "With God, all things are possible." **Song:** "Beautiful Ohio," words by Ballard MacDonald and music by Mary Earl. **Bird:** cardinal. **Flower:** red carnation. **Fossil:** *Trilobite isotelus.* **Gemstone:** flint. **Insect:** ladybug. **Mammal:** white-tailed deer. **Reptile:** black racer snake. **Tree:** Ohio buckeye.

Natural features

Land area: 44,825 sq mi, 116,096 sq km. **Highest point:** Campbell Hill, 472 m (1,549 ft). **Largest lake:** Grand Lake St. Marys. **Major rivers:** Ohio, Maumee, Cuyahoga, Miami, Scioto. **Natural regions:** the Appalachian Plateau, eastern half of the state, includes the Southern New York Section to the north and the Kanawha Section to the east; the Central Lowlands, western half of the state, includes the Eastern Lake Section in the northwest corner, the Till Plains in the central region, and the Lexington Plain in the southwest. **Land use:** agricultural, 42.5%; forest, 27.3%; other, 30.2%.

People

Population (2009): 11,542,645; persons per sq mi 257.5, persons per sq km 99.4. **Vital statistics** (2007; per 1,000 population): birth rate, 13.2; death

For details about state governments, see pages 608–613; for energy data, see pages 627–628.

rate, 9.3; marriage rate, 6.2; divorce rate, 3.3. **Major cities** (2008): **Columbus 754,885;** Cleveland 433,748; Cincinnati 333,336; Toledo 293,201; Akron 207,510; Dayton 154,200.

Government

Statehood: entered the Union on 1 Mar 1803 as the 17th state. **State constitution:** adopted 1851. **Representation in US Congress:** 2 senators; 18 representatives. **Electoral college:** 20 votes. **Political divisions:** 88 counties.

Economy

Employment (2008): services 33.7%; finance, insurance, real estate 15.8%; trade 14.4%; government 12.4%; manufacturing 11.2%. **Production** (2008): finance, insurance, real estate 26.9%; services 17.9%; manufacturing 17.8%; trade 12.8%; government 11.5%. **Chief agricultural products:** *Crops:* corn (maize), soybeans, grapes, apples, tobacco, winter wheat, dairy products, eggs, greenhouse and nursery products. *Livestock:* cattle and calves, hogs, poultry, goats. **Chief manufactured products:** machinery and apparatus; nonelectrical machinery; food products; transportation equipment; fabricated metal products; base metals; chemical products; rubber products.

Internet resources: <http://consumer.discoverohio. com>; <www.ohio.gov>.

Did you know■ Cambridge, Ohio's own John Glenn is famous for having been the first American astronaut to orbit Earth and later for serving four terms as a US Senator from Ohio. Less known is the fact that in late 1998 Glenn returned to space on the space shuttle *Discovery,* at 77 becoming the oldest person ever to travel in space.

Oklahoma

Name: Oklahoma, from two Choctaw Indian words: *okla,* meaning "people," and *humma,* meaning "red." **Nickname:** Sooner State. **Capital:** Oklahoma City. **Rank:** population: 28th; area: 19th. **Motto:** "Labor omnia vincit" ("Labor conquers all things"). **Song:** "Oklahoma," words by Oscar Hammerstein and music by Richard Rodgers. **Bird:** scissor-tailed flycatcher. **Fish:** white, or sand, bass. **Flower:** mistletoe. **Insect:** honeybee. **Mammal:** bison. **Reptile:** collared lizard (also known as the mountain boomer). **Rock:** rose rock. **Tree:** redbud.

Natural features

Land area: 69,898 sq mi, 181,035 sq km. **Mountain ranges:** Ouachita, Arbuckle, Wichita, Sandstone Hills. **Highest point:** Black Mesa, 1,516 m (4,973 ft). **Largest lake:** Lake Eufaula. **Major rivers:** Arkansas, Red, Canadian. **Natural regions:** Great Plains Province, panhandle region, includes the High Plains to the west and the Plains Border to the east; Central Lowland, covering most of the state, includes the Osage Plains in the central region; West Gulf Coastal Plain, southeastern corner; Oua-

chita Province, east-central region, includes the Arkansas Valley in the center and the Ouachita Mountains to the south; Ozark Plateaus, northeast corner, include the Boston Mountains and Springfield-Salem Plateaus. **Land use:** pasture, 31.6%; agricultural, 20.1%; forest, 16.5%; other, 31.8%.

People

Population (2009): 3,687,050; persons per sq mi 52.7, persons per sq km 20.4. **Vital statistics** (2007; per 1,000 population): birth rate, 15.2; death rate, 10.0; marriage rate, 7.3; divorce rate, 5.2. **Major cities** (2008): **Oklahoma City 551,789;** Tulsa 385,635; Norman 106,957; Broken Arrow 92,931; Lawton 90,091.

Government

Statehood: entered the Union on 16 Nov 1907 as the 46th state. **State constitution:** adopted 1907. **Representation in US Congress:** 2 senators; 5 representatives. **Electoral college:** 7 votes. **Political divisions:** 77 counties.

Economy

Employment (2008): services 30.2%; government 16.5%; finance, insurance, real estate 13.1%; trade 13.1%; manufacturing 7.2%. **Production** (2008): finance, insurance, real estate 17.9%; government 15.7%; services 15.7%; mining 14.3%; trade 11.6%. **Chief agricultural products:** *Crops:* wheat, sorghum, soybeans, cotton, dairy products. *Livestock:* cattle and calves, poultry, hogs and pigs. **Chief manufactured products:** electronics and electrical equipment; telecommunications equipment; transportation equipment; food products; refined petroleum products.

Internet resources: <www.travelok.com>; <www. ok.gov>.

Oregon

Name: Oregon, thought to be of Native American origin. **Nickname:** Beaver State. **Capital:** Salem. **Rank:** population: 27th; area: 10th. **Motto:** "Alis volat propiis" ("She flies with her own wings"). **Song:** "Oregon, My Oregon," words by J.A. Buchanan and music by Henry B. Murtagh. **Bird:** western meadowlark. **Fish:** chinook salmon. **Flower:** Oregon grape. **Gemstone:** Oregon sunstone. **Insect:** Oregon swallowtail. **Mammal:** beaver. **Rock:** thunder egg. **Tree:** Douglas fir.

Natural features

Land area: 97,047 sq mi, 251,351 sq km. **Mountain ranges:** Coast, Klamath, Cascade, Blue, Wallowa. **Highest point:** Mt. Hood, 3,425 m (11,239 ft). **Largest lake:** Upper Klamath Lake. **Major rivers:** Snake, Owyhee, Columbia, Coquille. **Natural regions:** northern Rocky Mountains, northeastern corner, include the Blue Mountain Section; Columbia Plateaus, north and north-central region, include the Walla Walla Plateau in the central region, Harney Section to the south, and Payette Section to the southeast; Basin and Range Province, south-central border, includes the Great Basin; Cascade Sierra Mountains, west central region, include the Middle and Southern Cascades; Pacific

Border Province, western coast, includes the Klamath Mountains to the south, the Oregon Coast Range in the center and north, and the Puget Trough to the east. **Land use:** forest, 20.5%; pasture, 15.1%; agricultural, 6.0%; other, 58.4%.

People

Population (2009): 3,825,657; persons per sq mi 39.4, persons per sq km 15.2. **Vital statistics** (2007; per 1,000 population): birth rate, 13.2; death rate, 8.4; marriage rate, 7.8; divorce rate, 4.0. **Major cities** (2008): Portland 557,706; **Salem 153,435;** Eugene 150,104; Gresham 101,221; Hillsboro 93,638.

Government

Statehood: entered the Union on 14 Feb 1859 as the 33rd state. **State constitution:** adopted 1857. **Representation in US Congress:** 2 senators; 5 representatives. **Electoral college:** 7 votes. **Political divisions:** 36 counties.

Economy

Employment (2008): services 32.7%; finance, insurance, real estate 15.9%; trade 14.4%; government 12.6%; manufacturing 9.0%. **Production** (2008): finance, insurance, real estate 25.3%; manufacturing 18.7%; services 17.0%; government 12.8%; trade 11.9%. **Chief agricultural products:** *Crops:* horticultural and nursery products, Christmas trees, pears, cherries, apples, hazelnuts, potatoes, mint, hops, sugar beets. *Livestock:* cattle and calves, horses, mink, poultry, sheep and lambs. *Fish catch:* tuna, salmon, shellfish, crab, shrimp. **Chief manufactured products:** lumber and wood products; food products; aircraft and spacecraft; semiconductors; computers.

Internet resources: <www.traveloregon.com>; <www.oregon.gov>.

Pennsylvania

Name: Pennsylvania, named for Adm. Sir William Penn, father of the territory's founder, William Penn, and also including the Latin term *sylvania* ("woodlands"). **Nickname:** Keystone State. **Capital:** Harrisburg. **Rank:** population: 6th; area: 33rd. **Motto:** "Virtue, liberty, and independence." **Song:** "Pennsylvania," words and music by Eddie Khoury and Ronnie Bonner. **Bird:** ruffled grouse. **Fish:** brook trout. **Flower:** mountain laurel. **Fossil:** *Phacops rana.* **Insect:** firefly. **Mammal:** white-tailed deer. **Tree:** hemlock.

Natural features

Land area: 46,056 sq mi, 119,284 sq km. **Mountain ranges:** Appalachian, Allegheny. **Highest point:** Mt. Davis, 979 m (3,213 ft). **Largest lake:** Raystown Lake. **Major rivers:** Delaware, Lehigh, Schuylkill, Susquehanna, Ohio. **Natural regions:** Central Lowland, Eastern Lake Section, extreme northwestern edge; Appalachian Plateaus, including the Southern New York, Allegheny Mountain, and Kanawha sections, western

half of state; Valley and Ridge Province, central region, including portions of the Appalachian Mountains; Piedmont Province, comprising the Piedmont Lowlands and Upland, southeast corner; Coastal Plain, extreme southeast edge; New England Province, New England Upland Section, east-central border. **Land use:** forest, 53.9%; agricultural, 17.7%; other, 28.4%.

People

Population (2009): 12,604,767; persons per sq mi 273.7, persons per sq km 105.7. **Vital statistics** (2007; per 1,000 population): birth rate, 12.1; death rate, 10.1; marriage rate, 5.7; divorce rate, 2.8. **Major cities** (2008): Philadelphia 1,447,395; Pittsburgh 310,037; Allentown 107,250; Erie 103,817; Reading 80,506; **Harrisburg 47,148.**

Government

Statehood: entered the Union on 12 Dec 1787 as the 2nd state. **State constitution:** adopted 1968. **Representation in US Congress:** 2 senators, 19 representatives. **Electoral college:** 21 votes. **Political divisions:** 67 counties.

Economy

Employment (2008): services 35.5%; finance, insurance, real estate 17.2%; trade 14.3%; government 11.0%; manufacturing 9.1%. **Production** (2008): finance, insurance, real estate 29.7%; services 19.8%; manufacturing 13.6%; trade 12.0%; government 9.8%. **Chief agricultural products:** *Crops:* mushrooms, apples, tobacco, grapes, peaches, cut flowers, dairy products. *Livestock:* cattle and calves, poultry, pigs, horses. **Chief manufactured products:** electronics; telecommunications equipment; semiconductors; chemical products; food products; base metals; machinery and apparatus; transportation equipment; paper products.

Internet resources: <www.visitpa.com>; <www.pa.gov>.

Rhode Island

Name: Rhode Island, from the Greek island of Rhodes or the Dutch name *Roodt Eyland* ("Red Island"). **Nicknames:** Little Rhody; Ocean State. **Capital:** Providence. **Rank:** population: 43rd; area: 50th. **Motto:** "Hope." **Song:** "Rhode Island's It for Me," words by Charlie Hall and music by Maria Day. **Bird:** Rhode Island Red chicken. **Flower:** violet. **Mineral:** bowenite. **Rock:** cumberlandite.

Natural features

Land area: 1,223 sq mi, 3,168 sq km. **Highest point:** Jerimoth Hill, 247 m (812 ft). **Largest lake:** Scituate Reservoir. **Major rivers:** Blackstone, Pawtuxet, Pawcatuck. **Natural regions:** the entire state is part of the New England Province, subdivided into the New England Upland (western two-thirds) and the Seaboard Lowland (eastern third). **Land use:** forest, 45.9%; agricultural, 2.5%; other, 51.6%.

For details about state governments, see pages 608–613; for energy data, see pages 627–628.

People

Population (2009): 1,053,209; persons per sq mi 861.2, persons per sq km 332.5. Vital statistics (2007; per 1,000 population): birth rate, 11.7; death rate, 9.2; marriage rate, 6.4; divorce rate, 2.8. Major cities (2008): Providence 171,557; Warwick 84,483; Cranston 79,980; Pawtucket 71,765; East Providence 48,480.

Government

Statehood: entered the Union on 29 May 1790 as the 13th state. State constitution: adopted 1986. Representation in US Congress: 2 senators; 2 representatives. Electoral college: 4 votes. Political divisions: 5 counties.

Economy

Employment (2008): services 38.5%; finance, insurance, real estate 17.9%; trade 12.8%; government 12.2%; manufacturing 8.2%. Production (2008): finance, insurance, real estate 34.0%; services 20.5%; government 12.9%; trade 10.9%; manufacturing 9.8%. Chief agricultural products: Crops: apples, peaches, dairy products, eggs, potatoes. Livestock: poultry, cattle and calves, sheep and lambs. Fish catch: shellfish. Chief manufactured products: jewelry; silverware; textiles; fabricated metal products; electrical equipment; machinery and apparatus; surgical instruments; plastics.

Internet resources: <www.visitrhodeisland.com>; <www.ri.gov>.

South Carolina

Name: South Carolina, named in honor of Charles I of England. Nickname: Palmetto State. Capital: Columbia. Rank: population: 24th; area: 40th. Mottoes: "Animis opibusque parati" ("Prepared in mind and resources"); Dum Spiro Spero (While I Breathe, I Hope). Songs: "Carolina," words by Henry Timrod and music by Anne Custis Burgess; "South Carolina on My Mind," words and music by Hank Martin and Buzz Arledge. Amphibian: spotted salamander. Bird: Carolina wren. Fish: striped bass. Flower: Carolina jessamine. Gemstone: amethyst. Insect: Carolina mantid. Mammal: white-tailed deer. Reptile: loggerhead turtle. Rock: blue granite. Tree: palmetto.

Natural features

Land area: 31,118 sq mi, 80,595 sq km. Mountain range: Blue Ridge. Highest point: Sassafras Mountain, 1,085 m (3,560 ft). Largest lake: Lake Marion. Major rivers: Pee Dee, Savannah, Ashley, Combahee, Edisto. Natural regions: Coastal Plain covers the eastern two-thirds of the state and includes the Sea Island Section in the central region; Piedmont Province extends across the central and western region and includes the Piedmont Upland; Blue Ridge Province covers the far northwestern corner and includes the Southern Section. Land use: forest, 56.0%; agricultural, 11.9%; other, 32.1%.

People

Population (2009): 4,561,242; persons per sq mi 146.6, persons per sq km 56.6. Vital statistics

(2007; per 1,000 population): birth rate, 14.3; death rate, 9.0; marriage rate, 7.1; divorce rate, 3.3. Major cities (2008): Columbia 127,029; Charleston 111,978; North Charleston 94,407; Rock Hill 67,339; Mount Pleasant 65,472.

Government

Statehood: entered the Union on 23 May 1788 as the 8th state. State constitution: adopted 1895. Representation in US Congress: 2 senators; 6 representatives. Electoral college: 8 votes. Political divisions: 46 counties.

Economy

Employment (2008): services 33.7%; government 15.6%; trade 14.1%; finance, insurance, real estate 14.0%; manufacturing 9.7%. Production (2008): finance, insurance, real estate 21.3%; services 17.6%; government 17.3%; manufacturing 16.1%; trade 13.6%. Chief agricultural products: Crops: tobacco, cotton, barley, peanuts (groundnuts), peaches, apples, pecans, sweet potatoes, snap beans, dairy products. Livestock: cattle and calves, chickens, pigs. Fish catch: marine fish, oysters, clams, shrimp. Chief manufactured products: chemical products, including pharmaceuticals and fertilizers; textiles; wearing apparel; machinery and apparatus; plastics and rubber products; paper and paperboard; electronics and electrical equipment; transportation equipment; lumber.

Internet resources: <www.discoversouthcarolina.com>; <www.sc.gov>.

South Dakota

Name: South Dakota, from the Dakota division of the Sioux, the Native American tribe that inhabited the plains before the arrival of Europeans; dakota may be the Sioux word for "friend." Nickname: Mount Rushmore State. Capital: Pierre. Rank: population: 46th; area: 17th. Motto: "Under God the people rule." Song: "Hail! South Dakota," words and music by Deecort Hammitt. Bird: Chinese ring-necked pheasant. Fish: walleye. Flower: pasque. Fossil: triceratops. Gemstone: Fairburn agate. Insect: honeybee. Mammal: coyote. Mineral: rose quartz. Tree: Black Hills spruce.

Natural features

Land area: 77,117 sq mi, 199,732 sq km. Mountain range: Black Hills. Highest point: Harney Peak, 2,207 m (7,242 ft). Largest lake: Lake Thompson. Major rivers: Big Sioux, Vermillion, James, Grand, Moreau. Natural regions: the Central Lowland, eastern third of the state, includes the Dissected Till Plains along the eastern edge and the Western Lake Section at the center; the Great Plains Province, western two-thirds of the state; the Black Hills, far west; the High Plains, southern border; the Missouri Plateau, west. Land use: pasture, 44.7%; agricultural, 34.6%; forest, 1.0%; other, 19.7%.

People

Population (2009): 812,383; persons per sq mi 10.5, persons per sq km 4.1. Vital statistics (2007; per 1,000 population): birth rate, 15.4; death rate, 8.6; marriage rate, 7.7; divorce rate, 3.1. Major cities

(2008): Sioux Falls 154,997; Rapid City 65,491; Aberdeen 24,460; Watertown 20,488; Brookings 19,865; **Pierre 13,899.**

Government

Statehood: entered the Union on 2 Nov 1889 as the 40th state. **State constitution:** adopted 1889. **Representation in US Congress:** 2 senators; 1 representative. **Electoral college:** 3 votes. **Political divisions:** 66 counties.

Economy

Employment (2008): services 30.6%; trade 15.1%; government 14.4%; finance, insurance, real estate 14.2%; manufacturing 7.9%. **Production** (2008): finance, insurance, real estate 27.9%; services 16.8%; government 12.3%; trade 12.2%; manufacturing 9.6%. **Chief agricultural products:** Crops: corn (maize), wheat, sunflowers, dairy products, eggs, flaxseed, barley, rye. Livestock: cattle and calves, pigs, sheep and lambs. **Chief manufactured products:** machinery and apparatus; office machinery; computers; food products; electronics; printing and publishing; lumber; fabricated metal products; medical instruments; jewelry.

Internet resources: <www.travelsd.com>; <www.sd.gov>.

 **Did you know?** The state of Tennessee was once called Franklin. Settlers from the east moved into the area in 1768, and by 1777 the territory had become Washington County, a part of North Carolina. In 1784 some of the settlers declared themselves independent of North Carolina and formed the State of Franklin, adopting their own constitution.

Tennessee

Name: Tennessee, from *Tanasi,* a Cherokee Indian village. **Nickname:** Volunteer State. **Capital:** Nashville. **Rank:** population: 17th; area: 35th. **Motto:** "Agriculture and commerce." **Songs:** "My Homeland, Tennessee," words by Nell Grayson Taylor and music by Roy Lamont Smith; "When It's Iris Time in Tennessee," words and music by Willa Mae Waid; "The Tennessee Waltz," words and music by Redd Stewart and Pee Wee King; "Rocky Top," words and music by Boudleaux and Felice Bryant; "The Pride of Tennessee," words and music by Fred Congdon, Thomas Vaughn, and Carol Elliot. **Amphibian:** cave salamander. **Bird:** mockingbird. **Fish:** largemouth bass; channel catfish. **Flower:** iris. **Gemstone:** river pearl. **Insects:** firefly; ladybug. **Mammal:** raccoon. **Reptile:** box turtle. **Rocks:** limestone; agate. **Tree:** tulip poplar.

Natural features

Land area: 42,143 sq mi, 109,150 sq km. **Mountain ranges:** Unaka, Great Smoky. **Highest point:** Clingmans Dome, 2,025 m (6,643 ft). **Largest lake:** Reelfoot. **Major rivers:** Tennessee, Cumberland, Mississippi. **Natural regions:** Blue Ridge Province, eastern border; Valley and Ridge Province, extending from southwest to northeast; Appalachian Plateau, central,

running from south to north, includes the Cumberland Plateau Section in the center and the Cumberland Mountain Section at the northern end; Interior Low Plateau, west central, includes the Nashville Basin and Highland Rim Section. **Land use:** forest, 44.3%; agricultural, 17.6%; other, 38.1%.

People

Population (2009): 6,296,254; persons per sq mi 149.4, persons per sq km 57.7. **Vital statistics** (2007; per 1,000 population): birth rate, 14.1; death rate, 9.3; marriage rate, 10.6; divorce rate, 4.9. **Major cities** (2008): Memphis 669,651; **Nashville 596,462;** Knoxville 184,802; Chattanooga 170,880; Clarksville 119,735.

Government

Statehood: entered the Union on 1 Jun 1796 as the 16th state. **State constitution:** adopted 1870. **Representation in US Congress:** 2 senators; 9 representatives. **Electoral college:** 11 votes. **Political divisions:** 95 counties.

Economy

Employment (2008): services 33.3%; trade 14.8%; finance, insurance, real estate 14.1%; government 12.1%; manufacturing 10.0%. **Production** (2008): finance, insurance, real estate 22.7%; services 21.5%; manufacturing 16.1%; trade 14.9%; government 11.3%. **Chief agricultural products:** Crops: cotton, tobacco, peaches, apples, tomatoes, snap beans, honey, dairy products, wheat, sorghum. Livestock: cattle and calves, poultry, hogs, sheep and lambs. Fish catch: catfish, trout. **Chief manufactured products:** transportation equipment, including motor vehicles, aircraft parts, and boats; chemical products; printing and publishing; electronics; lumber; paper products; wearing apparel; surgical instruments and supplies.

Internet resources: <www.tnvacation.com>; <www.tn.gov>.

Texas

Name: Texas, from the Caddo Indian word *thecas,* meaning "allies" or "friends." **Nickname:** Lone Star State. **Capital:** Austin. **Rank:** population: 2nd; area: 2nd. **Motto:** "Friendship." **Song:** "Texas, Our Texas," words and music by William J. Marsh and Gladys Yoakum Wright. **Bird:** mockingbird. **Fish:** Guadalupe bass. **Flower:** bluebonnet. **Fossil:** pleurocoelus. **Gemstone:** Texas blue topaz. **Insect:** monarch butterfly. **Mammal:** Mexican free-tailed bat (flying); longhorn (large); armadillo (small). **Reptile:** horned lizard. **Rock:** petrified palmwood. **Tree:** pecan.

Natural features

Land area: 266,853 sq mi, 691,146 sq km. **Mountain ranges:** Rocky, Guadalupe. **Highest point:** Guadalupe Peak, 2,667 m (8,749 ft). **Largest lake:** Caddo Lake. **Major rivers:** Red, Trinity, Brazos, Colorado, Rio Grande. **Natural regions:** Coastal Plain, southern and eastern regions, includes the west

For details about state governments, see pages 608–613; for energy data, see pages 627–628.

Gulf Coastal Plain near the east-central coast; Central Lowland, north central, includes the Osage Plains; Great Plains Province, extending from the panhandle across most of central and western Texas, includes the Edwards Plateau to the south, Pecos Valley to the west, High Plains to the north, and Central Texas Section; Basin and Range Province, extreme western region, comprises the Mexican Highland to the south and the Sacramento Section to the north. **Land use:** pasture, 56.2%; agricultural, 14.9%; forest, 6.2%; other, 22.7%.

People

Population (2009): 24,782,302; persons per sq mi 92.9, persons per sq km 35.9. **Vital statistics** (2007; per 1,000 population): birth rate, 17.1; death rate, 6.7; marriage rate, 7.5; divorce rate, 3.3. **Major cities** (2008): Houston 2,242,193; San Antonio 1,351,305; Dallas 1,279,910; **Austin 757,688;** Fort Worth 703,073; El Paso 613,190; Arlington 374,417; Corpus Christi 286,462.

Government

Statehood: entered the Union on 29 Dec 1845 as the 28th state. **State constitution:** adopted 1876. **Representation in US Congress:** 2 senators; 32 representatives. **Electoral college:** 34 votes. **Political divisions:** 254 counties.

Economy

Employment (2008): services 31.0%; finance, insurance, real estate 16.6%; trade 14.2%; government 13.4%; construction 7.4%. **Production** (2008): finance, insurance, real estate 22.4%; services 14.4%; manufacturing 13.0%; trade 12.1%; mining 11.3%. **Chief agricultural products:** *Crops:* cotton, apples, greenhouse and nursery products, corn (maize), sorghum, wheat, dairy products, eggs, rice. *Livestock:* cattle and calves, pigs, chickens. *Fish catch:* shrimp. **Chief manufactured products:** refined petroleum products; food products; computers; electronics; chemical products; plastics; wearing apparel; wood products; paper products; nonelectrical machinery; fabricated metal products; transportation equipment, including aerospace products and parts, aircraft parts, and motor vehicle parts.

Internet resources: <www.traveltex.com>; <www.texas.gov>.

Utah

Name: Utah, named for the Ute Indian tribe; the word *ute* means "people of the mountains." **Nickname:** Beehive State. **Capital:** Salt Lake City. **Rank:** population: 34th; area: 13th. **Motto:** "Industry." **Song:** "Utah, This Is the Place," words by Sam and Gary Francis and music by Gary Francis. **Bird:** California seagull. **Fish:** Bonneville cutthroat trout. **Flower:** sego lily. **Fossil:** allosaurus. **Gemstone:** topaz. **Insect:** honeybee. **Mammal:** Rocky Mountain elk. **Mineral:** copper. **Rock:** coal. **Tree:** blue spruce.

Natural features

Land area: 84,899 sq mi, 219,887 sq km. **Mountain ranges:** Uinta, Wasatch, Rocky. **Highest point:** Kings

Peak, 4,123 m (13,528 ft). **Largest lake:** Great Salt Lake. **Major rivers:** Colorado, Green, Sevier. **Natural regions:** Basin and Range Province, western half of the state, includes the Great Salt Lake Desert and Bonneville Salt Flats to the north and the Great Basin to the south; Middle Rocky Mountains, northeast; Colorado Plateaus, east-central and southeast regions, include the Grand Canyon Section to the south, the High Plateaus of Utah and Canyon Lands in the center, the Navajo Section in the extreme southeast corner, and the Uinta Basin to the north. **Land use:** pasture, 19.6%; forest, 3.5%; agricultural, 3.1%; other, 73.8%.

People

Population (2009): 2,784,572; persons per sq mi 32.8, persons per sq km 12.7. **Vital statistics** (2007; per 1,000 population): birth rate, 20.8; death rate, 5.3; marriage rate, 8.6; divorce rate, 3.4. **Major cities** (2008): **Salt Lake City 181,698;** West Valley City 123,447; Provo 118,581; West Jordan 104,447; Sandy 96,660.

Government

Statehood: entered the Union on 4 Jan 1896 as the 45th state. **State constitution:** adopted 1895. **Representation in US Congress:** 2 senators; 3 representatives. **Electoral college:** 5 votes. **Political divisions:** 29 counties.

Economy

Employment (2008): services 29.1%; finance, insurance, real estate 20.0%; trade 14.2%; government 13.5%; manufacturing 7.9%. **Production** (2008): finance, insurance, real estate 28.8%; services 15.9%; government 13.8%; trade 12.3%; manufacturing 11.9%. **Chief agricultural products:** *Crops:* peaches, cherries, onions, dairy products. *Livestock:* cattle and calves, sheep and lambs, mink, poultry. *Fish catch:* trout. **Chief manufactured products:** machinery and apparatus; computers; office machinery; transportation equipment, including aerospace products, missile parts, and motor vehicle parts; surgical tools and electromedical equipment; food products.

Internet resources: <www.utah.com>; <www.utah.gov>.

Vermont

Name: Vermont, from the French words *vert* and *mont,* meaning "green mountains." **Nickname:** Green Mountain State. **Capital:** Montpelier. **Rank:** population: 49th; area: 43rd. **Motto:** "Freedom and unity." **Song:** "These Green Mountains," words and music by Diane Martin. **Bird:** hermit thrush. **Flower:** red clover. **Insect:** honeybee. **Mammal:** Morgan horse. **Tree:** sugar maple.

Natural features

Land area: 9,615 sq mi, 24,903 sq km. **Mountain ranges:** Green, Appalachian, Hoosac, Taconic. **Highest point:** Mt. Mansfield, 1,339 m (4,393 ft). **Largest lake:** Lake Champlain. **Major rivers:** Lamoille, Winooski, Otter Creek, Poultney, White. **Nat-**

ural regions: the New England Province, eastern two-thirds of the state, includes the Taconic Section to the south, the Green Mountain Section in the center, the New England Upland Section along the east-central edge, and the White Mountain Section in the far northeast corner; the St. Lawrence Valley, western edge of the state, includes the Champlain Section in the central portion; the Valley and Ridge Province, small section along the west-central edge, includes the Hudson Valley. Land use: forest, 67.1%; agricultural, 9.5%; other, 23.4%.

People

Population (2009): 621,760; persons per sq mi 64.7, persons per sq km 25.0. Vital statistics (2007; per 1,000 population): birth rate, 10.5; death rate, 8.3; marriage rate, 8.6; divorce rate, 3.8. Major cities (2008): Burlington 38,897; South Burlington 17,574; Rutland 16,742; Essex Junction 9,056; Barre 8,837; Montpelier 7,760.

Government

Statehood: entered the Union on 4 Mar 1791 as the 14th state. State constitution: adopted 1793. Representation in US Congress: 2 senators; 1 representative. Electoral college: 3 votes. Political divisions: 14 counties.

Economy

Employment (2008): services 36.2%; trade 14.2%; government 13.1%; finance, insurance, real estate 12.9%; manufacturing 8.9%. Production (2008): finance, insurance, real estate 24.5%; services 22.2%; government 13.9%; trade 12.9%; manufacturing 11.4%. Chief agricultural products: *Crops:* apples, honey, greenhouse and nursery products, Christmas trees, maple syrup, dairy products, eggs. *Livestock:* cattle and calves, chickens, turkeys, sheep and lambs, horses. Chief manufactured products: electronics and electrical equipment; fabricated metal products; nonelectrical machinery; paper products; printing and publishing; food products; transportation equipment; lumber and wood products.

Internet resources: <www.travel-vermont.com>; <www.vermont.gov>.

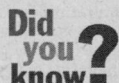 **Did you know?** Hampton Roads, Virginia, witnessed a battle on 9 Mar 1862 between USS *Monitor* and CSS *Virginia* (formerly USS *Merrimack*). The battle, which ended in a draw, featured the first combat between two iron-armored ships and ushered in the age of modern naval warfare.

Virginia

Name: Virginia, named in honor of Elizabeth I of England, known as the Virgin Queen. Nickname: Old Dominion. Capital: Richmond. Rank: population: 12th; area: 36th. Motto: "Sic semper tyrannis" ("Thus ever to tyrants"). Song: "Carry Me Back to Old Virginia," words and music by James B. Bland. Bird: cardinal. Fish: brook trout. Flower:

dogwood. Fossil: *Chesapecten jeffersonius.* Insect: tiger swallowtail butterfly. Tree: dogwood.

Natural features

Land area: 40,600 sq mi, 105,154 sq km. Mountain ranges: Blue Ridge, Appalachian. Highest point: Mt. Rogers, 1,746 m (5,729 ft). Largest lake: Smith Mountain Lake. Major rivers: Potomac, Shenandoah, James, Roanoke. Natural regions: Coastal Plain, eastern region below the Potomac River; Piedmont Province, extending from the south-central border up to the border with Maryland, includes the Piedmont Upland and Piedmont Lowlands; Blue Ridge Province, west of the Piedmont Province; Valley and Ridge region, covering most of western Virginia, includes the Shenandoah Valley and Allegheny, Shenandoah, and Appalachian mountains; Appalachian Plateau, extreme western tip of the state, includes the Cumberland Mountain and Kanawha sections. Land use: forest, 48.7%; agricultural, 10.6%; other, 40.7%.

People

Population (2009): 7,882,590; persons per sq mi 194.2, persons per sq km 75.0. Vital statistics (2007; per 1,000 population): birth rate, 14.1; death rate, 7.5; marriage rate, 7.5; divorce rate, 3.8. Major cities (2008): Virginia Beach 433,746; Norfolk 234,220; Chesapeake 220,111; Richmond 202,002; Newport News 179,614; Hampton 145,494; Alexandria 143,885; Portsmouth 100,577.

Government

Statehood: entered the Union on 26 Jun 1788 as the 10th state. State constitution: adopted 1970. Representation in US Congress: 2 senators; 11 representatives. Electoral college: 13 votes. Political divisions: 95 counties.

Economy

Employment (2008): services 30.1%; finance, insurance, real estate 20.2%; government 17.7%; trade 12.9%; construction 6.7%. Production (2008): finance, insurance, real estate 34.1%; government 18.4%; services 14.9%; trade 9.9%; transportation, public utilities 9.1%. Chief agricultural products: *Crops:* tobacco, soybeans, peanuts (groundnuts), cotton, apples, tomatoes, wheat, potatoes, honey. *Livestock:* chickens, turkeys, pigs, cattle and calves, sheep and lambs. *Fish catch:* clams, soft-shell and blue crabs, oysters, trout, catfish, hybrid striped bass. Chief manufactured products: electronics and electrical equipment; paper products; tobacco products; plastics and rubber products; chemical products; food products; printing and publishing.

Internet resources: <www.virginia.org>; <www.virginia.gov>.

Washington

Name: Washington, named in honor of George Washington. Nickname: Evergreen State. Capital: Olympia. Rank: population: 13th; area: 21st. Motto: "Alki" ("By and by"). Song: "Washington My

Home," words and music by Helen Davis. **Bird:** willow goldfinch. **Fish:** steelhead trout. **Flower:** coast rhododendron. **Fossil:** Columbian mammoth. **Gemstone:** petrified wood. **Insect:** green darner dragonfly. **Tree:** western hemlock.

Natural features

Land area: 68,097 sq mi, 176,370 sq km. **Mountain ranges:** Olympic, Cascade, Blue. **Highest point:** Mt. Rainier, 4,392 m (14,410 ft). **Largest lake:** Moses Lake. **Major rivers:** Columbia, Pend Oreille, Snake, Yakima. **Natural regions:** Pacific Border Province, western quarter of the state, includes the Olympic Mountains to the west and the Puget Trough to the east; Cascade-Sierra Mountains, running north to south down center of state, include the Northern and Middle Cascades; Northern Rocky Mountains, northeast corner; Columbia Plateaus, eastern, central, and southern regions, include the Walla Walla Plateau in the center and the Blue Mountain Section in the southeast corner. **Land use:** forest, 28.9%; agricultural, 14.7%; pasture, 13.3%; other, 43.1%.

People

Population (2009): 6,664,195; persons per sq mi 97.9, persons per sq km 37.8. **Vital statistics** (2007; per 1,000 population): birth rate, 13.8; death rate, 7.3; marriage rate, 6.5; divorce rate, 4.5. **Major cities** (2008): Seattle 598,541; Spokane 202,319; Tacoma 197,181; Vancouver 163,186; Bellevue 123,771; **Olympia 45,322.**

Government

Statehood: entered the Union on 11 Nov 1889 as the 42nd state. **State constitution:** adopted 1889. **Representation in US Congress:** 2 senators; 9 representatives. **Electoral college:** 11 votes. **Political divisions:** 39 counties.

Economy

Employment (2008): services 29.9%; finance, insurance, real estate 17.0%; government 15.6%; trade 13.8%; manufacturing 7.7%. **Production** (2008): finance, insurance, real estate 27.5%; services 16.4%; government 14.5%; trade 13.1%; transportation, public utilities 11.8%. **Chief agricultural products:** *Crops:* apples, peaches, pears, cherries, grapes, apricots, raspberries, asparagus, sweet corn, mint. *Livestock:* cattle and calves, chickens, turkeys, horses. *Fish catch:* oysters, clams, mussels, crab, shrimp, geoduck, sea cucumbers, salmon. **Chief manufactured products:** aerospace equipment; food products; forest products; advanced medical and technology products; aluminum products.

Internet resources: <www.experiencewa.com>; <http://access.wa.gov>.

West Virginia

Name: West Virginia, named in honor of Elizabeth I of England, known as the Virgin Queen. **Nickname:** Mountain State. **Capital:** Charleston. **Rank:** population: 37th; area: 41st. **Motto:** "Montani semper liberi" ("Mountaineers are always free"). **Songs:** "This Is My West Virginia," words and music by Iris Bell; "West Virginia, My Home Sweet Home," words and music by Julian G. Hearne, Jr.; "The West Virginia Hills," words by Ellen King and music by H.E. Engle. **Bird:** cardinal. **Fish:** brook trout. **Flower:** rhododendron. **Gemstone:** West Virginia fossil coral. **Insect:** monarch butterfly. **Mammal:** black bear. **Tree:** sugar maple.

Natural features

Land area: 24,230 sq mi, 62,755 sq km. **Mountain ranges:** Appalachian, Allegheny. **Highest point:** Spruce Knob, 1,482 m (4,863 ft). **Largest lake:** Summersville Lake. **Major rivers:** Ohio, Big Sandy, Guyandotte, Great Kanawha, Little Kanawha. **Natural regions:** the Valley and Ridge Province, eastern edge of the state, includes portions of the Shenandoah Mountains; the remainder of the state consists of the Appalachian Plateaus and includes the Kanawha Section to the south, and the Allegheny Mountains in the northeast. **Land use:** forest, 68.1%; agricultural, 5.3%; other, 26.6%.

People

Population (2009): 1,819,777; persons per sq mi 75.1, persons per sq km 29.0. **Vital statistics** (2007; per 1,000 population): birth rate, 12.1; death rate, 11.6; marriage rate, 7.2; divorce rate, 5.0. **Major cities** (2008): **Charleston 50,302;** Huntington 49,185; Parkersburg 31,611; Morgantown 29,642; Wheeling 28,913.

Government

Statehood: entered the Union on 20 Jun 1863 as the 35th state. **State constitution:** adopted 1872. **Representation in US Congress:** 2 senators; 3 representatives. **Electoral college:** 5 votes. **Political divisions:** 55 counties.

Economy

Employment (2008): services 33.1%; government 16.7%; trade 14.8%; finance, insurance, real estate 10.8%; manufacturing 6.3%. **Production** (2008): government 17.8%; services 17.7%; finance, insurance, real estate 17.4%; trade 12.1%; manufacturing 10.7%. **Chief agricultural products:** *Crops:* apples, tobacco, peaches, dairy products. *Livestock:* cattle and calves, sheep and lambs, poultry. **Chief manufactured products:** chemical products; automobile parts; base metals; fabricated metal products; glassware; computer software; wood products; electrical equipment; machinery and apparatus.

Internet resources: <www.wvtourism.com>; <www.wv.gov>.

Wisconsin

Name: Wisconsin, an anglicized version of a French rendering of the Algonquian Indian name *Meskousing,* said to mean "this stream of red stone." **Nickname:** Badger State. **Capital:** Madison. **Rank:** population: 20th; area: 22nd. **Motto:** "Forward." **Song:**

"On, Wisconsin," words and music by William T. Purdy. **Bird:** robin. **Fish:** muskellunge (muskie). **Flower:** wood violet. **Fossil:** trilobite. **Insect:** honeybee. **Mammal:** badger. **Mineral:** galena. **Rock:** red granite. **Tree:** sugar maple.

Natural features

Land area: 65,498 sq mi, 169,639 sq km. **Mountain ranges:** Baraboo, Rib, Gogebic. **Highest point:** Timms Hill, 595 m (1,952 ft). **Largest lake:** Lake Winnebago. **Major rivers:** Wisconsin, St. Croix, Rock, Mississippi, Namekagon. **Natural regions:** Superior Upland, northern half of the state, divided into highland and lowland sections; Central Lowland, southern half of the state, divided into the Wisconsin Driftless Section to the west and the Eastern Lake Section to the east, with a section of the Till Plains occupying a small area at the southern border. **Land use:** forest, 40.4%; agricultural, 28.7%; other, 30.9%.

People

Population (2009): 5,654,774; persons per sq mi 86.3, persons per sq km 33.3. **Vital statistics** (2007; per 1,000 population): birth rate, 13.0; death rate, 8.3; marriage rate, 5.8; divorce rate, 2.9. **Major cities** (2008): Milwaukee 604,477; **Madison 231,916;** Green Bay 101,025; Kenosha 96,950; Racine 82,196.

Government

Statehood: entered the Union on 29 May 1848 as the 30th state. **State constitution:** adopted 1848. **Representation in US Congress:** 2 senators; 8 representatives. **Electoral college:** 10 votes. **Political divisions:** 72 counties.

Economy

Employment (2008): services 31.3%; trade 14.6%; finance, insurance, real estate 14.4%; manufacturing 14.1%; government 11.9%. **Production** (2008): finance, insurance, real estate 25.7%; manufacturing 20.3%; services 17.2%; trade 11.7%; government 11.0%. **Chief agricultural products:** *Crops:* dairy products, corn (maize), honey, maple syrup, potatoes, strawberries, cherries, cranberries, Christmas trees, mint oil. *Livestock:* cattle and calves, hogs, mink. *Fish catch:* bass, trout, pike. **Chief manufactured products:** food products; beer; machinery and apparatus; paper products; fabricated metal products; transportation equipment; household appliances.

Internet resources: <www.travelwisconsin.com>; <www.wisconsin.gov>.

Wyoming

Name: Wyoming, from a Delaware Indian word meaning "land of vast plains." **Nicknames:** Equality State; Cowboy State. **Capital:** Cheyenne. **Rank:** population: 50th; area: 9th. **Motto:** "Equal rights." **Song:** "Wyoming," words by Charles E. Winter and music by George E. Knapp. **Bird:** meadowlark. **Fish:**

cutthroat trout. **Flower:** Indian paintbrush. **Fossil:** *Knightia.* **Gemstone:** jade. **Mammal:** bison. **Reptile:** horned toad. **Tree:** plains cottonwood.

Natural features

Land area: 97,813 sq mi, 253,335 sq km. **Mountain ranges:** Rocky, Big Horn, Grand Teton, Wind River, Continental Divide, Sierra Madre, Washakie. **Highest point:** Gannett Peak, 4,207 m (13,804 ft). **Largest lake:** Yellowstone Lake. **Major rivers:** Snake, Colorado, Green, Columbia. **Natural regions:** Great Plains Province, eastern third of the state, includes the Black Hills in the northeast corner, the High Plains in the southwest corner, and the Missouri Plateau in the center; Wyoming Basin, central and southern regions; Southern Rocky Mountains, southern border; Middle Rocky Mountains, northwest third of the state, also cover a small area on the southern border; Northern Rocky Mountains, extreme northwestern tip of the state. **Land use:** pasture, 44.0%; agricultural, 3.5%; forest, 1.5%; other, 51.0%.

People

Population (2009): 544,270; persons per sq mi 5.6, persons per sq km 2.1. **Vital statistics** (2007; per 1,000 population): birth rate, 15.1; death rate, 8.2; marriage rate, 9.3; divorce rate, 5.5. **Major cities** (2008): Cheyenne **56,915;** Casper 54,047; Laramie 27,664; Gillette 26,871; Rock Springs 20,200.

Government

Statehood: entered the Union on 10 Jul 1890 as the 44th state. **State constitution:** adopted 1889. **Representation in US Congress:** 2 senators; 1 representative. **Electoral college:** 3 votes. **Political divisions:** 23 counties.

Economy

Employment (2008): services 26.0%; government 17.8%; finance, insurance, real estate 13.1%; trade 12.8%; construction 9.5%. **Production** (2008): mining 33.2%; finance, insurance, real estate 12.9%; government 12.7%; transportation, public utilities 11.5%; services 10.7%. **Chief agricultural products:** *Crops:* wheat, barley, sugar beets, corn (maize). *Livestock:* cattle and calves, sheep and lambs. **Chief manufactured products:** refined petroleum products; lumber and wood products; food products; fabricated metal products.

Internet resources: <www.wyomingtourism.org>; <www.wyoming.gov>.

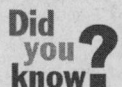
Did you know? Wyoming is the home of Shoshone National Forest, the oldest national forest in the United States (declared in 1891). Yellowstone National Park, the oldest national park in the world and one of the largest, was established by Congress in 1872 and also lies mostly within the boundaries of Wyoming.

For details about state governments, see pages 608–613; for energy data, see pages 627–628.

State Government

Governors of US States and Territories

Governors of New Hampshire and Vermont serve two-year terms; all others serve four-year terms. Parties: Democratic (D); Republican (R); New Progressive (NP); Covenant (C). Sources: National Governors Association; Council of State Governments.

STATE	GOVERNOR	IN OFFICE SINCE	PRESENT TERM EXPIRES
Alabama	Bob Riley (R)	January 2003	January 2011
Alaska	Sean R. Parnell (R)[1]	July 2009	December 2010*
Arizona	Jan Brewer (R)[2]	January 2009	January 2011*
Arkansas	Mike Beebe (D)	January 2007	January 2011*
California	Arnold Schwarzenegger (R)[3]	November 2003	January 2011
Colorado	Bill Ritter (D)	January 2007	January 2011*
Connecticut	M. Jodi Rell (R)[4]	July 2004	January 2011*
Delaware	Jack Markell (D)	January 2009	January 2013*
Florida	Charlie Crist (R)	January 2007	January 2011*
Georgia	Sonny Perdue (R)	January 2003	January 2011
Hawaii	Linda Lingle (R)	December 2002	December 2010
Idaho	C.L. "Butch" Otter (R)	January 2007	January 2011*
Illinois	Pat Quinn (D)[5]	January 2009	January 2011*
Indiana	Mitch Daniels (R)	January 2005	January 2013
Iowa	Chet Culver (D)	January 2007	January 2011*
Kansas	Mark Parkinson (D)[6]	April 2009	January 2011*
Kentucky	Steve Beshear (D)	December 2007	December 2011*
Louisiana	Bobby Jindal (R)	January 2008	January 2012*
Maine	John E. Baldacci (D)	January 2003	January 2011
Maryland	Martin O'Malley (D)	January 2007	January 2011*
Massachusetts	Deval Patrick (D)	January 2007	January 2011*
Michigan	Jennifer Granholm (D)	January 2003	January 2011
Minnesota	Tim Pawlenty (R)	January 2003	January 2011*
Mississippi	Haley Barbour (R)	January 2004	January 2012
Missouri	Jay Nixon (D)	January 2009	January 2013*
Montana	Brian Schweitzer (D)	January 2005	January 2013
Nebraska	Dave Heineman (R)[7]	January 2005	January 2011*
Nevada	Jim Gibbons (R)	January 2007	January 2011*
New Hampshire	John Lynch (D)	January 2005	January 2011*
New Jersey	Christopher J. Christie (R)	January 2010	January 2014*
New Mexico	Bill Richardson (D)	January 2003	January 2011
New York	David A. Paterson (D)[8]	March 2008	January 2011*
North Carolina	Beverly Perdue (D)	January 2009	January 2013*
North Dakota	John Hoeven (R)	December 2000	December 2012*
Ohio	Ted Strickland (D)	January 2007	January 2011*
Oklahoma	Brad Henry (D)	January 2003	January 2011
Oregon	Ted Kulongoski (D)	January 2003	January 2011
Pennsylvania	Edward G. Rendell (D)	January 2003	January 2011
Rhode Island	Don Carcieri (R)	January 2003	January 2011
South Carolina	Mark Sanford (R)	January 2003	January 2011
South Dakota	Mike Rounds (R)	January 2003	January 2011
Tennessee	Phil Bredesen (D)	January 2003	January 2011
Texas	Rick Perry (R)[9]	December 2000	January 2011*
Utah	Gary Herbert (R)[10]	August 2009	January 2011*
Vermont	Jim Douglas (R)	January 2003	January 2011*
Virginia	Robert McDonnell (R)	January 2010	January 2014
Washington	Chris Gregoire (D)	January 2005	January 2013*
West Virginia	Joe Manchin III (D)	January 2005	January 2013
Wisconsin	Jim Doyle (D)	January 2003	January 2011*
Wyoming	Dave Freudenthal (D)	January 2003	January 2011

TERRITORY	GOVERNOR	IN OFFICE SINCE	PRESENT TERM EXPIRES
American Samoa	Togiola T.A. Tulafono (D)[11]	April 2003	January 2013
Guam	Felix Perez Camacho (R)	January 2003	January 2011
Northern Mariana Islands	Benígno Fitial (C)	January 2006	January 2015
Puerto Rico	Luis G. Fortuño (R) (NP)	January 2009	January 2013*
Virgin Islands	John deJongh, Jr. (D)	January 2007	January 2011*

Present governor is eligible for reelection.

Governors of US States and Territories (continued)

[1]*Lieut. Gov. Sean R. Parnell became governor on 26 Jul 2009 following Sarah Palin's resignation.* [2]*Secretary of State Jan Brewer became governor on 21 Jan 2009 following Janet Napolitano's appointment to the office of US secretary of homeland security.* [3]*Arnold Schwarzenegger was elected in October 2003 following the recall of former governor Gray Davis. Gov. Schwarzenegger was elected to a full term in November 2006.* [4]*Lieut. Gov. M. Jodi Rell became governor on 1 Jul 2004 following John G. Rowland's resignation. Gov. Rell was elected to a full term in November 2006.* [5]*Lieut. Gov. Patrick Quinn became governor on 29 Jan 2009 following Rod Blagojevich's removal from office.* [6]*Lieut. Gov. Mark Parkinson became governor on 28 Apr 2009 following Kathleen Sebelius's appointment to the office of US secretary of health and human services.* [7]*Lieut. Gov. Dave Heineman became governor on 21 Jan 2005 following Mike Johanns's appointment to the office of US secretary of agriculture. Gov. Heineman was elected to a full term in November 2006.* [8]*Lieut. Gov. David A. Paterson became governor in March 2008 following Eliot Spitzer's resignation.* [9]*Lieut. Gov. Rick Perry became governor in December 2000 following George W. Bush's election as president of the United States. Gov. Perry was elected to a full term in November 2002.* [10]*Lieut. Gov. Gary Herbert became governor on 10 Aug 2009 following the appointment of Jon M. Huntsman, Jr., as ambassador to China.* [11]*Lieut. Gov. Togiola T.A. Tulafono became governor in April 2003 following the death of Gov. Tauese Sunia. Gov. Tulafono was elected to a full term in November 2004.*

State Officers and Legislatures

Sources: Web sites of the individual states; The Book of the States, vol. 42; and the CSG State Directory, published by the Council of State Governments. Legislature figures are as of March 2010. N/A means not available.

STATE/OFFICE	OFFICEHOLDER	PAY[1]
Alabama		
Governor	Bob Riley (R)	US$112,895
Lieut. Gov.	Jim Folsom, Jr. (D)	US$73,488
Sec. of State	Beth Chapman (R)	US$79,580
Atty. Gen.	Troy King (R)	US$168,003
Treasurer	Kay Ivey (R)	US$79,580
Legislature		
Senate	Dem: 21; Rep: 14	
House	Dem: 60; Rep: 45	
Alaska		
Governor	Sean R. Parnell (R)	US$125,000
Lieut. Gov.	Craig Campbell (R)	US$100,000
Sec. of State[2]		
Atty. Gen.	Daniel S. Sullivan	US$135,000
Treasurer[3]	Jerry Burnett (Deputy Treasury Commissioner)	US$123,456
Legislature		
Senate	Dem: 10; Rep: 10	
House	Dem: 18; Rep: 22	
Arizona		
Governor	Jan Brewer (R)	US$95,000
Lieut. Gov.[4]		
Sec. of State	Ken Bennett (R)	US$70,000
Atty. Gen.	Terry Goddard (D)	US$90,000
Treasurer	Dean Martin (R)	US$70,000
Legislature		
Senate	Dem: 12; Rep: 18	
House	Dem: 25; Rep: 35	
Arkansas		
Governor	Mike Beebe (D)	US$87,352
Lieut. Gov.	Bill Halter (D)	US$42,219
Sec. of State	Charlie Daniels (D)	US$54,594
Atty. Gen.	Dustin McDaniel (D)	US$72,794
Treasurer	Martha A. Shoffner (D)	US$54,594
General Assembly		
Senate	Dem: 27; Rep: 8	
House	Dem: 71; Rep: 28; Green: 1	
California		
Governor	Arnold Schwarzenegger (R)	US$173,987
Lieut. Gov.	Abel Maldonado (R)	US$130,490
Sec. of State	Debra Bowen (D)	US$130,490
Atty. Gen.	Edmund G. Brown, Jr. (D)	US$151,127

STATE/OFFICE	OFFICEHOLDER	PAY[1]
California (continued)		
Treasurer	Bill Lockyer (D)	US$139,189
Legislature		
Senate	Dem: 25; Rep: 14; vacant: 1	
Assembly	Dem: 49; Rep: 29; Ind.: 1; vacant: 1	
Colorado		
Governor	Bill Ritter (D)	US$90,000
Lieut. Gov.	Barbara O'Brien (D)	US$68,500
Sec. of State	Bernie Buescher (D)	US$68,500
Atty. Gen.	John W. Suthers (R)	US$80,000
Treasurer	Cary Kennedy (D)	US$68,500
General Assembly		
Senate	Dem: 21; Rep: 14	
House	Dem: 38; Rep: 27	
Connecticut		
Governor	M. Jodi Rell (R)	US$150,000
Lieut. Gov.	Michael C. Fedele (R)	US$110,000
Sec. of State	Susan Bysiewicz (D)	US$110,000
Atty. Gen.	Richard Blumenthal (D)	US$110,000
Treasurer	Denise L. Nappier (D)	US$110,000
General Assembly		
Senate	Dem: 24; Rep: 12	
House	Dem: 114; Rep: 37	
Delaware		
Governor	Jack Markell (D)	US$171,000
Lieut. Gov.	Matthew Denn (D)	US$74,345
Sec. of State	Jeffrey Bullock (D)	US$120,755
Atty. Gen.	Joseph Biden III (D)	US$137,425
Treasurer	Velda Jones-Potter (D)	US$107,300
General Assembly		
Senate	Dem: 15; Rep: 6	
House	Dem: 24; Rep: 17	
Florida		
Governor	Charlie Crist (R)	US$130,273
Lieut. Gov.	Jeffrey D. Kottkamp (R)	US$124,851
Sec. of State	Dawn Roberts (interim)	US$120,000
Atty. Gen.	Bill McCollum (R)	US$128,972
Treasurer[3]	Alex Sink (Chief Financial Officer)	US$128,972
Legislature		
Senate	Dem: 14; Rep: 26	
House	Dem: 44; Rep: 76	

State Officers and Legislatures (continued)

STATE/OFFICE	OFFICEHOLDER	PAY[1]
Georgia		
Governor	Sonny Perdue (R)	US$139,339
Lieut. Gov.	Casey Cagle (R)	US$91,609
Sec. of State	Brian Kemp (R)	US$123,636
Atty. Gen.	Thurbert E. Baker (D)	US$137,791
Treasurer[3]	W. Daniel Ebersole	US$130,927
	(Dir., Office of Treasury and Fiscal Services)	
General Assembly		
Senate	Dem: 22; Rep: 34	
House	Dem: 74; Rep: 105; Ind.: 1	
Hawaii		
Governor	Linda Lingle (R)	US$117,312
Lieut. Gov.	James R. Aiona, Jr. (R)	US$114,420
Sec. of State[2]		
Atty. Gen.	Mark J. Bennett (R)	US$114,420
Treasurer[3]	Georgina K. Kawamura	US$108,972
	(Director of Finance)	
Legislature		
Senate	Dem: 23; Rep: 2	
House	Dem: 45; Rep: 6	
Idaho		
Governor	C.L. "Butch" Otter (R)	US$115,348
Lieut. Gov.	Brad Little (R)	US$30,400
Sec. of State	Ben Ysursa (R)	US$93,756
Atty. Gen.	Lawrence Wasden (R)	US$103,984
Treasurer	Ron G. Crane (R)	US$93,756
Legislature		
Senate	Dem: 7; Rep: 28	
House	Dem: 18; Rep: 52	
Illinois		
Governor	Pat Quinn (D)	US$177,500
Lieut. Gov.	vacant	US$135,700
Sec. of State	Jesse White (D)	US$156,600
Atty. Gen.	Lisa Madigan (D)	US$156,600
Treasurer	Alexi Giannoulias (D)	US$130,800
General Assembly		
Senate	Dem: 37; Rep: 22	
House	Dem: 70; Rep: 48	
Indiana		
Governor	Mitch Daniels (R)	US$95,000
Lieut. Gov.	Becky Skillman (R)	US$79,172
Sec. of State	Todd Rokita (R)	US$68,772
Atty. Gen.	Greg Zoeller (R)	US$82,734
Treasurer	Richard E. Mourdock (R)	US$68,772
General Assembly		
Senate	Dem: 17; Rep: 33	
House	Dem: 52; Rep: 48	
Iowa		
Governor	Chet Culver (D)	US$130,000
Lieut. Gov.	Patty Judge (D)	US$103,212
Sec. of State	Michael A. Mauro (D)	US$103,212
Atty. Gen.	Tom Miller (D)	US$123,669
Treasurer	Michael L. Fitzgerald (D)	US$103,212
General Assembly		
Senate	Dem: 32; Rep: 18	
House	Dem: 56; Rep: 44	
Kansas		
Governor	Mark Parkinson (D)	US$110,707
Lieut. Gov.	Troy Findley (D)	US$100,000
Sec. of State	Chris Biggs (D)	US$86,003

STATE/OFFICE	OFFICEHOLDER	PAY[1]
Kansas (continued)		
Atty. Gen.	Stephen Six (D)	US$98,901
Treasurer	Dennis McKinney	US$82,563
Legislature		
Senate	Dem: 9; Rep: 31	
House	Dem: 49; Rep: 76	
Kentucky		
Governor	Steve Beshear (D)	US$145,885
Lieut. Gov.	Daniel Mongiardo (D)	US$108,720
Sec. of State	Trey Grayson (R)	US$108,720
Atty. Gen.	Jack Conway (D)	US$108,720
Treasurer	Todd Hollenbach (D)	US$108,720
General Assembly		
Senate	Dem: 17; Rep: 20; Ind.: 1	
House	Dem: 65; Rep: 35	
Louisiana		
Governor	Bobby Jindal (R)	US$130,000
Lieut. Gov.	Scott Angelle (interim)	US$115,000
Sec. of State	Jay Dardenne (R)	US$115,000
Atty. Gen.	James D. Caldwell (D)	US$115,000
Treasurer	John Kennedy (R)	US$115,000
Legislature		
Senate	Dem: 24 Rep: 15	
House	Dem: 52; Rep: 50; Ind: 3	
Maine		
Governor	John E. Baldacci (D)	US$70,000
Lieut. Gov.[5]		
Sec. of State	Matthew Dunlap (D)	US$83,844
Atty. Gen.	Janet T. Mills (D)	US$92,248
Treasurer	David G. Lemoine (D)	US$83,844
Legislature		
Senate	Dem: 20; Rep: 15	
House	Dem: 96; Rep: 54; unenrolled: 1	
Maryland		
Governor	Martin O'Malley (D)	US$150,000
Lieut. Gov.	Anthony G. Brown (D)	US$125,000
Sec. of State	John McDonough (D)	US$87,500
Atty. Gen.	Douglas F. Gansler (D)	US$125,000
Treasurer	Nancy K. Kopp (D)	US$125,000
General Assembly		
Senate	Dem: 33; Rep: 14	
House	Dem: 104; Rep: 36; Ind.: 1	
Massachusetts		
Governor	Deval Patrick (D)	US$140,535
Lieut. Gov.	Timothy Murray (D)	US$124,920
Sec. of State	William F. Galvin (D)	US$130,916
Atty. Gen.	Martha Coakley (D)	US$133,644
Treasurer	Timothy Cahill (D)	US$130,916
General Court (legislature)		
Senate	Dem: 35; Rep: 5	
House	Dem: 143; Rep: 16; Ind.: 1	
Michigan		
Governor	Jennifer Granholm (D)	US$177,000
Lieut. Gov.	John D. Cherry, Jr. (D)	US$123,900
Sec. of State	Terri Lynn Land (R)	US$124,900
Atty. Gen.	Mike Cox (R)	US$124,900
Treasurer	Robert J. Kleine	US$174,204
Legislature		
Senate	Dem: 16; Rep: 22	
House	Dem: 66; Rep: 43; vacant: 1	

State Officers and Legislatures (continued)

STATE/OFFICE	OFFICEHOLDER	PAY[1]
Minnesota		
Governor	Tim Pawlenty (R)	US$120,303
Lieut. Gov.	Carol Molnau (R)	US$78,197
Sec. of State	Mark Ritchie (D)	US$90,227
Atty. Gen.	Lori Swanson (D)	US$114,288
Treasurer[3]	Tom J. Hanson	US$108,388
	(Commissioner of Finance)	
Legislature		
Senate	Dem: 46; Rep: 21	
House	Dem: 87; Rep: 47	
Mississippi		
Governor	Haley Barbour (R)	US$122,160
Lieut. Gov.	Phil Bryant (R)	US$61,714
Sec. of State	C. Delbert Hosemann, Jr. (R)	US$90,000
Atty. Gen.	Jim Hood (D)	US$108,960
Treasurer	Tate Reeves (R)	US$90,000
Legislature		
Senate	Dem: 27; Rep: 25	
House	Dem: 74; Rep: 48	
Missouri		
Governor	Jay Nixon (D)	US$133,821
Lieut. Gov.	Peter Kinder (R)	US$86,484
Sec. of State	Robin Carnahan (D)	US$107,746
Atty. Gen.	Chris Koster (D)	US$116,437
Treasurer	Clint Zweifel (D)	US$107,746
General Assembly		
Senate	Dem: 11; Rep: 23	
House	Dem: 74; Rep: 88; vacant: 1	
Montana		
Governor	Brian Schweitzer (D)	US$100,121
Lieut. Gov.	John Bohlinger (R)	US$79,007
Sec. of State	Linda McCulloch (D)	US$79,129
Atty. Gen.	Steve Bullock (D)	US$89,602
Treasurer[3]	Janet Kelly (Dir., Dept. of Administration)	US$96,967
Legislature		
Senate	Dem: 23; Rep: 27	
House	Dem: 50; Rep: 50	
Nebraska		
Governor	Dave Heineman (R)	US$105,000
Lieut. Gov.	Rick Sheehy (R)	US$75,000
Sec. of State	John A. Gale (R)	US$85,000
Atty. Gen.	Jon Bruning (R)	US$95,000
Treasurer	Shane Osborn (R)	US$85,000
Legislature (unicameral)	49 nonpartisan members	
Nevada		
Governor	Jim Gibbons (R)	US$141,000
Lieut. Gov.	Brian K. Krolicki (R)	US$60,000
Sec. of State	Ross Miller (D)	US$97,000
Atty. Gen.	Catherine Cortez Masto (D)	US$133,000
Treasurer	Kate Marshall (D)	US$97,000
Legislature		
Senate	Dem: 12; Rep: 9	
Assembly	Dem: 28; Rep: 14	
New Hampshire		
Governor	John Lynch (D)	US$113,834
Lieut. Gov.[5]		
Sec. of State	William Gardner (D)	US$104,364
Atty. Gen.	Michael Delaney (D)	US$110,114

STATE/OFFICE	OFFICEHOLDER	PAY[1]
New Hampshire (continued)		
Treasurer	Catherine Provencher	US$104,364
General Court (legislature)		
Senate	Dem: 14; Rep: 10	
House	Dem: 225; Rep: 175	
New Jersey		
Governor	Christopher J. Christie (R)	US$175,000
Lieut. Gov.	Kim Guadagno (R)	US$141,000
Sec. of State[2]		
Atty. Gen.	Paula T. Dow (D)	US$141,000
Treasurer	Andrew P. Sidamon-Eristoff (acting)	US$141,000
Legislature		
Senate	Dem: 23; Rep: 17	
General Assembly	Dem: 47; Rep: 33	
New Mexico		
Governor	Bill Richardson (D)	US$110,000
Lieut. Gov.	Diane Denish (D)	US$85,000
Sec. of State	Mary Herrera (D)	US$85,000
Atty. Gen.	Gary K. King (D)	US$95,000
Treasurer	James B. Lewis (D)	US$85,000
Legislature		
Senate	Dem: 27; Rep: 15	
House	Dem: 45; Rep: 25	
New York		
Governor	David A. Paterson (D)	US$179,000
Lieut. Gov.	Richard Ravitch (D)	US$151,500
Sec. of State	Lorraine Cortés-Vázquez (D)	US$120,800
Atty. Gen.	Andrew M. Cuomo (D)	US$151,500
Treasurer	Aida Brewer	US$127,000
Legislature		
Senate	Dem: 32; Rep: 30	
Assembly	Dem: 105; Rep: 43; Ind.: 2	
North Carolina		
Governor	Beverly Perdue (D)	US$139,590
Lieut. Gov.	Walter Dalton (D)	US$123,198
Sec. of State	Elaine F. Marshall (D)	US$123,198
Atty. Gen.	Roy Cooper (D)	US$123,198
Treasurer	Jane Cowell (D)	US$123,198
General Assembly		
Senate	Dem: 30; Rep: 20	
House	Dem: 68; Rep: 52	
North Dakota		
Governor	John Hoeven (R)	US$105,036
Lieut. Gov.	Jack Dalrymple (R)	US$81,540
Sec. of State	Alvin A. Jaeger (R)	US$83,556
Atty. Gen.	Wayne Stenehjem (R)	US$91,716
Treasurer	Kelly Schmidt (R)	US$78,900
Legislative Assembly		
Senate	Dem: 21; Rep: 26	
House	Dem: 36; Rep: 58	
Ohio		
Governor	Ted Strickland (D)	US$144,269
Lieut. Gov.	Lee Fisher (D)	US$142,501
Sec. of State	Jennifer Brunner (D)	US$109,554
Atty. Gen.	Richard Cordray (D)	US$109,554
Treasurer	Kevin L. Boyce	US$109,554
General Assembly		
Senate	Dem: 12; Rep: 21	
House	Dem: 53; Rep: 46	

State Officers and Legislatures (continued)

STATE/OFFICE	OFFICEHOLDER	PAY[1]
Oklahoma		
Governor	Brad Henry (D)	US$147,000
Lieut. Gov.	Jari Askins (D)	US$114,713
Sec. of State	M. Susan Savage (D)	US$94,500
Atty. Gen.	W.A. Drew Edmondson (D)	US$132,850
Treasurer	Scott Meacham (D)	US$114,713
Legislature		
Senate	Dem: 22; Rep: 26	
House	Dem: 40; Rep: 61	
Oregon		
Governor	Ted Kulongoski (D)	US$93,600
Lieut. Gov.[4]		
Sec. of State	Kate Brown (D)	US$72,000
Atty. Gen.	John R. Kroger (D)	US$77,200
Treasurer	Ben Westlund (D)	US$72,000
Legislative Assembly		
Senate	Dem: 18; Rep: 12	
House	Dem: 36; Rep: 24	
Pennsylvania		
Governor	Edward G. Rendell (D)	US$174,914
Lieut. Gov.	Joseph B. Scarnati (R)	US$146,926
Sec. of State	Pedro A. Cortés (D)	US$125,939
Atty. Gen.	Tom Corbett (R)	US$145,529
Treasurer	Robert McCord (D)	US$145,529
General Assembly		
Senate	Dem: 20; Rep: 30	
House	Dem: 103; Rep: 97; vacant: 3	
Rhode Island		
Governor	Don Carcieri (R)	US$117,817
Lieut. Gov.	Elizabeth H. Roberts (D)	US$99,214
Sec. of State	A. Ralph Mollis (D)	US$99,214
Atty. Gen.	Patrick C. Lynch (D)	US$105,416
Treasurer	Frank T. Caprio (D)	US$99,214
General Assembly		
Senate	Dem: 33; Rep: 4; Ind.: 1	
House	Dem: 69; Rep: 6	
South Carolina		
Governor	Mark Sanford (R)	US$106,078
Lieut. Gov.	André Bauer (R)	US$100,000
Sec. of State	Mark Hammond (R)	US$92,007
Atty. Gen.	Henry McMaster (R)	US$92,007
Treasurer	Converse Chellis (R)	US$92,007
General Assembly		
Senate	Dem: 19; Rep: 27	
House	Dem: 51; Rep: 73	
South Dakota		
Governor	Mike Rounds (R)	US$115,331
Lieut. Gov.	Dennis Daugaard (R)	US$17,699
Sec. of State	Chris Nelson (R)	US$78,363
Atty. Gen.	Martin Jackley (R)	US$97,928
Treasurer	Vernon L. Larson (R)	US$78,363
Legislature		
Senate	Dem: 14; Rep: 21	
House	Dem: 24; Rep: 46	
Tennessee		
Governor	Phil Bredesen (D)	US$170,340
Lieut. Gov.[6]	Ron Ramsey (R)	US$57,027
Sec. of State	Tre Hargett (R)	US$180,000
Atty. Gen.	Robert E. Cooper, Jr. (D)	US$165,336
Treasurer	David H. Lillard, Jr.	US$180,000

STATE/OFFICE	OFFICEHOLDER	PAY[1]
Tennessee (continued)		
General Assembly		
Senate	Dem: 14; Rep: 19	
House	Dem: 48; Rep: 51	
Texas		
Governor	Rick Perry (R)	US$150,000
Lieut. Gov.	David Dewhurst (R)	US$7,200
Sec. of State	Esperanza Andrade	US$125,880
Atty. Gen.	Greg Abbott (R)	US$150,000
Treasurer[3]	Susan Combs (R) (Comptroller)	US$150,000
Legislature		
Senate	Dem: 12; Rep: 19	
House	Dem: 73; Rep: 77	
Utah		
Governor	Gary Herbert (R)	US$109,900
Lieut. Gov.	Greg Bell (R)	US$104,405
Sec. of State[2]		
Atty. Gen.	Mark Shurtleff (R)	US$104,405
Treasurer	Richard K. Ellis (R)	US$104,405
Legislature		
Senate	Dem: 8; Rep: 21	
House	Dem: 22; Rep: 53	
Vermont		
Governor	Jim Douglas (R)	US$142,542
Lieut. Gov.	Brian Dubie (R)	US$60,507
Sec. of State	Deborah L. Markowitz (D)	US$90,376
Atty. Gen.	William H. Sorrell (D)	US$108,202
Treasurer	Jeb Spaulding (D)	US$90,376
General Assembly		
Senate	Dem: 23; Rep: 7	
House	Dem: 95; Rep: 48; Ind: 2; Progressive: 5	
Virginia		
Governor	Robert McDonnell (R)	US$175,000
Lieut. Gov.	Bill Bolling (R)	US$36,321
Sec. of State	Katherine K. Hanley (D)	US$152,793
Atty. Gen.	Ken Cuccinelli (R)	US$150,000
Treasurer	Manju Ganeriwala	US$149,761
General Assembly		
Senate	Dem: 22; Rep: 18	
House	Dem: 39; Rep: 59; Ind: 2	
Washington		
Governor	Chris Gregoire (D)	US$166,891
Lieut. Gov.	Brad Owen (D)	US$93,948
Sec. of State	Sam Reed (R)	US$116,950
Atty. Gen.	Rob McKenna (R)	US$151,718
Treasurer	James L. McIntire (D)	US$116,950
Legislature		
Senate	Dem: 31; Rep: 18	
House	Dem: 61; Rep: 37	
West Virginia		
Governor	Joe Manchin III (D)	US$150,000
Lieut. Gov.[7]	Earl Ray Tomblin (D)	N/A
Sec. of State	Natalie Tennant (D)	US$95,000
Atty. Gen.	Darrell V. McGraw, Jr. (D)	US$95,000
Treasurer	John D. Perdue (D)	US$95,000
Legislature		
Senate	Dem: 26; Rep: 8	
House	Dem: 71; Rep: 29	

State Officers and Legislatures (continued)

STATE/OFFICE	OFFICEHOLDER	PAY[1]	STATE/OFFICE	OFFICEHOLDER	PAY[1]
Wisconsin			**Wyoming**		
Governor	Jim Doyle (D)	US$137,092	Governor	Dave Freudenthal (D)	US$105,000
Lieut. Gov.	Barbara Lawton (D)	US$72,394	Lieut. Gov.[4]		
Sec. of State	Douglas La Follette (D)	US$65,079	Sec. of State	Max Maxfield (R)	US$92,000
Atty. Gen.	J.B. Van Hollen (R)	US$133,033	Atty. Gen.	Bruce A. Salzburg (D)	US$137,150
Treasurer	Dawn Marie Sass (D)	US$65,079	Treasurer	Joseph B. Meyer (R)	US$92,000
Legislature			Legislature		
Senate	Dem: 18; Rep: 15		Senate	Dem: 7; Rep: 23	
Assembly	Dem: 52; Rep: 46; Ind.: 1		House	Dem: 19; Rep: 41	

[1]The salary rates are from March 2010.   [2]The lieutenant governor serves as secretary of state.   [3]No official state treasurer; the official in charge of the general treasury performs duties.   [4]The secretary of state assumes duties of lieutenant governor.   [5]No official lieutenant governor; the president of the Senate succeeds the governor.   [6]In Tennessee the speaker of the Senate and the lieutenant governor are one and the same.   [7]In West Virginia the president of the Senate and the lieutenant governor are one and the same.

United States Cities

US Urban Growth, 1850–2009

Source: US Census Bureau.

RANK	CITY	1850	1900	1950	1990	2000	2009
1	New York NY[1]	515,547	3,437,202	7,891,957	7,322,564	8,008,278	8,391,881
2	Los Angeles CA	1,610	102,479	1,970,358	3,485,398	3,694,820	3,831,868
3	Chicago IL	29,963	1,698,575	3,620,962	2,783,726	2,896,016	2,851,268
4	Houston TX	2,396	44,633	596,163	1,630,553	1,953,631	2,257,926
5	Phoenix AZ		5,544	106,818	983,403	1,321,045	1,601,587
6	Philadelphia PA[1]	121,376	1,293,697	2,071,605	1,585,577	1,517,550	1,547,297
7	San Antonio TX	3,488	53,321	408,442	935,933	1,144,646	1,373,668
8	San Diego CA		17,700	334,387	1,110,549	1,223,400	1,306,301
9	Dallas TX		42,638	434,462	1,006,877	1,188,580	1,299,543
10	San Jose CA		21,500	95,280	782,248	894,943	964,695
11	Detroit MI	21,019	285,704	1,849,568	1,027,974	951,270	910,920
12	San Francisco CA[1]	34,776	342,782	775,357	723,959	776,733	815,358
13	Jacksonville FL	1,045	28,429	204,517	635,230	735,617	813,518
14	Indianapolis IN[1]	8,091	169,164	427,173	731,726[2]	781,870[2]	807,584[2]
15	Austin TX	629	22,258	132,459	465,622	656,562	786,382
16	Columbus OH	17,882	125,560	375,901	632,910	711,470	769,360
17	Fort Worth TX		26,688	278,778	447,619	534,694	727,575
18	Charlotte NC	1,065	18,091	134,042	395,934	540,828	709,441
19	Memphis TN	8,841	102,320	396,000	610,337	650,100	676,640
20	Boston MA	136,881	560,892	801,444	574,283	589,141	645,169
21	Baltimore MD	169,054	508,957	949,708	736,014	651,154	637,418
22	El Paso TX		15,906	130,485	515,342	563,662	620,447
23	Seattle WA		80,671	467,591	516,259	563,374	617,334
24	Denver CO[1]		133,859	415,786	467,610	554,636	610,345
25	Nashville TN[1]	10,165	80,865	174,307	488,374[2]	545,524[2]	605,473

[1]Cities with boundaries contiguous with their respective counties (year consolidated): New York (1683), Philadelphia (1854), San Francisco (1856), Indianapolis (1970), and Denver (1902).   [2]Figure represents the "balance," or the population of the consolidated city minus any semi-incorporated places located within the consolidated city.

Fifteen Fastest-Growing Cities in the US

Based on a population of 100,000 or more. Source: US Census Bureau.

CITY	POPULATION 1 APR 2000	POPULATION 1 JUL 2009	CHANGE (%)
Frisco TX	33,695	102,412	+203.9
McKinney TX	54,319	127,671	+135.0
North Las Vegas NV	115,531	224,387	+94.2
Gilbert AZ	114,702	217,285	+89.4
Port St. Lucie FL	88,471	154,410	+74.5

Fifteen Fastest-Growing Cities in the US (continued)

CITY	1 APR 2000	1 JUL 2009	CHANGE (%)
Victorville CA	64,058	110,921	+73.2
Round Rock TX	61,467	105,412	+71.5
Elk Grove CA	81,096	135,228	+66.8
Cape Coral FL	102,467	154,202	+50.5
Miramar FL	72,739	109,176	+50.1
Murfreesboro TN	70,139	105,209	+50.0
Peoria AZ	108,749	162,740	+49.6
Denton TX	82,686	122,830	+48.5
Henderson NV	175,484	256,445	+46.1
Irvine CA	144,146	209,716	+45.5

Fifteen Cities with the Greatest Population Losses in the US

Based on a population of 100,000 or more. Source: US Census Bureau.

CITY	POPULATION 1 APR 2000	1 JUL 2009	CHANGE (%)	CITY	POPULATION 1 APR 2000	1 JUL 2009	CHANGE (%)
New Orleans LA	484,674	354,850	−26.8	Mobile AL	204,214	193,171	−5.4
Flint MI	124,943	111,475	−10.8	Syracuse NY	146,464	138,560	−5.4
Cleveland OH	477,463	431,363	−9.7	Birmingham AL	242,451	230,130	−5.1
Buffalo NY	292,648	270,240	−7.7	Lansing MI	119,357	113,810	−4.6
Dayton OH	166,210	153,857	−7.4	Akron OH	217,106	207,216	−4.6
Pittsburgh PA	334,438	311,647	−6.8	Detroit MI	951,270	910,920	−4.2
Jackson MS	185,786	175,021	−5.8	Evansville IN	121,651	116,584	−4.2
Rochester NY	219,782	207,294	−5.7				

Racial Makeup of the Fifteen Largest US Cities

Information is given in percent of the total population. The Hispanic or Latino category is listed for comparative purposes even though Hispanic or Latino people may be of any race; thus, the rows of racial percentages will not add up to 100 if the Hispanic or Latino entries are included. Data are preliminary.
Source: US Census Bureau, *2008 American Community Survey.*

CITY	WHITE	BLACK OR AFRICAN AMERICAN	AMERICAN INDIAN AND ALASKA NATIVE	ASIAN	NATIVE HAWAIIAN AND OTHER PACIFIC ISLANDER	SOME OTHER RACE	TWO OR MORE RACES	HISPANIC OR LATINO	TOTAL POPULATION
New York NY	45.7	25.6	0.4	11.9	—	13.9	2.4	27.7	8,363,710
Los Angeles CA	51.6	9.8	0.7	10.4	0.2	24.5	2.7	49.1	3,803,383
Chicago IL	44.9	34.6	0.3	4.9	—	13.5	1.8	28.1	2,741,455
Houston TX	55.6	23.6	0.4	5.5	—	13.7	1.1	42.7	2,023,601
Phoenix AZ	80.3	5.6	1.8	2.4	0.2	7.5	2.2	43.0	1,525,257
Philadelphia PA	42.4	43.4	0.4	5.5	—	6.3	1.9	11.3	1,447,395
San Antonio TX	77.4	6.5	0.7	2.0	0.1	10.7	2.7	61.4	1,292,997
San Diego CA	68.6	6.6	0.8	15.2	0.6	4.6	3.7	27.7	1,266,963
Dallas TX	59.2	22.6	0.4	2.7	0.1	13.6	1.5	44.6	1,227,082
San Jose CA	49.3	3.1	0.5	30.8	0.2	12.9	3.1	31.9	916,715
Jacksonville FL	62.2	30.1	0.4	3.6	0.1	1.6	2.0	6.4	811,953
San Francisco CA	54.7	6.2	0.4	31.2	0.5	3.6	3.4	14.1	808,976
Indianapolis IN	66.5	26.1	0.1	1.7	—	3.3	2.3	7.4	798,594
Austin TX	68.2	8.0	0.3	5.6	—	15.5	2.4	35.4	777,783
Detroit MI	11.1	82.7	0.3	0.8	—	3.6	1.4	6.9	777,493

— Less than 0.05 percent.   *Detail may not add to total given because of rounding.*

Area and Zip Codes Web Sites

US telephone area codes and postal codes change frequently to accommodate telecommunications user patterns and expansions and shifts in patterns of business and residential development. Check local listings to determine whether to dial "1" before dialing outside of the area code or to dial the area code as well as the telephone number when dialing within the area code.
Area codes: <www.nanpa.com>.
Zip codes: <http://zip4.usps.com/zip4/welcome.jsp>.

United States Law and Crime

State Crime Rates, 2001–08

Estimates of crimes reported to the police per 100,000 population.

STATE	2001[1] TOTAL	2002 TOTAL	2003 TOTAL	2004 TOTAL	2005 TOTAL	2006 TOTAL	2007 TOTAL	2008 TOTAL
AL	4,319	4,465	4,475	4,452	4,324	4,361	4,420	4,536
AK	4,236	4,310	4,360	4,018	4,244	4,293	4,041	3,584
AZ	6,077	6,386	6,147	5,845	5,351	5,129	4,897	4,738
AR	4,134	4,158	4,088	4,512	4,585	4,519	4,483	4,339
CA	3,903	3,944	4,006	3,971	3,849	3,703	3,556	3,444
CO	4,219	4,348	4,299	4,293	4,436	3,843	3,354	3,192
CT	3,118	2,997	2,984	2,913	2,833	2,785	2,656	2,757
DE	4,053	3,939	4,090	3,732	3,744	4,099	4,059	4,289
DC[2]	7,710	8,022	7,489	6,230	6,206	6,162	6,328	6,542
FL	5,570	5,421	5,188	4,891	4,716	4,698	4,812	4,830
GA	4,646	4,507	4,715	4,722	4,621	4,360	4,394	4,494
HI	5,386	6,044	5,547	5,047	5,048	4,512	4,498	3,844
ID	3,133	3,173	3,175	3,039	2,955	2,666	2,486	2,330
IL[3]	4,098	4,016	3,844	3,729	3,632	3,561	3,469	3,458
IN	3,831	3,750	3,708	3,723	3,780	3,817	3,730	3,670
IA	3,301	3,448	3,254	3,176	3,125	3,086	2,910	2,705
KS	4,321	4,087	4,408	4,349	4,174	4,175	4,131	3,788
KY	2,938[3]	2,903[3]	2,759[3]	2,783	2,797	2,808	2,813	2,880
LA	5,338	5,098	4,948	5,049	4,278	4,691	4,806	4,479
ME	2,688	2,656	2,559	2,514	2,525	2,634	2,547	2,570
MD	4,867	4,747	4,503	4,341	4,247	4,159	4,073	4,146
MA	3,099	3,094	3,036	2,919	2,821	2,838	2,823	2,849
MI	4,082	3,874	3,790	3,548	3,643	3,775	3,602	3,436
MN[3]	3,584	3,535	3,376	3,309	3,381	3,391	3,325	3,113
MS	4,185	4,159	4,031	3,774	3,539	3,507	3,492	3,225
MO	4,776	4,602	4,575	4,395	4,453	4,372	4,243	4,168
MT	3,689	3,513	3,461	3,230	3,424	2,941	3,053	2,861
NE	4,330	4,257	4,046	3,830	3,710	3,623	3,464	3,182
NV	4,266	4,498	4,903	4,823	4,848	4,830	4,528	4,172
NH	2,322	2,220	2,203	2,207	1,928	2,013	2,029	2,249
NJ	3,225	3,024	2,914	2,785	2,688	2,643	2,542	2,620
NM	5,324	5,078	4,756	4,885	4,851	4,580	4,390	4,559
NY	2,925	2,804	2,715	2,641	2,554	2,488	2,393	2,392
NC	4,938	4,721	4,725	4,608	4,543	4,596	4,554	4,511
ND	2,418	2,406	2,190	1,996	2,076	2,128	2,032	2,061
OH	4,178	4,107	3,984	4,015	4,014	4,029	3,798	3,760
OK	4,607	4,743	4,818	4,743	4,551	4,102	4,026	3,969
OR	5,044	4,868	5,061	4,929	4,687	3,952	3,814	3,539
PA	2,961	2,841	2,828	2,826	2,842	2,883	2,778	2,820
RI	3,685	3,589	3,281	3,131	2,970	2,814	2,850	3,090
SC	4,753	5,297	5,328	5,289	5,101	5,008	5,060	4,964
SD	2,332	2,279	2,177	2,106	1,952	1,791	1,822	1,847
TN	5,153	5,019	5,080	5,002	5,028	4,888	4,842	4,765
TX	5,153	5,190	5,153	5,035	4,862	4,598	4,632	4,494
UT	4,243	4,452	4,505	4,322	4,096	3,741	3,735	3,579
VT	2,769	2,530	2,343	2,420	2,400	2,441	2,447	2,674
VA	3,178	3,140	3,000	2,953	2,921	2,760	2,736	2,774
WA	5,152	5,107	5,102	5,193	5,239	4,826	4,364	4,090
WV	2,560	2,515	2,594	2,777	2,898	2,901	2,800	2,842
WI	3,321	3,253	3,101	2,873	2,902	3,102	3,129	3,030
WY	3,518	3,581	3,578	3,564	3,385	3,220	3,105	2,949
US	4,161	4,119	4,067	3,983	3,899	3,808	3,730	3,668

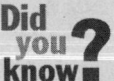

Did you know? Rudolph the Red-Nosed Reindeer made his debut as part of a promotional campaign for Chicago's Montgomery Ward department stores in 1939. The song "Rudolph the Red-Nosed Reindeer," based on a poem written by Montgomery Ward ad copywriter Robert L. May, did not become popular until Gene Autry's hit recording 10 years later. Rudolph's name was originally proposed to be Rollo or Reginald.

State Crime Rates, 2001–08 (continued)

2008 CRIME RATES IN DETAIL

	VIOLENT CRIME RATES					PROPERTY CRIME RATES			
STATE	MURDER[4]	FORCIBLE RAPE	AGGRAVATED ASSAULT	ROBBERY	TOTAL[5]	BURGLARY	LARCENY/ THEFT	MOTOR VEHICLE THEFT	TOTAL[5]
AL	7.6	34.7	253	158	453	1,081	2,713	289	4,083
AK	4.1	64.3	490	94.0	652	472	2,222	239	2,932
AZ	6.3	25.7	266	149	447	869	2,850	573	4,291
AR	5.7	48.9	353	95.8	503	1,180	2,427	228	3,835
CA	5.8	24.2	285	189	504	647	1,769	524	2,940
CO	3.2	42.5	229	68.1	343	572	2,003	274	2,849
CT	3.5	19.3	164	112	298	429	1,774	256	2,459
DE	6.5	41.9	444	211	703	774	2,520	291	3,585
DC[2]	31.4	31.4	626	749	1,438	640	3,372	1,092	5,105
FL	6.4	32.6	452	198	689	1,028	2,766	347	4,141
GA	6.6	22.7	271	179	479	1,039	2,568	409	4,016
HI	1.9	28.3	158	84.3	273	728	2,445	399	3,571
ID	1.5	36.2	175	15.8	229	440	1,552	110	2,101
IL[3]	6.1	31.9	301	186	525	612	2,068	253	2,933
IN	5.1	27.0	184	118	334	763	2,299	274	3,336
IA	2.5	29.6	210	41.6	284	548	1,729	144	2,421
KS	4.0	42.5	304	60.1	411	700	2,413	264	3,377
KY	4.6	33.0	94	165	296	676	1,729	180	2,584
LA	11.9	27.9	480	136	656	982	2,529	312	3,823
ME	2.4	28.5	61.4	25.3	118	495	1,868	89.3	2,452
MD	8.8	20.0	365	234	628	690	2,378	450	3,518
MA	2.6	26.7	311	109	449	556	1,649	196	2,400
MI	5.4	45.0	322	130	502	742	1,831	362	2,935
MN[3]	2.1	34.6	146	80.0	263	506	2,152	193	2,851
MS	8.1	30.3	144	103	285	886	1,839	216	2,940
MO	7.7	27.3	344	125	504	775	2,538	351	3,664
MT	2.4	30.4	208	17.8	258	344	2,096	163	2,603
NE	3.8	32.7	194	72.8	304	492	2,152	235	2,879
NV	6.3	42.4	427	249	725	929	1,907	612	3,448
NH	1.0	29.7	94.7	31.8	157	326	1,661	105	2,092
NJ	4.3	12.9	163	146	327	465	1,596	232	2,293
NM	7.2	57.4	476	110	650	1,094	2,412	403	3,909
NY	4.3	14.4	216	163	398	337	1,527	129	1,994
NC	6.5	24.8	281	155	467	1,210	2,544	290	4,044
ND	0.5	36.2	119	11.2	167	328	1,429	138	1,894
OH	4.7	38.5	142	163	348	893	2,271	248	3,412
OK	5.8	40.2	380	101	527	963	2,181	299	3,442
OR	2.2	30.5	155	69.7	257	551	2,432	299	3,282
PA	5.6	27.9	225	152	410	471	1,759	181	2,410
RI	2.8	26.4	137	83.7	249	547	1,989	305	2,841
SC	6.8	36.6	539	147	730	1,026	2,814	394	4,234
SD	3.2	53.7	130	14.9	201	302	1,244	100	1,646
TN	6.6	33.2	509	174	722	1,046	2,687	309	4,043
TX	5.6	32.9	314	155	508	946	2,689	351	3,986
UT	1.4	32.6	136	51.9	222	537	2,558	263	3,357
VT	2.7	20.4	98.3	14.3	136	557	1,887	94.2	2,539
VA	4.7	22.6	133	95.7	256	412	1,936	171	2,518
WA	2.9	40.1	191	96.9	331	801	2,525	433	3,758
WV	3.3	20.0	202	49.0	274	610	1,782	177	2,569
WI	2.6	19.9	160	91.1	274	488	2,063	205	2,756
WY	1.9	33.8	180	16.1	232	410	2,173	134	2,717
Total US	5.4	29.3	275	145	455	731	2,167	315	3,213

[1]This table does not include the murder and nonnegligent homicides that occurred because of the terrorist attacks of 11 Sep 2001. [2]Includes reported offenses at the National Zoo and, from 2002, offenses reported by the Metro Transit Police. [3]Data are estimated or incomplete. [4]Includes nonnegligent manslaughter. [5]Detail may not add to total given because of rounding.

Source: US Bureau of Justice Statistics, <http://bjsdata.ojp.usdoj.gov/dataonline>.

Crime in the US, 1989–2008

This table presents the number of crimes reported in the seven categories that, with arson, are known as Part I crimes and are used by the Federal Bureau of Investigation to assess trends in criminality in the country.
Source: Federal Bureau of Investigation.

		VIOLENT CRIME			PROPERTY CRIME		
YEAR	MURDER[1]	FORCIBLE RAPE	ROBBERY	AGGRAVATED ASSAULT	BURGLARY	LARCENY/ THEFT	MOTOR VEHICLE THEFT
1989	21,500	94,504	578,326	951,707	3,168,170	7,872,442	1,564,800
1990	23,438	102,555	639,271	1,054,863	3,073,909	7,945,670	1,635,907
1991	24,703	106,593	687,732	1,092,739	3,157,150	8,142,228	1,661,738
1992	23,760	109,062	672,478	1,126,974	2,979,884	7,915,199	1,610,834
1993	24,526	106,014	659,870	1,135,607	2,834,808	7,820,909	1,563,060
1994	23,326	102,216	618,949	1,113,179	2,712,774	7,879,812	1,539,287
1995	21,606	97,470	580,509	1,099,207	2,593,784	7,997,710	1,472,441
1996	19,645	96,252	535,594	1,037,049	2,506,400	7,904,685	1,394,238
1997	18,208	96,153	498,534	1,023,201	2,460,526	7,743,760	1,354,189
1998	16,974	93,144	447,186	976,583	2,332,735	7,376,311	1,242,781
1999	15,522	89,411	409,371	911,740	2,100,739	6,955,520	1,152,075
2000	15,586	90,178	408,016	911,706	2,050,992	6,971,590	1,160,002
2001	16,037	90,863	423,557	909,023	2,116,531	7,092,267	1,228,391
2002	16,204	95,136	420,637	894,348	2,151,875	7,052,922	1,246,096
2003	16,528	93,883	414,235	859,030	2,154,834	7,026,802	1,261,226
2004	16,148	95,089	401,470	847,381	2,144,446	6,937,089	1,237,851
2005	16,692	93,934	417,122	862,947	2,154,126	6,776,807	1,235,226
2006	17,034	92,455	447,403	860,853	2,183,746	6,607,013	1,192,809
2007	16,929	90,427	445,125	855,856	2,179,140	6,568,572	1,095,769
2008	16,272	89,000	441,855	834,885	2,222,196	6,588,873	956,846

Crime trends: percent change in number of offenses[2]

		VIOLENT CRIME			PROPERTY CRIME		
YEARS COMPARED	MURDER[1]	FORCIBLE RAPE	ROBBERY	AGGRAVATED ASSAULT	BURGLARY	LARCENY/ THEFT	MOTOR VEHICLE THEFT
2008/2007	−3.9	−1.6	−0.7	−2.5	+2.0	+0.3	−12.7
2008/2004	+0.8	−6.4	+10.1	−1.5	+3.6	−5.0	−22.7
2008/1999	+4.8	−0.5	+7.9	−8.4	+5.8	−5.3	−16.9

[1]Includes the crime of nonnegligent manslaughter.   [2]A minus sign indicates a decrease in crime; a plus sign indicates an increase.

US Cities with Most and Fewest Violent Crimes

This table ranks cities with populations greater than 100,000 by the number of violent crimes reported during 2009.
Source: Federal Bureau of Investigation, *Preliminary Annual Uniform Crime Report, January to December 2009.*

CITIES	VIOLENT CRIMES[1]	MURDER	FORCIBLE RAPE	ROBBERY	AGGRAVATED ASSAULT	BURGLARY	LARCENY/ THEFT	CAR THEFT
Most Violent Crimes								
New York NY	46,357	471	832	18,597	26,457	18,780	112,526	10,694
Houston TX	25,593	287	823	11,367	13,116	29,279	77,058	14,596
Los Angeles CA	22,454	313	863	11,136	10,142	16,603	52,027	17,040
Philadelphia PA	19,163	302	896	9,037	8,928	10,969	37,941	6,978
Detroit MI	17,553	361	335	5,749	11,108	18,742	18,369	13,163
Las Vegas NV	13,039	111	698	4,495	7,735	13,512	25,229	8,927
Memphis TN	12,047	132	378	4,137	7,400	13,935	29,030	4,193
Dallas TX	10,221	166	485	5,501	4,069	19,428	41,481	10,455
Baltimore MD	9,664	238	158	3,707	5,561	7,798	16,741	4,624
Phoenix AZ	8,730	122	522	3,757	4,329	16,281	39,643	9,693
Fewest Violent Crimes								
Frisco TX	104	2	13	13	76	357	1,621	74
Surprise AZ	111	1	9	37	64	532	1,706	167
Murrieta CA	119	0	17	34	68	472	884	153
Temecula CA	127	1	15	59	52	576	1,574	220
Round Rock TX	128	1	23	32	72	412	2,255	105
Amherst NY	129	1	7	46	75	238	1,844	48

US Cities with Most and Fewest Violent Crimes (continued)

CITIES	VIOLENT CRIMES[1]	MURDER	FORCIBLE RAPE	ROBBERY	AGGRAVATED ASSAULT	BURGLARY	LARCENY/ THEFT	CAR THEFT
Fewest Violent Crimes (continued)								
Cary NC	132	0	12	48	72	469	1,454	83
Irvine CA	151	3	26	54	68	477	2,359	150
Simi Valley CA	155	2	10	51	92	375	1,508	114
Orange CA	160	2	11	68	79	431	1,959	235

[1]Data for overall incidents of violent crimes are composites of data for murder, forcible rape, robbery, and aggravated assault. Data are not available for Chicago IL or Naperville IL, on the list for most and fewest violent crimes, respectively, in recent years.

Total Arrests in the US, 2008

Estimates for the year 2008. Source: Federal Bureau of Investigation, Crime in the United States, 2008.

TYPE OF CRIME	NUMBER OF ARRESTS
violent crime	
aggravated assault	429,969
robbery	129,403
forcible rape	22,584
murder and nonnegligent manslaughter	12,955
violent crime total	**594,911**
property crime	
larceny/theft	1,266,706
burglary	308,479
motor vehicle theft	98,035
arson	14,125
property crime total	**1,687,345**
other crime types	
drug abuse violations	1,702,537
driving under the influence	1,483,396
other assaults	1,298,342
disorderly conduct	685,985
liquor laws	625,939

TYPE OF CRIME	NUMBER OF ARRESTS
other crime types (continued)	
drunkenness	611,069
vandalism	285,012
fraud	234,199
weapons (carrying, possessing, etc.)	179,661
curfew and loitering law violations	133,063
offenses against the family and children	118,419
stolen property (buying, receiving, possessing)	111,319
runaways	109,225
forgery and counterfeiting	90,127
sex offenses (except forcible rape and prostitution)	79,914
prostitution and commercialized vice	75,004
vagrancy	33,852
embezzlement	21,402
gambling	9,811
suspicion (not included in total)	1,650
all other offenses (except traffic)	3,835,083
total arrests	**14,005,615**

US State and Federal Prison Population

Source: US Bureau of Justice Statistics.

STATE	NUMBER OF PRISONERS				% CHANGE (31 DEC 2007 TO 31 DEC 2008)
	31 DEC 1980	31 DEC 1990	31 DEC 2007	31 DEC 2008	
Alabama	6,543	15,665	29,412	30,508	+3.7
Alaska[1]	822	2,622	5,167	5,014	−3.0
Arizona[2]	4,372	14,261	37,746	39,589	+4.9
Arkansas	2,911	7,322	14,314	14,716	+2.8
California	24,569	97,309	174,282	173,670	−0.4
Colorado	2,629	7,671	22,841	23,274	+1.9
Connecticut[1]	4,308	10,500	20,924	20,661	−1.3
Delaware[1]	1,474	3,471	7,276	7,075	−2.8
Florida	20,735	44,387	98,219	102,388	+4.2
Georgia[2]	12,178	22,411	54,256	52,719	−2.8
Hawaii[1]	985	2,533	5,978	5,955	−0.4
Idaho	817	1,961	7,319	7,290	−0.4
Illinois	11,899	27,516	45,215	45,474	+0.6
Indiana	6,683	12,736	27,132	28,322	+4.4
Iowa[2]	2,481	3,967	8,732	8,766	+0.4
Kansas	2,494	5,775	8,696	8,539	−1.8
Kentucky	3,588	9,023	22,457	21,706	−3.3
Louisiana	8,889	18,599	37,540	38,381	+2.2
Maine	814	1,523	2,148	2,195	+2.2
Maryland	7,731	17,848	23,433	23,324	−0.5
Massachusetts	3,185	8,345	11,436	11,408	−0.2

US State and Federal Prison Population (continued)

STATE	NUMBER OF PRISONERS 31 DEC 1980	31 DEC 1990	31 DEC 2007	31 DEC 2008	% CHANGE (31 DEC 2007 TO 31 DEC 2008)
Michigan	15,124	34,267	50,233	48,738	−3.0
Minnesota	2,001	3,176	9,468	9,406	−0.7
Mississippi	3,902	8,375	22,431	22,754	+1.4
Missouri	5,726	14,943	29,857	30,186	+1.1
Montana	739	1,425	3,462	3,607	+4.2
Nebraska	1,446	2,403	4,505	4,520	+0.3
Nevada	1,839	5,322	13,400	12,743	−4.9
New Hampshire	326	1,342	2,943	2,904	−1.3
New Jersey	5,884	21,128	26,827	25,953	−3.3
New Mexico	1,279	3,187	6,466	6,402	−1.0
New York	21,815	54,895	62,620	60,347	−3.6
North Carolina	15,513	18,411	37,970	39,482	+4.0
North Dakota	253	483	1,416	1,452	+2.5
Ohio	13,489	31,822	50,731	51,686	+1.9
Oklahoma	4,796	12,285	25,849	25,864	+0.1
Oregon	3,177	6,492	13,948	14,167	+1.6
Pennsylvania	8,171	22,290	45,969	50,147	+9.1
Rhode Island[1]	813	2,392	4,018	4,045	+0.7
South Carolina	7,862	17,319	24,239	24,326	+0.4
South Dakota	635	1,341	3,311	3,342	+0.9
Tennessee	7,022	10,388	26,267	27,228	+3.7
Texas	29,892	50,042	171,790	172,506	+0.4
Utah	932	2,496	6,515	6,546	+0.5
Vermont[1]	480	1,049	2,145	2,116	−1.4
Virginia	8,920	17,593	38,069	38,276	+0.5
Washington	4,399	7,995	17,772	17,926	+0.9
West Virginia	1,257	1,565	6,056	6,059	0.0
Wisconsin	3,980	7,465	23,743	23,380	−1.5
Wyoming	534	1,110	2,084	2,084	0.0
state	305,458	708,393	1,398,627	1,409,166	+0.8
federal[3]	24,363	65,526	199,618	201,280	+0.8
US total	329,821	773,919	1,598,245	1,610,446	+0.8

[1]Jails and prisons are part of an integrated system. Data include total jail and prison populations.   [2]Population figures are based on custody counts.   [3]As of the end of 2001, when the transfer of responsibility for sentenced felons from the District of Columbia to the Federal Bureau of Prisons was completed, the District of Columbia no longer operates a prison system, and its prisoners are from that date forward included in federal data only.

Directors of the Federal Bureau of Investigation (FBI)

The FBI evolved from an unnamed force appointed by Attorney General Charles J. Bonaparte on 26 Jul 1908. It is the unit of the Department of Justice responsible for investigating foreign intelligence and terrorist activities and violations of federal criminal law. The president appoints the director of the FBI with confirmation from the Senate. Since J. Edgar Hoover's tenure, a director's term may not exceed 10 years. Acting directors are not included in this table.

NAME	DATES OF SERVICE	NAME	DATES OF SERVICE
Stanley Finch	26 Jul 1908–30 Apr 1912	Clarence M. Kelley	9 Jul 1973–15 Feb 1978
Alexander Bruce Bielaski	30 Apr 1912–10 Feb 1919	William H. Webster	23 Feb 1978–25 May 1987
		William S. Sessions	2 Nov 1987–19 Jul 1993
William J. Flynn	1 Jul 1919–21 Aug 1921	Louis J. Freeh	1 Sep 1993–25 Jun 2001
William J. Burns	22 Aug 1921–14 Jun 1924	Robert S. Mueller, III	4 Sep 2001–
J. Edgar Hoover	10 Dec 1924–2 May 1972		

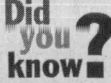

Did you know? The first woman in the United States to earn a Ph.D. degree was Helen Magill White. After graduating as part of the first class of Swarthmore College (Pennsylvania), she earned a doctorate in Greek from Boston University in 1877, with a dissertation on Greek drama. She received her doctorate 16 years after the first US Ph.D.'s were conferred on men (by Yale University).

United States Society

Average US Family Size, 1950–2008

Source: Statistical Abstract of the United States: 2010.

YEAR	NUMBER OF FAMILIES ('000)	PEOPLE PER FAMILY (AVERAGE)	YEAR	NUMBER OF FAMILIES ('000)	PEOPLE PER FAMILY (AVERAGE)	YEAR	NUMBER OF FAMILIES ('000)	PEOPLE PER FAMILY (AVERAGE)
1950	39,303	3.54	1970	51,586	3.58	1990	66,090	3.17
1955	41,951	3.59	1975	55,712	3.42	1995	69,305	3.19
1960	45,111	3.67	1980	59,550	3.29	2000	72,025	3.17
1965	47,956	3.70	1985	62,706	3.23	2008	77,873	3.15

US Population by Age, 2010

Numbers are in thousands ('000). Source: US Census Bureau. Detail may not add to total given because of rounding.

AGE	POPULATION NUMBER	(%)	AGE	POPULATION NUMBER	(%)
under 5 years	21,099,521	6.8	55 to 64 years	36,274,842	11.7
5 to 9 years	20,885,755	6.7	65 to 74 years	21,462,599	7.0
10 to 14 years	20,395,334	6.6	75 years and over	18,766,113	5.9
15 to 19 years	21,769,824	7.0	total population	310,232,863	100
20 to 24 years	21,779,480	7.0			
25 to 34 years	41,817,605	13.5	under 20 years	84,150,434	27.1
35 to 44 years	41,277,055	13.3	20 years and over	226,082,429	72.9
45 to 54 years	44,704,735	14.4	65 years and over	40,228,712	13.0

Living Arrangements of Children Under 18 in the US, 2009

Numbers in thousands ('000). Hispanics may be of any race. Detail may not add to total given because of rounding. Source: US Census Bureau.

LIVING IN HOUSEHOLD WITH	RACE/ETHNICITY ALL RACES	WHITE	BLACK	HISPANIC
both parents	51,836	42,645	4,281	11,241
mother only	16,912	9,930	5,645	4,070
father only	2,504	1,920	378	413
neither parent	2,979	1,758	932	637
total	74,231	56,253	11,236	16,361

Children Under 18 in the US Living Below the Poverty Level, 1985–2008

Numbers are in thousands ('000). Hispanics may be of any race. N/A means not available. Source: US Census Bureau. For the definition of the poverty level, see <www.census.gov/hhes/www/poverty/povdef.html>.

	% OF CHILDREN BELOW THE POVERTY LEVEL					NUMBER OF CHILDREN BELOW THE POVERTY LEVEL				
YEAR	ALL[1]	WHITE[2]	BLACK	ASIAN/ PACIFIC ISLANDER	HISPANIC	ALL[1]	WHITE[2]	BLACK	ASIAN/ PACIFIC ISLANDER	HISPANIC
1985	20.7	12.8	43.6	N/A	40.3	13,010	5,745	4,157	N/A	2,606
1986	20.5	13.0	43.1	N/A	37.7	12,876	5,789	4,148	N/A	2,507
1987	20.3	11.8	45.1	23.5	39.3	12,843	5,230	4,385	455	2,670
1988	19.5	11.0	43.5	24.1	37.6	12,455	4,888	4,296	474	2,631
1989	19.6	11.5	43.7	19.8	36.2	12,590	5,110	4,375	392	2,603
1990	20.6	12.3	44.8	17.6	38.4	13,431	5,532	4,550	374	2,865
1991	21.8	13.1	45.9	17.5	40.4	14,341	5,918	4,755	360	3,094
1992	22.3	13.2	46.6	16.4	40.0	15,294	6,017	5,106	363	3,637
1993	22.7	13.6	46.1	18.2	40.9	15,727	6,255	5,125	375	3,873
1994	21.8	12.5	43.8	18.3	41.5	15,289	5,823	4,906	318	4,075
1995	20.8	11.2	41.9	19.5	40.0	14,665	5,115	4,761	564	4,080
1996	20.5	11.1	39.9	19.5	40.3	14,463	5,072	4,519	571	4,237
1997	19.9	11.4	37.2	20.3	36.8	14,113	5,204	4,225	628	3,972
1998	18.9	10.6	36.7	18.0	34.4	13,467	4,822	4,151	564	3,837
1999	16.9	9.4	33.2	11.9	30.3	12,280	4,155	3,813	381	3,693

Children Under 18 in the US Living Below the Poverty Level, 1985–2008 (continued)

	% OF CHILDREN BELOW THE POVERTY LEVEL				NUMBER OF CHILDREN BELOW THE POVERTY LEVEL				
YEAR	ALL[1]	WHITE[2]	BLACK	ASIAN/ PACIFIC ISLANDER	HISPANIC	ALL[1]	WHITE[2]	BLACK	ASIAN/ PACIFIC ISLANDER	HISPANIC
2000	16.2	9.1	31.2	12.7	28.4	11,587	4,018	3,581	420	3,522
2001	16.3	9.5	30.2	11.5	28.0	11,733	4,194	3,492	369	3,570
2002	16.7	9.4	32.3	12.2	28.6	12,133	4,090	3,645	351	3,782
2003	17.6	9.8	34.1	12.7	29.7	12,866	4,233	3,877	377	4,077
2004	17.8	10.5	33.7	10.1	28.9	13,041	4,519	3,788	305	4,098
2005	17.6	10.0	34.5	11.0	28.3	12,896	4,254	3,841	333	4,143
2006	17.4	10.0	33.4	12.5	26.9	12,827	4,208	3,777	391	4,072
2007	18.0	10.1	34.5	12.5	28.6	13,324	4,255	3,904	398	4,482
2008	19.0	10.6	34.7	15.5	30.6	14,068	4,364	3,878	514	5,010

[1]Includes other and unclassified. [2]Excludes Hispanic population.

US Adoptions of Foreign-Born Children

Adoptions of foreign children by US citizens are tracked by the number of immigrant visas issued to orphans entering the US. Source: US Department of State.

TOP 10 COUNTRIES OF ORIGIN	ADOPTIONS FISCAL YEAR 2008	2009	TOP 10 COUNTRIES OF ORIGIN	ADOPTIONS FISCAL YEAR 2008	2009	TOTAL FOREIGN ADOPTIONS FISCAL YEAR	ADOPTIONS
1 China	3,911	3,001	6 Ukraine	490	610	2004	22,990
2 Ethiopia	1,724	2,277	7 Vietnam	748	481	2005	22,734
3 Russia	1,857	1,586	8 Haiti	301	330	2006	20,680
4 Rep. of Korea	1,065	1,080	9 India	308	297	2007	19,609
5 Guatemala	4,122	756	10 Kazakhstan	380	295	2008	17,475
						2009	12,753

US Nursing Home Population

The data in these tables were gathered through interviews conducted for the most recent National Nursing Home Survey (2004) and through the publication *Health, United States, 2009*. Only those residents who described themselves as being of one race are included. Data on residents under the age of 65 are not available. Detail may not add to total given because of rounding.

Source: US National Center for Health Statistics.

AGE AT INTERVIEW	TOTAL RESIDENTS	%	GENDER (2004) MALE	%	FEMALE	%
65–74	174,100	13.2	75,400	22.4	98,800	10.1
75–84	468,700	35.6	140,900	41.8	327,800	33.4
85 and older	674,500	51.2	120,600	35.8	553,900	56.5
total	1,317,300	100.0	336,900	100.0	980,400	100.0

	RACE (2004) WHITE	%	BLACK	%
65–74	134,200	11.7	34,500	23.7
75–84	405,800	35.3	54,600	37.6
85 and older	608,900	53.0	56,300	38.7
total	1,148,900	100.0	145,400	100.0

	RESIDENT LOCATION (1999) NORTHEAST	%	MIDWEST	%	SOUTH	%	WEST	%
65–74	46,400	12.1	58,900	11.8	63,400	11.9	26,100	12.1
75–84	118,500	30.9	153,200	30.8	179,100	33.7	66,800	31.1
85 and older	184,300	48.1	241,100	48.4	237,700	44.7	94,000	43.7
total	383,400	100.0	498,200	100.0	531,500	100.0	215,200	100.0

	RESIDENT LOCATION (2008) NORTHEAST	%	MIDWEST	%	SOUTH	%	WEST	%
TOTAL RESIDENTS	331,590	23.5	409,195	29.0	480,309	34.0	191,446	13.6

Marital Status of US Population by Sex, 1950–2009

The data in this table are taken from surveys of individuals 18 or over conducted by the US Census Bureau and exclude members of the armed forces except those living off post or with their families on post. Data exclude Alaska and Hawaii prior to 1960. Detail may not add to total given because of rounding.
    Source: US Census Bureau.

	TOTAL						
	1950	1960	1970	1980	1990	2000	2009
Total individuals surveyed in hundred thousands ('000,000)	111.7	125.5	132.5	159.5	181.8	201.8	226.9
Percentage of individuals never married	22.8	22.0	16.2	20.3	22.2	23.9	26.1
Percentage of individuals married	67.0	67.3	71.7	65.5	61.9	59.5	55.0
Percentage of individuals widowed	8.3	8.4	8.9	8.0	7.6	6.8	6.3
Percentage of individuals divorced	1.9	2.3	3.2	6.2	8.3	9.8	10.2
Percentage of males never married	26.2	25.3	18.9	23.8	25.8	27.0	29.5
Percentage of males married	68.0	69.1	75.3	68.4	64.3	61.5	56.9
Percentage of males widowed	4.2	3.7	3.3	2.6	2.7	2.7	2.6
Percentage of males divorced	1.7	1.9	2.5	5.2	7.2	8.8	9.0
Percentage of females never married	11.1	12.3	13.7	17.1	18.9	21.1	22.8
Percentage of females married	37.6	42.6	68.5	63.0	18.9	57.6	53.3
Percentage of females widowed	7.0	8.3	13.9	12.8	12.1	10.5	9.8
Percentage of females divorced	1.2	1.7	3.9	7.1	9.3	10.8	11.4

Unmarried-Couple Households in the US

Data based on Current Population Survey or American Community Survey except for census years of 1960 and 1970. 2007 data shown separately. Numbers in thousands ('000). Source: Statistical Abstract of the United States: 2010.

YEAR	TOTAL US HOUSEHOLDS	UNMARRIED-COUPLE HOUSEHOLDS (OPPOSITE SEX)	% OF TOTAL HOUSEHOLDS	NO CHILDREN UNDER 15	WITH CHILDREN UNDER 15
1960 census	52,799	439	0.8	242	197
1970 census	63,401	523	0.8	327	196
1980	80,776	1,589	2.0	1,159	431
1985	86,789	1,983	2.3	1,380	603
1990	93,347	2,856	3.1	1,966	891
1995	98,990	3,668	3.7	2,349	1,319
2000	104,705	4,736	4.5	3,061	1,675

UNMARRIED-COUPLE HOUSEHOLDS	2007
male householder/female partner	2,834
male householder/male partner	396
female householder/female partner	358
female householder/male partner	2,622
unmarried-couple households	**6,210**
total households	**112,378**

United States Education

Educational Attainment in the US by Gender and Race

For persons ages 25 years old and older. Percentage rates for 1960, 1970, and 1980 are based on sample data from the decennial censuses. Rates for 1990, 2000, and 2008 are based on the Current Population Survey. N/A means not available.
    Source: US Census Bureau.

Educational Attainment in the US by Gender and Race (continued)

Percentage who had graduated from high school[1]

YEAR	ALL RACES[2]		WHITE		BLACK		ASIAN/PACIFIC ISLANDER		HISPANIC[3]	
	MALE	FEMALE	MALE	FEMALE	MALE	FEMALE	MALE	FEMALE	MALE	FEMALE
1960	39.5	42.5	41.6	44.7	18.2	21.8	N/A	N/A	N/A	N/A
1970	51.9	52.8	54.0	55.0	30.1	32.5	N/A	N/A	37.9	34.2
1980	67.3	65.8	69.6	68.1	50.8	51.5	N/A	N/A	67.3	65.8
1990	77.7	77.5	79.1	79.0	65.8	66.5	84.0	77.2	50.3	51.3
2000	84.2	84.0	84.8	85.0	78.7	78.3	88.2	83.4	56.6	57.5
2008	85.9	87.2	86.3	87.8	81.8	84.0	90.8	86.9	60.9	63.7

Percentage who had graduated from college[4]

YEAR	ALL RACES[2]		WHITE		BLACK		ASIAN/PACIFIC ISLANDER		HISPANIC[3]	
	MALE	FEMALE	MALE	FEMALE	MALE	FEMALE	MALE	FEMALE	MALE	FEMALE
1960	9.7	5.8	10.3	6.0	2.8	3.3	N/A	N/A	N/A	N/A
1970	13.5	8.1	14.4	8.4	4.2	4.6	N/A	N/A	7.8	4.3
1980	20.1	12.8	21.3	13.3	8.4	8.3	N/A	N/A	9.4	6.0
1990	24.4	18.4	25.3	19.0	11.9	10.8	44.9	35.4	9.8	8.7
2000	27.8	23.6	28.5	23.9	16.3	16.7	47.6	40.7	10.7	10.6
2008	30.1	28.8	30.5	29.1	18.7	20.4	55.8	49.8	12.6	14.1

[1]Through 1990, finished four years or more of high school. [2]Includes races not shown separately in the table.
[3]Hispanics may be of any race. [4]Through 1990, finished four years or more of college.

National Spelling Bee

A spelling bee is a contest in which players attempt to spell correctly and aloud words assigned them by an impartial judge. Competition may be individual, with players eliminated when they misspell a word and the last remaining player being the winner, or between teams, the winner being the team with the most players remaining at the close of the contest. The spelling bee is an old custom that was revived in schools in the United States in the late 19th century and enjoyed a great vogue there and in Great Britain. In the US, local, regional, and national competitions continue to be held annually. The US National Spelling Bee was begun by the Louisville *Courier-Journal* newspaper in 1925, and it was taken over by Scripps Howard, Inc., in 1941. To qualify, spellers (who are sponsored by an organization, usually a newspaper) must meet 12 requirements, including that they have neither reached their 16th birthday nor passed beyond the eighth grade.

National Spelling Bee Web site:
<www.spellingbee.com>.

YEAR	CHAMPION	WINNING WORD
1925	Frank Neuhauser, *Courier-Journal* (Louisville KY)	gladiolus
1926	Pauline Bell, *Courier-Journal* (Louisville KY)	cerise
1927	Dean Lucas, *Akron Beacon Journal* (Ohio)	abrogate
1928	Betty Robinson, *South Bend News-Tribune* (Indiana)	knack
1929	Virginia Hogan, *Omaha World-Herald* (Nebraska)	luxuriance
1930	Helen Jensen, *Des Moines Register & Tribune* (Iowa)	albumen
1931	Ward Randall, *White Hall Register-Republican* (Illinois)	foulard
1932	Dorothy Greenwald, *Des Moines Register & Tribune* (Iowa)	knack[1]
1933	Alma Roach, *Akron Beacon Journal* (Ohio)	torsion
1934	Sarah Wilson, *Portland Evening Express* (Maine)	brethren
1935	Clara Mohler, *Akron Beacon Journal* (Ohio)	intelligible
1936	Jean Trowbridge, *Des Moines Register & Tribune* (Iowa)	eczema
1937	Waneeta Beckley, *Courier-Journal* (Louisville KY)	promiscuous
1938	Marian Richardson, *Louisville Times* (Kentucky)	pronunciation
1939	Elizabeth Ann Rice, *Worcester Telegram & Gazette* (Massachusetts)	canonical
1940	Laurel Kuykendall, *Knoxville News-Sentinel* (Tennessee)	therapy[1]
1941	Louis Edward Sissman, *Detroit News* (Michigan)	chrysanthemum
1942	Richard Earnhart, *El Paso Herald-Post* (Texas)	sacrilegious
1943–45		not held
1946	John McKinney, *Des Moines Register & Tribune* (Iowa)	semaphore
1947	Mattie Lou Pollard, *Atlanta Journal* (Georgia)	chlorophyll
1948	Jean Chappelear, *Akron Beacon Journal* (Ohio)	psychiatry
1949	Kim Calvin, *Canton Repository* (Ohio)	onerous
1950	Diana Reynard, *Cleveland Press* (Ohio);	meticulosity[1]
	Colquitt Dean, *Atlanta Journal* (Georgia) (tied)	
1951	Irving Belz, *Memphis Press-Scimitar* (Tennessee)	insouciant

National Spelling Bee (continued)

YEAR	CHAMPION	WINNING WORD
1952	Doris Ann Hall, *Winston-Salem Journal* (North Carolina)	vignette
1953	Elizabeth Hess, *Arizona Republic* (Phoenix AZ)	soubrette
1954	William Cashore, *Norristown Times Herald* (Pennsylvania)	transept
1955	Sandra Sloss, *St. Louis Globe-Democrat* (Missouri)	crustaceology
1956	Melody Sachko, *Pittsburgh Press* (Pennsylvania)	condominium
1957	Sandra Owen, *Canton Repository* (Ohio);	schappe[2]
	Dana Bennett, *Rocky Mountain News* (Denver CO) (tied)	
1958	Jolitta Schlehuber, *Topeka Daily Capital* (Kansas)	syllepsis
1959	Joel Montgomery, *Rocky Mountain News* (Denver CO)	catamaran
1960	Henry Feldman, *Knoxville News-Sentinel* (Tennessee)	eudaemonic
1961	John Capehart, *Tulsa Tribune* (Oklahoma)	smaragdine
1962	Nettie Crawford, *El Paso Herald-Post* (Texas);	esquamulose[2]
	Michael Day, *St. Louis Democrat* (Missouri) (tied)	
1963	Glen Van Slyke III, *Knoxville News-Sentinel* (Tennessee)	equipage
1964	William Kerek, *Akron Beacon Journal* (Ohio)	sycophant
1965	Michael Kerpan, Jr., *Tulsa Tribune* (Oklahoma)	eczema
1966	Robert A. Wake, *Houston Chronicle* (Texas)	ratoon
1967	Jennifer Reinke, *Omaha World-Herald* (Nebraska)	chihuahua
1968	Robert L. Walters, *Topeka Daily Capital* (Kansas)	abalone
1969	Susan Yoachum, *Dallas Morning News* (Texas)	interlocutory
1970	Libby Childress, *Winston-Salem Journal & Sentinel* (North Carolina)	croissant
1971	Jonathan Knisely, *Philadelphia Bulletin* (Pennsylvania)	shalloon
1972	Robin Kral, *Lubbock Avalanche-Journal* (Texas)	macerate
1973	Barrie Trinkle, *Fort Worth Press* (Texas)	vouchsafe
1974	Julie Ann Junkin, *Birmingham Post-Herald* (Alabama)	hydrophyte
1975	Hugh Tosteson, *San Juan Star* (Puerto Rico)	incisor
1976	Tim Kneale, *Syracuse Herald Journal-American* (New York)	narcolepsy
1977	John Paola, *Pittsburgh Press* (Pennsylvania)	cambist
1978	Peg McCarthy, *Topeka Capital-Journal* (Kansas)	deification
1979	Katie Kerwin, *Rocky Mountain News* (Denver CO)	maculature
1980	Jacques Bailly, *Rocky Mountain News* (Denver CO)	elucubrate
1981	Paige Pipkin, *El Paso Herald-Post* (Texas)	sarcophagus
1982	Molly Dieveney, *Rocky Mountain News* (Denver CO)	psoriasis
1983	Blake Giddens, *El Paso Herald-Post* (Texas)	Purim
1984	Daniel Greenblatt, *Loudoun Times-Mirror* (Virginia)	luge
1985	Balu Natarajan, *Chicago Tribune* (Illinois)	milieu
1986	Jon Pennington, *Patriot News* (Harrisburg PA)	odontalgia
1987	Stephanie Petit, *Pittsburgh Press* (Pennsylvania)	staphylococci
1988	Rageshree Ramachandran, *Sacramento Bee* (California)	elegiacal
1989	Scott Isaacs, *Rocky Mountain News* (Denver CO)	spoliator
1990	Amy Marie Dimak, *Seattle Times* (Washington)	fibranne
1991	Joanne Lagatta, *Wisconsin State Journal* (Madison WI)	antipyretic
1992	Amanda Goad, *Richmond News Leader* (Virginia)	lyceum
1993	Geoff Hooper, *Commercial Appeal* (Memphis TN)	kamikaze
1994	Ned G. Andrews, *Knoxville News-Sentinel* (Tennessee)	antediluvian
1995	Justin Tyler Carroll, *Commercial Appeal* (Memphis TN)	xanthosis
1996	Wendy Guey, *Palm Beach Post* (Florida)	vivisepulture
1997	Rebecca Sealfon, *Daily News* (New York NY)	euonym
1998	Jody-Anne Maxwell, Phillips & Phillips Stationery Suppliers, Ltd. (Kingston, Jamaica)	chiaroscurist
1999	Nupur Lala, *Tampa Tribune* (Florida)	logorrhea
2000	George Abraham Thampy, *St. Louis Post-Dispatch* (Missouri)	demarche
2001	Sean Conley, *Aitkin Independent Age* (Minnesota)	succedaneum
2002	Pratyush Buddiga, *Rocky Mountain News* (Denver CO)	prospicience
2003	Sai R. Gunturi, *Dallas Morning News* (Texas)	pococurante
2004	David Tidmarsh, *South Bend Tribune* (Indiana)	autochthonous
2005	Anurag Kashyap, *San Diego Union-Tribune* (California)	appoggiatura
2006	Kerry Close, *Asbury Park Press/Home News Tribune* (New Jersey)	Ursprache
2007	Evan M. O'Dorney, *Contra Costa Times* (Walnut Creek CA)	serrefine
2008	Sameer Mishra, *Journal and Courier* (Lafayette IN)	guerdon
2009	Kavya Shivashankar, *Olathe News* (Kansas)	Laodicean
2010	Anamika Veeramani, *Plain Dealer* (Cleveland OH)	stromuhr

[1]*It has not been independently verified that this was the winning, or final, word.*   [2]*Neither winning contestant spelled the winning word correctly, and the contest was declared a draw.*

Business

All That Glitters May Not Make Your Fortune

by David von Drehle, TIME

One particularly grim day in the middle of the financial collapse, as the value of my retirement account plummeted like Wile E. Coyote off a cliff, my brother asked me if I had considered buying gold. Without thinking, I said, "I'm not quite ready to dig a bunker in the backyard." Which was a silly thing to say about a perfectly reasonable investment, one that has appealed to figures as diverse as Cleopatra, King Midas, the Rothschilds, and the villain in *Goldfinger*. On reflection, though, what struck me was that my brother immediately got what I was saying. Gold is an element—it's a commodity—but it is also, for many people, an extreme political statement. When you are no longer willing to buy anything they're telling you to, that's the time to buy gold. Don't hunker down for the apocalypse without it.

Gold is the color of anxiety, a hedge against fear. Its price tends to soar when times are stormy and crash when the rainbows reappear. Not surprisingly, when the subprime bubble burst in 2007, a 21st-century gold fever gripped the US and convulsed the globe, prompting buy orders from kitchen-table investors as well as high-flying traders. Profits have spiked at gold-mining companies.

High gold prices—north of US$1,100 per ounce, roughly double the pre-crisis price—have pried open jewelry boxes from coast to coast, as would-be sellers decide that the sentimental value of old gifts and by-gone bling is no match for quick cash. People have been trading in their rings, bracelets, necklaces, and watches at pawnshops, jewelry stores, and heavily promoted buying events in the conference rooms of suburban motels. Or you can monetize your memories in the comfort of your own living room, for just as suburban domesticity once begat the Tupperware party, fiscal chaos has now given us the gold party, at which friends gather to have their trinkets assayed by merchants bearing rolls of green.

There is nothing arbitrary about the grip of gold on the human imagination. It is an amazing metal. Gold can be pounded into a sheet so thin that light passes through it, yet the sheet doesn't crack. Gold can be stretched into wires thinner than a human hair, yet those wires still conduct electricity beautifully. Implant it in a human body in the form of a medical device, and it will resist the growth of bacteria. Gold is beautiful, pliable, ductile, strong. The Stone Age, Bronze Age, and Iron Age all came and went, but gold is forever. Contrast that with, say, collateralized debt obligations, whatever those are, or the concept of collecting insurance on bad investments made by other people—so-called credit-default swaps. In a world of unreal investments, reality must finally have its day, and there is nothing more real than periodic-table element No. 79—favored shelter from the financial storm.

This pattern is as old as legal tender: gold is the contrary indicator of peace and prosperity. And the reason for this relationship is simple. When it comes to money, gold is, well, the gold standard. As other forms of stored value—paper banknotes, government bonds, inked entries in bank ledgers—came into widespread use, they were understood to represent actual amounts of precious metal. Someone with a pocketful of paper could, if so moved, exchange it for actual gold. When times were good, very few people felt any desire to do so. Gold was heavy and cumbersome compared with paper money. However, when times looked bad, the abstract symbols of value tended to break away from the underlying metal, because a government facing a crisis could print banknotes or issue bonds a lot faster than it could find more gold. The result is inflation, which eats away at the value of money. A really badly run government, like those of Weimar Germany or modern-day Zimbabwe, might create so much money that it becomes virtually worthless; in Harare, you can meet homeless trillionaires. Gold, however, never goes to zero.

The US cut its last link to the gold standard in 1971, but it was effectively finished prior to World War I by a series of credit shortages that led to bank panics. Gold may be honest, and tangible, but it is not nearly as powerful an economic tool as the more abstract forms of money that have taken its place.

The miracles of the modern world weren't wrought by gold; they were wrought in large part by abstract money, because it has an attribute that gold can't mimic. It can grow. The Fed poured hundreds of billions of dollars into the economy to refloat it, backed not by gold but by the full faith and credit of the US.

If everybody had to carry bags of precious metal around to buy things or if every ledger entry on a banker's computer screen had to be backed by a gold bar in a vault somewhere, economies would grow a lot more slowly or, in a panic, they would shrink. On the other hand, this engine revs only if people have faith that those ledger entries, those pixels, those scraps of green paper, represent actual value. Abstract money is an awesome thing—as long as people believe in it. But suppose that belief were to collapse one day and all the customers of the bank tried to empty their accounts at once. They would discover that the money wasn't there.

As global finance has grown ever more complex, gold has become a badge of mistrust in the modern political economy. A stack of gold coins in your gun safe signals that you won't be caught flat-footed when FEMA opens concentration camps, or when the UN imposes the new world order. Gold dealers have clearly figured this out; they advertise heavily on the radio talk shows of such doomsday-minded libertarians as George Noory, Glenn Beck, Alex Jones, and G. Gordon Liddy.

The problem with doomsday investing is that it's difficult to cash out. And you can be wrong for decades. An ounce of gold sold for US$675 in January 1980. The price in January 2001: US$265. The price of gold hasn't gone up any lately, as the global economy slowly recovers, and central bankers are serene about inflation. According to a blog on the Wall Street Journal's Web site, gold has lost "luster" with China's government, and the International Monetary Fund is selling a big chunk of its stash. Is this the end of gold fever for now? That depends on which way the fear index goes. Here's something to watch, though: on some survivalist blogs, a debate has recently opened, led by skeptics questioning the utility of gold. The smart play for the well-prepared, they argue, is silver.

US Economy

Denominations of US Currency

PAPER MONEY

VALUE	PORTRAIT ON FRONT	DESIGN ON BACK	WHEN CIRCULATED
$1	George Washington	Great Seal of US	1929–
$2	Thomas Jefferson	Monticello	1929–75
$2	Thomas Jefferson	John Trumbull's *Signing of the Declaration of Independence*	1976–
$5[1]	Abraham Lincoln	Lincoln Memorial	2000–
$10[1]	Alexander Hamilton	US Treasury	2000–
$20[1]	Andrew Jackson	White House	1998–
$50[1]	Ulysses S. Grant	US Capitol	1997–
$100[1]	Benjamin Franklin	Independence Hall	1996–
$500	William McKinley	ornate figure of value	1929–69
$1,000	Grover Cleveland	ornate figure of value	1929–69
$5,000	James Madison	ornate figure of value	1929–69
$10,000	Salmon P. Chase	ornate figure of value	1929–69
$100,000[2]	Woodrow Wilson	ornate figure of value	—

[1]*Earlier versions issued starting in 1929 had same subjects as current version.*   [2]*Never issued to public.*

COINS

VALUE	PORTRAIT ON FRONT	DESIGN ON BACK	WHEN CIRCULATED
1¢	Abraham Lincoln	"one cent" and wheat	1909–58
1¢	Abraham Lincoln	Lincoln Memorial	1959–2008
1¢	Abraham Lincoln	scenes from Lincoln's life	2009
1¢	Abraham Lincoln	Union shield with scroll	2010
5¢	Thomas Jefferson	Monticello	1938–2003; 2006–
5¢	Thomas Jefferson	"Westward Journey" designs	2004–05
10¢	Franklin D. Roosevelt	torch	1946–
25¢	George Washington	eagle	1932–74; 1977–98
25¢ (bicentennial)	George Washington	colonial drummer	1975–76
25¢	George Washington	50 state designs	1999–2008
25¢	George Washington	Washington DC, US territories designs	2009
25¢	George Washington	national parks and sites designs	2010–21
50¢	John F. Kennedy	presidential seal	1964–74; 1977–
50¢ (bicentennial)	John F. Kennedy	Independence Hall	1975–76
$1	Dwight D. Eisenhower	eagle	1971–74; 1977–78
$1 (bicentennial)	Dwight D. Eisenhower	Liberty Bell and Moon	1975–76
$1	Susan B. Anthony	eagle	1979–80; 1999
$1	Sacagawea	eagle	2000–06
$1	Sacagawea	Native American farmer	2009
$1	presidential portraits	Statue of Liberty	2007–16

50 STATE QUARTERS PROGRAM

STATE	WHEN ISSUED	STATE	WHEN ISSUED	STATE	WHEN ISSUED
Alabama	2003	Louisiana	2002	Ohio	2002
Alaska	2008	Maine	2003	Oklahoma	2008
Arizona	2008	Maryland	2000	Oregon	2005
Arkansas	2003	Massachusetts	2000	Pennsylvania	1999
California	2005	Michigan	2004	Rhode Island	2001
Colorado	2006	Minnesota	2005	South Carolina	2000
Connecticut	1999	Mississippi	2002	South Dakota	2006
Delaware	1999	Missouri	2003	Tennessee	2002
Florida	2004	Montana	2007	Texas	2004
Georgia	1999	Nebraska	2006	Utah	2007
Hawaii	2008	Nevada	2006	Vermont	2001
Idaho	2007	New Hampshire	2000	Virginia	2000
Illinois	2003	New Jersey	1999	Washington	2007
Indiana	2002	New Mexico	2008	West Virginia	2005
Iowa	2004	New York	2001	Wisconsin	2004
Kansas	2005	North Carolina	2001	Wyoming	2007
Kentucky	2001	North Dakota	2006		

PRESIDENTIAL $1 COINS PROGRAM

2007	George Washington, John Adams, Thomas Jefferson, James Madison
2008	James Monroe, John Quincy Adams, Andrew Jackson, Martin Van Buren

Denominations of US Currency (continued)

PRESIDENTIAL $1 COINS PROGRAM (CONTINUED)

2009   William Henry Harrison, John Tyler, James K. Polk, Zachary Taylor
2010   Millard Fillmore, Franklin Pierce, James Buchanan, Abraham Lincoln

US Currency and Coins in Circulation

*Currency and coins outstanding and currency in circulation by denomination,
31 Dec 2009. Source: Treasury Bulletin, March 2010.*

	TOTAL CURRENCY AND COINS	CURRENCY	COINS[1]
amounts in circulation	$ 928,227,830,091	$ 888,323,196,122	$39,904,633,969
amounts held by:			
US Treasury	255,506,891	7,224,465	248,282,426
Federal Reserve Banks	195,194,491,924	193,141,389,957	2,053,101,967
total amounts outstanding	**1,123,677,828,906**	**1,081,471,810,544**	**42,206,018,362**

DENOMINATION	TOTAL CURRENCY IN CIRCULATION	FEDERAL RESERVE NOTES[2]	US NOTES	CURRENCY NO LONGER ISSUED
$1	$ 9,573,049,736	$ 9,430,501,798	$ 143,503	$142,404,435
$2	1,726,800,156	1,594,713,814	132,073,718	12,624
$5	11,196,491,570	11,061,401,145	108,646,510	26,443,915
$10	16,227,060,490	16,206,186,140	6,300	20,868,050
$20	127,546,114,720	127,526,003,340	3,840	20,107,540
$50	65,349,731,350	65,338,227,100	500	11,503,750
$100	656,390,796,000	656,368,790,400	—[3]	22,005,600
$500	142,257,500	142,049,500	5,500	202,500
$1,000	165,604,000	165,355,000	5,000	244,000
$5,000	1,780,000	1,710,000	—	70,000
$10,000	3,510,000	3,360,000	—	150,000
fractional notes[4]	600	—	90	510
total currency	**888,323,196,122**	**887,838,298,237**	**240,884,961**	**244,012,924**

[1]*Excludes coins sold to collectors at premium prices.*   [2]*Issued on or after 1 Jul 1929.*   [3]*Represents prior month adjustment.*   [4]*Represents value of certain partial denominations not presented for redemption.*

Energy

Energy Consumption by Source, 2008

*Figures represent '000,000,000,000 BTU.
Source: US Energy Information Administration, <www.eia.doe.gov>.*

	PETROLEUM	NATURAL GAS	COAL	HYDRO-ELECTRIC POWER[1, 2]	NUCLEAR ELECTRIC POWER[1]	TOTAL[1]
Alabama	598	420	843	41	360	2,132
Alaska	279	344	15	13	0	724
Arizona	576	410	459	65	281	1,578
Arkansas	376	238	279	32	162	1,149
California	3,736	2,521	63	270	375	8,492
Colorado	504	515	385	17	0	1,479
Conneticut	362	170	45	4	172	871
Delaware	128	50	61	0	0	302
District of Columbia	20	33	0	0	0	187
Florida	1,808	970	693	2	307	4,602
Georgia	1,029	437	886	22	341	3,133
Hawaii	245	3	20	1	0	344
Idaho	159	91	9	89	0	530
Illinois	1,367	1,015	1,103	2	1,004	4,043
Indiana	836	559	1,558	4	0	2,904
Iowa	428	324	485	10	47	1,235
Kansas	408	293	372	0	109	1,136
Kentucky	698	233	1,025	17	0	2,023
Louisiana	1,450	1,300	263	8	179	3,766
Maine	210	65	6	37	0	456
Maryland	535	203	309	16	151	1,489
Massachusetts	657	382	107	8	54	1,515
Michigan	913	797	800	13	331	3,027

Energy Consumption by Source, 2008 (continued)

	PETROLEUM	NATURAL GAS	COAL	HYDRO-ELECTRIC POWER[1,2]	NUCLEAR ELECTRIC POWER[1]	TOTAL[1]
Minnesota	739	411	359	7	137	1,875
Mississippi	430	364	177	0	98	1,240
Missouri	716	298	793	12	98	1,964
Montana	184	78	203	93	0	462
Nebraska	226	170	235	3	116	693
Nevada	271	275	89	20	0	777
New Hampshire	168	73	40	13	113	314
New Jersey	1,300	635	98	0	336	2,744
New Mexico	267	251	284	3	0	711
New York	1,560	1,205	229	250	445	4,064
North Carolina	953	250	795	30	420	2,700
North Dakota	141	66	425	13	0	428
Ohio	1,300	824	1,438	4	165	4,049
Oklahoma	572	691	392	30	0	1,609
Oregon	374	275	41	332	0	1,108
Pennsylvania	1,378	778	1,421	22	812	4,006
Rhode Island	97	91	0	[3]	0	218
South Carolina	560	176	446	15	558	1,692
South Dakota	117	65	43	29	0	292
Tennessee	763	239	644	49	301	2,331
Texas	5,499	3,656	1,606	16	430	11,835
Utah	291	237	396	5	0	806
Vermont	81	9	0	6	49	162
Virginia	939	311	415	12	286	2,611
Washington	804	307	95	779	85	2,067
West Virginia	273	120	956	12	0	851
Wisconsin	601	415	481	15	135	1,846
Wyoming	179	147	500	7	0	496
total[4]	38,102	23,847	22,385	2,446	8,458	101,468

[1]Data for 2007.   [2]Data do not include results from pumped-storage hydroelectricity.   [3]Negligible.   [4]Detail may not add to total given because of rounding and the inclusion of energy that has not been allocated to a state.

Travel and Tourism

Passports, Visas, and Immunizations

With certain exceptions, a **passport** (also called a passport book) is required by law for all US citizens, including infants, to travel outside the United States and its territories. The exceptions of travel without passport to Mexico, Canada, Bermuda, and countries in the Caribbean were eliminated in 2007 by implementation of the Western Hemisphere Travel Initiative. A wallet-sized **passport card** was created as a more convenient, less expensive alternative to the passport book for reentry only into the US from those formerly exempt areas. A new passport card costs US$55 for persons ages 16 and older and US$40 for those under 16; the renewal fee is US$30. Passports can be applied for at more than 9,400 passport acceptance facilities nationwide, including most government facilities. State Department passport agencies accept applications only by appointment, usually from those in need of expedited service (two weeks or less). Passport agencies are located in Aurora CO, Boston MA, Chicago IL, Dallas TX, Detroit MI, Honolulu HI, Houston TX, Los Angeles CA, Miami FL, Minneapolis MN, New Orleans LA, New York NY, Norwalk CT, Philadelphia PA, San Francisco CA, Seattle WA, Tucson AZ, and Washington DC. Everyone must apply in person for his or her first passport; those issued to persons ages 16 and older may be renewed by mail if the person's expiring passport is undamaged, is in his or her possession, and was issued no more than 15 years previously. Appropriate paperwork should be submitted several months in advance of planned travel to allow for processing. New passport fees total US$135 for persons ages 16 and older (US$110 application fee, US$25 execution fee) and US$105 for those under 16 (US$80 application fee, US$25 execution fee); expedited service is an additional US$60. Renewal fees are US$110 for adults; minors must reapply in person at the cost of US$105. Passports are mailed to applicants in about six weeks or about two weeks for rush service. The status of a passport application may be checked online at <http://travel.state.gov/passport/get/status/status_2567.html> or by contacting the National Passport Information Center at 1-877-487-2778 (toll-free; automated information; representatives are available weekdays 8 AM to 10 PM ET, except federal holidays).

Applying in person for a passport requires submission of an application form; proof of US citizenship, such as a certified birth certificate; proof of identity, such as a driver's license; two identical recent 2×2-inch photographs; a social security number; and all applicable fees. Options for proving identity or citizenship are listed on the State Department Web site. A passport is valid for 10 years, or 5 years if issued to a person age 15 or younger. Renewing by mail requires submission of an application form, the most recent passport, two identical photographs, and applicable fees. Frequent travelers may request a passport with extra pages. A pass-

Passports, Visas, and Immunizations (continued)

port that is lost or stolen in a foreign country must immediately be reported to local police and the nearest US embassy or consulate to allow for the citizen's reentry into the US. Replacing a lost or stolen passport requires completion of a form reporting the loss or theft and an application for a new passport, as well as the usual documentation, photographs, and fees.

Visas. A visa is usually a stamp placed on a US passport by a foreign country's officials allowing the passport owner to visit that country. It is the traveler's responsibility to check visa regulations and obtain visas where necessary before traveling to a foreign country. Visas may be acquired from the embassy or consulate of the intended destination and can be applied for by mail. Processing fees vary among countries.

Immunizations. Under regulations adopted by the World Health Organization, some countries require International Certificates of Vaccination against yellow fever. Other immunizations, such as those for tetanus and polio, should also be up-to-date. Preventive measures for malaria are recommended for some destinations. There are no immunization requirements for returning to the United States. Many countries require HIV/AIDS testing for work, study, or residence permits or for long-term stays.

For passport information, forms, and office locations, access the State Department Web site at <http://travel.state.gov/passport>. Entry requirements for foreign countries, including necessity of visas, immunizations, and HIV testing, are available at <http://travel.state.gov/travel/cis_pa_tw/cis/cis_1765.html>. Additional information on required or recommended health care measures can be obtained from the Centers for Disease Control and Prevention (CDC) at <www.cdc.gov/travel> or by calling 1-800-CDC-INFO; also helpful are local health departments and the Government Printing Office publication *Health Information for International Travel,* available at the CDC Web site.

Travelers to and from the US

Data for 2002 showed that overseas travel to the US dropped significantly during 2002, primarily as a response to the terrorist attacks of 11 Sep 2001. Since then, however, travel has rebounded at varying levels. Data for 2009 for all US resident travel to specific overseas countries are not available, but data for air travel to the various regions, as well as to Mexico and Canada, are presented below. Source: US Department of Commerce, International Trade Administration, Office of Travel and Tourism Industries.

TOP COUNTRIES OF ORIGIN FOR VISITORS TO THE US (2009)

		% CHANGE FROM 2008
UK	3,899,167	−14.6
Japan	2,918,268	−10.2
Germany	1,686,825	−5.4
France	1,204,490	−3.2
Brazil	892,611	+16.0
Italy	753,310	−3.4
Republic of Korea	743,846	−2.0
Australia	723,576	+4.9
China[1]	640,840	+1.3
Spain	596,766	−9.4
total overseas	**23,756,184**	**−6.3**
Canada	17,964,454	−5.0
Mexico	13,164,000	−3.8
total worldwide	**54,884,638**	**−5.3**

REGIONAL DESTINATION OF US AIR TRAVELERS ABROAD (2009)

		% CHANGE FROM 2008
Europe	11,929,977	−4.0
Caribbean	5,515,526	−2.1
Asia	5,265,778	−4.0
South America	2,566,726	+1.2
Central America	2,524,852	−1.6
Middle East	1,204,885	+41.4
Oceania	784,025	+2.6
Africa	397,204	+25.2
total overseas	**30,188,973**	**−1.3**
Mexico	5,249,810	−10.5
Canada	3,280,508	−8.6
total worldwide	**38,719,291**	**−3.3**

TOP 10 STATES AND CITIES VISITED BY OVERSEAS VISITORS (2009)[2]

STATE	VISITORS/ IN THOUSANDS ('000)	% CHANGE FROM 2008	CITY	VISITORS/ IN THOUSANDS ('000)	% CHANGE FROM 2008
New York	8,006	−4.8	New York NY	7,792	−5.1
Florida	5,274	+0.5	Miami FL	2,661	+2.9
California	4,632	−12.5	Los Angeles CA	2,518	−9.7
Nevada	1,900	−9.7	Orlando FL	2,399	−1.4
Hawaii	1,853	+1.5	San Francisco CA	2,233	−14.4
Massachusetts	1,259	−0.6	Las Vegas NV	1,853	−8.6
Illinois	1,164	−18.0	Washington DC	1,544	+5.0
Guam[3]	1,140	−4.3	Honolulu HI	1,497	0.1
New Jersey	926	−10.9	Boston MA	1,140	+2.2
Texas	903	−17.2	Chicago IL	1,117	−18.3

[1]*Data for China include Hong Kong.*   [2]*Excludes Canadian and Mexican visitors to the US.*   [3]*Guam is a US territory. If Guam were excluded, Pennsylvania would rank 10th on the list with about 879,000 overseas visitors.*

Customs Exemptions

Upon returning to the US from a foreign country, travelers must pay duty on items acquired outside the US if the value of the items is greater than the allowable exemption. The general exemption is US$800 per person, but it can also be US$200 or US$1,600, depending on the country or countries visited. Exemptions apply if the items are in the traveler's possession, are for the traveler's own use, and are declared to US Customs. The traveler must also have been out of the country for at least 48 hours (unless returning from Mexico or the US Virgin Islands) and must not have used any part of the exemption within the past 30 days; if one or both of these requirements does not apply, the allowable exemption drops to US$200 per person and includes additional restrictions. The general exemption of US$800 includes no more than 200 previously exported cigarettes, 100 cigars, and no more than one liter of alcoholic beverages. Cuban tobacco products are prohibited. Family members may combine their total exemptions in a joint declaration except under the US$200 exemption. The US$800 exemption also applies to travelers returning from any of 28 countries and dependencies in the Caribbean Basin or Andean Region but may include two liters of alcoholic beverages, as long as one of the liters was produced in one of these. The 28 countries and dependencies are Antigua and Barbuda, Aruba, The Bahamas, Barbados, Belize, Bolivia, the British Virgin Islands, Colombia, Costa Rica, Dominica, the Dominican Republic, Ecuador, El Salvador, Grenada, Guatemala, Guyana, Haiti, Honduras, Jamaica, Montserrat, the Netherlands Antilles, Nicaragua, Panama, Peru, Saint Kitts and Nevis, Saint Lucia, Saint Vincent and the Grenadines, and Trinidad and Tobago. A US$1,600 exemption applies to travelers returning from a trip that included the US Virgin Islands, American Samoa, or Guam and includes 1,000 cigarettes and five liters of alcoholic beverages; of this amount, 800 cigarettes and one liter of alcohol must be from one of the US islands. The US$1,600 exemption also applies to multi-country travel (such as a cruise) to a US possession and any of the 28 Caribbean Basin and Andean Region countries and dependencies, as long as no more than US$800 worth of goods was purchased in those locations.

Gifts valued at US$100 or less (US$200 or less for gifts sent from American Samoa, Guam, or the US Virgin Islands) may be sent to the US without duty as long as no single person receives more than this value within 24 hours. Alcoholic beverages may not be sent by mail; tobacco and alcohol-based perfumes worth more than US$5 are not included in the exemption. Travelers may ship goods home for personal use without duty if the value of the goods is US$200 or less and no single person receives more than this value within a day. This exemption increases to US$800 for goods from one of the 28 countries listed above and to US$1,600 for goods from American Samoa, Guam, or the US Virgin Islands.

Customs information is available from the Customs and Border Protection Web site at: <www.cbp.gov/xp/cgov/travel>.

US State Department Travel Warnings

The State Department issues Travel Warnings when it is believed best for Americans to avoid certain countries in the interest of safety. It also releases Travel Alerts of more short-term hazards, such as terrorist threats or political coups, that may endanger American travelers; these include an expiration date when the announcement need no longer be heeded. The department also makes available Consular Information Sheets for all countries, which may discuss safety conditions not severe enough to require a travel warning. Current information can be found at <http://travel.state.gov>.

Travel Warnings were in effect on 14 Jul 2010 for: Afghanistan, Algeria, Burundi, the Central African Republic, Chad, Colombia, Côte d'Ivoire, the Democratic Republic of the Congo, Eritrea, Georgia, Guinea, Haiti, Iran, Iraq, Israel (including the West Bank and the Gaza Strip), Kenya, Lebanon, Mali, Mauritania, Mexico, Nepal, Niger, Nigeria, Pakistan, the Philippines, Saudi Arabia, Somalia, Sudan, Uzbekistan, and Yemen.

Travel Alerts in effect on the same day and set to expire on various dates from July through December 2010 included advisories for Jamaica and South Africa and general notices alerting US citizens to the dangers of typhoon season in East Asia and the west and central Pacific Ocean and to hurricane season in the Atlantic and Pacific oceans, the Caribbean Sea, and the Gulf of Mexico. A worldwide caution on the continuing threat of terrorist acts and violence against Americans was also in effect.

Employment

US Employment by Gender and Occupation

Detail may not add to total given because of rounding. Source: US Bureau of Labor Statistics.

OCCUPATION	WORKERS 16 YEARS AND OLDER (NUMBERS IN '000)					
	TOTAL		MEN		WOMEN	
	2008	2009	2008	2009	2008	2009
management, professional, and related occupations	52,761	52,219	25,948	25,385	26,813	26,833
management, business, and financial-operations occupations	22,059	21,529	12,647	12,330	9,412	9,199
management occupations	15,852	15,447	9,925	9,674	5,926	5,773
business and financial-operations occupations	6,207	6,082	2,721	2,655	3,486	3,426

US Employment by Gender and Occupation (continued)

| OCCUPATION | WORKERS 16 YEARS AND OLDER (NUMBERS IN '000) | | | | | |
| | TOTAL | | MEN | | WOMEN | |
	2008	2009	2008	2009	2008	2009
management, professional, and related occupations (cont.)						
professional and related occupations	30,702	30,690	13,301	13,056	17,401	17,634
computer and mathematical occupations	3,676	3,481	2,765	2,618	911	863
architecture and engineering occupations	2,931	2,740	2,536	2,363	395	377
life, physical, and social-science occupations	1,307	1,328	704	707	603	621
community and social-services occupations	2,293	2,341	909	868	1,383	1,474
legal occupations	1,671	1,710	803	859	867	851
education, training, and library occupations	8,605	8,627	2,234	2,221	6,371	6,407
arts, design, entertainment, sports, and media occupations	2,820	2,724	1,471	1,453	1,349	1,271
health-care-practitioner and technical occupations	7,399	7,738	1,878	1,968	5,521	5,770
service occupations	24,451	24,598	10,471	10,521	13,980	14,077
health-care-support occupations	3,212	3,309	359	350	2,853	2,959
protective-service occupations	3,047	3,164	2,352	2,457	695	707
food-preparation and serving-related occupations	7,824	7,733	3,443	3,422	4,381	4,310
building- and grounds-cleaning and maintenance occupations	5,445	5,349	3,254	3,186	2,192	2,163
personal-care and service occupations	4,923	5,043	1,064	1,106	3,859	3,937
sales and office occupations	35,544	33,787	13,067	12,498	22,477	21,289
sales and related occupations	16,295	15,641	8,221	7,880	8,073	7,761
office and administrative-support occupations	19,249	18,146	4,845	4,618	14,404	13,527
natural-resources, construction, and maintenance occupations	14,806	13,323	14,181	12,735	626	587
farming, fishing, and forestry occupations	988	926	780	736	208	190
construction and extraction occupations	8,667	7,439	8,448	7,248	219	191
installation, maintenance, and repair occupations	5,152	4,957	4,953	4,751	199	206
production, transportation, and material-moving occupations	17,800	15,951	13,820	12,530	3,980	3,421
production occupations	8,973	7,654	6,313	5,502	2,661	2,152
transportation and material-moving occupations	8,827	8,297	7,507	7,028	1,319	1,269
total	145,362	139,877	77,486	73,670	67,876	66,208

US Federal Minimum Wage Rates, 1954–2010

The table shows the actual minimum wage for the year in question and the value of that minimum wage adjusted for inflation in the year 2010. Source: US Department of Labor.

| | minimum wage | | | minimum wage | | | minimum wage | |
YEAR	US DOLLARS	2010 DOLLARS	YEAR	US DOLLARS	2010 DOLLARS	YEAR	US DOLLARS	2010 DOLLARS
1954	0.75	6.07	1959	1.00	7.48	1964	1.25	8.78
1955	0.75	0.00	1960	1.00	7.35	1965	1.25	8.64
1956	1.00	8.00	1961	1.15	8.37	1966	1.25	8.40
1957	1.00	7.74	1962	1.15	8.29	1967	1.40	9.12
1958	1.00	7.53	1963	1.25	8.89	1968	1.60	10.01

US Federal Minimum Wage Rates, 1954–2010 (continued)

	minimum wage			minimum wage			minimum wage	
YEAR	US DOLLARS	2010 DOLLARS	YEAR	US DOLLARS	2010 DOLLARS	YEAR	US DOLLARS	2010 DOLLARS
1969	1.60	9.49	1983	3.35	7.32	1997	5.15	6.98
1970	1.60	8.97	1984	3.35	7.02	1998	5.15	6.88
1971	1.60	8.60	1985	3.35	6.78	1999	5.15	6.73
1972	1.60	8.33	1986	3.35	6.65	2000	5.15	6.51
1973	1.60	7.84	1987	3.35	6.42	2001	5.15	6.33
1974	2.00	8.83	1988	3.35	6.16	2002	5.15	6.23
1975	2.10	8.49	1989	3.35	5.88	2003	5.15	6.09
1976	2.30	8.80	1990	3.80	6.33	2004	5.15	5.93
1977	2.30	8.26	1991	4.25	6.79	2005	5.15	5.74
1978	2.65	8.85	1992	4.25	6.59	2006	5.15	5.56
1979	2.90	8.69	1993	4.25	6.40	2007	5.85	6.14
1980	3.10	8.19	1994	4.25	6.24	2008	6.55	6.62
1981	3.35	8.02	1995	4.25	6.07	2009	7.25	7.35
1982	3.35	7.56	1996	4.75	6.59	2010	7.25	7.25

US Workers Earning the Minimum Wage

This table refers to wage and salary workers who were paid hourly rates in 2009, excluding the incorporated self-employed. The prevailing federal minimum wage was US$6.55/hour until 24 Jul 2009 and US$7.25 thereafter. Workers earning less than minimum wage may have been working in jobs that are exempted from the minimum-wage provision of the Fair Labor Standards Act. Numbers are in thousands ('000).

Source: US Bureau of Labor Statistics.

WORKER CHARACTERISTICS	TOTAL NUMBER OF WORKERS	BELOW MINIMUM WAGE	AT MINIMUM WAGE	TOTAL NUMBER OF WORKERS AT OR BELOW MINIMUM WAGE	
				NUMBER	%
age					
16–24 years	14,389	1,229	508	1,737	12.1
25 years and over	58,222	1,363	472	1,835	3.2
total (16 years and over)	72,611	2,592	980	3,572	4.9
men					
16–24 years	7,045	460	214	674	9.6
25 years and over	28,140	530	154	684	2.4
16 years and over	35,185	990	368	1,358	3.9
women					
16–24 years	7,344	769	295	1,064	14.5
25 years and over	30,082	833	318	1,151	3.8
16 years and over	37,426	1,603	612	2,215	5.9
race and Hispanic or Latino ethnicity[1]					
white (16 years and over)	58,633	2,094	763	2,857	4.9
black (16 years and over)	9,269	327	168	495	5.3
Asian (16 years and over)	2,718	96	21	117	4.3
Hispanic or Latino (16 years and over)	12,740	439	183	622	4.9
full- and part-time workers[2]					
full-time	52,454	952	320	1,272	2.4
part-time	20,027	1,625	656	2,281	11.4

[1]Hispanics may be of any race and are also included in white, black, and Asian population groups. For this reason, data within this category do not add up to total.   [2]Full- and part-time workers are distinguished by the number of hours worked. These data do not add up to total because of a small number of multiple jobholders whose status on the principal job is unknown.

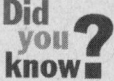

Did you know?   The Michelin guides were initiated by André Michelin, whose aim was to promote tourism by car and thus to support his tire company. His first *Red Guide* (1900) listed French towns of interest that were large enough to contain hotels and garages. It included the prototypical rating symbols for which Michelin became famous. A select number of restaurants that provide "cooking worth a special journey" are indicated by the presence of three stars.

Median Income by Educational and Social Variables

This table refers to persons who worked full-time throughout the year and are 15 years old and older as of March of the following year. Median income dollar amounts are not adjusted for inflation. N/A means not available. Source: US Census Bureau.

	median income (US$) males				median income (US$) females			
	1980	1990	2000	2008	1980	1990	2000	2008
full-time workers	19,173	28,979	38,891	47,779	11,591	20,591	29,123	36,688
educational level[1]								
less than 9th grade	N/A	10,319	14,131	17,043	N/A	6,268	8,546	10,625
9th to 12th grade (no diploma)	N/A	14,736	18,915	20,845	N/A	7,055	10,063	11,904
high school graduate	N/A	21,546	27,480	30,879	N/A	10,818	15,153	18,293
some college (no degree)	N/A	26,591	33,319	37,297	N/A	13,963	20,166	23,252
associate degree	N/A	29,358	38,026	42,608	N/A	17,364	23,124	27,715
bachelor's degree	N/A	36,067	49,080	57,278	N/A	20,967	30,418	36,294
master's degree	N/A	43,125	59,732	70,973	N/A	29,747	40,619	48,000
professional degree	N/A	63,741	83,701	100,000	N/A	34,064	46,084	58,364
doctoral degree	N/A	51,845	71,271	90,575	N/A	37,242	51,460	60,619
race and origin[2,3]								
white	13,328	21,170	29,797	35,120	4,947	10,317	16,079	20,950
white (non-Hispanic)	13,681	21,958	31,508	37,409	4,980	10,581	16,665	21,749
black	8,009	12,868	21,343	25,254	4,580	8,328	15,881	20,197
Hispanic origin	9,659	13,470	19,498	24,003	4,405	7,532	12,248	16,417
age[2]								
15 to 24 years	4,597	6,319	9,546	10,778	3,124	4,902	7,360	8,901
25 to 34 years	15,580	21,393	30,254	33,415	6,973	12,589	21,049	25,553
35 to 44 years	20,037	29,773	37,922	44,189	6,465	14,504	22,077	27,371
45 to 54 years	19,974	31,007	41,039	45,540	6,403	14,230	23,732	28,236
55 to 64 years	15,914	24,804	34,189	41,757	4,926	9,400	16,920	25,515
65 years and over	7,339	14,183	19,411	25,503	4,226	8,044	11,023	14,559
all workers over age 14	12,530	20,293	28,343	33,161	4,920	10,070	16,063	20,867

[1]The income figures for the various educational levels are for workers 25 years old and over. Before 1991, the level of education categories used by the US Census Bureau differed from the categories presented in this table. Because of this, the 1980 figures for the median income by educational level are not completely comparable with the figures for later years. The figures presented in the 1990 column for educational levels are actually for 1991, the first year the educational categories listed in this table were used by the US Census Bureau. [2]The figures presented in the 1980 column for race and origin and age pertain to civilian workers only. [3]Hispanic people may be of any race.

The 20 US Metropolitan Areas with the Highest Average Annual Per Capita Incomes

Personal income is income received from all sources, including wages and salaries, property rental, transfers, and interest and dividends. Source: US Bureau of Economic Analysis.

METROPOLITAN AREA	ANNUAL INCOME (US$) 2007	2008[1]	INCOME CHANGE (%)	METROPOLITAN AREA	ANNUAL INCOME (US$) 2007	2008[1]	INCOME CHANGE (%)
Bridgeport, CT[2]	81,576	82,266	0.8	Trenton-Ewing, NJ	52,255	54,200	3.7
Naples, FL[3]	63,276	64,349	1.7	Boulder, CO	51,388	52,719	2.6
San Francisco, CA[4]	60,983	61,747	1.3	Napa, CA	51,218	52,418	2.3
Sebastian, FL[5]	59,419	61,274	3.1	Seattle-Tacoma-Bellevue, WA	49,401	50,471	2.2
San Jose, CA[6]	59,338	58,802	−0.9	Barnstable, MA	47,640	49,979	4.9
Midland, TX	52,974	57,615	8.8	Hartford, CT[10]	48,330	49,129	1.7
Washington, DC, VA, MD, WV[7]	54,971	56,510	2.8	Santa Barbara, CA[11]	47,302	48,693	2.9
				Santa Cruz–Watsonville, CA	48,337	48,647	0.6
Casper, WY	52,543	55,736	6.1	Bradenton-Sarasota-Venice, FL	48,255	48,536	0.6
Boston, MA, NH[8]	53,443	55,023	3.0				
New York, NY, NJ, PA[9]	52,855	54,222	2.6	Houston, TX[12]	46,471	48,259	3.8

[1]Preliminary. [2]Includes Stamford and Norwalk. [3]Includes Marco Island. [4]Includes Oakland and Fremont. [5]Includes Vero Beach. [6]Includes Sunnyvale and Santa Clara. [7]Includes Arlington and Alexandria. [8]Includes Cambridge and Quincy. [9]Includes northern New Jersey and Long Island. [10]Includes West Hartford and East Hartford. [11]Includes Santa Maria and Goleta. [12]Includes Sugar Land and Baytown.

US Civilian Federal Employment

Source: Statistical Abstract of the United States: 2010.

AGENCIES	1970	1980	1990	2000	2008
legislative branch	29,939	39,710	37,495	31,157	29,919
judicial branch	6,879	15,178	23,605	32,186	33,682
executive branch	2,829,495	2,820,978	3,067,167	2,644,758	2,666,440[1]
Executive Office of the President	997	1,886	1,731	1,658	1,717
executive departments	1,772,363	1,716,970	2,065,542	1,592,200	1,740,979[1]
State	40,042	23,497	25,288	27,983	35,779
Treasury	90,683	124,663	158,655	143,508	111,335
Defense	1,169,173	960,116	1,034,152	676,268	682,142
Justice	40,075	56,327	83,932	125,970	107,970
Interior	71,671	77,357	77,679	73,818	70,515
Agriculture	114,309	129,139	122,594	104,466	98,720
Commerce	36,124	48,563	69,920	47,652	41,339
Labor	10,928	23,400	17,727	16,040	16,269
Health and Human Services	110,186	155,662	123,959	62,605	62,344
Housing and Urban Development	15,046	16,964	13,596	10,319	9,599
Transportation	66,970	72,361	67,364	63,598	54,676
Energy	7,156	21,557	17,731	15,692	14,857
Education	0	7,364	4,771	4,734	4,210
Veterans Affairs	169,241	228,285	248,174	219,547	265,390
Homeland Security	0	0	0	0	165,839
independent agencies[2,3]	1,056,135	1,102,122	999,894	1,050,900	923,744
Board of Governors of the Federal Reserve System	N/A	N/A	1,525	2,372	1,873
Environmental Protection Agency	0	14,715	17,123	18,036	18,127
Equal Employment Opportunity Commission	797	3,515	2,880	2,780	2,209
Federal Communications Commission	N/A	N/A	1,778	1,965	1,809
Federal Deposit Insurance Corporation	2,462	3,520	17,641	6,958	4,726
Federal Trade Commission	N/A	N/A	988	1,019	1,131
General Services Administration[4]	37,661	37,654	20,277	14,334	11,929
National Aeronautics and Space Administration	30,674	23,714	24,872	18,819	18,531
National Archives and Records Administration	N/A	N/A	3,120	2,702	3,068
National Labor Relations Board	N/A	N/A	2,263	2,054	1,670
National Science Foundation	N/A	N/A	1,318	1,247	1,383
Nuclear Regulatory Commission	0	3,283	3,353	2,858	3,833
Office of Personnel Management	5,513	8,280	6,636	3,780	5,375
Peace Corps	N/A	N/A	1,178	1,065	1,035
Railroad Retirement Board	N/A	N/A	1,772	1,176	977
Securities and Exchange Commission	N/A	N/A	2,302	2,955	3,562
Small Business Administration	4,397	5,804	5,128	4,150	3,813
Smithsonian Institution	2,547	4,403	5,092	5,065	4,929
Social Security Administration	N/A	N/A	N/A	64,474	62,337
Tennessee Valley Authority	23,785	51,714	28,392	13,145	11,727
US Information Agency	10,156	8,138	8,555	2,436	2,052
US International Development Cooperation Agency	14,493	6,152	4,698	2,552	2,515
US Postal Service	721,183	660,014	816,886	860,726	744,405
total, all agencies[2]	2,866,313	2,875,866	3,128,267	2,708,101	2,730,040[1]

N/A means not available.　[1]Detail does not add to total given because of a statistical discrepancy.　[2]Includes other agencies not shown separately.　[3]The Defense Intelligence Agency was excluded as of November 1984 and the National Imagery and Mapping Agency as of October 1996. Entries for 1990, 2000, and 2008 exclude the Central Intelligence Agency and the National Security Agency.　[4]Entries for 1970 and 1980 include the National Archives and Records Administration, which became an independent agency in 1985.

Strikes and Lockouts in the US

Strikes and lockouts are referred to as work stoppages by the Bureau of Labor Statistics. This table covers work stoppages since 1952 involving 1,000 workers or more. The number of workers and stoppages are for stoppages begun during that year. The number of days of work lost pertains to all strikes or lockouts in effect during the year, whether they began in that year or not. Percentage of working time pertains to all workers except those employed in private households, forestry, or fisheries. A minus sign (−) indicates a percentage less than 0.005.

Source: US Bureau of Labor Statistics.

Strikes and Lockouts in the US (continued)

YEAR	strikes and lockouts NUMBER	WORKERS INVOLVED ('000)	work time lost DAYS LOST ('000)	% OF WORKING TIME	YEAR	strikes and lockouts NUMBER	WORKERS INVOLVED ('000)	work time lost DAYS LOST ('000)	% OF WORKING TIME
1952	470	2,746	48,820	0.38	1981	145	729	16,908	0.07
1953	437	1,623	18,130	0.14	1982	96	656	9,061	0.04
1954	265	1,075	16,630	0.13	1983	81	909	17,461	0.08
1955	363	2,055	21,180	0.16	1984	62	376	8,499	0.04
1956	287	1,370	26,840	0.20	1985	54	324	·7,079	0.03
1957	279	887	10,340	0.07	1986	69	533	11,861	0.05
1958	332	1,587	17,900	0.13	1987	46	174	4,481	0.02
1959	245	1,381	60,850	0.43	1988	40	118	4,381	0.02
1960	222	896	13,260	0.09	1989	51·	452	16,996	0.07
1961	195	1,031	10,140	0.07	1990	44	185	5,926	0.02
1962	211	793	11,760	0.08	1991	40	392	4,584	0.02
1963	181	512	10,020	0.07	1992	35	364	3,989	0.01
1964	246	1,183	16,220	0.11	1993	35	182	3,981	0.01
1965	268	999	15,140	0.10	1994	45	322	5,021	0.02
1966	321	1,300	16,000	0.10	1995	31	192	5,771	0.02
1967	381	2,192	31,320	0.18	1996	37	273	4,889	0.02
1968	392	1,855	35,367	0.20	1997	29	339	4,497	0.01
1969	412	1,576	29,397	0.16	1998	34	387	5,116	0.02
1970	381	2,468	52,761	0.29	1999	17	73	1,996	0.01
1971	298	2,516	35,538	0.19	2000	39	394	20,419	0.06
1972	250	975	16,764	0.09	2001	29	99	1,151	–
1973	317	1,400	16,260	0.08	2002	19	46	660	–
1974	424	1,796	31,809	0.16	2003	14	129	4,091	0.01
1975	235	965	17,563	0.09	2004	17	171	3,344	.0.01
1976	231	1,519	23,962	0.12	2005	22	100	1,736	0.01
1977	298	1,212	21,258	0.10	2006	20	70	2,688	0.01
1978	219	1,006	23,774	0.11	2007	21	189	1,265	–
1979	235	1,021	20,409	0.09	2008	15	72	1,954	0.01
1980	187	795	20,844	0.09	2009	5	13	124	–

US Trade Union Membership

Numbers are in thousands ('000). N/A means not available. Source: US Bureau of Labor Statistics.

YEAR	NUMBER OF UNION MEMBERS	% OF TOTAL LABOR FORCE	YEAR	NUMBER OF UNION MEMBERS	% OF TOTAL LABOR FORCE	YEAR	NUMBER OF UNION MEMBERS	% OF TOTAL LABOR FORCE
1900[1]	791	N/A	1940	8,717	26.9	1980	20,095	23.0
1905	1,918	N/A	1945	14,322	35.5	1985	16,996	18.0
1910	2,116	N/A	1950	14,300[3]	31.5	1990	16,740	16.1
1915	2,560	N/A	1955	16,802	33.2	1995	16,360	14.9
1920	5,034	N/A	1960	17,049	31.4	2000	·16,258	13.5
1925	3,566	N/A	1965	17,299	28.4	2005	15,685	12.5
1930[2]	3,401	11.6	1970	19,381	27.4	2008	·16,098	12.4
1935	3,584	13.2	1977[4]	19,335	23.8	2009	15,327	12.3

[1]Data from 1900 to 1925 include Canadian members whose union headquarters were in the US. [2]Agricultural workers were not included as part of the total labor force for the years from 1930 to 1970. [3]Rounded to nearest hundred thousand. [4]Data for 1975 are not available. Data for 1977 on include only employed union members.

US Unemployment Rates

Unemployment rates of the civilian labor force ages 16 years and older. Source: US Bureau of Labor Statistics.

YEAR	UNEMPLOYMENT RATE (%)	YEAR	UNEMPLOYMENT RATE (%)	YEAR	UNEMPLOYMENT RATE (%)	YEAR	UNEMPLOYMENT RATE (%)
1950	5.3	1956	4.1	1962	5.5	1968	3.6
1951	3.3	1957	4.3	1963	5.7	1969	3.5
1952	3.0	1958	6.8	1964	5.2	1970	4.9
1953	2.9	1959	5.5	1965	4.5	1971	5.9
1954	5.5	1960	5.5	1966	3.8	1972	5.6
1955	4.4	1961	6.7	1967	3.8	1973	4.9

US Unemployment Rates (continued)

YEAR	UNEMPLOYMENT RATE (%)	YEAR	UNEMPLOYMENT RATE (%)	YEAR	UNEMPLOYMENT RATE (%)	YEAR	UNEMPLOYMENT RATE (%)
1974	5.6	1983	9.6	1992	7.5	2001	4.7
1975	8.5	1984	7.5	1993	6.9	2002	5.8
1976	7.7	1985	7.2	1994	6.1	2003	6.0
1977	7.1	1986	7.0	1995	5.6	2004	5.5
1978	6.1	1987	6.2	1996	5.4	2005	5.1
1979	5.8	1988	5.5	1997	4.9	2006	4.6
1980	7.1	1989	5.3	1998	4.5	2007	4.6
1981	7.6	1990	5.6	1999	4.2	2008	5.8
1982	9.7	1991	6.8	2000	4.0	2009	9.3

Social Characteristics of the Unemployed in the US

Unemployment as a percentage of the civilian labor force. Source: US Bureau of Labor Statistics.

SOCIAL CHARACTERISTICS	UNEMPLOYMENT RATES BY YEAR (%)									
	1975	1980	1985	1990	1995	2000	2005	2007	2008	2009
age (both sexes)										
16 and over[1]	19.9	17.8	18.6	15.5	17.3	13.1	5.1	4.6	5.8	9.3
25–54[2]	6.0	5.1	5.6	4.4	4.3	3.0	4.1	3.7	4.8	8.3
sex (16 years and older)[3]										
men	6.8	5.9	6.2	5.0	4.8	3.3	5.1	4.7	6.1	10.3
women	8.0	6.4	6.6	4.9	4.9	3.6	5.1	4.5	5.4	8.1
race/ethnicity										
white	7.8	6.3	6.2	4.8	4.9	3.5	4.4	4.1	5.2	8.5
black	14.8	14.3	15.1	11.4	10.4	7.6	10.0	8.3	10.1	14.8
Hispanic[4]	12.2	10.1	10.5	8.2	9.3	5.7	6.0	5.6	7.6	12.1
overall unemployment	8.5	7.1	7.2	5.6	5.6	4.0	5.1	4.6	5.8	9.3

[1]*Data for ages 16–19 until 2005.*   [2]*Data for ages 25 and older until 2005.*   [3]*Data for ages 20 years and older until 2005.*   [4]*Hispanics may be of any race and are included in both the white and black racial categories in this table.*

US Work-Related Fatalities by Cause

Totals for major categories may include some subcategories not listed in the table. Detail may not add to total given because of rounding. Source: US Bureau of Labor Statistics.

CAUSE OF FATALITY	2001–05 NUMBER (AVG.)	2008 NUMBER	(%)
transportation incidents	**2,451**	**2,053**	**40.5**
highway	1,394	1,149	22.7
collision between vehicles, mobile equipment	686	562	11.1
moving in same direction	151	144	2.8
moving in opposite directions, oncoming	254	191	3.8
moving in intersection	137	123	2.4
vehicle struck stationary object or equipment	336	314	6.2
noncollision	335	264	5.2
jackknifed or overturned—no collision	274	230	4.5
nonhighway (farm, industrial premises)	335	283	5.6
overturned	175	151	3.0
worker struck by a vehicle	369	322	6.3
railway accident	60	34	0.7
water vehicle accident	82	75	1.5
aircraft accident	206	189	3.7
assaults and violent acts	**850**	**794**	**15.7**
homicides	602	517	10.2
shooting	465	413	8.1
stabbing	60	32	0.6
self-inflicted injury	207	251	4.9

US Work-Related Fatalities by Cause (continued)

CAUSE OF FATALITY	2001-05 NUMBER (AVG.)	2008 NUMBER	(%)
contact with objects and equipment	952	923	18.2
struck by object	560	508	10.0
struck by falling object	345	349	6.9
struck by flying object	50	50	1.0
caught in or compressed by equipment or objects	256	299	5.9
caught in running equipment or machinery	128	109	2.1
caught in or crushed in collapsing materials	118	101	2.0
falls	763	680	13.4
fall to lower level	669	576	11.4
fall from ladder	125	116	2.3
fall from roof	154	121	2.4
fall from scaffold, staging	87	68	1.3
fall on same level	73	84	1.7
exposure to harmful substances or environments	498	432	8.5
contact with electric current	265	192	3.8
contact with overhead power lines	118	102	2.0
contact with temperature extremes	44	35	0.7
exposure to caustic, noxious, or allergenic substances	114	127	2.5
inhalation of substance	56	56	1.1
oxygen deficiency	74	77	1.5
drowning, submersion	54	59	1.2
fires and explosions	174	173	3.4
total	5,704	5,071	100

Consumer Prices

The consumer price index (CPI) is used as an indicator of price changes in the goods and services purchased by US consumers. The information provided below is based on the purchases of a specific group of urban consumers who serve as a sample population representing more than 80% of the total US population. Each annual CPI is compared with the average index level of 100, which is a base number that represents the average price level for the 36-month period covering the years 1982, 1983, and 1984. A minus sign indicates a decrease.

Source: US Bureau of Labor Statistics.

US Consumer Price Index, 1913—2009

This table presents the annual change in the Consumer Price Index (CPI) since 1913.

YEAR	ANNUAL CPI	% ANNUAL CHANGE IN CPI	YEAR	ANNUAL CPI	% ANNUAL CHANGE IN CPI	YEAR	ANNUAL CPI	% ANNUAL CHANGE IN CPI
1913	9.9		1929	17.1	0.0	1945	18.0	2.3
1914	10.0	1.0	1930	16.7	-2.3	1946	19.5	8.3
1915	10.1	1.0	1931	15.2	-9.0	1947	22.3	14.4
1916	10.9	7.9	1932	13.7	-9.9	1948	24.1	8.1
1917	12.8	17.4	1933	13.0	-5.1	1949	23.8	-1.2
1918	15.1	18.0	1934	13.4	3.1	1950	24.1	1.3
1919	17.3	14.6	1935	13.7	2.2	1951	26.0	7.9
1920	20.0	15.6	1936	13.9	1.5	1952	26.5	1.9
1921	17.9	-10.5	1937	14.4	3.6	1953	26.7	0.8
1922	16.8	-6.1	1938	14.1	-2.1	1954	26.9	0.7
1923	17.1	1.8	1939	13.9	-1.4	1955	26.8	-0.4
1924	17.1	0.0	1940	14.0	0.7	1956	27.2	1.5
1925	17.5	2.3	1941	14.7	5.0	1957	28.1	3.3
1926	17.7	1.1	1942	16.3	10.9	1958	28.9	2.8
1927	17.4	-1.7	1943	17.3	6.1	1959	29.1	0.7
1928	17.1	-1.7	1944	17.6	1.7	1960	29.6	1.7

US Consumer Price Index, 1913–2009 (continued)

YEAR	ANNUAL CPI	% ANNUAL CHANGE IN CPI	YEAR	ANNUAL CPI	% ANNUAL CHANGE IN CPI	YEAR	ANNUAL CPI	% ANNUAL CHANGE IN CPI
1961	29.9	1.0	1978	65.2	7.6	1995	152.4	2.8
1962	30.2	1.0	1979	72.6	11.3	1996	156.9	3.0
1963	30.6	1.3	1980	82.4	13.5	1997	160.5	2.3
1964	31.0	1.3	1981	90.9	10.3	1998	163.0	1.6
1965	31.5	1.6	1982	96.5	6.2	1999	166.6	2.2
1966	32.4	2.9	1983	99.6	3.2	2000	172.2	3.4
1967	33.4	3.1	1984	103.9	4.3	2001	177.1	2.8
1968	34.8	4.2	1985	107.6	3.6	2002	179.9	1.6
1969	36.7	5.5	1986	109.6	1.9	2003	184.0	2.3
1970	38.8	5.7	1987	113.6	3.6	2004	188.9	2.7
1971	40.5	4.4	1988	118.3	4.1	2005	195.3	3.4
1972	41.8	3.2	1989	124.0	4.8	2006	201.6	3.2
1973	44.4	6.2	1990	130.7	5.4	2007	207.3	2.8
1974	49.3	11.0	1991	136.2	4.2	2008	215.3	3.8
1975	53.8	9.1	1992	140.3	3.0	2009	214.5	-0.4
1976	56.9	5.8	1993	144.5	3.0			
1977	60.6	6.5	1994	148.2	2.6			

US Consumer Price Indexes by Item Group, 1975–2009

Source: US Bureau of Labor Statistics.

ITEM GROUP	CONSUMER PRICE INDEX								
	1975	1980	1985	1990	1995	2000	2005	2008	2009
all items	53.8	82.4	107.6	130.7	152.4	172.2	195.3	215.3	214.5
commodities	58.2	86.0	105.4	122.8	136.4	149.2	160.2	174.8	169.7
energy	42.1	86.0	101.6	102.1	105.2	124.6	177.1	236.7	193.1
food	59.8	86.8	105.6	132.4	148.4	167.8	190.7	214.1	218.0
shelter	48.8	81.0	109.8	140.0	165.7	193.4	224.4	246.7	249.4
transportation	50.1	83.1	106.4	120.5	139.1	153.3	173.9	195.5	179.3
medical care	47.5	74.9	113.5	162.8	220.5	260.8	323.2	364.1	375.6
apparel	72.5	90.9	105.0	124.1	132.0	129.6	119.5	118.9	120.1

ITEM GROUP	% CHANGE IN CPI[1]								
	1975	1980	1985	1990	1995	2000	2005	2008	2009
all items	9.1	13.5	3.6	5.4	2.8	3.4	3.4	3.8	-0.4
commodities	8.8	12.3	2.1	5.2	1.9	3.3	3.6	4.3	-2.9
energy	10.5	30.9	0.7	8.3	0.6	16.9	17.0	13.9	-18.4
food	8.5	8.6	2.3	5.8	2.8	2.3	2.4	5.5	1.8
shelter	9.9	17.6	5.6	5.4	3.2	3.3	2.6	2.5	1.1
transportation	9.4	17.9	2.6	5.6	3.6	6.2	6.6	5.9	-8.3
medical care	12.0	11.0	6.3	9.0	4.5	4.1	4.2	3.7	3.2
apparel	4.5	7.1	2.8	4.6	-1.0	-1.3	-0.7	-0.1	1.0

[1]*Annual percent change from the preceding year.*

US Budget
US Public Debt

In order to fund governmental operations, the Department of the Treasury borrows money by selling Treasury bills, US savings bonds, and other securities to the public. The money borrowed by the Treasury is referred to as the public debt. A broader measure of the federal debt is known as the gross federal debt. It consists of the public debt plus money borrowed by federal agencies. The GDP is the gross domestic product.

Source: US Office of Management and Budget.

END OF FISCAL YEAR	PUBLIC DEBT (IN US$ MILLIONS)	% OF GDP	GROSS FEDERAL DEBT (IN US$ MILLIONS)	% OF GDP	END OF FISCAL YEAR	PUBLIC DEBT (IN US$ MILLIONS)	% OF GDP	GROSS FEDERAL DEBT (IN US$ MILLIONS)	% OF GDP
1940	42,772	44.2	50,696	52.4	1960	236,840	45.6	290,525	56.0
1950	219,023	80.1	256,853	93.9	1970	283,198	28.0	380,921	37.6

US Public Debt (continued)

END OF FISCAL YEAR	PUBLIC DEBT (IN US$ MILLIONS)	% OF GDP	GROSS FEDERAL DEBT (IN US$ MILLIONS)	% OF GDP	END OF FISCAL YEAR	PUBLIC DEBT (IN US$ MILLIONS)	% OF GDP	GROSS FEDERAL DEBT (IN US$ MILLIONS)	% OF GDP
1980	711,923	26.1	909,041	33.3	2007	5,035,129	36.8	8,950,744	65.5
1990	2,411,558	42.0	3,206,290	55.9	2008	5,428,619	37.9	9,654,436	67.5
2000	3,409,804	35.1	5,628,700	58.0	2009	5,856,153	39.0	10,413,414	69.3

US Governmental Spending, 1800–2009

Entries for the years prior to 1933 are based on the administrative budget concept rather than on the unified budget concept. For a discussion of the unified budget concept and related topics, see <www.fms.treas.gov/bulletin/b2010_1ffotxt.doc>. The figures are in thousands ('000). A minus sign indicates a deficit.

Source: US Office of Management and Budget.

YEAR[1]	FEDERAL INCOME	FEDERAL SPENDING	SURPLUS OR DEFICIT	YEAR[1]	FEDERAL INCOME	FEDERAL SPENDING	SURPLUS OR DEFICIT
1800	10,849	10,786	63	1848	35,736	45,377	−9,641
1801	12,935	9,395	3,541	1849	31,208	45,052	−13,844
1802	14,996	7,862	7,134	1850	43,603	39,543	4,060
1803	11,064	7,852	3,212	1851	52,559	47,709	4,850
1804	11,826	8,719	3,107	1852	49,847	44,195	5,652
1805	13,561	10,506	3,054	1853	61,587	48,184	13,403
1806	15,560	9,804	5,756	1854	73,800	58,045	15,755
1807	16,398	8,354	8,044	1855	65,351	59,743	5,608
1808	17,061	9,932	7,128	1856	74,057	69,571	4,486
1809	7,773	10,281	−2,507	1857	68,965	67,796	1,170
1810	9,384	8,157	1,228	1858	46,655	74,185	−27,530
1811	14,424	8,058	6,365	1859	53,486	69,071	−15,585
1812	9,801	20,281	−10,480	1860	56,065	63,131	−7,066
1813	14,340	31,682	−17,341	1861	41,510	66,547	−25,037
1814	11,182	34,721	−23,539	1862	51,987	474,762	−422,774
1815	15,729	32,708	−16,979	1863	112,697	714,741	−602,043
1816	47,678	30,587	17,091	1864	264,627	865,323	−600,696
1817	33,099	21,844	11,255	1865	333,715	1,297,555	−963,841
1818	21,585	19,825	1,760	1866	558,033	520,809	37,223
1819	24,603	21,464	3,140	1867	490,634	357,543	133,091
1820	17,881	18,261	−380	1868	405,638	377,340	28,298
1821	14,573	15,811	−1,237	1869	370,944	322,865	48,078
1822	20,232	15,000	5,232	1870	411,255	309,654	101,602
1823	20,541	14,707	5,834	1871	383,324	292,177	91,147
1824	19,381	20,327	−945	1872	374,107	277,518	96,589
1825	21,841	15,857	5,984	1873	333,738	290,345	43,393
1826	25,260	17,036	8,225	1874	304,979	302,634	2,345
1827	22,966	16,139	6,827	1875	288,000	274,623	13,377
1828	24,764	16,395	8,369	1876	294,096	265,101	28,995
1829	24,828	15,203	9,624	1877	281,406	241,334	40,072
1830	24,844	15,143	9,701	1878	257,764	236,964	20,800
1831	28,527	15,248	13,279	1879	273,827	266,948	6,879
1832	31,866	17,289	14,577	1880	333,527	267,643	65,884
1833	33,948	23,018	10,931	1881	360,782	260,713	100,069
1834	21,792	18,628	3,164	1882	403,525	257,981	145,544
1835	35,430	17,573	17,857	1883	398,288	265,408	132,879
1836	50,827	30,868	19,959	1884	348,520	244,126	104,394
1837	24,954	37,243	−12,289	1885	323,691	260,227	63,464
1838	26,303	33,865	−7,562	1886	336,440	242,483	93,957
1839	31,483	26,899	4,584	1887	371,403	267,932	103,471
1840	19,480	24,318	−4,837	1888	379,266	267,925	111,341
1841	16,860	26,566	−9,706	1889	387,050	299,289	87,761
1842	19,976	25,206	−5,230	1890	403,081	318,041	85,040
1843	8,303	11,858	−3,555	1891	392,612	365,774	26,839
1844	29,321	22,338	6,984	1892	354,938	345,023	9,914
1845	29,970	22,937	7,033	1893	385,820	383,478	2,342
1846	29,700	27,767	1,933	1894	306,355	367,525	−61,170
1847	26,496	57,281	−30,786	1895	324,729	356,195	−31,466

US Governmental Spending, 1800–2009 (continued)

YEAR[1]	FEDERAL INCOME	FEDERAL SPENDING	SURPLUS OR DEFICIT	YEAR[1]	FEDERAL INCOME	FEDERAL SPENDING	SURPLUS OR DEFICIT
1896	338,142	352,179	−14,037	1954	69,701,000	70,855,000	−1,154,000
1897	347,722	365,774	−18,052	1955	65,451,000	68,444,000	−2,993,000
1898	405,321	443,369	−38,047	1956	74,587,000	70,640,000	3,947,000
1899	515,961	605,072	−89,112	1957	79,990,000	76,578,000	3,412,000
1900	567,241	520,861	46,380	1958	79,636,000	82,405,000	−2,769,000
1901	587,685	524,617	63,068	1959	79,249,000	92,098,000	−12,849,000
1902	562,478	485,234	77,244	1960	92,492,000	92,191,000	301,000
1903	561,881	517,006	44,875	1961	94,388,000	97,723,000	−3,335,000
1904	541,087	583,660	−42,573	1962	99,676,000	106,821,000	−7,146,000
1905	544,275	567,279	−23,004	1963	106,560,000	111,316,000	−4,756,000
1906	594,984	570,202	24,782	1964	112,613,000	118,528,000	−5,915,000
1907	665,860	579,129	86,732	1965	116,817,000	118,228,000	−1,411,000
1908	601,862	659,196	−57,334	1966	130,835,000	134,532,000	−3,698,000
1909	604,320	693,744	−89,423	1967	148,822,000	157,464,000	−8,643,000
1910	675,512	693,617	−18,105	1968	152,973,000	178,134,000	−25,161,000
1911	701,833	691,202	10,631	1969	186,882,000	183,640,000	3,242,000
1912	692,609	689,881	2,728	1970	192,807,000	195,649,000	−2,842,000
1913	714,463	714,864	−401	1971	187,139,000	210,172,000	−23,033,000
1914	725,117	725,525	−408	1972	207,309,000	230,681,000	−23,373,000
1915	683,417	746,093	−62,676	1973	230,799,000	245,707,000	−14,908,000
1916	761,445	712,967	48,478	1974	263,224,000	269,359,000	−6,135,000
1917	1,100,500	1,953,857	−853,357	1975	279,090,000	332,332,000	−53,242,000
1918	3,645,240	12,677,359	−9,032,120	1976	298,060,000	371,792,000	−73,732,000
1919	5,130,042	18,492,665	−13,362,623	TQ	81,232,000	95,975,000	−14,744,000
1920	6,648,898	6,357,677	291,222	1977	355,559,000	409,218,000	−53,659,000
1921	5,570,790	5,061,785	509,005	1978	399,561,000	458,746,000	−59,185,000
1922	4,025,901	3,289,404	736,496	1979	463,302,000	504,028,000	−40,726,000
1923	3,852,795	3,140,287	712,508	1980	517,112,000	590,941,000	−73,830,000
1924	3,871,214	2,907,847	963,367	1981	599,272,000	678,241,000	−78,968,000
1925	3,640,805	2,923,762	717,043	1982	617,766,000	745,743,000	−127,977,000
1926	3,795,108	2,929,964	865,144	1983	600,562,000	808,364,000	−207,802,000
1927	4,012,794	2,857,429	1,155,365	1984	666,486,000	851,853,000	−185,367,000
1928	3,900,329	2,961,245	939,083	1985	734,088,000	946,396,000	−212,308,000
1929	3,861,589	3,127,199	734,391	1986	769,215,000	990,430,000	−221,215,000
1930	4,057,884	3,320,211	737,673	1987	854,353,000	1,004,082,000	−149,728,000
1931	3,115,557	3,577,434	−461,877	1988	909,303,000	1,064,455,000	−155,152,000
1932	1,923,892	4,659,182	−2,735,290	1989	991,190,000	1,143,646,000	−152,456,000
1933	1,996,844	4,598,496	−2,601,652	1990	1,031,969,000	1,253,165,000	−221,195,000
1934	2,955,000	6,541,000	−3,586,000	1991	1,055,041,000	1,324,369,000	−269,328,000
1935	3,609,000	6,412,000	−2,803,000	1992	1,091,279,000	1,381,655,000	−290,376,000
1936	3,923,000	8,228,000	−4,304,000	1993	1,154,401,000	1,409,489,000	−255,087,000
1937	5,387,000	7,580,000	−2,193,000	1994	1,258,627,000	1,461,877,000	−203,250,000
1938	6,751,000	6,840,000	−89,000	1995	1,351,830,000	1,515,802,000	−163,972,000
1939	6,295,000	9,141,000	−2,846,000	1996	1,453,062,000	1,560,535,000	−107,473,000
1940	6,548,000	9,468,000	−2,920,000	1997	1,579,292,000	1,601,250,000	−21,958,000
1941	8,712,000	13,653,000	−4,941,000	1998	1,721,798,000	1,652,585,000	69,213,000
1942	14,634,000	35,137,000	−20,503,000	1999	1,827,454,000	1,701,891,000	125,563,000
1943	24,001,000	78,555,000	−54,554,000	2000	2,025,218,000	1,788,773,000	236,445,000
1944	43,747,000	91,304,000	−47,557,000	2001	1,991,194,000	1,863,770,000	127,424,000
1945	45,159,000	92,712,000	−47,553,000	2002	1,853,173,000	2,010,970,000	−157,797,000
1946	39,296,000	55,232,000	−15,936,000	2003	1,782,342,000	2,157,637,000	−375,295,000
1947	38,514,000	34,496,000	4,018,000	2004	1,880,071,000	2,292,215,000	−412,144,000
1948	41,560,000	29,764,000	11,796,000	2005	2,153,859,000	2,472,205,000	−318,346,000
1949	39,415,000	38,835,000	580,000	2006	2,407,254,000	2,655,435,000	−248,181,000
1950	39,443,000	42,562,000	−3,119,000	2007	2,568,239,000	2,730,241,000	−162,002,000
1951	51,616,000	45,514,000	6,102,000	2008	2,521,175,000	2,931,222,000	−410,047,000
1952	66,167,000	67,686,000	−1,519,000	2009	2,699,947,000	3,107,355,000	−407,408,000
1953	69,608,000	76,101,000	−6,493,000				

[1]The fiscal year ended on 31 December for the budgets from 1800 to 1842. It ended on 30 June for the budgets from 1844 through 1976 and on 30 September from fiscal year 1977. The budget figures for 1843 are for the period from 1 January to 30 June. The third quarter of 1976 was budgeted separately because of the change in the fiscal year calendar. It is referred to as the Transition Quarter (TQ).

Annual National Average Terms on Conventional Single-Family Mortgages, 1980–2008

Source: Federal Housing Finance Board Monthly Interest Rate Survey.

YEAR	CONTRACT INTEREST RATE (%)	INITIAL FEES AND CHARGES (%)	EFFECTIVE INTEREST RATE (%)	TERM TO MATURITY (YEARS)	MORTGAGE AMOUNT (US$'000)	PURCHASE PRICE (US$'000)	LOAN-TO-PRICE RATIO (%)
1980	12.46	1.97	12.84	27.2	51.7	73.4	72.9
1981	14.39	2.39	14.91	26.4	53.7	76.3	73.1
1982	14.73	2.65	15.31	25.6	55.0	78.4	72.9
1983	12.26	2.39	12.73	26.0	59.9	83.1	74.5
1984	11.99	2.57	12.48	26.8	64.5	86.6	77.0
1985	11.17	2.51	11.64	25.9	70.2	96.1	75.8
1986	9.79	2.21	10.18	25.6	79.3	110.6	74.1
1987	8.95	2.08	9.30	26.8	89.1	121.8	75.2
1988	8.98	1.96	9.30	27.7	97.4	131.6	76.0
1989	9.81	1.87	10.13	27.7	104.5	142.8	74.8
1990	9.74	1.79	10.05	27.0	104.0	142.6	74.7
1991	9.07	1.58	9.34	26.5	106.3	146.7	74.4
1992	7.83	1.58	8.11	25.4	108.7	146.4	76.6
1993	6.93	1.20	7.13	25.5	107.0	143.1	77.2
1994	7.31	1.10	7.49	27.1	109.9	142.0	79.9
1995	7.69	0.97	7.85	27.4	110.4	142.8	79.9
1996	7.58	0.97	7.74	26.9	118.7	155.1	79.0
1997	7.52	0.98	7.68	27.5	126.6	164.5	79.4
1998	6.97	0.85	7.10	27.8	131.8	173.4	78.9
1999	7.14	0.74	7.25	28.2	139.3	184.2	78.5
2000	7.86	0.67	7.96	28.7	148.3	198.9	77.8
2001	6.94	0.53	7.03	27.6	155.7	215.5	76.2
2002	6.44	0.46	6.51	27.3	163.4	231.2	75.1
2003	5.67	0.37	5.73	26.8	167.9	243.4	73.5
2004	5.68	0.40	5.74	27.9	185.5	262.0	74.9
2005	5.85	0.38	5.90	28.5	211.9	299.8	74.7
2006	6.52	0.41	6.58	29.0	222.3	306.4	76.5
2007	6.43	0.48	6.50	29.3	224.5	300.4	79.4
2008	6.06	0.54	6.14	28.4	219.1	304.6	76.7

US Bankruptcy Filings

This table shows the number of business and nonbusiness (consumer) bankruptcy filings in the US since 1980. Bankruptcy is intended to give debtors a fresh start in managing their resources by cancelling many of their debts through a court order called a "discharge." It is also meant to give creditors a fair share of the money that the debtors can afford to pay back.

Businesses may file for bankruptcy under chapter 11 of the Internal Revenue Code. Chapter 11 offers protection from creditor demands to a business in debt so that its officers and managers have time to reorganize in order to fulfill obligations to creditors. In some instances, creditors may receive dollar-for-dollar what the business owes them, plus interest. In others, the creditor may receive only pennies on the owed dollar.

Individuals may file for bankruptcy under either chapter 7 of the Internal Revenue Code (under which debtors may liquidate assets with the supervision of a trustee in order to receive a nearly immediate discharge of debts) or chapter 13 (under which the debtor enters into a payment plan to repay debt out of future earnings over a three-to-five-year period, with the oversight of a trustee).

Source: American Bankruptcy Institute.

YEAR	TOTAL FILINGS	BUSINESS FILINGS	CONSUMER FILINGS	CONSUMER FILINGS AS A PERCENTAGE OF TOTAL FILINGS%
1980	331,264	43,694	287,570	86.81%
1985	412,510	71,277	341,233	82.72%
1990	782,960	64,853	718,107	91.72%
1995	926,601	51,959	874,642	94.39%
2000	1,253,444	35,472	1,217,972	97.17%
2001	1,492,129	40,099	1,452,030	97.31%
2002	1,577,651	38,540	1,539,111	97.56%
2003	1,660,245	35,037	1,625,208	97.89%
2004	1,597,462	34,317	1,563,145	97.85%
2005	2,078,415	39,201	2,039,214	98.11%
2006	617,660	19,695	597,965	96.81%
2007	850,912	28,322	822,590	96.67%
2008	1,117,771	43,546	1,074,225	96.10%
2009	1,473,675	60,837	1,412,838	95.87%

US Taxes

US Federal Taxation Structure

This table shows the range of income taxes for various types of households in each tax bracket. In 2010 the standard deductions for most filers were US$5,700 for those submitting returns under status "single" and status "married filing separately," US$8,400 for those filing under status "head of household," and US$11,400 for those submitting returns under status "married filing jointly" or "qualifying widow(er) with dependent child." Source: US Department of the Treasury, Internal Revenue Service.

Single — Schedule X

IF TAXABLE INCOME

IS OVER	BUT NOT OVER	THEN THE TAX IS	PLUS	OF THE AMOUNT OVER
US$0	US$8,375	—	10%	US$0
US$8,375	US$34,000	US$837.50	15%	US$8,375
US$34,000	US$82,400	US$4,681.25	25%	US$34,000
US$82,400	US$171,850	US$16,781.25	28%	US$82,400
US$171,850	US$373,650	US$41,827.25	33%	US$171,850
US$373,650	—	US$108,421.25	35%	US$373,650

Married Filing Jointly or Qualifying Widow(er) — Schedule Y-1

IF TAXABLE INCOME

IS OVER	BUT NOT OVER	THEN THE TAX IS	PLUS	OF THE AMOUNT OVER
US$0	US$16,750	—	10%	US$0
US$16,750	US$68,000	US$1,675.00	15%	US$16,750
US$68,000	US$137,300	US$9,362.50	25%	US$68,000
US$137,300	US$209,250	US$26,687.50	28%	US$137,300
US$209,250	US$373,650	US$46,833.50	33%	US$209,250
US$373,650	—	US$101,085.50	35%	US$373,650

Married Filing Separately — Schedule Y-2

IF TAXABLE INCOME

IS OVER	BUT NOT OVER	THEN THE TAX IS	PLUS	OF THE AMOUNT OVER
US$0	US$8,375	—	10%	US$0
US$8,375	US$34,000	US$837.50	15%	US$8,375
US$34,000	US$68,650	US$4,681.25	25%	US$34,000
US$68,650	US$104,625	US$13,343.75	28%	US$68,650
US$104,625	US$186,825	US$23,416.75	33%	US$104,625
US$186,825	—	US$50,542.75	35%	US$186,825

Head of Household — Schedule Z

IF TAXABLE INCOME

IS OVER	BUT NOT OVER	THEN THE TAX IS	PLUS	OF THE AMOUNT OVER
US$0	US$11,950	—	10%	US$0
US$11,950	US$45,550	US$1,195.00	15%	US$11,950
US$45,550	US$117,650	US$6,235.00	25%	US$45,550
US$117,650	US$190,550	US$24,260.00	28%	US$117,650
US$190,550	US$373,650	US$44,672.00	33%	US$190,550
US$373,650	—	US$105,095.00	35%	US$373,650

Individual Income Taxes by US State

This table shows tax rates as of 1 Jan 2010 for tax year 2010. Tax rates are given in percentages; income brackets and personal exemptions are given in US$.
Source: Federation of Tax Administrators, <www.taxadmin.org/fta/rate/ind_inc.html>.

STATE	TAX RATES		NUMBER OF	INCOME BRACKETS		PERSONAL EXEMPTIONS			FEDERAL TAX
	LOW	HIGH	BRACKETS	LOW	HIGH	SINGLE	JOINT	DEPENDENTS	DEDUCTIBLE
AL	2.0	5.0	3	500[1]	3,000[1]	1,500	3,000	300	yes
AK	no state income tax								
AZ	2.59	4.54	5	10,000[1]	150,000[1]	2,100	4,200	2,300	
AR[2]	1.0	7.0[3]	6	3,899[1]	32,600[1]	23[4]	46[4]	23[4]	
CA[2]	1.25	9.55[5]	6	7,300[1]	47,900[1]	98[4]	196[4]	98[4]	
CO	4.63		1	—flat rate—		—none—			
CT	3.0	6.5	3	10,000[1]	500,001[1]	13,000[6]	26,000[6]	0	
DE	2.2	6.95	6	5,000	60,001	110[4]	220[4]	110[4]	
DC	4.0	8.5	3	10,000	40,000	1,675	3,350	1,675	
FL	no state income tax								
GA	1.0	6.0	6	750[7]	7,000[7]	2,700	5,400	3,000	
HI	1.4	11.00	12	2,400[1]	200,001[1]	1,040	2,080	1,040	

Individual Income Taxes by US State (continued)

STATE	TAX RATES LOW	TAX RATES HIGH	NUMBER OF BRACKETS	INCOME BRACKETS LOW	INCOME BRACKETS HIGH	PERSONAL EXEMPTIONS SINGLE	JOINT	DEPENDENTS	FEDERAL TAX DEDUCTIBLE
ID[2]	1.6	7.8	8	1,320[8]	26,418[8]	3,650[9]	7,300[9]	3,650[9]	
IL	3.0		1	——flat rate——		2,000	4,000	2,000	
IN	3.4		1	——flat rate——		1,000	2,000	1,000	
IA[2]	0.36	8.98	9	1,407	63,316	40[4]	80[4]	40[4]	yes
KS	3.5	6.45	3	15,000[1]	30,000[1]	2,250	4,500	2,250	
KY	2.0	6.0	6	3,000	75,000	20[4]	40[4]	20[4]	
LA	2.0	6.0	3	12,500[1]	50,000[1]	4,500[10]	9,000[10]	1,000[10]	yes
ME[2]	2.0	8.5	4	4,949[1]	19,750[1]	2,850	5,700	2,850	
MD	2.0	6.25	8	1,000	1,000,001	2,400	4,800	2,400	
MA[2]	5.3		1	——flat rate——		4,400	8,800	1,000	
MI[2]	4.35		1	——flat rate——		3,300	6,600	3,300	
MN[2]	5.35	7.85	3	22,770[11]	74,781[11]	3,650[9]	7,300[9]	3,650[9]	
MS	3.0	5.0	3	5,000	10,000	6,000	12,000	1,500	
MO	1.5	6.0	10	1,000	9,000	2,100	4,200	1,200	yes[12]
MT[2]	1.0	6.9	7	2,600	15,401	2,110	4,220	2,110	yes[12]
NE[2]	2.56	6.84	4	2,400[13]	27,001[13]	118[4]	236[4]	118[4]	
NV	no state income tax								
NH	state income tax is limited to dividends and interest income only								
NJ	1.4	10.75	8	20,000[14]	1,000,000[14]	1,000	2,000	1,500	
NM	1.7	4.9	4	5,500[15]	16,000[15]	3,650[9]	7,300[9]	3,650[9]	
NY	4.0	8.97	7	8,000[16]	500,000[16]	0	0	1,000	
NC	6.0	7.75[17]	3	12,750[17]	60,000[17]	3,650[9]	7,300[9]	3,650[9]	
ND[2]	1.84	4.86	5	34,000[18]	373,650[18]	3,650[9]	7,300[9]	3,650[9]	
OH[2]	0.618	6.24	9	5,000	200,000	1,550[19]	3,100[19]	1,550[19]	
OK	0.5	5.50[20]	7	1,000[20]	8,701[20]	1,000	2,000	1,000	
OR[2]	5.0	11.0	5	2,000[1]	250,000[1]	176[4]	352[4]	176[4]	yes[12]
PA	3.07		1	——flat rate——		——none——			
RI	3.8	9.9[21]	5	33,500[21]	372,950[21]	3,650[9]	7,300[9]	3,650[9]	
SC[2]	0.0	7.0	6	2,740	13,701	3,650[9]	7,300[9]	3,650[9]	
SD	no state income tax								
TN	state income tax is limited to dividends and interest income only								
TX	no state income tax								
UT	5.0		1	——flat rate——		22	22	22	
VT[2]	3.55	8.95	5	33,950[23]	372,951[23]	3,650[9]	7,300[9]	3,650[9]	
VA	2.0	5.75	4	3,000	17,000	930	1,860	930	
WA	no state income tax								
WV	3.0	6.5	5	10,000	60,000	2,000	4,000	2,000	
WI[2]	4.6	7.75	5	10,220[24]	225,001[24]	700	1,400	700	
WY	no state income tax								

[1]For joint returns, the taxes are twice the tax imposed on half the income. [2]Sixteen states have statutory provision for automatic adjustment of tax brackets, personal exemption, or standard deductions to the rate of inflation. Massachusetts, Michigan, Nebraska, and Ohio index the personal exemption amounts only. [3]A special tax table is available for low-income taxpayers that reduces their tax payments. [4]Tax credits. [5]An additional 1% tax is imposed on taxable income over US$1 million. Tax rates are scheduled to fall by 0.25% after 2011. [6]Combined personal exemptions and standard deduction. An additional tax credit is allowed ranging from 75% to 0% based on state adjusted gross income. Exemption amounts are phased out for higher income taxpayers until they are eliminated for households earning over US$61,000. [7]The tax brackets reported are for single individuals. For married households, the same rates apply to income brackets ranging from US$1,000 to US$10,000. [8]A US$10 filing tax is charged for each return and a US$15 credit is allowed for each exemption. [9]These states allow personal exemption or standard deductions as provided in the Internal Revenue Code (IRC). [10]Combined personal exemption and standard deduction. [11]The tax brackets reported are for single individuals. For married couples filing jointly, the same rates apply for income under US$33,280 to over US$132,221. A 6.4% alternative minimum tax rate is also applicable. [12]Deduction is limited to US$10,000 for joint returns and US$5,000 for individuals in Missouri and Montana, and to US$5,600 in Oregon. [13]The tax brackets reported are for single individuals. For married couples filing jointly, the same rates apply for income under US$4,800 to over US$54,000. [14]The tax brackets reported are for single individuals. For married couples filing jointly, the same rates range from 1.4% to 10.75% (with 9 income brackets) applying to income brackets from US$20,000 to over US$1 million. [15]The tax brackets reported are for single individuals. For married couples filing jointly, the same rates apply for income under US$8,000 to over US$24,000. Married households filing separately pay the tax imposed on half the income. [16]The tax brackets reported are for single individuals. For married taxpayers, the same rates apply to income brackets ranging from US$16,000 to US$500,000. [17]The tax brackets reported are for single individuals. For married taxpayers, the same rates apply to income brackets ranging from US$21,250 to US$100,000. Lower exemption amounts are allowed for high-income taxpayers. For tax years 2009 and 2010, a surcharge that equals 2% of total liability for taxpayers with income over US$60,000 single filer (US$100,000 joint) and 3% of total liability for income over US$150,000 (US$250,000). [18]The tax brackets reported are for single individuals. For married taxpayers, the same rates apply to income brackets ranging from US$56,850 to US$373,650. An additional US$300 personal exemption is allowed for joint returns or unmarried

Individual Income Taxes by US State (continued)

head of households.   [19]Plus an additional US$20 per exemption tax credit.   [20]The rate range reported is for single persons. For married persons filing jointly, the same rates apply to income brackets ranging from US$2,000 to US$15,000.   [21]Or an alternative flat rate of 6.5%. Rates reported are for a single filer based on a tax of 25% of federal liability using IRC in 2001. For married taxpayers filing jointly, the same rates apply to income brackets ranging from US$56,700 to US$372,950.   [22]Tax credits are equal to 6% of federal standard/itemized deductions (without state taxes paid) and 75% of federal personal exemption amounts. The credit amount is phased out above US$12,000 in income (US$24,000 for joint returns).   [23]The tax brackets reported are for single individuals. For married couples filing jointly, the same rates apply for income under US$56,700 to over US$372,950. [24]The tax brackets reported are for single individuals. For married taxpayers, the same rates apply to income brackets ranging from US$13,620 to US$300,000.

World Economy

Standardized Unemployment Rates in Selected Developed Countries

Percentage of total labor force. N/A stands for not available. Sources: International Labour Organization; IMF, International Financial Statistics, May 2010.

COUNTRY	2005	2006	2007	2008	COUNTRY	2005	2006	2007	2008
Argentina	10.6	9.5	8.5	7.9	Japan	4.4	4.1	3.9	4.0
Australia	5.0	4.8	4.4	4.2	Korea, Rep. of	3.7	3.5	3.2	3.2
Brazil	9.3	8.4	8.2	7.9	Mexico	3.5	3.2	3.4	3.5
Canada	6.8	6.3	6.0	6.1	Russia	7.2	7.2	6.1	6.3
China	4.2	4.1	4.0	4.2	Saudi Arabia	N/A	6.3	5.6	5.0
France	8.9	8.8	8.0	7.4	South Africa	26.7	25.5	23.0	22.9
Germany	11.1	10.3	8.6	7.5	Turkey	10.3	9.9	10.3	11.0
India	N/A	N/A	N/A	N/A	UK	4.6	5.4	5.3	5.3
Indonesia	11.2	10.3	9.1	8.4	US	5.1	4.6	4.6	5.8
Italy	7.7	6.8	6.1	6.7	European Union	8.9	8.2	7.1	7.0

Consumer Price Change in Selected Countries

This table shows the change in consumer prices from the year previous, expressed in percent. The change in consumer prices is used as an indicator of inflation. An increase in percent from one year to the next indicates an increase in the overall price of certain goods and services purchased by the average consumer. A negative number indicates a decrease in consumer prices. N/A stands for not available. Source: International Monetary Fund, International Financial Statistics, May 2010.

COUNTRY	2006	2007	2008	2009	COUNTRY	2006	2007	2008	2009
Argentina	10.9	8.8	8.6	6.3	Japan	0.2	0.1	1.4	-1.4
Australia	3.5	2.3	4.4	1.8	Korea, Rep. of	2.2	2.5	4.7	2.8
Brazil	4.2	3.6	5.7	4.9	Mexico	3.6	4.0	5.1	5.3
Canada	2.0	2.1	2.4	0.3	Russia	9.7	9.0	14.1	11.7
China	1.5	4.8	5.9	-0.7	Saudi Arabia	2.2	4.2	9.9	5.1
France	1.7	1.5	2.8	0.1	South Africa	4.6	7.1	11.5	7.1
Germany	1.6	2.3	2.6	0.3	Turkey	10.5	8.8	10.4	6.3
India	5.8	6.4	8.4	10.9	UK	3.2	4.3	4.0	-0.6
Indonesia	13.1	6.3	10.1	4.6	US	3.2	2.9	3.8	-0.4
Italy	2.1	1.8	3.3	0.8	European Union	2.3	2.4	3.7	1.0

Real Gross Domestic Products of Selected Developed Countries

Percent annual change. N/A stands for not available. Source: IMF, International Financial Statistics, May 2010.

COUNTRY	2006	2007	2008	2009	COUNTRY	2006	2007	2008	2009
Argentina	8.5	9.4	8.2	0.8	Japan	2.0	2.4	-1.3	-5.3
Australia	2.6	4.8	2.6	1.4	Korea, Rep. of	5.2	5.3	2.5	0.2
Brazil	4.0	6.3	5.7	-0.3	Mexico	5.0	3.6	1.4	-7.2
Canada	2.9	2.6	0.4	-2.8	Russia	8.0	8.0	7.0	N/A
China	11.7	14.5	11.3	N/A	Saudi Arabia	3.2	3.4	4.7	N/A
France	2.2	2.4	0.5	-2.4	South Africa	5.6	5.8	4.1	-2.1
Germany	3.2	2.5	1.0	-5.1	Turkey	6.9	5.0	0.7	-5.3
India	9.7	10.1	8.1	9.2	UK	2.9	2.6	0.6	-5.3
Indonesia	5.5	6.6	6.8	N/A	US	2.7	2.2	0.4	-2.5
Italy	2.1	1.4	-1.4	-5.1	European Union	3.2	2.9	0.7	-4.2

Arts, Entertainment, & Leisure

The Growing Cult of the Celebrity Chef

by Lisa Abend, TIME

It's been a few decades since we started turning cooks into stars, and still the phenomenon continues to grow. These days, the Emerils, Marios, and Gordons of the world scarcely need the qualifier chef—they are celebrities, plain and simple. But between the television shows, the food festivals, the Vegas outposts, the spaghetti-sauce labels bearing their names and the fans rabidly tracking everything from new dishes to failed love affairs, it's easy to overlook the impact that fame has had on the once disparaged profession of cooking. In the Food Network era, the phenomenon of the celebrity chef has utterly transformed the restaurant industry and, in the process, changed the very nature of how we eat.

There's a reason restaurant food sales in the US have jumped from US$42.8 billion in 1970 to a projected US$520 billion in 2010, and it's not just that more women have entered the workforce. As best-selling food author Michael Pollan recently noted, the age of the TV chef has coincided with a dramatic decline in home cooking. Pollan argued that by making food a spectacle, shows like *Iron Chef* and *The F Word* have reinforced the message that cooking is best left to the professionals. By turning chefs into entertainers—whether performing onscreen or via the impeccable platings in their restaurants—we have widened the breach between ourselves and the once ordinary task of cooking.

And yet our alienation from food and its preparation is matched only by our obsession with it. Huge parts of the population now seek out artisanal cheeses at their local farmers' markets, and run-of-the-mill restaurants attempt to cater to their newly refined tastes, serving salads made of fancy lettuce. Lots of ordinary folk now aspire to have their own US$1,100 Thermomix food processor and blog about every course of every restaurant meal they eat. These trends are fed by chefs' newfound prominence but also prod them to attain ever greater influence. In a world in which what and how we eat have become fetishized, celebrity chefs are finding new ways to harness their star power—and not just to make money.

The term Foodie was coined in the early 1980s, at about the same time Wolfgang Puck began serving gourmet pizzas at his buzzy Spago restaurant in Los Angeles. But it took another decade before Puck really kicked off the celebrity phenomenon by turning his attention to the culinary desert that was Las Vegas. At the time, everyone thought he was crazy. Crazy, too, the cable channel (today's Food Network) that launched a few months later in 1993, in the remarkable belief that audiences would watch round-the-clock food programming.

It's not that there weren't famous cooks before then. As far back as the 19th century, Europe's aristocracy was agog about Marie-Antoine Carême's elaborate dishes. And within more recent memory, Julia Child used television to help turn America's housewives on to the glories of the French table and to turn herself into a star. But none of that comes close to the renown of today's celebrity chefs, which can be attributed not only to the multiple restaurants and bad-boy personas but also to the Food Network. Today the channel averages a million viewers a day and is so popular that in late May 2010 it launched a culinary spin-off called Cooking Channel, whose programming will include new shows with Bobby Flay and Emeril Lagasse. Culinary programs are also populating major networks like Fox, which in 2010 began airing its seventh season of *Hell's Kitchen*. In that show, Gordon Ramsay, the five-continent chef whose offscreen empire includes restaurants in Dubai and Cape Town, berates low-skill contestants into becoming better cooks. Ramsay and Bravo's popular *Top Chef* series have prompted NBC and CBS to prep their own reality-kitchen shows.

The Internet has also played an important role: on Web sites like Grub Street (1 million page views per day) and Eater (2 million), chef groupies can breathlessly track every charity event and opening—sometimes before the chef has gone public with the news. A whole subindustry of agents and publicists has sprung up to manage everything from a chef's media appearances to his hairstyle. And, yes, the chefs are mostly hes: although women are entering the profession in ever greater numbers, the vast majority of celebrity chefs are male.

All the fawning has propelled a profession once considered little better than servitude to the ranks of the glamorous and profitable. "I hate the word, but it's all about establishing a brand," says Mario Batali, whose endeavors include 15 restaurants, countless awards, a television show that had him tooling around Spain with Gwyneth Paltrow, and a full line of cookware products. "Because once you have that, all these other opportunities open up, and you have this giant soapbox."

Celebrity has had salutary effects on the profession of cooking as well. "Thirty years ago, most people who worked in restaurant kitchens had either just gotten out of the Army or were on their way to jail," says Batali. "Now you get all these people who went to college, then found their passion in cooking. The level is suddenly much higher because the people cooking are a lot smarter."

Most major culinary schools are going through an unprecedented growth spurt. For example, applications to the Culinary Institute of America, the premier cooking school in the US, have jumped 50% in the past six years. That may have something to do with the economy. At the venerable Cordon Bleu in Paris, communications director Sandra Messier notes, "we've seen a lot of students using their severance packages from their old jobs to pay tuition." Proof that in the US workforce, today's leftovers may be tomorrow's celebrity chefs.

Motion Pictures

Academy Awards (Oscars), 2009

The Academy of Motion Picture Arts and Sciences, formed in 1927, first awarded the Academy Awards of Merit in 1929. The ceremony is held early in the year following the release of films under consideration; the latest Oscars were awarded 7 Mar 2010 in Los Angeles. Award: gold-plated statuette of a man with a sword. **Academy of Motion Picture Arts and Sciences Web site: <www.oscars.org>.**

CATEGORY	WINNER
Motion picture of the year	*The Hurt Locker* (US; Kathryn Bigelow, Mark Boal, Nicolas Chartier, and Greg Shapiro, producers)
Director	Kathryn Bigelow (*The Hurt Locker,* US)
Actor	Jeff Bridges (*Crazy Heart,* US)
Actress	Sandra Bullock (*The Blind Side,* US)
Supporting actor	Christoph Waltz (*Inglourious Basterds,* US/Germany)
Supporting actress	Mo'Nique (*Precious: Based on the Novel "Push" by Sapphire,* US)
Foreign-language film	*El secreto de sus ojos* (*The Secret in Their Eyes*) (Argentina/Spain; Juan José Campanella, director)
Animated feature	*Up* (US; Pete Docter, director)
Animated short	*Logorama* (France; François Alaux, Hervé de Crécy, and Ludovic Houplain, directors)
Live-action short	*The New Tenants* (Denmark/US; Joachim Back, director)
Documentary feature	*The Cove* (US; Louie Psihoyos, director)
Documentary short	*Music by Prudence* (US/Zimbabwe; Roger Ross Williams, director)
Cinematography	Mauro Fiore (*Avatar,* US/UK)
Art direction	Rick Carter and Robert Stromberg, art direction; Kim Sinclair, set decoration (*Avatar,* US/UK)
Film editing	Bob Murawski and Chris Innis (*The Hurt Locker,* US)
Costume design	Sandy Powell (*The Young Victoria,* UK/US)
Makeup	Barney Burman, Mindy Hall, and Joel Harlow (*Star Trek,* US/Germany)
Original score	Michael Giacchino (*Up,* US)
Original song	"The Weary Kind (Theme from Crazy Heart)," Ryan Bingham and T Bone Burnett (*Crazy Heart,* US)
Sound mixing	Paul N.J. Ottosson and Ray Beckett (*The Hurt Locker,* US)
Sound editing	Paul N.J. Ottosson (*The Hurt Locker,* US)
Visual effects	Joe Letteri, Stephen Rosenbaum, Richard Baneham, and Andrew R. Jones (*Avatar,* US/UK)
Adapted screenplay	Geoffrey Fletcher (*Precious: Based on the Novel "Push" by Sapphire,* US)
Original screenplay	Mark Boal (*The Hurt Locker,* US)

Academy Awards (Oscars), 1928–2009

BEST PICTURE

1928	*Wings*
1929	*The Broadway Melody*
1930	*All Quiet on the Western Front*
1931	*Cimarron*
1932	*Grand Hotel*
1933	*Cavalcade*
1934	*It Happened One Night*
1935	*Mutiny on the Bounty*
1936	*The Great Ziegfeld*
1937	*The Life of Emile Zola*
1938	*You Can't Take It with You*
1939	*Gone with the Wind*
1940	*Rebecca*
1941	*How Green Was My Valley*
1942	*Mrs. Miniver*
1943	*Casablanca*
1944	*Going My Way*
1945	*The Lost Weekend*
1946	*The Best Years of Our Lives*
1947	*Gentleman's Agreement*
1948	*Hamlet*
1949	*All the King's Men*
1950	*All About Eve*
1951	*An American in Paris*

BEST PICTURE (CONTINUED)

1952	*The Greatest Show on Earth*
1953	*From Here to Eternity*
1954	*On the Waterfront*
1955	*Marty*
1956	*Around the World in 80 Days*
1957	*The Bridge on the River Kwai*
1958	*Gigi*
1959	*Ben-Hur*
1960	*The Apartment*
1961	*West Side Story*
1962	*Lawrence of Arabia*
1963	*Tom Jones*
1964	*My Fair Lady*
1965	*The Sound of Music*
1966	*A Man for All Seasons*
1967	*In the Heat of the Night*
1968	*Oliver!*
1969	*Midnight Cowboy*
1970	*Patton*
1971	*The French Connection*
1972	*The Godfather*
1973	*The Sting*
1974	*The Godfather Part II*

BEST PICTURE (CONTINUED)

1975	*One Flew Over the Cuckoo's Nest*
1976	*Rocky*
1977	*Annie Hall*
1978	*The Deer Hunter*
1979	*Kramer vs. Kramer*
1980	*Ordinary People*
1981	*Chariots of Fire*
1982	*Gandhi*
1983	*Terms of Endearment*
1984	*Amadeus*
1985	*Out of Africa*
1986	*Platoon*
1987	*The Last Emperor*
1988	*Rain Man*
1989	*Driving Miss Daisy*
1990	*Dances with Wolves*
1991	*The Silence of the Lambs*
1992	*Unforgiven*
1993	*Schindler's List*
1994	*Forrest Gump*
1995	*Braveheart*
1996	*The English Patient*
1997	*Titanic*
1998	*Shakespeare in Love*
1999	*American Beauty*

Academy Awards (Oscars), 1928–2009 (continued)

BEST PICTURE (CONTINUED)
2000 Gladiator
2001 A Beautiful Mind
2002 Chicago

BEST PICTURE (CONTINUED)
2003 The Lord of the Rings:
        The Return of the King
2004 Million Dollar Baby
2005 Crash

BEST PICTURE (CONTINUED)
2006 The Departed
2007 No Country for Old Men
2008 Slumdog Millionaire
2009 The Hurt Locker

BEST ACTOR
1928 Emil Jannings (The Last Command; The Way of All Flesh)
1929 Warner Baxter (In Old Arizona)
1930 George Arliss (Disraeli)
1931 Lionel Barrymore (A Free Soul)
1932 Wallace Beery (The Champ); Fredric March (Dr. Jekyll and Mr. Hyde) (tied)
1933 Charles Laughton (The Private Life of Henry VIII)
1934 Clark Gable (It Happened One Night)
1935 Victor McLaglen (The Informer)
1936 Paul Muni (The Story of Louis Pasteur)
1937 Spencer Tracy (Captains Courageous)
1938 Spencer Tracy (Boys Town)
1939 Robert Donat (Goodbye, Mr. Chips)
1940 James Stewart (The Philadelphia Story)
1941 Gary Cooper (Sergeant York)
1942 James Cagney (Yankee Doodle Dandy)
1943 Paul Lukas (Watch on the Rhine)
1944 Bing Crosby (Going My Way)
1945 Ray Milland (The Lost Weekend)
1946 Fredric March (The Best Years of Our Lives)
1947 Ronald Colman (A Double Life)
1948 Laurence Olivier (Hamlet)
1949 Broderick Crawford (All the King's Men)
1950 José Ferrer (Cyrano de Bergerac)
1951 Humphrey Bogart (The African Queen)
1952 Gary Cooper (High Noon)
1953 William Holden (Stalag 17)
1954 Marlon Brando (On the Waterfront)
1955 Ernest Borgnine (Marty)
1956 Yul Brynner (The King and I)
1957 Alec Guinness (The Bridge on the River Kwai)
1958 David Niven (Separate Tables)
1959 Charlton Heston (Ben-Hur)
1960 Burt Lancaster (Elmer Gantry)
1961 Maximilian Schell (Judgment at Nuremberg)
1962 Gregory Peck (To Kill a Mockingbird)
1963 Sidney Poitier (Lilies of the Field)
1964 Rex Harrison (My Fair Lady)
1965 Lee Marvin (Cat Ballou)
1966 Paul Scofield (A Man for All Seasons)
1967 Rod Steiger (In the Heat of the Night)
1968 Cliff Robertson (Charly)
1969 John Wayne (True Grit)
1970 George C. Scott (Patton) (declined)
1971 Gene Hackman (The French Connection)
1972 Marlon Brando (The Godfather) (declined)
1973 Jack Lemmon (Save the Tiger)
1974 Art Carney (Harry and Tonto)
1975 Jack Nicholson (One Flew Over the Cuckoo's Nest)
1976 Peter Finch (Network)[1]
1977 Richard Dreyfuss (The Goodbye Girl)
1978 Jon Voight (Coming Home)
1979 Dustin Hoffman (Kramer vs. Kramer)
1980 Robert De Niro (Raging Bull)
1981 Henry Fonda (On Golden Pond)
1982 Ben Kingsley (Gandhi)
1983 Robert Duvall (Tender Mercies)
1984 F. Murray Abraham (Amadeus)
1985 William Hurt (Kiss of the Spider Woman)

BEST ACTOR (CONTINUED)
1986 Paul Newman (The Color of Money)
1987 Michael Douglas (Wall Street)
1988 Dustin Hoffman (Rain Man)
1989 Daniel Day-Lewis (My Left Foot)
1990 Jeremy Irons (Reversal of Fortune)
1991 Anthony Hopkins (The Silence of the Lambs)
1992 Al Pacino (Scent of a Woman)
1993 Tom Hanks (Philadelphia)
1994 Tom Hanks (Forrest Gump)
1995 Nicolas Cage (Leaving Las Vegas)
1996 Geoffrey Rush (Shine)
1997 Jack Nicholson (As Good as It Gets)
1998 Roberto Benigni (Life Is Beautiful)
1999 Kevin Spacey (American Beauty)
2000 Russell Crowe (Gladiator)
2001 Denzel Washington (Training Day)
2002 Adrien Brody (The Pianist)
2003 Sean Penn (Mystic River)
2004 Jamie Foxx (Ray)
2005 Philip Seymour Hoffman (Capote)
2006 Forest Whitaker (The Last King of Scotland)
2007 Daniel Day-Lewis (There Will Be Blood)
2008 Sean Penn (Milk)
2009 Jeff Bridges (Crazy Heart)

BEST ACTRESS
1928 Janet Gaynor (7th Heaven; Street Angel; Sunrise)
1929 Mary Pickford (Coquette)
1930 Norma Shearer (The Divorcee)
1931 Marie Dressler (Min and Bill)
1932 Helen Hayes (The Sin of Madelon Claudet)
1933 Katharine Hepburn (Morning Glory)
1934 Claudette Colbert (It Happened One Night)
1935 Bette Davis (Dangerous)
1936 Luise Rainer (The Great Ziegfeld)
1937 Luise Rainer (The Good Earth)
1938 Bette Davis (Jezebel)
1939 Vivien Leigh (Gone with the Wind)
1940 Ginger Rogers (Kitty Foyle)
1941 Joan Fontaine (Suspicion)
1942 Greer Garson (Mrs. Miniver)
1943 Jennifer Jones (The Song of Bernadette)
1944 Ingrid Bergman (Gaslight)
1945 Joan Crawford (Mildred Pierce)
1946 Olivia de Havilland (To Each His Own)
1947 Loretta Young (The Farmer's Daughter)
1948 Jane Wyman (Johnny Belinda)
1949 Olivia de Havilland (The Heiress)
1950 Judy Holliday (Born Yesterday)
1951 Vivien Leigh (A Streetcar Named Desire)
1952 Shirley Booth (Come Back, Little Sheba)
1953 Audrey Hepburn (Roman Holiday)
1954 Grace Kelly (The Country Girl)
1955 Anna Magnani (The Rose Tattoo)
1956 Ingrid Bergman (Anastasia)
1957 Joanne Woodward (The Three Faces of Eve)
1958 Susan Hayward (I Want to Live!)
1959 Simone Signoret (Room at the Top)
1960 Elizabeth Taylor (Butterfield 8)
1961 Sophia Loren (Two Women)
1962 Anne Bancroft (The Miracle Worker)

Academy Awards (Oscars), 1928–2009 (continued)

BEST ACTRESS (CONTINUED)

1963   Patricia Neal (*Hud*)
1964   Julie Andrews (*Mary Poppins*)
1965   Julie Christie (*Darling*)
1966   Elizabeth Taylor (*Who's Afraid of Virginia Woolf?*)
1967   Katharine Hepburn (*Guess Who's Coming to Dinner*)
1968   Katharine Hepburn (*The Lion in Winter*); Barbra Streisand (*Funny Girl*) (tied)
1969   Maggie Smith (*The Prime of Miss Jean Brodie*)
1970   Glenda Jackson (*Women in Love*)
1971   Jane Fonda (*Klute*)
1972   Liza Minnelli (*Cabaret*)
1973   Glenda Jackson (*A Touch of Class*)
1974   Ellen Burstyn (*Alice Doesn't Live Here Anymore*)
1975   Louise Fletcher (*One Flew Over the Cuckoo's Nest*)
1976   Faye Dunaway (*Network*)
1977   Diane Keaton (*Annie Hall*)
1978   Jane Fonda (*Coming Home*)
1979   Sally Field (*Norma Rae*)
1980   Sissy Spacek (*Coal Miner's Daughter*)
1981   Katharine Hepburn (*On Golden Pond*)
1982   Meryl Streep (*Sophie's Choice*)
1983   Shirley MacLaine (*Terms of Endearment*)
1984   Sally Field (*Places in the Heart*)
1985   Geraldine Page (*The Trip to Bountiful*)
1986   Marlee Matlin (*Children of a Lesser God*)
1987   Cher (*Moonstruck*)
1988   Jodie Foster (*The Accused*)
1989   Jessica Tandy (*Driving Miss Daisy*)
1990   Kathy Bates (*Misery*)
1991   Jodie Foster (*The Silence of the Lambs*)
1992   Emma Thompson (*Howards End*)
1993   Holly Hunter (*The Piano*)
1994   Jessica Lange (*Blue Sky*)
1995   Susan Sarandon (*Dead Man Walking*)
1996   Frances McDormand (*Fargo*)
1997   Helen Hunt (*As Good as It Gets*)
1998   Gwyneth Paltrow (*Shakespeare in Love*)
1999   Hilary Swank (*Boys Don't Cry*)
2000   Julia Roberts (*Erin Brockovich*)
2001   Halle Berry (*Monster's Ball*)
2002   Nicole Kidman (*The Hours*)
2003   Charlize Theron (*Monster*)
2004   Hilary Swank (*Million Dollar Baby*)
2005   Reese Witherspoon (*Walk the Line*)
2006   Helen Mirren (*The Queen*)
2007   Marion Cotillard (*La Vie en rose*)
2008   Kate Winslet (*The Reader*)
2009   Sandra Bullock (*The Blind Side*)

BEST SUPPORTING ACTOR

1936   Walter Brennan (*Come and Get It*)
1937   Joseph Schildkraut (*The Life of Emile Zola*)
1938   Walter Brennan (*Kentucky*)
1939   Thomas Mitchell (*Stagecoach*)
1940   Walter Brennan (*The Westerner*)
1941   Donald Crisp (*How Green Was My Valley*)
1942   Van Heflin (*Johnny Eager*)
1943   Charles Coburn (*The More the Merrier*)
1944   Barry Fitzgerald (*Going My Way*)
1945   James Dunn (*A Tree Grows in Brooklyn*)
1946   Harold Russell (*The Best Years of Our Lives*)
1947   Edmund Gwenn (*Miracle on 34th Street*)
1948   Walter Huston (*The Treasure of the Sierra Madre*)

BEST SUPPORTING ACTOR (CONTINUED)

1949   Dean Jagger (*Twelve O'Clock High*)
1950   George Sanders (*All About Eve*)
1951   Karl Malden (*A Streetcar Named Desire*)
1952   Anthony Quinn (*Viva Zapata!*)
1953   Frank Sinatra (*From Here to Eternity*)
1954   Edmond O'Brien (*The Barefoot Contessa*)
1955   Jack Lemmon (*Mister Roberts*)
1956   Anthony Quinn (*Lust for Life*)
1957   Red Buttons (*Sayonara*)
1958   Burl Ives (*The Big Country*)
1959   Hugh Griffith (*Ben-Hur*)
1960   Peter Ustinov (*Spartacus*)
1961   George Chakiris (*West Side Story*)
1962   Ed Begley (*Sweet Bird of Youth*)
1963   Melvyn Douglas (*Hud*)
1964   Peter Ustinov (*Topkapi*)
1965   Martin Balsam (*A Thousand Clowns*)
1966   Walter Matthau (*The Fortune Cookie*)
1967   George Kennedy (*Cool Hand Luke*)
1968   Jack Albertson (*The Subject Was Roses*)
1969   Gig Young (*They Shoot Horses, Don't They?*)
1970   John Mills (*Ryan's Daughter*)
1971   Ben Johnson (*The Last Picture Show*)
1972   Joel Grey (*Cabaret*)
1973   John Houseman (*The Paper Chase*)
1974   Robert De Niro (*The Godfather Part II*)
1975   George Burns (*The Sunshine Boys*)
1976   Jason Robards (*All the President's Men*)
1977   Jason Robards (*Julia*)
1978   Christopher Walken (*The Deer Hunter*)
1979   Melvyn Douglas (*Being There*)
1980   Timothy Hutton (*Ordinary People*)
1981   John Gielgud (*Arthur*)
1982   Louis Gossett, Jr. (*An Officer and a Gentleman*)
1983   Jack Nicholson (*Terms of Endearment*)
1984   Haing S. Ngor (*The Killing Fields*)
1985   Don Ameche (*Cocoon*)
1986   Michael Caine (*Hannah and Her Sisters*)
1987   Sean Connery (*The Untouchables*)
1988   Kevin Kline (*A Fish Called Wanda*)
1989   Denzel Washington (*Glory*)
1990   Joe Pesci (*Goodfellas*)
1991   Jack Palance (*City Slickers*)
1992   Gene Hackman (*Unforgiven*)
1993   Tommy Lee Jones (*The Fugitive*)
1994   Martin Landau (*Ed Wood*)
1995   Kevin Spacey (*The Usual Suspects*)
1996   Cuba Gooding, Jr. (*Jerry Maguire*)
1997   Robin Williams (*Good Will Hunting*)
1998   James Coburn (*Affliction*)
1999   Michael Caine (*The Cider House Rules*)
2000   Benicio Del Toro (*Traffic*)
2001   Jim Broadbent (*Iris*)
2002   Chris Cooper (*Adaptation*)
2003   Tim Robbins (*Mystic River*)
2004   Morgan Freeman (*Million Dollar Baby*)
2005   George Clooney (*Syriana*)
2006   Alan Arkin (*Little Miss Sunshine*)
2007   Javier Bardem (*No Country for Old Men*)
2008   Heath Ledger (*The Dark Knight*)[1]
2009   Christoph Waltz (*Inglourious Basterds*)

BEST SUPPORTING ACTRESS

1936   Gale Sondergaard (*Anthony Adverse*)
1937   Alice Brady (*In Old Chicago*)
1938   Fay Bainter (*Jezebel*)
1939   Hattie McDaniel (*Gone with the Wind*)

Academy Awards (Oscars), 1928–2009 (continued)

BEST SUPPORTING ACTRESS (CONTINUED)

1940 Jane Darwell (*The Grapes of Wrath*)
1941 Mary Astor (*The Great Lie*)
1942 Teresa Wright (*Mrs. Miniver*)
1943 Katina Paxinou (*For Whom the Bell Tolls*)
1944 Ethel Barrymore (*None but the Lonely Heart*)
1945 Anne Revere (*National Velvet*)
1946 Anne Baxter (*The Razor's Edge*)
1947 Celeste Holm (*Gentleman's Agreement*)
1948 Claire Trevor (*Key Largo*)
1949 Mercedes McCambridge (*All the King's Men*)
1950 Josephine Hull (*Harvey*)
1951 Kim Hunter (*A Streetcar Named Desire*)
1952 Gloria Grahame (*The Bad and the Beautiful*)
1953 Donna Reed (*From Here to Eternity*)
1954 Eva Marie Saint (*On the Waterfront*)
1955 Jo Van Fleet (*East of Eden*)
1956 Dorothy Malone (*Written on the Wind*)
1957 Miyoshi Umeki (*Sayonara*)
1958 Wendy Hiller (*Separate Tables*)
1959 Shelley Winters (*The Diary of Anne Frank*)
1960 Shirley Jones (*Elmer Gantry*)
1961 Rita Moreno (*West Side Story*)
1962 Patty Duke (*The Miracle Worker*)
1963 Margaret Rutherford (*The V.I.P.s*)
1964 Lila Kedrova (*Zorba the Greek*)
1965 Shelley Winters (*A Patch of Blue*)
1966 Sandy Dennis (*Who's Afraid of Virginia Woolf?*)
1967 Estelle Parsons (*Bonnie and Clyde*)
1968 Ruth Gordon (*Rosemary's Baby*)
1969 Goldie Hawn (*Cactus Flower*)
1970 Helen Hayes (*Airport*)
1971 Cloris Leachman (*The Last Picture Show*)
1972 Eileen Heckart (*Butterflies Are Free*)
1973 Tatum O'Neal (*Paper Moon*)
1974 Ingrid Bergman (*Murder on the Orient Express*)
1975 Lee Grant (*Shampoo*)
1976 Beatrice Straight (*Network*)
1977 Vanessa Redgrave (*Julia*)
1978 Maggie Smith (*California Suite*)
1979 Meryl Streep (*Kramer vs. Kramer*)
1980 Mary Steenburgen (*Melvin and Howard*)
1981 Maureen Stapleton (*Reds*)
1982 Jessica Lange (*Tootsie*)
1983 Linda Hunt (*The Year of Living Dangerously*)
1984 Peggy Ashcroft (*A Passage to India*)
1985 Anjelica Huston (*Prizzi's Honor*)
1986 Dianne Wiest (*Hannah and Her Sisters*)
1987 Olympia Dukakis (*Moonstruck*)
1988 Geena Davis (*The Accidental Tourist*)
1989 Brenda Fricker (*My Left Foot*)
1990 Whoopi Goldberg (*Ghost*)
1991 Mercedes Ruehl (*The Fisher King*)
1992 Marisa Tomei (*My Cousin Vinny*)
1993 Anna Paquin (*The Piano*)
1994 Dianne Wiest (*Bullets over Broadway*)
1995 Mira Sorvino (*Mighty Aphrodite*)
1996 Juliette Binoche (*The English Patient*)
1997 Kim Basinger (*L.A. Confidential*)
1998 Judi Dench (*Shakespeare in Love*)
1999 Angelina Jolie (*Girl, Interrupted*)
2000 Marcia Gay Harden (*Pollock*)
2001 Jennifer Connelly (*A Beautiful Mind*)
2002 Catherine Zeta-Jones (*Chicago*)
2003 Renée Zellweger (*Cold Mountain*)
2004 Cate Blanchett (*The Aviator*)
2005 Rachel Weisz (*The Constant Gardener*)
2006 Jennifer Hudson (*Dreamgirls*)
2007 Tilda Swinton (*Michael Clayton*)

BEST SUPPORTING ACTRESS (CONTINUED)

2008 Penélope Cruz (*Vicky Cristina Barcelona*)
2009 Mo'Nique (*Precious: Based on the Novel "Push" by Sapphire*)

FOREIGN LANGUAGE FILM (AMERICAN TITLES)

1947 *Shoe-Shine*
1948 *Monsieur Vincent*
1949 *The Bicycle Thief*
1950 *The Walls of Malapaga*
1951 *Rashomon*
1952 *Forbidden Games*
1953 not awarded
1954 *Gate of Hell*
1955 *Samurai, the Legend of Musashi*
1956 *La Strada*
1957 *The Nights of Cabiria*
1958 *My Uncle*
1959 *Black Orpheus*
1960 *The Virgin Spring*
1961 *Through a Glass Darkly*
1962 *Sundays and Cybele*
1963 *Federico Fellini's 8½*
1964 *Yesterday, Today, and Tomorrow*
1965 *The Shop on Main Street*
1966 *A Man and a Woman*
1967 *Closely Watched Trains*
1968 *War and Peace*
1969 *Z*
1970 *Investigation of a Citizen Above Suspicion*
1971 *The Garden of the Finzi-Continis*
1972 *The Discreet Charm of the Bourgeoisie*
1973 *Day for Night*
1974 *Amarcord*
1975 *Dersu Uzala*
1976 *Black and White in Color*
1977 *Madame Rosa*
1978 *Get Out Your Handkerchiefs*
1979 *The Tin Drum*
1980 *Moscow Does Not Believe in Tears*
1981 *Mephisto*
1982 *To Begin Again*
1983 *Fanny & Alexander*
1984 *Dangerous Moves*
1985 *The Official Story*
1986 *The Assault*
1987 *Babette's Feast*
1988 *Pelle the Conqueror*
1989 *Cinema Paradiso*
1990 *Journey of Hope*
1991 *Mediterraneo*
1992 *Indochine*
1993 *Belle Epoque*
1994 *Burnt by the Sun*
1995 *Antonia's Line*
1996 *Kolya*
1997 *Character*
1998 *Life Is Beautiful*
1999 *All About My Mother*
2000 *Crouching Tiger, Hidden Dragon*
2001 *No Man's Land*
2002 *Nowhere in Africa*
2003 *The Barbarian Invasions*
2004 *The Sea Inside*
2005 *Tsotsi*
2006 *The Lives of Others*
2007 *The Counterfeiters*
2008 *Departures*
2009 *The Secret in Their Eyes*

Academy Awards (Oscars), 1928–2009 (continued)

DIRECTING

1928   Lewis Milestone (*Two Arabian Knights*); Frank Borzage (*7th Heaven*)
1929   Frank Lloyd (*The Divine Lady*)
1930   Lewis Milestone (*All Quiet on the Western Front*)
1931   Norman Taurog (*Skippy*)
1932   Frank Borzage (*Bad Girl*)
1933   Frank Lloyd (*Cavalcade*)
1934   Frank Capra (*It Happened One Night*)
1935   John Ford (*The Informer*)
1936   Frank Capra (*Mr. Deeds Goes to Town*)
1937   Leo McCarey (*The Awful Truth*)
1938   Frank Capra (*You Can't Take It with You*)
1939   Victor Fleming (*Gone with the Wind*)
1940   John Ford (*The Grapes of Wrath*)
1941   John Ford (*How Green Was My Valley*)
1942   William Wyler (*Mrs. Miniver*)
1943   Michael Curtiz (*Casablanca*)
1944   Leo McCarey (*Going My Way*)
1945   Billy Wilder (*The Lost Weekend*)
1946   William Wyler (*The Best Years of Our Lives*)
1947   Elia Kazan (*Gentleman's Agreement*)
1948   John Huston (*The Treasure of the Sierra Madre*)
1949   Joseph L. Mankiewicz (*A Letter to Three Wives*)
1950   Joseph L. Mankiewicz (*All About Eve*)
1951   George Stevens (*A Place in the Sun*)
1952   John Ford (*The Quiet Man*)
1953   Fred Zinnemann (*From Here to Eternity*)
1954   Elia Kazan (*On the Waterfront*)
1955   Delbert Mann (*Marty*)
1956   George Stevens (*Giant*)
1957   David Lean (*The Bridge on the River Kwai*)
1958   Vincente Minnelli (*Gigi*)
1959   William Wyler (*Ben-Hur*)
1960   Billy Wilder (*The Apartment*)
1961   Robert Wise, Jerome Robbins (*West Side Story*)
1962   David Lean (*Lawrence of Arabia*)
1963   Tony Richardson (*Tom Jones*)
1964   George Cukor (*My Fair Lady*)
1965   Robert Wise (*The Sound of Music*)
1966   Fred Zinnemann (*A Man for All Seasons*)
1967   Mike Nichols (*The Graduate*)
1968   Carol Reed (*Oliver!*)
1969   John Schlesinger (*Midnight Cowboy*)
1970   Franklin J. Schaffner (*Patton*)
1971   William Friedkin (*The French Connection*)
1972   Bob Fosse (*Cabaret*)
1973   George Roy Hill (*The Sting*)
1974   Francis Ford Coppola (*The Godfather Part II*)
1975   Milos Forman (*One Flew Over the Cuckoo's Nest*)
1976   John G. Avildsen (*Rocky*)
1977   Woody Allen (*Annie Hall*)
1978   Michael Cimino (*The Deer Hunter*)
1979   Robert Benton (*Kramer vs. Kramer*)
1980   Robert Redford (*Ordinary People*)
1981   Warren Beatty (*Reds*)
1982   Richard Attenborough (*Gandhi*)
1983   James L. Brooks (*Terms of Endearment*)
1984   Milos Forman (*Amadeus*)
1985   Sydney Pollack (*Out of Africa*)
1986   Oliver Stone (*Platoon*)
1987   Bernardo Bertolucci (*The Last Emperor*)
1988   Barry Levinson (*Rain Man*)
1989   Oliver Stone (*Born on the Fourth of July*)

DIRECTING (CONTINUED)

1990   Kevin Costner (*Dances with Wolves*)
1991   Jonathan Demme (*The Silence of the Lambs*)
1992   Clint Eastwood (*Unforgiven*)
1993   Steven Spielberg (*Schindler's List*)
1994   Robert Zemeckis (*Forrest Gump*)
1995   Mel Gibson (*Braveheart*)
1996   Anthony Minghella (*The English Patient*)
1997   James Cameron (*Titanic*)
1998   Steven Spielberg (*Saving Private Ryan*)
1999   Sam Mendes (*American Beauty*)
2000   Steven Soderbergh (*Traffic*)
2001   Ron Howard (*A Beautiful Mind*)
2002   Roman Polanski (*The Pianist*)
2003   Peter Jackson (*The Lord of the Rings: The Return of the King*)
2004   Clint Eastwood (*Million Dollar Baby*)
2005   Ang Lee (*Brokeback Mountain*)
2006   Martin Scorsese (*The Departed*)
2007   Joel Coen, Ethan Coen (*No Country for Old Men*)
2008   Danny Boyle (*Slumdog Millionaire*)
2009   Kathryn Bigelow (*The Hurt Locker*)

ADAPTED SCREENPLAY[2]

1928   Benjamin Glazer (*7th Heaven*)
1929   Hans Kraly (*The Patriot*)
1930   *no award given*
1931   Howard Estabrook (*Cimarron*)
1932   Edwin Burke (*Bad Girl*)
1933   Victor Heerman, Sarah Y. Mason (*Little Women*)
1934   Robert Riskin (*It Happened One Night*)
1935   Dudley Nichols (*The Informer*)[3] (declined)
1936   Pierre Collings, Sheridan Gibney (*The Story of Louis Pasteur*)[3]
1937   Norman Reilly Raine, Heinz Herald, Geza Herczeg (*The Life of Emile Zola*)[3]
1938   George Bernard Shaw, W.P. Lipscomb, Cecil Lewis, Ian Dalrymple (*Pygmalion*)[3]
1939   Sidney Howard (*Gone with the Wind*)[1,3]
1940   Donald Ogden Stewart (*The Philadelphia Story*)[3]
1941   Sidney Buchman, Seton I. Miller (*Here Comes Mr. Jordan*)[3]
1942   George Froeschel, James Hilton, Claudine West, Arthur Wimperis (*Mrs. Miniver*)[3]
1943   Julius J. Epstein, Philip G. Epstein, Howard Koch (*Casablanca*)[3]
1944   Frank Butler, Frank Cavett (*Going My Way*)[3]
1945   Charles Brackett, Billy Wilder (*The Lost Weekend*)[3]
1946   Robert E. Sherwood (*The Best Years of Our Lives*)[3]
1947   George Seaton (*Miracle on 34th Street*)[3]
1948   John Huston (*The Treasure of the Sierra Madre*)[3]
1949   Joseph L. Mankiewicz (*A Letter to Three Wives*)[3]
1950   Joseph L. Mankiewicz (*All About Eve*)[3]
1951   Michael Wilson, Harry Brown (*A Place in the Sun*)[3]
1952   Charles Schnee (*The Bad and the Beautiful*)[3]
1953   Daniel Taradash (*From Here to Eternity*)[3]
1954   George Seaton (*The Country Girl*)[3]
1955   Paddy Chayefsky (*Marty*)[3]
1956   James Poe, John Farrow, S.J. Perelman (*Around the World in 80 Days*)
1957   Michael Wilson[4], Carl Foreman[4] (Pierre Boulle, *The Bridge on the River Kwai*)

Academy Awards (Oscars), 1928–2009 (continued)

ADAPTED SCREENPLAY[2] (CONTINUED)

1958 Alan Jay Lerner (*Gigi*)
1959 Neil Paterson (*Room at the Top*)
1960 Richard Brooks (*Elmer Gantry*)
1961 Abby Mann (*Judgment at Nuremberg*)
1962 Horton Foote (*To Kill a Mockingbird*)
1963 John Osborne (*Tom Jones*)
1964 Edward Anhalt (*Becket*)
1965 Robert Bolt (*Doctor Zhivago*)
1966 Robert Bolt (*A Man for All Seasons*)
1967 Stirling Silliphant (*In the Heat of the Night*)
1968 James Goldman (*The Lion in Winter*)
1969 Waldo Salt (*Midnight Cowboy*)
1970 Ring Lardner, Jr. (*M*A*S*H*)
1971 Ernest Tidyman (*The French Connection*)
1972 Mario Puzo, Francis Ford Coppola (*The Godfather*)
1973 William Peter Blatty (*The Exorcist*)
1974 Francis Ford Coppola, Mario Puzo (*The Godfather Part II*)
1975 Lawrence Hauben, Bo Goldman (*One Flew Over the Cuckoo's Nest*)
1976 William Goldman (*All the President's Men*)
1977 Alvin Sargent (*Julia*)
1978 Oliver Stone (*Midnight Express*)
1979 Robert Benton (*Kramer vs. Kramer*)
1980 Alvin Sargent (*Ordinary People*)
1981 Ernest Thompson (*On Golden Pond*)
1982 Costa-Gavras, Donald Stewart (*Missing*)
1983 James L. Brooks (*Terms of Endearment*)
1984 Peter Shaffer (*Amadeus*)
1985 Kurt Luedtke (*Out of Africa*)
1986 Ruth Prawer Jhabvala (*A Room with a View*)
1987 Mark Peploe, Bernardo Bertolucci (*The Last Emperor*)
1988 Christopher Hampton (*Dangerous Liaisons*)
1989 Alfred Uhry (*Driving Miss Daisy*)
1990 Michael Blake (*Dances with Wolves*)
1991 Ted Tally (*The Silence of the Lambs*)
1992 Ruth Prawer Jhabvala (*Howards End*)
1993 Steven Zaillian (*Schindler's List*)
1994 Eric Roth (*Forrest Gump*)
1995 Emma Thompson (*Sense and Sensibility*)
1996 Billy Bob Thornton (*Sling Blade*)
1997 Brian Helgeland, Curtis Hanson (*L.A. Confidential*)
1998 Bill Condon (*Gods and Monsters*)
1999 John Irving (*The Cider House Rules*)
2000 Stephen Gaghan (*Traffic*)
2001 Akiva Goldsman (*A Beautiful Mind*)
2002 Ronald Harwood (*The Pianist*)
2003 Fran Walsh, Philippa Boyens, Peter Jackson (*The Lord of the Rings: The Return of the King*)
2004 Alexander Payne, Jim Taylor (*Sideways*)
2005 Larry McMurtry, Diana Ossana (*Brokeback Mountain*)
2006 William Monahan (*The Departed*)
2007 Joel Coen, Ethan Coen (*No Country for Old Men*)
2008 Simon Beaufoy (*Slumdog Millionaire*)
2009 Geoffrey Fletcher (*Precious: Based on the Novel "Push" by Sapphire*)

ORIGINAL SCREENPLAY[2]

1928 Ben Hecht (*Underworld*)[5]; Joseph Farnham (*The Fair Co-Ed*; *Laugh, Clown, Laugh*; *Telling the World*)[6]
1929 no award given
1930 Frances Marion (*The Big House*)

ORIGINAL SCREENPLAY[2] (CONTINUED)

1931 John Monk Saunders (*The Dawn Patrol*)[5]
1932 Frances Marion (*The Champ*)[5]
1933 Robert Lord (*One Way Passage*)[5]
1934 Arthur Caesar (*Manhattan Melodrama*)[5]
1935 Ben Hecht, Charles MacArthur (*The Scoundrel*)[5]
1936 Pierre Collings, Sheridan Gibney (*The Story of Louis Pasteur*)[5]
1937 William A. Wellman, Robert Carson (*A Star Is Born*)[5]
1938 Eleanore Griffin, Dore Schary (*Boys Town*)[5]
1939 Lewis R. Foster (*Mr. Smith Goes to Washington*)[5]
1940 Benjamin Glazer, John S. Toldy (*Arise, My Love*)[5]; Preston Sturges (*The Great McGinty*)[7]
1941 Harry Segall (*Here Comes Mr. Jordan*)[5]; Herman J. Mankiewicz, Orson Welles (*Citizen Kane*)[7]
1942 Emeric Pressburger (*Forty-Ninth Parallel*)[5]; Michael Kanin, Ring Lardner, Jr. (*Woman of the Year*)[7]
1943 William Saroyan (*The Human Comedy*)[5]; Norman Krasna (*Princess O'Rourke*)[7]
1944 Leo McCarey (*Going My Way*)[5]; Lamar Trotti (*Wilson*)[7]
1945 Charles G. Booth (*The House on 92nd Street*)[5]; Richard Schweizer (*Marie-Louise*)[7]
1946 Clemence Dane (*Vacation from Marriage*)[5]; Muriel Box, Sydney Box (*The Seventh Veil*)[7]
1947 Valentine Davies (*Miracle on 34th Street*)[5]; Sidney Sheldon (*The Bachelor and the Bobby-Soxer*)[7]
1948 Richard Schweizer, David Wechsler (*The Search*)[5]
1949 Douglas Morrow (*The Stratton Story*)[5]; Robert Pirosh (*Battleground*)[7]
1950 Edna Anhalt, Edward Anhalt (*Panic in the Streets*)[5]; Charles Brackett, Billy Wilder, D.M. Marshman, Jr. (*Sunset Blvd.*)[7]
1951 Paul Dehn, James Bernard (*Seven Days to Noon*)[5]; Alan Jay Lerner (*An American in Paris*)[7]
1952 Fredric M. Frank, Theodore St. John, Frank Cavett (*The Greatest Show on Earth*)[5]; T.E.B. Clarke (*The Lavender Hill Mob*)[7]
1953 Dalton Trumbo[4] (Ian McLellan Hunter, *Roman Holiday*)[5]; Charles Brackett, Walter Reisch, Richard L. Breen (*Titanic*)[7]
1954 Philip Yordan (*Broken Lance*)[5]; Budd Schulberg (*On the Waterfront*)[7]
1955 Daniel Fuchs (*Love Me or Leave Me*)[5]; William Ludwig, Sonya Levien (*Interrupted Melody*)[7]
1956 Dalton Trumbo[4] (as Robert Rich, *The Brave One*)[5]; Albert Lamorisse (*The Red Balloon*)[7]
1957 George Wells (*Designing Woman*)
1958 Nedrick Young[4] (as Nathan E. Douglas), Harold Jacob Smith (*The Defiant Ones*)
1959 Russell Rouse, Clarence Greene, Stanley Shapiro, Maurice Richlin (*Pillow Talk*)
1960 Billy Wilder, I.A.L. Diamond (*The Apartment*)
1961 William Inge (*Splendor in the Grass*)
1962 Ennio de Concini, Alfredo Giannetti, Pietro Germi (*Divorce—Italian Style*)
1963 James R. Webb (*How the West Was Won*)
1964 S.H. Barnett, Peter Stone, Frank Tarloff (*Father Goose*)
1965 Frederic Raphael (*Darling*)
1966 Claude Lelouch, Pierre Uytterhoeven (*A Man and a Woman*)

Academy Awards (Oscars), 1928–2009 (continued)

ORIGINAL SCREENPLAY[2] (CONTINUED)

1967 William Rose (Guess Who's Coming to Dinner)
1968 Mel Brooks (The Producers)
1969 William Goldman (Butch Cassidy and the Sundance Kid)
1970 Francis Ford Coppola, Edmund H. North (Patton)
1971 Paddy Chayefsky (The Hospital)
1972 Jeremy Larner (The Candidate)
1973 David S. Ward (The Sting)
1974 Robert Towne (Chinatown)
1975 Frank Pierson (Dog Day Afternoon)
1976 Paddy Chayefsky (Network)
1977 Woody Allen, Marshall Brickman (Annie Hall)
1978 Nancy Dowd, Waldo Salt, Robert C. Jones (Coming Home)
1979 Steve Tesich (Breaking Away)
1980 Bo Goldman (Melvin and Howard)
1981 Colin Welland (Chariots of Fire)
1982 John Briley (Gandhi)
1983 Horton Foote (Tender Mercies)
1984 Robert Benton (Places in the Heart)
1985 Earl W. Wallace, William Kelley, Pamela Wallace (Witness)
1986 Woody Allen (Hannah and Her Sisters)
1987 John Patrick Shanley (Moonstruck)
1988 Ronald Bass, Barry Morrow (Rain Man)
1989 Tom Schulman (Dead Poets Society)
1990 Bruce Joel Rubin (Ghost)
1991 Callie Khouri (Thelma & Louise)
1992 Neil Jordan (The Crying Game)
1993 Jane Campion (The Piano)
1994 Quentin Tarantino, Roger Avary (Pulp Fiction)
1995 Christopher McQuarrie (The Usual Suspects)
1996 Joel Coen, Ethan Coen (Fargo)
1997 Ben Affleck, Matt Damon (Good Will Hunting)
1998 Marc Norman, Tom Stoppard (Shakespeare in Love)
1999 Alan Ball (American Beauty)
2000 Cameron Crowe (Almost Famous)
2001 Julian Fellowes (Gosford Park)
2002 Pedro Almodóvar (Talk to Her)
2003 Sofia Coppola (Lost in Translation)
2004 Charlie Kaufman (Eternal Sunshine of the Spotless Mind)
2005 Paul Haggis, Bobby Moresco (Crash)
2006 Michael Arndt (Little Miss Sunshine)
2007 Diablo Cody (Juno)
2008 Dustin Lance Black (Milk)
2009 Mark Boal (The Hurt Locker)

CINEMATOGRAPHY

1928 Charles Rosher, Karl Struss (Sunrise)
1929 Clyde De Vinna (White Shadows in the South Seas)
1930 Joseph T. Rucker, Willard Van Der Veer (With Byrd at the South Pole)
1931 Floyd Crosby (Tabu)
1932 Lee Garmes (Shanghai Express)
1933 Charles Bryant Lang, Jr. (A Farewell to Arms)
1934 Victor Milner (Cleopatra)
1935 Hal Mohr (A Midsummer Night's Dream)
1936 Gaetano Gaudio (Anthony Adverse)
1937 Karl Freund (The Good Earth)
1938 Joseph Ruttenberg (The Great Waltz)
1939 Gregg Toland (Wuthering Heights)[8]; Ernest Haller, Ray Rennahan (Gone with the Wind)[9]
1940 George Barnes (Rebecca)[8]; Georges Perinal (The Thief of Bagdad)[9]

CINEMATOGRAPHY (CONTINUED)

1941 Arthur Miller (How Green Was My Valley)[8]; Ernest Palmer, Ray Rennahan (Blood and Sand)[9]
1942 Joseph Ruttenberg (Mrs. Miniver)[8]; Leon Shamroy (The Black Swan)[9]
1943 Arthur Miller (The Song of Bernadette)[8]; Hal Mohr, W. Howard Greene (The Phantom of the Opera)[9]
1944 Joseph LaShelle (Laura)[8]; Leon Shamroy (Wilson)[9]
1945 Harry Stradling (The Picture of Dorian Gray)[8]; Leon Shamroy (Leave Her to Heaven)[9]
1946 Arthur Miller (Anna and the King of Siam)[8]; Charles Rosher, Leonard Smith, Arthur Arling (The Yearling)[9]
1947 Guy Green (Great Expectations)[8]; Jack Cardiff (Black Narcissus)[9]
1948 William Daniels (The Naked City)[8]; Joseph Valentine, William V. Skall, Winton Hoch (Joan of Arc)[9]
1949 Paul C. Vogel (Battleground)[8]; Winton Hoch (She Wore a Yellow Ribbon)[9]
1950 Robert Krasker (The Third Man)[8]; Robert Surtees (King Solomon's Mines)[9]
1951 William C. Mellor (A Place in the Sun)[8]; Alfred Gilks, John Alton (An American in Paris)[9]
1952 Robert Surtees (The Bad and the Beautiful)[8]; Winton C. Hoch, Archie Stout (The Quiet Man)[9]
1953 Burnett Guffey (From Here to Eternity)[8]; Loyal Griggs (Shane)[9]
1954 Boris Kaufman (On the Waterfront)[8]; Milton Krasner (Three Coins in the Fountain)[9]
1955 James Wong Howe (The Rose Tattoo)[8]; Robert Burks (To Catch a Thief)[9]
1956 Joseph Ruttenberg (Somebody Up There Likes Me)[8]; Lionel Lindon (Around the World in 80 Days)[9]
1957 Jack Hildyard (The Bridge on the River Kwai)
1958 Sam Leavitt (The Defiant Ones)[8]; Joseph Ruttenberg (Gigi)[9]
1959 William C. Mellor (The Diary of Anne Frank)[8]; Robert L. Surtees (Ben-Hur)[9]
1960 Freddie Francis (Sons and Lovers)[8]; Russell Metty (Spartacus)[9]
1961 Eugen Shuftan (The Hustler)[8]; Daniel L. Fapp (West Side Story)[9]
1962 Jean Bourgoin, Walter Wottitz (The Longest Day)[8]; Fred A. Young (Lawrence of Arabia)[9]
1963 James Wong Howe (Hud)[8]; Leon Shamroy (Cleopatra)[9]
1964 Walter Lassally (Zorba the Greek)[8]; Harry Stradling (My Fair Lady)[9]
1965 Ernest Laszlo (Ship of Fools)[8]; Freddie Young (Doctor Zhivago)[9]
1966 Haskell Wexler (Who's Afraid of Virginia Woolf?)[8]; Ted Moore (A Man for All Seasons)[9]
1967 Burnett Guffey (Bonnie and Clyde)
1968 Pasqualino De Santis (Romeo and Juliet)
1969 Conrad Hall (Butch Cassidy and the Sundance Kid)
1970 Freddie Young (Ryan's Daughter)
1971 Oswald Morris (Fiddler on the Roof)
1972 Geoffrey Unsworth (Cabaret)
1973 Sven Nykvist (Cries and Whispers)
1974 Fred Koenekamp, Joseph Biroc (The Towering Inferno)
1975 John Alcott (Barry Lyndon)
1976 Haskell Wexler (Bound for Glory)

Academy Awards (Oscars), 1928–2009 (continued)

CINEMATOGRAPHY (CONTINUED)

1977 Vilmos Zsigmond (*Close Encounters of the Third Kind*)
1978 Nestor Almendros (*Days of Heaven*)
1979 Vittorio Storaro (*Apocalypse Now*)
1980 Geoffrey Unsworth[1], Ghislain Cloquet (*Tess*)
1981 Vittorio Storaro (*Reds*)
1982 Billy Williams, Ronnie Taylor (*Gandhi*)
1983 Sven Nykvist (*Fanny & Alexander*)
1984 Chris Menges (*The Killing Fields*)
1985 David Watkin (*Out of Africa*)
1986 Chris Menges (*The Mission*)
1987 Vittorio Storaro (*The Last Emperor*)
1988 Peter Biziou (*Mississippi Burning*)
1989 Freddie Francis (*Glory*)
1990 Dean Semler (*Dances with Wolves*)
1991 Robert Richardson (*JFK*)
1992 Philippe Rousselot (*A River Runs Through It*)
1993 Janusz Kaminski (*Schindler's List*)
1994 John Toll (*Legends of the Fall*)
1995 John Toll (*Braveheart*)
1996 John Seale (*The English Patient*)
1997 Russell Carpenter (*Titanic*)
1998 Janusz Kaminski (*Saving Private Ryan*)
1999 Conrad L. Hall (*American Beauty*)
2000 Peter Pau (*Crouching Tiger, Hidden Dragon*)
2001 Andrew Lesnie (*The Lord of the Rings: The Fellowship of the Ring*)
2002 Conrad L. Hall (*Road to Perdition*)[1]
2003 Russell Boyd (*Master and Commander: The Far Side of the World*)
2004 Robert Richardson (*The Aviator*)
2005 Dion Beebe (*Memoirs of a Geisha*)
2006 Guillermo Navarro (*Pan's Labyrinth*)
2007 Robert Elswit (*There Will Be Blood*)
2008 Anthony Dod Mantle (*Slumdog Millionaire*)
2009 Mauro Fiore (*Avatar*)

VISUAL EFFECTS[10]

1939 Fred Sersen (*The Rains Came*)
1940 Lawrence Butler (*The Thief of Bagdad*)
1941 Farciot Edouart, Gordon Jennings (*I Wanted Wings*)
1942 Farciot Edouart, Gordon Jennings, William L. Pereira (*Reap the Wild Wind*)
1943 Fred Sersen (*Crash Dive*)
1944 A. Arnold Gillespie, Donald Jahraus, Warren Newcombe (*Thirty Seconds Over Tokyo*)
1945 John P. Fulton (*Wonder Man*)
1946 Thomas Howard (*Blithe Spirit*)
1947 A. Arnold Gillespie, Warren Newcombe (*Green Dolphin Street*)
1948 Paul Eagler, J. McMillan Johnson, Russell Shearman, Clarence Slifer (*Portrait of Jennie*)
1949 *Mighty Joe Young*
1950 *Destination Moon*
1951 *When Worlds Collide*
1952 *Plymouth Adventure*
1953 *The War of the Worlds*
1954 *20,000 Leagues Under the Sea*
1955 *The Bridges at Toko-Ri*
1956 John Fulton (*The Ten Commandments*)
1957 [10]
1958 Tom Howard (*tom thumb*)
1959 A. Arnold Gillespie, Robert MacDonald (*Ben-Hur*)
1960 Gene Warren, Tim Baar (*The Time Machine*)
1961 Bill Warrington (*The Guns of Navarone*)
1962 Robert MacDonald (*The Longest Day*)

VISUAL EFFECTS[10] (CONTINUED)

1963 Emil Kosa, Jr. (*Cleopatra*)
1964 Peter Ellenshaw, Hamilton Luske, Eustace Lycett (*Mary Poppins*)
1965 John Stears (*Thunderball*)
1966 Art Cruickshank (*Fantastic Voyage*)
1967 L.B. Abbott (*Doctor Dolittle*)
1968 Stanley Kubrick (*2001: A Space Odyssey*)
1969 Robbie Robertson (*Marooned*)
1970 A.D. Flowers, L.B. Abbott (*Tora! Tora! Tora!*)
1971 Alan Maley, Eustace Lycett, Danny Lee (*Bedknobs and Broomsticks*)
1972 L.B. Abbott, A.D. Flowers (*The Poseidon Adventure*)
1974 Frank Brendel, Glen Robinson, Albert Whitlock (*Earthquake*)
1975 Albert Whitlock, Glen Robinson (*The Hindenburg*)
1976 Carlo Rambaldi, Glen Robinson, Frank Van der Veer (*King Kong*); L.B. Abbott, Glen Robinson, Matthew Yuricich (*Logan's Run*)
1977 John Stears, John Dykstra, Richard Edlund, Grant McCune, Robert Blalack (*Star Wars*)
1978 Les Bowie[1], Colin Chilvers, Denys Coop, Roy Field, Derek Meddings, Zoran Perisic (*Superman*)
1979 H.R. Giger, Carlo Rambaldi, Brian Johnson, Nick Allder, Denys Ayling (*Alien*)
1980 Brian Johnson, Richard Edlund, Dennis Muren, Bruce Nicholson (*The Empire Strikes Back*)
1981 Richard Edlund, Kit West, Bruce Nicholson, Joe Johnston (*Raiders of the Lost Ark*)
1982 Carlo Rambaldi, Dennis Muren, Kenneth F. Smith (*E.T.: The Extra-Terrestrial*)
1983 Richard Edlund, Dennis Muren, Ken Ralston, Phil Tippett (*Return of the Jedi*)
1984 Dennis Muren, Michael McAlister, Lorne Peterson, George Gibbs (*Indiana Jones and the Temple of Doom*)
1985 Ken Ralston, Ralph McQuarrie, Scott Farrar, David Berry (*Cocoon*)
1986 Robert Skotak, Stan Winston, John Richardson, Suzanne Benson (*Aliens*)
1987 Dennis Muren, William George, Harley Jessup, Kenneth Smith (*Innerspace*)
1988 Ken Ralston, Richard Williams, Edward Jones, George Gibbs (*Who Framed Roger Rabbit*)
1989 John Bruno, Dennis Muren, Hoyt Yeatman, Dennis Skotak (*The Abyss*)
1990 Eric Brevig, Rob Bottin, Tim McGovern, Alex Funke (*Total Recall*)
1991 Robert Skotak (*Terminator 2: Judgment Day*)
1992 Ken Ralston, Doug Chiang, Doug Smythe, Tom Woodruff, Jr. (*Death Becomes Her*)
1993 Dennis Muren, Stan Winston, Phil Tippett, Michael Lantieri (*Jurassic Park*)
1994 Ken Ralston, George Murphy, Stephen Rosenbaum, Allen Hall (*Forrest Gump*)
1995 Scott E. Anderson, Charles Gibson, Neal Scanlan, John Cox (*Babe*)
1996 Volker Engel, Douglas Smith, Clay Pinney, Joseph Viskocil (*Independence Day*)
1997 Robert Legato, Mark Lasoff, Thomas L. Fisher, Michael Kanfer (*Titanic*)
1998 Joel Hynek, Nicholas Brooks, Stuart Robertson, Kevin Mack (*What Dreams May Come*)

Academy Awards (Oscars), 1928–2009 (continued)

VISUAL EFFECTS[10] (CONTINUED)

1999 John Gaeta, Janek Sirrs, Steve Courtley, Jon Thum (*The Matrix*)

2000 John Nelson, Neil Corbould, Tim Burke, Rob Harvey (*Gladiator*)

2001 Jim Rygiel, Randall William Cook, Richard Taylor, Mark Stetson (*The Lord of the Rings: The Fellowship of the Ring*)

2002 Jim Rygiel, Joe Letteri, Randall William Cook, Alex Funke (*The Lord of the Rings: The Two Towers*)

2003 Jim Rygiel, Joe Letteri, Randall William Cook, Alex Funke (*The Lord of the Rings: The Return of the King*)

2004 John Dykstra, Scott Stokdyk, Anthony LaMolinara, John Frazier (*Spider-Man 2*)

2005 Joe Letteri, Brian Van't Hul, Christian Rivers, Richard Taylor (*King Kong*)

2006 John Knoll, Hal Hickel, Charles Gibson, Allen Hall (*Pirates of the Caribbean: Dead Man's Chest*)

2007 Michael Fink, Bill Westenhofer, Ben Morris, Trevor Wood (*The Golden Compass*)

2008 Eric Barba, Steve Preeg, Burt Dalton, Craig Barron (*The Curious Case of Benjamin Button*)

2009 Joe Letteri, Stephen Rosenbaum, Richard Baneham, Andrew R. Jones (*Avatar*)

MAKEUP

1981 Rick Baker (*An American Werewolf in London*)

1982 Sarah Monzani, Michele Burke (*Quest for Fire*)

1983 *no award given*

1984 Paul LeBlanc, Dick Smith (*Amadeus*)

1985 Michael Westmore, Zoltan Elek (*Mask*)

1986 Chris Walas, Stephan Dupuis (*The Fly*)

1987 Rick Baker (*Harry and the Hendersons*)

1988 Ve Neill, Steve La Porte, Robert Short (*Beetlejuice*)

1989 Manlio Rocchetti, Lynn Barber, Kevin Haney (*Driving Miss Daisy*)

1990 John Caglione, Jr., Doug Drexler (*Dick Tracy*)

1991 Stan Winston, Jeff Dawn (*Terminator 2: Judgment Day*)

1992 Greg Cannom, Michele Burke, Matthew W. Mungle (*Bram Stoker's Dracula*)

1993 Greg Cannom, Ve Neill, Yolanda Toussieng (*Mrs. Doubtfire*)

1994 Rick Baker, Ve Neill, Yolanda Toussieng (*Ed Wood*)

1995 Peter Frampton, Paul Pattison, Lois Burwell (*Braveheart*)

1996 Rick Baker, David LeRoy Anderson (*The Nutty Professor*)

1997 Rick Baker, David LeRoy Anderson (*Men in Black*)

1998 Jenny Shircore (*Elizabeth*)

1999 Christine Blundell, Trefor Proud (*Topsy-Turvy*)

2000 Rick Baker, Gail Ryan (*Dr. Seuss' How the Grinch Stole Christmas*)

2001 Peter Owen, Richard Taylor (*The Lord of the Rings: The Fellowship of the Ring*)

2002 John Jackson, Beatrice Alba (*Frida*)

2003 Richard Taylor, Peter King (*The Lord of the Rings: The Return of the King*)

2004 Valli O'Reilly, Bill Corso (*Lemony Snicket's A Series of Unfortunate Events*)

2005 Howard Berger, Tami Lane (*The Chronicles of Narnia: The Lion, the Witch, and the Wardrobe*)

MAKEUP (CONTINUED)

2006 David Martí, Montse Ribé (*Pan's Labyrinth*)

2007 Didier Lavergne, Jan Archibald (*La Vie en rose*)

2008 Greg Cannom (*The Curious Case of Benjamin Button*)

2009 Barney Burman, Mindy Hall, Joel Harlow (*Star Trek*)

ORIGINAL SCORE

1938 Erich Wolfgang Korngold (*The Adventures of Robin Hood*)

1939 Herbert Stothart (*The Wizard of Oz*)

1940 Leigh Harline, Paul J. Smith, Ned Washington (*Pinocchio*)

1941 Bernard Herrmann (*All That Money Can Buy*)

1942 Max Steiner (*Now, Voyager*)

1943 Alfred Newman (*The Song of Bernadette*)

1944 Max Steiner (*Since You Went Away*)

1945 Miklós Rózsa (*Spellbound*)

1946 Hugo Friedhofer (*The Best Years of Our Lives*)

1947 Miklós Rózsa (*A Double Life*)

1948 Brian Easdale (*The Red Shoes*)

1949 Aaron Copland (*The Heiress*)

1950 Franz Waxman (*Sunset Blvd.*)

1951 Franz Waxman (*A Place in the Sun*)

1952 Dimitri Tiomkin (*High Noon*)

1953 Bronislau Kaper (*Lili*)

1954 Dimitri Tiomkin (*The High and the Mighty*)

1955 Alfred Newman (*Love Is a Many-Splendored Thing*)

1956 Victor Young (*Around the World in 80 Days*)[1]

1957 Malcolm Arnold (*The Bridge on the River Kwai*)[11]

1958 Dimitri Tiomkin (*The Old Man and The Sea*)

1959 Miklós Rózsa (*Ben-Hur*)

1960 Ernest Gold (*Exodus*)

1961 Henry Mancini (*Breakfast at Tiffany's*)

1962 Maurice Jarre (*Lawrence of Arabia*)

1963 John Addison (*Tom Jones*)

1964 Richard M. Sherman, Robert B. Sherman (*Mary Poppins*)

1965 Maurice Jarre (*Doctor Zhivago*)

1966 John Barry (*Born Free*)

1967 Elmer Bernstein (*Thoroughly Modern Millie*)

1968 John Barry (*The Lion in Winter*)[12]; John Green (*Oliver!*)[13]

1969 Burt Bacharach (*Butch Cassidy and the Sundance Kid*)[12]; Lennie Hayton, Lionel Newman (*Hello, Dolly!*)[13]

1970 Francis Lai (*Love Story*); The Beatles (*Let It Be*)[14]

1971 Michel Legrand (*Summer of '42*)

1972 Charles Chaplin, Raymond Rasch[1], Larry Russell[1] (*Limelight*)

1973 Marvin Hamlisch (*The Way We Were*)

1974 Nino Rota, Carmine Coppola (*The Godfather Part II*)

1975 John Williams (*Jaws*)

1976 Jerry Goldsmith (*The Omen*)

1977 John Williams (*Star Wars*)

1978 Giorgio Moroder (*Midnight Express*)

1979 Georges Delerue (*A Little Romance*)

1980 Michael Gore (*Fame*)

1981 Vangelis (*Chariots of Fire*)

1982 John Williams (*E.T.: The Extra-Terrestrial*); Henry Mancini, Leslie Bricusse (*Victor/Victoria*)[14]

1983 Bill Conti (*The Right Stuff*); Michel Legrand, Alan Bergman, Marilyn Bergman (*Yentl*)[14]

Academy Awards (Oscars), 1928–2009 (continued)

ORIGINAL SCORE (CONTINUED)

1984 Maurice Jarre (A Passage to India); Prince (Purple Rain)[14]
1985 John Barry (Out of Africa)
1986 Herbie Hancock ('Round Midnight)
1987 Ryuichi Sakamoto, David Byrne, Cong Su (The Last Emperor)
1988 Dave Grusin (The Milagro Beanfield War)
1989 Alan Menken (The Little Mermaid)
1990 John Barry (Dances with Wolves)
1991 Alan Menken (Beauty and the Beast)
1992 Alan Menken (Aladdin)
1993 John Williams (Schindler's List)
1994 Hans Zimmer (The Lion King)
1995 Luis Enrique Bacalov (Il Postino)[12]; Alan Menken, Stephen Schwartz (Pocahontas)[15]
1996 Gabriel Yared (The English Patient)[12]; Rachel Portman (Emma)[15]
1997 James Horner (Titanic)[12]; Anne Dudley (The Full Monty)[15]
1998 Nicola Piovani (Life Is Beautiful)[12]; Stephen Warbeck (Shakespeare in Love)[15]
1999 John Corigliano (The Red Violin)
2000 Tan Dun (Crouching Tiger, Hidden Dragon)
2001 Howard Shore (The Lord of the Rings: The Fellowship of the Ring)
2002 Elliot Goldenthal (Frida)
2003 Howard Shore (The Lord of the Rings: The Return of the King)
2004 Jan A.P. Kaczmarek (Finding Neverland)
2005 Gustavo Santaolalla (Brokeback Mountain)
2006 Gustavo Santaolalla (Babel)
2007 Dario Marianelli (Atonement)
2008 A.R. Rahman (Slumdog Millionaire)
2009 Michael Giacchino (Up)

ORIGINAL SONG

1934 Con Conrad, Herb Magidson, "The Continental" (The Gay Divorcee)
1935 Harry Warren, Al Dubin, "Lullaby of Broadway" (Gold Diggers of 1935)
1936 Jerome Kern, Dorothy Fields, "The Way You Look Tonight" (Swing Time)
1937 Harry Owens, "Sweet Leilani" (Waikiki Wedding)
1938 Ralph Rainger, Leo Robin, "Thanks for the Memory" (The Big Broadcast of 1938)
1939 Harold Arlen, E.Y. Harburg, "Over the Rainbow" (The Wizard of Oz)
1940 Leigh Harline, Ned Washington, "When You Wish Upon a Star" (Pinocchio)
1941 Jerome Kern, Oscar Hammerstein II, "The Last Time I Saw Paris" (Lady Be Good)
1942 Irving Berlin, "White Christmas" (Holiday Inn)
1943 Harry Warren, Mack Gordon, "You'll Never Know" (Hello, Frisco, Hello)
1944 James Van Heusen, Johnny Burke, "Swinging on a Star" (Going My Way)
1945 Richard Rodgers, Oscar Hammerstein II, "It Might As Well Be Spring" (State Fair)
1946 Harry Warren, Johnny Mercer, "On the Atchison, Topeka, and the Santa Fe" (The Harvey Girls)
1947 Allie Wrubel, Ray Gilbert, "Zip-a-dee-doo-dah" (Song of the South)

ORIGINAL SONG (CONTINUED)

1948 Jay Livingston, Ray Evans, "Buttons and Bows" (The Paleface)
1949 Frank Loesser, "Baby, It's Cold Outside" (Neptune's Daughter)
1950 Ray Evans, Jay Livingston, "Mona Lisa" (Captain Carey, U.S.A.)
1951 Hoagy Carmichael, Johnny Mercer, "In The Cool, Cool, Cool of the Evening" (Here Comes the Groom)
1952 Dimitri Tiomkin, Ned Washington, "High Noon (Do Not Forsake Me, Oh My Darlin')" (High Noon)
1953 Sammy Fain, Paul Francis Webster, "Secret Love" (Calamity Jane)
1954 Jule Styne, Sammy Cahn, "Three Coins in the Fountain" (Three Coins in the Fountain)
1955 Sammy Fain, Paul Francis Webster, "Love Is a Many-Splendored Thing" (Love Is a Many-Splendored Thing)
1956 Jay Livingston, Ray Evans, "Whatever Will Be, Will Be (Que Sera, Sera)" (The Man Who Knew Too Much)
1957 James Van Heusen, Sammy Cahn, "All the Way" (The Joker Is Wild)
1958 Frederick Loewe, Alan Jay Lerner, "Gigi" (Gigi)
1959 James Van Heusen, Sammy Cahn, "High Hopes" (A Hole in the Head)
1960 Manos Hadjidakis, "Never on Sunday" (Never on Sunday)
1961 Henry Mancini, Johnny Mercer, "Moon River" (Breakfast at Tiffany's)
1962 Henry Mancini, Johnny Mercer, "Days of Wine and Roses" (Days of Wine and Roses)
1963 James Van Heusen, Sammy Cahn, "Call Me Irresponsible" (Papa's Delicate Condition)
1964 Richard M. Sherman, Robert B. Sherman, "Chim Chim Cher-ee" (Mary Poppins)
1965 Johnny Mandel, Paul Francis Webster, "The Shadow of Your Smile" (The Sandpiper)
1966 John Barry, Don Black, "Born Free" (Born Free)
1967 Leslie Bricusse, "Talk to the Animals" (Doctor Dolittle)
1968 Michel Legrand, Alan Bergman, Marilyn Bergman, "The Windmills of Your Mind" (The Thomas Crown Affair)
1969 Burt Bacharach, Hal David, "Raindrops Keep Fallin' On My Head" (Butch Cassidy and the Sundance Kid)
1970 Fred Karlin, Robb Royer (as Robb Wilson), James Griffin (as Arthur James), "For All We Know" (Lovers and Other Strangers)
1971 Isaac Hayes, "Theme from Shaft" (Shaft)
1972 Al Kasha, Joel Hirschhorn, "The Morning After" (The Poseidon Adventure)
1973 Marvin Hamlisch, Alan Bergman, Marilyn Bergman, "The Way We Were" (The Way We Were)
1974 Al Kasha, Joel Hirschhorn, "We May Never Love Like This Again" (The Towering Inferno)
1975 Keith Carradine, "I'm Easy" (Nashville)
1976 Barbra Streisand, Paul Williams, "Evergreen (Love Theme from A Star Is Born)" (A Star Is Born)

Academy Awards (Oscars), 1928–2009 (continued)

ORIGINAL SONG (CONTINUED)

1977 Joseph Brooks, "You Light Up My Life" (*You Light Up My Life*)

1978 Paul Jabara, "Last Dance" (*Thank God It's Friday*)

1979 David Shire, Norman Gimbel, "It Goes Like It Goes" (*Norma Rae*)

1980 Michael Gore, Dean Pitchford, "Fame" (*Fame*)

1981 Burt Bacharach, Carole Bayer Sager, Christopher Cross, Peter Allen, "Arthur's Theme (Best That You Can Do)" (*Arthur*)

1982 Jack Nitzsche, Buffy Sainte-Marie, Will Jennings, "Up Where We Belong" (*An Officer and a Gentleman*)

1983 Giorgio Moroder, Keith Forsey, Irene Cara, "Flashdance...What a Feeling" (*Flashdance*)

1984 Stevie Wonder, "I Just Called To Say I Love You" (*The Woman in Red*)

1985 Lionel Richie, "Say You, Say Me" (*White Nights*)

1986 Giorgio Moroder, Tom Whitlock, "Take My Breath Away" (*Top Gun*)

1987 Franke Previte, John DeNicola, Donald Markowitz, "(I've Had) The Time of My Life" (*Dirty Dancing*)

1988 Carly Simon, "Let the River Run" (*Working Girl*)

1989 Alan Menken, Howard Ashman, "Under the Sea" (*The Little Mermaid*)

1990 Stephen Sondheim, "Sooner or Later (I Always Get My Man)" (*Dick Tracy*)

1991 Alan Menken, Howard Ashman[1], "Beauty and the Beast" (*Beauty and the Beast*)

1992 Alan Menken, Tim Rice, "A Whole New World" (*Aladdin*)

1993 Bruce Springsteen, "Streets of Philadelphia" (*Philadelphia*)

ORIGINAL SONG (CONTINUED)

1994 Elton John, Tim Rice, "Can You Feel the Love Tonight" (*The Lion King*)

1995 Alan Menken, Stephen Schwartz, "Colors of the Wind" (*Pocahontas*)

1996 Andrew Lloyd Webber, Tim Rice, "You Must Love Me" (*Evita*)

1997 James Horner, Will Jennings, "My Heart Will Go On" (*Titanic*)

1998 Stephen Schwartz, "When You Believe" (*The Prince of Egypt*)

1999 Phil Collins, "You'll Be in My Heart" (*Tarzan*)

2000 Bob Dylan, "Things Have Changed" (*Wonder Boys*)

2001 Randy Newman, "If I Didn't Have You" (*Monsters, Inc.*)

2002 Eminem, Jeff Bass, Luis Resto, "Lose Yourself" (*8 Mile*)

2003 Fran Walsh, Howard Shore, Annie Lennox, "Into the West" (*The Lord of the Rings: The Return of the King*)

2004 Jorge Drexler, "Al otro lado del río" (*The Motorcycle Diaries*)

2005 Jordan Houston, Cedric Coleman, Paul Beauregard, "It's Hard Out Here for a Pimp" (*Hustle & Flow*)

2006 Melissa Etheridge, "I Need To Wake Up" (*An Inconvenient Truth*)

2007 Glen Hansard, Marketa Irglova, "Falling Slowly" (*Once*)

2008 A.R. Rahman, Gulzar, "Jai Ho" (*Slumdog Millionaire*)

2009 Ryan Bingham, T Bone Burnett, "The Weary Kind (Theme from Crazy Heart)" (*Crazy Heart*)

[1]*Posthumously.* [2]*The current screenplay categories were adopted for the 1957 awards. Until then, various separate writing awards were given for silent-film title writing, screenplay, story and screenplay, and motion picture story.* [3]*Screenplay (for script only).* [4]*Actual winner was blacklisted at the time of the award and the honored work was attributed to another name or person; pseudonym or nominal winner is listed in parentheses.* [5]*Motion picture story (for narrative only; also called original story).* [6]*Title writing.* [7]*Story and screenplay (for narrative and script; also called original screenplay).* [8]*Black and white.* [9]*Color.* [10]*Until 1963, both visual and sound effects were honored as special effects. Only those recipients honored for visual effects are listed here. In 1957 only a sound-effects engineer was honored.* [11]*Scoring.* [12]*Drama or not a musical.* [13]*Musical.* [14]*Song score.* [15]*Musical or comedy.*

Golden Globe Awards, 2009

The Hollywood Foreign Press Association, a group of film critics for publications outside the US, began awarding prizes for outstanding American motion pictures and acting in 1944 and created the Golden Globe Awards in 1945. Over the years the prizes have expanded from recognizing only motion pictures and acting to include directing, screenwriting, film music

scoring, foreign-language films, and television, as well as a number of other categories of achievement. The television network on which each winning series appears is given in parentheses. Prize: globe encircled by a strip of motion picture film, in gold.

Golden Globes/Hollywood Foreign Press Association Web site: <www.goldenglobes.org>.

Film

Drama	*Avatar* (US/UK; director, James Cameron)
Musical/comedy	*The Hangover* (US/Germany; director, Todd Phillips)
Director	James Cameron (*Avatar*, US/UK)
Actress, drama	Sandra Bullock (*The Blind Side*, US)
Actor, drama	Jeff Bridges (*Crazy Heart*, US)
Actress, musical/comedy	Meryl Streep (*Julie & Julia*, US)
Actor, musical/comedy	Robert Downey, Jr. (*Sherlock Holmes*, US)
Animated feature film	*Up* (US; director, Pete Docter)

Golden Globe Awards, 2009 (continued)

Film (continued)

Foreign-language film — *Das weisse Band—Eine deutsche Kindergeschichte* (*The White Ribbon*) (Austria/Germany/France/Italy; director, Michael Haneke)

Supporting actress — Mo'Nique (*Precious: Based on the Novel "Push" by Sapphire*, US)

Supporting actor — Christoph Waltz (*Inglourious Basterds*, US/Germany)

Screenplay — Jason Reitman and Sheldon Turner (*Up in the Air*, US)

Original score — Michael Giacchino (*Up*, US)

Original song — "I Want To Come Home" (*Everybody's Fine*, US/Italy); music and lyrics, Paul McCartney

Television

Drama series — *Mad Men* (AMC)

Actress, drama series — Julianna Margulies (*The Good Wife*)

Actor, drama series — Michael C. Hall (*Dexter*)

Musical/comedy series — *Glee* (FOX)

Actress, musical/comedy series — Toni Collette (*United States of Tara*)

Actor, musical/comedy series — Alec Baldwin (*30 Rock*)

Miniseries/movie made for TV — *Grey Gardens* (HBO)

Actress, miniseries/movie made for TV — Drew Barrymore (*Grey Gardens*)

Actor, miniseries/movie made for TV — Kevin Bacon (*Taking Chance*)

Supporting actress, series/miniseries/movie — Chloë Sevigny (*Big Love*)

Supporting actor, series/miniseries/movie — John Lithgow (*Dexter*)

Sundance Film Festival, 2010

Founded as the Utah/US Film Festival in Salt Lake City in 1978, the exhibition has traditionally focused on documentary and dramatic works from outside the Hollywood mainstream. It came under the auspices of actor Robert Redford's Sundance Institute in 1985 and is held every January in Park City UT.

Sundance Institute Web site: <www.sundance.org>.

Grand Jury Prize, drama — *Winter's Bone* (US; director, Debra Granik)

Grand Jury Prize, documentary — *Restrepo* (US; directors, Tim Hetherington and Sebastian Junger)

World Cinema Jury Prize, drama — *Animal Kingdom* (Australia; director, David Michôd)

World Cinema Jury Prize, documentary — *Det røde kapel* (*The Red Chapel*) (Denmark; director, Mads Brügger)

Audience Award, US drama — *Happythankyoumoreplease* (director, Josh Radnor)

Audience Award, US documentary — *Waiting for Superman* (director, Davis Guggenheim)

World Cinema Audience Award, drama — *Contracorriente* (*Undertow*) (Peru/Colombia; director, Javier Fuentes-León)

World Cinema Audience Award, documentary — *Waste Land* (Brazil/UK; director, Lucy Walker)

Directing Award, US drama — Eric Mendelsohn (*3 Backyards*)

Directing Award, US documentary — Leon Gast (*Smash His Camera*)

World Cinema Directing Award, drama — Juan Carlos Valdivia (*Zona sur* [*Southern District*], Bolivia)

World Cinema Directing Award, documentary — Christian Frei (*Space Tourists*, Switzerland)

Editing Award, US documentary — Ricki Stern and Anne Sundberg (*Joan Rivers: A Piece of Work*)

World Cinema Editing Award, documentary — Yael Hersonski (*A Film Unfinished,* Germany/Israel)

Cinematography Award, US drama — Zak Mulligan (*Obselidia*)

Cinematography Award, US documentary — Kirsten Johnson and Laura Poitras (*The Oath*)

World Cinema Cinematography Award, drama — Mariano Cohn and Gastón Duprat (*El Hombre de al lado* [*The Man Next Door*], Argentina)

World Cinema Cinematography Award, documentary — Ken Wardrop (*His & Hers,* Ireland)

Waldo Salt Screenwriting Award — Debra Granik and Anne Rosellini (*Winter's Bone*, US)

World Cinema Screenwriting Award — Juan Carlos Valdivia (*Zona sur* [*Southern District*], Bolivia)

Special Jury Prize, US drama — *Sympathy for Delicious* (director, Mark Ruffalo)

Special Jury Prize, US documentary — *GasLand* (director, Josh Fox)

World Cinema Special Jury Prize, drama (for breakout performance) — Tatiana Maslany (*Grown Up Movie Star*) (Canada; director, Adriana Maggs)

World Cinema Special Jury Prize, documentary — *Enemies of the People* (UK/Cambodia; directors, Rob Lemkin and Thet Sambath)

Jury Prize, US short filmmaking — *Drunk History: Douglass & Lincoln* (director, Jeremy Konner)

Sundance Film Festival, 2010 (continued)

International Jury Prize, short filmmaking	*The Six Fifty Dollar Man* (New Zealand; directors, Mark Albiston and Louis Sutherland)
Best of NEXT	*Homewrecker* (US; directors, Brad Barnes and Todd Barnes)
Alfred P. Sloan Prize	*Obselidia* (US; director, Diane Bell)

Toronto International Film Festival, 2009

Founded in 1976, the Toronto International Film Festival is one of North America's best-attended exhibitions and a frequent forum for the premieres of major feature films. The festival, held in September, awards seven prizes, three of which are for Canadian films.

Toronto International Film Festival Web site: <www.tiff.net>.

Canadian feature film	*Cairo Time* (director, Ruba Nadda)
Canadian first feature film	*The Wild Hunt* (director, Alexandre Franchi)
Canadian short film	*Danse Macabre* (director, Pedro Pires)
FIPRESCI Prize for Discovery	*The Man Beyond the Bridge* (India; director, Laxmikant Shetgaonkar)
FIPRESCI Prize for Special Presentations	*Hadewijch* (France; director, Bruno Dumont)
People's Choice Award	*Precious: Based on the Novel "Push" by Sapphire* (US; director, Lee Daniels)
People's Choice Award-Documentary	*The Topp Twins* (New Zealand; director, Leanne Pooley)
People's Choice Award–Midnight Madness	*The Loved Ones* (Australia; director, Sean Byrne)

Cannes International Film Festival, 2010

Established in 1946, the Cannes Festival is among the best-known and most influential film exhibitions in the world. An eight-member feature-film jury and a four-member short-film and Cinéfondation jury give awards to the best film (Palme d'Or) and other outstanding films (special jury prizes) in their respective categories. The Grand Prix goes to the feature film judged the most original, and the feature jury also chooses the winners of the performance, direction, and screenplay awards. The Caméra d'Or, for best first film, is awarded by a jury comprising film industry professionals and members of the moviegoing public. The Cinéfondation awards are for works of one hour or less by film-school students.

Cannes Festival Web site: <www.festival-cannes.fr>.

feature films ▶ **Palme d'Or:** *Lung Boonmee raluek chat* (*Uncle Boonmee Who Can Recall His Past Lives*) (UK/Thailand/France/Germany/Spain; director, Apichatpong Weerasethakul); ▶ **Grand Prix:** *Des hommes et des dieux* (*Of Gods and Men*) (France; director, Xavier Beauvois); ▶ **best actress:** Juliette Binoche (*Copie conforme* [*Certified Copy*], France/Italy); ▶ **best actor:** Javier Bardem (*Biutiful*, Spain/Mexico); Elio Germano (*La nostra vita* [*Our Life*], Italy/France); ▶ **best director:** Mathieu Amalric (*Tournée* [*On Tour*], France); ▶ **best screenplay:** Lee Chang-Dong (*Poetry*, Republic of Korea); ▶ **jury prize:** *Un Homme qui crie* (*A Screaming Man*) (France/Belgium/Chad; director, Mahamat-Saleh Haroun); ▶ **Caméra d'Or:** *Año bisiesto* (Mexico; director, Michael Rowe)

short films ▶ **Palme d'Or:** *Chienne d'histoire* (*Barking Island*) (France; director, Serge Avédikian)

Cinéfondation ▶ **1st prize:** *Taulukauppiaat* (*The Painting Sellers*) (Finland; director, Juho Kuosmanen); ▶ **2nd prize:** *Coucou-les-nuages* (*Anywhere Out of the World*) (France; director, Vincent Cardona); ▶ **3rd prize:** *Hinkerort zorasune* (*The Fifth Column*) (Lebanon/US; director, Vatche Boulghourjian); *Ja vec jesam sve ono sto zelim da imam* (*I Already Am Everything I Want To Have*) (Serbia; director, Dane Komljen)

Berlin International Film Festival, 2010

The Berlin International Film Festival (Internationale Filmfestspiele Berlin), held annually since its founding in West Berlin in 1951, comprises some 20 separate competitions and juries emphasizing aspects of both worldwide and German cinema, each with their own prizes. The International Jury, made up of film-industry figures from across the globe, selects the winners of the Golden and Silver Bears, the festival's top awards.

Berlin International Film Festival Web site: <www.berlinale.de>.

Golden Bear	*Bal* (*Honey*) (Turkey/Germany; director, Semih Kaplanoglu)
Jury Grand Prix (Silver Bear)	*Eu cand vreau sa fluier, fluier* (*If I Want To Whistle, I Whistle*) (Romania/Sweden; director, Florin Serban)
Silver Bear, director	Roman Polanski (*The Ghost Writer*, France/Germany/UK)
Silver Bear, actress	Shinobu Terajima (*Caterpillar*, Japan)
Silver Bear, actor	Grigory Dobrygin and Sergey Puskepalis (*Kak ya provel etim letom* [*How I Ended This Summer*], Russia)

Berlin International Film Festival, 2010 (continued)

Silver Bear, script	Wang Quan'an and Na Jin (*Tuan yuan* [*Apart Together*], China)
Silver Bear, artistic contribution	Pavel Kostomarov (cinematography) (*Kak ya provel etim letom* [*How I Ended This Summer*], Russia)
Alfred Bauer Prize (for a work of particular innovation)	*Eu cand vreau sa fluier, fluier* (*If I Want To Whistle, I Whistle*) (Romania/Sweden; director Florin Serban)
Ecumenical Jury prizes	Competition: *Bal* (*Honey*) (Turkey/Germany; director, Semih Kaplanoglu); Panorama: *Kawasakiho ruze* (*Kawasaki's Rose*) (Czech Republic; director, Jan Hrebejk); Forum: *Aisheen* (*Still Alive in Gaza*) (Qatar/Switzerland; director, Nicolas Wadimoff)
FIPRESCI prizes	Competition: *En familie* (*A Family*) (Denmark; director, Pernille Fischer Christensen); Panorama: *Parade* (Japan; director, Isao Yukisada); Forum: *El vuelco del cangrejo* (*Crab Trap*) (Colombia/France; director, Oscar Ruíz Navia)
Best First Feature Award	*Sebbe* (Sweden; director, Babak Najafi)

Worldwide Top-Grossing Films (Actual US Dollars)

As of 23 Aug 2010. Includes reissues. Source: <www.boxofficemojo.com>.

		ACTUAL US DOLLARS
1	*Avatar* (2009)	2,740,400,000
2	*Titanic* (1997)	1,843,200,000
3	*The Lord of the Rings: The Return of the King* (2003)	1,119,100,000
4	*Pirates of the Caribbean: Dead Man's Chest* (2006)	1,066,200,000
5	*Alice in Wonderland* (2010)	1,024,300,000
6	*The Dark Knight* (2008)	1,001,900,000
7	*Toy Story 3* (2010)	984,300,000
8	*Harry Potter and the Sorcerer's Stone* (2001)	974,700,000
9	*Pirates of the Caribbean: At World's End* (2007)	961,000,000
10	*Harry Potter and the Order of the Phoenix* (2007)	938,200,000
11	*Harry Potter and the Half-Blood Prince* (2009)	934,000,000
12	*The Lord of the Rings: The Two Towers* (2002)	925,300,000
13	*Star Wars: Episode I—The Phantom Menace* (1999)	924,300,000
14	*Shrek 2* (2004)	919,800,000
15	*Jurassic Park* (1993)	914,700,000
16	*Harry Potter and the Goblet of Fire* (2005)	895,900,000
17	*Spider-Man 3* (2007)	890,900,000
18	*Ice Age: Dawn of the Dinosaurs* (2009)	886,700,000
19	*Harry Potter and the Chamber of Secrets* (2002)	878,600,000
20	*The Lord of the Rings: The Fellowship of the Ring* (2001)	870,800,000

US Top-Grossing Films (Constant US Dollars, Estimated)

Admissions—the number of tickets sold to a movie—tell a different story from the raw dollars earned. While recent films have made hundreds of millions of dollars, only 2 of the top 10 films in terms of attendance were released after 1980. Includes reissues. Source: <www.boxofficemojo.com>.

		ADMISSIONS	2010 US DOLLARS	ACTUAL US DOLLARS
1	*Gone with the Wind* (1939)	202,044,600	1,606,254,800	198,676,459
2	*Star Wars* (1977)	178,119,600	1,416,050,800	460,998,007
3	*The Sound of Music* (1965)	142,415,400	1,132,202,200	158,671,368
4	*E.T.: The Extra-Terrestrial* (1982)	141,854,300	1,127,742,000	435,110,554
5	*The Ten Commandments* (1956)	131,000,000	1,041,450,000	65,500,000
6	*Titanic* (1997)	128,345,900	1,020,349,800	600,788,188
7	*Jaws* (1975)	128,078,800	1,018,226,600	260,000,000
8	*Doctor Zhivago* (1965)	124,135,500	986,876,900	111,721,910
9	*The Exorcist* (1973)	110,568,700	879,020,900	232,671,011
10	*Snow White and the Seven Dwarfs* (1937)	109,000,000	866,550,000	184,925,486

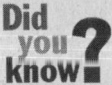
Did you know?

The Harry Potter films make up the most successful movie franchise of all time. As of July 2010, the films had brought in more than US$5,422,000,000 worldwide. The six-film franchise beat out the second-place franchise, the James Bond movies. The 23 films in the Bond franchise have made more than US$5,074,000,000. In the same month, it was announced that the *Saw* films had become the most successful horror film franchise in the world, taking in more than US$728,000,000 in worldwide box office receipts.

Top US DVD Sales, 2009

Source: <www.the-numbers.com>.

1	*Twilight*	11	*Bolt*
2	*Transformers: Revenge of the Fallen*	12	*X-Men Origins: Wolverine*
3	*Up*	13	*G.I. Joe: The Rise of Cobra*
4	*Madagascar: Escape 2 Africa*	14	*Taken*
5	*Harry Potter and the Half-Blood Prince*	15	*Gran Torino*
6	*Star Trek*	16	*Marley and Me*
7	*The Hangover*	17	*Beverly Hills Chihuahua*
8	*Monsters vs. Aliens*	18	*The Dark Knight*
9	*Ice Age: Dawn of the Dinosaurs*	19	*Paul Blart: Mall Cop*
10	*The Proposal*	20	*Hannah Montana: The Movie*

Television

Emmy Awards, 2010

The Academy of Television Arts and Sciences gave out its first awards for excellence in television, named the Emmys after the nickname of an early television camera part, for the 1948 season. In the ensuing decades, categories have evolved to include separate prime-time, daytime, and regional Emmy Awards. Award: statuette of a winged woman holding an atom.
Emmy Awards Web site: <http://www.emmys.tv/awards>.

Comedy: *Modern Family* (ABC)
Lead actor, comedy: Jim Parsons, *The Big Bang Theory* (CBS)
Lead actress, comedy: Edie Falco, *Nurse Jackie* (Showtime)
Supporting actor, comedy: Eric Stonestreet, *Modern Family* (ABC)
Supporting actress, comedy: Jane Lynch, *Glee* (FOX)
Drama: *Mad Men* (AMC)
Lead actor, drama: Bryan Cranston, *Breaking Bad* (AMC)
Lead actress, drama: Kyra Sedgwick, *The Closer* (TNT)

Supporting actor, drama: Aaron Paul, *Breaking Bad* (AMC)
Supporting actress, drama: Archie Panjabi, *The Good Wife* (CBS)
Miniseries: *The Pacific* (HBO)
Lead actor, miniseries or movie: Al Pacino, *You Don't Know Jack* (HBO)
Lead actress, miniseries or movie: Claire Danes, *Temple Grandin* (HBO)
Variety/music/comedy: *The Daily Show with Jon Stewart* (Comedy Central)
Nonfiction: *The National Parks: America's Best Idea* (PBS)

Emmy Awards, 1949–2010[1]

1949
Most popular program: *Pantomime Quiz*, KTLA
TV film: *Your Show Time: The Necklace*

1950
Live show: *The Ed Wynn Show*, KTTV
Kinescope show: *The Texaco Star Theater*, KNBH (NBC)
TV film: *The Life of Riley*, KNBH
Public service/cultural/educational: *Crusade in Europe*, KECA-TV/KTTV (ABC)
Children's: *Time for Beany*, KTLA

1951
Variety: *The Alan Young Show*, KTTV (CBS)
Drama: *Pulitzer Prize Playhouse*, KECA-TV (ABC)
Game/audience participation: *Truth or Consequences*, KTTV (CBS)
Children's: *Time for Beany*, KTLA
Educational: *KFI-TV University*, KFI-TV
Cultural: *Campus Chorus and Orchestra*, KTSL

1952
Variety: *Your Show of Shows* (NBC)
Comedy: *The Red Skelton Show* (NBC)
Drama: *Studio One* (CBS)

1953
Variety: *Your Show of Shows* (NBC)
Comedy: *I Love Lucy* (CBS)
Drama: *Robert Montgomery Presents* (NBC)
Mystery/action/adventure: *Dragnet* (NBC)
Public affairs: *See It Now* (CBS)
Audience participation/quiz/panel: *What's My Line?* (CBS)
Children's: *Time for Beany* (syndicated)

1954
Variety: *Omnibus* (CBS)
Comedy: *I Love Lucy* (CBS)
Drama: *The U.S. Steel Hour* (ABC)
Mystery/action/adventure: *Dragnet* (NBC)
Public affairs: *Victory at Sea* (NBC)
Audience participation/quiz/panel: *This Is Your Life* (NBC); *What's My Line?* (CBS)
Children's: *Kukla, Fran, and Ollie* (NBC)

1955
Variety: *Disneyland* (ABC)
Comedy: *Make Room for Daddy* (ABC)
Drama: *The U.S. Steel Hour* (ABC)
Mystery/intrigue: *Dragnet* (NBC)
Western/adventure: *Stories of the Century* (syndicated)

Emmy Awards, 1949–2010[1] (continued)

1955 (continued)
Cultural/religious/educational: *Omnibus* (CBS)
Audience participation/quiz/panel: *This Is Your Life* (NBC)
Children's: *Lassie* (CBS)

1956
Variety: *The Ed Sullivan Show* (CBS)
Comedy: *The Phil Silvers Show: You'll Never Get Rich* (CBS)
Drama: *Producers' Showcase* (NBC)
Action/adventure: *Disneyland* (ABC)
Music: *Your Hit Parade* (NBC)
Documentary: *Omnibus* (CBS)
Audience participation: *The $64,000 Question* (CBS)
Children's: *Lassie* (CBS)

1957
Series (½ hr. or less): *The Phil Silvers Show: You'll Never Get Rich* (CBS)
Series (1 hr. or more): *Caesar's Hour* (NBC)
New series: *Playhouse 90* (CBS)

1958
Musical/variety/audience participation/quiz: *The Dinah Shore Chevy Show* (NBC)
Comedy: *The Phil Silvers Show: You'll Never Get Rich* (CBS)
Drama, continuing: *Gunsmoke* (CBS)
Drama, anthology: *Playhouse 90* (CBS)
New series: *The Seven Lively Arts* (CBS)
Public service: *Omnibus* (ABC/NBC)

1959
Musical/variety: *The Dinah Shore Chevy Show* (NBC)
Comedy: *The Jack Benny Show* (CBS)
Drama (<1 hr.): *Alcoa-Goodyear Playhouse* (NBC)
Drama (1 hr.+): *Playhouse 90* (CBS)
Western: *Maverick* (ABC)
News reporting: *The Huntley-Brinkley Report* (NBC)
Public service: *Omnibus* (NBC)
Panel/quiz/audience participation: *What's My Line?* (CBS)

1960
Variety: *The Fabulous Fifties* (CBS)
Humor: *Art Carney Special* (NBC)
Drama: *Playhouse 90* (CBS)
News: *The Huntley-Brinkley Report* (NBC)
Public affairs/education: *The Twentieth Century* (CBS)
Children's: *Huckleberry Hound* (syndicated)

1961
Variety: *Astaire Time* (NBC)
Humor: *The Jack Benny Show* (CBS)
Drama: *Hallmark Hall of Fame: Macbeth* (NBC)
News: *The Huntley-Brinkley Report* (NBC)
Public affairs/education: *The Twentieth Century* (CBS)
Children's: "Aaron Copland's Birthday Party," *Young People's Concert* (CBS)
Program of the year: *Hallmark Hall of Fame: Macbeth* (NBC)

1962
Variety: *The Garry Moore Show* (CBS)
Humor: *The Bob Newhart Show* (NBC)
Drama: *The Defenders* (CBS)
News: *The Huntley-Brinkley Report* (NBC)

1962 (continued)
Educational/public affairs: *David Brinkley's Journal* (NBC)
Children's: *New York Philharmonic Young People's Concerts with Leonard Bernstein* (CBS)
Program of the year: *Hallmark Hall of Fame: Victoria Regina* (NBC)

1963
Variety: *The Andy Williams Show* (NBC)
Humor: *The Dick Van Dyke Show* (CBS)
Drama: *The Defenders* (CBS)
News: *The Huntley-Brinkley Report* (NBC)
Commentary/public affairs: *David Brinkley's Journal* (NBC)
Documentary: *The Tunnel* (NBC)
Panel/quiz/aud. particip.: *The G.E. College Bowl* (CBS)
Children's: *Walt Disney's Wonderful World of Color* (NBC)
Program of the year: *The Tunnel* (NBC)

1964
Variety: *The Danny Kaye Show* (CBS)
Comedy: *The Dick Van Dyke Show* (CBS)
Drama: *The Defenders* (CBS)
News reports: *The Huntley-Brinkley Report* (NBC)
Commentary/public affairs: "Cuba—Part I: The Bay of Pigs" and "Cuba—Part II: The Missile Crisis," *NBC White Paper* (NBC)
Documentary: *The Making of the President 1960* (ABC)
Children's: *Discovery '63–'64* (ABC)
Program of the year: *The Making of the President 1960* (ABC)

1965
Entertainment: *The Dick Van Dyke Show* (CBS); *Hallmark Hall of Fame: The Magnificent Yankee* (NBC); *My Name Is Barbra* (CBS); "What Is Sonata Form?," *New York Philharmonic Young People's Concerts with Leonard Bernstein* (CBS)
News/docu./info./sports: "I, Leonardo da Vinci," *Saga of Western Man* (ABC); *The Louvre* (NBC)

1966
Variety: *The Andy Williams Show* (NBC)
Comedy: *The Dick Van Dyke Show* (CBS)
Drama: *The Fugitive* (ABC)

1967
Variety: *The Andy Williams Show* (NBC)
Comedy: *The Monkees* (NBC)
Drama: *Mission: Impossible* (CBS)

1968
Musical/variety: *Rowan and Martin's Laugh-In* (NBC)
Comedy: *Get Smart* (NBC)
Drama: *Mission: Impossible* (CBS)

1969
Variety/musical: *Rowan and Martin's Laugh-In* (NBC)
Comedy: *Get Smart* (NBC)
Drama: *NET Playhouse* (NET)

1970
Variety/musical: *The David Frost Show* (syndicated)
Comedy: *My World and Welcome to It* (NBC)
Drama: *Marcus Welby, M.D.* (ABC)

Emmy Awards, 1949–2010[1] (continued)

1971
Comedy: *All in the Family* (CBS)
Drama: *The Bold Ones: The Senator* (NBC)
Variety, musical: *The Flip Wilson Show* (NBC)
Variety, talk: *The David Frost Show* (syndicated)
New series: *All in the Family* (CBS)

1972
Comedy: *All in the Family* (CBS)
Drama: *Masterpiece Theatre: Elizabeth R* (PBS)
Variety, musical: *The Carol Burnett Show* (CBS)
Variety, talk: *The Dick Cavett Show* (ABC)
New series: *Masterpiece Theatre: Elizabeth R* (PBS)

1973
Comedy: *All in the Family* (CBS)
Drama (continuing): *The Waltons* (CBS)
Drama/comedy (limited): *Masterpiece Theatre: Tom Brown's Schooldays* (PBS)
Variety, musical: *The Julie Andrews Hour* (ABC)
New series: *America* (NBC)

1974
Comedy: *M*A*S*H* (CBS)
Drama: *Masterpiece Theatre: Upstairs, Downstairs* (PBS)
Limited series: *Columbo* (NBC)
Music/variety: *The Carol Burnett Show* (CBS)

1975
Comedy: *The Mary Tyler Moore Show* (CBS)
Drama: *Masterpiece Theatre: Upstairs, Downstairs* (PBS)
Limited series: *Benjamin Franklin* (CBS)
Comedy-variety/music: *The Carol Burnett Show* (CBS)

1976
Comedy: *The Mary Tyler Moore Show* (CBS)
Drama: *Police Story* (NBC)
Limited series: *Masterpiece Theatre: Upstairs, Downstairs* (PBS)
Comedy-variety/music: *NBC's Saturday Night* (NBC)

1977
Comedy: *The Mary Tyler Moore Show* (CBS)
Drama: *Masterpiece Theatre: Upstairs, Downstairs* (PBS)
Limited series: *Roots* (ABC)
Comedy-variety/music: *Van Dyke and Company* (NBC)

1978
Comedy: *All in the Family* (CBS)
Drama: *The Rockford Files* (NBC)
Limited series: *Holocaust* (NBC)
Comedy-variety/music: *The Muppet Show* (syndicated)
Informational: *The Body Human* (CBS)

1979
Comedy: *Taxi* (ABC)
Drama: *Lou Grant* (CBS)
Limited series: *Roots: The Next Generations* (ABC)

1980
Comedy: *Taxi* (ABC)
Drama: *Lou Grant* (CBS)
Limited series: *Edward & Mrs. Simpson* (syndicated)

1981
Comedy: *Taxi* (ABC)
Drama: *Hill Street Blues* (NBC)
Limited series: *Shogun* (NBC)
Informational: *Steve Allen's Meeting of Minds* (PBS)

1982
Comedy: *Barney Miller* (ABC)
Drama: *Hill Street Blues* (NBC)
Limited series: *Marco Polo* (NBC)
Informational: *Creativity with Bill Moyers* (PBS)

1983
Comedy: *Cheers* (NBC)
Drama: *Hill Street Blues* (NBC)
Limited series: *Nicholas Nickleby* (syndicated)
Informational: *The Barbara Walters Specials* (ABC)

1984
Comedy: *Cheers* (NBC)
Drama: *Hill Street Blues* (NBC)
Limited series: *American Playhouse: Concealed Enemies* (PBS)
Informational: *A Walk Through the 20th Century with Bill Moyers* (PBS)

1985
Comedy: *The Cosby Show* (NBC)
Drama: *Cagney & Lacey* (CBS)
Limited series: *Masterpiece Theatre: The Jewel in the Crown* (PBS)
Informational: *The Living Planet: A Portrait of the Earth* (PBS)

1986
Comedy: *The Golden Girls* (NBC)
Drama: *Cagney & Lacey* (CBS)
Miniseries: *Peter the Great* (NBC)
Informational: *Great Performances: Laurence Olivier—A Life* (PBS); *Planet Earth* (PBS)

1987
Comedy: *The Golden Girls* (NBC)
Drama: *L.A. Law* (NBC)
Miniseries: *A Year in the Life* (NBC)
Informational: *Smithsonian World* (PBS); *American Masters: Unknown Chaplin* (PBS)

1988
Comedy: *The Wonder Years* (ABC)
Drama: *thirtysomething* (ABC)
Miniseries: *The Murder of Mary Phagan* (NBC)
Informational: *American Masters: Buster Keaton: A Hard Act To Follow* (PBS); *Nature* (PBS)

1989
Comedy: *Cheers* (NBC)
Drama: *L.A. Law* (NBC)
Miniseries: *War and Remembrance* (ABC)
Informational: *Nature* (PBS)

1990
Comedy: *Murphy Brown* (CBS)
Drama: *L.A. Law* (NBC)
Miniseries: *Drug Wars: The Camarena Story* (NBC)
Variety/music/comedy: *In Living Color* (Fox)
Informational: *Smithsonian World* (PBS)

Emmy Awards, 1949–2010[1] (continued)

1991
Comedy: *Cheers* (NBC)
Drama: *L.A. Law* (NBC)
Miniseries: *Separate but Equal* (ABC)
Informational: *The Civil War* (PBS)

1992
Comedy: *Murphy Brown* (CBS)
Drama: *Northern Exposure* (CBS)
Miniseries: *A Woman Named Jackie* (NBC)
Variety/music/comedy: *The Tonight Show Starring Johnny Carson* (NBC)
Informational: *MGM: When the Lion Roars* (TNT)

1993
Comedy: *Seinfeld* (NBC)
Drama: *Picket Fences* (CBS)
Miniseries: *Prime Suspect 2* (PBS)
Variety/music/comedy: *Saturday Night Live* (NBC)
Informational: *Healing and the Mind with Bill Moyers* (PBS)

1994
Comedy: *Frasier* (NBC)
Drama: *Picket Fences* (CBS)
Miniseries: *Prime Suspect 3* (PBS)
Variety/music/comedy: *Late Show with David Letterman* (CBS)
Informational: *Later with Bob Costas* (NBC)

1995
Comedy: *Frasier* (NBC)
Drama: *NYPD Blue* (ABC)
Miniseries: *Joseph* (TNT)
Variety/music/comedy: *The Tonight Show with Jay Leno* (NBC)
Informational: *Baseball* (PBS); *TV Nation* (NBC)

1996
Comedy: *Frasier* (NBC)
Drama: *ER* (NBC)
Miniseries: *Gulliver's Travels* (NBC)
Variety/music/comedy: *Dennis Miller Live* (HBO)
Informational: *Lost Civilizations* (NBC)

1997
Comedy: *Frasier* (NBC)
Drama: *Law & Order* (NBC)
Miniseries: *Prime Suspect 5: Errors of Judgment* (PBS)
Variety/music/comedy: *Tracey Takes On...* (HBO)
Informational: *Biography* (A&E); *The Great War and the Shaping of the 20th Century* (PBS)

1998
Comedy: *Frasier* (NBC)
Drama: *The Practice* (ABC)
Miniseries: *From the Earth to the Moon* (HBO)
Variety/music/comedy: *Late Show with David Letterman* (CBS)
Nonfiction: *The American Experience* (PBS)

1999
Comedy: *Ally McBeal* (Fox)
Drama: *The Practice* (ABC)
Miniseries: *Horatio Hornblower: The Even Chance* (A&E)
Variety/music/comedy: *Late Show with David Letterman* (CBS)
Nonfiction: *The American Experience* (PBS); *American Masters* (PBS)

2000
Comedy: *Will & Grace* (NBC)
Drama: *The West Wing* (NBC)
Miniseries: *The Corner* (HBO)
Variety/music/comedy: *Late Show with David Letterman* (CBS)
Nonfiction: *American Masters* (PBS)

2001
Comedy: *Sex and the City* (HBO)
Drama: *The West Wing* (NBC)
Miniseries: *Anne Frank* (ABC)
Variety/music/comedy: *Late Show with David Letterman* (CBS)
Nonfiction: *American Masters* (PBS)

2002
Comedy: *Friends* (NBC)
Drama: *The West Wing* (NBC)
Miniseries: *Band of Brothers* (HBO)
Variety/music/comedy: *Late Show with David Letterman* (CBS)
Nonfiction: *Biography* (A&E)

2003
Comedy: *Everybody Loves Raymond* (CBS)
Drama: *The West Wing* (NBC)
Miniseries: *Steven Spielberg Presents Taken* (Sci Fi)
Variety/music/comedy: *The Daily Show with Jon Stewart* (Comedy Central)
Nonfiction: *American Masters* (PBS)

2004
Comedy: *Arrested Development* (Fox)
Drama: *The Sopranos* (HBO)
Miniseries: *Angels in America* (HBO)
Variety/music/comedy: *The Daily Show with Jon Stewart* (Comedy Central)
Nonfiction: *American Masters* (PBS)

2005
Comedy: *Everybody Loves Raymond* (CBS)
Drama: *Lost* (ABC)
Miniseries: *Masterpiece Theatre: The Lost Prince* (PBS)
Variety/music/comedy: *The Daily Show with Jon Stewart* (Comedy Central)
Nonfiction: *Broadway: The American Musical* (PBS)

2006
Comedy: *The Office* (NBC)
Drama: *24* (Fox)
Miniseries: *Elizabeth I* (HBO)
Variety/music/comedy: *The Daily Show with Jon Stewart* (Comedy Central)
Nonfiction: *10 Days That Unexpectedly Changed America* (The History Channel)

2007
Comedy: *30 Rock* (NBC)
Drama: *The Sopranos* (HBO)
Miniseries: *Broken Trail* (AMC)
Variety/music/comedy: *The Daily Show with Jon Stewart* (Comedy Central)
Nonfiction: *Planet Earth* (Discovery Channel)

Emmy Awards, 1949–2010[1] (continued)

2008
Comedy: *30 Rock* (NBC)
Drama: *Mad Men* (AMC)
Miniseries: *John Adams* (HBO)
Variety/music/comedy: *The Daily Show with Jon Stewart* (Comedy Central)
Nonfiction: *American Masters* (PBS); *This American Life* (Showtime)

2009
Comedy: *30 Rock* (NBC)
Drama: *Mad Men* (AMC)
Miniseries: *Little Dorrit* (PBS)

2009 (continued)
Variety/music/comedy: *The Daily Show with Jon Stewart* (Comedy Central)
Nonfiction: *American Masters* (PBS)

2010
Comedy: *Modern Family* (ABC)
Drama: *Mad Men* (AMC)
Miniseries: *The Pacific* (HBO)
Variety/music/comedy: *The Daily Show with Jon Stewart* (Comedy Central)
Nonfiction: *The National Parks: America's Best Idea* (PBS)

[1]*From 1949 to 1958, awards were given for programs broadcast the previous year only; awards since have been given for programs broadcast in part of the previous year and in part of the year named.*

Theater

Tony Awards, 2010

The American Theatre Wing (ATW), established in 1939, created the Tony Awards, named for former ATW director Antoinette Perry, in 1947 to recognize distinguished achievement in the theater arts as presented on Broadway; since 1967 they have been presented in conjunction with the Broadway League (formerly the League of American Theatres and Producers), a trade association. Nominees are selected each May from among the year's new or newly revived Broadway shows; a body of some 700 current and former theater professionals, critics, and agents votes for the winners. The awards are presented in New York City in June. Prize: silver medallion, set in a base, depicting on one face the masks of tragedy and comedy and on the other the profile of Antoinette Perry.
Tony Awards Web site: <www.tonyawards.com>.

▶ **musical:** *Memphis* (book, Joe DiPietro; music, David Bryan; lyrics, Joe DiPietro and David Bryan); ▶ **play:** *Red* (playwright, John Logan); ▶ **revival of a musical:** *La Cage aux Folles* (book, Harvey Fierstein; music and lyrics, Jerry Herman); ▶ **revival of a play:** *Fences* (playwright, August Wilson); ▶ **book, musical:** *Memphis*; ▶ **score:** David Bryan (music) and Joe DiPietro and David Bryan (lyrics) (*Memphis*); ▶ **leading actress, musical:** Catherine Zeta-Jones (*A Little Night Music*); ▶ **leading actor, musical:** Douglas Hodge (*La Cage aux Folles*); ▶ **leading actress, play:** Viola Davis (*Fences*); ▶ **leading actor, play:** Denzel Washington (*Fences*); ▶ **featured actress, musical:** Katie Finneran (*Promises, Promises*); ▶ **featured actor, musical:** Levi Kreis (*Million Dollar Quartet*); ▶ **featured actress, play:** Scarlett Johansson (*A View from the Bridge*); ▶ **featured actor, play:** Eddie Redmayne (*Red*); ▶ **direction, musical:** Terry Johnson (*La Cage aux Folles*); ▶ **direction, play:** Michael Grandage (*Red*); ▶ **costume design, musical:** Marina Draghici (*Fela!*); ▶ **costume design, play:** Catherine Zuber (*The Royal Family*); ▶ **lighting design, musical:** Kevin Adams (*American Idiot*); ▶ **lighting design, play:** Neil Austin (*Red*); ▶ **scenic design, musical:** Christine Jones (*American Idiot*); ▶ **scenic design, play:** Christopher Oram (*Red*); ▶ **sound design, musical:** Robert Kaplowitz (*Fela!*); ▶ **sound design, play:** Adam Cork (*Red*); ▶ **orchestrations:** Daryl Waters and David Bryan (*Memphis*); ▶ **choreography:** Bill T. Jones (*Fela!*); ▶ **regional theater award:** The Eugene O'Neill Theater Center, Waterford CT; ▶ **lifetime achievement:** Alan Ayckbourn and Marian Seldes.

Tony Awards, 1947–2010

YEAR	BEST MUSICAL	BEST PLAY
1947	*not awarded*	*All My Sons* (Arthur Miller)[1]
1948	*not awarded*	*Mister Roberts* (Thomas Heggen and Joshua Logan)
1949	*Kiss Me, Kate* (book, Bella Spewack and Samuel Spewack; music and lyrics, Cole Porter)	*Death of a Salesman* (Arthur Miller)
1950	*South Pacific* (book, Oscar Hammerstein II and Joshua Logan; music, Richard Rodgers; lyrics, Oscar Hammerstein II)	*The Cocktail Party* (T.S. Eliot)
1951	*Guys and Dolls* (book, Jo Swerling and Abe Burrows; music and lyrics, Frank Loesser)	*The Rose Tattoo* (Tennessee Williams)
1952	*The King and I* (book and lyrics, Oscar Hammerstein II; music, Richard Rodgers)	*The Fourposter* (Jan de Hartog)

Tony Awards, 1947–2010 (continued)

YEAR	BEST MUSICAL	BEST PLAY
1953	*Wonderful Town* (book, Joseph Fields and Jerome Chodorov; music, Leonard Bernstein; lyrics, Betty Comden and Adolph Green)	*The Crucible* (Arthur Miller)
1954	*Kismet* (book, Charles Lederer and Luther Davis; music, Alexander Borodin; adaptation and lyrics, Robert Wright and George Forrest)	*The Teahouse of the August Moon* (John Patrick)
1955	*The Pajama Game* (book, George Abbott and Richard Bissell; music and lyrics, Richard Adler and Jerry Ross)	*The Desperate Hours* (Joseph Hayes)
1956	*Damn Yankees* (book, George Abbott and Douglass Wallop; music and lyrics, Richard Adler and Jerry Ross)	*The Diary of Anne Frank* (Frances Goodrich and Albert Hackett)
1957	*My Fair Lady* (book and lyrics, Alan Jay Lerner; music, Frederick Loewe)	*Long Day's Journey into Night* (Eugene O'Neill)
1958	*The Music Man* (book, Meredith Willson and Franklin Lacey; music and lyrics, Meredith Willson)	*Sunrise at Campobello* (Dore Schary)
1959	*Redhead* (book, Herbert Fields, Dorothy Fields, Sidney Sheldon, and David Shaw; music, Albert Hague; lyrics, Dorothy Fields)	*J.B.* (Archibald MacLeish)
1960	*The Sound of Music* (book, Howard Lindsay and Russel Crouse; music, Richard Rodgers; lyrics, Oscar Hammerstein II); *Fiorello!* (book, Jerome Weidman and George Abbott; music, Jerry Brock; lyrics, Sheldon Harnick) (tied)	*The Miracle Worker* (William Gibson)
1961	*Bye Bye Birdie* (book, Michael Stewart; music, Charles Strouse; lyrics, Lee Adams)	*Beckett* (Jean Anouilh, translated by Lucienne Hill)
1962	*How To Succeed in Business Without Really Trying* (book, Abe Burrows, Jack Weinstock, and Willie Gilbert; music and lyrics, Frank Loesser)	*A Man for All Seasons* (Robert Bolt)
1963	*A Funny Thing Happened on the Way to the Forum* (book, Burt Shevelove and Larry Gelbart; music and lyrics, Stephen Sondheim)	*Who's Afraid of Virginia Woolf?* (Edward Albee)
1964	*Hello, Dolly!* (book, Michael Stewart; music and lyrics, Jerry Herman)	*Luther* (John Osborne)
1965	*Fiddler on the Roof* (book, Joseph Stein; music, Jerry Bock; lyrics, Sheldon Harnick)	*The Subject Was Roses* (Frank Gilroy)
1966	*Man of La Mancha* (book, Dale Wasserman; music, Mitch Leigh; lyrics, Joe Darion)	*Marat/Sade* (Peter Weiss, translated by Geoffrey Skelton)
1967	*Cabaret* (book, Joe Masteroff; music, John Kander; lyrics, Fred Ebb)	*The Homecoming* (Harold Pinter)
1968	*Hallelujah, Baby!* (book, Arthur Laurents; music, Jule Styne; lyrics, Betty Comden and Adolph Green)	*Rosencrantz and Guildenstern Are Dead* (Tom Stoppard)
1969	*1776* (book, Peter Stone; music and lyrics, Sherman Edwards)	*The Great White Hope* (Howard Sackler)
1970	*Applause* (book, Betty Comden and Adolph Green; music, Charles Strouse; lyrics, Lee Adams)	*Borstal Boy* (Frank McMahon)
1971	*Company* (book, George Furth; music and lyrics, Stephen Sondheim)	*Sleuth* (Anthony Shaffer)
1972	*Two Gentlemen of Verona* (book, John Guare and Mel Shapiro; music, Galt MacDermot; lyrics, John Guare)	*Sticks and Bones* (David Rabe)
1973	*A Little Night Music* (book, Hugh Wheeler; music and lyrics, Stephen Sondheim)	*That Championship Season* (Jason Miller)
1974	*Raisin* (book, Robert Nemiroff and Charlotte Zaltzberg; music, Judd Woldin; lyrics, Robert Brittan)	*The River Niger* (Joseph A. Walker)
1975	*The Wiz* (book, William F. Brown; music and lyrics, Charlie Smalls)	*Equus* (Peter Shaffer)
1976	*A Chorus Line* (book, James Kirkwood and Nicholas Dante; music, Marvin Hamlisch; lyrics, Edward Kleban)	*Travesties* (Tom Stoppard)
1977	*Annie* (book, Thomas Meehan; music, Charles Strouse; lyrics, Martin Charnin)	*The Shadow Box* (Michael Christofer)
1978	*Ain't Misbehavin'* (book, Murray Horwitz and Richard Maltby, Jr.; music, Fats Waller; lyrics, Fats Waller and many others)	*Da* (Hugh Leonard)
1979	*Sweeney Todd* (book, Hugh Wheeler; music and lyrics, Stephen Sondheim)	*The Elephant Man* (Bernard Pomerance)
1980	*Evita* (book and lyrics, Tim Rice; music, Andrew Lloyd Webber)	*Children of a Lesser God* (Mark Medoff)
1981	*42nd Street* (book, Michael Stewart and Mark Bramble; music, Harry Warren; lyrics, Al Dubin)	*Amadeus* (Peter Shaffer)
1982	*Nine* (book, Arthur Kopit; music and lyrics, Maury Yeston)	*The Life and Adventures of Nicholas Nickleby* (David Edgar)
1983	*Cats* (book and lyrics, T.S. Eliot; music, Andrew Lloyd Webber)	*Torch Song Trilogy* (Harvey Fierstein)
1984	*La Cage aux folles* (book, Harvey Fierstein; music and lyrics, Jerry Herman)	*The Real Thing* (Tom Stoppard)
1985	*Big River* (book, William Hauptman; music and lyrics, Roger Miller)	*Biloxi Blues* (Neil Simon)
1900	*The Mystery of Edwin Drood* (book, music, and lyrics, Rupert Holmes)	*I'm Not Rappaport* (Herb Gardner)
1987	*Les Misérables* (book, Alain Boublil and Claude-Michel Schönberg; music, Claude-Michel Schönberg; lyrics, Herbert Kretzmer and Alain Boublil)	*Fences* (August Wilson)

Tony Awards, 1947–2010 (continued)

YEAR	BEST MUSICAL	BEST PLAY
1988	*The Phantom of the Opera* (book, Richard Stilgoe and Andrew Lloyd Webber; music, Andrew Lloyd Webber; lyrics, Charles Hart and Richard Stilgoe)	*M. Butterfly* (David Henry Hwang)
1989	*Jerome Robbins' Broadway* (compilation)	*The Heidi Chronicles* (Wendy Wasserstein)
1990	*City of Angels* (book, Larry Gelbart; music, Cy Coleman; lyrics, David Zippel)	*The Grapes of Wrath* (Frank Galati)
1991	*The Will Rogers Follies* (book, Peter Stone; music, Cy Coleman; lyrics, Betty Comden and Adolph Green)	*Lost in Yonkers* (Neil Simon)
1992	*Crazy for You* (book, Ken Ludwig; music and lyrics, George Gershwin and Ira Gershwin)	*Dancing at Lughnasa* (Brian Friel)
1993	*Kiss of the Spider Woman* (book, Terrence McNally; music, John Kander; lyrics, Fred Ebb)	*Angels in America: Millennium Approaches* (Tony Kushner)
1994	*Passion* (book, James Lapine; music and lyrics, Stephen Sondheim)	*Angels in America: Perestroika* (Tony Kushner)
1995	*Sunset Boulevard* (book and lyrics, Don Black and Christopher Hampton; music, Andrew Lloyd Webber)	*Love! Valour! Compassion!* (Terrence McNally)
1996	*Rent* (book, music, and lyrics, Jonathan Larson)	*Master Class* (Terrence McNally)
1997	*Titanic* (book, Peter Stone; music and lyrics, Maury Yeston)	*The Last Night of Ballyhoo* (Alfred Uhry)
1998	*The Lion King* (book, Roger Allers and Irene Mecchi; music and lyrics, Elton John, Tim Rice, and others)	*Art* (Yasmina Reza)
1999	*Fosse* (compilation)	*Side Man* (Warren Leight)
2000	*Contact* (book, John Weidman; music and lyrics, various artists)	*Copenhagen* (Michael Frayn)
2001	*The Producers* (book, Mel Brooks and Thomas Meehan; music and lyrics, Mel Brooks)	*Proof* (David Auburn)
2002	*Thoroughly Modern Millie* (book, Richard Morris and Dick Scanlan; music, Jeanine Tesori; lyrics, Dick Scanlan)	*The Goat, or Who Is Sylvia?* (Edward Albee)
2003	*Hairspray* (book, Mark O'Donnell and Thomas Meehan; music, Marc Shaiman; lyrics, Scott Wittman and Marc Shaiman)	*Take Me Out* (Richard Greenberg)
2004	*Avenue Q* (book, Jeff Whitty; music and lyrics, Robert Lopez and Jeff Marx)	*I Am My Own Wife* (Doug Wright)
2005	*Monty Python's Spamalot* (book, Eric Idle; music and lyrics, John Du Prez and Eric Idle)	*Doubt* (John Patrick Shanley)
2006	*Jersey Boys* (book, Marshall Brickman and Rick Elice; music, Bob Gaudio; lyrics, Bob Crewe)	*The History Boys* (Alan Bennett)
2007	*Spring Awakening* (book and lyrics, Steven Sater; music, Duncan Sheik)	*The Coast of Utopia* (Tom Stoppard)
2008	*In the Heights* (book, Quiara Alegría Hudes; music and lyrics, Lin-Manuel Miranda)	*August: Osage County* (Tracy Letts)
2009	*Billy Elliot: The Musical* (book and lyrics, Lee Hall; music, Elton John)	*God of Carnage* (Yasmina Reza)
2010	*Memphis* (book, Joe DiPietro; music, David Bryan; lyrics, Joe DiPietro and David Bryan)	*Red* (John Logan)

[1]Awarded to playwright for Best Author.

Longest-Running Broadway Shows

As of 23 Aug 2010. Source: *Internet Broadway Database, <www.ibdb.com>.*

	SHOW	RUN	PERFORMANCES		SHOW	RUN	PERFORMANCES
1	*The Phantom of the Opera*	1988–	9,379	6	*Chicago* (revival)	1996–	5,708
2	*Cats*	1982–2000	7,485	7	*Beauty and the Beast*	1994–2007	5,461
3	*Les Misérables*	1987–2003	6,680	8	*The Lion King*	1997–	5,293
4	*A Chorus Line*	1975–90	6,137	9	*Rent*	1996–2008	5,123
5	*Oh! Calcutta!* (revival)	1976–89	5,959	10	*Miss Saigon*	1991–2001	4,092

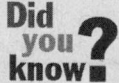

Did you know? Ava Gardner, who transformed herself from tomboyish farm girl into one of the most beautiful women in screen history, was given a screen test by MGM studios in 1941. In it, her lack of refinement was painfully evident and her thick southern drawl rendered much of what she said unintelligible. Upon seeing the test, studio chief Louis B. Mayer declared, "She can't act. She can't talk. She's terrific. Sign her."

Encyclopædia Britannica's 20 Notable US Theater Companies

COMPANY	LOCATION	ARTISTIC DIRECTOR (2010)
The Acting Company	New York NY	Margot Harley[1]
Actors Theatre of Louisville	Louisville KY	Marc Masterson
Alley Theatre	Houston TX	Gregory Boyd
American Conservatory Theater	San Francisco CA	Carey Perloff
American Repertory Theatre	Cambridge MA	Diane Paulus
Arena Stage	Washington DC	Molly Smith
Center Theatre Group	Los Angeles CA	Michael Ritchie
Chicago Shakespeare Theater	Chicago IL	Barbara Gaines
Denver Center Theatre Company	Denver CO	Kent Thompson
El Teatro Campesino	San Juan Bautista CA	Luis Valdez
Folger Theatre	Washington DC	Janet Alexander Griffin[2]
Goodman Theatre	Chicago IL	Robert Falls
Guthrie Theater	Minneapolis MN	Joe Dowling[3]
La Jolla Playhouse	La Jolla CA	Christopher Ashley
Long Wharf Theatre	New Haven CT	Gordon Edelstein
Oregon Shakespeare Festival	Ashland OR	Bill Rauch
The Public Theater	New York NY	Oskar Eustis
Seattle Repertory Theatre	Seattle WA	Jerry Manning
Steppenwolf Theatre Company	Chicago IL	Martha Lavey
Yale Repertory Theatre	New Haven CT	James Bundy

[1]*Producing artistic director.*   [2]*Artistic producer.*   [3]*Director.*

Music

Grammy Awards, 2009

The Grammys, first awarded in 1958, recognize excellence in the recording industry without regard to record sales or chart position. Nominees and winners are selected by the members of the National Academy of Recording Arts and Sciences according to the members' areas of expertise. In addition to the four general categories (record, album, and song of the year and best new artist) for which all members are eligible to vote, for 2009 there were 110 categories in 29 fields, of which Academy members were permitted to vote in no more than 8 fields. Prizes for works released 1 Oct 2008–31 Aug 2009 were awarded in Los Angeles on 31 Jan 2010. Prize: gold miniature phonograph.

Grammy Award Web site: <www.grammy.com>.

category: winner (performer in parentheses for songwriting/production awards)

▶ **record (single) of the year:** "Use Somebody," Kings of Leon; ▶ **album of the year:** *Fearless*, Taylor Swift; ▶ **song of the year:** "Single Ladies (Put a Ring on It)," Thaddis Harrell, Beyoncé Knowles, Terius Nash, and Christopher Stewart, songwriters (Beyoncé); ▶ **new artist:** Zac Brown Band; ▶ **pop vocal performance, female:** "Halo," Beyoncé; ▶ **pop vocal performance, male:** "Make It Mine," Jason Mraz; ▶ **pop vocal performance, duo/group:** "I Got a Feeling," The Black Eyed Peas; ▶ **pop vocal album:** *The E.N.D.*, The Black Eyed Peas; ▶ **pop vocal album, traditional:** *Michael Bublé Meets Madison Square Garden*, Michael Bublé; ▶ **rock vocal performance, solo:** "Working on a Dream," Bruce Springsteen; ▶ **rock vocal performance, duo/group:** "Use Somebody," Kings of Leon; ▶ **hard rock performance:** "War Machine," AC/DC; ▶ **metal performance:** "Dissident Aggressor," Judas Priest; ▶ **rock song:** "Use Somebody," Caleb Followill, Jared Followill, Matthew Followill, and Nathan Followill, songwriters (Kings of Leon); ▶ **rock album:** *21st Century Breakdown*, Green Day; ▶ **alternative music album:** *Wolfgang Amadeus Phoenix*, Phoenix; ▶ **R&B vocal performance, female:** "Single Ladies (Put a Ring on It)," Beyoncé; ▶ **R&B vocal performance, male:** "Pretty Wings," Maxwell; ▶ **R&B vocal performance, duo/group:** "Blame It," Jamie Foxx and T-Pain ▶ **R&B song:** "Single Ladies (Put a Ring on It)," Thaddis Harrell, Beyoncé Knowles, Terius Nash, and Christopher Stewart, songwriters (Beyoncé); ▶ **R&B album:** *Blacksummers' Night*, Maxwell; ▶ **R&B album, contemporary:** *I Am...Sasha Fierce*, Beyoncé; ▶ **rap performance, solo:** "D.O.A. (Death of Auto-Tune)," Jay-Z; ▶ **rap performance, duo/group:** "Crack a Bottle," Eminem, Dr. Dre, and 50 Cent; ▶ **rap song:** "Run This Town," Athanasios Alatas, Jeff Bhasker, Shawn Carter, Robyn Fenty, Kanye West, and Ernest Wilson, songwriters (Jay-Z, Rihanna, and Kanye West); ▶ **rap album:** *Relapse*, Eminem; ▶ **country vocal performance, female:** "White Horse," Taylor Swift; ▶ **country vocal performance, male:** "Sweet Thing," Keith Urban; ▶ **country vocal performance, duo/group:** "I Run to You," Lady Antebellum; ▶ **country song:** "White Horse," Liz Rose and Taylor Swift, songwriters (Taylor Swift); ▶ **country album:** *Fearless*, Taylor Swift; ▶ **bluegrass album:** *The Crow/New Songs for the Five-String Banjo*, Steve Martin; ▶ **new age album:** *Prayer for Compassion*, David Darling; ▶ **jazz album, contemporary:** *75*, Joe Zawinul & The Zawinul Syndicate; ▶ **jazz vocal album:** *Dedicated to You: Kurt Elling Sings the Music of Coltrane and Hartman*, Kurt Elling; ▶ **jazz instrumental solo:** Terence Blan-

Grammy Awards, 2009 (continued)

chard ("Dancin' 4 Chicken"); ▶ **jazz instrumental album:** *Five Peace Band–Live,* Chick Corea and John McLaughlin Five Peace Band; ▶ **jazz album, large ensemble:** *Book One,* New Orleans Jazz Orchestra; ▶ **jazz album, Latin:** *Juntos para siempre,* Bebo Valdés and Chucho Valdés; ▶ **gospel song:** "God in Me," Erica Campbell, Tina Campbell, and Warryn Campbell, songwriters (Mary Mary featuring Kierra "KiKi" Sheard); ▶ **gospel album, rock/rap:** *Live Revelations,* Third Day; ▶ **gospel album, pop/contemporary:** *The Power of One,* Israel Houghton; ▶ **gospel album, Southern/country/bluegrass:** *Jason Crabb,* Jason Crabb; ▶ **gospel album, traditional:** *Oh Happy Day,* various artists; ▶ **gospel album, contemporary R&B:** *Audience of One,* Heather Headley; ▶ **Latin album, pop:** *Sin frenos,* La Quinta Estación; ▶ **Latin album, rock/alternative/urban:** *Los de atras vienen conmigo,* Calle 13; ▶ **Latin album, tropical:** *Ciclos,* Luis Enrique; ▶ **regional Mexican album:** *Necesito de ti,* Vicente Fernández; ▶ **Tejano album:** *Borders y bailes,* Los Texmaniacs; ▶ **blues album, traditional:** *A Stranger Here,* Ramblin' Jack Elliott; ▶ **blues album, contemporary:** *Already Free,* The Derek Trucks Band; ▶ **folk album, traditional:** *High Wide & Handsome: The Charlie Poole Project;* Loudon Wainwright III; ▶ **folk album, contemporary:** *Townes,* Steve Earle; ▶ **Native American music album:** *Spirit Wind North,* Bill Miller; ▶ **Hawaiian music album:** *Masters of Hawaiian Slack Key Guitar, Volume 2,* various artists; ▶ **reggae album:** *Mind Control–Acoustic,* Stephen

Marley; ▶ **world music album, traditional:** *Douga Mansa,* Mamadou Diabate; ▶ **world music album, contemporary:** *Throw Down Your Heart: Tales from the Acoustic Planet, Vol. 3—Africa Sessions,* Béla Fleck; ▶ **spoken word album:** *Always Looking Up,* Michael J. Fox; ▶ **comedy album:** *A Colbert Christmas: The Greatest Gift of All!,* Stephen Colbert; ▶ **producer, nonclassical:** Brendan O'Brien; ▶ **producer, classical:** Steven Epstein; ▶ **classical album:** *Mahler: Symphony No. 8; Adagio from Symphony No. 10,* Michael Tilson Thomas, conductor; Andreas Neubronner, producer (San Francisco Symphony, Pacific Boychoir, San Francisco Girls Chorus, and San Francisco Symphony Chorus); ▶ **orchestral performance:** *Ravel: Daphis et Chloé,* Boston Symphony Orchestra and Tanglewood Festival Chorus; James Levine, conductor; ▶ **opera recording:** *Britten: Billy Budd,* Daniel Harding, conductor; Ian Bostridge, Neal Davies, Nathan Gunn, Jonathan Lemalu, Matthew Rose, and Gidon Saks, soloists; John Fraser, producer (London Symphony Orchestra and Gentlemen of the London Symphony Chorus); ▶ **chamber music performance:** *Intimate Letters,* Emerson String Quartet; ▶ **classical vocal performance:** *Verismo Arias,* Renée Fleming, soloist; ▶ **contemporary classical composition:** *Higdon, Jennifer: Percussion Concerto,* Jennifer Higdon, composer; ▶ **short-form music video:** "Boom Boom Pow," The Black Eyed Peas; Mathew Cullen and Mark Kudsi, directors; Javier Jimenez, Anna Joseph, and Patrick Nugent, producers

Grammy Awards, 1958–2009

The year denotes the period (from the fall of the previous year to the fall of the year named) for which the winning work or artist was recognized; the prizes are generally awarded during the following year.

YEAR	RECORD (SINGLE) OF THE YEAR	ALBUM OF THE YEAR	BEST NEW ARTIST
1958	"Nel blu dipinto di blu (Volare)," Domenico Modugno	*The Music from Peter Gunn,* Henry Mancini	*not awarded*
1959	"Mack the Knife," Bobby Darin	*Come Dance with Me,* Frank Sinatra	Bobby Darin
1960	"The Theme from *A Summer Place,*" Percy Faith	*The Button-Down Mind of Bob Newhart,* Bob Newhart	Bob Newhart
1961	"Moon River," Henry Mancini	*Judy at Carnegie Hall,* Judy Garland	Peter Nero
1962	"I Left My Heart in San Francisco," Tony Bennett	*The First Family,* Vaughn Meader	Robert Goulet
1963	"The Days of Wine and Roses," Henry Mancini	*The Barbra Streisand Album,* Barbra Streisand	Ward Swingle (The Swingle Singers)
1964	"The Girl from Ipanema," Stan Getz and Astrud Gilberto	*Getz/Gilberto,* Stan Getz and João Gilberto	The Beatles
1965	"A Taste of Honey," Herb Alpert	*September of My Years,* Frank Sinatra	Tom Jones
1966	"Strangers in the Night," Frank Sinatra	*A Man and His Music,* Frank Sinatra	*not awarded*
1967	"Up, Up, and Away," The 5th Dimension	*Sgt. Pepper's Lonely Hearts Club Band,* The Beatles	Bobbie Gentry
1968	"Mrs. Robinson," Simon & Garfunkel	*By the Time I Get to Phoenix,* Glen Campbell	José Feliciano
1969	"Aquarius/Let the Sunshine In," The 5th Dimension	*Blood, Sweat & Tears,* Blood, Sweat & Tears	Crosby, Stills & Nash
1970	"Bridge over Troubled Water," Simon & Garfunkel	*Bridge over Troubled Water,* Simon & Garfunkel	The Carpenters
1971	"It's Too Late," Carole King	*Tapestry,* Carole King	Carly Simon
1972	"The First Time Ever I Saw Your Face," Roberta Flack	*The Concert for Bangla Desh,* George Harrison and Friends	America
1973	"Killing Me Softly with His Song," Roberta Flack	*Innervisions,* Stevie Wonder	Bette Midler
1974	"I Honestly Love You," Olivia Newton-John	*Fulfillingness' First Finale,* Stevie Wonder	Marvin Hamlisch
1975	"Love Will Keep Us Together," Captain & Tennille	*Still Crazy After All These Years,* Paul Simon	Natalie Cole

Grammy Awards, 1958–2009 (continued)

YEAR	RECORD (SINGLE) OF THE YEAR	ALBUM OF THE YEAR	BEST NEW ARTIST
1976	"This Masquerade," George Benson	Songs in the Key of Life, Stevie Wonder	Starland Vocal Band
1977	"Hotel California," The Eagles	Rumours, Fleetwood Mac	Debby Boone
1978	"Just the Way You Are," Billy Joel	Saturday Night Fever, The Bee Gees	A Taste of Honey
1979	"What a Fool Believes," The Doobie Brothers	52nd Steet, Billy Joel	Rickie Lee Jones
1980	"Sailing," Christopher Cross	Christopher Cross, Christopher Cross	Christopher Cross
1981	"Bette Davis Eyes," Kim Carnes	Double Fantasy, John Lennon and Yoko Ono	Sheena Easton
1982	"Rosanna," Toto	Toto IV, Toto	Men at Work
1983	"Beat It," Michael Jackson	Thriller, Michael Jackson	Culture Club
1984	"What's Love Got To Do with It," Tina Turner	Can't Slow Down, Lionel Richie	Cyndi Lauper
1985	"We Are the World," USA for Africa	No Jacket Required, Phil Collins	Sade
1986	"Higher Love," Steve Winwood	Graceland, Paul Simon	Bruce Hornsby and the Range
1987	"Graceland," Paul Simon	The Joshua Tree, U2	Jody Watley
1988	"Don't Worry, Be Happy," Bobby McFerrin	Faith, George Michael	Tracy Chapman
1989	"Wind Beneath My Wings," Bette Midler	Nick of Time, Bonnie Raitt	Milli Vanilli (revoked)
1990	"Another Day in Paradise," Phil Collins	Back on the Block, Quincy Jones	Mariah Carey
1991	"Unforgettable," Natalie Cole with Nat King Cole	Unforgettable: With Love, Natalie Cole	Marc Cohn
1992	"Tears in Heaven," Eric Clapton	Unplugged, Eric Clapton	Arrested Development
1993	"I Will Always Love You," Whitney Houston	The Bodyguard, Whitney Houston	Toni Braxton
1994	"All I Wanna Do," Sheryl Crow	MTV Unplugged, Tony Bennett	Sheryl Crow
1995	"Kiss from a Rose," Seal	Jagged Little Pill, Alanis Morissette	Hootie and the Blowfish
1996	"Change the World," Eric Clapton	Falling into You, Celine Dion	LeAnn Rimes
1997	"Sunny Came Home," Shawn Colvin	Time Out of Mind, Bob Dylan	Paula Cole
1998	"My Heart Will Go On," Celine Dion	The Miseducation of Lauryn Hill, Lauryn Hill	Lauryn Hill
1999	"Smooth," Santana featuring Rob Thomas	Supernatural, Santana	Christina Aguilera
2000	"Beautiful Day," U2	Two Against Nature, Steely Dan	Shelby Lynne
2001	"Walk On," U2	O Brother, Where Art Thou?, various artists	Alicia Keys
2002	"Don't Know Why," Norah Jones	Come Away with Me, Norah Jones	Norah Jones
2003	"Clocks," Coldplay	Speakerboxxx/The Love Below, OutKast	Evanescence
2004	"Here We Go Again," Ray Charles and Norah Jones	Genius Loves Company, Ray Charles and various artists	Maroon 5
2005	"Boulevard of Broken Dreams," Green Day	How To Dismantle an Atomic Bomb, U2	John Legend
2006	"Not Ready To Make Nice," Dixie Chicks	Taking the Long Way, Dixie Chicks	Carrie Underwood
2007	"Rehab," Amy Winehouse	River: The Joni Letters, Herbie Hancock	Amy Winehouse
2008	"Please Read the Letter," Robert Plant and Alison Krauss	Raising Sand, Robert Plant and Alison Krauss	Adele
2009	"Use Somebody," Kings of Leon	Fearless, Taylor Swift	Zac Brown Band

Eurovision Song Contest

The European Broadcasting Union (EBU), an association of television and radio companies from Europe and the Mediterranean, began the Eurovision Song Contest in 1956. Each EBU member country, along with several provisional participants, can nominate one original song per year, with a maximum length of three minutes. The winner is selected based on votes from fans and juries in each participating country. Prize: crystal microphone. **Eurovision Song Contest Web site:** <www.eurovision.tv>.

YEAR	SONG, SONGWRITER(S) (PERFORMER, COUNTRY)
1956	"Refrain," Émile Gardaz, Géo Voumard (Lys Assia, Switzerland)
1957	"Net als toen," Willy van Hemert, Guus Jansen (Corry Brokken, Netherlands)

Eurovision Song Contest (continued)

YEAR   SONG, SONGWRITER(S) (PERFORMER, COUNTRY)
1958   "Dors mon amour," Pierre Delanoë, Hubert Giraud (André Claveau, France)
1959   "Een beetje," Willy van Hemert, Dick Schallies (Teddy Scholten, Netherlands)
1960   "Tom Pillibi," Pierre Cour, André Popp (Jacqueline Boyer, France)
1961   "Nous les amoureux," Jacques Datin, Maurice Vidalin (Jean-Claude Pascal, Luxembourg)
1962   "Un Premier amour," Rolande Valade, Claude Henri Vic (Isabelle Aubret, France)
1963   "Dansevise," Sejr Volmer-Sørensen, Otto Francker (Grethe and Jørgen Ingmann, Denmark)
1964   "Non ho l'étà," Nicola Salerno (Gigliola Cinquetti, Italy)
1965   "Poupée de cire, poupée de son," Serge Gainsbourg (France Gall, Luxembourg)
1966   "Merci chérie," Udo Jürgens, Thomas Hörbiger (Udo Jürgens, Austria)
1967   "Puppet on a String," Bill Martin, Phil Coulter (Sandie Shaw, United Kingdom)
1968   "La, la, la," Ramón Arcusa, Manuel de la Calva (Massiel, Spain)
1969   "Vivo cantando," Aniano Alcalde, Maria José de Cerato (Salomé, Spain); "Boom Bang-a-Bang," Peter Warne,
       Alan Moorhouse (Lulu, United Kingdom); "De troubadour," Lenny Kuhr, David Hartsena (Lenny Kuhr,
       Netherlands); "Un Jour, un enfant," Eddy Marnay, Emile Stern (Frida Boccara, France) (four-way tie)
1970   "All Kinds of Everything," Derry Lindsay, Jackie Smith (Dana, Ireland)
1971   "Un Banc, un arbre, une rue," Yves Dessca, Jean-Pierre Bourtayre (Séverine, Monaco)
1972   "Après toi," Klaus Munro, Yves Dessca, Mario Panas (Vicky Leandros, Luxembourg)
1973   "Tu te reconnaîtras," Vline Buggy, Claude Morgan (Anne-Marie David, Luxembourg)
1974   "Waterloo," Stikkan Anderson, Benny Andersson, Björn Ulvaeus (ABBA, Sweden)
1975   "Ding-a-Dong," Will Luikinga, Eddy Ouwens, Dick Bakker (Teach-In, Netherlands)
1976   "Save Your Kisses for Me," Tony Hiller, Lee Sheriden, Martin Lee (Brotherhood of Man, United Kingdom)
1977   "L'Oiseau et l'enfant," José Gracy, Jean-Paul Cara (Marie Myriam, France)
1978   "A-Ba-Ni-Bi," Ehud Manor, Nurit Hirsh (Izhar Cohen and the Alphabeta, Israel)
1979   "Hallelujah," Shimrit Orr, Kobi Oshrat (Gali Atari and Milk and Honey, Israel)
1980   "What's Another Year," Shay Healy (Johnny Logan, Ireland)
1981   "Making Your Mind Up," Andy Hill, John Danter (Bucks Fizz, United Kingdom)
1982   "Ein bisschen Frieden," Bernd Meinunger, Ralph Siegel (Nicole, West Germany)
1983   "Si la vie est cadeau," Alain Garcia, Jean-Pierre Millers (Corinne Hermès, Luxembourg)
1984   "Diggi-loo diggi-ley," Britt Lindeborg, Torgny Söderberg (Herrey's, Sweden)
1985   "La det swinge," Rolf Løvland (Bobbysocks, Norway)
1986   "J'aime la vie," Marino Atria, Jean-Pierre Furnémont, Angelo Crisci (Sandra Kim, Belgium)
1987   "Hold Me Now," Sean Sherrard (Johnny Logan, Ireland)
1988   "Ne partez pas sans moi," Nella Martinetti, Atilla Sereftug (Céline Dion, Switzerland)
1989   "Rock Me," Stevo Cvikich, Rajko Dujmich (Riva, Yugoslavia)
1990   "Insieme: 1992," Toto Cutugno (Toto Cutugno, Italy)
1991   "Fångad av en stormvind," Stephan Berg (Carola, Sweden)
1992   "Why Me," Sean Sherrard (Linda Martin, Ireland)
1993   "In Your Eyes," Jimmy Walsh (Niamh Kavanagh, Ireland)
1994   "Rock 'n' Roll Kids," Brendan Graham (Paul Harrington and Charlie McGettigan, Ireland)
1995   "Nocturne," Petter Skavlan, Rolf Løvland (Secret Garden, Norway)
1996   "The Voice," Brendan Graham (Eimear Quinn, Ireland)
1997   "Love Shine a Light," Kimberley Rew (Katrina and the Waves, United Kingdom)
1998   "Diva," Yoav Ginay (Dana International, Israel)
1999   "Take Me to Your Heaven," Gert Lengstrand (Charlotte Nilsson, Sweden)
2000   "Fly on the Wings of Love," Jørgen Olsen (Olsen Brothers, Denmark)
2001   "Everybody," Maian-Anna Kärmas, Ivar Must (Tanel Padar, Dave Benton, and 2XL, Estonia)
2002   "I Wanna," Marija Naumova, Marats Samauskis (Marie N, Latvia)
2003   "Every Way That I Can," Demir Demirkan, Sertab Erener (Sertab Erener, Turkey)
2004   "Wild Dances," Ruslana Lyzhichko, Aleksandr Ksenofontov (Ruslana, Ukraine)
2005   "My Number One," Christos Dantis, Natalia Germanou (Helena Paparizou, Greece)
2006   "Hard Rock Hallelujah," LORDI (LORDI, Finland)
2007   "Molitva," Sasa Milosevic Mare (Marija Serifovic, Serbia)
2008   "Believe," Dima Bilan, Jim Beanz (Dima Bilan, Russia)
2009   "Fairytale," Alexander Rybak (Alexander Rybak, Norway)
2010   "Satellite," Julie Frost, John Gordon (Lena, Germany)

Brit Awards, 2010

*The British Phonographic Industry, a trade association of record companies, established the Brit Awards in
1977 to recognize pop acts from Great Britain and abroad. Prize: statuette. Web site: <www.brits.co.uk>.*

British male solo artist: Dizzee Rascal
British female solo artist: Lily Allen
British breakthrough act: JLS
British group: Kasabian
MasterCard British album: Florence and the
   Machine, Lungs
British single: JLS, "Beat Again"

International male solo artist: Jay-Z
International female solo artist: Lady Gaga
International breakthrough act: Lady Gaga
International album: Jay-Z, The Blueprint 3
Outstanding contribution: Robbie Williams
Critics' choice: Ellie Goulding

Country Music Association Awards, 2009

The Country Music Association began its annual awards ceremony in 1967 and made it the first nationally televised music awards show the following year. Ceremonies are held in November. Prize: hand-blown crystal statuette. **Country Music Association Awards Web site:** <www.cmaawards.com>.

▸ **entertainer of the year:** Taylor Swift; ▸ **female vocalist of the year:** Taylor Swift; ▸ **male vocalist of the year:** Brad Paisley; ▸ **new artist of the year:** Darius Rucker; ▸ **vocal duo of the year:** Sugarland; ▸ **vocal group of the year:** Lady Antebellum; ▸ **album of the year:** *Fearless*, Taylor Swift; Nathan Chapman and Taylor Swift, producers; ▸ **song of the year:** "In Color" (Jamey Johnson), Jamey Johnson, Lee Thomas Miller, and James Otto, songwriters; ▸ **single of the year:** "I Run to You," Lady Antebellum; Victoria Shaw and Paul Worley, producers; ▸ **music video of the year:** "Love Story," Taylor Swift; Trey Fanjoy, director; ▸ **musical event of the year:** "Start a Band," Brad Paisley and Keith Urban; ▸ **musician of the year:** Mac McAnally (guitar)

All-Time Best-Selling Albums in the United States

As of June 2010. Album sales are given only to the nearest million units, and in the case of a tie albums are listed alphabetically. Source: Recording Industry Association of America (RIAA), <www.riaa.com>.

	ALBUM	ARTIST	YEAR		ALBUM	ARTIST	YEAR
1	Their Greatest Hits (1971–1975)	Eagles	1976	28	...Baby One More Time	Britney Spears	1999
	Thriller	Michael Jackson	1982		Backstreet Boys	Backstreet Boys	1997
3	untitled ("Led Zeppelin IV")	Led Zeppelin	1971		Bat out of Hell	Meat Loaf	1977
					Ropin' the Wind	Garth Brooks	1991
	The Wall	Pink Floyd	1979		Simon & Garfunkel's Greatest Hits	Simon & Garfunkel	1972
5	Back in Black	AC/DC	1980				
6	Double Live	Garth Brooks	1998	33	Greatest Hits 1974–1978	Steve Miller Band	1978
	Greatest Hits, Volume I & Volume II	Billy Joel	1985		Live/1975–85	Bruce Springsteen & the E Street Band	1986
8	Come On Over	Shania Twain	1997				
9	The Beatles ("The White Album")	The Beatles	1968		Millennium	Backstreet Boys	1999
	Rumours	Fleetwood Mac	1977		Purple Rain (soundtrack)	Prince and the Revolution	1984
11	Appetite for Destruction	Guns N' Roses	1987		Ten	Pearl Jam	1991
					Whitney Houston	Whitney Houston	1985
12	The Bodyguard (soundtrack)	Whitney Houston and various artists	1992	39	Abbey Road	The Beatles	1969
	Boston	Boston	1976		Breathless	Kenny G	1992
	No Fences	Garth Brooks	1990		Forrest Gump (soundtrack)	various artists	1994
15	Cracked Rear View	Hootie & the Blowfish	1994		Hot Rocks 1964–1971	The Rolling Stones	1972
	Greatest Hits	Elton John	1974		Hysteria	Def Leppard	1987
	Hotel California	Eagles	1976		Kenny Rogers' Greatest Hits	Kenny Rogers	1980
	Jagged Little Pill	Alanis Morissette	1995				
	1967–70	The Beatles	1973		Led Zeppelin II	Led Zeppelin	1969
	Physical Graffiti	Led Zeppelin	1975		No Jacket Required	Phil Collins	1985
21	Born in the U.S.A.	Bruce Springsteen	1984		Pieces of You	Jewel	1995
	Dark Side of the Moon	Pink Floyd	1973		Slippery When Wet	Bon Jovi	1986
	Greatest Hits	Journey	1988		II	Boyz II Men	1994
	Metallica	Metallica	1991		Wide Open Spaces	Dixie Chicks	1998
	1962–66	The Beatles	1973		The Woman in Me	Shania Twain	1995
	Saturday Night Fever (soundtrack)	The Bee Gees and various artists	1977		Yourself or Someone Like You	Matchbox 20	1996
	Supernatural	Santana	1999				

Rock and Roll Hall of Fame

Music-industry professionals established the Rock and Roll Hall of Fame Foundation in 1983 in order to "recognize the contributions of those who have had a significant impact on the evolution, development, and perpetuation of rock and roll." Performers are eligible for induction 25 years after the release of their first record. The foundation's nominating committee compiles an annual list of eligible artists and distrib-utes this list to about 1,000 rock experts throughout the world. Those performers receiving the highest number of votes, as well as at least 50% of the vote, are inducted. Special committees select inductees in other categories. Inductees for 2010 appear in **bold-face.**

Rock and Roll Hall of Fame and Museum Web site: <www.rockhall.com>.

Rock and Roll Hall of Fame (continued)

NAME (YEAR OF INDUCTION)

ABBA (2010)
AC/DC (2003)
Paul Ackerman[1] (1995)
Aerosmith (2001)
The Allman Brothers Band (1995)
Herb Alpert and Jerry Moss[2] (2006)
The Animals (1994)
Louis Armstrong[3] (1990)
Chet Atkins[4] (2002)
LaVern Baker (1991)
Hank Ballard (1990)
The Band (1994)
Dave Bartholomew[1] (1991)
Frank Barsalona[2] (2005)
Ralph Bass[1] (1991)
The Beach Boys (1988)
The Beatles (1988)
Jeff Beck (2009)
The Bee Gees (1997)
Benny Benjamin[4] (2003)
Chuck Berry (1986)
Bill Black[4] (2009)
Black Sabbath (2006)
Chris Blackwell[1] (2001)
Otis Blackwell[1] (2010)
Hal Blaine[4] (2000)
Bobby "Blue" Bland (1992)
Blondie (2006)
Booker T. and the MG's (1992)
David Bowie (1996)
Charles Brown[3] (1999)
James Brown (1986)
Ruth Brown (1993)
Jackson Browne (2004)
Buffalo Springfield (1997)
Solomon Burke (2001)
James Burton[4] (2001)
The Byrds (1991)
Johnny Cash (1992)
Ray Charles (1986)
Leonard Chess[1] (1987)
Charlie Christian[3] (1990)
Eric Clapton (2000)
Dick Clark[1] (1993)
The Clash (2003)
Jimmy Cliff (2010)
The Coasters (1987)
Eddie Cochran (1987)
Leonard Cohen (2008)
Nat King Cole[3] (2000)
Sam Cooke (1986)
Elvis Costello and the Attractions (2003)
Floyd Cramer[4] (2003)
Cream (1993)
Creedence Clearwater Revival (1993)
Crosby, Stills & Nash (1997)
Bobby Darin (1990)
The Dave Clark Five (2008)
Clive Davis[1] (2000)
Miles Davis (2006)
The Dells (2004)
Bo Diddley (1987)
Dion (1989)
Willie Dixon[3] (1994)

NAME (YEAR OF INDUCTION)

Fats Domino (1986)
Tom Donahue[1] (1996)
The Doors (1993)
Steve Douglas[4] (2003)
The Drifters (1988)
Bob Dylan (1988)
Eagles (1998)
Earth, Wind & Fire (2000)
Duane Eddy (1994)
Ahmet Ertegun[1] (1987)
Nesuhi Ertegun[2] (1991)
The Everly Brothers (1986)
Leo Fender[1] (1992)
The Flamingos (2001)
Fleetwood Mac (1998)
D.J. Fontana[4] (2009)
The Four Seasons (1990)
The Four Tops (1990)
Aretha Franklin (1987)
Alan Freed[1] (1986)
Milt Gabler[1] (1993)
Kenny Gamble and Leon Huff[1] (2008)
Marvin Gaye (1987)
David Geffen[1] (2010)
Genesis (2010)
Gerry Goffin and Carole King[1] (1990)
Berry Gordy, Jr.[1] (1988)
Bill Graham[1] (1992)
Grandmaster Flash and the Furious Five (2007)
Grateful Dead (1994)
Al Green (1995)
Ellie Greenwich and Jeff Barry[1] (2010)
Woody Guthrie[3] (1988)
Buddy Guy (2005)
Bill Haley (1987)
John Hammond[2] (1986)
George Harrison (2004)
Isaac Hayes (2002)
The Jimi Hendrix Experience (1992)
Billie Holiday[3] (2000)
Holland, Dozier, and Holland[1] (1990)
The Hollies (2010)
Buddy Holly (1986)
John Lee Hooker (1991)
Howlin' Wolf[3] (1991)
The Impressions (1991)
The Ink Spots[3] (1989)
The Isley Brothers (1992)
Mahalia Jackson[3] (1997)
Michael Jackson (2001)
Wanda Jackson[3] (2009)
The Jackson 5 (1997)
James Jamerson[4] (2000)
Elmore James[3] (1992)
Etta James (1993)
Jefferson Airplane (1996)
Billy Joel (1999)
Elton John (1994)
Little Willie John (1996)
Johnnie Johnson[4] (2001)
Robert Johnson[3] (1986)
Janis Joplin (1995)

NAME (YEAR OF INDUCTION)

Louis Jordan[3] (1987)
B.B. King (1987)
King Curtis[4] (2000)
The Kinks (1990)
Gladys Knight and the Pips (1996)
Leadbelly[3] (1988)
Led Zeppelin (1995)
Brenda Lee (2002)
Jerry Leiber and Mike Stoller[1] (1987)
John Lennon (1994)
Jerry Lee Lewis (1986)
Little Anthony and the Imperials (2009)
Little Richard (1986)
Little Walter (2008)
The Lovin' Spoonful (2000)
Frankie Lymon and the Teenagers (1993)
Lynyrd Skynyrd (2006)
Madonna (2008)
The Mamas and the Papas (1998)
Barry Mann and Cynthia Weil[1] (2010)
Bob Marley (1994)
Martha and the Vandellas (1995)
George Martin[1] (1999)
Curtis Mayfield (1999)
Paul McCartney (1999)
Clyde McPhatter (1987)
John Mellencamp (2008)
Metallica (2009)
Joni Mitchell (1997)
Bill Monroe[3] (1997)
The Moonglows (2000)
Scotty Moore[4] (2000)
Van Morrison (1993)
Jelly Roll Morton[3] (1998)
Syd Nathan[1] (1997)
Ricky Nelson (1987)
The O'Jays (2005)
Spooner Oldham[4] (2009)
Roy Orbison (1987)
The Orioles[3] (1995)
Mo Ostin[1] (2003)
Johnny Otis[1] (1994)
Earl Palmer[4] (2000)
Parliament-Funkadelic (1997)
Les Paul[3] (1988)
Carl Perkins (1987)
Tom Petty and the Heartbreakers (2002)
Sam Phillips[1] (1986)
Wilson Pickett (1991)
Pink Floyd (1996)
Gene Pitney (2002)
The Platters (1990)
The Police (2003)
Doc Pomus[1] (1992)
Elvis Presley (1986)
The Pretenders (2005)
Lloyd Price (1998)
Prince (2004)
Professor Longhair[3] (1992)
Queen (2001)
Ma Rainey[3] (1990)
Bonnie Raitt (2000)

Rock and Roll Hall of Fame (continued)

NAME (YEAR OF INDUCTION)	NAME (YEAR OF INDUCTION)	NAME (YEAR OF INDUCTION)
The Ramones (2002)	Patti Smith (2007)	The Velvet Underground (1996)
Otis Redding (1989)	The Soul Stirrers[3] (1989)	The Ventures (2008)
Jimmy Reed (1991)	Phil Spector[1] (1989)	Gene Vincent (1998)
R.E.M. (2007)	Dusty Springfield (1999)	T-Bone Walker[3] (1987)
The Righteous Brothers (2003)	Bruce Springsteen (1999)	Dinah Washington[3] (1993)
Smokey Robinson (1987)	The Staple Singers (1999)	Muddy Waters (1987)
Jimmie Rodgers[3] (1986)	Steely Dan (2001)	Jann S. Wenner[2] (2004)
The Rolling Stones (1989)	Seymour Stein[2] (2005)	Jerry Wexler[1] (1987)
The Ronettes (2007)	Jim Stewart[1] (2002)	The Who (1990)
Run-D.M.C. (2009)	Rod Stewart (1994)	Hank Williams[3] (1987)
Sam and Dave (1992)	**Jesse Stone[1] (2010)**	Bob Wills and His Texas
Santana (1998)	**The Stooges (2010)**	Playboys[3] (1999)
Pete Seeger[3] (1996)	The Supremes (1988)	Jackie Wilson (1987)
Bob Seger (2004)	Talking Heads (2002)	Bobby Womack (2009)
The Sex Pistols (2006)	James Taylor (2000)	Stevie Wonder (1989)
Del Shannon (1999)	The Temptations (1989)	Jimmy Yancey[3] (1986)
The Shirelles (1996)	Allen Toussaint[1] (1998)	The Yardbirds (1992)
Mort Shuman[1] (2010)	Traffic (2004)	Neil Young (1995)
Paul Simon (2001)	Big Joe Turner (1987)	The (Young) Rascals (1997)
Simon & Garfunkel (1990)	Ike and Tina Turner (1991)	Frank Zappa (1995)
Percy Sledge (2005)	U2 (2005)	ZZ Top (2004)
Sly and the Family Stone (1993)	Ritchie Valens (2001)	
Bessie Smith[3] (1989)	Van Halen (2007)	

[1]Ahmet Ertegun Award (nonperformers).   [2]Lifetime Achievement.   [3]Early Influences.   [4]Sidemen.

Encyclopædia Britannica's 20 World-Class Orchestras

ORCHESTRA	LOCATION	FOUNDED	MUSIC DIRECTOR OR CONDUCTOR (2010)
Berliner Philharmoniker	Berlin, Germany	1882	Simon Rattle
Boston Symphony Orchestra	Boston MA	1881	James Levine
Budapest Festival Orchestra	Budapest, Hungary	1983	Iván Fischer
Ceská Filharmonie	Prague, Czech Republic	1896	Eliahu Inbal
Chicago Symphony Orchestra	Chicago IL	1891	Riccardo Muti
Cleveland Orchestra	Cleveland OH	1918	Franz Welser-Möst
Gewandhaus zu Leipzig	Leipzig, Germany	1743	Riccardo Chailly
Koninklijk Concertgebouworkest	Amsterdam, Netherlands	1888	Mariss Jansons
London Symphony Orchestra	London, England	1904	Valery Gergiev
Los Angeles Philharmonic	Los Angeles CA	1919	Gustavo Dudamel
New York Philharmonic	New York NY	1842	Alan Gilbert
Orchestre Symphonique de Montréal	Montreal, QC, Canada	1934	Kent Nagano
Philadelphia Orchestra	Philadelphia PA	1900	Charles Dutoit[1]
Philharmonia Orchestra	London, England	1945	Esa-Pekka Salonen
Russian National Orchestra	Moscow, Russia	1990	Mikhail Pletnev
Saint Petersburg Philharmonic	Saint Petersburg, Russia	1882	Yury Temirkanov
San Francisco Symphony	San Francisco CA	1911	Michael Tilson Thomas
Staatskapelle Dresden	Dresden, Germany	1548	Fabio Luisi
Symphonieorchester des Bayerischen Rundfunks	Munich, Germany	1949	Mariss Jansons
Wiener Philharmoniker	Vienna, Austria	1842	guest conductors

[1]Chief conductor and artistic adviser. Yannick Nézet-Séguin will take over as music director in 2012.

Encyclopædia Britannica's Top 20 Opera Companies

COMPANY	LOCATION	FOUNDED	GENERAL OR ARTISTIC DIRECTOR (2010)
Bayerische Staatsoper	Munich, Germany	1653	Nikolaus Bachler
Bolshoi Opera	Moscow, Russia	1776	Makvala Kasrashvili
Canadian Opera Company	Toronto, ON, Canada	1950	Alexander Neef
De Nederlandse Opera	Amsterdam, Netherlands	1946	Pierre Audi
Deutsche Oper Berlin	Berlin, Germany	1912	Kirsten Harms
English National Opera	London, England	1931	John Berry

Encyclopædia Britannica's Top 20 Opera Companies (continued)

COMPANY	LOCATION	FOUNDED	GENERAL OR ARTISTIC DIRECTOR (2010)
Gran Teatre del Liceu	Barcelona, Spain	1847	Joan Francesc Marco
Lyric Opera of Chicago	Chicago IL	1954	William Mason
Mariinsky Theatre (Kirov Opera)	St. Petersburg, Russia	1783	Valery Gergiev
Metropolitan Opera	New York NY	1883	Peter Gelb
Opera Australia	Sydney, NSW, and Melbourne, VIC, Australia	1956	Lyndon Terracini
Opéra National de Paris	Paris, France	1669	Nicolas Joel
Royal Opera	London, England	1732	Tony Hall[1]
San Francisco Opera	San Francisco CA	1923	David Gockley
Staatsoper Hamburg	Hamburg, Germany	1678	Simone Young
Staatsoper Unter den Linden	Berlin, Germany	1742	Jürgen Flimm
Teatro alla Scala (La Scala)	Milan, Italy	1778	Stéphane Lissner
Teatro Real	Madrid, Spain	1850	Miguel Muñiz de las Cuevas
Théâtre Royal de la Monnaie	Brussels, Belgium	1700	Peter de Caluwe
Wiener Staatsoper	Vienna, Austria	1869	Ioan Holender

[1]Chief executive.

Arts and Letters Awards

Pulitzer Prizes

The Pulitzer Prizes are awarded annually by Columbia University, New York City, based on recommendations from the Pulitzer Prize Board, for works published or produced in the previous calendar year (for music, works must be performed or released between 16 January of the previous year and 15 January of the award year). The prizes, originally endowed by newspaper editor Joseph Pulitzer, were first awarded in 1917. There are currently 21 prizes presented. Most prizes include a US$10,000 cash award; the exception is the prize for public service in journalism, which is a gold medal.
Pulitzer Prize Web site: <www.pulitzer.org>.

Journalism, 2010

CATEGORY AND DESCRIPTION	WINNER	PUBLICATION	SUBJECT
Public Service: awarded to a newspaper for notable public service	staff	Bristol (VA) Herald Courier	investigation into the mismanagement of natural-gas royalties owed to local land owners
Breaking News Reporting: awarded for local reporting of breaking news	staff	Seattle Times	coverage of the slayings of four police officers and the subsequent 40-hour manhunt
Investigative Reporting: awarded to an individual or team for an investigative article or series	Barbara Laker and Wendy Ruderman	Philadelphia Daily News	exposure of a police narcotics squad whose corruption tainted hundreds of criminal cases
	Sheri Fink	ProPublica, in collaboration with New York Times Magazine	accounts the critical decisions of overworked doctors in a New Orleans LA-hospital cut off by Hurricane Katrina floods
Explanatory Reporting: awarded for clarification of a difficult subject through clear communication of in-depth knowledge	Michael Moss and staff	New York Times	examination of food safety issues, highlighting deficiencies in federal regulations
Local Reporting: awarded for consistent, intelligent coverage of a particular topic	Raquel Rutledge	Milwaukee Journal Sentinel	report on child-care fraud and abuse that endangered children and cost taxpayers hundreds of millions of dollars
National Reporting: awarded for coverage of national news	Matt Richtel and staff	New York Times	examination of the hazards of using electronic devices while driving
International Reporting: awarded for coverage of international news	Anthony Shadid	Washington Post	series on Iraq as the US exits and Iraqis are faced with the war's aftermath and an uncertain future

Journalism, 2010 (continued)

CATEGORY AND DESCRIPTION	WINNER	PUBLICATION	SUBJECT
Feature Writing: awarded for original and concise writing of quality	Gene Weingarten	*Washington Post*	portrait of parents whose children are accidentally killed when they are forgotten in cars
Commentary	Kathleen Parker	*Washington Post*	witty columns on a range of political and moral issues
Criticism	Sarah Kaufman	*Washington Post*	imaginative and insightful dance criticism
Editorial Writing: awarded for the ability to sway public opinion through solid reasoning, clear style, and "moral purpose"	Tod Robberson, Colleen McCain Nelson, and William McKenzie	*Dallas Morning News*	editorials on the glaring economic disparities between two sections of the city
Editorial Cartooning: awarded for creative cartoons that display editorial effectiveness and superior drawing	Mark Fiore	self syndicated, appearing on SFGate.com	sharp wit and complex subject matter in editorial animations
Breaking News Photography: awarded for single or group and color or black-and-white photographs of breaking news	Mary Chind	*Des Moines Register*	depiction of the daring rescue attempt of a woman trapped in the water beneath a dam
Feature Photography: awarded for single or group and color or black-and-white feature photographs	Craig F. Walker	*Denver Post*	photographic view of a teenager who joins the army during wartime in search of purpose and adulthood

Letters, Drama, and Music

Fiction
Awarded for a work of fiction, preferably about American life, by an American author.

YEAR	TITLE	AUTHOR	YEAR	TITLE	AUTHOR
1917	no award		1947	*All the King's Men*	Robert Penn Warren
1918	*His Family*	Ernest Poole	1948	*Tales of the South Pacific*	James A. Michener
1919	*The Magnificent Ambersons*	Booth Tarkington			
1920	no award		1949	*Guard of Honor*	James Gould Cozzens
1921	*The Age of Innocence*	Edith Wharton			
1922	*Alice Adams*	Booth Tarkington	1950	*The Way West*	A.B. Guthrie, Jr.
1923	*One of Ours*	Willa Cather	1951	*The Town*	Conrad Richter
1924	*The Able McLaughlins*	Margaret Wilson	1952	*The Caine Mutiny*	Herman Wouk
1925	*So Big*	Edna Ferber	1953	*The Old Man and the Sea*	Ernest Hemingway
1926	*Arrowsmith*	Sinclair Lewis (declined)			
			1954	no award	
1927	*Early Autumn*	Louis Bromfield	1955	*A Fable*	William Faulkner
1928	*The Bridge of San Luis Rey*	Thornton Wilder	1956	*Andersonville*	MacKinlay Kantor
			1957	no award	
1929	*Scarlet Sister Mary*	Julia Peterkin	1958	*A Death in the Family*[1]	James Agee
1930	*Laughing Boy*	Oliver Lafarge	1959	*The Travels of Jaimie McPheeters*	Robert Lewis Taylor
1931	*Years of Grace*	Margaret Ayer Barnes			
1932	*The Good Earth*	Pearl S. Buck	1960	*Advise and Consent*	Allen Drury
1933	*The Store*	T.S. Stribling	1961	*To Kill a Mockingbird*	Harper Lee
1934	*Lamb in His Bosom*	Caroline Miller	1962	*The Edge of Sadness*	Edwin O'Connor
1935	*Now in November*	Josephine Winslow Johnson	1963	*The Reivers*	William Faulkner
			1964	no award	
1936	*Honey in the Horn*	Harold L. Davis	1965	*The Keepers of the House*	Shirley Ann Grau
1937	*Gone with the Wind*	Margaret Mitchell	1966	*Collected Stories*	Katherine Anne Porter
1938	*The Late George Apley*	John Phillips Marquand			
1939	*The Yearling*	Marjorie Kinnan Rawlings	1967	*The Fixer*	Bernard Malamud
			1968	*The Confessions of Nat Turner*	William Styron
1940	*The Grapes of Wrath*	John Steinbeck	1969	*House Made of Dawn*	N. Scott Momaday
1941	no award		1970	*Collected Stories*	Jean Stafford
1942	*In This Our Life*	Ellen Glasgow	1971	no award	
1943	*Dragon's Teeth*	Upton Sinclair	1972	*Angle of Repose*	Wallace Stegner
1944	*Journey in the Dark*	Martin Flavin	1973	*The Optimist's Daughter*	Eudora Welty
1945	*A Bell for Adano*	John Hersey			
1946	no award		1974	no award	

Letters, Drama, and Music (continued)

<u>Fiction</u> (continued)

YEAR	TITLE	AUTHOR
1975	The Killer Angels	Michael Shaara
1976	Humboldt's Gift	Saul Bellow
1977	no award	
1978	Elbow Room	James Alan McPherson
1979	The Stories of John Cheever	John Cheever
1980	The Executioner's Song	Norman Mailer
1981	A Confederacy of Dunces[1]	John Kennedy Toole
1982	Rabbit Is Rich	John Updike
1983	The Color Purple	Alice Walker
1984	Ironweed	William Kennedy
1985	Foreign Affairs	Alison Lurie
1986	Lonesome Dove	Larry McMurtry
1987	A Summons to Memphis	Peter Taylor
1988	Beloved	Toni Morrison
1989	Breathing Lessons	Anne Tyler
1990	The Mambo Kings Play Songs of Love	Oscar Hijuelos
1991	Rabbit at Rest	John Updike
1992	A Thousand Acres	Jane Smiley
1993	A Good Scent from a Strange Mountain	Robert Olen Butler

YEAR	TITLE	AUTHOR
1994	The Shipping News	E. Annie Proulx
1995	The Stone Diaries	Carol Shields
1996	Independence Day	Richard Ford
1997	Martin Dressler: The Tale of an American Dreamer	Steven Millhauser
1998	American Pastoral	Philip Roth
1999	The Hours	Michael Cunningham
2000	Interpreter of Maladies	Jhumpa Lahiri
2001	The Amazing Adventures of Kavalier and Clay	Michael Chabon
2002	Empire Falls	Richard Russo
2003	Middlesex	Jeffrey Eugenides
2004	The Known World	Edward P. Jones
2005	Gilead	Marilynne Robinson
2006	March	Geraldine Brooks
2007	The Road	Cormac McCarthy
2008	The Brief Wondrous Life of Oscar Wao	Junot Díaz
2009	Olive Kitteridge	Elizabeth Strout
2010	Tinkers	Paul Harding

[1]Work published and prize awarded posthumously.

<u>Drama</u>
Awarded for a play, preferably about American life, by an American author.

YEAR	TITLE	AUTHOR
1917	no award	
1918	Why Marry?	Jesse Lynch Williams
1919	no award	
1920	Beyond the Horizon	Eugene O'Neill
1921	Miss Lulu Bett	Zona Gale
1922	Anna Christie	Eugene O'Neill
1923	Icebound	Owen Davis
1924	Hell-Bent fer Heaven	Hatcher Hughes
1925	They Knew What They Wanted	Sidney Howard
1926	Craig's Wife	George Kelly
1927	In Abraham's Bosom	Paul Green
1928	Strange Interlude	Eugene O'Neill
1929	Street Scene	Elmer L. Rice
1930	The Green Pastures	Marc Connelly
1931	Alison's House	Susan Glaspell
1932	Of Thee I Sing	George S. Kaufman, Morrie Ryskind, and Ira Gershwin
1933	Both Your Houses	Maxwell Anderson
1934	Men in White	Sidney Kingsley
1935	The Old Maid	Zoe Akins
1936	Idiot's Delight	Robert E. Sherwood
1937	You Can't Take It with You	Moss Hart and George S. Kaufman
1938	Our Town	Thornton Wilder
1939	Abe Lincoln in Illinois	Robert E. Sherwood
1940	The Time of Your Life	William Saroyan
1941	There Shall Be No Night	Robert E. Sherwood
1942	no award	
1943	The Skin of Our Teeth	Thornton Wilder
1944	no award	
1945	Harvey	Mary Chase

YEAR	TITLE	AUTHOR
1946	State of the Union	Russel Crouse and Howard Lindsay
1947	no award	
1948	A Streetcar Named Desire	Tennessee Williams
1949	Death of a Salesman	Arthur Miller
1950	South Pacific	Richard Rodgers, Oscar Hammerstein II, and Joshua Logan
1951	no award	
1952	The Shrike	Joseph Kramm
1953	Picnic	William Inge
1954	The Teahouse of the August Moon	John Patrick
1955	Cat on a Hot Tin Roof	Tennessee Williams
1956	The Diary of Anne Frank	Albert Hackett and Frances Goodrich
1957	Long Day's Journey into Night[1]	Eugene O'Neill
1958	Look Homeward, Angel	Ketti Frings
1959	J.B.	Archibald MacLeish
1960	Fiorello!	Jerome Weidman, George Abbott, Jerry Bock, and Sheldon Harnick
1961	All the Way Home	Tad Mosel
1962	How To Succeed in Business Without Really Trying	Frank Loesser and Abe Burrows
1963	no award	
1964	no award	

Letters, Drama, and Music (continued)

Drama (continued)

YEAR	TITLE	AUTHOR
1965	The Subject Was Roses	Frank D. Gilroy
1966	no award	
1967	A Delicate Balance	Edward Albee
1968	no award	
1969	The Great White Hope	Howard Sackler
1970	No Place To Be Somebody	Charles Gordone
1971	The Effect of Gamma Rays on Man-in-the-Moon Marigolds	Paul Zindel
1972	no award	
1973	That Championship Season	Jason Miller
1974	no award	
1975	Seascape	Edward Albee
1976	A Chorus Line	Michael Bennett, James Kirkwood, Nicholas Dante, Marvin Hamlisch, and Edward Kleban
1977	The Shadow Box	Michael Cristofer
1978	The Gin Game	Donald L. Coburn
1979	Buried Child	Sam Shepard
1980	Talley's Folly	Lanford Wilson
1981	Crimes of the Heart	Beth Henley
1982	A Soldier's Play	Charles Fuller
1983	'Night, Mother	Marsha Norman
1984	Glengarry Glen Ross	David Mamet
1985	Sunday in the Park with George	Stephen Sondheim and James Lapine

YEAR	TITLE	AUTHOR
1986	no award	
1987	Fences	August Wilson
1988	Driving Miss Daisy	Alfred Uhry
1989	The Heidi Chronicles	Wendy Wasserstein
1990	The Piano Lesson	August Wilson
1991	Lost in Yonkers	Neil Simon
1992	The Kentucky Cycle	Robert Schenkkan
1993	Angels in America: Millennium Approaches	Tony Kushner
1994	Three Tall Women	Edward Albee
1995	The Young Man from Atlanta	Horton Foote
1996	Rent[1]	Jonathan Larson
1997	no award	
1998	How I Learned To Drive	Paula Vogel
1999	Wit	Margaret Edson
2000	Dinner with Friends	Donald Margulies
2001	Proof	David Auburn
2002	Topdog/Underdog	Suzan-Lori Parks
2003	Anna in the Tropics	Nilo Cruz
2004	I Am My Own Wife	Doug Wright
2005	Doubt: A Parable	John Patrick Shanley
2006	no award	
2007	Rabbit Hole	David Lindsay-Abaire
2008	August: Osage County	Tracy Letts
2009	Ruined	Lynn Nottage
2010	Next to Normal	Tom Kitt and Brian Yorkey

[1] Awarded posthumously

History
Awarded for a work on the subject of American history.

YEAR	TITLE	AUTHOR
1917	With Americans of Past and Present Days	J.J. Jusserand
1918	History of the Civil War, 1861–1865	James Ford Rhodes
1919	no award	
1920	The War with Mexico, 2 vols.	Justin H. Smith
1921	The Victory at Sea	William Sowden Sims and Burton Jesse Hendrick
1922	The Founding of New England	James Truslow Adams
1923	The Supreme Court in United States History	Charles Warren
1924	The American Revolution: A Constitutional Interpretation	Charles Howard McIlwain
1925	History of the American Frontier	Frederic L. Paxson
1926	A History of the United States	Edward Channing
1927	Pinckney's Treaty	Samuel Flagg Bemis
1928	Main Currents in American Thought, 2 vols.	Vernon Louis Parrington

YEAR	TITLE	AUTHOR
1929	The Organization and Administration of the Union Army, 1861–1865	Fred Albert Shannon
1930	The War of Independence	Claude H. Van Tyne
1931	The Coming of the War, 1914	Bernadotte E. Schmitt
1932	My Experiences in the World War	John J. Pershing
1933	The Significance of Sections in American History[1]	Frederick J. Turner
1934	The People's Choice	Herbert Agar
1935	The Colonial Period of American History	Charles McLean Andrews
1936	A Constitutional History of the United States	Andrew C. McLaughlin
1937	The Flowering of New England, 1815–1865	Van Wyck Brooks
1938	The Road to Reunion, 1865–1900	Paul Herman Buck
1939	A History of American Magazines	Frank Luther Mott
1940	Abraham Lincoln: The War Years	Carl Sandburg

Letters, Drama, and Music (continued)

History (continued)

YEAR	TITLE	AUTHOR
1941	The Atlantic Migration, 1607–1860	Marcus Lee Hansen
1942	Reveille in Washington, 1860–1865	Margaret Leech
1943	Paul Revere and the World He Lived In	Esther Forbes
1944	The Growth of American Thought	Merle Curti
1945	Unfinished Business	Stephen Bonsal
1946	The Age of Jackson	Arthur M. Schlesinger, Jr.
1947	Scientists Against Time	James Phinney Baxter III
1948	Across the Wide Missouri	Bernard De Voto
1949	The Disruption of American Democracy	Roy Franklin Nichols
1950	Art and Life in America	Oliver W. Larkin
1951	The Old Northwest: Pioneer Period, 1815–1840	R. Carlyle Buley
1952	The Uprooted	Oscar Handlin
1953	The Era of Good Feelings	George Dangerfield
1954	A Stillness at Appomattox	Bruce Catton
1955	Great River: The Rio Grande in North American History	Paul Horgan
1956	The Age of Reform	Richard Hofstadter
1957	Russia Leaves the War: Soviet-American Relations, 1917–1920	George F. Kennan
1958	Banks and Politics in America	Bray Hammond
1959	The Republican Era: 1869–1901	Leonard D. White and Jean Schneider
1960	In the Days of McKinley	Margaret Leech
1961	Between War and Peace: The Potsdam Conference	Herbert Feis
1962	The Triumphant Empire: Thunder-Clouds Gather in the West, 1763–1766	Lawrence H. Gipson
1963	Washington, Village and Capital, 1800–1878	Constance McLaughlin Green
1964	Puritan Village: The Formation of a New England Town	Sumner Chilton Powell
1965	The Greenback Era	Irwin Unger
1966	The Life of the Mind in America[1]	Perry Miller
1967	Exploration and Empire: The Explorer and the Scientist in the Winning of the American West	William H. Goetzmann
1968	The Ideological Origins of the American Revolution	Bernard Bailyn
1969	Origins of the Fifth Amendment	Leonard W. Levy

YEAR	TITLE	AUTHOR
1970	Present at the Creation: My Years in the State Department	Dean Acheson
1971	Roosevelt: The Soldier of Freedom	James MacGregor Burns
1972	Neither Black nor White	Carl N. Degler
1973	People of Paradox: An Inquiry Concerning the Origins of American Civilization	Michael Kammen
1974	The Americans: The Democratic Experience	Daniel J. Boorstin
1975	Jefferson and His Time, vols. 1–5	Dumas Malone
1976	Lamy of Santa Fe	Paul Horgan
1977	The Impending Crisis, 1841–1867[2]	David M. Potter and Don E. Fehrenbacher
1978	The Visible Hand: The Managerial Revolution in American Business	Alfred D. Chandler, Jr.
1979	The Dred Scott Case	Don E. Fehrenbacher
1980	Been in the Storm So Long	Leon F. Litwack
1981	American Education: The National Experience, 1783–1876	Lawrence A. Cremin
1982	Mary Chesnut's Civil War	C. Vann Woodward[3]
1983	The Transformation of Virginia, 1740–1790	Rhys L. Isaac
1984	no award	
1985	Prophets of Regulation	Thomas K. McCraw
1986	The Heavens and the Earth: A Political History of the Space Age	Walter A. McDougall
1987	Voyagers to the West: A Passage in the Peopling of America on the Eve of the Revolution	Bernard Bailyn
1988	The Launching of Modern American Science, 1846–1876	Robert V. Bruce
1989	Battle Cry of Freedom: The Civil War Era	James M. McPherson
	Parting the Waters: America in the King Years, 1954–1963	Taylor Branch
1990	In Our Image: America's Empire in the Philippines	Stanley Karnow
1991	A Midwife's Tale	Laurel Thatcher Ulrich
1992	The Fate of Liberty: Abraham Lincoln and Civil Liberties	Mark E. Neely, Jr.
1993	The Radicalism of the American Revolution	Gordon S. Wood
1994	no award	
1995	No Ordinary Time: Franklin and Eleanor Roosevelt: The Home Front in World War II	Doris Kearns Goodwin

Letters, Drama, and Music (continued)

History (continued)

YEAR	TITLE	AUTHOR	YEAR	TITLE	AUTHOR
1996	William Cooper's Town: Power and Persuasion on the Frontier of the Early American Republic	Alan Taylor	2003	An Army at Dawn: The War in North Africa, 1942–1943	Rick Atkinson
1997	Original Meanings: Politics and Ideas in the Making of the Constitution	Jack N. Rakove	2004	A Nation Under Our Foot: Black Political Struggles in the Rural South from Slavery to the Great Migration	Steven Hahn
1998	Summer for the Gods: The Scopes Trial and America's Continuing Debate over Science and Religion	Edward J. Larson	2005	Washington's Crossing	David Hackett Fischer
			2006	Polio: An American Story	David M. Oshinsky
1999	Gotham: A History of New York City to 1898	Edwin G. Burrows and Mike Wallace	2007	The Race Beat: The Press, the Civil Rights Struggle, and the Awakening of a Nation	Gene Roberts and Hank Klibanoff
2000	Freedom from Fear: The American People in Depression and War, 1929–1945	David M. Kennedy	2008	What Hath God Wrought: The Transformation of America, 1815–1848	Daniel Walker Howe
2001	Founding Brothers: The Revolutionary Generation	Joseph J. Ellis	2009	The Hemingses of Monticello: An American Family	Annette Gordon-Reed
2002	The Metaphysical Club: A Story of Ideas in America	Louis Menand	2010	Lords of Finance: The Bankers Who Broke the World	Liaquat Ahamed

[1]Awarded posthumously.   [2]Potter died before completing the work; Fehrenbacher wrote the final chapters and edited it.   [3]Editor.

Biography or Autobiography
Awarded for a biography or autobiography by an American author.

YEAR	TITLE	AUTHOR	YEAR	TITLE	AUTHOR
1917	Julia Ward Howe	Laura Elizabeth Howe Richards and Maude Howe Elliott; assisted by Florence Howe Hall	1931	Charles W. Eliot	Henry James
			1932	Theodore Roosevelt	Henry F. Pringle
			1933	Grover Cleveland	Allan Nevins
			1934	John Hay	Tyler Dennett
			1935	R.E. Lee	Douglas S. Freeman
1918	Benjamin Franklin, Self-Revealed	William Cabell Bruce	1936	The Thought and Character of William James	Ralph Barton Perry
1919	The Education of Henry Adams[1]	Henry Adams			
1920	The Life of John Marshall, 4 vols.	Albert J. Beveridge	1937	Hamilton Fish	Allan Nevins
			1938	Andrew Jackson, 2 vols. Pedlar's Progress	Marquis James Odell Shepard
1921	The Americanization of Edward Bok	Edward Bok	1939	Benjamin Franklin	Carl Van Doren
1922	A Daughter of the Middle Border	Hamlin Garland	1940	Woodrow Wilson, Life and Letters, vols. 7 and 8	Ray Stannard Baker
1923	The Life and Letters of Walter H. Page	Burton J. Hendrick	1941	Jonathan Edward	Ola Elizabeth Winslow
1924	From Immigrant to Inventor	Michael Idvorsky Pupin	1942	Crusader in Crinoline	Forrest Wilson
1925	Barrett Wendell and His Letters	M.A. De Wolfe Howe	1943	Admiral of the Ocean Sea	Samuel Eliot Morison
1926	The Life of Sir William Osler, 2 vols.	Harvey Cushing	1944	The American Leonardo: The Life of Samuel F.B. Morse	Carleton Mabee
1927	Whitman	Emory Holloway			
1928	The American Orchestra and Theodore Thomas	Charles Edward Russell	1945	George Bancroft: Brahmin Rebel	Russell Blaine Nye
1929	The Training of an American: The Earlier Life and Letters of Walter H. Page	Burton J. Hendrick	1946	Son of the Wilderness	Linnie Marsh Wolfe
			1947	The Autobiography of William Allen White	William Allen White
1930	The Raven	Marquis James	1948	Forgotten First Citizen: John Bigelow	Margaret Clapp

Letters, Drama, and Music (continued)

Biography or Autobiography (continued)

YEAR	TITLE	AUTHOR
1949	Roosevelt and Hopkins	Robert E. Sherwood
1950	John Quincy Adams and the Foundations of American Foreign Policy	Samuel Flagg Bemis
1951	John C. Calhoun: American Portrait	Margaret Louise Coit
1952	Charles Evans Hughes	Merlo J. Pusey
1953	Edmund Pendleton, 1721–1803	David J. Mays
1954	The Spirit of St. Louis	Charles A. Lindbergh
1955	The Taft Story	William S. White
1956	Benjamin Henry Latrobe	Talbot Faulkner Hamlin
1957	Profiles in Courage	John F. Kennedy
1958	George Washington, 7 vols.[2]	Douglas Southall Freeman, John Alexander Carroll, and Mary Wells Ashworth
1959	Woodrow Wilson, American Prophet	Arthur Walworth
1960	John Paul Jones	Samuel Eliot Morison
1961	Charles Sumner and the Coming of the Civil War	David Herbert Donald
1962	no award	
1963	Henry James	Leon Edel
1964	John Keats	Walter Jackson Bate
1965	Henry Adams, 3 vols.	Ernest Samuels
1966	A Thousand Days	Arthur M. Schlesinger, Jr.
1967	Mr. Clemens and Mark Twain	Justin Kaplan
1968	Memoirs	George E. Kennan
1969	The Man from New York: John Quinn and His Friends	Benjamin Lawrence Reid
1970	Huey Long	T. Harry Williams
1971	Robert Frost: The Years of Triumph, 1915–1938	Lawrance Thompson
1972	Eleanor and Franklin	Joseph P. Lash
1973	Luce and His Empire	W.A. Swanberg
1974	O'Neill, Son and Artist	Louis Sheaffer
1975	The Power Broker: Robert Moses and the Fall of New York	Robert A. Caro
1976	Edith Wharton: A Biography	R.W.B. Lewis
1977	A Prince of Our Disorder: The Life of T.E. Lawrence	John E. Mack
1978	Samuel Johnson	Walter Jackson Bate
1979	Days of Sorrow and Pain: Leo Baeck and the Berlin Jews	Leonard Baker
1980	The Rise of Theodore Roosevelt	Edmund Morris

YEAR	TITLE	AUTHOR
1981	Peter the Great: His Life and World	Robert K. Massie
1982	Grant: A Biography	William McFeely
1983	Growing Up	Russell Baker
1984	Booker T. Washington: The Wizard of Tuskegee, 1901–1915	Louis R. Harlan
1985	The Life and Times of Cotton Mather	Kenneth Silverman
1986	Louise Bogan: A Portrait	Elizabeth Frank
1987	Bearing the Cross: Martin Luther King, Jr., and the Southern Christian Leadership Conference	David J. Garrow
1988	Look Homeward: A Life of Thomas Wolfe	David Herbert Donald
1989	Oscar Wilde[1]	Richard Ellmann
1990	Machiavelli in Hell	Sebastian de Grazia
1991	Jackson Pollock	Steven Naifeh and Gregory White Smith
1992	Fortunate Son: The Healing of a Vietnam Vet	Lewis B. Puller, Jr.
1993	Truman	David McCullough
1994	W.E.B. Du Bois: Biography of a Race, 1868–1919	David Levering Lewis
1995	Harriet Beecher Stowe: A Life	Joan D. Hedrick
1996	God: A Biography	Jack Miles
1997	Angela's Ashes: A Memoir	Frank McCourt
1998	Personal History	Katharine Graham
1999	Lindbergh	A. Scott Berg
2000	Vera (Mrs. Vladimir Nabokov)	Stacy Schiff
2001	W.E.B. Du Bois: The Fight for Equality and the American Century, 1919–1963	David Levering Lewis
2002	John Adams	David McCullough
2003	Master of the Senate	Robert A. Caro
2004	Khrushchev: The Man and His Era	William Taubman
2005	De Kooning: An American Master	Mark Stevens and Annalyn Swan
2006	American Prometheus: The Triumph and Tragedy	Kai Bird and Martin J. Sherwin
2007	The Most Famous Man in America: The Biography of Henry Ward Beecher	Debby Applegate
2008	Eden's Outcasts: The Story of Louisa May Alcott and Her Father	John Matteson
2009	American Lion: Andrew Jackson in the White House	Jon Meacham
2010	The First Tycoon: The Epic Life of Cornelius Vanderbilt	T.J. Stiles

[1]Awarded posthumously. [2]Freeman died in 1953 after completing vols. 1–6; Carroll and Ashworth continued his work with vol. 7.

Letters, Drama, and Music (continued)

Poetry
Awarded for a collection of original verse by an American author.

YEAR	TITLE	AUTHOR
1922	Collected Poems	Edwin Arlington Robinson
1923	The Ballad of the Harp-Weaver; A Few Figs from Thistles; eight sonnets in American Poetry, 1922: A Miscellany	Edna St. Vincent Millay
1924	New Hampshire: A Poem with Notes and Grace Notes	Robert Frost
1925	The Man Who Died Twice	Edwin Arlington Robinson
1926	What's O'Clock[1]	Amy Lowell
1927	Fiddler's Farewell	Leonora Speyer
1928	Tristram	Edwin Arlington Robinson
1929	John Brown's Body	Stephen Vincent Benét
1930	Selected Poems	Conrad Aiken
1931	Collected Poems	Robert Frost
1932	The Flowering Stone	George Dillon
1933	Conquistador	Archibald MacLeish
1934	Collected Verse	Robert Hillyer
1935	Bright Ambush	Audrey Wurdemann
1936	Strange Holiness	Robert P. Tristram Coffin
1937	A Further Range	Robert Frost
1938	Cold Morning Sky	Marya Zaturenska
1939	Selected Poems	John Gould Fletcher
1940	Collected Poems	Mark Van Doren
1941	Sunderland Capture	Leonard Bacon
1942	The Dust Which Is God	William Rose Benét
1943	A Witness Tree	Robert Frost
1944	Western Star[1]	Stephen Vincent Benét
1945	V-Letter and Other Poems	Karl Shapiro
1946	no award	
1947	Lord Weary's Castle	Robert Lowell
1948	The Age of Anxiety	W.H. Auden
1949	Terror and Decorum	Peter Viereck
1950	Annie Allen	Gwendolyn Brooks
1951	Complete Poems	Carl Sandburg
1952	Collected Poems	Marianne Moore
1953	Collected Poems, 1917–1952	Archibald MacLeish
1954	The Waking	Theodore Roethke
1955	Collected Poems	Wallace Stevens
1956	Poems: North & South—A Cold Spring	Elizabeth Bishop
1957	Things of This World	Richard Wilbur
1958	Promises: Poems 1954–1956	Robert Penn Warren
1959	Selected Poems, 1928–1958	Stanley Kunitz
1960	Heart's Needle	W.D. Snodgrass
1961	Times Three: Selected Verse from Three Decades	Phyllis McGinley
1962	Poems	Alan Dugan
1963	Pictures from Breughel[1]	William Carlos Williams
1964	At the End of the Open Road	Louis Simpson
1965	77 Dream Songs	John Berryman
1966	Selected Poems	Richard Eberhart
1967	Live or Die	Anne Sexton
1968	The Hard Hours	Anthony Hecht
1969	Of Being Numerous	George Oppen
1970	Untitled Subjects	Richard Howard
1971	The Carrier of Ladders	W.S. Merwin
1972	Collected Poems	James Wright
1973	Up Country	Maxine Kumin
1974	The Dolphin	Robert Lowell
1975	Turtle Island	Gary Snyder
1976	Self-Portrait in a Convex Mirror	John Ashbery
1977	Divine Comedies	James Merrill
1978	Collected Poems	Howard Nemerov
1979	Now and Then	Robert Penn Warren
1980	Selected Poems	Donald Justice
1981	The Morning of the Poem	James Schuyler
1982	The Collected Poems[2]	Sylvia Plath
1983	Selected Poems	Galway Kinnell
1984	American Primitive	Mary Oliver
1985	Yin	Carolyn Kizer
1986	The Flying Change	Henry Taylor
1987	Thomas and Beulah	Rita Dove
1988	Partial Accounts: New and Selected Poems	William Meredith
1989	New and Collected Poems	Richard Wilbur
1990	The World Doesn't End	Charles Simic
1991	Near Changes	Mona Van Duyn
1992	Selected Poems	James Tate
1993	The Wild Iris	Louise Glück
1994	Neon Vernacular: New and Selected Poems	Yusef Komunyakaa
1995	The Simple Truth	Philip Levine
1996	The Dream of the Unified Field	Jorie Graham
1997	Alive Together: New and Selected Poems	Lisel Mueller
1998	Black Zodiac	Charles Wright
1999	Blizzard of One	Mark Strand
2000	Repair	C.K. Williams
2001	Different Hours	Stephen Dunn
2002	Practical Gods	Carl Dennis
2003	Moy Sand and Gravel	Paul Muldoon
2004	Walking to Martha's Vineyard	Franz Wright
2005	Delights & Shadows	Ted Kooser
2006	Late Wife	Claudia Emerson
2007	Native Guard	Natasha Trethewey
2008	Time and Materials Failure	Robert Hass Philip Schultz
2009	The Shadow of Sirius	W.S. Merwin
2010	Versed	Rae Armantrout

[1]Awarded posthumously.   [2]Work published and prize awarded posthumously.

Letters, Drama, and Music (continued)

General Nonfiction
Awarded for a work of nonfiction, ineligible for any other category, by an American author.

YEAR	TITLE	AUTHOR
1962	The Making of the President, 1960	Theodore H. White
1963	The Guns of August	Barbara W. Tuchman
1964	Anti-intellectualism in American Life	Richard Hofstadter
1965	O Strange New World	Howard Mumford Jones
1966	Wandering Through Winter	Edwin Way Teale
1967	The Problem of Slavery in Western Culture	David Brion Davis
1968	Rousseau and Revolution: A History of Civilization in France, England, and Germany from 1756 and in the Remainder of Europe from 1715 to 1789	Will and Ariel Durant
1969	The Armies of the Night	Norman Mailer
	So Human an Animal	Rene Jules Dubos
1970	Gandhi's Truth	Erik H. Erikson
1971	The Rising Sun	John Toland
1972	Stilwell and the American Experience in China, 1911–1945	Barbara W. Tuchman
1973	Fire in the Lake: The Vietnamese and the Americans in Vietnam	Frances Fitzgerald
	Children of Crisis, vols. 2 and 3	Robert Coles
1974	The Denial of Death[1]	Ernest Becker
1975	Pilgrim at Tinker Creek	Annie Dillard
1976	Why Survive?: Being Old in America	Robert N. Butler
1977	Beautiful Swimmers	William W. Warner
1978	The Dragons of Eden	Carl Sagan
1979	On Human Nature	Edward O. Wilson
1980	Gödel, Escher, Bach: An Eternal Golden Braid	Douglas R. Hofstadter
1981	Fin-de-Siècle Vienna: Politics and Culture	Carl E. Schorske
1982	The Soul of a New Machine	Tracy Kidder
1983	Is There No Place on Earth for Me?	Susan Sheehan
1984	The Social Transformation of American Medicine	Paul Starr
1985	The Good War: An Oral History of World War Two	Studs Terkel
1986	Common Ground: A Turbulent Decade in the Lives of Three American Families	J. Anthony Lukas
	Move Your Shadow: South Africa, Black and White	Joseph Lelyveld
1987	Arab and Jew: Wounded Spirits in a Promised Land	David K. Shipler
1988	The Making of the Atomic Bomb	Richard Rhodes
1989	A Bright Shining Lie: John Paul Vann and America in Vietnam	Neil Sheehan

YEAR	TITLE	AUTHOR
1990	And Their Children After Them	Dale Maharidge and Michael Williamson
1991	The Ants	Bert Holldobler and Edward O. Wilson
1992	The Prize: The Epic Quest for Oil, Money, and Power	Daniel Yergin
1993	Lincoln at Gettysburg: The Words That Remade America	Garry Wills
1994	Lenin's Tomb: The Last Days of the Soviet Empire	David Remnick
1995	The Beak of the Finch: A Story of Evolution in Our Time	Jonathan Weiner
1996	The Haunted Land: Facing Europe's Ghosts After Communism	Tina Rosenberg
1997	Ashes to Ashes: America's Hundred-Year Cigarette War, the Public Health, and the Unabashed Triumph of Philip Morris	Richard Kluger
1998	Guns, Germs, and Steel: The Fates of Human Societies	Jared Diamond
1999	Annals of the Former World	John McPhee
2000	Embracing Defeat: Japan in the Wake of World War II	John W. Dower
2001	Hirohito and the Making of Modern Japan	Herbert P. Bix
2002	Carry Me Home: Birmingham, Alabama, the Climactic Battle of the Civil Rights Revolution	Diane McWhorter
2003	"A Problem from Hell": America and the Age of Genocide	Samantha Power
2004	Gulag: A History	Anne Applebaum
2005	Ghost Wars	Steve Coll
2006	Imperial Reckoning: The Untold Story of Britain's Gulag in Kenya	Caroline Elkins
2007	The Looming Tower: Al-Qaeda and the Road to 9/11	Lawrence Wright
2008	The Years of Extermination: Nazi Germany and the Jews, 1939–1945	Saul Friedländer
2009	Slavery by Another Name: The Re-Enslavement of Black Americans from the Civil War to World War II	Douglas A. Blackmon
2010	The Dead Hand: The Untold Story of the Cold War Arms Race and Its Dangerous Legacy	David E. Hoffman

[1]Awarded posthumously.

Letters, Drama, and Music (continued)

Music

Awarded for a musical piece of "significant dimension" composed by an American and first performed or recorded in the United States between 16 January of the previous year and 15 January of the year of the award.

YEAR	TITLE	COMPOSER
1943	Secular Cantata No. 2: A Free Song	William Schuman
1944	Symphony No. 4, Opus 34	Howard Hanson
1945	Appalachian Spring	Aaron Copland
1946	The Canticle of the Sun	Leo Sowerby
1947	Symphony No. 3	Charles Ives
1948	Symphony No. 3	Walter Piston
1949	music for the film Louisiana Story	Virgil Thomson
1950	The Consul	Gian Carlo Menotti
1951	Giants in the Earth	Douglas S. Moore
1952	Symphony Concertante	Gail Kubik
1953	no award	
1954	Concerto for Two Pianos and Orchestra	Quincy Porter
1955	The Saint of Bleecker Street	Gian Carlo Menotti
1956	Symphony No. 3	Ernst Toch
1957	Meditation on Ecclesiastics	Norman Dello Joio
1958	Vanessa	Samuel Barber
1959	Concerto for Piano and Orchestra	John LaMontaine
1960	Second String Quartet	Elliott Carter
1961	Symphony No. 7	Walter Piston
1962	The Crucible	Robert Ward
1963	Piano Concerto No. 1	Samuel Barber
1964	no award	
1965	no award	
1966	Variations for Orchestra	Leslie Bassett
1967	Quartet No. 3	Leon Kirchner
1968	Echoes of Time and the River	George Crumb
1969	String Quartet No. 3	Karel Husa
1970	Time's Encomium	Charles Wuorinen
1971	Synchronisms No. 6 for Piano and Electronic Sound	Mario Davidovsky
1972	Windows	Jacob Druckman
1973	String Quartet No. 3	Elliott Carter
1974	Notturno	Donald Martino
1975	From the Diary of Virginia Woolf	Dominick Argento
1976	Air Music	Ned Rorem
1977	Visions of Terror and Wonder	Richard Wernick
1978	Deja Vu for Percussion Quartet and Orchestra	Michael Colgrass
1979	Aftertones of Infinity	Joseph Schwantner
1980	In Memory of a Summer Day	David Del Tredici

YEAR	TITLE	COMPOSER
1981	no award	
1982	Concerto for Orchestra	Roger Sessions
1983	Symphony No. 1 (Three Movements for Orchestra)	Ellen Taaffe Zwilich
1984	"Canti del sole" for Tenor and Orchestra	Bernard Rands
1985	Symphony RiverRun	Stephen Albert
1986	Wind Quintet IV	George Perle
1987	The Flight into Egypt	John Harbison
1988	12 New Etudes for Piano	William Bolcom
1989	Whispers out of Time	Roger Reynolds
1990	"Duplicates": A Concerto for Two Pianos and Orchestra	Mel Powell
1991	Symphony	Shulamit Ran
1992	The Face of the Night, the Heart of the Dark	Wayne Peterson
1993	Trombone Concerto	Christopher Rouse
1994	Of Reminiscences and Reflections	Gunther Schuller
1995	Stringmusic	Morton Gould
1996	Lilacs, for Voice and Orchestra	George Walker
1997	Blood on the Fields	Wynton Marsalis
1998	String Quartet No. 2 (Musica Instrumentalis)	Aaron Jay Kernis
1999	Concerto for Flute, Strings, and Percussion	Melinda Wagner
2000	Life Is a Dream, Opera in Three Acts: Act II, Concert Version	Lewis Spratlan
2001	Symphony No. 2 for String Orchestra	John Corigliano
2002	Ice Field	Henry Brant
2003	On the Transmigration of Souls	John Adams
2004	Tempest Fantasy	Paul Moravec
2005	Second Concerto for Orchestra	Steven Stucky
2006	Piano Concerto: "Chiavi in mano"	Yehudi Wyner
2007	Sound Grammar	Ornette Coleman
2008	The Little Match Girl Passion	David Lang
2009	Double Sextet	Steve Reich
2010	Violin Concerto	Jennifer Higdon

Special Awards and Citations[1]

YEAR	RECIPIENT	FOR
1987	Joseph Pulitzer, Jr.	his contributions to journalism and letters
1992	Art Spiegelman	his graphic novel Maus

YEAR	RECIPIENT	FOR
1996	Herb Caen	his contributions as a voice of San Francisco

Letters, Drama, and Music (continued)

Special Awards and Citations[1] (continued)

YEAR	RECIPIENT	FOR
1998	George Gershwin[2]	centennial commemoration of his birth, celebrating his work in music
1999	Duke Ellington[2]	centennial commemoration of his birth, celebrating his life's work in music
2006	Edmund S. Morgan	his life's work as an American historian
	Thelonious Monk[2]	his contributions to jazz

YEAR	RECIPIENT	FOR
2007	Ray Bradbury	his contributions to science fiction and fantasy
	John Coltrane[2]	his contributions to jazz
2008	Bob Dylan	his profound influence on pop culture and American music
2010	Hank Williams[2]	his role, as a songwriter and performer, in advancing country music

[1]For the past 25 years.   [2]Awarded posthumously.

National Book Awards

In 1950 a consortium of publishing groups established the National Book Awards. The goals were to bring exceptional books written by Americans to the public's attention and to encourage reading. The number of award categories has varied from the inaugural 3 to as many as 28 in 1980. Today, the awards recognize achievements in four genres: fiction, nonfiction, poetry, and young people's literature. A five-member judging panel chooses a winner for each genre. Award: US$10,000 cash and a bronze sculpture.

Fiction

YEAR	TITLE	AUTHOR
1950	The Man with the Golden Arm	Nelson Algren
1951	The Collected Stories of William Faulkner	William Faulkner
1952	From Here to Eternity	James Jones
1953	Invisible Man	Ralph Ellison
1954	The Adventures of Augie March	Saul Bellow
1955	A Fable	William Faulkner
1956	Ten North Frederick	John O'Hara
1957	The Field of Vision	Wright Morris
1958	The Wapshot Chronicle	John Cheever
1959	The Magic Barrel	Bernard Malamud
1960	Goodbye, Columbus	Philip Roth
1961	The Waters of Kronos	Conrad Richter
1962	The Moviegoer	Walker Percy
1963	Morte d'Urban	J.F. Powers
1964	The Centaur	John Updike
1965	Herzog	Saul Bellow
1966	The Collected Stories of Katherine Anne Porter	Katherine Anne Porter
1967	The Fixer	Bernard Malamud
1968	The Eighth Day	Thornton Wilder
1969	Steps	Jerzy Kosinski
1970	Them	Joyce Carol Oates
1971	Mr. Sammler's Planet	Saul Bellow
1972	The Complete Stories	Flannery O'Connor
1973	Augustus	John Williams
	Chimera	John Barth
1974	A Crown of Feathers and Other Stories	Isaac Bashevis Singer
	Gravity's Rainbow	Thomas Pynchon
1975	Dog Soldiers: A Novel	Robert Stone
	The Hair of Harold Roux	Thomas Williams
1976	J.R.	William Gaddis
1977	The Spectator Bird	Wallace Stegner

Fiction (continued)

YEAR	TITLE	AUTHOR
1978	Blood Tie	Mary Lee Settle
1979	Going After Cacciato	Tim O'Brien
1980	Sophie's Choice[1]	William Styron
1981	Plains Song[1]	Wright Morris
1982	Rabbit Is Rich[1]	John Updike
1983	The Color Purple[1]	Alice Walker
1984	Victory over Japan: A Book of Stories	Ellen Gilchrist
1985	White Noise	Don DeLillo
1986	World's Fair	E.L. Doctorow
1987	Paco's Story	Larry Heinemann
1988	Paris Trout	Pete Dexter
1989	Spartina	John Casey
1990	Middle Passage	Charles Johnson
1991	Mating	Norman Rush
1992	All the Pretty Horses	Cormac McCarthy
1993	The Shipping News	E. Annie Proulx
1994	A Frolic of His Own	William Gaddis
1995	Sabbath's Theater	Philip Roth
1996	Ship Fever	Andrea Barrett
1997	Cold Mountain	Charles Frazier
1998	Charming Billy	Alice McDermott
1999	Waiting	Ha Jin
2000	In America	Susan Sontag
2001	The Corrections	Jonathan Franzen
2002	Three Junes	Julia Glass
2003	The Great Fire	Shirley Hazzard
2004	The News from Paraguay	Lily Tuck
2005	Europe Central	William T. Vollmann
2006	The Echo Maker	Richard Powers
2007	Tree of Smoke	Denis Johnson
2008	Shadow Country	Peter Matthiessen
2009	Let the Great World Spin	Colum McCann

Nonfiction

YEAR	TITLE	AUTHOR
1950	The Life of Ralph Waldo Emerson	Ralph L. Rusk
1951	Herman Melville	Newton Arvin
1952	The Sea Around Us	Rachel Carson
1953	The Course of Empire	Bernard A. De Voto

National Book Awards (continued)

Nonfiction (continued)

YEAR	TITLE	AUTHOR
1954	A Stillness at Appomattox	Bruce Catton
1955	The Measure of Man: On Freedom, Human Values, Survival, and the Modern Temper	Joseph Wood Krutch
1956	American in Italy	Herbert Kubly
1957	Russia Leaves the War	George F. Kennan
1958	The Lion and the Throne: The Life and Times of Sir Edward Coke (1552–1634)	Catherine Drinker Bowen
1959	Mistress to an Age: A Life of Madame de Staël	J. Christopher Herold
1960	James Joyce	Richard Ellmann
1961	The Rise and Fall of the Third Reich: A History of Nazi Germany	William L. Shirer
1962	The City in History: Its Origins, Its Transformations, and Its Prospects	Lewis Mumford
1963	Henry James, Vol. II: The Conquest of London (1870–1881); Vol. III: The Middle Years (1882–1895)	Leon Edel
1964	The Rise of the West: A History of the Human Community[2]	William H. McNeill
1965	The Life of Lenin[2]	Louis Fischer
1966	A Thousand Days: John F. Kennedy in the White House[2]	Arthur M. Schlesinger, Jr.
1967	The Enlightenment: An Interpretation, Vol. I[2]	Peter Gay
1968	Memoirs: 1925–1950[2]	George F. Kennan
1969	White over Black: American Attitudes Toward the Negro, 1550–1812[2]	Winthrop D. Jordan
1970	Huey Long[2]	T. Harry Williams
1971	Roosevelt: The Soldier of Freedom[2]	James MacGregor Burns
1972	Eleanor and Franklin: The Story of Their Relationship, Based on Eleanor Roosevelt's Private Papers[3]	Joseph P. Lash
1973	George Washington, Vol. IV: Anguish and Farewell, 1793–1799[3]	James Thomas Flexner
1974	Macaulay: The Shaping of the Historian[4]	John Clive
1975	The Life of Emily Dickinson[3]	Richard B. Sewall
1976	The Problem of Slavery in the Age of Revolution, 1770–1823[2]	David Brion Davis
1977	Norman Thomas: The Last Idealist[5]	W.A. Swanberg
1978	Samuel Johnson[5]	W. Jackson Bate
1979	Robert Kennedy and His Times[5]	Arthur M. Schlesinger, Jr.
1980	The Right Stuff[6]	Tom Wolfe
1981	China Men[6]	Maxine Hong Kingston
1982	The Soul of a New Machine[6]	Tracy Kidder
1983	China: Alive in the Bitter Sea[6]	Fox Butterfield
1984	Andrew Jackson and the Course of American Democracy, 1833–1845	Robert V. Remini
1985	Common Ground: A Turbulent Decade in the Lives of Three American Families	J. Anthony Lukas
1986	Arctic Dreams	Barry Lopez
1987	The Making of the Atomic Bomb	Richard Rhodes
1988	A Bright Shining Lie: John Paul Vann and America in Vietnam	Neil Sheehan
1989	From Beirut to Jerusalem	Thomas L. Friedman
1990	The House of Morgan: An American Banking Dynasty and the Rise of Modern Finance	Ron Chernow
1991	Freedom	Orlando Patterson
1992	Becoming a Man: Half a Life Story	Paul Monette
1993	United States: Essays, 1952–1992	Gore Vidal
1994	How We Die: Reflections on Life's Final Chapter	Sherwin B. Nuland
1995	The Haunted Land: Facing Europe's Ghosts After Communism	Tina Rosenberg
1996	An American Requiem: God, My Father, and the War That Came Between Us	James Carroll
1997	American Sphinx: The Character of Thomas Jefferson	Joseph J. Ellis
1998	Slaves in the Family	Edward Ball
1999	Embracing Defeat: Japan in the Wake of World War II	John W. Dower
2000	In the Heart of the Sea: The Tragedy of the Whaleship Essex	Nathaniel Philbrick
2001	The Noonday Demon: An Atlas of Depression	Andrew Solomon
2002	Master of the Senate: The Years of Lyndon Johnson	Robert A. Caro
2003	Waiting for Snow in Havana	Carlos Eire
2004	Arc of Justice: A Saga of Race, Civil Rights, and Murder in the Jazz Age	Kevin Boyle
2005	The Year of Magical Thinking	Joan Didion
2006	The Worst Hard Time: The Untold Story of Those Who Survived the Great American Dust Bowl	Timothy Egan
2007	Legacy of Ashes: The History of the CIA	Tim Weiner
2008	The Hemingses of Monticello: An American Family	Annette Gordon-Reed
2009	The First Tycoon: The Epic Life of Cornelius Vanderbilt	T.J. Stiles

Poetry

YEAR	TITLE	AUTHOR
1950	Paterson: Book III and Selected Poems	William Carlos Williams
1951	The Auroras of Autumn	Wallace Stevens
1952	Collected Poems	Marianne Moore

National Book Awards (continued)

Poetry (continued)

YEAR	TITLE	AUTHOR
1953	Collected Poems, 1917–1952	Archibald MacLeish
1954	Collected Poems	Conrad Aiken
1955	The Collected Poems of Wallace Stevens	Wallace Stevens
1956	The Shield of Achilles	W.H. Auden
1957	Things of This World: Poems	Richard Wilbur
1958	Promises: Poems, 1954–1956	Robert Penn Warren
1959	Words for the Wind: The Collected Verse of Theodore Roethke	Theodore Roethke
1960	Life Studies	Robert Lowell
1961	The Woman at the Washington Zoo	Randall Jarrell
1962	Poems	Alan Dugan
1963	Traveling Through the Dark	William Stafford
1964	Selected Poems	John Crowe Ransom
1965	The Far Field	Theodore Roethke
1966	Buckdancer's Choice: Poems	James Dickey
1967	Nights and Days	James Merrill
1968	The Light Around the Body: Poems	Robert Bly
1969	His Toy, His Dream, His Rest: 308 Dream Songs	John Berryman
1970	The Complete Poems	Elizabeth Bishop
1971	To See, To Take: Poems	Mona Van Duyn
1972	The Collected Poems of Frank O'Hara	Frank O'Hara
	Selected Poems	Howard Moss
1973	Collected Poems, 1951–1971	A.R. Ammons
1974	Diving into the Wreck: Poems, 1971–1972	Adrienne Rich
	The Fall of America: Poems of These States	Allen Ginsberg
1975	Presentation Piece	Marilyn Hacker
1976	Self-Portrait in a Convex Mirror: Poems	John Ashbery
1977	Collected Poems, 1930–1976	Richard Eberhart
1978	The Collected Poems of Howard Nemerov	Howard Nemerov
1979	Mirabell: Books of Number	James Merrill
1980	Ashes: Poems New & Old	Philip Levine
1981	The Need to Hold Still	Lisel Mueller
1982	Life Supports: New and Collected Poems	William Bronk
1983	Country Music: Selected Early Poems	Charles Wright
1984	Selected Poems	Galway Kinnell
1985	Yin	Carolyn Kizer
1986	The Flying Change	Henry Taylor
1987	Thomas and Beulah	Rita Dove
1988	Partial Accounts: New and Selected Poems	William Meredith
1989	New and Collected Poems	Richard Wilbur
1990	The World Doesn't End	Charles Simic
1991	What Work Is: Poems	Philip Levine
1992	New and Selected Poems	Mary Oliver
1993	Garbage	A.R. Ammons
1994	Worshipful Company of Fletchers: Poems	James Tate
1995	Passing Through: The Later Poems, New and Selected	Stanley Kunitz
1996	Scrambled Eggs & Whiskey: Poems, 1991–1995	Hayden Carruth
1997	Effort at Speech: New and Selected Poems	William Meredith
1998	This Time: New and Selected Poems	Gerald Stern
1999	Vice: New and Selected Poems	Ai
2000	Blessing the Boats: New and Selected Poems, 1988–2000	Lucille Clifton
2001	Poems Seven: New and Complete Poetry	Alan Dugan
2002	In the Next Galaxy	Ruth Stone
2003	The Singing	C.K. Williams
2004	Door in the Mountain: New and Collected Poems, 1965–2003	Jean Valentine
2005	Migration: New and Selected Poems	W.S. Merwin
2006	Splay Anthem	Nathaniel Mackey
2007	Time and Materials	Robert Hass
2008	Fire to Fire: New and Collected Poems	Mark Doty
2009	Transcendental Studies: A Trilogy	Keith Waldrop

Young People's Literature

YEAR	TITLE	AUTHOR
1969	Journey from Peppermint Street	Meindert De Jong
1970	A Day of Pleasure: Stories of a Boy Growing Up in Warsaw[7]	Isaac Bashevis Singer
1971	The Marvelous Misadventures of Sebastian[7]	Lloyd Alexander
1972	The Slightly Irregular Fire Engine; or, The Hithering Thithering Djinn[7]	Donald Barthelme
1973	The Farthest Shore[7]	Ursula Le Guin

National Book Awards (continued)

Young People's Literature (continued)

YEAR	TITLE	AUTHOR
1974	The Court of the Stone Children[7]	Eleanor Cameron
1975	M.C. Higgins, the Great[7]	Virginia Hamilton
1976	Bert Breen's Barn	Walter D. Edmonds
1977	The Master Puppeteer	Katherine Paterson
1978	The View from the Oak: The Private Worlds of Other Creatures	Judith and Herbert Kohl
1979	The Great Gilly Hopkins	Katherine Paterson
1980	A Gathering of Days: A New England Girl's Journal, 1830–32[8]	Joan W. Blos
1981	The Night Swimmers[9]	Betsy Byars
1982	Westmark[9]	Lloyd Alexander
1983	Homesick: My Own Story[9]	Jean Fritz
1996	Parrot in the Oven: Mi Vida	Victor Martinez
1997	Dancing on the Edge	Han Nolan
1998	Holes	Louis Sachar
1999	When Zachary Beaver Came to Town	Kimberly Willis Holt
2000	Homeless Bird	Gloria Whelan
2001	True Believer	Virginia Euwer Wolff
2002	The House of the Scorpion	Nancy Farmer
2003	The Canning Season	Polly Horvath
2004	The Godless	Pete Hautman
2005	The Penderwicks	Jeanne Birdsall
2006	The Astonishing Life of Octavian Nothing, Traitor to the Nation, Vol. 1: The Pox Party	M.T. Anderson
2007	The Absolutely True Diary of a Part-Time Indian	Sherman Alexie
2008	What I Saw and How I Lied	Judy Blundell
2009	Claudette Colvin: Twice Toward Justice	Phillip Hoose

[1]Fiction (Hardcover). [2]History and Biography (Nonfiction). [3]Biography. [4]History. [5]Biography and Autobiography. [6]General Nonfiction (Hardcover). [7]Children's Books. [8]Children's Books (Hardcover). [9]Children's Books, Fiction (Hardcover).

Newbery Medal

The American Library Association (ALA) began awarding the John Newbery Medal in 1922 to the author of the most distinguished American children's book of the previous year, as judged by the ALA's Children's Librarians' Section (now called the Association for Library Service to Children). Established at the suggestion of Frederic G. Melcher of the R.R. Bowker Publishing Company, the award is named for John Newbery, the 18th-century English publisher who was among the first to publish books exclusively for children. Prize: inscribed bronze medal.

ALA Newbery Medal Web site:
<www.ala.org/alsc/newbery.html>.

YEAR	TITLE	AUTHOR
1922	The Story of Mankind	Hendrik Willem van Loon
1923	The Voyages of Doctor Dolittle	Hugh Lofting
1924	The Dark Frigate	Charles Hawes
1925	Tales from Silver Lands	Charles Finger
1926	Shen of the Sea	Arthur Bowie Chrisman
1927	Smoky, the Cowhorse	Will James
1928	Gay Neck, the Story of a Pigeon	Dhan Gopal Mukerji
1929	The Trumpeter of Krakow	Eric P. Kelly
1930	Hitty, Her First Hundred Years	Rachel Field
1931	The Cat Who Went to Heaven	Elizabeth Coatsworth
1932	Waterless Mountain	Laura Adams Armer
1933	Young Fu of the Upper Yangtze	Elizabeth Lewis
1934	Invincible Louisa: The Story of the Author of Little Women	Cornelia Meigs
1935	Dobry	Monica Shannon
1936	Caddie Woodlawn	Carol Ryrie Brink

YEAR	TITLE	AUTHOR
1937	Roller Skates	Ruth Sawyer
1938	The White Stag	Kate Seredy
1939	Thimble Summer	Elizabeth Enright
1940	Daniel Boone	James Daugherty
1941	Call It Courage	Armstrong Sperry
1942	The Matchlock Gun	Walter Edmonds
1943	Adam of the Road	Elizabeth Janet Gray
1944	Johnny Tremain	Esther Forbes
1945	Rabbit Hill	Robert Lawson
1946	Strawberry Girl	Lois Lenski
1947	Miss Hickory	Carolyn Sherwin Bailey
1948	The Twenty-One Balloons	William Pène du Bois
1949	King of the Wind	Marguerite Henry
1950	The Door in the Wall	Marguerite de Angeli
1951	Amos Fortune, Free Man	Elizabeth Yates
1952	Ginger Pye	Eleanor Estes
1953	Secret of the Andes	Ann Nolan Clark
1954	...And Now Miguel	Joseph Krumgold
1955	The Wheel on the School	Meindert De Jong
1956	Carry On, Mr. Bowditch	Jean Lee Latham
1957	Miracles on Maple Hill	Virginia Sorenson

Newbery Medal (continued)

YEAR	TITLE	AUTHOR
1958	Rifles for Watie	Harold Keith
1959	The Witch of Blackbird Pond	Elizabeth George Speare
1960	Onion John	Joseph Krumgold
1961	Island of the Blue Dolphins	Scott O'Dell
1962	The Bronze Bow	Elizabeth George Speare
1963	A Wrinkle in Time	Madeleine L'Engle
1964	It's Like This, Cat	Emily Neville
1965	Shadow of a Bull	Maia Wojciechowska
1966	I, Juan de Pareja	Elizabeth Borton de Treviño
1967	Up a Road Slowly	Irene Hunt
1968	From the Mixed-Up Files of Mrs. Basil E. Frankweiler	E.L. Konigsburg
1969	The High King	Lloyd Alexander
1970	Sounder	William H. Armstrong
1971	Summer of the Swans	Betsy Byars
1972	Mrs. Frisby and the Rats of NIMH	Robert C. O'Brien
1973	Julie of the Wolves	Jean Craighead George
1974	The Slave Dancer	Paula Fox
1975	M.C. Higgins, the Great	Virginia Hamilton
1976	The Grey King	Susan Cooper
1977	Roll of Thunder, Hear My Cry	Mildred D. Taylor
1978	Bridge to Terabithia	Katherine Paterson
1979	The Westing Game	Ellen Raskin
1980	A Gathering of Days: A New England Girl's Journal, 1830–1832	Joan W. Blos
1981	Jacob Have I Loved	Katherine Paterson
1982	A Visit to William Blake's Inn: Poems for Innocent and Experienced Travelers	Nancy Willard
1983	Dicey's Song	Cynthia Voigt

YEAR	TITLE	AUTHOR
1984	Dear Mr. Henshaw	Beverly Cleary
1985	The Hero and the Crown	Robin McKinley
1986	Sarah, Plain and Tall	Patricia MacLachlan
1987	The Whipping Boy	Sid Fleischman
1988	Lincoln: A Photo-biography	Russell Freedman
1989	Joyful Noise: Poems for Two Voices	Paul Fleischman
1990	Number the Stars	Lois Lowry
1991	Maniac Magee	Jerry Spinelli
1992	Shiloh	Phyllis Reynolds Naylor
1993	Missing May	Cynthia Rylant
1994	The Giver	Lois Lowry
1995	Walk Two Moons	Sharon Creech
1996	The Midwife's Apprentice	Karen Cushman
1997	The View from Saturday	E.L. Konigsburg
1998	Out of the Dust	Karen Hesse
1999	Holes	Louis Sachar
2000	Bud, Not Buddy	Christopher Paul Curtis
2001	A Year Down Yonder	Richard Peck
2002	A Single Shard	Linda Sue Park
2003	Crispin: The Cross of Lead	Avi
2004	The Tale of Despereaux: Being the Story of a Mouse, a Princess, Some Soup, and a Spool of Thread	Kate DiCamillo
2005	Kira-Kira	Cynthia Kadohata
2006	Criss Cross	Lynne Rae Perkins
2007	The Higher Power of Lucky	Susan Patron
2008	Good Masters! Sweet Ladies! Voices from a Medieval Village	Laura Amy Schlitz
2009	The Graveyard Book	Neil Gaiman
2010	When You Reach Me	Rebecca Stead

Caldecott Medal

The American Library Association (ALA) awards the Caldecott Medal annually to "the artist of the most distinguished American picture book for children." It was established by the ALA in 1938 on the suggestion of Frederic G. Melcher, chairman of the board of the R.R. Bowker Publishing Company, and named for the 19th-century English illustrator Randolph Caldecott. If the author/reteller/translator/editor is someone other than the illustrator, that person's name appears in parentheses after that of the illustrator. Prize: inscribed bronze medal.

Web site: <www.ala.org/alsc/caldecott.html>.

YEAR	TITLE	ILLUSTRATOR
1938	Animals of the Bible: A Picture Book	Dorothy P. Lathrop (Helen Dean Fish)
1939	Mei Li	Thomas Handforth
1940	Abraham Lincoln	Ingri and Edgar Parin d'Aulaire
1941	They Were Strong and Good	Robert Lawson
1942	Make Way for Ducklings	Robert McCloskey
1943	The Little House	Virginia Lee Burton
1944	Many Moons	Louis Slobodkin (James Thurber)
1945	Prayer for a Child	Elizabeth Orton Jones (Rachel Field)
1946	The Rooster Crows	Maud and Miska Petersham
1947	The Little Island	Leonard Weisgard (Golden MacDonald, pseud. [Margaret Wise Brown])
1948	White Snow, Bright Snow	Roger Duvoisin (Alvin Tresselt)
1949	The Big Snow	Berta and Elmer Hader
1950	Song of the Swallows	Leo Politi
1951	The Egg Tree	Katherine Milhous

Caldecott Medal (continued)

YEAR	TITLE	ILLUSTRATOR
1952	Finders Keepers	Nicolas, pseud. (Nicholas Mordvinoff) (Will, pseud. [William Lipkind])
1953	The Biggest Bear	Lynd Ward
1954	Madeline's Rescue	Ludwig Bemelmans
1955	Cinderella, or the Little Glass Slipper	Marcia Brown (translated from Charles Perrault by Marcia Brown)
1956	Frog Went A-Courtin'	Feodor Rojankovsky (John Langstaff)
1957	A Tree Is Nice	Marc Simont (Janice Udry)
1958	Time of Wonder	Robert McCloskey
1959	Chanticleer and the Fox	Barbara Cooney (adapted from Chaucer's The Canterbury Tales by Barbara Cooney)
1960	Nine Days to Christmas	Marie Hall Ets (Marie Hall Ets and Aurora Labastida)
1961	Baboushka and the Three Kings	Nicolas Sidjakov (Ruth Robbins)
1962	Once a Mouse	Marcia Brown
1963	The Snowy Day	Ezra Jack Keats
1964	Where the Wild Things Are	Maurice Sendak
1965	May I Bring a Friend?	Beni Montresor (Beatrice Schenk de Regniers)
1966	Always Room for One More	Nonny Hogrogian (Sorche Nic Leodhas, pseud. [Leclair Alger])
1967	Sam, Bangs & Moonshine	Evaline Ness
1968	Drummer Hoff	Ed Emberley (Barbara Emberley)
1969	The Fool of the World and the Flying Ship	Uri Shulevitz (Arthur Ransome)
1970	Sylvester and the Magic Pebble	William Steig
1971	A Story, a Story	Gail E. Haley
1972	One Fine Day	Nonny Hogrogian
1973	The Funny Little Woman	Blair Lent (Arlene Mosel)
1974	Duffy and the Devil	Margot Zemach (Harve Zemach)
1975	Arrow to the Sun	Gerald McDermott
1976	Why Mosquitoes Buzz in People's Ears	Leo and Diane Dillon (Verna Aardema)
1977	Ashanti to Zulu: African Traditions	Leo and Diane Dillon (Margaret Musgrove)
1978	Noah's Ark	Peter Spier
1979	The Girl Who Loved Wild Horses	Paul Goble
1980	Ox-Cart Man	Barbara Cooney (Donald Hall)
1981	Fables	Arnold Lobel
1982	Jumanji	Chris Van Allsburg
1983	Shadow	Marcia Brown (translated from Blaise Cendrars by Marcia Brown)
1984	The Glorious Flight: Across the Channel with Louis Blériot	Alice and Martin Provensen
1985	Saint George and the Dragon	Trina Schart Hyman (Margaret Hodges)
1986	The Polar Express	Chris Van Allsburg
1987	Hey, Al	Richard Egielski (Arthur Yorinks)
1988	Owl Moon	John Schoenherr (Jane Yolen)
1989	Song and Dance Man	Stephen Gammell (Karen Ackerman)
1990	Lon Po Po: A Red-Riding Hood Story from China	Ed Young
1991	Black and White	David Macaulay
1992	Tuesday	David Wiesner
1993	Mirette on the High Wire	Emily Arnold McCully
1994	Grandfather's Journey	Allen Say (Walter Lorraine)
1995	Smoky Night	David Diaz (Eve Bunting)
1996	Officer Buckle and Gloria	Peggy Rathmann
1997	Golem	David Wisniewski
1998	Rapunzel	Paul O. Zelinsky
1999	Snowflake Bentley	Mary Azarian (Jacqueline Briggs Martin)
2000	Joseph Had a Little Overcoat	Simms Taback
2001	So You Want To Be President?	David Small (Judith St. George)
2002	The Three Pigs	David Wiesner
2003	My Friend Rabbit	Eric Rohmann
2004	The Man Who Walked Between the Towers	Mordicai Gerstein
2005	Kitten's First Full Moon	Kevin Henkes
2006	The Hello, Goodbye Window	Chris Raschka (Norton Juster)
2007	Flotsam	David Wiesner
2008	The Invention of Hugo Cabret	Brian Selznick
2009	The House in the Night	Beth Krommes (Susan Marie Swanson)
2010	The Lion & the Mouse	Jerry Pinkney

Coretta Scott King Award

Established in 1970, the Coretta Scott King Award honors outstanding African American authors and illustrators of books for young people. The books, which may be fiction or nonfiction, must be original works that portray some aspect of the black experience. In 1982 the award came under the aegis of the American Library Association. Only authors were eligible for the award until 1974, and no illustrator awards were given in 1975–1977 and 1985. Prize: citation, honorarium, and encyclopedia set.

Coretta Scott King Award Web site:
<www.ala.org/ala/emiert/corettascottking bookaward/corettascott.htm>.

1970   Lillie Patterson, *Martin Luther King, Jr.: Man of Peace*

1971   Charlemae Rollins, *Black Troubador: Langston Hughes*

1972   Elton C. Fax, *17 Black Artists*

1973   *I Never Had It Made: The Autobiography of Jackie Robinson*, as told to Alfred Duckett

1974   author: Sharon Bell Mathis, *Ray Charles;* illustrator: George Ford, *Ray Charles*

1975   author: Dorothy Robinson, *The Legend of Africana*

1976   author: Pearl Bailey, *Duey's Tale*

1977   author: James Haskins, *The Story of Stevie Wonder*

1978   author: Eloise Greenfield, *Africa Dream;* illustrator: Carole Byard, *Africa Dream*

1979   author: Ossie Davis, *Escape to Freedom;* illustrator: Tom Feelings, *Something on My Mind*

1980   author: Walter Dean Myers, *The Young Landlords;* illustrator: Carole Byard, *Cornrows*

1981   author: Sidney Poitier, *This Life;* illustrator: Ashley Bryan, *Beat the Story Drum, Pum-Pum*

1982   author: Mildred D. Taylor, *Let the Circle Be Unbroken;* illustrator: John Steptoe, *Mother Crocodiletexas tech*

1983   author: Virginia Hamilton, *Sweet Whispers, Brother Rush;* illustrator: Peter Mugabane, *Black Child*

1984   author: Lucille Clifton, *Everett Anderson's Goodbye;* illustrator: Pat Cummings, *My Mama Needs Me*

1985   author: Walter Dean Myers, *Motown and Didi*

1986   author: Virginia Hamilton, *The People Could Fly: American Black Folktales;* illustrator: Jerry Pinkney, *The Patchwork Quilt*

1987   author: Mildred Pitts Walter, *Justin and the Best Biscuits in the World;* illustrator: Jerry Pinkney, *Half a Moon and One Whole Star*

1988   author: Mildred D. Taylor, *The Friendship;* illustrator: John Steptoe, *Mufaro's Beautiful Daughters: An African Tale*

1989   author: Walter Dean Myers, *Fallen Angels;* illustrator: Jerry Pinkney, *Mirandy and Brother Wind*

1990   authors: Patricia C. and Frederick L. McKissack, *A Long Hard Journey: The Story of the Pullman Porter;* illustrator: Jan Spivey Gilchrist, *Nathaniel Talking*

1991   author: Mildred D. Taylor, *The Road to Memphis;* illustrators: Leo and Diahe Dillon, *Aida*

1992   author: Walter Dean Myers, *Now Is Your Time: The African American Struggle for Freedom;* illustrator: Faith Ringgold, *Tar Beach*

1993   author: Patricia C. McKissack, *Dark Thirty: Southern Tales of the Supernatural;* illustrator: Kathleen Atkins Wilson, *The Origin of Life on Earth: An African Creation Myth*

1994   author: Angela Johnson, *Toning the Sweep;* illustrator: Tom Feelings, *Soul Looks Back in Wonder*

1995   authors: Patricia C. and Frederick L. McKissack, *Christmas in the Big House, Christmas in the Quarters;* illustrator: James Ransome, *The Creation*

1996   author: Virginia Hamilton, *Her Stories;* illustrator: Tom Feelings, *The Middle Passage: White Ships/Black Cargo*

1997   author: Walter Dean Myers, *Slam;* illustrator: Jerry Pinkney, *Minty: A Story of Young Harriet Tubman*

1998   author: Sharon M. Draper, *Forged by Fire;* illustrator: Javaka Steptoe, *In Daddy's Arms I Am Tall: African Americans Celebrating Fathers*

1999   author: Angela Johnson, *Heaven;* illustrator: Michele Wood, *i see the rhythm*

2000   author: Christopher Paul Curtis, *Bud, Not Buddy;* illustrator: Brian Pinkney, *In the Time of the Drums*

2001   author: Jacqueline Woodson, *Miracle's Boys;* illustrator: Bryan Collier, *Uptown*

2002   author: Mildred D. Taylor, *The Land;* illustrator: Jerry Pinkney, *Goin' Someplace Special*

2003   author: Nikki Grimes, *Bronx Masquerade;* illustrator: E.B. Lewis, *Talkin' About Bessie: The Story of Aviator Elizabeth Coleman*

2004   author: Angela Johnson, *The First Part Last;* illustrator: Ashley Bryan, *Beautiful Blackbird*

2005   author: Toni Morrison, *Remember: The Journey to School Integration;* illustrator: Kadir Nelson, *Ellington Was Not a Street*

2006   author: Julius Lester, *Day of Tears: A Novel in Dialogue;* illustrator: Bryan Collier, *Rosa*

2007   author: Sharon Draper, *Copper Sun;* illustrator: Kadir Nelson, *Moses: When Harriet Tubman Led Her People to Freedom*

2008   author: Christopher Paul Curtis, *Elijah of Buxton;* illustrator: Ashley Bryan, *Let It Shine*

2009   author: Kadir Nelson, *We Are the Ship: The Story of Negro League Baseball;* illustrator: Floyd Cooper, *The Blacker the Berry*

2010   author: Vaunda Micheaux Nelson, *Bad News for Outlaws: The Remarkable Life of Bass Reeves, Deputy U.S. Marshal;* illustrator: Charles R. Smith, Jr., *My People*

Man Booker Prize

Awarded to the best full-length novel of the year written by a citizen of the Commonwealth or the Republic of Ireland and published in the UK between 1 October and 30 September. Prize: £50,000 (about US$75,000); each short-listed author receives £1,000 (about US$1,500). In 1993 Salman Rushdie was awarded the Booker of Bookers, a special award to mark 25 years of the Booker Prize, for *Midnight's Children*. In 2008 the Best of Bookers prize, to mark 40 years, was also won by Salman Rushdie's *Midnight's Children*. In 2005 the Man Booker International Prize was created, to be awarded biennially to a living writer for outstanding lifetime achievement. Prize: £60,000 (about US$90,000). Albanian novelist Ismail Kadare won the first Man Booker International Prize in 2005. Nigerian author Chinua Achebe won the second in 2007. Canadian short-story writer Alice Munro was awarded the third in 2009.
Web site: <www.themanbookerprize.com>.

YEAR	TITLE	AUTHOR	YEAR	TITLE	AUTHOR
1969	Something to Answer For	P.H. Newby	1989	The Remains of the Day	Kazuo Ishiguro
1970	The Elected Member	Bernice Rubens	1990	Possession	A.S. Byatt
1971	In a Free State	V.S. Naipaul	1991	The Famished Road	Ben Okri
1972	G.	John Berger	1992	The English Patient	Michael Ondaatje
1973	The Siege of Krishnapur	J.G. Farrell	1992	Sacred Hunger	Barry Unsworth
1974	The Conservationist	Nadine Gordimer	1993	Paddy Clarke Ha Ha Ha	Roddy Doyle
1974	Holiday	Stanley Middleton	1994	How Late It Was, How Late	James Kelman
1975	Heat and Dust	Ruth Prawer Jhabvala	1995	The Ghost Road	Pat Barker
1976	Saville	David Storey	1996	Last Orders	Graham Swift
1977	Staying On	Paul Scott	1997	The God of Small Things	Arundhati Roy
1978	The Sea, The Sea	Iris Murdoch	1998	Amsterdam	Ian McEwan
1979	Offshore	Penelope Fitzgerald	1999	Disgrace	J.M. Coetzee
1980	Rites of Passage	William Golding	2000	The Blind Assassin	Margaret Atwood
1981	Midnight's Children	Salman Rushdie	2001	True History of the Kelly Gang	Peter Carey
1982	Schindler's Ark	Thomas Keneally	2002	Life of Pi	Yann Martel
1983	Life and Times of Michael K	J.M. Coetzee	2003	Vernon God Little	DBC Pierre
1984	Hotel du Lac	Anita Brookner	2004	The Line of Beauty	Alan Hollinghurst
1985	The Bone People	Keri Hulme	2005	The Sea	John Banville
1986	The Old Devils	Kingsley Amis	2006	The Inheritance of Loss	Kiran Desai
1987	Moon Tiger	Penelope Lively	2007	The Gathering	Anne Enright
1988	Oscar and Lucinda	Peter Carey	2008	The White Tiger	Aravind Adiga
			2009	Wolf Hall	Hilary Mantel

Costa Book Awards

The Whitbread Book Awards were inaugurated in 1971, and in 2006 Britain's Costa chain of coffee shops took over the prize. Since 1985, awards have been given in five categories: Novel, First Novel, Biography, Poetry, and Children's. From these a panel of judges chooses one overall winner—the Costa Book of the Year. The total prize fund is £50,000 (about US$75,000): each of the category award winners receives £5,000 (about US$7,500), and the Book of the Year winner receives an additional £25,000 (about US$37,500).

This list includes Novel award winners from 1971 to 1984 and Book of the Year winners from 1985 to 2008.
Costa Book Awards Web site:
<www.costabookawards.com>.

YEAR	TITLE	AUTHOR	YEAR	TITLE	AUTHOR
1971	The Destiny Waltz	Gerda Charles	1985	Elegies	Douglas Dunn
1972	The Bird of Night	Susan Hill	1986	An Artist of the Floating World	Kazuo Ishiguro
1973	The Chip-Chip Gatherers	Shiva Naipaul	1987	Under the Eye of the Clock	Christopher Nolan
1974	The Sacred and Profane Love Machine	Iris Murdoch	1988	The Comforts of Madness	Paul Sayer
1975	Docherty	William McIlvanney	1989	Coleridge: Early Visions	Richard Holmes
1976	The Children of Dynmouth	William Trevor	1990	Hopeful Monsters	Nicholas Mosley
			1991	A Life of Picasso	John Richardson
1977	Injury Time	Beryl Bainbridge	1992	Swing Hammer Swing!	Jeff Torrington
1978	Picture Palace	Paul Theroux	1993	Theory of War	Joan Brady
1979	The Old Jest	Jennifer Johnston	1994	Felicia's Journey	William Trevor
1980	How Far Can You Go?	David Lodge	1995	Behind the Scenes at the Museum	Kate Atkinson
1981	Silver's City	Maurice Leitch	1996	The Spirit Level	Seamus Heaney
1982	Young Shoulders	John Wain	1997	Tales from Ovid	Ted Hughes
1983	Fools of Fortune	William Trevor	1998	Birthday Letters	Ted Hughes
1984	Kruger's Alp	Christopher Hope	1999	Beowulf	Seamus Heaney

Costa Book Awards (continued)

YEAR	TITLE	AUTHOR	YEAR	TITLE	AUTHOR
2000	*English Passengers*	Matthew Kneale	2004	*Small Island*	Andrea Levy
2001	*The Amber Spyglass*	Philip Pullman	2005	*Matisse: The Master*	Hilary Spurling
2002	*Samuel Pepys: The Unequalled Self*	Claire Tomalin	2006	*The Tenderness of Wolves*	Stef Penney
2003	*The Curious Incident of the Dog in the Night-Time*	Mark Haddon	2007	*Day*	A.L. Kennedy
			2008	*The Secret Scripture*	Sebastian Barry
			2009	*A Scattering*	Christopher Reid

Orange Prize for Fiction

Awarded to a work of published fiction written in English by a woman and published in the United Kingdom or Ireland. Prize: £30,000 (about US$45,000) and a bronze figurine called the "Bessie.". **Orange Prize for Fiction Web site:** <www.orangeprize.co.uk>.

YEAR	TITLE	AUTHOR	YEAR	TITLE	AUTHOR
1996	*A Spell of Winter*	Helen Dunmore	2005	*We Need To Talk About Kevin*	Lionel Shriver
1997	*Fugitive Pieces*	Anne Michaels	2006	*On Beauty*	Zadie Smith
1998	*Larry's Party*	Carol Shields	2007	*Half of a Yellow Sun*	Chimamanda Ngozi Adichie
1999	*A Crime in the Neighbourhood*	Suzanne Berne	2008	*The Road Home*	Rose Tremain
2000	*When I Lived in Modern Times*	Linda Grant	2009	*Home*	Marilynne Robinson
2001	*The Idea of Perfection*	Kate Grenville	2010	*The Lacuna*	Barbara Kingsolver
2002	*Bel Canto*	Ann Patchett			
2003	*Property*	Valerie Martin			
2004	*Small Island*	Andrea Levy			

Prix Goncourt

The Prix de l'Académie Goncourt was first awarded in 1903 from the estate of the brothers and French literary figures Edmond Huot de Goncourt (1822–1896) and Jules Huot de Goncourt (1830–1870) for a work of contemporary prose in French. Additional prizes have been awarded for such categories as best work of poetry, best first novel, and best biography. Prize: €10 (about US$12).

YEAR	TITLE	AUTHOR	YEAR	TITLE	AUTHOR
1903	*Force ennemie*	John-Antoine Nau	1924	*Le Chèvrefeuille; Le Purgatoire; Le Chapitre treize d'Athénée*	Thierry Sandre
1904	*La Maternelle*	Léon Frapié			
1905	*Les Civilisés*	Claude Farrère			
1906	*Dingley, l'illustre écrivain*	Jérôme and Jean Tharaud	1925	*Raboliot*	Maurice Genevoix
			1926	*Le Supplice de Phèdre*	Henry Deberly
1907	*Terres lorraines*	Emile Moselly	1927	*Jérôme, 60° latitude nord*	Maurice Bedel
1908	*Ecrit sur l'eau*	Francis de Miomandre	1928	*Un Homme se penche sur son passé*	Maurice Constantin-Weyer
1909	*En France*	Marius-Ary Leblond	1929	*L'Ordre*	Marcel Arland
1910	*De Goupil à Margot*	Louis Pergaud	1930	*Malaisie*	Henri Fauconnier
1911	*Monsieur des Lourdines*	Alphonse de Chateaubriant	1931	*Mal d'amour*	Jean Fayard
			1932	*Les Loups*	Guy Mazeline
1912	*Les Filles de la pluie*	André Savignon	1933	*La Condition humaine*	André Malraux
1913	*Le Peuple de la mer*	Marc Elder	1934	*Capitaine Conan*	Roger Vercel
1914	*L'Appel du sol*	Adrien Bertrand	1935	*Sang et lumières*	Joseph Peyré
1915	*Gaspard*	René Benjamin	1936	*L'Empreinte de Dieu*	Maxence van der Meersch
1916	*Le Feu*	Henri Barbusse			
1917	*La Flamme au poing*	Henri Malherbe	1937	*Faux passeports*	Charles Plisnier
1918	*Civilisation*	Georges Duhamel	1938	*L'Araigne*	Henri Troyat
1919	*A l'ombre des jeunes filles en fleur*	Marcel Proust	1939	*Les Enfants gâtés*	Philippe Hériat
			1940	*Les Grandes Vacances*	Francis Ambrière
1920	*Nene*	Ernest Pérochon	1941	*Vent de Mars*	Henri Pourrat
1921	*Batouala*	René Maran	1942	*Pareil à des enfants*	Bernard Marc
1922	*Le Vitriol de la lune; Le Martyre de l'obèse*	Henri Béraud	1943	*Passage de l'homme*	Marius Grout
			1944	*Le Premier Accroc coûte 200 francs*	Elsa Triolet
1923	*Rabevel; ou, le mal des ardents*	Lucien Fabre	1945	*Mon village à l'heure allemande*	Jean-Louis Bory

Prix Goncourt (continued)

YEAR	TITLE	AUTHOR
1946	*Histoire d'un fait divers*	Jean-Jacques Gautier
1947	*Les Forêts de la nuit*	Jean-Louis Curtis
1948	*Les Grandes Familles*	Maurice Druon
1949	*Week-end à Zuydcoote*	Robert Merle
1950	*Les Jeux sauvages*	Paul Colin
1951	*Le Rivage des Syrtes*	Julien Gracq (declined)
1952	*Léon Morin, prêtre*	Béatrice Beck
1953	*Les Bêtes; Le Temps des morts*	Pierre Gascar
1954	*Mandarins*	Simone de Beauvoir
1955	*Les Eaux mêlées*	Roger Ikor
1956	*Les Racines du ciel*	Romain Gary
1957	*La Loi*	Roger Vailland
1958	*Saint Germain; ou, la négociation*	Francis Walder
1959	*Le Dernier des justes*	André Schwartz-Bart
1960	*Dieu est né en exil*	Vintila Horia
1961	*La Pitié de Dieu*	Jean Cau
1962	*Les Bagages de sable*	Anna Langfus
1963	*Quand la mer se retire*	Armand Lanoux
1964	*L'État sauvage*	Georges Conchon
1965	*L'Adoration*	Jacques Borel
1966	*Oublier Palerme*	Edmonde Charles-Roux
1967	*La Marge*	André Pieyre de Mandiargues
1968	*Les Fruits de l'hiver*	Bernard Clavel
1969	*Creezy*	Félicien Marceau
1970	*Le Roi des Aulnes*	Michel Tournier
1971	*Les Bêtises*	Jacques Laurent
1972	*L'Épervier de Maheux*	Jean Carrière
1973	*L'Ogre*	Jacques Chessex
1974	*La Dentellière*	Pascal Lainé
1975	*La Vie devant soi*	Emile Ajar (declined)
1976	*Les Flamboyants*	Patrick Grainville
1977	*John l'enfer*	Didier Decoin
1978	*Rue des boutiques obscures*	Patrick Modiano
1979	*Pélagie-la-charrette*	Antonine Maillet
1980	*Le Jardin d'acclimatation*	Yves Navarre
1981	*Anne Marie*	Lucien Bodard
1982	*Dans la main de l'ange*	Dominique Fernandez
1983	*Les Égarés*	Frédérick Tristan
1984	*L'Amant*	Marguerite Duras
1985	*Les Noces barbares*	Yann Queffélec
1986	*Valet de nuit*	Michel Host
1987	*La Nuit sacrée*	Tahar Ben Jelloun
1988	*L'Exposition coloniale*	Erik Orsenna
1989	*Un Grand Pas vers le Bon Dieu*	Jean Vautrin
1990	*Les Champs d'honneur*	Jean Rouaud
1991	*Les Filles du calvaire*	Pierre Combescot
1992	*Texaco*	Patrick Chamoiseau
1993	*La Rocher de Tanios*	Amin Maalouf
1994	*Un Aller simple*	Didier van Cauwelaert
1995	*Le Testament français*	Andreï Makine
1996	*Le Chasseur zéro*	Pascale Roze
1997	*La Bataille*	Patrick Rambaud
1998	*Confidence pour confidence*	Paule Constant
1999	*Je m'en vais*	Jean Echenoz
2000	*Ingrid Caven*	Jean-Jacques Schuhl
2001	*Rouge Brésil*	Jean-Christophe Rufin
2002	*Les Ombres errantes*	Pascal Quignard
2003	*La Maîtresse de Brecht*	Jacques-Pierre Amette
2004	*Le Soleil des Scorta*	Laurent Gaudé
2005	*Trois jours chez ma mère*	François Weyergans
2006	*Les Bienveillantes*	Jonathan Littell
2007	*Alabama Song*	Gilles Leroy
2008	*Syngué sabour: pierre de patience*	Atiq Rahimi
2009	*Trois femmes puissantes*	Marie NDiaye

T.S. Eliot Prize

Great Britain's Poetry Book Society awards the T.S. Eliot Prize to the best new collection of poetry published in the UK or the Republic of Ireland during the preceding year. The prize is £15,000 (about US$22,500).

YEAR	WORK	AUTHOR	COUNTRY
1993	*First Language*	Ciaran Carson	Ireland
1994	*The Annals of Chile*	Paul Muldoon	United Kingdom
1995	*My Alexandria*	Mark Doty	United States
1996	*Subhuman Redneck Poems*	Les Murray	Australia
1997	*God's Gift to Women*	Don Paterson	United Kingdom
1998	*Birthday Letters*	Ted Hughes	United Kingdom
1999	*Billy's Rain*	Hugo Williams	United Kingdom
2000	*The Weather in Japan*	Michael Longley	United Kingdom
2001	*The Beauty of the Husband*	Anne Carson	Canada
2002	*Dart*	Alice Oswald	United Kingdom
2003	*Landing Light*	Don Paterson	United Kingdom
2004	*Reel*	George Szirtes	United Kingdom
2005	*Rapture*	Carol Ann Duffy	United Kingdom
2006	*District and Circle*	Seamus Heaney	Ireland
2007	*The Drowned Book*	Sean O'Brien	United Kingdom
2008	*Nigh-No-Place*	Jen Hadfield	United Kingdom
2009	*The Water Table*	Philip Gross	United Kingdom

Bollingen Prize in Poetry

The Bollingen Prize in Poetry is awarded biennially to the American poet whose work represents the highest achievement in the field of American poetry during the preceding two-year period. The committee considers published work, particularly work published during that preceding two-year period. Former winners of the US$100,000 prize are not eligible. **Web site:** <http://beinecke.library.yale.edu/bollingen>.

YEAR	POET	YEAR	POET	YEAR	POET
1948	Ezra Pound	1963	Robert Frost	1987	Stanley Kunitz
1949	Wallace Stevens	1965	Horace Gregory	1989	Edgar Bowers
1950	John Crowe Ransom	1967	Robert Penn Warren	1991	Laura Riding Jackson
1951	Marianne Moore	1969	John Berryman		Donald Justice
1952	Archibald MacLeish		Karl Shapiro	1993	Mark Strand
	William Carlos Williams	1971	Richard Wilbur	1995	Kenneth Koch
1953	W.H. Auden		Mona Van Duyn	1997	Gary Snyder
1954	Léonie Adams	1973	James Merrill	1999	Robert Creeley
	Louise Bogan	1975	A.R. Ammons	2001	Louise Glück
1955	Conrad Aiken	1977	David Ignatow	2003	Adrienne Rich
1956	Allen Tate	1979	W.S. Merwin	2005	Jay Wright
1957	E.E. Cummings	1981	May Swenson	2007	Frank Bidart
1958	Theodore Roethke		Howard Nemerov	2009	Allen Grossman
1959	Delmore Schwartz	1983	Anthony Hecht		
1960	Yvor Winters		John Hollander		
1961	Richard Eberhart	1985	John Ashbery		
	John Hall Wheelock		Fred Chappell		

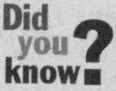

Did you know?

Although the belief in vampires was widespread throughout Asia and Europe, it was primarily a Slavic and Hungarian legend, with reports proliferating in Hungary from 1730 to 1735. As a result of Bram Stoker's novel *Dracula* (1897), the vampire—which leaves its burial place at night to drink the blood of humans—is, among the various demons of ancient folk tradition, the one that has enjoyed the most conspicuous literary and cinematic success in the 20th and 21st centuries.

Pritzker Architecture Prize

*The Pritzker Architecture Prize, awarded by the Hyatt Foundation since 1979, is given to an outstanding living architect for built work. Prize: US$100,000 and a bronze medallion. **Web site:** <www.pritzkerprize.com>.*

YEAR	NAME	COUNTRY	YEAR	NAME	COUNTRY
1979	Philip Johnson	United States	1996	Rafael Moneo	Spain
1980	Luis Barragán	Mexico	1997	Sverre Fehn	Norway
1981	James Stirling	Great Britain	1998	Renzo Piano	Italy
1982	Kevin Roche	United States	1999	Norman Foster	Great Britain
1983	I.M. Pei	United States	2000	Rem Koolhaas	Netherlands
1984	Richard Meier	United States	2001	Jacques Herzog	Switzerland
1985	Hans Hollein	Austria		Pierre de Meuron	Switzerland
1986	Gottfried Böhm	West Germany	2002	Glenn Murcutt	Australia
1987	Kenzo Tange	Japan	2003	Jørn Utzon	Denmark
1988	Gordon Bunshaft	United States	2004	Zaha Hadid	Great Britain
	Oscar Niemeyer	Brazil	2005	Thom Mayne	United States
1989	Frank O. Gehry	United States	2006	Paulo Mendes da Rocha	Brazil
1990	Aldo Rossi	Italy	2007	Richard Rogers	Great Britain
1991	Robert Venturi	United States	2008	Jean Nouvel	France
1992	Alvaro Siza	Portugal	2009	Peter Zumthor	Switzerland
1993	Fumihiko Maki	Japan	2010	Kazuyo Sejima	Japan
1994	Christian de Portzamparc	France		Ryue Nishizawa	Japan
1995	Tadao Ando	Japan			

Sport

Sport Coverage

The tables that follow contain information about the top contests of all the major sports that are international in character, as well as some professional and amateur sports that attract a huge national following—such as baseball in the United States and cricket in the United Kingdom, Australia, India, and the other Test match countries. In many sports the Olympic Games held every four years constitute the world championships; they are included in the listings below. In some cases circumstances such as marriage or divorce have changed the name of a winning athlete. The following tables give the name by which the athlete was known for the given year, resulting in instances in which the athlete may appear under two or more names in the same table. Similarly, if the citizenship of an athlete or name of the athlete's country changes, the tables reflect the accurate name for each given year.

Sporting Codes for Countries
Codes of the International Olympic Committee (IOC)

AFG	Afghanistan	CUB	Cuba	KAZ	Kazakhstan
AHO	Netherlands Antilles	CYP	Cyprus	KEN	Kenya
ALB	Albania	CZE	Czech Republic	KGZ	Kyrgyzstan
ALG	Algeria	DEN	Denmark	KIR	Kiribati
AND	Andorra	DJI	Djibouti	KOR	Korea, Republic of
ANG	Angola	DMA	Dominica		(South Korea)
ANT	Antigua and Barbuda	DOM	Dominican Republic	KOS	Kosovo
ARG	Argentina	ECU	Ecuador	KSA	Saudi Arabia
ARM	Armenia	EGY	Egypt	KUW	Kuwait
ARU	Aruba	ERI	Eritrea	LAO	Laos
ASA	American Samoa	ESA	El Salvador	LAT	Latvia
AUS	Australia	ESP	Spain	LBA	Libya
AUT	Austria	EST	Estonia	LBR	Liberia
AZE	Azerbaijan	ETH	Ethiopia	LCA	Saint Lucia
BAH	Bahamas, The	FIJ	Fiji	LES	Lesotho
BAN	Bangladesh	FIN	Finland	LIB	Lebanon
BAR	Barbados	FRA	France	LIE	Liechtenstein
BDI	Burundi	FSM	Micronesia, Federated	LTU	Lithuania
BEL	Belgium		States of	LUX	Luxembourg
BEN	Benin	GAB	Gabon	MAD	Madagascar
BER	Bermuda	GAM	Gambia, The	MAR	Morocco
BHU	Bhutan	GBR	Great Britain	MAS	Malaysia
BIH	Bosnia and Herzegovina	GBS	Guinea-Bissau	MAW	Malawi
BIZ	Belize	GEO	Georgia	MDA	Moldova
BLR	Belarus	GEQ	Equatorial Guinea	MDV	Maldives
BOL	Bolivia	GER	Germany	MEX	Mexico
BOT	Botswana	GHA	Ghana	MGL	Mongolia
BRA	Brazil	GRE	Greece	MHL	Marshall Islands
BRN	Bahrain	GRN	Grenada	MKD	Macedonia[1]
BRU	Brunei	GUA	Guatemala	MLI	Mali
BUL	Bulgaria	GUI	Guinea	MLT	Malta
BUR	Burkina Faso	GUM	Guam	MNE	Montenegro
CAF	Central African Republic	GUY	Guyana	MON	Monaco
CAM	Cambodia	HAI	Haiti	MOZ	Mozambique
CAN	Canada	HKG	Hong Kong	MRI	Mauritius
CAY	Cayman Islands	HON	Honduras	MTN	Mauritania
CGO	Congo, Republic of the	HUN	Hungary	MYA	Myanmar (Burma)
CHA	Chad	INA	Indonesia	NAM	Namibia
CHI	Chile	IND	India	NCA	Nicaragua
CHN	China	IRI	Iran	NED	Netherlands
CIV	Côte d'Ivoire	IRL	Ireland	NEP	Nepal
CMR	Cameroon	IRQ	Iraq	NGR	Nigeria
COD	Congo, Democratic	ISL	Iceland	NIG	Niger
	Republic of the	ISR	Israel	NOR	Norway
COK	Cook Islands	ISV	US Virgin Islands	NRU	Nauru
COL	Colombia	ITA	Italy	NZL	New Zealand
COM	Comoros	IVB	British Virgin Islands	OMA	Oman
CPV	Cape Verde	JAM	Jamaica	PAK	Pakistan
CRC	Costa Rica	JOR	Jordan	PAN	Panama
CRO	Croatia	JPN	Japan	PAR	Paraguay

Sporting Codes for Countries (continued)
Codes of the International Olympic Committee (IOC) (continued)

PER	Peru	SLE	Sierra Leone	TOG	Togo
PHI	Philippines	SLO	Slovenia	TPE	Taiwan
PLE	Palestine	SMR	San Marino	TRI	Trinidad and Tobago
PLW	Palau	SOL	Solomon Islands	TUN	Tunisia
PNG	Papua New Guinea	SOM	Somalia	TUR	Turkey
POL	Poland	SRB	Serbia	TUV	Tuvalu
POR	Portugal	SRI	Sri Lanka	UAE	United Arab Emirates
PRK	Korea, Democratic People's Republic of (North Korea)	STP	Sao Tome and Principe	UGA	Uganda
		SUD	Sudan	UKR	Ukraine
		SUI	Switzerland	URU	Uruguay
PUR	Puerto Rico	SUR	Suriname	USA	United States
QAT	Qatar	SVK	Slovakia	UZB	Uzbekistan
ROU	Romania	SWE	Sweden	VAN	Vanuatu
RSA	South Africa	SWZ	Swaziland	VEN	Venezuela
RUS	Russia	SYR	Syria	VIE	Vietnam
RWA	Rwanda	TAN	Tanzania	VIN	Saint Vincent and the Grenadines
SAM	Samoa	TGA	Tonga		
SEN	Senegal	THA	Thailand	YEM	Yemen
SEY	Seychelles	TJK	Tajikistan	ZAM	Zambia
SIN	Singapore	TKM	Turkmenistan	ZIM	Zimbabwe
SKN	Saint Kitts and Nevis	TLS	East Timor (Timor-Leste)		

Historical and Other Country Codes

ENG	England	GGY	Guernsey	TCH	Czechoslovakia
FRG	Germany, Federal Republic of (West Germany)	IMN	Isle of Man	UNT	Unified Team[2]
		JEY	Jersey	URS	USSR
GDR	German Democratic Republic (East Germany)	NIR	Northern Ireland	WAL	Wales
		SCO	Scotland	YUG	Yugoslavia

[1]*Macedonia is known by the IOC as the Former Yugoslav Republic of Macedonia.*   [2]*The Unified Team consisted of athletes from the Commonwealth of Independent States plus Georgia.*

The Olympic Games

By the 6th century BC several sporting festivals had achieved cultural importance in the Greek world. The most prominent among them were the Olympic Games at the city of Olympia, first recorded in 776 BC and held at four-year intervals thereafter. Those games, comprising many of the sports now included in the Summer Games, were abolished in AD 393 by the Roman emperor Theodosius I, probably because of their pagan associations.

In 1887 the 24-year-old French aristocrat and educator Pierre, baron de Coubertin, conceived the idea of reviving the Olympic Games and spent seven years gathering support for his plan. At an international congress in 1894, his plan was accepted and the International Olympic Committee (IOC) was founded. The first modern Olympic Games were held in Athens in April 1896, with some 300 representatives from 13 nations competing. The revival led to the formation of international amateur sports organizations and national Olympic committees throughout the world.

The IOC is responsible for maintaining the regular celebration of the games, seeing that the games are carried out in a spirit of peace and intercultural communication, and promoting amateur sport throughout the world. IOC members may not accept from the government of their country, or from any other entity, instructions that compromise their independence.

The Olympic Games have come to be regarded as the world's foremost sports competition. Before the 1970s the Games were officially limited to amateurs, but since that time many events have been opened to professional athletes. In 1924 the Winter Games were created, and in 1986 the IOC voted to alternate the Winter and Summer Games every two years, beginning in 1994.

The games were canceled during the two world wars (1916, 1940, and 1944) and have frequently served as venues for the expression of political dissent. China refused to participate in the Summer Games from 1956 until 1984 because of Taiwan's participation; 26 nations boycotted the games in 1976 over the participation of New Zealand, some of whose athletes had competed in apartheid-era South Africa; the United States and some 60 other countries boycotted the 1980 games in Moscow to protest the Soviet invasion of Afghanistan, and the Communist bloc and Cuba in turn boycotted the 1984 Los Angeles games.

In light of the IOC's declared independence from political and financial interests, in 1998 the world was shocked by allegations of widespread corruption within the committee. Several committee members, it was found, had accepted bribes to approve the bid of Salt Lake City UT as the site for the 2002 Winter Games. Impropriety was also alleged for several previous bid committees. The IOC responded by expelling six members and in 1999 announced a number of wide-ranging reforms.

IOC Web site: <www.olympic.org>.

Sites of the Modern Olympic Games

Summer Games

YEAR	LOCATION	YEAR	LOCATION	YEAR	LOCATION
1896	Athens, Greece	1948	London, England	1992	Barcelona, Spain
1900	Paris, France	1952	Helsinki, Finland	1996	Atlanta GA
1904	St. Louis MO	1956	Melbourne, VIC,	2000	Sydney, NSW, Australia
1908	London, England		Australia	2004	Athens, Greece
1912	Stockholm, Sweden	1960	Rome, Italy	2008	Beijing, China
1916	*not held*	1964	Tokyo, Japan	2012	*scheduled to be held 27*
1920	Antwerp, Belgium	1968	Mexico City, Mexico		*July–12 August,*
1924	Paris, France	1972	Munich, West Germany		*London, England*
1928	Amsterdam, Netherlands	1976	Montreal, QC, Canada	2016	*scheduled to be held*
1932	Los Angeles CA	1980	Moscow, USSR		*5–21 August,*
1936	Berlin, Germany	1984	Los Angeles CA		*Rio de Janeiro, Brazil*
1940–44	*not held*	1988	Seoul, Rep. of Korea		

Winter Games

YEAR	LOCATION	YEAR	LOCATION	YEAR	LOCATION
1924	Chamonix, France	1960	Squaw Valley CA	1994	Lillehammer, Norway
1928	St. Moritz, Switzerland	1964	Innsbruck, Austria	1998	Nagano, Japan
1932	Lake Placid NY	1968	Grenoble, France	2002	Salt Lake City UT
1936	Garmisch-Partenkirchen,	1972	Sapporo, Japan	2006	Turin, Italy
	Germany	1976	Innsbruck, Austria	2010	Vancouver, BC, Canada
1940–44	*not held*	1980	Lake Placid NY	2014	*scheduled to be held*
1948	St. Moritz, Switzerland	1984	Sarajevo, Yugoslavia		*7–23 February, Sochi,*
1952	Oslo, Norway	1988	Calgary, AB, Canada		*Russia*
1956	Cortina d'Ampezzo, Italy	1992	Albertville, France		

Summer Olympic Games

Gold-medal winners in all summer events since 1896. Note: East and West Germany fielded a joint all-Germany team in 1956, 1960, and 1964, abbreviated here as GER.

Archery

MEN'S INDIVIDUAL
1972   John Williams (USA)
1976   Darrell Pace (USA)
1980   Tomi Poikolainen (FIN)
1984   Darrell Pace (USA)
1988   Jay Barrs (USA)
1992   Sebastien Flute (FRA)
1996   Justin Huish (USA)
2000   Simon Fairweather (AUS)
2004   Marco Galiazzo (ITA)
2008   Viktor Ruban (UKR)

AU CORDON DORÉ (50 METERS)
1900   Henri Herouin (FRA)

AU CORDON DORÉ (33 METERS)
1900   Hubert van Innis (BEL)

AU CHAPELET (50 METERS)
1900   Eugène Mougin (FRA)

SUR LA PERCHE À LA HERSE
1900   Emmanuel Foulon (FRA)

AU CHAPELET (33 METERS)
1900   Hubert van Innis (BEL)

SUR LA PERCHE À LA PYRAMIDE
1900   Émile Grumiaux (FRA)

Archery (continued)

DOUBLE AMERICAN ROUND
1904   George Philip Bryant (USA)

(DOUBLE) YORK ROUND
1904   George Philip Bryant (USA)
1908   William Dod (GBR)

CONTINENTAL STYLE
1908   Eugène G. Grizot (FRA)

FIXED BIRD TARGET (SMALL)
1920   Edmond van Moer (BEL)

FIXED BIRD TARGET (LARGE)
1920   Édouard Cloetens (BEL)

MOVING BIRD TARGET (28 METERS)
1920   Hubert van Innis (BEL)

MOVING BIRD TARGET (33 METERS)
1920   Hubert van Innis (BEL)

MOVING BIRD TARGET (50 METERS)
1920   Julien Brulé (FRA)

WOMEN'S INDIVIDUAL
1972   Doreen Wilber (USA)
1976   Luann Ryon (USA)
1980   Ketevan Losaberidze (URS)
1984   Seo Hyang Soon (KOR)
1988   Kim Soo Nyung (KOR)

Summer Olympic Games (continued)

Archery (continued)

WOMEN'S INDIVIDUAL (CONTINUED)
1992	Cho Youn Jeong (KOR)
1996	Kim Kyung-Wook (KOR)
2000	Yun Mi-Jin (KOR)
2004	Park Sung Hyun (KOR)
2008	Zhang Juan Juan (CHN)

DOUBLE COLUMBIA ROUND
1904	Matilda Scott Howell (USA)

(DOUBLE) NATIONAL ROUND
1904	Matilda Scott Howell (USA)
1908	Sybil Fenton "Queenie" Newall (GBR)

MEN'S TEAM
1904	United States
1988	Republic of Korea
1992	Spain
1996	United States
2000	Republic of Korea
2004	Republic of Korea
2008	Republic of Korea

WOMEN'S TEAM
1904	United States
1988	Republic of Korea
1992	Republic of Korea
1996	Republic of Korea
2000	Republic of Korea
2004	Republic of Korea
2008	Republic of Korea

FIXED TARGET (2 EVENTS)
1920	Belgium

MOVING TARGET (28 METERS)
1920	The Netherlands

MOVING TARGET (33 METERS)
1920	Belgium

MOVING TARGET (50 METERS)
1920	Belgium

Association Football (Soccer)[1]

MEN
1900	Great Britain
1904	Canada
1908	Great Britain
1912	Great Britain
1920	Belgium
1924	Uruguay
1928	Uruguay
1936	Italy
1948	Sweden
1952	Hungary
1956	USSR
1960	Yugoslavia
1964	Hungary
1968	Hungary
1972	Poland
1976	East Germany
1980	Czechoslovakia
1984	France
1988	USSR
1992	Spain
1996	Nigeria
2000	Cameroon

Association Football (Soccer)[1] (continued)

MEN (CONTINUED)
2004	Argentina
2008	Argentina

WOMEN
1996	United States
2000	Norway
2004	United States
2008	United States

Athletics (Track and Field) (men)

60 METERS		SEC
1900	Alvin Kraenzlein (USA)	7
1904	Archie Hahn (USA)	7

100 METERS		SEC
1896	Thomas Burke (USA)	12.0
1900	Francis Jarvis (USA)	11.0
1904	Archie Hahn (USA)	11.0
1908	Reginald Walker (RSA)	10.8
1912	Ralph Craig (USA)	10.8
1920	Charles Paddock (USA)	10.8
1924	Harold Abrahams (GBR)	10.6
1928	Percy Williams (CAN)	10.8
1932	Eddie Tolan (USA)	10.3
1936	Jesse Owens (USA)	10.3
1948	Harrison Dillard (USA)	10.3
1952	Lindy Remigino (USA)	10.4
1956	Robert Morrow (USA)	10.5
1960	Armin Hary (GER)	10.2
1964	Robert Hayes (USA)	10.0
1968	James Hines (USA)	9.9
1972	Valery Borzov (URS)	10.14
1976	Hasely Crawford (TRI)	10.06
1980	Allan Wells (GBR)	10.25
1984	Carl Lewis (USA)	9.99
1988	Carl Lewis (USA)[2]	9.92
1992	Linford Christie (GBR)	9.96
1996	Donovan Bailey (CAN)	9.84
2000	Maurice Greene (USA)	9.87
2004	Justin Gatlin (USA)	9.85
2008	Usain Bolt (JAM)	9.69

200 METERS		SEC
1900	Walter Tewksbury (USA)	22.2
1904	Archie Hahn (USA)	21.6
1908	Robert Kerr (CAN)	22.6
1912	Ralph Craig (USA)	21.7
1920	Allen Woodring (USA)	22.0
1924	Jackson Scholz (USA)	21.6
1928	Percy Williams (CAN)	21.8
1932	Eddie Tolan (USA)	21.2
1936	Jesse Owens (USA)	20.7
1948	Melvin Patton (USA)	21.1
1952	Andy Stanfield (USA)	20.7
1956	Robert Morrow (USA)	20.6
1960	Livio Berruti (ITA)	20.5
1964	Henry Carr (USA)	20.3
1968	Tommie Smith (USA)	19.8
1972	Valery Borzov (URS)	20.00
1976	Donald Quarrie (JAM)	20.23
1980	Pietro Mennea (ITA)	20.19
1984	Carl Lewis (USA)	19.80
1988	Joe DeLoach (USA)	19.75
1992	Mike Marsh (USA)	20.01
1996	Michael Johnson (USA)	19.32
2000	Konstantinos Kenteris (GRE)	20.09

Summer Olympic Games (continued)

Athletics (Track and Field) (men) (continued)

200 METERS (CONTINUED)	SEC
2004 Shawn Crawford (USA)	19.79
2008 Usain Bolt (JAM)	19.30

400 METERS	SEC
1896 Thomas Burke (USA)	54.2
1900 Maxwell Long (USA)	49.4
1904 Harry Hillman (USA)	49.2
1908 Wyndham Halswelle (GBR)	50.0
1912 Charles Reidpath (USA)	48.2
1920 Bevil Rudd (RSA)	49.6
1924 Eric Liddell (GBR)	47.6
1928 Raymond Barbuti (USA)	47.8
1932 William Carr (USA)	46.2
1936 Archie Williams (USA)	46.5
1948 Arthur Wint (JAM)	46.2
1952 Vincent George Rhoden (JAM)	45.9
1956 Charles Jenkins (USA)	46.7
1960 Otis Davis (USA)	44.9
1964 Michael Larrabee (USA)	45.1
1968 Lee Evans (USA)	43.8
1972 Vincent Matthews (USA)	44.66
1976 Alberto Juantorena (CUB)	44.26
1980 Viktor Markin (URS)	44.60
1984 Alonzo Babers (USA)	44.27
1988 Steven Lewis (USA)	43.87
1992 Quincy Watts (USA)	43.50
1996 Michael Johnson (USA)	43.49
2000 Michael Johnson (USA)	43.84
2004 Jeremy Wariner (USA)	44.00
2008 LaShawn Merritt (USA)	43.75

800 METERS	MIN:SEC
1896 Edwin Flack (AUS)	2:11.0
1900 Alfred Tysoe (GBR)	2:01.2
1904 James Lightbody (USA)	1:56.0
1908 Melvin Sheppard (USA)	1:52.8
1912 James Edward Meredith (USA)	1:51.9
1920 Albert Hill (GBR)	1:53.4
1924 Douglas Lowe (GBR)	1:52.4
1928 Douglas Lowe (GBR)	1:51.8
1932 Thomas Hampson (GBR)	1:49.7
1936 John Woodruff (USA)	1:52.9
1948 Malvin Whitfield (USA)	1:49.2
1952 Malvin Whitfield (USA)	1:49.2
1956 Thomas Courtney (USA)	1:47.7
1960 Peter Snell (NZL)	1:46.3
1964 Peter Snell (NZL)	1:45.1
1968 Ralph Doubell (AUS)	1:44.3
1972 David Wottle (USA)	1:45.9
1976 Alberto Juantorena (CUB)	1:43.50
1980 Steven Ovett (GBR)	1:45.40
1984 Joaquim Cruz (BRA)	1:43.00
1988 Paul Ereng (KEN)	1:43.45
1992 William Tanui (KEN)	1:43.66
1996 Vebjoern Rodal (NOR)	1:42.58
2000 Nils Schumann (GER)	1:45.08
2004 Yury Borzakovsky (RUS)	1:44.45
2008 Wilfred Bungei (KEN)	1:44.65

1,500 METERS	MIN:SEC
1896 Edwin Flack (AUS)	4:33.2
1900 Charles Bennett (GBR)	4:06.2
1904 James Lightbody (USA)	4:05.4
1908 Melvin Sheppard (USA)	4:03.4
1912 Arnold Jackson (GBR)	3:56.8
1920 Albert Hill (GBR)	4:01.8
1924 Paavo Nurmi (FIN)	3:53.6

Athletics (Track and Field) (men) (continued)

1,500 METERS (CONTINUED)	MIN:SEC
1928 Harry Larva (FIN)	3:53.2
1932 Luigi Beccali (ITA)	3:51.2
1936 John Lovelock (NZL)	3:47.8
1948 Henry Eriksson (SWE)	3:49.8
1952 Joseph Barthel (LUX)	3:45.1
1956 Ronald Delany (IRL)	3:41.2
1960 Herbert Elliott (AUS)	3:35.6
1964 Peter Snell (NZL)	3:38.1
1968 Hezekiah Kipchoge Keino (KEN)	3:34.9
1972 Pekka Vasala (FIN)	3:36.3
1976 John Walker (NZL)	3:39.17
1980 Sebastian Coe (GBR)	3:38.40
1984 Sebastian Coe (GBR)	3:32.53
1988 Peter Rono (KEN)	3:35.96
1992 Fermin Cacho Ruiz (ESP)	3:40.12
1996 Noureddine Morceli (ALG)	3:35.78
2000 Noah Ngeny (KEN)	3:32.07
2004 Hicham El Guerrouj (MAR)	3:34.18
2008 winner stripped of medal	

5,000 METERS	MIN:SEC
1912 Hannes Kolehmainen (FIN)	14:36.6
1920 Joseph Guillemot (FRA)	14:55.6
1924 Paavo Nurmi (FIN)	14:31.2
1928 Vilho Ritola (FIN)	14:38.0
1932 Lauri Lehtinen (FIN)	14:30.0
1936 Gunnar Höckert (FIN)	14:22.2
1948 Gaston Reiff (BEL)	14:17.6
1952 Emil Zatopek (TCH)	14:06.6
1956 Vladimir Kuts (URS)	13:39.6
1960 Murray Halberg (NZL)	13:43.4
1964 Robert Keyser Schul (USA)	13:48.8
1968 Mohamed Gammoudi (TUN)	14:05.0
1972 Lasse Viren (FIN)	13:26.4
1976 Lasse Viren (FIN)	13:24.76
1980 Miruts Yifter (ETH)	13:21.00
1984 Said Aouita (MAR)	13:05.59
1988 John Ngugi (KEN)	13:11.70
1992 Dieter Baumann (GER)	13:12.52
1996 Venuste Niyongabo (BDI)	13:07.97
2000 Millon Wolde (ETH)	13:35.49
2004 Hicham El Guerrouj (MAR)	13:14.39
2008 Kenenisa Bekele (ETH)	12:57.82

5 MILES	MIN:SEC
1908 Emil Voigt (GBR)	25:11.2

10,000 METERS	MIN:SEC
1912 Hannes Kolehmainen (FIN)	31:20.8
1920 Paavo Nurmi (FIN)	31:45.8
1924 Vilho Ritola (FIN)	30:23.2
1928 Paavo Nurmi (FIN)	30:18.8
1932 Janusz Kusocinski (POL)	30:11.4
1936 Ilmari Salminen (FIN)	30:15.4
1948 Emil Zatopek (TCH)	29:59.6
1952 Emil Zatopek (TCH)	29:17.0
1956 Vladimir Kuts (URS)	28:45.6
1960 Pyotr Bolotnikov (URS)	28:32.2
1964 William Mills (USA)	28:24.4
1968 Nabiba Temu (KEN)	29:27.4
1972 Lasse Viren (FIN)	27:38.4
1976 Lasse Viren (FIN)	27:40.38
1980 Miruts Yifter (ETH)	27:42.70
1984 Alberto Cova (ITA)	27:47.54
1988 Brahim Boutaib (MAR)	27:21.46
1992 Khalid Skah (MAR)	27:46.70
1996 Haile Gebrselassie (ETH)	27:07.34

Summer Olympic Games (continued)

Athletics (Track and Field) (men) (continued)

10,000 METERS (CONTINUED) — MIN:SEC

		MIN:SEC
2000	Haile Gebrselassie (ETH)	27:18.20
2004	Kenenisa Bekele (ETH)	27:05.10
2008	Kenenisa Bekele (ETH)	27:01.17

MARATHON — HR:MIN:SEC

		HR:MIN:SEC
1896	Spiridon Louis (GRE)	2:58:50.0
1900	Michel Theato (FRA)	2:59:45.0
1904	Thomas Hicks (USA)	3:28:53.0
1908	John Hayes (USA)	2:55:18.4
1912	Kenneth McArthur (RSA)	2:36:54.8
1920	Hannes Kolehmainen (FIN)	2:32:35.8
1924	Albin Stenroos (FIN)	2:41:22.6
1928	Boughèra El Ouafi (FRA)	2:32:57.0
1932	Juan Carlos Zabala (ARG)	2:31:36.0
1936	Kitei Son (JPN)	2:29:19.2
1948	Delfo Cabrera (ARG)	2:34:51.6
1952	Emil Zatopek (TCH)	2:23:03.2
1956	Alain Mimoun-O-Kacha (FRA)	2:25:00.0
1960	Abebe Bikila (ETH)	2:15:16.2
1964	Abebe Bikila (ETH)	2:12:11.2
1968	Mamo Wolde (ETH)	2:20:26.4
1972	Frank Shorter (USA)	2:12:19.8
1976	Waldemar Cierpinski (GDR)	2:09:55.0
1980	Waldemar Cierpinski (GDR)	2:11:03.0
1984	Carlos Lopes (POR)	2:09:21.0
1988	Gelindo Bordin (ITA)	2:10:32.0
1992	Hwang Young-Cho (KOR)	2:13:23.0
1996	Josia Thugwane (RSA)	2:12:36.0
2000	Gezahgne Abera (ETH)	2:10:11.0
2004	Stefano Baldini (ITA)	2:10:55.0
2008	Samuel Kamau Wansiru (KEN)	2:06:32.0

110-METER HURDLES — SEC

		SEC
1896[3]	Thomas Curtis (USA)	17.6
1900	Alvin Kraenzlein (USA)	15.4
1904	Frederick Schule (USA)	16.0
1908	Forrest Smithson (USA)	15.0
1912	Frederick Kelly (USA)	15.1
1920	Earl Thomson (CAN)	14.8
1924	Daniel Kinsey (USA)	15.0
1928	Sydney Atkinson (RSA)	14.8
1932	George Saling (USA)	14.6
1936	Forrest Towns (USA)	14.2
1948	William Porter (USA)	13.9
1952	Harrison Dillard (USA)	13.7
1956	Lee Calhoun (USA)	13.5
1960	Lee Calhoun (USA)	13.8
1964	Hayes Wendell Jones (USA)	13.6
1968	Willie Davenport (USA)	13.3
1972	Rodney Milburn (USA)	13.24
1976	Guy Drut (FRA)	13.30
1980	Thomas Munkelt (GDR)	13.39
1984	Roger Kingdom (USA)	13.20
1988	Roger Kingdom (USA)	12.98
1992	Mark McKoy (CAN)	13.12
1996	Allen Johnson (USA)	12.95
2000	Anier Garcia (CUB)	13.00
2004	Liu Xiang (CHN)	12.91
2008	Dayron Robles (CUB)	12.93

200-METER HURDLES — SEC

		SEC
1900	Alvin Kraenzlein (USA)	25.4
1904	Harry Hillman (USA)	24.6

400-METER HURDLES — SEC

		SEC
1900	Walter Tewksbury (USA)	57.6
1904[4]	Harry Hillman (USA)	53.0

Athletics (Track and Field) (men) (continued)

400-METER HURDLES (CONTINUED) — SEC

		SEC
1908	Charles Bacon (USA)	55.0
1920	Frank Loomis (USA)	54.0
1924	Frederick Morgan Taylor (USA)	52.6
1928	David George Burghley (GBR)	53.4
1932	Robert Tisdall (IRL)	51.7
1936	Glenn Hardin (USA)	52.4
1948	Roy Cochran (USA)	51.1
1952	Charles Moore (USA)	50.8
1956	Glenn Davis (USA)	50.1
1960	Glenn Davis (USA)	49.3
1964	Warren Cawley (USA)	49.6
1968	David Hemery (GBR)	48.1
1972	John Akii-Bua (UGA)	47.82
1976	Edwin Moses (USA)	47.64
1980	Volker Beck (GDR)	48.70
1984	Edwin Moses (USA)	47.75
1988	Andre Phillips (USA)	47.19
1992	Kevin Young (USA)	46.78
1996	Derrick Adkins (USA)	47.54
2000	Angelo Taylor (USA)	47.50
2004	Felix Sánchez (DOM)	47.63
2008	Angelo Taylor (USA)	47.25

2,500-METER STEEPLECHASE — MIN:SEC

		MIN:SEC
1900	George Orton (USA)	7:34.4

2,590-METER STEEPLECHASE — MIN:SEC

		MIN:SEC
1904	James Lightbody (USA)	7:39.6

3,000-METER STEEPLECHASE — MIN:SEC

		MIN:SEC
1920	Percy Hodge (GBR)	10:00.4
1924	Vilho Ritola (FIN)	9:33.6
1928	Toivo Loukola (FIN)	9:21.8
1932	Volmari Iso-Hollo (FIN)	10:33.4[5]
1936	Volmari Iso-Hollo (FIN)	9:03.8
1948	Thore Sjöstrand (SWE)	9:04.6
1952	Horace Ashenfelter (USA)	8:45.4
1956	Christopher Brasher (GBR)	8:41.2
1960	Zdislaw Krzyszkowiak (POL)	8:34.2
1964	Gaston Roelants (BEL)	8:30.8
1968	Amos Biwott (KEN)	8:51.0
1972	Kipchoge Keino (KEN)	8:23.6
1976	Anders Gärderud (SWE)	8:08.02
1980	Bronislaw Malinowski (POL)	8:09.70
1984	Julius Korir (KEN)	8:11.80
1988	Julius Kariuki (KEN)	8:05.51
1992	Mathew Birir (KEN)	8:08.84
1996	Joseph Keter (KEN)	8:07.12
2000	Reuben Kosgei (KEN)	8:21.43
2004	Ezekiel Kemboi (KEN)	8:05.81
2008	Brimin Kiprop Kipruto (KEN)	8:10.34

3,200-METER STEEPLECHASE — MIN:SEC

		MIN:SEC
1908	Arthur Russell (GBR)	10:47.8

3,000 METERS (TEAM) (TEAM/INDIVIDUAL WINNER) — MIN:SEC

		MIN:SEC
1912	United States/Tell Berna	8:44.6
1920	United States/Horace Brown	8:45.4
1924	Finland/Paavo Nurmi	8:32

3 MILES (TEAM) (TEAM/INDIVIDUAL WINNER) — MIN:SEC

		MIN:SEC
1908	Great Britain/Joseph Deakin	14:39.6

5,000 METERS (TEAM) (TEAM/INDIVIDUAL WINNER) — MIN:SEC

		MIN:SEC
1900	Great Britain–Australia/Charles Bennett	15:20

Summer Olympic Games (continued)

Athletics (Track and Field) (men) (continued)

4 MILES (TEAM) (TEAM/INDIVIDUAL WINNER)		MIN:SEC
1904	United States/Arthur Newton	21:17.8

4 × 100-METER RELAY		SEC
1912	Great Britain	42.4
1920	United States	42.2
1924	United States	41.0
1928	United States	41.0
1932	United States	40.0
1936	United States	39.8
1948	United States	40.6
1952	United States	40.1
1956	United States	39.5
1960	Germany	39.5
1964	United States	39.0
1968	United States	38.2
1972	United States	38.19
1976	United States	38.33
1980	USSR	38.26
1984	United States	37.83
1988	USSR	38.19
1992	United States	37.40
1996	Canada	37.69
2000	United States	37.61
2004	Great Britain	38.07
2008	Jamaica	37.10

4 × 400-METER RELAY		MIN:SEC
1912	United States	3:16.6
1920	Great Britain	3:22.2
1924	United States	3:16.0
1928	United States	3:14.2
1932	United States	3:08.2
1936	Great Britain	3:09.0
1948	United States	3:10.4
1952	Jamaica	3:03.9
1956	United States	3:04.8
1960	United States	3:02.2
1964	United States	3:00.7
1968	United States	2:56.1
1972	Kenya	2:59.8
1976	United States	2:58.65
1980	USSR	3:01.08
1984	United States	2:57.91
1988	United States	2:56.16
1992	United States	2:55.74
1996	United States	2:55.99
2000	winner stripped of medal	
2004	United States	2:55.91
2008	United States	2:55.39

1,600-METER RELAY (200 × 200 × 400 × 800 METERS)		MIN:SEC
1908	United States	3:29.4

8,000-METER CROSS-COUNTRY		MIN:SEC
1920	Paavo Nurmi (FIN)	27:15

10,000-METER CROSS-COUNTRY		MIN:SEC
1924	Paavo Nurmi (FIN)	32:54.8

12,000-METER CROSS-COUNTRY		MIN:SEC
1912	Hannes Kolehmainen (FIN)	45:11.6

3,000-METER WALK		MIN:SEC
1920	Ugo Frigerio (ITA)	13:14.2

Athletics (Track and Field) (men) (continued)

3,500-METER WALK		MIN:SEC
1908	George Larner (GBR)	14:55

10,000-METER WALK		MIN:SEC
1912	George Goulding (CAN)	46:28.4
1920	Ugo Frigerio (ITA)	48:06.2
1924	Ugo Frigerio (ITA)	47:49.0
1948	John Mikaelsson (SWE)	45:13.2
1952	John Mikaelsson (SWE)	45:02.8

10-MILE WALK		HR:MIN:SEC
1908	George Larner (GBR)	1:15:57.4

20,000-METER WALK		HR:MIN:SEC
1956	Leonid Spirin (URS)	1:31:27.4
1960	Vladimir Golubnichy (URS)	1:34:07.2
1964	Kenneth Matthews (GBR)	1:29:34.0
1968	Vladimir Golubnichy (URS)	1:33:58.4
1972	Peter Frenkel (GDR)	1:26:42.6
1976	Daniel Bautista (MEX)	1:24:40.6
1980	Maurizio Damilano (ITA)	1:23:35.5
1984	Ernesto Canto (MEX)	1:23:13.0
1988	Jozef Pribilinec (TCH)	1:19:57.0
1992	Daniel Plaza Montero (ESP)	1:21:45.0
1996	Jefferson Pérez (ECU)	1:20:07.0
2000	Robert Korzeniowski (POL)	1:18:59.0
2004	Ivano Brugnetti (ITA)	1:19:40.0
2008	Valery Borchin (RUS)	1:19:01.0

50,000-METER WALK		HR:MIN:SEC
1932	Thomas Green (GBR)	4:50:10.0
1936	Harold Whitlock (GBR)	4:30:41.4
1948	John Ljunggren (SWE)	4:41:52.0
1952	Giuseppe Dordoni (ITA)	4:28:07.8
1956	Norman Read (NZL)	4:30:42.8
1960	Donald Thompson (GBR)	4:25:30.0
1964	Abdon Pamich (ITA)	4:11:12.4
1968	Christophe Höhne (GDR)	4:20:13.6
1972	Bernd Kannenberg (FRG)	3:56:11.6
1980	Hartwig Gauder (GDR)	3:49:24.0
1984	Raúl Gonzáles (MEX)	3:47:26.0
1988	Vyacheslav Ivanenko (URS)	3:38:29.0
1992	Andrey Perlov (UNT)	3:50:13.0
1996	Robert Korzeniowski (POL)	3:43:03.0
2000	Robert Korzeniowski (POL)	3:42:22.0
2004	Robert Korzeniowski (POL)	3:38:46.0
2008	Alex Schwazer (ITA)	3:37:09.0

HIGH JUMP		METERS
1896	Ellery Clark (USA)	1.81
1900	Irving Baxter (USA)	1.90
1904	Samuel Jones (USA)	1.80
1908	Harry Porter (USA)	1.90
1912	Alma Richards (USA)	1.93
1920	Richmond Landon (USA)	1.93
1924	Harold Osborn (USA)	1.98
1928	Robert King (USA)	1.94
1932	Duncan McNaughton (CAN)	1.97
1936	Cornelius Johnson (USA)	2.03
1948	John Winter (AUS)	1.98
1952	Walter Davis (USA)	2.04
1956	Charles Dumas (USA)	2.12
1960	Robert Shavlakadze (URS)	2.16
1964	Valery Brumel (URS)	2.18
1968	Richard Fosbury (USA)	2.24
1972	Yury Tarmak (URS)	2.23
1976	Jacek Wszola (POL)	2.25
1980	Gerd Wessig (GDR)	2.36

Summer Olympic Games (continued)

Athletics (Track and Field) (men) (continued)

HIGH JUMP (CONTINUED)		METERS
1984	Dietmar Mögenburg (FRG)	2.35
1988	Gennady Avdeyenko (URS)	2.38
1992	Javier Sotomayor (CUB)	2.34
1996	Charles Austin (USA)	2.39
2000	Sergey Klyugin (RUS)	2.35
2004	Stefan Holm (SWE)	2.36
2008	Andrey Silnov (RUS)	2.36

STANDING HIGH JUMP		METERS
1900	Ray Ewry (USA)	1.65
1904	Ray Ewry (USA)	1.60
1908	Ray Ewry (USA)	1.57
1912	Platt Adams (USA)	1.63

POLE VAULT		METERS
1896	William Welles Hoyt (USA)	3.30
1900	Irving Baxter (USA)	3.30
1904	Charles Dvorak (USA)	3.50
1908	Edward Cooke (USA); Alfred Gilbert (USA) (tied)	3.71
1912	Harry Babcock (USA)	3.95
1920	Frank Foss (USA)	4.09
1924	Lee Barnes (USA)	3.95
1928	Sabin Carr (USA)	4.20
1932	William Miller (USA)	4.31
1936	Earle Meadows (USA)	4.35
1948	Owen Guinn Smith (USA)	4.30
1952	Robert Richards (USA)	4.55
1956	Robert Richards (USA)	4.56
1960	Donald Bragg (USA)	4.70
1964	Fred Hansen (USA)	5.10
1968	Robert Seagren (USA)	5.40
1972	Wolfgang Nordwig (GDR)	5.50
1976	Tadeusz Slusarski (POL)	5.50
1980	Wladyslaw Kozakiewicz (POL)	5.78
1984	Pierre Quinon (FRA)	5.75
1988	Sergey Bubka (URS)	5.90
1992	Maksim Tarasov (UNT)	5.80
1996	Jean Galfione (FRA)	5.92
2000	Nick Hysong (USA)	5.90
2004	Timothy Mack (USA)	5.95
2008	Steve Hooker (AUS)	5.96

LONG JUMP		METERS
1896	Ellery Clark (USA)	6.35
1900	Alvin Kraenzlein (USA)	7.18
1904	Meyer Prinstein (USA)	7.34
1908	Francis Irons (USA)	7.48
1912	Albert Gutterson (USA)	7.60
1920	William Pettersson (SWE)	7.15
1924	William de Hart-Hubbard (USA)	7.44
1928	Edward Hamm (USA)	7.73
1932	Edward Gordon (USA)	7.64
1936	Jesse Owens (USA)	8.06
1948	Willie Steele (USA)	7.82
1952	Jerome Biffle (USA)	7.57
1956	Gregory Bell (USA)	7.83
1960	Ralph Boston (USA)	8.12
1964	Lynn Davies (GBR)	8.07
1968	Robert Beamon (USA)	8.90
1972	Randy Williams (USA)	8.24
1976	Arnie Robinson (USA)	8.35
1980	Lutz Dombrowski (GDR)	8.54
1984	Carl Lewis (USA)	8.54
1988	Carl Lewis (USA)	8.72
1992	Carl Lewis (USA)	8.67
1996	Carl Lewis (USA)	8.50

Athletics (Track and Field) (men) (continued)

LONG JUMP (CONTINUED)		METERS
2000	Ivan Pedroso (CUB)	8.55
2004	Dwight Phillips (USA)	8.59
2008	Irving Jahir Saladino Aranda (PAN)	8.34

STANDING LONG JUMP		METERS
1900	Ray Ewry (USA)	3.21
1904	Ray Ewry (USA)	3.47
1908	Ray Ewry (USA)	3.33
1912	Constantinos Tsiklitiras (GRE)	3.37

TRIPLE JUMP		METERS
1896	James Connolly (USA)	13.71
1900	Myer Prinstein (USA)	14.47
1904	Myer Prinstein (USA)	14.35
1908	Timothy Ahearne (GBR)	14.91
1912	Gustaf Lindblom (SWE)	14.76
1920	Vilho Tuulos (FIN)	14.50
1924	Anthony Winter (AUS)	15.53
1928	Mikio Oda (JPN)	15.21
1932	Chuhei Nambu (JPN)	15.72
1936	Naoto Tajima (JPN)	16.00
1948	Arne Åhman (SWE)	15.40
1952	Adhemar Ferreira da Silva (BRA)	16.22
1956	Adhemar Ferreira da Silva (BRA)	16.35
1960	Josef Szmidt (POL)	16.81
1964	Josef Szmidt (POL)	16.85
1968	Viktor Saneyev (URS)	17.39
1972	Viktor Saneyev (URS)	17.35
1976	Viktor Saneyev (URS)	17.29
1980	Jaak Uudmae (URS)	17.35
1984	Al Joyner (USA)	17.26
1988	Khristo Markov (BUL)	17.61
1992	Michael Conley (USA)	17.63
1996	Kenny Harrison (USA)	18.09
2000	Jonathan Edwards (GBR)	17.71
2004	Christian Olsson (SWE)	17.79
2008	Nelson Évora (POR)	17.67

STANDING TRIPLE JUMP		METERS
1900	Ray Ewry (USA)	10.58
1904	Ray Ewry (USA)	10.54

SHOT PUT		METERS
1896	Robert Garrett (USA)	11.22
1900	Richard Sheldon (USA)	14.10
1904	Ralph Rose (USA)	14.81
1908	Ralph Rose (USA)	14.21
1912	Patrick McDonald (USA)	15.34
1920	Frans Pörhölä (FIN)	14.81
1924	Lemuel Clarence Houser (USA)	14.99
1928	John Kuck (USA)	15.87
1932	Leo Sexton (USA)	16.00
1936	Hans Woellke (GER)	16.20
1948	Wilbur Thompson (USA)	17.12
1952	William Parry O'Brien (USA)	17.41
1956	William Parry O'Brien (USA)	18.57
1960	William Nieder (USA)	19.68
1964	Dallas Long (USA)	20.33
1968	Randy Matson (USA)	20.54
1972	Wladislaw Komar (POL)	21.18
1976	Udo Beyer (GDR)	21.05
1980	Vladimir Kiselyov (URS)	21.35
1984	Alessandro Andrei (ITA)	21.26
1988	Ulf Timmermann (GDR)	22.47
1992	Michael Stulce (USA)	21.70
1996	Randy Barnes (USA)	21.62
2000	Arsi Harju (FIN)	21.29

Summer Olympic Games (continued)

Athletics (Track and Field) (men) (continued)

SHOT PUT (CONTINUED)		METERS
2004	Yury Bilonog (UKR)	21.16
2008	Tomasz Majewski (POL)	21.51

SHOT PUT (TWO HANDS)		METERS
1912	Ralph Rose (USA)	27.7

DISCUS THROW		METERS
1896	Robert Garrett (USA)	29.15
1900	Rezso Bauer (HUN)	36.04
1904	Martin Sheridan (USA)	39.28
1908	Martin Sheridan (USA)	40.89
1912	Armas Taipale (FIN)	45.21
1920	Elmer Niklander (FIN)	44.68
1924	Lemuel Clarence Houser (USA)	46.15
1928	Lemuel Clarence Houser (USA)	47.32
1932	John Anderson (USA)	49.49
1936	Kenneth Carpenter (USA)	50.48
1948	Adolfo Consolini (ITA)	52.78
1952	Sim Iness (USA)	55.03
1956	Alfred Oerter (USA)	56.36
1960	Alfred Oerter (USA)	59.18
1964	Alfred Oerter (USA)	61.00
1968	Alfred Oerter (USA)	64.78
1972	Ludvig Danek (TCH)	64.40
1976	Mac Wilkins (USA)	67.50
1980	Viktor Rashchupkin (URS)	66.64
1984	Rolf Danneberg (FRG)	66.60
1988	Jürgen Schult (GDR)	68.82
1992	Romas Ubartas (LTU)	65.12
1996	Lars Riedel (GER)	69.40
2000	Virgilijus Alekna (LTU)	69.30
2004	Virgilijus Alekna (LTU)[2]	69.89
2008	Gerd Kanter (EST)	68.82

DISCUS (GREEK STYLE)		METERS
1908	Martin Sheridan (USA)	37.99

DISCUS (TWO HANDS)		METERS
1912	Armas Taipale (FIN)	82.86

HAMMER THROW		METERS
1900	John Flanagan (USA)	49.73
1904	John Flanagan (USA)	51.23
1908	John Flanagan (USA)	51.92
1912	Matthew McGrath (USA)	54.74
1920	Patrick Ryan (USA)	52.87
1924	Frederick Tootell (USA)	53.30
1928	Patrick O'Callaghan (IRL)	51.39
1932	Patrick O'Callaghan (IRL)	53.92
1936	Karl Hein (GER)	56.49
1948	Imre Nemeth (HUN)	56.07
1952	Jozsef Csermak (HUN)	60.34
1956	Harold Connolly (USA)	63.19
1960	Vasily Rudenkov (URS)	67.10
1964	Romuald Klim (URS)	69.74
1968	Gyula Zsivotzky (HUN)	73.36
1972	Anatoly Bondarchuk (URS)	75.50
1976	Yury Sedykh (URS)	77.52
1980	Yury Sedykh (URS)	81.80
1984	Juha Tiainen (FIN)	78.08
1988	Sergey Litvinov (URS)	84.80
1992	Andrey Abduvaliyev (UNT)	82.53
1996	Balazs Kiss (HUN)	81.24
2000	Szymon Ziolkowski (POL)	80.02
2004	Koji Murofushi (JPN)[2]	82.91
2008	Primoz Kozmus (SLO)	82.02

Athletics (Track and Field) (men) (continued)

JAVELIN THROW		METERS
1908	Eric Lemming (SWE)	54.83
1912	Eric Lemming (SWE)	60.64
1920	Jonni Myyrä (FIN)	65.78
1924	Jonni Myyrä (FIN)	62.96
1928	Erik Lundkvist (SWE)	66.60
1932	Matti Järvinen (FIN)	72.71
1936	Gerhard Stöck (GER)	71.84
1948	Kai Rautavaara (FIN)	69.77
1952	Cy Young (USA)	73.78
1956	Egil Danielson (NOR)	85.71
1960	Viktor Tsybulenko (URS)	84.64
1964	Pauli Nevala (FIN)	82.66
1968	Janis Lusis (URS)	90.10
1972	Klaus Wolfermann (FRG)	90.48
1976	Miklos Nemeth (HUN)	94.58
1980	Dainis Kula (URS)	91.20
1984	Arto Härkönen (FIN)	86.76
1988	Tapio Korjus (FIN)	84.28
1992	Jan Zelezny (TCH)	89.66
1996	Jan Zelezny (CZE)	88.16
2000	Jan Zelezny (CZE)	90.17
2004	Andreas Thorkildsen (NOR)	86.50
2008	Andreas Thorkildsen (NOR)	90.57

JAVELIN (FREESTYLE)		METERS
1908	Eric Lemming (SWE)	54.45

JAVELIN (TWO HANDS)		METERS
1912	Juho Saaristo (FIN)	109.42

56-LB WEIGHT THROW		METERS
1904	Étienne Desmarteau (CAN)	10.46
1920	Patrick McDonald (USA)	11.26

TUG-OF-WAR	
1900	Sweden-Denmark
1904	United States
1908	Great Britain
1912	Sweden
1920	Great Britain

TRIATHLON (LONG JUMP/SHOT PUT/100 YARDS)	
1904	Max Emmerich (USA)

PENTATHLON	
1912	Jim Thorpe (USA)[6]; Ferdinand Bie (NOR) (cowinners)
1920	Eero Lehtonen (FIN)
1924	Eero Lehtonen (FIN)

DECATHLON	
1904	Thomas Kiely (IRL)
1912	Jim Thorpe (USA)[6]; Hugo Wieslander (SWE) (cowinners)
1920	Helge Lövland (NOR)
1924	Harold Osborn (USA)
1928	Paavo Yrjölä (FIN)
1932	James Bausch (USA)
1936	Glenn Morris (USA)
1948	Robert Mathias (USA)
1952	Robert Mathias (USA)
1956	Milton Campbell (USA)
1960	Rafer Johnson (USA)
1964	Willi Holdorf (GER)
1968	William Toomey (USA)
1972	Nikolay Avilov (URS)
1976	Bruce Jenner (USA)

Summer Olympic Games (continued)

Athletics (Track and Field) (men) (continued)

DECATHLON (CONTINUED)

1980	Daley Thompson (GBR)	
1984	Daley Thompson (GBR)	
1988	Christian Schenk (GDR)	
1992	Robert Zmelik (TCH)	
1996	Dan O'Brien (USA)	
2000	Erki Nool (EST)	
2004	Roman Sebrle (CZE)	
2008	Bryan Clay (USA)	

Athletics (Track and Field) (women)

100 METERS   SEC

1928	Elizabeth Robinson (USA)	12.2
1932	Stanislawa Walasiewicz (POL)	11.9
1936	Helen Stephens (USA)	11.5
1948	Francina Blankers-Koen (NED)	11.9
1952	Marjorie Jackson (AUS)	11.5
1956	Elizabeth Cuthbert (AUS)	11.5
1960	Wilma Rudolph (USA)	11.0
1964	Wyomia Tyus (USA)	11.4
1968	Wyomia Tyus (USA)	11.0
1972	Renate Stecher (GDR)	11.07
1976	Annegret Richter (FRG)	11.08
1980	Lyudmila Kondratyeva (URS)	11.06
1984	Evelyn Ashford (USA)	10.97
1988	Florence Griffith Joyner (USA)	10.54
1992	Gail Devers (USA)	10.82
1996	Gail Devers (USA)	10.94
2000	*winner stripped of medal*	
2004	Yuliya Nesterenko (BLR)	10.93
2008	Shelly-Ann Fraser (JAM)	10.78

200 METERS   SEC

1948	Francina Blankers-Koen (NED)	24.4
1952	Marjorie Jackson (AUS)	23.7
1956	Elizabeth Cuthbert (AUS)	23.4
1960	Wilma Rudolph (USA)	24.0
1964	Edith Marie McGuire (USA)	23.0
1968	Irena Szewinska (POL)	22.5
1972	Renate Stecher (GDR)	22.40
1976	Bärbel Eckert (GDR)	22.37
1980	Bärbel Eckert-Wöckel (GDR)	22.03
1984	Valerie Brisco-Hooks (USA)	21.81
1988	Florence Griffith Joyner (USA)	21.34
1992	Gwen Torrence (USA)	21.81
1996	Marie-Jose Perec (FRA)	22.12
2000	Pauline Davis-Thompson (BAH)[6]	22.27
2004	Veronica Campbell (JAM)	22.05
2008	Veronica Campbell-Brown (JAM)	21.74

400 METERS   SEC

1964	Elizabeth Cuthbert (AUS)	52.0
1968	Colette Besson (FRA)	52.0
1972	Monika Zehrt (GDR)	51.08
1976	Irena Szewinska (POL)	49.29
1980	Marita Koch (GDR)	48.88
1984	Valerie Brisco-Hooks (USA)	48.83
1988	Olga Bryzgina (URS)	48.65
1992	Marie-Jose Perec (FRA)	48.83
1996	Marie-Jose Perec (FRA)	48.25
2000	Cathy Freeman (AUS)	49.11
2004	Tonique Williams-Darling (BAH)	49.41
2008	Christine Ohuruogu (GBR)	49.62

800 METERS   MIN:SEC

1928	Lina Radke-Batschauer (GER)	2:16.8
1960	Lyudmila Lysenko-Shevtsova (URS)	2:04.3
1964	Ann Packer (GBR)	2:01.1

Athletics (Track and Field) (women) (continued)

800 METERS (CONTINUED)   MIN:SEC

1968	Madeline Manning (USA)	2:00.9
1972	Hildegard Falck (FRG)	1:58.6
1976	Tatyana Kazankina (URS)	1:54.94
1980	Nadezhda Olizarenko (URS)	1:53.50
1984	Doina Melinte (ROM)	1:57.60
1988	Sigrun Wodars (GDR)	1:56.10
1992	Ellen van Langen (NED)	1:55.54
1996	Svetlana Masterkova (RUS)	1:57.73
2000	Maria Mutola (MOZ)	1:56.15
2004	Kelly Holmes (GBR)	1:56.38
2008	Pamela Jelimo (KEN)	1:54.87

1,500 METERS   MIN:SEC

1972	Lyudmila Bragina (URS)	4:01.4
1976	Tatyana Kazankina (URS)	4:05.48
1980	Tatyana Kazankina (URS)	3:56.56
1984	Gabriella Dorio (ITA)	4:03.25
1988	Paula Ivan (ROM)	3:53.96
1992	Hassiba Boulmerka (ALG)	3:55.30
1996	Svetlana Masterkova (RUS)	4:00.83
2000	Nouria Merah-Benida (ALG)	4:05.10
2004	Kelly Holmes (GBR)	3:57.90
2008	Nancy Jebet Langat (KEN)	4:00.23

3,000 METERS   MIN:SEC

1984	Maricica Puica (ROM)	8:35.96
1988	Tatyana Samolenko (URS)	8:26.53
1992	Yelena Romanova (UNT)	8:46.04

3,000-METER STEEPLECHASE   MIN:SEC

2008	Gulnara Samitova-Galkina (RUS)	8:58.81

5,000 METERS   MIN:SEC

1996	Wang Jungxia (CHN)	14:59.88
2000	Gabriela Szabo (ROM)	14:40.79
2004	Meseret Defar (ETH)	14:45.65
2008	Tirunesh Dibaba (ETH)	15:41.40

10,000 METERS   MIN:SEC

1988	Olga Bondarenko (URS)	31:05.21
1992	Derartu Tulu (ETH)	31:06.02
1996	Fernanda Ribeiro (POR)	31:01.63
2000	Derartu Tulu (ETH)	30:17.49
2004	Xing Huina (CHN)	30:24.36
2008	Tirunesh Dibaba (ETH)	29:54.66

MARATHON   HR:MIN:SEC

1984	Joan Benoit (USA)	2:24:52
1988	Rosa Mota (POR)	2:25:40
1992	Valentina Yegorova (UNT)	2:32:41
1996	Fatuma Roba (ETH)	2:26:05
2000	Naoko Takahashi (JPN)	2:23:14
2004	Mizuki Noguchi (JPN)	2:26:20
2008	Constantina Tomescu (ROM)	2:26:44

100-METER HURDLES[7]   SEC

1932	Mildred "Babe" Didrikson (USA)	11.7
1936	Trebisonda Valla (ITA)	11.7
1948	Francina Blankers-Koen (NED)	11.2
1952	Shirley Strickland de La Hunty (AUS)	10.9
1956	Shirley Strickland de La Hunty (AUS)	10.7
1960	Irina Press (URS)	10.8
1964	Karin Balzer (GER)	10.5
1968	Maureen Caird (AUS)	10.3
1972	Annelie Ehrhardt (GDR)	12.59
1976	Johanna Schaller (GDR)	12.77
1980	Vera Komisova (URS)	12.56

Summer Olympic Games (continued)

Athletics (Track and Field) (women) (continued)

100-METER HURDLES[7] (CONT.)		SEC
1984	Benita Fitzgerald-Brown (USA)	12.84
1988	Iordanka Donkova (BUL)	12.38
1992	Paraskevi Patoulidou (GRE)	12.64
1996	Ludmila Engquist (SWE)	12.58
2000	Olga Shishigina (KAZ)	12.65
2004	Joanna Hayes (USA)	12.37
2008	Dawn Harper (USA)	12.54

400-METER HURDLES		SEC
1984	Nawal el Moutawakel (MAR)	54.61
1988	Debra Flintoff-King (AUS)	53.17
1992	Sally Gunnell (GBR)	53.23
1996	Deon Hemmings (JAM)	52.82
2000	Irina Privalova (RUS)	53.02
2004	Fani Halkia (GRE)	52.82
2008	Melaine Walker (JAM)	52.64

4 × 100-METER RELAY		SEC
1928	Canada	48.4
1932	United States	47.0
1936	United States	46.9
1948	The Netherlands	47.5
1952	United States	45.9
1956	Australia	44.5
1960	United States	44.5
1964	Poland	43.6
1968	United States	42.8
1972	West Germany	42.81
1976	East Germany	42.55
1980	East Germany	41.60
1984	United States	41.65
1988	United States	41.98
1992	United States	42.11
1996	United States	41.95
2000	The Bahamas	41.95
2004	Jamaica	41.73
2008	Russia	42.31

4 × 400-METER RELAY		MIN:SEC
1972	East Germany	3:23.0
1976	East Germany	3:19.23
1980	USSR	3:20.2
1984	United States	3:18.29
1988	USSR	3:15.18
1992	Unified Team	3:20.20
1996	United States	3:20.91
2000	United States	3:22:62
2004	United States	3:19.01
2008	United States	3:18.54

10,000-METER WALK		MIN:SEC
1992	Chen Yueling (CHN)	44:32
1996	Yelena Nikolayeva (RUS)	41:49

20,000-METER WALK		HR:MIN:SEC
2000	Wang Liping (CHN)	1:29:05
2004	Athanasia Tsoumeleka (GRE)	1:29:12
2008	Olga Kaniskina (RUS)	1:26:31

HIGH JUMP		METERS
1928	Ethel Catherwood (CAN)	1.59
1932	Jean Shiley (USA)	1.66
1936	Ibolya Csak (HUN)	1.60
1948	Alice Coachman (USA)	1.68
1952	Esther Brand (RSA)	1.67
1956	Mildred Louise McDaniel (USA)	1.76
1960	Iolanda Balas (ROM)	1.85

Athletics (Track and Field) (women) (continued)

HIGH JUMP (CONTINUED)		METERS
1964	Iolanda Balas (ROM)	1.90
1968	Miloslava Rezkova (TCH)	1.82
1972	Ulrike Meyfarth (FRG)	1.92
1976	Rosemarie Ackermann (GDR)	1.93
1980	Sara Simeoni (ITA)	1.97
1984	Ulrike Meyfarth (FRG)	2.02
1988	Louise Ritter (USA)	2.03
1992	Heike Henkel (GER)	2.02
1996	Stefka Kostadinova (BUL)	2.05
2000	Yelena Yelesina (RUS)	2.01
2004	Yelena Slesarenko (RUS)	2.06
2008	Tia Hellebaut (BEL)	2.05

POLE VAULT		METERS
2000	Stacy Dragila (USA)	4.60
2004	Yelena Isinbayeva (RUS)	4.91
2008	Yelena Isinbayeva (RUS)	5.05

LONG JUMP		METERS
1948	Olga Gyarmati (HUN)	5.69
1952	Yvette Williams (NZL)	6.24
1956	Elzbieta Krzesinska (POL)	6.35
1960	Vera Krepkina (URS)	6.37
1964	Mary Rand (GBR)	6.76
1968	Viorica Viscopoleanu (ROM)	6.82
1972	Heidemarie Rosendahl (FRG)	6.78
1976	Angela Voigt (GDR)	6.72
1980	Tatyana Kolpakova (URS)	7.06
1984	Anisoara Stanciu (ROM)	6.96
1988	Jackie Joyner-Kersee (USA)	7.40
1992	Heike Drechsler (GER)	7.14
1996	Chioma Ajunwa (NGR)	7.12
2000	Heike Drechsler (GER)	6.99
2004	Tatyana Lebedeva (RUS)	7.07
2008	Maurren Higa Maggi (BRA)	7.04

TRIPLE JUMP		METERS
1996	Inessa Kravets (UKR)	15.33
2000	Tereza Marinova (BUL)	15.20
2004	Françoise Mbango Etone (CMR)	15.30
2008	Françoise Mbango Etone (CMR)	15.39

SHOT PUT		METERS
1948	Micheline Ostermeyer (FRA)	13.75
1952	Galina Zybina (URS)	15.28
1956	Tamara Tyshkevich (URS)	16.59
1960	Tamara Press (URS)	17.32
1964	Tamara Press (URS)	18.14
1968	Margitta Gummel (GDR)	19.61
1972	Nadezhda Chizhova (URS)	21.03
1976	Ivanka Khristova (BUL)	21.16
1980	Ilona Slupianek (GDR)	22.41
1984	Claudia Losch (FRG)	20.48
1988	Natalya Lisovskaya (URS)	22.24
1992	Svetlana Krivalyova (UNT)	21.06
1996	Astrid Kumbernuss (GER)	20.56
2000	Yanina Korolchik (BLR)	20.56
2004	Yumileidi Cumba (CUB)[2]	19.59
2008	Valerie Vili (NZL)	20.56

DISCUS THROW		METERS
1928	Halina Konopacka (POL)	39.62
1932	Lillian Copeland (USA)	40.58
1936	Gisela Mauermayer (GER)	47.63
1948	Micheline Ostermeyer (FRA)	41.92
1952	Nina Romashkova (URS)	51.42
1956	Olga Fikotova (TCH)	53.69

Summer Olympic Games (continued)

Athletics (Track and Field) (women) (continued)

DISCUS THROW (CONTINUED)		METERS
1960	Nina Ponomaryova-Romashkova (URS)	55.10
1964	Tamara Press (URS)	57.27
1968	Lia Manoliu (ROM)	58.28
1972	Faina Melnik (URS)	66.62
1976	Evelin Schlaak (GDR)	69.00
1980	Evelin Schlaak Jahl (GDR)	69.96
1984	Ria Stalman (NED)	65.36
1988	Martina Hellmann (GDR)	72.30
1992	Maritza Marten (CUB)	70.06
1996	Ilke Wyludda (GER)	69.66
2000	Ellina Zvereva (BLR)	68.40
2004	Natalya Sadova (RUS)	67.02
2008	Stephanie Brown Trafton (USA)	64.74

HAMMER THROW		METERS
2000	Kamila Skolimowska (POL)	71.16
2004	Olga Kuzenkova (RUS)	75.02
2008	Aksana Miankova (BLR)	76.34

JAVELIN THROW		METERS
1932	Mildred "Babe" Didrikson (USA)	43.68
1936	Tilly Fleischer (GER)	45.18
1948	Hermine Bauma (AUT)	45.57
1952	Dana Zatopkova (TCH)	50.47
1956	Inese Jaunzeme (URS)	53.86
1960	Elvira Ozolina (URS)	55.98
1964	Mihaela Penes (ROM)	60.54
1968	Angela Nemeth (HUN)	60.36
1972	Ruth Fuchs (GDR)	63.88
1976	Ruth Fuchs (GDR)	65.94
1980	María Colón (CUB)	68.40
1984	Tessa Sanderson (GBR)	69.56
1988	Petra Felke (GDR)	74.68
1992	Silke Renk (GER)	68.34
1996	Heli Rantanen (FIN)	67.94
2000	Trine Hattestad (NOR)	68.91
2004	Osleidys Menéndez (CUB)	71.53
2008	Barbora Spotakova (CZE)	71.42

HEPTATHLON[8]	
1964	Irina Press (URS)
1968	Ingrid Becker (FRG)
1972	Mary Peters (GBR)
1976	Siegrun Siegl (GDR)
1980	Nadezhda Tkachenko (URS)
1984	Glynis Nunn (AUS)
1988	Jackie Joyner-Kersee (USA)
1992	Jackie Joyner-Kersee (USA)
1996	Ghada Shouaa (SYR)
2000	Denise Lewis (GBR)
2004	Carolina Klüft (SWE)
2008	Nataliya Dobrynska (UKR)

Badminton

MEN'S SINGLES	
1992	Allan Budi Kusuma (INA)
1996	Poul-Erik Hoyer-Larsen (DEN)
2000	Ji Xinpeng (CHN)
2004	Taufik Hidayat (INA)
2008	Lin Dan (CHN)

MEN'S DOUBLES	
1992	Republic of Korea
1996	Indonesia
2000	Indonesia
2004	Republic of Korea
2008	Indonesia

Badminton (continued)

WOMEN'S SINGLES	
1992	Susi Susanti (INA)
1996	Bang Soo-Hyun (KOR)
2000	Gong Zhichao (CHN)
2004	Zhang Ning (CHN)
2008	Zhang Ning (CHN)

WOMEN'S DOUBLES	
1992	Republic of Korea
1996	China
2000	China
2004	China
2008	China

MIXED DOUBLES	
1996	Republic of Korea
2000	China
2004	China
2008	Republic of Korea

Baseball

1992	Cuba
1996	Cuba
2000	United States
2004	Cuba
2008	Republic of Korea

Basketball

MEN	
1936	United States
1948	United States
1952	United States
1956	United States
1960	United States
1964	United States
1968	United States
1972	USSR
1976	United States
1980	Yugoslavia
1984	United States
1988	USSR
1992	United States
1996	United States
2000	United States
2004	Argentina
2008	United States

WOMEN	
1976	USSR
1980	USSR
1984	United States
1988	United States
1992	Unified Team
1996	United States
2000	United States
2004	United States
2008	United States

Boxing[9]

48 KG (105.6 LB)	
1968	Francisco Rodríguez (VEN)
1972	Gyorgy Gedo (HUN)
1976	Jorge Hernández (CUB)
1980	Shamil Sabyrov (URS)
1984	Paul Gonzales (USA)
1988	Ivailo Khristov (BUL)
1992	Rogelio Marcelo (CUB)
1996	Daniel Petrov Bojilov (BUL)

Summer Olympic Games (continued)

Boxing[9] (continued)

48 KG (105.6 LB) (CONTINUED)

2000	Brahim Asloum (FRA)
2004	Yan Bhartelemy Varela (CUB)
2008	Zou Shiming (CHN)

51 KG (112 LB)

1904	George Finnegan (USA)
1920	Frank di Genaro (USA)
1924	Fidel La Barba (USA)
1928	Antal Kocsis (HUN)
1932	Istvan Enekes (HUN)
1936	Willi Kaiser (GER)
1948	Pascual Pérez (ARG)
1952	Nate Brooks (USA)
1956	Terence Spinks (GBR)
1960	Gyula Torok (HUN)
1964	Fernando Atzori (ITA)
1968	Ricardo Delgado (MEX)
1972	Georgi Kostadinov (BUL)
1976	Leo Randolph (USA)
1980	Petar Lesov (BUL)
1984	Steven McCrory (USA)
1988	Kim Kwang Sun (KOR)
1992	Chol Choi Su (PRK)
1996	Maikro Romero (CUB)
2000	Wijan Ponlid (THA)
2004	Yuriorkis Gamboa Toledano (CUB)
2008	Somjit Jongjohor (THA)

54 KG (118.8 LB)

1904	Oliver Kirk (USA)
1908	Henry Thomas (GBR)
1920	Clarence Walker (RSA)
1924	William Smith (RSA)
1928	Vittorio Tamagnini (ITA)
1932	Horace Gwynne (CAN)
1936	Ulderico Sergo (ITA)
1948	Tibor Csik (HUN)
1952	Pentti Hämäläinen (FIN)
1956	Wolfgang Behrendt (GER)
1960	Oleg Grigoryev (URS)
1964	Takao Sakurai (JPN)
1968	Valery Sokolov (URS)
1972	Orlando Martínez (CUB)
1976	Gu Yong Jo (PRK)
1980	Juan Hernández (CUB)
1984	Maurizio Stecca (ITA)
1988	Kennedy McKinney (USA)
1992	Joel Casamayor (CUB)
1996	Istvan Kovacs (HUN)
2000	Guillermo Rigondeaux Ortiz (CUB)
2004	Guillermo Rigondeaux Ortiz (CUB)
2008	Badar-Uugan Enkhbat (MGL)

57 KG (125.4 LB)

1904	Oliver Kirk (USA)
1908	Richard Gunn (GBR)
1920	Paul Fritsch (FRA)
1924	John Fields (USA)
1928	Lambertus van Kleveren (NED)
1932	Carmelo Robledo (ARG)
1936	Oscar Casanovas (ARG)
1948	Ernesto Formenti (ITA)
1952	Jan Zachara (TCH)
1956	Vladimir Safronov (URS)
1960	Francesco Musso (ITA)
1964	Stanislav Stepashkin (URS)
1968	Antonio Roldan (MEX)

Boxing[9] (continued)

57 KG (125.4 LB) (CONTINUED)

1972	Boris Kuznetsov (URS)
1976	Angel Herrera (CUB)
1980	Rudi Fink (GDR)
1984	Meldrick Taylor (USA)
1988	Giovanni Parisi (ITA)
1992	Andreas Tews (GER)
1996	Somluck Kamsing (THA)
2000	Bekzat Sattarkhanov (KAZ)
2004	Aleksey Tishchenko (RUS)
2008	Vasyl Lomachenko (UKR)

60 KG (132 LB)

1904	Harry Spanger (USA)
1908	Frederick Grace (GBR)
1920	Samuel Mosberg (USA)
1924	Hans Nielsen (DEN)
1928	Carlo Orlandi (ITA)
1932	Lawrence Stevens (RSA)
1936	Imre Harangi (HUN)
1948	Gerald Dreyer (RSA)
1952	Aureliano Bolognesi (ITA)
1956	Richard McTaggart (GBR)
1960	Kazimierz Pazdzior (POL)
1964	Jozef Grudzien (POL)
1968	Ronnie Harris (USA)
1972	Jan Szczepanski (POL)
1976	Howard Davis (USA)
1980	Angel Herrera (CUB)
1984	Pernell Whitaker (USA)
1988	Andreas Zuelow (GDR)
1992	Oscar De La Hoya (USA)
1996	Hocine Soltani (ALG)
2000	Mario Kindelan (CUB)
2004	Mario César Kindelan Mesa (CUB)
2008	Aleksey Tishchenko (RUS)

64 KG (140.8 LB)

1952	Charles Adkins (USA)
1956	Vladimir Engibaryan (URS)
1960	Bohumil Nemecek (TCH)
1964	Jerzy Kulej (POL)
1968	Jerzy Kulej (POL)
1972	Ray Seales (USA)
1976	Ray Leonard (USA)
1980	Patrizio Oliva (ITA)
1984	Jerry Page (USA)
1988	Vyacheslav Yanovsky (URS)
1992	Héctor Vinent (CUB)
1996	Héctor Vinent (CUB)
2000	Mahamadkadyz Abdullayev (UZB)
2004	Manus Boonjumnong (THA)
2008	Félix Díaz (DOM)

69 KG (151.8 LB)

1904	Albert Young (USA)
1920	Julius Schneider (CAN)
1924	Jean Delarge (BEL)
1928	Edward Morgan (NZL)
1932	Edward Flynn (USA)
1936	Sten Suvio (FIN)
1948	Julius Torma (TCH)
1952	Zygmunt Chychla (POL)
1956	Nicolae Linca (ROM)
1960	Giovanni Benvenuti (ITA)
1964	Marian Kasprzyk (POL)
1968	Manfred Wolke (GDR)
1972	Emilio Correa (CUB)

Summer Olympic Games (continued)

Boxing[9] (continued)

69 KG (151.8 LB) (CONTINUED)
1976	Jochen Bachfeld (GDR)
1980	Andres Aldama (CUB)
1984	Mark Breland (USA)
1988	Robert Wangila (KEN)
1992	Michael Carruth (IRL)
1996	Oleg Saytov (RUS)
2000	Oleg Saytov (RUS)
2004	Bakhtiyar Artayev (KAZ)
2008	Bakhyt Sarsekbayev (KAZ)

71 KG (156.2 LB)
1952	Laszlo Papp (HUN)
1956	Laszlo Papp (HUN)
1960	Wilbert McClure (USA)
1964	Boris Lagutin (URS)
1968	Boris Lagutin (URS)
1972	Dieter Kottysch (FRG)
1976	Jerzy Rybicki (POL)
1980	Armando Martínez (CUB)
1984	Frank Tate (USA)
1988	Park Si Hun (KOR)
1992	Juan Lemus (CUB)
1996	David Reid (USA)
2000	Yermakhan Ibraimov (KAZ)

75 KG (165 LB)
1904	Charles Mayer (USA)
1908	John Douglas (GBR)
1920	Harry Mallin (GBR)
1924	Harry Mallin (GBR)
1928	Piero Toscani (ITA)
1932	Carmen Barth (USA)
1936	Jean Despeaux (FRA)
1948	Laszlo Papp (HUN)
1952	Floyd Patterson (USA)
1956	Gennady Shatkov (URS)
1960	Edward Crook (USA)
1964	Valery Popenchenko (URS)
1968	Christopher Finnegan (GBR)
1972	Vyacheslav Lemeshev (URS)
1976	Michael Spinks (USA)
1980	Jose Gómez (CUB)
1984	Shin Joon Sup (KOR)
1988	Henry Maske (GDR)
1992	Ariel Hernández (CUB)
1996	Ariel Hernández (CUB)
2000	Jorge Gutiérrez (CUB)
2004	Gaydarbek Gaydarbekov (RUS)
2008	James Degale (GBR)

81 KG (178.2 LB)
1920	Edward Eagan (USA)
1924	Harry Mitchell (GBR)
1928	Viktor Avendano (ARG)
1932	David Carstens (RSA)
1936	Roger Michelot (FRA)
1948	George Hunter (RSA)
1952	Norvel Lee (USA)
1956	James Boyd (USA)
1960	Cassius Clay (USA)
1964	Cosimo Pinto (ITA)
1968	Dan Poznyak (URS)
1972	Mate Parlov (YUG)
1976	Leon Spinks (USA)
1980	Slobodan Kacar (YUG)
1984	Anton Josipovic (YUG)
1988	Andrew Maynard (USA)

Boxing[9] (continued)

81 KG (178.2 LB) (CONTINUED)
1992	Torsten May (GER)
1996	Vasily Zhirov (KAZ)
2000	Aleksandr Lebzyak (RUS)
2004	Andre Ward (USA)
2008	Zhang Xiaoping (CHN)

91 KG (200.2 LB)
1904	Samuel Berger (USA)
1908	Albert Oldman (GBR)
1920	Ronald Rawson (GBR)
1924	Otto Von Porat (NOR)
1928	Arturo Rodriguez (ARG)
1932	Alberto Santiago Lovell (ARG)
1936	Herbert Runge (GER)
1948	Rafael Iglesias (ARG)
1952	Edward Sanders (USA)
1956	Peter Rademacher (USA)
1960	Franco de Piccoli (ITA)
1964	Joseph Frazier (USA)
1968	George Foreman (USA)
1972	Teofilo Stevenson (CUB)
1976	Teofilo Stevenson (CUB)
1980	Teofilo Stevenson (CUB)
1984	Henry Tillman (USA)
1988	Ray Mercer (USA)
1992	Félix Savon (CUB)
1996	Félix Savon (CUB)
2000	Félix Savon (CUB)
2004	Odlanier Solis Fonte (CUB)
2008	Rakhim Chakhkiyev (RUS)

OVER 91 KG (200.2 LB)
1984	Tyrell Biggs (USA)
1988	Lennox Lewis (CAN)
1992	Roberto Balado (CUB)
1996	Vladimir Klichko (UKR)
2000	Audley Harrison (GBR)
2004	Aleksandr Povetkin (RUS)
2008	Roberto Cammarelle (ITA)

Canoeing (men)

KAYAK SINGLES (500 METERS)		MIN:SEC
1976	Vasile Diba (ROM)	1:46.41
1980	Vladimir Parfenovich (URS)	1:43.43
1984	Ian Ferguson (NZL)	1:47.84
1988	Zsolt Gyulay (HUN)	1:44.82
1992	Mikko Kolehmainen (FIN)	1:40.34
1996	Antonio Rossi (ITA)	1:37.423
2000	Knut Holmann (NOR)	1:57.847
2004	Adam van Koeverden (CAN)	1:37.919
2008	Ken Wallace (AUS)	1:37.252

KAYAK PAIRS (500 METERS)		MIN:SEC
1976	East Germany	1:35.87
1980	USSR	1:32.38
1984	New Zealand	1:34.21
1988	New Zealand	1:33.98
1992	Germany	1:29.84
1996	Germany	1:28.697
2000	Hungary	1:47.050
2004	Germany	1:27.040
2008	Spain	1:28.736

KAYAK SINGLES (1,000 METERS)		MIN:SEC
1936	Gregor Hradetzky (AUT)	4:22.90
1948	Gert Fredriksson (SWE)	4:33.20
1952	Gert Fredriksson (SWE)	4:07.90

Summer Olympic Games (continued)

Canoeing (men) (continued)

KAYAK SINGLES (1,000 METERS) (CONTINUED)		MIN:SEC
1956	Gert Fredriksson (SWE)	4:12.80
1960	Erik Hansen (DEN)	3:53.00
1964	Rolf Peterson (SWE)	3:57.13
1968	Mihaly Hesz (HUN)	4:03.58
1972	Aleksandr Shaparenko (URS)	3:48.06
1976	Rüdiger Helm (GDR)	3:48.20
1980	Rüdiger Helm (GDR)	3:48.77
1984	Alan Thompson (NZL)	3:45.73
1988	Gregory Barton (USA)	3:55.27
1992	Clint Robinson (AUS)	3:37.26
1996	Knut Holmann (NOR)	3:25.785
2000	Knut Holmann (NOR)	3:33.269
2004	Eirik Veraas Larsen (NOR)	3:25.897
2008	Tim Brabants (GBR)	3:26.323

KAYAK PAIRS (1,000 METERS)		MIN:SEC
1936	Austria	4:03.80
1948	Sweden	4:07.30
1952	Finland	3:51.10
1956	Germany	3:49.60
1960	Sweden	3:34.70
1964	Sweden	3:38.54
1968	USSR	3:37.54
1972	USSR	3:31.23
1976	USSR	3:29.01
1980	USSR	3:26.72
1984	Canada	3:24.22
1988	United States	3:32.42
1992	Germany	3:16.10
1996	Italy	3:09.190
2000	Italy	3:14.461
2004	Sweden	3:18.420
2008	Germany	3:11.809

KAYAK FOURS (1,000 METERS)		MIN:SEC
1964	USSR	3:14.67
1968	Norway	3:14.38
1972	USSR	3:14.02
1976	USSR	3:08.69
1980	East Germany	3:13.76
1984	New Zealand	3:02.28
1988	Hungary	3:00.20
1992	Germany	2:54.18
1996	Germany	2:51.528
2000	Hungary	2:55.188
2004	Hungary	2:56.919
2008	Belarus	2:55.714

KAYAK SINGLES (10,000 METERS)		MIN:SEC
1936	Ernst Krebs (GER)	46:01.6
1948	Gert Fredriksson (SWE)	50:47.7
1952	Thorvald Strömberg (FIN)	47:22.8
1956	Gert Fredriksson (SWE)	47:43.4

KAYAK PAIRS (10,000 METERS)		MIN:SEC
1936	Germany	41:45.0
1948	Sweden	46:09.4
1952	Finland	44:21.3
1956	Hungary	43:37.0

COLLAPSIBLE KAYAK SINGLES (10,000 METERS)		MIN:SEC
1936	Gregor Hradetzky (AUT)	50:01.2

COLLAPSIBLE KAYAK PAIRS (10,000 METERS)		MIN:SEC
1936	Sweden	45:48.9

Canoeing (men) (continued)

KAYAK SINGLES RELAY (1,500 METERS)		MIN:SEC
1960	Germany	7:39.43

SLALOM KAYAK SINGLES		
1972	Siegbert Horn (GDR)	
1992	Pierpaolo Ferrazzi (ITA)	
1996	Oliver Fix (GER)	
2000	Thomas Schmidt (GER)	
2004	Benoit Peschier (FRA)	
2008	Alexander Grimm (GER)	

CANADIAN SINGLES (500 METERS)		MIN:SEC
1976	Aleksandr Rogov (URS)	1:59.23
1980	Sergey Postrekin (URS)	1:53.37
1984	Larry Cain (CAN)	1:57.01
1988	Olaf Heukrodt (GDR)	1:56.42
1992	Nikolay Bukhalov (BUL)	1:51.15
1996	Martin Doktor (CZE)	1:49.934
2000	Gyorgy Kolonics (HUN)	2:24.813
2004	Andreas Dittmer (GER)	1:46.383
2008	Maksim Opalev (RUS)	1:47.140

CANADIAN PAIRS (500 METERS)		MIN:SEC
1976	USSR	1:45.81
1980	Hungary	1:43.39
1984	Yugoslavia	1:43.67
1988	USSR	1:41.77
1992	Unified Team	1:41.54
1996	Hungary	1:40.420
2000	Hungary	1:51.284
2004	China	1:40.278
2008	China	1:41.025

CANADIAN SINGLES (1,000 METERS)		MIN:SEC
1936	Francis Amyot (CAN)	5:32.10
1948	Josef Holecek (TCH)	5:42.00
1952	Josef Holecek (TCH)	4:56.30
1956	Leon Rottman (ROM)	5:05.30
1960	Janos Parti (HUN)	4:33.03
1964	Jürgen Eschert (GER)	4:35.14
1968	Tibor Tatai (HUN)	4:36.14
1972	Ivan Patzaichin (ROM)	4:08.94
1976	Matija Ljubek (YUG)	4:09.51
1980	Lyubomir Lyubenov (BUL)	4:12.38
1984	Ulrich Eicke (FRG)	4:06.32
1988	Ivans Klementyev (URS)	4:12.78
1992	Nikolay Bukhalov (BUL)	4:05.92
1996	Martin Doktor (CZE)	3:54.418
2000	Andreas Dittmer (GER)	3:54.379
2004	David Cal (ESP)	3:46.201
2008	Attila Sándor Vajda (HUN)	3:50.467

CANADIAN PAIRS (1,000 METERS)		MIN:SEC
1936	Czechoslovakia	4:50.10
1948	Czechoslovakia	5:07.10
1952	Denmark	4:38.30
1956	Romania	4:47.40
1960	USSR	4:17.04
1964	USSR	4:04.65
1968	Romania	4:07.18
1972	USSR	3:52.60
1976	USSR	3:52.76
1980	Romania	3:47.65
1984	Romania	3:40.60
1988	USSR	3:48.36
1992	Germany	3:37.42
1996	Germany	3:31.870
2000	Romania	3:37.355

Summer Olympic Games (continued)

Canoeing (men) (continued)

CANADIAN PAIRS (1,000 METERS) (CONTINUED)		MIN:SEC
2004	Germany	3:41.802
2008	Belarus	3:36.365

CANADIAN SINGLES (10,000 METERS)		MIN:SEC
1948	Frantisek Capek (TCH)	62:05.2
1952	Frank Havens (USA)	57:41.1
1956	Leon Rottman (ROM)	56:41.0

CANADIAN PAIRS (10,000 METERS)		MIN:SEC
1936	Czechoslovakia	50:35.5
1948	United States	55:55.4
1952	France	54:08.3
1956	USSR	54:02.4

SLALOM CANADIAN SINGLES
1972	Reinhard Eiben (GDR)
1992	Lukas Pollert (TCH)
1996	Michal Martikan (SVK)
2000	Tony Estanguet (FRA)
2004	Tony Estanguet (FRA)
2008	Michal Martikan (SVK)

SLALOM CANADIAN PAIRS
1972	East Germany
1992	United States
1996	France
2000	Slovakia
2004	Slovakia
2008	Slovakia

Canoeing (women)

KAYAK SINGLES (500 METERS)		MIN:SEC
1948	Karen Hoff (DEN)	2:31.90
1952	Sylvi Saimo (FIN)	2:18.40
1956	Yelizaveta Dementyeva (URS)	2:18.90
1960	Antonina Seredina (URS)	2:08.08
1964	Lyudmila Khvedosyuk (URS)	2:12.87
1968	Lyudmila Pinayeva-Khvedosyuk (URS)	2:11.09
1972	Yuliya Ryabchinskaya (URS)	2:03.17
1976	Carola Zirzow (GDR)	2:01.05
1980	Birgit Fischer (GDR)	1:57.96
1984	Agneta Andersson (SWE)	1:58.72
1988	Vanya Gecheva (BUL)	1:55.19
1992	Birgit Fischer Schmidt (GER)	1:51.60
1996	Rita Koban (HUN)	1:47.655
2000	Josefa Idem Guerrini (ITA)	2:13.848
2004	Natasa Janics (HUN)	1:47.741
2008	Inna Osypenko-Radomska (UKR)	1:50.673

KAYAK PAIRS (500 METERS)		MIN:SEC
1960	USSR	1:54.76
1964	Germany	1:56.95
1968	West Germany	1:56.44
1972	USSR	1:53.50
1976	USSR	1:51.15
1980	East Germany	1:43.88
1984	Sweden	1:45.25
1988	East Germany	1:43.46
1992	Germany	1:40.29
1996	Sweden	1:39.329
2000	Germany	1:56.996
2004	Hungary	1:38.101
2008	Hungary	1:41.308

KAYAK FOURS (500 METERS)		MIN:SEC
1984	Romania	1:38.34
1988	East Germany	1:40.78

Canoeing (women) (continued)

KAYAK FOURS (500 METERS) (CONTINUED)		MIN:SEC
1992	Hungary	1:38.32
1996	Germany	1:31.077
2000	Germany	1:34.532
2004	Germany	1:34.340
2008	Germany	1:32.231

SLALOM KAYAK SINGLES
1972	Angelika Bahmann (GDR)
1992	Elisabeth Micheler (GER)
1996	Stepanka Hilgertova (CZE)
2000	Stepanka Hilgertova (CZE)
2004	Elena Kaliska (SVK)
2008	Elena Kaliska (SVK)

Cricket
1900	Great Britain

Croquet
SINGLES (ONE BALL)
1900	Aumoitte (FRA)

SINGLES (TWO BALLS)
1900	Waydelick (FRA)

DOUBLES
1900	France

Cycling (men)
1,000-METER INDIVIDUAL SPRINT
1896[10]	Paul Masson (FRA)
1900[10]	Georges Taillandier (FRA)
1920	Mauritius Peeters (NED)
1924	Lucien Michard (FRA)
1928	Roger Beaufrand (FRA)
1932	Jacobus Van Egmond (NED)
1936	Toni Merkens (GER)
1948	Mario Ghella (ITA)
1952	Enzo Sacchi (ITA)
1956	Michel Rousseau (FRA)
1960	Sante Gaiardoni (ITA)
1964	Giovanni Pettenella (ITA)
1968	Daniel Morelon (FRA)
1972	Daniel Morelon (FRA)
1976	Anton Tkac (TCH)
1980	Lutz Hesslich (GDR)
1984	Mark Gorski (USA)
1988	Lutz Hesslich (GDR)
1992	Jens Fiedler (GER)
1996	Jens Fiedler (GER)
2000	Marty Nothstein (USA)
2004	Ryan Bayley (AUS)
2008	Chris Hoy (GBR)

1,000-METER TIME TRIAL		MIN:SEC
1896[11]	Paul Masson (FRA)	24.0
1928	Willy Falck-Hansen (DEN)	1:14.4
1932	Edgar Gray (AUS)	1:13.0
1936	Arie van Vliet (NED)	1:12.0
1948	Jacques Dupont (FRA)	1:13.5
1952	Russell Mockridge (AUS)	1:11.1
1956	Leandro Faggin (ITA)	1:09.8
1960	Sante Gaiardoni (ITA)	1:07.27
1964	Patrick Sercu (BEL)	1:09.59
1968	Pierre Trentin (FRA)	1:03.91
1972	Niels Fredborg (DEN)	1:06.44
1976	Klaus-Jürgen Grünke (GDR)	1:05.927
1980	Lothar Thoms (GDR)	1:02.955

Summer Olympic Games (continued)

Cycling (men) (continued)

1,000-METER TIME TRIAL (CONTINUED)	MIN:SEC
1984 Fredy Schmidtke (FRG)	1:06.104
1988 Aleksandr Kirichenko (URS)	1:04.499
1992 José Moreno (ESP)	1:03.342
1996 Florian Rousseau (FRA)	1:02.712
2000 Jason Queally (GBR)	1:01.609
2004 Chris Hoy (GBR)	1:00.711

1,500-METER TEAM PURSUIT
1900 United States

2,000 METERS
1904 Marcus Hurley (USA)

2,000-METER TANDEM
1908 France
1920 Great Britain
1924 France
1928 The Netherlands
1932 France
1936 Germany
1948 Italy
1952 Australia
1956 Australia
1960 Italy
1964 Italy
1968 France
1972 USSR

INDIVIDUAL PURSUIT
1964 Jiri Daler (TCH)
1968 Daniel Rebillard (FRA)
1972 Knut Knudsen (NOR)
1976 Gregor Braun (FRG)
1980 Robert Dill-Bondi (SUI)
1984 Steve Hegg (USA)
1988 Gintautas Umaras (URS)
1992 Christopher Boardman (GBR)
1996 Andrea Collinelli (ITA)
2000 Robert Bartko (GER)
2004 Bradley Wiggins (GBR)
2008 Bradley Wiggins (GBR)

TEAM PURSUIT
1908 Great Britain
1920 Italy
1924 Italy
1928 Italy
1932 Italy
1936 France
1948 France
1952 Italy
1956 Italy
1960 Italy
1964 Germany
1968 Denmark
1972 West Germany
1976 West Germany
1980 USSR
1984 Australia
1988 USSR
1992 Germany
1996 France
2000 Germany
2004 Australia
2008 Great Britain

Cycling (men) (continued)

5,000 METERS	MIN:SEC
1908 Benjamin Jones (GBR)	8:36.2

10,000 METERS	MIN:SEC
1896 Paul Masson (FRA)	17:54.2

20,000 METERS	MIN:SEC
1908 Charles Kingsbury (GBR)	34:13.6

50,000 METERS	HR:MIN:SEC
1920 Henry George (BEL)	1:16:43.2
1924 Jacobus Willems (NED)	1:18:24.0

100,000 METERS	HR:MIN:SEC
1896 Léon Flameng (FRA)	3:08:19.2
1908 Charles Bartlett (GBR)	2:41:48.6

ONE-QUARTER MILE (440 YARDS)	SEC
1904 Marcus Hurley (USA)	31.8

ONE-THIRD MILE (586⅔ YARDS)	SEC
1904 Marcus Hurley (USA)	43.8

ONE-LAP TIME TRIAL (660 YARDS)	SEC
1908 Victor Johnson (GBR)	51.2

ONE-HALF MILE (880 YARDS)	MIN:SEC
1904 Marcus Hurley (USA)	1:09.0

1 MILE	MIN:SEC
1904 Marcus Hurley (USA)	2:41.6

1-MILE 1-FURLONG (1,980-YARD) TEAM PURSUIT
1908 Great Britain

2 MILES	MIN:SEC
1904 Burton Downing (USA)	4:58.0

5 MILES	MIN:SEC
1904 Charles Schlee (USA)	13:08.2

25 MILES
1904 Burton Downing (USA)

12 HOURS
1896 Adolf Schmal (AUT)

INDIVIDUAL POINTS RACE
1984 Roger Ilegems (BEL)
1988 Dan Frost (DEN)
1992 Giovanni Lombardi (ITA)
1996 Silvio Martinello (ITA)
2000 Juan Llaneras (ESP)
2004 Mikhail Ignatyev (RUS)
2008 Joan Llaneras (ESP)

KEIRIN	SEC
2000 Florian Rousseau (FRA)	11.020
2004 Ryan Bayley (AUS)	10.601
2008 Chris Hoy (GBR)	10.450

MADISON
2000 Australia
2004 Australia
2008 Argentina

Summer Olympic Games (continued)

Cycling (men) (continued)

TEAM SPRINT

		SEC
2000	France	44.233
2004	Germany	43.980
2008	Great Britain	43.128

ROAD RACE (INDIVIDUAL)[12]

		HR:MIN:SEC
1896	Aristidis Konstantinidis (GRE)	3:22:31.0
1912	Rudolph Lewis (RSA)	10:42:39.0
1920	Harry Stenqvist (SWE)	4:40:01.8
1924	Armand Blanchonnet (FRA)	6:20:48.0
1928	Henry Hansen (DEN)	4:47:18.0
1932	Attilio Pavesi (ITA)	2:28:05.6
1936	Robert Charpentier (FRA)	2:33:05.0
1948	Jose Beyaert (FRA)	5:18:12.6
1952	Andre Noyelle (BEL)	5:06:03.4
1956	Ercole Baldini (ITA)	5:21:17.0
1960	Viktor Kapitonov (URS)	4:20:37.0
1964	Mario Zanin (ITA)	4:39:51.63
1968	Pierfranco Vianelli (ITA)	4:41:25.24
1972	Hennie Kuiper (NED)	4:14:37.0
1976	Bernt Johansson (SWE)	4:46:52.0
1980	Sergey Sukhoruchenkov (URS)	4:48:28.90
1984	Alexei Grewal (USA)	4:59:57.0
1988	Olaf Ludwig (GDR)	4:32:22.0
1992	Fabio Casartelli (ITA)	4:35:21.0
1996	Pascal Richard (SUI)	4:53:56.0
2000	Jan Ullrich (GER)	5:29:08.0
2004	Paolo Bettini (ITA)	5:41:44.0
2008	Samuel Sánchez (ESP)	6:23:49.0

ROAD RACE (TEAM)

		HR:MIN:SEC
1912	Sweden	44:35:33.6
1920	France	19:16:43.2
1924	France	19:30:14
1928	Denmark	15:09:14
1932	Italy	7:27:15.2
1936	France	7:39:16.2
1948	Belgium	15:58:17.4
1952	Belgium	15:20:46.6
1956	France	5:21:17

ROAD TIME TRIAL (INDIVIDUAL)

		HR:MIN:SEC
1996	Miguel Indurain (ESP)	1:04:05
2000	Vyacheslav Yekimov (RUS)	57:40.42
2004	Tyler Hamilton (USA)	57:31.74
2008	Fabian Cancellara (SUI)	1:02:11.43

ROAD TIME TRIAL (TEAM)

		HR:MIN:SEC
1960	Italy	2:14:33.53
1964	The Netherlands	2:26:31.19
1968	The Netherlands	2:07:49.06
1972	USSR	2:11:17.8
1976	USSR	2:08:53
1980	USSR	2:01:21.7
1984	Italy	1:58:28
1988	East Germany	1:57:47.7
1992	Germany	2:01:39

MOUNTAIN BIKE

		HR:MIN:SEC
1996	Bart Jan Brentjens (NED)	2:17:38
2000	Miguel Martinez (FRA)	2:09:2.50
2004	Julien Absalon (FRA)	2:15:02
2008	Julien Absalon (FRA)	1:55:59

MOTOCROSS/BMX

		SEC
2008	Maris Strombergs (LAT)	36.190

Cycling (women)

500-METER TIME TRIAL

		SEC
2000	Felicia Ballanger (FRA)	34.140
2004	Anna Meares (AUS)	53.016

1,000-METER INDIVIDUAL SPRINT

1988	Erika Salumae (URS)
1992	Erika Salumae (EST)
1996	Felicia Ballanger (FRA)
2000	Felicia Ballanger (FRA)
2004	Lori-Ann Muenzer (CAN)
2008	Victoria Pendleton (GBR)

INDIVIDUAL PURSUIT

1992	Petra Rossner (GER)
1996	Antonella Bellutti (ITA)
2000	Leontien Zijlaard–van Moorsel (NED)
2004	Sarah Ulmer (NZL)
2008	Rebecca Romero (GBR)

INDIVIDUAL POINTS RACE

1996	Nathalie Lancien (FRA)
2000	Antonella Bellutti (ITA)
2004	Olga Slyusareva (RUS)
2008	Marianne Vos (NED)

ROAD RACE (INDIVIDUAL)

		HR:MIN:SEC
1984	Connie Carpenter-Phinney (USA)	2:11:14.0
1988	Monique Knol (NED)	2:00:52.0
1992	Kathryn Watt (AUS)	2:04:42.0
1996	Jeannie Longo-Ciprelli (FRA)	2:36:13.0
2000	Leontien Zijlaard–van Moorsel (NED)	3:06:31
2004	Sara Carrigan (AUS)	3:24:24
2008	Nicole Cooke (GBR)	3:32:24

ROAD TIME TRIAL (INDIVIDUAL)

		MIN:SEC
1996	Zulfiya Zabirova (RUS)	36:40
2000	Leontien Zijlaard–van Moorsel (NED)	42:00.781
2004	Leontien Zijlaard–van Moorsel (NED)	31:11.53
2008	Kristin Armstrong (USA)	34:51.72

MOUNTAIN BIKE

		HR:MIN:SEC
1996	Paola Pezzo (ITA)	1:50:51
2000	Paola Pezzo (ITA)	1:49:24.38
2004	Gunn-Rita Dahle (NOR)	1:56:51
2008	Sabine Spitz (GER)	1:45:11

MOTOCROSS/BMX

		SEC
2008	Anne-Caroline Chausson (FRA)	35.976

Diving (men)

3-METER SPRINGBOARD DIVING

1908	Albert Zürner (GER)
1912	Paul Günther (GER)
1920	Louis Kuehn (USA)
1924	Albert White (USA)
1928	Peter Desjardins (USA)
1932	Michael Galitzen (USA)
1936	Richard Degener (USA)
1948	Bruce Harlan (USA)
1952	David Browning (USA)
1956	Robert Clotworthy (USA)
1960	Gary Tobian (USA)
1964	Kenneth Sitzberger (USA)
1968	Bernie Wrightson (USA)
1972	Vladimir Vasin (URS)

Summer Olympic Games (continued)

Diving (men) (continued)

3-METER SPRINGBOARD DIVING (CONTINUED)
1976 Philip Boggs (USA)
1980 Aleksandr Portnov (URS)
1984 Greg Louganis (USA)
1988 Greg Louganis (USA)
1992 Mark Edward Lenzi (USA)
1996 Xiong Ni (CHN)
2000 Xiong Ni (CHN)
2004 Peng Bo (CHN)
2008 He Chong (CHN)

10-METER PLATFORM (HIGH) DIVING
1904 George Sheldon (USA)
1908 Hjalmar Johansson (SWE)
1912 Erik Adlerz (SWE)
1920 Clarence Pinkston (USA)
1924 Albert White (USA)
1928 Peter Desjardins (USA)
1932 Harold Smith (USA)
1936 Marshall Wayne (USA)
1948 Samuel Lee (USA)
1952 Samuel Lee (USA)
1956 Joaquin Capilla Perez (MEX)
1960 Robert Webster (USA)
1964 Robert Webster (USA)
1968 Klaus Dibiasi (ITA)
1972 Klaus Dibiasi (ITA)
1976 Klaus Dibiasi (ITA)
1980 Falk Hoffman (GDR)
1984 Greg Louganis (USA)
1988 Greg Louganis (USA)
1992 Sun Shuwei (CHN)
1996 Dmitry Sautin (RUS)
2000 Tian Liang (CHN)
2004 Hu Jia (CHN)
2008 Matt Mitcham (AUS)

3-METER SYNCHRONIZED SPRINGBOARD DIVING
2000 China
2004 Greece
2008 China

10-METER SYNCHRONIZED PLATFORM (HIGH) DIVING
2000 Russia
2004 China
2008 China

PLUNGE FOR DISTANCE
1904 William Paul Dickey (USA)

PLAIN HIGH DIVING
1912 Erik Adlerz (SWE)
1920 Arvid Wallman (SWE)
1924 Richmond Eve (AUS)

Diving (women)

3-METER SPRINGBOARD DIVING
1920 Aileen Riggin (USA)
1924 Elizabeth Becker-Pinkton (USA)
1928 Helen Meany (USA)
1932 Georgia Coleman (USA)
1936 Marjorie Gestring (USA)
1948 Victoria Draves (USA)
1952 Patricia McCormick (USA)
1956 Patricia McCormick (USA)
1960 Ingrid Krämer-Engel-Gulbin (GER)
1964 Ingrid Krämer-Gulbin (GER)
1968 Sue Gossick (USA)

Diving (women) (continued)

3-METER SPRINGBOARD DIVING (CONTINUED)
1972 Micki King (USA)
1976 Jennifer Chandler (USA)
1980 Irina Kalinina (URS)
1984 Sylvie Bernier (CAN)
1988 Gao Min (CHN)
1992 Gao Min (CHN)
1996 Fu Mingxia (CHN)
2000 Fu Mingxia (CHN)
2004 Guo Jingjing (CHN)
2008 Guo Jingjing (CHN)

10-METER PLATFORM (HIGH) DIVING
1912 Greta Johansson (SWE)
1920 Stefani Fryland Clausen (DEN)
1924 Caroline Smith (USA)
1928 Elizabeth Anna Becker-Pinkston (USA)
1932 Dorothy Poynton (USA)
1936 Dorothy Poynton-Hill (USA)
1948 Victoria Draves (USA)
1952 Patricia McCormick (USA)
1956 Patricia McCormick (USA)
1960 Ingrid Krämer-Engel-Gulbin (GER)
1964 Lesley Leigh Bush (USA)
1968 Milena Duchkova (TCH)
1972 Ulrika Knape (SWE)
1976 Yelena Vaytsekhovskaya (URS)
1980 Martina Jäschke (GDR)
1984 Zhou Ji-Hong (CHN)
1988 Xu Yan-Mei (CHN)
1992 Fu Mingxia (CHN)
1996 Fu Mingxia (CHN)
2000 Laura Wilkinson (USA)
2004 Chantelle Newbery (AUS)
2008 Chen Ruolin (CHN)

3-METER SYNCHRONIZED SPRINGBOARD DIVING
2000 Russia
2004 China
2008 China

10-METER SYNCHRONIZED PLATFORM (HIGH) DIVING
2000 China
2004 China
2008 China

Equestrian Sports

GRAND PRIX (DRESSAGE) INDIVIDUAL	MOUNT
1912 Carl Bonde (SWE)	Emperor
1920 Janne Lundblad (SWE)	Uno
1924 Ernst Linder (SWE)	Piccolomini
1928 Carl Friedrich Freiherr von Langen-Parow (GER)	Draufgänger
1932 Xavier Lesage (FRA)	Taine
1936 Heinz Pollay (GER)	Kronos
1948 Hans Moser (SUI)	Hummer
1952 Henri St. Cyr (SWE)	Master Rufus
1956 Henri St. Cyr (SWE)	Juli
1960 Sergey Filatov (URS)	Absent
1964 Henri Chammartin (SUI)	Woermann
1968 Ivan Kizimov (URS)	Ikhor
1972 Liselott Linsenhoff (FRG)	Piaff
1976 Christine Stückelberger (SUI)	Granat
1980 Elisabeth Theurer (AUT)	Mon Cherie
1984 Reiner Klimke (FRG)	Ahlerich
1988 Nicole Uphoff (FRG)	Rembrandt 24
1992 Nicole Uphoff (GER)	Rembrandt 24
1996 Isabell Werth (GER)	Gigolo

Summer Olympic Games (continued)

Equestrian Sports (continued)

GRAND PRIX (DRESSAGE) INDIVIDUAL (CONTINUED)

		MOUNT
2000	Anky van Grunsven (NED)	Bonfire
2004	Anky van Grunsven (NED)	Salinero
2008	Anky van Grunsven (NED)	Keltec Salinero

GRAND PRIX (DRESSAGE) TEAM

1928	Germany
1932	France
1936	Germany
1948	France
1952	Sweden
1956	Sweden
1964	Germany
1968	West Germany
1972	USSR
1976	West Germany
1980	USSR
1984	West Germany
1988	West Germany
1992	Germany
1996	Germany
2000	Germany
2004	Germany
2008	Germany

GRAND PRIX (JUMPING) INDIVIDUAL

		MOUNT
1900	Aimé Haegeman (BEL)	Benton II
1912	Jean Cariou (FRA)	Mignon
1920	Tommaso Lequio di Assaba (ITA)	Trebecco
1924	Alphonse Gemuseus (SUI)	Lucette
1928	Frantisek Ventura (TCH)	Eliot
1932	Takeichi Nishi (JPN)	Uranus
1936	Kurt Hasse (GER)	Tora
1948	Humberto Mariles Cortés (MEX)	Arete
1952	Pierre Jonquères d'Oriola (FRA)	Ali Baba
1956	Hans-Günter Winkler (GER)	Halla
1960	Raimondo d'Inzeo (ITA)	Posillipo
1964	Pierre Jonquères d'Oriola (FRA)	Lutteur
1968	William Steinkraus (USA)	Snowbound
1972	Graziano Mancinelli (ITA)	Ambassador
1976	Alwin Schockemöhle (FRG)	Warwick Rex
1980	Jan Kowalczyk (POL)	Artemor
1984	Joe Fargis (USA)	Touch of Class
1988	Pierre Durand (FRA)	Jappeloup
1992	Ludger Beerbaum (GER)	Classic Touch
1996	Ulrich Kirchhoff (GER)	Jus des Pommes
2000	Jeroen Dubbeldam (NED)	Sjiem
2004	Rodrigo Pessoa (BRA)[2]	Baloubet du Rouet[2]
2008	Eric Lamaze (CAN)	Hickstead

GRAND PRIX (JUMPING) TEAM

1912	Sweden
1920	Sweden
1924	Sweden
1928	Spain
1936	Germany
1948	Mexico
1952	Great Britain
1956	Germany
1960	Germany
1964	Germany
1968	Canada
1972	West Germany
1976	France
1980	USSR
1984	United States
1988	West Germany
1992	The Netherlands

Equestrian Sports (continued)

GRAND PRIX (JUMPING) TEAM

1996	Germany
2000	Germany
2004	United States[2]
2008	United States

THREE-DAY EVENT (INDIVIDUAL)

		MOUNT
1912	Axel Nordlander (SWE)	Lady Artist
1920	Helmer Mörner (SWE)	Germania
1924	Adolph van der Voort van Zijp (NED)	Silver Piece
1928	Charles Pahud de Mortanges (NED)	Marcroix
1932	Charles Pahud de Mortanges (NED)	Marcroix
1936	Ludwig Stubbendorff (GER)	Nurmi
1948	Bernard Chevallier (FRA)	Aiglonne
1952	Hans von Blixen-Finecke, Jr. (SWE)	Jubal
1956	Petrus Kastenman (SWE)	Iluster
1960	Lawrence Morgan (AUS)	Salad Days
1964	Mauro Checcoli (ITA)	Surbean
1968	Jean-Jacques Goyon (FRA)	Pitou
1972	Richard Meade (GBR)	Laurieston
1976	Edmund Coffin (USA)	Bally-Cor
1980	Federico Euro Roman (ITA)	Rossinan
1984	Mark Todd (NZL)	Charisma
1988	Mark Todd (NZL)	Charisma
1992	Matthew Ryan (AUS)	Kibah Tic Toc
1996	Robert Blyth Tait (NZL)	Ready Teddy
2000	David O'Connor (USA)	Custom Made
2004	Leslie Law (GBR)	Shear L'Eau
2008	Hinrich Romeike (GER)	Marius

THREE-DAY EVENT (TEAM)

1912	Sweden
1920	Sweden
1924	The Netherlands
1928	The Netherlands
1932	United States
1936	Germany
1948	United States
1952	Sweden
1956	Great Britain
1960	Australia
1964	Italy
1968	Great Britain
1972	Great Britain
1976	United States
1980	USSR
1984	United States
1988	West Germany
1992	Australia
1996	Australia
2000	Australia
2004	France
2008	Germany

HIGH JUMP

		MOUNT
1900	Dominique Maximien Gardéres (FRA); Gian Giorgio Trissino (ITA) (tied)	Canela; Oreste

LONG JUMP

		MOUNT
1900	Constant van Langhendonck (BEL)	Extra Dry

FIGURE RIDING (INDIVIDUAL)

1920	T. Bouckaert (BEL)

FIGURE RIDING (TEAM)

1920	Belgium

Summer Olympic Games (continued)

Fencing (men)

FOIL (INDIVIDUAL)
1896 Eugène-Henri Gravelotte (FRA)
1900 Émile Coste (FRA)
1904 Ramón Fonst (CUB)
1912 Nedo Nadi (ITA)
1920 Nedo Nadi (ITA)
1924 Roger Ducret (FRA)
1928 Lucien Gaudin (FRA)
1932 Gustavo Marzi (ITA)
1936 Giulio Gaudini (ITA)
1948 Jehan Buhan (FRA)
1952 Christian d'Oriola (FRA)
1956 Christian d'Oriola (FRA)
1960 Viktor Zhdanovich (URS)
1964 Egon Franke (POL)
1968 Ion Drimba (ROM)
1972 Witold Woyda (POL)
1976 Fabio dal Zotto (ITA)
1980 Vladimir Smirnov (URS)
1984 Mauro Numa (ITA)
1988 Stefano Cerioni (ITA)
1992 Philippe Omnes (FRA)
1996 Alessandro Puccini (ITA)
2000 Kim Young Ho (KOR)
2004 Brice Guyart (FRA)
2008 Benjamin Philip Kleibrink (GER)

FOIL (TEAM)
1904 Cuba
1920 Italy
1924 France
1928 Italy
1932 France
1936 Italy
1948 France
1952 France
1956 Italy
1960 USSR
1964 USSR
1968 France
1972 Poland
1976 West Germany
1980 France
1984 Italy
1988 USSR
1992 Germany
1996 Russia
2000 France
2004 Italy

INDIVIDUAL FOIL, PROFESSIONAL (MASTERS)
1896 Leon Pyrgos (GRE)
1900 Lucien Mérignac (FRA)

INDIVIDUAL FOIL, JUNIOR
1904 Arthur Fox (USA)

ÉPÉE (INDIVIDUAL)
1900 Ramón Fonst (CUB)
1904 Ramón Fonst (CUB)
1908 Gaston Alibert (BEL)
1912 Paul Anspach (BEL)
1920 Armand Massard (FRA)
1924 Charles Delporte (BEL)
1928 Lucien Gaudin (FRA)
1932 Giancarlo Cornaggia-Medici (ITA)
1936 Franco Riccardi (ITA)
1948 Luigi Cantone (ITA)

ÉPÉE (INDIVIDUAL) (CONTINUED)
1952 Edoardo Mangiarotti (ITA)
1956 Carlo Pavesi (ITA)
1960 Giuseppe Delfino (ITA)
1964 Grigory Kriss (URS)
1968 Gyoso Kulcsar (HUN)
1972 Csaba Fenyvesi (HUN)
1976 Alexander Pusch (FRG)
1980 Johan Harmenberg (SWE)
1984 Philippe Boisse (FRA)
1988 Arnd Schmitt (FRG)
1992 Eric Srecki (FRA)
1996 Aleksandr Beketov (RUS)
2000 Pavel Kolobkov (RUS)
2004 Marcel Fischer (SUI)
2008 Matteo Tagliariol (ITA)

ÉPÉE (TEAM)
1908 France
1912 Belgium
1920 Italy
1924 France
1928 Italy
1932 France
1936 Italy
1948 France
1952 Italy
1956 Italy
1960 Italy
1964 Hungary
1968 Hungary
1972 Hungary
1976 Sweden
1980 France
1984 West Germany
1988 France
1992 Germany
1996 Italy
2000 Italy
2004 France
2008 France

INDIVIDUAL ÉPÉE, PROFESSIONAL (MASTERS)
1900 Albert Ayat (FRA)

INDIVIDUAL ÉPÉE, OPEN (AMATEUR AND MASTERS)
1900 Albert Ayat (FRA)

SABRE (INDIVIDUAL)
1896 Ioannis Georgiadis (GRE)
1900 Georges de la Falaise (FRA)
1904 Manuel Díaz (CUB)
1908 Jeno Fuchs (HUN)
1912 Jeno Fuchs (HUN)
1920 Nedo Nadi (ITA)
1924 Sandor Posta (HUN)
1928 Odon Vitez Tersztyanszky (HUN)
1932 Gyorgy Piller (HUN)
1936 Endre Kabos (HUN)
1948 Aladar Gerevich (HUN)
1952 Pal Kovacs (HUN)
1956 Rudolph Karpati (HUN)
1960 Rudolph Karpati (HUN)
1964 Tibor Pezsa (HUN)
1968 Jerzy Pawlowski (POL)
1972 Viktor Sidyak (URS)
1976 Viktor Krovopuskov (URS)
1980 Viktor Krovopuskov (URS)

Summer Olympic Games (continued)

Fencing (men) (continued)

SABRE (INDIVIDUAL) (CONTINUED)
1984 Jean-François Lamour (FRA)
1988 Jean-François Lamour (FRA)
1992 Bence Szabo (HUN)
1996 Stanislav Pozdnyakov (RUS)
2000 Mihai Claudiu Covaliu (ROM)
2004 Aldo Montano (ITA)
2008 Zhong Man (CHN)

SABRE (TEAM)
1908 Hungary
1912 Hungary
1920 Italy
1924 Italy
1928 Hungary
1932 Hungary
1936 Hungary
1948 Hungary
1952 Hungary
1956 Hungary
1960 Hungary
1964 USSR
1968 USSR
1972 Italy
1976 USSR
1980 USSR
1984 Italy
1988 Hungary
1992 Unified Team
1996 Russia
2000 Russia
2004 France
2008 France

INDIVIDUAL SABRE, PROFESSIONAL (MASTERS)
1900 Antonio Conte (ITA)

SINGLE STICK
1904 Albertson Van Zo Post (CUB)

Fencing (women)

FOIL (INDIVIDUAL)
1924 Ellen Osiier (DEN)
1928 Helene Mayer (GER)
1932 Ellen Preis (AUT)
1936 Ilona Schacherer-Elek (HUN)
1948 Ilona Elek (HUN)
1952 Irene Camber (ITA)
1956 Gillian Sheen (GBR)
1960 Adelheid Schmid (GER)
1964 Ildiko Ujlaki-Rejto (HUN)
1968 Yelena Novikova (URS)
1972 Antonella Ragno Lonzi (ITA)
1976 Ildiko Schwarczenberger (HUN)
1980 Pascale Trinquet (FRA)
1984 Jujie Luan (CHN)
1988 Anja Fichtel (FRG)
1992 Giovanna Trillini (ITA)
1996 Laura Gabriela Badea (ROM)
2000 Valentina Vezzali (ITA)
2004 Valentina Vezzali (ITA)
2008 Valentina Vezzali (ITA)

FOIL (TEAM)
1960 USSR
1964 Hungary
1968 USSR
1972 USSR

Fencing (women) (continued)

FOIL (TEAM) (CONTINUED)
1976 USSR
1980 France
1984 West Germany
1988 West Germany
1992 Italy
1996 Italy
2000 Italy
2008 Russia

ÉPÉE (INDIVIDUAL)
1996 Laura Flessel (FRA)
2000 Timea Nagy (HUN)
2004 Timea Nagy (HUN)
2008 Britta Heidemann (GER)

ÉPÉE (TEAM)
1996 France
2000 Russia
2004 Russia

SABRE (INDIVIDUAL)
2004 Mariel Zagunis (USA)
2008 Mariel Zagunis (USA)

SABRE (TEAM)
2008 Ukraine

Field Hockey

MEN
1908 Great Britain
1920 Great Britain
1928 India
1932 India
1936 India
1948 India
1952 India
1956 India
1960 Pakistan
1964 India
1968 Pakistan
1972 West Germany
1976 New Zealand
1980 India
1984 Pakistan
1988 Great Britain
1992 Germany
1996 The Netherlands
2000 The Netherlands
2004 Australia
2008 Germany

WOMEN
1980 Zimbabwe
1984 The Netherlands
1988 Australia
1992 Spain
1996 Australia
2000 Australia
2004 Germany
2008 The Netherlands

Golf

MEN, INDIVIDUAL
1900 Charles Sands (USA)
1904 George Lyon (CAN)

Summer Olympic Games (continued)

Golf (continued)

MEN, TEAM
1904   United States

WOMEN
1900   Margaret Abbott (USA)

Gymnastics (men)

COMBINED, OR ALL-AROUND (INDIVIDUAL)
1900   Gustave Sandras (FRA)
1904   Julius Lenhardt (USA)
1908   G. Alberto Braglia (ITA)
1912   G. Alberto Braglia (ITA)
1920   Giorgio Zampori (ITA)
1924   Leon Stukelj (YUG)
1928   Georges Miez (SUI)
1932   Romeo Neri (ITA)
1936   Karl-Alfred Schwarzmann (GER)
1948   Veikko Huhtanen (FIN)
1952   Viktor Chukarin (URS)
1956   Viktor Chukarin (URS)
1960   Boris Shakhlin (URS)
1964   Yukio Endo (JPN)
1968   Sawao Kato (JPN)
1972   Sawao Kato (JPN)
1976   Nikolay Andrianov (URS)
1980   Aleksandr Dityatin (URS)
1984   Koji Gushiken (JPN)
1988   Vladimir Artyomov (URS)
1992   Vitaly Shcherbo (UNT)
1996   Li Xiaosahuang (CHN)
2000   Aleksey Nemov (RUS)
2004   Paul Hamm (USA)
2008   Yang Wei (CHN)

COMBINED, OR ALL-AROUND (TEAM)
1920   Italy
1924   Italy
1928   Switzerland
1932   Italy
1936   Germany
1948   Finland
1952   USSR
1956   USSR
1960   Japan
1964   Japan
1968   Japan
1972   Japan
1976   Japan
1980   USSR
1984   United States
1988   USSR
1992   Unified Team
1996   Russia
2000   China
2004   Japan
2008   China

FLOOR EXERCISE
1932   Istvan Pelle (HUN)
1936   Georges Miez (SUI)
1948   Ferenc Pataki (HUN)
1952   William Thoresson (SWE)
1956   Valentin Muratov (URS)
1960   Nobuyuki Aihara (JPN)
1964   Franco Menichelli (ITA)
1968   Sawao Kato (JPN)
1972   Nikolay Andrianov (URS)
1976   Nikolay Andrianov (URS)

Gymnastics (men) (continued)

FLOOR EXERCISE (CONTINUED)
1980   Roland Brückner (GDR)
1984   Li Ning (CHN)
1988   Sergey Kharikov (URS)
1992   Li Xiaosahuang (CHN)
1996   Ioannis Melissanidis (GRE)
2000   Igors Vihrovs (LAT)
2004   Kyle Shewfelt (CAN)
2008   Zou Kai (CHN)

HORIZONTAL BAR
1896   Hermann Weingärtner (GER)
1904   Anton Heida (USA); Edward Henning (USA)
          (tied)
1924   Leon Stukelj (YUG)
1928   Georges Miez (SUI)
1932   Dallas Bixler (USA)
1936   Aleksanteri Saarvala (FIN)
1948   Josef Stalder (SUI)
1952   Jack Günthard (SUI)
1956   Takashi Ono (JPN)
1960   Takashi Ono (JPN)
1964   Boris Shakhlin (URS)
1968   Mikhail Voronin (URS); Akinori Nakayama
          (JPN) (tied)
1972   Mitsuo Tsukahara (JPN)
1976   Mitsuo Tsukahara (JPN)
1980   Stoyan Delchev (BUL)
1984   Shinji Morisue (JPN)
1988   Vladimir Artyomov (URS); Valery Lyukin (URS)
          (tied)
1992   Trent Dimas (USA)
1996   Andreas Wecker (GER)
2000   Aleksey Nemov (RUS)
2004   Igor Cassina (ITA)
2008   Zou Kai (CHN)

PARALLEL BARS
1896   Alfred Flatow (GER)
1904   George Eyser (USA)
1924   August Güttinger (SUI)
1928   Ladislav Vacha (TCH)
1932   Romeo Neri (ITA)
1936   Konrad Frey (GER)
1948   Michael Reusch (SUI)
1952   Hans Eugster (SUI)
1956   Viktor Chukarin (URS)
1960   Boris Shakhlin (URS)
1964   Yukio Endo (JPN)
1968   Akinori Nakayama (JPN)
1972   Sawao Kato (JPN)
1976   Sawao Kato (JPN)
1980   Aleksandr Tkachyov (URS)
1984   Bart Conner (USA)
1988   Vladimir Artyomov (URS)
1992   Vitaly Shcherbo (UNT)
1996   Rustam Sharipov (UKR)
2000   Li Xiaopeng (CHN)
2004   Valery Goncharov (UKR)
2008   Li Xiaopeng (CHN)

SIDE, OR POMMEL, HORSE
1896   Louis Zutter (SUI)
1904   Anton Heida (USA)
1924   Josef Wilhelm (SUI)
1928   Hermann Hänggi (SUI)
1932   Istvan Pelle (HUN)
1936   Konrad Frey (GER)

Summer Olympic Games (continued)

Gymnastics (men) (continued)

SIDE, OR POMMEL, HORSE (CONTINUED)

1948 Paavo Aaltonen (FIN); Veikko Huhtanen (FIN); Heikki Savolainen (FIN) (tied)
1952 Viktor Chukarin (URS)
1956 Boris Shakhlin (URS)
1960 Boris Shakhlin (URS); Eugen Ekman (FIN) (tied)
1964 Miroslav Cerar (YUG)
1968 Miroslav Cerar (YUG)
1972 Viktor Klimenko (URS)
1976 Zoltan Magyar (HUN)
1980 Zoltan Magyar (HUN)
1984 Li Ning (CHN); Peter Vidmar (USA) (tied)
1988 Lyubomir Geraskov (BUL); Zsolt Borkai (HUN); Dmitry Bilozerchev (URS) (tied)
1992 Vitaly Shcherbo (UNT); Pae Gil-su (PRK) (tied)
1996 Li Donghua (SUI)
2000 Marius Urzica (ROM)
2004 Teng Haibin (CHN)
2008 Xiao Qin (CHN)

LONG, OR VAULTING, HORSE

1896 Karl Schuhmann (GER)
1904 Anton Heida (USA); George Eyser (USA) (tied)
1924 Frank Kriz (USA)
1928 Eugen Mack (SUI)
1932 Savino Guglielmetti (ITA)
1936 Karl-Alfred Schnorzmann (GER)
1948 Paavo Johannes Aaltonen (FIN)
1952 Viktor Chukarin (URS)
1956 Valentin Muratov (URS); Helmut Bantz (GER) (tied)
1960 Takashi Ono (JPN); Boris Shakhlin (URS) (tied)
1964 Haruhiro Yamashita (JPN)
1968 Mikhail Voronin (URS)
1972 Klaus Köste (GDR)
1976 Nikolay Andrianov (URS)
1980 Nikolay Andrianov (URS)
1984 Lou Yun (CHN)
1988 Lou Yun (CHN)
1992 Vitaly Shcherbo (UNT)
1996 Aleksey Nemov (RUS)
2000 Gervasio Deferr (ESP)
2004 Gervasio Deferr (ESP)
2008 Leszek Blanik (POL)

RINGS

1896 Ioannis Mitropoulos (GRE)
1904 Hermann Glass (USA)
1924 Francesco Martino (ITA)
1928 Leon Stukelj (YUG)
1932 George Gulack (USA)
1936 Alois Hudec (TCH)
1948 Karl Frei (SUI)
1952 Grant Shaginyan (URS)
1956 Albert Azaryan (URS)
1960 Albert Azaryan (URS)
1964 Takuji Hayata (JPN)
1968 Akinori Nakayama (JPN)
1972 Akinori Nakayama (JPN)
1976 Nikolay Andrianov (URS)
1980 Aleksandr Dityatin (URS)
1984 Li Ning (CHN); Koji Gushiken (JPN) (tied)
1988 Holger Behrendt (GDR); Dmitry Bilozerchev (URS) (tied)
1992 Vitaly Shcherbo (UNT)
1996 Yury Chechi (ITA)

Gymnastics (men) (continued)

RINGS (CONTINUED)

2000 Szilveszter Csollany (HUN)
2004 Dimosthenis Tampakos (GRE)
2008 Chen Yibing (CHN)

TRAMPOLINE

2000 Aleksandr Moskalenko (RUS)
2004 Yury Nikitin (UKR)
2008 Lu Chunlong (CHN)

ROPE CLIMBING

1896 Nicolaos Andriakopoulos (GRE)
1904 George Eyser (USA)
1924 Bedrich Supcik (TCH)
1932 Raymond Bass (USA)

SWEDISH EXERCISES (TEAM)

1912 Sweden
1920 Sweden

OPTIONAL EXERCISES (TEAM)

1912 Norway
1920 Denmark
1932 United States

PARALLEL BARS (TEAM)

1896 Germany

HORIZONTAL BARS (TEAM)

1896 Germany

CLUB SWINGING

1904 Edward Hennig (USA)
1932 George Roth (USA)

TUMBLING

1932 Rowland Wolfe (USA)

COMBINED COMPETITION (7 APPARATUS)

1904 Anton Heida (USA)

COMBINED COMPETITION (9 EVENTS)

1904 Adolf Spinnler (SUI)

PRESCRIBED APPARATUS (TEAM)

1904 United States
1908 Sweden
1912 Italy
1952 Sweden
1956 Hungary

MASS EXERCISES (TEAM)

1952 Finland

SIDE HORSE (VAULTS)

1924 Albert Séguin (FRA)

Gymnastics (women)

COMBINED, OR ALL-AROUND (INDIVIDUAL)

1952 Mariya Gorokhovskaya (URS)
1956 Larisa Latynina (URS)
1960 Larisa Latynina (URS)
1964 Vera Caslavska (TCH)
1968 Vera Caslavska (TCH)
1972 Lyudmila Turishcheva (URS)
1976 Nadia Comaneci (ROM)
1980 Yelena Davydova (URS)
1984 Mary Lou Retton (USA)

Summer Olympic Games (continued)

Gymnastics (women) (continued)

COMBINED, OR ALL-AROUND (INDIVIDUAL) (CONTINUED)

1988	Yelena Shushunova (URS)
1992	Tatyana Gutsu (UNT)
1996	Liliya Podkopayeva (UKR)
2000	Simona Amanar (ROM)[2]
2004	Carly Patterson (USA)
2008	Nastia Liukin (USA)

COMBINED, OR ALL-AROUND (TEAM)

1928	The Netherlands
1936	Germany
1948	Czechoslovakia
1952	USSR
1956	USSR
1960	USSR
1964	USSR
1968	USSR
1972	USSR
1976	USSR
1980	USSR
1984	Romania
1988	USSR
1992	Unified Team
1996	United States
2000	Romania
2004	Romania
2008	China

BALANCE BEAM

1952	Nina Bocharova (URS)
1956	Agnes Keleti (HUN)
1960	Eva Bosakova (TCH)
1964	Vera Caslavska (TCH)
1968	Natalya Kuchinskaya (URS)
1972	Olga Korbut (URS)
1976	Nadia Comaneci (ROM)
1980	Nadia Comaneci (ROM)
1984	Ecaterina Szabo (ROM); Simona Pauca (ROM) (tied)
1988	Daniela Silivas (ROM)
1992	Tatyana Lysenko (UNT)
1996	Shannon Miller (USA)
2000	Liu Xuan (CHN)
2004	Catalina Ponor (ROM)
2008	Shawn Johnson (USA)

UNEVEN PARALLEL BARS

1952	Margit Korondi (HUN)
1956	Agnes Keleti (HUN)
1960	Polina Astakhova (URS)
1964	Polina Astakhova (URS)
1968	Vera Caslavska (TCH)
1972	Karin Janz (GDR)
1976	Nadia Comaneci (ROM)
1980	Maxi Gnauck (GDR)
1984	Julianne McNamara (USA); Ma Yanhong (CHN) (tied)
1988	Daniela Silivas (ROM)
1992	Li Lu (CHN)
1996	Svetlana Khorkina (RUS)
2000	Svetlana Khorkina (RUS)
2004	Emilie Lepennec (FRA)
2008	He Kexin (CHN)

VAULT

1952	Yekaterina Kalinchuk (URS)
1956	Larisa Latynina (URS)
1960	Margarita Nikolayeva (URS)

Gymnastics (women) (continued)

VAULT (CONTINUED)

1964	Vera Caslavska (TCH)
1968	Vera Caslavska (TCH)
1972	Karin Janz (GDR)
1976	Nelli Kim (URS)
1980	Natalya Shaposhnikova (URS)
1984	Ecaterina Szabo (ROM)
1988	Svetlana Boginskaya (URS)
1992	Henrietta Onodi (HUN); Lavinia Milosovici (ROM) (tied)
1996	Simona Amanar (ROM)
2000	Yelena Zamolodchikova (RUS)
2004	Monica Rosu (ROM)
2008	Hong Un Jong (PRK)

FLOOR EXERCISE

1952	Agnes Keleti (HUN)
1956	Larisa Latynina (URS); Agnes Keleti (HUN) (tied)
1960	Larisa Latynina (URS)
1964	Larisa Latynina (URS)
1968	Vera Caslavska (TCH); Larissa Petrik (URS) (tied)
1972	Olga Korbut (URS)
1976	Nelli Kim (URS)
1980	Nadia Comaneci (ROM); Nelli Kim (URS) (tied)
1984	Ecaterina Szabo (ROM)
1988	Daniela Silivas (ROM)
1992	Lavinia Milosovici (ROM)
1996	Liliya Podkopayeva (UKR)
2000	Yelena Zamolodchikova (RUS)
2004	Catalina Ponor (ROM)
2008	Sandra Izbasa (ROM)

RHYTHMIC GYMNASTICS (INDIVIDUAL)

1984	Lori Fung (CAN)
1988	Marina Lobatch (URS)
1992	Aleksandra Timoshenko (UNT)
1996	Yekaterina Serebryanskaya (UKR)
2000	Yuliya Barsukova (RUS)
2004	Alina Kabayeva (RUS)
2008	Yevgeniya Kanayeva (RUS)

RHYTHMIC GYMNASTICS (TEAM)

1996	Spain
2000	Russia
2004	Russia
2008	Russia

TRAMPOLINE

2000	Irina Karavayeva (RUS)
2004	Anna Dogonadze (GER)
2008	He Wenna (CHN)

HAND APPARATUS (TEAM)

1952	Sweden
1956	Hungary

Handball (team)

MEN

1936[13]	Germany
1972	Yugoslavia
1976	USSR
1980	East Germany
1984	Yugoslavia
1988	USSR
1992	Unified Team

Summer Olympic Games (continued)

Handball (team) (continued)

MEN (CONTINUED)

1996	Croatia
2000	Russia
2004	Croatia
2008	France

WOMEN

1976	USSR
1980	USSR
1984	Yugoslavia
1988	Republic of Korea
1992	Republic of Korea
1996	Denmark
2000	Denmark
2004	Denmark
2008	Norway

JEU DE PAUME (ROYAL TENNIS)

| 1908 | Jay Gould (USA) |

Judo (men)[14]

60 KG (132 LB)

1964	Takehide Nakatani (JPN)
1972	Takao Kawaguchi (JPN)
1976	Héctor Rodríguez (CUB)
1980	Thierry Rey (FRA)
1984	Shinji Hosokawa (JPN)
1988	Kim Jae-Yup (KOR)
1992	Nazim Guseynov (UNT)
1996	Tadahiro Nomura (JPN)
2000	Tadahiro Nomura (JPN)
2004	Tadahiro Nomura (JPN)
2008	Choi Min Ho (KOR)

66 KG (145.2 LB)

1980	Nikolay Solodukhin (URS)
1984	Yoshiyuki Matsuoka (JPN)
1988	Lee Kyung Ken (KOR)
1992	Rogerio Sampaio Cardoso (BRA)
1996	Udo Quellmalz (GER)
2000	Huseyin Ozkan (TUR)
2004	Masato Uchishiba (JPN)
2008	Masato Uchishiba (JPN)

73 KG (160.6 LB)

1972	Takao Kawaguchi (JPN)
1976	Héctor Rodríguez Torres (CUB)
1980	Ezio Gamba (ITA)
1984	Ahn Byeong Keun (KOR)
1988	Marc Alexandre (FRA)
1992	Toshihiko Koga (JPN)
1996	Kenzo Nakamura (JPN)
2000	Giuseppe Maddaloni (ITA)
2004	Lee Won Hee (KOR)
2008	Elnur Mammadli (AZE)

81 KG (178.2 LB)

1972	Toyojazu Nomura (JPN)
1976	Vladimir Nevzorov (URS)
1980	Shota Khabareli (URS)
1984	Frank Wieneke (FRG)
1988	Waldemar Legien (POL)
1992	Hidehiko Yoshida (JPN)
1996	Djamel Bouras (FRA)
2000	Makoto Takimoto (JPN)
2004	Ilias Iliadis (GRE)
2008	Ole Bischof (GER)

Judo (men)[14] (continued)

90 KG (198 LB)

1964	Isao Okano (JPN)
1972	Shinobu Sekine (JPN)
1976	Isamu Sonoda (JPN)
1980	Jürg Röthlisberger (SUI)
1984	Peter Seisenbacher (AUT)
1988	Peter Seisenbacher (AUT)
1992	Waldemar Legien (POL)
1996	Jeon Ki-Young (KOR)
2000	Mark Huizinga (NED)
2004	Zurab Zviadauri (GEO)
2008	Irakli Tsirekidze (GEO)

100 KG (220 LB)

1972	Shota Chochoshvili (URS)
1976	Kazuhiro Ninomiya (JPN)
1980	Robert van de Walle (BEL)
1984	Ha Young Zoo (KOR)
1988	Aurelio Miguel (BRA)
1992	Antal Kovacs (HUN)
1996	Pawel Nastula (POL)
2000	Kosei Inoue (JPN)
2004	Ihar Makarau (BLR)
2008	Tuvshinbayar Naidan (MGL)

OVER 100 KG (220+ LB)

1964	Isao Inokuma (JPN)
1972	Willem Ruska (NED)
1976	Sergey Novikov (URS)
1980	Angelo Parisi (FRA)
1984	Hitoshi Saito (JPN)
1988	Hitoshi Saito (JPN)
1992	David Khakhaleishvili (UNT)
1996	David Douillet (FRA)
2000	David Douillet (FRA)
2004	Keiji Suzuki (JPN)
2008	Satoshi Ishii (JPN)

OPEN (NO WEIGHT LIMIT)

1964	Antonius Johannes Geesink (NED)
1972	Willem Ruska (NED)
1976	Haruki Uemura (JPN)
1980	Dietmar Lorenz (GDR)
1984	Yasuhiro Yamashita (JPN)

Judo (women)[15]

48 KG (105.6 LB)

1992	Cecile Nowak (FRA)
1996	Kye Sun-Hi (PRK)
2000	Ryoko Tamura (JPN)
2004	Ryoko Tani (JPN)
2008	Alina Alexandra Dumitru (ROM)

52 KG (114.4 LB)

1992	Almudena Muñoz Martínez (ESP)
1996	Marie-Claire Restoux (FRA)
2000	Legna Verdecia (CUB)
2004	Xian Dongmei (CHN)
2008	Xian Dongmei (CHN)

57 KG (125.4 LB)

1992	Miriam Blasco Soto (ESP)
1996	Driulis González Morales (CUB)
2000	Isabel Fernández (ESP)
2004	Yvonne Bönisch (GER)
2008	Giulia Quintavalle (ITA)

Summer Olympic Games (continued)

Judo (women)[15] (continued)

63 KG (138.6 LB)
1992 Catherine Fleury-Vachon (FRA)
1996 Yuko Emoto (JPN)
2000 Severine Vandenhende (FRA)
2004 Ayumi Tanimoto (JPN)
2008 Ayumi Tanimoto (JPN)

70 KG (154 LB)
1992 Odalis Reve Jiménez (CUB)
1996 Cho Min-Sun (KOR)
2000 Sibelis Veranes (CUB)
2004 Masae Ueno (JPN)
2008 Masae Ueno (JPN)

78 KG (171.6 LB)
1992 Kim Mi-Jung (KOR)
1996 Ulla Werbrouck (BEL)
2000 Tang Lin (CHN)
2004 Noriko Anno (JPN)
2008 Yang Xiuli (CHN)

OVER 78 KG (171.6+ LB)
1992 Zhuang Xiaoyan (CHN)
1996 Sun Fuming (CHN)
2000 Yuan Hua (CHN)
2004 Maki Tsukada (JPN)
2008 Tong Wen (CHN)

Lacrosse
1904 Canada
1908 Canada

Modern Pentathlon

INDIVIDUAL (MEN)
1912 Gösta Lilliehöök (SWE)
1920 Gustaf Dyrssen (SWE)
1924 Bo Lindman (SWE)
1928 Sven Thofelt (SWE)
1932 Johan Oxenstierna (SWE)
1936 Gotthardt Handrick (GER)
1948 William Grut (SWE)
1952 Lars-Goran Hall (SWE)
1956 Lars-Goran Hall (SWE)
1960 Ferenc Nemeth (HUN)
1964 Ferenc Torok (HUN)
1968 Björn Ferm (SWE)
1972 Andras Balczo (HUN)
1976 Janusz Pyciak-Peciak (POL)
1980 Anatoly Starostin (URS)
1984 Daniele Masala (ITA)
1988 Janos Martinek (HUN)
1992 Arkadiusz Skrzypaszek (POL)
1996 Aleksandr Parygin (KAZ)
2000 Dmitry Svatkovsky (RUS)
2004 Andrey Moiseyev (RUS)
2008 Andrey Moiseyev (RUS)

INDIVIDUAL (WOMEN)
2000 Stephanie Cook (GBR)
2004 Zsuzsanna Voros (HUN)
2008 Lena Schöneborn (GER)

TEAM (MEN)
1952 Hungary
1956 USSR
1960 Hungary
1964 USSR
1968 Hungary

Modern Pentathlon (continued)

TEAM (MEN) (CONTINUED)
1972 USSR
1976 Great Britain
1980 USSR
1984 Italy
1988 Hungary
1992 Poland

Motorboat Racing

	BOAT
OPEN CLASS, 40 NAUTICAL MILES	
1908 Émile Thubron (FRA)	*Camille*
8-METER CLASS, 40 NAUTICAL MILES	
1908 Thomas Thornycroft, Bernard Redwood (GBR)	*Cyrinus*
UNDER 60-FOOT CLASS, 40 NAUTICAL MILES	
1908 Thomas Thornycroft, Bernard Redwood (GBR)	*Cyrinus*

Polo
1900 Great Britain–United States
1908 Great Britain
1920 Great Britain
1924 Argentina
1936 Argentina

Rackets

SINGLES
1908 Evan Noel (GBR)

DOUBLES
1908 Vane Pennell, John Jacob Astor (GBR)

Roque
1904 Charles Jacobus (USA)

Rowing (men)[16]

SINGLE SCULLS		MIN:SEC
1900	Henri Barrelet (FRA)	7:35.6
1904	Frank Greer (USA)	10:08.5
1908	Harry Blackstaffe (GBR)	9:26.0
1912	William Kinnear (GBR)	7:47.6
1920	John Kelly, Sr. (USA)	7:35.0
1924	Jack Beresford (GBR)	7:49.2
1928	Henry Pearce (AUS)	7:11.0
1932	Henry Pearce (AUS)	7:44.4
1936	Gustav Schäfer (GER)	8:21.5
1948	Mervyn Wood (AUS)	7:24.4
1952	Yury Tyukalov (URS)	8:12.8
1956	Vyacheslav Ivanov (URS)	8:02.5
1960	Vyacheslav Ivanov (URS)	7:13.96
1964	Vyacheslav Ivanov (URS)	8:22.51
1968	Henri-Jan Wienese (NED)	7:47.80
1972	Yury Malyshev (URS)	7:10.12
1976	Pertti Karppinen (FIN)	7:29.03
1980	Pertti Karppinen (FIN)	7:09.61
1984	Pertti Karppinen (FIN)	7:00.24
1988	Thomas Lange (GDR)	6:49.86
1992	Thomas Lange (GER)	6:51.40
1996	Xeno Mueller (SUI)	6:44.85
2000	Robert Waddell (NZL)	6:48.90
2004	Olaf Tufte (NOR)	6:49.30
2008	Olaf Tufte (NOR)	6:59.83

Summer Olympic Games (continued)

Rowing (men)[16] (continued)

DOUBLE SCULLS

		MIN:SEC
1904	United States	10:03.2
1920	United States	7:09.0
1924	United States	6:34.0
1928	United States	6:41.4
1932	United States	7:17.4
1936	Great Britain	7:20.8
1948	Great Britain	6:51.3
1952	Argentina	7:32.2
1956	USSR	7:24.0
1960	Czechoslovakia	6:47.50
1964	USSR	7:10.66
1968	USSR	6:51.82
1972	USSR	7:01.77
1976	Norway	7:13.20
1980	East Germany	6:24.33
1984	United States	6:36.87
1988	The Netherlands	6:21.13
1992	Australia	6:17.32
1996	Italy	6:16.98
2000	Slovenia	6:16.63
2004	France	6:29.00
2008	Australia	6:27.77

FOUR SCULLS

		MIN:SEC
1976	East Germany	6:18.65
1980	East Germany	5:49.81
1984	West Germany	5:57.55
1988	Italy	5:53.37
1992	Germany	5:45.17
1996	Germany	5:56.93
2000	Italy	5:45.56
2004	Russia	5:56.85
2008	Poland	5:41.33

LIGHTWEIGHT DOUBLE SCULLS

		MIN:SEC
1996	Switzerland	6:23.47
2000	Poland	6:21.75
2004	Poland	6:20.93
2008	Great Britain	6:10.99

PAIRS (WITHOUT COXSWAIN)

		MIN:SEC
1904	United States	10:57.0
1908	Great Britain	9:41.0
1924	The Netherlands	8:19.4
1928	Germany	7:06.4
1932	Great Britain	8:00.0
1936	Germany	8:16.1
1948	Great Britain	7:21.1
1952	United States	8:20.7
1956	United States	7:55.4
1960	USSR	7:02.01
1964	Canada	7:32.94
1968	East Germany	7:26.56
1972	East Germany	6:53.16
1976	East Germany	7:23.31
1980	East Germany	6:48.01
1984	Romania	6:45.39
1988	Great Britain	6:36.84
1992	Great Britain	6:27.72
1996	Great Britain	6:20.09
2000	France	6:32.97
2004	Australia	6:30.76
2008	Australia	6:37.44

PAIRS (WITH COXSWAIN)

		MIN:SEC
1900	The Netherlands–France	7:34.2
1920	Italy	7:56.0

Rowing (men)[16] (continued)

PAIRS (WITH COXSWAIN) (CONTINUED)

		MIN:SEC
1924	Switzerland	8:39.0
1928	Switzerland	7:42.6
1932	United States	8:25.8
1936	Germany	8:36.9
1948	Denmark	8:00.5
1952	France	8:28.6
1956	United States	8:26.1
1960	Germany	7:29.14
1964	United States	8:21.23
1968	Italy	8:04.81
1972	East Germany	7:17.25
1976	East Germany	7:58.99
1980	East Germany	7:02.54
1984	Italy	7:05.99
1988	Italy	6:58.79
1992	Great Britain	6:49.83

LIGHTWEIGHT FOURS (WITHOUT COXSWAIN)

		MIN:SEC
1996	Denmark	6:09.58
2000	France	6:01.68
2004	Denmark	6:01.39
2008	Denmark	5:47.76

FOURS (WITHOUT COXSWAIN)

		MIN:SEC
1900	France	7:11.0
1904	United States	9:53.8
1908	Great Britain	8:34.0
1920	Great Britain	7:08.6
1928	Great Britain	6:36.0
1932	Great Britain	6:58.2
1936	Germany	7:01.8
1948	Italy	6:39.0
1952	Yugoslavia	7:16.0
1956	Canada	7:08.8
1960	United States	6:26.26
1964	Denmark	6:59.30
1968	East Germany	6:39.18
1972	East Germany	6:24.27
1976	East Germany	6:37.42
1980	East Germany	6:08.17
1984	New Zealand	6:03.48
1988	East Germany	6:03.11
1992	Australia	5:55.04
1996	Australia	6:06.37
2000	Great Britain	5:56.24
2004	Great Britain	6:06.98
2008	Great Britain	6:06.57

FOURS (WITH COXSWAIN)

		MIN:SEC
1900	Germany	5:59.0
1912	Germany	6:59.4
1920	Switzerland	6:54.0
1924	Switzerland	7:18.4
1928	Italy	6:47.8
1932	Germany	7:19.0
1936	Germany	7:16.2
1948	United States	6:50.3
1952	Czechoslovakia	7:33.4
1956	Italy	7:19.4
1960	Germany	6:39.12
1964	Germany	7:00.44
1968	New Zealand	6:45.62
1972	West Germany	6:31.85
1976	USSR	6:40.22
1980	East Germany	6:14.51
1984	Great Britain	6:18.64

Summer Olympic Games (continued)

Rowing (men)[16] (continued)

FOURS (WITH COXSWAIN) (CONTINUED)

		MIN:SEC
1988	East Germany	6:10.74
1992	Romania	5:59.37

FOURS, INRIGGERS (WITH COXSWAIN)

		MIN:SEC
1912	Denmark	7:47.0

EIGHTS (WITH COXSWAIN)

		MIN:SEC
1900	United States	6:09.8
1904	United States	7:50.0
1908	Great Britain	7:52.0
1912	Great Britain	6:15.0
1920	United States	6:02.6
1924	United States	6:33.4
1928	United States	6:03.2
1932	United States	6:37.6
1936	United States	6:25.4
1948	United States	5:56.7
1952	United States	6:25.9
1956	United States	6:35.2
1960	Germany	5:57.18
1964	United States	6:18.23
1968	West Germany	6:07.00
1972	New Zealand	6:08.94
1976	East Germany	5:58.29
1980	East Germany	5:49.05
1984	Canada	5:41.32
1988	West Germany	5:46.05
1992	Canada	5:29.53
1996	The Netherlands	5:42.74
2000	Great Britain	5:33.08
2004	United States	5:42.48
2008	Canada	5:23.89

Rowing (women)[17]

SINGLE SCULLS

		MIN:SEC
1976	Christine Scheiblich (GDR)	4:05.56
1980	Sanda Toma (ROM)	3:40.69
1984	Valeria Racila (ROM)	3:40.68
1988	Jutta Behrendt (GDR)	7:47.19
1992	Elisabeta Lipa (ROM)	7:25.54
1996	Yekaterina Khodotovich (BLR)	7:32.21
2000	Yekaterina Khodotovich Karsten (BLR)	7:28.14
2004	Katrin Rutschow-Stomporowski (GER)	7:18.12
2008	Rumyana Neykova (BUL)	7:22.34

DOUBLE SCULLS

		MIN:SEC
1976	Bulgaria	3:44.36
1980	USSR	3:16.27
1984	Romania	3:26.75
1988	East Germany	7:00.48
1992	Germany	6:49.00
1996	Canada	6:56.84
2000	Germany	6:55.44
2004	New Zealand	7:01.79
2008	New Zealand	7:07.32

LIGHTWEIGHT DOUBLE SCULLS

		MIN:SEC
1996	Romania	7:12.78
2000	Romania	7:02.64
2004	Romania	6:56.05
2008	The Netherlands	6:54.74

Rowing (women)[17] (continued)

FOUR SCULLS

		MIN:SEC
1976	East Germany	3:29.99
1980	East Germany	3:15.32
1984	Romania	3:14.11
1988	East Germany	6:21.06
1992	Germany	6:20.18
1996	Germany	6:27.44
2000	Germany	6:19.58
2004	Germany	6:29.29
2008	China	6:16.06

PAIRS (WITHOUT COXSWAIN)

		MIN:SEC
1976	Bulgaria	4:01.22
1980	East Germany	3:30.49
1984	Romania	3:32.60
1988	Romania	7:28.13
1992	Canada	7:06.22
1996	Australia	7:01.39
2000	Romania	7:11.00
2004	Romania	7:06.55
2008	Romania	7:20.60

FOURS (WITH COXSWAIN)

		MIN:SEC
1976	East Germany	3:45.08
1980	East Germany	3:19.27
1984	Romania	3:19.3
1988	East Germany	6:56.0
1992[18]	Canada	6:30.85

EIGHTS (WITH COXSWAIN)

		MIN:SEC
1976	East Germany	3:33.32
1980	East Germany	3:03.32
1984	United States	2:59.80
1988	East Germany	6:15.17
1992	Canada	6:02.62
1996	Romania	6:19.73
2000	Romania	6:06.44
2004	Romania	6:17.70
2008	United States	6:05.34

Rugby Football

1900	France
1908	Australia
1920	United States
1924	United States

Sailing (Yachting)

BOARDSAILING (WINDGLIDER/DIVISION II) (OPEN)

1984	Stephan van den Berg (NED)
1988	Anthony Bruce Kendall (NZL)

BOARDSAILING (RS:X[19]) (MEN)

1992	Franck David (FRA)
1996	Nikolaos Kaklamanakis (GRE)
2000	Christoph Sieber (AUT)
2004	Gal Fridman (ISR)
2008	Tom Ashley (NZL)

BOARDSAILING (RS:X[19]) (WOMEN)

1992	Barbara Anne Kendall (NZL)
1996	Lee Lai Shan (HKG)
2000	Alessandra Sensini (ITA)

Summer Olympic Games (continued)

Sailing (Yachting) (continued)

BOARDSAILING (RS:X[19]) (WOMEN) (CONTINUED)
2004   Faustine Merret (FRA)
2008   Yin Jian (CHN)

SINGLE-HANDED DINGHY (LASER RADIAL) (WOMEN)
1992   Linda Andersen (NOR)
1996   Kristine Roug (DEN)
2000   Shirley Anne Robertson (GBR)
2004   Siren Sundby (NOR)
2008   Anna Tunnicliffe (USA)

SINGLE-HANDED DINGHY (LASER) (MEN[20])
1996   Robert Scheidt (BRA)
2000   Ben Ainslie (GBR)
2004   Robert Scheidt (BRA)
2008   Paul Goodison (GBR)

SINGLE-HANDED DINGHY (FINN[21]) (OPEN[22])
1924   Léon Huybrechts (BEL)
1928   Sven Thorell (SWE)
1932   Jacques Lebrun (FRA)
1936   Daniel Kagchelland (NED)
1948   Paul Elvström (DEN)
1952   Paul Elvström (DEN)
1956   Paul Elvström (DEN)
1960   Paul Elvström (DEN)
1964   Wilhelm Kuhweide (GER)
1968   Valentin Mankin (URS)
1972   Serge Maury (FRA)
1976   Jochen Schümann (GDR)
1980   Esko Rechardt (FIN)
1984   Russell Coutts (NZL)
1988   José Luis Doreste (ESP)
1992   José van der Ploeg (ESP)
1996   Mateusz Kusznierewicz (POL)
2000   Iain Percy (GBR)
2004   Ben Ainslie (GBR)
2008   Ben Ainslie (GBR)

DOUBLE-HANDED DINGHY (470) (MEN)
1976   West Germany
1980   Brazil
1984   Spain
1988   France
1992   Spain
1996   Ukraine
2000   Australia
2004   United States
2008   Australia

DOUBLE-HANDED DINGHY (470) (WOMEN)
1988   United States
1992   Spain
1996   Spain
2000   Australia
2004   Greece
2008   Australia

YNGLING (WOMEN)
2004   Great Britain
2008   Great Britain

HIGH-PERFORMANCE DINGHY (49ER) (OPEN)
2000   Finland
2004   Spain
2008   Denmark

Sailing (Yachting) (continued)

MULTIHULL (TORNADO) (OPEN)
1976   Great Britain
1980   Brazil
1984   New Zealand
1988   France
1992   France
1996   Spain
2000   Austria
2004   Austria
2008   Spain

FLEET/MATCH RACE KEELBOAT (SOLING) (OPEN)
1972   United States
1976   Denmark
1980   Denmark
1984   United States
1988   East Germany
1992   Denmark
1996   Germany
2000   Denmark

TWO-PERSON KEELBOAT (STAR) (MEN[23])
1932   United States
1936   Germany
1948   United States
1952   Italy
1956   United States
1960   USSR
1964   The Bahamas
1968   United States
1972   Australia
1980   USSR
1984   United States
1988   Great Britain
1992   United States
1996   Brazil
2000   United States
2004   Brazil
2008   Great Britain

40-METER CLASS
1920   Sweden

30-METER CLASS
1920   Sweden

12-METER CLASS
1920 (old)   Norway
1920 (new)   Norway

OVER-10-METER CLASS
1900   France
1908   Great Britain
1912   Norway

10-METER CLASS
1900   Germany
1912   Sweden
1920 (old)   Norway
1920 (new)   Norway

8-METER CLASS
1900   Great Britain
1908   Great Britain
1912   Norway
1920 (old)   Norway
1920 (new)   Norway
1924   Norway

Summer Olympic Games (continued)

Sailing (Yachting) (continued)

8-METER CLASS (CONTINUED)
1928   France
1932   United States
1936   Italy

7-METER CLASS
1908   Great Britain
1920 (old)   Great Britain

6.5-METER CLASS
1920 (new)   The Netherlands

6-METER CLASS
1900   Switzerland
1908   Great Britain
1912   France
1920 (old)   Belgium
1920 (new)   Norway
1924   Norway
1928   Norway
1932   Sweden
1936   Great Britain
1948   United States
1952   United States

5.5-METER CLASS
1952   United States
1956   Sweden
1960   United States
1964   Australia
1968   Sweden

18-FOOT CENTERBOARD BOAT
1920   Great Britain

12-FOOT CENTERBOARD BOAT
1920   The Netherlands
1924   Belgium

12-FOOT DINGHY
1928   Sweden

MONOTYPE CLASS
1932   France

MONOTYPE CLASS "NÜRNBERG"
1936   The Netherlands

SWALLOW
1948   Great Britain

FIREFLY
1948   Denmark

SHARPIE
1956   New Zealand

DRAGON
1948   Norway
1952   Norway
1956   Sweden
1960   Greece
1964   Denmark
1968   United States
1972   Australia

Sailing (Yachting) (continued)

TEMPEST
1972   USSR
1976   Sweden

FLYING DUTCHMAN
1960   Norway
1964   New Zealand
1968   Great Britain
1972   Great Britain
1976   West Germany
1980   Spain
1984   United States
1988   Denmark
1992   Spain

Shooting (men)
individual
TRAP (CLAY PIGEON)[24]
1900   Roger de Barbarin (FRA)
1908   Walter Ewing (CAN)
1912   James Graham (USA)
1920   Mark Arie (USA)
1924   Gyula Halasy (HUN)
1952   George Généreux (CAN)
1956   Galliano Rossini (ITA)
1960   Ion Dumitrescu (ROM)
1964   Ennio Mattarelli (ITA)
1968   John Braithwaite (GBR)
1972   Angelo Scalzone (ITA)
1976   Donald Haldeman (USA)
1980   Luciano Giovannetti (ITA)
1984   Luciano Giovannetti (ITA)
1988   Donald Monakov (URS)
1992   Petr Hrdlicka (TCH)
1996   Michael Constantine Diamond (AUS)
2000   Michael Constantine Diamond (AUS)
2004   Aleksey Alipov (RUS)
2008   David Kostelecky (CZE)

DOUBLE TRAP
1996   Russell Andrew Mark (AUS)
2000   Richard Faulds (GBR)
2004   Ahmed Almaktoum (UAE)
2008   Walton Eller (USA)

SKEET[25]
1968   Yevgeny Petrov (URS)
1972   Konrad Wirnhier (FRG)
1976   Josef Panacek (TCH)
1980   Hans Kjeld Rasmussen (DEN)
1984   Matthew Dryke (USA)
1988   Axel Wegner (GDR)
1992   Zhang Shan (CHN)
1996   Ennio Falco (ITA)
2000   Mykola Milchev (UKR)
2004   Andrea Benelli (ITA)
2008   Vincent Hancock (USA)

FREE PISTOL
1896   Sumner Paine (USA)
1900   Karl Konrad Röderer (SUI)
1912   Alfred Lane (USA)
1920   Carl Frederick (USA)
1936   Torsten Ullmann (SWE)
1948   Edwin Vásquez Cam (PER)
1952   Huelet Benner (USA)
1956   Pentti Tapio Linnosvuo (FIN)
1960   Aleksey Gushchin (URS)

Summer Olympic Games (continued)

Shooting (men) (continued)
individual (continued)

FREE PISTOL (CONTINUED)
1964	Väinö Johannes Markkanen (FIN)
1968	Grigory Kosykh (URS)
1976	Uwe Potteck (GDR)
1980	Aleksandr Melentev (URS)
1984	Xu Haifeng (CHN)
1988	Sorin Babii (ROM)
1992	Konstantin Lukachik (UNT)
1996	Boris Kokorev (RUS)
2000	Tanyu Kiryakov (BUL)
2004	Mikhail Nestruyev (RUS)
2008	Jin Jong Oh (KOR)

RAPID-FIRE PISTOL
1896	Joannis Phrangudis (GRE)
1900	Maurice Larrouy (FRA)
1908	Paul van Asbrock (BEL)
1912	Alfred Lane (USA)
1920	Guilherme Paraense (BRA)
1924	Henry Bailey (USA)
1932	Renzo Morigi (ITA)
1936	Cornelius van Oyen (GER)
1948	Karoly Takacs (HUN)
1952	Karoly Takacs (HUN)
1956	Stefan Petrescu (ROM)
1960	William McMillan (USA)
1964	Pentti Tapio Linnosvuo (FIN)
1968	Jozef Zapedzki (POL)
1972	Jozef Zapedzki (POL)
1976	Norbert Klaar (GDR)
1980	Corneliu Ion (ROM)
1984	Takeo Kamachi (JPN)
1988	Afanasy Kuzmin (URS)
1992	Ralf Schumann (GER)
1996	Ralf Schumann (GER)
2000	Sergey Alifirenko (RUS)
2004	Ralf Schumann (GER)
2008	Oleksandr Petriv (UKR)

SMALL-BORE RIFLE (PRONE)
1908	Arthur Ashton Carnell (GBR)
1912	Frederick Hird (USA)
1920	Lawrence Nuesslein (USA)
1924	Pierre Coquelin de Lisle (FRA)
1932	Bertil Rönnmark (SWE)
1936	Willy Røgeberg (NOR)
1948	Arthur Cook (USA)
1952	Iosif Sarbu (ROM)
1956	Gerald Ouellette (CAN)
1960	Peter Kohnke (GER)
1964	Laszlo Hammerl (HUN)
1968	Jan Kurka (TCH)
1972	Ho Jun Li (PRK)
1976	Karlheinz Smieszek (FRG)
1980	Karoly Varga (HUN)
1984	Edward Etzel (USA)
1988	Miroslav Varga (TCH)
1992	Lee Eun Chul (KOR)
1996	Christian Klees (GER)
2000	Jonas Edman (SWE)
2004	Matthew Emmons (USA)
2008	Artur Ayvazian (UKR)

SMALL-BORE RIFLE (3 POSITIONS)
1952	Erling Kongshaug (NOR)
1956	Anatoly Bogdanov (URS)
1960	Viktor Shamburkin (URS)

Shooting (men) (continued)
individual (continued)

SMALL-BORE RIFLE (3 POSITIONS) (CONTINUED)
1964	Lones Wesley Wigger (USA)
1968	Bernd Klingner (FRG)
1972	John Writer (USA)
1976	Lanny Bassham (USA)
1980	Viktor Vlasov (URS)
1984	Malcolm Cooper (GBR)
1988	Malcolm Cooper (GBR)
1992	Gratchia Petikian (UNT)
1996	Jean-Pierre Amat (FRA)
2000	Rajmond Debevec (SLO)
2004	Jia Zhanbo (CHN)
2008	Qiu Jian (CHN)

10-METER RUNNING (GAME) TARGET
1900	Louis Debray (FRA)
1972	Yakov Zhelezniak (URS)
1976	Aleksandr Gazov (URS)
1980	Igor Sokolov (URS)
1984	Li Yuwei (CHN)
1988	Tor Heiestad (NOR)
1992	Michael Jakosits (GER)
1996	Yang Ling (CHN)
2000	Yang Ling (CHN)
2004	Manfred Kurzer (GER)

AIR RIFLE
1984	Philippe Heberle (FRA)
1988	Goran Maksimovic (YUG)
1992	Yury Fedkin (UNT)
1996	Artyom Khadzhibekov (RUS)
2000	Cai Yalin (CHN)
2004	Zhu Quinan (CHN)
2008	Abhinav Bindra (IND)

AIR PISTOL
1988	Tanyu Kiryakov (BUL)
1992	Wang Yifu (CHN)
1996	Roberto di Donna (ITA)
2000	Franck Dumoulin (FRA)
2004	Wang Yifu (CHN)
2008	Pang Wei (CHN)

FREE RIFLE (300 METERS, 3 POSITIONS)
1908	Albert Helgerud (NOR)
1912	Paul René Colas (FRA)
1920	Morris Fisher (USA)
1924	Morris Fisher (USA)
1948	Emil Grünig (SUI)
1952	Anatoly Bogdanov (URS)
1956	Vasily Borisov (URS)
1960	Hubert Hammerer (AUT)
1964	Gary Lee Anderson (USA)
1968	Gary Lee Anderson (USA)
1972	Lones Wesley Wigger (USA)

ARMY RIFLE (300 METERS, 3 POSITIONS)
1896	Georgios Orphanidis (GRE)
1900	Emil Kellenberger (SUI)
1912	Sandor Prokop (HUN)

ARMY RIFLE (200 METERS)
1896	Pantelis Karasevdas (GRE)

FREE RIFLE (1,000 YARDS PRONE)
1908	Joshua Millner (GBR)

Summer Olympic Games (continued)

Shooting (men) (continued)
individual (continued)

FULL-BORE RIFLE (300 METERS STANDING)
1900   Lars Madsen (DEN)

FULL-BORE RIFLE (300 METERS KNEELING)
1900   Konrad Staeheli (SUI)

FULL-BORE RIFLE (300 METERS PRONE)
1900   Achille Paroche (FRA)

FULL-BORE RIFLE (300 METERS)
1900   Emil Kellenberger (SUI)

RIFLE (300 METERS, 2 POSITIONS)
1920   Morris Fisher (USA)

RIFLE (300 METERS STANDING)
1920   Carl Osburn (USA)

RIFLE (300 METERS PRONE)
1920   Otto Olsen (NOR)

RIFLE (600 METERS PRONE)
1920   Hugo Johansson (SWE)

6-MILLIMETER SMALL GUN (OPEN REAR SIGHT)
1900   C. Grosett (FRA)

SMALL-BORE RIFLE (VANISHING TARGET)
1908   William Styles (GBR)
1912   Wilhelm Carlberg (SWE)

SMALL-BORE RIFLE (MOVING TARGET)
1908   John Francis Fleming (GBR)

RUNNING DEER (100 METERS SINGLE SHOT)
1908   Oscar Swahn (SWE)
1912   Alfred Swahn (SWE)
1920   Otto Olsen (NOR)
1924   John Boles (USA)

RUNNING DEER (100 METERS DOUBLE SHOT)
1908   Walter Winans (USA)
1912   Ake Lundeberg (SWE)
1920   Ole Andreas Lilloe-Olsen (NOR)
1924   Ole Andreas Lilloe-Olsen (NOR)

RUNNING DEER (100 METERS SINGLE AND DOUBLE SHOT)
1952   John Larsen (NOR)
1956   Vitaly Romanenko (URS)

LIVE PIGEON
1900   Léon de Lunden (BEL)

GAME SHOOTING
1900   Donald Mackintosh (AUS)

MILITARY REVOLVER (25 METERS)
1896   John Paine (USA)

REVOLVER AND PISTOL
1900   Paul van Asbrock (BEL)
1908   Paul van Asbrock (BEL)
1912   Alfred Lane (USA)

Shooting (men) (continued)
individual (continued)

DUELING PISTOL
1912   Alfred Lane (USA)

team

FREE RIFLE (300 METERS)
1908   Norway
1912   Sweden

ARMY RIFLE (300 METERS)
1900   Norway

ARMY RIFLE (ALL-AROUND)
1900   United States
1908   United States
1912   United States

FULL-BORE RIFLE (300 METERS)
1900   Switzerland

SMALL-BORE RIFLE
1900   Great Britain
1908   Great Britain
1920   United States
1924   France

SMALL-BORE RIFLE (VANISHING TARGET)
1912   Sweden

RIFLE (600 METERS PRONE)
1920   United States

RIFLE (300 METERS, 2 POSITIONS)
1920   United States

RIFLE (300 METERS STANDING)
1920   Denmark

RIFLE (300 METERS PRONE)
1920   United States

RIFLE (ALL-AROUND)
1920   United States
1924   United States

RUNNING DEER (SINGLE SHOT)
1908   Sweden
1912   Sweden
1920   Norway
1924   Norway

RUNNING DEER (DOUBLE SHOT)
1920   Norway
1924   Great Britain

CLAY PIGEON
1900   Great Britain
1908   Great Britain
1912   United States
1920   United States
1924   United States

REVOLVER
1900   Switzerland

Summer Olympic Games (continued)

Shooting (men) (continued)
team (continued)
PISTOL
1920 United States
1924 United States

REVOLVER AND PISTOL
1900 United States
1908 United States
1912 United States
1920 United States

DUELING PISTOL
1912 Sweden

Shooting (women)
TRAP (CLAY PIGEON)
2000 Daina Gudzineviciute (LTU)
2004 Suzanne Balogh (AUS)
2008 Satu Mäkelä-Nummela (FIN)

DOUBLE TRAP
1996 Kimberly Rhode (USA)
2000 Pia Hansen (SWE)
2004 Kimberly Rhode (USA)

SKEET
2000 Zemfira Meftakhetdinova (AZE)
2004 Diana Igaly (HUN)
2008 Chiara Cainero (ITA)

PISTOL
1984 Linda Thom (CAN)
1988 Nino Salukvadze (URS)
1992 Marina Logvinenko (UNT)
1996 Li Duihong (CHN)
2000 Mariya Zdravkova Grozdeva (BUL)
2004 Mariya Zdravkova Grozdeva (BUL)
2008 Chen Ying (CHN)

SMALL-BORE RIFLE (3 POSITIONS)
1984 Wu Xiao-Xuan (CHN)
1988 Silvia Sperber (FRG)
1992 Launi Meili (USA)
1996 Aleksandra Ivosev (YUG)
2000 Renata Mauer (POL)
2004 Lyubov Galkina (RUS)
2008 Du Li (CHN)

AIR RIFLE
1984 Pat Spurgin (USA)
1988 Irina Chilova (URS)
1992 Yeo Kab Soon (KOR)
1996 Renata Mauer (POL)
2000 Nancy Johnson (USA)
2004 Du Li (CHN)
2008 Katerina Emmons (CZE)

AIR PISTOL
1988 Jasna Sekaric (YUG)
1992 Marina Logvinenko (UNT)
1996 Olga Klochneva (RUS)
2000 Tao Luna (CHN)
2004 Olena Kostevych (UKR)
2008 Guo Wenjun (CHN)

Softball
1996 United States
2000 United States

Softball (continued)
2004 United States
2008 Japan

Swimming (men)

50-METER FREESTYLE		SEC
1988	Matt Biondi (USA)	22.14
1992	Aleksandr Popov (UNT)	21.91
1996	Aleksandr Popov (RUS)	22.13
2000	Anthony Ervin (USA); Gary Hall, Jr. (USA) (tied)	21.98
2004	Gary Hall, Jr. (USA)	21.93
2008	César Cielo Filho (BRA)	21.30

100-METER FREESTYLE		MIN:SEC
1896	Alfred Hajos (HUN)	1:22.2
1904[26]	Zoltan Halmay (HUN)	1:02.8
1908	Charles Daniels (USA)	1:05.6
1912	Duke Paoa Kahanamoku (USA)	1:03.4
1920	Duke Paoa Kahanamoku (USA)	1:00.4
1924	Johnny Weissmuller (USA)	59.0
1928	Johnny Weissmuller (USA)	58.6
1932	Yasuji Miyazaki (JPN)	58.2
1936	Ferenc Csik (HUN)	57.6
1948	Walter Ris (USA)	57.3
1952	Clark Scholes (USA)	57.4
1956	Jon Henricks (AUS)	55.4
1960	John Devitt (AUS)	55.2
1964	Donald Schollander (USA)	53.4
1968	Michael Wenden (AUS)	52.2
1972	Mark Spitz (USA)	51.22
1976	Jim Montgomery (USA)	49.99
1980	Jörg Woithe (GDR)	50.40
1984	Ambrose Gaines (USA)	49.80
1988	Matt Biondi (USA)	48.63
1992	Aleksandr Popov (UNT)	49.02
1996	Aleksandr Popov (RUS)	48.74
2000	Pieter van den Hoogenband (NED)	48.30
2004	Pieter van den Hoogenband (NED)	48.17
2008	Alain Bernard (FRA)	47.21

100 METER FREESTYLE FOR SAILORS		MIN:SEC
1896	Ioannis Malokinis (GRE)	2:20.4

200-METER FREESTYLE		MIN:SEC
1900	Fred Lane (AUS)	2:25.2
1904[27]	Charles Daniels (USA)	2:44.2
1968	Michael Wenden (AUS)	1:55.2
1972	Mark Spitz (USA)	1:52.78
1976	Bruce Furniss (USA)	1:50.29
1980	Sergey Koplyakov (URS)	1:49.81
1984	Michael Gross (FRG)	1:47.44
1988	Duncan Armstrong (AUS)	1:47.25
1992	Yevgeny Sadovy (UNT)	1:46.70
1996	Danyon Loader (NZL)	1:47.63
2000	Pieter van den Hoogenband (NED)	1:45.35
2004	Ian Thorpe (AUS)	1:44.71
2008	Michael Phelps (USA)	1:42.96

400-METER FREESTYLE		MIN:SEC
1896[28]	Paul Neumann (AUT)	8:12.6
1904[29]	Charles Daniels (USA)	6:16.2
1908	Henry Taylor (GBR)	5:36.8
1912	George Hodgson (CAN)	5:24.4
1920	Norman Ross (USA)	5:26.8
1924	Johnny Weissmuller (USA)	5:04.2
1928	Victoriano Zorilla (ARG)	5:01.6
1932	Clarence Crabbe (USA)	4:48.4
1936	Jack Medica (USA)	4:44.5

Summer Olympic Games (continued)

Swimming (men) (continued)

400-METER FREESTYLE (CONTINUED)		MIN:SEC
1948	William Smith (USA)	4:41.0
1952	Jean Boiteux (FRA)	4:30.7
1956	Murray Rose (AUS)	4:27.3
1960	Murray Rose (AUS)	4:18.3
1964	Donald Schollander (USA)	4:12.2
1968	Michael Burton (USA)	4:09.0
1972	Bradford Cooper (AUS)[2]	4:00.27
1976	Brian Goodell (USA)	3:51.93
1980	Vladimir Salnikov (URS)	3:51.31
1984	George DiCarlo (USA)	3:51.23
1988	Uwe Dassler (GDR)	3:46.95
1992	Yevgeny Sadovy (UNT)	3:45.00
1996	Danyon Loader (NZL)	3:47.97
2000	Ian Thorpe (AUS)	3:40.59
2004	Ian Thorpe (AUS)	3:43.10
2008	Park Tae Hwan (KOR)	3:41.86

1,500-METER FREESTYLE		MIN:SEC
1896[30]	Alfred Hajos (HUN)	18:22.2
1900[31]	Johnny Arthur Jarvis (GBR)	13:40.2
1904[32]	Emil Rausch (GER)	27:18.2
1908	Henry Taylor (GBR)	22:48.4
1912	George Hodgson (CAN)	22:00.0
1920	Norman Ross (USA)	22:23.2
1924	Andrew Charlton (AUS)	20:06.6
1928	Arne Borg (SWE)	19:51.8
1932	Kusuo Kitamura (JPN)	19:12.4
1936	Noburu Terada (JPN)	19:13.7
1948	James McLane (USA)	19:18.5
1952	Ford Konno (USA)	18:30.0
1956	Murray Rose (AUS)	17:58.9
1960	John Konrads (AUS)	17:19.6
1964	Robert Windle (AUS)	17:01.7
1968	Michael Burton (USA)	16:38.9
1972	Michael Burton (USA)	15:52.58
1976	Brian Goodell (USA)	15:02.40
1980	Vladimir Salnikov (URS)	14:58.27
1984	Michael O'Brien (USA)	15:05.20
1988	Vladimir Salnikov (URS)	15:00.40
1992	Kieren Perkins (AUS)	14:43.48
1996	Kieren Perkins (AUS)	14:56.40
2000	Grant Hackett (AUS)	14:48.33
2004	Grant Hackett (AUS)	14:43.40
2008	Oussama Mellouli (TUN)	14:40.84

4,000-METER FREESTYLE		MIN:SEC
1900	Johnny Arthur Jarvis (GBR)	58:24

880-YARD FREESTYLE		MIN:SEC
1904	Emil Rausch (GER)	13:11.4

1-MILE FREESTYLE		MIN:SEC
1904	Emil Rausch (GER)	27:18.2

100-METER BUTTERFLY		SEC
1968	Douglas Russell (USA)	55.9
1972	Mark Spitz (USA)	54.27
1976	Matt Vogel (USA)	54.35
1980	Pär Arvidsson (SWE)	54.92
1984	Michael Gross (FRG)	53.08
1988	Anthony Nesty (SUR)	53.00
1992	Pablo Morales (USA)	53.32
1996	Denis Pankratov (RUS)	52.27
2000	Lars Frölander (SWE)	52.00
2004	Michael Phelps (USA)	51.25
2008	Michael Phelps (USA)	50.58

Swimming (men) (continued)

200-METER BUTTERFLY		MIN:SEC
1956	William Yorzyk (USA)	2:19.3
1960	Michael Troy (USA)	2:12.8
1964	Kevin Berry (AUS)	2:06.6
1968	Carl Robie (USA)	2:08.7
1972	Mark Spitz (USA)	2:00.70
1976	Mike Bruner (USA)	1:59.23
1980	Sergey Fesenko (URS)	1:59.76
1984	Jonathan Sieben (AUS)	1:57.04
1988	Michael Gross (FRG)	1:56.94
1992	Mel Stewart (USA)	1:56.26
1996	Denis Pankratov (RUS)	1:56.51
2000	Tom Malchow (USA)	1:55.35
2004	Michael Phelps (USA)	1:54.04
2008	Michael Phelps (USA)	1:52.03

100-METER BACKSTROKE		MIN:SEC
1904[33]	Walter Brack (GER)	1:16.8
1908	Arno Bieberstein (GER)	1:24.6
1912	Harry Hebner (USA)	1:21.2
1920	Warren Paoa Kealoha (USA)	1:15.2
1924	Warren Paoa Kealoha (USA)	1:13.2
1928	George Kojac (USA)	1:08.2
1932	Masaji Kiyokawa (JPN)	1:08.6
1936	Adolph Kiefer (USA)	1:05.9
1948	Allen Stack (USA)	1:06.4
1952	Yoshinobu Oyakawa (JPN)	1:05.4
1956	David Theile (AUS)	1:02.2
1960	David Theile (AUS)	1:01.9
1968	Roland Matthes (GDR)	58.7
1972	Roland Matthes (GDR)	56.58
1976	John Naber (USA)	55.49
1980	Bengt Baron (SWE)	56.53
1984	Richard Carey (USA)	55.79
1988	Daichi Suzuki (JPN)	55.05
1992	Mark Tewksbury (CAN)	53.98
1996	Jeff Rouse (USA)	54.10
2000	Lenny Krayzelburg (USA)	53.72
2004	Aaron Peirsol (USA)	54.06
2008	Aaron Peirsol (USA)	52.54

200-METER BACKSTROKE		MIN:SEC
1900	Ernst Hoppenberg (GER)	2:47.0
1964	Jed Graef (USA)	2:10.3
1968	Roland Matthes (GDR)	2:09.6
1972	Roland Matthes (GDR)	2:02.82
1976	John Naber (USA)	1:59.19
1980	Sandor Wladar (HUN)	2:01.93
1984	Richard Carey (USA)	2:00.23
1988	Igor Polyansky (URS)	1:59.37
1992	Martin López-Zubero (ESP)	1:58.47
1996	Brad Bridgewater (USA)	1:58.54
2000	Lenny Krayzelburg (USA)	1:56.76
2004	Aaron Peirsol (USA)	1:54.95
2008	Ryan Lochte (USA)	1:53.94

100-METER BREASTSTROKE		MIN:SEC
1968	Donald McKenzie (USA)	1:07.7
1972	Nobutaka Tagushi (JPN)	1:04.94
1976	John Hencken (USA)	1:03.11
1980	Duncan Goodhew (GBR)	1:03.34
1984	Steve Lundquist (USA)	1:01.65
1988	Adrian Moorhouse (GBR)	1:02.04
1992	Nelson Diebel (USA)	1:01.50
1996	Frederick Deburghgraeve (BEL)	1:00.65
2000	Domenico Fioravanti (ITA)	1:00.46
2004	Kosuke Kitajima (JPN)	1:00.08
2008	Kosuke Kitajima (JPN)	0:58.91

Summer Olympic Games (continued)

Swimming (men) (continued)

200-METER BREASTSTROKE

		MIN:SEC
1908	Frederick Holman (GBR)	3:09.2
1912	Walter Bathe (GER)	3:01.8
1920	Hakan Malmroth (SWE)	3:04.4
1924	Robert Skelton (USA)	2:56.6
1928	Yoshiyuki Tsuruta (JPN)	2:48.8
1932	Yoshiyuki Tsuruta (JPN)	2:45.4
1936	Tetsuo Hamuro (JPN)	2:42.5
1948	Joseph Verdeur (USA)	2:39.3
1952	John Davies (AUS)	2:34.4
1956	Masaru Furukawa (JPN)	2:34.7
1960	William Mulliken (USA)	2:37.4
1964	Ian O'Brien (AUS)	2:27.8
1968	Felipe Muñoz (MEX)	2:28.7
1972	John Hencken (USA)	2:21.55
1976	David Wilkie (GBR)	2:15.11
1980	Robertas Zulpa (URS)	2:15.85
1984	Victor Davis (CAN)	2:13.34
1988	Jozsef Szabo (HUN)	2:13.52
1992	Mike Barrowman (USA)	2:10.16
1996	Norbert Rozsa (HUN)	2:12.57
2000	Domenico Fioravanti (ITA)	2:10.87
2004	Kosuke Kitajima (JPN)	2:09.44
2008	Kosuke Kitajima (JPN)	2:07.64

400-METER BREASTSTROKE

		MIN:SEC
1904[34]	Georg Zacharias (GER)	7:23.6
1912	Walter Bathe (GER)	6:29.6
1920	Hakan Malmroth (SWE)	6:31.8

200-YARD RELAY

		MIN:SEC
1904	United States	2:04.6

200-METER INDIVIDUAL MEDLEY

		MIN:SEC
1968	Charles Hickcox (USA)	2:12.0
1972	Gunnar Larsson (SWE)	2:07.17
1984	Alex Baumann (CAN)	2:01.42
1988	Tamas Darnyi (HUN)	2:00.17
1992	Tamas Darnyi (HUN)	2:00.76
1996	Attila Czene (HUN)	1:59.91
2000	Massimiliano Rosolino (ITA)	1:58.98
2004	Michael Phelps (USA)	1:57.14
2008	Michael Phelps (USA)	1:54.23

400-METER INDIVIDUAL MEDLEY

		MIN:SEC
1964	Richard William Roth (USA)	4:45.4
1968	Charles Hickcox (USA)	4:48.4
1972	Gunnar Larsson (SWE)	4:31.98
1976	Rod Strachan (USA)	4:23.68
1980	Aleksandr Sidorenko (URS)	4:22.89
1984	Alex Baumann (CAN)	4:17.41
1988	Tamas Darnyi (HUN)	4:14.75
1992	Tamas Darnyi (HUN)	4:14.23
1996	Tom Dolan (USA)	4:14.90
2000	Tom Dolan (USA)	4:11.76
2004	Michael Phelps (USA)	4:08.26
2008	Michael Phelps (USA)	4:03.84

4 × 100-METER MEDLEY RELAY

		MIN:SEC
1960	United States	4:05.4
1964	United States	3:58.4
1968	United States	3:54.9
1972	United States	3:48.16
1976	United States	3:42.22
1980	Australia	3:45.70
1984	United States	3:39.30
1988	United States	3:36.93
1992	United States	3:36.93

Swimming (men) (continued)

4 × 100-METER MEDLEY RELAY (CONTINUED)

		MIN:SEC
1996	United States	3:34.84
2000	United States	3:33.73
2004	United States	3:30.68
2008	United States	3:29.34

4 × 100-METER FREESTYLE RELAY

		MIN:SEC
1964	United States	3:33.2
1968	United States	3:31.7
1972	United States	3:26.42
1984	United States	3:19.03
1988	United States	3:16.53
1992	United States	3:16.74
1996	United States	3:15.41
2000	Australia	3:13.67
2004	South Africa	3:13.17
2008	United States	3:08.24

4 × 200-METER FREESTYLE RELAY

		MIN:SEC
1908	Great Britain	10:55.6
1912	Australia	10:11.2
1920	United States	10:04.4
1924	United States	9:53.4
1928	United States	9:36.2
1932	Japan	8:58.4
1936	Japan	8:51.5
1948	United States	8:46.0
1952	United States	8:31.1
1956	Australia	8:23.6
1960	United States	8:10.2
1964	United States	7:52.1
1968	United States	7:52.3
1972	United States	7:35.78
1976	United States	7:23.22
1980	USSR	7:23.50
1984	United States	7:15.69
1988	United States	7:12.51
1992	Unified Team	7:11.95
1996	United States	7:14.84
2000	Australia	7:07.05
2004	United States	7:07.33
2008	United States	6:58.56

60-METER UNDERWATER

		MIN:SEC (UNDERWATER)
1900	Charles de Vendeville (FRA)	1:08.4

200-METER OBSTACLE

		MIN:SEC
1900	Frederick Lane (AUS)	2:38.4

10-KM OPEN-WATER MARATHON

		HR:MIN:SEC
2008	Maarten van der Weijden (NED)	1:51:51.6

Swimming (women)

50-METER FREESTYLE

		SEC
1988	Kristin Otto (GDR)	25.49
1992	Yang Wenyi (CHN)	24.79
1996	Amy Van Dyken (USA)	24.87
2000	Inge de Bruijn (NED)	24.32
2004	Inge de Bruijn (NED)	24.58
2008	Britta Steffen (GER)	24.06

100-METER FREESTYLE

		MIN:SEC
1912	Fanny Durack (AUS)	1:22.2
1920	Ethelda Bleibtrey (USA)	1:13.6
1924	Ethel Lackie (USA)	1:12.4
1928	Albina Osipowich (USA)	1:11.0
1932	Helene Madison (USA)	1:06.8
1936	Hendrika Mastenbroek (NED)	1:05.9

Summer Olympic Games (continued)

Swimming (women) (continued)

100-METER FREESTYLE (CONTINUED)		MIN:SEC
1948	Greta Andersen (DEN)	1:06.3
1952	Katalin Szoke (HUN)	1:06.8
1956	Dawn Fraser (AUS)	1:02.0
1960	Dawn Fraser (AUS)	1:01.2
1964	Dawn Fraser (AUS)	59.5
1968	Jan Henne (USA)	1:00.0
1972	Sandra Neilson (USA)	58.59
1976	Kornelia Ender (GDR)	55.65
1980	Barbara Krause (GDR)	54.79
1984	Carrie Steinseifer (USA); Nancy Hogshead (USA) (tied)	55.92
1988	Kristin Otto (GDR)	54.93
1992	Zhuang Yong (CHN)	54.64
1996	Le Jingyi (CHN)	54.50
2000	Inge de Bruijn (NED)	53.83
2004	Jodie Henry (AUS)	53.84
2008	Britta Steffen (GER)	53.12

200-METER FREESTYLE		MIN:SEC
1968	Debbie Meyer (USA)	2:10.5
1972	Shane Gould (AUS)	2:03.56
1976	Kornelia Ender (GDR)	1:59.26
1980	Barbara Krause (GDR)	1:58.33
1984	Mary Wayte (USA)	1:59.23
1988	Heike Friedrich (GDR)	1:57.65
1992	Nicole Haislett (USA)	1:57.90
1996	Claudia Poll (CRC)	1:58.16
2000	Susie O'Neill (AUS)	1:58.24
2004	Camelia Potec (ROM)	1:58.03
2008	Federica Pellegrini (ITA)	1:54.82

400-METER FREESTYLE		MIN:SEC
1920[35]	Ethelda Bleibtrey (USA)	4:34.0
1924	Martha Norelius (USA)	6:02.2
1928	Martha Norelius (USA)	5:42.8
1932	Helene Madison (USA)	5:28.5
1936	Hendrika Mastenbroek (NED)	5:26.4
1948	Ann Curtis (USA)	5:17.8
1952	Valeria Gyenge (HUN)	5:12.1
1956	Lorraine Crapp (AUS)	4:54.6
1960	Susan Christina von Saltza (USA)	4:50.6
1964	Virginia Duenkel (USA)	4:43.3
1968	Debbie Meyer (USA)	4:31.8
1972	Shane Gould (AUS)	4:19.04
1976	Petra Thümer (GDR)	4:09.89
1980	Ines Diers (GDR)	4:08.76
1984	Tiffany Cohen (USA)	4:07.10
1988	Janet Evans (USA)	4:03.85
1992	Dagmar Hase (GER)	4:07.18
1996	Michelle Smith (IRL)	4:07.25
2000	Brooke Bennett (USA)	4:05.80
2004	Laure Manaudou (FRA)	4:05.34
2008	Rebecca Adlington (GBR)	4:03.22

800-METER FREESTYLE		MIN:SEC
1968	Debbie Meyer (USA)	9:24.0
1972	Keena Rothhammer (USA)	8:53.68
1976	Petra Thümer (GDR)	8:37.14
1980	Michelle Ford (AUS)	8:28.90
1984	Tiffany Cohen (USA)	8:24.95
1988	Janet Evans (USA)	8:20.20
1992	Janet Evans (USA)	8:25.52
1996	Brooke Bennett (USA)	8:27.89
2000	Brooke Bennett (USA)	8:19.67
2004	Ai Shibata (JPN)	8:24.54
2008	Rebecca Adlington (GBR)	8:14.10

100-METER BUTTERFLY		MIN:SEC
1956	Shelley Mann (USA)	1:11.0
1960	Carolyn Schuler (USA)	1:09.5
1964	Sharon Stouder (USA)	1:04.7
1968	Lynette McClements (AUS)	1:05.5
1972	Mayumi Aoki (JPN)	1:03.34
1976	Kornelia Ender (GDR)	1:00.13
1980	Caren Metschuck (GDR)	1:00.42
1984	Mary Meagher (USA)	59.26
1988	Kristin Otto (GDR)	59.00
1992	Qian Hong (CHN)	58.62
1996	Amy Van Dyken (USA)	59.13
2000	Inge de Bruijn (NED)	56.61
2004	Petria Thomas (AUS)	57.72
2008	Lisbeth Lenton Trickett (AUS)	56.73

200-METER BUTTERFLY		MIN:SEC
1968	Aagje Kok (NED)	2:24.7
1972	Karen Moe (USA)	2:15.57
1976	Andrea Pollack (GDR)	2:11.41
1980	Ines Geissler (GDR)	2:10.44
1984	Mary Meagher (USA)	2:06.90
1988	Kathleen Nord (GDR)	2:09.51
1992	Summer Sanders (USA)	2:08.67
1996	Susie O'Neill (AUS)	2:07.76
2000	Misty Hyman (USA)	2:05.88
2004	Otylia Jedrzejczak (POL)	2:06.05
2008	Liu Zige (CHN)	2:04.18

100-METER BACKSTROKE		MIN:SEC
1924	Sybil Bauer (USA)	1:23.2
1928	Maria Braun (NED)	1:22.0
1932	Eleanor Holm (USA)	1:19.4
1936	Dina Senff (NED)	1:18.9
1948	Karen-Margrete Harup (DEN)	1:14.4
1952	Joan Harrison (RSA)	1:14.3
1956	Judith Grinham (GBR)	1:12.9
1960	Lynn Burke (USA)	1:09.3
1964	Cathy Ferguson (USA)	1:07.7
1968	Kaye Hall (USA)	1:06.2
1972	Melissa Belote (USA)	1:05.78
1976	Ulrike Richter (GDR)	1:01.83
1980	Rica Reinisch (GDR)	1:00.86
1984	Theresa Andrews (USA)	1:02.55
1988	Kristin Otto (GDR)	1:00.89
1992	Krisztina Egerszegi (HUN)	1:00.68
1996	Beth Botsford (USA)	1:01.19
2000	Diana Mocanu (ROM)	1:00.21
2004	Natalie Coughlin (USA)	1:00.37
2008	Natalie Coughlin (USA)	0:58.96

200-METER BACKSTROKE		MIN:SEC
1968	Pokey Watson (USA)	2:24.8
1972	Melissa Belote (USA)	2:19.19
1976	Ulrike Richter (GDR)	2:13.43
1980	Rica Reinisch (GDR)	2:11.77
1984	Jolanda De Rover (NED)	2:12.38
1988	Krisztina Egerszegi (HUN)	2:09.29
1992	Krisztina Egerszegi (HUN)	2:07.06
1996	Krisztina Egerszegi (HUN)	2:07.83
2000	Diana Mocanu (ROM)	2:08.16
2004	Kirsty Coventry (ZIM)	2:09.19
2008	Kirsty Coventry (ZIM)	2:05.24

100-METER BREASTSTROKE		MIN:SEC
1968	Djurdjica Bjedov (YUG)	1:15.8
1972	Cathy Carr (USA)	1:13.58
1976	Hannelore Anke (GDR)	1:11.16

Summer Olympic Games (continued)

Swimming (women) (continued)

100-METER BREASTSTROKE (CONTINUED)

		MIN:SEC
1980	Ute Geveniger (GDR)	1:10.22
1984	Petra van Staveren (NED)	1:09.88
1988	Tanya Dangalakova (BUL)	1:07.95
1992	Yelena Rudkovskaya (UNT)	1:08.00
1996	Penelope Heyns (RSA)	1:07.73
2000	Megan Quann (USA)	1:07.05
2004	Luo Xuejuan (CHN)	1:06.64
2008	Leisel Jones (AUS)	1:05.17

200-METER BREASTSTROKE

		MIN:SEC
1924	Lucy Morton (GBR)	3:33.2
1928	Hilde Schrader (GER)	3:12.6
1932	Claire Dennis (AUS)	3:06.3
1936	Hideko Maehata (JPN)	3:03.6
1948	Petronella van Vliet (NED)	2:57.2
1952	Eva Szekely (HUN)	2:51.7
1956	Ursula Happe (GER)	2:53.1
1960	Anita Lonsbrough (GBR)	2:49.5
1964	Galina Prozumenshchikova-Stepanova (URS)	2:46.4
1968	Sharon Wichman (USA)	2:44.4
1972	Beverley Whitfield (AUS)	2:41.71
1976	Marina Koshevaya (URS)	2:33.35
1980	Lina Kachushite (URS)	2:29.54
1984	Anne Ottenbrite (CAN)	2:30.38
1988	Silke Hörner (GDR)	2:26.71
1992	Kyoko Iwasaki (JPN)	2:26.65
1996	Penelope Heyns (RSA)	2:25.41
2000	Agnes Kovacs (HUN)	2:24.35
2004	Amanda Beard (USA)	2:23.37
2008	Rebecca Soni (USA)	2:20.22

200-METER INDIVIDUAL MEDLEY

		MIN:SEC
1968	Claudia Kolb (USA)	2:24.7
1972	Shane Gould (AUS)	2:23.07
1984	Tracy Caulkins (USA)	2:12.64
1988	Daniela Hunger (GDR)	2:12.59
1992	Lin Li (CHN)	2:11.65
1996	Michelle Smith (IRL)	2:13.93
2000	Yana Klochkova (UKR)	2:10.68
2004	Yana Klochkova (UKR)	2:11.14
2008	Stephanie Rice (AUS)	2:08.45

400-METER INDIVIDUAL MEDLEY

		MIN:SEC
1964	Donna De Varona (USA)	5:18.7
1968	Claudia Kolb (USA)	5:08.5
1972	Gail Neall (AUS)	5:02.97
1976	Ulrike Tauber (GDR)	4:42.77
1980	Petra Schneider (GDR)	4:36.29
1984	Tracy Caulkins (USA)	4:39.24
1988	Janet Evans (USA)	4:37.76
1992	Krisztina Egerszegi (HUN)	4:36.54
1996	Michelle Smith (IRL)	4:39.18
2000	Yana Klochkova (UKR)	4:33.59
2004	Yana Klochkova (UKR)	4:34.83
2008	Stephanie Rice (AUS)	4:29.45

4 × 100-METER MEDLEY RELAY

		MIN:SEC
1960	United States	4:41.1
1964	United States	4:33.9
1968	United States	4:28.3
1972	United States	4:20.75
1976	East Germany	4:07.95
1980	East Germany	4:06.67
1984	United States	4:08.34
1988	East Germany	4:03.74
1992	United States	4:02.54

Swimming (women) (continued)

4 × 100-METER MEDLEY RELAY (CONTINUED)

		MIN:SEC
1996	United States	4:02.88
2000	United States	3:58.30
2004	Australia	3:57.32
2008	Australia	3:52.69

4 × 100-METER FREESTYLE RELAY

		MIN:SEC
1912	Great Britain	5:52.8
1920	United States	5:11.6
1924	United States	4:58.8
1928	United States	4:47.6
1932	United States	4:38.0
1936	The Netherlands	4:36.0
1948	United States	4:29.2
1952	Hungary	4:24.4
1956	Australia	4:17.1
1960	United States	4:08.9
1964	United States	4:03.8
1968	United States	4:02.5
1972	United States	3:55.19
1976	United States	3:44.82
1980	East Germany	3:42.71
1984	United States	3:43.43
1988	East Germany	3:40.63
1992	United States	3:39.46
1996	United States	3:39.29
2000	United States	3:36.61
2004	Australia	3:35.94
2008	The Netherlands	3:33.76

4 × 200-METER FREESTYLE RELAY

		MIN:SEC
1996	United States	7:59.87
2000	United States	7:57.80
2004	United States	7:53.42
2008	Australia	7:44.31

10-KM OPEN-WATER MARATHON

		HR:MIN:SEC
2008	Larisa Ilchenko (RUS)	1:59:27.7

Synchronized Swimming

INDIVIDUAL

1984	Tracie Ruiz (USA)
1988	Carolyn Waldo (CAN)
1992	Kristen Babb-Sprague (USA); Sylvie Fréchette (CAN)[36]

DUET

1984	United States
1988	Canada
1992	United States
2000	Russia
2004	Russia
2008	Russia

TEAM

1996	United States
2000	Russia
2004	Russia
2008	Russia

Table Tennis (men)

SINGLES

1988	Yoo Nam Kyu (KOR)
1992	Jan-Ove Waldner (SWE)
1996	Liu Guoliang (CHN)
2000	Kong Linghui (CHN)
2004	Ryu Seung Min (KOR)
2008	Ma Lin (CHN)

Summer Olympic Games (continued)

Table Tennis (men) (continued)

TEAM

1988	China
1992	China
1996	China
2000	China
2004	China
2008	China

Table Tennis (women)

SINGLES

1988	Chen Jing (CHN)
1992	Deng Yaping (CHN)
1996	Deng Yaping (CHN)
2000	Wang Nan (CHN)
2004	Zhang Yining (CHN)
2008	Zhang Yining (CHN)

TEAM

1988	Republic of Korea
1992	China
1996	China
2000	China
2004	China
2008	China

Taekwondo (men)

58 KG (127.6 LB)

2000	Michail Mouroutsos (GRE)
2004	Chu Mu Yen (TPE)
2008	Guillermo Pérez (MEX)

68 KG (149.6 LB)

2000	Steven Lopez (USA)
2004	Hadi Saei Bonehkohal (IRI)
2008	Son Tae Jin (KOR)

80 KG (176 LB)

2000	Angel Valodia Matos (CUB)
2004	Steven Lopez (USA)
2008	Hadi Saei (IRI)

OVER 80 KG (176+ LB)

2000	Kim Kyong-Hun (KOR)
2004	Moon Sung Dae (KOR)
2008	Cha Dong Min (KOR)

Taekwondo (women)

49 KG (107.8 LB)

2000	Lauren Burns (AUS)
2004	Chen Shih Hsin (TPE)
2008	Wu Jingyu (CHN)

57 KG (125.4 LB)

2000	Jung Jae-Eun (KOR)
2004	Jang Ji Won (KOR)
2008	Lim Su Jeong (KOR)

67 KG (147.4 LB)

2000	Lee Sun-Hee (KOR)
2004	Luo Wei (CHN)
2008	Hwang Kyung Seon (KOR)

OVER 67 KG (147.4+ LB)

2000	Chen Zhong (CHN)
2004	Chen Zhong (CHN)
2008	María del Rosario Espinoza (MEX)

Tennis (men)

SINGLES

1896	John Pius Boland (GBR)
1900	Laurie Doherty (GBR)
1904	Beals Wright (USA)
1908	Josiah Ritchie (GBR)
1912	Charles Winslow (RSA)
1920	Louis Raymond (RSA)
1924	Vincent Richards (USA)
1988	Miloslav Mecir (TCH)
1992	Marc Rosset (SUI)
1996	Andre Agassi (USA)
2000	Yevgeny Kafelnikov (RUS)
2004	Nicolas Massu (CHI)
2008	Rafael Nadal (ESP)

DOUBLES

1896	John Pius Boland (GBR), Friedrich Thraun (GER)
1900	Laurie Doherty, Reggie Doherty (GBR)
1904	Edgar Leonard, Beals Wright (USA)
1908	George Hillyard, Reggie Doherty (GBR)
1912	Harold Kitson, Charles Winslow (RSA)
1920	Oswald Noel Turnbull, Max Woosnam (GBR)
1924	Frank Hunter, Vincent Richards (USA)
1988	Kenneth Flach, Robert Seguso (USA)
1992	Boris Becker, Michael Stich (GER)
1996	Todd Woodbridge, Mark Woodforde (AUS)
2000	Sebastien Lareau, Daniel Nestor (CAN)
2004	Fernando Gonzalez, Nicolas Massu (CHI)
2008	Roger Federer, Stanislas Wawrinka (SUI)

MIXED DOUBLES

1900	Charlotte Cooper, Reggie Doherty (GBR)
1912	Dora Köring, Heinrich Schomburgk (GER)
1920	Suzanne Lenglen, Max Décugis (FRA)
1924	Hazel Wightman, R. Norris Williams (USA)

Tennis (women)

SINGLES

1900	Charlotte Cooper (GBR)
1908	Dorothea Lambert Chambers (GBR)
1912	Marguerite Broquedis (FRA)
1920	Suzanne Lenglen (FRA)
1924	Helen Wills Moody (USA)
1988	Steffi Graf (FRG)
1992	Jennifer Capriati (USA)
1996	Lindsay Davenport (USA)
2000	Venus Williams (USA)
2004	Justine Henin-Hardenne (BEL)
2008	Yelena Dementyeva (RUS)

DOUBLES

1920	Winifred McNair, Kathleen McKane (GBR)
1924	Helen Wills Moody, Hazel Wightman (USA)
1988	Zina Garrison, Pam Shriver (USA)
1992	Gigi Fernández, Mary Joe Fernández (USA)
1996	Gigi Fernández, Mary Joe Fernández (USA)
2000	Serena Williams, Venus Williams (USA)
2004	Li Ting, Sun Tian Tian (CHN)
2008	Serena Williams, Venus Williams (USA)

Tennis—Covered Courts (Indoor Tennis)

MEN'S SINGLES

1908	Arthur Gore (GBR)
1912	Andre Gobert (FRA)

Summer Olympic Games (continued)

Tennis—Covered Courts (Indoor Tennis) (continued)
MEN'S DOUBLES
1908 Arthur Gore, Herbert Roper Barrett (GBR)
1912 Maurice Germot, André Gobert (FRA)

WOMEN'S SINGLES
1908 Gladys Eastlake-Smith (GBR)
1912 Edith Hannam (GBR)

MIXED DOUBLES
1912 Edith Hannam, Charles Dixon (GBR)

Triathlon (swim/bike/run) (men)
2000 Simon Whitfield (CAN)
2004 Hamish Carter (NZL)
2008 Jan Frodeno (GER)

Triathlon (swim/bike/run) (women)
2000 Brigitte McMahon (SUI)
2004 Kate Allen (AUT)
2008 Emma Snowsill (AUS)

Volleyball (men)
INDOOR
1964 USSR
1968 USSR
1972 Japan
1976 Poland
1980 USSR
1984 United States
1988 United States
1992 Brazil
1996 The Netherlands
2000 Yugoslavia
2004 Brazil
2008 United States

BEACH
1996 United States
2000 United States
2004 Brazil
2008 United States

Volleyball (women)
INDOOR
1964 Japan
1968 USSR
1972 USSR
1976 Japan
1980 USSR
1984 China
1988 USSR
1992 Cuba
1996 Cuba
2000 Cuba
2004 China
2008 Brazil

BEACH
1996 Brazil
2000 Australia
2004 United States
2008 United States

Water Polo (men)
1900 Great Britain
1904 United States
1908 Great Britain
1912 Great Britain

Water Polo (men) (continued)
1920 Great Britain
1924 France
1928 Germany
1932 Hungary
1936 Hungary
1948 Italy
1952 Hungary
1956 Hungary
1960 Italy
1964 Hungary
1968 Yugoslavia
1972 USSR
1976 Hungary
1980 USSR
1984 Yugoslavia
1988 Yugoslavia
1992 Italy
1996 Spain
2000 Hungary
2004 Hungary
2008 Hungary

Water Polo (women)
2000 Australia
2004 Italy
2008 The Netherlands

Weight Lifting (men)[37, 38]

56 KG (123.2 LB) — KG
1972	Zygmunt Smalcerz (POL)	337.5
1976	Aleksandr Varonin (URS)	242.5
1980	Kanybek Osmanaliyev (URS)	245.0
1984	Zeng Guoqiang (CHN)	235.0
1988	Sevdalin Marinov (BUL)	270.0
1992	Ivan Ivanov (BUL)	265.0
1996	Halil Mutlu (TUR)	287.5
2000	Halil Mutlu (TUR)	305.0
2004	Halil Mutlu (TUR)	295.0
2008	Long Qingquan (CHN)	292.0

62 KG (136.4 LB) — KG
1948	Joseph de Pietro (USA)	307.5
1952	Ivan Udodov (URS)	315.0
1956	Charles Vinci (USA)	342.5
1960	Charles Vinci (USA)	345.0
1964	Aleksey Vakhonin (URS)	357.5
1968	Mohammad Nassiri (IRI)	367.5
1972	Imre Foldi (HUN)	377.5
1976	Norair Nurikian (BUL)	262.5
1980	Daniel Núñez (CUB)	275.0
1984	Wu Shude (CHN)	267.5
1988	Oksen Mirzoyan (URS)[2]	292.5
1992	Chun Byung Kwan (KOR)	287.5
1996	Tang Ningsheng (CHN)	307.5
2000	Nikolay Pechalov (CRO)	325.0
2004	Shi Zhiyong (CHN)	325.0
2008	Zhang Xiangxiang (CHN)	319.0

69 KG (151.8 LB) — KG
1920	Frans de Haes (BEL)	220.0
1924	Pierino Gabetti (ITA)	402.5[39]
1928	Franz Andrysek (AUT)	287.5
1932	Raymond Suvigny (FRA)	287.5
1936	Anthony Terlazzo (USA)	312.5
1948	Mahmoud Fayad (EGY)	332.5
1952	Rafael Chimishkyan (URS)	337.5
1956	Isaac Berger (USA)	352.5
1960	Yevgeny Minayev (URS)	372.5

Summer Olympic Games (continued)

Weight Lifting (men)[37, 38] (continued)

69 KG (151.8 LB) (CONTINUED)

		KG
1964	Yoshinobu Miyake (JPN)	397.5
1968	Yoshinobu Miyake (JPN)	392.5
1972	Norair Nurikian (BUL)	402.5
1976	Nikolay Kolesnikov (URS)	285.0
1980	Viktor Mazin (URS)	290.0
1984	Chen Weiqiang (CHN)	282.5
1988	Naim Suleymanoglu (TUR)	342.5
1992	Naim Suleymanoglu (TUR)	320.0
1996	Naim Suleymanoglu (TUR)	335.0
2000	Galabin Boevski (BUL)	357.5
2004	Zhang Guozheng (CHN)	347.5
2008	Liao Hui (CHN)	348.0

70 KG (154 LB)

		KG
1920	Alfred Neyland (EST)	257.5
1924	Edmond Décottignies (FRA)	440.0[39]
1928	Kurt Helbig (GER); Hans Haas (AUT) (tied)	322.5
1932	René Duverger (FRA)	325.0
1936	Mohamed Ahmed Mesbah (EGY); Robert Fein (AUT) (tied)	342.5
1948	Ibrahim Shams (EGY)	360.0
1952	Tommy Kono (USA)	362.5
1956	Igor Rybak (URS)	380.0
1960	Viktor Bushuyev (URS)	397.5
1964	Waldemar Baszanowski (POL)	432.5
1968	Waldemar Baszanowski (POL)	437.5
1972	Mukharbi Kirzhinov (URS)	460.0
1976	Pyotr Korol (URS)[2]	305.0
1980	Yanko Rusev (BUL)	342.5
1984	Yao Jingyuan (CHN)	320.0
1988	Joachim Kunz (GDR)[2]	340.0
1992	Israil Militosyan (UNT)	337.5
1996	Zhan Xugang (CHN)	357.5

77 KG (169.4 LB)

		KG
1920	Henri Gance (FRA)	245.0
1924	Carlo Galimberti (ITA)	492.5[39]
1928	François Roger (FRA)	335.0
1932	Rudolf Ismayr (GER)	345.0
1936	Khadr el Thouni (EGY)	387.5
1948	Frank Spellman (USA)	390.0
1952	Peter George (USA)	400.0
1956	Fyodor Bogdanovsky (URS)	420.0
1960	Aleksandr Kurynov (URS)	437.5
1964	Hans Zdrazila (TCH)	445.0
1968	Viktor Kurentsov (URS)	475.0
1972	Iordan Bikov (BUL)	485.0
1976	Iordan Mitkov (BUL)	335.0
1980	Asen Zlatev (BUL)	360.0
1984	Karl-Heinz Radschinsky (FRG)	340.0
1988	Borislav Gidikov (BUL)	375.0
1992	Fyodor Kassapu (UNT)	357.5
1996	Pablo Lara (CUB)	367.5
2000	Zhan Xugang (CHN)	367.5
2004	Taner Sagir (TUR)	375.0
2008	Sa Jae Hyouk (KOR)	366.0

85 KG (187 LB)

		KG
1920	Ernest Cadine (FRA)	290.0
1924	Charles Rigoulot (FRA)	502.5[39]
1928	El Sayed Nosseir (EGY)	355.0
1932	Louis Hostin (FRA)	365.0
1936	Louis Hostin (FRA)	372.5
1948	Stanley Stanczyk (USA)	417.5
1952	Trofim Lomakin (URS)	417.5
1956	Tommy Kono (USA)	447.5

Weight Lifting (men)[37, 38] (continued)

85 KG (187 LB) (CONTINUED)

		KG
1960	Ireneusz Palinski (POL)	442.5
1964	Rudolph Plyukfelder (URS)	475.0
1968	Boris Selitsky (URS)	485.0
1972	Leif Jenssen (NOR)	507.5
1976	Valery Shary (URS)	365.0
1980	Yury Vardanyan (URS)	400.0
1984	Petre Becheru (ROM)	355.0
1988	Israil Arsamakov (URS)	377.5
1992	Pyrros Dimas (GRE)	370.0
1996	Pyrros Dimas (GRE)	392.5
2000	Pyrros Dimas (GRE)	390.0
2004	George Asanidze (GEO)	382.5
2008	Lu Yong (CHN)	394.0

94 KG (206.8 LB)

		KG
1952	Norbert Schemansky (USA)	445.0
1956	Arkady Vorobyev (URS)	462.5
1960	Arkady Vorobyev (URS)	472.5
1964	Vladimir Golovanov (URS)	487.5
1968	Kaarlo Kangasniemi (FIN)	517.5
1972	Andon Nikolov (BUL)	525.0
1976	David Rigert (URS)	382.5
1980	Peter Baczako (HUN)	377.5
1984	Nicu Vlad (ROM)	392.5
1988	Anatoly Khrapaty (URS)	412.5
1992	Kakhi Kakhiashvili (UNT)	412.5
1996	Aleksey Petrov (RUS)	402.5
2000	Akakios Kakhiashvilis (GRE)	405.0
2004	Milen Dobrev (BUL)	407.5
2008	Ilya Ilin (KAZ)	406.0

99 KG (217.8 LB)

		KG
1980	Ota Zaremba (TCH)	395.0
1984	Rolf Milser (FRG)	385.0
1988	Pavel Kuznetsov (URS)	425.0
1992	Viktor Tregubov (UNT)	410.0
1996	Akakios Kakhiashvilis (GRE)	420.0

105 KG (231 LB)

		KG
1972	Jan Talts (URS)	580.0
1976	Yury Zaytsev (URS)[2]	385.0
1980	Leonid Taranenko (URS)	422.5
1984	Norberto Oberburger (ITA)	390.0
1988	Yury Zakharevitch (URS)	455.0
1992	Ronny Weller (GER)	432.5
1996	Timur Taymazov (UKR)	430.0
2000	Hossein Tavakoli (IRI)	425.0
2004	Dmitry Berestov (RUS)	425.0
2008	Andrei Aramnau (BLR)	436.0

OVER 105 KG (231+ LB)

		KG
1920	Filippo Bottino (ITA)	265.5
1924	Giuseppe Tonani (ITA)	517.5[39]
1928	Josef Strassberger (GER)	372.5
1932	Jaroslav Skobia (TCH)	380.0
1936	Josef Manger (GER)	410.0
1948	John Davis (USA)	452.5
1952	John Davis (USA)	460.0
1956	Paul Anderson (USA)	500.0
1960	Yury Vlasov (URS)	537.5
1964	Leonid Zhabotinsky (URS)	572.5
1968	Leonid Zhabotinsky (URS)	572.5
1972	Vasily Alekseyev (URS)	640.0
1976	Vasily Alekseyev (URS)	440.0
1980	Sultan Rakhmanov (URS)	440.0
1984	Dinko Lukin (AUS)	412.5
1988	Aleksandr Kurlovich (URS)	462.5

Summer Olympic Games (continued)

Weight Lifting (men)[37, 38] (continued)

OVER 105 KG (231+ LB) (CONTINUED)   **KG**
1992	Aleksandr Kurlovich (UNT)	450.0
1996	Andrey Chemerkin (RUS)	457.5
2000	Hossein Reza Zadeh (IRI)	472.5
2004	Hossein Reza Zadeh (IRI)	472.5
2008	Matthias Steiner (GER)	461.0

ONE-HAND LIFT (UNLIMITED CLASS)   **KG**
1896	Launceston Elliot (GBR)	71.0

TWO-HAND LIFT (UNLIMITED CLASS)   **KG**
1896	Viggo Jensen (DEN)	111.5
1904	Perikles Kakousis (GRE)	111.7

ALL-AROUND DUMBBELLS (UNLIMITED CLASS)
1904	Oscar Osthoff (USA)

Weight Lifting (women)

48 KG (105.6 LB)   **KG**
2000	Tara Nott (USA)[2]	185.0
2004	Nurcan Taylan (TUR)	210.0
2008	Chen Xiexia (CHN)	212.0

53 KG (116.6 LB)   **KG**
2000	Yang Xia (CHN)	225.0
2004	Udomporn Polsak (THA)	222.5
2008	Prapawadee	221.0
	Jaroenrattanatarakoon (THA)	

58 KG (127.6 LB)   **KG**
2000	Soraya Jiménez Mendívil (MEX)	222.5
2004	Chen Yanqing (CHN)	237.5
2008	Chen Yanqing (CHN)	244.0

63 KG (138.6 LB)   **KG**
2000	Chen Xiaomin (CHN)	242.5
2004	Natalya Skakun (UKR)	242.5
2008	Pak Hyon Suk (PRK)	241.0

69 KG (151.8 LB)   **KG**
2000	Lin Weining (CHN)	242.5
2004	Liu Chunhong (CHN)	275.0
2008	Liu Chunhong (CHN)	286.0

75 KG (165 LB)   **KG**
2000	Maria Isabel Urrutia (COL)	245.0
2004	Pawina Thongsuk (THA)	272.5
2008	Cao Lei (CHN)	282.0

OVER 75 KG (165+ LB)   **KG**
2000	Ding Meiyuan (CHN)	300.0
2004	Tang Gonghong (CHN)	305.0
2008	Jang Mi Ran (KOR)	326.0

Wrestling—Freestyle (men)[37]

48 KG (105.6 LB)
1904	Robert Curry (USA)
1972	Roman Dmitriyev (URS)
1976	Khassan Issaev (BUL)
1980	Claudio Pollio (ITA)
1984	Robert Weaver (USA)
1988	Takashi Kobayashi (JPN)
1992	Kim Il (PRK)
1996	Kim Il (PRK)

Wrestling—Freestyle (men)[37] (continued)

55 KG (121 LB)
1904	George Mehnert (USA)
1948	Lennart Viitala (FIN)
1952	Hasan Gemici (TUR)
1956	Mirian Tsalkalamanidze (URS)
1960	Ahmet Bilek (TUR)
1964	Yoshikatsu Yoshida (JPN)
1968	Shigeo Nakata (JPN)
1972	Kiyomi Kato (JPN)
1976	Yuji Takada (JPN)
1980	Anatoly Beloglazov (URS)
1984	Saban Trstena (YUG)
1988	Mitsuru Sato (JPN)
1992	Li Hak-son (PRK)
1996	Valentin Iordanov (BUL)
2000	Namig Amdullayev (AZE)
2004	Mavlet Batirov (RUS)
2008	Henry Cejudo (USA)

60 KG (132 LB)
1904	Isidor "Jack" Niflot (USA)
1908	George Mehnert (USA)
1924	Kustaa Pihlajamäki (FIN)
1928	Kaarlo Maakinen (FIN)
1932	Robert Pearce (USA)
1936	Odon Zombory (HUN)
1948	Nasuh Akar (TUR)
1952	Shohachi Ishii (JPN)
1956	Mustafa Dagistanli (TUR)
1960	Terence McCann (USA)
1964	Yojiro Uetake (JPN)
1968	Yojiro Uetake (JPN)
1972	Hideaki Yanagida (JPN)
1976	Vladimir Yumin (URS)
1980	Sergey Beloglazov (URS)
1984	Hideaki Tomiyama (JPN)
1988	Sergey Beloglazov (URS)
1992	Alejandro Puerto Diaz (CUB)
1996	Kendall Cross (USA)
2000	Alireza Dabir (IRI)
2004	Yandro Miguel Quintana (CUB)
2008	Mavlet Batirov (RUS)

63 KG (138.6 LB)
1904	Benjamin Bradshaw (USA)
1908	George Dole (USA)
1920	Charles Ackerly (USA)
1924	Robin Reed (USA)
1928	Allie Morrison (USA)
1932	Hermanni Pihlajamäki (FIN)
1936	Kustaa Pihlajamäki (FIN)
1948	Gazanfer Bilge (TUR)
1952	Bayram Sit (TUR)
1956	Shozo Sasahara (JPN)
1960	Mustafa Dagistanli (TUR)
1964	Osamu Watanabe (JPN)
1968	Masaaki Kaneko (JPN)
1972	Zagalav Abdulbekov (URS)
1976	Yang Jung Mo (KOR)
1980	Magomedgasan Abushev (URS)
1984	Randy Lewis (USA)
1988	John Smith (USA)
1992	John Smith (USA)
1996	Tom Brands (USA)
2000	Murad Umakhanov (RUS)

Summer Olympic Games (continued)

Wrestling—Freestyle (men)[37] (continued)

66 KG (145.2 LB)

1904	Otto Roehm (USA)
1908	George de Relwyskow (GBR)
1920	Kaarlo "Kalle" Anttila (FIN)
1924	Russell Vis (USA)
1928	Osvald Käpp (EST)
1932	Charles Pacome (FRA)
1936	Karoly Karpati (HUN)
1948	Celal Atik (TUR)
1952	Olle Anderberg (SWE)
1956	Emamali Habibi (IRI)
1960	Shelby Wilson (USA)
1964	Enio Valchev Dimov (BUL)
1968	Abdollah Movahed (IRI)
1972	Dan Gable (USA)
1976	Pavel Pinigin (URS)
1980	Saipulla Absaldov (URS)
1984	You In Tak (KOR)
1988	Arsen Fadzayev (URS)
1992	Arsen Fadzayev (UNT)
1996	Vadim Bogiyev (RUS)
2000	Daniel Igali (CAN)
2004	Elbrus Tedeyev (UKR)
2008	Ramazan Sahin (TUR)

74 KG (162.8 LB)

1904	Charles Eriksen (USA)
1924	Hermann Gehri (SUI)
1928	Arvo Haavisto (FIN)
1932	Jack van Bebber (USA)
1936	Frank Lewis (USA)
1948	Yasar Dogu (TUR)
1952	William Smith (USA)
1956	Mitsuo Ikeda (JPN)
1960	Douglas Blubaugh (USA)
1964	Ismail Ogan (TUR)
1968	Mahmut Atalay (TUR)
1972	Wayne Wells (USA)
1976	Jiichiro Date (JPN)
1980	Valentin Raychev (BUL)
1984	David Schultz (USA)
1988	Kenneth Monday (USA)
1992	Park Jang Soon (KOR)
1996	Buvayasa Saytiyev (RUS)
2000	Brandon Slay (USA)[2]
2004	Buvayasa Saytiyev (RUS)
2008	Buvayasa Saytiyev (RUS)

84 KG (184.8 LB)

1908	Stanley Bacon (GBR)
1920	Eino Leino (FIN)
1924	Fritz Haggmann (SUI)
1928	Ernst Kyburz (SUI)
1932	Ivar Johansson (SWE)
1936	Émile Poilvé (FRA)
1948	Glen Brand (USA)
1952	David Tsimakurdze (URS)
1956	Nikola Stanchev (BUL)
1960	Hasan Gungor (TUR)
1964	Prodan Stoyanov Gardchev (BUL)
1968	Boris Gurevich (URS)
1972	Levan Tediashvili (URS)
1976	John Peterson (USA)
1980	Ismail Abilov (BUL)
1984	Mark Schultz (USA)
1988	Han Myung Woo (KOR)
1992	Kevin Jackson (USA)
1996	Khadshimurad Magomedov (RUS)

Wrestling—Freestyle (men)[37] (continued)

84 KG (184.8 LB) (CONTINUED)

2000	Adam Saytev (RUS)
2004	Cael Sanderson (USA)
2008	Revazi Mindorashvili (GEO)

90 KG (198.5 LB)

1920	Anders Larsson (SWE)
1924	John Franklin Spellman (USA)
1928	Thure Sjöstedt (SWE)
1932	Peter Mehringer (USA)
1936	Knut Fridell (SWE)
1948	Henry Wittenberg (USA)
1952	Bror Wiking Palm (SWE)
1956	Gholam-Reza Takhti (IRI)
1960	Ismet Atli (TUR)
1964	Aleksandr Medved (URS)
1968	Ahmet Ayuk (TUR)
1972	Ben Peterson (USA)
1976	Levan Tediashvili (URS)
1980	Sanasar Oganesyan (URS)
1984	Ed Banach (USA)
1988	Macharbek Khadartsev (URS)
1992	Macharbek Khadartsev (UNT)
1996	Rasul Khadem Azghadi (IRI)

96 KG (211.2 LB)

1896	Karl Schumann (GER)
1904	Bernhuff Hansen (USA)
1908	George O'Kelly (GBR)
1920	Robert Rothe (SUI)
1924	Harry Steele (USA)
1928	Johan Richthoff (SWE)
1932	Johan Richthoff (SWE)
1936	Kristjan Palusalu (EST)
1948	Gyula Bobis (HUN)
1952	Arsen Mekokishvili (URS)
1956	Hamit Kaplan (TUR)
1960	Wilfried Dietrich (GER)
1964	Aleksandr Ivanitsky (URS)
1968	Aleksandr Medved (URS)
1972	Ivan Yarygin (URS)
1976	Ivan Yarygin (URS)
1980	Ilya Mate (URS)
1984	Lou Banach (USA)
1988	Vasile Puscasu (ROM)
1992	Leri Khabelov (UNT)
1996	Kurt Angle (USA)
2000	Sagid Murtasaliyev (RUS)
2004	Khajimurat Gatsalov (RUS)
2008	Shirvani Muradov (RUS)

120 KG (264 LB)

1972	Aleksandr Medved (URS)
1976	Soslan Andiyev (URS)
1980	Soslan Andiyev (URS)
1984	Bruce Baumgartner (USA)
1988	David Gobedishvili (URS)
1992	Bruce Baumgartner (USA)
1996	Mahmut Demir (TUR)
2000	David Musulbes (RUS)
2004	Artur Taymazov (UZB)
2008	Artur Taymazov (UZB)

Wrestling—Freestyle (women)

48 KG (105.6 LB)

2004	Irini Merleni (UKR)
2008	Carol Huynh (CAN)

Summer Olympic Games (continued)

Wrestling—Freestyle (women) (continued)

55 KG (121 LB)
2004 Saori Yoshida (JPN)
2008 Saori Yoshida (JPN)

63 KG (138.6 LB)
2004 Kaori Icho (JPN)
2008 Kaori Icho (JPN)

72 KG (158 LB)
2004 Wang Xu (CHN)
2008 Wang Jiao (CHN)

Wrestling—Greco-Roman[37]

48 KG (105.6 LB)
1972 Gheorghe Berceanu (ROM)
1976 Aleksey Shumakov (URS)
1980 Zhaksylyk Ushkempirov (URS)
1984 Vincenzo Maenza (ITA)
1988 Vincenzo Maenza (ITA)
1992 Oleg Kucherenko (UNT)
1996 Sim Kwon-Ho (KOR)

55 KG (121 LB)
1948 Pietro Lombardi (ITA)
1952 Boris Gurevich (URS)
1956 Nikolay Solovyev (URS)
1960 Dumitru Pirvulescu (ROM)
1964 Tsutomu Hanahara (JPN)
1968 Petar Kirov (BUL)
1972 Petar Kirov (BUL)
1976 Vitaly Konstantinov (URS)
1980 Vakhtang Blagidze (URS)
1984 Atsuji Miyahara (JPN)
1988 Jon Ronningen (NOR)
1992 Jon Ronningen (NOR)
1996 Armen Nazaryan (ARM)
2000 Sim Kwon-Ho (KOR)
2004 Istvan Majoros (HUN)
2008 Nazyr Mankiyev (RUS)

60 KG (132 LB)
1924 Eduard Pütsep (EST)
1928 Kurt Leucht (GER)
1932 Jakob Brendel (GER)
1936 Marton Lorincz (HUN)
1948 Kurt Pettersen (SWE)
1952 Imre Hodos (HUN)
1956 Konstantin Vyrupayev (URS)
1960 Oleg Karavayev (URS)
1964 Masamitsu Ichiguchi (JPN)
1968 Janos Varga (HUN)
1972 Rustem Kazakov (URS)
1976 Pertti Ukkola (FIN)
1980 Shamil Serikov (URS)
1984 Pasquale Passarelli (FRG)
1988 Andras Sike (HUN)
1992 An Han Bong (KOR)
1996 Yury Melnichenko (KAZ)
2000 Armen Nazarian (BUL)
2004 Jung Ji Hyun (KOR)
2008 Islam-Beka Albiyev (RUS)

63 KG (138.6 LB)
1912 Kaarlo Koskelo (FIN)
1920 Oskar Friman (FIN)
1924 Kalle Anttila (FIN)
1928 Voldemar Väli (EST)
1932 Giovanni Gozzi (ITA)

Wrestling—Greco-Roman[37] (continued)

63 KG (138.6 LB) (CONTINUED)
1936 Yasar Erkan (TUR)
1948 Mehmet Oktav (TUR)
1952 Yakov Punkin (URS)
1956 Rauno Leonard Mäkinen (FIN)
1960 Muzahir Sille (TUR)
1964 Imre Polyak (HUN)
1968 Roman Rurua (URS)
1972 Georgi Markov (BUL)
1976 Kazimierz Lipien (POL)
1980 Stilianos Migiakis (GRE)
1984 Kim Weon Kee (KOR)
1988 Kamandar Madzhidov (URS)
1992 Akif Pirim (TUR)
1996 Wlodzimierz Zawadzki (POL)
2000 Varteres Samurgashev (RUS)

66 KG (145.2 LB)
1908 Enrico Porro (ITA)
1912 Eemil Väre (FIN)
1920 Eemil Väre (FIN)
1924 Oskar Friman (FIN)
1928 Lajos Keresztes (HUN)
1932 Erik Malmberg (SWE)
1936 Lauri Koskela (FIN)
1948 Karl Freij (SWE)
1952 Shazam Safin (URS)
1956 Kyösti Emil Lehtonen (FIN)
1960 Avtandil Koridze (URS)
1964 Kazim Ayvaz (TUR)
1968 Munji Mumemura (JPN)
1972 Shamil Khisamutdinov (URS)
1976 Suren Nalbandyan (URS)
1980 Stefan Rusu (ROM)
1984 Vlado Lisjak (YUG)
1988 Levon Dzhulfalakyan (URS)
1992 Attila Repka (HUN)
1996 Ryszard Wolny (POL)
2000 Filiberto Ascuy Aguilera (CUB)
2004 Farid Mansurov (AZE)
2008 Steeve Guénot (FRA)

74 KG (162.8 LB)
1932 Ivar Johansson (SWE)
1936 Rudolf Svedberg (SWE)
1948 Erik Gösta Andersson (SWE)
1952 Miklos Szilvasi (HUN)
1956 Mithat Bayrak (TUR)
1960 Mithat Bayrak (TUR)
1964 Anatoly Kolesov (URS)
1968 Rudolf Vesper (GDR)
1972 Viteslav Macha (TCH)
1976 Anatoly Bykov (URS)
1980 Ferenc Kocsis (HUN)
1984 Jouko Salomaki (FIN)
1988 Kim Young Nam (KOR)
1992 Mnatsakan Iskandaryan (UNT)
1996 Filiberto Ascuy Aguilera (CUB)
2000 Murat Kardanov (URS)
2004 Aleksandr Dokturishivili (UZB)
2008 Manuchar Kvirkelia (GEO)

84 KG (184.8 LB)
1908 Frithiof Martenson (SWE)
1912 Claes Johansson (SWE)
1920 Carl Westergren (SWE)
1924 Edward Westerlund (FIN)
1928 Väinö Kokkinen (FIN)

Summer Olympic Games (continued)

Wrestling—Greco-Roman[37] (continued)

84 KG (184.8 LB) (CONTINUED)

1932	Väinö Kokkinen (FIN)
1936	Ivar Johansson (SWE)
1948	Axel Grönberg (SWE)
1952	Axel Grönberg (SWE)
1956	Givi Kartoziya (URS)
1960	Dimitar Dobrev (BUL)
1964	Branislav Simic (YUG)
1968	Lothar Metz (GDR)
1972	Csaba Hegedus (HUN)
1976	Momir Petkovic (YUG)
1980	Gennady Korban (URS)
1984	Ion Draica (ROM)
1988	Mikhail Mamiashvili (URS)
1992	Peter Farkas (HUN)
1996	Hamza Yerlikaya (TUR)
2000	Hamza Yerlikaya (TUR)
2004	Aleksey Mishin (RUS)
2008	Andrea Minguzzi (ITA)

90 KG (198.5 LB)

1908	Verner Weckman (FIN)
1912	Anders Ahlgren (SWE)
1920	Claes Johansson (SWE)
1924	Carl Westergren (SWE)
1928	Ibrahim Moustafa (EGY)
1932	Rudolf Svensson (SWE)
1936	Axel Cadier (SWE)
1948	Karl-Erik Nilsson (SWE)
1952	Kelpo Olavi Gröndahl (FIN)
1956	Valentin Nikolayev (URS)
1960	Tevfik Kis (TUR)
1964	Boyan Radev (BUL)
1968	Boyan Radev (BUL)
1972	Valery Rezantsev (URS)
1976	Valery Rezantsev (URS)
1980	Norbert Nottny (HUN)
1984	Steven Fraser (USA)
1988	Atanas Komchev (BUL)

Wrestling—Greco-Roman[37] (continued)

90 KG (198.5 LB) (CONTINUED)

1992	Maik Bullmann (GER)
1996	Vyacheslav Oleynyk (UKR)

96 KG (211.2 LB)

1896	Karl Schumann (GER)
1908	Richard Weisz (HUN)
1912	Yrjö Saarela (FIN)
1920	Adolf Lindfors (FIN)
1924	Henri Deglane (FRA)
1928	Rudolf Svensson (SWE)
1932	Carl Westergren (SWE)
1936	Kristjan Palusalu (EST)
1948	Ahmet Kirecci (TUR)
1952	Johannes Kotkas (URS)
1956	Anatoly Parfenov (URS)
1960	Ivan Bogdan (URS)
1964	Istvan Kozma (HUN)
1968	Istvan Kozma (HUN)
1972	Nicolae Martinescu (ROM)
1976	Nikolay Balboshin (URS)
1980	Georgi Raikov-Petkov (BUL)
1984	Vasile Andrei (ROM)
1988	Andrzej Wronski (POL)
1992	Héctor Milian (CUB)
1996	Andrzej Wronski (POL)
2000	Mikael Ljungberg (SWE)
2004	Karam Ibrahim (EGY)
2008	Aslanbek Khushtov (RUS)

120 KG (264 LB)

1972	Anatoly Roshchin (URS)
1976	Aleksandr Kolchinsky (URS)
1980	Aleksandr Kolchinsky (URS)
1984	Jeffrey Blatnick (USA)
1988	Aleksandr Karelin (URS)
1992	Aleksandr Karelin (UNT)
1996	Aleksandr Karelin (RUS)
2000	Rulon Gardner (USA)
2004	Khasan Baroyev (RUS)
2008	Mijain López (CUB)

[1]The competitions in 1900 and 1904 are said to be unofficial. [2]Winner after disqualification of top finisher for drug use. [3]100-meter event. [4]Hurdles were 2′ 6″ high, not 3′. [5]An extra lap of 460 meters was run in error. [6]Jim Thorpe was stripped of his gold medals in 1913 when it was discovered he had briefly competed as a professional athlete; in 1982 his gold medals were restored, and he was declared "cowinner" of the events. [7]80 meters from 1932 to 1968. [8]Pentathlon from 1964 to 1980. [9]Weight classifications have been revised numerous times. [10]2,000-meter event. [11]333.3-meter event. [12]Distance has varied from 87 to 320 km. [13]Held outdoors. [14]Weight classifications were changed in 1980 and 1996. [15]Weight classifications were changed in 2000. [16]The distances in men's rowing events have varied from time to time. In 1904 it was 2 miles; in 1908, 1.5 miles; from 1912 to 1936, 2,000 meters; in 1948, 1 mile 350 yards; and since 1952, 2,000 meters (1 mile 427 yards). [17]The distance in women's rowing events was 1,000 meters until 1988, at which time it became 2,000 meters. [18]Without coxswain. [19]From 2004. [20]Open from 1996 to 2004. [21]From 1952. [22]Men-only from 1924 to 2004. [23]Open from 1932 to 2004. [24]Open from 1968 to 1992. [25]Open from 1968 to 1992. [26]100 yards. [27]220 yards. [28]500 meters. [29]440 yards. [30]1,200 meters. [31]1,000 meters. [32]1 mile. [33]100 yards. [34]440 yards. [35]300 meters. [36]Fréchette's gold medal awarded in 1993 on basis of error in scoring. [37]Weight classifications have been revised numerous times, most recently after the 1996 Games. [38]In 1976 the press lift was removed, weights given thereafter being the total for the clean and jerk and the snatch. [39]Total of five lifts.

Kano Jigoro (1860–1938) combined the knowledge of the old jujitsu schools of the Japanese samurai with the sporting ideology of the "muscular Christianity" movement and in 1882 founded his Kodokan School of judo (from the Chinese *jou-tao*, or *roudao*, meaning "gentle way"), the beginning of the sport in its modern form. By the 1960s judo associations had been established in most countries and affiliated to the International Judo Federation, which is headquartered in Budapest, Hungary.

Winter Olympic Games

Gold medalists in all winter events since 1908; winter sports were not included in the three Olympic Games before 1908, and separate Winter Games were not held until 1924. Note: East and West Germany fielded a joint all-Germany team in 1956, 1960, and 1964, abbreviated here as GER.

Biathlon (men)

10 KM

		MIN:SEC
1980	Frank Ullrich (GDR)	32:10.69
1984	Eirik Kvalfoss (NOR)	30:53.8
1988	Frank-Peter Rötsch (GDR)	25:08.1
1992	Mark Kirchner (GER)	26:02.3
1994	Sergey Chepikov (RUS)	28:07.0
1998	Ole Einar Bjørndalen (NOR)	27:16.2
2002	Ole Einar Bjørndalen (NOR)	24:51.3
2006	Sven Fischer (GER)	26:11.6
2010	Vincent Jay (FRA)	24:07.8

12.5-KM PURSUIT

		MIN:SEC
2002	Ole Einar Bjørndalen (NOR)	32:34.6
2006	Vincent Defrasne (FRA)	35:20.2
2010	Björn Ferry (SWE)	33:38.4

15-KM MASS START

		MIN:SEC
2006	Michael Greis (GER)	47:20.0
2010	Yevgeny Ustyugov (RUS)	35:35.7

20 KM

		HR:MIN:SEC
1960	Klas Lestander (SWE)	1:33:21.6
1964	Vladimir Melanin (URS)	1:20:26.8
1968	Magnar Solberg (NOR)	1:13:45.9
1972	Magnar Solberg (NOR)	1:15:55.50
1976	Nikolay Kruglov (URS)	1:14:12.26
1980	Anatoly Alyabyev (URS)	1:08:16.31
1984	Peter Angerer (FRG)	1:11:52.70
1988	Frank-Peter Rötsch (GDR)	56:33.3
1992	Yevgeny Redkin (UNT)	57:34.4
1994	Sergey Tarasov (RUS)	57:25.3
1998	Halvard Hanevold (NOR)	56:16.4
2002	Ole Einar Bjørndalen (NOR)	51:03.3
2006	Michael Greis (GER)	54:23.0
2010	Emil Hegle Svendsen (NOR)	48:22.5

4 × 7.5-KM RELAY

		HR:MIN:SEC
1968	USSR	2:13:02.4
1972	USSR	1:51:44.92
1976	USSR	1:57:55.64
1980	USSR	1:34:03.27
1984	USSR	1:38:51.70
1988	USSR	1:22:30.00
1992	Germany	1:24:43.5
1994	Germany	1:30:22.1
1998	Germany	1:19:43.3
2002	Norway	1:23:42.3
2006	Germany	1:21:51.5
2010	Norway	1:21:38.1

MILITARY SKI PATROL

1924	Switzerland
1928	Norway
1936	Italy
1948	Switzerland

DISTANCE SHOOTING

1936	Georg Edenhauser (AUT)

ICE SHOOTING (TEAM)

1936	Austria

TARGET SHOOTING

1936	Ignaz Reiterer (AUT)

Biathlon (women)

7.5 KM

		MIN:SEC
1992	Anfisa Restsova (UNT)	24:29.2
1994	Myriam Bédard (CAN)	26:08.8
1998	Galina Kukleva (RUS)	23:08.0
2002	Kati Wilhelm (GER)	20:41.4
2006	Florence Baverel-Robert (FRA)	22:31.4
2010	Anastazia Kuzmina (SVK)	19:55.6

10-KM PURSUIT

		MIN:SEC
2002	Olga Pyleva (RUS)	31:07.7
2006	Kati Wilhelm (GER)	36:43.6
2010	Magdalena Neuner (GER)	30:16.0

12.5-KM MASS START

		MIN:SEC
2006	Anna Carin Olofsson (SWE)	40:36.5
2010	Magdalena Neuner (GER)	35:19.6

15 KM

		MIN:SEC
1992	Antje Misersky (GER)	51:47.2
1994	Myriam Bédard (CAN)	52:06.6
1998	Ekaterina Dafovska (BUL)	54:52.0
2002	Andrea Henkel (GER)	47:29.1
2006	Svetlana Ishmuratova (RUS)	49:24.1
2010	Tora Berger (NOR)	40:52.8

4 × 6-KM RELAY[1]

		HR:MIN:SEC
1992	France	1:15:55.6
1994	Russia	1:47:19.5
1998	Germany	1:40:13.6
2002	Germany	1:27:55.0
2006	Russia	1:16:12.5
2010	Russia	1:09:36.3

Bobsled

TWO-MAN BOBSLED

		MIN:SEC
1932	United States	8:14.74
1936	United States	5:29.29
1948	Switzerland	5:29.2
1952	West Germany	5:24.54
1956	Italy	5:30.14
1964	Great Britain	4:21.90
1968	Italy	4:41.54
1972	West Germany	4:57.07
1976	East Germany	3:44.42
1980	Switzerland	4:09.36
1984	East Germany	3:25.56
1988	USSR	3:53.48
1992	Switzerland	4:03.26
1994	Switzerland	3:30.81
1998	Canada; Italy (tied)	3:37.24
2002	Germany	3:10.11
2006	Germany	3:43.38
2010	Germany	3:26.65

FOUR-MAN BOBSLED

		MIN:SEC
1924	Switzerland	5:45.54
1928[2]	United States	3:20.5
1932	United States	7:53.68
1936	Switzerland	5:19.85
1948	United States	5:20.1
1952	West Germany	5:07.84
1956	Switzerland	5:10.44
1964	Canada	4:14.46
1968	Italy	2:17.39

Winter Olympic Games (continued)

Bobsled (continued)

FOUR-MAN BOBSLED (CONTINUED)

		MIN:SEC
1972	Switzerland	4:43.07
1976	East Germany	3:40.43
1980	East Germany	3:59.92
1984	East Germany	3:20.22
1988	Switzerland	3:47.51
1992	Austria	3:53.90
1994	Germany	3:27.78
1998	Germany	2:39.41
2002	Germany	3:07.51
2006	Germany	3:40.42
2010	United States	3:24.46

TWO-WOMAN BOBSLED

		MIN:SEC
2002	United States	1:37.76
2006	Germany	3:49.98
2010	Canada	3:32.28

Curling

MEN

1924	Great Britain
1998	Switzerland
2002	Norway
2006	Canada
2010	Canada

WOMEN

1998	Canada
2002	Great Britain
2006	Sweden
2010	Sweden

Figure Skating

MEN'S SINGLES

1908	Ulrich Salchow (SWE)
1920	Gillis Gräfström (SWE)
1924	Gillis Gräfström (SWE)
1928	Gillis Gräfström (SWE)
1932	Karl Schäfer (AUT)
1936	Karl Schäfer (AUT)
1948	Richard Button (USA)
1952	Richard Button (USA)
1956	Hayes Alan Jenkins (USA)
1960	David Jenkins (USA)
1964	Manfred Schnelldorfer (GER)
1968	Wolfgang Schwarz (AUT)
1972	Ondrej Nepela (TCH)
1976	John Curry (GBR)
1980	Robin Cousins (GBR)
1984	Scott Hamilton (USA)
1988	Brian Boitano (USA)
1992	Viktor Petrenko (UNT)
1994	Aleksey Urmanov (RUS)
1998	Ilia Kulik (RUS)
2002	Aleksey Yagudin (RUS)
2006	Yevgeny Plushchenko (RUS)
2010	Evan Lysacek (USA)

WOMEN'S SINGLES

1908	Madge Syers (GBR)
1920	Magda Julin-Mauroy (SWE)
1924	Herma Planck-Szabo (AUT)
1928	Sonja Henie (NOR)
1932	Sonja Henie (NOR)
1936	Sonja Henie (NOR)
1948	Barbara Ann Scott (CAN)
1952	Jeannette Altwegg (GBR)
1956	Tenley Albright (USA)

Figure Skating (continued)

WOMEN'S SINGLES (CONTINUED)

1960	Carol Heiss (USA)
1964	Sjoukje Dijkstra (NED)
1968	Peggy Fleming (USA)
1972	Beatrix Schuba (AUT)
1976	Dorothy Hamill (USA)
1980	Annett Potzsch (GDR)
1984	Katarina Witt (GDR)
1988	Katarina Witt (GDR)
1992	Kristi Yamaguchi (USA)
1994	Oksana Bayul (UKR)
1998	Tara Lipinski (USA)
2002	Sarah Hughes (USA)
2006	Shizuka Arakawa (JPN)
2010	Kim Yu-Na (KOR)

PAIRS

1908	Anna Hübler, Heinrich Burger (GER)
1920	Ludoviga Jakobsson-Eilers, Walter Jakobsson (FIN)
1924	Helene Engelmann, Alfred Berger (AUT)
1928	Andrée Joly, Pierre Brunet (FRA)
1932	Andrée Brunet-Joly, Pierre Brunet (FRA)
1936	Maxi Herber, Ernst Baier (GER)
1948	Micheline Lannoy, Pierre Baugniet (BEL)
1952	Ria Falk, Paul Falk (FRG)
1956	Elisabeth Schwarz, Kurt Oppelt (AUT)
1960	Barbara Wagner, Robert Paul (CAN)
1964	Lyudmila Belousova, Oleg Protopopov (URS)
1968	Lyudmila Belousova, Oleg Protopopov (URS)
1972	Irina Rodnina, Aleksey Ulanov (URS)
1976	Irina Rodnina, Aleksandr Zaytsev (URS)
1980	Irina Rodnina, Aleksandr Zaytsev (URS)
1984	Yelena Valova, Oleg Vasilyev (URS)
1988	Yekaterina Gordeyeva, Sergey Grinkov (URS)
1992	Natalya Mishkutyonok, Artur Dmitriyev (UNT)
1994	Yekaterina Gordeyeva, Sergey Grinkov (RUS)
1998	Oksana Kazakova, Artur Dmitriyev (RUS)
2002	Yelena Berezhnaya, Anton Sikharulidze (RUS); Jamie Sale, David Pelletier (CAN) (shared)
2006	Tatyana Totmyanina, Maksim Marinin (RUS)
2010	Shen Xue, Zhao Hongbo (CHN)

ICE DANCING

1976	Lyudmila Pakhomova, Aleksandr Gorshkov (URS)
1980	Natalya Linichuk, Gennady Karponosov (URS)
1984	Jayne Torvill, Christopher Dean (GBR)
1988	Natalya Bestemyanova, Andrey Bukin (URS)
1992	Marina Klimova, Sergey Ponomarenko (UNT)
1994	Oksana Grishchuk, Yevgeny Platov (RUS)
1998	Oksana Grishchuk, Yevgeny Platov (RUS)
2002	Marina Anissina, Gwendal Peizerat (FRA)
2006	Tatyana Navka, Roman Kostomarov (RUS)
2010	Tessa Virtue, Scott Moir (CAN)

Ice Hockey

MEN

1920	Canada
1924	Canada
1928	Canada
1932	Canada
1936	Great Britain
1948	Canada
1952	Canada
1956	USSR
1960	United States

Winter Olympic Games (continued)

Ice Hockey (continued)

MEN (CONTINUED)

1964	USSR
1968	USSR
1972	USSR
1976	USSR
1980	United States
1984	USSR
1988	USSR
1992	Unified Team
1994	Sweden
1998	Czech Republic
2002	Canada
2006	Sweden
2010	Canada

WOMEN

1998	United States
2002	Canada
2006	Canada
2010	Canada

Luge

MEN'S SINGLES

		MIN:SEC
1964	Thomas Köhler (GER)	3:26.77
1968	Manfred Schmid (AUT)	2:52.48
1972	Wolfgang Schneidel (GDR)	3:27.58
1976	Detlef Guenther (GDR)	3:27.688
1980	Bernhard Glass (GDR)	2:54.796
1984	Paul Hildgartner (ITA)	3:04.258
1988	Jens Müller (GDR)	3:05.548
1992	Georg Hackl (GER)	3:02.363
1994	Georg Hackl (GER)	3:21.571
1998	Georg Hackl (GER)	3:18.436
2002	Armin Zöggeler (ITA)	2:57.941
2006	Armin Zöggeler (ITA)	3:26.088
2010	Felix Loch (GER)	3:13.085

MEN'S DOUBLES

		MIN:SEC
1964	Austria	1:41.62
1968	East Germany	1:35.85
1972	Italy; East Germany (tied)	1:28.35
1976	East Germany	1:25.604
1980	East Germany	1:19.331
1984	West Germany	1:23.620
1988	East Germany	1:31.940
1992	Germany	1:32.053
1994	Italy	1:36.720
1998	Germany	1:41.105
2002	Germany	1:26.082
2006	Austria	1:34.497
2010	Austria	1:22.705

WOMEN'S SINGLES

		MIN:SEC
1964	Ortrun Enderlein (GER)	3:24.67
1968	Erica Lechner (ITA)	2:29.37
1972	Anna-Maria Müller (GDR)	2:59.18
1976	Margit Schumann (GDR)	2:50.621
1980	Vera Zozulya (URS)	2:36.537
1984	Steffi Martin (GDR)	2:46.570
1988	Steffi Walter-Martin (GDR)	3:03.973
1992	Doris Neuner (AUT)	3:06.696
1994	Gerda Weissensteiner (ITA)	3:15.517
1998	Silke Kraushaar (GER)	3:23.779
2002	Sylke Otto (GER)	2:52.464
2006	Sylke Otto (GER)	3:07.979
2010	Tatjana Hüfner (GER)	2:46.524

Skeleton

MEN

		MIN:SEC
1928	Jennison Heaton (USA)	3:01.8
1948	Nino Bibbia (ITA)	5:23.2
2002	Jim Shea (USA)	1:41.96
2006	Duff Gibson (CAN)	1:55.88
2010	Jon Montgomery (CAN)	3:29.73

WOMEN

		MIN:SEC
2002	Tristan Gale (USA)	1:45.11
2006	Maya Pedersen (SUI)	1:59.83
2010	Amy Williams (GBR)	3:35.64

Alpine Skiing (men)

DOWNHILL

		MIN:SEC
1948	Henri Oreiller (FRA)	2:55.0
1952	Zeno Colò (ITA)	2:30.8
1956	Toni Sailer (AUT)	2:52.2
1960	Jean Vuarnet (FRA)	2:06.0
1964	Egon Zimmermann (AUT)	2:18.16
1968	Jean-Claude Killy (FRA)	1:59.85
1972	Bernhard Russi (SUI)	1:51.43
1976	Franz Klammer (AUT)	1:45.73
1980	Leonhard Stock (AUT)	1:45.50
1984	Bill Johnson (USA)	1:45.59
1988	Pirmin Zurbriggen (SUI)	1:59.63
1992	Patrick Ortlieb (AUT)	1:50.37
1994	Tommy Moe (USA)	1:45.75
1998	Jean-Luc Cretier (FRA)	1:50.11
2002	Fritz Strobl (AUT)	1:39.13
2006	Antoine Dénériaz (FRA)	1:48.80
2010	Didier Defago (SUI)	1:54.31

SLALOM

		MIN:SEC
1948	Edy Reinalter (SUI)	2:10.3
1952	Othmar Schneider (AUT)	2:00.0
1956	Toni Sailer (AUT)	3:14.7
1960	Ernst Hinterseer (AUT)	2:08.9
1964	Josef Stiegler (AUT)	2:21.13
1968	Jean-Claude Killy (FRA)	1:39.73
1972	Francisco Ochoa (ESP)	1:49.27
1976	Piero Gros (ITA)	2:03.29
1980	Ingemar Stenmark (SWE)	1:44.26
1984	Phil Mahre (USA)	1:39.41
1988	Alberto Tomba (ITA)	1:39.47
1992	Finn Christian Jagge (NOR)	1:44.39
1994	Thomas Stangassinger (AUT)	2:02.02
1998	Hans Petter Buraas (NOR)	1:49.31
2002	Jean-Pierre Vidal (FRA)	1:41.06
2006	Benjamin Raich (AUT)	1:43.14
2010	Giuliano Razzoli (ITA)	1:39.32

GIANT SLALOM

		MIN:SEC
1952	Stein Eriksen (NOR)	2:25.0
1956	Toni Sailer (AUT)	3:00.1
1960	Roger Staub (SUI)	1:48.3
1964	François Bonlieu (FRA)	1:46.71
1968	Jean-Claude Killy (FRA)	3:29.28
1972	Gustavo Thöni (ITA)	3:09.62
1976	Heini Hemmi (SUI)	3:26.97
1980	Ingemar Stenmark (SWE)	2:40.74
1984	Max Julen (SUI)	2:41.18
1988	Alberto Tomba (ITA)	2:06.37
1992	Alberto Tomba (ITA)	2:06.98
1994	Markus Wasmeier (GER)	2:52.46
1998	Hermann Maier (AUT)	2:38.51
2002	Stephan Eberharter (AUT)	2:23.28
2006	Benjamin Raich (AUT)	2:35.00
2010	Carlo Janka (SUI)	2:37.83

Winter Olympic Games (continued)

Alpine Skiing (men) (continued)

SUPERGIANT SLALOM	MIN:SEC
1988 Franck Piccard (FRA)	1:39.66
1992 Kjetil André Aamodt (NOR)	1:13.04
1994 Markus Wasmeier (GER)	1:32.53
1998 Hermann Maier (AUT)	1:34.82
2002 Kjetil André Aamodt (NOR)	1:21.58
2006 Kjetil André Aamodt (NOR)	1:30.65
2010 Aksel Lund Svindal (NOR)	1:30.34

ALPINE COMBINED[3]	MIN:SEC
1936 Franz Pfnür (GER)	
1948 Henri Oreiller (FRA)	
1972 Gustavo Thöni (ITA)	
1976 Gustavo Thöni (ITA)	
1988 Hubert Strolz (AUT)	
1992 Josef Polig (ITA)	
1994 Lasse Kjus (NOR)	3:17.53
1998 Mario Reiter (AUT)	3:08.06
2002 Kjetil André Aamodt (NOR)	3:17.56
2006 Ted Ligety (USA)	3:09.35
2010 Bode Miller (USA)	2:44.92

Alpine Skiing (women)

DOWNHILL	MIN:SEC
1948 Hedy Schlunegger (SUI)	2:28.3
1952 Trude Jochom-Beiser (AUT)	1:47.1
1956 Madeleine Berthod (SUI)	1:40.7
1960 Heidi Beibl (GER)	1:37.6
1964 Christl Haas (AUT)	1:55.39
1968 Olga Pall (AUT)	1:40.87
1972 Marie-Thérèse Nadig (SUI)	1:36.68
1976 Rosi Mittermaier (FRG)	1:46.16
1980 Annemarie Moser-Pröll (AUT)	1:37.52
1984 Michael Figini (SUI)	1:13.36
1988 Marina Kiehl (FRG)	1:25.86
1992 Kerrin Lee-Gartner (CAN)	1:52.55
1994 Katja Seizinger (GER)	1:35.93
1998 Katja Seizinger (GER)	1:28.29
2002 Carole Montillet (FRA)	1:39.56
2006 Michaela Dorfmeister (AUT)	1:56.49
2010 Lindsey Vonn (USA)	1:44.19

SLALOM	MIN:SEC
1948 Gretchen Fraser (USA)	1:57.2
1952 Andrea Lawrence-Mead (USA)	2:10.6
1956 Renée Colliard (SUI)	1:52.3
1960 Anne Heggtveit (CAN)	1:49.6
1964 Christine Goitschel (FRA)	1:29.86
1968 Marielle Goitschel (FRA)	1:59.85
1972 Barbara Cochran (USA)	1:31.24
1976 Rosi Mittermaier (FRG)	1:30.54
1980 Hanni Wenzel (LIE)	1:25.09
1984 Paoletta Magoni (ITA)	1:36.47
1988 Vreni Schneider (SUI)	1:36.69
1992 Petra Kronberger (AUT)	1:32.68
1994 Vreni Schneider (SUI)	1:56.01
1998 Hilde Gerg (GER)	1:32.40
2002 Janica Kostelic (CRO)	1:46.10
2006 Anja Pärson (SWE)	1:29.04
2010 Maria Riesch (GER)	1:42.89

GIANT SLALOM	MIN:SEC
1952 Andrea Lawrence-Mead (USA)	2:06.8
1956 Ossi Reichert (GER)	1:56.5
1960 Yvonne Rüegg (SUI)	1:39.9
1964 Marielle Goitschel (FRA)	1:52.24

Alpine Skiing (women) (continued)

GIANT SLALOM (CONTINUED)	MIN:SEC
1968 Nancy Greene (CAN)	1:51.97
1972 Marie-Thérèse Nadig (SUI)	1:29.90
1976 Kathy Kreiner (CAN)	1:29.13
1980 Hanni Wenzel (LIE)	2:41.66
1984 Debbie Armstrong (USA)	2:20.98
1988 Vreni Schneider (SUI)	2:06.49
1992 Pernilla Wiberg (SWE)	2:12.74
1994 Deborah Compagnoni (ITA)	2:30.97
1998 Deborah Compagnoni (ITA)	2:50.59
2002 Janica Kostelic (CRO)	2:30.01
2006 Julia Mancuso (USA)	2:09.19
2010 Viktoria Rebensburg (GER)	2:27.11

SUPERGIANT SLALOM	MIN:SEC
1988 Sigrid Wolf (AUT)	1:19.03
1992 Deborah Compagnoni (ITA)	1:21.22
1994 Diann Roffe-Steinrotter (USA)	1:22.15
1998 Picabo Street (USA)	1:18.02
2002 Daniela Ceccarelli (ITA)	1:13.59
2006 Michaela Dorfmeister (AUT)	1:32.47
2010 Andrea Fischbacher (AUT)	1:20.14

ALPINE COMBINED[3]	MIN:SEC
1936 Chrislt Cranz (GER)	
1948 Trude Beiser (AUT)	
1972 Annemarie Pröll (AUT)	
1976 Rosi Mittermaier (FRG)	
1988 Anita Wachter (AUT)	
1992 Petra Kronberger (AUT)	
1994 Pernilla Wiberg (SWE)	3:05.16
1998 Katja Seizinger (GER)	2:40.74
2002 Janica Kostelic (CRO)	2:43.28
2006 Janica Kostelic (CRO)	2:51.08
2010 Maria Riesch (GER)	2:09.14

Freestyle Skiing

MEN'S MOGULS
1992 Edgar Grospiron (FRA)
1994 Jean-Luc Brassard (CAN)
1998 Jonny Moseley (USA)
2002 Janne Lahtela (FIN)
2006 Dale Begg-Smith (AUS)
2010 Alexandre Bilodeau (CAN)

MEN'S AERIALS
1994 Andreas Schönbächler (SUI)
1998 Eric Bergoust (USA)
2002 Ales Valenta (CZE)
2006 Han Xiaopeng (CHN)
2010 Alexey Grishin (BLR)

MEN'S SKI CROSS
2010 Michael Schmid (SUI)

WOMEN'S MOGULS
1992 Donna Weinbrecht (USA)
1994 Stine Lise Hattestad (NOR)
1998 Tae Satoya (JPN)
2002 Kari Traa (NOR)
2006 Jennifer Heil (CAN)
2010 Hannah Kearney (USA)

WOMEN'S AERIALS
1994 Lina Cheryazova (UZB)
1998 Nikki Stone (USA)

Winter Olympic Games (continued)

Freestyle Skiing (continued)

WOMEN'S AERIALS (CONTINUED)
2002	Alisa Camplin (AUS)	
2006	Evelyne Leu (SUI)	
2010	Lydia Lassila (AUS)	

WOMEN'S SKI CROSS
2010	Ashleigh McIvor (CAN)	

Nordic Skiing (men)

1.5-KM CROSS-COUNTRY SPRINT
		MIN:SEC
2002	Tor Arne Hetland (NOR)	2:56.9
2006	Björn Lind (SWE)	2:26.5
2010	Nikita Kriyukov (RUS)	3:36.3

TEAM SPRINT
		MIN:SEC
2006	Sweden	17:02.9
2010	Norway	19:1.0

10-KM CROSS-COUNTRY
		MIN:SEC
1992	Vegard Ulvang (NOR)	27:36.0
1994	Bjørn Daehlie (NOR)	24:20.1
1998	Bjørn Daehlie (NOR)	27:24.5

15-KM CROSS-COUNTRY[4]
		HR:MIN:SEC
1924	Thorleif Haug (NOR)	1:14:31.0
1928	Johan Grøttumsbråten (NOR)	1:37:01.0
1932	Sven Utterström (SWE)	1:23:07.0
1936	Erik-August Larsson (SWE)	1:14:38.0
1948	Martin Lundström (SWE)	1:13:50.0
1952	Hallgeir Brenden (NOR)	1:01:34.0
1956	Hallgeir Brenden (NOR)	49:39.0
1960	Hakkon Brusveen (NOR)	51:55.5
1964	Eero Mäntyranta (FIN)	50:54.1
1968	Harald Grönningen (NOR)	47:54.2
1972	Sven-Ake Lundbäck (SWE)	45:28.24
1976	Nikolay Bazhukov (URS)	43:58.47
1980	Thomas Wassberg (SWE)	41:57.63
1984	Gunde Svan (SWE)	41:25.60
1988	Mikhail Devyatyarov (URS)	41:18.9
1998	Thomas Alsgaard (NOR)	39:13.7
2002	Andrus Veerpalu (EST)	37:07.4
2006	Andrus Veerpalu (EST)	38:01.3
2010	Dario Cologna (SUI)	33:36.3

COMBINED PURSUIT[5]
		HR:MIN:SEC
1992	Bjørn Daehlie (NOR)	1:05:37.9
1994	Bjørn Daehlie (NOR)	1:00:08.8
1998	Thomas Alsgaard (NOR)	1:07:01.7
2002	Thomas Alsgaard (NOR);	49:48.9
	Frode Estil (NOR) (tied)[6]	
2006	Yevgeny Dementyev (RUS)	1:17:00.8
2010	Marcus Hellner (SWE)	1:15:11.4

30-KM CROSS-COUNTRY
		HR:MIN:SEC
1956	Veikko Hakulinen (FIN)	1:44:06.0
1960	Sixten Jernberg (SWE)	1:51:03.9
1964	Eero Mäntyranta (FIN)	1:30:50.7
1968	Franco Nones (ITA)	1:35:39.2
1972	Vyacheslav Vedenin (URS)	1:36:31.15
1976	Sergey Savelyev (URS)	1:30:29.38
1980	Nikolay Zimyatov (URS)	1:27:02.80
1984	Nikolay Zimyatov (URS)	1:28:56.30
1988	Aleksey Prokourorov (URS)	1:24:26.3
1992	Vegard Ulvang (NOR)	1:22:27.8
1994	Thomas Alsgaard (NOR)	1:12:26.4
1998	Mika Myllylä (FIN)	1:33:56.0
2002	Christian Hoffmann (AUT)[6]	1:11:31.0

Nordic Skiing (men) (continued)

50-KM CROSS-COUNTRY
		HR:MIN:SEC
1924	Thorleif Haug (NOR)	3:44:32.0
1928	Per Erik Hedlund (SWE)	4:52:03.3
1932	Veli Saarinen (FIN)	4:28:00.0
1936	Elis Viklund (SWE)	3:30:11.0
1948	Nils Karlsson (SWE)	3:47:48.0
1952	Veikko Hakulinen (FIN)	3:33:33.0
1956	Sixten Jernberg (SWE)	2:50:27.0
1960	Kalevi Hämäläinen (FIN)	2:59:06.3
1964	Sixten Jernberg (SWE)	2:43:52.6
1968	Olle Ellefsäter (NOR)	2:28:45.8
1972	Pål Tyldum (NOR)	2:43:14.75
1976	Ivar Formo (NOR)	2:37:30.05
1980	Nikolay Zimyatov (URS)	2:27:24.60
1984	Thomas Wassberg (SWE)	2:15:55.80
1988	Gunde Svan (SWE)	2:04:30.9
1992	Bjørn Daehlie (NOR)	2:03:41.5
1994	Vladimir Smirnov (KAZ)	2:07:20.3
1998	Bjørn Daehlie (NOR)	2:05:08.2
2002	Mikhail Ivanov (RUS)[6]	2:06:20.8
2006	Giorgio Di Centa (ITA)	2:06:11.8
2010	Petter Northug (NOR)	2:05:35.5

4 × 10-KM RELAY
		HR:MIN:SEC
1936	Finland	2:41:33.0
1948	Sweden	2:32:08.0
1952	Finland	2:20:16.0
1956	USSR	2:15:30.0
1960	Finland	2:18:45.6
1964	Sweden	2:18:34.6
1968	Norway	2:08:33.5
1972	USSR	2:04:47.94
1976	Finland	2:07:59.72
1980	USSR	1:57:03.46
1984	Sweden	1:55:06.30
1988	Sweden	1:43:58.6
1992	Norway	1:39:26.0
1994	Italy	1:41:15.0
1998	Norway	1:40:55.7
2002	Norway	1:32:45.5
2006	Italy	1:43:45.7
2010	Sweden	1:45:05.4

SKI JUMPING (70 METERS)[7]
1924	Jacob Tullin Thams (NOR)
1928	Alf Andersen (NOR)
1932	Birger Ruud (NOR)
1936	Birger Ruud (NOR)
1948	Petter Hugsted (NOR)
1952	Arnfinn Bergmann (NOR)
1956	Antti Hyvärinen (FIN)
1960	Helmut Recknagel (GER)
1964	Veikko Kankkonen (FIN)
1968	Jiri Raska (TCH)
1972	Yukio Kasaya (JPN)
1976	Hans-Georg Aschenbach (GDR)
1980	Toni Innauer (AUT)
1984	Jens Weissflog (GDR)
1988	Matti Nykänen (FIN)

SKI JUMPING (95 METERS)[7]
1964	Toralf Engan (NOR)
1968	Vladimir Belousov (URS)
1972	Wojciech Fortuna (POL)
1976	Karl Schnabl (AUT)
1980	Jens Tormanen (FIN)
1984	Matti Nykänen (FIN)
1988	Matti Nykänen (FIN)

Winter Olympic Games (continued)

Nordic Skiing (men) (continued)

SKI JUMPING (95 METERS)[7] (CONTINUED)

1992	Ernst Vettori (AUT)
1994	Espen Bredesen (NOR)
1998	Jani Soininen (FIN)
2002	Simon Ammann (SUI)
2006	Lars Bystøl (NOR)
2010	Simon Ammann (SUI)

SKI JUMPING (125 METERS)[7]

1992	Toni Nieminen (FIN)
1994	Jens Weissflog (GER)
1998	Kazuyoshi Funaki (JPN)
2002	Simon Ammann (SUI)
2006	Thomas Morgenstern (AUT)
2010	Simon Ammann (SUI)

NORDIC COMBINED SPRINT (7.5 KM)[8]

2002	Samppa Lajunen (FIN)
2006	Felix Gottwald (AUT)

NORDIC COMBINED INDIVIDUAL NORMAL HILL[8]

2010	Jason Lamy Chappuis (FRA)

NORDIC COMBINED INDIVIDUAL LARGE HILL[8]

1924	Thorleif Haug (NOR)
1928	Johan Grøttumsbråten (NOR)
1932	Johan Grøttumsbråten (NOR)
1936	Oddbjörn Hagen (NOR)
1948	Heikki Hasu (FIN)
1952	Simon Slåttvik (NOR)
1956	Sverre Stenersen (NOR)
1960	Georg Thoma (GER)
1964	Tormod Knutsen (NOR)
1968	Franz Keller (FRG)
1972	Ulrich Wehling (GDR)
1976	Ulrich Wehling (GDR)
1980	Ulrich Wehling (GDR)
1984	Tom Sandberg (NOR)
1988	Hippolyt Kempf (SUI)
1992	Fabrice Guy (FRA)
1994	Fred Børre Lundberg (NOR)
1998	Bjarte Engen Vik (NOR)
2002	Samppa Lajunen (FIN)
2006	Georg Hettich (GER)
2010	Bill Demong (USA)

TEAM SKI JUMPING (125 METERS)[9]

1988	Finland
1992	Finland
1994	Germany
1998	Japan
2002	Germany
2006	Austria
2010	Austria

NORDIC COMBINED TEAM RELAY

1988	West Germany
1992	Japan
1994	Japan
1998	Norway
2002	Finland
2006	Austria
2010	Austria

Nordic Skiing (women)

1.5-KM CROSS-COUNTRY SPRINT

		MIN:SEC
2002	Yuliya Chepalova (RUS)	3:10.6
2006	Chandra Crawford (CAN)	2:12.3

Nordic Skiing (women) (continued)

1.5-KM CROSS-COUNTRY SPRINT (CONTINUED)

		MIN:SEC
2010	Marit Bjørgen (NOR)	3:39.2

TEAM SPRINT

		MIN:SEC
2006	Sweden	16:36.9
2010	Germany	18:03.7

5-KM CROSS-COUNTRY

		MIN:SEC
1964	Klavdiya Boyarskikh (URS)	17:50.5
1968	Toini Gustafsson (SWE)	16:45.2
1972	Galina Kulakova (URS)	17:00.50
1976	Helena Takalo (FIN)	15:48.69
1980	Raisa Smetanina (URS)	15:06.92
1984	Marja-Liisa Hämäläinen (FIN)	17:04.00
1988	Marjo Matikainen (FIN)	15:04.00
1992	Marjut Lukkarinen (FIN)	14:13.8
1994	Lyubov Yegorova (RUS)	14:08.8
1998	Larisa Lazutina (RUS)	17:39.9

10-KM CROSS-COUNTRY

		MIN:SEC
1952	Lydia Wideman (FIN)	41:40.0
1956	Lyubov Kozyreva (URS)	38:11.0
1960	Mariya Gusakova (URS)	39:46.6
1964	Klavdiya Boyarskikh (URS)	40:24.3
1968	Toini Gustafsson (SWE)	36:46.5
1972	Galina Kulakova (URS)	34:17.82
1976	Raisa Smetanina (URS)	30:13.41
1980	Barbara Petzold (GDR)	30:31.54
1984	Marja-Liisa Hämäläinen (FIN)	31:44.20
1988	Vida Ventsene (URS)	30:08.30
1998	Larisa Lazutina (RUS)	46:06.9
2002	Bente Skari (NOR)	28:05.6
2006	Kristina Smigun (EST)	27:51.4
2010	Charlotte Kalla (SWE)	24:58.4

COMBINED PURSUIT[10]

		MIN:SEC
1992	Lyubov Yegorova (UNT)	40:08.4
1994	Lyubov Yegorova (RUS)	41:38.1
1998	Larisa Lazutina (RUS)	46:06.9
2002	Beckie Scott (CAN)[6]	25:09.9
2006	Kristina Smigun (EST)	42:48.7
2010	Marit Bjørgen (NOR)	39:58.1

15-KM CROSS-COUNTRY

		MIN:SEC
1992	Lyubov Yegorova (UNT)	42:20.8
1994	Manuela Di Centa (ITA)	39:44.5
1998	Olga Danilova (RUS)	46:55.40
2002	Stefania Belmondo (ITA)	39:54.4

20-KM CROSS-COUNTRY

		HR:MIN:SEC
1984	Marja-Liisa Hämäläinen (FIN)	1:01:45.0
1988	Tamara Tikhonova (URS)	55:53.6

30-KM CROSS-COUNTRY

		HR:MIN:SEC
1992	Stefania Belmondo (ITA)	1:22:30.1
1994	Manuela Di Centa (ITA)	1:25:41.6
1998	Yuliya Chepalova (RUS)	1:22:01.5
2002	Gabriella Paruzzi (ITA)[6]	1:30:57.1
2006	Katerina Neumannova (CZE)	1:22:25.4
2010	Justyna Kowalczyk (POL)	1:30:33.7

4 × 5-KM RELAY[11]

		HR:MIN:SEC
1956	Finland	1:09:01.0
1960	Sweden	1:04:21.4
1964	USSR	59:20.2
1968	Norway	57:30.0
1972	USSR	48:46.15
1976	USSR	1:07:49.75

Winter Olympic Games (continued)

Nordic Skiing (women) (continued)

4 × 5-KM RELAY[11] (CONTINUED)

		HR:MIN:SEC
1980	East Germany	1:02:11.10
1984	Norway	1:06:49.70
1988	USSR	59:51.10
1992	Unified Team	59:34.8
1994	Russia	57:12.5
1998	Russia	55:13.5
2002	Germany	49:30.6
2006	Russia	54:47.7
2010	Norway	55:19.5

Sled-dog Race

1932	Emile St. Goddard (CAN)	

Snowboarding (men)

GIANT SLALOM

1998	Ross Rebagliati (CAN)
2002	Philipp Schoch (SUI)
2006	Philipp Schoch (SUI)
2010	Jasey Jay Anderson (CAN)

HALFPIPE

1998	Gian Simmen (SUI)
2002	Ross Powers (USA)
2006	Shaun White (USA)
2010	Shaun White (USA)

SNOWBOARDCROSS

2006	Seth Wescott (USA)
2010	Seth Wescott (USA)

Snowboarding (women)

GIANT SLALOM

1998	Karine Ruby (FRA)
2002	Isabelle Blanc (FRA)
2006	Daniela Meuli (SUI)
2010	Nicolien Sauerbreij (NED)

HALFPIPE

1998	Nicola Thost (GER)
2002	Kelly Clark (USA)
2006	Hannah Teter (USA)
2010	Torah Bright (AUS)

SNOWBOARDCROSS

2006	Tanja Frieden (SUI)
2010	Maelle Ricker (CAN)

Speed Skating (men)

500 METERS

		SEC
1924	Charles Jewtraw (USA)	44.0
1928	Clas Thunberg (FIN); Bernt Evensen (NOR) (tied)	43.4
1932	John Shea (USA)	43.4
1936	Ivar Ballangrud (NOR)	43.4
1948	Finn Helgesen (NOR)	43.1
1952	Kenneth Henry (USA)	43.2
1956	Yevgeny Grishin (URS)	40.2
1960	Yevgeny Grishin (URS)	40.2
1964	Richard McDermott (USA)	40.1
1968	Erhard Keller (FRG)	40.3
1972	Erhard Keller (FRG)	39.44
1976	Yevgeny Kulikov (URS)	39.17
1980	Eric Heiden (USA)	38.03
1984	Sergey Fokichev (URS)	38.19
1988	Uwe-Jens Mey (GDR)	36.45

Speed Skating (men) (continued)

500 METERS (CONTINUED)

		SEC
1992	Uwe-Jens Mey (GER)	37.14
1994	Aleksandr Golubyov (RUS)	36.33
1998	Hiroyasu Shimizu (JPN)	71.35[12]
2002	Casey Fitzrandolph (USA)	69.23[12]
2006	Joey Cheek (USA)	69.76[12]
2010	Mo Tae-Bum (KOR)	69.82[12]

1,000 METERS

		MIN:SEC
1976	Peter Mueller (USA)	1:19.32
1980	Eric Heiden (USA)	1:15.18
1984	Gaetan Boucher (CAN)	1:15.80
1988	Nikolay Gulyayev (URS)	1:13.03
1992	Olaf Zinke (GER)	1:14.85
1994	Dan Jansen (USA)	1:12.43
1998	Ids Postma (NED)	1:10.71
2002	Gerard van Velde (NED)	1:07.18
2006	Shani Davis (USA)	1:08.89
2010	Shani Davis (USA)	1:08.94

1,500 METERS

		MIN:SEC
1924	Clas Thunberg (FIN)	2:20.8
1928	Clas Thunberg (FIN)	2:21.1
1932	John Shea (USA)	2:57.5
1936	Charles Mathisen (NOR)	2:19.2
1948	Sverre Farstad (NOR)	2:17.6
1952	Hjalmar Andersen (NOR)	2:20.4
1956	Yury Mikhaylov (URS); Yevgeny Grishin (URS) (tied)	2:08.6
1960	Yevgeny Grishin (URS); Roald Aas (NOR) (tied)	2:10.4
1964	Ants Antson (URS)	2:10.3
1968	Cornelis Verkerk (NED)	2:03.4
1972	Ard Schenk (NED)	2:02.96
1976	Jan Egil Storholt (NOR)	1:59.38
1980	Eric Heiden (USA)	1:55.44
1984	Gaetan Boucher (CAN)	1:58.36
1988	André Hoffmann (GDR)	1:52.06
1992	Johann Olav Koss (NOR)	1:54.81
1994	Johann Olav Koss (NOR)	1:51.29
1998	Ådne Søndrål (NOR)	1:47.87
2002	Derek Parra (USA)	1:43.95
2006	Enrico Fabris (ITA)	1:45.97
2010	Mark Tuitert (NED)	1:45.57

5,000 METERS

		MIN:SEC
1924	Clas Thunberg (FIN)	8:39.0
1928	Ivar Ballangrud (NOR)	8:50.5
1932	Irving Jaffee (USA)	9:40.8
1936	Ivar Ballangrud (NOR)	8:19.6
1948	Reidar Liaklev (NOR)	8:29.4
1952	Hjalmar Andersen (NOR)	8:10.6
1956	Boris Shilkov (URS)	7:48.7
1960	Viktor Kosichkin (URS)	7:51.3
1964	Knut Johannesen (NOR)	7:38.4
1968	Fred Anton Maier (NOR)	7:22.4
1972	Ard Schenk (NED)	7:23.61
1976	Sten Stensen (NOR)	7:24.48
1980	Eric Heiden (USA)	7:02.29
1984	Thomas Gustafson (SWE)	7:12.28
1988	Thomas Gustafson (SWE)	6:44.63
1992	Geir Karlstad (NOR)	6:59.97
1994	Johann Olav Koss (NOR)	6:34.96
1998	Gianni Romme (NED)	6:22.20
2002	Jochem Uytdehaage (NED)	6:14.66
2006	Chad Hedrick (USA)	6:14.68
2010	Sven Kramer (NED)	6:14.60

Winter Olympic Games (continued)

Speed Skating (men) (continued)

10,000 METERS		MIN:SEC
1924	Julius Skutnabb (FIN)	18:04.8
1932	Irving Jaffee (USA)	19:13.6
1936	Ivar Ballangrud (NOR)	17:24.3
1948	Ake Seyffarth (SWE)	17:26.3
1952	Hjalmar Andersen (NOR)	16:45.8
1956	Sigvard Ericsson (SWE)	16:35.9
1960	Knut Johannesen (NOR)	15:46.6
1964	Jonny Nilsson (SWE)	15:50.1
1968	Johnny Höglin (SWE)	15:23.6
1972	Ard Schenk (NED)	15:01.35
1976	Piet Kleine (NED)	14:50.59
1980	Eric Heiden (USA)	14:28.13
1984	Igor Malkov (URS)	14:39.90
1988	Thomas Gustafson (SWE)	13:48.20
1992	Bart Veldkamp (NED)	14:12.12
1994	Johann Olav Koss (NOR)	13:30.55
1998	Gianni Romme (NED)	13:15.33
2002	Jochem Uytdehaage (NED)	12:58.92
2006	Bob de Jong (NED)	13:01.57
2010	Lee Seung-Hoon (KOR)	12:58.55

COMBINED SPEED SKATING	
1924	Clas Thunberg (FIN)

TEAM PURSUIT		MIN:SEC
2006	Italy	3:44.46
2010	Canada	3:41.37

Speed Skating (women)

500 METERS		SEC
1960	Helga Haase (GER)	45.9
1964	Lidiya Skoblikova (URS)	45.0
1972	Anne Henning (USA)	43.33
1976	Sheila Young (USA)	42.76
1980	Karin Enke (GDR)	41.78
1984	Christa Rothenburger (GDR)	41.02
1988	Bonnie Blair (USA)	39.10
1992	Bonnie Blair (USA)	40.33
1994	Bonnie Blair (USA)	39.25
1998	Catriona LeMay Doan (CAN)	76.60[12]
2002	Catriona LeMay Doan (CAN)	74.75[12]
2006	Svetlana Zhurova (RUS)	76.57[12]
2010	Lee Sang-Hwa (KOR)	76.09[12]

1,000 METERS		MIN:SEC
1960	Klara Guseva (URS)	1:34.1
1964	Lidiya Skoblikova (URS)	1:32.6
1968	Carolina Geijssen (NED)	1:32.6
1972	Monika Pflug (FRG)	1:31.40
1976	Tatyana Averina (URS)	1:28.43
1980	Natalya Petruseva (URS)	1:24.10
1984	Karin Enke (GDR)	1:21.61
1988	Christa Rothenburger (GDR)	1:17.65
1992	Bonnie Blair (USA)	1:21.90
1994	Bonnie Blair (USA)	1:18.74
1998	Marianne Timmer (NED)	1:16.51
2002	Chris Witty (USA)	1:13.83
2006	Marianne Timmer (NED)	1:16.05
2010	Christine Nesbitt (CAN)	1:16.56

1,500 METERS		MIN:SEC
1960	Lidiya Skoblikova (URS)	2:25.2
1964	Lidiya Skoblikova (URS)	2:22.6
1968	Kaija Mustonen (FIN)	2:22.4
1972	Dianne Holum (USA)	2:20.85

Speed Skating (women) (continued)

1,500 METERS (CONTINUED)		MIN:SEC
1976	Galina Stepanskaya (URS)	2:16.58
1980	Annie Borckink (NED)	2:10.95
1984	Karin Enke (GDR)	2:03.42
1988	Yvonne van Gennip (NED)	2:00.68
1992	Jacqueline Börner (GER)	2:05.87
1994	Emese Hunyady (AUT)	2:02.19
1998	Marianne Timmer (NED)	1:57.58
2002	Anni Friesinger (GER)	1:54.02
2006	Cindy Klassen (CAN)	1:55.27
2010	Ireen Wüst (NED)	1:56.89

3,000 METERS		MIN:SEC
1960	Lidiya Skoblikova (URS)	5:14.3
1964	Lidiya Skoblikova (URS)	5:14.9
1968	Johanna Schut (NED)	4:56.2
1972	Christina Baas-Kaiser (NED)	4:52.14
1976	Tatyana Averina (URS)	4:45.19
1980	Björg Eva Jensen (NOR)	4:32.13
1984	Andrea Schöne (GDR)	4:24.79
1988	Yvonne van Gennip (NED)	4:11.94
1992	Gunda Niemann (GER)	4:19.90
1994	Svetlana Bazhanova (RUS)	4:17.43
1998	Gunda Niemann-Stirnemann (GER)	4:07.29
2002	Claudia Pechstein (GER)	3:57.70
2006	Ireen Wüst (NED)	4:02.43
2010	Martina Sablikova (CZE)	4:02.53

5,000 METERS		MIN:SEC
1988	Yvonne van Gennip (NED)	7:14.13
1992	Gunda Niemann (GER)	7:31.57
1994	Claudia Pechstein (GER)	7:14.37
1998	Claudia Pechstein (GER)	6:59.61
2002	Claudia Pechstein (GER)	6:46.91
2006	Clara Hughes (CAN)	6:59.07
2010	Martina Sablikova (CZE)	6:50.91

TEAM PURSUIT		MIN:SEC
2006	Germany	3:01.25
2010	Germany	3:02.82

Short-Track Speed Skating (men)

500 METERS		SEC
1994	Chae Ji-Hoon (KOR)	43.45
1998	Takafumi Nishitani (JPN)	42.862
2002	Marc Gagnon (CAN)	41.802
2006	Apolo Anton Ohno (USA)	41.935
2010	Charles Hamelin (CAN)	40.981

1,000 METERS		MIN:SEC
1992	Kim Ki-Hoon (KOR)	1:30.76
1994	Kim Ki-Hoon (KOR)	1:34.57
1998	Kim Dong Sung (KOR)	1:32.428
2002	Steven Bradbury (AUS)	1:29.109
2006	Ahn Hyun Soo (KOR)	1:26.739
2010	Lee Jung-Su (KOR)	1:23.747

1,500 METERS		MIN:SEC
2002	Apolo Anton Ohno (USA)	2:18.541
2006	Ahn Hyun Soo (KOR)	2:25.341
2010	Lee Jung-Su (KOR)	2:17.611

5,000-METER RELAY		MIN:SEC
1992	Republic of Korea	7:14.02
1994	Italy	7:11.74
1998	Canada	7:06.075

Winter Olympic Games (continued)

Short-Track Speed Skating (men) (continued)

5,000-METER RELAY (CONTINUED)

		MIN:SEC
2002	Canada	6:51.579
2006	Republic of Korea	6:43.376
2010	Canada	6:44.224

Short-Track Speed Skating (women)

500 METERS

		SEC
1992	Cathy Turner (USA)	47.04
1994	Cathy Turner (USA)	45.98
1998	Annie Perreault (CAN)	46.568
2002	Yang Yang (A) (CHN)	44.187
2006	Wang Meng (CHN)	44.345
2010	Wang Meng (CHN)	43.048

1,000 METERS

		MIN:SEC
1994	Chun Lee-Kyung (KOR)	1:36.87
1998	Chun Lee-Kyung (KOR)	1:42.776
2002	Yang Yang (A) (CHN)	1:36.391
2006	Jin Sun Yu (KOR)	1:32.859

Short-Track Speed Skating (women) (continued)

1,000 METERS (CONTINUED)

		MIN:SEC
2010	Wang Meng (CHN)	1:29.213

1,500 METERS

		MIN:SEC
2002	Ko Gi-Hyun (KOR)	2:31.581
2006	Jin Sun Yu (KOR)	2:23.494
2010	Zhou Yang (CHN)	2:16.993

3,000-METER RELAY

		MIN:SEC
1992	Canada	4:36.62
1994	Republic of Korea	4:26.64
1998	Republic of Korea	4:16.260
2002	Republic of Korea	4:12.793
2006	Republic of Korea	4:17.040
2010	China	4:06.610

Winter Pentathlon[13]

1948	Gustav Lindh (SWE)

[1]In 1992 the relay was 3 × 7.5 km; from 1994 to 2002 it was 4 × 7.5 km.   [2]Five men.   [3]Competition scored on points until 1994.   [4]From 1924 to 1952, the event was 18 km.   [5]Results of a 10- or 15-km classical leg determine the starting order of a 10- or 15-km freestyle leg, the first finisher of which is the overall winner; each leg was 15 km in the 2010 Games.   [6]Winner after disqualification of top finisher for drug use.   [7]From 1924 to 1960 the jumping was held on one 70-meter hill. In 1964 there were two events, one on a 70-meter and the other on an 80-meter hill; from 1968 to 1988 there were 70-meter and 90-meter events; from 1992 to 2002 there were 90-meter and 120-meter events; and in 2006 there were 95-meter and 125-meter events.   [8]In 2010 the competition format was changed to consist of only individual normal hill and large hill.   [9]In 1988 the event was 90 meters; from 1992 to 2002 it was 120 meters.   [10]Results of a 5- or 7.5-km classical leg determine the starting order of a 5-, 7.5-, or 10-km freestyle leg, the first finisher of which is the overall winner; each leg was 7.5 km in the 2010 Games.   [11]From 1956 to 1972 the relay was 3 × 5 km.   [12]Combined time for two runs.   [13]Included elements of cross-country skiing, downhill skiing, shooting, fencing, and horse riding.

XXIX Summer Olympic Games (2008)

The XXIX Summer Games were held in Beijing, China, 8–24 Aug 2008. Since the games, several athletes have been stripped of medals for having failed drug tests. New medalists are shown in this table.

EVENT	GOLD MEDALIST	PERFORMANCE	SILVER MEDALIST	BRONZE MEDALIST
Archery				
Men's individual	Viktor Ruban (UKR)	113–112	Park Kyung Mo (KOR)	Bair Badenov (RUS)
Men's team	South Korea	227–225	Italy	China
Women's individual	Zhang Juan Juan (CHN)	110–109	Park Sung Hyun (KOR)	Yun Ok Hee (KOR)
Women's team	South Korea	224–215	China	France
Badminton				
Men's singles	Lin Dan (CHN)	21–12, 21–8	Chong Wei Lee (MAS)	Chen Lin (CHN)
Men's doubles	Indonesia	12–21, 21–11, 21–16	China	South Korea
Women's singles	Zhang Ning (CHN)	21–12, 10–21, 21–18	Xia Xingfang (CHN)	Maria Kristin Yulianti (INA)
Women's doubles	China	21–15, 21–13	South Korea	China
Mixed doubles	South Korea	21–11, 21–17	Indonesia	China
Baseball				
	South Korea	3–2	Cuba	United States
Basketball				
Men	United States	118–107	Spain	Argentina
Women	United States	92–65	Australia	Russia
Boxing[1]				
48 kg (105.6 lb)	Zou Shiming (CHN)		Serdamba Purevdorj (MGL)	Paddy Barnes (IRL); Yampier Hernández (CUB)
51 kg (112.2 lb)	Somjit Jongjohor (THA)		Andris Laffita Hernández (CUB)	Vincenzo Picardi (ITA); Georgy Balakshin (RUS)

XXIX Summer Olympic Games (2008) (continued)

EVENT	GOLD MEDALIST	PERFORMANCE	SILVER MEDALIST	BRONZE MEDALIST
Boxing[1] (continued)				
54 kg (118.8 lb)	Badar-Uugan Enkhbat (MGL)		Yankiel León Alarcón (CUB)	Veaceslav Gojan (MDA); Bruno Julie (MRI)
57 kg (125.4 lb)	Vasyl Lomachenko (UKR)		Khedafi Djelkhir (FRA)	Yakup Kilic (TUR); Shahin Imranov (AZE)
60 kg (132 lb)	Aleksey Tishchenko (RUS)		Daouda Sow (FRA)	Hrachik Javakhyan (ARM); Yordenis Ugás (CUB)
64 kg (140.8)	Félix Díaz (DOM)		Manus Boonjumnong (THA)	Alexis Vastine (FRA); Roniel Iglesias Sotolongo (CUB)
69 kg (151.8 lb)	Bakhyt Sarsekbayev (KAZ)		Carlos Banteaux Suárez (CUB)	Kim Jung Joo (KOR); Hanati Silamu (CHN)
75 kg (165 lb)	James Degale (GBR)		Emilio Correa Bayeaux (CUB)	Darren John Sutherland (IRL); Vijender Kumar (IND)
81 kg (178.2 lb)	Zhang Xiaoping (CHN)		Kenny Egan (IRL)	Yerkebulan Shynaliyev (KAZ); Tony Jeffries (GBR)
91 kg (200.2 lb)	Rakhim Chakhkiyev (RUS)		Clemente Russo (ITA)	Osmay Acosta Duarte (CUB); Deontay Wilder (USA)
91+ kg (200.2+ lb)	Roberto Cammarelle (ITA)		Zhang Zhilei (CHN)	David Price (GBR); Vyacheslav Glazkov (UKR)

Canoeing
Men

500-m kayak singles	Ken Wallace (AUS)	1 min 37.252 sec	Adam van Koeverden (CAN)	Tim Brabants (GBR)
1,000-m kayak singles	Tim Brabants (GBR)	3 min 26.323 sec	Eirik Verås Larsen (NOR)	Ken Wallace (AUS)
500-m kayak pairs	Spain	1 min 28.736 sec	Germany	Belarus
1,000-m kayak pairs	Germany	3 min 11.809 sec	Denmark	Italy
1,000-m kayak fours	Belarus	2 min 55.714 sec	Slovakia	Germany
Slalom kayak singles	Alexander Grimm (GER)	171.70 pt	Fabien Lefèvre (FRA)	Benjamin Boukpeti (TOG)
500-m Canadian singles	Maksim Opalev (RUS)	1 min 47.140 sec	David Cal (ESP)	Iurii Cheban (UKR)
1,000-m Canadian singles	Attila Sándor Vajda (HUN)	3 min 50.467 sec	David Cal (ESP)	Thomas Hall (CAN)
500-m Canadian pairs	China	1 min 41.025 sec	Russia	Germany
1,000-m Canadian pairs	Belarus	3 min 36.365 sec	Germany	Hungary
Slalom Canadian singles	Michal Martikan (SVK)	176.65 pt	David Florence (GBR)	Robin Bell (AUS)
Slalom Canadian pairs	Slovakia	190.82 pt	Czech Republic	Russia

Women

500-m kayak singles	Inna Osypenko-Radomska (UKR)	1 min 50.673 sec	Josefa Idem (ITA)	Katrin Wagner-Augustin (GER)
500-m kayak pairs	Hungary	1 min 41.308 sec	Poland	France
500-m kayak fours	Germany	1 min 32.231 sec	Hungary	Australia
Slalom kayak singles	Elena Kaliska (SVK)	192.64 pt	Jacqueline Lawrence (AUS)	Violetta Oblinger Peters (AUT)

Cycling
Men

Road race	Samuel Sánchez (ESP)	6 hr 23 min 49 sec	*medalist stripped of medal*	Fabian Cancellara (SUI)
Individual road time trial	Fabian Cancellara (SUI)	1 hr 2 min 11.43 sec	Gustav Larsson (SWE)	Levi Leipheimer (USA)
Individual pursuit	Bradley Wiggins (GBR)	4 min 16.977 sec	Hayden Roulston (NZL)	Steven Burke (GBR)
Team pursuit	Great Britain	3 min 53.314 sec	Denmark	New Zealand
Individual sprint	Chris Hoy (GBR)		Jason Kenny (GBR)	Mickaël Bourgain (FRA)

XXIX Summer Olympic Games (2008) (continued)

EVENT	GOLD MEDALIST	PERFORMANCE	SILVER MEDALIST	BRONZE MEDALIST
Cycling (continued)				
Men (continued)				
Team sprint	Great Britain	43.128 sec	France	Germany
Individual points race	Joan Llaneras (ESP)	60 pt	Roger Kluge (GER)	Chris Newton (GBR)
Madison	Argentina		Spain	Russia
Keirin	Chris Hoy (GBR)		Ross Edgar (GBR)	Kiyofumi Nagai (JPN)
Mountain bike	Julien Absalon (FRA)	1 hr 55 min 59 sec	Jean-Christophe Péraud (FRA)	Nino Schurter (SUI)
Motocross/BMX	Maris Strombergs (LAT)	36.190 sec	Mike Day (USA)	Donny Robinson (USA)
Women				
Road race	Nicole Cooke (GBR)	3 hr 32 min 24 sec	Emma Johansson (SWE)	Tatiana Guderzo (ITA)
Individual road time trial	Kristin Armstrong (USA)	34 min 51.72 sec	Emma Pooley (GBR)	Karin Thürig (SUI)
Individual pursuit	Rebecca Romero (GBR)	3 min 28.321 sec	Wendy Houvenaghel (GBR)	Lesya Kalitovska (UKR)
Individual sprint	Victoria Pendleton (GBR)		Anna Meares (AUS)	Guo Shuang (CHN)
Individual points race	Marianne Vos (NED)	30 pt	Yoanka González (CUB)	Leire Olaberria (ESP)
Mountain bike	Sabine Spitz (GER)	1 hr 45 min 11 sec	Maja Wloszczowska (POL)	Irina Kalentiyeva (RUS)
Motocross/BMX	Anne-Caroline Chausson (FRA)	35.976 sec	Laëtitia Le Corguillé (FRA)	Jill Kintner (USA)
Diving				
Men				
3-m springboard	He Chong (CHN)	572.90 pt	Alexandre Despatie (CAN)	Qin Kai (CHN)
10-m platform	Matt Mitcham (AUS)	537.95 pt	Zhou Luxin (CHN)	Gleb Galperin (RUS)
3-m synchronized springboard	China	469.08 pt	Russia	Ukraine
10-m synchronized platform	China	468.18 pt	Germany	Russia
Women				
3-m springboard	Guo Jingjing (CHN)	415.35 pt	Yuliya Pakhalina (RUS)	Wu Minxia (CHN)
10-m platform	Chen Ruolin (CHN)	447.70 pt	Émilie Heymans (CAN)	Wang Xin (CHN)
3-m synchronized springboard	China	343.50 pt	Russia	Germany
10-m synchronized platform	China	363.54 pt	Australia	Mexico
Equestrian				
Individual 3-day event	Hinrich Romeike (GER)		Gina Miles (USA)	Kristina Cook (GBR)
Team 3-day event	Germany		Australia	Great Britain
Individual dressage	Anky van Grunsven (NED)		Isabell Werth (GER)	Heike Kemmer (GER)
Team dressage	Germany		Netherlands	Denmark
Individual jumping	Eric Lamaze (CAN)		Rolf-Göran Bengtsson (SWE)	Beezie Madden (USA)
Team jumping	United States		Canada	Switzerland
Fencing				
Men				
Individual foil	Benjamin Philip Kleibrink (GER)		Yuki Ota (JPN)	Salvatore Sanzo (ITA)
Individual épée	Matteo Tagliariol (ITA)		Fabrice Jeannet (FRA)	José Luis Abajo (ESP)
Team épée	France		Poland	Italy
Individual sabre	Zhong Man (CHN)		Nicolas Lopez (FRA)	Mihai Covaliu (ROM)
Team sabre	France		United States	Italy
Women				
Individual foil	Valentina Vezzali (ITA)		Nam Hyun Hee (KOR)	Margherita Granbassi (ITA)
Team foil	Russia		United States	Italy
Individual épée	Britta Heidemann (GER)		Ana Maria Branza (ROM)	Ildikó Mincza-Nébald (HUN)
Individual sabre	Mariel Zagunis (USA)		Sada Jacobson (USA)	Becca Ward (USA)
Team sabre	Ukraine		China	United States

XXIX Summer Olympic Games (2008) (continued)

EVENT	GOLD MEDALIST	PERFORMANCE	SILVER MEDALIST	BRONZE MEDALIST
Field Hockey				
Men	Germany	1–0	Spain	Australia
Women	The Netherlands	2–0	China	Argentina
Gymnastics				
Men				
Team	China	286.125 pt	Japan	United States
All-around	Yang Wei (CHN)	94.575 pt	Kohei Uchimura (JPN)	Benoît Caranobe (FRA)
Floor exercise	Zou Kai (CHN)	16.050 pt	Gervasio Deferr (ESP)	Anton Golotsutskov (RUS)
Vault	Leszek Blanik (POL)	16.537 pt	Thomas Bouhail (FRA)	Anton Golotsutskov (RUS)
Pommel horse	Xiao Qin (CHN)	15.875 pt	Filip Ude (CRO)	Louis Smith (GBR)
Rings	Chen Yibing (CHN)	16.600 pt	Yang Wei (CHN)	Oleksandr Vorobiov (UKR)
Parallel bars	Li Xiaopeng (CHN)	16.450 pt	Yoo Won Chul (KOR)	Anton Fokin (UZB)
Horizontal bar	Zou Kai (CHN)	16.200 pt	Jonathan Horton (USA)	Fabian Hambüchen (GER)
Trampoline	Lu Chunlong (CHN)	41.00 pt	Jason Burnett (CAN)	Dong Dong (CHN)
Women				
Team	China	188.900 pt	United States	Romania
All-around	Nastia Liukin (USA)	63.325 pt	Shawn Johnson (USA)	Yang Yilin (CHN)
Floor exercise	Sandra Izbasa (ROM)	15.650 pt	Shawn Johnson (USA)	Nastia Liukin (USA)
Vault	Hong Un Jong (PRK)	15.650 pt	Oksana Chusovitina (GER)	Cheng Fei (CHN)
Uneven bars	He Kexin (CHN)	16.725 pt	Nastia Liukin (USA)	Yang Yilin (CHN)
Balance beam	Shawn Johnson (USA)	16.225 pt	Nastia Liukin (USA)	Cheng Fei (CHN)
Trampoline	He Wenna (CHN)	37.80 pt	Karen Cockburn (CAN)	Ekaterina Khilko (UZB)
Individual rhythmic	Yevgeniya Kanayeva (RUS)	75.500 pt	Inna Zhukova (BLR)	Anna Bessonova (UKR)
Team rhythmic	Russia	35.550 pt	China	Belarus
Handball (Team)				
Men	France	15–10, 13–13	Iceland	Spain
Women	Norway	18–13, 16–14	Russia	South Korea
Judo[1]				
Men				
60 kg (132 lb)	Choi Min Ho (KOR)		Ludwig Paischer (AUT)	Rishod Sobirov (UZB); Ruben Houkes (NED)
66 kg (145.2 lb)	Masato Uchishiba (JPN)		Benjamin Darbelet (FRA)	Yordanis Arencibia (CUB); Pak Chol Min (PRK)
73 kg (160.6 lb)	Elnur Mammadli (AZE)		Wang Ki Chun (KOR)	Rasul Boqiev (TJK); Leandro Guilheiro (BRA)
81 kg (178.2 lb)	Ole Bischof (GER)		Kim Jae Bum (KOR)	Tiago Camilo (BRA); Roman Gontiuk (UKR)
90 kg (198 lb)	Irakli Tsirekidze (GEO)		Amar Benikhlef (ALG)	Hesham Mesbah (EGY); Sergei Aschwanden (SUI)
100 kg (220 lb)	Tuvshinbayar Naidan (MGL)		Askhat Zhitkeyev (KAZ)	Movlud Miraliyev (AZE); Henk Grol (NED)
100+ kg (220+ lb)	Satoshi Ishii (JPN)		Abdullo Tangriev (UZB)	Oscar Brayson (CUB); Teddy Riner (FRA)
Women				
48 kg (105.6 lb)	Alina Alexandra Dumitru (ROM)		Yanet Bermoy (CUB)	Paula Belén Pareto (ARG); Ryoko Tani (JPN)
52 kg (114.4 lb)	Xian Dongmei (CHN)		An Kum Ae (PRK)	Soraya Haddad (ALG), Misato Nakamura (JPN)

XXIX Summer Olympic Games (2008) (continued)

EVENT	GOLD MEDALIST	PERFORMANCE	SILVER MEDALIST	BRONZE MEDALIST
Judo[1] (continued)				
Women (continued)				
57 kg (125.4 lb)	Giulia Quintavalle (ITA)		Deborah Gravenstijn (NED)	Ketleyn Quadros (BRA); Xu Yan (CHN)
63 kg (138.6 lb)	Ayumi Tanimoto (JPN)		Lucie Décosse (FRA)	Elisabeth Wille-boordse (NED); Won Ok Im (PRK)
70 kg (154 lb)	Masae Ueno (JPN)		Anaysi Hernández (CUB)	Ronda Rousey (USA); Edith Bosch (NED)
78 kg (171.6 lb)	Yang Xiuli (CHN)		Yalennis Castillo (CUB)	Jeong Gyeong Mi (KOR); Stéphanie Possamaï (FRA)
78+ kg (171.6 lb)	Tong Wen (CHN)		Maki Tsukada (JPN)	Lucija Polavder (SLO); Idalys Ortiz (CUB)
Modern Pentathlon				
Men	Andrey Moiseyev (RUS)		Edvinas Krungolcas (LTU)	Andrejus Zadneprovskis (LTU)
Women	Lena Schöneborn (GER)		Heather Fell (GBR)	Victoria Tereshuk (UKR)
Rowing				
Men				
Single sculls	Olaf Tufte (NOR)	6 min 59.83 sec	Ondrej Synek (CZE)	Mahe Drysdale (NZL)
Double sculls	Australia	6 min 27.77 sec	Estonia	Great Britain
Quadruple sculls	Poland	5 min 41.33 sec	Italy	France
Coxless pairs (oars)	Australia	6 min 37.44 sec	Canada	New Zealand
Coxless fours (oars)	Great Britain	6 min 06.57 sec	Australia	France
Eights	Canada	5 min 23.89 sec	Great Britain	United States
Lightweight double sculls	Great Britain	6 min 10.99 sec	Greece	Denmark
Lightweight fours	Denmark	5 min 47.76 sec	Poland	Canada
Women				
Single sculls	Rumyana Neykova (BUL)	7 min 22.34 sec	Michelle Guerette (USA)	Yekaterina Karsten (BLR)
Double sculls	New Zealand	7 min 07.32 sec	Germany	Great Britain
Quadruple sculls	China	6 min 16.06 sec	Great Britain	Germany
Coxless pairs (oars)	Romania	7 min 20.60 sec	China	Belarus
Eights	United States	6 min 05.34 sec	The Netherlands	Romania
Lightweight double sculls	The Netherlands	6 min 54.74 sec	Finland	Canada
Sailing				
Men's 470	Australia		Great Britain	France
Women's 470	Australia		The Netherlands	Brazil
Men's RS:X	Tom Ashley (NZL)		Julien Bontemps (FRA)	Shahar Zubari (ISR)
Women's RS:X	Yin Jian (CHN)		Alessandra Sensini (ITA)	Bryony Shaw (GBR)
Open Finn	Ben Ainslie (GBR)		Zach Railey (USA)	Guillaume Florent (FRA)
Women's Yngling	Great Britain		The Netherlands	Greece
Open 49er	Denmark		Spain	Germany
Men's Laser	Paul Goodison (GBR)		Vasilij Zbogar (SLO)	Diego Romero (ITA)
Women's Laser Radial	Anna Tunnicliffe (USA)		Gintare Volungeviciute (LTU)	Xu Lijia (CHN)
Men's Star	Great Britain		Brazil	Sweden
Open Tornado	Spain		Australia	Argentina
Shooting				
Men				
Rapid-fire pistol	Oleksandr Petriv (UKR)	780.2 pt[3]	Ralf Schumann (GER)	Christian Reitz (GER)
Free pistol	Jin Jong Oh (KOR)	660.4 pt	Tan Zongliang (CHN)	Vladimir Isakov (RUS)
Air pistol	Pang Wei (CHN)	688.2 pt	Jin Jong Oh (KOR)	Jason Turner (USA)
Small-bore (sport) rifle, 3 positions	Qiu Jian (CHN)	1272.5 pt	Jury Sukhorukov (UKR)	Rajmond Debevec (SLO)
Small-bore (sport) rifle, prone	Artur Ayvazian (UKR)	702.7 pt	Matthew Emmons (USA)	Warren Potent (AUS)

XXIX Summer Olympic Games (2008) (continued)

EVENT	GOLD MEDALIST	PERFORMANCE	SILVER MEDALIST	BRONZE MEDALIST
Shooting (continued				
Men (continued)				
Air rifle	Abhinav Bindra (IND)	700.5 pt	Zhu Qinan (CHN)	Henri Häkkinen (FIN)
Trap	David Kostelecky (CZE)	146.0 pt^3	Giovanni Pellielo (ITA)	Aleksey Alipov (RUS)
Double trap	Walton Eller (USA)	190.0 pt^3	Francesco D'Aniello (ITA)	Hu Binyuan (CHN)
Skeet	Vincent Hancock (USA)	145.0 pt^3	Tore Brovold (NOR)	Anthony Terras (FRA)
Women				
Pistol	Chen Ying (CHN)	793.4 pt^3	Gundegmaa Otryad (MGL)	Munkhbayar Dorj-suren (GER)
Air pistol	Guo Wenjun (CHN)	492.3 pt^3	Natalya Paderina (RUS)	Nino Salukvadze (GEO)
Small-bore (sport) rifle, 3 positions	Du Li (CHN)	690.3 pt^3	Katerina Emmons (CZE)	Eglis Yaima Cruz (CUB)
Air rifle	Katerina Emmons (CZE)	503.5 pt^3	Lyubov Galkina (RUS)	Snjezana Pejcic (CRO)
Trap	Satu Mäkelä-Nummela (FIN)	91.0 pt^3	Zuzana Stefecekova (SVK)	Corey Cogdell (USA)
Skeet	Chiara Cainero (ITA)	93.0 pt^3	Kimberly Rhode (USA)	Christina Brinker (GER)

Soccer (Association Football)				
Men	Argentina	1–0	Nigeria	Brazil
Women	United States	1–0	Brazil	Germany

Softball				
	Japan	3–1	United States	Australia

Swimming				
Men				
50-m freestyle	César Cielo Filho (BRA)	21.30 sec^3	Amaury Leveaux (FRA)	Alain Bernard (FRA)
100-m freestyle	Alain Bernard (FRA)	47.21 sec	Eamon Sullivan (AUS)	César Cielo Filho (BRA); Jason Lezak (USA) (tied)
200-m freestyle	Michael Phelps (USA)	1 min 42.96 sec^2	Park Tae Hwan (KOR)	Peter Vanderkaay (USA)
400-m freestyle	Park Tae Hwan (KOR)	3 min 41.86 sec	Zhang Lin (CHN)	Larsen Jensen (USA)
1,500-m freestyle	Oussama Mellouli (TUN)	14 min 40.84 sec	Grant Hackett (AUS)	Ryan Cochrane (CAN)
100-m backstroke	Aaron Peirsol (USA)	52.54 sec^2	Matt Grevers (USA)	Hayden Stoeckel (AUS); Arkady Vyat-chanin (RUS) (tied)
200-m backstroke	Ryan Lochte (USA)	1 min 53.94 sec^2	Aaron Peirsol (USA)	Arkady Vyatchanin (RUS)
100-m breaststroke	Kosuke Kitajima (JPN)	58.91 sec^2	Alexander Dale Oen (NOR)	Hugues Duboscq (FRA)
200-m breaststroke	Kosuke Kitajima (JPN)	2 min 07.64 sec^3	Brenton Rickard (AUS)	Hugues Duboscq (FRA)
100-m butterfly	Michael Phelps (USA)	50.58 sec^3	Milorad Cavic (SRB)	Andrew Lauterstein (AUS)
200-m butterfly	Michael Phelps (USA)	1 min 52.03 sec^2	László Cseh (HUN)	Takeshi Matsuda (JPN)
200-m individual medley	Michael Phelps (USA)	1 min 54.23 sec^2	László Cseh (HUN)	Ryan Lochte (USA)
400-m individual medley	Michael Phelps (USA)	4 min 03.84 sec^2	László Cseh (HUN)	Ryan Lochte (USA)
10-km open-water marathon	Maarten van der Weijden (NED)	1 hr 51 min 51.60 sec	David Davies (GBR)	Thomas Lurz (GER)
4 x 100-m freestyle relay	United States	3 min 08.24 sec^2	France	Australia
4 x 200-m freestyle relay	United States	6 min 58.56 sec^2	Russia	Australia
4 x 100-m medley relay	United States	3 min 29.34 sec^2	Australia	Japan
Women				
50 m freestyle	Britta Steffen (GER)	24.06 sec^3	Dara Torres (USA)	Cate Campbell (AUS)
100-m freestyle	Britta Steffen (GER)	53.12 sec^3	Lisbeth Lenton Trickett (AUS)	Natalie Coughlin (USA)

XXIX Summer Olympic Games (2008) (continued)

Swimming (continued)
Women (continued)

EVENT	GOLD MEDALIST	PERFORMANCE	SILVER MEDALIST	BRONZE MEDALIST
200-m freestyle	Federica Pellegrini (ITA)	1 min 54.82 sec[2]	Sara Isakovic (SLO)	Pang Jiaying (CHN)
400-m freestyle	Rebecca Adlington (GBR)	4 min 03.22 sec	Katie Hoff (USA)	Joanne Jackson (GBR)
800-m freestyle	Rebecca Adlington (GBR)	8 min 14.10 sec[2]	Alessia Filippi (ITA)	Lotte Friis (DEN)
100-m backstroke	Natalie Coughlin (USA)	58.96 sec	Kirsty Coventry (ZIM)	Margaret Hoelzer (USA)
200-m backstroke	Kirsty Coventry (ZIM)	2 min 05.24 sec[2]	Margaret Hoelzer (USA)	Reiko Nakamura (JPN)
100-m breaststroke	Leisel Jones (AUS)	1 min 05.17 sec[3]	Rebecca Soni (USA)	Mirna Jukic (AUT)
200-m breaststroke	Rebecca Soni (USA)	2 min 20.22 sec[2]	Leisel Jones (AUS)	Sara Nordenstam (NOR)
100-m butterfly	Lisbeth Lenton Trickett (AUS)	56.73 sec	Christine Magnuson (USA)	Jessicah Schipper (AUS)
200-m butterfly	Liu Zige (CHN)	2 min 04.18 sec[2]	Jiao Liuyang (CHN)	Jessicah Schipper (AUS)
200-m individual medley	Stephanie Rice (AUS)	2 min 08.45 sec[2]	Kirsty Coventry (ZIM)	Natalie Coughlin (USA)
400-m individual medley	Stephanie Rice (AUS)	4 min 29.45 sec[2]	Kirsty Coventry (ZIM)	Katie Hoff (USA)
10-km open-water marathon	Larisa Ilchenko (RUS)	1 hr 59 min 27.70 sec	Keri-Anne Payne (GBR)	Cassandra Patten (GBR)
4 x 100-m freestyle relay	The Netherlands	3 min 33.76 sec[3]	United States	Australia
4 x 200-m freestyle relay	Australia	7 min 44.31 sec[2]	China	United States
4 x 100-m medley relay	Australia	3 min 52.69 sec[2]	United States	China

Synchronized Swimming

Duet	Russia	99.251 pt	Spain	Japan
Team	Russia	99.500 pt	Spain	China

Table Tennis

Men's singles	Ma Lin (CHN)	11–9, 11–9, 6–11, 11–7, 11–9	Wang Hao (CHN)	Wang Liqin (CHN)
Men's team	China	3–0	Germany	South Korea
Women's singles	Zhang Yining (CHN)	8–11, 13–11, 11–8, 11–8, 11–3	Wang Nan (CHN)	Guo Yue (CHN)
Women's team	China	3–0	Singapore	South Korea

Taekwondo[1]
Men

58 kg (127.6 lb)	Guillermo Pérez (MEX)		Yulis Gabriel Mercedes (DOM)	Chu Mu-yen (TPE); Rohullah Nikpai (AFG)
68 kg (149.6 lb)	Son Tae Jin (KOR)		Mark Lopez (USA)	Sung Yu-chi (TPE); Servet Tazegul (TUR)
80 kg (176 lb)	Hadi Saei (IRI)		Mauro Sarmiento (ITA)	Steven Lopez (USA); Zhu Guo (CHN)
80+ kg (176+ lb)	Cha Dong Min (KOR)		Alexandros Nikolaidis (GRE)	Arman Chilmanov (KAZ); Chika Yagazie Chukwumerije (NGR)

Women

49 kg (107.8 lb)	Wu Jingyu (CHN)		Buttree Puedpong (THA)	Dalia Contreras Rivero (VEN); Daynellis Montejo (CUB)
57 kg (125.4 lb)	Lim Su Jeong (KOR)		Azize Tanrikulu (TUR)	Diana Lopez (USA); Martina Zubcic (CRO)
67 kg (147.4 lb)	Hwang Kyung Seon (KOR)		Karine Sergerie (CAN)	Gwladys Patience Epangue (FRA); Sandra Saric (CRO)
67+ kg (147.4+ lb)	María del Rosario Espinoza (MEX)		Nina Solheim (NOR)	Natalia Falavigna (BRA); Sarah Stevenson (GBR)

XXIX Summer Olympic Games (2008) (continued)

EVENT	GOLD MEDALIST	PERFORMANCE	SILVER MEDALIST	BRONZE MEDALIST
Tennis				
Men's singles	Rafael Nadal (ESP)	6–3, 7–6, 6–3	Fernando González (CHI)	Novak Djokovic (SRB)
Men's doubles	Switzerland	6–3, 6–4, 6–7, 6–3	Sweden	United States
Women's singles	Yelena Dementyeva (RUS)	3–6, 7–5, 6–3	Dinara Safina (RUS)	Vera Zvonareva (RUS)
Women's doubles	United States	6–2, 6–0	Spain	China

Track and Field (Athletics)

EVENT	GOLD MEDALIST	PERFORMANCE	SILVER MEDALIST	BRONZE MEDALIST
Men				
100 m	Usain Bolt (JAM)	9.69 sec[2]	Richard Thompson (TRI)	Walter Dix (USA)
200 m	Usain Bolt (JAM)	19.30 sec[2]	Shawn Crawford (USA)	Walter Dix (USA)
400 m	LaShawn Merritt (USA)	43.75 sec	Jeremy Wariner (USA)	David Neville (USA)
4 x 100-m relay	Jamaica	37.10 sec[2]	Trinidad and Tobago	Japan
4 x 400-m relay	United States	2 min 55.39 sec[3]	The Bahamas	Russia
800 m	Wilfred Bungei (KEN)	1 min 44.65 sec	Ismail Ahmed Ismail (SUD)	Alfred Kirwa Yego (KEN)
1,500 m	*winner stripped of medal*		Asbel Kipruto Kiprop (KEN)	Nicholas Willis (NZL)
5,000 m	Kenenisa Bekele (ETH)	12 min 57.82 sec[3]	Eliud Kipchoge (KEN)	Edwin Cheruiyot Soi (KEN)
10,000 m	Kenenisa Bekele (ETH)	27 min 01.17 sec[3]	Sileshi Sihine (ETH)	Micah Kogo (KEN)
Marathon	Samuel Kamau Wansiru (KEN)	2 hr 06 min 32 sec[3]	Jaouad Gharib (MAR)	Tsegay Kedebe (ETH)
110-m hurdles	Dayron Robles (CUB)	12.93 sec	David Payne (USA)	David Oliver (USA)
400-m hurdles	Angelo Taylor (USA)	47.25 sec	Kerron Clement (USA)	Bershawn Jackson (USA)
3,000-m steeple-chase	Brimin Kiprop Kipruto (KEN)	8 min 10.34 sec	Mahiedine Mekhissi-Benabbad (FRA)	Richard Kipkemboi Mateelong (KEN)
20,000-m walk	Valery Borchin (RUS)	1 hour 19 min 01 sec	Jefferson Pérez (ECU)	Jared Tallent (AUS)
50,000-m walk	Alex Schwazer (ITA)	3 hr 37 min 09 sec[3]	Jared Tallent (AUS)	Denis Nizhegorodov (RUS)
High jump	Andrey Silnov (RUS)	2.36 m	Germaine Mason (GBR)	Yaroslav Rybakov (RUS)
Long jump	Irving Jahir Saladino Aranda (PAN)	8.34 m	Khotso Mokoena (RSA)	Ibrahim Camejo (CUB)
Triple jump	Nelson Évora (POR)	17.67 m	Phillips Idowu (GBR)	Leevan Sands (BAH)
Pole vault	Steve Hooker (AUS)	5.96 m[3]	Yevgeny Lukyanenko (RUS)	Denys Yurchenko (UKR)
Shot put	Tomasz Majewski (POL)	21.51 m	Christian Cantwell (USA)	Andrei Mikhnevich (BLR)
Discus throw	Gerd Kanter (EST)	68.82 m	Piotr Malachowski (POL)	Virgilijus Alekna (LTU)
Javelin throw	Andreas Thorkildsen (NOR)	90.57 m[3]	Ainars Kovals (LAT)	Tero Pitkämäki (FIN)
Hammer throw	Primoz Kozmus (SLO)	82.02 m	Vadim Devyatovskiy (BLR)	Ivan Tsikhan (BLR)
Decathlon	Bryan Clay (USA)	8,791 pt	Andrei Krauchanka (BLR)	Leonel Suárez (CUB)
Women				
100 m	Shelly-Ann Fraser (JAM)	10.78 sec	Sherone Simpson (JAM); Kerron Stewart (JAM) (tied)	
200 m	Veronica Campbell-Brown (JAM)	21.74 sec	Allyson Felix (USA)	Kerron Stewart (JAM)
400 m	Christine Ohuruogu (GBR)	49.62 sec	Shericka Williams (JAM)	Sanya Richards (USA)
4 x 100-m relay	Russia	42.31 sec	Belgium	Nigeria
4 x 400-m relay	United States	3 min 18.54 sec	Russia	Jamaica
800 m	Pamela Jelimo (KEN)	1 min 54.87 sec	Janeth Jepkosgei Busienei (KEN)	Hasna Benhassi (MAR)
1,500 m	Nancy Jebet Langat (KEN)	4 min 00.23 sec	Iryna Lishchynska (UKR)	Nataliya Tobias (UKR)
5,000 m	Tirunesh Dibaba (ETH)	15 min 41.40 sec	Elvan Abeylegesse (TUR)	Meseret Defar (ETH)
10,000 m	Tirunesh Dibaba (ETH)	29 min 54.66 sec[3]	Elvan Abeylegesse (TUR)	Shalane Flanagan (USA)
Marathon	Constantina Tomescu (ROM)	2 hr 26 min 44 sec	Catherine Ndereba (KEN)	Zhou Chunxiu (CHN)
100-m hurdles	Dawn Harper (USA)	12.54 sec	Sally McLellan (AUS)	Priscilla Lopes Schliep (CAN)
400-m hurdles	Melaine Walker (JAM)	52.64 sec[3]	Sheena Tosta (USA)	Tasha Danvers (GBR)

XXIX Summer Olympic Games (2008) (continued)

EVENT	GOLD MEDALIST	PERFORMANCE	SILVER MEDALIST	BRONZE MEDALIST
Track and Field (Athletics) (continued)				
Women (continued)				
3,000-m steeplechase	Gulnara Samitova-Galkina (RUS)	8 min 58.81 sec^2	Eunice Jepkorir (ETH)	Yekaterina Volkova (RUS)
20-km walk	Olga Kaniskina (RUS)	1 hr 26 min 31 sec^3	Kjersti Tysse Plätzer (NOR)	Elisa Rigaudo (ITA)
High jump	Tia Hellebaut (BEL)	2.05 m	Blanka Vlasic (CRO)	Anna Chicherova (RUS)
Long jump	Maurren Higa Maggi (BRA)	7.04 m	Tatyana Lebedeva (RUS)	Blessing Okagbare (NGR)
Triple jump	Françoise Mbango Etone (CMR)	15.39 m^3	Tatyana Lebedeva (RUS)	Hrysopiyi Devetzi (GRE)
Pole vault	Yelena Isinbayeva (RUS)	5.05 m^2	Jennifer Stuczynski (USA)	Svetlana Feofanova (RUS)
Shot put	Valerie Vili (NZL)	20.56 m	Natallia Mikhnevich (BLR)	Nadzeya Ostapchuk (BLR)
Discus throw	Stephanie Brown Trafton (USA)	64.74 m	Yarelys Barrios (CUB)	Olena Antonova (UKR)
Javelin throw	Barbora Spotakova (CZE)	71.42 m	Mariya Abakumova (RUS)	Christina Obergfoll (GER)
Hammer throw	Aksana Miankova (BLR)	76.34 m^3	Yipsi Moreno (CUB)	Zhang Wenxiu (CHN)
Heptathlon	Nataliya Dobrynska (UKR)	6,733 pt	Hyleas Fountain (USA)	Tatyana Chernova (RUS)

Triathlon

Men	Jan Frodeno (GER)	1 hr 48 min 53.28 sec	Simon Whitfield (CAN)	Bevan Docherty (NZL)
Women	Emma Snowsill (AUS)	1 hr 58 min 27.66 sec	Vanessa Fernandes (POR)	Emma Moffatt (AUS)

Volleyball

Men's indoor	United States	20–25, 25–22, 25–21, 25–23, 25–23	Brazil	Russia
Women's indoor	Brazil	25–15, 18–25, 25–13, 25–21	United States	China
Men's beach	United States	23–21, 17–21, 15–4	Brazil	Brazil
Women's beach	United States	21–18, 21–18	China	China

Water Polo

Men	Hungary	14–10	United States	Serbia
Women	The Netherlands	9–8	United States	Australia

Weight Lifting

Men

56 kg (123.2 lb)	Long Qingquan (CHN)	292.0	Hoang Anh Tuan (VIE)	Eko Yuli Irawan (INA)
62 kg (136.4 lb)	Zhang Xiangxiang (CHN)	319.0 kg	Diego Salazar (COL)	Triyatno (INA)
69 kg (151.8 lb)	Liao Hui (CHN)	348.0 kg	Vencelas Dabaya-Tientcheu (FRA)	Tigran Gevorg Martirosyan (ARM)
77 kg (169.4 lb)	Sa Jae Hyouk (KOR)	366.0 kg	Li Hongli (CHN)	Gevorg Davtyan (ARM)
85 kg (187 lb)	Lu Yong (CHN)	394.0 kg	Andrei Rybakou (BLR)	Tigran Varban Martirosyan (ARM)
94 kg (206.8 lb)	Ilya Ilin (KAZ)	406.0 kg	Szymon Kolecki (POL)	Khadzhimurat Akkayev (RUS)
105 kg (231 lb)	Andrei Aramnau (BLR)	436.0 kg^2	Dmitry Klokov (RUS)	Dmitry Lapikov (RUS)
105+ kg (231+ lb)	Matthias Steiner (GER)	461.0 kg	Yevgeny Chigishev (RUS)	Viktors Scerbatihs (LAT)

Women

48 kg (105.6 lb)	Chen Xiexia (CHN)	212.0 kg^3	Sibel Ozkan (TUR)	Chen Wei-ling (TPE)
53 kg (116.6 lb)	Prapawadee Jaroenrattanatarakoon (THA)	221.0 kg	Yoon Jinhee (KOR)	Nastassia Novikava (BLR)
58 kg (127.6 lb)	Chen Yanqing (CHN)	244.0 kg^3	Marina Shainova (RUS)	O Jong Ae (PRK)
63 kg (138.6 lb)	Pak Hyon Suk (PRK)	241.0 kg	Irina Nekrassova (KAZ)	Lu Ying-chi (TPE)
69 kg (151.8 lb)	Liu Chunhong (CHN)	286.0 kg^2	Oksana Slivenko (RUS)	Natalya Davydova (UKR)
75 kg (165 lb)	Cao Lei (CHN)	282.0 kg^3	Alla Vazhenina (KAZ)	Nadezda Yevstyukhina (RUS)
75+ kg (165 lb)	Jang Mi Ran (KOR)	326.0 kg^2	Olha Korobka (UKR)	Mariya Grabovetskaya (KAZ)

XXIX Summer Olympic Games (2008) (continued)

EVENT	GOLD MEDALIST	SILVER MEDALIST	BRONZE MEDALIST
Wrestling[1]			
Freestyle			
Men			
55 kg (121 lb)	Henry Cejudo (USA)	Tomohiro Matsunaga (JPN)	Besik Kudukhov (RUS); Radoslav Velikov (BUL)
60 kg (132 lb)	Mavlet Batirov (RUS)	Vasyl Fedoryshyn (UKR)	Seyedmorad Mohammadi (IRI); Kenichi Yumoto (JPN)
66 kg (145.2 lb)	Ramazan Sahin (TUR)	Andriy Stadnik (UKR)	Sushil Kumar (IND); Otar Tushishvili (GEO)
74 kg (162.8 lb)	Buvaysaya Saytiyev (RUS)	Soslan Tigiev (UZB)	Murad Gaidarov (BLR); Kiril Terziev (BUL)
84 kg (184.8 lb)	Revazi Mindorashvili (GEO)	Yusup Abdusalomov (TJK)	Taras Danko (UKR); Georgy Ketoyev (RUS)
96 kg (211.2 lb)	Shirvani Muradov (RUS)	Taimuraz Tigiyev (KAZ)	Khetag Gazyumov (AZE); George Gogshelidze (GEO)
120+ kg (264 lb)	Artur Taymazov (UZB)	Bakhtiyar Akhmedov (RUS)	David Musulbes (SVK); Marid Mutalimov (KAZ)
Women			
48 kg (105.6 lb)	Carol Huynh (CAN)	Chiharu Icho (JPN)	Irini Merleni (UKR); Mariya Stadnik (AZE)
55 kg (121 lb)	Saori Yoshida (JPN)	Xu Li (CHN)	Jackeline Rentería (COL); Tonya Verbeek (CAN)
63 kg (138.6 lb)	Kaori Icho (JPN)	Alena Kartashova (RUS)	Randi Miller (USA); Yelena Shalygina (KAZ)
72 kg (158.4 lb)	Wang Jiao (CHN)	Stanka Zlateva (BUL)	Kyoko Hamaguchi (JPN); Agnieszka Wieszczek (POL)
Greco-Roman			
55 kg (121 lb)	Nazyr Mankiyev (RUS)	Rovshan Bayramov (AZE)	Roman Amoyan (ARM); Park Eun Chul (KOR)
60 kg (132 lb)	Islam-Beka Albiyev (RUS)	Vitaliy Rahimov (AZE)	Nurbakyt Tengizbayev (KAZ); Ruslan Tiumenbaev (KGZ)
66 kg (145.2 lb)	Steeve Guénot (FRA)	Kanatbek Begaliev (KGZ)	Mikhail Siamonau (BLR); Armen Vardanyan (UKR)
74 kg (162.8 lb)	Manuchar Kvirkelia (GEO)	Chang Yongxiang (CHN)	Christophe Guénot (FRA); Yavor Yanakiev (BUL)
84 kg (184.8 lb)	Andrea Minguzzo (ITA)	Zoltán Fodor (HUN)	Nazmi Avluca (TUR)
96 kg (211.2 lb)	Aslanbek Khushtov (RUS)	Mirko Englich (GER)	Asset Mambetov (KAZ); Adam Wheeler (USA)
120 kg (264 lb)	Mijain López (CUB)	Khasan Baroyev (RUS)	Mindaugas Mizgaitis (LTU); Yuri Patrikeev (ARM)

[1]Two bronze medals awarded in each weight division. [2]World record. [3]Olympic record.

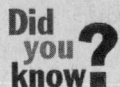

Gaylord Perry is a Hall of Fame pitcher who had 314 career wins and 3,534 strikeouts. He was also the first pitcher to win the Cy Young award in both the American and the National leagues (in 1972 and 1978, respectively). He declared in 1963, "They'll put a man on the moon before I hit a home run." Hours after Neil Armstrong set foot on the moon (20 Jul 1969), Perry hit the first home run of his major league career.

XXI Winter Olympic Games (2010)

The XXI Winter Games were held in Vancouver, BC, Canada, 12–28 Feb 2010.

EVENT	GOLD MEDALIST	PERFORMANCE	SILVER MEDALIST	BRONZE MEDALIST
Alpine Skiing				
Men				
Downhill	Didier Defago (SUI)	1 min 54.31 sec	Aksel Lund Svindal (NOR)	Bode Miller (USA)
Slalom	Giuliano Razzoli (ITA)	1 min 39.32 sec	Ivica Kostelic (CRO)	Andre Myhrer (SWE)
Giant slalom	Carlo Janka (SUI)	2 min 37.83 sec	Kjetil Jansrud (NOR)	Aksel Lund Svindal (NOR)
Supergiant slalom	Aksel Lund Svindal (NOR)	1 min 30.34 sec	Bode Miller (USA)	Andrew Weibrecht (USA)
Alpine combined	Bode Miller (USA)	2 min 44.92 sec	Ivica Kostelic (CRO)	Silvan Zurbriggen (SUI)
Women				
Downhill	Lindsey Vonn (USA)	1 min 44.19 sec	Julia Mancuso (USA)	Elisabeth Görgl (AUT)
Slalom	Maria Riesch (GER)	1 min 42.89 sec	Marlies Schild (AUT)	Sarka Zahrobska (CZE)
Giant slalom	Viktoria Rebensburg (GER)	2 min 27.11 sec	Tina Maze (SLO)	Elisabeth Görgl (AUT)
Supergiant slalom	Andrea Fischbacher (AUT)	1 min 20.14 sec	Tina Maze (SLO)	Lindsey Vonn (USA)
Alpine combined	Maria Riesch (GER)	2 min 09.14 sec	Julia Mancuso (USA)	Anja Pärson (SWE)
Nordic Skiing				
Men				
1.5-km sprint	Nikita Kriyukov (RUS)	3 min 36.3 sec	Aleksandr Panzhinskiy (RUS)	Petter Northug (NOR)
Team sprint	Øystein Pettersen, Petter Northug (NOR)	19 min 01.0 sec	Tim Tscharnke, Axel Teichmann (GER)	Nikolay Morilov, Aleksey Petukhov (RUS)
15-km classical	Dario Cologna (SUI)	33 min 36.3 sec	Pietro Piller Cottrer (ITA)	Lukas Bauer (CZE)
30-km pursuit	Marcus Hellner (SWE)	1 hr 15 min 11.4 sec	Tobias Angerer (GER)	Johan Olsson (SWE)
50-km freestyle, mass start	Petter Northug (NOR)	2 hr 5 min 35.5 sec	Axel Teichmann (GER)	Johan Olsson (SWE)
4 x 10-km relay	Sweden	1 hr 45 min 05.4 sec	Norway	Czech Republic
95-m ski jump	Simon Ammann (SUI)	276.5 pt	Adam Malysz (POL)	Gregor Schlierenzauer (AUT)
125-m ski jump	Simon Ammann (SUI)	283.6 pt	Adam Malysz (POL)	Gregor Schlierenzauer (AUT)
125-m team ski jump	Austria	1,107.9 pt	Germany	Norway
Nordic combined normal hill	Jason Lamy Chappuis (FRA)	25 min 01.1 sec	Johnny Spillane (USA)	Alessandro Pittin (ITA)
Nordic combined large hill	Bill Demong (USA)	24 min 46.9 sec	Johnny Spillane (USA)	Bernhard Gruber (AUT)
Nordic combined team relay	Austria	49 min 31.6 sec	United States	Germany
Women				
1.5-km sprint	Marit Bjørgen (NOR)	3 min 39.2 sec	Justyna Kowalczyk (POL)	Petra Majdic (SLO)
Team sprint	Evi Sachenbacher-Stehle, Claudia Nystad (GER)	18 min 03.7 sec	Charlotte Kalla, Anna Haag (SWE)	Irina Khazova, Nataliya Korosteleva (RUS)
10-km classical	Charlotte Kalla (SWE)	24 min 58.4 sec	Kristina Smigun-Vaehi (EST)	Marit Bjørgen (NOR)
15-km pursuit	Marit Bjørgen (NOR)	39 min 58.1 sec	Anna Haag (SWE)	Justyna Kowalczyk (POL)
30-km freestyle, mass start	Justyna Kowalczyk (POL)	1 hr 30 min 33.7 sec	Marit Bjørgen (NOR)	Aino-Kaisa Saarinen (FIN)
4 x 5-km relay	Norway	55 min 19.5 sec	Germany	Finland
Biathlon				
Men				
10 km	Vincent Jay (FRA)	24 min 07.8 sec	Emil Hegle Svendsen (NOR)	Jakov Fak (CRO)
12.5-km pursuit	Björn Ferry (SWE)	33 min 38.4 sec	Christoph Sumann (AUT)	Vincent Jay (FRA)
20 km	Emil Hegle Svendsen (NOR)	48 min 22.5 sec	Ole Einar Bjørndalen (NOR)[1], Sergey Novikov (BLR)[1]	

XXI Winter Olympic Games (2010) (continued)

EVENT	GOLD MEDALIST	PERFORMANCE	SILVER MEDALIST	BRONZE MEDALIST
Biathlon (continued)				
Men (continued)				
4 x 7.5-km relay	Norway	1 hr 21 min 38.1 sec	Austria	Russia
15-km mass start	Yevgeny Ustyugov (RUS)	35 min 35.7 sec	Martin Fourcade (FRA)	Pavol Hurajt (SVK)
Women				
7.5 km	Anastazia Kuzmina (SVK)	19 min 55.6 sec	Magdalena Neuner (GER)	Marie Dorin (FRA)
10-km pursuit	Magdalena Neuner (GER)	30 min 16.0 sec	Anastazia Kuzmina (SVK)	Marie-Laure Brunet (FRA)
15 km	Tora Berger (NOR)	40 min 52.8 sec	Elena Khrustaleva (KAZ)	Darya Domracheva (BLR)
4 x 6-km relay	Russia	1 hr 09 min 36.3 sec	France	Germany
12.5-km mass start	Magdalena Neuner (GER)	35 min 19.6 sec	Olga Zaitseva (RUS)	Simone Hauswald (GER)
Freestyle Skiing				
Men				
Moguls	Alexandre Bilodeau (CAN)	26.75 pt	Dale Begg-Smith (AUS)	Bryon Wilson (USA)
Aerials	Alexey Grishin (BLR)	248.41 pt	Jeret Peterson (USA)	Liu Zhongqing (CHN)
Ski cross	Michael Schmid (SUI)		Andreas Matt (AUT)	Audun Grønvold (NOR)
Women				
Moguls	Hannah Kearney (USA)	26.63 pt	Jennifer Heil (CAN)	Shannon Bahrke (USA)
Aerials	Lydia Lassila (AUS)	214.74 pt	Li Nina (CHN)	Guo Xinxin (CHN)
Ski cross	Ashleigh McIvor (CAN)		Hedda Berntsen (NOR)	Marion Josserand (FRA)
Snowboarding				
Men				
Giant slalom	Jasey Jay Anderson (CAN)		Benjamin Karl (AUT)	Mathieu Bozzetto (FRA)
Halfpipe	Shaun White (USA)	48.4 pt	Peetu Piiroinen (FIN)	Scott Lago (USA)
Snowboardcross	Seth Wescott (USA)		Mike Robertson (CAN)	Tony Ramoin (FRA)
Women				
Giant slalom	Nicolien Sauerbreij (NED)		Yekaterina Ilyukhina (RUS)	Marion Kreiner (AUT)
Halfpipe	Torah Bright (AUS)	45.0 pt	Hannah Teter (USA)	Kelly Clark (USA)
Snowboardcross	Maelle Ricker (CAN)		Deborah Anthonioz (FRA)	Olivia Nobs (SUI)
Figure Skating				
Men	Evan Lysacek (USA)	257.67 pt	Yevgeny Plushchenko (RUS)	Daisuke Takahashi (JPN)
Women	Kim Yu-Na (KOR)	228.56 pt	Mao Asada (JPN)	Joannie Rochette (CAN)
Pairs	Shen Xue, Zhao Hongbo (CHN)	216.57 pt	Pang Qing, Tong Jian (CHN)	Aliona Savchenko, Robin Szolkowy (GER)
Ice dancing	Tessa Virtue, Scott Moir (CAN)	221.57 pt	Meryl Davis, Charlie White (USA)	Oksana Domnina, Maksim Shabalin (RUS)
Speed Skating				
Men				
500 m	Mo Tae-Bum (KOR)	69.82 sec^2	Keiichiro Nagashima (JPN)	Joji Kato (JPN)
1,000 m	Shani Davis (USA)	1 min 08.94 sec	Mo Tae-Bum (KOR)	Chad Hedrick (USA)
1,500 m	Mark Tuitert (NED)	1 min 45.57 sec	Shani Davis (USA)	Havard Bokko (NOR)
5,000 m	Sven Kramer (NED)	6 min 14.60 sec^3	Lee Seung-Hoon (KOR)	Ivan Skobrev (RUS)
10,000 m	Lee Seung-Hoon (KOR)^4	12 min 58.55 sec^3	Ivan Skobrev (RUS)	Bob de Jong (NED)
Team pursuit	Canada	3 min 41.37 sec	United States	Netherlands

XXI Winter Olympic Games (2010) (continued)

EVENT	GOLD MEDALIST	PERFORMANCE	SILVER MEDALIST	BRONZE MEDALIST
Speed Skating (continued)				
Women				
500 m	Lee Sang-Hwa (KOR)	76.09 sec[2]	Jenny Wolf (GER)	Wang Beixing (CHN)
1,000 m	Christine Nesbitt (CAN)	1 min 16.56 sec	Annette Gerritsen (NED)	Laurine van Riessen (NED)
1,500 m	Ireen Wüst (NED)	1 min 56.89 sec	Kristina Groves (CAN)	Martina Sablikova (CZE)
3,000 m	Martina Sablikova (CZE)	4 min 02.53 sec	Stephanie Beckert (GER)	Kristina Groves (CAN)
5,000 m	Martina Sablikova (CZE)	6 min 50.91 sec	Stephanie Beckert (GER)	Clara Hughes (CAN)
Team pursuit	Germany	3 min 02.82 sec	Japan	Poland
Short-Track Speed Skating				
Men				
500 m	Charles Hamelin (CAN)	40.981 sec	Sung Si-Bak (KOR)	François-Louis Tremblay (CAN)
1,000 m	Lee Jung-Su (KOR)	1 min 23.747 sec[3]	Lee Ho-Suk (KOR)	Apolo Anton Ohno (USA)
1,500 m	Lee Jung-Su (KOR)	2 min 17.611 sec	Apolo Anton Ohno (USA)	J.R. Celski (USA)
5,000-m relay	Canada	6 min 44.224 sec	Republic of Korea	United States
Women				
500 m	Wang Meng (CHN)	43.048 sec	Marianne St-Gelais (CAN)	Arianna Fontana (ITA)
1,000 m	Wang Meng (CHN)	1 min 29.213 sec	Katherine Reutter (USA)	Park Seung-Hi (KOR)
1,500 m	Zhou Yang (CHN)	2 min 16.993 sec[3]	Lee Eun-Byul (KOR)	Park Seung-Hi (KOR)
3,000-m relay	China[4]	4 min 06.610 sec[5]	Canada	United States
Ice Hockey				
Men	Canada	6–1–0	United States	Finland
Women	Canada	5–0–0	United States	Finland
Curling				
Men	Canada	11–0–0	Norway	Switzerland
Women	Sweden	9–2–0	Canada	China
Bobsled				
Two-man	André Lange, Kevin Kuske (GER 1)	3 min 26.65 sec	Thomas Florschütz, Richard Adjei (GER 2)	Aleksandr Zoubkov, Aleksey Voyevoda (RUS 1)
Four-man	Steven Holcomb, Steve Mesler, Curtis Tomasevicz, Justin Olsen (USA 1)	3 min 24.46 sec	André Lange, Alexander Rödiger, Kevin Kuske, Martin Putze (GER 1)	Lyndon Rush, Chris Le Bihan, David Bissett, Lascelles Brown (CAN 1)
Two-woman	Kaillie Humphries, Heather Moyse (CAN 1)	3 min 32.28 sec	Helen Upperton, Shelley-Ann Brown (CAN 2)	Erin Pac, Elana Meyers (USA 2)
Luge				
Men's singles	Felix Loch (GER)	3 min 13.085 sec	David Möller (GER)	Armin Zöggeler (ITA)
Men's doubles	Andreas Linger, Wolfgang Linger (AUT 1)	1 min 22.705 sec	Andris Sics, Juris Sics (LAT 1)	Patric Leitner, Alexander Resch (GER 1)
Women's singles	Tatjana Hüfner (GER)	2 min 46.524 sec	Nina Reithmayer (AUT)	Natalie Geisenberger (GER)
Skeleton				
Men	Jon Montgomery (CAN)	3 min 29.73 sec	Martins Dukurs (LAT)	Aleksandr Tretyakov (RUS)
Women	Amy Williams (GBR)	3 min 35.64 sec	Kerstin Szymkowiak (GER)	Anja Huber (GER)

[1]Tied for silver; no bronze awarded.   [2]Time is combined total of two heats.   [3]Olympic record.   [4]Original winner disqualified.   [5]World record.

Special Olympics

The Special Olympics is an international program to provide individuals who have intellectual disabilities and are eight years of age or older with year-round sports training and athletic competition in a variety of Olympic-type summer and winter sports. Inaugurated in 1968, the Special Olympics is officially recognized by the International Olympic Committee. **International headquarters** are in Washington DC.

In June 1963, with support from the Joseph P. Kennedy, Jr., Foundation, **Eunice Kennedy Shriver** (sister of Pres. John F. Kennedy) started a summer day camp at her home in Rockville MD for children with mental retardation. The Kennedy Foundation promoted the creation of dozens of similar camps in the United States and Canada. Special awards were developed for physical achievements, and by 1968 Shriver had persuaded the Chicago Park District to join with the Foundation in sponsoring a "Special Olympics," held at Soldier Field on 20 July. About 1,000 athletes from 26 US states and Canada participated. The games were such a success that, in December, Special Olympics, Inc. (now **Special Olympics International**), was founded, with chapters in the United States, Canada, and France. The first International Winter Special Olympics Games were held 5–11 Feb 1977 (in Steamboat Springs CO). The number of participating countries proliferated so that by 2010 there were chapters in nearly 200 countries. More than 30,000 meets and tournaments are held worldwide each year, culminating in the Special Olympics World Games every two years, alternating between winter and summer sports.

Special Olympics Web site: <www.specialolympics.org>.

Automobile Racing

Of the various types of automobile races, the closed-circuit, or speedway, course was developed largely in the United States. The Indianapolis 500—now the premier Indy car event—was first run in 1911. A low-slung, fenderless (open-wheel) car—called an Indy car—is essential for this race; its suspension (i.e., its ability to hold the track) is as important to a car's performance as its turbocharged engine. Often the chassis manufacturer is different from the engine manufacturer, resulting in cars identified, for example, as a Brabham/Repco. In such cases the chassis maker is listed first, and the chassis maker receives any money or awards that the car may win.

Indy car racing began in 1909, when the American Automobile Association (AAA) began sponsoring a 24-race championship series, including three races at the newly opened Indianapolis Motor Speedway (IMS). In 1956 the AAA gave up its involvement with auto racing, and the United States Auto Club (**USAC**) was organized as the sport's governing body. In 1978 two race-car owners broke away from USAC to form a new organization, Championship Auto Racing Teams, Inc. (**CART**), which sponsored its own series of races. In 1980 CART and USAC joined to form the Championship Racing League, which dissolved after five races. In 1994 the IMS announced a new Indy Racing League (**IRL**) to oversee the Indianapolis 500 beginning in 1996 and a new series of IRL races (leading to an annual drivers' championship) separate from those sponsored by CART.

The standard cars used for Grand Prix road (i.e., closed-highway) racing are known as Formula One (or F-1) cars because they are built according to an evolving formula that was established after World War I by the Fédération Internationale de l'Automobile (**FIA**). Like the Indy car, the Formula One racer is open-wheeled and low-slung, but the F-1 is slightly smaller and more maneuverable.

There are approximately 18 Grand Prix events held worldwide throughout the year. Drivers compete for the **World Championship of Drivers** (inaugurated in 1950), receiving a total number of points based on their placement in each of the official Grand Prix events.

Many Grand Prix drivers participate in various endurance races, the most famous of which is the **Le Mans Grand Prix d'Endurance**, held on the 13.4-km (8.3-mi) Sarthe circuit, Le Mans, France.

Another type of popular racing event is the rally, which was established in 1907. More than 35 such competitions, raced over a specified route on public roads, take place yearly throughout the world. The classic occasion for rally racing is the **Rallye Automobile Monte-Carlo**, now started in various European cities with Monaco as its terminal point.

Stock-car racing, which began in the United States in the first half of the 20th century, involves the racing of commercial cars that have been altered to increase their speed and maneuverability. The National Association for Stock Car Auto Racing (**NASCAR**) was founded in 1947, and until 2004 it awarded the Winston Cup to the driver who had earned the greatest number of points in a series of official NASCAR Winston Cup events over the stock-car racing season. In 2004 the competition was renamed the Nextel Cup, and from 2008 it is known as the Sprint Cup. The **Daytona 500** is the premiere stock-car event.

Related Web sites: Champ Car: <www.champcarworldseries.com>; USAC: <www.usacracing.com>; IRL: <www.indycar.com>; FIA: <www.fia.com>; Automobile Club de Monaco <www.acm.mc>; NASCAR: <www.nascar.com>.

Formula One Grand Prix Race Results, 2009–10
The season for the Formula One Grand Prix circuit is March–November.

RACE	DATE	LOCALE	WINNER (COUNTRY)	TIME (HR.MIN.SEC)
European Grand Prix	23 Aug 2009	Valencia, Spain	Rubens Barrichello (BRA)	1:35:51.289
Belgian Grand Prix	30 Aug 2009	Spa-Francorchamps	Kimi Räikkönen (FIN)	1:23:50.995

Formula One Grand Prix Race Results, 2009–10 (continued)

RACE	DATE	LOCALE	WINNER (COUNTRY)	TIME (HR:MIN:SEC)
Italian Grand Prix	13 Sep 2009	Monza	Rubens Barrichello (BRA)	1:16:21.706
Singapore Grand Prix	27 Sep 2009	Singapore	Lewis Hamilton (GBR)	1:56:06.337
Japanese Grand Prix	4 Oct 2009	Suzuka	Sebastian Vettel (GER)	1:28:20.443
Brazilian Grand Prix	18 Oct 2009	São Paulo	Mark Webber (AUS)	1:32:23.081
Abu Dhabi Grand Prix	1 Nov 2009	Yas Marina	Sebastian Vettel (GER)	1:34:03.414
Bahrain Grand Prix	14 Mar 2010	Sakhir	Fernando Alonso (ESP)	1:39:20.396
Australian Grand Prix	28 Mar 2010	Melbourne	Jenson Button (GBR)	1:33:36.531
Malaysian Grand Prix	4 Apr 2010	Kuala Lumpur	Sebastian Vettel (GER)	1:33:48.412
Chinese Grand Prix	18 Apr 2010	Shanghai	Jenson Button (GBR)	1:46:42.163
Spanish Grand Prix	9 May 2010	Catalonia	Mark Webber (AUS)	1:35:44.101
Monaco Grand Prix	16 May 2010	Monte-Carlo	Mark Webber (AUS)	1:50:13.355
Turkish Grand Prix	30 May 2010	Istanbul	Lewis Hamilton (GBR)	1:28:47.620
Canadian Grand Prix	13 Jun 2010	Montreal	Lewis Hamilton (GBR)	1:33:53.456
European Grand Prix	27 Jun 2010	Valencia, Spain	Sebastian Vettel (GER)	1:40:29.571
British Grand Prix	11 Jul 2010	Silverstone	Mark Webber (AUS)	1:24:38.200
German Grand Prix	25 Jul 2010	Hockenheim	Fernando Alonso (ESP)	1:27:38.864

Indianapolis 500

There was no competition in 1917–18 and 1942–45. Won by an American racer except as indicated.

YEAR	WINNER	AVG. SPEED (MPH)	YEAR	WINNER	AVG. SPEED (MPH)	YEAR	WINNER	AVG. SPEED (MPH)
1911	Ray Harroun	74.602	1953	Bill Vukovich	128.740	1987	Al Unser	162.175
1912	Joe Dawson	78.719	1954	Bill Vukovich	130.840	1988	Rick Mears	144.809
1913	Jules Goux (FRA)	75.933	1955	Robert Sweikert	128.209	1989	Emerson Fitti-	167.581
1914	René Thomas (FRA)	82.474	1956	Pat Flaherty	128.490		paldi (BRA)	
			1957	Sam Hanks	135.601	1990	Arie Luyendyk	185.984
1915	Ralph DePalma	89.840	1958	Jimmy Bryan	133.791		(NED)	
1916[1]	Dario Resta (FRA)	84.001	1959	Rodger Ward	135.857	1991	Rick Mears	176.457
1919	Howdy Wilcox	88.050	1960	Jim Rathmann	138.767	1992	Al Unser, Jr.	134.479
1920	Gaston Chevrolet	88.618	1961	A.J. Foyt, Jr.	139.131	1993	Emerson Fitti-	157.207
1921	Tommy Milton	89.621	1962	Rodger Ward	140.293		paldi (BRA)	
1922	Jimmy Murphy	94.484	1963	Parnelli Jones	143.137	1994	Al Unser, Jr.	160.872
1923	Tommy Milton	90.954	1964	A.J. Foyt, Jr.	147.350	1995	Jacques Ville-	153.616
1924[2]	L.L. Corum, Joe Boyer	98.234	1965	Jim Clark (GBR)	150.686		neuve (CAN)	
			1966	Graham Hill (GBR)	144.317	1996	Buddy Lazier	147.956
1925	Peter DePaolo	101.127	1967	A.J. Foyt, Jr.	151.207	1997	Arie Luyendyk	145.827
1926[3]	Frank Lockhart	95.904	1968	Bobby Unser	152.882		(NED)	
1927	George Souders	97.545	1969	Mario Andretti	156.867	1998	Eddie Cheever, Jr.	145.155
1928	Louie Meyer	99.482	1970	Al Unser	155.749	1999	Kenny Bräck	153.176
1929	Ray Keech	97.585	1971	Al Unser	157.735		(SWE)	
1930	Billy Arnold	100.448	1972	Mark Donohue	162.962	2000	Juan Montoya	167.607
1931	Louis Schneider	96.629	1973[3]	Gordon Johncock	159.036		(COL)	
1932	Fred Frame	104.144				2001	Helio Castro-	153.601
1933	Louie Meyer	104.162	1974	Johnny Rutherford	158.589		neves (BRA)	
1934	Bill Cummings	104.863				2002	Helio Castro-	166.499
1935	Kelly Petillo	106.240	1975[3]	Bobby Unser	149.213		neves (BRA)	
1936	Louie Meyer	109.069	1976[3]	Johnny Rutherford	148.725	2003	Gil de Ferran	156.291
1937	Wilbur Shaw	113.580					(BRA)	
1938	Floyd Roberts	117.200	1977	A.J. Foyt, Jr.	161.331	2004[3]	Buddy Rice	138.518
1939	Wilbur Shaw	115.035	1978	Al Unser	161.363	2005	Dan Wheldon	157.603
1940	Wilbur Shaw	114.277	1979	Rick Mears	158.899		(GBR)	
1941[2]	Floyd Davis, Mauri Rose	115.117	1980	Johnny Rutherford	142.862	2006	Sam Hornish, Jr.	157.085
			1981	Bobby Unser	139.084	2007	Dario Franchitti	151.774
1946	George Robson	114.820	1982	Gordon Johncock	162.029		(GBR)	
1947	Mauri Rose	116.338				2008	Scott Dixon (NZL)	143.567
1948	Mauri Rose	119.814	1983	Tom Sneva	162.117	2009	Helio Castro-	150.318
1949	Bill Holland	121.327	1984	Rick Mears	163.612		neves (BRA)	
1950[3]	Johnnie Parsons	124.002	1985	Danny Sullivan	152.982	2010	Dario Franchitti	161.623
1951	Lee Wallard	126.244	1986	Bobby Rahal	170.722		(GBR)	
1952	Troy Ruttman	128.922						

[1]Scheduled 300-mile race. [2]First driver named started the race but was replaced during the race by the second driver named. [3]Race stopped because of rain (in 1926 after 400 miles, in 1950 after 345 miles, in 1973 after 332.5 miles, in 1975 after 435 miles, in 1976 after 255 miles, in 2004 after 450 miles, and in 2007 after 415 miles).

NASCAR Sprint Cup Champions

YEAR	WINNER	YEAR	WINNER	YEAR	WINNER	YEAR	WINNER
1949	Red Byron	1965	Ned Jarrett	1981	Darrell Waltrip	1997	Jeff Gordon
1950	Bill Rexford	1966	David Pearson	1982	Darrell Waltrip	1998	Jeff Gordon
1951	Herb Thomas	1967	Richard Petty	1983	Bobby Allison	1999	Dale Jarrett
1952	Tim Flock	1968	David Pearson	1984	Terry Labonte	2000	Bobby Labonte
1953	Herb Thomas	1969	David Pearson	1985	Darrell Waltrip	2001	Jeff Gordon
1954	Lee Petty	1970	Bobby Isaac	1986	Dale Earnhardt	2002	Tony Stewart
1955	Tim Flock	1971	Richard Petty	1987	Dale Earnhardt	2003	Matt Kenseth
1956	Buck Baker	1972	Richard Petty	1988	Bill Elliott	2004	Kurt Busch
1957	Buck Baker	1973	Benny Parsons	1989	Rusty Wallace	2005	Tony Stewart
1958	Lee Petty	1974	Richard Petty	1990	Dale Earnhardt	2006	Jimmie Johnson
1959	Lee Petty	1975	Richard Petty	1991	Dale Earnhardt	2007	Jimmie Johnson
1960	Rex White	1976	Cale Yarborough	1992	Alan Kulwicki	2008	Jimmie Johnson
1961	Ned Jarrett	1977	Cale Yarborough	1993	Dale Earnhardt	2009	Jimmie Johnson
1962	Joe Weatherly	1978	Cale Yarborough	1994	Dale Earnhardt		
1963	Joe Weatherly	1979	Richard Petty	1995	Jeff Gordon		
1964	Richard Petty	1980	Dale Earnhardt	1996	Terry Labonte		

Baseball

The sport of baseball—given its definitive form in the United States in the late 19th century—is popular throughout the world, though until 2006 it was organized internationally only for **Little League** players (children ages 5–18). Little League Baseball was founded in Pennsylvania in 1939. The first Little League World Series was in 1947, and the first Little League outside the US was organized in British Columbia in 1951. Baseball is especially popular in Japan and Latin America; it is also one of the national sports of the US.

On a **professional** level, the premier event of baseball in the US is the **World Series** of **Major League Baseball**, in which the first team to win four games wins the Series. In fact, the Series is not contested on an international level, but rather it is played between the leading team of the **National League** (NL; formed 1876) and the leading team of the **American League** (AL; formed 1900 and including, from 1977, one Canadian team). In 2006 the inaugural World Baseball Classic, a competition featuring national teams, was held in Japan, Puerto Rico, and the US. The team from Japan beat Cuba's team in the finals. The second competition, held in 2009, also was won by Japan, this time defeating Korea.

Professional baseball began in Japan in 1936. Teams are organized into two leagues of six teams each. The seven-game **Japan Series**, first played in 1950, is contested between the leading team of the Central League (CL) and the leading team of the Pacific League (PL). The modern **Caribbean Series** began in 1970 with the winning team from each league in the Dominican Republic, Mexico, Puerto Rico, and Venezuela.

Related Web sites:
Major League Baseball: <http://mlb.mlb.com/index.jsp>; Little League: <www.littleleague.org>.

Major League Baseball Final Standings, 2009

American League

East Division

CLUB	WON	LOST	GAMES BACK
New York[1]	103	59	—
Boston[1]	95	67	8
Tampa Bay	84	78	19
Toronto	75	87	28
Baltimore	64	98	39

Central Division

CLUB	WON	LOST	GAMES BACK
Minnesota[1]	87	76	—
Detroit	86	77	1
Chicago	79	83	7½
Cleveland	65	97	21½
Kansas City	65	97	21½

West Division

CLUB	WON	LOST	GAMES BACK
Los Angeles[1]	97	65	—
Texas	87	75	10
Seattle	85	77	12
Oakland	75	87	22

National League

East Division

CLUB	WON	LOST	GAMES BACK
Philadelphia[1]	93	69	—
Florida	87	75	6
Atlanta	86	76	7
New York	70	92	23
Washington	59	103	34

Central Division

CLUB	WON	LOST	GAMES BACK
St. Louis[1]	91	71	—
Chicago	83	78	7½
Milwaukee	80	82	11
Cincinnati	78	84	13
Houston	74	88	17
Pittsburgh	62	99	28½

West Division

CLUB	WON	LOST	GAMES BACK
Los Angeles[1]	95	67	—
Colorado[1]	92	70	3
San Francisco	88	74	7
San Diego	75	87	20
Arizona	70	92	25

[1]*Gained play-off berth.*

World Series

YEAR	WINNER	RUNNER-UP	RESULTS
1903	Boston Americans (AL)	Pittsburgh Pirates (NL)	5–3
1904	*not held*		
1905	New York Giants (NL)	Philadelphia Athletics (AL)	4–1
1906	Chicago White Sox (AL)	Chicago Cubs (NL)	4–2
1907	Chicago Cubs (NL)	Detroit Tigers (AL)	4–0[1]
1908	Chicago Cubs (NL)	Detroit Tigers (AL)	4–1
1909	Pittsburgh Pirates (NL)	Detroit Tigers (AL)	4–3
1910	Philadelphia Athletics (AL)	Chicago Cubs (NL)	4–1
1911	Philadelphia Athletics (AL)	New York Giants (NL)	4–2
1912	Boston Red Sox (AL)	New York Giants (NL)	4–3[1]
1913	Philadelphia Athletics (AL)	New York Giants (NL)	4–1
1914	Boston Braves (NL)	Philadelphia Athletics (AL)	4–0
1915	Boston Red Sox (AL)	Philadelphia Phillies (NL)	4–1
1916	Boston Red Sox (AL)	Brooklyn Robins (NL)	4–1
1917	Chicago White Sox (AL)	New York Giants (NL)	4–2
1918	Boston Red Sox (AL)	Chicago Cubs (NL)	4–2
1919	Cincinnati Reds (NL)	Chicago White Sox (AL)	5–3
1920	Cleveland Indians (AL)	Brooklyn Robins (NL)	5–2
1921	New York Giants (NL)	New York Yankees (AL)	5–3
1922	New York Giants (NL)	New York Yankees (AL)	4–0[1]
1923	New York Yankees (AL)	New York Giants (NL)	4–2
1924	Washington Senators (AL)	New York Giants (NL)	4–3
1925	Pittsburgh Pirates (NL)	Washington Senators (AL)	4–3
1926	St. Louis Cardinals (NL)	New York Yankees (AL)	4–3
1927	New York Yankees (AL)	Pittsburgh Pirates (NL)	4–0
1928	New York Yankees (AL)	St. Louis Cardinals (NL)	4–0
1929	Philadelphia Athletics (AL)	Chicago Cubs (NL)	4–1
1930	Philadelphia Athletics (AL)	St. Louis Cardinals (NL)	4–2
1931	St. Louis Cardinals (NL)	Philadelphia Athletics (AL)	4–3
1932	New York Yankees (AL)	Chicago Cubs (NL)	4–0
1933	New York Giants (NL)	Washington Senators (AL)	4–1
1934	St. Louis Cardinals (NL)	Detroit Tigers (AL)	4–3
1935	Detroit Tigers (AL)	Chicago Cubs (NL)	4–2
1936	New York Yankees (AL)	New York Giants (NL)	4–2
1937	New York Yankees (AL)	New York Giants (NL)	4–1
1938	New York Yankees (AL)	Chicago Cubs (NL)	4–0
1939	New York Yankees (AL)	Cincinnati Reds (NL)	4–0
1940	Cincinnati Reds (NL)	Detroit Tigers (AL)	4–3
1941	New York Yankees (AL)	Brooklyn Dodgers (NL)	4–1
1942	St. Louis Cardinals (NL)	New York Yankees (AL)	4–1
1943	New York Yankees (AL)	St. Louis Cardinals (NL)	4–1
1944	St. Louis Cardinals (NL)	St. Louis Browns (AL)	4–2
1945	Detroit Tigers (AL)	Chicago Cubs (NL)	4–3
1946	St. Louis Cardinals (NL)	Boston Red Sox (AL)	4–3
1947	New York Yankees (AL)	Brooklyn Dodgers (NL)	4–3
1948	Cleveland Indians (AL)	Boston Braves (NL)	4–2
1949	New York Yankees (AL)	Brooklyn Dodgers (NL)	4–1
1950	New York Yankees (AL)	Philadelphia Phillies (NL)	4–0
1951	New York Yankees (AL)	New York Giants (NL)	4–2
1952	New York Yankees (AL)	Brooklyn Dodgers (NL)	4–3
1953	New York Yankees (AL)	Brooklyn Dodgers (NL)	4–2
1954	New York Giants (NL)	Cleveland Indians (AL)	4–0
1955	Brooklyn Dodgers (NL)	New York Yankees (AL)	4–3
1956	New York Yankees (AL)	Brooklyn Dodgers (NL)	4–3
1957	Milwaukee Braves (NL)	New York Yankees (AL)	4–3
1958	New York Yankees (AL)	Milwaukee Braves (NL)	4–3
1959	Los Angeles Dodgers (NL)	Chicago White Sox (AL)	4–2
1960	Pittsburgh Pirates (NL)	New York Yankees (AL)	4–3
1961	New York Yankees (AL)	Cincinnati Reds (NL)	4–1
1962	New York Yankees (AL)	San Francisco Giants (NL)	4–3
1963	Los Angeles Dodgers (NL)	New York Yankees (AL)	4–0
1964	St. Louis Cardinals (NL)	New York Yankees (AL)	4–3
1965	Los Angeles Dodgers (NL)	Minnesota Twins (AL)	4–3
1966	Baltimore Orioles (AL)	Los Angeles Dodgers (NL)	4–0
1967	St. Louis Cardinals (NL)	Boston Red Sox (AL)	4–3
1968	Detroit Tigers (AL)	St. Louis Cardinals (NL)	4–3
1969	New York Mets (NL)	Baltimore Orioles (AL)	4–1
1970	Baltimore Orioles (AL)	Cincinnati Reds (NL)	4–1

World Series (continued)

YEAR	WINNER	RUNNER-UP	RESULTS
1971	Pittsburgh Pirates (NL)	Baltimore Orioles (AL)	4-3
1972	Oakland Athletics (AL)	Cincinnati Reds (NL)	4-3
1973	Oakland Athletics (AL)	New York Mets (NL)	4-3
1974	Oakland Athletics (AL)	Los Angeles Dodgers (NL)	4-1
1975	Cincinnati Reds (NL)	Boston Red Sox (AL)	4-3
1976	Cincinnati Reds (NL)	New York Yankees (AL)	4-0
1977	New York Yankees (AL)	Los Angeles Dodgers (NL)	4-2
1978	New York Yankees (AL)	Los Angeles Dodgers (NL)	4-2
1979	Pittsburgh Pirates (NL)	Baltimore Orioles (AL)	4-3
1980	Philadelphia Phillies (NL)	Kansas City Royals (AL)	4-2
1981	Los Angeles Dodgers (NL)	New York Yankees (AL)	4-2
1982	St. Louis Cardinals (NL)	Milwaukee Brewers (AL)	4-3
1983	Baltimore Orioles (AL)	Philadelphia Phillies (NL)	4-1
1984	Detroit Tigers (AL)	San Diego Padres (NL)	4-1
1985	Kansas City Royals (AL)	St. Louis Cardinals (NL)	4-3
1986	New York Mets (NL)	Boston Red Sox (AL)	4-3
1987	Minnesota Twins (AL)	St. Louis Cardinals (NL)	4-3
1988	Los Angeles Dodgers (NL)	Oakland Athletics (AL)	4-1
1989	Oakland Athletics (AL)	San Francisco Giants (NL)	4-0
1990	Cincinnati Reds (NL)	Oakland Athletics (AL)	4-0
1991	Minnesota Twins (AL)	Atlanta Braves (NL)	4-3
1992	Toronto Blue Jays (AL)	Atlanta Braves (NL)	4-2
1993	Toronto Blue Jays (AL)	Philadelphia Phillies (NL)	4-2
1994	*not held*		
1995	Atlanta Braves (NL)	Cleveland Indians (AL)	4-2
1996	New York Yankees (AL)	Atlanta Braves (NL)	4-2
1997	Florida Marlins (NL)	Cleveland Indians (AL)	4-3
1998	New York Yankees (AL)	San Diego Padres (NL)	4-0
1999	New York Yankees (AL)	Atlanta Braves (NL)	4-0
2000	New York Yankees (AL)	New York Mets (NL)	4-1
2001	Arizona Diamondbacks (NL)	New York Yankees (AL)	4-3
2002	Anaheim Angels (AL)	San Francisco Giants (NL)	4-3
2003	Florida Marlins (NL)	New York Yankees (AL)	4-2
2004	Boston Red Sox (AL)	St. Louis Cardinals (NL)	4-0
2005	Chicago White Sox (AL)	Houston Astros (NL)	4-0
2006	St. Louis Cardinals (NL)	Detroit Tigers (AL)	4-1
2007	Boston Red Sox (AL)	Colorado Rockies (NL)	4-0
2008	Philadelphia Phillies (NL)	Tampa Bay Rays (AL)	4-1
2009	New York Yankees (AL)	Philadelphia Phillies (NL)	4-2

[1]Plus one tied game.

Major League Baseball All-Time Records[1]

Research courtesy of Baseball Almanac, <www.baseball-almanac.com>.

	PLAYERS/TEAMS	NUMBER	SEASON/DATE
Individual career records			
Games played	Pete Rose	3,562	1963-86
Consecutive games played	Cal Ripken, Jr.	2,632	1982-98
Batting average[2]	Ty Cobb	.366	1905-28
Hits	Pete Rose	4,256	1963-86
Doubles	Tris Speaker	792	1907-28
Triples	Sam Crawford	309	1899-1917
Home runs	Barry Bonds	762	1986-2007
Runs	Rickey Henderson	2,295	1979-2003
Runs batted in	Hank Aaron	2,297	1954-76
Walks (batting)	Barry Bonds	2,558	1986-2007
Stolen bases	Rickey Henderson	1,406	1979-2003
Wins (pitching)	Cy Young	511	1890-1911
Earned run average[3]	Ed Walsh	1.82	1904-17
Strikeouts (pitching)	Nolan Ryan	5,714	1966-93
Saves	Trevor Hoffman[4]	591	1993-2009
No-hitters	Nolan Ryan	7	1966-93
Shutouts	Walter Johnson	110	1907-27
Wins (managing)	Connie Mack	3,731	1894-96; 1901-50

Major League Baseball All-Time Records[1] (continued)

	PLAYERS/TEAMS	NUMBER	SEASON/DATE
Individual season records			
Batting average[5]	Hugh Duffy	.440	1894
Hits	Ichiro Suzuki[4]	262	2004
Doubles	Earl Webb	67	1931
Triples	Chief Wilson	36	1912
Home runs	Barry Bonds	73	2001
Runs	Billy Hamilton	192	1894
Runs batted in	Hack Wilson	191	1930
Walks (batting)	Barry Bonds	232	2004
Stolen bases	Hugh Nicol	138	1887
Wins (pitching)	Charley Radbourn	59	1884
Earned run average[6]	Tim Keefe	0.86	1880
Strikeouts (pitching)	Matt Kilroy	513	1886
No-hitters	*4 players hold record*	2	
Saves	Francisco Rodriguez[4]	62	2008
Shutouts	George Bradley; Grover Alexander	16	1876; 1916
Individual game records[7]			
Hits	Wilbert Robinson; Rennie Stennett	7	10 Jun 1892; 16 Sep 1975
Doubles	*50 players hold record*	4	
Triples	George Strief; Bill Joyce	4	25 Jun 1885; 18 May 1897
Home runs	*15 players hold record*	4	
Runs	Guy Hecker	7	15 Aug 1886
Runs batted in	Jim Bottomley; Mark Whiten	12	16 Sep 1924; 7 Sep 1993
Walks (batting)	Walt Wilmot; Jimmie Foxx	6	22 Aug 1891; 16 Jun 1938
Stolen bases	George Gore; Billy Hamilton	7	25 Jun 1881; 31 Aug 1894
Strikeouts (pitching)	Roger Clemens (twice); Kerry Wood[4]	20	29 Apr 1986 and 18 Sep 1996; 6 May 1998
Team season records			
World Series titles	New York Yankees	26	
Consecutive World Series titles	New York Yankees	5	1949–53
Games won	Chicago Cubs; Seattle Mariners	116	1906; 2001
Highest winning percentage	St. Louis Maroons	.832 (94–19)	1884
Batting average	Philadelphia Phillies	.349	1894
Doubles	Texas Rangers	376	2008
Triples	Baltimore Orioles	153	1894
Home runs	Seattle Mariners	264	1997
Runs	Boston Beaneaters	1,220	1894
Runs batted in	Boston Beaneaters	1,043	1894
Walks (batting)	Boston Red Sox	835	1949
Stolen bases	Philadelphia Athletics	638	1887
Game records			
Highest combined score	Chicago Cubs versus Philadelphia Phillies	49 (26–23)	25 Aug 1922
Longest nine-inning game	New York Yankees versus Boston Red Sox	4 hr 45 min	18 Aug 2006
Longest extra-inning game (time)	Chicago White Sox versus Milwaukee Brewers	8 hr 6 min	9 May 1984
Longest extra-inning game (innings)	Brooklyn Dodgers versus Boston Braves	26 innings	1 May 1920

[1]*Through the end of the 2009 season.*   [2]*Minimum of 1,000 games played and 1,000 at-bats.*   [3]*Minimum of 2,000 innings pitched.*   [4]*Active in 2010.*   [5]*Minimum of 3.1 plate appearances per game played.*   [6]*Minimum of one inning pitched per game played.*   [7]*Nine-inning games only.*

Caribbean Series
Held since 1949. Table shows results for the past 20 years.

YEAR	WINNER	COUNTRY	YEAR	WINNER	COUNTRY
1991	Licey Tigers	DOM	1995	San Juan Senators	PUR
1992	Mayagüez Indians	PUR	1996	Culiacán Tomato Growers	MEX
1993	Santurce Crabbers	PUR	1997	Northern Eagles	DOM
1994	Licey Tigers	DOM	1998	Northern Eagles	DOM

Caribbean Series (continued)

YEAR	WINNER	COUNTRY	YEAR	WINNER	COUNTRY
1999	Licey Tigers	DOM	2005	Mazatlán Deer	MEX
2000	Santurce Crabbers	PUR	2006	Caracas Lions	VEN
2001	Cibao Eagles	DOM	2007	Cibao Eagles	DOM
2002	Culiacán Tomato Growers	MEX	2008	Licey Tigers	DOM
2003	Cibao Eagles	DOM	2009	Aragua Tigers	VEN
2004	Licey Tigers	DOM	2010	Escogido Lions	DOM

Japan Series

Held since 1950. Table shows results for the past 10 years.

YEAR	WINNER	RUNNER-UP	RESULTS
2000	Tokyo Yomiuri Giants (CL)	Fukuoka Daiei Hawks (PL)	4–2
2001	Yakult Swallows (CL)	Osaka Kintetsu Buffaloes (PL)	4–1
2002	Yomiuri Giants (CL)	Seibu Lions (PL)	4–0
2003	Fukuoka Daiei Hawks (PL)	Hanshin Tigers (CL)	4–3
2004	Seibu Lions (PL)	Chunichi Dragons (CL)	4–3
2005	Chiba Lotte Marines (PL)	Hanshin Tigers (CL)	4–0
2006	Hokkaido Nippon Ham Fighters (PL)	Chunichi Dragons (CL)	4–1
2007	Chunichi Dragons (CL)	Hokkaido Nippon Ham Fighters (PL)	4–1
2008	Saitama Seibu Lions (PL)	Yomiuri Giants (CL)	4–3
2009	Yomiuri Giants (CL)	Hokkaido Nippon Ham Fighters (PL)	4–2

Little League World Series

The Little League World Series, first called the National Little League Tournament, was established in 1947. Table shows results for past 10 years.

YEAR	WINNING TEAM/HOME	RUNNER-UP	SCORE
2001	Kitasuna/Tokyo (JPN)	Apopka National/Apopka FL	2–1
2002	Valley Sports American/Louisville KY	Sendai Higashi/Sendai (JPN)	1–0
2003	Musashi-Fuchu/Tokyo (JPN)	East Boynton Beach/Boynton Beach FL	10–1
2004	Pabao/Willemstad (AHO)	Conejo Valley/Thousand Oaks CA	5–2
2005	West Oahu/Ewa Beach HI	Pabao/Willemstad (AHO)	7–6
2006	Columbus Northern/Columbus GA	Kawaguchi/Kawaguchi City (JPN)	2–1
2007	Warner Robins American/Warner Robins GA	Tokyo Kitasuna/Tokyo (JPN)	3–2
2008	Waipio/Waipahu HI	Matamoros/Matamoros (MEX)	12–3
2009	Parkview/Chula Vista CA	Kuei-Shan/Taoyuan (TPE)	6–3
2010	Edogawa Minami/Tokyo (JPN)	Waipio/Waipahu HI	4–1

Basketball

American professional basketball is directed by the **National Basketball Association** (NBA; formed 1949). The NBA is divided into the Eastern and Western conferences (EC and WC; until 1970 the Eastern and Western divisions [ED and WD]), the top-ranking teams of which compete yearly for the championship. The NBA began the **Women's National Basketball Association** (WNBA), which is also divided into an Eastern and a Western Conference (EC and WC), in 1997.

Since the inclusion of basketball as an **Olympic sport** in 1936, the winners of the Olympic tournament have been considered by many to be the world champions. However, the **Fédération Internationale de Basketball** (FIBA; founded 1932) instituted world championships in 1950 for men and in 1953 for women. (Women's basketball was not admitted to the Olympics until 1976.) Amateur basketball in the United States is most closely followed at the **collegiate** level, where the most important event of the season is the **National Collegiate Athletic Association (NCAA) Championship.** The NCAA tournament was first contested in 1939 (by men's teams only). Women's college basketball was first played on an organized national level in 1972, under the auspices of the Association for Intercollegiate Athletics for Women (AIAW), which gave way in 1982 to the NCAA's first tournament for women.

Related Web sites: NBA: <www.nba.com>; WNBA: <www.wnba.com>; FIBA: <www.fiba.com>; NCAA: <www.ncaa.org>.

Did you know? The only man to hold managerial positions in both professional baseball and football was Hugo Bezdek. After coaching football at the collegiate level, Bezdek managed baseball's Pittsburgh Pirates from 1917 to 1919. He returned to college football (he was inducted into the College Football Hall of Fame in 1954) before coaching the Cleveland Rams in 1937 and 1938.

National Basketball Association Final Standings, 2009–10

EASTERN CONFERENCE

Atlantic Division				Central Division				Southeast Division			
TEAM	WON	LOST	GAMES BACK	TEAM	WON	LOST	GAMES BACK	TEAM	WON	LOST	GAMES BACK
Boston[1]	50	32	—	Cleveland[1]	61	21	—	Orlando[1]	59	23	—
Toronto	40	42	10	Milwaukee[1]	46	36	15	Atlanta[1]	53	29	6
New York	29	53	21	Chicago[1]	41	41	20	Miami[1]	47	35	12
Philadelphia	27	55	23	Indiana	32	50	29	Charlotte[1]	44	38	15
New Jersey	12	70	38	Detroit	27	55	34	Washington	26	56	33

WESTERN CONFERENCE

Northwest Division				Pacific Division				Southwest Division			
TEAM	WON	LOST	GAMES BACK	TEAM	WON	LOST	GAMES BACK	TEAM	WON	LOST	GAMES BACK
Denver[1]	53	29	—	L.A. Lakers[1]	57	25	—	Dallas[1]	55	27	—
Utah[1]	53	29	—	Phoenix[1]	54	28	3	San Antonio[1]	50	32	5
Portland[1]	50	32	3	L.A. Clippers	29	53	28	Houston	42	40	13
Oklahoma City[1]	50	32	3	Golden State	26	56	31	Memphis	40	42	15
Minnesota	15	67	38	Sacramento	25	57	32	New Orleans	37	45	18

[1]Gained play-off berth.

National Basketball Association Championship

SEASON	WINNER	RUNNER-UP	RESULTS
1949–50	Minneapolis Lakers (CD)[1]	Syracuse Nationals (ED)	4–2
1950–51	Rochester Royals (WD)	New York Knickerbockers (ED)	4–3
1951–52	Minneapolis Lakers (WD)	New York Knickerbockers (ED)	4–3
1952–53	Minneapolis Lakers (WD)	New York Knickerbockers (ED)	4–1
1953–54	Minneapolis Lakers (WD)	Syracuse Nationals (ED)	4–3
1954–55	Syracuse Nationals (ED)	Fort Wayne Pistons (WD)	4–3
1955–56	Philadelphia Warriors (ED)	Fort Wayne Pistons (WD)	4–1
1956–57	Boston Celtics (ED)	St. Louis Hawks (WD)	4–3
1957–58	St. Louis Hawks (WD)	Boston Celtics (ED)	4–2
1958–59	Boston Celtics (ED)	Minneapolis Lakers (WD)	4–0
1959–60	Boston Celtics (ED)	St. Louis Hawks (WD)	4–3
1960–61	Boston Celtics (ED)	St. Louis Hawks (WD)	4–1
1961–62	Boston Celtics (ED)	Los Angeles Lakers (WD)	4–3
1962–63	Boston Celtics (ED)	Los Angeles Lakers (WD)	4–2
1963–64	Boston Celtics (ED)	San Francisco Warriors (WD)	4–1
1964–65	Boston Celtics (ED)	Los Angeles Lakers (WD)	4–1
1965–66	Boston Celtics (ED)	Los Angeles Lakers (WD)	4–3
1966–67	Philadelphia 76ers (ED)	San Francisco Warriors (WD)	4–2
1967–68	Boston Celtics (ED)	Los Angeles Lakers (WD)	4–2
1968–69	Boston Celtics (ED)	Los Angeles Lakers (WD)	4–3
1969–70	New York Knickerbockers (EC)	Los Angeles Lakers (WC)	4–3
1970–71	Milwaukee Bucks (WC)	Baltimore Bullets (EC)	4–0
1971–72	Los Angeles Lakers (WC)	New York Knickerbockers (EC)	4–1
1972–73	New York Knickerbockers (EC)	Los Angeles Lakers (WC)	4–1
1973–74	Boston Celtics (EC)	Milwaukee Bucks (WC)	4–3
1974–75	Golden State Warriors (WC)	Washington Bullets (EC)	4–0
1975–76	Boston Celtics (EC)	Phoenix Suns (WC)	4–2
1976–77	Portland Trail Blazers (WC)	Philadelphia 76ers (EC)	4–2
1977–78	Washington Bullets (EC)	Seattle SuperSonics (WC)	4–3
1978–79	Seattle SuperSonics (WC)	Washington Bullets (EC)	4–1
1979–80	Los Angeles Lakers (WC)	Philadelphia 76ers (EC)	4–2
1980–81	Boston Celtics (EC)	Houston Rockets (WC)	4–2
1981–82	Los Angeles Lakers (WC)	Philadelphia 76ers (EC)	4–2
1982–83	Philadelphia 76ers (EC)	Los Angeles Lakers (WC)	4–0
1983–84	Boston Celtics (EC)	Los Angeles Lakers (WC)	4–3
1984–85	Los Angeles Lakers (WC)	Boston Celtics (EC)	4–2
1985–86	Boston Celtics (EC)	Houston Rockets (WC)	4–2
1986–87	Los Angeles Lakers (WC)	Boston Celtics (EC)	4–2
1987–88	Los Angeles Lakers (WC)	Detroit Pistons (EC)	4–3
1988–89	Detroit Pistons (EC)	Los Angeles Lakers (WC)	4–0
1989–90	Detroit Pistons (EC)	Portland Trail Blazers (WC)	4–1
1990–91	Chicago Bulls (EC)	Los Angeles Lakers (WC)	4–1

National Basketball Association Championship (continued)

SEASON	WINNER	RUNNER-UP	RESULTS
1991–92	Chicago Bulls (EC)	Portland Trail Blazers (WC)	4–2
1992–93	Chicago Bulls (EC)	Phoenix Suns (WC)	4–2
1993–94	Houston Rockets (WC)	New York Knickerbockers (EC)	4–3
1994–95	Houston Rockets (WC)	Orlando Magic (EC)	4–0
1995–96	Chicago Bulls (EC)	Seattle SuperSonics (WC)	4–2
1996–97	Chicago Bulls (EC)	Utah Jazz (WC)	4–2
1997–98	Chicago Bulls (EC)	Utah Jazz (WC)	4–2
1998–99	San Antonio Spurs (WC)	New York Knickerbockers (EC)	4–1
1999–2000	Los Angeles Lakers (WC)	Indiana Pacers (EC)	4–2
2000–01	Los Angeles Lakers (WC)	Philadelphia 76ers (EC)	4–1
2001–02	Los Angeles Lakers (WC)	New Jersey Nets (EC)	4–0
2002–03	San Antonio Spurs (WC)	New Jersey Nets (EC)	4–2
2003–04	Detroit Pistons (EC)	Los Angeles Lakers (WC)	4–1
2004–05	San Antonio Spurs (WC)	Detroit Pistons (EC)	4–3
2005–06	Miami Heat (EC)	Dallas Mavericks (WC)	4–2
2006–07	San Antonio Spurs (WC)	Cleveland Cavaliers (EC)	4–0
2007–08	Boston Celtics (EC)	Los Angeles Lakers (WC)	4–2
2008–09	Los Angeles Lakers (WC)	Orlando Magic (EC)	4–1
2009–10	Los Angeles Lakers (WC)	Boston Celtics (EC)	4–3

[1]*In its inaugural season, the NBA had a third division, the Central Division (CD).*

National Basketball Association All-Time Records[1]

	PLAYERS/TEAMS	NUMBER	SEASON/DATE
Individual career records			
Games played	Robert Parish	1,611	1976-77–1996-97
Points scored	Kareem Abdul-Jabbar	38,387	1969-70–1988-89
Most games, 50 or more points	Wilt Chamberlain	118	1959-60–1972-73
Most consecutive games, 10 or more points	Michael Jordan	866	25 Mar 1986–26 Dec 2001
Field goals attempted	Kareem Abdul-Jabbar	28,307	1969-70–1988-89
Field goals made	Kareem Abdul-Jabbar	15,837	1969-70–1988-89
Field-goal percentage[2]	Artis Gilmore	.599	1976-77–1987-88
Three-point field goals attempted	Reggie Miller	6,486	1987-88–2004-05
Three-point field goals made	Reggie Miller	2,560	1987-88–2004-05
Three-point field-goal percentage[3]	Steve Kerr	.454	1988-89–2002-03
Free throws attempted	Karl Malone	13,188	1985-86–2003-04
Free throws made	Karl Malone	9,787	1985-86–2003-04
Free-throw percentage[4]	Mark Price	.904	1986-87–1997-98
Assists	John Stockton	15,806	1984-85–2002-03
Rebounds	Wilt Chamberlain	23,924	1959-60–1972-73
Steals[5]	John Stockton	3,265	1984-85–2002-03
Blocked shots[5]	Hakeem Olajuwon	3,830	1984-85–2001-02
Personal fouls	Kareem Abdul-Jabbar	4,657	1969-70–1988-89
Wins (coaching)	Lenny Wilkens	1,332	1969-70–2004-05, except 1972–1974
Individual season records			
Points scored	Wilt Chamberlain	4,029	1961-62
Field goals attempted	Wilt Chamberlain	3,159	1961-62
Field goals made	Wilt Chamberlain	1,597	1961-62
Field-goal percentage	Wilt Chamberlain	.727	1972-73
Three-point field goals attempted	George McCloud	678	1995-96
Three-point field goals made	Ray Allen	269	2005-06
Three-point field-goal percentage	Kyle Korver	.536	2009-10
Free throws attempted	Wilt Chamberlain	1,363	1961-62
Free throws made	Jerry West	840	1965-66
Free-throw percentage	José Calderón	.981	2008-09
Assists	John Stockton	1,164	1990-91
Rebounds	Wilt Chamberlain	2,149	1960-61
Steals[5]	Alvin Robertson	301	1985-86
Blocked shots[5]	Mark Eaton	456	1984-85
Personal fouls	Darryl Dawkins	386	1983-84
Individual game records			
Points scored	Wilt Chamberlain	100	2 Mar 1962
Field goals attempted	Wilt Chamberlain	63	2 Mar 1962

National Basketball Association All-Time Records[1] (continued)

Individual game records (continued)

Field goals made	Wilt Chamberlain	36	2 Mar 1962
Three-point field goals attempted	Damon Stoudamire	21	15 Apr 2005
Three-point field goals made	Kobe Bryant;	12	7 Jan 2003;
	Donyell Marshall		13 Mar 2005
Free throws attempted	Wilt Chamberlain	34	22 Feb 1962
Free throws made	Wilt Chamberlain;	28	2 Mar 1962;
	Adrian Dantley		4 Jan 1984
Assists	Scott Skiles	30	30 Dec 1990
Rebounds	Wilt Chamberlain	55	24 Nov 1960
Steals[5]	Larry Kenon;	11	26 Dec 1976;
	Kendall Gill		3 Apr 1999
Blocked shots[5]	Elmore Smith	17	28 Oct 1973

Team records

Highest winning percentage (season)	Chicago Bulls	.878 (72–10)	1995–96
Consecutive games won	Los Angeles Lakers	33	5 Nov 1971–
			7 Jan 1972
Championships	Boston Celtics	17	
Consecutive championships	Boston Celtics	8	1959–66

Game records

Highest combined score	Detroit Pistons versus	370	13 Dec 1983
	Denver Nuggets	(186–184)	
Longest game (overtime periods)	Indianapolis Olympians versus	6	6 Jan 1951
	Rochester Royals		

[1]Through the end of the 2009–10 season.   [2]Minimum 2,000 made.   [3]Minimum 250 made.   [4]Minimum 1,200 made.   [5]Since 1973–74; before that season steals and blocked shots were not officially recorded by the NBA.

Women's National Basketball Association Championship

SEASON	WINNER	RUNNER-UP	RESULTS
1997	Houston Comets (EC)	New York Liberty (EC)	1–0
1998	Houston Comets (WC)	Phoenix Mercury (WC)	2–1
1999	Houston Comets (WC)	New York Liberty (EC)	2–1
2000	Houston Comets (WC)	New York Liberty (EC)	2–0
2001	Los Angeles Sparks (WC)	Charlotte Sting (EC)	2–0
2002	Los Angeles Sparks (WC)	New York Liberty (EC)	2–0
2003	Detroit Shock (EC)	Los Angeles Sparks (WC)	2–1
2004	Seattle Storm (WC)	Connecticut Sun (EC)	2–1
2005	Sacramento Monarchs (WC)	Connecticut Sun (EC)	3–1
2006	Detroit Shock (EC)	Sacramento Monarchs (WC)	3–2
2007	Phoenix Mercury (WC)	Detroit Shock (EC)	3–2
2008	Detroit Shock (EC)	San Antonio Silver Stars (WC)	3–0
2009	Phoenix Mercury (WC)	Indiana Fever (EC)	3–2

National Collegiate Athletic Association Basketball Championship—Men[1]

YEAR	WINNER	RUNNER-UP	SCORE	YEAR	WINNER	RUNNER-UP	SCORE
1939	Oregon	Ohio State	46–43	1955	San Francisco	La Salle	77–63
1940	Indiana	Kansas	60–42	1956	San Francisco	Iowa	83–71
1941	Wisconsin	Washington State	39–34	1957	North Carolina	Kansas	54–53
1942	Stanford	Dartmouth	53–38	1958	Kentucky	Seattle	84–72
1943	Wyoming	Georgetown	46–34	1959	California	West Virginia	71–70
1944	Utah	Dartmouth	42–40		(Berkeley)		
1945	Oklahoma A&M	New York	49–45	1960	Ohio State	California	75–55
1946	Oklahoma A&M	North Carolina	43–40			(Berkeley)	
1947	Holy Cross (MA)	Oklahoma	58–47	1961	Cincinnati	Ohio State	70–65
1948	Kentucky	Baylor	58–42	1962	Cincinnati	Ohio State	71–59
1949	Kentucky	Oklahoma State	46–36	1963	Loyola (IL)	Cincinnati	60–58
1950	City College of	Bradley	71–68	1964	UCLA	Duke	98–83
	New York			1965	UCLA	Michigan	91–80
1951	Kentucky	Kansas State	68–58	1966	Texas Western	Kentucky	72–65
1952	Kansas	St. John's (NY)	80–63	1967	UCLA	Dayton	79–64
1953	Indiana	Kansas	69–68	1968	UCLA	North Carolina	78–55
1954	La Salle	Bradley	92–76	1969	UCLA	Purdue	92–72

National Collegiate Athletic Association Basketball Championship—Men[1] (continued)

YEAR	WINNER	RUNNER-UP	SCORE	YEAR	WINNER	RUNNER-UP	SCORE
1970	UCLA	Jacksonville	80–69	1990	Nevada (Las Vegas)	Duke	103–73
1971	UCLA	Villanova	68–62	1991	Duke	Kansas	72–65
1972	UCLA	Florida State	81–76	1992	Duke	Michigan	71–51
1973	UCLA	Memphis State	87–66	1993	North Carolina	Michigan	77–71
1974	North Carolina State	Marquette	76–64	1994	Arkansas	Duke	76–72
				1995	UCLA	Arkansas	89–78
1975	UCLA	Kentucky	92–85	1996	Kentucky	Syracuse	76–67
1976	Indiana	Michigan	86–68	1997	Arizona	Kentucky	84–79
1977	Marquette	North Carolina	67–59	1998	Kentucky	Utah	78–69
1978	Kentucky	Duke	94–88	1999	Connecticut	Duke	77–74
1979	Michigan State	Indiana State	75–64	2000	Michigan State	Florida	89–76
1980	Louisville	UCLA	59–54	2001	Duke	Arizona	82–72
1981	Indiana	North Carolina	63–50	2002	Maryland	Indiana	64–52
1982	North Carolina	Georgetown	63–62	2003	Syracuse	Kansas	81–78
1983	North Carolina State	Houston	54–52	2004	Connecticut	Georgia Tech	82–73
				2005	North Carolina	Illinois	75–70
1984	Georgetown	Houston	84–75	2006	Florida	UCLA	73–57
1985	Villanova	Georgetown	66–64	2007	Florida	Ohio State	84–75
1986	Louisville	Duke	72–69	2008	Kansas	Memphis[2]	75–68
1987	Indiana	Syracuse	74–73	2009	North Carolina	Michigan State	89–72
1988	Kansas	Oklahoma	83–79	2010	Duke	Butler	61–59
1989	Michigan	Seton Hall	80–79				

[1]University Division 1957–73, Division I from 1974. [2]Stripped of this result in 2009 for NCAA rules violations.

National Collegiate Athletic Association Basketball Championship—Women[1]

YEAR	WINNER	RUNNER-UP	SCORE	YEAR	WINNER	RUNNER-UP	SCORE
1982	Louisiana Tech	Cheyney State	76–62	1997	Tennessee	Old Dominion	68–59
1983	Southern California	Louisiana Tech	69–67	1998	Tennessee	Louisiana Tech	93–75
1984	Southern California	Tennessee	72–61	1999	Purdue	Duke	62–45
1985	Old Dominion	Georgia	70–65	2000	Connecticut	Tennessee	71–52
1986	Texas	Southern California	97–81	2001	Notre Dame	Purdue	68–66
1987	Tennessee	Louisiana Tech	67–44	2002	Connecticut	Oklahoma	82–70
1988	Louisiana Tech	Auburn	56–54	2003	Connecticut	Tennessee	73–68
1989	Tennessee	Auburn	76–60	2004	Connecticut	Tennessee	70–61
1990	Stanford	Auburn	88–81	2005	Baylor	Michigan State	84–62
1991	Tennessee	Virginia	70–67	2006	Maryland	Duke	78–75
1992	Stanford	Western Kentucky	78–62	2007	Tennessee	Rutgers	59–46
1993	Texas Tech	Ohio State	84–82	2008	Tennessee	Stanford	64–48
1994	North Carolina	Louisiana Tech	60–59	2009	Connecticut	Louisville	76–54
1995	Connecticut	Tennessee	70–64	2010	Connecticut	Stanford	53–47
1996	Tennessee	Georgia	83–65				

[1]Division I.

FIBA World Championship—Men

YEAR	WINNER	RUNNER-UP	YEAR	WINNER	RUNNER-UP
1936[1]	United States	Canada	1978	Yugoslavia	USSR
1948[1]	United States	France	1980[1]	Yugoslavia	Italy
1950	Argentina	United States	1982	USSR	United States
1952[1]	United States	USSR	1984[1]	United States	Spain
1954	United States	Brazil	1986	United States	USSR
1956[1]	United States	USSR	1988[1]	USSR	Yugoslavia
1959	Brazil[2]	United States	1990	Yugoslavia	USSR
1960[1]	United States	USSR	1992[1]	United States	Croatia
1963	Brazil	Yugoslavia	1994	United States	Russia
1964[1]	United States	USSR	1996[1]	United States	Yugoslavia
1967	USSR	Yugoslavia	1998	Yugoslavia	Russia
1968[1]	United States	Yugoslavia	2000[1]	United States	France
1970	Yugoslavia	Brazil	2002	Yugoslavia	Argentina
1972[1]	USSR	United States	2004[1]	Argentina	Italy
1974	USSR	Yugoslavia	2006	Spain	Greece
1976[1]	United States	Yugoslavia	2008[1]	United States	Spain

[1]Olympic championships, recognized in this table as world championships (though not by FIBA). [2]Won by default.

FIBA World Championship—Women

YEAR	WINNER	RUNNER-UP	YEAR	WINNER	RUNNER-UP
1953	United States	Chile	1986	United States	USSR
1957	United States	USSR	1988[1]	United States	Yugoslavia
1959	USSR	Bulgaria	1990	United States	Yugoslavia
1964	USSR	Czechoslovakia	1992[1]	Unified Team	China
1967	USSR	Rep. of Korea	1994	Brazil	China
1971	USSR	Czechoslovakia	1996[1]	United States	Brazil
1975	USSR	Japan	1998	United States	Russia
1976[1]	USSR	United States	2000[1]	United States	Australia
1979	United States	Rep. of Korea	2002	United States	Russia
1980[1]	USSR	Bulgaria	2004[1]	United States	Australia
1983	USSR	United States	2006	Australia	Russia
1984[1]	United States	Rep. of Korea	2008[1]	United States	Australia

[1]Olympic championships, recognized in this table as world championships (though not by FIBA).

Bowling

The world governing body for bowling is the **Fédération Internationale des Quilleurs (FIQ)**. Since 1954 it has sponsored world bowling championships.

In the **United States,** men's bowling is governed by the **American Bowling Congress (ABC)**, which was founded in 1895 but became a constituent of the **United States Bowling Congress (USBC)** in 2004. In 1901 the first national championship was organized; in 1961 the yearly competition was split into two divisions—regular (for those with a combined average score of 851 or higher) and classic (for professionals). The classic division was discontinued in 1980. The **Women's International Bowling Congress (WIBC)** was organized in 1916 and sponsored an annual women's championship until 2004, when organizational mergers created the USBC. Competition takes place between teams, doubles, and singles. The all-events category is won by the individual who has the best score of nine games—three team, three doubles, and three singles scores. The Professional Bowlers Association (PBA) was established in 1958.

Related Web sites: FIQ: <www.fiq.org>; USBC: <www.bowl.com>; PBA: <www.pba.com>.

United States Bowling Congress Bowling Championships—Regular Division

Held since 1901. Table shows results for the past 10 years.

YEAR	SINGLES	SCORE	ALL-EVENTS	SCORE
2001	Nicholas Hoagland	798	D.J. Archer	2,219
2002	Mark Millsap	823	Stephen A. Hardy	2,279
2003	Ron Bahr	837	Steve Kloempken	2,215
2004[1]	John Janawicz	858	John Janawicz	2,224
2005	David Adam	791	Scott Craddock	2,131
2006	Wendy Macpherson	812	Dave A. Mitchell	2,189
2007	Frederick Aki	814	Mike Rose, Jr.	2,198
2008	Bryan Young	832	Jay Futrell	2,183
2009	Bo Goergen	862	Ron Vokes	2,321
2010	Terrence Syring	833	Matt McNiel	2,326

[1]Table shows American Bowling Congress winners through 2004 and USBC winners thereafter.

United States Bowling Congress Women's Bowling Championships—Classic Division

Held since 1916. Table shows results for the past 10 years.

YEAR	SINGLES	SCORE	ALL-EVENTS	SCORE
2001	Lisa Wagner	756	Jonquay Armon	2,044
2002	Theresa Smith	752	Cara Honeychurch	2,150
2003	Michelle Feldman	764	Michelle Feldman	2,048
2004[1]	Sharon Smith	754	Kim Adler	2,133
2005	Leanne Barrette	774	Leanne Barrette	2,231
2006	Karen Stroud	771	Karen Stroud	2,159
2007	Tiffany Stanbrough	745	Wendy Macpherson	2,161
2008	Corrine Ham	736	Liz Johnson	2,113

United States Bowling Congress Women's Bowling Championships—Classic Division (continued)

YEAR	SINGLES	SCORE	ALL-EVENTS	SCORE
2009	Michelle Feldman	816	Robin Romeo	2,172
2010	Krischna Howard	792	Jodi Woessner	2,330

[1]Table shows Women's International Bowling Congress winners through 2004 and USBC winners thereafter.

Cricket

Cricket is one of the **national sports** of England, and consequently it is played in nearly all the countries with which England has been associated. The world governing body is the **International Cricket Council** (ICC; founded as the Imperial Cricket Conference in 1909). The most important international cricket matches are the **Test matches**, which have been played since 1877. The Test-playing countries are England, Australia, South Africa (banned from international competition between about 1970 and 1992), West Indies (representing Barbados, Guyana, Jamaica, Trinidad and Tobago, and the Leeward and Windward islands), New Zealand, India, Pakistan, Sri Lanka, Zimbabwe (since 1992), and Bangladesh (since 2000).

The Test table is designed to be read from left to right across the columns. This will indicate, for example, that in Test match play against England, South Africa has won 26 games, has had 50 drawn matches, and has lost 54 games.

The **World Cup** is a quadrennial series of one-day, limited-overs competitions. It was first held in 1975.

International Cricket Council Web site: <www.icc-cricket.com>.

All-Time First-Class Test Cricket Standings (as of 30 Sep 2009)

	England			Australia			South Africa			West Indies			New Zealand		
	WINS	DRAWS	LOSSES	W	D	L	W	D	L	W	D	L	W	D	L
England v.	—	—	—	99	90	132	55	51	28	43	49#	53	45	41	8
Australia v.	132	90	99	—	—	—	47	18	18	50	23*	32	24	16	7
South Africa v.	28	51	55	18	18	47	—	—	—	14	5	3	20	11	4
West Indies v.	53	49#	43	32	23*	50	3	5	14	—	—	—	10	18†	9
New Zealand v.	8	41	45	7	16	24	4	11	20	9	18†	10	—	—	—
India v.	19	46	34	18	24*	34	5	7	11	11	41	30	15	24†	9
Pakistan v.	12	36	19‡	11	17	24	3	3	7	15	15	14	21	18	6
Sri Lanka v.	6	7	8	1	6	13	4	5	8	6	3	3	7	10	9
Zimbabwe v.	0	3	3	0	0	3	0	1	6	0	2	4	0	6	7
Bangladesh v.	0	0	4	0	0	4	0	0	8	2	1	3	0	1	7

	India			Pakistan			Sri Lanka			Zimbabwe			Bangladesh		
	WINS	DRAWS	LOSSES	W	D	L	W	D	L	W	D	L	W	D	L
England v.	34	46	19	19‡	36	12	8	7	6	3	3	0	4	0	0
Australia v.	34	24*	18	24	17	11	13	6	1	1	0	0	4	0	0
South Africa v.	11	7	5	7	3	3	8	5	4	6	1	0	8	0	0
West Indies v.	30	41	11	14	15	15	3	3	6	4	2	0	3	1	2
New Zealand v.	9	24†	15	6	18	21	9	10	7	7	6	0	7	1	0
India v.	—	—	—	9	38	12	11	13	5	7	2	2	4	1	0
Pakistan v.	12	38	9	—	—	—	15	13†	9	8	5†	2	6	0	0
Sri Lanka v.	5	13	11	9	13†	15	—	—	—	10	5	0	12	0	0
Zimbabwe v.	2	2	7	2	5†	8	0	5	10	—	—	—	4	3	1
Bangladesh v.	0	1	4	0	0	6	0	0	12	1	3	4	—	—	—

#Including two matches abandoned.   *Including one tie.   †Including one match abandoned.   ‡Including one forfeit.

Cycling

By all accounts, the greatest cycling event of all is the annual **Tour de France** road race (founded in 1903). It is raced in stages over a distance usually exceeding 3,500 km (2,175 mi). From 1911 to 1929, distances exceeded 5,300 km (3,290 mi). A Tour de France for women was first held in 1984, over an 18-stage course of 991 km (616 mi). In addition to this and a great number of other road races, there are yearly **road racing world championships.**

Track racing championships are also held. The oldest events of track racing are the **sprint** (in

Cycling (continued)

which only the last part of the race can actually be considered sprinting) and the **pursuit** (both a team and an individual event in which contestants start the race on opposite sides of the track and attempt to catch each other). **Mountain bike racing** and **cyclo-cross**, a cross-country bicycle race that requires cyclists to carry their bikes over parts of the course, developed in the latter part of the 20th century. World championships were established for these sports in 1997.

International Cycling Union (Union Cycliste Internationale—UCI) Web site: <www.uci.ch>.

Cycling Champions, 2009–10

In the case of multiday events, the concluding date is given.

EVENT	WINNER (COUNTRY)	DATE
World champions—mountain bikes		6 Sep 2009
Men		
Cross-country	Nino Schurter (SUI)	
Downhill	Steve Peat (GBR)	
Women		
Cross-country	Irina Kalentieva (RUS)	
Downhill	Emmeline Ragot (FRA)	
World champions—road		27 Sep 2009
Men		
Individual road race	Cadel Evans (AUS)	
Individual time trial	Fabian Cancellara (SUI)	
Women		
Individual road race	Tatiana Guderzo (ITA)	
Individual time trial	Kristin Armstrong (USA)	
World champions—cyclo-cross		31 Jan 2010
Men	Zdenek Stybar (CZE)	
Women	Marianne Vos (NED)	
World champions—track		28 Mar 2010
Men		
Individual pursuit	Taylor Phinney (USA)	
Individual sprint	Grégory Baugé (FRA)	
1-km time trial	Teun Mulder (NED)	
Points	Cameron Meyer (AUS)	
Team pursuit	Australia	
Team sprint	Germany	
Keirin	Chris Hoy (GBR)	
Madison	Leigh Howard, Cameron Meyer (AUS)	
Scratch	Alex Rasmussen (DEN)	
Omnium	Edward Clancy (GBR)	
Women		
Individual pursuit	Sarah Hammer (USA)	
Individual sprint	Victoria Pendleton (GBR)	
500-m time trial	Anna Meares (AUS)	
Points	Tara Whitten (CAN)	
Team pursuit	Australia	
Team sprint	Australia	
Keirin	Simona Krupeckaite (LTU)	
Scratch	Pascale Jeuland (FRA)	
Omnium	Tara Whitten (CAN)	
Major elite road-race winners		
Tour of Spain (Vuelta a España)	Alejandro Valverde Belmonte (ESP)	20 Sep 2009
Tour of Lombardy (Giro di Lombardia)	Philippe Gilbert (BEL)	17 Oct 2009
Milan–San Remo	Oscar Freire Gomez (ESP)	20 Mar 2010
Tour of Flanders (Ronde van Vlaanderen)	Fabian Cancellara (SUI)	4 Apr 2010
Paris–Roubaix	Fabian Cancellara (SUI)	11 Apr 2010
Tour of Romandie (Tour de Romandie)	Simon Spilak (SLO)	2 May 2010
Tour of Italy (Giro d'Italia)	Ivan Basso (ITA)	30 May 2010
Tour of Switzerland (Tour de Suisse)	Frank Schleck (LUX)	20 Jun 2010
Tour de France	Alberto Contador (ESP)	25 Jul 2010

Tour de France

YEAR	WINNER (COUNTRY)	LENGTH OF ROUTE (KM)	YEAR	WINNER (COUNTRY)	LENGTH OF ROUTE (KM)
1903	Maurice Garin (FRA)	2,428	1962	Jacques Anquetil (FRA)	4,274
1904	Henri Cornet (FRA)[1]	2,388	1963	Jacques Anquetil (FRA)	4,137
1905	Louis Trousselier (FRA)	2,975	1964	Jacques Anquetil (FRA)	4,504
1906	René Pottier (FRA)	4,637	1965	Felice Gimondi (ITA)	4,183
1907	Lucien Petit-Breton (FRA)	4,488	1966	Lucien Aimar (FRA)	4,303
1908	Lucien Petit-Breton (FRA)	4,487	1967	Roger Pingeon (FRA)	4,780
1909	François Faber (LUX)	4,507	1968	Jan Janssen (NED)	4,662
1910	Octave Lapize (FRA)	4,474	1969	Eddy Merckx (BEL)	4,110
1911	Gustave Garrigou (FRA)	5,344	1970	Eddy Merckx (BEL)	4,366
1912	Odile Defraye (BEL)	5,319	1971	Eddy Merckx (BEL)	3,689
1913	Philippe Thys (BEL)	5,387	1972	Eddy Merckx (BEL)	3,846
1914	Philippe Thys (BEL)	5,405	1973	Luis Ocaña (ESP)	4,140
1915–18	not held		1974	Eddy Merckx (BEL)	4,098
1919	Firmin Lambot (BEL)	5,560	1975	Bernard Thévenet (FRA)	4,000
1920	Philippe Thys (BEL)	5,519	1976	Lucien Van Impe (BEL)	4,050
1921	Léon Scieur (BEL)	5,484	1977	Bernard Thévenet (FRA)	4,098
1922	Firmin Lambot (BEL)	5,375	1978	Bernard Hinault (FRA)	3,920
1923	Henri Pélissier (FRA)	5,386	1979	Bernard Hinault (FRA)	3,719
1924	Ottavio Bottecchia (ITA)	5,425	1980	Joop Zoetemelk (NED)	3,948
1925	Ottavio Bottecchia (ITA)	5,430	1981	Bernard Hinault (FRA)	3,765
1926	Lucien Buysse (BEL)	5,745	1982	Bernard Hinault (FRA)	3,489
1927	Nicolas Frantz (LUX)	5,341	1983	Laurent Fignon (FRA)	3,568
1928	Nicolas Frantz (LUX)	5,377	1984	Laurent Fignon (FRA)	3,880
1929	Maurice De Waele (BEL)	5,286	1985	Bernard Hinault (FRA)	4,100
1930	André Leducq (FRA)	4,818	1986	Greg LeMond (USA)	4,091
1931	Antonin Magne (FRA)	5,095	1987	Stephen Roche (IRL)	4,100
1932	André Leducq (FRA)	4,520	1988	Pedro Delgado (ESP)	3,300
1933	Georges Speicher (FRA)	4,395	1989	Greg LeMond (USA)	3,215
1934	Antonin Magne (FRA)	4,363	1990	Greg LeMond (USA)	3,399
1935	Romain Maes (BEL)	4,338	1991	Miguel Indurain (ESP)	3,935
1936	Romain Maes (BEL)	4,442	1992	Miguel Indurain (ESP)	3,983
1937	Roger Lapébie (FRA)	4,415	1993	Miguel Indurain (ESP)	3,700
1938	Gino Bartali (ITA)	4,694	1994	Miguel Indurain (ESP)	3,978
1939	Sylvere Maes (BEL)	4,224	1995	Miguel Indurain (ESP)	3,635
1940–46	not held		1996	no winner[2]	3,764
1947	Jean Robic (FRA)	4,640	1997	Jan Ullrich (GER)	3,944
1948	Gino Bartali (ITA)	4,922	1998	Marco Pantani (ITA)	3,831
1949	Fausto Coppi (ITA)	4,808	1999	Lance Armstrong (USA)	3,687
1950	Ferdi Kubler (SUI)	4,775	2000	Lance Armstrong (USA)	3,663
1951	Hugo Koblet (SUI)	4,697	2001	Lance Armstrong (USA)	3,454
1952	Fausto Coppi (ITA)	4,807	2002	Lance Armstrong (USA)	3,272
1953	Louison Bobet (FRA)	4,479	2003	Lance Armstrong (USA)	3,428
1954	Louison Bobet (FRA)	4,469	2004	Lance Armstrong (USA)	3,391
1955	Louison Bobet (FRA)	4,855	2005	Lance Armstrong (USA)	3,608
1956	Roger Walkowiak (FRA)	4,496	2006	Óscar Pereiro (ESP)[3]	3,657
1957	Jacques Anquetil (FRA)	4,686	2007	Alberto Contador (ESP)	3,550
1958	Charly Gaul (LUX)	4,319	2008	Carlos Sastre (ESP)	3,554
1959	Federico Bahamontes (ESP)	4,355	2009	Alberto Contador (ESP)	3,445
1960	Gastone Nencini (ITA)	4,173	2010	Alberto Contador (ESP)	3,596
1961	Jacques Anquetil (FRA)	4,397			

[1]Maurice Garin (FRA), the tour's first champion, finished first in the 1904 race, as well, but was later disqualified for having eaten illegally and for other, suspected offenses.   [2]The victory for Bjarne Riis (DEN) was invalidated after he admitted to having used illegal performance-enhancing drugs.   [3]Floyd Landis (USA) was stripped of the title after he was found to have had illegal performance-enhancing drugs in his system.

Football

Many types of games are known as football, among them association football (also called soccer), gridiron football (also called American football), Canadian football (also called rugby football), Australian rules football (also called footy), and rugby union and rugby league football (also known as rugger). Each of these games is unique, though some—such as US football and Canadian football—bear more than a little resemblance.

American football professional. The National Football League (NFL) championship play-offs were organized in 1933. The American Football League

Football (continued)

(founded 1959) was a rival organization until 1970, when it merged with the NFL. The resulting reorganization added a few new teams (1976) and divided the reconstituted NFL into two conferences, the American Football Conference and the National Football Conference. (There have been several expansions since.) The play-off winner in each conference becomes that conference's representative in the Super Bowl, the final game of the professional football season.

American football—college. Historically the national champion of college football has been informally selected by two rival opinion polls—one based on a survey of collegiate football coaches (currently conducted by *USA Today*) and the other on a survey of sportswriters (conducted by the Associated Press [AP]). The AP sportswriters' poll began in 1936. The coaches' poll was begun in 1950 by the United Press (now United Press International [UPI]). Where polls designated different teams, both are listed. Desire for a clear-cut national champion led to the creation of the Bowl Championship Series (BCS) in 1999. The BCS uses a formula involving team records, strength of schedule, and rankings to determine the top two teams, who then meet in a national championship game. The site of the game annually shifts between the four major bowls—Fiesta, Orange, Rose, and Sugar. The first of the bowl games, the Rose Bowl, had its inaugural game in 1902 during the 12th annual Tournament of Roses festival in Pasadena CA. In 1935 the Sugar Bowl (played in New Orleans LA) and the Orange Bowl (played in Miami FL) were inaugurated. The Fiesta Bowl (played in Phoenix AZ) began play in 1971.

Canadian football—professional. The rules and organization of professional football in Canada have evolved gradually for well over 100 years based on the Canadian Rugby Union (formed in 1891). Until 1936 the game included intercollegiate teams. In 1958 the Canadian Football League was formed, dividing into two conferences, Eastern and Western. In 1981 these were renamed divisions. The two teams that win the division championships meet for the championship of the League, the Grey Cup (instituted in 1909). The intercollegiate teams withdrew from the Grey Cup competition in 1936, but the league did not become strictly professional until the mid-1950s.

Australian football—professional. Australian rules football, originally called Melbourne rules football, emerged in the state of Victoria in the late 1850s as a sporting alternative during the southern winter, when cricket was not played. The Victorian Football Association (formed in 1877) was supplanted by the Victorian Football League (formed in 1896), which was renamed the Australian Football League (AFL) in 1990 after two teams from outside Victoria were admitted in 1987. Currently, the eight AFL teams with the best records at the end of a 22-week season qualify for the play-offs. The first premiership Grand Final was played in 1886.

Association football. The game of association football is governed by the Fédération Internationale de Football Association (FIFA; founded 1904). The quadrennial FIFA World Cup (organized as the World Cup in 1930) was the first official internationally contested association football match. The popularity of the World Cup and, even earlier, the Copa América (1916) in South America led to the development of several regional cup competitions, including the European Champion Clubs' Cup (1955; discontinued after the 1992–93 season and superseded by the Union of European Football Associations [UEFA] Champions League), the Asian Cup (1956), the African Cup of Nations (1957), and the Libertadores de América Cup (1960). Competition for the FIFA Women's World Cup began in 1991. The Major League Soccer Cup in the US was launched in 1996.

Rugby union football. Rugby union football was open to amateurs only until 1995. The Six Nations Championship was first played in 1882 (as the Four Nations) and is now contested by England, Scotland, Wales, Ireland, France (since 1910), and Italy (since 2000). The international Test matches further include South Africa, New Zealand, and Australia. The International Amateur Rugby Fedpration (FIRA; now FIRA-AER) oversees rugby in 37 other (i.e., non-Test) countries. The chief international competition between rugby union clubs in the Southern Hemisphere is the tri-nation Super 14 (Super 10 from 1993 to 1995 and Super 12 from 1996 to 2005. Teams from Australia (four), South Africa (five), and New Zealand (five) play in a round-robin tournament; the four teams with the best records qualify for the semifinals. The World Cup, sponsored by the International Rugby Board (founded 1886), was inaugurated in 1987. The competition is held every four years.

Rugby league football. Rugby League World Cup competition began in 1954 between professionals from Australia, France, Great Britain, and New Zealand. In 1975–77 it was known as the International Championship. Competition was discontinued after 1977 but revived during the 1980s. The match has been held irregularly every few years.

Related Web sites: National Football League (NFL): <www.nfl.com>; Canadian Football League (CFL): <www.cfl.ca>; Australian Football League (AFL): <www.afl.com.au>; Fédération Internationale de Football Association (FIFA): <www.fifa.com>; Union of European Football Associations (UEFA): <www.uefa.com>; Major League Soccer (MLS): <www.mlsnet.com>; International Rugby Board (rugby union): <www.irb.com>; Rugby League International Federation: <www.rlif.org>; Super 14: <www.super14.com>.

National Football League Final Standings, 2009–10

American Football Conference

East Division			
TEAM	WON	LOST	TIED
New England[1]	10	6	0
New York Jets[1]	9	7	0
Miami	7	9	0
Buffalo	6	10	0

South Division			
TEAM	WON	LOST	TIED
Indianapolis[1]	14	2	0
Houston	9	7	0
Tennessee	8	8	0
Jacksonville	7	9	0

National Football League Final Standings, 2009–10 (continued)

American Football Conference (continued)

North Division

TEAM	WON	LOST	TIED
Cincinnati[1]	10	6	0
Baltimore[1]	9	7	0
Pittsburgh	9	7	0
Cleveland	5	11	0

West Division

TEAM	WON	LOST	TIED
San Diego[1]	13	3	0
Denver	8	8	0
Oakland	5	11	0
Kansas City	4	12	0

National Football Conference

East Division

TEAM	WON	LOST	TIED
Dallas[1]	11	5	0
Philadelphia[1]	11	5	0
New York Giants	8	8	0
Washington	4	12	0

South Division

TEAM	WON	LOST	TIED
New Orleans[1]	13	3	0
Atlanta	9	7	0
Carolina	8	8	0
Tampa Bay	3	13	0

North Division

TEAM	WON	LOST	TIED
Minnesota[1]	12	4	0
Green Bay[1]	11	5	0
Chicago	7	9	0
Detroit	2	14	0

West Division

TEAM	WON	LOST	TIED
Arizona[1]	10	6	0
San Francisco	8	8	0
Seattle	5	11	0
St. Louis	1	15	0

[1]Gained play-off berth.

Super Bowl

NFL-AFL championship 1966–70; NFL championship from 1970–71 season.

	SEASON	WINNER	RUNNER-UP	SCORE
I	1966–67	Green Bay Packers (NFL)	Kansas City Chiefs (AFL)	35–10
II	1967–68	Green Bay Packers (NFL)	Oakland Raiders (AFL)	33–14
III	1968–69	New York Jets (AFL)	Baltimore Colts (NFL)	16–7
IV	1969–70	Kansas City Chiefs (AFL)	Minnesota Vikings (NFL)	23–7
V	1970–71	Baltimore Colts (AFC)	Dallas Cowboys (NFC)	16–13
VI	1971–72	Dallas Cowboys (NFC)	Miami Dolphins (AFC)	24–3
VII	1972–73	Miami Dolphins (AFC)	Washington Redskins (NFC)	14–7
VIII	1973–74	Miami Dolphins (AFC)	Minnesota Vikings (NFC)	24–7
IX	1974–75	Pittsburgh Steelers (AFC)	Minnesota Vikings (NFC)	16–6
X	1975–76	Pittsburgh Steelers (AFC)	Dallas Cowboys (NFC)	21–17
XI	1976–77	Oakland Raiders (AFC)	Minnesota Vikings (NFC)	32–14
XII	1977–78	Dallas Cowboys (NFC)	Denver Broncos (AFC)	27–10
XIII	1978–79	Pittsburgh Steelers (AFC)	Dallas Cowboys (NFC)	35–31
XIV	1979–80	Pittsburgh Steelers (AFC)	Los Angeles Rams (NFC)	31–19
XV	1980–81	Oakland Raiders (AFC)	Philadelphia Eagles (NFC)	27–10
XVI	1981–82	San Francisco 49ers (NFC)	Cincinnati Bengals (AFC)	26–21
XVII	1982–83	Washington Redskins (NFC)	Miami Dolphins (AFC)	27–17
XVIII	1983–84	Los Angeles Raiders (AFC)	Washington Redskins (NFC)	38–9
XIX	1984–85	San Francisco 49ers (NFC)	Miami Dolphins (AFC)	38–16
XX	1985–86	Chicago Bears (NFC)	New England Patriots (AFC)	46–10
XXI	1986–87	New York Giants (NFC)	Denver Broncos (AFC)	39–20
XXII	1987–88	Washington Redskins (NFC)	Denver Broncos (AFC)	42–10
XXIII	1988–89	San Francisco 49ers (NFC)	Cincinnati Bengals (AFC)	20–16
XXIV	1989–90	San Francisco 49ers (NFC)	Denver Broncos (AFC)	55–10
XXV	1990–91	New York Giants (NFC)	Buffalo Bills (AFC)	20–19
XXVI	1991–92	Washington Redskins (NFC)	Buffalo Bills (AFC)	37–24
XXVII	1992–93	Dallas Cowboys (NFC)	Buffalo Bills (AFC)	52–17
XXVIII	1993–94	Dallas Cowboys (NFC)	Buffalo Bills (AFC)	30–13
XXIX	1994–95	San Francisco 49ers (NFC)	San Diego Chargers (AFC)	49–26
XXX	1995–96	Dallas Cowboys (NFC)	Pittsburgh Steelers (AFC)	27–17
XXXI	1996–97	Green Bay Packers (NFC)	New England Patriots (AFC)	35–21
XXXII	1997–98	Denver Broncos (AFC)	Green Bay Packers (NFC)	31–24
XXXIII	1998–99	Denver Broncos (AFC)	Atlanta Falcons (NFC)	34–19
XXXIV	1999–2000	St. Louis Rams (NFC)	Tennessee Titans (AFC)	23–16
XXXV	2000–01	Baltimore Ravens (AFC)	New York Giants (NFC)	34–7
XXXVI	2001–02	New England Patriots (AFC)	St. Louis Rams (NFC)	20–17
XXXVII	2002–03	Tampa Bay Buccaneers (NFC)	Oakland Raiders (AFC)	48–21

Super Bowl (continued)

	SEASON	WINNER	RUNNER-UP	SCORE
XXXVIII	2003–04	New England Patriots (AFC)	Carolina Panthers (NFC)	32–29
XXXIX	2004–05	New England Patriots (AFC)	Philadelphia Eagles (NFC)	24–21
XL	2005–06	Pittsburgh Steelers (AFC)	Seattle Seahawks (NFC)	21–10
XLI	2006–07	Indianapolis Colts (AFC)	Chicago Bears (NFC)	29–17
XLII	2007–08	New York Giants (NFC)	New England Patriots (AFC)	17–14
XLIII	2008–09	Pittsburgh Steelers (AFC)	Arizona Cardinals (NFC)	27–23
XLIV	2009–10	New Orleans Saints (NFC)	Indianapolis Colts (AFC)	31–17

American Professional Football All-Time Records[1]

Research courtesy of Football Almanac, <www.football-almanac.com>.

	PLAYERS/TEAMS	NUMBER	SEASON/DATE
Individual career records			
Total games	Morten Andersen	382	1982–2007, except 2005
Total points	Morten Andersen	2,544	1982–2007, except 2005
Touchdowns, total	Jerry Rice	208	1985–2004
Touchdowns, passing	Brett Favre	497	1991–2009
Touchdowns, receiving	Jerry Rice	197	1985–2004
Touchdowns, rushing	Emmitt Smith	164	1990–2004
Field goals made	Morten Andersen	565	1982–2007, except 2005
Extra points made (kicked)	George Blanda	943	1949–75, except 1959
Passing yardage	Brett Favre	69,329	1991–2009
Passing completions	Brett Favre	6,083	1991–2009
Receiving yardage	Jerry Rice	22,895	1985–2004
Rushing yardage	Emmitt Smith	18,355	1990–2004
Interceptions (defense)	Paul Krause	81	1964–79
Sacks (defense)[2]	Bruce Smith	200	1985–2003
Coaching, total wins	Don Shula	328	1963–95
Individual season records			
Total points	LaDainian Tomlinson	186	2006
Touchdowns, total	LaDainian Tomlinson	31	2006
Touchdowns, passing	Tom Brady	50	2007
Touchdowns, receiving	Randy Moss	23	2007
Touchdowns, rushing	LaDainian Tomlinson	28	2006
Field goals made	Neil Rackers	40	2005
Extra points made (kicked)	Stephen Gostkowski	74	2007
Passing yardage	Dan Marino	5,084	1984
Receiving yardage	Jerry Rice	1,848	1995
Rushing yardage	Eric Dickerson	2,105	1984
Interceptions (defense)	Dick Lane	14	1952
Sacks (defense)[2]	Michael Strahan	22.5	2001
Individual game records			
Total points	Ernie Nevers	40	28 Nov 1929
Touchdowns, total	Ernie Nevers; Dub Jones; Gale Sayers	6	28 Nov 1929; 25 Nov 1951; 12 Dec 1965
Touchdowns, passing	Sid Luckman; Adrian Burk; George Blanda; Y.A. Tittle; Joe Kapp	7	14 Nov 1943; 17 Oct 1954; 19 Nov 1961; 28 Oct 1962; 28 Sep 1969
Touchdowns, receiving	Bob Shaw; Kellen Winslow; Jerry Rice	5	2 Oct 1950; 22 Nov 1981; 14 Oct 1990
Touchdowns, rushing	Ernie Nevers	6	28 Nov 1929
Field goals made	Rob Bironas	8	21 Oct 2007
Longest field goal	Tom Dempsey; Jason Elam	63 yd	8 Nov 1970; 25 Oct 1998
Extra points made (kicked)	Pat Harder; Bob Waterfield; Charlie Gogolak	9	17 Oct 1948; 22 Oct 1950; 27 Nov 1966

American Professional Football All-Time Records[1] (continued)

	PLAYERS/TEAMS	NUMBER	SEASON/DATE
Individual game records (continued)			
Passing yardage	Norm Van Brocklin	554	28 Sep 1951
Receiving yardage	Willie Anderson	336	26 Nov 1989 (overtime)
Rushing yardage	Adrian Peterson	296	4 Nov 2007
Longest run from scrimmage	Tony Dorsett	99 yd	3 Jan 1983
Interceptions (defense)	*18 players hold record*	4	
Sacks (defense)[2]	Derrick Thomas	7	11 Nov 1990
Team season records			
League championships (including Super Bowls)	Green Bay Packers	12	
Super Bowl titles	Pittsburgh Steelers	6	
Consecutive Super Bowl titles	*7 teams hold record*	2	
Perfect regular season	New England Patriots;	16 wins	2007
	Miami Dolphins;	14 wins	1972
	Chicago Bears;	13 wins	1934
	Chicago Bears	11 wins	1942
Total points scored	New England Patriots	589	2007
Touchdowns, total	New England Patriots	75	2007
Touchdowns, passing	Indianapolis Colts	51	2004
Touchdowns, rushing	Green Bay Packers	36	1962
Field goals made	Arizona Cardinals	43	2005
Passing yardage	St. Louis Rams	5,232	2000
Rushing yardage	New England Patriots	3,165	1978
Game records			
Highest total score	Washington Redskins versus New York Giants	113 (72–41)	27 Nov 1966
Longest game	Miami Dolphins versus Kansas City Chiefs	82:40	25 Dec 1971 (two overtimes)

[1]Includes National Football League from 1920 through the 2009–10 season and American Football League from 1960 to 1969. [2]Since 1982; before that year sacks were not officially recorded by the NFL.

National Collegiate Athletic Association Football National Title[1]

SEASON	CHAMPION	SEASON	CHAMPION	SEASON	CHAMPION
1924–25	Notre Dame	1954–55	Ohio State (AP); UCLA (UP)	1978–79	Alabama (AP); Southern California (UPI)
1925–26	Dartmouth				
1926–27	Stanford	1955–56	Oklahoma	1979–80	Alabama
1927–28	Illinois	1956–57	Oklahoma	1980–81	Georgia
1928–29	Southern California	1957–58	Auburn (AP); Ohio State (UP)	1981–82	Clemson
1929–30	Notre Dame			1982–83	Penn State
1930–31	Notre Dame	1958–59	Louisiana State	1983–84	Miami (FL)
1931–32	Southern California	1959–60	Syracuse	1984–85	Brigham Young
1932–33	Michigan	1960–61	Minnesota	1985–86	Oklahoma
1933–34	Michigan	1961–62	Alabama	1986–87	Penn State
1934–35	Minnesota	1962–63	Southern California	1987–88	Miami (FL)
1935–36	Southern Methodist	1963–64	Texas	1988–89	Notre Dame
1936–37	Minnesota	1964–65	Alabama	1989–90	Miami (FL)
1937–38	Pittsburgh	1965–66	Alabama (AP); Michigan State (UPI)	1990–91	Colorado (AP); Georgia Tech (UPI)
1938–39	Texas Christian				
1939–40	Texas A&M	1966–67	Notre Dame	1991–92	Miami (FL) (AP); Washington (UPI)
1940–41	Minnesota	1967–68	Southern California		
1941–42	Minnesota	1968–69	Ohio State	1992–93	Alabama
1942–43	Ohio State	1969–70	Texas	1993–94	Florida State
1943–44	Notre Dame	1970–71	Nebraska (AP); Texas (UPI)	1994–95	Nebraska
1944–45	Army			1995–96	Nebraska
1945–46	Army	1971–72	Nebraska	1996–97	Florida
1946–47	Notre Dame	1972–73	Southern California	1997–98	Michigan (AP); Nebraska (USA Today/ESPN)
1947–48	Notre Dame	1973–74	Notre Dame (AP); Alabama (UPI)		
1948–49	Michigan				
1949–50	Notre Dame	1974–75	Oklahoma (AP); Southern California (UPI)	1998–99	Tennessee
1950–51	Oklahoma			1999–2000	Florida State
1951–52	Tennessee	1975–76	Oklahoma	2000–01	Oklahoma
1952–53	Michigan State	1976–77	Pittsburgh	2001–02	Miami (FL)
1953–54	Maryland	1977–78	Notre Dame	2002–03	Ohio State

National Collegiate Athletic Association Football National Title[1] (continued)

SEASON	CHAMPION	SEASON	CHAMPION	SEASON	CHAMPION
2003–04	Louisiana State (BCS); Southern California (AP)	2004–05	Southern California	2007–08	Louisiana State
		2005–06	Texas	2008–09	Florida
		2006–07	Florida	2009–10	Alabama

[1]*University Division 1956–73; Division I 1973–78; Division I-A 1978–2006; Football Bowl Subdivision from 2006.*

Rose Bowl

SEASON	WINNER	RUNNER-UP	SCORE	SEASON	WINNER	RUNNER-UP	SCORE
1901–02	Michigan	Stanford	49–0	1963–64	Illinois	Washington	17–7
1915–16	Washington State	Brown	14–0	1964–65	Michigan	Oregon State	34–7
				1965–66	UCLA	Michigan State	14–12
1916–17	Oregon	Pennsylvania	14–0				
1917–18	Mare Island[1]	Camp Lewis[2]	19–7	1966–67	Purdue	Southern California	14–13
1918–19	Great Lakes[3]	Mare Island[1]	17–0				
1919–20	Harvard	Oregon	7–6	1967–68	Southern California	Indiana	14–3
1920–21	California	Ohio State	28–0	1968–69	Ohio State	Southern California	27–16
1921–22	California	Washington and Jefferson	0–0	1969–70	Southern California	Michigan	10–3
1922–23	Southern California	Penn State	14–3	1970–71	Stanford	Ohio State	27–17
1923–24	Washington	Navy	14–14	1971–72	Stanford	Michigan	13–12
1924–25	Notre Dame	Stanford	27–10	1972–73	Southern California	Ohio State	42–17
1925–26	Alabama	Washington	20–19	1973–74	Ohio State	Southern California	42–21
1926–27	Alabama	Stanford	7–7				
1927–28	Stanford	Pittsburgh	7–6	1974–75	Southern California	Ohio State	18–17
1928–29	Georgia Tech	California	8–7	1975–76	UCLA	Ohio State	23–10
1929–30	Southern California	Pittsburgh	47–14	1976–77	Southern California	Michigan	14–6
1930–31	Alabama	Washington State	24–0	1977–78	Washington	Michigan	27–20
				1978–79	Southern California	Michigan	17–10
1931–32	Southern California	Tulane	21–12	1979–80	Southern California	Ohio State	17–16
1932–33	Southern California	Pittsburgh	35–0	1980–81	Michigan	Washington	23–6
1933–34	Columbia	Stanford	7–0	1981–82	Washington	Iowa	28–0
1934–35	Alabama	Stanford	29–13	1982–83	UCLA	Michigan	24–14
1935–36	Stanford	Southern Methodist	7–0	1983–84	UCLA	Illinois	45–9
1936–37	Pittsburgh	Washington	21–0	1984–85	Southern California	Ohio State	20–17
1937–38	California	Alabama	13–0	1985–86	UCLA	Iowa	45–28
1938–39	Southern California	Duke	7–3	1986–87	Arizona State	Michigan	22–15
1939–40	Southern California	Tennessee	14–0	1987–88	Michigan State	Southern California	20–17
1940–41	Stanford	Nebraska	21–13				
1941–42	Oregon State	Duke	20–16	1988–89	Michigan	Southern California	22–14
1942–43	Georgia	UCLA	9–0				
1943–44	Southern California	Washington	29–0	1989–90	Southern California	Michigan	17–10
1944–45	Southern California	Tennessee	25–0	1990–91	Washington	Iowa	46–34
1945–46	Alabama	Southern California	34–14	1991–92	Washington	Michigan	34–14
				1992–93	Michigan	Washington	38–31
1946–47	Illinois	UCLA	45–14	1993–94	Wisconsin	UCLA	21–16
1947–48	Michigan	Southern California	49–0	1994–95	Penn State	Oregon	38–20
				1995–96	Southern California	Northwestern	41–32
1948–49	Northwestern	California	20–14	1996–97	Ohio State	Arizona State	20–17
1949–50	Ohio State	California	17–14	1997–98	Michigan	Washington State	21–16
1950–51	Michigan	California	14–6				
1951–52	Illinois	Stanford	40–7	1998–99	Wisconsin	UCLA	38–31
1952–53	Southern California	Wisconsin	7–0	1999–2000	Wisconsin	Stanford	17–9
1953–54	Michigan State	UCLA	28–20	2000–01	Washington	Purdue	34–24
1954–55	Ohio State	Southern California	20–7	2001–02	Miami (FL)	Nebraska	37–14
				2002–03	Oklahoma	Washington State	34–14
1955–56	Michigan State	UCLA	17–14				
1956–57	Iowa	Oregon State	35–19	2003–04	Southern California	Michigan	28–14
1957–58	Ohio State	Oregon	10–7	2004–05	Texas	Michigan	38–37
1958–59	Iowa	California	38–12	2005–06	Texas	Southern California	41–38
1959–60	Washington	Wisconsin	44–8				
1960–61	Washington	Minnesota	17–7	2006–07	Southern California	Michigan	32–18
1961–62	Minnesota	UCLA	21–3	2007–08	Southern California	Illinois	49–17
1962–63	Southern California	Wisconsin	42–37	2008–09	Southern California	Penn State	38–24
				2009–10	Ohio State	Oregon	26–17

[1]*US Marine Corps team.*   [2]*US Army team.*   [3]*US Navy team.*

Orange Bowl

SEASON	WINNER	RUNNER-UP	SCORE	SEASON	WINNER	RUNNER-UP	SCORE
1934-35	Bucknell	Miami (FL)	26-0	1973-74	Penn State	Louisiana State	16-9
1935-36	Catholic	Mississippi	20-19	1974-75	Notre Dame	Alabama	13-11
1936-37	Duquesne	Mississippi State	13-12	1975-76	Oklahoma	Michigan	14-6
1937-38	Auburn	Michigan State	6-0	1976-77	Ohio State	Colorado	27-10
1938-39	Tennessee	Oklahoma	17-0	1977-78	Arkansas	Oklahoma	31-6
1939-40	Georgia Tech	Missouri	21-7	1978-79	Oklahoma	Nebraska	31-24
1940-41	Mississippi State	Georgetown	14-7	1979-80	Oklahoma	Florida State	24-7
1941-42	Georgia	Texas Christian	40-26	1980-81	Oklahoma	Florida State	18-17
1942-43	Alabama	Boston College	37-21	1981-82	Clemson	Nebraska	22-15
1943-44	Louisiana State	Texas A&M	19-14	1982-83	Nebraska	Louisiana State	21-20
1944-45	Tulsa	Georgia Tech	26-12	1983-84	Miami (FL)	Nebraska	31-30
1945-46	Miami (FL)	Holy Cross	13-6	1984-85	Washington	Oklahoma	28-17
1946-47	Rice	Tennessee	8-0	1985-86	Oklahoma	Penn State	25-10
1947-48	Georgia Tech	Kansas	20-14	1986-87	Oklahoma	Arkansas	42-8
1948-49	Texas	Georgia	41-28	1987-88	Miami (FL)	Oklahoma	20-14
1949-50	Santa Clara	Kentucky	21-13	1988-89	Miami (FL)	Nebraska	23-3
1950-51	Clemson	Miami (FL)	15-14	1989-90	Notre Dame	Colorado	21-6
1951-52	Georgia Tech	Baylor	17-14	1990-91	Colorado	Notre Dame	10-9
1952-53	Alabama	Syracuse	61-6	1991-92	Miami (FL)	Nebraska	22-0
1953-54	Oklahoma	Maryland	7-0	1992-93	Florida State	Nebraska	27-14
1954-55	Duke	Nebraska	34-7	1993-94	Florida State	Nebraska	18-16
1955-56	Oklahoma	Maryland	20-6	1994-95	Nebraska	Miami	24-17
1956-57	Colorado	Clemson	27-21	1995-96	Florida State	Notre Dame	31-26
1957-58	Oklahoma	Duke	48-21	1996-97	Nebraska	Virginia Tech	41-21
1958-59	Oklahoma	Syracuse	21-6	1997-98	Nebraska	Tennessee	42-17
1959-60	Georgia	Missouri	14-0	1998-99	Florida	Syracuse	31-10
1960-61	Missouri	Navy	21-14	1999-2000	Michigan	Alabama	35-34
1961-62	Louisiana State	Colorado	25-7	2000-01	Oklahoma	Florida State	13-2
1962-63	Alabama	Oklahoma	17-0	2001-02	Florida	Maryland	56-23
1963-64	Nebraska	Auburn	13-7	2002-03	Southern California	Iowa	38-17
1964-65	Texas	Alabama	21-17	2003-04	Miami (FL)	Florida State	16-14
1965-66	Alabama	Nebraska	39-28	2004-05	Southern California	Oklahoma	55-19
1966-67	Florida	Georgia Tech	27-12	2005-06	Penn State	Florida State	26-23
1967-68	Oklahoma	Tennessee	26-24	2006-07	Louisville	Wake Forest	24-13
1968-69	Penn State	Kansas	15-14	2007-08	Kansas	Virginia Tech	24-21
1969-70	Penn State	Missouri	10-3	2008-09	Virginia Tech	Cincinnati	20-7
1970-71	Nebraska	Louisiana State	17-12	2009-10	Iowa	Georgia Tech	24-14
1971-72	Nebraska	Alabama	38-6				
1972-73	Nebraska	Notre Dame	40-6				

Sugar Bowl

SEASON	WINNER	RUNNER-UP	SCORE	SEASON	WINNER	RUNNER-UP	SCORE
1934-35	Tulane	Temple	20-14	1957-58	Mississippi	Texas	39-7
1935-36	Texas Christian	Louisiana State	3-2	1958-59	Louisiana State	Clemson	7-0
1936-37	Santa Clara	Louisiana State	21-14	1959-60	Mississippi	Louisiana State	21-0
1937-38	Santa Clara	Louisiana State	6-0	1960-61	Mississippi	Rice	14-6
1938-39	Texas Christian	Carnegie Tech	15-7	1961-62	Alabama	Arkansas	10-3
1939-40	Texas A&M	Tulane	14-13	1962-63	Mississippi	Arkansas	17-13
1940-41	Boston College	Tennessee	19-13	1963-64	Alabama	Mississippi	12-7
1941-42	Fordham	Missouri	2-0	1964-65	Louisiana State	Syracuse	13-10
1942-43	Tennessee	Tulsa	14-7				
1943-44	Georgia Tech	Tulsa	20-18	1965-66	Missouri	Florida	20-18
1944-45	Duke	Alabama	29-26	1966-67	Alabama	Nebraska	34-7
1945-46	Oklahoma A&M	St. Mary's (CA)	33-13	1967-68	Louisiana State	Wyoming	20-13
1946-47	Georgia	North Carolina	20-10				
1947-48	Texas	Alabama	27-7	1968-69	Arkansas	Georgia	16-2
1948-49	Oklahoma	North Carolina	14-6	1969-70	Mississippi	Arkansas	27-22
1949-50	Oklahoma	Louisiana State	35-0	1970-71	Tennessee	Air Force	34-13
1950-51	Kentucky	Oklahoma	13-7	1971-72	Oklahoma	Auburn	40-22
1951-52	Maryland	Tennessee	28-13	1972-73	Oklahoma	Penn State	14-0
1952-53	Georgia Tech	Mississippi	24-7	1973-74	Notre Dame	Alabama	24-23
1953-54	Georgia Tech	West Virginia	42-19	1974-75	Nebraska	Florida	13-10
1954-55	Navy	Mississippi	21-0	1975-76	Alabama	Penn State	13-6
1955-56	Georgia Tech	Pittsburgh	7-0	1976-77	Pittsburgh	Georgia	27-3
1956-57	Baylor	Tennessee	13-7	1977-78	Alabama	Ohio State	35-6

Sugar Bowl (continued)

SEASON	WINNER	RUNNER-UP	SCORE	SEASON	WINNER	RUNNER-UP	SCORE
1978–79	Alabama	Penn State	14–7	1996–97	Florida	Florida State	52–20
1979–80	Alabama	Arkansas	24–9	1997–98	Florida State	Ohio State	31–14
1980–81	Georgia	Notre Dame	17–10	1998–99	Ohio State	Texas A&M	24–14
1981–82	Pittsburgh	Georgia	24–20	1999–2000	Florida State	Virginia Tech	46–29
1982–83	Penn State	Georgia	27–23	2000–01	Miami (FL)	Florida	37–20
1983–84	Auburn	Michigan	9–7	2001–02	Louisiana State	Illinois	47–34
1984–85	Nebraska	Louisiana State	28–10				
1985–86	Tennessee	Miami (FL)	35–7	2002–03	Georgia	Florida State	26–13
1986–87	Nebraska	Louisiana State	30–15	2003–04	Louisiana State	Oklahoma	21–14
1987–88	Auburn	Syracuse	16–16				
1988–89	Florida State	Auburn	13–7	2004–05	Auburn	Virginia Tech	16–13
1989–90	Miami (FL)	Alabama	33–25	2005–06	West Virginia	Georgia	38–35
1990–91	Tennessee	Virginia	23–22	2006–07	Louisiana State	Notre Dame	41–14
1991–92	Notre Dame	Florida	39–28				
1992–93	Alabama	Miami (FL)	34–13	2007–08	Georgia	Hawaii	41–10
1993–94	Florida	West Virginia	41–7	2008–09	Utah	Alabama	31–17
1994–95	Florida State	Florida	23–17	2009–10	Florida	Cincinnati	51–24
1995–96	Virginia Tech	Texas	28–10				

Fiesta Bowl

SEASON	WINNER	RUNNER-UP	SCORE	SEASON	WINNER	RUNNER-UP	SCORE
1971–72	Arizona State	Florida State	45–38	1990–91	Louisville	Alabama	34–7
1972–73	Arizona State	Missouri	49–35	1991–92	Penn State	Tennessee	42–17
1973–74	Arizona State	Pittsburgh	28–7	1992–93	Syracuse	Colorado	26–22
1974–75	Oklahoma State	Brigham Young	16–6	1993–94	Arizona	Miami (FL)	29–0
1975–76	Arizona State	Nebraska	17–14	1994–95	Colorado	Notre Dame	41–24
1976–77	Oklahoma	Wyoming	41–7	1995–96	Nebraska	Florida	62–24
1977–78	Penn State	Arizona State	42–30	1996–97	Penn State	Texas	38–15
1978–79	Arkansas	UCLA	10–10	1997–98	Kansas State	Syracuse	35–18
1979–80	Pittsburgh	Arizona	16–10	1998–99	Tennessee	Florida State	23–16
1980–81	Penn State	Ohio State	31–19	1999–2000	Nebraska	Tennessee	31–21
1981–82	Penn State	Southern California	26–10	2000–01	Oregon State	Notre Dame	41–9
				2001–02	Oregon	Colorado	38–16
1982–83	Arizona State	Oklahoma	32–21	2002–03	Ohio State	Miami (FL)	31–24
1983–84	Ohio State	Pittsburgh	28–23	2003–04	Ohio State	Kansas State	35–28
1984–85	UCLA	Miami (FL)	39–37	2004–05	Utah	Pittsburgh	35–7
1985–86	Michigan	Nebraska	27–23	2005–06	Ohio State	Notre Dame	34–20
1986–87	Penn State	Miami (FL)	14–10	2006–07	Boise State	Oklahoma	43–42
1987–88	Florida State	Nebraska	31–28	2007–08	West Virginia	Oklahoma	48–28
1988–89	Notre Dame	West Virginia	34–21	2008–09	Texas	Ohio State	24–21
1989–90	Florida State	Nebraska	41–17	2009–10	Boise State	Texas Christian	17–10

Heisman Trophy

The Heisman Trophy is named for John Heisman, former director of the Downtown Athletic Club in New York City. The trophy goes to the most outstanding college football player at the end of the football season each year.

Web site: <www.heisman.com>.

YEAR	WINNER	COLLEGE	POSITION	YEAR	WINNER	COLLEGE	POSITION
1935	Jay Berwanger	Chicago	HB	1950	Vic Janowicz	Ohio State	HB
1936	Larry Kelley	Yale	E	1951	Dick Kazmaier	Princeton	HB
1937	Clint Frank	Yale	HB	1952	Billy Vessels	Oklahoma	HB
1938	Davey O'Brien	Texas Christian	QB	1953	John Lattner	Notre Dame	HB
1939	Nile Kinnick	Iowa	HB	1954	Alan Ameche	Wisconsin	FB
1940	Tom Harmon	Michigan	HB	1955	Howard Cassady	Ohio State	HB
1941	Bruce Smith	Minnesota	HB	1956	Paul Hornung	Notre Dame	QB
1942	Frank Sinkwich	Georgia	HB	1957	John David Crow	Texas A&M	HB
1943	Angelo Bertelli	Notre Dame	QB	1958	Pete Dawkins	Army	HB
1944	Les Horvath	Ohio State	QB	1959	Billy Cannon	Louisiana State	HB
1945	Felix Blanchard	Army	FB	1960	Joe Bellino	Navy	HB
1946	Glenn Davis	Army	HB	1961	Ernie Davis	Syracuse	HB
1947	John Lujack	Notre Dame	QB	1962	Terry Baker	Oregon State	QB
1948	Doak Walker	Southern Methodist	HB	1963	Roger Staubach	Navy	QB
1949	Leon Hart	Notre Dame	E	1964	John Huarte	Notre Dame	QB

Heisman Trophy (continued)

YEAR	WINNER	COLLEGE	POSITION	YEAR	WINNER	COLLEGE	POSITION
1965	Mike Garrett	Southern California	HB	1988	Barry Sanders	Oklahoma State	RB
1966	Steve Spurrier	Florida	QB	1989	Andre Ware	Houston	QB
1967	Gary Beban	UCLA	QB	1990	Ty Detmer	Brigham Young	QB
1968	O.J. Simpson	Southern California	HB	1991	Desmond Howard	Michigan	WR
1969	Steve Owens	Oklahoma	HB	1992	Gino Torretta	Miami	QB
1970	Jim Plunkett	Stanford	QB	1993	Charlie Ward	Florida State	QB
1971	Pat Sullivan	Auburn	QB	1994	Rashaan Salaam	Colorado	TB
1972	Johnny Rodgers	Nebraska	RB	1995	Eddie George	Ohio State	RB
1973	John Cappelletti	Penn State	HB	1996	Danny Wuerffel	Florida	QB
1974	Archie Griffin	Ohio State	HB	1997	Charles Woodson	Michigan	DB
1975	Archie Griffin	Ohio State	HB	1998	Ricky Williams	Texas	RB
1976	Tony Dorsett	Pittsburgh	HB	1999	Ron Dayne	Wisconsin	RB
1977	Earl Campbell	Texas	HB	2000	Chris Weinke	Florida State	QB
1978	Billy Sims	Oklahoma	HB	2001	Eric Crouch	Nebraska	QB
1979	Charles White	Southern California	HB	2002	Carson Palmer	Southern California	QB
1980	George Rogers	South Carolina	HB	2003	Jason White	Oklahoma	QB
1981	Marcus Allen	Southern California	HB	2004	Matt Leinart	Southern California	QB
1982	Herschel Walker	Georgia	HB	2005	Reggie Bush	Southern California	RB
1983	Mike Rozier	Nebraska	HB	2006	Troy Smith	Ohio State	QB
1984	Doug Flutie	Boston College	QB	2007	Tim Tebow	Florida	QB
1985	Bo Jackson	Auburn	HB	2008	Sam Bradford	Oklahoma	QB
1986	Vinny Testaverde	Miami (FL)	QB	2009	Mark Ingram	Alabama	RB
1987	Tim Brown	Notre Dame	WR				

Canadian Football League Grey Cup

Held since 1909. Table shows results for the past 20 years.

YEAR	WINNER	RUNNER-UP	SCORE
1990	Winnipeg Blue Bombers (ED)	Edmonton Eskimos (WD)	50–11
1991	Toronto Argonauts (ED)	Calgary Stampeders (WD)	36–21
1992	Calgary Stampeders (WD)	Winnipeg Blue Bombers (ED)	24–10
1993	Edmonton Eskimos (WD)	Winnipeg Blue Bombers (ED)	33–23
1994	British Columbia Lions (WD)	Baltimore Stallions (ED)	26–23
1995[1]	Baltimore Stallions (SD)	Calgary Stampeders (ND)	37–20
1996	Toronto Argonauts (ED)	Edmonton Eskimos (WD)	43–37
1997	Toronto Argonauts (ED)	Saskatchewan Roughriders (WD)	47–23
1998	Calgary Stampeders (WD)	Hamilton Tiger-Cats (ED)	26–24
1999	Hamilton Tiger-Cats (ED)	Calgary Stampeders (WD)	32–21
2000	British Columbia Lions (WD)	Montreal Alouettes (ED)	28–26
2001	Calgary Stampeders (WD)	Winnipeg Blue Bombers (ED)	27–19
2002	Montreal Alouettes (ED)	Edmonton Eskimos (WD)	25–16
2003	Edmonton Eskimos (WD)	Montreal Alouettes (ED)	34–22
2004	Toronto Argonauts (ED)	British Columbia Lions (WD)	27–19
2005	Edmonton Eskimos (WD)	Montreal Alouettes (ED)	38–35
2006	British Columbia Lions (WD)	Montreal Alouettes (ED)	25–14
2007	Saskatchewan Roughriders (WD)	Winnipeg Blue Bombers (ED)	23–19
2008	Calgary Stampeders (WD)	Montreal Alouettes (ED)	22–14
2009	Montreal Alouettes (ED)	Saskatchewan Roughriders (WD)	28–27

[1]*In 1995 only, the divisions were reconfigured and renamed Northern and Southern in response to the inclusion of American teams in the CFL (1993–96).*

Australian Football League Final Standings, 2009[1]

Teams that qualified for play-offs only.

TEAM	WON	LOST	TIED	POINTS	TEAM	WON	LOST	TIED	POINTS
St. Kilda Saints	20	2	0	80	Adelaide Crows	14	8	0	56
Geelong Cats	18	4	0	72	Brisbane Lions	13	8	1	54
Western Bulldogs	15	7	0	60	Carlton Blues	13	9	0	52
Collingwood Magpies	15	7	0	60	Essendon Bombers	10	11	1	42

[1]*The Geelong Cats were the 2009 champions.*

Rugby World Cup

YEAR	WINNER	RUNNER-UP	SCORE	YEAR	WINNER	RUNNER-UP	SCORE
1987	New Zealand	France	29-9	1999	Australia	France	35-12
1991	Australia	England	12-6	2003	England	Australia	20-17
1995	South Africa	New Zealand	15-12	2007	South Africa	England	15-6

Rugby League World Cup

YEAR	WINNER	RUNNER-UP	SCORE	YEAR	WINNER	RUNNER-UP	SCORE
1954	Great Britain	France	16-12	1977[3]	Australia	Great Britain	13-12
1957	Australia	Great Britain	[1]	1988	Australia	New Zealand	25-12
1960	Great Britain	Australia	[1]	1992	Australia	Great Britain	10-6
1968	Australia	France	20-2	1995	Australia	England	16-8
1970	Australia	Great Britain	12-7	2000	Australia	New Zealand	40-12
1972	Great Britain	Australia	10-10[2]	2008	New Zealand	Australia	34-20
1975[3]	Australia	England	[1]				

[1]Tournament played without a grand final match; winner determined by match points.   [2]Great Britain won on match points.   [3]Called International Championship from 1975 to 1977.

Super 14 Rugby Final Standings, 2010[1]

Super 12 until 2006. Four points are awarded for a win and two for a draw; one bonus point is given for a loss by seven points or fewer and one for a team that scores four or more tries.

TEAM (COUNTRY)	POINTS	W	L	D	BONUS	TEAM (COUNTRY)	POINTS	W	L	D	BONUS
Bulls (RSA)	47	10	3	0	7	Hurricanes (NZL)	37	7	5	1	7
Stormers (RSA)	44	9	4	0	8	Sharks (RSA)	33	7	6	0	5
New South Wales	43	9	4	0	7	Central Cheetahs (RSA)	26	5	7	1	4
Waratahs (AUS)						Chiefs (NZL)	26	4	8	1	8
Crusaders (NZL)	41	8	4	1	7	Highlanders (NZL)	19	3	10	0	7
Queensland Reds (AUS)	39	8	5	0	7	Western Force (AUS)	19	4	9	0	3
Brumbies (AUS)	37	8	5	0	5	Lions (RSA)	5	0	13	0	5
Blues (NZL)	37	7	6	0	9						

[1]The Bulls were the 2010 champions.

Six Nations Championship

Held since 1883; Five Nations in 1910-31 and 1947-99. Round-robin tournament, usually ending in April.

YEAR	WINNER	YEAR	WINNER	YEAR	WINNER
1947	England; Wales[1]	1969	Wales[3]	1991	England[2,3]
1948	Ireland[2,3]	1970	France; Wales[1]	1992	England[2,3]
1949	Ireland[3]	1971	Wales[2,3]	1993	France
1950	Wales[2,3]	1972	not completed	1994	Wales
1951	Ireland	1973	quintuple tie	1995	England[2,3]
1952	Wales[2,3]	1974	Ireland	1996	England[3]
1953	England	1975	Wales	1997	France[2,5]
1954	England[3]; France; Wales[1]	1976	Wales[2,3]	1998	France[2,5]
1955	France; Wales[1]	1977	France[2,4]	1999	Scotland
1956	Wales	1978	Wales[2,3]	2000	England
1957	England[2,3]	1979	Wales[3]	2001	England
1958	England	1980	England[2,3]	2002	France[2,5]
1959	France	1981	France[2]	2003	England[2,3]
1960	England[3]; France[1]	1982	Ireland[3]	2004	France[2,6]
1961	France	1983	France; Ireland[1]	2005	Wales[2,3]
1962	France	1984	Scotland[2,3]	2006	France[6]
1963	England	1985	Ireland[3]	2007	France[6]
1964	Scotland; Wales[1]	1986	France; Scotland[1]	2008	Wales[2,3]
1965	Wales[3]	1987	France[2]	2009	Ireland[2,3]
1966	Wales	1988	France; Wales[1,3]	2010	France[2]
1967	France	1989	France		
1968	France[2]	1990	Scotland[2,3]		

[1]Tied.   [2]Grand Slam winner (defeats all other competitors).   [3]Triple Crown winner (Home Nation [England, Ireland, Scotland, Wales] that defeats all three other Home Nations).   [4]Triple Crown won by Wales.   [5]Triple Crown won by England.   [6]Triple Crown won by Ireland.

FIFA World Cup—Men

YEAR	WINNER	RUNNER-UP	SCORE	YEAR	WINNER	RUNNER-UP	SCORE
1930	Uruguay	Argentina	4–2	1978	Argentina	Netherlands	3–1
1934	Italy	Czechoslovakia	2–1	1982	Italy	West Germany	3–1
1938	Italy	Hungary	4–2	1986	Argentina	West Germany	3–2
1950	Uruguay	Brazil	2–1	1990	West Germany	Argentina	1–0
1954	West Germany	Hungary	3–2	1994	Brazil	Italy	0–0 (3–2[1])
1958	Brazil	Sweden	5–2	1998	France	Brazil	3–0
1962	Brazil	Czechoslovakia	3–1	2002	Brazil	Germany	2–0
1966	England	West Germany	4–2	2006	Italy	France	1–1 (5–3[1])
1970	Brazil	Italy	4–1	2010	Spain	Netherlands	1–0
1974	West Germany	Netherlands	2–1				

[1]Won in a penalty kick shoot-out.

FIFA World Cup—Women

YEAR	WINNER	RUNNER-UP	SCORE	YEAR	WINNER	RUNNER-UP	SCORE
1991	United States	Norway	2–1	2003	Germany	Sweden	2–1
1995	Norway	Germany	2–0	2007	Germany	Brazil	2–0
1999	United States	China	0–0 (5–4[1])				

[1]Won in a penalty kick shoot-out.

UEFA Champions League

Held since 1955 and known until 1992–93 as the European Champion Clubs' Cup; played on a knockout basis until 1992–93 and as a combination of group and knockout rounds since then. Table shows results for the past 20 years.

SEASON	WINNER (COUNTRY)	RUNNER-UP (COUNTRY)	SCORE
1990–91	FK Crvena Zvezda Beograd (YUG)	Olympique de Marseille (FRA)	0–0 (5–3[1])
1991–92	FC Barcelona (ESP)	Sampdoria UC (ITA)	1–0
1992–93	Olympique de Marseille (FRA)	AC Milan (ITA)	1–0
1993–94	AC Milan (ITA)	FC Barcelona (ESP)	4–0
1994–95	AFC Ajax (NED)	AC Milan (ITA)	1–0
1995–96	Juventus FC (ITA)	AFC Ajax (NED)	1–1 (4–2[1])
1996–97	BV Borussia Dortmund (GER)	Juventus FC (ITA)	3–1
1997–98	Real Madrid CF (ESP)	Juventus FC (ITA)	1–0
1998–99	Manchester United (ENG)	FC Bayern München (GER)	2–1
1999–2000	Real Madrid CF (ESP)	Valencia CF (ESP)	3–0
2000–01	FC Bayern München (GER)	Valencia CF (ESP)	1–1 (5–4[1])
2001–02	Real Madrid CF (ESP)	Bayer 04 Leverkusen (GER)	2–1
2002–03	AC Milan (ITA)	Juventus FC (ITA)	0–0 (3–2[1])
2003–04	FC Porto (POR)	AS Monaco (FRA)	3–0
2004–05	Liverpool FC (ENG)	AC Milan (ITA)	3–3 (3–2[1])
2005–06	FC Barcelona (ESP)	Arsenal FC (ENG)	2–1
2006–07	AC Milan (ITA)	Liverpool FC (ENG)	2–1
2007–08	Manchester United (ENG)	Chelsea FC (ENG)	1–1 (6–5[1])
2008–09	FC Barcelona (ESP)	Manchester United (ENG)	2–0
2009–10	FC Internazionale Milano (ITA)	FC Bayern München (GER)	2–0

[1]Won in a penalty kick shoot-out.

UEFA European Championship

YEAR	WINNER	RUNNER-UP	SCORE	YEAR	WINNER	RUNNER-UP	SCORE
1960	USSR	Yugoslavia	2–1	1988	Netherlands	USSR	2–0
1964	Spain	USSR	2–1	1992	Denmark	Germany	2–0
1968	Italy	Yugoslavia	2–0	1996	Germany	Czech Republic	2–1
1972	West Germany	USSR	3–0	2000	France	Italy	2–1
1976	Czechoslovakia	West Germany	2–2	2004	Greece	Portugal	1–0
1980	West Germany	Belgium	2–1	2008	Spain	Germany	1–0
1984	France	Spain	2–0				

UEFA Europa League

The UEFA Europa League is considered Europe's second most important football competition. Established in the 1971–72 season, the competition was restructured when the UEFA Cup Winners' Cup was abolished after the 1998–99 season and was named the UEFA Cup. Originally played on an entirely two-legged basis, since 1998 the competition has concluded with a single match. The competition is open to top- and second-ranked teams in each country's league as well as to the winners of domestic cups. The competition was renamed in 2010.

SEASON	WINNER (COUNTRY)	RUNNER-UP (COUNTRY)	SCORES
1971–72	Tottenham Hotspur FC (ENG)	Wolverhampton Wanderers FC (ENG)	2–1, 1–1
1972–73	Liverpool FC (ENG)	VfL Borussia Mönchengladbach (FRG)	3–0, 0–2
1973–74	Feyenoord (NED)	Tottenham Hotspur FC (ENG)	2–2, 2–0
1974–75	VfL Borussia Mönchengladbach (FRG)	FC Twente (NED)	0–0, 5–1
1975–76	Liverpool FC (ENG)	Club Brugge KV (BEL)	3–2, 1–1
1976–77	Juventus FC (ITA)	Athletic Club Bilbao (ESP)	1–0, 1–2
1977–78	PSV Eindhoven (NED)	SC Bastia (FRA)	0–0, 3–0
1978–79	VfL Borussia Mönchengladbach (FRG)	FK Crvena Zvezda Beograd (YUG)	1–1, 1–0
1979–80	Eintracht Frankfurt (FRG)	VfL Borussia Mönchengladbach (FRG)	2–3, 1–0
1980–81	Ipswich Town FC (ENG)	AZ Alkmaar (NED)	3–0, 2–4
1981–82	IFK Göteborg (SWE)	Hamburger SV (FRG)	1–0, 3–0
1982–83	RSC Anderlecht (BEL)	SL Benfica (POR)	1–0, 1–1
1983–84	Tottenham Hotspur FC (ENG)	RSC Anderlecht (BEL)	1–1, 1–1 (4–3[1])
1984–85	Real Madrid CF (ESP)	Videoton FCF (HUN)	3–0, 0–1
1985–86	Real Madrid CF (ESP)	1. FC Köln (FRG)	5–1, 0–2
1986–87	IFK Göteborg (SWE)	Dundee United FC (SCO)	1–0, 1–1
1987–88	Bayer 04 Leverkusen (FRG)	RCD Espanyol (ESP)	0–3, 3–0 (3–2[1])
1988–89	SSC Napoli (ITA)	VfB Stuttgart (FRG)	2–1, 3–3
1989–90	Juventus FC (ITA)	AC Fiorentina (ITA)	3–1, 0–0
1990–91	Internazionale FC (ITA)	AS Roma (ITA)	2–0, 0–1
1991–92	AFC Ajax (NED)	Torino Calcio (ITA)	2–2, 0–0
1992–93	Juventus FC (ITA)	BV Borussia Dortmund (GER)	3–1, 3–0
1993–94	Internazionale FC (ITA)	SV Austria Salzburg (AUT)	1–0, 1–0
1994–95	Parma AC (ITA)	Juventus FC (ITA)	1–0, 1–1
1995–96	FC Bayern München (GER)	FC Girondins de Bordeaux (FRA)	2–0, 3–1
1996–97	FC Schalke 04 (GER)	Internazionale FC (ITA)	1–0, 0–1 (4–1[1])
1997–98	Internazionale FC (ITA)	SS Lazio (ITA)	3–0
1998–99	Parma AC (ITA)	Olympique de Marseille (FRA)	3–0
1999–2000	Galatasaray SK (TUR)	Arsenal FC (ENG)	0–0 (4–1[1])
2000–01	Liverpool FC (ENG)	Deportivo Alavés (ESP)	5–4
2001–02	Feyenoord (NED)	BV Borussia Dortmund (GER)	3–2
2002–03	FC Porto (POR)	Celtic FC (SCO)	3–2[2]
2003–04	Valencia CF (ESP)	Olympique de Marseille (FRA)	2–0
2004–05	CSKA Moscow (RUS)	Sporting (POR)	3–1
2005–06	Sevilla FC (ESP)	Middlesbrough FC (ENG)	4–0
2006–07	Sevilla FC (ESP)	RCD Espanyol (ESP)	2–2 (3–1[1])
2007–08	FC Zenit St. Petersburg (RUS)	Rangers FC (SCO)	2–0
2008–09	Shakhtar Donetsk (UKR)	Werder Bremen (GER)	2–1[2]
2009–10	Club Atlético de Madrid (ESP)	Fulham FC (ENG)	2–1

[1]Won in a penalty kick shoot-out.   [2]Won on "silver goal" in overtime.

Copa Libertadores de América

Held since 1960. Table shows results for the past 20 years.

YEAR	WINNER (COUNTRY)	RUNNER-UP (COUNTRY)	SCORES
1991	Colo Colo (CHI)	Olímpia (PAR)	0–0, 3–0
1992	São Paulo (BRA)	Newell's Old Boys (ARG)	0–1, 1–0 (3–2[1])
1993	São Paulo (BRA)	Universidad Católica (CHI)	5–1, 0–2
1994	Vélez Sársfield (ARG)	São Paulo (BRA)	1–0, 0–1 (5–4[1])
1995	Grêmio (BRA)	Atlético Nacional (COL)	3–1, 1–1
1996	River Plate (ARG)	América de Cali (COL)	0–1, 2–0
1997	Cruzeiro (BRA)	Sporting Cristal (PER)	0–0, 1–0

Copa Libertadores de América (continued)

YEAR	WINNER (COUNTRY)	RUNNER-UP (COUNTRY)	SCORES
1998	Vasco da Gama (BRA)	Barcelona (ECU)	2-0, 2-1
1999	Palmeiras (BRA)	Deportiva Cali (COL)	0-1, 2-1 (4-3[1])
2000	Boca Juniors (ARG)	Palmeiras (BRA)	2-2, 0-0 (4-2[1])
2001	Boca Juniors (ARG)	Cruz Azul (MEX)	1-0, 0-1 (3-1[1])
2002	Olímpia (PAR)	São Caetano (BRA)	0-1, 2-1 (4-2[1])
2003	Boca Juniors (ARG)	Santos (BRA)	2-0, 3-1
2004	Once Caldas (COL)	Boca Juniors (ARG)	0-0, 1-1 (2-0[1])
2005	São Paulo (BRA)	Atlético Paranaense (BRA)	1-1, 4-0
2006	Internacional (BRA)	São Paulo (BRA)	2-1, 2-2
2007	Boca Juniors (ARG)	Grêmio (BRA)	3-0, 2-0
2008	Liga de Quito (ECU)	Fluminense (BRA)	4-2, 1-3 (3-1[1])
2009	Estudiantes de la Plata (ARG)	Cruzeiro (BRA)	0-0, 2-1
2010	Internacional (BRA)	Guadalajara (MEX)	2-1, 3-2

[1]Won in a penalty kick shoot-out.

Copa América

Held since 1916. Table shows results for past 20 years. The cup was contested by rounds in 1989 and 1991 (scores are shown here as winner's wins/losses/draws in final round) and by a final championship match from 1993.

YEAR	WINNER	RUNNER-UP	SCORE	YEAR	WINNER	RUNNER-UP	SCORE
1989	Brazil	Uruguay	3/0/0	1999	Brazil	Uruguay	3-0
1991	Argentina	Brazil	4/0/0	2001	Colombia	Mexico	1-0
1993	Argentina	Mexico	2-1	2003	postponed until 2004		
1995	Uruguay	Brazil	1-1 (4-2[1])	2004	Brazil	Argentina	2-2 (2-0[1])
1997	Brazil	Bolivia	3-1	2007	Brazil	Argentina	3-0

[1]Won in a penalty kick shoot-out.

Asian Cup

Scored on a points (percentage of wins) system until 1972.

YEAR	WINNER	RUNNER-UP	SCORE	YEAR	WINNER	RUNNER-UP	SCORE
1956	Rep. of Korea	Israel	83.3	1984	Saudi Arabia	China	2-0
1960	Rep. of Korea	Israel	100	1988	Saudi Arabia	Rep. of Korea	0-0 (4-3[1])
1964	Israel	India	100	1992	Japan	Saudi Arabia	1-0
1968	Iran	Burma	100	1996	Saudi Arabia	United Arab Emirates	0-0 (4-2[1])
1972	Iran	Rep. of Korea	2-1	2000	Japan	Saudi Arabia	1-0
1976	Iran	Kuwait	1-0	2004	Japan	China	3-1
1980	Kuwait	Rep. of Korea	3-0	2007	Iraq	Saudi Arabia	1-0

[1]Won in a penalty kick shoot-out.

Africa Cup of Nations

YEAR	WINNER	RUNNER-UP	SCORE	YEAR	WINNER	RUNNER-UP	SCORE
1957	Egypt	Ethiopia	4-0	1986	Egypt	Cameroon	0-0 (5-4[3])
1959	Egypt	The Sudan	2-1	1988	Cameroon	Nigeria	1-0
1962	Ethiopia	Egypt	4-2	1990	Algeria	Nigeria	1-0
1963	Ghana	The Sudan	3-0	1992	Côte d'Ivoire	Ghana	0-0 (11-10[3])
1965	Ghana	Tunisia	3-2	1994	Nigeria	Zambia	2-1
1968	Dem. Rep. of the Congo	Ghana	1-0	1996	South Africa	Tunisia	2-0
1970	The Sudan	Ghana	1-0	1998	Egypt	South Africa	2-0
1972	Rep. of the Congo	Mali	3-2	2000	Cameroon	Nigeria	2-2 (4-3[3])
1974	Zaire	Zambia	2-2, 2-0[1]	2002	Cameroon	Senegal	0-0 (3-2[3])
1976	Morocco	Guinea	1-1[2]	2004	Tunisia	Morocco	2-1
1978	Ghana	Uganda	2-0	2006	Egypt	Côte d'Ivoire	0-0 (4-2[3])
1980	Nigeria	Algeria	3-0	2008	Egypt	Cameroon	1-0
1982	Ghana	Libya	1-1 (7-6[3])	2010	Egypt	Ghana	1-0
1984	Cameroon	Nigeria	3-1				

[1]Game replayed.   [2]Won via group format.   [3]Won in a penalty kick shoot-out.

Major League Soccer Cup

YEAR	WINNER	RUNNER-UP	SCORE	YEAR	WINNER	RUNNER-UP	SCORE
1996	DC United	Los Angeles Galaxy	3–2 (OT)	2004	DC United	Kansas City Wizards	3–2
1997	DC United	Colorado Rapids	2–1				
1998	Chicago Fire	DC United	2–0	2005	Los Angeles Galaxy	New England Revolution	1–0 (OT)
1999	DC United	Los Angeles Galaxy	2–0				
2000	Kansas City Wizards	Chicago Fire	1–0	2006	Houston Dynamo	New England Revolution	1–1 (4–3[1])
2001	San Jose Earthquakes	Los Angeles Galaxy	2–1 (OT)	2007	Houston Dynamo	New England Revolution	2–1
2002	Los Angeles Galaxy	New England Revolution	1–0	2008	Columbus Crew	New York Red Bulls	3–1
2003	San Jose Earthquakes	Chicago Fire	4–2	2009	Real Salt Lake	Los Angeles Galaxy	1–1 (5–4[1])

[1]Won in a penalty kick shoot-out.

Golf

In **individual events**, three of the four major men's golf championships, the **US and British Open tournaments** and the **Professional Golfers' Association Championship**, are played annually at a variety of golf courses over 72 holes, and each is preceded by qualifying rounds. The fourth major, the invitational **Masters Tournament**, is held annually at the Augusta [GA] National Golf Course. Events for amateurs include the **US and British Amateur championships**. In 2007 the **Professional Golf Association** (PGA) inaugurated the **FedExCup**, a season-long competition in which players accumulate points based on their performances in various PGA events (including the more heavily weighted majors) and participate in a four-week playoff and a final Tour Championship.

Women's golf has been around nearly as long as men's golf, but until the late 1940s, it was limited to amateurs, with the **US and British Amateur championships** being the major tournaments. The **US Women's Open Championship** was started in 1946, and the **Ladies Professional Golf Association** (LPGA), which inaugurated the **LPGA Championship**, was formed in 1950. Since that time women's professional golf has flourished. In 1976 the **Women's British Open Championship** was added to the golf calendar, and in 1983 the Nabisco Dinah Shore (played since 1972 and renamed the **Kraft Nabisco Championship** in 2002) was designated the fourth women's major.

In **team events**, the **Ryder Cup** was originally a biennial match between the US and Great Britain, but beginning in 1979 it was expanded into a biennial match between the United States and Europe. Teams of British and US women golfers compete every two years for the **Curtis Cup**, which since 1964 has involved two days' play of three 18-hole foursomes and six 18-hole singles.

Related Web sites: United States Golf Association: <www.usga.org>; Professional Golf Association: <www.pgatour.com>; Ladies Professional Golf Association: <www.lpga.com>.

FedExCup

In 2007 the PGA inaugurated the FedExCup, a season-long competition in which players accumulate points based on their performances in various PGA events throughout the year. In a standard (non-major) tournament, for instance, 3,513 points are awarded, with the winner receiving 500 points, a runner-up receiving 300 points, and so on. The four major tournaments award 3,776 points, with 600 going to the winner. The cumulative total of points each player has received during the regular season determines that player's seed going into a four-tournament play-off at the end of the year, for which the top 125 players are eligible. A progressive cut through the first three of these play-off events determines the players who qualify for the final competition, the Tour Championship, which determines the FedExCup champion. The winner of each of the play-offs receives 2,500 points, the second-place finisher 1,500, and so on. The points are reset for the Tour Championship, with the leader at the end of the first three play-offs starting with 2,500 points, the player in second place receiving 2,250, and so on. The player with the most points at the end of the Tour Championship becomes the FedExCup champion and is awarded US$10 million, US$1 million of which is deferred into a retirement fund, making this the largest single bonus payout in professional sports. (In 2007 the entire US$10 million awarded to the winner was deferred.) Tiger Woods was the inaugural FedExCup champion. Vijay Singh of Fiji won the cup in 2008, and Woods repeated as champion in 2009.

Masters Tournament

Won by an American golfer except as indicated.

YEAR	WINNER	YEAR	WINNER	YEAR	WINNER
1934	Horton Smith	1937	Byron Nelson	1940	Jimmy Demaret
1935	Gene Sarazen	1938	Henry Picard	1941	Craig Wood
1936	Horton Smith	1939	Ralph Guldahl	1942	Byron Nelson

Masters Tournament (continued)

YEAR	WINNER	YEAR	WINNER	YEAR	WINNER
1943–45	*not held*	1967	Gay Brewer	1989	Nick Faldo (ENG)
1946	Herman Keiser	1968	Bob Goalby	1990	Nick Faldo (ENG)
1947	Jimmy Demaret	1969	George Archer	1991	Ian Woosnam (WAL)
1948	Claude Harmon	1970	Billy Casper	1992	Fred Couples
1949	Sam Snead	1971	Charles Coody	1993	Bernhard Langer (GER)
1950	Jimmy Demaret	1972	Jack Nicklaus	1994	José María Olazábal (ESP)
1951	Ben Hogan	1973	Tommy Aaron	1995	Ben Crenshaw
1952	Sam Snead	1974	Gary Player (RSA)	1996	Nick Faldo (ENG)
1953	Ben Hogan	1975	Jack Nicklaus	1997	Tiger Woods
1954	Sam Snead	1976	Raymond Floyd	1998	Mark O'Meara
1955	Cary Middlecoff	1977	Tom Watson	1999	José María Olazábal (ESP)
1956	Jack Burke	1978	Gary Player (RSA)	2000	Vijay Singh (FIJ)
1957	Doug Ford	1979	Fuzzy Zoeller	2001	Tiger Woods
1958	Arnold Palmer	1980	Seve Ballesteros (ESP)	2002	Tiger Woods
1959	Art Wall	1981	Tom Watson	2003	Mike Weir (CAN)
1960	Arnold Palmer	1982	Craig Stadler	2004	Phil Mickelson
1961	Gary Player (RSA)	1983	Seve Ballesteros (ESP)	2005	Tiger Woods
1962	Arnold Palmer	1984	Ben Crenshaw	2006	Phil Mickelson
1963	Jack Nicklaus	1985	Bernhard Langer (FRG)	2007	Zach Johnson
1964	Arnold Palmer	1986	Jack Nicklaus	2008	Trevor Immelman (RSA)
1965	Jack Nicklaus	1987	Larry Mize	2009	Ángel Cabrera (ARG)
1966	Jack Nicklaus	1988	Sandy Lyle (SCO)	2010	Phil Mickelson

United States Open Championship—Men
Won by an American golfer except as indicated.

YEAR	WINNER	YEAR	WINNER	YEAR	WINNER
1895	Horace Rawlins	1934	Olin Dutra	1975	Lou Graham
1896	James Foulis	1935	Sam Parks, Jr.	1976	Jerry Pate
1897	Joe Lloyd	1936	Tony Manero	1977	Hubert Green
1898	Fred Herd	1937	Ralph Guldahl	1978	Andy North
1899	Willie Smith	1938	Ralph Guldahl	1979	Hale Irwin
1900	Harry Vardon (ENG)	1939	Byron Nelson	1980	Jack Nicklaus
1901	Willie Anderson	1940	Lawson Little	1981	David Graham (AUS)
1902	Laurence Auchterlonie	1941	Craig Wood	1982	Tom Watson
1903	Willie Anderson	1942–45	*not held*	1983	Larry Nelson
1904	Willie Anderson	1946	Lloyd Mangrum	1984	Fuzzy Zoeller
1905	Willie Anderson	1947	Lew Worsham	1985	Andy North
1906	Alex Smith	1948	Ben Hogan	1986	Raymond Floyd
1907	Alex Ross	1949	Cary Middlecoff	1987	Scott Simpson
1908	Fred McLeod	1950	Ben Hogan	1988	Curtis Strange
1909	George Sargent	1951	Ben Hogan	1989	Curtis Strange
1910	Alex Smith	1952	Julius Boros	1990	Hale Irwin
1911	John J. McDermott	1953	Ben Hogan	1991	Payne Stewart
1912	John J. McDermott	1954	Ed Furgol	1992	Tom Kite
1913	Francis Ouimet	1955	Jack Fleck	1993	Lee Janzen
1914	Walter Hagen	1956	Cary Middlecoff	1994	Ernie Els (RSA)
1915	Jerome D. Travers	1957	Dick Mayer	1995	Corey Pavin
1916	Chick Evans	1958	Tommy Bolt	1996	Steve Jones
1917–18	*not held*	1959	Billy Casper	1997	Ernie Els (RSA)
1919	Walter Hagen	1960	Arnold Palmer	1998	Lee Janzen
1920	Edward Ray (ENG)	1961	Gene Littler	1999	Payne Stewart
1921	James M. Barnes	1962	Jack Nicklaus	2000	Tiger Woods
1922	Gene Sarazen	1963	Julius Boros	2001	Retief Goosen (RSA)
1923	Bobby Jones	1964	Ken Venturi	2002	Tiger Woods
1924	Cyril Walker	1965	Gary Player (RSA)	2003	Jim Furyk
1925	Willie MacFarlane, Jr.	1966	Billy Casper	2004	Retief Goosen (RSA)
1926	Bobby Jones	1967	Jack Nicklaus	2005	Michael Campbell (NZL)
1927	Tommy Armour	1968	Lee Trevino	2006	Geoff Ogilvy (AUS)
1928	Johnny Farrell	1969	Orville Moody	2007	Ángel Cabrera (ARG)
1929	Bobby Jones	1970	Tony Jacklin (ENG)	2008	Tiger Woods
1930	Bobby Jones	1971	Lee Trevino	2009	Lucas Glover
1931	Billy Burke	1972	Jack Nicklaus	2010	Graeme McDowell (NIR)
1932	Gene Sarazen	1973	Johnny Miller		
1933	John Goodman	1974	Hale Irwin		

British Open Tournament—Men

Won by an English golfer unless otherwise indicated.

YEAR	WINNER	YEAR	WINNER	YEAR	WINNER
1860	Willie Park, Sr. (SCO)	1908	James Braid (SCO)	1965	Peter Thomson (AUS)
1861	Tom Morris, Sr. (SCO)	1909	John H. Taylor	1966	Jack Nicklaus (USA)
1862	Tom Morris, Sr. (SCO)	1910	James Braid (SCO)	1967	Roberto de Vicenzo (ARG)
1863	Willie Park, Sr. (SCO)	1911	Harry Vardon (JEY)	1968	Gary Player (RSA)
1864	Tom Morris, Sr. (SCO)	1912	Ted Ray (JEY)	1969	Tony Jacklin
1865	Andrew Strath (SCO)	1913	John H. Taylor	1970	Jack Nicklaus (USA)
1866	Willie Park, Sr. (SCO)	1914	Harry Vardon (JEY)	1971	Lee Trevino (USA)
1867	Tom Morris, Sr. (SCO)	1915–19 *not held*		1972	Lee Trevino (USA)
1868	Tom Morris, Jr. (SCO)	1920	George Duncan (SCO)	1973	Tom Weiskopf (USA)
1869	Tom Morris, Jr. (SCO)	1921	Jock Hutchison (USA)	1974	Gary Player (RSA)
1870	Tom Morris, Jr. (SCO)	1922	Walter Hagen (USA)	1975	Tom Watson (USA)
1871	*not held*	1923	Arthur Havers	1976	Johnny Miller (USA)
1872	Tom Morris, Jr. (SCO)	1924	Walter Hagen (USA)	1977	Tom Watson (USA)
1873	Tom Kidd (SCO)	1925	James Barnes (USA)	1978	Jack Nicklaus (USA)
1874	Mungo Park (SCO)	1926	Bobby Jones (USA)	1979	Seve Ballesteros (ESP)
1875	Willie Park, Sr. (SCO)	1927	Bobby Jones (USA)	1980	Tom Watson (USA)
1876	Bob Martin (SCO)	1928	Walter Hagen (USA)	1981	Bill Rogers (USA)
1877	Jamie Anderson (SCO)	1929	Walter Hagen (USA)	1982	Tom Watson (USA)
1878	Jamie Anderson (SCO)	1930	Bobby Jones (USA)	1983	Tom Watson (USA)
1879	Jamie Anderson (SCO)	1931	Tommy Armour (USA)	1984	Seve Ballesteros (ESP)
1880	Robert Ferguson (SCO)	1932	Gene Sarazen (USA)	1985	Sandy Lyle (SCO)
1881	Robert Ferguson (SCO)	1933	Denny Shute (USA)	1986	Greg Norman (AUS)
1882	Robert Ferguson (SCO)	1934	Henry Cotton	1987	Nick Faldo
1883	Willie Fernie (SCO)	1935	Alfred Perry	1988	Seve Ballesteros (ESP)
1884	Jack Simpson (SCO)	1936	Alfred Padgham	1989	Mark Calcavecchia (USA)
1885	Bob Martin (SCO)	1937	Henry Cotton	1990	Nick Faldo
1886	David Brown (SCO)	1938	Reg A. Whitcombe	1991	Ian Baker-Finch (AUS)
1887	Willie Park, Jr. (SCO)	1939	Richard Burton	1992	Nick Faldo
1888	Jack Burns (SCO)	1940–45 *not held*		1993	Greg Norman (AUS)
1889	Willie Park, Jr. (SCO)	1946	Sam Snead (USA)	1994	Nick Price (ZIM)
1890	John Ball	1947	Fred Daly (NIR)	1995	John Daly (USA)
1891	Hugh Kirkaldy (SCO)	1948	Henry Cotton	1996	Tom Lehman (USA)
1892	Harold Hilton	1949	Bobby Locke (RSA)	1997	Justin Leonard (USA)
1893	William Auchterlonie (SCO)	1950	Bobby Locke (RSA)	1998	Mark O'Meara (USA)
1894	John H. Taylor	1951	Max Faulkner	1999	Paul Lawrie (SCO)
1895	John H. Taylor	1952	Bobby Locke (RSA)	2000	Tiger Woods (USA)
1896	Harry Vardon (JEY)	1953	Ben Hogan (USA)	2001	David Duval (USA)
1897	Harold Hilton	1954	Peter Thomson (AUS)	2002	Ernie Els (RSA)
1898	Harry Vardon (JEY)	1955	Peter Thomson (AUS)	2003	Ben Curtis (USA)
1899	Harry Vardon (JEY)	1956	Peter Thomson (AUS)	2004	Todd Hamilton (USA)
1900	John H. Taylor	1957	Bobby Locke (RSA)	2005	Tiger Woods (USA)
1901	James Braid (SCO)	1958	Peter Thomson (AUS)	2006	Tiger Woods (USA)
1902	Sandy Herd (SCO)	1959	Gary Player (RSA)	2007	Padraig Harrington (IRL)
1903	Harry Vardon (JEY)	1960	Kel Nagle (AUS)	2008	Padraig Harrington (IRL)
1904	Jack White (SCO)	1961	Arnold Palmer (USA)	2009	Stewart Cink (USA)
1905	James Braid (SCO)	1962	Arnold Palmer (USA)	2010	Louis Oosthuizen (RSA)
1906	James Braid (SCO)	1963	Bob Charles (NZL)		
1907	Arnaud Massy (FRA)	1964	Tony Lema (USA)		

US Professional Golfers' Association (PGA) Championship

Won by an American golfer except as indicated.

YEAR	WINNER	YEAR	WINNER	YEAR	WINNER
1916	James M. Barnes	1930	Tommy Armour	1943	*not held*
1917–18 *not held*		1931	Tom Creavy	1944	Bob Hamilton
1919	James M. Barnes	1932	Olin Dutra	1945	Byron Nelson
1920	Jock Hutchison	1933	Gene Sarazen	1946	Ben Hogan
1921	Walter Hagen	1934	Paul Runyan	1947	Jim Ferrier
1922	Gene Sarazen	1935	Johnny Revolta	1948	Ben Hogan
1923	Gene Sarazen	1936	Denny Shute	1949	Sam Snead
1924	Walter Hagen	1937	Denny Shute	1950	Chandler Harper
1925	Walter Hagen	1938	Paul Runyan	1951	Sam Snead
1926	Walter Hagen	1939	Henry Picard	1952	Jim Turnesa
1927	Walter Hagen	1940	Byron Nelson	1953	Walter Burkemo
1928	Leo Diegel	1941	Vic Ghezzi	1954	Chick Harbert
1929	Leo Diegel	1942	Sam Snead	1955	Doug Ford

US Professional Golfers' Association (PGA) Championship (continued)

YEAR	WINNER	YEAR	WINNER	YEAR	WINNER
1956	Jack Burke	1975	Jack Nicklaus	1994	Nick Price (ZIM)
1957	Lionel Hebert	1976	Dave Stockton	1995	Steve Elkington (AUS)
1958	Dow Finsterwald	1977	Lanny Wadkins	1996	Mark Brooks
1959	Bob Rosburg	1978	John Mahaffey	1997	Davis Love III
1960	Jay Hebert	1979	David Graham (AUS)	1998	Vijay Singh (FIJ)
1961	Jerry Barber	1980	Jack Nicklaus	1999	Tiger Woods
1962	Gary Player (RSA)	1981	Larry Nelson	2000	Tiger Woods
1963	Jack Nicklaus	1982	Raymond Floyd	2001	David Toms
1964	Bobby Nichols	1983	Hal Sutton	2002	Rich Beems
1965	Dave Marr	1984	Lee Trevino	2003	Shaun Micheel
1966	Al Geiberger	1985	Hubert Green	2004	Vijay Singh (FIJ)
1967	Don January	1986	Bob Tway	2005	Phil Mickelson
1968	Julius Boros	1987	Larry Nelson	2006	Tiger Woods
1969	Raymond Floyd	1988	Jeff Sluman	2007	Tiger Woods
1970	Dave Stockton	1989	Payne Stewart	2008	Padraig Harrington (IRL)
1971	Jack Nicklaus	1990	Wayne Grady (AUS)	2009	Y.E. Yang (KOR)
1972	Gary Player (RSA)	1991	John Daly	2010	Martin Kaymer (GER)
1973	Jack Nicklaus	1992	Nick Price (ZIM)		
1974	Lee Trevino	1993	Paul Azinger		

Kraft Nabisco Championship

Won by an American golfer except as indicated.

YEAR	WINNER	YEAR	WINNER	YEAR	WINNER
1972	Jane Blalock	1986	Pat Bradley	2000	Karrie Webb (AUS)
1973	Mickey Wright	1987	Betsy King	2001	Annika Sörenstam (SWE)
1974	Jo Ann Prentice	1988	Amy Alcott	2002	Annika Sörenstam (SWE)
1975	Sandra Palmer	1989	Juli Inkster	2003	Patricia Meunier-Lebouc
1976	Judy Rankin	1990	Betsy King		(FRA)
1977	Kathy Whitworth	1991	Amy Alcott	2004	Grace Park (KOR)
1978	Sandra Post	1992	Dottie Mochrie	2005	Annika Sörenstam (SWE)
1979	Sandra Post	1993	Helen Alfredsson (SWE)	2006	Karrie Webb (AUS)
1980	Donna Caponi	1994	Donna Andrews	2007	Morgan Pressel
1981	Nancy Lopez	1995	Nanci Bowen	2008	Lorena Ochoa (MEX)
1982	Sally Little (RSA)	1996	Patty Sheehan	2009	Brittany Lincicome
1983	Amy Alcott	1997	Betsy King	2010	Yani Tseng (TPE)
1984	Juli Inkster	1998	Pat Hurst		
1985	Alice Miller	1999	Dottie Pepper		

Ladies Professional Golf Association (LPGA) Championship

Won by an American golfer except as indicated.

YEAR	WINNER	YEAR	WINNER	YEAR	WINNER
1955	Beverly Hanson	1974	Sandra Haynie	1993	Patty Sheehan
1956	Marlene Hagge	1975	Kathy Whitworth	1994	Laura Davies (ENG)
1957	Louise Suggs	1976	Betty Burfeindt	1995	Kelly Robbins
1958	Mickey Wright	1977	Chako Higuchi	1996	Laura Davies (ENG)
1959	Betsy Rawls	1978	Nancy Lopez	1997	Chris Johnson
1960	Mickey Wright	1979	Donna Caponi	1998	Pak Se Ri (KOR)
1961	Mickey Wright	1980	Sally Little	1999	Juli Inkster
1962	Judy Kimball	1981	Donna Caponi	2000	Juli Inkster
1963	Mickey Wright	1982	Jan Stephenson (AUS)	2001	Karrie Webb (AUS)
1964	Mary Mills	1983	Patty Sheehan	2002	Pak Se Ri (KOR)
1965	Sandra Haynie	1984	Patty Sheehan	2003	Annika Sörenstam (SWE)
1966	Gloria Ehret	1985	Nancy Lopez	2004	Annika Sörenstam (SWE)
1967	Kathy Whitworth	1986	Pat Bradley	2005	Annika Sörenstam (SWE)
1968	Sandra Post	1987	Jane Geddes	2006	Pak Se Ri (KOR)
1969	Betsy Rawls	1988	Sherri Turner	2007	Suzann Pettersen (NOR)
1970	Shirley Englehorn	1989	Nancy Lopez	2008	Yani Tseng (TPE)
1971	Kathy Whitworth	1990	Beth Daniel	2009	Anna Nordqvist (SWE)
1972	Kathy Ahern	1991	Meg Mallon	2010	Cristie Kerr
1973	Mary Mills	1992	Betsy King		

United States Women's Open Championship

Won by an American golfer except as indicated.

YEAR	WINNER	YEAR	WINNER	YEAR	WINNER
1946	Patty Berg	1966	Sandra Spuzich	1988	Liselotte Neumann (SWE)
1947	Betty Jameson	1967	Catherine Lacoste	1989	Betsy King
1948	Babe Didrikson		(FRA)	1990	Betsy King
	Zaharias	1968	Susie Berning	1991	Meg Mallon
1949	Louise Suggs	1969	Donna Caponi	1992	Patty Sheehan
1950	Babe Didrikson	1970	Donna Caponi	1993	Lauri Merten
	Zaharias	1971	JoAnne Carner	1994	Patty Sheehan
1951	Betsy Rawls	1972	Susie Berning	1995	Annika Sörenstam (SWE)
1952	Louise Suggs	1973	Susie Berning	1996	Annika Sörenstam (SWE)
1953	Betsy Rawls	1974	Sandra Haynie	1997	Alison Nicholas (ENG)
1954	Babe Didrikson	1975	Sandra Palmer	1998	Pak Se Ri (KOR)
	Zaharias	1976	JoAnne Carner	1999	Juli Inkster
1955	Fay Crocker	1977	Hollis Stacy	2000	Karrie Webb (AUS)
1956	Kathy Cornelius	1978	Hollis Stacy	2001	Karrie Webb (AUS)
1957	Betsy Rawls	1979	Jerilyn Britz	2002	Juli Inkster
1958	Mickey Wright	1980	Amy Alcott	2003	Hilary Lunke
1959	Mickey Wright	1981	Pat Bradley	2004	Meg Mallon
1960	Betsy Rawls	1982	Janet Anderson	2005	Birdie Kim (KOR)
1961	Mickey Wright	1983	Jan Stephenson (AUS)	2006	Annika Sörenstam (SWE)
1962	Murle Breer	1984	Hollis Stacy	2007	Cristie Kerr
1963	Mary Mills	1985	Kathy Baker	2008	Inbee Park (KOR)
1964	Mickey Wright	1986	Jane Geddes	2009	Ji Eun-Hee (KOR)
1965	Carol Mann	1987	Laura Davies (ENG)	2010	Paula Creamer

Women's British Open Championship

Won by an English golfer unless otherwise indicated.

YEAR	WINNER	YEAR	WINNER	YEAR	WINNER
1976	Jenny Lee-Smith	1988	Corinne Dibnah (AUS)	2000	Sophie Gustafson (SWE)
1977	Vivien Saunders	1989	Jane Geddes (USA)	2001	Pak Se Ri (KOR)
1978	Janet Melville	1990	Helen Alfredsson (SWE)	2002	Karrie Webb (AUS)
1979	Alison Sheard (RSA)	1991	Penny Grice-Whittaker	2003	Annika Sörenstam (SWE)
1980	Debbie Massey (USA)	1992	Patty Sheehan (USA)	2004	Karen Stupples
1981	Debbie Massey (USA)	1993	Mardi Lunn (AUS)	2005	Jang Jeong (KOR)
1982	Marta Figueras-Dotti (ESP)	1994	Liselotte Neumann (SWE)	2006	Sherri Steinhauer (USA)
1983	*not held*	1995	Karrie Webb (AUS)	2007	Lorena Ochoa (MEX)
1984	Okamoto Ayako (JPN)	1996	Emilee Klein (USA)	2008	Ji Yai Shin (KOR)
1985	Betsy King (USA)	1997	Karrie Webb (AUS)	2009	Catriona Matthew (SCO)
1986	Laura Davies	1998	Sherri Steinhauer (USA)	2010	Yani Tseng (TPE)
1987	Alison Nicholas	1999	Sherri Steinhauer (USA)		

Ryder Cup

YEAR	RESULT	YEAR	RESULT
1927	United States 9½, Britain 2½	1973	United States 19, Britain 13
1929	Britain 7, United States 5	1975	United States 21, Britain 11
1931	United States 9, Britain 3	1977	United States 12½, Britain 7½
1933	Britain 6½, United States 5½	1979	United States 17, Europe 11
1935	United States 9, Britain 3	1981	United States 18½, Europe 9½
1937	United States 8, Britain 4	1983	United States 14½, Europe 13½
1939–45	*not held*	1985	Europe 16½, United States 11½
1947	United States 11, Britain 1	1987	Europe 15, United States 13
1949	United States 7, Britain 5	1989	Europe 14, United States 14
1951	United States 9½, Britain 2½	1991	United States 14½, Europe 13½
1953	United States 6½, Britain 5½	1993	United States 15, Europe 13
1955	United States 8, Britain 4	1995	Europe 14½, United States 13½
1957	Britain 7½, United States 4½	1997	Europe 14½, United States 13½
1959	United States 8½, Britain 3½	1999	United States 14½, Europe 13½
1961	United States 14½, Britain 9½	2001	*postponed until 2002*
1963	United States 23, Britain 9	2002	Europe 15½, United States 12½
1965	United States 19½, Britain 12½	2004	Europe 18½, United States 9½
1967	United States 23½, Britain 8½	2006	Europe 18½, United States 9½
1969	United States 16, Britain 16	2008	United States 16½, Europe 11½
1971	United States 18½, Britain 13½		

Curtis Cup

YEAR	RESULT	YEAR	RESULT
1932	United States 5½, Britain and Ireland 3½	1976	United States 11½, Britain and Ireland 6½
1934	United States 6½, Britain and Ireland 2½	1978	United States 12, Britain and Ireland 6
1936	United States[1] 4½, Britain and Ireland 4½	1980	United States 13, Britain and Ireland 5
1938	United States 5½, Britain and Ireland 3½	1982	United States 14½, Britain and Ireland 3½
1940–46	*not held*	1984	United States 9½, Britain and Ireland 8½
1948	United States 6½, Britain and Ireland 2½	1986	Britain and Ireland 13, United States 5
1950	United States 7½, Britain and Ireland 2½	1988	Britain and Ireland 11, United States 7
1952	Britain and Ireland 5, United States 4	1990	United States 14, Britain and Ireland 4
1954	United States 6, Britain and Ireland 3	1992	Britain and Ireland 10, United States 8
1956	Britain and Ireland 5, United States 4	1994	Britain and Ireland[1] 9, United States 9
1958	Britain and Ireland[1] 4½, United States 4½	1996	Britain and Ireland 11½, United States 6½
1960	United States 6½, Britain and Ireland 2½	1998	United States 10, Britain and Ireland 8
1962	United States 8, Britain and Ireland 1	2000	United States 10, Britain and Ireland 8
1964	United States 10½, Britain and Ireland 7½	2002	United States 11, Britain and Ireland 7
1966	United States 13, Britain and Ireland 5	2004	United States 10, Britain and Ireland 8
1968	United States 10½, Britain and Ireland 7½	2006	United States 11½, Britain and Ireland 6½
1970	United States 11½, Britain and Ireland 6½	2008	United States 13, Britain and Ireland 7
1972	United States 10, Britain and Ireland 8	2010	United States 12½, Britain and Ireland 7½
1974	United States 13, Britain and Ireland 5		

[1]*In case of a tie the defenders retain the cup.*

United States Amateur Championship—Men
Won by an American golfer except as indicated. Table shows results for the past 20 years.

YEAR	WINNER	YEAR	WINNER	YEAR	WINNER
1991	Mitch Voges	1998	Hank Kuehne	2005	Edoardo Molinari (ITA)
1992	Justin Leonard	1999	David Gossett	2006	Richie Ramsay (SCO)
1993	John Harris	2000	Jeff Quinney	2007	Colt Knost
1994	Tiger Woods	2001	Ben Dickerson	2008	Danny Lee (NZL)
1995	Tiger Woods	2002	Ricky Barnes	2009	Byeong-Hun An (KOR)
1996	Tiger Woods	2003	Nick Flanagan (AUS)	2010	Peter Uihlein
1997	Matt Kuchar	2004	Ryan Moore		

British Amateur Championship—Men
Held since 1885. Table shows results for the past 20 years. Won by an English golfer except as indicated.

YEAR	WINNER	YEAR	WINNER	YEAR	WINNER
1991	Gary Wolstenholme	1998	Sergio García (ESP)	2005	Brian McElhinney (IRL)
1992	Stephen Dundas (SCO)	1999	Graeme Storm	2006	Julien Guerrier (FRA)
1993	Ian Pyman	2000	Mikko Ilonen (FIN)	2007	Drew Weaver (USA)
1994	Lee James	2001	Michael Hoey (NIR)	2008	Reinier Saxton (NED)
1995	Gordon Sherry (SCO)	2002	Alejandro Larrazábal (ESP)	2009	Matteo Manassero (ITA)
1996	Warren Bledon	2003	Gary Wolstenholme	2010	Jin Jeong (KOR)
1997	Craig Watson (SCO)	2004	Stuart Wilson (SCO)		

United States Women's Amateur Championship
Held since 1895. Table shows results for the past 20 years. Won by an American golfer except as indicated.

YEAR	WINNER	YEAR	WINNER	YEAR	WINNER
1991	Amy Fruhwirth	1998	Grace Park	2004	Jane Park
1992	Vicki Goetze	1999	Dorothy Delasin	2005	Morgan Pressel
1993	Jill McGill	2000	Marcy Newton	2006	Kimberly Kim
1994	Wendy Ward	2001	Meredith Duncan	2007	María José Uribe (COL)
1995	Kelli Kuehne	2002	Becky Lucidi	2008	Amanda Blumenherst
1996	Kelli Kuehne	2003	Virada Nirapath-	2009	Jennifer Song
1997	Silvia Cavalleri (ITA)		pongporn (THA)	2010	Danielle Kang

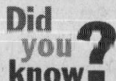
Did you know?

In the 1930s, radio announcers would often describe a football field as being divided into squares, thus aiding listeners in the visualization of the game. The area just in front of the goal posts, in modern parlance called the "red zone," was known then as "square one." From this usage comes the modern expression "back to square one."

Ladies' British Open Amateur Championship

Held since 1893. Table shows results for the past 20 years. Won by an English golfer except as indicated.

YEAR	WINNER	YEAR	WINNER	YEAR	WINNER
1991	Valerie Michaud	1998	Kim Rostron	2005	Louise Stahle (SWE)
1992	Bernille Pedersen (DEN)	1999	Marine Monnet (FRA)	2006	Belén Mozo (ESP)
1993	Catriona Lambert (SCO)	2000	Rebecca Hudson	2007	Carlota Ciganda (ESP)
1994	Emma Duggleby	2001	Marta Prieto (ESP)	2008	Anna Nordqvist (SWE)
1995	Julie Wade Hall	2002	Rebecca Hudson	2009	Azahara Muñoz (ESP)
1996	Kelli Kuehne (USA)	2003	Elisa Serramia (ESP)	2010	Kelly Tidy
1997	Alison Rose (SCO)	2004	Louise Stahle (SWE)		

Horse Racing

In the **oldest type** of horse racing, the rider sits astride the horse; in the other type of race, best known as **harness racing,** the driver sits in a sulky— a two-wheeled vehicle attached by shafts and traces to the horse. In the former type, a **Thoroughbred** horse is raced over either a track or a course of jumps and turns (**steeplechase**). Harness horses can be trotters or pacers and are Standardbred horses raced on a track.

The English Thoroughbred classics. The races are run by 3-year-old colts and fillies. **The Derby,** first run in 1780, is run at Epsom Downs, Surrey, over 1½ miles. **The Oaks** (for fillies only), also run at Epsom Downs, was first run in 1779; the oldest of the English races, however, is the **St. Leger** (1776). It is run over 1 mile 6½ furlongs at Doncaster, South Yorkshire. The **2,000 Guineas** (1809) is run over 1 mile at Newmarket, Suffolk. A horse that wins the Derby, the St. Leger, and the 2,000 Guineas all in one year is said to have won the **British Triple Crown.**

The American Thoroughbred classics. The **Kentucky Derby,** a **Triple Crown** event first run in 1875 and perhaps the best known of American horse races, is raced at Churchill Downs in Louisville KY, over a 10-furlong (1¼-mile) track. Another of the Triple Crown classics, the **Preakness Stakes,** was instituted in 1873; it is run over 9½ furlongs (1³⁄₁₆ miles) at Pimlico Race Track in Baltimore MD. The third Triple Crown event is the 12-furlong (1½-mile)

Belmont Stakes, established in 1867. It is run at Belmont Park Race Track, Long Island NY. All three events are for 3-year-old horses.

Australian Thoroughbred racing. The Victoria Racing Club's **Melbourne Cup,** first run in 1861, is one of the world's great handicap races. The day on which it is held (the first Tuesday in November) is a public holiday in Melbourne, VIC.

Dubai World Cup, first run in 1996, is the world's richest horse race ($6 million in 2007). The 2,000-m (about 1¼-mi) race is held on the dirt track at the Nad Al Sheba Racecourse in Dubai, United Arab Emirates, and is open to four-year-old and older Thoroughbred horses.

The **Grand National,** the world's most significant and widely followed **steeplechase** race, has been run annually at Aintree Racecourse near Liverpool, England, since 1839. The race, which includes 30 jumps, is run over a traditional distance of 4 miles 4 furlongs.

Harness racing. In the United States, the **Hambletonian Trot** is probably the most prestigious of harness races. It was established in 1926, was raced in New York, Kentucky, and Illinois, and is now run at the Meadowlands in New Jersey.

Related Web sites: US National Thoroughbred Racing Association: <www.ntra.com>; Fédération Equestre Internationale: <www.horsesport.org>; *Thoroughbred Times:* <www.thoroughbredtimes.com>; and *Racing Post:* <www.racingpost.co.uk>.

Major Thoroughbred Race Winners, 2009–10

United States

DATE	RACE	WINNER	JOCKEY
1 Aug 2009	Diana Stakes	Forever Together	Julien Leparoux
2 Aug 2009	Haskell Invitational Stakes	Rachel Alexandra	Calvin Borel
8 Aug 2009	Arlington Million Stakes	Gio Ponti	Ramon Dominguez
8 Aug 2009	Beverly D. Stakes	Dynaforce	Kent Desormeaux
8 Aug 2009	Bing Crosby Stakes	Zensational	Victor Espinoza
8 Aug 2009	Secretariat Stakes	Take the Points	Kent Desormeaux
8 Aug 2009	Test Stakes	Flashing	Richard Migliore
8 Aug 2009	Whitney Handicap	Bullsbay	Jeremy Rose
9 Aug 2009	Clement L. Hirsch Stakes	Zenyatta	Mike Smith
15 Aug 2009	Sword Dancer Invitational Stakes	Telling	Javier Castellano
16 Aug 2009	John C. Mabee Handicap	Magical Fantasy	Alex Solis
22 Aug 2009	Alabama Stakes	Careless Jewel	Robert Landry
22 Aug 2009	Del Mar Oaks	Internallyflawless	Garrett Gomez
29 Aug 2009	Ballerina Stakes	Music Note	Rajiv Maragh
29 Aug 2009	King's Bishop Stakes	Capt. Candyman Can	Javier Castellano
29 Aug 2009	Travers Stakes	Summer Bird	Kent Desormeaux
30 Aug 2009	Personal Ensign Stakes	Icon Project	Julien Leparoux
5 Sep 2009	Darley Debutante Stakes	Mi Sueno	Michael Baze
5 Sep 2009	Forego Stakes	Pyro	John Velazquez

Major Thoroughbred Race Winners, 2009–10 (continued)

United States (continued)

DATE	RACE	WINNER	JOCKEY
5 Sep 2009	Woodward Stakes	Rachel Alexandra	Calvin Borel
6 Sep 2009	Pacific Classic Stakes	Richard's Kid	Mike Smith
6 Sep 2009	Pat O'Brien Stakes	Zensational	Victor Espinoza
6 Sep 2009	Spinaway Stakes	Hot Dixie Chick	Robby Albarado
7 Sep 2009	Del Mar Futurity	Lookin At Lucky	Garrett Gomez
12 Sep 2009	Garden City Stakes	Miss World	Cornelio Velasquez
12 Sep 2009	Ruffian Handicap	Swift Temper	Alan Garcia
3 Oct 2009	Beldame Stakes	Music Note	Rajiv Maragh
3 Oct 2009	Flower Bowl Invitational Stakes	Pure Clan	Julien Leparoux
3 Oct 2009	Jockey Club Gold Cup Stakes	Summer Bird	Kent Desormeaux
3 Oct 2009	Joe Hirsch Turf Classic Invitational Stakes	Interpatation	Robby Albarado
3 Oct 2009	Vosburgh Stakes	Kodiak Kowboy	Shaun Bridgmohan
4 Oct 2009	Norfolk Stakes	Lookin At Lucky	Garrett Gomez
4 Oct 2009	Oak Leaf Stakes	Blind Luck	Tyler Baze
9 Oct 2009	Darley Alcibiades Stakes	Negligee	Rajiv Maragh
10 Oct 2009	Champagne Stakes	Homeboykris	Edgar Prado
10 Oct 2009	Dixiana Breeders' Futurity	Noble's Promise	Willie Martinez
10 Oct 2009	First Lady Stakes	Diamondrella	Rajiv Maragh
10 Oct 2009	Frizette Stakes	Devil May Care	John Velazquez
10 Oct 2009	Goodwood Stakes	Gitano Hernando	Kieren Fallon
10 Oct 2009	Jamaica Handicap	Take the Points	Edgar Prado
10 Oct 2009	Lady's Secret Stakes	Zenyatta	Mike Smith
10 Oct 2009	Shadwell Turf Mile Stakes	Court Vision	Robby Albarado
10 Oct 2009	Yellow Ribbon Stakes	Magical Fantasy	Alex Solis
11 Oct 2009	Clement L. Hirsch Memorial Turf Championship Stakes	Presious Passion	Elvis Trujillo
11 Oct 2009	Juddmonte Spinster Stakes	Mushka	Kent Desormeaux
17 Oct 2009	Queen Elizabeth II Challenge Cup Stakes	Hot Cha Cha	James Graham
24 Oct 2009	Frank J. De Francis Memorial Dash Stakes	Vineyard Haven	Alan Garcia
6 Nov 2009	Breeders' Cup Filly and Mare Sprint	Informed Decision	Julien Leparoux
6 Nov 2009	Breeders' Cup Filly and Mare Turf	Midday	Tom Queally
6 Nov 2009	Breeders' Cup Juvenile Fillies	She Be Wild	Julien Leparoux
6 Nov 2009	Breeders' Cup Ladies' Classic	Life Is Sweet	Garrett Gomez
7 Nov 2009	Breeders' Cup Classic	Zenyatta	Mike Smith
7 Nov 2009	Breeders' Cup Dirt Mile	Furthest Land	Julien Leparoux
7 Nov 2009	Breeders' Cup Juvenile	Vale of York	Ahmed Ajtebi
7 Nov 2009	Breeders' Cup Mile	Goldikova	Olivier Peslier
7 Nov 2009	Breeders' Cup Sprint	Dancing in Silks	Joel Rosario
7 Nov 2009	Breeders' Cup Turf	Conduit	Ryan Moore
27 Nov 2009	Citation Handicap	Fluke	Joe Talamo
28 Nov 2009	Cigar Mile Handicap	Kodiak Kowboy	Shaun Bridgmohan
28 Nov 2009	Gazelle Stakes	Flashing	Richard Migliore
28 Nov 2009	Matriarch Stakes	Ventura	Garrett Gomez
29 Nov 2009	Hollywood Derby	The Usual Q.T.	Victor Espinoza
19 Dec 2009	CashCall Futurity	Lookin At Lucky	Garrett Gomez
20 Dec 2009	Hollywood Starlet Stakes	Blind Luck	Rafael Bejarano
26 Dec 2009	La Brea Stakes	Evita Argentina	Joel Rosario
6 Feb 2010	Donn Handicap	Quality Road	John Velazquez
6 Feb 2010	Gulfstream Park Turf Handicap	Court Vision	Robby Albarado
6 Mar 2010	Santa Anita Handicap	Misremembered	Martin Garcia
20 Mar 2010	Florida Derby	Ice Box	Jose Lezcano
3 Apr 2010	Ashland Stakes	Evening Jewel	Kent Desormeaux
3 Apr 2010	Santa Anita Derby	Sidney's Candy	Joe Talamo
3 Apr 2010	Wood Memorial Stakes	Eskendereya	John Velazquez
8 Apr 2010	Vinery Madison Stakes	Dr. Zic	Kent Desormeaux
9 Apr 2010	Apple Blossom Handicap	Zenyatta	Mike Smith
9 Apr 2010	Maker's Mark Mile	Karelian	Julien Leparoux
10 Apr 2010	Arkansas Derby	Line of David	Jon Court
10 Apr 2010	Blue Grass Stakes	Stately Victor	Alan Garcia
30 Apr 2010	Kentucky Oaks	Blind Luck	Rafael Bejarano
1 May 2010	Humana Distaff	Mona de Momma	Joel Rosario
1 May 2010	Kentucky Derby[1]	Super Saver	Calvin Borel
1 May 2010	Woodford Reserve Turf Classic Stakes	General Quarters	Rafael Bejarano
15 May 2010	Preakness Stakes[1]	Lookin At Lucky	Martin Garcia
31 May 2010	Metropolitan Mile Handicap	Quality Road	John Velazquez
5 Jun 2010	Acorn Stakes	Champagne d'Oro	Martin Garcia
5 Jun 2010	Belmont Stakes[1]	Drosselmeyer	Mike Smith

Major Thoroughbred Race Winners, 2009–10 (continued)

United States (continued)

DATE	RACE	WINNER	JOCKEY
5 Jun 2010	Just a Game Handicap	Proviso	Mike Smith
5 Jun 2010	Manhattan Handicap	Winchester	Cornelio Velasquez
12 Jun 2010	Stephen Foster Handicap	Blame	Garrett Gomez
3 Jul 2010	United Nations Stakes	Chinchon	Garrett Gomez
10 Jul 2010	Hollywood Gold Cup Handicap	Awesome Gem	David Romero Flores
10 Jul 2010	Man o' War Stakes	Gio Ponti	Ramon Dominguez
10 Jul 2010	Princess Rooney Handicap	Jessica Is Back	Elvis Trujillo
24 Jul 2010	Eddie Read Stakes	The Usual Q.T.	Victor Espinoza
31 Jul 2010	Diana Stakes	Proviso	Mike Smith

Canada

2 Aug 2009	Breeders' Stakes	Perfect Shower	Jono Jones
20 Sep 2009	Woodbine Mile Stakes	Ventura	Garrett Gomez
17 Oct 2009	Canadian International Stakes	Champs Elysees	Garrett Gomez
17 Oct 2009	E.P. Taylor Stakes	Lahaleeb	William Buick
4 Jul 2010	Queen's Plate Stakes	Big Red Mike	Eurico Rosa da Silva
25 Jul 2010	Prince of Wales Stakes	Golden Moka	Anthony Stephen

England

18 Aug 2009	Juddmonte International Stakes	Sea The Stars	Mick Kinane
21 Aug 2009	Nunthorpe Stakes	Borderlescott	Neil Callan
12 Sep 2009	St. Leger Stakes[2]	Mastery	Ted Durcan
26 Sep 2009	Queen Elizabeth II Stakes	Rip Van Winkle	Johnny Murtagh
1 May 2010	2,000 Guineas[2]	Makfi	Christophe Lemaire
2 May 2010	1,000 Guineas	Special Duty	Stephane Pasquier
5 Jun 2010	The Derby[2]	Workforce	Ryan Moore
17 Jun 2010	Ascot Gold Cup	Rite of Passage	Pat Smullen
3 Jul 2010	Coral-Eclipse Stakes	Twice Over	Tom Queally
24 Jul 2010	King George VI and Queen Elizabeth Stakes	Harbinger	Olivier Peslier
28 Jul 2010	Sussex Stakes	Canford Cliffs	Richard Hughes

Ireland

5 Sep 2009	Irish Champion Stakes	Sea The Stars	Mick Kinane
12 Sep 2009	Irish St. Leger	Alandi	Mick Kinane
22 May 2010	Irish 2,000 Guineas	Canford Cliffs	Richard Hughes
23 May 2010	Irish 1,000 Guineas	Bethrah	Pat Smullen
27 Jun 2010	Irish Derby	Cape Blanco	Johnny Murtagh
18 Jul 2010	Irish Oaks	Snow Fairy	Ryan Moore

France

16 Aug 2009	Prix Jacques le Marois	Goldikova	Olivier Peslier
4 Oct 2009	Prix de l'Arc de Triomphe	Sea The Stars	Mick Kinane
4 Oct 2009	Prix Jean-Luc Lagardère (Grand Critérium)	Siyouni	Gerald Mosse
25 Oct 2009	Prix Royal-Oak	Ask	Ryan Moore
2 May 2010	Prix Ganay	Cutlass Bay	Maxime Guyon
16 May 2010	Poule d'Essai des Poulains	Lope de Vega	Maxime Guyon
16 May 2010	Poule d'Essai des Pouliches	Special Duty	Stephane Pasquier
23 May 2010	Prix Saint-Alary	Sarafina	Gerald Mosse
6 Jun 2010	Prix du Jockey Club	Lope de Vega	Maxime Guyon
13 Jun 2010	Prix de Diane	Sarafina	Christophe Lemaire
27 Jun 2010	Grand Prix de Saint-Cloud	Plumania	Olivier Peslier
14 Jul 2010	Grand Prix de Paris	Behkabad	Gerald Mosse

Germany

6 Sep 2009	Grosser Preis von Baden	Getaway	Adrie de Vries
27 Sep 2009	Preis von Europa	Jukebox Jury	Royston Ffrench
18 Jul 2010	Deutsches Derby	Buzzword	Royston Ffrench

Italy

8 May 2010	Derby Italiano	Worthadd	Mirco Demuro

Australia

17 Oct 2009	Caulfield Cup	Viewed	Brad Rawiller
24 Oct 2009	Cox Plate	So You Think	Glen Boss
3 Nov 2009	Melbourne Cup	Shocking	Corey Brown

Major Thoroughbred Race Winners, 2009–10 (continued)

United Arab Emirates

DATE	RACE	WINNER	JOCKEY
27 Mar 2010	Dubai Duty Free	Al Shemali	Royston Ffrench
27 Mar 2010	Dubai Golden Shaheen	Kinsale King	Garrett Gomez
27 Mar 2010	Dubai Sheema Classic	Dar Re Mi	William Buick
27 Mar 2010	Dubai World Cup	Gloria De Campeao	Tiago Pereira
27 Mar 2010	Godolphin Mile	Calming Influence	Ahmad Ajtebi
27 Mar 2010	UAE Derby	Musir	Christophe Soumillon

Japan

29 Nov 2009	Japan Cup	Vodka	Christophe Lemaire

Hong Kong

13 Dec 2009	Hong Kong Cup	Vision d'Etat	Olivier Peslier
28 Feb 2010	Hong Kong Gold Cup	Collection	Darren Beadman
25 Apr 2010	Queen Elizabeth II Cup	Viva Pataca	Weichong Marwing

Singapore

16 May 2010	International Cup	Lizard's Desire	Kevin Shea

[1]American Triple Crown race.   [2]British Triple Crown race.

Kentucky Derby

YEAR	HORSE	JOCKEY	YEAR	HORSE	JOCKEY
1875	Aristides	Oliver Lewis	1917	Omar Khayyam	Charles Borel
1876	Vagrant	Bobby Swim	1918	Exterminator	William Knapp
1877	Baden-Baden	William Walker	1919	Sir Barton	John Loftus
1878	Day Star	Jimmy Carter	1920	Paul Jones	Ted Rice
1879	Lord Murphy	Charlie Shauer	1921	Behave Yourself	Charles Thompson
1880	Fonso	George Garret Lewis	1922	Morvich	Albert Johnson
1881	Hindoo	James McLaughlin	1923	Zev	Earl Sande
1882	Apollo	Babe Hurd	1924	Black Gold	John D. Mooney
1883	Leonatus	William Donohue	1925	Flying Ebony	Earl Sande
1884	Buchanan	Isaac Murphy	1926	Bubbling Over	Albert Johnson
1885	Joe Cotton	Erskine Henderson	1927	Whiskery	Linus McAtee
1886	Ben Ali	Paul Duffy	1928	Reigh Count	Charles Lang
1887	Montrose	Isaac Lewis	1929	Clyde Van Dusen	Linus McAtee
1888	Macbeth II	George Covington	1930	Gallant Fox	Earl Sande
1889	Spokane	Thomas Kiley	1931	Twenty Grand	Charles Kurtsinger
1890	Riley	Isaac Murphy	1932	Burgoo King	Eugene James
1891	Kingman	Isaac Murphy	1933	Brokers Tip	Don Meade
1892	Azra	Alonzo Clayton	1934	Cavalcade	Mack Garner
1893	Lookout	Eddie Kunze	1935	Omaha	William Saunders
1894	Chant	Frank Goodale	1936	Bold Venture	Ira Hanford
1895	Halma	James Perkins	1937	War Admiral	Charles Kurtsinger
1896	Ben Brush	Willie Simms	1938	Lawrin	Eddie Arcaro
1897	Typhoon II	Fred Garner	1939	Johnstown	James Stout
1898	Plaudit	Willie Simms	1940	Gallahadion	Carroll Bierman
1899	Manuel	Fred Taral	1941	Whirlaway	Eddie Arcaro
1900	Lieut. Gibson	Jimmy Boland	1942	Shut Out	Wayne D. Wright
1901	His Eminence	James Winkfield	1943	Count Fleet	John Longden
1902	Alan-a-Dale	James Winkfield	1944	Pensive	Conn McCreary
1903	Judge Himes	Harold Booker	1945	Hoop Jr.	Eddie Arcaro
1904	Elwood	Frank Prior	1946	Assault	Warren Mehrtens
1905	Agile	Jack Martin	1947	Jet Pilot	Eric Guerin
1906	Sir Huon	Roscoe Troxler	1948	Citation	Eddie Arcaro
1907	Pink Star	Andy Minder	1949	Ponder	Steve Brooks
1908	Stone Street	Arthur Pickens	1950	Middleground	William Boland
1909	Wintergreen	Vincent Powers	1951	Count Turf	Conn McCreary
1910	Donau	Fred Herbert	1952	Hill Gail	Eddie Arcaro
1911	Meridian	George Archibald	1953	Dark Star	Henry Moreno
1912	Worth	Carroll Hugh Shilling	1954	Determine	Raymond York
1913	Donerail	Roscoe Goose	1955	Swaps	William Shoemaker
1914	Old Rosebud	John McCabe	1956	Needles	David Erb
1915	Regret	Joe Notter	1957	Iron Liege	William Hartack
1916	George Smith	John Loftus	1958	Tim Tam	Ismael Valenzuela

Kentucky Derby (continued)

YEAR	HORSE	JOCKEY	YEAR	HORSE	JOCKEY
1959	Tomy Lee	William Shoemaker	1985	Spend a Buck	Angel Cordero, Jr.
1960	Venetian Way	William Hartack	1986	Ferdinand	William Shoemaker
1961	Carry Back	John Sellers	1987	Alysheba	Chris McCarron
1962	Decidedly	William Hartack	1988	Winning Colors	Gary Stevens
1963	Chateaugay	Braulio Baeza	1989	Sunday Silence	Patrick Valenzuela
1964	Northern Dancer	William Hartack	1990	Unbridled	Craig Perret
1965	Lucky Debonair	William Shoemaker	1991	Strike the Gold	Chris Antley
1966	Kauai King	Don Brumfield	1992	Lil E. Tee	Pat Day
1967	Proud Clarion	Robert Ussery	1993	Sea Hero	Jerry Bailey
1968	Forward Pass	Ismael Valenzuela	1994	Go for Gin	Chris McCarron
1969	Majestic Prince	William Hartack	1995	Thunder Gulch	Gary Stevens
1970	Dust Commander	Mike Manganello	1996	Grindstone	Jerry Bailey
1971	Canonero II	Gustavo Avila	1997	Silver Charm	Gary Stevens
1972	Riva Ridge	Ron Turcotte	1998	Real Quiet	Kent Desormeaux
1973	Secretariat[1]	Ron Turcotte	1999	Charismatic	Chris Antley
1974	Cannonade	Angel Cordero, Jr.	2000	Fusaichi Pegasus	Kent Desormeaux
1975	Foolish Pleasure	Jacinto Vasquez	2001	Monarchos	Jorge Chávez
1976	Bold Forbes	Angel Cordero, Jr.	2002	War Emblem	Victor Espinoza
1977	Seattle Slew	Jean Cruguet	2003	Funny Cide	José Santos
1978	Affirmed	Steve Cauthen	2004	Smarty Jones	Stewart Elliott
1979	Spectacular Bid	Ronnie Franklin	2005	Giacomo	Mike Smith
1980	Genuine Risk	Jacinto Vasquez	2006	Barbaro	Edgar Prado
1981	Pleasant Colony	Jorge Velasquez	2007	Street Sense	Calvin Borel
1982	Gato del Sol	Eddie Delahoussaye	2008	Big Brown	Kent Desormeaux
1983	Sunny's Halo	Eddie Delahoussaye	2009	Mine That Bird	Calvin Borel
1984	Swale	Laffit Pincay, Jr.	2010	Super Saver	Calvin Borel

[1]*Fastest time—1 min 59⅖ sec.*

Preakness Stakes

YEAR	HORSE	JOCKEY	YEAR	HORSE	JOCKEY
1873	Survivor	George Barbee	1910	Layminster	Roy Estep
1874	Culpepper	William Donohue	1911	Watervale	Eddie Dugan
1875	Tom Ochiltree	Lloyd Hughes	1912	Colonel Holloway	Clarence Turner
1876	Shirley	George Barbee	1913	Buskin	James Butwell
1877	Cloverbrook	Cyrus Holloway	1914	Holiday	Andy Schuttinger
1878	Duke of Magenta	Cyrus Holloway	1915	Rhine Maiden	Douglas Hoffman
1879	Harold	Lloyd Hughes	1916	Damrosch	Linus McAtee
1880	Grenada	Lloyd Hughes	1917	Kalitan	Everett Haynes
1881	Saunterer	T. Costello	1918[1]	War Cloud;	John Loftus;
1882	Vanguard	T. Costello		Jack Hare, Jr.	Charles Peak
1883	Jacobus	George Barbee	1919	Sir Barton	John Loftus
1884	Knight of Ellerslie	S. Fisher	1920	Man o' War	Clarence Kummer
1885	Tecumseh	James McLaughlin	1921	Broomspun	Frank Coltiletti
1886	The Bard	S. Fisher	1922	Pillory	Louis Morris
1887	Dunboyne	William Donohue	1923	Vigil	Benny Marinelli
1888	Refund	Fred Littlefield	1924	Nellie Morse	John Merimee
1889	Buddhist	George Anderson	1925	Coventry	Clarence Kummer
1890	Montague	W. Martin	1926	Display	John Maiben
1891–93	not held		1927	Bostonian	Alf J. "Whitey" Abel
1894	Assignee	Fred Taral	1928	Victorian	Raymond Workman
1895	Belmar	Fred Taral	1929	Dr. Freeland	Louis Schaefer
1896	Margrave	Henry Griffin	1930	Gallant Fox	Earl Sande
1897	Paul Kauvar	T. Thorpe	1931	Mate	George Ellis
1898	Sly Fox	Willie Simms	1932	Burgoo King	Eugene James
1899	Half Time	R. Clawson	1933	Head Play	Charles Kurtsinger
1900	Hindus	H. Spencer	1934	High Quest	Robert Jones
1901	The Parader	Fred Landry	1935	Omaha	Willie Saunders
1902	Old England	L. Jackson	1936	Bold Venture	George Woolf
1903	Flocarline	W. Gannon	1937	War Admiral	Charles Kurtsinger
1904	Bryn Mawr	Eugene Hildebrand	1938	Dauber	Maurice Peters
1905	Cairngorm	W. Davis	1939	Challedon	George Seabo
1906	Whimsical	Walter Miller	1940	Bimelech	Fred A. Smith
1907	Don Enrique	G. Mountain	1941	Whirlaway	Eddie Arcaro
1908	Royal Tourist	Eddie Dugan	1942	Alsab	Basil James
1909	Effendi	Willie Doyle	1943	Count Fleet	John Longden

Preakness Stakes (continued)

YEAR	HORSE	JOCKEY	YEAR	HORSE	JOCKEY
1944	Pensive	Conn McCreary	1978	Affirmed	Steve Cauthen
1945	Polynesian	Wayne D. Wright	1979	Spectacular Bid	Ron Franklin
1946	Assault	Warren Mehrtens	1980	Codex	Angel Cordero, Jr.
1947	Faultless	Doug Dodson	1981	Pleasant Colony	Jorge Velasquez
1948	Citation	Eddie Arcaro	1982	Aloma's Ruler	Jack Kaenel
1949	Capot	Ted Atkinson	1983	Deputed Testamony	Donald Miller
1950	Hill Prince	Eddie Arcaro	1984	Gate Dancer	Angel Cordero, Jr.
1951	Bold	Eddie Arcaro	1985	Tank's Prospect[2]	Pat Day
1952	Blue Man	Conn McCreary	1986	Snow Chief	Alex Solis
1953	Native Dancer	Eric Guerin	1987	Alysheba	Chris McCarron
1954	Hasty Road	Johnny Adams	1988	Risen Star	Eddie Delahoussaye
1955	Nashua	Eddie Arcaro	1989	Sunday Silence	Patrick Valenzuela
1956	Fabius	William Hartack	1990	Summer Squall	Pat Day
1957	Bold Ruler	Eddie Arcaro	1991	Hansel	Jerry Bailey
1958	Tim Tam	Ismael Valenzuela	1992	Pine Bluff	Chris McCarron
1959	Royal Orbit	William Harmatz	1993	Prairie Bayou	Mike Smith
1960	Bally Ache	Robert Ussery	1994	Tabasco Cat	Pat Day
1961	Carry Back	John Sellers	1995	Timber Country	Pat Day
1962	Greek Money	John L. Rotz	1996	Louis Quatorze[2]	Pat Day
1963	Candy Spots	William Shoemaker	1997	Silver Charm	Gary Stevens
1964	Northern Dancer	William Hartack	1998	Real Quiet	Kent Desormeaux
1965	Tom Rolfe	Ron Turcotte	1999	Charismatic	Chris Antley
1966	Kauai King	Don Brumfield	2000	Red Bullet	Jerry Bailey
1967	Damascus	William Shoemaker	2001	Point Given	Gary Stevens
1968	Forward Pass	Ismael Valenzuela	2002	War Emblem	Victor Espinoza
1969	Majestic Prince	William Hartack	2003	Funny Cide	José Santos
1970	Personality	Eddie Belmonte	2004	Smarty Jones	Stewart Elliott
1971	Canonero II	Gustavo Avila	2005	Afleet Alex	Jeremy Rose
1972	Bee Bee Bee	Eldon Nelson	2006	Bernardini	Javier Castellano
1973	Secretariat	Ron Turcotte	2007	Curlin[2]	Robby Albarado
1974	Little Current	Miguel Rivera	2008	Big Brown	Kent Desormeaux
1975	Master Derby	Darrel McHague	2009	Rachel Alexandra	Calvin Borel
1976	Elocutionist	John Lively	2010	Lookin At Lucky	Martin Garcia
1977	Seattle Slew	Jean Cruguet			

[1]Run in two divisions in 1918 because of the large number of starters.   [2]Fastest time—1 min 53⅖ sec.

Belmont Stakes

YEAR	HORSE	JOCKEY	YEAR	HORSE	JOCKEY
1867	Ruthless	Gilbert Patrick	1894	Henry of Navarre	Willie Simms
1868	General Duke	Bobby Swim	1895	Belmar	Fred Taral
1869	Fenian	Charley Miller	1896	Hastings	Henry Griffin
1870	Kingfisher	Edward Brown	1897	Scottish Chieftain	J. Scherrer
1871	Harry Bassett	W. Miller	1898	Bowling Brook	Fred Littlefield
1872	Joe Daniels	James Rowe	1899	Jean Bereaud	R. Clawson
1873	Springbok	James Rowe	1900	Ildrim	Nash Turner
1874	Saxon	George Barbee	1901	Commando	H. Spencer
1875	Calvin	Bobby Swim	1902	Masterman	John Bullman
1876	Algerine	Billy Donohue	1903	Africander	John Bullman
1877	Cloverbrook	Cyrus Holloway	1904	Delhi	George Odom
1878	Duke of Magenta	Lloyd Hughes	1905	Tanya	Eugene Hildebrand
1879	Spendthrift	George Evans	1906	Burgomaster	Lucien Lyne
1880	Grenada	Lloyd Hughes	1907	Peter Pan	G. Mountain
1881	Saunterer	T. Costello	1908	Colin	Joe Notter
1882	Forester	James McLaughlin	1909	Joe Madden	Eddie Dugan
1883	George Kinney	James McLaughlin	1910	Sweep	James Butwell
1884	Panique	James McLaughlin	1911–12	not held	
1885	Tyrant	Paul Duffy	1913	Prince Eugene	Roscoe Troxler
1886	Inspector B	James McLaughlin	1914	Luke McLuke	Merritt Buxton
1887	Hanover	James McLaughlin	1915	The Finn	George Byrne
1888	Sir Dixon	James McLaughlin	1916	Friar Rock	Everett Haynes
1889	Eric	W. Hayward	1917	Hourless	James Butwell
1890	Burlington	Shelby Barnes	1918	Johren	Frank Robinson
1891	Foxford	Edward Garrison	1919	Sir Barton	John Loftus
1892	Patron	W. Hayward	1920	Man o' War	Clarence Kummer
1893	Comanche	Willie Simms	1921	Grey Lag	Earl Sande

Belmont Stakes (continued)

YEAR	HORSE	JOCKEY	YEAR	HORSE	JOCKEY
1922	Pillory	C.H. Miller	1967	Damascus	William Shoemaker
1923	Zev	Earl Sande	1968	Stage Door Johnny	Heliodoro Gustines
1924	Mad Play	Earl Sande	1969	Arts and Letters	Braulio Baeza
1925	American Flag	Albert Johnson	1970	High Echelon	John Rotz
1926	Crusader	Albert Johnson	1971	Pass Catcher	Walter Blum
1927	Chance Shot	Earl Sande	1972	Riva Ridge	Ron Turcotte
1928	Vito	Clarence Kummer	1973	Secretariat[1]	Ron Turcotte
1929	Blue Larkspur	Mack Garner	1974	Little Current	Miguel Rivera
1930	Gallant Fox	Earl Sande	1975	Avatar	William Shoemaker
1931	Twenty Grand	Charles Kurtsinger	1976	Bold Forbes	Angel Cordero, Jr.
1932	Faireno	Tom Malley	1977	Seattle Slew	Jean Cruguet
1933	Hurryoff	Mack Garner	1978	Affirmed	Steve Cauthen
1934	Peace Chance	Wayne D. Wright	1979	Coastal	Ruben Hernandez
1935	Omaha	Willie Saunders	1980	Temperence Hill	Eddie Maple
1936	Granville	James Stout	1981	Summing	George Martens
1937	War Admiral	Charles Kurtsinger	1982	Conquistador Cielo	Laffit Pincay, Jr.
1938	Pasteurized	James Stout	1983	Caveat	Laffit Pincay, Jr.
1939	Johnstown	James Stout	1984	Swale	Laffit Pincay, Jr.
1940	Bimelech	Fred A. Smith	1985	Creme Fraiche	Eddie Maple
1941	Whirlaway	Eddie Arcaro	1986	Danzig Connection	Chris McCarron
1942	Shut Out	Eddie Arcaro	1987	Bet Twice	Craig Perret
1943	Count Fleet	John Longden	1988	Risen Star	Eddie Delahoussaye
1944	Bounding Home	Gayle L. Smith	1989	Easy Goer	Pat Day
1945	Pavot	Eddie Arcaro	1990	Go and Go	Mick Kinane
1946	Assault	Warren Mehrtens	1991	Hansel	Jerry Bailey
1947	Phalanx	Ruperto Donoso	1992	A.P. Indy	Eddie Delahoussaye
1948	Citation	Eddie Arcaro	1993	Colonial Affair	Julie Krone
1949	Capot	Ted Atkinson	1994	Tabasco Cat	Pat Day
1950	Middleground	William Boland	1995	Thunder Gulch	Gary Stevens
1951	Counterpoint	David Gorman	1996	Editor's Note	Rene Douglas
1952	One Count	Eddie Arcaro	1997	Touch Gold	Chris McCarron
1953	Native Dancer	Eric Guerin	1998	Victory Gallop	Gary Stevens
1954	High Gun	Eric Guerin	1999	Lemon Drop Kid	José Santos
1955	Nashua	Eddie Arcaro	2000	Commendable	Pat Day
1956	Needles	David Erb	2001	Point Given	Gary Stevens
1957	Gallant Man	William Shoemaker	2002	Sarava	Edgar Prado
1958	Cavan	Pete Anderson	2003	Empire Maker	Jerry Bailey
1959	Sword Dancer	William Shoemaker	2004	Birdstone	Edgar Prado
1960	Celtic Ash	William Hartack	2005	Afleet Alex	Jeremy Rose
1961	Sherluck	Braulio Baeza	2006	Jazil	Fernando Jara
1962	Jaipur	William Shoemaker	2007	Rags to Riches	John Velazquez
1963	Chateaugay	Braulio Baeza	2008	Da' Tara	Alan Garcia
1964	Quadrangle	Manuel Ycaza	2009	Summer Bird	Kent Desormeaux
1965	Hail to All	John Sellers	2010	Drosselmeyer	Mike Smith
1966	Amberoid	William Boland			

[1]*Fastest time—2 min 24 sec.*

Triple Crown Champions—United States

YEAR	HORSE	YEAR	HORSE	YEAR	HORSE	YEAR	HORSE
1919	Sir Barton	1937	War Admiral	1946	Assault	1977	Seattle Slew
1930	Gallant Fox	1941	Whirlaway	1948	Citation	1978	Affirmed
1935	Omaha	1943	Count Fleet	1973	Secretariat		

Horse of the Year

A Horse of the Year was selected by the *Daily Racing Form* from 1936 to 1970 and by the Thoroughbred Racing Association beginning in 1950. From 1971 these two organizations, plus the National Turf Writers Association, founded the Eclipse Awards, of which the Horse of the Year is the most coveted.

YEAR	HORSE	YEAR	HORSE	YEAR	HORSE	YEAR	HORSE
1936	Granville	1940	Challedon	1944	Twilight Tear	1948	Citation
1937	War Admiral	1941	Whirlaway	1945	Busher	1949	Capot[1];
1938	Seabiscuit	1942	Whirlaway	1946	Assault		Coaltown[2]
1939	Challedon	1943	Count Fleet	1947	Armed	1950	Hill Prince

Horse of the Year (continued)

YEAR	HORSE	YEAR	HORSE	YEAR	HORSE	YEAR	HORSE
1951	Counterpoint	1965	Roman Brother[1];	1979	Affirmed	1995	Cigar
1952	One Count[1];		Moccasin[2]	1980	Spectacular Bid	1996	Cigar
	Native Dancer[2]	1966	Buckpasser	1981	John Henry	1997	Favorite Trick
1953	Tom Fool	1967	Damascus	1982	Conquistador Cielo	1998	Skip Away
1954	Native Dancer	1968	Dr. Fager	1983	All Along	1999	Charismatic
1955	Nashua	1969	Arts and Letters	1984	John Henry	2000	Tiznow
1956	Swaps	1970	Fort Marcy[1];	1985	Spend a Buck	2001	Point Given
1957	Bold Ruler[1];		Personality[2]	1986	Lady's Secret	2002	Azeri
	Dedicate[2]	1971	Ack Ack	1987	Ferdinand	2003	Mineshaft
1958	Round Table	1972	Secretariat	1988	Alysheba	2004	Ghostzapper
1959	Sword Dancer	1973	Secretariat	1989	Sunday Silence	2005	Saint Liam
1960	Kelso	1974	Forego	1990	Criminal Type	2006	Invasor
1961	Kelso	1975	Forego	1991	Black Tie Affair	2007	Curlin
1962	Kelso	1976	Forego	1992	A.P. Indy	2008	Curlin
1963	Kelso	1977	Seattle Slew	1993	Kotashaan	2009	Rachel
1964	Kelso	1978	Affirmed	1994	Holy Bull		Alexandra

[1]*Daily Racing Form.*   [2]*Thoroughbred Racing Association.*

2,000 Guineas
Held since 1809. Table shows the winners for the past 20 years.

YEAR	HORSE	JOCKEY	YEAR	HORSE	JOCKEY
1991	Mystiko	Michael Roberts	2001	Golan	Kieren Fallon
1992	Rodrigo de Triano	Lester Piggot	2002	Rock of Gibraltar	Johnny Murtagh
1993	Zafonic	Pat Eddery	2003	Refuse To Bend	Pat Smullen
1994	Mister Baileys	Jason Weaver	2004	Haafhd	Richard Hills
1995	Pennekamp	Thierry Jarnet	2005	Footstepsinthesand	Kieren Fallon
1996	Mark of Esteem	Frankie Dettori	2006	George Washington	Kieren Fallon
1997	Entrepreneur	Mick Kinane	2007	Cockney Rebel	Olivier Peslier
1998	King of Kings	Mick Kinane	2008	Henrythenavigator	Johnny Murtagh
1999	Island Sands	Frankie Dettori	2009	Sea The Stars	Mick Kinane
2000	King's Best	Kieren Fallon	2010	Makfi	Christophe Lemaire

The Derby
Held since 1780. Table shows the winners for the past 20 years.

YEAR	HORSE	JOCKEY	YEAR	HORSE	JOCKEY
1991	Generous	Alan Munro	2001	Galileo	Mick Kinane
1992	Dr Devious	John Reid	2002	High Chaparral	Johnny Murtagh
1993	Commander in Chief	Mick Kinane	2003	Kris Kin	Kieren Fallon
1994	Erhaab	Willie Carson	2004	North Light	Kieren Fallon
1995	Lammtarra	Walter R. Swinburn	2005	Motivator	Johnny Murtagh
1996	Shaamit	Michael Hills	2006	Sir Percy	Martin Dwyer
1997	Benny the Dip	Willie Ryan	2007	Authorized	Frankie Dettori
1998	High Rise	Olivier Peslier	2008	New Approach	Kevin Manning
1999	Oath	Kieren Fallon	2009	Sea The Stars	Mick Kinane
2000	Sinndar	Johnny Murtagh	2010	Workforce	Ryan Moore

St. Leger
Held since 1776. Table shows the winners for the past 20 years.

YEAR	HORSE	JOCKEY	YEAR	HORSE	JOCKEY
1991	Toulon	Pat Eddery	2001	Milan	Mick Kinane
1992	User Friendly	George Duffield	2002	Bollin Eric	Kevin Darley
1993	Bob's Return	Philip Robinson	2003	Brian Boru	Jamie Spencer
1994	Moonax	Pat Eddery	2004	Rule of Law	Kerrin McEvoy
1995	Classic Cliché	Frankie Dettori	2005	Scorpion	Frankie Dettori
1996	Shantou	Frankie Dettori	2006	Sixties Icon	Frankie Dettori
1997	Silver Patriarch	Pat Eddery	2007	Lucarno	Jimmy Fortune
1998	Nedawi	John Reid	2008	Conduit	Frankie Dettori
1999	Mutafaweq	Richard Hills	2009	Mastery	Ted Durcan
2000	Millenary	Richard Quinn	2010	Arctic Cosmos	William Buick

Triple Crown Champions—British

YEAR	WINNER	YEAR	WINNER	YEAR	WINNER	YEAR	WINNER
1853	West Australian	1891	Common	1900	Diamond Jubilee	1918	Gainsborough
1865	Gladiateur	1893	Isinglass	1903	Rock Sand	1935	Bahram
1866	Lord Lyon	1897	Galtee More	1915	Pommern	1970	Nijinsky
1886	Ormonde	1899	Flying Fox	1917	Gay Crusader		

Melbourne Cup

Held since 1861. Table shows the winners for the past 20 years.

YEAR	HORSE	JOCKEY	YEAR	HORSE	JOCKEY
1990	Kingston Rule	Darren Beadman	2000	Brew	Kerrin McEvoy
1991	Let's Elope	Steven King	2001	Ethereal	Scott Seamer
1992	Subzero	Greg Hall	2002	Media Puzzle	Damien Oliver
1993	Vintage Crop	Mick Kinane	2003	Makybe Diva	Glen Boss
1994	Jeune	Wayne Harris	2004	Makybe Diva	Glen Boss
1995	Doriemus	Damien Oliver	2005	Makybe Diva	Glen Boss
1996	Saintly	Darren Beadman	2006	Delta Blues	Yasunari Iwata
1997	Might and Power	Jim Cassidy	2007	Efficient	Michael Rodd
1998	Jezabeel	Chris Munce	2008	Viewed	Blake Shinn
1999	Rogan Josh	John Marshall	2009	Shocking	Corey Brown

Dubai World Cup

YEAR	HORSE	JOCKEY	YEAR	HORSE	JOCKEY
1996	Cigar	Jerry Bailey	2004	Pleasantly Perfect	Alex Solis
1997	Singspiel	Jerry Bailey	2005	Roses in May	John Velazquez
1998	Silver Charm	Gary Stevens	2006	Electrocutionist	Frankie Dettori
1999	Almutawakel	Richard Hills	2007	Invasor	Fernando Jara
2000	Dubai Millennium	Frankie Dettori	2008	Curlin	Robby Albarado
2001	Captain Steve	Jerry Bailey	2009	Well Armed	Aaron Gryder
2002	Street Cry	Jerry Bailey	2010	Gloria De Campeao	Tiago Pereira
2003	Moon Ballad	Frankie Dettori			

Hambletonian Trot

YEAR	HORSE	DRIVER	YEAR	HORSE	DRIVER
1926	Guy McKinney	Nat Ray	1956	The Intruder	Ned Bower
1927	Iosola's Worthy	Marvin Childs	1957	Hickory Smoke	John Simpson, Sr.
1928	Spencer	William H. Leese	1958	Emily's Pride	Flave Nipe
1929	Walter Dear	Walter Cox	1959	Diller Hanover	Frank Ervin
1930	Hanover's Bertha	Thomas Berry	1960	Blaze Hanover	Joseph O'Brien
1931	Calumet Butler	Richard D. McMahon	1961	Harlan Dean	James Arthur
1932	The Marchioness	William Caton	1962	A.C.'s Viking	Sanders Russell
1933	Mary Reynolds	Ben White	1963	Speedy Scot	Ralph Baldwin
1934	Lord Jim	Hugh M. Parshall	1964	Ayres	John Simpson, Sr.
1935	Greyhound	Scepter F. Palin	1965	Egyptian Candor	Adelbert Cameron
1936	Rosalind	Ben White	1966	Kerry Way	Frank Ervin
1937	Shirley Hanover	Henry Thomas	1967	Speedy Streak	Adelbert Cameron
1938	McLin Hanover	Henry Thomas	1968	Nevele Pride	Stanley Dancer
1939	Peter Astra	Hugh M. Parshall	1969	Lindy's Pride	Howard Beissinger
1940	Spencer Scott	Fred Egan	1970	Timothy T.	John Simpson, Sr.
1941	Bill Gallon	Lee Smith	1971	Speedy Crown	Howard Beissinger
1942	The Ambassador	Ben White	1972	Super Bowl	Stanley Dancer
1943	Volo Song	Ben White	1973	Flirth	Ralph Baldwin
1944	Yankee Maid	Henry Thomas	1974	Christopher T.	William Haughton
1945	Titan Hanover	Harry Pownall, Sr.	1975	Bonefish	Stanley Dancer
1946	Chestertown	Thomas Berry	1976	Steve Lobell	William Haughton
1947	Hoot Mon	Scepter F. Palin	1977	Green Speed	William Haughton
1948	Demon Hanover	Harrison Hoyt	1978	Speedy Somolli	Howard Beissinger
1949	Miss Tilly	Fred Egan	1979	Legend Hanover	George Sholty
1950	Lusty Song	Delvin Miller	1980	Burgomeister	William Haughton
1951	Mainliner	Guy Crippen	1981	Shiaway St. Pat	Ray Remmen
1952	Sharp Note	Bion Shively	1982	Speed Bowl	Tom Haughton
1953	Helicopter	Harry Harvey	1983	Duenna	Stanley Dancer
1954	Newport Dream	Adelbert Cameron	1984	Historic Freight	Ben Webster
1955	Scott Frost	Joseph O'Brien	1985	Prakas	William O'Donnell

Hambletonian Trot (continued)

YEAR	HORSE	DRIVER	YEAR	HORSE	DRIVER
1986	Nuclear Kosmos	Ulf Thoresen	1998	Muscles Yankee	John Campbell
1987	Mack Lobell	John Campbell	1999	Self Possessed	Michel Lachance
1988	Armbro Goal	John Campbell	2000	Yankee Paco	Trevor Ritchie
1989	Park Avenue Joe;	Ronald Waples;	2001	Scarlet Knight	Stefan Melander
	Probe (tied)	William Fahy	2002	Chip Chip Hooray	Eric Ledford
1990	Harmonious	John Campbell	2003	Amigo Hall	Michel Lachance
1991	Giant Victory	Jack Moiseyev	2004	Windsong's Legacy	Trond Smedshammer
1992	Alf Palema	Mickey McNichol	2005	Vivid Photo	Roger Hammer
1993	American Winner	Ron Pierce	2006	Glidemaster	John Campbell
1994	Victory Dream	Michel Lachance	2007	Donato Hanover	Ron Pierce
1995	Tagliabue	John Campbell	2008	Deweycheatumnhowe	Ray Schnittker
1996	Continentalvictory	Michel Lachance	2009	Muscle Hill	Brian Sears
1997	Malabar Man	Malvern Burroughs	2010	Muscle Massive	Ron Pierce

Ice Hockey

The **National Hockey League** (NHL), which was organized in Canada in 1917, welcomed the first US team, the Boston Bruins, in 1924. Since 1926 the symbol of supremacy in professional hockey has been the **Stanley Cup**, which is awarded to the winner of a play-off that concludes the NHL season. The Stanley Cup was presented to amateur champions from 1893 to 1925. The **World Hockey Championships**, contested by national teams and sponsored by the **International Ice Hockey Federation** (IIHF; founded 1908), have been held since 1930 for men and since 1990 for women.

Related Web sites: National Hockey League: <www.nhl.com>; International Ice Hockey Federation: <www.iihf.com>.

World Hockey Championship—Men

YEAR	WINNER	YEAR	WINNER	YEAR	WINNER	YEAR	WINNER
1920[1]	Canada	1953	Sweden	1973	USSR	1993	Russia
1924[1]	Canada	1954	USSR	1974	USSR	1994	Canada
1928[1]	Canada	1955	Canada	1975	USSR	1995	Finland
1930	Canada	1956[1]	USSR	1976	Czechoslovakia	1996	Czech Republic
1931	Canada	1957	Sweden	1977	Czechoslovakia	1997	Canada
1932[1]	Canada	1958	Canada	1978	USSR	1998	Sweden
1933	United States	1959	Canada	1979	USSR	1999	Czech Republic
1934	Canada	1960[1]	United States	1980	not held	2000	Czech Republic
1935	Canada	1961	Canada	1981	USSR	2001	Czech Republic
1936[1]	Great Britain	1962	Sweden	1982	USSR	2002	Slovakia
1937	Canada	1963	USSR	1983	USSR	2003	Canada
1938	Canada	1964[1]	USSR	1984	not held	2004	Canada
1939	Canada	1965	USSR	1985	Czechoslovakia	2005	Czech Republic
1940–46	not held	1966	USSR	1986	USSR	2006	Sweden
1947	Czechoslovakia	1967	USSR	1987	Sweden	2007	Canada
1948[1]	Canada	1968[1]	USSR	1988	not held	2008	Russia
1949	Czechoslovakia	1969	USSR	1989	USSR	2009	Russia
1950	Canada	1970	USSR	1990	Sweden	2010	Czech Republic
1951	Canada	1971	USSR	1991	Sweden		
1952[1]	Canada	1972[2]	Czechoslovakia	1992	Sweden		

[1]Olympic championships, recognized in this table as world championships. [2]In 1972 a separate world championship was held for the first time in an Olympic year.

World Hockey Championship—Women

YEAR	WINNER	YEAR	WINNER	YEAR	WINNER
1990	Canada	1997	Canada	2004	Canada
1991	not held	1998[1]	United States	2005	United States
1992	Canada	1999	Canada	2006[1]	Canada
1993	not held	2000	Canada	2007	Canada
1994	Canada	2001	Canada	2008	United States
1995	not held	2002[1]	Canada	2009	United States
1996	not held	2003	not held	2010[1]	Canada

[1]Olympic championships, recognized in this table as world championships.

National Hockey League Final Standings, 2009–10

EASTERN CONFERENCE

Northeast Division

	WON	LOST	OTL[1]
Buffalo[2]	45	27	10
Ottawa[2]	44	32	6
Boston[2]	39	30	13
Montreal[2]	39	33	10
Toronto	30	38	14

Atlantic Division

	WON	LOST	OTL[1]
New Jersey[2]	48	27	7
Pittsburgh[2]	47	28	7
Philadelphia[2]	41	35	6
New York Rangers	38	33	11
New York Islanders	34	37	11

Southeast Division

	WON	LOST	OTL[1]
Washington[2]	54	15	13
Atlanta	35	34	13
Carolina	35	37	10
Tampa Bay	34	36	12
Florida	32	37	13

WESTERN CONFERENCE

Central Division

	WON	LOST	OTL[1]
Chicago[2]	52	22	8
Detroit[2]	44	24	14
Nashville[2]	47	29	6
St. Louis	40	32	10
Columbus	32	35	15

Northwest Division

	WON	LOST	OTL[1]
Vancouver[2]	49	28	5
Colorado[2]	43	30	9
Calgary	40	32	10
Minnesota	38	36	8
Edmonton	27	47	8

Pacific Division

	WON	LOST	OTL[1]
San Jose[2]	51	20	11
Phoenix[2]	50	25	7
Los Angeles[2]	46	27	9
Anaheim	39	32	11
Dallas	37	31	14

[1]*Overtime losses, worth one point.*　　[2]*Gained play-off berth.*

Stanley Cup

YEAR	WINNER	RUNNER-UP	RESULTS
1893	Montreal Amateur Athletic Association	no challengers	
1894	Montreal Amateur Athletic Association	Ottawa Generals	2-0
1895	Montreal Victorias	no challengers	
1896	Winnipeg Victorias (Feb.); Montreal Victorias (Dec.)	Montreal Victorias (Feb.); Winnipeg Victorias (Dec.)	1-0; 1-0
1897	Montreal Victorias	Ottawa Capitals	1-0
1898	Montreal Victorias	no challengers	
1899	Montreal Victorias (Feb.); Montreal Shamrocks (March)	Winnipeg Victorias (Feb.); Queen's University (March)	2-0; 1-0
1900	Montreal Shamrocks	Winnipeg Victorias; Halifax Crescents	2-1; 2-0
1901	Winnipeg Victorias	Montreal Shamrocks	2-0
1902	Winnipeg Victorias (Jan.); Montreal Amateur Athletic Association (March)	Toronto Wellingtons (Jan.); Winnipeg Victorias (March)	2-0; 2-1
1903	Montreal Amateur Athletic Association (Feb.); Ottawa Silver Seven (March)	Winnipeg Victorias (Feb.); Montreal Victorias (March); Rat Portage Thistles (March)	2-1; 1-0; 2-0
1904	Ottawa Silver Seven	Winnipeg Rowing Club; Toronto Marlboros; Montreal Wanderers; Brandon Wheat Kings	2-1; 2-0; 0-0 (tie); 2-0
1905	Ottawa Silver Seven	Dawson City Nuggets; Rat Portage Thistles	2-0; 2-1
1906	Ottawa Silver Seven (Feb., March); Montreal Wanderers (March, Dec.)	Queen's University (Feb.); Smiths Falls (March); Ottawa Silver Seven (March); New Glasgow Cubs (Dec.)	2-0; 2-0; 1-1; 2-0
1907	Kenora Thistles (Jan.); Montreal Wanderers (March)	Montreal Wanderers (Jan.); Kenora Thistles (March)	2-0; 1-1
1908	Montreal Wanderers	Ottawa Victorias; Winnipeg Maple Leafs; Toronto Trolley Leaguers; Edmonton Eskimos	2-0; 2-0; 1-0; 1-1
1909	Ottawa Senators	no challengers	
1910	Ottawa Senators (Jan.); Montreal Wanderers (March)	Galt Professionals (Jan.); Edmonton Eskimos (Jan.); Berlin Union Jacks (March)	2-0; 2-0; 1-0
1911	Ottawa Senators	Port Arthur Bearcats; Galt Professionals	1-0; 1-0
1912	Quebec Bulldogs	Moncton Victorias	2-0
1913	Quebec Bulldogs[1]	Sydney Miners	2-0
1914	Toronto Blueshirts	Montreal Canadiens; Victoria Aristocrats	1-1; 3-0
1915	Vancouver Millionaires	Ottawa Senators	3-0
1916	Montreal Canadiens	Portland Rosebuds	3-2
1917	Seattle Metropolitans	Montreal Canadiens	3-1
1918	Toronto Arenas	Vancouver Millionaires	3-2
1919	no decision[2]		
1920	Ottawa Senators	Seattle Metropolitans	3-2

Stanley Cup (continued)

YEAR	WINNER	RUNNER-UP	RESULTS
1921	Ottawa Senators	Vancouver Millionaires	3-2
1922	Toronto St. Patricks	Vancouver Millionaires	3-2
1923	Ottawa Senators	Edmonton Eskimos	2-0
1924	Montreal Canadiens	Calgary Tigers	2-0
1925	Victoria Cougars	Montreal Canadiens	3-1
1926	Montreal Maroons	Victoria Cougars	3-1
1927	Ottawa Senators	Boston Bruins	2-0
1928	New York Rangers	Montreal Maroons	3-2
1929	Boston Bruins	New York Rangers	2-0
1930	Montreal Canadiens	Boston Bruins	2-0
1931	Montreal Canadiens	Chicago Black Hawks	3-2
1932	Toronto Maple Leafs	New York Rangers	3-0
1933	New York Rangers	Toronto Maple Leafs	3-1
1934	Chicago Black Hawks	Detroit Red Wings	3-1
1935	Montreal Maroons	Toronto Maple Leafs	3-0
1936	Detroit Red Wings	Toronto Maple Leafs	3-1
1937	Detroit Red Wings	New York Rangers	3-2
1938	Chicago Black Hawks	Toronto Maple Leafs	3-1
1939	Boston Bruins	Toronto Maple Leafs	4-1
1940	New York Rangers	Toronto Maple Leafs	4-2
1941	Boston Bruins	Detroit Red Wings	4-0
1942	Toronto Maple Leafs	Detroit Red Wings	4-3
1943	Detroit Red Wings	Boston Bruins	4-0
1944	Montreal Canadiens	Chicago Black Hawks	4-0
1945	Toronto Maple Leafs	Detroit Red Wings	4-3
1946	Montreal Canadiens	Boston Bruins	4-1
1947	Toronto Maple Leafs	Montreal Canadiens	4-2
1948	Toronto Maple Leafs	Detroit Red Wings	4-0
1949	Toronto Maple Leafs	Detroit Red Wings	4-0
1950	Detroit Red Wings	New York Rangers	4-3
1951	Toronto Maple Leafs	Montreal Canadiens	4-1
1952	Detroit Red Wings	Montreal Canadiens	4-0
1953	Montreal Canadiens	Boston Bruins	4-1
1954	Detroit Red Wings	Montreal Canadiens	4-3
1955	Detroit Red Wings	Montreal Canadiens	4-3
1956	Montreal Canadiens	Detroit Red Wings	4-1
1957	Montreal Canadiens	Boston Bruins	4-1
1958	Montreal Canadiens	Boston Bruins	4-2
1959	Montreal Canadiens	Toronto Maple Leafs	4-1
1960	Montreal Canadiens	Toronto Maple Leafs	4-0
1961	Chicago Black Hawks	Detroit Red Wings	4-2
1962	Toronto Maple Leafs	Chicago Black Hawks	4-2
1963	Toronto Maple Leafs	Detroit Red Wings	4-1
1964	Toronto Maple Leafs	Detroit Red Wings	4-3
1965	Montreal Canadiens	Chicago Black Hawks	4-3
1966	Montreal Canadiens	Detroit Red Wings	4-2
1967	Toronto Maple Leafs	Montreal Canadiens	4-2
1968	Montreal Canadiens	St. Louis Blues	4-0
1969	Montreal Canadiens	St. Louis Blues	4-0
1970	Boston Bruins	St. Louis Blues	4-0
1971	Montreal Canadiens	Chicago Black Hawks	4-3
1972	Boston Bruins	New York Rangers	4-2
1973	Montreal Canadiens	Chicago Black Hawks	4-2
1974	Philadelphia Flyers	Boston Bruins	4-2
1975	Philadelphia Flyers	Buffalo Sabres	4-2
1976	Montreal Canadiens	Philadelphia Flyers	4-0
1977	Montreal Canadiens	Boston Bruins	4-0
1978	Montreal Canadiens	Boston Bruins	4-2
1979	Montreal Canadiens	New York Rangers	4-1
1980	New York Islanders	Philadelphia Flyers	4-2
1981	New York Islanders	Minnesota North Stars	4-1
1982	New York Islanders	Vancouver Canucks	4-0
1983	New York Islanders	Edmonton Oilers	4-0
1984	Edmonton Oilers	New York Islanders	4-1
1985	Edmonton Oilers	Philadelphia Flyers	4-1
1986	Montreal Canadiens	Calgary Flames	4-1
1987	Edmonton Oilers	Philadelphia Flyers	4-3
1988	Edmonton Oilers	Boston Bruins	4-0

Stanley Cup (continued)

YEAR	WINNER	RUNNER-UP	RESULTS
1989	Calgary Flames	Montreal Canadiens	4–2
1990	Edmonton Oilers	Boston Bruins	4–1
1991	Pittsburgh Penguins	Minnesota North Stars	4–2
1992	Pittsburgh Penguins	Chicago Blackhawks	4–0
1993	Montreal Canadiens	Los Angeles Kings	4–1
1994	New York Rangers	Vancouver Canucks	4–3
1995	New Jersey Devils	Detroit Red Wings	4–0
1996	Colorado Avalanche	Florida Panthers	4–0
1997	Detroit Red Wings	Philadelphia Flyers	4–0
1998	Detroit Red Wings	Washington Capitals	4–0
1999	Dallas Stars	Buffalo Sabres	4–2
2000	New Jersey Devils	Dallas Stars	4–2
2001	Colorado Avalanche	New Jersey Devils	4–3
2002	Detroit Red Wings	Carolina Hurricanes	4–1
2003	New Jersey Devils	Mighty Ducks of Anaheim	4–3
2004	Tampa Bay Lightning	Calgary Flames	4–3
2005	*not held*		
2006	Carolina Hurricanes	Edmonton Oilers	4–3
2007	Anaheim Ducks	Ottawa Senators	4–1
2008	Detroit Red Wings	Pittsburgh Penguins	4–2
2009	Pittsburgh Penguins	Detroit Red Wings	4–3
2010	Chicago Blackhawks	Philadelphia Flyers	4–2

[1]*Though Victoria defeated Quebec in challenge games, Victoria's win was not officially recognized.*   [2]*Series between Montreal Canadiens and Seattle Metropolitans called off because of flu epidemic.*

Marathon

The marathon is a long-distance footrace first held at the revival of the Olympic Games at Athens in 1896. It commemorates the legendary feat of a Greek soldier who, in 490 BC, is supposed to have run from Marathon to Athens, a distance of about 40 km (25 mi), to bring news of the Athenian victory over the Persians. Appropriately, the first modern marathon winner in 1896 was a Greek, Spyridon Louis. In 1924 the **Olympic marathon distance** was standardized at 42,195 m, or 26 mi 385 yd. This was based on a decision of the British Olympic Committee to start the 1908 Olympic race from Windsor Castle and finish it in front of the royal box in the stadium at London. The marathon was added to the **women's Olympic program** in 1984. Because marathon courses are not of equal difficulty, the **International Association of Athletics Federations** (IAAF) does not list a world record for the event. One of the most coveted honors in marathon running is victory in the **Boston Marathon**, held annually since 1897. The **New York City Marathon** also attracts participants from many countries, as does the **Chicago Marathon**. Other popular marathons are held in London, Berlin, and Dublin.

  Related Web sites:
Boston Marathon: <www.bostonmarathon.org>;
New York City Marathon: <www.ingnycmarathon.org>;
Chicago Marathon: <www.chicagomarathon.com>.

Boston Marathon

Times are given in hours:minutes:seconds.

men

YEAR	WINNER	TIME	YEAR	WINNER	TIME
1897	John J. McDermott (USA)	2:55:10	1912	Michael J. Ryan (USA)	2:21:18
1898	Ronald J. McDonald (CAN)	2:42:00	1913	Fritz Carlson (USA)	2:25:14
1899	Lawrence J. Brignoli (USA)	2:54:38	1914	James Duffy (CAN)	2:25:01
1900	John J. Caffrey (CAN)	2:39:44	1915	Edouard Fabre (CAN)	2:31:41
1901	John J. Caffrey (CAN)	2:29:23	1916	Arthur V. Roth (USA)	2:27:16
1902	Sammy A. Mellor (USA)	2:43:12	1917	William K. Kennedy (USA)	2:28:37
1903	John C. Lorden (USA)	2:41:29	1918	*not held*	
1904	Michael Spring (USA)	2:39:04	1919	Carl W.A. Linder (USA)	2:29:13
1905	Frederick Lorz (USA)	2:38:25	1920	Peter Trivoulides (USA)	2:29:31
1906	Tim Ford (USA)	2:45:45	1921	Frank Zuna (USA)	2:18:57
1907	Thomas Longboat (CAN)	2:24:24	1922	Clarence H. DeMar (USA)	2:18:10
1908	Thomas P. Morrissey (USA)	2:25:43	1923	Clarence H. DeMar (USA)	2:23:47
1909	Henri Renaud (USA)	2:53:36	1924	Clarence H. DeMar (USA)	2:29:40
1910	Fred L. Cameron (CAN)	2:28:52	1925	Charles L. Mellor (USA)	2:33:06
1911	Clarence H. DeMar (USA)	2:21:39	1926	John C. Miles (CAN)	2:25:40

Boston Marathon (continued)

men (continued)

YEAR	WINNER	TIME	YEAR	WINNER	TIME
1927	Clarence H. DeMar (USA)	2:40:22	1969	Unetani Yoshiaki (JPN)	2:13:49
1928	Clarence H. DeMar (USA)	2:37:07	1970	Ron Hill (GBR)	2:10:30
1929	John C. Miles (CAN)	2:33:08	1971	Alvaro Mejia (COL)	2:18:45
1930	Clarence H. DeMar (USA)	2:34:48	1972	Olavi Suomalainen (FIN)	2:15:30
1931	James P. Hennigan (USA)	2:46:45	1973	Jon Anderson (USA)	2:16:03
1932	Paul DeBruyn (GER)	2:33:36	1974	Neil Cusack (USA)	2:13:39
1933	Leslie S. Pawson (USA)	2:31:01	1975	Bill Rodgers (USA)	2:09:55
1934	Dave Komonen (CAN)	2:32:53	1976	Jack Fultz (USA)	2:20:19
1935	John A. Kelley (USA)	2:32:07	1977	Jerome Drayton (CAN)	2:14:46
1936	Ellison M. Brown (USA)	2:33:40	1978	Bill Rodgers (USA)	2:10:13
1937	Walter Young (CAN)	2:33:20	1979	Bill Rodgers (USA)	2:09:27
1938	Leslie S. Pawson (USA)	2:35:34	1980	Bill Rodgers (USA)	2:12:11
1939	Ellison M. Brown (USA)	2:28:51	1981	Seko Toshihiko (JPN)	2:09:26
1940	Gerard Cote (CAN)	2:28:28	1982	Alberto Salazar (USA)	2:08:51
1941	Leslie S. Pawson (USA)	2:30:38	1983	Greg A. Meyer (USA)	2:09:00
1942	Joe Smith (USA)	2:26:51	1984	Geoff Smith (GBR)	2:10:34
1943	Gerard Cote (CAN)	2:28:25	1985	Geoff Smith (GBR)	2:14:05
1944	Gerard Cote (CAN)	2:31:50	1986	Robert de Castella (AUS)	2:07:51
1945	John A. Kelley (USA)	2:30:40	1987	Seko Toshihiko (JPN)	2:11:50
1946	Stylianos Kyriakides (GRE)	2:29:27	1988	Ibrahim Hussein (KEN)	2:08:43
1947	Suh Yun Bok (KOR)	2:25:39	1989	Abebe Mekonnen (ETH)	2:09:06
1948	Gerard Cote (CAN)	2:31:02	1990	Gelindo Bordin (ITA)	2:08:19
1949	Karl G. Leandersson (SWE)	2:31:50	1991	Ibrahim Hussein (KEN)	2:11:06
1950	Ham Kee Yong (KOR)	2:32:39	1992	Ibrahim Hussein (KEN)	2:08:14
1951	Tanaka Shigeki (JPN)	2:27:45	1993	Cosmas N'Deti (KEN)	2:09:33
1952	Doroteo Flores (GUA)	2:31:53	1994	Cosmas N'Deti (KEN)	2:07:15
1953	Yamada Keizo (JPN)	2:18:51	1995	Cosmas N'Deti (KEN)	2:09:22
1954	Veikko L. Karanen (FIN)	2:20:39	1996	Moses Tanui (KEN)	2:09:16
1955	Hamamura Hideo (JPN)	2:18:22	1997	Lameck Aguta (KEN)	2:10:34
1956	Antti Viskari (FIN)	2:14:14	1998	Moses Tanui (KEN)	2:07:34
1957	John J. Kelley (USA)	2:20:05	1999	Joseph Chebet (KEN)	2:09:52
1958	Franjo Mihalic (YUG)	2:25:54	2000	Elijah Lagat (KEN)	2:09:47
1959	Eino Oksanen (FIN)	2:22:42	2001	Lee Bong Ju (KOR)	2:09:43
1960	Paavo Kotila (FIN)	2:20:54	2002	Rodgers Rop (KEN)	2:09:02
1961	Eino Oksanen (FIN)	2:23:39	2003	Robert Kipkoech Cheruiyot (KEN)	2:10:11
1962	Eino Oksanen (FIN)	2:23:48	2004	Timothy Cherigat (KEN)	2:10:37
1963	Aurele Vandendriessche (BEL)	2:18:58	2005	Hailu Negussie (ETH)	2:11:45
1964	Aurele Vandendriessche (BEL)	2:19:59	2006	Robert Kipkoech Cheruiyot (KEN)	2:07:14
1965	Shigematsu Morio (JPN)	2:16:33	2007	Robert Kipkoech Cheruiyot (KEN)	2:14:13
1966	Kimihara Kenji (JPN)	2:17:11	2008	Robert Kipkoech Cheruiyot (KEN)	2:07:46
1967	David McKenzie (NZL)	2:15:45	2009	Deriba Merga (ETH)	2:08:42
1968	Amby Burfoot (USA)	2:22:17	2010	Robert Kiprono Cheruiyot (KEN)	2:05:52

women

YEAR	WINNER	TIME	YEAR	WINNER	TIME
1972	Nina Kuscsik (USA)	3:10:26	1992	Olga Markova (RUS)	2:23:43
1973	Jacqueline Hansen (USA)	3:05:59	1993	Olga Markova (RUS)	2:25:27
1974	Michiko Gorman (USA)	2:47:11	1994	Uta Pippig (GER)	2:21:45
1975	Liane Winter (FRG)	2:42:24	1995	Uta Pippig (GER)	2:25:11
1976	Kim Merritt (USA)	2:47:10	1996	Uta Pippig (GER)	2:27:12
1977	Michiko Gorman (USA)	2:46:22	1997	Fatuma Roba (ETH)	2:26:23
1978	Gayle S. Barron (USA)	2:44:52	1998	Fatuma Roba (ETH)	2:23:21
1979	Joan Benoit (USA)	2:35:15	1999	Fatuma Roba (ETH)	2:23:25
1980	Jacqueline Gareau (CAN)	2:34:28	2000	Catherine Ndereba (KEN)	2:26:11
1981	Allison Roe (NZL)	2:26:46	2001	Catherine Ndereba (KEN)	2:23:53
1982	Charlotte Teske (FRG)	2:29:33	2002	Margaret Okayo (KEN)	2:20:43
1983	Joan Benoit (USA)	2:22:42	2003	Svetlana Zakharova (RUS)	2:25:20
1984	Lorraine Moller (NZL)	2:29:28	2004	Catherine Ndereba (KEN)	2:24:27
1985	Lisa Larsen (USA)	2:34:06	2005	Catherine Ndereba (KEN)	2:25:13
1986	Ingrid Kristiansen (NOR)	2:24:55	2006	Rita Jeptoo (KEN)	2:23:38
1987	Rosa Mota (POR)	2:25:21	2007	Lidiya Grigoryeva (RUS)	2:29:18
1988	Rosa Mota (POR)	2:24:30	2008	Dire Tune (ETH)	2:25:25
1989	Ingrid Kristiansen (NOR)	2:24:33	2009	Salina Kosgei (KEN)	2:32:16
1990	Rosa Mota (POR)	2:25:23	2010	Teyba Erkesso (ETH)	2:26:11
1991	Wanda Panfil (POL)	2:24:18			

New York City Marathon

Times are given in hours:minutes:seconds.

YEAR	MEN	TIME	WOMEN	TIME
1970	Gary Muhrcke (USA)	2:31:38	*no finisher*	
1971	Norm Higgins (USA)	2:22:54	Beth Bonner (USA)	2:55:22
1972	Robert Karlin (USA)	2:27:52	Nina Kuscsik (USA)	3:08:41
1973	Tom Fleming (USA)	2:21:54	Nina Kuscsik (USA)	2:57:07
1974	Norbert Sander (USA)	2:26:30	Katherine Switzer (USA)	3:07:29
1975	Tom Fleming (USA)	2:19:27	Kim Merritt (USA)	2:46:14
1976	Bill Rodgers (USA)	2:10:09	Michiko Gorman (USA)	2:39:11
1977	Bill Rodgers (USA)	2:11:28	Michiko Gorman (USA)	2:43:10
1978	Bill Rodgers (USA)	2:12:12	Grete Waitz (NOR)	2:32:30
1979	Bill Rodgers (USA)	2:11:42	Grete Waitz (NOR)	2:27:33
1980	Alberto Salazar (USA)	2:09:41	Grete Waitz (NOR)	2:25:41
1981	Alberto Salazar (USA)	2:08:13	Allison Roe (NZL)	2:25:29
1982	Alberto Salazar (USA)	2:09:29	Grete Waitz (NOR)	2:27:14
1983	Rod Dixon (NZL)	2:08:59	Grete Waitz (NOR)	2:27:00
1984	Orlando Pizzolato (ITA)	2:14:53	Grete Waitz (NOR)	2:29:30
1985	Orlando Pizzolato (ITA)	2:11:34	Grete Waitz (NOR)	2:28:34
1986	Gianni Poli (ITA)	2:11:06	Grete Waitz (NOR)	2:28:06
1987	Ibrahim Hussein (KEN)	2:11:01	Priscilla Welch (GBR)	2:30:17
1988	Steve Jones (GBR)	2:08:20	Grete Waitz (NOR)	2:28:07
1989	Juma Ikangaa (TAN)	2:08:01	Ingrid Kristiansen (NOR)	2:25:30
1990	Douglas Wakiihuri (KEN)	2:12:39	Wanda Panfil (POL)	2:30:45
1991	Salvador Garcia (MEX)	2:09:28	Liz McColgan (GBR)	2:27:23
1992	Willie Mtolo (RSA)	2:09:29	Lisa Ondieki (AUS)	2:24:40
1993	Andrés Espinosa (MEX)	2:10:04	Uta Pippig (GER)	2:26:24
1994	German Silva (MEX)	2:11:21	Tegla Loroupe (KEN)	2:27:37
1995	German Silva (MEX)	2:11:00	Tegla Loroupe (KEN)	2:28:06
1996	Giacomo Leone (ITA)	2:09:54	Anuta Catuna (ROM)	2:28:18
1997	John Kagwe (KEN)	2:08:12	Franziska Rochat-Moser (SUI)	2:28:43
1998	John Kagwe (KEN)	2:08:45	Franca Fiacconi (ITA)	2:25:17
1999	Joseph Chebet (KEN)	2:09:14	Adriana Fernández (MEX)	2:25:06
2000	Abdelkhader El Mouaziz (MAR)	2:10:09	Lyudmila Petrova (RUS)	2:25:45
2001	Tesfaye Jifar (ETH)	2:07:43	Margaret Okayo (KEN)	2:24:21
2002	Rodgers Rop (KEN)	2:08:07	Joyce Chepchumba (KEN)	2:25:56
2003	Martin Lel (KEN)	2:10:30	Margaret Okayo (KEN)	2:22:31
2004	Hendrik Ramaala (RSA)	2:09:28	Paula Radcliffe (GBR)	2:23:10
2005	Paul Tergat (KEN)	2:09:30	Jelena Prokopcuka (LAT)	2:24:41
2006	Marílson Gomes dos Santos (BRA)	2:09:58	Jelena Prokopcuka (LAT)	2:25:05
2007	Martin Lel (KEN)	2:09:04	Paula Radcliffe (GBR)	2:23:09
2008	Marílson Gomes dos Santos (BRA)	2:08:43	Paula Radcliffe (GBR)	2:23:56
2009	Meb Keflezighi (USA)	2:09:15	Derartu Tulu (ETH)	2:28:52

Chicago Marathon

Times are given in hours:minutes:seconds.

YEAR	MEN	TIME	WOMEN	TIME
1977	Dan Cloeter (USA)	2:17:52	Dorothy Doolittle (USA)	2:50:47
1978	Mark Stanforth (USA)	2:19:20	Lynae Larson (USA)	2:59:25
1979	Dan Cloeter (USA)	2:23:20	Laura Michalek (USA)	3:15:45
1980	Frank Richardson (USA)	2:14:04	Sue Petersen (USA)	2:45:03
1981	Philip Coppess (USA)	2:16:13	Tina Gandy (USA)	2:49:39
1982	Greg Meyer (USA)	2:10:59	Nancy Conz (USA)	2:33:23
1983	Joseph Nzau (KEN)	2:09:44	Rosa Mota (POR)	2:31:12
1984	Steve Jones (GBR)	2:08:05	Rosa Mota (POR)	2:26:01
1985	Steve Jones (GBR)	2:07:13	Joan Benoit Samuelson (USA)	2:21:21
1986	Toshihiko Seko (JPN)	2:08:27	Ingrid Kristiansen (NOR)	2:27:08
1987	*not held*			
1988	Alejandro Cruz (MEX)	2:08:57	Lisa Weidenbach (USA)	2:29:17
1989	Paul Davis-Hale (GBR)	2:11:25	Lisa Weidenbach (USA)	2:28:15
1990	Martín Pitayo (MEX)	2:09:41	Aurora Cunha (POR)	2:30:11
1991	Joseildo Rocha (BRA)	2:14:33	Midde Hamrin-Senorski (SWE)	2:36:21
1992	José César de Souza (BRA)	2:16:14	Linda Somers (USA)	2:37:41
1993	Luiz Antônio dos Santos (BRA)	2:13:15	Ritva Lemettinen (FIN)	2:33:18
1994	Luiz Antônio dos Santos (BRA)	2:11:16	Kristy Johnston (USA)	2:31:34
1995	Eamonn Martin (GBR)	2:11:18	Ritva Lemettinen (FIN)	2:28:27
1996	Paul Evans (GBR)	2:08:52	Marian Sutton (GBR)	2:30:41
1997	Khalid Khannouchi (MAR)	2:07:10	Marian Sutton (GBR)	2:29:03

Chicago Marathon (continued)

YEAR	MEN	TIME	WOMEN	TIME
1998	Ondoro Osoro (KEN)	2:06:54	Joyce Chepchumba (KEN)	2:23:57
1999	Khalid Khannouchi (MAR)	2:05:42	Joyce Chepchumba (KEN)	2:25:59
2000	Khalid Khannouchi (USA)	2:07:01	Catherine Ndereba (KEN)	2:21:33
2001	Ben Kimondiu (KEN)	2:08:52	Catherine Ndereba (KEN)	2:18:47
2002	Khalid Khannouchi (USA)	2:05:56	Paula Radcliffe (GBR)	2:17:18
2003	Evans Rutto (KEN)	2:05:50	Svetlana Zakharova (RUS)	2:23:07
2004	Evans Rutto (KEN)	2:06:16	Constantina Tomescu-Dita (ROM)	2:23:45
2005	Felix Limo (KEN)	2:07:02	Deena Kastor (USA)	2:21:25
2006	Robert Kipkoech Cheruiyot (KEN)	2:07:35	Berhane Adere (ETH)	2:20:42
2007	Patrick Ivuti (KEN)	2:11:11	Berhane Adere (ETH)	2:33:49
2008	Evans Cheruiyot (KEN)	2:06:25	Lidiya Grigoryeva (RUS)	2:27:17
2009	Sammy Wanjiru (KEN)	2:05:41	Liliya Shobukhova (RUS)	2:25:56

Skiing

Although most of the events had been contested at the regional level since the mid-19th century, the first internationally organized **skiing championships** did not take place until 1924. From 1924 to 1931 only **Nordic** competition was involved; **Alpine** championship events were added to world competition in 1931 and to the Olympics in 1936. Except in Olympic years, the Nordic and Alpine championships are held separately and at different locations. **Events** include cross-country races, ski jumping, biathlon, and relay races (Nordic) and downhill and slalom skiing (Alpine). Since 1967, an **Alpine World Cup** has been presented to the competitor with the best combined downhill, slalom, giant slalom, and supergiant slalom (super-G) performance over a series of major contests. A **Nordic World Cup** for cross-country events has been awarded since 1979.

International Ski Federation (FIS) Web site: <www.fis-ski.com>.

Alpine Skiing World Championships—Men

Held since 1931. Table shows results for the past 20 years.

DOWNHILL
1991 Franz Heinzer (SUI)
1992[1] Patrick Ortlieb (AUS)
1993 Urs Lehmann (SUI)
1994[1] Tommy Moe (USA)
1995 *not held*
1996 Patrick Ortlieb (AUS)
1997 Bruno Kernen (SUI)
1998[1] Jean-Luc Cretier (FRA)
1999 Hermann Maier (AUT)
2001 Hannes Trinkl (AUT)
2002[1] Fritz Strobl (AUT)
2003 Michael Walchhofer (AUT)
2005 Bode Miller (USA)
2006[1] Antoine Déneriaz (FRA)
2007 Aksel Lund Svindal (NOR)
2009 John Kucera (CAN)
2010[1] Didier Defago (SUI)

COMBINED
1991 Stefan Eberharter (AUT)
1992[1] Josef Polig (ITA)
1993 Lasse Kjus (NOR)
1994[1] Lasse Kjus (NOR)
1995 *not held*
1996 Marc Girardelli (LUX)
1997 Kjetil André Aamodt (NOR)
1998[1] Mario Reiter (AUT)
1999 Kjetil André Aamodt (NOR)
2001 Kjetil André Aamodt (NOR)
2002[1] Kjetil André Aamodt (NOR)
2003 Bode Miller (USA)
2005 Benjamin Raich (AUT)
2006[1] Ted Ligety (USA)

COMBINED (CONTINUED)
2007 Daniel Albrecht (SUI)
2009 Aksel Lund Svindal (NOR)
2010[1] Bode Miller (USA)

SLALOM
1992[1] Finn Christian Jagge (NOR)
1993 Kjetil André Aamodt (NOR)
1994[1] Thomas Stangassinger (AUT)
1995 *not held*
1996 Alberto Tomba (ITA)
1997 Tom Stiansen (NOR)
1998[1] Hans Petter Buraas (NOR)
1999 Kalle Palander (FIN)
2001 Mario Matt (AUT)
2002[1] Jean-Pierre Vidal (FRA)
2003 Ivica Kostelic (CRO)
2005 Benjamin Raich (AUT)
2006[1] Benjamin Raich (AUT)
2007 Mario Matt (AUT)
2009 Manfred Pranger (AUT)
2010[1] Giuliano Razzoli (ITA)

GIANT SLALOM
1991 Rudolf Nierlich (AUT)
1992[1] Alberto Tomba (ITA)
1993 Kjetil André Aamodt (NOR)
1994[1] Markus Wasmeier (GER)
1995 *not held*
1996 Alberto Tomba (ITA)
1997 Michael von Grüningen (SUI)

GIANT SLALOM (CONTINUED)
1998[1] Hermann Maier (AUT)
1999 Lasse Kjus (NOR)
2001 Michael von Grüningen (SUI)
2002[1] Stephan Eberharter (AUT)
2003 Bode Miller (USA)
2005 Hermann Maier (AUT)
2006[1] Benjamin Raich (AUT)
2007 Aksel Lund Svindal (NOR)
2009 Carlo Janka (SUI)
2010[1] Carlo Janka (SUI)

SUPERGIANT SLALOM
1991 Stephan Eberharter (AUT)
1992[1] Kjetil André Aamodt (NOR)
1993 *not held*
1994[1] Markus Wasmeier (GER)
1995 *not held*
1996 Atle Skårdal (NOR)
1997 Atle Skårdal (NOR)
1998[1] Hermann Maier (AUT)
1999 Lasse Kjus (NOR), Hermann Maier (AUT) (tied)
2001 Daron Rahlves (USA)
2002[1] Kjetil André Aamodt (NOR)
2003 Stephan Eberharter (AUT)
2005 Bode Miller (USA)
2006[1] Kjetil André Aamodt (NOR)
2007 Patrick Staudacher (ITA)
2009 Didier Cuche (SUI)
2010[1] Aksel Lund Svindal (NOR)

[1]*Olympic champions, recognized in this table as world champions (though not by FIS).*

Alpine Skiing World Championships—Women

Held since 1931. Table shows results for the past 20 years.

DOWNHILL
1991   Petra Kronberger (AUT)
1992[1]   Kerrin Lee-Gartner (CAN)
1993   Kate Pace (CAN)
1994[1]   Katja Seizinger (GER)
1995   *not held*
1996   Picabo Street (USA)
1997   Hilary Lindh (USA)
1998[1]   Katja Seizinger (GER)
1999   Renate Götschl (AUT)
2001   Michaela Dorfmeister (AUT)
2002[1]   Carole Montillet (FRA)
2003   Mélanie Turgeon (CAN)
2005   Janica Kostelic (CRO)
2006[1]   Michaela Dorfmeister (AUT)
2007   Anja Pärson (SWE)
2009   Lindsey Vonn (USA)
2010[1]   Lindsey Vonn (USA)

COMBINED
1991   Chantal Bournissen (SUI)
1992[1]   Petra Kronberger (AUT)
1993   Miriam Vogt (GER)
1994[1]   Pernilla Wiberg (SWE)
1995   *not held*
1996   Pernilla Wiberg (SWE)
1997   Renate Götschl (AUT)
1998[1]   Katja Seizinger (GER)
1999   Pernilla Wiberg (SWE)
2001   Martina Ertl (GER)
2002[1]   Janica Kostelic (CRO)
2003   Janica Kostelic (CRO)
2005   Janica Kostelic (CRO)
2006[1]   Janica Kostelic (CRO)
2007   Anja Pärson (SWE)

COMBINED (CONTINUED)
2009   Kathrin Zettel (AUT)
2010[1]   Maria Riesch (GER)

SLALOM
1991   Vreni Schneider (SUI)
1992[1]   Petra Kronberger (AUT)
1993   Karin Buder (AUT)
1994[1]   Vreni Schneider (SUI)
1995   *not held*
1996   Pernilla Wiberg (SWE)
1997   Deborah Compagnoni (ITA)
1998[1]   Hilde Gerg (GER)
1999   Zali Steggall (AUS)
2001   Anja Pärson (SWE)
2002[1]   Janica Kostelic (CRO)
2003   Janica Kostelic (CRO)
2005   Janica Kostelic (CRO)
2006[1]   Anja Pärson (SWE)
2007   Sarka Zahrobska (CZE)
2009   Maria Riesch (GER)
2010[1]   Maria Riesch (GER)

GIANT SLALOM
1991   Pernilla Wiberg (SWE)
1992[1]   Pernilla Wiberg (SWE)
1993   Carole Merle (FRA)
1994[1]   Deborah Compagnoni (ITA)
1995   *not held*
1996   Deborah Compagnoni (ITA)
1997   Deborah Compagnoni (ITA)
1998[1]   Deborah Compagnoni (ITA)

GIANT SLALOM (CONTINUED)
1999   Alexandra Meissnitzer (AUT)
2001   Sonja Nef (SUI)
2002[1]   Janica Kostelic (CRO)
2003   Anja Pärson (SWE)
2005   Anja Pärson (SWE)
2006[1]   Julia Mancuso (USA)
2007   Nicole Hosp (AUT)
2009   Kathrin Hölzl (GER)
2010[1]   Viktoria Rebensburg (GER)

SUPERGIANT SLALOM
1991   Ulrike Maier (AUT)
1992[1]   Deborah Compagnoni (ITA)
1993   Katja Seizinger (GER)
1994[1]   Diann Roffe-Steinrotter (USA)
1995   *not held*
1996   Isolde Kostner (ITA)
1997   Isolde Kostner (ITA)
1998[1]   Picabo Street (USA)
1999   Alexandra Meissnitzer (AUT)
2001   Régine Cavagnoud (FRA)
2002[1]   Daniela Ceccarelli (ITA)
2003   Michaela Dorfmeister (AUT)
2005   Anja Pärson (SWE)
2006[1]   Michaela Dorfmeister (AUT)
2007   Anja Pärson (SWE)
2009   Lindsey Vonn (USA)
2010[1]   Andrea Fischbacher (AUT)

[1]*Olympic champions, recognized in this table as world champions (though not by FIS).*

Alpine World Cup

The winner is determined by the number of points awarded for finishes in various competitions during the season.

YEAR	MEN	WOMEN
1967	Jean-Claude Killy (FRA)	Nancy Greene (CAN)
1968	Jean-Claude Killy (FRA)	Nancy Greene (CAN)
1969	Karl Schranz (AUT)	Gertrude Gabl (AUT)
1970	Karl Schranz (AUT)	Michele Jacot (FRA)
1971	Gustavo Thöni (ITA)	Annemarie Pröll (AUT)
1972	Gustavo Thöni (ITA)	Annemarie Pröll (AUT)
1973	Gustavo Thöni (ITA)	Annemarie Pröll (AUT)
1974	Piero Gros (ITA)	Annemarie Moser-Pröll (AUT)
1975	Gustavo Thöni (ITA)	Annemarie Moser-Pröll (AUT)
1976	Ingemar Stenmark (SWE)	Rosi Mittermaier (FRG)
1977	Ingemar Stenmark (SWE)	Lise-Marie Morerod (SUI)
1978	Ingemar Stenmark (SWE)	Hanni Wenzel (LIE)
1979	Peter Luescher (SUI)	Annemarie Moser-Pröll (AUT)

YEAR	MEN	WOMEN
1980	Andreas Wenzel (LIE)	Hanni Wenzel (LIE)
1981	Phil Mahre (USA)	Marie-Thérèse Nadig (SUI)
1982	Phil Mahre (USA)	Erika Hess (SUI)
1983	Phil Mahre (USA)	Tamara McKinney (USA)
1984	Pirmin Zurbriggen (SUI)	Erika Hess (SUI)
1985	Marc Girardelli (LUX)	Michela Figini (SUI)
1986	Marc Girardelli (LUX)	Maria Walliser (SUI)
1987	Pirmin Zurbriggen (SUI)	Maria Walliser (SUI)
1988	Pirmin Zurbriggen (SUI)	Michela Figini (SUI)
1989	Marc Girardelli (LUX)	Vreni Schneider (SUI)
1990	Pirmin Zurbriggen (SUI)	Petra Kronberger (AUT)
1991	Marc Girardelli (LUX)	Petra Kronberger (AUT)
1992	Paul Accola (SUI)	Petra Kronberger (AUT)
1993	Marc Girardelli (LUX)	Anita Wachter (AUT)
1994	Kjetil André Aamodt (NOR)	Vreni Schneider (SUI)
1995	Alberto Tomba (ITA)	Vreni Schneider (SUI)
1996	Lasse Kjus (NOR)	Katja Seizinger (GER)

Alpine World Cup (continued)

YEAR	MEN	WOMEN	YEAR	MEN	WOMEN
1997	Luc Alphand (FRA)	Pernilla Wiberg (SWE)	2004	Hermann Maier (AUT)	Anja Pärson (SWE)
1998	Hermann Maier (AUT)	Katja Seizinger (GER)	2005	Bode Miller (USA)	Anja Pärson (SWE)
1999	Lasse Kjus (NOR)	Alexandra Meiss-	2006	Benjamin Raich (AUT)	Janica Kostelic (CRO)
		nitzer (AUT)	2007	Aksel Lund Svindal	Nicole Hosp (AUT)
2000	Hermann Maier (AUT)	Renate Götschl (AUT)		(NOR)	
2001	Hermann Maier (AUT)	Janica Kostelic (CRO)	2008	Bode Miller (USA)	Lindsey Vonn (USA)
2002	Stephan Eberharter	Michaela Dorf-	2009	Aksel Lund Svindal	Lindsey Vonn (USA)
	(AUT)	meister (AUT)		(NOR)	
2003	Stephan Eberharter	Janica Kostelic (CRO)	2010	Carlo Janka (SUI)	Lindsey Vonn (USA)
	(AUT)				

Nordic Skiing World Championships—Men

Held since 1924. Table shows results for the past 20 years.

INDIVIDUAL SPRINT
2001 Tor Arne Hetland (NOR)
2002[1] Tor Arne Hetland (NOR)
2003 Thobias Fredriksson
       (SWE)
2005 Vassily Rochev (RUS)
2006[1] Björn Lind (SWE)
2007 Jens Arne Svartedal (NOR)
2009 Ola Vigen Hattestad (NOR)
2010[1] Nikita Kriyukov (RUS)

10-KM CROSS-COUNTRY[2]
1991 Terje Langli (NOR)
1992[1] Vegard Ulvang (NOR)
1993 Sture Sivertsen (NOR)
1994[1] Bjørn Daehlie NOR)
1995 Vladimir Smirnov (KAZ)
1997 Bjørn Daehlie (NOR)
1998[1] Bjørn Daehlie (NOR)
1999 Mika Myllylä (FIN)

15-KM CROSS-COUNTRY[2, 3]
1991 Bjørn Daehlie (NOR)
1992[1] Bjørn Daehlie (NOR)
1993 Bjørn Daehlie (NOR)
1994[1] Bjørn Daehlie (NOR)
1995 Vladimir Smirnov (KAZ)
1997 Bjørn Daehlie (NOR)
1998[1] Thomas Alsgaard (NOR)
1999 Thomas Alsgaard (NOR)
2001 Per Elofsson (SWE)
2002[1] Andrus Veerpalu (EST)
2003 Axel Teichmann (GER)
2005 Pietro Piller Cottrer (ITA)
2006[1] Andrus Veerpalu (EST)
2007 Lars Berger (NOR)

15-KM CROSS-COUNTRY[2, 3] (CONT.)
2009 Andrus Veerpalu (EST)
2010[1] Dario Cologna (SUI)

COMBINED PURSUIT[2]
2001 Per Elofsson (SWE)
2002[1] Thomas Alsgaard (NOR),
       Frode Estil (NOR) (tied)
2003 Per Elofsson (SWE)
2005 Vincent Vittoz (FRA)
2006[1] Yevgeny Dementyev (RUS)
2007 Axel Teichmann (GER)
2009 Petter Northug (NOR)
2010[1] Marcus Hellner (SWE)

30-KM CROSS-COUNTRY
1991 Gunde Svan (SWE)
1992[1] Vegard Ulvang (NOR)
1993 Bjørn Daehlie (NOR)
1994[1] Thomas Alsgaard (NOR)
1995 Vladimir Smirnov (KAZ)
1997 Aleksey Prokurorov (RUS)
1998[1] Mika Myllylä (FIN)
1999 Mika Myllylä (FIN)
2001 Andrus Veerpalu (EST)
2002[1] Christian Hoffmann (AUT)
2003 Thomas Alsgaard (NOR)

50-KM CROSS-COUNTRY
1991 Torgny Mogren (SWE)
1992[1] Bjørn Daehlie (NOR)
1993 Torgny Mogren (SWE)
1994 Vladimir Smirnov (KAZ)
1995 Silvio Fauner (ITA)
1997 Mika Myllylä (FIN)
1998[1] Bjørn Daehlie (NOR)

50-KM CROSS-COUNTRY (CONT.)
1999 Mika Myllylä (FIN)
2001 Johann Mühlegg (ESP)
2002[1] Mikhail Ivanov (RUS)
2003 Martin Koukal (CZE)
2005 Frode Estil (NOR)
2006[1] Giorgio Di Centa (ITA)
2007 Odd-Bjørn Hjelmeset (NOR)
2009 Petter Northug (NOR)
2010[1] Petter Northug (NOR)

TEAM SPRINT
2005 Norway
2006[1] Sweden
2007 Italy
2009 Norway
2010[1] Norway

RELAY[4]
1991 Norway
1992[1] Norway
1993 Norway
1994[1] Italy
1995 Norway
1997 Norway
1998[1] Norway
1999 Austria
2001 Norway
2002[1] Norway
2003 Norway
2005 Norway
2006[1] Italy
2007 Norway
2009 Norway
2010[1] Sweden

[1]*Olympic champions, recognized in this table as world champions (though not by FIS).* [2]*From 1991 to 1999, the 10-km event was held in tandem with the 15-km event; one event featured classical and the other freestyle technique. Medals were awarded for both races. Beginning in 2001 this pursuit race (skiers competing directly against each other rather than against the clock) led to one medal being awarded upon winning. The 10-km was discontinued, and the 15-km became a stand-alone event featuring classical technique. In 2001–03 the pursuit race featured two 10-km races; since then, two 15-km races.* [3]*18-km cross-country through 1952; 15-km thereafter.* [4]*Military relay until 1939; 40-km relay in 1948 and thereafter.*

Nordic Skiing World Championships—Women

Held since 1952. Table shows results for the past 20 years.

INDIVIDUAL SPRINT
2001 Pirjo Manninen (FIN)
2002[1] Yuliya Chepalova (RUS)
2003 Marit Bjørgen (NOR)

INDIVIDUAL SPRINT (CONT.)
2005 Emilie Öhrstig (SWE)
2006[1] Chandra Crawford (CAN)
2007 Astrid Jacobsen (NOR)

INDIVIDUAL SPRINT (CONT.)
2009 Arianna Follis (ITA)
2010[1] Marit Bjørgen (NOR)

Nordic Skiing World Championships—Women (continued)

5-KM CROSS-COUNTRY[2]

1991	Trude Dybendahl (NOR)
1992[1]	Marjut Lukkarinen (FIN)
1993	Larisa Lazutina (RUS)
1994[1]	Lyubov Yegorova (RUS)
1995	Larisa Lazutina (RUS)
1997	Yelena Vyalbe (RUS)
1998[1]	Larisa Lazutina (RUS)
1999	Bente Martinsen (NOR)

10-KM CROSS-COUNTRY[2]

1991	Yelena Vyalbe (URS)
1992[1]	Lyubov Yegorova (UNT)
1993	Stefania Belmondo (ITA)
1994[1]	Lyubov Yegorova (RUS)
1995	Larisa Lazutina (RUS)
1997	Stefania Belmondo (ITA)
1998[1]	Larisa Lazutina (RUS)
1999	Stefania Belmondo (ITA)
2001	Bente Skari (NOR)
2002[1]	Bente Skari (NOR)
2003	Bente Skari (NOR)
2005	Katerina Neumannova (CZE)
2006[1]	Kristina Smigun (EST)
2007	Katerina Neumannova (CZE)
2009	Aino-Kaisa Saarinen (FIN)
2010[1]	Charlotte Kalla (SWE)

COMBINED PURSUIT[2]

2001	Virpi Kuitunen (FIN)
2002[1]	Beckie Scott (CAN)

COMBINED PURSUIT[2] (CONTINUED)

2003	Kristina Smigun (EST)
2005	Yuliya Chepalova (RUS)
2006[1]	Kristina Smigun (EST)
2007	Olga Zavyalova (RUS)
2009	Justyna Kowalczyk (POL)
2010[1]	Marit Bjørgen (NOR)

15-KM CROSS-COUNTRY

1991	Yelena Vyalbe (URS)
1992[1]	Lyubov Yegorova (URS)
1993	Yelena Vyalbe (RUS)
1994[1]	Manuela Di Centa (ITA)
1995	Larisa Lazutina (RUS)
1997	Yelena Vyalbe (RUS)
1998[1]	Olga Danilova (RUS)
1999	Stefania Belmondo (ITA)
2001	Bente Skari (NOR)
2002[1]	Stefania Belmondo (ITA)
2003	Bente Skari (NOR)

30-KM CROSS-COUNTRY

1991	Lyubov Yegorova (URS)
1992[1]	Stefania Belmondo (ITA)
1993	Stefania Belmondo (ITA)
1994[1]	Manuela Di Centa (ITA)
1995	Yelena Vyalbe (RUS)
1997	Yelena Vyalbe (RUS)
1998[1]	Yulia Chepalova (RUS)
1999	Larisa Lazutina (RUS)
2001	not held
2002[1]	Gabriella Paruzzi (ITA)
2003	Olga Savyalova (RUS)
2005	Marit Bjørgen (NOR)

30-KM CROSS-COUNTRY (CONTINUED)

2006[1]	Katerina Neumannova (CZE)
2007	Virpi Kuitunen (FIN)
2009	Justyna Kowalczyk (POL)
2010[1]	Justyna Kowalczyk (POL)

TEAM SPRINT

2005	Norway
2006[1]	Sweden
2007	Finland
2009	Finland
2010[1]	Germany

RELAY[3]

1991	USSR
1992[1]	Unified Team
1993	Russia
1994[1]	Russia
1995	Russia
1997	Russia
1998[1]	Russia
1999	Russia
2001	Russia
2002[1]	Germany
2003	Germany
2005	Norway
2006[1]	Russia
2007	Finland
2009	Finland
2010[1]	Norway

SKI JUMP

2009	Lindsey Van

[1]Olympic champions, recognized in this table as world champions (though not by FIS).   [2]From 1991 to 1999, the 5-km event was held in tandem with the 10-km event; one event featured classical and the other freestyle technique. Medals were awarded for both races. Beginning in 2001 this pursuit race (skiers competing directly against each other rather than against the clock) led to one medal being awarded upon winning. The 5-km was discontinued, and the 10-km became a stand-alone event featuring classical technique. In 2001–03 the pursuit race featured two 5-km races; since then, two 7.5-km races.   [3]15-km relay until 1974; 20-km in 1976 and thereafter.

Nordic Skiing World Championships—Nordic Combined

The Nordic combined involves a 10-km cross-country race and ski jumping.
Held since 1925. Table shows results for the past 20 years.

YEAR	COMBINED (NORMAL HILL)[1]	YEAR	COMBINED (LARGE HILL)[3]	YEAR	TEAM (CONTINUED)
1991	Fred Børre Lundberg (NOR)	1999	Bjarte Engen Vik (NOR)	1992[2]	Japan
1992[2]	Fabrice Guy (FRA)	2001	Marko Baacke (GER)	1993	Japan
1993	Kenji Ogiwara (JPN)	2002[2]	Samppa Lajunen (FIN)	1994[2]	Japan
1994[2]	Fred Børre Lundberg (NOR)	2003	Johnny Spillane (USA)	1995	Japan
1995	Fred Børre Lundberg (NOR)	2005	Ronny Ackermann (GER)	1997	Norway
1997	Kenji Ogiwara (JPN)	2006[2]	Felix Gottwald (AUT)	1998[2]	Norway
1998[2]	Bjarte Engen Vik (NOR)	2007	Hannu Manninen (FIN)	1999	Finland
1999	Bjarte Engen Vik (NOR)	2009	Bill Demong (USA)	2001	Norway
2001	Bjarte Engen Vik (NOR)	2010[2]	Bill Demong (USA)	2002[2]	Finland
2002[2]	Samppa Lajunen (FIN)			2003	Austria
2003	Ronny Ackermann (GER)	YEAR	MASS START	2005	Norway
2005	Ronny Ackermann (GER)	2009	Todd Lodwick (USA)	2006[2]	Austria
2006[2]	Georg Hettich (GER)			2007	Finland
2007	Ronny Ackermann (GER)	YEAR	TEAM	2009	Japan
2009	Todd Lodwick (USA)	1991	Austria	2010[2]	Austria
2010[2]	Jason Lamy Chappuis (FRA)				

[1]15-km cross-country race until 2009.   [2]Olympic champions, recognized in this table as world champions (though not by FIS).   [3]7.5-km cross-country race until 2009.

Nordic Skiing World Championships—Ski Jump

Men's events only. Held since 1924. Table shows results for the past 20 years.

YEAR	NORMAL HILL[1]	YEAR	LARGE HILL[3] (CONTINUED)	YEAR	TEAM JUMP (NORMAL HILL[1]) (CONTINUED)
1991	Heinz Kuttin (AUT)	1993	Espen Bredesen (NOR)		
1992[2]	Ernst Vettori (AUT)	1994[2]	Jens Weissflog (GER)	2006	*not held*
1993	Masahiko Harada (JPN)	1995	Tommy Ingebrigtsen (NOR)		
1994[2]	Espen Bredesen (NOR)	1997	Masahiko Harada (JPN)	YEAR	TEAM JUMP (LARGE HILL[3])
1995	Takanobu Okabe (JPN)	1998[2]	Kazuyoshi Funaki (JPN)	1991	Austria
1997	Janne Ahonen (FIN)	1999	Martin Schmitt (GER)	1992[2]	Finland
1998[2]	Jani Soininen (FIN)	2001	Martin Schmitt (GER)	1993	Norway
1999	Kazuyoshi Funaki (JPN)	2002[2]	Simon Ammann (SUI)	1994[2]	Germany
2001	Adam Malysz (POL)	2003	Adam Malysz (POL)	1995	Finland
2002[2]	Simon Ammann (SUI)	2005	Janne Ahonen (FIN)	1997	Finland
2003	Adam Malysz (POL)	2006[2]	Thomas Morgenstern (AUT)	1998[2]	Japan
2005	Rok Benkovic (SLO)	2007	Simon Ammann (SUI)	1999	Germany
2006[2]	Lars Bystøl (NOR)	2009	Andreas Kuettel (SUI)	2001	Germany
2007	Adam Malysz (POL)	2010[2]	Simon Ammann (SUI)	2002[2]	Germany
2009	Wolfgang Loitzl (AUT)			2003	Finland
2010[2]	Simon Ammann (SUI)	YEAR	TEAM JUMP (NORMAL HILL[1])	2005	Austria
		2001	Austria	2006[2]	Austria
YEAR	LARGE HILL[3]	2002	*not held*	2007	Austria
1991	Franci Petek (YUG)	2003	*not held*	2009	Austria
1992[2]	Toni Nieminen (FIN)	2005	Austria	2010[2]	Austria

[1]*The distance of the jump in the normal hill competition has varied over time; since 1992 it has been set at either 90 or 95 meters.* [2]*Olympic champions, recognized in this table as world champions (though not by FIS).* [3]*The distance of the jump in the large hill competition has varied over time; since 1992 it has been set at either 120 or 125 meters.*

Nordic World Cup

The winner is determined by the number of points awarded for finishes in various competitions during the season.

YEAR	MEN	WOMEN	YEAR	MEN	WOMEN
1979	Oddvar Braa (NOR)	Galina Kulakova (URS)	1996	Bjørn Daehlie (NOR)	Manuela Di Centa (ITA)
1980	*not held*		1997	Bjørn Daehlie (NOR)	Yelena Vyalbe (RUS)
1981	Aleksandr Zavyalov (URS)	Raisa Smetanina (URS)	1998	Thomas Alsgaard (NOR)	Larisa Lazutina (RUS)
1982	Bill Koch (USA)	Berit Aunli (NOR)	1999	Bjørn Daehlie (NOR)	Bente Martinsen (NOR)
1983	Aleksandr Zavyalov (URS)	Marja-Liisa Hämä-läinen (FIN)	2000	Johann Mühlegg (ESP)	Bente Skari-Martinsen (NOR)
1984	Gunde Svan (SWE)	Marja-Liisa Hämä-läinen (FIN)	2001	Per Elofsson (SWE)	Yuliya Chepalova (RUS)
1985	Gunde Svan (SWE)	Anette Boe (NOR)	2002	Per Elofsson (SWE)	Bente Skari (NOR)
1986	Gunde Svan (SWE)	Marjo Matikainen (FIN)	2003	Mathias Fredriksson (SWE)	Bente Skari (NOR)
1987	Torgny Mogren (SWE)	Marjo Matikainen (FIN)			
1988	Gunde Svan (SWE)	Marjo Matikainen (FIN)	2004	Rene Sommerfeldt (GER)	Gabriella Paruzzi (ITA)
1989	Gunde Svan (SWE)	Yelena Vyalbe (URS)	2005	Axel Teichmann (GER)	Marit Bjørgen (NOR)
1990	Vegard Ulvang (NOR)	Larisa Lazutina (URS)			
1991	Vladimir Smirnov (URS)	Yelena Vyalbe (URS)	2006	Tobias Angerer (GER)	Marit Bjørgen (NOR)
1992	Bjørn Daehlie (NOR)	Yelena Vyalbe (RUS)	2007	Tobias Angerer (GER)	Virpi Kuitunen (FIN)
1993	Bjørn Daehlie (NOR)	Lyudmila Yegorova (RUS)	2008	Lukas Bauer (CZE)	Virpi Kuitunen (FIN)
			2009	Dario Cologna (SUI)	Justyna Kowalczyk (POL)
1994	Vladimir Smirnov (KAZ)	Manuela Di Centa (ITA)			
1995	Bjørn Daehlie (NOR)	Yelena Vyalbe (RUS)	2010	Petter Northug (NOR)	Justyna Kowalczyk (POL)

Swimming

The **Fédération Internationale de Natation** (International Swimming Federation, FINA, still known by its French acronym that includes an "a" for "Amateur"; founded 1908) is the world governing body for amateur swimming. It held the first world swimming championships in 1973. After 1975 the FINA championships were held in non-Olympic, even-numbered years. (An exception was the 1991 championship that took place in Australia during the summer month of January.) Diving, synchronized (or synchro) swimming, and water polo events are included in the competition.

A distinction is made between **long-course** (50-m) and **short-course** (25-m) pools for purposes of record setting; world championships and other major contests were long held in 50-m pools, but now a separate short-course world championship and World Cup take place. **International Swimming Federation Web site:** <www.fina.org>.

World Swimming and Diving Championships—Men

swimming

50-M FREESTYLE
1986   Tom Jager (USA)
1991   Tom Jager (USA)
1994   Aleksandr Popov (RUS)
1998   Bill Pilczuk (USA)
2001   Anthony Ervin (USA)
2003   Aleksandr Popov (RUS)
2005   Roland Schoeman (RSA)
2007   Benjamin Wildman-
        Tobriner (USA)
2009   César Cielo Filho (BRA)

100-M FREESTYLE
1973   Jim Montgomery (USA)
1975   Andy Coan (USA)
1978   David McCagg (USA)
1982   Jörg Woithe (GDR)
1986   Matt Biondi (USA)
1991   Matt Biondi (USA)
1994   Aleksandr Popov (RUS)
1998   Aleksandr Popov (RUS)
2001   Anthony Ervin (USA)
2003   Aleksandr Popov (RUS)
2005   Filippo Magnini (ITA)
2007   Filippo Magnini (ITA)
2009   César Cielo Filho (BRA)

200-M FREESTYLE
1973   Jim Montgomery (USA)
1975   Tim Shaw (USA)
1978   Bill Forrester (USA)
1982   Michael Gross (FRG)
1986   Michael Gross (FRG)
1991   Giorgio Lamberti (ITA)
1994   Antti Kasvio (FIN)
1998   Michael Klim (AUS)
2001   Ian Thorpe (AUS)
2003   Ian Thorpe (AUS)
2005   Michael Phelps (USA)
2007   Michael Phelps (USA)
2009   Paul Biedermann (GER)

400-M FREESTYLE
1973   Rick DeMont (USA)
1975   Tim Shaw (USA)
1978   Vladimir Salnikov (URS)
1982   Vladimir Salnikov (URS)
1986   Rainer Henkel (FRG)
1991   Jörg Hoffmann (GER)
1994   Kieren Perkins (AUS)
1998   Ian Thorpe (AUS)
2001   Ian Thorpe (AUS)
2003   Ian Thorpe (AUS)
2005   Grant Hackett (AUS)
2007   Park Tae Hwan (KOR)
2009   Paul Biedermann (GER)

800-M FREESTYLE
2001   Ian Thorpe (AUS)
2003   Grant Hackett (AUS)
2005   Grant Hackett (AUS)
2007   Przemyslaw Stanczyk
        (POL)
2009   Zhang Lin (CHN)

1,500-M FREESTYLE
1973   Steve Holland (AUS)
1975   Tim Shaw (USA)

1,500-M FREESTYLE (CONTINUED)
1978   Vladimir Salnikov (URS)
1982   Vladimir Salnikov (URS)
1986   Rainer Henkel (FRG)
1991   Jörg Hoffmann (GER)
1994   Kieren Perkins (AUS)
1998   Grant Hackett (AUS)
2001   Grant Hackett (AUS)
2003   Grant Hackett (AUS)
2005   Grant Hackett (AUS)
2007   Mateusz Sawrymowicz
        (POL)
2009   Oussama Mellouli (TUN)

50-M BACKSTROKE
2001   Randall Bal (USA)
2003   Thomas Rupprath (GER)
2005   Aristeidis Grigoriadis (GRE)
2007   Gerhard Zandberg (RSA)
2009   Liam Tancock (GBR)

100-M BACKSTROKE
1973   Roland Matthes (GDR)
1975   Roland Matthes (GDR)
1978   Bob Jackson (USA)
1982   Dirk Richter (GDR)
1986   Igor Polyansky (URS)
1991   Jeff Rouse (USA)
1994   Martin López-Zubero
        (ESP)
1998   Lenny Krayzelburg (USA)
2001   Matt Welsh (AUS)
2003   Aaron Peirsol (USA)
2005   Aaron Peirsol (USA)
2007   Aaron Peirsol (USA)
2009   Junya Koga (JPN)

200-M BACKSTROKE
1973   Roland Matthes (GDR)
1975   Zoltán Verrasztó (HUN)
1978   Jesse Vassallo (USA)
1982   Rick Carey (USA)
1986   Igor Polyansky (URS)
1991   Martin López-Zubero
        (ESP)
1994   Vladimir Selkov (RUS)
1998   Lenny Krayzelburg (USA)
2001   Aaron Peirsol (USA)
2003   Aaron Peirsol (USA)
2005   Aaron Peirsol (USA)
2007   Ryan Lochte (USA)
2009   Aaron Peirsol (USA)

50-M BREASTSTROKE
2001   Oleg Lisogor (UKR)
2003   James Gibson (GBR)
2005   Mark Warnecke (GER)
2007   Oleg Lisogor (UKR)
2009   Cameron van der Burgh
        (RSA)

100-M BREASTSTROKE
1973   John Hencken (USA)
1975   David Wilkie (GBR)
1978   Walter Kusch (FRG)
1982   Steve Lundquist (USA)
1986   Victor Davis (CAN)
1991   Norbert Rózsa (HUN)

100-M BREASTSTROKE (CONTINUED)
1994   Norbert Rózsa (HUN)
1998   Fred Deburghgraeve (BEL)
2001   Roman Sloudnov (RUS)
2003   Kosuke Kitajima (JPN)
2005   Brendan Hansen (USA)
2007   Brendan Hansen (USA)
2009   Brenton Rickard (AUS)

200-M BREASTSTROKE
1973   David Wilkie (GBR)
1975   David Wilkie (GBR)
1978   Nick Nevid (USA)
1982   Victor Davis (CAN)
1986   József Szabó (HUN)
1991   Mike Barrowman (USA)
1994   Norbert Rózsa (HUN)
1998   Kurt Grote (USA)
2001   Brendan Hansen (USA)
2003   Kosuke Kitajima (JPN)
2005   Brendan Hansen (USA)
2007   Kosuke Kitajima (JPN)
2009   Daniel Gyurta (HUN)

50-M BUTTERFLY
2001   Geoff Huegill (AUS)
2003   Matt Welsh (AUS)
2005   Roland Schoeman (RSA)
2007   Roland Schoeman (RSA)
2009   Milorad Cavic (SRB)

100-M BUTTERFLY
1973   Bruce Robertson (CAN)
1975   Greg Jagenburg (USA)
1978   Joseph Bottom (USA)
1982   Matt Gribble (USA)
1986   Pablo Morales (USA)
1991   Anthony Nesty (SUR)
1994   Rafal Szukala (POL)
1998   Michael Klim (AUS)
2001   Lars Frölander (SWE)
2003   Ian Crocker (USA)
2005   Ian Crocker (USA)
2007   Michael Phelps (USA)
2009   Michael Phelps (USA)

200-M BUTTERFLY
1973   Robin Backhaus (USA)
1975   Bill Forrester (USA)
1978   Mike Bruner (USA)
1982   Michael Gross (FRG)
1986   Michael Gross (FRG)
1991   Melvin Stewart (USA)
1994   Denis Pankratov (RUS)
1998   Denys Silantyev (UKR)
2001   Michael Phelps (USA)
2003   Michael Phelps (USA)
2005   Pawel Korzeniowski (POL)
2007   Michael Phelps (USA)
2009   Michael Phelps (USA)

200-M INDIVIDUAL MEDLEY
1973   Gunnar Larsson (SWE)
1975   András Hargitay (HUN)
1978   Graham Smith (CAN)
1982   Aleksandr Sidorenko (URS)
1986   Tamás Darnyi (HUN)
1991   Tamás Darnyi (HUN)

World Swimming and Diving Championships—Men (continued)
swimming (continued)

200-M INDIVIDUAL MEDLEY (CONT.)
1994 Jani Sievinen (FIN)
1998 Marcel Wouda (NED)
2001 Massimiliano Rosolino (ITA)
2003 Michael Phelps (USA)
2005 Michael Phelps (USA)
2007 Michael Phelps (USA)
2009 Ryan Lochte (USA)

400-M INDIVIDUAL MEDLEY
1973 András Hargitay (HUN)
1975 András Hargitay (HUN)
1978 Jesse Vassallo (USA)
1982 Ricardo Prado (BRA)
1986 Tamás Darnyi (HUN)
1991 Tamás Darnyi (HUN)
1994 Tom Dolan (USA)
1998 Tom Dolan (USA)
2001 Alessio Boggiatto (ITA)
2003 Michael Phelps (USA)
2005 László Cseh (HUN)
2007 Michael Phelps (USA)
2009 Ryan Lochte (USA)

4 × 100-M FREESTYLE RELAY
1973 United States
1975 United States
1978 United States
1982 United States
1986 United States
1991 United States
1994 United States
1998 United States
2001 Australia
2003 Russia
2005 United States
2007 United States
2009 United States

4 × 200-M FREESTYLE RELAY
1973 United States
1975 West Germany
1978 United States
1982 United States
1986 East Germany
1991 Germany
1994 Sweden

4 × 200-M FREESTYLE RELAY (CONT.)
1998 Australia
2001 Australia
2003 Australia
2005 United States
2007 United States
2009 United States

4 × 100-M MEDLEY RELAY
1973 United States
1975 United States
1978 United States
1982 United States
1986 United States
1991 United States
1994 United States
1998 Australia
2001 Australia
2003 Australia
2005 Australia
2007 Australia
2009 United States

diving

1-M SPRINGBOARD
1991 Edwin Jongejans (NED)
1994 Evan Stewart (ZIM)
1998 Yu Zhuocheng (CHN)
2001 Wang Feng (CHN)
2003 Xu Xiang (CHN)
2005 Alexandre Despatie (CAN)
2007 Luo Yutong (CHN)
2009 Qin Kai (CHN)

3-M SPRINGBOARD
1973 Philip Boggs (USA)
1975 Philip Boggs (USA)
1978 Philip Boggs (USA)

3-M SPRINGBOARD (CONTINUED)
1982 Greg Louganis (USA)
1986 Greg Louganis (USA)
1991 Kent Ferguson (USA)
1994 Yu Zhuocheng (CHN)
1998 Dmitry Sautin (RUS)
2001 Dmitry Sautin (RUS)
2003 Aleksandr Dobrosok (RUS)
2005 Alexandre Despatie (CAN)
2007 Qin Kai (CHN)
2009 He Chong (CHN)

PLATFORM
1973 Klaus Dibiasi (ITA)
1975 Klaus Dibiasi (ITA)
1978 Greg Louganis (USA)
1982 Greg Louganis (USA)
1986 Greg Louganis (USA)
1991 Sun Shuwei (CHN)
1994 Dmitry Sautin (RUS)
1998 Dmitry Sautin (RUS)
2001 Tian Liang (CHN)
2003 Alexandre Despatie (CAN)
2005 Hu Jia (CHN)
2007 Gleb Galperin (RUS)
2009 Thomas Daley (GBR)

World Swimming and Diving Championships—Women
swimming

50-M FREESTYLE
1986 Tamara Costache (ROM)
1991 Zhuang Yong (CHN)
1994 Le Jingyi (CHN)
1998 Amy Van Dyken (USA)
2001 Inge de Bruijn (NED)
2003 Inge de Bruijn (NED)
2005 Lisbeth Lenton (AUS)
2007 Lisbeth Lenton (AUS)
2009 Britta Steffen (GER)

100-M FREESTYLE
1973 Kornelia Ender (GDR)
1975 Kornelia Ender (GDR)
1978 Barbara Krause (GDR)
1982 Birgit Meineke (GDR)
1986 Kristin Otto (GDR)
1991 Nicole Haislett (USA)
1994 Le Jingyi (CHN)
1998 Jenny Thompson (USA)
2001 Inge de Bruijn (NED)
2003 Hanna-Maria Seppälä (FIN)
2005 Jodie Henry (AUS)

100-M FREESTYLE (CONTINUED)
2007 Lisbeth Lenton (AUS)
2009 Britta Steffen (GER)

200-M FREESTYLE
1973 Keena Rothhammer (USA)
1975 Shirley Babashoff (USA)
1978 Cynthia Woodhead (USA)
1982 Annemarie Verstappen (NED)
1986 Heike Friedrich (GDR)
1991 Hayley Lewis (AUS)
1994 Franziska van Almsick (GER)
1998 Claudia Poll (CRC)
2001 Giaan Rooney (AUS)
2003 Alena Popchanka (BLR)
2005 Solenne Figues (FRA)
2007 Laure Manaudou (FRA)
2009 Federica Pellegrini (ITA)

400-M FREESTYLE
1973 Heather Greenwood (USA)
1975 Shirley Babashoff (USA)

400-M FREESTYLE (CONTINUED)
1978 Tracey Wickham (AUS)
1982 Carmela Schmidt (GDR)
1986 Heike Friedrich (GDR)
1991 Janet Evans (USA)
1994 Yang Aihua (CHN)
1998 Chen Yan (CHN)
2001 Yana Klochkova (UKR)
2003 Hannah Stockbauer (GER)
2005 Laure Manaudou (FRA)
2007 Laure Manaudou (FRA)
2009 Federica Pellegrini (ITA)

800-M FREESTYLE
1973 Novella Calligaris (ITA)
1975 Jenny Turrall (AUS)
1978 Tracey Wickham (AUS)
1982 Kim Linehan (USA)
1986 Astrid Strauss (GDR)
1991 Janet Evans (USA)
1994 Janet Evans (USA)
1998 Brooke Bennett (USA)
2001 Hannah Stockbauer (GER)

World Swimming and Diving Championships—Women (continued)
swimming (continued)

800-M FREESTYLE (CONTINUED)
2003   Hannah Stockbauer (GER)
2005   Kate Ziegler (USA)
2007   Kate Ziegler (USA)
2009   Lotte Friis (DEN)

1,500-M FREESTYLE
2001   Hannah Stockbauer (GER)
2003   Hannah Stockbauer (GER)
2005   Kate Ziegler (USA)
2007   Kate Ziegler (USA)
2009   Alessia Filippi (ITA)

50-M BREASTSTROKE
2001   Luo Xuejuan (CHN)
2003   Luo Xuejuan (CHN)
2005   Jade Edmistone (AUS)
2007   Jessica Hardy (USA)
2009   Yuliya Yefimova (RUS)

100-M BREASTSTROKE
1973   Renate Vogel (GDR)
1975   Hannelore Anke (GDR)
1978   Yuliya Bogdanova (URS)
1982   Ute Geweniger (GDR)
1986   Sylvia Gerasch (GDR)
1991   Linley Frame (AUS)
1994   Samantha Riley (AUS)
1998   Kristy Kowal (USA)
2001   Luo Xuejuan (CHN)
2003   Luo Xuejuan (CHN)
2005   Leisel Jones (AUS)
2007   Leisel Jones (AUS)
2009   Rebecca Soni (USA)

200-M BREASTSTROKE
1973   Renate Vogel (GDR)
1975   Hannelore Anke (GDR)
1978   Lina Kachushite (URS)
1982   Svetlana Varganova (URS)
1986   Silke Hörner (GDR)
1991   Yelena Volkova (URS)
1994   Samantha Riley (AUS)
1998   Agnes Kovacs (HUN)
2001   Agnes Kovacs (HUN)
2003   Amanda Beard (USA)
2005   Leisel Jones (AUS)
2007   Leisel Jones (AUS)
2009   Nadja Higl (SRB)

50-M BUTTERFLY
2001   Inge de Bruijn (NED)
2003   Inge de Bruijn (NED)
2005   Danni Miatke (AUS)
2007   Therese Alshammar (SWE)
2009   Marieke Guehrer (AUS)

100-M BUTTERFLY
1973   Kornelia Ender (GDR)
1975   Kornelia Ender (GDR)
1978   Joan Pennington (USA)
1982   Mary Meagher (USA)
1986   Kornelia Gressler (GDR)
1991   Qian Hong (CHN)
1994   Liu Limin (CHN)

100-M BUTTERFLY (CONTINUED)
1998   Jenny Thompson (USA)
2001   Petria Thomas (AUS)
2003   Jenny Thompson (USA)
2005   Jessicah Schipper (AUS)
2007   Lisbeth Lenton (AUS)
2009   Sarah Sjöström (SWE)

200-M BUTTERFLY
1973   Rosemarie Kother (GDR)
1975   Rosemarie Kother (GDR)
1978   Tracy Caulkins (USA)
1982   Ines Geissler (GDR)
1986   Mary T. Meagher (USA)
1991   Summer Sanders (USA)
1994   Liu Limin (CHN)
1998   Susie O'Neill (AUS)
2001   Petria Thomas (AUS)
2003   Otylia Jedrzejczak (POL)
2005   Otylia Jedrzejczak (POL)
2007   Jessicah Schipper (AUS)
2009   Jessicah Schipper (AUS)

50-M BACKSTROKE
2001   Haley Cope (USA)
2003   Nina Zhivanevskaya (ESP)
2005   Giaan Rooney (AUS)
2007   Leila Vaziri (USA)
2009   Zhao Jing (CHN)

100-M BACKSTROKE
1973   Ulrike Richter (GDR)
1975   Ulrike Richter (GDR)
1978   Linda Jezek (USA)
1982   Kristin Otto (GDR)
1986   Betsy Mitchell (USA)
1991   Krisztina Egerszegi (HUN)
1994   He Cihong (CHN)
1998   Lea Maurer (USA)
2001   Natalie Coughlin (USA)
2003   Antje Buschschulte (GER)
2005   Kirsty Coventry (ZIM)
2007   Natalie Coughlin (USA)
2009   Gemma Spofforth (GBR)

200-M BACKSTROKE
1973   Melissa Belote (USA)
1975   Birgit Treiber (GDR)
1978   Linda Jezek (USA)
1982   Cornelia Sirch (GDR)
1986   Cornelia Sirch (GDR)
1991   Krisztina Egerszegi (HUN)
1994   He Cihong (CHN)
1998   Roxana Maracineanu (FRA)
2001   Diana Mocanu (ROM)
2003   Katy Sexton (GBR)
2005   Kirsty Coventry (ZIM)
2007   Margaret Hoelzer (USA)
2009   Kirsty Coventry (ZIM)

200-M INDIVIDUAL MEDLEY
1973   Andrea Hubner (GDR)
1975   Kathy Heddy (USA)
1978   Tracy Caulkins (USA)
1982   Petra Schneider (GDR)
1986   Kristin Otto (GDR)

200-M INDIVIDUAL MEDLEY (CONT.)
1991   Lin Li (CHN)
1994   Lu Bin (CHN)
1998   Wu Yanyan (CHN)
2001   Martha Bowen (USA)
2003   Yana Klochkova (UKR)
2005   Katie Hoff (USA)
2007   Katie Hoff (USA)
2009   Ariana Kukors (USA)

400-M INDIVIDUAL MEDLEY
1973   Gudrun Wegner (GDR)
1975   Ulrike Tauber (GDR)
1978   Tracy Caulkins (USA)
1982   Petra Schneider (GDR)
1986   Kathleen Nord (GDR)
1991   Lin Li (CHN)
1994   Dai Guohong (CHN)
1998   Chen Yan (CHN)
2001   Yana Klochkova (UKR)
2003   Yana Klochkova (UKR)
2005   Katie Hoff (USA)
2007   Katie Hoff (USA)
2009   Katinka Hosszú (HUN)

4 × 100-M FREESTYLE RELAY
1973   East Germany
1975   East Germany
1978   United States
1982   East Germany
1986   East Germany
1991   United States
1994   China
1998   United States
2001   Germany
2003   United States
2005   Australia
2007   Australia
2009   The Netherlands

4 × 200-M FREESTYLE RELAY
1986   East Germany
1991   Germany
1994   China
1998   Germany
2001   Great Britain
2003   United States
2005   United States
2007   United States
2009   China

4 × 100-M MEDLEY RELAY
1973   East Germany
1975   East Germany
1978   United States
1982   East Germany
1986   East Germany
1991   United States
1994   China
1998   United States
2001   Australia
2003   China
2005   Australia
2007   Australia
2009   China

World Swimming and Diving Championships—Women (continued)
diving

1-M SPRINGBOARD
1991	Gao Min (CHN)
1994	Chen Lixia (CHN)
1998	Irina Lashko (RUS)
2001	Blythe Hartley (CAN)
2003	Irina Lashko (AUS)
2005	Blythe Hartley (CAN)
2007	He Zi (CHN)
2009	Yuliya Pakhalina (RUS)

3-M SPRINGBOARD
1973	Christa Kohler (GDR)
1975	Irina Kalinina (URS)
1978	Irina Kalinina (URS)
1982	Megan Neyer (USA)

3-M SPRINGBOARD (CONT.)
1986	Gao Min (CHN)
1991	Gao Min (CHN)
1994	Tan Shuping (CHN)
1998	Yuliya Pakhalina (RUS)
2001	Guo Jingjing (CHN)
2003	Guo Jingjing (CHN)
2005	Guo Jingjing (CHN)
2007	Guo Jingjing (CHN)
2009	Guo Jingjing (CHN)

PLATFORM
1973	Ulrika Knape (SWE)
1975	Janet Ely (USA)
1978	Irina Kalinina (URS)

PLATFORM (CONT.)
1982	Wendy Wyland (USA)
1986	Chen Lin (CHN)
1991	Fu Mingxia (CHN)
1994	Fu Mingxia (CHN)
1998	Olena Zhupina (UKR)
2001	Xu Mian (CHN)
2003	Emilie Heymans (CAN)
2005	Laura Wilkinson (USA)
2007	Wang Xin (CHN)
2009	Paola Espinosa (MEX)

Swimming World Records—Long Course (50 m)
Some records are awaiting FINA ratification as of 25 Aug 2010.

Men

EVENT	RECORD HOLDER (COUNTRY)	PERFORMANCE	DATE
50-m freestyle	César Cielo Filho (BRA)	20.91 sec	18 Dec 2009
100-m freestyle	César Cielo Filho (BRA)	46.91 sec	30 Jul 2009
200-m freestyle	Paul Biedermann (GER)	1 min 42.00 sec	28 Jul 2009
400-m freestyle	Paul Biedermann (GER)	3 min 40.07 sec	26 Jul 2009
800-m freestyle	Zhang Lin (CHN)	7 min 32.12 sec	29 Jul 2009
1,500-m freestyle	Grant Hackett (AUS)	14 min 34.56 sec	29 Jul 2001
50-m backstroke	Liam Tancock (GBR)	24.04 sec	2 Aug 2009
100-m backstroke	Aaron Peirsol (USA)	51.94 sec	8 Jul 2009
200-m backstroke	Aaron Peirsol (USA)	1 min 51.92 sec	31 Jul 2009
50-m breaststroke	Cameron van der Burgh (RSA)	26.67 sec	29 Jul 2009
100-m breaststroke	Brenton Rickard (AUS)	58.58 sec	27 Jul 2009
200-m breaststroke	Christian Sprenger (AUS)	2 min 07.31 sec	30 Jul 2009
50-m butterfly	Rafael Muñoz (ESP)	22.43 sec	5 Apr 2009
100-m butterfly	Michael Phelps (USA)	49.82 sec	1 Aug 2009
200-m butterfly	Michael Phelps (USA)	1 min 51.51 sec	29 Jul 2009
200-m individual medley	Ryan Lochte (USA)	1 min 54.10 sec	30 Jul 2009
400-m individual medley	Michael Phelps (USA)	4 min 03.84 sec	10 Aug 2008
4 × 100-m freestyle relay	United States (Michael Phelps, Garrett Weber-Gale, Cullen Jones, Jason Lezak)	3 min 08.24 sec	11 Aug 2008
4 × 200-m freestyle relay	United States (Michael Phelps, Ricky Berens, David Walters, Ryan Lochte)	6 min 58.55 sec	31 Jul 2009
4 × 100-m medley relay	United States (Aaron Peirsol, Eric Shanteau, Michael Phelps, David Walters)	3 min 27.28 sec	2 Aug 2009

Women

EVENT	RECORD HOLDER (COUNTRY)	PERFORMANCE	DATE
50-m freestyle	Britta Steffen (GER)	23.73 sec	2 Aug 2009
100-m freestyle	Britta Steffen (GER)	52.07 sec	31 Jul 2009
200-m freestyle	Federica Pellegrini (ITA)	1 min 52.98 sec	29 Jul 2009
400-m freestyle	Federica Pellegrini (ITA)	3 min 59.15 sec	26 Jul 2009
800-m freestyle	Rebecca Adlington (GBR)	8 min 14.10 sec	16 Aug 2008
1,500-m freestyle	Kate Ziegler (USA)	15 min 42.54 sec	17 Jun 2007
50-m backstroke	Zhao Jing (CHN)	27.06 sec	30 Jul 2009
100-m backstroke	Gemma Spofforth (GBR)	58.12 sec	28 Jul 2009
200-m backstroke	Kirsty Coventry (ZIM)	2 min 04.81 sec	1 Aug 2009
50-m breaststroke	Jessica Hardy (USA)	29.80 sec	7 Aug 2009
100-m breaststroke	Jessica Hardy (USA)	1 min 04.45 sec	7 Aug 2009
200-m breaststroke	Annamay Pierse (CAN)	2 min 20.12 sec	30 Jul 2009
50-m butterfly	Therese Alshammar (SWE)	25.07 sec	31 Jul 2009
100-m butterfly	Sarah Sjöström (SWE)	56.06 sec	27 Jul 2009
200-m butterfly	Zige Liu (CHN)	2 min 01.81 sec	21 Oct 2009
200-m individual medley	Ariana Kukors (USA)	2 min 06.15 sec	27 Jul 2009
400-m individual medley	Stephanie Rice (AUS)	4 min 29.45 sec	10 Aug 2008
4 × 100-m freestyle relay	Netherlands (Inge Dekker, Ranomi Kromowidjojo, Femke Heemskerk, Marleen Veldhuis)	3 min 31.72 sec	26 Jul 2009

Swimming World Records—Long Course (50 m) (continued)

Women (continued)

EVENT	RECORD HOLDER (COUNTRY)	PERFORMANCE	DATE
4 × 200-m freestyle relay	China (Yang Yu, Zhu Qian Wei, Liu Jing, Pang Jiaying)	7 min 42.08 sec	30 Jul 2009
4 × 100-m medley relay	China (Zhao Jing, Chen Huijia, Jiao Liuyang, Li Zhesi)	3 min 52.19 sec	1 Aug 2009

Swimming World Records—Short Course (25 m)

Some records are awaiting FINA ratification as of 25 Aug 2010.

Men

EVENT	RECORD HOLDER (COUNTRY)	PERFORMANCE	DATE
50-m freestyle	Roland Schoeman (RSA)	20.30 sec	8 Aug 2009
100-m freestyle	Amaury Leveaux (FRA)	44.94 sec	13 Dec 2008
200-m freestyle	Paul Biedermann (GER)	1 min 39.37 sec	15 Nov 2009
400-m freestyle	Paul Biedermann (GER)	3 min 32.77 sec	14 Nov 2009
800-m freestyle	Grant Hackett (AUS)	7 min 23.42 sec	20 Jul 2008
1,500-m freestyle	Grant Hackett (AUS)	14 min 10.10 sec	7 Aug 2001
50-m backstroke	Peter Marshall (USA)	22.61 sec	22 Nov 2009
100-m backstroke	Nick Thoman (USA)	48.94 sec	18 Dec 2009
200-m backstroke	Arkady Vyatchanin (RUS)	1 min 46.11 sec	15 Nov 2009
50-m breaststroke	Cameron van der Burgh (RSA)	25.25 sec	14 Nov 2009
100-m breaststroke	Cameron van der Burgh (RSA)	55.61 sec	15 Nov 2009
200-m breaststroke	Daniel Gyurta (HUN)	2 min 00.67 sec	13 Dec 2009
50-m butterfly	Steffen Deibler (GER)	21.80 sec	14 Nov 2009
100-m butterfly	Evgeny Korotyshkin (RUS)	48.48 sec	15 Nov 2009
200-m butterfly	Kaio Almeida (BRA)	1 min 49.11 sec	10 Nov 2009
100-m individual medley	Peter Mankoc (SLO)	50.76 sec	12 Dec 2009
200-m individual medley	Darian Townsend (RSA)	1 min 51.55 sec	15 Nov 2009
400-m individual medley	László Cseh (HUN)	3 min 57.27 sec	11 Dec 2009
4 × 100-m freestyle relay	United States (Nathan Adrian, Matt Grevers, Garrett Weber-Gale, Michael Phelps)	3 min 03.30 sec	19 Dec 2009
4 × 200-m freestyle relay	Canada (Colin Russell, Stefan Hirniak, Brent Hayden, Joel Greenshields)	6 min 51.05 sec	7 Aug 2009
4 × 100-m medley relay	Russia (Stanislav Donets, Sergei Geibel, Evgeny Korotyshkin, Danila Izotov)	3 min 19.16 sec	20 Dec 2009

Women

EVENT	RECORD HOLDER (COUNTRY)	PERFORMANCE	DATE
50-m freestyle	Marleen Veldhuis (NED)	23.25 sec	13 Apr 2008
100-m freestyle	Lisbeth Trickett (AUS)	51.01 sec	10 Aug 2009
200-m freestyle	Federica Pellegrini (ITA)	1 min 51.17 sec	13 Dec 2009
400-m freestyle	Joanne Jackson (GBR)	3 min 54.92 sec	8 Aug 2009
800-m freestyle	Alessia Filippi (ITA)	8 min 04.53 sec	12 Dec 2008
1,500-m freestyle	Lotte Friis (DEN)	15 min 28.65 sec	28 Nov 2009
50-m backstroke	Sanja Jovanovic (CRO)	25.70 sec	12 Dec 2009
100-m backstroke	Shiho Sakai (JPN)	55.23 sec	15 Nov 2009
200-m backstroke	Shiho Sakai (JPN)	2 min 00.18 sec	14 Nov 2009
50-m breaststroke	Jessica Hardy (USA)	28.80 sec	15 Nov 2009
100-m breaststroke	Rebecca Soni (USA)	1 min 02.70 sec	19 Dec 2009
200-m breaststroke	Rebecca Soni (USA)	2 min 14.57 sec	18 Dec 2009
50-m butterfly	Therese Alshammar (SWE)	24.38 sec	22 Nov 2009
100-m butterfly	Diane Bui-Duyet (FRA)	55.05 sec	12 Dec 2009
200-m butterfly	Zige Liu (CHN)	2 min 00.78 sec	15 Nov 2009
100-m individual medley	Hinkelien Schreuder (NED)	57.74 sec	15 Nov 2009
200-m individual medley	Julia Smit (USA)	2 min 04.60 sec	19 Dec 2009
400-m individual medley	Julia Smit (USA)	4 min 21.04 sec	18 Dec 2009
4 × 100-m freestyle relay	Netherlands (Hinkelien Schreuder, Ranomi Kromowidjojo, Inge Dekker, Marleen Veldhuis)	3 min 28.22 sec	19 Dec 2008
4 × 200-m freestyle relay	Netherlands (Inge Dekker, Femke Heemskerk, Marleen Veldhuis, Ranomi Kromowidjojo)	7 min 38.90 sec	9 Apr 2008
4 × 100-m medley relay	United States (Margaret Hoelzer, Jessica Hardy, Dana Vollmer, Amanda Weir)	3 min 47.97 sec	18 Dec 2009

Tennis

Four events dominate world championship tennis. The first of the traditional "Big Four," or "Grand Slam," events was the All-England Lawn Tennis Championships (better known as the Wimbledon Championships), founded in 1877. Its only event the first year was the men's singles championships; women first competed in 1884. Major tennis tournaments also sprang up in the United States (1881 for men; women's singles competition first officially added 1889), France (1891 for men; women's singles competition added 1897), and Australia (1905 for men; women's singles competition added 1922). Open tennis (open, that is, to both professionals and amateurs) became the rule in the Big Four tournaments in 1968. International team tennis was organized in 1900 with the institution of the Davis Cup. Men's teams competing for the Davis Cup play four singles matches and one doubles match in elimination rounds. The Wightman Cup was contested yearly between British and American women's teams from 1923 to 1989. The International Tennis Federation (ITF, formerly the International Lawn Tennis Federation; founded 1913) established the Federation Cup in 1963 (called the Fed Cup since 1994) for international women's team competition. It is decided by elimination rounds of two singles and one doubles contest.

Related Web sites: International Tennis Federation: <www.itftennis.com>; ATP (formerly Association of Tennis Professionals): <www.atpworldtour.com>; Women's Tennis Association: <www.wtatour.com>.

Australian Open Tennis Championships—Singles

YEAR	MEN	WOMEN
1905	Rodney Heath (AUS)	
1906	Tony Wilding (NZL)	
1907	Horace Rice (AUS)	
1908	Fred Alexander (USA)	
1909	Tony Wilding (NZL)	
1910	Rodney Heath (AUS)	
1911	Norman Brookes (AUS)	
1912	J. Cecil Parke (GBR)	
1913	E.F. Parker (AUS)	
1914	Pat O'Hara Wood (AUS)	
1915	Francis Lowe (GBR)	
1916–18	*not held*	
1919	A.R.F. Kingscote (GBR)	
1920	Pat O'Hara Wood (AUS)	
1921	Rhys Gemmell (AUS)	
1922	James Anderson (AUS)	Margaret Molesworth (AUS)
1923	Pat O'Hara Wood (AUS)	Margaret Molesworth (AUS)
1924	James Anderson (AUS)	Sylvia Lance (AUS)
1925	James Anderson (AUS)	Daphne Akhurst (AUS)
1926	John Hawkes (AUS)	Daphne Akhurst (AUS)
1927	Gerald Patterson (AUS)	Esna Boyd (AUS)
1928	Jean Borotra (FRA)	Daphne Akhurst (AUS)
1929	John Gregory (GBR)	Daphne Akhurst (AUS)
1930	Gar Moon (AUS)	Daphne Akhurst (AUS)
1931	Jack Crawford (AUS)	Coral Buttsworth (AUS)
1932	Jack Crawford (AUS)	Coral Buttsworth (AUS)
1933	Jack Crawford (AUS)	Joan Hartigan (AUS)
1934	Fred Perry (GBR)	Joan Hartigan (AUS)
1935	Jack Crawford (AUS)	Dorothy Round (GBR)
1936	Adrian Quist (AUS)	Joan Hartigan (AUS)
1937	Vivian McGrath (AUS)	Nancye Wynne (AUS)
1938	Don Budge (USA)	Dorothy Bundy (USA)
1939	John Bromwich (AUS)	Emily Westacott (AUS)
1940	Adrian Quist (AUS)	Nancye Wynne (AUS)
1941–45	*not held*	
1946	John Bromwich (AUS)	Nancye Wynne Bolton (AUS)
1947	Dinny Pails (AUS)	Nancye Wynne Bolton (AUS)
1948	Adrian Quist (AUS)	Nancye Wynne Bolton (AUS)
1949	Frank Sedgman (AUS)	Doris Hart (USA)
1950	Frank Sedgman (AUS)	Louise Brough (USA)
1951	Dick Savitt (USA)	Nancye Wynne Bolton (AUS)
1952	Ken McGregor (AUS)	Thelma Long (AUS)
1953	Ken Rosewall (AUS)	Maureen Connolly (USA)
1954	Mervyn Rose (AUS)	Thelma Long (AUS)
1955	Ken Rosewall (AUS)	Beryl Penrose (AUS)
1956	Lew Hoad (AUS)	Mary Carter (AUS)
1957	Ashley Cooper (AUS)	Shirley Fry (USA)
1958	Ashley Cooper (AUS)	Angela Mortimer (GBR)
1959	Alex Olmedo (PER)	Mary Carter-Reitano (AUS)

Australian Open Tennis Championships—Singles (continued)

YEAR	MEN	WOMEN
1960	Rod Laver (AUS)	Margaret Smith (AUS)
1961	Roy Emerson (AUS)	Margaret Smith (AUS)
1962	Rod Laver (AUS)	Margaret Smith (AUS)
1963	Roy Emerson (AUS)	Margaret Smith (AUS)
1964	Roy Emerson (AUS)	Margaret Smith (AUS)
1965	Roy Emerson (AUS)	Margaret Smith (AUS)
1966	Roy Emerson (AUS)	Margaret Smith (AUS)
1967	Roy Emerson (AUS)	Nancy Richey (USA)
1968	Bill Bowrey (AUS)	Billie Jean King (USA)
1969	Rod Laver (AUS)	Margaret Smith Court (AUS)
1970	Arthur Ashe (USA)	Margaret Smith Court (AUS)
1971	Ken Rosewall (AUS)	Margaret Smith Court (AUS)
1972	Ken Rosewall (AUS)	Virginia Wade (GBR)
1973	John Newcombe (AUS)	Margaret Smith Court (AUS)
1974	Jimmy Connors (USA)	Evonne Goolagong (AUS)
1975	John Newcombe (AUS)	Evonne Goolagong (AUS)
1976	Mark Edmondson (AUS)	Evonne Goolagong Cawley (AUS)
1977[1]	Roscoe Tanner (USA)	Kerry Reid (AUS)
1977[1]	Vitas Gerulaitis (USA)	Evonne Goolagong Cawley (AUS)
1978[2]	Guillermo Vilas (ARG)	Chris O'Neill (AUS)
1979[2]	Guillermo Vilas (ARG)	Barbara Jordan (USA)
1980[2]	Brian Teacher (USA)	Hana Mandlikova (TCH)
1981[2]	Johan Kriek (RSA)	Martina Navratilova (USA)
1982[2]	Johan Kriek (RSA)	Chris Evert Lloyd (USA)
1983[2]	Mats Wilander (SWE)	Martina Navratilova (USA)
1984[2]	Mats Wilander (SWE)	Chris Evert Lloyd (USA)
1985[2]	Stefan Edberg (SWE)	Martina Navratilova (USA)
1986	*not held*	
1987	Stefan Edberg (SWE)	Hana Mandlikova (TCH)
1988	Mats Wilander (SWE)	Steffi Graf (FRG)
1989	Ivan Lendl (TCH)	Steffi Graf (FRG)
1990	Ivan Lendl (TCH)	Steffi Graf (FRG)
1991	Boris Becker (GER)	Monica Seles (YUG)
1992	Jim Courier (USA)	Monica Seles (YUG)
1993	Jim Courier (USA)	Monica Seles (YUG)
1994	Pete Sampras (USA)	Steffi Graf (GER)
1995	Andre Agassi (USA)	Mary Pierce (FRA)
1996	Boris Becker (GER)	Monica Seles (USA)
1997	Pete Sampras (USA)	Martina Hingis (SUI)
1998	Petr Korda (CZE)	Martina Hingis (SUI)
1999	Yevgeny Kafelnikov (RUS)	Martina Hingis (SUI)
2000	Andre Agassi (USA)	Lindsay Davenport (USA)
2001	Andre Agassi (USA)	Jennifer Capriati (USA)
2002	Thomas Johansson (SWE)	Jennifer Capriati (USA)
2003	Andre Agassi (USA)	Serena Williams (USA)
2004	Roger Federer (SUI)	Justine Henin-Hardenne (BEL)
2005	Marat Safin (RUS)	Serena Williams (USA)
2006	Roger Federer (SUI)	Amélie Mauresmo (FRA)
2007	Roger Federer (SUI)	Serena Williams (USA)
2008	Novak Djokovic (SER)	Mariya Sharapova (RUS)
2009	Rafael Nadal (ESP)	Serena Williams (USA)
2010	Roger Federer (SUI)	Serena Williams (USA)

[1]*Tournament held in January and December.*   [2]*Tournament held in December rather than January.*

Australian Open Tennis Championships—Doubles

YEAR	MEN	WOMEN
1905	Tom Tachell, Randolph Lycett	
1906	Tony Wilding, Rodney Heath	
1907	Harry Parker, William Gregg	
1908	Fred Alexander, Alfred Dunlop	
1909	Ernie F. Parker, J.P. Keane	
1910	Horace Rice, Ashley Campbell	
1911	Rodney Heath, Randolph Lycett	
1912	J. Cecil Parke, Charles Dixon	
1913	Ernie F. Parker, Alf Hedemann	
1914	Ashley Campbell, Gerald Patterson	

Australian Open Tennis Championships—Doubles (continued)

YEAR	MEN	WOMEN
1915	Horace Rice, Clarrie Todd	
1916-18	*not held*	
1919	Pat O'Hara Wood, Ron Thomas	
1920	Pat O'Hara Wood, Ron Thomas	
1921	S.H. Eaton-Rice, Rhys Gemmell	
1922	Gerald Patterson, John Hawkes	Esne Boyd, Marjorie Mountain
1923	Pat O'Hara Wood, Bert St. John	Esne Boyd, Sylvia Lance
1924	Norman Brookes, James Anderson	Daphne Akhurst, Sylvia Lance
1925	Gerald Patterson, Pat O'Hara Wood	Daphne Akhurst, Sylvia Lance Harper
1926	Gerald Patterson, John Hawkes	Meryl O'Hara Wood, Esne Boyd
1927	Gerald Patterson, John Hawkes	Meryl O'Hara Wood, Louise Bickerton
1928	Jean Borotra, Jacques Brugnon	Daphne Akhurst, Esne Boyd
1929	Jack Crawford, Harry Hopman	Daphne Akhurst, Louise Bickerton
1930	Jack Crawford, Harry Hopman	Margaret Molesworth, Emily Hood
1931	Charles Donohoe, Ray Dunlop	Daphne Akhurst Cozens, Louise Bickerton
1932	Jack Crawford, Gar Moon	Coral Buttsworth, Marjorie Cox Crawford
1933	Ellsworth Vines, Keith Gledhill	Margaret Molesworth, Emily Hood Westacott
1934	Fred Perry, George Hughes	Margaret Molesworth, Emily Hood Westacott
1935	Jack Crawford, Vivian McGrath	Evelyn Dearman, Nancy Lyle
1936	Adrian Quist, D.P. Turnbull	Thelma Coyne, Nancye Wynne
1937	Adrian Quist, D.P. Turnbull	Thelma Coyne, Nancye Wynne
1938	Adrian Quist, John Bromwich	Thelma Coyne, Nancye Wynne
1939	Adrian Quist, John Bromwich	Thelma Coyne, Nancye Wynne
1940	Adrian Quist, John Bromwich	Thelma Coyne, Nancye Wynne
1941-45	*not held*	
1946	Adrian Quist, John Bromwich	Joyce Fitch, Mary Bevis
1947	Adrian Quist, John Bromwich	Thelma Coyne Long, Nancye Wynne Bolton
1948	Adrian Quist, John Bromwich	Thelma Coyne Long, Nancye Wynne Bolton
1949	Adrian Quist, John Bromwich	Thelma Coyne Long, Nancye Wynne Bolton
1950	Adrian Quist, John Bromwich	Louise Brough, Doris Hart
1951	Ken McGregor, Frank Sedgman	Thelma Coyne Long, Nancye Wynne Bolton
1952	Ken McGregor, Frank Sedgman	Thelma Coyne Long, Nancye Wynne Bolton
1953	Lew Hoad, Ken Rosewall	Maureen Connolly, Julia Sampson
1954	Rex Hartwig, Mervyn Rose	Mary Bevis Hawton, Beryl Penrose
1955	Vic Seixas, Tony Trabert	Mary Bevis Hawton, Beryl Penrose
1956	Lew Hoad, Ken Rosewall	Mary Bevis Hawton, Thelma Coyne Long
1957	Lew Hoad, Neale Fraser	Althea Gibson, Shirley Fry
1958	Ashley Cooper, Neale Fraser	Mary Bevis Hawton, Thelma Coyne Long
1959	Rod Laver, Robert Mark	Sandra Reynolds, Renee Schuurman
1960	Rod Laver, Robert Mark	Maria Bueno, Christine Truman
1961	Rod Laver, Robert Mark	Mary Reitano, Margaret Smith
1962	Roy Emerson, Neale Fraser	Robyn Ebbern, Margaret Smith
1963	Bob Hewitt, Fred Stolle	Robyn Ebbern, Margaret Smith
1964	Bob Hewitt, Fred Stolle	Judy Tegart, Lesley Turner
1965	John Newcombe, Tony Roche	Margaret Smith, Lesley Turner
1966	Roy Emerson, Fred Stolle	Carole Graebner, Nancy Richey
1967	John Newcombe, Tony Roche	Judy Tegart, Lesley Turner
1968	Dick Crealy, Allan Stone	Karen Krantzcke, Karrie Melville
1969	Roy Emerson, Rod Laver	Margaret Smith Court, Judy Tegart
1970	Bob Lutz, Stan Smith	Margaret Smith Court, Judy Tegart Dalton
1971	John Newcombe, Tony Roche	Margaret Smith Court, Evonne Goolagong
1972	Owen Davidson, Ken Rosewall	Kerry Harris, Helen Gourlay
1973	Mal Anderson, John Newcombe	Margaret Smith Court, Virginia Wade
1974	Ross Case, Geoff Masters	Evonne Goolagong, Peggy Michel
1975	John Alexander, Phil Dent	Evonne Goolagong, Peggy Michel
1976	John Newcombe, Tony Roche	Evonne Goolagong Cawley, Helen Gourlay
1977[1]	Arthur Ashe, Tony Roche	Dianne Fromholtz, Helen Gourlay
1977[1]	Allan Stone, Ray Ruffels	Evonne Goolagong Cawley, Helen Gourlay Cawley; Mona Guerrant, Kerry Reid[2]
1978[3]	Wojtek Fibak, Kim Warwick	Renata Tomanova, Betsy Nagelsen
1979[3]	Peter McNamara, Paul McNamee	Judy Chaloner, Dianne Evers
1980[3]	Kim Warwick, Mark Edmondson	Martina Navratilova, Betsy Nagelsen
1981[3]	Kim Warwick, Mark Edmondson	Kathy Jordan, Anne Smith
1982[3]	John Alexander, John Fitzgerald	Martina Navratilova, Pam Shriver
1983[3]	Mark Edmondson, Paul McNamee	Martina Navratilova, Pam Shriver
1984[3]	Mark Edmondson, Sherwood Stewart	Martina Navratilova, Pam Shriver
1985[3]	Paul Annacone, Christo van Rensburg	Martina Navratilova, Pam Shriver
1986	*not held*	

Australian Open Tennis Championships—Doubles (continued)

YEAR	MEN	WOMEN
1987	Stefan Edberg, Anders Järryd	Martina Navratilova, Pam Shriver
1988	Rick Leach, Jim Pugh	Martina Navratilova, Pam Shriver
1989	Rick Leach, Jim Pugh	Martina Navratilova, Pam Shriver
1990	Pieter Aldrich, Danie Visser	Jana Novotna, Helena Sukova
1991	Scott Davis, David Pate	Patty Fendick, Mary Joe Fernández
1992	Todd Woodbridge, Mark Woodforde	Arantxa Sánchez Vicario, Helena Sukova
1993	Danie Visser, Laurie Warder	Gigi Fernández, Natasha Zvereva
1994	Jacco Eltingh, Paul Haarhuis	Gigi Fernández, Natasha Zvereva
1995	Jared Palmer, Richey Reneberg	Arantxa Sánchez Vicario, Jana Novotna
1996	Stefan Edberg, Petr Korda	Arantxa Sánchez Vicario, Chanda Rubin
1997	Todd Woodbridge, Mark Woodforde	Martina Hingis, Natasha Zvereva
1998	Jonas Björkman, Jacco Eltingh	Martina Hingis, Mirjana Lucic
1999	Jonas Björkman, Patrick Rafter	Martina Hingis, Anna Kournikova
2000	Ellis Ferreira, Rick Leach	Lisa Raymond, Rennae Stubbs
2001	Jonas Björkman, Todd Woodbridge	Venus Williams, Serena Williams
2002	Mark Knowles, Daniel Nestor	Martina Hingis, Anna Kournikova
2003	Michaël Llodra, Fabrice Santoro	Venus Williams, Serena Williams
2004	Michaël Llodra, Fabrice Santoro	Virginia Ruano Pascual, Paola Suárez
2005	Wayne Black, Kevin Ullyett	Alicia Molik, Svetlana Kuznetsova
2006	Bob Bryan, Mike Bryan	Yan Zi, Zheng Jie
2007	Bob Bryan, Mike Bryan	Cara Black, Liezel Huber
2008	Jonathan Erlich, Andy Ram	Alona Bondarenko, Kateryna Bondarenko
2009	Bob Bryan, Mike Bryan	Venus Williams, Serena Williams
2010	Bob Bryan, Mike Bryan	Venus Williams, Serena Williams

[1]Tournament held in January and December.   [2]Tie; finals rained out.   [3]Tournament held in December rather than January.

French Open Tennis Championships—Singles

From 1891 to 1924, only members of French tennis clubs were eligible to play in the French Championships. The table shows the winners only since 1925, when the tournament was opened to international competition.

YEAR	MEN	WOMEN
1925	René Lacoste (FRA)	Suzanne Lenglen (FRA)
1926	Henri Cochet (FRA)	Suzanne Lenglen (FRA)
1927	René Lacoste (FRA)	Kornelia Bouman (NED)
1928	Henri Cochet (FRA)	Helen Wills (USA)
1929	René Lacoste (FRA)	Helen Wills (USA)
1930	Henri Cochet (FRA)	Helen Wills Moody (USA)
1931	Jean Borotra (FRA)	Cilly Aussem (GER)
1932	Henri Cochet (FRA)	Helen Wills Moody (USA)
1933	John Crawford (AUS)	Margaret Scriven (GBR)
1934	Gottfried von Cramm (GER)	Margaret Scriven (GBR)
1935	Fred Perry (GBR)	Hilde Sperling (DEN)
1936	Gottfried von Cramm (GER)	Hilde Sperling (DEN)
1937	Henner Henkel (GER)	Hilde Sperling (DEN)
1938	Don Budge (USA)	Simone Mathieu (FRA)
1939	Don McNeill (USA)	Simone Mathieu (FRA)
1940	*not held*	*not held*
1941	Bernard Destremau (FRA)	*not held*
1942	Bernard Destremau (FRA)	*not held*
1943	Yvon Petra (FRA)	*not held*
1944	Yvon Petra (FRA)	*not held*
1945	Yvon Petra (FRA)	*not held*
1946	Marcel Bernard (FRA)	Margaret Osborne (USA)
1947	Joseph Asboth (HUN)	Patricia Todd (USA)
1948	Frank Parker (USA)	Nelly Landry (BEL)
1949	Frank Parker (USA)	Margaret Osborne duPont (USA)
1950	Budge Patty (USA)	Doris Hart (USA)
1951	Jaroslav Drobny (TCH)	Shirley Fry (USA)
1952	Jaroslav Drobny (TCH)	Doris Hart (USA)
1953	Ken Rosewall (AUS)	Maureen Connolly (USA)
1954	Tony Trabert (USA)	Maureen Connolly (USA)
1955	Tony Trabert (USA)	Angela Mortimer (GBR)
1956	Lew Hoad (AUS)	Althea Gibson (USA)
1957	Sven Davidson (SWE)	Shirley Bloomer (GBR)

French Open Tennis Championships—Singles (continued)

YEAR	MEN	WOMEN
1958	Mervyn Rose (AUS)	Zsuzsi Kormoczi (HUN)
1959	Nicola Pietrangeli (ITA)	Christine Truman (GBR)
1960	Nicola Pietrangeli (ITA)	Darlene Hard (USA)
1961	Manuel Santana (ESP)	Ann Haydon (GBR)
1962	Rod Laver (AUS)	Margaret Smith (AUS)
1963	Roy Emerson (AUS)	Lesley Turner (AUS)
1964	Manuel Santana (ESP)	Margaret Smith (AUS)
1965	Fred Stolle (AUS)	Lesley Turner (AUS)
1966	Tony Roche (AUS)	Ann Haydon Jones (GBR)
1967	Roy Emerson (AUS)	Françoise Durr (FRA)
1968	Ken Rosewall (AUS)	Nancy Richey (USA)
1969	Rod Laver (AUS)	Margaret Smith Court (AUS)
1970	Jan Kodes (TCH)	Margaret Smith Court (AUS)
1971	Jan Kodes (TCH)	Evonne Goolagong (AUS)
1972	Andres Gimeno (ESP)	Billie Jean King (USA)
1973	Ilie Nastase (ROM)	Margaret Smith Court (AUS)
1974	Björn Borg (SWE)	Chris Evert (USA)
1975	Björn Borg (SWE)	Chris Evert (USA)
1976	Adriano Panatta (ITA)	Sue Barker (USA)
1977	Guillermo Vilas (ARG)	Mima Jausovec (YUG)
1978	Björn Borg (SWE)	Virginia Ruzici (ROM)
1979	Björn Borg (SWE)	Chris Evert Lloyd (USA)
1980	Björn Borg (SWE)	Chris Evert Lloyd (USA)
1981	Björn Borg (SWE)	Hana Mandlikova (TCH)
1982	Mats Wilander (SWE)	Martina Navratilova (USA)
1983	Yannick Noah (FRA)	Chris Evert Lloyd (USA)
1984	Ivan Lendl (TCH)	Martina Navratilova (USA)
1985	Mats Wilander (SWE)	Chris Evert Lloyd (USA)
1986	Ivan Lendl (TCH)	Chris Evert Lloyd (USA)
1987	Ivan Lendl (TCH)	Steffi Graf (FRG)
1988	Mats Wilander (SWE)	Steffi Graf (FRG)
1989	Michael Chang (USA)	Arantxa Sánchez Vicario (ESP)
1990	Andres Gómez (ECU)	Monica Seles (YUG)
1991	Jim Courier (USA)	Monica Seles (YUG)
1992	Jim Courier (USA)	Monica Seles (YUG)
1993	Sergi Bruguera (ESP)	Steffi Graf (GER)
1994	Sergi Bruguera (ESP)	Arantxa Sánchez Vicario (ESP)
1995	Thomas Muster (AUT)	Steffi Graf (GER)
1996	Yevgeny Kafelnikov (RUS)	Steffi Graf (GER)
1997	Gustavo Kuerten (BRA)	Iva Majoli (CRO)
1998	Carlos Moya (ESP)	Arantxa Sánchez Vicario (ESP)
1999	Andre Agassi (USA)	Steffi Graf (GER)
2000	Gustavo Kuerten (BRA)	Mary Pierce (FRA)
2001	Gustavo Kuerten (BRA)	Jennifer Capriati (USA)
2002	Albert Costa (ESP)	Serena Williams (USA)
2003	Juan Carlos Ferrero (ESP)	Justine Henin-Hardenne (BEL)
2004	Gastón Gaudio (ARG)	Anastasiya Myskina (RUS)
2005	Rafael Nadal (ESP)	Justine Henin-Hardenne (BEL)
2006	Rafael Nadal (ESP)	Justine Henin-Hardenne (BEL)
2007	Rafael Nadal (ESP)	Justine Henin (BEL)
2008	Rafael Nadal (ESP)	Ana Ivanovic (SRB)
2009	Roger Federer (SUI)	Svetlana Kuznetsova (RUS)
2010	Rafael Nadal (ESP)	Francesca Schiavone (ITA)

French Open Tennis Championships—Doubles

YEAR	MEN	WOMEN
1925	Jean Borotra, René Lacoste	Suzanne Lenglen, Didi Vlasto
1926	Vincent Richards, Howard Kinsey	Suzanne Lenglen, Didi Vlasto
1927	Henri Cochet, Jacques Brugnon	Irene Peacock, Bobby Heine
1928	Jean Borotra, Jacques Brugnon	Phoebe Watson, Eileen Bennett
1929	Jean Borotra, René Lacoste	Lili de Alvarez, Kea Bouman
1930	Henri Cochet, Jacques Brugnon	Helen Wills Moody, Elizabeth Ryan
1931	George Lott, John Van Ryn	Eileen Whittingstall, Betty Nuthall
1932	Henri Cochet, Jacques Brugnon	Helen Wills Moody, Elizabeth Ryan
1933	Pat Hughes, Fred Perry	Simone Mathieu, Elizabeth Ryan
1934	Jean Borotra, Jacques Brugnon	Simone Mathieu, Elizabeth Ryan
1935	Jack Crawford, Adrian Quist	Margaret Scriven, Kay Stammers

French Open Tennis Championships—Doubles (continued)

YEAR	MEN	WOMEN
1936	Jean Borotra, Marcel Bernard	Simone Mathieu, Billie Yorke
1937	Gottfried von Cramm, Henner Henkel	Simone Mathieu, Billie Yorke
1938	Bernard Destremau, Yvon Petra	Simone Mathieu, Billie Yorke
1939	Don McNeill, Charles Harris	Simone Mathieu, Jadwiga Jedrzejowska
1940–45	not held	
1946	Marcel Bernard, Yvon Petra	Louise Brough, Margaret Osborne
1947	Eustace Fannin, Eric Sturgess	Louise Brough, Margaret Osborne
1948	Lennart Bergelin, Jaroslav Drobny	Doris Hart, Patricia Todd
1949	Pancho Gonzáles, Frank Parker	Louise Brough, Margaret Osborne duPont
1950	Billy Talbert, Tony Trabert	Doris Hart, Shirley Fry
1951	Ken McGregor, Frank Sedgman	Doris Hart, Shirley Fry
1952	Ken McGregor, Frank Sedgman	Doris Hart, Shirley Fry
1953	Lew Hoad, Ken Rosewall	Doris Hart, Shirley Fry
1954	Vic Seixas, Tony Trabert	Maureen Connolly, Nell Hopman
1955	Vic Seixas, Tony Trabert	Beverly Fleitz, Darlene Hard
1956	Don Candy, Robert Perry	Angela Buxton, Althea Gibson
1957	Mal Anderson, Ashley Cooper	Shirley Bloomer, Darlene Hard
1958	Ashley Cooper, Neale Fraser	Rosie Reyes, Yola Ramirez
1959	Nicola Pietrangeli, Orlando Sirola	Sandra Reynolds, Renee Schuurman
1960	Roy Emerson, Neale Fraser	Maria Bueno, Darlene Hard
1961	Roy Emerson, Rod Laver	Sandra Reynolds, Renee Schuurman
1962	Roy Emerson, Neale Fraser	Sandra Reynolds Price, Renee Schuurman
1963	Roy Emerson, Manuel Santana	Ann Haydon Jones, Renee Schuurman
1964	Roy Emerson, Ken Fletcher	Margaret Smith, Lesley Turner
1965	Roy Emerson, Fred Stolle	Margaret Smith, Lesley Turner
1966	Clark Graebner, Dennis Ralston	Margaret Smith, Judy Tegart
1967	John Newcombe, Tony Roche	Françoise Durr, Gail Sherriff
1968	Ken Rosewall, Fred Stolle	Françoise Durr, Ann Haydon Jones
1969	John Newcombe, Tony Roche	Françoise Durr, Ann Haydon Jones
1970	Ilie Nastase, Ion Tiriac	Françoise Durr, Gail Chanfreau
1971	Arthur Ashe, Marty Riessen	Françoise Durr, Gail Chanfreau
1972	Bob Hewitt, Frew McMillan	Billie Jean King, Betty Stove
1973	John Newcombe, Tom Okker	Margaret Smith Court, Virginia Wade
1974	Dick Crealy, Onny Parun	Chris Evert, Olga Morozova
1975	Brian Gottfried, Raúl Ramírez	Chris Evert, Martina Navratilova
1976	Fred McNair, Sherwood Stewart	Fiorella Bonicelli, Gail Lovera
1977	Brian Gottfried, Raúl Ramírez	Regina Marsikova, Pam Teeguarden
1978	Hank Pfister, Gene Mayer	Mima Jausovec, Virginia Ruzici
1979	Sandy Mayer, Gene Mayer	Wendy Turnbull, Betty Stove
1980	Victor Amaya, Hank Pfister	Kathy Jordan, Anne Smith
1981	Heinz Günthardt, Balázs Taróczy	Rosalyn Fairbank, Tanya Harford
1982	Sherwood Stewart, Ferdi Taygan	Martina Navratilova, Anne Smith
1983	Anders Järryd, Hans Simonsson	Rosalyn Fairbank, Candy Reynolds
1984	Henri Leconte, Yannick Noah	Martina Navratilova, Pam Shriver
1985	Kim Warwick, Mark Edmondson	Martina Navratilova, Pam Shriver
1986	John Fitzgerald, Tomas Smid	Martina Navratilova, Andrea Temesvari
1987	Robert Seguso, Anders Järryd	Martina Navratilova, Pam Shriver
1988	Emilio Sánchez, Andres Gómez	Martina Navratilova, Pam Shriver
1989	Jim Grabb, Patrick McEnroe	Larisa Savchenko, Natasha Zvereva
1990	Sergio Casal, Emilio Sánchez	Jana Novotna, Helena Sukova
1991	John Fitzgerald, Anders Järryd	Gigi Fernández, Jana Novotna
1992	Jacob Hlasek, Marc Rosset	Gigi Fernández, Natasha Zvereva
1993	Luke Jensen, Murphy Jensen	Gigi Fernández, Natasha Zvereva
1994	Byron Black, Jonathan Stark	Gigi Fernández, Natasha Zvereva
1995	Jacco Eltingh, Paul Haarhuis	Gigi Fernández, Natasha Zvereva
1996	Yevgeny Kafelnikov, Daniel Vacek	Lindsay Davenport, Mary Joe Fernández
1997	Yevgeny Kafelnikov, Daniel Vacek	Gigi Fernández, Natasha Zvereva
1998	Jacco Eltingh, Paul Haarhuis	Martina Hingis, Jana Novotna
1999	Mahesh Bhupathi, Leander Paes	Venus Williams, Serena Williams
2000	Todd Woodbridge, Mark Woodforde	Martina Hingis, Mary Pierce
2001	Mahesh Bhupathi, Leander Paes	Virginia Ruano Pascual, Paola Suárez
2002	Yevgeny Kafelnikov, Paul Haarhuis	Virginia Ruano Pascual, Paola Suárez
2003	Bob Bryan, Mike Bryan	Kim Clijsters, Ai Sugiyama
2004	Xavier Malisse, Olivier Rochus	Virginia Ruano Pascual, Paola Suárez
2005	Jonas Björkman, Max Mirnyi	Virginia Ruano Pascual, Paola Suárez
2006	Jonas Björkman, Max Mirnyi	Lisa Raymond, Samantha Stosur
2007	Mark Knowles, Daniel Nestor	Alicia Molik, Mara Santangelo
2008	Pablo Cuevas, Luis Horna	Anabel Medina Garrigues, Virginia Ruano Pascual

French Open Tennis Championships—Doubles (continued)

YEAR	MEN	WOMEN
2009	Lukas Dlouhy, Leander Paes	Anabel Medina Garrigues, Virginia Ruano Pascual
2010	Nenad Zimonjic, Daniel Nestor	Venus Williams, Serena Williams

All-England (Wimbledon) Tennis Championships—Singles

YEAR	MEN	WOMEN
1877	Spencer Gore (GBR)	
1878	Frank Hadow (GBR)	
1879	John Hartley (GBR)	
1880	John Hartley (GBR)	
1881	William Renshaw (GBR)	
1882	William Renshaw (GBR)	
1883	William Renshaw (GBR)	
1884	William Renshaw (GBR)	Maud Watson (GBR)
1885	William Renshaw (GBR)	Maud Watson (GBR)
1886	William Renshaw (GBR)	Blanche Bingley (GBR)
1887	Herbert Lawford (GBR)	Lottie Dod (GBR)
1888	Ernest Renshaw (GBR)	Lottie Dod (GBR)
1889	William Renshaw (GBR)	Blanche Bingley Hillyard (GBR)
1890	William Hamilton (GBR)	Lena Rice (GBR)
1891	Wilfred Baddeley (GBR)	Lottie Dod (GBR)
1892	Wilfred Baddeley (GBR)	Lottie Dod (GBR)
1893	Joshua Pim (GBR)	Lottie Dod (GBR)
1894	Joshua Pim (GBR)	Blanche Bingley Hillyard (GBR)
1895	Wilfred Baddeley (GBR)	Charlotte Cooper (GBR)
1896	Harold Mahony (GBR)	Charlotte Cooper (GBR)
1897	Reggie Doherty (GBR)	Blanche Bingley Hillyard (GBR)
1898	Reggie Doherty (GBR)	Charlotte Cooper (GBR)
1899	Reggie Doherty (GBR)	Blanche Bingley Hillyard (GBR)
1900	Reggie Doherty (GBR)	Blanche Bingley Hillyard (GBR)
1901	Arthur Gore (GBR)	Charlotte Cooper Sterry (GBR)
1902	Laurie Doherty (GBR)	Muriel Robb (GBR)
1903	Laurie Doherty (GBR)	Dorothea Douglass (GBR)
1904	Laurie Doherty (GBR)	Dorothea Douglass (GBR)
1905	Laurie Doherty (GBR)	May Sutton (USA)
1906	Laurie Doherty (GBR)	Dorothea Douglass (GBR)
1907	Norman Brookes (AUS)	May Sutton (USA)
1908	Arthur Gore (GBR)	Charlotte Cooper Sterry (GBR)
1909	Arthur Gore (GBR)	Dora Boothby (GBR)
1910	Tony Wilding (NZL)	Dorothea Lambert Chambers (GBR)
1911	Tony Wilding (NZL)	Dorothea Lambert Chambers (GBR)
1912	Tony Wilding (NZL)	Ethel Larcombe (GBR)
1913	Tony Wilding (NZL)	Dorothea Lambert Chambers (GBR)
1914	Norman Brookes (AUS)	Dorothea Lambert Chambers (GBR)
1915–18	*not held*	
1919	Gerald Patterson (AUS)	Suzanne Lenglen (FRA)
1920	Bill Tilden (USA)	Suzanne Lenglen (FRA)
1921	Bill Tilden (USA)	Suzanne Lenglen (FRA)
1922	Gerald Patterson (AUS)	Suzanne Lenglen (FRA)
1923	Bill Johnston (USA)	Suzanne Lenglen (FRA)
1924	Jean Borotra (FRA)	Kathleen McKane (GBR)
1925	René Lacoste (FRA)	Suzanne Lenglen (FRA)
1926	Jean Borotra (FRA)	Kathleen McKane Godfree (GBR)
1927	Henri Cochet (FRA)	Helen Wills (USA)
1928	René Lacoste (FRA)	Helen Wills (USA)
1929	Henri Cochet (FRA)	Helen Wills (USA)
1930	Bill Tilden (USA)	Helen Wills Moody (USA)
1931	Sidney Wood (USA)	Cilly Aussem (GER)
1932	Ellsworth Vines (USA)	Helen Wills Moody (USA)
1933	Jack Crawford (AUS)	Helen Wills Moody (USA)
1934	Fred Perry (GBR)	Dorothy Round (GBR)
1935	Fred Perry (GBR)	Helen Wills Moody (USA)
1936	Fred Perry (GBR)	Helen Jacobs (USA)
1937	Don Budge (USA)	Dorothy Round (GBR)
1938	Don Budge (USA)	Helen Wills Moody (USA)
1939	Bobby Riggs (USA)	Alice Marble (USA)
1940–45	*not held*	
1946	Yvon Petra (FRA)	Pauline Betz (USA)

All-England (Wimbledon) Tennis Championships—Singles (continued)

YEAR	MEN	WOMEN
1947	Jack Kramer (USA)	Margaret Osborne (USA)
1948	Bob Falkenburg (USA)	Louise Brough (USA)
1949	Ted Schroeder (USA)	Louise Brough (USA)
1950	Budge Patty (USA)	Louise Brough (USA)
1951	Dick Savitt (USA)	Doris Hart (USA)
1952	Frank Sedgman (AUS)	Maureen Connolly (USA)
1953	Vic Seixas (USA)	Maureen Connolly (USA)
1954	Jaroslav Drobny (TCH)	Maureen Connolly (USA)
1955	Tony Trabert (USA)	Louise Brough (USA)
1956	Lew Hoad (AUS)	Shirley Fry (USA)
1957	Lew Hoad (AUS)	Althea Gibson (USA)
1958	Ashley Cooper (AUS)	Althea Gibson (USA)
1959	Alex Olmedo (PER)	Maria Bueno (BRA)
1960	Neale Fraser (AUS)	Maria Bueno (BRA)
1961	Rod Laver (AUS)	Angela Mortimer (GBR)
1962	Rod Laver (AUS)	Karen Susman (USA)
1963	Chuck McKinley (USA)	Margaret Smith (AUS)
1964	Roy Emerson (AUS)	Maria Bueno (BRA)
1965	Roy Emerson (AUS)	Margaret Smith (AUS)
1966	Manuel Santana (ESP)	Billie Jean King (USA)
1967	John Newcombe (AUS)	Billie Jean King (USA)
1968	Rod Laver (AUS)	Billie Jean King (USA)
1969	Rod Laver (AUS)	Ann Jones (GBR)
1970	John Newcombe (AUS)	Margaret Smith Court (AUS)
1971	John Newcombe (AUS)	Evonne Goolagong (AUS)
1972	Stan Smith (USA)	Billie Jean King (USA)
1973	Jan Kodes (TCH)	Billie Jean King (USA)
1974	Jimmy Connors (USA)	Chris Evert (USA)
1975	Arthur Ashe (USA)	Billie Jean King (USA)
1976	Björn Borg (SWE)	Chris Evert (USA)
1977	Björn Borg (SWE)	Virginia Wade (GBR)
1978	Björn Borg (SWE)	Martina Navratilova (TCH)
1979	Björn Borg (SWE)	Martina Navratilova (USA)
1980	Björn Borg (SWE)	Evonne Goolagong Cawley (AUS)
1981	John McEnroe (USA)	Chris Evert Lloyd (USA)
1982	Jimmy Connors (USA)	Martina Navratilova (USA)
1983	John McEnroe (USA)	Martina Navratilova (USA)
1984	John McEnroe (USA)	Martina Navratilova (USA)
1985	Boris Becker (FRG)	Martina Navratilova (USA)
1986	Boris Becker (FRG)	Martina Navratilova (USA)
1987	Pat Cash (AUS)	Martina Navratilova (USA)
1988	Stefan Edberg (SWE)	Steffi Graf (GDR)
1989	Boris Becker (FRG)	Steffi Graf (GDR)
1990	Stefan Edberg (SWE)	Martina Navratilova (USA)
1991	Michael Stich (GER)	Steffi Graf (GER)
1992	Andre Agassi (USA)	Steffi Graf (GER)
1993	Pete Sampras (USA)	Steffi Graf (GER)
1994	Pete Sampras (USA)	Conchita Martínez (ESP)
1995	Pete Sampras (USA)	Steffi Graf (GER)
1996	Richard Krajicek (NED)	Steffi Graf (GER)
1997	Pete Sampras (USA)	Martina Hingis (SUI)
1998	Pete Sampras (USA)	Jana Novotna (CZE)
1999	Pete Sampras (USA)	Lindsay Davenport (USA)
2000	Pete Sampras (USA)	Venus Williams (USA)
2001	Goran Ivanisevic (CRO)	Venus Williams (USA)
2002	Lleyton Hewitt (AUS)	Serena Williams (USA)
2003	Roger Federer (SUI)	Serena Williams (USA)
2004	Roger Federer (SUI)	Mariya Sharapova (RUS)
2005	Roger Federer (SUI)	Venus Williams (USA)
2006	Roger Federer (SUI)	Amélie Mauresmo (FRA)
2007	Roger Federer (SUI)	Venus Williams (USA)
2008	Rafael Nadal (ESP)	Venus Williams (USA)
2009	Roger Federer (SUI)	Serena Williams (USA)
2010	Rafael Nadal (ESP)	Serena Williams (USA)

All-England (Wimbledon) Tennis Championships—Doubles

YEAR	MEN	WOMEN
1879	L.R. Erskine, H. Lawford	
1880	William Renshaw, Ernest Renshaw	
1881	William Renshaw, Ernest Renshaw	
1882	J.T. Hartley, R.T. Richardson	
1883	C.W. Grinstead, C.E. Welldon	
1884	William Renshaw, Ernest Renshaw	
1885	William Renshaw, Ernest Renshaw	
1886	William Renshaw, Ernest Renshaw	
1887	Herbert Wilberforce, P.B. Lyon	
1888	William Renshaw, Ernest Renshaw	
1889	William Renshaw, Ernest Renshaw	
1890	Joshua Pim, F.O. Stoker	
1891	Wilfred Baddeley, Herbert Baddeley	
1892	E.W. Lewis, H.S. Barlow	
1893	Joshua Pim, F.O. Stoker	
1894	Wilfred Baddeley, Herbert Baddeley	
1895	Wilfred Baddeley, Herbert Baddeley	
1896	Wilfred Baddeley, Herbert Baddeley	
1897	Reggie Doherty, Laurie Doherty	
1898	Reggie Doherty, Laurie Doherty	
1899	Reggie Doherty, Laurie Doherty	
1900	Reggie Doherty, Laurie Doherty	
1901	Reggie Doherty, Laurie Doherty	
1902	Sidney Smith, Frank Riseley	
1903	Reggie Doherty, Laurie Doherty	
1904	Reggie Doherty, Laurie Doherty	
1905	Reggie Doherty, Laurie Doherty	
1906	Sidney Smith, Frank Riseley	
1907	Norman Brookes, Tony Wilding	
1908	Tony Wilding, M.J.G. Ritchie	
1909	Arthur Gore, H. Roper Barrett	
1910	Tony Wilding, M.J.G. Ritchie	
1911	André Gobert, Max Decugis	
1912	H. Roper Barrett, Charles Dixon	
1913	H. Roper Barrett, Charles Dixon	Winifred McNair, Dora Boothby
1914	Norman Brookes, Tony Wilding	Elizabeth Ryan, Agatha Morton
1915–18	not held	
1919	R.V. Thomas, Pat O'Hara Wood	Suzanne Lenglen, Elizabeth Ryan
1920	Richard Williams, Chuck Garland	Suzanne Lenglen, Elizabeth Ryan
1921	Randolph Lycett, Max Woosnam	Suzanne Lenglen, Elizabeth Ryan
1922	James Anderson, Randolph Lycett	Suzanne Lenglen, Elizabeth Ryan
1923	Leslie Godfree, Randolph Lycett	Suzanne Lenglen, Elizabeth Ryan
1924	Frank Hunter, Vincent Richards	Hazel Wightman, Helen Wills
1925	Jean Borotra, René Lacoste	Suzanne Lenglen, Elizabeth Ryan
1926	Henri Cochet, Jacques Brugnon	Mary Browne, Elizabeth Ryan
1927	Bill Tilden, Frank Hunter	Helen Wills, Elizabeth Ryan
1928	Henri Cochet, Jacques Brugnon	Peggy Saunders, Phoebe Watson
1929	Wilmer Allison, John Van Ryn	Peggy Saunders Michell, Phoebe Watson
1930	Wilmer Allison, John Van Ryn	Helen Wills Moody, Elizabeth Ryan
1931	George Lott, John Van Ryn	Phyllis Mudford, Dorothy Barron
1932	Jean Borotra, Jacques Brugnon	Doris Metaxa, Josane Sigart
1933	Jean Borotra, Jacques Brugnon	Simone Mathieu, Elizabeth Ryan
1934	George Lott, Lester Stoefen	Simone Mathieu, Elizabeth Ryan
1935	Adrian Quist, Jack Crawford	Freda James, Kay Stammers
1936	Pat Hughes, Raymond Tuckey	Freda James, Kay Stammers
1937	Don Budge, Gene Mako	Simone Mathieu, Billie Yorke
1938	Don Budge, Gene Mako	Sarah Palfrey Fabyan, Alice Marble
1939	Bobby Riggs, Elwood Cooke	Sarah Palfrey Fabyan, Alice Marble
1940–45	not held	
1946	Jack Kramer, Tom Brown	Louise Brough, Margaret Osborne
1947	Jack Kramer, Bob Falkenburg	Patricia Todd, Doris Hart
1948	John Bromwich, Frank Sedgman	Louise Brough, Margaret Osborne duPont
1949	Pancho Gonzáles, Frank Parker	Louise Brough, Margaret Osborne duPont
1950	Adrian Quist, John Bromwich	Louise Brough, Margaret Osborne duPont
1951	Ken McGregor, Frank Sedgman	Doris Hart, Shirley Fry
1952	Ken McGregor, Frank Sedgman	Doris Hart, Shirley Fry
1953	Lew Hoad, Ken Rosewall	Doris Hart, Shirley Fry
1954	Rex Hartwig, Mervyn Rose	Louise Brough, Margaret Osborne duPont

All-England (Wimbledon) Tennis Championships—Doubles (continued)

YEAR	MEN	WOMEN
1955	Rex Hartwig, Lew Hoad	Angela Mortimer, Anne Shilcock
1956	Lew Hoad, Ken Rosewall	Angela Buxton, Althea Gibson
1957	Budge Patty, Gardnar Mulloy	Althea Gibson, Darlene Hard
1958	Sven Davidson, Ulf Schmidt	Maria Bueno, Althea Gibson
1959	Roy Emerson, Neale Fraser	Jeanne Arth, Darlene Hard
1960	Rafael Osuna, Dennis Ralston	Maria Bueno, Darlene Hard
1961	Roy Emerson, Neale Fraser	Karen Hantze, Billie Jean Moffitt
1962	Bob Hewitt, Fred Stolle	Karen Hantze Susman, Billie Jean Moffitt
1963	Rafael Osuna, Antonio Palafox	Maria Bueno, Darlene Hard
1964	Bob Hewitt, Fred Stolle	Margaret Smith, Leslie Turner
1965	John Newcombe, Tony Roche	Maria Bueno, Billie Jean Moffitt
1966	John Newcombe, Ken Fletcher	Maria Bueno, Nancy Richey
1967	Bob Hewitt, Frew McMillan	Billie Jean King, Rosemary Casals
1968	John Newcombe, Tony Roche	Billie Jean King, Rosemary Casals
1969	John Newcombe, Tony Roche	Margaret Smith Court, Judy Tegart
1970	John Newcombe, Tony Roche	Billie Jean King, Rosemary Casals
1971	Roy Emerson, Rod Laver	Billie Jean King, Rosemary Casals
1972	Bob Hewitt, Frew McMillan	Billie Jean King, Betty Stove
1973	Jimmy Connors, Ilie Nastase	Billie Jean King, Rosemary Casals
1974	John Newcombe, Tony Roche	Evonne Goolagong, Peggy Michel
1975	Vitas Gerulaitis, Sandy Mayer	Ann Kiyomura, Kazuko Sawamatsu
1976	Brian Gottfried, Raúl Ramírez	Chris Evert, Martina Navratilova
1977	Ross Case, Geoff Masters	Helen Gourlay Cawley, Joanne Russell
1978	Bob Hewitt, Frew McMillan	Kerry Reid, Wendy Turnbull
1979	John McEnroe, Peter Fleming	Billie Jean King, Martina Navratilova
1980	Peter McNamara, Paul McNamee	Kathy Jordan, Anne Smith
1981	John McEnroe, Peter Fleming	Martina Navratilova, Pam Shriver
1982	Peter McNamara, Paul McNamee	Martina Navratilova, Pam Shriver
1983	John McEnroe, Peter Fleming	Martina Navratilova, Pam Shriver
1984	John McEnroe, Peter Fleming	Martina Navratilova, Pam Shriver
1985	Heinz Günthardt, Balázs Taróczy	Kathy Jordan, Elizabeth Smylie
1986	Joakim Nyström, Mats Wilander	Martina Navratilova, Pam Shriver
1987	Robert Seguso, Ken Flach	Claudia Kohde-Kilsch, Helena Sukova
1988	Robert Seguso, Ken Flach	Steffi Graf, Gabriela Sabatini
1989	John Fitzgerald, Anders Järryd	Jana Novotna, Helena Sukova
1990	Rick Leach, Jim Pugh	Jana Novotna, Helena Sukova
1991	John Fitzgerald, Anders Järryd	Larisa Savchenko, Natasha Zvereva
1992	John McEnroe, Michael Stich	Gigi Fernández, Natasha Zvereva
1993	Todd Woodbridge, Mark Woodforde	Gigi Fernández, Natasha Zvereva
1994	Todd Woodbridge, Mark Woodforde	Gigi Fernández, Natasha Zvereva
1995	Todd Woodbridge, Mark Woodforde	Arantxa Sánchez Vicario, Jana Novotna
1996	Todd Woodbridge, Mark Woodforde	Helena Sukova, Martina Hingis
1997	Todd Woodbridge, Mark Woodforde	Gigi Fernández, Natasha Zvereva
1998	Jacco Eltingh, Paul Haarhuis	Martina Hingis, Jana Novotna
1999	Mahesh Bhupathi, Leander Paes	Lindsay Davenport, Corina Morariu
2000	Todd Woodbridge, Mark Woodforde	Venus Williams, Serena Williams
2001	Donald Johnson, Jared Palmer	Lisa Raymond, Rennae Stubbs
2002	Jonas Björkman, Todd Woodbridge	Venus Williams, Serena Williams
2003	Jonas Björkman, Todd Woodbridge	Kim Clijsters, Ai Sugiyama
2004	Jonas Björkman, Todd Woodbridge	Cara Black, Rennae Stubbs
2005	Stephen Huss, Wesley Moodie	Cara Black, Liezel Huber
2006	Bob Bryan, Mike Bryan	Yan Zi, Zheng Jie
2007	Arnaud Clément, Michaël Llodra	Cara Black, Liezel Huber
2008	Daniel Nestor, Nenad Zimonjic	Venus Williams, Serena Williams
2009	Daniel Nestor, Nenad Zimonjic	Venus Williams, Serena Williams
2010	Jürgen Melzer, Philipp Petzschner	Vania King, Yaroslava Shvedova

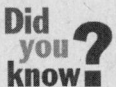

Did you know? The longest match in the history of professional tennis was contested at the All-England (Wimbledon) Tennis Championships in 2010. The first-round match, featuring American Jon Isner and Frenchman Nicolas Mahut, was played over three days and lasted more than 11 hours, four and a half hours longer than the previous record holder. There were 980 points played; 215 aces were served; and the final score was 6–4, 3–6, 6–7, 7–6, 70–68. The fifth set alone, stretching more than eight hours, would have set a new duration world record.

United States Open Tennis Championships—Singles

YEAR	MEN	WOMEN
1881	Richard Sears (USA)	
1882	Richard Sears (USA)	
1883	Richard Sears (USA)	
1884	Richard Sears (USA)	
1885	Richard Sears (USA)	
1886	Richard Sears (USA)	
1887	Richard Sears (USA)	Ellen Hansell (USA)
1888	Henry Slocum, Jr. (USA)	Bertha Townsend (USA)
1889	Henry Slocum, Jr. (USA)	Bertha Townsend (USA)
1890	Oliver Campbell (USA)	Ellen Roosevelt (USA)
1891	Oliver Campbell (USA)	Mabel Cahill (USA)
1892	Oliver Campbell (USA)	Mabel Cahill (USA)
1893	Robert Wrenn (USA)	Aline Terry (USA)
1894	Robert Wrenn (USA)	Helen Helwig (USA)
1895	Fred Hovey (USA)	Juliette Atkinson (USA)
1896	Robert Wrenn (USA)	Elisabeth Moore (USA)
1897	Robert Wrenn (USA)	Juliette Atkinson (USA)
1898	Malcom Whitman (USA)	Juliette Atkinson (USA)
1899	Malcom Whitman (USA)	Marion Jones (USA)
1900	Malcom Whitman (USA)	Myrtle McAteer (USA)
1901	William Larned (USA)	Elisabeth Moore (USA)
1902	William Larned (USA)	Marion Jones (USA)
1903	Laurie Doherty (GBR)	Elisabeth Moore (USA)
1904	Holcombe Ward (USA)	May Sutton (USA)
1905	Beals Wright (USA)	Elisabeth Moore (USA)
1906	Bill Clothier (USA)	Helen Homans (USA)
1907	William Larned (USA)	Evelyn Sears (USA)
1908	William Larned (USA)	Maud Barger-Wallach (USA)
1909	William Larned (USA)	Hazel Hotchkiss (USA)
1910	William Larned (USA)	Hazel Hotchkiss (USA)
1911	William Larned (USA)	Hazel Hotchkiss (USA)
1912	Maurice McLoughlin (USA)	Mary Browne (USA)
1913	Maurice McLoughlin (USA)	Mary Browne (USA)
1914	R. Norris Williams (USA)	Mary Browne (USA)
1915	Bill Johnston (USA)	Molla Bjurstedt (NOR)
1916	R. Norris Williams (USA)	Molla Bjurstedt (NOR)
1917	Lindley Murray (USA)	Molla Bjurstedt (NOR)
1918	Lindley Murray (USA)	Molla Bjurstedt (NOR)
1919	Bill Johnston (USA)	Hazel Hotchkiss Wightman (USA)
1920	Bill Tilden (USA)	Molla Bjurstedt Mallory (USA)
1921	Bill Tilden (USA)	Molla Bjurstedt Mallory (USA)
1922	Bill Tilden (USA)	Molla Bjurstedt Mallory (USA)
1923	Bill Tilden (USA)	Helen Wills (USA)
1924	Bill Tilden (USA)	Helen Wills (USA)
1925	Bill Tilden (USA)	Helen Wills (USA)
1926	René Lacoste (FRA)	Molla Bjurstedt Mallory (USA)
1927	René Lacoste (FRA)	Helen Wills (USA)
1928	Henri Cochet (FRA)	Helen Wills (USA)
1929	Bill Tilden (USA)	Helen Wills (USA)
1930	John Doeg (USA)	Betty Nuthall (GBR)
1931	Ellsworth Vines (USA)	Helen Wills Moody (USA)
1932	Ellsworth Vines (USA)	Helen Jacobs (USA)
1933	Fred Perry (GBR)	Helen Jacobs (USA)
1934	Fred Perry (GBR)	Helen Jacobs (USA)
1935	Wilmer Allison (USA)	Helen Jacobs (USA)
1936	Fred Perry (GBR)	Alice Marble (USA)
1937	Don Budge (USA)	Anita Lizana (CHI)
1938	Don Budge (USA)	Alice Marble (USA)
1939	Bobby Riggs (USA)	Alice Marble (USA)
1940	Don McNeill (USA)	Alice Marble (USA)
1941	Bobby Riggs (USA)	Sarah Palfrey Cooke (USA)
1942	Ted Schroeder (USA)	Pauline Betz (USA)
1943	Joe Hunt (USA)	Pauline Betz (USA)
1944	Frank Parker (USA)	Pauline Betz (USA)
1945	Frank Parker (USA)	Sarah Palfrey Cooke (USA)
1946	Jack Kramer (USA)	Pauline Betz (USA)
1947	Jack Kramer (USA)	Louise Brough (USA)
1948	Pancho Gonzáles (USA)	Margaret du Pont (USA)

United States Open Tennis Championships—Singles (continued)

YEAR	MEN	WOMEN
1949	Pancho Gonzáles (USA)	Margaret du Pont (USA)
1950	Arthur Larsen (USA)	Margaret du Pont (USA)
1951	Frank Sedgman (AUS)	Maureen Connolly (USA)
1952	Frank Sedgman (AUS)	Maureen Connolly (USA)
1953	Tony Trabert (USA)	Maureen Connolly (USA)
1954	Vic Seixas (USA)	Doris Hart (USA)
1955	Tony Trabert (USA)	Doris Hart (USA)
1956	Ken Rosewall (AUS)	Shirley Fry (USA)
1957	Mal Anderson (AUS)	Althea Gibson (USA)
1958	Ashley Cooper (AUS)	Althea Gibson (USA)
1959	Neale Fraser (AUS)	Maria Bueno (BRA)
1960	Neale Fraser (AUS)	Darlene Hard (USA)
1961	Roy Emerson (AUS)	Darlene Hard (USA)
1962	Rod Laver (AUS)	Margaret Smith (AUS)
1963	Rafael Osuna (MEX)	Maria Bueno (BRA)
1964	Roy Emerson (AUS)	Maria Bueno (BRA)
1965	Manuel Santana (ESP)	Margaret Smith (AUS)
1966	Fred Stolle (AUS)	Maria Bueno (BRA)
1967	John Newcombe (AUS)	Billie Jean King (USA)
1968[1]	Arthur Ashe (USA)	Virginia Wade (GBR); Margaret Smith Court (AUS)
1969[1]	Rod Laver (AUS); Stan Smith (USA)	Margaret Smith Court (AUS)
1970	Ken Rosewall (AUS)	Margaret Smith Court (AUS)
1971	Stan Smith (USA)	Billie Jean King (USA)
1972	Ilie Nastase (ROM)	Billie Jean King (USA)
1973	John Newcombe (AUS)	Margaret Smith Court (AUS)
1974	Jimmy Connors (USA)	Billie Jean King (USA)
1975	Manuel Orantes (ESP)	Chris Evert (USA)
1976	Jimmy Connors (USA)	Chris Evert (USA)
1977	Guillermo Vilas (ARG)	Chris Evert (USA)
1978	Jimmy Connors (USA)	Chris Evert (USA)
1979	John McEnroe (USA)	Tracy Austin (USA)
1980	John McEnroe (USA)	Chris Evert Lloyd (USA)
1981	John McEnroe (USA)	Tracy Austin (USA)
1982	Jimmy Connors (USA)	Chris Evert Lloyd (USA)
1983	Jimmy Connors (USA)	Martina Navratilova (USA)
1984	John McEnroe (USA)	Martina Navratilova (USA)
1985	Ivan Lendl (TCH)	Hana Mandlikova (TCH)
1986	Ivan Lendl (TCH)	Martina Navratilova (USA)
1987	Ivan Lendl (TCH)	Martina Navratilova (USA)
1988	Mats Wilander (SWE)	Steffi Graf (FRG)
1989	Boris Becker (FRG)	Steffi Graf (FRG)
1990	Pete Sampras (USA)	Gabriela Sabatini (ARG)
1991	Stefan Edberg (SWE)	Monica Seles (YUG)
1992	Stefan Edberg (SWE)	Monica Seles (YUG)
1993	Pete Sampras (USA)	Steffi Graf (GER)
1994	Andre Agassi (USA)	Arantxa Sánchez Vicario (ESP)
1995	Pete Sampras (USA)	Steffi Graf (GER)
1996	Pete Sampras (USA)	Steffi Graf (GER)
1997	Patrick Rafter (AUS)	Martina Hingis (SUI)
1998	Patrick Rafter (AUS)	Lindsay Davenport (USA)
1999	Andre Agassi (USA)	Serena Williams (USA)
2000	Marat Safin (RUS)	Venus Williams (USA)
2001	Lleyton Hewitt (AUS)	Venus Williams (USA)
2002	Pete Sampras (USA)	Serena Williams (USA)
2003	Andy Roddick (USA)	Justine Henin-Hardenne (BEL)
2004	Roger Federer (SUI)	Svetlana Kuznetsova (RUS)
2005	Roger Federer (SUI)	Kim Clijsters (BEL)
2006	Roger Federer (SUI)	Mariya Sharapova (RUS)
2007	Roger Federer (SUI)	Justine Henin (BEL)
2008	Roger Federer (SUI)	Serena Williams (USA)
2009	Juan Martín Del Potro (ARG)	Kim Clijsters (BEL)
2010	Rafael Nadal (ESP)	Kim Clijsters (BEL)

[1]In 1968 and 1969 both amateur and open championships were held. Ashe won both men's competitions in 1968; Smith won the amateur championship in 1969. Court won the women's amateur competition in 1968 and both championships in 1969. Thereafter the championships were open.

United States Open Tennis Championships—Doubles

YEAR	MEN	WOMEN
1881	Clarence Clark, Fred Taylor	
1882	Richard Sears, James Dwight	
1883	Richard Sears, James Dwight	
1884	Richard Sears, James Dwight	
1885	Richard Sears, Joseph Clark	
1886	Richard Sears, James Dwight	
1887	Richard Sears, James Dwight	
1888	Oliver Campbell, Valentine Hall	
1889	Henry Slocum, Howard Taylor	Bertha Townsend, Margarette Ballard
1890	Valentine Hall, Clarence Hobart	Ellen Roosevelt, Grace Roosevelt
1891	Oliver Campbell, Robert Huntington	Mabel Cahill, Mrs. W. Fellowes Morgan
1892	Oliver Campbell, Robert Huntington	Mabel Cahill, Adeline McKinley
1893	Clarence Hobart, Fred Hovey	Aline Terry, Hattie Butler
1894	Clarence Hobart, Fred Hovey	Helen Helwig, Juliette Atkinson
1895	Malcom Chace, Robert Wrenn	Helen Helwig, Juliette Atkinson
1896	Carr Neel, Samuel Neel	Elisabeth Moore, Juliette Atkinson
1897	Leo Ware, George Sheldon	Juliette Atkinson, Kathleen Atkinson
1898	Leo Ware, George Sheldon	Juliette Atkinson, Kathleen Atkinson
1899	Holcombe Ward, Dwight Davis	Jane Craven, Myrtle McAteer
1900	Holcombe Ward, Dwight Davis	Edith Parker, Hallie Champlin
1901	Holcombe Ward, Dwight Davis	Juliette Atkinson, Myrtle McAteer
1902	Reggie Doherty, Laurie Doherty	Juliette Atkinson, Marion Jones
1903	Reggie Doherty, Laurie Doherty	Elisabeth Moore, Carrie Neely
1904	Holcombe Ward, Beals Wright	Mary Sutton, Miriam Hall
1905	Holcombe Ward, Beals Wright	Helen Homans, Carrie Neely
1906	Holcombe Ward, Beals Wright	Mrs. L.S. Coe, Mrs. D.S. Platt
1907	Fred Alexander, Harold Hackett	Marie Weimer, Carrie Neely
1908	Fred Alexander, Harold Hackett	Evelyn Sears, Margaret Curtis
1909	Fred Alexander, Harold Hackett	Hazel Hotchkiss, Edith Rotch
1910	Fred Alexander, Harold Hackett	Hazel Hotchkiss, Edith Rotch
1911	Raymond Little, Gustave Touchard	Hazel Hotchkiss, Eleanora Sears
1912	Maurice McLoughlin, Thomas Bundy	Dorothy Green, Mary Browne
1913	Maurice McLoughlin, Thomas Bundy	Mary Browne, Mrs. R.H. Williams
1914	Maurice McLoughlin, Thomas Bundy	Mary Browne, Mrs. R.H. Williams
1915	William Johnston, Clarence Griffin	Hazel Hotchkiss Wightman, Eleanora Sears
1916	William Johnston, Clarence Griffin	Molla Bjurstedt, Eleanora Sears
1917	Fred Alexander, Harold Throckmorton	Molla Bjurstedt, Eleanora Sears
1918	Bill Tilden, Vincent Richards	Marion Zinderstein, Eleanor Goss
1919	Norman Brookes, Gerald Patterson	Marion Zinderstein, Eleanor Goss
1920	William Johnston, Clarence Griffin	Marion Zinderstein, Eleanor Goss
1921	Bill Tilden, Vincent Richards	Mary Browne, Mrs. R.H. Williams
1922	Bill Tilden, Vincent Richards	Marion Zinderstein Jessup, Helen Wills
1923	Bill Tilden, Brian Norton	Kathleen McKane, Phyllis Covell
1924	Howard Kinsey, Robert Kinsey	Hazel Hotchkiss Wightman, Helen Wills
1925	Richard Williams, Vincent Richards	Mary Browne, Helen Wills
1926	Richard Williams, Vincent Richards	Elizabeth Ryan, Eleanor Goss
1927	Bill Tilden, Frank Hunter	Kathleen McKane Godfree, Ermyntrude Harvey
1928	George Lott, John Hennessey	Hazel Hotchkiss Wightman, Helen Wills
1929	George Lott, John Doeg	Phoebe Watson, Peggy Michell
1930	George Lott, John Doeg	Betty Nuthall, Sarah Palfrey
1931	Wilmer Allison, John Van Ryn	Betty Nuthall, Eileen Whittingstall
1932	Ellsworth Vines, Keith Gledhill	Helen Jacobs, Sarah Palfrey
1933	George Lott, Lester Stoefen	Betty Nuthall, Freda James
1934	George Lott, Lester Stoefen	Helen Jacobs, Sarah Palfrey
1935	Wilmer Allison, John Van Ryn	Helen Jacobs, Sarah Palfrey Fabyan
1936	Don Budge, Gene Mako	Marjorie Van Ryn, Carolin Babcock
1937	Gottfried von Cramm, Henner Henkel	Sarah Palfrey Fabyan, Alice Marble
1938	Don Budge, Gene Mako	Sarah Palfrey Fabyan, Alice Marble
1939	Adrian Quist, John Bromwich	Sarah Palfrey Fabyan, Alice Marble
1940	Jack Kramer, Ted Schroeder	Sarah Palfrey Fabyan, Alice Marble
1941	Jack Kramer, Ted Schroeder	Sarah Palfrey Cooke, Margaret Osborne
1942	Gardnar Mulloy, Billy Talbert	Louise Brough, Margaret Osborne
1943	Jack Kramer, Frank Parker	Louise Brough, Margaret Osborne
1944	Don McNeill, Bob Falkenburg	Louise Brough, Margaret Osborne
1945	Gardnar Mulloy, Billy Talbert	Louise Brough, Margaret Osborne
1946	Gardnar Mulloy, Billy Talbert	Louise Brough, Margaret Osborne
1947	Jack Kramer, Ted Schroeder	Louise Brough, Margaret Osborne
1948	Gardnar Mulloy, Billy Talbert	Louise Brough, Margaret Osborne du Pont

United States Open Tennis Championships—Doubles (continued)

YEAR	MEN	WOMEN
1949	John Bromwich, Billy Sidwell	Louise Brough, Margaret Osborne du Pont
1950	John Bromwich, Frank Sedgman	Louise Brough, Margaret Osborne du Pont
1951	Ken McGregor, Frank Sedgman	Doris Hart, Shirley Fry
1952	Mervyn Rose, Vic Seixas	Doris Hart, Shirley Fry
1953	Rex Hartwig, Mervyn Rose	Doris Hart, Shirley Fry
1954	Vic Seixas, Tony Trabert	Doris Hart, Shirley Fry
1955	Kosei Kamo, Atushi Miyagi	Louise Brough, Margaret Osborne du Pont
1956	Lew Hoad, Ken Rosewall	Louise Brough, Margaret Osborne du Pont
1957	Ashley Cooper, Neale Fraser	Louise Brough, Margaret Osborne du Pont
1958	Alex Olmedo, Hamilton Richardson	Jeanne Arth, Darlene Hard
1959	Roy Emerson, Neale Fraser	Jeanne Arth, Darlene Hard
1960	Roy Emerson, Neale Fraser	Maria Bueno, Darlene Hard
1961	Charles McKinley, Dennis Ralston	Darlene Hard, Lesley Turner
1962	Rafael Osuna, Antonio Palafox	Maria Bueno, Darlene Hard
1963	Charles McKinley, Dennis Ralston	Robyn Ebbern, Margaret Smith
1964	Charles McKinley, Dennis Ralston	Karen Susman, Billie Jean Moffitt
1965	Roy Emerson, Fred Stolle	Carole Caldwell Graebner, Nancy Richey
1966	Roy Emerson, Fred Stolle	Maria Bueno, Nancy Richey
1967	John Newcombe, Tony Roche	Billie Jean Moffitt King, Rosemary Casals
1968[1]	Robert Lutz, Stan Smith	Maria Bueno, Margaret Smith Court
1969[1]	Ken Rosewall, Fred Stolle;	Françoise Durr, Darlene Hard;
	Dick Crealy, Allan Stone	Margaret Smith Court, Virginia Wade
1970	Pierre Barthes, Niki Pilic	Margaret Smith Court, Judy Dalton
1971	John Newcombe, Roger Taylor	Rosemary Casals, Judy Dalton
1972	Cliff Drysdale, Roger Taylor	Françoise Durr, Betty Stove
1973	Owen Davidson, John Newcombe	Margaret Smith Court, Virginia Wade
1974	Robert Lutz, Stan Smith	Billie Jean King, Rosemary Casals
1975	Jimmy Connors, Ilie Nastase	Margaret Smith Court, Virginia Wade
1976	Tom Okker, Marty Riessen	Delina Boshoff, Ilana Kloss
1977	Bob Hewitt, Frew McMillan	Martina Navratilova, Betty Stove
1978	Robert Lutz, Stan Smith	Billie Jean King, Martina Navratilova
1979	John McEnroe, Peter Fleming	Wendy Turnbull, Betty Stove
1980	Robert Lutz, Stan Smith	Billie Jean King, Martina Navratilova
1981	John McEnroe, Peter Fleming	Kathy Jordan, Anne Smith
1982	Kevin Curren, Steve Denton	Rosemary Casals, Wendy Turnbull
1983	John McEnroe, Peter Fleming	Martina Navratilova, Pam Shriver
1984	John Fitzgerald, Tomas Smid	Martina Navratilova, Pam Shriver
1985	Robert Seguso, Ken Flach	Claudia Kohde-Kilsch, Helena Sukova
1986	Andres Gómez, Slobodan Zivojinovic	Martina Navratilova, Pam Shriver
1987	Stefan Edberg, Anders Järryd	Martina Navratilova, Pam Shriver
1988	Sergio Casal, Emilio Sánchez	Gigi Fernández, Robin White
1989	John McEnroe, Mark Woodforde	Martina Navratilova, Hana Mandlikova
1990	Pieter Aldrich, Danie Visser	Martina Navratilova, Gigi Fernández
1991	John Fitzgerald, Anders Järryd	Pam Shriver, Natasha Zvereva
1992	Jim Grabb, Richey Reneberg	Gigi Fernández, Natasha Zvereva
1993	Ken Flach, Rick Leach	Arantxa Sánchez Vicario, Helena Sukova
1994	Jacco Eltingh, Paul Haarhuis	Arantxa Sánchez Vicario, Jana Novotna
1995	Todd Woodbridge, Mark Woodforde	Gigi Fernández, Natasha Zvereva
1996	Todd Woodbridge, Mark Woodforde	Gigi Fernández, Natasha Zvereva
1997	Yevgeny Kafelnikov, Daniel Vacek	Lindsay Davenport, Jana Novotna
1998	Sandon Stolle, Cyril Suk	Martina Hingis, Jana Novotna
1999	Sébastien Lareau, Alex O'Brien	Venus Williams, Serena Williams
2000	Lleyton Hewitt, Max Mirnyi	Julie Halard-Decugis, Ai Sugiyama
2001	Wayne Black, Kevin Ullyet	Lisa Raymond, Rennae Stubbs
2002	Mahesh Bhupathi, Max Mirnyi	Virginia Ruano Pascual, Paola Suárez
2003	Jonas Björkman, Todd Woodbridge	Virginia Ruano Pascual, Paola Suárez
2004	Mark Knowles, Daniel Nestor	Virginia Ruano Pascual, Paola Suárez
2005	Bob Bryan, Mike Bryan	Lisa Raymond, Samantha Stosur
2006	Martin Damm, Leander Paes	Nathalie Dechy, Vera Zvonareva
2007	Simon Aspelin, Julian Knowle	Nathalie Dechy, Dinara Safina
2008	Bob Bryan, Mike Bryan	Cara Black, Liezel Huber
2009	Lukas Dlouhy, Leander Paes	Venus Williams, Serena Williams
2010	Bob Bryan, Mike Bryan	Vania King, Yaroslava Shvedova

[1]In 1968 and 1969 both amateur and open championships were held. Lutz and Smith won both men's competitions in 1968; Crealy and Stone took the men's amateur championships in 1969. Bueno and Court won both women's competitions in 1968; Court and Wade took the women's amateur championships in 1969. Thereafter the championships were open.

Davis Cup

YEAR	WINNER	RUNNER-UP	RESULTS	YEAR	WINNER	RUNNER-UP	RESULTS
1900	United States	British Isles[1]	3-0	1960	Australia	Italy	4-1
1901	*not held*			1961	Australia	Italy	5-0
1902	United States	British Isles[1]	3-2	1962	Australia	Mexico	5-0
1903	British Isles[1]	United States	4-1	1963	United States	Australia	3-2
1904	British Isles[1]	Belgium	5-0	1964	Australia	United States	3-2
1905	British Isles[1]	United States	5-0	1965	Australia	Spain	4-1
1906	British Isles[1]	United States	5-0	1966	Australia	India	4-1
1907	Australasia[2]	British Isles[1]	3-2	1967	Australia	Spain	4-1
1908	Australasia[2]	United States	3-2	1968	United States	Australia	4-1
1909	Australasia[2]	United States	5-0	1969	United States	Romania	5-0
1910	*not held*			1970	United States	West Germany	5-0
1911	Australasia[2]	United States	5-0	1971	United States	Romania	3-2
1912	British Isles[1]	Australasia[2]	3-2	1972	United States	Romania	3-2
1913	United States	Great Britain	3-2	1973	Australia	United States	5-0
1914	Australasia[2]	United States	3-2	1974	South Africa	India	[3]
1915-18	*not held*			1975	Sweden	Czechoslovakia	3-2
1919	Australasia[2]	Great Britain	4-1	1976	Italy	Chile	4-1
1920	United States	Australasia[2]	5-0	1977	Australia	Italy	3-1
1921	United States	Japan	5-0	1978	United States	Great Britain	4-1
1922	United States	Australasia[2]	4-1	1979	United States	Italy	5-0
1923	United States	Australasia[2]	4-1	1980	Czecho-slovakia	Italy	4-1
1924	United States	Australia	5-0	1981	United States	Argentina	3-1
1925	United States	France	5-0	1982	United States	France	4-1
1926	United States	France	4-1	1983	Australia	Sweden	3-2
1927	France	United States	3-2	1984	Sweden	United States	4-1
1928	France	United States	4-1	1985	Sweden	West Germany	3-2
1929	France	United States	3-2	1986	Australia	Sweden	3-2
1930	France	United States	4-1	1987	Sweden	India	5-0
1931	France	Great Britain	3-2	1988	West Germany	Sweden	4-1
1932	France	United States	3-2	1989	West Germany	Sweden	3-2
1933	Great Britain	France	3-2	1990	United States	Australia	3-2
1934	Great Britain	United States	4-1	1991	France	United States	3-1
1935	Great Britain	United States	5-0	1992	United States	Switzerland	3-1
1936	Great Britain	Australia	3-2	1993	Germany	Australia	4-1
1937	United States	Great Britain	4-1	1994	Sweden	Russia	4-1
1938	United States	Australia	3-2	1995	United States	Russia	3-2
1939	Australia	United States	3-2	1996	France	Sweden	3-2
1940-45	*not held*			1997	Sweden	United States	5-0
1946	United States	Australia	5-0	1998	Sweden	Italy	4-1
1947	United States	Australia	4-1	1999	Australia	France	3-2
1948	United States	Australia	5-0	2000	Spain	Australia	3-1
1949	United States	Australia	4-1	2001	France	Australia	3-2
1950	Australia	United States	4-1	2002	Russia	France	3-2
1951	Australia	United States	3-2	2003	Australia	Spain	3-1
1952	Australia	United States	4-1	2004	Spain	United States	3-2
1953	Australia	United States	3-2	2005	Croatia	Slovakia	3-2
1954	United States	Australia	3-2	2006	Russia	Argentina	3-2
1955	Australia	United States	5-0	2007	United States	Russia	4-1
1956	Australia	United States	5-0	2008	Spain	Argentina	3-1
1957	Australia	United States	3-2	2009	Spain	Czech Republic	5-0
1958	United States	Australia	3-2				
1959	Australia	United States	3-2				

[1]*Great Britain and Ireland.* [2]*Australia and New Zealand.* [3]*Won by forfeit; India withdrew from the final.*

Fed Cup

YEAR	WINNER	RUNNER-UP	RESULTS	YEAR	WINNER	RUNNER-UP	RESULTS
1963	United States	Australia	2-1	1971	Australia	Great Britain	3-0
1964	Australia	United States	2-1	1972	South Africa	Great Britain	2-1
1965	Australia	United States	2-1	1973	Australia	South Africa	3-0
1966	United States	West Germany	3-0	1974	Australia	United States	2-1
1967	United States	Great Britain	2-0	1975	Czechoslovakia	Australia	3-0
1968	Australia	Netherlands	3-0	1976	United States	Australia	2-1
1969	United States	Australia	2-1	1977	United States	Australia	2-1
1970	Australia	West Germany	3-0	1978	United States	Australia	2-1

Fed Cup (continued)

YEAR	WINNER	RUNNER-UP	RESULTS	YEAR	WINNER	RUNNER-UP	RESULTS
1979	United States	Australia	3–0	1995	Spain	United States	3–2
1980	United States	Australia	3–0	1996	United States	Spain	5–0
1981	United States	Great Britain	3–0	1997	France	Netherlands	4–1
1982	United States	West Germany	3–0	1998	Spain	Switzerland	3–2
1983	Czechoslovakia	West Germany	2–1	1999	United States	Russia	4–1
1984	Czechoslovakia	Australia	2–1	2000	United States	Spain	5–0
1985	Czechoslovakia	United States	2–1	2001	Belgium	Russia	2–1
1986	United States	Czechoslovakia	3–0	2002	Slovakia	Spain	3–1
1987	West Germany	United States	2–1	2003	France	United States	4–1
1988	Czechoslovakia	USSR	2–1	2004	Russia	France	3–2
1989	United States	Spain	3–0	2005	Russia	France	3–2
1990	United States	USSR	2–1	2006	Italy	Belgium	3–2
1991	Spain	United States	2–1	2007	Russia	Italy	4–0
1992	Germany	Spain	2–1	2008	Russia	Spain	4–0
1993	Spain	Australia	3–0	2009	Italy	United States	4–0
1994	Spain	United States	3–0				

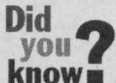

Did you know? The Barbie doll was fashioned after a German doll that was sold as a gag gift for men. Mattel owner Ruth Handler was traveling in Germany where she encountered the Bild Lilli doll, which was sold there at tobacco shops and in bars. She bought a doll for her daughter, Barbie, and gave one to the designers at Mattel. Mattel acquired the rights to Bild Lilli, and shortly thereafter, in 1959, Barbie was introduced in the United States.

Track & Field

The world governing body for track and field, or athletics, is the **International Association of Athletics Federations** (IAAF), founded in 1912. The sport includes relay running, a number of individual running, jumping, and throwing events, and one event (the decathlon for men and the heptathlon for women) that includes all three activities. The best-known competition for most track-and-field athletics is the **Olympic Games** held every four years. In 1983 the first officially recognized non-Olympic world athletics championships were held.

IAAF Web site: <www.iaaf.org>.

World Track & Field Championships—Men

100 M
1983	Carl Lewis (USA)
1987	Carl Lewis (USA)
1991	Carl Lewis (USA)
1993	Linford Christie (GBR)
1995	Donovan Bailey (CAN)
1997	Maurice Greene (USA)
1999	Maurice Greene (USA)
2001	Maurice Greene (USA)
2003	Kim Collins (SKN)
2005	Justin Gatlin (USA)
2007	Tyson Gay (USA)
2009	Usain Bolt (JAM)

200 M
1983	Calvin Smith (USA)
1987	Calvin Smith (USA)
1991	Michael Johnson (USA)
1993	Frank Fredericks (NAM)
1995	Michael Johnson (USA)
1997	Ato Boldon (TRI)
1999	Maurice Greene (USA)
2001	Konstadinos Kederis (GRE)
2003	John Capel (USA)
2005	Justin Gatlin (USA)
2007	Tyson Gay (USA)
2009	Usain Bolt (JAM)

400 M
1983	Bert Cameron (JAM)
1987	Thomas Schoenlebe (GDR)
1991	Antonio Pettigrew (USA)
1993	Michael Johnson (USA)
1995	Michael Johnson (USA)
1997	Michael Johnson (USA)
1999	Michael Johnson (USA)
2001	Avard Moncur (BAH)
2003	Tyree Washington (USA)
2005	Jeremy Wariner (USA)
2007	Jeremy Wariner (USA)
2009	LaShawn Merritt (USA)

800 M
1983	Willi Wülbeck (FRG)
1987	Billy Konchellah (KEN)
1991	Billy Konchellah (KEN)
1993	Paul Ruto (KEN)
1995	Wilson Kipketer (DEN)
1997	Wilson Kipketer (DEN)
1999	Wilson Kipketer (DEN)
2001	André Bucher (SUI)
2003	Djabir Saïd-Guerni (ALG)
2005	Rashid Ramzi (BRN)
2007	Alfred Kirwa Yego (KEN)
2009	Mbulaeni Mulaudzi (RSA)

1,500 M
1983	Steve Cram (GBR)
1987	Abdi Bile (SOM)
1991	Noureddine Morceli (ALG)
1993	Noureddine Morceli (ALG)
1995	Noureddine Morceli (ALG)
1997	Hicham El Guerrouj (MAR)
1999	Hicham El Guerrouj (MAR)
2001	Hicham El Guerrouj (MAR)
2003	Hicham El Guerrouj (MAR)
2005	Rashid Ramzi (BRN)
2007	Bernard Lagat (USA)
2009	Yusuf Saad Kamel (BRN)

5,000 M
1983	Eamonn Coghlan (IRL)
1987	Saïd Aouita (MAR)
1991	Yobes Ondieki (KEN)
1993	Ismael Kirui (KEN)
1995	Ismael Kirui (KEN)
1997	Daniel Komen (KEN)
1999	Salah Hissou (MAR)
2001	Richard Limo (KEN)
2003	Eliud Kipchoge (KEN)
2005	Benjamin Limo (KEN)
2007	Bernard Lagat (USA)
2009	Kenenisa Bekele (ETH)

World Track & Field Championships—Men (continued)

10,000 M

1983	Alberto Cova (ITA)
1987	Paul Kipkoech (KEN)
1991	Moses Tanui (KEN)
1993	Haile Gebrselassie (ETH)
1995	Haile Gebrselassie (ETH)
1997	Haile Gebrselassie (ETH)
1999	Haile Gebrselassie (ETH)
2001	Charles Kamathi (KEN)
2003	Kenenisa Bekele (ETH)
2005	Kenenisa Bekele (ETH)
2007	Kenenisa Bekele (ETH)
2009	Kenenisa Bekele (ETH)

STEEPLECHASE

1983	Patriz Ilg (FRG)
1987	Francesco Panetta (ITA)
1991	Moses Kiptanui (KEN)
1993	Moses Kiptanui (KEN)
1995	Moses Kiptanui (KEN)
1997	Wilson Boit Kipketer (KEN)
1999	Christopher Koskei (KEN)
2001	Reuben Kosgei (KEN)
2003	Saif Saaeed Shaheen (QAT)
2005	Saif Saaeed Shaheen (QAT)
2007	Brimin Kiprop Kipruto (KEN)
2009	Ezekiel Kemboi (KEN)

110-M HURDLES

1983	Greg Foster (USA)
1987	Greg Foster (USA)
1991	Greg Foster (USA)
1993	Colin Jackson (GBR)
1995	Allen Johnson (USA)
1997	Allen Johnson (USA)
1999	Colin Jackson (GBR)
2001	Allen Johnson (USA)
2003	Allen Johnson (USA)
2005	Ladji Doucouré (FRA)
2007	Liu Xiang (CHN)
2009	Ryan Brathwaite (BAR)

400-M HURDLES

1983	Edwin Moses (USA)
1987	Edwin Moses (USA)
1991	Samuel Matete (ZAM)
1993	Kevin Young (USA)
1995	Derrick Adkins (USA)
1997	Stéphane Diagana (FRA)
1999	Fabrizio Mori (ITA)
2001	Felix Sánchez (DOM)
2003	Felix Sánchez (DOM)
2005	Bershawn Jackson (USA)
2007	Kerron Clement (USA)
2009	Kerron Clement (USA)

MARATHON

1983	Robert de Castella (AUS)
1987	Douglas Wakiihuri (KEN)
1991	Hiromi Taniguchi (JPN)
1993	Mark Plaatjes (USA)
1995	Martín Fiz (ESP)
1997	Abel Antón (ESP)
1999	Abel Antón (ESP)
2001	Gezahegne Abera (ETH)
2003	Jaouad Gharib (MAR)
2005	Jaouad Gharib (MAR)
2007	Luke Kibet (KEN)
2009	Abel Kirui (KEN)

20-KM WALK

1983	Ernesto Canto (MEX)
1987	Maurizio Damilano (ITA)
1991	Maurizio Damilano (ITA)
1993	Valentí Massana (ESP)
1995	Michele Didoni (ITA)
1997	Daniel García (MEX)
1999	Ilya Markov (RUS)
2001	Roman Rasskazov (RUS)
2003	Jefferson Pérez (ECU)
2005	Jefferson Pérez (ECU)
2007	Jefferson Pérez (ECU)
2009	Valeriy Borchin (RUS)

50-KM WALK

1983	Ronald Weigel (GDR)
1987	Hartwig Gauder (GDR)
1991	Aleksandr Potashov (URS)
1993	Jesús Angel García (ESP)
1995	Valentin Kononen (FIN)
1997	Robert Korzeniowski (POL)
1999	Ivano Brugnetti (ITA)
2001	Robert Korzeniowski (POL)
2003	Robert Korzeniowski (POL)
2005	Sergey Kirdyapkin (RUS)
2007	Nathan Deakes (AUS)
2009	Sergey Kirdyapkin (RUS)

4 × 100-M RELAY

1983	United States
1987	United States
1991	United States
1993	United States
1995	Canada
1997	Canada
1999	United States
2001	South Africa
2003	United States
2005	France
2007	United States
2009	Jamaica

4 × 400-M RELAY

1983	USSR
1987	United States
1991	United Kingdom
1993	United States
1995	United States
1997	United States
1999	United States
2001	United States
2003	France
2005	United States
2007	United States
2009	United States

HIGH JUMP

1983	Gennady Avdeyenko (URS)
1987	Patrik Sjöberg (SWE)
1991	Charles Austin (USA)
1993	Javier Sotomayor (CUB)
1995	Troy Kemp (BAH)
1997	Javier Sotomayor (CUB)
1999	Vyacheslav Voronin (RUS)
2001	Martin Buss (GER)
2003	Jacques Freitag (RSA)
2005	Yuri Krymarenko (UKR)
2007	Donald Thomas (BAH)
2009	Yaroslav Rybakov (RUS)

POLE VAULT

1983	Sergey Bubka (URS)
1987	Sergey Bubka (URS)
1991	Sergey Bubka (URS)
1993	Sergey Bubka (UKR)
1995	Sergey Bubka (UKR)
1997	Sergey Bubka (UKR)
1999	Maksim Tarasov (RUS)
2001	Dmitri Markov (AUS)
2003	Giuseppe Gibilisco (ITA)
2005	Rens Blom (NED)
2007	Brad Walker (USA)
2009	Steven Hooker (AUS)

LONG JUMP

1983	Carl Lewis (USA)
1987	Carl Lewis (USA)
1991	Mike Powell (USA)
1993	Mike Powell (USA)
1995	Iván Pedroso (CUB)
1997	Iván Pedroso (CUB)
1999	Iván Pedroso (CUB)
2001	Iván Pedroso (CUB)
2003	Dwight Phillips (USA)
2005	Dwight Phillips (USA)
2007	Irving Saladino (PAN)
2009	Dwight Phillips (USA)

TRIPLE JUMP

1983	Zdzislaw Hoffman (POL)
1987	Khristo Markov (BUL)
1991	Kenny Harrison (USA)
1993	Mike Conley (USA)
1995	Jonathan Edwards (GBR)
1997	Yoelbi Quesada (CUB)
1999	Charles Michael Friedek (GER)
2001	Jonathan Edwards (GBR)
2003	Christian Olsson (SWE)
2005	Walter Davis (USA)
2007	Nelson Évora (POR)
2009	Phillips Idowu (GBR)

SHOT PUT

1983	Edward Sarul (POL)
1987	Werner Günthör (SUI)
1991	Werner Günthör (SUI)
1993	Werner Günthör (SUI)
1995	John Godina (USA)
1997	John Godina (USA)
1999	C.J. Hunter (USA)
2001	John Godina (USA)
2003	Andrey Mikhnevich (BLR)
2005	Adam Nelson (USA)
2007	Reese Hoffa (USA)
2009	Christian Cantwell (USA)

DISCUS THROW

1983	Imrich Bugar (TCH)
1987	Jürgen Schult (GDR)
1991	Lars Riedel (GER)
1993	Lars Riedel (GER)
1995	Lars Riedel (GER)
1997	Lars Riedel (GER)
1999	Anthony Washington (USA)
2001	Lars Riedel (GER)
2003	Virgilijus Alekna (LTU)
2005	Virgilijus Alekna (LTU)

World Track & Field Championships—Men (continued)

DISCUS THROW (CONTINUED)
2007   Gerd Kanter (EST)
2009   Robert Harting (GER)

HAMMER THROW
1983   Sergey Litvinov (URS)
1987   Sergey Litvinov (URS)
1991   Yury Sedykh (URS)
1993   Andrey Abduvaliyev (TJK)
1995   Andrey Abduvaliyev (TJK)
1997   Heinz Weis (GER)
1999   Karsten Kobs (GER)
2001   Szymon Ziolkowski (POL)
2003   Ivan Tikhon (BLR)
2005   Ivan Tikhon (BLR)
2007   Ivan Tikhon (BLR)
2009   Primoz Kozmus (SLO)

JAVELIN THROW
1983   Detlef Michel (GDR)
1987   Seppo Räty (FIN)
1991   Kimmo Kinnunen (FIN)
1993   Jan Zelezny (CZE)
1995   Jan Zelezny (CZE)
1997   Marius Corbett (RSA)
1999   Aki Parviainen (FIN)
2001   Jan Zelezny (CZE)
2003   Sergey Makarov (RUS)
2005   Andrus Varnik (EST)
2007   Tero Pitkämäki (FIN)
2009   Andreas Thorkildsen (NOR)

DECATHLON
1983   Daley Thompson (GBR)
1987   Torsten Voss (GDR)
1991   Dan O'Brien (USA)
1993   Dan O'Brien (USA)
1995   Dan O'Brien (USA)
1997   Tomas Dvorak (CZE)
1999   Tomas Dvorak (CZE)
2001   Tomas Dvorak (CZE)
2003   Tom Pappas (USA)
2005   Bryan Clay (USA)
2007   Roman Sebrle (CZE)
2009   Trey Hardee (USA)

Did you know? British monarch Charles II (reigned 1660–85) became known as "the father of the English turf" because of his passion for horse racing. He inaugurated the King's Plates, races for which prizes were awarded the winners, and he enjoyed racing horses himself. It was during the reign of Charles that the sport took on its nickname, "the sport of kings."

World Track & Field Championships—Women

100 M
1983   Marlies Göhr (GDR)
1987   Silke Gladisch (GDR)
1991   Katrin Krabbe (GER)
1993   Gail Devers (USA)
1995   Gwen Torrence (USA)
1997   Marion Jones (USA)
1999   Marion Jones (USA)
2001   Zhanna Pintusevich (UKR)
2003   Torri Edwards (USA)
2005   Lauryn Williams (USA)
2007   Veronica Campbell (JAM)
2009   Shelly-Ann Fraser (JAM)

200 M
1983   Marita Koch (GDR)
1987   Silke Gladisch (GDR)
1991   Katrin Krabbe (GER)
1993   Merlene Ottey (JAM)
1995   Merlene Ottey (JAM)
1997   Zhanna Pintusevich (UKR)
1999   Inger Miller (USA)
2001   Marion Jones (USA)
2003   Anastasiya Kapachin-
      skaya (RUS)
2005   Allyson Felix (USA)
2007   Allyson Felix (USA)
2009   Allyson Felix (USA)

400 M
1983   Jarmila Kratochvilova (TCH)
1987   Olga Bryzgina (URS)
1991   Marie-José Pérec (FRA)
1993   Jearl Miles (USA)
1995   Marie-José Pérec (FRA)
1997   Cathy Freeman (AUS)
1999   Cathy Freeman (AUS)
2001   Amy Mbacke Thiam (SEN)

400 M (CONTINUED)
2003   Ana Guevara (MEX)
2005   Tonique Williams-Darling
      (BAH)
2007   Christine Ohuruogu (GBR)
2009   Sanya Richards (USA)

800 M
1983   Jarmila Kratochvilova (TCH)
1987   Sigrun Wodars (GDR)
1991   Liliya Nurutdinova (URS)
1993   Maria Mutola (MOZ)
1995   Ana Quirot (CUB)
1997   Ana Quirot (CUB)
1999   Ludmila Formanova (CZE)
2001   Maria Mutola (MOZ)
2003   Maria Mutola (MOZ)
2005   Zulia Calatayud (CUB)
2007   Janeth Jepkosgei (KEN)
2009   Caster Semenya (RSA)

1,500 M
1983   Mary Decker (USA)
1987   Tatyana Samolenko (URS)
1991   Hassiba Boulmerka (ALG)
1993   Liu Dong (CHN)
1995   Hassiba Boulmerka (ALG)
1997   Carla Sacramento (POR)
1999   Svetlana Masterkova (RUS)
2001   Gabriela Szabo (ROM)
2003   Tatyana Tomashova (RUS)
2005   Tatyana Tomashova (RUS)
2007   Maryam Yusuf Jamal (BRN)
2009   Maryam Yusuf Jamal (BRN)

5,000 M[1]
1983   Mary Decker (USA)
1987   Tatyana Samolenko (URS)

5,000 M[1] (CONTINUED)
1991   Tatyana Dorovskikh (URS)
1993   Qu Yunxia (CHN)
1995   Sonia O'Sullivan (IRL)
1997   Gabriela Szabo (ROM)
1999   Gabriela Szabo (ROM)
2001   Olga Yegorova (RUS)
2003   Tirunesh Dibaba (ETH)
2005   Tirunesh Dibaba (ETH)
2007   Meseret Defar (ETH)
2009   Vivian Cheruiyot (KEN)

10,000 M
1987   Ingrid Kristiansen (NOR)
1991   Liz McColgan (GBR)
1993   Wang Junxia (CHN)
1995   Fernanda Ribeiro (POR)
1997   Sally Barsosio (KEN)
1999   Gete Wami (ETH)
2001   Derartu Tulu (ETH)
2003   Berhane Adere (ETH)
2005   Tirunesh Dibaba (ETH)
2007   Tirunesh Dibaba (ETH)
2009   Linet Chepkwemoi Masai
      (KEN)

STEEPLECHASE
2005   Dorcus Inzikuru (UGA)
2007   Yekaterina Volkova (RUS)
2009   Marta Domínguez (ESP)

100-M HURDLES
1983   Bettine Jahn (GDR)
1987   Ginka Zagorcheva (BUL)
1991   Ludmila Narozhilenko
      (URS)
1993   Gail Devers (USA)
1995   Gail Devers (USA)

World Track & Field Championships—Women (continued)

100-M HURDLES (CONTINUED)
1997 Ludmila Engquist (SWE)
1999 Gail Devers (USA)
2001 Anjanette Kirkland (USA)
2003 Perdita Felicien (CAN)
2005 Michelle Perry (USA)
2007 Michelle Perry (USA)
2009 Brigitte Foster-Hylton (JAM)

400-M HURDLES
1983 Yekaterina Fesenko (URS)
1987 Sabine Busch (GDR)
1991 Tatyana Ledovskaya (URS)
1993 Sally Gunnell (GBR)
1995 Kim Batten (USA)
1997 Nezha Bidouane (MAR)
1999 Daimí Pernía (CUB)
2001 Nezha Bidouane (MAR)
2003 Jana Pittman (AUS)
2005 Yuliya Pechonkina (RUS)
2007 Jana Rawlinson (AUS)
2009 Melanie Walker (JAM)

MARATHON
1983 Grete Waitz (NOR)
1987 Rosa Mota (POR)
1991 Wanda Panfil (POL)
1993 Asari Junko (JPN)
1995 Maria Machado (POR)
1997 Hiromi Suzuki (JPN)
1999 Jong Song Ok (PRK)
2001 Lidia Simon (ROM)
2003 Catherine Ndereba (KEN)
2005 Paula Radcliffe (GBR)
2007 Catherine Ndereba (KEN)
2009 Bai Xue (CHN)

10-KM WALK
1987 Irina Strakhova (URS)
1991 Alina Ivanova (URS)
1993 Sari Essayeh (FIN)
1995 Irina Stankina (RUS)
1997 Annarita Sidoti (ITA)

20-KM RACE WALK
1999 Liu Hongyu (CHN)
2001 Olimpiada Ivanova (RUS)
2003 Yelena Nikolayeva (RUS)
2005 Olimpiada Ivanova (RUS)
2007 Olga Kaniskina (RUS)
2009 Olga Kaniskina (RUS)

4 × 100-M RELAY
1983 East Germany
1987 United States
1991 Jamaica
1993 Russia
1995 United States
1997 United States
1999 Bahamas
2001 Germany
2003 France
2005 United States

4 × 100-M RELAY (CONTINUED)
2007 United States
2009 Jamaica

4 × 400-M RELAY
1983 East Germany
1987 East Germany
1991 USSR
1993 United States
1995 United States
1997 Germany
1999 Russia
2001 Jamaica
2003 United States
2005 Russia
2007 United States
2009 United States

HIGH JUMP
1983 Tamara Bykova (URS)
1987 Stefka Kostadinova (BUL)
1991 Heike Henkel (GER)
1993 Ioamnet Quintero (CUB)
1995 Stefka Kostadinova (BUL)
1997 Hanne Haugland (NOR)
1999 Inga Babakova (UKR)
2001 Hestrie Cloete (RSA)
2003 Hestrie Cloete (RSA)
2005 Kajsa Bergqvist (SWE)
2007 Blanka Vlasic (CRO)
2009 Blanka Vlasic (CRO)

POLE VAULT
1999 Stacy Dragila (USA)
2001 Stacy Dragila (USA)
2003 Svetlana Feofanova (RUS)
2005 Yelena Isinbayeva (RUS)
2007 Yelena Isinbayeva (RUS)
2009 Anna Rogowska (POL)

LONG JUMP
1983 Heike Daute (GDR)
1987 Jackie Joyner-Kersee (USA)
1991 Jackie Joyner-Kersee (USA)
1993 Heike Drechsler (GER)
1995 Fiona May (ITA)
1997 Ludmila Galkina (RUS)
1999 Niurka Montalvo (ESP)
2001 Fiona May (ITA)
2003 Eunice Barber (FRA)
2005 Tianna Madison (USA)
2007 Tatyana Lebedeva (RUS)
2009 Brittney Reese (USA)

TRIPLE JUMP
1993 Anna Biryukova (RUS)
1995 Inessa Kravets (UKR)
1997 Sarka Kasparkova (CZE)
1999 Paraskevi Tsiamita (GRE)
2001 Tatyana Lebedeva (RUS)
2003 Tatyana Lebedeva (RUS)
2005 Trecia Smith (JAM)
2007 Yargelis Savigne (CUB)
2009 Yargelis Savigne (CUB)

SHOT PUT
1983 Helena Fibingerova (TCH)
1987 Natalya Lisovskaya (URS)
1991 Huang Zhihong (CHN)
1993 Huang Zhihong (CHN)
1995 Astrid Kumbernuss (GER)
1997 Astrid Kumbernuss (GER)
1999 Astrid Kumbernuss (GER)
2001 Yanina Korolchik (BLR)
2003 Svetlana Krivelyova (RUS)
2005 Nadezhda Ostapchuk (BLR)
2007 Valerie Vili (NZL)
2009 Valerie Vili (NZL)

DISCUS THROW
1983 Martina Opitz (GDR)
1987 Martina Hellmann (GDR)
1991 Tsvetanka Khristova (BUL)
1993 Olga Burova (RUS)
1995 Ellina Zvereva (BLR)
1997 Beatrice Faumuina (NZL)
1999 Franka Dietzsch (GER)
2001 Ellina Zvereva (BLR)
2003 Irina Yachenko (BLR)
2005 Franka Dietzsch (GER)
2007 Franka Dietzsch (GER)
2009 Dani Samuels (AUS)

HAMMER THROW
1999 Mihaela Melinte (ROM)
2001 Yipsi Moreno (CUB)
2003 Yipsi Moreno (CUB)
2005 Olga Kuzenkova (RUS)
2007 Betty Heidler (GER)
2009 Anita Wlodarczyk (POL)

JAVELIN THROW
1983 Tiina Lillak (FIN)
1987 Fatima Whitbread (GBR)
1991 Xu Demei (CHN)
1993 Trine Hattestad (NOR)
1995 Natalya Shikolenko (BLR)
1997 Trine Hattestad (NOR)
1999 Mirela Tzelili (GRE)
2001 Osleidys Menéndez (CUB)
2003 Mirela Manjani (GRE)
2005 Osleidys Menéndez (CUB)
2007 Barbora Spotakova (CZE)
2009 Steffi Nerius (GER)

HEPTATHLON
1983 Ramona Neubert (GDR)
1987 Jackie Joyner-Kersee (USA)
1991 Sabine Braun (GER)
1993 Jackie Joyner-Kersee (USA)
1995 Ghada Shouaa (SYR)
1997 Sabine Braun (GER)
1999 Eunice Barber (FRA)
2001 Yelena Prokhorova (RUS)
2003 Carolina Klüft (SWE)
2005 Carolina Klüft (SWE)
2007 Carolina Klüft (SWE)
2009 Jessica Ennis (GBR)

¹3,000 m until 1995.

Outdoor Track & Field World Records

Men

EVENT	RECORD HOLDER (COUNTRY)	PERFORMANCE	DATE
100 m	Usain Bolt (JAM)	9.58 sec	16 Aug 2009
200 m	Usain Bolt (JAM)	19.19 sec	20 Aug 2009
400 m	Michael Johnson (USA)	43.18 sec	26 Aug 1999
800 m	David Lekuta Rudisha (KEN)[1]	1 min 41.09 sec	22 Aug 2010
1,000 m	Noah Ngeny (KEN)	2 min 11.96 sec	5 Sep 1999
1,500 m	Hicham El Guerrouj (MAR)	3 min 26.00 sec	14 Jul 1998
1 mile	Hicham El Guerrouj (MAR)	3 min 43.13 sec	7 Jul 1999
3,000 m	Daniel Komen (KEN)	7 min 20.67 sec	1 Sep 1996
5,000 m	Kenenisa Bekele (ETH)	12 min 37.35 sec	31 May 2004
10,000 m	Kenenisa Bekele (ETH)	26 min 17.53 sec	26 Aug 2005
Marathon[2]	Haile Gebrselassie (ETH)	2 hr 3 min 59 sec	28 Sep 2008
110-m hurdles	Dayron Robles (CUB)	12.87 sec	12 Jun 2008
400-m hurdles	Kevin Young (USA)	46.78 sec	6 Aug 1992
20-km walk	Vladimir Kanaykin (RUS)	1 hr 17 min 16 sec	29 Sep 2007
50-km walk	Denis Nizhegorodov (RUS)	3 hr 34 min 14 sec	11 May 2008
Steeplechase	Saif Saaeed Shaheen (QAT)	7 min 53.63 sec	3 Sep 2004
4 × 100-m relay	Jamaica	37.10 sec	22 Aug 2008
4 × 400-m relay	United States	2 min 54.29 sec	22 Aug 1993
High jump	Javier Sotomayor (CUB)	2.45 m (8 ft ½ in)	27 Jul 1993
Long jump	Mike Powell (USA)	8.95 m (29 ft 4½ in)	30 Aug 1991
Triple jump	Jonathan Edwards (GBR)	18.29 m (60 ft ¼ in)	7 Aug 1995
Pole vault	Sergey Bubka (UKR)	6.14 m (20 ft 1¾ in)	31 Jul 1994
Shot put	Randy Barnes (USA)	23.12 m (75 ft 10¼ in)	20 May 1990
Discus throw	Jürgen Schult (GDR)	74.08 m (243 ft)	6 Jun 1986
Hammer throw	Yuriy Sedykh (URS)	86.74 m (284 ft 7 in)	30 Aug 1986
Javelin throw	Jan Zelezny (CZE)	98.48 m (323 ft 1 in)	25 May 1996
Decathlon	Roman Sebrle (CZE)	9,026 points	27 May 2001

Women

EVENT	RECORD HOLDER (COUNTRY)	PERFORMANCE	DATE
100 m	Florence Griffith-Joyner (USA)	10.49 sec	16 Jul 1988
200 m	Florence Griffith-Joyner (USA)	21.34 sec	29 Sep 1988
400 m	Marita Koch (GDR)	47.60 sec	6 Oct 1985
800 m	Jarmila Kratochvilova (TCH)	1 min 53.28 sec	26 Jul 1983
1,000 m	Svetlana Masterkova (RUS)	2 min 28.98 sec	23 Aug 1996
1,500 m	Qu Yunxia (CHN)	3 min 50.46 sec	11 Sep 1993
1 mile	Svetlana Masterkova (RUS)	4 min 12.56 sec	14 Aug 1996
3,000 m	Wang Junxia (CHN)	8 min 6.11 sec	13 Sep 1993
5,000 m	Tirunesh Dibaba (ETH)	14 min 11.15 sec	6 Jun 2008
10,000 m	Wang Junxia (CHN)	29 min 31.78 sec	8 Sep 1993
Marathon[2]	Paula Radcliffe (GBR)	2 hr 15 min 25 sec	13 Apr 2003
100-m hurdles	Yordanka Donkova (BUL)	12.21 sec	20 Aug 1988
400-m hurdles	Yuliya Pechonkina (RUS)	52.34 sec	8 Aug 2003
20-km walk	Olimpiada Ivanova (RUS)	1 hr 25 min 41 sec	7 Aug 2005
Steeplechase	Gulnara Samitova-Galkina (RUS)	8 min 58.81 sec	17 Aug 2008
4 × 100-m relay	East Germany	41.37 sec	6 Oct 1985
4 × 400-m relay	USSR	3 min 15.17 sec	1 Oct 1988
High jump	Stefka Kostadinova (BUL)	2.09 m (6 ft 10¼ in)	30 Aug 1987
Long jump	Galina Chistyakova (URS)	7.52 m (24 ft 8¼ in)	11 Jun 1988
Triple jump	Inessa Kravets (UKR)	15.50 m (50 ft 10¼ in)	10 Aug 1995
Pole vault	Yelena Isinbayeva (RUS)	5.06 m (16 ft 7¼ in)	28 Aug 2009
Shot put	Natalya Lisovskaya (URS)	22.63 m (74 ft 3 in)	7 Jun 1987
Discus throw	Gabriele Reinsch (GDR)	76.80 m (252 ft)	9 Jul 1988
Hammer throw	Anita Wlodarczyk (POL)	78.30 m (256 ft 11 in)	6 Jun 2010
Javelin throw	Barbora Spotakova (CZE)	72.28 m (237 ft 2 in)	13 Sep 2008
Heptathlon	Jackie Joyner-Kersee (USA)	7,291 points	24 Sep 1988
Decathlon	Austra Skujyte (LTU)	8,358 points	15 Apr 2005

[1]*Awaiting IAAF ratification as of 25 Aug 2010.* [2]*Not an officially ratified event; best performance on record.*

Indoor Track & Field World Records

Men

EVENT	RECORD HOLDER (COUNTRY)	PERFORMANCE	DATE
50 m	Donovan Bailey (CAN)	5.56 sec	9 Feb 1996
60 m	Maurice Greene (USA)	6.39 sec	3 Feb 1998

Indoor Track & Field World Records

Men (continued)

EVENT	RECORD HOLDER (COUNTRY)	PERFORMANCE	DATE
200 m	Frank Fredericks (NAM)	19.92 sec	18 Feb 1996
400 m	Kerron Clement (USA)	44.57 sec	12 Mar 2005
800 m	Wilson Kipketer (DEN)	1 min 42.67 sec	9 Mar 1997
1,000 m	Wilson Kipketer (DEN)	2 min 14.96 sec	20 Feb 2000
1,500 m	Hicham El Guerrouj (MAR)	3 min 31.18 sec	2 Feb 1997
1 mile	Hicham El Guerrouj (MAR)	3 min 48.45 sec	12 Feb 1997
3,000 m	Daniel Komen (KEN)	7 min 24.90 sec	6 Feb 1998
5,000 m	Kenenisa Bekele (ETH)	12 min 49.60 sec	20 Feb 2004
50-m hurdles	Mark McKoy (CAN)	6.25 sec	5 Mar 1986
60-m hurdles	Colin Jackson (GBR)	7.30 sec	6 Mar 1994
5,000-m walk	Mikhail Shchennikov (RUS)	18 min 07.08 sec	14 Feb 1995
4 × 200-m relay	Great Britain and Northern Ireland	1 min 22.11 sec	3 Mar 1991
4 × 400-m relay	United States	3 min 02.83 sec	7 Mar 1999
4 × 800-m relay	United States	7 min 13.94 sec	6 Feb 2000
High jump	Javier Sotomayor (CUB)	2.43 m (7 ft 11½ in)	4 Mar 1989
Long jump	Carl Lewis (USA)	8.79 m (28 ft 10 in)	27 Jan 1984
Triple jump	Teddy Tamgho (FRA)	17.90 m (58 ft 9 in)	14 Mar 2010
Pole vault	Sergey Bubka (UKR)	6.15 m (20 ft 2¼ in)	21 Feb 1993
Shot put	Randy Barnes (USA)	22.66 m (74 ft 4¼ in)	20 Jan 1989
Heptathlon	Ashton Eaton (USA)[1]	6,499 points	13 Mar 2010

Women

EVENT	RECORD HOLDER (COUNTRY)	PERFORMANCE	DATE
50 m	Irina Privalova (RUS)	5.96 sec	9 Feb 1995
60 m	Irina Privalova (RUS)	6.92 sec	11 Feb 1993
200 m	Merlene Ottey (JAM)	21.87 sec	13 Feb 1993
400 m	Jarmila Kratochvilova (TCH)	49.59 sec	7 Mar 1982
800 m	Jolanda Ceplak (SLO)	1 min 55.82 sec	3 Mar 2002
1,000 m	Maria Mutola (MOZ)	2 min 30.94 sec	25 Feb 1999
1,500 m	Yelena Soboleva (RUS)	3 min 58.28 sec	18 Feb 2006
1 mile	Doina Melinte (ROU)	4 min 17.14 sec	9 Feb 1990
3,000 m	Meseret Defar (ETH)	8 min 23.72 sec	3 Feb 2007
5,000 m	Meseret Defar (ETH)	14 min 24.37 sec	18 Feb 2009
50-m hurdles	Cornelia Oschkenat (GDR)	6.58 sec	20 Feb 1988
60-m hurdles	Susanna Kallur (SWE)	7.68 sec	10 Feb 2008
3,000-m walk	Claudia Stef (ROU)	11 min 40.33 sec	30 Jan 1999
4 × 200-m relay	Russia	1 min 32.41 sec	29 Jan 2005
4 × 400-m relay	Russia	3 min 23.37 sec	28 Jan 2006
4 × 800-m relay	Russia	8 min 12.41 sec	28 Feb 2010
High jump	Kajsa Bergqvist (SWE)	2.08 m (6 ft 10 in)	4 Feb 2006
Long jump	Heike Drechsler (GDR)	7.37 m (24 ft 2¼ in)	13 Feb 1988
Triple jump	Tatyana Lebedeva (RUS)	15.36 m (50 ft 4¾ in)	6 Mar 2004
Pentathlon	Irina Belova (UNT)	4,991 points	15 Feb 1992
Pole vault	Yelena Isinbayeva (RUS)	5.00 m (16 ft 4¾ in)	15 Feb 2009
Shot put	Helena Fibingerova (TCH)	22.50 m (73 ft 9¾ in)	19 Feb 1977

[1]Awaiting IAAF ratification as of 25 Aug 2010.

Volleyball

World volleyball championships for men were inaugurated in 1949. Women's competition began in 1952. These biennial championships are organized by the Fédération Internationale de Volleyball (FIVB; founded 1947). Indoor volleyball has been included in the Olympic Games since 1964 and beach volleyball since 1996.

FIVB Web site: <www.fivb.org>.

Volleyball World Championships

YEAR	MEN	WOMEN	YEAR	MEN	WOMEN
1949	USSR		1964[1]	USSR	Japan
1952	USSR	USSR	1966	Czechoslovakia	not held
1956	Czechoslovakia	USSR	1967	not held	Japan
1960	USSR	USSR	1968[1]	USSR	USSR
1962	USSR	Japan	1970	East Germany	USSR

Volleyball World Championships (continued)

YEAR	MEN	WOMEN	YEAR	MEN	WOMEN
1972[1]	Japan	USSR	1990	Italy	USSR
1974	Poland	Japan	1992[1]	Brazil	Cuba
1976[1]	Poland	Japan	1994	Italy	Cuba
1978	USSR	Cuba	1996[1]	Netherlands	Cuba
1980[1]	USSR	USSR	1998	Italy	Cuba
1982	USSR	China	2000[1]	Yugoslavia	Cuba
1984[1]	United States	China	2002	Brazil	Italy
1986	United States	China	2004[1]	Brazil	China
1988[1]	United States	USSR	2006	Brazil	Russia
			2008[1]	United States	Brazil

[1]Olympic champions, recognized in this table as world champions (though not by FIVB).

Beach Volleyball World Championships

Beach volleyball world championships, organized by the **Fédération Internationale de Volleyball**, were inaugurated in 1997 with teams of two, who compete biennially for their share of US$1 million. Beach volleyball has been included in the Olympic Games since 1996. **FIVB Web site:** <www.fivb.org>.

YEAR	MEN	WOMEN
1996[1]	Karch Kiraly/Kent Steffes (USA)	Jackie Silva/Sandra Pires (BRA)
1997	Guilherme Marques/Para Ferreira (BRA)	Jackie Silva/Sandra Pires (BRA)
1999	Emanuel Rego/José Loiola (BRA)	Shelda Bede/Adriana Behar (BRA)
2000[1]	Dain Blaton/Eric Fonoimoana (USA)	Natalie Cook/Kerri-Ann Pottharst (AUS)
2001	Mariano Baracetti/Martín Conde (ARG)	Shelda Bede/Adriana Behar (BRA)
2003	Emanuel Rego/Ricardo Santos (BRA)	Misty May/Kerri Walsh (USA)
2004[1]	Emanuel Rego/Ricardo Santos (BRA)	Misty May/Kerri Walsh (USA)
2005	Marcio Araujo/Fabio Magalhães (BRA)	Misty May-Treanor/Kerri Walsh (USA)
2007	Phil Dalhausser/Todd Rogers (USA)	Misty May-Treanor/Kerri Walsh (USA)
2008[1]	Phil Dalhausser/Todd Rogers (USA)	Misty May-Treanor/Kerri Walsh (USA)
2009	Julius Brink/Jonas Reckermann (GER)	Jen Kessy/April Ross (USA)

[1]Olympic champions, recognized in this table as world champions.

Weight Lifting

World weight lifting is overseen by the International Weightlifting Federation (IWF; founded 1905). The first **men's international weight lifting competition** was held in London in 1891; the sport was also included in the first modern Olympic Games, in Athens in 1896. By the 1930s championship events consisted of the snatch, clean and jerk, and press (which was eliminated in 1972).

Women's world championships have been held since 1987, and women's competition was added to the Olympics in 2000. In 1998 the IWF established **new weight classes** (eight for men and seven for women) as well as a new world standard for each class in determining world records.

IWF Web site: <www.iwf.net>.

World Weight Lifting Champions, 2009

	Men	
WEIGHT CLASS	WINNER (COUNTRY)	PERFORMANCE
56 kg (123 lb)	Long Qingquan (CHN)	292 kg (644 lb)
62 kg (137 lb)	Ding Jianjun (CHN)	316 kg (697 lb)
69 kg (152 lb)	Liao Hui (CHN)	346 kg (763 lb)
77 kg (170 lb)	Lu Xiaojun (CHN)	378 kg (833 lb)
85 kg (187 lb)	Lu Yong (CHN)	383 kg (844 lb)
94 kg (207 lb)	Vladimir Sedov (KAZ)	402 kg (886 lb)
105 kg (231 lb)	Marcin Dolega (POL)	421 kg (928 lb)
105+ kg (231+ lb)	An Yong Kwon (KOR)	445 kg (981 lb)

World Weight Lifting Champions, 2009 (continued)

Women

WEIGHT CLASS	WINNER (COUNTRY)	PERFORMANCE
48 kg (106 lb)	Wang Mingjuan (CHN)	208 kg (459 lb)
53 kg (117 lb)	Zulfiya Chinshanlo (KAZ)	219 kg (483 lb)
58 kg (128 lb)	Li Xueying (CHN)	239 kg (527 lb)
63 kg (139 lb)	Maiya Maneza (KAZ)	246 kg (542 lb)
69 kg (152 lb)	Nazik Avdalyan (ARM)	266 kg (586 lb)
75 kg (165 lb)	Svetlana Podobedova (KAZ)	292 kg (644 lb)
75+ kg (165+ lb)	Jang Mi Ran (KOR)	323 kg (712 lb)

Weight Lifting World Records

Total weight for snatch and clean-and-jerk lifts.

Men

WEIGHT CLASS	RECORD HOLDER (COUNTRY)	PERFORMANCE	DATE
56 kg (123 lb)	Halil Mutlu (TUR)	305 kg (672 lb)	16 Sep 2000
62 kg (137 lb)	Zhang Jie (CHN)	326 kg (719 lb)	28 Apr 2008
69 kg (152 lb)	Galabin Boevski (BUL)	357 kg (787 lb)	24 Nov 1999
77 kg (170 lb)	Lu Xiaojun (CHN)	378 kg (833 lb)	24 Nov 2009
85 kg (187 lb)	Lu Yong (CHN);	394 kg (869 lb)	15 Aug 2008;
	Andrei Rybakov (BLR)		15 Aug 2008
94 kg (207 lb)	Akakios Kakiasvilis (GRE)	412 kg (908 lb)	27 Nov 1999
105 kg (231.5 lb)	Andrei Aramnau (BLR)	436 kg (961 lb)	18 Aug 2008
105+ kg (231.5+ lb)	Hossein Rezazadeh (IRI)	472 kg (1041 lb)	26 Sep 2000

Women

WEIGHT CLASS	RECORD HOLDER (COUNTRY)	PERFORMANCE	DATE
48kg (106 lb)	Yang Lian (CHN)	217 kg (478 lb)	1 Oct 2006
53 kg (117 lb)	Qiu Hongxia (CHN)	226 kg (498 lb)	2 Oct 2006
58 kg (128 lb)	Chen Yanqing (CHN)	251 kg (553 lb)	3 Dec 2006
63 kg (139 lb)	Liu Haixia (CHN)	257 kg (567 lb)	23 Sep 2007
69 kg (152 lb)	Liu Chunhong (CHN)	286 kg (631 lb)	13 Aug 2008
75 kg (165 lb)	Svetlana Podobedova (RUS)	292 kg (644 lb)	28 Nov 2009
75+ kg (165+ lb)	Jang Mi Ran (KOR)	326 kg (719 lb)	16 Aug 2008

INDEX

Page numbers in **boldface** indicate main subject references; references in *italics* indicate illustrations. Photographs are on plates 1–16 after page 480, flags of the world are on plates 17–22, and maps of the world are on plates 23–32.